LITERARY MARKET PLACE™

LMP 2025

Literary Market Place™
85th Edition

Publisher
Thomas H. Hogan

Senior Director, ITI Reference Group
Owen O'Donnell

Managing Editor
Karen Hallard

Assistant Editor
Karen DiDario

Tampa Operations:

Manager, Tampa Editorial Operations
Debra James

Project Coordinator, Tampa Editorial
Carolyn Victor

Graphics & Production:

Production Manager
Tiffany Chamenko

Production
Dana Stevenson
Jackie Crawford

LITERARY MARKET PLACE™

LMP 2025

THE DIRECTORY OF THE AMERICAN
BOOK PUBLISHING INDUSTRY WITH
INDUSTRY INDEXES

Volume

Published by

Information Today, Inc.
143 Old Marlton Pike
Medford, NJ 08055-8750
Phone: (609) 654-6266
Fax: (609) 654-4309
E-mail (Orders): custserv@infotoday.com
Web site: www.infotoday.com
Copyright 2024, Information Today, Inc. All Rights Reserved

ISSN 0000-1155
ISBN 978-1-57387-604-9 (set)
Library of Congress Catalog Card Number 41-51571

COPYRIGHT ©2024 INFORMATION TODAY, INC. All rights reserved. No part of this publication may be reproduced, stored in a retrieval system, or transmitted, in any form or by any means, electronic, mechanical, photocopy, recording or otherwise without the prior written permission of the publisher.

Information Today, Inc. uses reasonable care to obtain accurate and timely information. However, Information Today, Inc. disclaims any liability to any party for any loss or damage caused by errors or omissions in *Literary Market Place*™ whether or not such errors or omissions result from negligence, accident or any other cause.

Information Today, Inc.
143 Old Marlton Pike
Medford, NJ 08055-8750
Phone: 800-300-9868 (Customer Service)
         800-409-4929 (Editorial)
Fax: 609-654-4309
E-mail (orders): custserv@infotoday.com
Web Site: www.infotoday.com

Printed in the United States of America

CONTENTS

VOLUME 1

Preface ix
Abbreviations & Acronyms xi

BOOK PUBLISHERS
U.S. Publishers 1
    U.S. Publishers — Geographic Index 239
    U.S. Publishers — Type of Publication Index 247
    U.S. Publishers — Subject Index 277
Imprints, Subsidiaries & Distributors 333
Canadian Publishers 395

EDITORIAL SERVICES & AGENTS
    Editorial Services — Activity Index 429
Editorial Services 435
Literary Agents 447
Illustration Agents 485
Lecture Agents 487

ASSOCIATIONS, EVENTS, COURSES & AWARDS
    Book Trade & Allied Associations — Index 489
Book Trade & Allied Associations 493
Foundations 525
    Calendar of Book Trade & Promotional Events — Alphabetical Index of Sponsors 527
    Calendar of Book Trade & Promotional Events — Alphabetical Index of Events 531
Calendar of Book Trade & Promotional Events 535
Writers' Conferences & Workshops 553
Courses for the Book Trade 561
Awards, Prize Contests, Fellowships & Grants 569

BOOKS & MAGAZINES FOR THE TRADE
Reference Books for the Trade 681
Magazines for the Trade 699

INDEXES
Company Index 709
Personnel Index 785
Publishers Toll Free Directory 1079
Index to Sections 1089

VOLUME 2

Preface ix
Abbreviations & Acronyms xi

ADVERTISING, MARKETING & PUBLICITY

Advertising Agencies 1099
    Promotional Printing & Allied Services — Activity Index 1101
Promotional Printing & Allied Services 1103
Public Relations Services 1107
Direct Mail Specialists 1115
Mailing, Duplicating & Fax Services 1117
Mailing List Brokers & Services 1119
    Columnists & Commentators — Subject Index 1123
Columnists & Commentators 1125
Book Review Syndicates 1127
Book Review & Index Journals & Services 1129
Book Exhibits 1139
Book Clubs 1141
Book Lists & Catalogs 1145
Serials Featuring Books 1147
News Services & Feature Syndicates 1189
Radio, TV & Cable Networks 1193
Radio Programs Featuring Books 1197
TV Programs Featuring Books 1201

BOOK MANUFACTURING

Complete Book Manufacturing 1207
    Prepress Services Index 1217
Prepress Services 1221
    Printing, Binding & Book Finishing Index 1235
Printing, Binding & Book Finishing 1247
    Manufacturing Materials Index 1263
Manufacturing Materials 1265
    Manufacturing Services & Equipment Index 1275
Manufacturing Services & Equipment 1277

SALES & DISTRIBUTION

Book Distributors & Sales Representatives 1285
    Wholesalers — Activity Index 1305
Wholesalers 1311
Prebinders to Schools & Libraries 1325
Book Exporters & Importers 1327
Export Representatives 1331
Shipping Services 1333
Shipping Suppliers 1337

SERVICES & SUPPLIERS

Consultants — Activity Index 1339
Consultants 1343
Book Producers 1353
Publishing Systems, Services & Technology Index 1359
Publishing Systems, Services & Technology 1363
Employment Agencies 1381
Clipping Bureaus 1383
Typing & Word Processing Services 1385
Translators & Interpreters — Source Language Index 1387
Translators & Interpreters — Target Language Index 1393
Translators & Interpreters 1399
Artists & Art Services — Activity Index 1407
Artists & Art Services 1411
Photographers 1419
Stock Photo Agencies 1427

INDEXES

Company Index 1433
Personnel Index 1465
Index to Sections 1541

Preface

The 2025 edition marks the 85th annual publication of *Literary Market Place*™—the leading directory of the American and Canadian book publishing industry. Covering publishers and literary agents to manufacturers and shipping services, *LMP* is the most comprehensive directory of its kind. The revised 2025 edition contains almost 7,500 entries. Of these listings 1,973 are publishers—including Canadian houses. Together with its companion publication, *International Literary Market Place*™, these directories cover the global book publishing industry.

Organization & Content
Volume 1 covers core publishing industry information: Book Publishers; Editorial Services and Agents; Associations, Events, Courses and Awards; and Books and Magazines for the Trade.

Volume 2 contains information on service providers and suppliers to the publishing industry. Advertising, Marketing and Publicity; Book Manufacturing; Sales and Distribution; and Services and Suppliers can be found in this volume.

Entries generally contain name, address, telephone and other telecommunications data, key personnel, company reportage, branch offices, brief statistics and descriptive annotations. Where applicable, Standard Address Numbers (SANs) have been included. SANs are unique numbers assigned to the addresses of publishers, wholesalers and booksellers. Publishers' entries also contain their assigned ISBN prefixes. Both the SAN and ISBN systems are administered by R.R. Bowker LLC.

Indexes
In addition to the numerous section-specific indexes appearing throughout, each volume of *LMP* contains four indexes that reference listings appearing in that volume. The Industry Indexes cover two distinct areas of data: a Company Index that includes the name, address, communications information and page reference for company listings and a separate Personnel Index that includes the main personnel associated with each entry as well as the page reference. Also included in each volume is an Index to Sections for quickly finding specific categories of information.

A Note to Authors
Prospective authors seeking a publisher should be aware that there are publishers who, as a condition for publishing and marketing an individual's work, may require a significant sum of money be paid to the publisher. This practice is known by a number of terms including author subsidized publishing, author investment, and co-operative publishing. Before entering an agreement involving such a payment, the author is advised to make a careful investigation to determine the standing of the publisher's imprint in the industry.

Similarly, authors seeking literary representation are advised that some agents request a nominal reading fee that may be applied to the agent's commission upon representation. Other agencies may charge substantially higher fees which may not be applicable to a future commission and which are not refundable. The recommended course is to first send a query letter with an outline, sample chapter, and a self-addressed stamped envelope (SASE). Should an agent express interest in handling the manuscript, full details of fees and commissions should be obtained in writing before the complete manuscript is sent. Should an agency require significant advance payment from an author, the author is cautioned to make a careful investigation to determine the agency's standing in the industry before entering an agreement. The author should always retain a copy of the manuscript in his or her possession.

Occasionally, the editors of *LMP* will receive complaints against publishers or agents listed in the work. If, after investigation and review, the editors determine that the complaints are significant and justified, we may exclude the company or individual in question. However, the absence of a listing in *LMP* for any particular publisher or agent should not be construed as a judgment on the legitimacy or integrity of that organization or individual.

Compilation
LMP is updated throughout the year via a number of methods. A request for updated information is sent to current entrants to corroborate and update the information contained on our database. All updates received are edited for the next product release. Those entrants who do not respond to our request may be verified through telephone interviews or online research. Entrants who cannot be verified or who fall short of entry criteria are dropped from the current edition.

Information for new listings is gathered in a similar method. Possible new listings are identified through ongoing research, or when a listing request is received either from the organization itself or from a third party. If sufficient information is not initially gathered to create a listing, a data collection form is provided to the organization to submit essential listing information.

Updated information or suggestions for new listings can be submitted by mail to:

Literary Market Place
Information Today, Inc.
121 Chanlon Rd, Suite G-20
New Providence, NJ 07974-2195

An updating method using the Internet is also available for *LMP* listings:

Visit the *Literary Market Place* web site to update an *LMP* listing. **Literarymarketplace.com** allows you the opportunity to provide new information for a listing by clicking on the "Update or Correct Your Entry" option. The Feedback option on the home page of the web site can be used to suggest new entries as well.

Related Services

Literary Market Place, along with its companion volume *International Literary Market Place*, is available through the Internet at **www.literarymarketplace.com**. Designed to give users simple, logical access to the information they require, the site offers users the choice of searching for data alphabetically, geographically, by type, or by subject. Continuously updated by Information Today's team of editors, this is a truly enhanced version of the *LMP* and *ILMP* databases, incorporating features that make "must-have" information easily available.

Arrangements for placing advertisements in *LMP* can be coordinated through Customer Service by telephone at 609-654-6266, or by e-mail at custserv@infotoday.com.

Your feedback is important to us. We strongly encourage you to contact us with suggestions or comments on the print edition of *LMP*, or its web site. Our editorial office can be reached by telephone at 800-409-4929 (press 3) or 908-219-0277, or by e-mail at khallard@infotoday.com.

The editors would like to thank those entrants who took the time to respond to our requests for current information.

Abbreviations & Acronyms

The following is a list of acronyms & abbreviations used throughout *LMP*.

AALA - Association of American Literary Agents
AB - Alberta
Acct(s) - Account(s)
Acctg - Accounting
Acq(s) - Acquisition(s)
Ad - Advertising
Admin - Administrative, Administration, Administrator
Aff - Affairs
AK - Alaska
AL - Alabama
appt - appointment
Apt - Apartment
AR - Arkansas
Assoc - Associate
Asst - Assistant
AV - Audiovisual
Ave - Avenue
AZ - Arizona

B&W - Black & White
BC - British Columbia
Bd - Board
bio - biography
BISAC - Book Industry Standards and Communications
Bldg - Building
Blvd - Boulevard
Br - Branch
Busn - Business

CA - California
CEO - Chief Executive Officer
CFO - Chief Financial Officer
Chmn - Chairman
Chpn - Chairperson
CIO - Chief Information Officer
Circ - Circulation
CN - Canada
CO - Colorado
Co(s) - Company(-ies)
Co-edns - Co-editions
Coll(s) - College(s)
Comm - Committee
Commun(s) - Communication(s)
Comp - Compiler
Compt - Comptroller
Cont - Controller
Contrib - Contributing
COO - Chief Operating / Operations Officer
Coord - Coordinator
Corp - Corporate, Corporation
Coun - Counsel
CT - Connecticut
Ct - Court
CTO - Chief Technical / Technology Officer

Ctr - Center
Curr - Current
Cust - Customer
CZ - Canal Zone

DC - District of Columbia
DE - Delaware
Dept - Department
Devt - Development
Dir(s) - Director(s)
Dist - Distributed, Distribution, Distributor
Div - Division
Dom - Domestic
Dr - Drive

ed - edition
Ed(s) - Editor(s)
Edit - Editorial
Educ - Education, Educational
El-hi - Elementary-High School
Elem - Elementary
Ency - Encyclopedia
Eng - English
Engg - Engineering
Engr - Engineer
Equip - Equipment
ESL - English as a Second Language
Est - Established
EVP - Executive Vice President
exc - except
Exec - Executive
Expwy - Expressway
ext - extension

Fed - Federal
Fin - Finance, Financial
fl - floor
FL - Florida
Freq - Frequency
Fwy - Freeway

GA - Georgia
Gen - General
Govt - Government
GU - Guam

HD - High-definition
HI - Hawaii
HR - Human Resources
HS - High School
Hwy - Highway

IA - Iowa
ID - Idaho
IL - Illinois
Illus - Illustrator
IN - Indiana
Inc - Incorporated

indiv(s) - individual(s)
Indus - Industrial, Industry
Info - Information
Instl - Institutional
Instn(s) - Institution(s)
Instrl - Instructional
Intl - International
ISBN - International Standard Book Number
ISSN - International Standard Serial Number
IT - Information Technology

Jr - Junior
Jt - Joint
Juv - Juvenile

K - Kindergarten
KS - Kansas
KY - Kentucky

LA - Louisiana
Lang(s) - Language(s)
Lib(s) - Library(-ies)
Libn - Librarian
Lit - Literature

MA - Massachusetts
MB - Manitoba
MD - Maryland
Mdse - Merchandise
Mdsg - Merchandising
ME - Maine
Med - Medical
memb(s) - member(s)
Metro - Metropolitan
Mfg - Manufacturing
Mgmt - Management
Mgr - Manager
MI - Michigan
Mkt(s) - Market(s)
Mktg - Marketing
MN - Minnesota
Mng - Managing
MO - Missouri
mo - month
MS - Mississippi
ms(s) - manuscript(s)
MT - Montana

Natl - National
NB - New Brunswick
NC - North Carolina
ND - North Dakota
NE - Nebraska
NH - New Hampshire
NJ - New Jersey
NL - Newfoundland and Labrador
NM - New Mexico
No - Number

ABBREVIATIONS & ACRONYMS

NS - Nova Scotia
NT - Northwest Territories
NU - Nunavut
NV - Nevada
NY - New York

Off(s) - Office(s)
Offr - Officer
OH - Ohio
OK - Oklahoma
ON - Ontario
Oper(s) - Operation(s)
OR - Oregon

PA - Pennsylvania
Pbk(s) - Paperback(s)
PE - Prince Edward Island
Perms - Permissions
Photo - Photograph
Photog - Photographer, Photography
Pkwy - Parkway
pp - pages
PR - Public Relations
PR - Puerto Rico
Pres - President
Proc - Processing
Prod(s) - Product(s)
Prodn - Production
Prodr - Producer
Prof - Professional, Professor
Prog(s) - Program(s)
Proj(s) - Project(s)
Promo(s) - Promotion(s)
Prop - Proprietor
Pub Aff - Public Affairs

Publg - Publishing
Publr - Publisher
Pubn(s) - Publication(s)
Purch - Purchasing

QC - Quebec

R&D - Research & Development
Rd - Road
Ref - Reference
Reg - Region
Regl - Regional
Rel - Relations
Rep(s) - Representative(s)
Res - Research
RI - Rhode Island
Rm - Room
Rte - Route
Rts - Rights

SAN - Standard Address Number
SASE - Self-Addressed Stamped Envelope
SC - South Carolina
Sci - Science
SD - South Dakota
Secy - Secretary
Serv(s) - Service(s)
SK - Saskatchewan
Soc - Social, Sociology
Spec - Special
Sq - Square
Sr - Senior
St - Saint, Street
Sta - Station
Ste - Sainte

Subn(s) - Subscription(s)
Subs - Subsidiary
Supv - Supervisor
SVP - Senior Vice President
Synd - Syndicated, Syndication

Tech - Technical
Technol - Technology
Tel - Telephone
Terr - Terrace
TN - Tennessee
Tpke - Turnpike
Treas - Treasurer
TX - Texas

UK - United Kingdom
Univ - University
unsol - unsolicited
UT - Utah

V - Vice
VA - Virginia
VChmn - Vice Chairman
VI - Virgin Islands
vol(s) - volume(s)
VP - Vice President
VT - Vermont

WA - Washington
WI - Wisconsin
WV - West Virginia
WY - Wyoming

yr - year
YT - Yukon Territory

Advertising, Marketing & Publicity

Advertising Agencies

Listed here are the principal agencies for book industry advertising.

Accurate Writing & More
16 Barstow Lane, Hadley, MA 01035
Tel: 413-586-2388
Web Site: www.accuratewriting.com; frugalmarketing.com
Key Personnel
Owner & Dir: Shel Horowitz *E-mail:* shel@principledprofit.com
Dir: Dina Friedman
Founded: 1981
Copywriting of book covers, print & radio ads, direct mail pieces, press releases, fliers, brochures, catalog & web page copy, newsletters, other promotional materials. Marketing strategy development emphasizing low cost, high return strategies.
Book Publishing Account(s): All Books; Arts & Farces; Asalako Press; Author House; Autodidactic Press; AWM Books; Bialkin Books; BJB Publishing; bookbrowse.com; Construction Trades Press; CS Publishing; Dr Ivan Delman; Emerald Wave; Enterprise Publishing; Equestrian Press; Equilibrium Press; Firstbooks; ForeWord Magazine; Freedom Publishing; Golden Healing Publishing; Gwent Press; Hope Springs Press; Humble Press; Images from the Past; Inmark Associates; Kitchen Cupboard Press; Liam Works; Life Words; Love Gifts Publishing; Marketing Sherpa; Mindfulness Press; Nehemia & Solomon; Persolog GmbH; Pineapplesoft; Prism Publishing; sitesell.com; Six Strings Press; Space Link Books; United Graphics; Walking Tree Press; John Wiley & Sons; WordMate
Magazine Account(s): Cooperative Life; Related Matters
Other Account(s): adjunction.com; Asian Arts & Antiques; Bart's Homemade; Blue Ridge Office Products; The Body Works; Cate Cummings Book Publicist; Dependable Business Alternatives; Energy Management Consultants; FinancialPlanningforNurses.com; 1stBooks.com; Dr Dan Garfield; Gray Panthers of Brooklyn; Image Marketing; Independent Consultants Network; The Informer; Jones Town & Country Realty; Lorna Kepes; MASSAID; Dr Jonathan Miller; M2 Presswire.net; Naturally First; People Speak; prowebguide.com; Quest Group; Radwell Communications; Ragan Communications; Real Estate Org.com; Rhode Island Folk Music Society; Tom Russell & Associates; Roger Salloom; The Tea House; Hollis Thomases Publicist; Turning Tide Productions; U Mass Family Business Center; Union Car Wash; White Lotus Home

Backe Communications
Radnor Corporate Ctr, Bldg 3, Suite 101, 100 Matson Ford Rd, Radnor, PA 19087
Tel: 610-947-6900
Web Site: www.backemarketing.com
Key Personnel
Pres & CEO: John E Backe *Tel:* 610-947-6900 ext 6901 *E-mail:* jebacke@backemarketing.com
SVP, Client Servs & Strategy: Malcolm Brown *Tel:* 610-947-6900 ext 6904
Full service agency serving the advertising, public relations & corporate communications needs of clients in publishing, healthcare, pharmaceutical, education, high-tech, travel, insurance & other fields. Services include direct mail programs from concept development through list purchases & printing, college adoption programs, journal ads & outserts, complete campaigns & publicity.
Book Publishing Account(s): Dorchester Publishing; McGraw-Hill; Turner White Communications; John Wiley & Sons Inc
Magazine Account(s): Philadelphia Magazine
Other Account(s): Aegis Therapies (Beverly Enterprises); Airgas; Amplifier Research Corp; Alfred Angelo; Arcadia University; Avalon Carpet Tile and Flooring; Berwick Offray LLC; The Bryn Mawr Trust Company; C&D Technologies; Harriet Carter; Charming Shoppes/Fashion Bug; Christiana Care Health System; Civil War Trust; M Cohen & Sons; Comcast; Community Energy; Conrail; Crozer-Keystone Health System; CSS Industries Inc; CVM Engineers; DIA-Drug Information Association; EMC Technology Inc; Eureka Educational Products; Exelon Enterprises; Five Below; Fresh Finds; Gesu School; GlaxoSmithKline; Gloucester County; Haverford Trust; Hill's Main Line Seafood; Independence Visitor Center; Industry Sales Tax Solutions; The Iron Shop; Johnson & Johnson; KidsPeace; The Kirschner Center; Luggage Online; Lutron; Montgomery County Community College; New Wind Energy; Norfolk Southern Corp; Novartis; Omnicare CR; PECO; Peirce-Phelps Viking Culinary Arts Center; Pennsylvania College of Optometry; Philadelphia Zoo; Pizza Hut; The PMA Insurance Group; PNC Asset Management; Portescap; PQ Corp; Robinson Luggage; Rossi Shoe Service; SCA Personal Care; SCP Private Equity Partners; SunGard Data Systems; Susquehanna International Group LLP; TEMEX; Tredegar Performance Films; Triton PCS/SunCom; University of New Haven; Wissahickon Mountain Spring Water; Wyeth

Ted Barkus Co Inc
8017 Anderson St, Philadelphia, PA 19118
Key Personnel
Pres: Allen E Barkus *E-mail:* a.barkus-tbc@att.net
Founded: 1958
Advertising & promotion, public relations.
Magazine Account(s): Travelore Report
Other Account(s): Amana; Bulova; Eureka; Toshiba; Unilever

DJD/Golden Advertising
145 W 28 St, 12th fl, New York, NY 10001
Tel: 212-366-5033 *Fax:* 212-243-5044
E-mail: call@djdgolden.com
Web Site: www.djdgolden.com
Key Personnel
Partner: Marcia Golden *E-mail:* mgolden@djdgolden.com; Dominique Pasqua; Malcolm Petrook; Courtney St Clement
Want to improve sales? Our cost-effective, high response public relations, direct mail & print advertising for campaigns or projects generate business. Just ask our clients. Full service agency with clients nationwide. Also collateral, sales tools, media kits, incentive programs & sales meeting/trade show presentations.
Book Publishing Account(s): Crain Communications Inc; R R Bowker
Magazine Account(s): Business Insurance
Other Account(s): Standard Rate & Data Service

Franklin Advertising Associates Inc
441 Main St, Yarmouth Port, MA 02675
Mailing Address: PO Box 161, Yarmouth Port, MA 02675
Tel: 508-362-7472
E-mail: contact@franklinad.com
Web Site: www.franklinad.com
Key Personnel
Pres: Martin A Summerfield
Founded: 1970
Full service advertising agency.
Book Mfg Account(s): Bound-to-Stay-Bound Books Inc

The Gate Worldwide
71 Fifth Ave, 8th fl, New York, NY 10003
Tel: 212-508-3400 *Fax:* 212-508-3402 (cgi)
E-mail: contact@thegateworldwide.com
Web Site: thegateworldwide.com
Key Personnel
Chief Creative Offr: David Bernstein *Tel:* 212-508-3445 *E-mail:* david.bernstein@thegateworldwide.com
Pres: Beau Fraser *E-mail:* beau.fraser@thegateworldwide.com

ADVERTISING AGENCIES

Financial advertising.
Book Publishing Account(s): Executive Reports Corp; Parker Publishing Company; Prentice-Hall

Julie A Laitin Enterprises Inc
160 West End Ave, Suite 23N, New York, NY 10023
Tel: 917-841-8566
E-mail: info@julielaitin.com
Web Site: www.julielaitin.com
Key Personnel
Pres: Julie A Laitin *E-mail:* jlaitin@julielaitin.com
SVP: Cynthia Amorese
Sr Writer: Ravelle Brickman
Acct Mgr: Martha Hall
Founded: 1982
Full service public relations & marketing. Specialize in healthcare.
Other Account(s): AbelsonTaylor Inc; Closerlook; Flashpoint Medica; HCB Health; MicroMass Communications; Strikeforce; Triple Threat Communications

LK Advertising Agency
Subsidiary of The Linick Group Inc
Linick Bldg, 7 Putter Lane, Middle Island, NY 11953
Mailing Address: PO Box 102, Middle Island, NY 11953-0102
Tel: 631-924-3888; 631-924-8555; 631-604-8599
E-mail: topmarketingadvisor@gmail.com; linickgroup@gmail.com
Key Personnel
Pres: Andrew S Linick, PhD
 E-mail: linickgroup@gmail.com
EVP & Mktg Res Mgr: Roger Dextor
Dir, Spec Projs: Barbara Deal
Copy Chief: Kelly Boyles
Full service creative services: Internet & brand development, consulting, advertising, marketing from initial idea & design through complete fulfillment in the areas of consumer, business & trade. Planning, design, copy & production. Complete art, design & graphics. 12-month direct marketing action/business plans; innovative copy, layout & design through production; business/consumer/trade launch packages for all publishers (newsletters, magazines, books); specialize in circulation promotion, club & continuity plans, mail order selling, creative copy for two-step inquiry/lead generation & conversion packages, trial subscriptions, soft & hard offers, printed premiums, bouncebacks & package inserts & more. Interactive e-direct mail campaigns. Provides comprehensive graphic redesign/new web site content development, interactive services with web site marketing makeover advice for first-time authors, self-publishers, professionals & entrepreneurs. Specializes in online advertising/PR, links to top search engines, consulting on a 100% satisfaction guarantee. Free site evaluation marketing checklist (a $250 value) for LMP readers.
Book Publishing Account(s): American Health Institute; Casino Digest; Copywriter's Council of America; Creative Management Resources Inc; Epic Publishing LLC; Gruman Data Systems Inc; International Hair Research Center; Maclean Authors.com; National Learning Corp; New World Press Books.com; Newsletter Communications Corp; Northern Mortgage Funding Inc; Passport International of New York; Pharmco Inc; The Practical Gourmet
Book Mfg Account(s): B P Publishing Inc; Kroma Lithographers; LK Litho
Magazine Account(s): American Karate; The American Traveler; Combat Karate; Epicurean.com; Epicurean-Traveler.com; Food & Wine; Karate International; Ninja; Official Karate Magazine; The Practical Gourmet; Total Fitness; Travel International
Other Account(s): All Recipes.com; AloeProductsCenter.com; Ambrosia Catering; Casino Digest; Creative Management Resources Inc; The Direct Mail/Mail Order Guild; First-Time Home Buyers Helpline™; Grumman Corp; International Hair Research Center; National Association of Photo Sellers (NAPS); Newsletter Communications Corp; Northern Mortgage Funding Inc; officialkaratemag.com; Passport International of New York; Pharmco Inc; Rand Group Inc; Travel, Tourism, Transportation & Hospitality Advice Line™; whistlekick.com

Donya Melanson Associates
5 Bisson Lane, Merrimac, MA 01860
Tel: 978-346-9240 *Fax:* 978-346-8345
E-mail: dmelanson@dmelanson.com
Web Site: www.dmelanson.com
Key Personnel
Principal: Donya Melanson
Corporate communications, graphic design, advertising, image building.
Book Publishing Account(s): Copley Custom Publishing Group; TechMark; US Department of Agriculture (USDA); US Geological Survey (USGS)
Other Account(s): Cambridge College; The Commonwealth of Massachusetts; Federal Geographic Data Committee (FGDC)

Preston Kelly
222 First Ave NE, Minneapolis, MN 55413
Tel: 612-843-4000 *Fax:* 612-843-3900
E-mail: iconicideas@prestonkelly.com
Web Site: prestonkelly.com
Key Personnel
Pres: Chuck Kelly *Tel:* 612-843-3999
 E-mail: chuck@prestonkelly.com
EVP & Creative Dir: Chris Preston
Full service advertising & public relations agency.
Other Account(s): Be The Match; HealthPartners; Mall of America; Minnesota Zoo; Physicians Mutual; Piper Jaffray; Roundy's Supermarkets Inc; STAGG Chili; Taco John's; Valley Fresh; Wipfli CPAs and Consultants; YMCA

Roth Advertising Inc
PO Box 96, Sea Cliff, NY 11579
Tel: 516-674-8603 *Fax:* 516-368-3885
Web Site: www.rothadvertising.com
Key Personnel
Founder: Charles A Roth *E-mail:* charles@rothadvertising.com
Pres: Daniel J Roth *E-mail:* dan@rothadvertising.com
Founded: 1971
An advertising & marketing services agency for book publishers with special emphasis on the trade, institutional & consumer religious markets.
Book Publishing Account(s): Association of Theological Booksellers; Baylor University Press; BlueBridge; Chicken Soup for the Soul; The Christophers; Convivium Press; Fortress Press; HarperOne; New City Press; Orbis Books; Pauline Books & Media; Paulist Press; Westminster John Knox Press
Magazine Account(s): Commonwealth; Harvard Divinity Bulletin; The Tablet Publishing Co Ltd
Other Account(s): Association of Catholic Publishers; Catholic Media Association (CMA)
Membership(s): Association of Catholic Publishers Inc

The Souza Agency Inc
PO Box 128, Annapolis, MD 21401-0128
Tel: 410-573-1300 *Fax:* 410-573-1305
E-mail: info@souza.com
Web Site: www.souza.com
Key Personnel
Founder: Anthony Souza
Mng Dir: Roseanne Souza
Founded: 1982
Strategic spirit solutions, advertising, marketing & publishing.

Tri-Media Integrated Marketing Technologies Inc
1027 Pelham St, Unit 2, Fonthill, ON L0S 1E0, Canada
Mailing Address: 1027 S Pelham Rd, Unit 2, Welland, ON L3C 3E2, Canada
E-mail: think@tri-media.com
Web Site: tri-media.com
Key Personnel
Founder & CEO: Albert Iannantuono
 E-mail: alberti@tri-media.com
Dir, Creative & Strategy: Nader Ashway
 E-mail: nader@tri-media.com
Dir, Sales: Jim Durkee *E-mail:* jimd@tri-media.com
Dir, Solutions Architect: Rob Martinelli
 E-mail: robm@tri-media.com
Founded: 1986
Integrated marketing communications.

Verso Advertising Inc
79 Madison Ave, 8th fl, New York, NY 10016
Tel: 212-292-2990
Web Site: www.versoadvertising.com
Key Personnel
Pres: Martha Stillman Otis *E-mail:* martha@versoadvertising.com
VP, Group Dir: Jennifer Pasanen
VP, Acct Supv: Christian Toth
Founded: 1989
Full service advertising agency specializing in book publishing.
Book Publishing Account(s): Avon; Basic Books; Berkley Publishing Group; Crown Publishing Group; Dey Street; Dutton; Ecco; Farrar, Straus & Giroux, LLC; HarperCollins; HarperCollins Children's Books; HarperOne; HarperPerennial; Harvard University Press; Henry Holt; Houghton Mifflin Harcourt; Kensington Publishing; Macmillan Children's; William Morrow; W W Norton & Company Inc; Penguin Academic; Penguin Young Readers Group; Putnam; Thames & Hudson; Tor Books; Vintage/Anchor; Workman; Yale University Press
Other Account(s): Association of American Publishers (AAP); Books for a Better Life

Wunderman
Member of WPP Group
3 Columbus Circle, New York, NY 10019
Tel: 212-941-3000
Web Site: www.wunderman.com
Key Personnel
Pres: Jamie Gallo
Chief Creative Offr: Sami Thessman
Integrated marketing services firm with particular emphasis on customer relationship management; direct mail promotion, strong analytics around managing customer data; deliver Internet services, not only web design but e-business strategies; teleservices & database marketing.
Other Account(s): AARP; AT&T; Burger King®; Chevron Corporation; Citigroup Inc; Claro; Colgate-Palmolive Company; Cox Communications Inc; Diageo; EA; Ford; Jaguar Cars; Kraft Foods Inc; L'Oréal; Land Rover; Lufthansa; Microsoft Corporation; Morgan Stanley; MSN; Nationwide; Natura; Nike Inc; Nintendo®; Nokia; Novartis; Novo Nordisk®; Rogers Communications, Inc; Southern California Edison; Telefonica SA; Time Warner; Xerox

Promotional Printing & Allied Services — Activity Index

BINDERS
BR Printers, pg 1103
Linda Kittlitz & Associates, pg 1104
OneTouchPoint, pg 1105
Presskits, pg 1105
Universal Bindery (Sask) Ltd, pg 1105
Universal|Wilde, pg 1105
Viridiam LLC, pg 1106
Whitman Printing & Creative Services LLC, pg 1106

BINDING
BR Printers, pg 1103
Century Direct Solutions LLC, pg 1103
CG Book Printers, pg 1103
Fairfield Marketing Group Inc, pg 1104
The Hibbert Group, pg 1104
OneTouchPoint, pg 1105
V G Reed & Sons Inc, pg 1105
St Joseph Communications-Print Group, pg 1105
Universal|Wilde, pg 1105

BOOKLETS
BR Printers, pg 1103
CG Book Printers, pg 1103
Cypress House, pg 1104
Graphic Litho, pg 1104
Linda Kittlitz & Associates, pg 1104
OneTouchPoint, pg 1105
The Printer, pg 1105
The John Roberts Company, pg 1105
Tribal Print Source, pg 1105
TWIG One Stop, pg 1105
Universal|Wilde, pg 1105
Viridiam LLC, pg 1106
Whitman Printing & Creative Services LLC, pg 1106

BROCHURES, PAMPHLETS
appatura™, A Broadridge Company, pg 1103
Arrow Graphics Inc, pg 1103
BR Printers, pg 1103
Century Direct Solutions LLC, pg 1103
CG Book Printers, pg 1103
The Colad Group LLC, pg 1103
CRW Graphics Communications, pg 1103
Cypress House, pg 1104
Fairfield Marketing Group Inc, pg 1104
Graphic Litho, pg 1104
The Hibbert Group, pg 1104
The Horah Group, pg 1104
Inland Press, pg 1104
Intellicor Communications LLC, pg 1104
Linda Kittlitz & Associates, pg 1104
OneTouchPoint, pg 1105
The Printer, pg 1105
Progress Printing Plus, pg 1105
The John Roberts Company, pg 1105
St Joseph Communications-Print Group, pg 1105
Separa Color, pg 1105
Tribal Print Source, pg 1105
TWIG One Stop, pg 1105
Universal|Wilde, pg 1105
Viridiam LLC, pg 1106
Whitman Printing & Creative Services LLC, pg 1106

DIE-CUTTING
CG Book Printers, pg 1103
City Diecutting Inc, pg 1103
The Colad Group LLC, pg 1103
CRW Graphics Communications, pg 1103
Stephen Gould Corp, pg 1104
Graphic Litho, pg 1104
The Hibbert Group, pg 1104
The Horah Group, pg 1104
The Printer, pg 1105
Progress Printing Plus, pg 1105
The John Roberts Company, pg 1105
Viridiam LLC, pg 1106
Whitman Printing & Creative Services LLC, pg 1106

DISPLAYS
City Diecutting Inc, pg 1103
The Colad Group LLC, pg 1103
Fairfield Marketing Group Inc, pg 1104
Stephen Gould Corp, pg 1104
Graphic Litho, pg 1104
Hannecke Display Systems Inc, pg 1104
Tribal Print Source, pg 1105
Whitman Printing & Creative Services LLC, pg 1106

EDUCATIONAL KITS
BR Printers, pg 1103
City Diecutting Inc, pg 1103
Cypress House, pg 1104
Graphic Litho, pg 1104
Linda Kittlitz & Associates, pg 1104
Tribal Print Source, pg 1105
Universal|Wilde, pg 1105
Whitman Printing & Creative Services LLC, pg 1106

ENGRAVING
CRW Graphics Communications, pg 1103
Regal Press, pg 1105
Whitman Printing & Creative Services LLC, pg 1106

FOLDERS
BR Printers, pg 1103
CG Book Printers, pg 1103
Graphic Litho, pg 1104
Linda Kittlitz & Associates, pg 1104
OneTouchPoint, pg 1105
Presskits, pg 1105
The Printer, pg 1105
The John Roberts Company, pg 1105
Separa Color, pg 1105
Tribal Print Source, pg 1105
TWIG One Stop, pg 1105
Universal Bindery (Sask) Ltd, pg 1105
Universal|Wilde, pg 1105
Viridiam LLC, pg 1106
Whitman Printing & Creative Services LLC, pg 1106

IMPRINTING
Fairfield Marketing Group Inc, pg 1104
The Hibbert Group, pg 1104
Linda Kittlitz & Associates, pg 1104
Tribal Print Source, pg 1105
TWIG One Stop, pg 1105
Universal|Wilde, pg 1105
Viridiam LLC, pg 1106

MOUNTING & FINISHING
City Diecutting Inc, pg 1103
Graphic Litho, pg 1104
Tribal Print Source, pg 1105

PHOTOGRAPHY
AP Images, pg 1103
Linda Kittlitz & Associates, pg 1104
The Printer, pg 1105
RRD Manchester, pg 1105

POSTERS
Arrow Graphics Inc, pg 1103
BR Printers, pg 1103
CG Book Printers, pg 1103
City Diecutting Inc, pg 1103
The Colad Group LLC, pg 1103
CRW Graphics Communications, pg 1103
Stephen Gould Corp, pg 1104
Graphic Litho, pg 1104
The Horah Group, pg 1104
The Printer, pg 1105
The John Roberts Company, pg 1105
Separa Color, pg 1105
Tribal Print Source, pg 1105
TWIG One Stop, pg 1105
Universal|Wilde, pg 1105
Viridiam LLC, pg 1106
Whitman Printing & Creative Services LLC, pg 1106

PRINTING
appatura™, A Broadridge Company, pg 1103
Bolger Vision Beyond Print, pg 1103
BR Printers, pg 1103
Century Direct Solutions LLC, pg 1103
CG Book Printers, pg 1103
City Diecutting Inc, pg 1103
Cliff Digital, pg 1103
The Colad Group LLC, pg 1103
CRW Graphics Communications, pg 1103
RR Donnelley Marketing Solutions, pg 1104
Double Envelope, pg 1104
Fairfield Marketing Group Inc, pg 1104
Graphic Litho, pg 1104
The Hibbert Group, pg 1104
The Horah Group, pg 1104
Inland Press, pg 1104
Intellicor Communications LLC, pg 1104
Interprint Web Printing, pg 1104
Linda Kittlitz & Associates, pg 1104
OneTouchPoint, pg 1105
The Printer, pg 1105
Progress Printing Plus, pg 1105
V G Reed & Sons Inc, pg 1105
Regal Press, pg 1105
St Joseph Communications-Print Group, pg 1105
Tribal Print Source, pg 1105
TWIG One Stop, pg 1105
Universal|Wilde, pg 1105
Viridiam LLC, pg 1106
Whitman Printing & Creative Services LLC, pg 1106

PROMOTIONAL BOXES
City Diecutting Inc, pg 1103
Graphic Litho, pg 1104
Linda Kittlitz & Associates, pg 1104
The John Roberts Company, pg 1105
Tribal Print Source, pg 1105
Universal|Wilde, pg 1105
Whitman Printing & Creative Services LLC, pg 1106

SILK SCREEN
City Diecutting Inc, pg 1103
Cliff Digital, pg 1103
CRW Graphics Communications, pg 1103
Stephen Gould Corp, pg 1104
Linda Kittlitz & Associates, pg 1104
TWIG One Stop, pg 1105

PROMOTIONAL PRINTING & ALLIED SERVICES — ACTIVITY INDEX

SLIP CASES
City Diecutting Inc, pg 1103
Linda Kittlitz & Associates, pg 1104
Whitman Printing & Creative Services LLC, pg 1106

TYPOGRAPHY
appatura™, A Broadridge Company, pg 1103
Arrow Graphics Inc, pg 1103
CG Book Printers, pg 1103
Cliff Digital, pg 1103
CRW Graphics Communications, pg 1103
Cypress House, pg 1104
Fairfield Marketing Group Inc, pg 1104
Linda Kittlitz & Associates, pg 1104
RRD Manchester, pg 1105
TWIG One Stop, pg 1105
UniversalIWilde, pg 1105
Whitman Printing & Creative Services LLC, pg 1106

VARNISHING
CG Book Printers, pg 1103
CRW Graphics Communications, pg 1103
Graphic Litho, pg 1104
UniversalIWilde, pg 1105
Viridiam LLC, pg 1106
Whitman Printing & Creative Services LLC, pg 1106

Promotional Printing & Allied Services

The following firms are active in the production of promotional material–direct mail pieces, posters, displays, etc. For lists of book compositors, printers and binders, see the sections entitled **Prepress Services** and **Printing, Binding & Book Finishing**.

AP Images
Division of Associated Press (AP)
200 Liberty St, New York, NY 10281
Toll Free Tel: 844-777-2006
E-mail: info@ap.org
Web Site: newsroom.ap.org/editorial-photos-videos/home
News & historical photographs. Assignment photography, domestic & foreign. Digital photo transmission to & from most locations; online photo archive.

appatura™, A Broadridge Company
Division of Broadridge Financial Solutions Inc
65 Challenger Rd, Suite 400, Ridgefield Park, NJ 07660
Tel: 201-508-6000 Toll Free Tel: 800-277-2155
E-mail: contactus@appatura.com
Web Site: www.appatura.com
Key Personnel
CEO: Richard Plotka
CIO: Faisal Fareed
Chief Prod Offr: Harsh Choudhary
Chief Strategy Offr: John Closson
Head, Fin: Alpha Diarra
Full services direct marketing company including: desktop publishing/electronic prepress, digital-on-demand print, offset print, automated mailing & literature fulfillment from data to distribution.

Arrow Graphics Inc
PO Box 380291, Cambridge, MA 02238
E-mail: info@arrow1.com
Web Site: www.arrow1.com
Key Personnel
Pres: Alvart Badalian
Sr Graphic/Pubn Designer: Aramais Andonian
Founded: 1988
Complete book production services with state-of-the-art electronic design & publishing capabilities: copy-editing; indexing; typesetting & composition; typography; design & art direction from concept to finished product; printing; consultation; project management. Novels, poetry, monographs, self-help, how-to, guides, ebooks & children's picture books. From ms to camera-ready to bound book, serving the publishing industry & self-publishing community. Call or write for free information, or visit our web site.

Bolger Vision Beyond Print
3301 Como Ave SE, Minneapolis, MN 55414-2809
Tel: 651-645-6311 Toll Free Tel: 866-264-3287
E-mail: contact@bolgerinc.com
Web Site: www.bolgerinc.com
Key Personnel
CEO: Dik Bolger E-mail: dbolger@bolgerinc.com
Mktg Mgr: Kristen Stradinger
 E-mail: kstradinger@bolgerinc.com
Founded: 1934
Full service commercial printer, digital printing, print on demand, variable print, technology solutions, mailing, fulfillment & distribution. Specialty products include college publications, catalogs, marketing product brochures, direct mail, luxury print.

BR Printers
665 Lenfest Rd, San Jose, CA 95133
Tel: 408-278-7711 Fax: 408-929-8062
E-mail: info@brprinters.com
Web Site: www.brprinters.com
Key Personnel
Pres: Adam DeMaestri E-mail: adam@brprinters.com
VP & Chief Strategy Offr: David Gall
SVP, Sales: Derek Giulianelli Tel: 303-916-5346 (cell) E-mail: derek@brprinters.com
VP, Fin: Carina Follante
VP, KY Off: Chris Gerhold
Dir, HR: Kathryn Torre
Gen Mgr, CA Off: James Barrios
Founded: 1992
Leading provider of digital printing products. Based in San Jose, CA, with a production facility in Independence, KY & mailing & fulfillment operation in Denver, CO. The company's product portfolio includes self-publishing solutions, print-on-demand, short run publications, web-to-print, rebinds, wide format, promotional products, direct e-mail, fulfillment & other digital printing solutions.
Branch Office(s)
10154 Toebben Dr, Independence, KY 41051

Century Direct Solutions LLC
15 Enter Lane, Islandia, NY 11749
Tel: 212-763-0600
E-mail: contact@centurydirect.net
Web Site: www.centurydirect.net
Key Personnel
VP, Sales & Busn Devt: Martin A Rego
 E-mail: regom@centurydirect.net
Founded: 1932
Direct mail, newsletters, publications & catalogs are our specialty; electronic prepress, full binding, in-house lettershop.
Membership(s): Direct Mail Fundraisers Association (DMFA); Greater Hudson Valley Postal Customers Council; Greater New York Postal Customers Council; Hudson Valley Direct Marketing Association

CG Book Printers
Division of Corporate Graphics Commercial (CGC)
1750 Northway Dr, North Mankato, MN 56003
Tel: 507-388-3300 Toll Free Tel: 800-729-7575
 Fax: 507-386-6350
E-mail: cgbooks@corpgraph.com
Web Site: www.corpgraph.com
Key Personnel
Pres: Dan Kvasnicka Tel: 507-386-6340
 Fax: 507-344-5548 E-mail: dekvasnicka@corpgraph.com
Sales Exec, Book Mfg Sales: Mike Schmitt
 Tel: 507-386-6349 E-mail: mjschmitt@corpgraph.com
Founded: 1989
CG Book Printers currently provides book manufacturing services for publishers who sell product to school library & trade markets. In addition, we offer fulfillment services for those publishers wishing to maintain their inventories in the same location where their books are manufactured.
We bind books in hard case & paperback formats. We use Smyth sewn, side sew & adhesive bound for hard case trade or library bound books & section sew, or adhesive bind for paperback books.

City Diecutting Inc
Affiliate of Bookdisplays LLC
One Cory Rd, Morristown, NJ 07960
Tel: 973-270-0370 Fax: 973-270-0369
E-mail: sales@bookdisplays.com
Web Site: www.bookdisplays.com
Key Personnel
Pres & CEO: Eric De Vos E-mail: edevos@bookdisplays.com
VP, Sales: Frank Matonti E-mail: fmatonti@bookdisplays.com
Founded: 1989
Retail point of purchase corrugated displays for books & AV materials. In-stock displays for most standard trim sizes. 4-color branding on headers/risers. Custom displays for national rollouts.
Membership(s): American Booksellers Association (ABA); Independent Book Publishers Association (IBPA)

Cliff Digital
14700 S Main St, Gardena, CA 90248
Tel: 310-323-5600 Toll Free Tel: 866-429-2242
 Fax: 310-400-3090
E-mail: cliff@cliffdigital.com
Web Site: www.cliffdigital.com
Key Personnel
Owner: Dave Thomas
Prodn Mgr: Paolo Johnson
Large format printer, banners, murals, vinyl decals, prototype products, backdrops, t-shirts, movie props, screen printing & design.

The Colad Group LLC
693 Seneca St, 5th fl, Buffalo, NY 14210
Tel: 716-961-1776 Toll Free Tel: 800-950-1755
 Fax: 716-961-1753
E-mail: info@colad.com
Web Site: www.colad.com
Key Personnel
Pres: Todd Anson
Founded: 1947
Printer of film laminated paperboard products; also specializes in turned edge binders.

Corporate Graphics Book Printers, see CG Book Printers

CRW Graphics Communications
9100 Pennsauken Hwy, Pennsauken, NJ 08110
Tel: 856-662-9111 Toll Free Tel: 800-820-3000
 Fax: 856-665-1789
E-mail: info@crwgraphics.com
Web Site: www.crwgraphics.com
Key Personnel
Pres: David Carpenter
EVP: George Slater
VP, Sales & Mktg: Will Glassman
 E-mail: wglassman@crwgraphics.com
Cust Serv Mgr: Rich Quigley E-mail: rquigley@crwgraphics.com
High quality, multicolor sheetfed printing for promotional materials & short-medium run books, journals, magazines & book covers/jackets. In-house bindery with hand assembly, die-cutting

& Ultra-Kote UV coating. Prepress services include extensive electronic & conventional capabilities: type, comp, color separations, DTP service bureau, with digitally imposed output. Three shift conventional make-up & stripping, Opticopy & Misomex imposing. Full range of direct digital & film based proofing. Specialize in getting you from desktop to press with all your book & book promotional projects. Expert technical support & customer service.

Cypress House
Imprint of Comp-Type Inc
155 Cypress St, Suite A, Fort Bragg, CA 95437
Tel: 707-964-9520 *Toll Free Tel:* 800-773-7782
 Fax: 707-964-7531
E-mail: office@cypresshouse.com
Web Site: www.cypresshouse.com
Key Personnel
Pres: Cynthia Frank *E-mail:* cynthia@cypresshouse.com
Mng Ed: Joe Shaw *E-mail:* joeshaw@cypresshouse.com
Founded: 1986
Complete editorial, design, production, marketing & promotion services to independent publishers. Promotional services offered are typography, print brokering, editorial, copywriting, copy-editing & publicity.

RR Donnelley Marketing Solutions
35 W Wacker Dr, Chicago, IL 60601
Toll Free Tel: 800-742-4455
Web Site: www.rrd.com/services/marketing
Key Personnel
Pres, Mktg Solutions: Doug Ryan
A premier provider of sophisticated direct mail programs. We specialize in highly customized 1-to-1 communications, advanced production technology, project management & direct marketing services. RR Donnelley can help you break out of everyday direct mail to produce results beyond expected. From strategy & design to execution, RR Donnelley offers the knowledge that delivers.

Double Envelope
Subsidiary of BSC Ventures LLC
7702 Plantation Rd, Roanoke, VA 24019
Toll Free Tel: 800-800-9007
E-mail: inquire@double-envelope.com
Web Site: www.double-envelope.com
Key Personnel
Pres & CEO: Brian Sass
EVP, Opers: Jonathan M Peyton
EVP, Sales: John Draper
Gen Mgr: Bill Howell
Founded: 1917
Manufacturing of commercial, custom printed & specialty envelopes for the transactional & direct mail industries.
Branch Office(s)
2500 NE 39 Ave, Gainesville, FL 32609, Gen Mgr: Wayne Honeycutt *Toll Free Tel:* 800-543-5275
100 Woodhull Dr, Angola, IN 46703, Gen Mgr: Richard R McElrath *Toll Free Tel:* 800-466-9653
532 E 25 St, Baltimore, MD 21218, Gen Mgr: Lisa Kline *Toll Free Tel:* 800-822-6537

Fairfield Marketing Group Inc
Subsidiary of FMG Inc
830 Sport Hill Rd, Easton, CT 06112-1241
E-mail: info@fairfieldmarketing.com
Key Personnel
Pres & CEO: Edward P Washchilla, Jr
 E-mail: ed@fairfieldmarketing.com
Founded: 1986
Specialists in mailing list brokerage & list management services. FMG clients rely on us for annual direct marketing programs. We are customer driven & accommodate. Specialty services: custom designed account management; expedient list rental approval; monthly usage reports; market & account analyses; fulfillment, mailing & mail response services; freelance art work; graphic design; advertising & promotional copywriting; binding services; lettershop services; computer services. FMG is a full service direct mail marketing firm.
Membership(s): American Booksellers Association (ABA); Bridgeport Regional Business Council (BRBC); Education Market Association; United States Chamber of Commerce (USCC)

Stephen Gould Corp
35 S Jefferson Rd, Whippany, NJ 07981
Tel: 973-428-1500; 973-428-1510
E-mail: info@stephengould.com
Web Site: www.stephengould.com
Key Personnel
CEO: Michael Golden
CFO: Anthony Lupo
Pres: Justin Golden
EVP: John Golden
Cont: Kim Ings
Dir, Info Systems: Nanette Rosenbaum
Dir, Opers: Jason Rosario
Founded: 1939
Manufacturers & designers of corrugated & chipboard displays. Die-cutting, letterpress, offset, posters, silk screen, decorative foam.

Graphic Litho
Division of High Speed Process Printing Corp
130 Shepard St, Lawrence, MA 01843
Tel: 978-683-2766 *Fax:* 978-681-7588
E-mail: sales@graphiclitho.com
Web Site: www.graphiclitho.com
Key Personnel
Pres: Ralph E Wilbur
Founded: 1960
Services provided include printing & mailing of promotional literature, POP, book stands & displays, backlit displays, large store & window signage, life-size standees. Our products are produced on presses & equipment capable of printing sheet sizes up to 54 x 77 inches & folding sheet sizes up to 44 x 76 inches.
Membership(s): Print Services & Distribution Association (PSDA); Printing Industries of New England (PINE); PRINTING United Alliance

Hannecke Display Systems Inc
210 Grove St, Franklin, MA 02038
Tel: 774-235-2329
E-mail: info@hannecke.com
Web Site: www.hannecke.com
Key Personnel
Owner & CEO: Cuno Von Olenhusen
Design & manufacture patented point of purchase & in-store display systems for books & magazines, audio & video cassettes, CD & boxed software & other packaged products.

The Hibbert Group
400 Pennington Ave, Trenton, NJ 08650
Tel: 609-394-7500 *Toll Free Tel:* 888-HIBBERT (442-2378)
E-mail: info@hibbertgroup.com
Web Site: hibbert.com
Key Personnel
Co-Chmn & CEO: Timothy J Moonan
Co-Chmn & SVP, Sales & Mktg: Thomas J Moonan
Cont, Fin: Zobeida Madera-Zapf
SVP, Fin: George Dowbnia
SVP, IT: Kenneth J Swiatkowski
SVP, Sales: Michelle Spedding
VP, Cust & IT: Hussain Moochalla
VP, HR: Reney Cherian
VP, IT: Fran Kerr
In-house digital & offset print applications; product fulfillment.
Branch Office(s)
1100 US Hwy 130, Robbinsville, NJ 08691 (dist ctr)
19521 E 32 Pkwy, Aurora, CO 80011-8141 (dist ctr)
890 Ships Landing Way, New Castle, DE 19720 (dist ctr)

The Horah Group
Subsidiary of Personalized Mobile LLC
351 Manville Rd, Suite 105, Pleasantville, NY 10570
Tel: 914-495-3200 *Fax:* 914-769-8802
Web Site: www.horah.com
Key Personnel
Pres: Richard Goldsmith *E-mail:* dgoldsmith@horah.com
Founded: 1981
Direct marketing production agency; full service lettershop.

Inland Press
Subsidiary of Detroit Legal News
2001 W Lafayette Blvd, Detroit, MI 48216
Tel: 313-961-6000
Web Site: www.inlandpress.com
Key Personnel
Pres & CEO: Bradley L Thompson, II
 E-mail: bthompson@inlandpress.com
CFO: Steve Fowler *E-mail:* sfowler@inlandpress.com
Founded: 1895
Commercial printing & publisher.
Membership(s): Book Manufacturers' Institute (BMI); Great Lakes Graphics Association (GLGA); PRINTING United Alliance

Intellicor Communications LLC
330 Eden Rd, Lancaster, PA 17601
Toll Free Tel: 800-233-0107
Web Site: www.intellicor.com
Commercial printing, mailing & marketing.

Interprint Web Printing
Subsidiary of Morten Inc
12350 US 19 N, Clearwater, FL 33764
Tel: 727-531-8957 *Toll Free Tel:* 800-749-5152
 Fax: 727-536-0647
E-mail: info@interprintwebprinting.com
Web Site: www.interprintwebprinting.com
Key Personnel
CEO: Scott J Morten
Founded: 1965
Commercial printing: sheetfed & heat-set, web offset; magazine printing, catalog & direct mail.
Membership(s): Printing Industries of Florida (PIF)

Linda Kittlitz & Associates
193 Coleridge St, San Francisco, CA 94110-5112
Tel: 415-550-8898 *Toll Free Tel:* 800-550-8898
 Fax: 415-550-7975
Web Site: www.lkandassociates.com
Key Personnel
Owner: Linda G Kittlitz *E-mail:* linda@lkandassociates.com
Founded: 1990
Promotional products distributor, packaging, printing, embroidery & graphic design. Products include T-shirts, caps, pens, key tags, sports balls & embroidery.
Membership(s): Promotional Marketing Association of California (PMANC); Promotional Products Association International (PPAI); Visual Media Alliance (VMA)

Neibauer Press
20 Industrial Dr, Warminster, PA 18974
Tel: 215-322-6200 *Fax:* 215-322-2495

E-mail: sales@neibauer.com
Web Site: www.neibauer.com
Key Personnel
VP: Ruth Neibauer-Baker *Tel:* 215-322-6216
    E-mail: ruth@neibauer.com
Founded: 1955
Full service, family owned printing & publishing company. Services include copy & design, direct mail printing, shipping, warehousing, pick & pack & fulfillment.

OneTouchPoint
1225 Walnut Ridge Dr, Hartland, WI 53029
Tel: 262-369-6000 *Toll Free Tel:* 800-332-2348
    Fax: 262-369-5647
E-mail: info@1touchpoint.com
Web Site: www.1touchpoint.com
Key Personnel
CEO: Dave Holland
Dir, Mktg & Sales Opers: Carey Howard
Founded: 1982
Online & offline marketing execution capabilities combined with an adaptive technology interface & a national tem of solution innovators & domain experts to help companies across industry sectors create consistent & meaningful engagements with end consumers regardless of channel, medium or location. We produce & distribute beautifully crafted print, point of purchase, campaign & promotional materials, as easily as we can create targeted, personalized outreach based on customer value or lifecycle stage.
Branch Office(s)
5241 Voges Rd, Madison, WI 53718 *Tel:* 608-838-9147
525 W Alameda Dr, Suite 101, Tempe, AZ 85282, Contact: James Parker *Tel:* 480-966-4003 *Fax:* 480-966-4016
5280 Joliet St, Denver, CO 80239 *Tel:* 303-227-1400
1441 Western Ave, Cincinnati, OH 45214
    Tel: 513-421-1600
8410-B Tuscany Way, Austin, TX 78754
    Tel: 512-454-6874

Presskits
Subsidiary of Ardmore Graphic Services Inc
PO Box 71, East Walpole, MA 02032
Toll Free Tel: 800-472-3497
E-mail: files@presskits.com; team@presskits.com
Web Site: presskits.com
Key Personnel
Owner & Pres: Tom Spiegel
Founded: 1986
Manufacturer of pocket folders, video sleeves, CD & disk mailers, packaging, portfolios, three-ring binders & sales kits for solutions to your packaging & folder needs.

The Printer
2810 Cowell Blvd, Davis, CA 95618
Tel: 530-753-2519 *Fax:* 530-753-2528
E-mail: info@the-printer.net
Web Site: the-printer.net
Key Personnel
Owner & Estimator: Howard Galbreath
Founded: 1966
Offset sheetfed & digital printing.
Membership(s): National Foundation of Independent Businesses (NFIB)

Progress Printing Plus
2677 Waterlick Rd, Lynchburg, VA 24502
Tel: 434-239-9213 *Toll Free Tel:* 800-572-7804
    Fax: 434-832-7573
E-mail: info@progressprintplus.com
Web Site: www.progressprintplus.com
Key Personnel
Pres: Michael Thornton *E-mail:* mthornton@progressprintplus.com
Dir, Busn Devt: Gerald Bowles
    E-mail: gbowles@progressprintplus.com
Founded: 1962
Brochures, catalogs, publications, pamphlets, die-cutting & general commercial printing.

V G Reed & Sons Inc
1002 S 12 St, Louisville, KY 40210-1302
Toll Free Tel: 800-635-9788 *Fax:* 502-560-0197
Web Site: www.vgreed.com
Key Personnel
Pres: Bobby Reed, Sr
VP, Natl Sales: Scott W Reed
Founded: 1938
Full service provider of print & fulfillment for the pharmaceutical, manufacturing, consumer products, financial services & healthcare industries. ISO 9001-2015 certified & cGMP compliant.

Regal Press
79 Astor Ave, Norwood, MA 02062
Tel: 781-769-3900 *Toll Free Tel:* 800-447-3425
    Fax: 781-769-7361
E-mail: info@regalpress.com
Web Site: www.regalpress.com
Key Personnel
VP, Sales: Mike Simone *E-mail:* msimone@regalpress.com
Commercial printer. Offset printing, digital printing, thermography, foil stamping, embossing, engraving & custom products.

The John Roberts Company
9687 East River Rd NW, Minneapolis, MN 55433
Tel: 763-755-5500 *Toll Free Tel:* 800-551-1534
    Fax: 763-755-0394
E-mail: success@johnroberts.com
Web Site: www.johnroberts.com; www.facebook.com/TheJohnRobertsCompany
Key Personnel
CEO: Michael Keene *Tel:* 763-754-4401
    E-mail: mrk@johnroberts.com
CFO: Mike Thews *Tel:* 763-754-4303
    E-mail: thews@johnroberts.com
Pres: Marnie Janezich *Tel:* 763-754-4327
    E-mail: marnie.keene@johnroberts.com
Cont: Chantelle Butcher *Tel:* 763-754-4333
    E-mail: chantelle.butcher@johnroberts.com
EVP, Sales: Mark Carlson *Tel:* 763-754-4404
    E-mail: mark.carlson@johnroberts.com
VP, Opers: Scott Zorn *Tel:* 763-754-4416
    E-mail: scott.zorn@johnroberts.com
Dir, Client Servs: Emily Schultz *Tel:* 763-754-4445 *E-mail:* emily.schultz@johnroberts.com
Dir, HR: Debby Boyd *Tel:* 763-754-4366
    E-mail: dboyd@johnroberts.com
Dir, Mktg: Kyle Kennedy *Tel:* 763-754-4364
    E-mail: kyle.kennedy@johnroberts.com
Founded: 1951
Full service commercial, catalog & direct response printing company. Specialize in inserts, catalogs, corporate collateral annual reports, brochures & direct mail, direct to plate, 6-color sheetfed & web printing, die-cutting, full bindery, mailing services, fulfillment services.

RRD Manchester
151 Red Stone Rd, Manchester, CT 06042
Tel: 860-649-5570 *Fax:* 860-649-7800
Web Site: www.rrdonnelley.com/commercial-print/location/rr-donnelley-manchester
Printing & typography.

St Joseph Communications-Print Group
50 Macintosh Blvd, Concord, ON L4K 4P3, Canada
Tel: 905-660-3111
E-mail: marketing@stjoseph.com
Web Site: stjoseph.com
Key Personnel
Pres: John Gagliano
EVP, Sales & Mktg: Ray D'Antonio
VP & Gen Mgr: Ryan Anderson
Camera, film stripping, saddlestitch & perfect binding, shrink wrapping & mailing. Involved in the production of magazines, booklets, catalogs & advertising material; creative market research.
Branch Office(s)
119 Snow Blvd, Concord, ON L4K 4N9, Canada
    Tel: 905-695-8544
1165 Kenaston St, Ottawa, ON K1G 6S1, Canada
    Tel: 613-729-4303

Scott Publications Inc
2145 W Sherman Blvd, Norton Shores, MI 49441
Tel: 231-755-2200 *Toll Free Tel:* 866-733-9382
    Fax: 231-755-1003
E-mail: contactus@scottpublications.com
Web Site: scottpublications.com
Key Personnel
Pres: Robert H Keessen *E-mail:* rkeessen@scottpublications.com
Publr: Ruth M Keessen
Ed: Kelly Herrold *E-mail:* kherrold@scottpublications.com
Founded: 2001
Publish craft magazines & books.

Separa Color
6951 Oran Circle, Buena Park, CA 90621
Tel: 818-988-2882 *Toll Free Tel:* 800-859-0629
    Fax: 818-988-3882
E-mail: sales@separacolor.com
Web Site: www.separacolor.com; www.simplybrochures.com; www.simplycatalogs.com; www.simplypostcards.com
Key Personnel
Pres: David C Field

Tribal Print Source
Division of Southern California Tribal Chairman's Association
36146 Pala Temecula Rd, Bldg J, Pala, CA 92059
Mailing Address: 35008 Pala Temecula Rd, PMB 436, Pala, CA 92059
Tel: 760-597-2650
E-mail: sales@tribalprintsource.com
Web Site: www.tribalprintsource.com
Founded: 2003

TWIG One Stop
10444 White Pinto Ct, Lake Worth, FL 33449
Tel: 561-588-0244 *Toll Free Tel:* 855-894-4178
E-mail: info@twigonestop.com
Web Site: www.twigonestop.com
Key Personnel
Owner: Ike Thaler *E-mail:* ike@twigonestop.com
Founded: 1997
Full service promotional company specializing in: full color printing, graphic design, direct mail services & promotional items.

Universal Bindery (Sask) Ltd
516-A Duchess St, Saskatoon, SK S7K 0R1, Canada
Tel: 306-652-8313 *Toll Free Tel:* 888-JOE-MENU (563-6368) *Fax:* 306-244-2994
E-mail: gib@unibindery.com
Key Personnel
Pres: Gilbert Davis
Founded: 1966

Universal|Wilde
26 Dartmouth St, Westwood, MA 02090
Tel: 781-251-2700 *Fax:* 781-251-2613
Web Site: www.universalwilde.com
Key Personnel
Pres & CEO: Stephen Flood
COO: Christopher Armstrong
CFO: Joe Musanti
VP, HR: Jennifer MacAskill

PROMOTIONAL PRINTING & ALLIED SERVICES

VP, Sales: Jim Bailey
Mktg Mgr: Ryan Collins
Founded: 1958
Full service marketing communications company that can deliver end-to-end solutions: creative services. integrated print, lettershop/direct mail services, fulfillment & distribution services. Also premiums & incentives for trade show giveaways, gift with purchase, direct mail programs & advertising specialties.
Branch Office(s)
403 VFW Dr, Rockland, MA 02370 *Tel:* 781-871-7744 *Fax:* 781-878-2967
48 Third Ave, Somerville, MA 02143 *Tel:* 617-591-3000 *Fax:* 617-591-3091

Viridiam LLC
3030 Lowell Dr, Green Bay, WI 54311
Tel: 920-465-3030 *Toll Free Tel:* 800-829-6555
Web Site: www.viridiam.com
Key Personnel
VP, Sales: Rob Butler
Filing products, custom index tabs, print services & marketing services.

Whitman Printing & Creative Services LLC
PO Box 1681, Batavia, NY 14020
Tel: 516-294-5350 *Fax:* 516-294-5239
E-mail: info@whitmanprinting.com
Web Site: www.whitmanprinting.com

Key Personnel
Owner: Rebecca L Almeter *E-mail:* becky@whitmanprinting.com
Founded: 1996
Print services company that specializes in direct mail & printing solutions.
Membership(s): Direct Marketing Club of New York (DMCNY); Mailing & Fulfillment Service Association (MFSA); Print Services & Distribution Association (PSDA)

Public Relations Services

The public relations firms listed below handle book and library accounts and can undertake special campaigns for publishers and authors.

Accurate Writing & More
16 Barstow Lane, Hadley, MA 01035
Tel: 413-586-2388
Web Site: www.accuratewriting.com; frugalmarketing.com
Key Personnel
Owner & Dir: Shel Horowitz *E-mail:* shel@principledprofit.com
Dir: Dina Friedman
Founded: 1981
Press releases, public service announcements, public relations strategy, online public relations, client biographies, backgrounders, media kits, pitch letters, web page content & newsletters & marketing plans.
Publishing Account(s): All Books; Arts & Farces; Asalako Press; Author House; Autodidactic Press; AWM Books; Bialkin Books; BJB Publishing; Construction Trades Press; CS Publishing; Dr Ivan Delman; Emerald Wave; Enterprise Publishing; Equestrian Press; Equilibrium Press; 1stBooks.com; Freedom Publishing; Golden Healing Publishing; Green Island Audio Books; Gwent Press; Hope Springs Press; Humble Press; Images from the Past; Inmark Associates; Jenkins Group; Kitchen Cupboard Press; Liam Works; Life Tools Press; Life Words; MarketingSherpa.com; Maverick Spirit Press; Mindblazer.com; Mindfulness Press; Nehemia & Solomon; Peanut Butter & Jelly Press; Persolog GmbH; Pineapplesoft; Prism Publishing; Publishinggame.com; Related Matters Newsletter; Six Strings Press; Space Link Books; United Graphics; Walking Tree Press; John Wiley & Sons; WordMate

Alice B Acheson
Unit of Acheson-Greub Inc
PO Box 735, Friday Harbor, WA 98250
Tel: 360-378-5850 *Fax:* 360-378-2815
E-mail: aliceba7@gmail.com
Web Site: sites.google.com/view/alice-b-acheson
Founded: 1981
Consultation in all aspects of publicity (launching, reviews, interviews, press materials) & marketing for publishers, booksellers & authors. Specialize in assisting authors & independent presses enter the mainstream +/or improve expertise through enhanced contacts, timing, positioning, rights sales & distribution. Former recipient of the Literary Market Place Award Honoring Excellence in Book Publishing, Outside Services - Advertising/Promotion/Publicity.
Publishing Account(s): Mountain Dog Books; New Libri Press; Thoughtcatcher Publishing
Membership(s): Independent Book Publishers Association (IBPA); Pacific Northwest Booksellers Association (PNBA); Pacific Northwest Writers Association; Publishers' Publicity Association

Antonia Hall Communications
9663 Santa Monica Blvd, No 1128, Beverly Hills, CA 90210
Tel: 707-234-9738
E-mail: ahcassociates@gmail.com
Web Site: www.antoniahallcommunications.com
Key Personnel
Founder & Principal: Antonia Hall
Founded: 1996
Provides services for authors, filmmakers, politicians, philanthropists & other visionaries. We have garnered media attention on top radio & television shows & in the most influential newspapers, magazines & blogs. We also offer event planning & product launches. We successfully blend creative strategies & knowledgeable expertise for all of your promotional needs: publicity services, social media campaigns, search engine optimization (SEO) enhanced copywriting, marketing materials & superior customer service.
Publishing Account(s): Berrett-Koehler Publishers; CreateSpace; DVG Publishing; Estrella Catarina; Findhorn Press; Quest Books; Winter Goose Publications
Membership(s): Book Promotion Forum

Ascot Media Group Inc
PO Box 2394, Friendswood, TX 77549
Tel: 832-334-2733 *Toll Free Tel:* 800-854-1134
Toll Free Fax: 800-854-2207
Web Site: www.ascotmedia.com
Key Personnel
CEO: Trish Stevens *E-mail:* tstevens@ascotmediagroup.com
Mgmt: Vivian Franco *E-mail:* vfranco@ascotmediagroup.com; Kim McCall *E-mail:* kmccall@ascotmediagroup.com
Founded: 2003
PR services for authors & publishers include TV & radio interviews; reviews & articles in newspapers & magazines; Internet viral campaigns.

Stephanie Barko Literary Publicist
Austin, TX 78737
E-mail: stephanie@stephaniebarko.com
Web Site: www.stephaniebarko.com; www.diybookplatform.com
Key Personnel
Principal: Stephanie Barko
Founded: 2006
Custom book publicity for adult nonfiction & historical fiction publishers & authors. Debut authors welcome. Specializations in history, memoir, career, 19th century historicals & western themes & spiritual subjects: platform development, pre-publication endorsement acquisition, pre- & post-publication review requests, virtual tours, media pitching, event scheduling, press release creation & launch, electronic press kits & integrated online campaigns. Traditional, hybrid & Indie publication tracks accepted.
Publishing Account(s): CreateSpace; Ingram
Membership(s): Independent Book Publishers Association (IBPA); PEN America; Story Circle Network; Writer's League of Texas

Ted Barkus Co Inc
8017 Anderson St, Philadelphia, PA 19118
Key Personnel
Pres: Allen E Barkus *E-mail:* a.barkus-tbc@att.net
Founded: 1958
Write & distribute press releases, write & edit newsletters; offer creative & production services for promotional brochures & mailers; direct response formats; arrange media interviews, newspaper, magazine, radio & television ads.

The Blaine Group Inc
8665 Wilshire Blvd, No 301, Beverly Hills, CA 90211
Tel: 310-360-1499 *Fax:* 310-360-1498
Web Site: www.blainegroupinc.com
Key Personnel
Pres & CEO: Devon Blaine *E-mail:* devon@blainegroupinc.com
Founded: 1975
National, regional & local promotional campaigns & tours for authors & publishers, involving all media outlets. Includes publicity, advertising & marketing.
Publishing Account(s): Failure: When You Have Nothing You Have Everything; ID; SNIFF; Why Black & Brown Entrepreneurs Fail (To Win); Why Entrepreneurs Fail (To Win); Why Women Entrepreneurs Fail (To Win)

C Blohm & Associates Inc
5999 Monona Dr, Monona, WI 53716-3531
Tel: 608-216-7300
E-mail: hello@cblohm.com
Web Site: www.cblohm.com
Key Personnel
Pres & CEO: Charlene Blohm *Tel:* 608-216-7300 ext 17 *E-mail:* charlene@cblohm.com
VP: Emily Embury
Strategy Dir: Saul Hafenbredl
Acct Mgr: Chloe Dechow
Founded: 1991
Public relations & digital marketing agency for education & special needs industries. With extensive experience in marketing, sales, advertising & public relations, the firm handles both print & electronic educational publishers that produce content for preschool through college. Client services include media & public relations, market positioning & planning, advertising & sales collateral development, case studies, visibility campaigns, conference presentations & awards consultation.

Book Publishers Network
817 238 St SE, Suite G, Bothell, WA 98021
Mailing Address: PO Box 2256, Bothell, WA 98041
Tel: 425-483-3040 *Fax:* 425-483-3098
Web Site: www.bookpublishersnetwork.com
Key Personnel
Pres: Sheryn Hara *E-mail:* sheryn@bookpublishersnetwork.com
Founded: 1984
Publishing consultant in the areas of: editing, cover design, book design & layout, reviews, distribution, literary agent referral, media, publicity, book tours, etc.
Membership(s): Book Publishers of the Northwest (BPNW); Independent Book Publishers Association (IBPA)

Brickman Marketing
395 Del Monte Ctr, No 250, Monterey, CA 93940
Tel: 831-594-1500
E-mail: brickman@brickmanmarketing.com
Web Site: www.brickmanmarketing.com
Key Personnel
Owner & Pres: Wendy Brickman
Founded: 1990
Award-winning firm providing cost-effective public relations & marketing services.

Brody Public Relations
145 Kingwood Stockton Rd, Stockton, NJ 08559-1711

PUBLIC RELATIONS SERVICES

Tel: 908-295-0600
Web Site: www.brodypr.com
Key Personnel
Pres: Beth Brody *E-mail:* beth@brodypr.com
Founded: 1988
Full service national & local publicity for publishers, authors, speakers, products & services. Specialize in self-help, healthcare, consumer, music, arts, entertainment & business fields. Offer cost-effective placement, author tours & use of continually updated media list, including TV, radio, cable, online syndicated columnists, wire services, newspapers & magazines. Develop special events, contests & in-store appearances.
Publishing Account(s): Bantam Doubleday Dell; Berkley Publishing; Full Moon Publishing; Marquis Who's Who; Martindale-Hubbell®; Peterson's Publishing; Random House; Rock Hill Press; Thunders Mouth Press; Tower Hill Press; Villard Books; Wiley

Rosalie Brody
360 E 72 St, New York, NY 10021
Tel: 212-988-8951
Key Personnel
Owner & Pres: Rosalie Brody Feder
  E-mail: roz360b@yahoo.com
Full service national & local publicity, public relations & promotion campaigns for publishers, authors, associations & foundations. Complete author tours, preparation of press materials for print media, radio & TV interviews, press conferences, bookstore promotion, convention planning & special events.

Casemate | IPM
Division of Casemate Group
1950 Lawrence Rd, Havertown, PA 19083
Tel: 610-853-9131 *Fax:* 610-853-9146
E-mail: casemate@casematepublishers.com
Web Site: www.casemateipm.com
Founded: 1995
Full service sales & marketing for publishers: overall market planning, advertising, publicity, direct mail, trade representation.
Publishing Account(s): Allison & Busby; Artvoices Art Books; Ayebia Clarke Publishing; Big Sky Publishing; Black Knight Books; Briza Publications; Capital Books; Carnegie Publishing; Choc Lit; Classics Illustrated; CP Press; Enodare; Grub Street Cookery; Historika; Jackson Westgate Publishing Group; JJ Books; Kashi House; Kolibri Languages; Leading Authorities Press; Liberties Press; Litera Publications; Medina Publishing; New Africa Books; Penguin Random House South Africa; Protea Boekhuis; Publishing 451; Real Reads; Struik Inspirational Gifts; George F Thompson; Tilde Publishing & Distribution; UCT Publications; University of Buckingham Press; Waverly Lee Media; White Owl

Clear Concepts
1329 Federal Ave, Suite 6, Los Angeles, CA 90025
Tel: 323-285-0325
Key Personnel
Owner: Karen Kleiner
Founded: 1986
Research, media planning, writing & distribution of press releases.

Communication Matters
48 Aylmer Ave, Ottawa, ON K1S 2X1, Canada
Tel: 613-233-5423
Web Site: www.communicationmatters.ca
Key Personnel
Pres: Elaine Kenney *E-mail:* ekenney@communicationmatters.ca
Founded: 1991

Publicity, publishing, writing/editing & marketing; arranging publicity through radio, TV & print media; preparing people for interviews; publishing services include editing & design, print & project management; press releases, business & personal profiles & human interest stories.
Membership(s): Book Promoters Association of Canada; National Press Club (NPC); Saskatchewan Writers Guild

Cook Public Relations
3251 Spear Ave, Arcata, CA 95521
Tel: 707-630-3597; 415-302-1752 (cell)
Web Site: www.cookpr.com
Key Personnel
Owner & Pres: Sharon Cook *Tel:* 415-302-1752 (cell) *E-mail:* sharon@cookpr.com
Founded: 1986
Book publicity.
Publishing Account(s): Defy Your DNA/Dr Stephan Shrewsbury; Anne Geddes Collection; McGraw-Hill "The Wine Lovers Healthy Weight Loss Plan"; Media Arts Group Inc/Thomas Kinkade; Miramax/Hyperion/The Lightning Thief; Salt Kills/Dr Surender Neravetla; Sterling Publishing Co Inc, NY/"New Testament Code"; Watkins Publishing/London "Civilization One"

Dougherty and Associates Public Relations
1303 Caldwell Mountain Rd, Hot Springs, NC 28743
Tel: 828-622-3285 *Fax:* 828-622-3285
E-mail: dougherty1515@gmail.com
Web Site: doughertyandassociatespr.com
Key Personnel
Pres: Michael J Dougherty
Founded: 2002 (reestablished)
Specializing in literary PR (publishing, authors, corporate & personal representation), Michael Dougherty has 35+ years experience in the publishing industry. He is formerly Exec Dir of Publicity at Jeremy P Tarcher & Dir of Mktg-Sales-Publicity at Renaissance Media Inc/Audio Renaissance.
Publishing accounts include major houses as well as smaller niche publishers. Worked with authors including Maya Angelou, Tom Wolfe, Gore Vidal, M Scott Peck, Arianna Huffington, Joseph Wambaugh, Nancy Reagan, Dick Morris, Ben Stein, Morley Winograd/Mike Hais, Tracey A Benson, Daniel Beunza, Ken Follett, Larry King, & dozens of others.
Publishing Account(s): Arcadia Books Ltd; Harvard Education Press; Kube Publishing/London; Princeton University Press; Rutgers University Press

Eileen Duhne Public Relations
203-B Picnic Ave, San Rafael, CA 94901
Tel: 415-459-2573 *Fax:* 415-459-2573
E-mail: eduhne@comcast.net
Web Site: eduhne.com
Founded: 1993
Public relations, marketing & publishing services for authors & publishers. Services include advertising, national publicity, author tours. Specialize in general trade, pop culture, environmental, photography & health/spirituality.

Ekus Group LLC
57 North St, Hatfield, MA 01038
Tel: 413-247-9325
E-mail: info@ekusgroup.com
Web Site: ekusgroup.com
Key Personnel
Pres & Lead Agent: Sally Ekus *E-mail:* sally@ekusgroup.com
Founded: 1982
Represents a diversified selection of cookbooks, restaurants, food personalities & food products. Full service culinary agency specializing

ADVERTISING, MARKETING

in talent & literary representation. Support & advance the careers of culinary professionals around the globe. Identify high profile publishing, media & endorsement opportunities for clients. Offer specialized media training programs for authors. Offer personalized, detail-oriented literary services (for cookbooks, health & women's nonfiction topics only) to more than 150 authors, many of whom have published multiple books.
Publishing Account(s): Abrams; Artisan; Chronicle Books; Grand Central; Houghton Mifflin Harcourt; William Morrow; Penguin Publishing Group; Quirk; Regan Books; Robert Rose; Running Press; Simon & Schuster; Stewart, Tabori & Chang; Ten Speed Press; University of Florida Press; University of North Carolina Press; Workman Publishing
Membership(s): Chefs Collaborative; International Association of Culinary Professionals (IACP); Women Presidents' Organization

Linda Fairchild & Company LLC
101 Lucas Valley Rd, Suite 363, San Rafael, CA 94903
Tel: 415-336-6407
Web Site: www.lindafairchild.com
Key Personnel
Agent & Founder: Linda Fairchild
  E-mail: linda@lindafairchild.com
Founded: 2002
Supports illustrators, authors & emerging writers in need of personal branding & publicity in traditional & social media. We create a marketing plan & actively promote our authors through book signings & personal appearances. Our focus is on the timeliness of the subject matter as it relates to issues & themes of our time. We draw our audiences into a larger discussion beyond the specific works in order to maximize the visibility of our clients.

Fairfield Marketing Group Inc
Subsidiary of FMG Inc
830 Sport Hill Rd, Easton, CT 06112-1241
E-mail: info@fairfieldmarketing.com
Key Personnel
Pres & CEO: Edward P Washchilla, Jr
  E-mail: ed@fairfieldmarketing.com
Founded: 1986
Specialists in mailing list brokerage & list management services. FMG clients rely on us for annual direct marketing programs. We are customer driven & accommodate. Specialty services: custom designed account management; expedient list rental approval; monthly usage reports; market & account analyses; fulfillment, mailing & mail response services; freelance art work; graphic design; advertising & promotional copywriting; binding services; lettershop services; computer services. FMG is a full service direct mail marketing firm.
Membership(s): American Booksellers Association (ABA); Bridgeport Regional Business Council (BRBC); Education Market Association; United States Chamber of Commerce (USCC)

Bryan Farrish Marketing
1828 Broadway, 2nd fl, Santa Monica, CA 90404
Tel: 310-998-8305
E-mail: airplay@radio-media.com
Web Site: www.radio-media.com
Key Personnel
Owner: Bryan Farrish
Promoter: Nerry Berry
Founded: 1998
Radio publicity (radio interview) booking.

Flynn Media
1233 Fitzwater St, Philadelphia, PA 19147
Tel: 215-772-3048
Web Site: www.flynnmedia.com

& PUBLICITY

Founder: Erin Flynn Jay *E-mail:* erin@flynnmedia.com
Founded: 2001
Offer writing, editing & public relations services representing authors & speakers.

Gail Leondar Public Relations
19 Belknap St, Arlington, MA 02474
Tel: 781-648-1658
Web Site: www.glprbooks.com
Key Personnel
Principal: Peter Bermudes *E-mail:* peter@glprbooks.com
Founded: 1992
Publicity for books & authors. Specialize in progressive books.

Sandra Goroff & Associates
42 Waterfall Dr, Suite L, Canton, MA 02021
Tel: 617-750-0555
E-mail: sgma@aol.com
Web Site: www.sandragoroff.com
Key Personnel
Founder & Pres: Sandra Goroff
National & local public relations, publicity campaigns & promotional marketing for publishers, books, authors & personalities. Brand & new product launches for publishers. Radio & television placement, print interviews, book review coverage, special events & consulting services.

Susannah Greenberg Public Relations
41 Old Brook Rd, Dix Hills, NY 11746
Tel: 646-801-7477
E-mail: publicity@bookbuzz.com
Web Site: bookbuzz.com; linkedin.com/in/susannahgreenberg; www.facebook.com/SusannahGreenbergPublicRelations; x.com/SueGreenbergPR
Key Personnel
Founder & Pres: Susannah Greenberg
Represents publishers, authors & book industry organizations throughout North America. Susannah works with clients to secure media placements (features, interviews, reviews & mentions) in TV, radio, print & Internet. She researches media outlets, writes press releases & pitch letters, creates online press kits & works to optimize her clients' social media presence by advising them on platforms & content strategy.
Publishing Account(s): Albert Whitman & Co.; Book Industry Study Group; Chronicle Books; Hazelden Publishing; hoopla; Women's National Book Association
Membership(s): Women's Media Group; Women's National Book Association (WNBA)

Gulotta Communications Inc
321 Walnut St, Newton, MA 02460
Tel: 617-630-9286 *Fax:* 978-733-6162
Web Site: www.booktours.com
Key Personnel
Pres: Victor Gulotta *E-mail:* victor@booktours.com
Founded: 1993
Offers full service book promotion & publicity for authors & publishers seeking online, broadcast & print media exposure. In addition a full array of powerful marketing services are available including direct mail, print & broadcast advertising & web marketing. Founder & president Victor Gulotta has been publicizing books for more than three decades & has worked with such authors as Isaac Asimov, Jonathan Kozol, Margaret Thatcher, Richard Brodie, Thomas Szasz, James Randi, Martin Gardner, Gloria Nagy, Ken Fisher, Baxter Black, Nicholas Basbanes, Henry David Abraham, Karen Kondazian & Stewart E Weisberg.

Publishing Account(s): Atlantic Monthly Press; Avon; Columbia University Press; Crown; HarperCollins; Harvard University Press; Little, Brown; M E Sharpe; Oxford University Press; Simon & Schuster; Ten Speed Press; University of Massachusetts Press; Wiley; William Morrow

Kathryn Hall, Publicist
Los Lunas, NM 87031
E-mail: khpbooks@gmail.com
Web Site: www.kathrynhallpublicist.com; www.linkedin.com/in/kathrynhallpr
Founded: 1980
Kathryn Hall, Publicist is a longstanding boutique firm that specializes in working primarily with innovative thought leaders & grounded early adopters who are authors of nonfiction books, particularly business titles. Media placement is secured across platforms including print, podcasts, broadcast & online social media. All socially responsible projects considered. She has served as a book publicist for such authors as Marshall Goldsmith, Rich Karlgaard, Bob Burg, Shakti Gawain & Dan Millman.
Publishing Account(s): Berrett-Koehler Publishers Inc; Marshall Goldsmith; HarperCollins; Jossey-Bass; Rich Karlgaard; Harvey Mackay; New World Library; Viking Penguin

The Hendra Agency Inc
142 Sterling Place, Brooklyn, NY 11217-3307
Tel: 718-622-3232 *Fax:* 718-622-3322
Key Personnel
Pres: Barbara J Hendra
Acct Exec: Jan Andrew
Founded: 1979
Full service national & local publicity, public relations & promotion campaigns for book & computer publishers & authors. TV, radio, online & newspaper interviews & reviews, advertising, press kits & materials, parties & specialized promotions & complete marketing services. Major trade & business publisher & author accounts.
Membership(s): Publishers' Publicity Association

Hill+Knowlton Strategies
237 Park Ave, 4th fl, New York, NY 10017
Tel: 212-885-0300
Web Site: www.hkstrategies.com
Key Personnel
Global Chmn & CEO: Jack Martin *Tel:* 212-885-0372
Global COO & VChmn: Mark Thorne
Chief Global Strategist, CEO & Group SJR: Alexander Jutkowitz *Tel:* 212-885-0606
Global Gen Coun: Meredith Marks
Chief Content & Communs Offr: Leslie Cauley
Global Busn Devt & Client Servs: Scott Pollard *Tel:* 212-885-0315 *E-mail:* scott.pollard@hkstrategies.com
Global Head, Talent: Kate Augustine
Global public relations & integrated communications agency.
Branch Office(s)
3200 Bristol St, Suite 300, Costa Mesa, CA 92626 *Tel:* 949-223-2300
6300 Wilshire Blvd, 10th fl, Los Angeles, CA 90048 *Tel:* 310-633-9400
60 Green St, San Francisco, CA 94111 *Tel:* 415-281-7120
607 14 St NW, Suite 300, Washington, DC 20005 *Tel:* 202-333-7400
255 Alhambra Circle, Suite 330, Miami, FL 33134 *Tel:* 305-443-5454
215 S Monroe St, Suite 703, Tallahassee, FL 32301 *Tel:* 850-222-4100
201 E Kennedy Blvd, Suite 1611, Tampa, FL 33602 *Tel:* 813-221-0030
222 Merchandise Mart Plaza, Suite 275, Chicago, IL 60654 *Tel:* 312-255-1200

500 W Fifth St, Suite 1000, Austin, TX 78701 *Tel:* 512-474-8848
500 N Akard St, Suite 2125, Dallas, TX 75201 *Tel:* 214-363-3990
708 S Main St, Suite 200, Houston, TX 77002 *Tel:* 713-752-1900
Julia Industrial Park, 791 "C" St, San Juan, PR 00920 *Tel:* 787-474-2525

Hilsinger-Mendelson West Inc
115 N Kings Rd, Los Angeles, CA 90048
Tel: 323-931-5335 (text only)
E-mail: hmiwest@aol.com
Web Site: www.hilsingermendelson.com
Key Personnel
CEO: Judy Hilsinger
Pres & COO: Sandi Mendelson *Tel:* 212-725-7707 *Fax:* 212-725-7708 *E-mail:* smendelson@hmieast.com
Sr Publicist: Margaret Rogalski
Digital Media Mgr: Amrit Judge
Off Mgr: Renee Gulotta
Publicity Mgr: Emily Willette
Founded: 1983
Preeminent bi-coastal, full service public relations & publicity (national & regional), providing authors, publishers & corporations with press kit materials; national & local media tours; brand-building strategies & campaigns; organization of events. More than 25 years experience with an unprecedented track record of more than 100 national bestsellers in the past decade.
Branch Office(s)
Hilsinger-Mendelson East, 226 Fifth Ave, 4th fl, New York, NY 10001 *Tel:* 212-725-7707 *Fax:* 212-725-7708 *E-mail:* hmi@hmieast.com

HJMT Public Relations Inc
3280 Sunrise Hwy, Suite 296, Wantagh, NY 11793
Tel: 516-661-2800
E-mail: info@hjmt.com
Web Site: www.hjmt.com
Key Personnel
CEO: Hilary Topper
EVP: Lisa Gordon
Content Developer: David Parmet
Graphic & Web Design: Jonathan Gicewicz
Founded: 1992
Boutique public relations, event planning, social media & graphic design agency.

HurleyMedia LLC
1477 Canyon Rd, Santa Fe, NM 87501
Tel: 505-603-6392
Web Site: www.hurleymedia.com
Key Personnel
Owner: Joanna Thorne Hurley *E-mail:* jth@hurleymedia.com
Founded: 1994
We offer full service packaging for photography & art books from concept through publication, including editorial, design, production, as well as placement with a suitable publisher/distributor, marketing & publicity as needed to supplement publisher's efforts.

Integrated PR Agency (IPR)
Penthouse, 9025 Wilshire Blvd, Suite 500, Beverly Hills, CA 90211
Tel: 310-858-8230
Web Site: www.integrated-pr.com
Key Personnel
Owner & Founder: Monique Moss
  E-mail: monique@integrated-pr.com
Founded: 2010
Leading full service PR agency.

Jane Wesman Public Relations Inc
322 Eighth Ave, Suite 1702, New York, NY 10001
Tel: 212-620-4080 *Fax:* 212-620-0370
Web Site: www.wesmanpr.com

PUBLIC RELATIONS SERVICES

Key Personnel
Pres: Jane Wesman *Tel:* 212-620-4080 ext 11
  E-mail: jane@wesmanpr.com
Dir, Publicity: Andrea J Stein *Tel:* 212-620-4080 ext 15
Soc Media Mgr: Sarah Kelley
Graphic Design Coord: Victoria Lau
Create high impact book publicity campaigns that build name recognition & generates sales. Specialize in obtaining national media coverage on TV & radio, in newspapers & magazines including author interviews, feature stories & book reviews. Also generate in-depth Internet publicity including online video interviews & podcasts & produce television & radio satellite tours. Other services include the creation of written press materials, author media training & interview preparation & the dissemination of publicity information to booksellers.
Publishing Account(s): Barricade Books; Center Street/Hachette; Crown Business; Free Press; Grand Central Publishing; HarperCollins; Jossey-Bass; Lifetree Media; McGraw-Hill; Thomas Nelson Inc; Palgrave; Portfolio; St Martin's Press; Select Books; Simon & Schuster; Waterside Productions; Wiley
Membership(s): ArtTable; National Association of Women Business Owners (NAWBO); Publishers' Publicity Association; Women's Media Group

K H Marketing Communications
16205 NE Sixth St, Bellevue, WA 98008
Tel: 425-269-7411 (cell)
Key Personnel
Owner & Pres: Kathy D Hoggan
  E-mail: kdhoggan@aol.com
Founded: 1991
Marketing select titles to the book trade & to niche markets outside the book trade; creating catalogs; writing back cover & promo copy; generating publicity for titles, authors & publishers; securing rights for compilation publications & sourcing content.
Publishing Account(s): Current Inc; NTC/Contemporary Publishing; Palmer/Pletsch Publishers; Portland Press; Reading A-Z; Sea Hill Press; Washington State University; West 175 Publishers; The Wright Group Inc

Kelley & Hall Book Publicity
5 Briar Lane, Marblehead, MA 01945
Tel: 617-680-1976 *Fax:* 781-631-5959
Web Site: www.kelleyandhall.com
Key Personnel
Partner: Jocelyn Kelley *E-mail:* jocelyn@kelleyandhall.com; Megan Kelley Hall; Gloria Kelley
Founded: 2004
Full service agency providing public relations & promotional services for the publishing industry including authors, publishers, independent book producers, self-published authors & author associations for fiction & nonfiction titles. Produce creative & comprehensive online & print media kits which will secure timely news stories & book review coverage. Specialize in creating innovative article ideas. Publicity campaigns include national & local media coverage, features in newspaper & magazines as well as Internet promotion, publicity & social networking. Custom proposals will be sent upon request.

Kreab
House of Sweden, Suite 504, 2900 "K" St NW, Washington, DC 20007
Tel: 202-536-1590
E-mail: washingtondc@kreab.com
Web Site: www.kreab.com/washington-dc
Key Personnel
Mng Partner: Tapio Christiansen *Tel:* 202-536-1591 *E-mail:* tchristiansen@kreabgavinanderson.com
Sr Advisor: Richard J Wolff *Tel:* 646-283-3423
  E-mail: rwolff@kreabgavinanderson.com
Corporate, financial, public relations, public affairs, crisis management, special events, health care & other key areas of public relations. Owned by Magnora, Omnicom/DAS & multiple other partners. Offices located worldwide.

The Literary Media & Publishing Consultants
1815 Wynnewood Rd, Philadelphia, PA 19151
Tel: 215-877-2012
Key Personnel
CEO: Vanesse Lloyd-Sgambati
  E-mail: vlloydsgam@aol.com
Founded: 1992
Specialize in publishing ventures as well as promotion of African American & women authors; consultant to publishers, authors & corporate entities that are interested in literacy; development of children's book fairs.
Publishing Account(s): Doubleday Basic Books; Running Press; Smiley Group

Litzky PR
33-41 Newark St, 5th fl, Hoboken, NJ 07030
Tel: 201-222-9118
E-mail: inquiries@litzkypr.com
Web Site: litzkypr.com
Key Personnel
Pres: Josslynne Welch
VP, Client Servs: Kaylie Easton
VP, Strategy: Beth Zimmerling
Acct Dir: Christie Ziv
Creative Dir: Tara Wood
Founded: 1988
Strategy & positioning, brand building, integrated campaigns, strategic partnerships, global network, corporate communications, media relations, trade relations, affiliate public relations, influencer marketing, celebrity engagement, events & activations, product launches, thought leadership, storytelling, creative executions, copywriting, media training, measurement & reporting, book publicity.
Partner of the Worldcom Public Relations Group.
Publishing Account(s): Disney Publishing Worldwide; National Geographic
Membership(s): Agency Management Institute (AMI)

Litzky Public Relations, see Litzky PR

LPR, see Litzky PR

Susan Magrino Agency
352 Park Ave S, 6th fl, New York, NY 10010
Tel: 212-957-3005 *Fax:* 212-957-4071
E-mail: info@smapr.com
Web Site: www.smapr.com
Key Personnel
Pres: Ms Allyn Magrino
EVP: Leigh Ann Ambrosi
Acct Dir: Mary Blanton Ogushwitz
Full service public relations; specialize in television, magazines, travel, beauty & fitness, lifestyle & design, foods & restaurant.

Scott Manning & Associates
2 Horatio St, Suite 16G, New York, NY 10014
Tel: 603-491-0995
Web Site: www.scottmanningpr.com
Key Personnel
Owner: Scott Manning *E-mail:* scott@scottmanningpr.com
Publicity Mgr: Abigail Welhouse
Founded: 1995
Public relations & marketing consulting for authors & literary organizations.
Publishing Account(s): Grove Atlantic

ADVERTISING, MARKETING

Branch Office(s)
20 Main St, Box 417, Hancock, NH 03449
Membership(s): Publishers' Publicity Association

Media Connect
Division of Finn Partners
1675 Broadway, New York, NY 10019
Tel: 212-715-1600
Web Site: www.media-connect.com
Key Personnel
Mng Dir: David Hahn *Tel:* 212-593-5847
  E-mail: david.hahn@finnpartners.com
SVP & Dir, MC en Espanol: Deborah Kohan
  E-mail: deborahk@finnpartners.com
SVP & Dir, MC Satellite: Kristin Clifford
  E-mail: kristin@finnpartners.com
Dir, MC Faith: Sharon Farnell *E-mail:* sharonf@finnpartners.com
Publicity Mgr: Adrienne Fontaine *Tel:* 212-593-6309 *E-mail:* adrienne.fontaine@finnpartners.com
Founded: 1962
Full service national & local publicity campaigns for authors & publishers. Nonfiction & fiction, hardcover, trade, ebooks, audiobooks & paperback; TV, radio, digital media, social media & newspaper interviews in person or by phone, syndicate radio & TV interviews to newsrooms nationwide. Arrange press conferences; train authors & write their press kits. All work done on a pay-for-success basis. Specialize in media, radio & print promotions & arranging satellite media tours & TV production worldwide. Morning Drive Radio Tours®; blogging, podcasts & college media tours.
Publishing Account(s): BenBella Books; Grand Central Publishing; Greenleaf Book Group; HarperBusiness; HarperCollins; HarperSanFrancisco; Harvard University Press; Hay House; Houghton Mifflin Harcourt Publishing Company; Knopf; Little, Brown; McGraw-Hill; Milkweed Editions; Morgan James Publishers; National Geographic; W W Norton & Company Inc; Pantheon; Pocket; Random House; St Martin's; Scribners; Simon & Schuster; Sports Illustrated; Thomas Nelson; TOR/Forge; Touchstone; John Wiley; Zondervan

Media Masters Publicity
61 Depot St, Tryon, NC 28782
Tel: 828-859-9456
E-mail: info@mmpublicity.com
Web Site: www.mmpublicity.com
Key Personnel
Sr Partner: Tracey Daniels *E-mail:* tracey@mmpublicity.com
Founded: 1998
Full service literary publicity agency. Specialize in publicity for children's & teen books, cookbooks & lifestyle titles. Personalized service for every client with emphasis on procuring quality media results. Services: implementing & executing national & local media campaigns, author tours & appearances, TV & radio satellite tours, press kit design & consulting. Per-project or retainer services. Client list includes large & small publishing houses.
Branch Office(s)
6106 Majestic Pines Dr, Kingwood, TX 77345, Partner: Karen Wadsworth *Tel:* 617-869-5854
  E-mail: karen@mmpublicity.com
Membership(s): The American Library Association (ALA); Society of Children's Book Writers & Illustrators (SCBWI); Young Adult Library Services Association (YALSA)

Media Relations Agency
Division of Kocina Marketing Cos
350 W Burnsville Pkwy, Suite 350, Burnsville, MN 55337
Tel: 952-697-5220 *Fax:* 952-697-3256
Web Site: www.publicity.com

& PUBLICITY

Key Personnel
Founder & CEO: Lonny Kocina
Partner & COO: Heather Champine
   E-mail: heather@mediarelations.com
Founded: 1988
Traditional print, online print, TV & radio broadcasting. Electronic & print media placements on a performance basis; charge is per placement secured. Also develop web sites & handle sports marketing projects.

Monteiro & Co Inc
301 E 57 St, 4th fl, New York, NY 10022
Tel: 212-832-8183
Web Site: www.monteiroandco.com
Key Personnel
Pres: Barbara Monteiro *E-mail:* bam@monteiroandco.com
Publicist: Connie Perry
Publicity & marketing services for nonfiction books, authors & magazines. Specialize in political books, business publications, biographies & economics books.
Publishing Account(s): Bill Janeway/Cambridge; Barbara Kahn/Norton; Paul Krugman/NY Times; Ian Mitroff/Palgrave
Membership(s): Publishers' Publicity Association

Multicultural Marketing Resources Inc
720 Greenwich St, No 7T, New York, NY 10014
Tel: 212-242-3351
Web Site: www.multicultural.com
Key Personnel
Pres: Lisa Skriloff *E-mail:* lisa@multicultural.com
Founded: 1994
Public relations & marketing services for diversity experts/authors in marketing to multicultural customers.
Publishing Account(s): Multicultural Marketing News; Multicultural Speakers Showcase; Multicultural Travel News; The Source Book of Multicultural Experts

Music City Arts Network
PO Box 843, Brentwood, TN 37024
Toll Free Tel: 888-80-SHINE (807-4463)
E-mail: info@musiccityarts.net
Web Site: www.musiccityartsupdate.com; www.shinetimebooks.com
Key Personnel
Owner & Pres: Chuck Whiting
   E-mail: chucwhit@usit.net
Founded: 1993
Full service communications firm offering services such as writing, editing, media placement, on-air interview placements, research, public relations plan development, song & jingle selection, book development, digital marketing, photography, event planning, etc.
Publishing Account(s): The Littlest Star: A Musical Story; Music City Arts Update; The Ryman Diaries; Shine Time Records & Books; John & Lillie Spreckels: Diaries, Desserts & San Diego Dreams; Wordabulous!: Celebrating the Positive Power of Words
Membership(s): The American Society of Composers, Authors and Publishers (ASCAP); Association for Education in Journalism and Mass Communication (AEJMC); Broadcast Music Inc (BMI); Country Music Association (CMA); National Songwriters Association International (NSAI); Recording Academy (NARAS)

Nissen Public Relations LLC
18 Bank St, Suite 101, Summit, NJ 07901
Tel: 908-376-6470
E-mail: info@nissenpr.com
Web Site: www.nissenpr.com
Key Personnel
Founder & Book Publicist: Rob Nissen
Founded: 2000
Full service book publicity & book marketing firm that specializes in nonfiction categories with an emphasis on business, politics, history, biography, health, current affairs, lifestyle & science. Work with a variety of trade publishers & authors, managing everything from multi-city tours to online campaigns, creating a customized publicity strategy for each title. Our campaigns generate coverage in a wide variety of mainstream & niche media sources. Also offer professional copywriting services, press release distribution, online promotion & arrange speaking tours, lectures & book signing events.
Membership(s): Publishers' Publicity Association

The Nolan/Lehr Group Inc
214 W 29 St, Suite 1002, New York, NY 10001
Tel: 212-967-8200
E-mail: dblehr@cs.com
Web Site: www.nolanlehrgroup.com
Key Personnel
Pres: Donald B Lehr *Tel:* 917-304-4058
   E-mail: donald@nolanlehrgroup.com
Off Mgr: Jennifer Alperen
Founded: 1972
Full service national public relations office for authors, publishers, trade associations, foundations, organizations & services. Specialize in general nonfiction, reference & religion. Creation & production of press releases, press kits & other collateral materials. Interviews booked in all national & local print & broadcast media, live, satellite, online & telephone. Offer press conferences, in-city promotions, special events, publication day parties & events, consultation services, photography. Work closely with the author & publisher.

Caroline O'Connell Communications
11275 La Maida St, Suite 200, North Hollywood, CA 91601-4514
E-mail: oconnellpr@aol.com
Web Site: www.oconnellcommunications.com
Key Personnel
Owner & Pres: Caroline O'Connell
Founded: 1990
Full service public relations firm for publishers & authors since 1990, that conducts national & local tours with an emphasis on the West Coast. Arrange press conferences, train authors & prepare media kits. Specialize in business, beauty, education & political books.

Over the River Public Relations LLC
116 Gladwin Ave, Leonia, NJ 07605
Tel: 201-503-1321
E-mail: info@otrpr.com
Web Site: www.otrpr.com
Key Personnel
Founder & Pres: Rachel Tarlow Gul
   E-mail: rachel@otrpr.com; Jennifer Richards
   E-mail: jennifer@jrichardspr.com
Founded: 2000
Full service national & local publicity campaigns for publishers & authors of fiction, nonfiction, hardcover trade & mass market. Services include press kit development, radio, TV, print & Internet media tours, book signings. Work with many publishers, big & small, as well as directly with authors.
Publishing Account(s): Amazon Crossing; Dreamscape Media; Fordham University Press; HarperCollins; Lake Union; Montlake; Recorded Books; Red Hen Press; Simon & Schuster; Thomas & Mercer; Viking

PadillaCRT
1101 W River Pkwy, Suite 400, Minneapolis, MN 55415
Tel: 612-455-1700 *Fax:* 612-455-1060
Web Site: www.padillacrt.com

PUBLIC RELATIONS SERVICES

Key Personnel
Chair & CEO: Lynn Casey
Chief Creative Offr: Heath Ruddick
EVP: Marian Briggs; Matt Kucharski
SVP: Kathy Burnham; Riff Yeager
VP, Creative Opers: Jennifer Iwanicki
Founded: 1961
Full service public relations firm with expertise in national media placement, author tours & special event planning & promotion. Specialize in business book promotion.
Branch Office(s)
4 World Trade Center, 150 Greenwich St, 48th fl, New York, NY 10007, EVP & Mng Dir: Greg Tarmin *Tel:* 212-229-0500 *Fax:* 212-229-2925
101 W Commerce Rd, Richmond, VA 22314, Pres: Mark Raper *Tel:* 804-675-8100

Page Turner Publicity
8785 SW 28 St, Miami, FL 33165
Tel: 949-254-3214
E-mail: pgturnerpub@aol.com
Web Site: www.pageturnerpublicity.com
Key Personnel
Owner & Pres: Javier Perez
Founded: 2003
Full service literary publicity firm. Provides personalized hands-on public relations services to the publishing industry. Our experienced staff works closely with both individual authors & publishers to create optimal media campaigns for books of all genres. We listen closely to a client's goals & expectations & then plan & execute tailored, strategic publicity plans to meet them. Services include designing creative & well-produced press kits, planning author tours, arranging book signings, speaking engagements & literary events, securing book reviews & articles from traditional print media across the country & online sites, scheduling national & local television, radio & podcast interviews.
Membership(s): Florida Authors & Publishers Association Inc (FAPA); Publishers Association of Los Angeles; South Florida Writers Association

Parkhurst Communications Inc
11 Riverside Dr, Suite 1-TW, New York, NY 10023
Tel: 212-362-9722
Web Site: www.parkhurstcommunications.com
Key Personnel
Pres: William Parkhurst *E-mail:* billparkhurst@parkhurstcommunications.com
Collaborative Partnership & Sr Trainer: Nanette DeWester
Founded: 1981
Communications & media training, presentation skills programs, business writing & leadership workshops. Clients include legendary authors, corporate & nonprofit organizations & major publishers.
Membership(s): Association for Talent Development (ATD); National Speakers Association (NSA); Publishers' Publicity Association

Phoenix Media
29 Miriam Dr, Matawan, NJ 07747
Tel: 732-441-1519 *Fax:* 732-566-1913
Web Site: www.phoenixmediapr.com
Key Personnel
Pres: Donna Gould *E-mail:* donnagould@sprintmail.com
Founded: 1997
Full service publicity & public relations company. Specialize in radio campaigns, publicity campaigns, national interview campaigns for authors, products & corporations.
Publishing Account(s): Atria Books; Avery Books; Broadway Books; Element Books; The Free Press; Gotham Books; HarperCollins; Hylas Publishing; McGraw-Hill Publishers; Pen-

guin Publishing Group; Prentice Hall; Putnam Publishing; Random House; Rutgers University Press; St Martin's Press; Simon & Schuster; Warner Books; Workman Publishing
Membership(s): Publishers' Publicity Association

Porter Novelli
Division of Omnicom Group Inc
195 Broadway, 17th fl, New York, NY 10007
Tel: 212-601-8000
Web Site: www.porternovelli.com
Key Personnel
CFO & Pres, Global Busn Opers: Patrick Resk
Chief Mktg Offr: Kate Cusick
Mng Dir: Kyle Farnham
Founded: 1972

PR by the Book LLC
PO Box 6226, Round Rock, TX 78683
Tel: 512-501-4399 *Fax:* 512-501-4399
E-mail: info@prbythebook.com
Web Site: www.prbythebook.com
Key Personnel
CEO/Chief Publicity Strategist: Marika Flatt
 E-mail: marika@prbythebook.com
COO: Doug Flatt
Sr Publicist: Judy McDonough
Publicist: Leslie Barrett
Founded: 2002
Media relations & social media services for authors, publishers & small businesses. Provide services including full scale publicity campaigns, tour city campaigns, radio or online only blog tours & various other a la carte publicity projects.
Publishing Account(s): B&H Publishing Group; DK Books; Insight Editions; Patagonia Books; Wiley
Membership(s): Independent Book Publishers Association (IBPA); Writer's League of Texas

PR Newswire
Subsidiary of Cision Ltd
350 Hudson St, Suite 300, New York, NY 10014-4504
Toll Free Tel: 888-776-0942; 800-776-8090
 Toll Free Fax: 800-793-9313
E-mail: mediainquiries@prnewswire.com
Web Site: www.prnewswire.com
Key Personnel
CIO: Robert Coppola
Chief HR Offr: Whitney Benner
Pres, Americas: Jason Edelboim
Founded: 1954
Transmits the full texts of press releases simultaneously & within minutes to more than 2,000 news media across the country; News Lines provide national, regional, state or local coverage & international distribution to any country in the world. Also can be ordered. Newswire offers a number of special services: The Feature News Line, for next-day delivery of feature news; PR/TV News Line, reaching editors at 600 TV stations nationwide; EntertaiNET, a wire directly to the desks of entertainment editors & PRN Facsimile Services, for simultaneous fax transmissions to clients' proprietary lists; Fax-on-Demand Service allows clients to store a document of any length for automatic retrieval by any caller & deliverable to any fax machine worldwide. Financial news is transmitted directly to the investment community via the Investors Research Wire & through various specialized databases. A range of Internet-based audio & video services are also available.
Branch Office(s)
303 Second St, 9th fl, San Francisco, CA 94107
 Toll Free Tel: 866-732-1382
2901 28 St, Suite 100, Santa Monica, CA 90405
 Toll Free Tel: 866-732-1382

1515 Wynkoop St, Denver, CO 80202 *Toll Free Tel:* 866-732-1382
180 N Stetson Ave, Suite 1350, Chicago, IL 60601 *Toll Free Tel:* 866-732-1382
12051 Indian Creek Ct, Beltsville, MD 20705 *Toll Free Tel:* 800-378-7112
4041 Jefferson Plaza NE, Suite 100, Albuquerque, NM 87109 *Toll Free Tel:* 866-732-1382 *Fax:* 201-942-7020
1300 E Ninth St, Suite 700, Cleveland, OH 44114 *Toll Free Tel:* 800-826-3133

PR/PR Public Relations
2301 Hickory Lane, Orlando, FL 32803
Tel: 407-895-8800
Web Site: www.prpr.net
Key Personnel
Pres & Owner: Russell Trahan *E-mail:* russell@prpr.net
Specialize in nonfiction authors.

Press Box Publicity
3920 Duncan Dr, Boca Raton, FL 33434
Tel: 912-658-7860
E-mail: sportspr@smithpublicity.com
Web Site: pressboxpublicity-smithpublicity.com
Key Personnel
Pres: Adam Rifenberick
Founded: 2004
Sports media book publicist & public relations services for print & broadcast media.

Publicis North America
1675 Broadway, New York, NY 10009
Tel: 212-474-5000
Web Site: www.publicisna.com
Key Personnel
CEO: Carla Serrano *E-mail:* carla.serrano@publicisna.com
Chief Creative Offr: Andy Bird
Chief Digital Offr: Dawn Winchester
Chief Mktg Offr: Jamie Rosen *E-mail:* jamie.rosen@publicisna.com
Founded: 1993
Full service public relations firm.
Branch Office(s)
500 Corporate Pkwy, Suite 140, Buffalo, NY 14226 *Tel:* 716-626-4433
2001 The Embarcadero, San Francisco, CA 94133, Mng Dir: Julie Liss *Tel:* 415-293-2001 *E-mail:* julie.liss@riney.com
168 N Ninth, Suite 250, Boise, ID 83702, Mng Dir: Christal Gammill *Tel:* 208-395-8300 *E-mail:* christal.gammill@publicisna.com
2909 Hennepin Ave S, Minneapolis, MN 55408 *Tel:* 612-822-2960
325 Arlington Ave, Suite 700, Charlotte, NC 28203 *Tel:* 704-344-7900
2828 Routh St, Suite 300, Dallas, TX 75201 *Tel:* 214-749-0080
7300 Lone Star Dr, No 200, Plano, TX 75024 *Tel:* 469-366-2550
424 Second Ave W, Seattle, WA 98119, Pres: Melissa Nelson *Tel:* 206-285-2222 *E-mail:* melissa.nelson@publicisna.com
111 Queen St E, Suite 200, Toronto, ON M5C 1S2, Canada, Chief Mktg Offr: Brett McIntosh *Tel:* 416-925-7733
One Riverside Dr W, Windsor, ON N9A 5K3, Canada *Tel:* 519-252-9479
3530 Blvd St-Laurent, Montreal, QC H2X 2V1, Canada, Pres: Rachelle Claveau *Tel:* 514-285-1414 *E-mail:* rachelle.claveau@publicisna.com

Renaissance Consultations
PO Box 561, Auburn, CA 95604
Tel: 530-362-1339
E-mail: info@marketingandpr.com
Web Site: www.MarketingAndPR.com
Key Personnel
Owner & Dir, Media Rel: Ms S A "Sam" Jernigan *E-mail:* sam@marketingandpr.com

Founded: 1998
With over a decade of experience in the publishing trenches, we offer a menu of writing, book development & marketing strategies for authors wanting to pursue traditional or self-publishing routes. With a comprehensive array of services & a customized approach to each project we accept, authors can choose precisely the type of assistance they need in advancing the journey of getting their book to its intended audience.
Publishing Account(s): Author's Publishing Cooperative; Next Hat Press; Zumaya Publishing
Membership(s): National Writers Union (NWU)

Rivendell Media Inc
1248 Rte 22 W, Mountainside, NJ 07092
Tel: 908-232-2021 ext 200 *Fax:* 908-232-0521
E-mail: info@rivendellmedia.com; sales@rivendellmedia.com
Web Site: www.rivendellmedia.com
Key Personnel
Pres & CEO: Todd Evans *Tel:* 908-232-2021 ext 210 *E-mail:* todd@rivendellmedia.com
Specialize in LGBT media placement.

Sherri Rosen Publicity Intl NYC
454 Manhattan Ave, Suite 3-J, New York, NY 10026
Tel: 917-699-1284
E-mail: sherri@sherrirosen.com
Web Site: www.sherrirosen.com
Key Personnel
Pres: Sherri Rosen
Founded: 1999
Specialize in literary publicity with emphasis on sex, inspirational, spirituality & relationships - science fiction, published or self-published works. Work with authors in US & globally.
Publishing Account(s): Inspirational Publicity
Membership(s): National Writers Union (NWU)

Ruder Finn Inc
425 E 53 St, New York, NY 10022
Tel: 212-593-6400
E-mail: info@ruderfinn.com
Web Site: www.ruderfinn.com
Key Personnel
CEO: Kathy Bloomgarden, PhD
Chief Innovation Offr: Michael Schubert
EVP, Storytelling & Media: Rachel Spielman
Dir, Mktg & Communs: Sarah Coles *E-mail:* coless@ruderfinn.com
Promote books, especially mass market, cultural & art books & have media tours as well as a division that designs art books.
Branch Office(s)
600 California St, 11th fl, San Francisco, CA 94108, Global Head, Technol: Robin Kim *Tel:* 628-235-2101 *E-mail:* kimr@ruderfinn.com
East Lake Villas, E-101, 35 Dongzhimenwai Main St, 100027 Dongcheng District, Beijing, China, SVP & Gen Mgr: Judy Guo *Tel:* (010) 6462 7321 *Fax:* (010) 6462 7327 *E-mail:* judy.guo@rfcomms.com
Overseas Chinese Village, 3 Peace Rd, Guangzhou 510095, China, VP & Gen Mgr: Grace Liang *Tel:* (020) 8349 5783 *Fax:* (020) 8359 9685 *E-mail:* liangg@ruderfinnasia.com
Base Bldg, 9th fl, No 45, N Caoxi Rd, Xuhui District, Shanghai, China, SVP & Gen Mgr: Tony Dong *Tel:* (021) 5383 1188 *Fax:* (021) 6248 3176 *E-mail:* dongt@ruderfinnasia.com
24/F Neich Tower, 128 Gloucester Rd, Hong Kong, Hong Kong, SVP & Gen Mgr: Paul Yang *Tel:* 2521 0800 *Fax:* 2521 7088 *E-mail:* yangp@ruderfinnasia.com
Unit 001A, Tower B, Ground fl, Global Business Park, MG Rd, Gurgaon, Haryana 122 002, India, SVP & Gen Mgr: Jefferson Hou *Tel:* (0124) 4264343 *E-mail:* houj@ruderfinnasia.com

114 Lavender St, No 14-01 CT Hub 2, Singapore 338729, Singapore, SVP & Gen Mgr: Poh Leng Yu *Tel:* 6235 4495 *Fax:* 6235 7796 *E-mail:* yupl@ruderfinnasia.com
The Salisbury, 29 Finsbury Circus, London EC2M 7AQ, United Kingdom, Mng Dir: Nick Leonard *Tel:* (020) 7438 3050 *Fax:* (020) 7438 3083 *E-mail:* nleonard@ruderfinn.co.uk

Susan Schwartzman Public Relations
88 Kings Way, Pawling, NY 12564
Toll Free Tel: 877-833-4276 *Toll Free Fax:* 877-833-4276
E-mail: susan@susanschwartzmanpublicity.com
Web Site: www.susanschwartzmanpublicity.com
Founded: 1992
Full service publicity firm for publishers & authors. Publicity campaigns include national & local television & radio, author tours, feature stories in newspapers & magazines, review coverage, Online publicity, press kits & consulting. Represent literary & commercial fiction as well as nonfiction titles covering a broad range of subjects: memoirs, self-help, dating, baby boomer topics, social issues, parenting, current affairs, politics, environmental, history, food, sports & business. Extensive experience promoting award-winning cookbooks.
Membership(s): Publishers' Publicity Association

SSPR LLC
One Northfield Plaza, Suite 400, Northfield, IL 60093
Toll Free Tel: 800-287-2279
Web Site: www.sspr.com
Key Personnel
CEO: Heather Kelly
Founded: 1978
Create press releases, arrange national newspaper, magazine, radio & TV, newsletter interviews. Contacts with approximately 100 radio stations for phone interviews; trade shows.
Branch Office(s)
20 N Wacker Dr, Suite 4100, Chicago, IL 60606, Contact: Mellony Vasquez *Tel:* 847-955-0700
715 Bryant St, Suite 201, San Francisco, CA 94107, Contact: Kasey Thomas
105 E Moreno Ave, Suite 101, Colorado Springs, CO 80903, Contact: Kristen Broyles
1880 JFK Blvd, Suite 404, Philadelphia, PA 19103, Contact: Nicole Paleologus

StarGroup International Inc
1194 Old Dixie Hwy, Suite 201, West Palm Beach, FL 33413
Tel: 561-547-0667
E-mail: info@stargroupinternational.com
Web Site: stargroupinternational.com
Key Personnel
Pres & CEO: Brenda Star *E-mail:* brenda@stargroupinternational.com
Creative Dir: Mel Abfier
Internet Mktg Coord: Butch Butler
Mktg, Media & Web Site Devt: Rusty Durham
Media Specialist: Sam Smyth
Founded: 1993
Book Production: concept development, ghostwriting, editing, illustration, design, print promotion & distribution (all projects, fee based).
Membership(s): The Association of Publishers for Special Sales (APSS); Florida Authors & Publishers Association Inc (FAPA); Independent Book Publishers Association (IBPA)

Story Monsters LLC
4696 W Tyson St, Chandler, AZ 85226-2903
Tel: 480-940-8182 *Fax:* 480-940-8787
Web Site: www.StoryMonsters.com; www.StoryMonstersInk.com; www.AuthorBookings.com; www.partnershippublishing.com; www.StoryMonstersBookAwards.com
Key Personnel
Pres: Linda F Radke *E-mail:* Linda@StoryMonsters.com
Founded: 1985
Marketing & national publicity, media kit production, book trailers, audiobook production, web site development, distribution & printing, specialized promotion for children's books, co-opportunities in advertising & catalogues, bookmarks & workshops, Indie film contest entries, social media management, educational outreach & consulting services.
Publishing Account(s): Dr Nicolas Bazan; Jana Bommersbach; Betsy Coffeen; Alex Cord; Carol Hageman; Linda Harkey; Dr Rick Niece; Kathy Peach; Sharon Ritt; Conrad J Storad
Membership(s): Arizona Professional Writers (APW); Book Publicists of Southern California (BPSC); The Children's Book Council (CBC); Independent Book Publishers Association (IBPA); Local First Arizona; National Federation of Press Women; Society of Children's Book Writers & Illustrators (SCBWI)

Story Monsters Press, see Story Monsters LLC

T C Public Relations
One N La Salle St, Suite 600, Chicago, IL 60602
Tel: 312-422-1333
Web Site: www.tcpr.net
Key Personnel
Pres: Thomas Ciesielka *E-mail:* tc@tcpr.net
Publicist: Lori Solyom
Specialize in business, legal & book public relations.

Tandem Literary
28 Clinton Rd, Glen Ridge, NJ 07028
Tel: 212-629-1990 *Fax:* 212-629-1990
Web Site: tandemliterary.com
Key Personnel
Pres & Dir, Mktg: Meg Walker *E-mail:* meg@tandemliterary.com
Pres & Dir, Publicity: Gretchen Koss *E-mail:* gretchenkoss@tandemliterary.com
Founded: 2009
Author tours, pitch book review & features editors, national & local broadcast media, arrange radio interviews, press materials & pitch online media including blogs, social networking & online marketing.

To Press & Beyond
7507 Summersun Dr, Browns Summit, NC 27214
Tel: 805-570-8275
E-mail: info@topressandbeyond.com
Web Site: www.topressandbeyond.com
Key Personnel
Pres, Proj Ed & Prodn Coord: Gail M Kearns *E-mail:* gail@topressandbeyond.com
Art Dir & Proj Mgr: Penelope C Paine *E-mail:* pennypaine@aol.com
Copy Ed & Proofreader: Isabella Piestrzynska
Founded: 2001
Book publishing consulting & support services. We shepherd your print +/or ebook through writing, editing, design & layout, printing, distribution, sales & marketing & promotion, both in trade & niche markets & on the Web. We have worked with over 400 authors & independent publishers worldwide. You can contact Gail Kearns for a half-hour gratis phone consult about your project.
Membership(s): The Association of Publishers for Special Sales (APSS); Independent Book Publishers Association (IBPA)

Warwick Associates
18340 Sonoma Hwy, Sonoma, CA 95476
Tel: 707-939-9212 *Fax:* 707-938-3515
E-mail: warwick@vom.com
Web Site: www.warwickassociates.com
Key Personnel
Pres: Simon Warwick-Smith
Founded: 1985
Full service television, radio, print & web publicity service for publishers & authors, nationally, regionally & locally. Services include developing & implementing strategic advertising & publicity campaigns; coaching authors on presentation; arranging book signings & lectures; creating press kits, newsletters & feature oriented articles; eliciting pre-publication & post-publication reviews; keeping book distribution reps informed of publisher & author activities. Conference organization available. Specialize in spirituality & celebrity publicity.
Publishing Account(s): Associated Publishers Group; Blake Publishing (UK); Brad Blanton, PhD; Nicholas Brealey Publishing (UK); Business Outreach; Call Sign Press; Career Press; Celebrity Placement Services; Center for Conscious Evolution; Claremont Publishing; Daimon Verlag (Switzerland); C W Daniels Pty Ltd (UK); Dunhill Publishing; Earth Heart Publishing; Eckankar; Feterson Press; Flaming Rose Press; W Foulsham Pty Ltd (UK); Gateway Books (UK); Global Pacific Records; Grail Foundation Press (Germany); Hawk Press; Barbara Marx Hubbard; Inner Traditions, International; Investment Publishing House; Learning & Integration Inc; Lindesfarne; Barry Long Books (Australia); Mandeville Press/John-Roger; Mashiyach Ministries; Ralph Metzner PhD; Midpoint Trade Books; New Knowledge Library; New Page Books; Noetic Sciences; Origin Press; Phoenix Rising; Pluto Project; Power Press; St Lynn's Press; Seekers Press; Seti Institute; Silver Light Publications; Soka Gakkai International; Tharpa Publishing (UK); Torchlight Publishing; Unity School of Christianity; Valhalla Press; Vorco Publishing; Waveside Press

Weber Shandwick
909 Third Ave, New York, NY 10022
Tel: 212-445-8000 *Fax:* 212-445-8001
Web Site: www.webershandwick.com
Key Personnel
Chmn: Jack Leslie *E-mail:* jleslie@webershandwick.com
CEO: Andy Polansky *E-mail:* apolansky@webershandwick.com
Pres: Gail Heimann *E-mail:* gheimann@webershandwick.com
Founded: 1921
Full service public relations firm with additional expertise in high tech broadcast communications, promotions & healthcare.

Skye Wentworth Public Relations
23A Durham Point Rd, Durham, NH 03824
Tel: 978-462-4453
E-mail: skyewentworth@gmail.com
Web Site: www.skyewentworth.org/wordpress; www.skyewentworth.org
Key Personnel
Book Publicist: Skye Wentworth
Founded: 2000
Book publicity.

Meryl Zegarek Public Relations Inc
255 W 108 St, Suite 9D1, New York, NY 10025
Tel: 917-493-3601
Web Site: www.mzpr.com
Key Personnel
Pres: Meryl Zegarek *E-mail:* mz@mzpr.com
Founded: 2000
A full service public relations & publicity company with specialties in books, authors, publishing, comprehensive campaigns for traditionally published & self-published authors, media tours, web promotions, as well as consulting on publicity book proposals & marketing.

Direct Mail Specialists

Listed below are selected firms that are experienced in handling various aspects of direct mail promotion of books.

A B Data Ltd
600 A B Data Dr, Milwaukee, WI 53217
Tel: 414-961-6400 *Toll Free Tel:* 866-217-4470
Fax: 414-961-2674
E-mail: info@abdata.com; consulting@abdata.com
Web Site: www.abdata.com
Key Personnel
Pres: Thomas R Glenn
Co-Mng Dir: Bruce Arbit; Charles Pruitt
Branch Office(s)
915 15 St NW, Suite 300, Washington, DC 20005
 Tel: 202-618-2900
5080 PGA Blvd, Suite 209, Palm Beach Gardens, FL 33418 *Tel:* 561-336-1801
19 Weissburg St, Tel Aviv 69358, Israel *Tel:* (03) 720-8782
Membership(s): Association of National Advertisers Inc (ANA)

American International Distribution Corp (AIDC)
82 Winter Sport Lane, Williston, VT 05495
Mailing Address: PO Box 80, Williston, VT 05495-0080
Tel: 802-862-0095 *Toll Free Tel:* 800-678-2432
 Fax: 802-864-7749
Web Site: www.aidcvt.com
Key Personnel
Pres & CEO: Marilyn McConnell
Dir, Opers: Michael Pelland
Founded: 1986
Complete direct mail specialists, call center, subscription, continuity, list maintenance, order fulfillment, credit/collections, data management, online capable, Pubnet, Advantis, Internet, web site hosting & development, subscription standing order, periodicals.
Membership(s): Book Industry Study Group (BISG); Independent Publisher's Guild (IPG)

appatura™, A Broadridge Company
Division of Broadridge Financial Solutions Inc
65 Challenger Rd, Suite 400, Ridgefield Park, NJ 07660
Tel: 201-508-6000 *Toll Free Tel:* 800-277-2155
E-mail: contactus@appatura.com
Web Site: www.appatura.com
Key Personnel
CEO: Richard Plotka
CIO: Faisal Fareed
Chief Prod Offr: Harsh Choudhary
Chief Strategy Offr: John Closson
Head, Fin: Alpha Diarra
From data to distribution; overall market plan: copy, design, art, list consultation, printing, literature distribution, computer services, personalized communication, all mailing services.

Casemate | IPM
Division of Casemate Group
1950 Lawrence Rd, Havertown, PA 19083
Tel: 610-853-9131 *Fax:* 610-853-9146
E-mail: casemate@casematepublishers.com
Web Site: www.casemateipm.com
Founded: 1995
Full service marketing for book publishers, including: complete direct mail campaigns from concept through production & monitoring results, catalog production, publicity campaigns, trade sales distribution & special sales, web site print-on-demand.

CCG Marketing Solutions
Subsidiary of Corporate Mailings Inc
14 Henderson Dr, West Caldwell, NJ 07006
Tel: 973-808-0009
E-mail: info@corpcomm.com
Web Site: home.corpcomm.com
Founded: 1965
Full service marketing support company offering creative services, printing, lettershop/direct mail services & fulfillment. Branch office in Towaco, NJ.

Century Direct Solutions LLC
15 Enter Lane, Islandia, NY 11749
Tel: 212-763-0600
E-mail: contact@centurydirect.net
Web Site: www.centurydirect.net
Key Personnel
VP, Sales & Busn Devt: Martin A Rego
 E-mail: regom@centurydirect.net
Founded: 1932
Direct mail, newsletters, publications & catalogs, in-house lettershop. Electronic prepress; sheetfed offset printing in 2- & 4-colors; complete bindery; envelope printing, data processing, inkjet & laser imaging, warehousing, shipping & fulfillment.
Membership(s): Direct Mail Fundraisers Association (DMFA); Greater Hudson Valley Postal Customers Council; Greater New York Postal Customers Council; Hudson Valley Direct Marketing Association

CG Book Printers
Division of Corporate Graphics Commercial (CGC)
1750 Northway Dr, North Mankato, MN 56003
Tel: 507-388-3300 *Toll Free Tel:* 800-729-7575
 Fax: 507-386-6350
E-mail: cgbooks@corpgraph.com
Web Site: www.corpgraph.com
Key Personnel
Pres: Dan Kvasnicka *Tel:* 507-386-6340
 Fax: 507-344-5548 *E-mail:* dekvasnicka@corpgraph.com
Sales Exec, Book Mfg Sales: Mike Schmitt
 Tel: 507-386-6349 *E-mail:* mjschmitt@corpgraph.com
Founded: 1989
CG Book Printers currently provides book manufacturing services for publishers who sell product to school library & trade markets. In addition, we offer fulfillment services for those publishers wishing to maintain their inventories in the same location where their books are manufactured.
We bind books in hard case & paperback formats. We use Smyth sewn, side sew & adhesive bound for hard case trade or library bound books & section sew, or adhesive bind for paperback books.

Clarity Output Solutions (COS)
860 Honeyspot Rd, Stratford, CT 06615
Tel: 203-378-6200 *Toll Free Tel:* 800-414-1624
E-mail: info@clarityosl.com
Web Site: www.clarityosl.com
Key Personnel
VP, Sales: Jack Flaherty
Founded: 1984
Payment processing, transaction processing, Internet inquiry handling & fulfillment, managed database services, letter, statement, imaging & mailing services.

Conrad Direct Inc
800 Kinderkamack Rd, Suite 307N, Oradell, NJ 07649
Tel: 201-567-3200 *Fax:* 201-567-1530
E-mail: listinfo@conraddirect.com
Web Site: www.conraddirect.com
Key Personnel
CEO: Barbara Schonwald *E-mail:* bschonwald@conraddirect.com
COO: Steve Maier
Co-Pres: Tom Colwell; Sharon Traina
Founded: 1982
Mailing list brokers & marketing consultants to book publishers & cataloguers who advertise via direct mail also to consumer & business magazine publishers & nonprofit organizations.
Membership(s): Association of National Advertisers Inc (ANA); Direct Marketing Association of Washington

Content Critical Solutions Inc
10 Fifth St, 2nd fl, Valley Stream, NY 11581
Tel: 201-528-2777
E-mail: info@contentcritical.com
Web Site: www.contentcritical.com
Key Personnel
COO: Frederick Van Alstyne
CTO: John Slaney
VP, Client Servs: Daniel O'Connell
VP, Opers: Mario Ragusa
Provides creation, production, digital & conventional printing, fulfillment & electronic delivery of customized & personalized communications.
Branch Office(s)
227 N Rte 303, Congers, NY 10920 (processing ctr)
550 W Sunrise Blvd, Fort Lauderdale, FL 33311 (processing ctr)
121 Moonachi Ave, Moonachi, NJ 07074 (Northeast regional headquarters) *E-mail:* sales_info@contentcritical.com

Corporate Graphics Book Printers, see CG Book Printers

Demand Marketing
377 Fisher Rd, Suite D, Grosse Pointe, MI 48230
Tel: 313-823-8598 *Toll Free Tel:* 888-977-2256
E-mail: info@create-demand.com
Web Site: www.create-demand.com
Key Personnel
Pres: William Patterson
Founded: 2003
Direct & database marketing agency. DM strategy, data analytics, database development & creative execution (mail, e-mail, web, telemarketing), outbound business-to-business telemarketing/call center.
Membership(s): Direct Marketing Agency Council; Direct Marketing Association of Detroit

Double Envelope
Subsidiary of BSC Ventures LLC
7702 Plantation Rd, Roanoke, VA 24019
Toll Free Tel: 800-800-9007
E-mail: inquire@double-envelope.com

DIRECT MAIL SPECIALISTS

Web Site: www.double-envelope.com
Key Personnel
Pres & CEO: Brian Sass
EVP, Opers: Jonathan M Peyton
EVP, Sales: John Draper
Gen Mgr: Bill Howell
Founded: 1917
Manufacturing of commercial, custom printed & specialty envelopes for the transactional & direct mail industries.
Branch Office(s)
2500 NE 39 Ave, Gainesville, FL 32609, Gen Mgr: Wayne Honeycutt *Toll Free Tel:* 800-543-5275
100 Woodhull Dr, Angola, IN 46703, Gen Mgr: Richard R McElrath *Toll Free Tel:* 800-466-9653
532 E 25 St, Baltimore, MD 21218, Gen Mgr: Lisa Kline *Toll Free Tel:* 800-822-6537

Fairfield Marketing Group Inc
Subsidiary of FMG Inc
830 Sport Hill Rd, Easton, CT 06112-1241
E-mail: info@fairfieldmarketing.com
Key Personnel
Pres & CEO: Edward P Washchilla, Jr
 E-mail: ed@fairfieldmarketing.com
Founded: 1986
Mailing list brokerage & list management services. FMG clients rely on us for annual direct marketing programs. We are customer driven & accomodate. Specialty services: custom designed account management; expedient list rental approval; monthly usage reports; market & account analyses; fulfillment, mailing & mail response services; freelance art work; graphic design; advertising & promotional copywriting; binding services; lettershop services; computer services. FMG is a full service direct mail marketing firm.
Membership(s): American Booksellers Association (ABA); Bridgeport Regional Business Council (BRBC); Education Market Association; United States Chamber of Commerce (USCC)

The Hibbert Group
400 Pennington Ave, Trenton, NJ 08650
Tel: 609-394-7500 *Toll Free Tel:* 888-HIBBERT (442-2378)
E-mail: info@hibbertgroup.com
Web Site: hibbert.com
Key Personnel
Co-Chmn & CEO: Timothy J Moonan
Co-Chmn & SVP, Sales & Mktg: Thomas J Moonan
Cont, Fin: Zobeida Madera-Zapf
SVP, Fin: George Dowbnia
SVP, IT: Kenneth J Swiatkowski
SVP, Sales: Michelle Spedding
VP, Cust & IT: Hussain Moochalla
VP, HR: Reney Cherian
VP, IT: Fran Kerr
Integrated communications & marketing solutions, inquiry programs, rebate programs, mailing list maintenance, collating, inserting, shrink packaging, assembling & mailing, warehousing, fulfillment, distribution, inventory control & inkjet imaging.
Branch Office(s)
1100 US Hwy 130, Robbinsville, NJ 08691 (dist ctr)
19521 E 32 Pkwy, Aurora, CO 80011-8141 (dist ctr)
890 Ships Landing Way, New Castle, DE 19720 (dist ctr)

IBPA, see The Independent Book Publishers Association (IBPA)

The Independent Book Publishers Association (IBPA)
1020 Manhattan Beach Blvd, Suite 204, Manhattan Beach, CA 90266
Tel: 310-546-1818
E-mail: info@ibpa-online.org
Web Site: www.ibpa-online.org
Key Personnel
Chair: Tieshena Davis
CEO: Andrea Fleck-Nisbet *E-mail:* andrea@ibpa-online.org
COO: Terry Nathan *E-mail:* terry@ibpa-online.org
Chief Content Offr: Lee Wind *E-mail:* lee@ibpa-online.org
Dir, Mktg & Communs: Adeline Lui
 E-mail: adeline@ibpa-online.org
Vendor Rel Mgr: Louis Force Torres
 E-mail: louis@ibpa-online.org
Founded: 1983 (as Publishers Association of Southern California)
Nonprofit association of independent book publishers offering marketing, education & advocacy.
Membership(s): American Booksellers Association (ABA); The American Library Association (ALA); Book Industry Study Group (BISG)

MDR, A Dun & Bradstreet Division
Division of Dun & Bradstreet Inc
5335 Gate Pkwy, Jacksonville, FL 32256
Tel: 973-921-5500 *Toll Free Tel:* 800-333-8802
E-mail: mdrinfo@dnb.com
Web Site: mdreducation.com
Founded: 1969
Marketing information & services for the K-12, higher education, library, early childhood & related education markets. Powered by the most complete, current & accurate education databases available in the industry, MDR provides e-mail contacts & deployment, direct mail lists, sales contact & lead solutions, along with web & social media marketing services.

Donya Melanson Associates
5 Bisson Lane, Merrimac, MA 01860
Tel: 978-346-9240 *Fax:* 978-346-8345
E-mail: dmelanson@dmelanson.com
Web Site: www.dmelanson.com
Key Personnel
Principal: Donya Melanson
Advertising & design services, web site development, copywriting, mail list research & purchase, production, printing & mailing.

Neibauer Press
20 Industrial Dr, Warminster, PA 18974
Tel: 215-322-6200 *Fax:* 215-322-2495
E-mail: sales@neibauer.com
Web Site: www.neibauer.com
Key Personnel
VP: Ruth Neibauer-Baker *Tel:* 215-322-6216
 E-mail: ruth@neibauer.com
Founded: 1955
Full service, family owned printing & publishing company. Services include mail preparation, mailing list rentals & maintenance, expert postal data services, direct mail printing, EDDM mailings, shipping, warehousing, pick & pack & fulfillment.

Sterling Fulfillment
100 Quentin Roosevelt Blvd, Suite 205, Garden City, NY 11530
Tel: 516-758-2000
Web Site: sterlingfulfillment.com
Key Personnel
Pres: Donna Garda
Founded: 2017
Packaging & assembly services, direct mailing (from postcards to self-mailers & catalogs), printing services, warehousing & logistics.

Swan Packaging Fulfillment Inc
Unit of QuickBox Fulfillment
415 Hamburg Tpke, Wayne, NJ 07470
Tel: 973-790-0990 *Fax:* 973-790-0216
Web Site: www.swanpackaging.com
Key Personnel
Pres: Timothy S Werkley *Tel:* 973-790-8417
Founded: 1986
Provides third party order fulfillment (pick & pack) & contract packaging services (kit assembly, automated book cartoning & shrink-wrapping). Specialize in book packaging & fulfillment & ship via all carriers, including USPS bulk mail. Operate from a 125,000 sq ft facility located approximately 20 miles west of New York City.
Membership(s): Direct Marketing Club of New York (DMCNY); FMA

Tribal Print Source
Division of Southern California Tribal Chairman's Association
36146 Pala Temecula Rd, Bldg J, Pala, CA 92059
Mailing Address: 35008 Pala Temecula Rd, PMB 436, Pala, CA 92059
Tel: 760-597-2650
E-mail: sales@tribalprintsource.com
Web Site: www.tribalprintsource.com
Founded: 2003
Print pieces are customized by our powerful variable data software engine, enabling each individual piece to be custom tailored in both image & text for each recipient.

Universal|Wilde
26 Dartmouth St, Westwood, MA 02090
Tel: 781-251-2700 *Fax:* 781-251-2613
Web Site: www.universalwilde.com
Key Personnel
Pres & CEO: Stephen Flood
COO: Christopher Armstrong
CFO: Joe Musanti
VP, HR: Jennifer MacAskill
VP, Sales: Jim Bailey
Mktg Mgr: Ryan Collins
Founded: 1958
Communications platform Xccelerate™ for distribution & fulfillment. 15,000 orders fulfilled per week, each with multiple components, as well as on demand output. At peak capacity, we handle more than 50,000 orders, including bulk orders, pick/pack kits, on demand enrollment kits & booklets. Our distribution team processes up to 3 million pieces per day, using multi-list handling, perfect matching systems, read & print capabilities, Intelligent Mail® barcode, commingling & entry point deliver & on-site postal verification.
Branch Office(s)
403 VFW Dr, Rockland, MA 02370 *Tel:* 781-871-7744 *Fax:* 781-878-2967
48 Third Ave, Somerville, MA 02143 *Tel:* 617-591-3000 *Fax:* 617-591-3091

Yeck Brothers Co
2222 Arbor Blvd, Dayton, OH 45439
Tel: 937-294-4000 (ext 207) *Toll Free Tel:* 800-417-2767
E-mail: direct@yeck.com
Web Site: www.yeck.com
Key Personnel
Dir, Mktg & Creative Servs: Sherry Hang
Graphic Art Servs Mgr: Adam Smith
Founded: 1938
Database marketing & list purchase; strategic planning; copywriting; direct mail; e-mail marketing; printing; mailing production; fulfillment; shipping; hand & automated inserting & assembly; ID cards.
Membership(s): Epicomm

Mailing, Duplicating & Fax Services

ABDI Inc
16 Avenue "A", Leetsdale, PA 15056
Toll Free Tel: 800-796-6471 *Fax:* 412-741-4161
E-mail: e-fulfillment@abdintl.com
Web Site: www.abdi-ecommerce10.com/abdintl; www.abdintl.com/abdintl
Key Personnel
CEO: Michael D Cheteyan, II
Pres: Judy G Cheteyan *E-mail:* j.cheteyan@abdintl.com
VP, Fin & IT: Bryan A Cox
Gen Opers Mgr: Ericka D Giles
Produce high quality, efficient & cost-effective B&W article reprints & standards printing with a turnaround time of 5 days or less for associations & the publishing community. Our services contribute to your success by enhancing your total quality service to your members/customers while drastically reducing your overall printing costs.

American International Distribution Corp (AIDC)
82 Winter Sport Lane, Williston, VT 05495
Mailing Address: PO Box 80, Williston, VT 05495-0080
Tel: 802-862-0095 *Toll Free Tel:* 800-678-2432
Fax: 802-864-7749
Web Site: www.aidcvt.com
Key Personnel
Pres & CEO: Marilyn McConnell
Dir, Opers: Michael Pelland
Founded: 1986
Lettershop, call center, telemarketing, computer services, online ordering, subscription, continuity; direct marketing service, distribution & fulfillment, web hosting & development.
Membership(s): Book Industry Study Group (BISG); Independent Publisher's Guild (IPG)

appatura™, A Broadridge Company
Division of Broadridge Financial Solutions Inc
65 Challenger Rd, Suite 400, Ridgefield Park, NJ 07660
Tel: 201-508-6000 *Toll Free Tel:* 800-277-2155
E-mail: contactus@appatura.com
Web Site: www.appatura.com
Key Personnel
CEO: Richard Plotka
CIO: Faisal Fareed
Chief Prod Offr: Harsh Choudhary
Chief Strategy Offr: John Closson
Head, Fin: Alpha Diarra
Founded: 1949
Document management; from data to distribution, on demand printing. Personalized computer letters, mailing list enhancement, offset printing; literature distribution & fulfillment; manual & machine inserting, all mailing services.

CDS Global
Subsidiary of Hearst Corp
1901 Bell Ave, Des Moines, IA 50315-1099
Tel: 515-247-7500 *Toll Free Tel:* 866-897-7987
E-mail: salesinfo@cds-global.com
Web Site: www.cds-global.com
Key Personnel
Chmn & CEO: Malcolm Netburn
CFO: Paul Polus
SVP, Global Opers: Nancy Gessmann
Subscription fulfillment, merge/purge, list maintenance & management, demographic segmentation, product fulfillment, printing services, lettershop, telemarketing.
Branch Office(s)
1550 E Washington Ave, Des Moines, IA 50036
2005 Lakewood Dr, Boone, IA 50036
25 Main Place, Suite 125, Council Bluffs, IA 51503
3107 Shelby St, Harlan, IA 51537
411 E South St, Tipton, IA 52772
1600 36 St, West Des Moines, IA 50266
1419 W Fifth St, Wilton, IA 52778
2286 Crosswind Dr, Suite A, Prescott, AZ 86301
Hearst Tower, 300 W 57 St, 10th fl, New York, NY 10019
12401 Research Blvd, Bldg 1, Suite 420, Austin, TX 78759
261-265 Chalmers St, Suite 401, Level 4, Redfern, NSW 2016, Australia *Tel:* (02) 8296 5400 *E-mail:* sales@cds-global.com.au
Tower House, Sovereign Park, Lathkill St, Market Harborough, Leics LE16 9EF, United Kingdom *Tel:* (01858) 468811 *E-mail:* sales@cdsglobal.co.uk *Web Site:* www.cdsglobal.co.uk

Century Direct Solutions LLC
15 Enter Lane, Islandia, NY 11749
Tel: 212-763-0600
E-mail: contact@centurydirect.net
Web Site: www.centurydirect.net
Key Personnel
VP, Sales & Busn Devt: Martin A Rego
E-mail: regom@centurydirect.net
Founded: 1932
Completely automated lettershop, including inkjetting, data processing, laser imaging, automatic insertion, line-stamp affixing, computerized enhancement for maximum postal discounts, fulfillment; also 2- & 4-color sheetfed printing, envelope printing & electronic prepress.
Membership(s): Direct Mail Fundraisers Association (DMFA); Greater Hudson Valley Postal Customers Council; Greater New York Postal Customers Council; Hudson Valley Direct Marketing Association

Clarity Output Solutions (COS)
860 Honeyspot Rd, Stratford, CT 06615
Tel: 203-378-6200 *Toll Free Tel:* 800-414-1624
E-mail: info@clarityosl.com
Web Site: www.clarityosl.com
Key Personnel
VP, Sales: Jack Flaherty
Founded: 1984
Payment processing, transaction processing, Internet inquiry handling & fulfillment, managed database services, letter, statement, imaging & mailing services.

Fairfield Marketing Group Inc
Subsidiary of FMG Inc
830 Sport Hill Rd, Easton, CT 06112-1241
E-mail: info@fairfieldmarketing.com
Key Personnel
Pres & CEO: Edward P Washchilla, Jr
E-mail: ed@fairfieldmarketing.com
Founded: 1986
Mailing list brokerage & list management services. FMG clients rely on us for annual direct marketing programs. We are customer driven & accomodate. Specialty services: custom designed account management; expedient list rental approval; monthly usage reports; market & account analyses; fulfillment, mailing & mail response services; freelance art work; graphic design; advertising & promotional copywriting; binding services; lettershop services; computer services. FMG is a full service direct mail marketing firm.
Membership(s): American Booksellers Association (ABA); Bridgeport Regional Business Council (BRBC); Education Market Association; United States Chamber of Commerce (USCC)

First Choice Copy
5208 Grand Ave, Maspeth, NY 11378
Tel: 718-381-1480 (ext 200) *Toll Free Tel:* 800-222-COPY (222-2679)
Web Site: www.firstchoice-copy.com
Key Personnel
Owner & Pres: Joe Meisner *Tel:* 718-381-1480 ext 212 *E-mail:* jmeisner@nyc.rr.com
Short run perfect-bound books. Full 600 DPI resolution & full cover covers. Serving the publishing industry for reprints & short run book printing, all electronically printed. Nation's leading service bureau for on demand printing utilizing state-of-the-art equipment including a fully networked Xerox Docutech, 9 5090s, color equipment - 2 Canon 800s & 500, networked to the Fiery & full in-house bindery. Most electronic media accepted. Postscript file preferred, but will accept source applications too. Shop runs 24/7. Free pick up & delivery for jobs over $300. Average turnaround 3-5 days.

Global Order Fulfillment, see ABDI Inc

The Hibbert Group
400 Pennington Ave, Trenton, NJ 08650
Tel: 609-394-7500 *Toll Free Tel:* 888-HIBBERT (442-2378)
E-mail: info@hibbertgroup.com
Web Site: hibbert.com
Key Personnel
Co-Chmn & CEO: Timothy J Moonan
Co-Chmn & SVP, Sales & Mktg: Thomas J Moonan
Cont, Fin: Zobeida Madera-Zapf
SVP, Fin: George Dowbnia
SVP, IT: Kenneth J Swiatkowski
SVP, Sales: Michelle Spedding
VP, Cust & IT: Hussain Moochalla
VP, HR: Reney Cherian
VP, IT: Fran Kerr
Complete database management, CRM, multi-channel engagement, direct mail, promotion & mailing services, printing & fulfillment.
Branch Office(s)
1100 US Hwy 130, Robbinsville, NJ 08691 (dist ctr)
19521 E 32 Pkwy, Aurora, CO 80011-8141 (dist ctr)
890 Ships Landing Way, New Castle, DE 19720 (dist ctr)

PMSI Direct
242 Old New Brunswick Rd, Suite 350, Piscataway, NJ 08854
Tel: 732-465-1570 *Toll Free Tel:* 800-238-1316
Web Site: www.pmsidirect.com
Key Personnel
COO: Mark Corsi
Founded: 1984
Complete lettershop & direct marketing support services.

PremierIMS Inc
11101 Ella Blvd, Houston, TX 77067

MAILING, DUPLICATING & FAX SERVICES

Tel: 832-608-6400 *Fax:* 832-608-6420
E-mail: info@premier-ims.com
Web Site: www.premier-ims.com
Key Personnel
Founder & CEO: Norm Pegram
Pres: Geno Baiamonte
VP, Sales: Max Noble
Founded: 2008
Digital & offset printing, direct mailing services, fulfillment & distribution.

ProFAX Inc
20 Max Ave, Hicksville, NY 11801-1419
Toll Free Tel: 877-942-8100
E-mail: sales@profax.com
Web Site: www.profax.com
Key Personnel
Pres: Ralph Potente
Founded: 1989
Provides fax broadcasting services.

SGW Integrated Marketing Communications Inc
219 Changebridge Rd, Montville, NJ 07045
Tel: 973-299-8000
E-mail: info@sgw.com
Web Site: www.sgw.com
Key Personnel
CEO: Dave Scelba
Pres & COO: Frank Giarratano
Founded: 1986
Branding, advertising, PR & social media design, video, web site design, search engine optimization (SEO), media planning.

Streem Communications LLC
Division of Cleo Communications
4949 Harrison Ave, Rockford, IL 61107
Mailing Address: PO Box 15835, Loves Park, IL 61132-5835
Tel: 815-282-7695 *Toll Free Tel:* 800-325-7732
Fax: 815-639-8931 *Toll Free Fax:* 888-435-2348
E-mail: streemsales@cleo.com; sales@cleo.com
Web Site: www.streem.net
Key Personnel
CEO: Mahesh Rajasekharan, PhD
Fax on demand & fax broadcasting services.

Valid USA
1011 Warrenville Rd, Suite 450, Lisle, IL 60532
Tel: 630-852-8200 *Toll Free Tel:* 800-773-1588 (cust serv); 855-825-4387 (sales)
Web Site: www.valid.com
Services to direct database marketing organizations, including: address & data hygiene such as NCOA, DSF, DPV, LACS, SuiteLink; merge/purge (consumer, business & Canadian); business intelligence; database design, development & support; marketing automation solutions; direct mail printing; personalization (up to 600 dpi); finishing, mailing & commingling; plastic card manufacturing & personalization.

Mailing List Brokers & Services

Mailing list brokers have lists of almost every conceivable type. Names in all trades and professions can be purchased for circulation at a wide range of prices. These firms often handle mailing services as well.

ACT ONE Mailing List Services Inc
237 Washington St, 2nd fl, Marblehead, MA 01945-3334
Tel: 781-639-1919 *Toll Free Tel:* 800-ACT-LIST (228-5478) *Fax:* 781-639-2733
E-mail: info@act1lists.com
Web Site: www.act1lists.com
Key Personnel
Pres & CEO: Steven M Cushinsky
 E-mail: stevec@act1lists.com
Full service mailing, telemarketing, fax & e-mail list compiler, broker & manager.

Acxiom
301 E Dave Ward Dr, Conway, AR 72032
Toll Free Tel: 888-322-9466
Web Site: www.acxiom.com
Key Personnel
CEO: Dennis Self
CIO: Janet Cinfio
Founded: 1969
Provides a comprehensive global suite of consumer insights in the market, allowing you to build premier data lists for powerful digital & offline acquisition campaigns & strategies.
Branch Office(s)
1901 Butterfield Rd, Suite 900, Downers Grove, IL 60515
100 W 33 St, 10th fl, New York, NY 10001
River Place Corporate Park 3, 6500 River Place Blvd, Bldg 3, Suite 300, Austin, TX 78730

ALC Inc
750 College Rd E, Suite 201, Princeton, NJ 08540
Tel: 609-580-2800 *Toll Free Tel:* 800-252-5478 *Fax:* 609-580-2888
E-mail: info@alc.com
Web Site: www.alc.com
Key Personnel
CEO: Rick Erwin
Pres & COO: Susan Rice Rappaport
 E-mail: susan.rice.rappaport@alc.com
CFO: Peter Derosa *E-mail:* peter.derosa@alc.com
Pres, ALC Digital: Gregg Galletta *E-mail:* gregg.galletta@alc.com
Pres, Data Mgmt: Britt Vatne *E-mail:* britt.vatne@alc.com
Pres, Smart Data Solutions: Fran Green
 E-mail: fran.green@alc.com
EVP, Info Technol: Patricia Stecher *E-mail:* pat.stecher@alc.com
EVP, Strategic Planning: Bryan MacDonald
 E-mail: bryan.macdonald@alc.com
SVP, Data Acq: Tom Fleming *E-mail:* tom.fleming@alc.com; Rachel Mercer
 E-mail: rachel.mercer@alc.com
VP, Database Servs: Michael Reckinger
 E-mail: michael.reckinger@alc.com
Mng Partner, Data Acq: David Dotson
 E-mail: david.dotson@alc.com
Mailing list manager, broker, compiler.
Branch Office(s)
770 Tamalpais Dr, Suite 204, Corte Madera, CA 94925, Contact: Laurie Cole *Tel:* 415-886-6107
 E-mail: laurie.cole@alc.com
11670 Fountains Dr, Suite 200, Maple Grove, MN 55369, Contact: Tom Fleming *Tel:* 763-400-7665 *E-mail:* tom.fleming@alc.com
539 Bielenberg Dr, Suite 200, Woodbury, MN 55125, Contact: Michael Reckinger *Tel:* 651-264-3052 *E-mail:* michael.reckinger@alc.com
120 White Plains Rd, Suite 205, Tarrytown, NY 10591, Contact: Britt Vatne *Tel:* 914-524-5400 *Fax:* 914-524-5290 *E-mail:* britt.vatne@alc.com
1125 S Ball St, Suite 104, Grapevine, TX 76051, Contact: Holly Hammond *Tel:* 972-871-2828 *Fax:* 972-871-2929 *E-mail:* holly.hammond@alc.com
99 Trophy Club Dr, Trophy Club, TX 76262, Contact: David Dotson *Tel:* 817-742-0758 *Fax:* 817-887-2444 *E-mail:* david.dotson@alc.com

American List Counsel Inc, see ALC Inc

Best Mailing Lists Inc
7507 E Tanque Verde Rd, Tucson, AZ 85715
Toll Free Tel: 800-692-2378 *Fax:* 520-885-3100
E-mail: best@bestmailing.com
Web Site: www.bestmailing.com
Key Personnel
Founder & CEO: Karen J Kirsch
EVP: Herbert Kirsch
Founded: 1984
Direct marketing, e-mail marketing, printing & telemarketing.

CDS Global
Subsidiary of Hearst Corp
1901 Bell Ave, Des Moines, IA 50315-1099
Tel: 515-247-7500 *Toll Free Tel:* 866-897-7987
E-mail: salesinfo@cds-global.com
Web Site: www.cds-global.com
Key Personnel
Chmn & CEO: Malcolm Netburn
CFO: Paul Polus
SVP, Global Opers: Nancy Gessmann
Subscription fulfillment, merge/purge, list maintenance & management, demographic segmentation, product fulfillment, printing services, lettershop, telemarketing.
Branch Office(s)
1550 E Washington Ave, Des Moines, IA 50036
2005 Lakewood Dr, Boone, IA 50036
25 Main Place, Suite 125, Council Bluffs, IA 51503
3107 Shelby St, Harlan, IA 51537
411 E South St, Tipton, IA 52772
1600 36 St, West Des Moines, IA 50266
1419 W Fifth St, Wilton, IA 52778
2286 Crosswind Dr, Suite A, Prescott, AZ 86301
Hearst Tower, 300 W 57 St, 10th fl, New York, NY 10019
12401 Research Blvd, Bldg 1, Suite 420, Austin, TX 78759
261-265 Chalmers St, Suite 401, Level 4, Redfern, NSW 2016, Australia *Tel:* (02) 8296 5400 *E-mail:* sales@cdsglobal.com.au
Tower House, Sovereign Park, Lathkill St, Market Harborough, Leics LE16 9EF, United Kingdom *Tel:* (01858) 468811 *E-mail:* sales@cdsglobal.co.uk *Web Site:* www.cdsglobal.co.uk

Cross Country Computer Corp
250 Carleton Ave, East Islip, NY 11730-1240
Tel: 631-334-1810
E-mail: inquiry@crosscountrycomputer.com
Web Site: www.crosscountrycomputer.com
Key Personnel
Founder: Dick Berger *E-mail:* dberger@crosscountrycomputer.com
Principal/Pres & CEO: Thomas Berger
 E-mail: tberger@crosscountrycomputer.com
Principal/EVP: Elisa Berger, PhD
 E-mail: eberger@crosscountrycomputer.com
EVP & Chief Security Offr: Dave Love
 E-mail: dlove@crosscountrycomputer.com
VP, Client Servs: Joan Redwood
 E-mail: jredwood@crosscountrycomputer.com
VP, Fin & HR: Irene Lory *E-mail:* ilory@crosscountrycomputer.com
Dir, Database Architecture: Harvey Cooper
 E-mail: hcooper@crosscountrycomputer.com
Dir, IT: Anita Inkles *E-mail:* ainkles@crosscountrycomputer.com
Mgr, Prodn: Nick Mattina *E-mail:* nmattina@crosscountrycomputer.com
Founded: 1975
Service bureau specializing in database design & maintenance, desktop database systems, data enhancement, profiling, response analysis, modeling, merge/purge, CASS certification, postal presorting, NCOA, list rental fulfillment, data entry & e-mail broadcasting.
Membership(s): Association of National Advertisers Inc (ANA); Direct Marketing Club of New York (DMCNY)

Data Axle
13155 Noel Rd, Suite 1750, Dallas, TX 75240
Toll Free Tel: 866-DATAXLE (328-2953)
E-mail: sales@data-axle.com; corporate.communications@data-axle.com
Web Site: www.data-axle.com
Founded: 1917
Mailing list selection, compilation & brokerage for direct mail & telemarketing campaigns. Lists include businesses, S&P Big Business companies & their executives, professional offices, institutions, key executives, families by age & income, mail order buyers, association members & publication subscription lists. Free catalog. On-site data processing services.
Branch Office(s)
125 S Wacker, Suite 1700, Chicago, IL 60606
1523 S Bell Ave, Ames, IA 50010
20 Burlington Mall Rd, Suite 300, Burlington, MA 01803
1550 Utica Ave S, No 500, Minneapolis, MN 55416
1020 E First St, Papillion, NE 68046
10 Vose Farm Rd, Peterbough, NH 03458
155 W 23 St, New York, NY 10011
2 Blue Hill Plaza, 3rd fl, Pearl River, NY 10956
4 International Dr, Suite 210, Rye Brook, NY 10573
421 SW Sixth Ave, Suite 400, Portland, OR 97204
2930 Westlake Ave N, Seattle, WA 98109
4001 S Business Park Ave, Marshfield, WI 54449
1290 Central Pkwy W, No 500, Mississauga, ON L5C 4R3, Canada

Dunhill International List Co Inc
6400 Congress Ave, Suite 1750, Boca Raton, FL 33487-2898
Tel: 561-998-7800 *Toll Free Tel:* 800-DUNHILL (386-4455) *Fax:* 561-998-7880
E-mail: dunhill@dunhillintl.com
Web Site: www.dunhills.com
Key Personnel
Owner & Pres: Robert Dunhill *E-mail:* robert@dunhillintl.com

VP, Opers: Cindy Dunhill *Tel:* 561-998-7800 ext 6422 *E-mail:* cindy@dunhillintl.com
VP, Sales: Candy Dunhill *Tel:* 561-998-7800 ext 6424 *E-mail:* candy@dunhillintl.com
Mktg Dir: Lisa Martino *Tel:* 561-998-7800 ext 6421 *E-mail:* lisa@dunhillintl.com
Sr Acct Exec: Greg D'Aquila *Tel:* 561-998-7800 ext 6436 *E-mail:* gdaquila@dunhillintl.com; Chrissi Milano *Tel:* 561-998-7800 ext 6434 *E-mail:* chrissi@dunhillintl.com
Prodn Mgr: Mary Reed *E-mail:* mary@dunhillintl.com
Founded: 1938
Mailing, phone & e-mail lists of domestic & international business firms & executives in all SIC categories including retailers, wholesalers, manufacturers, science & engineering. 120 million families by age, income, etc. Choose from 20,000 categories. Other services provided include: e-mail broadcasting, printing & mailing, e-mail & phone appending & digital display advertising.
Membership(s): Florida Direct Marketing Association

Fairfield Marketing Group Inc
Subsidiary of FMG Inc
830 Sport Hill Rd, Easton, CT 06112-1241
E-mail: info@fairfieldmarketing.com
Key Personnel
Pres & CEO: Edward P Washchilla, Jr
  E-mail: ed@fairfieldmarketing.com
Founded: 1986
Mailing list brokerage & list management services. FMG clients rely on us for annual direct marketing programs. We are customer driven & accommodate. Specialty services: custom designed account management; expedient list rental approval; monthly usage reports; market & account analyses; fulfillment, mailing & mail response services; freelance art work; graphic design; advertising & promotional copywriting; binding services; lettershop services; computer services. FMG is a full service direct mail marketing firm.
Membership(s): American Booksellers Association (ABA); Bridgeport Regional Business Council (BRBC); Education Market Association; United States Chamber of Commerce (USCC)

Lake Group Media Inc
One Byram Brook Place, Armonk, NY 10504
Tel: 914-925-2400 *Fax:* 914-925-2499
Web Site: www.lakegroupmedia.com
Key Personnel
CEO: Ryan Lake *E-mail:* ryan.lake@lakegroupmedia.com
COO: Karen Lake *E-mail:* karen.lake@lakegroupmedia.com
SVP: Joe Robinson *E-mail:* joe.robinson@lakegroupmedia.com
Mng Dir: Heather Maylander *E-mail:* heather.maylander@lakegroupmedia.com
Mailing list brokers & managers, database marketing consultants, interactive marketing.

Lawyers & Judges Publishing Co Inc
917 N Swan Rd, Suite 300, Tucson, AZ 85711
Mailing Address: PO Box 30040, Tucson, AZ 85751-0040
Tel: 520-323-1500 *Fax:* 520-323-0055
E-mail: sales@lawyersandjudges.com
Web Site: www.lawyersandjudges.com
Key Personnel
Pres & Publr: Steve Weintraub
Founded: 1963
Lists of mail order buyers of products & publications. Response lists of personal injury attorneys, accountants & financial institutions & insurance claims adjusters, police, accident reconstructionists.

Listco Direct Marketing
1276 46 St, Brooklyn, NY 11219
Tel: 718-871-8400 *Fax:* 718-871-7692
E-mail: info@listcodirect.com
Web Site: www.listcodirect.com
Key Personnel
Pres: Meyer Eckstein
VP: Shlomo Eckstein
Acct Exec: Blima Salczer
List Broker: Simon Winkler
Bookkeeping: Devoiry Horowitz
Full service direct marketing, creative concepts, copy, design, typesetting, full service printing, binding, computer & database services, list marketing & maintenance, merge/purge, list brokerage & management, complete lettershop services.

Marketry Inc
1420 NW Gilman Blvd, No 2558, Issaquah, WA 98027
Tel: 425-451-1262 *Toll Free Tel:* 800-346-2013
Web Site: www.marketry.com
Key Personnel
Pres: Greg Swent *E-mail:* greg@marketry.com
Founded: 1980
Direct mailing lists, opt-in e-mail lists, online media brokerage, database creation & consulting.

MCH Strategic Data
Division of MCH Inc
601 E Marshall St, Sweet Springs, MO 65351
Mailing Address: PO Box 295, Sweet Springs, MO 65351
Toll Free Tel: 800-776-6373
E-mail: sales@mchdata.com
Web Site: www.mchdata.com
Key Personnel
Pres: Amy Rambo
CEO: Peter Long
CIO: Kelly Holder
VP, Mktg: Angela Ridpath
Founded: 1928
Leading provider of data & technology solutions. MCH's commitment to providing superior solutions is evidenced by ongoing investment & development in people, data, technology & services. Those services range from purchasing or leasing data, database integration & development, custom analytics & data technology solutions.

MDR, A Dun & Bradstreet Division
Division of Dun & Bradstreet Inc
5335 Gate Pkwy, Jacksonville, FL 32256
Tel: 973-921-5500 *Toll Free Tel:* 800-333-8802
E-mail: mdrinfo@dnb.com
Web Site: mdreducation.com
Founded: 1969
Marketing information & services for the K-12, higher education, library, early childhood & related education markets. Powered by the most complete, current & accurate education databases available in the industry, MDR provides e-mail contacts & deployment, direct mail lists, sales contact & lead solutions, along with web & social media marketing services.

MSC Lists
PO Box 32510, Minneapolis, MN 55432
Tel: 763-502-8819
Key Personnel
Contact: Ann Herrin; Jim Lance
List broker & manager.

Neibauer Press
20 Industrial Dr, Warminster, PA 18974
Tel: 215-322-6200 *Fax:* 215-322-2495
E-mail: sales@neibauer.com
Web Site: www.neibauer.com
Key Personnel
VP: Ruth Neibauer-Baker *Tel:* 215-322-6216
  E-mail: ruth@neibauer.com
Founded: 1955
Mail preparation, mailing list rentals & maintenance, EDDM mailings.

Special Libraries Association (SLA)
7918 Jones Branch Dr, Suite 300, McLean, VA 22102
Tel: 703-647-4900 *Fax:* 703-506-3266
E-mail: info@sla.org; sla@sla.org
Web Site: www.sla.org
Key Personnel
Mng Dir/VP, Communities & Programming: Monica Evans-Lombe *E-mail:* mevans-lombe@sla.org
Founded: 1909
Addresses of SLA member librarians provided for the promotion of products & services used by specialized libraries & information centers & their clients. Subject interests as well as geographic selections are available.

Specialist Marketing Services Inc
777 Terrace Ave, Suite 401, Hasbrouck Heights, NJ 07604
Tel: 201-865-5800
E-mail: info@sms-inc.com
Web Site: www.sms-inc.com
Key Personnel
Chmn: Lon Mandell *E-mail:* lonman@sms-inc.com
CFO: Nora Bush
CTO: Bruce Sherman
EVP, Cust Acq & Strategic Devt: Susan Giampietro
EVP, Data Div: Joanne Adams
VP, Sales: Kathy Hermann *Tel:* 201-865-5800 ext 2230 *E-mail:* kathyher@sms-inc.com
Founded: 1987
List broker of identified mail order buyers of books, magazines & merchandise. Specialize in general merchandise, culture, executive, health, garden & gifts, self-improvement & juvenile. Custom compilations in all fields including business, professional, cultural & consumer markets. Professional list management of direct mail & mail order buyer lists. Computerization, marketing & maintenance of direct mail lists & mail order buyers & subscribers.
Branch Office(s)
2000 Glades Rd, Suite 406, Boca Raton, FL 33431 *Tel:* 561-416-2888 *E-mail:* fl@sms-inc.com
80 South St, Milford, NH 03055, Contact: Jeremy Johnson *Tel:* 201-865-5800 *E-mail:* milford@sms-inc.com
640 Johnson Ave, Suite GL-001, Bohemia, NY 11716 *Tel:* 631-787-3007 *E-mail:* li@sms-inc.com
520 Columbia Dr, Suite 206, Johnson City, NY 13790 *Tel:* 607-770-1985 *E-mail:* ny@sms-inc.com
Philadelphia Technology Park, 4775 League Island Blvd, Philadelphia, PA 19112 *Toll Free Tel:* 888-656-1689 *E-mail:* philly@sms-inc.com

Worldata
3000 N Military Trail, Boca Raton, FL 33431-6321
Tel: 561-393-8200 *Toll Free Tel:* 800-331-8102
E-mail: hello@worldata.com
Web Site: www.worldata.com
Key Personnel
Pres & CEO: Jay Schwedelson *E-mail:* jays@worldata.com
Founded: 1975
The leader in information marketing services, providing postal, e-mail & telemarketing database services & interactive marketing solutions all housed under one roof, with a client

base that reads like a who's who in the direct/interactive marketing community.
Membership(s): Association of National Advertisers Inc (ANA); NEPA

Columnists & Commentators — Subject Index

ANIMALS, PETS
Wilson Casey, "Trivia" Guinness World Record Holder, pg 1125
Amy E Farrar, pg 1125
Vick Mickunas, pg 1126

ART, ANTIQUES
Adler, Corey, Issac, pg 1125
Wilson Casey, "Trivia" Guinness World Record Holder, pg 1125
Carla Demers, pg 1125
Maria Liberati, pg 1126
Vick Mickunas, pg 1126
Mary Mueller, pg 1126

AUTOMOTIVE
Wilson Casey, "Trivia" Guinness World Record Holder, pg 1125

BOOKS
Diane Abrams, pg 1125
Adler, Corey, Issac, pg 1125
Jane Adler, pg 1125
Wilson Casey, "Trivia" Guinness World Record Holder, pg 1125
Leon Collins, pg 1125
Steve Corey, pg 1125
Carla Demers, pg 1125
Amy E Farrar, pg 1125
Gayle Feldman, pg 1125
Jill Kramer - Best of Books, pg 1126
Maria Liberati, pg 1126
Vick Mickunas, pg 1126
Ruth & Robert Reld, pg 1126
Bruce E Southworth Reviews, pg 1126
Hope Strong, pg 1126

BUSINESS, FINANCE
Wilson Casey, "Trivia" Guinness World Record Holder, pg 1125
Gayle Feldman, pg 1125
Bruce Hoffman, pg 1125
Vick Mickunas, pg 1126
Eric Tyson, pg 1126

CONSUMER EDUCATION
Wilson Casey, "Trivia" Guinness World Record Holder, pg 1125
Bruce Hoffman, pg 1125
Linda King, pg 1125
Vick Mickunas, pg 1126
Mary Mueller, pg 1126
Eric Tyson, pg 1126

FASHION
Diane Abrams, pg 1125
Wilson Casey, "Trivia" Guinness World Record Holder, pg 1125
Maria Liberati, pg 1126
Vick Mickunas, pg 1126
Hope Strong, pg 1126

FILM, RADIO, TV, VIDEO
Diana Barth, pg 1125
Wilson Casey, "Trivia" Guinness World Record Holder, pg 1125
Carla Demers, pg 1125
Maria Liberati, pg 1126
Vick Mickunas, pg 1126

FOOD, WINE
Adler, Corey, Issac, pg 1125
Wilson Casey, "Trivia" Guinness World Record Holder, pg 1125
Maria Liberati, pg 1126
Vick Mickunas, pg 1126
Ruth & Robert Reld, pg 1126
Hope Strong, pg 1126
Margaret Swaine, pg 1126

GARDENING, PLANTS
Jane Adler, pg 1125
Wilson Casey, "Trivia" Guinness World Record Holder, pg 1125
Maria Liberati, pg 1126
Vick Mickunas, pg 1126
Mary Mueller, pg 1126

GENERAL COMMENTARY
David Bouchier, pg 1125
Wilson Casey, "Trivia" Guinness World Record Holder, pg 1125
Amy E Farrar, pg 1125
Gayle Feldman, pg 1125
Linda King, pg 1125
Judith Martin, pg 1126
Vick Mickunas, pg 1126

HEALTH, NUTRITION
Diane Abrams, pg 1125
Jane Adler, pg 1125
Diana Barth, pg 1125
Wilson Casey, "Trivia" Guinness World Record Holder, pg 1125
Amy E Farrar, pg 1125
Joe & Teresa Graedon, pg 1125
Maria Liberati, pg 1126
Vick Mickunas, pg 1126

HOUSE & HOME
Wilson Casey, "Trivia" Guinness World Record Holder, pg 1125
Carla Demers, pg 1125
Maria Liberati, pg 1126
Vick Mickunas, pg 1126
Mary Mueller, pg 1126
Hope Strong, pg 1126
Eric Tyson, pg 1126

HUMOR
David Bouchier, pg 1125
Wilson Casey, "Trivia" Guinness World Record Holder, pg 1125
Judith Martin, pg 1126
Vick Mickunas, pg 1126
Mary Mueller, pg 1126

INSPIRATIONAL
Wilson Casey, "Trivia" Guinness World Record Holder, pg 1125
Vick Mickunas, pg 1126
Mary Mueller, pg 1126

MUSIC, DANCE, THEATER
Adler, Corey, Issac, pg 1125
Jane Adler, pg 1125
Diana Barth, pg 1125
Wilson Casey, "Trivia" Guinness World Record Holder, pg 1125
Steve Corey, pg 1125
Carla Demers, pg 1125
Vick Mickunas, pg 1126
Alex Ross, pg 1126
Matt Stewart, pg 1126

NATIONAL & WORLD AFFAIRS
Wilson Casey, "Trivia" Guinness World Record Holder, pg 1125
Amy E Farrar, pg 1125
Vick Mickunas, pg 1126

PERSONAL ADVICE, COUNSELING
Wilson Casey, "Trivia" Guinness World Record Holder, pg 1125
Judith Martin, pg 1126
Vick Mickunas, pg 1126
Mary Mueller, pg 1126

PERSONALITIES
Diana Barth, pg 1125
Wilson Casey, "Trivia" Guinness World Record Holder, pg 1125
Maria Liberati, pg 1126
Vick Mickunas, pg 1126

PHOTOGRAPHY
Adler, Corey, Issac, pg 1125
Wilson Casey, "Trivia" Guinness World Record Holder, pg 1125
Carla Demers, pg 1125
Vick Mickunas, pg 1126
Mary Mueller, pg 1126

POLITICS
Wilson Casey, "Trivia" Guinness World Record Holder, pg 1125
Bruce Hoffman, pg 1125
Vick Mickunas, pg 1126

SCIENCE, TECHNOLOGY
Wilson Casey, "Trivia" Guinness World Record Holder, pg 1125
Leon Collins, pg 1125
Steve Corey, pg 1125
Amy E Farrar, pg 1125
Vick Mickunas, pg 1126

SPORTS, RECREATION
Wilson Casey, "Trivia" Guinness World Record Holder, pg 1125
Vick Mickunas, pg 1126
Margaret Swaine, pg 1126

TRAVEL, RESORTS
Adler, Corey, Issac, pg 1125
Jane Adler, pg 1125
Diana Barth, pg 1125
Wilson Casey, "Trivia" Guinness World Record Holder, pg 1125
Steve Corey, pg 1125
Amy E Farrar, pg 1125
Foster Travel Publishing, pg 1125
Maria Liberati, pg 1126
Vick Mickunas, pg 1126
Ruth & Robert Reld, pg 1126
Margaret Swaine, pg 1126

Columnists & Commentators

Prior to this section is a list of columnists and commentators classified by their special interests. For related information, see **Radio Programs Featuring Books, TV Programs Featuring Books** and **Book Review Syndicates**.

Letters in parentheses indicate type(s) of media:

(P)–Press (R)–Radio (TV)–Television

Publishers, authors and other correspondents are advised that only the U.S. Postal Service can deliver to Post Office Boxes.

Diane Abrams (P)
Whitegate Features Syndicate
Division of Whitegate International Corp
71 Faunce Dr, Providence, RI 02906
Tel: 401-274-2149
Web Site: www.whitegatefeatures.com
Key Personnel
Pres: Ed Isaac
Mgr: Mari Howard
Founded: 1988
Health, beauty, fashion, reviews, beauty products, clothing, spas, exercise equipment, interviews.

Adler, Corey, Issac (P-TV)
Whitegate Features Syndicate
Division of Whitegate International Corp
71 Faunce Dr, Providence, RI 02906
Tel: 401-274-2149
Web Site: www.whitegatefeatures.com
Key Personnel
Pres: Ed Isaac
Mgr: Mari Howard
Founded: 1988
Anything anyone would ever do when they travel.

Jane Adler (P-TV)
Whitegate Features Syndicate
Division of Whitegate International Corp
71 Faunce Dr, Providence, RI 02906
Tel: 401-274-2149
Web Site: www.whitegatefeatures.com
Key Personnel
Pres: Ed Isaac
Mgr: Mari Howard
Founded: 1988
Three columns; indoor gardening, relationships/self-help, medical, health & travel, writes & reviews products & interviews.

Diana Barth (P)
535 W 51 St, Suite 3-A, New York, NY 10019
Tel: 212-307-5465
E-mail: diabarth99@gmail.com
Columns on performing arts, TV, film & personalities. Book, theatre & film reviews.

David Bouchier (R)
David Bouchier's Commentary on WSHU
PO Box 763, Stony Brook, NY 11790
Tel: 631-751-2660
E-mail: davidbouchier5@gmail.com
Founded: 1992
WSHU, Public Radio, Fairfield, CT (weekly/humor).

Wilson Casey, "Trivia" Guinness World Record Holder (P)
TrivGuy Wilson Casey
282 Spring Dr, Spartanburg, SC 29302
Tel: 864-621-7129
E-mail: trivguy@bellsouth.net; wc@triviaguy.com
Web Site: www.triviaguy.com; www.patreon.com/triviaguy
Founded: 2000
"Trivia" Guiness World Record holder's "TrivGuy" column, provides trivia columns to newspapers & other media; 6 multiple choice questions with answers syndicated daily (7x/week); Also have a weekly version. King Features Syndicate nationally distributes Wilson Casey's "Bible Trivia" column once a week. Columns run the gamut of category appeal & are available 365 days per year in over 500 papers. Nationwide references. Free trial available.

Leon Collins (P)
Whitegate Features Syndicate
Division of Whitegate International Corp
71 Faunce Dr, Providence, RI 02906
Tel: 401-274-2149
Web Site: www.whitegatefeatures.com
Key Personnel
Pres: Ed Isaac
Mgr: Mari Howard
Founded: 1988
Science.

Steve Corey (P)
Whitegate Features Syndicate
Division of Whitegate International Corp
71 Faunce Dr, Providence, RI 02906
Tel: 401-274-2149
Web Site: www.whitegatefeatures.com
Key Personnel
Pres: Ed Isaac
Mgr: Mari Howard
Founded: 1988
Computer software review; everything in computers: software, hardware, books, gadgets, etc. Also travel column.

Carla Demers (P)
Whitegate Features Syndicate
Division of Whitegate International Corp
71 Faunce Dr, Providence, RI 02906
Tel: 401-274-2149
Web Site: www.whitegatefeatures.com
Key Personnel
Pres: Ed Isaac
Mgr: Mari Howard
Founded: 1988
Art review, crafts & craft materials, photography.

Amy E Farrar (P)
Farrar Writing & Editing
4638 Manchester Rd, Mound, MN 55364
Tel: 952-451-5982
E-mail: amyfarrar@mchsi.com
Web Site: www.writeandedit.net
Founded: 1999
Independent freelance writer & editor for book publishers & individuals. Author of *Global Warming: Essential Viewpoints*, *The Indispensable Field Guide to Freelance Writing*, *ADHD* & *A Jersey Girl's Guide to the Universe: A Memoir*. Primary topics are environment, health, medical & travel.

Gayle Feldman (P)
The Bookseller
131 E 74 St, New York, NY 10021
Tel: 212-772-8265 *Fax:* 212-517-4020
E-mail: feldmangayle@gmail.com
Web Site: www.gaylefeldman.com; www.thebookseller.com
US correspondent for *The Bookseller*; features & reviews for other print & online publications.

Foster Travel Publishing (P)
1623 Martin Luther King Jr Way, Berkeley, CA 94709
Tel: 510-549-2202
Web Site: www.fostertravel.com
Key Personnel
Owner & Pres: Lee Foster *E-mail:* lee@fostertravel.com
Founded: 1972
Travel column available from web site. Full text travel writing photography on 200 destinations worldwide. Reports on essence-of-the destination. Weekly travel commentary blog.
Membership(s): American Society of Media Photographers (ASMP); Bay Area Independent Publishers Association (BAIPA); Bay Area Travel Writers; Society of American Travel Writers (SATW)

Joe & Teresa Graedon (P-R)
King Features Syndicate
Division of Hearst Corp
300 W 57 St, 41st fl, New York, NY 10019
Toll Free Tel: 800-708-7311 (FL edit)
Web Site: www.kingfeatures.com; www.peoplespharmacy.com.
Syndicated; "The People's Pharmacy", pharmacology column & podcast; provides health, pharmaceutical & nutrition information; alternative therapies including herbs & home remedies.

Bruce Hoffman (P)
Whitegate Features Syndicate
Division of Whitegate International Corp
71 Faunce Dr, Providence, RI 02906
Tel: 401-274-2149
Web Site: www.whitegatefeatures.com
Key Personnel
Pres: Ed Isaac
Mgr: Mari Howard
Founded: 1988
Everything to do with business & finance: books & interviews.

Linda King (P)
Whitegate Features Syndicate
Division of Whitegate International Corp
71 Faunce Dr, Providence, RI 02906
Tel: 401-274-2149
Web Site: www.whitegatefeatures.com
Key Personnel
Pres: Ed Isaac
Mgr: Mari Howard

COLUMNISTS & COMMENTATORS

Founded: 1988
Interviews, current events, senior topics & book reviews.

Jill Kramer - Best of Books (P)
Whitegate Features Syndicate
Division of Whitegate International Corp
71 Faunce Dr, Providence, RI 02906
Tel: 401-274-2149
Web Site: www.whitegatefeatures.com
Key Personnel
Pres: Ed Isaac
Mgr: Mari Howard
Best of books.

Maria Liberati (P-R-TV)
The Basic Art of Italian Cooking
1250 Bethlehem Pike, Unit 241, Hatfield, PA 19440
Tel: 215-436-9524
E-mail: maria@marialiberati.com
Web Site: www.marialiberati.com
"Maria & Co," "Maria Liberati's The Basic Art of Italian Cooking™" & "Maria Liberati Show" podcast.

Judith Martin (P)
Andrews McMeel Syndication
Division of Andrews McMeel Universal
1130 Walnut St, Kansas City, MO 64106-2109
Tel: 816-581-7300 *Toll Free Tel:* 800-255-6734
Web Site: syndication.andrewsmcmeel.com
"Miss Manners" advice & etiquette column, print & online.

Vick Mickunas (R)
The Book Nook
4805 Meredith Rd, Yellow Springs, OH 45387
Tel: 937-767-1396
E-mail: vick@vickmickunas.com
Web Site: www.wyso.org/show/book-nook
Founded: 1994
Independent radio producer & author interviewer. Airs Sat 7-8 AM, Sun 10:30-11 AM (ET) on WYSO public radio. WYSO is a 50,000 watt National Public Radio affiliate that serves southwest Ohio.

Mary Mueller (P)
516 Bartram Rd, Moorestown, NJ 08057
Tel: 856-778-4769
E-mail: mamam49@aol.com
"Soup's On!" & "Letters to a Friend." More topics: marriage enrichment, spiritual, parenting-keeping teenagers off drugs. Also provides freelance proofreading services.
Please send free review copies for possible review in small local media outlets.

The People's Pharmacy, see Joe & Teresa Graedon

Ruth & Robert Reld (P)
Whitegate Features Syndicate
Division of Whitegate International Corp
71 Faunce Dr, Providence, RI 02906
Tel: 401-274-2149
Web Site: www.whitegatefeatures.com
Key Personnel
Pres: Ed Isaac
Mgr: Mari Howard
Founded: 1990
Fine dining, restaurant reviews & food & wine ratings. Also review cooking products, cooking equipment, recipes & recipe books.

Alex Ross (P)
The New Yorker
One World Trade Center, New York, NY 10007
Tel: 212-286-2860 *Toll Free Tel:* 800-444-7570
Web Site: www.newyorker.com/contributors/alex-ross; www.therestisnoise.com
Reviews & analyses of musical events, classical & opera.

Bruce E Southworth Reviews (P-TV)
1621 Lafond Ave, St Paul, MN 55104-2212
Tel: 651-808-1099
E-mail: mnbookcritic@yahoo.com
Key Personnel
Owner & Principal: Bruce E Southworth
Freelance for several newspapers, magazines & Internet sites. Co-produced a cable television program "Speaking of Mysteries", featuring interviews.

Matt Stewart (P)
Whitegate Features Syndicate
Division of Whitegate International Corp
71 Faunce Dr, Providence, RI 02906
Tel: 401-274-2149
Web Site: www.whitegatefeatures.com
Key Personnel
Pres: Ed Isaac
Mgr: Mari Howard
Founded: 1988
Music (including classical music), CD & equipment reviews.

Hope Strong (P)
Whitegate Features Syndicate
Division of Whitegate International Corp
71 Faunce Dr, Providence, RI 02906
Tel: 401-274-2149
Web Site: www.whitegatefeatures.com
Key Personnel
Pres: Ed Isaac
Mgr: Mari Howard
Founded: 1988
"Strong Style"- anything with new ways to live. Lifestyles & decorating.

Margaret Swaine (P)
2 Hawthorn Gardens, Unit 4, Toronto, ON M4W 1P3, Canada
Tel: 416-961-5328
E-mail: m.swaine@rogers.com
Web Site: www.margaretswaine.com
Founded: 1979
Restaurants & travel, ski, golf & spa. Online column appears in print & online for Best Health Magazine, Ensemble Travel Magazine, National Post, Ottawa Citizen, Travel Industry Today, Zoomer Magazine, Kawartha Magazine, Air Canada Vacations, Global Gourmet & WestJet Vacations.

Eric Tyson (P)
King Features Syndicate
300 W 57 St, 15th fl, New York, NY 10019-5238
Toll Free Tel: 800-708-7311 (FL edit)
E-mail: eric@erictyson.com
Web Site: www.erictyson.com
Key Personnel
Pres: CJ Kettler
SVP, Content Dist: Roland Hamilton
SVP, Gen Mgr & Global Head, Licensing: Carla Silva
Investor's Guide.

Book Review Syndicates

Publishers, authors and other correspondents are advised that only the U.S. Postal Service can deliver to Post Office Boxes.

BookPage®
2143 Belcourt Ave, Nashville, TN 37212
Tel: 615-292-8926 *Fax:* 615-292-8249
Web Site: bookpage.com
Key Personnel
Pres & Publr: Michael A Zibart
   E-mail: michael@bookpage.com
Publr & Ed-in-Chief: Trisha Ping
Assoc Publr: Julia Steele
Deputy Ed: Cat Acree
Mktg Mgr: Mary Claire Zibart *E-mail:* mary@bookpage.com
Prodn Mgr: Penny Childress
Founded: 1988
Monthly book review publication distributed through subscribing bookstores & public libraries.
Books Reviewed: 1,000

Literary Features Syndicate
88 Briarcliff Rd, Larchmont, NY 10538
Tel: 914-834-7480
Key Personnel
Ed: Barbara Basbanes Richter *E-mail:* barbara.basbanes@gmail.com
Reviewer: Nicholas A Basbanes
Young Adult Book Reviewer: Nicole Basbanes Claire
Founded: 1991
Reviews of the best new books, author reviews & news in the world of books.
Books Reviewed: 200

Rainbo Electronic Reviews
5405 Cumberland Rd, Minneapolis, MN 55410
Tel: 612-408-4057
Web Site: www.rainboreviews.com
Key Personnel
Ed: Richard Trethewey *E-mail:* editor@rainboreviews.com
Founded: 1980
Reviews are seen on web site; books (computer, mysteries, nonfiction, fiction, children's & cookbooks); video & audiobooks.
Books Reviewed: 350

United Press International (UPI)
Subsidiary of News World Communications
1133 19 St NW, Suite 800, Washington, DC 20036
Tel: 202-898-8000
E-mail: media@upi.com
Web Site: www.upi.com
Key Personnel
Pres: Nicholas Chiaia
Founded: 1907
News, TV, radio, sports & features.
Branch Office(s)
1200 N Federal Hwy, Suite 200, Boca Raton, FL 33432

Book Review & Index Journals & Services

In order to obtain copyright registration, two copies of every book published in the United States must be sent to the Library of Congress, U.S. Copyright Office, 101 Independence Avenue SE, Washington, DC 20559-6000. All copyrighted materials are then reviewed for eligibility for Library of Congress (LC) cataloging and subsequent listings in the National Union Catalog of Manuscript Collections (NUCMC), the Library's MARC system and other cataloging aids.

In addition to the review sources listed here, one will find reviewers listed in the sections **Magazines for the Trade** (volume 1), **Serials Featuring Books, Radio Programs Featuring Books** and **TV Programs Featuring Books**.

Publishers, authors and other correspondents are advised that only the U.S. Postal Service can deliver to Post Office Boxes.

Abridged Readers' Guide to Periodical Literature
Grey House Publishing Inc™
4919 Rte 22, Amenia, NY 12501
Mailing Address: PO Box 56, Amenia, NY 12501-0056
Tel: 518-789-8700 Toll Free Tel: 800-562-2139
Fax: 518-789-0556
E-mail: books@greyhouse.com
Web Site: greyhouse.com
Smaller subset of Readers' Guide to Periodical Literature. Comprehensive indexing of 72 of the most popular general-interest periodicals published in the US & Canada.
Frequency: 2 paperback issues, March & Sept plus library-bound annual cumulation in Jan
$295
ISSN: 0001-334X

African American Review (AAR)
Johns Hopkins University Press
c/o St Louis University, 317 Adorjan Hall, 3800 Lindell Blvd, St Louis, MO 63108
Tel: 314-977-3688
Web Site: afamreview.org
Subscription Address: Johns Hopkins University Press, Journals Div, PO Box 19966, Baltimore, MD 21211-0966 Tel: 410-516-6987
Toll Free Tel: 800-548-1784 Fax: 410-516-3866
E-mail: jrnlcirc@press.jhu.edu Web Site: www.press.jhu.edu/journals/african-american-review
Key Personnel
Mng Ed: Aileen M Keenan E-mail: aileen.keenan@slu.edu
Ed: Nathan L Grant
Scholarly aggregation of insightful essays on African American literature, theatre, film, the visual arts & culture; interviews; poetry; fiction; book reviews. AAR has featured renowned writers & cultural critics including Trudier Harris, Arnold Rampersad, Hortense Spillers, Amiri Baraka, Cyrus Cassells, Rita Dove, Charles Johnson, Cheryl Wall & Toni Morrison. The official publication of the Modern Language Association's LLC African American Forum, AAR fosters a vigorous conversation among writers & scholars in the arts, humanities & social sciences.
First published 1967
Frequency: Quarterly
Number of pages: 150
Circulation: 1,750
$45/yr indivs US, $55/yr (online), $140/yr instns US (print)
ISSN: 1062-4783
Books Reviewed: 40/yr

American Book Publishing Record® Monthly
Grey House Publishing Inc™
4919 Rte 22, Amenia, NY 12501
Mailing Address: PO Box 56, Amenia, NY 12501-0056
Tel: 518-789-8700 Toll Free Tel: 800-562-2139
Fax: 518-789-0556
E-mail: books@greyhouse.com
Web Site: greyhouse.com
Access to the newest cataloging records from the Library of Congress.
Frequency: Monthly
Number of pages: 3,500
$765/yr
ISSN: 0002-7707

American Book Review
University of Nebraska Press
c/o University of Houston-Victoria College of Liberal Arts & Sciences, 3007 N Ben Wilson St, Victoria, TX 77901
Tel: 361-248-8245
E-mail: abr@americanbookreview.org; americanbookreview@uhv.org; americanbookreview@gmail.com
Web Site: americanbookreview.org
Subscription Address: PO Box 880630, Lincoln, NE 68588-0630 Tel: 402-472-5988
E-mail: journals@unl.edu
Key Personnel
Ed-in-Chief: Dr Jeffrey R Di Leo
Mng Ed: Jake Snyder
Sr Ed: Jeffrey A Sartain
Edit Assoc: Orlando Di Leo
Reviews of fiction, poetry & criticism from small, regional, university, ethnic, avant-garde & women's presses.
First published 1977
Frequency: Quarterly
Number of pages: 32
Circulation: 5,000
$18/issue, $62/yr indivs, $140/yr instns
ISSN: 0149-9408
Books Reviewed: 240/yr

American Journal of Philology
Johns Hopkins University Press
2715 N Charles St, Baltimore, MD 21218-4363
SAN: 202-7348
Tel: 410-516-6987 (journal orders outside US & CN) Toll Free Tel: 800-548-1784 (journal orders) Fax: 410-578-2865 (journal orders)
E-mail: jrnlcirc@jh.edu (journal orders)
Web Site: www.press.jhu.edu/journals/american-journal-philology
Key Personnel
Ed: Rosa Andujar
Book Review Ed: Tom Hawkins E-mail: hawkins.312@osu.edu
The journal that has helped shape American classical scholarship. It has achieved worldwide recognition as a forum for international exchange among classicists & philologists.
Also available online (ISSN: 1086-3168).
First published 1880
Frequency: Quarterly
Number of pages: 176
Circulation: 208
Indivs: $50/yr print, $60/yr online; Instns: $240/yr print
ISSN: 0002-9475
Books Reviewed: 10

American Quarterly
Johns Hopkins University Press
2715 N Charles St, Baltimore, MD 21218-4363
SAN: 202-7348
Tel: 410-516-6987 (journal orders outside US & CN) Toll Free Tel: 800-548-1784 (journal orders) Fax: 410-578-2865 (journal orders)
E-mail: jrnlcirc@jh.edu (journal orders)
Web Site: www.americanquarterly.org; www.press.jhu.edu/journals/american-quarterly
Key Personnel
Mng Ed: Lilly Fisher
Ed: Mari Yoshihara
Book Review Ed: Alyosha Goldstein
E-mail: agoldstein@unm.edu; Britt Rusert
E-mail: brusert@afroam.umass.edu
The official publication of the American Studies Association, serving as a guide to studies in the culture of the US. Available to members only.
Also available online (ISSN: 1080-6490).
First published 1949
Frequency: Quarterly
Number of pages: 252
Circulation: 1,356
$230/yr instns print
ISSN: 0003-0678
Books Reviewed: 2-4/issue

The ANNALS of The American Academy of Political & Social Science
SAGE Publishing
2455 Teller Rd, Thousand Oaks, CA 91320
Toll Free Tel: 800-818-7243 Toll Free Fax: 800-583-2665
E-mail: journals@sagepub.com
Web Site: www.sagepub.com
Key Personnel
Exec Ed: Thomas A Kecskemethy
Organized Dec 14, 1889 to promote the progress of political & social science, especially through publications & meetings. The Academy seeks to gather & present reliable information to assist the public in forming an intelligent & accurate judgment.
Also available online (ISSN: 1552-3349).
First published 1889
Frequency: 6 issues/yr
Circulation: 4,800
Indivs: $46 paper, $68 hardcover, $155/yr print; Instl: $278 paper, $313 hardcover, $1,313/yr online, $1,545 print paper & online, $1,743 print hardcover & online
ISSN: 0002-7162

AudioFile®
AudioFile® Publications Inc
37 Silver St, Portland, ME 04101
Tel: 207-774-7563 Toll Free Tel: 800-506-1212
Fax: 207-775-3744
E-mail: info@audiofilemagazine.com
Web Site: www.audiofilemagazine.com
Key Personnel
Founder & Ed: Robin F Whitten E-mail: robin@audiofilemagazine.com

Publr: Michele L Cobb *E-mail:* michele@audiofilemagazine.com
Art Dir: Jennifer Steele
Mng Ed: Jennifer M Dowell *E-mail:* jennifer@audiofilemagazine.com
Review Ed: Elizabeth K Dodge
Edit Asst: Alisha Langerman; Joanne Simonean
Audiobook reviews & recommendations. Focus on the listening experience & the unique aspects of the audio performance. Reviews published weekly on web site. Also narrator & author profiles. Award exceptional performances with AudioFile's Earphone Awards.
First published 1992
Frequency: 6 issues/yr
Number of pages: 72
Circulation: 20,000
$19.95/yr, $26.95/2 yrs, $60/yr (prof subn with annual "Audiobook Reference Guide"); $10/issue
ISSN: 1063-0244
Books Reviewed: 2,500/yr

BC BookWorld
Subsidiary of BC Bookworld Productions Ltd
PO Box 93536, Vancouver, BC V6E 4L7, Canada
Tel: 604-736-4011 *Fax:* 604-736-4011
E-mail: bookworld@telus.net
Web Site: www.bcbookworld.com
Key Personnel
Publr: Beverly Cramp
News & photos of BC books & authors.
First published 1987
Frequency: Quarterly
Circulation: 30,000
$25/yr, $40/2 yrs
ISSN: 1701-5405
Books Reviewed: 100/issue, 400/yr

Bellevue Literary Review
149 E 23 St, Suite 1516, New York, NY 10010
Tel: 917-375-5790
E-mail: info@BLReview.org
Web Site: www.BLReview.org
Key Personnel
Ed-in-Chief: Dr Danielle Ofri
Mng Ed: Stacy Bodziak
Assoc Ed: Kate Falvey
Fiction Ed: Suzanne McConnell
Asst Fiction Ed: Doris W Cheng
Asst Nonfiction Ed: Scott Oglesby; Alanna Weissman
Asst Poetry Ed: Linda Harris Dolan; Saleem Hue Penny
Edit Asst: Rosalind Aparicio-Ramirez; Amanda Chen
Editors invite submissions of previously unpublished works of fiction, creative nonfiction & poetry that touch upon relationships to the human body, illness, health & healing. We encourage creative interpretations of these themes. Interested in high-quality literary writing.
First published 2001
Frequency: 2 issues/yr
Number of pages: 192
Circulation: 3,000
$25/yr
ISSN: 1537-5048
Books Reviewed: 1/issue

Book Review Index, see Gale Literature: Book Review Index

Bookforum
The Nation Co LLC
520 Eighth Ave, 21st fl, New York, NY 10018
E-mail: editors@bookforum.com; advertising@bookforum.com; circulation@bookforum.com
Web Site: www.bookforum.com; subscriptions.bookforum.com
Key Personnel
Ad Dir: Suzette Cabildo
Ed-in-Chief: Michael Miller
Book reviews on politics, culture & the arts.
First published 1984
Frequency: Quarterly
$30/yr digital, $40/yr print & digital

Booklist
The American Library Association (ALA)
225 N Michigan Ave, Suite 1300, Chicago, IL 60601
SAN: 201-0062
Tel: 312-944-6780 *Toll Free Tel:* 800-545-2433 *Fax:* 312-440-9374
E-mail: info@booklistonline.com; ala@ala.org
Web Site: www.booklistonline.com; www.ala.org
Subscription Address: PO Box 37014, Boone, IA 50037-0014 *Toll Free Tel:* 888-350-0949
Key Personnel
Publr & Ed: George Kendall *Tel:* 800-545-2433 ext 5717 *E-mail:* gkendall@ala.org
Prodn Dir: Ben Segedin *E-mail:* bsegedin@ala.org
Sr Ed, Adult Books: Annie Bostrom *E-mail:* abostrom@ala.org
Sr Ed, Books for Youth: Ronny Khuri *E-mail:* rkhuri@ala.org; Maggie Reagan *E-mail:* mreagan@ala.org; Julia Smith *E-mail:* jsmith@ala.org
Sr Ed, Collection Mgmt & Lib Outreach: Susan Maguire *E-mail:* smaguire@ala.org
Ed, Adult Books: Donna Seaman *E-mail:* dseaman@ala.org
Ed, Books for Youth: Sarah Hunter *E-mail:* shunter@ala.org
Prodn Ed: Carlos Orellana *E-mail:* corellana@ala.org
Mktg Mgr: Grace Rosean *E-mail:* grosean@ala.org
Periodicals & Subns Mgr: Dan Kaplan *E-mail:* dkaplan@ala.org
Review adult, young adult & juvenile books (most before publication); media, including videos, DVDs, audios & audiobooks, encyclopedias, dictionaries & other reference works including online databases.
Frequency: Semimonthly (exc monthly July & Aug); 22 issues/yr
Circulation: 12,250
$9/issue, $184.95/yr, $309.95/2 yrs, $439.95/3 yrs, $224.95/yr foreign
ISSN: 0006-7385
Books Reviewed: 8,000/yr

Boston Review
Boston Critic Inc
PO Box 390568, Cambridge, MA 02139
Tel: 617-356-8198
E-mail: review@bostonreview.net; customerservice@bostonreview.net
Web Site: bostonreview.net
Key Personnel
Publr & Co-Ed-in-Chief: Deborah Chasman
Assoc Publr: Jasmine Parmley
Co-Ed-in-Chief: Joshua Cohen
Exec Ed: Matt Lord
Asst Ed: Cameron Avery
Circ Mgr: Irina Costache *E-mail:* irina@bostonreview.net
Fin Mgr: Anthony DeMusis, III
Magazine of culture & politics. Books reviewed bimonthly in print & online.
First published 1975
Frequency: Quarterly
Number of pages: 64
Circulation: 10,000
$19.95/issue print, $15.95/issue digital, $50/yr print, $35/yr digital
ISSN: 0734-2306

Bulletin of the American Schools of Oriental Research (BASOR)
American Society of Overseas Research (ASOR)
James F Strange Ctr, 209 Commerce St, Alexandria, VA 22314
Tel: 703-789-9229; 703-789-9230 (pubns) *Fax:* 617-353-6575
E-mail: basor@asor.org; info@asor.org; publications@asor.org
Web Site: www.asor.org
Key Personnel
Ed: Susan Cohen; Marwan Kilani; Jana Mynarova; Regine Pruzsinszky
First published 1919
Frequency: 2 issues/yr
Number of pages: 120
Circulation: 1,700
Free to membs
ISSN: 0003-097X
Books Reviewed: 9

Bulletin of the History of Medicine
Johns Hopkins University Press
2715 N Charles St, Baltimore, MD 21218-4363
SAN: 202-7348
Tel: 410-516-6987 (journal orders outside US & CN) *Toll Free Tel:* 800-548-1784 (journal orders) *Fax:* 410-578-2865 (journal orders)
E-mail: bhm@jhmi.edu; jrnlcirc@jh.edu (journal orders)
Web Site: www.press.jhu.edu/journals/bulletin-history-medicine
Key Personnel
Ed: Jeremey A Greene; Alisha Rankin; Gabriela Soto Laveaga
Assoc Ed: Carolyn McLaughlin
Official publication of the American Association for the History of Medicine (AAHM) & Johns Hopkins Institute of the History of Medicine. Also available online (ISSN: 1086-3176).
Frequency: Quarterly
Number of pages: 255
Circulation: 881
Indivs: $50/yr print, $65/yr online; Instns: $225/yr print
ISSN: 0007-5140
Books Reviewed: 100

Callaloo
Johns Hopkins University Press
2715 N Charles St, Baltimore, MD 21218-4363
SAN: 202-7348
Tel: 410-516-6987 (journal orders outside US & CN) *Toll Free Tel:* 800-548-1784 (journal orders) *Fax:* 410-578-2865 (journal orders)
E-mail: jrnlcirc@jh.edu (journal orders)
Web Site: www.press.jhu.edu/journals/callaloo
Key Personnel
Mng Ed: Kelley A Robbins
Ed: Charles Henry Rowell
A journal of literature, art & culture of the African Diaspora. Also available online (ISSN: 1080-6512).
Frequency: Quarterly
Number of pages: 300
Circulation: 204
Indivs: $65/yr print, $75/yr online; Instns: $235/yr print
ISSN: 0161-2492
Books Reviewed: 12

The Bulletin of the Center for Children's Books
Johns Hopkins University Press
2715 N Charles St, Baltimore, MD 21218-4363
SAN: 202-7348
Tel: 410-516-6900; 410-516-6987 (journal orders outside US & CN); 217-244-0324 (bulletin info) *Toll Free Tel:* 800-548-1784 (journal orders) *Fax:* 410-516-6968; 410-578-2865 (journal orders)

E-mail: bccb@illinois.edu; jlorder@jhupress.jhu.edu
Web Site: www.press.jhu.edu/journals/bulletin-center-childrens-books
Key Personnel
Ed: Deborah Stevenson
Review juvenile books.
First published 1947
Frequency: 11 issues/yr
Number of pages: 40
Circulation: 1,000
$55/yr indivs, $120/yr instns (print or online)
ISSN: 0008-9036
Books Reviewed: 900/yr

Children's Bookwatch
Midwest Book Review
278 Orchard Dr, Oregon, WI 53575-1129
Tel: 608-835-7937
E-mail: mbr@execpc.com
Web Site: www.midwestbookreview.com
Key Personnel
Ed-in-Chief: James A Cox
Review large & small press publications: audio cassettes, videos, young adult/children's books, fiction, general interest nonfiction, CD music & children's educational CD-ROMs.
First published 1990
Frequency: Monthly
Number of pages: 8
Circulation: 32,000
Free online
ISSN: 0896-4521
Books Reviewed: 70/issue

Choice
Association of College & Research Libraries (ACRL)
Division of The American Library Association (ALA)
575 Main St, Suite 300, Middletown, CT 06457
Tel: 860-347-6933; 847-504-8803 (subns)
   Toll Free Tel: 844-291-0455 (subns) *Fax:* 860-346-8586
E-mail: acrlsubscriptions@omeda.com; support@acrlchoice.freshdesk.com
Web Site: www.ala.org/acrl-choice; www.choice360.org
Key Personnel
Publr & Ed: Rachel Hendrick *E-mail:* rhendrick@ala.org
Edit Dir: Bill Mickey *E-mail:* bmickey@ala.org
Dir, Info & Prodn Servs: Lisa M Gross
   E-mail: lgross@ala.org
Ad Sales Mgr: Pamela Marino *E-mail:* pmarino@ala.org
Mktg & Publicity Mgr: Deb Villavicencio-Eschinger *E-mail:* dvillavicencio@ala.org
High-quality evaluations of nonfiction academic writing. Bibliographic reference & recommendation for both collection development & individual research. Contains over 200,000 reviews of academic monographs & serves 2,400 institutions worldwide. Available online as *Choice Reviews Online.*
First published 1964
Frequency: Monthly
Circulation: 2,400
$555/yr US, $596/yr CN & Mexico, $715/yr foreign
ISSN: 0009-4978
Books Reviewed: 4,200/yr

Chronicles: A Magazine of American Culture
The Charlemagne Institute
8011 34 Ave S, Suite C11, Bloomington, MN 55425
Web Site: www.chroniclesmagazine.org
Subscription Address: PO Box 3247, Northbrook, IL 60065-9968 *Toll Free Tel:* 800-877-5459
Key Personnel
Exec Ed: Edward Welsch

Book reviews, political, economic & social criticism.
First published 1977
Frequency: Monthly
Number of pages: 52
Circulation: 7,500
$44.99/yr, $79.99/2 yrs, $104.99/3 yrs
ISSN: 0887-5731
Books Reviewed: 7/issue (3 in-depth, 4 in-brief)

Communication Abstracts
EBSCO Information Services
10 Estes St, Ipswich, MA 01938
Tel: 978-356-6500 *Toll Free Tel:* 800-653-2726
   Fax: 978-356-6565
E-mail: information@ebsco.com
Web Site: www.ebsco.com
Key Personnel
Pres & CEO: Tim Collins *E-mail:* tcollins@ebsco.com
EVP, Mktg, Sales, PR & Strategic Partnerships: Sam Brooks *E-mail:* sbrooks@ebsco.com
Sr Communs Specialist: Karena Donnelly
   E-mail: kdonnelly@ebsco.com
Provides coverage of recent literature in all areas of communication studies (both mass & interpersonal). Includes expanded coverage of new communications technologies.
First published 1978
Frequency: 6 issues/yr
Circulation: 1,300

Current Biography
Grey House Publishing Inc™
4919 Rte 22, Amenia, NY 12501
Mailing Address: PO Box 56, Amenia, NY 12501-0056
Tel: 518-789-8700 *Toll Free Tel:* 800-562-2139
   Fax: 518-789-0556
E-mail: books@greyhouse.com
Web Site: greyhouse.com
Offers 16-18 biographical, up-to-date profiles of accomplished & rising stars of politics, industry, entertainment & the arts from the US & around the world.
First published 1940
Frequency: 11 issues/yr
$199/yr, $185/2 yrs, $165/3 yrs
ISSN: 0011-3344

Dayton Daily News
Cox Media Group Ohio
Unit of Cox Media (Atlanta)
4805 Meredith Rd, Yellow Springs, OH 45387
Tel: 937-767-1396
Key Personnel
Book Reviewer: Vick Mickunas *E-mail:* vick@vickmickunas.com
Vick Mickunas is the author of regular reviews in the print version of the *Dayton Daily News* & other Cox Ohio newspapers. His reviews are also published on the Cox Ohio web sites.
First published 2004
Circulation: 192,000 (Sun)
ISSN: 0890-8931

Diacritics
Johns Hopkins University Press
2715 N Charles St, Baltimore, MD 21218-4363
SAN: 202-7348
Tel: 410-516-6987 (journal orders outside US & CN) *Toll Free Tel:* 800-548-1784 (journal orders) *Fax:* 410-578-2865 (journal orders)
E-mail: jrnlcirc@jh.edu (journal orders)
Web Site: www.press.jhu.edu/journals/diacritics
Key Personnel
Mng Ed: Hannah Miller
Ed: Andrea Bachner
A preeminent forum for exchange among literary theorists, critics & philosophers. Each issue features articles in which contributors compare & analyze books on particular theoretical works & develop their own positions on the theses, methods & theoretical implications of these works.
Also available online (ISSN: 1080-6539).
First published 1971
Frequency: Quarterly
Number of pages: 80
Circulation: 98
Indivs: $40/yr print, $45/yr online; Instns: $155/yr print
ISSN: 0300-7162
Books Reviewed: 5

ELH, see English Literary History (ELH)

English Literary History (ELH)
Johns Hopkins University Press
2715 N Charles St, Baltimore, MD 21218-4363
SAN: 202-7348
Tel: 410-516-6987 (journal orders outside US & CN) *Toll Free Tel:* 800-548-1784 (journal orders) *Fax:* 410-578-2865 (journal orders)
E-mail: jrnlcirc@jh.edu (journal orders)
Web Site: www.press.jhu.edu/journals/elh
Key Personnel
Mng Ed: Carolina Fautsch
Sr Ed: Jeanne-Marie Jackson
Essays on English language literature & on cultural forms & contexts related to those writings.
Also available online (ISSN: 1080-6547).
First published 1934
Frequency: Quarterly
Number of pages: 256
Circulation: 238
Indivs: $50/yr print, $60/yr online; Instns: $280/yr print
ISSN: 0013-8304

Film Quarterly
University of California Press
Journals & Digital Publishing, 155 Grand Ave, Suite 400, Oakland, CA 94612-3758
E-mail: info@filmquarterly.org; customerservice@ucpress.edu
Web Site: www.filmquarterly.org; online.ucpress.edu/fq
Subscription Address: MPS North America LLC, 941 W Morse Blvd, Suite 100, Winter Park, FL 32789 *Toll Free Tel:* 866-978-5898 *Fax:* 484-302-4348 *E-mail:* ucpress@mpslimited.com
Web Site: mps-ucpress.com
Key Personnel
Ed: J M Tyree
Book Review Ed: Nilo Couret *E-mail:* ncouret@umich.edu
Ed-at-Large: B Ruby Rich
Academic journal of film, television & video, theory & criticism. Also includes reviews of current & recent books.
Also available online (ISSN: 1533-8630).
First published 1945
Frequency: Quarterly
Number of pages: 125
Circulation: 1,000
Indivs: $52/yr online, $67/yr print & online; Students: $31/yr online; Instns: $304/yr online, $419/yr print & online
ISSN: 0015-1386
Books Reviewed: 30/yr

First Things: A Journal of Religion, Culture & Public Life
Institute on Religion & Public Life
9 E 40 St, 10th fl, New York, NY 10016
Tel: 212-627-1985 *Fax:* 212-627-2184
E-mail: ft@firstthings.com
Web Site: www.firstthings.com
Subscription Address: PO Box 8509, Big Sandy, TX 75755-9955 *Toll Free Tel:* 877-905-9920
Key Personnel
Ed: R R Reno
Monthly journal of religion & public life.

First published 1991
Frequency: Monthly (10/yr; 2 double issues, June/July & Aug/Sept)
Circulation: 30,000
$24.99/yr online, $60/yr print & online
ISSN: 1047-5141
Books Reviewed: 5-6 major reviews/issue (50-60/yr)

Forecast
Baker & Taylor LLC
2550 W Tyvola Rd, Suite 300, Charlotte, NC 28217
Mailing Address: PO Box 6885, Bridgewater, NJ 08807-0855
Tel: 704-998-3100 *Toll Free Tel:* 800-775-1800 (info servs); 800-775-1700 (cust serv)
Toll Free Fax: 866-557-3396 (cust serv)
E-mail: btinfo@baker-taylor.com
Web Site: www.baker-taylor.com
Key Personnel
Dir, Mdsg, Ad Sales & Edit: Lynn Bond
Ed: Charles Pizar
Mktg Specialist: Donna Heffner
Promotes new & forthcoming adult hardcover, paperback & spoken word audio titles. Digital only.
First published 1969
Frequency: Monthly
Number of pages: 87
Free

Foreword Reviews
Division of Foreword Magazine Inc
12935 W Bay Shore Rd, Suite 380, Traverse City, MI 49684
Tel: 231-933-3699
Web Site: www.forewordreviews.com
Key Personnel
Publr: Victoria Sutherland *E-mail:* victoria@forewordreviews.com
Assoc Publr: Barbara Hodge *E-mail:* barbara@forewordreviews.com
Ed-in-Chief: Michelle Anne Schingler
E-mail: mschingler@forewordreviews.com
Mng Ed: Matt Sutherland *E-mail:* matt@forewordreviews.com
Review source covering independent & university presses only. Sent to booksellers & librarians across the country. Also available online & major newsstands.
First published 1998
Frequency: 6 issues/yr
Number of pages: 68
Circulation: 30,000
$5.99 each, $29.95/yr, $59.95/yr intl
ISSN: 1099-2642
Books Reviewed: 100/issue

Forthcoming Books™
Grey House Publishing Inc™
4919 Rte 22, Amenia, NY 12501
Mailing Address: PO Box 56, Amenia, NY 12501-0056
Tel: 518-789-8700 *Toll Free Tel:* 800-562-2139
Fax: 518-789-0556
E-mail: books@greyhouse.com
Web Site: greyhouse.com
Lists just-published & to-be-published books, with ISBNs & US Library of Congress numbers.
First published 1966
Frequency: Quarterly
Number of pages: 900
$675/yr
ISSN: 0015-8119

Gale Literature: Book Review Index
Formerly Book Review Index
Gale
Division of Cengage Learning
27555 Executive Dr, Suite 270, Farmington Hills, MI 48331
SAN: 213-4373
Toll Free Tel: 800-877-4253 *Toll Free Fax:* 877-363-4253
E-mail: gale.customerexperience@cengage.com
Web Site: www.gale.com/c/literature-book-review-index
Key Personnel
Sr Media & PR Mgr, Corp Communs: Kayla Siefker
Online database provides access to reviews of books, periodicals, books on tape & electronic media representing a wide range of popular, academic & professional interests. Contains the entire backfile of *Book Review Index* print content from 1965 to present. Easily searchable by author, date, illustrator, audiobook reader, review length, reading level, review source, review type, reviewer, title & title of review.
First published 1965

Harvard Educational Review
Harvard Education Publishing Group
Division of Harvard Graduate School of Education
8 Story St, 1st fl, Cambridge, MA 02138
Tel: 617-495-3432 *Toll Free Tel:* 888-437-1437 (orders) *Fax:* 617-496-3584
Web Site: hepg.org/her-home/home
Key Personnel
Ed-in-Chief: Jayne M Fargnoli
E-mail: jayne_fargnoli@harvard.edu
Dir, Sales, Mktg & Busn Devt: Kelly Fattman
E-mail: kelly_fattman@gse.harvard.edu
Ms Subns & Rts & Perms: Laura Clos
E-mail: laura_clos@harvard.edu
Scholarly opinion & research in the field of education. Readers include professional educators & researchers, school & college administrators; college, university, school & public libraries.
Also available online (ISSN: 1943-5045).
First published 1931
Frequency: Quarterly
Circulation: 2,700 paid
Individuals (print & online): $61/yr US, $84/yr CN, $102/yr intl; Individuals (online only): $41/yr; Institutions (print & online): $435/yr US, $450/yr CN, $508/yr intl; Institutions (online only): $397/yr
ISSN: 0017-8055
Books Reviewed: 12/yr

The Henry James Review
Johns Hopkins University Press
2715 N Charles St, Baltimore, MD 21218-4363
SAN: 202-7348
Tel: 410-516-6987 (journal orders outside US & CN) *Toll Free Tel:* 800-548-1784 (journal orders) *Fax:* 410-578-2865 (journal orders)
E-mail: jrnlcirc@jh.edu (journal orders)
Web Site: www.press.jhu.edu/journals/henry-james-review
Key Personnel
Mng Ed: B Joanne Webb
Ed: Greg Zacharias
Book Review Ed: Miroslawa Buchholz
Publishes spirited critical essays & reviews of this major American writer by noted critics, bringing together contemporary scholarly, critical & theoretical work. Individual subscriptions include membership in the Henry James Society.
Also available online (ISSN: 1080-6555).
Frequency: 3 issues/yr
Number of pages: 108
Circulation: 129
Indivs: $40/yr print, $50/yr online; Instns: $150/yr print
ISSN: 0273-0340
Books Reviewed: 5

The Historical Novels Review
Historical Novel Society
PO Box 1146, Jacksonville, AL 36265
E-mail: reviews@historicalnovelsociety.org; contact@historicalnovelsociety.org
Web Site: historicalnovelsociety.org
Key Personnel
Publr: Richard Lee *E-mail:* richard@historicalnovelsociety.org
Mng Ed: Bethany Latham *E-mail:* blatham@jsu.edu
Book Review Ed: Sarah Johnson
E-mail: sljohnson2@eiu.edu
Features Ed: Lucinda Byatt *E-mail:* textline13@gmail.com
US Membership Contact: Bethany Latham
Reviews currently published historical fiction from the US & Great Britain.
First published 1997
Frequency: Quarterly
Number of pages: 64
Circulation: 1,400
$50/yr
ISSN: 1471-7492
Books Reviewed: 1,200/yr

History: Reviews of New Books
Taylor & Francis Inc
530 Walnut St, Suite 850, Philadelphia, PA 19106
Tel: 215-625-8900 (ext 4) *Toll Free Tel:* 800-354-1420 *Fax:* 215-207-0050; 215-207-0046 (cust serv)
E-mail: historyreviews@taylorandfrancis.com; support@tandfonline.com
Web Site: www.tandfonline.com
Lets readers know what's new in current scholarship on historical topics. Covers all geographic areas & time periods, from ancient times to present. The reviews outline & evaluate the author's arguments, describe the sources used in the research & place the book in the context of other scholarship.
Also available online (ISSN: 1930-8280).
First published 1972
Frequency: 6 issues/yr
Number of pages: 40
Circulation: 400
$144/yr indivs (print & online), $441/yr instns (print & online), $386/yr instns (online only)
ISSN: 0361-2759
Books Reviewed: 150/yr

The Horn Book Magazine
Horn Book Inc
7858 Industrial Pkwy, Plain City, OH 43064
Toll Free Tel: 800-325-9558
E-mail: info@hbook.com
Web Site: www.hbook.com
Subscription Address: PO Box 460965, Escondido, CA 92046 *Toll Free Tel:* 877-523-6072 *Fax:* 760-738-4805 *E-mail:* hbmsubs@pcspublink.com
Key Personnel
Group Publr: Rebecca T Miller *Tel:* 646-380-0738 *E-mail:* rmiller@mediasourceinc.com
Ed-in-Chief: Elissa Gershowitz
E-mail: egershowitz@hbook.com
Reviews Ed: Kitty Flynn *E-mail:* kflynn@hbook.com
Asst Ed: Monica de los Reyes
E-mail: mdelosreyes@hbook.com
Children's literature journal featuring reviews, essays, columns, interviews with authors, illustrators & current announcements.
First published 1924
Frequency: 6 issues/yr
Number of pages: 128
Circulation: 5,500
$72/yr
ISSN: 0018-5078
Books Reviewed: Approximately 600/yr

Human Rights Quarterly
Johns Hopkins University Press

2715 N Charles St, Baltimore, MD 21218-4363
SAN: 202-7348
Tel: 410-516-6987 (journal orders outside US & CN) *Toll Free Tel:* 800-548-1784 (journal orders) *Fax:* 410-578-2865 (journal orders)
E-mail: jrnlcirc@jh.edu (journal orders)
Web Site: www.press.jhu.edu/journals/human-rights-quarterly
Key Personnel
Ed-in-Chief: Bert Lockwood
Mng Ed: M Kenzie Poole
Book Review Ed: Madison Yoder
Deputy Ed: Jacob Katz Cogan
Provides insight into complex human rights issues through current research policy, analysis & philosophical essays.
Also available online (ISSN: 1085-794X).
Frequency: Quarterly
Number of pages: 232
Circulation: 261
Indivs: $50/yr print, $60/yr online; Instns: $280/yr print
ISSN: 0275-0392
Books Reviewed: 12

ICSID Review: Foreign Investment Law Journal
Oxford University Press USA
4000 CentreGreen Way, Suite 310, Cary, NC 27513
Toll Free Tel: 800-852-7323 (option 1)
E-mail: jnls.cust.serv@oup.com
Web Site: academic.oup.com/icsidreview
Key Personnel
Ed-in-Chief: Prof Campbell McLachlan; Martina Polasek
Assoc Ed, Book Reviews: Dr Gloria M Alvarez; Kiran Gore
The only journal devoted exclusively to foreign investment law & international investment dispute settlement for legal & business professionals.
Also available online (ISSN: 2049-1999).
Frequency: 3 issues/yr
Number of pages: 248
Circulation: 707
Indivs: $130/yr print; Instns: $437/yr print, $473/yr print & online, $357/yr online only
ISSN: 0258-3690
Books Reviewed: 5

International Leads (IL)
International Relations Round Table (IRRT)
Unit of The American Library Association (ALA)
225 N Michigan Ave, Suite 1300, Chicago, IL 60601
Tel: 312-944-6780 *Toll Free Tel:* 800-545-2433 *Fax:* 312-440-9374
E-mail: ala.intl.leads@gmail.com; ala@ala.org
Web Site: www.ala.org/rt/irrt/intlleads/internationalleads; www.ala.org/rt/irrt; www.ala.org
Key Personnel
Ed: Rebecca Miller; Florence Mugambi
Reviews works dealing with librarianship in countries other than the US, with international library & information science agencies & activities.
Frequency: Quarterly
Circulation: 850
ISSN: 0892-4546

Internet Bookwatch
Midwest Book Review
278 Orchard Dr, Oregon, WI 53575-1129
Tel: 608-835-7937
E-mail: mbr@execpc.com
Web Site: www.midwestbookreview.com
Key Personnel
Ed-in-Chief: James A Cox
Review large & small press publications: audio cassettes, videos, books, fiction, general interest nonfiction, CD music & children's educational CD-ROMs.
First published 1995
Frequency: Monthly
Number of pages: 80
Circulation: 32,000
Free online
Books Reviewed: 200

James, Henry Review, see The Henry James Review

Jeunesse: Young People, Texts, Cultures
University of Toronto Press
5201 Dufferin St, Toronto, ON M3H 5T8, Canada
Tel: 416-667-7777 (ext 7971)
E-mail: journals@utpress.utoronto.ca
Web Site: www.utpjournals.press/jeunesse
Key Personnel
Lead Ed: Sarah Olive
Scholar-led, interdisciplinary, peer-reviewed, bilingual academic journal. The mandate of the journal is to publish research on & to provide a form for discussion about cultural productions for, by & about young people.
Also available online (ISSN: 1920-261X).
First published 2009
Frequency: 2 issues/yr
Circulation: 300
$66/yr indiv (online & print)
ISSN: 1920-2601
Books Reviewed: 5-10/issue

Journal of Cuneiform Studies (JCS)
American Society of Overseas Research (ASOR)
James F Strange Ctr, 209 Commerce St, Alexandria, VA 22314
Tel: 703-789-9229; 703-789-9230 (pubns)
E-mail: info@asor.org; publications@asor.org
Web Site: www.asor.org
Key Personnel
Ed: Paul Delnero; Petra M Goedegebuure; Seth Richardson
First published 1947
Frequency: Annual
Number of pages: 144
Circulation: 650
Free to membs
ISSN: 0022-0256
Books Reviewed: 3

Journal of Modern Greek Studies
Johns Hopkins University Press
2715 N Charles St, Baltimore, MD 21218-4363
SAN: 202-7348
Tel: 410-516-6987 (journal orders outside US & CN) *Toll Free Tel:* 800-548-1784 (journal orders) *Fax:* 410-578-2865 (journal orders)
E-mail: jrnlcirc@jh.edu (journal orders)
Web Site: www.press.jhu.edu/journal-modern-greek-studies
Key Personnel
Ed: Artemis Leontis
Book Review Ed, Arts & Humanities: Frank L Hess
Book Review Ed, Soc & Behavioral Sci: Konstantina Zanou
Only scholarly journal to focus exclusively on Greek culture, literature & politics from the late Byzantine period to the present. Official publication of the Modern Greek Studies Association (MGSA).
Also available online (ISSN: 1086-3265).
Frequency: 2 issues/yr
Circulation: 350
Indivs: $50/yr print, $55/yr online; Instns: $160/yr print
ISSN: 0738-1727
Books Reviewed: 5

Kirkus
Kirkus Media LLC
1140 Broadway, Suite 802, New York, NY 10001
E-mail: customercare@kirkus.com
Web Site: www.kirkusreviews.com
Subscription Address: 2600 Via Fortuna, Suite 130, Austin, TX 78746 *Toll Free Tel:* 800-316-9361
Key Personnel
Publr & CEO: Meg LaBorde Kuehn
Chief Mktg Offr: Sarah Kalina *E-mail:* skalina@kirkus.com
Pres, Indie: Chaya Schechner *E-mail:* cschechner@kirkus.com
Ed-in-Chief: Tom Beer *E-mail:* tbeer@kirkus.com
Fiction Ed: Laurie Muchnick *Tel:* 212-209-1531 ext 25 *E-mail:* lmuchnick@kirkus.com
Nonfiction Ed: John McMurtrie
Young Readers Ed: Mahnaz Dar *E-mail:* mdar@kirkus.com; Laura Simeon *E-mail:* lsimeon@kirkus.com
Critical prepublication reviews of fiction, nonfiction, children's, young adult & self-published books. Issued to libraries, producers, periodicals, publishers, agents, booksellers & individuals. For all review submissions, please see www.kirkusreviews.com/about/publisher-submission-guidelines (page is updated often).
First published 1933
Frequency: Semimonthly
Number of pages: 180
Circulation: 12,000
Rates upon request
ISSN: 0042-6598
Books Reviewed: 10,000/yr

LARB Quarterly Journal
Los Angeles Review of Books
6671 Sunset Blvd, Suite 1521, Los Angeles, CA 90028
Tel: 323-952-3950
E-mail: info@lareviewofbooks.org; editorial@lareviewofbooks.org
Web Site: lareviewofbooks.org
Key Personnel
Publr & Ed-in-Chief: Tom Lutz *E-mail:* tom@lareviewofbooks.org
Mng Dir: Jessica Kubinec *E-mail:* jessica@lareviewofbooks.org
Exec Ed: Boris Dralyuk *E-mail:* boris@lareviewofbooks.org
Mng Ed: Medaya Ocher *E-mail:* medaya@lareviewofbooks.org
Literary journal featuring original art, essays, poetry & fiction.
First published 2013
Frequency: Quarterly
Number of pages: 144
Circulation: 1,250
$10/mo or $100/yr (LARB membership)

Leading Edge Express
Leading Edge Review
3651 Robin Lane, Minnetonka, MN 55503
Tel: 952-217-4665
Web Site: www.leadingedgereview.com
Key Personnel
Founder & Publr: Sheila K Andersen *E-mail:* sheila@leadingedgereview.com
Digital platform that sends custom e-blasts to the inboxes of thousands of body/mind/spirit & independent US & Canadian booksellers & their customers.
First published 1988
Frequency: Weekly
Circulation: 5,000
$450 per e-blast

Library Bookwatch
Midwest Book Review
278 Orchard Dr, Oregon, WI 53575-1129
Tel: 608-835-7937
E-mail: mbr@execpc.com
Web Site: www.midwestbookreview.com

Key Personnel
Ed-in-Chief: James A Cox
Review large & small press publications: audiocassettes, videos, books, fiction, general interest nonfiction, CD music & children's educational CD-ROMs.
First published 1992
Frequency: Monthly
Number of pages: 12
Circulation: 32,000
Free online
Books Reviewed: 75

Library Journal
Media Source Inc
123 William St, Suite 802, New York, NY 10038
Tel: 646-380-0700 *Toll Free Tel:* 800-588-1030
 Fax: 646-380-0756
E-mail: ljinfo@mediasourceinc.com
Web Site: www.libraryjournal.com
Key Personnel
Pres & CEO: Steve Zales *Tel:* 614-873-7940 *E-mail:* szales@mediasourceinc.com
Group Publr: Rebecca T Miller *Tel:* 646-380-0738 *E-mail:* rmiller@mediasourceinc.com
Ed-in-Chief: Hallie Rich
Mng Ed: Bette-Lee Fox *Tel:* 646-380-0717 *E-mail:* blfox@mediasourceinc.com
Reviews Ed: Neal Wyatt
Reviews over 8,000 books, audiobooks, DVDs, databases & web sites annually & provides coverage of technology, management, policy & other professional concerns through our print journal, weekly newsletters, online reporting & digital & live events. Over 75,000 library directors, administrators & staff in public, academic & special libraries read *Library Journal*.
First published 1876
Frequency: Semimonthly (exc monthly during Jan, July, Aug & Dec)
Number of pages: 104
Circulation: 12,000
$157.99/yr US, $199.99/yr CN & Mexico, $219.99/yr foreign
ISSN: 0363-0277
Books Reviewed: 5,000

The Lion and the Unicorn
Johns Hopkins University Press
2715 N Charles St, Baltimore, MD 21218-4363
SAN: 202-7348
Tel: 410-516-6987 (journal orders outside US & CN) *Toll Free Tel:* 800-548-1784 (journal orders) *Fax:* 410-578-2865 (journal orders)
E-mail: jrnlcirc@jh.edu (journal orders)
Web Site: www.press.jhu.edu/journals/lion-and-unicorn
Key Personnel
Ed: David L Russell; Karin E Westman; Naomi J Wood
Book Review Ed: Victoria Smith; Anastasia Ulanowicz
Theme & genre-centered journal of international scope, committed to a serious discussion of literature for children.
Also available online (ISSN: 1080-6563).
Frequency: 3 issues/yr
Number of pages: 160
Circulation: 124
Indivs: $40/yr print, $50/yr online; Instns: $155/yr print
ISSN: 0147-2593
Books Reviewed: 6

Literature & Medicine
Johns Hopkins University Press
2715 N Charles St, Baltimore, MD 21218-4363
SAN: 202-7348
Tel: 410-516-6987 (journal orders outside US & CN) *Toll Free Tel:* 800-548-1784 (journal orders) *Fax:* 410-578-2865 (journal orders)
E-mail: jrnlcirc@jh.edu (journal orders)
Web Site: www.press.jhu.edu/journals/literature-and-medicine
Key Personnel
Exec Ed: Michael Blackie
Mng Ed: Anna Fenton-Hathaway
Book Review Ed: Travis Chi Wing Lau
Peer-reviewed journal publishing scholarship that explores representational & cultural practices concerning health care & the body.
Also available online (ISSN: 1080-6571).
First published 1982
Frequency: 2 issues/yr
Number of pages: 164
Circulation: 104
Indivs: $40/yr print, $45/yr online; Instns: $130/yr print
ISSN: 0278-9671
Books Reviewed: 5

Management Communication Quarterly (MCQ)
SAGE Publishing
2455 Teller Rd, Thousand Oaks, CA 91320
Toll Free Tel: 800-818-7243 *Toll Free Fax:* 800-583-2665
E-mail: journals@sagepub.com
Web Site: www.sagepub.com
Key Personnel
Ed: Matthew Koschmann
Book Review Assoc Ed: Brett Robertson
Brings together communication research from a wide variety of fields, with a focus on organizational & managerial practice. Includes book reviews & notes from professionals in the field. Online only.
Frequency: Quarterly
$1,154/yr instns, $180/yr indivs
ISSN: 1552-6798

MBR Bookwatch
Midwest Book Review
278 Orchard Dr, Oregon, WI 53575-1129
Tel: 608-835-7937
E-mail: mbr@execpc.com
Web Site: www.midwestbookreview.com
Key Personnel
Ed-in-Chief: James A Cox
Review large & small press publications: audiocassettes, videos, books, fiction, general interest nonfiction, CD music & educational CD-ROMs.
First published 1997
Frequency: Monthly
Number of pages: 50
Circulation: 32,000
Free online
Books Reviewed: 200

Medievalia et Humanistica: Studies in Medieval & Renaissance Culture
Rowman & Littlefield
4501 Forbes Blvd, Suite 200, Lanham, MD 20706
SAN: 208-5143
Tel: 301-459-3366; 717-794-3800 (cust serv) *Toll Free Tel:* 800-462-6420 (ext 3024, cust serv) *Fax:* 301-429-5748; 717-794-3803 (cust serv) *Toll Free Fax:* 800-338-4550 (cust serv)
E-mail: customercare@rowman.com
Web Site: rowman.com
Key Personnel
Sales Dir: Sheila Burnett *Tel:* 301-459-3366 ext 5606 *E-mail:* sburnett@rowman.com
Reviews new, critical & scholarly books in all areas of Medieval & Renaissance studies. Includes annual list of outstanding books.
First published 1943
Frequency: Annual
Number of pages: 168
Circulation: 2,000
$90 hardcover, $85 ebook

ISSN: 0076-6127
Books Reviewed: 35/yr

The Midwest Book Review
Midwest Book Review
278 Orchard Dr, Oregon, WI 53575-1129
Tel: 608-835-7937
E-mail: mbr@execpc.com; mwbookrevw@aol.com
Web Site: www.midwestbookreview.com
Key Personnel
Ed-in-Chief: James A Cox
Book review publisher.
First published 1980
Frequency: Monthly
Circulation: 32,000
Free online
Books Reviewed: 700

MLN, see Modern Language Notes (MLN)

Modern Language Notes (MLN)
Johns Hopkins University Press
2715 N Charles St, Baltimore, MD 21218-4363
SAN: 202-7348
Tel: 410-516-6987 (journal orders outside US & CN) *Toll Free Tel:* 800-548-1784 (journal orders) *Fax:* 410-578-2865 (journal orders)
E-mail: jrnlcirc@jh.edu (journal orders)
Web Site: www.press.jhu.edu/journals/mln
Key Personnel
Comparative Lit Ed: Anne Eakin Moss; Yi-Ping Ong
French Ed: Wilda Anderson; Daniel Desormeaux; Stephen G Nichols; Elena Russo; Derek Schilling
German Ed: Christiane Frey; Rochelle Tobias
Hispanic Ed: Sara Castro-Klaren; William Egginton; Eduardo Gonzalez; Becquer Seguin
Italian Ed: Laura Di Bianco; Arielle Saiber; Bernadette Wegenstein
Contemporary continental criticism in Italian, Hispanic, German, French & comparative literature.
Also available online (ISSN: 1080-6598).
Frequency: 5 issues/yr
Number of pages: 256
Circulation: 140
Indivs: $50/yr print, $60/yr online; Instns: $275/yr print
ISSN: 0026-7910
Books Reviewed: 12

Mystery Readers Journal
Mystery Readers International
7155 Marlborough Terr, Berkeley, CA 94705
Tel: 510-845-3600
Web Site: www.mysteryreaders.org
Key Personnel
Ed: Janet A Rudolph *E-mail:* janet@mysteryreaders.org
Assoc Ed: Kate Derie
Thematic mystery review periodical. Each issue contains articles, reviews & author essays on a specific theme (i.e. art mysteries, historical mysteries & sports mysteries).
First published 1983
Frequency: Quarterly
Number of pages: 88
Circulation: 2,000
$39/yr, $50/yr overseas airmail, $15/pdf download
ISSN: 1043-3473
Books Reviewed: 2,000

New Haven Review
The Institute Library
55 Elmwood Rd, New Haven, CT 06515
Tel: 203-494-7018
Web Site: www.newhavenreview.com
Key Personnel
Publr: Nichole Gleisner *E-mail:* nichole.gleisner@gmail.com

Publishes reviews, essays, poems, fiction & occasional pieces by writers who live in the New Haven area & elsewhere. Solicits contributions but welcomes unsol submissions. Pay for full story or article $500 & $25 per poem. Favor will be shown to articles & book reviews that, in form, subject matter, or authorial background, can claim a credible connection to New Haven & its broader environs, but not an absolute necessity.
First published 2007
Frequency: 2 issues/yr
Number of pages: 160
Circulation: 500
$20/yr, $30/2 yrs
ISSN: 1940-8714
Books Reviewed: 2/issue

New Literary History
Johns Hopkins University Press
2715 N Charles St, Baltimore, MD 21218-4363
SAN: 202-7348
Tel: 410-516-6987 (journal orders outside US & CN) *Toll Free Tel:* 800-548-1784 (journal orders) *Fax:* 410-578-2865 (journal orders)
E-mail: jrnlcirc@jh.edu (journal orders)
Web Site: www.press.jhu.edu/journals/new-literary-history
Key Personnel
Mng Ed: Mollie H Washburne
Ed: Bruce Holsinger
Focuses on theory & interpretation of literary change, definition of literary periods & the evolution of styles, conventions & genres.
Also available online (ISSN: 1080-661X).
Frequency: Quarterly
Number of pages: 220
Circulation: 233
Indivs: $50/yr print, $60/yr online; Instns: $260/yr print
ISSN: 0028-6087

The New York Review of Science Fiction
Subsidiary of Burrowing Wombat Press
206 Valentine St, Yonkers, NY 10704-1814
Tel: 914-965-4861
Web Site: www.nyrsf.com
Key Personnel
Publr: Kevin Maroney *E-mail:* kjm@panix.com
Review journal devoted to speculative fiction.
First published 1988
Frequency: Monthly
Number of pages: 32
Circulation: 300
$3/issue; $30/yr (bulk) US
ISSN: 1052-9438
Books Reviewed: 5/issue; 60/yr

The New York Times Book Review
The New York Times Co
620 Eighth Ave, 5th fl, New York, NY 10018
Tel: 212-556-1234 *Toll Free Tel:* 800-631-2580 (subns)
E-mail: bookreview@nytimes.com; books@nytimes.com
Web Site: www.nytimes.com
Key Personnel
Mng Ed: David Kelly
Asst Mng Ed: Sam Sifton
Deputy Ed: Tina Jordan
Sr Ed: Gregory Cowles; Emily Eakin
Sr Staff Ed: Jennifer Harlan
Books Ed: Gilbert Cruz
Narrative Features Ed: Elisabeth Egan
Preview Ed: MJ Franklin; Neima Jahromi; Dave Kim; Sadie Stein
Contributing Essayist: Jennifer Wilson
Critic-at-Large: AO Scott
Review books & essays related to publishing & published in the US & available through general interest bookstores. By subscription only.
$4/wk US, $4.95/wk CN, $5.50/wk foreign
ISSN: 0028-7806

North Carolina Literary Review (NCLR)
East Carolina University/North Carolina Literary & Historical Association/University of North Carolina Press
East Carolina University, English Dept, ECU Mailstop 555 English, Greenville, NC 27858-4353
Tel: 252-328-1537 *Fax:* 252-328-4889
E-mail: nclrstaff@ecu.edu
Web Site: nclr.ecu.edu
Key Personnel
Mng Ed: Lyra Thomas
Ed: Margaret Bauer *E-mail:* bauerm@ecu.edu
Articles, essays, interviews, fiction/poetry by & about North Carolina writers & literature, culture & history. Essay reviews only; excerpts from forthcoming books when relevant & appropriate. *North Carolina Literary Review Online* also available quarterly.
First published 1992
Frequency: Annual
Number of pages: 200
Circulation: 750
$18/yr indiv, $30/2 yrs indiv, $27/yr instl, $50/2 yrs instl
ISSN: 1063-0724
Books Reviewed: 8-12/yr

Paper Brigade
Jewish Book Council
520 Eighth Ave, 4th fl, New York, NY 10018
Tel: 212-201-2920 *Fax:* 212-532-4952
E-mail: info@jewishbooks.org
Web Site: www.jewishbookcouncil.org
Key Personnel
Exec Dir: Carol Kaufman
Assoc Dir: Miri Pomerantz Dauber
Edit Dir: Carol E Kaufman
Mng Ed: Becca Kantor *E-mail:* becca@jewishbooks.org
Children's & Young Adult Ed: Ms Michal Hoschander Malen
Articles, interviews, personal essays, fiction, poetry, photography & illustrations that, together, highlight the breadth & diversity of Jewish books today.
Frequency: Annual
Number of pages: 200
$25 US, $46 foreign

Pennsylvania Literary Journal (PLJ)
Anaphora Literary Press
1108 W Third St, Quanah, TX 79252
Tel: 470-289-6395
Web Site: anaphoraliterary.com/journals/plj
Key Personnel
Dir & Ed-in-Chief: Anna Faktorovich, PhD *E-mail:* director@anaphoraliterary.com
Scholarly & creative journal, which publishes researched essays, short fiction, poems, nonfiction, personal essays, interviews, book reviews & other works. An extensive book review section is included in every issue. Special issues range from Interviews with Best-Selling Young Adult Writers, British Literature, New Historicism, New Formalism & editing technique. It is cataloged in the *MLA International Bibliography*, the *MLA Directory of Periodicals*, *Genamics JournalSeek* & *Duotrope's Digest*. PLJ has published works by & interviews with New York Times bestselling writers like Larry Niven & Cinda Williams Chima. Only e-mailed submissions accepted.
First published 2009
Frequency: 3 issues/yr
Number of pages: 200
Circulation: 20 copies/issue, plus EBSCO & ProQuest online viewing
$75/yr US, $100/yr elsewhere
ISSN: 2151-3066
Books Reviewed: 20 books/issue, 60 books/yr

Philosophy and Literature
Johns Hopkins University Press
2715 N Charles St, Baltimore, MD 21218-4363
SAN: 202-7348
Tel: 410-516-6987 (journal orders outside US & CN) *Toll Free Tel:* 800-548-1784 (journal orders) *Fax:* 410-578-2865 (journal orders)
E-mail: philandlit@bard.edu; jrnlcirc@jh.edu (journal orders)
Web Site: www.press.jhu.edu/journals/philosophy-and-literature
Key Personnel
Mng Ed: Cynthia Werthamer
Ed: Garry L Hagberg
Explores the dialogue between literary & philosophical studies. A constant source of fresh, stimulating ideas in aesthetics, theory of criticism & more in an assortment of lively articles, essays & reviews.
Also available online (ISSN: 1086-329X).
Frequency: 2 issues/yr
Number of pages: 250
Circulation: 131
Indivs: $40/yr print, $50/yr online; Instns: $155/yr print
ISSN: 0190-0013
Books Reviewed: 60

Poetry Flash
1450 Fourth St, Suite 4, Berkeley, CA 94710
Tel: 510-525-5476
Web Site: www.poetryflash.org
Key Personnel
Publr, Exec Dir & Ed: Joyce Jenkins *E-mail:* editor@poetryflash.org
Assoc Ed: Richard Silberg
Publishes online quality reviews, poems, interviews, essays & book trade & submission & award information for all creative writers. Although poetry is the editorial focus, interviews with prose writers & reviews of fiction & literary nonfiction are featured. Sponsors the annual Northern California Book Awards.
First published 1972
Distributed free primarily on the West Coast

ProtoView
Ringgold Inc
7515 NE Ambassador Place, Suite A, Portland, OR 97220
Tel: 503-281-9230
E-mail: info@protoview.com
Web Site: www.protoview.com
Key Personnel
Ed: Eithne O'Leyne *E-mail:* eithne.oleyne@ringgold.com
Subscription database incorporating Reference & Research & *SciTech Book News*. Abstracts, bibliographic & expanded metadata on scholarly works in all media. ProtoView content licensed to discovery channels, including vendors & related products owned by Baker & Taylor, ProQuest, Gale/Cengage & others.
ISSN: 2372-3424

Publishers Weekly
PWxyz LLC
49 W 23 St, 9th fl, New York, NY 10010
Tel: 212-377-5500 *Fax:* 212-377-2733
Web Site: www.publishersweekly.com
Key Personnel
Pres & COO, BookLife: Carl Pritzkat *E-mail:* cpritzkat@publishersweekly.com
Publr & CEO, BookLife: Cevin Bryerman *Tel:* 917-941-1879 *E-mail:* cbryerman@publishersweekly.com
SVP & Edit Dir: Jonathan Segura *E-mail:* jsegura@publishersweekly.com

SVP & Children's Book Ed: Diane Roback
  E-mail: roback@publishersweekly.com
VP, Opers: Ryk Hsieh *E-mail:* rhsieh@publishersweekly.com
VP, Sales & Assoc Publr: Joe Murray
  E-mail: jmurray@publisherswekly.com
Pres: George Slowik, Jr *E-mail:* george@publishersweekly.com
Art Dir: Clive Chiu *E-mail:* cchiu@publishersweekly.com
Dir, Branded Content: Rachel Deahl
  E-mail: rdeahl@publishersweekly.com
Dir, Digital Opers: Michael Morris
  E-mail: mmorris@publishersweekly.com
Dir, Mktg: Krista Rafanello *E-mail:* krafanello@publishersweekly.com
Reviews Dir: David Adams *E-mail:* dadams@publishersweekly.com
Exec Ed: Andrew R Albanese
  E-mail: aalbanese@publishersweekly.com
Mng Ed: Daniel Berchenko *E-mail:* dberchenko@publishersweekly.com
Sr Bookselling & Intl News Ed: Ed Nawotka
  E-mail: enawotka@publishersweekly.com
Sr Digital & News Ed: John Maher
  E-mail: jmaher@publishersweekly.com
Sr Ed: Adam Boretz *E-mail:* aboretz@publishersweekly.com
Sr Reviews Ed, Children's: Amanda Bruns
  E-mail: abruns@publishersweekly.com
Digital & News Ed: Emell Adolphus
  E-mail: eadolphus@publishersweekly.com
Ed, BookLife: Matia Burnett *E-mail:* mburnett@publishersweekly.com
Features Ed: Carolyn Juris *E-mail:* cjuris@publishersweekly.com
Religion Ed: Emma Koonse *E-mail:* ekoonse@publishersweekly.com
Reviews Ed: Phoebe Cramer *E-mail:* pcramer@publishersweekly.com; Marc Greenawalt *E-mail:* mgreenawalt@publishersweekly.com; Meg Lemke *E-mail:* mlemke@publishersweekly.com; Maya C Popa *E-mail:* mpopa@publishersweekly.com; Carliann Rittman *E-mail:* crittman@publishersweekly.com; David Varno *E-mail:* dvarno@publishersweekly.com; Vanessa Willoughby *E-mail:* vwilloughby@publishersweekly.com
Reviews Ed, BookLife: Alan Scherstuhl
  E-mail: ascherstuhl@publishersweekly.com
Reviews Ed, Children's: Amanda Ramirez
  E-mail: aramirez@publishersweekly.com
Ed-at-Large: Louisa Ermelino
  E-mail: lermelino@publishersweekly.com
Deputy Children's Book Ed: Emma Kantor
  E-mail: ekantor@publishersweekly.com
Ed-at-Large: Jim Milliot *E-mail:* jmilliot@publishersweekly.com
Copy Chief: Robby Ritacco *E-mail:* rritacco@publishersweekly.com
Mktg Mgr: Stacey Gill *E-mail:* sgill@publishersweekly.com
Licensing, Rts & Perms: Christi Cassidy
  E-mail: ccassidy@publishersweekly.com
International news magazine of book publishing & bookselling.
Digital ISSN: 2150-4008.
First published 1872
Frequency: Weekly (51 issues/yr)
Circulation: 64,000 print + digital
Print, digital & online: $289.99/yr US, $339.99/yr CN; Digital & online: $229.99/yr US & CN
ISSN: 0000-0019
Books Reviewed: 9,000/yr

Publishing Trends
Market Partners International Inc
232 Madison Ave, Suite 1400, New York, NY 10016
Tel: 212-447-0855 *Fax:* 212-447-0785
E-mail: info@publishingtrends.com
Web Site: www.marketpartnersinternational.com; www.publishingtrends.com
Key Personnel
Dir: Amy Rhodes; Lorraine W Shanley
Web site on news & opinion on the changing world of publishing.
Frequency: Weekly
Free online

QBR The Black Book Review
QBR
591 Warburton Ave, Unit 170, Hastings-on-Hudson, NY 10706
Tel: 914-231-6778
Web Site: www.qbr.com
Key Personnel
Dir: Max Rodriguez *E-mail:* mrod@qbr.com
Online review of African-American books & producer of the Harlem Book Fair.

Readers' Guide to Periodical Literature
Grey House Publishing Inc™
4919 Rte 22, Amenia, NY 12501
Mailing Address: PO Box 56, Amenia, NY 12501-0056
Tel: 518-789-8700 *Toll Free Tel:* 800-562-2139 *Fax:* 518-789-0556
E-mail: books@greyhouse.com
Web Site: greyhouse.com
Each issue indexes more than 40,000 individual articles. The cumulative library-bound annual includes over 2,500 pages, indexing over 160,000 articles published throughout the year.
First published 1900
Frequency: 3 paperback issues, March-Sept plus library-bound annual cumulation in Jan
Number of pages: 800
$495
ISSN: 0034-0464

Reference & User Services Quarterly, see RUSQ: A Journal of Reference and User Experience

Retailing Insight Magazine
New Way Publishing LLC
PO Box 12252, Charlotte, NC 28220
E-mail: circ@retailinginsight.com
Web Site: retailinginsight.com
Key Personnel
Ed-in-Chief: Roberta Gazzarolle
Trade magazine for retail stores selling books, music & giftware for the body, mind & spirit.
Frequency: 6 issues/yr
Circulation: 17,000
Free to qualified retailers
ISSN: 2372-7977
Books Reviewed: 15/issue, 105/yr

Reviewer Bookwatch
Midwest Book Review
278 Orchard Dr, Oregon, WI 53575-1129
Tel: 608-835-7937
E-mail: mbr@execpc.com
Web Site: www.midwestbookreview.com
Key Personnel
Ed-in-Chief: James A Cox
Review large & small press publications: audiocassettes, videos, books, fiction, general interest nonfiction, CD music & children's educational CD-ROMs.
First published 1992
Frequency: Monthly
Number of pages: 50
Circulation: 32,000
Free online
Books Reviewed: 200

Reviews in American History
Johns Hopkins University Press
2715 N Charles St, Baltimore, MD 21218-4363
SAN: 202-7348
Tel: 410-516-6987 (journal orders outside US & CN) *Toll Free Tel:* 800-548-1784 (journal orders) *Fax:* 410-578-2865 (journal orders)
E-mail: jrnlcirc@jh.edu (journal orders)
Web Site: www.press.jhu.edu/journals/reviews-american-history
Key Personnel
Mng Ed: Rose Curtin
Ed: Ari Kelman
Comprehensive evaluations of important new books in all areas of American history.
Also available online (ISSN: 1080-6628).
Frequency: Quarterly
Number of pages: 192
Circulation: 476
Indivs: $45/yr print, $55/yr online; Instns: $220/yr print
ISSN: 0048-7511
Books Reviewed: 120/yr

RUSQ: A Journal of Reference and User Experience
Formerly Reference & User Services Quarterly
Reference & User Services Association (RUSA)
Division of The American Library Association (ALA)
225 N Michigan Ave, Suite 1300, Chicago, IL 60601
SAN: 201-0062
Tel: 312-280-4395 *Toll Free Tel:* 800-545-2433 *Fax:* 312-280-5273
E-mail: rusq@ala.org
Web Site: www.ala.org/rusa/rusq-journal
Key Personnel
Exec Dir: Bill Ladewski *E-mail:* bladewski@ala.org
Open access journal.
Frequency: Quarterly
ISSN: 2163-5242
Books Reviewed: 35-40

School Library Journal
Media Source Inc
123 William St, Suite 802, New York, NY 10038
Tel: 646-380-0752 *Toll Free Tel:* 800-595-1066 *Fax:* 646-380-0756
E-mail: slj@mediasourceinc.com; sljsubs@pcspublink.com
Web Site: www.slj.com; www.facebook.com/schoollibraryjournal; x.com/sljournal
Subscription Address: PO Box 461119, Escondido, CA 92046
Key Personnel
Group Publr: Rebecca T Miller *Tel:* 646-380-0738 *E-mail:* rmiller@mediasourceinc.com
Reviews Dir: Kiera Parrott *E-mail:* kparrott@mediasourceinc.com
Ed-in-Chief: Kathy Ishizuka *E-mail:* kishizuka@mediasourceinc.com
Mng Ed, SLJ Reviews: Luann Toth *Tel:* 646-380-0749 *E-mail:* ltoth@mediasourceinc.com
Articles about library service to children & young adults; reviews of new books & multimedia products for children & young adults by school & public librarians.
Frequency: Monthly
Number of pages: 115
Circulation: 38,000
$15/issue newsstand; Indivs: $136.99/yr (print or digital), $159.99/yr (print & digital); Instns: $136.99/yr (print only), $249.99/yr (digital only), $349.99/yr (print & digital)
ISSN: 0362-8930
Books Reviewed: 4,500/yr, including 360 for young adults & 1,000 reviews for multimedia products

Small Press Bookwatch
Midwest Book Review
278 Orchard Dr, Oregon, WI 53575-1129
Tel: 608-835-7937

E-mail: mbr@execpc.com
Web Site: www.midwestbookreview.com
Key Personnel
Ed-in-Chief: James A Cox
Review small press publications: audiocassettes, videos, books, fiction, general interest nonfiction & CD music.
First published 1997
Frequency: Monthly
Number of pages: 20
Circulation: 32,000
Free online
Books Reviewed: 70

Sunday San Francisco Chronicle Book Review
San Francisco Chronicle
Subsidiary of Hearst Communications Inc
901 Mission St, San Francisco, CA 94103
Tel: 415-777-1111 *Toll Free Tel:* 866-732-4766
Web Site: www.sfgate.com
Key Personnel
Ed-in-Chief: Grant Marek *E-mail:* grant.marek@sfgate.com
Mng Ed: Katie Dowd *E-mail:* katie.dowd@sfgate.com
Broad-based daily newspaper with daily book review column & Sunday book review section; reviews of hardcover, softcover, nonfiction, fiction, poetry, children's books, literary guide; interviews; best sellers list; industry news; essays.
Frequency: Weekly

Theatre Journal
Johns Hopkins University Press
2715 N Charles St, Baltimore, MD 21218-4363
SAN: 202-7348
Tel: 410-516-6987 (journal orders outside US & CN) *Toll Free Tel:* 800-548-1784 (journal orders) *Fax:* 410-578-2865 (journal orders)
E-mail: tjbooks@athe.org; jrnlcirc@jh.edu (journal orders)
Web Site: www.press.jhu.edu/journals/theatre-journal
Key Personnel
Mng Ed: Aileen Keenan
Ed: Laura Edmondson; Ariel Nereson
Book Review Ed: Gwyneth Shanks

Official publication of the Association for Theatre in Higher Education (ATHE). One of the most authoritative & useful publications in theatre studies. Features scholarly articles that are on the cutting edge of theatre, dance & performance studies, focusing on historiographical, cultural +/or theoretical analyses in both national & transnational contexts.
Also available online (ISSN: 1086-332X).
Frequency: Quarterly
Number of pages: 152
Circulation: 614
Indivs: $50/yr print, $60/yr online; Instns: $200/yr print
ISSN: 0192-2882
Books Reviewed: 12

Washington Monthly
Washington Monthly Publishing LLC
1200 18 St NW, Suite 330, Washington, DC 20036
Tel: 202-955-9010 *Toll Free Tel:* 855-492-1648 (subns) *Fax:* 202-955-9011
E-mail: editors@washingtonmonthly.com
Web Site: washingtonmonthly.com
Key Personnel
Art Dir: Amy Swan
Dir, Fin: Terri Wallace
Deputy Dir: Alice J Gallin-Dwyer
Ed-in-Chief: Paul Glastris
Exec Ed, Digital: Matthew Cooper
Mng Ed: Amy M Stackhouse
Sr Ed: Phillip Longman
Review political & public policy books.
First published 1969
Frequency: 5 issues/yr
Number of pages: 64
Circulation: 15,000 paid, 3,000 controlled
$5.95/issue, $19.95/yr indiv, $39.95/yr foreign
ISSN: 0043-0633
Books Reviewed: 50/yr

Wisconsin Bookwatch
Midwest Book Review
278 Orchard Dr, Oregon, WI 53575-1129
Tel: 608-835-7937
E-mail: mbr@execpc.com
Web Site: www.midwestbookreview.com

Key Personnel
Ed-in-Chief: James A Cox
Review large & small press publications: audiocassettes, videos, books, fiction, general interest nonfiction, CD music & children's educational CD-ROMs.
First published 1990
Frequency: Monthly
Number of pages: 12
Circulation: 32,000
Free online
Books Reviewed: 70

World Literature Today
University of Oklahoma
630 Parrington Oval, Suite 110, Norman, OK 73019-4033
Tel: 405-325-4531
E-mail: wlt@ou.edu
Web Site: www.worldliteraturetoday.org
Key Personnel
Exec Dir: Robert Con Davis-Undiano
 E-mail: rcdavis@ou.edu
Asst Dir & Ed-in-Chief: Daniel Simon
 E-mail: dsimon@ou.edu
Art Dir: Parker Buske *E-mail:* pbuske@ou.edu
Mktg Dir, Progs & Devt: Terri D Stubblefield
 E-mail: tdstubb@ou.edu
Mng Ed: Michelle Johnson *E-mail:* lmjohnson@ou.edu
Book Reviews Ed: Robert Vollmar
 E-mail: robvollmar@ou.edu
Circ & Accts Specialist: Kay Blunck
 E-mail: kblunck@ou.edu
Critical essays & reviews covering all the major & most of the smaller languages & literatures of the world.
Also available online (ISSN: 1945-8134).
First published 1927
Frequency: 6 issues/yr
Number of pages: 80
Circulation: 300,000
Indivs: $45/yr US, $55/yr CN, $75/yr elsewhere (print), $30/yr (online); Instns: $170/yr US, $245/yr CN, $265/yr elsewhere (print), $155/yr (online)
ISSN: 0196-3570
Books Reviewed: 1,200

Book Exhibits

AIGA, the professional association for design
228 Park Ave S, Suite 58603, New York, NY 10003
Tel: 212-807-1990
E-mail: general@aiga.org
Web Site: www.aiga.org
Key Personnel
COO: Amy Chapman *Tel:* 212-710-3137
Exec Dir: Bennie F Johnson *Tel:* 212-710-3100
Dir, Digital Opers: Tiia Schurig *Tel:* 212-710-3134
Dir, Mktg: Michelle Koenigsknecht *Tel:* 212-710-3138
National nonprofit membership organization for graphic design professionals that sponsors competitions & major exhibits annually, including book shows & communication graphics. Exhibits & the work of two award recipients are published in *Graphic Design USA* (annual). Exhibits circulate for small rental fee.

The American Collective Stand®
277 White St, Buchanan, NY 10511
Tel: 914-739-7500 *Toll Free Tel:* 800-462-7687
Fax: 914-739-7575
Web Site: www.americancollectivestand.com
Key Personnel
Pres: Janet Fritsch *Tel:* 734-677-0955
  E-mail: janet@americancollectivestand.com
EVP: Jon Malinowski *E-mail:* jon@americancollectivestand.com
A US collective of individual stands representing all segments of publishing, book trade & electronic sectors for selling & buying rights & making strategic distribution alliances. Check out our database of Participant Profiles including key contact people, e-mails, available rights & other important information on our web site (www.amerciancollectivestand.com) to the right person & do business at International Book Fairs such as Frankfurt, London & Beijing.

American Institute of Graphic Arts, see AIGA, the professional association for design

Children's Books USA Inc
Subsidiary of Foreword Magazine Inc
425 Boardman Ave, Traverse City, MI 49684
Tel: 231-933-3699
E-mail: info@childrensbooksusa.com
Web Site: www.childrensbooksusa.com
Key Personnel
Mng Dir: Matt Sutherland; Victoria Sutherland
Organize & manage American collective exhibit at Bologna Children's Book Fair. An all-inclusive turnkey service. We arrange for space, signage, decoration, shipping, customs, loading & unloading.

The Combined Book Exhibit®
277 White St, Buchanan, NY 10511
Tel: 914-739-7500 *Toll Free Tel:* 800-462-7687
  Fax: 914-739-7575
E-mail: info@combinedbook.com
Web Site: www.combinedbook.com; www.cbedatabase.com
Key Personnel
Pres: Jon Malinowski *E-mail:* jon@combinedbook.com
Dir, Busn Devt: Chris Malinowski *E-mail:* chris@combinedbook.com
Mktg Coord: Claribel Ortega *E-mail:* claribel@combinedbook.com
Founded: 1933
Organize combined book & multimedia exhibits for publishers worldwide covering books, periodicals, audio, video & ebooks. Areas covered include library, academic education, trade & international markets. Upwards of 20 major conferences & trade shows scheduled.

Exhibit Promotions Plus Inc
11620 Vixens Path, Ellicott City, MD 21042-1539
Tel: 410-997-0763
E-mail: exhibit@epponline.com
Web Site: www.epponline.com
Key Personnel
Founder & Pres: Harve C Horowitz, Esq
CFO: Eileen S Horowitz
Sr Mgr, Cust Rel: Kelly K Marshall
Founded: 1969
Scholarly association representation; Generate program & journal advertising in conjunction with international, national, regional & state exhibits in subject-arranged collections. Catalog for each meeting with emphasis on titles authored by members of sponsoring association. Marketing & managing trade shows for nonprofit associations. Total convention management company including site selection/hotel contracting.

National Association of Book Entrepreneurs (NABE)
PO Box 606, Cottage Grove, OR 97424
Tel: 541-942-7455 *Fax:* 541-942-7455
E-mail: nabe@bookmarketingprofits.com
Web Site: www.bookmarketingprofits.com
Key Personnel
Exec Dir: Al Galasso
Founded: 1980
Combined book displays, North American Bookdealers Exchange Book Showcase, at various regional & national trade shows including mail order, business, gift shop, premium & school product shows.

The Scholar's Choice
6300 W Port Bay Rd, Suite 101, Wolcott, NY 14590
Tel: 315-905-4208
E-mail: information@scholarschoice.com
Web Site: www.scholarschoice.com
Key Personnel
Owner: Thomas Prins *E-mail:* tom@scholarschoice.com
Promote & market scholarly books through exhibits. More than 100 academic conferences scheduled in the humanities & human sciences.

Book Clubs

Included below are a variety of book clubs. Letters in parenthesis indicate the type of club.

(A)–Adult   (J)–Juvenile   (A-J)–Adult & Juvenile

Arrow (grades 4-6) (J)
Scholastic School Reading Events
Division of Scholastic Inc
557 Broadway, New York, NY 10012
Tel: 212-343-6100; 573-632-1632 (PR, US territories, US military bases) *Toll Free Tel:* 800-541-1097 (US) *Toll Free Fax:* 800-223-4011
E-mail: bookclubs@scholastic.com
Web Site: clubs.scholastic.com
Key Personnel
Pres, Scholastic School Reading Events: Sasha Quinton
Since 1948, Scholastic Book Clubs has inspired kids to love reading by making it easy & affordable for them to choose their very own books. The Scholastic Book Clubs flyers, both in print & digitally, offer a wide range of age-appropriate books handpicked by our editors. At prices starting as low as just $1, these flyers make it possible for kids of all income levels & from every part of the country to have access to great books & build their own home collections.
Publication(s): Monthly book catalogs for early childhood to middle school (sold exclusively in the school market).

Audiobooks.com, an RBmedia company (A)
935 Sheldon Ct, Burlington, ON L7L 5K6, Canada
E-mail: customerservice@audiobooks.com
Web Site: www.audiobooks.com
Key Personnel
Gen Mgr: Ian Small
Established: 2012
App-based audiobook subscription service.
Branch Office(s)
2225 Kenmore Ave, Suite 122, Buffalo, NY 14207-1359

Children's Braille Book Club (J)
National Braille Press
88 Saint Stephen St, Boston, MA 02115-4312
Tel: 617-266-6160 *Toll Free Tel:* 800-548-7323 (cust serv) *Fax:* 617-437-0456
E-mail: contact@nbp.org
Web Site: www.nbp.org
Key Personnel
Pres: Brian A MacDonald *E-mail:* bmacdonald@nbp.org
VP, Braille Pubns: Tony Grima *Tel:* 617-266-6160 ext 429 *E-mail:* agrima@nbp.org
Children's print-braille books, PreK-3rd grade.
Number of Members: 2,951

Club Leo (Spanish & bilingual books for all grades) (J)
Scholastic School Reading Events
Division of Scholastic Inc
557 Broadway, New York, NY 10012
Tel: 212-343-6100; 573-632-1632 (PR, US territories, US military bases) *Toll Free Tel:* 800-541-1097 (US) *Toll Free Fax:* 800-223-4011
E-mail: bookclubs@scholastic.com
Web Site: clubs.scholastic.com
Key Personnel
Pres, Scholastic School Reading Events: Sasha Quinton
Since 1948, Scholastic Book Clubs has inspired kids to love reading by making it easy & affordable for them to choose their very own books. The Scholastic Book Clubs flyers, both in print & digitally, offer a wide range of age-appropriate books handpicked by our editors. At prices starting as low as just $1, these flyers make it possible for kids of all income levels & from every part of the country to have access to great books & build their own home collections.
Publication(s): Monthly book catalogs for early childhood to middle school (sold exclusively in the school market).

Conservative Book Club (A)
Townhall Media
300 New Jersey Ave NW, Suite 500, Washington, DC 20001
Tel: 202-216-0601
Web Site: www.conservativebookclub.com
Key Personnel
VP, Brand Opers: Storm Paglia *E-mail:* storm.paglia@townhallmedia.com
Digital Media Sales Rep: Anne H Pelczar *E-mail:* anne.pelczar@salemwebnetwork.com
Established: 1964
Conservative books on politics, economics, defense, religion, social issues, home school, history & entertainment.
Number of Members: 50,000

Crafter's Choice® (A)
Bookspan LLC
34 W 27 St, 10th fl, New York, NY 10001
Tel: 716-250-5700 (cust serv) *Toll Free Tel:* 866-250-3166
E-mail: customer.service@crafterschoice.com
Web Site: www.crafterschoice.com
The number one crafting club in America featuring a variety of crafts such as quilting, knitting, scrapbooking & more.
Publication(s): *Crafter's Choice*

Doubleday Book Club® (A)
Bookspan LLC
34 W 27 St, 10th fl, New York, NY 10001
Tel: 716-250-5700 (cust serv)
E-mail: customer.service@doubledaybookclub.com; member.services@doubledaybookclub.com
Web Site: doubledaybookclub.com
Established: 1930
The best in women's fiction, suspense & romance at great prices.

Doubleday Large Print Book Club® (A)
Bookspan LLC
34 W 27 St, 10th fl, New York, NY 10001
Tel: 716-250-5700 (cust serv)
E-mail: customer.service@doubledaylargeprint.com
Web Site: doubledaylargeprint.com
Established: 1985
Bestsellers, nonfiction, reference, Christian titles, etc all in fine large print editions. Most books are NAVH compliant.
Publication(s): *The Doubleday Large Print Monthly Magazine*

5th Grade Book Club (J)
Scholastic School Reading Events
Division of Scholastic Inc
557 Broadway, New York, NY 10012
Tel: 212-343-6100; 573-632-1632 (PR, US territories, US military bases) *Toll Free Tel:* 800-541-1097 (US) *Toll Free Fax:* 800-223-4011
E-mail: bookclubs@scholastic.com
Web Site: clubs.scholastic.com
Key Personnel
Pres, Scholastic School Reading Events: Sasha Quinton
Since 1948, Scholastic Book Clubs has inspired kids to love reading by making it easy & affordable for them to choose their very own books. The Scholastic Book Clubs flyers, both in print & digitally, offer a wide range of age-appropriate books handpicked by our editors. At prices starting as low as just $1, these flyers make it possible for kids of all income levels & from every part of the country to have access to great books & build their own home collections.
Publication(s): Monthly book catalogs for early childhood to middle school (sold exclusively in the school market).

Firefly (PreK-K) (J)
Scholastic School Reading Events
Division of Scholastic Inc
557 Broadway, New York, NY 10012
Tel: 212-343-6100; 573-632-1632 (PR, US territories, US military bases) *Toll Free Tel:* 800-541-1097 (US) *Toll Free Fax:* 800-223-4011
E-mail: bookclubs@scholastic.com
Web Site: clubs.scholastic.com
Key Personnel
Pres, Scholastic School Reading Events: Sasha Quinton
Since 1948, Scholastic Book Clubs has inspired kids to love reading by making it easy & affordable for them to choose their very own books. The Scholastic Book Clubs flyers, both in print & digitally, offer a wide range of age-appropriate books handpicked by our editors. At prices starting as low as just $1, these flyers make it possible for kids of all income levels & from every part of the country to have access to great books & build their own home collections.
Publication(s): Monthly book catalogs for early childhood to middle school (sold exclusively in the school market).

1st Grade Book Club (J)
Scholastic School Reading Events
Division of Scholastic Inc
557 Broadway, New York, NY 10012
Tel: 212-343-6100; 573-632-1632 (PR, US territories, US military bases) *Toll Free Tel:* 800-541-1097 (US) *Toll Free Fax:* 800-223-4011
E-mail: bookclubs@scholastic.com
Web Site: clubs.scholastic.com
Key Personnel
Pres, Scholastic School Reading Events: Sasha Quinton
Since 1948, Scholastic Book Clubs has inspired kids to love reading by making it easy & affordable for them to choose their very own books. The Scholastic Book Clubs flyers, both in print & digitally, offer a wide range of age-

BOOK CLUBS

appropriate books handpicked by our editors. At prices starting as low as just $1, these flyers make it possible for kids of all income levels & from every part of the country to have access to great books & build their own home collections.
Publication(s): Monthly book catalogs for early childhood to middle school (sold exclusively in the school market).

4th Grade Book Club (J)
Scholastic School Reading Events
Division of Scholastic Inc
557 Broadway, New York, NY 10012
Tel: 212-343-6100; 573-632-1632 (PR, US territories, US military bases) *Toll Free Tel:* 800-541-1097 (US) *Toll Free Fax:* 800-223-4011
E-mail: bookclubs@scholastic.com
Web Site: clubs.scholastic.com
Key Personnel
Pres, Scholastic School Reading Events: Sasha Quinton
Since 1948, Scholastic Book Clubs has inspired kids to love reading by making it easy & affordable for them to choose their very own books. The Scholastic Book Clubs flyers, both in print & digitally, offer a wide range of age-appropriate books handpicked by our editors. At prices starting as low as just $1, these flyers make it possible for kids of all income levels & from every part of the country to have access to great books & build their own home collections.
Publication(s): Monthly book catalogs for early childhood to middle school (sold exclusively in the school market).

The Good Cook® (A)
Bookspan LLC
34 W 27 St, 10th fl, New York, NY 10001
Tel: 716-250-5700 (cust serv) *Toll Free Tel:* 866-250-3166
E-mail: customer.service@thegoodcook.com
Web Site: thegoodcook.com
Established: 1971
Cookbooks by TV chefs & others, for gourmets & beginners.
Publication(s): *The Good Cook*

History Book Club® (A)
Bookspan LLC
34 W 27 St, 10th fl, New York, NY 10001
Tel: 716-250-5700 (cust serv)
E-mail: member.services@historybookclub.com
Web Site: www.historybookclub.com
Established: 1947
Adult nonfiction; history, world affairs, biography.
Publication(s): *History Book Club Catalogue* (every 3 weeks)

Honeybee (ages 2-4) (J)
Scholastic School Reading Events
Division of Scholastic Inc
557 Broadway, New York, NY 10012
Tel: 212-343-6100; 573-632-1632 (PR, US territories, US military bases) *Toll Free Tel:* 800-541-1097 (US) *Toll Free Fax:* 800-223-4011
E-mail: bookclubs@scholastic.com
Web Site: clubs.scholastic.com
Key Personnel
Pres, Scholastic School Reading Events: Sasha Quinton
Since 1948, Scholastic Book Clubs has inspired kids to love reading by making it easy & affordable for them to choose their very own books. The Scholastic Book Clubs flyers, both in print & digitally, offer a wide range of age-appropriate books handpicked by our editors. At prices starting as low as just $1, these flyers make it possible for kids of all income levels & from every part of the country to have access to great books & build their own home collections.
Publication(s): Monthly book catalogs for early childhood to middle school (sold exclusively in the school market).

Inchworm (ages 3-5) (J)
Scholastic School Reading Events
Division of Scholastic Inc
557 Broadway, New York, NY 10012
Tel: 212-343-6100; 573-632-1632 (PR, US territories, US military bases) *Toll Free Tel:* 800-541-1097 (US) *Toll Free Fax:* 800-223-4011
E-mail: bookclubs@scholastic.com
Web Site: clubs.scholastic.com
Key Personnel
Pres, Scholastic School Reading Events: Sasha Quinton
Since 1948, Scholastic Book Clubs has inspired kids to love reading by making it easy & affordable for them to choose their very own books. The Scholastic Book Clubs flyers, both in print & digitally, offer a wide range of age-appropriate books handpicked by our editors. At prices starting as low as just $1, these flyers make it possible for kids of all income levels & from every part of the country to have access to great books & build their own home collections.
Publication(s): Monthly book catalogs for early childhood to middle school (sold exclusively in the school market).

Junior Library Guild (J)
7858 Industrial Pkwy, Plain City, OH 43064
Tel: 614-733-0312 *Toll Free Tel:* 800-491-0174 *Fax:* 614-733-0501 *Toll Free Fax:* 800-827-3080
E-mail: editorial@juniorlibraryguild.com
Web Site: www.juniorlibraryguild.com
Key Personnel
Edit Dir: Susan Marston *Tel:* 646-380-0701
Established: 1929
Children's book service for libraries featuring new hardcover books for PreK-12. Thirty monthly selections. Monthly catalogue with authors'/illustrators' bios & reviews curriculum indications.
Branch Office(s)
123 William St, Suite 802, New York, NY 10038

Kindergarten Book Club (J)
Scholastic School Reading Events
Division of Scholastic Inc
557 Broadway, New York, NY 10012
Tel: 212-343-6100; 573-632-1632 (PR, US territories, US military bases) *Toll Free Tel:* 800-541-1097 (US) *Toll Free Fax:* 800-223-4011
E-mail: bookclubs@scholastic.com
Web Site: clubs.scholastic.com
Key Personnel
Pres, Scholastic School Reading Events: Sasha Quinton
Since 1948, Scholastic Book Clubs has inspired kids to love reading by making it easy & affordable for them to choose their very own books. The Scholastic Book Clubs flyers, both in print & digitally, offer a wide range of age-appropriate books handpicked by our editors. At prices starting as low as just $1, these flyers make it possible for kids of all income levels & from every part of the country to have access to great books & build their own home collections.
Publication(s): Monthly book catalogs for early childhood to middle school (sold exclusively in the school market).

Library of Science® Book Club (A)
Bookspan LLC
34 W 27 St, 10th fl, New York, NY 10001
Tel: 716-250-5700 (cust serv)

ADVERTISING, MARKETING

E-mail: customer.service@libraryofscience.net
Web Site: www.libraryofscience.net
Books for the professional scientist & the informed layperson on the mathematical, physical, life & earth sciences.

The Literary Guild® (A)
Bookspan LLC
34 W 27 St, 10th fl, New York, NY 10001
Tel: 716-250-5700 (cust serv) *Toll Free Tel:* 866-284-3202
E-mail: member.services@literaryguild.com
Web Site: literaryguild.com
Established: 1927
Offer a variety of genres including fiction, nonfiction, history, biography, self-help & cookbooks.

Lucky (grades 2-3) (J)
Scholastic School Reading Events
Division of Scholastic Inc
557 Broadway, New York, NY 10012
Tel: 212-343-6100; 573-632-1632 (PR, US territories, US military bases) *Toll Free Tel:* 800-541-1097 (US) *Toll Free Fax:* 800-223-4011
E-mail: bookclubs@scholastic.com
Web Site: clubs.scholastic.com
Key Personnel
Pres, Scholastic School Reading Events: Sasha Quinton
Since 1948, Scholastic Book Clubs has inspired kids to love reading by making it easy & affordable for them to choose their very own books. The Scholastic Book Clubs flyers, both in print & digitally, offer a wide range of age-appropriate books handpicked by our editors. At prices starting as low as just $1, these flyers make it possible for kids of all income levels & from every part of the country to have access to great books & build their own home collections.
Publication(s): Monthly book catalogs for early childhood to middle school (sold exclusively in the school market).

Maryheart Crusaders Inc (A)
531 W Main St, Meriden, CT 06451-2707
Tel: 203-238-9735 *Toll Free Tel:* 800-879-1957 (orders only) *Fax:* 203-235-0059
E-mail: maryheart@msn.com
Web Site: www.maryheartcrusaders.com
Key Personnel
Pres: Louise D'Angelo *Tel:* 203-235-5979
Mgr, Book Dept: Theresa Perrotti
Mgr, Candle Dept: Michael D'Angelo
Catholic religious goods store.
Number of Members: 2,222
Publication(s): *The Catholic Answer to the Jehovah's Witnesses*; *The Catholic Answer to the Jehovah's Witnesses (Spanish ed)*; *Come Climb the Ladder & Rejoice Vol I*; *Come Climb the Ladder & Rejoice Vol II*; *Come Home the Door Is Open*; *The Triumph of the Immaculate Heart of Mary: Visions of the Golden Lady of Happiness*

Metaphysical Book Club (A)
Warwick Press
18340 Sonoma Hwy, Sonoma, CA 95476
Tel: 707-939-9212 *Fax:* 707-938-3515
E-mail: warwick@vom.com
Web Site: www.warwickassociates.com
Key Personnel
Pres: Simon Warwick-Smith
Established: 1985

Military Book Club® (A)
Bookspan LLC
34 W 27 St, 10th fl, New York, NY 10001
Tel: 716-250-5700 (cust serv)
E-mail: customer.service@militarybookclub.com
Web Site: www.militarybookclub.com

Established: 1990
Book club for military, history & warfare enthusiasts.

Mystery Guild® (A)
Bookspan LLC
34 W 27 St, 10th fl, New York, NY 10001
Tel: 716-250-5700 (cust serv)
E-mail: customer.service@mysteryguild.com
Web Site: mysteryguild.com
Established: 1948
Serving the needs of mystery fans & the mystery community.

Next Chapter Book Club (NCBC) (A-J)
5909 Cleveland Ave, Columbus, OH 43231
Toll Free Tel: 800-674-8390
E-mail: info@nextchapterbookclub.org
Web Site: nextchapterbookclub.org
Key Personnel
Founder: Thomas Fish, PhD *E-mail:* tfish@nextchapterbookclub.org
Exec Dir: Desi Doolin
Established: 2002
Community-based reading program for adolescents & adults with intellectual & developmental disabilities. Network includes 300 book clubs in 31 states, 4 Canadian provinces & 3 European countries.
Number of Members: 2,000

One Spirit® (A)
Bookspan LLC
34 W 27 St, 10th fl, New York, NY 10001
Tel: 716-250-5700 (cust serv) *Toll Free Tel:* 866-250-3166
E-mail: customer.service@onespirit.com
Web Site: www.onespirit.com
Established: 1995
Resource for spirit, mind & body.
Publication(s): *The One Spirit Review*

Roots & Rhythm Inc (A)
PO Box 837, El Cerrito, CA 94530
Tel: 510-965-9503 *Toll Free Tel:* 888-ROOTS-66 (766-8766) *Fax:* 510-526-9001
E-mail: roots@toast.net
Web Site: www.rootsandrhythm.com
Key Personnel
Owner: Frank Scott; Nancy Scott-Noennig
Mail order: records, cassettes, CDs, discs, books & videos.
Publication(s): *Roots & Rhythm Newsletter* (5-7 issues/yr)

Science Fiction Book Club® (A)
Bookspan LLC
34 W 27 St, 10th fl, New York, NY 10001
Tel: 716-250-5700 (cust serv)
E-mail: customer.service@sfbc.com; member.services@sfbc.com
Web Site: sfbc.com
Established: 1953
Science fiction, fantasy, horror & graphic novels.

2nd Grade Book Club (J)
Scholastic School Reading Events
Division of Scholastic Inc
557 Broadway, New York, NY 10012
Tel: 212-343-6100; 573-632-1632 (PR, US territories, US military bases) *Toll Free Tel:* 800-541-1097 (US) *Toll Free Fax:* 800-223-4011
E-mail: bookclubs@scholastic.com
Web Site: clubs.scholastic.com
Key Personnel
Pres, Scholastic School Reading Events: Sasha Quinton
Since 1948, Scholastic Book Clubs has inspired kids to love reading by making it easy & affordable for them to choose their very own books. The Scholastic Book Clubs flyers, both in print & digitally, offer a wide range of age-appropriate books handpicked by our editors. At prices starting as low as just $1, these flyers make it possible for kids of all income levels & from every part of the country to have access to great books & build their own home collections.
Publication(s): Monthly book catalogs for early childhood to middle school (sold exclusively in the school market).

SeeSaw (K-1) (J)
Scholastic School Reading Events
Division of Scholastic Inc
557 Broadway, New York, NY 10012
Tel: 212-343-6100; 573-632-1632 (PR, US territories, US military bases) *Toll Free Tel:* 800-541-1097 (US) *Toll Free Fax:* 800-223-4011
E-mail: bookclubs@scholastic.com
Web Site: clubs.scholastic.com
Key Personnel
Pres, Scholastic School Reading Events: Sasha Quinton
Since 1948, Scholastic Book Clubs has inspired kids to love reading by making it easy & affordable for them to choose their very own books. The Scholastic Book Clubs flyers, both in print & digitally, offer a wide range of age-appropriate books handpicked by our editors. At prices starting as low as just $1, these flyers make it possible for kids of all income levels & from every part of the country to have access to great books & build their own home collections.
Publication(s): Monthly book catalogs for early childhood to middle school (sold exclusively in the school market).

Simply Audiobooks, see Audiobooks.com, an RBmedia company

TAB (grades 6 & up) (J)
Scholastic School Reading Events
Division of Scholastic Inc
557 Broadway, New York, NY 10012
Tel: 212-343-6100; 573-632-1632 (PR, US territories, US military bases) *Toll Free Tel:* 800-541-1097 (US) *Toll Free Fax:* 800-223-4011
E-mail: bookclubs@scholastic.com
Web Site: clubs.scholastic.com
Key Personnel
Pres, Scholastic School Reading Events: Sasha Quinton
Since 1948, Scholastic Book Clubs has inspired kids to love reading by making it easy & affordable for them to choose their very own books. The Scholastic Book Clubs flyers, both in print & digitally, offer a wide range of age-appropriate books handpicked by our editors. At prices starting as low as just $1, these flyers make it possible for kids of all income levels & from every part of the country to have access to great books & build their own home collections.
Publication(s): Monthly book catalogs for early childhood to middle school (sold exclusively in the school market).

TEENS (grades 7 & up) (J)
Scholastic School Reading Events
Division of Scholastic Inc
557 Broadway, New York, NY 10012
Tel: 212-343-6100; 573-632-1632 (PR, US territories, US military bases) *Toll Free Tel:* 800-541-1097 (US) *Toll Free Fax:* 800-223-4011
E-mail: bookclubs@scholastic.com
Web Site: clubs.scholastic.com
Key Personnel
Pres, Scholastic School Reading Events: Sasha Quinton
Since 1948, Scholastic Book Clubs has inspired kids to love reading by making it easy & affordable for them to choose their very own books. The Scholastic Book Clubs flyers, both in print & digitally, offer a wide range of age-appropriate books handpicked by our editors. At prices starting as low as just $1, these flyers make it possible for kids of all income levels & from every part of the country to have access to great books & build their own home collections.
Publication(s): Monthly book catalogs for early childhood to middle school (sold exclusively in the school market).

3rd Grade Book Club (J)
Scholastic School Reading Events
Division of Scholastic Inc
557 Broadway, New York, NY 10012
Tel: 212-343-6100; 573-632-1632 (PR, US territories, US military bases) *Toll Free Tel:* 800-541-1097 (US) *Toll Free Fax:* 800-223-4011
E-mail: bookclubs@scholastic.com
Web Site: clubs.scholastic.com
Key Personnel
Pres, Scholastic School Reading Events: Sasha Quinton
Established: 1948
Since 1948, Scholastic Book Clubs has inspired kids to love reading by making it easy & affordable for them to choose their very own books. The Scholastic Book Clubs flyers, both in print & digitally, offer a wide range of age-appropriate books handpicked by our editors. At prices starting as low as just $1, these flyers make it possible for kids of all income levels & from every part of the country to have access to great books & build their own home collections.
Publication(s): Monthly book catalogs for early childhood to middle school (sold exclusively in the school market).

We Need Diverse Books Older (grades 3-6) (J)
Scholastic School Reading Events
Division of Scholastic Inc
557 Broadway, New York, NY 10012
Tel: 212-343-6100; 573-632-1632 (PR, US territories, US military bases) *Toll Free Tel:* 800-541-1097 (US) *Toll Free Fax:* 800-223-4011
E-mail: bookclubs@scholastic.com
Web Site: clubs.scholastic.com
Key Personnel
Pres, Scholastic School Reading Events: Sasha Quinton
Since 1948, Scholastic Book Clubs has inspired kids to love reading by making it easy & affordable for them to choose their very own books. The Scholastic Book Clubs flyers, both in print & digitally, offer a wide range of age-appropriate books handpicked by our editors. At prices starting as low as just $1, these flyers make it possible for kids of all income levels & from every part of the country to have access to great books & build their own home collections.
Publication(s): Monthly book catalogs for early childhood to middle school (sold exclusively in the school market).

We Need Diverse Books Younger (Kindergarten-grade 2) (J)
Scholastic School Reading Events
Division of Scholastic Inc
557 Broadway, New York, NY 10012
Tel: 212-343-6100; 573-632-1632 (PR, US territories, US military bases) *Toll Free Tel:* 800-541-1097 (US) *Toll Free Fax:* 800-223-4011
E-mail: bookclubs@scholastic.com
Web Site: clubs.scholastic.com
Key Personnel
Pres, Scholastic School Reading Events: Sasha Quinton
Since 1948, Scholastic Book Clubs has inspired kids to love reading by making it easy & af-

BOOK CLUBS

fordable for them to choose their very own books. The Scholastic Book Clubs flyers, both in print & digitally, offer a wide range of age-appropriate books handpicked by our editors. At prices starting as low as just $1, these flyers make it possible for kids of all income levels & from every part of the country to have access to great books & build their own home collections.

Publication(s): Monthly book catalogs for early childhood to middle school (sold exclusively in the school market).

Book Lists & Catalogs

Many organizations compile book lists and catalogs throughout the year, including lists of religious books, juvenile books, bestsellers, international topics, etc. This is not an inclusive list, but it is representative of the various fields. The lists outlined below vary greatly in format and scope.

Letters in parenthesis indicate type of book list:

(A)–Adult   (J)–Juvenile   (A-J)–Adult & Juvenile

Further information concerning children's book lists may be obtained from The Children's Book Council, 54 West 39th Street, 14th floor, New York, NY 10018; The American Library Association, 225 N Michigan Avenue, Suite 1300, Chicago, IL 60601; and the Center for Children's Books, 501 East Daniel Street, Champaign, IL 61820.

AAAS, see American Association for the Advancement of Science (AAAS)

Adoption Book Catalog (A-J)
Affiliate of Tapestry Books
131 John Muir Dr, Amherst, NY 14228
Tel: 716-639-3900 *Toll Free Tel:* 866-691-3300
E-mail: info@tapestrybooks.com
Web Site: www.tapestrybooks.com
Key Personnel
Contact: Chris Fancher *E-mail:* chris@adoptionstar.com
Mail order catalog containing books for children & adults about adoption, infertility & related subjects.

American Association for the Advancement of Science (AAAS) (A-J)
1200 New York Ave NW, Washington, DC 20005
Tel: 202-326-6400 *Fax:* 202-371-9526
Web Site: www.aaas.org
Key Personnel
CEO: Sudip Parikh
Chief Communs Offr: Tal Woliner
CFO: Tanisha Lewis
Chief Prog Offr: Julia MacKenzie
Founded: 1848
Science Books & Films (journal); SB&F Online; Inquiry in the Library; SB&F, Best Books for Children printed annually. Healthy People 2010 Library Initiative.

Anti-Defamation League (A-J)
605 Third Ave, New York, NY 10158-3560
Tel: 212-885-7700
Web Site: www.adl.org
Key Personnel
CEO: Jonathan Greenblatt
General & specialized books, pamphlets, reports, children's plays & stories, ethnic studies, posters, bibliographies & audio-visual materials dealing with human relations. Specialize in prejudice & discrimination, Jewish-Christian relations, Jews & Judaism, multicultural education, Israel & the Middle East, anti-Semitism, the Holocaust.

Association for Childhood Education International (A)
1875 Connecticut Ave NW, 10th fl, Washington, DC 20009
Tel: 202-372-9986 *Toll Free Tel:* 800-423-3563
E-mail: headquarters@acei.org
Web Site: acei.org
Key Personnel
Exec Dir: Diane Whitehead
Dir, Pubns & Webmaster: Anne Watson Bauer
Founded: 1892

Association of professionals concerned with the health, education & well being of children, infancy through early adolescence.
Publish *Childhood Education: Innovations* bi-monthly journal.

Association for Library Service to Children (ALSC) (J)
Division of The American Library Association (ALA)
225 N Michigan Ave, Suite 1300, Chicago, IL 60601
Tel: 312-280-2163 *Toll Free Tel:* 800-545-2433
Fax: 312-280-5271
E-mail: alsc@ala.org
Web Site: www.ala.org/alsc
Key Personnel
Exec Dir: Alena Rivers *Tel:* 800-545-2433 ext 5866 *E-mail:* arivers@ala.org
Awards Coord: Jordan Dubin *Tel:* 800-545-2433 ext 5839 *E-mail:* jdubin@ala.org
Prog Coord: Ann Michaud *Tel:* 800-545-2433 ext 2166 *E-mail:* amichaud@ala.org
Membership/Mktg Specialist: Elizabeth Serrano *Tel:* 800-545-2433 ext 2164 *E-mail:* eserrano@ala.org
Caldecott Medal Books: complete list of medal-winning picture books.
Newbery Medal Books: complete list of books awarded this medal for literature. Notable books, software, videos & recordings for children.

Baker & Taylor LLC (A)
2550 W Tyvola Rd, Suite 300, Charlotte, NC 28217
Tel: 704-998-3100 *Toll Free Tel:* 800-775-1800 (info servs) *Fax:* 704-998-3319
Toll Free Fax: 800-775-2600
E-mail: btinfo@baker-taylor.com
Web Site: www.baker-taylor.com
Key Personnel
EVP & Gen Mgr: Amandeep Kochar
EVP, Opers: Gary Dayton
Founded: 1828
Baker & Taylor Inc (www.baker-taylor.com) is an aggregator & distributor of books, digital content & entertainment products. The company leverages its unsurpassed worldwide distribution network to deliver rich content in multiple formats, anytime & anywhere. Baker & Taylor offers cutting-edge digital media services & innovative technology platforms to thousands of publishers & libraries worldwide. Baker & Taylor also offers industry-leading customized library services. Baker & Taylor is proud to power Blio (blioreader.com), a flexible engaging & revolutionary e-reading application.
Branch Office(s)
Commerce Service Center, 251 Mount Olive Church Rd, Dept R, Commerce, GA 30599 *Tel:* 706-335-5000 *Toll Free Tel:* 800-775-1200

Momence Service Center, 501 S Gladiolus St, Momence, IL 60954, VP, Opers/Gen Mgr: Terrell Osborne *Tel:* 815-802-2444 *Toll Free Tel:* 800-775-2300
Pittsburgh Service Center, 875 Greentree Rd, Suite 678, Pittsburgh, PA 15220 *Tel:* 412-787-8890 *Toll Free Tel:* 800-775-2600
Membership(s): The American Library Association (ALA); Book Industry Study Group (BISG)

Bank Street Book Store (J)
Division of Bank Street College of Education
2780 Broadway, New York, NY 10025
Tel: 212-678-1654 *Fax:* 212-316-7026
E-mail: books@bankstreet.edu
Web Site: www.bankstreetbooks.com
Key Personnel
Mgr: Caitlyn Morrissey *E-mail:* cmorrissey@bankstreet.edu
Founded: 1970
Juvenile books, educational games, audio & videocassettes, early childhood education & CD-ROMs.

The Children's Book Council (CBC) (J)
54 W 39 St, 14th fl, New York, NY 10018
E-mail: cbc.info@cbcbooks.org
Web Site: www.cbcbooks.org
Key Personnel
Exec Dir: Carl Lennertz *E-mail:* carl.lennertz@cbcbooks.org
Assoc Exec Dir: Shaina Birkhead *E-mail:* shaina.birkhead@cbcbooks.org
Annual Bibliographies: *Children's Choices*, a child-selected bibliography; *Notable Social Studies Trade Books for Young People*; *Outstanding Science Trade Books for Students K-12*; *Best STEM Books*, recommendations to educators, librarians, parents & guardians for the best children's books with STEM content; *Beyond: Advanced Reader List*, helps adults recommend age appropriate titles that will challenge advanced readers; *Building a Home Library*, guidance to parents, grandparents & others interested in assembling an at-home library for the kids in their care.
Catalog: Reading encouragement materials & select publications & products for library & education professionals.

DeVorss & Co (A-J)
1100 Flynn Rd, Unit 104, Camarillo, CA 93012
Mailing Address: PO Box 1389, Camarillo, CA 93011-1389
Tel: 805-322-9010 *Toll Free Tel:* 800-843-5743
Fax: 805-322-9011
E-mail: service@devorss.com
Web Site: www.devorss.com
Key Personnel
Pres: Gary R Peattie *Tel:* 805-322-9010 ext 14 *E-mail:* gpeattie@devorss.com
Founded: 1929

BOOK LISTS & CATALOGS

Metaphysical, spiritual, inspirational, self-help, body/mind/spirit, New Thought. Annual *DeVorss Publications Catalog*. Announcements of new books as available.

Horn Book Inc (A)
300 The Fenway, Suite P-311, Palace Road Bldg, Boston, MA 02115
Tel: 617-278-0225 *Toll Free Tel:* 888-628-0225
Fax: 617-278-6062
E-mail: info@hbook.com
Web Site: www.hbook.com
Key Personnel
Group Publr: Rebecca T Miller *Tel:* 646-380-0738 *E-mail:* rmiller@mediasourceinc.com
Founded: 1924
Review publications: *The Horn Book Magazine* & *The Horn Book Guide to Children's & Young Adult Books*.

Jewish Book Council (A)
520 Eighth Ave, 4th fl, New York, NY 10018
Tel: 212-201-2920 *Fax:* 212-532-4952
E-mail: info@jewishbooks.org
Web Site: www.jewishbookcouncil.org
Key Personnel
Exec Dir: Carol Kaufman
Assoc Dir: Miri Pomerantz Dauber
Prog Dir: Evie Saphire-Bernstein *E-mail:* evie@jewishbooks.org
Founded: 1944
Building Your Home Jewish Library: A Beginner's List; *Jewish Book Annual Vol 53*; *Jewish Book Fair List 1997*; *Jewish Book Month Kit*, Nov 14-Dec 14, 1998; National Jewish Book Awards: A List of Books That Received Awards from 1949-1996; A Selected Bibliography; annotated bibliographies: *Anti-Semitism*; *Guide to Books on Death & Bereavement for Adults & Children*; *How To Organize A Jewish Library*; *Israel*; *The Reality*; *Jerusalem 3000*; *Jewish History*; *Jewish Life Cycle Events*; *Jewish Story Collections*; *Jewish Women*.

NameBank International (A)
1001 Cathedral St, Baltimore, MD 21201
Tel: 410-864-0854 *Fax:* 410-864-0837
E-mail: lists@namebank.com
Web Site: www.namebank.com
Key Personnel
Dir: Jenelle Ketcham *Tel:* 410-864-0840
  E-mail: jketcham@namebank.com
Founded: 1980
Health, investments & travel, mailing lists. Caters mainly to senior citizens.

National Council of Teachers of English (NCTE) (A-J)
340 N Neil St, Suite 104, Champaign, IL 61820
Tel: 217-328-3870 *Toll Free Tel:* 877-369-6283 (cust serv) *Fax:* 217-328-9645
E-mail: customerservice@ncte.org; permissions@ncte.org
Web Site: ncte.org
Key Personnel
Exec Dir: Emily Kirkpatrick
Sr Books Ed: Kurt Austin *Tel:* 217-278-3619
  E-mail: kaustin@ncte.org
Media Sales: Liz Barrett *E-mail:* ebarrett@townsend-group.com
Founded: 1911
Professional learning books for teachers; college, el-hi lists; lists of teachers by name; publishers of 11 periodicals, a national newspaper & national standards for teachers of English & language arts.

ProtoView (A)
Division of Ringgold Inc
7515 NE Ambassador Place, Suite A, Portland, OR 97220
Tel: 503-281-9230
E-mail: info@protoview.com
Web Site: www.protoview.com
Key Personnel
Pres, Ringgold Inc: Laura Cox
Chief Mktg Offr, Ringgold Inc: Jay Henry
Ed: Eithne O'Leyne
Founded: 1975 (as Book News Inc)
Ringgold's ProtoView service is centered around professionally-written abstracts & metadata of new titles, content which is supplied back to the publisher & sent to the discovery services used in academic settings. ProtoView abstracts & metadata are used in librarian- & public-facing resources offered by ProQuest, EBSCO, GOBI® Library Solutions from EBSCO, Baker & Taylor & Gale/Cengage. ProtoView author affiliations incorporate the Ringgold ID & institutional records from Ringgold's Identify database, expanding the data applications possible for any publisher using both services.

Trade Commission in Miami, Embassy of Spain in the US (A-J)
2655 Le Juene Rd, Suite 1114, Miami, FL 33134
Tel: 305-446-4387 *Fax:* 305-446-2602
E-mail: info@newspanishbooks.com
Web Site: www.newspanishbooks.us
Produces *New Spanish Books*, an annual online compilation/guide to current Spanish titles, selected by a panel of experts from the US, with rights available for translation in the US. Includes up-to-date information about the Spanish publishing scene, translation grants, Spanish literary prizes, recent translations, news & events in the US & more.

Upstart Books™ (A-J)
Division of Demco Inc
PO Box 7488, Madison, WI 53707
Tel: 608-241-1201 *Toll Free Tel:* 800-356-1200 (orders); 800-962-4463 (cust serv)
Toll Free Fax: 800-245-1329 (orders)
E-mail: custserv@demco.com; order@demco.com
Web Site: www.demco.com/upstart
Key Personnel
Prod Devt Mgr, Lib Mkts: Heidi Green

Serials Featuring Books

The listings below outline a selected list of general interest and specialty periodicals that feature book reviews and/or articles on books and authors. The list also includes periodicals used for book-related advertising and reference purposes. The types of periodicals included are magazines, newspapers, newspaper magazine sections, newsletters & online publications.

Newspaper editions in this section are indicated as follows: (d) daily; (m) morning; (e) evening; (Sat) Saturday; (Sun) Sunday.

Magazines for the book publishing trade may be found in **Magazines for the Trade** (volume 1). Additionally, journals and services involved in book reviews can be found in **Book Review and Index Journals & Services**.

For a comprehensive international directory of periodicals, see *Ulrich's Periodicals Directory* (online only, compiled by ProQuest LLC, part of Clarivate PLC, 789 East Eisenhower Parkway, Ann Arbor, MI 48108), which lists magazines by subject and includes notations indicating those that carry book reviews.

Abilene Reporter-News
Published by Gannett Co Inc
101 Cypress St, Abilene, TX 79601
Mailing Address: PO Box 30, Abilene, TX 79604
Tel: 325-673-4271 *Toll Free Tel:* 844-900-7098 (sales)
E-mail: publishme@reporternews.com
Web Site: www.reporternews.com
Key Personnel
News Dir/Ed: Greg Jaklewicz *Tel:* 325-676-6764
  E-mail: greg.jaklewicz@reporternews.com
Sunday page, syndicated.
First published 1881
Frequency: Daily
Circulation: 40,000 (d); 50,000 (Sun)
$1.50/daily, $2/Sun

Academe: Magazine of the AAUP
Published by American Association of University Professors (AAUP)
1133 19 St NW, Suite 200, Washington, DC 20036
Tel: 202-737-5900 *Toll Free Tel:* 800-424-2973
Fax: 202-737-5526
E-mail: academe@aaup.org
Web Site: www.aaup.org
Key Personnel
Dir, External Rel: Gwendolyn Bradley
  E-mail: gbradley@aaup.org
Mng Ed: Michael Ferguson *E-mail:* mferguson@aaup.org
Book Review Ed: Michael DeCesare
  E-mail: mdecesare@aaup.org
Journal of higher education from a faculty perspective. No unsol mss, query first.
First published 1915
Book Use: Reviews
Frequency: 6 issues/yr
Avg pages per issue: 56
Circulation: 44,000
Free to membs, $92/yr domestic nonmembs, $97/yr foreign nonmembs
ISSN: 0190-2946
Sell back issues
Avg reviews per issue: 3
Trim Size: 8 1/4 x 10 7/8
Ad Rates: Full page $3,075, 1/2 page $1,880
Ad Closing Date(s): 1 1/2 months before cover date

The Ada News
Published by CNHI LLC
116 N Broadway, Ada, OK 74820
Tel: 580-332-4433 *Fax:* 580-332-8734
E-mail: news@theadanews.com
Web Site: www.theadanews.com
Key Personnel
Publr: Mark Millsap *E-mail:* mark@normantranscript.com
Local community newspaper. Occasional book reviews & author interviews.
Circulation: 5,000 (Tues-Sat)

Advisor Today
Published by National Association of Insurance & Financial Advisors (NAIFA)
2901 Telestar Ct, Falls Church, VA 22042-1205
Tel: 703-770-8100 *Toll Free Tel:* 877-TO-NAIFA (866-2432)
E-mail: membersupport@naifa.org
Web Site: www.advisortoday.com
Key Personnel
Ed-in-Chief: Ayo Mseka *Tel:* 703-770-8204
  E-mail: amseka@naifa.org
Pubn & Circ Coord: Tara Heuser *Tel:* 703-770-8207 *E-mail:* theuser@naifa.org
News & how-to articles for the professional life & health insurance agent & financial planner. No unsol mss, query first.
First published 1906
Frequency: 6 issues/yr
Avg pages per issue: 100
Circulation: 40,000
Free to membs, $50/yr indivs, $60/yr instns, $100/yr intl
ISSN: 1529-823X
Buy illustrations & photographs; Sell back issues

The Advocate
Published by Capital City Press LLC
10705 Rieger Rd, Baton Rouge, LA 70809
Tel: 225-388-0200 (circ); 225-388-0315 (newsroom) *Toll Free Tel:* 800-960-6397 (in Louisiana)
E-mail: newstips@theadvocate.com
Web Site: theadvocate.com
Key Personnel
Publr: Dan Shea
Features Ed: Karen Martin *Tel:* 225-388-0378
  E-mail: kmartin@theadvocate.com
Travel, puzzles, hobbies, art reviews, books & authors, entertainment, history & features.
Frequency: Daily
Digital & print: $14.95/mo (Sat & Sun), $24.95/mo (Mon-Sun); digital only: $9.99/mo

Afro-American Newspaper
1531 S Edgewood St, Baltimore, MD 21227
Tel: 410-554-8277 (edit); 410-554-8200 (subns)
  Toll Free Fax: 877-570-9297
E-mail: editor@afro.com; subs@afro.com
Web Site: www.afro.com
Key Personnel
Pres: Benjamin Murphy Phillips, IV
VP, Mktg & Technol: Kevin Peck
Publr: Frances Murphy Draper
Dir, Opers: Andre R Draper
Mng Ed: Tiffany Ginyard
Ed: Sean Yoes *E-mail:* syoes@afro.com
General interest newspaper targeted for African-American audience. Reviews done in-house, occasional author interviews.
First published 1892
Frequency: Monthly
$20/yr digital only, $70/yr print & digital

AGNI Magazine
Published by Boston University
236 Bay State Rd, Boston, MA 02215
E-mail: agni@bu.edu
Web Site: www.bu.edu/agni
Key Personnel
Ed: Sven Birkerts
Sr Ed: William Pierce
New literary fiction, poetry & essays by emerging & established writers. Accept unsol mss. For submission policy, see www.agnionline.bu.edu/submit.
First published 1972
Frequency: 2 issues/yr
Avg pages per issue: 240
Circulation: 4,000
$23/yr
ISSN: 0191-3352
Trim Size: 8 1/2 x 5 3/8
Ad Rates: Full page $500, 1/2 page $350
Ad Closing Date(s): Feb 5 & Aug 1

Akron Beacon Journal
Published by GateHouse Media LLC
44 E Exchange St, Akron, OH 44328
Tel: 330-996-3000
Web Site: www.ohio.com
Key Personnel
Pres & Publr: Bill Albrecht *Tel:* 330-996-3782
  E-mail: balbrecht@gatehousemedia.com
Ed: Michael Shearer *Tel:* 330-996-3750
  E-mail: mshearer@thebeaconjournal.com
Book reviews in-house, through syndication & other outside sources; occasional author interviews. Sunday pages.
Circulation: 70,000 (m); 100,000 (Sun)
Digital & print: $9.99/mo (Sat & Sun), $19.50/mo (Mon-Sun); digital only: $9.99/mo

Albuquerque Journal
Published by Albuquerque Publishing Co
7777 Jefferson NE, Albuquerque, NM 87109
Tel: 505-823-3800; 505-823-4400 (circ)
  Toll Free Tel: 800-990-5765; 800-577-8683 (subscriber servs)
Web Site: www.abqjournal.com
Key Personnel
Ed-in-Chief: Karen Moses *Tel:* 505-823-3803
  E-mail: kmoses@abqjournal.com
Mng Ed: Dan Herrera *Tel:* 505-823-3810
  E-mail: dherrera@abqjournal.com
Occasional book reviews.
Circulation: 304,224 (d); 379,315 (Sun)
Digital & print: $12/mo (Sun only), $15.50/mo (Fri-Sun), $20.50/mo (Mon-Sun); digital only: $10/mo

Alexandria Daily Town Talk
Published by Gannett Co Inc
PO Box 7558, Alexandria, LA 71306
Tel: 318-487-6397
E-mail: editor@thetowntalk.com

Web Site: www.thetowntalk.com
Weekly page book reviews, author interviews; in-house & syndicated reviews.
First published 1883
Circulation: 41,000 (d)

Alfred Hitchcock's Mystery Magazine
Published by Dell Magazines
Division of Penny Publications LLC
44 Wall St, Suite 904, New York, NY 10005-2401
Tel: 212-686-7188 *Toll Free Tel:* 800-220-7443 (corp sales) *Fax:* 212-480-5751
E-mail: alfredhitchcockmm@dellmagazines.com
Web Site: www.alfredhitchcockmysterymagazine.com
Subscription Address: Dell Magazines Direct, 6 Prowitt St, Norwalk, CT 06855-1220
Key Personnel
Ed: Linda Landrigan
Asst Mktg Mgr: Monique St Paul
Short stories of mystery, crime & detection, short-short contest, puzzle & book reviews.
First published 1956
Frequency: 6 issues/yr
Avg pages per issue: 192
Circulation: 90,000
$34.97/yr, $63.97/2 yrs, $59.94/yr intl, $35.88/yr digital
ISSN: 0002-5224
Avg reviews per issue: 4
Trim Size: 5 7/8 x 8 1/2
Ad Rates: 4-color back cover $1,800, B&W page $1,000, B&W 1/2 page-horizontal $600
Ad Closing Date(s): 3 months before sale date

Amarillo Globe News
Published by GateHouse Media LLC
600 S Tyler, Suite 103, Amarillo, TX 79101
Tel: 806-376-4488
Web Site: www.amarillo.com
Key Personnel
Regl Exec Ed: Jill Nevels-Haun *E-mail:* jnevels-haun@lubbockonline.com
One page weekly, in-house & through syndication; occasional author interviews.
Circulation: Globe: 55,000 (e); Sun Globe News: 65,000
Digital & print: $14.25/4 wks (Sun only), $19.09/4 wks (Fri-Sun), $22.50/4 wks (Mon-Sat), $23.45/4 wks (Mon-Sun); digital only: $9.99/mo

American Educator
Published by American Federation of Teachers
555 New Jersey Ave NW, Washington, DC 20001
Tel: 202-879-4420
E-mail: ae@aft.org
Web Site: www.aft.org/ae
Key Personnel
Art Dir: Jennifer Chang
Mng Ed: Jennifer Dubin
Graphic Designer: Jennifer Barney
Articles on education, labor, politics & social commentary. Includes news, book reviews & features for teachers at all grade levels, preschool through college & university.
First published 1977
Frequency: Quarterly
Avg pages per issue: 40
Circulation: 900,000
$10/yr nonmembs
ISSN: 0148-432X
Trim Size: 8 1/4 x 10 7/8

The American Legion Magazine
Published by The American Legion
700 N Pennsylvania St, Indianapolis, IN 46204
Mailing Address: PO Box 1055, Indianapolis, IN 46206
Tel: 317-630-1272
E-mail: magazine@legion.org

Web Site: www.legion.org
Subscription Address: Box 1954, Indianapolis, IN 46206
Key Personnel
Dir: Jeff Stoffer
Ad Mgr: Diane M Andretti *E-mail:* dandretti@legion.org
Contains feature articles that address a compelling issue in American society. Issues relating to veterans affairs, the US military, national security, foreign affairs, American values & patriotism often are preferred. Also publish selected general-interest articles & question & answer interviews with prominent national & world figures. Articles are not required to have a military angle. We make all assignments based on a 300-word query letter. Prefer to work with published/established writers.
First published 1919
Book Use: Occasional excerpts
Frequency: Monthly
Avg pages per issue: 56
Circulation: 1,600,000 paid
Free to membs, $6/yr surviving spouses, $15/yr nonmembs, $21/yr foreign
ISSN: 0086-1234
Buy nonfiction, cartoons; Sell back issues
Trim Size: 7 3/4 x 10 1/2
Ad Rates: B&W page $50,095, 4-color page $68,000
Ad Closing Date(s): 1st day of 2nd month preceding issue date

American Letters & Commentary (AL&C)
Subsidiary of University of Texas at San Antonio, Dept of English
One UTSA Circle, San Antonio, TX 78249-0643
E-mail: amerletters@satx.rr.com
Web Site: www.amletters.org
Key Personnel
Co-Ed: Catherine Kasper; David Ray Vance
For submission policy, see guidelines on our web site.

American Press
4900 Hwy 90 E, Lake Charles, LA 70615
Mailing Address: PO Box 2893, Lake Charles, LA 70602
Tel: 337-433-3000 *Fax:* 337-494-4070
E-mail: news@americanpress.com
Web Site: www.americanpress.com
Key Personnel
Book Review Ed: Donna Price
Sunday book reviews; occasional local author interviews.
Circulation: 29,000 (d); 32,000 (Sun)
$.50/daily, $1.25/Sun

American Scientist
Published by Sigma Xi, The Scientific Research Society
Cape Fear Bldg, Suite 300, 3200 Chapel Hill Nelson Hwy, Research Triangle Park, NC 27709-0013
Tel: 919-549-4691 *Toll Free Tel:* 800-282-0444 *Fax:* 919-549-0090
E-mail: editors@amscionline.org
Web Site: www.americanscientist.org
Key Personnel
Art Dir: Barbara Aulicino
Dir, Digital Features: Katie L Burke
Ed-in-Chief: Fenella Saunders
Mng Ed: Stacey Lutkoski
Reports on recent research in pure & applied sciences; written for scientists in all disciplines.
First published 1913
Frequency: 6 issues/yr
Circulation: 55,000 paid
Print only: $30/yr, $54/2 yrs; print & digital: $36/yr, $66/2 yrs
ISSN: 0003-0996
Buy art & cartoons; Sell back issues

Trim Size: 8 3/16 x 10 7/8
Ad Rates: B&W page $2,900, 4-color page $4,000
Ad Closing Date(s): 1st of month, 2 months prior to publication

American Songwriter
Published by ForASong Media LLC
PO Box 330249, Nashville, TN 37203
Tel: 615-321-6096
Web Site: americansongwriter.com
Subscription Address: PO Box 90187, Long Beach, CA 90809 *Toll Free Tel:* 888-881-5861
E-mail: americansongwriter@pfsmag.com
Key Personnel
Publr: Albie Del Favero *Tel:* 615-321-6096 ext 105 *E-mail:* adelfavero@americansongwriter.com
Ed-in-Chief: Caine O'Rear
Asst Ed: Brittney McKenna *E-mail:* bmckenna@americansongwriter.com
American Songwriter Magazine covers every aspect of the craft & art of songwriting, from how & why writers give birth to their songs, to engaging & informative assessments of our songwriting culture as a whole. The magazine provides in-depth interviews with up-&-coming, established & legendary songwriters; discussions on performance rights organizations & copyright law; & interviews with publishers, producers, A&R executives & other industry representatives who have something of interest to say to our readers. American Songwriter strives to serve as the unparalleled source of inspiration for passionate music fans & songwriters alike, by exploring all genres of music. Also available online.
First published 1984
Book Use: Reviews, might excerpt if appropriate
Frequency: 6 issues/yr
Circulation: 30,000
$2.49/mo, $24.95/yr
ISSN: 0896-8993
Sell articles, ad reprints & back issues

The American Spectator
Published by The American Spectator Foundation
122 S Royal St, Suite 1, Alexandria, VA 22314
Tel: 703-807-2011
E-mail: editor@spectator.org
Web Site: spectator.org
Key Personnel
Publr: Melissa Mackenzie
Edit Dir: Wladyslaw Pleszczynski
Ed-in-Chief: R Emmett Tyrrell, Jr
Occasional book reviews & articles featuring books. Online only.
First published 1924

AMG/Parade
Published by Athlon Media Group
60 E 42 St, Suite 820, New York, NY 10165
Tel: 212-478-1910
E-mail: info@amgparade.com
Web Site: athlonmediagroup.com
Key Personnel
Pres & CEO: Chuck Allen
CFO: Mary Lee Vanderkooi
Chief Revenue Offr Brand Sales: Amy Chernoff
EVP, New Ventures & Busn Devt: Tracey Altman
SVP & Chief Content Offr: Lisa Delaney
SVP & Chief Digital Offr: Michael McCracken
SVP & Chief Mktg Offr, Digital: Monique Kakar
General interest publication for a mass audience with editorial content on people, education, Washington & Hollywood, science & medicine & changing tastes & trends.
First published 1941
Frequency: Weekly
Circulation: 18,000,000
Trim Size: 8.250 x 9.375
Ad Rates: B&W page $584,800, 4-color page $722,800

The Amherst News
Published by SaltWire Network
2717 Joseph Howe Dr, Halifax, NS B3J 2T2, Canada
Mailing Address: PO Box 610, Halifax, NS B3J 2T2, Canada
Tel: 902-664-1260
Web Site: www.thecumberlandnewsnow.com
Key Personnel
Mng Ed: Darrell Cole *E-mail:* darrell.cole@amherstnews.ca
In-house, syndicated, author interviews.
First published 1893
$1.85/wk

Analog Science Fiction & Fact
Published by Dell Magazines
Division of Penny Publications LLC
44 Wall St, Suite 904, New York, NY 10005
Toll Free Tel: 800-220-7443 (corp sales)
E-mail: analogsf@dellmagazines.com
Web Site: www.analogsf.com
Subscription Address: Dell Magazines Direct, 6 Prowitt St, Norwalk, CT 06855-1220, Contact: Lisa Begley *Tel:* 203-866-6688 ext 204 *Fax:* 203-854-5962 *E-mail:* lbegley@pennypublications.net
Key Personnel
Ed: Trevor Quachri
Publishes 7-9 science fiction stories per issue, fact articles & book review.
First published 1930
Book Use: Reviews, excerpts & serializations
Frequency: 6 double issues/yr
Avg pages per issue: 144
Circulation: 32,900
$34.97/yr, $46.97/yr intl, $63.97/2 yrs, $87.97/2 yrs intl, $35.88/yr digital
ISSN: 1059-2113
Buy freelance fiction, poetry & cartoons; Sell back issues
Trim Size: 5 7/8 x 8 1/2
Ad Rates: B&W page $1,000, 4-color back cover $1,800
Ad Closing Date(s): 3 months before sale date

Anchorage Daily News
Published by Alaska Daily News LLC
300 W 31 Ave, Anchorage, AK 99503
Tel: 907-257-4200; 907-257-4400 (subns)
 Toll Free Tel: 800-478-4200 (AK only); 866-528-0236 (subns)
E-mail: letters@adn.com
Web Site: www.adn.com
Key Personnel
Pres & CEO: Ryan Binkley *E-mail:* ryan@adn.com
Publr: Andy Pennington *Tel:* 907-257-4210
 E-mail: apennington@adn.com
Ed: David Hulen *Tel:* 907-257-4596
 E-mail: dhulen@adn.com
Reviews books by Alaskan authors or on topics of specific interest to Alaskans.
First published 1946
Frequency: Daily (Mon-Fri & Sun)
Digital & print: $11.49/mo (Sun only), $16.95/mo (Thurs, Fri & Sun), $24.95/mo (Mon-Fri & Sun); digital only: $11.99/mo, $119.90/yr

Anniston Star
Published by Consolidated Publishing Co
4305 McClellan Blvd, Anniston, AL 36206
Tel: 256-236-1551 *Fax:* 256-241-1970
E-mail: news@annistonstar.com
Web Site: www.annistonstar.com
Key Personnel
Publr: Josephine Ayers
Exec Ed: Anthony Cook
Mng Ed: Ben Cunningham
 E-mail: bcunningham@annistonstar.com

Every Sunday, Life & Arts section, occasional author interviews; book reviews every Sunday in Coffee Break section.
Circulation: 30,000
$.75/daily, $2/Sun; digital & print: $9.25/mo (Sun only), $9.50/mo (Wed-Sat), $11.25/mo (Fri-Sun), $16.25/mo (Wed-Sun); digital only: $7.99/mo, $69.99/yr

The Antigonish Review
Published by St Francis Xavier University
PO Box 5000, Antigonish, NS B2G 2W5, Canada
Tel: 902-867-3962 *Fax:* 902-867-5563
E-mail: tar@stfx.ca
Web Site: www.antigonishreview.com
Key Personnel
Mng Ed: Thomas Hodd
Book Reviews Ed: Leo Furey
Literary journal.
First published 1970
Frequency: Quarterly
Avg pages per issue: 144
Circulation: 1,000
$75/yr print, $140/2 yrs, $20/back issue; $30/yr digital, $45/2 yrs, $10/back issue (if available)
ISSN: 0003-5662
Avg reviews per issue: 4
Ad Rates: Full page $300, 1/2 page $150

Archaeology
Published by Archaeological Institute of America
36-36 33 St, Long Island City, NY 11106
Tel: 718-472-3050 *Toll Free Tel:* 877-275-9782 (subns) *Fax:* 718-472-3051
E-mail: editorial@archaeology.org; general@archaeology.org
Web Site: www.archaeology.org; www.archaeological.org
Subscription Address: PO Box 433091, Palm Coast, FL 32164 *Tel:* 386-246-0414 *Toll Free Tel:* 877-ARKY-SUB (275-9782)
 E-mail: subscription@archaeology.org
Key Personnel
Publr: Kevin Quinlan *Tel:* 857-305-9354
 E-mail: kquinlan@archaeological.org
Ed-in-Chief: Jarrett A Lobell *Tel:* 718-472-3050 ext 4908 *E-mail:* jarrett@archaeology.org
Deputy Ed: Eric A Powell *E-mail:* eric@archaeology.org
Sr Ed: Benjamin Leonard *E-mail:* ben@archaeology.org; Daniel Weiss *E-mail:* daniel@archaeology.org
Contains articles written by freelance science writers & professionals edited to meet the needs of the general reader; excavation reports, recent discoveries & special studies of ancient cultures. No unsol mss, query first.
First published 1948
Book Use: Review new titles
Frequency: 6 issues/yr
Avg pages per issue: 72
Circulation: 225,000 paid
$14.97/yr US or digital only, $29.97/yr CN & intl
ISSN: 0003-8113
Sell articles, ad reprints & back issues
Trim Size: 8 x 10 1/2
Ad Closing Date(s): 30 days prior to sale date

Argus Leader
Published by Gannett Co Inc
200 S Minnesota Ave, Sioux Falls, SD 57104
Tel: 605-331-2200; 605-331-2222; 605-331-2300 (newsroom) *Toll Free Tel:* 800-952-0127 (cust serv)
Web Site: www.argusleader.com
Key Personnel
News Dir: Cory Myers *E-mail:* ctmyers@argusleader.com
Occasionally local, in-house & other sources. Occasional author interviews. Weekly book section-Sunday.

The Arizona Daily Star
Published by Lee Enterprises Inc
4850 S Park Ave, Tucson, AZ 85714
Tel: 520-573-4142 *Toll Free Tel:* 800-695-4492 (cust serv)
E-mail: metro@tucson.com; circulation@tucson.com
Web Site: tucson.com
Key Personnel
Pres & Publr: John D'Orlando *Tel:* 520-573-4215
 E-mail: jdorlando@tucson.com
Sunday page reviews, in-house & through syndication; occasional author interviews.
Circulation: 160,587 (d); 234,163 (Sun)
Digital & print: $14.99/mo (Sun only, Sat & Sun, Wed & Sun or Wed, Sat & Sun), $23.99/mo (Wed-Sun), $24.99/mo (Mon-Sun)

The Arizona Republic
Published by Gannett Co Inc
200 E Van Buren St, Phoenix, AZ 85004
Tel: 602-444-8000 *Toll Free Tel:* 800-331-9303 (delivery); 800-332-6733 (subns)
E-mail: azrepubliccustomerservice@gannett.com; newsubs@azcentral.com
Web Site: www.azcentral.com
Key Personnel
Edit Dir: Philip Boas *E-mail:* phil.boas@arizonarepublic.com
Features Dir: Rebecca Bartkowski
 E-mail: rebecca.bartkowski@gannett.com
Exec Ed: Greg Burton *E-mail:* greg.burton@azcentral.com
Pages produced in-house, through syndication & by other sources. Author interviews & book reviews.
Circulation: 488,000 (m); 603,500 (Sun)
Digital & print: $18/mo (Wed & Sun), $27/mo (Wed & Fri-Sun), $32/mo (Mon-Sun); digital only: $9.99/mo

Arkansas Democrat-Gazette
Published by Arkansas Democrat-Gazette Inc
Subsidiary of Wehco Media
121 E Capitol Ave, Little Rock, AR 72201
Mailing Address: PO Box 2221, Little Rock, AR 72203
Tel: 501-378-3400 *Toll Free Tel:* 800-482-1121 (subns) *Fax:* 501-372-4765
Web Site: www.arkansasonline.com
Key Personnel
Publr: Walter E Hussman, Jr
Mng Ed: David Baily *Tel:* 501-378-3594
Moviestyle Ed/Columnist: Phillip Martin
 Tel: 501-378-3473 *E-mail:* pmartin@arkansasonline.com
Book reviews & occasional author interviews.
Frequency: Daily
Circulation: 182,212 (d); 274,494 (Sun)
$34/mo
ISSN: 1060-4332

Army Magazine
Published by Association of the US Army
2425 Wilson Blvd, Arlington, VA 22201
Tel: 703-841-4300 *Toll Free Tel:* 800-336-4570
Web Site: www.ausa.org
Key Personnel
Art Dir: Sam Votsis *E-mail:* svotsis@ausa.org
Ed-in-Chief: Rick Maze *E-mail:* rmaze@ausa.org
Mng Ed: Elizabeth Rathbun *E-mail:* lrathbun@ausa.org
Military-oriented.
First published 1904
Book Use: Reviews
Frequency: Monthly
Avg pages per issue: 64
Circulation: 100,000 paid
Free to membs
ISSN: 0004-2455
Buy freelance, nonfiction, art, cartoons; Sell back issues
Trim Size: 8 1/8 x 10 7/8

Ad Rates: B&W page $9,950 (1x), 4-color page $11,485 (1x)
Ad Closing Date(s): 1st of month preceding publication

Art in America
Published by ArtNews Media/Penske Media Corp
475 Fifth Ave, New York, NY 10017
Tel: 212-398-1690 *Toll Free Tel:* 800-925-8059 (subns)
E-mail: ads@artmediaholdings.com
Web Site: www.artinamericamagazine.com
Key Personnel
Dir, Mktg: Vajra Kingsley *E-mail:* vkingsley@artmediaholdings.com
Ed: William S Smith
Comprehensive reporting & commentary on major achievements & events throughout the art world, particularly in painting, sculpture, photos & prints; includes numerous reproductions.
First published 1913
Book Use: Departmentalized book reviews, exhibition reviews & news columns
Frequency: Monthly
Avg pages per issue: 120
Circulation: 45,000
$79/yr, $110/yr CN, $127/yr intl
ISSN: 0004-3214
Buy freelance nonfiction; Sell articles & ad reprints, back issues
Trim Size: 9 x 10 7/8
Ad Rates: B&W page $6,409, 4-color page $8,236
Ad Closing Date(s): see Media Kit on web site

Artesia Daily Press
503 W Main St, Artesia, NM 88210
Mailing Address: PO Box 190, Artesia, NM 88211-0190
Tel: 575-746-3524 *Fax:* 575-746-8795
Web Site: www.artesianews.com
Key Personnel
Publr: Danny Scott *E-mail:* danny@artesianews.com
Local news in print & online.
Frequency: Daily (Tues-Fri & Sun)
Circulation: 3,200 (Tues-Fri); 3,500 (Sun)
$.50/issue (Tues-Fri), $1/issue (Sun), $6.75/mo local print, $8/mo electronic

Asbury Park Press
Published by Gannett Co Inc
3600 Hwy 66, Neptune, NJ 07754
Mailing Address: PO Box 1550, Neptune, NJ 07754
Tel: 732-922-6000 *Toll Free Tel:* 800-822-9770
E-mail: newstips@app.com
Web Site: www.app.com
Key Personnel
VP, News: Hollis R Towns
Exec Ed: Paul D'Ambrosio
Regl Features Planner: Bill Canacci
Sunday edition includes books page; occasional author interviews.
Circulation: 159,705 (e); 223,833 (Sun)
Digital & print: $16/mo (Fri & Sun), $19/mo (Fri-Sun), $28/mo (Mon-Sun)

The Asheville Citizen-Times
Published by Gannett Co Inc
14 O Henry Ave, Asheville, NC 28801
Mailing Address: PO Box 2090, Asheville, NC 28802-2090
Tel: 828-252-5611 *Toll Free Tel:* 800-672-2472
E-mail: news@citizen-times.com
Web Site: www.citizen-times.com
Key Personnel
News Dir: Katie Wadington *Tel:* 828-232-5429 *E-mail:* kwadington@citizen-times.com
Sunday in *Leisure* section; frequent author interviews.
First published 1870

Circulation: 75,000 (d); 82,000 (Sun)
$1/daily, $2/Sun
Avg reviews per issue: 2

Asimov's Science Fiction
Published by Dell Magazines
Division of Penny Publications LLC
44 Wall St, Suite 904, New York, NY 10005-2401
Tel: 212-686-7188 *Toll Free Tel:* 800-220-7443 (corp sales) *Fax:* 212-480-5751
E-mail: asimovs@dellmagazines.com; customerservice@pennypublications.com
Web Site: www.asimovs.com
Subscription Address: Dell Magazines Direct, 6 Prowitt St, Norwalk, CT 06855-1220
Key Personnel
Pres: Peter Kanter
SVP: Bruce W Sherbow
Dir, Mktg, E-Commerce & Brand Licensing: Abigail Browning
Sr Art Dir: Victoria Green
Ed: Sheila Williams *Tel:* 212-686-7188 ext 2323 *E-mail:* swilliams@dellmagazines.net
Circ Servs & Subns: Sandy Marlowe
Features science fiction & fantasy.
First published 1977
Book Use: Short stories
Frequency: 6 double issues/yr
Avg pages per issue: 208
Circulation: 62,600
$34.97/yr, $46.97/yr intl, $63.97/2 yrs, $87.97/2 yrs intl, $35.88/yr digital only
ISSN: 1055-2146
Buy freelance fiction & poetry; Sell back issues
Trim Size: 8 1/2 x 5 3/8
Ad Rates: B&W page $1,800, 4-color back cover $3,240 (rates include ads in both Asimov's Science Fiction & Analog Science Fiction & Fact)
Ad Closing Date(s): 3 months before sale date

Athens Messenger
Published by Adams Publishing Group
9300 Johnson Rd, Athens, OH 45701
Tel: 740-592-6612
E-mail: info@athensmessenger.com; subscriptions@athensmessenger.com
Web Site: www.athensmessenger.com
Key Personnel
Publr: Mark Cohen *E-mail:* mark.cohen@adamspg.com
Ad Dir: Amanda Montgomery *E-mail:* amontgomery@adamspg.com
Ed: Tyler Buchanan *E-mail:* tbuchanan@athensmessenger.com
In-house reviews with authors with a local connection & those with Ohio interests. Monthly local author interviews.
First published 1904
Circulation: 10,000 (d); 12,000 (Sun)

Atlanta Journal-Constitution
Subsidiary of Cox Media Group LLC
223 Perimeter Center Pkwy, Atlanta, GA 30346-1301
Tel: 404-526-5151 *Fax:* 404-526-5746
E-mail: customercare@ajc.com
Web Site: www.ajc.com
Key Personnel
Publr: Donna B Hall
Sr Features Ed: Nicole D Smith *E-mail:* nicole.smith@ajc.com
Ed: Kevin Riley *Tel:* 404-526-2161 *E-mail:* kriley@ajc.com
Weekly column, in-house & through syndication, with frequent author interviews.
First published 1868
Circulation: 427,300 (Mon-Thurs); 485,300 (Fri); 515,700 (Sat); 693,500 (Sun)
Digital & print: $12.99/mo (Sun only), $24.99/mo (Mon-Sun); digital only: $4.99/mo

The Atlantic
Published by Atlantic Monthly Group LLC
600 New Hampshire Ave NW, Washington, DC 20037
Tel: 202-266-6000
Web Site: www.theatlantic.com
Subscription Address: PO Box 37564, Boone, IA 50037-0564 *Tel:* 515-237-3670 (intl) *Toll Free Tel:* 800-234-2411 *E-mail:* theatlantic@cdsfulfillment.com
Key Personnel
Chmn: David G Bradley
VChmn: Peter Lattman
Pres: Bob Cohn
Creative Dir: Peter Mendelsund
Ed-in-Chief: Jeffrey Goldberg
Exec Ed: Adrienne LaFrance
Sr Ed: Lenika Cruz; Jenisha Watts
Sr Ed, Books: Boris Kachka
Literary Ed: Ann Hulbert
Assoc Ed: Maya Chung; Emma Sarappo
Staff Writer: Gal Beckerman
Public affairs, politics & the arts. Considers unsol mss, either fiction or nonfiction & poetry. Ad closing date & trim sizes information available at advertising.theatlantic.com.
First published 1857
Frequency: 10 issues/yr
Avg pages per issue: 130
Circulation: 496,000
$24.50/yr print or digital, $34.50/yr print & digital
ISSN: 0276-9077
Buy freelance fiction, nonfiction & poetry

Augusta Chronicle
Published by GateHouse Media LLC
725 Broad St, Augusta, GA 30901
Tel: 706-724-0851 *Toll Free Tel:* 866-249-8223
Web Site: www.augustachronicle.com
Key Personnel
News Ed: Mike Wynn *Tel:* 706-823-3218 *E-mail:* mike.wynn@augustachronicle.com
Sunday book page.
Digital & print: $18.42/mo (Sun only), $19.37/mo (Fri-Sun), $31.43/mo (Mon-Sun); digital only: $9.95/mo, $99.50/yr

Austin American-Statesman
Published by GateHouse Media LLC
305 S Congress Ave, Austin, TX 78704
Mailing Address: PO Box 670, Austin, TX 78767
Tel: 512-445-4040 *Toll Free Tel:* 800-445-9898 (cust serv) *Fax:* 512-445-3679
E-mail: customercare@statesman.com
Web Site: www.statesman.com
Key Personnel
Exec Features Ed: Sharon Chapman *Tel:* 512-445-3647 *E-mail:* schapman@statesman.com
Weekly book page, in-house & through syndication. Occasional author interviews.
First published 1871
Circulation: 130,000 (d); 191,000 (Sun)
Digital & print: $29.99/mo (Sun only), $70.99/mo (Mon-Sun); digital only: $19.99/mo

Avenue Magazine
Published by Cohen Media Publications LLC
750 Lexington Ave, 16th fl, New York, NY 10022
E-mail: editorial@avenuemagazine.com
Web Site: avenuemagazine.com
Key Personnel
Publr: Spencer Sharp
Creative Dir: Courtney Gooch
Prodn Dir: Jessica Lee
Ed-in-Chief: Ben Widdicombe
Deputy & Mng Ed: Angela M H Schuster
Literary Ed: Celia McGee
New York focused lifestyle magazine including book reviews & power lists of literary arts professionals.

First published 1976
Frequency: 6 issues/yr

The Baltimore Sun
Published by Baltimore Sun Media Group
Subsidiary of Tribune Publishing Co
300 E Cromwell St, Baltimore, MD 21230
Tel: 410-332-6000 *Toll Free Tel:* 800-829-8000
Fax: 410-332-6455
E-mail: newstips@baltimoresun.com
Web Site: www.baltimoresun.com
Key Personnel
Publr & Ed-in-Chief: Trif Alatzas *E-mail:* trif.alatzas@baltsun.com
Mng Ed: Sam Davis *E-mail:* sdavis@baltsun.com
Sunday, 2 pages, 4-5 reviews per week in-house & freelance. Occasional author interviews.
First published 1837
Circulation: 270,000 (d); 420,000 (Sun)
$6.93/wk digital

Bangor Daily News
Published by Bangor Publishing Co
One Merchants Plaza, Bangor, ME 04401
Mailing Address: PO Box 1329, Bangor, ME 04402
Tel: 207-990-8000 *Toll Free Tel:* 800-432-7964 (ME only)
Web Site: www.bangordailynews.com
Key Personnel
Publr: Richard J Warren
Mng Ed: Dan MacLeod *Tel:* 207-990-8260
  E-mail: dmacleod@bangordailynews.com
Sr Ed, Features: Sarah Walker Caron *Tel:* 207-990-8120 *E-mail:* scaron@bangordailynews.com
First published 1889
Circulation: 35,000 (m); 45,000 (Sat)
Digital & print: $24.25/mo (Mon-Sat); digital only: $8.43/mo, $93.90/yr

Barrow News-Journal
Published by MainStreet Newspapers Inc
33 Lee St, Jefferson, GA 30549
Mailing Address: PO Box 908, Jefferson, GA 30549
Tel: 706-367-5233 *Fax:* 706-367-8056
E-mail: news@barrowjournal.com
Web Site: www.barrowjournal.com
Key Personnel
Co-Publr: Mike Buffington; Scott Buffington
Ed: Chris Bridges *E-mail:* editor@barrowjournal.com
First published 1893
Frequency: Wed & Sun
Circulation: 15,800 (Wed); 4,400 (Sun)
$45/yr print & digital
Ad Rates: $9.20/retail, $9.45/classified

Battle Creek Enquirer
Published by Gannett Co Inc
77 E Michigan Ave, Suite 101, Battle Creek, MI 49017-3093
Tel: 269-964-7161; 269-966-0672
  Toll Free Tel: 800-333-4139
E-mail: battlecreekenquirer@gannett.com; bceeditors@battlecreekenquirer.com
Web Site: www.battlecreekenquirer.com
Weekly (2-3 reviews); Sunday page, syndicated reviews.
Circulation: 30,000 (e); 38,000 (Sun)
$1/daily, $2/Sun
New York Rep(s): Gannett Media Sales

The Bay City Times
Published by MLive Media Group
810 N Water St, Bay City, MI 48708
Tel: 989-895-8551; 989-671-1201
  Toll Free Tel: 800-878-1400 *Fax:* 989-895-5910
E-mail: bcnews@mlive.com
Web Site: www.mlive.com/bay-city

Key Personnel
Ed: Clark Hughes *E-mail:* chughes3@mlive.com
Weekly page. Book reviews through syndication; author interviews from AP.
Circulation: 35,000 (e); 44,000 (Sun)
$11.52/4 wks (Sun only, home delivery)
Avg reviews per issue: 4

The Beachcomber
Published by The SandPaper Inc
1816 Long Beach Blvd, Surf City, NJ 08008
Tel: 609-494-5900 *Fax:* 609-494-1437
E-mail: beachcomberlbi@gmail.com
Web Site: thesandpaper.net
Key Personnel
Publr: Curt Travers
Off Mgr: Lee Little
Occasional book reviews.
Frequency: 6 issues/yr
Avg pages per issue: 48
Free

Beaufort Gazette
Published by The McClatchy Co
10 Buck Island Rd, Bluffton, SC 29910
Mailing Address: PO Box 5727, Hilton Head Island, SC 29938
Tel: 843-706-8140 *Toll Free Tel:* 877-706-8100
Web Site: www.islandpacket.com
Key Personnel
Publr: Rodney Mahone *E-mail:* rmahone@mcclatchy.com
Sr Ed: Liz Farrell *E-mail:* lfarrell@islandpacket.com
First published 1897
$12.99/mo digital, $129.99/yr

The Beaumont Enterprise
Published by Hearst Newspapers
Division of Hearst Corp
380 Main St, Beaumont, TX 77701
Mailing Address: PO Box 3071, Beaumont, TX 77704-3071
Tel: 409-833-3311
E-mail: localnews@beaumontenterprise.com
Web Site: www.beaumontenterprise.com
Key Personnel
Publr: Mark Adkins *Tel:* 409-838-2898
  E-mail: madkins@beaumontenterprise.com
Mng Ed: Ashley Sanders *Tel:* 409-838-2860
  E-mail: arsanders@beaumontenterprise.com
Ed: Timothy M Kelly *Tel:* 409-838-2801
  E-mail: tkelly@hearstnp.com
Sunday, books page & reviews.
Circulation: 65,000 (d); 75,000 (Sun)
$3.88/wk (Sun print & electronic)

Birmingham News
Published by Alabama Media Group
Unit of Advance Local Media LLC
1731 First Ave N, Birmingham, AL 35203
Tel: 205-325-4444 *Toll Free Tel:* 800-568-4123
E-mail: customercare@bhamnews.com; life@al.com
Web Site: www.al.com/birmingham
Books & Alabama author info.
Print & digital: $18.07/mo (Sun), $24.09/mo (Wed & Sun), $30.12/mo (Wed, Fri & Sun); unlimited digital only $19.99/mo

The Bismarck Tribune
Published by Lee Enterprises Inc
707 E Front Ave, Bismarck, ND 58504
Mailing Address: PO Box 5516, Bismarck, ND 58506-5516
Tel: 701-223-2500 *Fax:* 701-223-2063
E-mail: news@bismarcktribune.com
Web Site: bismarcktribune.com
Key Personnel
Publr: Gary Adkisson *Tel:* 701-250-8299
  E-mail: gary.adkisson@bismarcktribune.com

Ad Dir: Lisa Weisz *Tel:* 701-250-8232
  E-mail: lisa.weisz@bismarcktribune.com
Circ Dir: Bural Coffey *Tel:* 701-250-8203
  E-mail: bural.coffey@bismarcktribune.com
Ed: Amy Dalrymple *Tel:* 701-250-8267
  E-mail: amy.dalrymple@bismarcktribune.com
Occasional, local author interviews & book reviews.
First published 1873
Circulation: 30,100
$5/mo digital basic, $9.99/mo digital plus, $22/mo silver, $37/mo gold, $46/mo platinum

The Blade
Published by Block Communications Inc
541 N Superior St, Toledo, OH 43660
Tel: 419-724-6000
Web Site: www.toledoblade.com
Key Personnel
Publr & Ed-in-Chief: John R Block
Dir, Mktg: Luann Sharp
Exec Ed: Kurt Franck
Mng Ed: Dave Murray
Frequency: Daily
Avg pages per issue: 40
Circulation: 52,000 (d); 80,000 (Sun)
$1/daily, $3/Sun

Borrow County News, see Barrow News-Journal

The Boston Globe Sunday Magazine
Published by Boston Globe Media Partners LLC
One Exchange Place, 2nd fl, Boston, MA 02109
Tel: 617-929-2955 *Toll Free Tel:* 888-MY-GLOBE (694-5623, subns)
E-mail: magazine@globe.com
Web Site: www.bostonglobe.com/magazine
Key Personnel
Ed: Veronica Chao *E-mail:* veronica.chao@globe.com
General interest; excerpts.
First published 1872
Book Use: Excerpts
Frequency: Weekly
Circulation: 754,000
$5/wk print (Sun only), $27.72/mo digital

The Boston Globe/The Boston Sunday Globe
Published by Boston Globe Media Partners LLC
One Exchange Place, 2nd fl, Boston, MA 02109
Mailing Address: PO Box 55819, Boston, MA 02205-5819
Tel: 617-929-7400 *Toll Free Tel:* 888-MY-GLOBE (694-5623, subns)
E-mail: customerservice@globe.com
Web Site: www.bostonglobe.com
Key Personnel
Publr: John Henry
Mng Ed: Jennifer Peter *Tel:* 617-929-3148
  E-mail: jennifer.peter@globe.com
Ed: Brian McGrory *Tel:* 617-929-3059
  E-mail: mcgrory@globe.com
Sr Deputy Mng Ed: Mark S Morrow *Tel:* 617-929-7129 *E-mail:* mark.morrow@globe.com
Deputy Mng Ed, Local News & Features: Felice Belman *Tel:* 617-929-7496 *E-mail:* felice.belman@globe.com
Deputy Mng Ed, Print & Opers: David Dahl
  Tel: 617-929-2809 *E-mail:* dahl@globe.com
Daily & Sunday, in-house & other sources, frequent author interviews, book excerpts.
First published 1872
Digital & print: $9.50/wk (Sat & Sun), $14.34/wk (Mon-Sun); print only: $5/wk (Sun only), $7.50/wk (Sat & Sun)

Boston Herald
Published by MediaNews Group Inc
100 Grossman Dr, 4th fl, Braintree, MA 02184
Tel: 617-426-3000 *Toll Free Tel:* 800-882-1211 (subns)
Web Site: www.bostonherald.com

Key Personnel
Ed-in-Chief: Joe Sciacca
In-house & freelance, daily, Sunday section; frequent author interviews.
Circulation: 108,548 (d); 85,398 (Sat); 81,925 (Sun)
Digital & print: $18/4 wks (Sun only), $63/4 wks (Mon-Sun); digital only: $9.98/4 wks
ISSN: 0738-5854

Boston Magazine
Published by Metro Corp
300 Massachusetts Ave, Boston, MA 02115
Tel: 617-262-9700 *Fax:* 617-262-4925; 617-267-1774 (edit)
E-mail: editor@bostonmagazine.com
Web Site: www.bostonmagazine.com
Key Personnel
Publr: Lynne Montesanto *Tel:* 617-275-2006
 E-mail: lmontesanto@bostonmagazine.com
Assoc Publr: Christina Miller *Tel:* 617-974-8431
 E-mail: cmiller@bostonmagazine.com
Ed-in-Chief: Chris Bogel
Exec Ed: Brittany Jasnoff
Mng Ed: Angela Mats
Covers issues confronting Boston metropolitan area, including politics, lifestyles, business trends, youth scene & sociological currents; culture, sports, entertainment reviews, fashion, dining & travel.
First published 1962
Book Use: Reviews
Frequency: Monthly
Avg pages per issue: 190
Circulation: 75,000
$15/yr, $25/2 yrs
Buy nonfiction; Sell article & ad reprints, back issues
Trim Size: 8 x 10 1/2

Bostonia
Published by Boston University
985 Commonwealth Ave, Boston, MA 02215
Tel: 617-353-3081 *Fax:* 617-353-6488
E-mail: bostonia@bu.edu
Web Site: www.bu.edu/bostonia
Key Personnel
Asst VP & Exec Ed: Doug Most *Tel:* 617-353-6190 *E-mail:* dmost@bu.edu
Mng Ed: Cynthia Buccini *Tel:* 617-353-5840
 E-mail: cbuccini@bu.edu
Alumni magazine of Boston University.
First published 1900
Book Use: Reviews, excerpts
Frequency: 3 issues/yr
Avg pages per issue: 88
Circulation: 240,000
Free to alumni
ISSN: 0164-1441
Trim Size: 8 1/8 x 10 7/8

Boys' Life, see Scout Life

Bozeman Daily Chronicle
Published by Big Sky Publishing
Division of Pioneer News Group
2820 W College St, Bozeman, MT 59718
Mailing Address: PO Box 1190, Bozeman, MT 59771-1190
Tel: 406-587-4491 *Fax:* 406-587-7995
E-mail: citydesk@dailychronicle.com
Web Site: www.bozemandailychronicle.com
Key Personnel
Publr: Mark Dobie *Tel:* 406-582-2626
 E-mail: mdobie@dailychronicle.com
Mng Ed: Nick Ehli *Tel:* 406-582-2647
 E-mail: nehli@dailychronicle.com
Asst Mng Ed: Ted Sullivan *Tel:* 406-582-2659
 E-mail: tsullivan@dailychronicle.com
City Ed: Michael Wright *Tel:* 406-582-2638
 E-mail: mwright@dailychronicle.com

In-house & through syndication; occasional author interviews.
Avg pages per issue: 90
Circulation: 15,000
Digital & print: $11.70/mo (Sun only), $14.30/mo (Fri-Sun), $16.90/mo (Tues-Sun)

Brandon Sun
Division of FP Canadian Newspapers
501 Rosser Ave, Brandon, MB R7A 0K4, Canada
Tel: 204-727-2451 *Toll Free Tel:* 877-786-2472 (rural); 866-438-8186 *Fax:* 204-571-7430 (edit)
E-mail: opinion@brandonsun.com; circ@brandonsun.com
Web Site: www.brandonsun.com
Key Personnel
Publr: Jim Mihaly *Tel:* 204-571-7401
 E-mail: jmihaly@brandonsun.com
Sales & Mktg Dir: Glen Parker *Tel:* 204-571-7424 *E-mail:* gparker@brandonsun.com
Ed: Matt Goerzen *Tel:* 204-571-7445
 E-mail: mgoerzen@brandonsun.com
Kids book reviews biweekly, in-house & through syndication; occasional author interviews.
First published 1882
Frequency: Daily (Mon-Sat)
Circulation: 18,027
Digital & print: $56.21/3 mos, $108.19/6 mos, $214.57/yr plus tax; digital only: $11.83/mo plus tax

Brick - A Literary Journal
Box 609, Sta P, Toronto, ON M5S 2Y4, Canada
Tel: 416-593-9684
E-mail: info@brickmag.com
Web Site: www.brickmag.com
Key Personnel
Publr: Laurie D Graham
Mng Ed: Allison LaSorda
Ed: Dionne Brand; David Chariandy; Michael Helm; Liz Johnston; Martha Sharpe; Rebecca Silver Slayter; Madeleine Thien
A twice yearly feast of the best literary nonfiction in English. Nonfiction submissions only. See web site for details.
First published 1977
Frequency: 2 issues/yr
Avg pages per issue: 168
Circulation: 5,500
$25/yr CN, $26/yr US, $30/yr intl
ISSN: 0382-8565
Trim Size: 8 x 8 1/2
Ad Rates: B&W full page $800, 1/2 page $550, 1/4 page $325
Ad Closing Date(s): April 2 for May release, Oct 2 for Nov release

BRIDES
Published by Dotdash
1500 Broadway, 6th fl, New York, NY 10036
Tel: 212-204-4000 *Toll Free Tel:* 800-456-6162 (subns)
E-mail: editors@brides.com; bricustserv@cdsfulfillment.com
Web Site: www.brides.com; www.dotdash.com/our-brands
Key Personnel
Exec Dir: Lisa Harman Gooder
Services magazine for brides-to-be, grooms, families & friends. Information on planning weddings, relationships, trousseau, honeymoons & new homes.
First published 1934
Book Use: Reviews

British Heritage Travel
Published by Kliger Heritage Media
201 E 87 St, Suite 23C, New York, NY 10128
Toll Free Tel: 877-843-8862
E-mail: info@britishheritage.com; memberservices@britishheritage.com
Web Site: britishheritage.com

Subscription Address: PO Box 579, Palm Coast, FL 32142-0579
Key Personnel
CEO: Jack Kliger
British travel, history, life & culture. Includes book reviews & information on British literary figures.
First published 1976
Book Use: Reviews & videos
Frequency: 6 issues/yr
Avg pages per issue: 68
Circulation: 20,000
$29.95/yr US, $41.95/yr CN & intl
ISSN: 0195-2633
Trim Size: 9 x 10.875
Ad Rates: 4-color full page $3,000

Brockville Recorder & Times
Published by Postmedia Network Inc
2479 Parkedale Ave, Brockville, ON K6V 3H2, Canada
Tel: 613-342-4441
Web Site: www.recorder.ca
Key Personnel
Media Sales Dir: Kerry Sammon *Tel:* 613-342-4441 ext 500267 *E-mail:* ksammon@postmedia.com
Edit: Ron Zajac *Tel:* 613-342-4441 ext 500245
 E-mail: rzajac@postmedia.com
Daily syndication & occasional author interviews.
First published 1821
Circulation: 15,100 (e)
$14.99/4 wks, $3.99/mo digital

Buffalo News
One News Plaza, Buffalo, NY 14203
Mailing Address: PO Box 100, Buffalo, NY 14240
Tel: 716-849-4444; 716-842-1111
 Toll Free Tel: 800-777-8640 *Fax:* 716-856-5150
E-mail: subscriberservices@buffnews.com
Web Site: www.buffalonews.com
Key Personnel
Arts & Books Ed: Jeff Simon *Tel:* 716-849-4438
 E-mail: jsimon@buffnews.com
In-house reviews weekly, multiple pages, occasional author interviews.
Circulation: 250,300 (d), 338,800 (Sun)
$13/mo digital, $11.75/mo print & digital (Sun only)

The Burlington Free Press
Published by Gannett Co Inc
100 Bank St, Suite 700, Burlington, VT 05401
Tel: 802-863-3441 *Toll Free Tel:* 800-427-3126
 Fax: 802-660-1802
E-mail: metro@burlingtonfreepress.com
Web Site: www.burlingtonfreepress.com
Key Personnel
Pres: Jim Fogler *Tel:* 802-660-1800
Exec Ed: Emilie Stigliani *Tel:* 802-660-1897
 E-mail: estigliani@freepressmedia.com
In-house & through syndication; biweekly author interviews.
Circulation: 41,901 (d); 47,566 (Sun)
New York Rep(s): Gannett Media Sales

Calgary Herald
Published by Postmedia Network Inc
215 16 St SE, Calgary, AB T2E 7P5, Canada
Tel: 403-235-7100 *Toll Free Tel:* 800-372-9219
E-mail: mysubscription@calgaryherald.com
Web Site: calgaryherald.com
Key Personnel
Mng Dir: Martin Hudson *Tel:* 403-235-7257
 E-mail: mhudson@postmedia.com
Ed (Arts & Life, Travel, Features): Michele Jarvie
 E-mail: mjarvie@postmedia.com
Book reviews in "Arts" section.
First published 1883

Campus Technology
Published by 1105 Media Inc
6300 Canoga Ave, Suite 1150, Woodland Hills, CA 91367
Tel: 818-734-1520 *Fax:* 818-734-1522
Web Site: campustechnology.com
Key Personnel
Pres & Group Publr: Kevin O'Grady
  E-mail: kogrady@1105media.com
Edit Dir, Educ: David Nagel *E-mail:* dnagel@1105media.com
Exec Ed: Rhea Kelly *Tel:* 818-814-5347
  E-mail: rkelly@1105media.com
Focused exclusively on the use of technology across all areas of higher education.
First published 2004
Frequency: 6 issues/yr digital, 3 issues/yr print
Avg pages per issue: 72
Circulation: 40,709
Free for those who qualify
ISSN: 1553-7544
Buy freelance, nonfiction, art & cartoons; Sell articles & ad reprints, back issues
Trim Size: 8 1/4 x 11
Ad Closing Date(s): 4 weeks prior to publication date

Cape Cod Times
Published by GateHouse Media LLC
319 Main St, Hyannis, MA 02601
Tel: 508-775-1200 *Fax:* 508-771-3292
Web Site: www.capecodonline.com; capecodtimes.com
Key Personnel
Books Ed: Gwenn Friss *Tel:* 508-862-1155
  E-mail: gfriss@capecodonline.com
Sunday page; book reviews in-house, through syndication, wire service; biweekly author interviews. Tend to concentrate on bestsellers & general audience books; of particular interest: nature (especially nonfiction) & science, environment, self-help, quality fiction.
Circulation: 49,850 (m); 60,600 (Sun)

The Capital Gazette
Published by Baltimore Sun Media Group
Subsidiary of Tribune Publishing Co
PO Box 6727, Annapolis, MD 21401
Tel: 410-268-5000; 410-268-7000 (classified); 410-268-4800 (circ) *Fax:* 410-280-5953 (newsroom); 410-268-4643
Web Site: www.capitalgazette.com
Key Personnel
Ed: Rick Hutzell *Tel:* 410-280-5938
  E-mail: rhutzell@capgaznews.com
Sunday paper, in-house & through syndication. Local author interviews only.
Circulation: 50,000
$2.99/wk print & digital, $1.99/wk digital

Catholic Digest
Published by Bayard Inc
One Montauk Ave, Suite 200, New London, CT 06320
Tel: 860-437-3012
E-mail: queries@catholicdigest.com
Web Site: www.catholicdigest.com
Subscription Address: PO Box 291826, Kettering, OH 45429 *Toll Free Tel:* 800-678-2836
Key Personnel
Mng Ed: Paul McKibben *E-mail:* pmckibben@bayard-inc.com
General interest Catholic family magazine. No unsol mss.
First published 1936
Book Use: Excerpts & reviews
Frequency: 9 issues/yr
Avg pages per issue: 128
Circulation: 150,000
$19.95/yr, $35.95/2 yrs, $51/3 yrs
ISSN: 0008-7998
Buy freelance nonfiction, art
Trim Size: 6 x 9
Ad Rates: 4-color page $3,700

The Cedar Rapids Gazette
Published by The Gazette Co
500 Third Ave SE, Cedar Rapids, IA 52401
Tel: 319-398-8211; 319-398-8333
  Toll Free Tel: 800-397-8333 (subns)
E-mail: customercare@thegazette.com
Web Site: thegazette.com
Key Personnel
Exec Ed: Zack Kucharski *Tel:* 319-398-8219
  E-mail: zack.kucharski@thegazette.com
Occasional section cover story, with color artwork, weekly page review, in-house & through syndication; occasional author interviews.
Circulation: 140,000 (d); 150,000 (Sun)
Digital & print: $35.40/13 wks (Sun only), $80.50/13 wks (Mon-Sun); print only: $22.10/13 wks (Sun only); digital only: $9.97/mo

Charleston Gazette-Mail
Published by HD Media Company LLC
1001 Virginia St E, Charleston, WV 25301
Tel: 304-348-5140; 304-348-4800 (subns)
  Toll Free Tel: 888-259-8867 (subns)
E-mail: support@wvgazettemail.com
Web Site: www.wvgazettemail.com
Key Personnel
Publr: Jim Heady
Features Ed: Maria Young *Tel:* 304-348-5115
  E-mail: maria.young@wvgazettemail.com
Occasional column, in-house & through syndication.
Circulation: 54,554 (m); 107,903 (Sun)
$1/daily, $2/Sun

The Charlotte Observer
Published by The McClatchy Co
550 S Caldwell St, Charlotte, NC 28202
Tel: 704-358-5000 *Toll Free Tel:* 800-532-5350 (cust serv)
Web Site: www.charlotteobserver.com/entertainment/books
Key Personnel
Publr: Rodney Mahone *E-mail:* rmahone@mcclatchy.com
Exec Ed: Sherry Chisenhall *E-mail:* schisenhall@charlotteobserver.com
Mng Ed: Taylor Batten *Tel:* 704-358-5934
  E-mail: tbatten@charlotteobserver.com
Book reviews & author interviews.
First published 1886
Digital & print: $55.77/13 wks (Sun only), $83.66/13 wks (Wed & Fri-Sun), $111.54/13 wks (Mon-Sun); digital only: $12.99/mo
Avg reviews per issue: 4-5

Chattanooga Times Free Press
Published by Chattanooga Publishing Co Inc
400 E 11 St, Chattanooga, TN 37403
Tel: 423-756-6900
Web Site: www.timesfreepress.com
Key Personnel
Pres: Jeff DeLoach
Ed & Dir, Content: Allison Gerber
  E-mail: agerber@timesfreepress.com
Occasional author interviews & book reviews.
Digital & print: $20/mo (Sun), $34/mo (Mon-Sun)

The Chicago Magazine
Published by Tribune Publishing Co
160 N Stetson Ave, 4th fl, Chicago, IL 60601
Tel: 312-222-8999 *Toll Free Tel:* 800-999-0879
E-mail: letters@chicagomag.com; chicago@emailcustomerservice.com
Web Site: www.chicagomag.com; www.chicagotribune.com
Key Personnel
Publr & Ed-in-Chief: Susanna Homan
  E-mail: susanna@chicagomag.com
Exec Ed: Terrance Noland *E-mail:* tnoland@chicagomag.com
Culture Ed: Tal Rosenberg *E-mail:* trosenberg@chicagomag.com
General interest newspaper magazine with Chicago & Midwest focus. Books & readings info in "Arts & Culture" section.
Book Use: Excerpts & photo essays
Frequency: 11 issues/yr
Circulation: 1,167,000
$19.90/yr, $28/2 yrs, $36/3 yrs, $9.99/yr digital
Trim Size: 7 x 10 1/2

Chicago Reader
Published by Sun-Times Media LLC
30 N Racine Ave, Suite 300, Chicago, IL 60607
Tel: 312-222-6920
E-mail: mail@chicagoreader.com
Web Site: www.chicagoreader.com
Key Personnel
Creative Dir: Vince Cerasani
Ed: Jake Malooley *E-mail:* kmalooley@chicagoreader.com
Freelance source; occasional book reviews, long essays, occasional local author. Also available online.
First published 1971
Frequency: Weekly
Circulation: 90,000
Free
ISSN: 1096-6919

Chicago Tribune
Published by Chicago Tribune Media Group (CTMG)
Subsidiary of Tribune Publishing Co
160 N Stetson Ave, Chicago, IL 60601
Toll Free Tel: 800-974-7520
E-mail: editor@chicagotribune.com
Web Site: www.chicagotribune.com
Key Personnel
Publr & Ed-in-Chief: R Bruce Dold
Mng Ed, Content: Peter Kendall
  E-mail: pkendall@chicagotribune.com
One review daily, Sunday 8-10 reviews. In-house & freelance reviewers.
First published 1847
Circulation: 740,154 (d); 675,065 (Sat); 1,137,447 (Sun)
Digital & print: $64.87/13 wks (Mon-Sun), $19.92/8 wks (Sun only); digital only: $7.96/4 wks

The Chippewa Herald
Published by Lee Enterprises Inc
321 Frenette Dr, Chippewa Falls, WI 54729
Mailing Address: PO Box 69, Chippewa Falls, WI 54729
Tel: 715-723-5515 *Toll Free Tel:* 800-236-5515; 866-477-0648 (classifieds) *Fax:* 715-723-9644
Web Site: www.chippewa.com
Key Personnel
Publr: Josh Trust *E-mail:* josh.trust@lee.net
Ed: John Casper *E-mail:* john.casper@lee.net
Infrequent & in-house reviews.
Circulation: 4,000
$5/mo digital basic, $3/13 wks digital plus, $29/26 wks digital plus, $24/mo full access (silver), $39.75/mo full access (platinum)

Christian New Age Quarterly
PO Box 276, Clifton, NJ 07015-0276
E-mail: info@christiannewage.com
Web Site: www.christiannewage.com

Key Personnel
Ed: Catherine Groves
Reviewer: Joanne Winetzki
Authentic dialogue between Christians & New Agers. Content examines Christianity & the New Age movement with special regard to contrasts & similarities. No simultaneous submissions. Writers' guidelines: send SASE or visit www.christiannewage.com.
First published 1989
Book Use: Reviews; request reviewers address before sending review copies
Frequency: Quarterly
Avg pages per issue: 20
$3.50/issue, $5/issue foreign, $12.50/yr, $18.50/yr foreign
ISSN: 0899-7292
Buy nonfiction; Sell back issues ($3.50)
Trim Size: 7 x 8 1/2
Ad Rates: B&W/color page $45
Ad Closing Date(s): Jan 1, April 1, July 1, Oct 1

The Christian Science Monitor
210 Massachusetts Ave, Boston, MA 02115
Tel: 617-450-2300 *Toll Free Tel:* 800-288-7090
E-mail: customerservice@csmonitor.com
Web Site: www.csmonitor.com
Subscription Address: PO Box 6074, Harlan, IA 51593 *Toll Free Tel:* 800-456-2220 (US); 800-333-2777 (CN) *E-mail:* csmonitorcustserv@cdsfulfillment.com
Key Personnel
Mng Ed: Amelia Newcomb
Books Ed: April Austin
Ed: Mark Sappenfield
Reviews of hardcover fiction & nonfiction. Bestseller lists for fiction & nonfiction, children's books, poetry & religion throughout the year.
First published 1908
Frequency: Daily
$11/mo digital, $15/mo print & digital

The Chronicle-Herald
Published by SaltWire Network
2717 Joseph Howe Dr, Halifax, NS B3J 2T2, Canada
Tel: 902-426-2811 *Toll Free Tel:* 800-563-1187 *Fax:* 902-426-1158
E-mail: reception@herald.ca
Web Site: www.thechronicleherald.ca
Key Personnel
Contact: Allison Lawlor
Sunday, books page; in-house, freelance & occasionally syndicated column; frequent author interviews.
Frequency: Daily (Mon-Sat)
Circulation: 100,000 (d)
Digital & print: $4.20/wk (Sat only), $6.30/wk (Mon-Sat); digital only: $14.99/mo

Chronicle-Journal
Subsidiary of Continental Newspapers (Canada) Ltd
75 S Cumberland St, Thunder Bay, ON P7B 1A3, Canada
Tel: 807-343-6200
E-mail: circulation@chroniclejournal.com
Web Site: www.chroniclejournal.com
Key Personnel
Publr & Gen Mgr: Clint Harris *E-mail:* charris@chroniclejournal.com
Mng Ed: Greg Giddens *E-mail:* ggiddens@chroniclejournal.com
Book page, one per week, in-house & by syndication; frequent author interviews; book reviews.
Avg pages per issue: 28
Circulation: 24,600 (d); 24,400 (Sat); 21,500 (Sun)
$1/daily, $1.50/Sat

Chronicles: A Magazine of American Culture
Published by The Charlemagne Institute
8011 34 Ave S, Suite C11, Bloomington, MN 55425
Web Site: www.chroniclesmagazine.org
Subscription Address: PO Box 3247, Northbrook, IL 60065-9968 *Toll Free Tel:* 800-877-5459
Key Personnel
Exec Ed: Edward Welsch
Essays & reviews on various aspects of American Culture including literature, popular culture, education & social issues. No unsol mss, query first.
First published 1977
Frequency: Monthly
Avg pages per issue: 52
Circulation: 7,500
$44.99/yr, $79.99/2 yrs, $104.99/3 yrs
ISSN: 0887-5731
Buy freelance fiction, nonfiction, poetry, art & cartoons; Sell articles & ad reprints, back issues
Avg reviews per issue: 3 in-depth, 4 in-brief
Trim Size: 8 3/8 x 10 7/8
Ad Rates: B&W page $650, 4-color page $1,134
Ad Closing Date(s): 8 weeks prior to release date

Cincinnati Enquirer
Published by Gannett Co Inc
312 Elm St, Cincinnati, OH 45202
Tel: 513-721-2700 *Toll Free Tel:* 800-876-4500 (subns); 877-513-7355 (cust serv)
Web Site: www.cincinnati.com
Key Personnel
Pres: Eddie Tyner *Tel:* 513-768-8500
E-mail: president@enquirer.com
Exec Ed: Beryl Love *Tel:* 513-768-8551
E-mail: blove@enquirer.com
Use wire reviews & no longer write reviews in-house. Pitches must have a local/greater Cincinnati connection, which would include authors coming here on tour.
Circulation: 201,200 (d); 330,000 (Sun)

Civil Engineering
Published by American Society of Civil Engineers (ASCE)
1801 Alexander Bell Dr, Reston, VA 20191
Tel: 703-295-6300 *Toll Free Tel:* 800-548-ASCE (548-2723)
E-mail: ascelibrary@asce.org
Web Site: www.asce.org/cemagazine
Key Personnel
Ed-in-Chief: Laurie Shuster *E-mail:* lshuster@asce.org
Ad Dir: Dianne Vance *E-mail:* dvance@asce.org
Art Dir: Jeff Roth *E-mail:* jroth@asce.org
Mng Ed: Margaret Mitchell *E-mail:* mmitchell@asce.org
Sr Ed/Features Mgr: Robert L Reid
E-mail: rreid@asce.org
Sr Ed: Catherine A Cardno, PhD
E-mail: ccardno@asce.org
Prodn Mgr: Sean Richardson
E-mail: srichardson@asce.org
Directed toward the civil, structural & environmental design engineers in the engineering construction market. No unsol mss, query first.
First published 1930
Book Use: Book listings, occasional reviews; general interest engineering/design/planning books
Frequency: Monthly
Avg pages per issue: 120
Circulation: 140,000
Free to membs
ISSN: 0885-7024
Sell articles & ad reprints, back issues
Trim Size: 7 7/8 x 10 7/8
Ad Rates: B&W page $11,650, 4-color page $14,395

Clarion-Ledger
Published by Gannett Co Inc
201 S Congress St, Jackson, MS 39201
Tel: 601-961-7000 *Toll Free Tel:* 877-850-5343
E-mail: letters@jackson.gannett.com
Web Site: www.clarionledger.com
Key Personnel
Exec Ed: Sam R Hall *Tel:* 601-961-7163
E-mail: srhall@jackson.gannett.com
Features Ed: Stephen Ward *E-mail:* sward2@jackson.gannett.com
Sunday in *Artist Leisure* section. Reviews in-house/freelance, occasional author interviews.
First published 1837
Circulation: 39,133 (d & Sat)

Cleveland Daily Banner
Published by Cleveland Newspapers Inc
1505 25 St NW, Cleveland, TN 37311
Mailing Address: PO Box 3600, Cleveland, TN 37320-3600
Tel: 423-472-5041 *Fax:* 423-476-1046; 423-614-6529 (newsroom)
E-mail: news@clevelandbanner.com
Web Site: www.clevelandbanner.com
Key Personnel
Publr & Ed: Ralph C Baldwin, Jr
Daily book reviews, in-house & through syndication; author interviews.
Circulation: 11,000 (e); 13,000 (Sun)
$75/yr

College Spotlight
Published by College & Career Press LLC
PO Box 300484, Chicago, IL 60630
Tel: 773-718-0366 *Fax:* 773-718-0366
Web Site: www.ccpnewsletters.com/college-spotlight
Key Personnel
Publr & Mng Ed: Andrew Morkes
E-mail: amorkes@chicagopa.com
College, high school & career guidance librarian. Books on college & career exploration.
First published 2002
Frequency: 9 issues/yr
Avg pages per issue: 10
$29.99/yr, $54.99/2 yrs, $79.99/3 yrs
ISSN: 1525-4313
Trim Size: 8 1/2 x 11

Colorado Springs Gazette
Published by Clarity Media
30 E Pikes Peak Ave, Suite 100, Colorado Springs, CO 80903
Tel: 719-632-5511 (advert) *Toll Free Tel:* 866-632-6397 (cust serv) *Fax:* 719-636-0202
E-mail: customercare@gazette.com
Web Site: www.gazette.com
Key Personnel
Publr: Dan Steever *Tel:* 719-636-0104
E-mail: dan.steever@gazette.com
Mng Ed: Jim Trotter *Tel:* 719-636-0251
E-mail: jim.trotter@gazette.com
Ed: Vince Bzdek *Tel:* 719-636-0273
E-mail: vince.bzdek@gazette.com
Weekly author interviews on Sunday books page.
Circulation: 89,000 (d); 138,900 (Sun)
$1.50/Sun

Columbia Missourian
Published by Missourian Publishing Association
Subsidiary of University of Missouri
Lee Hills Hall, 221 S Eighth St, Columbia, MO 65201
Mailing Address: PO Box 917, Columbia, MO 65205
Tel: 573-882-5700; 573-882-5720 (newsroom)
E-mail: news@columbiamissourian.com
Web Site: www.columbiamissourian.com
Key Personnel
Exec Ed: Ruby L Bailey *Tel:* 573-882-6695
E-mail: baileyru@missouri.edu
Mng Ed: Jeanne Abbott *Tel:* 573-882-5741
E-mail: abbottjm@missouri.edu
First published 1908
Frequency: Daily (exc Mon & Sat)

Circulation: 5,574
$5.95/mo digital, $7.95/mo print & digital

The Columbus Dispatch
Published by GateHouse Media LLC
62 E Broad St, Columbus, OH 43216
Tel: 614-461-5200 *Toll Free Tel:* 877-734-7728 (cust serv)
Web Site: www.dispatch.com
Key Personnel
Ed: Alan D Miller *E-mail:* amiller@dispatch.com
Book Ed: Becky Kover *E-mail:* bkover@dispatch.com
Asst Features Ed: Ryan E Smith *E-mail:* rsmith@dispatch.com
Book news & reviews, author interviews.
Circulation: 248,200 (m); 385,200 (Sun)
Digital & print: $71.37/13 wks (Sat & Sun), $94.77/13 wks (Mon-Sun); digital only: $7.99/mo

The Columbus Ledger Enquirer Newspapers
Published by The McClatchy Co
945 Broadway, Suite 102, Columbus, GA 31901
Tel: 706-324-5526 *Toll Free Tel:* 800-282-7859
Web Site: www.ledger-enquirer.com
Key Personnel
Gen Mgr & VP, Ad: Ross McDuffie *Tel:* 706-571-8615 *E-mail:* rmcduffie@ledgerenquirer.com
Reviews appear sporadically.
Circulation: 25,750 (d); 33,600 (Sun)
Digital & print: $42.12/13 wks (Wed & Sun), $63.18/13 wks (Thurs-Sun), $84.24/13 wks (Mon-Sun); digital only: $8.99/mo, $129.99/yr

Commentary
Published by Commentary Inc
561 Seventh Ave, 16th fl, New York, NY 10018
Tel: 212-891-1400 *Toll Free Tel:* 800-829-6270 (subns) *Fax:* 212-891-6700
E-mail: service@commentarymagazine.com; ads@commentarymagazine.com; submissions@commentarymagazine.com
Web Site: www.commentarymagazine.com
Key Personnel
Publr: Carol Moskot
Opers Dir: Stephanie Roberts *E-mail:* sroberts@commentarymagazine.com
Sr Ed: Abe Greenwald
Ed: John Podhoretz
Analyses of current events with an emphasis on politics, social policy & culture, with special interest in Jewish affairs.
First published 1945
Book Use: Reviews & excerpts
Frequency: Monthly
Avg pages per issue: 72
Circulation: 26,000 paid
$5.95/issue, $29.99/yr print US, $19.99/yr digital US, CN & intl
ISSN: 0010-2601
Buy fiction, nonfiction, no poetry, art, cartoons; Sell articles
Avg reviews per issue: 6
Ad Rates: B&W page $3,430, 4-color page $5,100
Ad Closing Date(s): 20th of the 2nd month preceding month of issue

The Commercial Appeal
Published by Gannett Co Inc
495 Union Ave, Memphis, TN 38103
Tel: 901-529-2345 *Toll Free Tel:* 844-900-7099 (subns)
Web Site: www.commercialappeal.com
Key Personnel
Exec Ed: Mark Russell *E-mail:* mark.russell@commercialappeal.com

Pop Culture Ed: John Beifuss *E-mail:* john.beifuss@commercialappeal.com
Sunday, one page, in-house, through syndication & other sources. Occasional author interviews.

Concord Monitor
Published by Newspapers of New England (NNE)
One Monitor Dr, Concord, NH 03302
Mailing Address: PO Box 1177, Concord, NH 03302-1177
Tel: 603-224-5301 *Fax:* 603-228-5856
Web Site: www.concordmonitor.com
Key Personnel
Ed-in-Chief: Steve Leone
Mng Ed: Jonathan Van Fleet
Gen Mgr: Ernesto Burden
Book page on Sundays; occasional regional author interviews; in-house book reviews; features.
Circulation: 22,000 (e)
Digital & print: $22/4 wks, $260/yr (Mon-Sun), $156/yr (Sun only); digital only: $10.99/mo, $104/yr

Conde Nast Traveler
Published by Conde Nast
One World Trade Center, 26th fl, New York, NY 10007-0090
Tel: 212-286-2860 *Toll Free Tel:* 800-777-0700 (subns)
E-mail: letters@condenasttraveler.com
Web Site: www.cntraveler.com; www.condenast.com
Key Personnel
Ed-in-Chief: Melinda Stevens
Mng Ed: Paula Maynard
Contains travel, dining, entertainment, fashion, business articles of interest to affluent travelers.
First published 1987
Book Use: Excerpts
Frequency: Monthly
Avg pages per issue: 125
Circulation: 814,833
$10/yr, $15/2 yrs (print & digital)
Sell article & ad reprints, back issues
Ad Rates: 4-color full page $154,353, 1/2 page $100,303, 1/3 page $61,709

The Connecticut Post
Published by Hearst Newspapers
Division of Hearst Corp
1057 Broad St, Bridgeport, CT 06604
Tel: 203-330-6248; 203-333-6688 (cust serv) *Fax:* 203-738-1230 (edit)
Web Site: www.ctpost.com
Key Personnel
Edit Page Ed: Hugh Bailey *Tel:* 203-842-2546
Asst Mng Ed: Ralph Hohman
Arts & Entertainment Ed: Patrick Quinn *Tel:* 203-842-2553 *E-mail:* pquinn@ctpost.com
Sunday column; frequent author interviews; area authors.
Circulation: 77,239 (d); 88,583 (Sun)
Digital & print: $2.99/wk (Sun only), $7.99/wk (Mon-Sun); digital only: $3.50/wk

Cornwall Standard-Freeholder
Published by Postmedia Network Inc
1150 Montreal Rd, Cornwall, ON K6H 1E2, Canada
Tel: 613-933-3160
Web Site: www.standard-freeholder.com
Key Personnel
Ad Dir: Kerry Sammon *Tel:* 613-933-3160 ext 508246 *E-mail:* ksammon@postmedia.com
Regl Mng Ed: Hugo Rodrigues *Tel:* 613-933-3160 ext 508225 *E-mail:* hrodrigues@postmedia.com
First published 1846
Frequency: Daily
Circulation: 5,780 (d); EMC-Thurs non-subscribers 20,000

$1.25
Trim Size: Broadsheet

Corpus Christi Caller-Times
Published by Gannett Co Inc
820 N Lower Broadway, Corpus Christi, TX 78401
Mailing Address: PO Box 9136, Corpus Christi, TX 78468-9136
Tel: 361-884-2011 *Toll Free Tel:* 800-827-2011; 844-900-7096
E-mail: caller-times@gannett.com
Web Site: www.caller.com
Key Personnel
News Dir: Mary Ann Beckett *Tel:* 361-886-3623 *E-mail:* maryann.beckett@caller.com
Ed: Tim Archuleta *E-mail:* tim.archuleta@caller.com
Sunday page produced in-house, by syndication & through various wire services. Occasional author interviews.
First published 1883
Circulation: 68,028 (d); 94,415 (Sun)

Cosmopolitan
Published by Hearst Communications Inc
Division of Hearst Magazines
300 W 57 St, New York, NY 10019-3787
Tel: 212-649-2000; 212-649-3570 (edit off)
E-mail: cosmo_letters@hearst.com
Web Site: www.cosmopolitan.com; www.hearst.com
Subscription Address: PO Box 6000, Harlan, IA 51593
Key Personnel
SVP & Publg Dir: Nancy Berger *Tel:* 212-841-8495 *E-mail:* nberger@hearst.com
Assoc Publr & Ad: Stacy Nathan *Tel:* 212-649-3984 *E-mail:* snathan@hearst.com
Ed-in-Chief: Jessica Pels
Edited for young women interested in self-improvement with articles on careers, clothes, beauty, travel, entertainment, the arts, relationships, men & sex.
First published 1886
Book Use: Reviews of books periodically
Frequency: Monthly
Avg pages per issue: 344
Circulation: 2,700,000
$4.99/issue, $12/yr, $22/2 yrs, $6/6 mos (digital)
ISSN: 0010-9541
Buy fiction & nonfiction; Sell articles & ad reprints, back issues
Trim Size: 7 3/4 x 10 7/8
Ad Rates: B&W page $251,000, 4-color page $313,750

Courier-Journal
Published by Gannett Co Inc
525 W Broadway, Louisville, KY 40202
Mailing Address: PO Box 740031, Louisville, KY 40201-7431
Tel: 502-582-4011 *Toll Free Tel:* 800-866-2211 (cust serv)
Web Site: www.courier-journal.com
Key Personnel
News Dir: Mike Trautmann *Tel:* 502-582-4295 *E-mail:* mtrautmann@courier-journal.com
Ed: Richard A Green *Tel:* 502-582-4642 *E-mail:* rgreen@gannett.com
Sunday book section.
First published 1867

Courier-Post
Published by Gannett Co Inc
301 Cuthbert Blvd, Cherry Hill, NJ 08002
Mailing Address: PO Box 5300, Cherry Hill, NJ 08034
Tel: 856-663-6000
E-mail: cpfeat@courierpostonline.com
Web Site: www.courierpostonline.com

SERIALS FEATURING BOOKS

Key Personnel
Audience Engagement/Features Ed: Tammy Paolino *Tel:* 856-486-2477 *E-mail:* tpaolino@gannettnj.com
Saturday, in-house & Gannett News Service. Occasional author interviews.
First published 1875
Circulation: 104,565 (e); 100,755 (Sat); 105,000 (Sun)
$12/mo (Sun only), $16/mo (Thurs-Sun), $23/mo (Mon-Sun)

CRA Today
Published by Christian Retail Association Inc (CRA)
200 West Bay Dr, Largo, FL 33770
Tel: 727-596-7625 *Toll Free Tel:* 800-868-4388 *Fax:* 727-593-3523 *Toll Free Fax:* 855-815-9277
E-mail: service@munce.com
Web Site: www.christianretailassociation.org
Key Personnel
Pres: Bob Munce
VP: Marti Munce
Content Dir: Sue Brewer
Creative Dir: Mike Solava
Ed: Andrea Stock
Ad: Christy Dollins *E-mail:* christy.dollins@munce.com
Educate retailers & inform them of upcoming Christian products. Available online.
First published 2019
Frequency: Quarterly
Free to membs

Cricket
Published by The Cricket Magazine Group
Subsidiary of Cricket Media Inc
1751 Pinnacle Dr, Suite 600, McLean, VA 22102
Tel: 312-701-1720; 703-885-3400
E-mail: help@cricketmedia.com
Web Site: shop.cricketmedia.com; cricketmedia.com
Publishes high quality fiction & classic literature & nonfiction stories on culture, history, science & the arts. *Cricket* magazine is aimed at young readers ages 9-14.
First published 1973
Book Use: We consider previously published children's books for possible reprint or excerption in our magazines
Frequency: 9 issues/yr
Avg pages per issue: 48
Circulation: 50,000
$33.95/yr print, $9.99/yr digital, $39.95/yr print & digital
ISSN: 0090-6034
Sell back issues
Avg reviews per issue: 4

Cruising World
Published by Bonnier Corp
460 N Orlando Ave, Suite 200, Winter Park, FL 32789
Tel: 407-571-4914 *Toll Free Tel:* 866-436-2461 *Fax:* 401-845-5180
E-mail: editor@cruisingworld.com
Web Site: www.cruisingworld.com
Subscription Address: PO Box 420235, Palm Coast, FL 32142-0235
Key Personnel
Group Publr: Sally Helme *E-mail:* sally.helme@bonniercorp.com
Ed-in-Chief: Mark Pillsbury *E-mail:* mark.pillsbury@cruisingworld.com
Deals with cruising in mid-sized sailboats; readership is upper middle class professionals. See submission policies & guidelines on web site.
First published 1974
Book Use: Reviews & excerpts
Frequency: Monthly
Circulation: 130,000 paid

$7/issue, $28/yr, $44/yr CN, $60/yr intl
ISSN: 0098-3519
Buy nonfiction; Sell articles, ad reprints & back issues
Trim Size: 8 x 10 3/4
Ad Rates: B&W page $23,000, 4-color page $28,180
Ad Closing Date(s): see web site

The Daily Gleaner
Published by Brunswick News Inc (BNI)
71 Alison Blvd, Fredericton, NB E3C 2N5, Canada
Tel: 506-452-6671 *Toll Free Tel:* 800-222-9710
E-mail: customerservice@brunswicknews.com
Web Site: tj.news/dailygleaner
Book reviews in-house; occasional author interviews.
First published 1881
Frequency: Daily
Circulation: 29,000 (d)
$25.99/mo print & digital

Daily Hampshire Gazette
Published by Newspapers of New England (NNE)
115 Conz St, Northampton, MA 01060
Tel: 413-584-5000
E-mail: circulation@gazettenet.com; newsroom@gazettenet.com (news & press releases)
Web Site: www.gazettenet.com
Key Personnel
Publr: Michael Moses *Tel:* 413-585-3462 *E-mail:* mmoses@gazettenet.com
Arts Ed: Steve Pfarrer *Tel:* 413-584-5000 ext 262 *E-mail:* spfarrer@gazettenet.com
Wednesday page, in-house & through syndication. Occasional Saturday reviews. Weekly author interviews.
Circulation: 20,500 (d)
$19.60/4 wks print & digital, $8.25/mo digital only
Avg reviews per issue: 2

Daily Inter Lake
Published by Hagadone Corp
727 E Idaho St, Kalispell, MT 59901
Mailing Address: PO Box 7610, Kalispell, MT 59904
Tel: 406-755-7000 *Fax:* 406-758-4481 (news); 406-752-6114
E-mail: newsed@dailyinterlake.com
Web Site: www.dailyinterlake.com
Key Personnel
Publr: Rick Weaver *Tel:* 406-758-4444 *E-mail:* rvweaver@dailyinterlake.com
Mng Ed: Matt Baldwin *Tel:* 406-758-4447 *E-mail:* mbaldwin@dailyinterlake.com
Occasional in-house book reviews & author interviews in the Arts, etc section.
Circulation: 14,500 (d); 15,000 (Sun)
$22.68/4 wks print & digital, $12.80/4 wks digital only

Daily News
813 College St, Bowling Green, KY 42102
Mailing Address: PO Box 90012, Bowling Green, KY 42102-9012
Tel: 270-783-3200 (circ); 270-781-1700
E-mail: editor@bgdailynews.com
Web Site: www.bgdailynews.com
Key Personnel
Co-Publr & Pres: Pipe Gaines
Co-Publr: Scott Gaines
Gen Mgr: Kent O'Toole *E-mail:* kotoole@bgdailynews.com
Mng Ed: Daniel Pike *Tel:* 270-783-3235 *E-mail:* dpike@bgdailynews.com
Ed: Steve Gaines *E-mail:* sgaines@bgdailynews.com

ADVERTISING, MARKETING

In-house book reviews every Sunday, one page.
Digital & print: $8.99/mo (Sun only), $15/mo (Sun only postal), $17.99/mo (Mon-Sun), $29/mo (Mon-Sun postal); digital only: $8.99/mo

Daily News
Published by Tribune Publishing Co
4 New York Plaza, New York, NY 10004
Tel: 212-210-2100
E-mail: customerservice@nydailynews.com
Web Site: www.nydailynews.com
Key Personnel
Ed-in-Chief: Robert York *E-mail:* ryork@nydailynews.com
Sunday in "Now" section, in-house; frequent book features.
Frequency: Daily
Circulation: 602,857 (d); 644,766 (Sun)
Digital & print: $2.49/wk (Fri-Sun), $4.99/wk (Mon-Sun); digital only: $1.99/wk

The Daily Post-Athenian
Published by Adams Publishing Group
320 S Jackson St, Athens, TN 37303
Mailing Address: PO Box 340, Athens, TN 37371-0340
Tel: 423-745-5664 *Fax:* 423-745-8295
E-mail: news@dailypostathenian.com; circulation@dailypostathenian.com
Web Site: www.dailypostathenian.com
Key Personnel
Publr/Ad Dir: Jeff Schumacher *E-mail:* jeff.schumacher@dailypostathenian.com
Ed: Dewey Morgan *E-mail:* dewey.morgan@dailypostathenian.com
In-house book reviews biweekly in entertainment section; occasional author interviews.
First published 1848
Frequency: 5 days/wk
Circulation: 7,265 (d); 7,671 (weekend)
$130/yr print & online, $9.50/mo digital

Daily Press
Published by Daily Press Media Group
Subsidiary of Tribune Publishing Co
703 Mariners Row, Newport News, VA 23606
Tel: 757-247-4600; 757-247-4800 (circ)
Toll Free Tel: 800-543-8908
E-mail: customerservice@dailypress.com
Web Site: www.dailypress.com
Key Personnel
Mng Ed: Ryan Gilchrest *Tel:* 757-247-4673 *E-mail:* rgilchrest@dailypress.com
Features Ed: Andi Petrini *Tel:* 757-247-4643 *E-mail:* apetrini@dailypress.com
In-house, Sunday page; occasional author interviews.
First published 1896
Circulation: 40,000 (d); 82,509 (Sun)

The Daily Sentinel
Subsidiary of Southern News Inc
4920 Colonial Dr, Nacogdoches, TX 75961
Mailing Address: PO Box 630068, Nacogdoches, TX 75693-0068
Tel: 936-564-8361 *Fax:* 936-560-4267
E-mail: news@dailysentinel.com
Web Site: dailysentinel.com
Key Personnel
Publr & Ed: Debi Ryan *Tel:* 936-558-3206 *E-mail:* dryan@dailysentinel.com
In-house & syndicated book reviews weekly on Sunday; frequent author interviews.
Avg pages per issue: 32
Circulation: 6,000 (d); 6,200 (Sun)
$1/daily; $2/Sun

The Daily Times
Published by Adams Publishing Group
307 E Harper Ave, Maryville, TN 37803

Tel: 865-981-1100; 865-981-1140 (newsroom)
Fax: 865-981-1175 (newsroom)
E-mail: editor@thedailytimes.com
Web Site: www.thedailytimes.com
Key Personnel
Publr: Carl Esposito Tel: 865-981-1137
Ed: J Todd Foster Tel: 865-981-1139
  E-mail: todd.foster@thedailytimes.com
Occasional author interviews; book reviews.
First published 1883
Circulation: 13,000 (d)
$1.50/daily, $2/Sun

The Dallas Morning News
Published by A H Belo Corp
1954 Commerce St, Dallas, TX 75201
Tel: 214-977-8222 Toll Free Tel: 800-925-1500
E-mail: customercare@dallasnews.com
Web Site: www.dallasnews.com
Key Personnel
VP & Ed: Mike Wilson E-mail: mikewilson@dallasnews.com
Mng Ed: Keith Campbell E-mail: kcampbell@dallasnews.com
Publish book reviews from established network of freelance critics. We do not accept unsol reviews.
Circulation: 200,000 (d); 300,000 (Sun)
$2.49/daily, $3.79/Sun; digital only: $6.89/wk; digital & print (Sun only): $64.87/13 wks, $103.74/26 wks, $155.48/yr; digital & print (Wed-Sun): $77.87/13 wks, $129.74/26 wks, $207.48/yr; digital & print (Mon-Sun): $90.87/13 wks, $155.74/26 wks, $259.48/yr
ISSN: 1553-846X

Dayton Daily News
Published by Cox Media Group Ohio
1611 S Main St, Dayton, OH 45409-2547
Tel: 937-222-5700; 937-225-2000 (Cox)
  Toll Free Tel: 888-397-6397 Fax: 937-225-2241
E-mail: customercare@daytondailynews.com
Web Site: www.daytondailynews.com
Key Personnel
Ed-in-Chief: Rob Rohr
Sr Ed: Ron Rollins Tel: 937-225-2165
  E-mail: rollins@coxinc.com
Books featured in Sunday weekly section, in-house, through syndication & other sources, feature author interviews.
Circulation: 180,000 (e); 230,000 (Sun)
$10.62/wk (Mon-Sun), $7.87/wk (Thurs-Sun), $3.99/wk (Sun only)
ISSN: 0897-0920

Decatur Daily
Published by Tennessee Valley Printing
201 First Ave SE, Decatur, AL 35609
Mailing Address: PO Box 2213, Decatur, AL 35609-2213
Tel: 256-353-4612; 256-340-2410 (circ)
  Toll Free Tel: 888-353-4612 Fax: 256-340-2392
E-mail: news@decaturdaily.com
Web Site: www.decaturdaily.com
Key Personnel
Publr: Clint Shelton Tel: 256-340-2465
  E-mail: clint.shelton@decaturdaily.com
Online Mng Ed: Bruce McLellan Tel: 256-340-2431 E-mail: bruce.mclellan@decaturdaily.com
In-house & other; book reviews, "Sunday Bookpage".
First published 1912
Circulation: 25,000

Delaware State News
Subsidiary of Independent Newsmedia Inc USA
110 Galaxy Dr, Dover, DE 19901
Tel: 302-674-3600; 302-741-8298 (cust serv)
E-mail: readerservices@newszap.com; newsroom@newszap.com
Web Site: delawarestatenews.net

Key Personnel
Publr: Darel La Prade E-mail: dlaprade@newszap.com
Ed: Andrew West
Occasional local author interviews.
First published 1953
Frequency: Daily
Circulation: 12,000 (Mon & Sat); 17,000 (Tues, Thurs & Fri); 35,000 (Wed); 23,600 (Sun)
Digital & print: $7.99/mo (Sun only), $17.99/mo (Mon-Sun); digital only: $5.99/mo
Trim Size: 10 3/4 x 12 1/4
Ad Rates: $2,386 per page/Wed & Sun; $1,988 per page/weekday

Delta Democrat Times
Division of Emmerich Newspapers
988 N Broadway, Greenville, MS 38701
Mailing Address: PO Box 1618, Greenville, MS 38701
Tel: 662-335-1155 Fax: 662-335-2860
E-mail: ddtnews@ddtonline.com
Web Site: www.ddtonline.com
Key Personnel
Publr & Ed: Jon Alverson Tel: 662-378-0761
  E-mail: jalverson@ddtonline.com
Occasional column & author interviews; in-house.
First published 1868
Frequency: Daily (Tues-Sat)
Circulation: 3,500
$78/6 mos, $156/yr

Democrat & Chronicle
Published by Gannett Co Inc
245 E Main St, Rochester, NY 14604
Tel: 585-232-7100 Toll Free Tel: 800-790-9565 (cust serv)
Web Site: www.democratandchronicle.com
Key Personnel
Ed: Mike Kilian Tel: 585-258-2220
  E-mail: mkilian@gannett.com
Exec Admin Asst: Tamra Springer Tel: 585-258-2221 E-mail: tspringer@gannett.com
Daily, in-house, through syndication & other sources; occasional author interviews.
Frequency: Daily
Circulation: 177,000 (d); 207,600 (Sat); 245,800 (Sun)
$1.50/daily, $3/Sun

The Denver Post
Published by MediaNews Group Inc
101 W Colfax Ave, Denver, CO 80202-5177
Tel: 303-954-1000; 303-954-1010; 303-832-3232 (cust serv) Toll Free Tel: 800-336-7678
E-mail: memberservices@denverpost.com; newsroom@denverpost.com
Web Site: www.denverpost.com
Key Personnel
Ed: Lee Ann Colacioppo Tel: 303-954-1754
  E-mail: lcolacioppo@denverpost.com
Features Ed: Barbara Ellis Tel: 303-954-1751
  E-mail: bellis@denverpost.com
Eight-page tabloid pull-out, "Books & Authors" each Sunday, occasional reviews daily; weekly author interview/feature; up to 6 feature reviews; columnists cover mysteries, children's books, regional interest/local history & science fiction/fantasy each month; occasional reviews of current audiobooks; "Footnotes", also weekly, brief reviews of 3-5 books; in-house & wire services; book review through syndication & by freelancers.
Circulation: 518,000 (d); 858,000 (Sun)
Digital & print: $7.58/mo (Sun & holidays), $8.67/mo (Wed & Sun), $30.33/mo (Mon-Sun); digital only: $11.99/mo

The Des Moines Register & The Des Moines Sunday Register
Published by Gannett Co Inc
400 Locust St, Suite 500, Des Moines, IA 50309
Tel: 515-284-8000 Toll Free Tel: 877-424-0225 (delivery cust serv) Fax: 515-286-2504
E-mail: metroiowa@dmreg.com
Web Site: www.desmoinesregister.com
Key Personnel
Exec Ed: Carol Hunter Tel: 515-284-8545
  E-mail: chunter@dmreg.com
Occasional author interviews. Book review in-house, through syndication & freelance.
Circulation: 84,500 (d); 146,500 (Sun)

The Desert Sun
Published by Gannett Co Inc
750 N Gene Autry Trail, Palm Springs, CA 92262
Tel: 760-322-8889 Toll Free Tel: 800-834-6052 (circ)
E-mail: thedesertsun@gannett.com
Web Site: www.mydesert.com
Key Personnel
Exec Ed: Julie Makinen Tel: 760-778-4511
  E-mail: julie.makinen@desertsun.com
Mng Ed: Kate Franco Tel: 760-778-4688
  E-mail: kate.franco@desertsun.com
Book reviews in-house & through syndication; some author interviews.
First published 1927
Circulation: 60,000 (d & Sat); 72,000 (Sun)

Detroit Free Press
Published by Gannett Co Inc
160 W Fort St, Detroit, MI 48226
Tel: 313-222-6400; 313-222-6610 (features)
  Toll Free Tel: 800-395-3300 (cust serv)
  Fax: 313-223-4726 (features)
E-mail: features@freepress.com; cserv@michigan.com
Web Site: www.freep.com
Key Personnel
Ed & VP: Peter Bhatia E-mail: pbhatia@freepress.com
Arts & Entertainment Ed: Steve Byrne
  E-mail: spbyrne@freepress.com
Weekly, in-house; frequent author interviews; book review special section annually.
Circulation: 380,000 (m); 750,000 (Sun)

The Detroit News
Published by Michigan.com
160 W Fort St, Detroit, MI 48226
Tel: 313-222-2480 Fax: 313-496-5249
Web Site: www.detroitnews.com
Key Personnel
Publr & Ed: Jonathan Wolman Tel: 313-222-2110
  E-mail: jon.wolman@detroitnews.com
Mng Ed: Gary Miles Tel: 313-222-2594
  E-mail: gmiles@detroitnews.com
Asst Mng Ed, Features: Felecia Henderson
  Tel: 313-222-2557 E-mail: fhenderson@detroitnews.com
Edit Page Ed: Nolan Finley Tel: 313-222-2064
  E-mail: nolan.finley@detroitnews.com
Book reviews, author interviews.
Circulation: 300,000 (d); 700,000 (Sun)

Le Devoir
Published by Le Devoir Inc
Subsidiary of L'Imprimerie Populaire Inc
1265 Berri St, 8th fl, Montreal, QC H2L 4X4, Canada
Tel: 514-985-3333 Fax: 514-985-3340
E-mail: redaction@ledevoir.com
Web Site: www.ledevoir.com
Key Personnel
VP, Devt: Christianne Benjamin
Publr & Ed: Brian Myles
Saturday book review section; in-house & through syndication; weekly author interviews.
Frequency: Weekly
Avg pages per issue: 20
Circulation: 29,000 (d); 45,000 (Sat)
$2.83 (Sat)

Down East Magazine
Published by Down East Enterprise Inc
680 Commercial St (US Rte 1), Rockport, ME 04856
SAN: 208-6301
Mailing Address: PO Box 679, Camden, ME 04843
Tel: 207-594-9544 *Toll Free Tel:* 800-766-1670
E-mail: editorial@downeast.com
Web Site: www.downeast.com
Key Personnel
Ed-in-Chief: Brian Kevin *E-mail:* bkevin@downeast.com
Features articles & columns which concentrate on Maine's heritage, contemporary events & newsmakers. Occasional features on Maine authors.
First published 1954
Book Use: Reviews, occasional excerpts
Frequency: Monthly
Avg pages per issue: 180
Circulation: 100,000 paid
$19.99/yr digital, $34/yr print, $39/yr digital & print
ISSN: 0012-5776
Buy freelance nonfiction; Sell articles, ad reprints & back issues

Duluth News Tribune
Published by Forum Communications Co
424 W First St, Duluth, MN 55802
Tel: 218-723-5281 *Fax:* 218-723-5295
E-mail: news@duluthnews.com
Web Site: www.duluthnewstribune.com
Key Personnel
Publr: Neal Ronquist *Tel:* 218-723-5235
Mng Ed: Andrew Krueger *Tel:* 218-720-4102
Arts & Entertainment Reporter: Christa Lawler *Tel:* 218-879-5536
No reviews; short synopses (2-4) on Sundays of books on regional interest.
Book Use: Local author reviews
Circulation: 40,106 (d); 60,480 (Sun)
$1.25/daily, $2/Sun

Duncan Banner
1001 W Elm Ave, Duncan, OK 73534
Mailing Address: PO Box 1268, Duncan, OK 73534-1268
Tel: 580-255-5354 *Fax:* 580-255-8889
E-mail: editor@duncanbanner.com
Web Site: www.duncanbanner.com
Key Personnel
Publr: Mark Millsap *E-mail:* mark@normantranscript.com
Ad Mgr: Crystal Childers *E-mail:* addirector@duncanbanner.com
Two each Sunday-Education section; in-house or syndicated; infrequent local author interviews.
First published 1892
Frequency: Daily exc Mon & Sat
Circulation: 10,000 (e)
$14.99/mo print & digital, $11.99/mo digital only

East Valley Tribune
Division of 10/13 Communications
1620 W Fountainhead Pkwy, Suite 219, Tempe, AZ 85282
Tel: 480-898-6500; 480-898-5641 *Fax:* 480-898-5606
E-mail: customercare@evtrib.com
Web Site: www.eastvalleytribune.com
Key Personnel
Publr: Steve Strickbine
Opers Mgr: Chuck Morales *Tel:* 480-898-5690 *E-mail:* chuck@timespublications.com
Weekly one page, through syndication & other sources. Author interviews.
First published 1891
Frequency: Weekly (Sun print)
Circulation: 140,000 (Sun)
Free

Edmonton Journal
Published by Postmedia Network Inc
10006 101 St, Edmonton, AB T5J 0S1, Canada
Tel: 780-429-5100 *Toll Free Tel:* 800-249-4695 (subns)
E-mail: city@edmontonjournal.com
Web Site: www.edmontonjournal.com
Key Personnel
Features Ed: Liane Faulder *Tel:* 780-429-5294 *E-mail:* lfaulder@postmedia.com
Book reviews in-house & through freelancers; frequent author interviews.
First published 1903
Frequency: Daily (Mon-Sat)
Circulation: 172,078 (e); 212,923 (Sat)
Digital & print: $21.67/mo (Sat only), $39/mo (Mon-Sat); digital only: $9.95/mo, $99.99/yr; e-paper: $9.99/mo

The El Paso Times
Published by Gannett Co Inc
500 W Overland Dr, Suite 150, El Paso, TX 79901
Tel: 915-546-6100; 915-546-6119 (newsroom) *Toll Free Tel:* 800-351-1677 (cust serv) *Fax:* 915-546-6284; 915-546-6415 (newsroom)
E-mail: elpasotimes@gannett.com
Web Site: www.elpasotimes.com
Key Personnel
Ed: Zahira Torres *Tel:* 915-546-6155 *E-mail:* ztorres@elpasotimes.com
Prodn Gen Mgr: Patsy Hernandez *Tel:* 915-546-6182 *E-mail:* phernandez@elpasotimes.com
Sunday reviews & columns; occasional author interviews; book reviews in-house & by syndication.
First published 1881
Circulation: 45,000 (d); 50,000 (Sun)

Ellery Queen's Mystery Magazine
Published by Dell Magazines
Division of Penny Publications LLC
44 Wall St, Suite 904, New York, NY 10005-2401
Tel: 212-686-7188 *Toll Free Tel:* 800-220-7443 (corp sales) *Fax:* 212-480-5751
E-mail: elleryqueenmm@dellmagazines.com; advertising@pennypublications.com
Web Site: www.elleryqueenmysterymagazine.com
Subscription Address: Dell Magazines Direct, 6 Prowitt St, Norwalk, CT 06855-1220
Tel: 203-866-6688 *Toll Free Tel:* 800-220-7443 *Fax:* 203-854-5962
Key Personnel
Pres: Peter Kanter
Sr Art Dir: Victoria Green
Dir, Mktg, E-Commerce & Brand Licensing: Abigail Browning
Ed: Janet Hutchings
Sr Asst Ed: Jackie Sherbow
Asst Mktg Mgr: Monique St Paul
Book Reviewer: Steve Steinbock
Contains 18-20 short stories of mystery, crime & detection, most never published before. No e-mail submissions. Only submit by online submission manager.
First published 1941
Book Use: Book Reviews
Frequency: 6 issues/yr
Avg pages per issue: 192
Circulation: 100,000
$34.97/yr, $63.97/2 yrs, $59.94/yr intl, $35.88/yr digital
ISSN: 0013-6328
Buy freelance fiction, short humorous verse & mystery/crime related cartoons; Sell back issues
Avg reviews per issue: 10
Trim Size: 5 7/8 x 8 1/2
Ad Rates: 4-color back cover $1,800, B&W page $1,000, B&W 1/2 page-horizontal $600
Ad Closing Date(s): 3 months before sale date

The Emporia Gazette
Published by White Corp Media Inc
517 Merchant St, Emporia, KS 66801
Tel: 620-342-4800 *Fax:* 620-342-8108
E-mail: news@emporia.com
Web Site: www.emporiagazette.com
Subscription Address: PO Drawer C, Emporia, KS 66801
Key Personnel
Publr & Ed: Christopher Walker *E-mail:* walker@emporia.com
Features/Edit Ed: Regina Murphy *E-mail:* regina@emporia.com
Weekly, in-house; occasional author interviews.
First published 1895
Circulation: 10,000 (e)
$9.50/mo, $28.48/3 mos, $54.11/6 mos, $108.23/yr

English Journal
Published by National Council of Teachers of English (NCTE)
340 N Neil St, Suite 104, Champaign, IL 61820
Tel: 217-328-3870 *Toll Free Tel:* 877-369-6283 (cust serv) *Fax:* 217-328-9645
E-mail: englishjournal@ncte.org
Web Site: ncte.org
Key Personnel
Ed: Toby Emert; R Joseph Rodriguez
Prodn Ed: Rona Smith
Journal of ideas for English language arts teachers in junior & senior high schools & middle schools. Presents information on the teaching of writing & reading, literature & language. Includes information on how teachers are applying practices, research & multimodal literacies in their classrooms.
First published 1912
Book Use: Reviews of young adult literature & professional books
Frequency: 6 issues/yr
Avg pages per issue: 128
Circulation: 9,000 paid
$12.50/yr student & emeritus, $25/yr membs, $75/yr nonmembs & instns, add $8 foreign, membership is required for indiv subns
ISSN: 0013-8274
Trim Size: 8 1/4 x 10 7/8
Ad Rates: B&W page $2,140, 4-color page $2,750
Ad Closing Date(s): 1st of 2nd month prior to publication

The Enterprise
Published by GateHouse Media LLC
5 Cohannet St, Taunton, MA 02780
Tel: 508-427-4000
E-mail: newsroom@enterprisenews.com
Web Site: www.enterprisenews.com
Key Personnel
VP, News: Lisa Strattan *E-mail:* pub@wickedlocal.com
City Ed: Rebecca Hyman *E-mail:* rhyman@gatehousemedia.com
Sunday; in-house, syndicated.
Frequency: Daily
Circulation: 47,000 (e & Sat); 58,000 (Sun)
Digital & print: $24/12 wks (Sun only), $48/12 wks (Mon-Sun); digital only: $9.95/mo, $99.95/yr
ISSN: 0744-2114

Entertainment Weekly
Published by Meredith Corporation
11766 Wilshire Blvd, Los Angeles, CA 90025
Web Site: ew.com; www.meredith.com/brand/entertainmentweekly
Key Personnel
Ed-in-Chief: J D Heyman
Brand Sales Dir: Ellie Duque *Tel:* 310-268-7206 *E-mail:* ellie.duque@meredith.com

The Erie Times-News
Published by GateHouse Media LLC
205 W 12 St, Erie, PA 16534
Tel: 814-870-1600
Web Site: goerie.com
Key Personnel
Pres & Publr: Terry Cascioli *Tel:* 814-870-1612
 E-mail: tcascioli@timesnews.com
Exec Ed: Matt Martin *Tel:* 814-870-1704
 E-mail: matt.martin@timesnews.com
Three days per week on Op-Ed page; Sunday page & column. In-house. Occasionally syndicated column. Galleys & review copies of books are encouraged; especially interested in books with a connection to the Erie, PA region.
Circulation: 39,935 (d); 54,329 (Sun)
Digital & print: $27.30/13 wks (Sun only), $48.10/13 wks (Mon-Sun); digital only: $4.99/mo, $29.99/yr

Esquire Magazine
Published by Hearst Communications Inc
Division of Hearst Magazines
300 W 57 St, New York, NY 10019-3787
Tel: 212-649-4020 (edit off); 212-649-2000
E-mail: editor@esquire.com
Web Site: www.esquire.com; www.hearst.com
Subscription Address: PO Box 6093, Harlan, IA 51593
Key Personnel
Exec Dir, Mktg: Jason Graham
Ed-in-Chief: Michael Sebastian
Articles of information & counsel for men on a broad range of subjects including politics, business, sports & the arts. Features include fiction, fashion, personal finance & health.
First published 1933
Book Use: Reviews
Frequency: 8 issues/yr
Avg pages per issue: 200
Circulation: 750,000 paid
$6.99/issue US, $15/yr, $25/2 yrs
ISSN: 0014-0791
Buy freelance fiction, nonfiction & art; Sell articles & ad reprints, back issues
Trim Size: 9 x 10 3/4
Ad Rates: B&W page $97,495, 4-color page $144,860
Ad Closing Date(s): 45 days prior to sale date

ESSENCE Magazine
Published by ESSENCE Communications Inc
241 37 St, 4th fl, Brooklyn, NY 11232
Toll Free Tel: 800-274-9398 (subns)
Web Site: www.essence.com
Key Personnel
Chief Content & Creative Offr: Moana Luu
How-to information directed toward Black women. Covers health, beauty, fashion, food, business, parenting, the arts & travel. Feature articles include celebrity interviews, current events & fitness. Also available online. No unsol mss, query first.
First published 1970
Book Use: Reviews & excerpts
Frequency: Monthly
Avg pages per issue: 130
Circulation: 1,078,000 paid
$4.99/issue, $10/yr print & digital
ISSN: 0014-0880
Buy freelance fiction, nonfiction, art; Sell articles & ad reprints, back issues
Trim Size: 8 x 10 1/2

The Express-Times
Published by PennLive LLC
18 Centre Sq, Easton, PA 18042
Tel: 610-258-7171 *Fax:* 610-258-7130
E-mail: news@lehighvalleylive.com
Web Site: www.lehighvalleylive.com/expresstimes
Key Personnel
Mng Prodr: Nick Falsone *Tel:* 610-553-3312
 E-mail: nfalsone@lehighvalleylive.com
Produced in-house & from other sources. Focus is on local authors (Lehigh Valley, PA & Western NJ).
Circulation: 50,000

Farm Journal
Published by Farm Journal Media
30 S 15 St, Suite 900, Philadelphia, PA 19102
Mailing Address: PO Box 958, Mexico, MO 65265
Tel: 573-581-9641 (edit requests)
 Toll Free Tel: 800-331-9310 (subns) *Fax:* 573-581-9646
E-mail: editors@farmjournal.com; customerservice@farmjournal.com
Web Site: www.agweb.com/farmjournal; www.farmjournal.com
Key Personnel
CEO: Andy Weber
Pres & COO: Steve Custer
Mng Ed: Katie Humphreys *E-mail:* khumphreys@farmjournal.com
Ed: Rhond Brooks *E-mail:* rbrooks@farmjournal.com
Practical information on crops & livestock. Emphasis on agricultural production, technology & policy.
First published 1877
Book Use: Occasional reviews
Frequency: 14 issues/yr
Avg pages per issue: 80
Circulation: 345,085
$29.95/yr, $60/yr intl
ISSN: 0014-8008
Trim Size: 7 3/4 x 10 1/2
Ad Closing Date(s): 5 to 6 weeks prior to mailing

Fayetteville Observer
Published by GateHouse Media LLC
458 Whitfield St, Fayetteville, NC 28306
Mailing Address: PO Box 849, Fayetteville, NC 28302
Tel: 910-323-4848 *Toll Free Tel:* 800-682-3476
E-mail: customerservice@fayobserver.com
Web Site: www.fayobserver.com
Key Personnel
Publr: Robert Gruber *Tel:* 910-486-3501
 E-mail: bgruber@fayobserver.com
Exec Ed: Matt Leclercq *Tel:* 910-486-3551
 E-mail: mleclercq@fayobserver.com
Lifestyle & Sports Ed: Monica Holland *Tel:* 910-486-3518 *E-mail:* mholland@fayobserver.com
Sunday page, column & occasional author interviews; book reviews in-house & syndicated.
Circulation: 88,000 (m); 92,000 (Sun)
Digital & print: $9.40/mo (Mon-Sun); digital only: $12.95/mo, $79.95/yr

Field & Stream®
Published by Bonnier Corp
Division of The Bonnier Group
2 Park Ave, New York, NY 10016
Tel: 386-447-6355
E-mail: fsletters@bonniercorp.com
Web Site: www.fieldandstream.com
Subscription Address: PO Box 420235, Palm Coast, FL 32142-0235 *Toll Free Tel:* 800-289-0639
Key Personnel
CEO: David Ritchie
Ed-in-Chief: Colin Kearns
Mng Ed: Jean McKenna *Tel:* 212-779-5000 ext 5290
Deputy Ed: Slaton L White
Articles on hunting & fishing, including humor, profiles, how-to, gear reviews, news & essays. Unsol mss accepted, but prefer queries.
First published 1895
Frequency: 6 issues/yr
Avg pages per issue: 100
Circulation: 1,250,000 paid
$7.99/issue, $10/yr US, $26/yr CN, $40/yr foreign
ISSN: 8755-8599
Buy freelance, nonfiction, art, cartoons, photographs
Trim Size: 8 x 10 1/2
Ad Rates: B&W full page $105,200, 4-color full page $131,500
Ad Closing Date(s): 1st of 2nd month preceding issue

The Flint Journal
Published by MLive Media Group
540 Saginaw St, Suite 101, Flint, MI 48502
Tel: 810-766-6280; 810-766-6100
 Toll Free Tel: 800-878-1400
E-mail: customercare@mlive.com; flnews@mlive.com; advertise@mlive.com
Web Site: www.mlive.com/flint
Sunday page, in-house; occasional author interviews on Lifestyle page.
Frequency: 4 issues/wk
$4.99/wk (print & digital)

Florida Sportsman
Published by Outdoor Sportsman Group
3725 SE Ocean Blvd, Suite 202, Stuart, FL 34996
Tel: 772-219-7400 *Toll Free Tel:* 800-274-6386 (subn only)
Web Site: www.floridasportsman.com
Key Personnel
Publr: Blair Wickstrom *E-mail:* blair@floridasportsman.com
Ed: Jeff Weakley *E-mail:* jeff@floridasportsman.com
How-to & where-to about fishing, boating & outdoor activity in Florida & the islands.
First published 1969
Frequency: Monthly
Avg pages per issue: 120
Circulation: 77,058
$15/yr
ISSN: 0015-3885
Buy nonfiction, occasional fiction; Sell articles, ad reprints & back issues
Trim Size: 8 x 10 7/8
Ad Rates: 4-color page $6,500
Ad Closing Date(s): 45 days prior to cover month

The Florida Times-Union
Published by GateHouse Media LLC
One Independent Dr, Suite 200, Jacksonville, FL 32202
Tel: 904-359-4111
E-mail: newstips@jacksonville.com
Web Site: jacksonville.com
Key Personnel
Sales Dir: Liz Borten *Tel:* 904-359-4099
 E-mail: lborten@jacksonville.com
Ed: Mary Kelli Palka *Tel:* 904-359-4107
 E-mail: mpalka@jacksonville.com
Jack (Fri weekend magazine).
First published 1883
Circulation: 96,968 (d); 155,087 (Sun)
Digital only: $9.99/mo, $59.99/yr; see web site for print subn rates

Florida Today
Published by Gannett Co Inc
One Gannett Plaza, PO Box 419000, Melbourne, FL 32940-9000
Tel: 321-242-3500 *Fax:* 321-242-6601
E-mail: letters@floridatoday.com
Web Site: www.floridatoday.com

Key Personnel
Exec Ed: Mara Bellaby *Tel:* 321-242-3573
 E-mail: mbellaby@floridatoday.com
Highlights local authors online.
Circulation: 100,000

Fort Worth Star-Telegram
Published by The McClatchy Co
808 Throckmorton St, Fort Worth, TX 76102
Mailing Address: PO Box 1870, Fort Worth, TX 76101
Tel: 817-390-7400 *Toll Free Tel:* 800-776-7827 (cust serv)
E-mail: paper@star-telegram.com
Web Site: www.star-telegram.com
Key Personnel
Publr: Ryan Mote *Tel:* 817-390-7454
 E-mail: rmote@star-telegram.com
Exec Ed: Steve Coffman *Tel:* 817-390-7704
 E-mail: scoffman@star-telegram.com
Two or three pages in Sunday newspaper & daily book reviews; in-house & through syndication; news feature on authors; regular author interviews.
First published 1909
Digital & print: $52/13 wks (Wed & Sun), $79.30/13 wks (Wed-Sun), $92.30/13 wks (Mon-Sun); digital only: $9.99/mo

The Forum
Published by Forum Communications Co
101 Fifth St N, Fargo, ND 58102
Mailing Address: PO Box 2020, Fargo, ND 58107-2020
Tel: 701-235-7311 *Fax:* 701-241-5406
E-mail: letters@forumcomm.com; news@forumcomm.com; inforum@fccinteractive.com
Web Site: www.inforum.com
Key Personnel
Ed: Matthew Von Pinnon *Tel:* 701-241-5579
 E-mail: mvonpinnon@forumcomm.com
Deputy Ed: Danielle Teigen *Tel:* 701-451-5709
 E-mail: danielle.teigen@forumcomm.com
Sunday in *Entertainment* section; in-house & by AP; through syndication.
Frequency: Daily
Circulation: 53,000 (d); 67,000 (Sun)
Digital & print: $15.64/mo (weekend), $21.97/mo (Mon-Sun); digital only: $9.99/mo

The Free Lance-Star
1340 Central Park Blvd, Suite 100, Fredericksburg, VA 22401-4940
Tel: 540-374-5400
Web Site: www.fredericksburg.com
Key Personnel
Ed: Phil Jenkins *Tel:* 540-374-5422
 E-mail: pjenkins@freelancestar.com
In-house & other weekly one-page reviews, style section does author interviews.
Circulation: 27,000
$2/daily, $3/Sun, $21.67/mo digital & print (Mon-Sun)

The Fresno Bee
Published by The McClatchy Co
1626 "E" St, Fresno, CA 93786
Tel: 559-441-6111 *Toll Free Tel:* 800-877-3400
Web Site: www.fresnobee.com
Key Personnel
Pres & Publr: Ken Riddick *Tel:* 559-441-6060
 E-mail: kriddick@fresnobee.com
SVP & Exec Ed: Jim Boren *Tel:* 559-441-6307
 E-mail: jboren@fresnobee.com
SVP, Sales & Strategic Mktg: John Coakley *Tel:* 559-441-6143 *E-mail:* jcoakley@fresnobee.com
Mng Ed: John Rich *Tel:* 559-441-6663
 E-mail: jrich@fresnobee.com
Sunday Page, plus 2-3 wire reviews per week; in-house & through syndication, mostly local author interviews.

First published 1922
Circulation: 110,167 (d); 162,989 (Sun)

Gaffney Ledger
1604 W Floyd Baker Blvd, Gaffney, SC 29341
Mailing Address: PO Box 670, Gaffney, SC 29342
Tel: 864-489-1131 *Fax:* 864-487-7667
Web Site: www.gaffneyledger.com
Key Personnel
Publr: Cody Sossamon *E-mail:* cody@gaffneyledger.com
Ed: Klonie Jordan *E-mail:* editor@gaffneyledger.com
Lifestyles/Features: Abbie Sossamon
 E-mail: abbie@gaffneyledger.com
In-house, syndicated & other book reviews periodically; occasional author interviews.
First published 1894
Frequency: 3 issues/wk (Mon, Wed & Fri)
Circulation: 9,200
$2/single issue online only, $65/yr print or online, $77/yr print & online

The Georgia Review
Published by University of Georgia
320 S Jackson St, Athens, GA 30602
Tel: 706-542-3481 *Toll Free Tel:* 800-542-3481
E-mail: garev@uga.edu
Web Site: thegeorgiareview.com
Key Personnel
Dir & Ed: Gerald Maa
National Magazine Award-winning literary journal that publishes short stories, poems, essays, reviews & art. Submission guidelines on web site.
Membership(s): Community of Literary Magazines & Presses (CLMP).
First published 1947
Frequency: Quarterly
Avg pages per issue: 200
Circulation: 2,500
$15/issue, $40/yr
ISSN: 0016-8386
Avg reviews per issue: 3-4
Trim Size: 7 x 10
Ad Rates: Full page $325, 1/2 page $200
Ad Closing Date(s): Jan 15, April 15, July 15, Oct 15

Glamour
Published by Conde Nast
One World Trade Center, 26th fl, New York, NY 10007-0090
Tel: 212-286-2860; 515-243-3273 (subns)
 Toll Free Tel: 800-274-7410 (subns)
E-mail: glamourpublicity@condenast.com
Web Site: www.glamour.com; www.condenast.com
Key Personnel
Chief Busn Offr: Susan Plagemann
Creative Dir: Nathalie Kirsheh
Ed-in-Chief: Samantha Barry
Contains articles & features on fashion, beauty, health, travel, lifestyle, entertainment, auto, diet & fitness, careers for young women, ages 18-34. Digital only.
First published 1939
Free

Glendale News-Press
Published by Times Community News
Subsidiary of Los Angeles Times
453 S Spring St, 3rd fl, Los Angeles, CA 90013
Tel: 818-637-3200 *Fax:* 818-790-5690 (newsroom)
E-mail: gnp@latimes.com
Web Site: www.latimes.com/socal/glendale-news-press
Key Personnel
Exec Ed: John Canalis *Tel:* 717-966-4607
 E-mail: john.canalis@latimes.com

Mng Ed: Carol Cormaci *Tel:* 818-495-4156
 E-mail: carol.cormaci@latimes.com
Book reviews, local author interviews only. Saturday entertainment tabloid, the *Living* section; in-house & through syndication. Occasional cover story (page 1) on books & authors; also excerpts. Only run news happening in Glendale, CA.
First published 1905
Frequency: Daily
Circulation: 20,000 (d)
Digital & print: $2.49/wk (Sun only), $4.99/wk (Mon-Sun); digital only: $1.99/wk

The Globe & Mail
351 King St, E, Toronto, ON M5A 0N1, Canada
Tel: 416-585-5000
E-mail: books@globeandmail.com
Web Site: www.globeandmail.com
Key Personnel
Publr & CEO: Phillip Crawley
Ed-in-Chief: David Walmsley *Tel:* 416-585-5000 ext 5300
Books Ed: Mark Medley *E-mail:* mmedley@globeandmail.com
Saturday, 24 pages, freelance review. Frequent author interviews; produce a separate book review section every week.
Circulation: 330,600 (d)
$9.44/wk, $5.24/Sat only

Golf Digest
Published by Discovery Inc
One World Trade Center, 27th fl, New York, NY 10007-0090
Toll Free Tel: 800-313-0337 (cust serv)
E-mail: editors@golfdigest.com
Web Site: golfdigest.com
Subscription Address: PO Box 37065, Boone, IA 50037-0065 *Toll Free Tel:* 800-PAR-GOLF (727-4653)
Key Personnel
Publr: Dan Robertson
Ed-in-Chief: Jerry Tarde
Ed, Golf Digest Resource Ctr: Cliff Schrock
Devoted to special interest service articles helping readers to play better golf & enjoy the sport more. No unsol mss, query first.
First published 1950
Book Use: Reviews in annual roundup; excerpts
Frequency: Monthly
Avg pages per issue: 150
Circulation: 1,200,000
$19.99/yr print or digital, $29.99/yr print & digital
ISSN: 0017-176X
Buy freelance fiction, poetry, photos, art & cartoons; Sell articles, ad reprints & back issues
Trim Size: 9 x 10.875
Ad Rates: B&W page $84,000, 1/2 page $54,600, 4-color page $120,000, 1/2 page $78,000

Good Housekeeping
Published by Hearst Communications Inc
Division of Hearst Magazines
300 W 57 St, New York, NY 10019-3787
Tel: 212-649-2200; 212-649-2000
E-mail: feedback@goodhousekeeping.com
Web Site: www.goodhousekeeping.com; www.hearst.com
Subscription Address: PO Box 6000, Harlan, IA 51593 *E-mail:* ghkcustserv@cdsfulfillment.com
Key Personnel
SVP & Group Publg Dir: Patricia Haegele
Digital Dir: Lauren Matthews
Ed-in-Chief: Jane Francisco
Contains articles of interest to homemakers, half of whom also work outside the home. Topics include food, fashion, decorating, beauty, diet, health, interpersonal relations, social problems, personalities, fiction, current affairs.
First published 1885
Frequency: Monthly

Grand Forks Herald
Published by Forum Communications Co
375 Second Ave N, Grand Forks, ND 58203
Tel: 701-780-1100 *Toll Free Tel:* 800-477-6572 (ND, SD, MN & MT) *Fax:* 701-780-1123
Web Site: www.grandforksherald.com
Key Personnel
Publr: Korrie Wenzel *Tel:* 701-780-1103
  E-mail: kwenzel@gfherald.com
Weekly book page produced through various sources. Author interviews, in-house & through syndication, appear sporadically.
$17.25/mo (Mon-Sun print & digital all-access), $11.50/mo (Fri-Sun print), $6.95/mo (digital all-access)
Avg reviews per issue: 7

The Grand Rapids Press
Published by MLive Media Group
169 Monroe NW, Suite 100, Grand Rapids, MI 49503
Tel: 616-222-5400 *Toll Free Tel:* 800-878-1411 (subns)
E-mail: grnews@mlive.com; advertise@mlive.com
Web Site: www.mlive.com/grand-rapids
Subscription Address: Advance Central Services, 3102 Walker Ridge Dr, Walker, MI 48544
Key Personnel
VP, Content: John Hiner
Sunday page, in-house & through syndication; occasional author interviews.
Circulation: 133,107 (d); 182,252 (Sun)
Digital & print: $3.99/wk (Sun only), $4.49/wk (Thurs & Sun), $4.99/wk (Tues, Thurs & Sun); digital only: $4.99/wk

The Graphic Leader
Published by Postmedia Network Inc
c/o Postmedia Network, 365 Bloor St E, Toronto, ON M4W 3L4, Canada
Tel: 204-857-3427
Web Site: thegraphicleader.com
Key Personnel
Ed: Brian Oliver *E-mail:* boliver@postmedia.com
Occasional column; author interviews.
First published 1895
Frequency: Weekly
Avg pages per issue: 32
Circulation: 10,000

The Greenville News
Published by Gannett Co Inc
32 E Broad St, Greenville, SC 29601
Mailing Address: PO Box 1688, Greenville, SC 29602-1688
Toll Free Tel: 800-736-7136
E-mail: customercare@greenvillenews.com
Web Site: www.greenvilleonline.com
Key Personnel
Exec Ed: Katrice Hardy *Tel:* 864-298-4165
  E-mail: khardy1@greenvillenews.com
Weekly through syndication; author interviews.
Circulation: 95,008 (d); 128,784 (Sun)
$15/mo (Sun only), $29/mo (Mon-Sun)

GROUP Magazine
Published by Group Publishing Inc
1515 Cascade Ave, Loveland, CO 80538
Tel: 970-669-3836 *Toll Free Tel:* 800-447-1070
  Fax: 970-292-4373
E-mail: info@group.com
Web Site: www.group.com
Key Personnel
Exec Ed: Rick Lawrence *E-mail:* rlawrence@group.com
Youth ministry, youth ministers.
First published 1974
Book Use: Reviews of youth ministry resources
Frequency: Quarterly
Avg pages per issue: 100
Free
ISSN: 0163-8971
Buy nonfiction & cartoons
Trim Size: 8 x 10 3/4; live area 7 x 10

Hadassah Magazine
Published by Hadassah, The Women's Zionist Organization of America Inc
40 Wall St, 8th fl, New York, NY 10005
Tel: 212-451-6289 *Toll Free Tel:* 800-664-5646 (subns)
E-mail: magazine@hadassah.org
Web Site: www.hadassahmagazine.org
Key Personnel
Exec Ed: Lisa Hostein *Tel:* 212-451-6292
Deputy Ed: Libby Barnea *Tel:* 212-451-6285
Ad Mgr: Celia Weintrob *Tel:* 212-451-6283
  E-mail: cweintrob@hadassah.org
Deals with social, economic, political & cultural issues in the US & the spiritual & economic development of Israel. Articles, stories, reviews & interviews with an appeal to an educated Jewish reader.
First published 1914
Frequency: 6 issues/yr
Avg pages per issue: 76
Circulation: 255,000 paid
$4/issue, $36/yr, $39/yr foreign
ISSN: 0017-6516
Buy freelance fiction, nonfiction, art & cartoons; Sell back issues up to one year if available. Do not provide reprints
Trim Size: 7 7/8 x 10 1/2; 1/8 bleed for all sides
Ad Rates: B&W page $7,750; 4-color page $9,900
Ad Closing Date(s): 5 weeks prior to issue date

The Hamilton Spectator
Published by Metroland Media Group Ltd
Subsidiary of Torstar Corp
44 Frid St, Hamilton, ON L8N 3G3, Canada
Tel: 905-526-3333 *Fax:* 905-526-0147 (busn off); 905-526-1395 (news); 905-521-8986 (entertainment/edit)
Web Site: www.thespec.com/hamilton-whatson/books
Key Personnel
Publr: Neil Oliver *E-mail:* noliver@metroland.com
Mng Ed: Howard Elliott *E-mail:* helliott@thespec.com; Jim Poling *E-mail:* jpoling@thespec.com
Features book reviews, news & releases from the writing community in Hamilton & worldwide.
Circulation: 120,000
$9.03/mo digital

Harper's Bazaar
Published by Hearst Communications Inc
Division of Hearst Magazines
300 W 57 St, New York, NY 10019-3787
Tel: 212-903-5000; 212-903-5061 (edit); 212-903-5398 (publg)
Web Site: www.harpersbazaar.com; www.hearst.com
Subscription Address: PO Box 6000, Harlan, IA 51593
Key Personnel
VP, Publr & Chief Revenue Offr: Carol A Smith
Ed-in-Chief: Samira Nasr
Edited for women interested in fashion & beauty; also for the professional fashion designer & retailer. Includes travel articles, profiles & interviews.
First published 1867
Book Use: Fashion
Frequency: Monthly
Avg pages per issue: 325
Circulation: 734,504
$4.99/issue, $10/yr, $15/2 yrs, $20/3 yrs
ISSN: 0017-7873
Trim Size: 8 1/4 x 11 1/8
Ad Rates: 4-color page $134,270
Ad Closing Date(s): 5th of the 2nd month of preceding issue

Harper's Magazine
Published by Harper's Magazine Foundation
666 Broadway, 11th fl, New York, NY 10012
Tel: 212-420-5720 *Toll Free Tel:* 800-444-4653
  Fax: 212-228-5889
E-mail: helpdesk@harpers.org; harpersmagazine@cdsfulfillment.com
Web Site: www.harpers.org
Subscription Address: PO Box 6237, Harlan, IA 51593-1737
Key Personnel
Pres & Publr: John R MacArthur
VP & Gen Mgr: Lynn Carlson *E-mail:* lynn@harpers.org
VP, Ad: Jocelyn D Giannini
VP, Circ: Shawn D Green
VP, Mktg & Communs: Giulia Melucci
Art Dir: Kathryn Humphries
Deputy Art Dir: Maria Dubon
Mng Ed: Will Augerot
Deputy Ed: Will Stephenson
Sr Ed: Joanna Biggs; Elena Saavedra Buckley; Joe Kloc; Katherine Ryder
Contains short fiction as well as articles on literature, politics, science, education, the arts, entertainment & business for an informed audience. Accept very few unsol mss. Submit in writing. Send queries with a SASE to editorial department.
First published 1850
Book Use: Excerpts & essay-reviews
Frequency: Monthly
Avg pages per issue: 96
Circulation: 105,000 paid
$6.99/issue, $30/yr, $33/yr CN, $50/yr foreign
ISSN: 0017-789X
Buy freelance fiction, nonfiction, poetry, art & cartoons; Sell articles & ad reprints, back issues
Avg reviews per issue: 6-8
Trim Size: 8 x 10.75
Ad Rates: B&W page $8,795, 4-color page $13,645
Ad Closing Date(s): 12th of 2nd month preceding issue date

The Hartford Courant
Published by Tribune Publishing Co
285 Broad St, Hartford, CT 06115
Tel: 860-525-5555 (cust serv); 860-241-6200
E-mail: custserv@courant.com
Web Site: www.courant.com; www.ctnow.com
Key Personnel
Publr & Ed-in-Chief: Andrew Julien
  E-mail: ajulien@courant.com
Dir, Content: Richard Green *E-mail:* rgreen@courant.com
Features Ed: Cindy Kuse *E-mail:* ckuse@courant.com
Digital & print: $2.49/wk (Sun only), $4.99/wk (Mon-Sun); digital only: $1.99/wk
ISSN: 1047-4153

Harvard Magazine
Published by Harvard Magazine Inc
7 Ware St, Cambridge, MA 02138-4037
Tel: 617-495-5746; 617-496-9780 *Fax:* 617-495-0324
E-mail: customerservice@harvardmag.com
Web Site: www.harvardmagazine.com
Key Personnel
Publr: Irina Kuksin *E-mail:* irina_kuksin@harvard.edu

Dir, Fundraising & Circ: Felecia Carter
 E-mail: felecia_carter@harvard.edu
Mng Ed: Jonathan S Shaw E-mail: jon_shaw@harvard.edu
Sr Ed: Jean Martin E-mail: jean_martin@harvard.edu
Ed: John S Rosenberg E-mail: john_rosenberg@harvard.edu
General interest material devoted to Harvard-related subjects & aimed at sharing the wealth of Harvard; contains articles about the Harvard community, its intellectual life & people. Books must be by Harvard students, graduates (any Harvard school) or faculty, or about Harvard-related subjects, higher education, Harvard graduates.
First published 1898
Book Use: Reviews, listings & occasional author profiles; excerpts-all require some Harvard connection
Frequency: 6 issues/yr
Avg pages per issue: 116
Circulation: 258,000
$27/yr US, $35/yr CN, $45/yr Mexico, $55/yr intl
Buy freelance, nonfiction; Sell back issues
Trim Size: 8 3/8 x 10 1/2
Ad Rates: See media kit for national & regional rates
Ad Closing Date(s): 15th of 2nd month preceding publication

Herald-Dispatch
Published by HD Media Company LLC
347 Braley Rd, Huntington, WV 25705
Mailing Address: PO Box 2017, Huntington, WV 25720
Tel: 304-526-4000 (operator) Toll Free Tel: 800-444-2446 (newsroom); 800-955-6110 (display & retail ad)
Web Site: www.herald-dispatch.com
Key Personnel
VP & Ad Dir: Jerry Briggs Tel: 304-526-2820
 E-mail: jwbriggs@hdmediallc.com
Ed: Jeff Rider Tel: 304-348-4815 E-mail: jrider@hdmediallc.com
Circ & Mktg Specialist: Savannah Carr Tel: 304-437-8083 E-mail: scarr@hdmediallc.com
In-house & through syndication; occasional interviews with local authors.
Circulation: 10,172 (d); 12,200 (Sat)

Herald News
Published by North Jersey Media Group
One Garret Mountain Plaza, Woodland Park, NJ 07424
Mailing Address: PO Box 471, Woodland Park, NJ 07424-0471
Tel: 973-569-7000 Toll Free Tel: 888-282-3422 Fax: 973-569-7037
E-mail: northjerseymediagroup@gannett.com
Web Site: www.northjersey.com
Occasional column; in-house, syndicated & through wire services; occasional author interviews.
Circulation: 50,000 (m)
Digital & print: $18/mo (Thurs & Sun), $32/mo (Mon-Sun); digital only: $9.99/mo

Herald News
Published by GateHouse Media LLC
207 Pocasset St, Fall River, MA 02722
Tel: 508-676-8211 Fax: 508-324-4047
E-mail: news@heraldnews.com
Web Site: www.heraldnews.com
Key Personnel
Pres & Group Publr: Peter Mayer
Dir, Content & Interactive: Jon Root
 E-mail: jroot@heraldnews.com
Ed-in-Chief: Lynne Sullivan Tel: 508-676-2534
 E-mail: lsullivan@heraldnews.com
Occasional column; in-house & through syndication, occasional author interviews & book reviews; Sunday book review page.
Circulation: 38,000 (d); 38,100 (Sun)
Digital & print: $24/12 wks (Sun only), $48/12 wks (Mon-Sun); digital only: $9.95/mo, $99.95/yr

The Herald-Sun Newspapers
Published by Durham Herald Co Inc
1530 N Gregson St, Suite 2A, Durham, NC 27701
Tel: 919-419-6500 Toll Free Tel: 800-522-4205
E-mail: news@heraldsun.com
Web Site: www.heraldsun.com
Key Personnel
Exec Ed: Robyn Tomlin Tel: 919-829-4806
Mng Ed: Jane Elizabeth Tel: 919-836-5909
Author interviews & book reviews.
Circulation: 40,000 (m); 55,000 (Sun)
Digital & print: $34.94/13 wks (Wed & Sun), $69.88/13 wks (Mon-Fri & Sun); digital only: $8.99/mo, $129.99/yr

The Hibbing Daily Tribune
Published by Adams Publishing Group
2142 First Ave, Hibbing, MN 55746
Mailing Address: PO Box 38, Hibbing, MN 55746-0038
Tel: 218-262-1011 Fax: 218-262-4318
E-mail: news@hibbingdailytribune.net
Web Site: hibbingmn.com
Key Personnel
News Asst: Connie Dickson; Hannah White
In-house, syndicated & other book reviews in space available in Accent section, reviews with excerpts, reproduction of jacket cover or author photo, occasional author interviews.
First published 1893
Frequency: Daily (Tues-Sun print & Mon e-edition)
Circulation: 10,000
$3.45/wk carrier, $3.61/wk mail, $3.95/wk motor route

The High Point Enterprise
Published by HP Enterprise Inc
213 Woodbine St, High Point, NC 27260
Tel: 336-888-3500 Fax: 336-888-0809
Web Site: www.hpenews.com; www.facebook.com/hpenterprise
Key Personnel
Publr: Nancy Baker E-mail: nbaker@hpenews.com
Ad Dir: David Jones E-mail: djones@hpenews.com
Ed: Megan Ward E-mail: mward@hpenews.com
Weekly, wire copy, syndicated; occasional local author interviews.
Circulation: 50,000 (d)
Print & e-edition: $16.24/mo (Mon-Sun); full digital access (no print): $10/mo

The Hollywood Reporter
Published by Prometheus Global Media LLC
5700 Wilshire Blvd, Suite 500, Los Angeles, CA 90036
Tel: 323-525-2000; 323-525-2150 (subns); 323-525-2130 (edit); 323-525-2013 (ad)
Toll Free Tel: 866-525-2150 (subns)
E-mail: thrnews@thr.com
Web Site: www.hollywoodreporter.com
Key Personnel
EVP/Group Publr, Entertainment Group: Lynne Segall
Exec Creative Dir: Shanti Marlar
News Dir: Erik Hayden
Exec Mng Ed: Sudie Redmond
Edit Dir: Matthew Belloni
Exec Ed, Features: Stephen Galloway
The oldest weekly entertainment trade publication, delivers the business of entertainment, including motion pictures, TV, home video, music, convergence, the crafts & production facilities servicing those media to over 100,000 readers in 64 countries.
First published 1930
Print & iPad: $99/yr, $249/yr intl; digital all access: $129/yr; print & digital all access: $199/yr, $299/yr intl
ISSN: 0018-3660

The Honolulu Star-Advertiser
Published by Oahu Publications Inc
Subsidiary of Black Press Ltd
7 Waterfront Plaza, Suite 210, 500 Ala Moana Blvd, Honolulu, HI 96813
Tel: 808-529-4747 Fax: 808-529-4750
E-mail: citydesk@staradvertiser.com
Web Site: www.staradvertiser.com
Key Personnel
Pres & Publr: Dennis Francis Tel: 808-529-4700
VP & Ed: Frank Bridgewater Tel: 808-529-4791
 E-mail: fbridgewater@staradvertiser.com
Mng Ed, Spec Sections: Clarke Reilly Tel: 808-529-4742 E-mail: creilly@staradvertiser.com
Book reviews.
First published 2010
Frequency: Daily
Circulation: 130,000 (e)
Digital & print: $28.15/mo (Wed-Sun), $42.25/mo (Mon-Sun); digital only: $21.95/mo

House Beautiful
Published by Hearst Communications Inc
Division of Hearst Magazines
300 W 57 St, 27th fl, New York, NY 10019-3787
Tel: 212-903-5206; 212-903-5005 (publg)
Web Site: www.housebeautiful.com; www.hearst.com
Subscription Address: PO Box 6000, Harlan, IA 51593
Key Personnel
Edit Dir: Joanna Saltz
Sr Features Ed: Emma Bazilian
Articles on architecture, decorating, home furnishings, design, practical home planning & maintenance. Also covers travel, entertainment, gardening & food.
First published 1896
Frequency: 10 issues/yr
Avg pages per issue: 176
Circulation: 804,917
$4.99/issue, $10/yr, $15/2 yrs
ISSN: 0018-6422
Trim Size: 8 1/4 x 10 7/8
Ad Rates: 4-color full page $182,590, 1/2 page $118,685

Houston Chronicle
Published by Houston Chronicle Publishing Co
Division of Hearst Newspapers
4747 Southwest Fwy, Houston, TX 77027
Mailing Address: PO Box 4260, Houston, TX 77210-4260
Tel: 713-220-7171 Fax: 713-362-3575
Web Site: www.houstonchronicle.com
Key Personnel
Chmn: Jack Sweeney
Pres & Publr: John McKeon
Ed & EVP: Nancy Barnes
Exec Ed, Opinions & Editorials: Jeff Cohen
Books Ed: Alyson Ward Tel: 713-362-7128
 E-mail: alyson.ward@chron.com
Entertainment Ed: Robert Morast
News Ed: Lisa Gray
Sunday in Zest magazine; book reviews in-house, freelancers & academic sources. Frequent author interviews Sunday.
First published 1901

Huntsville Times
Published by Alabama Media Group
Unit of Advance Local Media LLC

200 Westside Sq, Suite 100, Huntsville, AL 35801
Tel: 256-532-4000 *Toll Free Tel:* 800-239-5271
E-mail: advertise@al.com; marketing@al.com
Web Site: www.al.com/huntsville; www.alabamamediagroup.com
Subscription Address: PO Box 1487, West Sta, Huntsville, AL 35807
Key Personnel
Pres: Tom Bates *E-mail:* tbates@al.com
In-house & through syndication; author interviews.
Circulation: 40,000 (Wed/Fri); 60,433 (Sun)
Digital & print: $4.17/wk (Sun only), $5.56/wk (Wed & Sun), $6.95/wk (Wed, Fri & Sun); digital only: $4.61/wk

Idaho State Journal
Published by Adams Publishing Group
305 S Arthur St, Pocatello, ID 83204
Mailing Address: PO Box 431, Pocatello, ID 83204-0431
Tel: 208-232-4161 *Fax:* 208-233-8007
E-mail: newsroom@journalnet.com
Web Site: www.idahostatejournal.com
Key Personnel
Mng Ed: Ian Fennell *Tel:* 208-239-3121
    E-mail: ifennell@journalnet.com
Occasional author interviews; in-house & by syndicate; occasional reviews & excerpts.
Circulation: 17,000 (e); 18,500 (Sun)
Digital & print: $9.10/mo (Sun only), $12.39/mo (Thurs, Fri & Sun), $14.77/mo (Tues-Fri & Sun); digital only: $9.10/mo

The Independent Record
Published by Lee Enterprises Inc
PO Box 4249, Helena, MT 59604
Tel: 406-447-4000 *Toll Free Tel:* 800-523-2272
    Fax: 406-447-4052
Web Site: helenair.com
Key Personnel
Publr: Anita Fasbender *Tel:* 406-447-4012
    E-mail: anita.fasbender@helenair.com
Ed: Jesse Chaney *Tel:* 406-447-4074
    E-mail: jesse.chaney@helenair.com
Weekly book page-wire & reviews.
Circulation: 14,500 (m); 15,000 (Sun)
$5/mo digital basic, $9.99/mo digital plus

Indianapolis Star/News
Published by Gannett Co Inc
130 S Meridian St, Indianapolis, IN 46225
Mailing Address: PO Box 145, Indianapolis, IN 46206-0145
Tel: 317-444-4000 (call ctr) *Toll Free Tel:* 888-357-7827
E-mail: indianapolisstar@gannett.com
Web Site: www.indystar.com
Key Personnel
VP, Sales: David Hakanson
Sr News Dir: Ginger Rough
Exec Ed: Ronnie Ramos *Tel:* 317-444-6166
    E-mail: ronnie.ramos@indystar.com
Weekly book reviews; 200 reviews/yr, in-house; occasional author interviews.
Circulation: 557,990
ISSN: 1930-2533

Inland Valley Daily Bulletin
Published by Southern California News Group
9616 Archibald Ave, Suite 100, Rancho Cucamonga, CA 91730
Tel: 909-987-6397
E-mail: service@langnews.com
Web Site: www.dailybulletin.com
Key Personnel
Pres & Publr: Ron Hasse *Tel:* 818-713-3883
    E-mail: publisher@scng.com
Exec Ed: Frank Pine *Tel:* 909-483-9360
    E-mail: editor@scng.com
Author interviews if local.

First published 1882
Circulation: 49,899 (d); 54,401 (Sun)
Digital & print: $12.50/4 wks (Sun only), $15/4 wks (Thurs-Sun, $25/4 wks (Mon-Sun)

Iowa City Press-Citizen
Published by Gannett Co Inc
123 N Linn St, Suite 2-E, Iowa City, IA 52245
Mailing Address: PO Box 2480, Iowa City, IA 52244-2480
Tel: 319-337-3181 *Toll Free Tel:* 877-424-0071
E-mail: customerservice@press-citizen.com
Web Site: www.press-citizen.com
Key Personnel
Sales Mgr: Michael Vitti *Tel:* 319-339-7350
    E-mail: mvitti@press-citizen.com
Reviews books in-house & through syndication.
Circulation: 14,000; 10,000 paid

Island Packet
Published by The McClatchy Co
10 Buck Island Rd, Bluffton, SC 29910
Mailing Address: PO Box 5727, Hilton Head Island, SC 29938
Tel: 843-706-8140 *Toll Free Tel:* 877-706-8100
Web Site: www.islandpacket.com
Key Personnel
Publr: Rodney Mahone *E-mail:* rmahone@mcclatchy.com
Gen Mgr & Exec Ed: Brian Tolley
    E-mail: btolley@islandpacket.com
Sr Ed: Liz Farrell *E-mail:* lfarrell@islandpacket.com
Weekly in-house, syndicated & wire service book reviews, "Book Page" author interviews.
First published 1897
$12.99/mo digital, $129.99/yr

The Jackson Sun
Published by Gannett Co Inc
245 W Lafayette St, Jackson, TN 38301
Tel: 731-427-3333 *Toll Free Tel:* 800-372-3922
Web Site: www.jacksonsun.com
In-house, through syndication & other outside sources, book signings & previews.
Circulation: 30,000 (weekly); 35,000 (Sun)
Digital & print: $16/mo (Wed & Sun), $26/mo (Mon-Sun); digital only: $10/mo

The Jersey Journal
Published by The Evening Journal Association
One Harmon Plaza, Suite 1010, Secaucus, NJ 07094
Tel: 201-653-1000
Web Site: www.jjournal.com
Key Personnel
Publr: David Blomquist *E-mail:* dblomquist@jjournal.com
VP & Ed: Margaret Schmidt *Tel:* 201-217-2480
    E-mail: margaret.schmidt@jjournal.com
Mng Ed: Ron Zeitlinger *Tel:* 201-217-2429
    E-mail: ron.zeitlinger@jjournal.com
Occasional story; occasional local book review.
Circulation: 20,000 (d)
$1/day

Johnson City Press
Published by Sandusky Newspaper Group
204 W Main St, Johnson City, TN 37604
Mailing Address: PO Box 1717, Johnson City, TN 37605-1717
Tel: 423-929-3111 *Fax:* 423-929-7484
E-mail: circulation@johnsoncitypress.com
Web Site: www.johnsoncitypress.com
Key Personnel
Publr: Rick Thomason *Tel:* 423-722-0501
    E-mail: rthomason@johnsoncitypress.com
Daily, in-house & syndicated; AP wire & *The New York Times*. Occasional author interviews.

Circulation: 32,000 (m); 35,000 (Sun)
Print: $11.70/mo (Wed & Sun), $10.83/mo (Fri-Sun); digital only $13.55/mo; digital & print: $14.30/mo (Mon-Sun)

Journal & Courier
Published by Gannett Co Inc
823 Park East Blvd, Suite C, Lafayette, IN 47905
Tel: 765-423-5511 *Toll Free Tel:* 800-456-3223
Web Site: www.jconline.com
Key Personnel
Ed & News Dir: Carol Bangert
    E-mail: cbangert@gannett.com
Prodr: Joseph Mutascio *E-mail:* jmutascio@gannett.com
Daily newspaper; infrequent book reviews, in-house; infrequent author interviews.
Circulation: 37,000 (d); 44,000 (Sun)
$.75/daily, $1.75/Sun

The Journal Gazette
Published by Fort Wayne Newspapers
Affiliate of Ogden Newspapers
600 W Main St, Fort Wayne, IN 46802-1498
Tel: 260-461-8773 (newsroom); 260-461-8519 (subscriber info) *Toll Free Tel:* 800-324-0505 (circ) *Fax:* 260-461-8648 (newsroom)
E-mail: jgnews@jg.net
Web Site: www.journalgazette.net
Key Personnel
Publr: Julie Inskeep *Tel:* 260-461-8490
    E-mail: jinskeep@jg.net
Mng Ed: Jim Touvell *Tel:* 260-461-8629
    E-mail: jtouvell@jg.net
Ed: Sherry Skufca *Tel:* 260-461-8201
    E-mail: sskufca@jg.net
Edit Page Ed: Karen Francisco *Tel:* 260-461-8206
    E-mail: kfrancisco@jg.net
Book reviews.
Circulation: 41,000 (m); 71,000 (Sun)
$22.95/mo (daily print), $16.70/mo (Fri-Sun print), $10.85/mo (Sun only print), $20/mo (digital)

The Journal News
Published by Gannett Co Inc
1133 Westchester Ave, Suite N-110, White Plains, NY 10604
Tel: 914-694-9300 *Toll Free Tel:* 800-942-1010 (subns)
E-mail: westchesterthejournalnews@gannett.com
Web Site: www.lohud.com
Key Personnel
News Dir: Mary Dolan *E-mail:* mdolan@lohud.com
Community Content Ed: Karen Croke
    E-mail: kcroke1@lohud.com
Sunday page in Leisure section "Living Section" in-house & through syndication & wire services. Print-on-demand or self-published books are not reviewed.
Circulation: 87,205 (d); 104,652 (Sun)

Journal of Marketing
Published by American Marketing Association
130 E Randolph St, 22nd fl, Chicago, IL 60601
Tel: 312-542-9000 *Toll Free Tel:* 800-AMA-1150 (262-1150)
E-mail: jom@ama.org; amasubs@subscriptionoffice.com
Web Site: www.ama.org/journal-of-marketing
Key Personnel
VP, Pubns: David W Stewart
Ed-in-Chief: Christine Moorman
Develops & disseminates knowledge about real-world marketing questions useful to scholars, educators, managers, policy makers, consumers & other societal stakeholders around the world. It is the premier outlet for substantive research in marketing.
First published 1936
Frequency: 6 times/yr

Avg pages per issue: 144
Circulation: 8,200
Indivs: $41/issue, $171/yr online only, $186/yr print only, $190/yr print & online; Instns: $82/issue, $449/yr print or online only, $540/yr print & online
ISSN: 0022-2429 (print); 1547-7185 (online)
Sell articles, ad reprints & back issues

Journal of Marketing Research
Published by American Marketing Association
130 E Randolph St, 22nd fl, Chicago, IL 60601
Tel: 312-542-9000 *Toll Free Tel:* 800-AMA-1150 (262-1150)
E-mail: jmr@ama.org; amasubs@subscriptionoffice.com
Web Site: www.ama.org
Key Personnel
VP, Pubns: David W Stewart
Ed: Rajdeep Grewal
Articles representing the entire spectrum of topics in marketing. It welcomes diverse theoretical perspectives & a wide variety of data & methodological approaches. Seeks papers that make methodological, substantive +/or theoretical contributions. Empirical studies in papers that seek to make a theoretical +/or substantive contribution may involve experimental +/or observational designs & rely on primary data (including qualitative date) +/or secondary data (including meta-analytic data sets).
First published 1964
Frequency: 6 times/yr
Avg pages per issue: 128
Circulation: 4,400
Indivs: $41/issue, $171/yr online only, $186/yr print only, $190/yr print & online; Instns: $82/issue, $449/yr print or online only, $540/yr print & online
ISSN: 0022-2437 (print); 1547-7193 (online)
Sell articles, ad reprints & back issues

Journal Star
Published by GateHouse Media LLC
One News Plaza, Peoria, IL 61643
Tel: 309-686-3000 *Toll Free Tel:* 800-322-0804 (cust serv) *Fax:* 309-686-3296
E-mail: news@pjstar.com
Web Site: www.pjstar.com
Key Personnel
Pres & Publr: Paul Gaier *Tel:* 309-686-3005
 E-mail: pgaier@gatehousemedia.com
Exec Ed: Dennis Anderson *Tel:* 309-686-3159
 E-mail: danderson@pjstar.com
Occasional author interviews; in-house & syndicated.
First published 1855
Circulation: 70,000 (d); 90,000 (Sun)
Digital & print: $32.50/13 wks (Sun only), $41.60/13 wks (weekend), $78/13 wks (Mon-Sun); digital only: $4.99/mo, $34.99/yr

The Kansas City Star
Published by The McClatchy Co
1601 McGee St, Kansas City, MO 64108
Tel: 816-234-4636 *Toll Free Tel:* 877-962-7827 (subns)
Web Site: www.kansascity.com
Key Personnel
VP & Ed: Mike Fannin *Tel:* 816-234-4345
 E-mail: mfannin@kcstar.com
Mng Ed: Greg Farmer *Tel:* 816-234-4321
 E-mail: gfarmer@kcstar.com
Weekly books page, daily features page; staff freelance & wire sources; reviews & author interviews. Self-published print & ebooks rarely considered for review or mention.
Circulation: 216,000 (m); 275,000 (Sat); 325,000 (Sun)
Digital & print: $8.91/wk (Mon-Sun), $7.81/wk (Wed-Sun), $5.61/wk (Wed & Sun); digital only: $12.99/mo

Kentucky Living
Published by Kentucky Electric Cooperatives
PO Box 32170, Louisville, KY 40232-2170
Tel: 502-815-6337 *Toll Free Tel:* 800-595-4846 *Fax:* 502-459-1611
E-mail: news@kentuckyliving.com
Web Site: www.kentuckyliving.com
Key Personnel
Mng Ed: Joel Sams *E-mail:* jsams@kentuckyliving.com
Ed: Shannon Brock *E-mail:* sbrock@kentuckyliving.com
Kentucky feature magazine.
First published 1948
Book Use: Notice of new Kentucky books, Kentucky authors & excerpts
Frequency: Monthly
Avg pages per issue: 64
Circulation: 478,000
$15/yr, $25/3 yrs
ISSN: 1043-853X
Buy nonfiction; Sell back issues
Trim Size: 8 x 10 1/2
Ad Rates: 4-color page $10,369, 1/2 page $6,221, 1/4 page $3,087

Kentucky New Era
Published by New Era
1618 E Ninth St, Hopkinsville, KY 44240
Mailing Address: PO Box 729, Hopkinsville, KY 42241
Tel: 270-886-4444 *Fax:* 270-887-3222
E-mail: editor@kentuckynewera.com
Web Site: www.kentuckynewera.com
Key Personnel
Pres: Chuck Henderson *E-mail:* chenderson@kentuckynewera.com
Publr: Taylor Wood Hayes *E-mail:* twhayes@kentuckynewera.com
Dir, Sales & Mktg: Ted Jatczak
 E-mail: tjatczak@kentuckynewera.com
In-house occasional, syndicated; occasional local author interviews.
First published 1869
Frequency: Daily (Mon-Sat)
Circulation: 14,000 (d)
Print: $14/mo, $40/3 mos, $76/6 mos, $296/yr; online: $14/mo, $42/3 mos, $84/6 mos, $164.85/yr

The Kingston Whig-Standard
Published by Postmedia Network Inc
6 Cataraqui St, Kingston, ON K7L 4Z7, Canada
Tel: 613-544-5000
Web Site: www.thewhig.com
Key Personnel
Ed-in-Chief: Steve Serviss *E-mail:* steve.serviss@postmedia.com
Weekly book reviews tabloid; syndicated & freelance in-house. Occasional author interviews & freelance.
Frequency: Daily (Tues-Sat)
Circulation: 23,686 (d)
$22/4 wks, $3.99/mo digital
ISSN: 1197-4397
Avg reviews per issue: 3

Kiplinger's Personal Finance Magazine
Published by The Kiplinger Washington Editors Inc
1100 13 St NW, Suite 750, Washington, DC 20005
Tel: 202-887-6400 *Toll Free Tel:* 800-544-0155 (subn servs) *Toll Free Fax:* 888-547-5464 (spec issues)
E-mail: sub.services@kiplinger.com
Web Site: www.kiplinger.com
Key Personnel
Exec Ed: Anne Kates Smith
Mng Ed: Barbara Hoch Marcus
Sr Ed: Eileen Ambrose; Jane Bennett Clark; Sandra Block; Jeffrey R Kosnett

Ed-at-Large: Janet Bodnar
For general, adult audience interested in personal finance topics, especially investing & money management.
First published 1947
Frequency: Monthly
Avg pages per issue: 100
Circulation: 600,000
$7/issue, $12/yr print & digital
Sell article & ad reprints, back issues
Trim Size: 7.875 x 10.5
Ad Rates: 4-color page $66,801, 2/3 page $53,123, 1/2 page $46,788, 1/3 page $33,422
Ad Closing Date(s): 5-6 weeks preceding publication

Kitsap Sun
Published by Gannett Co Inc
545 Fifth St, Bremerton, WA 98337
Mailing Address: PO Box 259, Bremerton, WA 98337
Tel: 360-792-8558; 360-792-9222 (circ) *Toll Free Tel:* 844-900-7106
E-mail: sunnews@kitsapsun.com
Web Site: www.kitsapsun.com
Key Personnel
Ed: David Nelson *Tel:* 360-415-2679
 E-mail: david.nelson@kitsapsun.com
Weekly book reviews.
Circulation: 20,000
Digital & print: $14/mo (Sun only), $23/mo (Mon-Sun); digital only: $10/mo

The Knoxville News-Sentinel
Published by Gannett Co Inc
2332 News Sentinel Dr, Knoxville, TN 37921-5761
Tel: 865-523-3131 *Toll Free Tel:* 844-900-7097 (cust serv)
E-mail: features@knoxnews.com
Web Site: www.knoxnews.com
Key Personnel
Exec Ed: Joel Christopher *Tel:* 865-342-6300
 E-mail: jchristo@gannett.com
Book reviews & occasional author interviews.
$9.99/mo

LA Times, see Los Angeles Times

The Lakeville Journal
Published by The Lakeville Journal Co LLC
64 Rte 7 N, Falls Village, CT 06039
Mailing Address: PO Box 1688, Lakeville, CT 06039
Tel: 860-435-9873
E-mail: editor@lakevillejournal.com; compass@lakevillejournal.com
Web Site: www.tricornernews.com/lakevillagejournal
Key Personnel
Publr & Ed-in-Chief: Janet Manko
 E-mail: publisher@lakevillejournal.com
Exec Ed, Spec Sections: Cynthia Hochswender
 E-mail: cynthiah@lakevillejournal.com
Art & entertainment section with book reviews.
First published 1897
Frequency: Weekly
Circulation: 4,800 paid
$28/yr web only, $53/yr print inside Litchfield County, $38/yr digital

Lansing State Journal
Published by Gannett Co Inc
300 S Washington Sq, Suite 300, Lansing, MI 48933
Tel: 517-377-1000 *Toll Free Tel:* 800-234-1719
E-mail: lansingstatejournal@gannett.com (cust serv)
Web Site: www.lsj.com

& PUBLICITY

Key Personnel
Exec Ed: Stephanie Angel *Tel:* 517-377-1076
 E-mail: sangel@lsj.com
Circulation: 75,000 (d); 94,000 (Sun)

Las Vegas Magazine
Published by Greenspun Media Group
2275 Corporate Circle, Suite 300, Henderson, NV 89074
Tel: 702-383-7185; 702-990-2550 (corp)
E-mail: gmginfo@gmgvegas.com
Web Site: www.lasvegasmagazine.com
Key Personnel
Publr: Jamal Parker *E-mail:* jamal.parker@gmgvegas.com
Mng Ed: Nina King
Ed: Ken Miller
Assoc Ed: Kiko Miyasato
Entertainment/TV-Tour Guide & in-room hotel resort publication.
Frequency: Weekly
Circulation: 139,047
Free
Trim Size: 8 1/4 x 10 3/4
Ad Rates: Full page $5,256, 1/2 page horizontal $3,055, 1/3 page square $2,472
Ad Closing Date(s): 3rd Wednesday before issue date

Las Vegas Review-Journal
Published by Las Vegas Review-Journal Inc
1111 W Bonanza Rd, Las Vegas, NV 89106
Mailing Address: PO Box 70, Las Vegas, NV 89125-0070
Tel: 702-383-0211; 702-383-0264 (newsroom)
Web Site: www.lvrj.com
Key Personnel
Publr & Ed: J Keith Moyer *Tel:* 707-477-3829
 E-mail: kmoyer@reviewjournal.com
Exec Ed: Glenn Cook *Tel:* 702-387-2906
 E-mail: gcook@reviewjournal.com
Mng Ed: Anastasia Hendrix *Tel:* 702-383-0232
 E-mail: ahendrix@reviewjournal.com
Sunday column on Southwestern books, reviews; through syndication.
Circulation: 174,127 (d); 200,955 (Sun)
Digital & print: $5.99/mo (Sun only), $8.99/mo (Thurs-Sun), $9.99/mo (Mon-Sun); digital only: $8.99/mo, $89/yr

Las Vegas Weekly
Published by Greenspun Media Group
2275 Corporate Circle, Suite 300, Henderson, NV 89074
Tel: 702-990-2550 *Fax:* 702-383-7264
E-mail: letters@lasvegassun.com
Web Site: www.lasvegasweekly.com
Key Personnel
Pres & Ed, Las Vegas Sun: Brian Greenspun
Ed: Spencer Patterson
Thursday in-house & through syndication; occasional author interviews.
Circulation: 45,000 (e); 235,000 (Sun)
First copy free, additional copies $2
Avg reviews per issue: 4
Trim Size: 10 1/2 x 13 1/2
Ad Rates: Full page $4,056, 1/2 page $2,108

The Lewiston Tribune
Published by Tribune Publishing Co
505 Capital St, Lewiston, ID 83501
Mailing Address: PO Box 957, Lewiston, ID 83501
Tel: 208-743-9411 *Toll Free Tel:* 800-745-9411 (ID & WA only) *Fax:* 208-746-1185
E-mail: city@lmtribune.com
Web Site: lmtribune.com
Key Personnel
Mktg Dir: Doug Bauer *Tel:* 208-848-2269
 E-mail: dbauer@lmtribune.com
Mng Ed: Craig Clohessy *Tel:* 208-848-2251
 E-mail: cclohessy@lmtribune.com

Friday page; occasional author interviews; in-house, through syndication & other sources.
First published 1892
Frequency: Daily
Circulation: 21,000 (m); 24,000 (Sun)

The Lexington Herald-Leader
Published by The McClatchy Co
100 Midland Ave, Lexington, KY 40508-1943
Tel: 859-231-3100
Web Site: www.kentucky.com
Key Personnel
Exec Ed & Gen Mgr: Peter Baniak *Tel:* 859-231-3446 *E-mail:* pbaniak@herald-leader.com
Sunday, one page syndicated in-house books of regional & local interest.
Circulation: 159,826 (d); 190,057 (Sun)
Digital & print: $55.12/13 wks (Sat & Sun), $96.46/13 wks (Mon-Sun); digital only: $12.99/mo, $129.99/yr

Liguorian
Published by Liguori Publications
One Liguori Dr, Liguori, MO 63057-1000
Tel: 636-464-2500 *Toll Free Tel:* 866-848-2492
E-mail: liguorian@sfsdayton.com (cust serv)
Web Site: www.liguorian.org
Key Personnel
Pres & Publr: Fr Byron Miller
Mng Ed: Elizabeth Herzing-Gebhart *Tel:* 636-223-1538 *E-mail:* eherzing@liguori.org
Religious publication for people of all ages with Catholic (Christian) convictions; advertising accepted; do not consider previously published material or simultaneous submissions. Contact editor for submission guidelines at liguorianeditor@liguori.org.
First published 1913
Book Use: Reviews
Frequency: 10 issues/yr
Avg pages per issue: 44
Circulation: 50,000 paid
$25/yr print & digital
Buy freelance fiction & nonfiction
Avg reviews per issue: 3-4
Ad Rates: See web site for media kit or contact adsales@liguori.org

Living Lutheran
Published by Augsburg Fortress Publishers
8765 W Higgins Rd, 5th fl, Chicago, IL 60631-4183
Tel: 773-380-2540 *Toll Free Tel:* 800-638-3522 *Fax:* 773-380-2409
E-mail: livinglutheran@elca.org
Web Site: www.livinglutheran.org
Subscription Address: PO Box 1209, Minneapolis, MN 55440-1209 *Toll Free Tel:* 800-328-4648 *E-mail:* subscriptions@1517.media
Key Personnel
Ed: Jennifer Younker
Content Ed: Megan Brandsrud; John Potter; Erin Strybis
Ad: Ben Bitner
General interest magazine of the Evangelical Lutheran Church in America. No unsol mss, query first.
First published 1987
Book Use: Books column & reviews, articles
Frequency: Monthly
Avg pages per issue: 60
Circulation: 135,802
$1.66/issue, $19.95/yr, $31.95/2 yrs, $41.95/3 yrs
ISSN: 0024-743X
Buy nonfiction, art & cartoons; Sell back issues
Trim Size: 8 x 10 1/2
Ad Rates: Full page $4,050, 2-page spread $8,100
Ad Closing Date(s): 8 weeks before cover date

The London Free Press
Published by Postmedia Network Inc

SERIALS FEATURING BOOKS

210 Dundas St, Suite 201, London, ON N6A 5J3, Canada
Tel: 519-679-1111 *Fax:* 519-667-4523
Web Site: www.lfpress.com
Key Personnel
Entertainment, Travel, Life Ed: Barbara Taylor
 Tel: 519-667-5468 *E-mail:* btaylor@postmedia.com
Saturday pages, in-house & by freelancers, occasional author interviews.
First published 1849
Frequency: Daily (Mon-Sat)
Circulation: 105,000 (d); 135,000 (Sat)
Print: $14/4 wks (Sat only), $24/4 wks (Mon-Sat); digital: $9.99/mo

Long Beach Press-Telegram, see Press-Telegram

Los Angeles Magazine
Published by Engine Vision Media
644 S Figueroa St, Los Angeles, CA 90017
Tel: 949-862-1133
E-mail: subscriptions@lamag.com; letters@lamag.com
Web Site: www.lamag.com
Key Personnel
Pres & Publr: Christopher Gialanella
 E-mail: cgialanella@lamag.com
Ed-in-Chief: Shirley Halperin
Mng Ed: Eric Mercado
Covers life in Southern California. Features on people, food, culture, arts & entertainment, fashion, lifestyle & news.
First published 1961
Frequency: Monthly
Avg pages per issue: 350
Circulation: 140,000 paid
ISSN: 1522-9149 (print); 2996-3354 (online)
Trim Size: 8 x 10 1/2

Los Angeles Times
2300 E Imperial Hwy, El Segundo, CA 90245
Tel: 213-237-5000 *Fax:* 213-237-3535
E-mail: customerservice@latimes.com
Web Site: www.latimes.com
Key Personnel
Exec Chmn: Patrick Soon-Shiong, MD
Publr & CEO: Chris Argentieri
Exec Ed: Norman Pearlstine
Mng Ed: Scott Kraft
Deputy Mng Ed: Julia Turner
Book Club Ed: Donna Wares
Daily newspaper with reviews daily & Sunday. Reviews in-house, by freelancers & by syndication.
First published 1881
Frequency: Daily
Circulation: 1,253,849 (Sun); 907,997 (Mon-Sat)
Digital & print: $4/wk (Sun only), $15/wk (Mon-Sun); digital only: $6.93/wk

Lubbock Avalanche-Journal
Published by GateHouse Media LLC
710 Avenue "J", Lubbock, TX 79401
Tel: 806-762-8844
Web Site: www.lubbockonline.com
Key Personnel
Mng Ed: Adam Young *Tel:* 806-766-8717
 E-mail: ayoung@lubbockonline.com
Daily in Arts Section; book reviews; in-house & through syndication; occasional author interviews.
Circulation: 68,000 (d); 79,000 (Sun)
Digital & print: $12.95/4 wks (Sun only), $14.95/4 wks (Fri-Sun), $22.75/4 wks (Mon-Sun); digital only: $9.99/mo, $78.87/yr

The Magazine Antiques
Published by Brant Publications Inc
315 W 36 St, New York, NY 10018
Tel: 646-992-3840 *Toll Free Tel:* 800-925-9271 (subns)

E-mail: tmacustserv@cdsfulfillment.com; tmaedit@themagazineantiques.com
Web Site: www.themagazineantiques.com
Key Personnel
Publr: Don Sparacin Tel: 646-992-3857
E-mail: don@themagazineantiques.com
Mng Ed: Katherine Lanza
Sr Ed: Sammy Dalati
Ed: Gregory Cerio
Features furniture, painting, sculpture, prints, glass & textiles. Columns discuss current exhibitions, recent museum acquisitions & book reviews.
First published 1922
Book Use: Book reviews
Frequency: 6 issues/yr
Avg pages per issue: 151
Circulation: 30,000
$24.95/yr, $58.80/yr CN, $69.95/yr intl
ISSN: 0161-9284
Buy freelance nonfiction; Sell articles, ad reprints & back issues
Trim Size: 8 1/2 x 10 7/8
Ad Rates: 4-color page $4,230
Ad Closing Date(s): 25th of month 2 months previous to publishing date

The Magazine of Fantasy & Science Fiction
Published by Spilogale Inc
PO Box 3447, Hoboken, NJ 07030
Tel: 201-876-2551
E-mail: fandsf@aol.com
Web Site: www.fandsf.com
Key Personnel
Publr: Gordon Van Gelder
Asst Publr: Barbara J Norton
Ed: Sheree Renee Thomas
Fantasy & science fiction; regular departments on science, film, television, cartoons, short stories. Accepted unsol mss typed on clean white bond, double-spaced, with 1-inch margins. Put your name on each page & include SASE or submit online at submissions.cfinlay.com/fsf. Do not accept simultaneous submissions.
First published 1949
Book Use: Reviews & serialized novels
Frequency: 6 issues/yr
Avg pages per issue: 260
Circulation: 30,000 paid
$10.99/issue, $65.94/yr, $85.94/yr foreign
ISSN: 0024-984X
Buy freelance fiction, nonfiction, poetry, art & cartoons; Sell back issues
Avg reviews per issue: 2 book review columns/issue
Trim Size: 5 1/4 x 7 5/8
Ad Rates: B&W page $1,310, 4-color back cover (no 4 only) $3,575
Ad Closing Date(s): 20th of 3rd month preceding publication. Nov/Dec issue published Nov 1, closes Aug 20

Mansfield News Journal
Published by Gannett Co Inc
70 W Fourth St, Mansfield, OH 44903
Tel: 419-522-3311 Toll Free Tel: 877-424-0216 (cust serv)
Web Site: www.mansfieldnewsjournal.com
Key Personnel
Ed: David Yonke E-mail: dyonke@gannett.com
Syndicate & in-house; weekly column; occasional rare author interviews.
Circulation: 36,000 (d); 48,700 (Sun)
Digital & print: $15/mo (Thurs-Sun), $23/mo (Mon-Sun); digital only: $9.99/mo

Marietta Daily Journal
Published by Times-Journal Inc
47 Waddell St SE, Marietta, GA 30060
Mailing Address: PO Box 449, Marietta, GA 30061
Tel: 770-428-9411; 770-795-5000 Fax: 770-422-9533
E-mail: mdjnews@mdjonline.com; customerservice@mdjonline.com
Web Site: www.mdjonline.com
Key Personnel
Publr: Otis Brumby, III E-mail: otis@mdjonline.com
VP, Content: J K Murphy Tel: 770-428-9411 ext 207 E-mail: jkmurphy@mdjonline.com
Gen Mgr: Lee B Garrett Tel: 770-428-9411 ext 301 E-mail: lgarrett@mdjonline.com
Sr Ed: Jon Gillooly Tel: 770-428-9411 ext 211 E-mail: jgillooly@mdjonline.com
Features Ed: Katy Ruth Camp Tel: 770-428-9411 ext 222 E-mail: krcamp@mdjonline.com
Occasional book reviews.
Circulation: 20,000 (d); 21,000 (Sun)
$9.99/mo

Marin Independent Journal
Published by MediaNews Group Inc
4000 Civic Center Dr, Suite 301, San Raphael, CA 94903
Tel: 415-883-8600 Fax: 415-382-7209
E-mail: calendar@marinij.com
Web Site: www.marinij.com
Key Personnel
Lifestyles Ed: Vicki Larson Tel: 415-382-7286 E-mail: lifestyles@marinij.com
In-house & through syndication. Frequent Marin author interviews.
First published 1861
Circulation: 40,000 (e)
Digital & print: $52/13 wks (Sun only), $96/8 wks (Thurs-Sun), $112/8 wks (Mon-Sun); digital only: $9.95/mo

Men's Journal
Published by American Media Inc
4 New York Plaza, New York, NY 10004
Tel: 212-484-1616 Toll Free Tel: 800-677-6367 (cust serv) Fax: 212-484-3429
Web Site: www.mensjournal.com
Key Personnel
Chief Content Offr: Greg Emmanuel
Chief Revenue Offr: Jay Gallagher Tel: 212-484-1799 E-mail: jay.gallagher@mensjournal.com
Men's magazine for sports, travel, fitness & adventure.
First published 1992
Frequency: Monthly
Circulation: 1,000,000
$24.95/2 yrs print or digital
ISSN: 1063-4657
Trim Size: 8 1/4 x 10 7/8
Ad Rates: B&W full page $183,465, 1/2 page $110,090; 4-color full page $204,685, 1/2 page $122,325

The Miami Herald
Published by The McClatchy Co
3511 NW 91 Ave, Miami, FL 33172
Tel: 305-350-2111 Toll Free Tel: 800-843-4372 (subns)
Web Site: www.miamiherald.com
Key Personnel
Pres & Publr: Aminda "Mindy" Marques Gonzales Tel: 305-376-3429
Mng Ed: Rick Hirsch Tel: 305-376-3504
Features Ed: Kendall Hamersly Tel: 305-376-3667 E-mail: khamersly@miamiherald.com
Book pages in "Sunday in South Florida" section; in-house, syndicate & other sources, frequent author interviews & book features; Friday children's book feature.
First published 1903
Circulation: 450,000 (d); 550,000 (Sun)
Digital & print: $83.46/13 wks (Thurs-Sun), $111.28/13 wks (Mon-Sun); digital only: $12.99/mo, $129.99/yr

Michigan Quarterly Review
Published by University of Michigan
3277 Angell Hall, 435 S State St, Ann Arbor, MI 48109-1003
Tel: 734-764-9265
E-mail: mqr@umich.edu
Web Site: www.michiganquarterlyreview.com
Key Personnel
Mng Ed: Aaron J Stone
Asst Mng Ed: Monet Cooper
Ed: Khaled Mattawa
Journal of literature & the humanities.
First published 1962
Frequency: Quarterly
Avg pages per issue: 200
Circulation: 1,000
$10/issue
ISSN: 0026-2420 (print); 1558-7266 (online)
Trim Size: 6 x 9

The Middletown Press
Published by Hearst Newspapers
Division of Hearst Corp
100 Gando Dr, New Haven, CT 06513
Tel: 860-347-3331
E-mail: editor@middletownpress.com
Web Site: www.middletownpress.com
Key Personnel
Mng Ed: Cassandra Day Tel: 860-685-9125 E-mail: cassandra.day@hearstmediact.com
Daily, in-house syndication; locally oriented book reviews in Weekend section.
Frequency: Daily
Circulation: 8,500 (d); 21,038 (Sun)
$3/wk digital

Milwaukee Journal/Sentinel
Published by Gannett Co Inc
PO Box 371, Milwaukee, WI 53201
Tel: 414-224-2000 Toll Free Tel: 844-900-7103 (cust serv) Fax: 414-224-2133
E-mail: jsfeat@journalsentinel.com; milwaukeejournalsentinel@gannett.com
Web Site: www.jsonline.com
Key Personnel
SVP & Ed: George Stanley Tel: 414-224-2248 E-mail: george.stanley@jrn.com
Book reviews & occasional author interviews.
Circulation: 220,000 (e); 490,000 (Sun)
$9.99/mo digital

Moberly Monitor-Index
218 N Williams St, Moberly, MO 65270
Tel: 660-263-4123 Fax: 660-263-3626
Web Site: www.moberlymonitor.com
Key Personnel
Publr: Mike Murphy
First published 1869
Frequency: Daily
Avg pages per issue: 14
Circulation: 3,000 (d)
$14.73/mo
Ad Closing Date(s): 9 AM 2 days before publication

The Modesto Bee
Published by The McClatchy Co
948 11 St, 3rd fl, Modesto, CA 95354
Tel: 209-578-2000 Toll Free Tel: 800-776-4233
E-mail: customerservice@modbee.com
Web Site: modbee.com
Key Personnel
Sr Ed: Carlos Virgen
Infrequently, Sundays. In-house & through syndication. Occasional author interviews.
First published 1884
Circulation: 60,595 (d); 72,680 (Sun)
Digital & print: $49.10/13 wks (Wed & Sun), $63.13/13 wks (Fri-Sun), $84.17/13 wks (Mon-Sun); digital only: $12.99/mo, $129.99/yr

Moment Magazine
Published by The Center for Creative Change
Washington, DC 20016
Tel: 202-363-6422 *Toll Free Tel:* 800-777-1005 (cust serv) *Fax:* 202-362-2514
E-mail: editor@momentmag.com
Web Site: www.momentmag.com
Key Personnel
Ed-in-Chief & CEO: Nadine Epstein
Focuses on Jewish life, including social, religion, political science, history, arts & lifestyle. No unsol mss, query first.
First published 1975
Book Use: Reviews; author interviews
Frequency: 6 issues/yr
Avg pages per issue: 80
Circulation: 90,000 print/mo
$23.95/yr, $33.95/2 yrs
ISSN: 0099-0280
Sell back issues
Trim Size: 8 1/8 x 10 1/2
Ad Rates: Full page $3,640. Discounts for university presses
Ad Closing Date(s): 5th of month preceding issue

Monadnock Ledger-Transcript
Published by Newspapers of New England (NNE)
20 Grove St, Peterborough, NH 03458
Mailing Address: PO Box 36, Peterborough, NH 03458-0036
Tel: 603-924-7172 *Fax:* 603-924-3681
E-mail: news@ledgertranscript.com
Web Site: www.ledgertranscript.com
Key Personnel
Publr: Heather McKernan *Tel:* 603-924-7172 ext 222 *E-mail:* hmckernan@ledgertranscript.com
Ed: Ben Conant *Tel:* 603-924-7172 ext 226 *E-mail:* bconant@ledgertranscript.com
Reviews for weekly paper. Book reviews in-house. Occasionally author interviews; only review books with a local connection (i.e. local authors, books about the local area or writing authors involved in a local reading).
Frequency: 2 issues/wk (Tues & Thurs)
Digital & print: $8.04/mo (in state mail), $11.49/mo (out of state mail); digital only: $5.99/mo

The Montgomery Advertiser
Published by Gannett Co Inc
425 Molton St, Montgomery, AL 36104
Tel: 334-262-1611 *Toll Free Tel:* 877-424-0007 (subns)
E-mail: newstips@montgomeryadvertiser.com
Web Site: www.montgomeryadvertiser.com
Key Personnel
Exec Ed: Bro Krift *E-mail:* bkrift@montgomeryadvertiser.com
Sunday page, in-house, syndicated & by other sources; occasional author interviews.
First published 1829
Full access $20/mo (Mon-Sun), $18/mo (Wed-Sun), $10/mo (Sun & Wed) or digital only

Montreal Gazette
Published by Postmedia Network Inc
1010 Sainte-Catherine St W, Suite 200, Montreal, QC H3B 5L1, Canada
Tel: 514-987-2222; 514-987-2400 (reader sales & serv) *Toll Free Tel:* 800-361-8478 (ext 2400, reader sales & serv) *Fax:* 514-987-2640
E-mail: letters@thegazette.canwest.com
Web Site: montrealgazette.com
Key Personnel
Mng Ed: Basem Boshra *Tel:* 514-987-2628 *E-mail:* bboshra@postmedia.com
Deputy Mng Ed: Jeff Blond *Tel:* 514-987-2486 *E-mail:* jblond@postmedia.com
Ed: Lucinda Chodan *Tel:* 514-987-2508 *E-mail:* lchodan@postmedia.com
Monthly tabloid, in-house, syndication & freelancers, author interviews.
First published 1778
Frequency: Daily (Mon-Sat)
Avg pages per issue: 16
Circulation: 140,000 (m); 170,000 (Sat); 135,000 (Sun)
Digital only: $9.95/mo; e-paper: $9.99/mo; digital & print: $18/mo (Sat only), $30/mo (Mon-Sat)

The Morning Call
Published by The Morning Call Inc
Subsidiary of Tribune Publishing Co
101 N Sixth St, Allentown, PA 18101
Mailing Address: PO Box 1260, Allentown, PA 18105
Tel: 610-820-6566 *Fax:* 610-820-6693
E-mail: news@mcall.com
Web Site: www.mcall.com
Key Personnel
Ed-in-Chief: Theresa Rang *E-mail:* terry.rang@mcall.com
Content Ed, Entertainment & Life: Craig Larimer *E-mail:* clarimer@mcall.com
Sunday, in-house & by freelancers, feature occasional local author interviews.
First published 1883
Frequency: Daily
Circulation: 79,726 (d); 127,517 (Sat); 187,000 (Sun)
Digital & print: $2.49/wk (Sun only), $4.99/wk (Mon-Sun); digital only: $1.99/wk
Avg reviews per issue: 3

Morning Times
Published by Morning Times Inc
201 N Lehigh Ave, Sayre, PA 18840
Tel: 570-888-9643 *Fax:* 570-888-6463
E-mail: editor@morning-times.com
Web Site: www.morning-times.com
Key Personnel
Publr: Kelly Luvison *E-mail:* kluvison@morning-times.com
Mng Ed: Pat McDonald
Daily newspaper, book reviews weekly, in-house syndicated & other sources.
First published 1891
Frequency: Daily
Circulation: 10,000
Online only: $2/day, $15/mo, $24/3 mos, $79/yr; home delivery: $40/13 wks, $79/26 wks, $142/yr; mail delivery: $50/13 wks, $100/26 wks, $195/yr

Mother Earth News
Published by Ogden Publications Inc
1503 SW 42 St, Topeka, KS 66609-1265
Tel: 785-274-4365 *Toll Free Tel:* 800-234-3368 *Fax:* 785-274-4305
E-mail: customerservice@motherearthnews.com
Web Site: www.motherearthnews.com
Key Personnel
Publr: Bill Uhler
Mng Ed: Amanda Sorell
Lead Ed: Karmin Garrison
Sustainable living magazine containing book reviews & articles of interest to active, educated people interested in self-sufficiency through renewable energy sources & lifestyles, with articles on ecology, do-it-yourself projects, gardening, natural health, green transportation, modern homesteading, sustainable farming & real food.
First published 1970
Frequency: 2 issues/mo
Circulation: 1,000,000
$7.50/issue; digital: $19.95/yr; digital & print: $39.95/yr, $47.95/yr CN, $52.95/yr foreign
ISSN: 0027-1535
Buy freelance nonfiction & art; Sell articles, reprints & back issues
Trim Size: 8 x 10 1/2

Mother Jones
Published by Foundation for National Progress
222 Sutter St, Suite 600, San Francisco, CA 94108
Mailing Address: PO Box 584, San Francisco, CA 94104-0584
Tel: 415-321-1700 *Toll Free Tel:* 800-438-6656
E-mail: backtalk@motherjones.com (comments to ed)
Web Site: www.motherjones.com
Key Personnel
CEO: Monika Bauerlein
Publr: Steven Katz
Ed-in-Chief: Clara Jeffery
Investigative reporting, national political news, features on important contemporary issues & commentary.
First published 1976
Book Use: Reviews & excerpts for a well-educated, affluent, politically liberal audience
Frequency: 6 issues/yr
Avg pages per issue: 100
Circulation: 200,000 paid
Print only: $12/yr US, $27/yr CN, $32/yr intl; print & digital: $18/yr US, $33/yr CN, $38/yr intl; digital only: $12/yr
ISSN: 0362-8841
Buy nonfiction, art & cartoons; Sell articles & reprints, back issues
Trim Size: 8 x 10 1/2
Ad Rates: B&W page $10,595, 4-color page $14,125

The Nation
Published by The Nation Co LLC
520 Eighth Ave, 21st fl, New York, NY 10018
Tel: 212-209-5400 *Toll Free Tel:* 800-333-8536 (cust serv) *Fax:* 212-982-9000
E-mail: subscription@thenation.com; adsales@thenation.com
Web Site: www.thenation.com
Key Personnel
Pres: Bhaskar Sunkara
Publr & Edit Dir: Katrina Vanden Heuvel
Assoc Publr, Ad: Suzette Cabildo *E-mail:* scabildo@thenation.com
Mng Ed: Rose D'Amora
Literary Ed: David Marcus
Assoc Literary Ed: Kevin Lozano
Politics, arts, foreign affairs, education & law. See magazine section *Books & the Arts*.
First published 1865
Book Use: Reviews
Frequency: Monthly
Avg pages per issue: 40
Circulation: 80,000
$9.99/issue; digital only: $24.95/yr, $3.99/mo; print & digital: $29.95/yr; add $26 for CN & $59 for overseas
ISSN: 0027-8378 (print); 2769-9684 (online)
Buy nonfiction, poetry & art (no fiction); Sell back issues
Trim Size: 7 1/8 x 9 3/4

National Defense Magazine
Published by National Defense Industrial Association (NDIA)
2101 Wilson Blvd, Suite 700, Arlington, VA 22201-3061
Tel: 703-522-1820
Web Site: www.nationaldefensemagazine.org
Key Personnel
Ed-in-Chief: Stew Magnuson *Tel:* 703-247-2545 *E-mail:* smagnuson@ndia.org
Mng Ed: Jon Harper *Tel:* 703-247-2542 *E-mail:* jharper@ndia.org
Creative Dir: Brian Taylor *Tel:* 703-247-2546 *E-mail:* btaylor@ndia.org
Sales Dir: Kathleen Kenney *Tel:* 703-247-2576 *E-mail:* kkenney@ndia.org
Technical, military & management articles & departments for military & industrial audience, including those in federal government. North American industrial base, acquisition officers in industry & military. No unsol mss, query first.

First published 1920
Frequency: Monthly
Circulation: total qualified 83,768; qualified paid 56,412
$5/issue, $40/yr, $45/yr foreign
ISSN: 0092-1491
Sell articles, ad reprints & back issues
Ad Rates: B&W page $6,665, 4-color page $8,580
Ad Closing Date(s): 8th of month preceding cover date

National Post
Published by Postmedia Network Inc
365 Bloor St E, 3rd fl, Toronto, ON M4W 3L4, Canada
Tel: 416-383-2300 *Toll Free Tel:* 800-267-6568
Fax: 416-383-2305
Web Site: nationalpost.com
Key Personnel
SVP, Content (Natl Post): Gerry Nott
Exec Prod, Features: Dustin Parks
E-mail: dparks@postmedia.com
Ed-in-Chief: Anne Marie Owens
Books Ed: Paul Taunton *Tel:* 416-645-8816
E-mail: ptaunton@postmedia.com

National Review
Published by National Review Inc
19 W 44 St, Suite 1701, New York, NY 10036
Tel: 212-679-7330 *Toll Free Tel:* 800-464-5526 (cust serv)
E-mail: letters@nationalreview.com
Web Site: www.nationalreview.com
Subscription Address: PO Box 433015, Palm Coast, FL 32143-3015
Key Personnel
Publr: E Garrett Bewkes, IV
Sales Dir: Jim Fowler *Tel:* 212-849-2843
E-mail: jfowler@nationalreview.com
Mng Ed: Jason Lee Steorts
Ed: Richard Lowry
Literary Ed: Katherine Howell
Conservative opinion; reports & analyzes national & international developments; includes: articles, editorials, social commentary, book & movie reviews & arts & manners.
First published 1955
Book Use: Reviews, commentary
Frequency: 24 issues/yr
Avg pages per issue: 64
Circulation: 160,000 paid
$59.99/yr print, $99/yr digital, $130/yr print & digital
ISSN: 0028-0038
Buy freelance fiction, nonfiction, poetry, art & cartoons; Sell back issues & reprints
Trim Size: 8 1/4 x 10 3/4
Ad Rates: B&W page $8,640, 4-color page $12,100
Ad Closing Date(s): 4 weeks preceding cover date

National Wildlife
Published by National Wildlife Federation
11100 Wildlife Center Dr, Reston, VA 20190-5362
Mailing Address: PO Box 1583, Merrifield, VA 22116-1583
Tel: 703-438-6000 *Toll Free Tel:* 800-822-9919 (membership)
E-mail: info@nwf.org
Web Site: www.nwf.org/magazines/national-wildlife
Key Personnel
Edit Dir: Jennifer Wehunt *E-mail:* nweditor@nwf.org
Nature & environment for a general audience.
First published 1962
Book Use: Occasional excerpts
Frequency: 6 issues/yr
Avg pages per issue: 52
Donation basis
ISSN: 0028-0402
Buy freelance, art & nonfiction; Sell back issues
Trim Size: 8 x 10 1/2

Nature
Published by Springer Nature
One New York Plaza, Suite 4500, New York, NY 10004-1562
Tel: 212-726-9200 *Toll Free Tel:* 888-331-6288
Fax: 212-696-9006
E-mail: feedback@nature.com
Web Site: www.nature.com
Subscription Address: Hampshire Intl Busn Park, Cromwell Place, Lime Tree Way, Basingstoke, Hants RG24 8YJ, United Kingdom
E-mail: subscriptions@nature.com
Key Personnel
VP, Magazines & Edit: Stephen Pincock
Ed-in-Chief: Magdalena Skipper
Mng Dir: Dean Sanderson
Sr Ed, Biology: Noah Gray
Books & Arts Ed: Barbara Kiser
Journal of original scientific research articles & letters, review articles, news of science in universities, industry & government; book reviews, correspondence & opinion. Available in print & online.
First published 1869
Book Use: Weekly review section
Frequency: 51 issues/yr
Circulation: 65,500 paid
Print & online: $199/yr indivs, $119/yr students
ISSN: 0028-0836 (print); 1476-4687 (online)
Sell articles, ad reprints & back issues
Trim Size: 8 1/4 x 11
Ad Rates: B&W page $12,015, 4-color page $14,410
Ad Closing Date(s): Film & camera ready material - 17 days prior to cover date

Nevada Magazine
Division of Nevada Department of Tourism & Cultural Affairs
401 N Carson St, Carson City, NV 89701
Tel: 775-687-0610 *Toll Free Tel:* 855-729-7117
Fax: 775-687-6159
E-mail: editor@nevadamagazine.com
Web Site: nevadamagazine.com
Key Personnel
Publr: Janet M Geary *Tel:* 775-687-0603
E-mail: jmgeary@nevadamagazine.com
Art Dir: Kippy Spilker *Tel:* 775-687-0606
E-mail: kspilker@nevadamagazine.com
Ed: Megg Mueller *Tel:* 775-687-0602
E-mail: mmueller@nevadamagazine.com
Ad & Mktg Mgr: Adele Hoppe *Tel:* 775-687-0605 *E-mail:* ahoppe@nevadamagazine.com
Circ Mgr: Carrie Roussel *Tel:* 775-687-0610
E-mail: carrie@nevadamagazine.com
For Nevada tourists & residents. Focuses on travel, recreation, Nevada dining, nature & entertainment.
First published 1936
Book Use: Reviews & excerpts on Nevada topics
Frequency: 6 issues/yr
Avg pages per issue: 80
Circulation: 20,000 paid
$9.95/yr digital, $21.95/yr print, $26.95/yr print & digital
ISSN: 0199-1248
Buy nonfiction; Sell back issues
Trim Size: 8 3/8 x 10 7/8
Ad Rates: 4-color page $4,000
Ad Closing Date(s): 1-2 months prior to issue

The New Criterion
Published by The Foundation for Cultural Review Inc
900 Broadway, Suite 602, New York, NY 10003
Tel: 212-247-6980 *Fax:* 212-247-3127
Web Site: www.newcriterion.com
Subscription Address: PO Box 3000, Denville, NJ 07834 *Toll Free Tel:* 800-783-4903
Key Personnel
Publr & Ed: Roger Kimball
Exec Ed: James Panero
Contains literary & cultural essays & poetry.
First published 1982
Book Use: Reviews
Frequency: Monthly (exc July & Aug)
Avg pages per issue: 80
Circulation: 7,000 paid
$7.75/issue, $48/yr, $62/yr CN, $70/yr foreign
ISSN: 0734-0222
Sell back issues ($12)
Ad Closing Date(s): 10th of each month prior to issue date

New Hampshire Sunday News & Union Leader
Published by Union Leader Corp
100 William Loeb Dr, Manchester, NH 03108-9555
Mailing Address: PO Box 9555, Manchester, NH 03108-9555
Tel: 603-668-4321
E-mail: news@unionleader.com
Web Site: www.unionleader.com
Key Personnel
Publr: Joe McQuaid *Tel:* 603-668-4321 ext 554
E-mail: publisher@unionleader.com
Mng Ed: Matt Sartwell *E-mail:* msartwell@unionleader.com
Exec Ed: Trent Spiner *E-mail:* tspiner@unionleader.com
HR Mgr: Sarah Neveu *Tel:* 603-668-4321 ext 296
E-mail: sneveu@unionleader.com
PR Mgr: Stephanie Baxter *Tel:* 603-668-4321 ext 506 *E-mail:* sbaxter@unionleader.com
Travel articles, building & repair sections; book reviews, arts & entertainment all in separate sections on Sunday. Looking for freelance articles.
First published 1863
Circulation: 90,000 (Sun)
$14.95/mo

New Haven Register
Published by Hearst Newspapers
Division of Hearst Corp
100 Gando Dr, New Haven, CT 06513
Tel: 203-789-5200 *Toll Free Tel:* 888-969-0949
Fax: 203-789-5705
E-mail: subscriptions@nhregister.com
Web Site: www.nhregister.com
Key Personnel
Exec Ed: Helen Bennett Harvey *Tel:* 203-789-5730 *E-mail:* helen.bennett@hearstmediact.com
Asst Mng Ed: Viktoria Sundqvist *Tel:* 860-685-9130 *E-mail:* viktoria.sundqvist@hearstmediact.com
Syndicated Sunday in *Arts & Leisure* section; in-house & weekly author interviews.
Circulation: 80,000 (m); 110,000 (Sun)
Digital & print: $2.99/wk (Sun only), $7.99/wk (Mon-Sun); digital only: $3/wk

New Mexico Magazine
Published by State of New Mexico
Lew Wallace Bldg, 495 Old Santa Fe Trail, Santa Fe, NM 87501
Tel: 505-827-7447 *Toll Free Tel:* 800-898-6639 (subns only)
E-mail: ask@nmmagazine.com; nm.magazine@state.nm.us
Web Site: www.newmexico.com/nmmagazine
Subscription Address: PO Box 12002, Sante Fe, NM 87504-9794
Key Personnel
Mng Ed & Soc Media Dir: Kate Nelson *Tel:* 505-476-0203 *E-mail:* kate.nelson@state.nm.us
Exec Ed: John Clary Davies *Tel:* 505-231-3759
E-mail: john.davies@state.nm.us
Sr Ed: Alicia Ines Guzman *Tel:* 505-490-0284
E-mail: alicia.guzman@state.nm.us

Circ Mgr: Kurt Coey *Tel:* 505-827-6387
E-mail: kurt.coey@state.nm.us
Stories & color photography on people, places, events, history, prehistory, art, architecture & food of interest to residents, visitors & students of the Southwest & New Mexico. No unsol mss, query first.
First published 1923
Frequency: Monthly
Avg pages per issue: 78
Circulation: 70,000
$25.95/yr, $45.95/yr CN & foreign
ISSN: 0028-6249
Buy fiction, nonfiction; Sell back issues
Trim Size: 8 1/4 x 10 3/4
Ad Closing Date(s): 2 months preceding publication

The New Orleans Advocate, see The Times-Picayune | The New Orleans Advocate

The New Republic
Published by Lake Avenue Publishing
One Union Sq W, New York, NY 10003
Tel: 646-779-8000 *Toll Free Tel:* 800-827-1289 (cust serv)
E-mail: letters@tnr.com (ms & letters to ed submissions); poetry@tnr.com (poetry submissions)
Web Site: newrepublic.com
Key Personnel
Publr & CEO: Michael Caruso
   E-mail: mcaruso@tnr.com
Edit Dir: Emily Cooke *E-mail:* emily@tnr.com
Ed-in-Chief: Win McCormack
Mng Ed: Lorraine Cademartori
   E-mail: lcademartori@tnr.com
Ed-at-Large: Chris Lehmann
Journal of opinion which includes literary criticism as well as arts & culture.
First published 1914
Book Use: Reviews
Frequency: 10 issues/yr
Avg pages per issue: 44
Circulation: 40,000 paid
$20/yr digital, $30/yr print & digital
ISSN: 0028-6583
Buy nonfiction, poetry & art; Sell articles & ad reprints, back issues (syndicated)
Trim Size: 8 x 10 1/2
Ad Rates: B&W full page $6,340, 4-color full page $9,060
Ad Closing Date(s): 4 weeks preceding cover dates, see web site

New Spanish Books
Published by Trade Commission in Miami, Embassy of Spain in the US
2655 Le Juene Rd, Suite 1114, Miami, FL 33134
Tel: 305-446-4387 *Fax:* 305-446-2602
E-mail: info@newspanishbooks.com
Web Site: www.newspanishbooks.us
Annual online compilation/guide to current Spanish titles, selected by a panel of experts from the US, with rights available for translation in the US. Includes up-to-date information about the Spanish publishing scene, translation grants, Spanish literary prizes, recent translations, news & events in the US & more.

New York Daily News, see Daily News

New York Magazine
Published by New York Media LLC
75 Varick St, 4th fl, New York, NY 10013
Tel: 212-508-0700 *Toll Free Tel:* 800-678-0900 (subns)
E-mail: contactus@nymag.com
Web Site: nymag.com
Key Personnel
Mng Ed: Anne Clarke
Books Ed: Maris Kreizman
Prodn Coord: Gail Smith *E-mail:* gail.smith@nymag.com
Book Critic: Andrea Long Chu; Christian Lorentzen
Biweekly. Deals with contemporary lifestyles & personalities in the New York metropolitan area. Covers politics, business, fine arts, entertainment, home furnishings, food, wine & fashion.
First published 1968
Frequency: 29 issues/yr
Avg pages per issue: 140
Circulation: 378,757
$5/mo digital, $70/yr print & digital
ISSN: 0028-7369
Buy art, nonfiction; Sell articles & back issues
Trim Size: 7 7/8 x 10 1/2
Ad Rates: See web site
Ad Closing Date(s): 2 weeks prior to on sale date

New York Post Inc
Published by NYP Holdings Inc
Division of Newscorp
1211 Avenue of the Americas, New York, NY 10036-8790
Tel: 212-930-8000 *Toll Free Tel:* 800-552-7678 (cust serv)
E-mail: slareau@nypost.com
Web Site: www.nypost.com
Key Personnel
Group VP, Ad: Patrick Judge
Natl Ad: Scott Lareau *E-mail:* slareau@nypost.com
Reviews in-house, through syndication & other outside sources.
Circulation: 428,238 (d)
$2.50/wk (Sat & Sun or Fri-Sun), $4.99/wk (Mon-Fri or Mon-Sun)

The New York Review of Books
Published by NYREV Inc
435 Hudson St, Suite 300, New York, NY 10014-3994
Tel: 212-757-8070 *Fax:* 212-333-5374
E-mail: mail@nybooks.com
Web Site: www.nybooks.com
Subscription Address: PO Box 9310, Big Sandy, TX 75755-9310 *Toll Free Tel:* 800-354-0050
   E-mail: nyrsub@nybooks.info *Web Site:* www.nybooks.com
Key Personnel
Publr: Mr Rea S Hederman
Exec Ed: Jana Prikryl
Sr Ed: Hugh Eakin; Gabriel Winslow-Yost
Ed: Emily Greenhouse
Prodn Ed: Daniel Drake
Ed-at-Large: Daniel Mendelsohn
Off Mgr: Diane Seltzer *E-mail:* dseltzer@nybooks.com
Literary journal. Articles by American & European writers.
First published 1963
Book Use: Essay-length book reviews
Frequency: 20 issues/yr
Avg pages per issue: 64
Circulation: 134,503
$8.95/issue, $74.95/yr
ISSN: 0028-7504
Sell $15/back issue within the US, $25/back issue outside the US
Trim Size: 10 3/4 x 14 5/8
Ad Rates: B&W page $13,775, 4-color page $15,841
Ad Closing Date(s): 37 days prior to cover date

The New York Times
Published by The New York Times Co
620 Eighth Ave, New York, NY 10018
Tel: 212-556-1234 *Toll Free Tel:* 800-698-4637 (cust serv)
E-mail: books@nytimes.com
Web Site: www.nytimes.com
Key Personnel
Exec Ed: Dean Baquet
Sr Staff Ed: Lauren Christensen
Books Ed: Gilbert Cruz
Children's Book Ed: Jennifer Krauss
Op-Ed Ed: Jim Dao; Vanessa Mobley
Deputy Ed, News & Features: Juliana Barbassa
Book Critic: Dwight Garner; Alexandra Jacobs; Molly Young
Nonfiction Critic: Jennifer Ildiko Szalai
Daily column; Sunday section.
Circulation: 1,718,400 (Sun)
Digital & print: $10/wk (Sat & Sun), $11/wk (Fri-Sun), $12/wk (Mon-Fri), $18/wk (Mon-Sun); digital only: $4/mo

The New York Times Book Review
Published by The New York Times Co
620 Eighth Ave, 5th fl, New York, NY 10018
Tel: 212-556-1234 *Toll Free Tel:* 800-631-2580 (subns)
E-mail: bookreview@nytimes.com; books@nytimes.com
Web Site: www.nytimes.com
Key Personnel
Mng Ed: David Kelly
Asst Mng Ed: Sam Sifton
Deputy Ed: Tina Jordan
Sr Ed: Gregory Cowles; Emily Eakin
Sr Staff Ed: Jennifer Harlan
Books Ed: Gilbert Cruz
Narrative Features Ed: Elisabeth Egan
Preview Ed: MJ Franklin; Neima Jahromi; Dave Kim; Sadie Stein
Contributing Essayist: Jennifer Wilson
Critic-at-Large: AO Scott
Review books & essays related to publishing & published in the US & available through general interest bookstores. By subscription only.
$4/wk US, $4.95/wk CN, $5.50/wk foreign
ISSN: 0028-7806

The New Yorker
Published by Conde Nast
One World Trade Center, 38th fl, New York, NY 10007-0090
Tel: 212-286-2860; 515-243-3273 (subns)
Toll Free Tel: 800-444-7570
E-mail: fiction@newyorker.com (fiction submissions); TNY_shouts@advancemags.com (Shouts & Murmurs submissions)
Web Site: www.newyorker.com; www.condenast.com
Key Personnel
Ed: David Remnick
Fiction Ed: Deborah Treisman
Poetry Ed: Kevin Young
Story Ed: Namara Smith
Staff Writer: Kathryn Schulz; Parul Sehgal; Katy Waldman
Discusses current ideas & events, combining domestic & international news analysis with cartoons, criticism of sports, fashion & arts, biographical profiles, short fiction & poetry. Carries entertainment guide for New York. Send fiction & Shouts & Murmurs submissions by e-mail as noted above. Poetry submissions via Submittable only, see web site. No unsol Talk of the Town stories or other nonfiction. No unsol submissions by fax accepted.
First published 1925
Book Use: Reviews
Frequency: Weekly
Avg pages per issue: 112
Circulation: 1,035,428
$1/wk
ISSN: 0028-792X
Trim Size: 7 7/8 x 10 3/4
Ad Rates: 4-color full page $180,343, 1/2 page $108,169

The News & Observer
Published by The News & Observer Publishing Co
421 Fayetteville St, Suite 104, Raleigh, NC 27601
Tel: 919-829-4500 *Toll Free Tel:* 800-522-4205 (cust serv)
E-mail: customerservice@newsobserver.com
Web Site: www.newsobserver.com
Key Personnel
Mng Ed: Jane Elizabeth *Tel:* 919-836-5909
  E-mail: jelizabeth@newsobserver.com
Features Ed: Jessica Banov *Tel:* 919-829-4831
  E-mail: jbanov@newsobserver.com
Sunday, two-page review section; column by J Peder Zane; occasional author interviews.
Circulation: 165,000 (m); 205,000 (Sun)
Digital: $12.99/mo, $129.99/yr

News & Record
Published by BH Media Group Inc
200 E Market St, Greensboro, NC 27401
Tel: 336-373-7000; 336-274-5476 (subns)
  Toll Free Tel: 800-553-6880
E-mail: feedback@greensboro.com; subscriberservices@greensboro.com
Web Site: www.greensboro.com
Key Personnel
Publr: Alton Brown *Tel:* 336-727-7349
  E-mail: abrown@wsjournal.com
Mng Ed: Cindy Loman *Tel:* 336-373-7212
  E-mail: cindy.lowman@greensboro.com
Edit Page Ed: Allen Johnson *Tel:* 336-373-7010
  E-mail: allen.johnson@greensboro.com
Once a week; occasional author interviews, separate book page. Book reviews in-house, syndicated & through other outside sources.
Circulation: 60,000 (m); 70,000 (Sun)
Digital & print: $11.10/mo (Wed-Sun), $13.23/mo (Sun only), $27.89/mo (Mon-Sun); digital only: $8.95/mo

The News-Star
Published by Gannett Co Inc
411 N Fourth St, Monroe, LA 71201
Tel: 318-322-5161 *Toll Free Tel:* 800-259-7788; 877-424-0036 (cust serv)
Web Site: www.thenewsstar.com
Key Personnel
Ed: Barbara Leader *Tel:* 318-362-0262
Occasional weekly column.
Frequency: Daily
Circulation: 22,000 (d); 26,000 (Sun)
Digital & print: $12/mo (Sun only), $24/mo (Mon-Sun); digital only: $9.99/mo

The News-Times
Published by Hearst Newspapers
Division of Hearst Corp
333 Main St, Danbury, CT 06810
Tel: 203-744-5100 *Fax:* 203-792-8730 (edit)
Web Site: www.newstimes.com
Key Personnel
Features Ed: Linda Tuccio-Koonz *Tel:* 203-731-3330 *E-mail:* lkoonz@newstimes.com
Especially interested in Connecticut authors & women's issues in general. Food trends, local arts, local pop culture, music, theater, home decor & fashion (need Connecticut angle).
Book Use: Book reviews, author interviews; Sunday features, travel, trends, food, cooking
Frequency: Daily
Circulation: 38,000
$3.50/wk digital

The News Tribune
Published by The McClatchy Co
1950 S State St, Tacoma, WA 98405
Tel: 253-597-8742 *Fax:* 253-597-8274
Web Site: www.thenewstribune.com
Key Personnel
Pres & Publr: Rebecca Poynter *Tel:* 253-597-8554
  E-mail: rebecca.poynter@thenewstribune.com
Ed & VP, News: Dale Phelps *Tel:* 253-597-8681
  E-mail: dale.phelps@thenewstribune.com
Local Sales Dir: Rob White *Tel:* 253-597-8407
  E-mail: rob.white@thenewstribune.com
Sunday; book review off the wire & freelance; local columnist who writes book reviews with a national & local focus; literary calendar of book signings; bestseller lists featured.
Circulation: 38,762 (d); 87,332 (Sun)
Digital & print: $26/13 wks (Sun only), $45.50/13 wks (Fri-Sun), $71.50/13 wks (Mon-Sun); digital only: $12.99/mo, $129.99/yr

News Tribune
Published by Central Missouri Newspapers Inc
210 Monroe St, Jefferson City, MO 65101
Tel: 573-636-3131
E-mail: editor@newstribune.com
Web Site: www.newstribune.com
Key Personnel
Mng Ed: Gary Castor *Tel:* 573-761-0255
  E-mail: gary@newstribune.com
Frequency: Daily
Circulation: 2,700 (m); 17,000 (e); 24,300 (Sun)
$21/mo print & digital

Newsday
Published by Newsday Media Group
235 Pinelawn Rd, Melville, NY 11747
Tel: 631-843-2700 *Toll Free Tel:* 800-639-7329 (cust care)
Web Site: www.newsday.com
Key Personnel
Ed: Deborah Henley *E-mail:* editor@newsday.com
Sunday review section; weekly author interviews; in-house & freelance.
Circulation: 404,542 (d); 476,723 (Sun)
Digital & print: $1.99 wk (Sun only), $5.99/wk (Mon-Sun); digital only: $3.49/wk

Newsweek
Published by Newsweek Media Group
33 Whitehall St, New York, NY 10004
Tel: 646-867-7100
E-mail: enquiries@newsweek.com; support@newsweek.com
Web Site: www.newsweek.com
Key Personnel
Global Ed-in-Chief: Nancy Cooper
Edit Dir: Hank Gilman
Mng Ed: Melissa Jewsbury
Weekly news magazine, (in print, online & on mobile devices), features news & commentary on the week's developments in the nation & the world. Articles cover national & international affairs, science, sports, business, medicine, religion, entertainment & the arts. International editions also available.
First published 1933
Book Use: Reviews, excerpts
Frequency: Weekly
Avg pages per issue: 105
$99/yr print or digital, $129/yr print & digital
ISSN: 0028-9604
Buy nonfiction, poetry, art, cartoons; Sell articles, ad reprints & back issues
Trim Size: 8 1/8 x 10 1/2

The North Platte Telegraph
Published by BH Media Group Inc
621 N Chestnut St, North Platte, NE 69101
Mailing Address: PO Box 370, North Platte, NE 69103-0370
Tel: 308-532-6000 *Toll Free Tel:* 800-753-7092 *Fax:* 308-532-9268
E-mail: editor@nptelegraph.com
Web Site: www.nptelegraph.com
Key Personnel
Publr: Dee Klein *Tel:* 308-535-4708
  E-mail: dklein@nptelegraph.com
Mng Ed: Joan von Kampen *Tel:* 308-535-4707
  E-mail: joan.vonkampen@nptelegraph.com
Frequent Western author interviews & book reviews.
Circulation: 8,100
$6.50/mo digital, $22.94/mo digital & print, $35.97/mo digital & print (mail delivery)

Nutrition Health Review
Published by Matrix Medical Communications
1595 Paoli Pike, Suite 201, West Chester, PA 19380
Tel: 464-266-0702 *Toll Free Tel:* 866-325-9975; 866-325-9907 *Fax:* 464-266-0726
E-mail: info@matrixmedcom.com
Web Site: nutritionhealthreview.com
Key Personnel
Dir: Joseph Scullin *E-mail:* jscullin@matrixmedcom.com
Mng Ed: Julia Eckert *E-mail:* jeckert@matrixmedcom.com
Publishes a variety of evidence-based research articles aimed at educating the public on a wide range of topics related to nutrition & diet, physical fitness & exercise & overall general wellness. Published in partnership with the Vegetus Foundation.
First published 1975
Frequency: 6 issues/yr
Avg pages per issue: 20
Circulation: 6,000
$18/yr
ISSN: 0164-7202
Trim Size: 11 x 17

Ocala Star-Banner
Published by GateHouse Media LLC
2121 SW 19 Avenue Rd, Ocala, FL 34471
Tel: 352-867-4010 *Toll Free Tel:* 800-541-2172
E-mail: osbletters@starbanner.com
Web Site: www.ocala.com
Key Personnel
Publr: Robin Quillon
Mng Ed: Jim Ross *E-mail:* jim.ross@starbanner.com
Circulation: 45,000
Digital & print: $78/13 wks (Sun only), $143/13 wks (Thurs-Sun), $169/13 wks (Mon-Sun); digital only: $12.95/mo

Ohio Magazine
Published by Great Lakes Publishing
1422 Euclid Ave, Suite 730, Cleveland, OH 44115
Tel: 614-461-5083 (sales); 216-771-2833
  Toll Free Tel: 800-210-7293 (cust care)
E-mail: editorial@ohiomagazine.com
Web Site: www.ohiomagazine.com
Key Personnel
Pres: Lute Harmon, Jr
Assoc Publr & Ad Dir: Karen Matusoff
Dir, Prodn: Steven A Zemanek
Sr Ed: Linda Feagler
Ed: Jim Vickers
Covers general Ohio topics for upscale audience. Occasional stories about Ohio authors.
First published 1978
Book Use: Reviews & excerpts
Frequency: Monthly
Avg pages per issue: 132
Circulation: 52,424
$17.98/yr, $29.97/2 yrs, $38.83/3 yrs
ISSN: 0279-3504
Buy Ohio-related nonfiction, essays & art; Sell articles & back issues

The Oklahoman
Published by Oklahoma Publishing Co
100 W Main, Suite 100, Oklahoma City, OK 73102
Mailing Address: PO Box 25125, Oklahoma City, OK 73125

& PUBLICITY

Tel: 405-475-3311; 405-478-7171 (cust serv)
Toll Free Tel: 877-987-2737
Web Site: oklahoman.com
Key Personnel
Publr & Ed: Kelly Dyer Fry *E-mail:* kfry@oklahoman.com
Features Ed: Matthew Price *E-mail:* mprice@oklahoman.com
Sunday column & review page; in-house; occasional author interviews.
Circulation: 226,059 (m); 214,746 (Sat); 333,000 (Sun)
Digital & print: $2.77/wk (Wed & Sun), $4.50/wk (Mon-Sun); digital only: $9.99/mo
Avg reviews per issue: 6-8

The Olympian
Published by The McClatchy Co
522 Franklin St SE, Olympia, WA 98501
Tel: 360-754-5400 *Fax:* 360-357-0202
E-mail: news@theolympian.com
Web Site: www.theolympian.com
Key Personnel
Exec Ed: Dusti Demarest *Tel:* 360-357-0206 *E-mail:* ddemarest@theolympian.com
Sunday page, new book review.
Circulation: 25,455 (m); 30,007 (Sun)
Digital & print: $26/13 wks (Sun only), $45.50/13 wks (Fri-Sun), $71.50/13 wks (Mon-Sun); digital only: $12.99/mo, $129.99/yr

Omaha World-Herald Sunday Arts Section
Published by BH Media Group Inc
1314 Douglas St, Suite 700, Omaha, NE 68102
Tel: 402-444-1000 *Toll Free Tel:* 800-BUG-NEWS (284-6397)
E-mail: news@owh.com
Web Site: www.omaha.com
Key Personnel
Pres & Publr: Todd Sears *Tel:* 402-444-1179 *E-mail:* todd.sears@owh.com
Exec Ed: Melissa Matczak *Tel:* 402-444-1088 *E-mail:* melissa.matczak@owh.com
Sunday, 1 page, reviews by syndication & in-house, frequent author interviews.
Circulation: 95,616 paid
Digital & print: $19.50/mo (Sun only), $23.84/mo (Fri-Sun), $49.95/mo (Mon-Sun); digital only: $9.95/mo, $99.95/yr

The Orange County Register
Published by MediaNews Group Inc
2190 S Towne Centre Place, Anaheim, CA 92806
Tel: 714-796-7000
Web Site: www.ocregister.com
Subscription Address: Box 11626, Santa Ana, CA 92701
Key Personnel
Pres & Publr: Ron Hasse *Tel:* 818-713-3883 *E-mail:* publisher@scng.com
VP, Opers: John Merendino *E-mail:* jmerendino@scng.com
Exec Ed: Frank Pine *Tel:* 909-483-9360 *E-mail:* editor@scng.com
Dir, Circ: Kat Wang *E-mail:* kwang@scng.com
Sunday, 2 pages; book reviews in-house, through syndication & freelance; author interviews 4-5 times per month.
Frequency: Daily
Circulation: 236,770 (d); 299,339 (Sun)
Digital & print: $12.50/4 wks (Sun only), $15/4 wks (Thurs-Sun), $25/4 wks (Mon-Sun); digital only: $10/4 wks

The Oregonian
Published by Oregonian Media Group
1500 SW First Ave, Portland, OR 97201
Tel: 503-221-8240 (subns); 503-221-8481 (ad)
Toll Free Tel: 800-452-1420 (outside OR)
Web Site: oregonlive.com
Key Personnel
Ed & VP, Content: Therese Bottomly *Tel:* 503-221-8434 *E-mail:* tbottomly@oregonian.com
Mng Prodr: Kjerstin Gabrielson *Tel:* 503-412-7012 *E-mail:* kgabrielson@oregonian.com
In-house & freelance, Sunday book section; frequent author interviews & book reviews.
First published 1850
Circulation: 354,000 (d); 440,000 (Sun)
Digital & print: $4.99/wk (Wed & Sun), $6/wk (Wed & Fri-Sun); digital only: $6/wk

The Orlando Sentinel
Published by Tribune Publishing Co
633 N Orange Ave, Orlando, FL 32801
Tel: 407-420-5000
Web Site: www.orlandosentinel.com
Key Personnel
Publr & Gen Mgr: Nancy A Meyer *E-mail:* nmeyer@tribpub.com
Ed-in-Chief: Julie Anderson *E-mail:* janderson@sunsentinel.com
Mng Ed: Roger Simmons *E-mail:* rsimmons@orlandosentinel.com
Syndicated; in-house. Frequent author interviews & book blog.
First published 1876
Circulation: 300,000 (d & Sat); 400,000 (Sun)
Digital & print: $2.49/wk (Thurs & Sun), $4.99/wk (Mon-Sun); digital only: $1.99/wk

Ottawa Citizen
Published by Postmedia Network Inc
1101 Baxter Rd, Box 5020, Ottawa, ON K2C 3M4, Canada
Tel: 613-829-9100; 613-596-3664 (newsroom); 613-596-3590 (ad); 613-596-1950 (reader sales & serv) *Toll Free Tel:* 800-267-6100 (reader sales & serv); 888-744-3725 (classified)
E-mail: subscriberservices@ottawacitizen.com (reader sales & serv)
Web Site: ottawacitizen.com
Key Personnel
Ed: Michelle Richardson *Tel:* 613-726-5960 *E-mail:* mirichardson@postmedia.com
Deputy Ed: Chris Aung-Thwin *Tel:* 343-998-6066 *E-mail:* caungthwin@postmedia.com
Edit Pages Ed: Christina Spencer *Tel:* 613-596-3559 *E-mail:* cspencer@postmedia.com
Dir, Fin: Shirley Tam *Tel:* 613-596-3597 *E-mail:* stam@ottawacitizen.com
Weekly hardcover & paperback reviews, with in-house & freelance children's book column & weekly author interviews. Pre-Christmas book review section, extra pages Spring & Fall.
Print, digital & e-paper: $26/mo (Fri & Sat), $39/mo (Mon-Sat); digital only: $9.95/mo; e-paper only: $9.99/mo
ISSN: 0839-3222

Outdoor Life®
Published by Bonnier Corp
Division of The Bonnier Group
2 Park Ave, New York, NY 10016
Tel: 212-779-5000
Web Site: www.outdoorlife.com
Subscription Address: PO Box 6364, Harlan, IA 51593-1864 *Tel:* 515-237-3697 *Toll Free Tel:* 800-365-1580 *E-mail:* odlcustserv@cdsfulfillment.com *Web Site:* www.outdoorlife.com/cs
Key Personnel
Group Edit Dir: Anthony Licata
Mng Ed: Jean McKenna *Tel:* 212-779-5000 ext 5290
Articles on hunting, fishing, conservation, gun dogs, humor; for the outdoor sports person & family. No unsol mss, query first.
First published 1898
Frequency: 10 issues/yr
Circulation: 750,000
$12/yr US, $26/yr CN, $40/yr intl

SERIALS FEATURING BOOKS

Buy freelance, nonfiction, art, photos & illustrations
Trim Size: 7 7/8 x 10 1/2
Ad Rates: B&W full page $53,200, 4-color full page $66,150
Ad Closing Date(s): See www.outdoorlife.com/advertising

Outside Magazine
Published by Outside Integrated Media LLC
Outside Plaza, 400 Market St, Santa Fe, NM 87501
Tel: 505-989-7100 *Fax:* 505-989-4700
Web Site: www.outsideonline.com
Subscription Address: PO Box 6228, Harlan, IA 51593-1728 *Toll Free Tel:* 800-678-1131 *E-mail:* oumcustserv@cdsfulfillment.com
Key Personnel
Ed-in-Chief: Lawrence J Burke
Ed: Christopher Keyes *E-mail:* ckeyes@outsideim.com
Contemporary lifestyles for active adults; features sports, fitness, photography, adventure, travel & portraits of men & women adventurers; reviews wildlife, outdoor sports gear & clothing, product news, destination/travel options & environmental & political issues.
First published 1976
Book Use: Reviews & excerpts
Frequency: Monthly
Circulation: 675,000 paid
$24/yr, $36/2 yrs print & digital
ISSN: 0278-1433
Buy freelance nonfiction & art; Sell back issues
Trim Size: 8 x 10 7/8
Ad Rates: B&W page $98,190, full color page $101,750
Ad Closing Date(s): Last week in the month

Pacific Northwest Magazine
Published by The Seattle Times
1000 Denny Way, Seattle, WA 98109
Mailing Address: PO Box 70, Seattle, WA 98111
Tel: 206-464-2111 *Toll Free Tel:* 800-542-0820 (cust serv)
E-mail: customerservice@seattletimes.com
Web Site: www.seattletimes.com/pacific-nw-magazine
Key Personnel
Magazine Ed: Bill Reader *Tel:* 206-464-2416 *E-mail:* breader@seattletimes.com
Assoc Ed: Sandy Dunham *Tel:* 206-464-2252 *E-mail:* sdunham@seattletimes.com
Sunday general interest regional magazine, 1-2 book sections per year; author profiles.
Circulation: 821,800
Digital & print: $3.99/wk (Sun only), $8.70/wk (Mon-Sun); digital only: $4.99/wk
Ad Rates: Full page $6,880, 1/2 page $3,665
Ad Closing Date(s): 20 days prior to publication date

The Palm Beach Post
Published by GateHouse Media LLC
2751 S Dixie Hwy, West Palm Beach, FL 33405
Tel: 561-820-4663 *Toll Free Tel:* 800-926-7678
E-mail: breakingnews@pbpost.com
Web Site: www.palmbeachpost.com
Key Personnel
Mng Ed: Nicholas Moschella *Tel:* 561-820-4441 *E-mail:* nmoschella@pbpost.com
Culture Ed: Larry Aydlette *Tel:* 561-820-4436 *E-mail:* laydlette@pbpost.com
In-house & through syndication. Author interviews.
First published 1916
Circulation: 220,000
Digital & print: $3.45/wk (Sun only), $7.38/wk (Mon-Sun)
ISSN: 1528-5758

Palo Alto Weekly
Published by Embarcadero Media
450 Cambridge Ave, Palo Alto, CA 94306
Tel: 650-326-8210 *Fax:* 650-326-3928
E-mail: editor@paweekly.com
Web Site: www.paloaltoonline.com
Key Personnel
Pres & Publr: William S Johnson *Tel:* 650-223-6505 *E-mail:* bjohnson@paweekly.com
Arts & Entertainment Ed: Karla Kane *Tel:* 650-223-6517
News weekly serving Palo Alto, Stanford University, Menlo Park, Los Altos Hills, Portola Valley, CA; monthly book section.
First published 1979
Frequency: Weekly (Fri)
Circulation: 37,000

Parade Magazine, see AMG/Parade

Parents Magazine
Published by Meredith Corporation
225 Liberty St, New York, NY 10281
Toll Free Tel: 800-727-3682 (subns)
E-mail: pmmcustserv@cdsfulfillment.com (subns)
Web Site: www.parents.com
Key Personnel
Exec Ed: Julia Dennison
Deputy Ed: Melissa Bykofsky
Features Ed: Anna Halkidis
Contains articles on family formation & growth for young mothers, with features on food, home, beauty, fashion, child development, marriage, work, money, health, fathers, education.
First published 1926
Book Use: Reviews of adult & juvenile fiction
Frequency: Monthly
Avg pages per issue: 225
Circulation: 2,200,000
$9.98/yr
ISSN: 0161-4193
Buy nonfiction & art; no unsol mss, query first
Trim Size: 7 7/8 x 10 1/2
Ad Rates: B&W full page $198,700, 4-color full page $254,400
Ad Closing Date(s): 15th of month, 2 months prior to issue date

The Paris Review
Published by The Paris Review Foundation
544 W 27 St, New York, NY 10001
Tel: 212-343-1333
E-mail: queries@theparisreview.org
Web Site: www.theparisreview.org
Subscription Address: PO Box 8524, Big Sandy, TX 75755-8524 *Tel:* 903-636-1118 *Toll Free Tel:* 866-354-0212 *E-mail:* subscriptions@theparisreview.org
Key Personnel
Publr: Mona Simpson
Publg Dir: Lori Dorr *E-mail:* ldorr@theparisreview.org
Digital Dir: Craig Teicher
Mng Ed: Hasan Altaf
Ed: Emily Stokes
Poetry Ed: Vijay Seshadri
Literary quarterly dedicated to bringing the works of new & established writers to the critical attention of an educated audience. See web site for submission policy.
First published 1953
Book Use: Excerpts
Frequency: Quarterly
Avg pages per issue: 200
Circulation: 23,000
$49/yr US, $54/yr CN, $64/yr foreign
ISSN: 0031-2037
Sell back issues
Trim Size: 9 1/4 x 6 1/8
Ad Rates: B&W full page $3,000, 4-color full page $4,500

The Pasadena Citizen
Published by Hearst Newspapers
c/o Houston Chronicle, PO Box 4260, Houston, TX 77210
Tel: 713-362-7211
E-mail: help@chron.com
Web Site: www.chron.com/neighborhood/pasadena
Key Personnel
Ed: Greg May *Tel:* 713-362-4013 *E-mail:* greg.may@chron.com
Division of the *Houston Chronicle*.

Pasatiempo, The Santa Fe New Mexican
Published by The New Mexican Inc
150 Washington Ave, Santa Fe, NM 87501
Mailing Address: PO Box 2048, Santa Fe, NM 87504-2021
Tel: 505-983-3303
Web Site: www.santafenewmexican.com/pasatiempo/
Key Personnel
Ed: Carolyn Graham *E-mail:* cgraham@sfnewmexican.com
Arts & entertainment magazine included with Friday edition of The Santa Fe New Mexican. 1-2 author interviews per week, in-house book reviews.
Frequency: Weekly
Circulation: 27,000
$1/daily, $1.25/Sun & Fri
Avg reviews per issue: 3

The Patriot Ledger
Published by GateHouse Media LLC
400 Crown Colony Dr, Quincy, MA 02169-0916
Mailing Address: PO Box 699159, Quincy, MA 02269-9159
Tel: 617-786-7000; 617-786-7026 *Fax:* 617-786-7335
E-mail: features@ledger.com
Web Site: www.patriotledger.com
Key Personnel
Mng Ed: Ken Johnson *Tel:* 617-786-7052 *E-mail:* kenjohnson@patriotledger.com
Features Ed: Dana Barbuto *Tel:* 617-786-7074 *E-mail:* dbarbuto@ledger.com
Weekly, in-house & through syndication. Weekly author interviews occasionally.
Circulation: 50,000 (e); 60,000 (Sat)
Digital & print: $24/12 wks (Sat only), $48/12 wks (Mon-Sat); e-paper: $95/yr; digital only: $9.95/mo

Pennsylvania Literary Journal (PLJ)
Published by Anaphora Literary Press
1108 W Third St, Quanah, TX 79252
Tel: 470-289-6395
Web Site: anaphoraliterary.com/journals/plj
Key Personnel
Dir & Ed-in-Chief: Anna Faktorovich, PhD *E-mail:* director@anaphoraliterary.com
Scholarly & creative journal, which publishes researched essays, short fiction, poems, nonfiction, personal essays, interviews, book reviews & other works. An extensive book review section is included in every issue. Special issues range from Interviews with Best-Selling Young Adult Writers, British Literature, New Historicism, New Formalism & editing technique. It is cataloged in the *MLA International Bibliography*, the *MLA Directory of Periodicals*, *Genamics JournalSeek* & *Duotrope's Digest*. PLJ has published works by & interviews with New York Times bestselling writers like Larry Niven & Cinda Williams Chima. Only e-mailed submissions accepted.
First published 2009
Frequency: 3 issues/yr
Avg pages per issue: 200
Circulation: 20 copies/issue, plus EBSCO & ProQuest online viewing
$75/yr US, $100/yr elsewhere

ISSN: 2151-3066
Avg reviews per issue: 20 books/issue, 60 books/yr
Trim Size: 6 x 9

Pensacola News Journal
Published by Gannett Co Inc
2 N Palasox St, Pensacola, FL 32502
Tel: 850-435-8500 *Toll Free Tel:* 877-424-0028 (cust serv)
E-mail: online@pnj.com
Web Site: www.pnj.com
Key Personnel
Publr: Lisa Reese *Tel:* 850-435-8565
Exec Ed: Lisa Nellessen Savage *Tel:* 850-435-8514 *E-mail:* lnelless@gannett.com
Produced in-house with occasional author interviews. Local weekend entertainment in *Weekender* magazine inserted in Friday daily paper.
Circulation: 42,000 (d); 52,000 (Sun)

Penthouse
Published by Penthouse World Digital LLC
8944 Mason Ave, Chatsworth, CA 91311
E-mail: letters@penthouse.com; support@penthouse.zendesk.com
Web Site: penthousemagazine.com
Articles range from contemporary comment to photographic essays on beautiful women. Features interviews, sports, humor, politics, national & international issues.
First published 1965
Frequency: 6 issues/yr
Print: $13.99/newsstand issue, $24.95/yr, $36.95/yr intl; $42.95/2 yrs, $66.95/2 yrs intl; digital: $9.99/issue, $24.99/yr, $39.99/2 yrs
ISSN: 0090-2020
Sell reprints & back issues

People
Published by Meredith Corporation
225 Liberty St, New York, NY 10281
Tel: 212-522-1212 *Toll Free Tel:* 877-604-6512 (cust serv)
Web Site: www.people.com
Subscription Address: PO Box 60001, Tampa, FL 33660-0001 *Toll Free Tel:* 800-541-9000
Key Personnel
SVP & Publr: Cece Ryan *Tel:* 212-522-7130 *E-mail:* cece.ryan@meredith.com
VP & Assoc Publr: Lana Lorusso *Tel:* 212-522-7130 *E-mail:* cece.ryan@meredith.com
Exec Ed, Books: Kate Tuttle
Personality journalism, focusing on the pacesetters of the news, film & TV, the arts & sciences, as well as ordinary people in extraordinary circumstances.
First published 1974
Frequency: Weekly
Avg pages per issue: 126
Circulation: 3,400,000
$5.99/issue
ISSN: 0093-7673
Sell articles & ad reprints, back issues
Trim Size: 7 7/8 x 10 1/2
Ad Rates: B&W page $282,100, 4-color page $402,900 (non-bleed)
Ad Closing Date(s): 5 weeks before issue date

The Peterborough Examiner
Published by Metroland Media Group Ltd
Subsidiary of Torstar Corp
60 Hunter St E, Peterborough, ON K9H 1G5, Canada
Tel: 705-745-4641
Web Site: www.peterboroughexaminer.com
Key Personnel
Ad Dir: Michael Everson *Tel:* 705-745-4641 ext 2431 *E-mail:* michael.everson@peterboroughdaily.com
Mng Ed: Kennedy Gordon *Tel:* 705-745-4641 ext 2438 *E-mail:* kennedy.gordon@peterboroughdaily.com

Occasional interviews with local authors, wire service-Canadian Press.
Circulation: 23,000 (e)

Phi Delta Kappan
Published by PDK International
1820 N Fort Myer Dr, Suite 320, Arlington, VA 22209
Mailing Address: PO Box 13090, Arlington, VA 22219
Tel: 812-339-1156 *Toll Free Tel:* 800-766-1156 *Fax:* 812-339-0018
E-mail: kappan@pdkintl.org
Web Site: kappanonline.org; www.pdkintl.org; journals.sagepub.com/home/pdk
Key Personnel
Ed-in-Chief: Teresa Preston *E-mail:* tpreston@pdkintl.org
Mng Ed: Kathleen Vail
Creative Servs Mgr: Justine Hirshfeld *Tel:* 571-207-9677 *E-mail:* jhirshfeld@pdkintl.org
Creative Servs Specialist: Linda Fisher
Edit Specialist: Mary Stegmeir
Contains articles on research, policy & practice in K-12 education.
First published 1915
Book Use: Occasional excerpts
Frequency: 8 issues/yr
Avg pages per issue: 80
Circulation: 18,000
Institutional: $170 print only, $147 online only, $173 print & online, $23 single print issue
ISSN: 0031-7217 (print); 1940-6487 (online)
Buy nonfiction, art & cartoons; Sell ad, full-text electronic versions of articles, back issues
Trim Size: 8 3/8 x 10 7/8
Ad Rates: B&W page $3,889, 4-color page $4,545, see media kit on web site for all ad options

Physics Today
Published by AIP Publishing LLC
One Physics Ellipse, College Park, MD 20740-3843
Tel: 301-209-3040; 516-576-2270 (circ) *Fax:* 301-209-0842; 516-349-9704 (circ)
E-mail: help@aip.org; pteditors@aip.org (subns)
Web Site: www.aip.org; pubs.aip.org/physicstoday
Key Personnel
Art Dir: Donna Padian
Ed-in-Chief: Charles Day *E-mail:* cday@aip.org
Mng Ed: Richard J Fitzgerald *E-mail:* rjf@aip.org
Articles & news of interest to professional physicists, astrophysicists, geophysicists & those with a general interest in physical science. Content includes commentaries, book reviews & coverage of the latest research & science policy developments.
First published 1948
Book Use: Regular reviews & books received lists; occasional excerpts
Frequency: Monthly
Avg pages per issue: 80
Circulation: 123,000 paid
$25/yr nonmembs, free to membs
ISSN: 0031-9228
Buy cartoons; Sell articles & back issues
Trim Size: 8 x 10 1/2
Ad Rates: B&W page $10,970, 4-color per page add $1,600
Ad Closing Date(s): 1st of month preceding publication

Pittsburgh Post-Gazette
Published by PG Publishing Co
Division of Block Communications Inc
358 North Shore Dr, Pittsburgh, PA 15212
Tel: 412-263-1100 *Toll Free Tel:* 800-228-6397 (cust serv); 855-743-6763 (subns)
Web Site: www.post-gazette.com
Key Personnel
Publr & Ed-in-Chief: John Robinson Block
Exec Ed: Keith C Burris
Columnist/Book Review Ed: Tony Norman
Column weekly, in-house reviewers; syndicated & author interviews on a regular basis.
Circulation: 244,000 (d); 430,000 (Sun)
$2/issue, $4/issue (Sun); digital & print: $5.50/wk (Sun only), $6/wk (Thurs, Fri & Sun); digital only: $11.96/4 wks
Avg reviews per issue: 1 (Tues), 3 (Sun)

The Plain Dealer
Published by Advance Ohio
4800 Tiedeman Rd, Brooklyn, OH 44144
Tel: 216-999-5000 *Toll Free Tel:* 800-362-0727
E-mail: marketing@advance-ohio.com
Web Site: www.advance-ohio.com; www.plaindealer.com
Key Personnel
Pres & Ed: George Rodrigue *Tel:* 216-999-4373 *E-mail:* grodrigue@plaind.com
Daily review & 2 pages Sunday, in-house. Frequent author interviews; Christmas book review incorporated in gift-giving section; children's & adults; bestseller list on Sunday.
Circulation: 900,000

Playboy
Published by Playboy Enterprises Inc
10960 Wilshire Blvd, Suite 2200, Los Angeles, CA 90024
Tel: 310-424-1800 *Toll Free Tel:* 800-511-2457 (cust serv)
E-mail: playboy@netbillingsupport.com
Web Site: www.playboy.com; www.playboyenterprises.com
Key Personnel
CEO: Ben Kohn
Chief Creative Offr: Cooper Hefner
CFO & COO: David Isreal
Chief Mktg Offr: Jared Dougherty
Entertainment magazine for men, offering fiction, serious & satirical articles, sports, interviews, cartoons, picture stories of attractive women & reviews of features on fashion, food, merchandise & travel.
First published 1953
Frequency: Quarterly
Avg pages per issue: 220
$24.99/issue print, $7.99/issue digital, $24.99/yr digital only, $39.99/yr print & digital
ISSN: 0032-1478
Trim Size: 9 x 10 3/8
Ad Rates: B&W full page $64,660, 1/2 page $38,770; 4-color full page $90,540, 1/2 page $58,840

Plays, The Drama Magazine for Young People
Published by Sterling Partners Inc
897 Washington St, No 600160, Newton, MA 02460
Tel: 617-630-9100 *Fax:* 617-630-9101
E-mail: customerservice@playsmagazine.com
Web Site: www.playsmagazine.com
Key Personnel
Ed: Elizabeth Preston *E-mail:* lpreston@playsmagazine.com
One-act plays & programs for school age actors & audiences. Online only.
First published 1941
Frequency: 7 issues/yr
Avg pages per issue: 48
Circulation: 500
$69/yr
ISSN: 0032-1540
Buy freelance play scripts; Sell play reprints, back issues (subscribers only)

Popular Mechanics
Published by Hearst Communications Inc
300 W 57 St, New York, NY 10019-3787
Tel: 212-649-2000 *Toll Free Tel:* 800-333-4948 (subns & cust serv)
E-mail: popcustserv@cdsfulfillment.com
Web Site: www.popularmechanics.com; www.hearst.com
Subscription Address: PO Box 6093, Harlan, IA 51593
Key Personnel
Edit Dir: Bill Strickland
Contains ideas & information on automobiles, home building & maintenance, boating & outdoor recreation, science, hi-fi & electronics, computer, telecommunications, sports.
First published 1902
Book Use: Occasional reviews
Frequency: 6 issues/yr
Avg pages per issue: 191
Circulation: 5,069,000
$5.99/issue, $40/yr print & digital, $4/mo digital only
ISSN: 0032-4558 (print); 2769-8637 (online)
Trim Size: 7 x 10
Ad Rates: 4-color page $120,940, 1/2 page $68,940
Ad Closing Date(s): 6 weeks before issue date

Popular Science®
Published by Bonnier Corp
Division of The Bonnier Group
2 Park Ave, 9th fl, New York, NY 10016
Tel: 212-779-5000 *Fax:* 212-779-5108
E-mail: letters@popsci.com
Web Site: www.popsci.com
Subscription Address: PO Box 6364, Harlan, IA 51593-1864
Key Personnel
Exec Dir, Brand Mktg: Beth Hetrick
Group Edit Dir: Anthony Licata
Creative Dir: Pete Sucheski
Ed-in-Chief: Joe Brown
Exec Ed: Kevin Gray
Mng Ed: Corinne Iozzio
Sr Ed: Sophie Brushwick
Assoc Ed: Mary Beth Griggs
Feature articles on science & technology including space & aviation, electronics products, computer, automotive products, car tests & housing products. No unsol mss, query first.
First published 1872
Book Use: Occasional reviews, excerpts
Frequency: Quarterly
Avg pages per issue: 100
Circulation: 1,250,000
$7.99/issue, $10/yr US, $18/yr CN, $24/yr intl
ISSN: 0161-7370
Buy nonfiction, art, cartoons; Sell article & ad reprints, back issues
Trim Size: 7 3/8 x 10 1/2
Ad Rates: B&W page $63,450, 4-color page $89,820 + 10% (for a bleed)
Ad Closing Date(s): 45 days prior to sale date

Port Arthur News
Published by Carpenter Newsmedia
2349 Memorial Blvd, Port Arthur, TX 77640
Tel: 409-721-2400; 409-729-6397
E-mail: panews@panews.com (edit)
Web Site: www.panews.com
Key Personnel
Publr: Rich Macke *E-mail:* rich.macke@panews.com
Ed: Ken Stickney *E-mail:* ken.stickney@panews.com
In-house reviews & occasional author interviews.
First published 1897
Digital & print: $52/yr (Sat only), $131.88/yr (Tues-Sat); digital only: $9.99/mo, $29.97/3 mos, $119.88/yr

The Portland Press Herald/Maine Sunday Telegram
Published by Maine Today Media Inc
One City Ctr, 5th fl, Portland, ME 04101
Mailing Address: PO Box 1460, Portland, ME 04104-5009

Tel: 207-791-6000 (subns); 207-791-6650
 Toll Free Tel: 800-442-6036 (within ME)
 Fax: 207-791-6920
E-mail: online@mainetoday.com; circulation@mainetoday.com
Web Site: www.pressherald.com
Key Personnel
Publr & CEO: Lisa DeSisto *Tel:* 207-791-6630
 E-mail: lisa@mainetoday.com
Exec Ed: Cliff Schechtman *Tel:* 207-791-6693
 E-mail: cschechtman@mainetoday.com
Mng Ed: Steve Greenlee *Tel:* 207-791-6301
 E-mail: sgreenlee@pressherald.com
Sunday, book reviews through syndication & other sources.
Circulation: 46,751 (d); 56,756 (Sun)
$11.99/mo digital

The Post & Courier
Published by Evening Post Industries
134 Columbus St, Charleston, SC 29403-4800
Tel: 843-577-7111; 843-853-POST (853-7678)
 Fax: 843-937-5579
E-mail: features@postandcourier.com
Web Site: www.postandcourier.com
Key Personnel
Publr: P J Browning *E-mail:* pbrowning@postandcourier.com
Ad Pres: Scott Embry *Tel:* 843-937-5405
 E-mail: sembry@postandcourier.com
Edit Page Ed: Rick Nelson *Tel:* 843-937-5701
 E-mail: rnelson@postandcourier.com
Features Ed: Lauren Sausser *Tel:* 843-937-5598
 E-mail: lsausser@postandcourier.com
Sunday page *Post & Courier*, in-house & syndicated column; occasional author interviews.
First published 1803
Circulation: 1,800,000/mo
$12.95/mo digital, $27.50/mo digital & print

The Post-Standard
Published by Advance Media New York
220 S Warren St, Syracuse, NY 13202
Tel: 315-470-0032; 315-470-6397 (cust serv)
E-mail: info@advancemediany.com
Web Site: www.syracuse.com
Subscription Address: PO Box 9001048, Louisville, KY 40290-1048
Key Personnel
Life & Culture Ed: Chris Baker *Tel:* 315-345-6260 (cell) *E-mail:* cbaker@syracuse.com
Periodic, in-house & through syndication. Frequent regional interviews. Book review page-previews of books written by or directed to Central New Yorkers.
Print & online: Tues, Thurs & Sun $25.99/mo, Thurs & Sun $20.99/mo, Sun only $18.99/mo; Online only: $22.99/mo
Trim Size: 8 x 10 1/2

The Press & Sun Bulletin
Published by Gannett Co Inc
33 Lewis Rd, Suite 9, Binghamton, NY 13905
Mailing Address: PO Box 1270, Binghamton, NY 13902-1270
Tel: 607-798-1234 *Toll Free Tel:* 800-253-5343 (subns)
E-mail: pressandsun@gannett.com
Web Site: www.pressconnects.com
Key Personnel
Exec Ed: Kevin Hogan *E-mail:* khogan@gannett.com
Daily community in-house & by syndication. Occasional author interviews.
Frequency: Daily
Circulation: 38,234 (m); 53,944 (Sun)

The Press Democrat
Division of Sonoma Media Investments LLC
427 Mendocino Ave, Santa Rosa, CA 95401
Tel: 707-521-5235; 707-526-8585 (newsroom)
 Toll Free Tel: 800-675-5056 (newsroom)
 Fax: 707-521-5330 (newsroom)
E-mail: info@pressdemocrat.com
Web Site: www.pressdemocrat.com
Key Personnel
Features Ed: Corinne Asturias *E-mail:* corinne.asturias@pressdemocrat.com
Sunday page; in-house, through syndication & by other sources; twice monthly author interviews.
First published 1857
Circulation: 97,000 (m); 103,000 (Sun)
Digital & print: $17/mo (Sun only), $28/mo (Mon-Sun); digital only: $12/mo

The Press of Atlantic City
Published by BH Media Group Inc
1000 W Washington Ave, Pleasantville, NJ 08232
Tel: 609-272-7000 *Toll Free Tel:* 877-773-7724
 Fax: 609-272-7224
E-mail: spage@pressofac.com
Web Site: www.pressofatlanticcity.com
Key Personnel
Exec Ed & VP, News: Kris Worrell *Tel:* 609-272-7277 *E-mail:* kworrell@pressofac.com
Mng Ed: Buzz Keough *Tel:* 609-272-7238
 E-mail: bkeough@pressofac.com
Sunday page, in-house & through syndication; occasional author interviews.
Circulation: 90,000 (m); 105,000 (Sun)
Digital & print: $9.50/mo (Sun only), $16.25/mo (Thurs-Sun or Mon-Sun); digital only: $6.95/mo
Avg reviews per issue: 6

Press-Register
Published by Alabama Media Group
Unit of Advance Local Media LLC
18 S Royal St, Mobile, AL 36602
Tel: 251-219-5400 *Toll Free Tel:* 800-239-1340
E-mail: circulationcs@press-register.com
Web Site: www.al.com
Sunday page. In-house & through syndication; author interviews.
First published 1813
$18.07/mo digital & Sun print, $19.99/mo digital only

Press-Telegram
Published by Digital First Media
727 Pine Ave, Long Beach, CA 90813
Tel: 562-435-1161; 562-499-1222 (subns); 562-499-1382 (ad sales)
E-mail: ptnews@presstelegram.com
Web Site: www.presstelegram.com
Key Personnel
Group Pres & Publr: Ron Hasse *E-mail:* ron.hasse@socalnewsgroup.com
Exec Ed: Frank Pine *Tel:* 909-483-9360
 E-mail: frank.pine@socalnewsgroup.com
City Ed: Melissa Evans *Tel:* 562-499-1280
 E-mail: mevans@scng.com
Columnist: Tim Grobaty *Tel:* 562-714-2116
 E-mail: tgrobaty@scng.com
Weekly page, in-house & by syndication. Occasional author interviews.
First published 1897
Circulation: 20,432 (d); 34,605 (Sun)
$20/8 wks

The Progressive
Published by The Progressive Inc
931 E Main St, Suite 10, Madison, WI 53703
Tel: 608-257-4626 *Toll Free Tel:* 800-827-0555
E-mail: editorial@progressive.org
Web Site: www.progressive.org
Subscription Address: PO Box 1021, Madison, WI 53701
Key Personnel
Publr: Norman Stockwell
Sr Ed: Emilio Leanza
Web Ed: Delaney Nelson
Assoc Ed: Michaela Brant
Contains investigative reporting, analysis & commentary on major issues of political, economic & social concern.
First published 1909
Book Use: Reviews
Frequency: 6 issues/yr
Avg pages per issue: 72
Circulation: 20,000 paid
$5.95/issue, $29.70/yr, $50/yr instns
ISSN: 0033-0736
Buy nonfiction, poetry & art; Sell articles, back issues
Trim Size: 8 3/8 x 10 7/8
Ad Rates: Color full page $3,500, color back cover $4,000
Ad Closing Date(s): 20th of each published month

Psychology Today
Published by Sussex Publishers LLC
115 E 23 St, 9th fl, New York, NY 10010
Tel: 212-260-7210 *Toll Free Tel:* 800-234-8361 (subns) *Fax:* 212-260-7566
E-mail: sales@psychologytoday.com; subscriptions@psychologytoday.com
Web Site: www.psychologytoday.com
Key Personnel
CEO: Jo Colman
EVP & Publr: John Thomas
 E-mail: johnthomas@psychologytoday.com
Ed-in-Chief: Kaja Perina
Deputy Ed: Lybi Ma
Psychological information & media insight for the general audience. Covers personal relations, family issues, human behavior, pop culture, media, neuropsychology. Includes editorials, queries for writers, interviews, research news; extensive news & feature articles, very little fiction or poetry. No unsol mss, query first.
First published 1967
Frequency: 6 issues/yr
Avg pages per issue: 92
Circulation: 250,000
$29.97/yr, $37.97/yr CN, $49.99/yr foreign
ISSN: 0033-3107
Buy freelance nonfiction, art & fiction; Sell articles & back issues
Trim Size: 8 x 10 1/2
Ad Rates: B&W full page $13,755, 1/2 page $7,875, 4-color full page $20,055, 1/2 page $11,550
Ad Closing Date(s): 2 months before issue date, beginning of month

Queen's Quarterly
Published by Queen's University
Stauffer Library, Rm 215, 101 Union St, Kingston, ON K7L 2N9, Canada
Tel: 613-533-2667
E-mail: queens.quarterly@queensu.ca
Web Site: www.queensu.ca/quarterly
Key Personnel
Exec Ed: James Carson
Busn Mgr: Penny Roantree
First published 1893
Frequency: Quarterly
Avg pages per issue: 160
Circulation: 3,000
$10/issue, $30/yr CN, $35/yr US & foreign
ISSN: 0033-6041
Trim Size: 6 x 9

Rain Taxi Review of Books
Published by Rain Taxi
PO Box 3840, Minneapolis, MN 55403
E-mail: info@raintaxi.com
Web Site: www.raintaxi.com
Key Personnel
Art Dir: Kelly Everding
Ed: Eric Lorberer

Publishes original work by writers in all stages of their careers. Books are considered in the categories of poetry, fiction, literary nonfiction, art & graphic novels. Occasional reviews of children's & young adult books, audio books & chapbooks. No electronic files. Only printed books (finished books or bound galleys) are accepted for consideration.
Frequency: Quarterly
$16/yr, $28/2 yrs domestic; $25/yr, $45/2 yrs CN & Mexico; $45/yr, $80/2 yrs overseas

Reactor
Published by Tor Publishing Group
120 Broadway, New York, NY 10271
Web Site: reactormag.com
Key Personnel
Mng Ed: Bridget McGovern
Sr Books Ed & Publicity Coord: Christina Orlando *E-mail:* christina.orlando@reactormag.com
Sr Ed, Features: Leah Schnelbach
Sr Ed, News & Entertainment: Emmet Asher-Perrin *E-mail:* emmet.asherperrin@reactormag.com
Sr Prodn Ed: Stefan Raets
Articles, essays, etc on genre fiction & related pop culture literature. Publishes new original short fiction, as well as daily commentary on science fiction, fantasy & related subjects. Available online only.
First published 2008
Free

Reader's Digest
Published by Trusted Media Brands Inc
750 Third Ave, 3rd fl, New York, NY 10017
SAN: 212-4416
Tel: 914-238-1000 *Toll Free Tel:* 877-732-4438 (cust serv)
E-mail: customercare@trustedmediabrands.com
Web Site: www.rd.com; www.trustedmediabrands.com/brands/readers-digest
Key Personnel
Chief Admin Offr: Dean Durbin
Chief Content Offr: Bruce Kelley
SVP, Sales & Mktg: John Boland *Tel:* 646-518-4252 *E-mail:* john.boland@trustedmediabrands.com
Dir, PR: Becky Wisdom *E-mail:* becky.wisdom@trustedmediabrands.com
Sr Prodn Mgr: Leslie Kogan *Tel:* 914-244-5433 *E-mail:* leslie.kogan@trustedmediabrands.com
Contains general interest, nonfiction reading for the entire family. The balance are articles condensed from other publications; a condensation of a current book is carried in each issue.
First published 1922
Book Use: Excerpts
Frequency: 10 issues/yr
Avg pages per issue: 214
Circulation: 3,000,000
$3.99/issue, $10/yr, $15/2 yrs (includes digital)
ISSN: 0034-0375
Buy freelance, nonfiction, art & cartoons; Sell article & reprints, back issues
Trim Size: 5.187 x 7.25
Ad Rates: 4-color full page $77,660, 1/2 page $46,650; B&W full page $68,170, 1/2 page $40,920

The Record
Published by Metroland Media Group Ltd
Subsidiary of Torstar Corp
160 King St E, Kitchener, ON N2G 4E5, Canada
Tel: 519-894-2250; 519-894-3000 (cust serv)
Toll Free Tel: 800-265-8261; 800-210-5210 (cust serv)
Web Site: www.therecord.com
Key Personnel
Publr: Donna Luelo *Tel:* 519-895-5500
Ed-in-Chief: Jim Poling *Tel:* 519-895-5600
City Ed: Neil Ballantyne *Tel:* 519-895-5633 *E-mail:* nballantyne@therecord.com
Saturday page; in-house & syndicated, in-house book reviewers, plus occasional outside book reviews.
Circulation: 60,000
Digital, print & e-edition: $2.52/wk (Fri & Sat), $3.84/wk (Mon-Sat); digital only: $7.99/mo; e-edition (Mon-Sat): $9.99/mo

The Record
Published by Glacier Ventures International
6 Mallory, Sherbrooke, QC J1M 2E2, Canada
Tel: 819-569-9525 *Fax:* 819-569-6345
Web Site: www.sherbrookerecord.com
Key Personnel
Publr & Mng Ed: Sharon McCully *E-mail:* outletjournal@sympatico.ca
First published 1897
Frequency: Daily (Mon-Fri)
Circulation: 4,100 (e)
Digital only: $11.25/mo, $125/yr; print only: $50.59/3 mos, $97.73/6 mos, $178.21/yr; digital & print: $55.59/3 mos, $102.73/6 mos, $183.21/yr

The Record
Published by North Jersey Media Group
Subsidiary of Gannett Co Inc
One Garret Mountain Plaza, Woodland Park, NJ 07424
Mailing Address: PO Box 471, Woodland Park, NJ 07424-0471
Tel: 973-569-7000; 973-585-5633 (cust serv)
Toll Free Tel: 888-282-3422 *Fax:* 973-569-7037
E-mail: northjerseymediagroup@gannett.com
Web Site: www.northjersey.com
Key Personnel
Ed: Daniel Sforza *E-mail:* dsforza@northjersey.com
Magazines & Features Writer: Kimberly Wilson *E-mail:* wilsonk@northjersey.com
In-house & through syndication; author interviews when warranted.
Circulation: 177,969 (d); 192,817 (Sun)

The Record
Published by MediaNews Group Inc
7 Wells St, Suite 103, Saratoga Springs, NY 12866
Tel: 518-270-1200 *Fax:* 518-583-8014
E-mail: newsroom@troyrecord.com
Web Site: www.troyrecord.com
Key Personnel
Publr: Kevin Corrado *E-mail:* kcorrado@medianewsgroup.com
City Ed: Nicholas Buonanno *E-mail:* nbuonanno@digitalfirstmedia.com
Irregular book reviews in-house.
First published 1896
Circulation: 20,000
Digital & print: $59.15/13 wks (Thurs, Fri & Sun), $91.55/13 wks (Mon-Sun); digital only: $12/mo

Record-Journal
Published by The Record-Journal Publishing Co
500 S Broad St, 2nd fl, Meriden, CT 06450
Tel: 203-235-1661; 203-634-3933 (cust serv)
Fax: 203-639-0210 (edit); 203-235-4048 (ad)
E-mail: newsroom@record-journal.com
Web Site: www.myrecordjournal.com
Key Personnel
Pres & Publr: Eliot C White *Tel:* 203-317-2350 *E-mail:* ewhite@thewesterlysun.com
EVP & Asst Publr: Elizabeth White *Tel:* 203-317-2226 *E-mail:* lwhite@record-journal.com
SVP & Ed: Ralph Tomaselli *Tel:* 203-317-2220 *E-mail:* rtomaselli@record-journal.com
Mng Ed: Eric Cotton *Tel:* 203-317-2344 *E-mail:* ecotton@record-journal.com
Frequency: Daily
Circulation: 30,855 (d); 30,961 (Sun)
$37/mo print & digital, $15.99/mo digital only

Red Deer Advocate
Published by Black Press Group Ltd
2950 Bremner Ave, Red Deer, AB T4R 1M9, Canada
Tel: 403-343-2400
E-mail: editorial@reddeeradvocate.com
Web Site: www.reddeeradvocate.com
Key Personnel
Publr: Mary Kemmis *Tel:* 403-314-4311 *E-mail:* mkemmis@reddeeradvocate.com
Mng Ed: David Marsden *Tel:* 403-314-4324 *E-mail:* david.marsden@reddeeradvocate.com
Occasional local & visiting author interviews. Book reviews in-house & syndicated. Sunday edition "Red Deer Life" distributed free to households in Red Deer.
Circulation: 23,300 (d)
$15/mo

Redbook
Published by Hearst Communications Inc
Division of Hearst Magazines
300 W 57 St, 22nd fl, New York, NY 10019-3787
Tel: 212-649-3463 (edit); 212-649-3330 (publg/ad)
E-mail: redbook@hearst.com
Web Site: www.redbookmag.com; www.hearst.com
Key Personnel
Edit Dir: Jane Francisco
Articles on beauty, parenting, relationships, health & fitness. Online presence only.
First published 1903
ISSN: 0034-2106

Regina Leader-Post
Published by Postmedia Network Inc
PO Box 2020, Regina, SK S4P 3G4, Canada
Tel: 306-781-5211 *Toll Free Tel:* 800-667-8751 (subns) *Fax:* 306-657-6438
Web Site: www.leaderpost.com
Key Personnel
Mng Ed: Tim Switzer *Tel:* 306-781-5223 *E-mail:* tswitzer@postmedia.com
Ed: Heather Persson *Tel:* 306-657-6315 *E-mail:* hpersson@postmedia.com
Weekly half-page; in-house & through syndication. Occasional author interviews.
Circulation: 62,000
Digital & print: $15/mo (Sat only), $28/mo (Mon-Sat); digital only: $9.95/mo

The Register-Guard
Published by GateHouse Media LLC
3500 Chad Dr, Suite 600, Eugene, OR 97408
Tel: 541-485-1234
Web Site: www.registerguard.com
Key Personnel
Publr: Shanna Cannon *Tel:* 541-338-2525 *E-mail:* scannon@registerguard.com
First published 1867
Frequency: Daily
Digital & print: $32/mo (Fri-Sun), $48/mo (Mon-Sun); digital only: $12.95/mo
ISSN: 0739-8557
Avg reviews per issue: 60

The Register-Mail
Published by GateHouse Media LLC
140 S Prairie St, No 539, Galesburg, IL 61401
Tel: 309-343-7181 *Toll Free Tel:* 800-747-7181
E-mail: news@register-mail.com
Web Site: www.galesburg.com
Key Personnel
Publr: David Adams *Tel:* 309-343-7181 ext 286 *E-mail:* dadams@gatehousemedia.com
Features Ed: Robyn Gautschy *Tel:* 309-343-7181 ext 265 *E-mail:* rgautschy@gatehousemedia.com

Occasional column, books & travel.
Circulation: 10,000 (e)
Digital & print: $24.91/mo; digital only: $6.99/mo, $69.99/yr

The Republican
Published by MassLive LLC
1350 Main St, Springfield, MA 01103
Tel: 413-788-1000; 413-788-1200 (newsroom)
  Fax: 413-788-1301 (newsroom)
E-mail: masslivesales@masslive.com
Web Site: www.masslivemedia.com/republican
Key Personnel
Publr & CEO: George Arwady *Tel:* 413-788-1312
  E-mail: garwady@repub.com
Pres: David Starr *Tel:* 413-788-1040
  E-mail: dstarr@repub.com
VP & Asst to Publr: Robyn A Newhouse
  Tel: 413-788-1021 *E-mail:* rnewhouse@repub.com
Opers Dir: Tom Sewall *E-mail:* tsewall@repub.com
Ad Dir: Mark A French *Tel:* 413-788-1108
  E-mail: mfrench@repub.com
Exec Ed: Wayne E Phaneuf *Tel:* 413-788-1315
  E-mail: wphaneuf@repub.com
Mng Ed: Cynthia Simison *Tel:* 413-788-1214
  E-mail: csimison@repub.com
Book page in Sunday edition. Occasional author interviews.
$10.90/wk print & digital (Mon-Sun), $3.90/wk (Thurs & Sun); $40/mo digital

Richmond Times-Dispatch
Published by BH Media Group Inc
300 E Franklin St, Richmond, VA 23219
Tel: 804-649-6000 *Toll Free Tel:* 800-468-3382
Web Site: www.richmond.com
Key Personnel
Mng Ed: Mike Szvetitz *E-mail:* mszvetitz@timesdispatch.com
Sunday (Times-Dispatch); in-house, freelance & occasional author interviews.
Circulation: 89,401 (d); 120,280 (Sun)
Digital & print: $44/mo (Sun only), $50/mo (Thurs-Sun), $70/mo (Mon-Sun); digital only: $11.99/mo, $144/yr

The Roanoke Times
Published by BH Media Group Inc
201 Campbell Ave SW, Roanoke, VA 24011
Mailing Address: PO Box 2491, Roanoke, VA 24010-2491
Tel: 540-981-3211 (cust serv); 540-981-3340 (newsroom) *Toll Free Tel:* 800-346-1234 (cust serv)
E-mail: letters@roanoke.com
Web Site: www.roanoke.com
Key Personnel
Publr: Terry Jamerson *E-mail:* terry.jamerson@roanoke.com
Newsroom Mgr: Karen Belcher *E-mail:* karen.belcher@roanoke.com
Weekly page in-house.
First published 1886
Circulation: 163,000 (d); 230,000 (Sun)
Digital & print: $8.88/mo (Sun only), $13.31/mo (Fri-Sun), $16.90/mo (Mon-Sun); digital & e-edition: $8.95/mo, $100/yr

Rocky Mount Telegram
Division of Cook Communications
1151 Falls Rd, Suite 2008, Rocky Mount, NC 27804
Mailing Address: PO Box 1080, Rocky Mount, NC 27802
Tel: 252-366-8190; 252-329-9505 (cust care)
Web Site: www.rockymounttelegram.com
Key Personnel
Publr: Kyle Stephens *Tel:* 252-366-8146
  E-mail: kstephens@rmtelegram.com

Ed: Gene Metrick *Tel:* 252-366-8141
  E-mail: gmetrick@rmtelegram.com
Daily page, syndicated & in-house; occasional author interviews.
Circulation: 10,047 (e); 12,664 (Sun)
$5/mo digital, $16/mo print (home delivery), $25/mo print (mail delivery)

Rolling Stone
Published by Penske Media Corp
Subsidiary of Penske Business Media LLC
475 Fifth Ave, New York, NY 10017
Tel: 212-484-1616
E-mail: rseditors@rollingstone.com
Web Site: www.rollingstone.com
Subscription Address: PO Box 62230, Tampa, FL 33662
Key Personnel
Pres: Gus Wenner
Ed: Jason Fine
Sr Writer: David Fricke
General interest magazine covering modern American culture, politics & art with special interest in music. Review rock history books & rock biographies.
First published 1967
Book Use: Some reviews, some excerpts
Frequency: 12 issues/yr
Avg pages per issue: 92
Circulation: 670,671 paid
$9.99/issue, $49.95/yr print, $59.95/yr print & digital
ISSN: 0035-791X
Buy freelance, nonfiction & art
Trim Size: 9.6875 x 11.75
Ad Rates: B&W full page $209,945, 1/2 page $125,965, 4-color full page $233,270, 1/2 page $139,965
Ad Closing Date(s): Varies

Ruralite
Published by Ruralite Services Inc
5605 NE Elam Young Pkwy, Hillsboro, OR 97124
Tel: 503-357-2105
E-mail: info@ruralite.org
Web Site: www.ruralite.org
Key Personnel
Mng Ed: Leon Espinoza *E-mail:* editor@ruralite.org
First published 1954
Frequency: Monthly
Avg pages per issue: 32
Circulation: 326,050
$15/yr, $20/yr foreign
Buy freelance nonfiction
Trim Size: 8 3/8 x 10 3/4
Ad Rates: B&W page $7,090, 4-color page $8,150
Ad Closing Date(s): 20th of month, 2 months prior to issue date

Rutland Online Herald
Published by Brunswick Publishing LLC
77 Grove St, Suite 102, Rutland, VT 05701
Mailing Address: PO Box 668, Rutland, VT 05702-0668
Tel: 802-747-6121; 802-747-6131 (cust serv)
  Toll Free Tel: 800-498-4296 (VT); 800-776-5512 (outside VT)
E-mail: customerservices@rutlandherald.com
Web Site: www.rutlandherald.com
Key Personnel
Gen Mgr: Rob Mitchell *Tel:* 802-774-3028
  E-mail: rob.mitchell@rutlandherald.com
Author interviews.
First published 1794
Frequency: Daily (Tues-Sat)
$22.92/mo digital & print, $9/2 wks digital only

The Sacramento Bee
Published by The McClatchy Co

2100 "Q" St, Sacramento, CA 95816
Mailing Address: PO Box 15779, Sacramento, CA 95852
Tel: 916-321-1000 *Toll Free Tel:* 800-284-3233
Web Site: www.sacbee.com
Key Personnel
Mng Ed: Scott Lebar *Tel:* 916-321-1182
  E-mail: slebar@sacbee.com
4-6 reviews; reviews & features about authors also run during the week in the scene section; book reviews in-house & through syndication; author interviews; books & media published in Monday's paper, highlights 4 new books each week (hardcover & paperback).
First published 1857
Circulation: 163,482 (d); 177,626 (Sun)
Digital & print: $56.39/13 wks (Sun only), $84.59/13 wks (Fri-Sun), $112.79/13 wks (Mon-Sun); digital only: $12.99/mo, $129.99/yr

SAIL Magazine
Published by Cruz Bay Publishing Inc
Subsidiary of Active Interest Media (AIM)
10 Bokum Rd, Essex, CT 06426-1185
Mailing Address: 23a Glendale St, Salem, MA 01970
Tel: 860-767-3200 *Fax:* 860-767-1048
E-mail: sailmail@sailmagazine.com
Web Site: www.sailmagazine.com
Subscription Address: PO Box 37274, Boone, IA 50037-0274 *Tel:* 386-447-6318 *Toll Free Tel:* 800-745-7245 *E-mail:* salcustserv@cdsfulfillment.com
Key Personnel
Group Publr: Bob Bauer *E-mail:* bbauer@aimmedia.com
Art Dir: Steve Jylkka *E-mail:* sjylkka@aimmedia.com
Ed-in-Chief: Peter Nielsen *E-mail:* pnielsen@sailmagazine.com
Exec Ed: Adam Cort *E-mail:* acort@sailmagazine.com
Information on all aspects of recreational sailing including cruising, racing & equipment.
First published 1970
Book Use: Reviews, excerpts
Frequency: Monthly
Avg pages per issue: 100
Circulation: 68,000
$15/yr plus postage US, $30/yr CN, $42/yr foreign
ISSN: 0036-2700
Sell articles, ad reprints, back issues
Trim Size: 9 x 10 7/8
Ad Rates: B&W full page $10,970, 4-color full page $15,675

St Anthony Messenger
Published by Franciscan Friars of St John the Baptist Province
28 W Liberty St, Cincinnati, OH 45202-6498
Tel: 513-241-5615 *Toll Free Tel:* 800-488-0488
E-mail: sam@cambeywest.com
Web Site: info.franciscanmedia.org/st-anthony-messenger
Key Personnel
Publr: Daniel Kroger, OFM
Art Dir: Mary Catherine Kozusko
Mng Ed: Daniel Imwalle
Franciscan Ed: Pat McCloskey
For Catholic families; written to help people live a Christian life.
First published 1893
Book Use: 60-72 reviews & 2 excerpts per year
Frequency: Monthly
Avg pages per issue: 60
Circulation: 55,000
$39/yr US, $69/yr CN & foreign
ISSN: 0036-276X
Buy freelance fiction, nonfiction, poetry, art & cartoons & photos; Sell articles & ad reprints, back issues

Trim Size: 8.125 x 10.75
Ad Rates: Full page $3,500, 1/2 page $2,100

St Louis Post-Dispatch
Published by Lee Enterprises Inc
900 N Tucker Blvd, St Louis, MO 63101
Tel: 314-340-8000; 314-340-8888 (cust serv)
Toll Free Tel: 800-365-0820
E-mail: service@stltoday.com
Web Site: www.stltoday.com
Key Personnel
Dir, PR: Tracy Rouch *Tel:* 314-340-8903
  E-mail: trouch@post-dispatch.com
Ed-in-Chief: Gilbert Bailon *Tel:* 314-340-8387
  E-mail: gbailon@post-dispatch.com
Book Ed: Jane Henderson *Tel:* 314-340-8107
  E-mail: jhenderson@post-dispatch.com
Go! Entertainment section with book reviews & book blog.
Circulation: 394,900 (d); 485,800 (Sun)
Digital & print: $23.75/mo (Sun only), $51/mo (Thurs-Sun), $61.75/mo (Mon-Sun); digital only: $9.99/mo

St Paul Pioneer Press
Published by Digital First Media
10 River Park Plaza, Suite 700, St Paul, MN 55107
Toll Free Tel: 800-950-9080
E-mail: letters@pioneerpress.com; customerservice@pioneerpress.com
Web Site: www.twincities.com
Key Personnel
Books Ed: Mary Ann Grossmann *Tel:* 651-228-5574 *E-mail:* mgrossmann@pioneerpress.com
Ed: Mike Burbach *Tel:* 651-228-5544
  E-mail: mburbach@pioneerpress.com
Sunday pages, in-house & through syndication & outside sources. Author interviews conducted by staff several times monthly.
Circulation: 191,155 (d); 248,660 (Sun)
Digital & print: $8/mo (Sun only), $10/mo (Thurs & Sun), $18/mo (Mon-Sun); digital only: $10/mo
ISSN: 0892-1083

St Thomas Times-Journal
Published by Postmedia Network Inc
PO Box 82, St Thomas, ON N5P 3T5, Canada
Tel: 519-631-2790
Web Site: www.stthomastimesjournal.com
Key Personnel
Publr & Ad Sales Mgr: Linda LeBlanc
  E-mail: linda.leblanc@sunmedia.ca
In-house book reviews that appear irregularly.
Frequency: Daily (Tues-Fri)
Circulation: 1,550 (e)
$22.99/mo

The Salem News
Published by North of Boston Media Group
Subsidiary of CNHI LLC
32 Dunham Rd, Beverly, MA 01915
Tel: 978-922-1234 *Fax:* 978-927-4524
E-mail: sn@salemnews.com
Web Site: www.salemnews.com
Key Personnel
Publr: Karen Andreas *Tel:* 978-946-2241
  E-mail: kandreas@salemnews.com
Mng Ed: Cheryl Richardson *Tel:* 978-338-2664
  E-mail: crichardson@salemnews.com
Ed: David Olson *Tel:* 978-338-2531
  E-mail: dolson@salemnews.com
News Ed: Helen Gifford *Tel:* 978-338-2508
  E-mail: hgifford@salemnews.com
Edit Asst: Joann Mackenzie *Tel:* 978-338-2670
  E-mail: jomackenzie@salemnews.com
Frequency: Daily (Mon-Sat)
Circulation: 31,077 (e)
$54/8 wks print & digital, $36/8 wks digital only

Salisbury Post
131 W Innes St, Salisbury, NC 28144
Mailing Address: PO Box 4639, Salisbury, NC 28145-4639
Tel: 704-633-8950 *Fax:* 704-639-0003
E-mail: news@salisburypost.com
Web Site: www.salisburypost.com
Key Personnel
Book Review Ed: Deirdre Parker Smith
  E-mail: deirdre.smith@salisburypost.com
In-house, syndicated & freelance book reviews, one-page, weekly, occasional author interviews.
Circulation: 17,000 (d)
$.75/daily; $1.25/Sun

The Salt Lake Tribune
90 S 400 W, Suite 700, Salt Lake City, UT 84101
Tel: 801-257-8742 *Fax:* 801-257-8800
E-mail: newsroom@sltrib.com; features@sltrib.com
Web Site: www.sltrib.com
Key Personnel
Owner & Publr: Paul Huntsman
Ed: Jennifer Napier-Pearce
Arts & Living Ed: Anna Cekola *Tel:* 801-257-8769
Sunday arts section; produced in-house & through syndication, author interviews twice a month.
First published 1871
Circulation: 79,998 (d); 81,262 (Sat); 98,232 (Sun)
Print only: $66/12 wks (Sun only), $73.20/12 wks (Fri-Sun), $90/12 wks (Mon-Sun); digital & print: $71.04/12 wks (Sun only), $78.24/12 wks (Fri-Sun), $95.04/12 wks (Mon-Sun); digital only: $7.99/mo
ISSN: 0746-3502
Avg reviews per issue: 1-2

The San Angelo Standard Times
Published by Gannett Co Inc
34 W Harris Ave, San Angelo, TX 76903
Mailing Address: PO Box 5111, San Angelo, TX 76902-5111
Toll Free Tel: 800-588-1884
E-mail: standard@gosanangelo.com
Web Site: www.gosanangelo.com
Key Personnel
Ed & News Dir: Jen Killin-Guadarrama *Tel:* 325-659-8249 *E-mail:* jennifer.killin@gosanangelo.com
Occasionally in-house & by syndication; author interviews.
Circulation: 35,612 (m); 38,512 (Sat); 41,578 (Sun)
Digital & print: $17/mo (Wed & Sun), $23/mo (Mon-Sun); digital only: $9.99/mo

San Antonio Express-News
Published by Hearst Newspapers
Division of Hearst Corp
301 Avenue "E", San Antonio, TX 78205
Mailing Address: PO Box 2171, San Antonio, TX 78297-2171
Tel: 210-250-3000 *Toll Free Tel:* 800-456-7411
E-mail: citydesk@express-news.net
Web Site: www.expressnews.com; www.mysanantonio.com
Key Personnel
COO: Susan Pape
VP & Ed: Marc Duvoisin *E-mail:* marc.duvoisin@express-news.net
Features Ed: Emily Spicer *E-mail:* espicer@express-news.net
Sunday Insight.
Circulation: 296,000 (d); 200,000 (Sat); 420,000 (Sun)
Digital & print: $3.99/wk (Sun only), $9.99/wk (Mon-Sun); digital only: $9.99/mo

The San Diego Union-Tribune
Published by The San Diego Union-Tribune LLC
600 B St, No 1201, San Diego, CA 92101
Mailing Address: PO Box 120191, San Diego, CA 92112-0191
Tel: 619-293-1211
E-mail: local@sduniontribune.com
Web Site: www.sandiegouniontribune.com/entertainment/books
Key Personnel
Publr & Ed-in-Chief: Jeff Light *Tel:* 619-293-1201 *E-mail:* jeff.light@sduniontribune.com
Mng Ed: Lora Cicalo *Tel:* 619-293-1376
  E-mail: lora.cicalo@sduniontribune.com
Online book reviews & bestselling books.
Frequency: Daily
Circulation: 183,000 (d); 268,000 (Sun)
Digital & print: $2.49/wk (Sun only), $4.99/wk (Mon-Sun); digital only: $1.99/wk

San Francisco Chronicle
Published by Hearst Newspapers
Division of Hearst Corp
901 Mission St, San Francisco, CA 94103
Tel: 415-777-1111 *Toll Free Tel:* 800-499-5700
E-mail: books@sfchronicle.com; feedback@sfchronicle.com
Web Site: www.sfchronicle.com; www.sfgate.com
Subscription Address: PO Box 80083, Prescott, AZ 86304-8083
Key Personnel
Deputy Mng Ed, Features: Kitty Morgan
  E-mail: kmorgan@sfchronicle.com
Sr Arts & Entertainment Ed: Robert Morast
  E-mail: robert.morast@sfchronicle.com
In-house & freelance reviews & occasional author interviews.
First published 1865
Circulation: 167,602 (d); 252,088 (Sun)
Print only: $5.65/wk (Sun only), $8.70/wk (Mon-Sun); digital & print: $6.50/wk (Sun only), $14.60/wk (Mon-Sun); digital only: $12.60/wk
ISSN: 1932-8672

San Francisco Examiner
835 Market St, Suite 550, San Francisco, CA 94103
Tel: 415-359-2600 *Fax:* 415-359-2766
E-mail: info@sfexaminer.com
Web Site: www.sfexaminer.com
Key Personnel
Arts & Entertainment Ed: Leslie Katz *Tel:* 415-359-2727 *E-mail:* lkatz@sfexaminer.com
San Francisco local author interviews.
First published 1865
Frequency: 3 issues/wk (print ed Sun, Wed & Thurs)
Circulation: 255,000
Free
Ad Rates: See media kit online

The SandPaper
Published by The SandPaper Inc
1816 Long Beach Blvd, Surf City, NJ 08008
Tel: 609-494-5900 *Fax:* 609-494-1437
E-mail: beachcomberlbi@gmail.com
Web Site: thesandpaper.net
Key Personnel
Publr: Curt Travers
Off Mgr: Lee Little
Regular book reviews of Jersey Shore books. Tabloid newspaper format.
Frequency: Weekly
Avg pages per issue: 80
Circulation: 30,000
Free

Santa Barbara News-Press
Published by Ampersand Publishing LLC
715 Anacapa St, Santa Barbara, CA 93101
Mailing Address: PO Box 1359, Santa Barbara, CA 93102-1359
Tel: 805-564-5200; 805-966-7171 (subns)
Fax: 805-966-6258
E-mail: news@newspress.com

Web Site: www.newspress.com
Key Personnel
Co-Publr: Wendy McCaw *Tel:* 805-564-5165
 E-mail: wmccaw@newspress.com; Arthur von Wisenberger *E-mail:* avw@newspress.com
Weekly page, in-house, through syndication & wire services; very occasional author interviews.
First published 1855
Circulation: 55,000 (d); 57,608 (Sun)
Digital & print: $4.50/wk (Fri-Sun), $8.50/wk (Mon-Sun); digital only: $60/yr

Santa Cruz County Sentinel
Published by Santa Cruz Sentinel Publishers Co
Affiliate of Media News Group
324 Encinal St, Santa Cruz, CA 95060
Tel: 831-423-4242
E-mail: newsroom@santacruzsentinel.com
Web Site: www.santacruzsentinel.com
Key Personnel
Publr & Ed: Gary Omernick *Tel:* 831-706-3228
 E-mail: gomernick@santacruzsentinel.com
Mng Ed: Melissa Murphy *Tel:* 831-706-3252
 E-mail: mmurphy@santacruzsentinel.com
Lifestyles Ed: Anthony Solis *Tel:* 831-706-3259
 E-mail: tsolis@santacruzsentinel.com
No local book reviews; author interviews in features section & weekly entertainment book column; through syndication.
Circulation: 20,000 (e); 24,500 (Sun)
Digital & print: $2.30/wk (Sun only), $3.80/wk (Thurs, Fri & Sun), $5.50/wk (Mon-Sun)

Santa Maria Times
Published by Lee Enterprises Inc
3200 Skyway Dr, Santa Maria, CA 93455
Tel: 805-925-2691 *Toll Free Tel:* 888-422-8822
 Fax: 805-928-5657
Web Site: santamariatimes.com
Key Personnel
Publr: Cynthia Schur *Tel:* 805-739-2154
 E-mail: cschur@leecentralcoastnews.com
Mng Ed: Marga Cooley *Tel:* 805-739-2143
 E-mail: mcooley@leecentralcoastnews.com
Ed: Emily Slater *Tel:* 805-739-2217
 E-mail: eslater@leecentralcoastnews.com
Reviews appear online; local author interviews; in-house syndicated.
First published 1882
Circulation: 22,000 (d & Sun)
Digital & print: $21.25/mo silver option, $38/mo platinum option; digital only: $5/mo basic, $9.99/mo plus

Saskatoon StarPhoenix
Published by Postmedia Network Inc
204 Fifth Ave N, Saskatoon, SK S7K 2P1, Canada
Tel: 306-657-6231 *Toll Free Tel:* 800-667-2002
 Fax: 306-657-6437
E-mail: citydesk@thestarphoenix.com
Web Site: www.thestarphoenix.com
Key Personnel
Ed: Heather Persson *Tel:* 306-657-6315
 E-mail: hpersson@postmedia.com
Mktg: Hilary Klassen *Tel:* 306-657-6322
 E-mail: hiklassen@postmedia.com
One Saturday page, in-house & by outside sources; author interviews weekly.
First published 1902
Frequency: Daily (Mon-Sat)
Circulation: 63,000 (m)
Digital & print: $18/mo (Sat only), $30/mo (Mon-Sat); digital only: $9.95/mo; e-paper: $9.99/mo
ISSN: 0832-4174

Savannah Morning News
Published by GateHouse Media LLC
1375 Chatham Pkwy, Savannah, GA 31405
Mailing Address: PO Box 1088, Savannah, GA 31402-1088
Tel: 912-236-9511 *Toll Free Tel:* 888-348-3309 (cust care)
E-mail: news@savannahnow.com
Web Site: savannahnow.com
Key Personnel
Publr: Michael C Traynor *Tel:* 912-652-0268
Mktg & Events Dir: Megan Miller *Tel:* 912-652-0445 *E-mail:* megan.miller@savannahnow.com
Exec Ed: Susan Catron
Sunday page, in-house & other sources. Occasional author interviews.
First published 1850
Frequency: Daily
Digital & print: $14.92/mo (Sun only), $14.96/mo (Fri-Sun), $17.66/mo (Mon-Sun); digital only: $12.95/mo, $99.50/yr

SchoolArts Magazine
Published by Davis Publications Inc
50 Portland St, Worcester, MA 01608
Tel: 508-754-7201 *Toll Free Tel:* 800-533-2847 (ext 220, cust serv); 800-533-2847 (ext 219, ad) *Fax:* 508-753-3834; 508-791-0779 (edit)
E-mail: contactus@schoolartsmagazine.com
Web Site: www.davisart.com
Key Personnel
Pres: Julian Wade *E-mail:* jwade@davisart.com
Art Dir: Julia Wade *E-mail:* juliawade@davisart.com
Dir, Mktg: Toni Henneman *E-mail:* thenneman@davisart.com
Sr Ed: Missy Nicholson *E-mail:* mnicholson@davisart.com
Ed: Nancy Walkup *E-mail:* nwalkup@davisart.com
Natl Sales Mgr: Scott Benson *E-mail:* sbenson@davisart.com
Art education lesson plans for all levels, from elementary through post-secondary & college.
First published 1901
Frequency: 10 issues/yr (Sept-June)
Avg pages per issue: 72
Circulation: 24,000 paid; 700 controlled
$24.95/yr, $39.95/2 yrs, $49.95/3 yrs
ISSN: 0036-6463
Trim Size: 8 1/8 x 10 7/8
Ad Rates: B&W page $1,813, 4-color page additional $550
Ad Closing Date(s): 5-6 weeks before issue date

ScienceNews
Published by Society for Science & the Public
1719 "N" St NW, Washington, DC 20036
Tel: 202-785-2255 *Toll Free Tel:* 800-552-4412 (subns)
E-mail: editors@sciencenews.org
Web Site: www.sciencenews.org
Subscription Address: PO Box 292255, Kettering, OH 45429-0255
Key Personnel
Publr: Maya Ajmera
Ed-in-Chief: Nancy Shute
Mng Ed, Magazine: Erin Wayman
 E-mail: ewayman@sciencenews.org
For scientists & those interested in the latest developments in science, medicine & technology. No unsol mss.
First published 1922
Book Use: Listings with brief reviews
Frequency: 26 issues/yr
Avg pages per issue: 36
Circulation: 113,629 paid
$50/yr membs print & digital, $25/yr digital only
ISSN: 0036-8423
Sell article & ad reprints; sell back issues at $5/issue
Trim Size: 8 1/4 x 10 1/2
Ad Rates: 4-color page $4,000
Ad Closing Date(s): 5 weeks advance of issue date

Scientific American™
Published by Scientific American Inc
Division of Springer Nature America Inc
One New York Plaza, 46th fl, New York, NY 10004
Tel: 212-451-8200 *Toll Free Tel:* 800-333-1199 (cust serv)
E-mail: editors@sciam.com
Web Site: www.scientificamerican.com
Subscription Address: PO Box 3187, Harlan, IA 51537 *Toll Free Tel:* 800-333-1199
 E-mail: scacustserv@cdsfulfillment.com
Key Personnel
Pres: Kimberly Lau
SVP & Ed-in-Chief: Mariette DiChristina
VP, Magazines & Edit: Stephen Pincock
Head, Communs: Rachel Scheer
Mng Ed: Curtis Brainard
Chief Features Ed: Seth Fletcher
Magazine of discovery & innovation for decision-makers in industry, government & universities. Available in print & online. No unsol mss, query first.
First published 1845
Book Use: One major review, 3-4 brief reviews
Frequency: Monthly
Avg pages per issue: 120
Circulation: 350,000 paid worldwide
$34.99/yr print & digital, $39.99/yr digital & 4 yr archive, $99/yr print, digital & full archive, $199.99/yr unlimited
ISSN: 0036-8733
Sell articles, ad reprints & back issues
Trim Size: 8 1/8 x 10 3/4
Ad Rates: B&W full page $34,200, 4-color full page $51,266; see web site for complete list of ad rates

Scout Life
Formerly Boys' Life
Published by Scouting America/Boy Scouts of America
1325 W Walnut Hill Lane, Irving, TX 95015
Toll Free Tel: 866-584-6589 (subns)
Web Site: scoutlife.org
Subscription Address: PO Box 152401, Irving, TX 75015-2401 *Tel:* 972-580-2366
Key Personnel
Natl Sales Dir: Nicole Cosme *Tel:* 720-291-9208
 E-mail: nicole.cosme@scouting.org
Mng Ed: Paula Murphey
Client Servs Specialist: Bria Cavitt *Tel:* 972-580-2431 *E-mail:* bria.cavitt@scouting.org
Premiere magazine for kids, tweens & teens with active lifestyles, featuring award-winning editorial, pictorials, comics, games & movie reviews, buying guides, fiction & more.
First published 1911
Book Use: Reviews & excerpts
Frequency: Monthly
Avg pages per issue: 60
Circulation: 800,000 paid
$4.95/issue, $24/yr
ISSN: 0006-8608
Sell articles & ad reprints, back issues
Trim Size: 8 x 10 1/2
Ad Rates: Full page 4-color bleed $52,765 (open gross rate)
Ad Closing Date(s): 1 1/2 months prior to issue date

The Seattle Times
Published by Seattle Times Co
1000 Denny Way, Seattle, WA 98109
Mailing Address: PO Box 70, Seattle, WA 98111
Tel: 206-464-2111; 206-464-2121 (cust serv); 206-464-2200 (newsroom) *Toll Free Tel:* 800-542-0820 (cust serv)
Web Site: www.seattletimes.com
Key Personnel
Mng Ed: Ray Rivera *Tel:* 206-652-6521
Features Ed: Stefanie Loh *Tel:* 206-464-8994

Sunday, in-house, syndicate & freelancers. Frequent author interviews.
Frequency: Daily
Circulation: 236,563 (d); 232,580 (Sat); 504,993 (Sun)

Seattle Weekly
Published by Sound Publishing Inc
11630 Slater Ave NE, Suite 8/9, Kirkland, WA 98034
Tel: 206-623-0500
E-mail: info@seattleweekly.com
Web Site: www.seattleweekly.com
Key Personnel
Ed: Andy Hobbs *E-mail:* ahobbs@soundpublishing.com
Digital only. Book reviews & author interviews & stories.
First published 1976
$39.99/yr

Self
Published by Conde Nast
One World Trade Center, 26th fl, New York, NY 10007-0090
Tel: 212-286-2860; 515-243-3273 (subns)
   Toll Free Tel: 800-274-6111 (subns)
E-mail: letters@self.com; slfcustserv@cdsfulfillment.com
Web Site: www.self.com
Key Personnel
Chief Revenue & Mktg Offr: Pamela Drucker Mann
Ed-in-Chief: Carolyn Kylstra
Chief Busn Offr: Eric Gillin
Articles pertaining to the physical, emotional, cultural, financial & sexual well-being of women. Digital only format.
First published 1979
Book Use: Excerpts
Frequency: Monthly
Circulation: 1,420,858

Seventeen Magazine
Published by Hearst Communications Inc
Division of Hearst Magazines
300 W 57 St, 17th fl, New York, NY 10019-3787
Tel: 212-649-2000
E-mail: mail@seventeen.com
Web Site: www.seventeen.com; www.hearst.com
Key Personnel
Exec Dir: Kristin Koch
Articles on fashion, beauty, food & issues, fiction for female teenage audience. Digital only.
First published 1944

Sierra
Published by Sierra Club
2101 Webster St, Suite 1300, Oakland, CA 94612
Tel: 415-977-5691
E-mail: sierra.magazine@sierraclub.org
Web Site: www.sierraclub.org/sierra
Key Personnel
Ed-in-Chief: Jason Mark
Sr Ed: Paul Rauber
Contains articles on conservation, natural history, outdoor recreation & the environmental movement for Sierra Club members & others. Accepts clips if available. No e-mail queries.
First published 1893
Book Use: Reviews & excerpts
Frequency: 6 issues/yr
Avg pages per issue: 100
Circulation: 517,000 paid
ISSN: 0161-7362
Buy freelance nonfiction; Sell back issues
Avg reviews per issue: 3
Trim Size: 8 x 10 3/4

Simcoe Reformer
Published by Postmedia Network Inc
50 Gilbertson Dr, Simcoe, ON N3Y 4L2, Canada
Tel: 519-426-5710
E-mail: reformer.newsroom@sunmedia.ca
Web Site: www.simcoereformer.ca
Key Personnel
Mng Ed: Kim Novak *E-mail:* knovak@postmedia.com
Daily newspaper.
Circulation: 9,800
$14.99/4 wks print, $3.99/mo digital

Sioux City Journal
Published by Sioux City Newspapers Inc
Division of Lee Enterprises Inc
515 Pavonia St, Sioux City, IA 51101
Tel: 712-293-4250 *Toll Free Tel:* 800-397-9820
   Fax: 712-293-4211
Web Site: siouxcityjournal.com
Subscription Address: PO Box 118, Sioux City, IA 51102
Key Personnel
Ed: Bruce Miller *E-mail:* bmiller@siouxcityjournal.com
Includes weekly entertainment section. Author interviews weekly.
Frequency: Daily
Circulation: 58,000 (d); 57,000 (Sat); 60,000 (Sun)
$5/mo digital basic, $9.99/mo digital plus

Ski®
Published by Active Interest Media (AIM)
5720 Flatiron Pkwy, Boulder, CO 80301
Tel: 303-253-6300 *Toll Free Tel:* 800-678-0817 (subns)
E-mail: editor@skimag.com
Web Site: www.skimag.com
Key Personnel
Dir, Mktg & Busn Devt: Amy Lewis
   E-mail: alewis@aimmedia.com
Industry Sales Dir: Ginna Larson
   E-mail: glarson@aimmedia.com
Western Sales Dir: Al Crolius *E-mail:* acrolius@aimmedia.com
Gen Mgr: David Perry
Contains articles on technique, equipment, resorts & experiences of interest to skiers, real estate, kids gear & reviews. No unsol mss, query first.
First published 1936
Frequency: 6 issues/yr
Avg pages per issue: 150
Circulation: 300,000
$10/yr US, $20/yr CN, $30/yr intl
ISSN: 0037-6159
Buy nonfiction; Sell articles, ad reprints & back issues
Trim Size: 8 1/2 x 10 7/8
Ad Rates: 4-color page $24,500

Sky & Telescope
Published by American Astronomical Society
90 Sherman St, Suite A, Cambridge, MA 02140
Tel: 617-864-7360 *Toll Free Tel:* 866-644-1377
   Fax: 617-864-6117
E-mail: info@skyandtelescope.com
Web Site: www.skyandtelescope.com
Key Personnel
Ed-in-Chief: Peter Tyson
Sr Ed: Kelly Beatty; Alan M MacRobert
Assoc Ed: S N "Jr" Johnson-Roehr; Sean Walker
News Ed: Monica Young
Observing Ed: Diana Hannikainen
Sci Ed: Camille Carlile
Written for those interested in astronomy, space science, observatories, planetariums, telescope making & celestial events.
First published 1941
Book Use: Reviews & advertisements
Frequency: Monthy
Avg pages per issue: 84
Circulation: 71,017
$5.99/issue, $37.95/yr, $49.95/yr CN, $61.95/yr foreign
ISSN: 0037-6604
Buy nonfiction, art & cartoons; Sell articles, ad reprints & back issues
Trim Size: 8 3/8 x 10 1/2
Ad Rates: 4-color page $6,000

Smithsonian
Published by Smithsonian Institution
PO Box 37012, MRC 513, Washington, DC 20013-7012
Tel: 202-633-6090
E-mail: smithsonianmagazine@si.edu
Web Site: www.smithsonianmag.com; www.facebook.com/smithsonianmagazine
Subscription Address: PO Box 62060, Tampa, FL 33662-0608 *Tel:* 810-910-3609 *Toll Free Tel:* 800-766-2149 *E-mail:* smithsonian@customersvc.com
Key Personnel
Dir, Edit Opers: Debra Rosenberg
Art Dir: Maria G Keehan
Deputy Ed: Terence Monmaney
Sr Ed: Kathleen M Burke; T A Frail; Arik Gabbai; Jenni Rothenberg-Gritz; April White
Examines the quality of modern life in terms of the cultural, intellectual, social & physical environment. All web-based submission process - must submit via web site, www.smithsonian.mag.com/contact-us. Also available electronically.
First published 1970
Book Use: Nonfiction reviews & excerpts & first serial excerpts only
Frequency: 10 issues/yr
Avg pages per issue: 104
Circulation: 1,800,000 paid
$12/yr US, $25/yr CN, $38/yr foreign
ISSN: 0037-7333
Buy nonfiction; Sell back issues
Trim Size: 7 7/8 x 10 1/2 x 10 7/8
Ad Rates: B&W full page $108,979, 2-color full page $134,900, 4-color full page $159,600
Ad Closing Date(s): 10th of the month, 2 months preceding issue date

Sojourners Magazine
Published by Sojourners
408 "C" St NE, Washington, DC 20002
Tel: 202-328-8842 *Toll Free Tel:* 800-714-7474 (ad sales) *Fax:* 202-328-8757
E-mail: sojourners@sojo.net; magsubs@sojo.net (subns)
Web Site: www.sojo.net
Key Personnel
Ed: Julie Polter
Sr Assoc Ed: Jenna Barnett; Rose Marie Berger
Ecumenical Christian magazine offering an alternative perspective on matters of faith, politics & culture today. The mission of Sojourners magazine is to articulate the biblical call to social justice, inspiring hope & faith-rooted action. For writers' guidelines, see submission policy at www.sojo.net/writers.
First published 1971
Book Use: Reviews
Frequency: 11 issues/yr
Avg pages per issue: 52
Circulation: 20,000
$3.95/issue digital, $5.95/issue print, $29.95/yr digital, $39.95/yr US, $49.95/yr CN, $59.95/yr foreign print & digital
ISSN: 1550-1140
Buy nonfiction, poetry, art & cartoons; Sell article & ad reprints, back issues, resource guides, books
Trim Size: 8 3/16 x 10 7/8
Ad Rates: 4-color page $2,500, 1/2 page $1,600
Ad Closing Date(s): Approximately 10th of 3rd month prior to issue date

SERIALS FEATURING BOOKS

South Bend Tribune
Published by Schurz Communications Inc
225 W Colfax Ave, South Bend, IN 46626
Tel: 574-235-6161 *Fax:* 574-236-1765
E-mail: sbtnews@sbtinfo.com; sbtcustserv@press-one.com
Web Site: www.southbendtribune.com
Key Personnel
Publr: Sally Brown
VP, Publg: Cory Bollinger
VP, Ad: Shelley Chakan
Exec Ed: Alan Achkar *E-mail:* aachkar@sbtinfo.com
Sunday page, in-house & wire service; author interviews several times a month - mainly wire service interviews - local angle preferred, but not required for in-house interviews.
Circulation: 65,000 (e); 90,000 (Sun)
$24.70/mo (Mon-Sun print & digital), $13/mo (Sat & Sun print & digital), $11.27/mo (Sun only print & digital), $.99/wk (digital only)

South Florida Sun Sentinel, see Sun Sentinel

Southern Living
Published by Meredith Corporation
4100 Old Montgomery Hwy, Birmingham, AL 35209-5713
Tel: 205-445-6000
Web Site: www.southernliving.com
Subscription Address: PO Box 37508, Boone, IA 50037-0508 *Toll Free Tel:* 800-272-4101
E-mail: slvcustserv@cdsfulfillment.com
Key Personnel
Publr: Deirdre Finnegan *Tel:* 212-455-1276
E-mail: deirdre.finnegan@meredith.com
Service publication about the American South. Reviews & author interviews are all staff-written. No unsol mss, query first.
First published 1966
Book Use: Reviews & interviews with authors of southern books
Frequency: Monthly
Avg pages per issue: 200
Circulation: 2,800,000
$4.99/issue, $14.95/yr
Buy nonfiction; Sell articles & back issues
Trim Size: 8 x 10 1/2
Ad Rates: 4-color full page $277,800, 2/3 page $213,000, 1/2 page $173,700, 1/3 page $125,100

The Spokesman-Review
Published by Cowles Publishing Co
999 W Riverside Ave, Spokane, WA 99201
Mailing Address: PO Box 2160, Spokane, WA 99210-2160
Tel: 509-459-5400 (newsroom); 509-747-4422 (cust serv) *Fax:* 509-459-5098
E-mail: features@spokesman.com
Web Site: www.spokesman.com
Key Personnel
Ed: Rob Curley *Tel:* 509-459-5030
E-mail: robc@spokesman.com
Features Ed: Carolyn Lamberson *Tel:* 509-459-5068
Sunday page; in-house & through syndication. Author interviews, 3 or more a month.
First published 1883
Circulation: 110,000 (d); 140,000 (Sun)
Digital & print: $12.99/mo (Mon-Sun); digital only: $9.99/mo

Sports Afield
Published by Field Sports Publishing
15621 Chemical Lane, Suite A, Huntington Beach, CA 92649
Tel: 714-373-4910 *Toll Free Tel:* 800-451-4788
E-mail: info@sportsafield.com; letters@sportsafield.com
Web Site: sportsafield.com

Key Personnel
Dir, Sales: James C Reed *Tel:* 208-520-1600
E-mail: jreed@sportsafield.com
Sales & Licensing Exec: Kim Gattone *Tel:* 406-925-3062 *E-mail:* kgattone@sportsafield.com
Ed-in-Chief: Diana Rupp
Big-game hunting adventure stories & hunting destinations. Submission guidelines available on web site.
First published 1887
Book Use: Reviews in monthly almanac section; occasional excerpts
Frequency: 6 issues/yr
Avg pages per issue: 90
$34.97/yr, $59.97/2 yrs
ISSN: 0038-8149 (print); 6062-1859 (online)
Buy freelance, nonfiction, art & photography; Sell back issues
Trim Size: 8 1/4 x 10 7/8
Ad Rates: 4-color page $5,200, 1/2 page $3,200, 1/4 page $1,900

The Springfield News-Leader
Published by Gannett Co Inc
651 Boonville Ave, Springfield, MO 65806
Tel: 417-836-1100
Web Site: www.news-leader.com
Key Personnel
News Dir: Cheryl Whitsitt *E-mail:* cwhitsitt@gannett.com
Weekly page, in-house & through syndication; rare author interviews.
First published 1867
Circulation: 35,000 (Mon-Sat); 45,000 (Sun)

Standard-Examiner
Published by The Ogden Newspapers Inc
332 Standard Way, Ogden, UT 84404
Mailing Address: PO Box 12790, Ogden, UT 84412-2790
Tel: 801-625-4200; 801-625-4400
Toll Free Tel: 800-651-2105
E-mail: customerservice@standard.net
Web Site: www.standard.net
Key Personnel
Exec Ed: Jordan Carroll *Tel:* 801-625-4210
E-mail: jcarroll@standard.net
City Ed: Jessica Kokesh *Tel:* 801-625-4229
E-mail: jkokesh@standard.net
Columnist: Mark Saal *Tel:* 801-625-4272
E-mail: msaal@standard.net
Author interviews (local writers & well known writers visiting the area).
First published 1888
Circulation: 280,000/wk
Print: $6.50/mo (Sun only), $9.75/mo (Fri-Sun), $15.16/mo (Mon-Sun); digital: $9.99/mo

The Standard Times
Published by South Coast Media Group
Subsidiary of GateHouse Media LLC
25 Elm St, New Bedford, MA 02740
Tel: 508-997-7411 *Toll Free Tel:* 800-445-7482 (subns) *Fax:* 508-997-7491
Web Site: www.southcoasttoday.com
Key Personnel
Circ Serv Dir: Chad Campbell
Circ Serv Mgr: Mark Foisy *Tel:* 508-979-4400
E-mail: mfoisy@s-t.com
News Ed: Jennifer Driscoll *Tel:* 508-979-4466
E-mail: jdriscoll@s-t.com
Frequency: Daily
Circulation: 24,000 (d & Sat); 30,000 (Sun)
Digital & print: $26/13 wks (Sun only), $52/13 wks (Mon-Sun); digital only: $12/mo

The Star-Ledger
Published by NJ Advance Media
One Star Ledger Plaza, Newark, NJ 07102
Tel: 973-392-4040 (edit) *Toll Free Tel:* 888-STAR-LEDGER (782-7533 cust serv)
E-mail: custserv@starledger.com

ADVERTISING, MARKETING

Web Site: www.nj.com/starledger
Key Personnel
VP, Opers: Stephen Leotsakos
E-mail: sleotsakos@starledger.com
Publr & Ed: Richard Vezza *Tel:* 973-836-4906
E-mail: rvezza@starledger.com
Gen Mgr: John F Dennan *E-mail:* jdennan@starledger.com
Weekly, in-house book reviews & features.
$19.99/wk (7-day digital only), $3.95/wk (Sun & Thurs print & digital), $5.25/wk (Thurs-Sun print & digital), $7.95/wk (7-day print & digital)

Star Magazine
Published by American Media Inc
4 New York Plaza, New York, NY 10004
Tel: 212-545-4800
Web Site: starmagazine.com
Key Personnel
SVP & Group Publr: Neil Goldstein
E-mail: ngoldstein@amilink.com
Ed-in-Chief: James Heidenry
Assoc Publr, Mktg: Pamela Madden
E-mail: pmadden@amilink.com
Weekly book reviews, in-house & syndicated, local author interviews, local bestseller list & calendar of book-related events.
Frequency: Weekly
Circulation: 165,000 (Sun)
Ad Rates: B&W 2/3 page $98,770, 1/3 page $49,390; 4-color full page $137,155, 1/2 page $82,310

Star Tribune
Published by StarTribune Media Co LLC
650 Third Ave S, Suite 1300, Minneapolis, MN 55488
Tel: 612-673-4000
Web Site: www.startribune.com/variety/books
Key Personnel
Books Ed: Chris Hewitt *Tel:* 612-673-4367
E-mail: chris.hewitt@startribune.com
Book reviews, author interviews, book award announcements.
First published 1867
Frequency: Daily
Circulation: 106,758 (d); 224,142 (Sun)
ISSN: 0895-2825

The State
Published by The State Media Co
Subsidiary of The McClatchy Co
1401 Shop Rd, Columbia, SC 29201-4843
Tel: 803-771-6161 *Toll Free Tel:* 800-888-5353; 800-888-3566 (cust serv)
E-mail: state@thestate.com
Web Site: www.thestate.com
Key Personnel
Publr: Rodney Mahone *E-mail:* rmahone@mcclatchy.com
Exec Ed: Brian Tolley *E-mail:* btolley@thestate.com
Sr Ed: Paul Osmundson *E-mail:* posmundson@thestate.com
Sunday page, in-house; frequent author interviews.
First published 1891
Frequency: Daily
Circulation: 115,000 (d); 130,000 (Sun)
$16.99/mo digital

The State Journal
Published by Frankfort Newsmedia LLC
1216 Wilkinson Blvd, Frankfort, KY 40601
Tel: 502-227-4556 *Fax:* 502-227-2831
E-mail: news@state-journal.com
Web Site: www.state-journal.com
Key Personnel
Publr: Steve Stewart *Tel:* 502-209-6994
E-mail: steve.stewart@state-journal.com
News Ed: Chanda Veno *Tel:* 502-209-6299
E-mail: chanda.veno@state-journal.com

First published 1902
Circulation: 10,000 (d); 12,000 (Sun)

The State Journal-Register
Published by GateHouse Media LLC
PO Box 219, Springfield, IL 62705-0219
Tel: 217-788-1300
E-mail: sjr@sj-r.com
Web Site: www.sj-r.com
Key Personnel
Gen Mgr & Ad Dir: Eugene Jackson
  E-mail: ejackson@sj-r.com
Sunday page, in-house & by syndication. Infrequent author interviews.
Frequency: Daily
Circulation: 50,000 (Sun)
Digital & print: $9.13/mo (Sun only), $19.12/mo (Mon-Sun); digital only: $5.99/mo, $39.99/yr

Staten Island Advance
Published by SILive.com
950 W Fingerboard Rd, Staten Island, NY 10305
Tel: 718-981-1234; 718-816-3900 (cust serv)
E-mail: editor@siadvance.com
Web Site: www.silive.com
Key Personnel
Publr: Caroline Diamond Harrison
Exec Ed: Brian J Laline *E-mail:* laline@siadvance.com
Edit Page Ed: Mark Hanley *E-mail:* hanley@siadvance.com
Circ Mgr: Richard Salerno *E-mail:* salerno@siadvance.com
Sunday in "Arts & Ideas" section; in-house & by syndication.
Digital & print: $18/mo (Thurs-Sun), $25.78/mo (Mon-Sun); digital only: $19.99/mo

Statesville Record & Landmark
Published by BH Media Group Inc
222 E Broad St, Statesville, NC 28677
Tel: 704-873-1451 *Fax:* 704-872-3150
E-mail: news@statesville.com; circulation@statesville.com
Web Site: www.statesville.com
Key Personnel
Publr: Eric Millsap
Daily page.
Circulation: 15,600 (d); 14,900 (Sat); 16,600 (Sun)
Digital & print: $5.32/mo (Sun only), $9.62/mo (Mon-Sat), $16.50/mo (Mon-Sun); digital only: $7.95/mo, $79.95/yr

Sun Journal
Published by The Lewiston Sun Journal
Division of Sun Media Group
104 Park St, Lewiston, ME 04240
Mailing Address: PO Box 4400, Lewiston, ME 04243-4400
Tel: 207-784-5411 *Toll Free Tel:* 800-482-0753
  Fax: 207-777-3436
E-mail: circulation@sunjournal.com
Web Site: www.sunjournal.com
Key Personnel
Exec Ed: Judith Meyer *Tel:* 207-689-2902
  E-mail: jmeyer@sunjournal.com
Reviews of books about the state of Maine.
Circulation: 31,422 (d); 31,505 (Sun)
Digital & print: $10.60/4 wks (Sun only), $14.60/4 wks (Thurs-Sun), $19.60/4 wks (Mon-Sun); digital only: $11.96/4 wks

Sun Sentinel
Published by Tribune Publishing Co
333 SW 12 Ave, Deerfield Beach, FL 33442
Tel: 954-356-4000; 954-375-2018 (cust serv)
E-mail: customerservice@sunsentinel.com
Web Site: www.sun-sentinel.com
Key Personnel
Dir, Content/Entertainment: Melina I De Rose
  E-mail: mderose@sunsentinel.com
Ed-in-Chief: Julie Anderson *E-mail:* janderson@sunsentinel.com
Mng Ed: Gretchen Day-Bryant
  E-mail: gdaybryant@sunsentinel.com
Sunday page. Feature author interviews frequently; book reviews in-house, through syndication & freelance.
First published 1910

Sunset
Published by Sunset Publishing Corp
Subsidiary of Regent LLC
9720 Wilshire Blvd, Suite 600, Beverly Hills, CA 90212
Tel: 510-858-3400 *Toll Free Tel:* 800-777-0117 (subns); 877-297-7138 (cust serv)
E-mail: customerservice@sunset.com
Web Site: www.sunset.com
Subscription Address: PO Box 3228, Harlan, IA 51593 *Toll Free Tel:* 800-777-0117
Key Personnel
Ed-in-Chief: Matt Bean
Exec Ed: Hugh Garvey
Guide to the Western states; covers travel, food & entertaining, home & building, gardening, outdoor living.
First published 1898
Book Use: Occasional reviews
Frequency: Monthly
Avg pages per issue: 120
Circulation: 1,000,000
$20/yr all access print & digital (US only)
ISSN: 0039-5404
Sell back issues
Trim Size: 8 3/8 x 10 1/2
Ad Closing Date(s): 7 weeks preceding issue date

Tallahassee Democrat
Published by Gannett Co Inc
277 N Magnolia Dr, Tallahassee, FL 32301
Tel: 850-599-2100 *Toll Free Tel:* 800-999-2271 (subns)
E-mail: letters@tallahassee.com
Web Site: www.tallahassee.com
Key Personnel
Pres & Publr: Skip Foster *Tel:* 850-599-2126
Exec Ed: William Hatfield *Tel:* 850-599-2177
Sunday weekly, in-house, through syndicated wire service & other sources.
Circulation: 56,000 (m); 78,000 (Sun)
Digital & print: $4.30/mo (Sun only), $13/mo (Mon-Sun)

Tampa Bay Times
Published by Times Publishing Co
490 First Ave S, St Petersburg, FL 33701
Mailing Address: PO Box 1121, St Petersburg, FL 33731-1121
Tel: 727-893-8111 *Toll Free Tel:* 800-888-7012
  Fax: 727-893-8675
E-mail: custserv@tampabay.com
Web Site: www.tampabay.com
Key Personnel
Chmn & CEO: Paul Tash *Tel:* 727-893-8887
  Fax: 727-892-2328 *E-mail:* ptash@tampabay.com
EVP & Gen Mgr: Joe De Luca *Tel:* 813-226-3307 *E-mail:* jdeluca@tampabay.com
VP & CFO: Andy Corty *Tel:* 727-893-8204
  Fax: 727-822-5083 *E-mail:* acorty@tampabay.com
VP & Ed: Neil Brown *Tel:* 727-893-8441
  E-mail: nbrown@tampabay.com
VP, Ad & Mktg: Bruce Faulmann *Tel:* 727-893-8984 *Fax:* 727-892-2328 *E-mail:* bfaulmann@tampabay.com
Exec Ed: Mark Katches *Tel:* 727-893-8441
  E-mail: markkatches@tampabay.com
Sunday, in-house; occasional author interviews.
Circulation: 181,280 (d); 294,483 (Sun)
Digital & print: $7.75/mo (Sun only), $14.75/mo (Mon-Sun); digital only: $7.75/mo

Technology Review
Published by MIT
One Main St, 13th fl, Cambridge, MA 02142
Tel: 617-475-8000 *Toll Free Tel:* 800-877-5230 (subns)
E-mail: customer-service@technologyreview.com
Web Site: www.technologyreview.com
Subscription Address: 235 Pine St, San Francisco, CA 94104 *Tel:* 415-659-2980
Key Personnel
Publr & CEO: Elizabeth Bransom-Boudreau
Ed-in-Chief: Gideon Lichfield
Deputy Ed: Michael Reilly
Mng Ed: Timothy Maher
Ed-at-Large: David Rotman
MIT's national magazine on emerging technology. No unsol mss, query first.
First published 1899
Book Use: Reviews & excerpts
Frequency: 6 issues/yr
Avg pages per issue: 80
Circulation: 177,436 paid
$35.95/yr digital, $55.95/yr print, $79.95/yr print & digital
ISSN: 0040-1692
Buy freelance fiction, nonfiction; Sell articles & ad reprints, back issues
Trim Size: 8 3/16 x 10 1/2
Ad Rates: B&W full page $21,056, 4-color full page $28,075
Ad Closing Date(s): 5 weeks prior to cover date

The Telegram
Published by SaltWire Network
36 Austin St, St John's, NL A1B 4C2, Canada
Mailing Address: PO Box 8660, Sta A, St John's, NL A1B 3T7, Canada
Tel: 709-364-6300 *Toll Free Tel:* 888-333-8840 (circ) *Fax:* 709-364-3939
E-mail: telegram@thetelegram.com; circ@thetelegram.com
Web Site: www.thetelegram.com
Key Personnel
Sr Mng Ed: Steve Bartlett *E-mail:* steve.bartlett@thetelegram.com
Night Ed: Mark Vaughan-Jackson *E-mail:* mark.vaughan-jackson@thetelegram.com
Atlantic Regl Columnist: Russell Wangersky
  E-mail: russell.wangersky@thetelegram.com
Daily, in-house & through wire services; occasional author interviews; book reviews; publish book lists from public library.
First published 1879
Circulation: 40,000 (e); 60,000 (weekend)
Digital & print: $19.99/mo (Fri & Sat), $26.07/mo (Mon-Sat); digital only: $14.99/mo

Telegram & Gazette/Sunday Telegram
Published by GateHouse Media LLC
100 Front St, Worcester, MA 01615
Mailing Address: PO Box 15012, Worcester, MA 01615-0012
Tel: 508-793-9200 *Toll Free Tel:* 800-922-8200
  Fax: 508-793-9281
E-mail: newstips@telegram.com
Web Site: www.telegram.com
Key Personnel
Pres: Paul Provost *Tel:* 508-793-9111
  E-mail: paul.provost@telegram.com
Exec Ed: Dave Nordman *Tel:* 508-793-9375
  E-mail: david.nordman@telegram.com
Syndicated book reviews; holiday roundups.
Digital & print: $26/13 wks (Sun only), $39/13 wks (Thurs-Sun), $52/13 wks (Mon-Sun); digital only: $39.99/yr

The Telegraph
Published by The McClatchy Co
1675 Montpelier Ave, Macon, GA 31201
Tel: 478-744-4200 *Toll Free Tel:* 800-342-5845 (GA only) *Fax:* 478-744-4385
Web Site: www.macon.com

Key Personnel
Sr Ed: Sundra Hominik *Tel:* 478-744-4345
 E-mail: shominik@macon.com
Deputy Ed: Lauren Gorla *Tel:* 478-744-4292
 E-mail: lgorla@macon.com
Sunday full-page reviews written in-house, by freelancers & wire service. Occasional author interviews.
First published 1826
Circulation: 60,000 (m); 75,000 (Sun)
Digital & print: $42.12/13 wks (Wed & Sun), $56.16/13 wks (Thurs-Sun), $84.24/13 wks (Mon-Sun); digital only: $8.99/mo, $129.99/yr

The Telegraph Journal
Published by Brunswick News Inc (BNI)
210 Crown St, St John, NB E2L 2X7, Canada
Mailing Address: PO Box 2350, St John, NB E2L 3V8, Canada
Tel: 506-859-4900 *Toll Free Tel:* 800-295-8665
 Fax: 506-633-6758
Web Site: tj.news
Key Personnel
Publr: James Irving
Ed-in-Chief: Wendy Metcalfe
Mng Ed: Jack Poirier
Sr Ed: Marie Sutherland
Weekly reviews (Sat), local author interviews.
First published 1862
Circulation: 40,000
$1/daily, $1.70/Sat, $25.99/mo
Avg reviews per issue: 5

The Tennessean
Published by Gannett Co Inc
1801 West End, 17th fl, Nashville, TN 37203
Tel: 612-259-8300 *Toll Free Tel:* 800-342-8237
E-mail: customer@tennessean.com
Web Site: www.tennessean.com
Key Personnel
Exec Ed: Maria DeVarenne
 E-mail: mdevarenne@tennessean.com
General news/info, profiles, occasional reviews.
Circulation: 190,000 (d); 234,000 (Sat); 285,000 (Sun)

Texas Monthly
Published by Texas Monthly LLC
PO Box 1569, Austin, TX 78767-1569
Tel: 512-320-6900 *Toll Free Tel:* 800-759-2000 (orders) *Fax:* 512-476-9007
E-mail: subscription@texasmonthly.com
Web Site: www.texasmonthly.com
Key Personnel
Dir, Edit Opers: Anna Walsh *E-mail:* awalsh@texasmonthly.com
Creative Dir: Emily Kimbro *E-mail:* ekimbro@texasmonthly.com
Mktg Dir: Hannah Vickers *E-mail:* hvickers@texasmonthly.com
Ed-in-Chief: Dan Goodgame
 E-mail: dgoodgame@texasmonthly.com
Sr Exec Ed: Mimi Swartz *E-mail:* mswartz@texasmonthly.com
Deputy Ed: Ross McCammon
 E-mail: rmccammon@texasmonthly.com
Book reviews, profiles & interviews that capture the diverse voices adding to the rich literary tradition of Texas.
First published 1973
Frequency: Monthly
Circulation: 300,000
$9.99/issue, $25/yr print, $30/yr digital, $45/yr print & digital
ISSN: 0148-7736 (print); 2163-3274 (online)
Sell articles, ad reprints & back issues
Trim Size: 8 1/8 x 10 1/2
Ad Closing Date(s): 25th of the second month preceding issue date

Time Magazine
Published by Time USA LLC
225 Liberty St, New York, NY 10281
E-mail: editors@time.com
Web Site: time.com
Key Personnel
Ed-in-Chief & CEO: Edward Felsenthal
Deputy Ed: Sam Jacobs; Eben Shapiro
Assoc Audience Engagement Ed: Annabel Gutterman *E-mail:* annabel.gutterman@time.com
Covers national & international news organized by departments including art, behavior, books, business, cinema, design, education, environment, law, modern living, music, nation, press, religion, theater, video & world.
First published 1923
Book Use: Reviews
Frequency: Weekly
Avg pages per issue: 82
Circulation: 2,000,000
$5.99/issue, $12/yr
ISSN: 0040-781X
Ad Rates: B&W page $172,400, 4-color page $265,100

Time Out!
Published by Daily Herald
Subsidiary of Paddock Publications Inc
95 W Algonquin Rd, Arlington Heights, IL 60005
Mailing Address: PO Box 280, Arlington Heights, IL 60006-0280
Tel: 847-427-4300
E-mail: news@dailyherald.com
Web Site: www.dailyherald.com
Key Personnel
Chmn, Publr & CEO: Douglas K Ray *Tel:* 847-427-4510 *E-mail:* dray@dailyherald.com
Metro Ed: Lisa Miner *Tel:* 847-427-4516
 E-mail: lminer@dailyherald.com
Tabloid section in the *Daily Herald* print newspaper & e-edition. Reviews, in-house & syndicated, author interviews.
Frequency: Weekly (Fri)
Avg reviews per issue: 1 or 2
Ad Closing Date(s): Mon-Sat issues 5 pm 3 days prior, Sun 5 pm Tues prior

The Times
Published by Gannett Co Inc
401 Market St, Suite 1500, Shreveport, LA 71101-6911
Tel: 318-459-3200 *Toll Free Tel:* 866-979-6397 (cust serv)
Web Site: www.shreveporttimes.com
Key Personnel
Circ Dir: Kevin Welsh *E-mail:* kwelsh@gannett.com
Ed: Scott Ferrell *E-mail:* scott.ferrell@shreveporttimes.com
Book reviews; author news.
Circulation: 139,000 (m); 169,000 (Sun)

The Times Argus
Published by Vermont Community Media LLC
47 N Main St, Suite 200, Barre, VT 05641
Tel: 802-479-0191 *Toll Free Tel:* 800-776-5512
 Fax: 802-479-4096
E-mail: news@timesargus.com; customerservices@timesargus.com
Web Site: www.timesargus.com
First published 1897
Frequency: Daily (Tues-Sat)
Circulation: 10,000 (e)

Times Colonist
Division of Glacier Community Media
2621 Douglas St, Victoria, BC V8T 4M2, Canada
Tel: 250-380-5211
E-mail: customerservice@timescolonist.com
Web Site: www.timescolonist.com
Key Personnel
Publr & Ed: Dave Obee *Tel:* 250-380-5201
 E-mail: dobee@timescolonist.com
Book Columnist: Adrian Chamberlin
Monitor (Sun), Arts section (Fri); in-house & through syndication. Occasional author interviews.
Frequency: Daily (Tues-Sun)
Circulation: 55,000 (d); 70,000 (Sun)
Digital & print: $22.50/mo (Fri-Sun), $26/mo (Tues-Sun)

The Times-Picayune | The New Orleans Advocate
Published by NOLA Media Group
840 St Charles Ave, New Orleans, LA 70130
Tel: 504-636-7400 *Toll Free Tel:* 800-960-6397
E-mail: newstips@theadvocate.com; subscriberservices@theadvocate.com
Web Site: www.nola.com
Key Personnel
Mng Ed: Fred Kalmbach *Tel:* 225-388-0313
 E-mail: fkalmbach@theadvocate.com
Ed: Peter Kovacs *Tel:* 225-388-0277
 E-mail: pkovacs@theadvocate.com
Digital & print: $14.95/mo (Sat & Sun), $24.95/mo (Mon-Sun); digital only: $9.99/mo

The Times Union
Published by Hearst Newspapers
Division of Hearst Corp
645 Albany Shaker Rd, Albany, NY 12211
Mailing Address: PO Box 15000, Albany, NY 12212
Tel: 518-454-5694 *Fax:* 515-454-5628
E-mail: tucitydesk@timesunion.com
Web Site: www.timesunion.com
Key Personnel
Publr & CEO: George R Hearst, III
 E-mail: ghearst@timesunion.com
VP & Ed: Rex Smith *E-mail:* rsmith@timesunion.com
VP, Ad: Tom Eason *E-mail:* teason@timesunion.com
Sr Ed, Features: Gary Hahn *E-mail:* ghahn@timesunion.com
Sr Ed, Local News: Casey Seiler
 E-mail: cseiler@timesunion.com
Sr Ed, News: Lisa Robert Lewis *E-mail:* llewis@timesunion.com
Features Ed: Sara Tracey *E-mail:* stracey@timesunion.com
Occasional author interviews.
$2/wk Sun print & digital, $1.50/wk digital only

Today's Christian Woman
Published by Christianity Today International
465 Gundersen Dr, Carol Stream, IL 60188-2498
Tel: 630-260-6200 *Toll Free Tel:* 877-247-4787 (cust serv)
E-mail: tcw@christianitytoday.com
Web Site: www.todayschristianwoman.com
Mission is to challenge & equip women to love God more deeply & live fearlessly for his kingdom. Online only.
First published 2012
Book Use: Reviews published online
Free
Buy freelance nonfiction; Sell back issues, downloadable PDFs

Topeka Capital-Journal
Published by GateHouse Media LLC
100 SE Ninth St, Suite 500, Topeka, KS 66612-1213
Tel: 785-295-1111 *Toll Free Tel:* 800-291-3914
Web Site: cjonline.com
Key Personnel
Publr: Stephen Wade *Tel:* 785-295-1115
 E-mail: stephen.wade@cjonline.com
Ed & VP, Audience Devt: Tomari Quinn
 E-mail: tomari.quinn@cjonline.com
Dir, Digital Sales: Terri Benson *E-mail:* terri.benson@cjonline.com
Sunday column, occasional author interviews.
First published 1879
Frequency: Daily

The Toronto Star
Published by Toronto Star Newspapers Ltd
One Yonge St, Toronto, ON M5E 1E6, Canada
Tel: 416-367-2000 *Fax:* 416-869-4328
E-mail: city@thestar.ca
Web Site: www.thestar.com
Key Personnel
Publr: John Boynton
Ed: Irene Gentle
Edit Writer: Dianne Rinehart
Weekend section, reviews & column in "Book" section; in-house & other sources. Frequent author interviews.
Circulation: 193,050 (d); 290,153 (Sat); 185,159 (Sun)
Digital & e-paper: $5.30/wk; digital, e-paper & print: $5.49/wk (weekend), $6.90/wk (Mon-Sun); digital only: $19.99/mo

Toronto Sun
Published by Postmedia Network Inc
365 Bloor St E, 6th fl, Toronto, ON M4W 3L4, Canada
Tel: 416-947-2222; 416-383-2300 *Fax:* 416-947-1664 (newsroom)
E-mail: torsun.citydesk@sunmedia.ca
Web Site: www.torontosun.com
Key Personnel
Deputy Ed: Kevin Hann *E-mail:* khann@postmedia.com
Entertainment Ed: Mark Daniell *E-mail:* mdaniell@postmedia.com
One page; in-house; frequent author interviews.
Circulation: 250,000 (d); 450,000 (Sun)
Digital, e-paper & print: $16/4 wks (Sun only), $30/4 wks (Mon-Sun); digital or e-paper: $9.99/mo, $99.99/yr

Town & Country
Published by Hearst Communications Inc
Division of Hearst Magazines
300 W 57 St, New York, NY 10019-3787
Tel: 212-903-5000; 212-649-2000
Toll Free Tel: 800-289-8696 (subns)
E-mail: tnc@hearst.com
Web Site: www.townandcountrymag.com; www.hearst.com
Subscription Address: PO Box 6000, Harlan, IA 51593
Key Personnel
Publr & Chief Revenue Offr: Jennifer Leven Bruno
Ed-in-Chief: Stellene Volandes
For the affluent; covers travel, the home, personalities, fashion, beauty, food & other subjects.
First published 1846
Book Use: Reviews & excerpts, author profiles
Frequency: Monthly
Avg pages per issue: 230
Circulation: 464,330 paid & verified
$6.99/issue, $10/yr, $20/2 yrs, $25/3 yrs
ISSN: 0040-9952
Sell articles & ad reprints, back issues
Trim Size: 8.75 x 10.875
Ad Rates: B&W page $97,360, 4-color page $125,270
Ad Closing Date(s): 20th of 2nd month preceding issue date

The Town Talk, see Alexandria Daily Town Talk

Travel + Leisure
Published by Time Inc Affluent Media Group
225 Liberty St, New York, NY 10281
Tel: 212-522-1212 *Toll Free Tel:* 800-888-8728 (cust serv)
Web Site: www.travelandleisure.com
Subscription Address: Box 62160, Tampa, FL 33662 *Tel:* 813-979-6625
Key Personnel
Ed-in-Chief: Nathan Lump
Exec Ed: Jesse Ashlock
Mng Ed: Laura Teusink *E-mail:* laura.teusink@travelandleisure.com
Offers insider access to destination around the globe with a signature mix of smart advice, immersive photography & expert reporting on hotels, food, design, style, culture & trends.
First published 1971
Book Use: Reviews
Frequency: Monthly
Avg pages per issue: 200
Circulation: 953,484 paid & verified
$5.99/issue, $45/yr US, $57/yr CN
ISSN: 0041-2007
Buy freelance nonfiction & art; Sell articles, ad reprints & back issues
Trim Size: 8 x 10 1/2
Ad Rates: B&W page $111,100, 4-color page $163,300
Ad Closing Date(s): 2 months preceding issue date

Traverse, Northern Michigan's Magazine
Published by MyNorth Media
125 Park St, Suite 155, Traverse City, MI 49684
Tel: 231-941-8174 *Toll Free Tel:* 800-678-3416
E-mail: sales@traversemagazine.com
Web Site: mynorth.com
Key Personnel
Mktg Dir: Erin Lutke *Tel:* 231-941-5976
Sales Dir: Julie Parker *E-mail:* jparker@mynorth.com
Ed: Emily Tyra
Regional, highlighting the history, culture, people & natural beauty of northern Michigan.
First published 1981
Book Use: Excerpts
Frequency: Monthly
Avg pages per issue: 110
Circulation: 24,000
$24/yr
ISSN: 0746-2735
Buy fiction, nonfiction, poetry, art & cartoons; Sell ad reprints & back issues
Trim Size: 8 1/4 x 10 7/8
Ad Rates: 4-color full page $3,230
Ad Closing Date(s): 6 weeks prior to cover date

Tribune-Review
Published by Trib Total Media
622 Cabin Hill Dr, Greensburg, PA 15601
Tel: 724-836-6675 (newsroom) *Toll Free Tel:* 800-909-8742 (cust serv)
E-mail: gtrcity@tribweb.com
Web Site: www.triblive.com
Key Personnel
Exec Mng Ed: Jerry DeFlitch *E-mail:* jdeflitch@tribweb.com
Exec Ed: Susan K McFarland *E-mail:* smcfarland@tribweb.com
Features Ed: Jonna Miller *E-mail:* jonnamiller@tribweb.com
Sunday page in style section; in-house author.
First published 1974
Circulation: 120,000
Print & digital: $5/mo, $60/yr (Sun only), $6/mo, $72.80/yr (Thurs & Sun), $12/mo, $144/yr (Mon-Sun); digital only: $8/mo, $96/yr

Tricycle: The Buddhist Review
Published by The Tricycle Foundation
89 Fifth Ave, Suite 301, New York, NY 10003
Tel: 212-929-0320 *Toll Free Tel:* 800-873-9871 (cust serv & subns)
E-mail: editorial@tricycle.org; tricycle@gpr4ads.com (ad rates)
Web Site: www.tricycle.org
Key Personnel
Publr & Ed: James Shaheen
Features Ed: Andrew Cooper
Explores the intersection of Buddhism & western culture. All subscriptions are payable through company web site. No unsol mss, query first via web site only. No e-mail queries accepted.
First published 1991
Frequency: Quarterly
Avg pages per issue: 120
Circulation: 30,000
$49/yr digital, $59/yr print & digital
ISSN: 1055-484X
Avg reviews per issue: 1-2
Trim Size: 8 1/4 x 10 7/8
Ad Closing Date(s): Nov (Winter), Feb (Spring), May (Summer), Aug (Fall)

Tulsa World
Published by BH Media Group Inc
315 S Boulder Ave, Tulsa, OK 74103
Mailing Address: PO Box 1770, Tulsa, OK 74102
Tel: 918-581-8400
E-mail: letters@tulsaworld.com
Web Site: www.tulsaworld.com
Subscription Address: PO Box 85048, Richmond, VA 23261-5048
Key Personnel
Pres & Publr: Gloria Fletcher
Exec Ed: Susan Ellerbach *E-mail:* susan.ellerbach@tulsaworld.com
Sunday, publishing notes on paperbacks, weekly books column page of reviews, page of book news; in-house & syndicated book reviews. Frequent author interviews.
Circulation: 144,000 (d), 207,000 (Sun)
Digital & print: $21.67/mo (Wed & Sun), $34.67/mo (Wed & Fri-Sun), $43.45/mo (Mon-Sun); digital only: $5.95/mo, $59.95/yr

TV Guide Magazine
Published by TV Guide Magazine LLC
Subsidiary of NTVB Media
50 Rockefeller Plaza, 14th fl, New York, NY 10020
Mailing Address: PO Box 37360, Boone, IA 50099-0360
Toll Free Tel: 800-866-1400 (cust serv)
E-mail: letters@tvgm.com
Web Site: www.tvguidemagazine.com; www.tvinsider.com
TV, cable & pay-TV reporting. No unsol mss, query first.
First published 1953
Book Use: Excerpts of TV-related material
Frequency: 26 issues/yr
Avg pages per issue: 88
Circulation: 1,100,000
$4.99/issue
Buy nonfiction; Sell articles & ad reprints
Trim Size: 7 x 10
Ad Rates: B&W full page $97,700, 4-color full page $119,100

Tyler Morning Telegraph - Courier-Times-Telegraph
Published by M Roberts Media
410 W Erwin St, Tyler, TX 75702
Tel: 903-597-8111
E-mail: opinion@tylerpaper.com; news@tylerpaper.com
Web Site: tylerpaper.com
Key Personnel
Publr & Chief Revenue Offr: Justin Wilcox *Tel:* 903-596-6299
Ed: Emily Guevara *Tel:* 903-596-6281 *E-mail:* eguevara@tylerpaper.com
Sunday, in-house; occasional local author interviews.
First published 1929
Circulation: 22,556 (m); 47,568 (Sun)

Unity Magazine
Published by Unity Worldwide Ministries
1901 NW Blue Pkwy, Unity Village, MO 64065-0001
Tel: 816-524-3550 *Toll Free Tel:* 800-248-6489 (cust serv)
E-mail: unity@unityonline.org
Web Site: www.unity.org/publications/unity-magazine
Key Personnel
Ed: Katy Koontz *E-mail:* umageditor@unityonline.org
Contains articles on healing, metaphysics, prosperity, prayer & spirituality; advertising included. First published as *Modern Thought*.
First published 1889
Frequency: 6 issues/yr
Avg pages per issue: 44
Circulation: 16,000 paid
$6.95/issue, $21.95/yr, $36.95/yr foreign
ISSN: 0162-3567
Buy nonfiction
Avg reviews per issue: 4
Trim Size: 8 1/2 x 11
Ad Rates: See media kit on web site

US Catholic
Published by Claretian Publications
205 W Monroe St, 9th fl, Chicago, IL 60606
Tel: 312-544-8191
E-mail: editors@uscatholic.org
Web Site: www.uscatholic.org; claretians.org
Subscription Address: PO Box 1201, Skogie, IL 60076-1021 *Toll Free Tel:* 800-328-6515
Key Personnel
Ed-in-Chief: Fr John J Molyneux
Mng Ed: Emily Sanna
General interest publication about Catholic faith & life.
First published 1963
Book Use: Reviews
Frequency: Monthly
Avg pages per issue: 52
Circulation: 13,000 paid
US: $30/yr, $50/2 yrs, $70/3 yrs; CN & foreign: $40/yr, $60/2 yrs, $80/3 yrs (print & digital)
ISSN: 0041-7548
Buy freelance fiction, nonfiction, art & cartoons, poetry; Sell back issues & reprints
Avg reviews per issue: 3
Trim Size: 8 1/4 x 10 3/8
Ad Rates: 4-color full page $1,900, 1/2 page $1,325
Ad Closing Date(s): 60 days preceding issue date

US News & World Report Magazine
Published by US News & World Report
1050 Thomas Jefferson St NW, 4th fl, Washington, DC 20007
Tel: 202-955-2225
Web Site: www.usnews.com
Key Personnel
Ed & Chief Content Offr: Brian Kelly
E-mail: bkelly@usnews.com
Analysis of important national & world news for an affluent, well-educated audience. Digital only.
First published 1933

Us Weekly
Published by American Media Inc
4 New York Plaza, New York, NY 10004
Tel: 212-545-4800
E-mail: letters@usmagazine.com
Web Site: www.usmagazine.com
Key Personnel
EVP & Chief Revenue Offr: Victoria Lasdon Rose *Tel:* 212-484-3424 *E-mail:* victoria.rose@usmagazine.com
Head, Integrated Sales: Brian Kennedy
E-mail: brian.kennedy@usmagazine.com

Brief articles on entertainment personalities; heavy photographic content; all color.
First published 1977
Frequency: Weekly
Avg pages per issue: 80
Circulation: 1,950,000
$5.99/issue print or digital, $72/yr digital, $81/yr print
ISSN: 0147-510X
Avg reviews per issue: 2-4
Trim Size: 7 3/4 x 10 1/2
Ad Rates: B&W full page $260,640, 1/2 page $156,384, 4-color full page $289,595, 1/2 page $173,757
Ad Closing Date(s): Mon closing 4 weeks prior to issue date

USA Today
Published by Gannett Co Inc
7950 Jones Branch Dr, McLean, VA 22108-0605
Tel: 703-854-3400 *Toll Free Tel:* 800-872-0001
Web Site: www.usatoday.com
Key Personnel
Pres & Publr: Maribel Perez Wadsworth
Ed-in-Chief: Nicole Carroll
Friday page; in-house & freelance. Occasional author interviews.
First published 1982
Circulation: 2,300,000 (d); 2,600,000 (Fri)
$9.99/mo e-newspaper, $4.99/mo digital

Utne Reader
Published by Ogden Publications
Subsidiary of Ogden News
1503 SW 42 St, Topeka, KS 66609-1265
Toll Free Tel: 800-736-8863 (cust serv); 800-678-5779; 800-736-8863 (utne reader) *Fax:* 785-274-4305
E-mail: editor@utne.com; customerservice@ogdenpubs.com (subns)
Web Site: www.utne.com
Key Personnel
Publr: Bill Uhler
Ed: Chris Williams
Reprints the best articles from some 1,300 alternative publications. The magazine provides coverage missing from the mainstream, including emerging trends & alternative views on everything from politics & pop culture to the environment & economy. The magazine educates & activates & is aimed at people passionate about living at the forefront of progressive culture. For submissions policy, see guidelines on web site. No phone queries.
First published 1984
Book Use: Reviews, excerpts
Frequency: Quarterly
Avg pages per issue: 100
Circulation: 127,500
$6.99/issue, $39.96/yr US print & digital, $50/yr CN, prepaid in US funds, $55/yr (air mail) foreign prepaid in US funds
ISSN: 1544-2225
Buy freelance art; Sell back issues
Trim Size: 8 x 10 1/2

The Valley Advocate
Published by Newspapers of New England (NNE)
115 Conz St, Northampton, MA 01060
Mailing Address: PO Box 477, Northampton, MA 01061
Tel: 413-584-5000
E-mail: editor@valleyadvocate.com
Web Site: www.valleyadvocate.com
Key Personnel
Ed: Dave Eisenstadter *E-mail:* deisen@valleyadvocate.com
Syndicated book reviews once or twice a month, occasional author interviews.
Frequency: Weekly
Circulation: 55,000
Free

Vancouver Sun
Published by Postmedia Network Inc
400-2985 Virtual Way, Vancouver, BC V5M 4X7, Canada
Tel: 604-605-2000 *Fax:* 604-605-2323
E-mail: subscribe@vancouversun.com
Web Site: www.vancouversun.com
Key Personnel
Ed-in-Chief: Harold Munro *Tel:* 604-605-2185
E-mail: hmunro@postmedia.com
Mng Ed: Valerie Casselton *Tel:* 604-605-2125
E-mail: vcasselton@postmedia.com
Features Ed: Hardip Johal *Tel:* 604-605-2047
E-mail: hjohal@postmedia.com
Book reviews & author interviews.
First published 1912
Frequency: Daily (Mon-Sat)
Circulation: 208,675 (Sat)
$39/mo

Vanity Fair
Published by Conde Nast
One World Trade Center, 41st fl, New York, NY 10007-0090
Tel: 212-286-2860; 515-243-3273 (subns)
Toll Free Tel: 800-365-0635 (subns)
E-mail: letters@vf.com
Web Site: www.vanityfair.com; www.condenast.com
Key Personnel
CEO, Conde Nast: Roger Lynch
Chief Busn Offr: Chris Mitchell
Chief Revenue & Mktg Offr: Pamela Drucker Mann
Ed-in-Chief: Radhika Jones
Literature, the arts, politics & popular culture.
First published 1983
Book Use: Excerpts
Frequency: Monthly
Avg pages per issue: 125
Circulation: 1,197,922
Digital & print: $49.99/yr US, $59.99/yr CN, $68/yr foreign; digital only: $29.99/yr
Trim Size: 8 x 10 7/8
Ad Rates: 4-color full page $235,652, 1/2 page $149,471

Variety
Published by Penske Media Corp
11175 Santa Monica Blvd, Los Angeles, CA 90025
Tel: 323-617-9100 *Toll Free Tel:* 800-552-3632
E-mail: variety@pubservice.com; news@variety.com
Web Site: www.variety.com
Key Personnel
Chief Mktg Offr: Dea Lawrence
Group Publr & Chief Revenue Offr: Michelle Sobrino-Sterns
SVP: Timothy M Gray
VP & Exec Ed: Steven Gaydos
Assoc Publr: Donna Pennestri
Exec Ed: Ramin Setoodeh
Mng Ed: Joe Bel Bruno
Co Ed-in-Chief: Claudia Eller; Andrew Wallenstein
Mng Ed, Television: Cynthia Littleton
B2B publication for the entertainment industry.
First published 1905
Frequency: 48 issues/yr
Circulation: 40,000
$109/yr print, $129/yr print +/or digital US, $299/yr print & digital CN, $129/yr digital only CN & intl, $349/yr print & digital intl
ISSN: 0042-2738

VFW Magazine
Published by Veterans of Foreign Wars of the US
406 W 34 St, Suite 523, Kansas City, MO 64111
Tel: 816-756-3390 *Fax:* 816-968-1169
E-mail: magazine@vfw.org
Web Site: www.vfw.org/media-and-events/vfw-magazine

Key Personnel
Publr & Ed-in-Chief: Timothy K Dyhouse
 E-mail: tdyhouse@vfw.org
Art Dir: Lauren Goldman *E-mail:* lgoldman@vfw.org
Sr Ed: Janie Dyhouse *E-mail:* jdyhouse@vfw.org
Assoc Ed: Kari Williams *E-mail:* kwilliams@vfw.org
Sr Writer: Dave Spiva *E-mail:* dspiva@vfw.org
Articles of current interest to veterans; for VFW members. Includes book reviews. No unsol mss, query first.
First published 1904
Book Use: Excerpts
Frequency: 10 issues/yr
Avg pages per issue: 56
Circulation: 1,300,000 paid
Free to VFW membs, $15/yr nonmembs, $20/yr foreign
ISSN: 0161-8598
Buy freelance nonfiction, art; Sell articles & ad reprints, back issues
Ad Rates: B&W full page $29,830, 4-color full page $37,755
Ad Closing Date(s): see web site for dates

Victoria Advocate
311 E Constitution St, Victoria, TX 77901
Mailing Address: PO Box 1518, Victoria, TX 77902
Tel: 361-574-1222 (newsroom); 361-575-1451
 Toll Free Tel: 800-365-5779 (cust serv)
 Fax: 361-574-1220 (newsroom); 361-574-1225
E-mail: feedback@vicad.com
Web Site: www.victoriaadvocate.com
Key Personnel
Publr & Ed: Chris Cobler *Tel:* 361-574-1271
 E-mail: ccobler@vicad.com
Mng Ed: Becky Cooper *Tel:* 361-574-1285
 E-mail: bcooper@vicad.com
Features Ed: Elena Watts *Tel:* 361-580-6585
 E-mail: ewatts@vicad.com
Sunday, book reviews in-house & through syndication.
First published 1846
Circulation: 40,100 (d); 42,300 (Sun)
Digital & print: $8.99/4 wks (Sun only), $15/4 wks (Mon-Sun); digital only: $15/4 wks; print only: $24.25/4 wks (Mon-Sat)

The Virginian-Pilot
Published by Tribune Publishing Co
150 W Brambleton Ave, Norfolk, VA 23510
Tel: 757-446-9000
Web Site: pilotonline.com
Key Personnel
Mng Ed: Ryan Gilchrest *E-mail:* rgilchrest@dailypress.com
Books Ed: Erica Smith *Tel:* 757-446-2354
 E-mail: erica.smith@pilotonline.com
Sundays, 1 1/2 pages. Rare feature stories on writers. Often carry syndicated reviews. Reviews written by freelancers. Columns weekly, by alternating freelancers - one on children's & young adult, the other on adult titles.
First published 1865
Circulation: 199,800 (m); 228,600 (Sat); 238,600 (Sun)
$1.50/Sun; digital only: $1.99/wk; digital & print: $4.99/wk (Mon-Sun)

Vogue
Published by Conde Nast
One World Trade Center, 26th fl, New York, NY 10007-0090
Tel: 212-286-2860; 515-243-3273 (subns)
 Toll Free Tel: 800-234-2347 (subns); 800-405-8085 (intl subns)
E-mail: contact@vogue.com
Web Site: www.vogue.com; www.condenast.com

Key Personnel
Chief Busn Offr: Susan Plagemann
 E-mail: susan_plagemann@condenast.com
Ed-in-Chief: Anna Wintour
Mgr, Sales Opers: Nina Capaccione
 E-mail: nina_capaccione@condenast.com
Covers fashion, beauty, health, fitness, travel, entertainment & other areas of interest to women.
First published 1892
Book Use: Monthly book reviews
Frequency: Monthly
Avg pages per issue: 428
Circulation: 1,267,754
$21.99/yr US, $50/yr CN, $70/yr intl
ISSN: 0042-8000
Trim Size: 8 x 10 7/8
Ad Rates: 4-color full page $196,535, 1/2 page $132,687

The Wall Street Journal, A News Corp Co
Published by Dow Jones & Company
1211 Avenue of the Americas, 8th fl, New York, NY 10036
Tel: 212-416-3000; 609-514-0870
 Toll Free Tel: 800-369-2834; 800-568-7625 (cust support)
E-mail: wsjsupport@wsj.com
Web Site: www.wsj.com; www.dowjones.com
Subscription Address: 200 Burnett Rd, Chicopee, MA 01020
Key Personnel
Publr: Almar Latour
Ed-in-Chief: Matt Murray
Ed, "Five Best" Column: Brenda Cronin
Gen Mgr: Aaron Kissel
Features: Michael W Miller
Reporter, Book Publg: Jeffrey Trachtenberg
Reporter, News & Magazine Publg: Alexandra Bruell
In-house & other sources; rare author interviews.
First published 1889
Frequency: 6 days/wk (Mon-Fri & combined Sat/Sun weekend ed)
Circulation: 1,011,200
$43/mo classic print, $39/mo all access digital, $45/mo print & digital
Avg reviews per issue: 1
Ad Rates: B&W page $277,200, 1/2 page $138,600, color page $354,823.27, 1/2 page $198,709.39 (natl rates)

Walla Walla Union-Bulletin
112 S First Ave, Walla Walla, WA 99362
Mailing Address: PO Box 1358, Walla Walla, WA 99362-0306
Tel: 509-525-3300; 509-525-3301 (cust serv)
 Toll Free Tel: 800-423-5617
E-mail: news@wwub.com
Web Site: www.union-bulletin.com
Key Personnel
Publr: Brian Hunt *Tel:* 509-526-8331
Ed: Dian Ver Valen *Tel:* 509-526-8320
 E-mail: dianvervalen@wwub.com
Ed, Marquee: Annie Charnley Eveland *Tel:* 509-526-8313 *E-mail:* annieeveland@wwub.com
Arts & Entertainment (Thursday) distributed weekly in the area. Reviews (freelancers), syndicated, occasional local author interviews.
First published 1934
Frequency: Daily (Mon-Fri & Sun)
Avg pages per issue: 16
Circulation: 10,000
Print only: $6.50/mo (Sun only), $14.30/mo (Mon-Fri), $15.60/mo (Mon-Fri & Sun); digital only: $15.60/mo
Avg reviews per issue: 1

Washington Monthly
Published by Washington Monthly Publishing LLC
1200 18 St NW, Suite 330, Washington, DC 20036

Tel: 202-955-9010 *Toll Free Tel:* 855-492-1648 (subns) *Fax:* 202-955-9011
E-mail: editors@washingtonmonthly.com
Web Site: washingtonmonthly.com
Key Personnel
Art Dir: Amy Swan
Dir, Fin: Terri Wallace
Deputy Dir: Alice J Gallin-Dwyer
Ed-in-Chief: Paul Glastris
Exec Ed, Digital: Matthew Cooper
Mng Ed: Amy M Stackhouse
Sr Ed: Phillip Longman
Fresh look at government, public policy, current news, cultural issues.
First published 1969
Book Use: Reviews & excerpts
Frequency: 5 issues/yr
Avg pages per issue: 64
Circulation: 15,000 paid; 3,000 controlled
$5.95/issue, $19.95/yr indiv, $39.95/yr foreign
ISSN: 0043-0633
Sell articles, back issues & college guide
Avg reviews per issue: 10
Trim Size: 8 3/8 x 10 7/8
Ad Rates: 4-color full page $2,850, cover 2 $4,050, cover 3 $3,550, cover 4 $4,050

The Washington Post Magazine
Published by The Washington Post Co
One Franklin Sq, 1301 "K" St NW, Washington, DC 20071
Tel: 202-334-7585 *Toll Free Tel:* 800-477-4679
E-mail: wpmagazine@washpost.com
Web Site: www.washingtonpost.com/lifestyle/magazine
Key Personnel
Exec Features Ed: Liz Seymour
Deputy Features Ed: Mitch Rubin
Ed: Richard Just
Deputy Ed: David Rowell
Books Ed: John Williams
Aims to tell stories about the Washington area through long-form narrative journalism.
First published 1986
Book Use: Excerpts & adaptations
Frequency: Weekly (Sun)
Circulation: 1,267,759

The Washington Times
Published by The Washington Times Corp
3600 New York Ave NE, Washington, DC 20002
Tel: 202-636-3000
E-mail: circulation@washingtontimes.com
Web Site: www.washingtontimes.com
Key Personnel
Pres & Exec Ed: Christopher Dolan *Tel:* 202-636-3183 *E-mail:* cdolan@washingtontimes.com
Books Ed: Carol Herman
In-house, freelance & other sources. Book section Mon-Fri. Occasional author interviews.
Circulation: 100,000 (d)
$99.95/yr print or digital, $12.95/mo digital only
Avg reviews per issue: 12

Washingtonian
Published by Washingtonian Media Inc
1828 "L" St NW, Suite 200, Washington, DC 20036
Tel: 202-296-3600 (edit & busn); 202-296-1246 (print & online ad); 202-296-7580 (classified); 202-296-0715 (subns)
E-mail: editorial@washingtonian.com; subscriptions@washingtonian.com
Web Site: www.washingtonian.com
Subscription Address: The Washingtonian Subscription Service, PO Box 5530, Harlan, IA 51593-1030
Key Personnel
Pres & CEO: Catherine Merrill Williams
COO: Michael Johnson
Publr: Susan Farkas *E-mail:* sfarkas@washingtonian.com

SERIALS FEATURING BOOKS

Ad Dir: Kristen Anderson *E-mail:* kanderson@washingtonian.com
Prodn Dir: Cathy Dobos *E-mail:* cdobos@washingtonian.com
Exec Ed: Sherri Dalphonse *E-mail:* sdalphonse@washingtonian.com
Sr Mng Ed: William O'Sullivan
 E-mail: bosullivan@washingtonian.com
Articles Ed: Kristen Hinman
Ed: Michael Schaffer
Prodn Mgr: Sarah Rina Huang
Features matters of general interest for residents of the DC area.
First published 1965
Book Use: Washington-related excerpts
Frequency: Monthly
Avg pages per issue: 160
Circulation: 113,009 paid
$18/yr print & digital, $9.99/yr digital only
ISSN: 0043-0897
Buy freelance nonfiction & art; Sell back issues
Ad Rates: 4-color page $22,400
Ad Closing Date(s): 2 months preceding publication date

Watertown Daily Times
Published by Johnson Newspaper Corp
260 Washington St, Watertown, NY 13601
Tel: 315-782-1000 *Toll Free Tel:* 800-642-6222
 Fax: 315-661-2523 (newsroom); 315-661-2520 (busn off)
E-mail: news@wdt.net
Web Site: www.nny360.com
Key Personnel
Mng Ed: Alec Johnson *Tel:* 315-661-2351
 E-mail: aej@wdt.net
Features Ed: Christina Knott *Tel:* 315-661-2397
 E-mail: cknott@wdt.net
Weekly half-page devoted to books, through syndication & weekly author interviews; produce own magazine section.
First published 1861
Frequency: Daily (Tues-Sun)
Circulation: 37,000 (d); 40,000 (Sun)
Digital & print: $20.35/mo (Fri-Sun), $25.11/mo (Tues-Sat), $26.85/mo (Tues-Sun); digital only: $9.99/mo, $119.88/yr

Welland Tribune
Published by Metroland Media Group Ltd
Subsidiary of Torstar Corp
55 King St, Suite 600, St Catharines, ON L2R 3H5, Canada
Tel: 905-440-2516
E-mail: tribunecirc@niagaradailies.com (cust serv)
Web Site: www.wellandtribune.ca
Key Personnel
Group Dir, Media Sales: Jay Allin *Tel:* 905-225-1614 *E-mail:* jallin@starmetrolandmedia.com
Ed-in-Chief: Angus Scott *Tel:* 905-225-1625
 E-mail: angus.scott@niagaradailies.com
Occasionally, in-house; local author interviews covering the Niagara area; also syndicated.
Circulation: 16,500 (m)
$3.25/wk (Thurs-Sat), $5.21/wk (Mon-Sat), $5.99/4 wks e-paper

The Whitehorse Star
Published by Whitehorse Star Ltd
2149 Second Ave, Whitehorse, YT Y1A 1C5, Canada
Tel: 867-667-4481 *Fax:* 867-668-7130
E-mail: letters@whitehorsestar.com
Web Site: www.whitehorsestar.com
Key Personnel
Publr: Ms Jackie Pierce
Ed: Jim Butler
One column every Friday edition; author interviews.

Circulation: 5,100 (e)
$1/issue (Mon & Wed), $1.25/issue (Fri), $15/mo full digital & archives

The Wichita Eagle
Published by The McClatchy Co
330 N Mead St, Wichita, KS 67202
Tel: 316-268-6000 *Toll Free Tel:* 800-200-6627 (subns)
Web Site: www.kansas.com
Key Personnel
Exec Ed: Michael Roehrman *Tel:* 316-269-6753
One Sunday page, syndicated.
Circulation: 70,000 (d); 110,000 (Sun)
Digital & print: $41.93/13 wks (Sun only), $102.02/13 wks (Mon-Fri & Sun); digital only: $12.99/mo, $129.99/yr
Avg reviews per issue: 4

Wichita Falls Times Record News
Published by Gannett Co Inc
1301 Lamar St, Wichita Falls, TX 76301
Mailing Address: PO Box 120, Wichita Falls, TX 76307-0120
Tel: 940-767-8341 *Toll Free Tel:* 800-627-1646
Web Site: www.timesrecordnews.com
Key Personnel
Ed: Deanna Watson *E-mail:* deanna.watson@timesrecordnews.com
Weekly broadsheet, in-house & through syndication; occasional author interviews; Sunday books page.
Circulation: 16,000 (d); 18,000 (Sun)

Willamette Week
Published by City of Roses Newspaper Co
2220 NW Quimby St, Portland, OR 97210
Tel: 503-243-2122
Web Site: www.wweek.com
Key Personnel
Publr & Ed: Mark Zusman *E-mail:* mzusman@wweek.com
Arts & Culture Ed: Matthew Singer
 E-mail: msinger@wweek.com
First published 1974
Frequency: Weekly
Circulation: 70,000
Free

The Wilson Quarterly
Published by Woodrow Wilson International Center for Scholars
One Woodrow Wilson Plaza, 1300 Pennsylvania Ave NW, Washington, DC 20004-3027
E-mail: wq@wilsoncenter.org
Web Site: wilsonquarterly.com
Key Personnel
Busn Dir: Suzanne Napper
Digital Communs & Mktg Dir: Lauren Booth
Mng Ed: Stephanie Bowen
Provides unique insight, deep dives & fresh takes on developments in politics, culture, foreign affairs, history, the environment & more. Selected e-mail submissions will be considered.
First published 1976
Frequency: Quarterly
ISSN: 0363-3276 (print); 2328-529X (online)
Buy nonfiction, multimedia

Windsor Star
Published by Postmedia Network Inc
300 Oulette Ave, Windsor, ON N9A 7B4, Canada
Tel: 519-225-5711 *Toll Free Tel:* 800-265-5647 (CN only) *Fax:* 519-255-5515
Web Site: www.windsorstar.com
Key Personnel
Mng Ed: Craig Pearson *Tel:* 519-255-5767
 E-mail: cpearson@postmedia.com
Saturday page, in-house; monthly author interviews.
First published 1918

ADVERTISING, MARKETING

Circulation: 81,000 (d); 95,700 (Sat)
$30/mo (Tues-Sat); digital & print: $18/mo (Sat only); digital only: $9.95/mo, $99.99/yr; e-paper: $1.99/issue, $9.99/mo, $99.99/yr
ISSN: 0839-2277

Winnipeg Free Press
Published by FP Newspapers Inc
1355 Mountain Ave, Winnipeg, MB R2X 3B6, Canada
Tel: 204-697-7000 *Toll Free Tel:* 800-542-8900
 Fax: 204-697-7412
E-mail: letters@freepress.mb.ca
Web Site: www.winnipegfreepress.com
Key Personnel
Publr: Bob Cox *Tel:* 204-697-7547 *E-mail:* bob.cox@freepress.mb.ca
Literary Ed: Ben MacPhee-Sigurdson *Tel:* 204-697-7307 *E-mail:* ben.macphee-sigurdson@freepress.mb.ca
Feature author interviews; in-house book & freelance reviews. Books section runs every Saturday in the Weekend Review section.
Circulation: 125,000 (d); 162,000 (Sat)
Digital & print: $4.96/wk (Sat only), $8.72/wk (Mon-Sat); digital only: $3.92/wk
Avg reviews per issue: 8-9

Winston-Salem Journal
Published by BH Media Group Inc
418 N Marshall St, Winston-Salem, NC 27102
Mailing Address: PO Box 3159, Winston-Salem, NC 27102
Tel: 336-727-7211 *Toll Free Tel:* 800-642-0925
E-mail: contact@wsjournal.com
Web Site: www.journalnow.com
Key Personnel
Weekend Ed: Jon Jimison *Tel:* 336-727-7287
 E-mail: jjimison@wsjournal.com
Sunday book review, in-house & by freelancers. Several author interviews per year via features.
First published 1897
Circulation: 95,992 (m); 102,000 (Sun)
Digital & print: $19.15/mo (Sun only), $23.50/mo (Mon, Sat & Sun), $38.48/mo (Mon-Sun); digital only: $8.95/mo

Wisconsin State Journal
Published by Capital Newspapers
Division of Lee Enterprises Inc
1901 Fish Hatchery Rd, Madison, WI 53713
Mailing Address: PO Box 8056, Madison, WI 53708
Tel: 608-252-6100; 608-252-6200
 Toll Free Tel: 800-362-8333 (cust serv & circ)
E-mail: wsjcity@madison.com
Web Site: madison.com/wsj
Key Personnel
Publr: Tom Wiley *E-mail:* twiley@madison.com
Ed: John Smalley *Tel:* 608-252-6104
 E-mail: jsmalley@madison.com
Sunday page, features, columns; in-house & other book reviews. Author interviews.
Circulation: 108,000 (d); 114,000 (Sat); 161,000 (Sun)
$5/mo digital access
ISSN: 0749-405X

Words Without Borders
147 Prince St, Brooklyn, NY 11201
E-mail: submissions@wordswithoutborders.org
Web Site: www.wordswithoutborders.org
Key Personnel
Exec Dir: Elisabeth Jaquette
Digital Dir & Sr Ed: Eric M B Becker
Edit Dir: Susan Harris
Books Ed: Adam Dalva
Asst Ed & Devt Coord: Nina Perrotta
Translation, publication & promotion of the best international literature. English translations of contemporary fiction, nonfiction & poetry,

as well as reviews of thought-provoking new books in translation. Available online.
First published 2003
Frequency: Monthly
Free

Working Mother
Published by Working Mother Network
Division of Bonnier Corp
2 Park Ave, 9th fl, New York, NY 10016
Tel: 212-779-5000
Web Site: www.workingmother.com
Key Personnel
Editor-in-Chief: Meredith Bodgas
   E-mail: meredith.bodgas@workingmother.com
Creative Dir: Cara Reynoso *E-mail:* cara.reynoso@workingmother.com
Sr Ed: Audrey Goodson Kingo *E-mail:* audrey.kingo@workingmother.com
Assoc Publr: Olivia Kopchik *E-mail:* olivia.kopchik@workingmother.com
Contains articles & information for working mothers with children at home. Features articles & columns on money management, family relationships, health care, personal fulfillment, cooking & entertainment, business & careers, child development & humor. No unsol mss, query first.
First published 1979
Book Use: Reviews & excerpts
Frequency: Quarterly
Avg pages per issue: 53
Circulation: 750,000 paid
$3.99/issue, $9.97/yr, $12.97/3 yrs, $19.97/yr (USD) CN, $29.97/yr foreign
Buy nonfiction; Sell back issues $7 includes shipping & handling
Trim Size: 7 7/8 x 10 1/2
Ad Rates: B&W full page $61,010; 4-color full page $71,870

Wyoming Tribune-Eagle
Published by Adams Publishing Group
702 W Lincolnway, Cheyenne, WY 82001
Tel: 307-634-3361 *Toll Free Tel:* 800-561-6268
   Fax: 307-633-3189 (newsroom); 307-633-3191
E-mail: customerservice@wyomingnews.com
Web Site: www.wyomingnews.com
Key Personnel
Mng Ed: Brian Martin *Tel:* 307-633-3120
   E-mail: bmartin@wyomingnews.com
Asst Mng Ed: Erica Klimt *Tel:* 307-633-3129
   E-mail: eklimt@wyomingnews.com
Features Ed: Ellen Fike *Tel:* 307-633-3135
   E-mail: efike@wyomingnews.com
In-house & through syndication: "To Do" entertainment section, Fri-Sun; occasional author interviews.
Frequency: Daily (Tues-Sun)
Circulation: 14,000 (d); 14,750 (Sun)
$100/6 mos, $182/yr, $95/yr digital

Yachting®
Published by Bonnier Corp
Division of The Bonnier Group
460 N Orlando Ave, Suite 200, Winter Park, FL 32789
Tel: 407-571-4914
Web Site: www.yachtingmagazine.com
Subscription Address: PO Box 6364, Harlan, IA 51593 *Tel:* 515-237-3697 (intl) *Toll Free Tel:* 800-999-0869
Key Personnel
Publr: David Carr *Tel:* 954-594-7655
   E-mail: david.carr@bonniercorp.com
Ed-in-Chief: Patrick Sciacca *E-mail:* editor@yachtingmagazine.com
Mktg & Events Mgr: Deborah Velez *Tel:* 407-571-4839 *E-mail:* deborah.velez@bonniercorp.com
For those interested in pleasure boats & luxury yachts; articles on large power & sailing vessels, yachting events & marine equipment.
First published 1907
Frequency: Monthly
Avg pages per issue: 250
Circulation: 93,736 paid
$7/issue, $16/yr, $39/yr CN, $62/yr intl
Buy nonfiction & photos of interest to yachtsmen; Sell article & ad reprints, back issues
Trim Size: 8 3/8 x 10 7/8
Ad Rates: B&W page $36,410, 4-color page $40,010
Ad Closing Date(s): 45 days prior to sale date

Yankee Magazine
Published by Yankee Publishing Inc
1121 Main St, Dublin, NH 03444
Mailing Address: PO Box 520, Dublin, NH 03444
Tel: 603-563-8111
Web Site: newengland.com
Subscription Address: PO Box 420235, Palm Coast, FL 32142-0235 *Toll Free Tel:* 800-288-4284
Key Personnel
Pres: Jamie Trowbridge
VP & Publr: Brook Holmberg
VP, Sales: J D Hale, Jr
Ed-in-Chief: Judson Hale
Ed: Mel Allen
New England's magazine with regional stories covering food, travel, home, garden & other topics.
First published 1935
Book Use: Reviews & excerpts of titles that deal with New England
Frequency: 6 issues/yr
Avg pages per issue: 128
Circulation: 282,000 paid
$4.99/issue, $24/yr
ISSN: 0044-0191
Buy freelance fiction, nonfiction, photography
Trim Size: 7 3/4 x 10 1/2

Zest Magazine
Published by Houston Chronicle Publishing Co
Subsidiary of Hearst Corp
4747 Southwest Fwy, Houston, TX 77027
Mailing Address: PO Box 4260, Houston, TX 77210-4260
Tel: 713-220-7171 *Fax:* 713-362-3575
Web Site: www.houstonchronicle.com
Key Personnel
Chmn: Jack Sweeney
Books Ed: Alyson Ward *Tel:* 713-362-7128
   E-mail: alyson.ward@chron.com
Circulation: 825,000

News Services & Feature Syndicates

A & A
Division of Abramson & Abramson
PO Box 16223, Albuquerque, NM 87191-6223
Tel: 505-518-3939
E-mail: aaartwork@aol.com; aaauthor@aol.com
Web Site: www.elaineabramson.com
Key Personnel
Pres: Elaine Sandra Abramson
EVP: Martin Stanley Abramson
Founded: 1967
Syndicate *Appraisals by Abramson*, an appraisal column; *Pattern Craft by A & A*, craft & sewing patterns with instructions; *The Golden Gourmets*, cartoons & stories; *Those Characters From Cowtown*, cartoons; *The RomantiCats*, cartoons; *COW-TOWN*, cartoons; *Party Gators*, cartoons; *The Frisky Investigators*, cartoons; *The Star Staples*, cartoons; *The Collegiate Crunchies*, cartoons; *The Culinary Court*, cartoons; *The Artists' World*, column dealing with problems the artist faces such as health insurance, copyrights, etc. *The Collegiate Crunchies, The RomantiCats & COW-TOWN* appearing on the Pixelon Network, *Rufus & Mary*, cartoons; *Kaya, the Lucky Lab*; *Myschevious Animals*; *Tummy Ticklers*, cartoons; *From Fat to Fabulous: A Lifestyle Guide for Restaurant Lovers*. All submissions must be through a recognized agent. All unagented submissions are returned unopened. No unsol submissions. Author or artist must have credentials in subject applying to write or illustrate. We license our work out & also provide art & author services.
Membership(s): Best of Missouri Hands; Chesterfield Writers Guild; Composers, Authors & Artists of America; Creative Coalition; Croak & Dagger New Mexico; Electronically Published Internet Connection (EPIC); Graphic Artists Guild; Greater St Louis Art Association (GSLAA); Greater St Louis Artists Guild; Maryland Art League; Midwest Independent Booksellers Association (MIBA); Mystery Writers of America (MWA); National Association of Memoir Writers (NAMW); National Association of Television Program Executives Inc (NATPE); National League of American Pen Women; National Writers Association (NWA); National Writers Union (NWU); New Mexico Book Co-op; North Texas Writers Group; Publishers Association of the West (PubWest); Romance Writers of America (RWA); Romance Writers of America (RWA), Kiss of Death Chapter; St Louis Writers Guild; Sisters in Crime; Society of Children's Book Writers & Illustrators (SCBWI); Southern Independent Booksellers Alliance (SIBA); South-West Writers; Texas Association of Motion Media Professionals (TAMMP); Thriller Writers of America; Writers Under the Arch

American Urban Radio Networks (AURN)
938 Penn Ave, Suite 701, Pittsburgh, PA 15222-3811
Tel: 412-456-4099 *Fax:* 412-456-4077
Web Site: www.aurn.com
Key Personnel
SVP, Prog Opers & Affiliations: Lenore Williams *Tel:* 412-456-4098 *E-mail:* lwilliams@aurn.com
Founded: 1972
Entertainment, sports, news; 450 subscribers; movie reviews.
Branch Office(s)
932 W Madison, Chicago, IL 60607, Exec Sales Dir, Western Reg: Stephen Bates *Tel:* 312-558-1906 *E-mail:* sbates@aurn.com
112 W 34 St, Suite 2110, New York, NY 10120, Pres, Sales: Andy Anderson *Tel:* 212-883-2117 *Fax:* 212-687-3792 *E-mail:* aanderson@aurn.com

Andrews McMeel Syndication
1130 Walnut St, Kansas City, MO 64106-2109
Tel: 816-581-7300 *Toll Free Tel:* 800-255-6734
Web Site: syndication.andrewsmcmeel.com
Key Personnel
CEO, Andrews McMeel Universal: Kirsty Melville
VP & Mng Ed: Sue Roush *Tel:* 816-581-7320 *E-mail:* sroush@amuniversal.com
VP, Sales: John Vivona *Tel:* 816-581-7350 *E-mail:* salesdirector@amuniversal.com
Founded: 1970
Newspaper syndication (columnists, cartoons, comic strips).

Associated Press (AP)
200 Liberty St, New York, NY 10281
Tel: 212-621-1500
E-mail: info@ap.org
Web Site: www.ap.org
Key Personnel
Pres & CEO: Gary Pruitt
Ed-at-Large: Jerry Schwartz
Multimedia news service.
Number of Subscribers: 10,000

Ashleigh Brilliant Enterprises
117 W Valerio St, Santa Barbara, CA 93101
Tel: 805-682-0531
Web Site: www.ashleighbrilliant.com
Key Personnel
Pres: Ashleigh Brilliant *E-mail:* ashleigh@west.net
Founded: 1967
Panel feature; accept unsol mss.

Broadcast Wire & Audio
Subsidiary of The Canadian Press/La Presse Canadienne
c/o The Canadian Press, 36 King St E, Toronto, ON M5C 2L9, Canada
Tel: 416-507-2126 *Toll Free Tel:* 800-434-7578 (CN only) *Fax:* 416-364-1325
E-mail: broadcast@thecanadianpress.com
Web Site: www.thecanadianpress.com
Key Personnel
Dir, Broadcasting: Rose Kingdon
Data & audio news agency serving Canadian broadcasters providing regional, national & international news, weather, sports & features & alphanumeric cable TV information displays to Canada's major CATV operators.
Number of Subscribers: 400

Business Wire
Division of Berkshire Hathaway Co
101 California St, 20th fl, San Francisco, CA 94111
Tel: 415-986-4422 *Toll Free Tel:* 800-227-0845
E-mail: info@businesswire.com
Web Site: www.businesswire.com
Key Personnel
SVP, Global Media: Neil Hershberg
VP, Digital Strategy: Michael Toner
VP, Prod Mgmt: Galina Patil
Dir, Prod Mktg Mgmt: Serena Ehrlich
Dir, Tradeshow & Event Servs: Jim Liebenau
Founded: 1961
Business Wire electronically disseminates some 1,000 full-text news releases daily to the media, the Internet, online services & databases & the global investment community in 150 countries in 45 languages. The company's multi-channel delivery network, with access to some 60 international & national news agencies, financial information providers & web-based news services throughout North America, Europe, Asia, Latin America, the Middle East & Africa, provides real-time, simultaneous access to key audiences – the news media, trade publications, institutional & individual investors, business-to-business decision-makers & consumers. Business Wire has 24 US offices, Paris, Frankfurt, London, Brussels, Tokyo & Sydney offices & reciprocal offices throughout the world.
Branch Office(s)
40 E 52 St, 14th fl, New York, NY 10022 *Tel:* 212-752-9600 *Toll Free Tel:* 800-221-2462

California Focus, see Southern California Focus

The Canadian Press/La Presse Canadienne
36 King St E, Toronto, ON M5C 2L9, Canada
Tel: 416-364-0321 *Fax:* 416-364-0207 (newsroom)
E-mail: sales@thecanadianpress.com
Web Site: www.thecanadianpress.com
Key Personnel
CEO: Malcolm Kirk
Ed-in-Chief: Stephen Meurice
Founded: 1917
News-gathering agency. Provides content licensing services, custom content production services, real-time & archival database services, media monitoring services, newsfeed syndication services & publishes *The Canadian Press Stylebook* & *Caps & Spelling*.
Number of Subscribers: 600

Capitol News Service
Division of Metropolitan News
530 Bercut Dr, Suite E, Sacramento, CA 95811
Tel: 916-445-6336
E-mail: sacramentobulletin@gmail.com
Web Site: www.mnc.net/capitol.htm
Key Personnel
Ed: Dan Gougherty
Government & politics.

Congressional Quarterly Roll Call, see CQ Roll Call

Continental Features/Continental News Service
501 W Broadway, Plaza A, PMB 265, San Diego, CA 92101
Tel: 858-492-8696
E-mail: info@continentalnewsservice.com; continentalnewstime@gmail.com
Web Site: www.continentalnewsservice.com
Key Personnel
Pres & Ed-in-Chief: Gary P Salamone
Founded: 1981
Captioned photos on the *News Story of the Day*; country/background profiles; interview articles with national officials & international figures: *News Tip of the Month*. Market editorial commentary/analysis produced in-house. Publish children's newspaper, *Kids Newstime* & periodic national news magazine *Continental Newstime*, specializing in covering the unreported & under-reported world & national news, with

NEWS SERVICES & FEATURE SYNDICATES

238,000 multimedia, biweekly advertising circulation. Publishes a Northern California community newspaper & special complimentary, online Washington, DC, Chicago, Miami, Seattle, Boston, Anchorage, Atlanta, Honolulu, San Diego, Rochester (NY), Minneapolis & Houston news editions, on a rotational basis. Accept submissions with SASE; no unsol mss, query first; photos should be screened or half-toned (no negatives). CF/CNS is interested in adding substantially to our group of sponsored feature writers & feature cartoonists.

CQ Roll Call
Subsidiary of FiscalNote
1201 Pennsylvania Ave NW, Suite 600, Washington, DC 20004
Tel: 202-650-6500; 202-650-6511 (subns); 202-650-6621 (cust serv) *Toll Free Tel:* 800-432-2250; 800-678-8511 (subns)
E-mail: customerservice@cqrollcall.com
Web Site: cqrollcall.com; www.rollcall.com
Key Personnel
Publr: Josh Resnik
VP & Ed: Ed Timms
Mng Ed, Audience: John Helton
Asst Mng Ed, Prodn: George LeVines
Sr Staff Ed: Andrew Menezes
Design Ed: Chris Hale
Deputy Ed, News: Jason Dick
Deputy Ed, Visual Reporting: Gillian Roberts
Founded: 1955
Journals & newsletters on Congress, legislation, politics & national affairs; online products.

Crain Communications Inc
1155 Gratiot Ave, Detroit, MI 48207-2732
Tel: 313-446-6000 *Fax:* 313-446-0383
E-mail: info@crain.com
Web Site: crain.com
Key Personnel
Chmn: Keith Crain
Chief HR Offr: Nikki Kallek
CFO: Bob Recchia
CIO: Anthony Diponio
Pres & COO: K C Crain
SVP: Christopher Crain
VP & Gen Coun: Peter Grantz
Mng Dir, Audience, Prod & Mktg: Bonnie Roche
Dir, Procurement & Facilities: Eric Walters
Founded: 1916
Business media company with 56 business, trade & consumer brands in North America, Europe & Asia. Print publications, web sites, digital newsletters, webinars, direct mail, mobile apps, research, white papers & more.
Branch Office(s)
400 Continental Blvd, 6th fl, El Segundo, CA 90245-5074 *Tel:* 310-426-2470
1975 W El Camino Real, Suite 304, Mountain View, CA 94040-2218 *Tel:* 650-390-6200
601 13 St NW, Suite 9000 S, Washington, DC 20005-6714
150 N Michigan Ave, Chicago, IL 60601 *Tel:* 312-649-5200
685 Third Ave, New York, NY 10017-4024 *Tel:* 212-210-0100
1725 Merriman Rd, Suite 300, Akron, OH 44313-9006 *Tel:* 330-836-9180
700 W St Clair Ave, Suite 310, Cleveland, OH 44113-1256 *Tel:* 216-522-1383
Crain Communications GmbH, Technopark Oberpfaffenhofen, Argelsrieder Feld 13, 82234 Oberpfaffenhofen, Germany *Tel:* (0815) 390 7400
11 Ironmonger Lane, London EC2Y 8EY, United Kingdom *Tel:* (020) 7194 7570

Creators Syndicate
737 Third St, Hermosa Beach, CA 90254
Tel: 310-337-7003
E-mail: info@creators.com
Web Site: www.creators.com
Key Personnel
Founder & CEO: Rick Newcombe
Pres & COO: Jack Newcombe
Newspaper columns, comics, editorial cartoons & puzzles, all daily & weekly newspapers. Accept unsol mss.

The Cricket Letter Inc
Subsidiary of Cricket Communications Inc
PO Box 527, Ardmore, PA 19003-0527
Tel: 610-924-9158 *Fax:* 610-924-9159
E-mail: crcktinc@aol.com
Key Personnel
VP, Cricket Communications Inc & Publr/Ed-in-Chief, The Cricket Letter: Mark E Battersby *Tel:* 610-924-9157 *E-mail:* mebatt12@earthlink.net
Publr, Cricket Communications Inc: J D Krickett
Tax, financial, real estate, business editorial of interest to foreign investors. No unsol mss, query first.
Number of Subscribers: 7,325

Gannett News Service
Unit of Gannett Co Inc
7950 Jones Branch Dr, McLean, VA 22107-0150
Tel: 703-854-6000
E-mail: pr@gannett.com
Web Site: www.gannett.com
Key Personnel
Pres & CEO: Bob Dickey
Newswire to newspapers.

Gracenote, a Nielsen Company
2000 Powell St, Suite 1500, Emeryville, CA 94608
Tel: 510-428-7200
Web Site: www.gracenote.com
Key Personnel
Chief Content Offr: Atul Phadnis
Chief Prod Offr: Simon Adams
Chief Revenue Offr: Amilcar Perez
CTO: Kay Johansson
Pres: Karthik Rao
SVP, Busn Devt & Strategy: Ginger Bushell
SVP, Mktg & Communs: Graham McKenna
Electronic data & technology company powering music services, consumer electronics companies, automakers, media companies & cable/satellite operators.
Branch Office(s)
6255 Sunset Blvd, Los Angeles, CA 90028 *Tel:* 323-817-3505
40 Media Dr, Queensbury, NY 12804 *Tel:* 518-792-9914
211 Horseshoe Lake Dr, Halifax, NS B3S 0B9, Canada *Tel:* 902-835-3320
Av del Libertador 6350, Piso 6, C1428ART Buenos Aires, Argentina
Macquarie Park, Level 1, Bldg B, 11 Talavera Rd, Sydney, NSW 2113, Australia *Tel:* (02) 8397 7014
Rua George Ohm, 230-Torre A, 20° andar, Brooklin, 04576-020 Sao Paulo-SP, Brazil *Tel:* (011) 4420 9000 ext 9091
Gracenote GmbH, St-Martin-Str 61, 81669 Munich, Germany *Tel:* (089) 961183-0
Todi Estate, 2nd fl, B Wing, Lower Parel (W), Mumbai, Maharashtra 400 013, India
Gracenote KK, Shibuya Place 8F, 1-10-5 Dogenzaka, Shibuya-ku, Tokyo 150-0043, Japan *Tel:* (03) 3464-7785
Plot No 885, Amman, Wadi Sagra, Block 7, Bldg No 106, Off No 182, 8th fl, City Plazza, Amman 05047, Jordan
Millenium Tower, 13th fl, Radarweg 29, 1043 NX Amsterdam, Netherlands *Tel:* (020) 680 2560
Binnenwal 2, 3432 GH Nieuwegein, Netherlands *Tel:* (030) 600-71-71 *Fax:* (030) 600-71-77

ADVERTISING, MARKETING

Gracenote Korea Ltd, Seoul City Tower, Bldg 22F, 110, Huam-ro, Jung-gu, Seoul 04637, South Korea *Tel:* (02) 598-5857 *Fax:* (02) 798-5854

Hearst Newspapers
Division of Hearst Corp
300 W 57 St, New York, NY 10019
Tel: 212-649-2000
Web Site: www.hearst.com/newspapers
Key Personnel
Pres: Jeffrey M Johnson
Pres, Digital Media: Robertson Barrett
SVP & CFO: Barnabas Kui
SVP, Circ: Paul Barbetta
EVP: John C McKeon
EVP, Ad Sales: Mike DeLuca
Publishes 24 daily & 60 weekly newspapers.

Inman
Division of Inman Group Inc
1400 Village Square Blvd, Suite 3-80368, Tallahassee, FL 32312
Tel: 510-658-9252 *Toll Free Tel:* 800-775-4662 (cust support)
E-mail: customerservice@inman.com
Web Site: www.inman.com
Key Personnel
Founder: Brad Inman
CEO: Emily Paquette
Real estate features; 10 or 12 columns; electronic newspaper for real estate professionals.

Jewish Telegraphic Agency
24 W 30 St, 4th fl, New York, NY 10001
Tel: 646-778-5520
E-mail: info@70facesmedia.org
Web Site: www.jta.org; www.70facesmedia.org
Key Personnel
VP, Fin: Lee Silverstein
Ed-in-Chief: Andy Silow-Carroll
Founded: 1917
Jewish news & features.

Keister-Williams Newspaper Services Inc
PO Box 8187, Charlottesville, VA 22906
Tel: 434-293-4709 *Toll Free Tel:* 800-293-4709
E-mail: kw@kwnews.com
Web Site: www.kwnews.com
Key Personnel
Pres: Ky Lindsay
VP, Mktg: Meta L Nay
Busn Mgr: Carol Lindsay
Founded: 1984
Religion feature provided to newspapers.

Keystone Press Agency Inc
Subsidiary of Zuma Press
408 N El Camino Real, San Clemente, CA 92672
Tel: 949-481-3747 *Fax:* 949-481-3941
E-mail: info@keystonepictures.com
Web Site: www.keystonepictures.com
Key Personnel
Owner: Scott McKiernan *E-mail:* scott@keystonepictures.com
Founded: 1892
Picture archive.

King Features Syndicate
Subsidiary of Hearst Corp
300 W 57 St, New York, NY 10019-5238
Tel: 212-969-7550 *Toll Free Tel:* 800-526-5464
Web Site: www.kingfeatures.com
Key Personnel
Pres: C J Kettler
VP & Gen Mgr: Keith McCloat
Dir, Ad & PR: Beth Nock
Pubns Dir & Ed: Chris Rithcreek
Gen Mgr: Carla Silva
Founded: 1915

Columns, comic strips, cartoon panels, puzzles for newspaper use. Accept unsol column samples with cover letter, send to submissions editor in New York. Send copies as original material will not be returned. Visit web site for further information.

Kiplinger's Personal Finance/The Kiplinger Washington Editors Inc
1100 13 St NW, Suite 750, Washington, DC 20005-4364
Tel: 202-887-6400 *Toll Free Tel:* 800-544-0155 (cust serv)
E-mail: feedback@kiplinger.com
Web Site: www.kiplinger.com
Key Personnel
Ed: Mark Solherm
Off Mgr: Glen Mayers
Founded: 1947
Monthly personal finance/consumer magazine. No unsol mss, query first.
Number of Subscribers: 600,000

Merrell Enterprises
3542 E State Rte 73, Waynesville, OH 45068
Tel: 202-265-1925 *Fax:* 513-855-4277
Web Site: www.merrellenterprises.com
Key Personnel
Pres: Jesse H Merrell *E-mail:* jesse@jessehmerrell.com
Religious & political columns.

Metro Editorial Services
Division of Metro Creative Graphics Inc
519 Eighth Ave, New York, NY 10018
Tel: 212-947-5100 (ext 253, outside US & CN)
Toll Free Tel: 800-223-1600
E-mail: service@metro-email.com
Web Site: www.mcg.metrocreativeconnection.com
Key Personnel
Mng Ed: Andrew Griffin *E-mail:* agriffin@metro-email.com
Founded: 1903
Consumer editorial features distributed to 10,000 newspapers nationwide.

Military Update
PO Box 231111, Centreville, VA 20120-1111
Tel: 703-830-6863
E-mail: milupdate@aol.com
Web Site: www.militaryupdate.com
Key Personnel
News Columnist: Tom Philpott
Founded: 1994
Weekly military news column; 40 daily newspapers near military bases.

New Dimensions Radio
Subsidiary of New Dimensions Foundation
143 Colgan Ave, Suite 1103, Santa Rosa, CA 95404
Tel: 707-468-5215
E-mail: info@newdimensions.org
Web Site: www.newdimensions.org
Key Personnel
Co-Founder, Creative Prodr & Host: Justine Toms
Founded: 1973
Positive options & solutions for the future & personal growth. Topics include social changes & the arts & humanities as applied to everyday life; 40,000 subscribers; accept submissions; no unsol mss; query first. Heard in 300 communities in the US by over 1.5 million listeners.

The New York Times Licensing Group
Division of The New York Times Co
620 Eighth Ave, 20th fl, New York, NY 10018
Tel: 212-556-1927
E-mail: nytlg-sales@nytimes.com
Web Site: nytlicensing.com
Key Personnel
VP, Global Sales: Alice Ting *Tel:* 212-556-5967
E-mail: alicet@nytimes.com
Exec Dir, US/CN & Global Mktg: Aidan McNutty *Tel:* 212-556-4015 *E-mail:* mcnulaj@nytimes.com
Mng Ed, News Serv: Ray Krueger
E-mail: krueger@nytimes.com
Deliver Times journalism & curated content for publications & organizations of all sizes. Offers access to current & archival material across an extensive range of subjects. Content types include text, photo journalism, dynamic infographics, podcasts & video. All packages are rights-cleared & integrated with features to make them instantly available to global audiences.

NYT Licensing, see The New York Times Licensing Group

Post Bulletin Co LLC
Subsidiary of Small Newspaper Group
18 First Ave SE, Rochester, MN 55903
Tel: 507-285-7600 *Toll Free Tel:* 800-562-1758
E-mail: news@postbulletin.com
Web Site: www.postbulletin.com
Key Personnel
News Ed: Brian Sander *Tel:* 507-281-7420
E-mail: sander@postbulletin.com
News & Life Ed: Jeff Pieters *Tel:* 507-285-7748
E-mail: jpieters@postbulletin.com
One-panel cartoons, editorial cartoons, columns & approximately 500 various newspapers/publications. Send resume with 12 clippings of work, either columns or cartoons & send SASE for reply.
Number of Subscribers: 43,000

Press Associates Union News Service
4000 Cathedral Ave NW, No 535B, Washington, DC 20016
Tel: 312-806-4825
E-mail: paiunionnews@gmail.com
Key Personnel
Pres & Ed: Mark Gruenberg
Founded: 1955
Legislative, economic, political & social issues, job safety & health. No unsol mss, query first.
Number of Subscribers: 110
Membership(s): International Labor Communications Association (ILCA)

Quiz Features
PO Box 42222, Northwest Sta, Washington, DC 20015-0822
Tel: 202-966-0025 *Fax:* 202-966-0025
Key Personnel
Author & Gen Mgr: Donald Saltz
Founded: 1966
Daily Trivia Quiz: "Check Your Knowledge" & "Why That Expression?". Also theme quizzes & weekly "News Quiz".

Religion News Service
Subsidiary of Religion News Foundation
c/o University of Missouri's Journalism School, 30 Neff Annex, Columbia, MO 65211
Tel: 573-884-1327
E-mail: info@religionnews.com
Web Site: www.religionnews.com
Key Personnel
Publr & CEO: Thomas L Gallagher
Ed-in-Chief: Bob Smietana *E-mail:* bob.smietana@religionnews.com
Mng Ed: Paul O'Donnell *E-mail:* paul.odonnell@religionnews.com
Founded: 1934
Worldwide coverage of domestic & foreign religious news & photos; features. Uses news stories & news features; query first; prefer experienced journalists. Dist by Universal Press Syndicate & Canadian Press.

70 Faces Media, see Jewish Telegraphic Agency

Southern California Focus
1720 Oak St, Santa Monica, CA 90405
Tel: 310-452-3918
Web Site: www.californiafocus.net
Key Personnel
Owner & Author: Thomas D Elias
E-mail: tdelias@aol.com
Founded: 1972
California public affairs column.
Number of Subscribers: 93
Membership(s): Los Angeles Press Club

Thomson Reuters
3 Times Sq, New York, NY 10036
Tel: 646-223-4000; 646-223-6100 (edit); 646-223-6000 (newsroom)
Web Site: www.thomsonreuters.com
Key Personnel
Pres & CEO: Steve Hasker
COO, Cust Mkts: Brian Peccarelli
COO, Opers & Enablement: Neil Masterson
Chief of Staff: Carla Jones
Pres, Reuters News: Michael Friedenberg
EVP & Chief People Offr: Mary Alice Vuicic
EVP & Gen Coun: Deirdre Stanley
SVP & Head, Corp Fin: Mike Eastwood
Ed-in-Chief, Reuters News: Stephen J Adler
Founded: 1851
Global news service.

The Tribune News Service
Division of Tribune Content Agency
160 N Stetson Ave, Chicago, IL 60601
Tel: 312-222-4131
E-mail: tcanews@trbpub.com
Web Site: www.mctdirect.com; tribunecontentagency.com/tribune-news-service
Key Personnel
VP, Opers: Jack Barry *Tel:* 312-222-2193
E-mail: jbarry@tribpub.com
Sales Dir: Rick DeChantal *Tel:* 312-222-4544
E-mail: rdechantal@tribpub.com
Assoc Ed: Zach Finken *Tel:* 312-527-8756
E-mail: zfinken@tribpub.com; Emily Rosenbaum *Tel:* 312-222-4423 *E-mail:* erosenbaum@tribpub.com
Founded: 1973
Insightful coverage of politics & breaking news; lifestyle & entertainment reports; sports & business; compelling photography & useful graphics. Experienced editors deliver material from 70 leading companies, including the Los Angeles Times, Chicago Tribune, Miami Herald, The Dallas Morning News, Seattle Times & the Philadelphia Inquirer.

United Press International (UPI)
Subsidiary of News World Communications
1133 19 St NW, Suite 800, Washington, DC 20036
Tel: 202-898-8000
E-mail: media@upi.com
Web Site: www.upi.com
Key Personnel
Pres: Nicholas Chiaia
Founded: 1907
News, news picture & feature service.
Branch Office(s)
1200 N Federal Hwy, Suite 200, Boca Raton, FL 33432

Washington Post News Service with Bloomberg News
1301 "K" St NW, Washington, DC 20071
Tel: 202-334-7666

NEWS SERVICES & FEATURE SYNDICATES

E-mail: syndication@washpost.com
Web Site: www.washingtonpost.com/syndication
Key Personnel
Dir, Mktg & Technol: Robert S Cleland
Edit Dir: Richard Aldacushion
Mng Ed: Effie Dawson
Founded: 1962
Supplemental news service (subscribers only); no unsol mss.
Number of Subscribers: 644

Whitegate Features Syndicate
Division of Whitegate International Corp
71 Faunce Dr, Providence, RI 02906
Tel: 401-274-2149
E-mail: whitegate.featuressyndicate@gmail.com
Web Site: www.whitegatefeatures.com
Key Personnel
Pres: Ed Isaac
VP: Steve Corey
Talent Dir & Mgr, Spec Projs: Eve Green
Mgr: Mari Howard
Newspaper features & cartoons. Subscribers all around world. Every newspaper submitted; each columnist has own set number of newspapers. Accept unsol mss, but do not return submissions, do not send SASE.

Wingo LLC
Subsidiary of AmeriMarketing/Wingo LLC
12161 Ken Adams Way, Wellington, FL 33414
Tel: 561-379-2635
E-mail: sat@amerimarketing.com
Web Site: www.wingopromo.com; www.amerimarketing.com
Key Personnel
Owner & VP: Scott Thompson
VP: Daryl Thompson
Founded: 1981
Promote market games to increase newspaper circulation; 40 subscribers, promotional printing service, direct response printing.

Radio, TV & Cable Networks

A+E Networks®
235 E 45 St, New York, NY 10017
Tel: 212-210-1400 *Fax:* 212-210-9755
Web Site: www.aenetworks.com; x.com/aenetworks; www.facebook.com/AENetworks
Key Personnel
Pres: Paul Buccieri
EVP, Corp Communs: Michael Feeney
  E-mail: michael.feeney@aenetworks.com
Exec Asst: Mark Silverman *E-mail:* mark.silverman@aenetworks.com
Founded: 1984
Global content company comprised of some of the most popular & culturally relevant brands in media including A&E®, BIOGRAPHY®, Blaze™, Crime+Investigation®, FYI™, HISTORY®, HISTORY2™, Lifetime®, LMN™ & VICE TV®. A+E Networks' portfolio extends across platforms & genres, with a long-form production division, A+E Studios™; unscripted production unit, A+E Originals™; film division, A&E IndieFilms®; full service digital storytelling hub, 45th & Dean™; strategic investment division, A+E Ventures™; A+E Digital®, encompassing watch apps, games & SVOD initiatives including Lifetime Movie Club & HISTORY Vault. A+E Networks' channels & branded programming reach more than 335 million households in over 200 territories in 42 languages. A+E Networks has offices in the US, UK, Germany, Italy, Japan, Korea & Singapore. A+E Networks is a joint venture With Hearst Communications & Disney–ABC Television Group, a unit of The Walt Disney Company.

ABC Television Network
Subsidiary of The Walt Disney Co
47 W 66 St, New York, NY 10023
Tel: 818-460-7477
Web Site: abc.go.com
Key Personnel
CEO, The Walt Disney Co: Bob Iger
Pres, ABC: Karey Burke
Sr EVP & Corp Communs Offr, The Walt Disney Co: Zenia Mucha
Sr EVP & Gen Coun: Alan N Braverman
Network programming.

AMC
Subsidiary of AMC Networks Inc
11 Penn Plaza, 18th fl, New York, NY 10001
Tel: 212-324-8500
E-mail: amccustomerservice@amc.com
Web Site: www.amc.com
Key Personnel
Pres: Sarah Barnett
EVP, PR: Marnie Black *Tel:* 917-542-6361
Founded: 1984
Twenty-four hour movie based network dedicated to the American movie fan. A network that reaches 86 million homes, offers a comprehensive library of popular movies & a critically acclaimed slate of movie based original programming.

Bonneville International Corp
Subsidiary of Deseret Management Corp
Broadcast House, 55 N 300 W, Salt Lake City, UT 84101-3502
Tel: 801-575-5555
Web Site: bonneville.com
Key Personnel
Pres: Darrell Brown
CFO & SVP: Kent Nate
Founded: 1964
Broadcasting company consisting of 21 radio stations & an NBC affiliate TV station.

Cable One
210 E Earll Dr, Phoenix, AZ 85012
Tel: 602-364-6000
Web Site: www.cableone.net
Key Personnel
Pres & CEO: Julie M Laulis
CFO & SVP: Steven S Cochran
COO: Michael E Bowker
VP, Fin & Treas: Raymond L Storck, Jr
Founded: 1986
Leading broadband communications provider serving more than 800,000 residential & business customers in 21 states. Cable One provides customers with a wide array of connectivity & entertainment services, including high-speed Internet & advanced Wi-Fi solutions, cable television & phone service. Cable One Business provides scalable & cost-effective products for businesses ranging in size from small to mid-market, in addition to enterprise, wholesale & carrier customers.

The California Channel
1121 "L" St, Suite 110, Sacramento, CA 95814
Tel: 916-444-9792 *Fax:* 916-444-9812
E-mail: contact_us@calchannel.com
Web Site: www.calchannel.com
Key Personnel
Pres: John Hancock
Founded: 1989
Independent public affairs cable network for the state of California, modeled after the national C-SPAN network. 5.8 million subscribers. The network's core programming is gavel-to-gavel coverage of California Senate & Assembly floor sessions, committee hearings, state press conferences & other special events. California broadcast area only.

Canal SUR
Unit of SUR LLC
2105 NW 102 Ave, 3rd fl, Miami, FL 33172-2217
Tel: 305-227-6000 *Fax:* 305-554-6776
E-mail: info@condista.com
Web Site: www.canalsur.com
Key Personnel
Pres: Arturo Delgado
Founded: 1992
Live daily newscasts from the leading Latin American broadcasting networks. Journalistic & public opinion programs with in-depth coverage of current affairs from each country. The most popular game, comedy, variety show, sports & children programming from Latin America. 4,500,000 subscribers; 4 affiliates. Broadcast nationwide within the US.

CBS Television Network
Subsidiary of Paramount Global
51 W 52 St, New York, NY 10019-6188
Tel: 212-975-4321
Web Site: www.cbs.com
Key Personnel
Pres, CBS Corporation: Joseph Ianniello
EVP & Chief Communs Offr, CBS Corporation: Dana McClintock *E-mail:* dlmcclintock@cbs.com
EVP, Chief Res & Analytics Offr: Radha Subramanyam
Founded: 1928
Radio, cable & TV broadcasting.

City University Television (CUNY TV)
365 Fifth Ave, Suite 1400, New York, NY 10016
Tel: 212-817-7575 *Fax:* 212-251-0826
Web Site: www.cuny.tv
Key Personnel
Exec Dir: Gail Yancosek
Founded: 1985
University cable television channel serving over 7.3 million subscribers with educational, cultural, international & university based programming. Broadcasting in the 5 boroughs of New York City.

Comcast Cable Communications LLC
Division of Comcast Corp
Comcast Ctr, 1701 John F Kennedy Blvd, Philadelphia, PA 19103
Tel: 215-286-1700
E-mail: comcast_communications@comcast.com
Web Site: www.xfinity.com
Key Personnel
Pres: Mike Cavanagh
Sr EVP, Comcast Corp: Stephen B Burke
Founded: 1963
Operates cable television systems which serve approximately 22 million subscribers nationwide.

Cox Communications Inc
Subsidiary of Cox Enterprises Inc
6205-B Peachtree Dunwoody Rd, Atlanta, GA 30328
Tel: 404-843-5897 *Toll Free Tel:* 888-566-7751
E-mail: coxcorp.customerrelations@cox.com
Web Site: www.cox.com
Key Personnel
Exec Dir, Media Rel: Todd Smith *Tel:* 404-269-3124 *E-mail:* todd.smith@cox.com
Provider of digital cable television, telecommunications & home automation services. Cox serves approximately 6 million residences & businesses in the US.

The Crime Channel
310 N Indian Hills Blvd, Suite 214, Claremont, CA 91711
Tel: 760-360-9986
E-mail: crimechannel@dc.rr.com
Web Site: www.thecrimechannel.com
Key Personnel
Pres: Arnie Frank
Entertaining, informational & educational programs, all crime related. Series, documentaries & motion pictures. Broadcast throughout the US.

E! Entertainment Television LLC
Division of NBCUniversal
100 Universal City Plaza, Universal City, CA 91608
Tel: 323-954-2400 *Toll Free Tel:* 833-888-2726 (cust serv)
E-mail: customerservice@eentertainment.com
Web Site: www.eonline.com
Twenty-four hour coverage of entertainment news & events; 98.6 million viewers; long-form programming; telecast nationwide; programming seen in 130 countries internationally.

ESPN Inc
ESPN Plaza, Bristol, CT 06010

RADIO, TV & CABLE NETWORKS

Tel: 860-766-2000
E-mail: hello@espn.com
Web Site: www.espn.com
Key Personnel
EVP & CFO: Bryan Castellani
Pres: Jimmy Pitaro
SVP, Sales & Mktg: Patricia S Betron
VP, Communs: Katina Arnold
VP, Sales Communs: Cindy Freed
Founded: 1979
One of the most widely distributed cable networks, reaching more than 90 million homes. ESPN is America's #1 source for sports programming, airing more that 5,100 live +/or original hours of programming annually, including Monday Night Football, MLB, NBA, WNBA, college football, men's & women's college basketball, the X Games, the Great Outdoor Games. Its programming philosophy is to present a wide variety of exclusive, high-quality, innovative & in-depth sports events including both the marquee & narrow-interest; sports news, most notably the Emmy Award-winning SportsCenter & Outside the Lines.

In Touch Ministries
PO Box 7900, Atlanta, GA 30357
Tel: 770-451-1001 Toll Free Tel: 800-789-1473
Web Site: www.intouch.org
Key Personnel
Host: Dr Charles Stanley
Founded: 1988
Dr Charles Stanley can be heard on SiriusXM FamilyTalk (Christian teaching & talk) channel 161.

INSP LLC
PO Box 7750, Charlotte, NC 28241-7750
Tel: 803-578-1000 Fax: 803-578-1735
E-mail: info@insp.com
Web Site: www.insp.com
Key Personnel
Chmn & CEO: David Cerullo
COO: Dale S Ardizzone
CFO: Robert Brace
EVP, Corp Communs & Res: John E Roos
EVP, Worldwide Sales: Marc Favaro
SVP, Programming: Doug Butts
VP, Opers-Media Communs: Brack Rogers
Founded: 1990
24/7 general entertainment to 80 million US households via 2,800 cable systems; Dish Network, CVS, DirectTV & telcos.

KTTV-Fox 11
Division of Fox Television Stations LLC
1999 S Bundy Dr, Los Angeles, CA 90025
Tel: 310-584-2000
Web Site: foxla.com
Key Personnel
VP, News Dir: Kris Knutsen
Broadcast television station.

Minnesota Public Radio
480 Cedar St, St Paul, MN 55101
Tel: 651-290-1500 Toll Free Tel: 800-228-7123 (membs) Fax: 651-290-1188
E-mail: mail@mpr.org
Web Site: www.mpr.org
Key Personnel
CEO: Jon McTaggart
SVP & Chief Busn Devt Offr: Timothy T Roesler
 E-mail: troesler@americanpublicmedia.org
Founded: 1967
Regional public radio network of 45 stations in Minnesota, North & South Dakota, Wisconsin & Michigan. Three services: news, classical, The Current. More than 900,000 listeners, almost 100,000 members.

National Broadcasting Co (NBC)
Division of NBCUniversal
30 Rockefeller Plaza, New York, NY 10112
Tel: 212-664-4444
Web Site: www.nbc.com
Key Personnel
Exec VP, NBCUniversal: Adam Miller

National Public Radio
1111 N Capitol St NE, Washington, DC 20002
Tel: 202-513-2000 Fax: 202-513-3329
E-mail: mediarelations@npr.org
Web Site: www.npr.org
Key Personnel
Pres & CEO: Jarl Mohn
SVP, News & Edit Dir: Nancy Barnes
Exec Dir, Media Rel: Isabel Lara Tel: 202-513-2300
Program producer & distributor, as well as a membership organization with more than 770 member stations; news & information & cultural programming, broadcast nationwide.

NBCUniversal Telemundo Enterprises
Division of NBCUniversal
Telemundo Ctr, One Telemundo Way, Miami, FL 33182
Tel: 786-585-7000
Web Site: www.telemundo.com
Key Personnel
CFO: Amanda Calpin
VP, Ad Sales: Gian Pablo Kates
VP, Network Partnerships: Gerry Rojas
World-class media company leading the industry in production & distribution of high-quality Spanish language content to US Hispanics & audiences around the world. Telemundo Network features original Spanish language entertainment, news & sports content reaching 94% of US Hispanic TV households in 210 markets through 30 local stations, 51 affiliates & its national feed. Telemundo also owns WKAQ, a television station that serves viewers in Puerto Rico.

New England Sports Network (NESN)
480 Arsenal St, Bldg 1, Watertown, MA 02472
Tel: 617-536-9233 Fax: 617-536-7814
E-mail: sports@nesn.com
Web Site: www.nesn.com
Key Personnel
PR Mgr: Gary Roy
Founded: 1984
Most watched regional sports network in New England with 4 million subscribers. NESN is owned by the Boston Red Sox & Boston Bruins.

Premiere Networks Inc
Subsidiary of iHeartMedia Inc
15260 Ventura Blvd, Sherman Oaks, CA 91403
Tel: 818-377-5300
E-mail: feedback@premierenetworks.com
Web Site: www.premierenetworks.com
Key Personnel
Dir, Busn Opers: Michael Kindhart
PR Dir: Rachel Nelson Tel: 818-461-8057
Founded: 1987
Syndicated talk radio with over 6,000 affiliates reaching 245 million people monthly. Broadcast area, around the world via satellite & Internet. Coast to Coast AM is hosted by Art Bell & George Noory. Monthly, 4-color magazine After Dark uses freelance material from writers.
Branch Office(s)
3495 Piedmont Rd, Bldg 12, Suite 300, Atlanta, GA 30305 Tel: 404-365-4387
233 N Michigan Ave, Suite 2800, Chicago, IL 60611 Tel: 312-540-2921
27675 Halsted Rd, Farmington Hills, MI 48331 Tel: 248-324-5444
1270 Avenue of the Americas, New York, NY 10020 Tel: 212-445-3900

ADVERTISING, MARKETING

125 W 55 St, 4th fl, New York, NY 10019
801 Woodridge Center Dr, Charlotte, NC 28217
 Tel: 704-714-9444
14001 N Dallas Pkwy, Suite 300, Dallas, TX 75240 Tel: 972-239-6220

Public Broadcasting Service
2100 Crystal Dr, Arlington, VA 22202-3785
Tel: 703-739-5000
E-mail: corporatesecretary@pbs.org
Web Site: www.pbs.org
Key Personnel
Pres & CEO: Paula Kerger
Founded: 1969
There are 350 member stations nationally.

The EW Scripps Co
2800 Scripps Ctr, 312 Walnut St, Cincinnati, OH 45202
Tel: 513-977-3000 Toll Free Tel: 800-888-3000
Web Site: www.scripps.com
Key Personnel
Pres & CEO: Adam Symson
Pres, Local Media: Brian Lawlor
EVP & CFO: Lisa Knutson
EVP & Gen Coun: Bill Appleton
Deputy Gen Coun & Chief Ethics Offr: David Giles
SVP, Cont & Treas: Doug Lyons
SVP, Natl Media: Laura Tomlin
VP & Chief Diversity Offr: Danyelle ST Wright
VP & CIO: Bob Carson
VP & Corp Secy: Julie McGehee
VP, Audit & Compliance: Mark Koors
VP, Corp Communs & Investor Rel: Carolyn Micheli
VP, Strategy & Corp Devt: Robin Davis
VP, Strategy, New Busn & Corp Dev: Robert Kalutkiewicz
Television broadcasting.

Service Electric Cable TV Inc
2260 Avenue "A", Bethlehem, PA 18017
Tel: 610-865-9100 Toll Free Tel: 800-232-9100 (PA)
E-mail: office@sectv.com
Web Site: www.sectv.com
Key Personnel
Pres: John M Walson
VP & Cont: Joe Macus
Gen Mgr: John Capparell
Founded: 1948
Cable TV systems, phone & Internet.

Spectrum
Division of Charter Communications Inc
400 Washington Blvd, Stamford, CT 06902
Web Site: www.spectrum.com; www.facebook.com/Spectrum
TV, Internet, voice services & cell phone service to residential & business customers.

Superadio Networks
Division of Access.1 Communications Corp
112 W 34 St, Suite 2110, New York, NY 10120
Tel: 212-714-1000 Fax: 212-643-3871
Web Site: www.superadio.com
Key Personnel
CEO: Chelsey Maddox-Dorsey
Pres: Eric Faison Tel: 212-609-1168
 E-mail: eric@superadio.com
Network Affiliate Coord: Shawnjua Kelley Tel: 212-714-1000 ext 265
 E-mail: affiliaterelations@superadio.com
Founded: 1988
Produce & distribute marquee radio programs including shows in the urban, urban adult, mainstream top 40, rhythmic, talk, country, hot AC, rock, dance, alternative, gospel & oldies format.
Branch Office(s)
241 Boston Post Rd W, Marlborough, MA 01752,

Dist Mgr: Dianne Cook *Tel:* 508-620-0006
Fax: 952-556-9375 *E-mail:* dianne@superadio.com

Syfy
Division of NBCUniversal
30 Rockefeller Plaza, New York, NY 10112
Tel: 212-664-4444
E-mail: feedback@syfy.com
Web Site: www.syfy.com
Key Personnel
EVP, Mktg & Digital, USA Network & Syfy: Alexandra Shapiro
Founded: 1992
Science fiction, science fact, fantasy & horror. 94 million subscribers in US; broadcasts internationally.

TBS Inc, see Turner Broadcasting System Inc, A WarnerMedia Company

TCM, see Turner Classic Movies (TCM)

Telemundo, see NBCUniversal Telemundo Enterprises

Turner Broadcasting System Inc, A WarnerMedia Company
One CNN Center, Atlanta, GA 30303-2720
Tel: 404-827-1700
E-mail: turner.info@turner.com
Web Site: www.turner.com
Key Personnel
Pres: David Levy
EVP, Global Chief Communs Offr & Corp Mktg Offr: Molly Battin
EVP & Gen Coun: Louise Sams
EVP & Global Chief HR Offr: Angela Santone
Admin Offr: Pascal Descroches
Founded: 1976
Global entertainment, sports & news company. Turner owns & operates brands including Adult Swim, Bleacher Report, Boomerang, Cartoon Network, CNN, ELEAGUE, FilmStruck, Great Big Story, HLN, iStreamPlanet, Super Deluxe, TBS, Turner Classic Movies (TCM), TNT, truTV & Turner Sports.

Turner Classic Movies (TCM)
Subsidiary of Warner Bros Discovery Inc
230 Park Ave S, New York, NY 10003
Tel: 404-885-5535 (TCM); 212-548-5555 (Warner Bros)
Web Site: www.tcm.com; www.wbd.com/our-brands
Key Personnel
PR Mgr: Taryn Jacobs *Tel:* 404-885-0114
E-mail: taryn.jacobs@wbd.com
Founded: 1994
Classic movie network, uncut & commercial-free.

Univision Networks
Division of Univision Communications Inc
605 Third Ave, 12th fl, New York, NY 10158-5200
Tel: 212-455-5200
Web Site: www.univision.com
Key Personnel
CEO: Vincent Sadusky
CFO: Peter H Lori
Pres & COO: Jessica Rodriguez
Pres, Ad Sales & Mktg: Steve Mandala
US Hispanic cable network delivering broad-based, family oriented programming (including sports, music, classic movies, novelas, variety & news, children's programming & bilingual block) in Spanish language; 1,866 affiliates, nationwide.
Branch Office(s)
2323 Bryan St, Suite 1900, Dallas, TX 75201
Tel: 214-758-2300

USA Network
Division of NBCUniversal
30 Rockefeller Plaza, 21st fl, New York, NY 10112
Tel: 212-413-5000
Web Site: www.usanetwork.com
Founded: 1971
Cable television leader in original series & home to blockbuster theatrical films, acquired television series & entertainment events.

The Weather Channel (TWC) Television Network
Subsidiary of Weather Group Television LLC
300 Interstate N Pkwy, Atlanta, GA 30339
Tel: 770-226-0000
Web Site: weathergroup.com
Key Personnel
Communs Mgr: Katie Shuford *E-mail:* katie.shuford@weathergroup.com
Founded: 1982
24-hour all-weather satellite television programming service with 100 million subscribers. International, national, regional & local weather conditions & forecasts, shown nationwide.

WKTX AM830 & NBN-Radio/TV (Nationality Broadcasting Network)
Division of NBN Productions
11906 Madison Ave, Lakewood, OH 44107
Tel: 216-221-0330 *Fax:* 216-221-3638
Key Personnel
Prog Dir: Jack Cory
Opers Mgr: Jim Georgiades
International programming with affiliates of Scola Satellite & Cox Cable broadcast in Northeastern Ohio; 18 million subscribers, North American continent; news & entertainment.
Branch Office(s)
178 N Mecca, Cortland, OH 44410

Xfinity, see Comcast Cable Communications LLC

Radio Programs Featuring Books

Listed here are radio programs that deal with books and authors. Programs are listed alphabetically by program name. Some are hosted by established critics who devote their entire program to reviews of current books; others feature books only occasionally. Also see the sections **Columnists & Commentators** and **TV Programs Featuring Books**.

AirTalk with Larry Mantle
KPCC-FM
Division of Southern California Public Radio (SCPR)
474 S Raymond Ave, Pasadena, CA 91105
Tel: 626-583-5100 *Fax:* 626-583-5101
E-mail: airtalk@kpcc.org
Web Site: www.kpcc.org
Key Personnel
Sr Prodr: Fiona Ng
Host: Larry Mantle
Newstalk, interviews, call-ins.
Air Time: Mon-Fri 10 AM-noon

All About Books
KUCV-FM - NET Radio
1800 N 33 St, Lincoln, NE 68503
Tel: 402-472-6141 *Toll Free Tel:* 888-638-7346
 Fax: 402-472-1785
E-mail: radio@netnebraska.org
Web Site: www.netnebraska.org/radio
Key Personnel
Prodr: Jeff Smith *Tel:* 402-470-6370
 E-mail: jsmith@netnebraska.org
Weekly program about books.
Air Time: Wed 10 AM

All Sides
WOSU-FM
Division of Ohio State University
2400 Olentangy River Rd, Columbus, OH 43210-1027
Tel: 614-292-9678 (ext 49784)
E-mail: allsides@wosu.org
Web Site: www.wosu.org
Key Personnel
Host: Ann Fisher
Call in; National Public Radio affiliate, politics, history, English language, science. Books featured are primarily nonfiction.
Air Time: Mon-Fri 10 AM-noon (ET)

All Things Considered
National Public Radio
1111 N Capitol St NE, Washington, DC 20002
Tel: 202-513-2000
Web Site: www.npr.org
Key Personnel
Host: Audie Cornish; Ailsa Chang; Ari Shapiro; Mary Louise Kelly
Debut Date: 1971
News & information, current issues, book reviews & author interviews broadcast on stations nationwide at various times. See web site for list of stations & times.
Air Time: Daily

Amazon Country
WXPN-FM 88.5
Division of University of Pennsylvania
3025 Walnut St, Philadelphia, PA 19104
Tel: 215-898-6677 *Fax:* 215-898-0707
E-mail: wxpndesk@xpn.org; amazon@xpn.org
Web Site: www.xpn.org
Key Personnel
Host & Prodr: Debra D'Alessandro
Gen Mgr: Roger La May
Debut Date: 1974
Lesbian & feminist music & public affairs.
Air Time: Sun 11 AM-noon

Background Briefing
KPFK-FM (Pacifica)
Member of Pacifica Foundation
3729 Cahuenga Blvd W, North Hollywood, CA 91604
Tel: 818-985-2711 *Fax:* 818-763-7526
E-mail: comments@kpfk.org
Web Site: www.kpfk.org
Key Personnel
Host & Prodr: Ian Masters *E-mail:* icmasters@gmail.com
Interviews on world affairs.
Air Time: Mon-Thurs 5-6 PM, Sun 11 AM-noon

Beneath the Surface
KPFK-FM (Pacifica)
Member of Pacifica Foundation
3729 Cahuenga Blvd W, North Hollywood, CA 91604
Tel: 818-985-2711 *Fax:* 818-763-7526
E-mail: comments@kpfk.org
Web Site: www.kpfk.org
Key Personnel
Exec Prodr: Robert Brenner
Host: Suzi Weissman
Current issues, news & author interviews.
Air Time: Sun 10-11 AM

Between the Covers
KBOO-FM
20 SE Eighth Ave, Portland, OR 97214
Tel: 503-231-8032 *Fax:* 503-231-7145
E-mail: amnews@kboo.org
Web Site: www.kboo.fm/program/between-covers
Interviews with locally & nationally known fiction & nonfiction authors. Numerous hosts.
Air Time: 1st, 2nd & 4th Thurs 11-11:30 AM, 3rd & 5th Thurs 11 AM-noon

Book Bits
WTBF-AM/FM
Division of Troy Broadcasting Corp
67 W Court Sq, Troy, AL 36081
Tel: 334-566-0300 *Fax:* 334-566-5689
E-mail: wtbfdoc@yahoo.com
Web Site: www.wtbfradio.com
Key Personnel
Opers & Prog Mgr: Dave Kirby
Debut Date: 1985
Daily 3-minute book reviews.

The Book Nook
WYSO
Affiliate of National Public Radio
150 E South College St, Yellow Springs, OH 45387
Mailing Address: 4805 Meredith Rd, Yellow Springs, OH 45387
Tel: 937-767-6420 *Fax:* 937-769-1382
Web Site: www.wyso.org/show/book-nook
Key Personnel
Prodr & Host: Vick Mickunas *Tel:* 937-767-1396
 E-mail: vick@vickmickunas.com
Debut Date: 1994
Author interviews on a wide range of topics. The program covers fiction & nonfiction book titles.
Do not send any mail to WYSO. All book submissions must be sent to the mailing address.
WYSO is a National Public Radio affiliate that serves 14 counties in southwest Ohio.
Air Time: Sat 7-8 AM, Sun 10:30-11 AM (ET)

The Book Show
WAMC Northeast Public Radio
318 Central Ave, Albany, NY 12206
Mailing Address: PO Box 66600, Albany, NY 12206
Tel: 518-465-5233 *Toll Free Tel:* 800-323-9262
E-mail: book@wamc.org; mail@wamc.org
Web Site: www.wamc.org
Key Personnel
Host: Joe Donahue
Author/host interviews regarding their books, lives & their craft. A celebration of both reading & writers.
Air Time: Syndicated by National Productions (WAMC) & varies by station

Boston Sunday Review
WBZ-FM
Subsidiary of Beasley Media Group
55 Morissey Blvd, Boston, MA 02125
Tel: 617-746-1400 *Fax:* 617-746-1402
Web Site: www.985thesportshub.com
Key Personnel
Prodr: Tracy Clements *E-mail:* tclements@985thesportshub.com
Host: Mat Schaffer
General interest talk show & author interviews.
Air Time: Sun 6-8 AM

Charlie Brennan Show
KMOX-AM
Division of Entercom Communications Corp
1220 Olive St, 3rd fl, St Louis, MO 63103-2301
Tel: 314-621-2345 *Fax:* 314-588-1234
E-mail: kmoxnews@kmox.com
Web Site: kmox.radio.com/shows/charlie-brennan-show
Key Personnel
Host: Charles Brennan *E-mail:* charles.brennan@entercom.com
Interviews, phone-ins, issues of the day.
Air Time: Mon-Fri 8:30-11 AM

Chuck & Kelly in the Morning
WGY-AM
Division of iHeartMedia Inc
Riverhill Ctr, 1203 Troy-Schenectady Rd, Latham, NY 12110-1046
Tel: 518-452-4800
Web Site: www.wgy.com
Key Personnel
Host: Chuck Custer *E-mail:* chuck@wgy.com; Kelly Stevens *E-mail:* kelly@wgy.com
Book reviews, interviews & entertainment.
Air Time: Mon-Fri 5:30-9 AM

Cityscape
WFUV-FM
Affiliate of Fordham University
Fordham University, 441 E Fordham Rd, Keating Hall, Rm B-12, Bronx, NY 10458-9993
Tel: 718-817-4550
E-mail: thefolks@wfuv.org; cityscapewfuv@gmail.com
Web Site: www.wfuv.org

Key Personnel
Prodr, News & Pub Aff Dir: George Bodarky
  E-mail: gbodarky@wfuv.org
Urban issues, environment, literature, arts, human rights.
Air Time: Sun 6:30-7 AM

Community Spotlight
WESB-107.5 FM
Division of WESB Inc
1490 Saint Francis Dr, Bradford, PA 16701
Tel: 814-368-4141 *Fax:* 814-368-3180
E-mail: 1490@wesb.com
Web Site: www.wesb.com
Key Personnel
Pres & Gen Mgr: Don Fredeen
  E-mail: dfredeen@wesb.com
Host & Prodr: Anne Holliday
Talk show featuring community leaders, best-selling authors, actors & politicians.
Air Time: Fri 9:30 AM

Cover to Cover Open Book
KPFA-FM
Affiliate of Pacifica Foundation
1929 Martin Luther King Jr Way, Berkeley, CA 94704
Tel: 510-848-6767 *Fax:* 510-848-3812
E-mail: comments@kpfa.org
Web Site: www.kpfa.org
Key Personnel
Coord: Richard Wolinsky *E-mail:* richwol@well.com
Host: Reyna Cowan *E-mail:* reynacowan@gmail.com; Jack Foley *E-mail:* jandafoley@sbcglobal.net; Jovelyn Richards *E-mail:* jovelynrichards@aol.com; Nina Serrano *E-mail:* ninaserrano34@gmail.com
Weekly interviews with poets, performance artist, film-makers, novelists & storytellers. The first week of every month is a combined one-hour program featuring Jack Foley & Nina Serrano. The second week is hosted by Nina Serrano, Poet 2 Poet. The third week is hosted by Jovelyn Richards, Jovelyn's Bistro. The fourth week is hosted by Reyna Cowan, Frame to Frame. The fifth week (if there is one) is hosted again by Jovelyn Richards, Jovelyn's Bistro.
Air Time: Wed 3:30 PM, first Wed of the month 3-4 PM

Extension 720 with Justin Kaufmann
WGN-AM
Division of Nexstar Media Group Inc
303 E Wacker Dr, 18th fl, Chicago, IL 60601
Tel: 312-222-4700
E-mail: comments@wgnradio.com
Web Site: www.wgnradio.com
Key Personnel
Host: Justin Kaufmann
General interest talk & interviews.
Air Time: Mon-Fri 7-10 PM

Gwin Faulconer-Lippert Show
KTOK-AM
Subsidiary of iHeartMedia Inc
1900 Northwest Expwy, Suite 1000, Oklahoma City, OK 73118
Tel: 405-840-5271; 405-841-0200
Web Site: ktok.iheart.com
Various topics.
Air Time: Sun 8 PM

Forum
KQED-FM
Affiliate of National Public Radio
2601 Mariposa St, San Francisco, CA 94110
Tel: 415-553-2135 *Toll Free Tel:* 866-733-6786 (call-in) *Fax:* 415-553-2174
E-mail: forum@kqed.org
Web Site: www.kqed.org/forum

Key Personnel
Prodr: Judy Campbell
Host: Mina Kim; Michael Krasny
Community concerns, consumer issues & interviews.
Air Time: Mon-Fri 9-10 AM & 10-11 AM (two segments)

Fresh Air
WHYY-FM
Affiliate of National Public Radio
Independence Mall West, 150 N Sixth St, Philadelphia, PA 19106
Tel: 215-351-1200
E-mail: talkback@whyy.org
Web Site: www.whyy.org/programs/fresh-air
Key Personnel
Host & Exec Prodr: Terry Gross
Exec Prodr: Danny Miller
Prodr: Sam Briger; Amy Salit
Talk show; arts, popular culture & entertainment. Author interviews & book material. Broadcast nationally via National Public Radio.
Air Time: Check newspaper listing or web site

Lewis Burke Frumkes Show
WPAT-AM
Affiliate of Multicultural Radio Broadcasting Inc
27 Williams St, 11th fl, New York, NY 10005
Tel: 212-966-1059
Web Site: www.wpat930am.com
Key Personnel
Host & Prodr: Lewis Burke Frumkes
  E-mail: lewisfrumkes@gmail.com
Interviews with high profile people in arts & sciences.
Air Time: Sun 8-8:30 PM

Garage Logic
Hubbard Interactive
3415 University Ave SE, St Paul, MN 55114
Tel: 651-632-6646 *Fax:* 651-647-2932
Web Site: garagelogic.com/authors-corner
Key Personnel
Host: Joe Soucheray
Current topics podcast. Author's Corner feature on web site.

Steve Gruber
WAAM Talk 1600
4230 Packard Rd, Ann Arbor, MI 48108-1597
Tel: 734-971-1600 *Fax:* 734-973-2916
Web Site: www.waamradio.com
Key Personnel
News & Opers Dir: Dan Martin *Tel:* 734-971-1600 ext 15 *E-mail:* dan@waamradio.com
Gen Mgr & Sales Mgr: Theron Hughes *Tel:* 734-971-1600 ext 14 *E-mail:* x@waamradio.com
News, interviews, political talk show.
Air Time: Mon-Fri 6-9 AM

Roger Hedgecock Report
KFMB-760 AM
Division of TEGNA Media
7677 Engineer Rd, San Diego, CA 92111
Tel: 858-292-7600
E-mail: rogerhedgecock@gmail.com
Web Site: 760kfmb.com
Key Personnel
Host: Roger Hedgecock
Talk show. Politics, current events, occasional author interviews.
Air Time: Mon-Fri 7:30 AM, 12:30 PM, 3:30 PM & 5 PM

The Tom Kearney Show
WPTF-680 AM
Division of Curtis Media Group
3012 Highwoods Blvd, Suite 201, Raleigh, NC 27604
Tel: 919-790-9392 (busn); 919-860-9783 (studio)

Web Site: wptf.com/tom-kearney
Key Personnel
Host: Tom Kearney
Debut Date: 1988
General interest, various topics.
Air Time: Mon-Fri 9-10 PM

KOMO-1000 News
KOMO-AM Radio
Division of Sinclair Broadcast Group Inc
140 Fourth Ave N, Seattle, WA 98109
Tel: 206-404-5666
E-mail: editor@komoradio.com
Web Site: www.komonews.com
Key Personnel
Prog Dir: Rick Van Cise
News, current events.
Air Time: Mon-Sun all day

Mark Levin Show
WTVN-AM 610
Division of iHeartMedia Inc
2323 W Fifth Ave, Suite 200, Columbus, OH 43204
Tel: 614-486-6101
Web Site: 610wtvn.iheart.com; www.marklevinshow.com
Key Personnel
Host: Mark Levin
Talk show; includes interviews & call-ins.
Air Time: Mon-Fri 10 PM-midnight

LNK Today
KLIN-AM
Division of NRG Media
4343 "O" St, Lincoln, NE 68510
Tel: 402-475-4567 *Fax:* 402-479-1411
E-mail: news@klin.com
Web Site: www.klin.com
Key Personnel
Host: Jack Mitchell *E-mail:* jackm@klin.com
Local news, talk & interviews.
Air Time: Mon-Fri 6-9 AM

Maryland Today
WPOC-FM
Subsidiary of iHeartMedia Inc
711 W 40 St, Suite 350, Baltimore, MD 21211
Tel: 410-366-7600
Web Site: www.wpoc.com
Public affairs program, including author interviews.
Air Time: Sun 6-6:30 AM

Metroscope
KGON-FM, KFXX-1080-AM
Division of Entercom Communications Corp
0700 SW Bancroft St, Portland, OR 97239
Tel: 503-223-1441 *Fax:* 503-223-6909
E-mail: metroscope@entercom.com
Web Site: www.metroscopepdx.com
Key Personnel
Pub Aff Dir/Host: Preston Hiefield
Public affairs & news program; local concerns & issues. Also features authors & artists.
Air Time: Sun 6 AM (KGON-FM); Sun 10 PM (KFXX-1080-AM)

Dori Monson Show
KIRO-FM
Division of Bonneville International Corp
1820 Eastlake Ave E, Seattle, WA 98102
Tel: 206-726-7000 *Toll Free Tel:* 800-756-5476
Web Site: www.mynorthwest.com/category/the-dori-monson-show
Key Personnel
Prog Dir: Ryan Maguire *E-mail:* rmaguire@bonneville.com
Host: Dori Monson *E-mail:* dmonson@bonneville.com

Pop culture, politics & sports, talk show; author interviews.
Air Time: Mon-Fri noon-3 PM

Morning Edition
National Public Radio
1111 N Capitol St NE, Washington, DC 20002
Tel: 202-513-2000 *Fax:* 202-513-3329
Web Site: www.npr.org
Key Personnel
Host/Correspondent: David Greene
Host: Steve Inskeep; Noel King; Rachel Martin
Debut Date: 1979
News & information, used live or rebroadcast by over 600 National Public Radio stations; author interviews & book talk when relevant.
Air Time: Mon-Fri 5-9 AM (ET)

Morning Edition
KUHF-FM
Affiliate of National Public Radio
University of Houston, 4343 Elgin St, Houston, TX 77204-0887
Tel: 713-748-8888
E-mail: news@houstonpublicmedia.org
Web Site: www.npr.org/programs/morning-edition
Key Personnel
Dir, News & Pub Aff: Dave Fehling
 E-mail: dfehling@houstonpublicmedia.org
Debut Date: 1979
Local news inserts.
Air Time: Mon-Fri 5-9 AM

Morning News with Larry Richert & John Shumway
KDKA-Radio AM 1020
Division of Entercom Communications Corp
Foster Plaza, Bldg 5, 651 Holiday Dr, Pittsburgh, PA 15220
Tel: 412-920-9400
E-mail: newsdesk@kdka.com
Web Site: kdkaradio.radio.com
Key Personnel
Prog Dir: Jim Graci
Host: Larry Richert; John Shumway
Current events & news.
Air Time: Mon-Fri 6-10 AM

The Morning Show with Dave Lee
WCCO-AM
Division of Entercom Communications Corp
625 Second Ave S, Minneapolis, MN 55402
Tel: 612-370-0611; 651-989-9226 (studio/contest)
E-mail: newstips@wccoradio.com
Web Site: wccoradio.radio.com
Key Personnel
Host: Dave Lee
Air Time: Mon-Fri 5-9 AM

New Letters on the Air
New Letters Quarterly Magazine
Division of University of Missouri-Kansas City
UMKC, University House, 5101 Rockhill Rd, Kansas City, MO 64110-2499
Tel: 816-235-1159 *Toll Free Tel:* 888-LIT-AIRS (548-2477)
E-mail: radio@newletters.org
Web Site: www.newletters.org
Key Personnel
Ed-in-Chief: Robert Stewart *E-mail:* stewartr@umkc.edu
Prodr & Host: Angela Elam *E-mail:* elama@umkc.edu
Asst Prodr: Jamie Walsh *E-mail:* walshjm@umkc.edu
Debut Date: 1977
29-minute public radio program featuring interviews with or public readings by creative writers-poets, novelists, essayists, dramatists-talking about the creative process & their work. Available to any public radio station; recent programs can be heard free online at www.newletters.org or older archive interviews can be purchased through the web site. New Letters on the Air has been on the public airwaves since 1977, making it public radio's longest continuously-running literary program.
Air Time: Public Radio Satellite Service (PRSS) feed on Content Depot 1 PM (ET). Selected programs available at www.prx.org. Digital download available for stations not connected to the satellite (e-mail Jamie Welsh for details)

Nightside with Dan Rea
WBZ-AM
Subsidiary of iHeartMedia Inc
One Cabot Rd, Suite 320, Medford, MA 02155
Tel: 617-254-1030
Web Site: wbznewsradio.iheart.com/featured/nightside-with-dan-rea
General interest talk & political issues.
Air Time: Mon-Fri 8 PM-midnight

On My Mind
WAMU-FM
Affiliate of American University Radio
4401 Connecticut Ave NW, Washington, DC 20008
Mailing Address: 4400 Massachusetts Ave NW, Washington, DC 20016-8082
Tel: 202-854-8851
E-mail: drpodcast@wamu.org
Web Site: dianerehm.org
Key Personnel
Prodr: Sandra Baker; Alison Brody; Rebecca Kaufman
Host: Diane Rehm
Debut Date: 1984
Conversations with newsmakers, writers, artists & thinkers on a variety of issues.

On The Bookshelf
WTBF-AM/FM
Division of Troy Broadcasting Corp
67 W Court Sq, Troy, AL 36081
Tel: 334-566-0300 *Fax:* 334-566-5689
E-mail: wtbfdoc@yahoo.com
Web Site: www.wtbfradio.com
Key Personnel
Opers & Prog Mgr: Dave "Doc" Kirby
Debut Date: 1992
Interviews with book authors (30 minutes).
Air Time: Sun 11:30 AM-noon (970 AM & 96.3 FM); Sun 9:30-10 AM (94.7 FM)

On-the-Go
KGO810
Division of Cumulus Media Inc
750 Battery St, 2nd fl, San Francisco, CA 94111
Tel: 415-808-0810 (call-in show hotline); 415-995-5735 (mktg/promo) *Fax:* 415-954-8700
Web Site: www.kgoradio.com
Key Personnel
Host: John Hamilton *E-mail:* johnhamiltonotg@gmail.com
Travel & leisure.
Air Time: Sun 9-10 AM

Penny for Your Thoughts
WDWS-AM
15 Main St, Champaign, IL 61820
Tel: 217-351-5300
E-mail: talk@wdws.com; newsroom@wdws.com
Web Site: www.wdws.com
Key Personnel
Host: Brian Barnhart
Talk, call-ins & entertainment. Also as podcast.
Air Time: Mon-Fri 9-11 AM

Radio Times
WHYY-FM
Affiliate of National Public Radio
Independence Mall West, 150 N Sixth St, Philadelphia, PA 19106
Tel: 215-351-1200
E-mail: talkback@whyy.org
Web Site: www.whyy.org/programs/radio-times
Key Personnel
Host & Exec Prodr: Marty Moss-Coane
Talk & interviews; general interest.
Air Time: Mon-Fri 10-11 AM

The Mark Reardon Show
KMOX-AM
Division of Entercom Communications Corp
1220 Olive St, 3rd fl, St Louis, MO 63103-2301
Tel: 314-621-2345 *Fax:* 314-588-1234
E-mail: kmoxnews@kmox.com
Web Site: kmox.radio.com/shows/mark-reardon-show
Key Personnel
Host: Mark Reardon *E-mail:* mark.reardon@entercom.com
Interviews, phone-ins & issues of the day.
Air Time: Mon-Fri 2-4 PM

Joel Riley Show
WTVN-AM 610
Division of iHeartMedia Inc
2323 W Fifth Ave, Suite 200, Columbus, OH 43204
Tel: 614-486-6101
Web Site: 610wtvn.iheart.com
Key Personnel
Host: Joel Riley *E-mail:* joelriley@iheartmedia.com
Talk show, includes interviews.
Air Time: Mon-Fri 5:35-9 AM

Ross Files
KIRO-FM
Division of Bonneville International Corp
1820 Eastlake Ave E, Seattle, WA 98102
Tel: 206-726-7000 *Toll Free Tel:* 800-756-5476
Web Site: www.mynorthwest.com/category/dave-ross-blog
Key Personnel
Prog Dir: Ryan Maguire *E-mail:* rmaguire@bonneville.com
Host: Dave Ross
News/issues talk show, author interviews.
Air Time: Mon-Fri 5 AM-noon

St Louis on the Air
KWMU-FM/St Louis Public Radio
Affiliate of National Public Radio
St Louis Public Radio, 3651 Olive St, St Louis, MO 63108
Tel: 314-516-5968 *Fax:* 314-516-5993
E-mail: news@stlpublicradio.org
Web Site: www.stlpublicradio.org
Key Personnel
Prodr: Alex Heuer *E-mail:* heueral@umsl.edu
News, talk & information.
Air Time: Mon-Fri noon-1 PM; rebroadcast 10-11 PM

Sports to the Max
WCCO-AM
Division of Entercom Communications Corp
625 Second Ave S, Minneapolis, MN 55402
Tel: 612-370-0611; 651-989-9226 (studio/contest)
Web Site: wccoradio.radio.com
Key Personnel
Host: Mike Max
Sports talk & interviews.
Air Time: Mon-Fri 6:30-9 PM

Street Soldiers
KMEL-FM
Subsidiary of iHeartMedia Inc
340 Townsend St, San Francisco, CA 94107
Tel: 415-538-1061
Web Site: www.kmel.com

RADIO PROGRAMS FEATURING BOOKS

Key Personnel
Prog Dir: Don Parker *E-mail:* donparker@iheartmedia.com
Host: Dr Joe Marshall
Interview format; public interest & public affairs. Live.
Air Time: Sun 8-10 PM

The Sunday Journal
KOST-103.5 FM
Subsidiary of iHeartMedia Inc
3400 W Olive Ave, Suite 550, Burbank, CA 91505
Tel: 818-559-2252
E-mail: info@kost1035.com
Web Site: kost1035.iheart.com
Key Personnel
Dir, Mktg & Promos: Ilene Woodbury
Host: Kari Steele *E-mail:* karisteele@iheartmedia.com
Public affairs show.
Air Time: Sun 6-7 AM

Sunday Morning Magazine
WKRQ-FM
Division of Hubbard Radio LLC
2060 Redding Rd, Cincinnati, OH 45202
Tel: 513-699-5102 *Fax:* 513-699-5000
Web Site: www.wkrq.com
Key Personnel
Host: Rodney Lear *E-mail:* rlear@hubbardinteractive.com
Varies; news & talk, current events & features; relevant author interviews.
Air Time: Sun 7-8 AM

That's Life with Mark Snyder
PMPNetwork Inc
PO Box 639, East Sandwich, MA 02537-0639
Tel: 781-341-8332
Web Site: www.pmpnetwork.com
Key Personnel
CEO, PMPNetwork.com & Interviewer: Mark Snyder *E-mail:* mark@pmpnetwork.com
Prodr: Rod Belmont *E-mail:* rod@pmpnetwork.com; Irwin Marx *E-mail:* irwin@pmpnetwork.com
Internet celebrity interview show.
Air Time: Varies

Think
KERA-FM
Affiliate of National Public Radio
3000 Harry Hines Blvd, Dallas, TX 75201
Tel: 214-871-1390 *Toll Free Tel:* 800-933-5372 *Fax:* 214-754-0635
E-mail: think@kera.org
Web Site: think.kera.org
Key Personnel
Sr Prodr: Stephen Becker *E-mail:* sbecker@kera.org
Host: Krys Boyd
Debut Date: 2006
General interest topics; politics, current events, historical nonfiction, science, language, society & culture; authors interviewed. Live, call-in.
Air Time: Mon-Thurs noon-1 PM

Today's Black Woman (TBW)
1720 Mars Hill Rd, Suite 8-253, Acworth, GA 30101
Tel: 404-697-0104
E-mail: tbwradioshow@gmail.com
Web Site: www.jenniferkeitt.com
Key Personnel
Host: Jennifer Keitt
Issues & information of interest to Black women.

Tolbert & Lund
KNBR-AM
Division of Cumulus Media Inc
750 Battery St, 3rd fl, San Francisco, CA 94111
Tel: 415-995-6800 *Fax:* 415-995-6867
Web Site: www.knbr.com/shows/tom-tolbert
Key Personnel
Radio Prodr: Brian Smith
Prog Dir: Jeremiah Crowe *E-mail:* jeremiah.crowe@cumulus.com
Promos Dir: Jennifer Violet Kennedy
Host: John Lund; Tom "Mr T" Tolbert *E-mail:* mrt@knbr.com
Sports talk show; interviews.
Air Time: Mon-Fri 3-7 PM

Total Information AM
KMOX-AM
Division of Entercom Communications Corp
1220 Olive St, 3rd fl, St Louis, MO 63103-2301
Tel: 314-621-2345 *Fax:* 314-588-1234
E-mail: kmoxnews@kmox.com
Web Site: kmox.radio.com/shows/total-information-am
Key Personnel
Host: Tom Ackerman; Michael Calhoun; Debbie Monterrey *E-mail:* debbie.monterrey@entercom.com
Early day rise & shine, news, features, interviews, sports, traffic & weather.
Air Time: Mon-Fri 5-8:30 AM

Twin Cities News Talk
KTLK-1130 AM
Division of iHeartMedia Inc
1600 Utica Ave S, Suite 500, Minneapolis, MN 55416
Tel: 952-417-3000
Web Site: twincitiesnewstalk.iheart.com
Author interviews relevant to news on regular daily newscasts.

WBAL News Now
WBAL-AM
Division of Hearst Corp
3800 Hooper Ave, Baltimore, MD 21211
Tel: 410-467-3000
E-mail: mdnewsnow@wbal.com
Web Site: www.wbal.com
Key Personnel
Host: Bryan Nehman
Prodr: Malarie Pinkard *E-mail:* mpinkard@hearst.com; Jacob Young *E-mail:* jlyoung@hearst.com
Telephone interviews on a variety of subjects.
Air Time: Mon-Fri 5-9 AM

Weekend All Things Considered
National Public Radio
1111 N Capitol St NE, Washington, DC 20002
Tel: 202-513-2000 *Fax:* 202-513-3329
Web Site: www.npr.org
Key Personnel
Host: Michel Martin
News & information, current issues.
Air Time: Sat & Sun 5-6 PM

Weekend Edition Saturday
National Public Radio
1111 N Capitol St NE, Washington, DC 20002
Tel: 202-513-2000 *Fax:* 202-513-3329
Web Site: www.npr.org
Key Personnel
Host: Scott Simon
Debut Date: 1986
News & information, authors & writers.
Air Time: Sat 8-10 AM (ET)

Weekend Edition Sunday
National Public Radio
1111 N Capitol St NE, Washington, DC 20002
Tel: 202-513-2000 *Fax:* 202-513-3329
Web Site: www.npr.org
Key Personnel
Host: Lulu Garcia-Navarro
Debut Date: 1987
News & information, author & writer interviews.
Air Time: Sun 8-10 AM (ET)

The John Williams Show
WGN-AM
Subsidiary of Nexstar Media Group Inc
303 E Wacker Dr, 18th fl, Chicago, IL 60601
Tel: 312-981-7200
Web Site: www.wgnradio.com
Key Personnel
Prodr: Pete Zimmerman
Host: John Williams *E-mail:* johnwilliams@wgnradio.com
General talk show.
Air Time: Mon-Fri 10 AM-2 PM

Worldview
WBEZ-FM
Affiliate of Chicago Public Media Inc
848 E Grand Ave, Chicago, IL 60611
Tel: 312-948-4600
E-mail: worldview@wbez.org; news@wbez.org
Web Site: www.wbez.org
Key Personnel
Sr Prodr: Steve Bynum
Host: Jerome McDonnell
Focus on international news & international affairs interviews. Also features art, activism & social movements in Chicago.
Air Time: Mon-Fri noon-1 PM

WTOP News
WTOP-AM/FM
Division of Hubbard Radio LLC
5425 Wisconsin Ave, Chevy Chase, MD 20815
Tel: 202-895-5000
E-mail: newsroom@wtopnews.com
Web Site: wtop.com
Key Personnel
Dir, News & Programming: Mike McMearty *Tel:* 202-895-5039 *E-mail:* mmcmearty@wtop.com
Gen Mgr: Joel Oxley *Tel:* 202-895-5012 *E-mail:* joxley@wtop.com
All news format.

Your Legal Rights
KALW-FM
Affiliate of National Public Radio
500 Mansell St, San Francisco, CA 94134
Tel: 415-841-4121 *Fax:* 415-841-4125
E-mail: kalw@kalw.org
Web Site: www.kalw.org/programs/your-legal-rights
Key Personnel
Host: Jeff Hayden
Practical information on legal & consumer affairs; interview authors of relevant books. Live in Bay Area; call-in show.
Air Time: Wed 7-8 PM

TV Programs Featuring Books

Listed here are adult & juvenile TV programs that deal with books and authors. Programs are listed alphabetically by program name. Some are hosted by established critics who devote their entire program to reviews of current books; others mention books only occasionally. Also see the sections **Columnists & Commentators** and **Radio Programs Featuring Books**.

ABC2 News: Good Morning Maryland
WMAR-TV (ABC)
Member of Scripps TV Station Group
6400 York Rd, Baltimore, MD 21212
Tel: 410-377-2222
Web Site: www.wmar2news.com
Key Personnel
Morning Prodr: Calvin Johnson
Host: Jamie Costello; Christian Schaffer
News, author interviews.
Air Time: 4:30 AM & 7 AM

Action News 5
WMC-TV (NBC)
Division of Gray Television
1960 Union Ave, Memphis, TN 38104
Tel: 901-726-0416 (newsroom); 901-726-0555
  Fax: 901-278-7633
E-mail: news@wmctv.com; desk@wmctv.com
Web Site: www.wmctv.com
Key Personnel
News Dir: Gregg Phillips *E-mail:* gphillips@
  wmctv.com
Opers Mgr: Brent Green *E-mail:* bgreen@wmctv.
  com
Anchor: Joe Birch; Kym Clark
News & information.
Air Time: Mon-Sun 4-7 AM, noon-1 PM, 3-3:30
  PM, 6-6:30 PM, 10-10:30 PM

After Words
Cable-Satellite Public Affairs Network (C-SPAN2
  Book TV)
400 N Capitol St NW, Suite 650, Washington,
  DC 20001
Tel: 202-737-3220 *Fax:* 202-737-0580
E-mail: booktv@c-span.org
Web Site: www.c-span.org; booktv.org
Key Personnel
Sr Exec Prodr: Peter Slen
After Words is Book TV's newest author interview series. Each week nonfiction writers are interviewed by a guest host.
Air Time: Sat 10 PM (ET), Sun 9 PM (ET), Mon
  midnight (ET) on Book TV on C-SPAN2

AM Northwest
KATU-TV (ABC)
Division of Sinclair Broadcast Group Inc
2153 NE Sandy Blvd, Portland, OR 97232
Tel: 503-231-4610; 503-231-4222 *Fax:* 503-231-
  4626
E-mail: amnw@katu.com
Web Site: katu.com
Key Personnel
Host: Helen Raptis
Debut Date: 1976
Live author & entertainment interviews.
Air Time: Mon-Fri 9-10 AM

Awareness
WIS-TV (NBC)
Division of Gray Television
1111 Bull St, Columbia, SC 29201
Tel: 803-799-1010 *Fax:* 803-758-1278
Web Site: www.wistv.com
Key Personnel
Host: Leland Pinder
Minority issues.
Air Time: Sun 11-11:30 PM

Bay Area Focus
KBCW-TV
855 Battery St, San Francisco, CA 94111
Tel: 415-765-8144
Web Site: sanfrancisco.cbslocal.com/category/
  bayareafocus
Key Personnel
Host: Michelle Griego
Public affairs-news/talk, Bay Area issues, politics,
  authors, celebrities, national issues.
Air Time: Sun 8 AM

Black Renaissance
KBCW-TV
855 Battery St, San Francisco, CA 94111
Tel: 415-765-8144
Web Site: cwsanfrancisco.cbslocal.com/category/
  black-renaissance
Key Personnel
Prodr: Jan Mabry
News/interview show focused on arts & culture,
  race relations, politics & all other issues of interest to African Americans.
Air Time: Sun 11 AM (every 3rd week)

The Black Voice
KRIV-TV
Subsidiary of Fox Television Stations LLC
4261 Southwest Fwy, Houston, TX 77027
Tel: 713-479-2600; 713-479-2801 (newsroom)
  Fax: 713-479-2859 (newsroom)
Web Site: www.fox26houston.com
Key Personnel
Host: Jose Grinan *E-mail:* jose.grinan@foxtv.com
Public affairs program focusing on issues facing
  the Black community.

Books & The World
Cape Cod Writers Center
919 Main St, Osterville, MA 02655
Mailing Address: PO Box 408, Osterville, MA
  02655
Tel: 508-420-0200
E-mail: writers@capecodwriterscenter.org
Web Site: capecodwriterscenter.org
Key Personnel
Exec Dir: Nancy Rubin Stuart
Host: Madeline Holt
Debut Date: 1978
One of the longest running, cable access, author
  interview TV programs in New England & on
  YouTube. Two authors, including locally, nationally & internationally known writers, are
  recorded at the Cape Cod Community Media Center in Dennis Port. Recordings appear
  on local access stations on Cape Cod, Massachusetts & in the region & available for authors to have shown everywhere in the US.
Air Time: Locally controlled

CBS News Sunday Morning
CBS News
Division of Paramount Global
Box O, 524 W 57 St, New York, NY 10019
Tel: 212-975-3247
E-mail: sundays@cbsnews.com
Web Site: www.cbsnews.com/sunday-morning
Key Personnel
Exec Prodr: Rand Morrison
Sr Prodr: Gavin Boyle; Amy Rosner; Jason Sacca

90 minute news program highlighting the arts.
Air Time: Sun 9-10:30 AM

CBS 6 News at Noon
WTVR-TV (CBS)
Division of Local TV LLC
3301 W Broad St, Richmond, VA 23230
Tel: 804-254-3600 *Fax:* 804-254-3697
E-mail: newstips@wtvr.com
Web Site: www.wtvr.com
Key Personnel
Gen Mgr: Stephen Hayes *E-mail:* shayes@wtvr.
  com
Anchor: Cheryl Miller *E-mail:* cmiller@wtvr.com
Debut Date: 1948
Talk show; news & interviews.
Air Time: Mon-Fri noon-12:30 PM

CBS13 News at Noon
KOVR-TV
Subsidiary of CBS Television Stations
2713 KOVR Dr, West Sacramento, CA 95605
Tel: 916-374-1313 *Fax:* 916-374-1304
E-mail: news@kovr.com
Web Site: www.kovr.com
Key Personnel
News Dir: Mike Dello Stritto
News, features, inserts & general interest interviews.
Air Time: Mon-Fri noon-12:30 PM

Channel 9 News
WCPO-TV (ABC)
Subsidiary of EW Scripps Co
1720 Gilbert Ave, Cincinnati, OH 45202
Tel: 513-721-9900 *Fax:* 513-721-6032
E-mail: newsdesk@wcpo.com
Web Site: www.wcpo.com
Key Personnel
Anchor/Host: Timyka Artist *E-mail:* timyka.
  artist@wcpo.com
Air Time: Sun 8-9 AM

Daybreak
WFAA-TV
Subsidiary of TEGNA Media
606 Young St, Dallas, TX 75202-4810
Tel: 214-748-9631 *Fax:* 214-977-6585
E-mail: news8@wfaa.com
Web Site: www.wfaa.com
Key Personnel
Exec Prodr: Sheena Autin
Anchor: Ron Corning *E-mail:* rcorning@wfaa.
  com
News.
Air Time: Mon-Fri 5-7 AM

Eyewitness Morning News
WWL-TV (CBS)
Subsidiary of TEGNA Media
1024 N Rampart St, New Orleans, LA 70116
Tel: 504-529-6298 *Fax:* 504-529-6472
E-mail: pressrelease@wwltv.com
Web Site: www.wwltv.com
Key Personnel
Prodr: Haleigh Wolfe *E-mail:* hwolfe@wwltv.com
Host: Eric Paulsen *E-mail:* epaulsen@wwltv.com;
  Sheba Turk *E-mail:* sturk@wwltv.com

TV PROGRAMS FEATURING BOOKS

Live morning news/interviews, entertainment, health & medical.
Air Time: Mon-Fri 4:30-9 AM

Eyewitness News at Noon
WCHS-TV (ABC)
Division of Sinclair Broadcast Group Inc
1301 Piedmont Rd, Charleston, WV 25301
Tel: 304-346-5358 *Fax:* 304-346-4765
E-mail: news@wchstv.com
Web Site: www.wchstv.com
Key Personnel
Dir: Matt Sampson
Prodr: Rachel Tarr
News & interviews.
Air Time: Mon-Fri noon-1 PM

Fox In The Morning
WJW-TV (Fox)
Subsidiary of Fox Broadcasting
5800 S Marginal Rd, Cleveland, OH 44103
Tel: 216-432-4077
Web Site: www.fox8cleveland.com
Key Personnel
Planning Prodr: Margaret Daykin
   E-mail: margaret.daykin@fox8.com
Anchor: Kristi Capel; Wayne Dawson; Stefani Schaefer
News interviews.
Air Time: Mon-Fri 4-10 AM

Fox 13 News
WTVT (FOX)
Division of Fox Television Stations LLC
3213 W Kennedy Blvd, Tampa, FL 33609
Mailing Address: PO Box 31113, Tampa, FL 33631-3113
Tel: 813-870-9630 (newsroom); 813-876-1313
   Fax: 813-871-3135 (news & sports)
E-mail: fox13tampanews@wtvt.com
Web Site: www.fox13news.com
Key Personnel
VP & News Dir: John Hoffman
VP & Gen Mgr: Jeff Maloney
Asst News Dir: Scott Jones
Anchor: Chris Cato; Linda Hurtado; Kelly Ring; Cynthia Smoot; Mark Wilson
Air Time: Mon-Fri 4-10 AM, noon-1 PM, 4-7 PM, 10 PM-midnight

FOX 26 Morning News
KRIV-TV
Subsidiary of Fox Television Stations LLC
4261 Southwest Fwy, Houston, TX 77027
Tel: 713-479-2600; 713-479-2801 (newsroom)
   Fax: 713-479-2859 (newsroom)
Web Site: www.fox26houston.com
Key Personnel
VP, Creative Servs & Programming: Ralph Rendon *E-mail:* ralph.rendon@foxtv.com
Sr Anchor: Jose Grinan *E-mail:* jose.grinan@foxtv.com
News format. Live.
Air Time: Mon-Fri 6-10 AM, Sat 5-8 AM, Sun 5-7 AM

FOX 26 News at Noon
KRIV-TV
Subsidiary of Fox Television Stations LLC
4261 Southwest Fwy, Houston, TX 77027
Tel: 713-479-2600; 713-479-2801 (newsroom)
   Fax: 713-479-2859 (newsroom)
Web Site: www.fox26houston.com
Key Personnel
Sr Anchor: Jose Grinan *E-mail:* jose.grinan@foxtv.com
News format. Live.
Air Time: Mon-Fri noon-12:30 PM

Fox 2 News-Live at 11
WJBK-TV
16550 W Nine Mile, Southfield, MI 48075
Mailing Address: PO Box 2000, Southfield, MI 48037-0200
Tel: 248-552-5103 *Fax:* 248-557-1199
E-mail: fox2newsdesk@foxtv.com
Web Site: www.fox2detroit.com
News & interviews with authors & others.
Air Time: Mon-Fri 11 AM-noon

Good Day Atlanta
WAGA-TV (Fox)
Subsidiary of Fox Television Stations LLC
1551 Briarcliff Rd NE, Atlanta, GA 30306
Tel: 404-875-5555
E-mail: gooddayatlanta@foxtv.com
Web Site: www.fox5atlanta.com
Key Personnel
Exec Prodr: Amy Oates Ranel
Anchor: Alyse Eady; Ron Gant; Buck Lanford; Sharon Lawson
News & interviews.
Air Time: Mon-Fri 4:30-10 AM

Good Day Tampa Bay
WTVT (FOX)
Division of Fox Television Stations LLC
3213 W Kennedy Blvd, Tampa, FL 33609
Mailing Address: PO Box 31113, Tampa, FL 33631-3113
Tel: 813-870-9630 (newsroom); 813-876-1313
   Fax: 813-871-3135 (news & sports)
E-mail: fox13tampanews@wtvt.com
Web Site: www.fox13news.com/good-day
Key Personnel
Exec Prodr: Laura Cross
News, entertainment, features, medical format, personal financial, women's issues, nutrition, retirement & parenting.
Air Time: Mon-Fri 4-10 AM, Sat & Sun 6-10 AM

Good Morning America
ABC News
Division of The Walt Disney Co
47 W 66 St, New York, NY 10023
Tel: 818-460-7477
Web Site: abc.go.com/shows/good-morning-america
Key Personnel
Sr Exec Prodr: Tom Cibrowski
Host: Robin Roberts; George Stephanopoulis
Interviews, features.
Air Time: Mon-Fri 7-9 AM

Good Morning Oklahoma
KTUL-TV (ABC)
Subsidiary of Sinclair Broadcast Group Inc
3333 S 29 West Ave, Tulsa, OK 74101
Tel: 918-445-8888 *Fax:* 918-445-9354
E-mail: news@ktul.com
Web Site: ktul.com/station/good-morning-oklahoma; www.ktul.com
Key Personnel
Dir, Broadcasting Opers: Roger Herring
   E-mail: rbherring@sbgtv.com
Wide range of topics & author interviews.
Air Time: Mon-Fri 5-7 AM

Good Morning Texas
WFAA-TV
Subsidiary of TEGNA Media
606 Young St, Dallas, TX 75202-4810
Tel: 214-748-9631 *Fax:* 214-977-6585
E-mail: news8@wfaa.com
Web Site: www.wfaa.com
Key Personnel
Prodr: Paige McCoy Smith
Host: Jane McGarry
Interviews talk show with various people.
Air Time: Mon-Fri 9-10 AM

ADVERTISING, MARKETING

Lynne Hayes-Freeland Show
KDKA-TV
Division of Paramount Global
420 Fort Duquesne Blvd, Suite 100, Pittsburgh, PA 15222
Tel: 412-575-2200
E-mail: newsdesk@kdka.com
Web Site: pittsburgh.cbslocal.com
Key Personnel
Prodr & Host: Lynne Hayes-Freeland
   E-mail: lhfreeland@kdka.com
Minority issues, general interest with minority angle. Taped Wednesday mornings.
Air Time: Sat 6:30 AM, Sun 6 AM

Herman & Sharron Show
WCLF-TV
Division of Christian Television Network
6922 142 Ave, Largo, FL 33771
Mailing Address: PO Box 6922, Clearwater, FL 33758
Tel: 727-535-5622 *Fax:* 727-531-2497
Web Site: www.ctnonline.com
Key Personnel
Host: Herman Bailey; Sharron Bailey
Talk show interviews.
Air Time: Mon-Fri 10 AM & 5 PM

Hola Houston
KRIV-TV
Subsidiary of Fox Television Stations LLC
4261 Southwest Fwy, Houston, TX 77027
Tel: 713-479-2600; 713-479-2801 (newsroom)
   Fax: 713-479-2859 (newsroom)
Web Site: www.fox26houston.com
Public affairs program focusing on issues facing the Hispanic community.

Homekeepers
WCLF-TV
Division of Christian Television Network
6922 142 Ave, Largo, FL 33771
Mailing Address: PO Box 6922, Clearwater, FL 33758
Tel: 727-535-5622 *Fax:* 727-531-2497
Web Site: www.ctnonline.com
Key Personnel
Host: Arthelene Rippy *E-mail:* arthelenerippy@gmail.com
Talk show for homemakers, cooking segment, some music.
Air Time: Mon-Fri 5:30 AM & 1 PM (ET)

In Depth
Cable-Satellite Public Affairs Network (C-SPAN2 Book TV)
400 N Capitol St NW, Suite 650, Washington, DC 20001
Tel: 202-737-3220 *Fax:* 202-737-0580
E-mail: booktv@c-span.org
Web Site: www.c-span.org; booktv.org
Key Personnel
Sr Exec Prodr: Peter Slen
Comprehensive, live 3 hour look at one authors work, with questions from viewers via phone & e-mail.
Air Time: First Sun of the month noon & 10 PM on Book TV on C-SPAN2

KRON 4 News at 5
KRON-TV
Subsidiary of Nexstar Broadcasting
900 Front St, 3rd fl, San Francisco, CA 94111
Tel: 415-441-4444; 415-561-8905 (news dept)
E-mail: 4listens@kron4.com
Web Site: www.kron4.com
Key Personnel
Anchor: Vicki Liviakis; Pam Moore
Assignment Ed: Tamara Berry *E-mail:* berry@kron.com
News & features.
Air Time: Mon-Fri 5-6 PM

& PUBLICITY

KRON 4 News at 6
KRON-TV
Subsidiary of Nextstar Broadcasting
900 Front St, 3rd fl, San Francisco, CA 94111
Tel: 415-441-4444; 415-561-8905 (news dept)
E-mail: 4listens@kron4.com
Web Site: www.kron4.com
Key Personnel
Anchor: Pam Moore; Ken Wayne
Assignment Ed: Tamara Berry *E-mail:* berry@kron.com
Hard news.
Air Time: Mon-Fri 6-7 PM

KRON 4 News at 10
KRON-TV
Subsidiary of Nextstar Broadcasting
900 Front St, 3rd fl, San Francisco, CA 94111
Tel: 415-441-4444; 415-561-8905 (news dept)
E-mail: 4listens@kron4.com
Web Site: www.kron4.com
Key Personnel
Anchor: Pam Moore; Ken Wayne
Assignment Ed: Tamara Berry *E-mail:* berry@kron.com
Local news.
Air Time: Mon-Fri 10-11 PM

KTVU Channel 2 News at Noon
KTVU Partnership
Affiliate of Fox Television Stations Inc
2 Jack London Sq, Oakland, CA 94607
Tel: 510-834-1212 *Fax:* 510-451-2610
E-mail: newstips@foxtv.com
Web Site: www.ktvu.com
Key Personnel
Anchor: Gasia Mikaelian
Assignment Mgr: Jay Martinez *E-mail:* jay.martinez@foxtv.com
News.
Air Time: Mon-Fri noon-12:30 PM

KTVU Channel 2 News at 6
KTVU Partnership
Affiliate of Fox Television Stations Inc
2 Jack London Sq, Oakland, CA 94607
Tel: 510-834-1212 *Fax:* 510-451-2610
E-mail: newstips@foxtv.com
Web Site: www.ktvu.com
Key Personnel
Host: Julie Haener; Frank Somerville
Assignment Mgr: Jay Martinez *E-mail:* jay.martinez@foxtv.com
Air Time: Mon-Fri 6-6:30 PM

Local 4 News at 5
WDIV-TV (NBC)
Subsidiary of Graham Media Group
550 W Lafayette Blvd, Detroit, MI 48226
Tel: 313-222-0500
E-mail: news@wdiv.com
Web Site: www.clickondetroit.com
Key Personnel
Prodr: Tim French
News, weather & sports.
Air Time: Mon-Fri 5-6:30 PM

Local 4 News at Noon
WDIV-TV (NBC)
Subsidiary of Graham Media Group
550 W Lafayette Blvd, Detroit, MI 48226
Tel: 313-222-0500
E-mail: news@wdiv.com
Web Site: www.clickondetroit.com
Key Personnel
Host: Errod Kasney; Rhonda Walker
News, weather, sports & interviews.
Air Time: Mon-Fri noon-12:30 PM

Meet the Press
NBC-TV
Division of NBCUniversal
4001 Nebraska Ave NW, Washington, DC 20016
Tel: 202-885-4598
E-mail: mtpnewsreleases@msnbc.com
Web Site: www.meetthepressnbc.com
Key Personnel
Exec Prodr: John Reiss
Host: Kristen Welker
Interviews with newsmakers; direct discussion & report.
Air Time: Sun 10:30 AM in Washington, DC & NY (check local listings elsewhere)

Midday News
WKYC-TV (NBC)
Subsidiary of TEGNA Media
1333 Lakeside Ave, Cleveland, OH 44114
Tel: 216-344-3333 *Fax:* 216-344-3314
E-mail: news@wkyc.com
Web Site: www.wkyc.com
Key Personnel
Anchor: Maureen Kyle *Tel:* 216-344-7444
News & interviews.
Air Time: Mon-Fri noon-12:30 PM

Midday News
WFAA-TV
Subsidiary of TEGNA Media
606 Young St, Dallas, TX 75202-4810
Tel: 214-748-9631 *Fax:* 214-977-6585
E-mail: news8@wfaa.com
Web Site: www.wfaa.com
Key Personnel
Anchor: Demetria Obilor; Kara Sewell
Air Time: Mon-Fri 11 AM-noon

Midday on 5
WPTV-NBC
Affiliate of Scripps Howard Broadcasting
1100 Banyan Blvd, West Palm Beach, FL 33401
Tel: 561-655-5455
E-mail: newstips@wptv.com
Web Site: www.wptv.com
News segment.
Air Time: Mon-Fri 11 AM-noon

Mornings on Two
KTVU Partnership
Affiliate of Fox Television Stations Inc
2 Jack London Sq, Oakland, CA 94607
Tel: 510-834-1212 *Fax:* 510-451-2610
E-mail: newstips@foxtv.com
Web Site: www.ktvu.com
Key Personnel
Anchor: Gasia Mikaelian; Dave Clark
Assignment Mgr: Jay Martinez *E-mail:* jay.martinez@foxtv.com
News & interviews.
Air Time: Mon-Fri 7-10 AM

News at 5
WCCO-TV
Division of Paramount Global
90 S 11 St, Minneapolis, MN 55403
Tel: 612-339-4444 *Fax:* 612-330-2767
E-mail: wcconewstips@cbs.com
Web Site: minnesota.cbslocal.com
Key Personnel
News Dir: Kari Patey
Newscasts.
Air Time: Mon-Fri 5-5:30 PM

News at 5, 6, 10 & 11 PM
WSVN-TV
Division of Sunbeam Television Corp
1401 79 Street Causeway, Miami, FL 33141
Tel: 305-751-6692 *Toll Free Tel:* 800-845-7777 (FL only)
E-mail: newsdesk@wsvn.com
Web Site: www.wsvn.com
Key Personnel
Anchor: Belkys Nerey; Craig Stevens
News, information & entertainment.
Air Time: Mon-Fri 5-11:30 PM

News at Noon
WSVN-TV
Division of Sunbeam Television Corp
1401 79 Street Causeway, Miami, FL 33141
Tel: 305-751-6692 *Toll Free Tel:* 800-845-7777 (FL only)
E-mail: newsdesk@wsvn.com
Web Site: www.wsvn.com
Key Personnel
Anchor: Christine Cruz
News.
Air Time: Mon-Fri noon-1 PM

News at Noon
WCCO-TV
Division of Paramount Global
90 S 11 St, Minneapolis, MN 55403
Tel: 612-339-4444 *Fax:* 612-330-2767
E-mail: wcconewstips@cbs.com
Web Site: minnesota.cbslocal.com
Key Personnel
News Dir: Kari Patey
Newscasts & interviews.
Air Time: Mon-Fri noon-12:30 PM

News Channel 8 at Noon
WTNH-8TV (ABC)
Subsidiary of Nexstar Media Group Inc
8 Elm St, New Haven, CT 06510
Tel: 203-784-8888 *Fax:* 203-787-9698
E-mail: news8@wtnh.com
Web Site: www.wtnh.com
Key Personnel
Anchor: Keith Kountz
News, features & interviews.
Air Time: Mon-Fri noon-12:30 PM

News Channel 5 Live on 5
WEWS-TV (ABC)
Member of Scripps TV Station Group
3001 Euclid Ave, Cleveland, OH 44115
Tel: 216-431-3700; 216-431-5555 *Fax:* 216-431-3666
E-mail: newsdesk@wews.com
Web Site: www.news5cleveland.com
News, information, entertainment. Live.
Air Time: Mon-Fri 5-6 PM

News Channel 7 at Noon
WSPA-TV (CBS)
Subsidiary of Nexstar Media Group Inc
250 International Dr, Spartanburg, SC 29303
Tel: 864-576-7777
E-mail: assignmentdesk@wspa.com
Web Site: wspa.com
Key Personnel
Anchor: Fred Cunningham
News-oriented.
Air Time: Mon-Fri noon-12:30 PM

News 5 at Noon
KCTV5
4500 Shawnee Mission Pkwy, Fairway, KS 66205
Tel: 913-677-5555 *Fax:* 913-677-7243
E-mail: kctv5@kctv5.com; newsdesk@kctv5.com
Web Site: www.kctv5.com
Key Personnel
Host: Carolyn Long
News & interviews.
Air Time: Mon-Fri noon-12:30 PM

News 4 at Noon
WBZ-TV
Division of CBS Television Stations
1170 Soldiers Field Rd, Boston, MA 02134
Tel: 617-787-7000 *Fax:* 617-787-7346

TV PROGRAMS FEATURING BOOKS

E-mail: newstips@wbzty.com
Web Site: www.wbztv.com; boston.cbslocal.com
Key Personnel
News Dir: Johnny Green
News & talk format.
Air Time: Mon-Fri noon-12:30 PM

News Six at Noon
WKMG-TV
Division of Graham Media Group
4466 John Young Pkwy, Orlando, FL 32804
Tel: 407-291-6000 *Fax:* 407-298-2122
E-mail: desk@wkmg.com
Web Site: www.clickorlando.com
Key Personnel
Anchor: Bridgett Ellison; Kirstin O'Connor; Justin Warmoth
Air Time: Mon-Fri noon-12:30 PM

Nightline
ABC News
Division of The Walt Disney Co
47 W 66 St, New York, NY 10023
Tel: 202-222-7777
Web Site: abcnews.go.com/nightline
Key Personnel
Exec Prodr: Steven Baker
Co-Anchor: Juju Chang; Dan Harris; Byron Pitts
In-depth coverage of topical news issues/events of the day.
Air Time: Mon-Fri 12:35 AM (ET) (check local listings in other time zones)

Noon News
KCRA-TV (NBC)
3 Television Circle, Sacramento, CA 95814-0794
Tel: 916-446-3333 *Fax:* 916-441-4050 (news); 916-325-3731 (gen)
Web Site: www.kcra.com
News & guest segments featuring authors, chefs & personalities in the public eye. Live.
Air Time: Mon-Fri noon-1 PM

Noon News
WRAL-TV (NBC)
Subsidiary of Capitol Broadcasting Co Inc
2619 Western Blvd, Raleigh, NC 27606
Mailing Address: PO Box 12000, Raleigh, NC 27605-2000
Tel: 919-821-8555 *Fax:* 919-821-8541
E-mail: assignmentdesk@wral.com
Web Site: www.wral.com
Key Personnel
Anchor: Jeff Hogan
News.
Air Time: Mon-Fri noon-1 PM

Noon News
WISH-TV
Subsidiary of Nexstar Media Group Inc
1950 N Meridian St, Indianapolis, IN 46202
Tel: 317-923-8888; 317-921-NEWS (921-6397, news hotline) *Fax:* 317-931-2242 (news); 317-926-1144 (sales)
E-mail: newsdesk@wishtv.com
Web Site: www.wishtv.com
Air Time: Mon-Fri 11 AM-noon

Noon Newscast
KSAT-TV (ABC)
Division of Graham Media Group
1408 N Saint Mary St, San Antonio, TX 78215
Tel: 210-351-1200
E-mail: news@ksat.com
Web Site: www.ksat.com
Key Personnel
News Dir: Bernice Kearney *E-mail:* bkearney@ksat.com
Assignment Mgr: Sean Talbot
News & interviews.
Air Time: Mon-Fri noon-1 PM

PBS News Hour
PBS-TV
3939 Campbell Ave, Arlington, VA 22206
Tel: 703-998-2150 *Fax:* 703-998-4151
E-mail: newsdesk@newshour.org
Web Site: www.pbs.org/newshour
Key Personnel
Exec Prodr: Sarah Just
Anchor & Mng Ed: Judy Woodruff
Nightly newscast including regular book reviews.
Air Time: Consult local PBS listings, time varies

The 700 Club
Division of The Christian Broadcasting Network
977 Centerville Tpke, Virginia Beach, VA 23463
Tel: 757-226-7000 *Fax:* 757-226-2017
Web Site: www.cbn.com; www.700club.com
Key Personnel
CEO: Gordon Robertson
Guest Booking: Molly Young
Host: Terry Meeuwsen; Pat Robertson
News, talk, inspiration.
Air Time: Mon-Fri 10-11 AM, 11 PM-midnight, 3-4 AM (ET) (ABC Family Channel) or check local listing

7 News at 11 AM
KMGH-TV (ABC)
123 Speer Blvd, Denver, CO 80203
Tel: 303-832-7777
E-mail: 7newsdesk@kmgh.com
Web Site: www.thedenverchannel.com
Key Personnel
Gen Mgr: Dean Littleton
News program with occasional author interviews.
Air Time: Mon-Fri 11 AM-noon

7 News at Noon
WHDH-TV
Subsidiary of Sunbeam Television Corp
7 Bulfinch Place, Boston, MA 02114
Tel: 617-725-0777
E-mail: newstips@whdh.com
Web Site: www.whdh.com
News.
Air Time: Mon-Fri noon-1 PM

7 News at 6
WHDH-TV
Subsidiary of Sunbeam Television Corp
7 Bulfinch Place, Boston, MA 02114
Tel: 617-725-0777
E-mail: newstips@whdh.com
Web Site: www.whdh.com
News.
Air Time: Mon-Fri 6-6:30 PM

Show Me St Louis
KSDK-TV (NBC)
Division of TEGNA Media
1000 Market St, St Louis, MO 63101
Tel: 314-421-5055 *Fax:* 314-444-5164
E-mail: smsl@ksdk.com
Web Site: www.ksdk.com
Key Personnel
Sr Prodr: Melissa Spears
Anchor: Dana Dean
Local news & interviews.
Air Time: Mon-Fri 10 PM

60 Minutes
CBS News
Division of Paramount Global
524 W 57 St, New York, NY 10019
Tel: 212-975-3247
E-mail: 60m@cbsnews.com
Web Site: www.cbsnews.com
Key Personnel
Exec Prodr: Bill Owens
Exec Ed: Tanya Simon

Correspondent: Steve Kroft; Scott Pelley; Lesley Stahl; L Jon Wertheim; Bill Whitaker
Debut Date: 1968
Television news magazine focusing on people & events in news & behind headlines.
Air Time: Sun 7-8 PM (ET)

Street Beat
CW50 (CBS)
26905 W Eleven Mile Rd, Southfield, MI 48033
Tel: 248-355-7000
E-mail: streetbeat@wkbdtv.com
Web Site: www.cw50detroit.com
Key Personnel
Dir, Programming & Community Affairs: Paul Prange *Tel:* 248-355-7012 *E-mail:* paprange@cbs.com
Current affairs featuring community & organization events. Books featured are of local interest to those living in Detroit area & throughout Michigan. Taped.
Air Time: Sat 8:30 AM

The Sunday Business Page
KDKA-TV
Division of Paramount Global
420 Fort Duquesne Blvd, Suite 100, Pittsburgh, PA 15222
Tel: 412-575-2200
E-mail: newsdesk@kdka.com
Web Site: pittsburgh.cbslocal.com
Key Personnel
Host: Jon Delano *E-mail:* jdelano@kdka.com
Business issues, computer news & programs. Taped.
Air Time: Sun 6:30 AM

Talk of the Town
WTVF-TV
474 James Robertson Pkwy, Nashville, TN 37219
Tel: 615-248-5214
Web Site: www.newschannel5.com
Key Personnel
Prodr & Host: Merryll Rose *E-mail:* meryll.rose@newschannel5.com
Host: Leland Statom
Topical interest, interviews & lifestyle entertainment.
Air Time: Mon-Fri 11-11:30 AM

Talkin' Pittsburgh
WPXI-TV (NBC)
4145 Evergreen Rd, Pittsburgh, PA 15214
Tel: 412-237-1100 *Fax:* 412-323-8097
Web Site: www.wpxi.com
Key Personnel
Prodr & Pub Aff Dir: Jonas Chaney *Tel:* 412-237-1491 *E-mail:* jchaney@wpxi.com
Talk show; public affairs, interviews.
Air Time: Wed 12:55 PM

The Ten O'Clock News
KTVU Partnership
Affiliate of Fox Television Stations Inc
2 Jack London Sq, Oakland, CA 94607
Tel: 510-834-1212 *Fax:* 510-451-2610
E-mail: newstips@foxtv.com
Web Site: www.ktvu.com
Key Personnel
Host: Julie Haener; Frank Somerville
Assignment Mgr: Jay Martinez *E-mail:* jay.martinez@foxtv.com
News.
Air Time: Mon-Fri 10-11 PM

Today
NBC-TV
Division of NBCUniversal
30 Rockefeller Plaza, New York, NY 10112
Tel: 212-664-4602
E-mail: todaystories@nbcuni.com
Web Site: www.today.com

Key Personnel
Exec Prodr: Libby Leist
Anchor: Savannah Guthrie; Hoda Kotb
Anchor, Weather & Features: Al Roker
News & features.
Air Time: Mon-Fri 7-11 AM

Today in St Louis
KSDK-TV (NBC)
Division of TEGNA Media
1000 Market St, St Louis, MO 63101
Tel: 314-421-5055 *Fax:* 314-444-5164
E-mail: newstips@ksdk.com
Web Site: www.ksdk.com
Key Personnel
Anchor: Allie Corey; Rene Knott
Local & national news & interviews.
Air Time: Mon-Fri 4-7 AM, Sat & Sun 6-7 AM & 9-10 AM

The Tonight Show Starring Jimmy Fallon
NBC-TV
Division of NBCUniversal
Studio 6B, 30 Rockefeller Plaza, New York, NY 10112
Tel: 212-664-4444
Web Site: www.nbc.com/the-tonight-show
Key Personnel
Host: Jimmy Fallon
Guest appearances & interviews, including authors.
Air Time: Mon-Fri 11:35 PM-12:35 AM (ET) (check local listings elsewhere)

12 About Town
WWBT-TV (NBC)
Division of Gray Television
5710 Midlothian Tpke, Richmond, VA 23225
Mailing Address: PO Box 12, Richmond, VA 23218-0012
Tel: 804-230-1212 *Fax:* 804-230-2789
E-mail: newsroom@nbc12.com
Web Site: www.nbc12.com
Key Personnel
VP & Gen Mgr: Mr Kym Grinnage
Entertainment topics for viewers in the area. Air time varies. A segment of 12 News at Noon.

12 News at Noon
WWBT-TV (NBC)
Division of Gray Television
5710 Midlothian Tpke, Richmond, VA 23225
Mailing Address: PO Box 12, Richmond, VA 23218-0012
Tel: 804-230-1212 *Fax:* 804-230-2789
E-mail: newsroom@nbc12.com
Web Site: www.nbc12.com
Key Personnel
VP & Gen Mgr: Mr Kym Grinnage
News, special features & interviews.
Air Time: Mon-Fri noon-12:30 PM

20/20
ABC News
Division of The Walt Disney Co
47 W 66 St, New York, NY 10023
Tel: 818-460-7477
Web Site: abcnews.go.com/2020
Key Personnel
Sr Exec Prodr: David Sloan
Anchor: David Muir; Amy Robach
News magazine, features & investigative reporting.
Air Time: Fri 9-10 PM (ET) (check local listings in other areas)

WAVY News 10 Midday
WAVY-TV (NBC)
Subsidiary of Nexstar Media Group Inc
300 Wavy St, Portsmouth, VA 23704
Tel: 757-393-1010
E-mail: newsdesk@wavy.com
Web Site: www.wavy.com
Key Personnel
VP & Gen Mgr: Carol Ward
Host: Katie Collett; Don Roberts
News, weather & sports.
Air Time: Mon-Fri noon-1 PM

WAVY News 10 Today
WAVY-TV (NBC)
Subsidiary of Nexstar Media Group Inc
300 Wavy St, Portsmouth, VA 23704
Tel: 757-393-1010
E-mail: newsdesk@wavy.com
Web Site: www.wavy.com
Key Personnel
VP & Gen Mgr: Carol Ward
Host: Katie Collett; Don Roberts
Live interviews, news & weather.
Air Time: Mon-Fri 4:30-7 AM

WIS News Midday
WIS-TV (NBC)
Division of Gray Television
1111 Bull St, Columbia, SC 29201
Tel: 803-799-1010 *Fax:* 803-758-1278
Web Site: www.wistv.com
Key Personnel
Host: Emily Scarlett; Greg Adaline
Talk show, news oriented; public affairs & interviews.
Air Time: Mon-Fri noon-12:30 PM

A Word on Words
WNPT-TV
161 Raines Ave, Nashville, TN 37203-5330
Tel: 615-259-9325
E-mail: tv8@wnpt.org
Web Site: awordonwords.org
Key Personnel
Host: J T Ellison; Mary Laura Philpott
Debut Date: 2015
Books & authors.
Air Time: Sun 10:26 AM & alternates on Thurs 7:26 PM

World News Tonight with David Muir
ABC News
Division of The Walt Disney Co
47 W 66 St, New York, NY 10023
Tel: 212-456-4040
Web Site: abc.go.com/shows/world-news-tonight
Key Personnel
Sr Exec Prodr: Almin Karamehmedovic
Anchor: David Muir
Hard news program.
Air Time: Mon-Fri 6:30-7 PM (ET)

Book Manufacturing

Complete Book Manufacturing

This section includes companies offering complete book manufacturing services. The descriptions of the services provided are paid components.

Many of the companies listed here have been recommended by the manufacturing departments of book publishers as being active and experienced in the production of books.

A-R Editions Inc
1600 Aspen Commons, Suite 100, Middleton, WI 53562
Tel: 608-836-9000 *Fax:* 608-831-8200
E-mail: info@areditions.com
Web Site: www.areditions.com
Key Personnel
Pres & CEO: Patrick Wall *Tel:* 608-203-2575
   E-mail: patrick.wall@areditions.com
Dir, Spec Projs: James Zychowicz *Tel:* 608-203-2580 *E-mail:* james.zychowicz@areditions.com
Founded: 1962
Membership(s): American Musicological Society (AMS); Audio Engineering Society Inc (AES); Music Library Association; Music Publishers Association (MPA)

ABDI Inc
16 Avenue "A", Leetsdale, PA 15056
Toll Free Tel: 800-796-6471 *Fax:* 412-741-4161
E-mail: e-fulfillment@abdintl.com
Web Site: www.abdi-ecommerce10.com/abdintl; www.abdintl.com/abdintl
Key Personnel
CEO: Michael D Cheteyan, II
Pres: Judy G Cheteyan *E-mail:* j.cheteyan@abdintl.com
VP, Fin & IT: Bryan A Cox
Gen Opers Mgr: Ericka D Giles
Founded: 1985
Turnaround: 8 Workdays
Print Runs: 50 min - 50,000 max

Adair Graphic Communications
Division of Printwell
26975 Northline Rd, Taylor, MI 48180
Tel: 734-941-6300 *Fax:* 734-942-0920
E-mail: adair@printwell.com
Web Site: www.adairgraphic.com
Key Personnel
Pres & CEO: Paul Borg
VP: Dennis Adair *E-mail:* dennis@adairgraphic.com
Founded: 1931
Turnaround: 10 Workdays
Print Runs: 500 min - 500,000 max

Adams Press
1712 Oakton St, Evanston, IL 60202
E-mail: info@adamspress.com
Key Personnel
Pres: James A Kepler *E-mail:* jkepler@adamspress.com
Founded: 1942
Turnaround: 20-25 Workdays
Print Runs: 100 min - 15,000 max (print; publish on demand available)

Membership(s): The Association of Publishers for Special Sales (APSS); Independent Book Publishers Association (IBPA); Independent Writers of Chicago (IWOC); Midwest Writers Association

AGS
Subsidiary of RR Donnelley
4590 Graphics Dr, White Plains, MD 20695
Tel: 301-843-1800 *Fax:* 301-843-6339
E-mail: info@ags.com
Web Site: www.ags.com
Key Personnel
Pres: Mike Donohue *E-mail:* mike.donohue@rrd.com
VP, Sales & Mktg: Alan Flint *E-mail:* aflint@ags.com
Founded: 1975
Print Runs: 50 min - 1,000,000 max
Membership(s): American Society of Association Executives™ (ASAE)

American Mathematical Society (AMS)
201 Charles St, Providence, RI 02904-2213
SAN: 201-1654
Tel: 401-455-4000 *Toll Free Tel:* 800-321-4267
   Fax: 401-331-3842; 401-455-4046 (cust serv)
E-mail: cust-serv@ams.org; ams@ams.org
Web Site: www.ams.org
Key Personnel
Exec Dir: Dr Catherine A Roberts
Publr: Dr Sergei Gelfand
Assoc Exec Dir: Dr Robert M Harrington
Assoc Exec Dir, Washington, DC: Dr Karen Saxe
Founded: 1888
Print Runs: 100 min - 10,000 max
Branch Office(s)
1527 18 St NW, Washington, DC 20036-1358 (govt rel & sci policy) *Tel:* 202-588-1100
   Fax: 202-588-1853 *E-mail:* amsdc@ams.org
Mathematical Reviews®, 416 Fourth St, Ann Arbor, MI 48103-4820 (edit) *Tel:* 734-996-5250
   Fax: 734-996-2916 *E-mail:* mathrev@ams.org
Secretary of the AMS - Society Governance, Dept of Computer Science, North Carolina State University, Box 8206, Raleigh, NC 27695-8206 *Tel:* 919-515-7863 *Fax:* 919-515-7896
   E-mail: secretary@ams.org
Membership(s): Society for Scholarly Publishing (SSP)

appatura™, A Broadridge Company
Division of Broadridge Financial Solutions Inc
65 Challenger Rd, Suite 400, Ridgefield Park, NJ 07660
Tel: 201-508-6000 *Toll Free Tel:* 800-277-2155
E-mail: contactus@appatura.com
Web Site: www.appatura.com

Key Personnel
CEO: Richard Plotka
CIO: Faisal Fareed
Chief Prod Offr: Harsh Choudhary
Chief Strategy Offr: John Closson
Head, Fin: Alpha Diarra
Founded: 1949
Print Runs: 1,000 min - 250,000 max

Aptara Inc
Subsidiary of iEnergizer
2901 Telestar Ct, Suite 522, Falls Church, VA 22042
Tel: 703-352-0001
E-mail: moreinfo@aptaracorp.com
Web Site: www.aptaracorp.com
Key Personnel
Pres: Samir Kakar
EVP, Fin & Cont: Prashant Kapoor
SVP, Busn & Contact Ctr Opers: Ashish Madan
Busn Devt: Michael Scott *E-mail:* michael.scott@aptaracorp.com
Founded: 1988
Branch Office(s)
150 California St, Suite 301, Newton, MA 02458
   Tel: 617-423-7755
11009 Metric Blvd, Bldg J, Suite 150, Austin, TX 78758 *Tel:* 512-876-5997
299 Elizabeth St, Level 1, Sydney 2000, Australia *Tel:* (02) 8251 0070
Tower 1 & 2, 8/100, Acharya Thulasi Rd (Shandy Rd), Pallavaram, Chennai 600 043, India *Tel:* (044) 22640676
No 2310, Doon Express Business Park, Saharanpur Rd, Bldg 2000, Dehradun 248 002, India *Tel:* (0135) 2644055
7B, Leela Infopark, Technopark, Trivandrum, Kerala 695 581, India *Tel:* (0471) 14063370
A-37, Sector-60, Noida 201 301, India
   Tel: (0120) 7182424
D-10, Sector-2, Noida 201 301, India *Tel:* (0120) 24423678
SEZ Bldg 4A, 1st fl, S P Infocity, Pune Saswad Rd, Phursungi, Pune 412 308, India *Tel:* (020) 66728000

Arbor Books
244 Madison Ave, Box 254, New York, NY 10016
Tel: 212-956-0950 *Toll Free Tel:* 877-822-2500
   Fax: 914-401-9385
E-mail: info@arborbooks.com; editorial@arborbooks.net
Web Site: www.arborbooks.com
Key Personnel
Owner: Joel Hochman *Tel:* 877-822-2502 *E-mail:* arborbooksjoel@aol.com; Larry Leichman *Tel:* 877-822-2504
   E-mail: arborbookslarry@aol.com

COMPLETE BOOK MANUFACTURING

Mktg Dir: Olga Vladi *E-mail:* floatinggal1@aol.com
Founded: 1992
Turnaround: 21 Workdays; 1-7 Workdays for art
Print Runs: 1 min - 1,000,000 max

Arbor Services, see Arbor Books

Arrow Graphics Inc
PO Box 380291, Cambridge, MA 02238
E-mail: info@arrow1.com
Web Site: www.arrow1.com
Key Personnel
Pres: Alvart Badalian
Sr Graphic/Pubn Designer: Aramais Andonian
Founded: 1988
Print Runs: 300 min - 25,000 max

Asia Pacific Offset Inc
1312 "Q" St NW, Suite B, Washington, DC 20009
Tel: 202-462-5436 *Toll Free Tel:* 800-756-4344 *Fax:* 202-986-4030
Web Site: www.asiapacificoffset.com
Key Personnel
Pres: Andrew Clarke *E-mail:* andrew@asiapacificoffset.com
Founded: 1997
Turnaround: 104 Workdays including color separation & shipping
Print Runs: 2,000 min
Branch Office(s)
870 Market St, Suite 801, San Francisco, CA 94102, Dir, Sales: Amy Armstrong *Tel:* 415-433-3488 *Fax:* 415-433-3489 *E-mail:* amy@asiapacificoffset.com
1768 Oakmont Ct, Ann Arbor, MI 48108, Dir, Sales: Dean Sherman *Tel:* 734-223-6218 *E-mail:* dean@asiapacificoffset.com
62 Rivington St, Suite 2B, New York, NY 10002, Dir, Sales & Mktg: Simona Jansons *Tel:* 212-941-8300 *Fax:* 212-941-9810 *E-mail:* simona@asiapacificoffset.com
16 Clements Dr, Avoca Beach, NSW 2251, Australia, Dir, Sales: Penny Crocker *Tel:* (02) 4832 6174 *E-mail:* penny@asiapacificoffset.com
57 Norfolk St, Ponsonby, Auckland 1021, New Zealand, Consultant: Barbara Nielsen *Tel:* (09) 378-4971 *E-mail:* barbara@asiapacificoffset.com
C/ Tamarit 104, esc D, entrance 2, 08015 Barcelona, Spain, Dir, Sales: Carlos Blavia *Tel:* 933278837 *Fax:* 933254826 *E-mail:* carlos@asiapacificoffset.com
20 Mortlake High St, London SW14 8JN, United Kingdom, Dir, Sales: Adrian Gatheroole *Tel:* (020) 3170 8700 *Fax:* (020) 3170 8704 *E-mail:* adrian@asiapacificoffset.com

Automated Graphic Systems, see AGS

B & Z Printing Inc
1300 E Wakeham Ave, Unit B, Santa Ana, CA 92705
Tel: 714-892-2000
Web Site: www.bandzprinting.com
Key Personnel
Pres: Frank Buono *E-mail:* frank@bandzprinting.com
Founded: 1984
Turnaround: 7-10 Workdays
Print Runs: 3,000 min

Balfour Commercial Printing
Formerly Taylor Specialty Books
Division of Balfour/Taylor
225 E John Carpenter Fwy, Tower 2, Suite 400, Irving, TX 75062
Tel: 214-819-8588 (cust serv)
E-mail: printing@balfour.com
Web Site: commercial-printing.balfour.com

Key Personnel
Acct Exec: Julie Kacala *E-mail:* julie.kacala@balfour.com
Founded: 1939
Turnaround: 30-35 Workdays
Print Runs: 250 min - 25,000 max

Bang Printing Co Inc
Division of CJK Group Inc
3323 Oak St, Brainerd, MN 56401
Tel: 218-829-2877 *Toll Free Tel:* 800-328-0450 *Fax:* 218-829-7145
E-mail: info@bangprinting.com
Web Site: www.bangprinting.com
Key Personnel
Pres: Todd Vanek *E-mail:* toddv@bangprinting.com
VP, Opers: Joe Saiko *E-mail:* joes@bangprinting.com
VP, Sales: Doug Walters *E-mail:* dougw@bangprinting.com
Founded: 1899
Turnaround: 10-25 Workdays
Print Runs: 1,000 min - 500,000 max

BBC, see Brown Book Co Ltd

Berryville Graphics
Member of Bertelsmann Printing Group
25 Jack Enders Blvd, Berryville, VA 22611
Tel: 540-955-2750 *Fax:* 540-955-2633
E-mail: info@bvgraphics.com
Web Site: www.bpg-usa.com
Key Personnel
CEO: Christof Ludwig
CFO: Denis Leite
CTO: Yannic Schroeder
Founded: 1956
Turnaround: 15 Workdays (initial orders); 6 Workdays (reprint orders); 4 Workdays (out of stock)
Print Runs: 1,500 min
Branch Office(s)
100 N Miller St, Fairfield, PA 17320 *Tel:* 717-549-4800
871 Baker St, Martinsburg, VA 25405 *Tel:* 681-247-3300

Blue Note Books, see Blue Note Publications Inc

Blue Note Publications Inc
721 North Dr, Suite D, Melbourne, FL 32934
Tel: 321-799-2583; 321-622-6289 *Toll Free Tel:* 800-624-0401 (orders) *Fax:* 321-799-1942; 321-622-6830
E-mail: bluenotebooks@gmail.com
Web Site: bluenotepublications.com
Key Personnel
Pres: Paul Maluccio
Founded: 1988
Turnaround: 20 Workdays
Print Runs: 25 min - 10,000 max (short run digital print-on-demand available)

BookLogix
1264 Old Alpharetta Rd, Alpharetta, GA 30005
SAN: 860-0376
Tel: 470-239-8547
E-mail: info@booklogix.com; publishing@booklogix.com; customerservice@booklogix.com
Web Site: www.booklogix.com
Key Personnel
CEO: Angela DeCaires
Founded: 2009

Bookmasters
Division of Baker & Taylor Publisher Services
30 Amberwood Pkwy, Ashland, OH 44805
Tel: 419-281-5100 *Toll Free Tel:* 800-537-6727 *Fax:* 419-281-0200

E-mail: info@btpubservices.com
Web Site: www.btpubservices.com
Key Personnel
Dir of Mfg: Brad Sharp *E-mail:* bsharp@bookmasters.com
Founded: 1972

Bradford & Bigelow Inc
3 Perkins Way, Newburyport, MA 01950-4007
Tel: 978-904-3100
E-mail: sales@bradford-bigelow.com
Web Site: www.bradford-bigelow.com
Key Personnel
CFO: Carmen Frederico
Pres: John Galligan
VP, Sales & Busn Devt: Bob Bradley *Tel:* 978-904-3108 *E-mail:* bbradley@bradford-bigelow.com
Founded: 1970
Turnaround: 10 Workdays
Print Runs: 50 min - 250,000 max
Membership(s): Book Manufacturers' Institute (BMI); PRINTING United Alliance

Brown Book Co Ltd
65 Crockford Blvd, Toronto, ON M1R 3B7, Canada
Tel: 416-504-9696 *Fax:* 416-504-9393
E-mail: bbc@brownbook.ca
Web Site: www.brownbook.ca
Key Personnel
Owner & Pres: Robert Brown
Opers Supv: Sharon Endugesick
Prodn Coord: Melissa Brown

C & C Offset Printing Co USA Inc
Subsidiary of C & C Joint Printing Co (HK) Ltd
70 W 36 St, Unit 10C, New York, NY 10018
Tel: 212-431-4210 *Toll Free Fax:* 866-540-4134
Web Site: www.ccoffset.com
Key Personnel
Dir & EVP, C & C Offset Printing Co (USA) Inc & C & C Offset Printing Co (NY) Inc, New York, NY: Simon Chan *E-mail:* schan@ccoffset.com
Sales Mgr, C & C Offset Printing Co (NY) Inc, New York, NY: Frances Harkness *E-mail:* fharkness@ccoffset.com; Timothy McNulty
CEO, C & C Joint Printing Co (HK) Ltd, Hong Kong: Jackson Leung
Deputy Gen Mgr, C & C Joint Printing Co (HK) Ltd, Hong Kong: Francis Ho; Kit Wong
Dir, C & C Offset Printing Co (France) Ltd: Michele Olson Niel *E-mail:* michele@candcoffset.fr
Pres, C & C Printing Japan Co Ltd, Tokyo, Japan: Yamamoto Masaaki
Dir, C & C Offset Printing Co (UK) Ltd: Tracy Broderick *E-mail:* tracy@candcoffset.co.uk
Sales Rep, Australian Off: Lena Frew *E-mail:* lena.frew@candcprinting.com
Founded: 1980
Turnaround: Varies
Print Runs: 2,000 min - 3,000,000 max (average book runs: 7,500-50,000)
Branch Office(s)
C & C Offset Printing Co Ltd (Australia Off), Lithocraft Graphics, 3-7 Permas Way, Truganina, Victoria 3029, Australia *Tel:* (0613) 8366 0200 *Fax:* (0613) 8366 0299
C & C Offset Printing Co (France) Ltd, 15, rue d'Aboukir, 75002 Paris, France *Tel:* 01 40 26 21 07 *Fax:* 01 44 76 08 96
C & C Offset Printing Co Ltd, C & C Bldg, 36 Ting Lai Rd, Tai Po, New Territories, Hong Kong (corp headquarters) *Tel:* 2666 4988 *Fax:* 2666 4938 *E-mail:* info@candcprinting.com *Web Site:* www.candcprinting.com
C & C Printing Japan Co Ltd, Tozaido Bldg, 3F, 2-6-12 Hitotsubashi, Chiyoda-ku, Tokyo 101-0003, Japan *Tel:* (03) 5216 4580 *Fax:* (03)

MANUFACTURING

5216 4610 *E-mail:* mail@candcprinting.co.jp
Web Site: www.candcprinting.co.jp
C & C Offset Printing Co (UK) Ltd, 75 Newman St, 3rd fl, London W1T 3EN, United Kingdom
Tel: (020) 7637 5033 *Fax:* (020) 7637 5044
E-mail: info@candcoffset.co.uk

C-M Books, see Cushing-Malloy Inc

Cenveo Inc
200 First Stamford Place, 2nd fl, Stamford, CT 06902
Tel: 203-595-3000 *Fax:* 203-595-3070
E-mail: info@cenveo.com
Web Site: www.cenveo.com
Key Personnel
CEO: Robert G Burton, Jr
CFO: Mark Hiltwein
Pres: Michael Burton
Founded: 1830
Turnaround: 10 Workdays
Print Runs: 1,500 min - 1,000,000 max

Cenveo St Louis
101 Workman Ct, Eureka, MO 63025
Tel: 314-966-2000 *Toll Free Tel:* 800-800-8845
Fax: 314-966-4725
Web Site: www.cenveo.com

CG Book Printers
Division of Corporate Graphics Commercial (CGC)
1750 Northway Dr, North Mankato, MN 56003
Tel: 507-388-3300 *Toll Free Tel:* 800-729-7575
Fax: 507-386-6350
E-mail: cgbooks@corpgraph.com
Web Site: www.corpgraph.com
Key Personnel
Pres: Dan Kvasnicka *Tel:* 507-386-6340
Fax: 507-344-5548 *E-mail:* dekvasnicka@corpgraph.com
Sales Exec, Book Mfg Sales: Mike Schmitt *Tel:* 507-386-6349 *E-mail:* mjschmitt@corpgraph.com
Founded: 1989
Print Runs: 50 min - 100,000 max

Codra Enterprises Inc
17692 Cowan, Suite 200, Irvine, CA 92614
Tel: 949-756-8400 *Toll Free Tel:* 888-992-6372
Fax: 949-756-8484
E-mail: codra@codra.com; sales@codra.com
Web Site: www.codra.com
Key Personnel
Pres: Gary Kim
Sales: Chris Scotti *Tel:* 949-322-5639
E-mail: chris@codra.com
Founded: 1985
Turnaround: 30-40 Workdays
Print Runs: 3,000 min - 3,000,000 max
Membership(s): Independent Publishers Association; Pacific Northwest Booksellers Association (PNBA); Publishers Association of the West (PubWest)

Color House Graphics Inc
3505 Eastern Ave SE, Grand Rapids, MI 49508
Toll Free Tel: 800-454-1916 *Fax:* 616-245-5494
Web Site: www.colorhousegraphics.com
Key Personnel
Pres: Steve Landheer
Gen Mgr: Phil Knight *E-mail:* pknight@colorhousegraphics.com
Founded: 1987
Turnaround: 5-20 Workdays
Print Runs: 1 min - 50,000 max (1-500 digital short-run, 500+ offset)
Membership(s): The Association of Publishers for Special Sales (APSS); Colorado Independent Publishers Association (CIPA); Evangelical Christian Publishers Association (ECPA);

Florida Authors & Publishers Association Inc (FAPA); Independent Book Publishers Association (IBPA); Printing Industries of Michigan Inc (PIM); Publishers Association of the West (PubWest)

ColorPage
Division of Tri-State Associated Services Inc
81 Ten Broeck Ave, Kingston, NY 12401
Tel: 845-331-7581 *Toll Free Tel:* 800-836-7581
Fax: 845-331-1571
E-mail: sales@colorpageonline.com
Web Site: www.colorpageonline.com
Key Personnel
Pres & Mktg Strategist/Consultant: Frank J Campagna, II *E-mail:* fcampagna@colorpageonline.com
Acct Mgr & Cont: Kathy Riggins
E-mail: kriggins@colorpageonline.com
Prodn Mgr: Randy Delanoy
Cust Serv Supv: Debbie Downes
E-mail: ddownes@colorpageonline.com
Founded: 1976
Turnaround: 10-15 Workdays
Print Runs: 25 min - 20,000 max

C Harrison Conroy Co Inc
501 Penman St, Charlotte, NC 28203
Tel: 704-358-0459 *Toll Free Tel:* 800-242-2789
Fax: 704-358-0459
E-mail: chcphoto@charrisonconroy.com
Web Site: www.charrisonconroy.com
Key Personnel
Pres: Hal Conroy
Founded: 1936

Consolidated Printers Inc
2630 Eighth St, Berkeley, CA 94710
Tel: 510-495-3113 (sales); 510-843-8565 (admin)
Web Site: www.consoprinters.com
Key Personnel
CEO: Lawrence A Hawkins
Founded: 1952
Turnaround: 2-20 Workdays
Print Runs: 2,000 min - 500,000 max

Corporate Graphics Book Printers, see CG Book Printers

The Country Press Inc
One Commercial Dr, Lakeville, MA 02347
Mailing Address: PO Box 489, Middleborough, MA 02346
Tel: 508-947-4485 *Toll Free Tel:* 888-343-2227
Fax: 508-947-8989
E-mail: info@countrypressinc.com
Web Site: www.countrypressprinting.com
Key Personnel
Pres: Mike Pinto
VP & Gen Mgr: George Medeiros
VP, Cust Opers: David Brooks
Founded: 1967
Turnaround: 3-7 Workdays
Print Runs: 11 min - 5,000 max

Crane Duplicating Service Inc
4915 Rattlesnake Hammock Rd, Suite 207, Naples, FL 34113
Tel: 305-280-6742 (help desk) *Fax:* 239-732-8415
E-mail: info@craneduplicating.com
Web Site: www.craneduplicating.com
Key Personnel
Pres & CEO: Richard W Price
Mgr, Cust Serv: Jean Fahr
Founded: 1955
Turnaround: 5-7 Workdays, Same day; 3 or 4 Workdays available at extra cost
Print Runs: 11 min - 50,000 max (5-7 Days for short runs)

COMPLETE BOOK MANUFACTURING

Crown Connect
250 W Rialto Ave, San Bernadino, CA 92408
Tel: 909-888-7531 *Fax:* 909-889-1639
E-mail: sales@crownconnect.com
Web Site: www.crownconnect.com
Key Personnel
CFO: Nicole Albright *Tel:* 909-888-7531 ext 204
Pres: Denny Shorett *Tel:* 909-888-7531 ext 225
VP, Opers: Ken Martin *Tel:* 909-888-7531 ext 206
Mgr, Busn Devt: Erin Warren *Tel:* 909-888-7531 ext 228
Prodn Mgr: Chris McPhate *Tel:* 909-888-7531 ext 214
Founded: 1970

Cushing-Malloy Inc
1350 N Main St, Ann Arbor, MI 48104-1045
Tel: 734-663-8554 *Fax:* 734-663-5731
Web Site: www.cushing-malloy.com; www.c-mbooks.com
Key Personnel
Chmn of the Bd: Connie M Cushing
E-mail: ccushing@cushing-malloy.com
VP of Sales: Tedd Litty *E-mail:* tlitty@cushing-malloy.com
Cust Serv/Sales: Adam Hieber *E-mail:* ahieber@cushing-malloy.com
Founded: 1948
Turnaround: 15-30 Workdays
Print Runs: 150 min - 50,000 max
Membership(s): Independent Book Publishers Association (IBPA); Publishers Association of the West (PubWest)

Data Reproductions Corp
4545 Glenmeade Lane, Auburn Hills, MI 48326
Tel: 248-371-3700 *Toll Free Tel:* 800-242-3114
Fax: 248-371-3710
Web Site: datarepro.com
Key Personnel
Pres: Dennis Kavanagh
Gen Mgr: Steve Olko
Acct Mgr: Kimberly Kavanagh *Tel:* 248-881-6518 (cell) *E-mail:* kkavanagh@datarepro.com
Sales Exec: Nick Janosi *Tel:* 734-426-1229
E-mail: njanosi@datarepro.com
Founded: 1967
Turnaround: 15 Workdays
Print Runs: 250 min - 100,000 max

Desktop Miracles Inc
112 S Main St, Suite 294, Stowe, VT 05672
Tel: 802-253-7900 *Toll Free Fax:* 888-293-2676
E-mail: info@desktopmiracles.com
Web Site: www.desktopmiracles.com
Key Personnel
Pres & CEO: Barry T Kerrigan *E-mail:* barry@desktopmiracles.com
VP: Virginia Kerrigan *E-mail:* virginia@desktopmiracles.com
Founded: 1994
Turnaround: 10-15 Workdays
Print Runs: 500 min

DNP America LLC
Subsidiary of Dai Nippon Printing Co Ltd
335 Madison Ave, 3rd fl, New York, NY 10017
Tel: 212-503-1060
E-mail: gps@dnp-g.com
Web Site: www.dnpamerica.com
Key Personnel
VP & Gen Mgr: Norikatsu Nakamura
Founded: 1976
Print Runs: 1,000 min
Branch Office(s)
2099 Gateway Place, Suite 490, San Jose, CA 95110 *Tel:* 408-735-8880
3858 Carson St, Suite 300, Torrance, CA 90503 *Tel:* 310-540-5123

RR Donnelley
35 W Wacker Dr, Chicago, IL 60601

COMPLETE BOOK MANUFACTURING

Toll Free Tel: 800-742-4455
Web Site: www.rrd.com
Key Personnel
Pres & CEO: Daniel L Knotts
Pres, Busn Servs: John Pecaric
Pres, Mktg Solutions: Doug Ryan
EVP & CFO: Terry D Peterson
EVP & CIO: Ken O'Brien
EVP & Chief HR Offr: Sheila Rutt
EVP & Chief Strategy & Transformation Offr: Elif Sagsen-Ercel
EVP, Gen Coun, Chief Compliance Offr & Corp Secy: Deborah Steiner
EVP, Dom Opers & Chief Supply Chain Offr: Glynn Perry
SVP & Chief Acctg Offr: Michael J Sharp
Founded: 1864
Turnaround: 3-6 Weeks
Print Runs: 3,000 min - 500,000 max
Branch Office(s)
955 Gateway Center Way, San Diego, CA 92102 *Tel:* 619-527-4600
40610 County Center Dr, Temecula, CA 92591 *Tel:* 951-296-2890
151 Red Stone Rd, Manchester, CT 06042 *Tel:* 860-649-5570
9125 Bachman Rd, Orlando, FL 32824 *Tel:* 407-859-2030
5800 Peachtree Rd, Atlanta, GA 30341 *Tel:* 770-458-6351
825 Riverside Pkwy, Suite 300, Austell, GA 30168 *Tel:* 770-948-1330
1750 Wallace Ave, St Charles, IL 60174 *Tel:* 630-313-7000
609 S Kirk Rd, St Charles, IL 60174 *Tel:* 630-762-7600
One Poplar Ave, Thurmont, MD 21788 *Tel:* 301-271-7171
65 Sprague St, Hyde Park, MA 02136 *Tel:* 617-360-2000
18780 W 78 St, Chanhassen, MN 55317 *Tel:* 952-937-9764
5500 12 Ave E, Shakopee, MN 55379 *Tel:* 952-941-7546
6305 Sunset Corporate Dr, Las Vegas, NV 89120 *Tel:* 702-949-8500
5 Henderson Dr, West Caldwell, NJ 07006 *Tel:* 973-882-7000
12301 Vance Davis Dr, Charlotte, NC 28269 *Tel:* 704-949-3568
One Litho Way, Durham, NC 27703 *Tel:* 919-596-3660
3801 Gantz Rd, Grove City, OH 43123 *Tel:* 614-539-5527
700 Nestle Way, Suite 200, Breinigsville, PA 18031 *Tel:* 610-391-3900
9985 Gantry Rd, Philadelphia, PA 19115 *Tel:* 215-671-9500
218 N Braddock Ave, Pittsburgh, PA 15208 *Tel:* 412-241-8200
1210 Key Rd, Columbia, SC 29201 *Tel:* 803-799-9550
1645 W Sam Houston Pkwy N, Houston, TX 77043 *Tel:* 713-468-7175
1550 Lakeway Dr, Suite 600, Lewisville, TX 75057 *Tel:* 972-353-7500
630 W 1000 N, Logan, UT 84321 *Tel:* 435-755-4000
201 E Progress Dr, West Bend, WI 53095 *Tel:* 262-338-6101
Membership(s): Association of American Publishers (AAP); Book Industry Study Group (BISG); Book Manufacturers' Institute (BMI)

W R Draper Co
Division of The Arthur Press (1978) Ltd
162 Norfinch Dr, Toronto, ON M3N 1X6, Canada
Tel: 416-663-6001 *Fax:* 416-663-6043
E-mail: info@arthurpress.com
Web Site: www.arthurpress.com
Key Personnel
Pres: Jeremy Thorn
Founded: 1954

Turnaround: 10 Workdays
Print Runs: 1,000 min - 75,000 max

Dunn & Co Inc
Affiliate of Legacy Publishing Group
75 Green St, Clinton, MA 01510
Mailing Address: PO Box 1185, Clinton, MA 01510
Tel: 978-368-8505 *Fax:* 978-368-7867
E-mail: info@booktrauma.com
Web Site: www.booktrauma.com
Key Personnel
Chmn: David M Dunn
Pres: Peter R Heelan
VP: Rocco Windover
Founded: 1976
Turnaround: 3-10 Workdays
Print Runs: 100 min

Ecological Fibers Inc
40 Pioneer Dr, Lunenburg, MA 01462
Tel: 978-537-0003 *Fax:* 978-537-2238
E-mail: info@ecofibers.com
Web Site: www.ecofibers.com
Key Personnel
Pres: John A Quill
VP, Sales: Dave Robbins *E-mail:* drobbins@ecofibers.com
Dir, Book Group Sales: Jim McCafferty *E-mail:* jmccafferty@ecofibers.com
Dir, Busn Opers: Joyce Hardell *E-mail:* joyce@ecofibers.com
Founded: 1972
Branch Office(s)
730 York Ave, Pawtucket, RI 02861 *Tel:* 401-725-9700 *Fax:* 401-724-4970
Membership(s): Book Manufacturers' Institute (BMI); Publishing Professionals Network (PPN)

Emprint®
5425 Florida Blvd, Baton Rouge, LA 70806
Tel: 225-923-2550 *Toll Free Tel:* 800-211-8335
Web Site: emprint.com
Key Personnel
CEO: Mr Courtney Westbrook
Pres & COO: Becky Vance *E-mail:* beckyv@emprint.com
Turnaround: 5 Workdays
Print Runs: 2 min - 125,000 max
Branch Office(s)
109 Research Dr, Harahan, LA 70123 *Tel:* 504-733-9654 *Toll Free Tel:* 877-568-1555 *Fax:* 504-733-8506
151 Southpark Rd, Suite 100, Lafayette, LA 70508 *Tel:* 337-839-9761 *Toll Free Tel:* 888-874-9761
2830 Breard St, Monroe, LA 71201 *Tel:* 318-387-1725 *Toll Free Tel:* 800-256-2259

Ferry Associates Inc
49 Fostertown Rd, Medford, NJ 08055
Tel: 609-953-1233 *Toll Free Tel:* 800-257-5258 *Fax:* 609-953-8637
Web Site: www.ferryassociates.com
Key Personnel
Pres: Kevin Ferry *E-mail:* kferry@ferryassociates.com
Founded: 1982
Turnaround: Standard 2 week delivery
Print Runs: 1,000 min - 10,000,000 max

First Choice Copy
5208 Grand Ave, Maspeth, NY 11378
Tel: 718-381-1480 (ext 200) *Toll Free Tel:* 800-222-COPY (222-2679)
Web Site: www.firstchoice-copy.com
Key Personnel
Owner & Pres: Joe Meisner *Tel:* 718-381-1480 ext 212 *E-mail:* jmeisner@nyc.rr.com
Turnaround: 3-5 Workdays

Flottman Co Inc
720 Centre View Blvd, Crestview Hills, KY 41017
Tel: 859-331-6636 *Fax:* 859-344-7085
E-mail: info@flottmanco.com
Web Site: www.flottmanco.com
Key Personnel
CEO: Sue F Steller *E-mail:* ssteller@flottmanco.com
VP & CFO: Peter Flottman
Founded: 1921

Four Colour Print Group
2410 Frankfort Ave, Louisville, KY 40206
Tel: 502-896-9644 *Fax:* 502-896-9594
E-mail: sales@fourcolour.com
Web Site: www.fourcolour.com
Key Personnel
Pres & CEO: George C Dick *Tel:* 502-896-9644 ext 303 *E-mail:* gdick@fourcolour.com
Prodn Dir: Amy Martin *Tel:* 502-896-9644 ext 315 *E-mail:* amartin@fourcolour.com
Prodn Mgr: Cindy Jones *Tel:* 502-896-9644 ext 310 *E-mail:* cjones@fourcolour.com
Founded: 1985
Turnaround: 90 Workdays
Print Runs: 1,000 min - 100,000 max
Branch Office(s)
FCI Digital, 2032 S Alex Rd, Suite A, West Carrollton, OH 45449 *Tel:* 931-859-9701 *Fax:* 931-859-9709 *E-mail:* sales@fcidigital.com *Web Site:* www.fcidigital.com

Friesens Corp
One Printers Way, Altona, MB R0G 0B0, Canada
Tel: 204-324-6401 *Fax:* 204-324-1333
E-mail: book_info@friesens.com
Web Site: www.friesens.com
Key Personnel
Pres & CEO: Chad Friesen
Gen Sales Mgr: Doug Symington *E-mail:* dougs@friesens.com
Founded: 1907
Turnaround: 3-4 Weeks
Print Runs: 250 min - 250,000 max (& more)
Membership(s): Book Manufacturers' Institute (BMI)

Fry Communications Inc
800 W Church Rd, Mechanicsburg, PA 17055
Tel: 717-766-0211 *Toll Free Tel:* 800-334-1429 *Fax:* 717-691-0341
E-mail: info@frycomm.com
Web Site: www.frycomm.com
Key Personnel
Chmn of the Bd: Henry Fry
CEO: Mike Lukas
CFO: Chris Wawrzyniak
CTO: David S Fry
VP, Sales: Kevin Quinn
Founded: 1934
Turnaround: 7-12 Workdays
Print Runs: 10,000 min - 2,000,000 max

Fundcraft Publishing
410 Hwy 72 W, Collierville, TN 38017
Mailing Address: PO Box 340, Collierville, TN 38027
Tel: 901-853-7070 *Toll Free Tel:* 800-853-1363 *Fax:* 901-853-6196
E-mail: info@fundcraft.com
Web Site: www.fundcraft.com
Key Personnel
Pres: Chris Bradley *E-mail:* cbradley@cookbooks.com
Publr: David Bradley
Turnaround: 40-60 Workdays
Print Runs: 100 min

G & H Soho Inc
413 Market St, Elmwood Park, NJ 07407
Tel: 201-216-9400 *Fax:* 201-216-1778

MANUFACTURING

E-mail: print@ghsoho.com
Web Site: www.ghsoho.com
Key Personnel
Pres: Gerry Burstein
Prodn Mgr: Jason Burstein
Founded: 1985
Turnaround: 3-40 Workdays
Print Runs: 5 min - 10,000 max
Membership(s): Association of Graphic Communications; Digital Printing Council; PRINTING United Alliance

GEX Inc
80 Conley's Grove Rd, Derry, NH 03038
Mailing Address: PO Box 613, Atkinson, NH 03811
Tel: 603-870-9292
Web Site: www.gexinc.com
Key Personnel
Pres: Gary Russell *E-mail:* gary.russell@gexinc.com
VP: Jim LaPierre
Founded: 1986

Giant Horse Printing Inc
1336 San Mateo Ave, South San Francisco, CA 94080
Tel: 650-875-7137 *Fax:* 650-875-7194
E-mail: info@gianthorse.com
Web Site: www.gianthorse.com
Key Personnel
Pres: Chiu Bing Ma
Founded: 1970
Turnaround: 7-10 Workdays
Print Runs: 1 min - 50,000 max

Global Order Fulfillment, see ABDI Inc

Graphic Connections Group LLC
174 Chesterfield Industrial Blvd, Chesterfield, MO 63005
Tel: 636-519-8320 *Toll Free Tel:* 800-378-0378
Fax: 636-519-8310
Web Site: www.gcfrog.com
Key Personnel
Owner & Pres: Jeff Charlton
VP, Mktg: Michael Hecht *E-mail:* mhecht@gcfrog.com
Turnaround: 5-7 Workdays from final proof authorization
Print Runs: 25 min - 2,500 max

Graphic Litho
Division of High Speed Process Printing Corp
130 Shepard St, Lawrence, MA 01843
Tel: 978-683-2766 *Fax:* 978-681-7588
E-mail: sales@graphiclitho.com
Web Site: www.graphiclitho.com
Key Personnel
Pres: Ralph E Wilbur
Founded: 1960
Print Runs: 1,000 min
Membership(s): Print Services & Distribution Association (PSDA); Printing Industries of New England (PINE); PRINTING United Alliance

Hess Print Solutions
Division of CJK Group Inc
3765 Sunnybrook Rd, Brimfield, OH 44240
Toll Free Tel: 800-678-1222
E-mail: info@hessprintsolutions.com
Web Site: www.hessprintsolutions.com
Key Personnel
Dir & VP: Burt Phillips
VP, IT: Douglas Holzschuh
Founded: 2006
Print Runs: 1,000 min
Membership(s): Book Manufacturers' Institute (BMI)

Hignell Book Printing Ltd
Division of Unigraphics Ltd
488 Burnell St, Winnipeg, MB R3G 2B4, Canada
Tel: 204-784-1030 *Toll Free Tel:* 800-304-5553
Fax: 204-774-4053
E-mail: books@hignell.mb.ca
Web Site: www.hignell.mb.ca
Key Personnel
Pres: Kevin Polley *E-mail:* kevin@unigraphics.mb.ca
VP & Gen Mgr: David Morcom *E-mail:* davem@unigraphics.mb.ca
Founded: 1908
Turnaround: 15 Workdays
Print Runs: 100 min - 10,000 max

The P A Hutchison Co
400 Penn Ave, Mayfield, PA 18433
SAN: 991-5559
Tel: 570-876-4560 *Toll Free Tel:* 800-USA-PRNT (872-7768) *Fax:* 570-876-4561
E-mail: sales@pahutch.com
Web Site: www.pahutch.com
Key Personnel
Pres & CEO: Chris Hutchison
Dir, Sales & Admin: Erin Jones
Founded: 1911
Turnaround: 3-20 Workdays
Print Runs: 10 min - 200,000 max (digital & conventional)

Imago
110 W 40 St, New York, NY 10018
Tel: 212-921-4411 *Fax:* 212-921-8226
E-mail: sales@imagousa.com
Web Site: www.imagousa.com
Key Personnel
Pres & CEO: Howard Musk *E-mail:* howardm@imagogroup.com
Founded: 1985
Turnaround: 5-10 Workdays for color separations; 4-6 Weeks for printing & binding
Print Runs: 3,000 min
Branch Office(s)
Imago West Coast, 23412 Moulton Pkwy, Suite 250, Laguna Hills, CA 92653 (sales), Contact: Tammy Simms *Tel:* 949-367-1635 *Fax:* 949-367-1639
Imago Australia, 10 Help St, Suite 27, Level 6, Chatswood, NSW 2067, Australia (sales) *Tel:* (04) 3753 3351 (cell); (04) 4806 8704 (cell) *E-mail:* sales@imagaoaus.com
Imago Brazil, Domiciano Rossi, 340 unid 154, 09726-121 Sao Bernardo do Campo, Brazil (sales) *Tel:* (011) 2306 8546; (011) 2306 8547 *E-mail:* imagobra@gmail.com
Imago Shenzhen, Rm 2511-2512, Block A, United Plaza No 5022, Bin He Rd, Fu Tian Centre District, Shenzhen 518033, China (prodn), Contact: Kendrick Cheung *Tel:* (0755) 8304 8899 *Fax:* (0755) 8251 4073 *E-mail:* enquiries@imago.com.hk
Imago France, 23 rue Lavoisier, 75008 Paris, France (sales) *Tel:* 01 45 26 47 74 *Fax:* 01 78 94 14 44 *E-mail:* sales@imagogroup.com
Imago Services (HK) Ltd, Unit B309, 1/F, New East Sun Industrial Bldg, 18 Shing Yip St, Kwun Tong, Hong Kong (prodn), Contact: Kendrick Cheung *Tel:* 2811 3316 *E-mail:* enquiries@imago.com.hk
Imago Productions (Malaysia) Pte Ltd, No 43, Taman Emas, Jl Utama 31, Telok Panglima Garang, 42500 Kuala Langot, Selangor, Malaysia (prodn, incorporating South Africa sales) *Tel:* (017) 4288771 (cell) *E-mail:* enquiries@imago.com.sg
Imago Publishing, Albury Ct, Albury Thame, Oxon OX9 2LP, United Kingdom (sales), Dir: Simon Rosenheim *Tel:* (01844) 337000 *Fax:* (01844) 339915 *E-mail:* sales@imago.co.uk *Web Site:* imagogroup.com

COMPLETE BOOK MANUFACTURING

InfinitPrint Solutions Inc
14 N Tenth St, Richmond, IN 47374
Tel: 765-962-1507 *Toll Free Tel:* 800-478-4885
Fax: 765-962-4997
E-mail: info@infinitprint.com
Web Site: infinitprint.com
Key Personnel
Pres: Michael D Gibbs *E-mail:* mike@infinitprint.com
Founded: 1972
Turnaround: 30 Workdays
Print Runs: 100 min - 5,000 max
Branch Office(s)
211 NW Seventh St, Richmond, IN 47374
Tel: 765-966-7130 *Fax:* 765-966-7131

Ironmark
9040 Junction Dr, Annapolis Junction, MD 20701
Toll Free Tel: 888-775-3737
E-mail: marketing@ironmarkusa.com
Web Site: ironmarkusa.com
Key Personnel
CEO: Scott Hargest *E-mail:* scott@ironmarkusa.com; Jeff Ostenso *E-mail:* jeff@ironmarkusa.com
Pres: Matt Marzullo *E-mail:* mmarzullo@ironmarkusa.com
SVP, Sales: Scott Kravitz *E-mail:* skravitz@ironmarkusa.com
VP, Opers: Chris Marzullo *E-mail:* cmarzullo@ironmarkusa.com
Sr Sales Exec: Larry Davis *E-mail:* ldavis@ironmarkusa.com
Founded: 1955
Turnaround: 20 Workdays, case bound; 10 Workdays, paperback; 15 Workdays, mechanically bound
Print Runs: 500 min - 500,000 max

Itzhack Shelomi Design
25 Cushman Rd, Scarsdale, NY 10583
Tel: 212-689-7469
E-mail: studio@ishelomi.com; studio@serifes.com
Web Site: www.ishelomi.com
Key Personnel
Owner & Creative Dir: Itzhack Shelomi
Founded: 1987

JP Graphics Inc
3001 E Venture Dr, Appleton, WI 54911
Tel: 920-733-4483 *Fax:* 920-733-1700
E-mail: support@jpinc.com
Web Site: www.jpinc.com; www.print.jpinc.com
Key Personnel
Pres: Rod Stoffel
Sales Mgr: Randy Hearley
Founded: 1969

King Printing
181 Industrial Ave E, Lowell, MA 01852-5147
Tel: 978-458-2345 *Fax:* 978-458-1441
E-mail: inquiries@kingprinting.com
Web Site: www.kingprinting.com; www.adibooks.com
Founded: 1978
Print Runs: 1 min - 10,000 max
Membership(s): Independent Book Publishers Association (IBPA); Printing Industries of New England (PINE); PRINTING United Alliance

Knepper Press Corp
2251 Sweeney Dr, Clinton, PA 15026
Tel: 724-899-4200 *Fax:* 724-899-1331
Web Site: www.knepperpress.com
Key Personnel
Chmn: Ted Ford *E-mail:* tedford@knepperpress.com
CFO: Jerry Sales *E-mail:* jerry.sales@knepperpress.com
Cont: Dawn Bates *E-mail:* dawn.bates@knepperpress.com

COMPLETE BOOK MANUFACTURING

Pres: Bob Hreha *E-mail:* bobhreha@knepperpress.com
Founded: 1873
Turnaround: 10-20 Workdays
Print Runs: 500 min - 25,000 max

Kromar Printing Ltd
725 Portage Ave, Winnipeg, MB R3G 0M8, Canada
Tel: 204-775-8721 *Fax:* 204-783-8985
E-mail: info@kromar.com
Web Site: www.kromar.com
Key Personnel
CEO: Jack Cohen
COO: Joseph Cohen *E-mail:* josephcohen@kromar.com
Founded: 1945
Turnaround: 15 Workdays
Print Runs: 500 min - 50,000 max
Branch Office(s)
130 Slater St, Ottawa, ON K1P 6E2, Canada
Tel: 613-563-7577 *Fax:* 613-594-8705
E-mail: kromar@kromar.com

Lake Book Manufacturing Inc
2085 N Cornell Ave, Melrose Park, IL 60160
Tel: 708-345-7000
E-mail: info@lakebook.com
Web Site: www.lakebook.com
Key Personnel
Pres & COO: Dan Genovese
VP, Fin & CFO: Bob Flatow
VP & Gen Mgr: Bill Richards
VP, Mfg: Steve Quagliato
VP, Opers: Bill Flavin
VP, Sales & Mktg: Nick Vergoth
VP, Technol: Paul Genovese

Leo Paper USA
Division of Leo Paper Group
1180 NW Maple St, Suite 102, Issaquah, WA 98027
Tel: 425-646-8801 *Fax:* 425-646-8805
E-mail: info@leousa.com
Web Site: www.leopaper.com
Key Personnel
Pres: Behzad Pakzad
Founded: 1982
Turnaround: 30-40 Workdays
Print Runs: 3,500 min - 2,000,000 max
Branch Office(s)
286 Fifth Ave, 6th fl, New York, NY 10001, Contact: John DiMasi *Tel:* 917-305-0708 *Fax:* 917-305-0709 *E-mail:* info@leousanewyork.com

Lidec Inc
800, blvd Industriel, bureau 202, St-Jean-sur-Richlieu, QC J3B 8G4, Canada
Tel: 514-843-5991 *Toll Free Tel:* 800-350-5991 (CN only) *Fax:* 514-843-5252
E-mail: lidec@lidec.qc.ca
Web Site: www.lidec.qc.ca
Founded: 1965

Lightning Source LLC
Subsidiary of Ingram Content Group LLC
1246 Heil Quaker Blvd, La Vergne, TN 37086
Tel: 615-793-5000 (Ingram) *Toll Free Tel:* 800-378-5508; 800-509-4156 (cust serv)
E-mail: lsicustomersupport@ingramcontent.com; contentacquisitioninquiries@ingramcontent.com
Web Site: www.ingramcontent.com/publishers/print
Key Personnel
Chief Content Offr: Phil Ollila
CFO: Brian Dauphin
Chief Logistics Offr, Global Opers: John F Secrest
Sr Key Acct Mgr: Liz Hunter
Key Acct Sales Mgr: Ali Galbraith
Mgr, Content Acqs Sales: Alicia Samuel

Mgr, Trade Sales: Caitlin Kleinschmidt
Supv, Content Acq Sales: Bailey Davis
Founded: 1997

Lo Gatto Bookbinding
390 Paterson Ave, East Rutherford, NJ 07073
Tel: 201-438-4344 *Fax:* 201-438-1775
E-mail: bookbindin@aol.com
Key Personnel
Contact: Michael Lo Gatto
Founded: 1967
Turnaround: 7-10 Workdays

Lumina Datamatics Inc
600 Cordwainer Dr, Unit 103, Norwell, MA 02061
Tel: 508-746-0300 *Fax:* 508-746-3233
E-mail: marketing@luminad.com
Web Site: luminadatamatics.com
Key Personnel
EVP, Busn Devt: Jack Mitchell
EVP, Solutions, Transitions & US Opers: Sandeep Dhawan
Founded: 2005
Branch Office(s)
c/o Arnecke Sibeth Distribution, Rechtsanwaelte Steuerberater Partnergesellschaft mdB, Gueterplatz 1, 60327 Frankfurt am Main, Germany *Tel:* (06155) 862 99-0 *Fax:* (06155) 862 99-19
Ascendas International Tech Park, 12th fl, Phase II (Crest), CSIR Rd, Taramani, Chennai 600 113, India *Tel:* (044) 4017 6000; (044) 4017 6001
Santosh Raj Plaza, 1st fl, Subburaman St, Gandhi Nagar, 12/9, St, Shenoy Nagar, Madurai 625 020, India
Andheri (E), Unit 117-120, SDF - IV, SEEPZ - SEZ, Mumbai 400 096, India *Tel:* (022) 4034 0515; (022) 4034 0508 *Fax:* (022) 2829 1673
Off No 47/1, 7th fl, Tower-B, A-41, Correnthum Tower, Sector-62, Noida 201 301, India
Plot No 29-34, East Coast Rd, Saram Revenue Village, Oulgaret Municipality, Lawspet Post, Puducherry 605 008, India *Tel:* (0413) 226 4500
No 10, Vazhudavoor Rd, Pettaiyanchathiram, Thattanchavadi, Puducherry 605 009, India *Tel:* (0413) 401 1635
Apple One Equicom Tower, 11th fl, Mindanao Ave Corner Biliran St, Central (pob), Cebu Business Park, 6000 Cebu City, Cebu, Philippines
c/o SOPHI Outsourcing Inc, G/F DBPI IT Plaza, Calindagan, 6200 Dumaguete City, Negros Oriental, Philippines
Brixham Laboratory, Brixham, Devon TQ5 8BA, United Kingdom
Lumina Datamatics UK Ltd, 153 Milton Keynes Business Ctr, Linford Wood, Milton Keynes MK14 6GD, United Kingdom

Maple Press
480 Willow Springs Lane, York, PA 17406
Mailing Address: PO Box 2695, York, PA 17405-2695
Tel: 717-764-5911 *Toll Free Tel:* 800-999-5911 *Fax:* 717-764-4702
E-mail: sales@maplepress.com
Web Site: www.maplepress.com
Key Personnel
Pres: James S Wisotzkey
VP, Opers: Chris Benyovszky
VP, Sales: Bob Bethune
VP, Sales & Mktg: Andrew J Van Sprang *E-mail:* vansprang@maplepress.com
Founded: 1901
Print Runs: 25 min - 200,000 max
Branch Office(s)
92 Rockvale Rd, Tewksbury, MA 01876, VP, Sales: Bob Bethune *Tel:* 978-858-0900

Fax: 978-858-0920 *E-mail:* bethune@maplepress.com
Membership(s): Book Industry Study Group (BISG); Book Manufacturers' Institute (BMI)

Maracle Inc
1156 King St E, Oshawa, ON L1H 1H8, Canada
Tel: 905-723-3438 *Toll Free Tel:* 800-558-8604 *Fax:* 905-723-1759
E-mail: hello@maracleinc.com
Web Site: www.maracleinc.com
Key Personnel
Pres: George Sittlinger *Tel:* 905-723-3438 ext 236
Dir, Opers: Nadene D Aldred
Sales & Busn Devt Mgr: Brian Ostrander *Tel:* 905-723-3438 ext 272
E-mail: bostrander@maracleinc.com
Founded: 1920
Turnaround: 10 Workdays
Print Runs: 500 min - 500,000 max
Membership(s): Book Manufacturers' Institute (BMI); Canadian Book Manufacturer Association; Canadian Society of Association Executives (CSAE); Ontario Printing & Imaging Association; PRINTING United Alliance

Marrakech Express Inc
720 Wesley Ave, No 10, Tarpon Springs, FL 34689
Tel: 727-942-2218 *Toll Free Tel:* 800-940-6566 *Fax:* 727-937-4758
E-mail: print@marrak.com
Web Site: www.marrak.com
Key Personnel
CEO: Peter Henzell
Prodn Mgr: Steen Sigmund
Sales/Estimator: Shirley Copperman
Founded: 1976
Turnaround: 7-10 Workdays
Print Runs: 500 min - 1,000,000 max

Maverick Publications LLC
131 NE Fifth St, Prineville, OR 97754
Mailing Address: PO Box 5007, Bend, OR 97708
Tel: 541-382-6978
E-mail: moreinfo@maverickbooks.com
Web Site: maverickbooks.com
Key Personnel
Owner: Gary Asher
Founded: 1967
Turnaround: 25 Workdays
Print Runs: 100 min - 20,000 max

McClain Printing Co
212 Main St, Parsons, WV 26287-1033
Mailing Address: PO Box 403, Parsons, WV 26287-0403
Tel: 304-478-2881 *Toll Free Tel:* 800-654-7179 *Fax:* 304-478-4658
E-mail: mcclain@mcclainprinting.com
Web Site: www.mcclainprinting.com
Key Personnel
Pres: Kenneth E Smith
VP, Publg: Michelle McKinnie
Founded: 1958
Turnaround: 90-120 Workdays
Print Runs: 250 min - 10,000 max

Meadows Design Office
3800 Yuma St NW, Washington, DC 20016
Tel: 202-966-6007
E-mail: mdo@mdomedia.com
Key Personnel
Pres & Creative Dir: Marc Meadows *E-mail:* marc@mdomedia.com
Curator & Image Res: Amy Meadows
Founded: 1981
Print Runs: 100 min - 100,000 max
Membership(s): AIGA, the professional association for design; Type Directors Club

Moran Printing Inc, see Emprint®

MANUFACTURING

Morris Press Cookbooks®
Division of Morris Printing Group Inc
3212 E Hwy 30, Kearney, NE 68847
Mailing Address: PO Box 2110, Kearney, NE 68848-2110
Tel: 308-236-7888; 308-234-1385
Toll Free Tel: 800-445-6621 *Fax:* 308-234-3969
E-mail: cookbook@morriscookbooks.com
Web Site: www.morriscookbooks.com
Founded: 1933
Print Runs: 200 min - 50,000 max

Nissha USA Inc
Division of Nissha Co Ltd
1051 Perimeter Dr, Suite 600, Schaumburg, IL 60173
Tel: 847-413-2665 *Fax:* 847-413-4085
Web Site: www.nissha.com
Key Personnel
Chmn: Junya Suzuki
Dir & CEO: Hiroyuki Uenishi
Founded: 1993

OGM USA
4333 46 St, Suite F2, Sunnyside, NY 11104
Tel: 212-964-2430
Web Site: www.ogm.it
Key Personnel
Chmn, CEO & Sales Rep: Rino Varrasso
 E-mail: rvarrasso@ogm-usa.com
Founded: 1974
Turnaround: 30 Workdays
Print Runs: 1,000 min - 3,000,000 max

Omnipress
2600 Anderson St, Madison, WI 53704
Tel: 608-246-2600 *Toll Free Tel:* 800-828-0305
E-mail: justask@omnipress.com
Web Site: www.omnipress.com
Key Personnel
VP, Prodn: Greg Hubbard *Tel:* 608-778-6863
Dir, Mkt Devt: Dan Loomis
Dir, Mktg: Tracy Grzybowski
Dir, Servs: Rob Bossingham
Gen Mgr: Jonny Popp *Tel:* 608-215-9650
Founded: 1977
Turnaround: 5 Workdays
Print Runs: 1 min - 5,000 max

OneTouchPoint
1225 Walnut Ridge Dr, Hartland, WI 53029
Tel: 262-369-6000 *Toll Free Tel:* 800-332-2348
 Fax: 262-369-5647
E-mail: info@1touchpoint.com
Web Site: www.1touchpoint.com
Key Personnel
CEO: Dave Holland
Dir, Mktg & Sales Opers: Carey Howard
Founded: 1982
Turnaround: order processing: within 8 hours; digital printing: 24-48 hours after proof approval; press: 7 days after proof approval
Print Runs: 1 min - 500,000 max
Branch Office(s)
5241 Voges Rd, Madison, WI 53718 *Tel:* 608-838-9147
525 W Alameda Dr, Suite 101, Tempe, AZ 85282, Contact: James Parker *Tel:* 480-966-4003 *Fax:* 480-966-4016
5280 Joliet St, Denver, CO 80239 *Tel:* 303-227-1400
1441 Western Ave, Cincinnati, OH 45214 *Tel:* 513-421-1600
8410-B Tuscany Way, Austin, TX 78754 *Tel:* 512-454-6874

Overseas Printing Corporation
Division of InnerWorkings Inc
4040 Civic Center Dr, Suite 200, San Rafael, CA 94903
Tel: 415-500-8331 *Fax:* 415-835-9899
Web Site: www.overseasprinting.com
Key Personnel
Sr Prodn Mgr: Shaun Garrett *E-mail:* sgarrett@inwk.com
Founded: 1972
Turnaround: 8-12 Weeks

Paraclete Press Inc
100 Southern Eagle Cartway, Brewster, MA 02631
SAN: 282-1508
Mailing Address: PO Box 1568, Orleans, MA 02653-1568
Tel: 508-255-4685 *Toll Free Tel:* 800-451-5006
E-mail: customerservice@paracletepress.com
Web Site: www.paracletepress.com
Key Personnel
Design & Web Site Servs: Paul Tingley
 E-mail: pault@paracletepress.com
Founded: 1981
Turnaround: 20 Workdays
Print Runs: 500 min - 15,000 max
Membership(s): Association of Catholic Publishers Inc; Evangelical Christian Publishers Association (ECPA)

Patterson Printing Co
1550 Territorial Rd, Benton Harbor, MI 49022
Tel: 269-925-2177
E-mail: sales@patterson-printing.com
Web Site: patterson-printing.com
Founded: 1956
Print Runs: 250 min

PCA Printing, see Printing Corporation of the Americas Inc

POD Print
2012 E Northern St, Wichita, KS 67216
Tel: 316-522-5599 *Toll Free Tel:* 800-767-6066
E-mail: info@podprint.com
Web Site: www.podprint.com
Key Personnel
Owner: Grace Rishel; Jim Rishel
Prodn Opers Mgr: Traci Grote *E-mail:* tgrote@podprint.com
Founded: 1978
Print Runs: 1 min - 25,000 max (every service offered on-demand)
Membership(s): Print Services & Distribution Association (PSDA); PRINTING United Alliance

Printing Corporation of the Americas Inc
620 SW 12 Ave, Pompano Beach, FL 33069
Tel: 954-781-8100 *Toll Free Tel:* 866-721-1PCA (721-1722)
Web Site: pcaprintingplus.com
Key Personnel
Pres: Buddy Tuchman
Sales Mgr: Steven Konecky *E-mail:* steven@pcaprinting.com
Founded: 1980
Turnaround: 5-10 Workdays
Print Runs: 500 min - 100,000 max

PrintWest
1111 Eighth Ave, Regina, SK S4R 1C9, Canada
Tel: 306-525-2304 *Toll Free Tel:* 800-236-6438
 Fax: 306-757-2439
E-mail: general@printwest.com
Web Site: www.printwest.com
Key Personnel
Pres & Dir, Opers: Corie Triffo
VP, Sales & Mktg: Ken Benson
Founded: 1992
Turnaround: 15 Workdays
Print Runs: 1,000 min - 100,000 max

Progress Printing Plus
2677 Waterlick Rd, Lynchburg, VA 24502

COMPLETE BOOK MANUFACTURING

Tel: 434-239-9213 *Toll Free Tel:* 800-572-7804
 Fax: 434-832-7573
E-mail: info@progressprintplus.com
Web Site: www.progressprintplus.com
Key Personnel
Pres: Michael Thornton *E-mail:* mthornton@progressprintplus.com
Dir, Busn Devt: Gerald Bowles
 E-mail: gbowles@progressprintplus.com
Founded: 1962
Turnaround: 7-9 Workdays after final proof approval
Print Runs: 5,000 min - 500,000 max

Publishers Book Bindery (NY)
250 W 16 St, 4th fl, New York, NY 10011
Tel: 917-497-2950
Key Personnel
Pres: Ed Goldman
Founded: 1946
Print Runs: 100 min - 50,000 max

Publishers' Graphics LLC
131 Fremont St, Chicago, IL 60185
Tel: 630-221-1850
E-mail: contactpg@pubgraphics.com
Web Site: pubgraphics.com
Key Personnel
Pres: Nick A Lewis *E-mail:* nlewis@pubgraphics.com
VP: Kathleen Lewis *E-mail:* kmlewis@pubgraphics.com
Founded: 1996
Turnaround: 2-8 Workdays
Print Runs: 1 min - 20,000 max
Branch Office(s)
3777 Rider Trail S, St Louis, MO 63045
Tel: 314-739-3777 *Fax:* 314-739-1436
Sales Office(s): Louisville, KY, VP, Sales: Cara Lahey *Tel:* 630-291-4867 *E-mail:* clahey@pubgraphics.com

Sheridan GR
Division of CJK Group Inc
5100 33 St SE, Grand Rapids, MI 49512
Tel: 616-957-5100
Web Site: www.sheridan.com
Key Personnel
VP, Sales: Joe Thomson *E-mail:* joe.thomson@sheridan.com
Cust Serv Mgr: Tanya Eldred *E-mail:* tanya.eldred@sheridan.com
Estimating & Purch Mgr: Steve DeWeerd
 E-mail: steve.deweerd@sheridan.com
Plant Mgr: Jason Nelson *E-mail:* jason.nelson@sheridan.com
Founded: 1884
Print Runs: 1 min - 100,000 max

Sheridan MI
Division of CJK Group Inc
613 E Industrial Dr, Chelsea, MI 48118
Tel: 734-475-9145
Web Site: www.sheridan.com
Key Personnel
Pres: Paul Bozuwa *E-mail:* paul.bozuwa@sheridan.com
VP, Book Sales: Joe Thomson *E-mail:* joe.thomson@sheridan.com
VP, Fin: Nicole Mummert *E-mail:* nicole.mummert@sheridan.com
VP, HR: Ken Rapp *E-mail:* ken.rapp@sheridan.com
VP, Opers: Paul Loy *E-mail:* paul.loy@sheridan.com
Cust Serv Mgr: Ed Blissick *E-mail:* ed.blissick@sheridan.com
Direct Sales Rep: Jessica Ansorge *Tel:* 734-385-1544 *E-mail:* jessica.ansorge@sheridan.com; Kathy Brown *Tel:* 734-385-1540 *E-mail:* kathy.brown@sheridan.com; rebecca Humrich *Tel:* 734-385-1543 *E-mail:* rebecca.humrich@sheridan.com; Jennifer Riemen-

schneider *Tel:* 734-385-1533 *E-mail:* jennifer.riemenschneider@sheridan.com
Founded: 1950

Sheridan Saline
Division of CJK Group Inc
960 Woodland Dr, Saline, MI 48176
Tel: 734-429-5411
Web Site: www.sheridan.com
Key Personnel
Pres: Paul Bozuwa *E-mail:* paul.bozuwa@sheridan.com
SVP, Opers: Paul Loy *E-mail:* paul.loy@sheridan.com
Gen Mgr: Ron Vollink *E-mail:* ron.vollink@sheridan.com
Plant Mgr: Jim Clark *E-mail:* jim.clark@sheridan.com
HR Mgr: Betty Salow *E-mail:* betty.salow@sheridan.com
Chief Sales Offr: Todd Vanek *E-mail:* todd.vanek@sheridan.com
VP, Book Group Sales: Joe Thomson *E-mail:* joe.thomson@sheridan.com
Cust Serv Mgr & Dir, West Reg Sales: Jonnie Bryant *E-mail:* jonnie.bryant@sheridan.com
Sr Sales Exec: David Hilberer *E-mail:* david.hilberer@sheridan.com
North Central/Greater Chicago Sales Mgr: Marc Moore *E-mail:* marc.moore@sheridan.com
Founded: 1975
Print Runs: 24 min - 100,000 max

Signature Book Printing Inc
8041 Cessna Ave, Gaithersburg, MD 20879
Tel: 301-258-8353
E-mail: book@sbpbooks.com
Web Site: sbpbooks.com
Key Personnel
Pres: Phil Nanzetta
Off Mgr: Linda Wood
Founded: 1986
Print Runs: 500 min - 20,000 max

Smith & Sons Printers Inc
6403 Rutledge Pike, Knoxville, TN 37924
Tel: 865-523-1419
Web Site: www.ssprintinc.com
Key Personnel
Owner: Stephen Ownby *E-mail:* stephen@ssprint.com
Founded: 1979
Print Runs: 250 min - 100,000 max

Spectrum PrintGroup Inc
1535 Farmer's Lane, Suite 254, Santa Rosa, CA 95405
Tel: 707-542-6044 *Toll Free Tel:* 888-340-6049 *Fax:* 707-542-6045
E-mail: sales@spectrumprintgroup.com
Web Site: www.spectrumprintgroup.com
Key Personnel
Pres: Duncan McCallum *Tel:* 707-542-6044 ext 102 *E-mail:* duncan@spectrumprintgroup.com
Busn Devt Mgr: Elise Gochberg *Tel:* 415-461-1130 *E-mail:* elise@spectrumprintgroup.com
Founded: 1985
Print Runs: 500 min - 100,000 max

Sterling Pierce Co Inc
395 Atlantic Ave, East Rockaway, NY 11518
Tel: 516-593-1170 *Fax:* 516-593-1401
Web Site: www.sterlingpierce.com
Key Personnel
Owner & Pres: William Burke
Mgr: Steven Cieslicki *E-mail:* scieslicki@sterlingpierce.com
Founded: 1980
Turnaround: 5-7 Workdays
Print Runs: 5 min - 5,000 max

Sun Graphics LLC
1818 Broadway, Parsons, KS 67357
Toll Free Tel: 800-835-0588 *Fax:* 620-421-2089
E-mail: info@sun-graphics.com
Web Site: www.sun-graphics.com
Key Personnel
VP, Mktg: John Hammett *Tel:* 918-695-2267 *E-mail:* jhammett@sun-graphics.com
VP, Sales: John Hohenshell *Tel:* 913-257-9420 *E-mail:* jhohenshell@sun-graphics.com
Commercial Sales & Book Div Sales: Melody Morris *Tel:* 620-660-0614 *E-mail:* mmorris@sun-graphics.com
Founded: 1998
Turnaround: 10-15 Workdays
Print Runs: 500 min - 50,000 max
Membership(s): Independent Book Publishers Association (IBPA); Publishers Association of the West (PubWest)

John S Swift Co Inc
999 Commerce Ct, Buffalo Grove, IL 60089
Tel: 847-465-3300 *Fax:* 847-465-3309
Web Site: www.johnswiftprint.com
Key Personnel
Pres: John S Swift *E-mail:* jss@johnswiftprint.com
Founded: 1912
Turnaround: 5 Workdays & up
Print Runs: 10 min - 100,000 max
Branch Office(s)
John S Swift Print of NJ Inc, 375 North St, Unit N, Teterboro, NJ 07608, Contact: Rick Frydrych *Tel:* 201-678-3232 *Fax:* 201-378-3001 *E-mail:* rickfry@johnswiftprint.com

Taylor Specialty Books, see Balfour Commercial Printing

Toof American Digital
4222 Pilot Dr, Memphis, TN 38118
Tel: 901-274-3632 *Toll Free Tel:* 800-722-4772
Web Site: www.toofamericandigital.com
Key Personnel
Pres: Stillman McFadden
Founded: 1864
Turnaround: 60 Workdays
Print Runs: 2,000 min - 500,000 max

Versa Press Inc
1465 Spring Bay Rd, East Peoria, IL 61611-9788
Tel: 309-822-8272 *Toll Free Tel:* 800-447-7829 *Fax:* 309-822-8141
Web Site: www.versapress.com
Key Personnel
Chmn: Joseph F Kennell
Pres: Steven J Kennell
Sales Mgr: Matthew Kennell *E-mail:* mkennell@versapress.com
Founded: 1937
Turnaround: 20 Workdays
Print Runs: 500 min - 50,000 max
Membership(s): Book Manufacturers' Institute (BMI)

Vicks Lithograph & Printing Corp
5166 Commercial Dr, Yorkville, NY 13495
Tel: 315-736-9344
E-mail: info@vicks.biz
Web Site: www.vicks.biz
Key Personnel
CEO: Dwight E Vicks, III
Founded: 1918
Turnaround: 10 Workdays
Print Runs: 1 min - 100,000 max
Membership(s): Book Manufacturers' Institute (BMI); PRINTING United Alliance

Walker360
2501 Fifth Ave E, Montgomery, AL 36107
Tel: 334-832-4975
E-mail: info@walker360.com
Web Site: walker360.com
Key Personnel
Pres: Taylor Blackwell *E-mail:* taylor@walker360.com
Cont: Estella Riley *E-mail:* estella@walker360.com
IT Dir: Connie Manoliu *E-mail:* connie@walker360.com

Walsworth
306 N Kansas Ave, Marceline, MO 64658
Toll Free Tel: 800-265-6795
Web Site: www.walsworth.com; www.walsworthhistorybooks.com
Key Personnel
CEO: Don O Walsworth
COO: Jim Mead
Pres: Don Walsworth, Jr
VP, Mktg & Communs: Kristin Mateski *E-mail:* kristin.mateski@walsworth.com
Founded: 1937
Turnaround: 4 Weeks
Print Runs: 1,000 min - 500,000 max
Branch Office(s)
803 S Missouri Ave, Marceline, MO 64658 (printing & bindery facility)
Donning Co Publishers, 731 S Brunswick St, Brookfield, MO 64628 *Tel:* 660-675-5570 *Web Site:* www.donning.com
The Ovid Bell Press, 1201 Bluff St, Fulton, MO 65251-0370 *Toll Free Tel:* 800-835-8919 *Web Site:* www.ovidbell.com
903 E 104 St, Suite 700, Kansas City, MO 64131 (yearbook sales & mktg facility) *Toll Free Tel:* 800-369-2965
7300 W 110 St, Suite 600, Overland Park, KS 66210 (sales & mktg)
2180 Maiden Lane, St Joseph, MI 49085 (printing & bindery facility) *Toll Free Tel:* 888-563-3220
656 S Douglas St, Ripon, WI 54971 (printing & bindery facility)

Walter's Publishing
Division of Taylor Corp
1750 Northway Dr, North Mankato, MN 56003
Toll Free Tel: 800-447-3274
E-mail: info@walterspublishing.com
Web Site: www.walterspublishing.com
Key Personnel
Pres: Carolynn McCourtney
VP, Mktg: Jennifer Stein
Founded: 1939

Webcom Inc
Division of Marquis Book Printing Inc
3480 Pharmacy Ave, Toronto, ON M1W 2S7, Canada
Tel: 416-496-1000 *Toll Free Tel:* 800-665-9322 *Fax:* 416-496-1537
E-mail: webcom@webcomlink.com
Web Site: www.webcomlink.com
Key Personnel
Pres & CEO: Mike Collinge
Dir of HR & Cust Serv: Rhonda Suurd
Dir of Sales: Marc Doucet
Founded: 1975
Turnaround: 15 Workdays
Print Runs: 50 min - 100,000 max
Sales Office(s): 65 Spring Valley Ave, River Edge, NJ 07661, Sales: Susan Ginch *Tel:* 201-262-4301 *Fax:* 201-262-6375 *E-mail:* susan.ginch@webcomlink.com
Membership(s): Book Manufacturers' Institute (BMI); Canadian Book & Periodical Council; PRINTING United Alliance

Webcrafters Inc
2211 Fordem Ave, Madison, WI 53704
Tel: 608-244-3561 *Toll Free Tel:* 800-356-8200 *Fax:* 608-244-5120
E-mail: info@webcrafters-inc.com
Web Site: www.webcrafters-inc.com

MANUFACTURING

Key Personnel
CEO: Chris Kurtzman
VP, Div Dir: Brad Koch
Membership(s): Book Manufacturers' Institute (BMI)

Whitehall Printing Co
4244 Corporate Sq, Naples, FL 34104
Tel: 239-643-6464 *Toll Free Tel:* 800-321-9290
 Fax: 239-643-6439
E-mail: info@whitehallprinting.com
Web Site: www.whitehallprinting.com
Key Personnel
Chmn: Mike Hirsch
Pres: Jeff Hirsch
VP: Emil G Hirsch
Founded: 1959
Turnaround: 10-15 Business days
Print Runs: 250 min - 50,000 max

Worzalla
3535 Jefferson St, Stevens Point, WI 54481
Tel: 715-344-9608 *Fax:* 715-344-2578
Web Site: www.worzalla.com
Key Personnel
Chmn of the Bd: Charles Nason
Pres: James Fetherston
VP, Fin: Samuel Crockett
VP, Opers: Brian McManus
VP, Sales & Chief Mktg Offr: Richard Letchinger
Cust Serv Mgr: Kim Deuel
Field Sales: Rodger Beyer
Founded: 1892
Turnaround: 20 Workdays
Print Runs: 50 min - 1,000,000 max
Sales Office(s): 4819 W Berteau Ave, Chicago, IL 60641, Contact: Tim Taylor *Tel:* 773-383-7892
 E-mail: ttaylor@worzalla.com
2231 Morris Ave, Suite 3, Union, NJ 07083, Contact: Edmund Corvelli, III *Tel:* 201-749-7995
 E-mail: ecorvelli@worzalla.com
222 W 37 St, 10th fl, New York, NY 10018, Contact: Sam Gallucci *Tel:* 201-851-3292
 E-mail: sgallucci@worzalla.com
Membership(s): Book Manufacturers' Institute (BMI)

Yurchak Printing Inc
920 Links Ave, Landisville, PA 17538
Tel: 717-399-0209
E-mail: ypi.info@yurchak.com
Web Site: www.yurchak.com
Key Personnel
Founder & CEO: John Yurchak, Jr
Pres: John W Yurchak
VP, Opers: Jason Yurchak
Dir, Busn Devt: Randy Boyer
Founded: 1998
Turnaround: 5-20 Workdays
Print Runs: 1 min - 1,500 max
Membership(s): International Printers' Network (IPN)

Prepress Services Index

ART & DESIGN

Adams Design, pg 1221
Adams Press, pg 1221
AJP Communications Inc, pg 1221
All Craft Digital Inc, pg 1221
Allard Inc, pg 1221
American Mathematical Society (AMS), pg 1221
appatura™, A Broadridge Company, pg 1221
Aptara Inc, pg 1222
Aquent LLC, pg 1222
Arbor Books, pg 1222
Arrow Graphics Inc, pg 1222
Art Related Technology Inc, pg 1222
The Bear Wallow Publishing Co, pg 1222
David Berman Communications, pg 1222
Blue Note Publications Inc, pg 1223
BookComp Inc, pg 1223
Bookmasters, pg 1223
BookWise Design, pg 1223
Burmar Technical Corp, pg 1223
BW&A Books Inc, pg 1223
Cenveo St Louis, pg 1223
CG Book Printers, pg 1223
Circle Graphics Inc, pg 1223
Coach House Printing, pg 1223
ColorPage, pg 1223
Communicorp Inc, pg 1224
Concord Editorial & Design LLC, pg 1224
Corporate Disk Co, pg 1224
Crown Connect, pg 1224
Custom Studios, pg 1224
Cypress House, pg 1224
Data Index Inc, pg 1224
Delmas Typesetting Inc, pg 1224
Desktop Miracles Inc, pg 1224
diacriTech Inc, pg 1224
Didona Design, pg 1224
dix! Digital Prepress Inc, pg 1225
DNP America LLC, pg 1225
W R Draper Co, pg 1225
The Font Bureau Inc, pg 1225
Leanne Franson, pg 1225
Fry Communications Inc, pg 1225
G & H Soho Inc, pg 1226
GEX Inc, pg 1226
Celia Godkin, pg 1226
Goose River Press, pg 1226
GraphiColor Corp, pg 1226
Graphics Two, pg 1226
GW Inc, pg 1226
HBP Inc, pg 1226
Heidelberg Graphics, pg 1226
Hennegan Co, pg 1226
Worth Higgins & Associates Inc, pg 1226
Infinity Graphics, pg 1227
Innovative Design & Graphics, pg 1227
International Press Publication Inc, pg 1227
Interstate Printing Co, pg 1227
Itzhack Shelomi Design, pg 1227
Jenkins Group Inc, pg 1227
Kachergis Book Design Inc, pg 1227
Knepper Press Corp, pg 1227
Lachina Creative, pg 1227
The Lexington Press Inc, pg 1228
Lowe Graphics & Printing, pg 1228
Lumina Datamatics Inc, pg 1228
Mandel Graphic Solution, pg 1228
Maracle Inc, pg 1228
McClain Printing Co, pg 1228
Meadows Design Office, pg 1228
MPS North America LLC, pg 1228
Myriddian LLC, pg 1228
Neibauer Press, pg 1229
NETS, pg 1229
Newgen North America Inc, pg 1229
North Market Street Graphics (NMSG), pg 1229
OEC Graphics Inc, pg 1229
Paraclete Press Inc, pg 1229
POD Print, pg 1229
PrintWest, pg 1229
Pro-Composition Inc, pg 1229
Progressive Publishing Services (PPS), pg 1230
Pronk Media Inc, pg 1230
Publication Identification & Processing Systems, pg 1230
Publishing Data Management Inc, pg 1230
Reno Typographers, pg 1230
The Renton Printery Inc, pg 1230
Scribe Inc, pg 1230
SGS International LLC, pg 1230
Shepherd Inc, pg 1231
Six Red Marbles LLC, pg 1231
Smith & Sons Printers Inc, pg 1231
Smith-Edwards-Dunlap Co, pg 1231
Southeastern Printing Co, pg 1231
Barbara Spurll Illustration, pg 1231
Square Two Design Inc, pg 1231
Sun Graphics LLC, pg 1231
Swordsmith Productions, pg 1231
Symmetry Creative Production, pg 1232
Texas Graphic Resource Inc, pg 1232
Times Printing LLC, pg 1232
Toof American Digital, pg 1232
Tukaiz LLC, pg 1232
ViaTech Publishing Solutions Inc, pg 1232
Fred Weidner & Daughter Printers, pg 1232
WeMakeBooks.ca, pg 1232
Westchester Publishing Services, pg 1233
Whitehall Printing Co, pg 1233
Windhaven®, pg 1233
X-Height Studio, pg 1233

COLOR SEPARATIONS

Adams Press, pg 1221
All Craft Digital Inc, pg 1221
Ambassador Press Inc, pg 1221
American Mathematical Society (AMS), pg 1221
Aptara Inc, pg 1222
Aquent LLC, pg 1222
Asia Pacific Offset Inc, pg 1222
Bang Printing Co Inc, pg 1222
Blanks Printing & Imaging Inc, pg 1222
Bookmasters, pg 1223
The Bureau, pg 1223
C & C Offset Printing Co USA Inc, pg 1223
CG Book Printers, pg 1223
Coach House Printing, pg 1223
ColorPage, pg 1223
Colour Technologies, pg 1223
Coral Graphic Services Inc, pg 1224
Cypress House, pg 1224
Darwill, pg 1224
Datacolor, pg 1224
diacriTech Inc, pg 1224
DNP America LLC, pg 1225
RR Donnelley, pg 1225
W R Draper Co, pg 1225
Dual Graphics, pg 1225
FCI Digital, pg 1225
Fry Communications Inc, pg 1225
G & H Soho Inc, pg 1226
GEX Inc, pg 1226
GHP, pg 1226
GLS Companies, pg 1226
GraphiColor Corp, pg 1226
HBP Inc, pg 1226
Hennegan Co, pg 1226
Worth Higgins & Associates Inc, pg 1226
Imago, pg 1226
Infinity Graphics, pg 1227
Interstate Printing Co, pg 1227
Jenkins Group Inc, pg 1227
Knepper Press Corp, pg 1227
Lake Book Manufacturing Inc, pg 1227
Leo Paper USA, pg 1228
Lumina Datamatics Inc, pg 1228
Maracle Inc, pg 1228
McClain Printing Co, pg 1228
Neibauer Press, pg 1229
NETS, pg 1229
North American Color Inc, pg 1229
North Market Street Graphics (NMSG), pg 1229
OEC Graphics Inc, pg 1229
OGM USA, pg 1229
O'Neil Digital Solutions LLC, pg 1229
Overseas Printing Corporation, pg 1229
Printing Corporation of the Americas Inc, pg 1229
Reno Typographers, pg 1230
SGS International LLC, pg 1230
Shepherd Inc, pg 1231
Six Red Marbles LLC, pg 1231
Smith-Edwards-Dunlap Co, pg 1231
Southeastern Printing Co, pg 1231
John S Swift Co Inc, pg 1231
Texas Graphic Resource Inc, pg 1232
Toof American Digital, pg 1232
Tukaiz LLC, pg 1232
UniversallWilde, pg 1232
Versa Press Inc, pg 1232
Fred Weidner & Daughter Printers, pg 1232
Whitehall Printing Co, pg 1233
Widen Enterprises Inc, pg 1233
Worzalla, pg 1233

COMPUTERIZED TYPESETTING

A-R Editions Inc, pg 1221
Adair Graphic Communications, pg 1221
Adams Design, pg 1221
Adams Press, pg 1221
AJP Communications Inc, pg 1221
All Craft Digital Inc, pg 1221
American Mathematical Society (AMS), pg 1221
Apex CoVantage, pg 1221
appatura™, A Broadridge Company, pg 1221
Aptara Inc, pg 1222
Aquent LLC, pg 1222
Arbor Books, pg 1222
Arrow Graphics Inc, pg 1222
Art Related Technology Inc, pg 1222
Bang Printing Co Inc, pg 1222
The Bear Wallow Publishing Co, pg 1222
David Berman Communications, pg 1222
Berryville Graphics, pg 1222
Blue Note Publications Inc, pg 1223
BookComp Inc, pg 1223
Bookmasters, pg 1223
Burmar Technical Corp, pg 1223
BW&A Books Inc, pg 1223
Cape Cod Compositors Inc, pg 1223
CG Book Printers, pg 1223
Cimarron Design, pg 1223
Circle Graphics Inc, pg 1223
Clare Printing, pg 1223
Coach House Printing, pg 1223
ColorPage, pg 1223
Concord Editorial & Design LLC, pg 1224
Cookbook Publishers Inc, pg 1224
Corporate Disk Co, pg 1224
Crown Connect, pg 1224
Custom Studios, pg 1224
Cypress House, pg 1224
Delmas Typesetting Inc, pg 1224
Desktop Miracles Inc, pg 1224
diacriTech Inc, pg 1224
dix! Digital Prepress Inc, pg 1225
RR Donnelley, pg 1225
W R Draper Co, pg 1225
Emprint®, pg 1225
Fairfield Marketing Group Inc, pg 1225
Ferry Associates Inc, pg 1225
Frederic Printing, pg 1225
Fry Communications Inc, pg 1225
G & H Soho Inc, pg 1226
GEX Inc, pg 1226
Goose River Press, pg 1226
Graphics Two, pg 1226
HBP Inc, pg 1226
Heidelberg Graphics, pg 1226
Worth Higgins & Associates Inc, pg 1226
The P A Hutchison Co, pg 1226
Infinity Graphics, pg 1227
Innodata Inc, pg 1227
Innovative Design & Graphics, pg 1227
Interstate Printing Co, pg 1227
Itzhack Shelomi Design, pg 1227
Jenkins Group Inc, pg 1227
JP Graphics Inc, pg 1227
Kachergis Book Design Inc, pg 1227
Kappa Graphics LLP, pg 1227
Knepper Press Corp, pg 1227
Lachina Creative, pg 1227
Lake Book Manufacturing Inc, pg 1227
The Lane Press Inc, pg 1227
Larson Texts Inc, pg 1227
Leo Paper USA, pg 1228

PREPRESS SERVICES INDEX

The Lexington Press Inc, pg 1228
Lowe Graphics & Printing, pg 1228
Lumina Datamatics Inc, pg 1228
Maracle Inc, pg 1228
McClain Printing Co, pg 1228
Meadows Design Office, pg 1228
Miles 33 International LLC, pg 1228
MPS North America LLC, pg 1228
Myriddian LLC, pg 1228
NETS, pg 1229
Newgen North America Inc, pg 1229
North Market Street Graphics (NMSG), pg 1229
OEC Graphics Inc, pg 1229
Pantagraph Printing, pg 1229
POD Print, pg 1229
PrairieView Press, pg 1229
Pro-Composition Inc, pg 1229
Publishing Data Management Inc, pg 1230
Reno Typographers, pg 1230
The Renton Printery Inc, pg 1230
Scribe Inc, pg 1230
Shepherd Inc, pg 1231
Smith & Sons Printers Inc, pg 1231
Smith-Edwards-Dunlap Co, pg 1231
Southeastern Printing Co, pg 1231
John S Swift Co Inc, pg 1231
Swordsmith Productions, pg 1231
Thistle Printing Ltd, pg 1232
Times Citizen Communication Inc, pg 1232
Times Printing LLC, pg 1232
Toof American Digital, pg 1232
TotalWorks™ Inc, pg 1232
Townsend Communications Inc, pg 1232
Tukaiz LLC, pg 1232
UniversallWilde, pg 1232
Viridiam LLC, pg 1232
Walsworth, pg 1232
Fred Weidner & Daughter Printers, pg 1232
WeMakeBooks.ca, pg 1232
Westchester Publishing Services, pg 1233
Whitehall Printing Co, pg 1233
Windhaven®, pg 1233
Writer's Relief, Inc, pg 1233
X-Height Studio, pg 1233

DATA PROCESSING SERVICES

Adams Design, pg 1221
Adams Press, pg 1221
American International Distribution Corp (AIDC), pg 1221
Apex CoVantage, pg 1221
Aquent LLC, pg 1222
Cenveo St Louis, pg 1223
ColorPage, pg 1223
Corporate Disk Co, pg 1224
Custom Studios, pg 1224
Cypress House, pg 1224
Data Conversion Laboratory Inc (DCL), pg 1224
Delmas Typesetting Inc, pg 1224
Fairfield Marketing Group Inc, pg 1225
Fry Communications Inc, pg 1225
Goose River Press, pg 1226
Innodata Inc, pg 1227
Interstate Printing Co, pg 1227
Lumina Datamatics Inc, pg 1228
Maracle Inc, pg 1228
MBA Computer Service, pg 1228
Myriddian LLC, pg 1228
O'Neil Digital Solutions LLC, pg 1229
POD Print, pg 1229

Publishing Data Management Inc, pg 1230
Scribe Inc, pg 1230
Shepherd Inc, pg 1231
Windhaven®, pg 1233

FOREIGN LANGUAGE COMPOSITION

A-R Editions Inc, pg 1221
Apex CoVantage, pg 1221
appatura™, A Broadridge Company, pg 1221
Aptara Inc, pg 1222
Aquent LLC, pg 1222
David Berman Communications, pg 1222
BookComp Inc, pg 1223
Circle Graphics Inc, pg 1223
Crown Connect, pg 1224
Custom Studios, pg 1224
Delmas Typesetting Inc, pg 1224
diacriTech Inc, pg 1224
dix! Digital Prepress Inc, pg 1225
RR Donnelley, pg 1225
W R Draper Co, pg 1225
GEX Inc, pg 1226
GW Inc, pg 1226
Innodata Inc, pg 1227
International Press Publication Inc, pg 1227
Itzhack Shelomi Design, pg 1227
Larson Texts Inc, pg 1227
Leo Paper USA, pg 1228
Linguistic Systems Inc (LSI), pg 1228
Lumina Datamatics Inc, pg 1228
Maracle Inc, pg 1228
Meadows Design Office, pg 1228
Miles 33 International LLC, pg 1228
MPS North America LLC, pg 1228
NETS, pg 1229
North Market Street Graphics (NMSG), pg 1229
Progressive Publishing Services (PPS), pg 1230
Publishing Data Management Inc, pg 1230
Scribe Inc, pg 1230
Shepherd Inc, pg 1231
Six Red Marbles LLC, pg 1231
Thistle Printing Ltd, pg 1232
Viridiam LLC, pg 1232
WeMakeBooks.ca, pg 1232
Windhaven®, pg 1233
X-Height Studio, pg 1233

INDEXING

A-R Editions Inc, pg 1221
A to Z Indexing & Bibliographic Services, pg 1221
Access Points Indexing, pg 1221
Adams Press, pg 1221
Allex Indexing, pg 1221
American Mathematical Society (AMS), pg 1221
Apex CoVantage, pg 1221
Aptara Inc, pg 1222
Aquent LLC, pg 1222
BookComp Inc, pg 1223
Bookmasters, pg 1223
ColorPage, pg 1223
Concord Editorial & Design LLC, pg 1224
Crown Connect, pg 1224
Custom Studios, pg 1224
Cypress House, pg 1224
Delmas Typesetting Inc, pg 1224
Desktop Miracles Inc, pg 1224
diacriTech Inc, pg 1224
dix! Digital Prepress Inc, pg 1225

East Mountain Editing Services, pg 1225
Fry Communications Inc, pg 1225
G & H Soho Inc, pg 1226
GEX Inc, pg 1226
GW Inc, pg 1226
Molly Hall, pg 1226
HBP Inc, pg 1226
Heidelberg Graphics, pg 1226
Herr's Indexing Service, pg 1226
Worth Higgins & Associates Inc, pg 1226
Innodata Inc, pg 1227
Interstate Printing Co, pg 1227
Jenkins Group Inc, pg 1227
Lachina Creative, pg 1227
Leo Paper USA, pg 1228
Lumina Datamatics Inc, pg 1228
MPS North America LLC, pg 1228
Myriddian LLC, pg 1228
NETS, pg 1229
Newgen North America Inc, pg 1229
North Market Street Graphics (NMSG), pg 1229
Progressive Publishing Services (PPS), pg 1230
Publishing Data Management Inc, pg 1230
Reno Typographers, pg 1230
Ross Gage Inc, pg 1230
Schoolhouse Indexing, pg 1230
Schroeder Indexing Services, pg 1230
Scribe Inc, pg 1230
Shepherd Inc, pg 1231
Texas Graphic Resource Inc, pg 1232
Viridiam LLC, pg 1232
Fred Weidner & Daughter Printers, pg 1232
WeMakeBooks.ca, pg 1232
WordCo Indexing Services Inc, pg 1233
X-Height Studio, pg 1233

MATHEMATICS & CHEMISTRY COMPOSITION

Adams Design, pg 1221
American Mathematical Society (AMS), pg 1221
Apex CoVantage, pg 1221
Aptara Inc, pg 1222
Aquent LLC, pg 1222
BookComp Inc, pg 1223
Bookmasters, pg 1223
Burmar Technical Corp, pg 1223
Circle Graphics Inc, pg 1223
Crown Connect, pg 1224
Delmas Typesetting Inc, pg 1224
diacriTech Inc, pg 1224
RR Donnelley, pg 1225
Fry Communications Inc, pg 1225
GEX Inc, pg 1226
GW Inc, pg 1226
Interstate Printing Co, pg 1227
Lachina Creative, pg 1227
Larson Texts Inc, pg 1227
The Lexington Press Inc, pg 1228
Lumina Datamatics Inc, pg 1228
Miles 33 International LLC, pg 1228
MPS North America LLC, pg 1228
NETS, pg 1229
Newgen North America Inc, pg 1229
Pro-Composition Inc, pg 1229
Scribe Inc, pg 1230
Shepherd Inc, pg 1231
Six Red Marbles LLC, pg 1231

Thistle Printing Ltd, pg 1232
Townsend Communications Inc, pg 1232
X-Height Studio, pg 1233

MUSIC COMPOSITION

A-R Editions Inc, pg 1221
Aptara Inc, pg 1222
Aquent LLC, pg 1222
W R Draper Co, pg 1225
Leo Paper USA, pg 1228
MPS North America LLC, pg 1228
PrairieView Press, pg 1229
Shepherd Inc, pg 1231
Townsend Communications Inc, pg 1232

NON-ROMAN ALPHABETS

A-R Editions Inc, pg 1221
Adams Design, pg 1221
American Mathematical Society (AMS), pg 1221
Apex CoVantage, pg 1221
appatura™, A Broadridge Company, pg 1221
Aptara Inc, pg 1222
Aquent LLC, pg 1222
Arrow Graphics Inc, pg 1222
Berryville Graphics, pg 1222
BookComp Inc, pg 1223
Concord Editorial & Design LLC, pg 1224
Crown Connect, pg 1224
Custom Studios, pg 1224
Delmas Typesetting Inc, pg 1224
dix! Digital Prepress Inc, pg 1225
RR Donnelley, pg 1225
Leo Paper USA, pg 1228
Linguistic Systems Inc (LSI), pg 1228
MPS North America LLC, pg 1228
NETS, pg 1229
Publishing Data Management Inc, pg 1230
Scribe Inc, pg 1230
Shepherd Inc, pg 1231
Townsend Communications Inc, pg 1232
Windhaven®, pg 1233

PRODUCTION SERVICES

A-R Editions Inc, pg 1221
Adams Design, pg 1221
Adams Press, pg 1221
Allard Inc, pg 1221
Ambassador Press Inc, pg 1221
American Mathematical Society (AMS), pg 1221
Apex CoVantage, pg 1221
appatura™, A Broadridge Company, pg 1221
Aptara Inc, pg 1222
Aquent LLC, pg 1222
Arbor Books, pg 1222
Arrow Graphics Inc, pg 1222
Balfour Commercial Printing, pg 1222
The Bear Wallow Publishing Co, pg 1222
David Berman Communications, pg 1222
Berryville Graphics, pg 1222
Bindagraphics Inc, pg 1222
Blue Note Publications Inc, pg 1223
BookComp Inc, pg 1223
Bookmasters, pg 1223
BookWise Design, pg 1223
The Bureau, pg 1223

MANUFACTURING

Burmar Technical Corp, pg 1223
BW&A Books Inc, pg 1223
C & C Offset Printing Co USA Inc, pg 1223
Cape Cod Compositors Inc, pg 1223
Cenveo St Louis, pg 1223
CG Book Printers, pg 1223
Circle Graphics Inc, pg 1223
ColorPage, pg 1223
Concord Editorial & Design LLC, pg 1224
Corporate Disk Co, pg 1224
Crown Connect, pg 1224
Custom Studios, pg 1224
Cypress House, pg 1224
Datacolor, pg 1224
Delmas Typesetting Inc, pg 1224
Desktop Miracles Inc, pg 1224
diacriTech Inc, pg 1224
dix! Digital Prepress Inc, pg 1225
DNP America LLC, pg 1225
W R Draper Co, pg 1225
Edison Lithograph & Printing Corp, pg 1225
Fry Communications Inc, pg 1225
G & H Soho Inc, pg 1226
GEX Inc, pg 1226
Goose River Press, pg 1226
Graphics Two, pg 1226
GW Inc, pg 1226
Heidelberg Graphics, pg 1226
Worth Higgins & Associates Inc, pg 1226
The P A Hutchison Co, pg 1226
Imago, pg 1226
Infinity Graphics, pg 1227
Innodata Inc, pg 1227
Jenkins Group Inc, pg 1227
Kachergis Book Design Inc, pg 1227
Lachina Creative, pg 1227
Lake Book Manufacturing Inc, pg 1227
Larson Texts Inc, pg 1227
Leo Paper USA, pg 1228
The Lexington Press Inc, pg 1228
Lumina Datamatics Inc, pg 1228
Maracle Inc, pg 1228
McClain Printing Co, pg 1228
Meadows Design Office, pg 1228
Melissa Data Corp, pg 1228
MPS North America LLC, pg 1228
Myriddian LLC, pg 1228
NETS, pg 1229
Newgen North America Inc, pg 1229
North Market Street Graphics (NMSG), pg 1229
OEC Graphics Inc, pg 1229
O'Neil Digital Solutions LLC, pg 1229
Overseas Printing Corporation, pg 1229
The Ovid Bell Press Inc, pg 1229
POD Print, pg 1229
PrairieView Press, pg 1229
Printing Corporation of the Americas Inc, pg 1229
Pro-Composition Inc, pg 1229
Progress Printing Plus, pg 1230
Progressive Publishing Services (PPS), pg 1230
Pronk Media Inc, pg 1230
Publishing Data Management Inc, pg 1230
Reno Typographers, pg 1230
Scribe Inc, pg 1230
SGS International LLC, pg 1230
Shepherd Inc, pg 1231
Signature Book Printing Inc, pg 1231
Six Red Marbles LLC, pg 1231
Southeastern Printing Co, pg 1231
John S Swift Co Inc, pg 1231
Swordsmith Productions, pg 1231
Symmetry Creative Production, pg 1232
Texas Graphic Resource Inc, pg 1232
Thistle Printing Ltd, pg 1232
Times Printing LLC, pg 1232
Toof American Digital, pg 1232
Tukaiz LLC, pg 1232
UniversallWilde, pg 1232
Versa Press Inc, pg 1232
Walsworth, pg 1232
Fred Weidner & Daughter Printers, pg 1232
WeMakeBooks.ca, pg 1232
Westchester Publishing Services, pg 1233
Whitehall Printing Co, pg 1233
Windhaven®, pg 1233
Writer's Relief, Inc, pg 1233
X-Height Studio, pg 1233

PROOFING

Adair Graphic Communications, pg 1221
Adams Design, pg 1221
Adams Press, pg 1221
Ambassador Press Inc, pg 1221
American Mathematical Society (AMS), pg 1221
Apex CoVantage, pg 1221
Aptara Inc, pg 1222
Aquent LLC, pg 1222
Arbor Books, pg 1222
Asia Pacific Offset Inc, pg 1222
Balfour Commercial Printing, pg 1222
Bang Printing Co Inc, pg 1222
Berryville Graphics, pg 1222
BookComp Inc, pg 1223
Bookmasters, pg 1223
The Bureau, pg 1223
Burmar Technical Corp, pg 1223
C & C Offset Printing Co USA Inc, pg 1223
Cape Cod Compositors Inc, pg 1223
Cenveo St Louis, pg 1223
CG Book Printers, pg 1223
Coach House Printing, pg 1223
ColorPage, pg 1223
Colour Technologies, pg 1223
Concord Editorial & Design LLC, pg 1224
Coral Graphic Services Inc, pg 1224
Corporate Disk Co, pg 1224
Courier Printing, pg 1224
Crown Connect, pg 1224
Custom Studios, pg 1224
Cypress House, pg 1224
Desktop Miracles Inc, pg 1224
diacriTech Inc, pg 1224
dix! Digital Prepress Inc, pg 1225
RR Donnelley, pg 1225
W R Draper Co, pg 1225
FCI Digital, pg 1225
Fry Communications Inc, pg 1225
G & H Soho Inc, pg 1226
GEX Inc, pg 1226
Goose River Press, pg 1226
Heidelberg Graphics, pg 1226
Hennegan Co, pg 1226
Worth Higgins & Associates Inc, pg 1226
Innodata Inc, pg 1227
Interstate Printing Co, pg 1227
Ironmark, pg 1227
Jenkins Group Inc, pg 1227
Lachina Creative, pg 1227
Lake Book Manufacturing Inc, pg 1227
Leo Paper USA, pg 1228
Linguistic Systems Inc (LSI), pg 1228
Lumina Datamatics Inc, pg 1228
Maracle Inc, pg 1228
McClain Printing Co, pg 1228
MPS North America LLC, pg 1228
Myriddian LLC, pg 1228
NETS, pg 1229
Newgen North America Inc, pg 1229
Nissha USA Inc, pg 1229
North Market Street Graphics (NMSG), pg 1229
OEC Graphics Inc, pg 1229
OGM USA, pg 1229
O'Neil Digital Solutions LLC, pg 1229
Overseas Printing Corporation, pg 1229
PrairieView Press, pg 1229
Pro-Composition Inc, pg 1229
Progress Printing Plus, pg 1230
Progressive Publishing Services (PPS), pg 1230
Publishing Data Management Inc, pg 1230
Reno Typographers, pg 1230
Scribe Inc, pg 1230
SGS International LLC, pg 1230
Shepherd Inc, pg 1231
Six Red Marbles LLC, pg 1231
Sun Graphics LLC, pg 1231
John S Swift Co Inc, pg 1231
Swordsmith Productions, pg 1231
Symmetry Creative Production, pg 1232
Texas Graphic Resource Inc, pg 1232
Thistle Printing Ltd, pg 1232
Toof American Digital, pg 1232
Townsend Communications Inc, pg 1232
Tukaiz LLC, pg 1232
Versa Press Inc, pg 1232
Fred Weidner & Daughter Printers, pg 1232
WeMakeBooks.ca, pg 1232
Whitehall Printing Co, pg 1233
Windhaven®, pg 1233
Worzalla, pg 1233
Writer's Relief, Inc, pg 1233
X-Height Studio, pg 1233

SCIENTIFIC COMPOSITION

Adams Design, pg 1221
Allard Inc, pg 1221
American Mathematical Society (AMS), pg 1221
Apex CoVantage, pg 1221
Aptara Inc, pg 1222
Aquent LLC, pg 1222
BookComp Inc, pg 1223
Bookmasters, pg 1223
Burmar Technical Corp, pg 1223
Circle Graphics Inc, pg 1223
Crown Connect, pg 1224
diacriTech Inc, pg 1224
W R Draper Co, pg 1225
Fry Communications Inc, pg 1225
GEX Inc, pg 1226
GW Inc, pg 1226
Innodata Inc, pg 1227
Lachina Creative, pg 1227
Miles 33 International LLC, pg 1228
MPS North America LLC, pg 1228
Myriddian LLC, pg 1228
NETS, pg 1229
Newgen North America Inc, pg 1229
Pro-Composition Inc, pg 1229

PREPRESS SERVICES INDEX

Progressive Publishing Services (PPS), pg 1230
Scribe Inc, pg 1230
Shepherd Inc, pg 1231
Six Red Marbles LLC, pg 1231
Townsend Communications Inc, pg 1232
Windhaven®, pg 1233
X-Height Studio, pg 1233

UPC & BAR CODE SERVICES

Adams Design, pg 1221
Adams Press, pg 1221
Barcode Graphics Inc, pg 1222
Bookmasters, pg 1223
C & C Offset Printing Co USA Inc, pg 1223
CG Book Printers, pg 1223
Circle Graphics Inc, pg 1223
ColorPage, pg 1223
Concord Editorial & Design LLC, pg 1224
Custom Studios, pg 1224
Cypress House, pg 1224
Data Index Inc, pg 1224
Desktop Miracles Inc, pg 1224
G & H Soho Inc, pg 1226
Goose River Press, pg 1226
Heidelberg Graphics, pg 1226
Infinity Graphics, pg 1227
Jenkins Group Inc, pg 1227
Lake Book Manufacturing Inc, pg 1227
McClain Printing Co, pg 1228
POD Print, pg 1229
Product Identification & Processing Systems Inc, pg 1230
Publication Identification & Processing Systems, pg 1230
Sun Graphics LLC, pg 1231
Symbology Inc, pg 1232
WeMakeBooks.ca, pg 1232
Whitehall Printing Co, pg 1233
Windhaven®, pg 1233

WORD PROCESSING INTERFACE

A-R Editions Inc, pg 1221
Adams Design, pg 1221
Adams Press, pg 1221
All Craft Digital Inc, pg 1221
Allard Inc, pg 1221
American Mathematical Society (AMS), pg 1221
Apex CoVantage, pg 1221
appatura™, A Broadridge Company, pg 1221
Aptara Inc, pg 1222
Aquent LLC, pg 1222
Art Related Technology Inc, pg 1222
Bang Printing Co Inc, pg 1222
David Berman Communications, pg 1222
Blue Note Publications Inc, pg 1223
Bookmasters, pg 1223
The Bureau, pg 1223
Burmar Technical Corp, pg 1223
CG Book Printers, pg 1223
Circle Graphics Inc, pg 1223
Coach House Printing, pg 1223
ColorPage, pg 1223
Crown Connect, pg 1224
Custom Studios, pg 1224
diacriTech Inc, pg 1224
W R Draper Co, pg 1225
Fry Communications Inc, pg 1225
G & H Soho Inc, pg 1226
GEX Inc, pg 1226

PREPRESS SERVICES INDEX

Goose River Press, pg 1226
Heidelberg Graphics, pg 1226
Worth Higgins & Associates Inc, pg 1226
Infinity Graphics, pg 1227
Innodata Inc, pg 1227
Jenkins Group Inc, pg 1227
Knepper Press Corp, pg 1227
The Lexington Press Inc, pg 1228
Lumina Datamatics Inc, pg 1228
Maracle Inc, pg 1228
Myriddian LLC, pg 1228
NETS, pg 1229
Newgen North America Inc, pg 1229
North Market Street Graphics (NMSG), pg 1229
Pro-Composition Inc, pg 1229
Publishing Data Management Inc, pg 1230
The Renton Printery Inc, pg 1230
Scribe Inc, pg 1230
Shepherd Inc, pg 1231
Southeastern Printing Co, pg 1231
John S Swift Co Inc, pg 1231
Swordsmith Productions, pg 1231
Texas Graphic Resource Inc, pg 1232
Thistle Printing Ltd, pg 1232
Times Printing LLC, pg 1232
Westchester Publishing Services, pg 1233
Windhaven®, pg 1233
Writer's Relief, Inc, pg 1233
X-Height Studio, pg 1233

Prepress Services

The list below includes companies offering a variety of prepress services, including indexing, data processing, color separations, art and design, word processing interface, proofreading, production and various composition and typesetting services. The descriptions of the services provided are paid components.

For additional companies and individuals providing indexing and/or proofing services, see **Editorial Services** (volume 1). Additionally, companies and individuals providing art and design services can be found in **Artists & Art Services**.

A-R Editions Inc
1600 Aspen Commons, Suite 100, Middleton, WI 53562
Tel: 608-836-9000 *Fax:* 608-831-8200
E-mail: info@areditions.com
Web Site: www.areditions.com
Key Personnel
Pres & CEO: Patrick Wall *Tel:* 608-203-2575 *E-mail:* patrick.wall@areditions.com
Dir, Publg Servs: Lance Ottman *E-mail:* lance.ottman@areditions.com
Dir, Spec Projs: James Zychowicz *Tel:* 608-203-2580 *E-mail:* james.zychowicz@areditions.com
Founded: 1962

A to Z Indexing & Bibliographic Services
20 St James Rd, Shrewsbury, MA 01545
Tel: 508-842-5602
Web Site: sites.google.com/site/atozindexing
Key Personnel
Owner: Kathleen Rocheleau *E-mail:* kathleen.rocheleau@gmail.com
Founded: 1994

Access Points Indexing
PO Box 1155, Hood River, OR 97031
Tel: 541-806-5436
Web Site: www.accesspointsindexing.com
Key Personnel
Owner: Mary Harper *E-mail:* mary@accesspointsindexing.com
Founded: 2005
Membership(s): American Society for Indexing (ASI)

Ace Pro Inc, see Progressive Publishing Services (PPS)

Adair Graphic Communications
Division of Printwell
26975 Northline Rd, Taylor, MI 48180
Tel: 734-941-6300 *Fax:* 734-942-0920
E-mail: adair@printwell.com
Web Site: www.adairgraphic.com
Key Personnel
Pres & CEO: Paul Borg
VP: Dennis Adair *E-mail:* dennis@adairgraphic.com
Founded: 1931
Turnaround: 15 Workdays

Adams Design
4493 Horseshoe Bend, Murrells Inlet, SC 29576
Tel: 843-655-7097
E-mail: sa@stephenadamsdesign.com
Web Site: www.stephenadamsdesign.com
Key Personnel
Pres: Stephen Adams *E-mail:* sa@rof.net
Founded: 1990
Turnaround: 7 Workdays

Adams Press
1712 Oakton St, Evanston, IL 60202
E-mail: info@adamspress.com
Key Personnel
Pres: James A Kepler *E-mail:* jkepler@adamspress.com

Founded: 1942
Turnaround: 20-25 Workdays
Membership(s): The Association of Publishers for Special Sales (APSS); Independent Book Publishers Association (IBPA); Independent Writers of Chicago (IWOC); Midwest Writers Association

AJP Communications Inc
95 Macdonald Ave, Burnaby, BC V5C 4M4, Canada
Tel: 604-879-5880
E-mail: info@ajpcommunications.com
Web Site: www.ajpcommunications.com
Key Personnel
Creative Dir: Amy Pon
Founded: 1998

All Craft Digital Inc
289-C Skidmores Rd, Deer Park, NY 11729
Tel: 631-254-8495 *Fax:* 631-254-8496
Key Personnel
Pres: Jason Buser
Founded: 1970
Turnaround: 1 Workday

Allard Inc
4601 50 St, Suite 204, Lubbock, TX 79414
Tel: 214-736-4983
E-mail: info@allardinc.com
Web Site: www.allardinc.com
Key Personnel
Pres: Mike Bean
Founded: 1978

Allex Indexing
6039 Sunshine Dr, Ferndale, WA 98248-9234
Tel: 360-778-1308
Web Site: www.indexpert.com
Key Personnel
Indexer: Wendy Allex *E-mail:* wendy@indexpert.com
Founded: 2000
Membership(s): American Society for Indexing (ASI)

amb™, see Ambassador Press Inc

Ambassador Press Inc
1400 Washington Ave N, Minneapolis, MN 55411
Tel: 612-521-0123
E-mail: info@ambpress.com
Web Site: www.ambpress.com
Key Personnel
Co-Owner, Pres & CEO: Candice Engle-Fieldman
Co-Owner & EVP: Harold Engle
Founded: 1960
Turnaround: 3 Workdays

American International Distribution Corp (AIDC)
82 Winter Sport Lane, Williston, VT 05495
Mailing Address: PO Box 80, Williston, VT 05495-0080
Tel: 802-862-0095 *Toll Free Tel:* 800-678-2432 *Fax:* 802-864-7749

Web Site: www.aidcvt.com
Key Personnel
Pres & CEO: Marilyn McConnell
Dir, Opers: Michael Pelland
Founded: 1986
BISAC compatible software
Membership(s): Book Industry Study Group (BISG); Independent Publisher's Guild (IPG)

American Mathematical Society (AMS)
201 Charles St, Providence, RI 02904-2213
SAN: 201-1654
Tel: 401-455-4000 *Toll Free Tel:* 800-321-4267 *Fax:* 401-331-3842; 401-455-4046 (cust serv)
E-mail: cust-serv@ams.org; ams@ams.org
Web Site: www.ams.org
Key Personnel
Exec Dir: Dr Catherine A Roberts
Publr: Dr Sergei Gelfand
Assoc Exec Dir: Dr Robert M Harrington
Assoc Exec Dir, Washington, DC: Dr Karen Saxe
Founded: 1888
Turnaround: 7 Workdays
Branch Office(s)
1527 18 St NW, Washington, DC 20036-1358 (govt rel & sci policy) *Tel:* 202-588-1100 *Fax:* 202-588-1853 *E-mail:* amsdc@ams.org
Mathematical Reviews®, 416 Fourth St, Ann Arbor, MI 48103-4820 (edit) *Tel:* 734-996-5250 *Fax:* 734-996-2916 *E-mail:* mathrev@ams.org
Secretary of the AMS - Society Governance, Dept of Computer Science, North Carolina State University, Box 8206, Raleigh, NC 27695-8206 *Tel:* 919-515-7863 *Fax:* 919-515-7896 *E-mail:* secretary@ams.org
Membership(s): Society for Scholarly Publishing (SSP)

Apex CoVantage
4045 Sheridan Ave, No 266, Miami Beach, FL 33140
Tel: 703-709-3000 *Fax:* 703-709-8242
E-mail: info@apexcovantage.com
Web Site: www.apexcovantage.com
Key Personnel
Co-Founder & CEO: Dr Shashikant Gupta
Co-Founder & COO: Margaret Gupta
Pres, Content Solutions: Pardha Karamsetty
Founded: 1988
Membership(s): Society for Scholarly Publishing (SSP); Software & Information Industry Association (SIIA)

appatura™, A Broadridge Company
Division of Broadridge Financial Solutions Inc
65 Challenger Rd, Suite 400, Ridgefield Park, NJ 07660
Tel: 201-508-6000 *Toll Free Tel:* 800-277-2155
E-mail: contactus@appatura.com
Web Site: www.appatura.com
Key Personnel
CEO: Richard Plotka
CIO: Faisal Fareed
Chief Prod Offr: Harsh Choudhary
Chief Strategy Offr: John Closson
Head, Fin: Alpha Diarra
Founded: 1949

PREPRESS SERVICES

Aptara Inc
Subsidiary of iEnergizer
2901 Telestar Ct, Suite 522, Falls Church, VA 22042
Tel: 703-352-0001
E-mail: moreinfo@aptaracorp.com
Web Site: www.aptaracorp.com
Key Personnel
Pres: Samir Kakar
EVP, Fin & Cont: Prashant Kapoor
SVP, Busn & Contact Ctr Opers: Ashish Madan
Busn Devt: Michael Scott *E-mail:* michael.scott@aptaracorp.com
Founded: 1988
Branch Office(s)
150 California St, Suite 301, Newton, MA 02458 *Tel:* 617-423-7755
11009 Metric Blvd, Bldg J, Suite 150, Austin, TX 78758 *Tel:* 512-876-5997
299 Elizabeth St, Level 1, Sydney 2000, Australia *Tel:* (02) 8251 0070
Tower 1 & 2, 8/100, Acharya Thulasi Rd (Shandy Rd), Pallavaram, Chennai 600 043, India *Tel:* (044) 22640676
No 2310, Doon Express Business Park, Saharanpur Rd, Bldg 2000, Dehradun 248 002, India *Tel:* (0135) 2644055
7B, Leela Infopark, Technopark, Trivandrum, Kerala 695 581, India *Tel:* (047) 14063370
A-37, Sector-60, Noida 201 301, India *Tel:* (0120) 7182424
D-10, Sector-2, Noida 201 301, India *Tel:* (0120) 24423678
SEZ Bldg 4A, 1st fl, S P Infocity, Pune Saswad Rd, Phursungi, Pune 412 308, India *Tel:* (020) 66728000

Aquent LLC
101 W Elm St, Suite 300, Conshohocken, PA 19428-2075
Tel: 610-828-0900 *Toll Free Fax:* 877-303-5224
E-mail: questions@aquent.com
Web Site: aquentstudios.com; aquent.com
Key Personnel
Mgr: Kelly Griffin
Founded: 1986

Arbor Books
244 Madison Ave, Box 254, New York, NY 10016
Tel: 212-956-0950 *Toll Free Tel:* 877-822-2500 *Fax:* 914-401-9385
E-mail: info@arborbooks.com; editorial@arborbooks.net
Web Site: www.arborbooks.com
Key Personnel
Owner: Joel Hochman *Tel:* 877-822-2502 *E-mail:* arborbooksjoel@aol.com; Larry Leichman *Tel:* 877-822-2504 *E-mail:* arborbookslarry@aol.com
Mktg Dir: Olga Vladi *E-mail:* floatinggal1@aol.com
Founded: 1992
BISAC compatible software
Turnaround: 21 Workdays; 1-7 Workdays for art

Arbor Services, see Arbor Books

Arrow Graphics Inc
PO Box 380291, Cambridge, MA 02238
E-mail: info@arrow1.com
Web Site: www.arrow1.com
Key Personnel
Pres: Alvart Badalian
Sr Graphic/Pubn Designer: Aramais Andonian
Founded: 1988

Art Related Technology Inc
4 Brattle St, Rm 305, Cambridge, MA 02138
Tel: 617-661-1225 *Fax:* 617-491-0618
E-mail: artinc@artrelated.com

Web Site: www.artrelated.com
Key Personnel
Art Dir: Marvin Mortee
Founded: 1983

Asia Pacific Offset Inc
1312 "Q" St NW, Suite B, Washington, DC 20009
Tel: 202-462-5436 *Toll Free Tel:* 800-756-4344 *Fax:* 202-986-4030
Web Site: www.asiapacificoffset.com
Key Personnel
Pres: Andrew Clarke *E-mail:* andrew@asiapacificoffset.com
Founded: 1997
Turnaround: 105 Workdays including color separation & shipping
Branch Office(s)
870 Market St, Suite 801, San Francisco, CA 94102, Dir, Sales: Amy Armstrong *Tel:* 415-433-3488 *Fax:* 415-433-3489 *E-mail:* amy@asiapacificoffset.com
1768 Oakmont Ct, Ann Arbor, MI 48108, Dir, Sales: Dean Sherman *Tel:* 734-223-6218 *E-mail:* dean@asiapacificoffset.com
62 Rivington St, Suite 2B, New York, NY 10002, Dir, Sales & Mktg: Simona Jansons *Tel:* 212-941-8300 *Fax:* 212-941-9810 *E-mail:* simona@asiapacificoffset.com
16 Clements Dr, Avoca Beach, NSW 2251, Australia, Dir, Sales: Penny Crocker *Tel:* (02) 4382 6174 *E-mail:* penny@asiapacificoffset.com
57 Norfolk St, Ponsonby, Auckland 1021, New Zealand, Consultant: Barbara Nielsen *Tel:* (09) 378-4971 *E-mail:* barbara@asiapacificoffset.com
C/ Tamarit 104, esc D, entrance 2, 08015 Barcelona, Spain, Dir, Sales: Carlos Blavia *Tel:* 933278837 *Fax:* 933254826 *E-mail:* carlos@asiapacificoffset.com
20 Mortlake High St, London SW14 8JN, United Kingdom, Dir, Sales: Adrian Gatheroole *Tel:* (020) 3170 8700 *Fax:* (020) 3170 8704 *E-mail:* adrian@asiapacificoffset.com

Balfour Commercial Printing
Formerly Taylor Specialty Books
Division of Balfour/Taylor
225 E John Carpenter Fwy, Tower 2, Suite 400, Irving, TX 75062
Tel: 214-819-8588 (cust serv)
E-mail: printing@balfour.com
Web Site: commercial-printing.balfour.com
Key Personnel
Acct Exec: Julie Kacala *E-mail:* julie.kacala@balfour.com
Founded: 1939
Turnaround: 30-35 Workdays

Bang Printing Co Inc
Division of CJK Group Inc
3323 Oak St, Brainerd, MN 56401
Tel: 218-829-2877 *Toll Free Tel:* 800-328-0450 *Fax:* 218-829-7145
E-mail: info@bangprinting.com
Web Site: www.bangprinting.com
Key Personnel
Pres: Todd Vanek *E-mail:* toddv@bangprinting.com
VP, Opers: Joe Saiko *E-mail:* joes@bangprinting.com
VP, Sales: Doug Walters *E-mail:* dougw@bangprinting.com
Founded: 1899
Turnaround: 10-25 Workdays

Barcode Graphics Inc
25 Brodie Dr, Unit 5, Richmond Hill, ON L4B 3K7, Canada
Tel: 905-770-1154 *Toll Free Tel:* 800-263-3669 (orders) *Fax:* 905-787-1575
E-mail: info@barcodegraphics.com

Web Site: www.barcodegraphics.com
Key Personnel
Pres: John Herzig *E-mail:* jherzig@barcodegraphics.com
Founded: 1982

The Bear Wallow Publishing Co
809 S 12 St, La Grande, OR 97850
Tel: 541-962-7864
Web Site: www.bear-wallow.com
Key Personnel
Co-Owner: Cathy Gildemeister; Jerry Gildemeister *E-mail:* j-c@bear-wallow.com
Founded: 1976

David Berman Communications
340 Selby Ave, Ottawa, ON K2A 3X6, Canada
Tel: 613-728-6777 *Toll Free Tel:* 800-665-1809
E-mail: info@davidberman.com
Web Site: www.wcag2.com
Key Personnel
Pres: David Berman
Founded: 1984
Branch Office(s)
182 Pearson Ave, Toronto, ON M6R 1G5, Canada *Fax:* 416-532-7786
969 Second St SE, Charlottesville, VA 22902
6 Jl 14/7, Petaling Jaya Selangor, 46100 Kuala Lumpur, Malaysia

Berryville Graphics
Member of Bertelsmann Printing Group
25 Jack Enders Blvd, Berryville, VA 22611
Tel: 540-955-2750 *Fax:* 540-955-2633
E-mail: info@bvgraphics.com
Web Site: www.bpg-usa.com
Key Personnel
CEO: Christof Ludwig
CFO: Denis Leite
CTO: Yannic Schroeder
Founded: 1956
Turnaround: 15 Workdays (initial orders); 6 Workdays (reprint orders); 4 Workdays (out of stock)
Branch Office(s)
100 N Miller St, Fairfield, PA 17320 *Tel:* 717-549-4800
871 Baker St, Martinsburg, VA 25405 *Tel:* 681-247-3300

Bindagraphics Inc
2701 Wilmarco Ave, Baltimore, MD 21223-9922
Tel: 410-362-7200 *Toll Free Tel:* 800-326-0300 *Fax:* 410-362-7233
E-mail: info@bindagraphics.com
Web Site: www.bindagraphics.com
Key Personnel
Owner & Pres: Matt Anson
Founded: 1974
Turnaround: Same day & longer
Branch Office(s)
Bindagraphics South Inc, 100 N Pendleton S, High Point, NC 27260 *Tel:* 336-431-6200 *Fax:* 410-431-6232
Membership(s): PRINTING United Alliance

Blanks Printing & Imaging Inc
2343 N Beckley Ave, Dallas, TX 75208
Tel: 214-741-3905 *Toll Free Tel:* 800-325-7651
E-mail: sales@blanks.com
Web Site: www.blanks.com
Key Personnel
CFO: Doug Heyerdahl *E-mail:* cfo@blanks.com
Pres: Leron Blanks *E-mail:* lblanks@blanks.com
VP: Jeff Blanks *E-mail:* jblanks@blanks.com
VP, Sales & Mktg: Mark Connor *E-mail:* mconnor@blanks.com
Opers Mgr: Jan Thornton *E-mail:* jthornton@blanks.com
Founded: 1941

Blue Note Books, see Blue Note Publications Inc

MANUFACTURING

Blue Note Publications Inc
721 North Dr, Suite D, Melbourne, FL 32934
Tel: 321-799-2583; 321-622-6289
 Toll Free Tel: 800-624-0401 (orders) *Fax:* 321-799-1942; 321-622-6830
E-mail: bluenotebooks@gmail.com
Web Site: bluenotepublications.com
Key Personnel
Pres: Paul Maluccio
Founded: 1988
Turnaround: 20 Workdays

BookComp Inc
6124 Belmont Ave NE, Belmont, MI 49306
Tel: 616-774-9700
E-mail: production@bookcomp.com
Web Site: www.bookcomp.com
Key Personnel
Pres: Jon F Dertien *E-mail:* jd@bookcomp.com
Prodn Mgr: JoAnn Sikkes
Edit: Nicholle Robertson *E-mail:* nicholle@bookcomp.com
Founded: 1989
Turnaround: 10 Workdays
Membership(s): American Association of University Presses (AAUP)

Bookmasters
Division of Baker & Taylor Publisher Services
30 Amberwood Pkwy, Ashland, OH 44805
Tel: 419-281-5100 *Toll Free Tel:* 800-537-6727 *Fax:* 419-281-0200
E-mail: info@btpubservices.com
Web Site: www.btpubservices.com
Key Personnel
Dir of Mfg: Brad Sharp *E-mail:* bsharp@bookmasters.com
Founded: 1972
BISAC compatible software

BookWise Design
29089 SW Costa Circle W, Wilsonville, OR 97070
Tel: 503-542-3551 *Toll Free Tel:* 800-697-9833
Web Site: bookwisedesign.com
Key Personnel
Partner & Art Dir: Shannon Bodie
 E-mail: shannon@bookwisedesign.com
Partner & Creative Consultant: Bob Swingle
 Tel: 503-542-3550
Proj Mgr: Jann Armstrong *Tel:* 509-675-3440
 E-mail: jann@bookwisedesign.com
Founded: 1985

The Bureau
Division of The Vomela Companies
2354 English St, Maplewood, MN 55109
Tel: 612-788-1000; 612-432-3516 (sales)
 Toll Free Tel: 800-788-9536 *Fax:* 612-788-7792
E-mail: sales@thebureau.com
Web Site: www.thebureau.com
Key Personnel
Pres & CEO: Mark Auth
VP, Sales & Busn Devt: Tim Dobratz
 E-mail: tim.dobratz@vomela.com
Gen Mgr: John Henderson
Natl Acct Sales Rep: Mike Schreiner
Turnaround: 3-5 Workdays

Burmar Technical Corp
106 Ransom Ave, Sea Cliff, NY 11579
Tel: 516-484-6000 *Fax:* 516-484-6356
Web Site: burmar.net
Key Personnel
Pres: Christine Jensen *E-mail:* christine.jensen@burmar.net
Founded: 1954

BW&A Books Inc
112 W McClanahan St, Oxford, NC 27565
Tel: 919-956-9111 *Fax:* 919-956-9112
E-mail: bwa@bwabooks.com
Web Site: www.bwabooks.com
Key Personnel
Pres & Designer: Chris Crochetiere
 E-mail: chris@bwabooks.com
VP & Designer: Julie Allred *E-mail:* julie@bwabooks.com
Founded: 1988
Turnaround: Varies

C & C Offset Printing Co USA Inc
Subsidiary of C & C Joint Printing Co (HK) Ltd
70 W 36 St, Unit 10C, New York, NY 10018
Tel: 212-431-4210 *Toll Free Fax:* 866-540-4134
Web Site: www.ccoffset.com
Key Personnel
Dir & EVP, C & C Offset Printing Co (USA) Inc & C & C Offset Printing Co (NY) Inc, New York, NY: Simon Chan *E-mail:* schan@ccoffset.com
Sales Mgr, C & C Offset Printing Co (NY) Inc, New York, NY: Frances Harkness
 E-mail: fharkness@ccoffset.com; Timothy McNulty
CEO, C & C Joint Printing Co (HK) Ltd, Hong Kong: Jackson Leung
Deputy Gen Mgr, C & C Joint Printing Co (HK) Ltd, Hong Kong: Francis Ho; Kit Wong
Dir, C & C Offset Printing Co (France) Ltd: Michele Olson Niel *E-mail:* michele@candcoffset.fr
Pres, C & C Printing Japan Co Ltd, Tokyo, Japan: Yamamoto Masaaki
Dir, C & C Offset Printing Co (UK) Ltd: Tracy Broderick *E-mail:* tracy@candcoffset.co.uk
Sales Rep, Australian Off: Lena Frew
 E-mail: lena.frew@candcprinting.com
Founded: 1980
Turnaround: Varies
Branch Office(s)
C & C Offset Printing Co Ltd (Australia Off), Lithocraft Graphics, 3-7 Permas Way, Truganina, Victoria 3029, Australia *Tel:* (613) 8366 0200 *Fax:* (613) 8366 0299
C & C Offset Printing Co (France) Ltd, 15, rue d'Aboukir, 75002 Paris, France *Tel:* 01 40 26 21 07 *Fax:* 01 44 76 08 96
C & C Offset Printing Co Ltd, C & C Bldg, 36 Ting Lai Rd, Tai Po, New Territories, Hong Kong (corp headquarters) *Tel:* 2666 4988 *Fax:* 2666 4938 *E-mail:* info@candcprinting.com *Web Site:* www.candcprinting.com
C & C Printing Japan Co Ltd, Tozaido Bldg, 3F, 2-6-12 Hitotsubashi, Chiyoda-ku, Tokyo 101-0003, Japan *Tel:* (03) 5216 4580 *Fax:* (03) 5216 4610 *E-mail:* mail@candcprinting.co.jp *Web Site:* www.candcprinting.co.jp
C & C Offset Printing Co (UK) Ltd, 75 Newman St, 3rd fl, London W1T 3EN, United Kingdom *Tel:* (020) 7637 5033 *Fax:* (020) 7637 5044 *E-mail:* info@candcoffset.co.uk

Cape Cod Compositors Inc
811 Washington St, Suite 2, Pembroke, MA 02359-2333
Tel: 781-826-2100
Key Personnel
Pres: Missy Garnett *E-mail:* mg@capecodcompositors.com
Sr Assoc: Joanne Jesse
Cust Serv: Tami Trask
Founded: 1986

Cenveo St Louis
101 Workman Ct, Eureka, MO 63025
Tel: 314-966-2000 *Toll Free Tel:* 800-800-8845 *Fax:* 314-966-4725
Web Site: www.cenveo.com

CG Book Printers
Division of Corporate Graphics Commercial (CGC)

PREPRESS SERVICES

1750 Northway Dr, North Mankato, MN 56003
Tel: 507-388-3300 *Toll Free Tel:* 800-729-7575 *Fax:* 507-386-6350
E-mail: cgbooks@corpgraph.com
Web Site: www.corpgraph.com
Key Personnel
Pres: Dan Kvasnicka *Tel:* 507-386-6340 *Fax:* 507-344-5548 *E-mail:* dekvasnicka@corpgraph.com
Sales Exec, Book Mfg Sales: Mike Schmitt *Tel:* 507-386-6349 *E-mail:* mjschmitt@corpgraph.com
Founded: 1989

Cimarron Design
8285 Kincross Dr, Boulder, CO 80301-4228
Tel: 303-530-1785
Web Site: www.cimarrondesign.com
Key Personnel
Owner: Troy Scott Parker *E-mail:* tsparker@cimarrondesign.com
Founded: 1989
Turnaround: 5-15 Workdays

Circle Graphics Inc
316 Main St, Suite 1C, Reisters Town, MD 21136
Tel: 410-833-2200
E-mail: production@circleusa.com
Web Site: www.circleusa.com
Key Personnel
Pres: Richard Berkowitz
Consultant: Jay Berkowitz; Frank Dunn
Founded: 1974

Clare Printing
206 S Keystone Ave, Sayre, PA 18840
Tel: 570-888-2244
E-mail: hr@clareprint.com
Web Site: www.clareprint.com
Key Personnel
Pres: Ian Clare
Prodn Mgr: Alicia Blokzyl
Founded: 1903

Coach House Printing
80 bpNichol Lane, Toronto, ON M5S 3J4, Canada
Tel: 416-979-2217 *Toll Free Tel:* 800-367-6360 (outside Toronto) *Fax:* 416-977-1158
E-mail: mail@chbooks.com
Web Site: www.chbooks.com
Key Personnel
Publr: Stan Bevington *E-mail:* stan@chbooks.com
Edit Dir: Alana Wilcox *E-mail:* alana@chbooks.com
Prodn Mgr: John De Jesus *E-mail:* john@chbooks.com
Founded: 1965
Turnaround: 14 Workdays

ColorPage
Division of Tri-State Associated Services Inc
81 Ten Broeck Ave, Kingston, NY 12401
Tel: 845-331-7581 *Toll Free Tel:* 800-836-7581 *Fax:* 845-331-1571
E-mail: sales@colorpageonline.com
Web Site: www.colorpageonline.com
Key Personnel
Pres & Mktg Strategist/Consultant: Frank J Campagna, II *E-mail:* fcampagna@colorpageonline.com
Acct Mgr & Cont: Kathy Riggins
 E-mail: kriggins@colorpageonline.com
Prodn Mgr: Randy Delanoy
Cust Serv Supv: Debbie Downes
 E-mail: ddownes@colorpageonline.com
Founded: 1976
Turnaround: 10-15 Workdays

Colour Technologies
Division of CJ Graphics Inc

1223

PREPRESS SERVICES

560 Hensall Circle, Mississauga, ON L5A 1Y1, Canada
Tel: 416-588-0808
E-mail: info@cjgraphics.com
Web Site: www.cjgraphics.com/services/prepress
Key Personnel
Owner: Jay Mandarino

Communicorp Inc
Subsidiary of Aflac Inc
1001 Lockwood Ave, Columbus, GA 31999
Tel: 706-324-1182
E-mail: mktech@communicorp.com
Web Site: www.communicorp.com
Key Personnel
Pres & CEO: Eric Seldon
VP: Mike Thomas
Sr Mgr, Prodn Servs: Jason Lansdon
Sr Mgr, Sales & Mktg Servs: John Shutter *Tel:* 706-763-2912 *E-mail:* jshutter@communicorp.com
Founded: 1981
Branch Office(s)
100 Galleria Pkwy, Suite 450, Atlanta, GA 30339
Tel: 770-541-4515 *Toll Free Tel:* 800-775-7998

Concord Editorial & Design LLC
9450 SW Gemini Dr, Suite 68669, Beaverton, OR 97008
Tel: 616-827-7537 *Fax:* 616-825-6048
E-mail: info@concordeditorial.com
Web Site: www.concordeditorial.com
Key Personnel
Pres & Proj Dir: David Fideler, PhD
Founded: 2005
Turnaround: 10 Workdays

Cookbook Publishers Inc
11633 W 83 Terr, Lenexa, KS 66285
Mailing Address: PO Box 15920, Lenexa, KS 66285-5920
Tel: 913-492-5900 *Toll Free Tel:* 800-227-7282 *Fax:* 913-492-5947
E-mail: info@cookbookpublishers.com
Web Site: www.cookbookpublishers.com
Key Personnel
Pres: Kevin Naughton
New Busn Devt: Stephanie Jones
Founded: 1947
Turnaround: 5-30 Workdays

Coral Graphic Services Inc
Member of Bertelsmann Printing Group
840 S Broadway, Hicksville, NY 11801
Tel: 516-576-2100 *Fax:* 516-576-2168
E-mail: info@coralgraphics.com
Web Site: www.bpg-usa.com
Key Personnel
CEO: Christof Ludwig
CFO: Denis Leite
CTO: Yannic Schroeder
Founded: 1982
Branch Office(s)
25 Jack Enders Blvd, Berryville, VA 22611
Tel: 540-955-2750 *Fax:* 540-955-9164
Membership(s): Association of the Graphic Arts (AGA); PRINTING United Alliance

Corporate Disk Co
4610 Prime Pkwy, McHenry, IL 60050-7005
Tel: 815-331-6000 *Toll Free Tel:* 800-634-3475 *Fax:* 815-331-6030
E-mail: info@disk.com
Web Site: www.disk.com
Key Personnel
Owner & VP, Sales: Joe D Foley *Tel:* 815-331-6000 ext 233 *E-mail:* jfoley@disk.com
Founded: 1984

Corporate Graphics Book Printers, see CG Book Printers

Courier Printing
Division of RR Donnelley
One Courier Place, Smyrna, TN 37167
Tel: 615-355-4000 *Toll Free Tel:* 800-467-0444 *Fax:* 615-355-4088
Web Site: www.courierprinting.com
Key Personnel
Pres: Michelle Yun
Turnaround: 5-15 Workdays

Crown Connect
250 W Rialto Ave, San Bernadino, CA 92408
Tel: 909-888-7531 *Fax:* 909-889-1639
E-mail: sales@crownconnect.com
Web Site: www.crownconnect.com
Key Personnel
CFO: Nicole Albright *Tel:* 909-888-7531 ext 204
Pres: Denny Shorett *Tel:* 909-888-7531 ext 225
VP, Opers: Ken Martin *Tel:* 909-888-7531 ext 206
Mgr, Busn Devt: Erin Warren *Tel:* 909-888-7531 ext 228
Prodn Mgr: Chris McPhate *Tel:* 909-888-7531 ext 214
Founded: 1970

Custom Studios
Subsidiary of Nationwide Custom Services Inc
77 Main St, Tappan, NY 10983
Tel: 845-365-0414 *Toll Free Tel:* 800-631-1362 *Fax:* 845-365-0864
E-mail: customusa@aol.com
Web Site: customstudios.com
Key Personnel
Owner & Pres: Norman Shaifer
VP: Helen Newman; Harry Title
Founded: 1960

Cypress House
Imprint of Comp-Type Inc
155 Cypress St, Suite A, Fort Bragg, CA 95437
Tel: 707-964-9520 *Toll Free Tel:* 800-773-7782 *Fax:* 707-964-7531
E-mail: office@cypresshouse.com
Web Site: www.cypresshouse.com
Key Personnel
Pres: Cynthia Frank *E-mail:* cynthia@cypresshouse.com
Mng Ed: Joe Shaw *E-mail:* joeshaw@cypresshouse.com
Founded: 1986
Turnaround: 60 Workdays
Membership(s): American Booksellers Association (ABA); Bay Area Independent Publishers Association (BAIPA); California Independent Booksellers Alliance (CALIBA); Independent Book Publishers Association (IBPA); Pacific Northwest Booksellers Association (PNBA)

Darwill
11900 W Roosevelt Rd, Hillside, IL 60162
Tel: 708-236-4900 *Fax:* 708-236-5820
E-mail: info@darwill.net
Web Site: www.darwill.com
Key Personnel
Pres & Co-CEO: Brandon Van Dyke; Troy Van Dyke
Founded: 1951

Data Conversion Laboratory Inc (DCL)
61-18 190 St, Suite 205, Fresh Meadows, NY 11365
Tel: 718-357-8700 *Toll Free Tel:* 800-321-2816 (provider problems)
E-mail: info@dclab.com
Web Site: www.dataconversionlaboratory.com
Key Personnel
Pres: Mark Gross
COO: Amy Williams
CFO: Judy Gross
CIO: Tammy Bilitzky

BOOK

Chief Revenue Offr: Jeff Wood
CTO & Dir, Res: Mike Gross
Natl Sales Dir: Brian Trombley
Sales Dir, Publg: Amber Watson
Founded: 1981
Membership(s): American Institute of Architects (AIA); Association for Enterprise Integration (AFEI/CALS); Association of American Publishers (AAP); Graphic Communications Association (GCA); Society for Scholarly Publishing (SSP)

Data Index Inc
13713 NW Indian Springs Dr, Vancouver, WA 98685
Tel: 425-760-9193
Web Site: www.dataindex.com
Key Personnel
Pres: John Oglesby *E-mail:* joglesby@dataindex.com
Gen Mgr: Michelle Dufour
Founded: 1985
Turnaround: Quote specific for pressure sensitive labels; 1 Workday for ISBN or UPC digital files
Membership(s): American Society for Quality (ASQ)

Datacolor
5 Princess Rd, Lawrenceville, NJ 08648
Tel: 609-924-2189 *Toll Free Tel:* 800-982-6496 (support) *Fax:* 609-895-7414
E-mail: marketing@datacolor.com
Web Site: www.datacolor.com
Key Personnel
Sr Mktg Mgr: Patricia Shenk *E-mail:* pshenk@datacolor.com
Founded: 1970

Delmas Typesetting Inc
461 Hilldale Dr, Ann Arbor, MI 48105
Tel: 734-662-8899
E-mail: delmastype@comcast.net
Web Site: www.delmastype.com
Key Personnel
Pres: William Kalvin
Founded: 1979

Desktop Miracles Inc
112 S Main St, Suite 294, Stowe, VT 05672
Tel: 802-253-7900 *Toll Free Fax:* 888-293-2676
E-mail: info@desktopmiracles.com
Web Site: www.desktopmiracles.com
Key Personnel
Pres & CEO: Barry T Kerrigan *E-mail:* barry@desktopmiracles.com
VP: Virginia Kerrigan *E-mail:* virginia@desktopmiracles.com
Founded: 1994
Turnaround: 10-15 Workdays

diacriTech Inc
4 S Market St, 4th fl, Boston, MA 02109
Tel: 617-600-3366 *Fax:* 617-848-2938
Web Site: www.diacritech.com
Key Personnel
EVP: Madhu Rajamani *E-mail:* madhu@diacritech.com
Dir, Prodn & Edit Servs: Maureen Ross *E-mail:* m.ross@diacritech.com
Founded: 1997

Didona Design
160 Grandview Rd, Ardmore, PA 19003
Tel: 610-649-3110
E-mail: didona@didonadesign.com
Web Site: www.didonadesign.com
Key Personnel
Pres: Lawrence R Didona
Mktg Mgr: Cathy Didona
Founded: 2000

MANUFACTURING

PREPRESS SERVICES

dix! Digital Prepress Inc
8462 Wayfarer Dr, Cicero, NY 13039
Tel: 315-288-5888 *Fax:* 315-288-5898
E-mail: info@dixtype.com
Web Site: www.dixtype.com
Key Personnel
Pres: Scott Wenger *E-mail:* swenger@dixtype.com
Acct Exec, Sales & Mktg: Kelly Farley
  E-mail: kfarley@dixtype.com
Founded: 1923

DNP America LLC
Subsidiary of Dai Nippon Printing Co Ltd
335 Madison Ave, 3rd fl, New York, NY 10017
Tel: 212-503-1060
E-mail: gps@dnp-g.com
Web Site: www.dnpamerica.com
Key Personnel
VP & Gen Mgr: Norikatsu Nakamura
Founded: 1976
Turnaround: 30-60 Workdays
Branch Office(s)
2099 Gateway Place, Suite 490, San Jose, CA 95110 *Tel:* 408-735-8880
3858 Carson St, Suite 300, Torrance, CA 90503 *Tel:* 310-540-5123

RR Donnelley
35 W Wacker Dr, Chicago, IL 60601
Toll Free Tel: 800-742-4455
Web Site: www.rrd.com
Key Personnel
Pres & CEO: Daniel L Knotts
Pres, Busn Servs: John Pecaric
Pres, Mktg Solutions: Doug Ryan
EVP & CFO: Terry D Peterson
EVP & CIO: Ken O'Brien
EVP & Chief HR Offr: Sheila Rutt
EVP & Chief Strategy & Transformation Offr: Elif Sagsen-Ercel
EVP, Gen Coun, Chief Compliance Offr & Corp Secy: Deborah Steiner
EVP, Dom Opers & Chief Supply Chain Offr: Glynn Perry
SVP & Chief Acctg Offr: Michael J Sharp
Founded: 1864
Turnaround: 3-6 Weeks
Branch Office(s)
955 Gateway Center Way, San Diego, CA 92102 *Tel:* 619-527-4600
40610 County Center Dr, Temecula, CA 92591 *Tel:* 951-296-2890
151 Red Stone Rd, Manchester, CT 06042 *Tel:* 860-649-5570
9125 Bachman Rd, Orlando, FL 32824 *Tel:* 407-859-2030
5800 Peachtree Rd, Atlanta, GA 30341 *Tel:* 770-458-6351
825 Riverside Pkwy, Suite 300, Austell, GA 30168 *Tel:* 770-948-1330
1750 Wallace Ave, St Charles, IL 60174 *Tel:* 630-313-7000
609 S Kirk Rd, St Charles, IL 60174 *Tel:* 630-762-7600
One Poplar Ave, Thurmont, MD 21788 *Tel:* 301-271-7171
65 Sprague St, Hyde Park, MA 02136 *Tel:* 617-360-2000
18780 W 78 St, Chanhassen, MN 55317 *Tel:* 952-937-9764
5500 12 Ave E, Shakopee, MN 55379 *Tel:* 952-941-7546
6305 Sunset Corporate Dr, Las Vegas, NV 89120 *Tel:* 702-949-8500
5 Henderson Dr, West Caldwell, NJ 07006 *Tel:* 973-882-7000
12301 Vance Davis Dr, Charlotte, NC 28269 *Tel:* 704-949-3568
One Litho Way, Durham, NC 27703 *Tel:* 919-596-3660
3801 Gantz Rd, Grove City, OH 43123 *Tel:* 614-539-5527
700 Nestle Way, Suite 200, Breinigsville, PA 18031 *Tel:* 610-391-3900
9985 Gantry Rd, Philadelphia, PA 19115 *Tel:* 215-671-9500
218 N Braddock Ave, Pittsburgh, PA 15208 *Tel:* 412-241-8200
1210 Key Rd, Columbia, SC 29201 *Tel:* 803-799-9550
1645 W Sam Houston Pkwy N, Houston, TX 77043 *Tel:* 713-468-7175
1550 Lakeway Dr, Suite 600, Lewisville, TX 75057 *Tel:* 972-353-7500
630 W 1000 N, Logan, UT 84321 *Tel:* 435-755-4000
201 E Progress Dr, West Bend, WI 53095 *Tel:* 262-338-6101
Membership(s): Association of American Publishers (AAP); Book Industry Study Group (BISG); Book Manufacturers' Institute (BMI)

W R Draper Co
Division of The Arthur Press (1978) Ltd
162 Norfinch Dr, Toronto, ON M3N 1X6, Canada
Tel: 416-663-6001 *Fax:* 416-663-6043
E-mail: info@arthurpress.com
Web Site: www.arthurpress.com
Key Personnel
Pres: Jeremy Thorn
Founded: 1954
Turnaround: 10 Workdays

Dual Graphics
370 Cliffwood Park, Brea, CA 92821
Tel: 714-990-3700 *Fax:* 714-990-6818
Web Site: www.dualgraphics.com
Key Personnel
Pres & CEO: Jim Joyce
Cont: Jamie Bengard
VP, Opers: Tom Dupuis
Sales Mgr: Craig Evans
Founded: 1906

East Mountain Editing Services
PO Box 1895, Tijeras, NM 87059-1895
Tel: 505-281-8422
Web Site: www.spanishindexing.com
Key Personnel
Mgr: Francine Cronshaw *E-mail:* cronshaw@nmia.com
Founded: 1992
Turnaround: 9 Workdays
Membership(s): American Society for Indexing (ASI)

Edison Lithograph & Printing Corp
3725 Tonnelle Ave, North Bergen, NJ 07047-2421
Tel: 201-902-9191 *Fax:* 201-902-0475
E-mail: info@edisonlitho.com
Web Site: www.edisonlitho.com
Key Personnel
COO: Joseph Ostreicher
Founded: 1958

Emprint®
5425 Florida Blvd, Baton Rouge, LA 70806
Tel: 225-923-2550 *Toll Free Tel:* 800-211-8335
Web Site: emprint.com
Key Personnel
CEO: Mr Courtney Westbrook
Pres & COO: Becky Vance *E-mail:* beckyv@emprint.com
Turnaround: 5 Workdays
Branch Office(s)
109 Research Dr, Harahan, LA 70123 *Tel:* 504-733-9654 *Toll Free Tel:* 877-568-1555 *Fax:* 504-733-8506
151 Southpark Rd, Suite 100, Lafayette, LA 70508 *Tel:* 337-839-9761 *Toll Free Tel:* 888-874-9761
2830 Breard St, Monroe, LA 71201 *Tel:* 318-387-1725 *Toll Free Tel:* 800-256-2559

Fairfield Marketing Group Inc
Subsidiary of FMG Inc
830 Sport Hill Rd, Easton, CT 06112-1241
E-mail: info@fairfieldmarketing.com
Key Personnel
Pres & CEO: Edward P Washchilla, Jr
  E-mail: ed@fairfieldmarketing.com
Founded: 1986
Turnaround: 5-10 Workdays
Membership(s): American Booksellers Association (ABA); Bridgeport Regional Business Council (BRBC); Education Market Association; United States Chamber of Commerce (USCC)

FCI Digital
Subsidiary of Four Colour Print Group
2032 S Alex Rd, Suite A, West Carrollton, OH 45449
Tel: 937-859-9701
Web Site: www.fcidigital.com
Key Personnel
Gen Mgr: Steve Orf *E-mail:* steveo@fcidigital.com
Founded: 1989
Turnaround: 2 Workdays

Ferry Associates Inc
49 Fostertown Rd, Medford, NJ 08055
Tel: 609-953-1233 *Toll Free Tel:* 800-257-5258 *Fax:* 609-953-8637
Web Site: www.ferryassociates.com
Key Personnel
Pres: Kevin Ferry *E-mail:* kferry@ferryassociates.com
Founded: 1982
Turnaround: Standard 2 week delivery

The Font Bureau Inc
Affiliate of Type Network
151 Beach Rd, Vineyard Haven, MA 02568
E-mail: info@fontbureau.com
Web Site: fontbureau.typenetwork.com
Key Personnel
Founder: David Berlow; Roger Black
Gen Mgr: Sam Berlow
Founded: 1989
Turnaround: 1 Workday

Leanne Franson
4 Poplar Ave, Martensville, SK S0K 2T0, Canada
Mailing Address: PO Box 1327, Martensville, SK S0K 2T0, Canada
Tel: 514-432-4170
E-mail: leanne@leannefranson.com
Web Site: www.leannefranson.com
Founded: 1991
Turnaround: 3-7+ Workdays
Membership(s): Picture Book Artists Association (PBAA)

Frederic Printing
Subsidiary of RR Donnelley
14701 E 38 Ave, Aurora, CO 80011-1215
Tel: 303-371-7990 *Fax:* 303-371-7959
Web Site: www.fredericprinting.com
Key Personnel
Pres: Kurt Hamlin *Tel:* 303-418-6208
Founded: 1878

Fry Communications Inc
800 W Church Rd, Mechanicsburg, PA 17055
Tel: 717-766-0211 *Toll Free Tel:* 800-334-1429 *Fax:* 717-691-0341
E-mail: info@frycomm.com
Web Site: www.frycomm.com
Key Personnel
Chmn of the Bd: Henry Fry
CEO: Mike Lukas
CFO: Chris Wawrzyniak

PREPRESS SERVICES

CTO: David S Fry
VP, Sales: Kevin Quinn
Founded: 1934
Turnaround: 7-12 Workdays

G & H Soho Inc
413 Market St, Elmwood Park, NJ 07407
Tel: 201-216-9400 *Fax:* 201-216-1778
E-mail: print@ghsoho.com
Web Site: www.ghsoho.com
Key Personnel
Pres: Gerry Burstein
Prodn Mgr: Jason Burstein
Founded: 1985
Turnaround: 3-40 Workdays
Membership(s): Association of Graphic Communications; Digital Printing Council; PRINTING United Alliance

GEX Inc
80 Conley's Grove Rd, Derry, NH 03038
Mailing Address: PO Box 613, Atkinson, NH 03811
Tel: 603-870-9292
Web Site: www.gexinc.com
Key Personnel
Pres: Gary Russell *E-mail:* gary.russell@gexinc.com
VP: Jim LaPierre
Founded: 1986

GHP
475 Heffernan Dr, West Haven, CT 06516
Tel: 203-479-7500 *Fax:* 203-479-7575
Web Site: www.ghpmedia.com
Key Personnel
CEO: John Robinson *E-mail:* john.robinson@ghpmedia.com
Partner: Fred Hoxsie *E-mail:* fred.hoxsie@ghpmedia.com
VP, Sales: Steve Bortner *E-mail:* steve.bortner@ghpmedia.com
Founded: 1991
Turnaround: 2-3 Workdays

GLS Companies
1280 Energy Park Dr, St Paul, MN 55108-5106
Tel: 651-644-3000 *Toll Free Tel:* 800-655-9405
Web Site: www.glsmn.com
Key Personnel
Chmn: Gary Garner
CFO: Scott Richardson
CTO: Frank Powell
VP, Opers: Steve Kirk
VP, Sales: Todd Matuska
Mktg Dir: Jim Benedict *E-mail:* jim.benedict@glsmn.com
Founded: 1947
Branch Office(s)
6845 Winnetka Circle, Brooklyn Park, MN 55428-1537 *Tel:* 763-535-7277 *Toll Free Tel:* 888-646-7277

Celia Godkin
Mod 6, Comp 12, 10 James St, Frankville, ON K0E 1H0, Canada
Tel: 613-275-7204
E-mail: celia@godkin.ca
Web Site: www.celiagodkin.com
Founded: 1983
Membership(s): The Botanical Artists of Canada; Canadian Society of Children's Authors Illustrators & Performers (CANSCAIP); The Writers' Union of Canada

Goose River Press
3400 Friendship Rd, Waldoboro, ME 04572-6337
Tel: 207-832-6665
E-mail: gooseriverpress@gmail.com
Web Site: gooseriverpress.com

Key Personnel
Owner & Ed: Deborah J Benner
Founded: 1999
Turnaround: 20-40 Workdays
Membership(s): Maine Writers & Publishers Alliance (MWPA); Waldoboro Business Association

Graphic World Inc, see GW Inc

GraphiColor Corp
Division of Allegra Princeton
3490 N Mill Rd, Vineland, NJ 08360
Tel: 856-691-2507 *Toll Free Tel:* 800-552-2507 *Fax:* 856-696-3229
Web Site: www.graphicolorcorp.com
Key Personnel
Pres: Robert W Stenger, Jr *Tel:* 856-691-2507 ext 111 *E-mail:* bob@graphicolorcorp.com
Founded: 1919

Graphics Two
819 S Main St, Burbank, CA 91506
Tel: 818-841-4922
Key Personnel
Owner: Bert Johnson *E-mail:* cabert@aol.com; Jeanne Vlazny
Founded: 1973

GW Inc
2290 Ball Dr, St Louis, MO 63146
Tel: 314-567-9854
E-mail: media@gwinc.com
Web Site: www.gwinc.com
Key Personnel
CEO: Kevin Arrow
EVP: Andy Vosburgh
VP, Content Opers: Suzanne Kastner
Branch Office(s)
GW Tech Pvt Ltd, D-152, Mohali Bypass Rd, Phase 8, Sector 73, Chandigarh 140 308, India *Tel:* (0172) 415 1335

Molly Hall
4338 Mitchell St, Philadelphia, PA 19128
Tel: 215-970-1837
E-mail: mollyhallindexer@hotmail.com
Founded: 1995
Turnaround: 5 Workdays

HBP Inc
952 Frederick St, Hagerstown, MD 21740
Tel: 301-733-2000 *Toll Free Tel:* 800-638-3508 *Fax:* 301-733-6586
E-mail: contactus@hbp.com
Web Site: www.hbp.com
Key Personnel
Owner & Pres: John Snyder
VP, Busn Devt & Mktg: Ilene Lerner *Tel:* 703-289-9038 *E-mail:* ilerner@hbp.com
Founded: 1903
Turnaround: 4-7 Workdays
Sales Office(s): 2818 Fallfax Dr, Falls Church, VA 22042 *Tel:* 703-289-9000
Membership(s): CUA; Printing & Graphics Association MidAtlantic (PGAMA); Printing Industries of Virginia (PIVA); PRINTING United Alliance

Heidelberg Graphics
2 Stansbury Ct, Chico, CA 95928
SAN: 211-5654
Tel: 530-342-6582 *Fax:* 530-342-6582
E-mail: heidelberggraphics@gmail.com; service@heidelberggraphics.com
Web Site: www.heidelberggraphics.com
Key Personnel
Owner & Pres: Larry S Jackson
Founded: 1972
Turnaround: 15-30 Workdays

Hennegan Co
Division of RR Donnelley
7455 Empire Dr, Florence, KY 41042
Tel: 859-282-3600 *Fax:* 859-282-3601
Founded: 1885

Herr's Indexing Service
76-340 Kealoha St, Kailua Kona, HI 96740-2915
Tel: 808-365-4348
Web Site: www.herrsindexing.com
Key Personnel
Owner: Linda Herr Hallinger
 E-mail: lindahallinger@gmail.com
Founded: 1944
Membership(s): American Society for Indexing (ASI); Editorial Freelancers Association (EFA)

Worth Higgins & Associates Inc
8770 Park Central Dr, Richmond, VA 23227-1146
Tel: 804-264-2304 *Toll Free Tel:* 800-883-7768 *Fax:* 804-264-5733
E-mail: contact@whaprint.com
Web Site: www.worthhiggins.com
Key Personnel
CEO: Rick La Reau
Pres & COO: Benny Bowman *E-mail:* b.bowman@whaprint.com
VP, Sales: Brian Losch *E-mail:* blosch@whaprint.com
Dir, Corp Communs: Scott Hudson *E-mail:* shudson@whaprint.com
Founded: 1970

The P A Hutchison Co
400 Penn Ave, Mayfield, PA 18433
SAN: 991-5559
Tel: 570-876-4560 *Toll Free Tel:* 800-USA-PRNT (872-7768) *Fax:* 570-876-4561
E-mail: sales@pahutch.com
Web Site: www.pahutch.com
Key Personnel
Pres & CEO: Chris Hutchison
Dir, Sales & Admin: Erin Jones
Founded: 1911
Turnaround: 3-20 Workdays

Imago
110 W 40 St, New York, NY 10018
Tel: 212-921-4411 *Fax:* 212-921-8226
E-mail: sales@imagousa.com
Web Site: www.imagousa.com
Key Personnel
Pres & CEO: Howard Musk *E-mail:* howardm@imagogroup.com
Founded: 1985
Turnaround: 5-10 Workdays for color separations; 4-6 Weeks for printing & binding
Branch Office(s)
Imago West Coast, 23412 Moulton Pkwy, Suite 250, Laguna Hills, CA 92653 (sales), Contact: Tammy Simms *Tel:* 949-367-1635 *Fax:* 949-367-1639
Imago Australia, 10 Help St, Suite 27, Level 6, Chatswood, NSW 2067, Australia (sales) *Tel:* (04) 3753 3351 (cell); (04) 4806 8704 (cell) *E-mail:* sales@imagaoaus.com
Imago Brazil, Domiciano Rossi, 340 unid 154, 09726-121 Sao Bernardo do Campo, Brazil (sales) *Tel:* (011) 2306 8546; (011) 2306 8547 *E-mail:* imagobra@gmail.com
Imago Shenzhen, Rm 2511-2512, Block A, United Plaza No 5022, Bin He Rd, Fu Tian Centre District, Shenzhen 518033, China (prodn), Contact: Kendrick Cheung *Tel:* (0755) 8304 8899 *Fax:* (0755) 8251 4073 *E-mail:* enquiries@imago.com.hk
Imago France, 23 rue Lavoisier, 75008 Paris, France (sales) *Tel:* 01 45 26 47 74 *Fax:* 01 78 94 14 44 *E-mail:* sales@imagogroup.com
Imago Services (HK) Ltd, Unit B309, 1/F, New East Sun Industrial Bldg, 18 Shing Yip St, Kwun Tong, Hong Kong (prodn),

MANUFACTURING

Contact: Kendrick Cheung *Tel:* 2811 3316
E-mail: enquiries@imago.com.hk
Imago Productions (Malaysia) Pte Ltd, No 43, Taman Emas, Jl Utama 31, Telok Panglima Garang, 42500 Kuala Langot, Selangor, Malaysia (prodn, incorporating South Africa sales) *Tel:* (017) 4288771 (cell)
E-mail: enquiries@imago.com.sg
Imago Publishing, Albury Ct, Albury Thame, Oxon OX9 2LP, United Kingdom (sales), Dir: Simon Rosenheim *Tel:* (01844) 337000 *Fax:* (01844) 339935 *E-mail:* sales@imago.co.uk *Web Site:* imagogroup.com

Infinity Graphics
2277 Science Pkwy, Suite 5, Okemos, MI 48864
Tel: 517-349-4635 *Toll Free Tel:* 800-292-2633 *Fax:* 517-349-7608
E-mail: barcode@infinitygraphics.com
Web Site: www.infinitygraphics.com
Key Personnel
Owner & Partner: Brian Perry
Owner, Partner & Bar Code Specialist: Suzette Perry
Founded: 1972
Turnaround: Same day for bar codes, 1-2 weeks book design, 4-6 weeks books
Membership(s): Independent Book Publishers Association (IBPA)

Innodata Inc
55 Challenger Rd, Suite 202, Ridgefield Park, NJ 07660
Tel: 201-371-8000 *Toll Free Tel:* 877-454-8400
E-mail: info@innodata.com; marketing@innodata.com
Web Site: innodata.com
Key Personnel
Pres & CEO: Jack S Abuhoff
EVP & COO: Ashok Kumar Mishra
SVP & Gen Coun: Amy Agress
SVP, Prod Innovation: R Douglas Kemp
Founded: 1988
Turnaround: As little as 12 hours
Membership(s): The Association for Work Process Improvement; Association of American Publishers Professional & Scholarly Publishing Division; Center for Information Development & Content Management Strategies (CIDM); International Association of Outsourcing Professionals (IAOP); National Federation of Abstracting and Information Services (NFAIS); Society for Technical Communication (STC); Society of Knowledge Based Publishers (SKBP); Software & Information Industry Association (SIIA)

Innovative Design & Graphics
1327 Greenleaf St, Evanston, IL 60202
Tel: 847-475-7772 *Fax:* 847-475-7784
E-mail: info@idgevanston.com
Web Site: www.idgevanston.com
Key Personnel
Owner: Tim Sonder *E-mail:* tim@idgevanston.com
Founded: 1981
Membership(s): Chicago Creative Coalition; Promotional Products Association International (PPAI)

International Press Publication Inc
Spadina Rd, Richmond Hill, ON L4B 3C5, Canada
Tel: 905-883-0343
E-mail: sales@ippbooks.com
Web Site: www.ippbooks.com; www.facebook.com/ippbooks; x.com/ippbooks2
Key Personnel
Pres: Bali Sethi

Founded: 1976
Membership(s): The American Library Association (ALA); Children's Literature Association (ChLA); Ontario Library Association

Interstate Printing Co
2002 N 16 St, Omaha, NE 68110
Tel: 402-341-8028 *Toll Free Tel:* 800-788-4177
Web Site: www.interstateprinting.com
Founded: 1917
Turnaround: 7 Workdays

Ironmark
9040 Junction Dr, Annapolis Junction, MD 20701
Toll Free Tel: 888-775-3737
E-mail: marketing@ironmarkusa.com
Web Site: ironmarkusa.com
Key Personnel
CEO: Scott Hargest *E-mail:* scott@ironmarkusa.com; Jeff Ostenso *E-mail:* jeff@ironmarkusa.com
Pres: Matt Marzullo *E-mail:* mmarzullo@ironmarkusa.com
SVP, Sales: Scott Kravitz *E-mail:* skravitz@ironmarkusa.com
VP, Opers: Chris Marzullo *E-mail:* cmarzullo@ironmarkusa.com
Sr Sales Exec: Larry Davis *E-mail:* ldavis@ironmarkusa.com
Founded: 1955
Turnaround: 20 Workdays, case bound; 10 Workdays, paperback; 15 Workdays, mechanically bound

Itzhack Shelomi Design
25 Cushman Rd, Scarsdale, NY 10583
Tel: 212-689-7469
E-mail: studio@ishelomi.com; studio@serifes.com
Web Site: www.ishelomi.com
Key Personnel
Owner & Creative Dir: Itzhack Shelomi
Founded: 1987

Jenkins Group Inc
1129 Woodmere Ave, Suite B, Traverse City, MI 49686
Tel: 231-933-0445; 213-883-5365
E-mail: info@jenkinsgroupinc.com
Web Site: www.jenkinsgroupinc.com
Key Personnel
CEO: Jerrold R Jenkins *Tel:* 231-933-0445 ext 1008 *E-mail:* jrj@jenkinsgroupinc.com
Pres & COO: James Kalajian *Tel:* 231-933-0445 ext 1006 *E-mail:* jjk@jenkinsgroupinc.com
Ed, Independent Publisher Online: Jim Barnes *E-mail:* editor@independentpublisher.com
Book Prodn Mgr: Leah Nicholson *Tel:* 231-933-0445 ext 1015 *E-mail:* lnicholson@jenkinsgroupinc.com
Founded: 1989

JP Graphics Inc
3001 E Venture Dr, Appleton, WI 54911
Tel: 920-733-4483 *Fax:* 920-733-1700
E-mail: support@jpinc.com
Web Site: www.jpinc.com; www.print.jpinc.com
Key Personnel
Pres: Rod Stoffel
Sales Mgr: Randy Hearley
Founded: 1969

Kachergis Book Design Inc
575 Stone Wall Rd, Pittsboro, NC 27312
Tel: 919-656-7632
E-mail: goodbooks@kachergisbookdesign.com
Web Site: www.kachergisbookdesign.com
Key Personnel
Pres: Anne Kachergis
Founded: 1980

PREPRESS SERVICES

Kappa Graphics LLP
Division of Kappa Printing Management Associates LLC (KPMA)
50 Rock St, Hughestown, PA 18640
Tel: 570-655-9681 *Toll Free Tel:* 800-236-4396 (sales)
E-mail: weborders@kappapma.com
Web Site: www.kappapma.com/kappagraphics; kappapuzzles.com
Key Personnel
CEO: Nick Karabots
Pres: Thomas Simunek
Founded: 1906

Knepper Press Corp
2251 Sweeney Dr, Clinton, PA 15026
Tel: 724-899-4200 *Fax:* 724-899-1331
Web Site: www.knepperpress.com
Key Personnel
Chmn: Ted Ford *E-mail:* tedford@knepperpress.com
CFO: Jerry Sales *E-mail:* jerry.sales@knepperpress.com
Cont: Dawn Bates *E-mail:* dawn.bates@knepperpress.com
Pres: Bob Hreha *E-mail:* bobhreha@knepperpress.com
Founded: 1873
Turnaround: 10-20 Workdays

Lachina Creative
Formerly Lachina Precision Graphics Services
3693 Green Rd, Cleveland, OH 44122
Tel: 216-292-7959
E-mail: info@lachina.com
Web Site: www.lachina.com
Key Personnel
Pres: Jeff Lachina *E-mail:* jlachina@lachina.com
Dir, Prodn Servs: Whitney Philipp *E-mail:* wphilipp@lachina.com
Dir, Proj Mgmt Off: Shawn Vazinski *E-mail:* svazinski@lachina.com
Founded: 1978

Lachina Precision Graphics Services, see Lachina Creative

Lake Book Manufacturing Inc
2085 N Cornell Ave, Melrose Park, IL 60160
Tel: 708-345-7000
E-mail: info@lakebook.com
Web Site: www.lakebook.com
Key Personnel
Pres & COO: Dan Genovese
VP, Fin & CFO: Bob Flatow
VP & Gen Mgr: Bill Richards
VP, Mfg: Steve Quagliato
VP, Opers: Bill Flavin
VP, Sales & Mktg: Nick Vergoth
VP, Technol: Paul Genovese

The Lane Press Inc
87 Meadowland Dr, South Burlington, VT 05403
Mailing Address: PO Box 130, Burlington, VT 05402
Tel: 802-863-5555 *Toll Free Tel:* 877-300-5933 *Fax:* 802-264-1485
E-mail: sales@lanepress.com
Web Site: www.lanepress.com
Key Personnel
Edit Dir: Beth Renaud
Founded: 1904

Larson Texts Inc
1762 Norcross Rd, Erie, PA 16510
Tel: 814-824-6365 *Toll Free Tel:* 800-530-2355 *Fax:* 814-824-6377
Web Site: www.larsontexts.com
Key Personnel
CEO: Matt Totske
IT Mgr: Kathleen Williams

PREPRESS SERVICES

Leo Paper USA
Division of Leo Paper Group
1180 NW Maple St, Suite 102, Issaquah, WA 98027
Tel: 425-646-8801 *Fax:* 425-646-8805
E-mail: info@leousa.com
Web Site: www.leopaper.com
Key Personnel
Pres: Behzad Pakzad
Founded: 1982
Turnaround: 30-40 Workdays
Branch Office(s)
286 Fifth Ave, 6th fl, New York, NY 10001, Contact: John DiMasi *Tel:* 917-305-0708 *Fax:* 917-305-0709 *E-mail:* info@leousanewyork.com

The Lexington Press Inc
15 Meriam St, Lexington, MA 02420
Mailing Address: PO Box 51, Lexington, MA 02420-0001
Tel: 781-862-8900 *Fax:* 781-861-0375
Web Site: www.lexingtonpress.com
Key Personnel
Pres: Robert F Sacco *E-mail:* bob@lexingtonpress.com
Founded: 1955

Linguistic Systems Inc (LSI)
260 Franklin St, Suite 230, Boston, MA 02110
Tel: 617-528-7400
E-mail: clientservice@linguist.com
Web Site: www.linguist.com
Key Personnel
Founder & Pres: Martin Roberts
Founded: 1967
Membership(s): American Translators Association (ATA); Association of Language Companies (ALC); Globalization & Localization Association (GALA)

Lowe Graphics & Printing
Division of E T Lowe Publishing Co
220 Great Circle Rd, Suite 122, Nashville, TN 37228
Tel: 615-242-6649 *Fax:* 615-254-8867
Web Site: www.etlowe.com
Key Personnel
Pres: Albert E Ambrose, Jr *E-mail:* albert@etlowe.com
VP, Prodn: Charles Sutherland *E-mail:* charles@etlowe.com
Founded: 1906

Lumina Datamatics Inc
600 Cordwainer Dr, Unit 103, Norwell, MA 02061
Tel: 508-746-0300 *Fax:* 508-746-3233
E-mail: marketing@luminad.com
Web Site: luminadatamatics.com
Key Personnel
EVP, Busn Devt: Jack Mitchell
EVP, Solutions, Transitions & US Opers: Sandeep Dhawan
Founded: 2005
Branch Office(s)
c/o Arnecke Sibeth Distribution, Rechtsanwaelte Steuerberater Partnerschaftsgesellschaft mdB, Gueterplatz 1, 60327 Frankfurt am Main, Germany *Tel:* (06155) 862 99-0 *Fax:* (06155) 862 99-19
Ascendas International Tech Park, 12th fl, Phase II (Crest), CSIR Rd, Taramani, Chennai 600 113, India *Tel:* (044) 4017 6000; (044) 4017 6001
Santosh Raj Plaza, 1st fl, Subburaman St, Gandhi Nagar, 12/9, St, Shenoy Nagar, Madurai 625 020, India

Andheri (E), Unit 117-120, SDF - IV, SEEPZ - SEZ, Mumbai 400 096, India *Tel:* (022) 4034 0515; (022) 4034 0508 *Fax:* (022) 2829 1673
Off No 47/1, 7th fl, Tower-B, A-41, Corrrenthum Tower, Sector-62, Noida 201 301, India
Plot No 29-34, East Coast Rd, Saram Revenue Village, Oulgaret Municipality, Lawspet Post, Puducherry 605 008, India *Tel:* (0413) 226 4500
No 10, Vazhudavoor Rd, Pettaiyanchathiram, Thattanchavadi, Puducherry 605 009, India *Tel:* (0413) 401 1635
Apple One Equicom Tower, 11th fl, Mindanao Ave Corner Biliran St, Central (pob), Cebu Business Park, 6000 Cebu City, Cebu, Philippines
c/o SOPHI Outsourcing Inc, G/F DBPI IT Plaza, Calindagan, 6200 Dumaguete City, Negros Oriental, Philippines
Brixham Laboratory, Brixham, Devon TQ5 8BA, United Kingdom
Lumina Datamatics UK Ltd, 153 Milton Keynes Business Ctr, Linford Wood, Milton Keynes MK14 6GD, United Kingdom

Mandel Graphic Solution
727 W Glendale Ave, Suite 100, Milwaukee, WI 53209
Tel: 414-271-6970 *Fax:* 414-386-4660
E-mail: info@mandelcompany.com
Web Site: www.mandelcompany.com
Key Personnel
Pres: Rick Mandel *E-mail:* rick.mandel@mandelcompany.com
Founded: 1892

Maracle Inc
1156 King St E, Oshawa, ON L1H 1H8, Canada
Tel: 905-723-3438 *Toll Free Tel:* 800-558-8604
Fax: 905-723-1759
E-mail: hello@maracleinc.com
Web Site: www.maracleinc.com
Key Personnel
Pres: George Sittlinger *Tel:* 905-723-3438 ext 236
Dir, Opers: Nadene D Aldred
Sales & Busn Devt Mgr: Brian Ostrander *Tel:* 905-723-3438 ext 272
E-mail: bostrander@maracleinc.com
Founded: 1920
Turnaround: 10 Workdays
Membership(s): Book Manufacturers' Institute (BMI); Canadian Book Manufacturer Association; Canadian Society of Association Executives (CSAE); Ontario Printing & Imaging Association; PRINTING United Alliance

MBA Computer Service
1920 Lookout Dr, North Mankato, MN 56003
Tel: 507-625-3797
Key Personnel
Pres: DeMar Borth *E-mail:* demar@abdobooks.com

McClain Printing Co
212 Main St, Parsons, WV 26287-1033
Mailing Address: PO Box 403, Parsons, WV 26287-0403
Tel: 304-478-2881 *Toll Free Tel:* 800-654-7179
Fax: 304-478-4658
E-mail: mcclain@mcclainprinting.com
Web Site: www.mcclainprinting.com
Key Personnel
Pres: Kenneth E Smith
VP, Publg: Michelle McKinnie
Founded: 1958
Turnaround: 90-120 Workdays

Meadows Design Office
3800 Yuma St NW, Washington, DC 20016
Tel: 202-966-6007
E-mail: mdo@mdomedia.com

Key Personnel
Pres & Creative Dir: Marc Meadows *E-mail:* marc@mdomedia.com
Curator & Image Res: Amy Meadows
Founded: 1981

Melissa Data Corp
22382 Avenida Empresa, Rancho Santa Margarita, CA 92688-2112
Tel: 949-858-3000 *Toll Free Tel:* 800-800-6245
E-mail: info@melissadata.com
Web Site: www.melissadata.com
Key Personnel
Founder & Pres: Raymond F Melissa *E-mail:* raymond@melissadata.com
Founded: 1985
Turnaround: 2 Workdays
Branch Office(s)
150 Grossman Dr, Suite 208, Braintree, MA 02184-4902
29100 SW Town Center Loop W, Suite 250, Wilsonville, OR 97070-9315

Miles 33 International LLC
Subsidiary of Miles 33 Ltd
40 Richards Ave, Norwalk, CT 06854
Tel: 203-838-2333 *Fax:* 203-838-4473
E-mail: info@miles33.com
Web Site: www.miles33.com
Key Personnel
VP, US Opers: Jeff Malik

Moran Printing Inc, see Emprint®

MPS North America LLC
Subsidiary of MPS Ltd
5728 Major Blvd, Suite 528, Orlando, FL 32819
Tel: 407-472-1280 *Toll Free Tel:* 866-978-1008
Fax: 212-981-2983
E-mail: marketing@mpslimited.com
Web Site: www.mpslimited.com
Founded: 1973
Branch Office(s)
1901 S Fourth St, Suite 222, Effingham, IL 62401
477 Madison Ave, 6th fl, New York, NY 10022
1822 E NC Hwy 54, Suite 120, Durham, NC 27713-3210
MPS Ltd, HMG Ambassador, 137 Residency Rd, Bangalore 560 025, India *Tel:* (080) 4178 4242 *Fax:* (080) 4178 4222
MPS Ltd, RR Towers, Super A, 16/17 TVK Industrial Estate, Guindy, Chennai 600 032, India *Tel:* (044) 4916 2222 *Fax:* (044) 4916 2225
MPS Ltd, 33 IT Park, Sahastradhara Rd, Dehradun 248 001, India *Tel:* (0135) 6677 954
MPS Ltd, 709 DLI Corporate Greens, Sector 74A, Narsinghpur, Gurugram 122 004, India *Tel:* (0124) 661 3134
MPS Interactive Systems, GRM Tech Bldg, 2nd fl, Plot No DH-6/29, Action Area-1, Rajarhat, New Town, Kolkata, West Bengal 700 156, India *Tel:* (033) 66111500
MPS Interactive Systems, The Great Oasis, D-13, 2nd fl, Marol Industrial Estate, Andheri (E), Mumbai 400 093, India *Tel:* (022) 6643 8100 *Fax:* (022) 6643 8800
MPS Ltd, C35, Sector 62, Noida 201 307, India (corp off) *Tel:* (0120) 4599750 *Fax:* (0120) 4021280
Membership(s): Publishing Professionals Network (PPN)

Myriddian LLC
8510 Corridor Rd, Suite 100, Savage, MD 20763
Tel: 443-285-0271 (cell)
E-mail: info@myriddian.com
Web Site: www.myriddian.com
Key Personnel
CTO: Jason Myers
Founded: 2010

MANUFACTURING

BISAC compatible software
Turnaround: 10 Workdays

NAC, see North American Color Inc

Neibauer Press
20 Industrial Dr, Warminster, PA 18974
Tel: 215-322-6200 *Fax:* 215-322-2495
E-mail: sales@neibauer.com
Web Site: www.neibauer.com
Key Personnel
VP: Ruth Neibauer-Baker *Tel:* 215-322-6216
 E-mail: ruth@neibauer.com
Founded: 1955

NETS
Division of Newgen North America Inc
2714 Bee Caves Rd, Suite 201, Austin, TX 78746-5682
Web Site: www.netype.com
Founded: 1940
Branch Office(s)
60/3 Lattice Bridge Rd, Thiruvanmiyur, Chennai, India *Tel:* (044) 4348 0800 *Fax:* (044) 2443 0740

New England Typographic Service, see NETS

Newgen North America Inc
Subsidiary of Newgen KnowledgeWorks
2714 Bee Cave Rd, Suite 201, Austin, TX 78746
Tel: 512-478-5341 *Fax:* 512-476-4756
E-mail: sales@newgen.co
Web Site: www.newgen.co
Key Personnel
Pres: Maran Elancheran *E-mail:* maran@newgen.co
EVP: Tej PS Sood *E-mail:* tej@newgen.co
Founded: 1955

Nissha USA Inc
Subsidiary of Nissha Co Ltd
1051 Perimeter Dr, Suite 600, Schaumburg, IL 60173
Tel: 847-413-2665 *Fax:* 847-413-4085
Web Site: www.nissha.com
Key Personnel
Chmn: Junya Suzuki
Dir & CEO: Hiroyuki Uenishi
Founded: 1993

North American Color Inc
5960 S Sprinkle Rd, Portage, MI 49002
Tel: 269-323-0552 *Toll Free Tel:* 800-537-8296
 Fax: 269-323-0190
E-mail: info@nac-mi.com
Web Site: www.nac-mi.com
Key Personnel
VP, Accts: Susan Blesch *E-mail:* sblesch@nac-mi.com
Opers Mgr: Tim Leto
Founded: 1981
Turnaround: 1-3 Workdays
Membership(s): Epicomm; Graphic Artists Guild; International Publishers Association (IPA); PRINTING United Alliance

North Market Street Graphics (NMSG)
Affiliate of Archetype Inc
317 N Market St, Lancaster, PA 17603
Tel: 717-392-7438
E-mail: mail@nmsgbooks.com
Web Site: www.nmsgbooks.com
Key Personnel
Owner: Elizabeth Andes; LeRoy R Stipe, Jr
VP, Sales: Lainey Wolfe
Dir, Prepress Opers: Dennis Bicksler
Prepress Mgr: Dean Brian
Founded: 1988

OEC Graphics Inc
555 W Waukau Ave, Oshkosh, WI 54902
Tel: 920-235-7770 *Fax:* 920-235-2252
Web Site: www.oecgraphics.com
Key Personnel
CEO: Jack Schloesser *E-mail:* jack.schloesser@oecgraphics.com
Pres: Jeff Schloesser *E-mail:* jeff.schloesser@oecgraphics.com
VP, Mktg & Communs: Jennifer Navin
 E-mail: jennifer.navin@oecgraphics.com
Founded: 1912
Branch Office(s)
909 S Perkins St, Appleton, WI 54914 *Tel:* 920-832-4044 *Fax:* 920-832-4080
33288 Central Ave, Union City, CA 94587
 Tel: 510-240-6970
7630 S Quincy St, Willowbrook, IL 60527
 Tel: 630-455-6700 *Fax:* 630-455-6703
Membership(s): Flexographic Technical Association (FTA)

OGM USA
4333 46 St, Suite F2, Sunnyside, NY 11104
Tel: 212-964-2430
Web Site: www.ogm.it
Key Personnel
Chmn, CEO & Sales Rep: Rino Varrasso
 E-mail: rvarrasso@ogm-usa.com
Founded: 1974
Turnaround: 30 Workdays

O'Neil Digital Solutions LLC
12655 Beatrice St, Los Angeles, CA 90066
Tel: 310-448-6400
E-mail: sales@oneildata.com
Web Site: www.oneildata.com
Key Personnel
Pres & COO: Terry Chan
EVP, Sales & Mktg: Mark Rosson
Dir, HR: LaDonna Wise
Founded: 1973
Turnaround: 3-10 Workdays

Overseas Printing Corporation
Division of InnerWorkings Inc
4040 Civic Center Dr, Suite 200, San Rafael, CA 94903
Tel: 415-500-8331 *Fax:* 415-835-9899
Web Site: www.overseasprinting.com
Key Personnel
Sr Prodn Mgr: Shaun Garrett *E-mail:* sgarrett@inwk.com
Founded: 1972
Turnaround: 8-12 Weeks

The Ovid Bell Press Inc
Subsidiary of Walsworth Publishing Co
1201 Bluff St, Fulton, MO 65251
Mailing Address: PO Box 370, Fulton, MO 65251-0370
Tel: 573-642-2256 *Toll Free Tel:* 800-835-8919
E-mail: sales@ovidbell.com
Web Site: ovidbell.com
Key Personnel
CFO: Jill Custard *E-mail:* jillcustard@ovidbell.com
Pres: Troy Williams *Tel:* 573-310-2599
 E-mail: troywilliams@ovidbell.com
VP, Sales & Mktg: David O'Donley *Tel:* 573-310-2630 *E-mail:* david@ovidbell.com
Plant Mgr: Kevin Werdehausen *Tel:* 573-310-2598
 E-mail: kevin.werdehausen@ovidbell.com
Founded: 1927
Turnaround: 5 Workdays

Pantagraph Printing
217 W Jefferson St, Bloomington, IL 61701
Mailing Address: PO Box 1406, Bloomington, IL 61702-1406
Tel: 309-829-1071

PREPRESS SERVICES

E-mail: queries1@pantagraphprinting.com
Web Site: www.pantagraphprinting.com
Key Personnel
Pres: Mike Dolan
Founded: 1889

Paraclete Press Inc
100 Southern Eagle Cartway, Brewster, MA 02631
SAN: 282-1508
Mailing Address: PO Box 1568, Orleans, MA 02653-1568
Tel: 508-255-4685 *Toll Free Tel:* 800-451-5006
E-mail: customerservice@paracletepress.com
Web Site: www.paracletepress.com
Key Personnel
Design & Web Site Servs: Paul Tingley
 E-mail: pault@paracletepress.com
Founded: 1981
Turnaround: 5 Workdays or more
Membership(s): Association of Catholic Publishers Inc; Evangelical Christian Publishers Association (ECPA)

PCA Printing, see Printing Corporation of the Americas Inc

PIPS Inc, see Product Identification & Processing Systems Inc

POD Print
2012 E Northern St, Wichita, KS 67216
Tel: 316-522-5599 *Toll Free Tel:* 800-767-6066
E-mail: info@podprint.com
Web Site: www.podprint.com
Key Personnel
Owner: Grace Rishel; Jim Rishel
Prodn Opers Mgr: Traci Grote *E-mail:* tgrote@podprint.com
Founded: 1978
Turnaround: 1-5 days
Membership(s): Print Services & Distribution Association (PSDA); PRINTING United Alliance

PrairieView Press
625 Seventh St, Gretna, MB R0G 0V0, Canada
Mailing Address: PO Box 460, Gretna, MB R0G 0V0, Canada
Tel: 204-327-6543 *Toll Free Tel:* 800-477-7377
 Toll Free Fax: 866-480-0253
Web Site: prairieviewpress.com
Key Personnel
Owner & Pres: Chester Goossen
Founded: 1968

Printing Corporation of the Americas Inc
620 SW 12 Ave, Pompano Beach, FL 33069
Tel: 954-781-8100 *Toll Free Tel:* 866-721-1PCA (721-1722)
Web Site: pcaprintingplus.com
Key Personnel
Pres: Buddy Tuchman
Sales Mgr: Steven Konecky *E-mail:* steven@pcaprinting.com
Founded: 1980
Turnaround: 5-10 Workdays

PrintWest
1111 Eighth Ave, Regina, SK S4R 1C9, Canada
Tel: 306-525-2304 *Toll Free Tel:* 800-236-6438
 Fax: 306-757-2439
E-mail: general@printwest.com
Web Site: www.printwest.com
Key Personnel
Pres & Dir, Opers: Corie Triffo
VP, Sales & Mktg: Ken Benson
Founded: 1992
Turnaround: 15 Workdays

Pro-Composition Inc
2501 Catherine St, Suite 3, York, PA 17408

PREPRESS SERVICES

Tel: 717-965-9872
Web Site: www.pro-composition.com
Key Personnel
Pres: Jodi Brenner E-mail: jbrenner@pro-composition.com
Founded: 1979
Turnaround: 5-10 Workdays

Product Identification & Processing Systems Inc
10 Midland Ave, Suite M-02, Port Chester, NY 10573-5911
Tel: 212-996-6000 Toll Free Tel: 888-783-7439 Fax: 212-410-7477 Toll Free Fax: 800-241-PIPS (241-7477)
E-mail: info@pips.com
Web Site: www.pips.com
Key Personnel
VP: Randy Wright
Founded: 1978
BISAC compatible software
Turnaround: Same day
Branch Office(s)
8532 Sanford Dr, Richmond, VA 23228-2813 Tel: 804-264-4434 Toll Free Tel: 888-373-0028
E-mail: infova@pips.com
Membership(s): Book Industry Study Group (BISG)

Progress Printing Plus
2677 Waterlick Rd, Lynchburg, VA 24502
Tel: 434-239-9213 Toll Free Tel: 800-572-7804 Fax: 434-832-7573
E-mail: info@progressprintplus.com
Web Site: www.progressprintplus.com
Key Personnel
Pres: Michael Thornton E-mail: mthornton@progressprintplus.com
Dir, Busn Devt: Gerald Bowles
E-mail: gbowles@progressprintplus.com
Prepress Coord: Clay Atkins E-mail: catkins@progressprintplus.com; David Shelton E-mail: dshelton@progressprintplus.com; Stacy Wilson E-mail: swilson@progressprintplus.com
Founded: 1962
Turnaround: 7-9 Workdays after final proof approval

Progressive Publishing Services (PPS)
555 Ryan Run Rd, Suite B, York, PA 17404
Tel: 717-764-5908 Fax: 717-764-5530
E-mail: info@pps-ace.com
Web Site: www.pps-ace.com
Key Personnel
VP: Darby Jo Campbell E-mail: dcampbell@pps-ace.com
Dir: Crystal Clifton E-mail: cclifton@pps-ace.com
Founded: 2015

Pronk Media Inc
16 Glen Davis Crescent, Toronto, ON M4E 1X5, Canada
Tel: 416-716-9660 (cell)
E-mail: info@pronk.com; hello@pronk.com
Web Site: www.pronk.com; www.h5engines.com; www.html5alive.com
Key Personnel
Pres: Gord Pronk E-mail: gord@pronk.com
Founded: 1981 (as Pronk & Associates Inc)

Publication Identification & Processing Systems
Division of Product Identification & Processing Systems Inc
10 Midland Ave, Suite M-02, Port Chester, NY 10573
Tel: 212-996-6000 Toll Free Tel: 888-783-7439 Fax: 212-410-7477 Toll Free Fax: 800-241-7477
E-mail: info@pips.com

Web Site: www.pips.com
Key Personnel
VP: George Wright, IV Tel: 212-996-6000 ext 110 E-mail: gw4@pips.com
Founded: 1978
BISAC compatible software
Turnaround: Same day
Branch Office(s)
8532 Sanford Dr, Richmond, VA 23228 Tel: 804-264-4434 Toll Free Tel: 888-373-0028
E-mail: infova@pips.com
Membership(s): Book Industry Study Group (BISG)

Publishing Data Management Inc
39 Broadway, 28th fl, New York, NY 10006
Tel: 212-673-3210 Fax: 212-673-3390
E-mail: info@pubdata.com
Web Site: www.pubdata.com
Key Personnel
Pres: Addison Roverano E-mail: addison@pubdata.com
Founded: 1970
Turnaround: 1 hour-3 Workdays

Reno Typographers
1020 S Rock Blvd, Suite C, Reno, NV 89502
Tel: 775-852-8800
E-mail: info@renotype.com; work@renotype.com
Web Site: www.renotype.com
Key Personnel
Owner & Pres: Kurt Hoge
Founded: 1979

The Renton Printery Inc
315 S Third St, Renton, WA 98057-2028
Tel: 425-235-1776
E-mail: info@rentonprintery.com
Web Site: www.rentonprintery.com
Key Personnel
Pres & CEO: Richard Sweeney
Founded: 1959

Ross Gage Inc
8502 Brookville Rd, Indianapolis, IN 46239
Tel: 317-283-2323 Toll Free Tel: 800-799-2323 Fax: 317-931-2108
E-mail: info@rossgage.com
Web Site: www.rossgage.com
Key Personnel
Pres: Thomas W Ross E-mail: tomross@rossgage.com
VP: Bill Main E-mail: bmain@rossgage.com
Opers Coord/Cust Serv: Carol Eads E-mail: ceads@rossgage.com
Founded: 1972

Schoolhouse Indexing
10-B Parade Ground Rd, Etna, NH 03750
Tel: 603-359-5826
Web Site: schoolhouseindexing.com
Key Personnel
Owner & Indexer: Christine Hoskin E-mail: christine@schoolhousefarm.net
Membership(s): American Society for Indexing (ASI)

Schroeder Indexing Services
23 Camilla Pink Ct, Bluffton, SC 29909
Tel: 843-705-9779; 843-415-3900 (cell)
E-mail: sanindex@schroederindexing.com
Web Site: www.schroederindexing.com
Key Personnel
Owner & CEO: Sandi Schroeder
Membership(s): American Society for Indexing (ASI)

Scribe Inc
765 S Front St, Philadelphia, PA 19147
Tel: 215-336-5094; 215-336-5095
E-mail: contact@scribenet.com

Web Site: www.scribenet.com
Key Personnel
Pres: David Alan Rech Tel: 215-336-5094 ext 105 E-mail: drech@scribenet.com
Founded: 1993
BISAC compatible software
Turnaround: 2 days-2 weeks
Branch Office(s)
3758 SW 30 Ave, Fort Lauderdale, FL 33312

SGS International LLC
Division of Sgsco
626 W Main St, Suite 500, Louisville, KY 40202
Tel: 502-637-5443
E-mail: info@sgsco.com
Web Site: www.sgsintl.com
Key Personnel
CEO: Piyush Chaudhari
COO: Hoyoung Pak
Chief HR Offr: Andrew Tidwell
Pres, Design & Digital: Rob McCarthy
Pres, Global Accts: Julien Tessier
VP, Gen Coun & Secy: Justin Schauer
Founded: 1946
Branch Office(s)
7435 Empire Dr, Florence, KY 41042 Tel: 859-525-1190 Fax: 859-647-8205
3449 Technology Dr, Suite 311, Nokomis, FL 34275 Tel: 941-932-2177
3045 Chastain Meadows Pkwy, Suite 200, Marietta, GA 30066 Tel: 678-354-4800
1032 W Fulton Market, Suite 100, Chicago, IL 60607 Tel: 312-575-0700
150 Corporate Dr, Elgin, IL 60123 Tel: 847-695-9515
1720 W Detweiller Dr, Peoria, IL 61615 Tel: 309-692-1530
607 Jonesboro Rd, West Monroe, LA 71292 Tel: 318-322-0518
2125 E Lincoln St, Birmingham, MI 48009 Tel: 248-594-1818
2006 Cole St, Birmingham, MI 48009 Tel: 248-594-1818
9300 Winnetka Ave N, Brooklyn Park, MN 55445 Tel: 763-488-5700
2130 Kratky Rd, St Louis, MO 63114 Tel: 314-968-6800
252 W 37 St, 8th fl, New York, NY 10018 Tel: 646-561-0100
33 E 17 St, New York, NY 10003 Tel: 212-242-8787
333 Westchester Ave, Suite W1100, White Plains, NY 10604 Tel: 914-750-4217
4322 Piedmont Pkwy, Greensboro, NC 27410 Tel: 336-369-4700
535 Wilmer Ave, Cincinnati, OH 45226 Tel: 513-321-7500
1108 Broadway St, Cincinnati, OH 45202
3091 Mayfield Rd, Suite 210, Cleveland Heights, OH 44118
2781 Roberts Ave, Philadelphia, PA 19129 Tel: 215-843-2243
1000 Cliff Mine, Suite 360, Pittsburgh, PA 15275 Tel: 412-787-1283
68 Cumberland St, Suite 200, Woonsocket, RI 02895 Tel: 401-531-2300
1101 E Arapaho Rd, Suite 220, Richardson, TX 75081 Tel: 214-565-9000
5301 Lewis Rd, Sandston, VA 23150 Tel: 804-226-2490
1518 First Ave S, Suite 601, Seattle, WA 98134 Tel: 206-305-7366
119 N McCarthy Rd, Suite A, Appleton, WI 54913 Tel: 920-996-9055
W234 N2091 Ridgeview Pkwy Ct, Suite 400, Waukesha, WI 53188 Tel: 262-549-6890
521 Nottinghill Rd, Suite 5, London, ON N6K 4L4, Canada Tel: 519-668-0520
2620 Slough St, Mississauga, ON L4T 3T2, Canada Tel: 905-405-1555
7687 Bath Rd, Mississauga, ON L4T 3T1, Canada Tel: 905-364-3200
2 Dorchester Ave, Toronto, ON M8Z 4W3, Canada Tel: 416-252-9331

MANUFACTURING

14 Dorchester Ave, Toronto, ON M8Z 4W3, Canada *Tel:* 416-622-1005
559 College St, Suite 301, Toronto, ON M6G 1A9, Canada *Tel:* 416-535-4131
18 Dorchester Ave, Toronto, ON M8Z 4W3, Canada *Tel:* 416-252-9503
6300 Avenue du Parc, Suite 300, Montreal, QC H2V 4H8, Canada *Tel:* 514-426-5608
Juan F Segui 4646, 6° piso, C1425ADF Buenos Aires, Argentina *Tel:* (0114) 776-4847
Av Brigadeiro Faria Lima, 1478 CJ 513, Jardim Paulistano, 01451-001 Sao Paulo-SP, Brazil *Tel:* (011) 3032-1260
Rua do Rocio 423, Suite 212, Vila Olimpia, Sao Paulo-SP, Brazil *Tel:* (011) 3842-8687
1055 W Zhonshan Rd 302, Bldg A, Shanghai, China
Suite 601, Bldg 7, Bridge 8, 10 Jianguo Middle Rd, Shanghai 200025, China *Tel:* (021) 6135-5960
Zhuoyue Times Plaza, Units 02-04, 14th fl, 4068 Yitian Rd, Futian CBD, Shenzhen 518048, China *Tel:* (0755) 8371-7701
Oficentro Trilogia Edificio 1, Oficina 114, Escazu San Jose, Costa Rica *Tel:* 2228-0242
49 Blvd du General Martial Valin, 75015 Paris, France *Tel:* 01 45 58 80 00
Pier F, Franziusstr 6, 60314 Frankfurt am Main, Germany *Tel:* (0160) 5396246
Ginza Plaza, Rm 2015, Level 21, 2A-2H Sai Yeung Choi St S, Mong Kok, Kowloon, Hong Kong *Tel:* 3767 9700
1st fl, Om Sadan, Mehra Estate, LBS Marg Vikhroli (West), Mumbai 400 079, India *Tel:* (022) 42008585
Allahabad Bank Bldg, 2nd fl, 98 Mecricar Rd, Puram Coimbatore, Tamil Nadu 641 002, India
10, Sangothipalayam, Arasur Coimbatore, Tamil Nadu 641 407, India *Tel:* 9003825891
Victoria House, 8e etage, St Louis St, Port Louis, Mauritius *Tel:* 211 6360
125, route Menagerie, Port Louis, Mauritius *Tel:* 230 211 90 15
Km 8 letra C Carretera Libre a Celaya, Fraccionamiento Industrial Balvanera, 76900 Corregidora, QRO, Mexico *Tel:* (01442) 245-2525
Andres Bello No 45 Piso 8, Colonia Polanco Chapultepec, 11560 Mexico, CDMX, Mexico *Tel:* (0155) 250-2121
Herengracht 598-600, 1017 CJ Amsterdam, Netherlands *Tel:* (020) 3034-589
Citynet Bldg 1, 183 Epifanio de los Santos Ave, 1555 Mandaluyong, Metro Manila, Philippines *Tel:* (02) 910-5058
59 New Bridge Rd, Singapore 059405, Singapore
34 Petain Rd, Singapore 208101, Singapore *Tel:* 6513 9689
77 Kampong Bahru Rd, No 02-01, Singapore 169376, Singapore *Tel:* 6224 2152
Carrer Laurea Miro, 153, 2°1a, 08950 Esplugues de Llobregat, Barcelona, Spain *Tel:* 934 809 841
Place Saint-Francois 2, 1003 Lausanne, Switzerland *Tel:* (021) 552 22 00
Fort Dunlop, Unit 101, Birmingham, West Midlands B24 9FD, United Kingdom *Tel:* (0121) 740-0247
Off 9, Orchid Rd, Hessle, East Riding, Yorks HU13 0DH, United Kingdom *Tel:* (01482) 225835
Brewery House, The Maltings, Silvester St, Hull HU1 3HA, United Kingdom *Tel:* (01482) 973000
Citadel Trading Park, Citadel Way, Garrison Rd, Hull HU9 1TQ, United Kingdom *Tel:* (01482) 225835
91-94 Lower Marsh, London SE1 7AB, United Kingdom *Tel:* (020) 7202 4720
Morley House, 6 Nottingham St, London W1U 5EJ, United Kingdom *Tel:* (020) 7224 0874
South Suffolk Business Ctr, Unit 9, Alexandra Rd, Sudbury CO10 2ZX, United Kingdom *Tel:* (01787) 464234
Salterbeck Trading Estate, Harrington, Workington, Cumbria CA14 5BX, United Kingdom *Tel:* (01946) 833600

Shepherd Inc
2223 Key Way Dr, Suite B, Dubuque, IA 52002
Tel: 563-584-0500
Web Site: www.shepherd-inc.com
Key Personnel
Prodn Mgr: Deb Leibfried
Founded: 1989

Signature Book Printing Inc
8041 Cessna Ave, Gaithersburg, MD 20879
Tel: 301-258-8353
E-mail: book@sbpbooks.com
Web Site: sbpbooks.com
Key Personnel
Pres: Phil Nanzetta
Off Mgr: Linda Wood
Founded: 1986

Six Red Marbles LLC
101 Station Landing, Medford, MA 02155
Tel: 857-588-9000
E-mail: info@sixredmarbles.com
Web Site: www.sixredmarbles.com
Key Personnel
CEO: David Goodman
Chief Mktg & Admin Offr: Robin Zaccardo
EVP, Busn Devt: John Kenney
EVP, Opers: Michele Baird
SVP, Fin: Meg Trant
SVP, Prodn: Alexandre Vallette
SVP, Technol: Chris Kaefer
VP, Busn Devt: Cary Drake
VP, Learning Strategy: Kelvin Bentley
Exec Dir, Humanities: Bill Scroggie
Exec Dir, STEM: Joyce Spangler
Founded: 1996
Branch Office(s)
4030 W Braker Lane, Bldg 3, Suite 350, Austin, TX 78759 *Tel:* 512-372-4800
209 Austine Dr, Suite 115, Brattleboro, VT 05301 *Tel:* 410-527-1606
Jouve India Pvt Ltd, 1st fl, No 1415, No 283/1B2, Old Mahabalipuram Rd, Kottivakkam, Chennai 600 041, India *Tel:* (044) 40205300
The Great Eastern Ctr, 2nd fl, 70, Nehru Place, Delhi 110 019, India *Tel:* (011) 42636116

Smith & Sons Printers Inc
6403 Rutledge Pike, Knoxville, TN 37924
Tel: 865-523-1419
Web Site: www.ssprintinc.com
Key Personnel
Owner: Stephen Ownby *E-mail:* stephen@ssprint.com
Founded: 1979

Smith-Edwards-Dunlap Co
2867 E Allegheny Ave, Philadelphia, PA 19134
Tel: 215-425-8800 *Toll Free Tel:* 800-829-0020 *Fax:* 215-425-9715
E-mail: sales@sed.com
Web Site: www.sed.com
Key Personnel
Pres: Jonathan Shapiro
Sales Mgr: Fred Binder
Founded: 1880

Southeastern Printing Co
3601 SE Dixie Hwy, Stuart, FL 34997
Tel: 772-287-2141 *Toll Free Tel:* 800-226-8221 *Fax:* 772-288-3988
E-mail: sales@seprint.com
Web Site: www.seprint.com

PREPRESS SERVICES

Key Personnel
Pres: Don Mader
Founded: 1924
Turnaround: 20-40 Workdays
Branch Office(s)
950 SE Eighth St, Hialeah, FL 33010 *Tel:* 305-885-8707 *Fax:* 305-888-9903 *E-mail:* info@seprint.com
Sales Office(s): 6001 Park of Commerce Blvd, Suite 200, Boca Raton, FL 33487 *Tel:* 561-998-0870

Southern Graphic Systems LLC, see SGS International LLC

Barbara Spurll Illustration
160 Browning Ave, Toronto, ON M4K 1W5, Canada
Tel: 416-594-6594 *Toll Free Tel:* 800-989-3123
Web Site: www.barbaraspurll.com
Key Personnel
Prop: Barbara Spurll *E-mail:* barbara@barbaraspurll.com
Founded: 1975
Membership(s): Canadian Association of Professional Image Creators (CAPIC); Canadian Society of Children's Authors Illustrators & Performers (CANSCAIP)

Square Two Design Inc
2325 Third St, Suite 305, San Francisco, CA 94107
Tel: 415-437-3888
E-mail: info@square2.com
Web Site: www.square2.com
Key Personnel
Pres & Creative Dir: Eddie Lee
Founded: 1991
Branch Office(s)
No 8 Hua Jia Di Nan Jie, Chao Yang District, Beijing 100102, China, Pres: Min Wang *Tel:* (01350) 1084-543 *E-mail:* mwang@square2.com

Sun Graphics LLC
1818 Broadway, Parsons, KS 67357
Toll Free Tel: 800-835-0588 *Fax:* 620-421-2089
E-mail: info@sun-graphics.com
Web Site: www.sun-graphics.com
Key Personnel
VP, Mktg: John Hammett *Tel:* 918-695-2267 *E-mail:* jhammett@sun-graphics.com
VP, Sales: John Hohenshell *Tel:* 913-257-9420 *E-mail:* jhohenshell@sun-graphics.com
Commercial Sales & Book Div Sales: Melody Morris *Tel:* 620-660-0614 *E-mail:* mmorris@sun-graphics.com
Founded: 1998
Turnaround: 15-20 Workdays
Membership(s): Independent Book Publishers Association (IBPA); Publishers Association of the West (PubWest)

John S Swift Co Inc
999 Commerce Ct, Buffalo Grove, IL 60089
Tel: 847-465-3300 *Fax:* 847-465-3309
Web Site: www.johnswiftprint.com
Key Personnel
Pres: John S Swift *E-mail:* jss@johnswiftprint.com
Founded: 1912
Turnaround: 5 Workdays
Branch Office(s)
John S Swift Print of NJ Inc, 375 North St, Unit N, Teterboro, NJ 07608, Contact: Rick Frydrych *Tel:* 201-678-3232 *Fax:* 201-378-3001 *E-mail:* rickfry@johnswiftprint.com

Swordsmith Productions
PO Box 242, Pomfret, CT 06258
Tel: 860-208-4829

PREPRESS SERVICES

E-mail: information@swordsmith.com
Web Site: www.swordsmith.com
Key Personnel
Pres: Leigh Grossman
Founded: 1994
Turnaround: 3-6 Workdays for coding & tagging; 10-15 Workdays for other editorial production

Symbology Inc
7351 Kirkwood Lane N, Suite 126, Maple Grove, MN 55369
Tel: 763-315-8080 Toll Free Tel: 800-328-2612
  Fax: 763-315-8088
E-mail: clientservices@symbology.com; sales@symbology.com
Web Site: www.symbology.com
Key Personnel
Pres: Jeff Gossen E-mail: jgossen@symbology.com
VP, Sales & Mktg: John Gorowsky
  E-mail: jgorowsky@symbology.com
Founded: 1980
Membership(s): The American Library Association (ALA)

Symmetry Creative Production
1300 S Grove Ave, Suite 103, Barrington, IL 60010
Tel: 847-382-8750
E-mail: information@symmetrycp.com
Web Site: www.symmetrycp.com
Key Personnel
Owner & Partner: Roger Tillander Tel: 847-382-7530
Owner & Exec Dir, Edit: Mary Beth Gasiorowski Tel: 847-382-7550
Owner & Prodn: John F Deady Tel: 847-382-7577
Dir, Art, Design & Photog: Beth Morrison Tel: 847-382-7540
Acct Exec: Mike Tambellini Tel: 847-382-7610
Founded: 2002

Taylor Specialty Books, see Balfour Commercial Printing

Texas Graphic Resource Inc
1234 Round Table Dr, Dallas, TX 75247
Tel: 214-630-2800 Fax: 214-630-0713
E-mail: info@texasgraphics.com
Web Site: www.texasgraphics.com
Founded: 1907

Thistle Printing Ltd
Division of DATA Communications Management Corp
35 Mobile Dr, Toronto, ON M4A 2P6, Canada
Tel: 416-288-1288 Fax: 416-288-0737
E-mail: sales@thistleprinting.com
Web Site: www.thistleprinting.com
Key Personnel
Gen Mgr: Mike Branov
Founded: 1931

Times Citizen Communication Inc
Division of Spokesman Press
406 Stevens St, Iowa Falls, IA 50126
Tel: 641-648-2521 Toll Free Tel: 800-798-2691
  Fax: 641-648-4765
E-mail: tcc@iafalls.com
Web Site: timescitizen.com
Key Personnel
Dir, Local Media: Tony Baranowski
Founded: 1974

Times Printing LLC
Division of Kappa Printing Management Associates LLC (KPMA)
100 Industrial Dr, Random Lake, WI 53075
Tel: 920-994-4396 Toll Free Tel: 800-236-4396 (sales)

E-mail: info@kappapma.com
Web Site: www.kappapma.com
Founded: 1918
Turnaround: 5-10 Workdays

Toof American Digital
4222 Pilot Dr, Memphis, TN 38118
Tel: 901-274-3632 Toll Free Tel: 800-722-4772
Web Site: www.toofamericandigital.com
Key Personnel
Pres: Stillman McFadden
Founded: 1864
Turnaround: 80 Workdays

TotalWorks™ Inc
420 W Huron St, Chicago, IL 60654
Tel: 773-489-4313
E-mail: production@totalworks.net
Web Site: www.totalworks.net
Key Personnel
Principal, Pres & CEO: Gail Ludewig
Principal & EVP: Bruce Jensen
VP, Sales & Mktg: Louise Pauly
Founded: 1927
Turnaround: 2 Workdays
Membership(s): Women's Business Enterprise Network (WBENC)

Townsend Communications Inc
20 E Gregory Blvd, Kansas City, MO 64114
Tel: 816-361-0616
Web Site: www.townsendcommunications.com; www.townsendprint.com
Key Personnel
Pres: Guy Townsend, III
VP: Joe Chambers
Founded: 1964

Tukaiz LLC
2917 N Latoria Lane, Franklin Park, IL 60131
Tel: 847-455-1588; 847-288-4968 (sales)
  Toll Free Tel: 800-543-2674
E-mail: contacttukaiz@tukaiz.com
Web Site: www.tukaiz.com
Key Personnel
Founder & Mng Dir: Frank Defino, Sr
VP, Mng Dir & CFO: Christopher Calabra
VP & Mng Dir: Daniel Defino; Frank Defino, Jr
Founded: 1963

Universal|Wilde
26 Dartmouth St, Westwood, MA 02090
Tel: 781-251-2700 Fax: 781-251-2613
Web Site: www.universalwilde.com
Key Personnel
Pres & CEO: Stephen Flood
COO: Christopher Armstrong
CFO: Joe Musanti
VP, HR: Jennifer MacAskill
VP, Sales: Jim Bailey
Mktg Mgr: Ryan Collins
Founded: 1958
Branch Office(s)
403 VFW Dr, Rockland, MA 02370 Tel: 781-871-7744 Fax: 781-878-2967
48 Third Ave, Somerville, MA 02143 Tel: 617-591-3000 Fax: 617-591-3091

Versa Press Inc
1465 Spring Bay Rd, East Peoria, IL 61611-9788
Tel: 309-822-8272 Toll Free Tel: 800-447-7829
  Fax: 309-822-8141
Web Site: www.versapress.com
Key Personnel
Chmn: Joseph F Kennell
Pres: Steven J Kennell
Sales Mgr: Matthew Kennell E-mail: mkennell@versapress.com
Founded: 1937

Turnaround: 20 Workdays
Membership(s): Book Manufacturers' Institute (BMI)

ViaTech Publishing Solutions Inc
11935 N Stemmons Fwy, Dallas, TX 75234
Tel: 214-827-8151
E-mail: marketing@viatechpub.com
Web Site: www.viatech.io
Key Personnel
CEO: Michael Bertuch
VP, Global Sales: Tom Bergenholtz
Founded: 1928
Turnaround: 5-20 Workdays
Branch Office(s)
8857 Alexander Rd, Batavia, NY 14020
5668 E 61 St, Commerce, CA 90040
5021 Old Dixie Rd, Forest Park, GA 30297
Kingston Business Park, Kingston Bagpuize, Abingdon, Oxon OX13 5FE, United Kingdom Tel: (01865) 822170
Membership(s): Book Manufacturers' Institute (BMI)

Viridiam LLC
3030 Lowell Dr, Green Bay, WI 54311
Tel: 920-465-3030 Toll Free Tel: 800-829-6555
Web Site: www.viridiam.com
Key Personnel
VP, Sales: Rob Butler
Founded: 1888
Turnaround: 15 Workdays
Membership(s): Book Manufacturers' Institute (BMI)

Walsworth
306 N Kansas Ave, Marceline, MO 64658
Toll Free Tel: 800-265-6795
Web Site: www.walsworth.com; www.walsworthhistorybooks.com
Key Personnel
CEO: Don O Walsworth
COO: Jim Mead
Pres: Don Walsworth, Jr
VP, Mktg & Communs: Kristin Mateski
  E-mail: kristin.mateski@walsworth.com
Founded: 1937
Branch Office(s)
803 S Missouri Ave, Marceline, MO 64658 (printing & bindery facility)
Donning Co Publishers, 731 S Brunswick St, Brookfield, MO 64628 Tel: 660-675-5570 Web Site: www.donning.com
The Ovid Bell Press, 1201 Bluff St, Fulton, MO 65251-0370 Toll Free Tel: 800-835-8919 Web Site: www.ovidbell.com
7300 W 110 St, Suite 600, Overland Park, KS 66210 (sales & mktg)
2180 Maiden Lane, St Joseph, MI 49085 (printing & bindery facility)
656 S Douglas St, Ripon, WI 54971 (printing & bindery facility)

Fred Weidner & Daughter Printers
99 Hudson St, 5th fl, New York, NY 10013
Tel: 646-706-5180
E-mail: info@fwdprinters.com
Web Site: www.fwdprinters.com
Key Personnel
Pres: Cynthia Weidner E-mail: cynthia@fwdprinters.com
Creative Dir: Carol Mittelsdorf E-mail: carol@fwdprinters.com
Founded: 1860
Turnaround: 5-10 Workdays

WeMakeBooks.ca
Division of Heidy Lawrance Associates
238 Willowdale Ave, North York, ON M2N 4Z5, Canada
Tel: 416-733-1827 Fax: 416-733-7663
Web Site: www.wemakebooks.ca

MANUFACTURING

Key Personnel
Owner: Heidy Lawrance *E-mail:* heidy@wemakebooks.ca
Founded: 1988

Westchester Publishing Services
4 Old Newtown Rd, Danbury, CT 06810
Tel: 203-791-0080 *Fax:* 203-791-9286
E-mail: info@westchesterpubsvcs.com
Web Site: www.westchesterpublishingservices.com
Key Personnel
Founder & Chmn: Dennis Pistone
Pres & CEO: Paul J Crecca *E-mail:* paul.crecca@westchesterpubsvcs.com
Chief Revenue Offr: Tyler M Carey *Tel:* 203-658-6581 *E-mail:* tyler.carey@westchesterpubsvcs.com
Dir, Edit Servs: Susan Baker *Tel:* 203-791-0080 ext 103 *E-mail:* susan.baker@westchesterpubsvcs.com
Dir, Opers: Terry Colosimo *E-mail:* terry.colosimo@westchesterpubsvcs.com
Dir, Technol: Michael Jon Jensen
  E-mail: michael.jensen@westchesterpubsvcs.com
Busn Devt Mgr: Tim Cross *E-mail:* tim.cross@westchesterpubsvcs.com
Key Accts Mgr: William Foley *Tel:* 203-791-0080 ext 104 *E-mail:* bill.foley@westchesterpubsvcs.com
Prodn Mgr, Journals Servs: Celeste Bilyard *E-mail:* celeste.bilyard@westchesterpubsvcs.com
Founded: 1969
Turnaround: 5 Workdays

Whitehall Printing Co
4244 Corporate Sq, Naples, FL 34104
Tel: 239-643-6464 *Toll Free Tel:* 800-321-9290
  Fax: 239-643-6439
E-mail: info@whitehallprinting.com
Web Site: www.whitehallprinting.com
Key Personnel
Chmn: Mike Hirsch
Pres: Jeff Hirsch
VP: Emil G Hirsch
Founded: 1959
Turnaround: 10-15 Business days

Widen Enterprises Inc
6911 Mangrove Lane, Madison, WI 53713
Tel: 608-222-1296 *Toll Free Tel:* 800-444-2828
E-mail: marketing@widen.com
Web Site: www.widen.com
Key Personnel
CEO: Matthew Gonnering
CFO: Michael Kiesler
VP, Cust Devt: Brian Becker
VP, Mktg & Cust Experience: Jake Athey
VP, Prod Mgmt: Deanna Ballew
Dir, Creative & Brand Strategy: Nina Brakel-Schutt
Dir, Premedia Opers: Debby Leisner
Founded: 1948
Branch Office(s)
Aldgate Tower, 2 Leman St, London E1 8FA, United Kingdom *Tel:* (020) 3890 6777

B Williams & Associates, see BW&A Books Inc

Windhaven®
466 Rte 10, Orford, NH 03777
Tel: 603-512-9251 (cell)
E-mail: info@windhavenpress.com
Web Site: www.windhavenpress.com
Key Personnel
Dir & Ed: Nancy C Hanger *E-mail:* nhanger@windhavenpress.com
Ed & Consultant: Andrew V Phillips
  E-mail: andrew@windhavenpress.com
Founded: 1985
Turnaround: 3-5 days book design; 5-7 days typesetting; 7-14 days proofing; 2-4 weeks full production
Membership(s): Editorial Freelancers Association (EFA); National Writers Union (NWU)

WordCo Indexing Services Inc
66 Franklin St, Norwich, CT 06360
E-mail: office@wordco.com
Web Site: www.wordco.com
Key Personnel
Founder & CEO: Stephen Ingle *E-mail:* sringle@wordco.com
Proj Coord: Amy Moriarty *E-mail:* amoriarty@wordco.com
Founded: 1988

PREPRESS SERVICES

Turnaround: 5-15 Workdays
Membership(s): American Society for Indexing (ASI)

Worzalla
3535 Jefferson St, Stevens Point, WI 54481
Tel: 715-344-9608 *Fax:* 715-344-2578
Web Site: www.worzalla.com
Key Personnel
Chmn of the Bd: Charles Nason
Pres: James Fetherston
VP, Fin: Samuel Crockett
VP, Opers: Brian McManus
VP, Sales & Chief Mktg Offr: Richard Letchinger
Cust Serv Mgr: Kim Deuel
Field Sales: Rodger Beyer
Founded: 1892
Turnaround: 20 Workdays
Sales Office(s): 4819 W Berteau Ave, Chicago, IL 60641, Contact: Tim Taylor *Tel:* 773-383-7892 *E-mail:* ttaylor@worzalla.com
2231 Morris Ave, Suite 3, Union, NJ 07083, Contact: Edmund Corvelli, III *Tel:* 201-749-7995 *E-mail:* ecorvelli@worzalla.com
222 W 37 St, 10th fl, New York, NY 10018, Contact: Sam Gallucci *Tel:* 201-851-3292 *E-mail:* sgallucci@worzalla.com
Membership(s): Book Manufacturers' Institute (BMI)

Writer's Relief, Inc
18766 John J Williams Hwy, Unit 4, Box 335, Rehoboth Beach, DE 19971
Toll Free Tel: 866-405-3003 *Fax:* 201-641-1253
E-mail: info@writersrelief.com
Web Site: www.WritersRelief.com
Key Personnel
Pres: Ronnie L Smith *E-mail:* ronnie@wrelief.com

X-Height Studio
83 High St, Milford, MA 01757
Tel: 508-478-3897 *Toll Free Tel:* 888-474-8973
E-mail: info@x-heightstudio.com
Web Site: www.x-heightstudio.com
Key Personnel
Founder & Owner: Cecile Kaufman
Founded: 1999
Membership(s): Editorial Freelancers Association (EFA); Graphic Artists Guild

Printing, Binding & Book Finishing Index

ADHESIVE BINDING - HARD

AcmeBinding, pg 1247
Adams Press, pg 1247
American Mathematical Society (AMS), pg 1247
Arbor Books, pg 1248
Berryville Graphics, pg 1248
Bookmasters, pg 1249
BookMobile, pg 1249
Bookshelf Bindery Ltd, pg 1249
BR Printers, pg 1249
Bridgeport National Bindery Inc, pg 1249
Cenveo St Louis, pg 1250
CG Book Printers, pg 1250
Color House Graphics Inc, pg 1250
Corporate Disk Co, pg 1251
Cushing-Malloy Inc, pg 1251
Data Reproductions Corp, pg 1251
DeHART's Media Services Inc, pg 1251
Dekker Bookbinding Inc, pg 1251
DNP America LLC, pg 1252
RR Donnelley, pg 1252
W R Draper Co, pg 1252
Eckhart & Company Inc, pg 1253
Four Colour Print Group, pg 1253
Friesens Corp, pg 1253
G & H Soho Inc, pg 1253
Goose River Press, pg 1254
Gorham Printing, pg 1254
HF Group LLC, pg 1254
Imago, pg 1254
Impressions Inc, pg 1255
Ironmark, pg 1255
Lake Book Manufacturing Inc, pg 1255
Leo Paper USA, pg 1256
Long's Roullet Bookbinders Inc, pg 1256
Maple Press, pg 1256
Marquis Book Printing Inc, pg 1256
Marrakech Express Inc, pg 1256
McClain Printing Co, pg 1257
OGM USA, pg 1257
Overseas Printing Corporation, pg 1257
Publishers Book Bindery (NY), pg 1258
Publishers' Graphics LLC, pg 1258
Reindl Bindery Co Inc, pg 1259
Roswell Bookbinding, pg 1259
Sheridan GR, pg 1259
Sheridan MI, pg 1259
Sheridan Saline, pg 1260
Southeastern Printing Co, pg 1260
Spectrum PrintGroup Inc, pg 1260
Sun Graphics LLC, pg 1260
Total Printing Systems, pg 1261
Turtleback Books, pg 1261
Universal Bookbindery Inc, pg 1261
VeronaLibri, pg 1261
Versa Press Inc, pg 1261
VIP Digital Print Center, pg 1262
Wallaceburg Bookbinding & Mfg Co Ltd, pg 1262
Walsworth, pg 1262
Webcom Inc, pg 1262
Fred Weidner & Daughter Printers, pg 1262
Wert Bookbinding Inc, pg 1262
Whitehall Printing Co, pg 1262
Worzalla, pg 1262

ADHESIVE BINDING - SOFT

AcmeBinding, pg 1247
Action Printing, pg 1247
Adair Graphic Communications, pg 1247
Adams Press, pg 1247
AGS, pg 1247
American Mathematical Society (AMS), pg 1247
an ICON Company LLC, pg 1247
Arbor Books, pg 1248
B & Z Printing Inc, pg 1248
Bang Printing Co Inc, pg 1248
Beidel Printing House Inc, pg 1248
Berryville Graphics, pg 1248
Bethany Press International Inc, pg 1248
Bindagraphics Inc, pg 1248
The Bindery Inc, pg 1249
Blitzprint Inc, pg 1249
Bookmasters, pg 1249
BookMobile, pg 1249
Bookshelf Bindery Ltd, pg 1249
BR Printers, pg 1249
Bridgeport National Bindery Inc, pg 1249
The Bureau, pg 1249
C & C Offset Printing Co USA Inc, pg 1249
Cenveo St Louis, pg 1250
CG Book Printers, pg 1250
Coach House Printing, pg 1250
Color House Graphics Inc, pg 1250
ColorPage, pg 1250
Copycats, pg 1251
Corporate Disk Co, pg 1251
The Country Press Inc, pg 1251
Crane Duplicating Service Inc, pg 1251
Cushing-Malloy Inc, pg 1251
Data Reproductions Corp, pg 1251
DeHART's Media Services Inc, pg 1251
Dekker Bookbinding Inc, pg 1251
DNP America LLC, pg 1252
Docunet Corp, pg 1252
RR Donnelley, pg 1252
W R Draper Co, pg 1252
Dunn & Co Inc, pg 1252
Eckhart & Company Inc, pg 1253
Emprint®, pg 1253
Fenway Group, pg 1253
First Choice Copy, pg 1253
Four Colour Print Group, pg 1253
Friesens Corp, pg 1253
Fry Communications Inc, pg 1253
G & H Soho Inc, pg 1253
Goose River Press, pg 1254
Gorham Printing, pg 1254
Great Lakes Bindery Inc, pg 1254
Hess Print Solutions, pg 1254
Imago, pg 1254
Impressions Inc, pg 1255
Infinity Graphics, pg 1255
Ironmark, pg 1255
Knepper Press Corp, pg 1255
Lake Book Manufacturing Inc, pg 1255
Leo Paper USA, pg 1256
Letterhead Press Inc (LPI), pg 1256
Maple Press, pg 1256
Maracle Inc, pg 1256
Marquis Book Printing Inc, pg 1256
Marrakech Express Inc, pg 1256
Martin Printing Co Inc, pg 1257
McClain Printing Co, pg 1257
Nissha USA Inc, pg 1257
Noble Book Press Corp, pg 1257
OGM USA, pg 1257
OneTouchPoint, pg 1257
Overseas Printing Corporation, pg 1257
Patterson Printing Co, pg 1258
POD Print, pg 1258
Print It Plus, pg 1258
The Printer, pg 1258
Printing Corporation of the Americas Inc, pg 1258
Publishers Book Bindery (NY), pg 1258
Puritan Press Inc, pg 1258
Quantum Group, pg 1259
Reindl Bindery Co Inc, pg 1259
Roswell Bookbinding, pg 1259
Sheridan GR, pg 1259
Sheridan MI, pg 1259
Sheridan PA, pg 1259
Sheridan Saline, pg 1260
Signature Book Printing Inc, pg 1260
Southeastern Printing Co, pg 1260
Spectrum PrintGroup Inc, pg 1260
Sun Graphics LLC, pg 1260
John S Swift Co Inc, pg 1260
Toof American Digital, pg 1261
Total Printing Systems, pg 1261
Universal Bookbindery Inc, pg 1261
VeronaLibri, pg 1261
Versa Press Inc, pg 1261
Vicks Lithograph & Printing Corp, pg 1262
VIP Digital Print Center, pg 1262
Walsworth, pg 1262
Webcom Inc, pg 1262
Fred Weidner & Daughter Printers, pg 1262
Whitehall Printing Co, pg 1262
Worzalla, pg 1262

BOOK PRINTING - HARDBOUND

AcmeBinding, pg 1247
Adams Press, pg 1247
AGS, pg 1247
American Mathematical Society (AMS), pg 1247
appatura™, A Broadridge Company, pg 1248
Arbor Books, pg 1248
Asia Pacific Offset Inc, pg 1248
Balfour Commercial Printing, pg 1248
Beidel Printing House Inc, pg 1248
Berryville Graphics, pg 1248
Bethany Press International Inc, pg 1248
Blue Note Publications Inc, pg 1249
BookBaby, pg 1249
BookFactory, pg 1249
Bookmasters, pg 1249
BookMobile, pg 1249
BR Printers, pg 1249
Bridgeport National Bindery Inc, pg 1249
C & C Offset Printing Co USA Inc, pg 1249
Cenveo St Louis, pg 1250
CG Book Printers, pg 1250
CJK, pg 1250
Clare Printing, pg 1250
Coach House Printing, pg 1250
Codra Enterprises Inc, pg 1250
Color House Graphics Inc, pg 1250
ColorPage, pg 1250
Corporate Disk Co, pg 1251
Cushing-Malloy Inc, pg 1251
Data Reproductions Corp, pg 1251
DeHART's Media Services Inc, pg 1251
Dekker Bookbinding Inc, pg 1251
DNP America LLC, pg 1252
RR Donnelley, pg 1252
Four Colour Print Group, pg 1253
Friesens Corp, pg 1253
G & H Soho Inc, pg 1253
GHP, pg 1253
Global Interprint Inc, pg 1253
Goose River Press, pg 1254
Gorham Printing, pg 1254
Graphic Litho, pg 1254
Heidelberg Graphics, pg 1254
Imago, pg 1254
Infinity Graphics, pg 1255
Ironmark, pg 1255
La Crosse Graphics Inc, pg 1255
Lake Book Manufacturing Inc, pg 1255
Leo Paper USA, pg 1256
Lightning Source LLC, pg 1256
Maple Press, pg 1256
Marquis Book Printing Inc, pg 1256
Marrakech Express Inc, pg 1256
McClain Printing Co, pg 1257
Morris Printing Group Inc, pg 1257
Morris Publishing®, pg 1257
Nissha USA Inc, pg 1257
Noble Book Press Corp, pg 1257
OGM USA, pg 1257
Outskirts Press Inc, pg 1257
Overseas Printing Corporation, pg 1257
Printing Corporation of the Americas Inc, pg 1258
Progress Printing Plus, pg 1258
Publishers Book Bindery (NY), pg 1258
Puritan Press Inc, pg 1258
Scientific Bindery Inc, pg 1259
Sheridan GR, pg 1259
Sheridan MI, pg 1259
Sheridan Saline, pg 1260
Signature Book Printing Inc, pg 1260
Smith & Sons Printers Inc, pg 1260
Southeastern Printing Co, pg 1260
Spectrum PrintGroup Inc, pg 1260
Sun Graphics LLC, pg 1260
Taylor Communications Inc, pg 1261
Toof American Digital, pg 1261
Total Printing Systems, pg 1261
VeronaLibri, pg 1261
Versa Press Inc, pg 1261
Walsworth, pg 1262
Webcrafters Inc, pg 1262
Fred Weidner & Daughter Printers, pg 1262
Whitehall Printing Co, pg 1262
Worzalla, pg 1262

PRINTING, BINDING & BOOK FINISHING INDEX

BOOK PRINTING - MASS MARKET

Action Printing, pg 1247
Adams Press, pg 1247
Arbor Books, pg 1248
Asia Pacific Offset Inc, pg 1248
Berryville Graphics, pg 1248
Bethany Press International Inc, pg 1248
Blue Note Publications Inc, pg 1249
Bookmasters, pg 1249
BR Printers, pg 1249
C & C Offset Printing Co USA Inc, pg 1249
CG Book Printers, pg 1250
Codra Enterprises Inc, pg 1250
Color House Graphics Inc, pg 1250
Corporate Disk Co, pg 1251
Cushing-Malloy Inc, pg 1251
Data Reproductions Corp, pg 1251
Dekker Bookbinding Inc, pg 1251
DNP America LLC, pg 1252
G & H Soho Inc, pg 1253
Graphic Litho, pg 1254
Infinity Graphics, pg 1255
Lake Book Manufacturing Inc, pg 1255
Leo Paper USA, pg 1256
Marquis Book Printing Inc, pg 1256
Marrakech Express Inc, pg 1256
McClain Printing Co, pg 1257
Morris Publishing®, pg 1257
Printing Corporation of the Americas Inc, pg 1258
Sheridan GR, pg 1259
Signature Book Printing Inc, pg 1260
John S Swift Co Inc, pg 1260
Total Printing Systems, pg 1261
Townsend Communications Inc, pg 1261
Webcom Inc, pg 1262
Fred Weidner & Daughter Printers, pg 1262
Whitehall Printing Co, pg 1262
Worzalla, pg 1262

BOOK PRINTING - PROFESSIONAL

AcmeBinding, pg 1247
Action Printing, pg 1247
Adair Graphic Communications, pg 1247
Adams Press, pg 1247
AGS, pg 1247
an ICON Company LLC, pg 1247
appatura™, A Broadridge Company, pg 1248
Arbor Books, pg 1248
Asia Pacific Offset Inc, pg 1248
Berryville Graphics, pg 1248
Blitzprint Inc, pg 1249
BookFactory, pg 1249
Bookmasters, pg 1249
BookMobile, pg 1249
BR Printers, pg 1249
Cenveo St Louis, pg 1250
CG Book Printers, pg 1250
CJK, pg 1250
Codra Enterprises Inc, pg 1250
Color House Graphics Inc, pg 1250
Corporate Disk Co, pg 1251
Cushing-Malloy Inc, pg 1251
Data Reproductions Corp, pg 1251
DeHART's Media Services Inc, pg 1251
Dekker Bookbinding Inc, pg 1251
DNP America LLC, pg 1252
RR Donnelley, pg 1252
W R Draper Co, pg 1252
Dunn & Co Inc, pg 1252
Fenway Group, pg 1253
Four Colour Print Group, pg 1253
Friesens Corp, pg 1253
G & H Soho Inc, pg 1253
GHP, pg 1253
Goose River Press, pg 1254
Gorham Printing, pg 1254
Graphic Litho, pg 1254
Heidelberg Graphics, pg 1254
Hignell Book Printing Ltd, pg 1254
Imago, pg 1254
Infinity Graphics, pg 1255
Ironmark, pg 1255
Lake Book Manufacturing Inc, pg 1255
Maple Press, pg 1256
Maracle Inc, pg 1256
Marquis Book Printing Inc, pg 1256
Marrakech Express Inc, pg 1256
McClain Printing Co, pg 1257
Morris Publishing®, pg 1257
O'Neil Digital Solutions LLC, pg 1257
OneTouchPoint, pg 1257
Outskirts Press Inc, pg 1257
Patterson Printing Co, pg 1258
POD Print, pg 1258
Printing Corporation of the Americas Inc, pg 1258
Puritan Press Inc, pg 1258
V G Reed & Sons Inc, pg 1259
Sheridan GR, pg 1259
Sheridan MI, pg 1259
Sheridan Saline, pg 1260
Signature Book Printing Inc, pg 1260
Southeastern Printing Co, pg 1260
Spectrum PrintGroup Inc, pg 1260
Sun Graphics LLC, pg 1260
John S Swift Co Inc, pg 1260
Thistle Printing Ltd, pg 1261
Times Printing LLC, pg 1261
Total Printing Systems, pg 1261
Townsend Communications Inc, pg 1261
Tribal Print Source, pg 1261
VeronaLibri, pg 1261
Vicks Lithograph & Printing Corp, pg 1262
VIP Digital Print Center, pg 1262
Walsworth, pg 1262
Webcom Inc, pg 1262
Fred Weidner & Daughter Printers, pg 1262
Whitehall Printing Co, pg 1262
Worzalla, pg 1262

BOOK PRINTING - SOFTBOUND

AcmeBinding, pg 1247
Action Printing, pg 1247
Adair Graphic Communications, pg 1247
Adams Press, pg 1247
AGS, pg 1247
American Mathematical Society (AMS), pg 1247
an ICON Company LLC, pg 1247
appatura™, A Broadridge Company, pg 1248
Arbor Books, pg 1248
Asia Pacific Offset Inc, pg 1248
B & Z Printing Inc, pg 1248
Bang Printing Co Inc, pg 1248
Beidel Printing House Inc, pg 1248
Berryville Graphics, pg 1248
Bethany Press International Inc, pg 1248
Blitzprint Inc, pg 1249
Blue Note Publications Inc, pg 1249
BookBaby, pg 1249
BookFactory, pg 1249
Bookmasters, pg 1249
BookMobile, pg 1249
BR Printers, pg 1249
Bridgeport National Bindery Inc, pg 1249
C & C Offset Printing Co USA Inc, pg 1249
Canterbury Press, pg 1250
Cenveo St Louis, pg 1250
CG Book Printers, pg 1250
CJK, pg 1250
Clare Printing, pg 1250
Coach House Printing, pg 1250
Codra Enterprises Inc, pg 1250
Color House Graphics Inc, pg 1250
ColorPage, pg 1250
Consolidated Printers Inc, pg 1251
Cookbook Publishers Inc, pg 1251
Copycats, pg 1251
Corporate Disk Co, pg 1251
The Country Press Inc, pg 1251
Crane Duplicating Service Inc, pg 1251
Cushing-Malloy Inc, pg 1251
Data Reproductions Corp, pg 1251
DeHART's Media Services Inc, pg 1251
Dekker Bookbinding Inc, pg 1251
Diversified Printing Services Inc, pg 1252
DNP America LLC, pg 1252
Docunet Corp, pg 1252
RR Donnelley, pg 1252
W R Draper Co, pg 1252
Dunn & Co Inc, pg 1252
Emprint®, pg 1253
Fenway Group, pg 1253
Friesens Corp, pg 1253
Fry Communications Inc, pg 1253
G & H Soho Inc, pg 1253
GHP, pg 1253
Global Interprint Inc, pg 1253
GLS Companies, pg 1254
Goose River Press, pg 1254
Gorham Printing, pg 1254
Graphic Litho, pg 1254
Heidelberg Graphics, pg 1254
Hess Print Solutions, pg 1254
Worth Higgins & Associates Inc, pg 1254
The P A Hutchison Co, pg 1254
Imago, pg 1254
InfinitPrint Solutions Inc, pg 1255
Infinity Graphics, pg 1255
Ironmark, pg 1255
Kappa Graphics LLP, pg 1255
Knepper Press Corp, pg 1255
La Crosse Graphics Inc, pg 1255
Lake Book Manufacturing Inc, pg 1255
Leo Paper USA, pg 1256
Lightning Source LLC, pg 1256
Maple Press, pg 1256
Maracle Inc, pg 1256
Marquis Book Printing Inc, pg 1256
Marrakech Express Inc, pg 1256
McClain Printing Co, pg 1257
Morris Publishing®, pg 1257
Nissha USA Inc, pg 1257
Noble Book Press Corp, pg 1257
OGM USA, pg 1257
O'Neil Digital Solutions LLC, pg 1257
OneTouchPoint, pg 1257
Outskirts Press Inc, pg 1257
Overseas Printing Corporation, pg 1257
Panaprint Inc, pg 1258
Patterson Printing Co, pg 1258
POD Print, pg 1258
Print It Plus, pg 1258
The Printer, pg 1258
Printing Corporation of the Americas Inc, pg 1258
Progress Printing Plus, pg 1258
Puritan Press Inc, pg 1258
V G Reed & Sons Inc, pg 1259
RISO Inc, pg 1259
Scientific Bindery Inc, pg 1259
Sheridan GR, pg 1259
Sheridan MI, pg 1259
Sheridan Saline, pg 1260
Signature Book Printing Inc, pg 1260
Smith & Sons Printers Inc, pg 1260
Southeastern Printing Co, pg 1260
Spectrum PrintGroup Inc, pg 1260
Stephenson Printing, pg 1260
Sterling Pierce Co Inc, pg 1260
Sun Graphics LLC, pg 1260
John S Swift Co Inc, pg 1260
Taylor Communications Inc, pg 1261
Times Printing LLC, pg 1261
Toof American Digital, pg 1261
Total Printing Systems, pg 1261
Townsend Communications Inc, pg 1261
Tribal Print Source, pg 1261
VeronaLibri, pg 1261
Versa Press Inc, pg 1261
Vicks Lithograph & Printing Corp, pg 1262
VIP Digital Print Center, pg 1262
Walsworth, pg 1262
Webcom Inc, pg 1262
Webcrafters Inc, pg 1262
Fred Weidner & Daughter Printers, pg 1262
Whitehall Printing Co, pg 1262
Worzalla, pg 1262
Yurchak Printing Inc, pg 1262

BOUND GALLEYS

AcmeBinding, pg 1247
AGS, pg 1247
American Mathematical Society (AMS), pg 1247
Arbor Books, pg 1248
Asia Pacific Offset Inc, pg 1248
Beidel Printing House Inc, pg 1248
Berryville Graphics, pg 1248
Bethany Press International Inc, pg 1248
Blitzprint Inc, pg 1249
Bookmasters, pg 1249
BookMobile, pg 1249
BR Printers, pg 1249
Bridgeport National Bindery Inc, pg 1249
CG Book Printers, pg 1250
Color House Graphics Inc, pg 1250
ColorPage, pg 1250
Copycats, pg 1251
The Country Press Inc, pg 1251
Crane Duplicating Service Inc, pg 1251
DeHART's Media Services Inc, pg 1251
Dekker Bookbinding Inc, pg 1251
RR Donnelley, pg 1252
W R Draper Co, pg 1252
Dunn & Co Inc, pg 1252
Fry Communications Inc, pg 1253
G & H Soho Inc, pg 1253
Goose River Press, pg 1254
Infinity Graphics, pg 1255
Leo Paper USA, pg 1256
Lightning Source LLC, pg 1256
Outskirts Press Inc, pg 1257
Roswell Bookbinding, pg 1259
Sterling Pierce Co Inc, pg 1260
Sun Graphics LLC, pg 1260
John S Swift Co Inc, pg 1260
Total Printing Systems, pg 1261

MANUFACTURING

PRINTING, BINDING & BOOK FINISHING INDEX

Fred Weidner & Daughter Printers, pg 1262
Whitehall Printing Co, pg 1262
Yurchak Printing Inc, pg 1262

BURST BINDING

Adams Press, pg 1247
Arbor Books, pg 1248
Asia Pacific Offset Inc, pg 1248
Berryville Graphics, pg 1248
The Bureau, pg 1249
Cenveo St Louis, pg 1250
Dekker Bookbinding Inc, pg 1251
Dunn & Co Inc, pg 1252
Friesens Corp, pg 1253
Fry Communications Inc, pg 1253
Lake Book Manufacturing Inc, pg 1255
Maple Press, pg 1256
Roswell Bookbinding, pg 1259
Sheridan MI, pg 1259
Specialty Finishing Group, pg 1260
Walsworth, pg 1262
Webcom Inc, pg 1262
Fred Weidner & Daughter Printers, pg 1262
Worzalla, pg 1262

CALENDAR PRINTING

Action Printing, pg 1247
Ambassador Press Inc, pg 1247
Arbor Books, pg 1248
Asia Pacific Offset Inc, pg 1248
Bang Printing Co Inc, pg 1248
Beidel Printing House Inc, pg 1248
Birmingham Printing & Publishing Inc, pg 1249
BR Printers, pg 1249
C & C Offset Printing Co USA Inc, pg 1249
Canterbury Press, pg 1250
Cenveo St Louis, pg 1250
CG Book Printers, pg 1250
CJK, pg 1250
Clare Printing, pg 1250
Codra Enterprises Inc, pg 1250
ColorPage, pg 1250
Coral Graphic Services Inc, pg 1251
Corporate Disk Co, pg 1251
DeHART's Media Services Inc, pg 1251
DNP America LLC, pg 1252
Docunet Corp, pg 1252
RR Donnelley, pg 1252
W R Draper Co, pg 1252
Dual Graphics, pg 1252
Dunn & Co Inc, pg 1252
Dupli Envelope & Graphics Corp, pg 1252
Fenway Group, pg 1253
Ferry Associates Inc, pg 1253
Four Colour Print Group, pg 1253
Friesens Corp, pg 1253
Fry Communications Inc, pg 1253
G & H Soho Inc, pg 1253
Global Interprint Inc, pg 1253
GLS Companies, pg 1254
Goose River Press, pg 1254
Graphic Litho, pg 1254
Hess Print Solutions, pg 1254
Worth Higgins & Associates Inc, pg 1254
Hignell Book Printing Ltd, pg 1254
Imago, pg 1254
Impressions Inc, pg 1255
Infinity Graphics, pg 1255
La Crosse Graphics Inc, pg 1255
Leo Paper USA, pg 1256
Marquis Book Printing Inc, pg 1256
Marrakech Express Inc, pg 1256
Martin Printing Co Inc, pg 1257

McClain Printing Co, pg 1257
Morris Printing Group Inc, pg 1257
Nissha USA Inc, pg 1257
OGM USA, pg 1257
Overseas Printing Corporation, pg 1257
POD Print, pg 1258
PrairieView Press, pg 1258
Print It Plus, pg 1258
The Printer, pg 1258
Printing Corporation of the Americas Inc, pg 1258
Progress Printing Plus, pg 1258
Puritan Press Inc, pg 1258
Quantum Group, pg 1259
Signature Print Services, pg 1260
Smith-Edwards-Dunlap Co, pg 1260
Southeastern Printing Co, pg 1260
Spectrum PrintGroup Inc, pg 1260
Stephenson Printing, pg 1260
John S Swift Co Inc, pg 1260
Times Printing LLC, pg 1261
Townsend Communications Inc, pg 1261
Tribal Print Source, pg 1261
VeronaLibri, pg 1261
Webcom Inc, pg 1262
Fred Weidner & Daughter Printers, pg 1262
Worzalla, pg 1262

CASEBINDING

AcmeBinding, pg 1247
Adams Press, pg 1247
American Mathematical Society (AMS), pg 1247
Arbor Books, pg 1248
Asia Pacific Offset Inc, pg 1248
Balfour Commercial Printing, pg 1248
Bang Printing Co Inc, pg 1248
Berryville Graphics, pg 1248
BookBaby, pg 1249
BookFactory, pg 1249
Bookmasters, pg 1249
BookMobile, pg 1249
Bookshelf Bindery Ltd, pg 1249
BR Printers, pg 1249
Bridgeport National Bindery Inc, pg 1249
C & C Offset Printing Co USA Inc, pg 1249
Cenveo St Louis, pg 1250
CG Book Printers, pg 1250
CJK, pg 1250
Coach House Printing, pg 1250
Color House Graphics Inc, pg 1250
Corporate Disk Co, pg 1251
Cushing-Malloy Inc, pg 1251
Data Reproductions Corp, pg 1251
DeHART's Media Services Inc, pg 1251
Dekker Bookbinding Inc, pg 1251
DNP America LLC, pg 1252
RR Donnelley, pg 1252
W R Draper Co, pg 1252
Eckhart & Company Inc, pg 1253
Four Colour Print Group, pg 1253
Friesens Corp, pg 1253
G & H Soho Inc, pg 1253
Goose River Press, pg 1254
Gorham Printing, pg 1254
HF Group LLC, pg 1254
Imago, pg 1254
Impressions Inc, pg 1255
Ironmark, pg 1255
Lake Book Manufacturing Inc, pg 1255
Leo Paper USA, pg 1256
Lo Gatto Bookbinding, pg 1256
Long's Roullet Bookbinders Inc, pg 1256

Maple Press, pg 1256
Marquis Book Printing Inc, pg 1256
Marrakech Express Inc, pg 1256
Martin Printing Co Inc, pg 1257
McClain Printing Co, pg 1257
Multi-Reliure, pg 1257
NAPCO Inc, pg 1257
Nissha USA Inc, pg 1257
Noble Book Press Corp, pg 1257
OGM USA, pg 1257
Overseas Printing Corporation, pg 1257
POD Print, pg 1258
Printing Corporation of the Americas Inc, pg 1258
Publishers Book Bindery (NY), pg 1258
Puritan Press Inc, pg 1258
Quality Bindery Services Inc, pg 1259
Reindl Bindery Co Inc, pg 1259
Roswell Bookbinding, pg 1259
Sheridan GR, pg 1259
Sheridan MI, pg 1259
Sheridan Saline, pg 1260
Signature Book Printing Inc, pg 1260
Spectrum PrintGroup Inc, pg 1260
Sterling Pierce Co Inc, pg 1260
Sun Graphics LLC, pg 1260
Total Printing Systems, pg 1261
Turtleback Books, pg 1261
Universal Bookbindery Inc, pg 1261
VeronaLibri, pg 1261
Versa Press Inc, pg 1261
Viridiam LLC, pg 1262
Wallaceburg Bookbinding & Mfg Co Ltd, pg 1262
Fred Weidner & Daughter Printers, pg 1262
Wert Bookbinding Inc, pg 1262
Whitehall Printing Co, pg 1262
Worzalla, pg 1262
Yurchak Printing Inc, pg 1262

CATALOG PRINTING

Action Printing, pg 1247
Adair Graphic Communications, pg 1247
AGS, pg 1247
Ambassador Press Inc, pg 1247
American Mathematical Society (AMS), pg 1247
an ICON Company LLC, pg 1247
Arbor Books, pg 1248
Asia Pacific Offset Inc, pg 1248
B & Z Printing Inc, pg 1248
Bang Printing Co Inc, pg 1248
Bedford Printing Co, pg 1248
Birmingham Printing & Publishing Inc, pg 1249
Blitzprint Inc, pg 1249
Blue Ridge Printing Co, pg 1249
Bookmasters, pg 1249
BR Printers, pg 1249
C & C Offset Printing Co USA Inc, pg 1249
California Offset Printers Inc, pg 1250
Canterbury Press, pg 1250
Cenveo St Louis, pg 1250
CG Book Printers, pg 1250
CJK, pg 1250
Clare Printing, pg 1250
Clear Print, pg 1250
Codra Enterprises Inc, pg 1250
Color Graphic Press Inc, pg 1250
Color House Graphics Inc, pg 1250
ColorPage, pg 1250
Consolidated Printers Inc, pg 1251
Coral Graphic Services Inc, pg 1251
Corporate Disk Co, pg 1251

Courier Printing, pg 1251
Cushing-Malloy Inc, pg 1251
Data Reproductions Corp, pg 1251
DeHART's Media Services Inc, pg 1251
Dekker Bookbinding Inc, pg 1251
Democrat Printing & Lithographing Co, pg 1252
The Dingley Press, pg 1252
DNP America LLC, pg 1252
Docunet Corp, pg 1252
RR Donnelley, pg 1252
W R Draper Co, pg 1252
D3Logic Inc, pg 1252
Dual Graphics, pg 1252
EP Graphics, pg 1253
Fairfield Marketing Group Inc, pg 1253
Fenway Group, pg 1253
Fry Communications Inc, pg 1253
G & H Soho Inc, pg 1253
GHP, pg 1253
GLS Companies, pg 1254
Goose River Press, pg 1254
Gorham Printing, pg 1254
Graphic Litho, pg 1254
HBP Inc, pg 1254
Hennegan Co, pg 1254
Hess Print Solutions, pg 1254
Worth Higgins & Associates Inc, pg 1254
Hignell Book Printing Ltd, pg 1254
The P A Hutchison Co, pg 1254
Imago, pg 1254
Impressions Inc, pg 1255
Infinity Graphics, pg 1255
Ironmark, pg 1255
JP Graphics Inc, pg 1255
Knepper Press Corp, pg 1255
La Crosse Graphics Inc, pg 1255
Lake Book Manufacturing Inc, pg 1255
The Lane Press Inc, pg 1256
Leo Paper USA, pg 1256
Maracle Inc, pg 1256
Marquis Book Printing Inc, pg 1256
Marrakech Express Inc, pg 1256
Martin Printing Co Inc, pg 1257
McClain Printing Co, pg 1257
Morris Printing Group Inc, pg 1257
Nissha USA Inc, pg 1257
O'Neil Digital Solutions LLC, pg 1257
OneTouchPoint, pg 1257
Overseas Printing Corporation, pg 1257
The Ovid Bell Press Inc, pg 1257
Panaprint Inc, pg 1258
Patterson Printing Co, pg 1258
POD Print, pg 1258
Print It Plus, pg 1258
The Printer, pg 1258
Printing Corporation of the Americas Inc, pg 1258
ProductionPro, pg 1258
Progress Printing Plus, pg 1258
Puritan Press Inc, pg 1258
Quantum Group, pg 1259
V G Reed & Sons Inc, pg 1259
Sheridan GR, pg 1259
Sheridan Saline, pg 1260
Signature Book Printing Inc, pg 1260
Southeastern Printing Co, pg 1260
Stephenson Printing, pg 1260
Sun Graphics LLC, pg 1260
John S Swift Co Inc, pg 1260
Taylor Communications Inc, pg 1261
Times Printing LLC, pg 1261
Toof American Digital, pg 1261
Total Printing Systems, pg 1261

PRINTING, BINDING & BOOK FINISHING INDEX

Townsend Communications Inc, pg 1261
Tribal Print Source, pg 1261
VeronaLibri, pg 1261
Versa Press Inc, pg 1261
Walsworth, pg 1262
Webcom Inc, pg 1262
Webcrafters Inc, pg 1262
Fred Weidner & Daughter Printers, pg 1262
Whitehall Printing Co, pg 1262
Worzalla, pg 1262

COMIC BOOK PRINTING

Action Printing, pg 1247
Arbor Books, pg 1248
Asia Pacific Offset Inc, pg 1248
Birmingham Printing & Publishing Inc, pg 1249
Bookmasters, pg 1249
BR Printers, pg 1249
C & C Offset Printing Co USA Inc, pg 1249
Dekker Bookbinding Inc, pg 1251
DNP America LLC, pg 1252
Fry Communications Inc, pg 1253
G & H Soho Inc, pg 1253
Gorham Printing, pg 1254
Infinity Graphics, pg 1255
Lake Book Manufacturing Inc, pg 1255
Marquis Book Printing Inc, pg 1256
Marrakech Express Inc, pg 1256
Morris Publishing®, pg 1257
Patterson Printing Co, pg 1258
The Printer, pg 1258
John S Swift Co Inc, pg 1260
Times Printing LLC, pg 1261
Total Printing Systems, pg 1261
VeronaLibri, pg 1261
Walsworth, pg 1262
Fred Weidner & Daughter Printers, pg 1262
Whitehall Printing Co, pg 1262

DIE-CUTTING

Ambassador Press Inc, pg 1247
an ICON Company LLC, pg 1247
Anderberg Innovative Print Solutions, pg 1247
Apex Die Corp, pg 1248
Arbor Books, pg 1248
Asia Pacific Offset Inc, pg 1248
Bedford Printing Co, pg 1248
Beidel Printing House Inc, pg 1248
Bindagraphics Inc, pg 1248
Blanks Printing & Imaging Inc, pg 1249
The Bureau, pg 1249
C & C Offset Printing Co USA Inc, pg 1249
Canterbury Press, pg 1250
CG Book Printers, pg 1250
ColorPage, pg 1250
Communicorp Inc, pg 1250
C Harrison Conroy Co Inc, pg 1251
D C Graphics Inc, pg 1251
Dekker Bookbinding Inc, pg 1251
Diecrafters Inc, pg 1252
DNP America LLC, pg 1252
RR Donnelley, pg 1252
W R Draper Co, pg 1252
Dual Graphics, pg 1252
Dunn & Co Inc, pg 1252
Eckhart & Company Inc, pg 1253
Emprint®, pg 1253
Fairfield Marketing Group Inc, pg 1253
Four Colour Print Group, pg 1253
Friesens Corp, pg 1253

Fry Communications Inc, pg 1253
G & H Soho Inc, pg 1253
Garlich Printing Co, pg 1253
GHP, pg 1253
Graphic Composition Inc, pg 1254
Hennegan Co, pg 1254
Worth Higgins & Associates Inc, pg 1254
The P A Hutchison Co, pg 1254
Imago, pg 1254
Impressions Inc, pg 1255
Infinity Graphics, pg 1255
JP Graphics Inc, pg 1255
Kappa Graphics LLP, pg 1255
Knepper Press Corp, pg 1255
Labels Inc, pg 1255
Leo Paper USA, pg 1256
Letterhead Press Inc (LPI), pg 1256
Marquis Book Printing Inc, pg 1256
Marrakech Express Inc, pg 1256
McClain Printing Co, pg 1257
NAPCO Inc, pg 1257
Nissha USA Inc, pg 1257
OGM USA, pg 1257
OneTouchPoint, pg 1257
Overseas Printing Corporation, pg 1257
Patterson Printing Co, pg 1258
PBM Graphics Inc, an RR Donnelley Co, pg 1258
Pint Size Productions LLC, pg 1258
Print It Plus, pg 1258
The Printer, pg 1258
ProductionPro, pg 1258
Progress Printing Plus, pg 1258
Puritan Press Inc, pg 1258
Reindl Bindery Co Inc, pg 1259
Ross Gage Inc, pg 1259
Sheridan GR, pg 1259
Specialty Finishing Group, pg 1260
Springdale Bindery LLC, pg 1260
Sun Graphics LLC, pg 1260
Taylor Communications Inc, pg 1261
Times Printing LLC, pg 1261
Toof American Digital, pg 1261
TOP Engraving, pg 1261
VeronaLibri, pg 1261
Walker360, pg 1262
Fred Weidner & Daughter Printers, pg 1262
Worzalla, pg 1262

DIGITAL PRINTING

Absolut Color, pg 1247
AcmeBinding, pg 1247
Action Printing, pg 1247
Adams Press, pg 1247
an ICON Company LLC, pg 1247
Balfour Commercial Printing, pg 1248
Bamboo Ink, pg 1248
Bethany Press International Inc, pg 1248
Bookmasters, pg 1249
BR Printers, pg 1249
CG Book Printers, pg 1250
CJK, pg 1250
Communicorp Inc, pg 1250
Copycats, pg 1251
Cushing-Malloy Inc, pg 1251
Data Reproductions Corp, pg 1251
Dekker Bookbinding Inc, pg 1251
Docunet Corp, pg 1252
RR Donnelley, pg 1252
Drummond, pg 1252
D3Logic Inc, pg 1252
Dual Graphics, pg 1252
Fenway Group, pg 1253
Fry Communications Inc, pg 1253
G & H Soho Inc, pg 1253
Goose River Press, pg 1254

Gorham Printing, pg 1254
Graphic Composition Inc, pg 1254
Hignell Book Printing Ltd, pg 1254
InfinitPrint Solutions Inc, pg 1255
La Crosse Graphics Inc, pg 1255
Labels Inc, pg 1255
L+L Printers, pg 1256
Lawton Connect, pg 1256
Mandel Graphic Solution, pg 1256
Maple Press, pg 1256
Marquis Book Printing Inc, pg 1256
Morris Printing Group Inc, pg 1257
Neibauer Press, pg 1257
Omnipress, pg 1257
POD Print, pg 1258
Print It Plus, pg 1258
The Printer, pg 1258
ProductionPro, pg 1258
Publishers' Graphics LLC, pg 1258
Quantum Group, pg 1259
V G Reed & Sons Inc, pg 1259
Regal Press, pg 1259
The Renton Printery Inc, pg 1259
Shepherd Inc, pg 1259
Sheridan GR, pg 1259
Sheridan MI, pg 1259
Sheridan PA, pg 1259
Sheridan Saline, pg 1260
Smith-Edwards-Dunlap Co, pg 1260
Stephenson Printing, pg 1260
John S Swift Co Inc, pg 1260
Toof American Digital, pg 1261
Total Printing Systems, pg 1261
Tribal Print Source, pg 1261
Tukaiz LLC, pg 1261
UniversalIWilde, pg 1261
VIP Digital Print Center, pg 1262
Walker360, pg 1262

EDITION (HARDCOVER) BINDING

AcmeBinding, pg 1247
Adams Press, pg 1247
Arbor Books, pg 1248
Asia Pacific Offset Inc, pg 1248
Balfour Commercial Printing, pg 1248
Berryville Graphics, pg 1248
Bookmasters, pg 1249
Bookshelf Bindery Ltd, pg 1249
BR Printers, pg 1249
Bridgeport National Bindery Inc, pg 1249
C & C Offset Printing Co USA Inc, pg 1249
Cenveo St Louis, pg 1250
CG Book Printers, pg 1250
Cushing-Malloy Inc, pg 1251
DeHART's Media Services Inc, pg 1251
Dekker Bookbinding Inc, pg 1251
DNP America LLC, pg 1252
RR Donnelley, pg 1252
Four Colour Print Group, pg 1253
Friesens Corp, pg 1253
G & H Soho Inc, pg 1253
Goose River Press, pg 1254
Gorham Printing, pg 1254
The P A Hutchison Co, pg 1254
Imago, pg 1254
Impressions Inc, pg 1255
Ironmark, pg 1255
Lake Book Manufacturing Inc, pg 1255
Leo Paper USA, pg 1256
Lo Gatto Bookbinding, pg 1256
Long's Roullet Bookbinders Inc, pg 1256
Marquis Book Printing Inc, pg 1256
Marrakech Express Inc, pg 1256
McClain Printing Co, pg 1257
Nissha USA Inc, pg 1257

Noble Book Press Corp, pg 1257
OGM USA, pg 1257
Outskirts Press Inc, pg 1257
Overseas Printing Corporation, pg 1257
Printing Corporation of the Americas Inc, pg 1258
Publishers Book Bindery (NY), pg 1258
Reindl Bindery Co Inc, pg 1259
Roswell Bookbinding, pg 1259
Sheridan MI, pg 1259
Sheridan Saline, pg 1260
The Studley Press Inc, pg 1260
Total Printing Systems, pg 1261
Turtleback Books, pg 1261
Universal Bookbindery Inc, pg 1261
VeronaLibri, pg 1261
Fred Weidner & Daughter Printers, pg 1262
Wert Bookbinding Inc, pg 1262
Whitehall Printing Co, pg 1262
Worzalla, pg 1262

EMBOSSING

Adair Graphic Communications, pg 1247
Adams Press, pg 1247
Ambassador Press Inc, pg 1247
Anderberg Innovative Print Solutions, pg 1247
Apex Die Corp, pg 1248
Arbor Books, pg 1248
Asia Pacific Offset Inc, pg 1248
Balfour Commercial Printing, pg 1248
Bethany Press International Inc, pg 1248
Bindagraphics Inc, pg 1248
BookFactory, pg 1249
Bookmasters, pg 1249
BR Printers, pg 1249
C & C Offset Printing Co USA Inc, pg 1249
Canterbury Press, pg 1250
CG Book Printers, pg 1250
Color House Graphics Inc, pg 1250
C Harrison Conroy Co Inc, pg 1251
Coral Graphic Services Inc, pg 1251
Cushing-Malloy Inc, pg 1251
D C Graphics Inc, pg 1251
D&K Group Inc, pg 1251
Data Reproductions Corp, pg 1251
DeHART's Media Services Inc, pg 1251
Dekker Bookbinding Inc, pg 1251
Diecrafters Inc, pg 1252
DNP America LLC, pg 1252
RR Donnelley, pg 1252
W R Draper Co, pg 1252
Dual Graphics, pg 1252
Dunn & Co Inc, pg 1252
Eckhart & Company Inc, pg 1253
Four Colour Print Group, pg 1253
Friesens Corp, pg 1253
Fry Communications Inc, pg 1253
G & H Soho Inc, pg 1253
Garlich Printing Co, pg 1253
Gorham Printing, pg 1254
Graphic Composition Inc, pg 1254
Hennegan Co, pg 1254
Worth Higgins & Associates Inc, pg 1254
Hignell Book Printing Ltd, pg 1254
The P A Hutchison Co, pg 1254
Imago, pg 1254
Impressions Inc, pg 1255
Ironmark, pg 1255
ITW Foils, pg 1255
Kappa Graphics LLP, pg 1255
Knepper Press Corp, pg 1255
Lake Book Manufacturing Inc, pg 1255

MANUFACTURING

PRINTING, BINDING & BOOK FINISHING INDEX

Leo Paper USA, pg 1256
Letterhead Press Inc (LPI), pg 1256
Lo Gatto Bookbinding, pg 1256
Marquis Book Printing Inc, pg 1256
Marrakech Express Inc, pg 1256
Martin Printing Co Inc, pg 1257
McClain Printing Co, pg 1257
Multi-Reliure, pg 1257
Nissha USA Inc, pg 1257
OGM USA, pg 1257
PBM Graphics Inc, an RR Donnelley Co, pg 1258
The Printer, pg 1258
Printing Corporation of the Americas Inc, pg 1258
ProductionPro, pg 1258
Puritan Press Inc, pg 1258
Quantum Group, pg 1259
Regal Press, pg 1259
Roswell Bookbinding, pg 1259
Sheridan GR, pg 1259
Sheridan MI, pg 1259
Spectrum PrintGroup Inc, pg 1260
Spiral Binding LLC, pg 1260
Sun Graphics LLC, pg 1260
Taylor Communications Inc, pg 1261
Toof American Digital, pg 1261
TOP Engraving, pg 1261
Total Printing Systems, pg 1261
VeronaLibri, pg 1261
Versa Press Inc, pg 1261
Walsworth, pg 1262
Fred Weidner & Daughter Printers, pg 1262
Worzalla, pg 1262

ENGRAVING

Adams Press, pg 1247
Ambassador Press Inc, pg 1247
Arbor Books, pg 1248
Asia Pacific Offset Inc, pg 1248
BR Printers, pg 1249
Canterbury Press, pg 1250
D C Graphics Inc, pg 1251
Dekker Bookbinding Inc, pg 1251
DNP America LLC, pg 1252
W R Draper Co, pg 1252
G & H Soho Inc, pg 1253
Leo Paper USA, pg 1256
Lo Gatto Bookbinding, pg 1256
Long's Roullet Bookbinders Inc, pg 1256
Marquis Book Printing Inc, pg 1256
Marrakech Express Inc, pg 1256
McClain Printing Co, pg 1257
Perma Graphics, pg 1258
The Printer, pg 1258
Puritan Press Inc, pg 1258
Regal Press, pg 1259
TOP Engraving, pg 1261
Total Printing Systems, pg 1261
Fred Weidner & Daughter Printers, pg 1262

FILM LAMINATING

AcmeBinding, pg 1247
Action Printing, pg 1247
Adair Graphic Communications, pg 1247
Adams Press, pg 1247
Ambassador Press Inc, pg 1247
an ICON Company LLC, pg 1247
Any Laminating Service, pg 1247
Apex Die Corp, pg 1248
Arbor Books, pg 1248
Asia Pacific Offset Inc, pg 1248
Balfour Commercial Printing, pg 1248
Beidel Printing House Inc, pg 1248

Bethany Press International Inc, pg 1248
Bindagraphics Inc, pg 1248
Blitzprint Inc, pg 1249
BookBaby, pg 1249
Bookmasters, pg 1249
BR Printers, pg 1249
C & C Offset Printing Co USA Inc, pg 1249
Canterbury Press, pg 1250
Cenveo St Louis, pg 1250
CG Book Printers, pg 1250
CJK, pg 1250
Coach House Printing, pg 1250
Color House Graphics Inc, pg 1250
ColorPage, pg 1250
Cookbook Publishers Inc, pg 1251
Copycats, pg 1251
Coral Graphic Services Inc, pg 1251
Crane Duplicating Service Inc, pg 1251
Crown Roll Leaf Inc, pg 1251
Cushing-Malloy Inc, pg 1251
D&K Group Inc, pg 1251
Data Reproductions Corp, pg 1251
DeHART's Media Services Inc, pg 1251
Dekker Bookbinding Inc, pg 1251
DNP America LLC, pg 1252
RR Donnelley, pg 1252
W R Draper Co, pg 1252
Dunn & Co Inc, pg 1252
Eckhart & Company Inc, pg 1253
Fairfield Marketing Group Inc, pg 1253
Fenway Group, pg 1253
Four Colour Print Group, pg 1253
Friesens Corp, pg 1253
G & H Soho Inc, pg 1253
Goose River Press, pg 1254
Gorham Printing, pg 1254
Graphic Litho, pg 1254
Great Lakes Bindery Inc, pg 1254
Hess Print Solutions, pg 1254
Hignell Book Printing Ltd, pg 1254
The P A Hutchison Co, pg 1254
Imago, pg 1254
Impressions Inc, pg 1255
InfinitPrint Solutions Inc, pg 1255
Infinity Graphics, pg 1255
Ironmark, pg 1255
Kromar Printing Ltd, pg 1255
Lake Book Manufacturing Inc, pg 1255
Leo Paper USA, pg 1256
Letterhead Press Inc (LPI), pg 1256
Lightning Source LLC, pg 1256
Maple Press, pg 1256
Maracle Inc, pg 1256
Marquis Book Printing Inc, pg 1256
Marrakech Express Inc, pg 1256
Martin Printing Co Inc, pg 1257
McClain Printing Co, pg 1257
Morris Printing Group Inc, pg 1257
NAPCO Inc, pg 1257
Nissha USA Inc, pg 1257
OGM USA, pg 1257
Patterson Printing Co, pg 1258
Perma Graphics, pg 1258
POD Print, pg 1258
PrairieView Press, pg 1258
Printing Corporation of the Americas Inc, pg 1258
Pro Laminators, pg 1258
Puritan Press Inc, pg 1258
Quantum Group, pg 1259
The Renton Printery Inc, pg 1259
Sheridan GR, pg 1259
Sheridan MI, pg 1259
Sheridan Saline, pg 1260
Signature Book Printing Inc, pg 1260
Southeastern Printing Co, pg 1260

Spectrum PrintGroup Inc, pg 1260
Spiral Binding LLC, pg 1260
Sun Graphics LLC, pg 1260
Toof American Digital, pg 1261
Total Printing Systems, pg 1261
Tribal Print Source, pg 1261
Universal Bookbindery Inc, pg 1261
VeronaLibri, pg 1261
Vicks Lithograph & Printing Corp, pg 1262
Walsworth, pg 1262
Webcom Inc, pg 1262
Fred Weidner & Daughter Printers, pg 1262
Whitehall Printing Co, pg 1262
Worzalla, pg 1262
Yurchak Printing Inc, pg 1262

FOILING

AcmeBinding, pg 1247
Adams Press, pg 1247
Ambassador Press Inc, pg 1247
an ICON Company LLC, pg 1247
Anderberg Innovative Print Solutions, pg 1247
Apex Die Corp, pg 1248
APG Group, pg 1248
Arbor Books, pg 1248
Asia Pacific Offset Inc, pg 1248
Balfour Commercial Printing, pg 1248
Bethany Press International Inc, pg 1248
Bindagraphics Inc, pg 1248
BookFactory, pg 1249
Bookmasters, pg 1249
Bookshelf Bindery Ltd, pg 1249
C & C Offset Printing Co USA Inc, pg 1249
Canterbury Press, pg 1250
CG Book Printers, pg 1250
CJK, pg 1250
C Harrison Conroy Co Inc, pg 1251
Coral Graphic Services Inc, pg 1251
Corporate Disk Co, pg 1251
Crown Roll Leaf Inc, pg 1251
Cushing-Malloy Inc, pg 1251
D C Graphics Inc, pg 1251
DeHART's Media Services Inc, pg 1251
Dekker Bookbinding Inc, pg 1251
Diecrafters Inc, pg 1252
DNP America LLC, pg 1252
RR Donnelley, pg 1252
W R Draper Co, pg 1252
Eckhart & Company Inc, pg 1253
Fairfield Marketing Group Inc, pg 1253
Four Colour Print Group, pg 1253
Friesens Corp, pg 1253
Fry Communications Inc, pg 1253
G & H Soho Inc, pg 1253
Garlich Printing Co, pg 1253
Gorham Printing, pg 1254
Graphic Composition Inc, pg 1254
Hennegan Co, pg 1254
Worth Higgins & Associates Inc, pg 1254
Hignell Book Printing Ltd, pg 1254
Imago, pg 1254
Impressions Inc, pg 1255
Ironmark, pg 1255
ITW Foils, pg 1255
Kappa Graphics LLP, pg 1255
Knepper Press Corp, pg 1255
Labels Inc, pg 1255
Lake Book Manufacturing Inc, pg 1255
Leo Paper USA, pg 1256
Letterhead Press Inc (LPI), pg 1256
Maple Press, pg 1256
Marquis Book Printing Inc, pg 1256

Marrakech Express Inc, pg 1256
Martin Printing Co Inc, pg 1257
McClain Printing Co, pg 1257
Morris Printing Group Inc, pg 1257
Multi-Reliure, pg 1257
Nissha USA Inc, pg 1257
Patterson Printing Co, pg 1258
PBM Graphics Inc, an RR Donnelley Co, pg 1258
PrairieView Press, pg 1258
The Printer, pg 1258
ProductionPro, pg 1258
Puritan Press Inc, pg 1258
Quality Bindery Services Inc, pg 1259
Quantum Group, pg 1259
Regal Press, pg 1259
Reindl Bindery Co Inc, pg 1259
Roswell Bookbinding, pg 1259
Sheridan GR, pg 1259
Sheridan MI, pg 1259
Specialty Finishing Group, pg 1260
Spectrum PrintGroup Inc, pg 1260
Spiral Binding LLC, pg 1260
Sun Graphics LLC, pg 1260
Taylor Communications Inc, pg 1261
Toof American Digital, pg 1261
Total Printing Systems, pg 1261
Tribal Print Source, pg 1261
VeronaLibri, pg 1261
Versa Press Inc, pg 1261
Walsworth, pg 1262
Fred Weidner & Daughter Printers, pg 1262
Worzalla, pg 1262

GILDING

AcmeBinding, pg 1247
APG Group, pg 1248
Arbor Books, pg 1248
Asia Pacific Offset Inc, pg 1248
Bookmasters, pg 1249
C & C Offset Printing Co USA Inc, pg 1249
Cushing-Malloy Inc, pg 1251
Dekker Bookbinding Inc, pg 1251
DNP America LLC, pg 1252
RR Donnelley, pg 1252
Four Colour Print Group, pg 1253
G & H Soho Inc, pg 1253
Imago, pg 1254
Lake Book Manufacturing Inc, pg 1255
Leo Paper USA, pg 1256
Marquis Book Printing Inc, pg 1256
McClain Printing Co, pg 1257
Nissha USA Inc, pg 1257
Quantum Group, pg 1259
Sheridan GR, pg 1259
VeronaLibri, pg 1261
Fred Weidner & Daughter Printers, pg 1262

GLUE OR PASTE BINDING

Action Printing, pg 1247
Adams Press, pg 1247
AGS, pg 1247
American Mathematical Society (AMS), pg 1247
an ICON Company LLC, pg 1247
Arbor Books, pg 1248
Asia Pacific Offset Inc, pg 1248
B & Z Printing Inc, pg 1248
Bindagraphics Inc, pg 1248
Blitzprint Inc, pg 1249
Bookmasters, pg 1249
Bookshelf Bindery Ltd, pg 1249
BR Printers, pg 1249

1239

PRINTING, BINDING & BOOK FINISHING INDEX

C & C Offset Printing Co USA Inc, pg 1249
DeHART's Media Services Inc, pg 1251
Dekker Bookbinding Inc, pg 1251
DNP America LLC, pg 1252
Eckhart & Company Inc, pg 1253
Fenway Group, pg 1253
G & H Soho Inc, pg 1253
Garlich Printing Co, pg 1253
Gorham Printing, pg 1254
The P A Hutchison Co, pg 1254
Imago, pg 1254
Impressions Inc, pg 1255
Infinity Graphics, pg 1255
Lake Book Manufacturing Inc, pg 1255
Leo Paper USA, pg 1256
Letterhead Press Inc (LPI), pg 1256
Marquis Book Printing Inc, pg 1256
OGM USA, pg 1257
PBM Graphics Inc, an RR Donnelley Co, pg 1258
POD Print, pg 1258
Puritan Press Inc, pg 1258
Specialty Finishing Group, pg 1260
Springdale Bindery LLC, pg 1260
John S Swift Co Inc, pg 1260
Townsend Communications Inc, pg 1261
Walsworth, pg 1262
Fred Weidner & Daughter Printers, pg 1262

GRAVURE

Arbor Books, pg 1248
Crown Roll Leaf Inc, pg 1251
Dekker Bookbinding Inc, pg 1251
DNP America LLC, pg 1252
Nissha USA Inc, pg 1257
Fred Weidner & Daughter Printers, pg 1262

HAND BOOKBINDING

AcmeBinding, pg 1247
an ICON Company LLC, pg 1247
Arbor Books, pg 1248
BR Printers, pg 1249
Bridgeport National Bindery Inc, pg 1249
The Bureau, pg 1249
C & C Offset Printing Co USA Inc, pg 1249
Jerilyn Glenn Davis, pg 1251
RR Donnelley, pg 1252
Drummond, pg 1252
Eckhart & Company Inc, pg 1253
HF Group LLC, pg 1254
Imago, pg 1254
Impressions Inc, pg 1255
Leo Paper USA, pg 1256
Lo Gatto Bookbinding, pg 1256
Marquis Book Printing Inc, pg 1256
Marrakech Express Inc, pg 1256
McClain Printing Co, pg 1257
Nissha USA Inc, pg 1257
OneTouchPoint, pg 1257
Overseas Printing Corporation, pg 1257
Quality Bindery Services Inc, pg 1259
Roswell Bookbinding, pg 1259
Sun Graphics LLC, pg 1260
John S Swift Co Inc, pg 1260
Total Printing Systems, pg 1261
Universal Bookbindery Inc, pg 1261
VeronaLibri, pg 1261
Wallaceburg Bookbinding & Mfg Co Ltd, pg 1262

Fred Weidner & Daughter Printers, pg 1262
Wert Bookbinding Inc, pg 1262

HOLOGRAMS

Arbor Books, pg 1248
Crown Roll Leaf Inc, pg 1251
Dekker Bookbinding Inc, pg 1251
DNP America LLC, pg 1252
Imago, pg 1254
Impressions Inc, pg 1255
ITW Foils, pg 1255
Letterhead Press Inc (LPI), pg 1256
PBM Graphics Inc, an RR Donnelley Co, pg 1258
Sun Graphics LLC, pg 1260
Fred Weidner & Daughter Printers, pg 1262

JOURNAL PRINTING

Action Printing, pg 1247
Adams Press, pg 1247
AGS, pg 1247
American Mathematical Society (AMS), pg 1247
Arbor Books, pg 1248
Asia Pacific Offset Inc, pg 1248
Birmingham Printing & Publishing Inc, pg 1249
Bookmasters, pg 1249
BR Printers, pg 1249
C & C Offset Printing Co USA Inc, pg 1249
Canterbury Press, pg 1250
CG Book Printers, pg 1250
Clare Printing, pg 1250
Coach House Printing, pg 1250
Color House Graphics Inc, pg 1250
ColorPage, pg 1250
Copycats, pg 1251
Corporate Disk Co, pg 1251
Crane Duplicating Service Inc, pg 1251
Cushing-Malloy Inc, pg 1251
Data Reproductions Corp, pg 1251
Dekker Bookbinding Inc, pg 1251
Democrat Printing & Lithographing Co, pg 1252
DNP America LLC, pg 1252
Docunet Corp, pg 1252
RR Donnelley, pg 1252
W R Draper Co, pg 1252
EP Graphics, pg 1253
Fairfield Marketing Group Inc, pg 1253
Fenway Group, pg 1253
Fry Communications Inc, pg 1253
G & H Soho Inc, pg 1253
GHP, pg 1253
GLS Companies, pg 1254
Gorham Printing, pg 1254
HBP Inc, pg 1254
Hignell Book Printing Ltd, pg 1254
The P A Hutchison Co, pg 1254
Imago, pg 1254
Infinity Graphics, pg 1255
Ironmark, pg 1255
The Lane Press Inc, pg 1256
Leo Paper USA, pg 1256
Maracle Inc, pg 1256
Marquis Book Printing Inc, pg 1256
Marrakech Express Inc, pg 1256
McClain Printing Co, pg 1257
Overseas Printing Corporation, pg 1257
The Ovid Bell Press Inc, pg 1257
Patterson Printing Co, pg 1258
The Printer, pg 1258
Printing Corporation of the Americas Inc, pg 1258
Puritan Press Inc, pg 1258

V G Reed & Sons Inc, pg 1259
Sheridan GR, pg 1259
Sheridan MI, pg 1259
Sheridan PA, pg 1259
Sheridan Saline, pg 1260
Signature Book Printing Inc, pg 1260
Smith-Edwards-Dunlap Co, pg 1260
Southeastern Printing Co, pg 1260
Spectrum PrintGroup Inc, pg 1260
Sterling Pierce Co Inc, pg 1260
Times Printing LLC, pg 1261
Total Printing Systems, pg 1261
Tribal Print Source, pg 1261
Versa Press Inc, pg 1261
Vicks Lithograph & Printing Corp, pg 1262
VIP Digital Print Center, pg 1262
Webcom Inc, pg 1262
Fred Weidner & Daughter Printers, pg 1262
Whitehall Printing Co, pg 1262
Yurchak Printing Inc, pg 1262

LETTERPRESS

Ambassador Press Inc, pg 1247
APG Group, pg 1248
Arbor Books, pg 1248
Beidel Printing House Inc, pg 1248
BR Printers, pg 1249
CG Book Printers, pg 1250
C Harrison Conroy Co Inc, pg 1251
Dekker Bookbinding Inc, pg 1251
W R Draper Co, pg 1252
Fairfield Marketing Group Inc, pg 1253
Ferry Associates Inc, pg 1253
Fry Communications Inc, pg 1253
Hignell Book Printing Ltd, pg 1254
Impressions Inc, pg 1255
Marquis Book Printing Inc, pg 1256
Marrakech Express Inc, pg 1256
The Printer, pg 1258
Progress Printing Plus, pg 1258
Tribal Print Source, pg 1261
VIP Digital Print Center, pg 1262
Fred Weidner & Daughter Printers, pg 1262

LITHO PRINTING

an ICON Company LLC, pg 1247
APG Group, pg 1248
Bedford Printing Co, pg 1248
Bethany Press International Inc, pg 1248
CG Book Printers, pg 1250
Cushing-Malloy Inc, pg 1251
Dekker Bookbinding Inc, pg 1251
Fenway Group, pg 1253
Graphic Litho, pg 1254
Hignell Book Printing Ltd, pg 1254
Impressions Inc, pg 1255
Lake Book Manufacturing Inc, pg 1255
Marrakech Express Inc, pg 1256
The Printer, pg 1258
Quantum Group, pg 1259
The Renton Printery Inc, pg 1259
John S Swift Co Inc, pg 1260
Tribal Print Source, pg 1261

LOOSELEAF BINDING

AcmeBinding, pg 1247
Action Printing, pg 1247
Adair Graphic Communications, pg 1247
AGS, pg 1247
American Mathematical Society (AMS), pg 1247
an ICON Company LLC, pg 1247

BOOK

Arbor Books, pg 1248
Asia Pacific Offset Inc, pg 1248
Bindagraphics Inc, pg 1248
The Bindery Inc, pg 1249
Bookshelf Bindery Ltd, pg 1249
BR Printers, pg 1249
Canterbury Press, pg 1250
Copycats, pg 1251
Cushing-Malloy Inc, pg 1251
Data Reproductions Corp, pg 1251
DeHART's Media Services Inc, pg 1251
DNP America LLC, pg 1252
Docunet Corp, pg 1252
RR Donnelley, pg 1252
Dunn & Co Inc, pg 1252
Eckhart & Company Inc, pg 1253
Fenway Group, pg 1253
Fry Communications Inc, pg 1253
G & H Soho Inc, pg 1253
Great Lakes Bindery Inc, pg 1254
Holmberg Co Inc, pg 1254
The P A Hutchison Co, pg 1254
Imago, pg 1254
Impressions Inc, pg 1255
Infinity Graphics, pg 1255
Ironmark, pg 1255
Leo Paper USA, pg 1256
The Lexington Press Inc, pg 1256
Lo Gatto Bookbinding, pg 1256
Maracle Inc, pg 1256
Marquis Book Printing Inc, pg 1256
NAPCO Inc, pg 1257
Omnipress, pg 1257
OneTouchPoint, pg 1257
Patterson Printing Co, pg 1258
POD Print, pg 1258
Print It Plus, pg 1258
Printing Corporation of the Americas Inc, pg 1258
Puritan Press Inc, pg 1258
Quantum Group, pg 1259
Roswell Bookbinding, pg 1259
Scientific Bindery Inc, pg 1259
Sheridan MI, pg 1259
Sheridan Saline, pg 1260
Signature Book Printing Inc, pg 1260
Southeastern Printing Co, pg 1260
Specialty Finishing Group, pg 1260
Spiral Binding LLC, pg 1260
Sun Graphics LLC, pg 1260
Times Printing LLC, pg 1261
Toof American Digital, pg 1261
Total Printing Systems, pg 1261
TSO General Corp, pg 1261
Universal Bookbindery Inc, pg 1261
Versa Press Inc, pg 1261
ViaTech Publishing Solutions Inc, pg 1261
VIP Digital Print Center, pg 1262
Viridiam LLC, pg 1262
Wallaceburg Bookbinding & Mfg Co Ltd, pg 1262
Fred Weidner & Daughter Printers, pg 1262
Whitehall Printing Co, pg 1262
Yurchak Printing Inc, pg 1262

MANUAL PRINTING

Action Printing, pg 1247
Adair Graphic Communications, pg 1247
AGS, pg 1247
Ambassador Press Inc, pg 1247
American Mathematical Society (AMS), pg 1247
an ICON Company LLC, pg 1247
Arbor Books, pg 1248
Asia Pacific Offset Inc, pg 1248
Bang Printing Co Inc, pg 1248

MANUFACTURING

Birmingham Printing & Publishing Inc, pg 1249
Blitzprint Inc, pg 1249
Blue Note Publications Inc, pg 1249
Blue Ridge Printing Co, pg 1249
BR Printers, pg 1249
C & C Offset Printing Co USA Inc, pg 1249
Canterbury Press, pg 1250
CG Book Printers, pg 1250
CJK, pg 1250
Clare Printing, pg 1250
Coach House Printing, pg 1250
Codra Enterprises Inc, pg 1250
Color House Graphics Inc, pg 1250
ColorPage, pg 1250
Consolidated Printers Inc, pg 1251
Cookbook Publishers Inc, pg 1251
Copycats, pg 1251
The Country Press Inc, pg 1251
Courier Printing, pg 1251
Cushing-Malloy Inc, pg 1251
Data Reproductions Corp, pg 1251
DeHART's Media Services Inc, pg 1251
Dekker Bookbinding Inc, pg 1251
DNP America LLC, pg 1252
Docunet Corp, pg 1252
RR Donnelley, pg 1252
W R Draper Co, pg 1252
Dunn & Co Inc, pg 1252
Emprint®, pg 1253
Fairfield Marketing Group Inc, pg 1253
Ferry Associates Inc, pg 1253
Fry Communications Inc, pg 1253
G & H Soho Inc, pg 1253
Goose River Press, pg 1254
Gorham Printing, pg 1254
HBP Inc, pg 1254
Hess Print Solutions, pg 1254
The P A Hutchison Co, pg 1254
Impressions Inc, pg 1255
Infinity Graphics, pg 1255
Ironmark, pg 1255
Lake Book Manufacturing Inc, pg 1255
The Lexington Press Inc, pg 1256
Maracle Inc, pg 1256
Marquis Book Printing Inc, pg 1256
Marrakech Express Inc, pg 1256
McClain Printing Co, pg 1257
OneTouchPoint, pg 1257
Overseas Printing Corporation, pg 1257
Patterson Printing Co, pg 1258
POD Print, pg 1258
Print It Plus, pg 1258
Printing Corporation of the Americas Inc, pg 1258
Puritan Press Inc, pg 1258
V G Reed & Sons Inc, pg 1259
Sheridan GR, pg 1259
Sheridan MI, pg 1259
Sheridan Saline, pg 1260
Signature Print Services, pg 1260
Southeastern Printing Co, pg 1260
Sun Graphics LLC, pg 1260
John S Swift Co Inc, pg 1260
Times Printing LLC, pg 1261
Toof American Digital, pg 1261
Total Printing Systems, pg 1261
Townsend Communications Inc, pg 1261
Tribal Print Source, pg 1261
VeronaLibri, pg 1261
Versa Press Inc, pg 1261
VIP Digital Print Center, pg 1262
Viridian LLC, pg 1262
Webcom Inc, pg 1262
Fred Weidner & Daughter Printers, pg 1262
Whitehall Printing Co, pg 1262

MAP PRINTING

Action Printing, pg 1247
Ambassador Press Inc, pg 1247
an ICON Company LLC, pg 1247
Arbor Books, pg 1248
Asia Pacific Offset Inc, pg 1248
Birmingham Printing & Publishing Inc, pg 1249
BR Printers, pg 1249
C & C Offset Printing Co USA Inc, pg 1249
Canterbury Press, pg 1250
Cenveo St Louis, pg 1250
DeHART's Media Services Inc, pg 1251
DNP America LLC, pg 1252
RR Donnelley, pg 1252
W R Draper Co, pg 1252
Edison Lithograph & Printing Corp, pg 1253
G & H Soho Inc, pg 1253
Graphic Litho, pg 1254
Impressions Inc, pg 1255
La Crosse Graphics Inc, pg 1255
Leo Paper USA, pg 1256
Maracle Inc, pg 1256
Martin Printing Co Inc, pg 1257
Printing Corporation of the Americas Inc, pg 1258
Southeastern Printing Co, pg 1260
Stephenson Printing, pg 1260
John S Swift Co Inc, pg 1260
Times Printing LLC, pg 1261
Townsend Communications Inc, pg 1261
VeronaLibri, pg 1261
Webcrafters Inc, pg 1262
Fred Weidner & Daughter Printers, pg 1262

MCCAIN SEWN BINDING

Arbor Books, pg 1248
Asia Pacific Offset Inc, pg 1248
Bang Printing Co Inc, pg 1248
CG Book Printers, pg 1250
DNP America LLC, pg 1252
RR Donnelley, pg 1252
W R Draper Co, pg 1252
Eckhart & Company Inc, pg 1253
Four Colour Print Group, pg 1253
Friesens Corp, pg 1253
G & H Soho Inc, pg 1253
Hignell Book Printing Ltd, pg 1254
Lake Book Manufacturing Inc, pg 1255
Marrakech Express Inc, pg 1256
McClain Printing Co, pg 1257
Overseas Printing Corporation, pg 1257
Publishers Book Bindery (NY), pg 1258
Puritan Press Inc, pg 1258
Reindl Bindery Co Inc, pg 1259
Roswell Bookbinding, pg 1259
Sheridan GR, pg 1259
Southeastern Printing Co, pg 1260
Walsworth, pg 1262
Fred Weidner & Daughter Printers, pg 1262
Worzalla, pg 1262

METAL COMPOSITION

Arbor Books, pg 1248
Dekker Bookbinding Inc, pg 1251
Democrat Printing & Lithographing Co, pg 1252
W R Draper Co, pg 1252
ITW Foils, pg 1255
Smith & Sons Printers Inc, pg 1260
Fred Weidner & Daughter Printers, pg 1262

NOTCH BINDING

AcmeBinding, pg 1247
Action Printing, pg 1247
Adams Press, pg 1247
AGS, pg 1247
Arbor Books, pg 1248
Asia Pacific Offset Inc, pg 1248
Bindagraphics Inc, pg 1248
Blitzprint Inc, pg 1249
Bookshelf Bindery Ltd, pg 1249
C & C Offset Printing Co USA Inc, pg 1249
Canterbury Press, pg 1250
Cenveo St Louis, pg 1250
ColorPage, pg 1250
Cushing-Malloy Inc, pg 1251
Data Reproductions Corp, pg 1251
Dekker Bookbinding Inc, pg 1251
DNP America LLC, pg 1252
RR Donnelley, pg 1252
Dunn & Co Inc, pg 1252
Four Colour Print Group, pg 1253
Friesens Corp, pg 1253
Goose River Press, pg 1254
Hignell Book Printing Ltd, pg 1254
Imago, pg 1254
Ironmark, pg 1255
Lake Book Manufacturing Inc, pg 1255
Leo Paper USA, pg 1256
Long's Roullet Bookbinders Inc, pg 1256
Maple Press, pg 1256
Maracle Inc, pg 1256
Marquis Book Printing Inc, pg 1256
Marrakech Express Inc, pg 1256
Nissha USA Inc, pg 1257
Overseas Printing Corporation, pg 1257
Patterson Printing Co, pg 1258
Publishers Book Bindery (NY), pg 1258
Puritan Press Inc, pg 1258
Roswell Bookbinding, pg 1259
Sheridan GR, pg 1259
Sheridan MI, pg 1259
Sheridan PA, pg 1259
Sheridan Saline, pg 1260
Specialty Finishing Group, pg 1260
Spectrum PrintGroup Inc, pg 1260
John S Swift Co Inc, pg 1260
Total Printing Systems, pg 1261
Wallaceburg Bookbinding & Mfg Co Ltd, pg 1262
Walsworth, pg 1262
Fred Weidner & Daughter Printers, pg 1262
Worzalla, pg 1262

OFFSET PRINTING - SHEETFED

Absolut Color, pg 1247
Action Printing, pg 1247
Adair Graphic Communications, pg 1247
Adams Press, pg 1247
AGS, pg 1247
Ambassador Press Inc, pg 1247
American Mathematical Society (AMS), pg 1247
an ICON Company LLC, pg 1247
Anderberg Innovative Print Solutions, pg 1247
Angstrom Graphics Print, pg 1247
APG Group, pg 1248
Arbor Books, pg 1248
Asia Pacific Offset Inc, pg 1248

PRINTING, BINDING & BOOK FINISHING INDEX

Bamboo Ink, pg 1248
Bang Printing Co Inc, pg 1248
Bedford Printing Co, pg 1248
Beidel Printing House Inc, pg 1248
Birmingham Printing & Publishing Inc, pg 1249
Blanks Printing & Imaging Inc, pg 1249
Blue Note Publications Inc, pg 1249
Blue Ridge Printing Co, pg 1249
Bookmasters, pg 1249
BR Printers, pg 1249
The Bureau, pg 1249
C & C Offset Printing Co USA Inc, pg 1249
Canterbury Press, pg 1250
Cenveo Inc, pg 1250
Cenveo St Louis, pg 1250
CG Book Printers, pg 1250
CJK, pg 1250
Clare Printing, pg 1250
Clear Print, pg 1250
Coach House Printing, pg 1250
Color Graphic Press Inc, pg 1250
Color House Graphics Inc, pg 1250
ColorPage, pg 1250
Communicorp Inc, pg 1250
C Harrison Conroy Co Inc, pg 1251
Copycats, pg 1251
Coral Graphic Services Inc, pg 1251
Corporate Disk Co, pg 1251
Courier Printing, pg 1251
Crane Duplicating Service Inc, pg 1251
Cushing-Malloy Inc, pg 1251
Data Reproductions Corp, pg 1251
DeHART's Media Services Inc, pg 1251
Democrat Printing & Lithographing Co, pg 1252
DNP America LLC, pg 1252
RR Donnelley, pg 1252
Drummond, pg 1252
D3Logic Inc, pg 1252
Dual Graphics, pg 1252
Dunn & Co Inc, pg 1252
Dupli Envelope & Graphics Corp, pg 1252
Edison Lithograph & Printing Corp, pg 1253
Emprint®, pg 1253
EP Graphics, pg 1253
Fairfield Marketing Group Inc, pg 1253
Fenway Group, pg 1253
Ferry Associates Inc, pg 1253
Four Colour Print Group, pg 1253
Frederic Printing, pg 1253
Friesens Corp, pg 1253
Fry Communications Inc, pg 1253
Fuse Graphics, pg 1253
G & H Soho Inc, pg 1253
GHP, pg 1253
Global Interprint Inc, pg 1253
GLS Companies, pg 1254
Goose River Press, pg 1254
Graphic Composition Inc, pg 1254
Graphic Litho, pg 1254
GraphiColor Corp, pg 1254
HBP Inc, pg 1254
Heidelberg Graphics, pg 1254
Hennegan Co, pg 1254
Hess Print Solutions, pg 1254
Worth Higgins & Associates Inc, pg 1254
Hignell Book Printing Ltd, pg 1254
The P A Hutchison Co, pg 1254
Imago, pg 1254
Impressions Inc, pg 1255
InfinitPrint Solutions Inc, pg 1255
Infinity Graphics, pg 1255
Interstate Printing Co, pg 1255
Ironmark, pg 1255
JP Graphics Inc, pg 1255

1241

PRINTING, BINDING & BOOK FINISHING INDEX

Kappa Graphics LLP, pg 1255
Knepper Press Corp, pg 1255
Kromar Printing Ltd, pg 1255
La Crosse Graphics Inc, pg 1255
Lake Book Manufacturing Inc, pg 1255
L+L Printers, pg 1256
Lawton Connect, pg 1256
Lee Publications, pg 1256
Leo Paper USA, pg 1256
The Lexington Press Inc, pg 1256
Manroland Inc, pg 1256
Maple Press, pg 1256
Maracle Inc, pg 1256
Marquis Book Printing Inc, pg 1256
Marrakech Express Inc, pg 1256
Martin Printing Co Inc, pg 1257
The Master's Press, pg 1257
McClain Printing Co, pg 1257
Morris Printing Group Inc, pg 1257
Neibauer Press, pg 1257
Nissha USA Inc, pg 1257
Noble Book Press Corp, pg 1257
OGM USA, pg 1257
Omnipress, pg 1257
OneTouchPoint, pg 1257
Overseas Printing Corporation, pg 1257
Panaprint Inc, pg 1258
Patterson Printing Co, pg 1258
PBM Graphics Inc, an RR Donnelley Co, pg 1258
Pint Size Productions LLC, pg 1258
PrairieView Press, pg 1258
Print It Plus, pg 1258
The Printer, pg 1258
Printing Corporation of the Americas Inc, pg 1258
Progress Printing Plus, pg 1258
Publishers' Graphics LLC, pg 1258
Puritan Press Inc, pg 1258
Quantum Group, pg 1259
V G Reed & Sons Inc, pg 1259
Regal Press, pg 1259
St Joseph Communications-Print Group, pg 1259
Sheridan GR, pg 1259
Sheridan MI, pg 1259
Sheridan PA, pg 1259
Sheridan Saline, pg 1260
Signature Book Printing Inc, pg 1260
Smith & Sons Printers Inc, pg 1260
Smith-Edwards-Dunlap Co, pg 1260
Southeastern Printing Co, pg 1260
Spectrum PrintGroup Inc, pg 1260
Stephenson Printing, pg 1260
Sun Graphics LLC, pg 1260
John S Swift Co Inc, pg 1260
Thistle Printing Ltd, pg 1261
Times Printing LLC, pg 1261
Toof American Digital, pg 1261
Total Printing Systems, pg 1261
TSO General Corp, pg 1261
Tukaiz LLC, pg 1261
UniversallWilde, pg 1261
VeronaLibri, pg 1261
Versa Press Inc, pg 1261
Vicks Lithograph & Printing Corp, pg 1262
VIP Digital Print Center, pg 1262
Viridiam LLC, pg 1262
Walker360, pg 1262
Walsworth, pg 1262
Webcom Inc, pg 1262
Fred Weidner & Daughter Printers, pg 1262
Whitehall Printing Co, pg 1262
Worzalla, pg 1262
Yurchak Printing Inc, pg 1262

OFFSET PRINTING - WEB

Absolut Color, pg 1247
Action Printing, pg 1247
Adair Graphic Communications, pg 1247
Adams Press, pg 1247
AGS, pg 1247
Anderberg Innovative Print Solutions, pg 1247
Angstrom Graphics Print, pg 1247
APG Group, pg 1248
Arbor Books, pg 1248
Asia Pacific Offset Inc, pg 1248
B & Z Printing Inc, pg 1248
Bamboo Ink, pg 1248
Berryville Graphics, pg 1248
Bethany Press International Inc, pg 1248
Bookmasters, pg 1249
BR Printers, pg 1249
The Bureau, pg 1249
C & C Offset Printing Co USA Inc, pg 1249
California Offset Printers Inc, pg 1250
Cenveo Inc, pg 1250
CJK, pg 1250
Consolidated Printers Inc, pg 1251
Continental Web Press Inc, pg 1251
Corporate Disk Co, pg 1251
Courier Printing, pg 1251
Data Reproductions Corp, pg 1251
Democrat Printing & Lithographing Co, pg 1252
DNP America LLC, pg 1252
RR Donnelley, pg 1252
D3Logic Inc, pg 1252
Dual Graphics, pg 1252
EP Graphics, pg 1253
Fairfield Marketing Group Inc, pg 1253
Ferry Associates Inc, pg 1253
Frederic Printing, pg 1253
Friesens Corp, pg 1253
Fry Communications Inc, pg 1253
G & H Soho Inc, pg 1253
GLS Companies, pg 1254
Goose River Press, pg 1254
Heidelberg Graphics, pg 1254
Hennegan Co, pg 1254
Hess Print Solutions, pg 1254
The P A Hutchison Co, pg 1254
Imago, pg 1254
Interstate Printing Co, pg 1255
Ironmark, pg 1255
Kappa Graphics LLP, pg 1255
Lake Book Manufacturing Inc, pg 1255
The Lane Press Inc, pg 1256
Lee Publications, pg 1256
Manroland Inc, pg 1256
Maple Press, pg 1256
Maracle Inc, pg 1256
Marquis Book Printing Inc, pg 1256
Marrakech Express Inc, pg 1256
Martin Printing Co Inc, pg 1257
Nissha USA Inc, pg 1257
OneTouchPoint, pg 1257
The Ovid Bell Press Inc, pg 1257
Pacific Publishing Co Inc, pg 1258
Panaprint Inc, pg 1258
Patterson Printing Co, pg 1258
PBM Graphics Inc, an RR Donnelley Co, pg 1258
Printing Corporation of the Americas Inc, pg 1258
Progress Printing Plus, pg 1258
V G Reed & Sons Inc, pg 1259
St Joseph Communications-Print Group, pg 1259
Shepherd Inc, pg 1259
Sheridan GR, pg 1259
Sheridan MI, pg 1259
Sheridan NH, pg 1259
Sheridan Saline, pg 1260
Smith & Sons Printers Inc, pg 1260
Spectrum PrintGroup Inc, pg 1260
Stephenson Printing, pg 1260
Sun Graphics LLC, pg 1260
John S Swift Co Inc, pg 1260
Times Printing LLC, pg 1261
Toof American Digital, pg 1261
Total Printing Systems, pg 1261
Townsend Communications Inc, pg 1261
Trend Offset Printing Services, pg 1261
Vicks Lithograph & Printing Corp, pg 1262
Walsworth, pg 1262
Webcom Inc, pg 1262
Webcrafters Inc, pg 1262
Fred Weidner & Daughter Printers, pg 1262
Whitehall Printing Co, pg 1262
Worzalla, pg 1262

ON DEMAND PRINTING

AcmeBinding, pg 1247
Adams Press, pg 1247
AGS, pg 1247
APG Group, pg 1248
Arbor Books, pg 1248
Asia Pacific Offset Inc, pg 1248
Bethany Press International Inc, pg 1248
Blitzprint Inc, pg 1249
BookBaby, pg 1249
BookFactory, pg 1249
Bookmasters, pg 1249
BR Printers, pg 1249
Bridgeport National Bindery Inc, pg 1249
Canterbury Press, pg 1250
CG Book Printers, pg 1250
ColorPage, pg 1250
Copycats, pg 1251
Corporate Disk Co, pg 1251
The Country Press Inc, pg 1251
Cushing-Malloy Inc, pg 1251
DeHART's Media Services Inc, pg 1251
Dekker Bookbinding Inc, pg 1251
Docunet Corp, pg 1252
RR Donnelley, pg 1252
Dupli Envelope & Graphics Corp, pg 1252
EP Graphics, pg 1253
Fenway Group, pg 1253
First Choice Copy, pg 1253
Friesens Corp, pg 1253
Fry Communications Inc, pg 1253
G & H Soho Inc, pg 1253
Garlich Printing Co, pg 1253
Goose River Press, pg 1254
Heidelberg Graphics, pg 1254
Infinity Graphics, pg 1255
L+L Printers, pg 1256
Lightning Source LLC, pg 1256
Maple Press, pg 1256
Marquis Book Printing Inc, pg 1256
Marrakech Express Inc, pg 1256
The Master's Press, pg 1257
O'Neil Digital Solutions LLC, pg 1257
OneTouchPoint, pg 1257
Outskirts Press Inc, pg 1257
PBM Graphics Inc, an RR Donnelley Co, pg 1258
POD Print, pg 1258
Print It Plus, pg 1258
The Printer, pg 1258
Publishers' Graphics LLC, pg 1258

BOOK

Sheridan MI, pg 1259
Sheridan PA, pg 1259
Signature Print Services, pg 1260
Spectrum PrintGroup Inc, pg 1260
Stephenson Printing, pg 1260
Sun Graphics LLC, pg 1260
John S Swift Co Inc, pg 1260
Taylor Communications Inc, pg 1261
Total Printing Systems, pg 1261
VIP Digital Print Center, pg 1262
Walsworth, pg 1262
Wert Bookbinding Inc, pg 1262
Yurchak Printing Inc, pg 1262

PERFECT (ADHESIVE) BINDING

Absolut Color, pg 1247
AcmeBinding, pg 1247
Action Printing, pg 1247
Adair Graphic Communications, pg 1247
Adams Press, pg 1247
AGS, pg 1247
Ambassador Press Inc, pg 1247
American Mathematical Society (AMS), pg 1247
an ICON Company LLC, pg 1247
Arbor Books, pg 1248
Asia Pacific Offset Inc, pg 1248
B & Z Printing Inc, pg 1248
Bang Printing Co Inc, pg 1248
Beidel Printing House Inc, pg 1248
Berryville Graphics, pg 1248
Bindagraphics Inc, pg 1248
The Bindery Inc, pg 1249
Blitzprint Inc, pg 1249
BookBaby, pg 1249
Bookmasters, pg 1249
BookMobile, pg 1249
BR Printers, pg 1249
Bradford & Bigelow Inc, pg 1249
Bridgeport National Bindery Inc, pg 1249
Canterbury Press, pg 1250
Cenveo Inc, pg 1250
Cenveo St Louis, pg 1250
CG Book Printers, pg 1250
CJK, pg 1250
Clare Printing, pg 1250
Coach House Printing, pg 1250
Color House Graphics Inc, pg 1250
ColorPage, pg 1250
Communicorp Inc, pg 1250
Consolidated Printers Inc, pg 1251
Copycats, pg 1251
Corporate Disk Co, pg 1251
The Country Press Inc, pg 1251
Crane Duplicating Service Inc, pg 1251
Cushing-Malloy Inc, pg 1251
Data Reproductions Corp, pg 1251
DeHART's Media Services Inc, pg 1251
Dekker Bookbinding Inc, pg 1251
Democrat Printing & Lithographing Co, pg 1252
DNP America LLC, pg 1252
Docunet Corp, pg 1252
RR Donnelley, pg 1252
W R Draper Co, pg 1252
Dual Graphics, pg 1252
Dunn & Co Inc, pg 1252
Eckhart & Company Inc, pg 1253
Emprint®, pg 1253
EP Graphics, pg 1253
Fenway Group, pg 1253
First Choice Copy, pg 1253
Four Colour Print Group, pg 1253
Frederic Printing, pg 1253
Friesens Corp, pg 1253
Fry Communications Inc, pg 1253

1242

MANUFACTURING

PRINTING, BINDING & BOOK FINISHING INDEX

G & H Soho Inc, pg 1253
GHP, pg 1253
Goose River Press, pg 1254
Gorham Printing, pg 1254
Graphic Composition Inc, pg 1254
Great Lakes Bindery Inc, pg 1254
HBP Inc, pg 1254
Hennegan Co, pg 1254
Hess Print Solutions, pg 1254
Hignell Book Printing Ltd, pg 1254
The P A Hutchison Co, pg 1254
Imago, pg 1254
Impressions Inc, pg 1255
InfinitPrint Solutions Inc, pg 1255
Infinity Graphics, pg 1255
Interstate Printing Co, pg 1255
Ironmark, pg 1255
JP Graphics Inc, pg 1255
Kappa Graphics LLP, pg 1255
Kromar Printing Ltd, pg 1255
La Crosse Graphics Inc, pg 1255
Lake Book Manufacturing Inc, pg 1255
The Lane Press Inc, pg 1256
Leo Paper USA, pg 1256
Letterhead Press Inc (LPI), pg 1256
Lightning Source LLC, pg 1256
Maple Press, pg 1256
Maracle Inc, pg 1256
Marquis Book Printing Inc, pg 1256
Marrakech Express Inc, pg 1256
Martin Printing Co Inc, pg 1257
McClain Printing Co, pg 1257
Morris Printing Group Inc, pg 1257
Morris Publishing®, pg 1257
Multi-Reliure, pg 1257
Nissha USA Inc, pg 1257
Noble Book Press Corp, pg 1257
OGM USA, pg 1257
Omnipress, pg 1257
OneTouchPoint, pg 1257
Overseas Printing Corporation, pg 1257
The Ovid Bell Press Inc, pg 1257
Panaprint Inc, pg 1258
Patterson Printing Co, pg 1258
PBM Graphics Inc, an RR Donnelley Co, pg 1258
POD Print, pg 1258
Print It Plus, pg 1258
The Printer, pg 1258
Printing Corporation of the Americas Inc, pg 1258
ProductionPro, pg 1258
Progress Printing Plus, pg 1258
Publishers Book Bindery (NY), pg 1258
Publishers' Graphics LLC, pg 1258
Puritan Press Inc, pg 1258
Quality Bindery Services Inc, pg 1259
Quantum Group, pg 1259
V G Reed & Sons Inc, pg 1259
Reindl Bindery Co Inc, pg 1259
The Renton Printery Inc, pg 1259
Roswell Bookbinding, pg 1259
Sheridan GR, pg 1259
Sheridan MI, pg 1259
Sheridan PA, pg 1259
Sheridan Saline, pg 1260
Signature Book Printing Inc, pg 1260
Signature Print Services, pg 1260
Smith & Sons Printers Inc, pg 1260
Specialty Finishing Group, pg 1260
Spectrum PrintGroup Inc, pg 1260
Stephenson Printing, pg 1260
The Studley Press Inc, pg 1260
Sun Graphics LLC, pg 1260
John S Swift Co Inc, pg 1260
Times Printing LLC, pg 1261
Toof American Digital, pg 1261
Total Printing Systems, pg 1261

TSO General Corp, pg 1261
Turtleback Books, pg 1261
Universal Bookbindery Inc, pg 1261
VeronaLibri, pg 1261
Versa Press Inc, pg 1261
Vicks Lithograph & Printing Corp, pg 1262
VIP Digital Print Center, pg 1262
Walker360, pg 1262
Walsworth, pg 1262
Webcom Inc, pg 1262
Webcrafters Inc, pg 1262
Fred Weidner & Daughter Printers, pg 1262
Whitehall Printing Co, pg 1262
Worzalla, pg 1262
Yurchak Printing Inc, pg 1262

PHOTOCOMPOSITION

Action Printing, pg 1247
Adair Graphic Communications, pg 1247
Adams Press, pg 1247
AGS, pg 1247
American Mathematical Society (AMS), pg 1247
appatura™, A Broadridge Company, pg 1248
Arbor Books, pg 1248
Birmingham Printing & Publishing Inc, pg 1249
Blue Note Publications Inc, pg 1249
Clare Printing, pg 1250
Coach House Printing, pg 1250
ColorPage, pg 1250
Dekker Bookbinding Inc, pg 1251
dix! Digital Prepress Inc, pg 1252
RR Donnelley, pg 1252
W R Draper Co, pg 1252
Edison Lithograph & Printing Corp, pg 1253
G & H Soho Inc, pg 1253
GHP, pg 1253
Infinity Graphics, pg 1255
Knepper Press Corp, pg 1255
Leo Paper USA, pg 1256
Maracle Inc, pg 1256
Marquis Book Printing Inc, pg 1256
McClain Printing Co, pg 1257
PrairieView Press, pg 1258
Print It Plus, pg 1258
Publishing Data Management Inc, pg 1258
Quantum Group, pg 1259
The Renton Printery Inc, pg 1259
Southeastern Printing Co, pg 1260
The Studley Press Inc, pg 1260
John S Swift Co Inc, pg 1260
Thistle Printing Ltd, pg 1261
Times Printing LLC, pg 1261
Toof American Digital, pg 1261
TotalWorks™ Inc, pg 1261
VeronaLibri, pg 1261
Walsworth, pg 1262
Webcom Inc, pg 1262
Fred Weidner & Daughter Printers, pg 1262

PLASTIC COMB BINDING

Action Printing, pg 1247
Adams Press, pg 1247
AGS, pg 1247
Ambassador Press Inc, pg 1247
American Mathematical Society (AMS), pg 1247
Arbor Books, pg 1248
Asia Pacific Offset Inc, pg 1248
B & Z Printing Inc, pg 1248
Bang Printing Co Inc, pg 1248
Bindagraphics Inc, pg 1248

The Bindery Inc, pg 1249
Blitzprint Inc, pg 1249
Bookmasters, pg 1249
BR Printers, pg 1249
C & C Offset Printing Co USA Inc, pg 1249
Canterbury Press, pg 1250
CG Book Printers, pg 1250
CJK, pg 1250
Color House Graphics Inc, pg 1250
ColorPage, pg 1250
Cookbook Publishers Inc, pg 1251
Copycats, pg 1251
Corporate Disk Co, pg 1251
Cushing-Malloy Inc, pg 1251
Data Reproductions Corp, pg 1251
DeHART's Media Services Inc, pg 1251
Dekker Bookbinding Inc, pg 1251
DNP America LLC, pg 1252
RR Donnelley, pg 1252
W R Draper Co, pg 1252
Dunn & Co Inc, pg 1252
Dupli Envelope & Graphics Corp, pg 1252
Eckhart & Company Inc, pg 1253
EP Graphics, pg 1253
Fenway Group, pg 1253
First Choice Copy, pg 1253
Four Colour Print Group, pg 1253
Frederic Printing, pg 1253
Friesens Corp, pg 1253
Goose River Press, pg 1254
Great Lakes Bindery Inc, pg 1254
Hignell Book Printing Ltd, pg 1254
The P A Hutchison Co, pg 1254
Imago, pg 1254
Impressions Inc, pg 1255
InfinitPrint Solutions Inc, pg 1255
Infinity Graphics, pg 1255
Ironmark, pg 1255
L+L Printers, pg 1256
Leo Paper USA, pg 1256
Letterhead Press Inc (LPI), pg 1256
The Lexington Press Inc, pg 1256
Lo Gatto Bookbinding, pg 1256
Maracle Inc, pg 1256
Marquis Book Printing Inc, pg 1256
Marrakech Express Inc, pg 1256
McClain Printing Co, pg 1257
Morris Printing Group Inc, pg 1257
Morris Publishing®, pg 1257
Nissha USA Inc, pg 1257
OneTouchPoint, pg 1257
Patterson Printing Co, pg 1258
POD Print, pg 1258
PrairieView Press, pg 1258
Print It Plus, pg 1258
The Printer, pg 1258
Printing Corporation of the Americas Inc, pg 1258
Puritan Press Inc, pg 1258
Quality Bindery Services Inc, pg 1259
Quantum Group, pg 1259
Reindl Bindery Co Inc, pg 1259
The Renton Printery Inc, pg 1259
Sheridan GR, pg 1259
Sheridan MI, pg 1259
Sheridan Saline, pg 1260
Signature Book Printing Inc, pg 1260
Smith & Sons Printers Inc, pg 1260
Southeastern Printing Co, pg 1260
Specialty Finishing Group, pg 1260
Spectrum PrintGroup Inc, pg 1260
Spiral Binding LLC, pg 1260
Springdale Bindery LLC, pg 1260
Sun Graphics LLC, pg 1260
John S Swift Co Inc, pg 1260
Times Printing LLC, pg 1261
Toof American Digital, pg 1261
Total Printing Systems, pg 1261

TSO General Corp, pg 1261
Universal Bookbindery Inc, pg 1261
VeronaLibri, pg 1261
Versa Press Inc, pg 1261
Vicks Lithograph & Printing Corp, pg 1262
VIP Digital Print Center, pg 1262
Viridiam LLC, pg 1262
Walsworth, pg 1262
Fred Weidner & Daughter Printers, pg 1262
Whitehall Printing Co, pg 1262
Worzalla, pg 1262
Yurchak Printing Inc, pg 1262

SADDLE STITCH BINDING

Absolut Color, pg 1247
Action Printing, pg 1247
Adair Graphic Communications, pg 1247
Adams Press, pg 1247
AGS, pg 1247
Ambassador Press Inc, pg 1247
American Mathematical Society (AMS), pg 1247
an ICON Company LLC, pg 1247
Anderberg Innovative Print Solutions, pg 1247
Arbor Books, pg 1248
Asia Pacific Offset Inc, pg 1248
B & Z Printing Inc, pg 1248
Balfour Commercial Printing, pg 1248
Bang Printing Co Inc, pg 1248
Beidel Printing House Inc, pg 1248
Bindagraphics Inc, pg 1248
Blitzprint Inc, pg 1249
BookFactory, pg 1249
Bookmasters, pg 1249
BR Printers, pg 1249
Bradford & Bigelow Inc, pg 1249
The Bureau, pg 1249
C & C Offset Printing Co USA Inc, pg 1249
Canterbury Press, pg 1250
Cenveo St Louis, pg 1250
CG Book Printers, pg 1250
CJK, pg 1250
Clare Printing, pg 1250
Color House Graphics Inc, pg 1250
ColorPage, pg 1250
Consolidated Printers Inc, pg 1251
Cookbook Publishers Inc, pg 1251
Copycats, pg 1251
Corporate Disk Co, pg 1251
The Country Press Inc, pg 1251
Courier Printing, pg 1251
Crane Duplicating Service Inc, pg 1251
Cushing-Malloy Inc, pg 1251
Data Reproductions Corp, pg 1251
DeHART's Media Services Inc, pg 1251
Dekker Bookbinding Inc, pg 1251
Democrat Printing & Lithographing Co, pg 1252
DNP America LLC, pg 1252
Docunet Corp, pg 1252
RR Donnelley, pg 1252
W R Draper Co, pg 1252
Drummond, pg 1252
Dual Graphics, pg 1252
Dunn & Co Inc, pg 1252
EP Graphics, pg 1253
Fairfield Marketing Group Inc, pg 1253
Fenway Group, pg 1253
First Choice Copy, pg 1253
Four Colour Print Group, pg 1253
Friesens Corp, pg 1253
Fry Communications Inc, pg 1253

1243

PRINTING, BINDING & BOOK FINISHING INDEX — BOOK

G & H Soho Inc, pg 1253
Garlich Printing Co, pg 1253
GHP, pg 1253
Global Interprint Inc, pg 1253
GLS Companies, pg 1254
Goose River Press, pg 1254
Graphic Composition Inc, pg 1254
Graphic Litho, pg 1254
HBP Inc, pg 1254
Hennegan Co, pg 1254
Hess Print Solutions, pg 1254
Worth Higgins & Associates Inc, pg 1254
Hignell Book Printing Ltd, pg 1254
The P A Hutchison Co, pg 1254
Imago, pg 1254
Impressions Inc, pg 1255
InfinitPrint Solutions Inc, pg 1255
Infinity Graphics, pg 1255
Ironmark, pg 1255
JP Graphics Inc, pg 1255
Kappa Graphics LLP, pg 1255
Knepper Press Corp, pg 1255
Kromar Printing Ltd, pg 1255
La Crosse Graphics Inc, pg 1255
Lake Book Manufacturing Inc, pg 1255
L+L Printers, pg 1256
The Lane Press Inc, pg 1256
Leo Paper USA, pg 1256
Letterhead Press Inc (LPI), pg 1256
The Lexington Press Inc, pg 1256
Maracle Inc, pg 1256
Marquis Book Printing Inc, pg 1256
Marrakech Express Inc, pg 1256
Martin Printing Co Inc, pg 1257
McClain Printing Co, pg 1257
Morris Printing Group Inc, pg 1257
Morris Publishing®, pg 1257
Nissha USA Inc, pg 1257
Noble Book Press Corp, pg 1257
OGM USA, pg 1257
Omnipress, pg 1257
OneTouchPoint, pg 1257
Overseas Printing Corporation, pg 1257
The Ovid Bell Press Inc, pg 1257
Panaprint Inc, pg 1258
Patterson Printing Co, pg 1258
PBM Graphics Inc, an RR Donnelley Co, pg 1258
POD Print, pg 1258
PrairieView Press, pg 1258
Print It Plus, pg 1258
The Printer, pg 1258
Printing Corporation of the Americas Inc, pg 1258
ProductionPro, pg 1258
Progress Printing Plus, pg 1258
Publishers' Graphics LLC, pg 1258
Puritan Press Inc, pg 1258
Quality Bindery Services Inc, pg 1259
Quantum Group, pg 1259
V G Reed & Sons Inc, pg 1259
The Renton Printery Inc, pg 1259
Roswell Bookbinding, pg 1259
Sheridan GR, pg 1259
Sheridan MI, pg 1259
Sheridan PA, pg 1259
Sheridan Saline, pg 1260
Signature Book Printing Inc, pg 1260
Signature Print Services, pg 1260
Smith & Sons Printers Inc, pg 1260
Smith-Edwards-Dunlap Co, pg 1260
Southeastern Printing Co, pg 1260
Spectrum PrintGroup Inc, pg 1260
Springdale Bindery LLC, pg 1260
Stephenson Printing, pg 1260
Sterling Pierce Co Inc, pg 1260
Sun Graphics LLC, pg 1260
John S Swift Co Inc, pg 1260

Thistle Printing Ltd, pg 1261
Times Printing LLC, pg 1261
Toof American Digital, pg 1261
Total Printing Systems, pg 1261
Townsend Communications Inc, pg 1261
VeronaLibri, pg 1261
Versa Press Inc, pg 1261
Vicks Lithograph & Printing Corp, pg 1262
VIP Digital Print Center, pg 1262
Viridiam LLC, pg 1262
Walker360, pg 1262
Walsworth, pg 1262
Webcom Inc, pg 1262
Webcrafters Inc, pg 1262
Fred Weidner & Daughter Printers, pg 1262
Worzalla, pg 1262
Yurchak Printing Inc, pg 1262

SHORT RUN PRINTING

AcmeBinding, pg 1247
Action Printing, pg 1247
Adair Graphic Communications, pg 1247
Adams Press, pg 1247
AGS, pg 1247
Ambassador Press Inc, pg 1247
American Mathematical Society (AMS), pg 1247
an ICON Company LLC, pg 1247
appatura™, A Broadridge Company, pg 1248
Arbor Books, pg 1248
Asia Pacific Offset Inc, pg 1248
Balfour Commercial Printing, pg 1248
Bang Printing Co Inc, pg 1248
Bedford Printing Co, pg 1248
Beidel Printing House Inc, pg 1248
Bethany Press International Inc, pg 1248
Birmingham Printing & Publishing Inc, pg 1249
Blitzprint Inc, pg 1249
Blue Note Publications Inc, pg 1249
Blue Ridge Printing Co, pg 1249
BookFactory, pg 1249
Bookmasters, pg 1249
BookMobile, pg 1249
BR Printers, pg 1249
Bridgeport National Bindery Inc, pg 1249
California Offset Printers Inc, pg 1250
Canterbury Press, pg 1250
Cenveo St Louis, pg 1250
CG Book Printers, pg 1250
CJK, pg 1250
Clare Printing, pg 1250
Coach House Printing, pg 1250
Color Graphic Press Inc, pg 1250
Color House Graphics Inc, pg 1250
ColorPage, pg 1250
Cookbook Publishers Inc, pg 1251
Copycats, pg 1251
Corporate Disk Co, pg 1251
The Country Press Inc, pg 1251
Crane Duplicating Service Inc, pg 1251
Cushing-Malloy Inc, pg 1251
Data Reproductions Corp, pg 1251
DeHART's Media Services Inc, pg 1251
Dekker Bookbinding Inc, pg 1251
DNP America LLC, pg 1252
Docunet Corp, pg 1252
RR Donnelley, pg 1252
W R Draper Co, pg 1252
Dunn & Co Inc, pg 1252

Dupli Envelope & Graphics Corp, pg 1252
Eckhart & Company Inc, pg 1253
Edison Lithograph & Printing Corp, pg 1253
Emprint®, pg 1253
EP Graphics, pg 1253
Fairfield Marketing Group Inc, pg 1253
Fenway Group, pg 1253
First Choice Copy, pg 1253
Four Colour Print Group, pg 1253
Friesens Corp, pg 1253
G & H Soho Inc, pg 1253
GHP, pg 1253
Global Interprint Inc, pg 1253
Goose River Press, pg 1254
Gorham Printing, pg 1254
HBP Inc, pg 1254
Heidelberg Graphics, pg 1254
Hess Print Solutions, pg 1254
Hignell Book Printing Ltd, pg 1254
The P A Hutchison Co, pg 1254
InfinitPrint Solutions Inc, pg 1255
Infinity Graphics, pg 1255
Interstate Printing Co, pg 1255
Ironmark, pg 1255
Knepper Press Corp, pg 1255
Lake Book Manufacturing Inc, pg 1255
L+L Printers, pg 1256
The Lexington Press Inc, pg 1256
Lightning Source LLC, pg 1256
Maple Press, pg 1256
Maracle Inc, pg 1256
Marquis Book Printing Inc, pg 1256
Marrakech Express Inc, pg 1256
Martin Printing Co Inc, pg 1257
The Master's Press, pg 1257
McClain Printing Co, pg 1257
Morris Printing Group Inc, pg 1257
Morris Publishing®, pg 1257
Neibauer Press, pg 1257
Nissha USA Inc, pg 1257
Noble Book Press Corp, pg 1257
Omnipress, pg 1257
O'Neil Digital Solutions LLC, pg 1257
OneTouchPoint, pg 1257
Outskirts Press Inc, pg 1257
Overseas Printing Corporation, pg 1257
Patterson Printing Co, pg 1258
POD Print, pg 1258
The Printer, pg 1258
Printing Corporation of the Americas Inc, pg 1258
Publishers Book Bindery (NY), pg 1258
Puritan Press Inc, pg 1258
Quantum Group, pg 1259
The Renton Printery Inc, pg 1259
RISO Inc, pg 1259
Roswell Bookbinding, pg 1259
Sheridan MI, pg 1259
Sheridan PA, pg 1259
Sheridan Saline, pg 1260
Signature Book Printing Inc, pg 1260
Smith & Sons Printers Inc, pg 1260
Southeastern Printing Co, pg 1260
Spectrum PrintGroup Inc, pg 1260
Stephenson Printing, pg 1260
Sterling Pierce Co Inc, pg 1260
Sun Graphics LLC, pg 1260
John S Swift Co Inc, pg 1260
Thistle Printing Ltd, pg 1261
Times Printing LLC, pg 1261
Total Printing Systems, pg 1261
Townsend Communications Inc, pg 1261
Versa Press Inc, pg 1261
VIP Digital Print Center, pg 1262

Viridiam LLC, pg 1262
Walsworth, pg 1262
Webcom Inc, pg 1262
Webcrafters Inc, pg 1262
Fred Weidner & Daughter Printers, pg 1262
Wert Bookbinding Inc, pg 1262
Whitehall Printing Co, pg 1262
Worzalla, pg 1262
Yurchak Printing Inc, pg 1262

SIDE STITCH BINDING

Adair Graphic Communications, pg 1247
Adams Press, pg 1247
an ICON Company LLC, pg 1247
Arbor Books, pg 1248
Asia Pacific Offset Inc, pg 1248
Bookshelf Bindery Ltd, pg 1249
BR Printers, pg 1249
The Bureau, pg 1249
C & C Offset Printing Co USA Inc, pg 1249
CG Book Printers, pg 1250
Clare Printing, pg 1250
ColorPage, pg 1250
Copycats, pg 1251
Corporate Disk Co, pg 1251
Data Reproductions Corp, pg 1251
DeHART's Media Services Inc, pg 1251
Democrat Printing & Lithographing Co, pg 1252
DNP America LLC, pg 1252
Docunet Corp, pg 1252
RR Donnelley, pg 1252
W R Draper Co, pg 1252
Dunn & Co Inc, pg 1252
Fenway Group, pg 1253
First Choice Copy, pg 1253
Four Colour Print Group, pg 1253
Friesens Corp, pg 1253
G & H Soho Inc, pg 1253
Hennegan Co, pg 1254
HF Group LLC, pg 1254
The P A Hutchison Co, pg 1254
Imago, pg 1254
Impressions Inc, pg 1255
Infinity Graphics, pg 1255
Ironmark, pg 1255
Knepper Press Corp, pg 1255
La Crosse Graphics Inc, pg 1255
Lake Book Manufacturing Inc, pg 1255
L+L Printers, pg 1256
Leo Paper USA, pg 1256
Letterhead Press Inc (LPI), pg 1256
The Lexington Press Inc, pg 1256
Marrakech Express Inc, pg 1256
Martin Printing Co Inc, pg 1257
McClain Printing Co, pg 1257
Nissha USA Inc, pg 1257
OGM USA, pg 1257
Omnipress, pg 1257
OneTouchPoint, pg 1257
Overseas Printing Corporation, pg 1257
POD Print, pg 1258
PrairieView Press, pg 1258
The Printer, pg 1258
Printing Corporation of the Americas Inc, pg 1258
Publishers Book Bindery (NY), pg 1258
Puritan Press Inc, pg 1258
Reindl Bindery Co Inc, pg 1259
Southeastern Printing Co, pg 1260
Spectrum PrintGroup Inc, pg 1260
Springdale Bindery LLC, pg 1260
Sun Graphics LLC, pg 1260
Thistle Printing Ltd, pg 1261
Total Printing Systems, pg 1261

MANUFACTURING

PRINTING, BINDING & BOOK FINISHING INDEX

Turtleback Books, pg 1261
VeronaLibri, pg 1261
Fred Weidner & Daughter Printers, pg 1262
Yurchak Printing Inc, pg 1262

SMYTH-TYPE SEWN BINDING

AcmeBinding, pg 1247
Adams Press, pg 1247
an ICON Company LLC, pg 1247
Arbor Books, pg 1248
Asia Pacific Offset Inc, pg 1248
Balfour Commercial Printing, pg 1248
Bang Printing Co Inc, pg 1248
Beidel Printing House Inc, pg 1248
Bindagraphics Inc, pg 1248
BookFactory, pg 1249
Bookmasters, pg 1249
Bookshelf Bindery Ltd, pg 1249
C & C Offset Printing Co USA Inc, pg 1249
Cenveo St Louis, pg 1250
CG Book Printers, pg 1250
CJK, pg 1250
Color House Graphics Inc, pg 1250
Corporate Disk Co, pg 1251
Cushing-Malloy Inc, pg 1251
Data Reproductions Corp, pg 1251
Dekker Bookbinding Inc, pg 1251
DNP America LLC, pg 1252
RR Donnelley, pg 1252
W R Draper Co, pg 1252
Eckhart & Company Inc, pg 1253
Four Colour Print Group, pg 1253
Friesens Corp, pg 1253
G & H Soho Inc, pg 1253
Goose River Press, pg 1254
Hignell Book Printing Ltd, pg 1254
The P A Hutchison Co, pg 1254
Imago, pg 1254
Impressions Inc, pg 1255
Ironmark, pg 1255
Lake Book Manufacturing Inc, pg 1255
Leo Paper USA, pg 1256
Maple Press, pg 1256
Maracle Inc, pg 1256
Marrakech Express Inc, pg 1256
McClain Printing Co, pg 1257
Nissha USA Inc, pg 1257
OGM USA Inc, pg 1257
Overseas Printing Corporation, pg 1257
Printing Corporation of the Americas Inc, pg 1258
Publishers Book Bindery (NY), pg 1258
Puritan Press Inc, pg 1258
Quality Bindery Services Inc, pg 1259
Reindl Bindery Co Inc, pg 1259
Roswell Bookbinding, pg 1259
Sheridan GR, pg 1259
Sheridan MI, pg 1259
Sheridan Saline, pg 1260
Spectrum PrintGroup Inc, pg 1260
Sun Graphics LLC, pg 1260
Toof American Digital, pg 1261
Universal Bookbindery Inc, pg 1261
VeronaLibri, pg 1261
Versa Press Inc, pg 1261
Walsworth, pg 1262
Fred Weidner & Daughter Printers, pg 1262
Wert Bookbinding Inc, pg 1262
Whitehall Printing Co, pg 1262
Worzalla, pg 1262

SPECIALTY BINDING

AcmeBinding, pg 1247
Adams Press, pg 1247
AGS, pg 1247
Ambassador Press Inc, pg 1247
an ICON Company LLC, pg 1247
APG Group, pg 1248
Arbor Books, pg 1248
Asia Pacific Offset Inc, pg 1248
Bindagraphics Inc, pg 1248
The Bindery Inc, pg 1249
Bookshelf Bindery Ltd, pg 1249
BR Printers, pg 1249
Bridgeport National Bindery Inc, pg 1249
C & C Offset Printing Co USA Inc, pg 1249
Cenveo St Louis, pg 1250
Dekker Bookbinding Inc, pg 1251
RR Donnelley, pg 1252
W R Draper Co, pg 1252
Dunn & Co Inc, pg 1252
Eckhart & Company Inc, pg 1253
Four Colour Print Group, pg 1253
Friesens Corp, pg 1253
G & H Soho Inc, pg 1253
Global Interprint Inc, pg 1253
HF Group LLC, pg 1254
Imago, pg 1254
Impressions Inc, pg 1255
Lake Book Manufacturing Inc, pg 1255
Leo Paper USA, pg 1256
Letterhead Press Inc (LPI), pg 1256
Lo Gatto Bookbinding, pg 1256
Marquis Book Printing Inc, pg 1256
Marrakech Express Inc, pg 1256
Overseas Printing Corporation, pg 1257
Patterson Printing Co, pg 1258
Pint Size Productions LLC, pg 1258
Printing Corporation of the Americas Inc, pg 1258
Publishers Book Bindery (NY), pg 1258
Puritan Press Inc, pg 1258
Quantum Group, pg 1259
Reindl Bindery Co Inc, pg 1259
Roswell Bookbinding, pg 1259
Specialty Finishing Group, pg 1260
Styled Packaging LLC, pg 1260
John S Swift Co Inc, pg 1260
VeronaLibri, pg 1261
Fred Weidner & Daughter Printers, pg 1262
Wert Bookbinding Inc, pg 1262

SPIRAL BINDING

Action Printing, pg 1247
Adams Press, pg 1247
AGS, pg 1247
Ambassador Press Inc, pg 1247
an ICON Company LLC, pg 1247
Arbor Books, pg 1248
Asia Pacific Offset Inc, pg 1248
B & Z Printing Inc, pg 1248
Bang Printing Co Inc, pg 1248
Beidel Printing House Inc, pg 1248
Bindagraphics Inc, pg 1248
The Bindery Inc, pg 1249
Blitzprint Inc, pg 1249
Blue Note Publications Inc, pg 1249
Bookmasters, pg 1249
BookMobile, pg 1249
BR Printers, pg 1249
C & C Offset Printing Co USA Inc, pg 1249
Canterbury Press, pg 1250
CJK, pg 1250
Color House Graphics Inc, pg 1250
ColorPage, pg 1250
Cookbook Publishers Inc, pg 1251
Copycats, pg 1251
Corporate Disk Co, pg 1251
Cushing-Malloy Inc, pg 1251
Data Reproductions Corp, pg 1251
DeHART's Media Services Inc, pg 1251
Dekker Bookbinding Inc, pg 1251
DNP America LLC, pg 1252
Docunet Corp, pg 1252
RR Donnelley, pg 1252
W R Draper Co, pg 1252
Eckhart & Company Inc, pg 1253
Fairfield Marketing Group Inc, pg 1253
Fenway Group, pg 1253
First Choice Copy, pg 1253
Four Colour Print Group, pg 1253
Frederic Printing, pg 1253
Friesens Corp, pg 1253
G & H Soho Inc, pg 1253
Goose River Press, pg 1254
Gorham Printing, pg 1254
Great Lakes Bindery Inc, pg 1254
Hignell Book Printing Ltd, pg 1254
Imago, pg 1254
Impressions Inc, pg 1255
InfinitPrint Solutions Inc, pg 1255
Infinity Graphics, pg 1255
Ironmark, pg 1255
L+L Printers, pg 1256
Leo Paper USA, pg 1256
Letterhead Press Inc (LPI), pg 1256
Maracle Inc, pg 1256
Marquis Book Printing Inc, pg 1256
Marrakech Express Inc, pg 1256
Martin Printing Co Inc, pg 1257
McClain Printing Co, pg 1257
Morris Printing Group Inc, pg 1257
Morris Publishing®, pg 1257
Nissha USA Inc, pg 1257
Omnipress, pg 1257
OneTouchPoint, pg 1257
Overseas Printing Corporation, pg 1257
POD Print, pg 1258
Printing Corporation of the Americas Inc, pg 1258
Puritan Press Inc, pg 1258
Quality Bindery Services Inc, pg 1259
Quantum Group, pg 1259
The Renton Printery Inc, pg 1259
Sheridan GR, pg 1259
Sheridan MI, pg 1259
Sheridan Saline, pg 1260
Signature Book Printing Inc, pg 1260
Smith & Sons Printers Inc, pg 1260
Southeastern Printing Co, pg 1260
Specialty Finishing Group, pg 1260
Spectrum PrintGroup Inc, pg 1260
Spiral Binding LLC, pg 1260
Sun Graphics LLC, pg 1260
John S Swift Co Inc, pg 1260
Times Printing LLC, pg 1261
Toof American Digital, pg 1261
Total Printing Systems, pg 1261
Tribal Print Source, pg 1261
VeronaLibri, pg 1261
Versa Press Inc, pg 1261
Vicks Lithograph & Printing Corp, pg 1262
VIP Digital Print Center, pg 1262
Walker360, pg 1262
Walsworth, pg 1262
Webcom Inc, pg 1262
Webcrafters Inc, pg 1262
Fred Weidner & Daughter Printers, pg 1262
Worzalla, pg 1262
Yurchak Printing Inc, pg 1262

STRUCK-IMAGE COMPOSITION

Arbor Books, pg 1248
DeHART's Media Services Inc, pg 1251
Dekker Bookbinding Inc, pg 1251
W R Draper Co, pg 1252
Townsend Communications Inc, pg 1261
Fred Weidner & Daughter Printers, pg 1262

TEXTBOOK PRINTING - COLLEGE

AcmeBinding, pg 1247
Action Printing, pg 1247
Adair Graphic Communications, pg 1247
Adams Press, pg 1247
AGS, pg 1247
Arbor Books, pg 1248
Asia Pacific Offset Inc, pg 1248
Blitzprint Inc, pg 1249
Bookmasters, pg 1249
BR Printers, pg 1249
Cenveo St Louis, pg 1250
CJK, pg 1250
Corporate Disk Co, pg 1251
Cushing-Malloy Inc, pg 1251
Data Reproductions Corp, pg 1251
DeHART's Media Services Inc, pg 1251
Dekker Bookbinding Inc, pg 1251
DNP America LLC, pg 1252
RR Donnelley, pg 1252
W R Draper Co, pg 1252
Dunn & Co Inc, pg 1252
Fairfield Marketing Group Inc, pg 1253
Friesens Corp, pg 1253
Global Interprint Inc, pg 1253
Goose River Press, pg 1254
Gorham Printing, pg 1254
Graphic Litho, pg 1254
Hess Print Solutions, pg 1254
Hignell Book Printing Ltd, pg 1254
The P A Hutchison Co, pg 1254
Impressions Inc, pg 1255
Infinity Graphics, pg 1255
Ironmark, pg 1255
JP Graphics Inc, pg 1255
Lightning Source LLC, pg 1256
Maple Press, pg 1256
Maracle Inc, pg 1256
Marquis Book Printing Inc, pg 1256
Marrakech Express Inc, pg 1256
McClain Printing Co, pg 1257
Noble Book Press Corp, pg 1257
OneTouchPoint, pg 1257
Patterson Printing Co, pg 1258
POD Print, pg 1258
Sheridan MI, pg 1259
Sheridan Saline, pg 1260
Southeastern Printing Co, pg 1260
Spectrum PrintGroup Inc, pg 1260
Sun Graphics LLC, pg 1260
Total Printing Systems, pg 1261
Versa Press Inc, pg 1261
VIP Digital Print Center, pg 1262
Walsworth, pg 1262
Webcom Inc, pg 1262
Webcrafters Inc, pg 1262
Fred Weidner & Daughter Printers, pg 1262
Whitehall Printing Co, pg 1262

TEXTBOOK PRINTING - EL-HI

AcmeBinding, pg 1247
Action Printing, pg 1247

PRINTING, BINDING & BOOK FINISHING INDEX

Adams Press, pg 1247
AGS, pg 1247
Arbor Books, pg 1248
Asia Pacific Offset Inc, pg 1248
Blitzprint Inc, pg 1249
Bookmasters, pg 1249
BR Printers, pg 1249
Cenveo St Louis, pg 1250
CJK, pg 1250
Corporate Disk Co, pg 1251
Cushing-Malloy Inc, pg 1251
Data Reproductions Corp, pg 1251
DeHART's Media Services Inc, pg 1251
Dekker Bookbinding Inc, pg 1251
DNP America LLC, pg 1252
RR Donnelley, pg 1252
W R Draper Co, pg 1252
Dunn & Co Inc, pg 1252
Fairfield Marketing Group Inc, pg 1253
Friesens Corp, pg 1253
Global Interprint Inc, pg 1253
Gorham Printing, pg 1254
Graphic Litho, pg 1254
Hess Print Solutions, pg 1254
Hignell Book Printing Ltd, pg 1254
The P A Hutchison Co, pg 1254
Imago, pg 1254
Infinity Graphics, pg 1255
JP Graphics Inc, pg 1255
Maracle Inc, pg 1256
Marquis Book Printing Inc, pg 1256
Marrakech Express Inc, pg 1256
McClain Printing Co, pg 1257
OneTouchPoint, pg 1257
Patterson Printing Co, pg 1258
Sheridan MI, pg 1259
Sheridan Saline, pg 1260
Southeastern Printing Co, pg 1260
Spectrum PrintGroup Inc, pg 1260
Sun Graphics LLC, pg 1260
Total Printing Systems, pg 1261
Versa Press Inc, pg 1261
VIP Digital Print Center, pg 1262
Walsworth, pg 1262
Webcom Inc, pg 1262
Webcrafters Inc, pg 1262
Fred Weidner & Daughter Printers, pg 1262
Whitehall Printing Co, pg 1262

WIRE-O BINDING

Absolut Color, pg 1247
Action Printing, pg 1247
Adair Graphic Communications, pg 1247
Adams Press, pg 1247
AGS, pg 1247
Ambassador Press Inc, pg 1247
Arbor Books, pg 1248
Asia Pacific Offset Inc, pg 1248
Bang Printing Co Inc, pg 1248
Beidel Printing House Inc, pg 1248
Bindagraphics Inc, pg 1248
The Bindery Inc, pg 1249
Blitzprint Inc, pg 1249
BookFactory, pg 1249
Bookmasters, pg 1249
BR Printers, pg 1249
C & C Offset Printing Co USA Inc, pg 1249
Canterbury Press, pg 1250
CG Book Printers, pg 1250
CJK, pg 1250
Coach House Printing, pg 1250
Color House Graphics Inc, pg 1250
ColorPage, pg 1250
C Harrison Conroy Co Inc, pg 1251
Cookbook Publishers Inc, pg 1251
Copycats, pg 1251
Corporate Disk Co, pg 1251
Cushing-Malloy Inc, pg 1251
Data Reproductions Corp, pg 1251
DeHART's Media Services Inc, pg 1251
DNP America LLC, pg 1252
RR Donnelley, pg 1252
W R Draper Co, pg 1252
Dunn & Co Inc, pg 1252
Eckhart & Company Inc, pg 1253
EP Graphics, pg 1253
Fenway Group, pg 1253
Four Colour Print Group, pg 1253
G & H Soho Inc, pg 1253
Global Interprint Inc, pg 1253
Goose River Press, pg 1254
Gorham Printing, pg 1254
Graphic Composition Inc, pg 1254
Great Lakes Bindery Inc, pg 1254
Hignell Book Printing Ltd, pg 1254
The P A Hutchison Co, pg 1254
Imago, pg 1254
Impressions Inc, pg 1255
InfinitPrint Solutions Inc, pg 1255
Ironmark, pg 1255
L+L Printers, pg 1256
Leo Paper USA, pg 1256
Letterhead Press Inc (LPI), pg 1256
Maracle Inc, pg 1256
Marquis Book Printing Inc, pg 1256
Marrakech Express Inc, pg 1256
Martin Printing Co Inc, pg 1257
McClain Printing Co, pg 1257
Multi-Reliure, pg 1257
Nissha Inc, pg 1257
OGM USA, pg 1257
Omnipress, pg 1257
OneTouchPoint, pg 1257
Overseas Printing Corporation, pg 1257
Patterson Printing Co, pg 1258
PBM Graphics Inc, an RR Donnelley Co, pg 1258
POD Print, pg 1258
Printing Corporation of the Americas Inc, pg 1258
Publishers Book Bindery (NY), pg 1258
Quality Bindery Services Inc, pg 1259
Quantum Group, pg 1259
Reindl Bindery Co Inc, pg 1259
The Renton Printery Inc, pg 1259
Roswell Bookbinding, pg 1259
Sheridan GR, pg 1259
Sheridan MI, pg 1259
Sheridan Saline, pg 1260
Signature Print Services, pg 1260
Southeastern Printing Co, pg 1260
Specialty Finishing Group, pg 1260
Spectrum PrintGroup Inc, pg 1260
Spiral Binding LLC, pg 1260
Springdale Bindery LLC, pg 1260
Sun Graphics LLC, pg 1260
John S Swift Co Inc, pg 1260
Times Printing LLC, pg 1261
Toof American Digital, pg 1261
Total Printing Systems, pg 1261
Universal Bookbindery Inc, pg 1261
VeronaLibri, pg 1261
Versa Press Inc, pg 1261
VIP Digital Print Center, pg 1262
Viridiam LLC, pg 1262
Walker360, pg 1262
Walsworth, pg 1262
Webcom Inc, pg 1262
Webcrafters Inc, pg 1262
Fred Weidner & Daughter Printers, pg 1262
Whitehall Printing Co, pg 1262
Worzalla, pg 1262

WORKBOOK PRINTING

AcmeBinding, pg 1247
Action Printing, pg 1247
Adair Graphic Communications, pg 1247
Adams Press, pg 1247
AGS, pg 1247
Ambassador Press Inc, pg 1247
an ICON Company LLC, pg 1247
appatura™, A Broadridge Company, pg 1248
Arbor Books, pg 1248
Asia Pacific Offset Inc, pg 1248
Bang Printing Co Inc, pg 1248
Blitzprint Inc, pg 1249
Blue Note Publications Inc, pg 1249
Bookmasters, pg 1249
BR Printers, pg 1249
Canterbury Press, pg 1250
Cenveo St Louis, pg 1250
CG Book Printers, pg 1250
CJK, pg 1250
Clear Print, pg 1250
Color House Graphics Inc, pg 1250
ColorPage, pg 1250
Consolidated Printers Inc, pg 1251
Copycats, pg 1251
Corporate Disk Co, pg 1251
The Country Press Inc, pg 1251
Courier Printing, pg 1251
Cushing-Malloy Inc, pg 1251
Data Reproductions Corp, pg 1251
Dekker Bookbinding Inc, pg 1251
DNP America LLC, pg 1252
Docunet Corp, pg 1252
W R Draper Co, pg 1252
Dunn & Co Inc, pg 1252
Fairfield Marketing Group Inc, pg 1253
Fenway Group, pg 1253
Friesens Corp, pg 1253
Fry Communications Inc, pg 1253
G & H Soho Inc, pg 1253
GHP, pg 1253
Goose River Press, pg 1254
Gorham Printing, pg 1254
Graphic Litho, pg 1254
Hess Print Solutions, pg 1254
Hignell Book Printing Ltd, pg 1254
The P A Hutchison Co, pg 1254
Impressions Inc, pg 1255
InfinitPrint Solutions Inc, pg 1255
Infinity Graphics, pg 1255
Ironmark, pg 1255
JP Graphics Inc, pg 1255
Knepper Press Corp, pg 1255
The Lexington Press Inc, pg 1256
Maracle Inc, pg 1256
Marquis Book Printing Inc, pg 1256
Marrakech Express Inc, pg 1256
McClain Printing Co, pg 1257
Noble Book Press Corp, pg 1257
OneTouchPoint, pg 1257
Overseas Printing Corporation, pg 1257
Panaprint Inc, pg 1258
Patterson Printing Co, pg 1258
POD Print, pg 1258
The Printer, pg 1258
Printing Corporation of the Americas Inc, pg 1258
Quantum Group, pg 1259
RISO Inc, pg 1259
Sheridan GR, pg 1259
Sheridan MI, pg 1259
Sheridan Saline, pg 1260
Signature Book Printing Inc, pg 1260
Smith & Sons Printers Inc, pg 1260
Southeastern Printing Co, pg 1260
Sun Graphics LLC, pg 1260
John S Swift Co Inc, pg 1260
Times Printing LLC, pg 1261
Toof American Digital, pg 1261
Total Printing Systems, pg 1261
Tribal Print Source, pg 1261
Versa Press Inc, pg 1261
Vicks Lithograph & Printing Corp, pg 1262
VIP Digital Print Center, pg 1262
Webcom Inc, pg 1262
Webcrafters Inc, pg 1262
Fred Weidner & Daughter Printers, pg 1262
Whitehall Printing Co, pg 1262
Worzalla, pg 1262
Yurchak Printing Inc, pg 1262

Printing, Binding & Book Finishing

This section includes companies offering printing, binding and/or book finishing services. The descriptions of the services provided are paid components.

Many of the companies listed have been recommended by the manufacturing departments of book publishers as being active and experienced in the production of books.

Absolut Color
109 W 27 St, New York, NY 10001
Tel: 212-868-0404
E-mail: info@absolutcolor.com
Web Site: www.absolutcolor.com
Key Personnel
Pres: Dan Shill
VP: Peter Gordon
Founded: 1960
Turnaround: 1 Workday

AcmeBinding
Division of HF Group LLC
8844 Mayfield Rd, Chesterland, OH 44026
Tel: 440-729-9411 *Toll Free Tel:* 888-485-5415
 Fax: 440-729-9415
Web Site: www.acmebinding.com
Key Personnel
VP & Gen Mgr: Jim Bratton *E-mail:* jbratton@hfgroup.com
Plant Mgr: Dave Lair *E-mail:* dlair@hfgroup.com
Off Mgr/Cust Serv: Rick Burkhart
 E-mail: rburkhart@hfgroup.com
Founded: 1821
Turnaround: 20 Workdays
Print Runs: 1 min - 100,000 max (max for printing, not binding - binding, no limits for quantity)
Branch Office(s)
1010 N Sycamore St, North Manchester, IN 46962, Pres: Jim Heckman *Tel:* 260-982-2107 *Toll Free Tel:* 800-334-3628 *Fax:* 260-982-1130 *E-mail:* jheckman@hfgroup.com
92 Cambridge St, Charlestown, MA 02129-0212, Pres & COO: Paul Parisi *Tel:* 617-242-1100 *Toll Free Tel:* 800-242-1821 *Fax:* 617-242-3764 *E-mail:* pparisi@hfgroup.com
6204 Corporate Park Dr, Browns Summit, NC 27214-9745, VP & Gen Mgr: Scott May *Tel:* 336-931-0800 *Toll Free Tel:* 800-444-7534 *Fax:* 336-931-0711 *E-mail:* smay@hfgroup.com
340 First St, Utica, NE 68456, Gen Mgr: Damon Osborne *Tel:* 402-534-2261 *Toll Free Tel:* 800-869-0420 *Fax:* 402-534-2761 *E-mail:* dosborne@hfgroup.com
45 N Main St, Unit 528, Hatfield, PA 19440 (transportation hub), Off Mgr: Andy Selheimer *Tel:* 215-855-2293 *E-mail:* aselheimer@hfgroup.com
105 W Thomas St, Atlanta, TX 75551-2736 (transportation hub) *Tel:* 260-982-2107 *Fax:* 260-982-1130
Membership(s): The American Library Association (ALA); Book Manufacturers' Institute (BMI); Printing Industries of New England (PINE); PRINTING United Alliance

Action Printing
Division of Gannett Corp
N6637 Rolling Meadows Dr, Fond du Lac, WI 54937
Mailing Address: PO Box 1955, Fond du Lac, WI 54936-1955
Tel: 920-907-7820
E-mail: info@actionprinting.com
Web Site: www.actionprinting.com
Key Personnel
Gen Mgr: Darwin Bethke *E-mail:* dbethke@actionprinting.com
Natl Acct Mgr: Adam Kempf *E-mail:* akempf@actionprinting.com
Press & Bindery Mgr: Brian Thiede
 E-mail: bthiede@actionprinting.com
Founded: 1970
Turnaround: 10 Workdays
Print Runs: 500 min - 250,000 max
Membership(s): Great Lakes Graphics Association (GLGA); PRINTING United Alliance

Adair Graphic Communications
Division of Printwell
26975 Northline Rd, Taylor, MI 48180
Tel: 734-941-6300 *Fax:* 734-942-0920
E-mail: adair@printwell.com
Web Site: www.adairgraphic.com
Key Personnel
Pres & CEO: Paul Borg
VP: Dennis Adair *E-mail:* dennis@adairgraphic.com
Founded: 1931
Turnaround: 10 Workdays
Print Runs: 500 min - 500,000 max

Adams Press
1712 Oakton St, Evanston, IL 60202
E-mail: info@adamspress.com
Key Personnel
Pres: James A Kepler *E-mail:* jkepler@adamspress.com
Founded: 1942
Turnaround: 30-45 Workdays
Print Runs: 100 min
Membership(s): The Association of Publishers for Special Sales (APSS); Independent Book Publishers Association (IBPA); Independent Writers of Chicago (IWOC); Midwest Writers Association

AGS
Subsidiary of RR Donnelley
4590 Graphics Dr, White Plains, MD 20695
Tel: 301-843-1800 *Fax:* 301-843-6339
E-mail: info@ags.com
Web Site: www.ags.com
Key Personnel
Pres: Mike Donohue *E-mail:* mike.donohue@rrd.com
VP, Sales & Mktg: Alan Flint *E-mail:* aflint@ags.com
Founded: 1975
Print Runs: 50 min - 1,000,000 max
Membership(s): American Society of Association Executives™ (ASAE)

amb™, see Ambassador Press Inc

Ambassador Press Inc
1400 Washington Ave N, Minneapolis, MN 55411
Tel: 612-521-0123
E-mail: info@ambpress.com
Web Site: www.ambpress.com
Key Personnel
Co-Owner, Pres & CEO: Candice Engle-Fieldman
Co-Owner & EVP: Harold Engle
Founded: 1960
Turnaround: 3 Workdays
Print Runs: 100 min - 500,000 max

American Mathematical Society (AMS)
201 Charles St, Providence, RI 02904-2213
SAN: 201-1654
Tel: 401-455-4000 *Toll Free Tel:* 800-321-4267
 Fax: 401-331-3842; 401-455-4046 (cust serv)
E-mail: cust-serv@ams.org; ams@ams.org
Web Site: www.ams.org
Key Personnel
Exec Dir: Dr Catherine A Roberts
Publr: Dr Sergei Gelfand
Assoc Exec Dir: Dr Robert M Harrington
Assoc Exec Dir, Washington, DC: Dr Karen Saxe
Founded: 1888
Print Runs: 100 min - 10,000 max
Branch Office(s)
1527 18 St NW, Washington, DC 20036-1358 (govt rel & sci policy) *Tel:* 202-588-1100 *Fax:* 202-588-1853 *E-mail:* amsdc@ams.org
Mathematical Reviews®, 416 Fourth St, Ann Arbor, MI 48103-4820 (edit) *Tel:* 734-996-5250 *Fax:* 734-996-2916 *E-mail:* mathrev@ams.org
Secretary of the AMS - Society Governance, Dept of Computer Science, North Carolina State University, Box 8206, Raleigh, NC 27695-8206 *Tel:* 919-515-7863 *Fax:* 919-515-7896 *E-mail:* secretary@ams.org
Membership(s): Society for Scholarly Publishing (SSP)

an ICON Company LLC
401 Harper Ave SW, Lenoir, NC 28645
Tel: 828-758-7260 *Fax:* 828-754-6353
E-mail: info@lenoirprinting.com
Web Site: lenoirprinting.com
Key Personnel
Pres: Jeffrey R Chrisman
Turnaround: 8-10 Workdays

Anderberg Innovative Print Solutions
6999 Oxford St, St Louis Park, MN 55426
Tel: 952-848-7300 *Toll Free Tel:* 800-231-9777
 Fax: 952-920-1103
E-mail: sales@anderbergprint.com
Web Site: www.anderbergprint.com
Key Personnel
Owner: Greg Anderberg; Paul Anderberg
Founded: 1971

Angstrom Graphics Print
Division of Angstrom Group
4437 E 49 St, Cleveland, OH 44125
Tel: 216-271-5300 *Toll Free Tel:* 800-634-1262
E-mail: info@angstromgraphics.com
Web Site: www.angstromgraphics.com
Key Personnel
Chmn & CEO: Wayne Angstrom
Mng Dir: Mark Angstrom
Founded: 1918
Branch Office(s)
7060 W State Rd 84, Suite 1, Davie, FL 33317 *Tel:* 954-926-5000

Any Laminating Service
13214 Crenshaw Blvd, Gardena, CA 90249
Tel: 310-464-8885 *Toll Free Tel:* 800-400-3105
E-mail: quoterequest@anylam.com
Web Site: anylam.com
Key Personnel
Owner & Pres: Jim Rosenberger

PRINTING, BINDING & BOOK FINISHING

Founded: 1977
Turnaround: 2-3 Workdays
Print Runs: 100 min - 30,000 max
Membership(s): Digital Print Industry Association; PRINTING United Alliance

Apex Die Corp
840 Cherry Lane, San Carlos, CA 94070
Tel: 650-592-6350 *Fax:* 650-592-5315
E-mail: info@apexdie.com
Web Site: www.apexdie.com
Key Personnel
VP, Fin & CFO: Eva Cummings *Tel:* 650-592-6350 ext 231 *E-mail:* ecummings@apexdie.com
Pres & Prod Mgr: Teddee Cullen *Tel:* 650-592-6350 ext 262 *E-mail:* tedcullen@apexdie.com
Founded: 1956
Membership(s): Foil & Specialty Effects Association (FSEA); PRINTING United Alliance

APG Group
235 Homestead Place, Suite 1A, Park Ridge, NJ 07656
Tel: 201-420-8501
Web Site: www.apggroupinc.com
Key Personnel
Owner: Arlene Packles *E-mail:* arlene@apggroupinc.com
Founded: 1994

appatura™, A Broadridge Company
Division of Broadridge Financial Solutions Inc
65 Challenger Rd, Suite 400, Ridgefield Park, NJ 07660
Tel: 201-508-6000 *Toll Free Tel:* 800-277-2155
E-mail: contactus@appatura.com
Web Site: www.appatura.com
Key Personnel
CEO: Richard Plotka
CIO: Faisal Fareed
Chief Prod Offr: Harsh Choudhary
Chief Strategy Offr: John Closson
Head, Fin: Alpha Diarra
Founded: 1949
Print Runs: 1,000 min - 250,000 max

Arbor Books
244 Madison Ave, Box 254, New York, NY 10016
Tel: 212-956-0950 *Toll Free Tel:* 877-822-2500
Fax: 914-401-9385
E-mail: info@arborbooks.com; editorial@arborbooks.net
Web Site: www.arborbooks.com
Key Personnel
Owner: Joel Hochman *Tel:* 877-822-2502 *E-mail:* arborbooksjoel@aol.com; Larry Leichman *Tel:* 877-822-2504 *E-mail:* arborbookslarry@aol.com
Mktg Dir: Olga Vladi *E-mail:* floatinggal1@aol.com
Founded: 1992
Turnaround: 21 Workdays; 1-7 Workdays for art
Print Runs: 1 min - 1,000,000 max

Arbor Services, see Arbor Books

Asia Pacific Offset Inc
1312 "Q" St NW, Suite B, Washington, DC 20009
Tel: 202-462-5436 *Toll Free Tel:* 800-756-4344
Fax: 202-986-4030
Web Site: www.asiapacificoffset.com
Key Personnel
Pres: Andrew Clarke *E-mail:* andrew@asiapacificoffset.com
Founded: 1997
Turnaround: 105 Workdays including color separation & shipping
Print Runs: 2,000 min

Branch Office(s)
870 Market St, Suite 801, San Francisco, CA 94102, Dir, Sales: Amy Armstrong *Tel:* 415-433-3488 *Fax:* 415-433-3489 *E-mail:* amy@asiapacificoffset.com
1768 Oakmont Ct, Ann Arbor, MI 48108, Dir, Sales: Dean Sherman *Tel:* 734-223-6218 *E-mail:* dean@asiapacificoffset.com
62 Rivington St, Suite 2B, New York, NY 10002, Dir, Sales & Mktg: Simona Jansons *Tel:* 212-941-8300 *Fax:* 212-941-9810 *E-mail:* simona@asiapacificoffset.com
16 Clements Dr, Avoca Beach, NSW 2251, Australia, Dir, Sales: Penny Crocker *Tel:* (02) 4382 6174 *E-mail:* penny@asiapacificoffset.com
57 Norfolk St, Ponsonby, Auckland 1021, New Zealand, Consultant: Barbara Nielsen *Tel:* (09) 378-4971 *E-mail:* barbara@asiapacificoffset.com
C/ Tamarit 104, esc D, entrance 2, 08015 Barcelona, Spain, Dir, Sales: Carlos Blavia *Tel:* 933278837 *Fax:* 933254826 *E-mail:* carlos@asiapacificoffset.com
20 Mortlake High St, London SW14 8JN, United Kingdom, Dir, Sales: Adrian Gatheroole *Tel:* (020) 3170 8700 *Fax:* (020) 3170 8704 *E-mail:* adrian@asiapacificoffset.com

Automated Graphic Systems, see AGS

B & Z Printing Inc
1300 E Wakeham Ave, Unit B, Santa Ana, CA 92705
Tel: 714-892-2000
Web Site: www.bandzprinting.com
Key Personnel
Pres: Frank Buono *E-mail:* frank@bandzprinting.com
Founded: 1984
Turnaround: 7-10 Workdays
Print Runs: 3,000 min

Balfour Commercial Printing
Formerly Taylor Specialty Books
Division of Balfour/Taylor
225 E John Carpenter Fwy, Tower 2, Suite 400, Irving, TX 75062
Tel: 214-819-8588 (cust serv)
E-mail: printing@balfour.com
Web Site: commercial-printing.balfour.com
Key Personnel
Acct Exec: Julie Kacala *E-mail:* julie.kacala@balfour.com
Founded: 1939
Turnaround: 30-35 Workdays
Print Runs: 250 min - 25,000 max

Bamboo Ink
807 Oliver Hill Way, Richmond, VA 23219
Mailing Address: PO Box 398, Richmond, VA 23218-0398
Tel: 804-230-4515
E-mail: info@bambooink.com
Web Site: www.bambooink.com
Key Personnel
Owner & Sales: Robert Rhodes *E-mail:* bob@bambooink.com
Cust Serv: Brooke Rhodes *E-mail:* brooke@bambooink.com

Bang Printing Co Inc
Division of CJK Group Inc
3323 Oak St, Brainerd, MN 56401
Tel: 218-829-2877 *Toll Free Tel:* 800-328-0450
Fax: 218-829-7145
E-mail: info@bangprinting.com
Web Site: www.bangprinting.com
Key Personnel
Pres: Todd Vanek *E-mail:* toddv@bangprinting.com

VP, Opers: Joe Saiko *E-mail:* joes@bangprinting.com
VP, Sales: Doug Walters *E-mail:* dougw@bangprinting.com
Founded: 1899
Turnaround: 10-25 Workdays
Print Runs: 1,000 min - 500,000 max

Bedford Printing Co
1501 S Blount St, Raleigh, NC 27603
Mailing Address: PO Box 28617, Raleigh, NC 27611
Tel: 919-832-3973 *Fax:* 919-755-0204
Web Site: www.bedfordprinting.com
Key Personnel
Owner & Pres: Roger L Jones *E-mail:* rjones@bedfordprinting.com
Founded: 1975
Print Runs: 1 min - 1,000,000 max
Membership(s): PICA

Beidel Printing House Inc
Division of White Mane Publishing Co Inc
225 S Fayette St, Shippensburg, PA 17257
Mailing Address: PO Box 708, Shippensburg, PA 17257-0708
Tel: 717-532-5063 *Fax:* 717-532-2502
E-mail: customerservice@dreamprint.com
Web Site: dreamprint.com
Key Personnel
VP & Ed: Harold Collier
VP, Opers: Thomas M Fritz
Founded: 1917

Berryville Graphics
Member of Bertelsmann Printing Group
25 Jack Enders Blvd, Berryville, VA 22611
Tel: 540-955-2750 *Fax:* 540-955-2633
E-mail: info@bvgraphics.com
Web Site: www.bpg-usa.com
Key Personnel
CEO: Christof Ludwig
CFO: Denis Leite
CTO: Yannic Schroeder
Founded: 1956
Turnaround: 15 Workdays (initial orders); 6 Workdays (reprint orders); 4 Workdays (out of stock)
Print Runs: 1,500 min
Branch Office(s)
100 N Miller St, Fairfield, PA 17320 *Tel:* 717-549-4800
871 Baker St, Martinsburg, VA 25405 *Tel:* 681-247-3300

Bethany Press International Inc
6820 W 115 St, Bloomington, MN 55438
Tel: 952-914-7400 *Toll Free Tel:* 888-717-7400
Fax: 952-914-7410
E-mail: info@bethanypress.com
Web Site: www.bethanypress.com
Key Personnel
Pres & CEO: Pete Larson
Founded: 1997

Bindagraphics Inc
2701 Wilmarco Ave, Baltimore, MD 21223-9922
Tel: 410-362-7200 *Toll Free Tel:* 800-326-0300
Fax: 410-362-7233
E-mail: info@bindagraphics.com
Web Site: www.bindagraphics.com
Key Personnel
Owner & Pres: Matt Anson
Founded: 1974
Turnaround: Same day & longer
Branch Office(s)
Bindagraphics South Inc, 100 N Pendleton S, High Point, NC 27260 *Tel:* 336-431-6200 *Fax:* 410-431-6232
Membership(s): PRINTING United Alliance

MANUFACTURING

PRINTING, BINDING & BOOK FINISHING

The Bindery Inc
8201 Brooklyn Blvd, Brooklyn Park, MN 55445
Tel: 763-201-2800 *Toll Free Tel:* 800-851-6598
  Fax: 763-201-2790
E-mail: info@thebinderymn.com
Web Site: www.thebinderymn.com
Key Personnel
Pres & CEO: Rob Stire *E-mail:* rstire@
  thebinderymn.com
VP, Opers: Mat Browne *Tel:* 763-201-2723
  E-mail: mbrowne@thebinderymn.com
Founded: 1974
Membership(s): Epicomm; PRINTING United
  Alliance

Birmingham Printing & Publishing Inc
3101 Sixth Ave S, Birmingham, AL 35233
Mailing Address: PO Box 131298, Birmingham,
  AL 35213-6298
Tel: 205-251-5113 *Toll Free Tel:* 888-276-1192
  Fax: 205-251-2222
E-mail: sales@bhamprinting.com
Web Site: bhamprinting.com
Founded: 1910

Blanks Printing & Imaging Inc
2343 N Beckley Ave, Dallas, TX 75208
Tel: 214-741-3905 *Toll Free Tel:* 800-325-7651
E-mail: sales@blanks.com
Web Site: www.blanks.com
Key Personnel
CFO: Doug Heyerdahl *E-mail:* cfo@blanks.com
Pres: Leron Blanks *E-mail:* lblanks@blanks.com
VP: Jeff Blanks *E-mail:* jblanks@blanks.com
VP, Sales & Mktg: Mark Connor
  E-mail: mconnor@blanks.com
Opers Mgr: Jan Thornton *E-mail:* jthornton@
  blanks.com
Founded: 1941

Blitzprint Inc
1235 64 Ave SE, Suite 1, Calgary, AB T2H 2J7,
  Canada
Toll Free Tel: 866-479-3248 *Fax:* 403-253-5642
E-mail: books@blitzprint.com
Web Site: www.blitzprint.com
Key Personnel
Pres: Kevin Lanuke
Founded: 1999
Turnaround: 15-20 business days
Print Runs: 25 min - 1,000 max
Membership(s): The Association of Book Publish-
  ers of British Columbia (ABPBC)

Blue Note Books, see Blue Note Publications Inc

Blue Note Publications Inc
721 North Dr, Suite D, Melbourne, FL 32934
Tel: 321-799-2583; 321-622-6289
Toll Free Tel: 800-624-0401 (orders) *Fax:* 321-
  799-1942; 321-622-6830
E-mail: bluenotebooks@gmail.com
Web Site: bluenotepublications.com
Key Personnel
Pres: Paul Maluccio
Founded: 1988
Turnaround: 20 Workdays
Print Runs: 25 min - 10,000 max

Blue Ridge Printing Co
544 Haywood Rd, Asheville, NC 28806
Tel: 828-254-1000 *Toll Free Tel:* 800-633-4298
  Fax: 828-252-6455
E-mail: info@brprinting.com
Web Site: www.brprinting.com
Key Personnel
Pres: Bruce Fowler *Tel:* 828-254-1000 ext 238
  E-mail: bruce_f@brprinting.com
Dir, Sustainability & Sr Buyer: Allen Fowler
  Tel: 828-254-1000 ext 249 *E-mail:* allen_f@
  brprinting.com

Founded: 1974
Turnaround: 10 Workdays
Print Runs: 1,000 min

BookBaby
Division of DIY Media Inc
7905 N Crescent Blvd, Pennsauken, NJ 08110
Tel: 856-460-8069 *Toll Free Tel:* 877-961-6878
E-mail: info@bookbaby.com
Web Site: www.bookbaby.com/book-printing
Founded: 2011

BookFactory
2302 S Edwin C Moses Blvd, Dayton, OH 45417
Tel: 937-226-7100 *Toll Free Tel:* 877-431-2665
  Fax: 614-388-5635
E-mail: sales@bookfactory.com
Web Site: www.bookfactory.com
Key Personnel
Sales Mgr: Tessin Farmer
Founded: 2002
Turnaround: 20 Workdays after approval
Print Runs: 25 min - 3,000 max

Bookmasters
Division of Baker & Taylor Publisher Services
30 Amberwood Pkwy, Ashland, OH 44805
Tel: 419-281-5100 *Toll Free Tel:* 800-537-6727
  Fax: 419-281-0200
E-mail: info@btpubservices.com
Web Site: www.btpubservices.com
Key Personnel
Dir of Mfg: Brad Sharp *E-mail:* bsharp@
  bookmasters.com
Founded: 1972

BookMobile
5120 Cedar Lake Rd, Minneapolis, MN 55416
Tel: 763-398-0030 *Toll Free Tel:* 844-488-4477
  Fax: 763-398-0198
Web Site: www.bookmobile.com
Key Personnel
Founder & CEO: Don Leeper
Dir, Sales & Mktg: Nicole Baxter *Tel:* 763-398-
  0030 ext 126 *E-mail:* nbaxter@bookmobile.
  com
Founded: 1982
Turnaround: 10 Workdays or less
Print Runs: 25 min - 3,000 max

Bookshelf Bindery Ltd
22 Secord Dr, Unit 16, St Catharines, ON L2N
  1K8, Canada
Tel: 905-934-2801
E-mail: bookshelfbindery@bellnet.ca
Key Personnel
Pres: Cam Gregory
Founded: 1914
Turnaround: 15 Workdays
Print Runs: 1 min - 5,000 max

BR Printers
665 Lenfest Rd, San Jose, CA 95133
Tel: 408-278-7711 *Fax:* 408-929-8062
E-mail: info@brprinters.com
Web Site: www.brprinters.com
Key Personnel
Pres: Adam DeMaestri *E-mail:* adam@brprinters.
  com
VP & Chief Strategy Offr: David Gall
SVP, Sales: Derek Giulianelli *Tel:* 303-916-5346
  (cell) *E-mail:* derek@brprinters.com
VP, Fin: Carina Follante
VP, KY Off: Chris Gerhold
Dir, HR: Kathryn Torre
Gen Mgr, CA Off: James Barrios
Founded: 1992
Turnaround: 3-5 Workdays

Print Runs: 1 min - 10,000 max
Branch Office(s)
10154 Toebben Dr, Independence, KY 41051
  Tel: 859-292-1700 *Fax:* 859-292-1710

Bradford & Bigelow Inc
3 Perkins Way, Newburyport, MA 01950-4007
Tel: 978-904-3100
E-mail: sales@bradford-bigelow.com
Web Site: www.bradford-bigelow.com
Key Personnel
CFO: Carmen Frederico
Pres: John Galligan
VP, Sales & Busn Devt: Bob Bradley *Tel:* 978-
  904-3108 *E-mail:* bbradley@bradford-bigelow.
  com
Founded: 1970
Turnaround: 10 Workdays
Print Runs: 50 min - 250,000 max
Membership(s): Book Manufacturers' Institute
  (BMI); PRINTING United Alliance

Bridgeport National Bindery Inc
662 Silver St, Agawam, MA 01001
Mailing Address: PO Box 289, Agawam, MA
  01001-0289
Tel: 413-789-1981 *Toll Free Tel:* 800-223-5083
E-mail: info@bnbindery.com
Web Site: www.bnbindery.com
Key Personnel
Pres: James M Larsen
EVP: Bruce F Jacobsen
VP, Print on Demand Div: Kent Larson
Founded: 1947
Turnaround: 2-5 Workdays
Print Runs: 1 min - 1,000 max
Membership(s): Book Manufacturers' Institute
  (BMI)

The Bureau
Division of The Vomela Companies
2354 English St, Maplewood, MN 55109
Tel: 612-788-1000; 612-432-3516 (sales)
  Toll Free Tel: 800-788-9536 *Fax:* 612-788-7792
E-mail: sales@thebureau.com
Web Site: www.thebureau.com
Key Personnel
Pres & CEO: Mark Auth
VP, Sales & Busn Devt: Tim Dobratz
  E-mail: tim.dobratz@vomela.com
Gen Mgr: John Henderson
Natl Acct Sales Rep: Mike Schreiner

C & C Offset Printing Co USA Inc
Subsidiary of C & C Joint Printing Co (HK) Ltd
70 W 36 St, Unit 10C, New York, NY 10018
Tel: 212-431-4210 *Toll Free Fax:* 866-540-4134
Web Site: www.ccoffset.com
Key Personnel
Dir & EVP, C & C Offset Printing Co (USA)
  Inc & C & C Offset Printing Co (NY) Inc,
  New York, NY: Simon Chan *E-mail:* schan@
  ccoffset.com
Sales Mgr, C & C Offset Printing Co (NY)
  Inc, New York, NY: Frances Harkness
  E-mail: fharkness@ccoffset.com; Timothy Mc-
  Nulty
CEO, C & C Joint Printing Co (HK) Ltd, Hong
  Kong: Jackson Leung
Deputy Gen Mgr, C & C Joint Printing Co (HK)
  Ltd, Hong Kong: Francis Ho; Kit Wong
Dir, C & C Offset Printing Co (France) Ltd:
  Michele Olson Niel *E-mail:* michele@
  candcoffset.fr
Pres, C & C Printing Japan Co Ltd, Tokyo,
  Japan: Yamamoto Masaaki
Dir, C & C Offset Printing Co (UK) Ltd: Tracy
  Broderick *E-mail:* tracy@candcoffset.co.uk
Sales Rep, Australian Off: Lena Frew
  E-mail: lena.frew@candcprinting.com
Founded: 1980
Turnaround: Varies

1249

PRINTING, BINDING & BOOK FINISHING

Print Runs: 2,000 min - 3,000,000 max (average book runs: 7,500-50,000)
Branch Office(s)
C & C Offset Printing Co Ltd (Australia Off), Lithocraft Graphics, 3-7 Permas Way, Truganina, Victoria 3029, Australia *Tel:* (0613) 8366 0200 *Fax:* (0613) 8366 0299
C & C Offset Printing Co (France) Ltd, 15, rue d'Aboukir, 75002 Paris, France *Tel:* 01 40 26 21 07 *Fax:* 01 44 76 08 96
C & C Offset Printing Co Ltd, C & C Bldg, 36 Ting Lai Rd, Tai Po, New Territories, Hong Kong (corp headquarters) *Tel:* 2666 4988 *Fax:* 2666 4938 *E-mail:* info@candcprinting.com *Web Site:* www.candcprinting.com
C & C Printing Japan Co Ltd, Tozaido Bldg, 3F, 2-6-12 Hitotsubashi, Chiyoda-ku, Tokyo 101-0003, Japan *Tel:* (03) 5216 4580 *Fax:* (03) 5216 4610 *E-mail:* mail@candcprinting.co.jp *Web Site:* www.candcprinting.co.jp
C & C Offset Printing Co (UK) Ltd, 75 Newman St, 3rd fl, London W1T 3EN, United Kingdom *Tel:* (020) 7637 5033 *Fax:* (020) 7637 5044 *E-mail:* info@candcoffset.co.uk

C-M Books, see Cushing-Malloy Inc

California Offset Printers Inc
Division of COP Communications
620 W Elk Ave, Glendale, CA 91204
Tel: 818-291-1100 *Toll Free Tel:* 800-280-6446
 Fax: 818-291-1192
E-mail: info@copcomms.com
Web Site: www.copprints.com
Key Personnel
Pres & CEO: William Rittwage
 E-mail: brittwage@copprints.com
Founded: 1963
Turnaround: 5 Workdays
Print Runs: 10,000 min - 250,000 max
Membership(s): APALA; Epicomm; Printing Industries Association Inc of Southern California (PIASC); Western Fulfillment Management Association (WFMA); Western Publishing Association (WPA)

Canterbury Press
120 Interstate N Pkwy E, Suite 200, Atlanta, GA 30339
Tel: 770-952-8309 *Fax:* 770-952-4623
E-mail: sales@canterburypress.net
Web Site: canterburypress.net
Key Personnel
Contact: Jim Solmson *E-mail:* jsolmson@canterburypress.net
Founded: 1950
Membership(s): Printing & Imaging Association of Georgia (PIAG); PRINTING United Alliance

Cenveo Inc
200 First Stamford Place, 2nd fl, Stamford, CT 06902
Tel: 203-595-3000 *Fax:* 203-595-3070
E-mail: info@cenveo.com
Web Site: www.cenveo.com
Key Personnel
CEO: Robert G Burton, Jr
CFO: Mark Hiltwein
Pres: Michael Burton
Founded: 1830
Turnaround: 10 Workdays
Print Runs: 1,500 min - 1,000,000 max

Cenveo St Louis
101 Workman Ct, Eureka, MO 63025
Tel: 314-966-2000 *Toll Free Tel:* 800-800-8845
 Fax: 314-966-4725
Web Site: www.cenveo.com

CG Book Printers
Division of Corporate Graphics Commercial (CGC)
1750 Northway Dr, North Mankato, MN 56003
Tel: 507-388-3300 *Toll Free Tel:* 800-729-7575
 Fax: 507-386-6350
E-mail: cgbooks@corpgraph.com
Web Site: www.corpgraph.com
Key Personnel
Pres: Dan Kvasnicka *Tel:* 507-386-6340
 Fax: 507-344-5548 *E-mail:* dekvasnicka@corpgraph.com
Sales Exec, Book Mfg Sales: Mike Schmitt *Tel:* 507-386-6349 *E-mail:* mjschmitt@corpgraph.com
Founded: 1989
Print Runs: 50 min - 100,000 max

CJK
3962 Virginia Ave, Cincinnati, OH 45227
Tel: 513-271-6035 *Toll Free Tel:* 800-598-7808
 Fax: 513-271-6082
E-mail: info@cjkusa.com
Web Site: www.cjkusa.com
Key Personnel
CEO: Tim Ruppert *E-mail:* truppert@cjkusa.com
Founded: 1872
Turnaround: 10-20 Workdays
Print Runs: 1,000 min - 500,000 max
Sales Office(s): Gulf Coast Sales, Tallahassee, FL *Tel:* 850-668-6788 *Fax:* 850-681-6778
Cincinnati (OH) Sales, Contact: Chris Casey *Tel:* 513-271-6035 ext 277 *Toll Free Tel:* 800-598-7808 *Fax:* 513-271-6082 *E-mail:* ccasey@cjkusa.com
Dayton (OH)/Northern OH/Michigan Sales, Contact: Patrick Latham *Tel:* 513-271-6035 ext 241 *Toll Free Tel:* 800-598-7808 *Fax:* 513-271-6082 *E-mail:* platham@cjkusa.com
Tennessee/Carolinas Sales, Morristown, TN, Contact: Bill White *Tel:* 423-748-0201 *Fax:* 423-585-0915 *E-mail:* bwhite@cjkusa.com
Membership(s): PRINTING United Alliance

CJK Print Possibilities, see CJK

Clare Printing
206 S Keystone Ave, Sayre, PA 18840
Tel: 570-888-2244
E-mail: hr@clareprint.com
Web Site: www.clareprint.com
Key Personnel
Pres: Ian Clare
Prodn Mgr: Alicia Blokzyl
Founded: 1903
Print Runs: 50 min - 10,000 max

Clear Print
9025 Fullbright Ave, Chatsworth, CA 91311
Tel: 818-709-1220 *Fax:* 818-709-1320
E-mail: info@clearprint.com; sales@clearprint.com
Web Site: www.clearprint.com
Key Personnel
Pres: Geoffrey Pick *E-mail:* geoff@clearprint.com
Founded: 1980

Coach House Printing
80 bpNichol Lane, Toronto, ON M5S 3J4, Canada
Tel: 416-979-2217 *Toll Free Tel:* 800-367-6360 (outside Toronto) *Fax:* 416-977-1158
E-mail: mail@chbooks.com
Web Site: www.chbooks.com
Key Personnel
Publr: Stan Bevington *E-mail:* stan@chbooks.com
Edit Dir: Alana Wilcox *E-mail:* alana@chbooks.com
Prodn Mgr: John De Jesus *E-mail:* john@chbooks.com
Founded: 1965

Turnaround: 14 Workdays
Print Runs: 200 min - 2,000 max

Codra Enterprises Inc
17692 Cowan, Suite 200, Irvine, CA 92614
Tel: 949-756-8400 *Toll Free Tel:* 888-992-6372
 Fax: 949-756-8484
E-mail: codra@codra.com; sales@codra.com
Web Site: www.codra.com
Key Personnel
Pres: Gary Kim
Sales: Chris Scotti *Tel:* 949-322-5639
 E-mail: chris@codra.com
Founded: 1985
Turnaround: 30-40 Workdays
Print Runs: 3,000 min - 3,000,000 max
Membership(s): Independent Publishers Association; Pacific Northwest Booksellers Association (PNBA); Publishers Association of the West (PubWest)

Color Graphic Press Inc
42 Main St, Nyack, NY 10960
Tel: 845-535-3444 *Fax:* 845-535-3446
E-mail: info@cgpny.com
Web Site: www.cgpny.com
Key Personnel
Pres: Paul Rochman
Founded: 1969

Color House Graphics Inc
3505 Eastern Ave SE, Grand Rapids, MI 49508
Toll Free Tel: 800-454-1916 *Fax:* 616-245-5494
Web Site: www.colorhousegraphics.com
Key Personnel
Pres: Steve Landheer
Gen Mgr: Phil Knight *E-mail:* pknight@colorhousegraphics.com
Founded: 1987
Turnaround: 5-20 Workdays
Print Runs: 1 min - 50,000 max (10-500 digital short-run, 500+ offset)
Membership(s): The Association of Publishers for Special Sales (APSS); Colorado Independent Publishers Association (CIPA); Evangelical Christian Publishers Association (ECPA); Florida Authors & Publishers Association Inc (FAPA); Independent Book Publishers Association (IBPA); Printing Industries of Michigan Inc (PIM); Publishers Association of the West (PubWest)

ColorPage
Division of Tri-State Associated Services Inc
81 Ten Broeck Ave, Kingston, NY 12401
Tel: 845-331-7581 *Toll Free Tel:* 800-836-7581
 Fax: 845-331-1571
E-mail: sales@colorpageonline.com
Web Site: www.colorpageonline.com
Key Personnel
Pres & Mktg Strategist/Consultant: Frank J Campagna, II *E-mail:* fcampagna@colorpageonline.com
Acct Mgr & Cont: Kathy Riggins
 E-mail: kriggins@colorpageonline.com
Prodn Mgr: Randy Delanoy
Cust Serv Supv: Debbie Downes
 E-mail: ddownes@colorpageonline.com
Founded: 1976
Turnaround: 10-15 Workdays
Print Runs: 25 min - 20,000 max

Communicorp Inc
Subsidiary of Aflac Inc
1001 Lockwood Ave, Columbus, GA 31999
Tel: 706-324-1182
E-mail: mktech@communicorp.com
Web Site: www.communicorp.com
Key Personnel
Pres & CEO: Eric Seldon
VP: Mike Thomas
Sr Mgr, Prodn Servs: Jason Lansdon

MANUFACTURING — PRINTING, BINDING & BOOK FINISHING

Sr Mgr, Sales & Mktg Servs: John Shutter *Tel:* 706-763-2912 *E-mail:* jshutter@communicorp.com
Founded: 1981
Branch Office(s)
100 Galleria Pkwy, Suite 450, Atlanta, GA 30339 *Tel:* 770-541-4515 *Toll Free Tel:* 800-775-7998

C Harrison Conroy Co Inc
501 Penman St, Charlotte, NC 28203
Tel: 704-358-0459 *Toll Free Tel:* 800-242-2789 *Fax:* 704-358-0459
E-mail: chcphoto@charrisonconroy.com
Web Site: www.charrisonconroy.com
Key Personnel
Pres: Hal Conroy
Founded: 1936

Consolidated Printers Inc
2630 Eighth St, Berkeley, CA 94710
Tel: 510-495-3113 (sales); 510-843-8565 (admin)
Web Site: www.consoprinters.com
Key Personnel
CEO: Lawrence A Hawkins
Founded: 1952
Turnaround: 2-20 Workdays
Print Runs: 2,000 min - 500,000 max

Continental Web Press Inc
1430 Industrial Dr, Itasca, IL 60143-1858
Tel: 630-773-1903
E-mail: inquiries@continentalweb.com
Web Site: www.continentalweb.com
Key Personnel
Pres & CEO: Diane Field
VP: Ken Field, Sr
VP, Busn Devt: Ken Field, Jr
Founded: 1973

Cookbook Publishers Inc
11633 W 83 Terr, Lenexa, KS 66285
Mailing Address: PO Box 15920, Lenexa, KS 66285-5920
Tel: 913-492-5900 *Toll Free Tel:* 800-227-7282 *Fax:* 913-492-5947
E-mail: info@cookbookpublishers.com
Web Site: www.cookbookpublishers.com
Key Personnel
Pres: Kevin Naughton
New Busn Devt: Stephanie Jones
Founded: 1947
Turnaround: 30-60 Workdays
Print Runs: 100 min - 50,000 max

Copycats
216 E 45 St, 10th fl, New York, NY 10017
Tel: 212-557-2111 *Toll Free Tel:* 800-404-2679 *Fax:* 212-557-2039
E-mail: client@copycats.com
Web Site: www.copycats.com
Key Personnel
COO: Robert Stor *E-mail:* rstor@copycats.com
Founded: 1984
Turnaround: 3 Workdays
Print Runs: 1 min - 5,000 max
Membership(s): Epicomm

Coral Graphic Services Inc
Member of Bertelsmann Printing Group
840 S Broadway, Hicksville, NY 11801
Tel: 516-576-2100 *Fax:* 516-576-2168
E-mail: info@coralgraphics.com
Web Site: www.bpg-usa.com
Key Personnel
CEO: Christof Ludwig
CFO: Denis Leite
CTO: Yannic Schroeder
Founded: 1982

Branch Office(s)
25 Jack Enders Blvd, Berryville, VA 22611
Tel: 540-955-2750 *Fax:* 540-955-9164
Membership(s): Association of the Graphic Arts (AGA); PRINTING United Alliance

Corporate Disk Co
4610 Prime Pkwy, McHenry, IL 60050-7005
Tel: 815-331-6000 *Toll Free Tel:* 800-634-3475 *Fax:* 815-331-6030
E-mail: info@disk.com
Web Site: www.disk.com
Key Personnel
Owner & VP, Sales: Joe D Foley *Tel:* 815-331-6000 ext 233 *E-mail:* jfoley@disk.com
Founded: 1984
Turnaround: 24 hours-3 weeks

Corporate Graphics Book Printers, see CG Book Printers

The Country Press Inc
One Commercial Dr, Lakeville, MA 02347
Mailing Address: PO Box 489, Middleborough, MA 02346
Tel: 508-947-4485 *Toll Free Tel:* 888-343-2227 *Fax:* 508-947-8989
E-mail: info@countrypressinc.com
Web Site: www.countrypressprinting.com
Key Personnel
Pres: Mike Pinto
VP & Gen Mgr: George Medeiros
VP, Cust Opers: David Brooks
Founded: 1967
Print Runs: 11 min - 5,000 max

Courier Printing
Division of RR Donnelley
One Courier Place, Smyrna, TN 37167
Tel: 615-355-4000 *Toll Free Tel:* 800-467-0444 *Fax:* 615-355-4088
Web Site: www.courierprinting.com
Key Personnel
Pres: Michelle Yun
Turnaround: 5-15 Workdays
Print Runs: 2,500 min - 500,000 max

Crane Duplicating Service Inc
4915 Rattlesnake Hammock Rd, Suite 207, Naples, FL 34113
Tel: 305-280-6742 (help desk) *Fax:* 239-732-8415
E-mail: info@craneduplicating.com
Web Site: www.craneduplicating.com
Key Personnel
Pres & CEO: Richard W Price
Mgr, Cust Serv: Jean Fahr
Founded: 1955
Turnaround: 5-7 Workdays; Same day, 3 or 4 Workdays available at extra cost depending upon book
Print Runs: 11 min - 50,000 max

Crown Roll Leaf Inc
91 Illinois Ave, Paterson, NJ 07503
Tel: 973-742-4000 *Toll Free Tel:* 800-631-3831 *Fax:* 973-742-0219
Web Site: www.crownrollleaf.com
Key Personnel
CEO: George Waitts
Founded: 1971

Cushing-Malloy Inc
1350 N Main St, Ann Arbor, MI 48104-1045
Tel: 734-663-8554 *Fax:* 734-663-5731
Web Site: www.cushing-malloy.com; www.c-mbooks.com
Key Personnel
Chmn of the Bd: Connie M Cushing *E-mail:* ccushing@cushing-malloy.com
VP of Sales: Tedd Litty *E-mail:* tlitty@cushing-malloy.com

Cust Serv/Sales: Adam Hieber *E-mail:* ahieber@cushing-malloy.com
Founded: 1948
Turnaround: 15-30 Workdays
Print Runs: 150 min - 50,000 max
Membership(s): Independent Book Publishers Association (IBPA); Publishers Association of the West (PubWest)

D C Graphics Inc
59 Central Ave, Suite 15, Farmingdale, NY 11735
Tel: 631-777-3100 *Fax:* 631-777-7899
E-mail: prepress@dcgraphicsinc.com
Web Site: www.dcgraphicsinc.com
Key Personnel
Pres: Eugene Prohaske
VP: Christine Brandon
Founded: 1994
Turnaround: 1 Workday
Membership(s): Association of Graphic Solutions Providers

D&K Group Inc
1795 Commerce Dr, Elk Grove Village, IL 60007
Tel: 847-956-0160; 847-956-4757 (tech support) *Toll Free Tel:* 800-632-2314 *Fax:* 847-956-8214
E-mail: info@dkgroup.net
Web Site: www.dkgroup.com
Key Personnel
Pres: Karl Singer
VP, Sales & Mktg: Tom Pidgeon *E-mail:* tom.pidgeon@dkgroup.net
Mktg Communs Specialist: Brian Biegel *E-mail:* brian.biegel@dkgroup.net
Founded: 1979

Data Reproductions Corp
4545 Glenmeade Lane, Auburn Hills, MI 48326
Tel: 248-371-3700 *Toll Free Tel:* 800-242-3114 *Fax:* 248-371-3710
Web Site: datarepro.com
Key Personnel
Pres: Dennis Kavanagh
Gen Mgr: Steve Olko
Acct Mgr: Kimberly Kavanagh *Tel:* 248-881-6518 (cell) *E-mail:* kkavanagh@datarepro.com
Sales Exec: Nick Janosi *Tel:* 734-426-1229 *E-mail:* njanosi@datarepro.com
Founded: 1967
Turnaround: 15 Workdays
Print Runs: 250 min - 100,000 max

Jerilyn Glenn Davis
Cathedral Sta, Box 1712, New York, NY 10025
Tel: 212-889-2239
E-mail: jdavisbook@gmail.com

DeHART's Media Services Inc
6586 Whitbourne Dr, San Jose, CA 95120
Tel: 408-768-1575
Web Site: www.deharts.com
Key Personnel
Pres: Don DeHart *E-mail:* don@deharts.com
Founded: 1972
Turnaround: 7-15 Workdays (short run); 30 Workdays (over 1,000)
Print Runs: 25 min - 10,000 max
Membership(s): Independent Book Publishers Association (IBPA); PRINTING United Alliance

Dekker Bookbinding Inc
2941 Clydon Ave SW, Grand Rapids, MI 49519
Tel: 616-538-5160 *Toll Free Tel:* 800-299-BIND (299-2463)
E-mail: hello@dekkerbook.com
Web Site: www.dekkerbook.com
Key Personnel
Pres: Chris Dekker
VP: Corbin Dekker
Founded: 1928
Turnaround: 14 Workdays

PRINTING, BINDING & BOOK FINISHING

Print Runs: 100 min - 100,000 max
Membership(s): Forest Stewardship Council US (FSC-US); Printing Industries of Michigan Inc (PIM); PRINTING United Alliance

Democrat Printing & Lithographing Co
6401 Lindsey Rd, Little Rock, AR 72206
Toll Free Tel: 800-622-2216 *Fax:* 501-907-7953
Web Site: democratprinting.com
Key Personnel
Chmn of the Bd: Frank Parke, III
CEO: Haynes Whitney
Pres: Thomas Whitney
Founded: 1871
Turnaround: 6 Workdays
Print Runs: 10,000 min - 250,000 max

Diecrafters Inc
1349 S 55 Ct, Cicero, IL 60804-1211
Tel: 708-656-3336 *Fax:* 708-656-3386
E-mail: info@diecrafters.com
Web Site: www.diecrafters.com
Key Personnel
Pres: Robert Windler
Founded: 1947

The Dingley Press
119 Lisbon St, Lisbon, ME 04250
Tel: 207-353-4151 *Toll Free Tel:* 800-317-4574
Fax: 207-353-9886
E-mail: info@dingley.com
Web Site: www.dingley.com
Key Personnel
Pres & CEO: Eric Lane *E-mail:* elane@dingley.com
VP, Fin: Neal Poston *E-mail:* nposton@dingley.com
VP, Sales & Mktg: Jim Gibbs *E-mail:* jgibbs@dingley.com
Founded: 1928
Print Runs: 300,000 min - 5,000,000 max

Diversified Printing Services Inc
3425 Cherokee Ave, Columbus, GA 31906
Tel: 706-323-2759 *Toll Free Fax:* 888-410-5502
Web Site: www.1dps.com
Key Personnel
Owner: Brad Wheeler *E-mail:* bw@1dps.com
Founded: 1969
Turnaround: 24 hours

dix! Digital Prepress Inc
8462 Wayfarer Dr, Cicero, NY 13039
Tel: 315-288-5888 *Fax:* 315-288-5898
E-mail: info@dixtype.com
Web Site: www.dixtype.com
Key Personnel
Pres: Scott Wenger *E-mail:* swenger@dixtype.com
Acct Exec, Sales & Mktg: Kelly Farley *E-mail:* kfarley@dixtype.com
Founded: 1923
Turnaround: 2-10 Workdays

DNP America LLC
Subsidiary of Dai Nippon Printing Co Ltd
335 Madison Ave, 3rd fl, New York, NY 10017
Tel: 212-503-1060
E-mail: gps@dnp-g.com
Web Site: www.dnpamerica.com
Key Personnel
VP & Gen Mgr: Norikatsu Nakamura
Founded: 1976
Turnaround: 30-60 Workdays
Branch Office(s)
2099 Gateway Place, Suite 490, San Jose, CA 95110 *Tel:* 408-735-8880
3858 Carson St, Suite 300, Torrance, CA 90503 *Tel:* 310-540-5123

Docunet Corp
2435 Xenium Lane N, Plymouth, MN 55441
Tel: 763-475-9600 *Toll Free Tel:* 800-936-2863
Fax: 763-475-1516
E-mail: print@docunetworks.com
Web Site: www.docunetworks.com
Key Personnel
Partner: Wendy Morical *E-mail:* wnm@docunetworks.com; Brant Nelson
Founded: 1991
Print Runs: 1 min - 5,000 max
Membership(s): Print Industry of Minnesota (PIMN); Women's Business Enterprise Network (WBENC)

RR Donnelley
35 W Wacker Dr, Chicago, IL 60601
Toll Free Tel: 800-742-4455
Web Site: www.rrd.com
Key Personnel
Pres & CEO: Daniel L Knotts
Pres, Busn Servs: John Pecaric
Pres, Mktg Solutions: Doug Ryan
EVP & CFO: Terry D Peterson
EVP & CIO: Ken O'Brien
EVP & Chief HR Offr: Sheila Rutt
EVP & Chief Strategy & Transformation Offr: Elif Sagsen-Ercel
EVP, Gen Coun, Chief Compliance Offr & Corp Secy: Deborah Steiner
EVP, Dom Opers & Chief Supply Chain Offr: Glynn Perry
SVP & Chief Acctg Offr: Michael J Sharp
Founded: 1864
Turnaround: 3-6 Weeks
Print Runs: 3,000 min - 500,000 max
Branch Office(s)
955 Gateway Center Way, San Diego, CA 92102 *Tel:* 619-527-4600
40610 County Center Dr, Temecula, CA 92591 *Tel:* 951-296-2890
151 Red Stone Rd, Manchester, CT 06042 *Tel:* 860-649-5570
9125 Bachman Rd, Orlando, FL 32824 *Tel:* 407-859-2030
5800 Peachtree Rd, Atlanta, GA 30341 *Tel:* 770-458-6351
825 Riverside Pkwy, Suite 300, Austell, GA 30168 *Tel:* 770-948-1330
1750 Wallace Ave, St Charles, IL 60174 *Tel:* 630-313-7000
609 S Kirk Rd, St Charles, IL 60174 *Tel:* 630-762-7600
One Poplar Ave, Thurmont, MD 21788 *Tel:* 301-271-7171
65 Sprague St, Hyde Park, MA 02136 *Tel:* 617-360-2000
18780 W 78 St, Chanhassen, MN 55317 *Tel:* 952-937-9764
5500 12 Ave E, Shakopee, MN 55379 *Tel:* 952-941-7546
6305 Sunset Corporate Dr, Las Vegas, NV 89120 *Tel:* 702-949-8500
5 Henderson Dr, West Caldwell, NJ 07006 *Tel:* 973-882-7000
12301 Vance Davis Dr, Charlotte, NC 28269 *Tel:* 704-949-3568
One Litho Way, Durham, NC 27703 *Tel:* 919-596-3660
3801 Gantz Rd, Grove City, OH 43123 *Tel:* 614-539-5527
700 Nestle Way, Suite 200, Breinigsville, PA 18031 *Tel:* 610-391-3900
9985 Gantry Rd, Philadelphia, PA 19115 *Tel:* 215-671-9500
218 N Braddock Ave, Pittsburgh, PA 15208 *Tel:* 412-241-8200
1210 Key Rd, Columbia, SC 29201 *Tel:* 803-799-9550
1645 W Sam Houston Pkwy N, Houston, TX 77043 *Tel:* 713-468-7175
1550 Lakeway Dr, Suite 600, Lewisville, TX 75057 *Tel:* 972-353-7500
630 W 1000 N, Logan, UT 84321 *Tel:* 435-755-4000
201 E Progress Dr, West Bend, WI 53095 *Tel:* 262-338-6101
Membership(s): Association of American Publishers (AAP); Book Industry Study Group (BISG); Book Manufacturers' Institute (BMI)

W R Draper Co
Division of The Arthur Press (1978) Ltd
162 Norfinch Dr, Toronto, ON M3N 1X6, Canada
Tel: 416-663-6001 *Fax:* 416-663-6043
E-mail: info@arthurpress.com
Web Site: www.arthurpress.com
Key Personnel
Pres: Jeremy Thorn
Founded: 1954
Turnaround: 10 Workdays
Print Runs: 1,000 min - 75,000 max

Drummond
5664 New Peachtree Rd, Atlanta, GA 30341
Tel: 678-597-1050 *Fax:* 678-597-1051
E-mail: info@drummond.com
Web Site: pgc-atl.com
Key Personnel
Pres, Atlanta Div: Gene Hindman

D3Logic Inc
89 Commercial Way, East Providence, RI 02915
Tel: 401-435-4300 *Toll Free Tel:* 844-385-5388
E-mail: contact@d3-inc.com
Web Site: www.d3-inc.com
Key Personnel
Pres: Ralph R Delmonico, Jr
Branch Office(s)
D3 Synergy LLC, 399 River Rd, Hudson, MA 01749 *Tel:* 508-281-7800

Dual Graphics
370 Cliffwood Park, Brea, CA 92821
Tel: 714-990-3700 *Fax:* 714-990-6818
Web Site: www.dualgraphics.com
Key Personnel
Pres & CEO: Jim Joyce
Cont: Jamie Bengard
VP, Opers: Tom Dupuis
Sales Mgr: Craig Evans
Founded: 1906

Dunn & Co Inc
Affiliate of Legacy Publishing Group
75 Green St, Clinton, MA 01510
Mailing Address: PO Box 1185, Clinton, MA 01510
Tel: 978-368-8505 *Fax:* 978-368-7867
E-mail: info@booktrauma.com
Web Site: www.booktrauma.com
Key Personnel
Chmn: David M Dunn
Pres: Peter R Heelan
VP: Rocco Windover
Turnaround: 3-10 Workdays
Print Runs: 100 min

Dupli Envelope & Graphics Corp
6761 Thompson Rd N, Syracuse, NY 13211
Tel: 315-472-1316 *Toll Free Tel:* 800-724-2477
E-mail: sales@duplionline.com; orders@duplionline.com
Web Site: www.duplionline.com
Key Personnel
Pres: J Kemper Matt, Jr *Tel:* 315-234-7241 *E-mail:* kemper@duplionline.com
NY Regl Sales Mgr: Matthew J Oliver *Tel:* 315-234-7246 *E-mail:* moliver@duplionline.com
Founded: 1965
Print Runs: 1,000 min - 1,000,000 max

MANUFACTURING

Branch Office(s)
124 Francis Ave, Newington, CT 06111 *Toll Free Tel:* 800-666-6847
2533 Yellow Springs Rd, Malvern, PA 19355 *Toll Free Tel:* 800-726-7599

Eckhart & Company Inc
4011 W 54 St, Indianapolis, IN 46254
Tel: 317-347-2665 *Toll Free Tel:* 800-443-3791
Fax: 317-347-2666
E-mail: info@eckhartandco.com
Web Site: www.eckhartandco.com
Key Personnel
Pres: Chris Eckhart *Tel:* 317-347-2660
 E-mail: chriseckhart@eckhartandco.com
Plant Mgr: Gary Neidlinger *Tel:* 317-347-2669
 E-mail: garyneidlinger@eckhartandco.com
Founded: 1918
Turnaround: 10-15 Workdays
Membership(s): Print Image International

Edison Lithograph & Printing Corp
3725 Tonnelle Ave, North Bergen, NJ 07047-2421
Tel: 201-902-9191 *Fax:* 201-902-0475
E-mail: info@edisonlitho.com
Web Site: www.edisonlitho.com
Key Personnel
COO: Joseph Ostreicher
Founded: 1958

Emprint®
5425 Florida Blvd, Baton Rouge, LA 70806
Tel: 225-923-2550 *Toll Free Tel:* 800-211-8335
Web Site: emprint.com
Key Personnel
CEO: Mr Courtney Westbrook
Pres & COO: Becky Vance *E-mail:* beckyv@emprint.com
Turnaround: 5 Workdays
Print Runs: 2 min - 125,000 max
Branch Office(s)
109 Research Dr, Harahan, LA 70123 *Tel:* 504-733-9654 *Toll Free Tel:* 877-568-1555 *Fax:* 504-733-8506
151 Southpark Rd, Suite 100, Lafayette, LA 70508 *Tel:* 337-839-9761 *Toll Free Tel:* 888-874-9761
2830 Breard St, Monroe, LA 71201 *Tel:* 318-387-1725 *Toll Free Tel:* 800-256-2259

EP Graphics
Division of Dynamic Resource Group
169 S Jefferson St, Berne, IN 46711
Tel: 260-589-2145 *Toll Free Tel:* 877-589-2145 *Fax:* 260-589-2810
Web Site: www.epgraphics.com
Key Personnel
CEO: Tyler Kitt
Founded: 1925
Turnaround: 15 Workdays
Print Runs: 25,000 min - 500,000 max

Fairfield Marketing Group Inc
Subsidiary of FMG Inc
830 Sport Hill Rd, Easton, CT 06112-1241
E-mail: info@fairfieldmarketing.com
Key Personnel
Pres & CEO: Edward P Waschilla, Jr
 E-mail: ed@fairfieldmarketing.com
Founded: 1986
Turnaround: 1-7 Workdays
Print Runs: 2,500 min - 10,000,000 max
Membership(s): American Booksellers Association (ABA); Bridgeport Regional Business Council (BRBC); Education Market Association; United States Chamber of Commerce (USCC)

Fenway Group
870 Commonwealth Ave, Boston, MA 02215
Tel: 617-226-1900 *Fax:* 617-226-1901
E-mail: info@fenwaycommunications.com
Web Site: www.fenway-group.com
Key Personnel
Founder, Pres & Creative Dir: Rick Sands
 E-mail: rsands@sandscreativegroup.com
Founded: 1993
Print Runs: 1 min (no max)
Membership(s): Printing Industries of New England (PINE); PRINTING United Alliance

Ferry Associates Inc
49 Fostertown Rd, Medford, NJ 08055
Tel: 609-953-1233 *Toll Free Tel:* 800-257-5258
Fax: 609-953-8637
Web Site: www.ferryassociates.com
Key Personnel
Pres: Kevin Ferry *E-mail:* kferry@ferryassociates.com
Founded: 1982
Turnaround: Standard 2 week delivery
Print Runs: 1,000 min - 10,000,000 max

First Choice Copy
5208 Grand Ave, Maspeth, NY 11378
Tel: 718-381-1480 (ext 200) *Toll Free Tel:* 800-222-COPY (222-2679)
Web Site: www.firstchoice-copy.com
Key Personnel
Owner & Pres: Joe Meisner *Tel:* 718-381-1480 ext 212 *E-mail:* jmeisner@nyc.rr.com
Turnaround: 3-5 Workdays

Four Colour Print Group
2410 Frankfort Ave, Louisville, KY 40206
Tel: 502-896-9644 *Fax:* 502-896-9594
E-mail: sales@fourcolour.com
Web Site: www.fourcolour.com
Key Personnel
Pres & CEO: George C Dick *Tel:* 502-896-9644 ext 303 *E-mail:* gdick@fourcolour.com
Prodn Dir: Amy Martin *Tel:* 502-896-9644 ext 315 *E-mail:* amartin@fourcolour.com
Prodn Mgr: Cindy Jones *Tel:* 502-896-9644 ext 310 *E-mail:* cjones@fourcolour.com
Founded: 1985
Turnaround: 90 Workdays
Print Runs: 25 min - 100,000 max (digital printing 25-250 copies; offset printing 250-25,000 copies; web printing 25,000-100,000 copies)
Branch Office(s)
FCI Digital, 2032 S Alex Rd, Suite A, West Carrollton, OH 45449 *Tel:* 931-859-9701 *Fax:* 931-859-9709 *E-mail:* sales@fcidigital.com *Web Site:* www.fcidigital.com

Frederic Printing
Subsidiary of RR Donnelley
14701 E 38 Ave, Aurora, CO 80011-1215
Tel: 303-371-7990 *Fax:* 303-371-7959
Web Site: www.fredericprinting.com
Key Personnel
Pres: Kurt Hamlin *Tel:* 303-418-6208
Founded: 1878

Friesens Corp
One Printers Way, Altona, MB R0G 0B0, Canada
Tel: 204-324-6401 *Fax:* 204-324-1333
E-mail: book_info@friesens.com
Web Site: www.friesens.com
Key Personnel
Pres & CEO: Chad Friesen
Gen Sales Mgr: Doug Symington
 E-mail: dougs@friesens.com
Founded: 1907
Turnaround: 3-4 Weeks
Print Runs: 250 min - 250,000 max (& more)
Membership(s): Book Manufacturers' Institute (BMI); PRINTING United Alliance

PRINTING, BINDING & BOOK FINISHING

Fry Communications Inc
800 W Church Rd, Mechanicsburg, PA 17055
Tel: 717-766-0211 *Toll Free Tel:* 800-334-1429
Fax: 717-691-0341
E-mail: info@frycomm.com
Web Site: www.frycomm.com
Key Personnel
Chmn of the Bd: Henry Fry
CEO: Mike Lukas
CFO: Chris Wawrzyniak
CTO: David S Fry
VP, Sales: Kevin Quinn
Founded: 1934
Turnaround: 7-12 Workdays
Print Runs: 10,000 min - 2,000,000 max

Fuse Graphics
1800 Sandy Plains Pkwy, Suite 124, Marietta, GA 30066
Tel: 770-499-7777 *Fax:* 770-499-7778
E-mail: info@fusegraphicsatlanta.com
Web Site: www.fusegraphicsatlanta.com
Key Personnel
Owner & CEO: Kelly Carlin
Owner & Pres: James J Carlin
Founded: 1988
Turnaround: 5-7 Workdays

G & H Soho Inc
413 Market St, Elmwood Park, NJ 07407
Tel: 201-216-9400 *Fax:* 201-216-1778
E-mail: print@ghsoho.com
Web Site: www.ghsoho.com
Key Personnel
Pres: Gerry Burstein
Prodn Mgr: Jason Burstein
Founded: 1985
Turnaround: 3-40 Workdays
Print Runs: 25 min - 10,000 max
Membership(s): Association of Graphic Communications; Digital Printing Council; PRINTING United Alliance

Garlich Printing Co
525 Rudder Rd, St Louis, MO 63026
Tel: 636-349-8000 *Toll Free Tel:* 844-449-4752
Fax: 636-349-8080
E-mail: customerservice@garlich.com
Web Site: www.garlich.com
Key Personnel
Pres: Brad Garlich *E-mail:* bgarlich@garlich.com
VP, Fin & Admin: Greg Garlich
 E-mail: ggarlich@garlich.com
VP, Prodn: Don Hockenbury
 E-mail: dhockenbury@garlich.com
Founded: 1928

GHP
475 Heffernan Dr, West Haven, CT 06516
Tel: 203-479-7500 *Fax:* 203-479-7575
Web Site: www.ghpmedia.com
Key Personnel
CEO: John Robinson *E-mail:* john.robinson@ghpmedia.com
Partner: Fred Hoxsie *E-mail:* fred.hoxsie@ghpmedia.com
VP, Sales: Steve Bortner *E-mail:* steve.bortner@ghpmedia.com
Founded: 1991
Turnaround: 5-7 Workdays

Global Interprint Inc
800 Warrington Rd, Santa Rosa, CA 95403
Tel: 707-545-1220 *Fax:* 707-545-1210
Web Site: www.globalinterprint.com
Key Personnel
Gen Mgr: Augusta Cobar *E-mail:* augusta@globalinterprint.com
Founded: 1979

PRINTING, BINDING & BOOK FINISHING

GLS Companies
1280 Energy Park Dr, St Paul, MN 55108-5106
Tel: 651-644-3000 *Toll Free Tel:* 800-655-9405
Web Site: www.glsmn.com
Key Personnel
Chmn: Gary Garner
CFO: Scott Richardson
CTO: Frank Powell
VP, Opers: Steve Kirk
VP, Sales: Todd Matuska
Mktg Dir: Jim Benedict *E-mail:* jim.benedict@glsmn.com
Founded: 1947
Print Runs: 1,000 min
Branch Office(s)
6845 Winnetka Circle, Brooklyn Park, MN 55428-1537 *Tel:* 763-535-7277 *Toll Free Tel:* 888-646-7277 *Fax:* 763-535-7322

Goose River Press
3400 Friendship Rd, Waldoboro, ME 04572-6337
Tel: 207-832-6665
E-mail: gooseriverpress@gmail.com
Web Site: gooseriverpress.com
Key Personnel
Owner & Ed: Deborah J Benner
Founded: 1999
Turnaround: 7-28 Workdays
Print Runs: 50 min - 10,000 max
Membership(s): Maine Writers & Publishers Alliance (MWPA); Waldoboro Business Association

Gorham Printing
3718 Mahoney Dr, Centralia, WA 98531
Tel: 360-623-1323 *Toll Free Tel:* 800-837-0970
E-mail: info@gorhamprinting.com
Web Site: www.gorhamprinting.com
Key Personnel
Owner: Kurt Gorham
Co-Owner: Norma Gorham
Gen Mgr: Garrett Borden
Book Designer: Kathy Campbell
Founded: 1977
Turnaround: 2-3 weeks softbound, 6-7 weeks hardbound
Print Runs: 25 min - 2,000 max
Membership(s): Association of Personal Historians

Graphic Composition Inc
N1246 Technical Dr, Greenville, WI 54942
Tel: 920-757-6977 *Toll Free Tel:* 800-262-8973
Fax: 920-757-9266
E-mail: socialmedia@graphiccomp.com
Web Site: www.graphiccomp.com
Key Personnel
Pres: Mark Jungen
Founded: 1946

Graphic Litho
Division of High Speed Process Printing Corp
130 Shepard St, Lawrence, MA 01843
Tel: 978-683-2766 *Fax:* 978-681-7588
E-mail: sales@graphiclitho.com
Web Site: www.graphiclitho.com
Key Personnel
Pres: Ralph E Wilbur
Founded: 1960
Print Runs: 1,000 min
Membership(s): Print Services & Distribution Association (PSDA); Printing Industries of New England (PINE); PRINTING United Alliance

GraphiColor Corp
Division of Allegra Princeton
3490 N Mill Rd, Vineland, NJ 08360
Tel: 856-691-2507 *Toll Free Tel:* 800-552-2507
Fax: 856-696-3229
Web Site: www.graphicolorcorp.com
Key Personnel
Pres: Robert W Stenger, Jr *Tel:* 856-691-2507 ext 111 *E-mail:* bob@graphicolorcorp.com
Founded: 1919

Great Lakes Bindery Inc
3741 Linden Ave SE, Wyoming, MI 49548
Tel: 616-245-5264 *Fax:* 616-245-5883
E-mail: jeremy@greatlakesbindery.com
Web Site: www.greatlakesbindery.com
Key Personnel
Pres: Steve Landheer
Gen Mgr & Sales Rep: Matt Landheer *E-mail:* matt@greatlakesbindery.com
Plant Mgr: Brian Willemstyn
Founded: 1978
Print Runs: (call for information)

HBP Inc
952 Frederick St, Hagerstown, MD 21740
Tel: 301-733-2000 *Toll Free Tel:* 800-638-3508 *Fax:* 301-733-6586
E-mail: contactus@hbp.com
Web Site: www.hbp.com
Key Personnel
Owner & Pres: John Snyder
VP, Busn Devt & Mktg: Ilene Lerner *Tel:* 703-289-9038 *E-mail:* ilerner@hbp.com
Founded: 1903
Turnaround: 4-7 Workdays
Print Runs: 1 min - 250,000 max
Sales Office(s): 2818 Fallfax Dr, Falls Church, VA 22042 *Tel:* 703-894-3700
Membership(s): CUA; Printing & Graphics Association MidAtlantic (PGAMA); Printing Industries of Virginia (PIVA); PRINTING United Alliance

Heidelberg Graphics
2 Stansbury Ct, Chico, CA 95928
SAN: 211-5654
Tel: 530-342-6582 *Fax:* 530-342-6582
E-mail: heidelberggraphics@gmail.com; service@heidelberggraphics.com
Web Site: www.heidelberggraphics.com
Key Personnel
Owner & Pres: Larry S Jackson
Founded: 1972
Turnaround: 15-60 Workdays
Print Runs: 5 min - 50,000 max

Hennegan Co
Division of RR Donnelley
7455 Empire Dr, Florence, KY 41042
Tel: 859-282-3600 *Fax:* 859-282-3601
Founded: 1885

Hess Print Solutions
Division of CJK Group Inc
3765 Sunnybrook Rd, Brimfield, OH 44240
Toll Free Tel: 800-678-1222
E-mail: info@hessprintsolutions.com
Web Site: www.hessprintsolutions.com
Key Personnel
Dir & VP: Burt Phillips
VP, IT: Douglas Holzschuh
Founded: 2006
Membership(s): Book Manufacturers' Institute (BMI)

HF Group LLC
8844 Mayfield Rd, Chesterland, OH 44026
Tel: 440-729-2445; 440-729-9411 (bindery)
E-mail: custservice-oh@hfgroup.com
Web Site: www.hfgroup.com
Key Personnel
CEO: Jay Fairfield *Tel:* 440-729-2445 ext 4 *E-mail:* jayfairfield@hfgroup.com
VP & Gen Mgr: Jim Bratton *E-mail:* jbratton@hfgroup.com
Founded: 1821
Turnaround: 14-28 Workdays
Branch Office(s)
1010 N Sycamore St, North Manchester, IN 46962, Pres: Jim Heckman *Tel:* 260-982-2107 *E-mail:* jheckman@hfgroup.com
92 Cambridge St, Charlestown, MA 02129-0212, VP: John Parisi *Tel:* 617-242-1100 *E-mail:* jparisi@hfgroup.com
340 First St, Utica, NE 68456, Gen Mgr: Damon Osborne *Tel:* 402-534-2261 *E-mail:* dosborne@hfgroup.com
6204 Corporate Park Dr, Browns Summit, NC 27214-9745, Contact: Eric Fairfield *Tel:* 336-931-0800 *E-mail:* efairfield@hfgroup.com
45 N Main St, Unit 528, Hatfield, PA 19440 (transportation hub) *Tel:* 215-855-2293
105 W Thomas St, Atlanta, TX 75551-2736 (transportation hub) *Tel:* 260-982-2107 *Fax:* 260-982-1130

Worth Higgins & Associates Inc
8770 Park Central Dr, Richmond, VA 23227-1146
Tel: 804-264-2304 *Toll Free Tel:* 800-883-7768 *Fax:* 804-264-5733
E-mail: contact@whaprint.com
Web Site: www.worthhiggins.com
Key Personnel
Pres & COO: Benny Bowman *E-mail:* b.bowman@whaprint.com
VP, Sales: Brian Losch *E-mail:* blosch@whaprint.com
Dir, Corp Communs: Scott Hudson *E-mail:* shudson@whaprint.com
Founded: 1970
Print Runs: 500 min - 10,000 max

Hignell Book Printing Ltd
Division of Unigraphics Ltd
488 Burnell St, Winnipeg, MB R3G 2B4, Canada
Tel: 204-784-1030 *Toll Free Tel:* 800-304-5553 *Fax:* 204-774-4053
E-mail: books@hignell.mb.ca
Web Site: www.hignell.mb.ca
Key Personnel
Pres: Kevin Polley *E-mail:* kevin@unigraphics.mb.ca
VP & Gen Mgr: David Morcom *E-mail:* davem@unigraphics.mb.ca
Founded: 1908
Turnaround: 15 Workdays
Print Runs: 100 min - 10,000 max

Holmberg Co Inc
4155 Berkshire Lane N, Minneapolis, MN 55446-3814
Tel: 763-559-4155 *Toll Free Tel:* 800-328-5101
E-mail: customerservice@holmberg.com
Web Site: www.holmberg.com
Key Personnel
Natl Acct Mgr: Lynnette Hawkinson *Tel:* 800-328-5101 ext 2020 *E-mail:* lhawkinson@holmberg.com
Founded: 1958

The P A Hutchison Co
400 Penn Ave, Mayfield, PA 18433
SAN: 991-5559
Tel: 570-876-4560 *Toll Free Tel:* 800-USA-PRNT (872-7768) *Fax:* 570-876-4561
E-mail: sales@pahutch.com
Web Site: www.pahutch.com
Key Personnel
Pres & CEO: Chris Hutchison
Dir, Sales & Admin: Erin Jones
Founded: 1911
Turnaround: 3-20 Workdays
Print Runs: 10 min - 500,000 max (digital & conventional)

Imago
110 W 40 St, New York, NY 10018

MANUFACTURING

Tel: 212-921-4411 *Fax:* 212-921-8226
E-mail: sales@imagousa.com
Web Site: www.imagousa.com
Key Personnel
Pres & CEO: Howard Musk *E-mail:* howardm@imagogroup.com
Founded: 1985
Turnaround: 5-10 Workdays for color separations; 4-6 Weeks for printing & binding
Print Runs: 3,000 min
Branch Office(s)
Imago West Coast, 23412 Moulton Pkwy, Suite 250, Laguna Hills, CA 92653 (sales), Contact: Tammy Simms *Tel:* 949-367-1635 *Fax:* 949-367-1639
Imago Australia, 10 Help St, Suite 27, Level 6, Chatswood, NSW 2067, Australia (sales) *Tel:* (04) 3753 3351 (cell); (04) 4806 8704 (cell) *E-mail:* sales@imagaoaus.com
Imago Brazil, Domiciano Rossi, 340 unid 154, 09726-121 Sao Bernardo do Campo, Brazil (sales) *Tel:* (011) 2306 8546; (011) 2306 8547 *E-mail:* imagobra@gmail.com
Imago Shenzhen, Rm 2511-2512, Block A, United Plaza No 5022, Bin He Rd, Fu Tian Centre District, Shenzhen 518033, China (prodn), Contact: Kendrick Cheung *Tel:* (0755) 8304 8899 *Fax:* (0755) 8251 4073 *E-mail:* enquiries@imago.com.hk
Imago France, 23 rue Lavoisier, 75008 Paris, France (sales) *Tel:* 01 45 26 47 74 *Fax:* 01 78 94 14 44 *E-mail:* sales@imagogroup.com
Imago Services (HK) Ltd, Unit B309, 1/F, New East Sun Industrial Bldg, 18 Shing Yip St, Kwun Tong, Hong Kong (prodn), Contact: Kendrick Cheung *Tel:* 2811 3316 *E-mail:* enquiries@imago.com.hk
Imago Productions (Malaysia) Pte Ltd, No 43, Taman Emas, Jl Utama 31, Telok Panglima Garang, 42500 Kuala Langot, Selangor, Malaysia (prodn, incorporating South Africa sales) *Tel:* (017) 4288771 (cell) *E-mail:* enquiries@imago.com.sg
Imago Publishing, Albury Ct, Albury Thame, Oxon OX9 2LP, United Kingdom (sales), Dir: Simon Rosenheim *Tel:* (01844) 337000 *Fax:* (01844) 339935 *E-mail:* sales@imago.co.uk *Web Site:* imagogroup.com

Impressions Inc
1050 Westgate Dr, St Paul, MN 55114
Tel: 651-646-1050 *Toll Free Tel:* 800-251-4285
Fax: 651-646-7228
E-mail: info@i-i.com
Web Site: www.i-i.com
Key Personnel
CEO: Mike Jorgensen
VP, Packaging: Dave Bade
Sales & Mktg Mgr: Jenna Hazaert *Tel:* 651-917-1394
Founded: 1967
Turnaround: 7-10 Workdays
Branch Office(s)
235 Eastgate Dr SE, Hutchinson, MN 55350
Membership(s): Advertising Federation of Minnesota; Advertising Specialty Institute (ASI); American Marketing Association; Institute of Packaging Professionals; ISO; Private Label Manufacturers Association

InfinitPrint Solutions Inc
14 N Tenth St, Richmond, IN 47374
Tel: 765-962-1507 *Toll Free Tel:* 800-478-4885
Fax: 765-962-4997
E-mail: info@infinitprint.com
Web Site: infinitprint.com
Key Personnel
Pres: Michael D Gibbs *E-mail:* mike@infinitprint.com
Founded: 1972
Turnaround: 30 Workdays

Print Runs: 50 min - 5,000 max
Branch Office(s)
211 NW Seventh St, Richmond, IN 47374
Tel: 765-966-7130 *Fax:* 765-966-7131

Infinity Graphics
2277 Science Pkwy, Suite 5, Okemos, MI 48864
Tel: 517-349-4635 *Toll Free Tel:* 800-292-2633
Fax: 517-349-7608
E-mail: barcode@infinitygraphics.com
Web Site: www.infinitygraphics.com
Key Personnel
Owner & Partner: Brian Perry
Owner, Partner & Bar Code Specialist: Suzette Perry
Founded: 1972
Turnaround: 3-4 Weeks
Print Runs: 1 min - 10,000 max
Membership(s): Independent Book Publishers Association (IBPA)

Interstate Printing Co
2002 N 16 St, Omaha, NE 68110
Tel: 402-341-8028 *Toll Free Tel:* 800-788-4177
Web Site: www.interstateprinting.com
Founded: 1917
Turnaround: 7 Workdays
Print Runs: 500 min

Ironmark
9040 Junction Dr, Annapolis Junction, MD 20701
Toll Free Tel: 888-775-3737
E-mail: marketing@ironmarkusa.com
Web Site: ironmarkusa.com
Key Personnel
CEO: Scott Hargest *E-mail:* scott@ironmarkusa.com; Jeff Ostenso *E-mail:* jeff@ironmarkusa.com
Pres: Matt Marzullo *E-mail:* mmarzullo@ironmarkusa.com
SVP, Sales: Scott Kravitz *E-mail:* skravitz@ironmarkusa.com
VP, Opers: Chris Marzullo *E-mail:* cmarzullo@ironmarkusa.com
Sr Sales Exec: Larry Davis *E-mail:* ldavis@ironmarkusa.com
Founded: 1955
Turnaround: 20 Workdays, case bound; 10 Workdays, paperback; 15 Workdays, mechanically bound
Print Runs: 500 min - 500,000 max

ITW Foils
Division of Illinois Tool Works
5 Malcolm Hoyt Dr, Newburyport, MA 01950
Tel: 978-225-8200 *Toll Free Tel:* 800-942-9995
Fax: 978-462-0831
E-mail: info@itwsf.com
Web Site: www.itwfoils.com
Founded: 1926

JP Graphics Inc
3001 E Venture Dr, Appleton, WI 54911
Tel: 920-733-4483 *Fax:* 920-733-1700
E-mail: support@jpinc.com
Web Site: www.jpinc.com; www.print.jpinc.com
Key Personnel
Pres: Rod Stoffel
Sales Mgr: Randy Hearley
Founded: 1969

Kappa Graphics LLP
Division of Kappa Printing Management Associates LLC (KPMA)
50 Rock St, Hughestown, PA 18640
Tel: 570-655-9681 *Toll Free Tel:* 800-236-4396 (sales)
E-mail: weborders@kappapma.com
Web Site: www.kappapma.com/kappagraphics; kappapuzzles.com

PRINTING, BINDING & BOOK FINISHING

Key Personnel
CEO: Nick Karabots
Pres: Thomas Simunek
Founded: 1906
Print Runs: 30,000 min - 500,000 max

Knepper Press Corp
2251 Sweeney Dr, Clinton, PA 15026
Tel: 724-899-4200 *Fax:* 724-899-1331
Web Site: www.knepperpress.com
Key Personnel
Chmn: Ted Ford *E-mail:* tedford@knepperpress.com
CFO: Jerry Sales *E-mail:* jerry.sales@knepperpress.com
Cont: Dawn Bates *E-mail:* dawn.bates@knepperpress.com
Pres: Bob Hreha *E-mail:* bobhreha@knepperpress.com
Founded: 1873
Turnaround: 10-20 Workdays
Print Runs: 500 min - 50,000 max

The C J Krehbiel Company, see CJK

Kromar Printing Ltd
725 Portage Ave, Winnipeg, MB R3G 0M8, Canada
Tel: 204-775-8721 *Fax:* 204-783-8985
E-mail: info@kromar.com
Web Site: www.kromar.com
Key Personnel
CEO: Jack Cohen
COO: Joseph Cohen *E-mail:* josephcohen@kromar.com
Founded: 1945
Turnaround: 15 Workdays
Print Runs: 500 min - 50,000 max
Branch Office(s)
130 Slater St, Ottawa, ON K1P 6E2, Canada
Tel: 613-563-7577 *Fax:* 613-594-8705
E-mail: kromar@kromar.com

La Crosse Graphics Inc
3025 East Ave S, La Crosse, WI 54601
Tel: 608-788-2500 *Toll Free Tel:* 800-832-2503
Fax: 608-788-2660
Web Site: www.lacrossegraphics.com
Key Personnel
Pres: Tim Morgan
VP, Opers: Dianna Clements *Tel:* 608-788-2500 ext 202 *E-mail:* dclements@lacrossegraphics.com
VP, Sales: Heath Tschumper *Tel:* 608-788-2500 ext 203 *E-mail:* htschumper@lacrossegraphics.com
Purchasing Mgr: Shawn Wortman *Tel:* 608-788-2500 ext 206 *E-mail:* swortman@lacrossegraphics.com
Founded: 1987

Labels Inc
10 Merrill Industrial Dr, Hampton, NH 03842
Tel: 603-929-3088 *Toll Free Tel:* 800-852-2357
Fax: 603-929-7305
E-mail: sales@labelsinc.com
Web Site: www.labelsinc.com
Key Personnel
VP, Sales & Mktg: Chris Snow
Founded: 1975

Lake Book Manufacturing Inc
2085 N Cornell Ave, Melrose Park, IL 60160
Tel: 708-345-7000
E-mail: info@lakebook.com
Web Site: www.lakebook.com
Key Personnel
Pres & COO: Dan Genovese
VP, Fin & CFO: Bob Flatow
VP & Gen Mgr: Bill Richards
VP, Mfg: Steve Quagliato

PRINTING, BINDING & BOOK FINISHING

VP, Opers: Bill Flavin
VP, Sales & Mktg: Nick Vergoth
VP, Technol: Paul Genovese

L+L Printers
6200 Yarrow Dr, Carlsbad, CA 92011
Tel: 760-438-3456; 760-477-0321 *Fax:* 760-929-0853
E-mail: info@llprinters.com
Web Site: www.llprinters.com
Key Personnel
Partner & CEO: Bill Anderson
Partner & Pres, Mktg & Sales: Joel Green
Partner & VP, Sales: Alan Peel; Dirk Williams
COO: Frank Scorzelli
Founded: 1959
Branch Office(s)
8221 Arjons Dr, Suite E, San Diego, CA 92126
  Tel: 858-859-9044 *Fax:* 858-571-7352

The Lane Press Inc
87 Meadowland Dr, South Burlington, VT 05403
Mailing Address: PO Box 130, Burlington, VT 05402
Tel: 802-863-5555 *Toll Free Tel:* 877-300-5933
  Fax: 802-264-1485
E-mail: sales@lanepress.com
Web Site: www.lanepress.com
Key Personnel
Edit Dir: Beth Renaud
Founded: 1904

Lawton Connect
649 Triumph Ct, Orlando, FL 32805
Tel: 407-260-0400 *Toll Free Tel:* 877-330-1900
  Fax: 407-260-1321
E-mail: hello@lawtonconnect.com
Web Site: www.lawtonconnect.com
Key Personnel
Pres & CEO: Kimberly Lawton-Koon
  E-mail: kimberly@lawtonconnect.com
VP: Tyler Koon *E-mail:* ty@lawtonconnect.com
Founded: 1900
Turnaround: 3-5 Workdays

Lee Publications
Division of Stry-Lenkoff Co LLC
1100 W Broadway, Louisville, KY 40203
Mailing Address: PO Box 32120, Louisville, KY 40232-2120
Tel: 502-587-6804 *Toll Free Tel:* 800-626-8247
  Fax: 502-587-6822
E-mail: info@leemagicpen.com
Web Site: www.leemagicpen.com
Key Personnel
CEO: Rick Herndon

Lenoir Printing Solutions, see an ICON Company LLC

Leo Paper USA
Division of Leo Paper Group
1180 NW Maple St, Suite 102, Issaquah, WA 98027
Tel: 425-646-8801 *Fax:* 425-646-8805
E-mail: info@leousa.com
Web Site: www.leopaper.com
Key Personnel
Pres: Behzad Pakzad
Founded: 1982
Turnaround: 40 Workdays
Print Runs: 3,500 min - 2,000,000 max
Branch Office(s)
286 Fifth Ave, 6th fl, New York, NY 10001, Contact: John DiMasi *Tel:* 917-305-0708 *Fax:* 917-305-0709 *E-mail:* info@leousanewyork.com

Letterhead Press Inc (LPI)
16800 W Ryerson Rd, New Berlin, WI 53151
Tel: 262-787-1717 *Fax:* 262-787-1710; 262-787-7315 (estimating)
E-mail: contact@letterhead-press.com
Web Site: www.letterheadpress.com
Key Personnel
Pres: Michael Graf
VP, Sales & Mktg: Dick Reindl *E-mail:* dick@letterhead-press.com
Founded: 1984
Print Runs: 1 min - 10,000,000 max
Membership(s): Foil & Specialty Effects Association (FSEA); Great Lakes Graphics Association (GLGA); PRINTING United Alliance

The Lexington Press Inc
15 Meriam St, Lexington, MA 02420
Mailing Address: PO Box 51, Lexington, MA 02420-0001
Tel: 781-862-8900 *Fax:* 781-861-0375
Web Site: www.lexingtonpress.com
Key Personnel
Pres: Robert F Sacco *E-mail:* bob@lexingtonpress.com
Founded: 1955
Print Runs: 50 min - 1,000 max

Lightning Source LLC
Subsidiary of Ingram Content Group LLC
1246 Heil Quaker Blvd, La Vergne, TN 37086
Tel: 615-793-5000 (Ingram) *Toll Free Tel:* 800-378-5508; 800-509-4156 (cust serv)
E-mail: lsicustomersupport@ingramcontent.com
Web Site: www.ingramcontent.com/publishers/print
Key Personnel
Chief Content Offr: Phil Ollila
CFO: Brian Dauphin
Chief Logistics Offr, Global Opers: John F Secrest
Sr Key Acct Mgr: Liz Hunter
Key Acct Sales Mgr: Ali Galbraith
Mgr, Content Acqs Sales: Alicia Samuel
Mgr, Trade Sales: Caitlin Kleinschmidt
Supv, Content Acq Sales: Bailey Davis
Founded: 1997

Lo Gatto Bookbinding
390 Paterson Ave, East Rutherford, NJ 07073
Tel: 201-438-4344 *Fax:* 201-438-1775
E-mail: bookbindin@aol.com
Key Personnel
Contact: Michael Lo Gatto
Founded: 1967
Turnaround: 10 Workdays

Long's Roullet Bookbinders Inc
2800 Monticello Ave, Norfolk, VA 23504
Tel: 757-623-4244 *Fax:* 757-627-1404
E-mail: bindlrbi@gmail.com
Web Site: longs-roullet.com
Key Personnel
Pres: Alain Roullet
VP: Eileen Roullet
Founded: 1975

Mandel Graphic Solution
727 W Glendale Ave, Suite 100, Milwaukee, WI 53209
Tel: 414-271-6970 *Fax:* 414-386-4660
E-mail: info@mandelcompany.com
Web Site: www.mandelcompany.com
Key Personnel
Pres: Rick Mandel *E-mail:* rick.mandel@mandelcompany.com
Founded: 1892

Manroland Inc
Subsidiary of Manroland Sheetfed GmbH
800 E Oak Hill Dr, Westmont, IL 60559
Tel: 630-920-2000
E-mail: info.us@manrolandsheetfed.com
Web Site: manrolandsheetfed.com
Key Personnel
CEO: Sean Springett

Maple Press
480 Willow Springs Lane, York, PA 17406
Mailing Address: PO Box 2695, York, PA 17405-2695
Tel: 717-764-5911 *Toll Free Tel:* 800-999-5911
  Fax: 717-764-4702
E-mail: sales@maplepress.com
Web Site: www.maplepress.com
Key Personnel
Pres: James S Wisotzkey
VP, Opers: Chris Benyovszky
VP, Sales: Bob Bethune
VP, Sales & Mktg: Andrew J Van Sprang
  E-mail: vansprang@maplepress.com
Founded: 1901
Print Runs: 25 min - 200,000 max
Branch Office(s)
92 Rockvale Rd, Tewksbury, MA 01876, VP, Sales: Bob Bethune *Tel:* 978-858-0900 *Fax:* 978-858-0920 *E-mail:* bethune@maplepress.com
Membership(s): Book Industry Study Group (BISG); Book Manufacturers' Institute (BMI)

Maracle Inc
1156 King St E, Oshawa, ON L1H 1H8, Canada
Tel: 905-723-3438 *Toll Free Tel:* 800-558-8604
  Fax: 905-723-1759
E-mail: hello@maracleinc.com
Web Site: www.maracleinc.com
Key Personnel
Pres: George Sittlinger *Tel:* 905-723-3438 ext 236
Dir, Opers: Nadene D Aldred
Sales & Busn Devt Mgr: Brian Ostrander *Tel:* 905-723-3438 ext 272
  E-mail: bostrander@maracleinc.com
Founded: 1920
Turnaround: 10 Workdays
Print Runs: 500 min - 500,000 max
Membership(s): Book Manufacturers' Institute (BMI); Canadian Book Manufacturer Association; Canadian Society of Association Executives (CSAE); Ontario Printing & Imaging Association; PRINTING United Alliance

Marquis Book Printing Inc
Division of Lakeside Book Co
350, rue des Entrepreneurs, Montmagny, QC G5V 4T1, Canada
Tel: 418-246-5666 *Toll Free Tel:* 855-566-1937; 800-246-2468
E-mail: marquis@marquisbook.com
Web Site: www.marquislivre.com; www.marquisbook.com
Key Personnel
Pres & CEO: Serge Loubier
VP, Sales: Pierre Frechette
Founded: 1937
Turnaround: 5-10 Workdays
Print Runs: 1 min - 1,000,000 max (1/1, 2/2 + 4/4)
Sales Office(s): 2700 rue Rachel E, No 100, Montreal, QC H2H 1S7, Canada *Tel:* 514-954-1131
  Toll Free Tel: 877-594-1364

Marrakech Express Inc
720 Wesley Ave, No 10, Tarpon Springs, FL 34689
Tel: 727-942-2218 *Toll Free Tel:* 800-940-6566
  Fax: 727-937-4758
E-mail: print@marrak.com
Web Site: www.marrak.com
Key Personnel
CEO: Peter Henzell
Prodn Mgr: Steen Sigmund
Sales/Estimator: Shirley Copperman
Founded: 1976
Turnaround: 7-10 Workdays
Print Runs: 500 min - 1,000,000 max

MANUFACTURING

PRINTING, BINDING & BOOK FINISHING

Martin Printing Co Inc
1765 Powdersville Rd, Easley, SC 29642
Mailing Address: PO Box 69, Easley, SC 29641
Toll Free Tel: 888-985-7330 *Fax:* 864-859-8620
E-mail: info@martinprinting.com
Web Site: www.martinprinting.com
Key Personnel
Pres: William Ragsdale
VP, Sales & Mktg: Craig Ragsdale
    E-mail: craig@martinprinting.com
Founded: 1902
Turnaround: 5-7 Workdays
Print Runs: 500 min - 1,000,000 max
Branch Office(s)
1743 Powdersville Rd, Easley, SC 29642 (prodn facility)
Membership(s): PICA

The Master's Press
14550 Midway Rd, Dallas, TX 75244
Tel: 972-387-0046 *Fax:* 972-404-0317
Web Site: www.themasterspress.com
Key Personnel
Pres: Charlene Sims *E-mail:* char@themasterspress.com
Gen Mgr: Aaron Cottle *E-mail:* aaron@themasterspress.com
Founded: 1976
Turnaround: 1-3 Workdays
Print Runs: 25 min - 25,000 max
Membership(s): National Foundation of Independent Businesses (NFIB); Print Image International; PRINTING United Alliance

McClain Printing Co
212 Main St, Parsons, WV 26287-1033
Mailing Address: PO Box 403, Parsons, WV 26287-0403
Tel: 304-478-2881 *Toll Free Tel:* 800-654-7179
    Fax: 304-478-4658
E-mail: mcclain@mcclainprinting.com
Web Site: www.mcclainprinting.com
Key Personnel
Pres: Kenneth E Smith
VP, Publg: Michelle McKinnie
Founded: 1958
Turnaround: 90-120 Workdays
Print Runs: 250 min - 10,000 max

Moran Printing Inc, see Emprint®

Morris Printing Group Inc
3212 E Hwy 30, Kearney, NE 68847
Mailing Address: PO Box 2110, Kearney, NE 68848-2110
Tel: 308-236-7888 *Toll Free Tel:* 800-650-7888
    Fax: 308-237-0263
Web Site: www.morrisprintinggroup.com
Key Personnel
Owner: Scott Morris
VP, Opers: Ryan Morris
Founded: 1933
Turnaround: 5-15 Workdays
Print Runs: 25 min - 5,000 max

Morris Publishing®
Division of Morris Printing Group Inc
3212 E Hwy 30, Kearney, NE 68847
Mailing Address: PO Box 2110, Kearney, NE 68848-2110
Tel: 308-236-7888 *Toll Free Tel:* 800-650-7888
    Fax: 308-237-0263
E-mail: publish@morrispublishing.com
Web Site: www.morrispublishing.com
Key Personnel
Mgr: Gerald Bergstrom
Founded: 1994
Turnaround: 20-30 Workdays
Print Runs: 25 min - 5,000 max

Multi-Reliure
2112 Ave de la Transmission, Shawinigan, QC G9N 8N8, Canada
Tel: 819-537-6008 *Toll Free Tel:* 888-735-4873
    Fax: 819-537-4598
E-mail: info@multi-reliure.com; administration@multi-reliure.com
Web Site: www.multireliure.com
Key Personnel
Gen Mgr: Yvon Sauvageau *Tel:* 888-735-4873 ext 28 *E-mail:* ysauvageau@multi-reliure.com
Prodn Dir: Patrick Paquet *Tel:* 888-735-4873 ext 22 *E-mail:* ppaquet@multi-reliure.com
Prodn Coord: Sonia Paquet *Tel:* 888-735-4873 ext 23 *E-mail:* spaquet@multi-reliure.com
Admin & HR: Melanie Ethier *Tel:* 888-735-4873 ext 21
Founded: 1988

NAPCO Inc
120 Trojan Ave, Sparta, NC 28675
Mailing Address: PO Box 1029, Sparta, NC 28675-1029
Tel: 336-372-5228 *Toll Free Tel:* 800-854-8621
    Fax: 336-372-8602
E-mail: info@napcousa.com
Web Site: www.napcousa.com
Key Personnel
Cont: Kathy Royal
Pres & CEO: James R Proffit
EVP: Jerry Pearce
Founded: 1977

Neibauer Press
20 Industrial Dr, Warminster, PA 18974
Tel: 215-322-6200 *Fax:* 215-322-2495
E-mail: sales@neibauer.com
Web Site: www.neibauer.com
Key Personnel
VP: Ruth Neibauer-Baker *Tel:* 215-322-6216
    E-mail: ruth@neibauer.com
Founded: 1955

Nissha USA Inc
Subsidiary of Nissha Co Ltd
1051 Perimeter Dr, Suite 600, Schaumburg, IL 60173
Tel: 847-413-2665 *Fax:* 847-413-4085
Web Site: www.nissha.com
Key Personnel
Chmn: Junya Suzuki
Dir & CEO: Hiroyuki Uenishi
Founded: 1993

Noble Book Press Corp
211 Ditmas Ave, Brooklyn, NY 11218
Tel: 718-435-9321 *Fax:* 718-435-0464
Key Personnel
Pres: Philip B Weinreich *E-mail:* pwnoble@aol.com
Founded: 1981
Turnaround: 12-17 Workdays
Print Runs: 500 min - 100,000 max

OGM USA
4333 46 St, Suite F2, Sunnyside, NY 11104
Tel: 212-964-2430
Web Site: www.ogm.it
Key Personnel
Chmn, CEO & Sales Rep: Rino Varrasso
    E-mail: rvarrasso@ogm-usa.com
Founded: 1974
Turnaround: 30 Workdays
Print Runs: 75 min - 300,000 max

Omnipress
2600 Anderson St, Madison, WI 53704
Tel: 608-246-2600 *Toll Free Tel:* 800-828-0305
E-mail: justask@omnipress.com
Web Site: www.omnipress.com
Key Personnel
VP, Prodn: Greg Hubbard *Tel:* 608-778-6863
Dir, Mkt Devt: Dan Loomis
Dir, Mktg: Tracy Grzybowski
Dir, Servs: Rob Bossingham
Gen Mgr: Jonny Popp *Tel:* 608-215-9650
Founded: 1977
Turnaround: 5 Workdays
Print Runs: 1 min - 5,000 max

O'Neil Digital Solutions LLC
12655 Beatrice St, Los Angeles, CA 90066
Tel: 310-448-6400
E-mail: sales@oneildata.com
Web Site: www.oneildata.com
Key Personnel
Pres & COO: Terry Chan
EVP, Sales & Mktg: Mark Rosson
Dir, HR: LaDonna Wise
Founded: 1973
Turnaround: 3-10 Workdays
Print Runs: 500 min

OneTouchPoint
1225 Walnut Ridge Dr, Hartland, WI 53029
Tel: 262-369-6000 *Toll Free Tel:* 800-332-2348
    Fax: 262-369-5647
E-mail: info@1touchpoint.com
Web Site: www.1touchpoint.com
Key Personnel
CEO: Dave Holland
Dir, Mktg & Sales Opers: Carey Howard
Founded: 1982
Turnaround: order processing: within 8 hours; digital printing: 24-48 hours after proof approval; press: 7-10 days after proof approval
Print Runs: 1 min - 500,000 max
Branch Office(s)
5241 Voges Rd, Madison, WI 53718 *Tel:* 608-838-9147
525 W Alameda Dr, Suite 101, Tempe, AZ 85282, Contact: James Parker *Tel:* 480-966-4003 *Fax:* 480-966-4016
5280 Joliet St, Denver, CO 80239 *Tel:* 303-227-1400
1441 Western Ave, Cincinnati, OH 45214 *Tel:* 513-421-1600
8410-B Tuscany Way, Austin, TX 78754 *Tel:* 512-454-6874

Outskirts Press Inc
10940 S Parker Rd, Suite 515, Parker, CO 80134
Toll Free Tel: 888-OP-BOOKS (672-6657)
    Toll Free Fax: 888-208-8601
E-mail: info@outskirtspress.com
Web Site: www.outskirtspress.com
Key Personnel
CEO: Jeanine Sampson
CFO & CTO: Lynn Sampson
Pres & Chief Mktg Offr: Brent Sampson
Founded: 2003
Turnaround: 35 Workdays
Print Runs: 1 min (no max)

Overseas Printing Corporation
Division of InnerWorkings Inc
4040 Civic Center Dr, Suite 200, San Rafael, CA 94903
Tel: 415-500-8331 *Fax:* 415-835-9899
Web Site: www.overseasprinting.com
Key Personnel
Sr Prodn Mgr: Shaun Garrett *E-mail:* sgarrett@inwk.com
Founded: 1972
Turnaround: 8-12 Weeks
Print Runs: 1,000 min

The Ovid Bell Press Inc
Subsidiary of Walsworth Publishing Co
1201 Bluff St, Fulton, MO 65251

PRINTING, BINDING & BOOK FINISHING

Mailing Address: PO Box 370, Fulton, MO 65251-0370
Tel: 573-642-2256 *Toll Free Tel:* 800-835-8919
E-mail: sales@ovidbell.com
Web Site: ovidbell.com
Key Personnel
CFO: Jill Custard *E-mail:* jillcustard@ovidbell.com
Pres: Troy Williams *Tel:* 573-310-2599
 E-mail: troywilliams@ovidbell.com
VP, Sales & Mktg: David O'Donley *Tel:* 573-310-2630 *E-mail:* david@ovidbell.com
Plant Mgr: Kevin Werdehausen *Tel:* 573-310-2598
 E-mail: kevin.werdehausen@ovidbell.com
Founded: 1927
Turnaround: 5 Workdays
Print Runs: 5,000 min - 150,000 max

Pacific Publishing Co Inc
636 Alaska St S, Seattle, WA 98108
Mailing Address: PO Box 80156, Seattle, WA 98108
Tel: 206-461-1300
E-mail: ppcinfo@nwlink.com; ppccirc@nwlink.com; ppcbind@nwlink.com
Web Site: pacificpublishingcompany.com
Key Personnel
Pres & CEO: Peter Bernard
Dir, Opers: Richard Fazakerley *Tel:* 206-461-1282
 E-mail: opsmanager@nwlink.com
Dir, Sales & Mktg: Tammy Knaggs *Tel:* 206-461-1322 *E-mail:* ppcadmanager@nwlink.com
Gen Mgr: Robert Munford *Tel:* 206-461-1304
Opers Supv: Steve Yip *Tel:* 206-461-1287
Print Runs: 3,000 min - 100,000 max

Panaprint Inc
7979 NE Industrial Blvd, Macon, GA 31216
Tel: 478-788-0676 *Toll Free Tel:* 800-622-0676
 Fax: 478-788-4276
Web Site: www.panaprint.com
Key Personnel
Pres: Wanzie Collins *E-mail:* wcollins@panaprint.com
Sales: Byron Prickett *E-mail:* bprickett@panaprint.com
Founded: 1973
Turnaround: 10-20 Workdays
Membership(s): Epicomm; PRINTING United Alliance

Patterson Printing Co
1550 Territorial Rd, Benton Harbor, MI 49022
Tel: 269-925-2177
E-mail: sales@patterson-printing.com
Web Site: patterson-printing.com
Founded: 1956
Print Runs: 250 min

PBM Graphics Inc, an RR Donnelley Co
3700 S Miami Blvd, Durham, NC 27703
Tel: 919-544-6222 *Toll Free Tel:* 800-849-8100
 Fax: 919-544-6695
E-mail: info@pbmgraphics.com
Web Site: pbmgraphics.com

PCA Printing, see Printing Corporation of the Americas Inc

Perma Graphics
1356 S Jason St, Denver, CO 80223
Tel: 303-477-2070
E-mail: info@perma-graphics.com
Web Site: www.perma-graphics.com
Key Personnel
Owner: Erin Pfister
Founded: 1974

Pint Size Productions LLC
5745 Main St, Amherst, NY 14221
Tel: 716-204-3353
E-mail: sales@pintsizeproductions.com
Web Site: www.pintsizeproductions.com
Key Personnel
Pres & Creative Dir: Terry Ortolani
 E-mail: tortolani@pintsizeproductions.com
Founded: 2001
Print Runs: 2,500 min (no max)

POD Print
2012 E Northern St, Wichita, KS 67216
Tel: 316-522-5599 *Toll Free Tel:* 800-767-6066
E-mail: info@podprint.com
Web Site: www.podprint.com
Key Personnel
Owner: Grace Rishel; Jim Rishel
Prodn Opers Mgr: Traci Grote *E-mail:* tgrote@podprint.com
Founded: 1978
Print Runs: 1 min - 25,000 max (every service offered on-demand)
Membership(s): Print Services & Distribution Association (PSDA); PRINTING United Alliance

PrairieView Press
625 Seventh St, Gretna, MB R0G 0V0, Canada
Mailing Address: PO Box 460, Gretna, MB R0G 0V0, Canada
Tel: 204-327-6543 *Toll Free Tel:* 800-477-7377
 Toll Free Fax: 866-480-0253
Web Site: prairieviewpress.com
Key Personnel
Owner & Pres: Chester Goossen
Founded: 1968

Print It Plus
11420 Okeechobee Blvd, Royal Palm Beach, FL 33411
Tel: 561-790-0884 *Fax:* 561-790-9378
E-mail: info@printitplus.com
Web Site: printitplus.com
Key Personnel
Pres & CEO: David Leland *E-mail:* dave@printitplus.com
Mktg Mgr: Kimberly Leland *E-mail:* kim@printitplus.com
Founded: 1988
Membership(s): Florida Graphics Alliance (FGA); Print Image International

The Printer
2810 Cowell Blvd, Davis, CA 95618
Tel: 530-753-2519 *Fax:* 530-753-2528
E-mail: info@the-printer.net
Web Site: the-printer.net
Key Personnel
Owner & Estimator: Howard Galbreath
Founded: 1966
Print Runs: 1 min - 100,000 max
Membership(s): National Foundation of Independent Businesses (NFIB)

Printing Corporation of the Americas Inc
620 SW 12 Ave, Pompano Beach, FL 33069
Tel: 954-781-8100 *Toll Free Tel:* 866-721-1PCA (721-1722)
Web Site: pcaprintingplus.com
Key Personnel
Pres: Buddy Tuchman
Sales Mgr: Steven Konecky *E-mail:* steven@pcaprinting.com
Founded: 1980
Turnaround: 5-10 Workdays
Print Runs: 500 min - 100,000 max

Pro Laminators
1511 Avco Blvd, Sellersburg, IN 47172
Mailing Address: PO Box 274, Sellersburg, IN 47172-0274
Tel: 812-246-0900 *Toll Free Tel:* 800-357-6812
 Fax: 812-246-1900
E-mail: customerservice@prolaminators.com
Web Site: prolaminators.com
Key Personnel
Pres: Karen Haywood
Mgr: Jack Haywood *E-mail:* jack@prolaminators.com
Sales: Doug Hamilton *E-mail:* dough@prolaminators.com
Founded: 1984
Membership(s): PRINTING United Alliance

ProductionPro
246 Park St, Bensenville, IL 60106
Tel: 847-696-1600
E-mail: sales@productionpro.com; graphics@productionpro.com
Web Site: www.productionpro.com
Key Personnel
Owner: Douglas Tello *Tel:* 847-696-1600 ext 101
 E-mail: douglas@productionpro.com
Founded: 1992

Progress Printing Plus
2677 Waterlick Rd, Lynchburg, VA 24502
Tel: 434-239-9213 *Toll Free Tel:* 800-572-7804
 Fax: 434-832-7573
E-mail: info@progressprintplus.com
Web Site: www.progressprintplus.com
Key Personnel
Pres: Michael Thornton *E-mail:* mthornton@progressprintplus.com
Dir, Busn Devt: Gerald Bowles
 E-mail: gbowles@progressprintplus.com
Founded: 1962
Turnaround: 7-9 Workdays after final proof approval
Print Runs: 5,000 min - 500,000 max

Publishers Book Bindery (NY)
250 W 16 St, 4th fl, New York, NY 10011
Tel: 917-497-2950
Key Personnel
Pres: Ed Goldman
Founded: 1946
Print Runs: 100 min - 50,000 max

Publishers' Graphics LLC
131 Fremont St, Chicago, IL 60185
Tel: 630-221-1850
E-mail: contactpg@pubgraphics.com
Web Site: pubgraphics.com
Key Personnel
Pres: Nick A Lewis *E-mail:* nlewis@pubgraphics.com
VP: Kathleen Lewis *E-mail:* kmlewis@pubgraphics.com
Founded: 1996
Turnaround: 2-8 Workdays
Print Runs: 1 min - 20,000 max
Branch Office(s)
3777 Rider Trail S, St Louis, MO 63045
 Tel: 314-739-3777 *Fax:* 314-739-1436
Sales Office(s): Louisville, KY, VP, Sales: Cara Lahey *Tel:* 630-291-4867 *E-mail:* clahey@pubgraphics.com

Publishing Data Management Inc
39 Broadway, 28th fl, New York, NY 10006
Tel: 212-673-3210 *Fax:* 212-673-3390
E-mail: info@pubdata.com
Web Site: www.pubdata.com
Key Personnel
Pres: Addison Roverano *E-mail:* addison@pubdata.com
Founded: 1970
Turnaround: 1 Hour-3 Workdays

Puritan Press Inc
Division of Puritan Capital
95 Runnells Bridge Rd, Hollis, NH 03049-6565
Tel: 603-889-4500 *Toll Free Tel:* 800-635-6302
 Fax: 603-889-6551
E-mail: print@puritancapital.com

MANUFACTURING

PRINTING, BINDING & BOOK FINISHING

Web Site: www.puritanpress.com
Key Personnel
Owner & Pres: Kurt A Peterson *E-mail:* kurt@puritancapital.com
Owner & VP: Michael Ames *E-mail:* michael@puritancapital.com; Jay Stewart *E-mail:* jay@puritancapital.com
Founded: 1976
Turnaround: 21 Workdays
Print Runs: 25 min - 25,000 max
Membership(s): Printing Industries of New England (PINE); PRINTING United Alliance

Quality Bindery Services Inc
501 Amherst St, Buffalo, NY 14207
Tel: 716-883-5185 *Toll Free Tel:* 888-883-1266
Fax: 716-883-1598
E-mail: info@qualitybindery.com
Web Site: www.qualitybindery.com
Key Personnel
Partner: David Borics; Charles Stachowiak, Jr
Pres: Kathleen Hartmans *E-mail:* kathie@qualitybindery.com
Founded: 1993
Turnaround: 1-3 Workdays
Print Runs: 1 min (no max)
Membership(s): PRINTING United Alliance

Quantum Group
6511 Oakton St, Morton Grove, IL 60053
Tel: 847-967-3600 *Fax:* 847-967-3610
E-mail: info@quantumgroup.com
Web Site: www.quantumgroup.com
Key Personnel
CEO: Cheryl Kahanec
Founded: 1992
Membership(s): Great Lakes Graphics Association (GLGA); PRINTING United Alliance

V G Reed & Sons Inc
1002 S 12 St, Louisville, KY 40210-1302
Toll Free Tel: 800-635-9788 *Fax:* 502-560-0197
Web Site: www.vgreed.com
Key Personnel
Pres: Bobby Reed, Sr
VP, Natl Sales: Scott W Reed
Founded: 1938
Turnaround: 7-10 Workdays

Regal Press
79 Astor Ave, Norwood, MA 02062
Tel: 781-769-3900 *Toll Free Tel:* 800-447-3425
Fax: 781-769-7361
E-mail: info@regalpress.com
Web Site: www.regalpress.com
Key Personnel
VP, Sales: Mike Simone *E-mail:* msimone@regalpress.com

Reindl Bindery Co Inc
W194 N11381 McCormick Dr, Germantown, WI 53022
Tel: 262-293-1444 *Toll Free Tel:* 800-878-1121
Fax: 262-293-1445
E-mail: info@reindlbindery.com
Web Site: www.reindlbindery.com
Key Personnel
Pres: David C Reindl *E-mail:* david_reindl@reindlbindery.com
Founded: 1978
Print Runs: 1 min

The Renton Printery Inc
315 S Third St, Renton, WA 98057-2028
Tel: 425-235-1776
E-mail: info@rentonprintery.com
Web Site: www.rentonprintery.com
Key Personnel
Pres & CEO: Richard Sweeney
Founded: 1959

Turnaround: 2-7 Workdays
Print Runs: 1 min

RISO Inc
Subsidiary of RISO Kagaku Corp
10 State St, Suite 201, Woburn, MA 01801-2105
Tel: 978-777-7377 *Toll Free Tel:* 800-942-7476 (cust support)
Web Site: us.riso.com
Key Personnel
Pres & CEO: Koji Sonobe
VP & CFO: Alex Olshan
VP, Corp Planning: Sho Fujiwara
Founded: 1986

Ross Gage Inc
8502 Brookville Rd, Indianapolis, IN 46239
Tel: 317-283-2323 *Toll Free Tel:* 800-799-2323
Fax: 317-931-2108
E-mail: info@rossgage.com
Web Site: www.rossgage.com
Key Personnel
Pres: Thomas W Ross *E-mail:* tomross@rossgage.com
VP: Bill Main *E-mail:* bmain@rossgage.com
Opers Coord/Cust Serv: Carol Eads *E-mail:* ceads@rossgage.com
Founded: 1973

Roswell Bookbinding
2614 N 29 Ave, Phoenix, AZ 85009
Tel: 602-272-9338 *Toll Free Tel:* 888-803-8883
Fax: 602-272-9786
Web Site: www.roswellbookbinding.com
Key Personnel
Pres: Michael Roswell
Trade Div Cust Serv Dir: Jim Menke
Specialty Div Mgr: Kortez Brown
Trade Prodn Mgr: Bryan Way
Specialty Div Estimating: Steve Jones
Trade Div Estimating: Nancy Scherba
Founded: 1960
Turnaround: 20 Workdays
Print Runs: 1 min - 1,000,000 max

St Joseph Communications-Print Group
50 Macintosh Blvd, Concord, ON L4K 4P3, Canada
Tel: 905-660-3111
E-mail: marketing@stjoseph.com
Web Site: stjoseph.com
Key Personnel
Pres: John Gagliano
EVP, Sales & Mktg: Ray D'Antonio
VP & Gen Mgr: Ryan Anderson
Branch Office(s)
119 Snow Blvd, Concord, ON L4K 4N9, Canada
Tel: 905-695-8544
1165 Kenaston St, Ottawa, ON K1G 6S1, Canada
Tel: 613-729-4303

Scientific Bindery Inc
8052 Monticello Ave, Suite 206, Skokie, IL 60076
Mailing Address: PO Box 377, Highland Park, IL 60035-6377
Tel: 847-329-0510 *Fax:* 847-329-0608
E-mail: info@scientificbindery.com
Web Site: www.scientificbindery.com
Key Personnel
Owner & Pres: Diane Czerwinski
Founded: 1912
Turnaround: 14-28 Workdays
Print Runs: 50 min - 15,000 max

Shepherd Inc
2223 Key Way Dr, Suite B, Dubuque, IA 52002
Tel: 563-584-0500
Web Site: www.shepherd-inc.com

Key Personnel
Prodn Mgr: Deb Leibfried
Founded: 1989

Sheridan GR
Division of CJK Group Inc
5100 33 St SE, Grand Rapids, MI 49512
Tel: 616-957-5100
Web Site: www.sheridan.com
Key Personnel
VP, Sales: Joe Thomson *E-mail:* joe.thomson@sheridan.com
Cust Serv Mgr: Tanya Eldred *E-mail:* tanya.eldred@sheridan.com
Estimating & Purch Mgr: Steve DeWeerd *E-mail:* steve.deweerd@sheridan.com
Plant Mgr: Jason Nelson *E-mail:* jason.nelson@sheridan.com
Founded: 1884
Turnaround: 2-5 Workdays
Print Runs: 1 min - 100,000 max

Sheridan MI
Division of CJK Group Inc
613 E Industrial Dr, Chelsea, MI 48118
Tel: 734-475-9145
Web Site: www.sheridan.com
Key Personnel
Pres: Paul Bozuwa *E-mail:* paul.bozuwa@sheridan.com
VP, Book Sales: Joe Thomson *E-mail:* joe.thomson@sheridan.com
VP, Fin: Nicole Mummert *E-mail:* nicole.mummert@sheridan.com
VP, HR: Ken Rapp *E-mail:* ken.rapp@sheridan.com
VP, Opers: Paul Loy *E-mail:* paul.loy@sheridan.com
Cust Serv Mgr: Ed Blissick *E-mail:* ed.blissick@sheridan.com
Direct Sales Rep: Jessica Ansorge *Tel:* 734-385-1544 *E-mail:* jessica.ansorge@sheridan.com; Kathy Brown *Tel:* 734-385-1540 *E-mail:* kathy.brown@sheridan.com; Rebecca Humrich *Tel:* 734-385-1543 *E-mail:* rebecca.humrich@sheridan.com; Jennifer Riemenschneider *Tel:* 734-385-1533 *E-mail:* jennifer.riemenschneider@sheridan.com
Founded: 1950

Sheridan NH
Division of CJK Group Inc
69 Lyme Rd, Hanover, NH 03755
Tel: 603-643-2220
Web Site: www.sheridan.com
Key Personnel
Pres: Paul Bozuwa *E-mail:* paul.bozuwa@sheridan.com
VP, Fin: Nicole Mummert *E-mail:* nicole.mummert@sheridan.com
VP, HR: Ken Rapp *E-mail:* ken.rapp@sheridan.com
VP, Opers: Paul Loy *E-mail:* paul.loy@sheridan.com
VP, Sales: Mike Klauer *E-mail:* mike.klauer@sheridan.com
Founded: 1843 (as The Dartmouth Press)
Print Runs: 5,000 min - 100,000 max (average press run: 20,000)
Membership(s): PRINTING United Alliance

Sheridan PA
Division of CJK Group Inc
450 Fame Ave, Hanover, PA 17331
Tel: 717-632-3535 *Toll Free Tel:* 800-352-2210
Fax: 717-633-8900
Web Site: www.sheridan.com
Key Personnel
Pres: Paul Bozuwa *E-mail:* paul.bozuwa@sheridan.com
VP, Fin: Nicole Mummert *E-mail:* nicole.mummert@sheridan.com

PRINTING, BINDING & BOOK FINISHING

VP, Opers: Paul Loy *E-mail:* paul.loy@sheridan.com
VP, Sales: Michael Klauer *E-mail:* mike.klauer@sheridan.com
Dir, Cust Serv: Ed Blissick *E-mail:* ed.blissick@sheridan.com
Technol Dir: Eric Biggins *E-mail:* eric.biggins@sheridan.com
Mgr, Sheridan Content Solutions: Amy Schriver *E-mail:* amy.schriver@sheridan.com
Founded: 1915
Turnaround: 7-10 Workdays
Print Runs: 1 min - 15,000 max (1 is for Digital Print on Demand Printing)
Membership(s): International Printers' Network (IPN)

Sheridan Saline
Division of CJK Group Inc
960 Woodland Dr, Saline, MI 48176
Tel: 734-429-5411
Web Site: www.sheridan.com
Key Personnel
Pres: Paul Bozuwa *E-mail:* paul.bozuwa@sheridan.com
SVP, Opers: Paul Loy *E-mail:* paul.loy@sheridan.com
Gen Mgr: Ron Vollink *E-mail:* ron.vollink@sheridan.com
Plant Mgr: Jim Clark *E-mail:* jim.clark@sheridan.com
HR Mgr: Betty Salow *E-mail:* betty.salow@sheridan.com
Chief Sales Offr: Todd Vanek *E-mail:* todd.vanek@sheridan.com
VP, Book Group Sales: Joe Thomson *E-mail:* joe.thomson@sheridan.com
Cust Serv Mgr & Dir, West Reg Sales: Jonnie Bryant *E-mail:* jonnie.bryant@sheridan.com
Sr Sales Exec: David Hilberer *E-mail:* david.hilberer@sheridan.com
North Central/Greater Chicago Sales Mgr: Marc Moore *E-mail:* marc.moore@sheridan.com
Founded: 1975
Print Runs: 24 min - 100,000 max

Signature Book Printing Inc
8041 Cessna Ave, Gaithersburg, MD 20879
Tel: 301-258-8353
E-mail: book@sbpbooks.com
Web Site: sbpbooks.com
Key Personnel
Pres: Phil Nanzetta
Off Mgr: Linda Wood
Founded: 1986
Print Runs: 500 min - 20,000 max

Signature Print Services
3565 Sierra Rd, San Jose, CA 95132
Mailing Address: PO Box 32464, San Jose, CA 95152-2464
Tel: 408-213-3393 *Fax:* 408-213-3399
Web Site: www.signatureprint.com
Key Personnel
Pres & CEO: Meifang Xu
Secy & Dir: Peter B Martin
Print Runs: 10 min - 25,000 max

Smith & Sons Printers Inc
6403 Rutledge Pike, Knoxville, TN 37924
Tel: 865-523-1419
Web Site: www.ssprintinc.com
Key Personnel
Owner: Stephen Ownby *E-mail:* stephen@ssprint.com
Founded: 1979
Print Runs: 250 min - 100,000 max

Smith-Edwards-Dunlap Co
2867 E Allegheny Ave, Philadelphia, PA 19134

Tel: 215-425-8800 *Toll Free Tel:* 800-829-0020 *Fax:* 215-425-9715
E-mail: sales@sed.com
Web Site: www.sed.com
Key Personnel
Pres: Jonathan Shapiro
Sales Mgr: Fred Binder
Founded: 1880

Southeastern Printing Co
3601 SE Dixie Hwy, Stuart, FL 34997
Tel: 772-287-2141 *Toll Free Tel:* 800-226-8221 *Fax:* 772-288-3988
E-mail: sales@seprint.com
Web Site: www.seprint.com
Key Personnel
Pres: Don Mader
Founded: 1924
Turnaround: 20-40 Workdays
Print Runs: 5,000 min - 100,000 max
Branch Office(s)
950 SE Eighth St, Hialeah, FL 33010 *Tel:* 305-885-8707 *Fax:* 305-888-9903 *E-mail:* info@seprint.com
Sales Office(s): 6001 Park of Commerce Blvd, Suite 200, Boca Raton, FL 33487 *Tel:* 561-998-0870

Specialty Finishing Group
1401 Kirk St, Elk Grove Village, IL 60007
Tel: 847-290-0110 *Fax:* 847-290-9404
Web Site: www.sfgrp.com
Key Personnel
Pres: Jim Gallo
Gen Mgr: Jamie Morris *E-mail:* jmorris@sfgrp.com
Founded: 1981
Membership(s): Chicago Association of Direct Marketing (CADM); Print Image International; PRINTING United Alliance

Spectrum PrintGroup Inc
1535 Farmer's Lane, Suite 254, Santa Rosa, CA 95405
Tel: 707-542-6044 *Toll Free Tel:* 888-340-6049 *Fax:* 707-542-6045
E-mail: sales@spectrumprintgroup.com
Web Site: www.spectrumprintgroup.com
Key Personnel
Pres: Duncan McCallum *Tel:* 707-542-6044 ext 102 *E-mail:* duncan@spectrumprintgroup.com
Busn Devt Mgr: Elise Gochberg *Tel:* 415-461-1130 *E-mail:* elise@spectrumprintgroup.com
Founded: 1985
Print Runs: 500 min - 100,000 max

Spiral Binding LLC
One Maltese Dr, Totowa, NJ 07511
Mailing Address: PO Box 286, Totowa, NJ 07511
Tel: 973-256-0666 *Toll Free Tel:* 800-631-3572 *Fax:* 973-256-5981
E-mail: customerservice@spiralbinding.com; international@spiralbinding.com (outside US)
Web Site: spiralbinding.com
Key Personnel
CEO: Robert Roth
Pres: Douglas Nash
Founded: 1932
Turnaround: 2-10 Workdays
Print Runs: 100 min
Branch Office(s)
431 Calle San Pablo, Camarillo, CA 93012 *Tel:* 805-482-9100 *Toll Free Fax:* 800-215-2463
835 Bonnie Lane, Elk Grove Village, IL 60007 *Tel:* 847-437-3700 *Fax:* 847-437-4155
253 N Grand Ave, Poughkeepsie, NY 12603 *Tel:* 845-471-3408
9200 Waterford Centre Blvd, Suite 550, Austin, TX 78758 *Tel:* 512-832-7902 *Fax:* 512-832-7982

Membership(s): Digital Solutions Cooperative (Dscoop); New Jersey Business & Industry Association (NJBIA); Printing Industries Alliance; PRINTING United Alliance

Springdale Bindery LLC
11411 Landan Lane, Cincinnati, OH 45246
Tel: 513-772-8500
E-mail: info@springdalebindery.com
Web Site: www.springdalebindery.com
Key Personnel
Pres: Steve DeHamer
Membership(s): National Foundation of Independent Businesses (NFIB); PRINTING United Alliance

Stephenson Printing
5731 General Washington Dr, Alexandria, VA 22312
Tel: 703-642-9000 *Toll Free Tel:* 800-336-4637 *Fax:* 703-354-0384
Web Site: www.stephensonprinting.com
Key Personnel
Pres: George W Stephenson
VP: Sandy Stephenson

Sterling Pierce Co Inc
395 Atlantic Ave, East Rockaway, NY 11518
Tel: 516-593-1170 *Fax:* 516-593-1401
Web Site: www.sterlingpierce.com
Key Personnel
Owner & Pres: William Burke
Mgr: Steven Cieslicki *E-mail:* scieslicki@sterlingpierce.com
Founded: 1980
Turnaround: 5-7 Workdays
Print Runs: 5 min - 5,000 max

The Studley Press Inc
151 E Housatonic St, Dalton, MA 01226
Mailing Address: PO Box 214, Dalton, MA 01227-0214
Tel: 413-684-0441 *Toll Free Tel:* 877-684-0441 *Fax:* 413-684-0220
Web Site: thestudleypress.com
Key Personnel
Owner: Suzanne K Salinetti *E-mail:* suzanne@thestudleypress.com
Founded: 1938
Print Runs: 100 min - 25,000 max

Styled Packaging LLC
PO Box 30299, Philadelphia, PA 19103-8299
Tel: 610-529-4122 *Fax:* 610-520-9662
Web Site: www.taylorbox.com
Key Personnel
Pres: William R Fenkel *E-mail:* jjibill@aol.com
Founded: 2003

Sun Graphics LLC
1818 Broadway, Parsons, KS 67357
Toll Free Tel: 800-835-0588 *Fax:* 620-421-2089
E-mail: info@sun-graphics.com
Web Site: www.sun-graphics.com
Key Personnel
VP, Mktg: John Hammett *Tel:* 918-695-2267 *E-mail:* jhammett@sun-graphics.com
VP, Sales: John Hohenshell *Tel:* 913-257-9420 *E-mail:* jhohenshell@sun-graphics.com
Commercial Sales & Book Div Sales: Melody Morris *Tel:* 620-660-0614 *E-mail:* mmorris@sun-graphics.com
Founded: 1998
Turnaround: 15-20 Workdays
Print Runs: 250 min - 100,000 max
Membership(s): Independent Book Publishers Association (IBPA); Publishers Association of the West (PubWest)

John S Swift Co Inc
999 Commerce Ct, Buffalo Grove, IL 60089

MANUFACTURING

PRINTING, BINDING & BOOK FINISHING

Tel: 847-465-3300 *Fax:* 847-465-3309
Web Site: www.johnswiftprint.com
Key Personnel
Pres: John S Swift *E-mail:* jss@johnswiftprint.com
Founded: 1912
Turnaround: 5 Workdays & up
Branch Office(s)
John S Swift Print of NJ Inc, 375 North St, Unit N, Teterboro, NJ 07608, Contact: Rick Frydrych *Tel:* 201-678-3232 *Fax:* 201-678-3001 *E-mail:* rickfry@johnswiftprint.com

Taylor Communications Inc
Subsidiary of Taylor Corp
1725 Roe Crest Dr, North Mankato, MN 56003
Toll Free Tel: 866-541-0937
Web Site: www.taylorcommunications.com
Key Personnel
CEO: Glen Taylor

Taylor Specialty Books, see Balfour Commercial Printing

Thistle Printing Ltd
Division of DATA Communications Management Corp
35 Mobile Dr, Toronto, ON M4A 2P6, Canada
Tel: 416-288-1288 *Fax:* 416-288-0737
E-mail: sales@thistleprinting.com
Web Site: www.thistleprinting.com
Key Personnel
Gen Mgr: Mike Branov
Founded: 1931

Times Printing LLC
Division of Kappa Printing Management Associates LLC (KPMA)
100 Industrial Dr, Random Lake, WI 53075
Tel: 920-994-4396 *Toll Free Tel:* 800-236-4396 (sales)
E-mail: info@kappapma.com
Web Site: www.kappapma.com
Founded: 1918
Turnaround: 5-10 Workdays
Print Runs: 5,000 min - 250,000 max

Toof American Digital
4222 Pilot Dr, Memphis, TN 38118
Tel: 901-274-3632 *Toll Free Tel:* 800-722-4772
Web Site: www.toofamericandigital.com
Key Personnel
Pres: Stillman McFadden
Founded: 1864
Turnaround: 80 Workdays
Print Runs: 2,000 min - 500,000 max

TOP Engraving
106 Windsor Way, Berkeley Heights, NJ 07922
Tel: 212-239-9170; 201-223-4800
Key Personnel
Pres: Shane Levin *E-mail:* shane@hapengraving.com
Founded: 1934
Turnaround: 5-7 Workdays

Total Printing Systems
Division of TPS Enterprises Inc
201 S Gregory Dr, Newton, IL 62448
Mailing Address: PO Box 375, Newton, IL 62448-0365
Tel: 618-783-2978 *Toll Free Tel:* 800-465-5200 *Fax:* 618-783-8407
E-mail: sales@tps1.com
Web Site: www.tps1.com
Key Personnel
Pres: Rick Lindemann *Tel:* 618-783-0501 *E-mail:* rick@tps1.com
Scheduling, VP: RJ Lindemann *Tel:* 618-783-0535 *E-mail:* rj@tps1.com
Inside Sales Mgr: Darrin Sappenfield *Tel:* 618-783-0529 *E-mail:* darrin@tps1.com
Mktg Mgr/Acct Rep: Meg Souza *Tel:* 618-783-0532 *E-mail:* meg@tps1.com
Natl Accts Mgr: Mike Ammirata *Tel:* 317-999-7575 *E-mail:* mjammirata@tps1.com
Acct Rep: Lori Perkins *Tel:* 618-783-0531 *E-mail:* lori@tps1.com
Founded: 1973
Turnaround: 3-10 Workdays
Print Runs: 1 min - 50,000 max (1-200 print-on-demand)
Membership(s): American Association of University Presses (AAUP); Evangelical Christian Publishers Association (ECPA); Independent Book Publishers Association (IBPA); Midwest Independent Publishing Association (MIPA); Print Services & Distribution Association (PSDA)

TotalWorks™ Inc
420 W Huron St, Chicago, IL 60654
Tel: 773-489-4313
E-mail: production@totalworks.net
Web Site: www.totalworks.net
Key Personnel
Principal, Pres & CEO: Gail Ludewig
Principal & EVP: Bruce Jensen
VP, Sales & Mktg: Louise Pauly
Founded: 1927
Membership(s): Women's Business Enterprise Network (WBENC)

Townsend Communications Inc
20 E Gregory Blvd, Kansas City, MO 64114
Tel: 816-361-0616
Web Site: www.townsendcommunications.com; www.townsendprint.com
Key Personnel
Pres: Guy Townsend, III
VP: Joe Chambers
Founded: 1964

Trend Offset Printing Services
3791 Catalina St, Los Alamitos, CA 90720
Tel: 562-598-2446 *Fax:* 562-493-6840 (sales); 562-430-2373
E-mail: salesca@trendoffset.com
Web Site: www.trendoffset.com
Key Personnel
Owner: Anthony Lienau; Robert Lienau, Jr
CEO: Todd Nelson
Founded: 1986

Tribal Print Source
Division of Southern California Tribal Chairman's Association
36146 Pala Temecula Rd, Bldg J, Pala, CA 92059
Mailing Address: 35008 Pala Temecula Rd, PMB 436, Pala, CA 92059
Tel: 760-597-2650
E-mail: sales@tribalprintsource.com
Web Site: www.tribalprintsource.com
Founded: 2003

TSO General Corp
79 Emjay Blvd, Brentwood, NY 11717
Tel: 631-952-5320 *Fax:* 631-952-5315
Web Site: www.tsogeneral.com
Key Personnel
Pres: Kirk Malandrakis *E-mail:* kmalan@tsogeneral.com
Founded: 1969
Turnaround: 5 Workdays
Print Runs: 100,000 min

Tukaiz LLC
2917 N Latoria Lane, Franklin Park, IL 60131
Tel: 847-455-1588; 847-288-4968 (sales)
Toll Free Tel: 800-543-2674
E-mail: contacttukaiz@tukaiz.com
Web Site: www.tukaiz.com
Key Personnel
Founder & Mng Dir: Frank Defino, Sr
VP, Mng Dir & CFO: Christopher Calabra
VP & Mng Dir: Daniel Defino; Frank Defino, Jr
Founded: 1963

Turtleback Books
Division of Perfection Learning
1000 N Second Ave, Logan, IA 51546-0500
Toll Free Tel: 800-831-4190 *Toll Free Fax:* 800-543-2745
E-mail: turtleback@perfectionlearning.com
Web Site: turtleback.perfectionlearning.com
Founded: 1961
Turnaround: 30 Workdays

Universal Bookbindery Inc
1200 N Colorado, San Antonio, TX 78207
Mailing Address: PO Box 7849, San Antonio, TX 78207
Tel: 210-734-9502 *Toll Free Tel:* 800-594-2015 *Fax:* 210-736-0867
E-mail: service@universalbookbindery.com
Web Site: www.universalbookbindery.com
Key Personnel
Cont: Cordell Reinhard *E-mail:* creinhard@universalbookbindery.com
Pres: Trip Worden *E-mail:* tworden@universalbookbindery.com
VP: Fred Daubert
Founded: 1923

Universal|Wilde
26 Dartmouth St, Westwood, MA 02090
Tel: 781-251-2700 *Fax:* 781-251-2613
Web Site: www.universalwilde.com
Key Personnel
Pres & CEO: Stephen Flood
COO: Christopher Armstrong
CFO: Joe Musanti
VP, HR: Jennifer MacAskill
VP, Sales: Jim Bailey
Mktg Mgr: Ryan Collins
Founded: 1958
Print Runs: 3,000 min - 100,000 max
Branch Office(s)
403 VFW Dr, Rockland, MA 02370 *Tel:* 781-871-7744 *Fax:* 781-878-2967
48 Third Ave, Somerville, MA 02143 *Tel:* 617-591-3000 *Fax:* 617-591-3091

VeronaLibri
124 Willowbrook Ave, Stamford, CT 06902
Tel: 203-614-8335
Web Site: www.veronalibri.com
Key Personnel
Sales Rep: Nancy Freeman *E-mail:* nancy.freeman@veronalibri.com

Versa Press Inc
1465 Spring Bay Rd, East Peoria, IL 61611-9788
Tel: 309-822-8272 *Toll Free Tel:* 800-447-7829 *Fax:* 309-822-8141
Web Site: www.versapress.com
Key Personnel
Chmn: Joseph F Kennell
Pres: Steven J Kennell
Sales Mgr: Matthew Kennell *E-mail:* mkennell@versapress.com
Founded: 1937
Turnaround: 20 Workdays
Print Runs: 500 min - 50,000 max
Membership(s): Book Manufacturers' Institute (BMI)

ViaTech Publishing Solutions Inc
11935 N Stemmons Fwy, Dallas, TX 75234
Tel: 214-827-8151
E-mail: marketing@viatechpub.com
Web Site: www.viatech.io

PRINTING, BINDING & BOOK FINISHING

Key Personnel
CEO: Michael Bertuch
VP, Global Sales: Tom Bergenholtz
Founded: 1928
Turnaround: 5-20 Workdays
Print Runs: 50 min - 1,000,000 max
Branch Office(s)
8857 Alexander Rd, Batavia, NY 14020
5668 E 61 St, Commerce, CA 90040
5021 Old Dixie Rd, Forest Park, GA 30297
Kingston Business Park, Kingston Bagpuize, Abingdon, Oxon OX13 5FE, United Kingdom *Tel:* (01865) 822170
Membership(s): Book Manufacturers' Institute (BMI)

Vicks Lithograph & Printing Corp
5166 Commercial Dr, Yorkville, NY 13495
Tel: 315-736-9344
E-mail: info@vicks.biz
Web Site: www.vicks.biz
Key Personnel
CEO: Dwight E Vicks, III
Founded: 1918
Turnaround: 10 Workdays
Print Runs: 1 min - 100,000 max
Membership(s): Book Manufacturers' Institute (BMI); PRINTING United Alliance

VIP Digital Print Center
Affiliate of The Millenium Group
200 Circle Dr N, Piscataway, NJ 08854
Tel: 732-469-5400 *Fax:* 732-469-8414
E-mail: info@vipcopycenter.com
Web Site: www.vipcopycenter.com
Key Personnel
VP: Joe Errico
Founded: 1986
Turnaround: 2-3 Workdays

Viridiam LLC
3030 Lowell Dr, Green Bay, WI 54311
Tel: 920-465-3030 *Toll Free Tel:* 800-829-6555
Web Site: www.viridiam.com
Key Personnel
VP, Sales: Rob Butler
Founded: 1888
Turnaround: 15 Workdays
Print Runs: 250 min
Membership(s): Book Manufacturers' Institute (BMI)

Walker360
2501 Fifth Ave E, Montgomery, AL 36107
Tel: 334-832-4975
E-mail: info@walker360.com
Web Site: walker360.com
Key Personnel
Pres: Taylor Blackwell *E-mail:* taylor@walker360.com
Cont: Estella Riley *E-mail:* estella@walker360.com
IT Dir: Connie Manoliu *E-mail:* connie@walker360.com

Wallaceburg Bookbinding & Mfg Co Ltd
95 Arnold St, Wallaceburg, ON N8A 3P3, Canada
Tel: 519-627-3552 *Toll Free Tel:* 800-214-BIND (214-2463) *Fax:* 519-627-6922
E-mail: helpdesk@wbmbindery.com
Web Site: www.wbmbindery.com
Key Personnel
Pres: Clarence Dykhouse
VP: Gerrit Dykhouse
Founded: 1958
Turnaround: 15-20 Workdays
Membership(s): Atlantic Provinces Library Association (APLA); Canadian Library Association (CLA); Michigan Library Association (MLA); National Information Standards Organization (NISO)

Walsworth
306 N Kansas Ave, Marceline, MO 64658
Toll Free Tel: 800-265-6795
Web Site: www.walsworth.com; www.walsworthhistorybooks.com
Key Personnel
CEO: Don O Walsworth
COO: Jim Mead
Pres: Don Walsworth, Jr
VP, Mktg & Communs: Kristin Mateski *E-mail:* kristin.mateski@walsworth.com
Founded: 1937
Print Runs: 100 min - 500,000 max
Branch Office(s)
803 S Missouri Ave, Marceline, MO 64658 (printing & bindery facility)
Donning Co Publishers, 731 S Brunswick St, Brookfield, MO 64628 *Tel:* 660-675-5570 *Web Site:* www.donning.com
The Ovid Bell Press, 1201 Bluff St, Fulton, MO 65251-0370 *Toll Free Tel:* 800-835-8919 *Web Site:* www.ovidbell.com
903 E 104 St, Suite 700, Kansas City, MO 64131 (yearbook sales & mktg facility) *Toll Free Tel:* 800-369-2965
7300 W 110 St, Suite 600, Overland Park, KS 66210 (sales & mktg)
2180 Maiden Lane, St Joseph, MI 49085 (printing & bindery facility) *Toll Free Tel:* 888-563-3220
656 S Douglas St, Ripon, WI 54971 (printing & bindery facility)

Webcom Inc
Division of Marquis Book Printing Inc
3480 Pharmacy Ave, Toronto, ON M1W 2S7, Canada
Tel: 416-496-1000 *Toll Free Tel:* 800-665-9322 *Fax:* 416-496-1537
E-mail: webcom@webcomlink.com
Web Site: www.webcomlink.com
Key Personnel
Pres & CEO: Mike Collinge
Dir of HR & Cust Serv: Rhonda Suurd
Dir of Sales: Marc Doucet
Founded: 1975
Turnaround: 15 Workdays
Print Runs: 50 min - 100,000 max
Sales Office(s): 65 Spring Valley Ave, River Edge, NJ 07661, Contact: Susan Ginch *Tel:* 201-262-4301 *Fax:* 201-262-6375 *E-mail:* susan.ginch@webcomlink.com
Membership(s): Book Manufacturers' Institute (BMI); Canadian Book & Periodical Council; PRINTING United Alliance

Webcrafters Inc
2211 Fordem Ave, Madison, WI 53704
Tel: 608-244-3561 *Toll Free Tel:* 800-356-8200 *Fax:* 608-244-5120
E-mail: info@webcrafters-inc.com
Web Site: www.webcrafters-inc.com
Key Personnel
CEO: Chris Kurtzman
VP, Div Dir: Brad Koch
Membership(s): Book Manufacturers' Institute (BMI)

Fred Weidner & Daughter Printers
99 Hudson St, 5th fl, New York, NY 10013
Tel: 646-706-5180
E-mail: info@fwdprinters.com
Web Site: www.fwdprinters.com
Key Personnel
Pres: Cynthia Weidner *E-mail:* cynthia@fwdprinters.com
Creative Dir: Carol Mittelsdorf *E-mail:* carol@fwdprinters.com
Founded: 1860
Turnaround: 5-10 Workdays
Print Runs: 1,000 min - 500,000 max

Wert Bookbinding Inc
9975 Allentown Blvd, Grantville, PA 17028
Tel: 717-469-0626 *Toll Free Tel:* 800-344-9378 *Fax:* 717-469-0629
E-mail: quotes@wertbookbinding.com
Web Site: www.wertbookbinding.com
Key Personnel
Owner: Kathryn E Wert
Pres: Gary L Wert *E-mail:* gary@wertbookbinding.com
VP & Treas: Rodney D Wert *E-mail:* rod@wertbookbinding.com
VP & Secy: Scott A Wert *E-mail:* scott@wertbookbinding.com
Founded: 1966
Turnaround: 7-28 Workdays
Print Runs: 1 min - 3,000 max
Membership(s): Book Manufacturers' Institute (BMI)

Whitehall Printing Co
4244 Corporate Sq, Naples, FL 34104
Tel: 239-643-6464 *Toll Free Tel:* 800-321-9290 *Fax:* 239-643-6439
E-mail: info@whitehallprinting.com
Web Site: www.whitehallprinting.com
Key Personnel
Chmn: Mike Hirsch
Pres: Jeff Hirsch
VP: Emil G Hirsch
Founded: 1959
Turnaround: 10-15 Business days
Print Runs: 250 min - 50,000 max

Worzalla
3535 Jefferson St, Stevens Point, WI 54481
Tel: 715-344-9608 *Fax:* 715-344-2578
Web Site: www.worzalla.com
Key Personnel
Chmn of the Bd: Charles Nason
Pres: James Fetherston
VP, Fin: Samuel Crockett
VP, Opers: Brian McManus
VP, Sales & Chief Mktg Offr: Richard Letchinger
Cust Serv Mgr: Kim Deuel
Field Sales: Rodger Beyer
Founded: 1892
Turnaround: 20 Workdays
Print Runs: 50 min - 1,000,000 max
Sales Office(s): 4819 W Berteau Ave, Chicago, IL 60641, Contact: Tim Taylor *Tel:* 773-383-7892 *E-mail:* ttaylor@worzalla.com
2231 Morris Ave, Suite 3, Union, NJ 07083, Contact: Edmund Corvelli, III *Tel:* 201-749-7995 *E-mail:* ecorvelli@worzalla.com
222 W 37 St, 10th fl, New York, NY 10018, Contact: Sam Gallucci *Tel:* 201-851-3292 *E-mail:* sgallucci@worzalla.com
Membership(s): Book Manufacturers' Institute (BMI)

Yurchak Printing Inc
920 Links Ave, Landisville, PA 17538
Tel: 717-399-0209
E-mail: ypi.info@yurchak.com
Web Site: www.yurchak.com
Key Personnel
Founder & CEO: John Yurchak, Jr
Pres: John W Yurchak
VP, Opers: Jason Yurchak
Dir, Busn Devt: Randy Boyer
Founded: 1998
Turnaround: 5-20 Workdays
Print Runs: 1 min - 1,500 max
Membership(s): International Printers' Network (IPN)

Manufacturing Materials Index

BINDING SUPPLIES

Adams Magnetic Products Co, pg 1265
CG Book Printers, pg 1265
Columbia Finishing Mills Inc, pg 1266
Conservation Resources International LLC, pg 1266
Coverline Inc, pg 1266
Cromwell Leather, pg 1266
Dikeman Laminating Corp, pg 1266
Ecological Fibers Inc, pg 1267
Eska USA BV Inc, pg 1267
FIM, pg 1267
Flock Tex Inc, pg 1267
H B Fuller Co, pg 1267
Gane Brothers & Lane Inc, pg 1267
Henkel Corp, pg 1268
Hollinger Metal Edge Inc, pg 1268
Holliston Holdings LLC, pg 1268
Kwikprint Manufacturing Co Inc, pg 1268
LBS, pg 1269
Mekatronics Inc, pg 1269
Neenah Inc, pg 1270
Iris Nevins Decorative Papers, pg 1270
Omniafiltra LLC, pg 1270
Peregrine Arts Bindery, pg 1270
PrairieView Press, pg 1270
Reichhold Inc, pg 1271
St Armand Paper Mill, pg 1271
Sepp Leaf Products Inc, pg 1271
Solar-Screen Co Inc, pg 1272
Styled Packaging LLC, pg 1272
Talas, pg 1272
The Thomas Tape & Supply Co Inc, pg 1272
Ulster Linen Co Inc, pg 1273
University Products Inc, pg 1273
Fred Weidner & Daughter Printers, pg 1273

BOOK COVERS

Ambassador Press Inc, pg 1265
Arbor Books, pg 1265
Balfour Commercial Printing, pg 1265
Bang Printing Co Inc, pg 1265
Bookmasters, pg 1265
Cenveo St Louis, pg 1265
CG Book Printers, pg 1265
ColorPage, pg 1265
Coral Graphic Services Inc, pg 1266
Cromwell Leather, pg 1266
D&K Group Inc, pg 1266
Dekker Bookbinding Inc, pg 1266
Desktop Miracles Inc, pg 1266
Dikeman Laminating Corp, pg 1266
DNP America LLC, pg 1266
W R Draper Co, pg 1267
Dunn & Co Inc, pg 1267
Ecological Fibers Inc, pg 1267
Flock Tex Inc, pg 1267
G & H Soho Inc, pg 1267
Gane Brothers & Lane Inc, pg 1267
Gould Paper Corp, pg 1267
HF Group LLC, pg 1268
Holliston Holdings LLC, pg 1268
Horizon Paper Co Inc, pg 1268
The P A Hutchison Co, pg 1268
Imago, pg 1268
Ironmark, pg 1268
Lake Book Manufacturing Inc, pg 1268
Larson Texts Inc, pg 1269
LBS, pg 1269
McClain Printing Co, pg 1269
Neenah Inc, pg 1270
OGM USA, pg 1270
Omniafiltra LLC, pg 1270
O'Neil Digital Solutions LLC, pg 1270
Patterson Printing Co, pg 1270
Peregrine Arts Bindery, pg 1270
PrairieView Press, pg 1270
Printing Corporation of the Americas Inc, pg 1270
PrintWest, pg 1270
Sheridan MI, pg 1271
Southeastern Printing Co, pg 1272
Spectrum PrintGroup Inc, pg 1272
Styled Packaging LLC, pg 1272
Times Printing LLC, pg 1272
Toof American Digital, pg 1272
TSO General Corp, pg 1272
Tukaiz LLC, pg 1273
University Products Inc, pg 1273
Versa Press Inc, pg 1273
Fred Weidner & Daughter Printers, pg 1273
Whitehall Printing Co, pg 1273

BOOK JACKETS

Ambassador Press Inc, pg 1265
Arbor Books, pg 1265
Balfour Commercial Printing, pg 1265
Bang Printing Co Inc, pg 1265
Bookmasters, pg 1265
Cenveo Inc, pg 1265
Cenveo St Louis, pg 1265
CG Book Printers, pg 1265
ColorPage, pg 1265
Coral Graphic Services Inc, pg 1266
D&K Group Inc, pg 1266
Dekker Bookbinding Inc, pg 1266
Desktop Miracles Inc, pg 1266
DNP America LLC, pg 1266
RR Donnelley, pg 1266
W R Draper Co, pg 1267
Dunn & Co Inc, pg 1267
Ecological Fibers Inc, pg 1267
Edison Lithograph & Printing Corp, pg 1267
G & H Soho Inc, pg 1267
Horizon Paper Co Inc, pg 1268
The P A Hutchison Co, pg 1268
Imago, pg 1268
Ironmark, pg 1268
Lake Book Manufacturing Inc, pg 1268
Larson Texts Inc, pg 1269
LBS, pg 1269
McClain Printing Co, pg 1269
Neenah Inc, pg 1270
OGM USA, pg 1270
O'Neil Digital Solutions LLC, pg 1270
Overseas Printing Corporation, pg 1270
The Ovid Bell Press Inc, pg 1270
Patterson Printing Co, pg 1270
Printing Corporation of the Americas Inc, pg 1270
Sheridan MI, pg 1271
Smith-Edwards-Dunlap Co, pg 1271
Southeastern Printing Co, pg 1272
Spectrum PrintGroup Inc, pg 1272
The Studley Press Inc, pg 1272
Styled Packaging LLC, pg 1272
Times Printing LLC, pg 1272
Toof American Digital, pg 1272
TSO General Corp, pg 1272
Tukaiz LLC, pg 1273
University Products Inc, pg 1273
Versa Press Inc, pg 1273
Fred Weidner & Daughter Printers, pg 1273
Whitehall Printing Co, pg 1273

PAPER MERCHANTS

Richard Bauer & Co Inc, pg 1265
Bulkley Dunton, pg 1265
Ecological Fibers Inc, pg 1267
Gould Paper Corp, pg 1267
Horizon Paper Co Inc, pg 1268
Lindenmeyr Book Publishing Papers, pg 1269
McManus & Morgan, pg 1269
Miami Wabash Paper LLC, pg 1269
Midland Paper, Packaging & Supplies, pg 1269
Pratt Paper Company LLC, pg 1270
Reichhold Inc, pg 1271
Roosevelt Paper Co, pg 1271
St Armand Paper Mill, pg 1271
Simon Miller Paper & Packaging, pg 1271
Spicers Paper, pg 1272
Veritiv™ Corporation, pg 1273
B W Wilson Paper Co Inc, pg 1273

PAPER MILLS

Domtar Paper Co LLC, pg 1266
Ecological Fibers Inc, pg 1267
Finch Paper LLC, pg 1267
French Paper, pg 1267
Gane Brothers & Lane Inc, pg 1267
Glatfelter, pg 1267
Gould Paper Corp, pg 1267
International Paper Co, pg 1268
Miami Wabash Paper LLC, pg 1269
Midwest Paper Group, pg 1270
Mohawk Fine Papers Inc, pg 1270
Monadnock Paper Mills Inc, pg 1270
Neenah Inc, pg 1270
Rayonier Advanced Materials, pg 1270
Resolute Forest Products, pg 1271
Rolland Enterprises, pg 1271
St Armand Paper Mill, pg 1271
Sappi Fine Paper North America, pg 1271
StoraEnso North American Sales Inc, pg 1272
Twin Rivers Paper Co, pg 1273

PRINTING INK

Sun Chemical Corp, pg 1272
Superior Printing Ink Co Inc, pg 1272
Xerox Corporation, pg 1273

1263

Manufacturing Materials

This section includes companies involved in the production of book manufacturing materials such as paper, book jacket and cover materials, binding supplies and printing inks. The descriptions of the services provided are paid components.

The paper merchants listed maintain stocks of book, offset and advertising paper and handle orders from the book trade. The names of the principal mills they represent for book paper have been included when the information was available.

Most paper mills manufacture many grades and kinds of paperboard, some as stock items, others on special order only. The paper is usually distributed through merchants although larger paper users sometimes contract for their requirements directly with the mills. The mills listed are among the major mills in this country supplying large quantities of paper to book publishers.

Adams Magnetic Products Co
888 N Larch Ave, Elmhurst, IL 60126-1133
Tel: 630-617-8880 *Toll Free Tel:* 800-747-7543 (sales) *Fax:* 630-617-8881 *Toll Free Fax:* 800-747-1323
E-mail: info@adamsmagnetic.com
Web Site: www.adamsmagnetic.com
Key Personnel
Pres: Scott Lewis
Dir, Mktg: Alice Martin *E-mail:* amartin@adamsmagnetic.com
Founded: 1950
Branch Office(s)
3198 Lionshead Ave, Carlsbad, CA 92010
2600 Ring Rd, Elizabethtown, KY 42701
  Tel: 270-763-9090 *Fax:* 270-763-0641
140A Metro Park, Suites 9 & 10, Rochester, NY 14623

amb™, see Ambassador Press Inc

Ambassador Press Inc
1400 Washington Ave N, Minneapolis, MN 55411
Tel: 612-521-0123
E-mail: info@ambpress.com
Web Site: www.ambpress.com
Key Personnel
Co-Owner, Pres & CEO: Candice Engle-Fieldman
Co-Owner & EVP: Harold Engle
Founded: 1960

Arbor Books
244 Madison Ave, Box 254, New York, NY 10016
Tel: 212-956-0950 *Toll Free Tel:* 877-822-2500
  Fax: 914-401-9385
E-mail: info@arborbooks.com; editorial@arborbooks.net
Web Site: www.arborbooks.com
Key Personnel
Owner: Joel Hochman *Tel:* 877-822-2502 *E-mail:* arborbooksjoel@aol.com;
  Larry Leichman *Tel:* 877-822-2504
  E-mail: arborbookslarry@aol.com
Mktg Dir: Olga Vladi *E-mail:* floatinggal1@aol.com
Founded: 1992

Arbor Services, see Arbor Books

Balfour Commercial Printing
Formerly Taylor Specialty Books
Division of Balfour/Taylor
225 E John Carpenter Fwy, Tower 2, Suite 400, Irving, TX 75062
Tel: 214-819-8588 (cust serv)
E-mail: printing@balfour.com
Web Site: commercial-printing.balfour.com
Key Personnel
Acct Exec: Julie Kacala *E-mail:* julie.kacala@balfour.com
Founded: 1939

Bang Printing Co Inc
Division of CJK Group Inc
3323 Oak St, Brainerd, MN 56401
Tel: 218-829-2877 *Toll Free Tel:* 800-328-0450
  Fax: 218-829-7145
E-mail: info@bangprinting.com
Web Site: www.bangprinting.com
Key Personnel
Pres: Todd Vanek *E-mail:* toddv@bangprinting.com
VP, Opers: Joe Saiko *E-mail:* joes@bangprinting.com
VP, Sales: Doug Walters *E-mail:* dougw@bangprinting.com
Founded: 1899

Richard Bauer & Co Inc
310 Cedar Lane, Teaneck, NJ 07666
Tel: 201-692-1005 *Toll Free Tel:* 800-995-7881
  Fax: 201-692-8626
E-mail: info@richardbauer.com
Web Site: www.richardbauer.com
Key Personnel
CEO: Robert Cipolaro
Founded: 1916
Book Paper Line(s) Sold: Abitibi; Badger; Finch Pruyn; Fraser; International; Miami Valley; Nashua; National Envelope; Riverside; Rolland; Wausau Paper
Cover Line(s) Sold: International; Wausau Paper

Bookmasters
Division of Baker & Taylor Publisher Services
30 Amberwood Pkwy, Ashland, OH 44805
Tel: 419-281-5100 *Toll Free Tel:* 800-537-6727
  Fax: 419-281-0200
E-mail: info@btpubservices.com
Web Site: www.btpubservices.com
Key Personnel
Dir of Mfg: Brad Sharp *E-mail:* bsharp@bookmasters.com
Founded: 1972

Bulkley Dunton
Division of Veritiv™ Corporation
One Penn Plaza, Suite 2814, 250 W 34 St, New York, NY 10119
Tel: 212-863-1800 *Toll Free Tel:* 800-347-9279
  Fax: 212-863-1872
Web Site: www.bulkleydunton.com
Key Personnel
SVP, Publg & Print Mgmt: John Biscanti
Dir of Sales: Terence Sheehy
Founded: 1833
Book Paper Line(s) Sold: Alberta Newsprint; American Eagle®; APC Paper Group; Appleton Coated; Asia Pulp and Paper; Boise Paper; Bollore Thin Papers; BPM Inc; Burgo; Canfor Premium One; Cascades; Catalyst; Chenming; Clearwater Paper; Coating Excellence Inc; Domtar; Dunn Paper; Evergreen Packaging; Expera Specialty Solutions; Finch Paper LLC; French Paper Co; Georgia Pacific; Glatfelter; International Paper; InterWrap Papers; Irving Paper; Kotkamills; Kruger Inc; Manchester Industries; Metsa Board; Mohawk Paper; Monadnock Paper Mills Inc; Neenah Paper; New Leaf Paper; Nippon Paper; NORPAC; Novolex™; Parenco; Port Hawkesbury Paper; Reich Paper; Resolute Forest Products; Sappi; Scheufelen North America; Soporcel; Stora Enso; Suzano Pulp and Paper; Twin Rivers Paper Company; UPM Paper; Verso Corp; Wausau Paper; West Linn Paper Co; WestRock; Yupo Corporation America
Branch Office(s)
7500 Amigos Ave, Downey, CA 90242 *Tel:* 562-922-7814
850 N Arlington Heights Rd, Suite 100, Itasca, IL 60143 *Tel:* 630-875-7037
7445 New Ridge Rd, Hanover, MD 21076
  Tel: 410-696-8500
4265 Trailer Dr, Charlotte, NC 28269 *Tel:* 704-599-6180
3120 N Marshall Rd, Appleton, WI 54915
  Tel: 920-749-2820 *Toll Free Tel:* 800-259-7974

Cenveo Inc
200 First Stamford Place, 2nd fl, Stamford, CT 06902
Tel: 203-595-3000 *Fax:* 203-595-3070
E-mail: info@cenveo.com
Web Site: www.cenveo.com
Key Personnel
CEO: Robert G Burton, Jr
CFO: Mark Hiltwein
Pres: Michael Burton
Founded: 1830

Cenveo St Louis
101 Workman Ct, Eureka, MO 63025
Tel: 314-966-2000 *Toll Free Tel:* 800-800-8845
  Fax: 314-966-4725
Web Site: www.cenveo.com

CG Book Printers
Division of Corporate Graphics Commercial (CGC)
1750 Northway Dr, North Mankato, MN 56003
Tel: 507-388-3300 *Toll Free Tel:* 800-729-7575
  Fax: 507-386-6350
E-mail: cgbooks@corpgraph.com
Web Site: www.corpgraph.com
Key Personnel
Pres: Dan Kvasnicka *Tel:* 507-386-6340
  Fax: 507-344-5548 *E-mail:* dekvasnicka@corpgraph.com
Sales Exec, Book Mfg Sales: Mike Schmitt
  Tel: 507-386-6349 *E-mail:* mjschmitt@corpgraph.com
Founded: 1989

ColorPage
Division of Tri-State Associated Services Inc
81 Ten Broeck Ave, Kingston, NY 12401
Tel: 845-331-7581 *Toll Free Tel:* 800-836-7581
  Fax: 845-331-1571

MANUFACTURING MATERIALS

E-mail: sales@colorpageonline.com
Web Site: www.colorpageonline.com
Key Personnel
Pres & Mktg Strategist/Consultant: Frank J Campagna, II *E-mail:* fcampagna@colorpageonline.com
Acct Mgr & Cont: Kathy Riggins
  E-mail: kriggins@colorpageonline.com
Prodn Mgr: Randy Delanoy
Cust Serv Supv: Debbie Downes
  E-mail: ddownes@colorpageonline.com
Founded: 1976

Columbia Finishing Mills Inc
135 Boundary Rd, Cornwall, ON K6H 5T3, Canada
Mailing Address: Box 546, Cornwall, ON K6H 5T3, Canada
Tel: 613-933-1462 *Toll Free Tel:* 800-267-9174 *Fax:* 613-933-7717 *Toll Free Fax:* 800-242-9174
E-mail: info@columbiafinishingmills.com
Web Site: www.columbiafinishingmills.com
Key Personnel
Pres: Brian Lynch
Sales Mgr: Dan Plourde

Conservation Resources International LLC
7350 Lockport Place, Suite A, Lorton, VA 22079
Tel: 703-321-7730 *Toll Free Tel:* 800-634-6932 *Fax:* 703-321-0629
E-mail: sales@conservationresources.com
Web Site: www.conservationresources.com
Key Personnel
COO: Catherine Hollinger
Pres: William K Hollinger, Jr
VP: Lavonia Hollinger
Membership(s): AIC

Coral Graphic Services Inc
Member of Bertelsmann Printing Group
840 S Broadway, Hicksville, NY 11801
Tel: 516-576-2100 *Fax:* 516-576-2168
E-mail: info@coralgraphics.com
Web Site: www.bpg-usa.com
Key Personnel
CEO: Christof Ludwig
CFO: Denis Leite
CTO: Yannic Schroeder
Founded: 1982
Branch Office(s)
25 Jack Enders Blvd, Berryville, VA 22611
  Tel: 540-955-2750 *Fax:* 540-955-9164
Membership(s): Association of the Graphic Arts (AGA); PRINTING United Alliance

Corporate Graphics Book Printers, see CG Book Printers

Coverline Inc
13 Spruce Pond Rd, Franklin, MA 02038
Tel: 508-528-8511 *Fax:* 508-528-6838
Key Personnel
Pres: Paul Langley *E-mail:* pglcov@comcast.net

Cromwell Leather
147 Palmer Ave, Mamaroneck, NY 10543
Tel: 914-381-0100 *Fax:* 914-381-0046
E-mail: sales@cromwellgroup.com
Web Site: www.cromwellgroup.com
Key Personnel
Pres: Thomas Fleisch
VP, Sales: Margaret Zulkowsky *E-mail:* mz@cromwellgroup.com

D&K Group Inc
1795 Commerce Dr, Elk Grove Village, IL 60007
Tel: 847-956-0160; 847-956-4757 (tech support)
  Toll Free Tel: 800-632-2314 *Fax:* 847-956-8214
E-mail: info@dkgroup.net
Web Site: www.dkgroup.com

Key Personnel
Pres: Karl Singer
VP, Sales & Mktg: Tom Pidgeon *E-mail:* tom.pidgeon@dkgroup.net
Mktg Communs Specialist: Brian Biegel
  E-mail: brian.biegel@dkgroup.net
Founded: 1979

Dekker Bookbinding Inc
2941 Clydon Ave SW, Grand Rapids, MI 49519
Tel: 616-538-5160 *Toll Free Tel:* 800-299-BIND (299-2463)
E-mail: hello@dekkerbook.com
Web Site: www.dekkerbook.com
Key Personnel
Pres: Chris Dekker
VP: Corbin Dekker
Founded: 1928
Membership(s): Forest Stewardship Council US (FSC-US); Printing Industries of Michigan Inc (PIM); PRINTING United Alliance

Desktop Miracles Inc
112 S Main St, Suite 294, Stowe, VT 05672
Tel: 802-253-7900 *Toll Free Tel:* 888-293-2676
E-mail: info@desktopmiracles.com
Web Site: www.desktopmiracles.com
Key Personnel
Pres & CEO: Barry T Kerrigan *E-mail:* barry@desktopmiracles.com
VP: Virginia Kerrigan *E-mail:* virginia@desktopmiracles.com
Founded: 1994

Dikeman Laminating Corp
181 Sargeant Ave, Clifton, NJ 07013
Tel: 973-473-5696 *Fax:* 973-473-2540
E-mail: office@dikemanlaminating.com
Web Site: dikemanlaminating.com
Key Personnel
Owner & Pres: Jeffrey W Snyder
Founded: 1949

DNP America LLC
Subsidiary of Dai Nippon Printing Co Ltd
335 Madison Ave, 3rd fl, New York, NY 10017
Tel: 212-503-1060
E-mail: gps@dnp-g.com
Web Site: www.dnpamerica.com
Key Personnel
VP & Gen Mgr: Norikatsu Nakamura
Founded: 1976
Branch Office(s)
2099 Gateway Place, Suite 490, San Jose, CA 95110 *Tel:* 408-735-8880
3858 Carson St, Suite 300, Torrance, CA 90503
  Tel: 310-540-5123

Domtar Paper Co LLC
Division of Domtar
234 Kingsley Park Dr, Fort Mill, SC 29715
Tel: 803-802-7500 *Toll Free Tel:* 877-877-4685
E-mail: communications@domtar.com; commercialprinting@domtar.com
Web Site: www.domtar.com
Key Personnel
Pres, Pulp & Paper: Michael Garcia
Media & Community Rel: Jan Martin *Tel:* 803-802-8027 *E-mail:* jan.martin@domtar.com
Founded: 1965
Book Paper Line(s) Milled: Century® Premium Opaque; Cougar® Digital; Cougar® Digital Color Copy; Cougar® Smooth; Cougar® Super Smooth; EarthChoice® Colors; EarthChoice® HOTS®; EarthChoice® Tradebook; Guardian® Opaque; Husky® Digital; Husky® Opaque Offset; Husky® Recycled Digital; Husky® Recycled Opaque Offset; HuskyJET®; HuskyJET® 7 pt Card; Lynx® Digital; Lynx® Digital Super Smooth; Lynx® Opaque Ultra™; LynxJET®; Printers Opaque; TitaniumJET™;

Vista® Opaque; Vista® Ultra; Xerox® Bold Digital®; Xerox® Revolution®
Cover Line(s) Milled: Century® Premium Opaque; Century® Premium Opaque Pharma; Century® Premium Pharma HiFold; Guardian® Opaque; Guardian® Opaque Pharma; Guardian® Pharma HiFold
Branch Office(s)
395 de Maisonneuve Blvd W, Montreal, QC H3A 1L6, Canada *Tel:* 514-848-5555

RR Donnelley
35 W Wacker Dr, Chicago, IL 60601
Toll Free Tel: 800-742-4455
Web Site: www.rrd.com
Key Personnel
Pres & CEO: Daniel L Knotts
Pres, Busn Servs: John Pecaric
Pres, Mktg Solutions: Doug Ryan
EVP & CFO: Terry D Peterson
EVP & CIO: Ken O'Brien
EVP & Chief HR Offr: Sheila Rutt
EVP & Chief Strategy & Transformation Offr: Elif Sagsen-Ercel
EVP, Dom Opers & Chief Supply Chain Offr: Glynn Perry
EVP, Gen Coun, Chief Compliance Offr & Corp Secy: Deborah Steiner
SVP & Chief Acctg Offr: Michael J Sharp
Founded: 1864
Branch Office(s)
955 Gateway Center Way, San Diego, CA 92102
  Tel: 619-527-4600
40610 County Center Dr, Temecula, CA 92591
  Tel: 951-296-2890
151 Red Stone Rd, Manchester, CT 06042
  Tel: 860-649-5570
9125 Bachman Rd, Orlando, FL 32824 *Tel:* 407-859-2030
5800 Peachtree Rd, Atlanta, GA 30341 *Tel:* 770-458-6351
825 Riverside Pkwy, Suite 300, Austell, GA 30168 *Tel:* 770-948-1330
1750 Wallace Ave, St Charles, IL 60174 *Tel:* 630-313-7000
609 S Kirk Rd, St Charles, IL 60174 *Tel:* 630-762-7600
One Poplar Ave, Thurmont, MD 21788 *Tel:* 301-271-7171
65 Sprague St, Hyde Park, MA 02136 *Tel:* 617-360-2000
18780 W 78 St, Chanhassen, MN 55317
  Tel: 952-937-9764
5500 12 Ave E, Shakopee, MN 55379 *Tel:* 952-941-7546
6305 Sunset Corporate Dr, Las Vegas, NV 89120
  Tel: 702-949-8500
5 Henderson Dr, West Caldwell, NJ 07006
  Tel: 973-882-7000
12301 Vance Davis Dr, Charlotte, NC 28269
  Tel: 704-949-3568
One Litho Way, Durham, NC 27703 *Tel:* 919-596-3660
3801 Gantz Rd, Grove City, OH 43123 *Tel:* 614-539-5527
700 Nestle Way, Suite 200, Breinigsville, PA 18031 *Tel:* 610-391-3900
9985 Gantry Rd, Philadelphia, PA 19115
  Tel: 215-671-9500
218 N Braddock Ave, Pittsburgh, PA 15208
  Tel: 412-241-8200
1210 Key Rd, Columbia, SC 29201 *Tel:* 803-799-9550
1645 W Sam Houston Pkwy N, Houston, TX 77043 *Tel:* 713-468-7175
1550 Lakeway Dr, Suite 600, Lewisville, TX 75057 *Tel:* 972-353-7500
630 W 1000 N, Logan, UT 84321 *Tel:* 435-755-4000
201 E Progress Dr, West Bend, WI 53095
  Tel: 262-338-6101
Membership(s): Association of American Publishers (AAP); Book Industry Study Group (BISG); Book Manufacturers' Institute (BMI)

MANUFACTURING

W R Draper Co
Division of The Arthur Press (1978) Ltd
162 Norfinch Dr, Toronto, ON M3N 1X6, Canada
Tel: 416-663-6001 *Fax:* 416-663-6043
E-mail: info@arthurpress.com
Web Site: www.arthurpress.com
Key Personnel
Pres: Jeremy Thorn
Founded: 1954

Dunn & Co Inc
Affiliate of Legacy Publishing Group
75 Green St, Clinton, MA 01510
Mailing Address: PO Box 1185, Clinton, MA 01510
Tel: 978-368-8505 *Fax:* 978-368-7867
E-mail: info@booktrauma.com
Web Site: www.booktrauma.com
Key Personnel
Chmn: David M Dunn
Pres: Peter R Heelan
VP: Rocco Windover
Founded: 1976

Ecological Fibers Inc
40 Pioneer Dr, Lunenburg, MA 01462
Tel: 978-537-0003 *Fax:* 978-537-2238
E-mail: info@ecofibers.com
Web Site: www.ecofibers.com
Key Personnel
Pres: John A Quill
VP, Sales: Dave Robbins *E-mail:* drobbins@ecofibers.com
Dir, Book Group Sales: Jim McCafferty *E-mail:* jmccafferty@ecofibers.com
Dir, Busn Opers: Joyce Hardell *E-mail:* joyce@ecofibers.com
Founded: 1972
Book Paper Line(s) Milled: Rainbow® 80 & 100 lb cream & white endleaf; Rainbow® 80 NASTA spec colored endleaf, side & spine material; Rainbow® 70 lb colored endleaf & side material
Cover Line(s) Milled: Arizona; Corona; Lumina Silver Pearlescent; Mirage; Mirage 325 gsm; Prestige; Rainbow® 17; Rainbow® 3; Rainbow® 9 Type II coated cover; Rainbow® Eco-Cover; Rainbow® Excel; Rainbow® LX; Ultima
Book Paper Line(s) Sold: Rainbow® 80 & 100 lb cream & white endleaf; Rainbow® 80 NASTA spec colored endleaf, side & spine material; Rainbow® 70 lb colored endleaf & side material
Branch Office(s)
730 York Ave, Pawtucket, RI 02861 *Tel:* 401-725-9700 *Fax:* 401-724-4970
Membership(s): Book Manufacturers' Institute (BMI); Publishing Professionals Network (PPN)

Edison Lithograph & Printing Corp
3725 Tonnelle Ave, North Bergen, NJ 07047-2421
Tel: 201-902-9191 *Fax:* 201-902-0475
E-mail: info@edisonlitho.com
Web Site: www.edisonlitho.com
Key Personnel
COO: Joseph Ostreicher
Founded: 1958

Eska USA BV Inc
Subsidiary of Eska BV (Netherlands)
1910 Campostella Rd, Chesapeake, VA 23324
Tel: 757-494-7330
E-mail: usa@eska.com
Web Site: www.eska.com
Key Personnel
Gen Mgr: Vincent Tophoff

FIM
18 Central Blvd, South Hackensack, NJ 07606
Tel: 201-549-1037
Web Site: www.fimheadbands.com
Key Personnel
Pres: Jon Weingarten
Dir, Mfg & Dist: Milt Wolfson
Sales/Serv: Mariluz Yambao

Finch Paper LLC
One Glen St, Glens Falls, NY 12801
Tel: 518-793-2541 *Toll Free Tel:* 800-833-9983
Fax: 518-743-9656
E-mail: info@finchpaper.com
Web Site: www.finchpaper.com
Key Personnel
Chmn & CEO: Debabrata Mukherjee *E-mail:* dmukherjee@finchpaper.com
Sales Dir, Eastern & Natl Accts: Ken Ritchie *Tel:* 516-375-0256 *E-mail:* ken.ritchie@finchpaper.com
Western Regl Sales Dir: Tom Dieckman *Tel:* 630-450-2064 *E-mail:* tom.dieckman@finchpaper.com
Founded: 1865
Book Paper Line(s) Milled: Alkaline base; Finch Fine; Casa Opaque Book; Finch Casa Opaque (recycled); Finch Digital Web XP; Finch Fine Soft White; Finch Inkjet Pi; Finch Opaque Book; Finch Vanilla Fine (natural white); Finch Vanilla Opaque (natural white)
Cover Line(s) Milled: Finch Casa Opaque Cover; Finch Fine Cover; Finch Fine Soft White Cover; Finch Opaque Cover; Finch Vanilla Fine Cover; Finch Vanilla Opaque Cover
Paper Type(s) Sold: Acid Free; Chlorine Free; Recycled; Uncoated Free Sheet
Membership(s): Book Manufacturers' Institute (BMI)

Flock Tex Inc
200 Founders Dr, Woonsocket, RI 02895
Tel: 401-765-2340 *Toll Free Tel:* 800-556-7286
Fax: 401-765-4915
Web Site: www.flocktex.com
Key Personnel
Owner & Pres: Edward T Abramek, Jr
VP: Brian Abramek; Gary Abramek *E-mail:* garya@flocktex.com
VP, Sales: Walter Armstrong
Founded: 1967

French Paper
100 French St, Niles, MI 49120
Tel: 269-683-1100 *Toll Free Tel:* 800-253-5952
E-mail: frenchassetorders@frenchpaper.com; frenchpaperco@gmail.com
Web Site: www.frenchpaper.com
Founded: 1871
Book Paper Line(s) Milled: Construction; acid-free paper available; Dur-O-Tone; Finch Digital; Glo-Tone; Kraft-Tone; Parchtone; Pop-Tone; Smart White; Speckletone; Vivitone

H B Fuller Co
1200 Willow Lake Blvd, St Paul, MN 55110-5146
Tel: 651-236-5900 *Toll Free Tel:* 888-423-8553
E-mail: inquiry@hbfuller.com
Web Site: www.hbfuller.com
Key Personnel
Pres & CEO: Jim Owens
EVP & COO: Ted Clark
EVP & CFO: John Corkrean
VP & Cont: Robert Martsching
VP & Treas: Heidi Weiler
VP, Gen Coun & Corp Secy: Timothy Keenan

G & H Soho Inc
413 Market St, Elmwood Park, NJ 07407
Tel: 201-216-9400 *Fax:* 201-216-1778
E-mail: print@ghsoho.com
Web Site: www.ghsoho.com

MANUFACTURING MATERIALS

Key Personnel
Pres: Gerry Burstein
Prodn Mgr: Jason Burstein
Founded: 1985
Membership(s): Association of Graphic Communications; Digital Printing Council; PRINTING United Alliance

Gane Brothers & Lane Inc
1400 Greenleaf Ave, Elk Grove Village, IL 60007
Tel: 847-593-3364 *Toll Free Tel:* 800-323-0596
Toll Free Fax: 800-784-2464
E-mail: sales@ganebrothers.com
Web Site: www.ganebrothers.com
Key Personnel
Owner & Pres: Glenn Brown
VP: Jack McLoraine
Founded: 1846

Glatfelter
Capitol Towers South, 4350 Congress St, Suite 600, Charlotte, NC 28209
Tel: 717-850-0170 *Toll Free Tel:* 866-744-7380
E-mail: info@glatfelter.com
Web Site: www.glatfelter.com
Key Personnel
Chmn & CEO: Dante C Parrini
SVP & Chief Commercial Offr: Chris W Astley
SVP & CFO: Samuel L Hillard
SVP, Integrated Global Supply Chain & IT: Wolfgang Laures
VP, Deputy Gen Coun & Corp Secy: Jill L Urey
VP, Fin & Chief Acctg Offr: David C Elder
VP, Global HR & Admin: Eileen L Beck
VP, Global Opers: Philippe Sevoz
Founded: 1864
Book Paper Line(s) Milled: Digibook; Ecolotext; Editors; EPA Reference; Glatfelter EndLeaf; Glatfelter Hi-Brite; Glatfelter Hi-Opaque; Glatfelter Offset; Natures; Restorecote; Spring Forge; Supple Opaque; Thor; Writers
Branch Office(s)
8201 Chad Colley Blvd, Fort Smith, AR 72916 (mfg) *Tel:* 479-242-0754 *E-mail:* info.ambu@glatfelter.com
351 Jesse Jewell Pkwy, Suite 301, Gainesville, GA 30501 (sales & dist) *Tel:* 770-536-2400
1680 rue Atmec, Gatineau, QC J8P 7G7, Canada (mfg) *Tel:* 819-669-8100
Membership(s): American Association of University Presses (AAUP); Association of American Publishers (AAP); Book Industry Study Group (BISG); Book Manufacturers' Institute (BMI); OTT.X

Gould Paper Corp
99 Park Ave, 10th fl, New York, NY 10016
Tel: 212-301-0000 *Toll Free Tel:* 800-221-3043
Fax: 212-481-0067
E-mail: info@gouldpaper.com
Web Site: www.gouldpaper.com
Key Personnel
Pres & CEO: David H Berkowitz
Founded: 1924
Book Paper Line(s) Sold: A B Massa; Abitibi; Appleton Papers; Beveridge; Cascade; Domtar; Evergreen Packaging; Finch Paper LLC; Fraser; Georgia-Pacific; Hazen; Kruger Inc; Lincoln; Manistique; Mohawk Paper; Potlach; St Mary's; Smart Papers; Stora Enso; Temboard; Wausau Paper; Whiting
Paper Type(s) Sold: Uncoated Groundwood
Branch Office(s)
Gould Paper South LLC, 10400 NW 21 St, Suite 104, Doral, FL 33172 *Tel:* 305-470-0003 *Fax:* 305-470-0088 *Web Site:* www.gouldsouth.com
Gould Publishing & Catalog, 25 East St, Winchester, MD 01890 *Tel:* 781-729-2059 *Toll Free Tel:* 800-882-2781 *Fax:* 781-721-1986

MANUFACTURING MATERIALS

Gould Paper Corp (Metro), 319 Ridge Rd, Dayton, NJ 08810 *Tel:* 732-248-7800 *Toll Free Tel:* 800-672-7379 *Fax:* 732-248-5981
Membership(s): National Paper Trade Association (NPTA)

Henkel Corp
One Henkel Way, Rocky Hill, CT 06067
Tel: 860-571-5100 *Fax:* 860-571-5465
E-mail: corp.info@henkel.com
Web Site: www.henkel-northamerica.com; www.henkel-adhesives.com
Founded: 1876

HF Group LLC
8844 Mayfield Rd, Chesterland, OH 44026
Tel: 440-729-2445; 440-729-9411 (bindery)
E-mail: custservice-oh@hfgroup.com
Web Site: www.hfgroup.com
Key Personnel
CEO: Jay Fairfield *Tel:* 440-729-2445 ext 4 *E-mail:* jayfairfield@hfgroup.com
VP & Gen Mgr: Jim Bratton *E-mail:* jbratton@hfgroup.com
Founded: 1821
Branch Office(s)
1010 N Sycamore St, North Manchester, IN 46962, Pres: Jim Heckman *Tel:* 260-982-2107 *E-mail:* jheckman@hfgroup.com
92 Cambridge St, Charlestown, MA 02129-0212, VP: John Parisi *Tel:* 617-242-1100 *E-mail:* jparisi@hfgroup.com
340 First St, Utica, NE 68456, Gen Mgr: Damon Osborne *Tel:* 402-534-2261 *E-mail:* dosborne@hfgroup.com
6204 Corporate Park Dr, Browns Summit, NC 27214-9745, Contact: Eric Fairfield *Tel:* 336-931-0800 *E-mail:* efairfield@hfgroup.com
45 N Main St, Unit 528, Hatfield, PA 19440 (transportation hub) *Tel:* 215-855-2293
105 W Thomas St, Atlanta, TX 75551-2736 (transportation hub) *Tel:* 260-982-2107 *Fax:* 260-982-1130

Hollinger Metal Edge Inc
9401 Northeast Dr, Fredricksburg, VA 22408
Tel: 540-898-7300 *Toll Free Tel:* 800-634-0491 *Toll Free Fax:* 800-947-8814
E-mail: info@hollingermetaledge.com
Web Site: www.hollingermetaledge.com
Key Personnel
Pres & CEO: Bob Henderson
Founded: 1945

Holliston Holdings LLC
Subsidiary of Holliston Mills
905 Holliston Mills Rd, Church Hill, TN 37642
Tel: 423-357-6141 *Toll Free Tel:* 800-251-0451; 800-251-0251 (cust serv) *Fax:* 423-357-8840 *Toll Free Fax:* 800-325-0351 (cust serv)
E-mail: custserv@holliston.com
Web Site: holliston.com
Key Personnel
Acct Exec: Jennifer Anderson
Founded: 1895
Cover Line(s) Milled: Arrestox®; Arrestox® Shimmer; Buckram® Lustre; Buckram® Roxite F; Kennett®; Linen-Set®; Luminaire®; Pearl Linen®; Pearl Linen® 2 Tone; Sturdite®
Membership(s): Book Manufacturers' Institute (BMI); Publishers Association of the West (PubWest)

Horizon Paper Co Inc
1010 Washington Blvd, Stamford, CT 06901
Tel: 203-358-0855 *Toll Free Tel:* 866-358-0855
E-mail: info@horizonpaper.com
Web Site: www.horizonpaper.com
Key Personnel
Chmn: Robert B Obernier
CEO: Jeffrey Hansen
Pres (Oak Park, IL off): Jeffrey A Hill
EVP, Sales: Matthew Asen
SVP, Sales: Michael P Hurley
VP, Sales: Mark Gerardi
Sales Mgr: Karl Pelikan
Sales: Thomas McGee
Founded: 1978
Book Paper Line(s) Sold: Alberta Newsprint; American Eagle®; APP; Burgo; Catalyst; Domtar; Evergreen Packaging; Finch Paper LLC; Inland Empire; Irving Paper; Kruger Inc; Lecta; Midwest Paper Group; Mitsubishi Paper Mills Ltd; ND Paper; New Indie/Catawaba; NORPAC; Pixelle Specialty Solutions™; Ponderay; Port Hawkesbury Paper; Rayonier Advanced Materials™; Resolute Forest Products; Rolland; Spruce Falls; Stora Enso; Suzano Pulp and Paper; Twin Rivers Paper Company; UPM Paper; Verso Corp; White Birch; Willamette Falls
Cover Line(s) Sold: Tembec; Verso Corp; WestRock

The P A Hutchison Co
400 Penn Ave, Mayfield, PA 18433
SAN: 991-5559
Tel: 570-876-4560 *Toll Free Tel:* 800-USA-PRNT (872-7768) *Fax:* 570-876-4561
E-mail: sales@pahutch.com
Web Site: www.pahutch.com
Key Personnel
Pres & CEO: Chris Hutchison
Dir, Sales & Admin: Erin Jones
Founded: 1911

Imago
110 W 40 St, New York, NY 10018
Tel: 212-921-4411 *Fax:* 212-921-8226
E-mail: sales@imagousa.com
Web Site: www.imagousa.com
Key Personnel
Pres & CEO: Howard Musk *E-mail:* howardm@imagogroup.com
Founded: 1985
Branch Office(s)
Imago West Coast, 23412 Moulton Pkwy, Suite 250, Laguna Hills, CA 92653 (sales), Contact: Tammy Simms *Tel:* 949-367-1635 *Fax:* 949-367-1639
Imago Australia, 10 Help St, Suite 27, Level 6, Chatswood, NSW 2067, Australia (sales) *Tel:* (04) 3753 3351 (cell); (04) 4806 8704 (cell) *E-mail:* sales@imagaoaus.com
Imago Brazil, Domiciano Rossi, 340 unid 154, 09726-121 Sao Bernardo do Campo, Brazil (sales) *Tel:* (011) 2306 8546; (011) 2306 8547 *E-mail:* imagobra@gmail.com
Imago Shenzhen, Rm 2511-2512, Block A, United Plaza No 5022, Bin He Rd, Fu Tian Centre District, Shenzhen 518033, China (prodn), Contact: Kendrick Cheung *Tel:* (0755) 8304 8899 *Fax:* (0755) 8251 4073 *E-mail:* enquiries@imago.com.hk
Imago France, 23 rue Lavoisier, 75008 Paris, France (sales) *Tel:* 01 45 26 47 74 *Fax:* 01 78 94 14 44 *E-mail:* sales@imagogroup.com
Imago Services (HK) Ltd, Unit B309, 1/F, New East Sun Industrial Bldg, 18 Shing Yip St, Kwun Tong, Hong Kong (prodn), Contact: Kendrick Cheung *Tel:* 2811 3316 *E-mail:* enquiries@imago.com.hk
Imago Productions (Malaysia) Pte Ltd, No 43, Taman Emas, Jl Utama 31, Telok Panglima Garang, 42500 Kuala Langot, Selangor, Malaysia (prodn, incorporating South Africa sales) *Tel:* (017) 4288771 (cell) *E-mail:* enquiries@imago.com.sg
Imago Publishing, Albury Ct, Albury Thame, Oxon OX9 2LP, United Kingdom (sales), Dir: Simon Rosenheim *Tel:* (01844) 337000 *Fax:* (01844) 339935 *E-mail:* sales@imago.co.uk *Web Site:* imagogroup.com

International Paper Co
6400 Poplar Ave, Memphis, TN 38197
Tel: 901-419-9000 *Toll Free Tel:* 800-207-4003
Web Site: www.internationalpaper.com; facebook.com/internationalpaper; x.com/intlpaperco
Key Personnel
Chmn & CEO: Mark S Sutton
SVP & CFO: Tim S Nicholls
SVP, Gen Coun & Corp Secy: Sharon R Ryan
SVP, Corp Devt: C Cato Ealy
SVP, HR & Global Citizenship: Thomas J Plath
SVP, Mfg, Technol, EHS & Global Sourcing: Tommy S Joseph
SVP, Papers (Americas): W Michael Amick, Jr
Founded: 1898
Book Paper Line(s) Milled: Accent Opaque; by George!; CutLess®; DataSpeed®; DRM®; Hammermill®; HP; Postmark; Springhill; Williamsburg
Cover Line(s) Milled: Accent Opaque; Accent Opaque Digital; Hammermill®; Springhill Digital Opaque; Springhill Opaque; Springhill Vellum Bristol
Paper Type(s) Sold: Acid Free; Book Offset; Chlorine Free; Recycled
Branch Office(s)
International Paper Europe, Middle East & Africa, Chaussee de la Hulpe, 166, 1170 Brussels, Belgium *Tel:* (02) 774-1211
International Paper Latin America, Ave Eng Luis Carlos Berrini, 04571-010 Sao Paulo-SP, Brazil *Tel:* 0800 70 30070
International Paper Asia, 17-18F, West Bldg Greenland Ctr, 600 Middle Longhua Rd, Shanghai 200032, China *Tel:* (021) 6113 3200
International Paper India, 603 6th fl, Swapnalok Complex, 92/93 Sarojini Devi Rd, Secunderabad 500 003, India *Tel:* (040) 4002 0263
International Paper Japan Ltd, Kamiyacho Sq, 9th fl, Azabudai 1-chome, Bldg 7-3, Minato-ku, Tokyo 106-0041, Japan *Tel:* (03) 3560 7410
Ave 5 de Febrero No 1351, Edificio Sequoia PB Zona, Zona Industrial Benito Juarez, 76120 Santiago de Queretaro, QRO, Mexico *Tel:* (01442) 427 6150

Ironmark
9040 Junction Dr, Annapolis Junction, MD 20701
Toll Free Tel: 888-775-3737
E-mail: marketing@ironmarkusa.com
Web Site: ironmarkusa.com
Key Personnel
CEO: Scott Hargest *E-mail:* scott@ironmarkusa.com; Jeff Ostenso *E-mail:* jeff@ironmarkusa.com
Pres: Matt Marzullo *E-mail:* mmarzullo@ironmarkusa.com
SVP, Sales: Scott Kravitz *E-mail:* skravitz@ironmarkusa.com
VP, Opers: Chris Marzullo *E-mail:* cmarzullo@ironmarkusa.com
Sr Sales Exec: Larry Davis *E-mail:* ldavis@ironmarkusa.com
Founded: 1955

Kwikprint Manufacturing Co Inc
4868 Victor St, Jacksonville, FL 32207
Tel: 904-737-3755 *Toll Free Tel:* 800-940-5945 *Fax:* 904-730-0349
E-mail: info@kwikprint.net
Web Site: www.kwik-print.com
Key Personnel
Pres: Jay D Cann, Jr

Lake Book Manufacturing Inc
2085 N Cornell Ave, Melrose Park, IL 60160
Tel: 708-345-7000
E-mail: info@lakebook.com
Web Site: www.lakebook.com
Key Personnel
Pres & COO: Dan Genovese
VP, Fin & CFO: Bob Flatow
VP & Gen Mgr: Bill Richards

MANUFACTURING

VP, Mfg: Steve Quagliato
VP, Opers: Bill Flavin
VP, Sales & Mktg: Nick Vergoth
VP, Technol: Paul Genovese

Larson Texts Inc
1762 Norcross Rd, Erie, PA 16510
Tel: 814-824-6365 *Toll Free Tel:* 800-530-2355
Fax: 814-824-6377
Web Site: www.larsontexts.com
Key Personnel
CEO: Matt Totske
IT Mgr: Kathleen Williams
Sr Researcher: Tim Larson
Founded: 1983

LBS
Division of Library Binding Service
1801 Thompson Ave, Des Moines, IA 50316-2751
Tel: 515-262-3191 *Toll Free Tel:* 800-247-5323
Toll Free Fax: 800-262-4091
E-mail: info@lbsbind.com
Web Site: www.lbsbind.com
Key Personnel
Pres & CEO: Rob Mauritz *Tel:* 515-299-7402
 E-mail: robm@lbsbind.com
COO: Steve Deaton *Tel:* 515-299-1022
 E-mail: steved@lbsbind.com
CFO: Derek Stocking *Tel:* 515-299-1007
 E-mail: dereks@lbsbind.com
SVP & Gen Mgr: Joe Dunham *Tel:* 515-299-7416
 E-mail: joed@lbsbind.com
SVP, Corp Devt & Culture: Chris Paxson
 E-mail: chrisp@lbsbind.com
Acct Mgr: Shelly Davis *Tel:* 877-301-7421
 E-mail: shellyd@lbsbind.com
Sales Rep: Tony Nelson *Tel:* 866-331-7431
 E-mail: tonyn@lbsbind.com
Founded: 1936
Cover Line(s) Sold: Advantage 9; Advantage 7; Algora; Arrestox® B-Cloth; Arrestox® Shimmer; Beaudiva; Buckram; C-1 Cloth; Canoso; Cezane; Chameleon; Chromo; Colibri; Colored Endleaf Paper; Cot-Linen; Diamond; Duo®; Dust; Eurobond®; euroBuckram; Excel-Tan®; Feincanvas; Fluctuations; Forest; Frankonia®; Hype; Imperial; Iris®; Ismara; Kashmir; Kennett®; Kensington® Leather; Leathers; Library SUMMIT™; Linen Buckram; Linen Set®; Lino; Lipare; Liv; Lizard; Luminaire™; Lustre; Manhattan; Maple; Marano; Masanti; Medusa; Merino; Natural Papers; Nomad; Ottawa; Padusa; Pearl Linen®; Pellana; Printa Offset; Rebel; Record; Reflections; Saffiano; Santina; Stingray; Sturdite®; Tango; Taratan II®; TexMex; Tsarina Crush; Velluto; Verona®; Walnut
Membership(s): Book Manufacturers' Institute (BMI)

Lindenmeyr Book Publishing Papers
Division of Central National Gottesman Inc
3 Manhattanville Rd, Purchase, NY 10577
Tel: 914-696-9300
Web Site: www.lindenmeyrbook.com
Key Personnel
Pres: Peter Harding
SVP: Tim Christie *Tel:* 914-696-9305
 E-mail: tchristie@lbppaper.com
Cust Serv Mgr: Michael A Yeager
 E-mail: myeager@lbppaper.com
Founded: 1859
Book Paper Line(s) Sold: Appleton; Domtar; Evergreen Packaging; Finch Pruyn; Georgia-Pacific; Glatfelter; International Paper; Kansaki; Kruger Inc; Madison International; Mohawk Paper; Monadnock Paper Mills Inc; Newton Falls; Plainwell; Rolland; Stora Enso; Tervakoski; Wausau Paper; Weyerhaeuser/NOR-PAC; Zanders
Cover Line(s) Sold: Eastex Inc; International Paper; Mead; Smart Papers; Temboard; UPM-Kymmene; Zanders
Paper Type(s) Sold: Book Offset; Coated Free Sheet; Coated Groundwood; Uncoated Free Sheet; Uncoated Groundwood
Membership(s): Association of American Publishers (AAP); Book Industry Study Group (BISG); Book Manufacturers' Institute (BMI); Publishing Professionals Network (PPN)

Lindenmeyr Paper, see Lindenmeyr Book Publishing Papers

McClain Printing Co
212 Main St, Parsons, WV 26287-1033
Mailing Address: PO Box 403, Parsons, WV 26287-0403
Tel: 304-478-2881 *Toll Free Tel:* 800-654-7179
 Fax: 304-478-4658
E-mail: mcclain@mcclainprinting.com
Web Site: www.mcclainprinting.com
Key Personnel
Pres: Kenneth E Smith
VP, Publg: Michelle McKinnie
Founded: 1958

McManus & Morgan
2506 W Seventh St, Los Angeles, CA 90057
Tel: 213-387-4433
Web Site: www.mcmanusandmorgan.com
Key Personnel
Owner: Gary Wolin *E-mail:* gary@mcmanusmorgan.com
Founded: 1923

Mekatronics Inc
85 Channel Dr, Port Washington, NY 11050
Tel: 516-883-6805 *Fax:* 516-883-6948
E-mail: office@mekatronicsinc.com
Web Site: mekatronicsinc.com
Key Personnel
Pres: Jack Bendror *E-mail:* jbendror@mekatronicsinc.com
Founded: 1960
Membership(s): The American Library Association (ALA)

Miami Wabash Paper LLC
Affiliate of Mafcote Inc
301 Wedcor Ave, Wabash, IN 46992
Tel: 260-563-4181 *Toll Free Tel:* 800-842-9112
 Fax: 219-563-2724
E-mail: miamivalley@mafcote.com
Web Site: www.mafcote.com
Key Personnel
Pres: Steven A Schulman
VP: Daryl Evans
Founded: 1965

Midland Paper, Packaging & Supplies
101 E Palatine Rd, Wheeling, IL 60090
Mailing Address: PO Box 9032, Wheeling, IL 60090-9032
Tel: 847-777-2700 *Toll Free Tel:* 800-323-8522; 888-564-3526 (cust serv) *Fax:* 847-403-6320 (cust serv)
E-mail: whl@midlandpaper.com; sales@midlandpaper.com; custservice@midlandpaper.com
Web Site: www.midlandpaper.com
Key Personnel
CEO: Mike Graves
EVP & CFO: Ralph DeLetto
EVP, Publg & Consulting: Jim O'Toole
Founded: 1907
Book Paper Line(s) Sold: BPM Inc; Catalyst; Cenveo; Clearwater Paper; CTI; Decorated; Domtar; FiberMark; French Paper Co; Kallima® Coated Cover C1S; Kallima® Coated Cover C2S; Kruger Inc; Mactac;

MANUFACTURING MATERIALS

Magic; Mohawk Paper; Moorim; Neenah Paper; Nekoosa; Pixelle Specialty Solutions™; Reich Paper; Resolute Forest Products; SIHL Inc; Teslin®; Verso Corp; Yupo Corporation America
Branch Office(s)
363 N Third St, Des Plaines, IL 60016 *Toll Free Tel:* 800-323-8522 *Fax:* 847-403-6302
 E-mail: des@midlandpaper.com
150 S Unit Dr, Normal, IL 61761 *Toll Free Tel:* 866-289-2974 *Toll Free Fax:* 866-289-2975
 E-mail: nml@midlandpaper.com
1801 Hollister Whitney Pkwy, Quincy, IL 62305 *Toll Free Tel:* 866-289-2974 *Fax:* 217-223-0905
 E-mail: qcy@midlandpaper.com
690 Southrock Dr, Rockford, IL 61102 *Toll Free Tel:* 800-929-3380 *Fax:* 847-403-6365
 E-mail: rok@midlandpaper.com
2050 W Iles Ave, Springfield, IL 62704 *Toll Free Tel:* 866-289-2974 *Fax:* 847-403-6385
 E-mail: spg@midlandpaper.com
2 Venture, Suite 455, Irvine, CA 92618 *Toll Free Tel:* 855-353-3922 *Fax:* 847-403-6303
 E-mail: nat@midlandpaper.com
CohereOne, 777 Grand Ave, Suite 204, San Rafael, CA 94901 *Tel:* 415-322-6986
 E-mail: info@cohereone.com
1375 Kings Hwy E, Suite 240, Fairfield, CT 06824 *Toll Free Tel:* 888-615-5551 *Fax:* 203-256-1548 *E-mail:* nat@midlandpaper.com
1140A Maxwell Ave, Evansville, IN 47711 *Toll Free Tel:* 888-260-5270 *Fax:* 847-403-6260
 E-mail: evn@midlandpaper.com
2363 Perry Rd, Suite 150, Plainfield, IN 46168 *Toll Free Tel:* 800-888-8291 *Fax:* 847-403-6308
 E-mail: ind@midlandpaper.com
801 S 19 St, West Des Moines, IA 50265 *Toll Free Tel:* 800-422-3174 *Fax:* 847-403-6305
 E-mail: dem@midlandpaper.com
14449 W 100 St, Lenexa, KS 66215 *Toll Free Tel:* 866-204-9700 *Fax:* 847-403-6278
 E-mail: len@midlandpaper.com
3805 Business Park Dr, Louisville, KY 40213 *Toll Free Tel:* 888-260-6398 *Fax:* 502-969-8177
 E-mail: lou@midlandpaper.com
30 Constitution Dr, Southborough, MA 01801 *Tel:* 847-777-2480 *E-mail:* nat@midlandpaper.com
1860 SE Elm St, Minneapolis, MN 55414 *Toll Free Tel:* 866-339-0414 *Fax:* 847-403-6886
 E-mail: mnp@midlandpaper.com
401 Hazelwood Logistics, Center Dr, Suite 500, St Louis, MO 63042 *Toll Free Tel:* 888-260-4105 *Fax:* 847-403-6380 *E-mail:* stl@midlandpaper.com
4363 W Calhoun St, Suite A, Springfield, MO 65802 *Toll Free Tel:* 888-832-8200 *Fax:* 847-403-6385 *E-mail:* spm@midlandpaper.com
40 Hillcrest Rd, Madison, NJ 07940 *Tel:* 847-777-2418 *E-mail:* nat@midlandpaper.com
440 Ivy Trails Dr, Cincinnati, OH 45244 *Toll Free Tel:* 855-549-2930 *Fax:* 847-403-6281
 E-mail: nat@midlandpaper.com
6749 E 12 St, Tulsa, OK 74112 *Toll Free Tel:* 888-260-5835 *Fax:* 847-403-6335
 E-mail: tul@midlandpaper.com
10200 Harwin Dr, Houston, TX 77036-1587 *Tel:* 713-995-9510 *Fax:* 281-530-9619
 E-mail: hou@midlandpaper.com
195 NE Gilman Blvd, Suite 201, Issaquah, WA 98027 *Toll Free Tel:* 855-900-2874 *Fax:* 847-403-6916 *E-mail:* nat@midlandpaper.com
4826 W Converters Dr, Appleton, WI 54913 *Toll Free Tel:* 800-242-3398 *Fax:* 847-403-6936
 E-mail: app@midlandpaper.com
1220 Femrite Dr, Suite 208, Madison, WI 53716 *Toll Free Tel:* 866-339-0406 *Fax:* 847-403-6350
 E-mail: mad@midlandpaper.com
8601 N 91 St, Milwaukee, WI 53224 *Toll Free Tel:* 800-242-8917 *Fax:* 847-403-6910
 E-mail: mke@midlandpaper.com
400 S 72 Ave, Wausau, WI 54401 *Toll Free Tel:* 800-688-1872 *Fax:* 847-403-6333
 E-mail: wsa@midlandpaper.com

MANUFACTURING MATERIALS

Midwest Paper Group
540 Prospect St, Combined Locks, WI 54113
Tel: 920-788-3550 *Toll Free Tel:* 800-828-1987
  Fax: 920-968-3950
Web Site: mwpaper.com
Key Personnel
VP, Publg Papers: Mike Baker *Tel:* 920-968-3801
Founded: 1907
Book Paper Line(s) Milled: Ethos Offset Smooth; Ethos Offset Vellum; Utopia Coated Matte; Utopia Matte Inkjet

Mohawk Fine Papers Inc
465 Saratoga St, Cohoes, NY 12047
Tel: 518-237-1740 *Toll Free Tel:* 800-THE-MILL
  (843-6455) *Fax:* 518-237-7394
Web Site: www.mohawkconnects.com
Key Personnel
Chmn & CEO: Thomas D O'Connor, Jr
COO: Bruce M Hogan
EVP & CFO: John P Macy
Chief Revenue Offr: Melissa Stevens
Chief Strategy Offr: Paul J Biesiadecki
Founded: 1931
Book Paper Line(s) Milled: Mohawk Carnival; Mohawk Everyday Digital Uncoated; Mohawk Loop; Mohawk Opaque; Mohawk Options; Mohawk Skytone; Mohawk Superfine; Mohawk Via; Strathmore Premium; Strathmore Writing
Cover Line(s) Milled: Mohawk Carnival; Mohawk Everyday Digital Uncoated; Mohawk Loop; Mohawk Opaque; Mohawk Options; Mohawk Skytone; Mohawk Superfine; Mohawk Via; Strathmore Premium; Strathmore Writing
Book Paper Line(s) Sold: Chromolux; Curious Collection; Keaykolour; Mohawk Paper; Strathmore
Cover Line(s) Sold: Chromolux; Curious Collection; Keaykolour; Mohawk Paper; Strathmore
Paper Type(s) Sold: Acid Free; Recycled

Monadnock Paper Mills Inc
117 Antrim Rd, Bennington, NH 03442-4205
Tel: 603-588-3311 *Toll Free Tel:* 800-221-2159
  (cust serv) *Fax:* 603-588-3158
E-mail: info@mpm.com
Web Site: www.mpm.com
Key Personnel
Dir, Mktg & Communs: Lisa Berghaum
Founded: 1819
Book Paper Line(s) Sold: Astrolite; Astrolite Digital+; Astrolite PC 100; Astrolite PC 100 Velvet C2S; Caress; Dulcet®
Cover Line(s) Sold: Astrolite; Astrolite Digital+; Astrolite PC 100; Astrolite PC 100 Velvet C2S; Caress; Dulcet®; Duraprint™
Membership(s): American Forest & Paper Association; University & College Designers Association

Neenah Inc
3460 Preston Ridge Rd, Suite 600, Alpharetta, GA 30005
Toll Free Tel: 800-344-5287
E-mail: publishing.team@neenah.com
Web Site: www.neenahperformance.com/products/neenah-performance/publishing-products
Key Personnel
Dir, Sales & Mktg: Melanie Calkins
Book Paper Line(s) Milled: Corvon®; HyFlex®; Kivar®; Kivarflex™; Lexide®; Lexotone®; Skivertex®
Branch Office(s)
5492 Bostwick St, Lowville, KY 13367
443B Shaker Rd, East Longmeadow, MA 01028
501 E Munising Ave, Munising, MI 49862
Bridge St, Brownville, NY 13615
45 N Fourth St, Quakertown, PA 18951
Membership(s): Book Manufacturers' Institute (BMI)

Iris Nevins Decorative Papers
PO Box 429, Johnsonburg, NJ 07846-0429
Tel: 908-813-8617
E-mail: irisnevins@verizon.net
Web Site: www.marblingpaper.com
Key Personnel
Owner: Iris Nevins
Founded: 1978

OGM USA
4333 46 St, Suite F2, Sunnyside, NY 11104
Tel: 212-964-2430
Web Site: www.ogm.it
Key Personnel
Chmn, CEO & Sales Rep: Rino Varrasso
  E-mail: rvarrasso@ogm-usa.com
Founded: 1974

Omniafiltra LLC
9567 Main St, Beaver Falls, NY 13305
Mailing Address: PO Box 410, Beaver Falls, NY 13305
Tel: 315-346-7300
Web Site: www.omniafiltra.it/inglese/default_en.html
Key Personnel
Mill Mgr: Scott Sauer
Busn Devt & Sales Mgr: Peter Gendreau
Founded: 1955

O'Neil Digital Solutions LLC
12655 Beatrice St, Los Angeles, CA 90066
Tel: 310-448-6400
E-mail: sales@oneildata.com
Web Site: www.oneildata.com
Key Personnel
Pres & COO: Terry Chan
EVP, Sales & Mktg: Mark Rosson
Dir, HR: LaDonna Wise
Founded: 1973

Overseas Printing Corporation
Division of InnerWorkings Inc
4040 Civic Center Dr, Suite 200, San Rafael, CA 94903
Tel: 415-500-8331 *Fax:* 415-835-9899
Web Site: www.overseasprinting.com
Key Personnel
Sr Prodn Mgr: Shaun Garrett *E-mail:* sgarrett@inwk.com
Founded: 1972

The Ovid Bell Press Inc
Subsidiary of Walsworth Publishing Co
1201 Bluff St, Fulton, MO 65251
Mailing Address: PO Box 370, Fulton, MO 65251-0370
Tel: 573-642-2256 *Toll Free Tel:* 800-835-8919
E-mail: sales@ovidbell.com
Web Site: ovidbell.com
Key Personnel
CFO: Jill Custard *E-mail:* jillcustard@ovidbell.com
Pres: Troy Williams *Tel:* 573-310-2599
  E-mail: troywilliams@ovidbell.com
VP, Sales & Mktg: David O'Donley *Tel:* 573-310-2630 *E-mail:* david@ovidbell.com
Plant Mgr: Kevin Werdehausen *Tel:* 573-310-2598
  E-mail: kevin.werdehausen@ovidbell.com
Founded: 1927

Patterson Printing Co
1550 Territorial Rd, Benton Harbor, MI 49022
Tel: 269-925-2177
E-mail: sales@patterson-printing.com
Web Site: patterson-printing.com
Founded: 1956

PCA Printing, see Printing Corporation of the Americas Inc

Peregrine Arts Bindery
7 Avenida Vista Grande, Suite B-7 119, Santa Fe, NM 87508
Tel: 505-466-0490
Web Site: www.peregrineartsbindery.etsy.com
Key Personnel
Pres: Katherine Loeffler

PrairieView Press
625 Seventh St, Gretna, MB R0G 0V0, Canada
Mailing Address: PO Box 460, Gretna, MB R0G 0V0, Canada
Tel: 204-327-6543 *Toll Free Tel:* 800-477-7377
  Toll Free Fax: 866-480-0253
Web Site: prairieviewpress.com
Key Personnel
Owner & Pres: Chester Goossen
Founded: 1968

Pratt Paper Company LLC
20 Davis Rd, Marblehead, MA 01945
Tel: 781-639-9450 *Fax:* 781-639-9452
Key Personnel
Pres & CEO: A Diehl Jenkins *E-mail:* djenkins@prattpaper.com
CFO: Drew J Lemieux
Founded: 1907
Book Paper Line(s) Sold: Finch Pruyn; Glatfelter; International Paper; Monadnock Paper Mills Inc; Rolland; Stora Enso; Tervakoski; UPM-Kymmene
Cover Line(s) Sold: Glatfelter; Monadnock Paper Mills Inc; Rolland; Stora Enso

Printing Corporation of the Americas Inc
620 SW 12 Ave, Pompano Beach, FL 33069
Tel: 954-781-8100 *Toll Free Tel:* 866-721-1PCA
  (721-1722)
Web Site: pcaprintingplus.com
Key Personnel
Pres: Buddy Tuchman
Sales Mgr: Steven Konecky *E-mail:* steven@pcaprinting.com
Founded: 1980

PrintWest
1111 Eighth Ave, Regina, SK S4R 1C9, Canada
Tel: 306-525-2304 *Toll Free Tel:* 800-236-6438
  Fax: 306-757-2439
E-mail: general@printwest.com
Web Site: www.printwest.com
Key Personnel
Pres & Dir, Opers: Corie Triffo
VP, Sales & Mktg: Ken Benson
Founded: 1992

Rayonier Advanced Materials
1301 Riverplace Blvd, Suite 2300, Jacksonville, FL 32207
Tel: 904-357-4600
Web Site: rayonieram.com
Key Personnel
Chmn, Pres & CEO: Paul G Boynton
SVP, Forest Prods, Paper & Board Busn: Chris Black
SVP, Mfg Opers: William R Manzer
Founded: 1937
Branch Office(s)
405 The West Mall, Suite 800, Toronto, ON M9C 5J1, Canada *Tel:* 416-775-2806 *Fax:* 416-621-3119
4 Place Ville-Marie, Suite 100, Montreal, QC H3B 2E7, Canada *Tel:* 514-871-0137 *Fax:* 514-397-0896
10 Gatineau Rd, PO Box 5000, Temiscaming, QC J0Z 3R0, Canada *Tel:* 819-627-4780 *Fax:* 819-627-1178
Sales Office(s): 4474 Savannah Hwy, Jesup, GA 31545, Contact: John Gegg *Tel:* 912-588-8007 *Fax:* 912-588-8300 *E-mail:* john.gegg@rayonieram.com

MANUFACTURING

Hotel Equatorial, Unit 804, Off Bldg, 65, Yanan Rd W, Shanghai 200040, China, Contact: Wu Yaodong *Tel:* (021) 6248-2510; (021) 6249-6127; (0139) 01764581 (cell) *Fax:* (021) 6248-8929 *E-mail:* yaodong.wu@rayonieram.com
Cross Off Uchisaiwaicho, 1-18-6, Nishishimbashi, Minato-ku, Tokyo 105-0003, Japan, Contact: Tatsuro Miyachi *Tel:* (03) 6457-9530; (070) 2810-9913 (cell) *Fax:* (03) 6457-9532 *E-mail:* tatsuro.miyachi@rayonieram.com

Reichhold Inc
1035 Swabia Ct, Durham, NC 27703
Mailing Address: PO Box 13582, Research Triangle Park, NC 27709
Tel: 919-990-7500 *Toll Free Tel:* 800-448-3482 *Fax:* 919-990-7749
Web Site: www.reichhold.com
Key Personnel
Pres & CEO: John Gaither
SVP, Corp Servs: Mitzi Van Leeuwen
Founded: 1927
Branch Office(s)
237 S Motor Ave, Azusa, CA 91702 *Tel:* 626-334-4974 *Fax:* 626-969-6978
54 Wamsley Rd, Jacksonville, FL 32254 *Tel:* 904-695-7500 *Fax:* 904-695-7517
425 S Pace Blvd, Pensacola, FL 32502 *Tel:* 850-433-7621 *Fax:* 850-433-7699
6350 E Collins Rd, Morris, IL 60450 *Tel:* 815-942-4600 *Fax:* 815-942-4722
249 Saint Louis Ave, Valley Park, MO 63088 *Tel:* 636-225-5226 *Fax:* 636-225-2954
1503 Haden Rd, Houston, TX 77015 *Tel:* 713-453-5431 *Fax:* 713-453-1093

Resolute Forest Products
111 Robert-Bourassa Blvd, Suite 5000, Montreal, QC H3C 2M1, Canada
Tel: 514-875-2160 *Toll Free Tel:* 800-361-2888
E-mail: info@resolutefp.com
Web Site: www.resolutefp.com
Key Personnel
Pres & CEO: Yves Laflamme
SVP & CFO: Jo-Ann Longworth
SVP, Corp Aff & Chief Legal Offr: Jacques Vachon
SVP, HR: Daniel Ouellet
SVP, Pulp & Paper Opers: Richard Tremblay
SVP, Pulp & Paper Sales & Mktg: John Lafave
SVP, Tissue Group: Patrice Minguez
Founded: 2011
Book Paper Line(s) Milled: Alternative Book; Alternative Book Cream; Alternative Offset; Alternative Opaque; Ecopaque Offset; Equal Book; Equal Offset; Resolute Connect; ResoluteBook 70; ResoluteBook 70 Cream; ResoluteBook 75; ResoluteBook 60; ResoluteBook 65; ResoluteLite; ResoluteSCA; ResoluteSCA+; ResoluteSCA++; ResoluteSCB; ResoluteSelect 70; ResoluteSelect 75; ResoluteSelect 65; ResoluteSNC
Book Paper Line(s) Sold: Alternative Book; Alternative Book Cream; Alternative Offset; Alternative Opaque; Ecopaque Offset; Equal Book; Equal Offset; Resolute Connect; ResoluteBook 70; ResoluteBook 70 Cream; ResoluteBook 75; ResoluteBook 60; ResoluteBook 65; ResoluteLite; ResoluteSCA; ResoluteSCA+; ResoluteSCA++; ResoluteSCB; ResoluteSelect 70; ResoluteSelect 75; ResoluteSelect 65; ResoluteSNC
Paper Type(s) Sold: Coated Mechanical No 4; Coated Mechanical No 5; Directory; Supercalendered; Uncoated Free Sheet; Uncoated Mechanical
Membership(s): American Forest & Paper Association; American Wood Council (AWC); Forest Products Association of Canada (FPAC); FPInnovations; Quebec Forest Industry Council (QFIC); Two Sides North America Inc

Rolland Enterprises
256 JB Rolland W, St-Jerome, QC J7Y 0L6, Canada
Toll Free Tel: 800-567-9872 (CN); 800-388-0882 (US)
E-mail: media@rollandinc.com; marketing@rollandinc.com
Web Site: www.rollandinc.com
Founded: 1882
Book Paper Line(s) Milled: Rolland Enviro® Book; Rolland Enviro® Opaque Offset; Rolland Enviro® Print; Rolland Enviro® Satin; Rolland HiBulk; Rolland Kraft®; Rolland Opaque®

Roosevelt Paper Co
One Roosevelt Dr, Mount Laurel, NJ 08054
Tel: 856-303-4100 *Toll Free Tel:* 800-523-3470 *Fax:* 856-642-1949
E-mail: marketing@rooseveltpaper.com
Web Site: www.rooseveltpaper.com
Key Personnel
Chmn & CEO: Ted Kosloff
CFO: Tony Janulewicz
CIO: John Gordon, Jr
Pres: David Kosloff
VP, Sales & Mktg: Dean T Egan
Sales Mgr: Dennis Carney
Founded: 1932
Branch Office(s)
5100 W 123 St, Alsip, IL 60803, Div Mgr: Donald Raugh *Tel:* 708-653-5121 *Toll Free Tel:* 800-323-1778 *Fax:* 708-653-3103
11001 Paper Blvd, Richwood, KY 41094-9341, Div Mgr: Donald Raugh *Tel:* 859-485-8100 *Toll Free Tel:* 800-354-9829 *Fax:* 859-485-9724

St Armand Paper Mill
3700 St Patrick, Montreal, QC H4E 1A2, Canada
Tel: 514-931-8338 *Fax:* 514-931-5953
Web Site: www.st-armand.com
Key Personnel
Prop: David Carruthers
VP: Denise Lapointe
Founded: 1979
Book Paper Line(s) Milled: Canal Paper; Old Masters
Cover Line(s) Milled: St Armand Colours
Membership(s): Alcuin Society; Canadian Bookbinders & Book Artists Guild (CBBAG); Pulp & Paper Technical Association of Canada (PAPTAC)

Sappi Fine Paper North America
Subsidiary of Sappi Ltd
255 State St, Boston, MA 02109
Tel: 617-423-7300 *Toll Free Tel:* 800-882-4332
E-mail: webqueriesna@sappi.com
Web Site: www.sappi.com/na
Key Personnel
Pres & CEO: Mike Haws
VP & CFO: Annette Luchene
VP, Graphics, Packaging & Specialties: Deece Hannigan
VP, HR & Gen Coun: Sarah Manchester
VP, Mfg: Mike Schultz
VP, Pulp Busn & Supply Chain: Anne Ayer
VP, Res, Devt & Sustainability: Beth Cormier
Founded: 1854 (as S D Warren Co which was acquired by Sappi in 1994)
Book Paper Line(s) Milled: EuroArt Plus (sheet); Flo (sheet, web & digital); Galerie Brite (web); Galerie Fine (web); Galerie Lite (web); McCoy (sheet, web & digital); Opus (sheet, web & digital); Opus PS (sheet & web); Somerset (web)
Cover Line(s) Milled: EuroArt Plus (sheet); Flo (sheet, web & digital); Galerie Brite (web); Galerie Fine (web); Galerie Lite (web); McCoy (sheet, web & digital); Opus (sheet, web & digital); Opus PS (sheet & web); Somerset (web)

MANUFACTURING MATERIALS

Sales Office(s): Western Region Sales Office, 333 S Anita Dr, Suite 840, Orange, CA 92868 *Tel:* 714-456-0600
Southern Region Sales Office, 3700 Mansell Rd, Suite 140, Alpharetta, GA 30322 *Tel:* 404-751-2600
Chicago Sales Office, 10600 W Higgins Rd, Suite 701, Rosemont, IL 60018 *Toll Free Tel:* 800-333-9855
Great Lakes Region Sales Office, 1717 Dixie Hwy, Suite 150B, Fort Wright, KY 41011 *Toll Free Tel:* 888-739-6601
Pulp Sales Office-North America, 20 N 22 St, Cloquet, MN 55720 *Tel:* 218-879-2300
Northern Region Sales Office, 287 Bowman Ave, Suite 225, Purchase, NY 10577-2544 *Tel:* 914-696-5544

Sepp Leaf Products Inc
381 Park Ave S, No 13, New York, NY 10016
Tel: 212-683-2840 *Fax:* 212-725-0308
E-mail: sales@seppleaf.com
Web Site: www.seppleaf.com
Key Personnel
Pres: Peter Sepp

Sheridan MI
Division of CJK Group Inc
613 E Industrial Dr, Chelsea, MI 48118
Tel: 734-475-9145
Web Site: www.sheridan.com
Key Personnel
Pres: Paul Bozuwa *E-mail:* paul.bozuwa@sheridan.com
VP, Book Sales: Joe Thomson *E-mail:* joe.thomson@sheridan.com
VP, Fin: Nicole Mummert *E-mail:* nicole.mummert@sheridan.com
VP, HR: Ken Rapp *E-mail:* ken.rapp@sheridan.com
VP, Opers: Paul Loy *E-mail:* paul.loy@sheridan.com
Cust Serv Mgr: Ed Blissick *E-mail:* ed.blissick@sheridan.com
Direct Sales Rep: Jessica Ansorge *Tel:* 734-385-1544 *E-mail:* jessica.ansorge@sheridan.com; Kathy Brown *Tel:* 734-385-1540 *E-mail:* kathy.brown@sheridan.com; Rebecca Humrich *Tel:* 734-385-1543 *E-mail:* rebecca.humrich@sheridan.com; Jennifer Riemenschneider *Tel:* 734-385-1533 *E-mail:* jennifer.riemenschneider@sheridan.com
Founded: 1950

Simon Miller Paper & Packaging
3409 W Chester Pike, Suite 204, Newton Square, PA 19073
Tel: 215-923-3600 *Toll Free Tel:* 800-642-1899 *Fax:* 610-355-9330
E-mail: info@simonmiller.com
Web Site: www.simonmiller.com
Key Personnel
Chmn & CEO: Henri C Levit *E-mail:* henri.levit@simonmiller.com
Dir, Opers: Jeffrey Levit
Dir, Sales & Mktg: G Scott Earls
Founded: 1926
Cover Line(s) Milled: New Age
Book Paper Line(s) Sold: Domtar; Finch Pruyn; Glatfelter; Manistique; Seaman; Stora
Paper Type(s) Sold: Acid Free; Recycled
Membership(s): Forest Stewardship Council US (FSC-US); National Paper Trade Association (NPTA); Two Sides North America Inc

Smith-Edwards-Dunlap Co
2867 E Allegheny Ave, Philadelphia, PA 19134
Tel: 215-425-8800 *Toll Free Tel:* 800-829-0020 *Fax:* 215-425-9715
E-mail: sales@sed.com
Web Site: www.sed.com
Key Personnel
Pres: Jonathan Shapiro

MANUFACTURING MATERIALS

Sales Mgr: Fred Binder
Founded: 1880

Solar-Screen Co Inc
53-11 105 St, Corona, NY 11368
Tel: 718-592-8222 *Toll Free Tel:* 800-347-6527
 Toll Free Fax: 888-271-0891
E-mail: solarscreen@prodigy.net
Web Site: www.solar-screen.com
Key Personnel
Pres: Miles Joseph
Founded: 1960

Southeastern Printing Co
3601 SE Dixie Hwy, Stuart, FL 34997
Tel: 772-287-2141 *Toll Free Tel:* 800-226-8221
 Fax: 772-288-3988
E-mail: sales@seprint.com
Web Site: www.seprint.com
Key Personnel
Pres: Don Mader
Founded: 1924
Branch Office(s)
950 SE Eighth St, Hialeah, FL 33010 *Tel:* 305-885-8707 *Fax:* 305-888-9903 *E-mail:* info@seprint.com
Sales Office(s): 6001 Park of Commerce Blvd, Suite 200, Boca Raton, FL 33487 *Tel:* 561-998-0870

Spectrum PrintGroup Inc
1535 Farmer's Lane, Suite 254, Santa Rosa, CA 95405
Tel: 707-542-6044 *Toll Free Tel:* 888-340-6049
 Fax: 707-542-6045
E-mail: sales@spectrumprintgroup.com
Web Site: www.spectrumprintgroup.com
Key Personnel
Pres: Duncan McCallum *Tel:* 707-542-6044 ext 102 *E-mail:* duncan@spectrumprintgroup.com
Busn Devt Mgr: Elise Gochberg *Tel:* 415-461-1130 *E-mail:* elise@spectrumprintgroup.com
Founded: 1985

Spicers Paper
Division of Central National Gottesman Inc
12310 E Slauson Ave, Santa Fe Springs, CA 90670
Toll Free Tel: 800-774-2377 *Fax:* 562-693-8339
Web Site: www.spicers.com
Key Personnel
Pres: Jan Gottesman
SVP: Rick Anderson
Book Paper Line(s) Milled: Moorim; Sappi
Cover Line(s) Milled: Clearwater; Moorim; MWV; Tango
Book Paper Line(s) Sold: CTI; Domtar; French Paper Co; Mohawk Paper; Neenah Paper; Sappi; Verso Corp; West Linn Paper Co; Yupo Corporation America
Cover Line(s) Sold: Appleton; Clearwater Paper; Tango
Paper Type(s) Sold: Acid Free; Book Offset; Chlorine Free; Coated Free Sheet; Coated Groundwood; Contract Embossings; Fancy; Printed; Recycled; Uncoated Free Sheet; Uncoated Groundwood
Branch Office(s)
47422 Kato Rd, Fremont, CA 94538, Contact: Jeff Jarvis *Tel:* 510-476-7700 *Fax:* 510-476-7755
105 S 41 Ave, Suite 2, Phoenix, AZ 85009, Contact: Kathy Markley *Tel:* 602-484-7337 *Fax:* 602-484-7388
14209 E 35 Place, Suite 103, Aurora, CO 80011, Contact: George Seymour *Tel:* 303-373-9655 *Fax:* 303-373-9658
320C Waiakamilo, Honolulu, HI 96817, Contact: Mr Jody Kadokawa *Tel:* 808-832-0001 *Fax:* 808-832-0016
4161 NE 189 Ave, Gresham, OR 97230 *Tel:* 503-405-0100 *Fax:* 503-405-0130

2454 S 3600 W, Suite A, West Valley City, UT 84119, Contact: Heath Lawrence *Tel:* 801-364-0113 *Fax:* 801-364-0302
21527 64 Ave S, Kent, WA 98032 *Tel:* 253-518-0030 *Fax:* 253-395-4849
Membership(s): National Paper Trade Association (NPTA); Visual Media Alliance (VMA)

StoraEnso North American Sales Inc
Canterbury Green, 201 Broad St, Stamford, CT 06901
Tel: 203-541-5100 *Fax:* 203-353-1143
Web Site: www.storaenso.com
Key Personnel
Pres: Peter Mersmann
Sales Dir, Paper: Courtney Wemyss *Tel:* 203-541-5194 *E-mail:* courtney.wemyss@storaenso.com
Book Paper Line(s) Milled: Belle; Bulky; Classic; Creamy; Lux; Lux Cream; Novel 80; Novel 76
Cover Line(s) Milled: LumiArt; LumiSilk; Novapress

The Studley Press Inc
151 E Housatonic St, Dalton, MA 01226
Mailing Address: PO Box 214, Dalton, MA 01227-0214
Tel: 413-684-0441 *Toll Free Tel:* 877-684-0441
 Fax: 413-684-0220
Web Site: thestudleypress.com
Key Personnel
Owner: Suzanne K Salinetti *E-mail:* suzanne@thestudleypress.com
Founded: 1938

Styled Packaging LLC
PO Box 30299, Philadelphia, PA 19103-8299
Tel: 610-529-4122 *Fax:* 610-520-9662
Web Site: www.taylorbox.com
Key Personnel
Pres: William R Fenkel *E-mail:* jjibill@aol.com
Founded: 2003

Sun Chemical Corp
Member of DIC Group
35 Waterview Blvd, Parsippany, NJ 07054-1285
Tel: 973-404-6000
E-mail: globalmarketing@sunchemical.com
Web Site: www.sunchemical.com
Key Personnel
Pres & CEO: Myron Petruch
Chief Admin Offr, Gen Coun & Secy: James R Van Horn
Founded: 1830
Branch Office(s)
135 W Lake St, Northlake, IL 60164 (North American inks)
5020 Spring Grove Ave, Cincinnati, OH 45232 (performance pigments)
Av Justino de Maio, 140 Guarulhos, 07222-000 Sao Paulo-SP, Brazil *Tel:* (011) 2462 2500 *Fax:* (011) 2462 2520
Leeuwenveldsweg 3-T, 1382 LV Weesp, Netherlands
Wexham Springs, Framewood Rd, Slough SL3 6PJ, United Kingdom *Tel:* (0203) 139 0000 *Fax:* (0203) 139 0001

Superior Printing Ink Co Inc
100 North St, Teterboro, NJ 07608
Tel: 201-478-5600 *Fax:* 201-478-5650
Web Site: www.superiorink.com
Key Personnel
CEO: Jeffrey I Simons
COO: Angel Torres
CFO: Peter Nunez
Founded: 1918
Branch Office(s)
666 E Linwood Ave, Maple Shade Township, NJ 08052 *Tel:* 856-482-9066
252 Wright St, Newark, NJ 07114 *Tel:* 973-824-0005

BOOK

2125 Yates Ave, Commerce, CA 90040 *Tel:* 323-767-2173 *Fax:* 323-767-2192
750 Sherman Ave, Hamden, CT 06514 *Tel:* 203-281-1921
1220 NW 23 Ave, Fort Lauderdale, FL 33311 *Tel:* 954-587-0780
7498 Fullerton St, Jacksonville, FL 32256 *Tel:* 904-538-0601
300-A Shirley Way, Atlanta, GA 30336 *Tel:* 404-691-6759
1125 Republic Dr, Addison, IL 60101 *Tel:* 630-543-9770
120 Forbes Blvd, Mansfield, MA 02048 *Tel:* 508-337-8181
255 E Main St, Marlborough, MA 01752 *Tel:* 508-481-5015
2483 Walden Ave, Cheektowaga, NY 14225 *Tel:* 716-685-6763
4020 Rozzelles Ferry Rd, Charlotte, NC 28216-3343 *Tel:* 704-399-2523
309 Gallimore Dairy Rd, Suite 104, Greensboro, NC 27409 *Tel:* 336-931-3100
4440 Creek Rd, Cincinnati, OH 45242 *Tel:* 513-221-4707
7655 Hub Pkwy, Suite 205, Cleveland, OH 44125 *Tel:* 216-328-1720
1481 Goodale Blvd, Columbus, OH 43212 *Tel:* 614-486-2100
2708 S 163 St, New Berlin, WI 53151 *Tel:* 262-796-1499
Membership(s): National Association of Printing Ink Manufacturers (NAPIM)

Talas
330 Morgan Ave, Brooklyn, NY 11211
Tel: 212-219-0770
E-mail: info@talasonline.com; support@talasonline.com
Web Site: www.talasonline.com
Key Personnel
Pres: Aarol Salik
VP: Jillian Salik
Founded: 1962

Taylor Specialty Books, see Balfour Commercial Printing

Technical Library Service Inc, see Talas

The Thomas Tape & Supply Co Inc
1713 Sheridan Ave, Springfield, OH 45505
Mailing Address: PO Box 207, Springfield, OH 45501-0207
Tel: 937-325-6414 *Fax:* 937-325-2850
Web Site: www.thomastape.com
Key Personnel
Pres: David Simonton *E-mail:* dave11@thomastape.com
Founded: 1894

Times Printing LLC
Division of Kappa Printing Management Associates LLC (KPMA)
100 Industrial Dr, Random Lake, WI 53075
Tel: 920-994-4396 *Toll Free Tel:* 800-236-4396 (sales)
E-mail: info@kappapma.com
Web Site: www.kappapma.com
Founded: 1918

Toof American Digital
4222 Pilot Dr, Memphis, TN 38118
Tel: 901-274-3632 *Toll Free Tel:* 800-722-4772
Web Site: www.toofamericandigital.com
Key Personnel
Pres: Stillman McFadden
Founded: 1864

TSO General Corp
79 Emjay Blvd, Brentwood, NY 11717
Tel: 631-952-5320 *Fax:* 631-952-5315
Web Site: www.tsogeneral.com

MANUFACTURING

Key Personnel
Pres: Kirk Malandrakis *E-mail:* kmalan@tsogeneral.com
Founded: 1969

Tukaiz LLC
2917 N Latoria Lane, Franklin Park, IL 60131
Tel: 847-455-1588; 847-288-4968 (sales)
Toll Free Tel: 800-543-2674
E-mail: contacttukaiz@tukaiz.com
Web Site: www.tukaiz.com
Key Personnel
Founder & Mng Dir: Frank Defino, Sr
VP, Mng Dir & CFO: Christopher Calabra
VP & Mng Dir: Daniel Defino; Frank Defino, Jr
Founded: 1963

Twin Rivers Paper Co
82 Bridge Ave, Madawaska, ME 04756
Tel: 207-728-3321 *Toll Free Tel:* 800-920-9988
Fax: 207-728-8701
E-mail: info@twinriverspaper.com
Web Site: www.twinriverspaper.com
Key Personnel
Pres: Ken Winterhalter
VP, Sales: Tony Rigelman *Tel:* 404-285-1864
E-mail: tony.rigelman@twinriverspaper.com
VP, Strategy & Mktg: Dave Deger *Tel:* 207-523-2355 *E-mail:* dave.deger@twinriverspaper.com

Ulster Linen Co Inc
383 Moffit Blvd, Islip, NY 11751
Tel: 631-859-5244 *Fax:* 631-859-4990
E-mail: sales@ulsterlinen.com
Web Site: www.ulsterlinen.com
Key Personnel
Dir: Joseph H Larmor
Sales Mgr: Jackie Mihaley
Founded: 1933

University Products Inc
517 Main St, Holyoke, MA 01040
Mailing Address: PO Box 101, Holyoke, MA 01041-0101
Tel: 413-532-3372 *Toll Free Tel:* 800-628-1912 (orders) *Fax:* 413-533-4743 *Toll Free Fax:* 800-532-9281
E-mail: info@universityproducts.com
Web Site: www.universityproducts.com
Key Personnel
VP & Gen Mgr: John A Dunphy
Mktg Mgr: Linda McInerney
Founded: 1968

Veritiv™ Corporation
1000 Abernathy Rd, Bldg 400, Suite 1700, Atlanta, GA 30328
Toll Free Tel: 844-VERITIV (837-4848); 866-714-8303 (packaging cust serv); 866-714-8306 (print cust serv)
E-mail: contactus@veritivcorp.com; media@veritivcorp.com
Web Site: www.veritivcorp.com
Key Personnel
CEO: Salvatore A Abbate
SVP & CFO: Eric J Guerin
SVP & Chief HR Offr: Dean A Adelman
SVP & CIO: Karen K Renner
SVP, Gen Coun & Corp Secy: Susan B Salyer
SVP, Facility Solutions, Digital & Mktg: Daniel B Calderwood
SVP, Packaging & Global Opers: Michael D Walkenhorst
SVP, Sales: Stephanie E Mayerle
VP, Corp Devt: Peter C Troup
Founded: 2014 (as a result of the merger of Unisource Worldwide Inc & xpedx)
Book Paper Line(s) Sold: Comet™; Econosource®; Endurance™; PoliPrint™; Seville™; Showcase™; Starbrite® Opaque Select; ViV™
Paper Type(s) Sold: Acid Free; Book Offset

Versa Press Inc
1465 Spring Bay Rd, East Peoria, IL 61611-9788
Tel: 309-822-8272 *Toll Free Tel:* 800-447-7829
Fax: 309-822-8141
Web Site: www.versapress.com
Key Personnel
Chmn: Joseph F Kennell
Pres: Steven J Kennell
Sales Mgr: Matthew Kennell *E-mail:* mkennell@versapress.com
Founded: 1937
Membership(s): Book Manufacturers' Institute (BMI)

Fred Weidner & Daughter Printers
99 Hudson St, 5th fl, New York, NY 10013
Tel: 646-706-5180
E-mail: info@fwdprinters.com
Web Site: www.fwdprinters.com
Key Personnel
Pres: Cynthia Weidner *E-mail:* cynthia@fwdprinters.com
Creative Dir: Carol Mittelsdorf *E-mail:* carol@fwdprinters.com
Founded: 1860

MANUFACTURING MATERIALS

Whitehall Printing Co
4244 Corporate Sq, Naples, FL 34104
Tel: 239-643-6464 *Toll Free Tel:* 800-321-9290
Fax: 239-643-6439
E-mail: info@whitehallprinting.com
Web Site: www.whitehallprinting.com
Key Personnel
Chmn: Mike Hirsch
Pres: Jeff Hirsch
VP: Emil G Hirsch
Founded: 1959

B W Wilson Paper Co Inc
2501 Brittons Hill Rd, Richmond, VA 23230
Tel: 804-358-6715 *Toll Free Tel:* 800-868-2868
Fax: 804-358-4742
E-mail: info@bwwilson.com; sales@bwwilson.com
Web Site: www.bwwilson.com
Key Personnel
Pres: Lawrence H Rauppius, Jr
Dir, Sales & Mktg: Phil L Knab
Founded: 1904
Branch Office(s)
1015 Cavalier Blvd, Chesapeake, VA 27215
Tel: 757-487-7700 *Toll Free Tel:* 800-277-1136
Fax: 757-485-0710
2817 Carroll Ave, Lynchburg, VA 24501
Tel: 434-847-5220 *Toll Free Tel:* 888-511-3072
Fax: 434-847-5265
1006 Hauerhill Rd, Baltimore, MD 21229
308 S Anthony St, Burlington, NC 27215
Tel: 336-226-3226 *Toll Free Tel:* 800-277-9895
Fax: 336-226-3127
1219-B S Brightleaf Blvd, Smithfield, NC 27577
Toll Free Tel: 800-868-2868 *Fax:* 804-358-4742
2969 N Seventh St, Harris, PA 17110

Xerox Corporation
201 Merritt 7, Norwalk, CT 06851-1056
Toll Free Tel: 800-835-6100 (cust serv)
Web Site: www.xerox.com
Key Personnel
CEO: Steven Bandrowczak
Corp EVP & CFO: Xavier Heiss
Chief Mktg Offr: Deena LaMarque Piquion
EVP & Pres, Americas: Joanne Collins Smee
Founded: 1906

Manufacturing Services & Equipment Index

BOOK MANUFACTURING EQUIPMENT

A-R Editions Inc, pg 1277
Agfa North America, pg 1277
Amergraph Corp, pg 1277
Anderson & Vreeland Inc, pg 1277
Association for PRINT Technologies (APTech), pg 1277
AVT Inc, pg 1277
AWT World Trade Inc, pg 1277
Baumfolder Corp, pg 1277
Book Automation Inc, pg 1278
Book Machine Sales Inc, pg 1278
Brackett Inc, pg 1278
Brandtjen & Kluge LLC, pg 1278
Bunting Magnetics Co, pg 1278
Busch LLC, pg 1278
CC1 Inc, pg 1278
CG Book Printers, pg 1278
Challenge Machinery Co, pg 1278
Clamco Corp, pg 1278
The Cleveland Vibrator Co, pg 1278
CONTECH (Converting Technologies), pg 1278
Craftsmen Machinery Co Inc, pg 1278
D&K Group Inc, pg 1279
Datalogic USA Inc, pg 1279
Douthitt Corp, pg 1279
Durr MEGTEC LLC, pg 1279
Eastman Kodak Co, pg 1279
EMT International Inc, pg 1279
Essex Products Group, pg 1279
Evergreen Engravers, pg 1279
Fujifilm North America Corporation, Graphic Systems Division, pg 1280
H B Fuller Co, pg 1280
GTI Graphic Technology Inc, pg 1280
Heidelberg USA Inc, pg 1280
Heraeus Noblelight America LLC, pg 1280
HID Ultraviolet LLC, pg 1280
Holo Image Technology Inc, pg 1280
I-Web, pg 1280
Koenig & Bauer (US) Inc, pg 1281
Lassco-Wizer Equipment & Supplies, pg 1281
MacDermid Graphics Solutions LLC, pg 1281
Magna Visual Inc, pg 1281
manroland Goss web systems Americas LLC, pg 1281
Manroland Inc, pg 1281
Maple Press, pg 1281
Markwith Tool Co Inc, pg 1281
Master Flo Technology Inc, pg 1281
Maxcess International, pg 1281
McClain Printing Co, pg 1282
Miles 33 International LLC, pg 1282
Muller Martini Corp, pg 1282
Neenah Inc, pg 1282
The Ohio Blow Pipe Co, pg 1282
On Demand Machinery, pg 1282
Pantone Inc, pg 1282
Printer's Repair Parts, pg 1282
Printing Research Inc (PRI), pg 1282
Sakurai USA Inc, pg 1282
Samuel Packaging Systems, pg 1282
Santec Corp, pg 1282
Schaefer Machine Co Inc, pg 1283
E C Schultz & Company Inc, pg 1283
SCREEN Americas, pg 1283
Simco-Ion, pg 1283
SITMA USA Inc, pg 1283
Specialty Product Technologies (SPT), pg 1283
Spraymation Inc, pg 1283
Standard Finishing Systems, pg 1283
Staplex® Electric Stapler Division, pg 1283
Stoesser Register Systems, pg 1283
Suspension Feeder, pg 1283
Taconic Wire, pg 1283
Tecnau Inc, pg 1283
Timsons Inc, pg 1283
Tobias Associates Inc, pg 1283
Tompkins Printing Equipment Co, pg 1283
Videojet Technologies Inc, pg 1284
Western Printing Machinery Co (WPM), pg 1284
X-Rite Inc, pg 1284
Yurchak Printing Inc, pg 1284

DISTRIBUTION & MAILING

A-R Editions Inc, pg 1277
Adair Graphic Communications, pg 1277
American Mathematical Society (AMS), pg 1277
Association for PRINT Technologies (APTech), pg 1277
Bookmasters, pg 1278
Century Direct Solutions LLC, pg 1278
CG Book Printers, pg 1278
Clare Printing, pg 1278
Crown Connect, pg 1279
RR Donnelley, pg 1279
Dynaric Inc, pg 1279
Fairfield Marketing Group Inc, pg 1280
Ferry Associates Inc, pg 1280
Four Colour Print Group, pg 1280
Fry Communications Inc, pg 1280
Gallus Group, pg 1280
HBP Inc, pg 1280
The P A Hutchison Co, pg 1280
International Press Publication Inc, pg 1281
Ironmark, pg 1281
Lake Book Manufacturing Inc, pg 1281
Maple Press, pg 1281
Marrakech Express Inc, pg 1281
McClain Printing Co, pg 1282
Nevada Publications, pg 1282
O'Neil Digital Solutions LLC, pg 1282
The Ovid Bell Press Inc, pg 1282
Patterson Printing Co, pg 1282
PrairieView Press, pg 1282
PrintWest, pg 1282
Publishers' Graphics LLC, pg 1282
SITMA USA Inc, pg 1283
Southeastern Printing Co, pg 1283
Spring Arbor Distributors Inc, pg 1283
Styled Packaging LLC, pg 1283
Times Printing LLC, pg 1283
Townsend Communications Inc, pg 1284
Tukaiz LLC, pg 1284
Videojet Technologies Inc, pg 1284
Webcom Inc, pg 1284
Webcrafters Inc, pg 1284
Fred Weidner & Daughter Printers, pg 1284
Yurchak Printing Inc, pg 1284

MANUFACTURING BROKERS OR BROKERING

A-R Editions Inc, pg 1277
The Bear Wallow Publishing Co, pg 1277
Bindery & Distribution Service Inc, pg 1277
Blue Note Publications Inc, pg 1278
Desktop Miracles Inc, pg 1279
Four Colour Print Group, pg 1280
Graphics Two, pg 1280
Heidelberg Graphics, pg 1280
Imago, pg 1281
McClain Printing Co, pg 1282
Overseas Printing Corporation, pg 1282
Publishers Book Bindery (NY), pg 1282
Sakurai USA Inc, pg 1282
Styled Packaging LLC, pg 1283
Videojet Technologies Inc, pg 1284
Fred Weidner & Daughter Printers, pg 1284

Manufacturing Services & Equipment

This section includes companies throughout the world offering manufacturing services. Services include distribution and mailing as well as companies that manufacture and distribute book manufacturing equipment, types and matrices. The descriptions of the services provided are paid components. For additional book distribution and mailing firms, see **Book Distributors & Sales Representatives** and **Shipping Services**.

A-R Editions Inc
1600 Aspen Commons, Suite 100, Middleton, WI 53562
Tel: 608-836-9000 *Fax:* 608-831-8200
E-mail: info@areditions.com
Web Site: www.areditions.com
Key Personnel
Pres & CEO: Patrick Wall *Tel:* 608-203-2575
    E-mail: patrick.wall@areditions.com
Dir, Spec Projs: James Zychowicz *Tel:* 608-203-2580 *E-mail:* james.zychowicz@areditions.com
Founded: 1962

Adair Graphic Communications
Division of Printwell
26975 Northline Rd, Taylor, MI 48180
Tel: 734-941-6300 *Fax:* 734-942-0920
E-mail: adair@printwell.com
Web Site: www.adairgraphic.com
Key Personnel
Pres & CEO: Paul Borg
VP: Dennis Adair *E-mail:* dennis@adairgraphic.com
Founded: 1931

Agfa-Gevaert Graphics Inc, see Agfa North America

Agfa North America
Unit of Agfa-Gevaert Group
580 Gotham Pkwy, Carlstadt, NJ 07072
Tel: 201-440-2500 *Toll Free Tel:* 888-274-8626 (cust serv)
E-mail: customercare.us@agfa.com
Web Site: www.agfa.com/printing/global/usa; www.agfa.com/printing/industrial; www.agfa.com/printing/large-format
Key Personnel
Global Head, Mergers & Acqs: Gunther Muertens
Dir, Strategic Busn Devt & Dist: Deborah Hutcheson *Tel:* 908-342-1797 *E-mail:* deborah.hutcheson@agfa.com
Sales Office(s): 10798 Catawba Ave, Fontana, CA 92337
665 Raco Dr, Suite C, Lawrenceville, GA 30046 (sales/dist ctr)
14360 SW 147 St, Lockport, IL 60491
22 Stauffer Industrial Park, DC5, Taylor, PA 18517
951 Valley View Lane, Suite 100, Irving, TX 75061

Amergraph Corp
Unit of HID Ultraviolet LLC
Rte 15, 520 Lafayette Rd, Sparta, NJ 07871
Tel: 973-383-8700 *Fax:* 973-383-9225
E-mail: sales@amergraph.com
Web Site: amergraph.com
Founded: 1975

American Mathematical Society (AMS)
201 Charles St, Providence, RI 02904-2213
SAN: 201-1654
Tel: 401-455-4000 *Toll Free Tel:* 800-321-4267
    Fax: 401-331-3842; 401-455-4046 (cust serv)
E-mail: cust-serv@ams.org; ams@ams.org
Web Site: www.ams.org
Key Personnel
Exec Dir: Dr Catherine A Roberts
Publr: Dr Sergei Gelfand
Assoc Exec Dir: Dr Robert M Harrington
Assoc Exec Dir, Washington, DC: Dr Karen Saxe
Founded: 1888
Branch Office(s)
1527 18 St NW, Washington, DC 20036-1358 (govt rel & sci policy) *Tel:* 202-588-1100 *Fax:* 202-588-1853 *E-mail:* amsdc@ams.org
Mathematical Reviews®, 416 Fourth St, Ann Arbor, MI 48103-4820 (edit) *Tel:* 734-996-5250 *Fax:* 734-996-2916 *E-mail:* mathrev@ams.org
Secretary of the AMS - Society Governance, Dept of Computer Science, North Carolina State University, Box 8206, Raleigh, NC 27695-8206 *Tel:* 919-515-7863 *Fax:* 919-515-7896 *E-mail:* secretary@ams.org
Membership(s): Society for Scholarly Publishing (SSP)

Anderson & Vreeland Inc
15348 US Hwy 127 EW, Bryan, OH 43506
Tel: 419-636-5002 *Toll Free Tel:* 866-282-7697; 888-832-1600 (CN) *Fax:* 419-636-4334
E-mail: info@andersonvreeland.com
Web Site: andersonvreeland.com
Key Personnel
Chmn & CEO: Howard Vreeland, Jr
Pres: Darin Lyon
VP: Joseph Anderson
Branch Office(s)
14106 Pontlavoy Ave, Santa Fe Springs, CA 90670 (warehouse), West Regl Warehouse Mgr: Ariel Hernandez *Toll Free Tel:* 800-446-7716 *E-mail:* ahernandez@andvre.com
2196 Sweetwater Industrial Blvd, Suite A, Lithia Springs, GA 30122 (warehouse), East Regl Warehouse Mgr: Lonnie Grieser *E-mail:* lgrieser@andvre.com
1000 Estes Ave, Elk Grove Village, IL 60007 (warehouse)
8 Evans St, Fairfield, NJ 07004 (warehouse), East Regl Warehouse Mgr: Lonnie Grieser *E-mail:* lgrieser@andvre.com
8200 Tristar Dr, Suite 100, Irving, TX 75063-2836 (warehouse), South Warehouse Mgr: Ted Strenk *E-mail:* tstrenk@andvre.com
530 Andover Park W, Tukwila, WA 98188 (warehouse), West Regl Warehouse Mgr: Ariel Hernandez *Toll Free Tel:* 800-446-7716 *E-mail:* ahernandez@andvre.com
719 Millennium Ct, De Pere, WI 54115 (warehouse), Midwest Regl Warehouse Mgr: Ted Strenk *Tel:* 920-347-6010 *E-mail:* tstrenk@andvre.com
1645 Cliveden Ave, Delta, BC V3M 6V5, Canada
1260 Lakeshore Rd E, Mississauga, ON L5E 3B8, Canada
5435 Rue Francois-Cusson, Lachine, QC H8T 3J4, Canada
Membership(s): Flexographic Technical Association (FTA)

Association for PRINT Technologies (APTech)
113 Seaboard Lane, Suite C-250, Franklin, TN 37067
Tel: 703-264-7200
E-mail: aptech@aptech.org
Web Site: printtechnologies.org
Key Personnel
Pres: Thayer Long *E-mail:* tlong@aptech.org
VP, Prog Devt: Julie Shaffer *E-mail:* jshaffer@aptech.org
Sr Dir, Communs: Jane Pratt *E-mail:* jpratt@aptech.org
Founded: 1933
Membership(s): American Society of Association Executives™ (ASAE); Council of Manufacturing Associations; International Association of Exhibitions and Events® (IAEE); National Association of Manufacturers (NAM)

AVT Inc
Subsidiary of Danaher Corp
8601 Dunwoody Place, Bldg 100, Suite 100, Sandy Springs, GA 30350
Tel: 770-541-9780
E-mail: support@avt-inc.com
Web Site: www.avt-inc.com
Branch Office(s)
AVT EMEA, Generaal Dewittelaan 9 Bus 3, 2800 Mechelen, Belgium *Tel:* (015) 56 03 80 *Fax:* (015) 55 39 97
AVT Ltd, 6 Hanagar St, 4527703 Hod Hasharon, Israel (headquarters) *Tel:* (09) 7614444 *Fax:* (09) 7614555

AWT World Trade Inc
Division of AWT World Trade Group
4321 N Knox Ave, Chicago, IL 60641-1906
Tel: 773-777-7100 *Fax:* 773-777-0909
E-mail: sales@awtworldtrade.com
Web Site: www.awt-gpi.com
Key Personnel
Owner: Michael Green
Branch Office(s)
8984 NW 105 Way, Medley, FL 33178 *Tel:* 305-887-7500 *Fax:* 305-887-2300
AWT World Trade Europe BV, Holland, Netherlands

Baumfolder Corp
Division of Heidelberg
1660 Campbell Rd, Sidney, OH 45365
Tel: 937-492-1281 *Toll Free Tel:* 800-543-6107 *Fax:* 937-492-7280
E-mail: baumfolder@baumfolder.com
Web Site: www.baumfolder.com
Key Personnel
Pres & CEO: Janice Benanzer
Founded: 1917
Membership(s): Association for Supply Chain Management (ASCM); Dayton Region Manufacturers Association (DRMA); Print Industries Market Information and Research Organization (PRIMIR)

The Bear Wallow Publishing Co
809 S 12 St, La Grande, OR 97850
Tel: 541-962-7864
Web Site: www.bear-wallow.com
Key Personnel
Co-Owner: Cathy Gildemeister; Jerry Gildemeister *E-mail:* j-c@bear-wallow.com
Founded: 1976

Bindery & Distribution Service Inc
9 Overbrook Rd, South Barrington, IL 60010
Tel: 312-550-7000 *Fax:* 847-842-8800

MANUFACTURING SERVICES & EQUIPMENT

Key Personnel
Pres: Dennis Uchimoto *E-mail:* uchimoto@aol.com
Founded: 1986

Blue Note Books, see Blue Note Publications Inc

Blue Note Publications Inc
721 North Dr, Suite D, Melbourne, FL 32934
Tel: 321-799-2583; 321-622-6289
   Toll Free Tel: 800-624-0401 (orders) *Fax:* 321-799-1942; 321-622-6830
E-mail: bluenotebooks@gmail.com
Web Site: bluenotepublications.com
Key Personnel
Pres: Paul Maluccio
Founded: 1988

Book Automation Inc
Division of Meccanotecnica Spa
458 Danbury Rd, Unit B10, New Milford, CT 06776
Tel: 860-354-7900 *Toll Free Tel:* 800-429-6305
E-mail: info@bookautomation.com
Web Site: www.bookautomation.com
Key Personnel
Pres: Manrico Caglioni
Founded: 1975

Book Machine Sales Inc
PO Box 297, Hamlin, PA 18427
Tel: 570-647-9111
Web Site: bookmachinesales.com
Key Personnel
Owner & Pres: Peter H Johnson *E-mail:* pete@bookmachinesales.com

Bookmasters
Division of Baker & Taylor Publisher Services
30 Amberwood Pkwy, Ashland, OH 44805
Tel: 419-281-5100 *Toll Free Tel:* 800-537-6727
   Fax: 419-281-0200
E-mail: info@btpubservices.com
Web Site: www.btpubservices.com
Key Personnel
Dir of Mfg: Brad Sharp *E-mail:* bsharp@bookmasters.com
Founded: 1972

Brackett Inc
7115 SE Forbes Ave, Topeka, KS 66619
Mailing Address: PO Box 19306, Topeka, KS 66619-0306
Tel: 785-862-2205 *Toll Free Tel:* 800-255-3506
   Fax: 785-862-1127
E-mail: brackett@brackett-inc.com; sales@brackett-inc.com
Web Site: brackett-inc.com
Key Personnel
Pres & CEO: J M "Mike" Murray
   E-mail: mmurray@brackett-inc.com
Founded: 1910

Brandtjen & Kluge LLC
539 Blanding Woods Rd, St Croix Falls, WI 54024
Tel: 715-483-3265 *Toll Free Tel:* 800-826-7320
   Fax: 715-483-1640
E-mail: sales@kluge.biz
Web Site: www.kluge.biz
Key Personnel
Pres: Michael C Aumann
Founded: 1919
Branch Office(s)
Kluge International, Springmill Industrial Estate, Unit 3, Avening Rd, Nailsworth, Glos GL6 0BS, United Kingdom *Tel:* (01453) 836 522 *Fax:* (01453) 836 009

Membership(s): Association for Print Technologies (APTech); Foil & Specialty Effects Association (FSEA); International Association of Diecutting & Diemaking (IADD)

Bunting Magnetics Co
500 S Spencer Rd, Newton, KS 67114
Mailing Address: PO Box 468, Newton, KS 67114-0468
Tel: 316-284-2020 *Toll Free Tel:* 800-835-2526; 877-576-0156 *Fax:* 316-283-4975
E-mail: bmc@buntingmagnetics.com
Web Site: www.buntingmagnetics.com
Key Personnel
Pres & CEO: Robert J Bunting, Sr
Gen Mgr: Robert Bunting, Jr
Prod Mgr: Barry Voorhees *E-mail:* bvoorhees@buntingmagnetics.com
Founded: 1959
Branch Office(s)
Flexible Die Division, 600 S Spencer Rd, Newton, KS 67114 *E-mail:* sales@flexdies.com *Web Site:* www.flexdies.com
Magnet Materials Division, 1150 Howard St, Elk Grove Village, IL 60007 *Tel:* 847-593-2060 *E-mail:* info@buymagnets.com *Web Site:* www.buymagnets.com
Bunting Magnetics Mexico S de RL de CV, Privada Liendo 708 Sur Despacho 4, Colonia Obispado, 64060 Monterey, NL, Mexico *Tel:* (0181) 8348 3943
Bunting Magnetics Europe Ltd, Northbridge Rd, Berkhamsted, Herts HP4 1EH, United Kingdom *Tel:* (01442) 87508 *E-mail:* sales@buntingeurope.com *Web Site:* www.buntingeurope.com

Busch LLC
516 Viking Dr, Virginia Beach, VA 23452
Tel: 757-463-7800 *Toll Free Tel:* 800-USA-PUMP (872-7867) *Fax:* 757-463-7407
E-mail: info@buschusa.com; marketing@buschusa.com
Web Site: www.buschvacuum.com/us
Key Personnel
Lead Prod Mktg Mgr: Antonio Mantilla
Founded: 1963
Sales Office(s): 373 Joseph Dr, South Elgin, IL 60177 *Tel:* 630-545-1310
39 Davis St, South Plainfield, NJ 07080 *Tel:* 908-561-3233
13123 NE David Circle, Portland, OR 97230 *Tel:* 408-782-0800
420 "E" St, Suite 4, Bayamon, PR 00959-1901 *Tel:* 787-798-5045
1100 E Howard Lane, Bldg 2, Suite 200, Austin, TX 78753 *Tel:* 512-835-0906
1901 S Starpoint Dr, Houston, TX 77032 *Tel:* 281-214-8400
Membership(s): Fab Owners Association (FOA); Facilities 450mm Consortium (F450C); Semiconductor Equipment & Materials International (SEMI)

CC1 Inc
170 West Rd, Suite 7, Portsmouth, NH 03801
Tel: 603-319-2000 *Fax:* 603-319-2200
E-mail: customerservice@cc1inc.com
Web Site: www.cc1inc.com
Founded: 1979

Century Direct Solutions LLC
15 Enter Lane, Islandia, NY 11749
Tel: 212-763-0600
E-mail: contact@centurydirect.net
Web Site: www.centurydirect.net
Key Personnel
VP, Sales & Busn Devt: Martin A Rego
   E-mail: regom@centurydirect.net
Founded: 1932
Membership(s): Direct Mail Fundraisers Association (DMFA); Greater Hudson Valley Postal Customers Council; Greater New York Postal Customers Council; Hudson Valley Direct Marketing Association

CG Book Printers
Division of Corporate Graphics Commercial (CGC)
1750 Northway Dr, North Mankato, MN 56003
Tel: 507-388-3300 *Toll Free Tel:* 800-729-7575
   Fax: 507-386-6350
E-mail: cgbooks@corpgraph.com
Web Site: www.corpgraph.com
Key Personnel
Pres: Dan Kvasnicka *Tel:* 507-386-6340
   Fax: 507-344-5548 *E-mail:* dekvasnicka@corpgraph.com
Sales Exec, Book Mfg Sales: Mike Schmitt *Tel:* 507-386-6349 *E-mail:* mjschmitt@corpgraph.com
Founded: 1989

Challenge Machinery Co
6125 Norton Center Dr, Norton Shores, MI 49441
Tel: 231-799-8484 *Fax:* 231-798-1275
E-mail: info@challengemachinery.com; sales@challengemachinery.com
Web Site: www.challengemachinery.com
Key Personnel
Pres & CEO: Tom Zant
Dir, Sales & Mktg: Britt Cary
Founded: 1870

Clamco Corp
Member of PAC Machinery Group
775 Berea Industrial Pkwy, Berea, OH 44017
Tel: 216-267-1911 *Toll Free Tel:* 800-985-9570
   (headquarters) *Fax:* 216-267-8713
E-mail: info@clamcopackaging.com
Web Site: www.pacmachinery.com/clamcopackaging
Key Personnel
Mgr: Rob Patton
Founded: 1946

Clare Printing
206 S Keystone Ave, Sayre, PA 18840
Tel: 570-888-2244
E-mail: hr@clareprint.com
Web Site: www.clareprint.com
Key Personnel
Pres: Ian Clare
Prodn Mgr: Alicia Blokzyl
Founded: 1903

The Cleveland Vibrator Co
2828 Clinton Ave, Cleveland, OH 44113
Tel: 216-241-7157 *Toll Free Tel:* 800-221-3298
   Fax: 216-241-3480
E-mail: sales@clevelandvibrator.com
Web Site: www.clevelandvibrator.com
Key Personnel
Gen Sales Mgr: Jack Steinbuch
Founded: 1923

CONTECH (Converting Technologies)
1756 S 151 St W, Goddard, KS 67052
Tel: 316-722-6907 *Fax:* 316-722-2976
E-mail: info@contechusa.com
Web Site: www.contechusa.com
Key Personnel
VP: Max Ogden *E-mail:* mogden@contechusa.com
Founded: 1980

Corporate Graphics Book Printers, see CG Book Printers

Craftsmen Machinery Co Inc
1257 Worcester Rd, Unit 167, Framingham, MA 01701

MANUFACTURING

Mailing Address: PO Box 2006, Framingham, MA 01703-2006
Tel: 508-376-2001 *Fax:* 508-376-2003
E-mail: sales@craftsmenmachinery.com
Web Site: www.craftsmenmachinery.com
Key Personnel
Pres: Sherwin Marks

Crown Connect
250 W Rialto Ave, San Bernadino, CA 92408
Tel: 909-888-7531 *Fax:* 909-889-1639
E-mail: sales@crownconnect.com
Web Site: www.crownconnect.com
Key Personnel
CFO: Nicole Albright *Tel:* 909-888-7531 ext 204
Pres: Denny Shorett *Tel:* 909-888-7531 ext 225
VP, Opers: Ken Martin *Tel:* 909-888-7531 ext 206
Mgr, Busn Devt: Erin Warren *Tel:* 909-888-7531 ext 228
Prodn Mgr: Chris McPhate *Tel:* 909-888-7531 ext 214
Founded: 1970

D&K Group Inc
1795 Commerce Dr, Elk Grove Village, IL 60007
Tel: 847-956-0160; 847-956-4757 (tech support)
Toll Free Tel: 800-632-2314 *Fax:* 847-956-8214
E-mail: info@dkgroup.net
Web Site: www.dkgroup.com
Key Personnel
Pres: Karl Singer
VP, Sales & Mktg: Tom Pidgeon *E-mail:* tom.pidgeon@dkgroup.net
Mktg Communs Specialist: Brian Biegel *E-mail:* brian.biegel@dkgroup.net
Founded: 1979

Datalogic USA Inc
959 Terry St, Eugene, OR 97402-9150
Tel: 541-683-5700 *Toll Free Tel:* 800-227-2633
Web Site: www.datalogic.com
Founded: 1969
Branch Office(s)
55 W Del Mar Blvd, Pasadena, CA 91105
5775 W Old Shakopee Rd, Suite 160, Bloomington, MN 55437
511 School House Rd, Telford, PA 18969-1196
144 Milestone Way, Greenville, SC 29615

Desktop Miracles Inc
112 S Main St, Suite 294, Stowe, VT 05672
Tel: 802-253-7900 *Toll Free Fax:* 888-293-2676
E-mail: info@desktopmiracles.com
Web Site: www.desktopmiracles.com
Key Personnel
Pres & CEO: Barry T Kerrigan *E-mail:* barry@desktopmiracles.com
VP: Virginia Kerrigan *E-mail:* virginia@desktopmiracles.com
Founded: 1994

RR Donnelley
35 W Wacker Dr, Chicago, IL 60601
Toll Free Tel: 800-742-4455
Web Site: www.rrd.com
Key Personnel
Pres & CEO: Daniel L Knotts
Pres, Busn Servs: John Pecaric
Pres, Mktg Solutions: Doug Ryan
EVP & CFO: Terry D Peterson
EVP & CIO: Ken O'Brien
EVP & Chief HR Offr: Sheila Rutt
EVP & Chief Strategy & Transformation Offr: Elif Sagsen-Ercel
EVP, Gen Coun, Chief Compliance Offr & Corp Secy: Deborah Steiner
EVP, Dom Opers & Chief Supply Chain Offr: Glynn Perry
SVP & Chief Acctg Offr: Michael J Sharp
Founded: 1864

Branch Office(s)
955 Gateway Center Way, San Diego, CA 92102
Tel: 619-527-4600
40610 County Center Dr, Temecula, CA 92591
Tel: 951-296-2890
151 Red Stone Rd, Manchester, CT 06042
Tel: 860-649-5570
9125 Bachman Rd, Orlando, FL 32824 *Tel:* 407-859-2030
5800 Peachtree Rd, Atlanta, GA 30341 *Tel:* 770-458-6351
825 Riverside Pkwy, Suite 300, Austell, GA 30168 *Tel:* 770-948-1330
1750 Wallace Ave, St Charles, IL 60174 *Tel:* 630-313-7000
609 S Kirk Rd, St Charles, IL 60174 *Tel:* 630-762-7600
One Poplar Ave, Thurmont, MD 21788 *Tel:* 301-271-7171
65 Sprague St, Hyde Park, MA 02136 *Tel:* 617-360-2000
18780 W 78 St, Chanhassen, MN 55317
Tel: 952-937-9764
5500 12 Ave E, Shakopee, MN 55379 *Tel:* 952-941-7546
6305 Sunset Corporate Dr, Las Vegas, NV 89120
Tel: 702-949-8500
5 Henderson Dr, West Caldwell, NJ 07006
Tel: 973-882-7000
12301 Vance Davis Dr, Charlotte, NC 28269
Tel: 704-949-3568
One Litho Way, Durham, NC 27703 *Tel:* 919-596-3660
3801 Gantz Rd, Grove City, OH 43123 *Tel:* 614-539-5527
700 Nestle Way, Suite 200, Breinigsville, PA 18031 *Tel:* 610-391-3900
9985 Gantry Rd, Philadelphia, PA 19115
Tel: 215-671-9500
218 N Braddock Ave, Pittsburgh, PA 15208
Tel: 412-241-8200
1210 Key Rd, Columbia, SC 29201 *Tel:* 803-799-9550
1645 W Sam Houston Pkwy N, Houston, TX 77043 *Tel:* 713-468-7175
1550 Lakeway Dr, Suite 600, Lewisville, TX 75057 *Tel:* 972-353-7500
630 W 1000 N, Logan, UT 84321 *Tel:* 435-755-4000
201 E Progress Dr, West Bend, WI 53095
Tel: 262-338-6101
Membership(s): Association of American Publishers (AAP); Book Industry Study Group (BISG); Book Manufacturers' Institute (BMI)

Douthitt Corp
245 Adair St, Detroit, MI 48207-4287
Tel: 313-259-1565 *Toll Free Tel:* 800-368-8448 *Fax:* 313-259-6806
E-mail: em@douthittcorp.com
Web Site: www.douthittcorp.com
Key Personnel
Natl Sales Mgr: Jim Primo

Durr MEGTEC LLC
Division of Duerr AG
830 Prosper St, DePere, WI 54115
Mailing Address: PO Box 5030, DePere, WI 54115-5030
Tel: 920-336-5715
E-mail: megtecinquiries@megtec.com
Web Site: www.durr-megtec.com
Key Personnel
SVP: Ken Zak
VP, Sales & Busn Devt: Rodney Schwartz
Founded: 1969
Branch Office(s)
Solvent Recovery Division, 1201 19 Place, No B301, Vero Beach, FL 32960 *Tel:* 772-567-1320
Solvent Recovery Division, 2120 Citygate Dr, Columbus, OH 43219 *Tel:* 614-324-2660

MANUFACTURING SERVICES & EQUIPMENT

MEGTEC TurboSonic Inc, 550 Parkside Dr, No A-14, Waterloo, ON N2L 5V4, Canada
Tel: 519-885-5513
MEGTEC Systems Australia Inc, 25, 21 Aristoc Rd, Glen Waverley, Victoria 3150, Australia
Tel: (03) 9574 7450
MEGTEC Systems (Shanghai) Ltd, No 125, Lane 1190, Jiujing Rd, Jiuting Town, Songjiang District, Shanghai 201615, China *Tel:* (021) 6769 7878
MEGTEC Systems SAS, Z I des Malines, 32 rue des Malines, 91090 Lisses, France *Tel:* 01 69 89 47 93
Duerr Systems AG, Honeywellstr 18, 63477 Maintal, Germany *Tel:* (06181) 94040
MEGTEC Systems India Pvt Ltd, Plot No 6/5, CTS No 8/5 Erandawana, near Nal-Stop, Karve Rd, behind Saraswat Bank, Pune 411 004, India *Tel:* (020) 2546 6610
MEGTEC Systems AB, Olskroksgatan 30, Box 6106, 40060 Gothenburg, Sweden *Tel:* (031) 65 78 00
MEGTEC Environmental Ltd, Unit 133, Bradley Hall Trading Estate, Bradley Lane, Standish Wigan WN6 0XQ, United Kingdom
Tel: (01257) 42 7070
Membership(s): Flexible Packaging Association (FPA)

Dynapar, see Specialty Product Technologies (SPT)

Dynaric Inc
5740 Bayside Rd, Virginia Beach, VA 23455
Tel: 757-363-5850 *Toll Free Tel:* 800-526-0827 *Fax:* 757-363-8016
E-mail: gd@dynaric.com; order@dynaric.com
Web Site: www.dynaric.com
Key Personnel
Pres: Joseph Martinez
Founded: 1973

Eastman Kodak Co
343 State St, Rochester, NY 14650
Tel: 585-724-4000 *Toll Free Tel:* 866-563-2533
Web Site: www.kodak.com
Key Personnel
Exec Chmn: Jim Continenza
SVP & Pres, Print Systems Div: John O'Grady
Dir, Communs: Nicholas Rangel *E-mail:* nicholas.rangel@kodak.com
Founded: 1880

EMT International Inc
780 Centerline Dr, Hobart, WI 54155
Tel: 920-468-5475 *Fax:* 920-468-7991
E-mail: info@emtinternational.com
Web Site: www.emtinternational.com
Key Personnel
EVP, Sales & Mktg: Jim Driscoll
Regl Mgr: Jeff Messenger

Essex Products Group
30 Industrial Park Rd, Centerbrook, CT 06409-0307
Tel: 860-767-7130 *Toll Free Tel:* 800-394-7130 *Fax:* 860-767-9137
E-mail: sales@epg-inc.com
Web Site: www.epg-inc.com
Key Personnel
Pres: Peter Griffin
Admin: Kaylynn Washington

Evergreen Engravers
Division of Diecraft Dispatch Inc
1819 S Central Ave, Suite 24, Kent, WA 98032
Tel: 253-852-6766 *Toll Free Tel:* 800-852-6766 *Fax:* 253-850-3944
E-mail: emboss@evergreenengravers.com
Web Site: www.evergreenengravers.com

MANUFACTURING SERVICES & EQUIPMENT

Key Personnel
Pres: Jeff Hilton
Founded: 1952

Fairfield Marketing Group Inc
Subsidiary of FMG Inc
830 Sport Hill Rd, Easton, CT 06112-1241
E-mail: info@fairfieldmarketing.com
Key Personnel
Pres & CEO: Edward P Washchilla, Jr
  E-mail: ed@fairfieldmarketing.com
Founded: 1986
Membership(s): American Booksellers Association (ABA); Bridgeport Regional Business Council (BRBC); Education Market Association; United States Chamber of Commerce (USCC)

Ferry Associates Inc
49 Fostertown Rd, Medford, NJ 08055
Tel: 609-953-1233 *Toll Free Tel:* 800-257-5258
  Fax: 609-953-8637
Web Site: www.ferryassociates.com
Key Personnel
Pres: Kevin Ferry *E-mail:* kferry@ferryassociates.com
Founded: 1982

Fife, see Maxcess International

Four Colour Print Group
2410 Frankfort Ave, Louisville, KY 40206
Tel: 502-896-9644 *Fax:* 502-896-9594
E-mail: sales@fourcolour.com
Web Site: www.fourcolour.com
Key Personnel
Pres & CEO: George C Dick *Tel:* 502-896-9644 ext 303 *E-mail:* gdick@fourcolour.com
Prodn Dir: Amy Martin *Tel:* 502-896-9644 ext 315 *E-mail:* amartin@fourcolour.com
Prodn Mgr: Cindy Jones *Tel:* 502-896-9644 ext 310 *E-mail:* cjones@fourcolour.com
Founded: 1985
Branch Office(s)
FCI Digital, 2032 S Alex Rd, Suite A, West Carrollton, OH 45449 *Tel:* 931-859-9701 *Fax:* 931-859-9709 *E-mail:* sales@fcidigital.com *Web Site:* www.fcidigital.com

Fry Communications Inc
800 W Church Rd, Mechanicsburg, PA 17055
Tel: 717-766-0211 *Toll Free Tel:* 800-334-1429
  Fax: 717-691-0341
E-mail: info@frycomm.com
Web Site: www.frycomm.com
Key Personnel
Chmn of the Bd: Henry Fry
CEO: Mike Lukas
CFO: Chris Wawrzyniak
CTO: David S Fry
VP, Sales: Kevin Quinn
Founded: 1934

Fujifilm North America Corporation, Graphic Systems Division
Division of Fujifilm Corporation
850 Central Ave, Hanover Park, IL 60133
Tel: 630-259-7200 *Toll Free Tel:* 800-877-0555
  Fax: 630-259-7078
Web Site: www.fujifilmusa.com/products/graphic_arts_printing/index.html; www.fujifilmusa.com
Founded: 1965
Branch Office(s)
2507 W Erie Dr, Suite 103, Tempe, AZ 85282
  Toll Free Tel: 800-279-1673 *Fax:* 602-437-8483
6200 Phyllis Dr, Cypress, CA 90630 *Tel:* 714-933-3300 *Toll Free Tel:* 800-879-2355
  Fax: 714-899-4707
30962 San Benito St, Hayward, CA 94544 *Toll Free Tel:* 800-734-8745 *Fax:* 510-266-0707

4424 Seaboard Rd, Suite C, Orlando, FL 32808, Regl Sales Mgr: Jim Kornmeyer *Toll Free Tel:* 800-940-6366 *Fax:* 407-898-0818
6810 Deerpath Rd, Suite 405, Elkridge, MD 21075, Regl Sales Mgr: Tony Aquino *Tel:* 301-317-7480 *Toll Free Tel:* 800-729-3600 *Fax:* 301-317-7480
France Avenue Business Park IV, 4001 Lakebreeze Ave N, Suite 400, Brooklyn Center, MN 55429-3860 *Tel:* 651-855-6000 *Toll Free Tel:* 800-758-8421 *Fax:* 651-855-6025
2001 NE 46 St, Suite 250, Kansas City, MO 64116, Regl Sales Mgr: John Steege *Tel:* 913-233-0355 *Toll Free Tel:* 800-776-4019 *Fax:* 913-233-0125
1100 King Georges Post Rd, Edison, NJ 08837, Regl Sales Mgr: Fred Heinkel *Tel:* 732-857-3280 *Fax:* 732-857-3470
1650 Magnolia Dr, Cincinnati, OH 45215, Regl Sales Mgr: Kurt Paskert *Toll Free Tel:* 800-582-7406 *Fax:* 513-563-0377
3926 Willow Lake Blvd, Memphis, TN 38118, Regl Sales Mgr: Tony Aquino *Toll Free Tel:* 800-365-2457 *Fax:* 901-795-1251
330 West Way Place, No 446, Arlington, TX 76018, Regl Sales Mgr: Bob O'Shea *Toll Free Tel:* 800-404-3228 *Fax:* 817-467-7351
1795 Fremont Dr, Salt Lake City, UT 84104 *Tel:* 801-975-1234 *Fax:* 801-972-3981
5103 "D" St NW, Suite 102, Auburn, WA 98001 *Toll Free Tel:* 800-628-0317 *Fax:* 253-852-4701 *Toll Free Fax:* 800-555-0776

H B Fuller Co
1200 Willow Lake Blvd, St Paul, MN 55110-5146
Tel: 651-236-5900 *Toll Free Tel:* 888-423-8553
E-mail: inquiry@hbfuller.com
Web Site: www.hbfuller.com
Key Personnel
Pres & CEO: Jim Owens
EVP & COO: Ted Clark
EVP & CFO: John Corkrean
VP & Cont: Robert Martsching
VP & Treas: Heidi Weiler
VP, Gen Coun & Corp Secy: Timothy Keenan

Gallus Group
Subsidiary of Heidelberg
One Ivybrook Blvd, Suite 180, Ivyland, PA 18974
Tel: 215-677-9600 *Fax:* 215-677-9700
E-mail: info@gallus-group.com
Web Site: gallus.contento.ch
Founded: 1980
Membership(s): Flexographic Technical Association (FTA); TLMI

Graphics Two
819 S Main St, Burbank, CA 91506
Tel: 818-841-4922
Key Personnel
Owner: Bert Johnson *E-mail:* cabert@aol.com; Jeanne Vlazny
Founded: 1973

GTI Graphic Technology Inc
211 Dupont Ave, Newburgh, NY 12550
Mailing Address: PO Box 3138, Newburgh, NY 12550-0651
Tel: 845-562-7066 *Fax:* 845-562-2543
E-mail: sales@gtilite.com
Web Site: www.gtilite.com
Key Personnel
Pres: Robert McCurdy
EVP: Louis Chappo
Sales & Mktg Coord: Linda Sutherland
Founded: 1975

HBP Inc
952 Frederick St, Hagerstown, MD 21740

Tel: 301-733-2000 *Toll Free Tel:* 800-638-3508
  Fax: 301-733-6586
E-mail: contactus@hbp.com
Web Site: www.hbp.com
Key Personnel
Owner & Pres: John Snyder
VP, Busn Devt & Mktg: Ilene Lerner *Tel:* 703-289-9038 *E-mail:* ilerner@hbp.com
Founded: 1903
Sales Office(s): 2818 Fallfax Dr, Falls Church, VA 22042 *Tel:* 703-289-9000
Membership(s): CUA; Printing & Graphics Association MidAtlantic (PGAMA); Printing Industries of Virginia (PIVA); PRINTING United Alliance

Heidelberg Graphics
2 Stansbury Ct, Chico, CA 95928
SAN: 211-5654
Tel: 530-342-6582 *Fax:* 530-342-6582
E-mail: heidelberggraphics@gmail.com; service@heidelberggraphics.com
Web Site: www.heidelberggraphics.com
Key Personnel
Owner & Pres: Larry S Jackson
Founded: 1972

Heidelberg USA Inc
Division of Heidelberg Druckmaschinen AG
1000 Gutenberg Dr, Kennesaw, GA 30144
Tel: 770-419-6500 *Toll Free Tel:* 800-437-7388
E-mail: info@heidelberg.com
Web Site: www.heidelberg.com/us
Key Personnel
Pres: Felix Mueller

Heraeus Noblelight America LLC
910 Clopper Rd, Gaithersburg, MD 20878-1361
Tel: 301-527-2660 *Toll Free Tel:* 888-276-8600
  Fax: 301-527-2661
E-mail: info.hna.uvp@heraeus.com
Web Site: www.heraeus-noblelight.com/uvamericas
Key Personnel
Pres: P K Swain
Dir, Sales: Kevin Joesel
Mktg Communs Mgr: Gina Gonzalez
Founded: 1971

HID Ultraviolet LLC
520 Lafayette Rd, Sparta, NJ 07871
Tel: 973-383-8535 *Fax:* 973-383-1606
E-mail: sales@hid.com
Web Site: www.hid.com
Founded: 1981

Holo Image Technology Inc
101 William Leigh Dr, Tullytown, PA 19007
Tel: 215-946-2190 *Fax:* 215-946-2129
E-mail: info@holoimagetechnology.com
Web Site: www.holoimagetechnology.com
Key Personnel
Pres: Tom Chiang
Founded: 1992
Membership(s): SPIE, The international society for optics and photonics

The P A Hutchison Co
400 Penn Ave, Mayfield, PA 18433
SAN: 991-5559
Tel: 570-876-4560 *Toll Free Tel:* 800-USA-PRNT (872-7768) *Fax:* 570-876-4561
E-mail: sales@pahutch.com
Web Site: www.pahutch.com
Key Personnel
Pres & CEO: Chris Hutchison
Dir, Sales & Admin: Erin Jones
Founded: 1911

I-Web
175 Bodwell St, Avon, MA 02322

MANUFACTURING

Tel: 508-580-5809 *Fax:* 508-580-5632
E-mail: info@iwebus.com
Web Site: iwebus.com
Key Personnel
Owner: Robert Williams *E-mail:* bwilliams@iwebus.com

Imago
110 W 40 St, New York, NY 10018
Tel: 212-921-4411 *Fax:* 212-921-8226
E-mail: sales@imagousa.com
Web Site: www.imagousa.com
Key Personnel
Pres & CEO: Howard Musk *E-mail:* howardm@imagogroup.com
Founded: 1985
Branch Office(s)
Imago West Coast, 23412 Moulton Pkwy, Suite 250, Laguna Hills, CA 92653 (sales), Contact: Tammy Simms *Tel:* 949-367-1635 *Fax:* 949-367-1639
Imago Australia, 10 Help St, Suite 27, Level 6, Chatswood, NSW 2067, Australia (sales) *Tel:* (04) 3753 3351 (cell); (04) 4806 8704 (cell) *E-mail:* sales@imagaoaus.com
Imago Brazil, Domiciano Rossi, 340 unid 154, 09726-121 Sao Bernardo do Campo, Brazil (sales) *Tel:* (011) 2306 8546; (011) 2306 8547 *E-mail:* imagobra@gmail.com
Imago Shenzhen, Rm 2511-2512, Block A, United Plaza No 5022, Bin He Rd, Fu Tian Centre District, Shenzhen 518033, China (prodn), Contact: Kendrick Cheung *Tel:* (0755) 8304 8899 *Fax:* (0755) 8251 4073 *E-mail:* enquiries@imago.com.hk
Imago France, 23 rue Lavoisier, 75008 Paris, France (sales) *Tel:* 01 45 26 47 74 *Fax:* 01 78 94 14 44 *E-mail:* sales@imagogroup.com
Imago Services (HK) Ltd, Unit B309, 1/F, New East Sun Industrial Bldg, 18 Shing Yip St, Kwun Tong, Hong Kong (prodn), Contact: Kendrick Cheung *Tel:* 2811 3316 *E-mail:* enquiries@imago.com.hk
Imago Productions (Malaysia) Pte Ltd, No 43, Taman Emas, Jl Utama 31, Telok Panglima Garang, 42500 Kuala Langot, Selangor, Malaysia (prodn, incorporating South Africa sales) *Tel:* (017) 4288771 (cell) *E-mail:* enquiries@imago.com.sg
Imago Publishing, Albury Ct, Albury Thame, Oxon OX9 2LP, United Kingdom (sales), Dir: Simon Rosenheim *Tel:* (01844) 337000 *Fax:* (01844) 339935 *E-mail:* sales@imago.co.uk *Web Site:* imagogroup.com

International Press Publication Inc
Spadina Rd, Richmond Hill, ON L4B 3C5, Canada
Tel: 905-883-0343
E-mail: sales@ippbooks.com
Web Site: www.ippbooks.com; www.facebook.com/ippbooks; x.com/ippbooks2
Key Personnel
Pres: Bali Sethi
Founded: 1976
Membership(s): The American Library Association (ALA); Children's Literature Association (ChLA); Ontario Library Association

Ironmark
9040 Junction Dr, Annapolis Junction, MD 20701
Toll Free Tel: 888-775-3737
E-mail: marketing@ironmarkusa.com
Web Site: ironmarkusa.com
Key Personnel
CEO: Scott Hargest *E-mail:* scott@ironmarkusa.com; Jeff Ostenso *E-mail:* jeff@ironmarkusa.com
Pres: Matt Marzullo *E-mail:* mmarzullo@ironmarkusa.com
SVP, Sales: Scott Kravitz *E-mail:* skravitz@ironmarkusa.com
VP, Opers: Chris Marzullo *E-mail:* cmarzullo@ironmarkusa.com
Sr Sales Exec: Larry Davis *E-mail:* ldavis@ironmarkusa.com
Founded: 1955

Koenig & Bauer (US) Inc
Member of KBA (Koenig & Bauer AG) Group
2555 Regent Blvd, Dallas, TX 75229
Mailing Address: PO Box 619006, Dallas, TX 75261
Tel: 469-532-8000 *Fax:* 469-532-8190
Web Site: us.koenig-bauer.com
Key Personnel
Pres & CEO: Mark Hischar *E-mail:* mark.hischar@koenig-bauer.com
SVP, Fin & CFO: Gerrit Zwergel *Tel:* 469-532-8050 *E-mail:* gerrit.zwergel@koenig-bauer.com
SVP, Mktg & Prod Mgmt: Eric Frank *Tel:* 469-532-8040 *E-mail:* eric.frank@koenig-bauer.com
SVP, Sheetfed Sales: Richard Dreshfield *Tel:* 469-532-8030 *E-mail:* richard.dreshfield@koenig-bauer.com
VP, Web & Specialty Press Div: Jeff Dietz *Tel:* 469-532-8029 *E-mail:* jeff.dietz@koenig-bauer.com
Branch Office(s)
Koenig & Bauer (CA) Inc, 181 Bay St, No 1800, Box 754, Toronto, ON M5J 2T9, Canada

Lake Book Manufacturing Inc
2085 N Cornell Ave, Melrose Park, IL 60160
Tel: 708-345-7000
E-mail: info@lakebook.com
Web Site: www.lakebook.com
Key Personnel
Pres & COO: Dan Genovese
VP, Fin & CFO: Bob Flatow
VP & Gen Mgr: Bill Richards
VP, Mfg: Steve Quagliato
VP, Opers: Bill Flavin
VP, Sales & Mktg: Nick Vergoth
VP, Technol: Paul Genovese

Lassco-Wizer Equipment & Supplies
Division of Woerner Industries
485 Hague St, Rochester, NY 14606-1296
Tel: 585-436-1934 *Toll Free Tel:* 800-854-6595 *Fax:* 585-464-8665
E-mail: info@lasscowizer.com; sales@lasscowizer.com
Web Site: www.lasscowizer.com
Key Personnel
Busn Mgr: Jennifer Weinschreider

MacDermid Graphics Solutions LLC
Division of Element Solutions
5210 Phillip Lee Dr, Atlanta, GA 30336
Tel: 404-696-4565 *Toll Free Tel:* 800-348-7201
E-mail: mpsproductinfo@macdermid.com
Web Site: graphics.macdermid.com
Key Personnel
Pres & COO: Scot Benson

Magna Visual Inc
28271 Cedar Park Blvd, Perrysburg, OH 43551
Tel: 314-843-9000 *Toll Free Tel:* 800-843-3399 *Fax:* 314-843-0000
E-mail: magna@magnavisual.com; mvsales@magnavisual.com
Web Site: www.magnavisual.com
Key Personnel
Co-Pres: Joseph L Young
Branch Office(s)
9400 Watson Rd, St Louis, MO 63126-1596

MAGPOWR®, see Maxcess International

manroland Goss web systems Americas LLC
121 Technology Dr, Durham, NH 03824

MANUFACTURING SERVICES & EQUIPMENT

Tel: 603-749-6600 *Toll Free Tel:* 800-323-1200 (parts & serv) *Fax:* 603-750-6860
E-mail: info@manrolandgoss.com
Web Site: www.manrolandgoss.com
Key Personnel
Mng Dir: Dave Soden
Branch Office(s)
Alois-Senefelder-Allee 1, 86153 Augsburg, Germany (world headquarters) *Tel:* (0821) 424-0 *Fax:* (0821) 424-33 03

Manroland Inc
Subsidiary of Manroland Sheetfed GmbH
800 E Oak Hill Dr, Westmont, IL 60559
Tel: 630-920-2000
E-mail: info.us@manrolandsheetfed.com
Web Site: manrolandsheetfed.com
Key Personnel
CEO: Sean Springett

Maple Press
480 Willow Springs Lane, York, PA 17406
Mailing Address: PO Box 2695, York, PA 17405-2695
Tel: 717-764-5911 *Toll Free Tel:* 800-999-5911 *Fax:* 717-764-4702
E-mail: sales@maplepress.com
Web Site: www.maplepress.com
Key Personnel
Pres: James S Wisotzkey
VP, Opers: Chris Benyovszky
VP, Sales: Bob Bethune
VP, Sales & Mktg: Andrew J Van Sprang *E-mail:* vansprang@maplepress.com
Founded: 1901
Branch Office(s)
92 Rockvale Rd, Tewksbury, MA 01876, VP, Sales: Bob Bethune *Tel:* 978-585-0900 *Fax:* 978-858-0920 *E-mail:* bethune@maplepress.com
Membership(s): Book Industry Study Group (BISG); Book Manufacturers' Institute (BMI)

Markwith Tool Co Inc
5261 State Rte 49 S, Greenville, OH 45331
Tel: 937-548-6808 *Fax:* 937-548-7051
Web Site: markwithtool.com
Key Personnel
Pres: Merlin Miller *E-mail:* merlin@markwithtool.com

Marrakech Express Inc
720 Wesley Ave, No 10, Tarpon Springs, FL 34689
Tel: 727-942-2218 *Toll Free Tel:* 800-940-6566 *Fax:* 727-937-4758
E-mail: print@marrak.com
Web Site: www.marrak.com
Key Personnel
CEO: Peter Henzell
Prodn Mgr: Steen Sigmund
Sales/Estimator: Shirley Copperman
Founded: 1976

Master Flo Technology Inc
154 Seale Rd, Wentworth, QC J8H 0G9, Canada
Tel: 450-533-0088 *Fax:* 450-533-4597
E-mail: info@mflo.com; sales@mflo.com
Web Site: www.mflo.com
Key Personnel
VP, Opers: Tim Duffy
Founded: 1984

Maxcess International
222 W Memorial Rd, Oklahoma City, OK 73114
Mailing Address: PO Box 26508, Oklahoma City, OK 73126
Tel: 405-755-1600 *Toll Free Tel:* 800-639-3433 *Fax:* 405-755-8425
E-mail: sales@maxcessintl.com
Web Site: www.maxcessintl.com

MANUFACTURING SERVICES & EQUIPMENT

Key Personnel
VP, Global Mktg & Devt: Sean Craig
Mktg Communs Mgr: Ben Bowlware
 E-mail: bbowlware@maxcessintl.com
Membership(s): Paper Industry Machine Association (PIMA); Technical Association of the Pulp & Paper Industry (TAPPI)

McClain Printing Co
212 Main St, Parsons, WV 26287-1033
Mailing Address: PO Box 403, Parsons, WV 26287-0403
Tel: 304-478-2881 *Toll Free Tel:* 800-654-7179
 Fax: 304-478-4658
E-mail: mcclain@mcclainprinting.com
Web Site: www.mcclainprinting.com
Key Personnel
Pres: Kenneth E Smith
VP, Publg: Michelle McKinnie
Founded: 1958

Miles 33 International LLC
Subsidiary of Miles 33 Ltd
40 Richards Ave, Norwalk, CT 06854
Tel: 203-838-2333 *Fax:* 203-838-4473
E-mail: info@miles33.com
Web Site: www.miles33.com
Key Personnel
VP, US Opers: Jeff Malik

Muller Martini Corp
456 Wheeler Rd, Hauppauge, NY 11788
Tel: 631-582-4343 *Toll Free Tel:* 888-268-5537
 Fax: 631-348-1961
E-mail: info@us.mullermartini.com
Web Site: www.mullermartiniusa.com
Key Personnel
Pres & CEO: Werner Naegeli *Tel:* 631-486-1351
Founded: 1946
Membership(s): Association for Print Technologies (APTech); Book Manufacturers' Institute (BMI)

Neenah Inc
3460 Preston Ridge Rd, Suite 600, Alpharetta, GA 30005
Toll Free Tel: 800-344-5287
E-mail: publishing.team@neenah.com
Web Site: www.neenahperformance.com/products/neenah-performance/publishing-products
Key Personnel
Dir, Sales & Mktg: Melanie Calkins
Branch Office(s)
5492 Bostwick St, Lowville, KY 13367
443B Shaker Rd, East Longmeadow, MA 01028
501 E Munising Ave, Munising, MI 49862
Bridge St, Brownville, NY 13615
45 N Fourth St, Quakertown, PA 18951
Membership(s): Book Manufacturers' Institute (BMI)

Nevada Publications
4135 Badger Circle, Reno, NV 89519
Tel: 775-747-0800
Web Site: nevadapublicationsonline.com
Key Personnel
Owner & Author: Stanley W Paher
 E-mail: swpaher@gmail.com
Founded: 1970

The Ohio Blow Pipe Co
446 E 131 St, Cleveland, OH 44108-1684
Tel: 216-681-7379 *Fax:* 216-681-7713
E-mail: sales@obpairsystems.com
Web Site: www.obpairsystems.com
Key Personnel
Pres & CEO: Edward G Fakeris
VP, Engg: Bill Roberts
Founded: 1932

On Demand Machinery
150 Broadway, Elizabeth, NJ 07206
Tel: 908-351-6906 *Fax:* 908-351-7156
E-mail: info@odmachinery.com
Web Site: www.odmachinery.com

O'Neil Digital Solutions LLC
12655 Beatrice St, Los Angeles, CA 90066
Tel: 310-448-6400
E-mail: sales@oneildata.com
Web Site: www.oneildata.com
Key Personnel
Pres & COO: Terry Chan
EVP, Sales & Mktg: Mark Rosson
Dir, HR: LaDonna Wise
Founded: 1973

Overseas Printing Corporation
Division of InnerWorkings Inc
4040 Civic Center Dr, Suite 200, San Rafael, CA 94903
Tel: 415-500-8331 *Fax:* 415-835-9899
Web Site: www.overseasprinting.com
Key Personnel
Sr Prodn Mgr: Shaun Garrett *E-mail:* sgarrett@inwk.com
Founded: 1972

The Ovid Bell Press Inc
Subsidiary of Walsworth Publishing Co
1201 Bluff St, Fulton, MO 65251
Mailing Address: PO Box 370, Fulton, MO 65251-0370
Tel: 573-642-2256 *Toll Free Tel:* 800-835-8919
E-mail: sales@ovidbell.com
Web Site: ovidbell.com
Key Personnel
CFO: Jill Custard *E-mail:* jillcustard@ovidbell.com
Pres: Troy Williams *Tel:* 573-310-2599
 E-mail: troywilliams@ovidbell.com
VP, Sales & Mktg: David O'Donley *Tel:* 573-310-2630 *E-mail:* david@ovidbell.com
Plant Mgr: Kevin Werdehausen *Tel:* 573-310-2598
 E-mail: kevin.werdehausen@ovidbell.com
Founded: 1927

Pantone Inc
Subsidiary of X-Rite Inc
590 Commerce Blvd, Carlstadt, NJ 07072-3098
Tel: 201-935-5500 *Toll Free Tel:* 888-800-9580
 Fax: 201-896-0242
E-mail: pantonesocial@pantone.com
Web Site: www.pantone.com
Key Personnel
Pres: Elley Cheng
Founded: 1963
Branch Office(s)
AXA Tower, Landmark East, 28th fl, 100 How Ming St, Suite 2801, Kwun Tong, Kowloon, Hong Kong *Fax:* 2885 8610 *Web Site:* www.pantone.com.hk
Pantone LLC, International House, Dover Place, Ashford, Kent TN23 1HU, United Kingdom *Tel:* (01233) 225450 *Web Site:* www.pantone.com.uk

Patterson Printing Co
1550 Territorial Rd, Benton Harbor, MI 49022
Tel: 269-925-2177
E-mail: sales@patterson-printing.com
Web Site: patterson-printing.com
Founded: 1956

PrairieView Press
625 Seventh St, Gretna, MB R0G 0V0, Canada
Mailing Address: PO Box 460, Gretna, MB R0G 0V0, Canada
Tel: 204-327-6543 *Toll Free Tel:* 800-477-7377
 Toll Free Fax: 866-480-0253
Web Site: prairieviewpress.com

Key Personnel
Owner & Pres: Chester Goossen
Founded: 1968

Printer's Repair Parts
2706 Edgington St, Franklin Park, IL 60131-3438
Tel: 847-288-9000 *Toll Free Tel:* 800-444-4338
 Fax: 847-288-9010
E-mail: prpsales@printersrepairparts.com
Web Site: www.printersrepairparts.com
Key Personnel
Sales Mgr: Ken Schelberger *Tel:* 847-228-9000 ext 1054 *E-mail:* ken@printersrepairparts.com

Printing Research Inc (PRI)
10760 Shady Trail, Suite 300, Dallas, TX 75220
Tel: 214-353-9000 *Toll Free Tel:* 800-627-5537 (US only) *Fax:* 214-357-5847
E-mail: info@superblue.net
Web Site: www.printingresearch.com; www.superblue.net
Key Personnel
Global Sales Dir: Phillip Jones *E-mail:* pjones@superblue.net
Founded: 1968

PrintWest
1111 Eighth Ave, Regina, SK S4R 1C9, Canada
Tel: 306-525-2304 *Toll Free Tel:* 800-236-6438
 Fax: 306-757-2439
E-mail: general@printwest.com
Web Site: www.printwest.com
Key Personnel
Pres & Dir, Opers: Corie Triffo
VP, Sales & Mktg: Ken Benson
Founded: 1992

Publishers Book Bindery (NY)
250 W 16 St, 4th fl, New York, NY 10011
Tel: 917-497-2950
Key Personnel
Pres: Ed Goldman
Founded: 1946

Publishers' Graphics LLC
131 Fremont St, Chicago, IL 60185
Tel: 630-221-1850
E-mail: contactpg@pubgraphics.com
Web Site: pubgraphics.com
Key Personnel
Pres: Nick A Lewis *E-mail:* nlewis@pubgraphics.com
VP: Kathleen Lewis *E-mail:* kmlewis@pubgraphics.com
Founded: 1996
Branch Office(s)
3777 Rider Trail S, St Louis, MO 63045
 Tel: 314-739-3777 *Fax:* 314-739-1436
Sales Office(s): Louisville, KY, VP, Sales: Cara Lahey *Tel:* 630-291-4867 *E-mail:* clahey@pubgraphics.com

Sakurai USA Inc
Subsidiary of Sakurai Graphic Systems Corp
1700 N Basswood Rd, Schaumburg, IL 60173
Tel: 847-490-9400 *Toll Free Tel:* 800-458-4720
 Fax: 847-490-4200
E-mail: inquiry@sakurai.com
Web Site: www.sakurai.com
Key Personnel
Pres: Ryuta Sakurai
VP: David Rose

Samuel Packaging Systems
4020 Gault Ave S, Fort Payne, AL 35967
Tel: 256-845-1928
Web Site: www.samuel.com

Santec Corp
84 Old Gate Lane, Milford, CT 06460
Tel: 203-878-1379 *Fax:* 203-876-0949
E-mail: info@santeccorp.com

MANUFACTURING

Web Site: www.santeccorp.com
Key Personnel
Pres: Laura M Lombardo
Opers Mgr: Vito Lombardo
Founded: 1983

Schaefer Machine Co Inc
200 Commercial Dr, Deep River, CT 06417
Tel: 860-526-4000 *Toll Free Tel:* 800-243-5143
 Fax: 860-526-4654
E-mail: schaefer@schaeferco.com
Web Site: www.schaeferco.com
Key Personnel
Pres: Robert Gammons

E C Schultz & Company Inc
333 Crossen Ave, Elk Grove Village, IL 60007-2001
Tel: 847-640-1190
E-mail: jobfiles@ecschultz.com
Web Site: www.ecschultz.com
Key Personnel
Pres: Michael Pautz
Founded: 1895
Membership(s): Foil & Specialty Effects Association (FSEA)

SCREEN Americas
Subsidiary of SCREEN Graphic & Precision Solutions
5110 Tollview Dr, Rolling Meadows, IL 60008-3715
Tel: 847-870-7400 *Toll Free Tel:* 800-372-7737
E-mail: info@screenamericas.com
Web Site: www.screenamericas.com
Key Personnel
Pres: Ken Ingram
Founded: 1967

Simco-Ion
Subsidiary of ITW Co
2257 N Penn Rd, Hatfield, PA 19440
Tel: 215-822-6401 *Toll Free Tel:* 800-203-3419
E-mail: customerservice@simco-ion.com
Web Site: www.simco-ion.com
Founded: 1936

SITMA USA Inc
Subsidiary of Sitma Machinery SpA
45 Empire Dr, St Paul, MN 55103-1856
Tel: 651-222-2324 *Fax:* 651-222-4652
E-mail: sales@sitma.com
Web Site: www.sitma.it
Key Personnel
Mng Dir: Kevin Curran
Founded: 1965

Southeastern Printing Co
3601 SE Dixie Hwy, Stuart, FL 34997
Tel: 772-287-2141 *Toll Free Tel:* 800-226-8221
 Fax: 772-288-3988
E-mail: sales@seprint.com
Web Site: www.seprint.com
Key Personnel
Pres: Don Mader
Founded: 1924
Branch Office(s)
950 SE Eighth St, Hialeah, FL 33010 *Tel:* 305-885-8707 *Fax:* 305-888-9903 *E-mail:* info@seprint.com
Sales Office(s): 6001 Park of Commerce Blvd, Suite 200, Boca Raton, FL 33487 *Tel:* 561-998-0870

Specialty Product Technologies (SPT)
2100 W Broad St, Elizabethtown, NC 28337
Tel: 910-862-2511 *Toll Free Tel:* 800-390-6405
 Fax: 910-879-5486 *Toll Free Fax:* 800-476-5463
E-mail: customer.service@sptech.com
Web Site: www.specialtyproducttechnologies.com

Key Personnel
Materials Mgr: Mike Warrick
Prod Mgr: Salvatore DeLuca
Founded: 1969

Spraymation Inc
Division of Spraymation Development Corp
4180 NW Tenth Ave, Fort Lauderdale, FL 33309
Tel: 954-484-9700 *Toll Free Tel:* 800-327-4985
 Fax: 954-301-0842
E-mail: orders@spraymation.com
Web Site: www.spraymation.com
Key Personnel
CEO: Grant Fitzwilliam
VP: Jim McMillen; Michael Moran
Founded: 1958

Spring Arbor Distributors Inc
Unit of Ingram Content Group LLC
One Ingram Blvd, La Vergne, TN 37086-1986
Toll Free Tel: 800-395-4340 *Toll Free Fax:* 800-876-0186
E-mail: customerservice@ingramcontent.com
Web Site: www.ingramcontent.com
Founded: 1978
Branch Office(s)
Indiana Distribution Center, 7315 Innovation Blvd, Fort Wayne, IN 46818-1371
Oregon Distribution Center, 201 Ingram Dr, Roseburg, OR 97471
Chambersburg Distribution Center, 1240 Ingram Dr, Chambersburg, PA 17202

Standard Finishing Systems
Division of Standard Duplicating Machines Corp
10 Connector Rd, Andover, MA 01810
Tel: 978-470-1920 *Toll Free Tel:* 877-404-4460
 Fax: 978-470-0819
E-mail: marketing@sdmc.com
Web Site: www.sdmc.com
Key Personnel
Dir, Mktg: Don Dubuque *E-mail:* don_dubuque@sdmc.com

Staplex® Electric Stapler Division
Division of The Staplex® Co Inc
777 Fifth Ave, Brooklyn, NY 11232-1626
Tel: 718-768-3333 *Toll Free Tel:* 800-221-0822
 Fax: 718-965-0750
E-mail: info@staplex.com
Web Site: www.staplex.com
Key Personnel
Sales Mgr: Doug Butler
Founded: 1949

Stoesser Register Systems
610 Whitetail Blvd, River Falls, WI 54022
Tel: 715-425-1900 *Toll Free Tel:* 888-407-4808
 Fax: 715-425-1901
E-mail: info@nela-usa.com
Web Site: www.nela-usa.com
Key Personnel
Inside Sales: Dave Kurz

Styled Packaging LLC
PO Box 30299, Philadelphia, PA 19103-8299
Tel: 610-529-4122 *Fax:* 610-520-9662
Web Site: www.taylorbox.com
Key Personnel
Pres: William R Fenkel *E-mail:* jjibill@aol.com
Founded: 2003

Suspension Feeder
Division of Roessner Holdings Inc
631 E Washington St, St Henry, OH 45883
Tel: 419-763-1571 *Toll Free Tel:* 888-210-9654
Web Site: www.suspensionfeeder.com
Key Personnel
Owner & Pres: Jeff Roessner
Founded: 1969

MANUFACTURING SERVICES & EQUIPMENT

Taconic Wire
250 Totoket Rd, North Branford, CT 06471
Tel: 203-484-2863 *Toll Free Tel:* 800-253-1450
 Fax: 203-484-2865
E-mail: sales@taconicwire.com; taconicwiresales@gmail.com
Web Site: www.taconicwire.com
Key Personnel
Pres: Angela Watrous *E-mail:* angela@taconicwire.com
VP, Sales & Mktg: Anthony Candelora *E-mail:* anthony@taconicwire.com
Sales & Cust Serv: Michele Pollock *E-mail:* michele@taconicwire.com

Tecnau Inc
4 Suburban Park Dr, Billerica, MA 01821
Tel: 978-608-0500 *Fax:* 978-608-0558
E-mail: info.us@tecnau.com
Web Site: www.tecnau.com
Key Personnel
District Sales Mgr: Chris Markley *Tel:* 610-469-2008 *E-mail:* cmarkley@tecnau.com
Founded: 2011 (from acquisition of Lasermax Roll Systems by Tecnau)
Branch Office(s)
Tecnau NV, Stoofstr 39/a, 1785 Merchtem, Belgium *Tel:* (0524) 82 444 *E-mail:* info@tecnau.com
Tecnau Ltd, North Bldg, Rm 200, 223 XiKang Rd, Jing An District, Shanghai 200040, China *Tel:* (0159) 00710147 *Fax:* (0216) 2898662 *E-mail:* info.cn@tecnau.com
Tecnau SRL, Via Torino, 603, 10015 Ivrea TO, Italy *Tel:* (0125) 63 16 78 *Fax:* (0125) 23 90 35 *E-mail:* info.it@tecnau.com
Tecnau Pte Ltd, Block 829, Jurong West St 81, No 03-314, Singapore 640829, Singapore *Tel:* 6793 9478 *Fax:* 6793 9476 *E-mail:* info.sg@tecnau.com
Tecnau AB, Langgatan 21, 341 32 Ljungby, Sweden *Tel:* (0372) 256 00 *Fax:* (0372) 828 37 *E-mail:* info.se@tecnau.com

Tidland, see Maxcess International

Times Printing LLC
Division of Kappa Printing Management Associates LLC (KPMA)
100 Industrial Dr, Random Lake, WI 53075
Tel: 920-994-4396 *Toll Free Tel:* 800-236-4396 (sales)
E-mail: info@kappapma.com
Web Site: www.kappapma.com
Founded: 1918

Timsons Inc
385 Crossen Ave, Elk Grove Village, IL 60007
Tel: 847-884-8611 *Fax:* 847-884-8676
E-mail: sales@timsonsinc.com
Web Site: www.timsonsinc.com
Key Personnel
VP, Opers: Nancy Panzarella *E-mail:* nancyp@timsonsinc.com
Founded: 1896

Tobias Associates Inc
50 Industrial Dr, Ivyland, PA 18974
Mailing Address: PO Box 2699, Ivyland, PA 18974
Tel: 215-322-1500 *Toll Free Tel:* 800-877-3367
 Fax: 215-322-1504
E-mail: sales@tobiasinc.com
Web Site: www.densitometer.com
Key Personnel
Pres: Eric Tobias
Founded: 1959

Tompkins Printing Equipment Co
5050 N Rose St, Schiller Park, IL 60176
Tel: 847-671-5050 *Fax:* 847-671-5538

1283

MANUFACTURING SERVICES & EQUIPMENT

E-mail: sales@tompkins.com
Web Site: www.tompkins.com
Key Personnel
Pres: Steve Tompkins
VP: Bill Tompkins
Founded: 1932

Townsend Communications Inc
20 E Gregory Blvd, Kansas City, MO 64114
Tel: 816-361-0616
Web Site: www.townsendcommunications.com; www.townsendprint.com
Key Personnel
Pres: Guy Townsend, III
VP: Joe Chambers
Founded: 1964

Tukaiz LLC
2917 N Latoria Lane, Franklin Park, IL 60131
Tel: 847-455-1588; 847-288-4968 (sales)
 Toll Free Tel: 800-543-2674
E-mail: contacttukaiz@tukaiz.com
Web Site: www.tukaiz.com
Key Personnel
Founder & Mng Dir: Frank Defino, Sr
VP, Mng Dir & CFO: Christopher Calabra
VP & Mng Dir: Daniel Defino; Frank Defino, Jr
Founded: 1963

Valley Roller, see Maxcess International

Videojet Technologies Inc
Subsidiary of Danaher Corp
1500 N Mittel Blvd, Wood Dale, IL 60191-1073
Tel: 630-860-7300 *Toll Free Tel:* 800-843-3610
 Toll Free Fax: 800-582-1343
E-mail: info@videojet.com
Web Site: www.videojet.com
Key Personnel
Sr Mktg Communs Specialist: Theresa DiCanio
 E-mail: theresa.dicanio@videojet.com
Founded: 1980

Webcom Inc
Division of Marquis Book Printing Inc
3480 Pharmacy Ave, Toronto, ON M1W 2S7, Canada
Tel: 416-496-1000 *Toll Free Tel:* 800-665-9322
 Fax: 416-496-1537
E-mail: webcom@webcomlink.com
Web Site: www.webcomlink.com
Key Personnel
Pres & CEO: Mike Collinge
Dir of HR & Cust Serv: Rhonda Suurd
Dir of Sales: Marc Doucet
Founded: 1975
Sales Office(s): 65 Spring Valley Ave, River Edge, NJ 07661, Contact: Susan Ginch
 Tel: 201-262-4301 *Fax:* 201-262-6375
 E-mail: susan.ginch@webcomlink.com
Membership(s): Book Manufacturers' Institute (BMI); Canadian Book & Periodical Council; PRINTING United Alliance

Webcrafters Inc
2211 Fordem Ave, Madison, WI 53704
Tel: 608-244-3561 *Toll Free Tel:* 800-356-8200
 Fax: 608-244-5120
E-mail: info@webcrafters-inc.com
Web Site: www.webcrafters-inc.com
Key Personnel
CEO: Chris Kurtzman
VP, Div Dir: Brad Koch
Membership(s): Book Manufacturers' Institute (BMI)

Webex, see Maxcess International

Fred Weidner & Daughter Printers
99 Hudson St, 5th fl, New York, NY 10013
Tel: 646-706-5180
E-mail: info@fwdprinters.com
Web Site: www.fwdprinters.com
Key Personnel
Pres: Cynthia Weidner *E-mail:* cynthia@fwdprinters.com
Creative Dir: Carol Mittelsdorf *E-mail:* carol@fwdprinters.com
Founded: 1860

Western Printing Machinery Co (WPM)
9228 Ivanhoe St, Schiller Park, IL 60176
Tel: 847-678-1740 *Fax:* 847-678-6176
E-mail: info@wpm.com
Web Site: www.wpm.com
Key Personnel
Pres & CEO: Paul Kapolnek
CFO: Kelvin O'Meara
Dir, Cust Servs: Renee Reckamp *Tel:* 847-994-8622
Founded: 1933
Membership(s): International Association of Diecutting & Diemaking (IADD)

X-Rite Inc
Subsidiary of Danaher Corp
4300 44 St SE, Grand Rapids, MI 49512
Tel: 616-803-2100 *Toll Free Tel:* 800-248-9748; 888-800-9580 (sales)
E-mail: info@xrite.com
Web Site: www.xrite.com
Key Personnel
CFO: Jeff McKee
CTO: Dr Francis Lamy
Pres: Ondrej Kruk
Founded: 1958

Yurchak Printing Inc
920 Links Ave, Landisville, PA 17538
Tel: 717-399-0209
E-mail: ypi.info@yurchak.com
Web Site: www.yurchak.com
Key Personnel
Founder & CEO: John Yurchak, Jr
Pres: John W Yurchak
VP, Opers: Jason Yurchak
Dir, Busn Devt: Randy Boyer
Founded: 1998
Membership(s): International Printers' Network (IPN)

Sales & Distribution

Book Distributors & Sales Representatives

Featuring freelance book salespersons who represent publishers in various parts of the country as well as publishers' distributors that, in addition to representing groups of smaller publishers throughout the United States and Canada, may also provide marketing and sales services.

Abraham Associates Inc
5120-A Cedar Lake Rd, Minneapolis, MN 55416
Tel: 952-927-7920 *Toll Free Tel:* 800-701-2489
Fax: 952-927-8089
E-mail: info@abrahamassociatesinc.com
Web Site: www.abrahamassociatesinc.com
Key Personnel
Founder: Stu Abraham *E-mail:* stu@abrahamassociatesinc.com
Owner: John Mesjak *E-mail:* john@abrahamassociatesinc.com
Sales Rep: Emily Johnson *E-mail:* emily@abrahamassociatesinc.com; Sandra Law *E-mail:* sandra@abrahamassociatesinc.com; Alice Mesjak *E-mail:* alice@abrahamassociatesinc.com
Off Mgr: Ted Seykora *E-mail:* ted@abrahamassociatesinc.com
Founded: 1992
Trade sales representatives.
Territory: Midwestern States

ACC Distribution Ltd
Division of ACC Art Books
6 W 18 St, Suite 4B, New York, NY 10011
Tel: 212-645-1111 *Toll Free Tel:* 800-252-5231
Fax: 716-242-4911
E-mail: ussales@accpublishinggroup.com
Web Site: www.accpublishinggroup.com/us
Key Personnel
VP & Gen Mgr: John Brancati
 E-mail: jbrancati@accpublishinggroup.com
Press: Jennifer Burch *E-mail:* jburch@accpublishinggroup.com
Represents over 150 publishing houses with distribution worldwide. Focus on antiques & decorative art books. Foreign office in the UK.
Distributor for ACC Art Books; ACC Editions; ACR Edition; John Adamson; Adler Planetarium & Astronomy; America's Greatest Brands; Anniversary Books; Archetype Books; Arkivia Books SRL; Arnoldsche Art Publishers; Art of Power Publishing; Artis; Artist Book Foundation; Artmedia; ArtPostAsia; Artpower International Publishers; Ashmolean Museum Publications; AV Edition; Barn Elms; Bauer & Dean; Belmont Press/Fiske & Freeman; Beta Plus Publishing; Bierke Publishing; Books & Projects; Brown & Brown; Callaway; Callwey Verlag; Cannibal/Hannibal; Carlton Books Ltd; Centro Di; Editions Cercle d'Art; Chameleon Books; Circa Press; Editions du Chene; William G Congdon Foundation; Congedo Editore; DAAB Media; De Menil Gallery; Diane de Selliers; Debrett's; Delius Klasing Verlag; Richard Dennis Publications; Duval & Hamilton; Editemos; Ediciones El Viso; Ediciones El Viso America; Emons; Fawn's Leap Publications; Fine Arts Society/Atelier Books; Floating World Editions; M Shafik Gabr; Gallimard; Gambero Rosso; Garden Art Press; Editions Gourcuff Gradenigo; Grayson Publishing; Guido Tomassi Editore; Hasson Editorial; Hathi Chiti/Shunya Inc; Heel Verlag; Hudson Hills Press LLC; The Images Publishing Group; Jaico Publishing House; Jensen Fine Arts; Johan & Levi SRL; Urban Juergensen; KMW Studio; LACMA; Edition Lammerhuber; Lange Uhren; Lannoo Publishers; London Editions Turkey Ltd; Luster; Macklowe Gallery; Mandragora SRL; Mapin Publishing; The Marg Foundation; Luca Maroni; Marquand Books; Merrick & Day; David Messum; Monaco Books; Andrea Monfried Editions; MT Train; Museum of Arts & Design; Museum of Brands; National Galleries of Scotland; National Museums of Scotland; New Cavendish; Nicolai; Niyogi Books; Editions Norma; North Carolina Museum of Art; Officina Libraria SRL; Orchid Press; Franco Cosimo Panini Editore SpA; Papadakis Publisher; Pelluceo; Grupo Penin; Plurabelle; Pointed Leaf Press; Quart Architektur; Red Dot; Ridgewood Publishing LLC; River Books; Roads Publishing; Roli Books; Rovakada; Royal Pavilion Libraries & Museums; San Diego Museum of Art; Scala Arts Publishers Inc; Shannongrove Press; Sieveking; Smallwood + Stewart; Spacemaker Press; Stichting Kunstboek; teNeues Verlag; Tf Editores; Third Millenium Publishing/Profile Books; Trilce Ediciones; Two Red Roses Foundation; 24 ORE Cultura; Vadehra Art Gallery; Vendage Press; Grafiche Vianello/Vianello Libri; Visionary World; Wartski; Watchprint; Watermark Press; WBooks Publishers; Winterthur Museum; Wonderland

Actar D
440 Park Ave S, 17th fl, New York, NY 10016
Tel: 212-966-2207
E-mail: salesnewyork@actar-d.com
Web Site: www.actar.com
Key Personnel
Pres: Brian Brash *E-mail:* brian.brash@actar-d.com
Founded: 2006
Distributor of architecture & design books.
Distributor for Applied Research & Design (CN & US); Architectural Association (worldwide); DOM Publishers (CN & US); Evolo (worldwide); Goff Books (CN & US); ORO Editions (CN & US); Yale School of Architecture (worldwide)
Territory: worldwide exc Europe

Les Messageries ADP
Subsidiary of Quebecor Media Inc
2315, rue de la Province, Longueuil, QC J4G 1G4, Canada
Tel: 450-640-1234 (commercial); 450-640-1237 (sales) *Toll Free Tel:* 800-771-3022 (commercial); 866-874-1237 (sales) *Fax:* 450-640-1251 (commercial); 450-674-6237 (sales) *Toll Free Fax:* 800-603-0433 (commercial); 866-874-6237 (sales)
E-mail: adpcommandes@messageries-adp.com
Web Site: www.messageries-adp.com
Key Personnel
SVP: Lyne Robitaille
Commercial Dir: Ronald Blouin
Gen Mgr: Charles Cusson
Founded: 1967
Represents Adventure Press; Les Editions Alaska Inc; L'Alchimiste Editions; Alire; Alma Ma Terre; Alter Real; Des Ameriques; Archipel; Atma; Atramenta; Aupel; De la Bagnole; Berlicoco; Boomerang Editeur Jeunesse; Bravo!; Marcel Broquet Editeur; Calligram; Catalogue Lsuk; CEC Parasco; Centre quebecois de lutte aux dependances; Chouette; Editions Cinq-Cygne; Couer de Pomme; Coup de Pouce; Crackboom!; Editions de l'ecole de Guerre; L'Ecrivain de l'Est; Fonfon; Fontea; Les Editions Goelette; La Griffe; H Tag Editions; Les Editions de l'Hexagone; Les Editions de l'Homme; Houle; Les Editions Inst-Art; Maison Jacynthe; Les Editions JCL; Jeux Ludex; Jobboom; Le Jour; Les Editions du Journal; Klorofil; Kmag; Michel Lafon; Michel Lafon Poche; Editions LaLucia; Peter Lang Group; Linda Leith Editions; Libre Expression; Livresque Edit; Les Editions Logiques; Le Maitre-Routier; Mega Editions; Albin Michel Jeunesse; Albin Michel Litterature; Modus Vivendi; Un Monde Different; Option Sante Editions; Origo; Orinha Media; Otherlands Editions; Perro Editeur; Petit homme; Groupe Phaneuf; Pratico-Pratiques; Presses Aventure; Prive; Publistar; Les Editions Quebec-Livres; Editions Michel Quintin; Recrealire; Recto-Verso; Rouge; Editions Caroline Roy; Selection du Reader's Digest; Editions La Semaine; Solaris; Something Else; Soulieres Editeur; Stanke; Alexandre Stanke Editions; Editions Theatre des Varietes (TDV); Trapeze; Trecarre; Editions du Tresor cache; Typo; Utilis; Velo Quebec; VLB Editeur; Voyel; Wilson & Lafleur; Z'Ailees
Territory: Canada (French-speaking)

Aeon Books
Affiliate of Aeon Group
PO Box 396, Accord, NY 12404-0396
Tel: 845-658-3068
E-mail: aeongroup@msn.com
Web Site: www.aeongroup.com
Founded: 1975
Distributor of books by author Patrizia Norelli-Bachelet.
Territory: USA

AIMS International Books Inc
7709 Hamilton Ave, Cincinnati, OH 45231

BOOK DISTRIBUTORS & SALES REPRESENTATIVES

Tel: 513-521-5590 Fax: 513-521-5592
E-mail: info@aimsbooks.com
Web Site: www.aimsbooks.com
Key Personnel
Pres: Georgia W Crowell
Secy & Treas: David Crowell
Distributes books in Spanish & other foreign languages.
Represents Another Language Press
Territory: Canada, USA

AKJ Education
4702 Benson Ave, Halethorpe, MD 21227
Tel: 410-242-1602 Toll Free Tel: 800-922-6066 Fax: 410-242-6107 Toll Free Fax: 888-770-2338
E-mail: info@akjeducation.com
Web Site: www.akjeducation.com
Key Personnel
Owner & Pres: Tim Thompson
Founded: 1974
Children's book distributor specializing in infant–12th grade educational sales & literacy programs. Also services literacy programs like Reading is Fundamental, Reach Out & Read & others.
Territory: USA
Membership(s): Educational Book & Media Association (EBMA); Reading Recovery Council of North America

Amazon Advantage, see Fulfillment by Amazon (FBA)

Amazon Fulfillment Services, see Fulfillment by Amazon (FBA)

American International Distribution Corp (AIDC)
82 Winter Sport Lane, Williston, VT 05495
Mailing Address: PO Box 80, Williston, VT 05495-0080
Tel: 802-862-0095 Toll Free Tel: 800-678-2432 Fax: 802-864-7749
Web Site: www.aidcvt.com
Key Personnel
Pres & CEO: Marilyn McConnell
Dir, Opers: Michael Pelland
Founded: 1986
Comprehensive order processing, payment processing, pick, pack, ship & processing, collection services; inventory receipt, management & preparation services; comprehensive data management & reporting via e-mail & web; membership & association services, subscription services; lettershop services, web site hosting & development.
Distributor for Air Age Media; American Agora Foundation; Belvoir Media Group; Berrett-Koehler Publishers; Business Expert Press; Chooseco; Crown House Publishers; The Geological Society of London; Hardspring Publishing; Height of Land Pubications; International Monetary Fund; Jolly Learning Ltd; Kugler Publications; MCC Magazines; Metropolis Magazine; Momentum Press; More Press; Morgan & Claypool Publishers; National Geographic; Outside Magazine; People's Medical Publishing House; Reef to Rainforest Media; Rethinking Schools; SAP Press; Society of Biblical Literature; Source Interlink Media; String Letter Publishing; Teachers College Press; Trusted Media Brands; Vermont Department of Health; Wine Enthusiast Magazine; Zeig, Tucker & Theisen
Membership(s): Book Industry Study Group (BISG); Independent Publisher's Guild (IPG)

APG Sales & Distribution
1501 County Hospital Rd, Nashville, TN 37218
Tel: 615-254-2488 Toll Free Tel: 800-327-5113 Toll Free Fax: 800-510-3650
Web Site: www.apg-sales.com
Sales, consultation & distribution group that services the book, gift & decorative accessories market nationwide.
Distributor for Aslan Publishing; Concept Inc; Foundation House Publishing
Represents Aequus Institute; Aristata Publishing; Aslan Publishing; Borgata Books; BTS Publishing; Celebrity Books; Compendium Inc; Eager Minds Press; Everywhere Press; Forrason Press; Foulsham; David Icke Books; Inclusive Books; Knowledge Products; Legacy Publishing; Life Action Press; Ned's Head Productions; Peace Publishing; Pers Publishing; Prelude Press/Mary Books; Recovery Communications; Rock House Way; Simple Dream Publishing; SOS Publishing; Summerjoy Press; Zoetic Publishing; Zulu Publishing
Territory: USA

Arrow Publications Inc
5270 N Park Place NE, Suite 114, Cedar Rapids, IA 52402
Tel: 319-395-7833 Toll Free Tel: 877-363-6889 Fax: 319-395-7353
Web Site: www.frangipane.org; www.arrowbookstore.com
Key Personnel
Mgr: Daniel Hite E-mail: daniel@frangipane.org
Publish & distribute Christian books & teaching materials.

Ars Medica, see RAmEx Ars Medica Inc

Art Media Resources Inc
1965 W Pershing Rd, Chicago, IL 60605
Tel: 312-663-5351 Fax: 312-663-5177
E-mail: paragon@paragonbook.com
Web Site: www.artmediaresources.com
Key Personnel
Owner: Amy Lee
Publishers & distributors of Asian art books.

Athena Productions Inc
2204 S Ashford Ct, Nashville, TN 37214
Tel: 305-807-8607
E-mail: atheprod@aol.com
Key Personnel
Pres: Athena Millas Kaiman
EVP: Ken Kaiman
Founded: 1969
Sales representatives & consultants. Foreign rights agency.
Represents Book Publishing Co; New Leaf Distributing Co; Square One Publishers
Territory: USA, worldwide
Membership(s): Independent Book Publishers Association (IBPA)

Auromere Inc
Division of Integral Yoga
2621 W Hwy 12, Lodi, CA 95242
Toll Free Tel: 800-735-4691
E-mail: contact@auromere.com
Web Site: www.auromere.com
Book distributor, importer & exporter of spiritual & classical Indian texts. Specialize in Sri Aurobindo & the Mother, yoga, health literature & children's books from India.
Territory: Canada, USA

AzureGreen
16 Bell Rd, Middlefield, MA 01243
Mailing Address: PO Box 48, Middlefield, MA 01243-0048
Tel: 413-623-2155 Fax: 413-623-2156
E-mail: azuregreen@azuregreen.com
Web Site: www.azuregreen.net

SALES

Key Personnel
Owner: Adair Cafarella E-mail: adair@abyssdistribution.com
Founded: 1986
Distributors of specialty books & gifts for spiritual seekers. Leaders in providing titles on: magick, wicca, tarot, New Age, goddess studies, herbs, healing, shamanism, Celtic lore, western mystery traditions, occult, ancient Egypt, magical children's stories & related subjects. Suppliers of merchandise to New Age retail stores & mail-order companies.

Baha'i Distribution Service (BDS)
Division of Baha'i Publishing Trust
1233 Central St, Evanston, IL 60201
Tel: 847-853-7899 Toll Free Tel: 800-999-9019
E-mail: bds@usbnc.org
Web Site: www.bahaibookstore.com
Key Personnel
Gen Mgr: Nat Yogachandra
Founded: 1902
Distributor of literature on or related to the Baha'i Faith.
Distributor for Baha'i Books UK; Baha'i Distribution Services of Australia; Baha'i Publishing Trust of the United States
Represents Baha'i Distribution Services of Canada; Oneworld Publications; Palabra Publications; George Ronald Publishers
Territory: worldwide

Baker & Taylor LLC
2550 W Tyvola Rd, Suite 300, Charlotte, NC 28217
Tel: 704-998-3100 Toll Free Tel: 800-775-1800 (info servs) Fax: 704-998-3319
E-mail: btinfo@baker-taylor.com
Web Site: www.baker-taylor.com
Key Personnel
EVP & Gen Mgr: Amandeep Kochar
EVP, Opers: Gary Dayton
Founded: 1828
Aggregator & distributor of books, digital content & entertainment products. The company leverages its unsurpassed worldwide distribution network to deliver rich content in multiple formats, anytime & anywhere. Offers cutting-edge digital media services & innovative technology platforms to thousands of publishers & libraries. Baker & Taylor also offers industry-leading customized library services. Baker & Taylor is proud to power Blio (blioreader.com), a flexible engaging & revolutionary e-reading application.
Branch Office(s)
Commerce Service Center, 251 Mount Olive Church Rd, Dept R, Commerce, GA 30599
Tel: 706-335-5000 Toll Free Tel: 800-775-1200
Momence Service Center, 501 S Gladiolus St, Momence, IL 60954, VP, Opers/Gen Mgr: Terrell Osborne Tel: 815-802-2444 Toll Free Tel: 800-775-2300
Pittsburgh Service Center, 875 Greentree Rd, Suite 678, Pittsburgh, PA 15220 Tel: 412-787-8890 Toll Free Tel: 800-775-2600
Territory: worldwide
Membership(s): The American Library Association (ALA); Book Industry Study Group (BISG)

Baker & Taylor Publisher Services
30 Amberwood Pkwy, Ashland, OH 44805
Tel: 567-215-0030 Toll Free Tel: 888-814-0208
E-mail: info@btpubservices.com; orders@btpubservices.com
Web Site: www.btpubservices.com
Key Personnel
SVP, Sales & Client Servs: Mark Suchomel
SVP, Opers: Bob Gospodarek
Trade Sales Dir: Deanna Meyerhoff
Founded: 2017

Baker & Taylor Publisher Services can efficiently get your books to market. For print books, in-house & contracted field sales professionals call on major industry buyers & we can help you reach independent bookstores, libraries, mass merchandisers & special markets. For eBooks, connect with Amazon, Barnes & Noble, Apple, Kobo & Overdrive. Also offers warehousing, commercial & direct-to-consumer fulfillment & online account management.

Balogh International Inc
1911 N Duncan Rd, Champaign, IL 61822
Tel: 217-355-9331 *Fax:* 217-355-9413
E-mail: balogh@balogh.com
Web Site: www.balogh.com
Key Personnel
Pres: Scott Michael Balogh *E-mail:* scott@balogh.com
Booksellers & distributors of international publishers.

BCH Fulfillment & Distribution
33 Oakland Ave, Harrison, NY 10528
Tel: 914-835-0015 *Toll Free Tel:* 800-431-1579
 Fax: 914-835-0398
E-mail: bookch@aol.com
Web Site: www.bookch.com
Key Personnel
Pres: Diane Musto
Founded: 1934
Represent over 700 self-publishers. Approved vendor for Ingram, Baker & Taylor, Amazon & Barnes & Noble.
Membership(s): Independent Book Publishers Association (IBPA)

Beacon Audiobooks
Subsidiary of Beacon Publishing Group
132 W 31 St, New York, NY 10001
Toll Free Tel: 800-817-8480
E-mail: info@beaconaudiobooks.com
Web Site: www.beaconaudiobooks.com
Specialize in narration & distribution of audiobooks worldwide.

Bernan
Imprint of Rowman & Littlefield Publishing Group
4501 Forbes Blvd, Suite 200, Lanham, MD 20706
Mailing Address: PO Box 191, Blue Ridge Summit, PA 17214-0191
Tel: 717-794-3800 (cust serv & orders)
 Toll Free Tel: 800-462-6420 (cust serv & orders) *Fax:* 717-794-3803 *Toll Free Fax:* 800-338-4550
E-mail: customercare@rowman.com
Web Site: rowman.com/page/bernan
Key Personnel
Mktg Mgr: Veronica M Dove *Tel:* 301-459-2255 ext 5716 *Fax:* 301-459-0056 *E-mail:* vdove@rowman.com
Founded: 1952
Standing order & one-time order service for US government publications.
Represents Government Printing Office; Library of Congress; National Technical Information Service (NTIS)

Bilingual Educational Services Inc
2514 S Grand Ave, Los Angeles, CA 90007
SAN: 169-0388
Tel: 213-749-6213 *Toll Free Tel:* 800-448-6032
Key Personnel
Pres: Jeff Penichet
Textbooks, books, posters, study prints & AV programs for bilingual & multicultural education.

Book Vine for Children
3980 Albany St, Suite 7, McHenry, IL 60050-8397
Tel: 815-363-8880 *Toll Free Tel:* 800-772-4220
 Fax: 815-363-8883
E-mail: info@bookvine.com
Web Site: www.bookvine.com
Key Personnel
Owner & Pres: Isabel Baker
Founded: 1989
Distributor of children's books.

B Broughton Co Ltd
322 Consumers Rd, North York, ON M2J 1P8, Canada
Tel: 416-690-4777 *Toll Free Tel:* 800-268-4449
 Fax: 416-690-5357
E-mail: sales@bbroughton.com
Web Site: www.bbroughton.com
Key Personnel
Owner & Pres: Brian Broughton *E-mail:* brian@bbroughton.com
Founded: 1970
Religious education books, AV & trade.
Distributor for Hermitage Art; Ignatius Press; Liturgical Press; Malhame Publishing; Our Sunday Visitor; Regina Press; Saint Mary's Press
Represents Hermitage Art; Ignatius Press; Liturgical Press; Malhame Publishing; Our Sunday Visitor; Regina Press; Saint Mary's Press
Territory: Canada
Membership(s): National Church Goods Association (NCGA)

Brunswick Books
14 Afton Ave, Toronto, ON M6J 1R7, Canada
Tel: 416-703-3598 *Fax:* 416-703-6561
E-mail: info@brunswickbooks.ca; orders@brunswickbooks.ca
Web Site: brunswickbooks.ca
Key Personnel
Pres: Lindsay Sharpe *E-mail:* lindsay@brunswickbooks.ca
Off Mgr: Michael Jackel *E-mail:* michael@brunswickbooks.ca
Founded: 1978
Sales & distribution.
Distributor for Baylor University Press; Between the Lines; Catholic University of America Press; Daraja Press; Demeter Press; Duke University Press; Fernwood Publishing; Georgetown University Press; Inanna Publications; Johns Hopkins University Press; Maryland Historical Society; Monthly Review Press; New Star Books; New York University Press; Pluto Books; Roseway Publishing; University of Massachusetts Press; University Press of Kentucky
Territory: Canada

Calvary Distribution
3232 W MacArthur Blvd, Santa Ana, CA 92704
Tel: 714-545-6548 *Toll Free Tel:* 800-444-7664
 Fax: 714-641-8201
E-mail: info@calvaryd.org
Web Site: www.calvaryd.org
Key Personnel
Purch: Megan Yorimitsu *E-mail:* megany@calvaryd.org
Religious book distributor.

Canadian Manda Group
664 Annette St, Toronto, ON M6S 2C8, Canada
Tel: 416-516-0911 *Fax:* 416-516-0917
 Toll Free Fax: 888-563-8327 (CN only)
E-mail: general@mandagroup.com; info@mandagroup.com
Web Site: www.mandagroup.com
Key Personnel
Pres & Partner: Nick Smith *Tel:* 416-516-0911 ext 236 *E-mail:* nsmith@mandagroup.com
VP & Partner: Carey Low *Tel:* 416-516-0911 ext 237 *E-mail:* clow@mandagroup.com
Founded: 1977
Sales agency of books, stationery & gift products offering renowned international & local publishers to retailers, libraries & wholesalers.

CannonBertelli LLC, see Parson Weems' Publisher Services LLC

Cardinal Publishers Group
2402 N Shadeland Ave, Suite A, Indianapolis, IN 46219
Tel: 317-352-8200 *Toll Free Tel:* 800-296-0481 (cust serv) *Fax:* 317-352-8202
E-mail: customerservice@cardinalpub.com
Web Site: cardinalpub.com
Key Personnel
Opers: Adriane Doherty *E-mail:* adoherty@cardinalpub.com
Cust Serv: Barbara Carter
Sales & Mktg: Thomas Doherty
 E-mail: tdoherty@cardinalpub.com
Founded: 2000
Provides full service book distribution to publishers throughout North America & beyond.
Distributor for AFN; AGA Institute Press; Akashic Media Enterprises; American Golfer; AMI Publishers; Archimedes Printing Shoppe; Ada Ari; Axel & Ash Journals; Birdzilla; Blue River Press; Body & Breath Inc; Buttercup Publishing; C C Fine Tea Books; Cali's Books; Crew Press; Crista Corp; CS Publishing; DeBenedictis Books; Dynamic Press Books; Eat Sleep Race; Emerald Career Publishing; EMS Publishing; Executive Suite Press; Les Giblin; Gluten Free RN; Great Day Press; Halfcourt Press; Terry Hutchens Publications; Indiana Landmarks; Jamenair Publishing; Jazzy Vegetarian; L & L Pardey Publications; La Luz Press Inc; Little Pineapple Press; MicMac Margins; Micro Publishing Media Inc; Meyer & Meyer Sport; Momentum Media; Mountainside MD Press; National Parks Conservation Association; Naturally Healthy Desserts; Paradise Cay; Peanut Bake Shop; PeopleSpeak; Pfunomenal Stories; Pilgrim Book Services; Pure Carbon Publishing; Quixotic Travel Guides; Resume Place Inc; Rite Site Custom Career Services; Rubber Ducky Press; Gretchen Rubin Media; Salut Studio Lifestyle Publishing; SJJ Inc; Strategic Media Books; 26Letters; Van Ryder Games; YinSights (Vancouver, BC)

Casemate | academic
Affiliate of Oxbow Books (UK)
1950 Lawrence Rd, Havertown, PA 19083
Tel: 610-853-9131 *Fax:* 610-853-9146
E-mail: info@casemateacademic.com
Web Site: www.oxbowbooks.com/dbbc
Key Personnel
SVP, US Dist Servs, Casemate Group: Michaela Goff
Group VP, Busn Devt: Curtis Key
VP, Busn Devt: Simone Drinkwater
Cust Serv Rep: Jen Romano
Distribution of academic, scholarly & specialist literature.
Distributor for Akanthina; American Numismatic Society; American Research Center in Sofia; American School of Classical Studies at Athens (ASCSA); American School of Prehistoric Research; American Society of Papyrologists; Ancient Egypt Research Associates; Anglo-Saxon Books; Archaeolingua; Archaeopress; Armatura Press; ASTENE; Ekdotike Athenon; Australian Centre for Ancient Numismatic Studies; Australian Centre for Egyptology; Australian Theological Forum; Axioma; Azimuth Editions; Bannerstone Press; Barkhuis; Bellview; British Academy; British Institute at Ankara; British Institute for the Study of Iraq; British Insti-

BOOK DISTRIBUTORS & SALES REPRESENTATIVES

tute in Eastern Africa; British Institute of Persian Studies; British Museum Press; British School at Athens; British School at Rome; Brown University, Department of Egyptology & Ancient Western Asian Studies; Bryn Mawr Archaeological Monographs; Butrint Foundation; Francis Cairns Publications; Cambridge Archaeological Unit; Cambridge Philological Society; Canterbury Archaeological Trust; CB Edizioni; Celtic Studies Publications; Christianity & Culture; Citeaux; Concordia University; Cotswold Archaeology; Council for British Archaeology; Council for British Research in the Levant; Countryside Books; Librairie Cybele; Cyclamen Press; Czech Institute of Egyptology; Discussions in Egyptology; East Anglian Archaeology; Edinburgh University, Department of Archaeology; Egyptological Seminar of New York; Etruscan Foundation; Ezekiel; Fine Arts Department of Thailand; Footwork; Friends of Canterbury Cathedral; Gibb Memorial Trust; Golden House Publications; Grant & Cutler (Foyles); Griffith Institute, University of Oxford; Halgo; Highfield Press; Hirmer Verlag; Illuminata; INSTAP Academic Press; Institute for Philosophical Research; Institute of Classical Archaeology; International Centre for Albanian Archaeology; International Monographs in Prehistory; Joukowsky Institute for Archaeology & the Ancient World, Brown University; Journal of Juristic Papyrology; Milton Keynes Archaeological Reports; Khalili Collections; Logogram Publishing; London Association of Classical Teachers Occasional Research Series (LACTOR); Lutterworth Press; Maney Publishing; McDonald Institute for Archaeological Research; Medina Publishing; Medstroms Bokforlag; Midsea Books; Mistra Estate; Museum of Fine Arts, Boston; Museum of London Archaeology (MoLA); Northcote House Publishers; Northgate Publishers; Ocarina Books; On-Site Archaeology; Onassis Foundation; Orcadian; Oriental Institute of the University of Chicago; Oxbow Books; Oxford Archaeology; Oxford Centre for Maritime Archaeology; Oxford University School of Archaeology; Pallas Athene; Peartree Publishing; Pierides Foundation; Pindar Press; Edizioni Polistampa; Portcullis Publishing; Pre-Construct Archaeology; Princeton University Library; Pro Calima Foundation; Ravenhall Books; Regatta Press; Riksantikvarieabetet (National Heritage Board of Sweden); Mary Rose Trust; Royal Commission on the Ancient & Historic Monuments of Scotland; Andrzej Rozwadowski; Rutherford Press; St George's Chapel; St John's College, Oxford; San Diego Museum of Man; Scientia; Sidestone Press; Siduri Books; Societas Archaeologica Upsaliensis; Society for Libyan Studies; Society for the Promotion of Roman Studies; Society of Antiquaries of London; Spire Books; SSEA-Benben Publications; Stacey International; Statens Maritima Museer; Franz Steiner Verlag; Stobart Davies; Stone Age Institute Press; Summanus; University College Cork, Ireland; University of Iceland Press; University of Leiden; Viking Ship Museum, Roskilde; Wessex Archaeology; Wiltshire Archaeological & Natural History Society; Windgather Press; York University Department of Archaeology
Territory: North America

Casemate | IPM
Division of Casemate Group
1950 Lawrence Rd, Havertown, PA 19083
Tel: 610-853-9131 *Fax:* 610-853-9146
E-mail: casemate@casematepublishers.com
Web Site: www.casemateipm.com
Key Personnel
SVP, US Dist Servs, Casemate Group:
  Michaela Goff *E-mail:* michaela.goff@casematepublishers.com
Founded: 1995

Provides sales, marketing & distribution services for book publishers, in both the academic & trade fields.
Distributor for ABK Publications; After the Battle; AFV Modeller; Air World; Alcemi; Ian Allan; American Educational Research Association; Andrea Press; Anomie Publishing; Anomie Special Projects; Anvil; Arabian Publishing Ltd; Arden; Arena Sport; Artists Bookworks; At Bay Press; Atebol; Ayebia Clarke Publishing; Azimuth Editions; Baker Street Press; Banovallum; Barzipan Publishing; Bauernfeind Press; Bauhan Publishing; BC Books; Bellagio Press; Big Sky Publishing; Birlinn Ltd; Blackman Associates; Blackstaff Press; Blueprint; Booth-Clibborn Editions; Brandon; Brookline Books; CAA Cymru; Carnegie Publishing; Caroline Press; Casemate; Classic Publications; Classics Illustrated Comics; Claymore Press; Collins Books; Colourpoint; Columba Books; Compendium; Cornucopia Books/Caique Publishing; Countryside Books; Crecy Publishing Ltd; Currach Books; Dalrymple & Verdun; John Donald; Dragon Press; Dufour Editions; Editions Hemeria; Editions Technip; Edizioni Polistampa; Eken Press; Eland Publishing; Enodare Ltd; Even Keel; Fernhurst Books; Flight Recorder; Fonthill Media; Formac Publishing; Fox Run Publishing; Frontline Books; Gill Books; Global Collective Publishers; Gomer Press; Green Bean Books; Greenhill Books; Gremese International; Gresley; Grove Street Books; Grub Street Cookery; Grub Street Publishing; Gwasg Carreg Gwalch; Gwasg y Bwthyn; Heimdal; Helion & Co; Hidden Europe Publications; Hikoki; Histoire & Collections; Historic New England; History West Midlands; Ice Publishing; Imperial War Museum; International Polar Institute; Jantar Publishing; JDF & Associates; Kasva Press; Key Publishing; Kitchen Press; Leda; Liberties Press; The Liffey Press; LIT Verlag; Lorimer; Johnny Magory; Mainline & Maritime; McNidder & Grace Ltd; Medina Publishing; Mercat Press; Mercier Press; Messenger Publications; Midland Publishing; Mimesis International; MMPBooks; Monroe Publications; Mortons Media; Musette Publishing; New England Historic Genealogical Society; New Island Books; New Welsh Review; The New York City Police Foundation; 9crows Publishing; Northumbria University Press; Nostalgia Road; The O'Brien Press; Origin; Papillote Press; Pen & Sword; Penguin Random House South Africa; Piano Nobile; Pikku Publishing; Playroom Press; Polaris; Polygon; Poster to Poster Publishing; Potomac Books; Protea Boekhuis; Quacks Books; Peter E Randall Publisher; Real Reads; Remember When; Riebel-Roque; Rily; Rinaldi Studio Press; Rock Foundations Press; Sabrestorm Publishing; Salmon Poetry; Sandstone Press; Savas Beatie; Savas Publishing; Seaforth Publishing; Sickle Moon; Silphium Press; Silver Link; Simply Media; Colin Smythe Ltd; Southbound; Specialty Press; Spink Books; Taj Books International; Tattered Flag; Tempest; 30 Degrees South Publishers; George F Thompson Publishing; Urdd Gobaith Cymru; Vagabond Voices; Veritas Books; Wharncliffe; White Owl; Wordwell Books; WorldChangers Media; Y Lolfa; Your Story Wizard

Catamount Content LLC
240 Cummings Rd, Montpelier, VT 05602
Tel: 917-512-1962
E-mail: info@catamountinternational.com
Web Site: catamountinternational.com
Key Personnel
Owner & Pres: Ethan Atkin *E-mail:* ethan.atkin@catamountcontent.com

Principal: Carlos Haase *E-mail:* carlosh@catamountinternational.com
Founded: 1994
Academic publishers' representation agency in Latin America/Caribbean, including partnerships with POD printer/distributors & digital aggregators.
Represents Academic Network of Latin & the Caribbean on China; American Meteorological Society; American Psychiatric Association Publishing; Arizona Center for Medieval & Rennaisance Studies; Asia Ink; Autumn House Press; Bard Graduate Center; Baseball Prospectus; Bodleian Library; Brandeis University Press; Brigham Young University Press; Burleigh Dodds Science Publishing; CABI; Cambridge University Press; Campus Compact; Campus Verlag GmbH; Carnegie Mellon University Press; Casemate | academic; CavanKerry Press; Concordia University Press; Conservation International; CSIRO; CSLI Publications; CSREA Press; Dalton Watson Fine Books; F A Davis Publishing; De Gruyter; Diaphanes; Eburon Academic Publishers; The Field Museum of Natural History; The French National Museum of Natural History; Gingko Library; The Grolier Club; gta Verlag; HAU Books; Haus Publishing; Hirmer Publishers; Paul Holberton Press; Holmes & Meier Publishers; Honk Kong University Museum of Art Gallery; Hong Kong University Press; Intellect Publishers; Island Press; Iter Press; The Jamestown Foundation; Karolinum Press; Mildren Lane Kemper Art Museum; Koc University Press; Leiden University Press; Lexington Books; McMullen Museum; Missouri Botanical Gardens Press; Missouri Historical Society; Museum of Modern Art in Warsaw; Museum Tusculanum Press; Myers Education Press; National Resource Center for First Year Experience; Neubaer Collegium; New Academic Science; New Issues Poetry; Newberry Library; Nova Science Publishers; NUS Press; NYU Press; Oberlin College; Omnidawn Publishing; Oxbow Books; Park Books; Prickly Paradigm Press; Princeton University Press; Reaktion Books; The Renaissance Society; Lynne Riener Publishers; J Ross Publishing; Rowman & Littlefield; Royal Botanical Gardens; Royal Collection Trust; SAIC; Scheidegger & Spiess; Scion Publishing; Seagull Books; SMArt University of Chicago; SOBO; Solar Books; Springer Publishing; Swan Isle Press; Tenov Books; Terra Foundation for American Art; Thorogood Publishing; Trentham Books; 2Leaf Press; UCL IOE Press; UCL Press; Unicorn Publishing Group; University College of Dublin Press; University of British Columbia Press; The University of Chicago Library; The University of Chicago Press; University of Cincinnati Press; University of Florida Press; University of London Press; University of Scranton Press; University of Texas Press; University of Wales Press; Whitewalls Inc; World Health Organization; World Scientific Publishing

Chesapeake & Hudson Inc
27 Jacks Shop Rd, Rochelle, VA 22738
Tel: 301-834-7170 *Toll Free Tel:* 800-231-4469
E-mail: office@cheshud.com
Web Site: www.cheshudinc.com
Key Personnel
Pres: Janine Jensen *E-mail:* janine@cheshud.com
VP, Opers: Steve Straw *E-mail:* steve@cheshud.com
Dir, Opers: Robin Bell *E-mail:* robin@cheshud.com
Cust Serv Mgr: Angie Nicewarner
  E-mail: angie@cheshud.com
Museum Accts: Laura Compton *E-mail:* laura@cheshud.com

Sales Rep: Alia Maria Almeida *E-mail:* alia@cheshud.com; Keith Arsenault *E-mail:* keith@cheshud.com
Sales Rep, Natl Accts: Meg Moster
  E-mail: meg@cheshud.com
Sales Asst: Jennifer Hawkinberry
  E-mail: jennifer@cheshud.com; Dawn Roseberry *E-mail:* dawn@cheshud.com
Founded: 1992
Publishers representatives.
Territory: Mid-Atlantic States, New England

Chicago Distribution Center (CDC)
Division of University of Chicago Press
11030 S Langley Ave, Chicago, IL 60628
Tel: 773-702-7010 *Toll Free Fax:* 800-621-8476
Web Site: press.uchicago.edu/cdc
Key Personnel
Exec Dir & Gen Mgr: Joseph D'Onofrio
Dir, Client Servs & Busn Opers: Saleem Dhamee *Tel:* 773-702-7014 *E-mail:* sdhamee@press.uchicago.edu
Dir, Dist & Warehouse Opers: Mark Stewart *Tel:* 773-702-7024 *E-mail:* mstewart@press.uchicago.edu
Accts Receivable Mgr: Cynthia Bastion *Tel:* 773-702-7164 *E-mail:* cab9@press.uchicago.edu
BiblioVault Mgr: Kate Davey *Tel:* 773-834-4417 *E-mail:* kdavey@press.uchicago.edu
Cust Serv Mgr: Karen Hyzy *Tel:* 773-702-7109 *E-mail:* khyzy@press.uchicago.edu
Info Systems Mgr: Christopher Jones *Tel:* 773-702-7229 *E-mail:* cjones@press.uchicago.edu
Inventory Control Mgr: Dennis Kraus *Tel:* 773-834-3499 *E-mail:* kraus@uchicago.edu
Returns Mgr: Jenn Stone *Tel:* 773-834-3687 *E-mail:* jstone@press.uchicago.edu
Royalty & Rts Mgr: Cassie Wisniewski *Tel:* 773-702-7062 *E-mail:* cwisniewski@press.uchicago.edu
Warehouse Asst Supv: Tammy Paul *Tel:* 773-702-7081 *E-mail:* tpaul@press.uchicago.edu
Warehouse Off Mgr: Gail Szwet *Tel:* 773-702-7080 *E-mail:* gszwet@press.uchicago.edu
Founded: 1991
CDC began in 1966 as a distributor for University of Chicago Press & in 1991 began offering distribution services to other university presses. Today CDC handles distribution for more than 100 publishers.
Distributor for ACMRS Publications; Aksant-Royal Netherlands; American Institute of Musicology; The American Library Association (ALA); American Meteorological Society; AmP Publishers; Amsterdam University Press; Arizona Center for Medieval & Renaissance Studies (ACMRS) Press; Association of College & Research Libraries (ACRL); Autumn House Press; Bard Graduate Center; Bayeux Arts; Bodleian Library; Brandeis University Press; Brigham Young University; Campus Verlag GmbH; Carnegie Mellon University Press; Casel; Catholic University Press; CavanKerry Press; Central Conference of American Rabbis/CCAR Press; Columbia College Chicago; CSLI Publications; DaltonWatson; Dana Press; Dartmouth College Press; diaphanes; Eburon Academic Publishers; Editorial Edinumen; EPFL Press; French National Museum of Natural History; Front Forty Press; Fum d'Estampa Press Ltd; Gallaudet University Press; J Paul Getty Trust; Gingko Library; Grolier Club; GTA Verlag Publishers; Guerra Edizioni; HAU; Haus Publishing; Hirmer Verlag; Hong Kong University Press; Intellect Ltd; Historic England Publishing; ISI Books; Island Press; Karolinum/Charles University Prague; Koc University Publishing (KUP); Leiden University Press; McGill-Queen's University Press; Michigan Publishing Services; Michigan State University Press; Missouri History Museum Press; MMA in Warsaw; Museum Tusculanum; National Journal Group; New Issues Poetry & Prose; Northern Illinois University Press; Northwestern University Press; NUS Press Singapore; Oberlin College Press; Ohio State University Press; Ohio University Press; Omnidawn Publishing; Oregon State University Press; Park Books; Parkhurst Brothers Inc; Parmenides Publishing; Passionaries Press; Penultimate Press Inc; Pluto Press; Policy Press at the University of Bristol; Prickly Paradigm; Reaktion Books Ltd; Research Publishers LLC; Royal Botanic Gardens, Kew; Royal Collection Trust; Russel Sage Foundation; St Augustine's Press; Scheiddegger & Spiess; School of the Art Institute of Chicago; Scion Publishing Ltd; Seagull Books; Sidewalks Books Co; Signature Books; Solar Books; Southern Illinois University Press; Swan Isle Press; Swedenborg Foundation Press; Temple University Press; Templeton Foundation Press; Tenov Books; 2Leaf Press; Unicorn Press Ltd; University College Dublin Press; University of Alabama Press; University of Alaska Press; University of Arizona Press; University of Arkansas Press; University of British Columbia Press; University of Chicago Department of Medicine; University of Chicago Press; University of Exeter Press; University of Illinois Press; University of Iowa Press; University of Michigan Press; University of Minnesota Press; University of Missouri Press; University of Nevada Press; University of North Texas Press; University of Scranton Press; University of Tennessee Press; University of Texas Press; University of Utah Press; University of Wales Press; University of Wisconsin Press; University Press of Colorado; Utah State University Press; Vu Boekhandel/Uitgeverij; West Virginia University Press; Westholme Publishing; WhiteWalls Inc; Wisconsin Historical Society; Zed Books

Consortium Book Sales & Distribution, an Ingram brand
The Keg House, Suite 101, 34 13 Ave NE, Minneapolis, MN 55413-1007
SAN: 200-6049
Tel: 612-746-2600 *Toll Free Tel:* 866-400-5351 (cust serv, Jackson, TN)
E-mail: cbsdinfo@ingramcontent.com
Web Site: www.cbsd.com
Key Personnel
Pres: Julie Schaper
VP, Sales: Jim Nichols
Client Rel: Lindsay Eidel
Natl Accts: Michael Croy; Elizabeth O'Bries; Jaime Starling
Founded: 1985
Provides full service distribution for independent publishers worldwide.
Distributor for Actar D; Agnes & Aubrey; AK Press; Albatros Media; AMMO Books LLC; And Other Stories; Anthology Editions; Arsenal Pulp Press; Artifice Press; Artvoices Books; Assembly Press; Association for Talent Development; Beehive Books; Behler Publications LLC; Bellevue Literary Press; Berbay Publishing; Biblioasis; Biteback Publishing Ltd; Bitmap Books Ltd; Bitter Lemon Press; Black Dog Press; Black Ocean; Blair; Bloodaxe Books; Blue Dot Kids Press; Blurring Books; BOA Editions Ltd; Marion Boyars Publishers Ltd; Braun Publishing AG; Breakaway Books; Bywater Books; CAEZIK; Carpet Bombing Culture; CarTech Inc (digital only); Cassava Republic Press; Catalyst Press; Central Recovery Press LLC; Charco Press; Chin Music Press Inc; Cicada Books; City Lights Publishers; CLASH Books; Coach House Books; Coffee House Press; Common Notions; Concord Theatricals; Conundrum Press; CONVOKE; Copper Canyon Press; Daylight Books; Deep Vellum Publishing; DENPA; Design Studio Press; DoppelHouse Press; Dottir Press; Paul Dry Books; Eighth Mountain Press; Etruscan Press; Eye of Newt; Feminist Press at CUNY; Fence Books; Feral House; Fitzcarraldo Editions; Floating World Comics; Floris Books; Gallic Books Ltd; Gentle Path Press; D Giles Ltd; Global Book Sales; Graphis; Green Card Voices; The Gryphon Press; h.f.ullmann publishing; Haymarket Books; Hazy Dell Press; Helvetiq; High Conflict Institute Press; Hoaki Books; Holy Cow! Press; Image Continuum Press; Immedium; Imperfect Publishing; Inhabit Education Books; Inhabit Media; Iron Circus Comics; J-Novel Club; Alice James Books; Kehrer Verlag; Kube Publishing Ltd; Lanternfish Press; Latticework Publishing Inc; Leapfrog Press; Learning Roots Ltd; Little Island Books; Lookout Books; Mandel Vilar Press; Manic D Press Inc; Warren Miller Co; Milo Books; Monkfish Book Publishing; National Association for the Education of Young Children; National Council of Teachers of English; Neem Tree Press; New Europe Books; New Internationalist; New Society Publishers; New Vessel Press; Nicolo Whimsey Press; Nightboat Books; 1984 Publishing; Nippan IPS; Not a Cult; NubeOcho; Open Letter; OR Books; Our World My Roots; Portage & Main Press; Process; Profile Books; Radius Books; Redleaf Press; River Horse Books; Rosarium Publishing; Sacred Bones Records; Salamander Street; Saqi Books; Saraband Ltd; Sarabande Books Inc; The School of Life; Secret Acres; Serpent's Tail; Simply Read Books; Six Foot Press; Skinner House Books; Small Beer Press; Stark Raving Group (digital only); Stone Bridge Press; Street Noise Books; Stripe Matter Inc; Talonbooks; Telegram Books; Tentai Books; Theatre Communications Group; Third Man Books; Third World Press; 3dtotal Publishing; Tiny Owl Publishing; Torrey House Press; Transit Books; Trigger Publishing; Trope Publishing Co; Turtle Point Press; Tyrant Books; Unbound; Uncivilized Books; Wave Books; White Pine Press; Wiener Schiller Productions Inc; Michael Wiese Productions; Willsow Ltd; Windhorse Publications; World Editions; Young Authors Publishing; Zephyr Press
Territory: worldwide
Membership(s): American Booksellers Association (ABA)

Continental Book Co Inc
7000 Broadway, Suite 102, Denver, CO 80221-2913
Tel: 303-289-1761 *Toll Free Fax:* 800-279-1764
E-mail: cbc@continentalbook.com
Web Site: www.continentalbook.com
Key Personnel
Dir: Linette Hayat *E-mail:* linette@continentalbook.com
Founded: 1961
Importers & distributors of language materials. Specialize in Spanish, French, German, Italian, Latin, Chinese, Arabic, Bilingual Spanish, Heritage Spanish, ELL, ESL, Common Core, English Novels, ASL, juvenile to advanced levels.
Territory: USA

Continental Sales Inc
213 W Main St, Barrington, IL 60010
Tel: 847-381-6530 *Fax:* 847-382-0385; 847-382-0419
Web Site: www.continentalsalesinc.com
Key Personnel
Pres: Ron Prazuch *E-mail:* prazur@wybel.com
Founded: 2001
Complete sales, marketing & distribution services for independent publishers. US coverage.
Represents Aveditions GmbH; Becker Joest Volk Verlag; Braun; Brunswick House; Callisto Publishing; Diamond Cutter; Editions Didier Millet; Hal Leonard; Links International; Mo-

mosa Publishing; New in Chess; Parker House; Pigna; Marco Polo; RSD Publishing; Regina Orthodox Press; Scientific Publishing; Seltmann & Sohne; Swedenborg Foundation; Templeton Foundation Press; Visual Profile Books; XPat Media/Scriptum
Membership(s): American Booksellers Association (ABA)

DAP, see Distributed Art Publishers Inc

Diamond Book Distributors (DBD)
Division of Geppi Family Enterprises
10150 York Rd, Hunt Valley, MD 21030
Tel: 443-318-8001; 443-318-8519 (cust serv)
E-mail: distribution@diamondbookdistributors.com; dbdreorders@diamondbookdistributors.com (orders); books@diamondbookdistributors.com (cust serv)
Web Site: diamondbookdistributors.com
Key Personnel
Pres: Tony Lutkus
VP, Sales & Busn Devt: Rich Johnson
VP, Publr Rel & Mktg: Emily Botica
Assoc Dir, Online Sales: Terry Helman
Mktg Mgr: Ashley Kronsberg
Sales Mgr: Stuart Carter; Devin Funches
Key Accts Mgr: Phil Gibson; Simon Byrne
Full service distribution to independent publishers of English-language graphic novels & manga, role playing games, prose novels & pop culture books & merchandise. Warehouse locations in Plattsburgh, NY; Olive Branch, MS; Runcorn, UK.
Distributor for A Wave Blue World; Ablaze; Abstract Studio; Action Lab; AdHouse Books; Aftershock; Alien Books; American Mythology; Apex Book Co; Asylum Press; Black Panel Press; Boom! Studios™; Curiosity Books™; Difference Engine; Digital Manga Publishing (DMP™); DSTLRY; Dynamite®; FairSquare Comics; Fantagraphics; 50 Amp Productions; Gemstone Publishing; Lev Gleason Publications Inc; Goodman Games; Graphic Mundi; Green Ronin Publishing; Gungnir; Hermes Press; Image; Kodansha; Lion Wing Publishing; Living the Line; Magma Comix; Magnetic Press; Manga Classics®; Net Comics; New Friday; Oni Press; Paizo®; Penguin Random House UK; Roll for Combat; Seismic Press; Soaring Penguin Press; Storm King Productions; TwoMorrows; Udon; Viz Media; Wizards of the Coast®; Yen Press™; Zenescope™; Zombie Love Studios

Diffusion Inter-Livres
Division of Ligue pour la Lecture de la Bible Inc
1701 Belleville, Lemoyne, QC J4P 3M2, Canada
Tel: 450-465-0037 *Toll Free Tel:* 866-465-5579
E-mail: interlivres@llbquebec.org
Web Site: www.inter-livres.ca
Key Personnel
Dir: Guillaume Duvieusart
Founded: 1982
Distribute religious books (French language).
Distributor for A Auderset; Editions du Cedre; De la Colline; Editions ELLB; Emmaus; Excelsis; Editions Exit; Famille Je t'aime; Farel; Editions Foi et Victoire; iCharacter; Editions Inspiration Publishings; Jeunesse en Mission; Ligue de Belgique; Ligue de Suisse; Editions Missionnaire Francophone; Editions Oladios; Parole de Vie; Editions Passiflores; Pretexte; Derek Prince Ministries France; Editions Raphael; Editions RDF; Editions sur Ses Traces
Territory: Canada, USA

Distribooks Inc
Subsidiary of MEP Inc
8154 N Ridgeway Ave, Skokie, IL 60076-2911
Tel: 847-676-1596 *Toll Free Fax:* 888-266-5713
E-mail: info@distribooks.com
Key Personnel
Pres: Nicolas Mengin
Dir, Mktg & Sales: Daniel Eastman
 E-mail: deastman@mep-inc.net
Sale of foreign language books to high schools, universities, bookstores, trade bookstores & libraries at trade discount. Branch office located in Boston, MA.
Represents Assimil; Book King International; ELI
Territory: USA

Distributed Art Publishers Inc
75 Broad St, Suite 630, New York, NY 10004
Tel: 212-627-1999 *Toll Free Tel:* 800-338-2665 (cust serv) *Fax:* 212-627-9484
E-mail: orders@dapinc.com
Web Site: www.artbook.com
Key Personnel
Pres & Publr: Sharon Helgason Gallagher
 E-mail: sgallagher@dapinc.com
SVP & Dir, Mktg & Admin: Avery Lozada
 Tel: 212-627-1999 ext 209 *E-mail:* alozada@dapinc.com
SVP & Sales Dir: Jane Brown *Tel:* 323-969-8985 *Fax:* 818-243-4676 *E-mail:* jbrown@dapinc.com
Dir, Opers: Carson Hall *Tel:* 212-627-1999 ext 206 *E-mail:* chall@dapinc.com
Dir, Publr Servs: Elizabeth Gaffin
 E-mail: elizabethg@dapinc.com
Key Accts & Spec Sales Mgr, NYC: Jamie Johnston *Tel:* 212-627-1999 ext 205
 E-mail: jjohnston@dapinc.com
Trade Sales Assoc: Clare Curry *E-mail:* ccurry@dapinc.com
Founded: 1990
Contemporary art, photography, design & aesthetic culture titles. Major international distributor of books, special editions & rare publications from major publishers, museums & cultural institutions.
Branch Office(s)
818 S Broadway, Suite 700, Los Angeles, CA 90014 (showroom, by appt only) *Tel:* 323-969-8958
Distributor for Actes Sud; T Adler Books; After 8 Books; Archive of Modern Conflict; Arquine; Edicions de Arrabal; Art / Books; Art Gallery of York University; Art Issues Press; Artspace Books; Aspen Art Museum; Atelier Editions; Atlas Press; August Editions; Badlands Unlimited; Baggu Corporation; Editions Xavier Barral; Benton Museum of Art at Pomona College; Blank Forms; BLUM Books; Bywater Bros Editions; Cabinet; Cahiers D'Art; Canada; Candela Books; Capricious Publishing; CARA; Carnegie Museum of Art; Carpenter Center for the Visual Arts; Center for Art, Design & Visual Culture, UMBC; Centre Pompidou; Circle Books; Edition Circle; Contemporary Art Museum, Houston; Contemporary Art Museum, St Louis; Cooper-Hewitt, Smithsonian Design Museum; Corraini Editions; Daba Press; Damiani; Dancing Foxes Press; DAP Publishing; Deitch Projects Archive; DelMonico Books; Delpire & Co; Deste Foundation for Contemporary Art; Dia Center for the Arts; Editions Dis Voir; The Drawing Center; Dumont; Dung Beetle; Dust to Digital; George Eastman House; Andrew Edlin Gallery; Derek Eller Gallery Inc; Design Museum; Dilecta; Eakins Press; Errant Bodies; Esopus; Exact Change; Exhibitions International; La Fabrica; Edition Patrick Frey; Fondation Cartier Pour L'Art Contemporain, Paris; Fondazione Prada; Forlaget Press; Four Corners Books; Fraenkel Gallery; FUEL; Fulgur Press; Fulton Ryder; Fundacion Juan March; Galerie Patrick Seguin; Glenstone Museum; Marian Goodman Gallery; Granary Books; Garth Greenan Gallery; Gray; Guggenheim; Hatje Cantz; Hauser & Wirth Publishers; Hayward Gallery Publishing; Heni Publishing; Hips Road/Tzadik; Holzwarth Publications; Hunters Point Press; ICA Philadelphia; Ice Plant; Image Text Ithaca Press; Independent Curators International (ICI); Inventory Press; Irish Museum of Modern Art; J&L Books; JBE Books; JRP|Editions; Judd Foundation; Kant; Kaph Books; Karma, New York; Kasmin; Kaya Press; Kerber Verlag; Kiito-San; Walther Koenig; David Kordansky Gallery; Kunsthaus Bregenz; Kunstinstituut Melly; Letterform Archive Books; Letter16 Press; Levy Gorvy Dayan; Lisson Gallery; Louisiana Museum of Modern Art; Ludion Publishers; Luma Arles; Magic Hour Press; MAMCO Geneva; Many Voices Press; Matthew Marks Gallery; Marquand Books; Marsilio Art; Marsilio Editori; MASP, Museu de Arte de Sao Paulo; MER Paper Kunsthalle; Metropolis Books; MFA Publications, Museum of Fine Arts, Boston; Nino Mier Gallery; Gregory R Miller & Co; Miller Institute for Contemporary Art at Carnegie Mellon University; Mirrorical Press; Mitchell-Innes & Nash; MoMA; MoMA PS1; Mousse Publishing; Lars Mueller Publishers; MW Editions; nai010 Publishers; National Gallery of Victoria; National Portrait Gallery; New Museum; Nieves; No More Rulers; Onomatopee; Osmos; Other Criteria Books; Pace Publishing; Pacific/Jeffrey Deitch; Parkett Publishers; Performa Publications; PictureBox; Pioneer Works; Poligrafa; Power Plant; Primary Information; Purple Martin Press; R & Company; Redstone Press; Reel Art Press; Regen Projects; Richter Verlag; Ridinghouse; RM; Roberts Projects; Thaddaeus Ropac; Royal Academy of Arts, London; Rubell Family Collection Contemporary Arts Foundation; Salon 94; Schaulager/Laurenz Foundation; Jordan Schnitzer Family Foundation; Set Margins'; Siglio; Silvana Editoriale; SITE Santa Fe; Skira; Soberscove Press; The Song Cave; Soul Jazz; Spector Books; Steidl; Bokfoerlaget Stolpe; Strandberg Publishing; Max Stroem; Swiss Institute Contemporary Art New York; TamTam Books; Testify Books; Thyssen-Bornemisza Museum; Torst; TPB Productions; Triple Canopy; Turner; Twin Palms Publishers; Ugly Duckling Presse; Um Yeah Arts; University Galleries of Illinois State University; University of California, Berkeley Art Museum and Pacific Rim Archive; Valiz; VFMK Verlag fuer Moderne Kunst; Violette Editions; Visionaire Publishing; Vitra Design; Wakefield Press; Walker Art Center; Andy Warhol Museum; Wasmuth; Weiss Publications; Wexner Center for the Arts; White Cube; Whitechapel Gallery; Wienand Verlag; Yerba Buena Center for the Arts
Territory: worldwide

Faherty & Associates Inc
Division of Left Coast Book Sales Inc
17548 Redfern Ave, Lake Oswego, OR 97035
Tel: 503-639-3113 *Fax:* 503-213-6168
E-mail: faherty@fahertybooks.com
Web Site: www.fahertybooks.com
Key Personnel
Owner, Opers: Ken Guerins *Tel:* 503-703-4597
 E-mail: ken@fahertybooks.com
Sales Coord & Online Accts: Shea Petty
 Tel: 503-597-2214 *E-mail:* shea@fahertybooks.com
Rep: Trevin Matlock *Tel:* 909-263-2346
 E-mail: trevin@fahertybooks.com; Richard McNeace *Tel:* 323-273-7763 *E-mail:* richard@fahertybooks.com; Joseph Tremblay *Tel:* 503-490-3141 *E-mail:* joe@fahertybooks.com
Commission based sales group.
Represents ACC Art Books; Actar D; Amber Lotus Publishing; APG Sales & Distribution; Applied Research + Design; Black Spring Press Group; Bloomsbury Academic; Book Art Bookmarks; Brilliance Publishing; Brunswick House Press; Carousel Calendars; Citation Me-

dia; Diamond Cutter Press; Discover Books LLC/Ciak Journals; DOM Publishers; Editions Didier Millet; Goldhawk International; Graphis; IRH Press; Island Press; Langenscheidt; Leuchtturm1917; Mack Books; Marco Polo Travel Publishing; McGraw-Hill Education; Momosa Publishing; National Book Network (NBN); New Harbinger Publications; New in Chess; ORO Editions; Paperblanks by Hartley & Marks; Phaidon Press; Punctum Books; Red Wheel/Weiser; Routledge (Taylor & Francis); RPD Publications; Rutgers University Press; Schiffer Publishing; Scientific Publishing; Sea Hill Press; Sellers Publishing; Semikolon; Sonicbond; Springer Nature; Stone Paper Notebooks; Tanooki Press; Templeton Foundation Press; teNeues Books & Stationery; TF Publishing; University of Texas Press; University Press of Kentucky; University Press of Mississippi; Visual Profile Books; XPat Media; Zoomikon
Territory: Alaska, Hawaii, 13 Western States
Membership(s): California Independent Booksellers Alliance (CALIBA); Mountains & Plains Booksellers Association (MPBA); Pacific Northwest Booksellers Association (PNBA); Southern California Children's Booksellers Association

Far Eastern Books
8889 Yonge St, Richmond Hill, ON L4C 0V3, Canada
SAN: 159-0227
Tel: 905-477-2900 Toll Free Tel: 800-291-8886
E-mail: books@febonline.com
Web Site: fareasternbooks.com
Key Personnel
Owner & Pres: Virender Malik
Founded: 1976
Distributor of books, periodicals & multimedia material in international languages including dual-language books, large print books, language learning material, dictionaries (adult & picture), DVDs, music CDs & talking books.
Represents Ferozsons; HarperCollins India; Ingram Yates; Magi; Mantra; Motilal Banarsidas Publishing House; Navbharat Sahitya Mandir; Penguin India; Scholastic India; R R Sheth & Co Pvt Ltd; Sterling; Tulika; Vani Publications
Territory: Australia, New Zealand, North America, South Africa

Fire Engineering Books & Videos
Clarion Events LLC, 110 S Hartford, Suite 220, Tulsa, OK 74120
Tel: 918-831-9421 Toll Free Tel: 800-752-9764
Fax: 918-831-9555
E-mail: info@fireengineeringbooks.com
Web Site: fireengineeringbooks.com
Key Personnel
Prodn Mgr: Tony Quinn
Publishes, produces & distributes training & instructional materials (books, videos, magazines, software) for firefighters.
Represents ASVP; Brady; Emergency Film Group; Idea Bank; IFSTA/Fire Protection Publications; ISFSI; Krieger; Macmillan; Mosby Yearbook
Territory: worldwide

Firefly Books Ltd
50 Staples Ave, Unit 1, Richmond Hill, ON L4B 0A7, Canada
Tel: 416-499-8412 Toll Free Tel: 800-387-6192 (CN); 800-387-5085 (US) Fax: 416-499-8313 Toll Free Fax: 800-450-0391 (CN); 800-565-6034 (US)
E-mail: service@fireflybooks.com
Web Site: www.fireflybooks.com
Key Personnel
Pres: Lionel Koffler
Dir, Foreign Rts, Licensing & Contracts: Parisa Michailidis Tel: 416-499-8412 ext 157
E-mail: parisa@fireflybooks.com
Founded: 1977
North American publisher & distributor of nonfiction adult & children's books.
Represents The Boston Mills Press; Cottage Life; Firefly Books; Fitzhenry & Whiteside Limited; Kiddy Chronicles Publishing; Mikaya Press; Robert Rose Inc
Territory: North America
Membership(s): American Booksellers Association (ABA); Association of Canadian Publishers (ACP)

Follett School Solutions Inc
Division of Francisco Partners
1340 Ridgeview Dr, McHenry, IL 60050
SAN: 169-1902
Tel: 815-759-1700 Toll Free Tel: 888-511-5114 (cust serv); 877-899-8550 (sales) Fax: 815-759-9831 Toll Free Fax: 800-852-5458
E-mail: info@follettlearning.com; customerservice@follett.com
Web Site: www.follettlearning.com; www.follett.com/prek12; www.titlewave.com
Key Personnel
CEO, Content: Britten Follett
CEO, Software: Paul Ilse
Sales Exec: Erica Moore
Suppliers of books (new & pre-owned), reference materials, digital resources, ebooks & AV materials to PreK-12 libraries, classrooms, learning centers & school districts.

Fotofolio
561 Broadway, New York, NY 10012
Tel: 212-226-0923 Toll Free Tel: 800-955-FOTO (955-3686)
E-mail: contact@fotofolio.com
Web Site: www.fotofolio.com
Key Personnel
Dir: Martin Bondell
Founded: 1975
Publishers & distributors of art & photographic postcards, note cards, boxed cards, holiday cards, posters, calendars, postcard books, books, art t-shirts & art coloring books, blank books & puzzles.
Represents Artkeeping (Spain); Artpost & Fotofolio; Bizarr (Germany); L M Kartenvertrieb (Germany); Point It (Germany); Polite (UK); Printed Matter (NY); Cheim Read Gallery; Reunion des Musees Nationoux (Nat'l Museums of France); Edition Toube (Germany)
Membership(s): American Booksellers Association (ABA); Museum Store Association (MSA)

Fujii Associates Inc
75 Sunny Hill Dr, Troy, MO 63379
Tel: 636-528-2546 Fax: 636-600-5153
Web Site: www.fujiiassociates.com
Key Personnel
Pres: Eric Heidemann
Mng Partner: Don Sturtz
Assoc: Jennifer Allen; Tom Bowen; Beth Chang; Mark Fleeman; Adrienne Franceschi; Andy Holcomb
Off Mgr: Kathy Bogs E-mail: kathybogs@fujiiassociates.com
Sales representatives.
Represents Abrams; Arte Publico Press; Baker & Taylor Publisher Services (select group of publrs); Brilliance Publishing; Capstone Press; Chico Bag; Chihuly Workshop; Childs Play; Chooseco; Familius; Flowerpot Press; Gardner; Gibbs Smith Publisher; Houghton Mifflin Harcourt; Interlink Publishing; Independent Publishers Group-Trade; Island Press; Jessica Kingsley Publishers; Kumon Publishing; Litographs; McGraw-Hill; Merrymakers Inc; Mountain Press; Mountaineers Books; Naval Institute Press; Octane; Peachtree Publishers; Scholastic/Grolier; Shelter Harbor Press; Sounds True; Sourcebooks; Sterling; TF Publishing; Tiger Tales; Time Home; UPG; US Games Systems; Workman; Zebra Publishing
Territory: Arkansas, Illinois, Indiana, Iowa, Kansas, Kentucky, Louisiana, Michigan, Minnesota, Missouri, Nebraska, North Dakota, Ohio, Oklahoma, South Dakota, Texas, Wisconsin

Fulfillment by Amazon (FBA)
Subsidiary of Amazon Services LLC
440 Terry Ave N, Seattle, WA 98109
Web Site: services.amazon.com; www.amazon.com/advantage
Founded: 2002
Amazon has the unique ability to match specialized, niche, or "hard-to-find" books with the customers most likely to purchase them & Amazon.com has a world-renowned reputation for service, reliability & security. Amazon.com Advantage is a consignment program that enables authors & publishers to list & sell their books on Amazon.com right alongside products that have massive marketing & distribution. The Advantage program provides a simple, efficient way to have a direct relationship with Amazon.com. The Advantage program includes listing your book in stock & ready to ship, the ability to control your detail page on Amazon.com, automatic reordering, sales & inventory reports, quick invoice-free payments, Search Inside the Book™ & hassle-free fulfillment to customers.
Territory: worldwide

Gaunt Inc
Gaunt Bldg, 3011 Gulf Dr, Holmes Beach, FL 34217
SAN: 202-9413
Tel: 941-778-5211 Toll Free Tel: 800-WGAUNT3 (942-8683) Fax: 941-778-5252
E-mail: info@gaunt.com
Web Site: www.gaunt.com
Founded: 1968
Law books: reprints, textbooks-college.

Gefen Books
Unit of Gefen Publishing House Ltd (Jerusalem, Israel)
c/o Storch, 255 Central Ave, B-206, Lawrence, NY 11559
Tel: 516-593-1234 Fax: 516-295-2739
E-mail: info@gefenpublishing.com
Web Site: www.gefenpublishing.com
Distributor & importer of Jewish books & Hebrew studies textbooks from Israel.

Genesis Marketing Group Inc
850 Wade Hampton Blvd, Bldg A, Suite 100, Greenville, SC 29609
Tel: 864-233-2651 Toll Free Tel: 800-627-2651 Toll Free Fax: 800-849-4363
E-mail: orders@genesislink.com
Web Site: www.genesislink.com
Key Personnel
CEO: Tim Morgan
Pres: David George Tel: 864-233-2651 ext 1605
Founded: 1970
Group of sales representatives to the Christian retail market.
Territory: worldwide

Girol Books Inc
PO Box 5473, LCD Merivale, Ottawa, ON K2C 3M1, Canada
Tel: 613-233-9044
E-mail: info@girol.com
Web Site: www.girol.com

BOOK DISTRIBUTORS & SALES REPRESENTATIVES

Key Personnel
Owner: Miguel Angel Giella; Peter Roster
Mgr: Leslie Roster *E-mail:* lroster@girol.com
Founded: 1975
Sales of books in Spanish & Portuguese from Spain, Portugal, Central & South America, plus North American books in Spanish.
Territory: worldwide

GoodMinds.com
Six Nations of the Grand River Territory, 188 Mohawk St, Brantford, ON N3S 2X2, Canada
Tel: 519-753-1185 *Toll Free Tel:* 877-862-8483 (CN & US) *Fax:* 519-751-3136
E-mail: helpme@goodminds.com
Web Site: www.goodminds.com
Key Personnel
Founder & Pres: Jeff Burnham
 E-mail: burnhamj@goodminds.com
Owner & Operator: Linda Burnham
Founded: 2000
Native American, Aboriginal, First Nations, Metis & Inuit books.
Territory: Canada, USA

Greenleaf Book Group LLC
PO Box 91869, Austin, TX 78709
Tel: 512-891-6100 *Fax:* 512-891-6150
E-mail: contact@greenleafbookgroup.com; orders@greenleafbookgroup.com; foreignrights@greenleafbookgroup.com; media@greenleafbookgroup.com
Web Site: greenleafbookgroup.com
Key Personnel
Founder: Clint Greenleaf
CEO: Tanya Hall
CFO: Brian Viktorin
COO: Carrie Jones
Dir, Consulting & Sales: Justin Branch
Founded: 1997
Publisher & distributor specializing in the development of independent authors & the growth of small presses. Our publishing model was designed to support independent authors & allow writers to retain the rights to their work & still compete with major publishing houses. We also distribute select titles from small & independent publishers to major trade outlets, including bookstores, libraries & airport retailers. We serve the small & independent publishing community by offering industry guidance, business development, production, distribution & marketing services.
Distributor for Thundersnow Publications; Western Classics
Membership(s): The American Library Association (ALA); The Association of Publishers for Special Sales (APSS); BookSense Publisher Partner; Independent Book Publishers Association (IBPA); National Speakers Association (NSA)

Greenleaf Book Group Press, see Greenleaf Book Group LLC

Hanser Publications LLC
Subsidiary of Carl Hanser Verlag GmbH & Co KG
c/o CFAS, 5667 Kyles Lane, Liberty Township, OH 45044
Toll Free Tel: 800-950-8977; 888-558-2632 (orders)
E-mail: info@hanserpublications.com
Web Site: www.hanserpublications.com
Premier source for plastics-related reference & educational materials in North America. Over 150 books written by industry experts are available.

HBG Productions/International Publishers Alliance
PO Box 5560, Chico, CA 95927-5560
Tel: 530-893-4699
Web Site: www.hbgproductions.com
Key Personnel
Exec Dir: Deanna Leah *E-mail:* deanna@hbgproductions.com
Founded: 1987
HBG Productions represents independent publishers & authors in the international marketplace. We specialize in hands-on representation of select books which are life-affirming & empowering. We bring your work to the attention of like-minded international publishers. In 2007 HBG Productions joined forces with International Publishers Alliance, founded in 1987 & they have been working together to represent creative works at book fairs & trade shows ever since. Our services include: author representation & coaching, foreign & translation rights negotiation, international trade show presentations, specializing in the Mind-Body-Spirit market.
Territory: worldwide
Membership(s): Book Publicists of Southern California (BPSC)

HFS
Division of Johns Hopkins University Press
2715 N Charles St, Baltimore, MD 21218
Mailing Address: PO Box 50370, Baltimore, MD 21211-4370
Tel: 410-516-6965 *Toll Free Tel:* 800-537-5487 (US & CN) *Fax:* 410-516-6998
E-mail: hfscustserv@jh.edu
Web Site: hfs.jhu.edu; www.hfsbooks.com
Key Personnel
Dir: Davida Breier *E-mail:* dgb@press.jhu.edu
Mgr: Terrence Melvin *E-mail:* tjm@press.jhu.edu
Founded: 1977
Order processing, collection management, warehousing & fulfillment for university presses & nonprofit institutions.
Distributor for The Catholic University of America Press; Central European University Press (CEU Press); Family Development Press; Georgetown University Press; Indiana University Press; Johns Hopkins University Press; Maryland Center for History & Culture; Maryland Historical Society; Modern Language Association of America (MLA); Mount Sinai Health System; Northeastern University Press; University of Alberta Press; University of South Carolina Press; University of Toronto Press; University of Washington Press; The University Press of Kentucky; UNO Press; Wayne State University Press; Wesleyan University Press

Hopkins Fulfillment Services, see HFS

Imprint Group
2070 Cherry St, Denver, CO 80207
Toll Free Tel: 800-738-3961 *Toll Free Fax:* 888-867-3869
Web Site: imprintgroupwest.com
Key Personnel
Group Co-Head: Derek Lawrence
 E-mail: derek@imprintgroupwest.com; Kurtis Lowe
Sales Rep: Suzi Hough; Kevin Peters; John Votaw
Founded: 1987
Commission sales group & publisher services.
Represents Adventure Publications; Angel City Press; Bower House; Brown Books; Candlewick; Cottage Door Press; EDC/Usborne/Kane Miller; John Fielder Publishing; Firefly Books; Kids Can Press; Microcosm Publishing; Midpoint Trade Books; Mountain Press; Norwood House Press; Peachtree Publishers; Peter Pauper Press; Scholastic Library Publishers; Sleeping Bear Press; Sourcebooks; Treasure Bay; Wiley
Territory: Alaska, Arizona, California, Colorado, Hawaii, Idaho, Montana, Nevada, New Mexico, Oregon, Utah, Washington, Wyoming
Membership(s): California Independent Booksellers Alliance (CALIBA); Mountains & Plains Independent Booksellers Association (MPIBA); National Association of Independent Publishers (NAIP); Pacific Northwest Booksellers Association (PNBA); Southern California Booksellers Association

Independent Publishers Group (IPG)
Division of Chicago Review Press
814 N Franklin St, Chicago, IL 60610
Tel: 312-337-0747 *Toll Free Tel:* 800-888-4741 (orders) *Fax:* 312-337-5985
E-mail: frontdesk@ipgbook.com; orders@ipgbook.com
Web Site: www.ipgbook.com
Key Personnel
Global CEO: Joe Matthews
Global CFO: Frank Autunnale
SVP, Intl Busn Devt: Brooke O'Donnell
VP & Dir, Natl Accts: Jeff Palicki *Tel:* 312-337-0747 ext 281
VP, Academic, Art & Prof Mkts: Paul Murphy
 Tel: 312-337-0747 ext 229
VP, Busn Devt: Alex Kampmann
VP, Busn Mgmt & Opers: Mark Noble
VP, Publr Devt, Publg & Licensing: Richard T Williams
VP, Sales: Tim McCall
Sr Dir, Mktg: Lauren Klouda
Dir, Academic, Lib & Educ Sales: Sharon Shell
Dir, Credit & Collections: Kristen Noon
Dir, HR: Alicia McCray
Dir, Opers: Amber McKown-Finken
Dir, Publicity: Candysse Miller
Dir, Spec Sales: Ilene Schreider
Sr Mgr, Supply Chain: Tashina Richardson
Accts Receivable Mgr: Walt Braley
Busn Devt Mgr: Sidney Thompson
Client Mgr, Fin Statements: Megan Trank
Cust Serv Mgr: David Gebhart
Data Mgr: Topher Bigelow
Digital Print Mgr: Qassye "Q" Inwood
Digital Servs Mgr: Casey Park
Lib & Educ Sales Mgr: Cynthia Murphy
Opers Mgr: Joshleigh Rowe-Richardson
Publr Devt Mgr: Anna Torres
Supply Chain Mgr: Betsy Rayas
Trade Sales Rep, Central: Travis Hale
Assoc Mktg Mgr: Chelsea Balesh; Stefani Szenda
Sr Digital Mktg Coord: Kara Brock
Sr Publr Devt Coord: Amy Everett
Digital Mktg Coord: Kenneth Duncan
HR Coord: Tatrianna Burnett
Sales Coord: Scott McWilliams; Jason Reasoner
Supply Chain Coord: Jacob Slater
Digital Servs Specialist: Emma Baietto
Sr Assoc, Digital Servs: Adam Barresse; Harlow Brightheart
Accts Payable Assoc: Mai Yang
Data Assoc: Huey Wells
Mktg Assoc: Serena Knudson; Bianca Rodriguez
Natl Accts, Sales Rep: Layne Ruda
Founded: 1971
Sales & distribution services for independent publishers.
Six distribution programs: IPG; Trafalgar Square Publishing; River North Editions; IPG Spanish Books; Art Stock Books; Small Press United.
Distributor for AA Publishing; Aalborg University Press; A&C Publishing; Aboriginal Studies Press; Academic Foundation; Academy & Finance; Academy of Nutrition & Dietics; Acapella Publishing; ACER Press; Addicus Books; African American Images; AH Comics Inc; AJR Publishing; Akiara Books; Alamo Press; Alazar Press; Alephactory Press; Alexandria Press; Ediciones Aljibe SL; All Clear Publishing; Allen & Unwin; ALM Media LLC; Editorial Alma; Ediciones Alpha Decay; Al-

terna; Amalion Publishing; Amazing People Worldwide; Amberley Publishing; American Academy of Pediatrics; American Cancer Society Inc; American Legacy Media; American Museum of Radio & Electricity; Ammonite Press; Analogue Media; Analytics Press; Angry Penguin Ltd; Annelidical Books; Annie's; Anqa Publishing; Arissa Media Group LLC; Arkin Publishing; Art on Dekz/Goodman; ASP-VUB Press; Aspen Books; Libros del Asteroide; A Thousand Words Press LLC; At Bay Press; Atelier Saint-Luc Press; Atelier26 Books; ATHLiTACOMiCS; Atlantic Books Ltd; Auckland University Press; AudKnits LLC; Aurora Publishers Inc; Austin Lamp Press; Autumn Hill Books; Awa Press; Ayurveda Holistic Center; Azure Moon Publishing; B Brothers Press; b small publishing; BackPage Books; Baha'i Publishing; Baker Street Press; Balance for Health Publishing; Balanced Living Press; Ball Publishing (BPU); Ball Publishing (CRP); Baraka Books; Ediciones Barataria; Barbican Press; Bay Otter Press; Bedazzled Ink Publishing; Bees Knees Books; Bella Figura Publications; Bella Musica Publishing; Belle Point Press; Belle Publishing LLC; Belly Song Press; Belt Publishing; Laurence Bennett; BennettKnepp Publishing; benton buckley books; Berbay Publishing; Berlinica; Bertz + Fischer Verlag; Bienville Ray LLC; Thom Bierdz Inc; Big Kid Science; BIICL; Birdsong Books; Birlinn Ltd; Black & White Publishing; Black Belt Communications; Black Heron Press; Black Lawrence Press; BlackBook Media Corp; Blackwater Press; Blackwell & Ruth Ltd; John Blake; Blink Publishing; Bloomin Books; Bloomsbury Professional; blue manatee press; Blume; BMG Books; Board & Bench Publishing; Bocconi University Press; Bonnier Publishing Australia; Bonnier Zaffre; Book Club Productions; Booklife; Bookmark Publishers; Bosco Publishing; Boutique of Quality Books; Bowhead Press; Bowman Sculpture; Boxing Clever Publishing; Boy's & Girl's Guide Books; The Brainstorm Co; Brand Nu Words; Bravebird Publishing; Breckling Press; Bright Ideas Publishing; British Library Publishing; Broken Shell Press; Brookside Press; Bucket Fillers; Budding Biologist; Bull City Press; Bull Publishing; Burnt Cheese Press; Butterfly Bliss Productions; By Architect Publications; Caboodle Books Ltd; Cadillac Press; Cadmos Verlag GmbH; Calithumpian Press; Campbell Hall Press; CAMRA Books; Cannonball Books; Canterbury University Press; La Caravane Publishing; Carcanet Press Ltd; Cardinal Rule Press; Cargo Publishing; Carlton Publishing Group; Carysfort Press Ltd; Editorial Casals; CAST Professional Publishing; Catbird Press; CBAY Books; CCC Publishing; Cedar Grove Publishing; Central Avenue Publishing; Chalk Hill Books; Change the Universe Press; Chase Sequence Co; Chawton House Press LLC; Chax Press; Cherry Red Books; Cherrytree Books; Chicago Children's Museum; Chicago International Poster Biennial Association; Chicago Review Press; Childhood Cancer Guides; ChiLiving Inc; Chirp Publishing; Cinco Tintas; Claeys & Casteels Publishing; Clarus Press Ltd; Co & Bear Productions UK Ltd; Code Babies Media; Cognella Press; Cohesion Press; Colorful Cities; Comma Press; Commonwealth Secretariat; Companion Press; Compass Publishing; Connell Publishing; Construction Trade Press; Contra; Conversation Arts Media; Ruth Beaumont Cook; Copenhagen Business School Press; Copernicus Center Press; Copper Ridge Press; Coralstone; Ediciones Corona Borealis; Corporativo V y T; Council Oak Books; Arthur Coyle Press; CPA911 Publishing; Craigmore Creations; Creative Noggin; Creotz; Critical Publishing; The Crossroad Publishing Co; Crown King Books; Crowood Press; CTO Editorial; Cupola Press;

Curtis Press; Cute Ediciones; Gus D'Angelo; de Monza; de Sitter Publications; Debrett's; Del Nuevo Extremo; Demeter Press; DesignerBooks; Deutscher Kunstverlag; Dhyanyoga Centers; Die Neue Sachlichkeit; Dike Publishers; Dine Out LLC; Diplomat Books; Discover Art; The Discovery Box; Disruption Books; Djoef Publishing; The Do-It-Yourself Florist Enterprises; do re mi Languages; dr.Herriot; Doodles Ave; Double Dove Press; Double-Barrelled Books; Draft2Digital; Drag City; Dragon Threads; Dragonfly Group; Dream Character Inc; Dreamspinner Press; DreamTitle Publishing; Duckbill Books; Dunedin Academic Press; Dunemere Books; e-artnow; Earnshaw Books; Edimat Libros; Educational Resources Ltd; Edward & Dee; Wm B Eerdmans Publishing Co; Egmont UK; Editorial Ekeka; Elder Signs Press; Elephant Rock Productions Inc; Eleven International Publishing; Elliott & Thompson; Elva Resa Publishing; Elysian Editions; Emmaus Academic; Enitharmon Press; Enterprise Publishing; Ess Ess Publications; Europa Law Publishing; evenSO Press LLC; Exile Editions; Experience Institute; Eye Books; EZChinesey.com; Fagbokforlaget; Fairyfaye Publications Ltd; Fanfare; Fantasmus; Fields Publishing; Fifth Star Press; Filbert Press; Adam Filippi; Filles Vertes Publishing; Finch Publishing; Fine Feather Press; Editorial Fineo; Firefly Press; Firehouse Publications; FireStarter Speaking & Consulting; Firewater Media Group; Fish Out of Water Books; Five Mile; 5m Publishing; Flashlight Press; Flora Publishing LLC; Fons Vitae; Footsteps Media; 45th Parallel Press; Four Courts Press; La Fragatina; Fragmenta Editorial; Free Association Books; Freight Books; Freizeit Publishers; Fremantle Press; Fresh Baby LLC; Fulcrum Publishing; Future House Publishing; Gainsborough House; Galt Publishing; Gao House Press; Garant Publishers; Garlic Press; Gateways Books & Tapes; Gathering Wave Press; The Gelofer Press; Gia Publications Inc; Gibson House Press; Gilgamesh Publishing; Gingerbread House; Glass Books Pty Ltd; Golden Pheasant Press; The Golden Sufi Center; Gomer Press Ltd; Good Luck Black Cat Books; GracePoint Publishing; Graffeg; Graffito Books; Granite Peak Publications; Grid Books; Griffin Publishers; Grimdark Magazine; Grip Press; G2 Entertainment; Gylendal Akademisk; Robert Hale; Hall & Stott Publishing Ltd; Handfinger Press; HarperCollins UK; Hart Publishing; Hawthorn Press; HCNY Press; Head of Zeus; Health Administration Press; Health Inspired Publishing; Heartstrings Press; Hesperus Press; Hide Stationery Ltd; High Rock Press; HighLine Editions; Lawrence Hill Books; Historical Society of Michigan; The History Press; Histria Books; Hodos Historia; Hogs Back Books; Holladay House; Holy Macro! Books; Holy Trinity Publications; Honeybee in the Garden; Honno Press; Hoover Institution Press; HopeRoad; House of Stratus; Huckleberry Sweet Pie Publishing Ltd; The Human Sciences Research Council; Hummingbird Press (worldwide exc Asia); Hunter Press; Huron Street Press; IAD Press; IFWG Publishing International; IHS Press; Ikeda Center for Peace Learning & Dialogue; Illumination Press; Image Comics; Imagine That UK; Michael Imhof Verlag; Editorial Impedimenta; Impossible Foods; InData Group Inc; Independent Institute; India Research Press; Indigo Press; Inhabit Media; Inner Coaching; Inscribe Digital Small Press United; INscribe UNassigned; Insight Press; Inspired Studios; Institute for Collaborative Communication; Institute of Art & Law; Institute of Economic Affairs; Interlude Press; International Courts Association; Intersentia; Into the Void; Intrigue Publishing LLC; Invisible Cities Press LLC; Irish Academic Press; Iskanchi Press; Islamic Texts So-

ciety; Istros Books; IWP Book Publishers; Jacana Media; Jam Graphics & Publishing; JB Max Publishing; Jora Books; Jordan Publishing Ltd; Just World Books; K F Enterprises; Editorial Kairos; KAMA Publishing; Karolinger Verlag; Keep It Simple Books; Kent Press; KettleDrummer Books; KiCam Projects; Kidsbooks; Knitbot; Kombi-Nation Sweden AB; Korero Books; Korero Press; KPO Creative LLC; Krittergitters; Kunati; Kuperard; Libros del Kultrum; Kyoto University Press; Laburnum Press; Lafayette Publishers; Lakeview Research; Lao Tse Press; Larkfield Publishing; Ediciones Larousse; Last Syllable Books; Ediciones Lea; Lectio Ediciones; Lectura Colaborativa; Leete's Island Books; Legend Times Group; La Librairie Parisienne; Libri Publishing; Liesl + Co; Life of Reiley; Light Beams Publishing; Linkgua; Lion Hudson; LIT Verlag; Little Hare; Little House Press; Little Island Books; Little Island Press; Little Lamb Books; Live Model Books LLC; Long Haul Press; Long Stride Books; Looking Glass Books Inc; Lost the Plot; Love the World Books; Lucky Bamboo Crafts; Lucky Sky Press; Lund Humphries; Machillock Publishing; MacIntyre Purcell Publishing; Madder; madebyfae; The Magenta Foundation; Mainstream Publishing; Maklu Publishers; Malpaso Editorial; Malt Shop Publishing; Malyszko Photography; Manitenahk Books; Manohar Books; Marion Street Press; Markelle Media; Marlor Press Inc; Marsh Hawk Press; Massey University Press; Mattamayura Press; Maverick Arts Publishing; Maximilian Verlag; Maximo Potencial; MC Press; Graham McDonald Stringed Instruments; Meg & Lucy Books; Melbourne University Press; Melbournestyle Books; Merlin Press; Robert G Merrick; Meteoor Books; Metro Publications; Micro Publishing Media; Middleway Press; Milet Publishing; Millfree Mursaps Media; Minted Prose LLC; Mira Vista Press; Missouri's Civil War Heritage Foundation; Ernest Mitchell Publishing; MMS Gold; modo Verlag; Momentum Press (Africa, Europe, Middle East & Oceania); Monash University Publishing; Monogatari Novels; Month9Books LLC; Moonlight Publishing; Moonstone Press LLC; Mortar & Press; Mo's Nose LLC; Mosaic Press; Motorcycle Misadventures; Mount Castle Co; Mountain Lake Press; Mountain Trail Press; Move Books; MR Publishing LLC; Museyon; Myrmidon Books; Mystic Productions Press; NADD; National Association of Home Builders; National Museum of Australia Press; Natural History Museum, London; NBM Publishing; NBS Publications; Nebulous Arts LLC; Nehora Press; Stephen L Nelson Inc; Neofelis Verlag; Netribution; Never Lose Heart LLC; New Century Publications; New Chapter Press; New India Publishing Agency (NIPA); New Island; New World Publishing; NewRoad Publishing; The Next Big Think; Next Step Test Preparation Publishing; Nite Owl Books; NNK Press; Noah Publications; Nordic Academic Press; Nordica Libros; Ediciones Norte; Northwestern Publishing House; Nostra Ediciones; Nourish Publishing; NSTA Kids; NTI Upstream; NW1 Books; Oak Grove Press; Oak Lane Press; Ediciones Obliciones Inc; Editorial Oceano de Mexico; Odyssey Books & Maps; Odyssey Publishing LLC; Old Bow Publishing; The Old Mill Press; Oldcastle Books Ltd; Edition Olms; Georg Olms Verlag AG; Michael O'Mara Books; Omnibus Press; On-Word Bound Books LLC; 121 Publications; Oni Press; Opal Publishing Co; Open Road Integrated Media; Orbit Media Studios Inc; Orenda Books; Otago University Press; Out of Your Mind...and Into the Marketplace™; Outlook Words & Art; Oval Books; Peter Owen Publishers; Oxford University Press (children's fiction); Ozone Zone Books; Paginas Libros de Magia; Paladin Communications; Palazzo

BOOK DISTRIBUTORS & SALES REPRESENTATIVES

Editions; Pallas Athene; Palm Island Press; Palmer/Pletsch Publishing; Palmyra Publishing; Pan Macmillan; Pandasaur Press; Pangolin London; Paper Books LLC; Paper Chase Farms Publishing Group; Paragon Garage Co Ltd; Parent Guide Books; Parenting Press; Pariyatti Publishing; Park Publishing Inc; Partera Press; Parthian Books Ltd; Pathfinder Equine Publications; Paths International Ltd; PatrickGeorge; Pavilion Books Group; Pavilion Publishing & Media; Editorial Pax Mexico; Peepal Tree Press Ltd; Pelican Book Group; Pendo Press; Penguin Books China; Penguin Books New Zealand; Penguin Random House Australia; Penguin UK; Penlight Publications; Penny Publishing; Editorial Periferica; Perronet Press; Personhood Press; The phazelFOZ Co (CN & US); Phoenix Yard Books; Pikku Publishing; Pimpernel Press Ltd; Pitch Publishing; Pitchstone Publishing; Plaid People Press; Plaintales Inc; The Plan Editions; Plaza y Valdes; PM Press; Poorhouse Publishing; Popular Kinetics Press; Portal Books; Posthuman Studios; Practical Psychology Press; Prakash Books India Pvt Ltd; Editorial Primapersona; Princeton Book Co; The Print Project; Prion; Prison Radio; Privateer Publications; Probitas Press; Project Management Institute; Psychodynamic Diagnostic Manual; PublikumArt; Pucci Books; Pucci Publishing; PuddleDancer Press; Pukka Publishing; Pumpkin House Ltd; Verlag Anton Pustet; The PuzzleWorks; Qi Works; Quarto Iberoamericana; Quiller Publishing; Quince & Co; Rabsel Editions; Racing Post Books; Marian Rae Publications; Ragged Bears; Rainbow Morning Music; Raincloud Press; Rakennustieto Publishing; Random House Australia Pty Ltd; Random House UK; Rawat Publications; RCR Creative Press; Reading Rainbow; ReadZone Books; Real African Publishers; Redbook Ediciones; RedDoor Publishing; Dietrich Reimer Verlag GmbH; Resonance House LLC; Reynolds Hearn (Cherry); RHINO Poetry; River Horse Press; Rivers Turn Press; ROCK International; Rockpool Publishing; Ediciones Rodeno; Rolling Homes Press; Ronsdale Press; Roof Books; Rosarium Publishing; Rosenberg Publishing; J Ross Publishing; Roundup Press; Rowhouse Publishing; Royal British Columbia Museum; Royal Collins Publishing Group; Royal Irish Academy; Ruka Press; Russell House Publishing Ltd; Sad Hill LLC; SAFE for Children Publishing; Saint Andrew's Press; St James's House; Salor Press; Salvia Press; Samfundslitteratur; Sandalwood Press; Sandorf Passage (North America & UK); Sandy Point Ink LLC; Santa Fe Writer's Project; Saraband; Scandinavia House Publishing; Schaffner Press; Schlebruegge Editor; Schnell und Steiner; Science Literacy Books; Scribble & Sons; Scribe Publications Pty Ltd; Scruffie Munster Media; Search Institute Press; Second Base Publishing; The Secret Mountain; Secret Passage Press; Sedro Publishing; See Sharp Press; Seemann Henschel; Self-Counsel Press; Selwa Press; Seren; Seven Gates Media; Shepheard-Walwyn Publishers; Sheldrake Press; Shinola; Shogam Publications; Siddha Yoga Publications; Signature Publishing Group; Silent 7 Publishing; Silk Web Publishing; Simax; Sinister Wisdom; Skeezel Press; Edition Skylight; Sladmore Gallery; The Sleepy Animals LLC; Slovart Publishing Ltd; Small Mountain Press; Smart Guide Publications Inc; Smoking Gun Publishing LLC; Society for Human Resource Management; Solana Press; Soluble LLC; Solum Forlag; Somogy Art Publishers; Soul Support; SourceAid LLC; Southeast Missouri State University Press; Souvenir Press; Spark Avenue; Specialty Press/ADD Warehouse; Spinifex Press; Spinning Wheel Press; Spiramus Press; Spy Publishing Ltd; Square Monkey Publishing; Staghorn Press; Starfish Bay Publishing; Dr Steven D Stark Podiatric Corp; Stone Skin Press; Stonemark Publishing; Strauss House Productions; Streamline Press; Suitcase Media International; Summersdale Publishers Ltd; SummitView Publishing Inc; Susaeta Ediciones SA; Sussex Academic Press; Symphony Space Inc; Tabula Books; Tamarisk Books LLC; Tango Books Ltd; Tantan Publishing; TCU Press (worldwide exc North America); Tell-A-Gram Publishing LLC; Temenos Press; Te Papa Press; Terrace Publishing; Thircuir; Thompson Mill Press; Thorntree Press; Three Pebble Press LLC; Thrums Books; Thule Ediciones; TI Inc Books; Tightrope Books; Tiller Publishing; Titiris; TJ Studios; TOKYOPOP GmbH; Top That Publishing US; Tortuga Press; Tot Toppers; Touche Publishing; Tracks Publishing; Tradart Institut; Trans Pacific Press; Transworld Publishers; Trellis Publishing; Triarchy Press Ltd; Tribeca View Press LLC; Trigger Publishing; Trine Day; Triplekite Publishing; Trism Books; Triumph Books; Troika Books; Tulip Books; Tumblehome Learning Inc; TuTu's Green World LLC; Tuva Publishing; Two Thousand Three Associates; UIT Cambridge Ltd; Umiya Publishing; Union Press; Universitas Press; Presses de l'Universite du Quebec; University of Hertfordshire Press; University of KwaZulu-Natal Press; University of New South Wales Press; University of Queensland Press; University Press of Southern Denmark; Upriver Press; Upstart Press; Urban Land Institute; Urbane Publications; Urim Publications; USNA Publishing Inc; USRSA; UWA Publishing; Vallentine Mitchell; Variant Press; Vegueta Ediciones; Vehicule Press; Velociteach; Vesuvian Media Group; Victoria University Press; Visual Steps Publishing; Wachholtz Verlag GmbH; Wacky Bee Books; Wake Forest University Press; Walnut Cracker Publishing LLC; Water Environment Federation; Weddle's LLC; Welsh Academic Press; Weslo Publishing; Whimsical Designs by CJ LLC; Whimspire Books; White Goat Press; Wienand Verlag; Wild Iris Publishing; Wild River Press; Wilkins Farago Pty Ltd; Wilkinson Publishing; Willow Tree Books; Wings Press; Wishland LLC; Wits University Press; Wolf Legal Publishers; Wolsak & Wynn Publishers Ltd; World Council of Churches; WorldRider Publishing & Press; Verlagshaus Wuerzburg; XRX Books; Yan Lei Press; You Can Publishing; Zophorus Books; ZuZu Petals Books
Territory: worldwide

Indigo Books & Music Inc
468 King St W, Suite 500, Toronto, ON M5V 1L8, Canada
Tel: 416-364-4499
E-mail: cisales@indigo.ca
Web Site: www.chapters.indigo.ca
Key Personnel
CEO: Heather Reisman
Chief Creative Offr: Scott Formby
EVP & CFO: Hugues Simard
EVP & Chief Mdsg Offr: Tod Morehead
EVP & CTO: Bo Parizadeh
EVP, E-Commerce & Chief Mktg Offr: Kristen Chapman
EVP, Gen Coun & Corp Secy: Kathleen Flynn
EVP, Retail & HR: Gil Dennis
Founded: 2001
Distributor for Audio & Video; Children's Book Store
Territory: Canada, USA

Ingram Content Group LLC
One Ingram Blvd, La Vergne, TN 37086-1986
Tel: 615-793-5000 Toll Free Tel: 800-937-8000 (retailers); 800-937-5300 (ext 1, libs)
E-mail: customerservice@ingramcontent.com
Web Site: www.ingramcontent.com
Key Personnel
Chmn: John Ingram
Pres & CEO: Shawn Morin
Chief Content Offr: Phil Ollila
CFO: Brian Dauphin
Chief HR Offr: Wayne Keegan
CIO: Steve Marshall
Chief Legal Offr: Kelly Arnold
Chief Logistics Offr: Shawn Everson
Chief Strategy & Devt Offr: Kent Freeman
Chief Venture Capital Offr: David Roland
VP & Cont: Tina Elmore
VP, Application Servs: William Daniel
VP, Credit: Roger Lee
VP, Community Rel: Emily Weiss
VP, Content Acq: Kelly Gallagher
VP, Digital Servs: Margaret Harrison
VP, HR: Jacqueline Letson
VP, Mktg: Brian McKinley
VP, Mdsg: Amy Cox Williams
VP, Opers: Chris Willis
VP, Retail Sales: Donald Roseman
Dir, Academic Servs: Kurt Hettler
Dir, Application Servs: Robert Barnard
Dir, Consumer Insights: Pete McCarthy
Dir, Consumer Mktg: Kim Schutte
Dir, Mass Merchandisers Sales: Lisa Tomasello
Dir, Natl Accts: Michael Bell
Dir, Sales Opers: Tammy Spurlock
Sales Dir: Sharon Swados
Sr Mgr, Content Acqs: John Hussey
Sr Mgr, Mktg Servs: Ann Zangri
Sr Mgr, PR & Communs: Kris Wiese
Lib Sales & Servs Mgr: Tricia Racke Bengel
Mgr, Client Rel: Louisa Brody
Prod Mktg Mgr: Catherine Robinson
Proj Mgr, Integration & Outsource: Sterling Crawford
Specialty Retail Mgr: Megan Smith
Sales & Support Rep, Mass Mdse Group: Tori Cushman
Founded: 1964
Comprehensive publishing industry services company that offers numerous solutions, including physical book distribution, print-on-demand & digital services. Ingram works closely with publishers, retailers, libraries & schools around the world to provide them with the right products & services to help them succeed in the dynamic & increasingly complex world of content publishing. Ingram's operating units are Ingram Book Group LLC, Lightning Source LLC, VitalSource Technologies LLC, Ingram International Inc, Ingram Library Services LLC, Spring Arbor Distributors Inc, Ingram Publisher Services LLC & Tennessee Book Co LLC.
Branch Office(s)
6050 Dana Way, Antioch, TN 37013
7315 Innovation Blvd, Fort Wayne, IN 46818
4260 Port Union Rd, Fairfield, OH 45011
201 Ingram Dr, Roseberg, OR 97470
860 Nestle Way, Breinigsville, PA 18031
1200 Ingram Dr, Chambersburg, PA 17202
Territory: worldwide

Ingram Publisher Services, an Ingram brand
Subsidiary of Ingram Content Group LLC
14 Ingram Blvd, Mail Stop 631, La Vergne, TN 37086
SAN: 631-8630
Tel: 615-793-5000 Toll Free Tel: 866-400-5351 (cust serv)
E-mail: ips@ingramcontent.com
Web Site: www.ingrampublisherservices.com
Key Personnel
VP & Gen Mgr: Meredith Greenhouse
VP: Nick Parker
Dir, Acqs: Gonzalo Ferreyra
Dir, Busn Opers: Alison Black
Dir, Mktg: Peter Antone
Sr Client Rel Mgr: Leah Rex McCracken
Client Rel Mgr: Sarah Armstrong
European Sales Mgr: Matthew Dickie
Mgr, Busn Opers Support: Kristal Smith
Mgr, Sales: Johanna Hynes

Mgr, Sales & Support: Leslie Jobson
Founded: 2004
Assist publishers in a variety of ways including sales, distribution & account management. Provides distribution to 220 countries & territories with 19 offices, distribution centers & manufacturing plants worldwide.
Distributor for Academic Studies Press; Actar D; Adaptive Studios; Advantage Media Group Inc; AMMO Books LLC; Anomaly Productions Inc; Anthology Editions; Apa Publications; Aperture; APL Publishing; Apollo Publishers; Applewood Books Inc; Arcas Publishing; Arundel Publishing; Australian Academic Press; Bella & Harry; BiggerPockets Publishing Inc; Blue Star Press; Books & Books; Bottom Dog Press; Burleigh Dodds Science Publishing; Calexia Press; Cambridge International Science; Carpet Bombing Culture; Chiltern Publishing (US & CN); Clovercroft Publishing; CN Times Books; Conari Press; Cooking Lab; Dabel Brothers Publishing; Dalkey Archive Press; Design Studio Press; The Do Book Co (CN & US); Dovetail Press; Drago Media; Dreamscape Media (audio); Dundurn Press; Elevate Publishing; The Enthusiast; Esri Press; Fodor's Travel; Fordham University Press; Le French Book; Future Horizons Inc; Gemma Open Door; GemmaMedia; Gestalten; Ghost Mountain Books; Gingko Press; Bruno Gmuender; Granta Books; Grim Oak Press; Hanser Publications LLC; Harriman House; Hodder Education; Hoffman Media; Ideapress Publishing; Imprint Academic; Indiana University Press; Inkshares; The Institution of Engineering & Technology; International Society for Technology in Education; Morgan James Publishing; Jumping Jack Press; Kogan Page; Danielle LaPorte Inc; Laughing Elephant; Wilfrid Laurier University Press; The Law School Admission Council; Lemniscaat USA; Liberty Fund Inc; Linden Publishing; Made for Success Publishing; Maiden Lane Press; Mandevilla Press; Mango Media; Mango Publishing; Warren Miller Co; Minnesota Historical Society Press; ML Books International; MONKEY; Montana Publishing; The Mother Co; Mouse Prints Press; Museum of Jewish Heritage; NewSouth Books; Nippan IPS; No Nonsense Fly Fishing; Nolo; NYU Press; Oceanview Publishing; Ooligan Press; O'Reilly Media; Outpost19 Books; Oxford University Press; Pajama Press; ParentMap; Parkstone Press; Perilous Worlds (US & CN); PIE International Inc; The Planning Shop; Plough Publishing House; Poisoned Pen Press; Popular Book Co; Ramsey Press; Recorded Books; Red Pen Press; Rocky Nook; Rosenfield Media: Two Waves Books & Digital Reality Checks; Rough Guides; RSC Publishing; St Lynn's Press; Susan Schadt Press; Schilt Publishing; Sensory Focus; Severn House Publishers; She Writes Press; Simply Read Books; SparkPress; Spring House Press; Tantor Media; Taschen America; Tate's Bake Shop; Taunton Press; Terra Galleria Press; Third World Press; Three Hands Press; The TMG Firm; Trope Reader; Turner Publishing Co; University of Regina Press; US News & World Report; VanitaBooks; VeloPress; Waterhouse Press; West Margin Press®; What on Earth Publishing; Michael Wiese Productions; Windsor Peak Press; XAMonline.com

Institute for the Study of Human Knowledge (ISHK)
1702-L Meridian Ave, No 266, San Jose, CA 95125-5586
Tel: 617-497-4124 *Toll Free Tel:* 800-222-4745 (orders) *Fax:* 617-500-0268 *Toll Free Fax:* 800-223-4200 (orders)
E-mail: ishkadm@aol.com; ishkbooks@aol.com (orders)
Web Site: www.ishk.com
Key Personnel
Founder & Pres: Robert Ornstein, PhD
Founded: 1969
Represents Hoopoe Books; Malor Books
Territory: Canada, Central America, Mexico, South America, USA

International Press Publication Inc
Spadina Rd, Richmond Hill, ON L4B 3C5, Canada
Tel: 905-883-0343
E-mail: sales@ippbooks.com
Web Site: www.ippbooks.com; www.facebook.com/ippbooks; x.com/ippbooks2
Key Personnel
Pres: Bali Sethi
Founded: 1976
Library & wholesale suppliers of all types of publications, directories, dictionaries, foreign language books. Supply to the book trade & to individuals.
Distributor for ABC-CLIO; ABC-CLIO/Greenwood; Academic Press; Addison Wesley Longman; Blackwell Publishers; Bowker; Cambridge University Press; Career Press; Contact Canada; CQ Press; CRC Press; CSA; Elsevier; Europa Publications; Ferguson; Gale Research Inc; Grey House; Harcourt; HarperCollins; Information Today, Inc; International Code Council (ICC); ISO; Jist; Kluwer Academic Publishers; Libraries Unlimited; Library of Congress (USA); Macmillan; McGraw-Hill; Mediacorp; MIT Press; Monarch; Nelson Stationery Office; W W Norton & Company Inc; Omnigraphics; Orderline; Oxford University Press; Palgrave; Pearson; Penguin Group (USA) LLC; Prentice Hall; Project Management Institute; Raincoast; Random House; Lynn Reiner; Routledge; Sage; Self-Counsel Press; Simon & Schuster; Springer Verlag; Taylor & Francis Group, an Informa Business (USA); Techstreet; Thames & Hudson; Thomson Publishing; Time Warner; United Nations Publishing; John Wiley & Sons; H W Wilson
Territory: worldwide
Membership(s): The American Library Association (ALA); Children's Literature Association (ChLA); Ontario Library Association

Jonathan David Publishers Inc
52 Tuscan Way, Suite 202-371, St Augustine, FL 32092
SAN: 169-5274
Tel: 718-456-8611
E-mail: customerservice@jdbooks.com
Web Site: www.jdbooks.com
Key Personnel
Cont: Carol A Zelezny
Pres & Edit Dir: David Kolatch
VP, Sales & Mktg: Marvin Sekler
Acct Exec: Barbara Burke
Founded: 1948
Nonfiction trade book publishing.
Territory: Australia, Canada, Israel, South Africa, UK, USA

The Karel/Dutton Group
San Francisco, CA 94121
Tel: 415-668-0829
Web Site: karelduttongroup.com
Key Personnel
Founding Partner: Howard Karel
Partner: Dory Dutton; Mark O'Neal; Lisa Solomon; Ellen Towell *E-mail:* ellentowell.kdg@gmail.com
Assoc: Domenica DeSalvo
Represents Abrams Publishing; Consortium; Distributed Art Publishers (DAP); 1517 Media - Broadleaf & Beaming Books; Gibbs Smith Publishing; Inner Traditions; Lerner; Llewellyn; Mountaineers; Pearson ITP; Pomegranate Art; SCB Distributors; University of Minnesota Press

Kitzmiller Sales & Marketing Co
35 Flint St, Suite 304, Salem, MA 01970-3264
Tel: 978-985-1144 (cell) *Fax:* 978-744-0232
E-mail: dnd.kitzmiller@gmail.com
Key Personnel
Pres: David E Kitzmiller
Founded: 1992
Remainder & bargain book specialist.
Represents Book Country Clearing House LLC; Nationwide Book Industries LLC
Territory: Connecticut, Maine, Massachusetts, New Hampshire, Rhode Island, Vermont

Lerner Publisher Services
Division of Lerner Publishing Group Inc
241 First Ave N, Minneapolis, MN 55401
Tel: 612-332-3344 *Toll Free Tel:* 800-328-4929 (orders) *Fax:* 612-215-6230
E-mail: info@lernerpublisherservices.com; custserve@lernerpublisherservices.com
Web Site: www.lernerpublisherservices.com
Key Personnel
EVP, Sales: David Wexler *E-mail:* dwexler@lernerpublisherservices.com
Distributes titles from high quality children's publishers to the school, library & retail markets.
Distributor for Andersen Press; Big & Small; Cheriton Children's Books; Creston Books; Flying Start Books; Full Tilt Press; Gecko Press; Hungry Tomato®; Intergalactic Afikoman; JR Comics®; Knowledge Books; Lantana Publishing; Live Oak Media; Lorimer Children & Teens; Maverick Arts Publishing; Mayo Clinic Press Kids; New Frontier Publishing; The Page Education Foundation; Planting People Growing Justice Press; Quarto Library; Red Chair Press; Ruby Tuesday Books; Scallywag Press; Soaring Kite Books; Walker Books Australia; We Do Listen Foundation
Territory: worldwide

Longleaf Services Inc
Affiliate of The University of North Carolina Press
116 S Boundary St, Chapel Hill, NC 27514-3808
SAN: 203-3151
Tel: 919-966-7449 *Toll Free Tel:* 800-848-6224 *Fax:* 919-962-2704 (24 hours)
Toll Free Fax: 800-272-6817 (24 hours)
E-mail: customerservice@longleafservices.org; orders@longleafservices.org
Web Site: longleafservices.org
Key Personnel
CEO: Clay Farr *Tel:* 919-962-0540 *E-mail:* clay.farr@longleafservices.org
Dir, Content Servs: Lisa Stallings *Tel:* 919-962-0544 *E-mail:* lisa.stallings@longleafservices.org
Dir, Edit, Design & Prodn: Chris Granville
Dir, Opers & Client Fulfillment Servs: Molly Koecher *Tel:* 919-445-8767 *E-mail:* molly.koecher@longleafservices.org
Credit Mgr: Terry Miles *Tel:* 919-296-8359 *E-mail:* tmiles@longleafservices.org
Founded: 2005
Cost-effective fulfillment services for university presses.
Distributor for Baylor University Press; Chemeketa Press; Clemson University Press; Cornell University Press (including Northern Illinois University Press imprint); Cork University Press; InterVarsity Press; Louisiana State University Press; Purdue University Press; Syracuse University Press; TCU Press; Texas Tech University Press; University of Calgary Press; University of Georgia Press; University of Manitoba Press; University of Nebraska Press (including Potomac Books imprint); Uni-

BOOK DISTRIBUTORS & SALES REPRESENTATIVES

versity of New Mexico Press; The University of North Carolina Press; University of Notre Dame Press; University of Oklahoma Press; University of Pittsburgh Press; University of the West Indies Press; University of Virginia Press; University Press of Kansas; Vanderbilt University Press

Maple Logistics Solutions
60 Grumbacher Rd, York, PA 17406
Mailing Address: PO Box 15100, York, PA 17405-7100
Tel: 717-764-4596
E-mail: info@maplesoln.com
Web Site: www.maplelogisticssolutions.com
Key Personnel
Pres: James S Wisotzkey
VP, Dist Opers: Chris Benyovszky
VP, Dist, Sales & Mktg: Andrew J Van Sprang
 E-mail: vansprang@maplepress.com
VP, Sales & Mktg: William S Long
 E-mail: long@maplepress.com
Warehousing, distribution, fulfillment, print-on-demand, drop shipping, invoicing & value added services.
Territory: North America, worldwide
Membership(s): Associated Warehouses Inc (AWI); Book Manufacturers' Institute (BMI); Council of Supply Chain Management Professionals (CSCMP); Distributors & Consolidators of America (DACA); Express Carriers Association (ECA); Warehousing Education and Research Council (WERC); World Trade Center Harrisburg

Matthews Book Co
11559 Rock Island Ct, Maryland Heights, MO 63043
SAN: 169-4316
Tel: 314-432-1400 *Toll Free Tel:* 800-633-2665
Fax: 314-432-7044 *Toll Free Fax:* 800-421-8816
E-mail: orders@mattmccoy.com
Web Site: www.matthewsbooks.com
Key Personnel
CEO: Linda Nash
Founded: 1889
Wholesale distributor of medical, nursing, allied health, dental, veterinary, scientific & technical books.
Represents Academic Press; Acindes; Addison-Wesley (Prentiss Hall Health); Advanced Medical Publishing; Airway Cam Technologies; Alert & Oriented Publishing; American Academy of Orthopaedic Surgeons; American Academy of Pediatrics; American College of Obstetricians & Gynecologists (ACOG); American College of Physicians (ACP); American Dietetic Association; American Hospital Association; American Institute of Cancer Research; American Medical Association; American Pharmaceutical Association (APhA); American Psychiatric Publishing Inc; American Psychological Association; American Public Health Association (Benenson); American Society for Microbiology; American Society of Health System Pharmacists (ASHP); American Wolf; Anadem Publishing Inc; Anatomical Chart Co (LWW); Annie Enterprises; Anshan Publishing; Anson Publishing LLC; Antimicrobial Therapy Inc; Anup Research; Apollos Voice; Appleton (Prentiss Hall Health); Applied Therapeutics Inc (LWW); Jason Aronson (Rowman Littlefield); Artech House; Arts End Books; Ashbury Press; Ashgate Publishing Co (Wiley); Aspen Publishers (Jones & Bartlett); Atheneum Press; Ausmed Publications; Baja Books; Bandido Books (HCPro); BarCharts Publishing Inc; Basic Books Inc; Birkhauser Boston Inc; BL Publishing Co; Blackwell Publishing (Wiley); Bontrager Publishing; Book Smythe; Books of Discover; Ken Bookstein; Borm Bruckmeier Publishing LLC; Brady (Prentice Hall Health); BrainX; Brookes Publishing (Paul H Brooks); Brunner Mazel Inc (Taylor & Francis); Bryan Edwards/Flash Anatomy; Butterworth (Elsevier); Butterworth-Heinemann; Cache River Press; Cambridge University Press; Canadian Nurses Association; Cardiotext; CCNM Press; Cengage; Chapman & Hall; Charles Press Publishers; Chicago Review Press; Clinical EKG Guide; Clinical Publishing; The Coding Institute; Cold Spring Harbor; Colon Publishing; Columbia University Press; Cover Publishing Co; CRC Press; Creative Healthcare; Cricket Science; Critical Care Research & Associates; Critical Concepts; Current Clinical Strategies; Current Medicine (Springer); Curties-Overzet; Dalhousie University (Midnight Medicine); Data Trace Publishing Co; Davies Publishing; Davis Associates; F A Davis; B C Decker; Marcel Dekker Inc; Dudley Delaney; Delmar Publishers (Cengage); Demos Publications Inc; Martin Dunitz (Taylor & Francis); E D Insight; Educational Communications; Edu Rad; Elsevier Science Publishing Co; Lawrence Erlbaum & Associates (LEA) (Taylor & Francis); Exam Master Corporation; Facts & Comparisons Inc; Family Health Publications; W H Freeman & Co; Futura Publishing Co Inc; Galen Press Ltd; Garland Publishing (Taylor & Francis); Gordon & Breach Science Publishers (Taylor & Francis); Greenbranch Publishing LLC; Greenwich Medical Media (Cambridge); Guilford Publications Inc; GW Medical Publishing (STM Learning); H & H Publications; H & H Publishing Co Inc; Hampton Medical; Hancock Surgical Consultants; Handbooks in Health Care Co (HHC); HarperCollins Publishers; Haworth Press; HC Pro (Opus Communications); Health Emergency Publishing; Health Leadership (J&B); Health Press International; Health Professions Institute; Health Professions Press; HIMSS; Hogrefe & Huber Publishers; Human Kinetics; Human Sciences Press Inc; Humana Press; I-Can; I D G Books (Wiley); Ideas2Pen; IGI Global; IMP Publishing; In the Spotlight; Informed/Creative Ventures; Ingenix; Inner Traditions International; Insight Therapeutics LLC; InterLingua Publishing; International Medical Publishers; International University Press; Interpretive Laboratory Data; IOS Press Inc; Iowa State University Press; IRL Press (Oxford); Isis Medical (Taylor & Francis); IWA Publishing; J & S Publishing Co; Jeff Computers; JLW Publications; Joint Commission Resources (JCR); Jones & Bartlett Publishing; Jossey-Bass Inc Publishers (Wiley); JP Medical; Karger; KG/EKG Press; Jessica Kingsley (Taylor & Francis); Kluwer Academic Publishers; Lander-Drysdale; LearningExpress; Lewis Publishers Inc (Taylor & Francis); Lexi-Comp Inc; Lippincott, Williams & Wilkins; Mainely Physical Therapy; Margol Publishing LLC; Maxwell Publishing Co; McGraw-Hill Inc; MD Pocket; MD2B; Medconsult Publishing; Medhumor Publications; Medical Group Management Association (MGMA); Medical Management Institute (MMI); Medical Surveillance; Medlearn; Medmaster Inc; Megabooks; Megusta Publishing; Merck & Co; Merriam-Webster; Milady; Minireview LLC; Miracle Press; MIT Press (selected titles); Modern Language Association; Morgan & Claypool Publishers; Morrow, William & Co Inc; Mountainside MD Press; Mudpiles.com; National Academy Press; National League for Nursing (Jones & Bartlett); National Nursing Review; National Safety Council (Jones & Bartlett); New Harbinger Publications; NNCC Inc; North Atlantic Books; W W Norton & Company Inc; Nursecom Inc; Nurse's Station; Nursing Education Consultants; Oakwood Publishing; OEM/Managed Medical Services; Ohio State University; Oncology Nursing Society (ONS); Open Heart Publishing; OPP Crunch; Optum; Osote Publishing; Oxford University Press Inc; Pan American Health Organization (PAHO); Parthenon Publications Group (Taylor & Francis); People's Medical Publishing House (PMPH); Pergamon Press Inc (Elsevier); Peterson's Guides Inc; Pharmaceutical Press; Physician Support Resources (PSR); Physician's Desk Reference (PDR); Physician's Press; Plenum Publishing Corp (Kluwer); Plural Publishing Inc; Pluribus Press (Precept); PMIC; Porter & Associates; Precept Press; Prentice Hall Health; Pro-Ed; Psych Products Press; Quintessence Publishing Co Inc; Quiz Me A&P; Radcliff Medical; Random House; Rapid Psychler Press; Raspberry Publishing Co; Remedica Publishing Ltd; RennieMatrix Inc; Reveneco; Review for Nurses Inc; Rheum Info; Rodram Corp Sa De CV; Routledge (Taylor & Francis); Rowman & Littlefield Publishers; Royal College of Physicians (American Psychiatric Publishing Inc); RSM Press; RuveneCo Publishing; St Lucie Press (CRC); St Martin's Press Inc; Scientific Publishing Ltd; Scrub Hill Press; Scymed Sa De Cv; Seak Inc; SFI Medical; Sigma Theta Tau International; Simon & Schuster; Simply Books; Sinauer & Associates; Slack Inc; SmartDraw.com; Sportsmed Press; Springer New York Inc; Springer Publishing Co Inc; Springhouse Publishing (LWW); Tarascon Publishing (J&B); Taylor & Francis Inc; Tell Me Press; Teton New Media; TFM Publishing; Therapeutic Articulations; Thieme Medical Publishers Inc; Transmedical Corp; VCH Publishers (Wiley); Visual-Edge; Waveland Press; Whurr Publishing (Wiley); John Wiley & Sons Inc; World Bank Publications; World Scientific Publishing; Wysteria Ltd
Territory: Puerto Rico, USA

McGarr & Associates
5692 Heathwood Ct, Covington, KY 41015
Tel: 859-356-9295 *Fax:* 859-356-7804
Key Personnel
Pres: William D McGarr *E-mail:* wdmcgarr@aol.com
Representing book publishers, calendars & audio, bookmarks, journals & other sidelines to bookstores, wholesaler & specialty accounts.
Territory: Illinois, Indiana, Iowa, Kansas, Kentucky, Michigan, Minnesota, Missouri, Nebraska, North Dakota, Ohio, South Dakota, West Virginia, Wisconsin

MEP Education
8154 N Ridgeway Ave, Skokie, IL 60076
Tel: 847-676-1596 *Fax:* 847-676-1195
E-mail: info@mep-inc.net
Web Site: www.mepeducation.net
Founded: 1856
Distribute imported foreign language (French, German, Italian, Spanish) materials; books, software, audio, video, periodicals, to schools, libraries, teachers & general public. Office of Publication of European Language Institute for ELI magazines. Also distribute for US & foreign publishers in ESL/bilingual & foreign language materials.
Territory: USA

Midpoint National Inc
1263 Southwest Blvd, Kansas City, KS 66103
Tel: 913-362-7400 *Toll Free Tel:* 800-228-4321
E-mail: info@midpt.com
Web Site: www.midpt.com
Key Personnel
Pres: Ron Freund
EVP: Kent Gedman
Founded: 1988
Full service order fulfillment operations for book publishers, direct marketers, continuity book clubs, video & audio tape suppliers. Fully conveyorized 60,000 square foot distribution center, shipping nationwide from a "Mid-

point USA" location. Services tailored to each client's needs include 800 number call center; complete or partial invoicing, accounting, credit management & collection; mailing list management; inventory reporting, computerized credit card authorization & processing; complete handling of returned merchandise; full pick, pack & ship capability ranging from individual consumer orders & small store retail shipments to truckload quantities.

Midpoint Trade Books
Division of Independent Publishers Group (IPG)
814 N Franklin St, Suite 100, Chicago, IL 60610
Tel: 312-337-0747 *Fax:* 312-337-5985
E-mail: orders@ipgbook.com
Web Site: www.midpointtrade.com
Key Personnel
Pres: Eric Kampmann *E-mail:* eric@midpointtrade.com
VP & Gen Mgr: Alex Kampmann *E-mail:* alex@midpointtrade.com
Mktg Mgr: Alison Kampmann
Natl Accts Mgr: William Huhn *E-mail:* bill@midpointtrade.com
Natl Sales Acct Mgr: Annette Hughes
Ebook Coord: Casey Park
Founded: 1996
Full service book distribution company. Provides an important new model of marketing & distribution for independent publishers, with hands-on sales management. Represents US, Canadian & UK publishers in the US market.
Distributor for AAPC Inc; AAPC Publishing; Active Planet Kids Inc; ACW Press; Adams Printing Press; Affinitas Publishing; Albion Press; Alexander & Smith Publishing; Alicon Holdings Ltd; Allen Lane; Alliance Quebecoise editeurs independants; American Series; Amphorae Publishing Group LLC; Anglican House Media Ministries Inc; Anglican House Publishers Inc; APC Books; Apostle Press; Appalachian Trail Conservancy; Archetype; Artemesia Publishing LLC; Artichoke Publishers; Ash Tree Publishing; Asphodel Press; Atomic Fez Publishing; Austin Macauley Publishers Ltd; Authority Press; AWSNA Publications; B-Strong LLC; Backcountry Publishing; Backpack Editions; Balfour Books; Barlow Publishing; Barrytown/Station Hill Press Inc; Beaufort Books; John Beaufoy Publishing; Becoming Journey LLC; Beijing Mediatime United Publishing Co Ltd; Believe Books LLC; Bellekeep Books; Benjamin Press; Ensign Benson Books LLC; Beyond Dreams Publishing Group; Big Mind Publishing; Big Tent Entertainment; Bitingduck Press; Black Heron Press; Black Moss Press; Blank Slate Communications LLC; Blank Slate Press; blewointment; Bluebonnet Kids; Bluefield Books; Book Publishers Network; Book Ripple; Bookhaven Press; Bookstorm; Boulder Publications; BP Books; Brand Artist Press; Robin Brass Studio Inc; Bridgeway Publishing; Broken Hill; Brolga Publishing; Buckingham Book Publishing Ltd; Buffalo Heritage Press; Burke Publishing; Byword Books; Caffeine Nights Publishing; Caitlin Press Inc; Callinectes Press; CamCat Publishing; Cameo Press; Canine Wellness LLC; Canon Publishers; Cappuccino Books Publishing; CareNet Pregnancy Centers; Casino Vacations Press Inc; CELA Publishing; Central Park Tutors; Changing Lives Press; Nina Charles LLC; Chef Media; China Resource Center Press; Chowder Inc; Chronology Books; Church Media; Cicerone Press Ltd; Circle Publishing; CJ Books; Clarens Publishing; Clarity Marketing USA LLC; Clean Teen Publishing; CLM Publishing; Clockwise Press; Clotho Press; CN Times Books Inc; Cogin Inc; Comfort Publishing LLC; Conquill Press; Convergence Press; Cool Titles; Corgi Bits; Cormorant Books; Cosmos Internet Sdn Bhd; Cosmos Press Inc; Courtright; David & Nicole Crank Ministries; Creality Publishing; Creative Production Services Inc; Crimson Tree Publishing; Cross House Books; Crow Flies Press; CS Media; Cuidono Press; CulturAle Press; Jean Cunningham Consulting; Curtis Christine Press; Jen Dafoe Publishing; Dagger Editions; Dalsimer Press Inc; Darton Longman & Todd Ltd; DC Books; DCDESIGN Books; Defiance Press; Difference Press; Don't Rent Inc; Dragon Door Publications; Dragon Moon Press; Dram Good Books; Dreams Shared Publications; Dreamtitle Publishing; Dunham Books; Early Learning Foundation; East End Press; eBury Press; Ecademy Press Ltd; EDGE Science Fiction & Fantasy Publishing; Editions Mundo; Editions Veritas Quebec; Elijah Books; Entangled Books; Executive Books; Expert Subjects LLC; Facing History & Ourselves; FAL Enterprises LLC; Family Health Publications; Famous Publishing; Fayetteville Mafia Press; The Fedd Agency; Fidelis Publishing; Fieldhouse; Fifth House Publishers; The Fine Print Press Ltd; First Base Sports; Fitch & Madison Publishers LLC; Fitzhenry & Whiteside Limited; Five Elements Press; 5Points Publishing; Five Wisdoms Press; Flowers in Bloom Publishing; Foragers Harvest Press; Forever Young Publishers; 498 Productions LLC; 4GenPress; Fortem Press; Foxglove Press; Fracas Press; Franklin Green Publishing LLC; Franklin Square Press; Frederick Fell Publishers Inc; FRI Research; Frigate Books; Front Porch Press; Frontrunner; Gateway Entertainment Inc; Gavia Books; Gazelles Inc; Gelos Publications; Genesis Publishing; Glass House Nocturnal; Glass House Press; GMF Publishing; Gold Star Publishing; Goldminds Publishing; Goodman Beck Publishing; Good2Go Kids; Jeff Gordon Inc; Great River Books; Green Jellybean Press; Green Kids Press LLC; Green Place Books; Green Sprouts; Green Writers Press; Grid Press; Guernica Editions; Habits of Health Press; Hamish Hamilton; Hank Enterprises LLC; Harbour; Harbour Publishing; Haute Life Press; HeartWork Publishing; Heaven's Library; Hellgate Press; HigherLife Publishing; Hiraeth Press; Histria Books; HL Special Ebook Imprint; HnL; Homebound Publications; Hometown Fanfare Publishing LLC; House of David Publishers; HPN Books; h2 press; Hummingbird Books; Hummingbird World Media; Ignatius Press; Illumify Media Global; Illumify Press; In-Depth Editions LLC; Incorgnito Publishing Press; Influence Publishing Inc; Influencers; Inked; Integrative Nutrition Inc; Interactive Publishing Corp; Isaac Publishing LLC; ISB Publishing; Island Heritage Publishing; JAFS Inc; JahBread LLC; JCC Press; JEC Press; Jinda Corp; John August Media LLC; Junction; Kalpa Tree Press; Kingdom Driven Publishing; Kinkajou Press; KMG Publishing; Knox Robinson Publishing; Kokoro; Koebele Weaver Enterprises; Krazy Coupon Lady LLC; Ladyslipper Press; Lagniappe Publishing; Lambert Hill; Lamplight Ministries Inc; Layla Dog Press; Leadership First; The Leading Edge Publishing Co; Level 4 Press Inc; Lexington Marshall Publishing LLC; Life Journey Publishing; Life's Plan Publishing; LifeBridge Books; Lifestyle Entrepreneurs Press; Lighthouse Press; Little Adventures; Little Bound Books; Living Clay; Living Waters Publications; London Wall Publishing; Lorimer Press; Lost Moose; Lotus Publications; Loving On Purpose; Luath Press Ltd; Luminescent Herbivore; Mad Norwegian Press; Magic Light Publishing; Magnificat; Managing Times Press; Marching Books; Barbara McLennan; Meerkat Press LLC; Mehta Publishers; Mentobe Press; Merril Press; Messenger International; Mile Oak Publishing Inc; Mr Mark's Classroom; Mitchell Street Press; Mithras Books; MKids; Mokum Media; Monkeyfeather; Moonshots Press; Brett Morgan Publishing; Motivating The Masses Press; Motivational Press; Moyer Bell; MP Publishing Ltd; Mutasian Entertainment LLC; Mwella Publishing; Myndset Press; New Atlantean Press; New Awareness Network; New Chapter Publisher; New Holland Publishers; NEWTYPE; Next; Next Century Publishing; NEXT SAS; NEXTBOOK Ltd; NEXTBOOK SAS; Nightwood; Nightwood Editions; 9 Heads Media Inc; NK Publications Inc; North Star Press of St Cloud; Notable Kids Publishing; Nunavut Arctic College; Obstacles Press; Oceanview Publishing; Old Dog Books; Olmstead Press; Olympic Press; 1-Take MultiMedia; Onward; Owl House Books; Paloma Books; PaperUp Publishing; Papier-Mache Press; Annika Parance Publishing; Park Avenue Press; PCG Business; PCG Kids; PCG Legacy; Pemmican Publications; Penguin; Penguin Ananda; Penguin Classics; Penguin Enterprise; Penguin Metro Reads; Penguin Modern Classics; Penguin Random House India Pvt Ltd; Penguin Studio; Penguin Young Adult; Penguin Zubaan; Penrhyn Press; Pentatonic Press; Perichoresis Press; Personal Power Press; Pilot Communications Group; Pinata Publishing; PMP; Pokeweed Press; Polar Horizons; Polaris Publications; Ponent Mon SL; Portfolio; Press Syndication Group; Primal Nutrition Inc; Primus Books; Printopya; Project Restored Press; Prolance; Promontory Press Inc; Puffin; Puffin Young Zubaan; Quinn & Associates Publishing & Consulting; Khalil Rafati; Ransom Note Press LLC; Ratna Sagar; Ratna Sagar P Ltd; Readers Legacy Inc; Reading With Peaches LLC; Real Magic Design LLC; Real Western; Rebel Press; Red Deer Press Inc; Red Press Ltd; Redwood Publishing LLC; Robert Reed Publishers; Reservoir Square Books; Retire Secure Press; Walter Reutiman Publishing; RFI Publishing; Risen Son Publishing LLC; River Publishing; Riverrun LLC; RLM Publishing; Rock Foundations Press; Rogue Bear Press; Rollerbird; Warren K Ross Jr; Roundup Press; Sandbox Publishing LLC; S&J Multimedia LLC; Sands Press; Satya House Publications; Jeff Schmidgall Ministries; Schoolside Press; Scribe Publishing Co; Search for the Truth Ministry; SelectBooks; Shadow Dragon Press; Shanghai Press; Sharitt Publications; Shobha De Books; Singing Turtle Press; Six Points Press; Smart Travel Press; Snow & Associates Inc; Soar in Trust; Solo Roma Inc; Sonflower Publishing Co; SOS Publishing; Space Goat Productions Inc; Sparrow Publishing; Special Yoga Publications; Spence City; Spencer Hill Contemporary; Spencer Hill Middle Grade; Spencer Hill Press; SSE Publishing; Star of Light Publications; The Star Trilogy; Steamboat Springs Publishing; Summer Fit Learning; Super Senses Productions; taotime verlag; Tatra Press; 10 Finger Press; 3 Dreams Creative Enterprises LLC; Thunder Bay Press Michigan; Tiara Publishing; Tiger Blood International; Times Media Group Inc; Timothy & Titus; Titletown Publishing LLC; TM Publishing; Today is the Day Publishing; Today's Books; Tomahawk Press; Top Executive Media; Topos Books; Totus Tuus Press; Tourist Town Guides; TreeGirl Studios LLC; Treehouse Publishing Group; Trifolium Books; Trinacria Editions LLC; True North Publishing; Trueface; Truth in Science; Tulip; 12 Pines Press; Under the Maple Tree Books; Vesst Investment Partnership LP; VESST Publishing; Veterans Publishing Inc; Viking; Vision Life Ministries International Inc; Vista Communications; Walrus Books; Wapner & Brent Books; Westminster Institute; Whitecap America; Whitecap Books Ltd; Why Not Books; Wild Thorn Publishing LLC; Buck Wilder Inc; Windhill Books LLC; Windsor-Brooke Books LLC; Dortha Withrow Books; WND

BOOK DISTRIBUTORS & SALES REPRESENTATIVES — SALES

Books; WND Films; World Ahead Publishing; X-Communication LLC
Territory: Canada, UK, USA, worldwide
Membership(s): American Booksellers Association (ABA); California Independent Booksellers Alliance (CALIBA); Great Lakes Independent Booksellers Association (GLIBA); Independent Book Publishers Association (IBPA); Mountains & Plains Booksellers Association (MPBA); New Atlantic Independent Booksellers Association (NAIBA); Pacific Northwest Booksellers Association (PNBA)

Miller Trade Book Marketing Inc
1426 W Carmen Ave, Chicago, IL 60640
Tel: 773-307-3446
Key Personnel
Pres: Bruce Miller *E-mail:* bruce@millertrade.com
Founded: 1985
Sales representative for midwest territory for book marketing.
Represents Duke University Press; Johns Hopkins University Press; Kent State University Press; Michigan State University Press; Minnesota Historical Society Press; Rutgers University Press; Springer Nature; Syracuse University Press; Temple University Press; University of Georgia Press; University of Iowa Press; University of Minnesota Press; University of Texas Press; University Press of Kansas; University Press of Kentucky; University Press of Mississippi; Wayne State University Press; Wisconsin Historical Society Press
Territory: Midwestern States
Membership(s): Great Lakes Independent Booksellers Association (GLIBA); Midwest Independent Booksellers Association (MIBA)

National Association of Book Entrepreneurs (NABE)
PO Box 606, Cottage Grove, OR 97424
Tel: 541-942-7455 *Fax:* 541-942-7455
E-mail: nabe@bookmarketingprofits.com
Web Site: www.bookmarketingprofits.com
Key Personnel
Exec Dir: Al Galasso
Founded: 1980
Book marketing consultations, publishing seminars, NABE Book Showcase combined book exhibits, mail order marketing through "Publishers Preview." Over 1,000 independent & small press publishers, electronic marketing service.
Distributor for Moore Publishing; Publishers Media
Territory: USA

National Book Network (NBN)
Subsidiary of Rowman & Littlefield Publishing Group
4501 Forbes Blvd, Suite 200, Lanham, MD 20706
Tel: 301-459-3366 *Toll Free Tel:* 800-462-6420 (orders only) *Fax:* 301-429-5746
Toll Free Fax: 800-338-4550 (orders only)
E-mail: customercare@nbnbooks.com
Web Site: www.nbnbooks.com
Key Personnel
CEO: Jed Lyons
COO: Robert S Marsh *E-mail:* rmarsh@rowman.com
SVP & CFO: Michael Lippenholz
  E-mail: mlippenholz@rowman.com
Pres: Jason Brockwell *E-mail:* jbrockwell@nbnbooks.com
VP, Opers: Mike Cornell *E-mail:* mcornell@nbnbooks.com
VP, Publr & Cust Servs: Carla Quental
  E-mail: cquental@nbnbooks.com
Dir, Sales Admin: Sylvia Williams
  E-mail: swilliams@nbnbooks.com

Intl Sales Dir: Les Petriw *E-mail:* lpetriw@nbnbooks.com
Mgr, Dist: Sue Bumbaugh *E-mail:* sbumbaugh@nbnbooks.com
Publr Servs Mgr: Karen Mattscheck
  E-mail: kmattscheck@nbnbooks.com
Founded: 1986
Sales, marketing & distribution for publishers to the trade.
Distribution center located in Blue Ridge Summit, PA.
Represents Active Parenting; Advantage Books; AEI Press; American Bar Association; Anness Publishing; Appalachian Mountain Club Books; Applause Theatre & Cinema Books; Aquila Polonica Publishing; Army War College; Association for Talent Development; Astragal Press; Astronaut Projects (BizBookLab LLC); August House; Axios Press; Backbeat Books; Bard Press; Baron Barclay Bridge; Barricade Books; Black Widow Press/Commonwealth Books Inc; Blacksmith Books; Blood Moon Productions; Blue Dome Press; Bnei Baruch/Laitman Kabbalah Publishers; Boone & Crockett Club; Bradt Travel Guides; Bragg/Health Science; Brewers Publications; Bristol Park Books; British American Publishing; Burford Books; C&T Publishing; Capizon Publishing; Cato Institute; Cinebook; Common Deer Press; Continental Sales Inc (CSI); Crimson Publishing; Crystal Clarity Publishers; D&B Publishing; Day Hike Books; Dharma Publishing; Dillman Karate International; Don't Eat Any Bugs Productions; Earthbound Sports; Everyman Chess; ExPress; Facts on Demand Press; Felony & Mayhem; Fitness Information Technology; Flower Press; Footprint Travel Guides; Garrett County Press; Glitterati Inc; Globe Pequot; Good Sam Club; Goofy Foot Press; Green Editorial; Green Lion Press; Harbor Press; Headwater Books; Himalayan Institute Press; Hobar Publications; Alan C Hood; A C Hubbard; Impact Publications; Jeffers Press; Jonglez Publishing; Jupitalia; Kidwick Books; Lake Isle Press; Larson Publications; Learning Express; Limelight Editions; Lost Classics Book Co; Lotus Press; Marshall Cavendish; McBooks Press; Axel Menges; Michelin Travel & Lifestyle; Milepost; Moffly Media; Mongoose Press; Monsoon Books; Mount Alpha Media; Mustang Publishing; New Academy Publishers; NewTrends Publishing Inc; NIMBUS; No Voice Unheard; Nomad Press; Oak Hill Publishing; Octobre LLC; Peak Performance Press; Phobos Books; Photo Tour Books Inc; Pigna; Pineapple Press; Pinter & Martin; Platypus Media/Science, Naturally; PopOut; Practising Law Institute; Prometheus Books; Quality Chess; Quiller Publishing Ltd; Radical Honesty Enterprises Inc; Rainforest Books; RAND Corp; Riverbend Publishing; Edward Everett Root; Rowman & Littlefield; Royal College of General Practitioners; Ryton Publications; Safari Press; Sausage Maker; Scientific Publishing; Seapoint Books & Media; Sentient Publications; Shalem Press; Smart Publications; Speechmark Publishing; Stoecklein Photography; The Story Plant; Survival Books Ltd; Trailblazer Publications; Tughra Books; Velocity Press; Vij Books India; Visions International Publishing; Waterford Press; Welcome Rain Publishers; Western Horseman; Whittles Publishing; Windsor Books; Windward Publishing; Wisdom Waters Press; Woodland Press; World Wisdom/Wisdom Tales; Yale University Art Gallery; YMAA Publication Center; Zeshan Qureshi
Territory: Australia, Caribbean, Central America, Mexico, New Zealand, South America, UK, USA
Membership(s): Independent Book Publishers Association (IBPA)

New Leaf Distributing Co
Subsidiary of Lotus Light Enterprises Inc
1085 E Lotus Dr, Silver Lake, WI 53170
SAN: 169-1449
Tel: 262-889-8501 (ext 162) *Toll Free Tel:* 800-326-2665 (orders) *Fax:* 262-889-8598
E-mail: orders@newleafdist.com
Key Personnel
Pres: Santosh Krinsky
Buyer: Denise Milano *E-mail:* denise@lotuspress.com
Founded: 1975
Serves publishers both inside & outside of New Leaf's usual Body, Mind & Spirit niche. Founded on the premise that in the present publishing environment, the traditional one size fits all distribution scheme may no longer meet the needs of many small presses. We offer a service that is uniquely flexible & designed to ensure that worthy books are presented effectively to important buyers. Additional services include ebook distribution, digital short run printing, plus freight consolidation & logistics for small publishers.
Distributor for Beech Hill Publishing; Blue Juice Comics; Brotherhood of Life; BurmanBooks Media Corp; George Cappannelli; Center for Touch Drawing; DBM Press; Enrealment Press; Expansion Publishing; Foundation for Inner Peace; Grail Press; Kitchen Sink Publishing (one title only); Pari Publishing; Promontory Press; Sky Grove; Sounding Light Publishing; Spiritual Journeys; Carl Studna; Sufi Ruhaniat International; Thoth Publications; TV Guestpert; Whitedove Press; World Tree Press; Zen Publications (one title only)

Northeast Publishers Reps
Montville Chase, 20 Davenport Rd, Montville, NJ 07045
Tel: 973-299-0085 *Fax:* 973-263-2363
E-mail: siraksirak@aol.com
Web Site: www.nepubreps.com
Key Personnel
Owner: James F Sirak
Sales Off Mgr: Mariel Dryl *Tel:* 973-625-3694
Contact: Beth Martin; Bill Palizzolo; Lisa Sirak
Founded: 1981
Sales organization that represents publishers & manufacturers to the book trade in the northeastern US.
Represents Artgame; Bar Charts Publishing; Earthbound Journals; EDC Publishing/Kane Miller; Enchanted World of Boxes; FoxMind; Fridolin; From There to Here Imports (FTTH); Gift Trenz; Gold Crest/Mighty Bright/With iT; Good Cause Greetings; Johns Hopkins/HFS Distribution; Lang Companies/Turner; Mark-My-Time; Masterpiece Puzzles; Sellers Publishing; Sourcebooks; 3 Oak Publishing; Tide-Mark Calendars; University of Hawaii Press; Waypoint Geographic; White Mountain Puzzles; Willow Creek
Territory: Mid-Atlantic States, New England
Membership(s): New Atlantic Independent Booksellers Association (NAIBA); New England Independent Booksellers Association (NEIBA)

OverDrive Inc
One OverDrive Way, Cleveland, OH 44125
Tel: 216-573-6886 *Fax:* 216-573-6888
E-mail: info@overdrive.com
Web Site: www.overdrive.com
Key Personnel
Pres & CEO: Steve Potash
COO: Lori Franklin
CFO: Greg Farmer
Chief Mktg Offr: Jennifer Leitman
EVP & Gen Coun: Erica Lazzaro
EVP, Content Group: Jason Tyrrell
VP, Content: Alexis Petric-Black
Intl Busn Devt Exec: Steve Rosato

& DISTRIBUTION

BOOK DISTRIBUTORS & SALES REPRESENTATIVES

Founded: 1986
Leading full service digital distributor of ebooks, audiobooks & other digital content.

Parson Weems' Publisher Services LLC
3811 Canterbury Rd, No 707, Baltimore, MD 21218
Tel: 914-948-4259 *Toll Free Fax:* 866-861-0337
E-mail: office@parsonweems.com
Web Site: www.parsonweems.com
Key Personnel
Partner/Owner & Sales Rep, Mid Atlantic Region: Eileen Bertelli *Tel:* 845-987-7233 *Fax:* 866-761-7112 *E-mail:* eileenbertelli@parsonweems.com
Partner: Chris Kerr *Tel:* 914-329-4961 *E-mail:* chriskerr@parsonweems.com
Mgr: Causten Stehle *Tel:* 914-948-4259 *Fax:* 866-861-0337
Sales Rep, Mid Atlantic Region: Jason Kincade *Tel:* 347-244-2165 *E-mail:* jasonkincade@parsonweems.com; Kevin Moran *Tel:* 848-303-4164 *E-mail:* kevinmoran@parsonweems.com
Sales Rep, New England & Mid Atlantic Region: Ryan O'Connor
Founded: 1997
Independent trade sales representatives & marketing consultants specializing in art & lifestyle illustrated books, business, travel, regional, reference, children's books, scholarly & professional, calendars, museum products, promotional books & note cards.
Represents Actar/ORO (New England only); Berghahn; Birkhauser (New England only); Bloomsbury Academic; Capstone; Casemate | IPM; Children's Press; Child's Play (New England only); ChooseCo; Consortium; Diamond Books; Familius; Fine Print Publishing; Gardner (New England only); Geotoys; Inner Traditions; Island Press; Jessica Kingsley Publishers; LSU Press; MACK Publications; McGraw-Hill Professional; Midpoint/Green Writers Press; Mountaineers Books; Naval Institute Press; Penn State University Press; Rutgers University Press; Shelter Harbor Press; Stillman & Birn; Stylus Publishing; University of Kansas Press; University of Pennsylvania Press; University of Tennessee Press; University of Toronto Press; University Press of Kentucky; Wayne State University Press
Territory: Connecticut, Delaware, District of Columbia, Maine, Maryland, Massachusetts, New Hampshire, New Jersey, New York, Pennsylvania, Rhode Island, Vermont, West Virginia
Membership(s): Association of Book Travelers; New Atlantic Independent Booksellers Association (NAIBA); New England Independent Booksellers Association (NEIBA)

Penguin Random House Canada, a Penguin Random House company
320 Front St W, Suite 1400, Toronto, ON M5V 3B6, Canada
SAN: 201-3975
Tel: 416-364-4449 *Toll Free Tel:* 888-523-9292 (cust serv) *Fax:* 416-598-7764
E-mail: customerservicescanada@penguinrandomhouse.com; publicitycanada@penguinrandomhouse.com; rightscanada@penguinrandomhouse.com
Web Site: www.penguinrandomhouse.ca
Key Personnel
CEO: Kristin Cochrane
CFO: Barry Gallant
Chief Strategy & Opers Offr: Robert Wheaton
Cont: Kwangu Mashumba
VP, Mktg & Communs: Beth Lockley
VP, Sales: Charidy Johnston
VP, Subs Rts: Adrienne Tang
Group Dir, Publicity & Mktg: Erin Kelly
Group Sales Dir: Val Gow
Sr Dir, Young Readers Group Sales: Kelly Glover
Dir, Data Sci (Global): Andrew Myrden
Dir, Lifestyle Mktg & Publicity: Michelle Arbus
Dir, Mktg & Publicity: Tonia Addison
Dir, Mktg & Publicity, Cookbooks & Lifestyle: Adria Iwasutiak
Dir, Online & Digital Sales: Taylor Berry
Dir, Sales Mgmt: Brent Richard
Dir, Wholesale & Spec Mkts Sales Strategy: Lavanya Narasimhan
Assoc Dir, Mktg: Beth Cockeram
Assoc Dir, Mktg & Publicity, Young Readers: Sylvia Chan
Head, Prodn: Carla Kean
Sr Contracts Mgr: Naomi Pinn
Sr Imprint Sales Mgr, Young Readers: Kathryn Rennie
Sr Mgr, Ad Servs: Dulce Rosales
Sr Mgr, Amazon Sales: Kelly Rankin
Sr Mgr, Children's Imprint Sales: Julie Forrest
Academic Sales Mgr: Melody Tacit
Busn Mgr: Anya Oberdorf
District Sales Mgr: Hala Kamaliddin
District Sales Mgr, Children's Independent & School Sales: Kyrell Grant
District Sales Mgr, Eastern CN: Linda Iarrera
Lib Sales Mgr, Children's Books, Manga & Graphic Novels: Krisztina Riez
Mgr, Busn Intelligence & Reporting: Jill Smith
Mgr, Comics & Specialty Category Sales: Nicole Alfaro
Mgr, Consumer Insights: Kirby Best
Mgr, Ebook & Digital Audiobook Sales & Mdsg: Sarah Seto
Mgr, Mktg & Publicity: Anais Loewen-Young
Mgr, Mktg & Publicity Opers: Emily Sheppard
Mgr, Publicity & Mktg: Danielle LeSage
Mgr, Spec Projs: Julia Hartland
Opers Mgr: Juan Aguilar; Francesca Conte
Publicity Mgr: Evan Munday
Royalty Accountant Mgr: Cheryl Nurse
Sales Mgr: Patrick Georges
Sales Mgr, Natl Accts: Karen Ma
Sr Publicist: Erin Bonner; Natasha Tsakiris
Sr Publicist, Lifestyle: Kelly Albert
Publicist: Chalista Andadari; Cameron Waller
Publicist, Lifestyle: Megan Konzelman; Aakanksha Malhotra
Publicist, Young Readers: Graciela Patron Colin
Mktg Specialist: Charlotte Nip; Dara Sheere
Mktg Analyst: Kirti Henry
Ad Coord: John Castillanes; Paola Gonzalez
Audiobooks Coord: Ankanee Lagunarajan
Communs Coord: Trudy Fegan
Events Coord: Farishteh Pavri
HR Coord: Ayomikun Taiwo
Intl Sales Coord: Alicia Edwards
Mktg & Publicity Coord: Megan Costa; Sabrina Papas; Taylor Rice
Mktg & Publicity Coord, Young Readers: Stephanie Ehmann
Off Servs Coord: Joey Arredondo
Online & Digital Sales Coord: Ellen Zhang
Opers Coord: Gautham Raja
Proj Coord, Mktg Design: Hailey LeBlanc
Sales Coord, Online Retail Ad & SEO: Zahra Abdi
Sales Coord, SEO & Ad: Kirsten Armstrong
Spec Mkts Coord: Dilara Kurtaran
Royalty Accountant: Sharon Ramsahai
Contracts Assoc: Jamie Steep
Mktg Assoc: Danya Elsayed
Prodn Assoc: Melanie Cheng; Rachel Guglielmelli
Rts Assoc: Catherine Ryoo
Group Asst, Mktg, Publicity & Communs: Supipi Weerasooriya
Data Scientist: Georgia Henry; Cecilia Yang
Help Desk Analyst: Ricky Utomo
Jr Fin Analyst: Farnaz Lilian
Sales, marketing, warehouse & accounting services for Bantam Press, Seal Books, Doubleday Canada, Knopf Canada, McClelland & Stewart, Vintage Canada, etc.
Distributor for Appetite by Random House; Bantam Press; Bond Street Books; Charlesbridge Publishing; Crown; Delacorte Press; Dell; Doubleday Canada; Emblem; Hamish Hamilton Canada; Knopf Canada; McClelland & Stewart; Penguin Canada; Penguin Random House Canada Young Readers; Penguin Teen; Puffin Canada; Random House Canada; Seal Books; Signal Books; Strange Light; Tundra Books; Viking Canada; Vintage Canada
Represents Doubleday Canada; Knopf Canada; Vintage Canada
Territory: Canada

Power Engineering Books Ltd
Division of Book Order Service of Canada
7 Perron St, St Albert, AB T8N 1E3, Canada
SAN: 115-4850
Tel: 780-458-3155; 780-459-2525
Toll Free Tel: 800-667-3155 *Fax:* 780-460-2530
E-mail: power@nucleus.com
Web Site: www.powerengbooks.com
Key Personnel
Dir: Kim Borle
Founded: 1973
Distributors of technical books, codes & standards to private individuals, trade shows & businesses in Canada.
Distributor for Reeds
Represents ACGIH®; American Petroleum Institute (API); American Society for Testing & Materials (ASTM); American Society of Mechanical Engineers (ASME); American Welding Society (AWS); Canadian Standards Association (CSA); DEWALT®; Institute of Electrical & Electronics Engineers (IEEE); Manufacturers Standardization Society of the Valve & Fittings Industry Inc; National Association of Corrosion Engineers (NACE); National Fire Protection Association (NFPA); National Research Council Canada (NRCC); RSMeans; Reeds
Territory: Canada

Printed Matter Inc
231 11 Ave, Ground fl, New York, NY 10001
Tel: 212-925-0325 *Fax:* 212-925-0464
E-mail: info@printedmatter.org
Web Site: www.printedmatter.org
Key Personnel
Exec Dir: Lesley A Martin
Bookstore & Dist Mgr: Craig Mathis
Founded: 1976
Nonprofit distributor of artists' books; more than 15,000 titles.
Territory: worldwide
Membership(s): Art Libraries Society (ARLIS)

Prologue Inc
Subsidiary of Groupe Renaud-Bray
3785, Rue La Fayette Ouest, Boisbriand, QC J7H 1N5, Canada
Tel: 450-434-0306 *Toll Free Tel:* 800-363-2864
Toll Free Tel: 800-361-8088 (cust serv)
E-mail: prologue@prologue.ca
Web Site: www.prologue.ca
Founded: 1976
Distributes books in Canada in French for children & adults.
Distributor for A Editeur; Alibi; Alisio; Alma; Alpha; Ancre de Marine; Andara; Animae; Ankama; Anspach Editions; Apogee; Aquarupella; Art & BD; L'Asiatheque; Assimil; Association Expeditions; Athena; Atlande; Avant Scene Opera/Premieres Loges; Marie Barbier; Les Bas-Bleus; Belin Editeur; Belin Education; Beliveau Editeur; La Belle Colere; Berger; Binge; Blake et Mortimer; Boomerang; Bornemann; Bouton d'or Acadie; Breal; Broquet; Budo; C Puzzle; Cafe Sale; Cahiers de l'Hotel de Galliffet; Cahiers de l'Iued; Callidor; Calligram; Campagne Premiere; CARD; Anne Carriere Editions; Cartovision; Cernunnos; Chalet; Champaka Brussels; Charleston; Chasse-Maree; Chateau d'Ame; Chronique

Editions; CIUSSS du Centre-Sud-de-l'Ile-de-Montreal; Cognito; Emmanuelle Collas; Collector BD; Colloidales; Cristel Editions; CSLI; Dargaud; Le Dauphin Blanc; De Mortagne; De Vinci Editions; Demi Lune; Le Dernier Havre; Desclee; Diva Romance; DLL Presse Editeur; D'Orbestier; Druide Editions; Druide Informatique; Ecrits des Forges; EDIFA; Edisens; Les Editeurs Reunis; Editions Accarias/L'Originel; Editions Amaterra; Editions Au Carre; Editions Charlevoix; Editions Cristal; Les Editions de la Gouttiere; Editions Defendu; Editions des Crepuscules; Editions des Falaises; Editions de l'Envolee; Les Editions de l'Individu; Les Editions de Saxe; Editions DIXIT; Les Editions do Expression; Editions du CHU Sainte-Justine; Editions du Cram; Editions du Parc en Face; Editions du Phoenix; Les Editions du Quebecois; Les Editions du Renouveau Quebecois; Les Editions du Soleil de Minuit; Editions du Tullinois; Les Editions Dupuis; Les Editions ETC; Editions Exclusif; Editions Fabulle; Les Editions Fei; Editions Fleurus; Editions FouLire; Editions Grandvaux; Editions Jeanne & Juliette; Editions La Grande Ourse; Editions Le Pommier; Editions Le Souffle d'or; Editions les Malins; Les Editions l'Interligne; Editions Lito; Editions Lux&Nox; Editions Mains Libres; Editions Marie-Claire; Editions Michel Quintin; Editions Nami; Editions Naturat; Editions Phidal; Editions Pierre de Taillac; Editions Pierre Tisseyre; Editions Pratiko; Les Editions RDL; Les Editions Reynald Goulet Inc; Editions Soteca; Editions Sully; Editions 365; Editions Touristiques du Quebec; Editions Trois-Pistoles; Editions Universitaires; Editions Vaudreuil; Editions Vial; Editions Vigot; Editions Yves Michel; Education 4 Peace; Eliott; EMS; ENI Editions; Entourage; Les Equateurs; Eveil Citoyen; Eveil Conscience; Eveil Nature; Evergreen; Expressmap; Fab; Fantask; Fantasy Dreams; Filature(s); Firefly Books; Fleurus Religion; Flic Flac; Fondation Urantia; Fragrances; Gladius Editions; La Grande Maree; Graph Zeppelin; Graton; Groupe Mame Liturgie; Le Guide de la Moto; Herscher; Historia; Huginn et Muninn; humenSciences; Imago; Impact Editions; Les Impatients; In Press; L'Inedite; Instituto Italiano; Interferences Editions; Invenire; IQRC; Jardin des Livres; Jouvence; K Puzzle; Kana; Kinaye; KM Editions; KO Editions; K6 Editions; Leduc Creatif; Leduc Graphic; Leduc Humor; Leduc.S; Leduc Societe; Libellus; La Librairie Vuibert; Lieux Dits; Little Urban; Locus Solus; Le Lombard; Lucis Trust; Lucky Comics; Lumiere d'El Morya; Luzerne Rousse; M Editeur; Macro Editions; Magnard Jeunesse; La Maison; Mama Editions; Mame Editions Universitaires; Mammouth Rose; Mango; Mango Jeunesse; Manokan; Mardaga; Marmaille et Cie; Marsu Productions; Massin; Media Participations; Medias Pouvoirs; Metamorphe; Michelin; Midi Trente Editions; Mijade; Max Milo Editions; Moelle Graphik; Mosquito; Mouvement Quebec Francais; Mouvement Quebec Independant (MQI); Mud Puddles; Mylene Arpin; Niffle; Nord-Sud; Nouvelles Editions de l'Arc; Novel; Now Future; Nuinui; Octave Editions; 123 Soleil; Onisep; Ouest & Cie; Ouest France; Les Ozalids d'Humensis; Papiers Musique; Papillon Rouge; Le Passe-Monde; Passes Composes; Performance Edition; Petites Pommes; Petites Pousses; Petits Genies; Piccolia Daphne; Pix'n Love Editions; Plein Jour; Pour la Science; Les Presses de l'Universite d'Ottawa; Presses de l'Universite du Quebec; Presses de l'Universite Laval; PUF; Qilinn; Que Sais-Je?; Ramsay Editions; Revue des Deux Mondes; Revues Humensis; Rose de la Fontaine; Rustica Editions; Rustikid; Guy Saint-Jean; Salamandre; Saltimbanque; Secret d'etoiles; Sedirep; Shoebox Media; Snag; SpiceBox; Studio Boule et Bill; Studyrama; Sud Ouest; Tabou; Tardy; Taschen; Tigre & Cie; Michelle Tisseyre Editeur; TJ Editions; Tom Pousse; Toundra; Ulisse Editions; Univers/Cite Mikael; Urban China; Urban Comics; Urban Link; Vagnon; Vagnon Jeunesse; Vega-Dupuis; La Ville Brule; Vilo Groupe; Voiles et Voiliers; WebTech Management; Yoyo Editions; Zephyr Editions
Territory: Canada

Publishers Group West (PGW), an Ingram brand
Division of Ingram Content Group LLC
1700 Fourth St, Berkeley, CA 94710
SAN: 202-8522
Tel: 510-809-3700 *Toll Free Tel:* 866-400-5351 (cust serv) *Fax:* 510-809-3777
E-mail: info@pgw.com
Web Site: www.pgw.com
Key Personnel
VP, Busn Devt: Kevin Votel *E-mail:* kevin.votel@ingramcontent.com
Founded: 1976
Marketing & distribution services for more than 100 independent publishers.
Branch Office(s)
154 W 14 St, 12th fl, New York, NY 10011 (natl accts off)
Distributor for A Public Space; Adventure Publications; AdventureKEEN; Aeon Books Ltd; Agate Digital; Agate Publishing; American Diabetes Association; Amherst Media; Annick Press; Augustus Publishing; Automatic Publishing; Aviation Supplies & Academics; Bailiwick Press; Baobab Press; Barbican Press; Beginning Press; Believer Magazine; Belt Publishing; Bilingual Books Inc; Black Classic Press; Black Sands Entertainment; Black Ship Publishing; Blast Books; Blizzard Entertainment LLC; Blue Dot Press; Bluebridge; The Book Peddlers; Breadpig; Breathing Books; Button Books; Cadmus Editions; Canongate Books; Cartoon Books; Carus Books; Chouette Publishing Inc; Cityfiles Press; Classical Comics; Clavis; Clerisy Press; Coconut Press; Columbia Global Reports; Come & Get It Publishing; Cool Tools Lab; Cornell Lab Publishing Group; Counterpoint; Creston Books; Crooked Lane Books; Cuento de Luz; Cune Press; Curiosity Books; Cursor; Deletrea; Destination Press; DeVorss & Co; Douglas & McIntyre; Dry Climate Studios; Dzanc Books; 826 Valencia; Encantos Media; Entrepreneur Press; Europa Editions; Faber & Faber; Fang Duff Kahn Publishers; Featherproof Books; Felony & Mayhem; Fig Tree Books; Figure 1 Publishing; Flesk Publications; Forest Avenue Press; Four Elephants Press; Four Winds Press; Fourth Chapter Books; Franklin Publishers; Frommer Media; Genesis Publications; Gibson House Press; Gingko Press; Peter Glickman Inc; Global Travel Publishers; Golden Notebook Press; Goosebottom Books; John Gray's Mars Venus LLC; Green Candy Press; Green City Books; Greystone Books; Groundwood Books; Grove/Atlantic Inc; Harbour Publishing; Hartley & Marks Publishers; Hawthorne Books; Healthy Travel Media; Heritage Builders; The Hero's Journal; Heyday; Hopscotch Press; House of Anansi Press; Hub City Press; Hundreds of Heads Books; Huntington Press; Icon Books; Imbrifex Books; In Easy Steps Ltd; Insight Press; Into Action Publications; Interlink Publishing; Invisible Publishing; Jawbone Press; Kalmbach Publishing; Kelcy Press; KO Kids Books; Laboratory Books; LARB Books; Leaf Storm Press; Let's Go Inc; London Town Press; Machines of Death; Mayo Clinic; McWitty Press; Medallion Media Group; Medicine Wheel Publishing; Menasha Ridge Press; Microcosm Publishing; Mighty Media Inc; Milkweed Editions; Minoan Moon Publishing; Missionday LLC; Morpheus International; Mount Vernon Press; M27 Editions LLC; Namaste Publishing; Namchak Publishing LLC; Nature Study Guides; Naval Institute Press; Need To Know; New World Library; NewSage Press; Nilgiri Press; Nolo Press Occidental; Nothing But The Truth Publishing; Open Court; OR Books; Osho Media International; Otter-Barry Books; Owlkids Books; Owners Manual Press; Page Two; Papaloa Press; Passporter Travel Press; Patagonia Books; PDR Consumer; PDR Network; Penngrove Publications; Penny Candy Books; Pharos Editions; Phoneme Media; Plexus Publishing; PM Press; Polis Books; Pomegranate Press; Pritzker Military; Public Lands Alliance; Quick American Archives; Raincoast Books; Rare Bird Books; RE/Search Publications; Readers to Eaters; Restless Books; Resurrection House; Ronin Publishing; Roundtree Press; Sandow Media; Santa Monica Press; ScienceWiz; Seven Footer Press; Shelter Publications; Shoemaker & Co; Sierra Club/Counterpoint; Soft Skull Press; Source Book Publications; Sudden Oak Books; Supercollege; Surrey Books; Synergetic Press; Tachyon Publications; Tahrike Tarsile Qur'an; TalentSmart; Tara Books; Three Rooms Press; Time Out; Tinderbox Press; Tinwood Books; Trafalgar Square Books; Travelers' Tales; Trinity University Press; Tuttle Publishing; Two Dollar Radio; Two Lines Press; 2.13.61; Udon Entertainment; Unbridled Books; Underwood Books; Unnamed Press; Unofficial Guides; Urantia Foundation; Val De Grace Books; Verse Chorus Press; Visible Ink Press; Waterford Press Inc; Watershed Media; Web of Life Children's Books; Wellstone Books; West Hills Press; Whereabouts Press; White Cloud Press; Wide World Publishing; Wild Strawberry Productions; Wilderness Press; Wildlands Press; Wine House Press; Yellow Pear Press; Rangjung Yeshe Publications; Yosemite Conservancy; You Live Right Publishing; Zakka Workshop
Territory: worldwide

QDS, see Quarto Distribution Services (QDS)

Quarto Distribution Services (QDS)
Division of Quarto Publishing Group USA
100 Cummings Ctr, Suite 265D, Beverly, MA 01915
Tel: 978-282-9590
E-mail: qds@quarto.com
Web Site: www.quartoknows.com/qds
Key Personnel
Dir, Dist Servs: John Groton *Tel:* 978-282-3562 *E-mail:* john.groton@quarto.com
Distributor for Brooklands Books Ltd; Clever Publishing; The Crowood Press Ltd; Enthusiast Books; Evro; Exisle Publishing Ltd; Haynes Publishing; Herridge & Sons Ltd; Icon Publishing Ltd; Jawbone Press; James Mann; Murdoch Books; Giorgio Nada Editore SRL; Orca Publishing; Porter Press; TPR; Veloce Publishing Ltd

R & R Book Co LLC
666 Godwin Ave, Suite 120-C, Midland Park, NJ 07432
Tel: 201-337-3400
Web Site: www.rrbookcompany.com
Key Personnel
Partner: Ruth Alden Hook *E-mail:* ruth@rrbookcompany.com
Founded: 2005
Publisher sales & marketing representatives.
Represents Actar Publishing; Child's Play; Firefly; Free Spirit; Gardner Publishing; Gryphon House; Holiday House; Peachtree; Pepin; Prestel; Ronnie Sellers Productions
Territory: USA

BOOK DISTRIBUTORS & SALES REPRESENTATIVES

Raincoast Books Distribution Ltd
2440 Viking Way, Richmond, BC V6V 1N2, Canada
SAN: 115-0871
Tel: 604-448-7100 Toll Free Tel: 800-663-5714 (CN only) Fax: 604-270-7161
Toll Free Fax: 800-565-3770
E-mail: info@raincoast.com; customerservice@raincoast.com
Web Site: www.raincoast.com/distribution
Key Personnel
CEO: John Sawyer E-mail: johns@raincoast.com
Head, Raincoast Books: Peter MacDougall E-mail: pete@raincoast.com
VP, Mktg: Jamie Broadhurst E-mail: jamie@raincoast.com
Founded: 1979
Distributor for Alma Books; Beginning Press; Bilingual Books; Bloomsbury; Chronicle Books; CollegeBoard; The Do Book Co; Drawn & Quarterly; Entangled Publishing; Familius; Farrar, Straus and Giroux; Feiwel & Friends; Figure 1; First Second; Flatiron Books; Graywolf Press; Hardie Grant; Henry Holt & Co; Houghton Mifflin Harcourt; Imprint; Laurence King; Kingfisher; Lonely Planet; Macmillan Audio; Macmillan Children's Publishing Group; Magnetic Poetry; Media Lab Books; Minotaur; Mountaineers Books; New Harbinger Publications; Osprey; Page Two; Papercutz; Picador; Priddy Books; Princeton Architectural Press; Quadrille; St Martin's Press; Gibbs Smith; Sourcebooks; The Tite Group; Tor/Forge; Twirl; Wattpad Books
Represents Alma Books; Beginning Press; Bilingual Books; Bloomsbury; Chronicle Books; CollegeBoard; The Creative Co; The Do Book Co; Drawn & Quarterly; Entangled Publishing; Familius; Farrar, Straus and Giroux; Feiwel & Friends; Figure 1; First Second; Flatiron Books; Graywolf Press; Hardie Grant; Henry Holt & Co; Houghton Mifflin Harcourt; Imprint; Laurence King; Kingfisher; Lonely Planet; Macmillan Audio; Macmillan Children's Publishing Group; Magnetic Poetry; Media Lab Books; Minotaur; Mountaineers Books; New Harbinger Publications; Osprey; Page Two; Papercutz; Picador; Priddy Books; Princeton Architectural Press; Quadrille; St Martin's Press; Gibbs Smith; Sourcebooks; The Tite Group; Tor/Forge; Twirl; Wattpad Books
Territory: Canada

RAM Publications & Distribution Inc
2525 Michigan Ave, Bldg A2, Santa Monica, CA 90404
Tel: 310-453-0043 Fax: 310-264-4888
E-mail: info@rampub.com; orders@rampub.com
Web Site: www.rampub.com
Key Personnel
Founder: Theresa Luisotti E-mail: theresa@rampub.com
Dir: Paul Schumacher E-mail: paul@rampub.com
Warehouse Mgr: John Melendez
Founded: 1984
Distributor for Alvar Aalto Foundation; AC Books; Arquine; Art 21 Inc; Armory Center for the Arts; Arvinius + Orfeus Publishing; Morris & Helen Belkin Art Gallery (University of British Columbia); BNN Inc; Book Works; Clouds; Eakins Press Foundation; Falkenstein Foundation; Fotohof Editions; Editions Patrick Frey; Inventory Press; Jap Sam Books; David Kordansky Gallery; LA Forum for Architecture & Urban Design; Los Angeles Contemporary Exhibitions (LACE); M/M (Paris); Museum of Contemporary Art; Nohara Co Ltd; Office for Discourse Engineering; Onomatopee; Oslo Editions; Passenger Books; Post Editions; Raking Leaves; Rice University Architectural Dept; Ridinghouse; Santa Barbara Museum of Art; Smart Art Press; Snoeck Verlag; Spector Books; Sternberg Press; Wright

RAmEx Ars Medica Inc
Subsidiary of Rampertab American Exports Inc
1714 S Westgate Ave, No 2, Los Angeles, CA 90025-3852
SAN: 631-6573
Tel: 310-826-4964 Toll Free Tel: 800-633-9281 Fax: 310-826-9674
E-mail: ars.medica@ramex.com
Web Site: www.ramex.com
Key Personnel
CEO: Ramesh Rampertab Tel: 310-826-3489 E-mail: zerohourzulu@yahoo.com
Founded: 1994
International distributor of medical multimedia products including CD-ROMs, videos, slides, books & other software. Products are for reference, teaching, training, administration & research. Represent over 500 medical publishers.
Represents Academic Press; ADAM; Addison Wesley; AHC; American Academy of Orthopaedic Surgeons; American Diabetes Association; American Hospital Association; American Psychiatric Publishing Inc; American Society of Health-System Pharmacists; Andromeda Software Inc; Aspen Publishers; ASTM International; Auerbach Publishers; Belson/Hanwright Video; Blackwell Science; Blanchard & Loeb Publishers; Butterworth-Heinemann; Canon Communications LLC; Cardionics; CG; Chapman & Hall/CRC; Churchill-Livingstone; Ciba Geigy; Clinics in Motion; Concept Media; CP Inc; CRC Press; Creative Educational Options LLC; Critical Concepts; CTT; Current Medicine Inc; Current Science Group; Database Publishing Group; FA Davis Co; Marcel Dekker; Delmar; DP; DxR Development Group Inc; Elsevier Science; Facts & Comparisons; FITNE Electronic Vision Inc; Fleetwood; Food Chemical News; Franklin Electronic Publishers; G W Medical Publishing; Garland Science Publishing; Graphic Education Corp; Grey House Publishing; Harcourt Health Sciences; Health Professions Press; Health Stream Inc; Mike Holt Publications; Humana Press; Icon Learning Systems; IM; Informa Healthcare; Ingenix; Intercollegiate Center for Nursing Education; International Thompson Publishing; Johns Hopkins University Press; Lange Video Production; Lewis Publishers; Lexi-Comp; LifeART; Lippincott Williams & Wilkins; Mayo Clinic Scientific Press; McGraw-Hill; Medcom-Trainex Inc; Medical Economics Co; Medical Multimedia Systems; Medicode; Medifor Inc; Meds Publishing; Merck; Miscellaneous Publishers; Mosby; National Technical Information Services; NEVCO; Novartis; Nursing Videos; Oxford University Press; Parthenon Publishing; Pearson Education; Pharmaceutical Press; Prentice Hall; Primal Pictures; Professional Pharmaceutical Index; Quality Medical Publishing; Reality Surgery; Relax Herbals & Exports Pvt Ltd; St Anthony Publishing; St Lucie Press; WB Saunders; Scientific American Medicine; Seak Inc; Silver Platter Information; Software & Medical Image SL; Spellex Corp; Springer-Verlag; Springhouse Publishing; Stedman's; Stethographics Inc; Stokes Publishing Co; Taylor & Francis; Thieme Medical Publishing; Thomson Healthcare; TVMED Corp; US Government Publications; US Pharmacopoeia; Vi Me S Publishing; Victory Technology; Virtual Learning Center; WebMD; John Wiley & Sons Publishing Inc; John Wiley Current Protocols; Yale/CAIM
Territory: worldwide

Readerlink Distribution Services LLC
1420 Kensington Rd, Suite 300, Oakbrook, IL 60523-2164
SAN: 169-197X
Tel: 708-547-4400 Toll Free Tel: 800-549-5389
E-mail: info@readerlink.com; marketingservices@readerlink.com
Web Site: www.readerlink.com
Key Personnel
Pres, Chmn & CEO: Dennis Abboud
EVP & COO: John Bode
EVP & Chief Mktg Offr: David Barker
SVP, Fin & Busn Analytics: Jeremy Armer
SVP, HR: Margarita Carrillo
SVP, Mktg: Kristin Bartelme
SVP, Mktg & Procurement: Corey Berger
SVP, Sales: David Travettoo
VP, Enterprise Analytics: Kyle Marx
VP, Prod Mgmt & Mktg: John Norris
Sr Dir, Field Serv: Rob Denney
Founded: 2011
Full service distributor of hardcover, trade & paperback books to non-trade channel booksellers in North America.
Branch Office(s)
812 SW Raintree Lane, Suite 6, Bentonville, AR 72712 Tel: 479-464-4932
50 S Tenth St, Suite 600, Minneapolis, MN 55403 Tel: 612-339-3249

Rights & Distribution Inc
7519 LaPaz Blvd, Suite C303, Boca Raton, FL 33433
Tel: 954-925-5242
E-mail: rightsinc@aol.com
Key Personnel
Pres & Publr: Donald L Lessne
Founded: 1943
The only company in the US that sells both foreign rights & handles all foreign distribution for our small & medium-sized publishers.
Distributor for Bancroft Press; Bartleby Press; Frederick Fell Publishers; Gulliver Publishing; YMAA Publication Center
Territory: USA, worldwide

St Catharines Museum
1932 Welland Canals Pkwy, RR 6, St Catharines, ON L2R 7K6, Canada
Mailing Address: PO Box 3012, St Catharines, ON L2R 7C2, Canada
Tel: 905-984-8880 Toll Free Tel: 800-305-5134 Fax: 905-984-6910
E-mail: museum@stcatharines.ca
Web Site: www.stcatharines.ca
Key Personnel
Supv, Historical Servs & Curator: Kathleen Powell
Publishing & retail sales.

Saunders Book Co
Division of Saunders Office & School Supplies Ltd
PO Box 308, Collingwood, ON L9Y 3Z7, Canada
Tel: 705-445-4777 Toll Free Tel: 800-461-9120 Fax: 705-445-9569 Toll Free Fax: 800-561-1763
E-mail: info@saundersbook.ca
Web Site: librarybooks.com
Key Personnel
Pres: John Saunders Fax: 705-445-5804 E-mail: johns@saundersbook.ca
VP, Direct Sales: James Saunders E-mail: jamess@saundersbook.ca
Dir, Mktg: Carol Saunders Tel: 800-461-9120 ext 2000 Fax: 705-445-5804 E-mail: carols@saundersbook.ca
Gen Mgr: Judy Purdy
Sales to schools, public libraries & school/library wholesalers.
Distributor for Mason Crest
Represents Amicus; Arcturus Publishing Ltd; Beech Street Books; Bellwether Media; Black Rabbit Books; Brown Bear Books; Cherry Lake Publishing; Creative Editions; Creative Education; Lerner Publishing Group Inc; Millbrook; Reference Point Press; Saddleback Ed-

BOOK DISTRIBUTORS & SALES REPRESENTATIVES — SALES

ucational Publishing; Smart Apple Media; 12-Story Press; 21st Century
Territory: Canada

SCB Distributors
Subsidiary of ABP Inc
15608 S New Century Dr, Gardena, CA 90248
Tel: 310-532-9400 *Toll Free Tel:* 800-729-6423
Fax: 310-532-7001
E-mail: scb@scbdistributors.com
Web Site: www.scbdistributors.com
Key Personnel
Pres: Aaron Silverman *E-mail:* aaron@scbdistributors.com
Gen Mgr: Victor Duran *E-mail:* victor@scbdistributors.com
Sales & Mktg Mgr: Gabriel Wilmoth *E-mail:* gabriel@scbdistributors.com
Full service distributor, fulfillment, order entry, national sales representation.
Distributor for Acrobat Books; Adventures Unlimited Press; Alchimia; Amok Books; Anacapa Press; Arcata Arts; Sherman Asher Publishing; Atides Publishing; Auad Publishing; Ayerware Publishing; Baby Tattoo Books; Bascom-Hall Publishing; BDSM Press; Belly Kids; BEST Life Media; Beyond Binary Books; Aaron Blake Publishers; Blenheim Press; Blind Eye Books; Blue Bird Press; Bluewater Productions; Bluewood Books; Braided Worlds Publishing; Bristol Books; Bullet Point Publishing; CCNM Press; Centrala; Chopra Center Press; Circlet Press Inc; Clarity Press Inc; CLU Press; Coffee Table Comics; CRCS Publications; Creation Books; Creation Oneiros; Cricket Feet Publishing; Daedalus Publishing; Daje Publishing; Damron Guides; Dancing Hands Music; Daniel & Daniel Publishers; Dark Dragon Books; Dedalus Ltd; Deicide Press; Devastator Press; Dokument Press; Down There Press; Dunhill Publishing; Editions Akileos; Ermor Enterprises; FAB Press; Fair Oaks Press; Food for Talk; Fox Music Books; Fox Women's Books; Freedom Press; From Here to Fame; Gatehouse Publishing; Ghost & Co; Glorian Publishing; Goliath Books; Gorsky Press; Gothic Image Publications; Grand Central Press; Greenery Press; Happy Hen Books; Headpress; Hohm Press; Hybrid Cinema; I Love Mel; IamCoach Publishing; Iam8bit Productions; Illustre Books; Infilpress; Ingenuity Press; Inner Health Books; Inner Travel Books; International Neighborhood; K Publications; Kahboom; Kalindi Press; Kingyo Press; Kontur Publishing; Kopetkai Press; Lange Media; Lasp Gasp; Lebowski Publishers; Herb Lester Associates; Lightpoint Press; Limehouse Books; Luxe City Guides; MapMania Publishing; Masteryear Publishing; McCarty PhotoWorks; Milk Mug Publishing; Mindpower Press; New Century Publishers; Nicotext; One Love Books; One Peace Books; Over & Above Creative; Overcup Press; Pacific Highlands Press; Penny-Ante Editions; Perseverance Press; Pet Friendly Publications; Pier 99 Publishing; Polair Publishing; Power Press; Quarry Press; Quintessential Healing Inc; Quotable Zodiac Publishing; Ram Publishing; Rankin Photography; Raw Vision; Resources for Infant Educators (RIE); Rock Out Books; Rock Point Press; Russell Enterprises Inc; RVP Publishers; Scratter & Pomace; Sedona Press; September Publishing; Shake It!; Shinbaku Books; Silver Lake Publishing; Soaring Penguin Press; Soundcheck Books; Steller Press; Street Smart Press; Sugoi Books; Sun Vision Press; Synergetic Press; Tallfellow Press; Tangent Books; Tavin Press; The Temple Publications; Terra Nova Books; Three Wings Press; Toddler Press; Twisted Spoon Press; Merlin Unwin Books; Vidov Publishing; Vision Sports Publishing; We Heard You Like Books; Wet Angel Books; Winged Horse Publishing; Wisdom Tree Publishers; Wizarding World Press; Wolf Creek Press; Wordslinger Press; Write Bloody Publishing
Territory: Canada, USA

Scholarly Book Services Inc
289 Bridgeland Ave, Unit 105, Toronto, ON M6A 1Z6, Canada
Toll Free Tel: 800-847-9736 *Toll Free Fax:* 800-220-9895
E-mail: customerservice@sbookscan.com
Web Site: www.sbookscan.com
Key Personnel
Pres & CEO: Laura Rust *E-mail:* laura@sbookscan.com
Distributors & sales representatives for university, literary & specialist presses in Canada.
Distributor for Boydell & Brewer Inc; Cork University Press; International Society for Technology in Education; Kent State University Press; Liberty Fund Books; Louisiana State University Press (CN only); Marquette University Press (CN only); Minnesota Historical Society Press; Naval Institute Press; Northwestern University Press; Notre Dame University Press; Ohio University Press; Oklahoma University Press; Polebridge Publishing; Purdue University Press (CN only); Rutgers University Press (CN only); Southern Illinois University Press (CN only); Syracuse University Press; Texas A&M University Press; University of Arkansas Press; University of Hawaii Press (CN only); University of Illinois Press (CN only); University of Missouri Press (CN only); University of Nevada Press (CN only); University of North Carolina Press (CN only); University of Pennsylvania Press (CN only); University of Pittsburgh Press (CN only); University of South Carolina Press (CN only); University of the West Indies; University of Virginia Press (CN only); University Press of Florida (CN only); University Press of Kansas; University Press of Mississippi (CN only); Vanderbilt University Press; Wayne State University Press (CN only); World Scientific Publishing (CN only)
Territory: Canada

Scholar's Choice Ltd
2323 Trafalgar St, London, ON N5Y 5S7, Canada
Mailing Address: PO Box 7214, London, ON N5Y 5S7, Canada
Tel: 519-453-7470 *Toll Free Tel:* 800-265-1095
Fax: 519-455-2853 *Toll Free Fax:* 800-363-3398 (CN only)
E-mail: sales@scholarschoice.ca
Web Site: www.scholarschoice.ca
Key Personnel
Pres: Scott Webster
Founded: 1952
Distributor & retailer of educational toys & teaching materials to parents, teachers & early childhood educators in Canada & around the world. 25 retail locations in Canada.
Distributor for Check & Double Check Workbooks; Scholar's Choice
Territory: North America

Scholastic Book Fairs®, see Scholastic School Reading Events

Scholastic School Reading Events
Division of Scholastic Inc
1080 Greenwood Blvd, Lake Mary, FL 32746
Tel: 407-829-8000 *Toll Free Tel:* 800-770-4662
Fax: 407-829-2600
E-mail: custservbf@scholasticbookfairs.com
Web Site: bookfairs.scholastic.com/content/fairs/home.html
Key Personnel
Pres, Scholastic School Reading Events: Sasha Quinton
VP, Busn Devt & Strategy: Ben Stone
VP, Fin: Phil Bernhardt
VP, Sales & Serv (North): Jeff Marty
VP, Sales & Serv (South): Shane Kyle
VP, Mktg: Laura Lundgren
VP, Prod Category Mgmt: Eric Compton
VP, Field Deployment & Optimization: Brian Carter
VP, HR: Tim Vuolo
Founded: 1981
Scholastic School Reading Events, in partnership with schools across the country, hosts more than 120,000 book-sale events each year, reaching more than 35 million children & their families in preschool-9th grade. Book Fairs provide students, teachers & parents access to thousands of affordable books & educational products & is responsible for putting more than 100 million books in the hands of children, helping to foster enthusiasm for reading & generating more than $200 million annually in fundraising for school projects & classroom materials.

Socadis Inc
Subsidiary of Groupe Madrigall
420 rue Stinson, Ville St-Laurent, QC H4N 3L7, Canada
Tel: 514-331-3300 *Toll Free Tel:* 800-361-2847
Fax: 514-745-3282; 514-331-8202 (major dist)
Toll Free Fax: 866-803-5422
E-mail: socinfo@socadis.com (cust serv); direction@socadis.com; salesgd@socadis.com (major dist)
Web Site: www.socadis.com
Key Personnel
Dir, Fin: Genevieve Castonguay
Founded: 1970
French language book distributor for 1,000 publishers.

Social Studies School Service
10200 Jefferson Blvd, PO Box 802, Culver City, CA 90232
Tel: 310-839-2436 *Toll Free Tel:* 800-421-4246 (US & CN) *Fax:* 310-839-2249
Toll Free Fax: 800-944-5432
E-mail: access@socialstudies.com; customerservice@socialstudies.com
Web Site: www.socialstudies.com
Key Personnel
CEO: David Weiner
CFO: Russell Kantor
Chief Learning Offr: Dr Aaron Willis
Art Dir: Mark Gutierrez
Dir, District Partnerships: Dr Montra L Rogers
Dir, Opers: Luis Castro
Mktg Dir: Nisreen Breik
Natl Sales Dir: Jennifer Carlson
Head, Content: Bill Walter
Founded: 1965
Provide a wide variety of supplementary curriculum materials to schools, including books, CD-ROMs, DVDs, software, charts, posters, maps, globes & atlases.

Southern Territory Associates
4508 64 St, Lubbock, TX 79414
E-mail: sta77@suddenlink.net
Web Site: www.southernterritory.com
Key Personnel
Pres: Geoff Rizzo *Tel:* 772-223-7776 *Fax:* 877-679-6913
Secy & Treas: Judy Stevenson
Assoc: Tom Caldwell *Tel:* 773-450-2695; Rayner Krause *Tel:* 972-618-1149 *Fax:* 972-618-1149; Teresa Rolfe Kravtin *Tel:* 706-882-9014 *Fax:* 706-882-4105; Angie Smits *Tel:* 336-574-1879 *Fax:* 336-275-3290
Founded: 1976
Represents Baker & Taylor Publisher Services (southeastern US & select southern states)

Territory: Alabama, Arkansas, Florida, Georgia, Louisiana, Mississippi, North Carolina, Oklahoma, South Carolina, Tennessee, Texas, Virginia

Southwest Book Co
Division of Scholastic School Reading Events
13003 Murphy Rd, Suite H1, Stafford, TX 77477-3934
Tel: 281-498-2603 *Fax:* 281-498-7566
Founded: 1980
Distribute paperbacks to book fairs & classrooms. Reading Is Fundamental programs.
Branch Office(s)
2956 Reward Lane, Dallas, TX 75220 *Tel:* 214-357-9656 *Fax:* 214-357-0222

Spring Arbor Distributors Inc
Unit of Ingram Content Group LLC
One Ingram Blvd, La Vergne, TN 37086-1986
Toll Free Tel: 800-395-4340 *Toll Free Fax:* 800-876-0186
E-mail: customerservice@ingramcontent.com
Web Site: www.ingramcontent.com
Founded: 1978
Distributor of Christian books, Bibles, music & video, to Christian retail stores.
Branch Office(s)
Indiana Distribution Center, 7315 Innovation Blvd, Fort Wayne, IN 46818-1371
Oregon Distribution Center, 201 Ingram Dr, Roseburg, OR 97471
Chambersburg Distribution Center, 1240 Ingram Dr, Chambersburg, PA 17202

Stylus Publishing LLC
22883 Quicksilver Dr, Sterling, VA 20166-2019
SAN: 299-1853
Tel: 703-661-1504 (edit & sales); 703-661-1581 (orders & cust serv); 703-996-1036
Toll Free Tel: 800-232-0223 (orders & cust serv) *Fax:* 703-661-1547; 703-661-1501 (orders & cust serv)
E-mail: stylusinfo@styluspub.com; stylusmail@styluspub.com (orders & cust serv)
Web Site: styluspub.com
Key Personnel
Pres & Publr: John von Knorring *E-mail:* jvk@styluspub.com
VP, Mktg & Publicity Mgr: Andrea Ciecierski *Tel:* 703-996-1036 *E-mail:* andrea@styluspub.com
Mktg Mgr, Educ & Higher Educ: Patricia Webb *E-mail:* patricia@styluspub.com
Sales & Mktg Admin: Jane Leathem *E-mail:* jane.leathem@styluspub.com
Founded: 1996
Publishes in higher education. Distributes books for trade, education, engineering, higher education, scholarly & professional markets in the following subjects: agriculture, business, education & public health.
Distributor for Baseball Prospectus; Cabi Books; Campus Compact; CSREA; Mercury Learning & Information; Myers Education Press; National Resource Center for The First-Year Experience & Students in Transition; Thorogood Publishing; Trentham Books Ltd; UCL IOE Press; World Health Organization (WHO)
Represents Baseball Prospectus; Cabi Books; Campus Compact; CSREA; Mercury Learning & Information; Myers Education Press; National Resource Center for The First-Year Experience & Students in Transition; Thorogood Publishing; Trentham Books Ltd; UCL IOE Press; World Health Organization (WHO)
Territory: North America, South America

Chip Taylor Communications, LLC
2 East View Dr, Derry, NH 03038
Tel: 603-434-9262 *Toll Free Tel:* 800-876-CHIP (876-2447) *Fax:* 603-425-1784
E-mail: info@chiptaylor.com
Web Site: www.chiptaylor.com
Key Personnel
Pres: Chip Taylor
Founded: 1985
Producer, distributor of 4,000+ exclusive DVDs, streaming digital files, videos, associated books, posters & CDs for educators, librarians, TV programmers & the home use markets.
Distributor for SquareOne Publishers Inc
Represents SquareOne Publishers Inc
Territory: worldwide
Membership(s): National Association of Television Program Executives Inc (NATPE)

Teacher's Discovery®
Division of American Eagle Co Inc
2741 Paldan Dr, Auburn Hills, MI 48326
Toll Free Tel: 800-TEACHER (832-2437)
Toll Free Fax: 800-287-4509
E-mail: help@teachersdiscovery.com; orders@teachersdiscovery.com
Web Site: www.teachersdiscovery.com
Key Personnel
Owner: Skip McWilliams
Dir, Mktg: Steve Giroux
Founded: 1968
Sell supplemental classroom teaching materials for Spanish, French, German, English & Social Studies. See www.vocesdigital.com for prize-winning digital courseware (e-textbooks).

Terry & Read LLC
4471 Dean Martin Dr, The Martin 3302, Las Vegas, NV 89103
Tel: 510-813-9854 *Toll Free Fax:* 866-214-4762
Key Personnel
Dir: David M Terry *E-mail:* dmterry@aol.com
Assoc: Alan Read
Founded: 1943
Represents Atlas Books; Babalu Inc; Brookings; Casemate; Catholic University Press; Holiday House; Johns Hopkins University Press; Illinois University Press; International Publishers Marketing (IPM); Jessica Kingsley; Louisiana State University Press; North Carolina University Press; Springer; Stylus Publications; Transaction Publishers; University of Georgia; University of Mississippi; University of Texas Press; University of Toronto; University of Wisconsin Press
Territory: Alaska, Arizona, California, Colorado, Hawaii, Idaho, Montana, Nevada, New Mexico, Oregon, Utah, Washington, Wyoming
Membership(s): American Booksellers Association (ABA)

David M Terry, see Terry & Read LLC

Tri-Fold Books
PO Box 534, King City, ON L7B 1A7, Canada
Tel: 905-726-0142
E-mail: info@trifoldbooks.com
Web Site: trifoldbooks.com
Key Personnel
Owner & Prop: Gabriele Freydank Edelstein
Founded: 1982
Distribution to book trade, institutions, schools & libraries. Mail order to general public.
Distributor for Bell Pond Books (USA); Bio-Dynamic Literature (USA); Claiview Book (UK); Floris Books (UK); Hawthorne Press (UK); Lindisfarne Books (USA); Rudolf Steiner Press (UK); SteinerBooks (USA); Temple Lodge Publishing (UK)
Represents Bell Pond Books (USA); Bio-Dynamic Literature (USA); Hawthorne Press (UK); Lindisfarne Books (USA); Rudolf Steiner Press (UK); SteinerBooks (USA); Temple Lodge Publishing (UK)
Territory: Canada

Two Rivers Distribution, an Ingram brand
Member of Ingram Publisher Services
1400 Broadway, Suite 520, New York, NY 10018
Toll Free Tel: 866-400-5351
E-mail: ips@ingramcontent.com (orders, independent bookstores & gift accts)
Web Site: www.tworiversdistribution.com
Key Personnel
Mgr, Client Rel: Louisa Brody; Jessica Morales
Founded: 1999
Sales, print, ebook & distribution services for independent publishers.
Branch Office(s)
IPS Jackson, 193 Edwards Dr, Jackson, TN 38301 (shipping) *Toll Free Tel:* 800-343-4499 *Toll Free Fax:* 800-351-5073
E-mail: ipsjacksonorders@ingramcontent.com
Distributor for Abbeville Press; American Academy of Pediatrics; Architecture/Interiors Press; Assouline; Bard Press; Bella Books; Black Dog Publishing Ltd London; Brisance Books Group; CompanionHouse; David & Charles Ltd; Distributed Art Publishers; Easton Studio Press; Encounter Books; Exisle Publishing; G Editions; Gemini Books Group; Girl Friday Books; David R Godine Inc; Hamilcar Publications; Handheld Press; Harvard Business Review Press; Hippocrene Books; Humanix Books; The Infatuation Inc; Justice Studios; LifeLines; Mayo Clinic Press; Melcher Media Inc; Merrell Publishers; The New Press; Park Avenue Publishers; Pear Press; Penguin Random House Grupo Editorial; Peterson's; Planeta Publishing Corp; Plata Publishing; Platform Books; Podium; RDA Press LLC; Regnery Publishing; Editorial Reverte SA; SelectBooks; Seven Press; Spiegel & Grau; Spry Publishing LLC; Starry Forest Books; Sungazer Publishing; Ta-Da! Language Productions; teNeues Publishing; Waterside Publishing; Welbeck Publishing Group; WS Publishing Group; ZAGAT Survey; Zando; Zibby Books
Territory: USA

P Tyrrell Associates
321 Monica Crescent, Burlington, ON L7N 1Z5, Canada
Tel: 289-937-6436 *Fax:* 905-639-2640
E-mail: pgtyrrell@cogeco.ca
Key Personnel
Prop: Paul Tyrrell
Founded: 1991
Agent representing educational publishers.
Represents Curriculum Associates; McGraw-Hill/Macmillan; SRA
Territory: Southwestern Ontario

Ulverscroft Large Print (USA) Inc
Member of The Ulverscroft Group
950A Union Rd, Suite 427, West Seneca, NY 14224
Mailing Address: PO Box 1230, West Seneca, NY 14224-1230
Tel: 716-674-4270; 905-637-8734 (CN)
Toll Free Tel: 800-955-9659; 888-860-3365 (CN) *Fax:* 716-674-4195; 905-333-6788 (CN)
E-mail: sales@ulverscroftusa.com; sales@ulverscroftcanada.com (CN)
Web Site: www.ulverscroft.com
Key Personnel
Dir: Charlene Kessel
Sales of large print books, unabridged & abridged audiobooks & CDs.

University of Toronto Press Guidance Centre
Division of University of Toronto Press
5201 Dufferin St, Toronto, ON M3H 5T8, Canada
Tel: 416-667-7791 *Toll Free Tel:* 800-565-9523 *Fax:* 416-667-7832 *Toll Free Fax:* 800-221-9985
E-mail: utpbooks@utpress.utoronto.ca
Web Site: www.utpguidancecentre.com

BOOK DISTRIBUTORS & SALES REPRESENTATIVES

Key Personnel
Mgr: Cindy Hall *Tel:* 416-667-8731
   E-mail: chall@utpress.utoronto.ca
Distributes a variety of resources in all areas of education for teachers, teacher educators, administrators, school board members, students & parents.
Distributor for Alta Book Centre; ALTA English Publishers; Boys Town Press; Brookes Publishing Co; Corwin; Gryphon House Inc; Guidance Centre; Kaplan Press; The Laboratory School at the Dr Eric Jackman Institute of Child Study, Ontario Institute for Studies in Education; NSTA Press; Pippin Publishing; Prometheus Nemesis Book Co; Rec Room Publishing; Teachers College Press; University of Toronto Press; University of Toronto Press, Higher Education Division; University of Toronto Press, Scholarly Publishing Division; Woodbine House
Territory: Canada

USCIB International Bookstore
Division of United States Council for International Business
1212 Avenue of the Americas, 21st fl, New York, NY 10036
Tel: 212-703-5066 *Fax:* 212-944-0012
E-mail: bookstore@uscib.org
Web Site: store.internationaltradebooks.org
Founded: 1980
International trade including banking, commercial trade terms, law & arbitration, counterfeiting & fraud, model commercial contracts to advertising & environmental matters.

West Virginia Book Co
1125 Central Ave, Charleston, WV 25302
Tel: 304-342-1848 *Fax:* 304-343-0594
E-mail: wvbooks@wvbookco.com
Web Site: www.wvbookco.com
Key Personnel
Owner: Bill Clements
Founded: 1995
Distributor of WV books.
Distributor for Elk River Press; Mountain Memories Books; Pictorial Histories Publishing Co; Quarrier Press

Worldwide Books
1001 W Seneca St, Ithaca, NY 14850-3342
Tel: 607-272-9200 *Toll Free Tel:* 800-473-8146 (US/CN orders only) *Fax:* 607-272-0239
E-mail: info@worldwide-artbooks.com
Web Site: www.worldwide-artbooks.com
Key Personnel
Pres: Mr Kelly M Fiske *E-mail:* fiske@worldwide-artbooks.com
Mgr, Exhibit Catalog Prog: Eileen Baker
   E-mail: ebaker@worldwide-artbooks.com
Mgr, Approval Plan Prog: David Fogel
   E-mail: dfogel@worldwide-artbooks.com
Founded: 1962
Library vendor specializing in the selection, review & distribution of museum & gallery exhibition catalogues from around the globe. Also supplying trade & university press books on art, architecture, design & photography. Approval plans available.
Membership(s): Art Libraries Society of North America (ARLIS/NA)

Wybel Marketing Group Inc
213 W Main St, Barrington, IL 60010
Tel: 847-382-0384; 847-382-0382
   Toll Free Tel: 800-323-5297 *Fax:* 847-382-0385
   Toll Free Fax: 800-595-5252
E-mail: bookreps@wybel.com
Key Personnel
Pres: Ronald J Prazuch *E-mail:* prazur@wybel.com
VP: Sheryl L Wybel *E-mail:* wybels@wybel.com
Assoc: Laurie Kendziora *E-mail:* lauriek@wybel.com; Bill McGarr *E-mail:* wdmgarr@aol.com
Founded: 1976
Sales representatives.
Territory: Midwestern States
Membership(s): American Booksellers Association (ABA); Midwest Independent Booksellers Association (MIBA)

Wholesalers — Activity Index

ACCOUNTS - BOOKSTORES

American International Distribution Corp (AIDC), pg 1311
Ariane Editions Inc, pg 1311
Art Consulting Scandinavia: Books on Art & Architecture, pg 1311
AzureGreen, pg 1311
BCH Fulfillment & Distribution, pg 1312
Benjamin News Group, pg 1312
Book Express, pg 1312
Book Sales, pg 1312
Bookazine Co Inc, pg 1312
B Broughton Co Ltd, pg 1313
The Children's Book Store Distribution (CBSD), pg 1313
China Books, pg 1313
Chinese Christian Mission Bookroom, pg 1313
CLC Ministries, pg 1313
Cooperative Etudiante de Polytechnique, pg 1314
Coronet Books Inc, pg 1314
De Ru's Fine Art, pg 1314
Devin-Adair Publishers/Seagrace Partners, pg 1314
DeVorss & Co, pg 1314
Distribooks Inc, pg 1314
Eaglecrafts Inc, pg 1314
East-West Health Arts, pg 1314
Eastern Book Co, pg 1314
Eastwind Books & Arts Inc, pg 1314
Edipresse Inc, pg 1314
Elder's Bookstore, pg 1315
European Books & Media, pg 1315
Fall River News Co Inc, pg 1315
Forest Sales & Distributing Co, pg 1315
GBS Books, pg 1315
Gem Guides Book Co, pg 1315
Dot Gibson Publications, pg 1315
Girol Books Inc, pg 1316
GoalsGuy Learning Systems, pg 1316
Harvard Art Museums, pg 1316
Ideal Foreign Books LLC, pg 1316
indiCo, pg 1316
Ingram Content Group LLC, pg 1316
Institute of Intergovernmental Relations, pg 1317
International Book Centre Inc, pg 1317
International Press Publication Inc, pg 1317
International Service Co, pg 1317
Iranbooks, pg 1317
The Islander Group, pg 1317
Israel's Judaica Center, pg 1317
Ketab Corp, pg 1317
Kinokuniya Bookstores of America Co Ltd, pg 1318
Lushena Books Inc, pg 1318
Metro 360, pg 1319
Montfort Publications, pg 1319
Motorbooks, pg 1319
National Book Network (NBN), pg 1319
National Learning Corp, pg 1319
The New England Mobile Book Fair®, pg 1319
New Leaf Distributing Co, pg 1319
Newborn Enterprises Inc (Altoona News Agency), pg 1319
North 49 Books, pg 1320
Pathway Book Service, pg 1320
Penfield Books, pg 1320
Redwing Book Co, pg 1320
Rising Sun Book Co, pg 1320
Rizzoli Bookstores, pg 1320
Richard Owen Roberts, Booksellers & Publishers, pg 1320
Rushmore News Inc, pg 1321
S & L Sales Co Inc, pg 1321
Sandhill Book Marketing Ltd, pg 1321
Schoenhof's Foreign Books Inc, pg 1321
Small Changes, pg 1321
SOM Publishing, pg 1321
Southern Wisconsin News Co, pg 1321
Spring Arbor Distributors Inc, pg 1322
Sunbelt Publications Inc, pg 1322
TEACH Services Inc, pg 1322
Upstart Books™, pg 1323
Valley News Co, pg 1323
Vedanta Book Center, pg 1323
VisionWorks, pg 1323
VistaBooks LLC, pg 1323
WeWrite LLC, pg 1323
Wilshire Book Co, pg 1323
Woodcrafters Lumber Sales Inc, pg 1323

ACCOUNTS - LIBRARIES

AKJ Education, pg 1311
American International Distribution Corp (AIDC), pg 1311
Ariane Editions Inc, pg 1311
Art Consulting Scandinavia: Books on Art & Architecture, pg 1311
Baker & Taylor LLC, pg 1312
BCH Fulfillment & Distribution, pg 1312
Beijing Book Co Inc, pg 1312
BMI Educational Services Inc, pg 1312
Bookazine Co Inc, pg 1312
Bound to Stay Bound Books Inc, pg 1312
Brodart Books & Library Services, pg 1313
B Broughton Co Ltd, pg 1313
Carolina Biological Supply Co, pg 1313
The Children's Book Store Distribution (CBSD), pg 1313
China Books, pg 1313
CLC Ministries, pg 1313
Coronet Books Inc, pg 1314
Devin-Adair Publishers/Seagrace Partners, pg 1314
DeVorss & Co, pg 1314
Distribooks Inc, pg 1314
Eaglecrafts Inc, pg 1314
Eastern Book Co, pg 1314
Eastwind Books & Arts Inc, pg 1314
Edipresse Inc, pg 1314
Elder's Bookstore, pg 1315
Emery-Pratt Co, pg 1315
Encyclopaedia Britannica Inc, pg 1315
European Books & Media, pg 1315
Fall River News Co Inc, pg 1315
Fennell Subscription Service Inc, pg 1315
Forest Sales & Distributing Co, pg 1315
GBS Books, pg 1315
Gem Guides Book Co, pg 1315
Girol Books Inc, pg 1316
GoalsGuy Learning Systems, pg 1316
GOBI® Library Solutions from EBSCO, pg 1316
Louis Goldberg Library Book Supplier, pg 1316
Harvard Art Museums, pg 1316
Historic Cherry Hill, pg 1316
Ideal Foreign Books LLC, pg 1316
Ingram Content Group LLC, pg 1316
Institute of Intergovernmental Relations, pg 1317
International Book Centre Inc, pg 1317
International Press Publication Inc, pg 1317
International Service Co, pg 1317
Interstate Books4School, pg 1317
Iranbooks, pg 1317
The Islander Group, pg 1317
The James & Law Co, pg 1317
Ketab Corp, pg 1317
Kinokuniya Bookstores of America Co Ltd, pg 1318
Learning World Inc, pg 1318
Lectorum Publications Inc, pg 1318
Library Bound Inc, pg 1318
The Library Services Centre, pg 1318
Lushena Books Inc, pg 1318
Mackin Educational Resources, pg 1318
Metro 360, pg 1319
Midwest Library Service, pg 1319
Motorbooks, pg 1319
National Book Network (NBN), pg 1319
National Learning Corp, pg 1319
Mrs Nelson's Library Services, pg 1319
New England Book Service Inc, pg 1319
The New England Mobile Book Fair®, pg 1319
Newborn Enterprises Inc (Altoona News Agency), pg 1319
Pannonia Bookstore, pg 1320
Paperbacks For Educators, pg 1320
Pathway Book Service, pg 1320
Paulist Press, pg 1320
The Penworthy Company LLC, pg 1320
Redwing Book Co, pg 1320
Rising Sun Book Co, pg 1320
Richard Owen Roberts, Booksellers & Publishers, pg 1320
S & L Sales Co Inc, pg 1321
Sandhill Book Marketing Ltd, pg 1321
Schoenhof's Foreign Books Inc, pg 1321
Schroeder's Book Haven, pg 1321
SOM Publishing, pg 1321
Southeastern Book Co, pg 1321
Spring Arbor Distributors Inc, pg 1322
Sunbelt Publications Inc, pg 1322
The Supreme Co, pg 1322
United Library Services Inc, pg 1323
Upstart Books™, pg 1323
Vedanta Book Center, pg 1323
WeWrite LLC, pg 1323
Whitehots Inc, pg 1323
Wilshire Book Co, pg 1323

ACCOUNTS - SCHOOLS

Adams Book Co Inc, pg 1311
AKJ Education, pg 1311
American International Distribution Corp (AIDC), pg 1311
Ariane Editions Inc, pg 1311
Art Consulting Scandinavia: Books on Art & Architecture, pg 1311
BCH Fulfillment & Distribution, pg 1312
BMI Educational Services Inc, pg 1312
Bookazine Co Inc, pg 1312
The Booksource Inc, pg 1312
Bound to Stay Bound Books Inc, pg 1312
Brodart Books & Library Services, pg 1313
B Broughton Co Ltd, pg 1313
Carolina Biological Supply Co, pg 1313
The Children's Book Store Distribution (CBSD), pg 1313
China Books, pg 1313
CLC Ministries, pg 1313
Coronet Books Inc, pg 1314
De Ru's Fine Art, pg 1314
Devin-Adair Publishers/Seagrace Partners, pg 1314
DeVorss & Co, pg 1314
Eaglecrafts Inc, pg 1314
East-West Health Arts, pg 1314
Eastern Book Co, pg 1314
Eastwind Books & Arts Inc, pg 1314
Edipresse Inc, pg 1314
Emery-Pratt Co, pg 1315
Encyclopaedia Britannica Inc, pg 1315
European Books & Media, pg 1315
Fall River News Co Inc, pg 1315
Fennell Subscription Service Inc, pg 1315
GBS Books, pg 1315
Girol Books Inc, pg 1316
Harvard Art Museums, pg 1316
Historic Cherry Hill, pg 1316
Ideal Foreign Books LLC, pg 1316
indiCo, pg 1316
International Book Centre Inc, pg 1317
International Press Publication Inc, pg 1317
Interstate Books4School, pg 1317
The Islander Group, pg 1317
Israel's Judaica Center, pg 1317
The James & Law Co, pg 1317
Kinokuniya Bookstores of America Co Ltd, pg 1318
Lectorum Publications Inc, pg 1318
The Library Services Centre, pg 1318

1305

WHOLESALERS — ACTIVITY INDEX / SALES

Mackin Educational Resources, pg 1318
Metro 360, pg 1319
Motorbooks, pg 1319
National Learning Corp, pg 1319
Mrs Nelson's Library Services, pg 1319
New England Book Service Inc, pg 1319
The New England Mobile Book Fair®, pg 1319
Newborn Enterprises Inc (Altoona News Agency), pg 1319
Osa's Ark Museum Shop, pg 1320
Paperbacks For Educators, pg 1320
Pathway Book Service, pg 1320
Paulist Press, pg 1320
The Penworthy Company LLC, pg 1320
Perma-Bound Books, pg 1320
Polybook Distributors, pg 1320
Redwing Book Co, pg 1320
Richard Owen Roberts, Booksellers & Publishers, pg 1320
S & L Sales Co Inc, pg 1321
San Diego Museum of Art, pg 1321
Schoenhof's Foreign Books Inc, pg 1321
Schroeder's Book Haven, pg 1321
Social Studies School Service, pg 1321
SOM Publishing, pg 1321
Southeastern Book Co, pg 1321
Sunbelt Publications Inc, pg 1322
The Supreme Co, pg 1322
Tennessee Book Co, pg 1322
United Library Services Inc, pg 1323
Upstart Books™, pg 1323
Vedanta Book Center, pg 1323
WeWrite LLC, pg 1323
Wilshire Book Co, pg 1323
Woodcrafters Lumber Sales Inc, pg 1323

APPROVAL PLANS

American International Distribution Corp (AIDC), pg 1311
Art Consulting Scandinavia: Books on Art & Architecture, pg 1311
Baker & Taylor LLC, pg 1312
Coronet Books Inc, pg 1314
Emery-Pratt Co, pg 1315
Girol Books Inc, pg 1316
GOBI® Library Solutions from EBSCO, pg 1316
International Press Publication Inc, pg 1317
Lectorum Publications Inc, pg 1318
Manning's Book & Prints, pg 1318
Midwest Library Service, pg 1319
Social Studies School Service, pg 1321
The Supreme Co, pg 1322

AV MATERIALS

Ancient Healing Ways, pg 1311
Art Consulting Scandinavia: Books on Art & Architecture, pg 1311
Baker & Taylor LLC, pg 1312
Beijing Book Co Inc, pg 1312
Bilingual Educational Services Inc, pg 1312
BMI Educational Services Inc, pg 1312
Carolina Biological Supply Co, pg 1313
The Children's Book Store Distribution (CBSD), pg 1313
East-West Health Arts, pg 1314
Emery-Pratt Co, pg 1315

Girol Books Inc, pg 1316
Glenbow Museum Shop, pg 1316
Ingram Content Group LLC, pg 1316
The Islander Group, pg 1317
Kinokuniya Bookstores of America Co Ltd, pg 1318
Library Bound Inc, pg 1318
The Library Services Centre, pg 1318
Le Messager Chretien (The Christian Messenger), pg 1319
Mrs Nelson's Library Services, pg 1319
Perma-Bound Books, pg 1320
Social Studies School Service, pg 1321
The Supreme Co, pg 1322

CATALOG CARDS & KITS

American International Distribution Corp (AIDC), pg 1311
Baker & Taylor LLC, pg 1312
Bilingual Educational Services Inc, pg 1312
BMI Educational Services Inc, pg 1312
Bound to Stay Bound Books Inc, pg 1312
China Books, pg 1313
Eastern Book Co, pg 1314
Emery-Pratt Co, pg 1315
GOBI® Library Solutions from EBSCO, pg 1316
Ingram Content Group LLC, pg 1316
The James & Law Co, pg 1317
Midwest Library Service, pg 1319
Mrs Nelson's Library Services, pg 1319
The Penworthy Company LLC, pg 1320
Perma-Bound Books, pg 1320
The Supreme Co, pg 1322

CATALOGING & PROCESSING

Baker & Taylor LLC, pg 1312
Bound to Stay Bound Books Inc, pg 1312
Brodart Books & Library Services, pg 1313
China Books, pg 1313
Emery-Pratt Co, pg 1315
GBS Books, pg 1315
GOBI® Library Solutions from EBSCO, pg 1316
Ingram Content Group LLC, pg 1316
Library Bound Inc, pg 1318
The Library Services Centre, pg 1318
Mackin Educational Resources, pg 1318
Midwest Library Service, pg 1319
The New England Mobile Book Fair®, pg 1319
The Penworthy Company LLC, pg 1320
Perma-Bound Books, pg 1320
Regent Book Co, pg 1320
The Supreme Co, pg 1322
United Library Services Inc, pg 1323

COMPUTER SOFTWARE

Beijing Book Co Inc, pg 1312
Bilingual Educational Services Inc, pg 1312

BMI Educational Services Inc, pg 1312
Carolina Biological Supply Co, pg 1313
Cheng & Tsui Co Inc, pg 1313
Christianbook Inc, pg 1313
Eastern Book Co, pg 1314
Eastwind Books & Arts Inc, pg 1314
Emery-Pratt Co, pg 1315
indiCo, pg 1316
Ingram Micro Inc, pg 1317
International Service Co, pg 1317
The James & Law Co, pg 1317
Kinokuniya Bookstores of America Co Ltd, pg 1318
Le Messager Chretien (The Christian Messenger), pg 1319
National Learning Corp, pg 1319
The Supreme Co, pg 1322
Teacher's Discovery®, pg 1322

DICTIONARIES & REFERENCE BOOKS

American International Distribution Corp (AIDC), pg 1311
Art Consulting Scandinavia: Books on Art & Architecture, pg 1311
Baker & Taylor LLC, pg 1312
Beijing Book Co Inc, pg 1312
Bernan, pg 1312
Bilingual Educational Services Inc, pg 1312
BMI Educational Services Inc, pg 1312
Bookazine Co Inc, pg 1312
The Booksource Inc, pg 1312
Bound to Stay Bound Books Inc, pg 1313
Brodart Books & Library Services, pg 1313
Carolina Biological Supply Co, pg 1313
Cheng & Tsui Co Inc, pg 1313
China Books, pg 1313
Christianbook Inc, pg 1313
Coronet Books Inc, pg 1314
De Ru's Fine Art, pg 1314
Distribooks Inc, pg 1314
Eastern Book Co, pg 1314
Eastwind Books & Arts Inc, pg 1314
Edipresse Inc, pg 1314
Les Editions Themis, pg 1315
Emery-Pratt Co, pg 1315
European Books & Media, pg 1315
GBS Books, pg 1315
Girol Books Inc, pg 1316
The Hubbard Co, pg 1316
Ideal Foreign Books LLC, pg 1316
indiCo, pg 1316
Ingram Content Group LLC, pg 1316
Institute of Intergovernmental Relations, pg 1317
International Book Centre Inc, pg 1317
International Press Publication Inc, pg 1317
International Service Co, pg 1317
Interstate Books4School, pg 1317
The James & Law Co, pg 1317
Kazi Publications Inc, pg 1317
Ketab Corp, pg 1317
Kinokuniya Bookstores of America Co Ltd, pg 1318
Learning World Inc, pg 1318
Lectorum Publications Inc, pg 1318
Mackin Educational Resources, pg 1318
Manning's Book & Prints, pg 1318
Metro 360, pg 1319

Midwest Library Service, pg 1319
National Learning Corp, pg 1319
The New England Mobile Book Fair®, pg 1319
Newborn Enterprises Inc (Altoona News Agency), pg 1319
North 49 Books, pg 1320
Paperbacks For Educators, pg 1320
Perma-Bound Books, pg 1320
Polybook Distributors, pg 1320
Rising Sun Book Co, pg 1320
S & L Sales Co Inc, pg 1321
Schoenhof's Foreign Books Inc, pg 1321
Scholastic School Reading Events, pg 1321
Schroeder's Book Haven, pg 1321
Southern Tier News Company, Inc, pg 1321
Southern Wisconsin News Co, pg 1321
Spring Arbor Distributors Inc, pg 1322
Sunbelt Publications Inc, pg 1322
The Supreme Co, pg 1322
Teacher's Discovery®, pg 1322
United Library Services Inc, pg 1323
Upstart Books™, pg 1323
Woodcrafters Lumber Sales Inc, pg 1323

DROP SHIPPING

American International Distribution Corp (AIDC), pg 1311
Art Consulting Scandinavia: Books on Art & Architecture, pg 1311
Baker & Taylor LLC, pg 1312
BCH Fulfillment & Distribution, pg 1312
BMI Educational Services Inc, pg 1312
Brodart Books & Library Services, pg 1313
CLC Ministries, pg 1313
Devin-Adair Publishers/Seagrace Partners, pg 1314
GoalsGuy Learning Systems, pg 1316
Harvard Art Museums, pg 1316
Ideal Foreign Books LLC, pg 1316
indiCo, pg 1316
International Press Publication Inc, pg 1317
International Service Co, pg 1317
The Islander Group, pg 1317
Lushena Books Inc, pg 1318
Mackin Educational Resources, pg 1318
Metro 360, pg 1319
National Learning Corp, pg 1319
Newborn Enterprises Inc (Altoona News Agency), pg 1319
Penfield Books, pg 1320
The Penworthy Company LLC, pg 1320
Polybook Distributors, pg 1320
Richard Owen Roberts, Booksellers & Publishers, pg 1320
Small Changes, pg 1321
Sunbelt Publications Inc, pg 1322
The Supreme Co, pg 1322
TEACH Services Inc, pg 1322
Upstart Books™, pg 1323
WeWrite LLC, pg 1323

FOREIGN LANGUAGE & BILINGUAL MATERIALS

Art Consulting Scandinavia: Books on Art & Architecture, pg 1311
Baker & Taylor LLC, pg 1312

& DISTRIBUTION

WHOLESALERS — ACTIVITY INDEX

Bilingual Educational Services Inc, pg 1312
Bound to Stay Bound Books Inc, pg 1312
Brodart Books & Library Services, pg 1313
Cheng & Tsui Co Inc, pg 1313
China Books, pg 1313
Chinese Christian Mission Bookroom, pg 1313
Continental Book Co Inc, pg 1314
Coronet Books Inc, pg 1314
Distribooks Inc, pg 1314
Eastern Book Co, pg 1314
Eastwind Books & Arts Inc, pg 1314
Edipresse Inc, pg 1314
Emery-Pratt Co, pg 1315
European Books & Media, pg 1315
GBS Books, pg 1315
Girol Books Inc, pg 1316
Ideal Foreign Books LLC, pg 1316
indiCo, pg 1316
Ingram Content Group LLC, pg 1316
Institute of Intergovernmental Relations, pg 1317
International Book Centre Inc, pg 1317
International Press Publication Inc, pg 1317
Iranbooks, pg 1317
The Islander Group, pg 1317
Israel's Judaica Center, pg 1317
The James & Law Co, pg 1317
Ketab Corp, pg 1317
Kinokuniya Bookstores of America Co Ltd, pg 1318
Lectorum Publications Inc, pg 1318
The Library Services Centre, pg 1318
Mackin Educational Resources, pg 1318
Le Messager Chretien (The Christian Messenger), pg 1319
National Learning Corp, pg 1319
Pannonia Bookstore, pg 1320
Perma-Bound Books, pg 1320
Schoenhof's Foreign Books Inc, pg 1321
Spring Arbor Distributors Inc, pg 1322
Sunbelt Publications Inc, pg 1322
Teacher's Discovery®, pg 1322
Vedanta Book Center, pg 1323
WeWrite LLC, pg 1323
Woodcrafters Lumber Sales Inc, pg 1323

GENERAL TRADE BOOKS - HARDCOVER

Adams Book Co Inc, pg 1311
American International Distribution Corp (AIDC), pg 1311
The Antiquarian Bookstore, pg 1311
Art Consulting Scandinavia: Books on Art & Architecture, pg 1311
Augsburg Fortress Publishers, Publishing House of the Evangelical Lutheran Church in America, pg 1311
Baker & Taylor LLC, pg 1312
BCH Fulfillment & Distribution, pg 1312
Beijing Book Co Inc, pg 1312
Book Express, pg 1312
Book Sales, pg 1312
Bookazine Co Inc, pg 1312
The Booksource Inc, pg 1312
Brodart Books & Library Services, pg 1313

Carolina Biological Supply Co, pg 1313
Wm Caxton Ltd - Bookseller & Publisher, pg 1313
Christianbook Inc, pg 1313
DeHoff Christian Bookstore, pg 1314
Devin-Adair Publishers/Seagrace Partners, pg 1314
DeVorss & Co, pg 1314
Eastern Book Co, pg 1314
Edipresse Inc, pg 1314
Elder's Bookstore, pg 1315
Emery-Pratt Co, pg 1315
Fall River News Co Inc, pg 1315
GBS Books, pg 1315
Gem Guides Book Co, pg 1315
Girol Books Inc, pg 1316
Glenbow Museum Shop, pg 1316
GoalsGuy Learning Systems, pg 1316
GOBI® Library Solutions from EBSCO, pg 1316
Historic Aviation Books, pg 1316
indiCo, pg 1316
Ingram Content Group LLC, pg 1316
International Press Publication Inc, pg 1317
International Service Co, pg 1317
Interstate Books4School, pg 1317
The James & Law Co, pg 1317
Kazi Publications Inc, pg 1317
Kinokuniya Bookstores of America Co Ltd, pg 1318
Learning World Inc, pg 1318
Library Bound Inc, pg 1318
The Library Services Centre, pg 1318
Lushena Books Inc, pg 1318
Mackin Educational Resources, pg 1318
Metro 360, pg 1319
Midwest Library Service, pg 1319
Motorbooks, pg 1319
National Book Network (NBN), pg 1319
The New England Mobile Book Fair®, pg 1319
New Leaf Distributing Co, pg 1319
Newborn Enterprises Inc (Altoona News Agency), pg 1319
North 49 Books, pg 1320
Paperbacks For Educators, pg 1320
Pathway Book Service, pg 1320
Polybook Distributors, pg 1320
Regent Book Co, pg 1320
Rising Sun Book Co, pg 1320
S & L Sales Co Inc, pg 1321
Schroeder's Book Haven, pg 1321
Sheriar Books, pg 1321
Social Studies School Service, pg 1321
Southern Tier News Company, Inc, pg 1321
Southern Wisconsin News Co, pg 1321
Spring Arbor Distributors Inc, pg 1322
Sunbelt Publications Inc, pg 1322
The Supreme Co, pg 1322
Swedenborg Foundation, pg 1322
Talas, pg 1322
TEACH Services Inc, pg 1322
Texas Art Supply, pg 1322
United Library Services Inc, pg 1323
Vedanta Book Center, pg 1323
WeWrite LLC, pg 1323
Woodcrafters Lumber Sales Inc, pg 1323

GOVERNMENT PUBLICATIONS

Beijing Book Co Inc, pg 1312
Bernan, pg 1312
Eastern Book Co, pg 1314
Emery-Pratt Co, pg 1315
William S Hein & Co Inc, pg 1316
International Press Publication Inc, pg 1317
International Service Co, pg 1317
Kinokuniya Bookstores of America Co Ltd, pg 1318
The Supreme Co, pg 1322
Woodcrafters Lumber Sales Inc, pg 1323

IMPORTS

Adams Book Co Inc, pg 1311
American International Distribution Corp (AIDC), pg 1311
Art Consulting Scandinavia: Books on Art & Architecture, pg 1311
Baker & Taylor LLC, pg 1312
Bernan, pg 1312
Coronet Books Inc, pg 1314
Crescent Imports, pg 1314
Eastern Book Co, pg 1314
Edipresse Inc, pg 1314
Emery-Pratt Co, pg 1315
European Books & Media, pg 1315
Girol Books Inc, pg 1316
Ideal Foreign Books LLC, pg 1316
International Press Publication Inc, pg 1317
International Service Co, pg 1317
Iranbooks, pg 1317
The Islander Group, pg 1317
Israel's Judaica Center, pg 1317
Ketab Corp, pg 1317
Kinokuniya Bookstores of America Co Ltd, pg 1318
Lectorum Publications Inc, pg 1318
Motorbooks, pg 1319
New Leaf Distributing Co, pg 1319
Schoenhof's Foreign Books Inc, pg 1321
United Library Services Inc, pg 1323
Vedanta Book Center, pg 1323
VisionWorks, pg 1323
Woodcrafters Lumber Sales Inc, pg 1323

JUVENILE & YOUNG ADULT BOOKS

AKJ Education, pg 1311
American Camp Association Inc, pg 1311
American International Distribution Corp (AIDC), pg 1311
Art Consulting Scandinavia: Books on Art & Architecture, pg 1311
Augsburg Fortress Publishers, Publishing House of the Evangelical Lutheran Church in America, pg 1311
Baker & Taylor LLC, pg 1312
Bilingual Educational Services Inc, pg 1312
BMI Educational Services Inc, pg 1312
Book Express, pg 1312
Book Sales, pg 1312
Bookazine Co Inc, pg 1312
The Booksource Inc, pg 1312
Bound to Stay Bound Books Inc, pg 1312
Brodart Books & Library Services, pg 1313
B Broughton Co Ltd, pg 1313

China Books, pg 1313
Christianbook Inc, pg 1313
CLC Ministries, pg 1313
DeVorss & Co, pg 1314
Eaglecrafts Inc, pg 1314
Eastern Book Co, pg 1314
Eastwind Books & Arts Inc, pg 1314
Edipresse Inc, pg 1314
Emery-Pratt Co, pg 1315
Forest Sales & Distributing Co, pg 1315
GBS Books, pg 1315
Gem Guides Book Co, pg 1315
Girol Books Inc, pg 1316
indiCo, pg 1316
Ingram Content Group LLC, pg 1316
Interstate Books4School, pg 1317
The Islander Group, pg 1317
The James & Law Co, pg 1317
Kazi Publications Inc, pg 1317
Kinokuniya Bookstores of America Co Ltd, pg 1318
Library Bound Inc, pg 1318
The Library Services Centre, pg 1318
Lushena Books Inc, pg 1318
Mackin Educational Resources, pg 1318
Metro 360, pg 1319
Midwest Library Service, pg 1319
National Learning Corp, pg 1319
Mrs Nelson's Library Services, pg 1319
The New England Mobile Book Fair®, pg 1319
New Leaf Distributing Co, pg 1319
Newborn Enterprises Inc (Altoona News Agency), pg 1319
North 49 Books, pg 1320
Ollis Book Co, pg 1320
Paperbacks For Educators, pg 1320
Pathway Book Service, pg 1320
Paulist Press, pg 1320
Penfield Books, pg 1320
The Penworthy Company LLC, pg 1320
Perma-Bound Books, pg 1320
Polybook Distributors, pg 1320
Regent Book Co, pg 1320
Rising Sun Book Co, pg 1320
S & L Sales Co Inc, pg 1321
Schoenhof's Foreign Books Inc, pg 1321
Scholastic School Reading Events, pg 1321
Social Studies School Service, pg 1321
Southern Tier News Company, Inc, pg 1321
Southern Wisconsin News Co, pg 1321
Spring Arbor Distributors Inc, pg 1322
Sunbelt Publications Inc, pg 1322
The Supreme Co, pg 1322
TEACH Services Inc, pg 1322
United Library Services Inc, pg 1323
WeWrite LLC, pg 1323
Woodcrafters Lumber Sales Inc, pg 1323

LARGE PRINT & BRAILLE MATERIALS

Baker & Taylor LLC, pg 1312
Brodart Books & Library Services, pg 1313
Eastern Book Co, pg 1314
Emery-Pratt Co, pg 1315

WHOLESALERS — ACTIVITY INDEX — SALES

Ingram Content Group LLC, pg 1316
International Service Co, pg 1317
The James & Law Co, pg 1317
The Library Services Centre, pg 1318
Mackin Educational Resources, pg 1318
Midwest Library Service, pg 1319
Spring Arbor Distributors Inc, pg 1322
WeWrite LLC, pg 1323

MAPS & ATLASES

Beijing Book Co Inc, pg 1312
Benjamin News Group, pg 1312
Bilingual Educational Services Inc, pg 1312
BMI Educational Services Inc, pg 1312
Carolina Biological Supply Co, pg 1313
Cheneliere Education Inc, pg 1313
China Books, pg 1313
Eastern Book Co, pg 1314
Eastwind Books & Arts Inc, pg 1314
Elder's Bookstore, pg 1315
Emery-Pratt Co, pg 1315
Fall River News Co Inc, pg 1315
Forest Sales & Distributing Co, pg 1315
Glenbow Museum Shop, pg 1316
indiCo, pg 1316
Ingram Content Group LLC, pg 1316
International Institute of Reflexology, pg 1317
International Press Publication Inc, pg 1317
International Service Co, pg 1317
The Islander Group, pg 1317
The James & Law Co, pg 1317
Kinokuniya Bookstores of America Co Ltd, pg 1318
Mackin Educational Resources, pg 1318
Manning's Book & Prints, pg 1318
The New England Mobile Book Fair®, pg 1319
S & L Sales Co Inc, pg 1321
Social Studies School Service, pg 1321
Southern Wisconsin News Co, pg 1321
Sunbelt Publications Inc, pg 1322
Teacher's Discovery®, pg 1322

MICROFORMS

Beijing Book Co Inc, pg 1312
Emery-Pratt Co, pg 1315
William S Hein & Co Inc, pg 1316
Kinokuniya Bookstores of America Co Ltd, pg 1318

ONLINE ORDERING

A-M Church Supply, pg 1311
American Camp Association Inc, pg 1311
American International Distribution Corp (AIDC), pg 1311
Art Consulting Scandinavia: Books on Art & Architecture, pg 1311
Baker & Taylor LLC, pg 1312
BCH Fulfillment & Distribution, pg 1312
BMI Educational Services Inc, pg 1312
Book Express, pg 1312

Brodart Books & Library Services, pg 1313
Christianbook Inc, pg 1313
Eastern Book Co, pg 1314
Emery-Pratt Co, pg 1315
Follett Higher Education Group, pg 1315
GBS Books, pg 1315
GOBI® Library Solutions from EBSCO, pg 1316
Ingram Content Group LLC, pg 1316
Kinokuniya Bookstores of America Co Ltd, pg 1318
The Library Services Centre, pg 1318
Mackin Educational Resources, pg 1318
Manning's Book & Prints, pg 1318
Le Messager Chretien (The Christian Messenger), pg 1319
Midwest Library Service, pg 1319
Mrs Nelson's Library Services, pg 1319
New Leaf Distributing Co, pg 1319
Paperbacks For Educators, pg 1320
Pathway Book Service, pg 1320
The Penworthy Company LLC, pg 1320
Perma-Bound Books, pg 1320
Sheriar Books, pg 1321
Spring Arbor Distributors Inc, pg 1322
Sunbelt Publications Inc, pg 1322
The Supreme Co, pg 1322
Upstart Books™, pg 1323
VisionWorks, pg 1323
Wilshire Book Co, pg 1323

OP SEARCH

The Antiquarian Bookstore, pg 1311
Art Consulting Scandinavia: Books on Art & Architecture, pg 1311
Wm Caxton Ltd - Bookseller & Publisher, pg 1313
Elder's Bookstore, pg 1315
Ingram Content Group LLC, pg 1316
International Press Publication Inc, pg 1317
International Service Co, pg 1317
Midwest Library Service, pg 1319
Richard Owen Roberts, Booksellers & Publishers, pg 1320

PAPERBACK BOOKS - MASS MARKET

Adams Book Co Inc, pg 1311
AKJ Education, pg 1311
American Camp Association Inc, pg 1311
The Antiquarian Bookstore, pg 1311
Augsburg Fortress Publishers, Publishing House of the Evangelical Lutheran Church in America, pg 1311
Baker & Taylor LLC, pg 1312
BCH Fulfillment & Distribution, pg 1312
BMI Educational Services Inc, pg 1312
Book Express, pg 1312
Bookazine Co Inc, pg 1312
The Booksource Inc, pg 1312
Brodart Books & Library Services, pg 1313
Wm Caxton Ltd - Bookseller & Publisher, pg 1313
Choice Books, pg 1313
Christianbook Inc, pg 1313
CLC Ministries, pg 1313

DeVorss & Co, pg 1314
Eastern Book Co, pg 1314
Edipresse Inc, pg 1314
Emery-Pratt Co, pg 1315
Fall River News Co Inc, pg 1315
Forest Sales & Distributing Co, pg 1315
GBS Books, pg 1315
Girol Books Inc, pg 1316
indiCo, pg 1316
Ingram Content Group LLC, pg 1316
International Institute of Reflexology, pg 1317
International Service Co, pg 1317
The James & Law Co, pg 1317
Kinokuniya Bookstores of America Co Ltd, pg 1318
Lectorum Publications Inc, pg 1318
The Library Services Centre, pg 1318
Lushena Books Inc, pg 1318
Mackin Educational Resources, pg 1318
Metro 360, pg 1319
Midwest Library Service, pg 1319
National Learning Corp, pg 1319
Mrs Nelson's Library Services, pg 1319
The New England Mobile Book Fair®, pg 1319
Newborn Enterprises Inc (Altoona News Agency), pg 1319
North 49 Books, pg 1320
Paperbacks For Educators, pg 1320
Polybook Distributors, pg 1320
Rising Sun Book Co, pg 1320
Richard Owen Roberts, Booksellers & Publishers, pg 1320
Rushmore News Inc, pg 1321
S & L Sales Co Inc, pg 1321
Scholastic School Reading Events, pg 1321
Social Studies School Service, pg 1321
Southern Tier News Company, Inc, pg 1321
Southern Wisconsin News Co, pg 1321
Spring Arbor Distributors Inc, pg 1322
The Supreme Co, pg 1322
TNG, pg 1322
United Library Services Inc, pg 1323
Vedanta Book Center, pg 1323
Woodcrafters Lumber Sales Inc, pg 1323

PAPERBACK BOOKS - TRADE

Adams Book Co Inc, pg 1311
AKJ Education, pg 1311
American International Distribution Corp (AIDC), pg 1311
Ancient Healing Ways, pg 1311
Ariane Editions Inc, pg 1311
Art Consulting Scandinavia: Books on Art & Architecture, pg 1311
Augsburg Fortress Publishers, Publishing House of the Evangelical Lutheran Church in America, pg 1311
Baker & Taylor LLC, pg 1312
BCH Fulfillment & Distribution, pg 1312
BMI Educational Services Inc, pg 1312
Book Express, pg 1312
Book Sales, pg 1312
Bookazine Co Inc, pg 1312
The Booksource Inc, pg 1312

Brodart Books & Library Services, pg 1313
B Broughton Co Ltd, pg 1313
Burlington News Agency Inc, pg 1313
Carolina Biological Supply Co, pg 1313
China Books, pg 1313
Choice Books, pg 1313
Christianbook Inc, pg 1313
CLC Ministries, pg 1313
DeHoff Christian Bookstore, pg 1314
Devin-Adair Publishers/Seagrace Partners, pg 1314
DeVorss & Co, pg 1314
Distribooks Inc, pg 1314
Eaglecrafts Inc, pg 1314
East-West Health Arts, pg 1314
Eastern Book Co, pg 1314
Edipresse Inc, pg 1314
Emery-Pratt Co, pg 1315
Fall River News Co Inc, pg 1315
Forest Sales & Distributing Co, pg 1315
GBS Books, pg 1315
Gem Guides Book Co, pg 1315
Girol Books Inc, pg 1316
Glenbow Museum Shop, pg 1316
GoalsGuy Learning Systems, pg 1316
GOBI® Library Solutions from EBSCO, pg 1316
Historic Aviation Books, pg 1316
Ideal Foreign Books LLC, pg 1316
indiCo, pg 1316
Ingram Content Group LLC, pg 1316
Interstate Books4School, pg 1317
The Islander Group, pg 1317
The James & Law Co, pg 1317
Kazi Publications Inc, pg 1317
Kinokuniya Bookstores of America Co Ltd, pg 1318
Lectorum Publications Inc, pg 1318
Library Bound Inc, pg 1318
The Library Services Centre, pg 1318
Lushena Books Inc, pg 1318
Mackin Educational Resources, pg 1318
Metro 360, pg 1319
Midwest Library Service, pg 1319
Motorbooks, pg 1319
National Book Co Inc, pg 1319
National Book Network (NBN), pg 1319
National Learning Corp, pg 1319
Mrs Nelson's Library Services, pg 1319
The New England Mobile Book Fair®, pg 1319
New Leaf Distributing Co, pg 1319
Newborn Enterprises Inc (Altoona News Agency), pg 1319
North 49 Books, pg 1320
Paperbacks For Educators, pg 1320
Pathway Book Service, pg 1320
Paulist Press, pg 1320
Penfield Books, pg 1320
Polybook Distributors, pg 1320
Redwing Book Co, pg 1320
Regent Book Co, pg 1320
Rising Sun Book Co, pg 1320
Richard Owen Roberts, Booksellers & Publishers, pg 1320
Rushmore News Inc, pg 1321
S & L Sales Co Inc, pg 1321
Sandhill Book Marketing Ltd, pg 1321
Scholastic School Reading Events, pg 1321
Schroeder's Book Haven, pg 1321
Sheriar Books, pg 1321

& DISTRIBUTION

Social Studies School Service, pg 1321
SOM Publishing, pg 1321
Southern Tier News Company, Inc, pg 1321
Southern Wisconsin News Co, pg 1321
Spring Arbor Distributors Inc, pg 1322
Sunbelt Publications Inc, pg 1322
The Supreme Co, pg 1322
Swedenborg Foundation, pg 1322
TEACH Services Inc, pg 1322
Texas Art Supply, pg 1322
TNG, pg 1322
United Library Services Inc, pg 1323
Upstart Books™, pg 1323
Vedanta Book Center, pg 1323
VisionWorks, pg 1323
VistaBooks LLC, pg 1323
WeWrite LLC, pg 1323
Wilshire Book Co, pg 1323
Woodcrafters Lumber Sales Inc, pg 1323

PERIODICALS

The Antiquarian Bookstore, pg 1311
Art Consulting Scandinavia: Books on Art & Architecture, pg 1311
Augsburg Fortress Publishers, Publishing House of the Evangelical Lutheran Church in America, pg 1311
Beijing Book Co Inc, pg 1312
Bernan, pg 1312
Bilingual Educational Services Inc, pg 1312
Burlington News Agency Inc, pg 1313
Wm Caxton Ltd - Bookseller & Publisher, pg 1313
China Books, pg 1313
Comag Marketing Group LLC (CMG), pg 1314
Eastern Book Co, pg 1314
Eastwind Books & Arts Inc, pg 1314
Les Editions Themis, pg 1315
Fall River News Co Inc, pg 1315
Fennell Subscription Service Inc, pg 1315
William S Hein & Co Inc, pg 1316
Ingram Content Group LLC, pg 1316
International Press Publication Inc, pg 1317
International Service Co, pg 1317
Kinokuniya Bookstores of America Co Ltd, pg 1318
Manning's Book & Prints, pg 1318
Metro 360, pg 1319
New Leaf Distributing Co, pg 1319
Newborn Enterprises Inc (Altoona News Agency), pg 1319
Pannonia Bookstore, pg 1320
Rushmore News Inc, pg 1321
Small Changes, pg 1321
Southern Tier News Company, Inc, pg 1321
Southern Wisconsin News Co, pg 1321
Spring Arbor Distributors Inc, pg 1322
Texas Bookman, pg 1322
TNG, pg 1322
Valley News Co, pg 1323

PREBINDING

AKJ Education, pg 1311
Baker & Taylor LLC, pg 1312
Bilingual Educational Services Inc, pg 1312
BMI Educational Services Inc, pg 1312
The Booksource Inc, pg 1312
Bound to Stay Bound Books Inc, pg 1312
Brodart Books & Library Services, pg 1313
Emery-Pratt Co, pg 1315
Metro 360, pg 1319
Midwest Library Service, pg 1319
Mrs Nelson's Library Services, pg 1319
The Penworthy Company LLC, pg 1320
Perma-Bound Books, pg 1320
The Supreme Co, pg 1322

REMAINDERS & OVERSTOCK

Mark A Adams Inc, pg 1311
Art Image Publications, pg 1311
C J Traders Inc, pg 1313
Christianbook Inc, pg 1313
Clear Concepts, pg 1314
Forest Sales & Distributing Co, pg 1315
indiCo, pg 1316
International Service Co, pg 1317
Maison de l'Education Inc, pg 1318
The Mazel Co, pg 1318
National Learning Corp, pg 1319
The New England Mobile Book Fair®, pg 1319
New Leaf Distributing Co, pg 1319
Promotional Book Co, pg 1320
Rising Sun Book Co, pg 1320
S & L Sales Co Inc, pg 1321
Schroeder's Book Haven, pg 1321
Southern Wisconsin News Co, pg 1321
Sunbelt Publications Inc, pg 1322
Texas Bookman, pg 1322
Upstart Books™, pg 1323
Warehouse Books Inc, pg 1323
Woodcrafters Lumber Sales Inc, pg 1323

SCHOLARLY BOOKS

American International Distribution Corp (AIDC), pg 1311
Art Consulting Scandinavia: Books on Art & Architecture, pg 1311
Augsburg Fortress Publishers, Publishing House of the Evangelical Lutheran Church in America, pg 1311
Baker & Taylor LLC, pg 1312
Beijing Book Co Inc, pg 1312
Bernan, pg 1312
Carolina Biological Supply Co, pg 1313
Cheng & Tsui Co Inc, pg 1313
Christianbook Inc, pg 1313
Coronet Books Inc, pg 1314
Eastern Book Co, pg 1314
Edipresse Inc, pg 1314
Les Editions Themis, pg 1315
Emery-Pratt Co, pg 1315
Feldheim Publishers, pg 1315
Girol Books Inc, pg 1316
GOBI® Library Solutions from EBSCO, pg 1316
Harvard Art Museums, pg 1316
indiCo, pg 1316
Ingram Content Group LLC, pg 1316
Institute of Intergovernmental Relations, pg 1317
International Press Publication Inc, pg 1317
International Service Co, pg 1317
Kazi Publications Inc, pg 1317
Kinokuniya Bookstores of America Co Ltd, pg 1318
Mackin Educational Resources, pg 1318
Midwest Library Service, pg 1319
The New England Mobile Book Fair®, pg 1319
Paulist Press, pg 1320
Redwing Book Co, pg 1320
Rising Sun Book Co, pg 1320
S & L Sales Co Inc, pg 1321
Schoenhof's Foreign Books Inc, pg 1321
Schroeder's Book Haven, pg 1321
Spring Arbor Distributors Inc, pg 1322
Sunbelt Publications Inc, pg 1322
The Supreme Co, pg 1322
Swedenborg Foundation, pg 1322
Texas Bookman, pg 1322
Upstart Books™, pg 1323

SCI-TECH & MEDICINE

American International Distribution Corp (AIDC), pg 1311
Baker & Taylor LLC, pg 1312
Beijing Book Co Inc, pg 1312
Bookazine Co Inc, pg 1312
Carolina Biological Supply Co, pg 1313
Coronet Books Inc, pg 1314
Eastern Book Co, pg 1314
Eastwind Books & Arts Inc, pg 1314
Edipresse Inc, pg 1314
Emery-Pratt Co, pg 1315
GOBI® Library Solutions from EBSCO, pg 1316
indiCo, pg 1316
Ingram Content Group LLC, pg 1316
International Press Publication Inc, pg 1317
International Service Co, pg 1317
Kinokuniya Bookstores of America Co Ltd, pg 1318
Learning World Inc, pg 1318
Login Canada, pg 1318
Midwest Library Service, pg 1319
Sunbelt Publications Inc, pg 1322
The Supreme Co, pg 1322

STANDING ORDERS & CONTINUATIONS

American International Distribution Corp (AIDC), pg 1311
Art Consulting Scandinavia: Books on Art & Architecture, pg 1311
Baker & Taylor LLC, pg 1312
Beijing Book Co Inc, pg 1312
Bernan, pg 1312
Brodart Books & Library Services, pg 1313
Eastern Book Co, pg 1314
Edipresse Inc, pg 1314
Emery-Pratt Co, pg 1315
GOBI® Library Solutions from EBSCO, pg 1316
Harvard Art Museums, pg 1316
William S Hein & Co Inc, pg 1316
indiCo, pg 1316
Ingram Content Group LLC, pg 1316
Institute of Intergovernmental Relations, pg 1317
International Press Publication Inc, pg 1317
International Service Co, pg 1317
Kinokuniya Bookstores of America Co Ltd, pg 1318
Metro 360, pg 1319
Midwest Library Service, pg 1319
Newborn Enterprises Inc (Altoona News Agency), pg 1319
Schoenhof's Foreign Books Inc, pg 1321
The Supreme Co, pg 1322
United Library Services Inc, pg 1323
Upstart Books™, pg 1323
Woodcrafters Lumber Sales Inc, pg 1323

TEXTBOOKS - ELEMENTARY

Adams Book Co Inc, pg 1311
American International Distribution Corp (AIDC), pg 1311
BMI Educational Services Inc, pg 1312
Carolina Biological Supply Co, pg 1313
Cheneliere Education Inc, pg 1313
Cheng & Tsui Co Inc, pg 1313
Christianbook Inc, pg 1313
Eastern Book Co, pg 1314
Eastwind Books & Arts Inc, pg 1314
Edipresse Inc, pg 1314
Emery-Pratt Co, pg 1315
Ideal Foreign Books LLC, pg 1316
International Book Centre Inc, pg 1317
International Service Co, pg 1317
The James & Law Co, pg 1317
Kazi Publications Inc, pg 1317
Kinokuniya Bookstores of America Co Ltd, pg 1318
Lectorum Publications Inc, pg 1318
National Learning Corp, pg 1319
Paperbacks For Educators, pg 1320
Polybook Distributors, pg 1320
Schoenhof's Foreign Books Inc, pg 1321
The Supreme Co, pg 1322
Teacher's Discovery®, pg 1322
Tennessee Book Co, pg 1322
Woodcrafters Lumber Sales Inc, pg 1323

TEXTBOOKS - SECONDARY

Adams Book Co Inc, pg 1311
American International Distribution Corp (AIDC), pg 1311
BMI Educational Services Inc, pg 1312
B Broughton Co Ltd, pg 1313
Carolina Biological Supply Co, pg 1313
Cheneliere Education Inc, pg 1313
Cheng & Tsui Co Inc, pg 1313
Eastern Book Co, pg 1314
Eastwind Books & Arts Inc, pg 1314
Edipresse Inc, pg 1314
Emery-Pratt Co, pg 1315
Girol Books Inc, pg 1316
Ideal Foreign Books LLC, pg 1316
International Book Centre Inc, pg 1317
International Press Publication Inc, pg 1317
International Service Co, pg 1317
The James & Law Co, pg 1317
Kazi Publications Inc, pg 1317

WHOLESALERS — ACTIVITY INDEX

Kinokuniya Bookstores of America Co Ltd, pg 1318
Lectorum Publications Inc, pg 1318
National Learning Corp, pg 1319
Paperbacks For Educators, pg 1320
Paulist Press, pg 1320
Polybook Distributors, pg 1320
Schoenhof's Foreign Books Inc, pg 1321
The Supreme Co, pg 1322
Teacher's Discovery®, pg 1322
Tennessee Book Co, pg 1322
Woodcrafters Lumber Sales Inc, pg 1323

TEXTBOOKS - COLLEGE

American International Distribution Corp (AIDC), pg 1311
Art Consulting Scandinavia: Books on Art & Architecture, pg 1311
Augsburg Fortress Publishers, Publishing House of the Evangelical Lutheran Church in America, pg 1311
Baker & Taylor LLC, pg 1312
Beijing Book Co Inc, pg 1312
Carolina Biological Supply Co, pg 1313
Cheneliere Education Inc, pg 1313
Cheng & Tsui Co Inc, pg 1313
Eastern Book Co, pg 1314
Eastwind Books & Arts Inc, pg 1314
Edipresse Inc, pg 1314
Emery-Pratt Co, pg 1315
Follett Higher Education Group, pg 1315
Girol Books Inc, pg 1316
Ideal Foreign Books LLC, pg 1316
indiCo, pg 1316
International Book Centre Inc, pg 1317
International Press Publication Inc, pg 1317
International Service Co, pg 1317
Kinokuniya Bookstores of America Co Ltd, pg 1318
Learning World Inc, pg 1318
Lectorum Publications Inc, pg 1318
MBS Textbook Exchange Inc, pg 1318
Midwest Library Service, pg 1319
National Book Co Inc, pg 1319
National Learning Corp, pg 1319
New England Book Service Inc, pg 1319
Paperbacks For Educators, pg 1320
Pathway Book Service, pg 1320
Paulist Press, pg 1320
Schoenhof's Foreign Books Inc, pg 1321
The Supreme Co, pg 1322
Teacher's Discovery®, pg 1322
Texas Book Co, pg 1322
Woodcrafters Lumber Sales Inc, pg 1323

UNIVERSITY PRESS BOOKS

Adams Book Co Inc, pg 1311
American International Distribution Corp (AIDC), pg 1311
Art Consulting Scandinavia: Books on Art & Architecture, pg 1311
Baker & Taylor LLC, pg 1312
Beijing Book Co Inc, pg 1312
Bookazine Co Inc, pg 1312
Brodart Books & Library Services, pg 1313
Carolina Biological Supply Co, pg 1313
Coronet Books Inc, pg 1314
De Ru's Fine Art, pg 1314
Eaglecrafts Inc, pg 1314
Eastern Book Co, pg 1314
Edipresse Inc, pg 1314
Les Editions Themis, pg 1315
Emery-Pratt Co, pg 1315
Forest Sales & Distributing Co, pg 1315
GoalsGuy Learning Systems, pg 1316
GOBI® Library Solutions from EBSCO, pg 1316
Harvard Art Museums, pg 1316
indiCo, pg 1316
Ingram Content Group LLC, pg 1316
International Book Centre Inc, pg 1317
International Press Publication Inc, pg 1317
International Service Co, pg 1317
Kazi Publications Inc, pg 1317
Kinokuniya Bookstores of America Co Ltd, pg 1318
Learning World Inc, pg 1318
Midwest Library Service, pg 1319
National Learning Corp, pg 1319
The New England Mobile Book Fair®, pg 1319
North 49 Books, pg 1320
Paperbacks For Educators, pg 1320
Pathway Book Service, pg 1320
Rising Sun Book Co, pg 1320
S & L Sales Co Inc, pg 1321
Schoenhof's Foreign Books Inc, pg 1321
Schroeder's Book Haven, pg 1321
Spring Arbor Distributors Inc, pg 1322
The Supreme Co, pg 1322
Woodcrafters Lumber Sales Inc, pg 1323

Wholesalers

Included is a partial list of active book wholesalers, including wholesale remainder dealers (buyers of bulk remainder stock from publishers and other sources). *The American Book Trade Directory* (Information Today, Inc., 121 Chanlon Road, Suite G-20, New Providence, NJ 07974-2195) lists wholesalers (including paperback wholesalers), jobbers and remainder houses in all fields. See also **Book Exporters & Importers**.

A-M Church Supply
3220 Bay Rd, Suite E, Saginaw, MI 48603
Tel: 989-249-9174 *Toll Free Tel:* 800-345-4694
Web Site: www.am-church.com
Key Personnel
Pres: Karrie Rapin-Klopp *E-mail:* rapin1974@yahoo.com
Founded: 1902
Religious goods, church supplies.
Number of Titles Warehoused: 300
Publication(s): *Annual catalog* (circ 1,200)

Adams Book Co Inc
80 Broad St, 5th fl, New York, NY 10004
Tel: 718-875-5464 *Toll Free Tel:* 800-221-0909
Fax: 718-852-3212 *Toll Free Fax:* 888-229-2650
E-mail: customerservice@adamsbook.com; orders@adamsbook.com; sales@adamsbook.com; returns@adamsbook.com
Web Site: www.adamsbook.com
Key Personnel
VP: Glen Schattner
Founded: 1945
Textbooks, paperbacks, digital books & ebooks; all subjects for elementary through high school & college.

Mark A Adams Inc
425 Riverside Dr, New York, NY 10025
Tel: 917-528-3459 *Fax:* 212-864-0416
E-mail: mark@markadamsinc.com
Technical & medical text remainders.

AKJ Education
4702 Benson Ave, Halethorpe, MD 21227
Tel: 410-242-1602 *Toll Free Tel:* 800-922-6066
Fax: 410-242-6107 *Toll Free Fax:* 888-770-2338
E-mail: info@akjeducation.com
Web Site: www.akjeducation.com
Key Personnel
Owner & Pres: Tim Thompson
Founded: 1974
Wholesaler of paperback books for schools & literacy programs.
Catalog available.
Number of Titles Warehoused: 25,000
Membership(s): Educational Book & Media Association (EBMA)

American Camp Association Inc
5000 State Rd 67 N, Martinsville, IN 46151-7902
Tel: 765-342-8456 *Toll Free Tel:* 800-428-2267
Fax: 765-342-2065
E-mail: contactus@acacamps.org
Web Site: www.acacamps.org
Key Personnel
Chief Prog Offr: Amy Katzenberger *Tel:* 765-349-3515 *E-mail:* akatzenberger@acacamps.org
Founded: 1910
Accreditation of children's camps; educational conferences & print resources (magazine & books), membership.
Catalog available.
Number of Titles Warehoused: 400

American International Distribution Corp (AIDC)
82 Winter Sport Lane, Williston, VT 05495
Mailing Address: PO Box 80, Williston, VT 05495-0080
Tel: 802-862-0095 *Toll Free Tel:* 800-678-2432
Fax: 802-864-7749
Web Site: www.aidcvt.com
Key Personnel
Pres & CEO: Marilyn McConnell
Dir, Opers: Michael Pelland
Founded: 1986
Fulfillment, credit, collections, reporting, customer service, data processing & subscriptions, continuity, call center, comprehensive suite of web services. Catalog available upon request.
Number of Titles Warehoused: 75,000
Membership(s): Book Industry Study Group (BISG); Independent Publisher's Guild (IPG)

Ancient Healing Ways
PO Box 459, Espanola, NM 87532
Tel: 505-747-2860 *Toll Free Tel:* 877-753-5351
Web Site: www.a-healing.com
Key Personnel
Owner & Pres: Siri Ram Singh
E-mail: sirirams@windstream.net
Founded: 1976
Health, yoga, herbs, teas, oils, organic foods bulk & packaged.
Catalog available.
Number of Titles Warehoused: 100

The Antiquarian Bookstore
1070 Lafayette Rd, US Rte 1, Portsmouth, NH 03801-5408
Tel: 603-436-7250
Web Site: www.antiquarianbookstore.com
Key Personnel
Mgr & Buyer: John W Foster
Founded: 1973
Rare books & periodicals.
Number of Titles Warehoused: 250,000

Ariane Editions Inc
1504-3460 Blvd St-Elzear W, Laval, QC H7P 0M7, Canada
Tel: 514-916-8809
E-mail: infor@editions-ariane.com
Web Site: www.editions-ariane.com
Key Personnel
Pres: Marc Vallee *E-mail:* marc@editions-ariane.com
Founded: 1994
Catalog available.
Number of Titles Warehoused: 350

Art Consulting Scandinavia: Books on Art & Architecture
25777 Punto de Vista Dr, Monte Nido, CA 91302-2155
Tel: 310-456-8762 *Fax:* 310-456-5714
E-mail: info@nordicartbooks.com
Web Site: www.nordicartbooks.com
Key Personnel
Owner: Lena Torslow Hansen
Founded: 1985
Importing & distributing of books on art & architecture & related subjects from Scandinavia. Catalogue available online.
Catalog available.
Number of Titles Warehoused: 4,000

Art Image Publications
Division of Beauchemin International Inc
PO Box 160, Derby Line, VT 05830
Toll Free Tel: 800-361-2598 *Toll Free Fax:* 800-559-2598
E-mail: customer.service@artimagepublications.com; info@artimagepublications.com
Web Site: www.artimagepublications.com
Key Personnel
Pres: Yvan Boulerice
Secy: Francoise Desjardins
Founded: 1998
Publisher & distributor. Art education, school books.
Catalog available.
Number of Titles Warehoused: 45

Augsburg Fortress Publishers, Publishing House of the Evangelical Lutheran Church in America
510 Marquette Ave S, Minneapolis, MN 55402
SAN: 169-4081
Mailing Address: PO Box 1209, Minneapolis, MN 55440-1209
Tel: 612-330-3300 *Toll Free Tel:* 800-426-0115 (ext 639, subns); 800-328-4648 (orders)
Fax: 612-330-3455 *Toll Free Fax:* 800-722-7766 (orders)
E-mail: customercare@augsburgfortress.org; copyright@augsburgfortress.org (reprint permission requests); info@augsburgfortress.org
Web Site: www.augsburgfortress.org; www.1517.media
Key Personnel
Pres & CEO: Tim Blevins *Tel:* 612-330-3300 ext 400 *E-mail:* blevinst@1517.media
VP & Publr, Sparkhouse: Tim Paulson
E-mail: paulsont@1517.media
Publr, Worship & Music: Suzanne Burke
E-mail: burkes@augsburgfortress.org
Perms, Pubns: Michael Moore *E-mail:* moorem@1517.media
Founded: 1855
Catalog available.
Number of Titles Warehoused: 1,200

AzureGreen
16 Bell Rd, Middlefield, MA 01243
Mailing Address: PO Box 48, Middlefield, MA 01243-0048
Tel: 413-623-2155 *Fax:* 413-623-2156
E-mail: azuregreen@azuregreen.com
Web Site: www.azuregreen.net
Key Personnel
Owner: Adair Cafarella *E-mail:* adair@abyssdistribution.com
Founded: 1986
Distributors of specialty books & gifts for spiritual seekers. Leaders in providing titles on: magic, wicca, tarot, New Age, goddess studies, herbs, healing, shamanism, Celtic lore, western mystery traditions, occult, ancient Egypt, magical children's stories & related subjects. Distribute mail-order catalog. Supply merchandise to New Age retail stores & mail-order companies.
Catalog available.
Number of Titles Warehoused: 2,500

WHOLESALERS — SALES

Baker & Taylor LLC
2550 W Tyvola Rd, Suite 300, Charlotte, NC 28217
Tel: 704-998-3100 *Toll Free Tel:* 800-775-1800 (info servs) *Fax:* 704-998-3319
E-mail: btinfo@baker-taylor.com
Web Site: www.baker-taylor.com
Key Personnel
EVP & Gen Mgr: Amandeep Kochar
EVP, Opers: Gary Dayton
Founded: 1828
Global information & entertainment services company that offers print & digital books & entertainment products along with value-added services to libraries & educational institutions. Based in Charlotte, NC, the company has been in existence for more than 180 years, developing long-term relationships with major suppliers, including book publishers, movie studios & music labels. Baker & Taylor maintains one of the largest combined in-stock book, video & music inventories in the US.
Branch Office(s)
Commerce Service Center, 251 Mount Olive Church Rd, Dept R, Commerce, GA 30599
Tel: 706-335-5000 *Toll Free Tel:* 800-775-1200
Momence Service Center, 501 S Gladiolus St, Momence, IL 60954, VP, Opers/Gen Mgr: Terrell Osborne *Tel:* 815-802-2444 *Toll Free Tel:* 800-775-2300
Pittsburgh Service Center, 875 Greentree Rd, Suite 678, Pittsburgh, PA 15220 *Tel:* 412-787-8890 *Toll Free Tel:* 800-775-2600
Membership(s): The American Library Association (ALA); Book Industry Study Group (BISG)

BCH Fulfillment & Distribution
33 Oakland Ave, Harrison, NY 10528
Tel: 914-835-0015 *Toll Free Tel:* 800-431-1579 *Fax:* 914-835-0398
E-mail: bookch@aol.com
Web Site: www.bookch.com
Key Personnel
Pres: Diane Musto
Founded: 1934
Distributor & small press fulfillment. Approved vendor for Ingram, Baker & Taylor, Amazon & Barnes & Noble.
Catalog available.
Number of Titles Warehoused: 5,000
Membership(s): Independent Book Publishers Association (IBPA)

Beaming Books, see Augsburg Fortress Publishers, Publishing House of the Evangelical Lutheran Church in America

Beijing Book Co Inc
Subsidiary of China National Publications Import & Export (Group) Co Ltd (People's Republic of China)
701 E Linden Ave, Linden, NJ 07036
Tel: 908-862-0909 *Fax:* 908-862-4201
E-mail: journals@cnpbbci.com
Key Personnel
Mgr: Donna Jacik
Founded: 1981
Export American publications (books, periodicals, other serials & government publications) to China for Chinese libraries. Purchase newspapers, music products, micro products, CD-ROM.

Benjamin News Group
1701 Rankin St, Missoula, MT 59808
Mailing Address: PO Box 16147, Missoula, MT 59808
Tel: 406-721-7801 *Toll Free Tel:* 800-823-6397 (MT only); 800-735-8557 (outside MT)
E-mail: customerservice@bngmsla.com
Web Site: www.bngmsla.com; www.facebook.com/Benjamin-News-Group-168874803126737/
Wholesale distributor of books, magazines & atlases.
Branch Office(s)
2701 N Van Marter, Spokane Valley, WA 99206
Tel: 509-928-0122 *Toll Free Tel:* 800-863-6278

Bernan
Imprint of Rowman & Littlefield Publishing Group
4501 Forbes Blvd, Suite 200, Lanham, MD 20706
Mailing Address: PO Box 191, Blue Ridge Summit, PA 17214-0191
Tel: 717-794-3800 (cust serv & orders)
Toll Free Tel: 800-462-6420 (cust serv & orders) *Fax:* 717-794-3803 *Toll Free Fax:* 800-338-4550
E-mail: customercare@rowman.com
Web Site: rowman.com/page/bernan
Key Personnel
Mktg Mgr: Veronica M Dove *Tel:* 301-459-2255 ext 5716 *Fax:* 301-459-0056 *E-mail:* vdove@rowman.com
Founded: 1952
Distributor of publications from the US government & intergovernmental agencies. Publisher of government-related reference works.
Catalog available.

Bilingual Educational Services Inc
2514 S Grand Ave, Los Angeles, CA 90007
SAN: 169-0388
Tel: 213-749-6213 *Toll Free Tel:* 800-448-6032
Key Personnel
Pres: Jeff Penichet
Founded: 1971
Textbooks, books, posters, study prints & AV programs for bilingual & multicultural education.
Number of Titles Warehoused: 5,000

BMI Educational Services Inc
26 Haypress Rd, Cranbury, NJ 08512
SAN: 169-4669
Mailing Address: PO Box 800, Dayton, NJ 08810-0800
Tel: 732-329-6991 *Toll Free Tel:* 800-222-8100 (orders only) *Fax:* 732-329-6994
Toll Free Fax: 800-986-9393 (orders only)
E-mail: info@bmionline.com
Web Site: bmionline.com
Key Personnel
Owner & Secy-Treas: Lynda Bradley
Pres: Jerry Wagner *E-mail:* jwagner@bmionline.com
Founded: 1964
Distributors of popular & classic fiction & non-fiction paperback titles for K-12, leveled book collections for schools, teacher's guides. Also offers book binding services.
Catalog available.
Number of Titles Warehoused: 10,000
Publication(s): *Catalogs for grades K-12*
Membership(s): International Literacy Association (ILA); National Council of Teachers of English (NCTE)

Book Express
Division of Raincoast Book Distribution Ltd
2440 Viking Way, Richmond, BC V6V 1N2, Canada
SAN: 115-0871
Tel: 604-448-7100 *Toll Free Tel:* 800-663-5714 *Fax:* 604-270-7161 *Toll Free Fax:* 800-565-3770
E-mail: info@raincoast.com
Web Site: www.raincoast.com
Key Personnel
CEO, Raincoast Books: John Sawyer
E-mail: johns@raincoast.com
Buyer: Debra Berglind
Founded: 1975
Book wholesaler. Trade wholesale in Canada.
Catalog available.
Number of Titles Warehoused: 5,000

Book Sales
Division of Quarto Publishing Group USA Inc
142 W 36 St, 4th fl, New York, NY 10018
SAN: 299-4062
Tel: 212-779-4971; 212-779-4972 *Fax:* 212-779-6058
Web Site: www.quartoknows.com
Key Personnel
Sales Dir: Steven Wilson *Tel:* 212-779-4973
E-mail: steve.wilson@quarto.com
Founded: 1952
Publisher & supplier of books to wholesalers, mail order companies & retail stores for over 60 years. In addition to books published, we are one of the largest purchasers of other publishers' remainder +/or overstock titles for resale at significantly reduced prices. Categories include novels, cookbooks, history, juvenile, Civil War, militaria, fine art, art instruction, how-to craft books, natural history, gardening & more.
Catalog available.
Membership(s): American Booksellers Association (ABA)

Bookazine Co Inc
75 Hook Rd, Bayonne, NJ 07002
SAN: 169-5665
Tel: 201-339-7777 *Toll Free Tel:* 800-221-8112 *Fax:* 201-339-7778
E-mail: info@bookazine.com
Web Site: www.bookazine.com
Key Personnel
Pres & CEO: Robert Kallman
COO: Richard Kallman
Pres, Sales: Cindy Raiton
VP, Mdse: Andrew Collings
VP, Dist: Allan Davis
Dir, Natl Accts: Steven Goldberg
Northeast Sales Dir: Josh Harwood
Mktg Mgr: Lani Buess
Founded: 1929
General book wholesaler to bookstores & libraries. Specialize in books of Jewish interest, Black interest books, juvenile books, gay-lesbian books, computer books, international services.
Number of Titles Warehoused: 80,000
Publication(s): *Gift Books for the Holidays*

The Booksource Inc
Division of GL group Inc
1230 Macklind Ave, St Louis, MO 63110
Tel: 314-647-0600 *Toll Free Tel:* 800-444-0435 *Fax:* 314-647-6850 *Toll Free Fax:* 800-647-1923
E-mail: service@booksource.com
Web Site: www.booksource.com
Key Personnel
Owner: Neil Jaffe *Tel:* 314-647-0600 ext 245
E-mail: njaffe@booksource.com
CEO: Gary Jaffe
Founded: 1974
K-12 school wholesaler, hardcover & paperbacks. Vinaclad, prebound paperback books.
Catalog available.
Number of Titles Warehoused: 30,000
Publication(s): *K-12 Education Catalog* (annual, circ 50,000); *Leveled Reading K-6 Catalog* (annual, circ 20,000)
Membership(s): Educational Book & Media Association (EBMA)

Bound to Stay Bound Books Inc
1880 W Morton Rd, Jacksonville, IL 62650
SAN: 169-1996

Tel: 217-245-5191 *Toll Free Tel:* 800-637-6586
Fax: 217-245-0424 *Toll Free Fax:* 800-747-7872
E-mail: btsb@btsb.com
Web Site: www.btsb.com
Key Personnel
Pres: Robert L Sibert
Founded: 1920
Prebinder of children's books which are sold to schools & libraries all over the country. Seasonal catalogs available.
Number of Titles Warehoused: 19,000

Broadleaf Books, see Augsburg Fortress Publishers, Publishing House of the Evangelical Lutheran Church in America

Brodart Books & Library Services
500 Arch St, Williamsport, PA 17701
Tel: 570-326-2461 *Toll Free Tel:* 800-233-8467
Fax: 570-651-1639 *Toll Free Fax:* 800-999-6799
E-mail: support@brodart.com
Web Site: www.brodartbooks.com
Key Personnel
Pres & CEO: George Coe
CFO: Richard Dill
VP, Books Div: Gretchen Herman
Founded: 1939
Delivers shelf-ready books, exclusively serving libraries. Professional selection & customized cataloging & processing are avilable for English & Spanish language titles.
Catalog available.
Number of Titles Warehoused: 1,000,000

B Broughton Co Ltd
322 Consumers Rd, North York, ON M2J 1P8, Canada
Tel: 416-690-4777 *Toll Free Tel:* 800-268-4449
Fax: 416-690-5357
E-mail: sales@bbroughton.com
Web Site: www.bbroughton.com
Key Personnel
Owner & Pres: Brian Broughton *E-mail:* brian@bbroughton.com
Founded: 1970
Religious education books, AV & trade.
Catalog available.
Number of Titles Warehoused: 6,000
Membership(s): National Church Goods Association (NCGA)

Burlington News Agency Inc
382 Hercules Dr, Suite 2, Colchester, VT 05446
Tel: 802-655-7000 *Fax:* 802-655-7002
E-mail: burlnews@aol.com
Key Personnel
Pres: Glenn E Murphy
VP: Brian T Murphy
Founded: 1942
Wholesaler & distributor of newspapers, magazines, paperback books & periodicals.

C J Traders Inc
555 Second Ave, Suite C700, Collegeville, PA 19426
Tel: 484-902-8057 *Fax:* 484-902-8093
E-mail: cjtraders714@gmail.com
Key Personnel
Pres: John Jacobs
Founded: 1995
Specialize in cookbooks, children's books, craft, gardening; hardcover, trade, fiction, nonfiction & textbooks.
Number of Titles Warehoused: 1,000

Carolina Biological Supply Co
2700 York Rd, Burlington, NC 27215-3398
Mailing Address: PO Box 6010, Burlington, NC 27216-6010
Tel: 336-586-4399 (intl sales); 336-538-6211
Toll Free Tel: 800-334-5551 *Fax:* 336-584-7686 (intl sales) *Toll Free Fax:* 800-222-7112
E-mail: quotations@carolina.com; product@carolina.com
Web Site: www.carolina.com
Key Personnel
Pres & CEO: Jim Parrish
VP: Bruce Wilcox *E-mail:* bruce.wilcox@carolina.com
HR Mgr: Jim Scruggs
Founded: 1927
Publish & distribute books, charts, audiovisuals, CD-ROMs.
Catalog available.
Number of Titles Warehoused: 1,700
Publication(s): *Carolina Tips* (quarterly, circ 100,000)

Wm Caxton Ltd - Bookseller & Publisher
12037 Hwy 42, Ellison Bay, WI 54210
SAN: 664-7901
Mailing Address: Box 220, Ellison Bay, WI 54210
Tel: 920-854-2955
Key Personnel
Owner: Kubet Luchterhand
Founded: 1986
Number of Titles Warehoused: 24

Cheneliere Education Inc
Division of TC Media Books Inc
5800, rue St Denis, bureau 900, Montreal, QC H2S 3L5, Canada
Tel: 514-273-1066 *Toll Free Tel:* 800-565-5531
Fax: 514-276-0324 *Toll Free Fax:* 800-814-0324
E-mail: info@cheneliere.ca
Web Site: www.cheneliere.ca
Key Personnel
Pres & Gen Mgr: Patrick Lutzy
VP, Prodn: Michel Carl Perron
E-mail: mcperron@cheneliere.ca
Founded: 1985
Publish & distribute.
Catalog available.
Number of Titles Warehoused: 2,500

Cheng & Tsui Co Inc
25 West St, 2nd fl, Boston, MA 02111-1213
Tel: 617-988-2400 *Toll Free Tel:* 800-554-1963
Fax: 617-426-3669
E-mail: service@cheng-tsui.com; orders@cheng-tsui.com; marketing@cheng-tsui.com
Web Site: www.cheng-tsui.com
Key Personnel
Pres: Jill Cheng
Founded: 1979
Distribute & publish Asian studies related textbooks, literature, software, DVDs & more.
Catalog available.

The Children's Book Store Distribution (CBSD)
Division of IDLA Associated Label Distribution
23 Griffin St, Waterdown, ON L0R 2H0, Canada
Mailing Address: PO Box 170, Waterdown, ON L0R 2H0, Canada
Tel: 905-690-9397 (ext 237) *Toll Free Tel:* 800-757-8372 (cust serv, CN & US) *Fax:* 905-690-3419
E-mail: info@childrensgroup.com; sales@idla.ca
Web Site: www.childrensgroup.com
Key Personnel
Sales: Judy Smyth
Founded: 1991
Children's audio recordings, teacher resource materials & DVDs.
Catalog available.
Number of Titles Warehoused: 2,000

China Books
Division of Sinomedia International Group
360 Swift Ave, Suite 48, South San Francisco, CA 94080
SAN: 169-0167
Fax: 650-872-7808
E-mail: editor.sinomedia@gmail.com
Key Personnel
Edit Dir: Chris Robyn *Tel:* 650-872-7718 ext 312
E-mail: chris@sinomediausa.com
Sales Mgr: Kelly Feng *Tel:* 650-872-7076 ext 310
E-mail: kelly@chinabooks.com
Founded: 1960
Publisher, distributor & importer of books from & about China.
Catalog available.
Number of Titles Warehoused: 3,000

China Books & Periodicals Inc, see China Books

Chinese Christian Mission Bookroom
1269 N McDowell Blvd, Petaluma, CA 94954-1133
Mailing Address: PO Box 750759, Petaluma, CA 94975-0759
Tel: 707-762-2688; 707-762-1314 *Fax:* 707-762-1713
E-mail: bookroom@ccmusa.org; ccm@ccmusa.org
Web Site: www.ccmusa.org; www.ccmbookroom.org
Key Personnel
Mgr: Jenny Sit
Founded: 1972
Chinese Bibles, Christian books & tracts, mail order service, Christian gift items.
Catalog available.

Choice Books
10100 Piper Lane, Bristow, VA 20136
Tel: 703-530-9993 *Fax:* 703-530-9983
E-mail: info@choicebooks.com
Web Site: www.choicebooks.com
Key Personnel
CEO: Joe Bacher
Prog Asst: E Dale Mast *E-mail:* dale.mast@choicebooks.com
Founded: 1962
Rack jobber/wholesale vendor of trade & mass market paperbacks.
Number of Titles Warehoused: 2,000

Christianbook Inc
140 Summit St, Peabody, MA 01960-5156
Mailing Address: PO Box 7000, Peabody, MA 01961-7000
Tel: 978-977-5060; 978-977-5000 (intl calls)
Toll Free Tel: 800-CHRISTIAN (247-4784)
Fax: 978-977-5010
E-mail: customer.service@christianbook.com
Web Site: www.christianbook.com
Key Personnel
Pres & CEO: Ray Hendrickson
COO: Kevin Hendrickson
EVP: Ken Davis
Dist Ctr Systems Mgr: Gary Lussier
Founded: 1978
Direct mail to individuals throughout the world. Religious reference, language, popular, youth counseling, sermon resources, Bibles, theological reference, juvenile, young adult books & videos.
Number of Titles Warehoused: 12,000

CLC Ministries
701 Pennsylvania Ave, Fort Washington, PA 19034
SAN: 169-7358
Mailing Address: PO Box 1449, Fort Washington, PA 19034-8499
Tel: 215-542-1240 *Toll Free Tel:* 800-659-1240
Fax: 215-542-7580

WHOLESALERS

E-mail: orders@clcpublications.com
Web Site: www.clcpublications.com
Key Personnel
Dir: Jim Pitman *E-mail:* jpitman@clcusa.org
Dist/Sales Dir: Charlie Hurd
Founded: 1941
Also sells to ministries.
Catalog available.
Number of Titles Warehoused: 440
Membership(s): EFMA

Clear Concepts
1329 Federal Ave, Suite 6, Los Angeles, CA 90025
Tel: 323-285-0325
Key Personnel
Owner: Karen Kleiner
Brokers remainders & overstock, books & audio, fiction & nonfiction. Subjects include children's, cookbooks, artbooks, how-to, health, reference books & best sellers. Prefers exclusive representation.

Comag Marketing Group LLC (CMG)
Division of The Jim Pattison Group
155 Village Blvd, Suite 300, Princeton, NJ 08540
Tel: 609-524-1800 *Fax:* 609-524-1629
Web Site: www.i-cmg.com
Key Personnel
Pres: James W Felts
EVP: Michael P Herrington
SVP: Robert F Brassell; Michael Gillen
Founded: 1919
Our client services team works with publishers on developing & implementing a targeted single-copy sales business plan. We act as the liaison between our publishers & all our channel partners (internal & external) to make sure that our clients' objectives are communicated & put into practice. Our goal is to exceed our clients' expectations every day.

Continental Book Co Inc
7000 Broadway, Suite 102, Denver, CO 80221-2913
Tel: 303-289-1761 *Toll Free Fax:* 800-279-1764
E-mail: cbc@continentalbook.com
Web Site: www.continentalbook.com
Key Personnel
Dir: Linette Hayat *E-mail:* linette@continentalbook.com
Founded: 1961
Distributors of French, Spanish, ELL, Italian, German, Arabic, Chinese, Heritage Spanish & American publications, imported & domestic, juvenile to advanced levels.
Catalog available.
Number of Titles Warehoused: 15,000

Cooperative Etudiante de Polytechnique
Pavillon Principal Local C-220, 2900 Edouard Mont Petit, Montreal, QC H3T 1J4, Canada
Mailing Address: CP 6079, Succursale Centre-Ville, Montreal, QC H3C 3A7, Canada
Tel: 514-340-4851 *Fax:* 514-340-4543
E-mail: andre.daneau@polymtl.ca
Web Site: www.coopoly.ca
Key Personnel
Bookstore Dir: Jacques Desharnais *Tel:* 514-340-4362 *E-mail:* jacques.desharnais@polymtl.ca
Gen Mgr: Yves Daigneault *Tel:* 514-340-5229 *E-mail:* yves.daigneault@polymtl.ca
Founded: 1944
Engineering publications.
Number of Titles Warehoused: 10,000

Coronet Books Inc
33 Ashley Dr, Schwenksville, PA 19473
SAN: 210-6043
Tel: 215-925-2762 *Fax:* 215-925-1912
Web Site: www.coronetbooks.com

Key Personnel
Pres: Ronald P Smolin
VP: Jeff Goldstein *E-mail:* jeffgolds@comcast.net
Founded: 1985

Crescent Imports
PO Box 721, Union City, CA 94587
Tel: 734-665-3492 *Toll Free Tel:* 800-521-9744
Fax: 734-677-1717
E-mail: message@crescentimports.com
Web Site: crescentimports.com; crescentimports.store
Key Personnel
Co-Owner: Gulshan Ibrahim; Sabir Ibrahim
Founded: 1978
Distribute books on Islamic religion & African-American literature, free catalog & Islamic supplies.
Catalog available.
Number of Titles Warehoused: 10,000

De Ru's Fine Art
Subsidiary of De Ru's Fine Arts Gallery
27762 Antonio Pkwy, No L1103, Ladeira Ranch, CA 92694
SAN: 216-3667
Tel: 714-349-8250
E-mail: derusfinearts@yahoo.com
Web Site: www.derusfinearts.com
Key Personnel
Owner: Clint McCall
Founded: 1969
Art gallery, art restoration, art reference books, library bound catalogs from museums & galleries dealing with early California art.
Number of Titles Warehoused: 20

DeHoff Christian Bookstore
749 NW Broad St, Murfreesboro, TN 37129
Tel: 615-893-8322 *Toll Free Tel:* 800-695-5385
Fax: 615-896-7447
E-mail: dehoffbooks@gmail.com
Web Site: www.dehoffpublications.com
Key Personnel
Owner & Mgr: Bonnie Fakes
Founded: 1939
Religious books, literature, workbooks & publications.
Catalog available.
Number of Titles Warehoused: 100

Devin-Adair Publishers/Seagrace Partners
525 Flagler Dr, Suite 15A, West Palm Beach, FL 33401
Tel: 561-909-7576 *Fax:* 718-359-8568
Key Personnel
VP: Roger H Lourie
Cust Serv Mgr: Chris Dowdell
Founded: 1911
Mail order & trade sales to libraries, retail stores, institutions, individuals & private organizations.
Catalog available.
Number of Titles Warehoused: 725
Membership(s): American Booksellers Association (ABA); Association of Research Libraries (ARL); Connecticut Business & Industry Association (CBIA)

DeVorss & Co
1100 Flynn Rd, Unit 104, Camarillo, CA 93012
SAN: 168-9886
Mailing Address: PO Box 1389, Camarillo, CA 93011-1389
Tel: 805-322-9010 *Toll Free Tel:* 800-843-5743
Fax: 805-322-9011
E-mail: service@devorss.com
Web Site: www.devorss.com
Key Personnel
Pres: Gary R Peattie *Tel:* 805-322-9010 ext 14 *E-mail:* gpeattie@devorss.com
Founded: 1929

SALES

Metaphysical, spiritual, inspirational, self-help, body/mind/spirit & New Thought books. Announcements of new books as available.
Catalog available.
Publication(s): *DeVorss Publications Catalog* (annual)

Distribooks Inc
Subsidiary of MEP Inc
8154 N Ridgeway Ave, Skokie, IL 60076-2911
Tel: 847-676-1596 *Fax:* 847-676-1195
Toll Free Fax: 888-266-5713
E-mail: info@distribooks.com; info@schoenhofs.com
Web Site: www.schoenhofs.com
Key Personnel
Pres: Nicolas Mengin
Dir, Mktg & Sales: Daniel Eastman *E-mail:* deastman@mep-inc.net
Founded: 1989
Foreign language book distributor. Branch office located in Boston, MA.
Catalog available.
Number of Titles Warehoused: 8,000

Eaglecrafts Inc
168 W 12 St, Ogden, UT 84404
SAN: 630-6381
Tel: 801-393-3991 *Fax:* 801-393-4647
E-mail: sales@eaglefeathertrading.com
Web Site: www.eaglefeathertrading.com
Key Personnel
Publr: Monte Smith
Sales Mgr: Sue Smith
Founded: 1972
Native American & early American frontier titles & related subjects: crafts, history & mountain men titles.
Catalog available.
Number of Titles Warehoused: 2,500

East-West Health Arts
45 Academy Circle, Oakland, NJ 07436-0945
Tel: 201-337-8787
Key Personnel
Owner: Martin S Ruback
Founded: 2006
Wholesale to New Age stores, massage schools & Judaica stores.

Eastern Book Co
7 Lincoln Ave, Scarborough, ME 04074
SAN: 169-3050
Tel: 207-856-1370 *Toll Free Tel:* 800-937-0331
Toll Free Fax: 800-214-3895
E-mail: info@ebc.com; sales@ebc.com
Web Site: www.ebc.com
Key Personnel
Owner: Stephen P Coyne
Founded: 1957
Wholesaler for all publishers to schools & libraries.
Number of Titles Warehoused: 15,000

Eastwind Books & Arts Inc
1435 Stockton St, San Francisco, CA 94133
SAN: 127-3159
Tel: 415-772-5888 *Fax:* 415-772-5885
E-mail: contact@eastwindbooks.com
Web Site: www.eastwindbooks.com
Key Personnel
Mgr: Cat Deng
Founded: 1978
Books on Asia, Asian-American, China in English +/or Chinese language.
Number of Titles Warehoused: 30,000
Membership(s): American Booksellers Association (ABA)

Edipresse Inc
945, ave Beaumont, Montreal, QC H3N 1W3, Canada

Tel: 514-273-6141 *Toll Free Tel:* 800-361-1043
 Fax: 514-273-7021
E-mail: information@edipresse.ca
Web Site: www.edipresse.ca
Key Personnel
Pres: Ms Leone Giannone Rameau
Gen Mgr: Pascal Chamaillard *Tel:* 514-273-6141 ext 203 *E-mail:* chamaillard@edipresse.ca
Founded: 1979
Distribute French books.
Number of Titles Warehoused: 24,000
Membership(s): Association des Distributeurs Exclusifs de Livres en Langue Francaise (ADELF)

Les Editions Themis
Faculte de droit, Universite de Montreal, CP 6128, Succursale Centreville, Montreal, QC H3C 3J7, Canada
Tel: 514-343-6627 *Fax:* 514-343-6779
E-mail: info@editionsthemis.com
Web Site: ssl.editionsthemis.com
Key Personnel
Pres: Stephane Rousseau *E-mail:* stephane.rousseau@umontreal.ca
Deputy Dir: Michel Morin *E-mail:* direction.rjtum@editionsthemis.com
Founded: 1969
Law books, reference books, journals & professional books.
Catalog available.
Number of Titles Warehoused: 100
Publication(s): *La Revue Juridique Themis* (3 issues/yr)

Elder's Bookstore
101 White Bridge Rd, Nashville, TN 37209
Tel: 615-352-1562
E-mail: info@eldersbookstore.com
Web Site: eldersbookstore.com
Key Personnel
Owner: Randy Elder
Founded: 1950
Book search; wholesale, retail, rare.
Number of Titles Warehoused: 60,000

Emery-Pratt Co
1966 W M 21, Owosso, MI 48867-1397
SAN: 170-1401
Tel: 989-723-5291 *Toll Free Tel:* 800-762-5683 (orders); 800-248-3887 (cust serv) *Fax:* 989-723-4677 *Toll Free Fax:* 800-523-6379 (cust serv)
E-mail: customer.service@emery-pratt.com
Web Site: www.emery-pratt.com
Key Personnel
Pres: Maurie Shattuck
Dir, Busn Devt: Byron Shattuck
Mktg Mgr: Mo Shattuck *E-mail:* mo.shattuck@emery-pratt.com
Book Buyer: Kathi Strong
Founded: 1873
Book distributors dedicated to meeting the needs of academic, public & hospital libraries & in turn, the communities they serve. Everything we do is designed around your needs. Have over 70,000 publishing sources to find any of the 3.4 million titles currently in print. Along with that, we have a wide range of services available to streamline operations saving you time & money.
Number of Titles Warehoused: 100,000
Publication(s): *New Titles Trade* (weekly); *Technical & Reference* (weekly)

Encyclopaedia Britannica Inc
325 N La Salle St, Suite 200, Chicago, IL 60654
Tel: 312-347-7000 (all other countries)
 Toll Free Tel: 800-323-1229 (US & CN)
 Fax: 312-294-2104
E-mail: contact@eb.com
Web Site: www.britannica.com
Key Personnel
Global CEO: Jorge Cauz
Global CFO: Steve Brodsky
EVP, Corp Secy & Gen Coun: Douglas Eveleigh
SVP & CFO: Jim Conners
SVP, Britannica Digital Learning Intl: Leah Mansoor
VP, Consumer Mkts: Chris Mayland
VP, Mktg & Channel Devt: Sal De Spirito
Founded: 1768

European Books & Media
6600 Shattuck Ave, Oakland, CA 94609
Tel: 510-922-9157
E-mail: info@europeanbook.com
Web Site: www.europeanbook.com
Key Personnel
Owner & Mng Memb: Nicolas Pellerin
 E-mail: nicolas.pellerin@europeanbook.com
Founded: 1963
Foreign language & bilingual materials. Specializes in French books. Online catalog.
Catalog available.
Number of Titles Warehoused: 100,000

Fall River News Co Inc
144 Robeson St, Fall River, MA 02720
Tel: 508-679-5266
E-mail: frnewsco@gmail.com
Key Personnel
Owner & Pres: David W Boland, III
Founded: 1935
Distribute mass market paperbacks, hardcovers, periodicals, maps, newspapers & atlases to convenience & drug stores, bookstores, schools, libraries, etc.
Membership(s): American Booksellers Association (ABA)

Philipp Feldheim Inc, see Feldheim Publishers

Feldheim Publishers
208 Airport Executive Park, Nanuet, NY 10954
SAN: 207-0545
Tel: 845-356-2282 *Toll Free Tel:* 800-237-7149 (orders) *Fax:* 845-425-1908
E-mail: sales@feldheim.com
Web Site: www.feldheim.com
Key Personnel
Pres: Yitzchak Feldheim
Mng Dir: Eli M Hollander *E-mail:* eli3@feldheim.com
Sales Mgr: Suzanne Brandt *E-mail:* suzanne@feldheim.com
Founded: 1939
Publishers & distributors of English language Judaica.
Catalog available.
Number of Titles Warehoused: 2,600

Fennell Subscription Service Inc
1002 W Michigan Ave, Jackson, MI 49202
Tel: 517-782-3132
Key Personnel
Pres: Reginald F Fennell
Founded: 1910
Ordering service & maintenance, magazines, newspapers.

1517 Media, see Augsburg Fortress Publishers, Publishing House of the Evangelical Lutheran Church in America

Follett Higher Education Group
3 Westbrook Corporate Ctr, Suite 200, Westchester, IL 60154
Tel: 708-884-0000 *Toll Free Tel:* 800-FOLLETT (365-5388)
Web Site: www.follett.com/higher-ed
Key Personnel
CEO, Follett: Emmanuel Kolady
Pres: Ryan Petersen
Founded: 1873
Wholesaler of new & used college textbooks.
Number of Titles Warehoused: 125,000

Forest Sales & Distributing Co
139 Jean Marie St, Reserve, LA 70084
SAN: 157-5511
E-mail: forestsales@juno.com
Key Personnel
Contact: Rob Schauffler
Founded: 1967
Wholesaler & distributor of primarily regional titles; cookbooks.
Catalog available.
Number of Titles Warehoused: 2,400
Membership(s): American Booksellers Association (ABA); New Orleans Gulf South Booksellers Association (NOGSBA)

Fortress Press, see Augsburg Fortress Publishers, Publishing House of the Evangelical Lutheran Church in America

GBS Books
2321 W Royal Palm Rd, Suite F, Phoenix, AZ 85021
Tel: 602-863-6000 *Toll Free Tel:* 800-851-6001
E-mail: gbsbooks@gbsbooks.com
Web Site: www.gbsbooks.com
Key Personnel
Book Buyer: Tammy Echter
Gen Mgr: Troy Williams
Mktg: Abigail Williams
Founded: 2013
Juvenile & young adult books, trade & mass market paperback books, library accounts.
Number of Titles Warehoused: 33,000
Membership(s): American Booksellers Association (ABA)

Gem Guides Book Co
1155 W Ninth St, Upland, CA 91786
Tel: 626-855-1611 *Toll Free Tel:* 800-824-5118 (orders) *Fax:* 626-855-1610
E-mail: info@gemguidesbooks.com; sales@gemguidesbooks.com (orders)
Web Site: www.gemguidesbooks.com
Key Personnel
Opers Mgr: Matt Warner
Ed: Nancy Fox
Off Mgr: Nannette Becerra
Sales: Michael Moran
Founded: 1965
Western publisher & distributor of regional titles on Western Americana, Native American, travel, outdoor, recreational prospecting, historical/ghost towns, railroads, rocks & minerals, jewelry making, bead crafts & New Age crystal.
Catalog available.
Number of Titles Warehoused: 1,000

Dot Gibson Publications
PO Box 117, Waycross, GA 31502
SAN: 200-4143
Tel: 912-285-2848 *Toll Free Tel:* 800-336-8095 (for orders) *Fax:* 912-285-2848
E-mail: info@dotgibson.com
Web Site: www.dotgibson.com
Key Personnel
CEO: Dot Gibson
Pres: N Gilbert Gibson, Jr
Founded: 1975
Distribution & publishing of cookbooks, giftbooks & children's books.
Catalog available.
Number of Titles Warehoused: 400
Publication(s): *Dot Gibson Bestsellers catalog* (annual); *Dot Gibson Bestsellers newsletter* (quarterly)

Gift of Words, see GBS Books

Girol Books Inc
PO Box 5473, LCD Merivale, Ottawa, ON K2C 3M1, Canada
Tel: 613-233-9044
E-mail: info@girol.com
Web Site: www.girol.com
Key Personnel
Owner: Miguel Angel Giella; Peter Roster
Mgr: Leslie Roster *E-mail:* lroster@girol.com
Founded: 1975
Importers & distributors of books in Spanish & Portuguese. Publishers of Latin American theater titles & theater criticism.

Glenbow Museum Shop
Division of Glenbow Museum
130 Ninth Ave SE, Calgary, AB T2G 0P3, Canada
SAN: 157-0048
Tel: 403-268-4119 *Fax:* 403-262-4045
E-mail: shop@glenbow.org
Web Site: www.glenbow.org
Key Personnel
Mgr: Cherry Deacon
Founded: 1957
Catalog production, nonfiction (native & Canadian titles) publications, maps, note cards & videos.
Number of Titles Warehoused: 100

GoalsGuy Learning Systems
36181 E Lake Rd, Suite 139, Palm Harbor, FL 34685
Toll Free Tel: 877-462-5748 *Fax:* 813-435-2022
Toll Free Fax: 877-903-2284
E-mail: info@goalsguy.com
Web Site: www.100daychallenge.com
Key Personnel
Owner: Gary Ryan Blair
Buy & sell books for corporate libraries nationwide.
Branch Office(s)
201 E Jefferson St, Suite 269, Fayetteville, NY 13066 *Tel:* 315-446-4960

GOBI® Library Solutions from EBSCO
Division of EBSCO Information Services
999 Maple St, Contoocook, NH 03229
SAN: 169-4510
Tel: 603-746-3102 *Toll Free Tel:* 800-258-3774 (US & CN) *Fax:* 603-746-5628
E-mail: information@ebsco.com
Web Site: gobi.ebsco.com
Key Personnel
COO: Darby Kopp
VP, Content Mgmt: Nat Bruning
VP, Fin & Acctg: Kate Hartnett
VP, Opers & Lean Mgmt: Jeffrey Pickert
VP, Strategic Projs, Consortia & Admin: Kristine Baker
Founded: 2015 (1971 as Yankee Book Peddler Inc)
Full service bookseller to libraries; monographic order fulfillment, series standing orders & approval plans. National library book jobber: university presses; university affiliated departments; scientific, technical & business publishers; medical publishers; societies; museums; trade; juvenile & young adult.
Publication(s): Dialogue: The Business of Publishing (Feb, June, Oct, circ 1,000)
Membership(s): Book Industry Study Group (BISG)

Louis Goldberg Library Book Supplier
45 Belvidere St, Nazareth, PA 18064
SAN: 169-7536
Tel: 610-759-9458
E-mail: orders@goldberg-books.com
Web Site: www.goldberg-books.com
Key Personnel
Owner: Dianne Duignam; Katherine Hoadley
Founded: 1951

Harvard Art Museums
32 Quincy St, Cambridge, MA 02138
Tel: 617-495-9400
Web Site: www.harvardartmuseums.org
Founded: 1901
Reproductions & bookshop.
Number of Titles Warehoused: 50

William S Hein & Co Inc
2350 N Forest Rd, Suite 10A, Getzville, NY 14068
Tel: 716-882-2600 *Toll Free Tel:* 800-828-7571
Fax: 716-883-8100
E-mail: mail@wshein.com; marketing@wshein.com; customerservice@wshein.com
Web Site: home.heinonline.org
Key Personnel
Chmn of the Bd: William S Hein, Jr
Pres & CEO: Shane Marmion
   E-mail: smarmion@wshein.com
VP, Sales & Mktg: Ben Boron *E-mail:* bboron@wshein.com
VP, Technol: Kyle Daving *E-mail:* kdaving@wshein.com
Sr Dir, Sales: Tim Hooge *E-mail:* thooge@wshein.com
Founded: 1961
Online publisher, law book publishers, legal periodicals, subscription, continuation, law libraries & micropublishers.
Catalog available.
Number of Titles Warehoused: 4,000
Membership(s): American Association of Law Libraries; American Bar Association (ABA); The American Library Association (ALA); Canadian Association of Law Libraries

HeinOnline, see William S Hein & Co Inc

Historic Aviation Books
Division of Sky Media LLC
640 Taft St NE, Minneapolis, MN 55413-2815
Tel: 612-206-3200 *Toll Free Tel:* 800-225-5575
Fax: 612-877-3160
E-mail: info@historicaviation.com; customerservice@historicaviation.com
Web Site: www.historicaviation.com
Key Personnel
Owner: Greg E Herrick
Founded: 1969
Aviation books, videos, art prints, models & kits, puzzles & games, calendars, apparel, software, home decor & accessories.
Number of Titles Warehoused: 1,000

Historic Cherry Hill
523 1/2 S Pearl St, Albany, NY 12202
SAN: 111-3178
Tel: 518-434-4791
E-mail: info@historiccherryhill.org
Web Site: www.historiccherryhill.org
Key Personnel
Pres: Maryrita Dobiel
Dir: Deborah Emmons-Andarawis
   E-mail: deborah@historiccherryhill.org
Founded: 1964
Historic house museum, tours, museum shop; publisher.
Number of Titles Warehoused: 5

The Hubbard Co
612 Clinton St, Defiance, OH 43512
Mailing Address: PO Drawer 100, Defiance, OH 43512
Tel: 419-784-4455 *Toll Free Tel:* 888-448-2227
Web Site: www.hubbardcompany.com
Key Personnel
Pres: Thomas K Hubbard *E-mail:* tom@hubbardcompany.com
Founded: 1906
Class record & plan books. Commercial printer.
Catalog available.
Membership(s): Epicomm

Ideal Foreign Books LLC
132-10 Hillside Ave, Richmond Hill, NY 11418
Tel: 718-297-7477 *Toll Free Tel:* 800-284-2490
Fax: 718-297-7645
E-mail: idealforeignbooks@att.net
Key Personnel
Owner & Pres: Alain Fetaya
Founded: 1977
Distribute foreign language books & materials, from elementary to college level, to bookstores, libraries & schools; specialize in French, Spanish, German & Italian.
Catalog available.
Number of Titles Warehoused: 1,500
Membership(s): National Association of College Stores (NACS)

Independent Campus Stores Collaborative, see indiCo

indiCo
Subsidiary of National Association of College Stores (NACS)
528 E Lorain St, Oberlin, OH 44074-1298
SAN: 169-6823
Toll Free Tel: 800-622-7498; 800-321-3883 (orders)
E-mail: cs@goindico.com; info@goindico.com; orders@goindico.com; service@goindico.com
Web Site: www.goindico.com
Founded: 1963
Wholesaler of trade paperbacks, mass market paperbacks, hardcovers, calendars, computer products & peripherals, remainders & assortments, textbooks.
Number of Titles Warehoused: 2,000,000

Ingram Content Group LLC
One Ingram Blvd, La Vergne, TN 37086-1986
Tel: 615-793-5000 *Toll Free Tel:* 800-937-8000 (retailers); 800-937-5300 (ext 1, libs)
E-mail: customerservice@ingramcontent.com
Web Site: www.ingramcontent.com
Key Personnel
Chmn: John Ingram
Pres & CEO: Shawn Morin
Chief Content Offr: Phil Ollila
CFO: Brian Dauphin
Chief HR Offr: Wayne Keegan
CIO: Steve Marshall
Chief Legal Offr: Kelly Arnold
Chief Logistics Offr: Shawn Everson
Chief Strategy & Devt Offr: Kent Freeman
Chief Venture Capital Offr: David Roland
VP & Cont: Tina Elmore
VP, Application Servs: William Daniel
VP, Community Rel: Emily Weiss
VP, Content Acq: Kelly Gallagher
VP, Credit: Roger Lee
VP, Digital Servs: Margaret Harrison
VP, HR: Jacqueline Letson
VP, Mktg: Brian McKinley
VP, Opers: Chris Willis
VP, Mdsg: Amy Cox Williams
VP, Retail Sales: Donald Roseman
Dir, Academic Servs: Kurt Hettler
Dir, Application Servs: Robert Barnard
Dir, Consumer Insights: Pete McCarthy
Dir, Consumer Mktg: Kim Schutte
Dir, Mass Merchandisers Sales: Lisa Tomasello
Dir, Natl Accts: Michael Bell
Dir, Sales Opers: Tammy Spurlock
Sales Dir: Sharon Swados
Sr Mgr, Content Acqs: John Hussey
Sr Mgr, Mktg Servs: Ann Zangri

Sr Mgr, PR & Communs: Kris Wiese
Sr Mgr, Specialty Retail: Lori Bowen
Lib Sales & Servs Mgr: Tricia Racke Bengel
Mgr, Client Rel: Louisa Brody
Prod Mktg Mgr: Catherine Robinson
Proj Mgr, Integration & Outsource: Sterling Crawford
Specialty Retail Mgr: Megan Smith
Sales & Support Rep, Mass Mdse Group: Tori Cushman
Founded: 1964
Wholesaler of trade books, audiobooks, calendars, interactive information & inventory systems & periodicals to retailers, libraries, specialty markets, higher education stores.
Number of Titles Warehoused: 500,000
Publication(s): *Advance* (monthly); *African American Connection* (3 issues/yr); *Business Connections* (2 issues/yr); *Calendar Catalog* (annual); *Children's Advance* (6 issues/yr); *Children's Backlist* (annual); *Christian Advance* (6 issues/yr); *Computer Books Catalog* (6 issues/yr); *Cooking Catalog* (annual); *Holiday* (annual); *Libros en Espanol* (annual); *Paperback Advance* (monthly); *Professional/Technical/Reference Cat* (2 issues/yr); *Spring/Summer* (annual); *Trade Books for the Class Room* (annual); *Travel* (2 issues/yr)
Branch Office(s)
6050 Dana Way, Antioch, TN 37013
7315 Innovation Blvd, Fort Wayne, IN 46818
4260 Port Union Rd, Fairfield, OH 45011
201 Ingram Dr, Roseberg, OR 97470
860 Nestle Way, Breinigsville, PA 18031
1200 Ingram Dr, Chambersburg, PA 17202

Ingram Micro Inc
3351 Michelson Dr, Suite 100, Irvin, CA 92612
Tel: 714-566-1000
E-mail: customerexperience@ingrammicro.com
Web Site: www.ingrammicro.com
Key Personnel
CEO: Alain Monie
CFO: Gina Mastantuono
EVP & Chief Info & Digital Offr: Tom Peck
EVP, Secy & Gen Coun: Augusto P Aragone
EVP, HR: Scott D Sherman
Founded: 1979
Full service distributor of microcomputer software, hardware, peripherals & accessories to resalers.
Number of Titles Warehoused: 4,500
Publication(s): *The Dealer Price Book* (quarterly); *The Ingram Journal* (weekly)
Branch Office(s)
1759 Wehrle Dr, Williamsville, NY 14221
Tel: 716-633-3600

Institute of Intergovernmental Relations
Queen's University, Robert Sutherland Hall, Rm 301, Kingston, ON K7L 3N6, Canada
Tel: 613-533-2080
E-mail: iigr@queensu.ca
Web Site: www.queensu.ca/iigr
Key Personnel
Dir: Dr Christian Leurpecht
Pubns Coord & Admin Secy: Mary Kennedy
Founded: 1965
Publish & distribute research & other scholarly work on Canadian federalism & intergovernmental relations as it affects public policy.
Number of Titles Warehoused: 115

International Book Centre Inc
2391 Auburn Rd, Shelby Township, MI 48317
SAN: 208-7022
Tel: 586-254-7230 *Fax:* 586-254-7230
E-mail: ibc@ibcbooks.com
Web Site: www.ibcbooks.com
Key Personnel
Owner: Doris Mukalla
Founded: 1974
Importer, distributor of foreign language books. Distribute Arabic language textbooks, dictionaries, imports to bookstores, libraries & schools; distributor of University of Michigan textbooks on Arabic languages & all Librairie du Liban publications (Beirut, Lebanon). Distributor of English language learning books.
Number of Titles Warehoused: 200

International Institute of Reflexology Inc
PO Box 12642, St Petersburg, FL 33733-2642
Tel: 727-343-4811
E-mail: info@reflexology-usa.net; orderdept@reflexology-usa.net
Web Site: reflexology-usa.net
Key Personnel
Pres: Gail Byers *E-mail:* gailbyers@reflexology-usa.net
Founded: 1975
Paperbacks, hardbound & charts.
Number of Titles Warehoused: 7

International Press Publication Inc
Spadina Rd, Richmond Hill, ON L4B 3C5, Canada
Tel: 905-883-0343
E-mail: sales@ippbooks.com
Web Site: www.ippbooks.com; www.facebook.com/ippbooks; x.com/ippbooks2
Key Personnel
Pres: Bali Sethi
Founded: 1976
Reference books, yearbooks, directories, language dictionaries, library sales, trade, government research, business libraries, mail order & subscriptions: international, US, UK, India, China, Hong Kong & Canada.
Number of Titles Warehoused: 100,000
Membership(s): The American Library Association (ALA); Children's Literature Association (ChLA); Ontario Library Association

International Service Co
International Service Bldg, 333 Fourth Ave, Indialantic, FL 32903-4295
SAN: 169-5134
Tel: 321-724-1443 *Fax:* 321-724-1443
Key Personnel
Pres: Dennis Samuels
Compt: F Schneider
Mng Dir: Katherine Swanberg
Coord Dir: Ann C Samuels
Shipping & Receiving Mgr: Larry A Whobrey
Systems Supv: Suzanne Jones
Admin Asst: Irene August
Asst to Pres: Robert Cohen
Founded: 1958
Exporters & importers of books, quantity & single copy, periodicals & school supplies, commissionaires.

Interstate Books4School
Division of Interstate Promotional Distributors Inc
201 E Badger Rd, Madison, WI 53713
Tel: 608-277-2407 *Toll Free Tel:* 800-752-3131
Fax: 608-277-2410
E-mail: sales@books4school.com
Web Site: www.books4school.com
Key Personnel
Pres: Marty Fields *Tel:* 608-277-2407 ext 14
E-mail: mfields@books4school.com
Founded: 1924
Hardback & paperback books. Distribution of paperback books to educational institutions, K-12. Catalog also available online.
Catalog available.
Number of Titles Warehoused: 12,000

Iranbooks
PO Box 30087, Bethesda, MD 20824
Tel: 301-718-8188 *Toll Free Tel:* 888-718-8188
Fax: 301-907-8707
E-mail: info@iranbooks.com
Web Site: www.iranbooks.com
Key Personnel
Mgr: Farhad Shirzad
Founded: 1979
Distribute for most Iranian publishers & Persian language publishers outside of Iran.

The Islander Group
269 Palii St, Mililani, HI 96789
Tel: 808-676-0116 *Toll Free Tel:* 877-828-4852
Fax: 808-676-5156
E-mail: customerservice@islandergroup.com
Web Site: www.islandergroup.com
Key Personnel
CEO: Jeff Swartz
Pres & COO: Steve Holmberg
Founded: 1976
Hardcover & quality paperback supplier of Hawaiian & Pacific titles to stores & libraries, children's books.
Catalog available.
Number of Titles Warehoused: 6,500

Israel's Judaica Center
441 Clark Ave W, Thornhill, ON L4J 6W7, Canada
Tel: 905-881-1010 *Toll Free Tel:* 877-511-1010
Fax: 905-881-1016
E-mail: contact@israelsjudaica.com; thornhill@israelsjudaica.com (retail store)
Web Site: www.israelsjudaica.com
Key Personnel
Pres: Joseph Segal *Tel:* 905-881-1010 ext 23
E-mail: jsegal@israelsjudaica.com
Founded: 1982
Books & gift retail & wholesale, Judaica.
Number of Titles Warehoused: 2,500
Branch Office(s)
1172 Eglinton Ave W, Toronto, ON M6C 2E3, Canada *E-mail:* eglinton@israelsjudaica.com

The James & Law Co
217 W Main St, Clarksburg, WV 26301
SAN: 169-894X
Tel: 304-624-7401 *Toll Free Tel:* 800-253-5428
Fax: 304-624-9331
E-mail: sales@jamesandlaw.com
Web Site: jamesandlaw.com
Key Personnel
Pres: George I Brown
VP & Retail Sales: Alice Godfrey
E-mail: agodfrey@jamesandlaw.com
Founded: 1905
Suppliers of hardcover & paperback trade books, school supplies, reference books & microcomputer software to libraries & schools.

Kazi Publications Inc
3023 W Belmont Ave, Chicago, IL 60618
Tel: 773-267-7001 *Fax:* 773-267-7002
E-mail: info@kazi.org
Web Site: www.kazi.org
Key Personnel
Pres: Liaquat Ali
Mktg Dir: Mary Bakhtiar
Founded: 1972
Islamic books & supplies; books on Islam & Muslim world; Sufism.
Catalog available.
Number of Titles Warehoused: 1,963
Publication(s): *Catalog of Books on Islam & the Muslim World* (2 issues/yr)

Ketab Corp
12701 Van Nuys Blvd, Unit H, Pacoima, CA 91331
Tel: 310-477-7477 *Toll Free Tel:* 800-FOR-IRAN (367-4726) *Fax:* 818-908-1457
E-mail: ketab1@ketab.com
Web Site: www.ketab.com

Key Personnel
Pres: Bijan Khalili
Founded: 1981
Distribute Persian books & books in English about Iran.
Catalog available.
Number of Titles Warehoused: 5,000

Kinokuniya Bookstores of America Co Ltd
Subsidiary of Kinokuniya Co Ltd (Japan)
1581 Webster St, San Francisco, CA 94115
SAN: 121-8441
Tel: 415-567-6787 *Fax:* 415-567-4109
E-mail: sales@kinokuniya.com; san_francisco@kinokuniya.com; bookwebusa@kinokuniya.com (cust serv)
Web Site: usa.kinokuniya.com
Founded: 1969
Retail & wholesale Japanese books & magazines.
Number of Titles Warehoused: 80,000
Branch Office(s)
Little Tokyo, 123 Astronaut E S Onizuka St, Los Angeles, CA 90012 *Tel:* 213-687-4480 *E-mail:* los_angeles@kinokuniya.com
Mitsuwa Marketplace, 3760 S Centinela Ave, Los Angeles, CA 90066 *Tel:* 310-482-3382 *E-mail:* santamonica@kinokuniya.com
Mitsuwa Marketplace, 675 Saratoga Ave, San Jose, CA 95129 *Tel:* 408-252-1300 *E-mail:* san_jose@kinokuniya.com
Mitsuwa Marketplace, 100 E Algonquin Rd, Arlington Heights, IL 60005 *Tel:* 847-427-2665 *E-mail:* chicago@kinokuniya.com
Mitsuwa Marketplace, 595 River Rd, Edgewater, NJ 07020 *Tel:* 201-496-6910 *E-mail:* nj@kinokuniya.com
1073 Avenue of the Americas, New York, NY 10018 *Tel:* 212-869-1700 *E-mail:* nyinfo@kinokuniya.com
Uwajimaya Plaza, 10500 SW Beaverton-Hillsdale Hwy, Beaverton, OR 97005 *Tel:* 503-641-6240 *E-mail:* beaverton@kinokuniya.com
6929 Airport Blvd, No 121, Austin, TX 78752 *Tel:* 512-291-2026 *E-mail:* austin@kinokuniya.com
Carrollton Town Ctr, 2540 Old Denton Rd, Suite 114, Carrollton, TX 75006 *Tel:* 214-731-6800 *E-mail:* carrollton@kinokuniya.com
Mitsuwa Marketplace, 100 Legacy Dr, Plano, TX 75023 *Tel:* 972-517-0226 *E-mail:* plano@kinokuniya.com
Uwajimaya Village, 525 S Weller St, Seattle, WA 98104 *Tel:* 206-587-2477 *E-mail:* seattle@kinokuniya.com

Learning World Inc
Subsidiary of Okhai Educational Inc
287 Wycliffe Ave, Vaughan, ON L4L 3N7, Canada
Key Personnel
Pres: Adam Okhai *E-mail:* ceo@tlcq.com
VP: Dr A Osman
Founded: 1884
Distributor of educational supplies, including law books & K-12 educational software.
Catalog available.
Number of Titles Warehoused: 730

Lectorum Publications Inc
10 New Maple Ave, Suite 303, Pine Brook, NJ 07058
Tel: 201-559-2200 *Toll Free Tel:* 800-345-5946
E-mail: lectorum@lectorum.com
Web Site: www.lectorum.com
Key Personnel
Pres & CEO: Alex Correa *E-mail:* acorrea@lectorum.com
Opers Mgr: Fernando Febus *E-mail:* ffebus@lectorum.com
Mgr, Collection Devt & Spec Sales: Marjorie Samper *E-mail:* msamper@lectorum.com
Mgr, Educ Sales, Schools & School Libs: Hilda Viskovic *E-mail:* hviskovic@lectorum.com
Public Lib Sales: Chastery Tiburcio *E-mail:* ctiburcio@lectorum.com
Cust Serv Mgr: Gladys Ochoa *E-mail:* gochoa@lectorum.com
Founded: 1960
America's oldest & largest distributor of children & adult books in Spanish, with titles from more than 500 domestic & foreign publishers. Lectorum serves schools & libraries, as well as the trade & various specialized markets, with the best selection of children's books in Spanish, including works originally written in Spanish, translations from other languages & the Spanish language editions of many popular children's books.
Catalog available.
Number of Titles Warehoused: 25,000

Library Bound Inc
100 Bathurst Dr, Unit 2, Waterloo, ON N2V 1V6, Canada
SAN: 116-9203
Tel: 519-885-3233 *Toll Free Tel:* 800-363-4728 *Fax:* 519-885-2662
Web Site: www.librarybound.com
Key Personnel
Pres: Heather Bindseil *E-mail:* heatherb@librarybound.com
COO: Duncan Hamilton *E-mail:* duncan@librarybound.com
Dir, Sales & Mktg: Terry Palmer *E-mail:* terry.palmer@librarybound.com
Music & Video Games Mgr: Tracy Reid *E-mail:* tracy@librarybound.com
Print Mgr: Ron Stadnik *E-mail:* ron@librarybound.com
Founded: 1993
National Canadian wholesaler for print materials & AV products to public libraries. Full cataloging including MARC records & customized processing available for all material types, print, bestsellers, audiobooks, CD music, DVD/Blu-ray & video games.
Catalog available.
Branch Office(s)
LBI West, 8370 Prince Edward St, Vancouver, BC V5X 3R9, Canada *Tel:* 604-434-5242 *Fax:* 604-434-5262
Membership(s): BCLA; Ontario Library Association

The Library Services Centre
131 Shoemaker St, Kitchener, ON N2E 3B5, Canada
SAN: 319-2024
Tel: 519-746-4420 *Toll Free Tel:* 800-265-3360 (CN only) *Fax:* 519-746-4425
Web Site: www.lsc.on.ca
Key Personnel
CEO: Michael Monahan
CFO: Kirk Oliver
CIO: Marta Gonzalez
VP, Sales & Mktg: Cecile Dillon
VP, Servs: Trish Hayes
Founded: 1985
Wholesalers.
Publication(s): *Spotlight* (irregular)

Login Canada
300 Saulteaux Crescent, Winnipeg, MB R3J 3T2, Canada
Tel: 204-837-2987 *Toll Free Tel:* 800-665-1148 (CN only) *Fax:* 204-837-3116
Toll Free Fax: 800-665-0103
E-mail: sales@lb.ca
Web Site: www.lb.ca
Key Personnel
Pres & CEO: Mark Champagne *E-mail:* markc@lb.ca
CFO: Sharon Murray *E-mail:* sho@lb.ca

Chief Mktg Offr: Russell Friesen *E-mail:* russellf@lb.ca
Founded: 1991
Health science books.
Number of Titles Warehoused: 30,000

Lushena Books Inc
607 Country Club Dr, Unit E, Bensenville, IL 60106
Tel: 630-238-8708 *Toll Free Tel:* 800-785-1545 *Fax:* 630-238-8824
E-mail: lushenabks@yahoo.com
Web Site: lushenabks.com
Key Personnel
Pres & Gen Mgr: Luther A Warner
Founded: 1988
African-American books to retailers.
Catalog available.
Number of Titles Warehoused: 1,000

Mackin Educational Resources
3505 County Rd 42 W, Burnsville, MN 55306
Tel: 952-895-9540 *Toll Free Tel:* 800-245-9540 *Fax:* 952-894-8806 *Toll Free Fax:* 800-369-5490
E-mail: mackin@mackin.com
Web Site: www.mackin.com
Key Personnel
Dir, Mktg & Communs: Troy Mikell *E-mail:* troy.mikell@mackin.com
PreK-12 book resellers.

Maison de l'Education Inc
10840 Ave Millen, Montreal, QC H2C 0A5, Canada
Tel: 514-384-4401 *Fax:* 514-384-4844
E-mail: librairie@maisondeleducation.com
Web Site: maisondeleducation.com
Key Personnel
Dir Gen: Danielle Dion
Founded: 1967
Bookstore & distributor.

Manning's Book & Prints
Subsidiary of Prints Old & Rare
580-M Crespi Dr, Pacifica, CA 94044
Tel: 415-621-3565 *Toll Free Tel:* 800-TRY-MAPS (879-6277) *Fax:* 650-355-1851
E-mail: staff@printsoldandrare.com; manningsbk@aol.com
Web Site: www.printsoldandrare.com
Key Personnel
Owner: Kathleen Manning
Founded: 1972
Buy, sell, rent old prints, maps, books; wholesale antique prints.
Catalog available.
Membership(s): Antiquarian Booksellers Association of America (ABAA)

The Mazel Co
31000 Aurora Rd, Solon, OH 44139-2769
Tel: 440-248-5200 *Toll Free Tel:* 800-443-4789 *Fax:* 440-349-1931
Web Site: www.themazelcompany.com
Closeout & remainder liquidator.
Branch Office(s)
1020 Taylor Station Rd, Suite A, Gahanna, OH 43230-6674 *Tel:* 614-239-2331 *Fax:* 614-239-2357
9555 Foster Ave, Suite 595, Schiller Park, IL 60176 *Tel:* 847-261-9680 *Fax:* 847-261-9679
230 Fifth Ave, Suite 918, New York, NY 10001-7704 *Tel:* 212-696-0200 *Fax:* 212-696-0073

MBS Textbook Exchange Inc
2711 W Ash, Columbia, MO 65203
Mailing Address: PO Box 637, Columbia, MO 65205-0637

Tel: 573-445-2243 *Toll Free Tel:* 800-325-0530 (textbook solutions); 800-325-4138 (bookstore systems) *Fax:* 573-446-5256
E-mail: cserv@mbsbooks.com
Web Site: www.mbsbooks.com
Key Personnel
Pres: Mark Henderson
VP, Sales & Mktg: Jeff Miller
Founded: 1973
College textbook wholesaler.

Le Messager Chretien (The Christian Messenger)
185 Gatineau Ave, Gatineau, QC J8T 4J7, Canada
Tel: 819-243-8880 *Toll Free Tel:* 800-263-8086 *Fax:* 819-243-1220
E-mail: info@messagerchretien.com
Web Site: www.messagerchretien.com
Key Personnel
Contact: Luc Deschenes
Founded: 1981
Christian books & Bibles.
Number of Titles Warehoused: 3,000
Branch Office(s)
1148 rue des Cascades, St-Hyacinthe, QC J2S 3G8, Canada, Contact: Marielle Charland
Tel: 450-774-8086 *Toll Free Tel:* 866-774-8086

Metro 360
120 Sinnott Rd, Scarborough, ON M1L 4N1, Canada
Tel: 416-752-8720 *Toll Free Tel:* 888-260-2208
Web Site: www.metro360.ca
Key Personnel
Pres & CEO: Daniel Shapiro
Founded: 1915
Wholesaler of magazines & books Branch offices in Calgary, Edmonton, Montreal, Regina, Saskatoon & Winnipeg.
Number of Titles Warehoused: 20,000

Midwest Library Service
11443 Saint Charles Rock Rd, Bridgeton, MO 63044
SAN: 169-4243
Tel: 314-739-3100 *Fax:* 314-739-1326
E-mail: mail@midwestls.com
Web Site: www.midwestls.com
Key Personnel
Pres: Howard N Lesser
VP: Herbert M Lesser
Gen Mgr: Trudy Barrett *E-mail:* barrett@midwestls.com
Book Buyer: Angie Schuler
Founded: 1959
Service to academic & public libraries for more than half a century. Complete order fulfillment is a paramount objective, coupled with prompt, personalized assistance from an expert staff of professionals. Midwest's comprehensive services, products & resources are all designed to improve your library's efficiency.
Number of Titles Warehoused: 75,000
Publication(s): *Choice's Outstanding Academic Titles Catalog*; *Sci-Tech-Health Sciences Catalog*; *University Press Catalog*; *University Press Law Catalog*
Membership(s): The American Library Association (ALA)

Montfort Publications
Division of Montfort Missionaries
26 S Saxon Ave, Bay Shore, NY 11706-8993
SAN: 169-5053
Tel: 631-665-0726; 631-666-7500 *Fax:* 631-665-0726
E-mail: info@montfortpublications.com
Web Site: www.montfortpublications.com
Key Personnel
Dir: Hugh Guillespie
Founded: 1947

Religious & Catholic books, devotional & theological, about Mariology & Marian spirituality only.
Catalog available.
Number of Titles Warehoused: 20

Motorbooks
Division of Quarto Publishing Group USA Inc
100 Cummings Ctr, Suite 265D, Beverly, MA 01915
Tel: 978-282-9590 *Toll Free Tel:* 800-759-0190 (orders)
Web Site: www.quartoknows.com/motorbooks
Key Personnel
SVP & Group Publg Dir, US: Winnie Prentiss *E-mail:* winnie.prentiss@quarto.com
Publr: Zack Miller *E-mail:* zack.miller@quarto.com
Sr Acqs Ed: Dennis Pernu *E-mail:* dennis.pernu@quarto.com
Mgr, Spec Mkt Sales: Nichole Schiele *E-mail:* nichole.schiele@quarto.com
Mktg Mgr: Steve Roth *E-mail:* steve.roth@quarto.com
Founded: 1965
Number of Titles Warehoused: 14,000

National Book Co Inc
Division of W W Norton & Company Inc
Keystone Industrial Park, Dunmore, PA 18512
SAN: 157-1869
Tel: 570-346-2029 *Toll Free Tel:* 800-233-4830
Founded: 1960
Fulfillment center; invoicing & shipping; specialize in college text & trade paperbacks.
Number of Titles Warehoused: 13,000

National Book Network (NBN)
Subsidiary of Rowman & Littlefield Publishing Group
4501 Forbes Blvd, Suite 200, Lanham, MD 20706
Tel: 301-459-3366 *Toll Free Tel:* 800-462-6420 (orders only) *Fax:* 301-429-5746
Toll Free Fax: 800-338-4550 (orders only)
E-mail: customercare@nbnbooks.com
Web Site: www.nbnbooks.com
Key Personnel
CEO: Jed Lyons
COO: Robert S Marsh *E-mail:* rmarsh@rowman.com
SVP & CFO: Michael Lippenholz *E-mail:* mlippenholz@rowman.com
Pres: Jason Brockwell *E-mail:* jbrockwell@nbnbooks.com
VP, Opers: Mike Cornell *E-mail:* mcornell@nbnbooks.com
VP, Publr & Cust Servs: Carla Quental *E-mail:* cquental@nbnbooks.com
Dir, Sales Admin: Sylvia Williams *E-mail:* swilliams@nbnbooks.com
Intl Sales Dir: Les Petriw *E-mail:* lpetriw@nbnbooks.com
Mgr, Dist: Sue Bumbaugh *E-mail:* sbumbaugh@nbnbooks.com
Publr Servs Mgr: Karen Mattscheck *E-mail:* kmattscheck@nbnbooks.com
Founded: 1986
National sales, marketing, order fulfillment, distribution & collections services for independent trade book publishers.
Distribution center located in Blue Ridge Summit, PA.
Number of Titles Warehoused: 25,000

National Learning Corp
212 Michael Dr, Syosset, NY 11791
Tel: 516-921-8888 *Toll Free Tel:* 800-632-8888 *Fax:* 516-921-8743
E-mail: info@passbooks.com
Web Site: www.passbooks.com

Key Personnel
Pres & CEO: Michael P Rudman
Founded: 1967
Educational, commercial, industrial & government sales.
Catalog available.
Number of Titles Warehoused: 6,000
Publication(s): *Passbooks*
Membership(s): Association of American Publishers (AAP)

Mrs Nelson's Library Services
Division of Mrs Nelson's Toy & Book Shop
1650 W Orange Grove Ave, Pomona, CA 91768
SAN: 168-9703
Tel: 909-397-7820 *Toll Free Tel:* 800-875-9911 *Fax:* 909-397-7833
E-mail: bookcompany@mrsnelsons.com
Web Site: www.mrsnelsons.com
Key Personnel
Pres: Judy Nelson
Mgr: Patrick Nelson *E-mail:* pnelson@mrsnelsons.com
Founded: 1985
Prebound novels, wholesale book orders & textbook rebinding.
Catalog available.
Membership(s): California School Library Association (CSLA)

New England Book Service Inc
7000 Vt Rte 17 W, Addison, VT 05491
Tel: 802-759-3000 *Toll Free Tel:* 800-356-5772 *Fax:* 802-759-3220
E-mail: nebs@together.net
Web Site: www.nebooks.com
Key Personnel
Pres: Fred Morrow
VP: Dee Morrow
Founded: 1959
Book service/book store. All books available.

The New England Mobile Book Fair®
241 Needham St, Newton, MA 02464
SAN: 169-3530
Tel: 617-527-5817; 617-964-7440
E-mail: customerservice@nebookfair.com
Web Site: nebookfair.com
Key Personnel
Owner: Tom Lyons
Founded: 1958
Juveniles, adult hardcovers, paperbacks, trade paperbacks & remaindered books.

New Leaf Distributing Co
Subsidiary of Lotus Light Enterprises Inc
1085 E Lotus Dr, Silver Lake, WI 53170
SAN: 169-1449
Tel: 262-889-8501 (ext 162) *Toll Free Tel:* 800-326-2665 (orders) *Fax:* 262-889-8598
E-mail: orders@newleafdist.com
Key Personnel
Pres: Santosh Krinsky
Buyer: Denise Milano *E-mail:* denise@lotuspress.com
Founded: 1975
Health & metaphysics.
Catalog available.
Number of Titles Warehoused: 30,000
Membership(s): American Booksellers Association (ABA)

Newborn Enterprises Inc (Altoona News Agency)
808 Green Ave, Altoona, PA 16601
Tel: 814-944-3593
Key Personnel
Pres: Barry Newborn
Wholesale distributor of magazines, books, newspapers & videos.

WHOLESALERS

North 49 Books
Division of Waldock Publishing Ltd
35 Prince Andrew Place, Toronto, ON M3C 2H2, Canada
SAN: 117-2689
Tel: 416-449-4000 *Toll Free Tel:* 800-490-4049
Fax: 416-449-9924 *Toll Free Fax:* 888-349-2221
E-mail: sales@north49books.com
Web Site: www.north49books.com
Key Personnel
Pres: Peter Mikos
Founded: 1992
Catalog available in Winter, Spring & Fall.
Catalog available.
Number of Titles Warehoused: 2,500

Ollis Book Co
28 E 35 St, Steger, IL 60475
SAN: 169-2224
Mailing Address: PO Box 258, Steger, IL 60475
Tel: 708-755-5151 *Toll Free Tel:* 800-323-0343 (natl) *Fax:* 708-755-5153
Key Personnel
Pres: Kenneth R Ollis
Founded: 1965
Juvenile books only.
Number of Titles Warehoused: 2,500

Osa's Ark Museum Shop
Division of The Martin and Osa Johnson Safari Museum Inc
111 N Lincoln Ave, Chanute, KS 66720
Tel: 620-431-2730 *Fax:* 620-431-2730
E-mail: osajohns@safarimuseum.com; osasark@yahoo.com
Web Site: www.safarimuseum.com
Key Personnel
Dir: Conrad G Froehlich
Mgr: Shirley Rogers-Naff
Founded: 1961
Wholesaler.
Number of Titles Warehoused: 20

Pannonia Bookstore
300 Sainte Clair Ave W, Suite 103, Toronto, ON M4V 1S4, Canada
Tel: 416-966-5156
E-mail: info@pannonia.ca
Web Site: www.pannonia.ca
Key Personnel
Owner: Zsolt Bede Fazekas; Hortenzia Papp
Founded: 1957
Subscriptions, mail order, retail.
Number of Titles Warehoused: 15,000

Paperbacks For Educators
426 W Front St, Washington, MO 63090
SAN: 103-3379
Tel: 314-960-3015
E-mail: paperbacks@usmo.com
Web Site: www.any-book-in-print.com
Key Personnel
Pres: David L Craig *E-mail:* davecraig@usmo.com
Founded: 1978
Wholesaler to schools. Specialize in counseling, bibliotherapy for children & teens, career, staff development, teacher resources & parenting.
Number of Titles Warehoused: 8,000

Pathway Book Service
Division of The No Tomorrow Book Co
34 Production Ave, Keene, NH 03431
SAN: 170-0545
Tel: 603-357-0236 *Toll Free Tel:* 800-345-6665
Fax: 603-965-2181
E-mail: pbs@pathwaybook.com
Web Site: www.pathwaybook.com
Key Personnel
Partner: George Corrette; Robert Zipoli

Founded: 1978
Complete distribution & fulfillment company distributing titles to all of the major wholesalers, including Ingram, Baker & Taylor, Barnes & Noble & Books-A-Million as well as Amazon & the popular online digital catalog used by bookstore buyers, Edelweiss+.
Number of Titles Warehoused: 8,200

Paulist Press
997 Macarthur Blvd, Mahwah, NJ 07430-9990
SAN: 202-5159
Tel: 201-825-7300 *Toll Free Tel:* 800-218-1903
Fax: 201-825-6921
E-mail: info@paulistpress.com; publicity@paulistpress.com
Web Site: www.paulistpress.com
Key Personnel
Pres & Publr: Rev Mark-David Janus, PhD
Founded: 1865
Religious & Catholic books.
Catalog available.
Number of Titles Warehoused: 1,650
Membership(s): Association of Catholic Publishers Inc

Penfield Books
215 Brown St, Iowa City, IA 52245
SAN: 221-6671
Tel: 319-337-9998 *Toll Free Tel:* 800-728-9998
Fax: 319-351-6846
E-mail: penfield@penfieldbooks.com; orders@penfieldbooks.com
Web Site: www.penfieldbooks.com
Founded: 1979
Publisher & distributor of cookbooks, ethnic cultural cookbooks, crafts & folk art & ethnic subjects.
Catalog available.
Number of Titles Warehoused: 200

The Penworthy Company LLC
219 N Milwaukee St, 4th fl, Milwaukee, WI 53202
Tel: 414-287-4600 *Toll Free Tel:* 800-262-2665
Fax: 414-287-4602
E-mail: info@penworthy.com
Web Site: www.penworthy.com
Key Personnel
Pres: Holly Ritz
EVP: Julie Plantz *Tel:* 414-287-4600 ext 211 *E-mail:* julie.plantz@penworthy.com
Founded: 1982
Prebinding; specialize in juvenile books.
Number of Titles Warehoused: 2,000

Perma-Bound Books
Division of Hertzberg-New Method Inc
617 E Vandalia Rd, Jacksonville, IL 62650
Tel: 217-243-5451 *Toll Free Tel:* 800-637-6581
Fax: 217-243-7505 *Toll Free Fax:* 800-551-1169
E-mail: books@perma-bound.com
Web Site: www.perma-bound.com
Key Personnel
Owner & Pres: James Orr
Founded: 1954
Bookbinding; education market; wholesale books K-12.
Catalog available.
Number of Titles Warehoused: 5,000,000
Branch Office(s)
PO Box 868, Sta Main, Peterborough, ON K9J 7A2, Canada *Tel:* 705-742-1513 *Toll Free Tel:* 800-461-1999 *Toll Free Fax:* 888-250-3811 *E-mail:* perma-bound.ca@sympatico.ca *Web Site:* www.perma-bound.com/canada

Polybook Distributors
Subsidiary of Main Street Book Shop Inc
501 Mamaroneck Ave, White Plains, NY 10605

SAN: 169-5568
Tel: 914-328-6346
Key Personnel
Owner & Pres: Daniel Makanoff
Founded: 1965
School book fairs, RIF distributor, rack jobbing.
Number of Titles Warehoused: 50,000

Promotional Book Co
Division of Strathearn Books Inc
12 Cranfield Rd, No 100, Toronto, ON M4B 3G8, Canada
Tel: 416-759-2226 *Fax:* 416-759-2150
Key Personnel
Pres: Ron Goelman *Tel:* 416-759-2226 ext 236
VP, Sales & Purch: Joan Rickerby *Tel:* 416-759-2226 ext 232 *E-mail:* joanr@promobookco.com
Founded: 1981
Remainders & overstock.

Redwing Book Co
202 Bendix St, Taos, NM 87571
Tel: 575-758-7758 *Toll Free Tel:* 800-873-3946 (US); 888-873-3947 (CN) *Fax:* 575-758-7768
E-mail: info@redwingbooks.com; custsrv@redwingbooks.com
Web Site: www.redwingbooks.com
Key Personnel
Pres & Publr: Robert Felt
Founded: 1973
Wholesale & direct mail, trade paperbacks & scholarly books; specialize in acupuncture & oriental medicine. Publish scholarly works in oriental medicine under the imprint Paradigm Publications. Distribute selected titles for a variety of publishers, US & foreign.
Number of Titles Warehoused: 1,500
Publication(s): *Redwing Reviews* (biennial, circ 50,000)

Regent Book Co
PO Box 37, Liberty Corner, NJ 07938
SAN: 169-4715
Tel: 973-574-7600 *Toll Free Tel:* 800-999-9554
Fax: 973-944-5073 *Toll Free Fax:* 888-597-3661
E-mail: info@regentbook.com
Web Site: www.regentbook.com
Key Personnel
Owner: Janice Zucker
VP: Josh Zucker
Founded: 1958
Juveniles (kits available), K-12, library bound juvenile books & cataloging services available.
Number of Titles Warehoused: 3,000

Rising Sun Book Co
1424 Stony Brook Rd, Stony Brook, NY 11790
Tel: 631-473-7000 *Fax:* 631-473-7447
Web Site: risingsunbook.com
Key Personnel
Pres: Arun Shanbhag *E-mail:* shanbhagarun@aol.com
Founded: 1983
Book wholesaler & exporter.
Number of Titles Warehoused: 10,000

Rizzoli Bookstores
1133 Broadway, New York, NY 10010
Tel: 212-759-2424 *Toll Free Tel:* 800-52-BOOKS (522-6657) *Fax:* 212-826-9754
Web Site: rizzolibookstore.com; www.rizzoliusa.com
Key Personnel
Chmn of the Bd: Marco Ausenda
Pres & CEO: Stefano Peccatori
Art books.

Richard Owen Roberts, Booksellers & Publishers
139 N Washington St, Wheaton, IL 60189
SAN: 239-4847

Mailing Address: PO Box 21, Wheaton, IL 60187-0021
Tel: 630-752-4122
E-mail: sales@rorbooks.com
Web Site: www.rorbooks.com
Key Personnel
Pres: Richard Owen Roberts
VP: Margaret J Roberts
Founded: 1961
Book distribution to stores, schools & libraries.
Number of Titles Warehoused: 51

Rushmore News Inc
924 E Saint Andrew, Rapid City, SD 57701
SAN: 169-7846
Tel: 605-342-2617 *Toll Free Tel:* 800-423-0501
Key Personnel
Gen Mgr: Michael Freese *E-mail:* mfrushmore@rushmore.com
Founded: 1956
Number of Titles Warehoused: 24,000

S & L Sales Co Inc
2165 Industrial Blvd, Waycross, GA 31503
Tel: 912-283-0210 *Toll Free Tel:* 800-243-3699
 Fax: 912-283-0261 *Toll Free Fax:* 800-736-7329
E-mail: sales@slsales.com
Web Site: slsales.com
Key Personnel
Pres: Rickey L Perritt
Founded: 1965
Remainders.
Number of Titles Warehoused: 25,000

San Diego Museum of Art
Balboa Park, 1450 El Prado, San Diego, CA 92112
SAN: 121-3679
Mailing Address: PO Box 122107, San Diego, CA 92112-2107
Tel: 619-232-7931
Web Site: www.sdmart.org
Key Personnel
Assoc Dir, Earned Income: Chacho Herman *E-mail:* cherman@sdmart.org
Publish, wholesale & retail.
Publication(s): *Exhibition Art Catalogs*

Sandhill Book Marketing Ltd
Millcreek Industrial Park, Unit 4, 3308 Appaloosa Rd, Kelowna, BC V1V 2W5, Canada
SAN: 115-2181
Tel: 250-491-1446 *Toll Free Tel:* 800-667-3848 (CN only) *Fax:* 250-491-4066
E-mail: info@sandhillbooks.com
Web Site: www.sandhillbooks.com
Key Personnel
Pres: Nancy Wise
Founded: 1984
Trade book distribution (no imprints from the US); specialty store, only carry Canadian titles/publishers.
Number of Titles Warehoused: 1,000

Schoenhof's Foreign Books Inc
Subsidiary of MEP Inc
76 A Mount Auburn St, Cambridge, MA 02138
SAN: 122-7963
Tel: 617-547-8855
E-mail: info@schoenhofs.com
Web Site: www.schoenhofs.com
Key Personnel
Pres: Nicolas Mengin
Mgr: Daniel Eastman
Founded: 1856
French, Spanish, German, Italian, Russian, Portuguese, Arabic, Slavic, Scandinavian, Greek & Latin literature, children's books & nonfiction. Dictionaries, audio courses & grammars in over 700 languages & dialects.
Number of Titles Warehoused: 75,000

Scholastic Book Fairs®, see Scholastic School Reading Events

Scholastic School Reading Events
Division of Scholastic Inc
1080 Greenwood Blvd, Lake Mary, FL 32746
Tel: 407-829-8000 *Toll Free Tel:* 800-770-4662
 Fax: 407-829-2600
E-mail: custservbf@scholasticbookfairs.com
Web Site: bookfairs.scholastic.com/content/fairs/home.html
Key Personnel
Pres, Scholastic School Reading Events: Sasha Quinton
VP, Busn Devt & Strategy: Ben Stone
VP, Fin: Phil Bernhardt
VP, Sales & Serv (North): Jeff Marty
VP, Sales & Serv (South): Shane Kyle
VP, Mktg: Laura Lundgren
VP, Prod Category Mgmt: Eric Compton
VP, Field Deployment & Optimization: Brian Carter
VP, HR: Tim Vuolo
Founded: 1981
Scholastic School Reading Events, in partnership with schools across the country, hosts more than 120,000 book-sale events each year, reaching more than 35 million children & their families in preschool-9th grade. Book Fairs provide students, teachers & parents access to thousands of affordable books & educational products & is responsible for putting more than 100 million books in the hands of children, helping to foster enthusiasm for reading & generating more than $200 million annually in fundraising for school projects & classroom materials.
Number of Titles Warehoused: 2,000

Schroeder's Book Haven
104 Michigan Ave, League City, TX 77573
SAN: 122-7998
Tel: 281-332-5226
E-mail: info@bookhaventexas.com
Web Site: www.bookhaventexas.com
Key Personnel
Mgr & Buyer: Bert Schroeder
Founded: 1968
Wholesale to schools & libraries.
Number of Titles Warehoused: 15,000

Seagrace Partners, see Devin-Adair Publishers/Seagrace Partners

SEBCO Books, see Southeastern Book Co

Sheriar Books
Formerly Sheriar Foundation Bookstore
603 Briarwood Dr, Myrtle Beach, SC 29572
SAN: 203-2457
Tel: 843-272-1339 *Fax:* 843-361-1747
Web Site: www.sheriarbooks.org
Key Personnel
Mgr: Laura Smith *E-mail:* laura@sheriarbooks.org
Founded: 1971
Publishes & distributes books by & about Meher Baba, videos, music & photos.
Catalog available.
Number of Titles Warehoused: 100

Sheriar Foundation Bookstore, see Sheriar Books

Small Changes
1418 NW 53 St, Seattle, WA 98107
Mailing Address: PO Box 70740, Seattle, WA 98127
Tel: 206-382-1980 *Fax:* 206-382-1514
E-mail: info@smallchanges.com
Web Site: www.smallchanges.com

Key Personnel
Owner: Shari Basom
Founded: 1977
Wholesale distribution magazines, calendars, natural foods stores.
Number of Titles Warehoused: 550
Membership(s): California Independent Booksellers Alliance (CALIBA); Pacific Northwest Booksellers Association (PNBA)

Social Studies School Service
10200 Jefferson Blvd, PO Box 802, Culver City, CA 90232
Tel: 310-839-2436 *Toll Free Tel:* 800-421-4246 (US & CN) *Fax:* 310-839-2249
 Toll Free Fax: 800-944-5432
E-mail: access@socialstudies.com; customerservice@socialstudies.com
Web Site: www.socialstudies.com
Key Personnel
CEO: David Weiner
CFO: Russell Kantor
Chief Learning Offr: Dr Aaron Willis
Art Dir: Mark Gutierrez
Dir, District Partnerships: Dr Montra L Rogers
Dir, Opers: Luis Castro
Mktg Dir: Nisreen Breik
Natl Sales Dir: Jennifer Carlson
Head, Content: Bill Walter
Founded: 1965
Provide a wide variety of supplementary curriculum materials to schools, including books, CD-ROMs, DVDs, software, charts, posters, maps, globes & atlases.
Catalog available.
Number of Titles Warehoused: 15,000

SOM Publishing
Division of School of Metaphysics
163 Moon Valley Rd, Windyville, MO 65783
SAN: 159-5423
Tel: 417-345-8411 *Fax:* 417-345-6668
E-mail: som@som.org; dreams@dreamschool.org
Web Site: www.som.org; www.dreamschool.org
Key Personnel
Pres: Dr Christine Spretnjak
Founded: 1973
Publishing & wholesale distribution.
Number of Titles Warehoused: 15,000

Southeastern Book Co
Division of Library Sales Inc
2001 SW 31 Ave, Pembroke Park, FL 33009
Tel: 954-985-9400 *Toll Free Tel:* 800-223-3251
 Fax: 954-987-2200
E-mail: staff@sebcobooks.com
Web Site: www.sebcobooks.com
Key Personnel
Pres: Dan Comer *E-mail:* dan@sebcobooks.com
Founded: 1984
Distributor of paperback classroom sets, library bound books & ebooks to schools & libraries.

Southern Tier News Company, Inc
353 Upper Oakwood Ave, Elmira Heights, NY 14903
Mailing Address: PO Box 2128, Elmira Heights, NY 14903-0128
Tel: 607-734-7108 *Toll Free Tel:* 888-287-4786
 Fax: 607-734-6825
Web Site: www.southerntiernews.com
Key Personnel
Pres: Jeff Rubin
Founded: 1909
Hardcover, trade paperback, mass market & educational paperbacks & newspapers, children's books & magazines. Periodical distribution.

Southern Wisconsin News Co
Subsidiary of Purnell Brothers Inc
58 Artisan Dr, Edgerton, WI 53534

Tel: 608-884-2600 *Fax:* 608-884-2636
Web Site: www.southernwisconsinnews.com
Key Personnel
Owner & Pres: Thomas Purnell
  E-mail: tpurnell@southernwisconsinnews.com
Founded: 1933
Wholesaler of magazines & books.
Number of Titles Warehoused: 4,000

Sparkhouse, see Augsburg Fortress Publishers, Publishing House of the Evangelical Lutheran Church in America

Sparkhouse Family, see Augsburg Fortress Publishers, Publishing House of the Evangelical Lutheran Church in America

Spring Arbor Distributors Inc
Unit of Ingram Content Group LLC
One Ingram Blvd, La Vergne, TN 37086-1986
Toll Free Tel: 800-395-4340 *Toll Free Fax:* 800-876-0186
E-mail: customerservice@ingramcontent.com
Web Site: www.ingramcontent.com
Founded: 1978
Distribute Christian books, Bibles, music & videos to Christian retail stores.
Number of Titles Warehoused: 260,000
Branch Office(s)
Indiana Distribution Center, 7315 Innovation Blvd, Fort Wayne, IN 46818-1371
Oregon Distribution Center, 201 Ingram Dr, Roseburg, OR 97471
Chambersburg Distribution Center, 1240 Ingram Dr, Chambersburg, PA 17202

Sunbelt Publications Inc
664 Marsat Ct, Suite A, Chula Vista, CA 91911
SAN: 630-0790
Tel: 619-258-4911 *Toll Free Tel:* 800-626-6579 (cust serv) *Fax:* 619-258-4916
E-mail: info@sunbeltpub.com; service@sunbeltpub.com
Web Site: sunbeltpublications.com
Key Personnel
CEO & Sales Mgr: Lisa Gulick
COO: Nichole Groschup-Black *E-mail:* nichole@sunbeltpub.com
CFO: Maria Groschup-Black *E-mail:* maria@sunbeltpub.com
Pubns Mgr: Debi Young *E-mail:* dyoung@sunbeltpub.com
Founded: 1984
Specialty wholesaler, distributor & publisher; regional reference & travel books on Southwest US & Baja, California; outdoor adventure, sports; natural history & science.
Catalog available.
Number of Titles Warehoused: 800
Membership(s): Association of Earth Science Editors (AESE); Independent Book Publishers Association (IBPA); Outdoor Writers Association of America (OWAA); Publishers Association of the West (PubWest)

The Supreme Co
Division of Supreme Company Wholesaler of Books Inc
1909 Lagneaux Rd, Lafayette, LA 70506
SAN: 631-3388
Tel: 337-453-1028 *Toll Free Fax:* 888-600-4180
E-mail: information@supremebooks.com
Web Site: www.supremebooks.com
Key Personnel
Pres: Sandra Curley
Founded: 1992
Wholesaler for all publishers to schools & libraries throughout the US & Canada. Distribute all hardbound & paperback titles, reference, audios & videos, music & software suitable to the library or school market. Library cataloging kits & cards, full book processing available. Able to supply almost any book in print.
Catalog available.
Number of Titles Warehoused: 150,000
Publication(s): *Books For Schools & Libraries* (annual catalog)

Swedenborg Foundation
320 N Church St, West Chester, PA 19380
SAN: 202-5280
Tel: 610-430-3222 *Toll Free Tel:* 800-355-3222 (cust serv) *Fax:* 610-430-7982
E-mail: info@swedenborg.com
Web Site: swedenborg.com
Key Personnel
Exec Dir: Morgan Beard *Tel:* 610-430-3222 ext 102 *E-mail:* mbeard@swedenborg.com
Mktg Coord: Amy Acquarola *Tel:* 610-430-3222 ext 103 *E-mail:* aacquarola@swedenborg.com
Founded: 1849
Publisher & wholesaler of theological works of Emanuel Swedenborg & related literature, as well as books on spiritual transformation.
Catalog available.
Number of Titles Warehoused: 190

Talas
330 Morgan Ave, Brooklyn, NY 11211
Tel: 212-219-0770
E-mail: info@talasonline.com; support@talasonline.com
Web Site: www.talasonline.com
Key Personnel
Pres: Aarol Salik
VP: Jillian Salik
Founded: 1962
Art & book conservation materials.
Number of Titles Warehoused: 50

TEACH Services Inc
11 Quartermaster Circle, Fort Oglethorpe, GA 30742-3886
SAN: 246-9863
Tel: 706-504-9192 *Toll Free Tel:* 800-367-1844 (sales) *Toll Free Fax:* 866-757-6023
E-mail: sales@teachservices.com; info@teachservices.com
Web Site: www.teachservices.com
Key Personnel
Owner & Pres: Timothy Hullquist *E-mail:* t.hullquist@teachservices.com
Publr & Opers Mgr: Bill Newman *E-mail:* b.newman@teachservices.com
Founded: 1984
Publisher & distributor of Seventh-Day Adventist books. Offer editing, design, typesetting & printing services.
Catalog available.
Number of Titles Warehoused: 2,500
Membership(s): Independent Book Publishers Association (IBPA)

Teacher's Discovery®
Division of American Eagle Co Inc
2741 Paldan Dr, Auburn Hills, MI 48326
Toll Free Tel: 800-TEACHER (832-2437)
Toll Free Fax: 800-287-4509
E-mail: help@teachersdiscovery.com; orders@teachersdiscovery.com
Web Site: www.teachersdiscovery.com
Key Personnel
Owner: Skip McWilliams
Dir, Mktg: Steve Giroux
Founded: 1968
Proprietary products; English, social studies, foreign language, science; full color maps.
Catalog available.

Technical Library Service Inc, see Talas

Tennessee Book Co
Subsidiary of Ingram Industries Inc
1550 Heil Quaker Blvd, La Vergne, TN 37086
SAN: 150-6897
Mailing Address: PO Box 3009, La Vergne, TN 37086-1986
Tel: 615-793-5040 *Toll Free Tel:* 800-456-0418 *Fax:* 615-213-9545
Web Site: www.tennesseebook.com
Key Personnel
VP & Gen Mgr: Todd Svec
Dir, Admin & Fin Servs: Mandy Bolin
Dir, Digital Solutions: Andrew McGarrity
Sr Mgr, Cust Success: Derrick Greer
Mgr, Cust Rel: Kellie Dumas
Mgr, Prod & Publr Rel: Carol Anne Brown
Founded: 1935
School book depository/wholesaler.

Texas Art Supply
2001 Montrose Blvd, Houston, TX 77006
Tel: 713-526-5221
E-mail: customerservice@texasart.com
Web Site: www.texasart.com
Founded: 1948
Wholesale books sold through retail bookstores & online.
Number of Titles Warehoused: 5,000
Branch Office(s)
1507 Baybrook Mall Dr, Friendswood, TX 77546 *Tel:* 281-486-9320
2237 S Voss, Houston, TX 77057 *Tel:* 713-780-0440
Membership(s): American Booksellers Association (ABA); Craft Hobby Association (CHA); NAMTA® - The International Art Materials Association; National Association of College Stores (NACS)

Texas Book Co
8501 Technology Circle, Greenville, TX 75402
Tel: 903-455-6969 *Toll Free Tel:* 800-527-1016
E-mail: customerservice@texasbook.com
Web Site: www.texasbook.com
Key Personnel
CEO: C Brent Dyer
Pres: Darren Croom
Dir, Campus Rel & Busn Devt: Stacy Dyer *E-mail:* sdyer@texasbook.com
Founded: 1975
Wholesale books.
Number of Titles Warehoused: 20,000

Texas Bookman
Division of Half Price Books, Records, Magazines Inc
2700 Lone Star Dr, Dallas, TX 75212
Tel: 214-678-6680 *Toll Free Tel:* 800-566-2665 *Fax:* 214-678-6699
E-mail: orders@texasbookman.com
Web Site: www.texasbookman.com
Key Personnel
Dir, Sales & Opers: Crystal Reyes *E-mail:* creyes@texasbookman.com
Sales: Mark Wren *E-mail:* mwren@texasbookman.com
Founded: 1983
Scholarly & general remainders.
Catalog available.
Number of Titles Warehoused: 2,000
Publication(s): *Catalog* (monthly); *E-mail* (monthly)
Membership(s): Museum Store Association (MSA)

TNG
Member of The Jim Pattison Group
3320 S Service Rd, Burlington, ON L7N 3M6, Canada
Toll Free Tel: 800-201-8127 *Toll Free Fax:* 877-664-9732
E-mail: cs@tng.com
Web Site: www.tng.com

Key Personnel
Pres, CN: Peter Olson
SVP: Scott Shepherd
VP, Purch: Carm Alfano
VP, Sales & Mktg: Rob Smith
Founded: 1914
Wholesaler of magazines & books.

United Library Services Inc
7140 Fairmount Dr SE, Calgary, AB T2H 0X4, Canada
SAN: 169-9342
Tel: 403-252-4426 *Toll Free Tel:* 888-342-5857 (CN only) *Fax:* 403-258-3426
Toll Free Fax: 800-661-2806 (CN only)
E-mail: info@uls.com
Web Site: www.uls.com
Key Personnel
Gen Mgr: Robin Hoogwerf *E-mail:* robin@uls.com
Mgr, Children's Books & Schools/French Book Buyer: Keitha Langston *E-mail:* klangston@uls.com
Mgr, Prod Devt: Jana Seshadri *E-mail:* jana@uls.com
Natl Sales Mgr: Ren Speer *E-mail:* rspeer@uls.com
Adult Book Buyer/ARP Mgmt: Nadia Fortuna *E-mail:* nadia@uls.com
Fin & Admin: Yolanda Arambarri *E-mail:* accounting@uls.com
Founded: 1939
Book wholesaler; automatic release plans & profile purchasing.
Catalog available.
Number of Titles Warehoused: 15,000
Publication(s): *Accelerated Reader*; *Adult Large Print* (monthly); *Alberta Education Authorized Novels & Nonfiction*; *Alberta Social Studies*; *Best New Books for Children & Young Adults* (daily); *Book Club Picks*; *First Nations Metis Inuit*; *French Collection-Children's*; *French Titles for Adults* (2 times/yr, Spring & Autumn); *Hotlist Catalogue*; *Levelled Books for Guided Reading*; *Nonfiction Reading Power: Teaching Students How to Think While They Read All Kinds of Information*; *Novel Sets*; *Reading Power: Teaching Students to Think While They Read*; *Super Forthcoming Catalogue*; *Top New Titles-Children's* (3 times/yr); *Top New Titles-Young Adult* (3 times/yr); *Top 10 Adult Paperback Bestsellers* (3 times/yr); *Young Reader's Choice Awards*
Branch Office(s)
101-B 3430 Brighton Ave, Burnaby, BC V5A 3H4, Canada, Showroom Mgr: Ria Bleumer
Tel: 604-421-1154 *Toll Free Tel:* 877-853-1200 (CN only) *Fax:* 604-421-2216
Toll Free Fax: 866-421-2216 (CN only)
E-mail: burnaby@uls.com
Membership(s): Association of Canadian Book Wholesalers; BCLA

Upstart Books™
Division of Demco Inc
PO Box 7488, Madison, WI 53707
Tel: 608-241-1201 *Toll Free Tel:* 800-356-1200 (orders); 800-962-4463 (cust serv)
Toll Free Fax: 800-245-1329 (orders)
E-mail: custserv@demco.com; order@demco.com
Web Site: www.demco.com/upstart

Key Personnel
Prod Devt Mgr, Lib Mkts: Heidi Green
Founded: 1956
Distributor of penworthy prebound books & library bound books.
Number of Titles Warehoused: 50
Membership(s): The American Library Association (ALA)

Valley News Co
1305 Stadium Rd, Mankato, MN 56001
Tel: 507-345-4819 *Fax:* 507-345-6793
Web Site: www.valleynewscompany.com
Key Personnel
Pres: Troy Leiferman *E-mail:* tleiferman@valleynewscompany.com
Gen Mgr: Paul Dirks *E-mail:* pauldirks@valleynewscompany.com
Off Mgr: Nancy Nickels *E-mail:* nnickels@valleynewscompany.com
Founded: 1940
Wholesale book & magazine distributor.

Vedanta Book Center
Subsidiary of Vivekananda Vedanta Society
14630 S Lemont Rd, Homer Glen, IL 60491
Tel: 708-301-9062 *Fax:* 708-301-9063
E-mail: info@chicagovedanta.org
Web Site: www.vedantabooks.com
Key Personnel
Mgr: Swami Ishatmananda
Founded: 1930
Retail & wholesale for nonprofit religious organizations.
Number of Titles Warehoused: 1,100

VisionWorks
PO Box 92, Greenfield, MA 01302
Tel: 413-772-6569 *Toll Free Tel:* 800-933-7326 (orders) *Fax:* 413-772-6559
E-mail: dreaming@changingworld.com
Web Site: www.changingworld.com
Key Personnel
Owner: Dick McLeester
Founded: 1986
Postcard & note card publisher; promotion & wholesale distribution for cards, books & calendars & bumper stickers.
Catalog available.
Number of Titles Warehoused: 400
Publication(s): *Annual catalog*

VistaBooks LLC
637 Blue Ridge Rd, Silverthorne, CO 80498-8931
Tel: 970-468-7673 *Fax:* 970-468-7673
E-mail: email@vistabooks.com
Web Site: www.vistabooks.com
Key Personnel
Partner & Ed: William R Jones
Founded: 1972
Catalog available.
Number of Titles Warehoused: 500

Warehouse Books Inc
1006 Ballantine Blvd, Norfolk, VA 23504
Tel: 757-627-4160
E-mail: sales@warehousebooksinc.com
Web Site: www.warehousebooksinc.com
Key Personnel
Owner: Marie Roukas

Founded: 1990
Buying & selling remainders.
Number of Titles Warehoused: 2,850

WeWrite LLC
11040 Alba Rd, Ben Lomond, CA 95005
Tel: 831-336-3382
E-mail: info@wewrite.net
Web Site: www.wewrite.net
Key Personnel
Pres & CEO: Delores L Palmer *E-mail:* dpalmer@wewrite.net
Dir, Mktg: Rickey Bowen *E-mail:* rbowen@wewrite.net
Ed: Jan Hansen *E-mail:* jhansen@wewrite.net
Founded: 1993
Regional & national publisher, book & interactive comic books created from workshop setting, by children for children. *We Write Kids!*™.
Catalog available.
Number of Titles Warehoused: 10

Whitehots Inc
205 Industrial Pkwy N, Unit 3, Aurora, ON L4G 4C4, Canada
Tel: 905-727-9188 *Toll Free Tel:* 888-567-9188 *Fax:* 905-727-8756 *Toll Free Fax:* 888-563-0020
E-mail: admin@whitehots.com
Web Site: www.whitehots.com
Key Personnel
CEO: Russ Culver *Tel:* 905-727-9188 ext 142 *E-mail:* rculver@whitehots.com
CFO: Sharon Culver *E-mail:* sculver@whitehots.com
Pres: Edmund Salt *E-mail:* esalt@whitehots.com
Natl Accts Mgr: Eleanor Heidt *E-mail:* eheidt@whitehots.com
Founded: 1987
Membership(s): Association of Canadian Book Wholesalers; Aurora Chamber of Commerce; Ontario Library Association; Vistage

Wilshire Book Co
22647 Ventura Blvd, Suite 314, Woodland Hills, CA 91364
SAN: 205-5368
Tel: 818-700-1522
E-mail: sales@mpowers.com
Web Site: www.mpowers.com
Key Personnel
Pres & Rts & Perms: Marcia Powers
Founded: 1967 (by Melvin Powers)
Psychological, self-help, motivational & inspirational books, adult fables, horses, bridge; mail order, business, advertising & marketing; originals & reprints.
Number of Titles Warehoused: 23

Woodcrafters Lumber Sales Inc
212 NE Sixth Ave, Portland, OR 97232-2976
Tel: 503-231-0226 *Toll Free Tel:* 800-777-3709
Fax: 503-232-0511
Web Site: www.woodcrafters.us
Key Personnel
Pres: Stephen Penberthy
Sales Mgr: Carl Paasche
Founded: 1973
Woodworking & wood titles.
Catalog available.
Number of Titles Warehoused: 1,465

Prebinders to Schools & Libraries

These firms handle prebound books, usually juvenile titles, for which publishers' bindings have been replaced by stronger bindings prior to sale to schools or libraries. Some of the firms handle only the titles listed in their own catalogs, which they usually purchase in sheets from the publishers and bind in quantity. Others will prebind any book on request, removing the publisher's case and replacing it with a stronger one.

Arizona Library Binding Service
1337 W McKinley, Phoenix, AZ 85007
Tel: 602-253-1861
E-mail: info@azlbinding.com
Key Personnel
VP: Greg Couturier; Ron Couturier
Founded: 1938
Binding of books & related work, some tradework oversewing & saddle (smyth) sewing. No perfect binding.

BMI Educational Services Inc
26 Haypress Rd, Cranbury, NJ 08512
SAN: 169-4669
Mailing Address: PO Box 800, Dayton, NJ 08810-0800
Tel: 732-329-6991 *Toll Free Tel:* 800-222-8100 (orders only) *Fax:* 732-329-6994
Toll Free Fax: 800-986-9393 (orders only)
E-mail: info@bmionline.com
Web Site: bmionline.com
Key Personnel
Owner & Secy-Treas: Lynda Bradley
Pres: Jerry Wagner *E-mail:* jwagner@bmionline.com
Founded: 1964
Complete prebinding service for all books; including mass market & trade paperback, dictionaries & reference books.
Catalog available.
Number of Titles Warehoused: 10,000
Membership(s): International Literacy Association (ILA); National Council of Teachers of English (NCTE)

Bound to Stay Bound Books Inc
1880 W Morton Rd, Jacksonville, IL 62650
SAN: 169-1996
Tel: 217-245-5191 *Toll Free Tel:* 800-637-6586 *Fax:* 217-245-0424 *Toll Free Fax:* 800-747-7872
E-mail: btsb@btsb.com
Web Site: www.btsb.com
Key Personnel
Pres: Robert L Sibert
Founded: 1920
Prebound books, grades K-12.
Catalog available.
Number of Titles Warehoused: 19,000

Bridgeport National Bindery Inc
662 Silver St, Agawam, MA 01001
Mailing Address: PO Box 289, Agawam, MA 01001-0289
Tel: 413-789-1981 *Toll Free Tel:* 800-223-5083
E-mail: info@bnbindery.com
Web Site: www.bnbindery.com
Key Personnel
Pres: James M Larsen
EVP: Bruce F Jacobsen
VP, Print on Demand Div: Kent Larson
Founded: 1947
Prebinding services (library bound), short run edition binding, print on demand (POD), textbook rebinding, conservation services.
Membership(s): Book Manufacturers' Institute (BMI)

Brodart Books & Library Services
500 Arch St, Williamsport, PA 17701
Tel: 570-326-2461 *Toll Free Tel:* 800-474-9816 *Fax:* 570-651-1639 *Toll Free Fax:* 800-999-6799
E-mail: support@brodart.com
Web Site: www.brodartbooks.com
Key Personnel
Pres & CEO: George Coe
CFO: Richard Dill
VP, Books Div: Gretchen Herman
Founded: 1939
Premier supplier of shelf-ready materials to libraries delivering carefully selected, cataloged & processed books. Today, Brodart offers state-of-the-art online tools, bibliographic services & consulting exclusively to libraries. Customers select from English language titles, Spanish language materials, plus audio & video products.
Catalog available.
Number of Titles Warehoused: 1,000,000

The Campbell-Logan Bindery Inc
7615 Baker St NE, Fridley, MN 55432
Tel: 612-332-1313 *Toll Free Tel:* 800-942-6224
E-mail: info@campbell-logan.com
Web Site: www.campbell-logan.com
Key Personnel
Pres: Greg Campbell *E-mail:* greg@campbell-logan.com
VP: Duncan Campbell *E-mail:* duncan@campbell-logan.com
Founded: 1949
Bookbinding, book design, art & design, edition hardcover binding, covers, paper & paper products, printing & publishing. Consulting to libraries.

Denver Bookbinding Co Inc
1401 W 47 Ave, Denver, CO 80211
Tel: 303-455-5521
E-mail: dbbc@denverbook.com; info@denverbook.com
Web Site: www.denverbook.com
Key Personnel
CEO: Gail Lindley
Founded: 1929
Bookbinder, leather binding, restorations & short run editions, book making kits, story making kits.
Catalog available.

HF Group LLC
8844 Mayfield Rd, Chesterland, OH 44026
Tel: 440-729-2445; 440-729-9411 (bindery)
E-mail: custservice-oh@hfgroup.com
Web Site: www.hfgroup.com
Key Personnel
CEO: Jay Fairfield *Tel:* 440-729-2445 ext 4 *E-mail:* jayfairfield@hfgroup.com
VP & Gen Mgr: Jim Bratton *E-mail:* jbratton@hfgroup.com
Founded: 1821
Prebinding, rebinding, binding of short runs.
Branch Office(s)
1010 N Sycamore St, North Manchester, IN 46962, Pres: Jim Heckman *Tel:* 260-982-2107 *E-mail:* jheckman@hfgroup.com
92 Cambridge St, Charlestown, MA 02129-0212, VP: John Parisi *Tel:* 617-242-1100 *E-mail:* jparisi@hfgroup.com
340 First St, Utica, NE 68456, Gen Mgr: Damon Osborne *Tel:* 402-534-2261 *E-mail:* dosborne@hfgroup.com
6204 Corporate Park Dr, Browns Summit, NC 27214-9745, Contact: Eric Fairfield *Tel:* 336-931-0800 *E-mail:* efairfield@hfgroup.com
45 N Main St, Unit 528, Hatfield, PA 19440 (transportation hub) *Tel:* 215-855-2293
105 W Thomas St, Atlanta, TX 75551-2736 (transportation hub) *Tel:* 260-982-2107 *Fax:* 260-982-1130

Houchen Bindery Ltd
340 First St, Utica, NE 68456
Tel: 402-534-2261 *Toll Free Tel:* 800-869-0420 *Fax:* 402-534-2761
E-mail: email@houchenbindery.com
Web Site: www.houchenbindery.com
Key Personnel
Pres: H Damon Osborne
VP, Opers: John C Salistean
Founded: 1935
Library, edition & comic book binding; repair & restoration services.
Branch Office(s)
University Bindery Div, 7917 Watson Rd, St Louis, MO 63119 *Tel:* 314-918-7017 *Fax:* 314-918-7133

International Service Co
International Service Bldg, 333 Fourth Ave, Indialantic, FL 32903-4295
SAN: 169-5134
Tel: 321-724-1443 *Fax:* 321-724-1443
Key Personnel
Pres: Dennis Samuels
Compt: F Schneider
Mng Dir: Katherine Swanberg
Coord Dir: Ann C Samuels
Shipping & Receiving Mgr: Larry A Whobrey
Systems Supv: Suzanne Jones
Asst to Pres: Robert Cohen
Admin Asst: Irene August
Founded: 1958
Exporter & importer of books, quantity & single copies; periodicals & school supplies; commissionaires.

Long's Roullet Bookbinders Inc
2800 Monticello Ave, Norfolk, VA 23504
Tel: 757-623-4244 *Fax:* 757-627-1404
E-mail: bindlrbi@gmail.com
Web Site: longs-roullet.com
Key Personnel
Pres: Alain Roullet
VP: Eileen Roullet
Founded: 1975
Library & edition binding.

The Penworthy Company LLC
219 N Milwaukee St, 4th fl, Milwaukee, WI 53202
Tel: 414-287-4600 *Toll Free Tel:* 800-262-2665 *Fax:* 414-287-4602
E-mail: info@penworthy.com
Web Site: www.penworthy.com
Key Personnel
Pres: Holly Ritz
EVP: Julie Plantz *Tel:* 414-287-4600 ext 211 *E-mail:* julie.plantz@penworthy.com

PREBINDERS TO SCHOOLS & LIBRARIES

Founded: 1982
Prebound juvenile books, cataloging, bar coding, complete processing.
Number of Titles Warehoused: 2,000

Perma-Bound Books
Division of Hertzberg-New Method Inc
617 E Vandalia Rd, Jacksonville, IL 62650
Tel: 217-243-5451 *Toll Free Tel:* 800-637-6581 *Fax:* 217-243-7505 *Toll Free Fax:* 800-551-1169
E-mail: books@perma-bound.com
Web Site: www.perma-bound.com
Key Personnel
Owner & Pres: James Orr
Founded: 1954
Prebinder of paperbacks & educational vendor of Perma-Bound books & related media.
Catalog available.
Number of Titles Warehoused: 5,000,000
Branch Office(s)
PO Box 868, Sta Main, Peterborough, ON K9J 7A2, Canada *Tel:* 705-742-1513 *Toll Free Tel:* 800-461-1999 *Toll Free Fax:* 888-250-3811 *E-mail:* perma-bound.ca@sympatico.ca *Web Site:* www.perma-bound.com/canada

Roswell Bookbinding
2614 N 29 Ave, Phoenix, AZ 85009
Tel: 602-272-9338 *Toll Free Tel:* 888-803-8883 *Fax:* 602-272-9786
Web Site: www.roswellbookbinding.com
Key Personnel
Pres: Michael Roswell
Trade Div Cust Serv Dir: Jim Menke
Specialty Div Mgr: Kortez Brown
Trade Prodn Mgr: Bryan Way
Specialty Div Estimating: Steve Jones
Trade Div Estimating: Nancy Scherba
Founded: 1960
Prebinders to schools & libraries, library binding, edition binding, specialty binding & book restoration.

Shaffner's Bindery
3305 Pattee Canyon Rd, Missoula, MT 59803
Tel: 406-251-2699
E-mail: shaffnersbindery@centric.net
Web Site: shaffnersbindery.com
Key Personnel
Owner: Carol Shaffner; Jeff Shaffner
Founded: 1965
Bookbinding, library rebinding & restoration.

Turtleback Books
Division of Perfection Learning
1000 N Second Ave, Logan, IA 51546-0500
Toll Free Tel: 800-831-4190 *Toll Free Fax:* 800-543-2745
E-mail: turtleback@perfectionlearning.com
Web Site: turtleback.perfectionlearning.com
Founded: 1961
Dedicated to providing children & adults with the most popular literature in a sturdy hardcover library binding created for the highly demanding school & library environment.

Wallaceburg Bookbinding & Mfg Co Ltd
95 Arnold St, Wallaceburg, ON N8A 3P3, Canada
Tel: 519-627-3552 *Toll Free Tel:* 800-214-BIND (214-2463) *Fax:* 519-627-6922
E-mail: helpdesk@wbmbindery.com
Web Site: www.wbmbindery.com
Key Personnel
Pres: Clarence Dykhouse
VP: Gerrit Dykhouse
Founded: 1967
Bookbinding, library binding, rare book restoration. Specialize in archival boxes.
Membership(s): Atlantic Provinces Library Association (APLA); Canadian Library Association (CLA); Michigan Library Association (MLA); National Information Standards Organization (NISO)

Book Exporters & Importers

For more complete lists of book exporters and importers, see the latest edition of *The American Book Trade Directory* (Information Today, Inc., 121 Chanlon Road, Suite G-20, New Providence, NJ 07974-2195).

AK Press
Subsidiary of AK Press Inc
370 Ryan Ave, Unit 100, Chico, CA 95973
Tel: 510-208-1700 *Fax:* 510-208-1701
E-mail: info@akpress.org; orders@akpress.org; sales@akpress.org
Web Site: www.akpress.org
Founded: 1994
Radical publishing & distribution.
Number of Titles Warehoused: 4,000

Amcorp Ltd
10 Norden Lane, Huntington Station, NY 11746
Tel: 631-271-0548 *Fax:* 631-549-8849
E-mail: amcorpltd@aol.com
Key Personnel
Pres: Durga Edson
VP: Chandru Mahtani; Lal Uttam
Founded: 1946
Exporters of all published materials to Hong Kong, Singapore, Philippines, Malaysia, Australia & India. Branch offices at Singapore Magazine Distributors, Singapore & Far East Media (HKG) Ltd, Hong Kong.

Auromere Inc
Division of Integral Yoga
2621 W Hwy 12, Lodi, CA 95242
SAN: 211-7207
Toll Free Tel: 800-735-4691
E-mail: contact@auromere.com
Web Site: www.auromere.com
Founded: 1974
Importers of spiritual & classical Indian texts. Specialize in Sri Aurobindo & the Mother, yoga, health literature & children's books from India.
Number of Titles Warehoused: 365

Avanti Enterprises Inc
18901 Springfield Ave, Flossmoor, IL 60422-1071
SAN: 158-3727
Tel: 630-850-3245 *Toll Free Tel:* 800-799-6464
Fax: 708-799-6474 *Toll Free Fax:* 877-799-6474
E-mail: sales@avantiusa.com
Web Site: www.avantiusa.com
Key Personnel
Pres: Nilima Kumar *E-mail:* kumar@avantiusa.com
Founded: 1971
Export wholesale book distribution, medical, fiction, nonfiction, children's, textbooks, maps, dictionaries, trade library; subscription agency; import from UK, Europe, Asia & India.
Number of Titles Warehoused: 175,000

Beijing Book Co Inc
Subsidiary of China National Publications Import & Export (Group) Co Ltd (People's Republic of China)
701 E Linden Ave, Linden, NJ 07036
Tel: 908-862-0909 *Fax:* 908-862-4201
E-mail: journals@cnpbbci.com
Key Personnel
Mgr: Donna Jacik
Founded: 1981
Export American publications (books, periodicals, other serials & government publications) to China for Chinese libraries. Purchase newspapers, music products, micro products, CD-ROM.

Bentley Publishers
Division of Robert Bentley Inc
1734 Massachusetts Ave, Cambridge, MA 02138-1804
SAN: 213-9839
Tel: 617-547-4170
E-mail: sales@bentleypubs.com
Web Site: www.bentleypublishers.com
Key Personnel
Chmn & Pres: Michael Bentley
Dir, Publg: Janet Barnes
Founded: 1949
Official factory automobile service manuals & other automobile manuals, sports car & automobile books; hardcover fiction reprints.
Number of Titles Warehoused: 8,100

Bookazine Co Inc
75 Hook Rd, Bayonne, NJ 07002
SAN: 169-5665
Tel: 201-339-7777 *Toll Free Tel:* 800-221-8112
Fax: 201-339-7778
E-mail: info@bookazine.com
Web Site: www.bookazine.com
Key Personnel
Pres & CEO: Robert Kallman
COO: Richard Kallman
Pres, Sales: Cindy Raiton
VP, Dist: Allan Davis
VP, Mdse: Andrew Collings
Dir, Natl Accts: Steven Goldberg
Northeast Sales Dir: Josh Harwood
Mktg Mgr: Lani Buess
Founded: 1929
Exporters of hardcover, paperback, computer books & audios to bookstores, schools & libraries.
Number of Titles Warehoused: 80,000

Cedar Fort Inc
2373 W 700 S, Suite 100, Springville, UT 84663
Tel: 801-489-4084 *Toll Free Tel:* 800-SKY-BOOK (759-2665)
E-mail: marketinginfo@cedarfort.com
Web Site: cedarfort.com
Key Personnel
CEO: Bryce Mortimer *Tel:* 801-489-9366
E-mail: bmortimer@cedarfort.com
CFO: Tanya Flynn *Tel:* 801-477-9022
E-mail: tflynn@cedarfort.com
EVP, Sales & Mktg, Acqs & Events: Dru Huffaker *Tel:* 801-477-9025 *E-mail:* dru@cedarfort.com
VP, Digital Sales & Mktg: Clint Hunter *Tel:* 801-477-9023 *E-mail:* chunter@cedarfort.com
Dir, Logistics: Bevan Olsen *Tel:* 801-477-9038
E-mail: bolsen@cedarfort.com
Dir, Sourcing: Kim Clemons *Tel:* 801-477-9029
E-mail: kclemons@cedarfort.com
Founded: 1986
Number of Titles Warehoused: 1,800

China Books
Division of Sinomedia International Group
360 Swift Ave, Suite 48, South San Francisco, CA 94080
SAN: 169-0167
Fax: 650-872-7808
E-mail: editor.sinomedia@gmail.com
Key Personnel
Edit Dir: Chris Robyn *Tel:* 650-872-7718 ext 312
E-mail: chris@sinomediausa.com
Sales Mgr: Kelly Feng *Tel:* 650-872-7076 ext 310
E-mail: kelly@chinabooks.com
Founded: 1960
Publisher & importer of books & periodicals in English from China (Foreign Language Press, etc). Subscription agents for Chinese periodicals in English & Chinese.
Number of Titles Warehoused: 5,000

China Books & Periodicals Inc, see China Books

Continental Book Co Inc
7000 Broadway, Suite 102, Denver, CO 80221-2913
Tel: 303-289-1761 *Toll Free Fax:* 800-279-1764
E-mail: cbc@continentalbook.com
Web Site: www.continentalbook.com
Key Personnel
Dir: Linette Hayat *E-mail:* linette@continentalbook.com
Founded: 1961
Importers & distributors of language materials. Specialize in Spanish, French, German, Italian, Latin, Chinese, Arabic, Bilingual Spanish, Heritage Spanish, ELL, ESL, Common Core, English Novels, ASL, juvenile to advanced levels.
Number of Titles Warehoused: 15,000

Crescent Imports
PO Box 721, Union City, CA 94587
Tel: 734-665-3492 *Toll Free Tel:* 800-521-9744
Fax: 734-677-1717
E-mail: message@crescentimports.com
Web Site: crescentimports.store; crescentimports.com
Key Personnel
Co-Owner: Gulshan Ibrahim; Sabir Ibrahim
Founded: 1978
Islamic books; free catalog upon request.
Number of Titles Warehoused: 10,000

Eastwind Books & Arts Inc
1435 Stockton St, San Francisco, CA 94133
SAN: 127-3159
Tel: 415-772-5888 *Fax:* 415-772-5885
E-mail: contact@eastwindbooks.com
Web Site: www.eastwindbooks.com
Key Personnel
Mgr: Cat Deng
Founded: 1978
Export & import, specialize in China or Asia-related titles.

European Books & Media
6600 Shattuck Ave, Oakland, CA 94609
Tel: 510-922-9157
E-mail: info@europeanbook.com
Web Site: www.europeanbook.com
Key Personnel
Owner & Mng Memb: Nicolas Pellerin
E-mail: nicolas.pellerin@europeanbook.com
Founded: 1963

BOOK EXPORTERS & IMPORTERS   SALES

Importer/distributor of French books.
Number of Titles Warehoused: 100,000

French & European Publications Inc
425 E 58 St, Suite 27-D, New York, NY 10022
Tel: 212-581-8810 *Fax:* 212-202-4356
E-mail: livresny@gmail.com; frenchbookstore@aol.com
Web Site: www.frencheuropean.com
Key Personnel
Pres: Emanuel Molho
Founded: 1928
Importers & exporters of language-learning books in all languages. Specialize in French & Spanish books & dictionaries in all languages.
Number of Titles Warehoused: 80,000
Membership(s): American Booksellers Association (ABA); National Association of College Stores (NACS)

Gefen Books
Unit of Gefen Publishing House Ltd (Jerusalem, Israel)
c/o Storch, 255 Central Ave, B-206, Lawrence, NY 11559
Tel: 516-593-1234 *Fax:* 516-295-2739
E-mail: info@gefenpublishing.com
Web Site: www.gefenpublishing.com
Distributor & North American importer of Jewish books & Hebrew studies textbooks from Israel.

Girol Books Inc
PO Box 5473, LCD Merivale, Ottawa, ON K2C 3M1, Canada
Tel: 613-233-9044
E-mail: info@girol.com
Web Site: www.girol.com
Key Personnel
Owner: Miguel Angel Giella; Peter Roster
Mgr: Leslie Roster *E-mail:* lroster@girol.com
Founded: 1975
Importers & distributors of books in Spanish & Portuguese. Publishers of Latin American theater titles & theater criticism.

Gurarys Books & Trade Inc, see Gurarys Israeli Trading Co Inc

Gurarys Israeli Trading Co Inc
724 Eastern Pkwy, Brooklyn, NY 11213
Tel: 718-493-5225
E-mail: hebbook@gmail.com
Key Personnel
Mgr: Hyam Lieberman

Haynes North America Inc
Division of InfoPro Digital
2801 Townsgate Rd, Suite 340, Westlake Village, CA 91361
Tel: 805-498-6703 *Toll Free Tel:* 800-4-HAYNES (442-9637) *Fax:* 805-498-2867
E-mail: customerservice.haynes@infopro-digital.com
Web Site: www.haynes.com
Key Personnel
Pres: Harvey Wolff
Mktg Dir: Jon Louie
Founded: 1960
Publisher & importer of books on domestic & foreign autos & motorcycles, historical & technical motoring. Export to all countries except England. Haynes Repair Manuals, Haynes DIY Repair Manuals, Chilton Repair Manuals, Clymer Repair Manuals & I&T Tractor Manuals.
Number of Titles Warehoused: 800

Haynes Repair Manuals, see Haynes North America Inc

Independent Publishers Group (IPG)
Division of Chicago Review Press
814 N Franklin St, Chicago, IL 60610
Tel: 312-337-0747 *Toll Free Tel:* 800-888-4741 (orders) *Fax:* 312-337-5985
E-mail: frontdesk@ipgbook.com; orders@ipgbook.com
Web Site: www.ipgbook.com
Key Personnel
Global CEO: Joe Matthews
Global CFO: Frank Autunnale
SVP, Intl Busn Devt: Brooke O'Donnell
VP & Dir, Natl Accts: Jeff Palicki *Tel:* 312-337-0747 ext 281
VP, Academic, Art & Prof Mkts: Paul Murphy *Tel:* 312-337-0747 ext 229
VP, Busn Devt: Alex Kampmann
VP, Busn Mgmt & Opers: Mark Noble
VP, Publr Devt, Publg & Licensing: Richard T Williams
VP, Sales: Tim McCall
Dir, Academic, Lib & Educ Sales: Sharon Shell
Dir, Credit & Collections: Kristen Noon
Dir, HR: Alicia McCray
Dir, Publicity: Candysse Miller
Dir, Spec Sales: Ilene Schreider
Sr Mgr, Supply Chain: Tashina Richardson
Accts Receivable Mgr: Walt Braley
Busn Devt Mgr: Sidney Thompson
Client Mgr, Fin Statements: Megan Trank
Data Mgr: Topher Bigelow
Digital Print Mgr: Qassye "Q" Inwood
Digital Servs Mgr: Casey Park
Lib & Educ Sales Mgr: Cynthia Murphy
Opers Mgr: Joshleigh Rowe-Richardson
Publr Devt Mgr: Anna Torres
Supply Chain Mgr: Betsy Rayas
Trade Sales Rep, Central: Travis Hale
Digital Mktg Coord: Kenneth Duncan
Supply Chain Coord: Jacob Slater
Digital Servs Specialist: Emma Baietto
Sr Assoc, Digital Servs: Adam Barresse; Harlow Brightheart
Accts Payable Assoc: Mai Yang
Data Assoc: Huey Wells
Mktg Assoc: Serena Knudson; Bianca Rodriguez
Founded: 1971
Exporter & importer.
Number of Titles Warehoused: 50,000

International Book Import Service Inc
161 Main St, Lynchburg, TN 37352-8300
SAN: 175-8179
Mailing Address: PO Box 8188, Lynchburg, TN 37352-8188
Tel: 931-759-7400 *Toll Free Tel:* 800-277-4247 *Fax:* 931-759-7555 *Toll Free Fax:* 866-277-2722
E-mail: ibis@ibiservice.com
Web Site: www.ibiservice.com
Key Personnel
Pres: Barbara L Patten
Founded: 1989
Import German, French & Italian books; can supply any title published in Germany, Switzerland, Austria, France & Italy.
Number of Titles Warehoused: 10,000
Membership(s): American Association of Teachers of German (AATG); National Association of College Stores (NACS)

International Institute of Reflexology Inc
PO Box 12642, St Petersburg, FL 33733-2642
Tel: 727-343-4811
E-mail: info@reflexology-usa.net; orderdept@reflexology-usa.net
Web Site: reflexology-usa.net
Key Personnel
Pres: Gail Byers *E-mail:* gailbyers@reflexology-usa.net
Export/import hardbound, paperbacks & charts.
Number of Titles Warehoused: 7

International Service Co
International Service Bldg, 333 Fourth Ave, Indialantic, FL 32903-4295
SAN: 169-5134
Tel: 321-724-1443 *Fax:* 321-724-1443
Key Personnel
Pres: Dennis Samuels
Compt: F Schneider
Mng Dir: Katherine Swanberg
Coord Dir: Ann C Samuels
Shipping & Receiving Mgr: Larry A Whobrey
Systems Supv: Suzanne Jones
Asst to Pres: Robert Cohen
Admin Asst: Irene August
Founded: 1958
Exporters & importers of books; quantity & single copy.

Iranbooks
PO Box 30087, Bethesda, MD 20824
Tel: 301-718-8188 *Toll Free Tel:* 888-718-8188 *Fax:* 301-907-8707
E-mail: info@iranbooks.com
Web Site: www.iranbooks.com
Key Personnel
Mgr: Farhad Shirzad
Founded: 1979
Import & distribute for most publishers from Iran.

The Islander Group
269 Palii St, Mililani, HI 96789
Tel: 808-676-0116 *Toll Free Tel:* 877-828-4852 *Fax:* 808-676-5156
E-mail: customerservice@islandergroup.com
Web Site: www.islandergroup.com
Key Personnel
CEO: Jeff Swartz
Pres & COO: Steve Holmberg
Founded: 1992
Wholesale distributor, specialize in Hawaiian & Pacific Rim material.
Number of Titles Warehoused: 6,000

Kazi Publications Inc
3023 W Belmont Ave, Chicago, IL 60618
Tel: 773-267-7001 *Fax:* 773-267-7002
E-mail: info@kazi.org
Web Site: www.kazi.org
Key Personnel
Pres: Liaquat Ali
Mktg Dir: Mary Bakhtiar
Founded: 1972
Number of Titles Warehoused: 1,963

kfa.org, see Krishnamurti Publications of America

Kinokuniya Bookstores of America Co Ltd
Subsidiary of Kinokuniya Co Ltd (Japan)
1581 Webster St, San Francisco, CA 94115
SAN: 121-8441
Tel: 415-567-6787 *Fax:* 415-567-4109
E-mail: sales@kinokuniya.com; san_francisco@kinokuniya.com; bookwebusa@kinokuniya.com (cust serv)
Web Site: usa.kinokuniya.com
Founded: 1969
Import & retail sales.
Number of Titles Warehoused: 80,000
Branch Office(s)
Little Tokyo, 123 Astronaut E S Onizuka St, Los Angeles, CA 90012 *Tel:* 213-687-4480 *E-mail:* los_angeles@kinokuniya.com
Mitsuwa Marketplace, 3760 S Centinela Ave, Los Angeles, CA 90066 *Tel:* 310-482-3382 *E-mail:* santamonica@kinokuniya.com
Mitsuwa Marketplace, 675 Saratoga Ave, San Jose, CA 95129 *Tel:* 408-252-1300 *E-mail:* san_jose@kinokuniya.com
Mitsuwa Marketplace, 100 E Algonquin Rd, Arlington Heights, IL 60005 *Tel:* 847-427-2665 *E-mail:* chicago@kinokuniya.com

Mitsuwa Marketplace, 595 River Rd, Edgewater, NJ 07020 *Tel:* 201-496-6910 *E-mail:* nj@kinokuniya.com
1073 Avenue of the Americas, New York, NY 10018 *Tel:* 212-869-1700 *E-mail:* nyinfo@kinokuniya.com
Uwajimaya Plaza, 10500 SW Beaverton-Hillsdale Hwy, Beaverton, OR 97005 *Tel:* 503-641-6240 *E-mail:* beaverton@kinokuniya.com
6929 Airport Blvd, No 121, Austin, TX 78752 *Tel:* 512-291-2026 *E-mail:* austin@kinokuniya.com
Carrollton Town Ctr, 2540 Old Denton Rd, Suite 114, Carrollton, TX 75006 *Tel:* 214-731-6800 *E-mail:* carrollton@kinokuniya.com
Mitsuwa Marketplace, 100 Legacy Dr, Plano, TX 75023 *Tel:* 972-517-0226 *E-mail:* plano@kinokuniya.com
Uwajimaya Village, 525 S Weller St, Seattle, WA 98104 *Tel:* 206-587-2477 *E-mail:* seattle@kinokuniya.com

Krishnamurti Publications of America
Division of Krishnamurti Foundation of America
1070 McAndrew Rd, Ojai, CA 93023
Mailing Address: PO Box 1560, Ojai, CA 93024
Tel: 805-646-2726
E-mail: kfa@kfa.org
Web Site: www.kfa.org
Key Personnel
Exec Dir: Jaap Sluijter
Pubns: Cory Fisher
Founded: 1999
Publisher & distributor of the books, CDs of the writings, talks & dialogues of author, educator & philosopher J Krishnamurti.
Number of Titles Warehoused: 200
Membership(s): American Booksellers Association (ABA); Independent Book Publishers Association (IBPA); Small Publishers Marketing Association

The Latin American Book Store Ltd
PO Box 7328, Redlands, CA 92375
Toll Free Tel: 800-645-4276 *Fax:* 909-335-9945
E-mail: libros@latinamericanbooks.com
Web Site: www.latinamericanbooks.com
Key Personnel
Contact: Alfonso Vijil
Founded: 1982
Importer of Latin American & Spanish academic publications.
Number of Titles Warehoused: 4,000

LEA Book Distributors, see LEA Libros de Espana y America

LEA Libros de Espana y America
170-23 83 Ave, Jamaica, NY 11432
SAN: 170-5407
Tel: 718-291-9891 *Fax:* 718-291-9830
E-mail: lea@leabooks.com; orders@leabooks.com
Web Site: www.leabooks.com
Key Personnel
Owner: Dr Angel Capellan
Founded: 1977
Service basis only. Specialize in sale of any type of book published in US for export to foreign academic institutions & bookstores; distribute to certain American publishers for American university libraries. Also import Spanish books from Spain, Latin America & Mexico for sale to American academic institutions & bookstores. Sale of CD-ROM multimedia products in Spanish to US markets. Audiobooks. Spanish literary videos.
Number of Titles Warehoused: 10,000
Membership(s): ABE

Motorbooks
Division of Quarto Publishing Group USA Inc
100 Cummings Ctr, Suite 265D, Beverly, MA 01915
Tel: 978-282-9590 *Toll Free Tel:* 800-759-0190 (orders)
Web Site: www.quartoknows.com/motorbooks
Key Personnel
SVP & Group Publg Dir, US: Winnie Prentiss *E-mail:* winnie.prentiss@quarto.com
Publr: Zack Miller *E-mail:* zack.miller@quarto.com
Sr Acqs Ed: Dennis Pernu *E-mail:* dennis.pernu@quarto.com
Mgr, Spec Mkt Sales: Nichole Schiele *E-mail:* nichole.schiele@quarto.com
Mktg Mgr: Steve Roth *E-mail:* steve.roth@quarto.com
Founded: 1965
Exporters & importers of European & British books; publish & distribute own books, transportation, military history & aviation books.
Number of Titles Warehoused: 9,000

OCS America Inc
Subsidiary of Overseas Courier Service Co Ltd (Japan)
195 Anderson Ave, Moonachie, NJ 07074
Tel: 201-460-2888 *Toll Free Tel:* 800-367-3405
E-mail: info@ocsworld.com
Web Site: www.ocsworld.com
Key Personnel
Pres & CEO: Tsukasa Shibata
Sales Rep: Edward Ho
Founded: 1957
Courier service worldwide; mailing service to Asian countries; subscription agency for Japanese publications.
Number of Titles Warehoused: 1,000

Pannonia Bookstore
300 Sainte Clair Ave W, Suite 103, Toronto, ON M4V 1S4, Canada
Tel: 416-966-5156
E-mail: info@pannonia.ca
Web Site: www.pannonia.ca
Key Personnel
Owner: Zsolt Bede Fazekas; Hortenzia Papp
Founded: 1957
Importers of books & periodicals on Hungary or published in Hungarian, including history, culture, music, geography, science, CDs & tapes, maps & playing cards.
Number of Titles Warehoused: 15,000

Redwing Book Co
202 Bendix St, Taos, NM 87571
Tel: 575-758-7758 *Toll Free Tel:* 800-873-3946 (US); 888-873-3947 (CN) *Fax:* 575-758-7768
E-mail: info@redwingbooks.com; custsrv@redwingbooks.com
Web Site: www.redwingbooks.com
Key Personnel
Pres & Publr: Robert Felt
Founded: 1973
Oriental traditional medicine, acupuncture, herbology, homeopathy, massage, dietary therapy, tai chi chuan.
Number of Titles Warehoused: 1,500

Rising Sun Book Co
1424 Stony Brook Rd, Stony Brook, NY 11790
Tel: 631-473-7000 *Fax:* 631-473-7447
Web Site: risingsunbook.com
Key Personnel
Pres: Arun Shanbhag *E-mail:* shanbhagarun@aol.com
Founded: 1983
Book wholesaler & exporter, domestic US.
Number of Titles Warehoused: 10,000

Schoenhof's Foreign Books Inc
Subsidiary of MEP Inc
76 A Mount Auburn St, Cambridge, MA 02138
SAN: 122-7963
Tel: 617-547-8855
E-mail: info@schoenhofs.com
Web Site: www.schoenhofs.com
Key Personnel
Pres: Nicolas Mengin
Mgr: Daniel Eastman
Founded: 1856
Importers & distributors of foreign language books in over 700 languages & dialects from 50 countries. Book listings available.
Number of Titles Warehoused: 75,000

Silvermine International Books LLC
25 Perry Ave, Suite 11, Norwalk, CT 06850
SAN: 760-6338
Tel: 203-451-2396
E-mail: info@jawilsons.com
Web Site: jawilsons.com/pages/who-we-are
Key Personnel
Pres: John Atkin *E-mail:* jatkin@silvermineinternational.com
Founded: 2006
Represents clients in the US market from all parts of the world. Specialize in academic, Spanish language, photography, engineering, reference, architectural & trade publications. Provide distribution, warehousing, fulfillment, ebook, sales & marketing services, online listings & sales, trade show displays & other support services.

Skylark Co Inc
PO Box 237043, New York, NY 10023-0028
Tel: 212-595-0700 *Fax:* 212-595-0700
Key Personnel
Pres: Brian Eskenazi *E-mail:* eskenazi@rcn.com
Founded: 1982
Exporters of books from all publishers. Buying service, shipping, banking, documentation & insurance.

Thinkers' Press Inc
1524 Le Claire St, Davenport, IA 52803
SAN: 176-4632
Tel: 563-271-6657
E-mail: info@chessbutler.com
Web Site: www.thinkerspressinc.com
Key Personnel
Pres & Busn Mgr: Bob Long
Founded: 1971
Specialize in books on chess.

Trophy Room Books
PO Box 3041, Agoura, CA 91376
Tel: 818-889-2469
E-mail: info@trophyroombooks.com
Web Site: www.trophyroombooks.com
Key Personnel
Co-Owner: Jim Herring; Ellen Herring
Founded: 1971
Antiquarian big game hunting.
Number of Titles Warehoused: 30
Membership(s): Antiquarian Booksellers Association of America (ABAA); Independent Book Publishers Association (IBPA); International League of Antiquarian Booksellers (ILAB)

Vedanta Book Center
Subsidiary of Vivekananda Vedanta Society
14630 S Lemont Rd, Homer Glen, IL 60491
Tel: 708-301-9062 *Fax:* 708-301-9063
E-mail: info@chicagovedanta.org
Web Site: www.vedantabooks.com
Key Personnel
Mgr: Swami Ishatmananda
Founded: 1930
Imported & US titles for nonprofit religious organizations.
Number of Titles Warehoused: 1,100

Export Representatives

International Service Co
International Service Bldg, 333 Fourth Ave, Indialantic, FL 32903-4295
SAN: 169-5134
Tel: 321-724-1443 *Fax:* 321-724-1443
Key Personnel
Pres: Dennis Samuels
Compt: F Schneider
Mng Dir: Katherine Swanberg
Coord Dir: Ann C Samuels
Shipping & Receiving Mgr: Larry A Whobrey
Systems Supv: Suzanne Jones
Asst to Pres: Robert Cohen
Admin Asst: Irene August
Founded: 1958
Exporter & importer of books, quantity & single copy; periodicals & school supplies; commissionaires. Specialize in science, technology & medicine.

Shipping Services

ABDI Inc
16 Avenue "A", Leetsdale, PA 15056
Toll Free Tel: 800-796-6471 *Fax:* 412-741-4161
E-mail: e-fulfillment@abdintl.com
Web Site: www.abdi-ecommerce10.com/abdintl; www.abdintl.com/abdintl
Key Personnel
CEO: Michael D Cheteyan, II
Pres: Judy G Cheteyan *E-mail:* j.cheteyan@abdintl.com
VP, Fin & IT: Bryan A Cox
Gen Opers Mgr: Ericka D Giles
Founded: 1985
Provide associations with highly responsive, member-focused order fulfillment, customer-client care call center, membership processing, e-commerce solutions, specialized web-enabled applications & variable data/digital printing. Based on your requirements, we use your association's or our specialized systems. Our primary goals are to help improve your member satisfaction & retention while reducing your overall costs.
BISAC compatible software

American International Distribution Corp (AIDC)
82 Winter Sport Lane, Williston, VT 05495
Mailing Address: PO Box 80, Williston, VT 05495-0080
Tel: 802-862-0095 *Toll Free Tel:* 800-678-2432 *Fax:* 802-864-7749
Web Site: www.aidcvt.com
Key Personnel
Pres & CEO: Marilyn McConnell
Dir, Opers: Michael Pelland
Founded: 1986
Order fulfillment, distribution, warehouse services, call center, computerized reporting, credit & collections, list maintenance, data management, lettershop, subscription, Pubnet, Advantis, web site hosting & development.
BISAC compatible software
Membership(s): Book Industry Study Group (BISG); Independent Publisher's Guild (IPG)

Baker & Taylor Publisher Services
30 Amberwood Pkwy, Ashland, OH 44805
Tel: 567-215-0030 *Toll Free Tel:* 888-814-0208
E-mail: info@btpubservices.com; orders@btpubservices.com
Web Site: www.btpubservices.com
Key Personnel
SVP, Sales & Client Servs: Mark Suchomel
SVP, Opers: Bob Gospodarek
Trade Sales Dir: Deanna Meyerhoff
Founded: 2017
Complete warehousing, shipping & order fulfillment. Our dedicated call center takes orders & ships products directly from our distribution centers. Baker & Taylor Publisher Services' online Publisher Dashboard allows you to access sales information, track inventory & place orders. Customized reports also available.

Books International Inc
22883 Quicksilver Dr, Dulles, VA 20166
Mailing Address: PO Box 605, Herndon, VA 20172-0605
Tel: 703-661-1500
E-mail: hdqtrs@booksintl.com
Web Site: booksintl.presswarehouse.com
Key Personnel
Pres: Vartan Ajamian
Dir, Busn Devt: Ellen Loerke *E-mail:* ellen.loerke@booksintl.com
Founded: 1984
Complete fulfillment services for medium & large-sized book publishers since 1984. Order processing, EDI, customer service, collections, royalties, commissions, reports, Internet access to live data, 24-hour turn-around, on-site digital printing (color & B&W) & digital content support. Ebook distribution direct from your web site. We ship worldwide. Call for a free estimate.
BISAC compatible software
Membership(s): American Association of University Presses (AAUP); Association of American Publishers (AAP)

Canon Business Process Services
Division of Canon USA Inc
261 Madison Ave, 3rd fl, New York, NY 10016
Tel: 212-502-2100 *Toll Free Tel:* 888-623-2668
E-mail: cbps-info@cbps.canon.com
Web Site: cbps.canon.com
Key Personnel
Pres & CEO: Joseph R Marciano
Canon leverages advanced technologies & solutions to deliver agility, exceptional workplace experiences & improved business performance. This includes Business Process Outsourcing (BPO), mailroom management, digital mailroom services, print center management, managed print services, facilities management, internal logistics & warehouse services, workplace experience services, document scanning, Robotic Process Automation (RPA) & intelligent automation.
BISAC compatible software

Courier Systems Inc
180 Pulaski St, Bayonne, NJ 07002
Tel: 201-432-0550 *Toll Free Tel:* 800-252-0353 *Fax:* 201-432-9686
E-mail: sales@csweb.biz
Web Site: www.csweb.biz
Key Personnel
Owner & Pres: Richard Murad *Tel:* 201-432-0550 ext 211 *E-mail:* rick.murad@csweb.biz
Warehousing, pick-pack shipping, trucking, import-export, hand assembly.
BISAC compatible software
Branch Office(s)
415 Bank St, Bridgeton, NJ 08302
45 Rosenhayn Ave, Bridgeton, NJ 08302, Contact: Tori Morris *Tel:* 856-455-3600 *Toll Free Tel:* 800-252-0353 *E-mail:* tori.morris@csweb.biz

Direct Link™ Worldwide Inc
Subsidiary of PostNord
700 Dowd Ave, Elizabeth, NJ 07201
Tel: 908-289-0703 *Fax:* 908-289-0705
E-mail: infousa@directlink.com
Web Site: www.directlink.com
Key Personnel
Natl VP, Sales: Paul Moser
Founded: 1986
Provider of international remail services.
BISAC compatible software
Branch Office(s)
LAX Processing Hub, 23803 Wilmington Ave, Carson, CA 90745 *Tel:* 424-450-1073

Disticor Magazine Distribution Services
Division of MicroVite Investments Ltd
1000 Thornton Rd S, Oshawa, ON L1J 7E2, Canada
Tel: 905-619-6565
Web Site: www.disticor.com; www.magamall.com
Key Personnel
CEO: John Lafranier *E-mail:* johnl@disticor.com
National distributor of newsstand publications.
BISAC compatible software

RR Donnelley & Sons Company
35 W Wacker Dr, Chicago, IL 60601
Tel: 312-326-8000 *Toll Free Tel:* 800-742-4455
Web Site: www.rrd.com
Key Personnel
Pres & CEO: Daniel L Knotts
Pres, Busn Servs: John Pecaric
Pres, Mktg Solutions: Doug Ryan
EVP & CIO: Ken O'Brien
EVP & CFO: Terry D Peterson
EVP & Chief Human Resources Offr: Sheila Rutt
EVP, Dom Opers & Chief Supply Chain Offr: Glynn Perry
EVP, Gen Coun, Chief Compliance Offr & Corp Secy: Deborah Steiner
EVP, Chief Strategy & Transformation Offr: Elif Sagsen-Ercel
SVP & Chief Acctg Offr: Michael J Sharp
Founded: 1864
Order processing; shrink wrapping, product assembly, pick-pack, mass mailing, drop & bulk shipping, warehousing & inventory control, customer service, royalties, credit & collections, trucking services.
BISAC compatible software

eFulfillment Service Inc
807 Airport Access Rd, Traverse City, MI 49686
Tel: 231-276-5057 *Toll Free Tel:* 866-922-6783
E-mail: sales@efulfillmentservice.com
Web Site: www.efulfillmentservice.com
Key Personnel
Pres: Steve Bulger
VP, Systems Devt: Jeff Dorsch
VP, Web Devt: Matt Burden
Dir, Expansion: Jason Lindberg
Off Servs & Purch Dir: Steve Sleder
Client Success Mgr: Angela Davenport
Cust Serv Mgr: Jennifer Robinson
Dist Ctr Mgr: JP LaRoche
HR Mgr: Merry Hawley
Sales & Client Care Mgr: Linda Sorna
Inventory Supv: Terry White
Outbound Freight Supv: Rachelle Lauzon
Prodn Supv: Veronica Freet
Receiving Supv: Christina Olmsted
Founded: 2001
Internet based order fulfillment services for book, tape, CD & DVD publishers.
BISAC compatible software
Membership(s): Better Business Bureau (BBB); Mailing & Fulfillment Service Association (MFSA)

FedEx Ground
Subsidiary of FedEx Corp
1000 FedEx Dr, Coraopolis, PA 15108
Mailing Address: PO Box 108, Coraopolis, PA 15230
Tel: 412-269-1000 *Toll Free Tel:* 800-762-3725
Web Site: www.fedex.com
Key Personnel
Pres & CEO: Henry J Maier
EVP & COO: Ward B Strang
EVP & CFO: Robert D Henning

SHIPPING SERVICES

Transport small packages, ground, US, Canada, Mexico.
BISAC compatible software

FedEx Supply Chain
Subsidiary of FedEx Corp
145 Lt George W Lee Ave, Memphis, TN 38103
Toll Free Tel: 800-677-3110
E-mail: fsc-leads@fedex.com
Web Site: www.fedex.com/en-us/logistics/supply-chain.html
Key Personnel
Pres: Scott Temple
Founded: 1898
Third-party logistics provider. Value-added warehousing & transportation services.
BISAC compatible software

Global Order Fulfillment, see ABDI Inc

Hassett Express
17W775 Butterfield Rd, Suite 109, Oakbrook Terrace, IL 60181
Tel: 630-530-6515 *Fax:* 630-530-6538
Web Site: www.hassettexpress.com
Key Personnel
Pres & CEO: Michelle Halkerston
SVP: Frank Borta; Dennis Cartwright
VP, Admin: Rosemary Giovannelli
VP, Logistics Servs: Matt Sherman
VP, Network Servs: Don Prentice
VP, Technol & Strategic Planning: Traci Richard
Founded: 1980
Specialize in the reliable transport of time-sensitive printed material & printing equipment. Experienced in wholesale/newsstand deliveries as well as subscriber deliveries drop shipped into USPS facilities around the country.
BISAC compatible software
Branch Office(s)
377 Meyer Rd, Bensenville, IL 60106 *Tel:* 630-758-3220
5214 W 104 St, Los Angeles, CA 90045 *Tel:* 310-645-4515
430 Plaza Dr, Suite A, College Park, GA 30349 *Tel:* 404-366-1448
625 Heron Dr, Swedesboro, NJ 08085 *Tel:* 856-467-5300

Integrated Distribution Services (IDS)
9431 AllPoints Pkwy, Plainfield, IN 46168
Toll Free Tel: 866-232-6533
E-mail: cwelch@idsfulfillment.com
Web Site: www.idsfulfillment.com
Key Personnel
CEO: Mark DeFabis
Pres, Warehousing & Fulfillment: Mike Jones
VP, Warehousing, Fulfillment & Busn Devt: Mike DeFabis
Founded: 1960
Third party logistics fulfillment services distribution provider for both direct to consumer & B2B shippers that utilizes the latest in automated warehouse technology & proven processes.
BISAC compatible software
Membership(s): DSA; International Warehouse Logistics Association (IWLA); Internet Assigned Numbers Authority (IANA); Toy International Association (TIA)

Kable Product Services Inc
4275 Thunderbird Lane, Fairfield, OH 45014
Tel: 513-671-2800
E-mail: info@kable.com
Web Site: www.kablefulfillment.com
Key Personnel
Dir, Sales & Mktg: Bowen Smith
Multichannel fulfillment & custom repackaging.

LSC Global Logistics
Division of LSC Communications LLC
10 New Maple Ave, Suite 304, Pine Brook, NJ 07058
Tel: 973-628-8800
Web Site: www.lsccom.com/clarkgroupinc
Leading independent third party logistics provider of value-added distribution, transportation management & international air & ocean freight forwarding services to the print media & other highly service sensitive industries.
Branch Office(s)
8200 Slausen Ave, Dock Door 26, Pico Rivera, CA 90660 *Tel:* 562-566-4562
8920 San Mateo Dr, Suite A, Laredo, TX 78045 *Tel:* 956-615-9107
Membership(s): Distripress

Magnum Book Services LLC
Division of The Magnum Group Ltd
180 Raritan Center Pkwy, Suite 105, Edison, NJ 08837
Tel: 908-349-2300
E-mail: info@magnumbookservices.com; usoffice@magnumbookservices.com
Web Site: www.magnumbookservices.com
Key Personnel
Pres: Scott B Bramson
Supplier of shipping & consolidation services to the global publishing industry. With office-depots in Edison, NJ & Essex, UK, plus our overseas partners we offer specific door-to-door services covering the US, Far East, Australasia & the UK, plus a fully integrated European network. Our emphasis is on total customer care, flexibility & resourcefulness to solve your shipping issues.
Branch Office(s)
Magnum Book Services Ltd, Unit 8, Repton Close, Burnt Mills Industrial Area, Basildon, Essex SS13 1LJ, United Kingdom (headquarters) *Tel:* (01268) 244 211 *E-mail:* ukoffice@magnumbookservices.com *Web Site:* www.facebook.com/magnumbookservices

Maple Logistics Solutions
60 Grumbacher Rd, York, PA 17406
Mailing Address: PO Box 15100, York, PA 17405-7100
Tel: 717-764-4596
E-mail: info@maplesoln.com
Web Site: www.maplelogisticssolutions.com
Key Personnel
Pres: James S Wisotzkey
VP, Dist Opers: Chris Benyovszky
VP, Dist, Sales & Mktg: Andrew J Van Sprang
E-mail: vansprang@maplepress.com
Warehousing, distribution, fulfillment, print-on-demand, drop-shipping, invoicing & value added services.
BISAC compatible software
Membership(s): Associated Warehouses Inc (AWI); Book Manufacturers' Institute (BMI); Council of Supply Chain Management Professionals (CSCMP); Distributors & Consolidators of America (DACA); Express Carriers Association (ECA); Warehousing Education and Research Council (WERC); World Trade Center Harrisburg

Neibauer Press
20 Industrial Dr, Warminster, PA 18974
Tel: 215-322-6200 *Fax:* 215-322-2495
E-mail: sales@neibauer.com
Web Site: www.neibauer.com
Key Personnel
VP: Ruth Neibauer-Baker *Tel:* 215-322-6216
E-mail: ruth@neibauer.com
Founded: 1955
Expert postal data services, shipping, warehousing, pick & pack, fulfillment.

SALES

Omeda
4 Overlook Point, Suite A2SE, Lincolnshire, IL 60069
Tel: 847-564-8900
E-mail: getstarted@omeda.com
Web Site: www.omeda.com
Key Personnel
Founder: Aaron Oberman
CFO: Alaine Kotze
Pres: James Capo
SVP, Audience Opers: Bryan Swartz
VP, Client Experience: Tony Napoleone
VP, HR: Diane Gaerlan
VP, Privacy & Data Governance: Bettina Lippisch
VP, Sales: Jared Thomas
VP, Technol: Tracy Rivas
VP, User Experience: Doug Gainous
Founded: 1980
Fulfillment & database management for business-to-business trade publications & business marketers.
BISAC compatible software
Branch Office(s)
One N Dearborn, Suite 750, Chicago, IL 60602 *Tel:* 312-312-2050

The Order Fulfillment Group
7313 Mayflower Park Dr, Zionsville, IN 46077
Tel: 317-733-7755
Web Site: www.tofg.com
Key Personnel
Owner & Pres: Tony Hughes *E-mail:* thughes@tofg.com
Founded: 1989
Complete fulfillment services for publishers including call center, cashiering, pick/pack, storage, kitting & online reports portal.
BISAC compatible software

PBD Worldwide Inc
Affiliate of Georgia School Book
1650 Bluegrass Lakes Pkwy, Alpharetta, GA 30004
Tel: 470-769-1000 *Toll Free Tel:* 866-998-4PBD (998-4723)
E-mail: sales.marketing@pbd.com; customerservice@pbd.com
Web Site: www.pbd.com
Key Personnel
Pres & CEO: Scott A Dockter
SVP & CFO: David S Ferguson
SVP: Gregory R Dockter
SVP, Client Rel: Brion Zaeh
SVP, Opers: Lisa Williams
VP/Cont: Jeff Wells
VP, Sales: Jan Jones
Mktg Mgr: Jeanna Akins
Founded: 1976
Fulfillment & distribution services for e-commerce companies, retailers, corporations, publishers, associations, nonprofits & faith-based organizations. Provides order fulfillment solutions for over 120 B2C & B2B clients that enable growth & streamline operations.
BISAC compatible software
Branch Office(s)
8215 Roswell Rd, Suite 925, Atlanta, GA 30350
3280 Summit Ridge Pkwy, Duluth, GA 30096, Dir, Opers: Tim Krupel *Tel:* 470-769-1300
905 Carlow Dr, Unit B, Bolingbrook, IL 60490 *Tel:* 470-769-1400
8779 Greenwood Place, Suite A, Savage, MD 20763 *Tel:* 470-769-1500
7055 S Decatur Blvd, No 180, Las Vegas, NV 89118

Publishers Storage & Shipping Corp
46 Development Rd, Fitchburg, MA 01420
Tel: 978-345-2121
Web Site: www.pssc.com
Key Personnel
Pres: Mike Seagram

VP, Massachusetts Opers: Carol Braman
Dir, Sales & Mktg: Pam Nuffer
Founded: 1974
Full order processing, warehousing & shipping services for small- & medium-sized publishers. Customer service: invoicing, web shopping cart integration, real time credit card processing, back orders, credit memos. Handle all types of published materials: books, calendars, CDs, back issues. Ship any quantity singles to thousands, domestic & foreign. Set assembly & shrink wrapping.
BISAC compatible software
Branch Office(s)
660 S Mansfield, Ypsilanti, MI 48197 *Tel:* 734-487-9720 SAN: 991-2665

Styled Packaging LLC
PO Box 30299, Philadelphia, PA 19103-8299
Tel: 610-529-4122 *Fax:* 610-520-9662
Web Site: www.taylorbox.com
Key Personnel
Pres: William R Fenkel *E-mail:* jjibill@aol.com
Founded: 2003
Design & manufacture slipcases, box sets, set-up-boxes, folding cartons, inserting; POP displays & corrugated packaging, plastic rigid & folding boxes, vacuum-formed components & custom packaging.
BISAC compatible software

Swan Packaging Fulfillment Inc
Unit of QuickBox Fulfillment
415 Hamburg Tpke, Wayne, NJ 07470
Tel: 973-790-0990 *Fax:* 973-790-0216
Web Site: www.swanpackaging.com
Key Personnel
Pres: Timothy S Werkley *Tel:* 973-790-8417
Founded: 1986
SPF provides third party fulfillment (pick-pack) & project packaging services (kit assembly, automated cartoning & shrink wrapping). Operate from a 125,000 sq ft facility located approximately 20 miles west of New York City.
BISAC compatible software
Membership(s): Direct Marketing Club of New York (DMCNY); FMA

UPS Supply Chain Solutions
12380 Morris Rd, Alpharetta, GA 30005
Tel: 913-693-6151 (outside US & CN)
Toll Free Tel: 800-742-5727 (US & CN)
Web Site: www.ups.com/us/en/supplychain/Home.page

Key Personnel
EVP & Pres Intl, Healthcare & Supply Chain Solutions: Kate Gutmann
Specialize in arranging consolidated ocean & air shipments for books, magazines & printed matter. Provide the export-import link between publishers, booksellers & distributors. Custom house brokers. Freight forwarders. Warehousemen.
BISAC compatible software

US Postal Service International Business Shipping
Division of US Postal Service
475 L'Enfant Plaza SW, Washington, DC 20260
Web Site: www.usps.com/business/international-shipping.htm
Founded: 2006
International mail & distribution.
BISAC compatible software

Value Added Resources
Subsidiary of Wilson Logistics Inc
7900 Rockville Rd, Indianapolis, IN 46214
Tel: 317-899-1000
E-mail: info@valueaddedres.com
Web Site: www.valueaddedres.com
Key Personnel
Owner: Scott Wilson *E-mail:* swilson@valueaddedres.com
Founded: 2005
Quality provider of fulfillment services to publishers, distributors & manufacturers. Over 13 years of experience in publishing distribution. Provide services such as order entry/customer service, pick/pack/shipping, kitting, display building, product labeling & shrink wrapping. Specialize in the small- to medium-size publisher who wants to be treated like they are our only client.
BISAC compatible software
Membership(s): Book Industry Study Group (BISG); Council of Supply Chain Management Professionals (CSCMP); Distribution Executive Interest Group (DEIG); Warehousing Education and Research Council (WERC)

Ware-Pak LLC
2427 Bond St, University Park, IL 60484
Tel: 708-534-2600
E-mail: sales@ware-pak.com
Web Site: www.ware-pak.com

Key Personnel
Pres: Corby Plechaty *E-mail:* cplechaty@ware-pak.com
VP: Matthew Kurtis *E-mail:* mkurtis@ware-pak.com
Busn Devt: Ysobel Schmidt *E-mail:* yschmidt@ware-pak.com
Founded: 1963
Complete fulfillment services for publishers including call center services, pick-pack fulfillment, storage, kit assembly & complete account information online, anytime, 24/7.
BISAC compatible software

Whitehurst & Clark Book Fulfillment
1200 County Rd, Rte 523, Flemington, NJ 08822
Tel: 908-782-2323 *Toll Free Tel:* 800-488-8040
E-mail: wcbooks@aol.com
Web Site: www.wcbks.com
Key Personnel
Pres: Bradley J Searles
IT Mgr: Jay Makuch
Plant Mgr: Elayne Suckno
Computerized order processing, customer service, sales analysis & inventory control. Complete warehousing for book publishers of all types including nonprofit associations & scientific. Full shrink wrapping operation. Pick, pack, shipping & pallet storage.
BISAC compatible software

Wood & Associates Direct Marketing Services Ltd
9-1410 Bayly St, Pickering, ON L1W 3R3, Canada
Tel: 905-831-2511
E-mail: clientservices@wood-and-associates.com
Web Site: www.wood-and-associates.com
Key Personnel
Owner & CEO: Ralph Bain
Founded: 1979
Digital print services, database programming, mail management, inventory management & parcel shipping.
BISAC compatible software
Membership(s): Canadian Federation for Independent Business (CFIB); Canadian Marketing Association (CMA); Canadian Society of Association Executives (CSAE); National Association of Major Mail Users (NAMMU); Scarborough Chamber of Commerce; Toronto Board of Trade

Shipping Suppliers

Citation Box & Paper Co
4700 W Augusta Blvd, Chicago, IL 60651-3397
Tel: 773-378-1400
E-mail: info@citationbox.com
Web Site: www.citationbox.com
Key Personnel
Pres: Tony Kostiuk
Founded: 1951
Corrugated boxes.
BISAC compatible software

The Gluefast Co Inc
3535 State Rte 66, Bldg No 1, Neptune, NJ 07753
Tel: 732-918-4600 *Toll Free Tel:* 800-242-7318
 Fax: 732-918-4646
E-mail: info@gluefast.com
Web Site: www.gluefast.com
Key Personnel
Pres: Lester Mallet *E-mail:* lmallet@gluefast.com
VP: Amy Altman *E-mail:* aaltman@gluefast.com
Gen Mgr: Joe Benenati *E-mail:* jbenenati@gluefast.com
Manufacturer of adhesives, liquid glues, manual & electric label gluers & moisteners as well as case making equipment & products for the wall art industry.
BISAC compatible software
Membership(s): PMMI: The Association for Packaging and Processing Technologies

Stephen Gould Corp
35 S Jefferson Rd, Whippany, NJ 07981
Tel: 973-428-1500; 973-428-1510
E-mail: info@stephengould.com
Web Site: www.stephengould.com
Key Personnel
CEO: Michael Golden
CFO: Anthony Lupo
Pres: Justin Golden
EVP: John Golden
Cont: Kim Ings
Dir, Info Systems: Nanette Rosenbaum
Dir, Opers: Jason Rosario
Founded: 1939
Design & manufacture corrugated & chipboard containers for book publishers & suppliers; die-cut specialties.
BISAC compatible software

Styled Packaging LLC
PO Box 30299, Philadelphia, PA 19103-8299
Tel: 610-529-4122 *Fax:* 610-520-9662
Web Site: www.taylorbox.com
Key Personnel
Pres: William R Fenkel *E-mail:* jjibill@aol.com
Founded: 2003
Design & manufacture slipcases, box sets, set-up-boxes, folding cartons, inserting; POP displays & corrugated packaging, plastic rigid & folding boxes, vacuum-formed components & custom packaging.
BISAC compatible software

Swan Packaging Fulfillment Inc
Unit of QuickBox Fulfillment
415 Hamburg Tpke, Wayne, NJ 07470
Tel: 973-790-0990 *Fax:* 973-790-0216
Web Site: www.swanpackaging.com
Key Personnel
Pres: Timothy S Werkley *Tel:* 973-790-8417
SPF provides third party pick-pack fulfillment services for B2C & B2B product marketers in the e-commerce & catalog markets, specializing in books, CDs, clothing, gifts & other products. Offers electronic order import & shipment confirmation export, returns processing, electronic reports & shipping via USPS, UPS & FedEx. 125,000 sq ft facility is located approximately 20 miles west of New York City & maintains secured client storage in flow racks, shelving & pallet storage environments. SPF also provides value-added packaging services such as kit assembly & automated packaging.
BISAC compatible software
Membership(s): Direct Marketing Club of New York (DMCNY); FMA

Services & Suppliers

Consultants — Activity Index

ADVERTISING, PROMOTION

Accurate Writing & More, pg 1343
AEI (Atchity Entertainment International Inc), pg 1343
Arbor Books, pg 1343
Audiobook Department, pg 1344
AuthorBytes, pg 1344
JB Bryans Literary, pg 1344
Casemate | IPM, pg 1344
City Diecutting Inc, pg 1344
Cohesion®, pg 1344
Concierge Marketing Inc, pg 1345
Copywriters' Council of America™ (CCA), pg 1345
Creative Direct Marketing Group Inc (CDMG), pg 1345
Creative Trust Inc, pg 1345
Cypress House, pg 1345
Jeff Davidson MBA, CMC, Breathing Space Institute, pg 1345
Exhibit Promotions Plus Inc, pg 1346
Linda Fairchild & Company LLC, pg 1346
Fairfield Marketing Group Inc, pg 1346
Figaro, pg 1346
Garvan Media, Management & Marketing Inc, pg 1347
International Transactions Inc, pg 1348
Jenkins Group Inc, pg 1348
Klopotek North America Inc, pg 1348
knk Software LP, pg 1348
Lorimer Literary Consulting, pg 1349
Media Masters Publicity, pg 1349
MGP Direct Inc, pg 1349
Open Horizons Publishing Co, pg 1350
Orobora Inc, pg 1350
Promote A Book Inc, pg 1350
ps ink LLC, pg 1350
Publishing Management Associates Inc, pg 1350
Purplegator, pg 1350
R J Promotions & Advertising, pg 1350
Sherri Rosen Publicity Intl NYC, pg 1350
Schnoll Media Consulting, pg 1351
SDP Publishing Solutions LLC, pg 1351
Story Monsters LLC, pg 1351
Tanenbaum International Literary Agency Ltd (TILA), pg 1351
To Press & Beyond, pg 1351
VillageSoup®, pg 1351
Warwick Associates, pg 1351
Weidner Communications International Inc, pg 1351
Fred Weidner & Daughter Printers, pg 1351
Westwind Communications, pg 1351
The Writers Lifeline Inc, a Story Merchant company, pg 1352

BOOK CLUBS

Agent Research & Evaluation Inc (AR&E), pg 1343
Altman Dedicated Direct, pg 1343
Arbor Books, pg 1343
Casemate | IPM, pg 1344
Concierge Marketing Inc, pg 1345
Copywriters' Council of America™ (CCA), pg 1345
Creative Direct Marketing Group Inc (CDMG), pg 1345
Jeff Davidson MBA, CMC, Breathing Space Institute, pg 1345
Double Play, pg 1346
Fairfield Marketing Group Inc, pg 1346
International Transactions Inc, pg 1348
Jenkins Group Inc, pg 1348
Open Horizons Publishing Co, pg 1350
Story Monsters LLC, pg 1351
To Press & Beyond, pg 1351
Warwick Associates, pg 1351

BUSINESS, FINANCE

Arbor Books, pg 1343
JB Bryans Literary, pg 1344
R E Carsch, MS-Consultant, pg 1344
Concierge Marketing Inc, pg 1345
Copywriters' Council of America™ (CCA), pg 1345
Cypress House, pg 1345
Peter L DeGiglio, pg 1345
Fairfield Marketing Group Inc, pg 1346
The Fisher Company, pg 1346
Albert Henderson, pg 1347
IP Royalty Auditors LLC, pg 1348
Kaplan/DeFiore Rights, pg 1348
knk Software LP, pg 1348
Lorimer Literary Consulting, pg 1349
MetaComet Systems, pg 1349
Orobora Inc, pg 1350
Paz & Associates: The Bookstore Training & Consulting Group, pg 1350
Schnoll Media Consulting, pg 1351
Scribe Inc, pg 1351

COMPUTER TECHNOLOGY

Agent Research & Evaluation Inc (AR&E), pg 1343
Applied Information Sciences Corp, pg 1343
Arbor Books, pg 1343
Copywriters' Council of America™ (CCA), pg 1345
Cypress House, pg 1345
Fairfield Marketing Group Inc, pg 1346
Albert Henderson, pg 1347
Innodata Inc, pg 1347
Klopotek North America Inc, pg 1348
knk Software LP, pg 1348
The Live Oak Press LLC, pg 1349
Lorimer Literary Consulting, pg 1349
Lumina Datamatics Inc, pg 1349
Mendon Associates Inc, pg 1349
MetaComet Systems, pg 1349
Orobora Inc, pg 1350
Publishing Management Associates Inc, pg 1350
Purplegator, pg 1350
Schnoll Media Consulting, pg 1351
Scribe Inc, pg 1351
Story Monsters LLC, pg 1351

ELECTRONIC PUBLISHING

Agent Research & Evaluation Inc (AR&E), pg 1343
Ampersand Inc/Professional Publishing Services, pg 1343
Aptara Inc, pg 1343
Arbor Books, pg 1343
Audiobook Department, pg 1344
JB Bryans Literary, pg 1344
CeciBooks Editorial & Publishing Consultation, pg 1344
Cohesion®, pg 1344
Concierge Marketing Inc, pg 1345
Copywriters' Council of America™ (CCA), pg 1345
Cypress House, pg 1345
Jeff Davidson MBA, CMC, Breathing Space Institute, pg 1345
Fairfield Marketing Group Inc, pg 1346
Figaro, pg 1346
G & H Soho Inc, pg 1346
Heidelberg Graphics, pg 1347
Albert Henderson, pg 1347
Idea Architects, pg 1347
Innodata Inc, pg 1347
Integra Software Services Inc, pg 1348
International Transactions Inc, pg 1348
The Live Oak Press LLC, pg 1349
Lumina Datamatics Inc, pg 1349
Open Book Systems Inc®, pg 1350
Orobora Inc, pg 1350
Law Office of Robert G Pimm Attorney at Law, pg 1350
ps ink LLC, pg 1350
Publishing Management Associates Inc, pg 1350
Schnoll Media Consulting, pg 1351
Scribe Inc, pg 1351
SDP Publishing Solutions LLC, pg 1351
Story Monsters LLC, pg 1351
To Press & Beyond, pg 1351
Warwick Associates, pg 1351
Writer's Relief, Inc, pg 1352

LEGAL SERVICES

Arbor Books, pg 1343
Copywriters' Council of America™ (CCA), pg 1345
Feigenbaum Publishing Consultants Inc, pg 1346
Law Offices of Lloyd J Jassin, pg 1348
David W Koehser Attorney at Law, pg 1349
Law Office of Robert G Pimm Attorney at Law, pg 1350
Nina J Reznick Esq, pg 1350
Warwick Associates, pg 1351

LIBRARIES

Agent Research & Evaluation Inc (AR&E), pg 1343
Arbor Books, pg 1343
JB Bryans Literary, pg 1344
R E Carsch, MS-Consultant, pg 1344
Casemate | IPM, pg 1344
Copywriters' Council of America™ (CCA), pg 1345
Cypress House, pg 1345
Double Play, pg 1346
Fairfield Marketing Group Inc, pg 1346
Albert Henderson, pg 1347
Innodata Inc, pg 1347
Jenkins Group Inc, pg 1348
The Live Oak Press LLC, pg 1349
Lumina Datamatics Inc, pg 1349
Media Masters Publicity, pg 1349
To Press & Beyond, pg 1351

LITERARY SCOUT

Arbor Books, pg 1343
Cat's Eye Consultancy, pg 1344
Del Commune Enterprises Inc, pg 1345

CONSULTANTS — ACTIVITY INDEX

Alanna Feldman Scouting, pg 1346
Franklin & Siegal Associates Inc, pg 1346
Liz Gately Book Scouting, pg 1347
International Transactions Inc, pg 1348
Jenkins Group Inc, pg 1348
Lorimer Literary Consulting, pg 1349
Stephanie Rogers & Associates, pg 1350
Bettina Schrewe Literary Scouting, pg 1351
Jane Starr Literary Scouts, pg 1351
Warwick Associates, pg 1351
Writer's Relief, Inc, pg 1352

MANAGEMENT

AEI (Atchity Entertainment International Inc), pg 1343
Aptara Inc, pg 1343
Arbor Books, pg 1343
JB Bryans Literary, pg 1344
R E Carsch, MS-Consultant, pg 1344
Cohesion®, pg 1344
Conspire Creative, pg 1345
Copywriters' Council of America™ (CCA), pg 1345
Cypress House, pg 1345
Jeff Davidson MBA, CMC, Breathing Space Institute, pg 1345
Peter L DeGiglio, pg 1345
Linda Fairchild & Company LLC, pg 1346
Fairfield Marketing Group Inc, pg 1346
Flannery Book Service, pg 1346
Fournies Associates, pg 1346
Garvan Media, Management & Marketing Inc, pg 1347
GGP Publishing Inc, pg 1347
Albert Henderson, pg 1347
The Idea Logical Co Inc, pg 1347
Integra Software Services Inc, pg 1348
International Transactions Inc, pg 1348
Javelin Group, pg 1348
Jenkins Group Inc, pg 1348
Kinokuniya Publications Service of New York (KPS-NY), pg 1348
knk Software LP, pg 1348
Lumina Datamatics Inc, pg 1349
Market Partners International Inc, pg 1349
Orobora Inc, pg 1350
Paz & Associates: The Bookstore Training & Consulting Group, pg 1350
ps ink LLC, pg 1350
Publishing Management Associates Inc, pg 1350
R J Promotions & Advertising, pg 1350
Judith Riven Literary Agent LLC, pg 1350
Stephanie Rogers & Associates, pg 1350
Schnoll Media Consulting, pg 1351
Scribe Inc, pg 1351
SDP Publishing Solutions LLC, pg 1351
Tanenbaum International Literary Agency Ltd (TILA), pg 1351
To Press & Beyond, pg 1351
The Writers Lifeline Inc, a Story Merchant company, pg 1352

MANUFACTURING, PRODUCTION

A-R Editions Inc, pg 1343
AEI (Atchity Entertainment International Inc), pg 1343
Aptara Inc, pg 1343
Arbor Books, pg 1343
Audiobook Department, pg 1344
JB Bryans Literary, pg 1344
City Diecutting Inc, pg 1344
Color House Graphics Inc, pg 1344
Concierge Marketing Inc, pg 1345
Conspire Creative, pg 1345
Copywriters' Council of America™ (CCA), pg 1345
Cypress House, pg 1345
Fairfield Marketing Group Inc, pg 1346
G & H Soho Inc, pg 1346
GGP Publishing Inc, pg 1347
Heidelberg Graphics, pg 1347
Albert Henderson, pg 1347
Imago, pg 1347
Innodata Inc, pg 1347
Integra Software Services Inc, pg 1348
Jenkins Group Inc, pg 1348
Klopotek North America Inc, pg 1348
knk Software LP, pg 1348
The Live Oak Press LLC, pg 1349
Lumina Datamatics Inc, pg 1349
Schnoll Media Consulting, pg 1351
Scribe Inc, pg 1351
SDP Publishing Solutions LLC, pg 1351
Story Monsters LLC, pg 1351
To Press & Beyond, pg 1351
Warwick Associates, pg 1351
Fred Weidner & Daughter Printers, pg 1351
The Writers Lifeline Inc, a Story Merchant company, pg 1352

MARKETING

Accurate Writing & More, pg 1343
Alice B Acheson, pg 1343
AEI (Atchity Entertainment International Inc), pg 1343
Agent Research & Evaluation Inc (AR&E), pg 1343
Altman Dedicated Direct, pg 1343
Ampersand Inc/Professional Publishing Services, pg 1343
Arbor Books, pg 1343
Audiobook Department, pg 1344
JB Bryans Literary, pg 1344
R E Carsch, MS-Consultant, pg 1344
Casemate | IPM, pg 1344
CeciBooks Editorial & Publishing Consultation, pg 1344
City Diecutting Inc, pg 1344
Concierge Marketing Inc, pg 1345
Conspire Creative, pg 1345
Copywriters' Council of America™ (CCA), pg 1345
Creative Direct Marketing Group Inc (CDMG), pg 1345
Cypress House, pg 1345
Jeff Davidson MBA, CMC, Breathing Space Institute, pg 1345
Exhibit Promotions Plus Inc, pg 1346
Linda Fairchild & Company LLC, pg 1346
Fairfield Marketing Group Inc, pg 1346
The French Publishers' Agency, pg 1346
Garvan Media, Management & Marketing Inc, pg 1347
Albert Henderson, pg 1347
HurleyMedia LLC, pg 1347
Idea Architects, pg 1347
The Idea Logical Co Inc, pg 1347
The Intermarketing Group-Art Licensing Agency, pg 1348
International Transactions Inc, pg 1348
Jenkins Group Inc, pg 1348
Klopotek North America Inc, pg 1348
knk Software LP, pg 1348
The Live Oak Press LLC, pg 1349
Lorimer Literary Consulting, pg 1349
Market Partners International Inc, pg 1349
Media Masters Publicity, pg 1349
MGP Direct Inc, pg 1349
Odyssey Books, pg 1349
Open Horizons Publishing Co, pg 1350
Orobora Inc, pg 1350
Paz & Associates: The Bookstore Training & Consulting Group, pg 1350
Promote A Book Inc, pg 1350
ps ink LLC, pg 1350
Publishing Management Associates Inc, pg 1350
Purplegator, pg 1350
R J Promotions & Advertising, pg 1350
Stephanie Rogers & Associates, pg 1350
Schnoll Media Consulting, pg 1351
SDP Publishing Solutions LLC, pg 1351
Story Monsters LLC, pg 1351
Tanenbaum International Literary Agency Ltd (TILA), pg 1351
To Press & Beyond, pg 1351
VillageSoup®, pg 1351
Warwick Associates, pg 1351
Weidner Communications International Inc, pg 1351
Wheatmark Inc, pg 1351
The Writers Lifeline Inc, a Story Merchant company, pg 1352
Writer's Relief, Inc, pg 1352

MERGERS, ACQUISITIONS

Agent Research & Evaluation Inc (AR&E), pg 1343
Arbor Books, pg 1343
JB Bryans Literary, pg 1344
Copywriters' Council of America™ (CCA), pg 1345
Peter L DeGiglio, pg 1345
Fairfield Marketing Group Inc, pg 1346
The Fisher Company, pg 1346
Garvan Media, Management & Marketing Inc, pg 1347
Albert Henderson, pg 1347
International Transactions Inc, pg 1348
JPMC Associates, pg 1348
Market Partners International Inc, pg 1349
ps ink LLC, pg 1350
Warwick Associates, pg 1351

PAPER, PAPER PRODUCTS

Arbor Books, pg 1343
Concierge Marketing Inc, pg 1345

SERVICES

Copywriters' Council of America™ (CCA), pg 1345
Fairfield Marketing Group Inc, pg 1346
The Intermarketing Group-Art Licensing Agency, pg 1348
Fred Weidner & Daughter Printers, pg 1351

PRINTING

AEI (Atchity Entertainment International Inc), pg 1343
Arbor Books, pg 1343
Beidel Printing House Inc, pg 1344
Color House Graphics Inc, pg 1344
Concierge Marketing Inc, pg 1345
Conspire Creative, pg 1345
Copywriters' Council of America™ (CCA), pg 1345
Cypress House, pg 1345
Fairfield Marketing Group Inc, pg 1346
G & H Soho Inc, pg 1346
GGP Publishing Inc, pg 1347
Heidelberg Graphics, pg 1347
Imago, pg 1347
Jenkins Group Inc, pg 1348
Publishing Management Associates Inc, pg 1350
Schnoll Media Consulting, pg 1351
SDP Publishing Solutions LLC, pg 1351
Story Monsters LLC, pg 1351
To Press & Beyond, pg 1351
Warwick Associates, pg 1351
Fred Weidner & Daughter Printers, pg 1351
The Writers Lifeline Inc, a Story Merchant company, pg 1352

PUBLISHING

Accurate Writing & More, pg 1343
Alice B Acheson, pg 1343
AEI (Atchity Entertainment International Inc), pg 1343
Agent Research & Evaluation Inc (AR&E), pg 1343
Ampersand Inc/Professional Publishing Services, pg 1343
Arbor Books, pg 1343
Audiobook Department, pg 1344
Beidel Printing House Inc, pg 1344
JB Bryans Literary, pg 1344
Cat's Eye Consultancy, pg 1344
CeciBooks Editorial & Publishing Consultation, pg 1344
Clear Concepts, pg 1344
Dwight Clough, pg 1344
Cohesion®, pg 1344
Concierge Marketing Inc, pg 1345
Conspire Creative, pg 1345
Copywriters' Council of America™ (CCA), pg 1345
Creative Trust Inc, pg 1345
Cypress House, pg 1345
Jeff Davidson MBA, CMC, Breathing Space Institute, pg 1345
Peter L DeGiglio, pg 1345
Steven Diamond Inc, pg 1345
Double Play, pg 1346
Embolden Media Group, pg 1346
Fairfield Marketing Group Inc, pg 1346
Figaro, pg 1346
The Fisher Company, pg 1346
The French Publishers' Agency, pg 1346
GGP Publishing Inc, pg 1347
Heidelberg Graphics, pg 1347
Albert Henderson, pg 1347

HurleyMedia LLC, pg 1347
Idea Architects, pg 1347
The Idea Logical Co Inc, pg 1347
Innodata Inc, pg 1347
Integra Software Services Inc, pg 1348
International Transactions Inc, pg 1348
IP Royalty Auditors LLC, pg 1348
Law Offices of Lloyd J Jassin, pg 1348
Jenkins Group Inc, pg 1348
JMW Group Inc, pg 1348
Klopotek North America Inc, pg 1348
knk Software LP, pg 1348
The Live Oak Press LLC, pg 1349
Lumina Datamatics Inc, pg 1349
Market Partners International Inc, pg 1349
Virginia McCullough, pg 1349
Media Masters Publicity, pg 1349
Odyssey Books, pg 1349
Open Horizons Publishing Co, pg 1350
Orobora Inc, pg 1350
Law Office of Robert G Pimm Attorney at Law, pg 1350
ps ink LLC, pg 1350

Publishing Management Associates Inc, pg 1350
Sherri Rosen Publicity Intl NYC, pg 1350
Scribe Inc, pg 1351
SDP Publishing Solutions LLC, pg 1351
Story Monsters LLC, pg 1351
To Press & Beyond, pg 1351
Warwick Associates, pg 1351
Fred Weidner & Daughter Printers, pg 1351
Wheatmark Inc, pg 1351
The Writers Lifeline Inc, a Story Merchant company, pg 1352
Writer's Relief, Inc, pg 1352

RECRUITER

Arbor Books, pg 1343
Cohesion®, pg 1344
ps ink LLC, pg 1350

RIGHTS, PERMISSIONS

Agent Research & Evaluation Inc (AR&E), pg 1343
Ampersand Inc/Professional Publishing Services, pg 1343
Arbor Books, pg 1343
JB Bryans Literary, pg 1344
Casemate | IPM, pg 1344
Cat's Eye Consultancy, pg 1344
Concierge Marketing Inc, pg 1345
Copyright Clearance Center Inc (CCC), pg 1345
Copywriters' Council of America™ (CCA), pg 1345
Cypress House, pg 1345
Jeff Davidson MBA, CMC, Breathing Space Institute, pg 1345
Steven Diamond Inc, pg 1345
Bob Erdmann, pg 1346
Taryn Fagerness Agency, pg 1346
Fairfield Marketing Group Inc, pg 1346
Feigenbaum Publishing Consultants Inc, pg 1346
GGP Publishing Inc, pg 1347
Heidelberg Graphics, pg 1347
Idea Architects, pg 1347
Integra Software Services Inc, pg 1348
The Intermarketing Group-Art Licensing Agency, pg 1348
International Literary Properties (ILP), pg 1348

International Transactions Inc, pg 1348
Law Offices of Lloyd J Jassin, pg 1348
Jenkins Group Inc, pg 1348
JMW Group Inc, pg 1348
Kaplan/DeFiore Rights, pg 1348
Klopotek North America Inc, pg 1348
Lumina Datamatics Inc, pg 1349
MetaComet Systems, pg 1349
Odyssey Books, pg 1349
Open Horizons Publishing Co, pg 1350
Law Office of Robert G Pimm Attorney at Law, pg 1350
Publishing Management Associates Inc, pg 1350
Nina J Reznick Esq, pg 1350
Scribe Inc, pg 1351
SDP Publishing Solutions LLC, pg 1351
Tanenbaum International Literary Agency Ltd (TILA), pg 1351
Warwick Associates, pg 1351

Consultants

This section includes firms and individuals who offer consultation on matters such as advertising and promotion, book production, finance, management, marketing and printing.

A-R Editions Inc
1600 Aspen Commons, Suite 100, Middleton, WI 53562
Tel: 608-836-9000 *Fax:* 608-831-8200
E-mail: info@areditions.com
Web Site: www.areditions.com
Key Personnel
Pres & CEO: Patrick Wall *Tel:* 608-203-2575
 E-mail: patrick.wall@areditions.com
Dir, Spec Projs: James Zychowicz *Tel:* 608-203-2580 *E-mail:* james.zychowicz@areditions.com
Founded: 1962
Complete production services & project management from editorial & design through typesetting, printing, art creation, indexing, printing & mailing for journal, book & magazine publishers; specialize in computerized music engraving, integration of music & text, foreign language, scientific & non-Roman alphabet. Typesetting on Mac/Quark systems. Disk conversion; automatic pagination; Postscript & PDF output; customized music engraving.

Accurate Writing & More
16 Barstow Lane, Hadley, MA 01035
Tel: 413-586-2388
Web Site: www.accuratewriting.com; frugalmarketing.com
Key Personnel
Owner & Dir: Shel Horowitz *E-mail:* shel@principledprofit.com
Dir: Dina Friedman
Founded: 1981
Marketing, promotion & advertising consulting emphasizing green & ethical practices & highest return for lowest cost. Also consulting to authors on traditional & independent publishing options, preparation of book proposals, vendor selection & project management for self-publishers.

Alice B Acheson
Unit of Acheson-Greub Inc
PO Box 735, Friday Harbor, WA 98250
Tel: 360-378-5850 *Fax:* 360-378-2815
E-mail: aliceba7@gmail.com
Web Site: sites.google.com/view/alice-b-acheson
Founded: 1981
Consultation in all aspects of publicity (launching, reviews, interviews, press materials) & marketing for publishers, booksellers & authors. Specialize in assisting authors & independent presses enter the mainstream +/or improve expertise through enhanced contacts, timing, positioning, rights sales & distribution.
Former recipient of the Literary Market Place Award Honoring Excellence in Book Publishing, Outside Services - Advertising/Promotion/Publicity.
Membership(s): Independent Book Publishers Association (IBPA); Pacific Northwest Booksellers Association (PNBA); Pacific Northwest Writers Association; Publishers' Publicity Association

AEI (Atchity Entertainment International Inc)
400 S Burnside Ave, Suite 11B, Los Angeles, CA 90036
Tel: 323-932-1685

Key Personnel
Chmn: Dr Kenneth Atchity *E-mail:* atchity@storymerchant.com
CEO: Ms Chi-Li Wong
Founded: 1996
Full service literary company that deals with editing & developing, book publishing, TV production, motion picture production, licensing & merchandising.
Sister companies: Atchity Productions; Story Merchant; Story Merchant Books; The Writer's Lifeline Inc.

Agent Research & Evaluation Inc (AR&E)
44 Park Rd, Woodbury, CT 06798
Tel: 203-586-1397
Web Site: www.agentresearch.org
Key Personnel
Pres: Beverly Swerling Martin *E-mail:* beverly@agentresearch.org
Founded: 1996
Directs you to the literary agents right for you, twentieth book or your first. We keep in contact by exchange of e-mail +/or telephone & use our wide experience to produce a highly individualized, nuanced & in-depth report with full data on the sales records of the recommended agents & how to design your approach to them. Author web sites: In this mass-media age, you now need three things to make it as an author, your own talent, the right literary agent & a successful web site. The Internet has become the most powerful tool for selling the maximum number of books to the widest possible readership & we're talking mainstream royalty-paying publishers, not self-publishing. We recommend developers & promoters of author web sites, without any kick-backs or finders fees.

Altman Dedicated Direct
853 Academy St, Rural Hall, NC 27045-9329
Tel: 336-969-9538 *Fax:* 336-969-9538
Web Site: www.altmandedicateddirect.com
Key Personnel
Pres: Shari Altman *E-mail:* saltman@altmandedicateddirect.com
Founded: 1999
Direct response marketing consultancy.

Ampersand Inc/Professional Publishing Services
515 Madison St, New Orleans, LA 70116
Tel: 312-280-8905 *Fax:* 312-944-1582
E-mail: info@ampersandworks.com
Web Site: www.ampersandworks.com
Key Personnel
Pres & Publr: Suzanne T Isaacs
Founded: 1995 (began consulting in 2005)
Provides a wide range of publishing services including private publishing. Branch office in Chicago, IL.
Membership(s): Association of Independent Authors (AIA); The Association of Publishers for Special Sales (APSS); Independent Book Publishers Association (IBPA); Society of Children's Book Writers & Illustrators (SCBWI)

Applied Information Sciences Corp
PO Box 9182, Calabasas, CA 91372-9182
Tel: 818-222-0926 *Fax:* 818-222-4329

E-mail: sales@aisciences.com
Web Site: www.aisciences.com; www.searchware.com
Key Personnel
Pres: Norm Mazer *E-mail:* nmazer@aisciences.com
Founded: 1984
Software products for companies selling books to libraries. Products include SmartSearch® Offline Sales Tool, SmartSearch® Web Module & VendorCat™ Book Processing Software. The SearchWare™ web site enables librarians to search multiple vendors to find just the right books. The SmartSearch® Web Module integrates into a vendor's web site & enables libraries to upload their collections, perform a complete collection analysis & create complete book lists that fill the libraries collection deficiencies within an overall budget. Consulting services include: central database creation & maintenance, upgrading & enhancing incomplete book data & custom software development.

Aptara Inc
Subsidiary of iEnergizer
2901 Telestar Ct, Suite 522, Falls Church, VA 22042
Tel: 703-352-0001
E-mail: moreinfo@aptaracorp.com
Web Site: www.aptaracorp.com
Key Personnel
Pres: Samir Kakar
EVP, Fin & Cont: Prashant Kapoor
SVP, Busn & Contact Ctr Opers: Ashish Madan
Busn Devt: Michael Scott *E-mail:* michael.scott@aptaracorp.com
Founded: 1988
Liaison for complete or any combination of production services, ranging from simple 1-color to complex 4-color projects. Copy-editing.
Branch Office(s)
150 California St, Suite 301, Newton, MA 02458
 Tel: 617-423-7755
11009 Metric Blvd, Bldg J, Suite 150, Austin, TX 78758 *Tel:* 512-876-5997
299 Elizabeth St, Level 1, Sydney 2000, Australia *Tel:* (02) 8251 0070
Tower 1 & 2, 8/100, Acharya Thulasi Rd (Shandy Rd), Pallavaram, Chennai 600 043, India *Tel:* (044) 22640676
No 2310, Doon Express Business Park, Saharanpur Rd, Bldg 2000, Dehradun 248 002, India *Tel:* (0135) 2644055
7B, Leela Infopark, Technopark, Trivandrum, Kerala 695 581, India *Tel:* (047) 14063370
A-37, Sector-60, Noida 201 301, India *Tel:* (0120) 7182424
D-10, Sector-2, Noida 201 301, India *Tel:* (0120) 24423678
SEZ Bldg 4A, 1st fl, S P Infocity, Pune Saswad Rd, Phursungi, Pune 412 308, India *Tel:* (020) 66728000

Arbor Books
244 Madison Ave, Box 254, New York, NY 10016
Tel: 212-956-0950 *Toll Free Tel:* 877-822-2500 *Fax:* 914-401-9385
E-mail: info@arborbooks.com; editorial@arborbooks.net
Web Site: www.arborbooks.com

CONSULTANTS

Key Personnel
Owner: Joel Hochman *Tel:* 877-822-2502 *E-mail:* arborbooksjoel@aol.com;
Larry Leichman *Tel:* 877-822-2504 *E-mail:* arborbookslarry@aol.com
Mktg Dir: Olga Vladi *E-mail:* floatinggal1@aol.com
Founded: 1992
Full service writing services & book production. Specialize in ghostwriting, editing, proofreading, developmental editing, promotional copy, cover design, printing, publishing & marketing. Arbor Books works for both corporations (business books, corporate histories, CEO bios) & individuals (novels - all genres: general fiction, young adult, mystery, crime, thrillers, horror, romance, science fiction, fantasy, litrpg, graphic novels, comic books, etc), memoirs, children's books, business books, how-to, inspiration, religious, Christian, Jewish, Islamic, Hindu, self-help, history, politics, humor, gay, etc. Services include supervised & insured ghostwriting, copy-editing, translation, proofreading, design (even the most complex, including model shoots, illustrations, photo reconstruction & manipulation, book jacket design, album cover & magazine design), word processing (including transcription), scanning, layout, typesetting, obtaining registrations & endorsements, B&W & 4-color printing, marketing, promotion & advertising. Creates logos, letterheads, annual reports, posters & promotional flyers. Self-publishing services include: Amazon book marketing, press kits, press releases, booking TV & radio programs, speaking tours & book signings & negotiating with producers & agents.

Arbor Services, see Arbor Books

Atchity Entertainment International Inc, see AEI (Atchity Entertainment International Inc)

ATS Mobile, see Purplegator

Audiobook Department
6429 N Talman Ave, Chicago, IL 60645
Tel: 773-312-0554
Web Site: www.judithwest.com
Key Personnel
Owner & Prodr: Judith West *E-mail:* judith@judithwest.com
Founded: 2000
Full service audiobook production, with a diverse talent pool & on-site production facilities. Special consulting for publishers new to audiobooks: from concept to design, through digital distribution & marketing pointers. Free estimates.
Membership(s): Audio Publishers Association; Chicago Women in Publishing

AuthorBytes
PO Box 382103, Cambridge, MA 02238-2103
Tel: 617-492-0442
E-mail: info@authorbytes.com
Web Site: www.authorbytes.com
Key Personnel
Founder: Steve Bennett
Founded: 2000
Web design, blogs, multimedia previews, social media consulting for authors.

Beidel Printing House Inc
Division of White Mane Publishing Co Inc
225 S Fayette St, Shippensburg, PA 17257
Mailing Address: PO Box 708, Shippensburg, PA 17257-0708
Tel: 717-532-5063 *Fax:* 717-532-2502
E-mail: customerservice@dreamprint.com
Web Site: dreamprint.com

Key Personnel
VP & Ed: Harold Collier
VP, Opers: Thomas M Fritz
Founded: 1917
Full service company.

JB Bryans Literary
7 Meetinghouse Ct, Indian Mills, NJ 08088
Tel: 609-922-0369
E-mail: info@brylit.com
Web Site: brylit.com
Key Personnel
Pres: John B Bryans *E-mail:* john@brylit.com
Founded: 2017
Provides strategic, customized consulting services that help independent, association, non-profit, corporate, niche & regional publishers & content developers succeed critically & commercially & avoid costly missteps. Innovative consulting modules cover: Publishing business models, sales strategy development, finding & serving profitable niche markets, customized social media marketing, affordable market & competitor research, shoe-stringing the startup, content & author acquisition strategies, building the evergreen backlist, content & subsidiary rights licensing, editorial services management, publication design & production, & strategic outsourcing.

R E Carsch, MS-Consultant
1453 Rhode Island St, San Francisco, CA 94107-3248
Tel: 415-533-8356 (cell)
E-mail: recarsch@mzinfo.com
Founded: 1973
Full range custom information services including library marketing; fiscal development; research organization; analytical reporting; publications development; space planning. Unique & rare collections development & management. Specialize in art, business, architecture & engineering, information literacy, philanthropy & funding development.

Casemate | IPM
Division of Casemate Group
1950 Lawrence Rd, Havertown, PA 19083
Tel: 610-853-9131 *Fax:* 610-853-9146
E-mail: casemate@casematepublishers.com
Web Site: www.casemateipm.com
Founded: 1995
Full service sales, marketing & distribution firm, offering strategic planning, direct mail, advertising & publicity campaigns, sales representation & POD on web site to book publishers.

Cat's Eye Consultancy
4120 Durham Ct, Eagan, MN 55122
Tel: 651-270-3190
Key Personnel
Independent Literary Consultant: Cassandra Faulkner *E-mail:* cjfaulkner243@gmail.com
Founded: 2014
Experienced consultant providing the following services: editing, copywriting, proofreading, research, indexing, database & library archiving, photography, copyright/Library of Congress, book fair/trade show coordination, author/artist relations.

CeciBooks Editorial & Publishing Consultation
7057 26 Ave NW, Seattle, WA 98117
Mailing Address: PO Box 17229, Seattle, WA 98127
E-mail: ceci@cecibooks.com
Web Site: www.cecibooks.com
Key Personnel
Owner: Ceci Miller *E-mail:* ceci@cecibooks.com
Founded: 1988

SERVICES

We provide expert publishing, writing, editing & editorial coaching services to authors & other professionals in the US & Canada. We offer a professional orientation to publishing, as well as effective, respectful coaching to develop a book & marketing strategy that expresses our client's highest intention. E-mail to set up a phone consultation.
Membership(s): The Authors Guild; Independent Book Publishers Association (IBPA); Northwest Editors Guild; Society of Children's Book Writers & Illustrators (SCBWI)

City Diecutting Inc
Affiliate of Bookdisplays LLC
One Cory Rd, Morristown, NJ 07960
Tel: 973-270-0370 *Fax:* 973-270-0369
E-mail: sales@bookdisplays.com
Web Site: www.bookdisplays.com
Key Personnel
Pres & CEO: Eric De Vos *E-mail:* edevos@bookdisplays.com
VP, Sales: Frank Matonti *E-mail:* fmatonti@bookdisplays.com
Founded: 1989
Retail point of purchase corrugated displays for books & AV materials. In-stock displays for most standard trim sizes. 4-color branding on headers/risers. Custom displays for national rollouts.
Membership(s): American Booksellers Association (ABA); Independent Book Publishers Association (IBPA)

Clear Concepts
1329 Federal Ave, Suite 6, Los Angeles, CA 90025
Tel: 323-285-0325
Key Personnel
Owner: Karen Kleiner
Communications consultant. Marketing plans, research, writing & editing.

Dwight Clough
PO Box 670, Wyocena, WI 53969
E-mail: lmp@dwightclough.com
Web Site: dwightclough.com
Founded: 1983
Serving authors, especially first-time authors & publishers, to help write & self-publish their books on Amazon.

Cohesion®
511 W Bay St, Suite 480, Tampa, FL 33606
Tel: 813-999-3111 *Toll Free Tel:* 866-727-6800
Web Site: www.cohesion.com
Key Personnel
CEO: John Owens
Chief Strategy Offr: John Larson
Founded: 1982
Complete book, journal, electronic & CD-ROM development & production services. Web design, content, development & production, project management, writing, editing (including online), indexing, proofreading, design & art management. XML-based production processes for both print & electronic products & content management support. Specialize in educational, reference, medical & allied health, computer science, law, physical & life sciences, engineering & technical.
Branch Office(s)
6760 Alexander Bell Dr, Suite 120, Columbia, MD 21046 *Toll Free Tel:* 800-560-0630
5151 Pfeiffer Rd, Suite 105, Cincinnati, OH 45242 *Tel:* 513-587-7700

Color House Graphics Inc
3505 Eastern Ave SE, Grand Rapids, MI 49508
Toll Free Tel: 800-454-1916 *Fax:* 616-245-5494
Web Site: www.colorhousegraphics.com

Key Personnel
Gen Mgr: Phil Knight *E-mail:* pknight@colorhousegraphics.com
Founded: 1987
CHG is a full service book manufacturing company.
Membership(s): The Association of Publishers for Special Sales (APSS); Colorado Independent Publishers Association (CIPA); Evangelical Christian Publishers Association (ECPA); Florida Authors & Publishers Association Inc (FAPA); Independent Book Publishers Association (IBPA); Printing Industries of Michigan Inc (PIM); Publishers Association of the West (PubWest)

Concierge Marketing Inc
4822 S 133 St, Omaha, NE 68137
Tel: 402-884-5995
Web Site: www.conciergemarketing.com
Key Personnel
Pres: Lisa K Pelto *E-mail:* lisa@conciergemarketing.com
Founded: 2004
Consultant for small publishers, illustrators, editorial, marketing & product development. Help independent authors become high quality publishers. Audio production, design & ebook programming.
Membership(s): American Advertising Federation (AAF); American Marketing Association; The Association of Publishers for Special Sales (APSS); Greater Omaha Chamber of Commerce; Independent Book Publishers Association (IBPA)

Conspire Creative
Division of Everything Goes Media LLC
Chicago, IL 60657
Tel: 773-562-5499
Web Site: www.conspirecreative.com
Key Personnel
Owner: Sharon Woodhouse *E-mail:* sharon@conspirecreative.com
Founded: 2005
Publishing consulting; author milestone & business coaching; project management for self-published books; entrepreneurial publishing, author public relations, web site & marketing support; e-mail advice on demand; print brokering.

Copyright Clearance Center Inc (CCC)
222 Rosewood Dr, Danvers, MA 01923
Tel: 978-750-8400 (sales); 978-646-2600 (cust serv)
E-mail: info@copyright.com
Web Site: www.copyright.com
Key Personnel
Pres & CEO: Tracey L Armstrong
EVP & CTO: Haralambos "Babis" Marmanis
VP, CFO & Treas: Richard A Ruf
VP & Gen Coun: Catherine Zaller Rowland
VP & Mng Dir: Emily Sheahan; Lauren Tulloch
VP, Client Engagement & Busn Devt: Kim Zwollo
VP, Enterprise Opers: Gretchen L Gasser-Ellis
VP, HR: Michele R Nivens
VP, Mktg: Ian Palmer
VP, Sales: Donna Pouliot
Exec Dir, Intl Rel: Michael Healy
Mng Dir, Busn Devt & Govt Rel: Roy S Kaufman
Founded: 1978
Leading global information solutions provider. Domain expertise in copyright, technology, content, PIDs, FAIR data principles, metadata & more.

Copywriters' Council of America™ (CCA)
Division of The Linick Group Inc
Linick Bldg, 7 Putter Lane, Middle Island, NY 11953
Mailing Address: PO Box 102, Middle Island, NY 11953-0102
Tel: 631-924-3888; 631-924-8555; 631-604-8599
E-mail: linickgroup@gmail.com
Key Personnel
Founder & CEO: Andrew S Linick, PhD *E-mail:* cca4dmcopy@gmail.com
Sr Consultant: Gaylen Andrews
Dir, Spec Projs: Barbara Deal
EVP & Creative Dir: Roger Dextor
Treas: Milt Sosinsky
Edit Dir: Kelly Boyles
Art Dir: Keith Yates
Photos: Johnathan Gerson; Laura Covas; Tim Deos
Founded: 1970
Free referral service to 35,000 independent full service consultative talent. Member consultants cover over 1,550 areas of expertise. Specialize in working with authors, Internet publishers & Infomarketers, advertising, direct marketing, public relations in-house & outside agencies; government agencies, profit & nonprofit associations, corporations, independent publishers, self-publishers, speakers, talent agencies, celebrities & entertainers, other consulting firms & professionals; developers of trade shows, webinars, seminars & workshops, meetings & conventions; book, video & continuity clubs. Call for CCA's Free InfoActive™ Marketing Communications Audit. Provides comprehensive graphic redesign/new web site content development, interactive services with web site marketing makeover advice for first-time authors, self-publishers, professionals & entrepreneurs. Specializes in online advertising/PR, links to top search engines, consulting on a 100% satisfaction guarantee. Free site evaluation marketing checklist (a $250 value) for LMP readers.
Branch Office(s)
7 Lincoln Ave, Smithtown, NY 11787
Membership(s): The Imaging Alliance

Creative Direct Marketing Group Inc (CDMG)
1313 Fourth Ave N, Nashville, TN 37208
Tel: 615-814-6633
Web Site: www.cdmginc.com
Key Personnel
Founder & CEO: Craig Huey
COO: Scott Sheppard
Pres: Caleb Huey *E-mail:* caleb@cdmginc.com
Art Dir: Suzanne Pfeil
Creative Dir: Brandon Brison
Dir, Busn Devt: Michael Oppenheimer *E-mail:* moppenheimer@cdmginc.com
Dir, Data & Audiences: Jeremiah Dart
Dir, Digital Media: Jorge Sandoval
Dir, Print & Prodn: Nancy Gullette
Full service, direct response advertising & digital marketing agency.

Creative Trust Inc
Division of Creative Trust Ventures
210 Jamestown Park Dr, Suite 200, Brentwood, TN 37027
Tel: 615-297-5010 *Fax:* 615-297-5020
E-mail: info@creativetrust.com
Web Site: creativetrust.com
Key Personnel
Founder & Pres: Daniel Raines
Mng Partner, Creative Trust Literary Group: Kathryn A Helmers
Founded: 1989
Literary representation.

Cypress House
Imprint of Comp-Type Inc
155 Cypress St, Suite A, Fort Bragg, CA 95437
Tel: 707-964-9520 *Toll Free Tel:* 800-773-7782
Fax: 707-964-7531
E-mail: office@cypresshouse.com
Web Site: www.cypresshouse.com
Key Personnel
Pres: Cynthia Frank *E-mail:* cynthia@cypresshouse.com
Mng Ed: Joe Shaw *E-mail:* joeshaw@cypresshouse.com
Founded: 1986
Project coordination, prepress, typesetting, page design, complete page make-up to camera ready, book cover preparation, color separations, cover design & layout, printer selection & supervision, press release development, solicitation & coordination of media interviews, press kit development, packaging & mailing review & advance copies.
Membership(s): American Booksellers Association (ABA); Bay Area Independent Publishers Association (BAIPA); California Independent Booksellers Alliance (CALIBA); Independent Book Publishers Association (IBPA); Pacific Northwest Booksellers Association (PNBA)

Jeff Davidson MBA, CMC, Breathing Space Institute
3202 Ruffin St, Raleigh, NC 27607
Tel: 919-932-1996
Web Site: www.breathingspace.com
Key Personnel
Founder & Exec Dir: Jeff Davidson *E-mail:* jeff@breathingspace.com
Founded: 1995
Promotion, marketing, publicity, foreign sales, book clubs, subsidiary sales, negotiations, second editions & ghostwriting.
Membership(s): Authors Registry; IMC; National Speakers Association (NSA); Triangle Area Freelancers

Peter L DeGiglio
6 Overlook Dr, Washingtonville, NY 10992
Tel: 914-850-3803
E-mail: pdegiglio@gmail.com
Founded: 2011
Consulting services to publishers, authors & agents with a full range of expertise in the areas of finance, strategic planning, mergers & acquisitions, building infrastructure & business development.

Del Commune Enterprises Inc
18 Bellport Lane, Bellport, NY 11713
Tel: 212-226-6664
E-mail: mail@dcescouts.com
Web Site: www.dcescouts.com
Key Personnel
Founder & Pres: Lauri del Commune
Sr Scout: Lindsey Milne
Founded: 1996
Book scouting agency & international consulting service within the US book publishing industry. Focus on adult trade (fiction & nonfiction) & young adult titles originating in the US.

Steven Diamond Inc
104 W 17 St, Suite 3-E, New York, NY 10011
Tel: 212-675-0723 *Fax:* 212-675-0762
E-mail: steven.diamond@verizon.net
Key Personnel
Pres: Steven Diamond
VP: Carol Poticny
Visual research of all kinds, with an emphasis on fine art, both painting & photography. In addition to the standard services we provide, we have our own fine art reference library on the premises.
Membership(s): American Society of Picture Professionals (ASPP)

CONSULTANTS | SERVICES

Double Play
303 Hillcrest Rd, Belton, MO 64012-1852
Tel: 816-651-7118
Key Personnel
Pres: Lloyd Johnson *E-mail:* wlloydj@yahoo.com
VP: Connie Johnson
Writing & research on baseball; baseball museum consultant.
Membership(s): Society for American Baseball Research

Embolden Media Group
PO Box 953607, Lake Mary, FL 32795-3607
E-mail: info@emboldenmediagroup.com
Web Site: emboldenmediagroup.com
Key Personnel
Founder & CEO: Jevon Bolden
Founded: 2017
Boutique book publishing consulting firm representing a diverse group of writers, speakers, activists, faith leaders & cultural influencers. Author coaching & development, content development services, author education events, e-courses, books & resources. Diversity, equity & inclusion consulting for publishing teams & associated organizations.

Bob Erdmann
1116 Oakmont Dr, No 6, Walnut Creek, CA 94595
Tel: 925-451-8201
E-mail: info@bob-erdmann.com; columbcomm@gmail.com
Founded: 1978
Full service foreign rights consultancy to publishers & self-published authors. Foreign rights agent.
Membership(s): The Association of Publishers for Special Sales (APSS); Independent Book Publishers Association (IBPA)

Exhibit Promotions Plus Inc
11620 Vixens Path, Ellicott City, MD 21042-1539
Tel: 410-997-0763
E-mail: exhibit@epponline.com
Web Site: www.epponline.com
Key Personnel
Founder & Pres: Harve C Horowitz, Esq
CFO: Eileen S Horowitz
Sr Mgr, Cust Rel: Kelly K Marshall
Founded: 1969
Advise publishers where to advertise & exhibit their books; advertising & exhibit representative for scholarly & other professional trade associations. Generate program & journal advertising in conjunction with international, national, regional & state exhibits in subject-arranged collections. Comprehensive convention management.

Taryn Fagerness Agency
4810 Point Fosdick Dr NW, PMB 34, Gig Harbor, WA 98335
Tel: 858-254-7711
E-mail: taryn@tarynfagernessagency.com
Web Site: www.tarynfagernessagency.com
Founded: 2009
Represents foreign subsidiary rights on behalf of North American literary agents.

Linda Fairchild & Company LLC
101 Lucas Valley Rd, Suite 363, San Rafael, CA 94903
Tel: 415-336-6407
Web Site: www.lindafairchild.com
Key Personnel
Agent & Founder: Linda Fairchild
   E-mail: linda@lindafairchild.com
Founded: 2002
We consult with writers & illustrators to prepare their work for publication & distribution.

Fairfield Marketing Group Inc
Subsidiary of FMG Inc
830 Sport Hill Rd, Easton, CT 06112-1241
E-mail: info@fairfieldmarketing.com
Key Personnel
Pres & CEO: Edward P Washchilla, Jr
   E-mail: ed@fairfieldmarketing.com
Founded: 1986
Mailing list brokerage & list management services. FMG clients rely on us for annual direct marketing programs. We are customer driven & accomodate. Specialty services: custom designed account management; expedient list rental approval; monthly usage reports; market & account analyses; fulfillment, mailing & mail response services; freelance art work; graphic design; advertising & promotional copywriting; binding services; lettershop services; computer services. FMG is a full service direct mail marketing firm.
Membership(s): American Booksellers Association (ABA); Bridgeport Regional Business Council (BRBC); Education Market Association; United States Chamber of Commerce (USCC)

Feigenbaum Publishing Consultants Inc
61 Bounty Lane, Jericho, NY 11753
Tel: 516-647-8314 (cell)
Key Personnel
Pres: Laurie Feigenbaum
   E-mail: lauriefeigenbaum@gmail.com
Founded: 1991
Contract review & negotiation; permissions clearance; general publishing advice. Trademark & copyright registrations. Reasonable hourly rate.

Alanna Feldman Scouting
4080 Via Marisol, Apt 135, Los Angeles, CA 90042
E-mail: info@afscouting.com
Web Site: www.afscouting.com
Key Personnel
Owner: Alanna Feldman
Sr Scout: Hannah Ekren
Assoc Scout: Andrew Dugan
Founded: 2017
Scout for international publishers & film/TV companies across most genres in the adult & children's markets.

Figaro
PO Box 848, Sharon, CT 06069
Tel: 860-248-8989; 860-364-0834
E-mail: design@figro.com
Web Site: www.figro.com
Key Personnel
Co-Pres & Creative Dir: Walter Schwarz
Co-Pres: Linda Swenson *E-mail:* ls@figro.com
Creative, editorial, production & photographic services for books, catalogs, promotional materials & packaging. Digital creation of text, art, maps, illustration & photos for current & out of print books. Consultation, graphic arts management & printing supervision. Web site development & maintenance. Photography of Suzanne Szasz & Ray Shorr.

The Fisher Company
PO Box 89578, Tucson, AZ 85752-9578
Tel: 520-547-2460
Web Site: www.thefishercompany.com
Key Personnel
Mng Dir: Howard W Fisher *E-mail:* howard.fisher@thefishercompany.com
Founded: 2002
Offers international mergers & acquisitions brokerage & business development consulting. We work with you to improve your financial capabilities & develop your company. We provide advice on how to increase your profitability & add value to your publishing companies.
Membership(s): Independent Book Publishers Association (IBPA); Publishers Association of the West (PubWest)

Flannery Book Service
20258 Hwy 18, Suite 430-436, Apple Valley, CA 92307
Toll Free Tel: 800-456-3400
Web Site: fbs-now.com
Key Personnel
Co-Founder & COO: Heath W Spurgeon
Co-Founder & CFO: Eve Flannery Toles
Management consultants for K-12 school curriculum print & digital material logistics (K-12 textbooks).

Fournies Associates
1226 NW 19 Terr, Delray Beach, FL 33445
Tel: 561-445-5102
Key Personnel
Partner: Sandra Fournies
Founded: 1972
Book publisher of professional books, behavioral science & business; management consultant.

Franklin & Siegal Associates Inc
40 Exchange Place, Suite 1703, New York, NY 10005
Tel: 212-868-6311
Web Site: www.franklinandsiegal.com
Key Personnel
Pres: Todd R Siegal *E-mail:* todd@franklinandsiegal.com
VP & Dir, Adult Scouting: Danny Yanez
Dir, Children's Scouting: Kalah McCaffrey
Dir, Film & TV Scouting: Lauren Hogan
Sr Literary Scout: Dorian Randall
Literary Scout: Brianna Zimmerman
Scout, Young Adult & Film: Chanelle Norman
Scout Asst: Emma Danz
Founded: 1992
Scouts for: Planeta (Brazil); Egmont (Bulgaria); Citic (China); Storyhouse Egmont (Croatia); Lindhardt & Ringhof & Carlsen (Denmark); WSOY/Kniga/Minerva (Finland); Flammarion/J'ai Lu & Nathan Jeunesse (France); Heyne Verlag & cbj (Germany); Yedioth (Israel); Sperling & Kupfer (Italy); Hayakawa (Japan); Munhakdonge (Korea); Unieboek/Spectrum & Van Holkema-Van Goor (Netherlands); Proszynski (Poland); Litera (Romania); MTS/Stroki (Russia); Grupo SM (Spain); China Times (Taiwan); Hodder & Stoughton/Sceptre, John Murray Press/Baskerville/Quercus, riverrun, Orion Publishing Group (UK).

The French Publishers' Agency
Affiliate of BIEF (Bureau International de L'Edition Francaise)
PO Box 140, New York, NY 10009
Tel: 212-254-4874
Web Site: www.frenchrights.com
Key Personnel
Dir: Alice Tassel
Founded: 1983
Represents French member publishers of BIEF.

G & H Soho Inc
413 Market St, Elmwood Park, NJ 07407
Tel: 201-216-9400 *Fax:* 201-216-1778
E-mail: print@ghsoho.com
Web Site: www.ghsoho.com
Key Personnel
Pres: Gerry Burstein
Prodn Mgr: Jason Burstein
Membership(s): Association of Graphic Communications; Digital Printing Council; PRINTING United Alliance

Garvan Media, Management & Marketing Inc
PO Box 737, Sandpoint, ID 83864
Tel: 208-265-1718
Web Site: facebook.com/stephen.b.garvan
Key Personnel
CEO & Expediter: Stephen Bond Garvan
Tel: 303-809-1676 (cell) *E-mail:* steve@garvanmarketing.com
Founded: 1997
Strategic marketing & business guidance & development, 20+ years independent. Formerly in marketing/sales management, national accounts at: Workman, Morrow, Fulcrum, Roberts Rinehart & IABC. Overall marketing, business development, forecasting, analysis, budgeting & list building. Soliciting & managing sales/distribution in the US, Canada, Europe, Australia & New Zealand. Former AAP Telemarketing Committee, NEIBA & Pub West Boards. Numerous music industry, civic, cultural & community boards. Works also to place & strategize marketing & sales for music-oriented books. Has extensive music industry experience & contacts.
Membership(s): Mountains & Plains Independent Booksellers Association (MPIBA); Pacific Northwest Booksellers Association (PNBA); Publishers Association of the West (PubWest); Southern Independent Booksellers Alliance (SIBA)

Liz Gately Book Scouting
36 W 37 St, Rm 408, New York, NY 10018
Tel: 212-244-1441
E-mail: liz@lizgately.com
Web Site: www.lizgately.com
Key Personnel
Owner & Scout, Adult Books: Liz Gately
Scout, Adult Books: Eve Gleichman; Hunter Simpson
Scout, Childrens & Young Adult Books: Cathrin Wirtz
Founded: 2010
Foreign scouting firm for adult & children's titles. Clients: HarperCollins (UK), Headline (UK), Rowohlt (Germany), Meulenhoff Boekerij (Holland), Edi8 (France), Piemme (Italy), Aboca (Italy), LeYa (Portugal), Maeva (Spain), Globo (Brazil), Lumen (Croatia), Nemira (Romania), Agora (Poland), Commonwealth Magazine (Taiwan), Horizon (China), The English Agency (Japan).

GGP Publishing Inc
Larchmont, NY 10538
Tel: 914-834-8896 *Fax:* 914-834-7566
Web Site: www.GGPPublishing.com
Key Personnel
Founder, Owner & Dir: Generosa Gina Protano
E-mail: GGProtano@GGPPublishing.com
Founded: 1991
Full service development house & packaging firm offering services from concept to finished electronic files/bound books to online distribution or for any one step of this publishing process. Specialize in educational publishing from K-12 to college/university to adult education. Have a niche in the writing, development, editing & production up to finished electronic files/bound books of textbooks & trade books for the study of foreign languages such as French, German, Italian, Latin, Portuguese & Spanish. Also translates complete/partial programs or cluster of books from English into any of these languages or from any of these languages into English, edit the translation for publication & set the edited translation into book form up to finished electronic files/bound books. Develop, edit, do art/design & production of different genres both for publishing houses as well as individuals who wish to self-publish. Has produced novels, memoirs & books in the fields of religion, psychology & culinary arts among others. Special interest in memoirs. Acts as literary agents & foreign publisher representatives.

Heidelberg Graphics
2 Stansbury Ct, Chico, CA 95928
SAN: 211-5654
Tel: 530-342-6582 *Fax:* 530-342-6582
E-mail: heidelberggraphics@gmail.com; service@heidelberggraphics.com
Web Site: www.heidelberggraphics.com
Key Personnel
Owner & Pres: Larry S Jackson
Founded: 1972
Promotion, printing & publishing consultants; complete book preparation; advisors to self-publishers; copyrights; desktop publishing, imagesetting & disk conversion to type.

Albert Henderson
655 West Ave, Milford, CT 06461-3003
Tel: 203-301-0791
E-mail: 70244.1532@compuserve.com
Writer, editor, reviewer & management consultant to publishers. Scholarly, professional, scientific, technical books & journals; operations, production, marketing, fulfillment, importing & exporting, mergers, acquisitions & sale of business. Bibliography on request.

HurleyMedia LLC
1477 Canyon Rd, Santa Fe, NM 87501
Tel: 505-603-6392
Web Site: www.hurleymedia.com
Key Personnel
Owner: Joanna Thorne Hurley *E-mail:* jth@hurleymedia.com
Founded: 1994
We offer full service packaging for photography & art books from concept through publication, including editorial, design, production, as well as placement with a suitable publisher/distributor, marketing & publicity as needed to supplement publisher's efforts.

Idea Architects
523 Swift St, Santa Cruz, CA 95060
Tel: 831-465-9565
Web Site: www.ideaarchitects.com
Key Personnel
Founder & Pres: Douglas Carlton Abrams
Dir, Author Success & Contracts Mgr: Ty Gideon Love
Dir, Community Engagement: Cody Love
Dir, Global Prospecting & Res: Boo Prince
Edit Dir: Sarah Rainone
Literary Agent: Sydney Rogers
Founded: 2001
Literary agency, book & media development agency for visionary authors.
IA True Division focuses on inspirational & compelling memories & true stories that have the power to change hearts & minds.

The Idea Logical Co Inc
300 E 51 St, Apt 17C, New York, NY 10017
Tel: 917-680-8598
E-mail: info@idealog.com
Web Site: www.idealog.com
Key Personnel
Founder & CEO: Mike Shatzkin *E-mail:* mike@idealog.com
Founded: 1979
Innovative consulting for all aspects of the global book business; specialties are digital strategy & digital change, creating new models, new technology integration & supply chain management.

Imago
110 W 40 St, New York, NY 10018
Tel: 212-921-4411 *Fax:* 212-921-8226
E-mail: sales@imagousa.com
Web Site: imagousa.com
Key Personnel
Pres & CEO: Howard Musk *E-mail:* howardm@imagogroup.com
Founded: 1985
Global print & production services with a network of production & sales offices across Southeast Asia, Europe & America. Areas of expertise include the production of conventional & novelty books, packaging, stationery, plush toys & board games.
Branch Office(s)
Imago West Coast, 23412 Moulton Pkwy, Suite 250, Laguna Hills, CA 92653 (sales), Contact: Tammy Simms *Tel:* 949-367-1635 *Fax:* 949-367-1639
Imago Australia, 10 Help St, Suite 27, Level 6, Chatswood, NSW 2067, Australia (sales) *Tel:* (04) 3753 3351 (cell); (04) 4806 8704 (cell) *E-mail:* sales@imagoaus.com
Imago Brazil, Domiciano Rossi, 340 unid 154, 09726-121 Sao Bernardo do Campo, Brazil (sales) *Tel:* (011) 2306 8546; (011) 2306 8547 *E-mail:* imagobra@gmail.com
Imago Shenzhen, Rm 2511-2512, Block A, United Plaza No 5022, Bin He Rd, Fu Tian Centre District, Shenzhen 518033, China (prodn), Contact: Kendrick Cheung *Tel:* (0755) 8304 8899 *Fax:* (0755) 8251 4073 *E-mail:* enquiries@imago.com.hk
Imago France, 23 rue Lavoisier, 75008 Paris, France (sales) *Tel:* 01 45 26 47 74 *Fax:* 01 78 94 14 44 *E-mail:* sales@imagogroup.com
Imago Services (HK) Ltd, Unit B309, 1/F, New East Sun Industrial Bldg, 18 Shing Yip St, Kwun Tong, Hong Kong (prodn), Contact: Kendrick Cheung *Tel:* 2811 3316 *E-mail:* enquiries@imago.com.hk
Imago Productions (Malaysia) Pte Ltd, No 43, Taman Emas, Jl Utama 31, Telok Panglima Garang, 42500 Kuala Langot, Selangor, Malaysia (prodn, incorporating South Africa sales) *Tel:* (017) 4288771 (cell) *E-mail:* enquiries@imago.com.sg
Imago Publishing, Albury Ct, Albury Thame, Oxon OX9 2LP, United Kingdom (sales), Dir: Simon Rosenheim *Tel:* (01844) 337000 *Fax:* (01844) 339935 *E-mail:* sales@imago.co.uk *Web Site:* imagogroup.com

Innodata Inc
55 Challenger Rd, Suite 202, Ridgefield Park, NJ 07660
Tel: 201-371-8000 *Toll Free Tel:* 877-454-8400
E-mail: info@innodata.com; marketing@innodata.com
Web Site: innodata.com
Key Personnel
Pres & CEO: Jack S Abuhoff
EVP & COO: Ashok Kumar Mishra
SVP & Gen Coun: Amy Agress
SVP, Prod Innovation: R Douglas Kemp
Founded: 1988
Innodata is a global services & technology solutions company. Our technology & services power leading information products & online retail destinations around the world. Our solutions help enterprises harness the power of digital data to reimagine how they operate & drive performance. We serve publishers, media & information companies, digital retailers, banks, insurance companies, government agencies & many other industries. We comprise a team of 5,000 diverse people in 8 countries who are dedicated to delivering services & solutions that help the world embrace digital data as a means of enhancing our lives & transforming our businesses. The company operates in 3 reporting segments: Digital Data Solutions (DDS), Innodata Data Solutions (IADS) & Media Intelligence Solutions (MIS).

CONSULTANTS

Headquartered in Northern New Jersey, Innodata has offices & operations in the US, Canada, Germany, India, Israel, Philippines, Sri Lanka & UK.
Membership(s): The Association for Work Process Improvement; Association of American Publishers Professional & Scholarly Publishing Division; Center for Information Development & Content Management Strategies (CIDM); International Association of Outsourcing Professionals (IAOP); National Federation of Abstracting and Information Services (NFAIS); Society for Technical Communication (STC); Society of Knowledge Based Publishers (SKBP); Software & Information Industry Association (SIIA)

Integra Software Services Inc
Division of Integra Software Services Pvt Ltd
2021 Midwest Rd, Suite 200, Oak Brook, IL 60523
Web Site: www.integranxt.com
Founded: 1991
Project management, development & production support for book publishers.

The Intermarketing Group-Art Licensing Agency
29 Holt Rd, Amherst, NH 03031
Tel: 603-672-0499
Key Personnel
Founder & Principal: Linda Gerson
Founded: 1985
Art licensing agency, marketing/sales & international trade.

International Literary Properties (ILP)
286 Madison Ave, New York, NY 10017
Tel: 646-202-1633 *Fax:* 212-967-0977
E-mail: contact@ilpliterary.com
Web Site: www.internationalliteraryproperties.com
Key Personnel
Exec Chmn: Ted Green
Pres & CEO: Scott Hoffman
CFO: Andrew Minkow
SVP, Fin Opers: Lan Wong
VP, Legal & Busn Aff, North America: Barbara Cohen
VP, Corp Devt: Polly Benton; Max Hinchcliffe
VP, Creative & Brand/Exec Prodr: Emma Bell
VP, Literary: Sarah Yake
VP, North American Acqs & Publg: Molly Cusick
Dir: Bob Benton
Acqs Analyst: Noah Goodman
Acquires all or partial rights to literary intellectual property, including books, plays & books of musicals.
Branch Office(s)
6 Fitzroy Sq, London W1T 5DX, United Kingdom, CEO, UK & Europe: Hilary Strong

International Transactions Inc
28 Alope Way, Gila, NM 88038
Mailing Address: PO Box 97, Gila, NM 88038
Tel: 845-373-9696 *Fax:* 480-393-5162
E-mail: info@internationaltransactions.us
Web Site: www.intltrans.com
Key Personnel
Pres: Peter Riva *E-mail:* priva@intltrans.com
Founded: 1975

IP Royalty Auditors LLC
316 Perkins Ave, Oceanside, NY 11572
Tel: 516-503-5985
E-mail: royalty@aol.com
Web Site: www.iproyaltyauditors.com
Key Personnel
Pres: Gail R Gross
Founded: 2008

Conduct on our clients behalf, systematic reviews of books & records to verify proper payment of royalties due to intellectual property owners, i.e., authors, agents, attorneys & publishers, on sales of intellectual properties including books, merchandise licenses, electronic audio & video sales & subsidiary rights. In addition, our services include valuation of intellectual property as well as book office royalty consulting.
Membership(s): American Book Producers Association (ABPA); The Authors Guild; National Women's Book Association; Textbook & Academic Authors Association (TAA)

Law Offices of Lloyd J Jassin
The Paramount Bldg, 1501 Broadway, 12th fl, New York, NY 10036
Tel: 212-354-4442
E-mail: jassin@copylaw.com
Web Site: www.copylaw.org
Founded: 1991
Draft & negotiate publishing agreements; work for hire; distribution; subsidiary rights; trademark registration; copyright termination; pre-publication review re: fair use, libel, invasion of privacy, right of publicity claims; film options; merchandise licensing claims; publishing consultant; literary agent.
Membership(s): The Authors Guild; Independent Book Publishers Association (IBPA)

Javelin Group
203 S Union St, Suite 200, Alexandria, VA 22314
Tel: 703-490-8845
E-mail: hello@javelindc.com
Web Site: javelindc.com
Key Personnel
Pres: Keith Urbahn *E-mail:* keith@javelindc.com
Founding Partner: Matt Latimer *E-mail:* matt@javelindc.com
Literary Agent/Foreign Rts Dir: Matt Carlini
Full service literary & communications firm. Representation, writing, editing & publicity.

Jenkins Group Inc
1129 Woodmere Ave, Suite B, Traverse City, MI 49686
Tel: 231-933-0445; 213-883-5365
E-mail: info@jenkinsgroupinc.com
Web Site: www.jenkinsgroupinc.com
Key Personnel
CEO: Jerrold R Jenkins *Tel:* 231-933-0445 ext 1008 *E-mail:* jrj@jenkinsgroupinc.com
Pres & COO: James Kalajian *Tel:* 231-933-0445 ext 1006 *E-mail:* jjk@jenkinsgroupinc.com
Book Prodn Mgr: Leah Nicholson *Tel:* 231-933-0445 ext 1015 *E-mail:* lnicholson@jenkinsgroupinc.com
Founded: 1988
Provide consulting services to Fortune 500 companies, associations, booksellers, publishers, corporations & organizations attempting to reach the publishing community. Unparalleled access & experience with all aspects of the publishing industry, providing knowledge for trade distributors & library wholesalers; assistance with galley presentation for pre-publication reviews; media publicity & promotion, literary agent acquisition; recommendations for public relations firms; contacts for book clubs, catalogs & corporate level bookstores; necessary information & guidance to assist independent publishers in building a presence within the industry.

JMW Group Inc
346 Rte 6, No 867, Mahopac, NY 10541
Tel: 914-841-7105 *Fax:* 914-248-8861
E-mail: jmwgroup@jmwgroup.net
Web Site: jmwforlife.com
Key Personnel
Pres & CEO: Patti DeMatteo

SERVICES

VP, Rts: Pete Allen
Dir, Licensing: Sara Castle
Founded: 1949
Licenses rights to nonfiction books & other copyrighted material in a range of subjects on a worldwide basis, including self-help, self-improvement & business.

JPMC Associates
7037 Snapdragon Dr, Carlsbad, CA 92011
Tel: 916-203-3693 *Fax:* 760-931-6878
E-mail: jpmcaso@aol.com
Key Personnel
Pres: Jim McGough
Founded: 1979

Kaplan/DeFiore Rights
47 E 19 St, 3rd fl, New York, NY 10003
Tel: 212-925-7244
Web Site: kaplanrights.com
Key Personnel
Dir: Linda Kaplan *Tel:* 212-925-7744 ext 106 *E-mail:* linda@defliterary.com
Offers publishers & literary agents full service international licensing solutions, including early proposal/ms reports, solicitation & negotiation of contracts, tax forms & financial analysis of royalty statements.

Kinokuniya Publications Service of New York (KPS-NY)
Subsidiary of Kinokuniya Co Ltd (Tokyo, Japan)
1073 Avenue of the Americas, New York, NY 10018-3701
Tel: 212-765-1465 *Fax:* 212-307-5593
E-mail: nyinfo@kinokuniya.com
Web Site: www.kinokuniya.co.jp; www.kinokuniya.com
Key Personnel
VP: Eigi Matsuoka
Bookstore, book & subscription agency, wholesaler.
Membership(s): Association of American Publishers (AAP)

Klopotek North America Inc
Division of Klopotek AG
19321 US Hwy 19 N, Suite 407, Clearwater, FL 33764
Tel: 973-331-1010
E-mail: info@klopotek.com
Web Site: www.klopotek.com
Founded: 1992
Leading supplier of software & consulting services for publishers of books & journals, print & online. Publishers rely on our programs to help them manage their business & achieve their goals. Delivers innovative solutions to publishers around the world. Our software supports the entire publishing value chain for print & digital products, including contracts, rights & royalties management, editorial planning, production management, product promotion, marketing, sales & distribution all the way through to order processing & customer service support.
Membership(s): Book Industry Study Group (BISG)

knk Software LP
Member of knk Group
89 Headquarters Plaza N, No 1478, Morristown, NJ 07960
Tel: 908-206-4599
E-mail: info@knk.com
Web Site: www.knkpublishingsoftware.com
Key Personnel
VP, Opers: Michael Fox
Regl Sales Dir: Alan Hirsch
Busn Devt Mgr: Steve Rutberg

Mktg Mgr: Oliver Holden *Tel:* 781-772-2213
  E-mail: oliver.holden@knk.com
Sales Mgr: Jason Spanos *Tel:* 206-769-9245
  E-mail: jason.spanos@knk.com
Founded: 1988
As an expert in the publishing industry, knk combines the strengths of a business consultancy & the solution expertise of a software company.
knk develops & markets knkPublishing - the only Microsoft certified publishing software in the world. knkPublishing combines the classical ERP functions (financial accounting, supply chain management & sales & marketing), with industry specific functions for modern publishers & media companies.

David W Koehser Attorney at Law
322 First Ave N, Suite 402, Minneapolis, MN 55401
Tel: 612-910-6468
E-mail: dk@dklex.com
Web Site: www.dklex.com
Founded: 1996
Law firm providing representation for copyrights, publishing agreements & agent agreements.

The Live Oak Press LLC
PO Box 60036, Palo Alto, CA 94306-0036
E-mail: info@liveoakpress.com
Web Site: www.liveoakpress.com
Key Personnel
Founder & Pres: David M Hamilton
Founded: 1982
Offers consulting & publishing services (editorial & production).
Membership(s): The American Library Association (ALA); Association of College & Research Libraries (ACRL); The Authors Guild; Book Club of California (BCC); Independent Book Publishers Association (IBPA); Publishing Professionals Network (PPN); Society for Scholarly Publishing (SSP)

Lorimer Literary Consulting
1524 SE 46 Ave, Suite A, Portland, OR 97215
Tel: 503-481-5847
E-mail: amnotice@yahoo.com
Key Personnel
Owner & Pres: Kevin L Faherty
Founded: 2003
Consultancy to independent authors, self-publishers, ms development, sales representative hiring & trade show participation. Over 25 years of publishing & sales experience, specialty sales & club penetration.

Lumina Datamatics Inc
600 Cordwainer Dr, Unit 103, Norwell, MA 02061
Tel: 508-746-0300 *Fax:* 508-746-3233
E-mail: marketing@luminad.com
Web Site: luminadatamatics.com
Key Personnel
EVP, Busn Devt: Jack Mitchell
EVP, Solutions, Transitions & US Opers: Sandeep Dhawan
Founded: 1974
Providing full service content creation, design/packaging & media delivery systems to publishers. Services include authoring/writing, editorial research & development, media development & production, editing, photo & text research/permissions, photography/photo shoot direction, indexing, proofreading, fact checking, design/design direction, art direction/editing, technical/illustrative art packages, photo manipulation & page make-up/composition services. Employs over 1,200 US & offshore resources specializing in content/media creation & make-up including file conversions/re-purposing & content management & delivery services. All services are offered both in the US & at offshore facilities. Areas of specialization include school, higher education & professional publishing: mathematics (grade school/algebra/calculus/physics), foreign language (French/Spanish/German/Italian), English & English composition, history, political science, science (chemistry/biology/astronomy), social studies, computer science, business (economics/finance/marketing), engineering & technical trades as well as professional/reference material. Products range from simple one-color ancillaries components to highly complex design & art intensive core content.
Branch Office(s)
c/o Arnecke Sibeth Distribution, Rechtsanwaelte Steuerberater Partnerschaftsgesellschaft mdB, Gueterplatz 1, 60327 Frankfurt am Main, Germany *Tel:* (06155) 862 99-0 *Fax:* (06155) 862 99-19
Ascendas International Tech Park, 12th fl, Phase II (Crest), CSIR Rd, Taramani, Chennai 600 113, India *Tel:* (044) 4017 6000; (044) 4017 6001
Santosh Raj Plaza, 1st fl, Subburaman St, Gandhi Nagar, 12/9, St, Shenoy Nagar, Madurai 625 020, India
Andheri (E), Unit 117-120, SDF - IV, SEEPZ - SEZ, Mumbai 400 096, India *Tel:* (022) 4034 0515; (022) 4034 0508 *Fax:* (022) 2829 1673
Off No 47/1, 7th fl, Tower-B, A-41, Correnthum Tower, Sector-62, Noida 201 301, India
Plot No 29-34, East Coast Rd, Saram Revenue Village, Oulgaret Municipality, Lawspet Post, Puducherry 605 008, India *Tel:* (0413) 226 4500
No 10, Vazhudavoor Rd, Pettaiyanchathiram, Thattanchavadi, Puducherry 605 009, India *Tel:* (0413) 401 1635
Apple One Equicom Tower, 11th fl, Mindanao Ave Corner Biliran St, Central (pob), Cebu Business Park, 6000 Cebu City, Cebu, Philippines
c/o SOPHI Outsourcing Inc, G/F DBPI IT Plaza, Calindagan, 6200 Dumaguete City, Negros Oriental, Philippines
Brixham Laboratory, Brixham, Devon TQ5 8BA, United Kingdom
Lumina Datamatics UK Ltd, 153 Milton Keynes Business Ctr, Linford Wood, Milton Keynes MK14 6GD, United Kingdom

Market Partners International Inc
232 Madison Ave, Suite 1400, New York, NY 10016
Tel: 212-447-0855 *Fax:* 212-447-0785
E-mail: info@marketpartnersinternational.com
Web Site: www.marketpartnersinternational.com
Key Personnel
Dir: Amy Rhodes; Lorraine W Shanley
Consulting services to adult & children's publishers, book clubs, retailers, packagers & institutions including a full range of online & retail marketing expertise, digital strategy, business & strategic planning, special sales, mergers & acquisitions & executive search. Publishers of www.PublishingTrends.com, a web site dedicated to the book publishing industry.
Member of the Publishers Lunch Club.
Membership(s): Book Industry Study Group (BISG); Women's Media Group

Virginia McCullough
2527 Telluride Trail, Suite D, Green Bay, WI 54313
Tel: 920-662-9633; 920-680-3232 (text)
E-mail: virginiaauthor47@gmail.com
Web Site: www.virginiamccullough.com
Publishing advice, ms critiques & edits.
Membership(s): The Authors Guild; Romance Writers of America (RWA); Women's Fiction Writers Association (WFWA)

Media Masters Publicity
61 Depot St, Tryon, NC 28782
Tel: 828-859-9456
E-mail: info@mmpublicity.com
Web Site: www.mmpublicity.com
Key Personnel
Sr Partner: Tracey Daniels *E-mail:* tracey@mmpublicity.com
Founded: 1998
Full service literary publicity agency. Specialize in publicity for children's & teen books, cookbooks & lifestyle titles. Personalized service for every client with emphasis on procuring quality media results. Services: implementing & executing national & local media campaigns, author tours & appearances, TV & radio satellite tours, press kit design & consulting. Per-project or retainer services. Client list includes large & small publishing houses.
Branch Office(s)
6106 Majestic Pines Dr, Kingwood, TX 77345, Partner: Karen Wadsworth *Tel:* 617-869-5854
E-mail: karen@mmpublicity.com
Membership(s): The American Library Association (ALA); Society of Children's Book Writers & Illustrators (SCBWI); Young Adult Library Services Association (YALSA)

Mendon Associates Inc
44 Glenwood Ave, Suite 210, Toronto, ON M6P 3C6, Canada
Tel: 416-239-9661 *Toll Free Tel:* 800-361-1325
E-mail: info@mendon.com
Web Site: www.mendon.com
Key Personnel
Owner & Partner: A Jorge de Mendonca
  E-mail: jd@mendon.com
Founded: 1983
Media research & computer consulting for publishers.

MetaComet Systems
29 College St, South Hadley, MA 01075
Tel: 413-536-5989
Web Site: www.metacomet.com
Key Personnel
COO: Khalid Elkalai *E-mail:* kelkalai@metacomet.com
Pres: David Marlin *E-mail:* dmarlin@metacomet.com
Founded: 2000
Leading provider of royalty automation solutions designed to reduce effort by 90% while reducing risk & improving author relations.
Membership(s): Audio Publishers Association; Book Industry Study Group (BISG); Evangelical Christian Publishers Association (ECPA); Independent Book Publishers Association (IBPA); Independent Publisher's Guild (IPG); Publishers Association of the West (PubWest)

MGP Direct Inc
17814 Shotley Bridge Place, Olney, MD 20832
Tel: 240-755-6976
Web Site: www.mgpdirect.com
Key Personnel
Pres & CEO: Roberta Rosenberg
  E-mail: roberta@mgpdirect.com
Founded: 1987
Marketing consulting & direct marketing & search engine optimization (SEO) copywriting services for print, electronic & web information publishers.

OBS, see Open Book Systems Inc®

Odyssey Books
Division of The Ciletti Publishing Group Inc
2421 Redwood Ct, Longmont, CO 80503
Tel: 720-494-1473 *Fax:* 720-494-1471
E-mail: books@odysseybooks.net
Key Personnel
Pres & Publr: Barbara Ciletti

Founded: 1995
Book publishers specializing in fiction & nonfiction. Subject areas include social science, adult nonfiction, children's books, gardening & crafts.
Membership(s): The American Library Association (ALA); APPL; International Association of Culinary Professionals (IACP); International Literacy Association (ILA); National Science Teachers Association (NSTA); Society of American Poets

Open Book Systems Inc®
21 Broadway, Suite 5, Rockport, MA 01966
Tel: 978-546-7346
E-mail: info@obs.com
Web Site: www.obs.com
Key Personnel
Pres: Laura Fillmore *E-mail:* laura@obs.com
Founded: 1982
Consult with publishers & educators on digital strategy. Specialize in: Standards & workflows for traditional & digital publishing; ebook conversion & distribution; sci-tech-medical (STM) & educational publishing; institutional sales & access; re-purposing of print & electronic content; backend content & digital asset management; proprietary code development; customization of open source software.
Membership(s): Book Industry Study Group (BISG); Independent Book Publishers Association (IBPA); Internet Society

Open Horizons Publishing Co
PO Box 271, Dolan Springs, NM 86441
Tel: 575-741-1581
E-mail: books@bookmarketingbestsellers.com
Web Site: bookmarketingbestsellers.com
Key Personnel
Owner & Publr: John Kremer
E-mail: johnkremer@bookmarket.com
Founded: 1982
Book marketing, publicity, direct marketing, pricing & general planning for book publishers of all sizes as well as for individual authors. Most consulting is done over the phone, but also provides on-site consulting services; book covers; news releases, Internet marketing.
Membership(s): The Association of Publishers for Special Sales (APSS); Independent Book Publishers Association (IBPA)

Orobora Inc
644 Greenville Ave, Suite 234, Staunton, VA 24401
Tel: 540-324-7023
E-mail: info@orobora.com
Web Site: orobora.com
Key Personnel
Pres: Steve O'Keefe *E-mail:* steve.okeefe@orobora.com
Founded: 1994
Provides online public relations for the publishing trade.
Membership(s): Independent Book Publishers Association (IBPA); International Association of Online Communicators (IAOC); Public Relations Society of America Inc (PRSA)

Paz & Associates: The Bookstore Training & Consulting Group
1417 Sadler Rd, No 274, Fernandina Beach, FL 32034
Tel: 904-277-2664 *Fax:* 904-261-6742
Web Site: www.pazbookbiz.com
Key Personnel
Owner & Partner: Donna Paz Kaufman
E-mail: dpaz@pazbookbiz.com
Partner: Mark Kaufman *E-mail:* mkaufman@pazbookbiz.com
Founded: 1992

Bookstore consultants with specialties in store design, inventory selection, marketing, staff training & business management. Also used by public libraries for design & marketing.
Membership(s): American Booksellers Association (ABA); American Institute of Architects (AIA); Association of Booksellers for Children; Women's National Book Association (WNBA)

Law Office of Robert G Pimm Attorney at Law
2977 Ygnacio Valley Rd, Suite 265, Walnut Creek, CA 94598-3535
Tel: 925-374-1442 *Fax:* 925-281-2888
Web Site: www.rgpimm.com
Key Personnel
Literary Attorney: Robert G Pimm *E-mail:* bob@rgpimm.com
Founded: 2001
Represents authors & publishers, artists & illustrators, agents, printers & other participants in the book industry. Areas of practice include copyright, trademark, trade secrets & contract negotiations in the book industry. Also, formation of book industry corporations & advising corporate directors & officers.
Membership(s): American Bar Association (ABA); Authors Alliance; The Authors Guild; California Lawyers for the Arts; National Writers Union (NWU)

Promote A Book Inc
1753 Rylie Ann Circle, South Jordan, UT 84095
Tel: 512-586-6073
Web Site: promoteabook.com
Key Personnel
Owner: Michael R Drew *E-mail:* michael@promoteabook.com
Book marketing, author video bio's, book video trailers, broadcast & syndication service.

Generosa Gina Protano Publishing, see GGP Publishing Inc

ps ink LLC
857 Post Rd, Suite 367, Fairfield, CT 06824
Tel: 203-331-6942
Web Site: www.ps-ink.com
Key Personnel
Mng Partner: Patty Sullivan *E-mail:* patty@ps-ink.com
Founded: 1999
Publishing solutions company offering consulting services, licensing, property development & book/series packaging. Client base includes educational & trade publishers, toy manufacturers, authors, illustrators & photographers as well as companies representing children's products & programs. Our expertise has its roots in the development of underlying intellectual properties with a focus on identifying ways to leverage those properties across multiple formats in print publishing, digital expression, licensed categories & other media.

Publishing Management Associates Inc
129 S Phelps Ave, Suite 312, Rockford, IL 61108
Tel: 815-398-8569 *Fax:* 815-398-8579
E-mail: pma@pma-inc.net
Web Site: www.pma-inc.net
Key Personnel
Pres: Richard A Vaughan
Founded: 1989
Publishing consulting firm providing marketing, advertising & business management services for a wide range of publications.

Purplegator
Formerly ATS Mobile
1055 Westlakes Dr, Berwyn, PA 19312
Tel: 610-688-6000 *Toll Free Tel:* 888-76-GATOR (764-2867)
Web Site: www.purplegator.com
Key Personnel
COO: Martin Birdsall
CFO: Emilie Smeltz
Pres & Dir, Mktg & Sales: Bob Bentz *Tel:* 610-513-0900 *E-mail:* bob@purplegator.com
Mktg Dir: Josh Moyer
Founded: 1989
Marketing services.

R J Promotions & Advertising
120 Holton Ave S, Hamilton, ON L8M 2L5, Canada
Tel: 905-548-0389
E-mail: rjpromo@cogeco.ca
Key Personnel
Mktg Consultant: Jacqueline Rotterman
Founded: 1984
Marketing & media plans, budgets; creative writing, art & logo designs; computer graphic design & production (Mac).

Nina J Reznick Esq
28 E Tenth St, New York, NY 10003
Tel: 212-473-6279
E-mail: ninarezesq@icloud.com
Founded: 1980
All legal work for writers & producers in all areas of the entertainment business with special emphasis on publishing, theatre, film & TV.
Membership(s): American Bar Association (ABA); National Lawyers Guild (NLG); New York State Bar Association

Judith Riven Literary Agent LLC
250 W 16 St, Suite 4F, New York, NY 10011
Key Personnel
Owner & Pres: Judith Riven
Founded: 1993
Advising & consulting writers on how to develop & strategize their careers.

Stephanie Rogers & Associates
Affiliate of Philipico Pictures Co
8737 Carlitas Joy Ct, Las Vegas, NV 89117
Tel: 702-255-9999
E-mail: sjrlion@aol.com; write2wow@aol.com
Web Site: www.write2wow.com
Key Personnel
Owner: Stephanie Rogers
Founded: 1980
Represent writers in film & TV. No unsol mss, screenplays or teleplays (must have industry referral/recommendation). We do not represent mss to publishers, only published books, screenplays & teleplays to the film & television trade along with writers for hire. No reading fee. Will accept query letters with a SASE & e-mail queries (without attachments).

Sherri Rosen Publicity Intl NYC
454 Manhattan Ave, Suite 3-J, New York, NY 10026
Tel: 917-699-1284
E-mail: sherri@sherrirosen.com
Web Site: www.sherrirosen.com
Key Personnel
Pres: Sherri Rosen
Founded: 1999
Publicity firm which gives a powerful voice to people doing great things in the world. Specialize in literary with emphasis on sex, spirituality & relationships, multicultural publicity, science fiction, Alzheimers', caregiving, foster care, sexual abuse & publicizing published or self-published books. Designs specific media lists for genre of clients. Created her own award-winning ebook *Give Me Your Truth* & author of award-winning *Publicity from the Trenches: For Published & Self-Published Authors*.
Membership(s): National Writers Union (NWU)

& SUPPLIERS / CONSULTANTS

Schnoll Media Consulting
1253 Springfield Ave, PMB 338, New Providence, NJ 07974
Tel: 908-522-3190 *Fax:* 908-273-2667
Web Site: www.schnollconsult.com
Key Personnel
Mng Dir: Steven Schnoll *E-mail:* steven@schnollconsult.com
Founded: 1998
Marketing technology issues, workflow, process control, printing, manufacturing & production.
Membership(s): Electronic Document Systems Foundation (EDSF); Epicomm; PRINTING United Alliance

Bettina Schrewe Literary Scouting
101 Fifth Ave, Suite 11B, New York, NY 10003
Tel: 212-414-2515
Web Site: www.bschrewe.com
Key Personnel
Scout: Amy Gordon *E-mail:* agordon@bschrewe.com; Alexandra Heimann *E-mail:* aheimann@bschrewe.com; Bettina Schrewe *E-mail:* bschrewe@bschrewe.com; Taylor Pisanie *E-mail:* tpisanie@bschrewe.com

Scribe Inc
765 S Front St, Philadelphia, PA 19147
Tel: 215-336-5094; 215-336-5095
E-mail: contact@scribenet.com
Web Site: www.scribenet.com
Key Personnel
Pres: David Alan Rech *Tel:* 215-336-5094 ext 105 *E-mail:* drech@scribenet.com
Founded: 1993
A full range of publishing services, including OCR/data conversion, editing, proofreading, design, typesetting, & ebook creation, with expertise in XML, Well-Formed Document Workflow, & staff training. Also helps publishers with accessible, multipurpose publishing.
Branch Office(s)
3758 SW 30 Ave, Fort Lauderdale, FL 33312

SDP Publishing Solutions LLC
36 Captain's Way, East Bridgewater, MA 02333
Tel: 617-775-0656
E-mail: info@sdppublishing.com
Web Site: sdppublishing.com
Key Personnel
Publr & Publg Consultant: Lisa Akoury-Ross *E-mail:* lross@sdppublishing.com
Founded: 2009
Offer consulting services in all related publishing aspects such as ms review of all genres. Offer editorial & ghostwriting services, international rights, custom book covers, interior design, marketing & distribution services. Offer publishing solutions for authors worldwide.
Membership(s): Independent Book Publishers Association (IBPA)

Jane Starr Literary Scouts
1350 Avenue of the Americas, Suite 1205, New York, NY 10019
Tel: 212-421-0777
E-mail: jane@janestarr.com
Key Personnel
Owner: Jane Starr
Jr Scout: Catalina Carret Aguero
Founded: 1995
An international scouting agency for: Allen & Unwin (Australia), Bastei Luebbe/Eichborn (Germany), Japan UNI Agency (Japan), Editions Michel Lafon (France), Newton Compton Editori (Italy), Vulkan Publishing (Serbia), Uitgeverij De Fontein (Netherlands), Vigmostad & Bjoerke (Norway), Atlantic Books (UK).

Story Monsters LLC
4696 W Tyson St, Chandler, AZ 85226-2903
Tel: 480-940-8182 *Fax:* 480-940-8787
Web Site: www.StoryMonsters.com; www.StoryMonstersInk.com; www.AuthorBookings.com; www.StoryMonstersBookAwards.com
Key Personnel
Pres: Linda F Radke *E-mail:* Linda@StoryMonsters.com
Founded: 1985
Offers consulting in book production, marketing, publicity, distribution, book trailers, social media, web sites & book ms evaluations. Story Monsters has been producing & marketing children's books since 1985 & has helped numerous authors achieve success. Story Monsters can help you avoid the inevitable pitfalls that frustrate even experienced writers.
Membership(s): Better Business Bureau (BBB); The Children's Book Council (CBC); Independent Book Publishers Association (IBPA); National Federation of Press Women

Story Monsters Press, see Story Monsters LLC

Tanenbaum International Literary Agency Ltd (TILA)
1035 Fifth Ave, Suite 15D, New York, NY 10028
Tel: 212-371-4120 *Fax:* 212-988-0457
E-mail: hello@tanenbauminternational.com
Web Site: tanenbauminternational.com
Key Personnel
Owner & Pres: Ann Tanenbaum
Ed/Assoc Agent: Kate Ellsworth
Agency Asst: Mary Noorlander
Founded: 1980
Provide comprehensive editorial guidance to help polish & refine work in-house & connect authors with trusted outside designers, illustrators & editors.

To Press & Beyond
7507 Summersun Dr, Browns Summit, NC 27214
Tel: 805-570-8275
E-mail: info@topressandbeyond.com
Web Site: www.topressandbeyond.com
Key Personnel
Pres, Proj Ed & Prodn Coord: Gail M Kearns *E-mail:* gail@topressandbeyond.com
Art Dir & Proj Mgr: Penelope C Paine *E-mail:* pennypaine@aol.com
Copy Ed & Proofreader: Isabella Piestrzynska
Founded: 2001
Book publishing consulting & support services. We shepherd your print +/or ebook through writing, editing, design & layout, printing, distribution, sales & marketing & promotion, both in trade & niche markets & on the Web. We have worked with over 400 authors & independent publishers worldwide. You can contact Gail Kearns for a half-hour gratis phone consult about your project.
Membership(s): The Association of Publishers for Special Sales (APSS); Independent Book Publishers Association (IBPA)

VillageSoup®
Unit of MaineStay Media
One Printinghouse Sq, Ellsworth, ME 04605
Tel: 207-594-4401
E-mail: info@villagesoup.com
Web Site: www.villagesoup.com; mainestaymedia.com
Key Personnel
Publr: Chris Crockett
Community Internet station & community newspaper; marketing, promotion & publishing consultants; combined editorial & visual services.

Warwick Associates
18340 Sonoma Hwy, Sonoma, CA 95476
Tel: 707-939-9212 *Fax:* 707-938-3515
E-mail: warwick@vom.com
Web Site: www.warwickassociates.com
Key Personnel
Pres: Simon Warwick-Smith
Founded: 1985
Consulting on all aspects of publishing, from sales & distribution, to marketing & publicity. Steps include creating a winning ms, cover & design, getting printed successfully, getting excellent distribution, the launch & managing sales (trade, special sales, foreign rights). Also offers guidance on reviews, interviews, press materials, getting national radio & TV for publishers & authors. One-stop shop for creating & implementing successful publishing strategies. Specializations include spirituality, business, how-to, nonfiction, celebrity autobiographies, sports & general trade. Expert witness on all aspects of publishing.

Weidner Communications International Inc
1468 Alton Way, Downingtown, PA 19335
Tel: 610-486-6525 *Fax:* 610-486-6527
Web Site: www.weidcom.com
Key Personnel
Pres: Matthew T Weidner *E-mail:* mtw@weidcom.com
Founded: 1982
Publisher's representatives for trade & professional journals.
Membership(s): NAPR

Fred Weidner & Daughter Printers
99 Hudson St, 5th fl, New York, NY 10013
Tel: 646-706-5180
E-mail: info@fwdprinters.com
Web Site: www.fwdprinters.com
Key Personnel
Pres: Cynthia Weidner *E-mail:* cynthia@fwdprinters.com
Creative Dir: Carol Mittelsdorf *E-mail:* carol@fwdprinters.com
Founded: 1860
Incorporated in 1860 in the city of Brooklyn, the Weidner family has, for five generations, provided complete printing & production services for small to medium volume buyers of printing who wish to have all their graphic needs conveniently met by one supplier.
Design, copy-editing & all types of printing, binding & die-cutting techniques can be readily utilized for everything from business cards to large runs of 4-color brochures & catalogues. Economy of scale is applied on continuous or repeated work.
Our unique & long-time trade arrangement with specialized firms in all parts of the country allow us to be competitive with the finest printing firms in the production of museum quality brochures & posters.
Call us & discover how the cumulative experience of a century & a half can benefit you.

Westwind Communications
1310 Maple St, Plymouth, MI 48170
Tel: 734-667-2090
Web Site: www.book-marketing-expert.com
Key Personnel
Pres: Scott Lorenz *E-mail:* scottlorenz@westwindcos.com
Founded: 1981
Book marketing, publicity & promotion.

Wheatmark Inc
2030 E Speedway Blvd, Suite 106, Tucson, AZ 85719
Tel: 520-798-0888 *Toll Free Tel:* 888-934-0888 *Fax:* 520-798-3394
E-mail: info@wheatmark.com
Web Site: www.wheatmark.com
Key Personnel
Pres & Founder: Sam Henrie *E-mail:* sam@wheatmark.com
VP: Atilla Vekony *E-mail:* atilla@wheatmark.com

CONSULTANTS

Dir, Mktg: Grael Norton *E-mail:* grael@wheatmark.com
Founded: 1999
Provider of editing, publishing & online marketing services to authors.
Membership(s): Independent Book Publishers Association (IBPA)

write 2 wow, see Stephanie Rogers & Associates

The Writers Lifeline Inc, a Story Merchant company
Subsidiary of Story Merchant
400 S Burnside Ave, Suite 11B, Los Angeles, CA 90036
Tel: 310-968-1607
Web Site: www.thewriterslifeline.com
Key Personnel
CEO: Kenneth Atchity, PhD *E-mail:* kja@thewriterslifeline.com
Mgr: Samantha Skelton *E-mail:* sam@storymerchant.com
Founded: 1996
A full service editorial company, providing nonfiction book writers, business, professional, technical & screenwriters with assistance in storytelling, mentoring, perfecting their style & craft, style-structure-concept-line editing, ghost-writing, publishing, consulting, development, translation, advertising & promotion, printing & self-publishing, distribution & research. Branch office in New York.
Sister companies: Atchity Productions; Story Merchant; Story Merchant Books.
Membership(s): The Authors Guild; National Academy of Television Arts & Sciences (NATAS); PEN America; Women in Film (WIF); Writers Guild of America (WGA)

Writer's Relief, Inc
18766 John J Williams Hwy, Unit 4, Box 335, Rehoboth Beach, DE 19971
Toll Free Tel: 866-405-3003 *Fax:* 201-641-1253
E-mail: info@writersrelief.com
Web Site: www.WritersRelief.com
Key Personnel
Pres: Ronnie L Smith *E-mail:* ronnie@wrelief.com
Founded: 1994
Free submission leads/guidelines. Cover/query letters. Join 60,000+ writers subscribing to *Submit Write Now!* Best for poetry, short prose, book projects.

Book Producers

Book producers (also called book packagers) provide publishers with complete book preparation services from outline to final book, sometimes including marketing and distribution services as well. Some of the book producers listed here are also book publishers and as such are listed in **U.S. Publishers** or **Canadian Publishers** (both in volume 1). For related listings, see **Editorial Services** (volume 1), **Consultants, Artists & Art Services, Complete Book Manufacturers** and **Prepress Services**.

Agincourt Press
25 Main St, Chatham, NY 12037
Tel: 518-392-2898
E-mail: aginpress@aol.com
Key Personnel
Pres: David Rubel
Founded: 1990
Book packager, adult & children's.
Number of titles produced annually: 1 Print

AGS BookWorks
Division of American Graphic Systems
PO Box 460313, San Francisco, CA 94146-0313
Tel: 415-285-8799
Web Site: www.agsbookworks.com
Key Personnel
Pres: Bill Yenne *E-mail:* bill_yenne@sbcglobal.net
Founded: 1981
High quality illustrated books for international trade publishers on subjects such as history, biography, natural history, transportation & pop culture. Company provides full service book production services & licenses its vast library of verbal & pictorial content to print & electronic publishers.
Number of titles produced annually: 1 Print

American BookWorks Corp
309 Florida Hill Rd, Ridgefield, CT 06877
Mailing Address: PO Box 294, Georgetown, CT 06829
Tel: 203-431-9620 *Fax:* 203-244-9522 (orders)
E-mail: info@abwcorporation.com
Key Personnel
Pres: Fred N Grayson
EVP & Gen Coun: Valerie Levy-Grayson
Founded: 1976
Package general, self-help & educational paperbacks, trade & mass market reference books, premiums, textbook supplements & ancillaries, review books (K-Graduate) & test preparation.
Number of titles produced annually: 10 Print

Aptara Inc
Subsidiary of iEnergizer
2901 Telestar Ct, Suite 522, Falls Church, VA 22042
Tel: 703-352-0001
E-mail: moreinfo@aptaracorp.com
Web Site: www.aptaracorp.com
Key Personnel
Pres: Samir Kakar
EVP, Fin & Cont: Prashant Kapoor
SVP, Busn & Contact Ctr Opers: Ashish Madan
Busn Devt: Michael Scott *E-mail:* michael.scott@aptaracorp.com
Founded: 1988
Liaison for complete or any combination of production services, ranging from simple 1-color to complex 4-color projects. Copy-editing.
Number of titles produced annually: 6 Print
Branch Office(s)
150 California St, Suite 301, Newton, MA 02458
Tel: 617-423-7755
11009 Metric Blvd, Bldg J, Suite 150, Austin, TX 78758 *Tel:* 512-876-5997
299 Elizabeth St, Level 1, Sydney 2000, Australia
Tel: (02) 8251 0070
Tower 1 & 2, 8/100, Acharya Thulasi Rd (Shandy Rd), Pallavaram, Chennai 600 043, India
Tel: (044) 22640676
No 2310, Doon Express Business Park, Saharanpur Rd, Bldg 2000, Dehradun 248 002, India
Tel: (0135) 2644055
7B, Leela Infopark, Technopark, Trivandrum, Kerala 695 581, India *Tel:* (047) 14063370
A-37, Sector-60, Noida 201 301, India
Tel: (0120) 7182424
D-10, Sector-2, Noida 201 301, India *Tel:* (0120) 24423678
SEZ Bldg 4A, 1st fl, S P Infocity, Pune Saswad Rd, Phursungi, Pune 412 308, India *Tel:* (020) 66728000

Arbor Books
244 Madison Ave, Box 254, New York, NY 10016
Tel: 212-956-0950 *Toll Free Tel:* 877-822-2500
Fax: 914-401-9385
E-mail: info@arborbooks.com; editorial@arborbooks.net
Web Site: www.arborbooks.com
Key Personnel
Owner: Joel Hochman *Tel:* 877-822-2502 *E-mail:* arborbooksjoel@aol.com;
Larry Leichman *Tel:* 877-822-2504
E-mail: arborbookslarry@aol.com
Mktg Dir: Olga Vladi *E-mail:* floatinggal1@aol.com
Founded: 1992
Full service writing services & book production. Specialize in ghostwriting, editing, proofreading, developmental editing, promotional copy, cover design, printing, publishing & marketing. Arbor Books works for both corporations (business books, corporate histories, CEO bios) & individuals (novels - all genres: general fiction, young adult, mystery, crime, thrillers, horror, romance, science fiction, fantasy, litrpg, graphic novels, comic books, etc), memoirs, children's books, business books, how-to, inspiration, religious, Christian, Jewish, Islamic, Hindu, self-help, history, politics, humor, gay, etc. Services include supervised & insured ghostwriting, copy-editing, translation, proofreading, design (even the most complex, including model shoots, illustrations, photo reconstruction & manipulation, book jacket design, album cover & magazine design), word processing (including transcription), scanning, layout, typesetting, obtaining registrations & endorsements, B&W & 4-color printing, marketing, promotion & advertising. Creates logos, letterheads, annual reports, posters & promotional flyers. Self-publishing services include: Amazon book marketing, press kits, press releases, booking TV & radio programs, speaking tours & book signings & negotiating with producers & agents.
Number of titles produced annually: 100 Print

Arbor Services, see Arbor Books

Archetype Press Inc
11272 N Meadow Sage Dr, Oro Valley, AZ 85737-7250
Tel: 302-249-5879
E-mail: archepress@aol.com
Key Personnel
Pres: Diane Maddex *E-mail:* dimaddex@gmail.com
Founded: 1990
Complete editorial services to bound books. Produces illustrated books, calendars & sidelines on lifestyles, architecture, design, the arts & American culture for trade publishers, museums, hotels & associations.
Number of titles produced annually: 5 Print

Arrow Graphics Inc
PO Box 380291, Cambridge, MA 02238
E-mail: info@arrow1.com
Web Site: www.arrow1.com
Key Personnel
Pres: Alvart Badalian
Sr Graphic/Pubn Designer: Aramais Andonian
Founded: 1988
Complete book production services with state-of-the-art electronic design & publishing capabilities: copy-editing; indexing; typesetting & page composition; typography; design & art direction from concept to finished product; printing; consultation; project management. Novels, poetry, monographs, self-help, how-to, guides, ebooks & children's picture books. From ms to camera-ready to bound book, serving the publishing industry & self-publishing community. Call or write for free information, or visit our web site.
Number of titles produced annually: 25 Print

Balfour Commercial Printing
Formerly Taylor Specialty Books
Division of Balfour/Taylor
225 E John Carpenter Fwy, Tower 2, Suite 400, Irving, TX 75062
Tel: 214-819-8588 (cust serv)
E-mail: printing@balfour.com
Web Site: commercial-printing.balfour.com
Key Personnel
Acct Exec: Julie Kacala *E-mail:* julie.kacala@balfour.com
Founded: 1939
Full service book & catalog manufacturer specializing in 4-color case bound books: juvenile, medical, trade, coffee table, oblong trims & 4-color catalogs. Full in-house bindery & case stamping/embossing capabilities with a "Can Do!" attitude.

BookComp Inc
6124 Belmont Ave NE, Belmont, MI 49306
Tel: 616-774-9700
E-mail: production@bookcomp.com
Web Site: www.bookcomp.com
Key Personnel
Pres: Jon F Dertien *E-mail:* jd@bookcomp.com
Prodn Mgr: JoAnn Sikkes
Founded: 1989
A privately owned company located in the greater Grand Rapids, MI area providing publishing service solutions for publishers of trade, professional & scholarly, scientific & university presses on a global scale.
Number of titles produced annually: 325 Print

BOOK PRODUCERS

Recent Title(s): *The Best Writing on Mathematics* (Princeton University Press); *Conflict in the Middle East* (ABC-CLIO); *The Pearl Harbor Secret* (ABC-CLIO); *Unmanning: How Humans, Machines and Media Perform Drone Warfare* (Rutgers University Press)
Membership(s): American Association of University Presses (AAUP)

Bowen Books LLC
971 First Ave, New York, NY 10022
Tel: 212-421-5797
E-mail: bowenbooks@aol.com
Key Personnel
Pres: Barbara Bowen
Founded: 1989
Books that provide insight into human potential, awareness & all areas of life improvement.

CG Book Printers
Division of Corporate Graphics Commercial (CGC)
1750 Northway Dr, North Mankato, MN 56003
Tel: 507-388-3300 *Toll Free Tel:* 800-729-7575
Fax: 507-386-6350
E-mail: cgbooks@corpgraph.com
Web Site: www.corpgraph.com
Key Personnel
Pres: Dan Kvasnicka *Tel:* 507-386-6340
Fax: 507-344-5548 *E-mail:* dekvasnicka@corpgraph.com
Sales Exec, Book Mfg Sales: Mike Schmitt
Tel: 507-386-6349 *E-mail:* mjschmitt@corpgraph.com
Founded: 1989
CG Book Printers currently provides book manufacturing services for publishers who sell product to school library & trade markets. In addition, we offer fulfillment services for those publishers wishing to maintain their inventories in the same location where their books are manufactured.
We bind books in hard case & paperback formats. We use Smyth sewn, side sew & adhesive bound for hard case trade or library bound books & section sew, or adhesive bind for paperback books.

Concord Editorial & Design LLC
9450 SW Gemini Dr, Suite 68669, Beaverton, OR 97008
Tel: 616-827-7537 *Fax:* 616-825-6048
E-mail: info@concordeditorial.com
Web Site: www.concordeditorial.com
Key Personnel
Pres & Proj Dir: David Fideler, PhD
Founded: 2005
Offers complete design, book production, prepress & editorial services for publishers at extremely competitive rates with over 25 years of experience. Produce both general trade, academic & highly illustrated titles through high-resolution, press-ready Adobe Acrobat files. We offer fast turnaround, free FTP sites for clients & guarantee total customer satisfaction.
Number of titles produced annually: 30 Print

Corporate Graphics Book Printers, see CG Book Printers

Dell Magazines
Division of Penny Publications LLC
6 Prowitt St, Norwalk, CT 06855
Tel: 203-866-6688 *Toll Free Tel:* 800-220-7443 (corp sales) *Fax:* 203-854-5962 (pubns)
E-mail: customerservice@pennypublications.com
Web Site: www.pennydellpuzzles.com
Key Personnel
Pres: Peter Kanter
SVP, Edit & Prod Devt: Christine Begley
SVP: Bruce W Sherbow

Dir, Mktg, E-Commerce & Brand Licensing: Abigail Browning
Founded: 1931
Packaging puzzle books compiled from 26 puzzle magazines & science fiction & mystery anthologies based on stories from 4 fiction magazines: *Alfred Hitchcock Mystery Magazine, Ellery Queen's Mystery Magazine, Asimov's Science Fiction, Analog Science Fiction & Fact*. Provide book packaging services for mass market paperbacks, promotional & trade books.
Number of titles produced annually: 6 Print

Desktop Miracles Inc
112 S Main St, Suite 294, Stowe, VT 05672
Tel: 802-253-7900 *Toll Free Fax:* 888-293-2676
E-mail: info@desktopmiracles.com
Web Site: www.desktopmiracles.com
Key Personnel
Pres & CEO: Barry T Kerrigan *E-mail:* barry@desktopmiracles.com
VP: Virginia Kerrigan *E-mail:* virginia@desktopmiracles.com
Founded: 1994
Full service book design & production studio for publishers large & small. Turnkey services from concept to editorial to design to production.

diacriTech Inc
4 S Market St, 4th fl, Boston, MA 02109
Tel: 617-600-3366 *Fax:* 617-848-2938
Web Site: www.diacritech.com
Key Personnel
EVP: Madhu Rajamani *E-mail:* madhu@diacritech.com
Dir, Prodn & Edit Servs: Maureen Ross *E-mail:* m.ross@diacritech.com
Founded: 1997
Specialize in meeting educational publishing needs. Full service development includes project management, editorial & content development services, print & digital production, art & prepress services. In-house staff of over 800 are experienced with all phases & disciplines of K-12, college & STM. Facilities in Boston, MA, Manchester, NH & in Chennai, Madurai & Kottayam, India.

Eriako Associates
1380 Morningside Way, Venice, CA 90291
Tel: 310-392-6537 *Fax:* 310-392-6537
E-mail: eriakoassociates@gmail.com
Key Personnel
CEO: Erika Fabian
Founded: 1972
Create & package illustrated books to invite investment to a country or profile a company, worldwide; travel, photography oriented guides & multicultural children's books based on the culture & customs of a variety of exotic countries. Package books of general interest & self-help.
Recent Title(s): *Driver to Sky*; *Liars' Paradise*; *Pro Ways to Great Photos*; *Stolen Minds* (Eriako Associates); *The Travel Photographer's Handbook* (Eriako Associates)
Membership(s): American Society of Media Photographers (ASMP); Independent Writers of Southern California; Publishers Association of Los Angeles

f-stop Fitzgerald Inc
88 James St, Rosendale, NY 12472
E-mail: fstopf@gmail.com
Key Personnel
CEO: Richard Minissali

SERVICES

Adult trade, travel, reference, sports, biography & photography.
Membership(s): American Book Producers Association (ABPA); Professional Photographers of America (PPA)

Linda Fairchild & Company LLC
101 Lucas Valley Rd, Suite 363, San Rafael, CA 94903
Tel: 415-336-6407
Web Site: www.lindafairchild.com
Key Personnel
Agent & Founder: Linda Fairchild *E-mail:* linda@lindafairchild.com
Founded: 2002
Recent Title(s): *Left Behind* (Fine Arts Press); *Primal Sound* (Fine Arts Press)

Figaro
PO Box 848, Sharon, CT 06069
Tel: 860-248-8989; 860-364-0834
E-mail: design@figro.com
Web Site: www.figro.com
Key Personnel
Co-Pres & Creative Dir: Walter Schwarz
Co-Pres: Linda Swenson *E-mail:* ls@figro.com
Copy-editing, design, page make-up, illustration & prepress.
Number of titles produced annually: 20 Print

Focus Strategic Communications Inc
15 Hunter Way, Brantford, ON N3T 6S3, Canada
Tel: 519-756-3265
E-mail: info@focussc.com
Web Site: www.focussc.com
Key Personnel
Dir: Adrianna Edwards *E-mail:* aedwards@focussc.com; Ron Edwards *E-mail:* redwards@focussc.com
Founded: 1988
North American full service book packaging firm providing complete book development & production, from original concept to finished product, both print & digital. Specialize in children's nonfiction books for the trade, library & classroom markets as well as educational materials such as K-12 classroom books & teacher resources. Innovative in assembling tailored & creative teams of experts to develop & produce superior products. Excellent track record & reputation.
Number of titles produced annually: 50 Print

G & H Soho Inc
413 Market St, Elmwood Park, NJ 07407
Tel: 201-216-9400 *Fax:* 201-216-1778
E-mail: print@ghsoho.com
Web Site: www.ghsoho.com
Key Personnel
Pres: Gerry Burstein
Prodn Mgr: Jason Burstein
Founded: 1985
Complete service, beginning with development through copy-editing & production editing. Text & cover design. Production service through bound books. Specialize in short run, on-demand book manufacturing with variable data.
Number of titles produced annually: 10 Print
Membership(s): Association of Graphic Communications; Digital Printing Council; PRINTING United Alliance

Garcia Publishing Services
830 Russell Rd, No 8, DeKalb, IL 60115
Tel: 815-338-5512
E-mail: garpubserv@aol.com
Key Personnel
Owner: Robert T Garcia
CFO: Nancy Garcia
Founded: 1991

Provides editorial, consulting & design services to presses throughout the US. Design books, magazines, advertising, catalogs, direct-mail pieces, flyers, corporate identity, etc. Manages the work of several freelance artists & designers during the course of any given year.
Number of titles produced annually: 12 Print
Recent Title(s): *Weinberg Tales* (American Fantasy Press)

GEX Inc
80 Conley's Grove Rd, Derry, NH 03038
Mailing Address: PO Box 613, Atkinson, NH 03811
Tel: 603-870-9292
Web Site: www.gexinc.com
Key Personnel
Pres: Gary Russell *E-mail:* gary.russell@gexinc.com
VP: Jim LaPierre
Founded: 1986
Full service educational publishing services company, providing content development, digital & production services to the world's foremost publishers. With over 30 years of experience, GEX designs courses, creates engaging content & provides services that deliver content to a variety of media with digital & print solutions.

GGP Publishing Inc
Larchmont, NY 10538
Tel: 914-834-8896 *Fax:* 914-834-7566
Web Site: www.GGPPublishing.com
Key Personnel
Founder, Owner & Dir: Generosa Gina Protano *E-mail:* GGProtano@GGPPublishing.com
Founded: 1991
Full service development house & packaging firm offering services from concept to finished electronic files/bound books to online distribution or for any one step of this publishing process. Specialize in educational publishing from K-12 to college/university to adult education. Have a niche in the writing, development, editing & production up to finished electronic files/bound books of textbooks & trade books for the study of foreign languages such as French, German, Italian, Latin, Portuguese & Spanish. Also translates complete/partial programs or cluster of books from English into any of these languages or from any of these languages into English, edit the translation for publication & set the edited translation into book form up to finished electronic files/bound books. Develop, edit, do art/design & production of different genres both for publishing houses as well as individuals who wish to self-publish. Has produced novels, memoirs & books in the fields of religion, psychology & culinary arts among others. Special interest in memoirs. Acts as literary agents & foreign publisher representatives.

P M Gordon Associates Inc
Affiliate of New Door Books
2115 Wallace St, Philadelphia, PA 19130
Tel: 215-769-2525
Web Site: www.pmgordonassociates.com
Key Personnel
Pres: Peggy M Gordon
VP: Douglas C Gordon *E-mail:* doug@newdoorbooks.com
Founded: 1982
Complete book production from copy-editing & design through bound books. Ms development & writing services also available.
Number of titles produced annually: 15 Print
Recent Title(s): *Foundations of International Macroeconomics* (MIT Press); *Practical Pulmonary Pathology* (Elsevier); *Right Off the Bat: Baseball, Cricket, Literature & Life* (Paul Dry Books)

Greenleaf Book Group LLC
PO Box 91869, Austin, TX 78709
Tel: 512-891-6100 *Fax:* 512-891-6150
E-mail: contact@greenleafbookgroup.com; orders@greenleafbookgroup.com; foreignrights@greenleafbookgroup.com; media@greenleafbookgroup.com
Web Site: greenleafbookgroup.com
Key Personnel
Founder: Clint Greenleaf
CEO: Tanya Hall
CFO: Brian Viktorin
COO: Carrie Jones
Art Dir: Neil Gonzalez
Dir, Consulting & Sales: Justin Branch
Prodn Mgr: Jen Glynn
Proj Mgr: Adrianna Hernandez; Leah Pierre; Benito Salazar; Brian Welch
Founded: 1997
Publisher & distributor specializing in the development of independent authors & the growth of small presses. Our publishing model was designed to support independent authors & allow writers to retain the rights to their work & still compete with major publishing houses. We also distribute select titles from small & independent publishers to major trade outlets, including bookstores, libraries & airport retailers. We serve the small & independent publishing community by offering industry guidance, business development, production, distribution & marketing services.
Number of titles produced annually: 100 Print
Membership(s): The American Library Association (ALA); Association of American Publishers (AAP); BookSense Publisher Partner; Independent Book Publishers Association (IBPA); National Speakers Association (NSA)

Greenleaf Book Group Press, see Greenleaf Book Group LLC

Integra Software Services Inc
Division of Integra Software Services Pvt Ltd
2021 Midwest Rd, Suite 200, Oak Brook, IL 60523
Web Site: www.integranxt.com
Founded: 1991
Project management, development & production support for book publishers. Full range of publishing services, including developmental editing, design, rights & permissions, photo research, copy-editing & indexing, proofreading, language polishing, typesetting, XML & conversion, illustrations & artwork, ebooks & digital services. Specialty areas are business & economics, computer science, mathematics, science, medical, English, education & history texts.
Number of titles produced annually: 150 Print
Membership(s): Chicago Women in Publishing

Jenkins Group Inc
1129 Woodmere Ave, Suite B, Traverse City, MI 49686
Tel: 231-933-0445; 213-883-5365
E-mail: info@jenkinsgroupinc.com
Web Site: www.jenkinsgroupinc.com
Key Personnel
CEO: Jerrold R Jenkins *Tel:* 231-933-0445 ext 1008 *E-mail:* jrj@jenkinsgroupinc.com
Pres & COO: James Kalajian *Tel:* 231-933-0445 ext 1006 *E-mail:* jjk@jenkinsgroupinc.com
Ed, Independent Publisher Online: Jim Barnes *E-mail:* editor@independentpublisher.com
Book Prodn Mgr: Leah Nicholson *Tel:* 231-933-0445 ext 1015 *E-mail:* lnicholson@jenkinsgroupinc.com
Founded: 1988
Provides complete project management, development & production services for authors, corporations, associations & foundations. We offer a comprehensive range of production & editorial services that include art & text design, ghostwriting, copy-editing, proofreading, research, layout, composition, printing & packaging. Audiobook & ebook production. Post-production services include fulfillment, distributing, marketing, publicity, consultation & an extensive special market sales program.
Number of titles produced annually: 60 Print

Lachina Creative
Formerly Lachina Precision Graphics Services
3693 Green Rd, Cleveland, OH 44122
Tel: 216-292-7959
E-mail: info@lachina.com
Web Site: www.lachina.com
Key Personnel
Pres: Jeff Lachina *E-mail:* jlachina@lachina.com
Dir, Prodn Servs: Whitney Philipp *E-mail:* wphilipp@lachina.com
Dir, Proj Mgmt Off: Shawn Vazinski *E-mail:* svazinski@lachina.com
Founded: 1978
Full service creative & business consulting agency that helps companies tackle creative, brand & business dilemmas with the right tools, methods & technology.
Number of titles produced annually: 50 Print

Lachina Precision Graphics Services, see Lachina Creative

Larson Texts Inc
1762 Norcross Rd, Erie, PA 16510
Tel: 814-824-6365 *Toll Free Tel:* 800-530-2355
Fax: 814-824-6377
Web Site: www.larsontexts.com
Key Personnel
CEO: Matt Totske
IT Mgr: Kathleen Williams
Sr Researcher: Tim Larson
Founded: 1983
Author & develop educational materials in print, interactive multimedia & web formats for the elementary through college markets with a primary focus on mathematical instruction.
Number of titles produced annually: 5 Print

The Learning Source Ltd
644 Tenth St, Brooklyn, NY 11215
E-mail: info@learningsourceltd.com
Web Site: www.learningsourceltd.com
Key Personnel
Dir: Gary Davis; Wendy Davis
Mng Ed: Brian Ableman
Founded: 1986
Provides a full range of book-producing activities from concept through ms, art & design to film & bound book. Specialty areas include classroom materials & trade reference.
Number of titles produced annually: 150 Print
Membership(s): ASCD; International Literacy Association (ILA); National Council for the Social Studies (NCSS); National Council of Teachers of English (NCTE); National Council of Teachers of Mathematics (NCTM)

The Philip Lief Group Inc (PLG)
2976 Pleasant Ridge Rd, Wingdale, NY 12594
Tel: 609-430-1000 *Fax:* 845-724-7139
E-mail: info@plg.us.com
Web Site: plg.us.com
Key Personnel
Pres: Philip Lief *Tel:* 609-430-1000 ext 108 *E-mail:* pl@plg.us.com
VP & Creative Dir: Sandy Davis *Tel:* 609-430-1000 ext 142
Admin: Megan Misiewicz *Tel:* 609-430-1000 ext 109 *E-mail:* megan@plg.us.com
Founded: 1978
Innovative content developer partnering with many Fortune 500 companies. Provides high

impact content that expands & supports brand & publisher goals. Strategically planned books & multimedia from original ideas & client concepts in all areas of nonfiction are developed to generate visibility & drive revenue. Brings together the best minds & creative talent to provide the perfect team for each project. Provides publishing solutions that enhance brand image, educate consumers & drive sales.
Number of titles produced annually: 10 Print
Recent Title(s): *Diet Smoothies: 168 Delicious Recipes* (Science-Smart)
Membership(s): Custom Publishing Council (CPC)

Lucia|Marquand, see Marquand Books

Lumina Datamatics Inc
600 Cordwainer Dr, Unit 103, Norwell, MA 02061
Tel: 508-746-0300 *Fax:* 508-746-3233
E-mail: marketing@luminad.com
Web Site: luminadatamatics.com
Key Personnel
EVP, Busn Devt: Jack Mitchell
EVP, Solutions, Transitions & US Opers: Sandeep Dhawan
Founded: 1974
Providing full service content creation, design/packaging & media delivery systems to publishers. Services include authoring/writing, editorial research & development, media development & production, editing, photo & text research/permissions, photography/photo shoot direction, indexing, proofreading, fact checking, design/design direction, art direction/editing, technical/illustrative art packages, photo manipulation & page make-up/composition services. Employs over 1,200 US & offshore resources specializing in content/media creation & make-up including file conversions/re-purposing & content management & delivery services. All services are offered both in the US & at offshore facilities. Areas of specialization include school, higher education & professional publishing: mathematics (grade school/algebra/calculus/physics), foreign language (French/Spanish/German/Italian), English & English composition, history, political science, science (chemistry/biology/astronomy), social studies, computer science, business (economics/finance/marketing), engineering & technical trades as well as professional/reference material. Products range from simple 1-color ancillaries components to highly complex design & art intensive core content.
Branch Office(s)
c/o Arnecke Sibeth Distribution, Rechtsanwaelte Steuerberater Partnerschaftsgesellschaft mdB, Gueterplatz 1, 60327 Frankfurt am Main, Germany *Tel:* (06155) 862 99-0 *Fax:* (06155) 862 99-19
Ascendas International Tech Park, 12th fl, Phase II (Crest), CSIR Rd, Taramani, Chennai 600 113, India *Tel:* (044) 4017 6000; (044) 4017 6001
Santosh Raj Plaza, 1st fl, Subburaman St, Gandhi Nagar, 12/9, St, Shenoy Nagar, Madurai 625 020, India
Andheri (E), Unit 117-120, SDF - IV, SEEPZ - SEZ, Mumbai 400 096, India *Tel:* (022) 4034 0515; (022) 4034 0508 *Fax:* (022) 2829 1673
Off No 47/1, 7th fl, Tower-B, A-41, Correnthum Tower, Sector-62, Noida 201 301, India
Plot No 29-34, East Coast Rd, Saram Revenue Village, Oulgaret Municipality, Lawspet Post, Puducherry 605 008, India *Tel:* (0413) 226 4500
No 10, Vazhudavoor Rd, Pettaiyanchathiram, Thattanchavadi, Puducherry 605 009, India *Tel:* (0413) 401 1635
Apple One Equicom Tower, 11th fl, Mindanao Ave Corner Biliran St, Central (pob), Cebu Business Park, 6000 Cebu City, Cebu, Philippines
c/o SOPHI Outsourcing Inc, G/F DBPI IT Plaza, Calindagan, 6200 Dumaguete City, Negros Oriental, Philippines
Brixham Laboratory, Brixham, Devon TQ5 8BA, United Kingdom
Lumina Datamatics UK Ltd, 153 Milton Keynes Business Ctr, Linford Wood, Milton Keynes MK14 6GD, United Kingdom

Marquand Books
Formerly Lucia|Marquand
3131 Western Ave, Suite 522, Seattle, WA 98121
Tel: 206-624-2030
Web Site: www.marquandbooks.com
Key Personnel
Pres & Creative Dir: Gina Broze *E-mail:* gina@marquandbooks.com
Design Dir: Tom Eykemans; Ryan Polich
Edit Dir: Melissa Duffes
Prodn Mgr: Lea Finger
Prodn Coord: Jeremy Linden
Founded: 1983
Art book packaging, editing, design, production; trade books, exhibition catalogs, museum collection handbooks. Develop fine art & illustrated books, delivering bound books or digital files.
Number of titles produced annually: 30 Print
Recent Title(s): *A Centennial Album: The Museum of Fine Arts, Houston*; *Artist Stories by Sanford Schwartz*; *Collidoscope: De La Torre Brothers Retro | Perspective*; *Fabricating Wilderness: The Habitat Dioramas of the Natural History Museum of Los Angeles County*; *George R Anthonisen: Meditations on the Human Condition*; *Nancy Callan: Forces at Play*; *Never Broken: Visualizing Lenape Histories*; *Nordic Utopia?: African Americans in the 20th Century*; *Out of Site: Survey Science and the Hidden West*; *The Phillip G Schrager Collection at the Joslyn Art Museum*; *Shinichi Sawada: Agents of Clay*; *Ulises Carrion: Bookworks and Beyond*

Maverick Publications LLC
131 NE Fifth St, Prineville, OR 97754
Mailing Address: PO Box 5007, Bend, OR 97708
Tel: 541-382-6978
E-mail: moreinfo@maverickbooks.com
Web Site: maverickbooks.com
Key Personnel
Owner: Gary Asher
Founded: 1967
Complete book production, ms to fulfillment, including design, computerized phototypesetting, mechanical editing, graphics, photography, laser color separations, layout, proofing, page proofs, printing & binding. Book & author promotional materials. Free consultation on marketing & distribution. Specialize in deluxe trade paperbacks, handcrafted hardbound editions, short, fast production runs.
Number of titles produced annually: 5 Print

Meadows Design Office
3800 Yuma St NW, Washington, DC 20016
Tel: 202-966-6007
E-mail: mdo@mdomedia.com
Key Personnel
Pres & Creative Dir: Marc Meadows *E-mail:* marc@mdomedia.com
Curator & Image Res: Amy Meadows
Founded: 1981
A full service graphic design firm. Design & production of books, book jackets, illustrated books, cookbooks & publications; consultation, art direction, design, layout, type specification & mechanical art. Specialize in trade & textbooks. Conceptualize & prepare mock-up covers & compositions & presentations & blads for publishers. State-of-the-art electronic publishing equipment & software. Typeset & produce multilingual editions of our book designs.
Recent Title(s): *Palace of State: A History of the Eisenhower Executive Office Building* (US Government Printing Office)
Membership(s): AIGA, the professional association for design; Type Directors Club

Melcher Media Inc
124 W 13 St, New York, NY 10011
Tel: 212-727-2322 *Fax:* 212-627-1973
E-mail: info@melcher.com
Web Site: www.melcher.com
Key Personnel
CEO: Charles Melcher
VP, COO: Bonnie Eldon *E-mail:* beldon@melcher.com
Prodn Mgr: Susan Lynch *E-mail:* slynch@melcher.com
Exec Ed: Lauren Nathan *E-mail:* lnathan@melcher.com
Ed: Megan Worman *E-mail:* mworman@melcher.com
Founded: 1994
Innovative content production company, producing innovative, award-winning books, apps, ebooks & other multimedia content on a wide range of subjects including photography, popular culture, art, music, cooking & the environment.
Number of titles produced annually: 20 Print
Recent Title(s): *An Inconvenient Sequel: Truth to Power* (Rodale Books); *Dear Evan Hansen: Through the Window* (Grand Central Publishing); *The Wisdom of Sundays* (Flatiron Books)

Mount Ida Press
111 Washington Ave, Albany, NY 12210-2203
Tel: 518-426-5935
E-mail: info@mountidapress.com
Web Site: www.mountidapress.com
Key Personnel
Pres: Diana S Waite
Founded: 1985
Complete book production & marketing plans for associations, corporations, universities, government agencies, public relations firms & small presses. Trade & scholarly books, guides, directories, conference proceedings, journals, premiums, corporate histories, local histories, calendars & commemorative publications.
Number of titles produced annually: 3 Print

OTTN Publishing
16 Risler St, Stockton, NJ 08559
Tel: 609-397-4005 *Toll Free Tel:* 866-356-6886 *Fax:* 609-397-4007
E-mail: inquiries@ottnpublishing.com; sales@ottnpublishing.com
Web Site: www.ottnpublishing.com
Key Personnel
Publr: Jim Gallagher *E-mail:* jgallagher@ottnpublishing.com
Founded: 1998
Provides a full range of editorial services, from developing book or series ideas to providing a finished product all at a reasonable price. This allows the publisher to avoid the cost of maintaining a large editorial staff, thereby freeing up resources for promotion, sales & distribution. Our in-house staff includes writers, editors, photo researchers, graphic artists, proofreaders & indexers.
Number of titles produced annually: 40 Print
Recent Title(s): *Girls Guides* (Eldorado Ink); *Scientists and Their Discoveries* (Mason Crest Publishers)

Parachute Publishing LLC
Division of Parachute Properties LLC
PO Box 320249, Fairfield, CT 06825

Tel: 203-255-1303
Key Personnel
Chmn & CEO: Joan Waricha *E-mail:* jwaricha@parachuteproperties.com
Founded: 1983
Children's & adult fiction & nonfiction: original books & series, books from licensed properties, coloring books & other licensed merchandise.
Number of titles produced annually: 100 Print
Membership(s): American Book Producers Association (ABPA); The Children's Book Council (CBC)

Generosa Gina Protano Publishing, see GGP Publishing Inc

The Pushpin Group Inc
38 W 26 St, New York, NY 10010
Tel: 212-529-7590
Web Site: www.pushpininc.com
Key Personnel
Co-Founder, Pres & Dir: Seymour Chwast *E-mail:* seymour@pushpininc.com
Founded: 1954
Full service book design & production, from concept to mechanicals. Handle a variety of genres, from graphic design texts & reference to children's books. Specialize in heavily illustrated books.
Recent Title(s): *At War With War* (7 Stories Press); *Bobo's Smile* (Creative Education); *Dante's Divine Comedy* (Boonesberry); *Get Dressed!* (Abrams); *Mr Merlin & the Turtle* (Greenwillow); *Moonride* (Houghton Mifflin Company); *My Daddy & Me* (Knopf Children's Books)

QBS Learning
242 W 30 St, Suite 1100, New York, NY 10001
Tel: 646-668-4645
E-mail: contact@qbslearning.com
Web Site: www.qbslearning.com
Key Personnel
Co-Founder & CEO: Hanut Singh
Co-Founder & Mng Dir: Brian Kobberger
CFO: Indrajeet Agrawal
EVP, Busn Devt: Michael Porter
VP, Edit: Jonathan Schmalzbach
VP, HR: Pallavi Verma
Dir, Intl: Reggie Chua Singh
Founded: 1983 (as Bill Smith Group)
Full service partner for educational publishers & instructional technology firms. More than 60 professionals in New York & Austin creating programs in American education. Provide end-to-end publishing solutions for early childhood through higher education publishing: both print & eMedia. Editorial, design, photo services & illustration, production & prepress, digital media.
Number of titles produced annually: 1,000 Print

Renaissance House
Imprint of Laredo Publishing Co
465 Westview Ave, Englewood, NJ 07631
Tel: 201-408-4048
Web Site: www.renaissancehouse.net
Key Personnel
Pres: Sam Laredo *E-mail:* laredo@laredopublishing.com
VP & Exec Ed: Raquel Benatar *E-mail:* raquel@renaissancehouse.net
Founded: 1991
Full service book producer company that takes projects from the conceptual, development, editorial, translation & production stages to the finished printed book. Short & long runs. Produces highly illustrated children's books, multicultural projects (ESL, SSL, bilingual) & educational materials. Specialize in Spanish & French. Represents more than 80 illustrators specializing in children's books & multicultural projects. Editorial, translation, illustrations, design & production services. Contact us for rights & availability on existing projects & titles.
Number of titles produced annually: 20 Print
Recent Title(s): *Black History, Tina & Gina Discover 12 People of Color*; *Cornelia Ladybug and Other Tales*; *Full of Empty*; *Green Not Greener*; *Luisita ad War/Lusita y la Guerra*; *Omani Kitty's Journey of Color*; *The Tenth Square*

Roundtable Press Inc
20 E Ninth St, New York, NY 10003
Tel: 917-597-2183
Web Site: www.roundtablepressinc.com
Key Personnel
Pres & Dir: Marsha Melnick *E-mail:* marsha@roundtablepressinc.com
Founded: 1981
Complete development of illustrated & non-illustrated nonfiction books; series & continuity programs; custom books for direct mail publishers, corporations & associations. Ideas developed with authors or clients. Specialize in trade books & popular reference on art & design, decorating & architecture, cooking, crafts, gardening, home improvement, health & fitness, nature & wildlife, American history, media tie-ins, popular culture, women's interests & parenting. Provide electronic files or bound books. Editorial & publishing consultants.
Number of titles produced annually: 10 Print
Membership(s): American Book Producers Association (ABPA)

Scarf Press
1385 Baptist Church Rd, Yorktown Heights, NY 10598
Tel: 914-245-7811
Key Personnel
Owner: Mark L Levine *E-mail:* mlevine@marklevine.us
Founded: 1979
Originate projects & deliver copy-edited ms on computer disks. Specialize in religious & reference books, trade books, premiums.
Recent Title(s): *The Complete Book of Bible Quotations*; *Negotiating a Book Contract: A Guide for Authors, Agents & Lawyers*

Schenkman Books Inc
145 Bethel Mountain Rd, Rochester, VT 05767
Mailing Address: PO Box 119, Rochester, VT 05767
Tel: 802-767-3104
E-mail: schenkmanbooks@gmail.com
Web Site: www.schenkmanbooks.com
Key Personnel
Pres: Joe Schenkman
VP & Penstroke Press Publr: Kathryn Schenkman *E-mail:* kms@penstrokepress.com
Founded: 1961
Academic nonfiction books.

Scribe Inc
765 S Front St, Philadelphia, PA 19147
Tel: 215-336-5094; 215-336-5095
E-mail: contact@scribenet.com
Web Site: www.scribenet.com
Key Personnel
Pres: David Alan Rech *Tel:* 215-336-5094 ext 105 *E-mail:* drech@scribenet.com
Founded: 1993
A full range of publishing services, including OCR/data conversion, editing, proofreading, design, typesetting, & ebook creation, with expertise in XML, Well-Formed Document Workflow, & staff training. Also helps publishers with accessible, multipurpose publishing.

Number of titles produced annually: 1,200 Print
Branch Office(s)
3758 SW 30 Ave, Fort Lauderdale, FL 33312

Shoreline Publishing Group LLC
125 Santa Rosa Place, Santa Barbara, CA 93109
Tel: 805-564-1004
E-mail: info@shorelinepublishing.com
Web Site: shorelinepublishing.com
Key Personnel
Edit Dir: James Buckley, Jr
Design Consultant: Thomas J Carling
Founded: 1999
Number of titles produced annually: 10 Print
Membership(s): American Book Producers Association (ABPA)

Sideshow Media LLC
315 St Johns Place, 1G, Brooklyn, NY 11238
Tel: 917-519-5335
E-mail: inquiries@sideshowbooks.com
Web Site: main.sideshowbooks.com
Key Personnel
Founding Partner: Daniel Tucker *E-mail:* dtucker@sideshowbooks.com
Founded: 2000
Full service print & digital book developer, producer & agent. Specialize in the visual & performing arts, history, pop culture & travel.
Recent Title(s): *Citizen Woman* (Prestel); *The Hamilton Collection* (Black Dog & Leventhal/Hachette); *The Lincoln Notebooks* (Black Dog & Leventhal/Hachette); *The Only Way Out is Through* (Blue Sky/Bonnier); *Subversive Cross Stitch Coloring & Activity Book* (Blue Sky/Bonnier)

Smallwood & Stewart Inc
5 E 20 St, New York, NY 10003
Tel: 212-505-3268
Web Site: www.smallwoodandstewart.com
Founded: 1980
Complete packaging of popular reference books, illustrated trade books & sidelines; producer of international co-editions. Specialize in decorating & design, home how-to, food & wine, weddings. Ideas developed with authors, editors & private clients. Custom publishing.
Number of titles produced annually: 10 Print

Stonesong
270 W 39 St, Suite 201, New York, NY 10018
Tel: 212-929-4600
E-mail: editors@stonesong.com
Web Site: www.stonesong.com
Key Personnel
Partner & Literary Agent: Alison Fargis
Partner & Prodn Servs: Ellen Scordato
EVP & Literary Agent: Judy Linden
Literary Agent & Contracts Mgr: Madelyn Burt
Literary Agent: Leila Campoli; Melissa Edwards; Alyssa Jennette
Literary Agent & Soc Media Coord: Kim Lindman
Literary Agent: Emmanuelle Morgan; Maria Ribas; Adrienne Rosado
Founded: 1979
Representing nonfiction & fiction, including middle grade, young adult & adult titles. Create & develop commercial nonfiction & popular reference books on many subjects: cooking, business, how-to, self-help, memoir, beauty & fashion. Complete trade hardcover, paperback & ebook development, from concept to delivery. Consultants on backlist exploitation, acquisitions, publicity planning & editorial systems. Custom publishing for professional associations & magazines.
Recent Title(s): *A Lady's Guide to Etiquette and Murder* (Kensington Publishing); *ALFA Series* (InterMix); *Become an American Ninja Warrior* (St Martin's Press); *Color Me Floral*:

BOOK PRODUCERS

Stunning Monochromatic Arrangements for Every Season (Chronicle Books); *Coloring in the Lions: Vintage Art from the Archives of The New York Public Library* (Holt); *The Cooks Atelier: Recipes, Techniques, and Stories from our French Cooking School* (Abrams); *Dosa Kitchen: Recipes for India's Favorite Street Food* (Clarkson Potter); *Favorite Recipes from Melissa Clark's Kitchen: Family Meals, Festive Gatherings, and Everything In-between* (Black Dog & Leventhal/Hachette); *Hardcore Carnivore: Cook Meat Like You Mean It* (Agate Surrey); *Hottest Heads of State* (Holt); *How to Get Sh*t Done: Why Women Need to Stop Doing Everything so They Can Achieve Anything* (North Star Way); *Italian Moms: Something Old, Something New* (Sterling Epicure); *Leaving Everest* (CreateSpace Independent Publishing Platform); *Love and Estrogen* (Amazon Original Stories); *Love and Lemons Meal Record and Market List* (Clarkson Potter); *The Memory of Forgotten Things* (Aladdin); *The Million-Dollar, One-Person Business: Make Great Money. Work the Way You Like. Have the Life You Want.* (Lorena Jones Books); *The Music of the Deep* (Lake Union Publishing); *Next is Now* (North Star Way); *On Pills and Needles: The Relentless Fight to Save My Son from Opiod Addiction* (Baker Books); *Once Upon a Chef, the Cookbook: 100 Tested, Perfected, and Family-Approved Recipes* (Chronicle Books); *The One-Bottle Cocktail* (Ten Speed Press); *Paris in Stride: An Insider's Walking Guide* (Rizzoli); *Pug Pals: Two's a Crowd* (Scholastic Press); *The Restaurant Diet: How to Eat Out Every Night and Still Lose Weight* (Mango); *Ruined Series* (Harper Teen); *Simply Vibrant: All-Day Vegetarian Recipes for Colorful Plant-Based Cooking* (Roost Books); *The Sister's Grimm Series: 10th Anniversary Edition* (Amulet Paperbacks); *Sweet Laurel: Recipes for Whole Food, Grain-Free Desserts* (Clarkson Potter); *The Vintage Baker* (Chronicle Books); *To Kill a Kingdom* (Feiwel & Friends); *When Likes Aren't Enough: A Crash Course in the Science of Happiness* (Grand Central Life & Style); *Where I Live* (Harper Teen); *Words That Built a Nation: Voices of Democracy That Have Shaped America's History* (Rodale Kids/Penguin Random House); *The World According to Rick* (Hachette)
Membership(s): American Book Producers Association (ABPA)

Story Monsters LLC
4696 W Tyson St, Chandler, AZ 85226-2903
Tel: 480-940-8182 *Fax:* 480-940-8787
Web Site: www.StoryMonsters.com
Key Personnel
Pres: Linda F Radke *E-mail:* Linda@StoryMonsters.com
Founded: 1985
Produce & market everything children's book related. Publisher of *Story Monsters Ink* literary magazine for children, parents & teachers.
Number of titles produced annually: 10 Print
Recent Title(s): *Markie the Magnificent*; *Nightwatchers*; *The Great Animal Escape*
Membership(s): Better Business Bureau (BBB); The Children's Book Council (CBC); Independent Book Publishers Association (IBPA); National Federation of Press Women

Story Monsters Press, see Story Monsters LLC

Sweetgrass Books
Division of Farcountry Press
2750 Broadway Ave, Helena, MT 59602
Mailing Address: PO Box 5630, Helena, MT 59604
Tel: 406-422-1255 *Toll Free Tel:* 800-821-3874
Web Site: sweetgrassbooks.com

Key Personnel
Dir, Pubns: Kathy Springmeyer *E-mail:* kathy@farcountrypress.com
Custom publishing division of Farcountry Press. Professional editorial, design, production, print management & distribution services.
Number of titles produced annually: 34 Print

Taylor Specialty Books, see Balfour Commercial Printing

To Press & Beyond
7507 Summersun Dr, Browns Summit, NC 27214
Tel: 805-570-8275
E-mail: info@topressandbeyond.com
Web Site: www.topressandbeyond.com
Key Personnel
Pres, Proj Ed & Prodn Coord: Gail M Kearns
 E-mail: gail@topressandbeyond.com
Art Dir & Proj Mgr: Penelope C Paine
 E-mail: pennypaine@aol.com
Copy Ed & Proofreader: Isabella Piestrzynska
Founded: 2001
Book publishing consulting & support services. We shepherd your print +/or ebook through writing, editing, design & layout, printing, distribution, sales & marketing & promotion, both in trade & niche markets & on the Web. We have worked with over 400 authors & independent publishers worldwide. You can contact Gail Kearns for a half-hour gratis phone consult about your project.
Number of titles produced annually: 15 Print
Recent Title(s): *Santa Ynez: A Novel* (Does Hill Publishing LLC); *Sentinel 10: The Edge of Destiny*
Membership(s): The Association of Publishers for Special Sales (APSS); Independent Book Publishers Association (IBPA)

VanDam Inc
The VanDam Bldg, 121 W 27 St, New York, NY 10001
Tel: 917-297-5445
E-mail: info@vandam.com
Web Site: www.vandam.com
Key Personnel
Pres/Creative Dir: Stephan Van Dam
 E-mail: stephan@vandam.com
VP, Soc Media: Patricia Grant *E-mail:* patricia.grant@vandam.com
Dir, Opers: Jessy Cerda *E-mail:* jessy@vandam.com
R&D: Jon Tyillian *E-mail:* jontyillian@vandam.com
Founded: 1985
Publisher, licensor & developer of UNFOLDS®, @tlas® & StreetSmart® brand maps, UNFOLDS® maps & book formats, extra-dimensional reference, travel & educational media; designer of multimedia reference in nature & science; designs & produces new multimedia book formats, direct mail premiums & custom specialties for publishers, government agencies & financial services companies.

Victory Productions Inc
55 Linden St, Worcester, MA 01609
Tel: 508-755-0051
E-mail: victory@victoryprd.com
Web Site: www.victoryprd.com
Key Personnel
Founder & CEO: Victoria Porras *E-mail:* victoria.porras@victoryprd.com
Exec Dir: Neil Saunders
Deputy Exec Dir & CFO: Raul Porras
Dir, Busn Devt: Charles Hartford *E-mail:* charles.hartford@victoryprd.com; Dan Souers *E-mail:* danner.souers@victoryprd.com
Dir, Educ Technol: Haris Papamichael
Dir, Prod Devt: Joel Gendler *E-mail:* joel.gendler@victoryprd.com

Dir, Strategic Technol: Owen Lawlor
Develops K-16 products for 21st century students. Content specialists develop STEM, ELA, ELL, social studies & modern language programs, high-stakes assessment items, performance tasks, knowledge graphs, Spanish content in all curriculum areas & translations in multiple languages. Instructional designers & digital learning experts develop online courses & interactive activities, including simulations, technology enhanced items (TEIs), complex digital learning objects (CDLOs) & games. metacog™, a Victory spinoff, instruments digital-learning objects to collect, analyze, record & report student data in easily understood visualizations. For more information, visit victoryprd.com & metacog.com.

VKH Media Resources
122 S Oneida Ave, Rhinelander, WI 54501
Tel: 715-499-6800 (cell)
Web Site: www.victoriahouston.com
Key Personnel
Author: Victoria Houston
 E-mail: victoriahouston72@gmail.com
Founded: 1996
Package trade books; nonfiction; fly-fishing, hunting, gardening & nature; mysteries.
Number of titles produced annually: 1 Print
Recent Title(s): *At the Edge of the Woods* (Crooked Lane Books); *Hidden in the Pines* (Crooked Lane Books); *Wolf Hollow* (Crooked Lane Books)
Membership(s): The Authors Guild; Mystery Writers of America (MWA)

Welcome Enterprises Inc
Imprint of Welcome Enterprises
50 Plaza St, No 7A, Brooklyn, NY 11238
Tel: 212-989-3200
Web Site: www.welcomeenterprisesinc.com
Key Personnel
Pres: H Clark Wakabayashi *E-mail:* clark@welcomeenterprisesinc.com
Publr: Lena Tabori *E-mail:* lena@welcomeenterprisesinc.com
Founded: 1980
Complete book production from concept to delivery of bound books. Specialize in visual books of all kinds for trade, hardcover & softcover; art, gift, photography/illustration, how-to. Services include packaging, agenting & distribution.
Number of titles produced annually: 3 Print
Recent Title(s): *The American Nurse* (Welcome Books); *Avedon at Work: In the American West* (University of Texas Press); *Disney's The Lion King: Twenty Years on Broadway and Around the World* (Disney Editions); *Grandmother Remembers: A Written Heirloom for My Grandchild* (Stewart, Tabori & Chang); *New York, New York* (Rizzoli)
Membership(s): American Book Producers Association (ABPA)

Wiley-Blackwell
111 River St, Suite 300, Hoboken, NJ 07030-5774
Tel: 201-748-6000 *Toll Free Tel:* 800-567-4797
Fax: 201-748-6088 *Toll Free Fax:* 800-565-6802
E-mail: info@wiley.com
Web Site: www.wiley.com
Medical meeting management & complete medical publishing facilities, from editing to marketing & worldwide distribution. Consultants available for all types of medical publications & symposia.

John Wiley & Sons Inc Scientific, Technical, Medical & Scholarly (STMS), see Wiley-Blackwell

Publishing Systems, Services & Technology Index

HARDWARE

CD-ROM MASTERING

CD ROM Inc, pg 1366
CD Solutions Inc, pg 1366
Disc Makers, pg 1367
DSM Producers Inc, pg 1368
Hedquist Productions Inc, pg 1370
Imago, pg 1370
LG Electronics USA, pg 1371
Lumina Datamatics Inc, pg 1372
Microboards Technology Inc, pg 1372
OneTouchPoint, pg 1374
Scribe Inc, pg 1376
Sony DADC US Inc, pg 1376

DISPLAY DEVICES

alfa CTP Systems Inc, pg 1364
Alps Alpine North America Inc, pg 1364
AZTEK Inc, pg 1365
Canvys® Visual Technology Solutions, pg 1365
Dell Wyse, pg 1367
Dotronix Technology Inc, pg 1368
Eizo Inc, pg 1368
Envision Peripherals Inc (EPI), pg 1368
HP Inc, pg 1370
Infocus® Corp, pg 1370
Kontron America Inc, pg 1371
LG Electronics USA, pg 1371
Matrox Graphics Inc, pg 1372
Planar, pg 1374
Rex Three Inc, pg 1375
Samsung Research America (SRA), pg 1376
Sceptre Inc, pg 1376
Scribe Inc, pg 1376
Sony Electronics Inc, pg 1376
Tamron USA Inc, pg 1377
Tatung Co of America Inc, pg 1377
Taylor Communications Inc, pg 1377
Unisys Corp, pg 1378
VITEC Multimedia, pg 1378
Z-Axis, pg 1378

INPUT DEVICES

Agfa North America, pg 1364
alfa CTP Systems Inc, pg 1364
Alps Alpine North America Inc, pg 1364
AZTEK Inc, pg 1365
BDT Products Inc, pg 1365
CD ROM Inc, pg 1366
Dynabook Americas Inc, pg 1368
Fujitsu Computer Products of America Inc, pg 1369
GTCO Calcomp, pg 1369
HP Inc, pg 1370
IMSI/Design LLC, pg 1370
Kensington Technology Group, pg 1371
Kontron America Inc, pg 1371
Lumina Datamatics Inc, pg 1372
Nissho Electronics USA Corp, pg 1373
Rex Three Inc, pg 1375
Scribe Inc, pg 1376
Tamron USA Inc, pg 1377

TEACH Services Inc, pg 1377
3M Touch Systems Inc, pg 1377
Videx Inc, pg 1378
VITEC Multimedia, pg 1378

INTERFACES

Aaron Marcus and Associates Inc, pg 1363
Agfa North America, pg 1364
alfa CTP Systems Inc, pg 1364
Apple Inc, pg 1364
Aptara Inc, pg 1364
AZTEK Inc, pg 1365
Data Connect/RelComm Inc, pg 1367
Envision Peripherals Inc (EPI), pg 1368
HP Inc, pg 1370
Kontron America Inc, pg 1371
OneTouchPoint, pg 1374
Rex Three Inc, pg 1375
RISO Inc, pg 1376
Scribe Inc, pg 1376
TEACH Services Inc, pg 1377

MODEMS

Apple Inc, pg 1364
Clerical Plus, pg 1366
Data Connect/RelComm Inc, pg 1367
HP Inc, pg 1370
Kontron America Inc, pg 1371
Lumina Datamatics Inc, pg 1372
Multi-Tech Systems Inc, pg 1373
Rex Three Inc, pg 1375
Scribe Inc, pg 1376
Western Telematic Inc (WTI), pg 1378

OCR

Alps Alpine North America Inc, pg 1364
DocuWare Corp, pg 1367
HP Inc, pg 1370
Nuance Communications Inc, pg 1373
Pivar Computing Services Inc, pg 1374
Scribe Inc, pg 1376
SENCOR International, pg 1376
TEACH Services Inc, pg 1377

PHOTOTYPESETTERS

Agfa Canada Inc, pg 1363
alfa CTP Systems Inc, pg 1364
Rex Three Inc, pg 1375
Scribe Inc, pg 1376

PLATFORMS

Agfa North America, pg 1364
Apple Inc, pg 1364
HP Inc, pg 1370
IBM Corp, pg 1370
NETS, pg 1373
Oracle America Inc, pg 1374
Sceptre Inc, pg 1376
Scribe Inc, pg 1376

PRINTERS (LASER & NON-IMPACT)

Advantage Laser Products Inc, pg 1363
Agfa Canada Inc, pg 1363
alfa CTP Systems Inc, pg 1364
AlphaGraphics Inc, pg 1364
Alps Alpine North America Inc, pg 1364
Mark Andy Inc, pg 1364
Apple Inc, pg 1364
AZTEK Inc, pg 1365
BDT Products Inc, pg 1365
Citizen Systems America Corp, pg 1366
Clerical Plus, pg 1366
Delphax Solutions Inc, pg 1367
Fairfield Marketing Group Inc, pg 1368
Figaro, pg 1368
GEI WideFormat, A Visual Edge Technology Company, pg 1369
HID Global, pg 1370
HP Inc, pg 1370
Kroy LLC, pg 1371
OKI Data Americas Inc, pg 1374
Printronix Inc, pg 1375
Printware LLC, pg 1375
Rex Three Inc, pg 1375
Ricoh Americas Corp, pg 1375
Rimage Corp, pg 1375
RISO Inc, pg 1376
Scribe Inc, pg 1376
Sharp Electronics Corp, pg 1376
Star Micronics America Inc, pg 1376
Taylor Communications Inc, pg 1377
TEACH Services Inc, pg 1377
UniNet Imaging Inc, pg 1378
Xante Corp, pg 1378

SCANNERS & DIGITIZERS

Agfa Canada Inc, pg 1363
Agfa North America, pg 1364
alfa CTP Systems Inc, pg 1364
Alps Alpine North America Inc, pg 1364
Mark Andy Inc, pg 1364
AZTEK Inc, pg 1365
The Crowley Co, pg 1367
ECRM Imaging Systems, pg 1368
Figaro, pg 1368
Fujitsu Computer Products of America Inc, pg 1369
GEI WideFormat, A Visual Edge Technology Company, pg 1369
GTCO Calcomp, pg 1369
HP Inc, pg 1370
iCAD Inc, pg 1370
Kroy LLC, pg 1371
Megavision Inc, pg 1372
Nissho Electronics USA Corp, pg 1373
OneTouchPoint, pg 1374
Rex Three Inc, pg 1375
Ricoh Americas Corp, pg 1375
RISO Inc, pg 1376
SCREEN Americas, pg 1376
Scribe Inc, pg 1376
Sharp Electronics Corp, pg 1376
TEACH Services Inc, pg 1377

Videotex Systems Inc, pg 1378
Videx Inc, pg 1378

OTHER

Alliance Storage Technologies Inc (ASTI), pg 1364
CD ROM Inc, pg 1366
The Crowley Co, pg 1367
Data Connect/RelComm Inc, pg 1367
DisplayMate Technologies Corp, pg 1367
Dukane Corp, Audio Visual Products Division, pg 1368
Follett School Solutions Inc, pg 1369
GEI WideFormat, A Visual Edge Technology Company, pg 1369
GTCO Calcomp, pg 1369
OMRON Microscan Systems Inc, pg 1374
PrimeArray Systems Inc, pg 1375
Scribe Inc, pg 1376
Star Micronics America Inc, pg 1376
Tatung Co of America Inc, pg 1377
WeWrite LLC, pg 1378

SOFTWARE

AD PLACEMENT

Conway Greene Co, pg 1366
DSM Producers Inc, pg 1368
Fairfield Marketing Group Inc, pg 1368
Lumina Datamatics Inc, pg 1372
Lynx Media Inc, pg 1372
Saferock, pg 1376

APP DEVELOPMENT

ACD Systems International Inc, pg 1363
DSM Producers Inc, pg 1368
GTxcel Inc, pg 1370
Myriddian LLC, pg 1373
North Atlantic Publishing Systems Inc, pg 1373
QualityLogic Inc, pg 1375
Scribe Inc, pg 1376
SumTotal Systems LLC, pg 1377

CD-ROM AUTHORING

Aaron Marcus and Associates Inc, pg 1363
CD ROM Inc, pg 1366
CD Solutions Inc, pg 1366
Conway Greene Co, pg 1366
Disc Makers, pg 1367
DSM Producers Inc, pg 1368
Eastgate Systems Inc, pg 1368
GEX Inc, pg 1369
ISOMEDIA Inc, pg 1371
Lachina Creative, pg 1371
Lumina Datamatics Inc, pg 1372
Microboards Technology Inc, pg 1372
MRC Medical Communications, pg 1373
OneTouchPoint, pg 1374
Pronk Media Inc, pg 1375
REX, pg 1375

PUBLISHING SYSTEMS, SERVICES & TECHNOLOGY INDEX — SERVICES

Scribe Inc, pg 1376
Sony DADC US Inc, pg 1376

CHART & GRAPH

Aaron Marcus and Associates Inc, pg 1363
AccuWeather Inc, pg 1363
Adobe Systems Inc, pg 1363
AZTEK Inc, pg 1365
BroadVision, pg 1365
Conway Greene Co, pg 1366
Corel Corporation, pg 1366
Figaro, pg 1368
GEX Inc, pg 1369
IMSI/Design LLC, pg 1370
Intex Solutions Inc, pg 1371
ISIS Papyrus America, pg 1371
Itzhack Shelomi Design, pg 1371
Lachina Creative, pg 1371
Lumina Datamatics Inc, pg 1372
Pronk Media Inc, pg 1375
Publishing Data Management Inc, pg 1375
Saferock, pg 1376
Scribe Inc, pg 1376
Three D Graphics Inc, pg 1377
Wasatch Computer Technology LLC, pg 1378

CLIP ART

A&L Express Corp, pg 1363
AZTEK Inc, pg 1365
BroadVision, pg 1365
Design Plus, pg 1367
Fairfield Marketing Group Inc, pg 1368
Getty Images Inc, pg 1369
IMSI/Design LLC, pg 1370
Lumina Datamatics Inc, pg 1372
Scribe Inc, pg 1376

COLOR SEPARATION

A&L Express Corp, pg 1363
Adobe Systems Inc, pg 1363
Amgraf Inc, pg 1364
Aptara Inc, pg 1364
AZTEK Inc, pg 1365
BroadVision, pg 1365
Fairfield Marketing Group Inc, pg 1368
Imago, pg 1370
Itzhack Shelomi Design, pg 1371
Lumina Datamatics Inc, pg 1372
Pronk Media Inc, pg 1375
Quark Software Inc, pg 1375
Rex Three Inc, pg 1375
Ricoh Americas Corp, pg 1375
Videotex Systems Inc, pg 1378

DRAW & PAINT

A&L Express Corp, pg 1363
Adobe Systems Inc, pg 1363
Autodesk Inc, pg 1365
AZTEK Inc, pg 1365
BroadVision, pg 1365
Corel Corporation, pg 1366
Digimage Arts, pg 1367
Engineered Software™, pg 1368
Fairfield Marketing Group Inc, pg 1368
Itzhack Shelomi Design, pg 1371
Lumina Datamatics Inc, pg 1372
Map Resources, pg 1372
Pronk Media Inc, pg 1375
Rex Three Inc, pg 1375
Scribe Inc, pg 1376
TEACH Services Inc, pg 1377
Wasatch Computer Technology LLC, pg 1378

EP UTILITY

Agfa North America, pg 1364
Corel Corporation, pg 1366
Design Science Inc (DSI), pg 1367
DSM Producers Inc, pg 1368
Electronics for Imaging Inc (EFI), pg 1368
Lachina Creative, pg 1371
QualityLogic Inc, pg 1375
Scribe Inc, pg 1376

FILE CONVERSION

Adobe Systems Inc, pg 1363
Agfa North America, pg 1364
Aptara Inc, pg 1364
AutoGraph International Inc (AGI), pg 1365
AZTEK Inc, pg 1365
Clerical Plus, pg 1366
Data Conversion Laboratory Inc (DCL), pg 1367
DSM Producers Inc, pg 1368
Electronics for Imaging Inc (EFI), pg 1368
Elixir Technologies Corp, pg 1368
Engineered Software™, pg 1368
Fairfield Marketing Group Inc, pg 1368
GEX Inc, pg 1369
Heidelberg Graphics, pg 1370
IMSI/Design LLC, pg 1370
Innodata Inc, pg 1370
Intex Solutions Inc, pg 1371
Lachina Creative, pg 1371
Lumina Datamatics Inc, pg 1372
Lynx Media Inc, pg 1372
MPS North America LLC, pg 1373
Myriddian LLC, pg 1373
OneTouchPoint, pg 1374
Pivar Computing Services Inc, pg 1374
Progressive Publishing Services (PPS), pg 1375
Pronk Media Inc, pg 1375
Publishing Data Management Inc, pg 1375
Rex Three Inc, pg 1375
Saferock, pg 1376
Scribe Inc, pg 1376
SENCOR International, pg 1376
Shepherd Inc, pg 1376
Stilo Corp, pg 1377
TEACH Services Inc, pg 1377
TeXnology Inc, pg 1377
Videotex Systems Inc, pg 1378

FONT EDITORS

Adobe Systems Inc, pg 1363
Agfa North America, pg 1364
Electronics for Imaging Inc (EFI), pg 1368
Elixir Technologies Corp, pg 1368
Fairfield Marketing Group Inc, pg 1368
Fontlab Ltd, pg 1369
ISIS Papyrus America, pg 1371
Lightning Source LLC, pg 1371
OneTouchPoint, pg 1374
Scribe Inc, pg 1376
TEACH Services Inc, pg 1377

FONTS & FACES

Adobe Systems Inc, pg 1363
Agfa North America, pg 1364
Azalea Software Inc, pg 1365
Corel Corporation, pg 1366
Design Plus, pg 1367
Electronics for Imaging Inc (EFI), pg 1368
Itzhack Shelomi Design, pg 1371
Linguist's Software, pg 1372
Monotype Imaging Inc, pg 1373
OneTouchPoint, pg 1374
Personal TeX Inc, pg 1374
Scribe Inc, pg 1376
Shepherd Inc, pg 1376
Treacyfaces Inc, pg 1377
Unitype LLC, pg 1378

PAGE COMPOSITION

Adobe Systems Inc, pg 1363
Agfa North America, pg 1364
Aptara Inc, pg 1364
AZTEK Inc, pg 1365
Brainworks Software, pg 1365
BroadVision, pg 1365
Charlesworth Author Services (USA) Inc, pg 1366
Dwight Clough, pg 1366
Conway Greene Co, pg 1366
Corder Associates Inc, pg 1366
Datalogics Inc, pg 1367
DSM Producers Inc, pg 1368
Electronics for Imaging Inc (EFI), pg 1368
Elixir Technologies Corp, pg 1368
Fairfield Marketing Group Inc, pg 1368
Figaro, pg 1368
GEX Inc, pg 1369
Heidelberg Graphics, pg 1370
IBM Corp, pg 1370
IMSI/Design LLC, pg 1370
Innodata Inc, pg 1370
ISIS Papyrus America, pg 1371
Itzhack Shelomi Design, pg 1371
KyTek Inc, pg 1371
Lachina Creative, pg 1371
Linguistic Systems Inc (LSI), pg 1372
Lumina Datamatics Inc, pg 1372
Maverick Publications LLC, pg 1372
Miles 33 International LLC, pg 1373
OneTouchPoint, pg 1374
Progressive Publishing Services (PPS), pg 1375
Pronk Media Inc, pg 1375
Publishing Data Management Inc, pg 1375
Quark Software Inc, pg 1375
Saferock, pg 1376
Scribe Inc, pg 1376
SDL, pg 1376
SENCOR International, pg 1376
Shepherd Inc, pg 1376
TEACH Services Inc, pg 1377
Writers' Supercenter, pg 1378

SGML PROGRAMS

Conway Greene Co, pg 1366
DSM Producers Inc, pg 1368
GEX Inc, pg 1369
Lumina Datamatics Inc, pg 1372
Pronk Media Inc, pg 1375
Publishing Data Management Inc, pg 1375
Saferock, pg 1376
Scribe Inc, pg 1376
SDL, pg 1376
SENCOR International, pg 1376
Stilo Corp, pg 1377

TEXT FORMATTERS

Agfa North America, pg 1364
Charlesworth Author Services (USA) Inc, pg 1366
Corder Associates Inc, pg 1366
Corel Corporation, pg 1366
DSM Producers Inc, pg 1368
Electronics for Imaging Inc (EFI), pg 1368
GEX Inc, pg 1369
ISIS Papyrus America, pg 1371
KyTek Inc, pg 1371
Linguistic Systems Inc (LSI), pg 1372
Lumina Datamatics Inc, pg 1372
North Atlantic Publishing Systems Inc, pg 1373
Progressive Publishing Services (PPS), pg 1375
Pronk Media Inc, pg 1375
Publishing Data Management Inc, pg 1375
Rex Three Inc, pg 1375
Ricoh Americas Corp, pg 1375
Saferock, pg 1376
Scribe Inc, pg 1376
SDL, pg 1376

TRACKING

DSM Producers Inc, pg 1368
Freestyle Software, pg 1369
Lightning Source LLC, pg 1371
Lynx Media Inc, pg 1372
Publishing Data Management Inc, pg 1375
Scribe Inc, pg 1376

WORD PROCESSING & TEXT EDITING

Adobe Systems Inc, pg 1363
Aptara Inc, pg 1364
Avery Dennison Corp, pg 1365
BroadVision, pg 1365
Charlesworth Author Services (USA) Inc, pg 1366
Clerical Plus, pg 1366
Dwight Clough, pg 1366
Conway Greene Co, pg 1366
Data Conversion Laboratory Inc (DCL), pg 1367
Design Science Inc (DSI), pg 1367
DSM Producers Inc, pg 1368
Eastgate Systems Inc, pg 1368
Fairfield Marketing Group Inc, pg 1368
GEX Inc, pg 1369
IBM Corp, pg 1370
Innodata Inc, pg 1370
Intex Solutions Inc, pg 1371
ISIS Papyrus America, pg 1371
Itzhack Shelomi Design, pg 1371
LexisNexis®, pg 1371
Linguistic Systems Inc (LSI), pg 1372
Linguist's Software, pg 1372
Lumina Datamatics Inc, pg 1372
Maverick Publications LLC, pg 1372
Nisus Software Inc, pg 1373
OneTouchPoint, pg 1374
Personal TeX Inc, pg 1374
Progressive Publishing Services (PPS), pg 1375
Publishing Data Management Inc, pg 1375
Rex Three Inc, pg 1375
Saferock, pg 1376
Scribe Inc, pg 1376
SENCOR International, pg 1376
Shepherd Inc, pg 1376
TEACH Services Inc, pg 1377
Unitype LLC, pg 1378
Writers' Supercenter, pg 1378

& SUPPLIERS

PUBLISHING SYSTEMS, SERVICES & TECHNOLOGY INDEX

OTHER

Aatrix Software Inc, pg 1363
AccuWeather Inc, pg 1363
ACD Systems International Inc, pg 1363
AdvantageCS, pg 1363
Agfa North America, pg 1364
Alliance Storage Technologies Inc (ASTI), pg 1364
Apple Inc, pg 1364
Autodesk Inc, pg 1365
Avanti Computer Systems Ltd, pg 1365
Azalea Software Inc, pg 1365
AZTEK Inc, pg 1365
BCC Software Inc, pg 1365
Claris International Inc, pg 1366
Claritas LLC, pg 1366
Corder Associates Inc, pg 1366
The Crowley Co, pg 1367
CyberWolf® Inc, pg 1367
Datalogics Inc, pg 1367
Decker Intellectual Properties Inc, pg 1367
Dell EMC, pg 1367
Digital Wisdom Inc, pg 1367
DSM Producers Inc, pg 1368
Eastgate Systems Inc, pg 1368
Evolution Computing Inc, pg 1368
Follett School Solutions Inc, pg 1369
Getty Images Inc, pg 1369
Global Graphics Software Inc, pg 1369
Indexing Research, pg 1370
Ingenta, pg 1370
Intex Solutions Inc, pg 1371
Intuit Inc, pg 1371
ISIS Papyrus America, pg 1371
Laplink Software Inc, pg 1371
Masque Publishing Inc, pg 1372
Meadows Publishing Solutions, pg 1372
Media Cybernetics Inc, pg 1372
Micro Focus, pg 1372
Naviga, pg 1373
NewTek Inc, pg 1373
Nuance Communications Inc, pg 1373
NWinds, pg 1374
Open Book Systems Inc®, pg 1374
O'Reilly Media Inc, pg 1374
PrimeArray Systems Inc, pg 1375
Rex Three Inc, pg 1375
Scribe Inc, pg 1376
SDL, pg 1376
Smart Communications Inc, pg 1376
Square Two Design Inc, pg 1376
Stilo Corp, pg 1377
TEACH Services Inc, pg 1377
Teledyne DALSA, pg 1377
Thomson Reuters, pg 1377
Transparent Language Inc, pg 1377
Ultimate TechnoGraphics Inc, pg 1378
Unisys Corp, pg 1378
UnitechEDI Inc, pg 1378
Unitype LLC, pg 1378
Vectorworks Inc, pg 1378
Videotex Systems Inc, pg 1378
Virginia Systems, pg 1378
VITEC Multimedia, pg 1378
Wasatch Computer Technology LLC, pg 1378
WeWrite LLC, pg 1378
Z-Axis, pg 1378
ZyLAB North America LLC, pg 1378

SYSTEMS

COMPOSITION

Agfa Canada Inc, pg 1363
Agfa North America, pg 1364
alfa CTP Systems Inc, pg 1364
AZTEK Inc, pg 1365
Brainworks Software, pg 1365
Datalogics Inc, pg 1367
DFI Technologies LLC, pg 1367
DSM Producers Inc, pg 1368
Eastgate Systems Inc, pg 1368
Elixir Technologies Corp, pg 1368
GEX Inc, pg 1369
Itzhack Shelomi Design, pg 1371
Lachina Creative, pg 1371
Linguistic Systems Inc (LSI), pg 1372
Lumina Datamatics Inc, pg 1372
Maverick Publications LLC, pg 1372
Miles 33 International LLC, pg 1373
Myriddian LLC, pg 1373
NETS, pg 1373
Progressive Publishing Services (PPS), pg 1375
PTC, pg 1375
Publishing Data Management Inc, pg 1375
Regent Press Printers & Publishers, pg 1375
Rex Three Inc, pg 1375
Saferock, pg 1376
Scribe Inc, pg 1376
SDL, pg 1376
SENCOR International, pg 1376
Shepherd Inc, pg 1376

CONVERSION

Agfa Canada Inc, pg 1363
Conway Greene Co, pg 1366
The Criterion Collection, pg 1366
Data Conversion Laboratory Inc (DCL), pg 1367
Elixir Technologies Corp, pg 1368
Fairfield Marketing Group Inc, pg 1368
Innodata Inc, pg 1370
Lightning Source LLC, pg 1371
Myriddian LLC, pg 1373
OneTouchPoint, pg 1374
Pivar Computing Services Inc, pg 1374
Progressive Publishing Services (PPS), pg 1375
Rex Three Inc, pg 1375
Saferock, pg 1376
Scribe Inc, pg 1376
SENCOR International, pg 1376
Shepherd Inc, pg 1376
TEACH Services Inc, pg 1377

DESKTOP PUBLISHING

Agfa Canada Inc, pg 1363
alfa CTP Systems Inc, pg 1364
Amgraf Inc, pg 1364
Art Related Technology Inc, pg 1365
AZTEK Inc, pg 1365
Brainworks Software, pg 1365
BroadVision, pg 1365
Canon USA Inc, pg 1365
CD ROM Inc, pg 1366
Clerical Plus, pg 1366
Conway Greene Co, pg 1366
Design Science Inc (DSI), pg 1367
DSM Producers Inc, pg 1368
Electronics for Imaging Inc (EFI), pg 1368
Fairfield Marketing Group Inc, pg 1368
GEX Inc, pg 1369
IBM Corp, pg 1370
Intex Solutions Inc, pg 1371
Itzhack Shelomi Design, pg 1371
Lachina Creative, pg 1371
Linguist's Software, pg 1372
Lumina Datamatics Inc, pg 1372
Maverick Publications LLC, pg 1372
Miles 33 International LLC, pg 1373
NWinds, pg 1374
OneTouchPoint, pg 1374
Personal TeX Inc, pg 1374
Progressive Publishing Services (PPS), pg 1375
PTC, pg 1375
Publishing Data Management Inc, pg 1375
Quark Software Inc, pg 1375
Rex Three Inc, pg 1375
Saferock, pg 1376
Samsung Research America (SRA), pg 1376
Scribe Inc, pg 1376
SDL, pg 1376
Shepherd Inc, pg 1376
Story Monsters LLC, pg 1377
TEACH Services Inc, pg 1377
Thistle Printing Ltd, pg 1377
TRUMATCH Inc, pg 1377

EDITING

Aaron Marcus and Associates Inc, pg 1363
Charlesworth Author Services (USA) Inc, pg 1366
Conway Greene Co, pg 1366
Design Science Inc (DSI), pg 1367
DSM Producers Inc, pg 1368
Elixir Technologies Corp, pg 1368
Foster Travel Publishing, pg 1369
Heidelberg Graphics, pg 1370
Innodata Inc, pg 1370
Lachina Creative, pg 1371
LexisNexis®, pg 1371
Linguistic Systems Inc (LSI), pg 1372
Lumina Datamatics Inc, pg 1372
Progressive Publishing Services (PPS), pg 1375
PTC, pg 1375
Publishing Data Management Inc, pg 1375
QualityLogic Inc, pg 1375
Saferock, pg 1376
Samsung Research America (SRA), pg 1376
Scribe Inc, pg 1376
Shepherd Inc, pg 1376
Story Monsters LLC, pg 1377
TEACH Services Inc, pg 1377

FONT EDITORS

Elixir Technologies Corp, pg 1368
Fairfield Marketing Group Inc, pg 1368
Itzhack Shelomi Design, pg 1371
Scribe Inc, pg 1376

FRONT END SYSTEMS

Agfa North America, pg 1364
alfa CTP Systems Inc, pg 1364
Brainworks Software, pg 1365
Esko USA, pg 1368
Fairfield Marketing Group Inc, pg 1368
Maverick Publications LLC, pg 1372
Megavision Inc, pg 1372
Miles 33 International LLC, pg 1373
OneTouchPoint, pg 1374
Saferock, pg 1376
Scribe Inc, pg 1376
SDL, pg 1376
Ultimate TechnoGraphics Inc, pg 1378

GRAPHIC SYSTEMS

A&L Express Corp, pg 1363
Aaron Marcus and Associates Inc, pg 1363
AccuWeather Inc, pg 1363
Agfa Canada Inc, pg 1363
Agfa North America, pg 1364
alfa CTP Systems Inc, pg 1364
Avanti Computer Systems Ltd, pg 1365
AZTEK Inc, pg 1365
BroadVision, pg 1365
Charlesworth Author Services (USA) Inc, pg 1366
Electronics for Imaging Inc (EFI), pg 1368
Fairfield Marketing Group Inc, pg 1368
Kroy LLC, pg 1371
Matrox Graphics Inc, pg 1372
Megavision Inc, pg 1372
Printware LLC, pg 1375
Rex Three Inc, pg 1375
Saferock, pg 1376
Samsung Research America (SRA), pg 1376
SCREEN Americas, pg 1376
Scribe Inc, pg 1376
Shepherd Inc, pg 1376
Square Two Design Inc, pg 1376

OTHER

A&L Express Corp, pg 1363
alfa CTP Systems Inc, pg 1364
Avanti Computer Systems Ltd, pg 1365
Datalogics Inc, pg 1367
Follett School Solutions Inc, pg 1369
GTI Graphic Technology Inc, pg 1370
ISIS Papyrus America, pg 1371
ISOMEDIA Inc, pg 1371
Multi-Tech Systems Inc, pg 1373
Nissho Electronics USA Corp, pg 1373
NWinds, pg 1374
Open Text Corp, pg 1374
Powis Parker Inc, pg 1374
Rex Three Inc, pg 1375
Roland DGA Corp, pg 1376
Saferock, pg 1376
Sceptre Inc, pg 1376
Scribe Inc, pg 1376
SDL, pg 1376

SERVICES

AUDIOBOOK PRODUCTION

Allusion Studios & Pure Wave Audio, pg 1364
American Artist Studio, pg 1364
The American Audio Prose Library Inc, pg 1364
Biblical Archaeology Society, pg 1365

PUBLISHING SYSTEMS, SERVICES & TECHNOLOGY INDEX

Hedquist Productions Inc, pg 1370
Labrecque Creative Sound, pg 1371
Love & Logic Institute Inc, pg 1372
Master Books®, pg 1372
Outskirts Press Inc, pg 1374
Paulist Press, pg 1374
Progressive Publishing Services (PPS), pg 1375
REX, pg 1375
The Sound Lab Inc, pg 1376
Story Monsters LLC, pg 1377
VO2 Mix Audio Post, pg 1378

CD-ROM

Aaron Marcus and Associates Inc, pg 1363
Acxiom, pg 1363
AGS, pg 1364
Allusion Studios & Pure Wave Audio, pg 1364
American Artist Studio, pg 1364
Aquent LLC, pg 1365
CD ROM Inc, pg 1366
CG Book Printers, pg 1366
Computer Analytics Corp, pg 1366
Conway Greene Co, pg 1366
Corporate Disk Co, pg 1366
Disc Makers, pg 1367
DSM Producers Inc, pg 1368
Fluke Networks, pg 1369
Imago, pg 1370
ISOMEDIA Inc, pg 1371
Labrecque Creative Sound, pg 1371
Lachina Creative, pg 1371
Lumina Datamatics Inc, pg 1372
Media Supply Inc, pg 1372
Microboards Technology Inc, pg 1372
MPS North America LLC, pg 1373
MRC Medical Communications, pg 1373
OneTouchPoint, pg 1374
PrimeArray Systems Inc, pg 1375
ProductionPro, pg 1375
Progressive Publishing Services (PPS), pg 1375
REX, pg 1375
Rimage Corp, pg 1375
Saferock, pg 1376
Scribe Inc, pg 1376
SENCOR International, pg 1376
Six Red Marbles LLC, pg 1376
Sony DADC US Inc, pg 1376
SumTotal Systems LLC, pg 1377

DESKTOP PUBLISHING

Aaron Marcus and Associates Inc, pg 1363
Adobe Systems Inc, pg 1363
alfa CTP Systems Inc, pg 1364
Aptara Inc, pg 1364
Aquent LLC, pg 1365
Arrow Graphics Inc, pg 1365
Art Related Technology Inc, pg 1365
Avery Dennison Corp, pg 1365
BroadVision, pg 1365

Burmar Technical Corp, pg 1365
CG Book Printers, pg 1366
Claritas LLC, pg 1366
Clerical Plus, pg 1366
Dwight Clough, pg 1366
Cohesion®, pg 1366
Computer Analytics Corp, pg 1366
Conway Greene Co, pg 1366
CRW Graphics Communications, pg 1367
Design Plus, pg 1367
First Choice Copy, pg 1368
GEX Inc, pg 1369
GTxcel Inc, pg 1370
Heidelberg Graphics, pg 1370
IMSI/Design LLC, pg 1370
Infinity Graphics, pg 1370
Lachina Creative, pg 1371
Laplink Software Inc, pg 1371
Linguistic Systems Inc (LSI), pg 1372
Lumina Datamatics Inc, pg 1372
Media Supply Inc, pg 1372
Medina Software Inc, pg 1372
Microsearch Corp, pg 1372
MPS North America LLC, pg 1373
NETS, pg 1373
New Riders Publishing, pg 1373
OneTouchPoint, pg 1374
Open Book Systems Inc®, pg 1374
Pivar Computing Services Inc, pg 1374
Progressive Publishing Services (PPS), pg 1375
Pronk Media Inc, pg 1375
Publishing Data Management Inc, pg 1375
Regent Press Printers & Publishers, pg 1375
Rex Three Inc, pg 1375
Saferock, pg 1376
Scribe Inc, pg 1376
SDL, pg 1376
SENCOR International, pg 1376
Shepherd Inc, pg 1376
Six Red Marbles LLC, pg 1376
Story Monsters LLC, pg 1377
Taylor Communications Inc, pg 1377
Thistle Printing Ltd, pg 1377

EBOOK CONVERSION

Biblical Archaeology Society, pg 1365
CG Book Printers, pg 1366
Dwight Clough, pg 1366
CyberWolf® Inc, pg 1367
GTxcel Inc, pg 1370
GW Inc, pg 1370
Heidelberg Graphics, pg 1370
Infinity Graphics, pg 1370
Lachina Creative, pg 1371
LanternMedia, pg 1371
LexisNexis®, pg 1371
Lightning Source LLC, pg 1371
NETS, pg 1373
New York Legal Publishing Corp, pg 1373

Open Book Systems Inc®, pg 1374
Outskirts Press Inc, pg 1374
ProductionPro, pg 1375
Progressive Publishing Services (PPS), pg 1375
Saferock, pg 1376
Scribe Inc, pg 1376
TEACH Services Inc, pg 1377
TeXnology Inc, pg 1377

SGML

Allied Vaughn, pg 1364
Aptara Inc, pg 1364
Aquent LLC, pg 1365
Conway Greene Co, pg 1366
Data Conversion Laboratory Inc (DCL), pg 1367
Design Science Inc (DSI), pg 1367
GEX Inc, pg 1369
Lumina Datamatics Inc, pg 1372
Miles 33 International LLC, pg 1373
MPS North America LLC, pg 1373
Progressive Publishing Services (PPS), pg 1375
PTC, pg 1375
Publishing Data Management Inc, pg 1375
Scribe Inc, pg 1376
SDL, pg 1376
SENCOR International, pg 1376
Six Red Marbles LLC, pg 1376

WEB DEVELOPMENT

Aaron Marcus and Associates Inc, pg 1363
Aquent LLC, pg 1365
Art Related Technology Inc, pg 1365
CD/Works, pg 1366
Cohesion®, pg 1366
Conway Greene Co, pg 1366
Corder Associates Inc, pg 1366
Cosmos Communications Inc, pg 1366
CRW Graphics Communications, pg 1367
Design Plus, pg 1367
Figaro, pg 1368
Follett School Solutions Inc, pg 1369
Foster Travel Publishing, pg 1369
GEX Inc, pg 1369
Infinity Graphics, pg 1370
Innodata Inc, pg 1370
Lachina Creative, pg 1371
Linguistic Systems Inc (LSI), pg 1372
Lumina Datamatics Inc, pg 1372
Medina Software Inc, pg 1372
Microsearch Corp, pg 1372
Miles 33 International LLC, pg 1373
MPS North America LLC, pg 1373
Myriddian LLC, pg 1373
OmniUpdate Inc, pg 1374
OneTouchPoint, pg 1374

Progressive Publishing Services (PPS), pg 1375
Pronk Media Inc, pg 1375
Publishing Data Management Inc, pg 1375
REX, pg 1375
Saferock, pg 1376
Scribe Inc, pg 1376
SENCOR International, pg 1376
Six Red Marbles LLC, pg 1376
Square Two Design Inc, pg 1376
Story Monsters LLC, pg 1377

OTHER

AccuWeather Inc, pg 1363
Acxiom, pg 1363
AGS, pg 1364
AlphaGraphics Inc, pg 1364
Aquent LLC, pg 1365
Art Related Technology Inc, pg 1365
Association for PRINT Technologies (APTech), pg 1365
BCC Software Inc, pg 1365
BJU Press, pg 1365
CD/Works, pg 1366
Cohesion®, pg 1366
Conway Greene Co, pg 1366
DCA Inc, pg 1367
Design Plus, pg 1367
Disc Makers, pg 1367
DSM Producers Inc, pg 1368
Eastgate Systems Inc, pg 1368
Fairfield Marketing Group Inc, pg 1368
Falcon Safety Products Inc, pg 1368
First Choice Copy, pg 1368
Fluke Networks, pg 1369
Follett School Solutions Inc, pg 1369
GSB Digital, pg 1369
GW Inc, pg 1370
Hedquist Productions Inc, pg 1370
Indexing Research, pg 1370
Ingenta, pg 1370
Innodata Inc, pg 1370
ISOMEDIA Inc, pg 1371
Knovel Corp, pg 1371
Love & Logic Institute Inc, pg 1372
Map Resources, pg 1372
Microboards Technology Inc, pg 1372
MPS North America LLC, pg 1373
NETS, pg 1373
New York Legal Publishing Corp, pg 1373
Outskirts Press Inc, pg 1374
ProductionPro, pg 1375
Progressive Publishing Services (PPS), pg 1375
ProQuest LLC, part of Clarivate PLC, pg 1375
Saferock, pg 1376
Scribe Inc, pg 1376
SDL, pg 1376
Six Red Marbles LLC, pg 1376
Chip Taylor Communications, LLC, pg 1377
Writers' Supercenter, pg 1378

Publishing Systems, Services & Technology

Companies that offer publishing systems, services or technology are listed alphabetically. Entries include company name and address, phone numbers, and personnel to contact to receive further information on products & services. The descriptions of company products and services are paid components.

Preceding this section is a classified index that identifies entrants by specialization. This index is divided into four major categories; Hardware, Software, Systems and Services. The categories are further subdivided by the type of hardware, software or systems produced (for example Input Devices and Page Composition) or the service provided. Company names may appear under more than one category.

A&L Express Corp
PO Box 790733, San Antonio, TX 78279-0733
Tel: 210-262-6633
E-mail: sales@arts-letters.com; support@arts-letters.com
Web Site: www.arts-letters.com

Aaron Marcus and Associates Inc
1196 Euclid Ave, Berkeley, CA 94708-1640
Tel: 510-599-3195 (cell) *Fax:* 510-527-1994
Web Site: www.bamanda.com
Key Personnel
Principal: Aaron Marcus *E-mail:* aaron.marcus@bamanda.com
Founded: 1982
Membership(s): AIGA, the professional association for design; Association for Computing Machinery (ACM); Special Interest Group for Computer Human Interaction (SIGCHI); User Experience Professionals Association (UXPA)

Aatrix Software Inc
2100 Library Circle, Grand Forks, ND 58201
Tel: 701-746-6801; 701-746-6814 (Windows); 701-746-6017 (MacIntosh) *Toll Free Tel:* 800-426-0854 (sales) *Fax:* 701-746-4393
E-mail: sales@aatrix.com; support@aatrix.com
Web Site: www.aatrix.com
Key Personnel
Pres & CEO: Steve Lunseth
Founded: 1986

ACCUMEN Book®, see CyberWolf® Inc

AccuWeather Inc
385 Science Park Rd, State College, PA 16803
Tel: 814-235-8600; 814-237-0309
E-mail: salesmail@accuweather.com; support@accuweather.com
Web Site: www.accuweather.com; corporate.accuweather.com
Key Personnel
Founder & CEO: Dr Joel N Myers *Tel:* 814-235-8537 *E-mail:* joel.myers@accuweather.com
COO: Evan Myers *Tel:* 814-235-8505
E-mail: evan.myers@accuweather.com
CFO: Edward Arditte *Tel:* 814-235-8650
E-mail: ed.arditte@accuweather.com
CTO: Chris Patti *Tel:* 814-235-8694
E-mail: chris.patti@accuweather.com
Pres: Steven Smith *Tel:* 814-235-8695
E-mail: steven.smith@accuweather.com
VP, Busn Servs & Gen Mgr, Enterprise Solutions: Jonathan Porter *Tel:* 814-235-8681
E-mail: jonathan.porter@accuweather.com
Founded: 1962
Branch Office(s)
100 N Broadway, Suite 750, Wichita, KS 67202
Tel: 316-266-8000
250 Greenwich St, Manhattan, NY 10006
Tel: 212-554-4750

ACD Systems International Inc
129-1335 Bear Mountain Pkwy, Victoria, BC V9B 6T9, Canada
Toll Free Tel: 800-949-1457
E-mail: sales@acdsee.com
Web Site: www.acdsee.com
Founded: 1994

Ace Pro Inc, see Progressive Publishing Services (PPS)

Acxiom
301 E Dave Ward Dr, Conway, AR 72032
Toll Free Tel: 888-322-9466
Web Site: www.acxiom.com
Key Personnel
CEO: Chad Engelgau
Founded: 1997
Branch Office(s)
1901 Butterfield Rd, Suite 900, Downers Grove, IL 60515
100 W 33 St, 10th fl, New York, NY 10001
River Place Corporate Park 3, 6500 River Place Blvd, Bldg 3, Suite 300, Austin, TX 78730

Adobe Systems Inc
345 Park Ave, San Jose, CA 95110-2704
Tel: 408-536-6000 *Fax:* 408-537-6000
Web Site: www.adobe.com
Key Personnel
Chmn, Pres & CEO: Shantanu Narayen
EVP & CFO: John Murphy
EVP & Chief Mktg Offr: Ann Lewnes
EVP & Gen Mgr, Digital Experience: Anil Chakravarthy
EVP & Gen Mgr, Digital Media: Bryan Lamkin
EVP, Creative Cloud & Chief Prod Offr: Scott Belsky
EVP, Employee Experience & Chief HR Offr: Gloria Chen
EVP, Gen Coun & Corp Secy: Dana Rao
EVP, Strategy & Growth & CTO: Abhay Parasnis
EVP, Worldwide Field Opers: Matt Thompson
Branch Office(s)
1250 53 St, Emeryville, CA 94608 *Tel:* 510-817-6300
3640 Holdrege Ave, Los Angeles, CA 90016
601 Townsend St, San Francisco, CA 94103
Tel: 415-832-2000 *Fax:* 415-832-2020
100 Hooper St, San Francisco, CA 94107
Tel: 415-832-4700
901 Mariners Island Blvd, San Mateo, CA 94404
429 Santa Monica Blvd, Suite 222, Santa Monica, CA 90401 *Tel:* 310-633-2631
707 17 St, Denver, CO 80202
300 New Jersey Ave NW, Washington, DC 20001
420 N Wabash Ave, Suite 700, Chicago, IL 60611 *Tel:* 312-764-5598
7878 Diamondback Dr, College Park, MD 20742
One Broadway, Cambridge, MA 02142
One Newton Place, 3rd fl, Newton, MA 02458
Tel: 617-766-2360
3900 Northwoods, 3rd fl, Arden Hills, MN 55112
Tel: 651-766-4700 *Fax:* 651-766-4750
275 Fair St, Kingston, NY 12401
1540 Broadway, 17th fl, New York, NY 10036
Tel: 212-471-0904 *Fax:* 212-471-0990
100 Fifth Ave, New York, NY 10011 *Tel:* 212-597-0504
114 Fifth Ave, 9th fl, New York, NY 10011
Tel: 646-264-9101
1500 SW First Ave, Portland, OR 97201
Tel: 503-889-2800
11501 Domain Dr, Suite 110, Austin, TX 78758
316 W 12 St, Austin, TX 78701
3900 Adobe Way, Lehi, UT 84043 *Tel:* 385-345-0000
1300 W Traverse Pkwy, Lehi, UT 84043
7930 Jones Branch Dr, 5th fl, McLean, VA 22102
Tel: 571-765-5400 *Fax:* 571-765-5450
801 N 34 St, Seattle, WA 98103 *Tel:* 206-675-7000
830 Fourth Ave S, Suite 400, Seattle, WA 98134
Tel: 206-675-7600
343 Preston St, Ottawa, ON K1S 1N4, Canada
Tel: 613-940-3676 *Fax:* 613-594-8886
225 King St W, 14th fl, Toronto, ON M5V 3M2, Canada *Tel:* 613-940-4134
281 Ruben Dario, 11580 Mexico, CDMX, Mexico *Tel:* (0155) 5283-2401 *Fax:* (0155) 5281-3384
Membership(s): Association of American Publishers (AAP)

Advantage Laser Products Inc
1840 Marietta Blvd NW, Atlanta, GA 30318
Tel: 404-351-2700 *Toll Free Tel:* 800-722-2804 (cust serv) *Fax:* 404-351-0911
Toll Free Fax: 800-871-3305
E-mail: sales@advlaser.com
Web Site: www.advlaser.com
Key Personnel
Pres: Brian Chaney *E-mail:* brian@advlaser.com
VP, Sales & Cust Serv: John Miller
E-mail: john@advlaser.com
Founded: 1987

AdvantageCS
3850 Ranchero Dr, Ann Arbor, MI 48108
Tel: 734-327-3600 *Fax:* 734-327-3620
E-mail: sales-na@advantagecs.com
Web Site: www.advantagecs.com
Key Personnel
VP: Daniel D Heffernan
Mktg Dir: Cynthia M Twiss *Tel:* 734-327-3651
E-mail: cindy.twiss@advantagecs.com
Founded: 1979
BISAC compatible software
Membership(s): Association for Audience Marketing Professionals (AAMP); Media & Content Marketing Association (MCMA); Society for Scholarly Publishing (SSP); World Association of News Publishers (WAN-IFRA)

Agfa Canada Inc
5975 Falbourne St, Unit 2, Mississauga, ON L5R 3V8, Canada
Tel: 905-361-6982 *Toll Free Tel:* 800-540-2432
Fax: 905-502-9360
E-mail: can.customercare@agfa.com (orders)
Web Site: www.agfa.com/printing/worldwide/north-south-america/canada
Founded: 1867
Branch Office(s)
250 First Gulf Blvd, Brampton, ON L6W 4T5, Canada (dist ctr)

1363

PUBLISHING SYSTEMS, SERVICES & TECHNOLOGY — SERVICES

Agfa-Gevaert Graphics Inc, see Agfa North America

Agfa North America
580 Gotham Pkwy, Carlstadt, NJ 07072
Tel: 201-440-2500 *Toll Free Tel:* 888-274-8626 (cust serv)
E-mail: customercare.us@agfa.com
Web Site: www.agfa.com/printing/global/usa; www.agfa.com/printing/industrial; www.agfa.com/printing/large-format
Key Personnel
Global Head, Mergers & Acqs: Gunther Muertens
Dir, Strategic Busn Devt & Dist: Deborah Hutcheson *Tel:* 908-342-1797 *E-mail:* deborah.hutcheson@agfa.com
Branch Office(s)
10798 Catawba Ave, Fontana, CA 92337
665 Raco Dr, Suite C, Lawrenceville, GA 30046 (sales/dist ctr)
14360 SW 147 St, Lockport, IL 60491
22 Stauffer Industrial Park, DC5, Taylor, PA 18517
951 Valley View Lane, Suite 100, Irving, TX 75061

AGS
Subsidiary of RR Donnelley
4590 Graphics Dr, White Plains, MD 20695
Tel: 301-843-1800 *Fax:* 301-843-6339
E-mail: info@ags.com
Web Site: www.ags.com
Key Personnel
Pres: Mike Donohue *E-mail:* mike.donohue@rrd.com
VP, Sales & Mktg: Alan Flint *E-mail:* aflint@ags.com
Founded: 1975
Membership(s): American Society of Association Executives™ (ASAE)

alfa CTP Systems Inc
Member of IPA Group
2503 Spring Ridge Dr, Unit D, Spring Grove, IL 60081
Tel: 815-474-7634
E-mail: info@alfactp.com
Web Site: www.alfactp.com
Key Personnel
CFO: Karen McAndrew
Pres: Tony Ford
VP, Opers: Keith Roeske *E-mail:* keith.roeske@alfactp.com
Founded: 2007
Branch Office(s)
229 Billerica Rd, Suite 4, Chelmsford, MA 01824-3632 (headquarters) *Tel:* 603-689-1101 *Fax:* 978-689-0870

Alliance Storage Technologies Inc (ASTI)
10045 Federal Dr, Colorado Springs, CO 80908
Tel: 719-593-7900 *Toll Free Tel:* 888-567-6332 *Fax:* 719-598-3472
E-mail: sales@astiusa.com; info@astiusa.com
Web Site: www.alliancestoragetechnologies.com
Key Personnel
CEO: Chris Carr
VP, Prod Devt: Tim Summers
Admin Dir: Fran Rogers
Worldwide Dir, Sales & Mktg: Bill Gallagher
Founded: 2003

Allied Vaughn
7600 Parklawn Ave, Suite 300, Minneapolis, MN 55435
SAN: 920-8089
Tel: 952-832-3100 *Toll Free Tel:* 800-323-0281 *Fax:* 952-832-3203
Web Site: www.alliedvaughn.com
Key Personnel
CEO: E David Willette
CTO: James Laib *E-mail:* jim.laib@alliedvaughn.com
Pres: Doug Olzenak
VP, Busn Devt: Mike Haney *E-mail:* mike.haney@alliedvaughn.com
VP, Retail Mgmt: Cindy Verant *E-mail:* cindy.verant@alliedvaughn.com
VP, Sales & Mktg: Richard Skillman *E-mail:* richard.skillman@alliedvaughn.com
Branch Office(s)
901 Bilter Rd, Suite 150, Aurora, IL 60502, Gen Mgr: Rick Polizzi *Tel:* 630-626-0215 *Toll Free Tel:* 800-759-4087 *Fax:* 630-892-2672 *E-mail:* rick.polizzi@alliedvaughn.com
11923 Brookfield, Livonia, MI 48150, Gen Mgr: Chris Barkoozis *Tel:* 734-462-5543 *Toll Free Tel:* 800-462-5543 *Fax:* 734-462-4004 *E-mail:* chris.barkoozis@alliedvaughn.com

Allusion Studios & Pure Wave Audio
Division of Allusion Enterprises
248 W Elm St, Tucson, AZ 85705
Tel: 520-622-3895 (Allusion Studios); 520-447-8116 (Pure Wave Audio)
E-mail: contact@allusionstudios.com
Web Site: www.allusionstudios.com; www.purewaveaudio.com
Key Personnel
Owner & Operator: Jim Pavett

AlphaGraphics Inc
Division of MBE Worldwide
143 Union Blvd, Suite 650, Lakewood, CO 80228
Toll Free Tel: 800-955-6246 *Fax:* 801-595-7270
E-mail: contactus@alphagraphics.com
Web Site: www.alphagraphics.com
Key Personnel
CEO: Paolo Fiorelli
CFO: Camden Hodge
Pres, COO & CTO: Ryan Farris
Gen Coun: Kathleen Panek
VP, Franchise Devt: Bill McPherson
VP, HR: McKenzie Perez
VP, Mktg: Stephanie Johnson
VP, Network Sales & Opers: Tom Kennedy
VP, Purch: Cory Sawatzki
VP, Technol: Ira Shapiro
Founded: 1970

Alps Alpine North America Inc
Subsidiary of Alps Alpine Co Ltd
3151 Jay St, Suite 101, Santa Clara, CA 95054
Tel: 408-361-6400; 408-226-7301 *Fax:* 408-980-9945; 408-226-7301
E-mail: alps-pr@jp.alps.com
Web Site: www.alpsalpine.com/na
Key Personnel
Pres: Toshihiro Kuriyqua
Founded: 1948
Branch Office(s)
1500 Altantic Blvd, Auburn Hills, MI 48326 *Tel:* 248-391-9950 *Fax:* 248-391-2500
4312 Tuller Rd, Dublin, OH 43017 *Tel:* 614-336-1400 *Fax:* 614-336-1426
7100 International Pkwy, Suite 100, McAllen, TX 78503 *Tel:* 956-217-6500 *Fax:* 956-994-1400
2509 152 Ave NE, Suite MEZZ-D, Redmond, WA 98052 *Tel:* 425-242-0343 *Fax:* 425-896-8616

AM+A, see Aaron Marcus and Associates Inc

American Artist Studio
1114 W 26 St, Erie, PA 16508-1518
Mailing Address: PO Box 131, Erie, PA 16512-0131
Tel: 814-455-4796
E-mail: skip@americanartiststudio.com
Web Site: americanartiststudio.com
Key Personnel
Owner: Skip Niebauer *E-mail:* skipniebauer@gmail.com
Founded: 1972

The American Audio Prose Library Inc
PO Box 842, Columbia, MO 65205
Tel: 573-449-7075
E-mail: aaplinc@centurytel.net
Key Personnel
Dir: Kay Callison
Founded: 1980

Amgraf Inc
1501 Oak St, Kansas City, MO 64108-1424
Tel: 816-474-4797 *Toll Free Tel:* 800-304-4797 (sales & mktg) *Fax:* 816-842-4477
E-mail: support@amgraf.com
Web Site: www.amgraf.com
Key Personnel
Pres & CEO: Frank Garner, III
VP, Software Devt: Robert Kisel
Chief Design Engr: Huver Hu
Major Accts Sales Mgr: Raymond L Garner
Mfg Mgr: Jonathan Garner
Training & Documentation Mgr: Debra Poll
Founded: 1976
Membership(s): Business Forms Management Association (BFMA); DSA; NASPO INTERNATIONAL; Print Services & Distribution Association (PSDA); Public Retiement Information Systems Management (PRISM)

Mark Andy Inc
18081 Chesterfield Airport Rd, Chesterfield, MO 63005
Tel: 636-532-4433 *Toll Free Tel:* 800-447-1231 *Toll Free Fax:* 800-447-1231
Web Site: www.presstek.com; markandy.com; shop.markandy.com
Key Personnel
VP, Offset Busn: Stuart Gallup
Dir, MAPP Offset Sales, North America: Ralph Jenkins
Dir, Presstek EAMER: Ian Pollock

AOC, see Envision Peripherals Inc (EPI)

Apple Inc
One Apple Park Way, Cupertino, CA 95014
Tel: 408-996-1010
Web Site: www.apple.com
Key Personnel
CEO: Tim Cook
COO: Jeff Williams
SVP & CFO: Luca Maestri
SVP & Gen Coun: Katherine Adams
SVP, Hardware Engg: Dan Riccio
SVP, Hardware Technol: Johnny Srouji
SVP, Internet Software & Servs: Eddy Cue
SVP, Machine Learning & AI Strategy: John Giannandrea
SVP, Opers: Sabih Khan
SVP, Retail & People: Deidre O'Brien
SVP, Software Engg: Craig Federighi
SVP, Worldwide Mktg: Philip W Schiller
VP, Corp Devt: Adrian Perica
VP, Environment, Policy & Social Initiatives: Lisa Jackson
VP, Mktg Communs: Tor Myhren

Aptara Inc
Subsidiary of iEnergizer
2901 Telestar Ct, Suite 522, Falls Church, VA 22042
Tel: 703-352-0001
E-mail: moreinfo@aptaracorp.com
Web Site: www.aptaracorp.com
Key Personnel
Pres: Samir Kakar
EVP, Fin & Cont: Prashant Kapoor

SVP, Busn & Contact Ctr Opers: Ashish Madan
Sr Dir, Edit: David George
Busn Devt: Michael Scott *E-mail:* michael.scott@aptaracorp.com
Founded: 1988
Branch Office(s)
150 California St, Suite 301, Newton, MA 02458
 Tel: 617-423-7755
11009 Metric Blvd, Bldg J, Suite 150, Austin, TX 78758 *Tel:* 512-876-5997
299 Elizabeth St, Level 1, Sydney 2000, Australia *Tel:* (02) 8251 0070
Tower 1 & 2, 8/100, Acharya Thulasi Rd (Shandy Rd), Pallavaram, Chennai 600 043, India *Tel:* (044) 22640676
No 2310, Doon Express Business Park, Saharanpur Rd, Bldg 2000, Dehradun 248 002, India *Tel:* (0135) 2644055
7B, Leela Infopark, Technopark, Trivandrum, Kerala 695 581, India *Tel:* (047) 14063370
A-37, Sector-60, Noida 201 301, India *Tel:* (0120) 7182424
D-10, Sector-2, Noida 201 301, India *Tel:* (0120) 24423678
SEZ Bldg 4A, 1st fl, S P Infocity, Pune Saswad Rd, Phursungi, Pune 412 308, India *Tel:* (020) 66728000

Aquent LLC
101 W Elm St, Suite 300, Conshohocken, PA 19428-2075
Tel: 610-828-0900 *Toll Free Fax:* 877-303-5224
E-mail: questions@aquent.com
Web Site: aquentstudios.com; aquent.com
Key Personnel
Mgr: Kelly Griffin
Founded: 1986

Arrow Graphics Inc
PO Box 380291, Cambridge, MA 02238
E-mail: info@arrow1.com
Web Site: www.arrow1.com
Key Personnel
Pres: Alvart Badalian
Sr Graphic/Pubn Designer: Aramais Andonian
Founded: 1988

Art Related Technology Inc
4 Brattle St, Rm 305, Cambridge, MA 02138
Tel: 617-661-1225 *Fax:* 617-491-0618
E-mail: artinc@artrelated.com
Web Site: www.artrelated.com
Key Personnel
Art Dir: Marvin Mortee

Association for PRINT Technologies (APTech)
113 Seaboard Lane, Suite C-250, Franklin, TN 37067
Tel: 703-264-7200
E-mail: aptech@aptech.org
Web Site: printtechnologies.org
Key Personnel
Pres: Thayer Long *E-mail:* tlong@aptech.org
VP, Prog Devt: Julie Shaffer *E-mail:* jshaffer@aptech.org
Sr Dir, Communs: Jane Pratt *E-mail:* jpratt@aptech.org
Founded: 1933
Membership(s): American Society of Association Executives™ (ASAE); Council of Manufacturing Associations; International Association of Exhibitions and Events® (IAEE); National Association of Manufacturers (NAM)

Autodesk Inc
111 McInnis Pkwy, San Rafael, CA 94903
Tel: 415-507-5000 *Fax:* 415-507-5100
Web Site: www.autodesk.com
Key Personnel
Pres & CEO: Andrew Anagnost
Founded: 1982

AutoGraph International Inc (AGI)
2500 Wilcrest Dr, Suite 324, Houston, TX 77042
Mailing Address: 650 W Bough Lane, Suite 150-117, Houston, TX 77024
Tel: 713-954-4848
E-mail: sales@myeasycopy.com
Web Site: myeasycopy.com
Founded: 1989

Automated Graphic Systems, see AGS

Avanti Computer Systems Ltd
Division of Ricoh Co Ltd
251 Consumers Rd, Suite 600, Toronto, ON M2J 4R3, Canada
Tel: 416-445-1722 *Toll Free Tel:* 800-482-2908
 Fax: 416-445-6319
E-mail: askavanti@avantisystems.com
Web Site: www.avantisystems.com
Key Personnel
VP, Sales: John Alden
Gen Mgr: Duncan Ellis
Founded: 1984
Membership(s): Association for Print Technologies (APTech); Epicomm; International Cooperation for Integration of Processes in Prepress, Press & Postpress Organization (CIP4); National State Printing Association (NSPA); PRINTING United Alliance

Avery Dennison Corp
207 N Goode Ave, 6th fl, Glendale, CA 91203-1222
Tel: 626-304-2000
Web Site: www.averydennison.com
Key Personnel
Chmn of the Bd, Pres & CEO: Mitch Butier
SVP & CFO: Greg Lovins
SVP & Chief HR Offr: Anne Hill
SVP, Gen Coun & Secy: Sue Miller
VP & CIO: Nick Colisto
VP, Strategy & Corp Devt: Danny Allouche
Founded: 1935
Branch Office(s)
224 Industrial Rd, Fitchburg, MA 01420 *Tel:* 508-383-0511 *Fax:* 508-879-4259

Azalea Software Inc
PO Box 16660, Seattle, WA 98116-0660
Tel: 206-341-9500; 206-336-9559 (software support); 206-336-9575 (sales & info) *Fax:* 206-299-5600
E-mail: salesinfo@azaleabarcodes.com
Web Site: www.azaleabarcodes.com
Key Personnel
Founder: Jerry Whiting
Pres: Miranda Pinero
Sales & Support: Scotty Carreiro
Founded: 1992

AZTEK Inc
13765-F Alton Pkwy, Irvine, CA 92618
Tel: 949-770-8787
E-mail: mail@aztek.com
Web Site: www.aztek.net
Founded: 1980

BCC Software Inc
75 Josons Dr, Rochester, NY 14623-3494
Toll Free Tel: 800-453-3130; 800-337-0442 (sales)
E-mail: marketing@bccsoftware.com
Web Site: www.bccsoftware.com
Key Personnel
CFO: Eric Narowski
Pres: Chris Lien
VP, Opers: Jim Mann
VP, Prod Strategy: Shawn Ryan
VP, Sales: Marcus Banks
Founded: 1978

BDT Products Inc
Division of BDT Media Automation GmbH
250 E Rincon St, Suite 101, Corona, CA 92879
Tel: 949-263-6363
Key Personnel
CEO: David St Clair *Tel:* 949-263-6363 ext 101
Founded: 1979

Biblical Archaeology Society
4710 41 St NW, Washington, DC 20016-1705
Tel: 202-364-3300 *Toll Free Tel:* 800-221-4644
 Fax: 202-364-2636
E-mail: info@biblicalarchaeology.org
Web Site: www.biblicalarchaeology.org
Key Personnel
Publr: Susan Laden
Mng Ed: Megan Sauter
Ed: Robert R Cargill
Prodn Mgr: Heather Metzger *Tel:* 202-364-3300 ext 236
Founded: 1974

BJU Press
Unit of BJU Education Group
1430 Wade Hampton Blvd, Greenville, SC 29609-5046
SAN: 223-7512
Tel: 864-770-1317; 864-546-4600
 Toll Free Tel: 800-845-5731
E-mail: bjupinfo@bjupress.com
Web Site: www.bjupress.com
Key Personnel
Pres: Bill Apelian
Exec Asst: Jennifer Headley

Brainworks Software
100 S Main St, Sayville, NY 11782
Tel: 631-563-5000 *Toll Free Tel:* 800-755-1111
 Fax: 631-563-6320
E-mail: info@brainworks.com; sales@brainworks.com; support@brainworks.com
Web Site: www.brainworks.com
Key Personnel
CEO: John Barry

BroadVision
Division of Aurea Inc
460 Seaport Ct, Suite 102, Redwood City, CA 94063
Tel: 650-331-1000
Web Site: www.broadvision.com
Key Personnel
Pres, CEO & Chmn of the Bd: Dr Pehong Chen
VP & Gen Mgr, Global Servs: Stefano Gargioli
VP, Engg: Yuk Chan
VP, Sales: Fadi Micaelian
Founded: 1993
Branch Office(s)
255 Bear Hill Rd, Waltham, MA 02451 *Tel:* 781-290-0710

Burmar Technical Corp
106 Ransom Ave, Sea Cliff, NY 11579
Tel: 516-484-6000 *Fax:* 516-484-6356
Web Site: burmar.net
Key Personnel
Pres: Christine Jensen *E-mail:* christine.jensen@burmar.net

Canon USA Inc
One Canon Park, Milville, NY 11747
Tel: 516-328-5000; 631-330-5000
Web Site: www.usa.canon.com
Key Personnel
Pres & CEO: Kazuto Ogawa

Canvys® Visual Technology Solutions
Division of Richardson Electronics
40W267 Keslinger Rd, LaFox, IL 60147

PUBLISHING SYSTEMS, SERVICES & TECHNOLOGY — SERVICES

Mailing Address: PO Box 393, LaFox, IL 60147-0393
Toll Free Tel: 888-735-7373 *Fax:* 630-208-2350
Web Site: www.canvys.com
Key Personnel
EVP & Gen Mgr: Jens Ruppert
VP, Global Engg: Brian Blanchett
Founded: 1992
Branch Office(s)
753 Forest St, Suite 100, Marlborough, MA 01752 *Tel:* 508-460-5400 *Toll Free Tel:* 800-291-1344 *Fax:* 508-460-5470

CD ROM Inc
3131 E Riverside Dr, Fort Myers, FL 33916
Tel: 239-332-2800 *Toll Free Tel:* 866-66-CDROM (662-3766)
E-mail: info@cdrominc.com
Web Site: www.cdrominc.com
Key Personnel
Owner & Pres: Roger Hutchison
Founded: 1988

CD Solutions Inc
100 W Monument St, Pleasant Hill, OH 45359
Mailing Address: PO Box 536, Pleasant Hill, OH 45359-0536
Tel: 937-676-2376 *Toll Free Tel:* 800-860-2376 *Fax:* 937-676-2478
E-mail: contact@cds.com
Web Site: www.cds.com
Key Personnel
Pres: Jerry Warner *E-mail:* jerryw@cds.com
Founded: 1993
Membership(s): International Disc Duplicating Association (IDDA)

CD/Works
Division of Zerious Electronic Publishing Corp
30 Doaks Lane, Marblehead, MA 01945
Tel: 978-922-4990 *Toll Free Tel:* 800-CDWORKS (239-6757) *Fax:* 978-922-5110
Web Site: www.cdworks.com
Key Personnel
Pres: Jeffrey Starfield *E-mail:* jbs@cdworks.com
Founded: 1993
Membership(s): International Disc Duplicating Association (IDDA)

CG Book Printers
Division of Corporate Graphics Commercial (CGC)
1750 Northway Dr, North Mankato, MN 56003
Tel: 507-388-3300 *Toll Free Tel:* 800-729-7575 *Fax:* 507-386-6350
E-mail: cgbooks@corpgraph.com
Web Site: www.corpgraph.com
Key Personnel
Pres: Dan Kvasnicka *Tel:* 507-386-6340 *Fax:* 507-344-5548 *E-mail:* dekvasnicka@corpgraph.com
Sales Exec, Book Mfg Sales: Mike Schmitt *Tel:* 507-386-6349 *E-mail:* mjschmitt@corpgraph.com
Founded: 1989

Charlesworth Author Services (USA) Inc
Unit of The Charlesworth Group (USA) Inc
c/o Suite 510 Constitution Place, 325 Chestnut St, Philadelphia, PA 19106
E-mail: usa@cwauthors.com
Web Site: www.cwauthors.com
Branch Office(s)
Charlesworth Author Services China, Room 1105, No 9 Bldg, Jianwai SOHO, No 39 Dongsanhuan Zhonglu, Chaoyang District, Beijing 100022, China *Tel:* (010) 5869 6201 *E-mail:* info@cwauthors.com.cn
Charlesworth Author Services UK, 250 Deighton Rd, Deighton, Huddersfield HD2 1JJ, United Kingdom *Tel:* (01484) 506250 *E-mail:* helpdesk@cwauthors.com

Citizen Systems America Corp
363 Van Ness Way, Suite 404, Torrance, CA 90501
Tel: 310-781-1460 *Toll Free Tel:* 800-421-6516
Web Site: www.citizen-systems.com
Key Personnel
Pres & CEO: Shuichi Ishiwata
Founded: 1930

Claris International Inc
Subsidiary of Apple Inc
5201 Patrick Henry Dr, Santa Clara, CA 95054
Tel: 408-727-8227 (sales & cust support) *Toll Free Tel:* 800-725-2747 (sales); 800-325-2747 (cust support) *Fax:* 408-987-7447
E-mail: claris_sales@claris.com
Web Site: www.claris.com
Key Personnel
CEO: Brad Freitag
Corp Coun & Secy: Sophia Yungen
VP, Engg: Peter Nelson
VP, Mktg: Britta Meyer Rock
VP, Prod Mgmt & Design: Srini Gurrapu
VP, Sales: Ryan McCann
VP, Worldwide Prod Release Engg: Lucy Chen
Founded: 1998
Branch Office(s)
20 Martin Place, Level 3, Sydney, NSW 2000, Australia *Tel:* (02) 8987 8300
B505 COFO Plaza, No 8 Jian Guo Men Nei Ave, Beijing 100005, China *Tel:* 400 601 5902
7 Place d'Iena, CS 81626, 75773 Paris Cedex 16, France *Tel:* 08 10 25 27 47
Katharina von Bora Str 3, 80333 Munich, Germany *Tel:* (089) 1 2089 5651
Roppongi Hills Mori Tower, 6-10-1 Roppongi, Minato-ku, Tokyo 106-6140, Japan *Tel:* (03) 4345 3333
2 Furzeground Way, Stockley Park, Uxbridge, Middx UB11 1BB, United Kingdom *Tel:* (020) 8268 6030

Claritas LLC
8044 Montgomery Rd, Suite 455, Cincinnati, OH 45236
Toll Free Tel: 888-981-0040
E-mail: findcustomers@claritas.com; marketing@claritas.com
Web Site: www.claritas.com
Key Personnel
CEO: Mike Nazzaro
COO: Karthik Iyer
Founded: 1971

Clerical Plus
97 Blueberry Lane, Shelton, CT 06484
Tel: 203-225-0879 *Fax:* 203-225-0879
E-mail: clericalplus@aol.com
Web Site: www.clericalplus.net
Key Personnel
Pres: Rose Brown
Founded: 1990

Dwight Clough
PO Box 670, Wyocena, WI 53969
E-mail: lmp@dwightclough.com
Web Site: dwightclough.com
Founded: 1983

Cohesion®
511 W Bay St, Suite 480, Tampa, FL 33606
Tel: 813-999-3111 *Toll Free Tel:* 866-727-6800
Web Site: www.cohesion.com
Key Personnel
CEO: John Owens
Chief Strategy Offr: John Larson
Founded: 1982
Branch Office(s)
6760 Alexander Bell Dr, Suite 120, Columbia, MD 21046 *Toll Free Tel:* 800-560-0630
5151 Pfeiffer Rd, Suite 105, Cincinnati, OH 45242 *Tel:* 513-587-7700

Computer Analytics Corp
999 E Touhy Ave, Suite 130, Des Plaines, IL 60018-2736
Tel: 847-297-5290 *Fax:* 847-297-8680
Web Site: www.cacorp.com
Key Personnel
Principal: Dale C Jessen *E-mail:* dale.jessen@cacorp.com; Jay Cosentino *E-mail:* jay.cosentino@cacorp.com; Kenneth R Kosnik *E-mail:* ken.kosnik@cacorp.com
Founded: 1976

Conway Greene Co
1400 E 30 St, Suite 402, Cleveland, OH 44114
Tel: 216-965-3195
Web Site: www.conwaygreene.com
Key Personnel
Principal: Barry Conway *E-mail:* bconway@conwaygreene.com

Corder Associates Inc
2602 W Baseline Rd, Suite 22, Mesa, AZ 85202
Mailing Address: PO Box 40518, Mesa, AZ 85274-0518
Tel: 480-752-8533 *Toll Free Tel:* 877-303-7575 *Fax:* 480-752-8534
E-mail: info@cordernet.com
Web Site: cordernet.com
Key Personnel
Pres: Kelly Corder
VP: Jennifer D Corder
Founded: 1991

Corel Corporation
1600 Carling Ave, Ottawa, ON K1Z 8R7, Canada
Toll Free Tel: 877-582-6735
Web Site: www.corel.com
Key Personnel
CEO: Christa Quarles
Chief Legal Offr: Connie Chen
Chief Mktg Offr: Michelle Chiantera
CFO: Brad Jewett
Chief Revenue Offr: Andrea Johnston
Chief Technol & Prod Offr: Prashant Ketkar
Founded: 1985

Corporate Disk Co
4610 Prime Pkwy, McHenry, IL 60050-7005
Tel: 815-331-6000 *Toll Free Tel:* 800-634-3475 *Fax:* 815-331-6030
E-mail: info@disk.com
Web Site: www.disk.com
Key Personnel
Owner & VP, Sales: Joe D Foley *Tel:* 815-331-6000 ext 233 *E-mail:* jfoley@disk.com
Founded: 1984

Corporate Graphics Book Printers, see CG Book Printers

Cosmos Communications Inc
11-05 44 Dr, Long Island City, NY 11101
Tel: 718-482-1800 *Toll Free Tel:* 800-223-5751 *Fax:* 718-482-1968
Web Site: www.cosmoscommunications.com
Key Personnel
CEO: Jack Weiss *E-mail:* jweiss@cosmoscommunications.com
Founded: 1933

The Criterion Collection
215 Park Ave S, 5th fl, New York, NY 10003
Tel: 212-756-8822
E-mail: suggestions@criterion.com
Web Site: www.criterion.com

Key Personnel
Contact: Jon Mulvaney *E-mail:* mulvaney@criterion.com
Founded: 1984

The Crowley Co
5111 Pegasus Ct, Suite M, Frederick, MD 21704
Tel: 240-215-0224 *Fax:* 240-215-0234
E-mail: webrequest@thecrowleycompany.com
Web Site: www.thecrowleycompany.com
Key Personnel
Pres & CEO: Pat Crowley *E-mail:* pat@thecrowleycompany.com
COO: Kevin Crowley
CFO: Jeffrey Manwiller
VP, Sales & Mktg: Matthew McCabe
    E-mail: mattm@thecrowleycompany.com
Dir, Admin: Debbie Harris *E-mail:* debbie@thecrowleycompany.com
Dir, Communs: Amanda Martinez
    E-mail: amandam@thecrowleycompany.com
Founded: 1980

CRW Graphics Communications
9100 Pennsauken Hwy, Pennsauken, NJ 08110
Tel: 856-662-9111 *Toll Free Tel:* 800-820-3000
    Fax: 856-665-1789
E-mail: info@crwgraphics.com
Web Site: www.crwgraphics.com
Key Personnel
Pres: David Carpenter
EVP: George Slater
VP, Sales & Mktg: Will Glassman
    E-mail: wglassman@crwgraphics.com
Cust Serv Mgr: Rich Quigley *E-mail:* rquigley@crwgraphics.com

CyberWolf® Inc
c/o 530-B Harkle Rd, Suite 100, Santa Fe, NM 87505
E-mail: sales@cyberwolf.com
Web Site: www.ebookdownloadservice.com
Key Personnel
Pres: Lawrence Wolf
Corp Secy: Linda Masco Wolf
Founded: 1988

Data Connect/RelComm Inc
Division of Data Connect Enterprise Inc
4868 Hwy 4, Suite G, Angels Camp, CA 95222
Tel: 301-924-7400 (ext 17) *Fax:* 301-924-7403
E-mail: sales@relcomm.com
Web Site: www.relcomm.com
Founded: 1989

Data Conversion Laboratory Inc (DCL)
61-18 190 St, Suite 205, Fresh Meadows, NY 11365
Tel: 718-357-8700 *Toll Free Tel:* 800-321-2816
    (provider problems)
E-mail: info@dclab.com
Web Site: www.dataconversionlaboratory.com
Key Personnel
Pres: Mark Gross
COO: Amy Williams
CFO: Judy Gross
CIO: Tammy Bilitzky
Chief Revenue Offr: Jeff Wood
CTO & Dir, Res: Mike Gross
Natl Sales Dir: Brian Trombley
Sales Dir, Publg: Amber Watson
Founded: 1981
Membership(s): American Institute of Architects (AIA); Association for Enterprise Integration (AFEI/CALS); Association of American Publishers (AAP); Graphic Communications Association (GCA); Society for Scholarly Publishing (SSP)

Datalogics Inc
101 N Wacker, Suite 1800, Chicago, IL 60606
Tel: 312-853-8200 *Fax:* 312-853-8282
E-mail: sales@datalogics.com; marketing@datalogics.com
Web Site: www.datalogics.com
Key Personnel
CEO: Kevin McNeill
CFO: Ruth Walker
CTO: Matt Zuznicki
VP, Sales: Maryanne Pavlin
Founded: 1967

DCA Inc
1515 E Pine St, Cushing, OK 74023
Tel: 918-225-0346 *Fax:* 918-225-1113
E-mail: sales@dcainc.com
Web Site: www.dcainc.com
Key Personnel
Chmn of the Bd & CEO: Doug Carson
Pres & COO: Mike Griffith
CTO: Henry Boon Kelly
Founded: 1988

Decker Intellectual Properties Inc
372 Richmond St W, Toronto, ON M5V 2L7, Canada
Tel: 905-522-8526 *Toll Free Tel:* 855-647-6511
E-mail: customercare@deckermed.com
Web Site: www.deckerip.com
Key Personnel
Chief Content Offr: Ryan T Decker
CTO: Jeffrey B Decker
BISAC compatible software
Branch Office(s)
516 Tennessee St, Memphis, TN 38103

DeckerMed, see Decker Intellectual Properties Inc

Dell EMC
Division of Dell Technologies
176 South St, Hopkinton, MA 01748
Tel: 508-435-1000 *Toll Free Tel:* 866-438-3622
Web Site: www.delltechnologies.com

Dell Wyse
Division of Dell Technologies
One Dell Way, Round Rock, TX 78682
Toll Free Tel: 866-438-3622 (sales)
Web Site: www.delltechnologies.com
Key Personnel
Chmn & CEO: Michael S Dell
VChmn & COO: Jeff Clarke
Chief Mktg Offr: Allison Dew

Delphax Solutions Inc
Unit of Air T Inc
2810 Argentia Rd, Unit 6, Mississauga, ON L5N 8L2, Canada
Toll Free Tel: 833-DELPHAX (335-7429)
Web Site: www.delphaxsolutions.com
Key Personnel
CEO: Richard Lee
Founded: 1981
Branch Office(s)
5000 W 36 St, Suite 130, Minneapolis, MN 55416 *Toll Free Tel:* 855-404-0026

Design Plus
1086 Main Rd, Aquebogue, NY 11931
Mailing Address: PO Box 1140, Aquebogue, NY 11931
Tel: 631-722-4384
E-mail: designplusonline@yahoo.com
Key Personnel
Creative Dir: Denise Lebrun
BISAC compatible software

Design Science Inc (DSI)
Division of Wiris
444 W Ocean Blvd, Suite 800, Long Beach, CA 90802
Tel: 562-432-2920 *Toll Free Tel:* 800-827-0685
    (US sales only) *Fax:* 562-624-2859
E-mail: info@wiris.com; sales@wiris.com; support@wiris.com
Web Site: www.dessci.com
Key Personnel
CEO: Robert Karmelich
Founded: 1986

DFI Technologies LLC
5501 Monte Claire Lane, Loomis, CA 95650
Tel: 916-568-1234
Web Site: dfitech.com
Key Personnel
Chmn & Pres: David Lu *E-mail:* david@dfitech.com
Founded: 1985

Digimage Arts
100 S Eighth Ave, Winterset, IA 50273
Tel: 515-462-1874
E-mail: geninfo@digimagearts.com
Web Site: www.digimagearts.com
Key Personnel
Pres: Wayne Davis
Founded: 1987

Digital Wisdom Inc
PO Box 11, Tappahannock, VA 22560-0011
Tel: 804-443-9000 *Toll Free Tel:* 800-800-8560
E-mail: info@digitalwisdom.net
Web Site: www.digiwis.com; www.mountainhighmaps.com
Key Personnel
Pres: David M Broad
Founded: 1992

Disc Makers
Division of DiY Media Group Inc
7905 N Crescent Blvd, Pennsauken, NJ 08110-1402
Tel: 856-663-9030 *Toll Free Tel:* 800-468-9353
    Fax: 856-661-3450
E-mail: info@discmakers.com
Web Site: www.discmakers.com
Key Personnel
EVP: David Olinsky
Founded: 1946
Membership(s): Content Delivery & Storage Association (CDSA); Recording Academy (NARAS); Society of Professional Audio Recording Services (SPARS)

DisplayMate Technologies Corp
PO Box 550, Amherst, NH 03031
Tel: 603-672-8500 *Toll Free Tel:* 800-932-6323
    (orders)
E-mail: info.dm@displaymate.com
Web Site: www.displaymate.com
Key Personnel
Founder, Pres & CEO: Dr Raymond Soneira
Founded: 1984

DocuWare Corp
4 Crotty Lane, Suite 200, New Windsor, NY 12553
Tel: 845-563-9045 *Toll Free Tel:* 888-565-5907
    Fax: 845-563-9046
E-mail: dwsales@docuware.com; support.americas@docuware.com
Web Site: www.docuware.com
Key Personnel
CFO: Paul Remington
VP, Prof Servs Americas: Brian Love
Mktg Communs Mgr: Mary K Williams *Tel:* 845-563-9045 ext 221 *E-mail:* mary.williams@docuware.com
Founded: 1988
Branch Office(s)
35 Thorpe Ave, Suite 201, Wallingford, CT

06492 *Tel:* 203-871-4984 *Fax:* 203-269-0322
E-mail: fortissupport@docuware.com
DocuWare SARL, 17 rue du Colisee, 75008 Paris, France *Tel:* 01 57 19 03 23 *E-mail:* infoline@docuware.com
DocuWare GmbH, Therese-Giehse-Platz 2, 82110 Germering, Germany (headquarters), Mng Dir: Juergen Biffar *Tel:* (089) 894433-0 *Fax:* (089) 8419966 *E-mail:* docuware@docuware.com
DocuWare SL, Casp, 90 3° 1a, 08010 Barcelona, Spain *Tel:* 933171771 *E-mail:* infoline@docuware.com
DocuWare Ltd, Chiltern Chambers, 37 St Peters Ave, Caversham, United Kingdom *Tel:* (0115) 7180353 *E-mail:* infoline@docuware.com

Dotronix Technology Inc
2420 Oakgreen Ave N, West Lakeland, MN 55082
Tel: 651-633-1742 *Fax:* 651-633-2152
E-mail: sales@dotronix.com
Web Site: dotronix.com
Key Personnel
Pres: Kurt Sadler *E-mail:* ksadler@dotronix.com

DSM Producers Inc
PO Box 1160, Marco Island, FL 34146-1160
Tel: 212-245-0006
Key Personnel
Owner & Pres: Suzan J Bader
Natl Sales Dir: Doris Kaufman
Founded: 1970
Membership(s): The American Society of Composers, Authors and Publishers (ASCAP); Broadcast Music Inc (BMI); SESAC

Dukane Corp, Audio Visual Products Division
Division of Dukane Corp
2900 Dukane Dr, St Charles, IL 60174
Tel: 630-584-2300 *Toll Free Tel:* 888-245-1966; 800-676-2487 (tech support) *Fax:* 630-584-5156
E-mail: avsales@dukane.com
Web Site: dukaneav.com
Key Personnel
Pres: James Locascio *E-mail:* jlocascio@dukane.com
Natl Sales Mgr: Scott Doornbos *Tel:* 800-269-9715 *E-mail:* sdoornbos@dukane.com
Founded: 1922

Dynabook Americas Inc
5241 California Ave, Suite 100, Irvine, CA 92617
Tel: 949-583-3000
Web Site: us.dynabook.com
Key Personnel
Media Rel: Eric Paulsen *E-mail:* eric.paulsen@dynabook.com

Eastgate Systems Inc
134 Main St, Watertown, MA 02472
Tel: 617-924-9044 *Toll Free Tel:* 800-562-1638
E-mail: info@eastgate.com
Web Site: www.eastgate.com
Key Personnel
Chief Scientist: Mark Bernstein
Founded: 1982

ECRM Imaging Systems
25 Commerce Way, North Andover, MA 01845-1002
Tel: 978-851-0207 *Toll Free Tel:* 800-537-ECRM (537-3176)
E-mail: sales@ecrm.com
Web Site: www.ecrm.com
Founded: 1969

Eizo Inc
5710 Warland Dr, Cypress, CA 90630
Tel: 562-431-5011 *Toll Free Tel:* 800-800-5202 *Fax:* 562-431-4811
E-mail: orders@eizo.com
Web Site: www.eizo.com
Key Personnel
VP, Sales: Dave Waletzki *Tel:* 888-925-6481
E-mail: david.waletzki@eizo.com
Mktg Coord: Julie De Anda *Tel:* 800-800-5202 ext 140 *E-mail:* julie.deanda@eizo.com
Founded: 1985

Electronics for Imaging Inc (EFI)
6750 Dumbarton Circle, Fremont, CA 94555
Tel: 650-357-3500 *Toll Free Tel:* 800-568-1917; 800-875-7117 (sales) *Fax:* 650-357-3907
E-mail: info@efi.com
Web Site: www.efi.com
Key Personnel
CEO: Guy Gecht
Chief Acctg Offr: Gene Zamiska
Chief Busn Devt Offr: Roy Douglass
CFO: Marc Olin
Chief HR Offr: Paul Sexton
CIO: Jill Norris
Chief Legal Offr: Alex K Grab
Chief Process Offr: Brandy Green
Chief Revenue Offr: Frank Mallozzi
CTO: Ghilad Dziesietnik
Chief of Staff: Vicki Sam
SVP & Gen Mgr, Fiery: Toby Weiss
SVP & Gen Mgr, Productivity Software: Gaby Matsliach
VP, Partner Alliance: Bernie Lepore
VP, Sales, Americas: Patrick Morrissey
VP, Sales, EMEA Opers: Paul Cripps
Founded: 1989
Branch Office(s)
15150 Avenue of Science, Suite 100, San Diego, CA 92128 *Tel:* 858-578-3550 *Fax:* 858-546-1401
9035 S Kyrene, Suite 106, Tempe, AZ 85284 *Tel:* 480-538-5800 *Fax:* 480-538-5882
5011 Gate Pkwy, Bldg 100, Suite 225, Jacksonville, FL 32256 *Tel:* 904-564-9690 *Fax:* 904-564-9691
4237 SW High Meadows Ave, Palm City, FL 34990 *Tel:* 772-220-7966
4955 Avalon Ridge Pkwy, Suite 300, Norcross, GA 30071 *Tel:* 770-448-9008 *Fax:* 770-448-3202
9 Aldrin Rd, Plymouth, MA 02360 *Tel:* 603-298-2490 *Fax:* 508-746-1569
1260 James L Hart Pkwy, Ypsilanti, MI 48197 *Tel:* 734-641-3062 *Fax:* 734-641-3065
1340 Corporate Center Curve, Eagan, MN 55121 *Tel:* 651-365-5300
8606 NW 107 Terr, Kansas City, MO 64153
79 E Wilder Rd, Lebanon, NH 03784 *Tel:* 603-298-2400 *Fax:* 603-298-2489
12 Innovation Way, Londondery, NH 03053 *Tel:* 603-279-4635 *Fax:* 603-279-6411
7 Campus Dr, 1st fl, Parsippany, NJ 07054 *Tel:* 973-451-7100 *Fax:* 973-451-7188
589 W Eighth Ave, 8th fl, New York, NY 10018 *Tel:* 212-629-9053 *Fax:* 212-629-9055
90 Earhart Dr, Suite 8, Williamsville, NY 14221 *Tel:* 716-631-3770 *Fax:* 716-631-3576
40 24 St, 1st fl, Pittsburgh, PA 15222 *Tel:* 412-456-1141 *Fax:* 412-456-1151
16825 48 Ave W, Suite 414, Lynnwood, WA 98037 *Tel:* 972-638-7490
121 Granton Dr, Unit 14, Richmond Hill, ON L4B 3N4, Canada *Tel:* 905-882-2500 *Fax:* 905-882-2535

Elixir Technologies Corp
1314 E Ojai Ave, Ojai, CA 93023
Tel: 805-641-5900 *Fax:* 805-648-9151
E-mail: info_us@elixir.com
Web Site: www.elixir.com
Key Personnel
CEO: Tarek Harry
Founded: 1985

Engineered Software™
PO Box 408, Grafton, MA 01519-0408
Tel: 336-299-4843
E-mail: info@engsw.com; sales@engsw.com
Web Site: www.engsw.com
Key Personnel
Pres & Dir, Software Devt: Todd Stanley

Envision Peripherals Inc (EPI)
490 N McCarthy Blvd, Suite 120, Milpitas, CA 95035
Web Site: us.aoc.com
Key Personnel
CEO: David Mo

Esko USA
Division of Danaher
8535 Gander Creek Dr, Miamisburg, OH 45342
Tel: 937-454-1721 *Toll Free Tel:* 800-743-7131 *Fax:* 937-454-1522
E-mail: info.usa@esko.com
Web Site: www.esko.com
Key Personnel
VP & Gen Mgr, North America: Stephen Bennett

Evolution Computing Inc
4228 E Andrea Dr, Cave Creek, AZ 85331
Tel: 602-299-1949
E-mail: support@fastcad.com; order_request@fastcad.com
Web Site: www.fastcad.com
Key Personnel
Owner: Michael Riddle
Tech Support: John Steen
Founded: 1985

Fairfield Marketing Group Inc
Subsidiary of FMG Inc
830 Sport Hill Rd, Easton, CT 06112-1241
E-mail: info@fairfieldmarketing.com
Key Personnel
Pres & CEO: Edward P Washchilla, Jr *E-mail:* ed@fairfieldmarketing.com
Founded: 1986
BISAC compatible software
Membership(s): American Booksellers Association (ABA); Bridgeport Regional Business Council (BRBC); Education Market Association; United States Chamber of Commerce (USCC)

Falcon Safety Products Inc
25 Imclone Dr, Branchburg, NJ 08876
Tel: 908-707-4900 *Toll Free Tel:* 800-332-5266
E-mail: marketing@falconsafety.com
Web Site: www.falconsafety.com
Key Personnel
Dir, Cust Serv: Trish Dupuis-Jones
Dir, Mktg: Jennifer Rappaport
Founded: 1953

Figaro
PO Box 848, Sharon, CT 06069
Tel: 860-248-8989; 860-364-0834
E-mail: design@figro.com
Web Site: www.figro.com
Key Personnel
Co-Pres & Creative Dir: Walter Schwarz
Co-Pres: Linda Swenson *E-mail:* ls@figro.com

FileMaker Inc, see Claris International Inc

First Choice Copy
5208 Grand Ave, Maspeth, NY 11378
Tel: 718-381-1480 (ext 200) *Toll Free Tel:* 800-222-COPY (222-2679)
Web Site: www.firstchoice-copy.com
Key Personnel
Owner & Pres: Joe Meisner *Tel:* 718-381-1480 ext 212 *E-mail:* jmeisner@nyc.rr.com

Fluke Networks
Division of Fluke Electronics Corp
6920 Seaway Blvd, Everett, WA 98203
Mailing Address: PO Box 777, Everett, WA 98206-0777
Tel: 425-446-5500; 425-446-4519 (sales & support) *Toll Free Tel:* 800-283-5853
E-mail: info@flukenetworks.com
Web Site: www.flukenetworks.com
Key Personnel
Pres, Fluke Corp: Marc Tremblay
VP, Mktg: Tom Roth
Founded: 1984

Follett School Solutions Inc
Division of Francisco Partners
1340 Ridgeview Dr, McHenry, IL 60050
SAN: 169-1902
Tel: 815-759-1700 *Toll Free Tel:* 888-511-5114 (cust serv); 877-899-8550 (sales) *Fax:* 815-759-9831 *Toll Free Fax:* 800-852-5458
E-mail: info@follettlearning.com; customerservice@follett.com
Web Site: www.follettlearning.com; www.follett.com/prek12; www.titlewave.com
Key Personnel
CEO, Content: Britten Follett
CEO, Software: Paul Ilse
Sales Exec: Erica Moore

Fontlab Ltd
403 S Lincoln St, Suite 4-51, Port Angeles, WA 98362
Tel: 301-560-3208 *Toll Free Tel:* 866-571-5039
E-mail: orders@fontlab.com; contact@fontlab.com
Web Site: www.fontlab.com
Key Personnel
Pres: Ted Harrison
VP & Lead Developer: Yuri Yarmola
Dir, Prods: Adam Twardoch
Founded: 1992

Foster Travel Publishing
1623 Martin Luther King Jr Way, Berkeley, CA 94709
Tel: 510-549-2202
Web Site: www.fostertravel.com
Key Personnel
Owner & Pres: Lee Foster *E-mail:* lee@fostertravel.com
Founded: 1972
Membership(s): American Society of Media Photographers (ASMP); Bay Area Independent Publishers Association (BAIPA); Bay Area Travel Writers; Society of American Travel Writers (SATW)

Freestyle Software
Unit of FOG Software
9 Campus Dr, Parsippany, NJ 07054
Toll Free Tel: 800-474-5760 *Fax:* 973-237-9043
E-mail: info@freestylesolutions.com
Web Site: www.freestylesolutions.com
Key Personnel
CEO: Fred Lizza
CFO: Paul Kincaid
VP, Cust Satisfaction: Tony Kyberd *E-mail:* tony.k@freestylesolutions.com
Founded: 1986

Fujitsu Computer Products of America Inc
Subsidiary of Fujitsu Ltd
1250 E Arques Ave, Sunnyvale, CA 94085-4701
Tel: 408-746-6000 *Toll Free Tel:* 800-626-4686
E-mail: scanner-sales@us.fujitsu.com
Web Site: www.fujitsu.com/us
Key Personnel
Pres & CEO: Yasunari Shimizu
SVP, Partner Alliance: Yasuhiko Nagaoka
SVP, Planning, Serv Opers & Logistics: Masanori Shibusawa
VP, Serv Opers & Logistics: Glenn Wood

GEI WideFormat, A Visual Edge Technology Company
3874 Highland Park NW, North Canton, OH 44720
Toll Free Tel: 800-842-8448 (serv); 888-722-6434 (sales)
E-mail: sales@geiwideformat.com
Web Site: www.geiwideformat.com; www.visualedgetechnology.com
Key Personnel
Dir, Mktg: Denise Dennewitz-Hobson
Founded: 1970
BISAC compatible software

Getty Images Inc
605 Fifth Ave S, Suite 400, Seattle, WA 98104
Tel: 206-925-5000 *Toll Free Tel:* 800-IMAGERY (462-4379); 888-888-5889
Web Site: www.gettyimages.com; www.gettyimages.com/customer-support; engage.gettyimages.com/media-inquiries
Key Personnel
CEO: Craig Peters
CEO, Unsplash: Mikael Cho
CFO: Jennifer Leyden
CTO: Nate Gandert
Chief Mktg & Revenue Offr: Gene Foca
Chief People Offr: Lizanne Vaughan
Chief Prod Offr: Grant Farhall
SVP & Gen Coun: Kjelti Kellough
SVP & Chief of Staff: Michael Teaster
SVP, Content: Ken Mainardis
SVP, Creative Content: Andrew Saunders
SVP, E-Commerce: Daine Weston
SVP, Strategic Devt: Peter Orlowsky
VP, Cust Serv: Matthew J "MJ" Richards
VP, Cust Success: Guy Thorneloe
VP, Sales (Americas): Katie Calhoun
VP, Sales (APAC): Mike Harris
VP, Sales (EMEA): Ken Levernz
VP, Sales Enablement & Opers: Rick Thompson
Founded: 1995
Branch Office(s)
6300 Wilshire Blvd, 16th fl, Los Angeles, CA 90048 *Tel:* 323-202-4200
55 E Monroe St, 17th fl, Chicago, IL 60603 *Tel:* 312-855-0055
195 Broadway, 10th fl, New York, NY 10007 *Tel:* 646-613-4000
Enrique Butty 275 Capital Federal, C1001AFA Buenos Aires, Argentina *Tel:* (011) 59842872
182-186 Blues Point Rd, Level 6, McMahons Point, Sydney, NSW 2060, Australia *Tel:* (02) 9004 2200
LocalMotive Crossing, 1240 20 Ave SE, 3rd fl, Calgary, AB T2G 1M8, Canada *Tel:* 403-265-3062
Unsplash, 5th fl, 400 McGill, Montreal, QC H2Y 2G1, Canada
No 48 Wangjing Xilu, Rm 12A01, Bldg 5, Chaoyang District, Beijing 100102, China *Tel:* (010) 8477 5185
Morning, Bureau 203, 34 rue Laffitte, 75009 Paris, France *Tel:* 01 55 33 66 00
Auenstr 5, 80469 Munich, Germany *Tel:* (089) 20 24 06 0
Off 25, 6/F Luk Kwok Ctr, 72 Gloucester Rd, Wan Chai, Hong Kong *Tel:* 2832 0900
Vaswani Chambers, 2nd fl 264-265, Dr Annie Besant Rd, Worli, Mumbai 400 030, India *Tel:* (022) 40734848
The Herbert Bldg, 1st fl, The Park, Carrickmines, Dublin 18 K8Y4, Ireland *Tel:* (01) 2462700
Via Sant Maria Valle 3, 2012 Milan MI, Italy *Tel:* (02) 36 02 1299
Jingumae Tower Bldg, Level 14, 1-5-8 Jingumae, Shibuya-ku, Tokyo 150-0001, Japan *Tel:* (050) 1790-3930
Varsovia 36, Piso 12 (1202), Colonia Juarez, Delegacion Cuauhtemoc, 06600 Mexico, CDMX, Mexico *Tel:* (0155) 41720159
Generator Level, 10/11 Britomart Place, Auckland CBD, Auckland 1010, New Zealand *Tel:* 0800 462 431
Concept Communications, Oscars Gate 30, 0352 Oslo, Norway *Tel:* 90 87 14 59
120 Robinson Rd, Off S1202, Singapore 068913, Singapore *Tel:* 6410 3300
Lexington, Paseo de la Castellana no 79, Plantas 4, 6, 7 & 8, 28046 Madrid, Spain *Tel:* 91 787 09 00
G Tower, Level 33, 9 Rama Rd, Huaykwang, Bangkok 10310, Thailand *Tel:* (02) 026 0745
Kolektif House, Esentepe Mah Talatpasa Caddesi, Harman Sokak No 5, Levent, Sisli, 34393 Istanbul, Turkey *Tel:* (0850) 441 0939
DSC Tower, Unit 601, Dubai Studio City, Dubai, United Arab Emirates *Tel:* (04) 597-3710
Duo, 6th fl S, 280 Bishopsgate, London EC2M 4AG, United Kingdom

GEX Inc
80 Conley's Grove Rd, Derry, NH 03038
Mailing Address: PO Box 613, Atkinson, NH 03811
Tel: 603-870-9292
Web Site: www.gexinc.com
Key Personnel
Pres: Gary Russell *E-mail:* gary.russell@gexinc.com
VP: Jim LaPierre
Founded: 1986

Global Graphics Software Inc
Subsidiary of Global Graphics PLC
5996 Clark Center Ave, Sarasota, FL 34238
Tel: 941-925-1303
E-mail: info@globalgraphics.com; sales@globalgraphics.com
Web Site: www.globalgraphics.com/globalgraphics-software
Founded: 1986
Branch Office(s)
Global Graphics KK, 610 AIOS Nagatacho Bldg, 2-17-17 Nagatacho Chiyoda-ku, Tokyo 100-0014, Japan *Tel:* (03) 6273-3198 *Fax:* (03) 6273-3197
Global Graphics Software Ltd, Cambourne Busn Park, Bldg 2030, Cambourne, Cambridge CB23 6DW, United Kingdom *Tel:* (01954) 283100
Membership(s): Association for Print Technologies (APTech); DDAP; ICC; PRINTING United Alliance

Graphic World Inc, see GW Inc

GSB Digital
33-01 Hunters Point Ave, Long Island City, NY 11101
Tel: 212-684-3600 *Fax:* 212-684-3613
E-mail: questions@gsbdigital.com
Web Site: www.gsbdigital.com
Key Personnel
Pres: Stephan S Steiner
Founded: 1991
Branch Office(s)
51 Madison Ave, No 3B, New York, NY 10010 *Tel:* 212-500-6503 *E-mail:* litigation@gsbdigital.com

GTCO Calcomp
Division of Turning Technologies LLC
14557 N 82 St, Scottsdale, AZ 85260
Tel: 480-443-2264 *Toll Free Tel:* 800-220-1137 *Fax:* 480-948-1751
E-mail: sales@gtcocalcomp.com
Web Site: www.gtcocalcomp.com
Key Personnel
Natl Acct Mgr: Markie Nielsen
Founded: 1975

PUBLISHING SYSTEMS, SERVICES & TECHNOLOGY — SERVICES

GTI Graphic Technology Inc
211 Dupont Ave, Newburgh, NY 12550
Mailing Address: PO Box 3138, Newburgh, NY 12550-0651
Tel: 845-562-7066 Fax: 845-562-2543
E-mail: sales@gtilite.com
Web Site: www.gtilite.com
Key Personnel
Pres: Robert McCurdy
EVP: Louis Chappo
Sales & Mktg Coord: Linda Sutherland

GTxcel Inc
144 Turnpike Rd, Suite 130, Southborough, MA 01772-2104
Toll Free Tel: 800-609-8994
E-mail: info@gtxcel.com
Web Site: www.gtxcel.com
Key Personnel
Pres & CEO: Peter Stilson
CFO: Robert Epping
EVP, Gen Mgr: Kim Keller
VP, Sales: Jim Clarke
Sr Dir, Digital Servs: Lauren Wine
Dir, Engg: Mohammad Salih
Founded: 1991

GW Inc
2290 Ball Dr, St Louis, MO 63146
Tel: 314-567-9854
E-mail: media@gwinc.com
Web Site: www.gwinc.com
Key Personnel
CEO: Kevin Arrow
EVP: Andy Vosburgh
VP, Content Opers: Suzanne Kastner
Branch Office(s)
GW Tech Pvt Ltd, D-152, Mohali Bypass Rd, Phase 8, Sector 73, Chandigarh 140 308, India
Tel: (0172) 415 1335

Hedquist Productions Inc
PO Box 1475, Fairfield, IA 52556
Tel: 641-472-6708
Web Site: www.hedquist.com
Key Personnel
Pres & Creative Dir: Jeffrey P Hedquist
  E-mail: jeffrey@hedquist.com
Founded: 1985

Heidelberg Graphics
2 Stansbury Ct, Chico, CA 95928
SAN: 211-5654
Tel: 530-342-6582 Fax: 530-342-6582
E-mail: heidelberggraphics@gmail.com; service@heidelberggraphics.com
Web Site: www.heidelberggraphics.com
Key Personnel
Owner & Pres: Larry S Jackson
Founded: 1972

HID Global
611 Center Ridge Dr, Austin, TX 78753
Tel: 512-776-9000 Toll Free Tel: 800-872-5359 (cust serv) Fax: 512-776-9930
E-mail: customerservice@hidglobal.com
Web Site: www.hidglobal.com
Key Personnel
Sr Dir, Corp Communs & Pub Aff: Anthony Petrucci E-mail: apetrucci@hidglobal.com
Founded: 1991 (as Hughes Identification Devices)

HP Inc
1501 Paige Mill Rd, Palo Alto, CA 94304-1112
Tel: 650-857-1501 Toll Free Tel: 800-282-6672
Web Site: www.hp.com
Key Personnel
Pres & CEO: Enrique Lores
CFO: Steve Fieler
Chief Commercial Offr: Christopher Schell
Chief Communs Offr: Karen Kahn
Chief HR Offr: Tracy Keogh
Chief Legal Offr & Pres, Strategy & Busn Mgmt: Kim M Rivera
Chief Mktg Offr: Vikrant Batra
Chief Supply Chain Offr: Antoine Simonnet
Chief Transformation Offr: Richard Bailey
Pres, Imaging, Printing Solutions: Tuan Tran
Pres, Personal Systems: Alex Cho
Founded: 1939
Branch Office(s)
10300 Energy Dr, Spring, TX 77389

IBM Corp
One New Orchard Rd, Armonk, NY 10504
Tel: 914-499-1900 Toll Free Tel: 800-426-4968
E-mail: askibm@vnet.ibm.com
Web Site: www.ibm.com
Key Personnel
CEO: Arvind Krishna
CIO: Fletcher Previn
Pres: Jim Whitehurst
SVP & CFO: James J Kavanaugh
SVP & Chief HR Offr: Diane Gherson
SVP & Gen Coun: Michelle H Browdy
SVP, Digital Sales & Chief Mktg Offr: Michelle Peluso
SVP, Global Mkts: Bridget van Kralingen

iCAD Inc
98 Spit Brook Rd, Suite 100, Nashua, NH 03062
Tel: 603-882-5200 Toll Free Tel: 866-280-2239
E-mail: sales@icadmed.com; support@icamed.com
Web Site: www.icadmed.com
Key Personnel
Exec Chmn & CEO: Michael Klein
CFO: R Scott Areglado
CTO: Jonathan Go
Pres: Stacey Stevens

Imago
110 W 40 St, New York, NY 10018
Tel: 212-921-4411 Fax: 212-921-8226
E-mail: sales@imagousa.com
Web Site: www.imagousa.com
Key Personnel
Pres & CEO: Howard Musk E-mail: howardm@imagogroup.com
Founded: 1985
Branch Office(s)
Imago West Coast, 23412 Moulton Pkwy, Suite 250, Laguna Hills, CA 92653 (sales), Contact: Tammy Simms Tel: 949-367-1635 Fax: 949-367-1639
Imago Australia, 10 Help St, Suite 27, Level 6, Chatswood, NSW 2067, Australia (sales) Tel: (04) 3753 3351 (cell); (04) 4806 8704 (cell) E-mail: sales@imagaoaus.com
Imago Brazil, Domiciano Rossi, 340 unid 154, 09726-121 Sao Bernardo do Campo, Brazil (sales) Tel: (011) 2306 8546; (011) 2306 8547 E-mail: imagobra@gmail.com
Imago Shenzhen, Rm 2511-2512, Block A, United Plaza No 5022, Bin He Rd, Fu Tian Centre District, Shenzhen 518033, China (prodn), Contact: Kendrick Cheung Tel: (0755) 8304 8899 Fax: (0755) 8251 4073 E-mail: enquiries@imago.com.hk
Imago France, 23 rue Lavoisier, 75008 Paris, France (sales) Tel: 01 45 26 47 74 Fax: 01 78 94 14 44 E-mail: sales@imagogroup.com
Imago Services (HK) Ltd, Unit B309, 1/F, New East Sun Industrial Bldg, 18 Shing Yip St, Kwun Tong, Hong Kong (prodn), Contact: Kendrick Cheung Tel: 2811 3316 E-mail: enquiries@imago.com.hk
Imago Productions (Malaysia) Pte Ltd, No 43, Taman Emas, Jl Utama 31, Telok Panglima Garang, 42500 Kuala Langot, Selangor, Malaysia (prodn, incorporating South Africa sales) Tel: (017) 4288771 (cell) E-mail: enquiries@imago.com.sg

Imago Publishing, Albury Ct, Albury Thame, Oxon OX9 2LP, United Kingdom (sales), Dir: Simon Rosenheim Tel: (01844) 337000 Fax: (01844) 339935 E-mail: sales@imago.co.uk Web Site: imagogroup.com

IMSI/Design LLC
384 Bel Marin Keys Blvd, No 150, Novato, CA 94949
Tel: 415-483-8000 Toll Free Tel: 800-833-8082 (sales)
E-mail: sales@imsidesign.com; support@imsidesign.com
Web Site: www.imsidesign.com
Key Personnel
Pres & CEO: Robert Mayer
Founded: 1983

Indexing Research
620 Park Ave, Suite 183, Rochester, NY 14607
Tel: 585-413-1819
E-mail: info@indexres.com
Web Site: www.indexres.com
Key Personnel
Owner: Frances S Lennie E-mail: flennie@indexres.com
Founded: 1986
Membership(s): American Society for Indexing (ASI); Australian and New Zealand Society of Indexers (ANZSI); Society of Indexers (UK)

Infinity Graphics
2277 Science Pkwy, Suite 5, Okemos, MI 48864
Tel: 517-349-4635 Toll Free Tel: 800-292-2633 Fax: 517-349-7608
E-mail: barcode@infinitygraphics.com
Web Site: www.infinitygraphics.com
Key Personnel
Owner & Partner: Brian Perry
Owner, Partner & Bar Code Specialist: Suzette Perry
Founded: 1972
BISAC compatible software
Membership(s): Independent Book Publishers Association (IBPA)

Infocus® Corp
13190 SW 68 Pkwy, Suite 120, Portland, OR 97223-8368
Tel: 503-207-4700 Toll Free Tel: 877-388-8360 (cust serv)
E-mail: salessupport@infocus.com
Web Site: www.infocus.com
Key Personnel
Pres: Liting Cai
Founded: 1986

Ingenta
317 George St, New Brunswick, NJ 08901
Tel: 732-563-9292 Fax: 732-563-9044
Web Site: www.ingenta.com
Key Personnel
CEO: Scott Winner
CFO & Secy: Jon Sheffield
Dir, Busn Growth: Heather Lantz
Head, Prof Servs: Matt Williams
Founded: 1998
Branch Office(s)
7 Bulfinch, Suite 202, Boston, MA 02114
313A, Zhongguancun Development Bldg, No 12, Shangdi Information Rd, Haidian District, Beijing 100085, China Tel: (010) 62961913
8100 Alec Issigonis Way, Oxford OX4 2HU, United Kingdom (headquarters), Sales Mgr: Claire Milburn Tel: (01865) 397800 Fax: (01865) 397801

Innodata Inc
55 Challenger Rd, Suite 202, Ridgefield Park, NJ 07660
Tel: 201-371-8000 Toll Free Tel: 877-454-8400

E-mail: info@innodata.com; marketing@innodata.com
Web Site: innodata.com
Key Personnel
Pres & CEO: Jack S Abuhoff
EVP & COO: Ashok Kumar Mishra
SVP & Gen Coun: Amy Agress
SVP, Prod Innovation: R Douglas Kemp
Founded: 1988
Membership(s): The Association for Work Process Improvement; Association of American Publishers Professional & Scholarly Publishing Division; Center for Information Development & Content Management Strategies (CIDM); International Association of Outsourcing Professionals (IAOP); National Federation of Abstracting and Information Services (NFAIS); Society for Technical Communication (STC); Society of Knowledge Based Publishers (SKBP); Software & Information Industry Association (SIIA)

International Business Machines Corp, see IBM Corp

Intex Solutions Inc
110 "A" St, Needham, MA 02494
Tel: 781-449-6222 *Fax:* 781-444-2318
E-mail: sales@intex.com
Web Site: www.intex.com
Key Personnel
VP, Sales: Jim Wilner
Founded: 1985

Intuit Inc
2700 Coast Ave, Mountain View, CA 94043
Tel: 650-944-6000 *Toll Free Tel:* 800-446-8848
E-mail: investor_relations@intuit.com
Web Site: www.intuit.com
Key Personnel
Founder & Chmn, Exec Comm: Scott Cook
Exec Chmn of the Bd: Brad Smith
CEO: Sasan Goodarzi *E-mail:* sasan_goodarzi@intuit.com
Chief Mktg Offr & Gen Mgr, Strategic Partnerships: Lara Balazs *E-mail:* lara_balazs@intuit.com
EVP & CFO: Michelle Clatterbuck *E-mail:* michelle_clatterbuck@intuit.com
EVP & CTO: Marianna Tessel *E-mail:* marianna_tessel@intuit.com
EVP & Chief Corp Strategy & Devt Offr: Anton Hanebrink *E-mail:* anton_hanebrink@intuit.com
EVP & Chief Cust Success Offr: Mark Notarainni *E-mail:* mark_notarainni@intuit.com
EVP & Chief Prod & Design Offr: Diego Rodriguez *E-mail:* diego_rodriguez@intuit.com
EVP & Chief People & Places Offr: Laura Fennell *E-mail:* laura_fennell@intuit.com
EVP & Gen Mgr, Consumer Group: Greg Johnson *E-mail:* greg_johnson@intuit.com
SVP, Gen Coun & Corp Secy: Kerry McLean *E-mail:* kerry_mclean@intuit.com
Sr Communs Mgr: Karen Nolan *Tel:* 650-944-6619 *E-mail:* karen_nolan@intuit.com
Founded: 1983

ISIS Papyrus America
Subsidiary of ISIS Information Systems GmbH
301 Bank St, South Lake, TX 76092
Tel: 817-416-2345 *Fax:* 817-416-1223
E-mail: info@isis-papyrus.com
Web Site: www.isis-papyrus.com
Key Personnel
CEO: Annmarie Pucher
Acct Mgr: Carol A Fiore *E-mail:* carol.fiore@isis-papyrus.com
Branch Office(s)
ISIS Papyrus Europe AG, Papyrus Platz 1, Brunn am Gebirge, 2345 Vienna, Austria (intl headquarters)
ISIS Papyrus Asia Pacific Pte Ltd, 29-01 Suntec City Tower 2, 9 Temasek Blvd, Singapore 038989, Singapore

ISOMEDIA Inc
12842 Interurban Ave S, Seattle, WA 98168
Tel: 425-869-5411 *Toll Free Tel:* 866-838-4389 (sales); 877-638-9277 (support) *Fax:* 425-869-9437
E-mail: sales@isomedia.com
Web Site: www.isomedia.com
Key Personnel
Pres & Chmn: Bruce Straughan
CEO & CTO: Steve Milton
Dir, Internet Opers: Dan Sivils
Founded: 1991

Itzhack Shelomi Design
25 Cushman Rd, Scarsdale, NY 10583
Tel: 212-689-7469
E-mail: studio@ishelomi.com; studio@serifes.com
Web Site: www.ishelomi.com
Key Personnel
Owner & Creative Dir: Itzhack Shelomi
Founded: 1987

JF Language LLC, see Unitype LLC

Kensington Technology Group
Division of ACCO Brands Inc
1500 Fashion Island Blvd, Suite 300, San Mateo, CA 94404-1595
Toll Free Tel: 800-535-4242
E-mail: globalmarketing@kensington.com
Web Site: www.kensington.com
Key Personnel
VP & Global Gen Mgr: Ben Thacker
Dir, US Mktg: Jeff Smith
Founded: 1981

Knovel Corp
Division of Elsevier Inc
230 Park Ave, 8th fl, New York, NY 10169
Tel: 212-309-8100
Web Site: app.knovel.com/kn
Founded: 1880
Membership(s): Special Libraries Association (SLA)

Kontron America Inc
Division of Kontron S&T AG
9477 Waples St, San Diego, CA 92121
Toll Free Tel: 888-294-4558 (sales); 800-480-0044 (cust serv, US only) *Fax:* 858-677-0898
E-mail: info@kontron.com
Web Site: www.kontron.com
Branch Office(s)
5020 Brandin Ct, Fremont, CA 94538 *Tel:* 510-284-1100 *Fax:* 510-284-1111
4555 Rue Ambroise-Lafortune, Boisbriand, QC J7H 0A4, Canada *Tel:* 450-437-5682 *Toll Free Tel:* 800-387-4222 *Fax:* 450-437-8053

Kroy LLC
3830 Kelley Ave, Cleveland, OH 44114
Tel: 216-426-5600 *Toll Free Fax:* 800-523-2881
E-mail: info@kroy.com; support@kroy.com
Web Site: www.kroy.com

KyTek Inc
PO Box 338, Weare, NH 03281
Tel: 603-529-2512
E-mail: sales@kytek.com
Web Site: www.kytek.com
Key Personnel
Pres: Keith Erf

Labrecque Creative Sound
2825 Main St, Becket, MA 01223
Key Personnel
Owner & Prodr: David Labrecque *Tel:* 520-240-6001 (cell)
Founded: 1993

Lachina Creative
Formerly Lachina Precision Graphics Services
3693 Green Rd, Cleveland, OH 44122
Tel: 216-292-7959
E-mail: info@lachina.com
Web Site: www.lachina.com
Key Personnel
Pres: Jeff Lachina *E-mail:* jlachina@lachina.com
Dir, Prodn Servs: Whitney Philipp *E-mail:* wphilipp@lachina.com
Dir, Proj Mgmt Off: Shawn Vazinski *E-mail:* svazinski@lachina.com
Founded: 1978

Lachina Precision Graphics Services, see Lachina Creative

LanternMedia
Division of Lantern Publishing & Media
128 Second Place, Garden Suite, Brooklyn, NY 11231
Tel: 212-414-2275
Web Site: www.lanternmedia.net
Key Personnel
Pres & Publr: Martin Rowe *E-mail:* martin@lanternbooks.com

Laplink Software Inc
600 108 Ave NE, Suite 610, Bellevue, WA 98004
Tel: 425-952-6000 *Toll Free Tel:* 800-LAPLINK (527-5465)
E-mail: info@laplink.com; sales@laplink.com
Web Site: web.laplink.com
Key Personnel
Chmn of the Bd & CEO: Thomas Koll
VP, Fin & COO: Randy Clark
VP & CTO: Jack Wilson
Founded: 1983

LexisNexis®
Division of RELX Group plc
9443 Springboro Pike, Dayton, OH 45342
Toll Free Tel: 800-227-9597
E-mail: information@lexisnexis.com
Web Site: www.lexisnexis.com

LG Electronics USA
Division of LG Electronics Inc
1000 Sylvan Ave, Englewood Cliffs, NJ 07632
Tel: 201-816-2000 *Toll Free Tel:* 800-243-0000 (cust serv)
Web Site: www.lg.com/us
Key Personnel
Pres & CEO: Thomas Yoon
Founded: 1958

Lightning Source LLC
Subsidiary of Ingram Content Group LLC
1246 Heil Quaker Blvd, La Vergne, TN 37086
Tel: 615-793-5000 (Ingram) *Toll Free Tel:* 800-378-5508; 800-509-4156 (cust serv)
E-mail: lsicustomersupport@ingramcontent.com
Web Site: www.ingramcontent.com/publishers/print
Key Personnel
Chief Content Offr: Phil Ollila
CFO: Brian Dauphin
Chief Logistics Offr, Global Opers: John F Secrest
Sr Key Acct Mgr: Liz Hunter
Key Acct Sales Mgr: Ali Galbraith
Mgr, Content Acqs Sales: Alicia Samuel
Mgr, Trade Sales: Caitlin Kleinschmidt
Supv, Content Acq Sales: Bailey Davis
Founded: 1997

PUBLISHING SYSTEMS, SERVICES & TECHNOLOGY — SERVICES

Linguistic Systems Inc (LSI)
260 Franklin St, Suite 230, Boston, MA 02110
Tel: 617-528-7400
E-mail: clientservice@linguist.com
Web Site: www.linguist.com
Key Personnel
Founder & Pres: Martin Roberts
Founded: 1967
Membership(s): American Translators Association (ATA); Association of Language Companies (ALC); Globalization & Localization Association (GALA)

Linguist's Software
300 Tineke Way, Travelers Rest, SC 29690-6903
Tel: 425-775-1130
E-mail: sales@linguistsoftware.com
Web Site: www.linguistsoftware.com
Key Personnel
Pres: Philip B Payne *E-mail:* phil@linguistsoftware.com
Founded: 1988

Love & Logic Institute Inc
2207 Jackson St, Suite 102, Golden, CO 80401-2300
Tel: 303-278-7552 *Toll Free Tel:* 800-338-4065
Fax: 303-278-3894 *Toll Free Fax:* 800-455-7557
E-mail: cservice@loveandlogic.com
Web Site: www.loveandlogic.com
Key Personnel
Opers Mgr: Kelly Borden *E-mail:* kellyb@loveandlogic.com
Founded: 1977

Lumina Datamatics Inc
600 Cordwainer Dr, Unit 103, Norwell, MA 02061
Tel: 508-746-0300 *Fax:* 508-746-3233
E-mail: marketing@luminad.com
Web Site: luminadatamatics.com
Key Personnel
EVP, Busn Devt: Jack Mitchell
EVP, Solutions, Transitions & US Opers: Sandeep Dhawan
Founded: 2005
Branch Office(s)
c/o Arnecke Sibeth Distribution, Rechtsanwaelte Steuerberater Partnerschaftsgesellschaft mdB, Gueterplatz 1, 60327 Frankfurt am Main, Germany *Tel:* (06155) 862 99-0 *Fax:* (06155) 862 99-19
Ascendas International Tech Park, 12th fl, Phase II (Crest), CSIR Rd, Taramani, Chennai 600 113, India *Tel:* (044) 4017 6000; (044) 4017 6001
Santosh Raj Plaza, 1st fl, Subburaman St, Gandhi Nagar, 12/9, St, Shenoy Nagar, Madurai 625 020, India
Andheri (E), Unit 117-120, SDF - IV, SEEPZ - SEZ, Mumbai 400 096, India *Tel:* (022) 4034 0515; (022) 4034 0508 *Fax:* (022) 2829 1673
Off No 47/1, 7th fl, Tower-B, A-41, Correnthum Tower, Sector-62, Noida 201 301, India
Plot No 29-34, East Coast Rd, Saram Revenue Village, Oulgaret Municipality, Lawspet Post, Puducherry 605 008, India *Tel:* (0413) 226 4500
No 10, Vazhudavoor Rd, Pettaiyanchathiram, Thattanchavadi, Puducherry 605 009, India *Tel:* (0413) 401 1635
Apple One Equicom Tower, 11th fl, Mindanao Ave Corner Biliran St, Central (pob), Cebu Business Park, 6000 Cebu City, Cebu, Philippines
c/o SOPHI Outsourcing Inc, G/F DBPI IT Plaza, Calindagan, 6200 Dumaguete City, Negros Oriental, Philippines

Brixham Laboratory, Brixham, Devon TQ5 8BA, United Kingdom
Lumina Datamatics UK Ltd, 153 Milton Keynes Business Ctr, Linford Wood, Milton Keynes MK14 6GD, United Kingdom

Lynx Media Inc
13654 Victory Blvd, No 282, Valley Glen, CA 91401
Tel: 818-761-5859 *Toll Free Tel:* 800-451-5969
Fax: 818-761-7099
E-mail: sales@lynxmedia.com
Web Site: www.lynxmedia.com
Key Personnel
Pres: Len Latimer
Founded: 1987

Map Resources
151 N Union St, No 4, Lambertville, NJ 08530
Mailing Address: PO Box 334, Lambertville, NJ 08530
Tel: 609-397-1611 *Toll Free Tel:* 800-334-4291
Fax: 609-751-9378
E-mail: info@mapresources.com; support@mapresources.com
Web Site: www.mapresources.com
Key Personnel
Owner: Barbara Fordyce
Founded: 1985

Masque Publishing Inc
8400 Park Meadows Dr, Lonetree, CO 80124
Tel: 303-290-9853 *Fax:* 303-290-6303
E-mail: support@masque.com
Web Site: www.masque.com
Key Personnel
Off Mgr: Beverly Scott *Tel:* 303-290-9853 ext 114
Founded: 1986

Master Books®
Imprint of New Leaf Publishing Group LLC
3142 Hwy 103 N, Green Forest, AR 72638
Mailing Address: PO Box 726, Green Forest, AR 72638
Tel: 870-438-5288 *Toll Free Tel:* 800-999-3777
E-mail: nlp@nlpg.com; sales@masterbooks.com
Web Site: www.masterbooks.com; www.nlpg.com
Key Personnel
Pres, New Leaf Publishing Group: Randy Pratt
Ed-in-Chief: Laura Welch
Edit Asst: Craig Froman
Founded: 1976

Matrox Graphics Inc
Division of Matrox
1055 Saint Regis Blvd, Dorval, QC H9P 2T4, Canada
Tel: 514-822-6000 *Toll Free Tel:* 800-361-1408 (sales) *Fax:* 514-822-6363
Web Site: www.matrox.com/graphics
Key Personnel
Busn Devt Mgr: Ron Berty
Founded: 1976

Maverick Publications LLC
131 NE Fifth St, Prineville, OR 97754
Mailing Address: PO Box 5007, Bend, OR 97708
Tel: 541-382-6978
E-mail: moreinfo@maverickbooks.com
Web Site: maverickbooks.com
Key Personnel
Owner: Gary Asher
Founded: 1967

Meadows Publishing Solutions
1320 Tower Rd, Schaumburg, IL 60173
Tel: 847-882-8202 *Fax:* 847-882-9494
E-mail: sales@meadowsps.com
Web Site: meadowsps.com

Key Personnel
Founder & Pres: John Kriho *E-mail:* jkriho@meadowsps.com
Founded: 1991 (as Meadows Information Systems Inc)

Media Cybernetics Inc
1700 Rockville Pike, Suite 240, Rockville, MD 20852
Tel: 301-495-3305 *Toll Free Tel:* 800-263-2088
E-mail: support@mediacy.com; marketing@mediacy.com
Web Site: www.mediacy.com
Key Personnel
Pres: Nick Beavers
Founded: 1981

Media Supply Inc
208 Philips Rd, Exton, PA 19341
Tel: 610-884-4400 *Toll Free Tel:* 800-944-4237
Fax: 610-884-4500
E-mail: info@mediasupply.com
Web Site: www.mediasupply.com
Key Personnel
VP: Frank Quinlisk
Founded: 1986

Medina Software Inc
1441 Oberlin Terr, Suite 1010, Lake Mary, FL 32746
Tel: 407-227-4112
Web Site: www.medinasoft.com
Key Personnel
CEO & Dir, Mktg: Carmen Medina
CFO: Jorge Medina *E-mail:* jm@medinasoft.com
Founded: 1985
Membership(s): Institute of Electrical and Electronics Engineers Inc (IEEE)

Megavision Inc
PO Box 60158, Santa Barbara, CA 93160
Tel: 805-964-1400 *Toll Free Tel:* 888-324-2580
E-mail: info@mega-vision.com
Web Site: www.mega-vision.com
Key Personnel
Pres: Ken Boydston
Sales & Mktg: Richard Chang *E-mail:* rchang@mega-vision.com
Founded: 1983

Micro Focus
One Irvington Ctr, 700 King Farm Blvd, Suite 125, Rockville, MD 20850-5736
Tel: 301-838-5000 *Toll Free Tel:* 877-686-9637
Web Site: www.microfocus.com
Founded: 1981

Microboards Technology Inc
8150 Mallory Ct, Chanhassen, MN 55317
Tel: 952-556-1600; 952-556-1639 (tech support)
Toll Free Tel: 800-646-8881 *Fax:* 952-556-1620
E-mail: sales@microboards.com
Web Site: www.microboards.com
Key Personnel
Dir, Opers: Dean Ditty
Sales Mgr: Brian Towey *E-mail:* briant@microboards.com
Founded: 1989

Microsearch Corp
101 Western Ave, Gloucester, MA 01930
Tel: 781-231-9991 *Toll Free Tel:* 800-895-0212
E-mail: info@microsearch.net
Web Site: www.microsearchcorporation.net
Key Personnel
CEO: Charles J Kelly *Tel:* 781-231-9991 ext 3 *E-mail:* chuck.kelly@microsearch.net
Pres & Mktg Dir: Susan Kelly *Tel:* 781-231-9991 ext 4

Dir, Electronic Publg: Josephine Sacco *Tel:* 781-231-9991 ext 6
Founded: 1995

Miles 33 International LLC
Subsidiary of Miles 33 Ltd
40 Richards Ave, Norwalk, CT 06854
Tel: 203-838-2333 *Fax:* 203-838-4473
E-mail: info@miles33.com
Web Site: www.miles33.com
Key Personnel
VP, US Opers: Jeff Malik

Monotype Imaging Inc
600 Unicorn Park Dr, Woburn, MA 01801
Tel: 781-970-6000
Web Site: www.monotype.com
Key Personnel
Pres & CEO: Scott Landers
Dir, Sales Opers: Kyle Jacobson
Branch Office(s)
12655 W Jefferson Blvd, Los Angeles, CA 90066
600 California St, San Francisco, CA 94108
6309 Monarch Park Place, Suite 102, Niwot, CO 80503
National Bldg, 125 S Clark St, Chicago, IL 60603
1370 Broadway, Suite 1450, New York, NY 10018
Corrientes 161, 2nd fl, Cordoba, Argentina
Monotype China, 16 XiXia Rd, FuHui Bldg, Suite 5-115, Shanghai 200120, China
Monotype GmbH, Spichernstr 2, 10777 Berlin, Germany
Prius Global & Universal, Tower-B, 2nd, 3rd & 4th fl, Plot No A-3, 4 & 5, Sector-125, Noida 201 301, India
Monotype KK, MG Ichigaya Bldg, 5th fl, 1-9 Gobancho, Chiyoda-ku, Tokyo 102-0076, Japan
Monotype Korea, 805 Seongji Heights 3-Cha Bldg, Yeoksam-dong, Gangnam-gu, Seoul 135-717, South Korea
The Tea Bldg, Unit 2.05, 56 Shoreditch High St, London E1 6JJ, United Kingdom

MPS North America LLC
Subsidiary of MPS Ltd
5728 Major Blvd, Suite 528, Orlando, FL 32819
Tel: 407-472-1280 *Toll Free Tel:* 866-978-1008
Fax: 212-981-2983
E-mail: marketing@mpslimited.com
Web Site: www.mpslimited.com
Founded: 1973
Branch Office(s)
1901 S Fourth St, Suite 222, Effingham, IL 62401
477 Madison Ave, 6th fl, New York, NY 10022 *Tel:* 407-472-1280
1822 E NC Hwy 54, Suite 120, Durham, NC 27713-3210
MPS Ltd, HMG Ambassador, 137 Residency Rd, Bangalore 560 025, India *Tel:* (080) 4178 4242 *Fax:* (080) 4178 4222
MPS Ltd, RR Towers, Super A, 16/17 TVK Industrial Estate, Guindy, Chennai 600 032, India *Tel:* (044) 4916 2222 *Fax:* (044) 4916 2225
MPS Ltd, 33 IT Park, Sahastradhara Rd, Dehradun 248 001, India *Tel:* (0135) 6677 954
MPS Ltd, 709 DLI Corporate Greens, Sector 74A, Narsinghpur, Gurugram 122 004, India *Tel:* (0124) 661 3134
MPS Interactive Systems, GRM Tech Bldg, 2nd fl, Plot No DH-6/29, Action Area-1, Rajarhat, New Town, Kolkata, West Bengal 700 156, India *Tel:* (033) 66111500
MPS Interactive Systems, The Great Oasis, D-13, 2nd fl, Marol Industrial Estate, Andheri (E), Mumbai 400 093, India *Tel:* (022) 6643 8100 *Fax:* (022) 6643 8800
MPS Ltd, C35, Sector 62, Noida 201 307, India (corp off) *Tel:* (0120) 4599750 *Fax:* (0120) 4021280
Membership(s): Publishing Professionals Network (PPN)

MRC Medical Communications
Division of MRC Media Group Co
12 Lincoln Blvd, Suite 103, Emerson, NJ 07630
Tel: 201-986-0247
E-mail: info@mrcmedical.net
Web Site: www.mrcmedical.net
Key Personnel
Pres & CEO: David J Rector
VP, New Busn Devt: Susan Rector
Founded: 1978

Multi-Tech Systems Inc
2205 Woodale Dr, Mounds View, MN 55112
Tel: 763-785-3500 *Toll Free Tel:* 800-328-9717
Fax: 763-785-9874
E-mail: info@multitech.com; sales@multitech.com; mtsmktg@multitech.com
Web Site: www.multitech.com
Key Personnel
Chmn: Patricia Sharma
CEO: Stefan Lindvall
CFO: Patrick Golden
EVP, Strategic Progs: Del Palacheck
VP, Mktg: Sara Brown
VP, Opers: Terry Boe
VP, Strategic Devt: Daniel Quant
Founded: 1970

Myriddian LLC
8510 Corridor Rd, Suite 100, Savage, MD 20763
Tel: 443-285-0271 (cell)
E-mail: info@myriddian.com
Web Site: www.myriddian.com
Key Personnel
CTO: Jason Myers
Founded: 2010
BISAC compatible software

Naviga
7900 International Dr, Suite 800, Bloomington, MN 55425
Tel: 651-639-0662
E-mail: info@navigaglobal.com
Web Site: www.navigaglobal.com
Key Personnel
CEO: Jeffrey Shine
Mktg Mgr: Ted Thomason *Tel:* 602-674-5800 ext 104 *E-mail:* ted.thomason@navigaglobal.com
Founded: 1985
Branch Office(s)
1652 Greenview Dr, Suite 220, Rochester, MN 55902 *Tel:* 609-466-5305
14614 N Kierland Blvd, S-270, Scottsdale, AZ 85254 *Tel:* 602-674-5800
6767 N Wickham Rd, Suite 111, Melbourne, FL 32940 *Tel:* 321-254-5559
302 Knights Run Ave, Suite 940, Tampa, FL 33602 *Tel:* 813-221-1600
One Van de Graaff Dr, Suite 205, Burlington, MA 01803
173 Parkland Plaza, Suite B, Ann Arbor, MI 48103 *Tel:* 734-887-4400
3 Becker Farm Rd, Suite 401, Roseland, NJ 07068 *Tel:* 973-422-0800
5625 FM 1960 Rd W, Suite 503, Houston, TX 77069 *Tel:* 281-537-6060
350 S 400 W, Suite 100, Lindon, UT 84042 *Tel:* 801-853-5000
3610 W 2100 S, Salt Lake City, UT 84120 *Tel:* 801-746-1542
Visionsvej 51, 9000 Aalborg, Denmark *Tel:* 96 31 42 00
Pieni Roobertinkatu 9, 00130 Helsinki, Finland *Tel:* (040) 0899637
Rheinstr 40-42, 64283 Darmstadt, Germany *Tel:* (06151) 27 76 652
Berga Alle 1, 254 52 Helsingborg, Sweden *Tel:* (042) 25 39 00
Sodra Langgatan 31, 392 32 Kalmar, Sweden *Tel:* (0480) 36 20 00
49-51 Eton St, Suite 5A, Sutherland, NSW 2232, Australia *Tel:* (02) 9810 6939

NETS
Division of Newgen North America Inc
2714 Bee Caves Rd, Suite 201, Austin, TX 78746-5682
Web Site: www.netype.com
Founded: 1940
Branch Office(s)
60/3 Lattice Bridge Rd, Thiruvanmiyur, Chennai, India *Tel:* (044) 4348 0800 *Fax:* (044) 2443 0740

New England Typographic Service, see NETS

New Riders Publishing
Division of Pearson Education Ltd
50 California St, 18th fl, San Francisco, CA 94111
Toll Free Tel: 800-428-5331 (cust serv)
E-mail: customer-service@informit.com; press@peachpit.com
Web Site: www.peachpit.com
Founded: 1986

New York Legal Publishing Corp
120 Broadway, Menands, NY 12204
Tel: 518-459-1100 *Toll Free Tel:* 800-541-2681
Fax: 518-459-9718
E-mail: info@nylp.com
Web Site: www.nylp.com
Key Personnel
Pres: Ernest Barvoets
VP: Alex Barvoets

NewTek Inc
5131 Beckwith Blvd, San Antonio, TX 78249
Tel: 210-370-8000 *Toll Free Tel:* 800-368-5441
Fax: 210-370-8001
E-mail: sales@newtek.com (cust serv)
Web Site: www.newtek.com
Key Personnel
Dir, PR: Scott Carroll *E-mail:* scarroll@newtek.com
Founded: 1986

Nissho Electronics USA Corp
The Concourse I, 226 Airport Pkwy, Suite 340, San Jose, CA 95110
Tel: 408-969-9700
E-mail: info@nelco.com
Web Site: www.nelco.com
Key Personnel
Pres: Mizuki Enomoto
Founded: 1985

Nisus Software Inc
PO Box 1302, Solana Beach, CA 92075-7302
Tel: 858-481-1477 *Fax:* 858-764-0573
E-mail: info@nisus.com; sales@nisus.com; customerservice@nisus.com
Web Site: www.nisus.com
Key Personnel
Founder, Pres & CEO: Jerzy Lewak, PhD
PR: Dave Larson *E-mail:* dave@nisus.com
Founded: 1983

North Atlantic Publishing Systems Inc
66 Commonwealth Ave, Concord, MA 01742
Tel: 978-371-8989
E-mail: naps@napsys.com
Web Site: www.napsys.com
Key Personnel
Pres: Peter Baumgartner *E-mail:* pjb@napsys.com
Founded: 1989

Nuance Communications Inc
One Wayside Rd, Burlington, MA 01803
Tel: 781-565-5000 *Toll Free Tel:* 800-654-1187 (cust serv); 888-372-1908 (orders)

PUBLISHING SYSTEMS, SERVICES & TECHNOLOGY

Web Site: www.nuance.com
Key Personnel
CEO: Mark Benjamin
EVP & CFO: Dan Tempesta
EVP & Chief People Offr: Beth Conway
EVP & CTO: Joe Petro
EVP & Gen Mgr, Healthcare Div: Diana Nole
SVP & CIO: Mark Sherwood
SVP, Corp Devt: David Garfinkel
Sr Communs Mgr: Katie Byrne *Tel:* 781-565-5290 *E-mail:* katie.byrne@nuance.com

NWinds
One Northgate Sq, Greensburg, PA 15601
Mailing Address: PO Box 1760, Greensburg, PA 15601
Tel: 724-838-8993 *Toll Free Fax:* 888-315-3711
E-mail: support@nwinds.com
Web Site: www.nwinds.com
Key Personnel
Pres & Programming Dir: Randolph S Krofick, PhD
Founded: 1987
Membership(s): American Society of Mechanical Engineers (ASME)

OBS, see Open Book Systems Inc®

OKI Data Americas Inc
Subsidiary of OKI Data Corp of Japan
8505 Freeport Pkwy, Suite 600, Irving, TX 75063
Tel: 972-815-4800 *Toll Free Tel:* 800-OKI-DATA (654-3282)
E-mail: support@okidata.com
Web Site: www.oki.com/us/printing
Key Personnel
Pres & CEO: Sergio Horikawa
Deputy Pres: Shigeaki Tadokoro
SVP, Fin & CFO: Takehito Katagiri
Dir, Channel Sales: Mark Hansinger
Founded: 1972
Branch Office(s)
2067 Wineridge Place, Suite C, Escondido, CA 92029
5000 Dearborn Circle, Suite 110, Mount Laurel, NJ 08054
5800 Hurontario St, Suite 1020, Mississauga, ON L5R 4B9, Canada *Tel:* 905-755-5800 *Fax:* 905-755-5840 *Web Site:* www.oki.com/ca

OmniUpdate Inc
1320 Flynn Rd, Suite 100, Camarillo, CA 93012
Tel: 805-484-9400 *Toll Free Tel:* 800-362-2605
E-mail: sales@omniupdate.com
Web Site: omniupdate.com
Key Personnel
Pres & CEO: Lance Merker
CFO: Gordon Dyer
Chief Mktg Offr: Owen Savage
COO: Peter DeVries
Chief Prod Architect: Yves Lempereur
Chief Revenue Offr: Mark Triest
VP, Cust Success: Dennis Esguerra
Sr Dir, Prod Mgmt: Kimberly Prieto
Dir, IT: Micah Roark
Dir, Prod Devt: Shahab Lashkari
Founded: 1982

OMRON Microscan Systems Inc
Division of OMRON Corp
700 SW 39 St, Suite 100, Renton, WA 98057
Tel: 425-226-5700 *Toll Free Tel:* 800-762-1149 *Fax:* 425-226-8250
E-mail: info@microscan.com
Web Site: www.microscan.com
Key Personnel
Pres & CEO: Andy Zosel
Founded: 1982
Branch Office(s)
486 Amherst St, Nashua, NH 03063 *Tel:* 603-598-8400 *Fax:* 603-821-6908

Rm 2211, Bank of China Tower, No 200, Yincheng Zhong Rd, Shanghai 200120, China *Tel:* 400 820 4535; (0186) 6621 9571 (cell)
E-mail: jdeng@microscan.com

OneTouchPoint
1225 Walnut Ridge Dr, Hartland, WI 53029
Tel: 262-369-6000 *Toll Free Tel:* 800-332-2348 *Fax:* 262-369-5647
E-mail: info@1touchpoint.com
Web Site: www.1touchpoint.com
Key Personnel
CEO: Dave Holland
Dir, Mktg & Sales Opers: Carey Howard
Founded: 1982
BISAC compatible software
Branch Office(s)
5241 Voges Rd, Madison, WI 53718 *Tel:* 608-838-9147
525 W Alameda Dr, Suite 101, Tempe, AZ 85282, Contact: James Parker *Tel:* 480-966-4003 *Fax:* 480-966-4016
5280 Joliet St, Denver, CO 80239 *Tel:* 303-227-1400
1441 Western Ave, Cincinnati, OH 45214 *Tel:* 513-421-1600
8410-B Tuscany Way, Austin, TX 78754 *Tel:* 512-454-6874

Open Book Systems Inc®
21 Broadway, Suite 5, Rockport, MA 01966
Tel: 978-546-7346
E-mail: info@obs.com
Web Site: www.obs.com
Key Personnel
Pres: Laura Fillmore *E-mail:* laura@obs.com
Founded: 1982
Membership(s): Book Industry Study Group (BISG); Independent Book Publishers Association (IBPA); Internet Society

Open Text Corp
275 Frank Tompa Dr, Waterloo, ON N2L 0A1, Canada
Tel: 519-888-7111 *Fax:* 519-888-0677
Web Site: opentext.com
Key Personnel
Vice Chair, CEO & CTO: Mark J Barrenechea
Chief HR Offr: Brian Sweeney
EVP & CFO: Madhu Ranganathan
EVP & Chief Prod Offr: Muhi Majzoub
EVP & Gen Mgr, SMB & Consumer: Craig Stilwell
EVP, Chief Legal Offr & Corp Devt: Gordon A Davies
EVP, Cust Opers: James McGourlay
EVP, Worldwide Sales: Simon "Ted" Harrison
SVP & CIO: David Jamieson
SVP & Chief Mktg Offr: Lou Blatt
SVP, Cloud Serv Delivery: Savinay Berry
SVP, Corp Devt: Douglas "Doug" M Parker
SVP, Partners & Alliances: Prentiss Donohue
SVP, Revenue Opers: Paul Duggan
Branch Office(s)
2655 N Sheridan Way, Suites 301 & 300, Mississauga, ON L5K 2N6, Canada
38 Leek Crescent, Richmond Hill, ON L4B 4N8, Canada *Tel:* 905-762-6001
75 Queen St, Suite 4400, Montreal, QC H3C 2N6, Canada *Tel:* 514-908-5406

Oracle America Inc
Unit of Oracle Corp
500 Oracle Pkwy, Redwood Shores, CA 94065
Tel: 650-506-7000 *Toll Free Tel:* 800-392-2999; 800-633-0738 (sales)
Web Site: www.oracle.com
Key Personnel
Exec Chmn of the Bd & CTO: Larry Ellison
VChmn of the Bd: Jeffrey O Henley
CEO: Safra A Catz
Founded: 1982

SERVICES

O'Reilly Media Inc
1005 Gravenstein Hwy N, Sebastopol, CA 95472
Tel: 707-827-7019 (cust support); 707-827-7000 *Toll Free Tel:* 800-889-8969; 800-998-9938 *Fax:* 707-829-0104; 707-824-8268
E-mail: orders@oreilly.com; support@oreilly.com
Web Site: www.oreilly.com
Key Personnel
Founder & CEO: Tim O'Reilly
Founded: 1978
Branch Office(s)
2 Ave de Lafayette, 6th fl, Boston, MA 02111 *Tel:* 617-354-5800 *Fax:* 617-661-1116

Outskirts Press Inc
10940 S Parker Rd, Suite 515, Parker, CO 80134
Toll Free Tel: 888-OP-BOOKS (672-6657) *Toll Free Fax:* 888-208-8601
E-mail: info@outskirtspress.com
Web Site: www.outskirtspress.com
Key Personnel
CEO: Jeanine Sampson
CFO & CTO: Lynn Sampson
Pres & Chief Mktg Offr: Brent Sampson
Founded: 2003
Membership(s): The Association of Publishers for Special Sales (APSS); Better Business Bureau (BBB); Colorado Independent Publishers Association (CIPA); Florida Writers Association; Independent Book Publishers Association (IBPA)

Paulist Press
997 Macarthur Blvd, Mahwah, NJ 07430-9990
SAN: 202-5159
Tel: 201-825-7300 *Toll Free Tel:* 800-218-1903 *Fax:* 201-825-6921
E-mail: info@paulistpress.com; publicity@paulistpress.com
Web Site: www.paulistpress.com
Key Personnel
Pres & Publr: Rev Mark-David Janus, PhD
Founded: 1865
Membership(s): Association of Catholic Publishers Inc

Personal TeX Inc
722 Lombard St, Suite 201, San Francisco, CA 94133
Tel: 415-296-7550 *Toll Free Tel:* 800-808-7906 *Fax:* 415-296-7501
E-mail: sales@pctex.com
Web Site: www.pctex.com
Key Personnel
Pres: Lance Carnes
Founded: 1985

Pivar Computing Services Inc
1500 Abbott Ct, Buffalo Grove, IL 60089
Tel: 847-478-8000 *Toll Free Tel:* 800-CONVERT (266-8378) *Fax:* 847-478-8750
Web Site: www.pivar.com
Key Personnel
Prod Mgr: Scott Johnson *E-mail:* scott@pivar.com
Founded: 1982

Planar
Subsidiary of Leyard International
1195 NW Compton Dr, Beaverton, OR 97006-1992
Tel: 503-748-1100 *Toll Free Tel:* 866-475-2627
E-mail: sales@planar.com
Web Site: www.planar.com
Key Personnel
EVP, Sales, Mktg & Prof Servs: Adam Schmidt
VP, Global Opers: Rob Baumgartner
Founded: 1983

Powis Parker Inc
2929 Fifth St, Berkeley, CA 94710

Tel: 510-848-2463 *Toll Free Tel:* 800-321-BIND (321-2463) *Fax:* 510-848-2169
E-mail: customerservice@powis.com
Web Site: www.powis.com
Key Personnel
Founder & Pres: Kevin Powis Parker
US Sales Dir: Bill Lawrence
Founded: 1983

Presstek LLC, see Mark Andy Inc

PrimeArray Systems Inc
1500 District Ave, Burlington, MA 01803
Tel: 978-455-9488 *Toll Free Tel:* 800-433-5133
E-mail: info@primearray.com; sales@primearray.com
Web Site: www.primearray.com
Key Personnel
Pres: Sean D Campbell

Printronix Inc
6440 Oak Canyon, Suite 200, Irvine, CA 92618
Tel: 714-368-2300 *Toll Free Tel:* 800-665-6210
Web Site: www.printronix.com
Key Personnel
CEO: Werner Heid
CFO: Mark Tobin
VP & Gen Mgr, Global Prods: Marlon Woolforde
VP, Americas Sales & Mktg: Ron Gillies
Founded: 1974

Printware LLC
Member of Vanguard Graphics International
2935 Waters Rd, Suite 160, St Paul, MN 55121-1523
Tel: 651-456-1400 *Fax:* 651-454-3684
E-mail: sales@printwarellc.com
Web Site: www.printwarellc.com
Key Personnel
Pres: Tim Murphy *Tel:* 651-456-1404
  E-mail: tim.murphy@printwarellc.com
Dir, Sales Opers: Bill Frederick *Tel:* 651-456-1418 *E-mail:* bill.frederick@printwarellc.com

ProductionPro
246 Park St, Bensenville, IL 60106
Tel: 847-696-1600
E-mail: sales@productionpro.com; graphics@productionpro.com
Web Site: www.productionpro.com
Key Personnel
Owner: Douglas Tello *Tel:* 847-696-1600 ext 101
  E-mail: douglas@productionpro.com
Founded: 1992

Progressive Publishing Services (PPS)
555 Ryan Run Rd, Suite B, York, PA 17404
Tel: 717-764-5908 *Fax:* 717-764-5530
E-mail: info@pps-ace.com
Web Site: www.pps-ace.com
Key Personnel
VP: Darby Jo Campbell *E-mail:* dcampbell@pps-ace.com
Dir: Crystal Clifton *E-mail:* cclifton@pps-ace.com
Founded: 2015

Pronk Media Inc
16 Glen Davis Crescent, Toronto, ON M4E 1X5, Canada
Tel: 416-715-9660 (cell)
E-mail: info@pronk.com; hello@pronk.com
Web Site: www.pronk.com; www.h5engines.com; www.html5alive.com
Key Personnel
Pres: Gord Pronk *E-mail:* gord@pronk.com
Founded: 1981 (as Pronk & Associates Inc)
BISAC compatible software

ProQuest LLC, part of Clarivate PLC
789 E Eisenhower Pkwy, Ann Arbor, MI 48108
Tel: 734-761-4700 *Toll Free Tel:* 800-521-0600; 877-779-6768 (sales)
E-mail: sales@proquest.com
Web Site: www.proquest.com
Key Personnel
SVP, Global Sales, Mktg & Cust Experience: James Holmes
Founded: 1872
Branch Office(s)
699 James L Hart Pkwy, Ypsilanti, MI 48197
7315 Innovation Blvd, Fort Wayne, IN 46818
800 S Tucker Dr, MLIC 1520, Tulsa, OK 74104
Unit 804, Tower E1, Beijing Oriental Plaza, No 1 E Chang An Ave, Dong Cheng District, Beijing 100738, China *Tel:* (010) 5977 6010 *Fax:* (010) 8460 8669
Taskoepruestr 1, 22761 Hamburg, Germany *Tel:* (040) 89 809 0 *Fax:* (040) 89 809 250
16A W Sq, 318 Hennessy Rd, Wanchai, Hong Kong *Tel:* 2836 5636 *Fax:* 2834 7133
315, AKD Tower, Near HUDA Off, Sector 14, Gurgaon 122 001, India *Tel:* (0124) 4100615
Mitsubishi Juko Yokohama Bldg, 3-3-1, Minatomirai, Nishi-ku, Yokohama-shi, Kanagawa 220-8401, Japan *Tel:* (045) 342 4780 *Fax:* (045) 342 4784
B909, Phileo Damansara 1, No 9 Jl 16/11, 46350 Petaling Jaya, Selangor, Malaysia *Tel:* (03) 7954 2880 *Fax:* (03) 7958 3446
Al-Thurayya II, Off 1304, PO Box 502568, Dubai, United Arab Emirates *Tel:* (04) 4331810 *Fax:* (04) 3697646
The Quorum, Barnwell Rd, Cambridge CB5 8SW, United Kingdom *Tel:* (01223) 215 512 *Fax:* (01223) 215 513
3 Dorset Rise, 5th fl, London EC4Y 8EN, United Kingdom *Tel:* (020) 7832 1700 *Fax:* (020) 7832 1710
Avon House, Headlands Business Park, Salisbury Rd, Ringwood, Hants BH24 3PB, United Kingdom *Tel:* (01425) 471160

PTC
121 Seaport Blvd, Boston, MA 02210
Tel: 781-370-5000 *Fax:* 781-370-6000
Web Site: www.ptc.com
Key Personnel
Pres & CEO: James Heppelman
EVP & CFO: Kristian Talvitie
EVP & Chief Cust Offr: Eduarda Camacho
EVP & Chief HR Offr: Jill Larsen
EVP & Chief Strategy Offr: Kathleen Mitford
EVP & Gen Coun: Aaron Von Staats
EVP & Pres, SaaS: Jon Hirschtick
EVP, Augmented Reality Prods: Mike Campbell
EVP, Prods: Kevin Wrenn
EVP, Sales & Commercial Mktg: Michael Ditullio
VP, Corp Communs: Jack McAvoy
  E-mail: jmcavoy@ptc.com
Dir, Corp Communs: Michelle Hopkins
  E-mail: mihopkins@ptc.com

Publishing Data Management Inc
39 Broadway, 28th fl, New York, NY 10006
Tel: 212-673-3210 *Fax:* 212-673-3390
E-mail: info@pubdata.com
Web Site: www.pubdata.com
Key Personnel
Pres: Addison Roverano *E-mail:* addison@pubdata.com
Founded: 1970

QualityLogic Inc
9576 W Emerald St, Boise, ID 83704
Tel: 208-424-1905
E-mail: info@qualitylogic.com
Web Site: www.qualitylogic.com
Key Personnel
Pres & CEO: Gary James

SVP, Engg: Steve Kang
Gen Mgr, Smart Grid: James Mater
Founded: 1986
Branch Office(s)
2245 First St, Suite 103, Simi Valley, CA 93065
4045 NW 64 St, Suite 120, Oklahoma City, OK 73116

Quark Software Inc
Chrysler Bldg, 405 Lexington Ave, 9th fl, New York, NY 10174
Toll Free Tel: 800-676-4575
Web Site: www.quark.com
Founded: 1981
Branch Office(s)
1600 Beltline Ave NE, Suite 210, Grand Rapids, MI 49525
QuarkXPress Publishing R&D (India) Pvt Ltd, A-45, Industrial Area, Phase-VIII-B, Mohali 160 059, India
5th fl, Block 3, 3 Custom House Plaza, Harbour Master Place, IFSC, Dublin 1 D01 VY76, Ireland

Regent Press Printers & Publishers
2747 Regent St, Berkeley, CA 94705
Tel: 510-845-1196
E-mail: regentpress@mindspring.com
Web Site: www.regentpress.net
Key Personnel
Owner, Publr & Mng Ed: Mark Weiman
Founded: 1978

REX
13431 SW Scotts Bridge Dr, Tigard, OR 97223-1609
Tel: 503-238-4525
E-mail: info@rexpost.com
Web Site: www.rexpost.com
Key Personnel
Pres & Chief Audio Engr: Russell Gorsline
Founded: 1972
Membership(s): Oregon Media Production Association (OMPA); Screen Actors Guild - American Federation of Television & Radio Artists (SAG-AFTRA)

Rex Three Inc
15431 SW 14 St, Sunrise, FL 33326
Tel: 954-388-8708 *Toll Free Tel:* 800-782-6509 *Fax:* 954-452-0569
Web Site: www.rex3.com
Key Personnel
VP, Sales: Alex Steuben
Founded: 1959

Ricoh Americas Corp
Subsidiary of Ricoh Co Ltd (Tokyo, Japan)
300 Eagleview Blvd, Exton, PA 19341
Tel: 610-296-8000 *Toll Free Tel:* 800-333-2679 (prod support); 800-637-4264 (sales)
Web Site: www.ricoh-usa.com
Key Personnel
Pres & CEO: Joji Tokunaga
SVP & CFO: Sven Adler
SVP, Busn Advancement: Dennis Dispenziere
SVP, Commercial & Indus Print: Gavin Jordan-Smith
SVP, Gen Coun & Secy: George Gowen
SVP, Strategic Planning Off: Shark Samejima
EVP, HR & Deputy Gen Mgr, Shared Servs: Donna Venable
Founded: 1962

Rimage Corp
Division of Equus Holdings Inc
201 General Mills Blvd, Golden Valley, MN 55427
Tel: 952-944-8144; 952-946-0004 (option 2, tech support) *Toll Free Tel:* 800-445-8288; 800-553-8312 (option 2, tech support)

PUBLISHING SYSTEMS, SERVICES & TECHNOLOGY — SERVICES

E-mail: sales@rimage.com
Web Site: www.rimage.com
Key Personnel
VP, Sales (Americas): Sean Gaafar
Founded: 1978
Branch Office(s)
Rimage Information Technology (Shanghai) Co Ltd, Rm No 206, 207, 2F, No 1, FuXing Zhong Rd, HuangPu District, Shanghai 200025, China *Tel:* (021) 5887 8905 *E-mail:* enterprise.sales@rimage.cn
Rimage Europe GmbH, Werner-von-Braun str 9, 63303 Dreieich-Offenthal, Germany *Tel:* (06074) 8521 0 *E-mail:* sales@rimage.de
Rimage Japan Co Ltd, 4F Arai No 38 Bldg, 2-7-1 Hamamatsu-cho, Minato-ku, Tokyo 105-0013, Japan *Tel:* (03) 6452 8780 *Fax:* (03) 6452 8785 *E-mail:* jsales@rimage.co.jp
Rimage Taiwan, 2F-1, No 115, sec 2, Keelung Rd, Taipei 11053, Taiwan *Tel:* (02) 2726 0100 *E-mail:* asia-sales@rimage.com

RISO Inc
Subsidiary of RISO Kagaku Corp
10 State St, Suite 201, Woburn, MA 01801-2105
Tel: 978-777-7377 *Toll Free Tel:* 800-942-7476 (cust support)
Web Site: us.riso.com
Key Personnel
Pres & CEO: Koji Sonobe
VP & CFO: Alex Olshan
VP, Corp Planning: Sho Fujiwara
Founded: 1986

Roland DGA Corp
Subsidiary of Roland Corporation of Japan
15363 Barranca Pkwy, Irvine, CA 92618-2216
Tel: 949-727-2100 *Toll Free Tel:* 800-542-2307 *Fax:* 949-727-2112
Web Site: www.rolanddga.com
Key Personnel
Pres & CEO: Andrew Oransky
Mktg Dir: Dan Wilson *E-mail:* dwilson@rolanddga.com
Founded: 1990

Saferock
75 Armour Place, Dumont, NJ 07628
Tel: 646-535-0110
E-mail: info@saferock.com
Web Site: saferockretail.com
Key Personnel
CEO: Shah Karim *E-mail:* shah@saferock.com
Founded: 1997

Samsung Research America (SRA)
Subsidiary of Samsung Electronics Co Ltd
665 Clyde Ave, Mountain View, CA 94043
Tel: 650-210-1001
E-mail: sra-contact-us@samsung.com
Web Site: www.sra.samsung.com
Key Personnel
Pres: Joon Lee
Founded: 1988
Branch Office(s)
18500 Von Karman Ave, Suite 700, Irvine, CA 92612
735 Battery St, San Francisco, CA 94111
27931 Smyth Dr, Valencia, CA 91355
3 Van De Graff Dr, Suite 4, Burlington, MA 01803
123 W 18 St, 7th fl, New York, NY 10011
6625 Excellence Way, Plano, TX 75023
101 College St, Toronto, ON M5G 1L7, Canada
1250 Rene-Levesque Blvd W, 37th fl, Montreal, QC H3B 4W8, Canada

Sceptre Inc
16800 Gale Ave, City of Industry, CA 91745
Tel: 626-369-3698 *Toll Free Tel:* 800-788-2878 *Fax:* 626-369-3488

E-mail: sceptrecs@sceptre.com; scp-marketing@sceptre.com; scp-sales@sceptre.com
Web Site: www.sceptre.com
Founded: 1984

SCREEN Americas
Subsidiary of SCREEN Graphic & Precision Solutions
5110 Tollview Dr, Rolling Meadows, IL 60008-3715
Tel: 847-870-7400 *Toll Free Tel:* 800-372-7737
E-mail: info@screenamericas.com
Web Site: www.screenamericas.com
Key Personnel
Pres: Ken Ingram
Founded: 1967

Scribe Inc
765 S Front St, Philadelphia, PA 19147
Tel: 215-336-5094; 215-336-5095
E-mail: contact@scribenet.com
Web Site: www.scribenet.com
Key Personnel
Pres: David Alan Rech *Tel:* 215-336-5094 ext 105 *E-mail:* drech@scribenet.com
Founded: 1993
BISAC compatible software
Branch Office(s)
3758 SW 30 Ave, Fort Lauderdale, FL 33312

SDL
201 Edgewater Dr, Suite 225, Wakefield, MA 01880
Tel: 781-756-4400 *Toll Free Tel:* 800-933-6910 (sales) *Fax:* 781-989-8199
Web Site: www.sdl.com

SENCOR International
445 Park Ave, 9th fl, New York, NY 10022
Tel: 212-980-6726
Web Site: www.sencorinternational.com
Key Personnel
CEO: George Martel *E-mail:* georgemartel@sencorinternational.com
Founded: 1984

Sharp Electronics Corp
Subsidiary of Sharp Corp
100 Paragon Dr, Montvale, NJ 07645
Toll Free Tel: 800-BE-SHARP (237-4277)
Web Site: www.sharpusa.com
Key Personnel
Pres & CEO: Mike Marusic
Founded: 1962

Shepherd Inc
2223 Key Way Dr, Suite B, Dubuque, IA 52002
Tel: 563-584-0500
Web Site: www.shepherd-inc.com
Key Personnel
Prodn Mgr: Deb Leibfried
Founded: 1989

Six Red Marbles LLC
101 Station Landing, Medford, MA 02155
Tel: 857-588-9000
E-mail: info@sixredmarbles.com
Web Site: www.sixredmarbles.com
Key Personnel
CEO: David Goodman
Chief Mktg & Admin Offr: Robin Zaccardo
EVP, Busn Devt: John Kenney
EVP, Opers: Michele Baird
SVP, Fin: Meg Trant
SVP, Prodn: Alexandre Vallette
SVP, Technol: Chris Kaefer
VP, Busn Devt: Cary Drake
VP, Learning Strategy: Kelvin Bentley
Exec Dir, Humanities: Bill Scroggie
Exec Dir, STEM: Joyce Spangler
Founded: 1996

BISAC compatible software
Branch Office(s)
4030 W Braker Lane, Bldg 3, Suite 350, Austin, TX 78759 *Tel:* 512-372-4800
209 Austine Dr, Suite 115, Brattleboro, VT 05301 *Tel:* 410-527-1606
Jouve India Pvt Ltd, 1st fl, No 1415, No 283/1B2, Old Mahabalipuram Rd, Kottivakkam, Chennai 600 041, India *Tel:* (044) 40205300
The Great Eastern Ctr, 2nd fl, 70, Nehru Place, Delhi 110 019, India *Tel:* (011) 42636116

Smart Communications Inc
641 Lexington Ave, 13th fl, New York, NY 10022
Tel: 212-486-1894
E-mail: info@smartny.com
Web Site: www.smartny.com
Key Personnel
Pres: John M Smart
BISAC compatible software

Sony DADC US Inc
Division of Sony Corp of America
1800 N Fruitridge Ave, Terre Haute, IN 47804
Tel: 818-462-8100
E-mail: sales@sonydadc.com
Web Site: www.sonydadc.com
Founded: 1983
Branch Office(s)
430 Gibraltar Dr, Bolingbrook, IL 60440 *Tel:* 630-739-8060
Membership(s): Association of National Advertisers Inc (ANA); Audio Publishers Association; Content Delivery & Storage Association (CDSA); The Digital Entertainment Group (DEG)

Sony Electronics Inc
Division of Sony Corp of America
16535 Via Esprillo, San Diego, CA 92127
Tel: 858-942-2400
E-mail: selpr@sony.com
Web Site: www.sony.com/all-electronics
Key Personnel
Head, Corp Communs: Rosemary Flynn

The Sound Lab Inc
3355 Bee Cave Rd, Bldg 7, Suite 701, Austin, TX 78746
Tel: 512-476-2122 *Fax:* 512-476-2127
E-mail: info@thesoundlabinc.com
Web Site: www.thesoundlabinc.com
Key Personnel
Owner: Steve Metz *E-mail:* steve@thesoundlabinc.com
Owner & Pres: Phil Mezzetti *E-mail:* phil@thesoundlabinc.com
Founded: 2002

Square Two Design Inc
2325 Third St, Suite 305, San Francisco, CA 94107
Tel: 415-437-3888
E-mail: info@square2.com
Web Site: www.square2.com
Key Personnel
Pres & Creative Dir: Eddie Lee
Founded: 1991
Branch Office(s)
No 8 Hua Jia Di Nan Jie, Chao Yang District, Beijing 100102, China, Pres: Min Wang *Tel:* (01350) 1084-543 *E-mail:* mwang@square2.com

Star Micronics America Inc
Subsidiary of Star Micronics Co Ltd
65 Clyde Rd, Suite G, Somerset, NJ 08873-3485
Tel: 848-216-3300 (sales) *Toll Free Tel:* 800-782-7636 *Fax:* 848-216-3222 (sales)
E-mail: sales@starmicronics.com
Web Site: www.starmicronics.com

Stilo Corp
1900 City Park Dr, Suite 504, Ottawa, ON K1J 1A3, Canada
Tel: 613-745-4242 *Fax:* 613-745-5560
E-mail: contact@stilo.com
Web Site: www.stilo.com
Key Personnel
CEO: Bryan Tipper
Branch Office(s)
Stilo International, Windmill Hill Business Park, Whitehill Way, Swindon SN5 6QR, United Kingdom (headquarters) *Tel:* (01793) 441 444 *Fax:* (01793) 441 644

Story Monsters LLC
4696 W Tyson St, Chandler, AZ 85226-2903
Tel: 480-940-8182 *Fax:* 480-940-8787
Web Site: www.StoryMonsters.com; www.StoryMonstersInk.com; www.StudioStoryMonster.com
Key Personnel
Pres: Linda F Radke *E-mail:* Linda@StoryMonsters.com
Founded: 1985

Story Monsters Press, see Story Monsters LLC

SumTotal Systems LLC
Division of Skillsoft Co
2850 NW 43 St, Suite 150, Gainesville, FL 32606
Tel: 352-264-2800 *Toll Free Tel:* 866-933-1416 *Fax:* 352-374-2257
E-mail: customersupport@sumtotalsystems.com
Web Site: www.sumtotalsystems.com
Key Personnel
Exec Chmn: Ronald Hovsepian
Chief Admin Offr: John Frederick
Chief Content Offr: Mark Onisk
CFO: Bobby Jenkins
Chief Mktg Offr: Michelle Boockoff-Bajdek
COO: Mike Pellegrino
CTO: Apratim Purakayastha
SVP, Global Sales: Ted Winslow
Branch Office(s)
1415 28 St, Suite 410, West Des Moines, IA 50266 *Tel:* 515-222-9903 *Fax:* 515-222-5920
10 Post Office Sq, Suite 800N, Boston, MA 02109 *Tel:* 857-317-7700
200 Summit Dr, 2nd fl, Burlington, MA 01803
600 Parsippany Rd, Parsippany, NJ 07054
1110 A Brookdale Ave, Cornwall, ON K6J 4P4, Canada
Three International Towers, Level 24, 300 Barangaroo Ave, Sydney, NSW 2000, Australia *Tel:* (02) 8067 8663
102-116 Rue Victor Hugo, 92300 Levallois Perret, France *Tel:* 01 70 37 53 18 *Fax:* 01 70 37 53 53 *Web Site:* www.sumtotalsystems.fr
SumTotal Systems GmbH, Berliner Allee 59, 40212 Duesseldorf, Germany *Tel:* (061) 55-60 52 91 *Fax:* (061) 55-60 51 00
Two International Finance Ctr, Level 19, 8 Finance St, Hong Kong, Hong Kong *Tel:* 2251 8926 *Fax:* 2251 8926
Mindspace Raheja IT Park, Maximus Towers, Bldg 2-B, 7th fl, Cyberabad, Hyderabad 500 081, India *Tel:* (040) 6695 0000
Urbanprem Shibuya Bldg 4F, 1-4-2, Shibuya, Shibuya-ku, Tokyo 150-0002, Japan *Tel:* (03) 6823 6400 *Fax:* (03) 6823 6401 *Web Site:* japan.sumtotalsystems.com
Suntec Tower Three, Level 42, 8 Temasek Blvd, Singapore 038988, Singapore *Tel:* 6866 3788

In der Luberzen 40, 8902 Undorf, Zurich, Switzerland *Tel:* (044) 744 47 42
5 Arlington Sq, 1st fl, Dawnshire Way, Bracknell RG12 1WA, United Kingdom *Tel:* (01276) 401950

Sunny Day Productions Inc, see REX

Tamron USA Inc
10 Austin Blvd, Commack, NY 11725
Tel: 631-858-8400 *Toll Free Tel:* 800-827-8880 *Fax:* 631-543-5666; 631-858-8462 (cust serv)
E-mail: custserv@tamron.com
Web Site: www.tamron-usa.com
Key Personnel
Pres & CEO: Greg Maniaci
SVP: Hidekazu Suzuki
VP, Mktg & Communs: Stacie Errera *E-mail:* errera@tamron.com
Dir, Fin: Hiroaki Katano *E-mail:* katano@tamron.com
Dir, Opers: Pat Simonetti *E-mail:* simonetti@tamron.com

Tatung Co of America Inc
Subsidiary of Tatung Co of Tawain
2850 El Presidio St, Long Beach, CA 90810
Tel: 310-637-2105
E-mail: service@tatungusa.com
Web Site: www.tatungusa.com
Key Personnel
CEO: Christina Sun
Founded: 1972

Chip Taylor Communications, LLC
2 East View Dr, Derry, NH 03038
Tel: 603-434-9262 *Toll Free Tel:* 800-876-CHIP (876-2447) *Fax:* 603-425-1784
E-mail: info@chiptaylor.com
Web Site: www.chiptaylor.com
Key Personnel
Pres: Chip Taylor
Founded: 1985
Membership(s): National Association of Television Program Executives Inc (NATPE)

Taylor Communications Inc
Subsidiary of Taylor Corp
1725 Roe Crest Dr, North Mankato, MN 56003
Toll Free Tel: 866-541-0937
Web Site: www.taylorcommunications.com
Key Personnel
CEO: Glen Taylor

TEACH Services Inc
11 Quartermaster Circle, Fort Oglethorpe, GA 30742-3886
SAN: 246-9863
Tel: 706-504-9192 *Toll Free Tel:* 800-367-1844 (sales) *Toll Free Fax:* 866-757-6023
E-mail: sales@teachservices.com; info@teachservices.com
Web Site: www.teachservices.com
Key Personnel
Owner & Pres: Timothy Hullquist *E-mail:* t.hullquist@teachservices.com
Publr & Opers Mgr: Bill Newman *E-mail:* b.newman@teachservices.com
Founded: 1984
BISAC compatible software
Membership(s): Independent Book Publishers Association (IBPA)

Teledyne DALSA
Subsidiary of Teledyne Technologies Inc
605 McMurray Rd, Waterloo, ON N2V 2E9, Canada
Tel: 519-886-6000 *Toll Free Tel:* 800-361-4914
Web Site: www.teledynedalsa.com

Key Personnel
Group Pres: Edwin Roks
Founded: 1979

TeXnology Inc
57 Longwood Ave, Brookline, MA 02446
Tel: 617-738-8029
Web Site: www.texnology.com
Key Personnel
Pres: Amy Hendrickson *E-mail:* amyh@texnology.com

Thistle Printing Ltd
Division of DATA Communications Management Corp
35 Mobile Dr, Toronto, ON M4A 2P6, Canada
Tel: 416-288-1288 *Fax:* 416-288-0737
E-mail: sales@thistleprinting.com
Web Site: www.thistleprinting.com
Key Personnel
Gen Mgr: Mike Branov
Founded: 1931

Thomson Reuters
Union Bank Bldg, 50 California St, San Francisco, CA 94111
Tel: 424-434-7000
E-mail: editorial.booking@tr.com
Web Site: www.thomsonreuters.com

Three D Graphics Inc
11340 W Olympic Blvd, Suite 352, Los Angeles, CA 90064
Tel: 310-231-3330 *Toll Free Tel:* 800-913-0008 *Fax:* 310-231-3303
E-mail: info@threedgraphics.com; orders@threedgraphics.com; sales@threedgraphics.com
Web Site: www.threedgraphics.com
Key Personnel
CEO: Elmer Easton
Founded: 1986

3M Touch Systems Inc
501 Griffin Brook Park Dr, Methuen, MA 01844
Tel: 978-659-9000
Web Site: www.3m.com/3m/en_us/touch-systems-us

Transparent Language Inc
12 Murphy Dr, Nashua, NH 03062
Tel: 603-262-6300 *Toll Free Tel:* 800-567-9619 (cust serv & sales)
E-mail: info@transparent.com; support@transparent.com (tech support)
Web Site: www.transparent.com
Key Personnel
Founder & CEO: Michael Quinlan
SVP & Gen Mgr: Chuck McGonagle
Founded: 1991

Treacyfaces Inc
43 Maltby Ave, West Haven, CT 06516
Mailing Address: PO Box 26036, West Haven, CT 06516-8036
Tel: 203-389-7037
Web Site: www.treacyfaces.com
Key Personnel
Pres & Dir, Typography: Joseph Treacy *E-mail:* jtreacy@treacyfaces.com
Founded: 1984

TRUMATCH Inc
PO Box 501, Water Mill, NY 11976-0501
Tel: 631-204-9100 *Toll Free Tel:* 800-TRU-9100 (878-9100 US & CN)
E-mail: info@trumatch.com
Web Site: www.trumatch.com
Key Personnel
Pres: Steven J Abramson *E-mail:* stevea@trumatch.com

VP: Jane E Nichols *E-mail:* janen@trumatch.com
Founded: 1990
Membership(s): PRINTING United Alliance

Ultimate TechnoGraphics Inc
480 Blvd St-Laurent, Suite 404, Montreal, QC H2Y 3Y7, Canada
Tel: 514-938-9050
E-mail: customerservice@imposition.com; marketing@imposition.com; sales@imposition.com
Web Site: www.imposition.com
Key Personnel
Pres & CEO: Julie Watson *Tel:* 514-938-9050 ext 226 *E-mail:* julie@imposition.com
Founded: 1989
Membership(s): Association for Print Technologies (APTech); Ghent Workgroup; International Cooperation for Integration of Processes in Prepress, Press & Postpress Organization (CIP4); NAGASA

UniNet Imaging Inc
3232 W El Segundo Blvd, Hawthorne, CA 90250
Tel: 424-675-3300 *Fax:* 424-675-3400
E-mail: sales@uninetimaging.com
Web Site: www.uninetimaging.com
Key Personnel
Pres: Nestor Saporiti
Corp Mktg Dir: Marcela Gasanz
 E-mail: marcelag@uninetimaging.com
Inside Sales Mgr: Karen Hughes *Tel:* 424-675-3300 ext 1109 *E-mail:* karenh@uninetimaging.com
Founded: 1995
Branch Office(s)
UniNet East Coast, 22 Old Dock Rd, Yaphank, NY 11980, Dir of Sales, North America: Craig Spooner *Tel:* 631-590-1040 ext 203 *Fax:* 603-218-3285 *E-mail:* craigs@uninetimaging.com

Unisys Corp
801 Lakeview Dr, Suite 100, Blue Bell, PA 19422
Tel: 215-274-2742
Web Site: www.unisys.com
Key Personnel
Chmn & CEO: Peter Altabef
Pres & COO: Eric Hutto
SVP & CFO: Mike Thomson
SVP & Chief HR Offr: Katie Ebrahimi
SVP & Chief Mktg Offr: Ann Sung Ruckstuhl
SVP & Pres, Global Sales: Jeff Renzi
SVP, Gen Coun & Secy: Gerald P Kenney
SVP, Prods & Platforms & CTO: Vishal Gupta
VP & Corp Cont: Erin Mannix
VP & Treas: Shalabh Gupta
Branch Office(s)
4750 Lindle Rd, Harrisburg, PA 17111 *Tel:* 717-561-7500
9701 Jeronimo Rd, Irvine, CA 92618 *Tel:* 949-380-5000
5451 Great America Pkwy, Suite 125, Santa Clara, CA 95054 *Tel:* 408-980-9526
Discovery Plaza, One Seventh St, Suite A, Augusta, GA 30901 *Tel:* 706-842-6191 *Fax:* 706-432-0534
Bishop Street Tower, 700 Bishop St, Suite 507, Honolulu, HI 96813
3199 Pilot Knob Rd, Eagan, MN 55121 *Tel:* 651-846-0006 *Fax:* 651-687-2985
10B Madison Ave Ext, Albany, NY 12203 *Tel:* 518-452-6100 *Fax:* 518-452-6196
55 Broad St, 7th fl, New York, NY 10004
2501 N Harwood St, Suite 1501, Dallas, TX 75201 *Tel:* 469-250-1620
480 N 2200 W, Salt Lake City, UT 84116 *Tel:* 801-594-4911 *Fax:* 801-594-5660
44664 Guilford Dr, Ashburn, VA 20147
1051 E Cary St, Suite 610, Richmond, VA 23219

UnitechEDI Inc
220 Winthrop St, Winthrop, MA 02152
Toll Free Tel: 800-330-4094
E-mail: info@unitechedi.com
Web Site: www.unitechedi.com
Key Personnel
Pres: Rich Vettel
Founded: 1995
Membership(s): Book Industry Study Group (BISG)

Unitype LLC
116-A Mockingbird Lane, Lockhart, TX 78644
Tel: 512-620-0384 *Toll Free Tel:* 800-697-9186
E-mail: info@unitype.com; sales@unitype.com; support@unitype.com
Web Site: www.unitype.com
Key Personnel
Pres: Mike Forgey

Vectorworks Inc
Subsidiary of Nemetschek Group
7150 Riverwood Dr, Columbia, MD 21046
Tel: 410-290-5114 *Toll Free Tel:* 888-646-4223 (sales) *Fax:* 410-290-7266
E-mail: sales@vectorworks.net
Web Site: www.vectorworks.net
Key Personnel
CEO: Dr Biplab Sarkar
CFO: Maria Bible
CIO: Paul Pharr
VP, Mktg: Jeremy Powell
VP, Prod Devt: Steve Johnson
VP, Sales: Nicole Davison
Founded: 1985

Videotex Systems Inc
10255 Miller Rd, Dallas, TX 75238
Tel: 972-231-9200 *Toll Free Tel:* 800-888-4336 *Fax:* 972-231-2420
E-mail: info@videotexsystems.com
Web Site: www.videotexsystems.com
Key Personnel
Pres: Bob Gillman *Tel:* 972-231-9200 ext 102 *E-mail:* gillman@videotexsystems.com

Videx Inc
1105 NE Circle Blvd, Corvallis, OR 97330
Tel: 541-738-5500; 541-738-0521 *Fax:* 541-752-5285
E-mail: sales@videx.com; support@videx.com
Web Site: www.videx.com
Key Personnel
Pres: Tammy Davis
Founded: 1979

Virginia Systems
5509 W Bay Ct, Midlothian, VA 23112
Tel: 804-739-3200 *Fax:* 804-739-8376
E-mail: sales@virginiasystems.com
Web Site: www.virginiasystems.com
Key Personnel
Pres: Philip Van Cleave *E-mail:* philip@virginiasystems.com
VP: Margaret Van Cleave
Founded: 1984

VITEC Multimedia
931 Benecia Ave, Sunnyvale, CA 94085
Tel: 650-230-2400 *Toll Free Tel:* 800-451-5101 *Fax:* 408-739-1706
E-mail: sunnyvale@vitec.com
Web Site: www.vitec.com
Founded: 1988
Branch Office(s)
3174 Marjan Dr, Atlanta, GA 30340 *Tel:* 404-320-0110 *Fax:* 404-320-3132 *E-mail:* atlanta@vitec.com

VO2 Mix Audio Post
116 Spadina Ave, Suite 208, Toronto, ON M5V 2K6, Canada
Tel: 416-603-3954 *Fax:* 416-603-3957
E-mail: info@vo2mix.ca
Web Site: www.vo2mix.ca
Key Personnel
Owner & Pres: Terry Wedel
Founded: 1999

Wasatch Computer Technology LLC
333 S 300 E, Salt Lake City, UT 84111
Tel: 801-575-8043
E-mail: subscription@wasatch.com
Web Site: www.wasatch.com

Western Telematic Inc (WTI)
5 Sterling, Irvine, CA 92618
Tel: 949-586-9950 *Toll Free Tel:* 800-854-7226
E-mail: info@wti.com
Web Site: www.wti.com
Key Personnel
CEO: Dan Morrison
Founded: 1964

WeWrite LLC
11040 Alba Rd, Ben Lomond, CA 95005
Tel: 831-336-3382
E-mail: info@wewrite.net
Web Site: www.wewrite.net
Key Personnel
Pres & CEO: Delores L Palmer
 E-mail: dpalmer@wewrite.net
Dir, Mktg: Rickey Bowen *E-mail:* rbowen@wewrite.net
Ed: Jan Hansen *E-mail:* jhansen@wewrite.net
Founded: 1993

Writers' Supercenter
560 Roland Dr, Norfolk, VA 23509
Tel: 757-515-4315
E-mail: writerspage@writerspage.com
Web Site: writersupercenter.com
Key Personnel
Pres: Irwin Berent
Founded: 2003

Xante Corp
2800 Dauphin St, Suite 100, Mobile, AL 36606
Tel: 251-473-6502; 251-473-4920 (tech support) *Fax:* 251-473-6503
Web Site: www.xante.com
Key Personnel
Pres & CEO: Robert C Ross, Jr
COO: Mark Swanzy
CFO: Mary Ann Harris
VP, Worldwide Mktg & Intl Sales: Mark Priede
Founded: 1989
Branch Office(s)
7920 Alta Sunrise Dr, Suite 110, Citrus Heights, CA 95610
Xante Europe BV, Ratio 39, 6921 RW Duiven, Netherlands *Tel:* (026) 319 3210 *Fax:* (026) 319 3211

Z-Axis
1916 Rte 96, Phelps, NY 14532
Tel: 315-548-5000 *Fax:* 315-548-5100
E-mail: sales@zaxis.net
Web Site: www.zaxis.net
Key Personnel
Pres: Michael Allen
Founded: 1989

ZyLAB North America LLC
7918 Jones Branch Dr, Suite 230, McLean, VA 22102-3366
Tel: 703-442-2400 *Toll Free Tel:* 866-995-2262 *Fax:* 703-991-2508
E-mail: info@zylab.com
Web Site: www.zylab.com
Key Personnel
EVP, North America: Nils Nugeren
Founded: 1983

Branch Office(s)
ZyLAB Technologies BV, Laarderhoogtweg 25, 1101 EB Amsterdam, Netherlands *Tel:* (020) 717 6500 *E-mail:* info@zylab.nl

Employment Agencies

The firms listed below specialize in the book publishing industry.

Aquent LLC
101 W Elm St, Suite 300, Conshohocken, PA 19428-2075
Tel: 610-828-0900 *Toll Free Fax:* 877-303-5224
E-mail: questions@aquent.com
Web Site: aquentstudios.com; aquent.com
Key Personnel
Mgr: Kelly Griffin
Founded: 1986 (as Aquent Inc in Massachusetts)
A professional services firm with a new way of thinking about business. Every service we provide, every solution we advance is driven by a mission to help clients work smarter & more efficiently, achieving greater business results. Our five areas of focus are: marketing & creative services; information technology; healthcare services; financial services; offshore publishing services.
Since 1986, at nearly 70 locations in 15 countries, Aquent has led the way in these fields with a pioneering approach to staffing, consulting, outsourcing & technology. Through more efficient use of people, processes & technology, Aquent partners with clients to optimize resources, improve productivity & maximize financial outcomes.

Association of Writers & Writing Programs (AWP)
440 Monticello Ave, Suite 1802, PMB 73708, Norfolk, VA 23510-2670
Tel: 240-696-7700
E-mail: awp@awpwriter.org; press@awpwriter.org
Web Site: www.awpwriter.org
Founded: 1967
Provides news, information & services for writers & teachers of creative writing. Publishes job list & provides job placement for writers. Advocates on behalf of freedom of expression & professional standards in academia. Conducts an annual competition for the publication of books in poetry, short fiction, creative nonfiction & the novel.
The Writer's Chronicle is published quarterly. *The Guide to Writing Programs* is the most comprehensive guide to creative writing programs in the US & Canada.

Bert Davis Executive Search Inc
555 Fifth Ave, Suite 302, New York, NY 10017
Tel: 212-838-4000
E-mail: info@bertdavis.com
Web Site: www.bertdavis.com
Key Personnel
Founder & Chmn: Bert Davis
Pres: James Conley
EVP: Jeanne Bertelle
SVP: Lauren Aaron; Kristi Johnston; Linda Rascher; Janine Subel
VP: John Tagler
Founded: 1977
The largest executive search firm handling senior-level recruitment for all areas of book publishing: sales, marketing, editorial, finance, design etc. Longtime history of placements in leading companies nationwide; confidential & thorough. President is a director of National Association of Executive Recruiters.

Choice Associates
501 Fifth Ave, Suite 1601, New York, NY 10017
Tel: 212-679-2434 *Fax:* 212-213-0984
E-mail: info@choicepersonnelinc.com
Web Site: www.choicepersonnelinc.com
Key Personnel
Founder & Principal: Steve Klein; Harold Robbins
Founded: 1974
Specialize in editorial, marketing, production, promotion, designers & sales.
Branch Office(s)
700 Veterans Hwy, Suite CL140, Hauppage, NY 11788 *Tel:* 631-617-6002

Cohesion®
511 W Bay St, Suite 480, Tampa, FL 33606
Tel: 813-999-3111 *Toll Free Tel:* 866-727-6800
Web Site: www.cohesion.com
Key Personnel
CEO: John Owens
Chief Strategy Offr: John Larson
Founded: 1982
Provides complete publications support & training. Places screened publications professionals in temporary & permanent positions. Provides start-to-finish editorial, production & design services on outsourcing/project basis. Offers workshops in print & interactive publications. Offers consulting services such as publications evaluations & electronic publishing. Industries served: computer industry, management & environmental consulting firms, book publishers, banks & government agencies. Geographic area served: US. Small, minority, woman-owned firms.
Branch Office(s)
6760 Alexander Bell Dr, Suite 120, Columbia, MD 21046 *Toll Free Tel:* 800-560-0630
5151 Pfeiffer Rd, Suite 105, Cincinnati, OH 45242 *Tel:* 513-587-7700

The Creative Group®, A Robert Half Company
Oliver Street Tower, 17th fl, 125 High St, Boston, MA 02110
Tel: 617-925-5754
Web Site: www.roberthalf.com/us/en/about/our-company/brands/creative-group
Placement of temporary & permanent writers, editors, proofreaders, desktop publishing professionals, designers, illustrators, web designers, web content developers, course developers, media buyers, brand managers & public relations specialists for all forms of creative & technical communications.

HumanEdge
30 Glenn St, Suite 401, White Plains, NY 10603
Tel: 914-428-2233 *Fax:* 914-428-5547
E-mail: info@humanedge.com
Web Site: www.humanedge.com
Key Personnel
Pres: Paul Schwabe
Founded: 1988
Working to create great hiring experiences for candidates & clients alike by applying our skills, energy, integrity & understanding of both individual needs & market forces to make the right match for all types of positions, including traditional contract assignments, career-changing direct searches & freelance gigs.
Branch Office(s)
144 E 44 St, Suite 705, New York, NY 10017 *Tel:* 212-986-6800; 212-779-3333 (client line)
33 Main St, 2nd fl, Newton, CT 06470 *Tel:* 203-792-8500 *Fax:* 203-792-8508
1100 Park Central Blvd S, Suite 3400, Pompano Beach, FL 33064 *Tel:* 954-236-6381 (client line)
201 Rte 17 N, Suite 605, Rutherford, NJ 07070 *Tel:* 201-939-9416 *Fax:* 201-939-0270
Membership(s): American Staffing Association (ASA); Business Council of Westchester (BCW); Staffing Industry Analysts (SIA)

Koller Search Partners
655 Third Ave, 24th fl, New York, NY 10017
Tel: 212-661-5250
E-mail: ksp@kollersearch.com
Web Site: www.kollersearch.com
Key Personnel
Founder & Mng Partner: Edward R Koller, Jr
E-mail: ekoller@kollersearch.com
Mng Partner: Karen Danziger
E-mail: kdanziger@kollersearch.com; Edward Koller, III *E-mail:* erkoller3@kollersearch.com
Executive recruitment in all aspects of book publishing, magazine publishing, direct marketing & electronic information publishing, as well as art & creative publishing.
Branch Office(s)
12655 W Jefferson Blvd, Los Angeles, CA 90066 *Tel:* 213-377-5664
600 California St, San Francisco, CA 94108 *Tel:* 415-964-5688

Lynne Palmer Executive Recruitment Inc
295 Madison Ave, Suite 701, New York, NY 10017
Tel: 212-883-0203 *Fax:* 212-883-0149
E-mail: careers@lpalmer.com
Web Site: www.lpalmer.com
Key Personnel
Owner & Pres: Susan Gordon
Executive search & recruitment within media/digital/publishing industry: including books, magazines, journals, newsletters & online media. Areas in which we recruit & place include administration, art, circulation, corporate communications, digital, design & production, editorial, finance, human resources, marketing, operations, public relations, sales & technology. Our nationwide clientele include: publishing, online educational, multimedia, medical communications & public relations firms.

Publications Professionals LLC
3603 Chain Bridge Rd, Suite A & B, Fairfax, VA 22030-3244
Tel: 703-934-4499 *Fax:* 703-591-7389
E-mail: info@pubspros.com
Web Site: www.pubspros.com
Key Personnel
Founder & CEO: Barbara B Hart
Pres: Linda L Stringer
Founded: 1988
Recruiters of permanent & temporary publication specialists. Pubs Pros, its staff & a roster of independent contractors handle production tasks for books, journals & reports. Clients are in the Washington, DC, metropolitan area; across the US & around the world.
Branch Office(s)
11215 Willamette Meridian Rd NW, Silverdale, WA 98383
Membership(s): Washington Publishers (WP); Women's National Book Association (WNBA)

EMPLOYMENT AGENCIES

Ribolow Associates Inc
1350 Avenue of the Americas, 2nd fl, New York, NY 10019
Tel: 212-575-2700 *Fax:* 646-496-9122
E-mail: ribolowstaffingservices@gmail.com
Web Site: www.ribolow.com
Key Personnel
Pres: Adele Ribolow *E-mail:* adeleribolow@gmail.com
Founded: 1960
Executive search & recruitment in all areas of publishing, advertising & new media: editorial, production, sales, marketing, finance, interactive, desktop & support staff. Permanent placement services.

Winston Personnel
Division of Winston Resources LLC
122 E 42 St, Suite 320, New York, NY 10168
Tel: 212-557-5000
Web Site: www.winstonresources.com
Key Personnel
Chmn: Sy Kaye
Pres: Gregg Kaye; Todd Kaye
Founded: 1967
Senior management, middle & junior level recruitment in magazine & book publishing, corporate communications & public relations; print production & graphics.
Branch Office(s)
1400 Old Country Rd, Suite 418, Westbury, NY 11590 *Tel:* 516-333-3222
50 Main St, 10th fl, White Plains, NY 10606 *Tel:* 914-682-2076
301 Rte 17 N, Main Lobby, Rutherford, NJ 07070 *Tel:* 201-460-9200

Clipping Bureaus

Magnolia Clipping Service
298 Commerce Park Dr, Suite A, Ridgeland, MS 39157
Tel: 601-856-0911 *Fax:* 601-856-3340
E-mail: mail@magnoliaclips.com
Web Site: magnoliaclips.com
Key Personnel
Owner: Dred Porter, Sr *E-mail:* dredportersr@magnoliaclips.com
VP & Dir, Print Monitoring: Joe Porter
  E-mail: joe@magnoliaclips.com
VP, Broadcast Div: Dred Porter, Jr
  E-mail: dredporterjr@magnoliaclips.com
Regional newspaper & magazine clipping service; broadcast monitoring service.

Metropolitan Newsclips Service Inc
1250 Hanley Industrial Ct, St Louis, MO 63144
Tel: 314-395-8917
E-mail: cheryllm@metronewsclips.com
Web Site: www.metronewsclips.com
Key Personnel
Pres: Cheryll A Meyer
Founded: 1985
Complete Missouri, regional, national print, online, broadcast & social media monitoring.
Membership(s): North American Conference of Press Clipping Services

Oklahoma Press Service Inc
Division of Oklahoma Press Association
3601 N Lincoln Blvd, Oklahoma City, OK 73105
Tel: 405-499-0020 *Toll Free Tel:* 888-815-2672
Web Site: www.okpress.com
Key Personnel
Mgr, Digital News Tracking: Keith Burgin
  Tel: 405-499-0024 *E-mail:* kburgin@okpress.com
Clipping service/news monitoring service.

Typing & Word Processing Services

The firms and individuals listed below provide typing, word processing or transcription services. For related listings, see **Editorial Services** (volume 1).

Archetype Inc
Affiliate of North Market Street Graphics (NMSG)
317 N Market St, Lancaster, PA 17603
Tel: 717-392-7438
E-mail: mail@nmsgbooks.com
Web Site: nmsgbooks.com
Key Personnel
Owner: Elizabeth Andes *E-mail:* landes@nmsgbooks.com; LeRoy R Stipe, Jr
Founded: 1983
Double keyboarding/verification of book mss, conversion & coding of disks, typesetting preparation & translation program for all major desktop & conventional front-end systems, large volume capacity. All related Macintosh services specializing in the book publishing market.

Arrow Graphics Inc
PO Box 380291, Cambridge, MA 02238
E-mail: info@arrow1.com
Web Site: www.arrow1.com
Key Personnel
Pres: Alvart Badalian
Sr Graphic/Pubn Designer: Aramais Andonian
Founded: 1988
Complete book production services with state-of-the-art electronic design & publishing capabilities: copy-editing; indexing; typesetting & page composition; typography; design & art direction from concept to finished product; printing; consultation; project management. Novels, poetry, monographs, self-help, how-to, guides, ebooks & children's picture books. From ms to camera-ready to bound book, serving the publishing industry & self-publishing community. Call or write for free information, or visit our web site.

Cynthia Barnhart
141 E 56 St, New York, NY 10022
Tel: 212-759-8037
E-mail: trans.action@verizon.net
Founded: 2000
Word processing mss, academic papers, market research, interviews, reports, legal documents. Transcription from digital audio files, tapes or longhand drafts.

Clotilde's Secretarial & Management Services
PO Box 871926, New Orleans, LA 70187
Tel: 504-242-2912; 504-266-9239 (cell) *Fax:* 504-242-2912
Key Personnel
Owner, Mgr, Writer & ESL Instructor: Elvira C Sylve *E-mail:* elcsy58@att.net
Researcher: Kelly M Sylve
Writer: Lillian Gail Tillman; Brenda Bailey, MLIS
Founded: 1989
Proofread journals, newsletters, research papers & medical documents. Specialize in preparing research papers, medical & legal documents. Write basic legal briefs & transcribe documents. Type reports, proposals & academic papers.
Membership(s): ProLiteracy

Mari Lynch Dehmler, see Fine Wordworking

Fine Wordworking
PO Box 3041, Monterey, CA 93942-3041
Tel: 831-375-6278
E-mail: info@finewordworking.com
Web Site: marilynch.com
Key Personnel
Owner: Mari Lynch Dehmler
Founded: 1981
Services for individuals, publishers & others. Offer editing for accuracy, clarity & effectiveness. Also special assignment writing, proofreading, other help. Confidential. Visit web site for testimonials & other info.

Mari Lynch, see Fine Wordworking

Peace Visions
18850 Vista del Canon, Suite A, Santa Clarita, CA 91321-4512
Tel: 661-251-6669 *Fax:* 661-251-6669
Key Personnel
Contact: Susie V Kaufman
E-mail: susievkaufman@gmail.com
Transcribing. Type/edit TV/film scripts, treatments, mss, theses/dissertations, reports, resumes, newsletters, correspondence. Proofreading (including web site content).

Scribe Inc
765 S Front St, Philadelphia, PA 19147
Tel: 215-336-5094; 215-336-5095
E-mail: contact@scribenet.com
Web Site: www.scribenet.com
Key Personnel
Pres: David Alan Rech *Tel:* 215-336-5094 ext 105
E-mail: drech@scribenet.com
Founded: 1993

A full range of publishing services, including OCR/data conversion, editing, proofreading, design, typesetting, & ebook creation, with expertise in XML, Well-Formed Document Workflow, & staff training. Also helps publishers with accessible, multipurpose publishing.
BISAC compatible software
Branch Office(s)
3758 SW 30 Ave, Fort Lauderdale, FL 33312

SENCOR International
445 Park Ave, 9th fl, New York, NY 10022
Tel: 212-980-6726
Web Site: www.sencorinternational.com
Key Personnel
CEO: George Martel *E-mail:* georgemartel@sencorinternational.com
Founded: 1984
Litigational & transactional document drafting & editing, contract abstracting, case summary writing, electronic document discovery & legal research & analysis comprise SENCOR's range of LPO capabilities. The company combines the domain knowledge of legal researchers & attorneys with the efficiency of in-house developed data acquisition & management tools to meet the knowledge requirements of clients in the legal industry. Among these are legal publishers & practitioners needing the latest information in case law, statutes or testimonies to win court battles.
Clients engaging in SENCOR BI work with IT & statistics professionals & domain experts in marketing, risk management, operations & finance. Aids companies in problem definition, data preparation, exploratory data analytics, descriptive & predictive modeling & the processing & deployment of results.
Also provides customized end-to-end content development & publishing solutions that span the range of information acquisition via research, content enhancement & publication in various formats including printed publications & electronic media.

WordPlayJane
21 Harrison St, Suite 3, New York, NY 10013
Tel: 646-370-9541 (cell)
Key Personnel
Contact: Jane Freeman *E-mail:* wordplayjane@yahoo.com
Founded: 1980
Ms preparation, fiction & nonfiction, ghostwriting, editing, writing coach & book illustration. References available.

Translators & Interpreters — Source Language Index

AFRIKAANS
A WordJourney Translation LLC, pg 1399
American Translation Partners Inc (ATP), pg 1399
Wanda J Boeke, pg 1400
East-West Concepts, pg 1400
iProbe Multilingual Solutions Inc, pg 1402
Linguistic Systems Inc (LSI), pg 1402
Link Translations Inc, pg 1403
Polyglot Communications Inc, pg 1403
Universe Technical Translation Inc, pg 1405

ALBANIAN
A WordJourney Translation LLC, pg 1399
AAA Fine Translation & Interpretation, pg 1399
American Translation Partners Inc (ATP), pg 1399
East-West Concepts, pg 1400
iProbe Multilingual Solutions Inc, pg 1402
Linguistic Systems Inc (LSI), pg 1402
Link Translations Inc, pg 1403
Polyglot Communications Inc, pg 1403
Rennert Translation Group, pg 1404
Universe Technical Translation Inc, pg 1405

ARABIC
A WordJourney Translation LLC, pg 1399
American Translation Partners Inc (ATP), pg 1399
Cross Cultural Communication Systems Inc, pg 1400
East-West Concepts, pg 1400
Eriksen Translations Inc, pg 1401
iProbe Multilingual Solutions Inc, pg 1402
The Language Center, pg 1402
Linguistic Systems Inc (LSI), pg 1402
Link Translations Inc, pg 1403
Polyglot Communications Inc, pg 1403
Rennert Translation Group, pg 1404
School of World Studies, pg 1404
Universe Technical Translation Inc, pg 1405

ARMENIAN
A WordJourney Translation LLC, pg 1399
American Translation Partners Inc (ATP), pg 1399
Cross Cultural Communication Systems Inc, pg 1400
East-West Concepts, pg 1400
iProbe Multilingual Solutions Inc, pg 1402

Linguistic Systems Inc (LSI), pg 1402
Polyglot Communications Inc, pg 1403
Rennert Translation Group, pg 1404
Universe Technical Translation Inc, pg 1405

BELARUSSIAN
A WordJourney Translation LLC, pg 1399
AAA Fine Translation & Interpretation, pg 1399
American Translation Partners Inc (ATP), pg 1399
East-West Concepts, pg 1400
iProbe Multilingual Solutions Inc, pg 1402
Linguistic Systems Inc (LSI), pg 1402
Polyglot Communications Inc, pg 1403
Universe Technical Translation Inc, pg 1405

BENGALI
A WordJourney Translation LLC, pg 1399
American Translation Partners Inc (ATP), pg 1399
Cross Cultural Communication Systems Inc, pg 1400
East-West Concepts, pg 1400
iProbe Multilingual Solutions Inc, pg 1402
Linguistic Systems Inc (LSI), pg 1402
Polyglot Communications Inc, pg 1403
Rennert Translation Group, pg 1404
Universe Technical Translation Inc, pg 1405

BULGARIAN
A WordJourney Translation LLC, pg 1399
AAA Fine Translation & Interpretation, pg 1399
American Translation Partners Inc (ATP), pg 1399
East-West Concepts, pg 1400
iProbe Multilingual Solutions Inc, pg 1402
Linguistic Systems Inc (LSI), pg 1402
Link Translations Inc, pg 1403
MediaLocate Inc, pg 1403
Polyglot Communications Inc, pg 1403
Rennert Translation Group, pg 1404
Universe Technical Translation Inc, pg 1405

BURMESE
A WordJourney Translation LLC, pg 1399
American Translation Partners Inc (ATP), pg 1399

East-West Concepts, pg 1400
iProbe Multilingual Solutions Inc, pg 1402
Linguistic Systems Inc (LSI), pg 1402
Polyglot Communications Inc, pg 1403

CATALAN
A WordJourney Translation LLC, pg 1399
AAA Fine Translation & Interpretation, pg 1399
American Translation Partners Inc (ATP), pg 1399
East-West Concepts, pg 1400
Mark Herman & Ronnie Apter, Translators, pg 1401
iProbe Multilingual Solutions Inc, pg 1402
Linguistic Systems Inc (LSI), pg 1402
Polyglot Communications Inc, pg 1403
Rennert Translation Group, pg 1404
Universe Technical Translation Inc, pg 1405

CHINESE
A WordJourney Translation LLC, pg 1399
American Translation Partners Inc (ATP), pg 1399
Cross Cultural Communication Systems Inc, pg 1400
East-West Concepts, pg 1400
Eriksen Translations Inc, pg 1401
iProbe Multilingual Solutions Inc, pg 1402
The Language Center, pg 1402
Linguistic Systems Inc (LSI), pg 1402
Link Translations Inc, pg 1403
MediaLocate Inc, pg 1403
Polyglot Communications Inc, pg 1403
Rennert Translation Group, pg 1404
School of World Studies, pg 1404
Translations.com, pg 1405
Universe Technical Translation Inc, pg 1405

CZECH
A WordJourney Translation LLC, pg 1399
American Translation Partners Inc (ATP), pg 1399
East-West Concepts, pg 1400
Mark Herman & Ronnie Apter, Translators, pg 1401
iProbe Multilingual Solutions Inc, pg 1402
The Language Center, pg 1402
Linguistic Systems Inc (LSI), pg 1402
Link Translations Inc, pg 1403
MediaLocate Inc, pg 1403
Polyglot Communications Inc, pg 1403

Rennert Translation Group, pg 1404
Universe Technical Translation Inc, pg 1405

DANISH
A WordJourney Translation LLC, pg 1399
AAA Fine Translation & Interpretation, pg 1399
American Translation Partners Inc (ATP), pg 1399
East-West Concepts, pg 1400
Eriksen Translations Inc, pg 1401
iProbe Multilingual Solutions Inc, pg 1402
Solveig Kjok, pg 1402
The Language Center, pg 1402
Linguistic Systems Inc (LSI), pg 1402
Link Translations Inc, pg 1403
MediaLocate Inc, pg 1403
Polyglot Communications Inc, pg 1403
Rennert Translation Group, pg 1404
Translations.com, pg 1405
Universe Technical Translation Inc, pg 1405

DUTCH
A WordJourney Translation LLC, pg 1399
AAA Fine Translation & Interpretation, pg 1399
American Translation Partners Inc (ATP), pg 1399
Wanda J Boeke, pg 1400
East-West Concepts, pg 1400
iProbe Multilingual Solutions Inc, pg 1402
The Language Center, pg 1402
Linguistic Systems Inc (LSI), pg 1402
Link Translations Inc, pg 1403
MediaLocate Inc, pg 1403
Polyglot Communications Inc, pg 1403
Rennert Translation Group, pg 1404
Translations.com, pg 1405
Universe Technical Translation Inc, pg 1405

ENGLISH
A WordJourney Translation LLC, pg 1399
AAA Fine Translation & Interpretation, pg 1399
Accredited Language Services (ALS), pg 1399
Veronika Albrecht-Rodrigues PhD, pg 1399
Marvelia Alpizar, pg 1399
American Language Services Inc (ALSi), pg 1399
American Translation Partners Inc (ATP), pg 1399
Auerbach International, pg 1400
Baker & Taylor Publisher Services, pg 1400
Calaf Communications, pg 1400

TRANSLATORS & INTERPRETERS — SOURCE LANGUAGE INDEX

Elizabeth Castaldini, pg 1400
Cross Cultural Communication Systems Inc, pg 1400
Cross Culture Communications, pg 1400
East-West Concepts, pg 1400
Ecegul (AJ) Elterman, pg 1401
Eriksen Translations Inc, pg 1401
French and English Communication Services LLC, pg 1401
Mayra E Garcia, pg 1401
German Language Services, pg 1401
GGP Publishing Inc, pg 1401
Rosanna M Giammanco Frongia PhD, pg 1401
Glasnost Communications, pg 1401
Andrew S Gordon, PhD, pg 1401
Regina Gorzkowska-Rossi, pg 1401
Joan E Howard, pg 1402
inlingua Translation Service, pg 1402
iProbe Multilingual Solutions Inc, pg 1402
IRCO-International Language Bank, pg 1402
Bruni Johnson, pg 1402
Solveig Kjok, pg 1402
The Language Center, pg 1402
Linguistic Systems Inc (LSI), pg 1402
Link Translations Inc, pg 1403
MediaLocate Inc, pg 1403
MEJ Personal Business Services Inc, pg 1403
Metro Translation Service, pg 1403
Passwords Communications Inc, pg 1403
Emmanuel X Pierreuse, pg 1403
Polyglot Communications Inc, pg 1403
Polyglot Translators, pg 1403
Louise B Popkin, pg 1403
Rennert Translation Group, pg 1404
Claudette Roland, pg 1404
Rosemoor House Translations, pg 1404
Richard Schneider Language Services (RSLS), pg 1404
School of World Studies, pg 1404
Schreiber Translations Inc (STI), pg 1404
Natalia V Sciarini, pg 1404
Boris Mark Silversteyn, pg 1404
Spanish/English Translation & Interpreting Services, pg 1404
Strictly Spanish Translations LLC, pg 1404
Szablya Consultants Inc, pg 1405
Johannes Tan, pg 1405
Teneo Linguistics Co LLC, pg 1405
Transimpex Translators, Interpreters, Editors, Consultants Inc, pg 1405
Translations.com, pg 1405
Translingua Associates Inc, pg 1405
Universe Technical Translation Inc, pg 1405
University Language Services (ULS), pg 1405
Liliana Valenzuela, pg 1405
Maria Lidia Wilczewski, pg 1406

ESPERANTO

A WordJourney Translation LLC, pg 1399
American Translation Partners Inc (ATP), pg 1399
East-West Concepts, pg 1400
iProbe Multilingual Solutions Inc, pg 1402
Polyglot Communications Inc, pg 1403

ESTONIAN

A WordJourney Translation LLC, pg 1399
American Translation Partners Inc (ATP), pg 1399
East-West Concepts, pg 1400
iProbe Multilingual Solutions Inc, pg 1402
Linguistic Systems Inc (LSI), pg 1402
MediaLocate Inc, pg 1403
Polyglot Communications Inc, pg 1403
Universe Technical Translation Inc, pg 1405

FINNISH

A WordJourney Translation LLC, pg 1399
American Translation Partners Inc (ATP), pg 1399
East-West Concepts, pg 1400
Eriksen Translations Inc, pg 1401
iProbe Multilingual Solutions Inc, pg 1402
The Language Center, pg 1402
Linguistic Systems Inc (LSI), pg 1402
MediaLocate Inc, pg 1403
Polyglot Communications Inc, pg 1403
Rennert Translation Group, pg 1404
Universe Technical Translation Inc, pg 1405

FLEMISH

A WordJourney Translation LLC, pg 1399
American Translation Partners Inc (ATP), pg 1399
Wanda J Boeke, pg 1400
East-West Concepts, pg 1400
iProbe Multilingual Solutions Inc, pg 1402
Linguistic Systems Inc (LSI), pg 1402
Polyglot Communications Inc, pg 1403
Rennert Translation Group, pg 1404
Universe Technical Translation Inc, pg 1405

FRENCH

A WordJourney Translation LLC, pg 1399
AAA Fine Translation & Interpretation, pg 1399
Accredited Language Services (ALS), pg 1399
Veronika Albrecht-Rodrigues PhD, pg 1399
American Translation Partners Inc (ATP), pg 1399
Auerbach International, pg 1400
Baker & Taylor Publisher Services, pg 1400
Bien Fait Translations, pg 1400
Wanda J Boeke, pg 1400
Robert Bononno, pg 1400
Alexandra Chciuk-Celt, pg 1400
Cross Cultural Communication Systems Inc, pg 1400
Cross Culture Communications, pg 1400
Marcia Nita Doron, pg 1400
East-West Concepts, pg 1400
Ecegul (AJ) Elterman, pg 1401
Eriksen Translations Inc, pg 1401
French and English Communication Services LLC, pg 1401
GGP Publishing Inc, pg 1401
Rosanna M Giammanco Frongia PhD, pg 1401
Diana Mara Henry, pg 1401
Mark Herman & Ronnie Apter, Translators, pg 1401
Joan E Howard, pg 1402
inlingua Translation Service, pg 1402
iProbe Multilingual Solutions Inc, pg 1402
IRCO-International Language Bank, pg 1402
Alicja T Kawecki, pg 1402
Solveig Kjok, pg 1402
The Language Center, pg 1402
Linguistic Systems Inc (LSI), pg 1402
Link Translations Inc, pg 1403
MediaLocate Inc, pg 1403
MEJ Personal Business Services Inc, pg 1403
Donald Nicholson-Smith, pg 1403
Passwords Communications Inc, pg 1403
Emmanuel X Pierreuse, pg 1403
Polyglot Communications Inc, pg 1403
Polyglot Translators, pg 1403
Rennert Translation Group, pg 1404
Claudette Roland, pg 1404
Richard Schneider Language Services (RSLS), pg 1404
School of World Studies, pg 1404
Schreiber Translations Inc (STI), pg 1404
Martin Sokolinsky, pg 1404
Szablya Consultants Inc, pg 1405
Joan Wagner Teller PhD, Translator, pg 1405
Teneo Linguistics Co LLC, pg 1405
Transimpex Translators, Interpreters, Editors, Consultants Inc, pg 1405
Translations.com, pg 1405
Translingua Associates Inc, pg 1405
Elizabeth Uhlig, pg 1405
Universe Technical Translation Inc, pg 1405
University Language Services (ULS), pg 1405
Glenn E Weisfeld PhD, pg 1405

GAELIC

A WordJourney Translation LLC, pg 1399
American Translation Partners Inc (ATP), pg 1399
East-West Concepts, pg 1400
iProbe Multilingual Solutions Inc, pg 1402
Linguistic Systems Inc (LSI), pg 1402
Polyglot Communications Inc, pg 1403

GEORGIAN

A WordJourney Translation LLC, pg 1399
American Translation Partners Inc (ATP), pg 1399
East-West Concepts, pg 1400
iProbe Multilingual Solutions Inc, pg 1402
Linguistic Systems Inc (LSI), pg 1402
Link Translations Inc, pg 1403
Polyglot Communications Inc, pg 1403
Universe Technical Translation Inc, pg 1405

GERMAN

A WordJourney Translation LLC, pg 1399
AAA Fine Translation & Interpretation, pg 1399
Accredited Language Services (ALS), pg 1399
Rodelinde Albrecht, pg 1399
Veronika Albrecht-Rodrigues PhD, pg 1399
American Translation Partners Inc (ATP), pg 1399
Auerbach International, pg 1400
Baker & Taylor Publisher Services, pg 1400
Wanda J Boeke, pg 1400
Alexandra Chciuk-Celt, pg 1400
Cross Cultural Communication Systems Inc, pg 1400
Cross Culture Communications, pg 1400
East-West Concepts, pg 1400
Ecegul (AJ) Elterman, pg 1401
Eriksen Translations Inc, pg 1401
German Language Services, pg 1401
GGP Publishing Inc, pg 1401
Mark Herman & Ronnie Apter, Translators, pg 1401
inlingua Translation Service, pg 1402
iProbe Multilingual Solutions Inc, pg 1402
IRCO-International Language Bank, pg 1402
Bruni Johnson, pg 1402
Solveig Kjok, pg 1402
Kenneth Kronenberg, pg 1402
The Language Center, pg 1402
Linguistic Systems Inc (LSI), pg 1402
Link Translations Inc, pg 1403
MediaLocate Inc, pg 1403
MEJ Personal Business Services Inc, pg 1403
Metro Translation Service, pg 1403
Polyglot Communications Inc, pg 1403
Polyglot Translators, pg 1403
Rennert Translation Group, pg 1404
Richard Schneider Language Services (RSLS), pg 1404
School of World Studies, pg 1404
Schreiber Translations Inc (STI), pg 1404
Lesley M Schuldt, pg 1404
Monika Shoffman-Graves, pg 1404
Martin Sokolinsky, pg 1404
Szablya Consultants Inc, pg 1405
Joan Wagner Teller PhD, Translator, pg 1405
Teneo Linguistics Co LLC, pg 1405
Transimpex Translators, Interpreters, Editors, Consultants Inc, pg 1405
Translations.com, pg 1405
Translingua Associates Inc, pg 1405
Elizabeth Uhlig, pg 1405
Universe Technical Translation Inc, pg 1405
University Language Services (ULS), pg 1405
Krishna Winston, pg 1406

GREEK

A WordJourney Translation LLC, pg 1399
AAA Fine Translation & Interpretation, pg 1399
American Translation Partners Inc (ATP), pg 1399

Cross Cultural Communication Systems Inc, pg 1400
East-West Concepts, pg 1400
iProbe Multilingual Solutions Inc, pg 1402
Linguistic Systems Inc (LSI), pg 1402
Link Translations Inc, pg 1403
MediaLocate Inc, pg 1403
Polyglot Communications Inc, pg 1403
Rennert Translation Group, pg 1404
Elizabeth Uhlig, pg 1405
Universe Technical Translation Inc, pg 1405

HEBREW
A WordJourney Translation LLC, pg 1399
AAA Fine Translation & Interpretation, pg 1399
American Translation Partners Inc (ATP), pg 1399
Cross Cultural Communication Systems Inc, pg 1400
Marcia Nita Doron, pg 1400
East-West Concepts, pg 1400
iProbe Multilingual Solutions Inc, pg 1402
Linguistic Systems Inc (LSI), pg 1402
Link Translations Inc, pg 1403
Polyglot Communications Inc, pg 1403
Rennert Translation Group, pg 1404
Monika Shoffman-Graves, pg 1404
Universe Technical Translation Inc, pg 1405

HINDI
A WordJourney Translation LLC, pg 1399
American Translation Partners Inc (ATP), pg 1399
Cross Cultural Communication Systems Inc, pg 1400
East-West Concepts, pg 1400
iProbe Multilingual Solutions Inc, pg 1402
Linguistic Systems Inc (LSI), pg 1402
Link Translations Inc, pg 1403
Polyglot Communications Inc, pg 1403
Rennert Translation Group, pg 1404
Universe Technical Translation Inc, pg 1405

HUNGARIAN
A WordJourney Translation LLC, pg 1399
AAA Fine Translation & Interpretation, pg 1399
American Translation Partners Inc (ATP), pg 1399
East-West Concepts, pg 1400
iProbe Multilingual Solutions Inc, pg 1402
The Language Center, pg 1402
Linguistic Systems Inc (LSI), pg 1402
Link Translations Inc, pg 1403
MediaLocate Inc, pg 1403
Polyglot Communications Inc, pg 1403
Rennert Translation Group, pg 1404
Szablya Consultants Inc, pg 1405
Universe Technical Translation Inc, pg 1405

ICELANDIC
A WordJourney Translation LLC, pg 1399
American Translation Partners Inc (ATP), pg 1399
East-West Concepts, pg 1400
iProbe Multilingual Solutions Inc, pg 1402
Linguistic Systems Inc (LSI), pg 1402
Polyglot Communications Inc, pg 1403
Universe Technical Translation Inc, pg 1405

INDONESIAN
A WordJourney Translation LLC, pg 1399
American Translation Partners Inc (ATP), pg 1399
East-West Concepts, pg 1400
iProbe Multilingual Solutions Inc, pg 1402
Linguistic Systems Inc (LSI), pg 1402
Link Translations Inc, pg 1403
MediaLocate Inc, pg 1403
Polyglot Communications Inc, pg 1403
Rennert Translation Group, pg 1404
Johannes Tan, pg 1405
Universe Technical Translation Inc, pg 1405

ITALIAN
A WordJourney Translation LLC, pg 1399
AAA Fine Translation & Interpretation, pg 1399
Accredited Language Services (ALS), pg 1399
American Translation Partners Inc (ATP), pg 1399
Anne Milano Appel, pg 1400
Auerbach International, pg 1400
Baker & Taylor Publisher Services, pg 1400
Robert Bononno, pg 1400
Cross Cultural Communication Systems Inc, pg 1400
Cross Culture Communications, pg 1400
East-West Concepts, pg 1400
Eriksen Translations Inc, pg 1401
GGP Publishing Inc, pg 1401
Rosanna M Giammanco Frongia PhD, pg 1401
Mark Herman & Ronnie Apter, Translators, pg 1401
inlingua Translation Service, pg 1402
iProbe Multilingual Solutions Inc, pg 1402
IRCO-International Language Bank, pg 1402
Alicja T Kawecki, pg 1402
The Language Center, pg 1402
Linguistic Systems Inc (LSI), pg 1402
Link Translations Inc, pg 1403
MediaLocate Inc, pg 1403
MEJ Personal Business Services Inc, pg 1403
Polyglot Communications Inc, pg 1403
Polyglot Translators, pg 1403
Rennert Translation Group, pg 1404
Rosemoor House Translations, pg 1404
Richard Schneider Language Services (RSLS), pg 1404
School of World Studies, pg 1404
Schreiber Translations Inc (STI), pg 1404
Teneo Linguistics Co LLC, pg 1405
Transimpex Translators, Interpreters, Editors, Consultants Inc, pg 1405
Translations.com, pg 1405
Translingua Associates Inc, pg 1405
Elizabeth Uhlig, pg 1405
Universe Technical Translation Inc, pg 1405
University Language Services (ULS), pg 1405

JAPANESE
A WordJourney Translation LLC, pg 1399
American Translation Partners Inc (ATP), pg 1399
Cross Cultural Communication Systems Inc, pg 1400
East-West Concepts, pg 1400
Eriksen Translations Inc, pg 1401
iProbe Multilingual Solutions Inc, pg 1402
The Language Center, pg 1402
Linguistic Systems Inc (LSI), pg 1402
Link Translations Inc, pg 1403
MediaLocate Inc, pg 1403
Metro Translation Service, pg 1403
Polyglot Communications Inc, pg 1403
Rennert Translation Group, pg 1404
Translations.com, pg 1405
Universe Technical Translation Inc, pg 1405

JAVANESE
A WordJourney Translation LLC, pg 1399
American Translation Partners Inc (ATP), pg 1399
East-West Concepts, pg 1400
iProbe Multilingual Solutions Inc, pg 1402
Linguistic Systems Inc (LSI), pg 1402
Polyglot Communications Inc, pg 1403

KHMER
A WordJourney Translation LLC, pg 1399
American Translation Partners Inc (ATP), pg 1399
Cross Cultural Communication Systems Inc, pg 1400
East-West Concepts, pg 1400
iProbe Multilingual Solutions Inc, pg 1402
Linguistic Systems Inc (LSI), pg 1402
Polyglot Communications Inc, pg 1403

KOREAN
A WordJourney Translation LLC, pg 1399
American Translation Partners Inc (ATP), pg 1399
Cross Cultural Communication Systems Inc, pg 1400
East-West Concepts, pg 1400
Eriksen Translations Inc, pg 1401
iProbe Multilingual Solutions Inc, pg 1402
The Language Center, pg 1402
Linguistic Systems Inc (LSI), pg 1402
Link Translations Inc, pg 1403
MediaLocate Inc, pg 1403
Polyglot Communications Inc, pg 1403
Rennert Translation Group, pg 1404
Translations.com, pg 1405
Universe Technical Translation Inc, pg 1405

KURDISH
A WordJourney Translation LLC, pg 1399
American Translation Partners Inc (ATP), pg 1399
East-West Concepts, pg 1400
iProbe Multilingual Solutions Inc, pg 1402
Polyglot Communications Inc, pg 1403
Universe Technical Translation Inc, pg 1405

LATIN
A WordJourney Translation LLC, pg 1399
AAA Fine Translation & Interpretation, pg 1399
American Translation Partners Inc (ATP), pg 1399
East-West Concepts, pg 1400
GGP Publishing Inc, pg 1401
Rosanna M Giammanco Frongia PhD, pg 1401
Mark Herman & Ronnie Apter, Translators, pg 1401
iProbe Multilingual Solutions Inc, pg 1402
Linguistic Systems Inc (LSI), pg 1402
Polyglot Communications Inc, pg 1403
Rennert Translation Group, pg 1404
Szablya Consultants Inc, pg 1405
Universe Technical Translation Inc, pg 1405

LATVIAN
A WordJourney Translation LLC, pg 1399
American Translation Partners Inc (ATP), pg 1399
East-West Concepts, pg 1400
iProbe Multilingual Solutions Inc, pg 1402
Linguistic Systems Inc (LSI), pg 1402
Link Translations Inc, pg 1403
MediaLocate Inc, pg 1403
Polyglot Communications Inc, pg 1403
Universe Technical Translation Inc, pg 1405

LITHUANIAN
A WordJourney Translation LLC, pg 1399
American Translation Partners Inc (ATP), pg 1399
East-West Concepts, pg 1400
iProbe Multilingual Solutions Inc, pg 1402
The Language Center, pg 1402
Linguistic Systems Inc (LSI), pg 1402
MediaLocate Inc, pg 1403
Polyglot Communications Inc, pg 1403

TRANSLATORS & INTERPRETERS — SOURCE LANGUAGE INDEX

Rennert Translation Group, pg 1404
Universe Technical Translation Inc, pg 1405

MACEDONIAN
A WordJourney Translation LLC, pg 1399
AAA Fine Translation & Interpretation, pg 1399
American Translation Partners Inc (ATP), pg 1399
East-West Concepts, pg 1400
iProbe Multilingual Solutions Inc, pg 1402
Linguistic Systems Inc (LSI), pg 1402
Link Translations Inc, pg 1403
MediaLocate Inc, pg 1403
Polyglot Communications Inc, pg 1403
Universe Technical Translation Inc, pg 1405

MALAGASY
A WordJourney Translation LLC, pg 1399
American Translation Partners Inc (ATP), pg 1399
East-West Concepts, pg 1400
iProbe Multilingual Solutions Inc, pg 1402
Polyglot Communications Inc, pg 1403
Universe Technical Translation Inc, pg 1405

MALAYALAM
A WordJourney Translation LLC, pg 1399
American Translation Partners Inc (ATP), pg 1399
East-West Concepts, pg 1400
iProbe Multilingual Solutions Inc, pg 1402
Polyglot Communications Inc, pg 1403
Universe Technical Translation Inc, pg 1405

MALAYSIAN
A WordJourney Translation LLC, pg 1399
American Translation Partners Inc (ATP), pg 1399
East-West Concepts, pg 1400
iProbe Multilingual Solutions Inc, pg 1402
Linguistic Systems Inc (LSI), pg 1402
MediaLocate Inc, pg 1403
Polyglot Communications Inc, pg 1403
Universe Technical Translation Inc, pg 1405

NEPALI
A WordJourney Translation LLC, pg 1399
American Translation Partners Inc (ATP), pg 1399
East-West Concepts, pg 1400
iProbe Multilingual Solutions Inc, pg 1402
Linguistic Systems Inc (LSI), pg 1402
Polyglot Communications Inc, pg 1403

NORWEGIAN
A WordJourney Translation LLC, pg 1399
AAA Fine Translation & Interpretation, pg 1399
American Translation Partners Inc (ATP), pg 1399
East-West Concepts, pg 1400
Eriksen Translations Inc, pg 1401
iProbe Multilingual Solutions Inc, pg 1402
Solveig Kjok, pg 1402
The Language Center, pg 1402
Linguistic Systems Inc (LSI), pg 1402
Link Translations Inc, pg 1403
MediaLocate Inc, pg 1403
Polyglot Communications Inc, pg 1403
Rennert Translation Group, pg 1404
Universe Technical Translation Inc, pg 1405

PERSIAN
A WordJourney Translation LLC, pg 1399
American Translation Partners Inc (ATP), pg 1399
Cross Cultural Communication Systems Inc, pg 1400
East-West Concepts, pg 1400
iProbe Multilingual Solutions Inc, pg 1402
Polyglot Communications Inc, pg 1403
Polyglot Translators, pg 1403
Universe Technical Translation Inc, pg 1405

POLISH
A WordJourney Translation LLC, pg 1399
AAA Fine Translation & Interpretation, pg 1399
American Translation Partners Inc (ATP), pg 1399
Alexandra Chciuk-Celt, pg 1400
Cross Cultural Communication Systems Inc, pg 1400
East-West Concepts, pg 1400
Regina Gorzkowska-Rossi, pg 1401
iProbe Multilingual Solutions Inc, pg 1402
Alicja T Kawecki, pg 1402
The Language Center, pg 1402
Linguistic Systems Inc (LSI), pg 1402
Link Translations Inc, pg 1403
MediaLocate Inc, pg 1403
Polyglot Communications Inc, pg 1403
Rennert Translation Group, pg 1404
Universe Technical Translation Inc, pg 1405
Maria Lidia Wilczewski, pg 1406

PORTUGUESE
A WordJourney Translation LLC, pg 1399
AAA Fine Translation & Interpretation, pg 1399
American Language Services Inc (ALSi), pg 1399
American Translation Partners Inc (ATP), pg 1399
Elizabeth Castaldini, pg 1400
Cross Cultural Communication Systems Inc, pg 1400
East-West Concepts, pg 1400
GGP Publishing Inc, pg 1401
iProbe Multilingual Solutions Inc, pg 1402
The Language Center, pg 1402
Linguistic Systems Inc (LSI), pg 1402
Link Translations Inc, pg 1403
MediaLocate Inc, pg 1403
Metro Translation Service, pg 1403
Polyglot Communications Inc, pg 1403
Rennert Translation Group, pg 1404
Translations.com, pg 1405
Elizabeth Uhlig, pg 1405
Universe Technical Translation Inc, pg 1405

PROVENCAL
A WordJourney Translation LLC, pg 1399
American Translation Partners Inc (ATP), pg 1399
East-West Concepts, pg 1400
Mark Herman & Ronnie Apter, Translators, pg 1401
iProbe Multilingual Solutions Inc, pg 1402
Polyglot Communications Inc, pg 1403

PUNJABI
A WordJourney Translation LLC, pg 1399
American Translation Partners Inc (ATP), pg 1399
Cross Cultural Communication Systems Inc, pg 1400
East-West Concepts, pg 1400
iProbe Multilingual Solutions Inc, pg 1402
Linguistic Systems Inc (LSI), pg 1402
Polyglot Communications Inc, pg 1403
Rennert Translation Group, pg 1404
Universe Technical Translation Inc, pg 1405

ROMANIAN
A WordJourney Translation LLC, pg 1399
AAA Fine Translation & Interpretation, pg 1399
American Translation Partners Inc (ATP), pg 1399
East-West Concepts, pg 1400
iProbe Multilingual Solutions Inc, pg 1402
Linguistic Systems Inc (LSI), pg 1402
Link Translations Inc, pg 1403
MediaLocate Inc, pg 1403
Polyglot Communications Inc, pg 1403
Rennert Translation Group, pg 1404
Universe Technical Translation Inc, pg 1405

RUSSIAN
A WordJourney Translation LLC, pg 1399
AAA Fine Translation & Interpretation, pg 1399
American Translation Partners Inc (ATP), pg 1399
Cross Cultural Communication Systems Inc, pg 1400
East-West Concepts, pg 1400
Glasnost Communications, pg 1401
Mark Herman & Ronnie Apter, Translators, pg 1401
iProbe Multilingual Solutions Inc, pg 1402
Alicja T Kawecki, pg 1402
The Language Center, pg 1402
Linguistic Systems Inc (LSI), pg 1402
Link Translations Inc, pg 1403
MediaLocate Inc, pg 1403
Polyglot Communications Inc, pg 1403
Rennert Translation Group, pg 1404
Marian Schwartz, pg 1404
Natalia V Sciarini, pg 1404
Christina Sever, pg 1404
Boris Mark Silversteyn, pg 1404
Martin Sokolinsky, pg 1404
Joan Wagner Teller PhD, Translator, pg 1405
Translations.com, pg 1405
Universe Technical Translation Inc, pg 1405

SERBO-CROATIAN
A WordJourney Translation LLC, pg 1399
AAA Fine Translation & Interpretation, pg 1399
American Translation Partners Inc (ATP), pg 1399
Cross Cultural Communication Systems Inc, pg 1400
iProbe Multilingual Solutions Inc, pg 1402
The Language Center, pg 1402
Linguistic Systems Inc (LSI), pg 1402
Link Translations Inc, pg 1403
MediaLocate Inc, pg 1403
Polyglot Communications Inc, pg 1403
Rennert Translation Group, pg 1404
Universe Technical Translation Inc, pg 1405

SINHALESE
A WordJourney Translation LLC, pg 1399
American Translation Partners Inc (ATP), pg 1399
East-West Concepts, pg 1400
iProbe Multilingual Solutions Inc, pg 1402
Linguistic Systems Inc (LSI), pg 1402
Polyglot Communications Inc, pg 1403

SLOVAK
A WordJourney Translation LLC, pg 1399
AAA Fine Translation & Interpretation, pg 1399
American Translation Partners Inc (ATP), pg 1399
East-West Concepts, pg 1400
iProbe Multilingual Solutions Inc, pg 1402
The Language Center, pg 1402
Linguistic Systems Inc (LSI), pg 1402
Link Translations Inc, pg 1403
MediaLocate Inc, pg 1403
Polyglot Communications Inc, pg 1403
Rennert Translation Group, pg 1404
Universe Technical Translation Inc, pg 1405

SLOVENE

A WordJourney Translation LLC, pg 1399
AAA Fine Translation & Interpretation, pg 1399
American Translation Partners Inc (ATP), pg 1399
East-West Concepts, pg 1400
iProbe Multilingual Solutions Inc, pg 1402
Linguistic Systems Inc (LSI), pg 1402
Polyglot Communications Inc, pg 1403

SPANISH

A WordJourney Translation LLC, pg 1399
AAA Fine Translation & Interpretation, pg 1399
Accredited Language Services (ALS), pg 1399
Marvelia Alpizar, pg 1399
American Language Services Inc (ALSi), pg 1399
American Translation Partners Inc (ATP), pg 1399
Auerbach International, pg 1400
Baker & Taylor Publisher Services, pg 1400
Calaf Communications, pg 1400
Alexandra Chciuk-Celt, pg 1400
Cross Cultural Communication Systems Inc, pg 1400
Cross Culture Communications, pg 1400
East-West Concepts, pg 1400
Eriksen Translations Inc, pg 1401
Mayra E Garcia, pg 1401
GGP Publishing Inc, pg 1401
Rosanna M Giammanco Frongia PhD, pg 1401
Andrew S Gordon, PhD, pg 1401
Rita Granda, pg 1401
Mark Herman & Ronnie Apter, Translators, pg 1401
Indexing by the Book, pg 1402
inlingua Translation Service, pg 1402
iProbe Multilingual Solutions Inc, pg 1402
IRCO-International Language Bank, pg 1402
Solveig Kjok, pg 1402
The Language Center, pg 1402
Linguistic Systems Inc (LSI), pg 1402
Link Translations Inc, pg 1403
MediaLocate Inc, pg 1403
MEJ Personal Business Services Inc, pg 1403
Metro Translation Service, pg 1403
Donald Nicholson-Smith, pg 1403
Passwords Communications Inc, pg 1403
Polyglot Communications Inc, pg 1403
Polyglot Translators, pg 1403
Louise B Popkin, pg 1403
Rennert Translation Group, pg 1404
Richard Schneider Language Services (RSLS), pg 1404
School of World Studies, pg 1404
Schreiber Translations Inc (STI), pg 1404
Monika Shoffman-Graves, pg 1404
Martin Sokolinsky, pg 1404
Spanish/English Translation & Interpreting Services, pg 1404
Strictly Spanish Translations LLC, pg 1404
Teneo Linguistics Co LLC, pg 1405
Transimpex Translators, Interpreters, Editors, Consultants Inc, pg 1405
Translations.com, pg 1405
Translingua Associates Inc, pg 1405
Elizabeth Uhlig, pg 1405
Universe Technical Translation Inc, pg 1405
University Language Services (ULS), pg 1405

SWAHILI

A WordJourney Translation LLC, pg 1399
American Translation Partners Inc (ATP), pg 1399
Cross Cultural Communication Systems Inc, pg 1400
East-West Concepts, pg 1400
iProbe Multilingual Solutions Inc, pg 1402
Linguistic Systems Inc (LSI), pg 1402
Polyglot Communications Inc, pg 1403
Rennert Translation Group, pg 1404
Universe Technical Translation Inc, pg 1405

SWEDISH

A WordJourney Translation LLC, pg 1399
AAA Fine Translation & Interpretation, pg 1399
American Translation Partners Inc (ATP), pg 1399
East-West Concepts, pg 1400
Eriksen Translations Inc, pg 1401
Indexing by the Book, pg 1402
iProbe Multilingual Solutions Inc, pg 1402
Solveig Kjok, pg 1402
The Language Center, pg 1402
Linguistic Systems Inc (LSI), pg 1402
Link Translations Inc, pg 1403
MediaLocate Inc, pg 1403
Polyglot Communications Inc, pg 1403
Rennert Translation Group, pg 1404
Translations.com, pg 1405
Universe Technical Translation Inc, pg 1405

TAGALOG

A WordJourney Translation LLC, pg 1399
American Translation Partners Inc (ATP), pg 1399
Cross Cultural Communication Systems Inc, pg 1400
East-West Concepts, pg 1400
iProbe Multilingual Solutions Inc, pg 1402
Linguistic Systems Inc (LSI), pg 1402
Link Translations Inc, pg 1403
Polyglot Communications Inc, pg 1403
Rennert Translation Group, pg 1404
Universe Technical Translation Inc, pg 1405

TAMIL

A WordJourney Translation LLC, pg 1399
American Translation Partners Inc (ATP), pg 1399
East-West Concepts, pg 1400
iProbe Multilingual Solutions Inc, pg 1402
Linguistic Systems Inc (LSI), pg 1402
Polyglot Communications Inc, pg 1403
Universe Technical Translation Inc, pg 1405

TELUGU

A WordJourney Translation LLC, pg 1399
American Translation Partners Inc (ATP), pg 1399
East-West Concepts, pg 1400
iProbe Multilingual Solutions Inc, pg 1402
Polyglot Communications Inc, pg 1403

THAI

A WordJourney Translation LLC, pg 1399
AAA Fine Translation & Interpretation, pg 1399
American Translation Partners Inc (ATP), pg 1399
Cross Cultural Communication Systems Inc, pg 1400
East-West Concepts, pg 1400
iProbe Multilingual Solutions Inc, pg 1402
Linguistic Systems Inc (LSI), pg 1402
Link Translations Inc, pg 1403
MediaLocate Inc, pg 1403
Polyglot Communications Inc, pg 1403
Rennert Translation Group, pg 1404
Universe Technical Translation Inc, pg 1405

TURKISH

A WordJourney Translation LLC, pg 1399
AAA Fine Translation & Interpretation, pg 1399
American Translation Partners Inc (ATP), pg 1399
Cross Cultural Communication Systems Inc, pg 1400
East-West Concepts, pg 1400
Ecegul (AJ) Elterman, pg 1401
iProbe Multilingual Solutions Inc, pg 1402
The Language Center, pg 1402
Linguistic Systems Inc (LSI), pg 1402
Link Translations Inc, pg 1403
MediaLocate Inc, pg 1403
Polyglot Communications Inc, pg 1403
Rennert Translation Group, pg 1404
Universe Technical Translation Inc, pg 1405

UKRAINIAN

A WordJourney Translation LLC, pg 1399
AAA Fine Translation & Interpretation, pg 1399
American Translation Partners Inc (ATP), pg 1399
East-West Concepts, pg 1400
Glasnost Communications, pg 1401
iProbe Multilingual Solutions Inc, pg 1402
Alicja T Kawecki, pg 1402
Linguistic Systems Inc (LSI), pg 1402
Link Translations Inc, pg 1403
Polyglot Communications Inc, pg 1403
Rennert Translation Group, pg 1404
Boris Mark Silversteyn, pg 1404
Universe Technical Translation Inc, pg 1405

URDU

A WordJourney Translation LLC, pg 1399
American Translation Partners Inc (ATP), pg 1399
Cross Cultural Communication Systems Inc, pg 1400
East-West Concepts, pg 1400
Eriksen Translations Inc, pg 1401
iProbe Multilingual Solutions Inc, pg 1402
Linguistic Systems Inc (LSI), pg 1402
Link Translations Inc, pg 1403
Polyglot Communications Inc, pg 1403
Rennert Translation Group, pg 1404
Universe Technical Translation Inc, pg 1405

VIETNAMESE

A WordJourney Translation LLC, pg 1399
American Translation Partners Inc (ATP), pg 1399
Cross Cultural Communication Systems Inc, pg 1400
East-West Concepts, pg 1400
iProbe Multilingual Solutions Inc, pg 1402
The Language Center, pg 1402
Linguistic Systems Inc (LSI), pg 1402
Link Translations Inc, pg 1403
MediaLocate Inc, pg 1403
Polyglot Communications Inc, pg 1403
Rennert Translation Group, pg 1404
Universe Technical Translation Inc, pg 1405

WELSH

A WordJourney Translation LLC, pg 1399
American Translation Partners Inc (ATP), pg 1399
East-West Concepts, pg 1400
iProbe Multilingual Solutions Inc, pg 1402
Polyglot Communications Inc, pg 1403
Universe Technical Translation Inc, pg 1405

YIDDISH

A WordJourney Translation LLC, pg 1399
AAA Fine Translation & Interpretation, pg 1399
American Translation Partners Inc (ATP), pg 1399
East-West Concepts, pg 1400
iProbe Multilingual Solutions Inc, pg 1402
Linguistic Systems Inc (LSI), pg 1402
Polyglot Communications Inc, pg 1403

TRANSLATORS & INTERPRETERS — SOURCE LANGUAGE INDEX

Rennert Translation Group, pg 1404
Universe Technical Translation Inc, pg 1405

Translators & Interpreters — Target Language Index

AFRIKAANS
A WordJourney Translation LLC, pg 1399
American Translation Partners Inc (ATP), pg 1399
East-West Concepts, pg 1400
iProbe Multilingual Solutions Inc, pg 1402
Linguistic Systems Inc (LSI), pg 1402
Link Translations Inc, pg 1403
Polyglot Communications Inc, pg 1403
Universe Technical Translation Inc, pg 1405

ALBANIAN
A WordJourney Translation LLC, pg 1399
AAA Fine Translation & Interpretation, pg 1399
American Translation Partners Inc (ATP), pg 1399
East-West Concepts, pg 1400
iProbe Multilingual Solutions Inc, pg 1402
Linguistic Systems Inc (LSI), pg 1402
Link Translations Inc, pg 1403
Polyglot Communications Inc, pg 1403
Rennert Translation Group, pg 1404
Universe Technical Translation Inc, pg 1405

ARABIC
A WordJourney Translation LLC, pg 1399
American Translation Partners Inc (ATP), pg 1399
Cross Cultural Communication Systems Inc, pg 1400
East-West Concepts, pg 1400
Eriksen Translations Inc, pg 1401
iProbe Multilingual Solutions Inc, pg 1402
The Language Center, pg 1402
Linguistic Systems Inc (LSI), pg 1402
Link Translations Inc, pg 1403
Polyglot Communications Inc, pg 1403
Rennert Translation Group, pg 1404
Universe Technical Translation Inc, pg 1405

ARMENIAN
A WordJourney Translation LLC, pg 1399
American Translation Partners Inc (ATP), pg 1399
Cross Cultural Communication Systems Inc, pg 1400
East-West Concepts, pg 1400
iProbe Multilingual Solutions Inc, pg 1402
Linguistic Systems Inc (LSI), pg 1402
Polyglot Communications Inc, pg 1403
Rennert Translation Group, pg 1404
Universe Technical Translation Inc, pg 1405

BELARUSSIAN
A WordJourney Translation LLC, pg 1399
AAA Fine Translation & Interpretation, pg 1399
American Translation Partners Inc (ATP), pg 1399
East-West Concepts, pg 1400
iProbe Multilingual Solutions Inc, pg 1402
Linguistic Systems Inc (LSI), pg 1402
Polyglot Communications Inc, pg 1403
Universe Technical Translation Inc, pg 1405

BENGALI
A WordJourney Translation LLC, pg 1399
American Translation Partners Inc (ATP), pg 1399
Cross Cultural Communication Systems Inc, pg 1400
East-West Concepts, pg 1400
iProbe Multilingual Solutions Inc, pg 1402
Linguistic Systems Inc (LSI), pg 1402
Polyglot Communications Inc, pg 1403
Rennert Translation Group, pg 1404
Universe Technical Translation Inc, pg 1405

BULGARIAN
A WordJourney Translation LLC, pg 1399
AAA Fine Translation & Interpretation, pg 1399
American Translation Partners Inc (ATP), pg 1399
East-West Concepts, pg 1400
iProbe Multilingual Solutions Inc, pg 1402
Linguistic Systems Inc (LSI), pg 1402
Link Translations Inc, pg 1403
MediaLocate Inc, pg 1403
Polyglot Communications Inc, pg 1403
Rennert Translation Group, pg 1404
Universe Technical Translation Inc, pg 1405

BURMESE
A WordJourney Translation LLC, pg 1399
American Translation Partners Inc (ATP), pg 1399
East-West Concepts, pg 1400
iProbe Multilingual Solutions Inc, pg 1402
Linguistic Systems Inc (LSI), pg 1402
Polyglot Communications Inc, pg 1403

CATALAN
A WordJourney Translation LLC, pg 1399
AAA Fine Translation & Interpretation, pg 1399
American Translation Partners Inc (ATP), pg 1399
East-West Concepts, pg 1400
iProbe Multilingual Solutions Inc, pg 1402
Linguistic Systems Inc (LSI), pg 1402
Polyglot Communications Inc, pg 1403
Rennert Translation Group, pg 1404
Universe Technical Translation Inc, pg 1405

CHINESE
A WordJourney Translation LLC, pg 1399
American Translation Partners Inc (ATP), pg 1399
Cross Cultural Communication Systems Inc, pg 1400
East-West Concepts, pg 1400
Eriksen Translations Inc, pg 1401
iProbe Multilingual Solutions Inc, pg 1402
The Language Center, pg 1402
Linguistic Systems Inc (LSI), pg 1402
Link Translations Inc, pg 1403
MediaLocate Inc, pg 1403
Polyglot Communications Inc, pg 1403
Rennert Translation Group, pg 1404
Translations.com, pg 1405
Universe Technical Translation Inc, pg 1405

CZECH
A WordJourney Translation LLC, pg 1399
American Translation Partners Inc (ATP), pg 1399
East-West Concepts, pg 1400
iProbe Multilingual Solutions Inc, pg 1402
The Language Center, pg 1402
Linguistic Systems Inc (LSI), pg 1402
Link Translations Inc, pg 1403
MediaLocate Inc, pg 1403
Polyglot Communications Inc, pg 1403
Rennert Translation Group, pg 1404
Universe Technical Translation Inc, pg 1405

DANISH
A WordJourney Translation LLC, pg 1399
AAA Fine Translation & Interpretation, pg 1399
American Translation Partners Inc (ATP), pg 1399
East-West Concepts, pg 1400
Eriksen Translations Inc, pg 1401
iProbe Multilingual Solutions Inc, pg 1402
The Language Center, pg 1402
Linguistic Systems Inc (LSI), pg 1402
Link Translations Inc, pg 1403
MediaLocate Inc, pg 1403
Polyglot Communications Inc, pg 1403
Rennert Translation Group, pg 1404
Translations.com, pg 1405
Universe Technical Translation Inc, pg 1405

DUTCH
A WordJourney Translation LLC, pg 1399
AAA Fine Translation & Interpretation, pg 1399
American Translation Partners Inc (ATP), pg 1399
East-West Concepts, pg 1400
iProbe Multilingual Solutions Inc, pg 1402
The Language Center, pg 1402
Linguistic Systems Inc (LSI), pg 1402
Link Translations Inc, pg 1403
MediaLocate Inc, pg 1403
Polyglot Communications Inc, pg 1403
Rennert Translation Group, pg 1404
Translations.com, pg 1405
Universe Technical Translation Inc, pg 1405

ENGLISH
A WordJourney Translation LLC, pg 1399
AAA Fine Translation & Interpretation, pg 1399
Accredited Language Services (ALS), pg 1399
Rodelinde Albrecht, pg 1399
Veronika Albrecht-Rodrigues PhD, pg 1399
Marvelia Alpizar, pg 1399
American Language Services Inc (ALSi), pg 1399
American Translation Partners Inc (ATP), pg 1399
Anne Milano Appel, pg 1400
Auerbach International, pg 1400
Baker & Taylor Publisher Services, pg 1400
Bien Fait Translations, pg 1400
Wanda J Boeke, pg 1400
Robert Bononno, pg 1400
Elizabeth Castaldini, pg 1400
Alexandra Chciuk-Celt, pg 1400

TRANSLATORS & INTERPRETERS — TARGET LANGUAGE INDEX

Cross Cultural Communication Systems Inc, pg 1400
Cross Culture Communications, pg 1400
Marcia Nita Doron, pg 1400
East-West Concepts, pg 1400
Ecegul (AJ) Elterman, pg 1401
Eriksen Translations Inc, pg 1401
French and English Communication Services LLC, pg 1401
Mayra E Garcia, pg 1401
German Language Services, pg 1401
GGP Publishing Inc, pg 1401
Rosanna M Giammanco Frongia PhD, pg 1401
Glasnost Communications, pg 1401
Andrew S Gordon, PhD, pg 1401
Regina Gorzkowska-Rossi, pg 1401
Rita Granda, pg 1401
Diana Mara Henry, pg 1401
Mark Herman & Ronnie Apter, Translators, pg 1401
Joan E Howard, pg 1402
Indexing by the Book, pg 1402
inlingua Translation Service, pg 1402
iProbe Multilingual Solutions Inc, pg 1402
IRCO-International Language Bank, pg 1402
Bruni Johnson, pg 1402
Alicja T Kawecki, pg 1402
Solveig Kjok, pg 1402
Kenneth Kronenberg, pg 1402
The Language Center, pg 1402
Linguistic Systems Inc (LSI), pg 1402
Link Translations Inc, pg 1403
MediaLocate Inc, pg 1403
MEJ Personal Business Services Inc, pg 1403
Metro Translation Service, pg 1403
Donald Nicholson-Smith, pg 1403
Passwords Communications Inc, pg 1403
Emmanuel X Pierreuse, pg 1403
Polyglot Communications Inc, pg 1403
Polyglot Translators, pg 1403
Louise B Popkin, pg 1403
Rennert Translation Group, pg 1404
Claudette Roland, pg 1404
Rosemoor House Translations, pg 1404
Richard Schneider Language Services (RSLS), pg 1404
School of World Studies, pg 1404
Schreiber Translations Inc (STI), pg 1404
Lesley M Schuldt, pg 1404
Marian Schwartz, pg 1404
Natalia V Sciarini, pg 1404
Christina Sever, pg 1404
Monika Shoffman-Graves, pg 1404
Boris Mark Silversteyn, pg 1404
Martin Sokolinsky, pg 1404
Spanish/English Translation & Interpreting Services, pg 1404
Strictly Spanish Translations LLC, pg 1404
Szablya Consultants Inc, pg 1405
Johannes Tan, pg 1405
Joan Wagner Teller PhD, Translator, pg 1405
Teneo Linguistics Co LLC, pg 1405
Transimpex Translators, Interpreters, Editors, Consultants Inc, pg 1405
Translations.com, pg 1405
Translingua Associates Inc, pg 1405
Elizabeth Uhlig, pg 1405
Universe Technical Translation Inc, pg 1405
University Language Services (ULS), pg 1405
Glenn E Weisfeld PhD, pg 1405
Maria Lidia Wilczewski, pg 1406
Krishna Winston, pg 1406

ESPERANTO

A WordJourney Translation LLC, pg 1399
American Translation Partners Inc (ATP), pg 1399
East-West Concepts, pg 1400
iProbe Multilingual Solutions Inc, pg 1402
Polyglot Communications Inc, pg 1403

ESTONIAN

A WordJourney Translation LLC, pg 1399
American Translation Partners Inc (ATP), pg 1399
East-West Concepts, pg 1400
iProbe Multilingual Solutions Inc, pg 1402
Linguistic Systems Inc (LSI), pg 1402
MediaLocate Inc, pg 1403
Polyglot Communications Inc, pg 1403
Universe Technical Translation Inc, pg 1405

FINNISH

A WordJourney Translation LLC, pg 1399
American Translation Partners Inc (ATP), pg 1399
East-West Concepts, pg 1400
Eriksen Translations Inc, pg 1401
iProbe Multilingual Solutions Inc, pg 1402
The Language Center, pg 1402
Linguistic Systems Inc (LSI), pg 1402
MediaLocate Inc, pg 1403
Polyglot Communications Inc, pg 1403
Rennert Translation Group, pg 1404
Universe Technical Translation Inc, pg 1405

FLEMISH

A WordJourney Translation LLC, pg 1399
American Translation Partners Inc (ATP), pg 1399
East-West Concepts, pg 1400
iProbe Multilingual Solutions Inc, pg 1402
Linguistic Systems Inc (LSI), pg 1402
Polyglot Communications Inc, pg 1403
Rennert Translation Group, pg 1404
Universe Technical Translation Inc, pg 1405

FRENCH

A WordJourney Translation LLC, pg 1399
AAA Fine Translation & Interpretation, pg 1399
Accredited Language Services (ALS), pg 1399
American Translation Partners Inc (ATP), pg 1399
Auerbach International, pg 1400
Baker & Taylor Publisher Services, pg 1400
Cross Cultural Communication Systems Inc, pg 1400
Cross Culture Communications, pg 1400
East-West Concepts, pg 1400
Eriksen Translations Inc, pg 1401
French and English Communication Services LLC, pg 1401
GGP Publishing Inc, pg 1401
Joan E Howard, pg 1402
inlingua Translation Service, pg 1402
iProbe Multilingual Solutions Inc, pg 1402
IRCO-International Language Bank, pg 1402
The Language Center, pg 1402
Linguistic Systems Inc (LSI), pg 1402
Link Translations Inc, pg 1403
MediaLocate Inc, pg 1403
MEJ Personal Business Services Inc, pg 1403
Emmanuel X Pierreuse, pg 1403
Polyglot Communications Inc, pg 1403
Polyglot Translators, pg 1403
Rennert Translation Group, pg 1404
Claudette Roland, pg 1404
Richard Schneider Language Services (RSLS), pg 1404
School of World Studies, pg 1404
Schreiber Translations Inc (STI), pg 1404
Teneo Linguistics Co LLC, pg 1405
Transimpex Translators, Interpreters, Editors, Consultants Inc, pg 1405
Translations.com, pg 1405
Translingua Associates Inc, pg 1405
Universe Technical Translation Inc, pg 1405
University Language Services (ULS), pg 1405

GAELIC

A WordJourney Translation LLC, pg 1399
American Translation Partners Inc (ATP), pg 1399
East-West Concepts, pg 1400
iProbe Multilingual Solutions Inc, pg 1402
Linguistic Systems Inc (LSI), pg 1402
Polyglot Communications Inc, pg 1403

GEORGIAN

A WordJourney Translation LLC, pg 1399
American Translation Partners Inc (ATP), pg 1399
East-West Concepts, pg 1400
iProbe Multilingual Solutions Inc, pg 1402
Linguistic Systems Inc (LSI), pg 1402
Link Translations Inc, pg 1403
Polyglot Communications Inc, pg 1403
Universe Technical Translation Inc, pg 1405

GERMAN

A WordJourney Translation LLC, pg 1399
AAA Fine Translation & Interpretation, pg 1399
Accredited Language Services (ALS), pg 1399
Veronika Albrecht-Rodrigues PhD, pg 1399
American Translation Partners Inc (ATP), pg 1399
Auerbach International, pg 1400
Baker & Taylor Publisher Services, pg 1400
Cross Cultural Communication Systems Inc, pg 1400
Cross Culture Communications, pg 1400
East-West Concepts, pg 1400
Ecegul (AJ) Elterman, pg 1401
Eriksen Translations Inc, pg 1401
German Language Services, pg 1401
GGP Publishing Inc, pg 1401
inlingua Translation Service, pg 1402
iProbe Multilingual Solutions Inc, pg 1402
IRCO-International Language Bank, pg 1402
Bruni Johnson, pg 1402
The Language Center, pg 1402
Linguistic Systems Inc (LSI), pg 1402
Link Translations Inc, pg 1403
MediaLocate Inc, pg 1403
MEJ Personal Business Services Inc, pg 1403
Metro Translation Service, pg 1403
Polyglot Communications Inc, pg 1403
Polyglot Translators, pg 1403
Rennert Translation Group, pg 1404
Richard Schneider Language Services (RSLS), pg 1404
School of World Studies, pg 1404
Schreiber Translations Inc (STI), pg 1404
Teneo Linguistics Co LLC, pg 1405
Transimpex Translators, Interpreters, Editors, Consultants Inc, pg 1405
Translations.com, pg 1405
Translingua Associates Inc, pg 1405
Universe Technical Translation Inc, pg 1405
University Language Services (ULS), pg 1405

GREEK

A WordJourney Translation LLC, pg 1399
AAA Fine Translation & Interpretation, pg 1399
American Translation Partners Inc (ATP), pg 1399
Cross Cultural Communication Systems Inc, pg 1400
East-West Concepts, pg 1400
iProbe Multilingual Solutions Inc, pg 1402
Linguistic Systems Inc (LSI), pg 1402
Link Translations Inc, pg 1403
MediaLocate Inc, pg 1403
Polyglot Communications Inc, pg 1403
Rennert Translation Group, pg 1404
Universe Technical Translation Inc, pg 1405

HEBREW

A WordJourney Translation LLC, pg 1399
AAA Fine Translation & Interpretation, pg 1399
American Translation Partners Inc (ATP), pg 1399

Cross Cultural Communication Systems Inc, pg 1400
East-West Concepts, pg 1400
iProbe Multilingual Solutions Inc, pg 1402
Linguistic Systems Inc (LSI), pg 1402
Link Translations Inc, pg 1403
Polyglot Communications Inc, pg 1403
Rennert Translation Group, pg 1404
School of World Studies, pg 1404
Universe Technical Translation Inc, pg 1405

HINDI

A WordJourney Translation LLC, pg 1399
American Translation Partners Inc (ATP), pg 1399
Cross Cultural Communication Systems Inc, pg 1400
East-West Concepts, pg 1400
iProbe Multilingual Solutions Inc, pg 1402
Linguistic Systems Inc (LSI), pg 1402
Link Translations Inc, pg 1403
Polyglot Communications Inc, pg 1403
Rennert Translation Group, pg 1404
School of World Studies, pg 1404
Universe Technical Translation Inc, pg 1405

HUNGARIAN

A WordJourney Translation LLC, pg 1399
AAA Fine Translation & Interpretation, pg 1399
American Translation Partners Inc (ATP), pg 1399
East-West Concepts, pg 1400
iProbe Multilingual Solutions Inc, pg 1402
The Language Center, pg 1402
Linguistic Systems Inc (LSI), pg 1402
Link Translations Inc, pg 1403
MediaLocate Inc, pg 1403
Polyglot Communications Inc, pg 1403
Rennert Translation Group, pg 1404
Szablya Consultants Inc, pg 1405
Universe Technical Translation Inc, pg 1405

ICELANDIC

A WordJourney Translation LLC, pg 1399
American Translation Partners Inc (ATP), pg 1399
East-West Concepts, pg 1400
iProbe Multilingual Solutions Inc, pg 1402
Linguistic Systems Inc (LSI), pg 1402
Polyglot Communications Inc, pg 1403
Universe Technical Translation Inc, pg 1405

INDONESIAN

A WordJourney Translation LLC, pg 1399
American Translation Partners Inc (ATP), pg 1399
East-West Concepts, pg 1400
iProbe Multilingual Solutions Inc, pg 1402
Linguistic Systems Inc (LSI), pg 1402
Link Translations Inc, pg 1403
MediaLocate Inc, pg 1403
Polyglot Communications Inc, pg 1403
Rennert Translation Group, pg 1404
Johannes Tan, pg 1405
Universe Technical Translation Inc, pg 1405

ITALIAN

A WordJourney Translation LLC, pg 1399
AAA Fine Translation & Interpretation, pg 1399
Accredited Language Services (ALS), pg 1399
American Translation Partners Inc (ATP), pg 1399
Auerbach International, pg 1400
Baker & Taylor Publisher Services, pg 1400
Cross Cultural Communication Systems Inc, pg 1400
Cross Culture Communications, pg 1400
East-West Concepts, pg 1400
Eriksen Translations Inc, pg 1401
GGP Publishing Inc, pg 1401
Rosanna M Giammanco Frongia PhD, pg 1401
inlingua Translation Service, pg 1402
iProbe Multilingual Solutions Inc, pg 1402
IRCO-International Language Bank, pg 1402
The Language Center, pg 1402
Linguistic Systems Inc (LSI), pg 1402
Link Translations Inc, pg 1403
MediaLocate Inc, pg 1403
MEJ Personal Business Services Inc, pg 1403
Polyglot Communications Inc, pg 1403
Polyglot Translators, pg 1403
Rennert Translation Group, pg 1404
Rosemoor House Translations, pg 1404
Richard Schneider Language Services (RSLS), pg 1404
School of World Studies, pg 1404
Schreiber Translations Inc (STI), pg 1404
Teneo Linguistics Co LLC, pg 1405
Transimpex Translators, Interpreters, Editors, Consultants Inc, pg 1405
Translations.com, pg 1405
Translingua Associates Inc, pg 1405
Universe Technical Translation Inc, pg 1405
University Language Services (ULS), pg 1405

JAPANESE

A WordJourney Translation LLC, pg 1399
American Translation Partners Inc (ATP), pg 1399
Cross Cultural Communication Systems Inc, pg 1400
East-West Concepts, pg 1400
Eriksen Translations Inc, pg 1401
iProbe Multilingual Solutions Inc, pg 1402
The Language Center, pg 1402
Linguistic Systems Inc (LSI), pg 1402
Link Translations Inc, pg 1403
MediaLocate Inc, pg 1403
Metro Translation Service, pg 1403
Polyglot Communications Inc, pg 1403
Rennert Translation Group, pg 1404
Translations.com, pg 1405
Universe Technical Translation Inc, pg 1405

JAVANESE

A WordJourney Translation LLC, pg 1399
American Translation Partners Inc (ATP), pg 1399
East-West Concepts, pg 1400
iProbe Multilingual Solutions Inc, pg 1402
Linguistic Systems Inc (LSI), pg 1402
Polyglot Communications Inc, pg 1403

KHMER

A WordJourney Translation LLC, pg 1399
American Translation Partners Inc (ATP), pg 1399
Cross Cultural Communication Systems Inc, pg 1400
East-West Concepts, pg 1400
iProbe Multilingual Solutions Inc, pg 1402
Linguistic Systems Inc (LSI), pg 1402
Polyglot Communications Inc, pg 1403

KOREAN

A WordJourney Translation LLC, pg 1399
American Translation Partners Inc (ATP), pg 1399
Cross Cultural Communication Systems Inc, pg 1400
East-West Concepts, pg 1400
Eriksen Translations Inc, pg 1401
iProbe Multilingual Solutions Inc, pg 1402
The Language Center, pg 1402
Linguistic Systems Inc (LSI), pg 1402
Link Translations Inc, pg 1403
MediaLocate Inc, pg 1403
Polyglot Communications Inc, pg 1403
Rennert Translation Group, pg 1404
Translations.com, pg 1405
Universe Technical Translation Inc, pg 1405

KURDISH

A WordJourney Translation LLC, pg 1399
American Translation Partners Inc (ATP), pg 1399
East-West Concepts, pg 1400
iProbe Multilingual Solutions Inc, pg 1402
Polyglot Communications Inc, pg 1403
Universe Technical Translation Inc, pg 1405

LATIN

A WordJourney Translation LLC, pg 1399
AAA Fine Translation & Interpretation, pg 1399
American Translation Partners Inc (ATP), pg 1399
East-West Concepts, pg 1400
GGP Publishing Inc, pg 1401
iProbe Multilingual Solutions Inc, pg 1402
Linguistic Systems Inc (LSI), pg 1402
Polyglot Communications Inc, pg 1403
Rennert Translation Group, pg 1404
Universe Technical Translation Inc, pg 1405

LATVIAN

A WordJourney Translation LLC, pg 1399
American Translation Partners Inc (ATP), pg 1399
East-West Concepts, pg 1400
iProbe Multilingual Solutions Inc, pg 1402
Linguistic Systems Inc (LSI), pg 1402
Link Translations Inc, pg 1403
MediaLocate Inc, pg 1403
Polyglot Communications Inc, pg 1403
Universe Technical Translation Inc, pg 1405

LITHUANIAN

A WordJourney Translation LLC, pg 1399
American Translation Partners Inc (ATP), pg 1399
East-West Concepts, pg 1400
iProbe Multilingual Solutions Inc, pg 1402
The Language Center, pg 1402
Linguistic Systems Inc (LSI), pg 1402
MediaLocate Inc, pg 1403
Polyglot Communications Inc, pg 1403
Rennert Translation Group, pg 1404
Universe Technical Translation Inc, pg 1405

MACEDONIAN

A WordJourney Translation LLC, pg 1399
AAA Fine Translation & Interpretation, pg 1399
American Translation Partners Inc (ATP), pg 1399
East-West Concepts, pg 1400
iProbe Multilingual Solutions Inc, pg 1402
Linguistic Systems Inc (LSI), pg 1402
Link Translations Inc, pg 1403
MediaLocate Inc, pg 1403
Polyglot Communications Inc, pg 1403
Universe Technical Translation Inc, pg 1405

MALAGASY

A WordJourney Translation LLC, pg 1399
American Translation Partners Inc (ATP), pg 1399
East-West Concepts, pg 1400

TRANSLATORS & INTERPRETERS — TARGET LANGUAGE INDEX

iProbe Multilingual Solutions Inc, pg 1402
Polyglot Communications Inc, pg 1403
Universe Technical Translation Inc, pg 1405

MALAYALAM

A WordJourney Translation LLC, pg 1399
American Translation Partners Inc (ATP), pg 1399
East-West Concepts, pg 1400
iProbe Multilingual Solutions Inc, pg 1402
Polyglot Communications Inc, pg 1403
Universe Technical Translation Inc, pg 1405

MALAYSIAN

A WordJourney Translation LLC, pg 1399
American Translation Partners Inc (ATP), pg 1399
East-West Concepts, pg 1400
iProbe Multilingual Solutions Inc, pg 1402
Linguistic Systems Inc (LSI), pg 1402
MediaLocate Inc, pg 1403
Polyglot Communications Inc, pg 1403
Universe Technical Translation Inc, pg 1405

NEPALI

A WordJourney Translation LLC, pg 1399
American Translation Partners Inc (ATP), pg 1399
East-West Concepts, pg 1400
iProbe Multilingual Solutions Inc, pg 1402
Linguistic Systems Inc (LSI), pg 1402
Polyglot Communications Inc, pg 1403

NORWEGIAN

A WordJourney Translation LLC, pg 1399
AAA Fine Translation & Interpretation, pg 1399
American Translation Partners Inc (ATP), pg 1399
East-West Concepts, pg 1400
Eriksen Translations Inc, pg 1401
iProbe Multilingual Solutions Inc, pg 1402
Solveig Kjok, pg 1402
The Language Center, pg 1402
Linguistic Systems Inc (LSI), pg 1402
Link Translations Inc, pg 1403
MediaLocate Inc, pg 1403
Polyglot Communications Inc, pg 1403
Rennert Translation Group, pg 1404
Universe Technical Translation Inc, pg 1405

PERSIAN

A WordJourney Translation LLC, pg 1399
American Translation Partners Inc (ATP), pg 1399

Cross Cultural Communication Systems Inc, pg 1400
East-West Concepts, pg 1400
iProbe Multilingual Solutions Inc, pg 1402
Polyglot Communications Inc, pg 1403
Polyglot Translators, pg 1403
Universe Technical Translation Inc, pg 1405

POLISH

A WordJourney Translation LLC, pg 1399
American Translation Partners Inc (ATP), pg 1399
Cross Cultural Communication Systems Inc, pg 1400
East-West Concepts, pg 1400
Regina Gorzkowska-Rossi, pg 1401
iProbe Multilingual Solutions Inc, pg 1402
The Language Center, pg 1402
Linguistic Systems Inc (LSI), pg 1402
Link Translations Inc, pg 1403
MediaLocate Inc, pg 1403
Polyglot Communications Inc, pg 1403
Rennert Translation Group, pg 1404
Universe Technical Translation Inc, pg 1405
Maria Lidia Wilczewski, pg 1406

PORTUGUESE

A WordJourney Translation LLC, pg 1399
AAA Fine Translation & Interpretation, pg 1399
American Language Services Inc (ALSi), pg 1399
American Translation Partners Inc (ATP), pg 1399
Elizabeth Castaldini, pg 1400
Cross Cultural Communication Systems Inc, pg 1400
East-West Concepts, pg 1400
GGP Publishing Inc, pg 1401
iProbe Multilingual Solutions Inc, pg 1402
The Language Center, pg 1402
Linguistic Systems Inc (LSI), pg 1402
Link Translations Inc, pg 1403
MediaLocate Inc, pg 1403
Metro Translation Service, pg 1403
Polyglot Communications Inc, pg 1403
Rennert Translation Group, pg 1404
Translations.com, pg 1405
Universe Technical Translation Inc, pg 1405

PROVENCAL

A WordJourney Translation LLC, pg 1399
American Translation Partners Inc (ATP), pg 1399
East-West Concepts, pg 1400
iProbe Multilingual Solutions Inc, pg 1402
Polyglot Communications Inc, pg 1403

PUNJABI

A WordJourney Translation LLC, pg 1399
American Translation Partners Inc (ATP), pg 1399

Cross Cultural Communication Systems Inc, pg 1400
East-West Concepts, pg 1400
iProbe Multilingual Solutions Inc, pg 1402
Linguistic Systems Inc (LSI), pg 1402
Polyglot Communications Inc, pg 1403
Rennert Translation Group, pg 1404
Universe Technical Translation Inc, pg 1405

ROMANIAN

A WordJourney Translation LLC, pg 1399
AAA Fine Translation & Interpretation, pg 1399
American Translation Partners Inc (ATP), pg 1399
East-West Concepts, pg 1400
iProbe Multilingual Solutions Inc, pg 1402
Linguistic Systems Inc (LSI), pg 1402
Link Translations Inc, pg 1403
MediaLocate Inc, pg 1403
Polyglot Communications Inc, pg 1403
Rennert Translation Group, pg 1404
Universe Technical Translation Inc, pg 1405

RUSSIAN

A WordJourney Translation LLC, pg 1399
AAA Fine Translation & Interpretation, pg 1399
American Translation Partners Inc (ATP), pg 1399
Cross Cultural Communication Systems Inc, pg 1400
East-West Concepts, pg 1400
Glasnost Communications, pg 1401
iProbe Multilingual Solutions Inc, pg 1402
The Language Center, pg 1402
Linguistic Systems Inc (LSI), pg 1402
Link Translations Inc, pg 1403
MediaLocate Inc, pg 1403
Polyglot Communications Inc, pg 1403
Rennert Translation Group, pg 1404
School of World Studies, pg 1404
Natalia V Sciarini, pg 1404
Boris Mark Silversteyn, pg 1404
Translations.com, pg 1405
Universe Technical Translation Inc, pg 1405

SERBO-CROATIAN

A WordJourney Translation LLC, pg 1399
AAA Fine Translation & Interpretation, pg 1399
American Translation Partners Inc (ATP), pg 1399
Cross Cultural Communication Systems Inc, pg 1400
iProbe Multilingual Solutions Inc, pg 1402
The Language Center, pg 1402
Linguistic Systems Inc (LSI), pg 1402
Link Translations Inc, pg 1403
MediaLocate Inc, pg 1403
Polyglot Communications Inc, pg 1403

Rennert Translation Group, pg 1404
Universe Technical Translation Inc, pg 1405

SINHALESE

A WordJourney Translation LLC, pg 1399
American Translation Partners Inc (ATP), pg 1399
East-West Concepts, pg 1400
iProbe Multilingual Solutions Inc, pg 1402
Linguistic Systems Inc (LSI), pg 1402
Polyglot Communications Inc, pg 1403

SLOVAK

A WordJourney Translation LLC, pg 1399
AAA Fine Translation & Interpretation, pg 1399
American Translation Partners Inc (ATP), pg 1399
East-West Concepts, pg 1400
iProbe Multilingual Solutions Inc, pg 1402
The Language Center, pg 1402
Linguistic Systems Inc (LSI), pg 1402
Link Translations Inc, pg 1403
MediaLocate Inc, pg 1403
Polyglot Communications Inc, pg 1403
Rennert Translation Group, pg 1404
Universe Technical Translation Inc, pg 1405

SLOVENE

A WordJourney Translation LLC, pg 1399
AAA Fine Translation & Interpretation, pg 1399
American Translation Partners Inc (ATP), pg 1399
East-West Concepts, pg 1400
iProbe Multilingual Solutions Inc, pg 1402
Linguistic Systems Inc (LSI), pg 1402
Polyglot Communications Inc, pg 1403

SPANISH

A WordJourney Translation LLC, pg 1399
AAA Fine Translation & Interpretation, pg 1399
Accredited Language Services (ALS), pg 1399
Marvelia Alpizar, pg 1399
American Language Services Inc (ALSi), pg 1399
American Translation Partners Inc (ATP), pg 1399
Auerbach International, pg 1400
Baker & Taylor Publisher Services, pg 1400
Calaf Communications, pg 1400
Cross Cultural Communication Systems Inc, pg 1400
Cross Culture Communications, pg 1400
East-West Concepts, pg 1400
Eriksen Translations Inc, pg 1401
Mayra E Garcia, pg 1401
GGP Publishing Inc, pg 1401
Andrew S Gordon, PhD, pg 1401

inlingua Translation Service, pg 1402
iProbe Multilingual Solutions Inc, pg 1402
IRCO-International Language Bank, pg 1402
The Language Center, pg 1402
Linguistic Systems Inc (LSI), pg 1402
Link Translations Inc, pg 1403
MediaLocate Inc, pg 1403
MEJ Personal Business Services Inc, pg 1403
Metro Translation Service, pg 1403
Passwords Communications Inc, pg 1403
Polyglot Communications Inc, pg 1403
Polyglot Translators, pg 1403
Louise B Popkin, pg 1403
Rennert Translation Group, pg 1404
Richard Schneider Language Services (RSLS), pg 1404
School of World Studies, pg 1404
Schreiber Translations Inc (STI), pg 1404
Spanish/English Translation & Interpreting Services, pg 1404
Strictly Spanish Translations LLC, pg 1404
Teneo Linguistics Co LLC, pg 1405
Transimpex Translators, Interpreters, Editors, Consultants Inc, pg 1405
Translations.com, pg 1405
Translingua Associates Inc, pg 1405
Universe Technical Translation Inc, pg 1405
University Language Services (ULS), pg 1405
Liliana Valenzuela, pg 1405

SWAHILI

A WordJourney Translation LLC, pg 1399
American Translation Partners Inc (ATP), pg 1399
Cross Cultural Communication Systems Inc, pg 1400
East-West Concepts, pg 1400
iProbe Multilingual Solutions Inc, pg 1402
Linguistic Systems Inc (LSI), pg 1402
Polyglot Communications Inc, pg 1403
Rennert Translation Group, pg 1404
Universe Technical Translation Inc, pg 1405

SWEDISH

A WordJourney Translation LLC, pg 1399
AAA Fine Translation & Interpretation, pg 1399
American Translation Partners Inc (ATP), pg 1399
East-West Concepts, pg 1400
Eriksen Translations Inc, pg 1401

iProbe Multilingual Solutions Inc, pg 1402
The Language Center, pg 1402
Linguistic Systems Inc (LSI), pg 1402
Link Translations Inc, pg 1403
MediaLocate Inc, pg 1403
Polyglot Communications Inc, pg 1403
Rennert Translation Group, pg 1404
Translations.com, pg 1405
Universe Technical Translation Inc, pg 1405

TAGALOG

A WordJourney Translation LLC, pg 1399
American Translation Partners Inc (ATP), pg 1399
Cross Cultural Communication Systems Inc, pg 1400
East-West Concepts, pg 1400
iProbe Multilingual Solutions Inc, pg 1402
Linguistic Systems Inc (LSI), pg 1402
Link Translations Inc, pg 1403
Polyglot Communications Inc, pg 1403
Rennert Translation Group, pg 1404
Universe Technical Translation Inc, pg 1405

TAMIL

A WordJourney Translation LLC, pg 1399
American Translation Partners Inc (ATP), pg 1399
East-West Concepts, pg 1400
iProbe Multilingual Solutions Inc, pg 1402
Linguistic Systems Inc (LSI), pg 1402
Polyglot Communications Inc, pg 1403
Universe Technical Translation Inc, pg 1405

TELUGU

A WordJourney Translation LLC, pg 1399
American Translation Partners Inc (ATP), pg 1399
East-West Concepts, pg 1400
iProbe Multilingual Solutions Inc, pg 1402
Polyglot Communications Inc, pg 1403

THAI

A WordJourney Translation LLC, pg 1399
AAA Fine Translation & Interpretation, pg 1399
American Translation Partners Inc (ATP), pg 1399

Cross Cultural Communication Systems Inc, pg 1400
East-West Concepts, pg 1400
iProbe Multilingual Solutions Inc, pg 1402
Linguistic Systems Inc (LSI), pg 1402
Link Translations Inc, pg 1403
MediaLocate Inc, pg 1403
Polyglot Communications Inc, pg 1403
Rennert Translation Group, pg 1404
Universe Technical Translation Inc, pg 1405

TURKISH

A WordJourney Translation LLC, pg 1399
AAA Fine Translation & Interpretation, pg 1399
American Translation Partners Inc (ATP), pg 1399
Cross Cultural Communication Systems Inc, pg 1400
East-West Concepts, pg 1400
Ecegul (AJ) Elterman, pg 1401
iProbe Multilingual Solutions Inc, pg 1402
The Language Center, pg 1402
Linguistic Systems Inc (LSI), pg 1402
Link Translations Inc, pg 1403
MediaLocate Inc, pg 1403
Polyglot Communications Inc, pg 1403
Rennert Translation Group, pg 1404
Universe Technical Translation Inc, pg 1405

UKRAINIAN

A WordJourney Translation LLC, pg 1399
AAA Fine Translation & Interpretation, pg 1399
American Translation Partners Inc (ATP), pg 1399
East-West Concepts, pg 1400
Glasnost Communications, pg 1401
iProbe Multilingual Solutions Inc, pg 1402
Linguistic Systems Inc (LSI), pg 1402
Link Translations Inc, pg 1403
Polyglot Communications Inc, pg 1403
Rennert Translation Group, pg 1404
Boris Mark Silversteyn, pg 1404
Universe Technical Translation Inc, pg 1405

URDU

A WordJourney Translation LLC, pg 1399
American Translation Partners Inc (ATP), pg 1399
Cross Cultural Communication Systems Inc, pg 1400

East-West Concepts, pg 1400
Eriksen Translations Inc, pg 1401
iProbe Multilingual Solutions Inc, pg 1402
Linguistic Systems Inc (LSI), pg 1402
Link Translations Inc, pg 1403
Polyglot Communications Inc, pg 1403
Rennert Translation Group, pg 1404
Universe Technical Translation Inc, pg 1405

VIETNAMESE

A WordJourney Translation LLC, pg 1399
American Translation Partners Inc (ATP), pg 1399
Cross Cultural Communication Systems Inc, pg 1400
East-West Concepts, pg 1400
iProbe Multilingual Solutions Inc, pg 1402
The Language Center, pg 1402
Linguistic Systems Inc (LSI), pg 1402
Link Translations Inc, pg 1403
MediaLocate Inc, pg 1403
Polyglot Communications Inc, pg 1403
Rennert Translation Group, pg 1404
Universe Technical Translation Inc, pg 1405

WELSH

A WordJourney Translation LLC, pg 1399
American Translation Partners Inc (ATP), pg 1399
East-West Concepts, pg 1400
iProbe Multilingual Solutions Inc, pg 1402
Polyglot Communications Inc, pg 1403
Universe Technical Translation Inc, pg 1405

YIDDISH

A WordJourney Translation LLC, pg 1399
AAA Fine Translation & Interpretation, pg 1399
American Translation Partners Inc (ATP), pg 1399
East-West Concepts, pg 1400
iProbe Multilingual Solutions Inc, pg 1402
Linguistic Systems Inc (LSI), pg 1402
Polyglot Communications Inc, pg 1403
Rennert Translation Group, pg 1404
Universe Technical Translation Inc, pg 1405

Translators & Interpreters

The two indexes preceding this section identify the source and target languages translated or interpreted by the entrants.

The American Translators Association (311 North Union Street, Suite 100, Alexandria, VA 22314) publishes the *Language Services Directory* (online), which contains information about the association's members and their specialties.

A WordJourney Translation LLC
PO Box 3181, Humble, TX 77347-3181
Tel: 281-813-1827 *Fax:* 832-213-2777
E-mail: word@wjtranslation.com
Web Site: www.awordjourneytranslation.com
Key Personnel
Head, Prodn: Virginia Potcoava *E-mail:* virginia@wjtranslation.com
Founded: 2013
Multilingual staff & linguists worldwide. Virginia Potcoava has years of experience in the translation industry with a multitude of resources for translators worldwide. Certified translators for over 100 different languages. Expertise includes the following industries: energy/oil & gas, legal, technical, compliance, human resources, business & economy/finance, marketing & health. Services include: certified translations, translation/editing of documents, web translations, localization services, video & audio translation, safety compliance translations. E-mail for quote. Sample translation (up to 300 words) can be provided. Also work with Translation Memory.
Source Language(s): Afrikaans, Albanian, Arabic, Armenian, Belarussian, Bengali, Bulgarian, Burmese, Catalan, Chinese, Czech, Danish, Dutch, English, Esperanto, Estonian, Finnish, Flemish, French, Gaelic, Georgian, German, Greek, Hebrew, Hindi, Hungarian, Icelandic, Indonesian, Italian, Japanese, Javanese, Khmer, Korean, Kurdish, Latin, Latvian, Lithuanian, Macedonian, Malagasy, Malayalam, Malaysian, Nepali, Norwegian, Persian, Polish, Portuguese, Provencal, Punjabi, Romanian, Russian, Serbo-Croatian, Sinhalese, Slovak, Slovene, Spanish, Swahili, Swedish, Tagalog, Tamil, Telugu, Thai, Turkish, Ukrainian, Urdu, Vietnamese, Welsh, Yiddish
Target Language(s): Afrikaans, Albanian, Arabic, Armenian, Belarussian, Bengali, Bulgarian, Burmese, Catalan, Chinese, Czech, Danish, Dutch, English, Esperanto, Estonian, Finnish, Flemish, French, Gaelic, Georgian, German, Greek, Hebrew, Hindi, Hungarian, Icelandic, Indonesian, Italian, Japanese, Javanese, Khmer, Korean, Kurdish, Latin, Latvian, Lithuanian, Macedonian, Malagasy, Malayalam, Malaysian, Nepali, Norwegian, Persian, Polish, Portuguese, Provencal, Punjabi, Romanian, Russian, Serbo-Croatian, Sinhalese, Slovak, Slovene, Spanish, Swahili, Swedish, Tagalog, Tamil, Telugu, Thai, Turkish, Ukrainian, Urdu, Vietnamese, Welsh, Yiddish
Membership(s): International Chamber of Commerce–Texas

AAA Fine Translation & Interpretation
3820 Bowne St, Flushing, NY 11354
Tel: 917-582-7456
Key Personnel
Proj Dir: Prof David Schultz
 E-mail: davidtrans123@gmail.com
Speedy translation, live interpretation & turnaround time at very reasonable rates.
Source Language(s): Albanian, Belarussian, Bulgarian, Catalan, Danish, Dutch, English, French, German, Greek, Hebrew, Hungarian, Italian, Latin, Macedonian, Norwegian, Polish, Portuguese, Romanian, Russian, Serbo-Croatian, Slovak, Slovene, Spanish, Swedish, Thai, Turkish, Ukrainian, Yiddish
Target Language(s): Albanian, Belarussian, Bulgarian, Catalan, Danish, Dutch, English, French, German, Greek, Hebrew, Hungarian, Italian, Latin, Macedonian, Norwegian, Portuguese, Romanian, Russian, Serbo-Croatian, Slovak, Slovene, Spanish, Swedish, Thai, Turkish, Ukrainian, Yiddish
Membership(s): American Literary Translators Association (ALTA)

Accredited Language Services (ALS)
15 Maiden Lane, Suite 308, New York, NY 10038
Toll Free Tel: 800-322-0284
E-mail: interpreting@accreditedlanguage.com; sales@accreditedlanguage.com; translation@accreditedlanguage.com; transcription@accreditedlanguage.com; multimedia@accreditedlanguage.com
Web Site: www.accreditedlanguage.com
Founded: 1983
Translation, interpreting, transcription, voiceovers, subtitling, typesetting, printing, graphic design & desktop publishing. Over 150 languages & dialects.
Source Language(s): English, French, German, Italian, Spanish
Target Language(s): English, French, German, Italian, Spanish

Rodelinde Albrecht
274 Bradley St, Lee, MA 01238
Tel: 413-243-4350
E-mail: rodelinde@gmail.com
Founded: 1979
Translation (fiction & nonfiction), German to English. Also provides editorial services.
Source Language(s): German
Target Language(s): English

Veronika Albrecht-Rodrigues PhD
PO Box 44, Lovell, ME 04051-0044
Tel: 207-925-3117
E-mail: vroni@fairpoint.net
Translator/cultural consultant. General fiction & nonfiction; arts, humanities, medicine, business, legal & general correspondence & documents. Specialize in translating literary & musical subjects & in editing/proofreading foreign language teaching materials, including software.
Source Language(s): English, French, German
Target Language(s): English, German

Marvelia Alpizar
PO Box 4013, Burbank, CA 91503
Tel: 213-986-8207
E-mail: malpizar@gmail.com
Dependable & accurate service in the following areas of specialization: medicine, entertainment, arts & humanities, social sciences, business, natural sciences, pure sciences & media.
Source Language(s): English, Spanish
Target Language(s): English, Spanish
Membership(s): National Association of Hispanic Journalists (NAHJ); Society of Professional Journalists (SPJ)

American Language Services Inc (ALSi)
110 Otis St, Cambridge, MA 02141
E-mail: info@alsiweb.us
Web Site: www.americanlanguageservices.us
Key Personnel
Founder & Owner: Gema M Schaff *E-mail:* gs@alsiweb.us
Legal & medical translations. Simultaneous, consecutive & sight translating. Popular languages are Spanish, Portuguese, Haitian Creole, Amharic & Cape Verde.
Source Language(s): English, Portuguese, Spanish
Target Language(s): English, Portuguese, Spanish
Membership(s): National Association of Judiciary Interpreters & Translators (NAJIT); New England Translators Association (NETA)

American Translation Partners Inc (ATP)
One Trowbridge Rd, Suite 340, Buzzards Bay, MA 02532
Tel: 508-823-8892 *Toll Free Tel:* 888-443-2376 (US only) *Fax:* 508-823-8854
E-mail: info@atptranslations.com; request@atptranslations.com
Web Site: atptranslations.com
Key Personnel
VP: Scott M Crystal
Founded: 1997
Interpretation & translation in over 150 language pairs. CCHI certified.
Source Language(s): Afrikaans, Albanian, Arabic, Armenian, Belarussian, Bengali, Bulgarian, Burmese, Catalan, Chinese, Czech, Danish, Dutch, English, Esperanto, Estonian, Finnish, Flemish, French, Gaelic, Georgian, German, Greek, Hebrew, Hindi, Hungarian, Icelandic, Indonesian, Italian, Japanese, Javanese, Khmer, Korean, Kurdish, Latin, Latvian, Lithuanian, Macedonian, Malagasy, Malayalam, Malaysian, Nepali, Norwegian, Persian, Polish, Portuguese, Provencal, Punjabi, Romanian, Russian, Serbo-Croatian, Sinhalese, Slovak, Slovene, Spanish, Swahili, Swedish, Tagalog, Tamil, Telugu, Thai, Turkish, Ukrainian, Urdu, Vietnamese, Welsh, Yiddish
Target Language(s): Afrikaans, Albanian, Arabic, Armenian, Belarussian, Bengali, Bulgarian, Burmese, Catalan, Chinese, Czech, Danish, Dutch, English, Esperanto, Estonian, Finnish, Flemish, French, Gaelic, Georgian, German, Greek, Hebrew, Hindi, Hungarian, Icelandic, Indonesian, Italian, Japanese, Javanese, Khmer, Korean, Kurdish, Latin, Latvian, Lithuanian, Macedonian, Malagasy, Malayalam, Malaysian, Nepali, Norwegian, Persian, Polish, Portuguese, Provencal, Punjabi, Romanian, Russian, Serbo-Croatian, Sinhalese, Slovak, Slovene, Spanish, Swahili, Swedish, Tagalog, Tamil, Telugu, Thai, Turkish, Ukrainian, Urdu, Vietnamese, Welsh, Yiddish
Membership(s): American Translators Association (ATA); Association of Language Companies (ALC); Association of Translation Companies (ATC); International Federation of Translators (FIT); International Medical Interpreters Association (IMIA); National Association of Judiciary Interpreters & Translators (NAJIT); National Council on Interpreting in Health Care (NCIHC)

TRANSLATORS & INTERPRETERS — SERVICES

Anne Milano Appel
1364 Virginia St, Alamo, CA 94507
Tel: 925-837-5203
E-mail: annemilanoappel@gmail.com; amappel@pacbell.net
Web Site: www.annemilanoappel.com
Founded: 1996
Literary translation.
Source Language(s): Italian
Target Language(s): English
Membership(s): American Literary Translators Association (ALTA); American Translators Association (ATA); The Authors Guild; Northern California Translators Association; PEN America; PEN Center USA West

Apter, Ronnie, see Mark Herman & Ronnie Apter, Translators

Auerbach International
Alameda, CA 94501
Tel: 415-592-0042 *Fax:* 415-592-0043
E-mail: translations@auerbach-intl.com
Web Site: www.auerbach-intl.com
Key Personnel
Pres: Philip B Auerbach *Tel:* 415-592-0042 ext 107
Founded: 1991
30+ years of experience translating into 120 languages & handling many types of books with professional linguists. Special prices available for publishers.
Source Language(s): English, French, German, Italian, Spanish
Target Language(s): English, French, German, Italian, Spanish

Baker & Taylor Publisher Services
30 Amberwood Pkwy, Ashland, OH 44805
Tel: 567-215-0030 *Toll Free Tel:* 888-814-0208
E-mail: info@btpubservices.com; orders@btpubservices.com
Web Site: www.btpubservices.com
Key Personnel
SVP, Sales & Client Servs: Mark Suchomel
SVP, Opers: Bob Gospodarek
Trade Sales Dir: Deanna Meyerhoff
Founded: 2017
Baker & Taylor Publisher Services offers translation services for all major languages, specializing in English-to-Spanish & Spanish-to-English translation.
Source Language(s): English, French, German, Italian, Spanish
Target Language(s): English, French, German, Italian, Spanish

Bien Fait Translations
104 Seascape, Laguna Niguel, CA 92677
Tel: 781-769-1637 *Toll Free Tel:* 866-243-6324
Web Site: www.bien-fait.com
Key Personnel
Translator: Bruce D Popp, PhD *E-mail:* bdpopp@bien-fait.com
Founded: 2002
Translate general interest & technical books in astronomy & astrophysics & shorter documents in other scientific & technical areas.
Source Language(s): French
Target Language(s): English
Membership(s): American Astronomical Society; American Translators Association (ATA); New England Translators Association (NETA)

Wanda J Boeke
26 Brown Rd, Corning, NY 14830
Tel: 607-207-2786
E-mail: wjboeke@gmail.com
Translation & copy-editing since 1979: book-length works, articles, reviews; young adult fiction & nonfiction, poetry; publicity texts; reader's reports; AV scripts. Specializing in arts & humanities, accounting, finance, health & medicine, natural sciences, social sciences, tourism & travel. Published NEA translation grant recipient; ATA & TTIG certified. Wide experience, quick turnaround, great result. Contact information updated at www.atanet.org.
Source Language(s): Afrikaans, Dutch, Flemish, French, German
Target Language(s): English
Membership(s): American Literary Translators Association (ALTA); American Translators Association (ATA)

Robert Bononno
109 E Second St, Apt 5, New York, NY 10009
Tel: 646-673-6102
E-mail: rbononno@twc.com
Web Site: www.robert-bononno.com
Fiction & nonfiction translation from the French by published translator & language consultant. NEA two-time translation grant winner. Over 30 years experience. Nonfiction topics covered include fine art, philosophy, film & television, history & fashion. Free price quote on request.
Source Language(s): French, Italian
Target Language(s): English
Membership(s): American Literary Translators Association (ALTA); American Translators Association (ATA); PEN America

Calaf Communications
Affiliate of Cambridge Brick House
10 Warwick Ct, Lawrence, MA 01841
Tel: 978-314-3125 *Fax:* 978-686-5960
Web Site: www.calafcommunications.com
Key Personnel
Principal Consultant: Dolores C Calaf
E-mail: dcalaf@calafcommunications.com
Founded: 1995
Marketing, community relations & media production specialized in reaching Latino/Hispanic/Spanish & the speaking market, cultural adapted campaigns. Special areas/topics include health, education & arts/culture.
Source Language(s): English, Spanish
Target Language(s): Spanish
Membership(s): New England Translators Association (NETA)

Elizabeth Castaldini
927 Winterlochen Dr, Greensboro, NC 27410
Tel: 646-247-3190
E-mail: eranhec@yahoo.com
Source Language(s): English, Portuguese
Target Language(s): English, Portuguese
Membership(s): National Language Service Corps (NLSC)

CCCS, see Cross Cultural Communication Systems Inc

Alexandra Chciuk-Celt
392 Maple St, West Hempstead, NY 11552
Tel: 516-485-5531
E-mail: languagelady@juno.com
Translating, consecutive & simultaneous interpreting. Specialize in law, poetry, social & artistic subjects, linguistics, psychology.
Source Language(s): French, German, Polish, Spanish
Target Language(s): English

Cross Cultural Communication Systems Inc
227 Garfield Ave, Suite B, Woburn, MA 01801
Mailing Address: PO Box 2308, Woburn, MA 01888-0508
Tel: 781-729-3736 *Toll Free Tel:* 888-678-CCCS (678-2227 out of state only) *Fax:* 781-729-1217
Web Site: www.cccsorg.com; www.embracingculture.com
Key Personnel
Pres & Owner: Zarita Araujo-Lane
E-mail: zaraujo_lane@embracingculture.com
Founded: 1996
Source Language(s): Arabic, Armenian, Bengali, Chinese, English, French, German, Greek, Hebrew, Hindi, Italian, Japanese, Khmer, Korean, Persian, Polish, Portuguese, Punjabi, Russian, Serbo-Croatian, Spanish, Swahili, Tagalog, Thai, Turkish, Urdu, Vietnamese
Target Language(s): Arabic, Armenian, Bengali, Chinese, English, French, German, Greek, Hebrew, Hindi, Italian, Japanese, Khmer, Korean, Persian, Polish, Portuguese, Punjabi, Russian, Serbo-Croatian, Spanish, Swahili, Tagalog, Thai, Turkish, Urdu, Vietnamese
Membership(s): American Translators Association (ATA); Association for Talent Development (ATD); California Healthcare Interpreters Association (CHIA); Conference of Interpreter Trainers (CIT); Florida Chapter of the American Translators Association (FLATA); Massachusetts Medical Interpreters Association (MMIA); Michigan Translators Interpreters Network; National Council on Interpreting in Health Care (NCIHC); New England Translators Association (NETA); New Hampshire Interpreters & Translators Organization (NHITO)

Cross Culture Communications
PO Box 141263, Dallas, TX 75214
Tel: 214-394-3000
E-mail: info@crossculturecommunications.com
Web Site: crossculturecommunications.com
Key Personnel
Co-Founder: Edward Retta *E-mail:* eretta@crossculturecommunications.com;
Marilyn Retta *E-mail:* mretta@crossculturecommunications.com
Founded: 1994
Cross cultural training & language services.
Source Language(s): English, French, German, Italian, Spanish
Target Language(s): English, French, German, Italian, Spanish
Membership(s): American Translators Association (ATA); National Association of Judiciary Interpreters & Translators (NAJIT)

Marcia Nita Doron
10 Millstone Dr, Concord, NH 03301
Tel: 508-735-3454 (cell)
Translating & editing.
Source Language(s): French, Hebrew
Target Language(s): English
Membership(s): National Capital Area Chapter/American Translators Association

East-West Concepts
PO Box 1435, Kapaa, HI 96746
Tel: 808-938-8410 *Fax:* 808-441-8121
Web Site: www.eastwestconcepts.com
Key Personnel
Opers Mgr: Krisztina Samu *E-mail:* krisztina@eastwestconcepts.com
Founded: 1989
Translation company, 260 different Source & Target languages. Also translates to & from Chamorro, Chuukese, Divehi, Dzongkha, Fijian, Hawaiian, Karen, Kongri, Luxembourgish, Marshallese, Samoan, Shan, Tibetan, Tongan, Yapese, Yi, Yupik & Zulu languages.
Source Language(s): Afrikaans, Albanian, Arabic, Armenian, Belarussian, Bengali, Bulgarian, Burmese, Catalan, Chinese, Czech, Danish, Dutch, English, Esperanto, Estonian, Finnish, Flemish, French, Gaelic, Georgian, German, Greek, Hebrew, Hindi, Hungarian, Icelandic, Indonesian, Italian, Japanese, Javanese, Khmer, Korean, Kurdish, Latin, Latvian, Lithuanian,

Macedonian, Malagasy, Malayalam, Malaysian, Nepali, Norwegian, Persian, Polish, Portuguese, Provencal, Punjabi, Romanian, Russian, Sinhalese, Slovak, Slovene, Spanish, Swahili, Swedish, Tagalog, Tamil, Telugu, Thai, Turkish, Ukrainian, Urdu, Vietnamese, Welsh, Yiddish
Target Language(s): Afrikaans, Albanian, Arabic, Armenian, Belarussian, Bengali, Bulgarian, Burmese, Catalan, Chinese, Czech, Danish, Dutch, English, Esperanto, Estonian, Finnish, Flemish, French, Gaelic, Georgian, German, Greek, Hebrew, Hindi, Hungarian, Icelandic, Indonesian, Italian, Japanese, Javanese, Khmer, Korean, Kurdish, Latin, Latvian, Lithuanian, Macedonian, Malagasy, Malayalam, Malaysian, Nepali, Norwegian, Persian, Polish, Portuguese, Provencal, Punjabi, Romanian, Russian, Sinhalese, Slovak, Slovene, Spanish, Swahili, Swedish, Tagalog, Tamil, Telugu, Thai, Turkish, Ukrainian, Urdu, Vietnamese, Welsh, Yiddish

Ecegul (AJ) Elterman
18 Sixteenth St, Bayville, NY 11709
Tel: 516-661-6525 (cell)
E-mail: ajelterman@mindspring.com
Translating & interpreting, proofreading, copyediting, transcribing, narrating & voice-over.
Source Language(s): English, French, German, Turkish
Target Language(s): English, German, Turkish
Membership(s): American Translators Association (ATA); National Association of Judiciary Interpreters & Translators (NAJIT); New York Circle of Translators

Eriksen Translations Inc
360 Court St, Unit 37, Brooklyn, NY 11231
Tel: 718-802-9010 *Fax:* 718-802-0041
Web Site: www.eriksen.com
Key Personnel
Pres & CEO: Vigdis Eriksen *E-mail:* vigdis.eriksen@eriksen.com
Dir, Sales: Will Lach
Founded: 1986
Translation, typesetting, web & multimedia localization, transcreation, voice-over & subtitling services in over 100 languages.
Source Language(s): Arabic, Chinese, Danish, English, Finnish, French, German, Italian, Japanese, Korean, Norwegian, Spanish, Swedish, Urdu
Target Language(s): Arabic, Chinese, Danish, English, Finnish, French, German, Italian, Japanese, Korean, Norwegian, Spanish, Swedish, Urdu
Membership(s): American Translators Association (ATA); Globalization & Localization Association (GALA); New York Circle of Translators

French and English Communication Services LLC
3104 E Camelback Rd, No 124, Phoenix, AZ 85016-4502
Tel: 602-870-1000
E-mail: RequestFAECS2008@cox.net
Web Site: www.FrenchAndEnglish.com
Key Personnel
Owner: Diane Goullard
Founded: 1984
French to English & English to French translation, proofreading, narrating.
Source Language(s): English, French
Target Language(s): English, French

Frongia, Rosanna M, see Rosanna M Giammanco Frongia PhD

Mayra E Garcia
313 Valley Ct, Sinking Spring, PA 19608
Tel: 803-422-5903
E-mail: mayra.garcia11@gmail.com
Speedy & accurate translation with areas of specialization in psychology, psychiatry, education, immigration, business, travel & general topics.
Source Language(s): English, Spanish
Target Language(s): English, Spanish
Membership(s): American Translators Association (ATA)

German Language Services
4752 41 Ave SW, Suite B, Seattle, WA 98116
Tel: 206-938-3600
E-mail: info@germanlanguageservices.com
Web Site: germanlanguageservices.com
Key Personnel
CEO: Maia Costa *E-mail:* maia@germanlanguageservices.com
Founded: 1979
Translation, interpreting, content writing, editing, localization & transcreation.
Source Language(s): English, German
Target Language(s): English, German
Membership(s): American Translators Association (ATA)

GGP Publishing Inc
Larchmont, NY 10538
Tel: 914-834-8896 *Fax:* 914-834-7566
Web Site: www.GGPPublishing.com
Key Personnel
Founder, Owner & Dir: Generosa Gina Protano *E-mail:* GGProtano@GGPPublishing.com
Founded: 1991
Full service development house & packaging firm offering services from concept to finished electronic files/bound books to online distribution or for any one step of this publishing process. Specialize in educational publishing from K-12 to college/university to adult education. Have a niche in the writing, development, editing & production up to finished electronic files/bound books of textbooks & trade books for the study of foreign languages such as French, German, Italian, Latin, Portuguese & Spanish. Also translates complete/partial programs or cluster of books from English into any of these languages or from any of these languages into English, edit the translation for publication & set the edited translation into book form up to finished electronic files/bound books. Develop, edit, do art/design & production of different genres both for publishing houses as well as individuals who wish to self-publish. Has produced novels, memoirs & books in the fields of religion, psychology & culinary arts among others. Special interest in memoirs. Acts as literary agents & foreign publisher representatives.
Source Language(s): English, French, German, Italian, Latin, Portuguese, Spanish
Target Language(s): English, French, German, Italian, Latin, Portuguese, Spanish

Rosanna M Giammanco Frongia PhD
Affiliate of Verbum Linguistic Services Inc
PO Box 810422, Boca Raton, FL 33481-0422
Tel: 718-619-2637 (cell)
E-mail: giammancorm@gmail.com
Translation, editing, consulting, abstracting, coordinating, research. Ability to handle large multi-language projects. All subjects; broad experience in academic texts, social sciences, Italy, legal, financial. Equipment: PC, laser printer, fax, modem, e-mail.
Source Language(s): English, French, Italian, Latin, Spanish
Target Language(s): English, Italian
Membership(s): American Translators Association (ATA); National Association of Judiciary Interpreters & Translators (NAJIT); New York Circle of Translators

Glasnost Communications
Tallberry Dr, Cincinnati, OH 45230
Tel: 513-231-3599
E-mail: glasnost@currently.com
Key Personnel
Interpreter/Translator: Alexander (Sasha) Etlin
Founded: 1995
Extensive translation & interpretation experience in many fields including business; manufacturing; agriculture; government, city services, urban planning; health care, public health, domestic violence, substance abuse; NGOs, social services; law, law enforcement; education; religion; environment; arts & culture; mass media.
Source Language(s): English, Russian, Ukrainian
Target Language(s): English, Russian, Ukrainian

Andrew S Gordon, PhD
1230 23 St NW, No 804, Washington, DC 20037
E-mail: andgordon@yahoo.com
Advertising, law, literature & politics. Certified interpreter/translator with 30 plus years experience. Professor Emeritus of Spanish language, literature & translation.
Source Language(s): English, Spanish
Target Language(s): English, Spanish
Membership(s): Modern Language Association (MLA)

Regina Gorzkowska-Rossi
3349 E Thompson St, Philadelphia, PA 19134
Tel: 267-535-1691
E-mail: proarterg@yahoo.com
Source Language(s): English, Polish
Target Language(s): English, Polish
Membership(s): American Literary Translators Association (ALTA)

Diane Goullard, see French and English Communication Services LLC

Rita Granda
466 Cambridge St, Peterborough, ON K9H 4T3, Canada
Tel: 705-748-0943
E-mail: rita@ritagranda.com
Web Site: www.ritagranda.com
Source Language(s): Spanish
Target Language(s): English
Membership(s): American Translators Association (ATA); Association of Translators & Interpreters of Ontario (ATIO)

Diana Mara Henry
51 Carbonneau Dr, Suite 3, Newport, VT 05855
Tel: 802-334-7054
E-mail: dhenry188@gmail.com
Web Site: www.natzweiler-struthof.com
Founded: 2000
Literary & historical translations; certificates; medical & general transcription & translation of conferences; interpretation for immigration hearings, legal & medical proceedings.
Source Language(s): French
Target Language(s): English

Mark Herman & Ronnie Apter, Translators
2222 Westview Dr, Nashville, TN 37212-4123
Tel: 615-942-8462
E-mail: mnh18@columbia.edu
Key Personnel
Partner: Ronnie Apter; Mark Herman
Founded: 1975
Translation into English of opera & drama for performance & poetry, ancient & modern.
Source Language(s): Catalan, Czech, French, German, Italian, Latin, Provencal, Russian, Spanish
Target Language(s): English
Membership(s): American Literary Translators Association (ALTA); American Translators Association (ATA)

TRANSLATORS & INTERPRETERS

Joan E Howard
51 Congress St, Augusta, ME 04330
Tel: 207-622-0580
E-mail: petiteplaisance@acadia.net
Founded: 1991
Translation & copy-editing.
Source Language(s): English, French
Target Language(s): English, French
Membership(s): Modern Language Association (MLA)

Indexing by the Book
5912 E Eastland St, Tucson, AZ 85711-4636
Tel: 520-405-8083
E-mail: indextran@cox.net
Web Site: www.indexingbythebook.com
Key Personnel
Indexer: Cynthia J Coan
Founded: 2003
Provide both indexing & translation services. Specialties in the translation field include medicine & law/patents.
Source Language(s): Spanish, Swedish
Target Language(s): English
Membership(s): American Literary Translators Association (ALTA); American Society for Indexing (ASI); American Translators Association (ATA)

inlingua Translation Service
95 Summit Ave, Summit, NJ 07901
Tel: 908-522-0622
E-mail: summit@inlingua.com
Web Site: www.inlingua.com
Key Personnel
Translation Coord: Sue Baldani
Translation & interpreting services to corporations & private individuals; provide language & intercultural training.
Source Language(s): English, French, German, Italian, Spanish
Target Language(s): English, French, German, Italian, Spanish

iProbe Multilingual Solutions Inc
145 W 30 St, 9th fl, New York, NY 10001
Tel: 212-489-6035 *Toll Free Tel:* 888-489-6035 *Fax:* 212-202-4790
E-mail: info@iprobesolutions.com
Web Site: iprobesolutions.com
Key Personnel
Founder & CEO: Julie H Setbon
  E-mail: setbon@iprobesolutions.com
Founded: 2001
iProbe provides pre-production, production, post-production support & foreign language versioning in 6,912 languages for broadcast, corporate, commercial & educational programming. Our specialty is the creation of multilingual media for print, industrial, broadcast, DVD, video tape, Internet & new media use.
Production, Post-Production & Localization Services: DVD authoring, duplication & replication; production; post-production; video & audio encoding; casting, dubbing & voice-overs; subtitling & captioning; transcription; graphic production; typesetting; desktop publishing (DTP) compositing; interpreting & simultaneous interpretation wireless equipment, rental & sales. Also provide publishers with scanning & OCR services in major languages including Russian (Cyrillic alphabet).
Source Language(s): Afrikaans, Albanian, Arabic, Armenian, Belarussian, Bengali, Bulgarian, Burmese, Catalan, Chinese, Czech, Danish, Dutch, English, Esperanto, Estonian, Finnish, Flemish, French, Gaelic, Georgian, German, Greek, Hebrew, Hindi, Hungarian, Icelandic, Indonesian, Italian, Japanese, Javanese, Khmer, Korean, Kurdish, Latin, Latvian, Lithuanian, Macedonian, Malagasy, Malayalam, Malaysian, Nepali, Norwegian, Persian, Polish, Portuguese, Provencal, Punjabi, Romanian, Russian, Serbo-Croatian, Sinhalese, Slovak, Slovene, Spanish, Swahili, Swedish, Tagalog, Tamil, Telugu, Thai, Turkish, Ukrainian, Urdu, Vietnamese, Welsh, Yiddish
Target Language(s): Afrikaans, Albanian, Arabic, Armenian, Belarussian, Bengali, Bulgarian, Burmese, Catalan, Chinese, Czech, Danish, Dutch, English, Esperanto, Estonian, Finnish, Flemish, French, Gaelic, Georgian, German, Greek, Hebrew, Hindi, Hungarian, Icelandic, Indonesian, Italian, Japanese, Javanese, Khmer, Korean, Kurdish, Latin, Latvian, Lithuanian, Macedonian, Malagasy, Malayalam, Malaysian, Nepali, Norwegian, Persian, Polish, Portuguese, Provencal, Punjabi, Romanian, Russian, Serbo-Croatian, Sinhalese, Slovak, Slovene, Spanish, Swahili, Swedish, Tagalog, Tamil, Telugu, Thai, Turkish, Ukrainian, Urdu, Vietnamese, Welsh, Yiddish

IRCO-International Language Bank
10301 NE Glisan St, Portland, OR 97220
Tel: 503-234-0068 (interpretation); 503-505-5186 (translation) *Fax:* 503-233-4724
E-mail: translation@ircoilb.org; interpretation@ircoilb.org
Web Site: www.irco.org/ilb
Key Personnel
Exec Dir: Lee Po Cha
Founded: 1976
Provide interpretation & translation services, specializing in refugee languages.
Source Language(s): English, French, German, Italian, Spanish
Target Language(s): English, French, German, Italian, Spanish
Membership(s): American Translators Association (ATA); International Medical Interpreters Association (IMIA); Northwest Translators & Interpreters Society (NOTIS)

Bruni Johnson
457 E Colfax St, Palatine, IL 60074
Tel: 847-359-6839 *Fax:* 847-359-7075
E-mail: brunijohnson@sbcglobal.net
Source Language(s): English, German
Target Language(s): English, German
Membership(s): American Translators Association (ATA)

Alicja T Kawecki
4-A Foxwood Dr, Apt D, Morris Plains, NJ 07950
Tel: 973-590-2236
E-mail: atkawecki@optonline.net
Technical & specialized materials.
Also translates from English into Polish.
Source Language(s): French, Italian, Polish, Russian, Ukrainian
Target Language(s): English
Membership(s): American Translators Association (ATA); The Institute of Linguists (England)

Solveig Kjok
520 Kingsland Ave, Brooklyn, NY 11222
Web Site: www.art-texts.plus; www.solkjok.info
Founded: 1984
Multilingual arts writer & visual artist.
Source Language(s): Danish, English, French, German, Norwegian, Spanish, Swedish
Target Language(s): English, Norwegian

Kenneth Kronenberg
51 Maple Ave, Cambridge, MA 02139
Tel: 617-868-8070
E-mail: mail@kfkronenberg.com
Web Site: www.kfkronenberg.com
Mr Kronenberg specializes in 19th- & 20th-century diaries & letters for publication & private clients; also Holocaust-related materials. His most recent books: Jorun Poettering *Migrating Merchants* (DeGruyter Oldenbourg, 2018); Michael North *The Baltic: A History* (Harvard University Press, 2015); Juergen Leonhardt *Latin: Story of a World Language* (Harvard University Press, 2013). Mr Kronenberg also translates in psychology/psychiatry: Karl Heinz Brisch *Treating Attachment Disorders* (Guilford Press, 2002, 2012 & 2023).
Source Language(s): German
Target Language(s): English

The Language Center
Division of The Center for Professional Advancement
62 Brunswick Woods Dr, East Brunswick, NJ 08816
Tel: 732-613-4554 *Fax:* 732-238-7659
Web Site: www.thelanguagectr.com
Key Personnel
VP & Dir: Mary Majkowski
  E-mail: marymajkowski@thelanguagectr.com
Proj Mgr: Grace Chio; Brian Vogel
Founded: 1967
Translation, editing, typesetting in all languages & printing services. Specialize in books, manuals, catalogs, brochures, periodicals, patents, correspondence, package inserts. Fields including, but not limited to pharmaceutical, medical, chemistry, technology, engineering, electronics, computers, manufacturing, law, government, politics, civics, publishing, advertising, marketing, travel & tourism. Also provide onsite & phone interpretation services.
Source Language(s): Arabic, Chinese, Czech, Danish, Dutch, English, Finnish, French, German, Hungarian, Italian, Japanese, Korean, Lithuanian, Norwegian, Polish, Portuguese, Russian, Serbo-Croatian, Slovak, Spanish, Swedish, Turkish, Vietnamese
Target Language(s): Arabic, Chinese, Czech, Danish, Dutch, English, Finnish, French, German, Hungarian, Italian, Japanese, Korean, Lithuanian, Norwegian, Polish, Portuguese, Russian, Serbo-Croatian, Slovak, Spanish, Swedish, Turkish, Vietnamese
Membership(s): American Translators Association, Translation Company Division (TCD); Association of Language Companies (ALC)

Linguistic Systems Inc (LSI)
260 Franklin St, Suite 230, Boston, MA 02110
Tel: 617-528-7400
E-mail: clientservice@linguist.com
Web Site: www.linguist.com
Key Personnel
Founder & Pres: Martin Roberts
Founded: 1967
Premier language translation services company. Provides exceptional translation & interpreting services for tens of thousands of clients across dozens of industries including medical, life sciences, technology, publishing, government & more. Ai Translate by LSI™ is Linguistic Systems' powerful, unique language translation solution. It offers best-in-class technology & security & the opportunity to select from 6 quality levels & up to 120 language pairs for optimum results.
Source Language(s): Afrikaans, Albanian, Arabic, Armenian, Belarussian, Bengali, Bulgarian, Burmese, Catalan, Chinese, Czech, Danish, Dutch, English, Estonian, Finnish, Flemish, French, Gaelic, Georgian, German, Greek, Hebrew, Hindi, Hungarian, Icelandic, Indonesian, Italian, Japanese, Javanese, Khmer, Korean, Latin, Latvian, Lithuanian, Macedonian, Malaysian, Nepali, Norwegian, Polish, Portuguese, Punjabi, Romanian, Russian, Serbo-Croatian, Sinhalese, Slovak, Slovene, Spanish, Swahili, Swedish, Tagalog, Tamil, Thai, Turkish, Ukrainian, Urdu, Vietnamese, Yiddish

Target Language(s): Afrikaans, Albanian, Arabic, Armenian, Belarussian, Bengali, Bulgarian, Burmese, Catalan, Chinese, Czech, Danish, Dutch, English, Estonian, Finnish, Flemish, French, Gaelic, Georgian, German, Greek, Hebrew, Hindi, Hungarian, Icelandic, Indonesian, Italian, Japanese, Javanese, Khmer, Korean, Latin, Latvian, Lithuanian, Macedonian, Malaysian, Nepali, Norwegian, Polish, Portuguese, Punjabi, Romanian, Russian, Serbo-Croatian, Sinhalese, Slovak, Slovene, Spanish, Swahili, Swedish, Tagalog, Tamil, Thai, Turkish, Ukrainian, Urdu, Vietnamese, Yiddish
Membership(s): American Translators Association (ATA); Association of Language Companies (ALC); Globalization & Localization Association (GALA)

Link Translations Inc
60 E 96 St, New York, NY 10128
Toll Free Tel: 866-866-5010
E-mail: info@link-translations.com
Web Site: www.link-translations.com
Key Personnel
Owner & Pres: Evren Ay
Sr Proj Mgr: Mustafa Cengiz
Proj Mgr: Oytun Tez
Jr Proj Mgr: Asli Merve Karabulut
Systems Engr: Kaan Daniel
Founded: 1995
Translation, interpretation & localization.
Source Language(s): Afrikaans, Albanian, Arabic, Bulgarian, Chinese, Czech, Danish, Dutch, English, French, Georgian, German, Greek, Hebrew, Hindi, Hungarian, Indonesian, Italian, Japanese, Korean, Latvian, Macedonian, Norwegian, Polish, Portuguese, Romanian, Russian, Serbo-Croatian, Slovak, Spanish, Swedish, Tagalog, Thai, Turkish, Ukrainian, Urdu, Vietnamese
Target Language(s): Afrikaans, Albanian, Arabic, Bulgarian, Chinese, Czech, Danish, Dutch, English, French, Georgian, German, Greek, Hebrew, Hindi, Hungarian, Indonesian, Italian, Japanese, Korean, Latvian, Macedonian, Norwegian, Polish, Portuguese, Romanian, Russian, Serbo-Croatian, Slovak, Spanish, Swedish, Tagalog, Thai, Turkish, Ukrainian, Urdu, Vietnamese
Membership(s): American Translators Association (ATA)

MediaLocate Inc
1200 Piedmont Ave, Pacific Grove, CA 93950
Tel: 831-655-7500
E-mail: info@medialocate.com
Web Site: www.medialocate.com
Key Personnel
CEO: Stephan Lins
CFO: Ilge Karancak
Dir, Proj Mgmt: Anne Thompson
Dir, Strategic Partnerships: Kurt Alexander
Localization, translation & interpretation services in more than 150 languages. Fields covered: Technology, marketing, life sciences, law, education, defense, hospitality & entertainment.
Source Language(s): Bulgarian, Chinese, Czech, Danish, Dutch, English, Estonian, Finnish, French, German, Greek, Hungarian, Indonesian, Italian, Japanese, Korean, Latvian, Lithuanian, Macedonian, Malaysian, Norwegian, Polish, Portuguese, Romanian, Russian, Serbo-Croatian, Slovak, Spanish, Swedish, Thai, Turkish, Vietnamese
Target Language(s): Bulgarian, Chinese, Czech, Danish, Dutch, English, Estonian, Finnish, French, German, Greek, Hungarian, Indonesian, Italian, Japanese, Korean, Latvian, Lithuanian, Macedonian, Malaysian, Norwegian, Polish, Portuguese, Romanian, Russian, Serbo-Croatian, Slovak, Spanish, Swedish, Thai, Turkish, Vietnamese
Membership(s): American Translators Association (ATA)

MEJ Personal Business Services Inc
245 E 116 St, New York, NY 10029
Tel: 212-426-6017 *Toll Free Tel:* 866-557-5336
Fax: 646-827-3628
E-mail: support@mejpbs.com
Web Site: www.mejpbs.com
Key Personnel
Pres: Melvin Johnson *E-mail:* mjohnson@mejpbs.com
Contact: Elizabeth Johnson *E-mail:* elizabeth@mejpbs.com
Full service language service provider. Over 140 languages. Medical & legal translations & tax preparation services.
Source Language(s): English, French, German, Italian, Spanish
Target Language(s): English, French, German, Italian, Spanish
Membership(s): American Translators Association (ATA)

Metro Translation Service
294 De Kalb Ave, Brooklyn, NY 11205
Tel: 917-558-0089 (cell)
E-mail: metrotourservice21@gmail.com
Web Site: metrotourservice.blogspot.com
Key Personnel
Contact: Mauricio Lorence
In business for more than 15 years providing skilled & accurate translations. Work with businesses & service industries. Languages are Spanish, Japanese, Portuguese, German & English. Also does tailored tours for executives & professionals.
Source Language(s): English, German, Japanese, Portuguese, Spanish
Target Language(s): English, German, Japanese, Portuguese, Spanish
Membership(s): Chicago Area Translators & Interpreters Association (CHICATA); Court Interpreters & Translators Association; New York Circle of Translators

Donald Nicholson-Smith
50 Plaza St E, Apt 1D, Brooklyn, NY 11238
Tel: 718-636-4732
E-mail: mnr.dns@verizon.net
Specialize in humanities, fiction, psychology & psychoanalysis.
Source Language(s): French, Spanish
Target Language(s): English
Membership(s): Translators Association (London)

Passwords Communications Inc
1804 21 St N, Arlington, VA 22209
Tel: 703-624-5953
E-mail: paellero@aol.com
Web Site: www.passwords-comm.com
Translation of fiction, nonfiction, poetry, children's literature & technical documentation.
Source Language(s): English, French, Spanish
Target Language(s): English, Spanish
Membership(s): American Literary Translators Association (ALTA); American Translators Association (ATA)

Emmanuel X Pierreuse
1830 Avenida del Mundo, Suite 412, Coronado, CA 92118
Tel: 619-435-3931; 619-508-1712 (cell)
E-mail: epierreuse@aol.com; franslations@aol.com
Web Site: franslations.wixsite.com/website
Founded: 1998
Translations & interpreting, consecutive & simultaneous.
Source Language(s): English, French
Target Language(s): English, French
Membership(s): American Translators Association (ATA)

Polyglot Communications Inc
PO Box 1962, Laguna Beach, CA 92652
Tel: 949-497-1544
E-mail: info@polyglot.us.com
Web Site: www.polyglot.us.com
Key Personnel
Pres & CEO: Arturo Valdivia
Founded: 1987
Translations, interpreters & voice-over narration in all languages.
Source Language(s): Afrikaans, Albanian, Arabic, Armenian, Belarussian, Bengali, Bulgarian, Burmese, Catalan, Chinese, Czech, Danish, Dutch, English, Esperanto, Estonian, Finnish, Flemish, French, Gaelic, Georgian, German, Greek, Hebrew, Hindi, Hungarian, Icelandic, Indonesian, Italian, Japanese, Javanese, Khmer, Korean, Kurdish, Latin, Latvian, Lithuanian, Macedonian, Malagasy, Malayalam, Malaysian, Nepali, Norwegian, Persian, Polish, Portuguese, Provencal, Punjabi, Romanian, Russian, Serbo-Croatian, Sinhalese, Slovak, Slovene, Spanish, Swahili, Swedish, Tagalog, Tamil, Telugu, Thai, Turkish, Ukrainian, Urdu, Vietnamese, Welsh, Yiddish
Target Language(s): Afrikaans, Albanian, Arabic, Armenian, Belarussian, Bengali, Bulgarian, Burmese, Catalan, Chinese, Czech, Danish, Dutch, English, Esperanto, Estonian, Finnish, Flemish, French, Gaelic, Georgian, German, Greek, Hebrew, Hindi, Hungarian, Icelandic, Indonesian, Italian, Japanese, Javanese, Khmer, Korean, Kurdish, Latin, Latvian, Lithuanian, Macedonian, Malagasy, Malayalam, Malaysian, Nepali, Norwegian, Persian, Polish, Portuguese, Provencal, Punjabi, Romanian, Russian, Serbo-Croatian, Sinhalese, Slovak, Slovene, Spanish, Swahili, Swedish, Tagalog, Tamil, Telugu, Thai, Turkish, Ukrainian, Urdu, Vietnamese, Welsh, Yiddish
Membership(s): American Translators Association (ATA)

Polyglot Translators
PO Box 30087, Bethesda, MD 20824
Fax: 301-907-8707
E-mail: info@polyglottranslators.com
Web Site: polyglottranslators.com
Founded: 1979
Translating from & into Middle-Eastern languages, including Dari/Farsi/Tajik, in all subjects.
Source Language(s): English, French, German, Italian, Persian, Spanish
Target Language(s): English, French, German, Italian, Persian, Spanish

Louise B Popkin
9 Cliff St, Apt 2, Arlington, MA 02476
Tel: 617-281-4649
E-mail: louise@louisebpopkin.com
Freelance literary translating (fiction, poetry, drama); certified English-Spanish & Spanish-English. Can check translations for accuracy & style.
Source Language(s): English, Spanish
Target Language(s): English, Spanish
Membership(s): American Literary Translators Association (ALTA); American Translators Association (ATA); New England Translators Association (NETA)

Pro Arte Associates, see Regina Gorzkowska-Rossi

Generosa Gina Protano Publishing, see GGP Publishing Inc

TRANSLATORS & INTERPRETERS

Rennert Translation Group
Division of Rennert International
12 E 41 St, New York, NY 10017
Tel: 212-867-8700
E-mail: translations@rennert.com
Web Site: rennerttranslations.com
Key Personnel
Pres: Cesar Rennert
Founded: 1973
Translation, transcreation, interpretation, desktop publishing, localization, dubbing, subtitling, transcription & cross-cultural consulting services.
Source Language(s): Albanian, Arabic, Armenian, Bengali, Bulgarian, Catalan, Chinese, Czech, Danish, Dutch, English, Finnish, Flemish, French, German, Greek, Hebrew, Hindi, Hungarian, Indonesian, Italian, Japanese, Korean, Latin, Lithuanian, Norwegian, Polish, Portuguese, Punjabi, Romanian, Russian, Serbo-Croatian, Slovak, Spanish, Swahili, Swedish, Tagalog, Thai, Turkish, Ukrainian, Urdu, Vietnamese, Yiddish
Target Language(s): Albanian, Arabic, Armenian, Bengali, Bulgarian, Catalan, Chinese, Czech, Danish, Dutch, English, Finnish, Flemish, French, German, Greek, Hebrew, Hindi, Hungarian, Indonesian, Italian, Japanese, Korean, Latin, Lithuanian, Norwegian, Polish, Portuguese, Punjabi, Romanian, Russian, Serbo-Croatian, Slovak, Spanish, Swahili, Swedish, Tagalog, Thai, Turkish, Ukrainian, Urdu, Vietnamese, Yiddish

Claudette Roland
Los Angeles, CA 90024
Tel: 310-266-6980
E-mail: claudette_roland@verizon.net
Founded: 1983
Source Language(s): English, French
Target Language(s): English, French
Membership(s): American Translators Association (ATA)

Rosemoor House Translations
Rosemoor House, 400 New Bedford Dr, Vallejo, CA 94591
Tel: 707-557-8595
Key Personnel
Owner: Kathryn D Marocchino
E-mail: marocchino@sbcglobal.net
Founded: 1988
Translation services; editorial language consultations; proofreading & editing; summaries of foreign language publications; review books for publishers; special assignment writing; professional tutoring in Italian, English & French; dubbing & film voice-overs; book translations, rewriting & indexing; abstracting; contracts & legal depositions; research, review documents for conferences; technical writing; cassette & dictaphone transcribing; audio & video translation. Specialize in: literature, history, banking & finance, electronics & electrotechnology, humanities, sociology & psychology, linguistics, pedagogy, pharmaceutics, psychiatry, biological sciences, commerce, business, law, mechanical engineering, computer science, semantics & philology, advertising & tourism.
Source Language(s): English, Italian
Target Language(s): English, Italian
Membership(s): American Translators Association (ATA); Northern California Translators Association

Richard Schneider Language Services (RSLS)
Division of MediaLocate Inc
1200 Piedmont Ave, Pacific Grove, CA 93950
Toll Free Tel: 800-500-5808
E-mail: service@idioms.com
Web Site: www.idioms.com

Key Personnel
CEO: Stephan Lins
CFO & Chief HR Offr: Ilge Karancak-Splane
Founded: 1980
Accurate language interpreting & translating services in over 170 different languages.
Source Language(s): English, French, German, Italian, Spanish
Target Language(s): English, French, German, Italian, Spanish
Membership(s): American Literary Translators Association (ALTA); American Translators Association (ATA); American Wholesale Booksellers Association (AWBA); Association of Language Companies (ALC); Better Business Bureau (BBB); Business for Social Responsibility (BSR); California Court Interpreters Association (CCIA); California Federation of Interpreters (CFI); Chicago Area Translators & Interpreters Association (CHICATA); Delaware Valley Translators Association (DVTA); Mid-America Chapter of the American Translators Association (MICATA); Northern Ohio Translators Association (NOTA); NYCTA; Society for Photographic Education (SPE); Southern California Area Translators Association (SCATIA)

School of World Studies
Affiliate of Virginia Commonwealth University
312 N Shafer St, Richmond, VA 23284-2021
Tel: 804-827-1111
Web Site: worldstudies.vcu.edu
Key Personnel
Dir: Amy Rector, PhD *E-mail:* alrector@vcu.edu
Translating & interpreting.
Source Language(s): Arabic, Chinese, English, French, German, Italian, Spanish
Target Language(s): English, French, German, Hebrew, Hindi, Italian, Russian, Spanish

Schreiber Translations Inc (STI)
51 Monroe St, Suite 101, Rockville, MD 20850
Tel: 301-424-7737 *Toll Free Tel:* 800-822-3213
Fax: 301-424-2336
E-mail: translation@schreibernet.com
Web Site: www.schreibernet.com
Key Personnel
Pres: Marla Schulman *E-mail:* mschulman@schreibernet.com
Founded: 1984
Technical, scientific & literary translation into & out of all languages, all subject matters, translator & interpreter services.
Source Language(s): English, French, German, Italian, Spanish
Target Language(s): English, French, German, Italian, Spanish
Membership(s): American Translators Association (ATA); Association of Language Companies (ALC)

Lesley M Schuldt
10153 Bellwether Lane, Lone Tree, CO 80124-5456
Tel: 303-619-0310
E-mail: stmbt97@aol.com
German translator.
Source Language(s): German
Target Language(s): English
Membership(s): American Literary Translators Association (ALTA); American Translators Association (ATA); American Translators Association, German Language Division (GLD); American Translators Association, Literary Division (LD); Professional Translators Association

Marian Schwartz
Austin, TX 78704
E-mail: marianschwartz@gmail.com
Web Site: www.marianschwartz.com
Founded: 1978

SERVICES

Russian literary translator: fiction, history, biography, criticism & fine art.
Source Language(s): Russian
Target Language(s): English
Membership(s): American Literary Translators Association (ALTA); Austin Area Translators & Interpreters Association (AATIA); PEN America

Natalia V Sciarini
219 New England Rd, Guilford, CT 06437
Tel: 203-314-7680
E-mail: sciarini2009@gmail.com
Source Language(s): English, Russian
Target Language(s): English, Russian

Christina Sever
PO Box 197, Corvallis, OR 97339
Tel: 541-753-3913 *Fax:* 541-757-0640
E-mail: csever17@yahoo.com
Founded: 1989
Translation, editing & Russian language research.
Source Language(s): Russian
Target Language(s): English
Membership(s): American Translators Association (ATA); Associated Linguists of Oregon

Monika Shoffman-Graves
70 Transylvania Ave, Key Largo, FL 33037
Tel: 305-451-1462
E-mail: mograv@gmail.com
Source Language(s): German, Hebrew, Spanish
Target Language(s): English

Boris Mark Silversteyn
700 Cocoanut Ave, Apt 210, Sarasota, FL 34236
Tel: 941-552-8310; 941-284-7282 (cell)
E-mail: bsilversteyn@comcast.net
Russian & Ukrainian translation & interpretation services.
Source Language(s): English, Russian, Ukrainian
Target Language(s): English, Russian, Ukrainian
Membership(s): American Translators Association (ATA)

Martin Sokolinsky
60 Pineapple St, Unit 1-F, Brooklyn, NY 11201
Tel: 718-643-2747
E-mail: cuddys1@verizon.net
Literary subjects, including fiction; interviews & contemporary affairs. Also reading for publishers.
Source Language(s): French, German, Russian, Spanish
Target Language(s): English

Spanish/English Translation & Interpreting Services
5704 SW 86 Dr, Gainesville, FL 32608-8536
Tel: 352-215-7200
Web Site: www.afn.org/~vanessa
Key Personnel
Bilingual Translator & Interpreter: Vanessa M Carbia *E-mail:* vcarbia@hotmail.com
Source Language(s): English, Spanish
Target Language(s): English, Spanish

SST, see Strictly Spanish Translations LLC

Strictly Spanish Translations LLC
Milford, OH 45150
E-mail: info@strictlyspanish.com; quotes@strictlyspanish.com
Web Site: www.strictlyspanish.com
Key Personnel
Sr Mng Dir & Edit Dir: Laura Leonhartsberger
Founded: 1990
Business-to-business Spanish translation agency.
Source Language(s): English, Spanish
Target Language(s): English, Spanish
Membership(s): American Translators Association (ATA)

TRANSLATORS & INTERPRETERS

Szablya Consultants Inc
5300 94 Ave NE, Apt 327, Seattle, WA 98105
Tel: 206-465-0482 (cell)
Web Site: www.helenmszablya.com
Key Personnel
Pres: Helen M Szablya *E-mail:* ilona.szablya@gmail.com
Founded: 1967 (incorporated in 1991)
Translation: books, documents, writing & lectures.
Source Language(s): English, French, German, Hungarian, Latin
Target Language(s): English, Hungarian
Membership(s): American Association of University Women; American Hungarian Federation (AHF); American Translators Association (ATA); The Authors Guild; Hungarian American Coalition; Northwest Translators & Interpreters Society (NOTIS)

Johannes Tan
16682 SW Henderson Ct, Beaverton, OR 97007
Tel: 503-642-2586 *Fax:* 503-642-2586
E-mail: jt@indotransnet.com
Web Site: www.indotransnet.com
Founded: 1993
One-stop English-Indonesian translation & interpreting services.
Source Language(s): English, Indonesian
Target Language(s): English, Indonesian
Membership(s): American Translators Association (ATA)

Joan Wagner Teller PhD, Translator
11625 SE Boise St, Unit 106, Portland, OR 97266-2281
Tel: 503-760-1320
E-mail: j-teller-11@alumni.uchicago.edu
Web Site: joantellertranslations.webs.com
Founded: 1976
Translations from Russian, German, French into English, with experience particularly in literature, mathematics, sports medicine & nutrition, education & psychology. Many published translations. Also many years of experience in evaluating & editing translations.
Source Language(s): French, German, Russian
Target Language(s): English

Teneo Linguistics Co LLC
3010 W Parkrow Dr, Pampego, TX 76013
Tel: 817-441-9974 *Fax:* 817-953-6424
E-mail: info@tlctranslation.com
Web Site: www.tlctranslation.com
Key Personnel
Founder: Hana Laurenzo
Founded: 2005
Source Language(s): English, French, German, Italian, Spanish
Target Language(s): English, French, German, Italian, Spanish
Membership(s): Metroplex Interpreters & Translators Association (MITA); National Association of Women Business Owners (NAWBO)

Transimpex Translators, Interpreters, Editors, Consultants Inc
2300 Main St, 9th fl, Kansas City, MO 64108
Mailing Address: 602 Fairway, Belton, MO 64012
Tel: 816-561-3777 *Fax:* 816-561-5515
E-mail: translations@transimpex.com
Web Site: www.transimpex.com
Key Personnel
Owner & Pres: Doris Ganser *E-mail:* doris@transimpex.com
VP & Exec Asst: Brian White *E-mail:* brian@transimpex.com
Proj Dir: Aleyois Silcott *E-mail:* aleyois@transimpex.com
Off Mgr: Petra Rudat
Founded: 1974
Translation, interpreting & international consultancy, editorial services, foreign language desktop publishing, audio, video.
Source Language(s): English, French, German, Italian, Spanish
Target Language(s): English, French, German, Italian, Spanish
Membership(s): Alliance Francaise; American Translators Association (ATA); German American Citizens Association (GACA); Germania Club of Greater Kansas City; International Trade Council of Greater Kansas City; Mid-America Chapter of the American Translators Association (MICATA)

Translations.com
1250 Broadway, 32nd fl, New York, NY 10001
Tel: 212-689-1616 *Fax:* 212-504-8057
E-mail: newyork@translations.com; info@translations.com
Web Site: translations.com
Key Personnel
Pres & CEO: Phil Shawe
COO: Roy B Trujillo
CFO: Steve Tondera
CIO: Yu-Kai Ng
Chief Revenue Offr: Kevin Obarski
CTO: Mark Hagerty
SVP: Matt Hauser; Dan O'Sullivan
SVP, Strategic Accts: Martha Ferro Geller
SVP, Technol: Keith Brazil
VP, Corp Devt: Michael Sank
VP, Sales: Tim Coughlin
Founded: 1992
Globalization management, web site localization, machine translation, content authoring & XML, translator tools & information rights management.
Source Language(s): Chinese, Danish, Dutch, English, French, German, Italian, Japanese, Korean, Portuguese, Russian, Spanish, Swedish
Target Language(s): Chinese, Danish, Dutch, English, French, German, Italian, Japanese, Korean, Portuguese, Russian, Spanish, Swedish

Translingua Associates Inc
630 Ninth Ave, Suite 708, New York, NY 10036
Tel: 212-697-2020 *Fax:* 212-697-2891
Web Site: www.translingua.com
Key Personnel
Pres & Mng Dir: Nicole Cee *E-mail:* nicole.cee@translingua.com
Founded: 1972
Translating & interpreting services in all languages.
Source Language(s): English, French, German, Italian, Spanish
Target Language(s): English, French, German, Italian, Spanish

TransPerfect, see Translations.com

Elizabeth Uhlig
6766 108 St, Suite D-27, Forest Hills, NY 11375
Tel: 718-896-4186
E-mail: elizabeth.uhlig7@gmail.com
Web Site: www.marble-house-editions.com
Founded: 1998
Translation of literature, children's books, poetry, nontechnical articles & educational materials.
Source Language(s): French, German, Greek, Italian, Portuguese, Spanish
Target Language(s): English
Membership(s): American Literary Translators Association (ALTA); American Translators Association (ATA); New York Circle of Translators

Universe Technical Translation Inc
9225 Katy Fwy, Suite 400, Houston, TX 77024
Tel: 713-827-8800 *Fax:* 713-464-5511
E-mail: universe@universe.us
Web Site: www.universetranslation.com
Key Personnel
Pres: Marion Rifkind
Founded: 1981
Translation, typesetting, desktop publishing, translation of web pages, printing & simultaneous telephone & consecutive interpreting in more than 60 languages. Also simultaneous interpreting equipment rental.
Source Language(s): Afrikaans, Albanian, Arabic, Armenian, Belarussian, Bengali, Bulgarian, Catalan, Chinese, Czech, Danish, Dutch, English, Estonian, Finnish, Flemish, French, Georgian, German, Greek, Hebrew, Hindi, Hungarian, Icelandic, Indonesian, Italian, Japanese, Korean, Kurdish, Latin, Latvian, Lithuanian, Macedonian, Malagasy, Malayalam, Malaysian, Norwegian, Persian, Polish, Portuguese, Punjabi, Romanian, Russian, Serbo-Croatian, Slovak, Spanish, Swahili, Swedish, Tagalog, Tamil, Thai, Turkish, Ukrainian, Urdu, Vietnamese, Welsh, Yiddish
Target Language(s): Afrikaans, Albanian, Arabic, Armenian, Belarussian, Bengali, Bulgarian, Catalan, Chinese, Czech, Danish, Dutch, English, Estonian, Finnish, Flemish, French, Georgian, German, Greek, Hebrew, Hindi, Hungarian, Icelandic, Indonesian, Italian, Japanese, Korean, Kurdish, Latin, Latvian, Lithuanian, Macedonian, Malagasy, Malayalam, Malaysian, Norwegian, Persian, Polish, Portuguese, Punjabi, Romanian, Russian, Serbo-Croatian, Slovak, Spanish, Swahili, Swedish, Tagalog, Tamil, Thai, Turkish, Ukrainian, Urdu, Vietnamese, Welsh, Yiddish
Membership(s): American Translators Association (ATA); Greater Houston Partnership; Houston Interpreters & Translators Association (HITA); US-Russia Chamber of Commerce (USRCC)

University Language Services (ULS)
Division of Accredited Language Services (ALS)
15 Maiden Lane, Suite 308, New York, NY 10038
Tel: 212-766-3920 *Toll Free Tel:* 800-419-4601
E-mail: clientservices@universitylanguage.com
Web Site: www.universitylanguage.com
Founded: 1983
Translation for course evaluation & academic credit, school applications & study abroad, professional licenses & fellowships.
Source Language(s): English, French, German, Italian, Spanish
Target Language(s): English, French, German, Italian, Spanish
Membership(s): American Translators Association (ATA); Chicago Area Translators & Interpreters Association (CHICATA); New York Circle of Translators; Society for Technical Communication (STC); Software & Information Industry Association (SIIA)

Liliana Valenzuela
1103 Maufrais St, Austin, TX 78703
Tel: 512-804-8141
E-mail: aguafuegolv@gmail.com
Web Site: www.lilianavalenzuela.com
Key Personnel
Agent: Stuart Bernstein
Founded: 1991
Literary translation services. Specialities include fiction, poetry, museum exhibitions & art catalogues. ATA certified.
Source Language(s): English
Target Language(s): Spanish
Membership(s): American Literary Translators Association (ALTA); American Translators Association (ATA); Austin Area Translators & Interpreters Association (AATIA)

Glenn E Weisfeld PhD
1326 Joliet Place, Detroit, MI 48207

TRANSLATORS & INTERPRETERS

Tel: 313-393-2403
E-mail: ad4297@wayne.edu
Web Site: www.clas.wayne.edu
Medical, biological & behavioral science literature.
Source Language(s): French
Target Language(s): English

Maria Lidia Wilczewski
228 SW Fernleaf Trail, Port St Lucie, FL 34953
Tel: 772-873-9803 *Fax:* 772-873-9803
E-mail: lidiaw@bellsouth.net
Translating, interpreting, editing, proofreading. Specialize in literary & technical material, natural sciences, computer application, business, legal.
Source Language(s): English, Polish
Target Language(s): English, Polish
Membership(s): American Translators Association (ATA); Colorado Translators Association

Krishna Winston
655 Bow Lane, Middletown, CT 06457
Tel: 860-347-0329; 860-918-8713 (cell)
E-mail: kwinston@wesleyan.edu
Non-technical translation.
Source Language(s): German
Target Language(s): English
Membership(s): American Association of Teachers of German (AATG); Modern Language Association (MLA); PEN International

Artists & Art Services — Activity Index

ART EDITING

A Good Thing Inc, pg 1411
Aptara Inc, pg 1411
Carol Bancroft & Friends, pg 1412
Big Vision Art + Design, pg 1412
theBookDesigners, pg 1412
Robert Cooney Graphic Design, pg 1413
diacriTech Inc, pg 1413
Emerson, Wajdowicz Studios Inc, pg 1414
Linda Fairchild & Company LLC, pg 1414
GEX Inc, pg 1414
GW Illustration & Design, pg 1414
Hermani & Sorrentino Design, pg 1415
Patti Isaacs Maps, Infographics, Writing, pg 1415
Lachina Creative, pg 1415
Meadows Design Office, pg 1416
Melissa Turk & the Artist Network, pg 1416
MPS North America LLC, pg 1416
Pronk Media Inc, pg 1417
Reynolds Design & Management, pg 1417
Round Table Companies, pg 1417
Shepherd Inc, pg 1417
Steeleworks, pg 1417
Story Monsters LLC, pg 1417
Wild West Communications Group, pg 1417

BOOK DESIGN

A & A, pg 1411
A Good Thing Inc, pg 1411
A-R Editions Inc, pg 1411
Abacus Graphics LLC, pg 1411
J Adel Art & Design, pg 1411
Aptara Inc, pg 1411
Arbor Books, pg 1411
Arrow Graphics Inc, pg 1412
The Association of Medical Illustrators (AMI), pg 1412
Baker & Taylor Publisher Services, pg 1412
Carol Bancroft & Friends, pg 1412
Karin Batten, pg 1412
Big Vision Art + Design, pg 1412
The Blue Mouse Studio, pg 1412
Bookcovers.com, pg 1412
theBookDesigners, pg 1412
BookWise Design, pg 1412
Burmar Technical Corp, pg 1412
By Design Communications, pg 1412
Robert Cooney Graphic Design, pg 1413
Cox-King Multimedia, pg 1413
Crawshaw Design, pg 1413
The Creative Group®, A Robert Half Company, pg 1413
Cypress House, pg 1413
Decode, Inc, pg 1413
Desktop Miracles Inc, pg 1413
diacriTech Inc, pg 1413
Digital Vista Inc, pg 1413
Spencer Drate, pg 1413
1106 Design LLC, pg 1414
Emerson, Wajdowicz Studios Inc, pg 1414
Entro Communications Inc, pg 1414
Linda Fairchild & Company LLC, pg 1414
Fairfield Marketing Group Inc, pg 1414
Figaro, pg 1414
Foster Covers, pg 1414
G & H Soho Inc, pg 1414
GEX Inc, pg 1414
Gore Studio Inc, pg 1414
Graphics International, pg 1414
Heidelberg Graphics, pg 1414
Hermani & Sorrentino Design, pg 1415
Itzhack Shelomi Design, pg 1415
Kachergis Book Design Inc, pg 1415
Lachina Creative, pg 1415
Lumina Datamatics Inc, pg 1415
Meadows Design Office, pg 1416
Melissa Turk & the Artist Network, pg 1416
Brian Thomas Merrill, pg 1416
Wendell Minor, pg 1416
Andrew Newman Design, pg 1416
North Market Street Graphics (NMSG), pg 1416
Pronk Media Inc, pg 1417
The Pushpin Group Inc, pg 1417
Reynolds Design & Management, pg 1417
Round Table Companies, pg 1417
Shepherd Inc, pg 1417
Snow Lion Graphics, pg 1417
Square Two Design Inc, pg 1417
Story Monsters LLC, pg 1417
Studio E Book Production, pg 1417
Stephen Tiano, pg 1417
Tyler Creative, pg 1417
Wild West Communications Group, pg 1417
Brice Wood, pg 1417

CALLIGRAPHY

Abacus Graphics LLC, pg 1411
Carol Bancroft & Friends, pg 1412
Emerson, Wajdowicz Studios Inc, pg 1414
G & H Soho Inc, pg 1414
Graphics International, pg 1414
Lumina Datamatics Inc, pg 1415
Melissa Turk & the Artist Network, pg 1416
Brian Thomas Merrill, pg 1416
Pronk Media Inc, pg 1417
Square Two Design Inc, pg 1417
Steeleworks, pg 1417
Wild West Communications Group, pg 1417

CARTOONS

A & A, pg 1411
A Good Thing Inc, pg 1411
Andrews McMeel Syndication, pg 1411
Aptara Inc, pg 1411
Arbor Books, pg 1411
Carol Bancroft & Friends, pg 1412
The Blue Mouse Studio, pg 1412
Leila Cabib, pg 1412
The Cartoon Bank, A New Yorker Magazine Company, pg 1413
The Creative Group®, A Robert Half Company, pg 1413
Desktop Miracles Inc, pg 1413
Fairfield Marketing Group Inc, pg 1414
Leanne Franson, pg 1414
Karen Karibian, pg 1415
Wayne Lim, pg 1415
Lumina Datamatics Inc, pg 1415
Melissa Turk & the Artist Network, pg 1416
Brian Thomas Merrill, pg 1416
MPS North America LLC, pg 1416
Pronk Media Inc, pg 1417
QBS Learning, pg 1417
Round Table Companies, pg 1417
Story Monsters LLC, pg 1417
Stan Tusan, pg 1417
Brice Wood, pg 1417

COVER DESIGN

A & A, pg 1411
A Good Thing Inc, pg 1411
Abacus Graphics LLC, pg 1411
Aptara Inc, pg 1411
Arrow Graphics Inc, pg 1412
The Association of Medical Illustrators (AMI), pg 1412
Baker & Taylor Publisher Services, pg 1412
Carol Bancroft & Friends, pg 1412
Big Vision Art + Design, pg 1412
The Blue Mouse Studio, pg 1412
BookBaby, pg 1412
Bookcovers.com, pg 1412
theBookDesigners, pg 1412
BookWise Design, pg 1412
Robert Cooney Graphic Design, pg 1413
Cox-King Multimedia, pg 1413
Cypress House, pg 1413
Desktop Miracles Inc, pg 1413
diacriTech Inc, pg 1413
Didona Design, pg 1413
Digital Vista Inc, pg 1413
Spencer Drate, pg 1413
1106 Design LLC, pg 1414
Emerson, Wajdowicz Studios Inc, pg 1414
Foster Covers, pg 1414
G & H Soho Inc, pg 1414
GEX Inc, pg 1414
Heidelberg Graphics, pg 1414
Hermani & Sorrentino Design, pg 1415
ITW Foils, pg 1415
Itzhack Shelomi Design, pg 1415
Kachergis Book Design Inc, pg 1415
Dimitri Karetnikov, pg 1415
Lachina Creative, pg 1415
Lumina Datamatics Inc, pg 1415
Meadows Design Office, pg 1416
Wendell Minor, pg 1416
MPS North America LLC, pg 1416
Andrew Newman Design, pg 1416
Robert Pizzo Illustration/Design, pg 1416
Pronk Media Inc, pg 1417
QBS Learning, pg 1417
Reynolds Design & Management, pg 1417
Round Table Companies, pg 1417
Shepherd Inc, pg 1417
Steeleworks, pg 1417
Story Monsters LLC, pg 1417
Stephen Tiano, pg 1417
Stan Tusan, pg 1417
Tyler Creative, pg 1417
Wild West Communications Group, pg 1417

ELECTRONIC LAYOUT

A Good Thing Inc, pg 1411
Barbara S Anderson, pg 1411
Aptara Inc, pg 1411
Arrow Graphics Inc, pg 1412
The Association of Medical Illustrators (AMI), pg 1412
Baker & Taylor Publisher Services, pg 1412
Carol Bancroft & Friends, pg 1412
Karin Batten, pg 1412
Big Vision Art + Design, pg 1412
theBookDesigners, pg 1412
BookWise Design, pg 1412
Cox-King Multimedia, pg 1413
Cypress House, pg 1413
Decode, pg 1413
Desktop Miracles Inc, pg 1413
1106 Design LLC, pg 1414
Emerson, Wajdowicz Studios Inc, pg 1414
G & H Soho Inc, pg 1414
Heidelberg Graphics, pg 1414
Hermani & Sorrentino Design, pg 1415
Kachergis Book Design Inc, pg 1415
Lachina Creative, pg 1415
Lumina Datamatics Inc, pg 1415
Meadows Design Office, pg 1416
Brian Thomas Merrill, pg 1416
MPS North America LLC, pg 1416
Pronk Media Inc, pg 1417
QBS Learning, pg 1417
Reynolds Design & Management, pg 1417
Shepherd Inc, pg 1417
Tyler Creative, pg 1417
Wild West Communications Group, pg 1417

FILM ANIMATION

The Association of Medical Illustrators (AMI), pg 1412
The Blue Mouse Studio, pg 1412
The Creative Group®, A Robert Half Company, pg 1413
Emerson, Wajdowicz Studios Inc, pg 1414
Fairfield Marketing Group Inc, pg 1414
International Mapping Associates, pg 1415
Karen Karibian, pg 1415
Lachina Creative, pg 1415
Lumina Datamatics Inc, pg 1415
Melissa Turk & the Artist Network, pg 1416
The Pushpin Group Inc, pg 1417
Square Two Design Inc, pg 1417
Brice Wood, pg 1417

ICON DESIGN

A Good Thing Inc, pg 1411
Aptara Inc, pg 1411
Carol Bancroft & Friends, pg 1412

ARTISTS & ART SERVICES — ACTIVITY INDEX

Big Vision Art + Design, pg 1412
theBookDesigners, pg 1412
BookWise Design, pg 1412
Cypress House, pg 1413
Emerson, Wajdowicz Studios Inc, pg 1414
GEX Inc, pg 1414
Hermani & Sorrentino Design, pg 1415
International Mapping Associates, pg 1415
Kachergis Book Design Inc, pg 1415
Karen Karibian, pg 1415
Lachina Creative, pg 1415
Melissa Turk & the Artist Network, pg 1416
Andrew Newman Design, pg 1416
Robert Pizzo Illustration/Design, pg 1416
Pronk Media Inc, pg 1417
QBS Learning, pg 1417
Wild West Communications Group, pg 1417

ILLUSTRATION

A & A, pg 1411
A Good Thing Inc, pg 1411
Abacus Graphics LLC, pg 1411
J Adel Art & Design, pg 1411
Barbara S Anderson, pg 1411
Aptara Inc, pg 1411
Arbor Books, pg 1411
Arrow Graphics Inc, pg 1412
The Association of Medical Illustrators (AMI), pg 1412
Carol Bancroft & Friends, pg 1412
Karin Batten, pg 1412
Big Vision Art + Design, pg 1412
The Blue Mouse Studio, pg 1412
theBookDesigners, pg 1412
Burmar Technical Corp, pg 1412
Leila Cabib, pg 1412
Cornell & Company, LLC, pg 1413
The Creative Group®, A Robert Half Company, pg 1413
Cypress House, pg 1413
Dan Daly, pg 1413
Desktop Miracles Inc, pg 1413
diacriTech Inc, pg 1413
Digital Vista Inc, pg 1413
1106 Design LLC, pg 1414
Emerson, Wajdowicz Studios Inc, pg 1414
Linda Fairchild & Company LLC, pg 1414
Fairfield Marketing Group Inc, pg 1414
Figaro, pg 1414
Leanne Franson, pg 1414
G & H Soho Inc, pg 1414
GEX Inc, pg 1414
GW Illustration & Design, pg 1414
Graphics International, pg 1414
Hermani & Sorrentino Design, pg 1415
Cathy Hull, pg 1415
International Mapping Associates, pg 1415
Patti Isaacs Maps, Infographics, Writing, pg 1415
Itzhack Shelomi Design, pg 1415
Karen Karibian, pg 1415
Lachina Creative, pg 1415
Wayne Lim, pg 1415
Lumina Datamatics Inc, pg 1415
Mapping Specialists Ltd, pg 1416
Maps by Mathison, pg 1416
Diane Maurer-Hand Marbled Papers, pg 1416
Melissa Turk & the Artist Network, pg 1416

Brian Thomas Merrill, pg 1416
Wendell Minor, pg 1416
MPS North America LLC, pg 1416
North Market Street Graphics (NMSG), pg 1416
Robert Pizzo Illustration/Design, pg 1416
Pointing Robot Studios, pg 1416
Pronk Media Inc, pg 1417
The Pushpin Group Inc, pg 1417
QBS Learning, pg 1417
Round Table Companies, pg 1417
Shepherd Inc, pg 1417
Snow Lion Graphics, pg 1417
Square Two Design Inc, pg 1417
Steeleworks, pg 1417
Story Monsters LLC, pg 1417
Stan Tusan, pg 1417
Wild West Communications Group, pg 1417
Brice Wood, pg 1417

JACKET DESIGN

A & A, pg 1411
A Good Thing Inc, pg 1411
Abacus Graphics LLC, pg 1411
J Adel Art & Design, pg 1411
Aptara Inc, pg 1411
Arbor Books, pg 1411
Arrow Graphics Inc, pg 1412
The Association of Medical Illustrators (AMI), pg 1412
Baker & Taylor Publisher Services, pg 1412
Carol Bancroft & Friends, pg 1412
Karin Batten, pg 1412
Big Vision Art + Design, pg 1412
The Blue Mouse Studio, pg 1412
theBookDesigners, pg 1412
BookWise Design, pg 1412
Robert Cooney Graphic Design, pg 1413
Cox-King Multimedia, pg 1413
Crawshaw Design, pg 1413
The Creative Group®, A Robert Half Company, pg 1413
Cypress House, pg 1413
Decode, Inc, pg 1413
Desktop Miracles Inc, pg 1413
diacriTech Inc, pg 1413
Didona Design, pg 1413
Digital Vista Inc, pg 1413
Spencer Drate, pg 1413
1106 Design LLC, pg 1414
Emerson, Wajdowicz Studios Inc, pg 1414
Entro Communications Inc, pg 1414
Fairfield Marketing Group Inc, pg 1414
Figaro, pg 1414
Foster Covers, pg 1414
G & H Soho Inc, pg 1414
Laurence Gartel, pg 1414
GEX Inc, pg 1414
Gore Studio Inc, pg 1414
Graphics International, pg 1414
Heidelberg Graphics, pg 1414
Hermani & Sorrentino Design, pg 1415
Itzhack Shelomi Design, pg 1415
Kachergis Book Design Inc, pg 1415
Lachina Creative, pg 1415
Lumina Datamatics Inc, pg 1415
Diane Maurer-Hand Marbled Papers, pg 1416
Meadows Design Office, pg 1416
Brian Thomas Merrill, pg 1416
Wendell Minor, pg 1416
Andrew Newman Design, pg 1416
Robert Pizzo Illustration/Design, pg 1416

Pronk Media Inc, pg 1417
The Pushpin Group Inc, pg 1417
QBS Learning, pg 1417
Reynolds Design & Management, pg 1417
Round Table Companies, pg 1417
Shepherd Inc, pg 1417
Square Two Design Inc, pg 1417
Steeleworks, pg 1417
Story Monsters LLC, pg 1417
Stephen Tiano, pg 1417
Stan Tusan, pg 1417
Tyler Creative, pg 1417
Wild West Communications Group, pg 1417
Brice Wood, pg 1417

LAYOUT

A & A, pg 1411
A Good Thing Inc, pg 1411
A-R Editions Inc, pg 1411
Abacus Graphics LLC, pg 1411
J Adel Art & Design, pg 1411
Barbara S Anderson, pg 1411
Aptara Inc, pg 1411
Arbor Books, pg 1411
Arrow Graphics Inc, pg 1412
The Association of Medical Illustrators (AMI), pg 1412
Baker & Taylor Publisher Services, pg 1412
Carol Bancroft & Friends, pg 1412
Karin Batten, pg 1412
Big Vision Art + Design, pg 1412
The Blue Mouse Studio, pg 1412
theBookDesigners, pg 1412
BookWise Design, pg 1412
By Design Communications, pg 1412
Robert Cooney Graphic Design, pg 1413
Cox-King Multimedia, pg 1413
The Creative Group®, A Robert Half Company, pg 1413
Cypress House, pg 1413
Decode, Inc, pg 1413
Desktop Miracles Inc, pg 1413
diacriTech Inc, pg 1413
1106 Design LLC, pg 1414
Emerson, Wajdowicz Studios Inc, pg 1414
Entro Communications Inc, pg 1414
Linda Fairchild & Company LLC, pg 1414
Fairfield Marketing Group Inc, pg 1414
Figaro, pg 1414
G & H Soho Inc, pg 1414
GEX Inc, pg 1414
Graphics International, pg 1414
Hermani & Sorrentino Design, pg 1415
Itzhack Shelomi Design, pg 1415
Lachina Creative, pg 1415
Linguistic Systems Inc (LSI), pg 1415
Lumina Datamatics Inc, pg 1415
Meadows Design Office, pg 1416
Brian Thomas Merrill, pg 1416
MPS North America LLC, pg 1416
Andrew Newman Design, pg 1416
Pronk Media Inc, pg 1417
The Pushpin Group Inc, pg 1417
QBS Learning, pg 1417
Reynolds Design & Management, pg 1417
Round Table Companies, pg 1417
Shepherd Inc, pg 1417
Square Two Design Inc, pg 1417
Story Monsters LLC, pg 1417
Stephen Tiano, pg 1417
Tyler Creative, pg 1417

Wild West Communications Group, pg 1417
Brice Wood, pg 1417

LETTERHEADS

A Good Thing Inc, pg 1411
Abacus Graphics LLC, pg 1411
J Adel Art & Design, pg 1411
Barbara S Anderson, pg 1411
Aptara Inc, pg 1411
Arbor Books, pg 1411
The Association of Medical Illustrators (AMI), pg 1412
Carol Bancroft & Friends, pg 1412
Karin Batten, pg 1412
Big Vision Art + Design, pg 1412
The Blue Mouse Studio, pg 1412
BookWise Design, pg 1412
By Design Communications, pg 1412
Robert Cooney Graphic Design, pg 1413
Crawshaw Design, pg 1413
The Creative Group®, A Robert Half Company, pg 1413
Cypress House, pg 1413
Decode, Inc, pg 1413
Didona Design, pg 1413
Spencer Drate, pg 1413
1106 Design LLC, pg 1414
Emerson, Wajdowicz Studios Inc, pg 1414
Entro Communications Inc, pg 1414
Fairfield Marketing Group Inc, pg 1414
Figaro, pg 1414
Graphics International, pg 1414
Hermani & Sorrentino Design, pg 1415
Cathy Hull, pg 1415
Itzhack Shelomi Design, pg 1415
Dimitri Karetnikov, pg 1415
Meadows Design Office, pg 1416
Brian Thomas Merrill, pg 1416
Andrew Newman Design, pg 1416
Robert Pizzo Illustration/Design, pg 1416
The Pushpin Group Inc, pg 1417
Round Table Companies, pg 1417
Square Two Design Inc, pg 1417
Story Monsters LLC, pg 1417
Wild West Communications Group, pg 1417
Brice Wood, pg 1417

LETTERING

A Good Thing Inc, pg 1411
Abacus Graphics LLC, pg 1411
Carol Bancroft & Friends, pg 1412
The Blue Mouse Studio, pg 1412
The Creative Group®, A Robert Half Company, pg 1413
Emerson, Wajdowicz Studios Inc, pg 1414
Entro Communications Inc, pg 1414
Fairfield Marketing Group Inc, pg 1414
G & H Soho Inc, pg 1414
Graphics International, pg 1414
Itzhack Shelomi Design, pg 1415
Melissa Turk & the Artist Network, pg 1416
Brian Thomas Merrill, pg 1416
Andrew Newman Design, pg 1416
Robert Pizzo Illustration/Design, pg 1416
Square Two Design Inc, pg 1417
Wild West Communications Group, pg 1417

LOGOS & CORPORATE IDENTITY

A Good Thing Inc, pg 1411
Abacus Graphics LLC, pg 1411
Aptara Inc, pg 1411
Arbor Books, pg 1411
The Association of Medical Illustrators (AMI), pg 1412
Karin Batten, pg 1412
Big Vision Art + Design, pg 1412
The Blue Mouse Studio, pg 1412
theBookDesigners, pg 1412
BookWise Design, pg 1412
By Design Communications, pg 1412
Robert Cooney Graphic Design, pg 1412
Crawshaw Design, pg 1413
The Creative Group®, A Robert Half Company, pg 1413
Cypress House, pg 1413
Decode, Inc, pg 1413
Digital Vista Inc, pg 1413
Spencer Drate, pg 1413
1106 Design LLC, pg 1414
Emerson, Wajdowicz Studios Inc, pg 1414
Entro Communications Inc, pg 1414
Linda Fairchild & Company LLC, pg 1414
Fairfield Marketing Group Inc, pg 1414
fd2s, pg 1414
Figaro, pg 1414
Graphics International, pg 1414
Hermani & Sorrentino Design, pg 1415
Cathy Hull, pg 1415
Itzhack Shelomi Design, pg 1415
Karen Karibian, pg 1415
Lachina Creative, pg 1415
Wayne Lim, pg 1415
Meadows Design Office, pg 1416
Brian Thomas Merrill, pg 1416
Andrew Newman Design, pg 1416
Robert Pizzo Illustration/Design, pg 1416
The Pushpin Group Inc, pg 1417
QBS Learning, pg 1417
Round Table Companies, pg 1417
Square Two Design Inc, pg 1417
Steeleworks, pg 1417
Story Monsters LLC, pg 1417
Tyler Creative, pg 1417
Wild West Communications Group, pg 1417
Brice Wood, pg 1417

MAP DESIGN

A Good Thing Inc, pg 1411
Abacus Graphics LLC, pg 1411
Carol Bancroft & Friends, pg 1412
Burmar Technical Corp, pg 1412
Emerson, Wajdowicz Studios Inc, pg 1414
Fairfield Marketing Group Inc, pg 1414
Figaro, pg 1414
G & H Soho Inc, pg 1414
General Cartography Inc, pg 1414
Graphics International, pg 1414
International Mapping Associates, pg 1415
Patti Isaacs Maps, Infographics, Writing, pg 1415
Kachergis Book Design Inc, pg 1415
Dimitri Karetnikov, pg 1415
Lachina Creative, pg 1415
Lumina Datamatics Inc, pg 1415
Mapping Specialists Ltd, pg 1416
Maps by Mathison, pg 1416
Meadows Design Office, pg 1416
Melissa Turk & the Artist Network, pg 1416
Andrew Newman Design, pg 1416
Pronk Media Inc, pg 1417
Square Two Design Inc, pg 1417
Wild West Communications Group, pg 1417

PASTE-UP

A & A, pg 1411
Barbara S Anderson, pg 1411
Aptara Inc, pg 1411
Arrow Graphics Inc, pg 1412
The Blue Mouse Studio, pg 1412
The Creative Group®, A Robert Half Company, pg 1413
D&D Sales & Printing, pg 1413
Fairfield Marketing Group Inc, pg 1414
G & H Soho Inc, pg 1414
Itzhack Shelomi Design, pg 1415
Linguistic Systems Inc (LSI), pg 1415
Lumina Datamatics Inc, pg 1415
Meadows Design Office, pg 1416
Pronk Media Inc, pg 1417
QBS Learning, pg 1417
Wild West Communications Group, pg 1417
Brice Wood, pg 1417

PICTORIAL STATISTICS

A Good Thing Inc, pg 1411
Abacus Graphics LLC, pg 1411
Aptara Inc, pg 1411
Burmar Technical Corp, pg 1412
The Creative Group®, A Robert Half Company, pg 1413
Emerson, Wajdowicz Studios Inc, pg 1414
GW Illustration & Design, pg 1414
Patti Isaacs Maps, Infographics, Writing, pg 1415
Kachergis Book Design Inc, pg 1415
Lachina Creative, pg 1415

POSTER DESIGN

A & A, pg 1411
A Good Thing Inc, pg 1411
Abacus Graphics LLC, pg 1411
J Adel Art & Design, pg 1411
Aptara Inc, pg 1411
Arbor Books, pg 1411
Arrow Graphics Inc, pg 1412
The Association of Medical Illustrators (AMI), pg 1412
Carol Bancroft & Friends, pg 1412
Karin Batten, pg 1412
Big Vision Art + Design, pg 1412
The Blue Mouse Studio, pg 1412
By Design Communications, pg 1412
Crawshaw Design, pg 1413
The Creative Group®, A Robert Half Company, pg 1413
Cypress House, pg 1413
Decode, Inc, pg 1413
Didona Design, pg 1413
Digital Vista Inc, pg 1413
Spencer Drate, pg 1413
1106 Design LLC, pg 1414
Emerson, Wajdowicz Studios Inc, pg 1414
Entro Communications Inc, pg 1414
Fairfield Marketing Group Inc, pg 1414
Figaro, pg 1414
Laurence Gartel, pg 1414
Gore Studio Inc, pg 1414
Graphics International, pg 1414
Hermani & Sorrentino Design, pg 1415
Itzhack Shelomi Design, pg 1415
Kachergis Book Design Inc, pg 1415
Karen Karibian, pg 1415
Lachina Creative, pg 1415
Meadows Design Office, pg 1416
Brian Thomas Merrill, pg 1416
Andrew Newman Design, pg 1416
Robert Pizzo Illustration/Design, pg 1416
Pronk Media Inc, pg 1417
The Pushpin Group Inc, pg 1417
Round Table Companies, pg 1417
Square Two Design Inc, pg 1417
Steeleworks, pg 1417
Story Monsters LLC, pg 1417
Tyler Creative, pg 1417
Wild West Communications Group, pg 1417
Brice Wood, pg 1417

PROTOTYPING

A Good Thing Inc, pg 1411
Aptara Inc, pg 1411
Carol Bancroft & Friends, pg 1412
Decode, Inc, pg 1413
Emerson, Wajdowicz Studios Inc, pg 1414
Lachina Creative, pg 1415
Pronk Media Inc, pg 1417
QBS Learning, pg 1417
Wild West Communications Group, pg 1417

RETOUCHING

A Good Thing Inc, pg 1411
Aptara Inc, pg 1411
The Association of Medical Illustrators (AMI), pg 1412
The Blue Mouse Studio, pg 1412
Colour Technologies, pg 1413
The Creative Group®, A Robert Half Company, pg 1413
CRW Graphics Communications, pg 1413
G & H Soho Inc, pg 1414
Gore Studio Inc, pg 1414
Graphics International, pg 1414
Dimitri Karetnikov, pg 1415
Lachina Creative, pg 1415
Lumina Datamatics Inc, pg 1415
Brian Thomas Merrill, pg 1416
MPS North America LLC, pg 1416
Andrew Newman Design, pg 1416
Square Two Design Inc, pg 1417
Tyler Creative, pg 1417
Wild West Communications Group, pg 1417

SILK SCREEN

Fairfield Marketing Group Inc, pg 1414

SPOT DRAWINGS

A & A, pg 1411
A Good Thing Inc, pg 1411
Abacus Graphics LLC, pg 1411
J Adel Art & Design, pg 1411
Aptara Inc, pg 1411
Carol Bancroft & Friends, pg 1412
Karin Batten, pg 1412
Big Vision Art + Design, pg 1412
The Blue Mouse Studio, pg 1412
Burmar Technical Corp, pg 1412
The Cartoon Bank, A New Yorker Magazine Company, pg 1413
The Creative Group®, A Robert Half Company, pg 1413
Cypress House, pg 1413
Dan Daly, pg 1413
1106 Design LLC, pg 1414
Emerson, Wajdowicz Studios Inc, pg 1414
Fairfield Marketing Group Inc, pg 1414
Leanne Franson, pg 1414
G & H Soho Inc, pg 1414
GW Illustration & Design, pg 1414
Graphics International, pg 1414
Hermani & Sorrentino Design, pg 1415
Dimitri Karetnikov, pg 1415
Lachina Creative, pg 1415
Lumina Datamatics Inc, pg 1415
Maps by Mathison, pg 1416
Melissa Turk & the Artist Network, pg 1416
Brian Thomas Merrill, pg 1416
MPS North America LLC, pg 1416
Andrew Newman Design, pg 1416
Robert Pizzo Illustration/Design, pg 1416
Pronk Media Inc, pg 1417
QBS Learning, pg 1417
Steeleworks, pg 1417
Story Monsters LLC, pg 1417
Stan Tusan, pg 1417
Wild West Communications Group, pg 1417
Brice Wood, pg 1417

TECHNICAL ILLUSTRATION

A Good Thing Inc, pg 1411
A-R Editions Inc, pg 1411
Abacus Graphics LLC, pg 1411
Aptara Inc, pg 1411
Arbor Books, pg 1411
The Association of Medical Illustrators (AMI), pg 1412
Carol Bancroft & Friends, pg 1412
theBookDesigners, pg 1412
Burmar Technical Corp, pg 1412
Cox-King Multimedia, pg 1413
The Creative Group®, A Robert Half Company, pg 1413
Figaro, pg 1414
G & H Soho Inc, pg 1414
GW Illustration & Design, pg 1414
Graphics International, pg 1414
International Mapping Associates, pg 1415
Itzhack Shelomi Design, pg 1415
Lachina Creative, pg 1415
Lumina Datamatics Inc, pg 1415
Mapping Specialists Ltd, pg 1416
Maps by Mathison, pg 1416
Melissa Turk & the Artist Network, pg 1416
MPS North America LLC, pg 1416
Pronk Media Inc, pg 1417
QBS Learning, pg 1417
Shepherd Inc, pg 1417
Story Monsters LLC, pg 1417
Brice Wood, pg 1417

TEMPLATING

A Good Thing Inc, pg 1411
Aptara Inc, pg 1411
Baker & Taylor Publisher Services, pg 1412
theBookDesigners, pg 1412
GEX Inc, pg 1414
Lachina Creative, pg 1415
MPS North America LLC, pg 1416

ARTISTS & ART SERVICES — ACTIVITY INDEX

Pronk Media Inc, pg 1417
QBS Learning, pg 1417

TRADEMARKS

A Good Thing Inc, pg 1411
Abacus Graphics LLC, pg 1411
Carol Bancroft & Friends, pg 1412
Karin Batten, pg 1412
The Blue Mouse Studio, pg 1412
Crawshaw Design, pg 1413
The Creative Group®, A Robert Half Company, pg 1413
Spencer Drate, pg 1413
Emerson, Wajdowicz Studios Inc, pg 1414
Fairfield Marketing Group Inc, pg 1414
Gore Studio Inc, pg 1414
Graphics International, pg 1414
Meadows Design Office, pg 1416
Andrew Newman Design, pg 1416
Round Table Companies, pg 1417
Square Two Design Inc, pg 1417
Wild West Communications Group, pg 1417
Brice Wood, pg 1417

TYPESETTING

A Good Thing Inc, pg 1411
A-R Editions Inc, pg 1411
Aptara Inc, pg 1411
Arbor Books, pg 1411
Arrow Graphics Inc, pg 1412
Baker & Taylor Publisher Services, pg 1412
theBookDesigners, pg 1412
BookWise Design, pg 1412
Burmar Technical Corp, pg 1412
Cox-King Multimedia, pg 1413
The Creative Group®, A Robert Half Company, pg 1413
Cypress House, pg 1413
D&D Sales & Printing, pg 1413
Desktop Miracles Inc, pg 1413
1106 Design LLC, pg 1414
Emerson, Wajdowicz Studios Inc, pg 1414
Fairfield Marketing Group Inc, pg 1414
G & H Soho Inc, pg 1414
GEX Inc, pg 1414
Heidelberg Graphics, pg 1414
Itzhack Shelomi Design, pg 1415
Kachergis Book Design Inc, pg 1415
Lachina Creative, pg 1415
Linguistic Systems Inc (LSI), pg 1415
Lumina Datamatics Inc, pg 1415
Meadows Design Office, pg 1416
MPS North America LLC, pg 1416
Pronk Media Inc, pg 1417
QBS Learning, pg 1417
Shepherd Inc, pg 1417
Story Monsters LLC, pg 1417
Studio E Book Production, pg 1417
Stephen Tiano, pg 1417
Wild West Communications Group, pg 1417

Artists & Art Services

See also **Promotional Printing & Allied Services** for producers of promotional materials.

A & A
Division of Abramson & Abramson
PO Box 16223, Albuquerque, NM 87191-6223
Tel: 505-518-3939
E-mail: aaartwork@aol.com; aaauthor@aol.com
Web Site: www.elaineabramson.com
Key Personnel
Pres: Elaine Sandra Abramson
EVP: Martin Stanley Abramson
Founded: 1967
Book design, cartoons, illustrations, character creation, licensing, jacket design, layout, paste-up, poster design & spot drawings. Also provide special assignment writing. All books are via mail order. Packages: Book, t-shirt, greeting card & plush toy, advertising art. Artwork by award-winning artist/author. Licensing fine art & cartoon characters. Also, art & contest judge, t-shirt, plush toy, greeting card & jewelry package design. Absolutely no unagented submissions. Submissions are not returned.
Membership(s): American Advertising Association; Best of Missouri Hands; Chesterfield Writers Guild; Composers, Authors & Artists of America; Creative Coalition; Electronically Published Internet Connection (EPIC); Graphic Artists Guild; Greater St Louis Art Association (GSLAA); Greater St Louis Artists Guild; Maryland Art League; Midwest Independent Booksellers Association (MIBA); Mystery Writers of America (MWA); National Association of Memoir Writers (NAMW); National Association of Television Program Executives Inc (NATPE); National League of American Pen Women; National Writers Association (NWA); National Writers Union (NWU); New Mexico Book Co-op; North Texas Writers Group; Publishers Association of the West (PubWest); Romance Writers of America (RWA); Romance Writers of America (RWA), Kiss of Death Chapter; St Louis Artists' Guild; St Louis Writers Guild; Sisters in Crime; Society of Children's Book Writers & Illustrators (SCBWI); Southern Independent Booksellers Alliance (SIBA); SouthWest Writers; Texas Association of Motion Media Professionals (TAMMP); Thriller Writers of America; Writers Under the Arch

A Good Thing Inc
333 E 79 St, New York, NY 10075
Tel: 212-687-8155
Web Site: www.facebook.com/agoodthinginc
Key Personnel
Pres: Aaron J Richman *E-mail:* arichman@agoodthingink.com
Founded: 1972
Book, illustration, jacket & poster design, layout, letterheads, spot drawings, packaging; trademarks; computer art.

A-R Editions Inc
1600 Aspen Commons, Suite 100, Middleton, WI 53562
Tel: 608-836-9000 *Fax:* 608-831-8200
E-mail: info@areditions.com
Web Site: www.areditions.com
Key Personnel
Pres & CEO: Patrick Wall *Tel:* 608-203-2575
E-mail: patrick.wall@areditions.com
Dir, Spec Projs: James Zychowicz *Tel:* 608-203-2580 *E-mail:* james.zychowicz@areditions.com
Mng Ed: Pamela Whitcomb *Tel:* 608-203-2565
E-mail: pamela.whitcomb@areditions.com
Founded: 1962
Complete production services & project management from editorial & design through typesetting, printing, art creation, indexing, printing & mailing for journal, book & magazine publishers; specialize in computerized music engraving; integration of music & text; foreign language, scientific & non-Roman alphabet. Typesetting on Mac/Quark systems. Disk conversion; automatic pagination; PostScript & PDF output; customized music engraving software for publishers; music typesetting.
Membership(s): American Musicological Society (AMS); Audio Engineering Society Inc (AES); Music Library Association; Music Publishers Association (MPA)

Abacus Graphics LLC
15179 Hunger Creek Lane, Bigfork, MT 59911-8313
Tel: 406-837-5776
Web Site: www.abacusgraphics.com
Key Personnel
Principal & Creative Dir: John R Webster
E-mail: jrw@abacusgraphics.com
Designer & Prodn Mgr & Off Mgr: Francesca Droll
Founded: 1979
Creative design specialists of award-winning, eye-catching image & marketing content. Web site design for businesses of all sizes. Hosting, search engine optimization (SEO), databases, exhibit booths, branding, business cards, flyers, Web hosting, etc. Traditional print materials & collateral.
Membership(s): Independent Book Publishers Association (IBPA)

J Adel Art & Design
586 Ramapo Rd, Teaneck, NJ 07666
Tel: 201-836-2606
E-mail: jadelnj@aol.com
Key Personnel
Creative Dir: Judith Adel
Founded: 1985
Complete graphic design services; book & jacket design, posters, letterheads & magazine design; fine art paintings-watercolors & oils.
Membership(s): Middletown Art Group; New Jersey Water Color Society

Barbara S Anderson
706 W Davis Ave, Ann Arbor, MI 48103-4855
Tel: 734-995-0125; 734-846-3864
E-mail: bsa@watercolorbarbara.com
Commissioned watercolor illustrations: houses, places; portraits in pencil. Newsletter design & page layout. Additional editorial services offered.
Membership(s): Ann Arbor Women Artists

Andrews McMeel Syndication
1130 Walnut St, Kansas City, MO 64106-2109
Tel: 816-581-7300 *Toll Free Tel:* 800-255-6734
Web Site: syndication.andrewsmcmeel.com
Key Personnel
CEO, Andrews McMeel Universal: Kirsty Melville
VP & Mng Ed: Sue Roush *Tel:* 816-581-7320
E-mail: sroush@amuniversal.com
VP, Sales: John Vivona *Tel:* 816-581-7350
E-mail: salesdirector@amuniversal.com
Founded: 1970
Provide a searchable database of popular cartoons such as Doonesbury, Garfield, For Better or For Worse, Non Sequitur, Marmaduke & Pearls Before Swine for reprinting in books, magazines & newsletters.

Aptara Inc
Subsidiary of iEnergizer
2901 Telestar Ct, Suite 522, Falls Church, VA 22042
Tel: 703-352-0001
E-mail: moreinfo@aptaracorp.com
Web Site: www.aptaracorp.com
Key Personnel
Pres: Samir Kakar
EVP, Fin & Cont: Prashant Kapoor
SVP, Busn & Contact Ctr Opers: Ashish Madan
Busn Devt: Michael Scott *E-mail:* michael.scott@aptaracorp.com
Founded: 1988
Liaison for complete or any combination of production services, ranging from simple 1-color to complex 4-color projects. Copy-editing.
Branch Office(s)
150 California St, Suite 301, Newton, MA 02458
Tel: 617-423-7755
11009 Metric Blvd, Bldg J, Suite 150, Austin, TX 78758 *Tel:* 512-876-5997
299 Elizabeth St, Level 1, Sydney 2000, Australia
Tel: (02) 8251 0070
Tower 1 & 2, 8/100, Acharya Thulasi Rd (Shandy Rd), Pallavaram, Chennai 600 043, India
Tel: (044) 22640676
No 2310, Doon Express Business Park, Saharanpur Rd, Bldg 2000, Dehradun 248 002, India
Tel: (0135) 2644055
7B, Leela Infopark, Technopark, Trivandrum, Kerala 695 581, India *Tel:* (047) 14063370
A-37, Sector-60, Noida 201 301, India
Tel: (0120) 7182424
D-10, Sector-2, Noida 201 301, India *Tel:* (0120) 24423678
SEZ Bldg 4A, 1st fl, S P Infocity, Pune Saswad Rd, Phursungi, Pune 412 308, India *Tel:* (020) 66728000

Arbor Books
244 Madison Ave, Box 254, New York, NY 10016
Tel: 212-956-0950 *Toll Free Tel:* 877-822-2500
Fax: 914-401-9385
E-mail: info@arborbooks.com; editorial@arborbooks.net
Web Site: www.arborbooks.com; www.arborghostwriters.com; www.arborservices.com
Key Personnel
Owner: Joel Hochman *Tel:* 877-822-2502 *E-mail:* arborbooksjoel@aol.com;
Larry Leichman *Tel:* 877-822-2504
E-mail: arborbookslarry@aol.com
Mktg Dir: Olga Vladi *E-mail:* floatinggal1@aol.com
Founded: 1992
Full service writing services & book production. Specialize in ghostwriting, editing, proofreading, developmental editing, promotional copy, cover design, printing, publishing & marketing. Arbor Books works for both corporations (business books, corporate histories, CEO bios) & individuals (novels - all genres: general fiction,

ARTISTS & ART SERVICES

young adult, mystery, crime, thrillers, horror, romance, science fiction, fantasy, litrpg, graphic novels, comic books, etc), memoirs, children's books, business books, how-to, inspiration, religious, Christian, Jewish, Islamic, Hindu, self-help, history, politics, humor, gay, etc. Services include supervised & insured ghost-writing, copy-editing, translation, proofreading, design (even the most complex, including model shoots, illustrations, photo reconstruction & manipulation, book jacket design, album cover & magazine design), word processing (including transcription), scanning, layout, typesetting, obtaining registrations & endorsements, B&W & 4-color printing, marketing, promotion & advertising. Creates logos, letterheads, annual reports, posters & promotional flyers. Self-publishing services include: Amazon book marketing, press kits, press releases, booking TV & radio programs, speaking tours & book signings & negotiating with producers & agents.

Arbor Services, see Arbor Books

Arrow Graphics Inc
PO Box 380291, Cambridge, MA 02238
E-mail: info@arrow1.com
Web Site: www.arrow1.com
Key Personnel
Pres: Alvart Badalian
Sr Graphic/Pubn Designer: Aramais Andonian
Founded: 1988
Complete book production services with state-of-the-art electronic design & publishing capabilities: copy-editing; indexing; typesetting & page composition; typography; design & art direction from concept to finished product; printing; consultation; project management. Novels, poetry, monographs, self-help, how-to, guides, ebooks & children's picture books. From ms to camera-ready to bound book, serving the publishing industry & self-publishing community. Call or write for information, or visit our web site.

The Association of Medical Illustrators (AMI)
201 E Main St, Suite 810, Lexington, KY 40507
Toll Free Tel: 866-393-4AMI (393-4264)
E-mail: hq@ami.org
Web Site: www.ami.org
Key Personnel
Exec Dir: Jennifer Duckworth
E-mail: jduckworth@amrms.com
Prog Mgr: Kaitlyn Mathews *E-mail:* kmathews@amrms.com
Film animation, illustration, layout, letterheads, logos & corporate identity, poster design, retouching & technical illustration.

Baker & Taylor Publisher Services
30 Amberwood Pkwy, Ashland, OH 44805
Tel: 567-215-0030 *Toll Free Tel:* 888-814-0208
E-mail: info@btpubservices.com; orders@btpubservices.com
Web Site: www.btpubservices.com
Key Personnel
SVP, Sales & Client Servs: Mark Suchomel
SVP, Opers: Bob Gospodarek
Trade Sales Dir: Deanna Meyerhoff
Founded: 2017
Whether print or ebook, Baker & Taylor Publisher Services provides interior & exterior art services, including cover design, interior design, layout & typesetting. Our designers are US based, formally trained in fine & commercial art, & specialize in everything from children's books to college texts. In addition, Baker & Taylor Publisher Services offers distribution & sales, warehousing & fulfillment.

Carol Bancroft & Friends
PO Box 2030, Danbury, CT 06813
Tel: 203-730-8270 *Fax:* 203-730-8275
E-mail: cbfriends@sbcglobal.net
Web Site: www.carolbancroft.net
Key Personnel
Owner: Joy Elton Tricarico
Founded: 1972
Represents many fine illustrators specializing in art for children of all ages. Servicing the publishing industry including, but not limited to: picture/mass market books & educational materials.
We work with packagers, studios, toy companies & corporations in addition to licensing art to related products. Promotional packets sent upon request.
Art services include illustration, full color & black line. Digital art also available.
Unsol artwork not accepted.
Membership(s): Graphic Artists Guild; Society of Children's Book Writers & Illustrators (SCBWI); Society of Illustrators

Karin Batten
463 West St, Suite C-617, New York, NY 10014
Tel: 917-405-3595
E-mail: karin.batten@gmail.com
Web Site: karinbatten.com
Electronic jacket, poster design, illustrations, drawings.

Big Vision Art + Design
251 Hwy 179, Creekside Plaza A1, Sedona, AZ 86336
Mailing Address: PO Box 1297, Sedona, AZ 86339
Tel: 928-202-6320
Web Site: www.bigvisionarts.com
Key Personnel
Illustrator & Designer: Pamela Becker
E-mail: pamela@bigvisionarts.com
Founded: 2012
Children's book illustrator & designer, print broker & fine artist.
Membership(s): Society of Children's Book Writers & Illustrators (SCBWI)

The Blue Mouse Studio
26829 37 St, Gobles, MI 49055
Tel: 269-628-5160
E-mail: frogville@earthlink.net
Key Personnel
Illus: Rex Schneider
Writer & Designer: Chris Buchman
Illustration, book design, cartoons, film animation, jacket design, layout, letterheads & lettering, logos & corporate identity, poster & cover design, spot drawings & trademarks; also storyboards, copywriting, research; film history, film presentation, computer graphics & coloring, photograph restoration, PowerPoint presentation, graphics for PowerPoint/DVD programs, DVD production & computer animation.

BookBaby
Division of DIY Media Inc
7905 N Crescent Blvd, Pennsauken, NJ 08110
Toll Free Tel: 877-961-6878
E-mail: info@bookbaby.com
Web Site: www.bookbaby.com/book-design
Founded: 2011
Custom book cover designs & interior formatting for printed books & ebooks.

Bookcovers.com
Subsidiary of Archer Ellison Inc
c/o Archer Ellison Inc, 7025 CR 46-A, Suite 1071, Lake Mary, FL 32746
Toll Free Tel: 800-449-4095 (ext 702)
Toll Free Fax: 800-366-4086
E-mail: info@bookcovers.com
Web Site: bookcovers.com
Key Personnel
Pres: Allen D'Angelo *E-mail:* allen@bookcovers.com
Founded: 1994
Book cover marketing expertise that translates into more book marketing methods.
Membership(s): Independent Book Publishers Association (IBPA)

theBookDesigners
454 Las Gallinas Ave, PMB 2015, San Rafael, CA 94903
Tel: 415-637-9550
E-mail: info@bookdesigners.com
Web Site: bookdesigners.com
Key Personnel
Co-Founder, Mgr & Cust Rel: Alan Dino Hebel
Co-Founder & Creative Dir: Ian Koviak
Founded: 2008
Help in every aspect of creating your book. Services include design (cover, jacket, interiors), concept development, visualizations, full editorial services, photography & custom illustrations.

BookWise Design
29089 SW Costa Circle W, Wilsonville, OR 97070
Tel: 503-542-3551 *Toll Free Tel:* 800-697-9833
Web Site: bookwisedesign.com
Key Personnel
Partner & Art Dir: Shannon Bodie
E-mail: shannon@bookwisedesign.com
Partner & Creative Consultant: Bob Swingle
Tel: 503-542-3550
Proj Mgr: Jann Armstrong *Tel:* 509-675-3440
E-mail: jann@bookwisedesign.com
Founded: 1992
Offer a full range of book services for every level of the publishing industry bringing years of experience, innovative design skills & personal attention to every project. Services include book covers & interiors, editorial services, web sites, flyers, brochures, bookmarks, postcards, advertisements, CD or audio packages, corporate identity & web design services.
Membership(s): Independent Book Publishers Association (IBPA)

Burmar Technical Corp
106 Ransom Ave, Sea Cliff, NY 11579
Tel: 516-484-6000 *Fax:* 516-484-6356
Web Site: burmar.net
Key Personnel
Pres: Christine Jensen *E-mail:* christine.jensen@burmar.net
Technical & illustrative illustrations; charts, graphs, maps & spot art using Macintosh systems. Complete desktop publishing service with full book experience. Math & other technical subjects a specialty. Design, art direction & production. Scanning, laser & color proofs. Special expertise in the el-hi & college publishing areas. Specialties: composition, desktop publishing & CD-ROM.

By Design Communications
144 W 27 St, 3rd fl (rear), New York, NY 10001
Tel: 212-366-1740
Key Personnel
Principal: Joelle Silverman Miller
Founded: 1990
A full service studio specializing in catalogs, brochures, newsletters, ads, annual reports, posters & other collateral pieces. Complete design, production, writing, editing & printing services provided.

Leila Cabib
8601 Buckhannon Dr, Potomac, MD 20854
Tel: 301-299-2659

E-mail: leila@leilacabib.com
Web Site: www.leilacabib.com
Cartoons, humorous illustrations & spot drawings.
Membership(s): Graphic Artists Guild

The Cartoon Bank, A New Yorker Magazine Company
Division of Conde Nast
One World Trade Center, 42nd fl, New York, NY 10007
Tel: 212-286-2860
E-mail: image_licensing@condenast.com; thenewyorkerinfo@condenast.com
Web Site: www.cartoonbank.com
Founded: 1925
Database of over 120,000 New Yorker cartoons.

Colour Technologies
Division of CJ Graphics Inc
560 Hensall Circle, Mississauga, ON L5A 1Y1, Canada
Tel: 416-588-0808
E-mail: info@cjgraphics.com
Web Site: www.cjgraphics.com/services/prepress
Key Personnel
Owner: Jay Mandarino
Prepress, wide format & color specialists.

Robert Cooney Graphic Design
PO Box 362, Half Moon Bay, CA 94019
Tel: 650-712-4400
Key Personnel
Principal: Robert Cooney
Founded: 1979
Art direction, graphic design, photo research & complete production services for books, publications & special projects.

Cornell & Company, LLC
44 Jog Hill Rd, Trumbull, CT 06611
Tel: 203-454-4210
Web Site: www.cornellandco.com
Key Personnel
Owner: Merial Cornell *E-mail:* merial@cornellandco.com
Founded: 1989
Professional illustrators specializing in children's book markets; educational, trade & mass market. Representing over 25 artists with a variety of styles & techniques.
Membership(s): Graphic Artists Guild; Society of Children's Book Writers & Illustrators (SCBWI)

Cox-King Multimedia
PO Box 909, Geneva, NY 14456
Tel: 315-719-0141
E-mail: info@ckmm.com
Web Site: www.ckmm.com
Key Personnel
Owner & Pres: Charles King
Founded: 1999
Editorial, proofreading, typesetting, book design & prepress services meeting the needs of a wide variety of fiction & nonfiction books. Traditional & on-demand workflows supported. Self-publishers need not inquire.

Crawshaw Design
120 Bayview Dr, San Rafael, CA 94901
Tel: 415-456-5544 *Fax:* 415-456-4319
Web Site: www.crawshawdesign.com
Key Personnel
Founder & Owner: Todd Crawshaw *E-mail:* todd@crawshawdesign.com
Founded: 1975
Book jacket & poster design, letterheads, logos & trademarks, web site design & development.
Membership(s): Executives Association of San Francisco (EASF)

The Creative Group®, A Robert Half Company
Oliver Street Tower, 17th fl, 125 High St, Boston, MA 02110
Tel: 617-925-5754
Web Site: www.roberthalf.com/us/en/about/our-company/brands/creative-group
Placement of temporary & permanent designers, illustrators, typographers, desktop publishing professionals & project managers for publishing, publications, marketing & all aspects of communications. Creative resource for concept development, writing, designing & project management through to final production.

CRW Graphics Communications
9100 Pennsauken Hwy, Pennsauken, NJ 08110
Tel: 856-662-9111 *Toll Free Tel:* 800-820-3000 *Fax:* 856-665-1789
E-mail: info@crwgraphics.com
Web Site: www.crwgraphics.com
Key Personnel
Pres: David Carpenter
EVP: George Slater
VP, Sales & Mktg: Will Glassman *E-mail:* wglassman@crwgraphics.com
Cust Serv Mgr: Rich Quigley *E-mail:* rquigley@crwgraphics.com
Founded: 1964
Highest quality commercial print services, fulfillment & direct mail. Includes database work, variable imaging, digital prepress & productions as well as conventional lithography. Work with artists & designers to refine their work to a commercially acceptable quality level.

Cypress House
Imprint of Comp-Type Inc
155 Cypress St, Suite A, Fort Bragg, CA 95437
Tel: 707-964-9520 *Toll Free Tel:* 800-773-7782 *Fax:* 707-964-7531
E-mail: office@cypresshouse.com
Web Site: www.cypresshouse.com
Key Personnel
Pres: Cynthia Frank *E-mail:* cynthia@cypresshouse.com
Mng Ed: Joe Shaw *E-mail:* joeshaw@cypresshouse.com
Founded: 1986
Provide complete editorial, design, production, marketing & promotion services to independent publishers. Editorial services include ms evaluation, editing, rewriting, proofreading. Production services include book, cover & page design. Marketing & promotion services for selected titles.
Membership(s): American Booksellers Association (ABA); Bay Area Independent Publishers Association (BAIPA); California Independent Booksellers Alliance (CALIBA); Independent Book Publishers Association (IBPA); Pacific Northwest Booksellers Association (PNBA)

Dan Daly
23 Limerock St, Camden, ME 04843-2116
Tel: 207-691-3061
E-mail: dan@dalyart.com
Web Site: www.dalyart.com
Expert based B&W, full color drawings & paintings of wildlife, fly-fishing, hunting & skiing. Cover illustration services.

D&D Sales & Printing
840 12 St NW, Mason City, IA 50401
Tel: 641-423-9487 *Toll Free Tel:* 800-325-5308 *Fax:* 641-423-3068
E-mail: ddsales.service@gmail.com
Web Site: www.ddsalesonline.com
Key Personnel
Owner: Dale Helgeland; Sue Helgeland; Dave Lane; Lisa Lane
Founded: 2005
Embossing dies, prepress camera work, stripping, screen printing, embroidery, offset printing (sheetfed).

Decode, Inc
1938 11 Ave E, Seattle, WA 98102
Tel: 206-343-9101
E-mail: books@decodebooks.com
Web Site: www.decodeinc.com; www.decodebooks.com
Key Personnel
Owner & Pres: John Jenkins, III
Owner & Partner: Stephen Lyons
Founded: 1991
Publish fine art photography monographs; providing innovative graphic & information design services for the educational publishing market.

Desktop Miracles Inc
112 S Main St, Suite 294, Stowe, VT 05672
Tel: 802-253-7900 *Toll Free Fax:* 888-293-2676
E-mail: info@desktopmiracles.com
Web Site: www.desktopmiracles.com
Key Personnel
Pres & CEO: Barry T Kerrigan *E-mail:* barry@desktopmiracles.com
VP: Virginia Kerrigan *E-mail:* virginia@desktopmiracles.com
Full service publishing design & production firm providing interior typesetting & jacket/cover design to publishing clients nationwide.

diacriTech Inc
4 S Market St, 4th fl, Boston, MA 02109
Tel: 617-600-3366 *Fax:* 617-848-2938
Web Site: www.diacritech.com
Key Personnel
EVP: Madhu Rajamani *E-mail:* madhu@diacritech.com
Dir, Prodn & Edit Servs: Maureen Ross *E-mail:* m.ross@diacritech.com
Founded: 1997
Art & design services for K-12, college, STM & trade publishers. Facilities in Boston, MA, Manchester, NH & in Chennai, Madurai & Kottayam, India.

Didona Design
160 Grandview Rd, Ardmore, PA 19003
Tel: 610-649-3110
E-mail: didona@didonadesign.com
Web Site: www.didonadesign.com
Key Personnel
Pres: Lawrence R Didona
Mktg Mgr: Cathy Didona
Founded: 2000
A graphic design studio that specializes in book cover & text design for many publishing companies large & small, as well as individual authors. With strong Photoshop expertise, we also offer digital image manipulation & collage.

Digital Vista Inc
24 Amity Place, Massapequa, NY 11758
Tel: 516-799-5277
E-mail: info@digitalvista.net
Web Site: www.digitalvista.net
Key Personnel
Owner: Rich Di Silvio
Founded: 1992
Creative cover design, illustration, jacket design, logos, poster design & new media.

Spencer Drate
119 W 80 St, Suite 1-F, New York, NY 10024-7134
Tel: 212-799-0535
E-mail: spencerdrate@yahoo.com
Key Personnel
Owner & Creative Dir: Spencer Drate
Creative Dir: Judith Salavetz

ARTISTS & ART SERVICES

Founded: 1989
Book jacket & book design, poster design, music design, letterheads, logos, promotional design, trademarks, corporate identity, design & other graphic areas.
Nominated for National Design Award.
Membership(s): AIGA, the professional association for design; Recording Academy (NARAS)

1106 Design LLC
1007 E Orange Dr, Phoenix, AZ 85014
Tel: 602-866-3226 *Fax:* 602-866-8166
E-mail: md@1106design.com
Web Site: 1106design.com
Key Personnel
Owner: Michele De Filippo
Founded: 2001
Quality book cover, interior design & production with 30 years experience.

Emerson, Wajdowicz Studios Inc
514 W 25 St, New York, NY 10001
Tel: 212-807-8144
E-mail: info@designews.com
Web Site: www.designews.com; www.facebook.com/DesignEWS; www.instagram.com/ewsdesign
Key Personnel
Founder & Creative Dir: Jurek Wajdowicz
Sr Art Dir & Principal: Lisa LaRochelle
Sr Designer: Yoko Yoshida-Carrera
Assoc: Manny Mendez; Teresa Olsen
Annual report, book, jacket & poster design, magazine & newspaper design & redesign, letterheads, photo editing, photography, trademarks, lettering, layout, corporate identity, art direction, annual reports & marketing & desktop publishing & web design.

Entro Communications Inc
33 Harbour Sq, Suite 202, Toronto, ON M5J 2G2, Canada
Tel: 416-368-6988 *Fax:* 416-368-5616
E-mail: toronto@entro.com
Web Site: www.entro.com
Key Personnel
Founding Partner: Andrew Kuzyk; Wayne McCutcheon
Graphic design & corporate identity, environmental graphics, wayfinding & signage.

Equator Graphics Inc, see International Mapping Associates

Linda Fairchild & Company LLC
101 Lucas Valley Rd, Suite 363, San Rafael, CA 94903
Tel: 415-336-6407
Web Site: www.lindafairchild.com
Key Personnel
Agent & Founder: Linda Fairchild
 E-mail: linda@lindafairchild.com
Founded: 2002

Fairfield Marketing Group Inc
Subsidiary of FMG Inc
830 Sport Hill Rd, Easton, CT 06112-1241
E-mail: info@fairfieldmarketing.com
Key Personnel
Pres & CEO: Edward P Washchilla, Jr
 E-mail: ed@fairfieldmarketing.com
Founded: 1986
Book design, cartoons, film animation, illustration, jacket design, layout, letterheads, lettering, map design, poster design, trademarks & typesetting.
Membership(s): American Booksellers Association (ABA); Bridgeport Regional Business Council (BRBC); Education Market Association; United States Chamber of Commerce (USCC)

fd2s
14205 N Motac Express, Suite 400F, Austin, TX 78728
Tel: 512-476-7733
Web Site: www.fd2s.com
Key Personnel
Founder & Principal: Steven L Stamper
 E-mail: sstamper@fd2s.com
Principal: Curtis Roberts
Founded: 1985
Experiential graphic design, wayfinding consulting, donor recognition, logos & corporate identity, branding & messaging.
Membership(s): Society for Experiential Graphic Design (SEGD)

Figaro
PO Box 848, Sharon, CT 06069
Tel: 860-248-8989; 860-364-0834
E-mail: design@figro.com
Web Site: www.figro.com
Key Personnel
Co-Pres & Creative Dir: Walter Schwarz
Co-Pres: Linda Swenson *E-mail:* ls@figro.com
Creative, editorial, production, photographic services for books, catalogs, promotional materials & packaging. Digital creation of text, art, maps, illustration & photos for current & out of print books. Consultation, graphic arts management & printing supervision. Web site development & maintenance. Photography of Suzanne Szasz & Ray Schorr.

45th Parallel Maps & Infographics, see Patti Isaacs Maps, Infographics, Writing

Foster Covers
1401 Wonder Way, Fairfield, IA 52556
Tel: 641-919-4367
E-mail: info@fostercovers.com
Web Site: www.fostercovers.com; www.facebook.com/bookcoverdesign
Key Personnel
Pres: George Foster *E-mail:* george@fostercovers.com
Founded: 1982
Book cover design & audio covers.

Leanne Franson
4 Poplar Ave, Martensville, SK S0K 2T0, Canada
Mailing Address: PO Box 1327, Martensville, SK S0K 2T0, Canada
Tel: 514-432-4170
E-mail: leanne@leannefranson.com
Web Site: www.leannefranson.com
Founded: 1991
Illustrate children's textbooks & trade books (picture books, children's novels) & magazines to client's spec, working in pen & ink (B&W) or colored acrylic inks & pencil (watercolor technique).
Membership(s): Picture Book Artists Association (PBAA)

G & H Soho Inc
413 Market St, Elmwood Park, NJ 07407
Tel: 201-216-9400 *Fax:* 201-216-1778
E-mail: print@ghsoho.com
Web Site: www.ghsoho.com
Key Personnel
Pres: Gerry Burstein
Prodn Mgr: Jason Burstein
Founded: 1985
Complete service, from copy-editing through production editing. Text & cover design, from rough layouts to final pages delivered on film or disk. Production service through bound books. Specialize in computer, technical & heavily illustrated books.
Membership(s): Association of Graphic Communications; Digital Print Industry Association; PRINTING United Alliance

Laurence Gartel
PO Box 4114, Deerfield Beach, FL 33442
Tel: 561-302-6774
E-mail: gartel@comcast.net
Web Site: gartelart.com
Multimedia & DVDs, computer graphic designs & illustrations, logos & text, digital photography & digital art.

General Cartography Inc
4 Estate Dr, Boynton Beach, FL 33436
Tel: 561-914-6323
E-mail: terradata@aol.com
Web Site: cartographybypaul.com
Key Personnel
Pres: Paul Pugliese
Founded: 1968
Maps.

GEX Inc
80 Conley's Grove Rd, Derry, NH 03038
Mailing Address: PO Box 613, Atkinson, NH 03811
Tel: 603-870-9292
Web Site: www.gexinc.com
Key Personnel
Pres: Gary Russell *E-mail:* gary.russell@gexinc.com
VP: Jim LaPierre
Full service educational publishing services company, providing content development, digital & production services to the world's foremost publishers. With over 30 years of experience, GEX designs courses, creates engaging content & provides services that deliver content to a variety of media with digital & print solutions.

Gore Studio Inc
101 Paxton Ct, Brentwood, TN 37027
Tel: 615-519-2262
E-mail: gorestudioinc@gmail.com
Web Site: www.gorestudio.com
Key Personnel
Pres: Bruce Gore
Book & bookcover design, electronic layout, letterheads, logos, trademarks & posters.

GW Illustration & Design
Subsidiary of GW Inc
2290 Ball Dr, St Louis, MO 63146
Tel: 314-567-9854
Web Site: www.gwinc.com
Key Personnel
CEO: Kevin Arrow
EVP: Mike Loomis
VP, Content Opers: Suzanne Kastner
Scanning & art rendering services for technical, medical & educational textbook art projects.

Graphics International
Division of Illustration Services Inc
20475 Bunker Hill Dr, Cleveland, OH 44126
Tel: 440-333-9988
Key Personnel
Pres: Don Izold *E-mail:* dlozi@aol.com
Founded: 1981
Precision B&W line illustration.

Heidelberg Graphics
2 Stansbury Ct, Chico, CA 95928
SAN: 211-5654
Tel: 530-342-6582 *Fax:* 530-342-6582
E-mail: heidelberggraphics@gmail.com; service@heidelberggraphics.com
Web Site: www.heidelberggraphics.com
Key Personnel
Owner & Pres: Larry S Jackson
Founded: 1972

Book design, layout & book publication. Consultant to self-publishers. Provide editing, word processing/typesetting, bar codes, Internet sales & copyright services.

Hermani & Sorrentino Design
404 Musgrave Rd, Salt Spring Island, BC V8K 1V5, Canada
Tel: 250-538-8426
E-mail: hermani2sorrentino@gmail.com
Web Site: www.hermanisorrentino.com
Key Personnel
Owner: Michela Sorrentino
Founded: 1993
Complete graphic design services including book design & illustrations.

Cathy Hull
180 E 79 St, New York, NY 10075
Tel: 212-772-7743 *Fax:* 212-535-1877
E-mail: cathy@cathyhull.com
Web Site: www.cathyhull.com
Freelance illustrator; specializes in conceptual illustration for editorial, advertising, corporate & institutional clients in the US, Europe & Japan. Services include illustration, logos & corporate identity, greeting cards, fun apparel & products.

International Mapping Associates
5300 Dorsey Hall Dr, Suite 201, Ellicott City, MD 21042
Tel: 443-367-0050
E-mail: frontdesk@internationalmapping.com
Web Site: internationalmapping.com
Key Personnel
Founder & Pres: Scott Edmonds
IT Dir: Thomas Frogh
Founded: 2000
Custom map design services for the publishing industry. Services include research, design, compilation & production of maps & information graphics for both print & electronic publishing. Offering a complete range of products including textbook maps, wall maps, travel guides, 2-D & 3-D maps, 3-D block diagrams, shaded relief, 3-D terrain models, map exhibits, virtual fly-thrus, animated & interactive maps, web maps & graphics.
Membership(s): International Map Industry Association (IMIA)

Patti Isaacs Maps, Infographics, Writing
Formerly 45th Parallel Maps & Infographics
13720 Paragon Ave N, Stillwater, MN 55082
Tel: 651-430-8127
Web Site: patti-isaacs.com
Key Personnel
Principal Cartographer: Patricia Isaacs
E-mail: isaacs.patti@gmail.com
Founded: 1990
Art production & management for digital & print applications. Developmental & technical art services, specializing in custom cartography, charts, graphs & diagrams for text & trade books, magazines, travel guides, museum & visitor center displays. We can take your project from research through design & production & can handle jobs from single piece to hundreds. Many subject areas: geography, geology & other earth sciences; history, anthropology & other social sciences; business, computer science, foreign languages. Major clients include McGraw-Hill, Houghton Mifflin, Cengage & university presses.
Membership(s): Minnesota Bookbuilders; Publishing Professionals Network (PPN)

ITW Foils
Division of Illinois Tool Works
5 Malcolm Hoyt Dr, Newburyport, MA 01950
Tel: 978-225-8200 *Toll Free Tel:* 800-942-9995 *Fax:* 978-462-0831
E-mail: info@itwsf.com
Web Site: www.itwfoils.com
Founded: 1926
Hotstamping foil.

Itzhack Shelomi Design
25 Cushman Rd, Scarsdale, NY 10583
Tel: 212-689-7469
E-mail: studio@ishelomi.com; studio@serifes.com
Web Site: www.ishelomi.com
Key Personnel
Owner & Creative Dir: Itzhack Shelomi
Founded: 1987
Design & production from children's to young adult publications: Storybooks, activity books, educational publications & games, packages for games, packages & sleeve cases for books, display cases, brochures, booklets, newsletters, etc. Handling design, pictures & illustrations editing, page composition & word processing for interior & cover, from the ms through full-color dummy-up to the final mechanical, in both English & Hebrew languages. Special custom-made typefaces & fonts for English & Hebrew languages; 3-D color comps for package's presentation. Fully equipped with the latest computer graphic technology.

Kachergis Book Design Inc
575 Stone Wall Rd, Pittsboro, NC 27312
Tel: 919-656-7632
E-mail: goodbooks@kachergisbookdesign.com
Web Site: www.kachergisbookdesign.com
Key Personnel
Pres: Anne Kachergis
Founded: 1980
Book & book cover design, electronic layout, letterheads, logos, trademarks & posters.

Dimitri Karetnikov
221 Ewell Ave, Gettesburg, PA 17325
Tel: 609-468-5627
E-mail: dkare@aol.com
Founded: 1983
Advising authors on illustration & graphic design. Illustration from concept through press-ready art. Wide variety of subject matter including medical & science illustrations for books, audiovisual presentations, web sites in a wide variety of graphic formats including Adobe Illustrator & PhotoShop.

Karen Karibian
444 Warren St, Apt 1450, Jersey City, NJ 07302
Tel: 914-564-4201
E-mail: karenesque2@aol.com; karenkaribian@gmail.com; karenessence@aol.com
Web Site: www.coroflot.com/karenessence/undercurrent-cartoons; www.karenessence.wix.com/undercurrentcartoons
Founded: 2000
Cartoons, illustrations & figure drawing; colorful, whimsical, humorous, festive & sublime. Available for licensing & branding. Artwork is under Karen Karibian & Undercurrent Cartoons.
Membership(s): Art Directors Club; Art on Call; Women in Animation

Lachina Creative
Formerly Lachina Precision Graphics Services
3693 Green Rd, Cleveland, OH 44122
Tel: 216-292-7959
E-mail: info@lachina.com
Web Site: www.lachina.com
Key Personnel
Pres: Jeff Lachina *E-mail:* jlachina@lachina.com
Dir, Prodn Servs: Whitney Philipp
E-mail: wphilipp@lachina.com
Dir, Proj Mgmt Off: Shawn Vazinski
E-mail: svazinski@lachina.com
Founded: 1978
Full service creative & business consulting agency that helps companies tackle creative, brand & business dilemmas with the right tools, methods & technology.

Lachina Precision Graphics Services, see Lachina Creative

Wayne Lim
2429 Clement St, No 2, San Francisco, CA 94121
Tel: 415-940-3868
E-mail: w_c_lim@yahoo.com
Founded: 1984
Draw cartoons/illustrations & logos for a wide audience.

Linguistic Systems Inc (LSI)
260 Franklin St, Suite 230, Boston, MA 02110
Tel: 617-528-7400
E-mail: clientservice@linguist.com
Web Site: www.linguist.com
Key Personnel
Founder & Pres: Martin Roberts
Founded: 1967
Leading language conversion company, specializing in the translation of books, periodicals, manuals & catalogs. For over 50 years the company has produced more than 2,000,000 pages of translation, covering 120 languages. LSI maintains a database of 7,500 carefully screened & certified translators for expertise in a broad spectrum of industrial & scientific subjects. Foreign language typesetting for print, web site & mobile apps & narration for video & multimedia programs are also available.
Membership(s): American Translators Association (ATA); Association of Language Companies (ALC); Globalization & Localization Association (GALA)

Lumina Datamatics Inc
600 Cordwainer Dr, Unit 103, Norwell, MA 02061
Tel: 508-746-0300 *Fax:* 508-746-3233
E-mail: marketing@luminad.com
Web Site: luminadatamatics.com
Key Personnel
EVP, Busn Devt: Jack Mitchell
EVP, Solutions, Transitions & US Opers: Sandeep Dhawan
Founded: 2005
Providing full service content creation, design/packaging & media delivery systems to publishers. Services include authoring/writing, editorial research & development, media development & production, editing, photo & text research/permissions, photography/photo shoot direction, indexing, proofreading, fact checking, design/design direction, art direction/editing, technical/illustrative art packages, photo manipulation & page makeup/composition services. Employs over 1,200 US & offshore resources specializing in content/media creation & make-up including file conversions/repurposing & content management & delivery services. All services are offered both in the US & at offshore facilities. Areas of specialization include school, higher education & professional publishing: mathematics (grade school/algebra/calculus/physics), foreign language (French/Spanish/German/Italian), English & English composition, history, political science, science (chemistry/biology/astronomy), social studies, computer science, business (economics/finance/marketing), engineering & technical trades as well as professional/reference material. Products range from simple one-color

ARTISTS & ART SERVICES / SERVICES

ancillaries components to highly complex design & art intensive core content.
Branch Office(s)
c/o Arnecke Sibeth Distribution, Rechtsanwaelte Steuerberater Partnerschaftsgesellschaft mdB, Gueterplatz 1, 60327 Frankfurt am Main, Germany *Tel:* (06155) 862 99-0 *Fax:* (06155) 862 99-19
Ascendas International Tech Park, 12th fl, Phase II (Crest), CSIR Rd, Taramani, Chennai 600 113, India *Tel:* (044) 4017 6000; (044) 4017 6001
Santosh Raj Plaza, 1st fl, Subburaman St, Gandhi Nagar, 12/9, St, Shenoy Nagar, Madurai 625 020, India
Andheri (E), Unit 117-120, SDF - IV, SEEPZ - SEZ, Mumbai 400 096, India *Tel:* (022) 4034 0515; (022) 4034 0508 *Fax:* (022) 2829 1673
Off No 47/1, 7th fl, Tower-B, A-41, Correnthum Tower, Sector-62, Noida 201 301, India
Plot No 29-34, East Coast Rd, Saram Revenue Village, Oulgaret Municipality, Lawspet Post, Puducherry 605 008, India *Tel:* (0413) 226 4500
No 10, Vazhudavoor Rd, Pettaiyanchathiram, Thattanchavadi, Puducherry 605 009, India *Tel:* (0413) 401 1635
Apple One Equicom Tower, 11th fl, Mindanao Ave Corner Biliran St, Central (pob), Cebu Business Park, 6000 Cebu City, Cebu, Philippines
c/o SOPHI Outsourcing Inc, G/F DBPI IT Plaza, Calindagan, 6200 Dumaguete City, Negros Oriental, Philippines
Brixham Laboratory, Brixham, Devon TQ5 8BA, United Kingdom
Lumina Datamatics UK Ltd, 153 Milton Keynes Business Ctr, Linford Wood, Milton Keynes MK14 6GD, United Kingdom

Mapping Specialists Ltd
3000 Cahill Main, Suite 220, Fitchburg, WI 53711
Tel: 608-274-4004 *Toll Free Tel:* 866-525-2298
E-mail: msl@mappingspecialists.com
Web Site: www.mappingspecialists.com
Key Personnel
Owner & Pres: David R Knipfer
Founded: 1984
Full service map program development, consultation services using the latest computer & animated techniques. Complete project coordination, design, in-house research, computer base generation, compilation, shaded relief & digital files. PC, Mac & CD-ROM output. Specialize in thematic mapping for textbooks, encyclopedias, reference, trade, travel guides, etc. Strong staff background in cartography, computer graphics, geography, art illustration, charts, graphs, history. In-house editing at every production stage with emphasis on technical, geographic, historical & thematic accuracy. Project manager works as part of client's team.

Maps by Mathison
PO Box 152, Spring Mills, PA 16875
Tel: 814-321-7571
E-mail: jcmaps6@gmail.com
Web Site: mapsbymathison.com
Key Personnel
Owner: Jeff Mathison
Founded: 1980
Create illustrated maps of real or fictional territory in a variety of styles.

Diane Maurer-Hand Marbled Papers
Subsidiary of Hand Marbled Papers
Water St, Spring Mills, PA 16875
Mailing Address: PO Box 78, Spring Mills, PA 16875-0078
Tel: 814-308-3685
E-mail: dkmaurer1@gmail.com
Web Site: dianemaurer.com
Illustration; jacket design. Specialize in hand-marbled papers, paste papers & handmade books.

Meadows Design Office
3800 Yuma St NW, Washington, DC 20016
Tel: 202-966-6007
E-mail: mdo@mdomedia.com
Key Personnel
Pres & Creative Dir: Marc Meadows
 E-mail: marc@mdomedia.com
Curator & Image Res: Amy Meadows
Founded: 1981
A full service graphic design firm. Design & production of books, book jackets, illustrated books, cookbooks, publications & promotional materials & sidelines; consultation, art direction, design, layout, type specification & mechanical art. Specialize in trade & text books. Conceptualize & prepare mock-up covers, compositions, presentations & blads for publishers. State-of-the-art electronic publishing equipment & software. Typeset & produce multilingual editions of our book designs.
Membership(s): AIGA, the professional association for design; Type Directors Club

Melissa Turk & the Artist Network
9 Babbling Brook Lane, Suffern, NY 10901
Tel: 845-368-8606
E-mail: melissa@melissaturk.com
Web Site: www.melissaturk.com
Key Personnel
Owner & Pres: Melissa Turk
Contact: Dorothy Ziff
Founded: 1986
Represents professional artists supplying quality illustration, calligraphy & cartography. Specialize in children's trade & educational illustration as well as natural science illustration (wildlife, botanical, medical, etc).
Membership(s): Graphic Artists Guild; Society of Children's Book Writers & Illustrators (SCBWI)

Brian Thomas Merrill
40 Vandale St, Putnam, CT 06260
Tel: 860-315-4638
E-mail: zangmerrill@yahoo.com
Desktop publishing, art & design: jackets, interiors, logos & corporate ID, ads, calligraphy, lettering, cartoons, illustration, letterheads, typesetting, photography.

Wendell Minor
15 Old North Rd, Washington, CT 06793
Mailing Address: PO Box 1135, Washington, CT 06793-0135
Tel: 860-868-9101
E-mail: wendell@minorart.com
Web Site: www.minorart.com
Key Personnel
Proj Coord: Florence Minor
Illustration & design for trade & juvenile books, from concept to electronic mechanical; jacket design & illustration; magazine illustration.

MPS North America LLC
Subsidiary of MPS Ltd
5728 Major Blvd, Suite 528, Orlando, FL 32819
Tel: 407-472-1280 *Toll Free Tel:* 866-978-1008 *Fax:* 212-981-2983
E-mail: marketing@mpslimited.com
Web Site: www.mpslimited.com
Founded: 1973
Technical, medical, situational, scientific & chemistry. We offer high quality art renderings, as well as full service typesetting & book production.
Branch Office(s)
1901 S Fourth St, Suite 222, Effingham, IL 62401
477 Madison Ave, 6th fl, New York, NY 10022
1822 E NC Hwy 54, Suite 120, Durham, NC 27713-3210
MPS Ltd, HMG Ambassador, 137 Residency Rd, Bangalore 560 025, India *Tel:* (080) 4178 4242 *Fax:* (080) 4178 4222
MPS Ltd, RR Towers, Super A, 16/17 TVK Industrial Estate, Guindy, Chennai 600 032, India *Tel:* (044) 4916 2222 *Fax:* (044) 4916 2225
MPS Ltd, 33 IT Park, Sahastradhara Rd, Dehradun 248 001, India *Tel:* (0135) 6677 954
MPS Ltd, 709 DLI Corporate Greens, Sector 74A, Narsinghpur, Gurugram 122 004, India *Tel:* (0124) 661 3134
MPS Interactive Systems, GRM Tech Bldg, 2nd fl, Plot No DH-6/29, Action Area-1, Rajarhat, New Town, Kolkata, West Bengal 700 156, India *Tel:* (033) 66111500
MPS Interactive Systems, The Great Oasis, D-13, 2nd fl, Marol Industrial Estate, Andheri (E), Mumbai 400 093, India *Tel:* (022) 6643 8100 *Fax:* (022) 6643 8800
MPS Ltd, C35, Sector 62, Noida 201 307, India (corp off) *Tel:* (0120) 4599750 *Fax:* (0120) 4021280
Membership(s): Publishing Professionals Network (PPN)

Andrew Newman Design
9509 W Lilac Rd, Escondido, CA 92026
Tel: 508-221-5101
E-mail: newmandesign@gmail.com
Web Site: www.andrewnewmandesign.com
Key Personnel
Owner: Andrew Newman
Founded: 1980
Award-winning graphic design studio knowledgeable in all areas of design & production for logotypes, advertising & promotional materials, web site design, cover design, illustration, art direction, package design, lettering & typeface design.

North Market Street Graphics (NMSG)
Affiliate of Archetype Inc
317 N Market St, Lancaster, PA 17603
Tel: 717-392-7438
E-mail: mail@nmsgbooks.com
Web Site: www.nmsgbooks.com
Key Personnel
Owner: Elizabeth Andes; LeRoy R Stipe, Jr
VP, Sales: Lainey Wolfe
Prepress services for book publishers including book design, double keyboarding/verify, Macintosh composition including creation of ebooks, page assembly, copy-editing, proofreading, PDF files, postscript, extensive art services & Epson proofing. All commonly used media available. ISDN, DSL electronic transmissions; archiving services.
Art services include: color separation with Photoshop adjustment, B&W scanning with Photoshop adjustment, art & output calibrated to printer specifications.

Robert Pizzo Illustration/Design
51 Somerset Rd, New Rochelle, NY 10804
Tel: 914-278-9252
E-mail: rp@robertpizzo.com
Web Site: www.robertpizzo.com
Corporate, advertising, editorial & stock illustration, children's books, infographic design.

Pointing Robot Studios
2 Englewood Dr, Suite D3, Harwich, MA 02645
Tel: 774-237-0690
Web Site: nedsonntag.com
Key Personnel
Owner: Ned Sonntag *E-mail:* nedso@comcast.net
Founded: 1971

Illustrator, cartoonist & science fiction writer. Betty Boop illustrator 1985-2016 for King Features Syndicate/Fleischer Studios. Services provided: Illustration; research; storyboards.

Pronk Media Inc
16 Glen Davis Crescent, Toronto, ON M4E 1X5, Canada
Tel: 416-716-9660 (cell)
E-mail: info@pronk.com; hello@pronk.com
Web Site: www.pronk.com; www.h5engines.com; www.html5alive.com
Key Personnel
Pres: Gord Pronk *E-mail:* gord@pronk.com
Founded: 1981 (as Pronk & Associates Inc)
Print design & production, including product conceptualization & prototypes, design & art direction, photo research & licensing, infographics, charts, graphs, technical art, page design, layout & production. Interactive content development, digital games, activities, animations & complete lessons for the classroom.

The Pushpin Group Inc
38 W 26 St, New York, NY 10010
Tel: 212-529-7590
Web Site: www.pushpininc.com
Key Personnel
Co-Founder, Pres & Dir: Seymour Chwast
  E-mail: seymour@pushpininc.com
Founded: 1954
Book jackets, poster design, illustration, letterheads, trademarks, packaging design, graphics, logo & corporate identity.
Membership(s): AIGA, the professional association for design; Art Directors Club of New York; Graphic Artists Guild

QBS Learning
242 W 30 St, Suite 1100, New York, NY 10001
Tel: 646-668-4645
E-mail: contact@qbslearning.com
Web Site: www.qbslearning.com
Key Personnel
Co-Founder & CEO: Hanut Singh
Co-Founder & Mng Dir: Brian Kobberger
CFO: Indrajeet Agrawal
EVP, Busn Devt: Michael Porter
VP, Edit: Jonathan Schmalzbach
VP, HR: Pallavi Verma
Dir, Intl: Reggie Chua Singh
Founded: 1983 (as Bill Smith Group)
Full development services for children's products. Editorial, photography, illustration, interior & cover design & production; web site design. Art buying illustration services, early childhood thru higher education.

Reynolds Design & Management
52 Piedmont Ave, Waltham, MA 02451-3015
Tel: 781-893-7464
E-mail: rdandm@comcast.net
Key Personnel
Owner: Christine Reynolds
Founded: 1986
Design, project management & production of company history books.
Membership(s): Letterpress Guild of New England; New England Museum Association; Society of Printers; Women's National Book Association (WNBA)

Round Table Companies
Subsidiary of Writers of the Round Table Press Inc
PO Box 1603, Deerfield, IL 60015
Toll Free Tel: 833-750-5683
Web Site: www.roundtablecompanies.com
Key Personnel
Founder & CEO: Corey Michael Blake
  E-mail: corey@roundtablecompanies.com
Dir, Stories & Learning: Kelsey Schurer
Company Integrator: Sunny DiMartino
  E-mail: sun@roundtablecompanies.com
Fin & HR: Andrea Yahr
Exec Asst: Liz Bauman
Founded: 2006
Writing, branding, printing, distribution, coaching & consulting, bringing culture to companies.

Shepherd Inc
2223 Key Way Dr, Suite B, Dubuque, IA 52002
Tel: 563-584-0500
Web Site: www.shepherd-inc.com
Key Personnel
Prodn Mgr: Deb Leibfried
Founded: 1989
A seasoned book production company that offers state-of-the-art electronic composition, full service project management. Experienced in producing texts in the college, school, professional, trade & reference fields. Shepherd is a schedule-oriented, cost-efficient & quality-conscious vendor.

Snow Lion Graphics
Division of SLG Books
PO Box 9465, Berkeley, CA 94709-0465
Tel: 510-525-1134; 510-816-2840 (cell)
E-mail: info@slgbooks.com
Web Site: www.slgbooks.com
Key Personnel
Pres & Dir: Roger Dale Williams *E-mail:* roger@slgbooks.com
Prodn Mgr: Frances Williams
Founded: 1986
Book design & illustrations, color separation & printing (books, calendars, posters, cards), publishing, book packaging.
Membership(s): Book Promotion Forum; The Imaging Alliance

Square Two Design Inc
2325 Third St, Suite 305, San Francisco, CA 94107
Tel: 415-437-3888
E-mail: info@square2.com
Web Site: www.square2.com
Key Personnel
Pres & Creative Dir: Eddie Lee
Founded: 1991
Corporate identity & web site design. Full service graphic design firm.
Branch Office(s)
No 8 Hua Jia Di Nan Jie, Chao Yang District, Beijing 100102, China, Pres: Min Wang
  Tel: (01350) 1084-543 *E-mail:* mwang@square2.com

Steeleworks
PO Box 4002, Philadelphia, PA 19118
Tel: 215-247-4619
Web Site: www.sarasteele.com
Key Personnel
Principal: Sara Steele *E-mail:* sara@sarasteele.com
Founded: 1983
Artist, art dealer, designer & art publisher.

Story Monsters LLC
4696 W Tyson St, Chandler, AZ 85226-2903
Tel: 480-940-8182 *Fax:* 480-940-8787
Web Site: www.StoryMonsters.com
Key Personnel
Pres: Linda F Radke *E-mail:* Linda@StoryMonsters.com
Founded: 1985
A team of talented graphic designers creating integrated, eye-catching designs to make our books stand out from the rest. Can provide cover design, format for interior pages, typesetting assistance, logo design, business cards or marketing materials. Just let us know what your needs are & we'll promptly provide a plan & an estimate.
Membership(s): Better Business Bureau (BBB); The Children's Book Council (CBC); Independent Book Publishers Association (IBPA); National Federation of Press Women

Story Monsters Press, see Story Monsters LLC

Studio E Book Production
PO Box 20005, Santa Barbara, CA 93120-0005
Tel: 805-683-6202 *Fax:* 805-683-6202
E-mail: queries@studio-e-books.com
Web Site: www.studio-e-books.com
Key Personnel
Prop: Eric C Larson *E-mail:* eric@studio-e-books.com
Founded: 1999
Book packaging, book design & typesetting.

Stephen Tiano
56 Tyler Dr, Riverhead, NY 11901
Tel: 631-284-3842; 631-764-2487 (cell) *Fax:* 631-284-3842
E-mail: stephen@stephentianobookdesign.com
Web Site: stephentianobookdesign.com
Founded: 1993
Book designer & page composition specialist. Specialize in memoirs, books on technical & scientific subjects filled with math, equations & tabular material. Also does page design & layout on children's picture & storybooks, as well as trade books loaded with photos & other art.
Membership(s): Editorial Freelancers Association (EFA)

Stan Tusan
105 Breckinridge Dr, Phoenix, OR 97535
Tel: 541-535-6791
E-mail: stantoon@charter.net
Web Site: www.stantoon.com
Digital artwork & design: humorous illustrations, children's educational books & materials, spot drawings; licensor.
Membership(s): National Cartoonist Society

Tyler Creative
1300 S Johnstone Ave, Bartlesville, OK 74003-5624
Tel: 918-527-6779
E-mail: info@tylercreative.com
Web Site: tylercreative.com
Key Personnel
Owner: Sherry L Stinson
Founded: 1994
A full service, award-winning graphic design & photography studio.
Membership(s): Graphic Artists Guild; National Association of Photoshop Professionals (NAPP); Professional Photographers of America (PPA)

Wild West Communications Group
PO Box 346, Homewood, CA 96141
Tel: 530-412-1096 *Fax:* 530-525-4559
Web Site: www.wildwest-tahoe.com
Key Personnel
Principal: Lolly Kupec *E-mail:* lk.wwcg@gmail.com
Pres: Edward Miller *E-mail:* em@wildwest-tahoe.com
Founded: 1977
Editorial services, book design jacket & poster design, layout, letterheads, logos & corporate identity, sales presentations, typesetting, voiceovers & narration.

Brice Wood
PO Box A, Jerome, AZ 86331
Tel: 928-634-3238

ARTISTS & ART SERVICES

E-mail: bricewood@yahoo.com
Web Site: www.bricewood.com
Artist: master draftsman. Design, illustration, photography, typography. Brochures to books. Computer graphics & electronic delivery.

Photographers

Listed below are photographers available for almost any type of assignment, although many of them are specialists in one field or another. Among these photographers and firms are many who maintain stock files of their own photos, whereas the section **Stock Photo Agencies** lists firms that represent several photographers and maintain stock photo files of their work.

Russell Abraham Photography
Jack London Sq, 309 Fourth St, Suite 108, Oakland, CA 94607
Tel: 510-333-6633
E-mail: ra@russellabraham.com
Web Site: russellabraham.com
Key Personnel
Owner & Photog: Russell Abraham
Founded: 1978
Membership(s): American Institute of Architects (AIA); American Society of Media Photographers (ASMP)

Accent Photography Ltd
1842 31 Ave SW, Calgary, AB T2T 1S7, Canada
Tel: 403-860-8588 *Toll Free Tel:* 877-470-4120
Fax: 403-271-4121
E-mail: info@calgaryphotographer.com
Web Site: www.accentphotography.ca
Key Personnel
Owner & Chief Photog: Lawrence De Pape
Founded: 1979
Portrait & commercial photography, photo restoration.
Membership(s): Alberta Professional Photographers Association (APPA); Wedding & Portrait Photographers International (WPPI)

Aerial Archives
Lakeport, CA 95453
Tel: 415-771-2555
E-mail: research@aerialarchives.com
Web Site: aerialarchives.com
Key Personnel
Dir & Photog: Herb Lingl *E-mail:* herb@aerialarchives.com
Founded: 1989
Aerial photography & aerial videography on assignment; large archive of current & historical aerial photography & satellite imagery.
File Begins: 1907
Membership(s): American Photographic Artists (APA); American Society of Media Photographers (ASMP); American Society of Picture Professionals (ASPP); Professional Aerial Photography Association (PAPA)

Airphoto
2311 S Prairie Ave, Pueblo, CO 81005
Tel: 719-542-5719
Web Site: airphotona.com; johnwark.com
Key Personnel
Owner: John Wark *E-mail:* john@johnwark.com
Founded: 1990
Comprehensive aerial stock photography of North America: urban, agricultural, industry, mining, marine, geology, environmental, national parks, transportation & US borders. Seven books on John Wark's aerial photography have been published.
Membership(s): American Society of Media Photographers (ASMP); American Society of Picture Professionals (ASPP); AOPA; Professional Aerial Photography Association (PAPA)

Atlanta Panorama
Division of ALPS Labs
c/o ALPS Labs, 2579 Lawrenceville Hwy, Suite B, Decatur, GA 30033
Tel: 404-872-2577 *Fax:* 404-872-0548
E-mail: alps007@mindspring.com
Web Site: www.alpslabs.com/PANO/index.htm
Key Personnel
Owner & Photog: George S Pearl *Tel:* 404-840-0834 (cell)
Founded: 1978
Professional panoramic photography & framing services.
Membership(s): American Society of Media Photographers (ASMP); International Virtual Reality Professionals Association (IVRPA)

Noella Ballenger & Associates
PO Box 457, La Canada, CA 91012
Tel: 818-954-0933 *Fax:* 818-954-0910
E-mail: noella1b@aol.com
Web Site: www.noellaballenger.com
Key Personnel
Owner & Photog: Noella Ballenger
Founded: 1984
Stock photography, text/photo packages. Provides online classes with one-on-one instruction & portfolio reviews. Contact directly.
Membership(s): American Society of Media Photographers (ASMP)

Frank Balthis Photography
PO Box 255, Davenport, CA 95017-0255
Tel: 805-770-3018; 831-426-8205
E-mail: frankbalthisphoto@gmail.com
Web Site: frankbalthis.photoshelter.com
Key Personnel
Owner & Photog: Frank S Balthis
Founded: 1980
Natural history & travel stock photo file. Photograph & publish natural history cards, books, postcards & photo magnets. Work closely with parks, interpretive associations, museums & galleries. Over 600 designs currently available.
Stock: 150,000 color transparencies; 35mm & medium formats; 20,000 B&W; 500,000 digital capture

Steve Banks Photographer
Subsidiary of Studio 6 Art
14822 Channel Lane, Santa Monica, CA 90402
Tel: 310-998-7062
E-mail: steve@studio6art.com
Web Site: www.studio6art.com
Founded: 2000
Photojournalist & fine art photographer; stock includes music, celebrities, sports, photographic essays & more.
File Begins: 1964
Membership(s): Recording Academy (NARAS)

Tim Barnwell Photography
10 Governors Ct, Asheville, NC 28805
Tel: 828-251-0040
E-mail: barnwellphoto@hotmail.com
Web Site: www.barnwellphoto.com
Key Personnel
Owner: Tim Barnwell
Founded: 1980
Professional photography for editorial & advertising clients. Book publishing under imprint; Numinous Editions. Author of fine books.

Tom Bean Photography
PO Box 1567, Flagstaff, AZ 86002-1567
Tel: 928-779-4381
E-mail: tom@tombean.com
Web Site: tombean.photoshelter.com
Key Personnel
Pres: Tom Bean
Assignment & stock photography. Stock includes travel & outdoor adventure, earth science, wildlife, Western landscapes & natural areas, with an emphasis on natural history.

Morton Beebe Photographer/Author
San Francisco, CA 94111
Tel: 415-362-6222; 415-706-0594 (cell)
E-mail: morton.beebe@gmail.com
Web Site: www.mortonbeebe.com
Key Personnel
Owner & Photog: Morton Beebe
Founded: 1962
Photographer & author. Current projects include editorial & advertising assignments, producing fine art prints for collectors & property developers & managing a large stock archive.
Membership(s): American Society of Media Photographers (ASMP); Bay Area Travel Writers; The Explorers Club

Miriam Berkley Photography
353 W 51 St, Suite 1-A/6, New York, NY 10019-6457
Tel: 212-246-7979
E-mail: miriam.berkley@mac.com; authorpix@aol.com
Web Site: www.PublishersMarketplace.com/members/MiriamBerkley; www.miriamberkley.com
Founded: 1986
Strong author portraits in color & B&W (35mm film & JPEGs). Now shooting entirely digitally. Large stock (approximately 1,500 names) of international author photographs, including Nobel Prize winners; special strengths: writers from Spain & Latin America; Scandinavia; mystery writers; some publishers & literary agents; publishing & literary events; digitally scan & transmit large number of artistic editorial images suitable for cover art or interiors. Also, since 2003, large stock of New York City images, as well as Paris, London, Stockholm, Mexico & Cuba.
File Begins: 1986
Stock: 150,000 B&W; 200,000 35mm color tranparencies & digital images
Membership(s): American Society of Media Photographers (ASMP); American Society of Picture Professionals (ASPP); The Authors Guild; Editorial Photographers (EP); Professional Women Photographers (PWP)

Jennifer Bishop Photography
843 W University Pkwy, Baltimore, MD 21210
Tel: 410-366-6662
Web Site: www.jenniferbishopphotography.com
Key Personnel
Owner & Photog: Jennifer Bishop
E-mail: jenb6@verizon.net
Assignment & stock photography.
Membership(s): American Society of Media Photographers (ASMP)

PHOTOGRAPHERS

Bondarenko Photography
Division of Image Hive LLC
210 S 41 St, Birmingham, AL 35222
Tel: 205-592-8319; 205-243-9910 (cell)
E-mail: info@bondarenkophoto.com
Web Site: www.bondarenkophoto.com
Key Personnel
Owner & Photog: Marc Bondarenko
Founded: 1981
Commercial photography studio working both in studio & on location worldwide.
Membership(s): American Advertising Federation (AAF); American Society of Media Photographers (ASMP)

Bradley Ireland Productions
c/o Sea Save Foundation, 20540 Pacific Coast Hwy, Malibu, CA 90265
Key Personnel
Owner & Photog: Georgienne Bradley; Jay Ireland
Founded: 1990
Video & still stock house-natural history/underwater specialty.

Art Brewer Photography LLC
25262 Mainsail Dr, Dana Point, CA 92629
Tel: 949-661-8930
E-mail: art@artbrewer.com
Web Site: www.artbrewer.com; www.artbrewergallery.com
Key Personnel
Owner & Photog: Art Brewer *Tel:* 949-230-8130 (cell)
Founded: 1981
Surf photography in a diverse array of publications.
File Begins: 1969

Tom Brownold Photography
801 W Summit Ave, Flagstaff, AZ 86001
Tel: 928-779-1583
E-mail: tbrownold@tombrownold.com
Web Site: www.tombrownold.com
Key Personnel
Owner: Tom Brownold
Founded: 1980
Landscapes, lifestyles, portraits, natural history of the US, Southwest parks & monuments, Alaska, Guatemala, Chile & Mexico. Portraiture & stock photography for advertising & editorial usage.
Natural history: Selected vertebrates in their natural environs; close-ups & scenic of wildflowers, dramatic landscapes of geologic & woodland varieties from desert to alpine; geology, earth science, weather, wildlife, flora; agriculture, forest management practices.
General stock: Archaeological sites, destination travel, indigenous culture; people of all ages engaged in daily life & outdoor sports activities (skiing, kayaking, swimming, track & field, ballooning); rock art.
File Begins: 1980
Membership(s): American Photographic Artists (APA)

Donna Brunet Macro Photography
PO Box 30123, Columbia, MO 65205-3123
Tel: 573-999-2178
Web Site: www.donnabrunet.com
Key Personnel
Owner: Donna Brunet *E-mail:* donna@donnabrunet.com
Founded: 2006
Provide insect photographs to publishers for textbooks, trade books, magazines & paper products. All images are identified to order & family with a significant number identified to genus or species. Images from over 60 insect families in 13 orders. In addition to insects, there are a limited number of plants, crustaceans & reptiles. A complete species list can be found on the web site.
File Begins: 2003

Cactus Clyde Productions
PO Box 3624, St Francisville, LA 70775-3624
Tel: 225-245-5008
E-mail: cactusclyd@aol.com
Web Site: www.cclockwood.com
Key Personnel
Owner: C C Lockwood
Founded: 1971
Available for worldwide natural history assignments; specialize in swamps & coastal marshes; outdoor, wildlife, underwater subjects & astrophotography.
File Begins: 1971
Stock: 100,000 35mm B&W & color transparencies; 34,000 Nikon digital raw images
Membership(s): American Society of Media Photographers (ASMP); North American Nature Photography Association (NANPA)

Michael Carpenter Photography
7704 Carrleigh Pkwy, Springfield, VA 22152-1304
Tel: 703-644-9666
Web Site: www.michaelcarpenterphotography.com
Key Personnel
Photog: Michael Carpenter
Corporate & editorial photographer. Serves clients in the Washington, DC area & nationally providing editorial, architectural & industrial location photography.

Celtic Castle Photography
1319 Hardys Creek Rd, Jonesville, VA 24263
Tel: 276-346-3625
E-mail: celticastlephotography@gmail.com
Web Site: www.celticastlephotography.com
Key Personnel
Pres: Dr John William O'Connor Sr, PhD
Contact: Kirsten O'Connor
Founded: 1982
High fashion, stock, commercial, portraits, industrial, children, digital.
File Begins: 1975
Membership(s): American Society of Media Photographers (ASMP)

Dwight Cendrowski Photography LLC
2870 Easy St, Ann Arbor, MI 48104-6532
Tel: 734-330-5230
Web Site: www.cendrowski.com
Key Personnel
Owner & Photog: Dwight Cendrowski *E-mail:* dwight@cendrowski.com
Founded: 1978
Corporate & editorial photography for national clients. Stock image file including, corporate/industrial, healthcare, lifestyle, academia & travel.
File Begins: 1978
Membership(s): American Society of Media Photographers (ASMP)

Brandon Cole Marine Photography
4917 N Boeing Rd, Spokane Valley, WA 99206
Tel: 509-535-3489
E-mail: brandoncole@msn.com
Web Site: www.brandoncole.com
Marine photographer.
File Begins: 1991
Stock: 155,000 35mm transparencies & digital captures select HD digital file

Bob Daemmrich Photography Inc
1122 Colorado St, Suite 2202, Austin, TX 78701
Tel: 512-469-9700
Web Site: www.bobphoto.com
Key Personnel
Owner & Photog: Bob Daemmrich *E-mail:* bob@bobphoto.com
VP, Mktg: Janis Daemmrich *E-mail:* janis@bobphoto.com
Founded: 1985
Editorial & stock photography assignment work, multicultural images.
File Begins: 1984
Agent(s): Alamy, 49 Flatbush Ave, No 130, Brooklyn, NY 11217 *Toll Free Tel:* 866-671-7305 (US); 866-331-4914 (CN) *E-mail:* sales@alamy.com *Web Site:* www.alamy.com; Getty Images, 605 Fifth Ave S, Suite 400, Seattle, WA 98104 *Tel:* 206-925-5000 *Web Site:* www.gettyimages.com
Membership(s): American Society of Media Photographers (ASMP)

Kent Dannen
1997 Big Owl Rd, Allenspark, CO 80510
Tel: 303-747-2047 *Fax:* 303-747-2016
E-mail: kent.dannen@yahoo.com
Nature, outdoor recreation, travel, dogs, scenics & energy. Available for assignments.
Stock: 50,000 35mm & 120mm, B&W & color, HD digital
Agent(s): Photo Researchers Inc

DANPHOTO, LLC
408 E Rte 66, Flagstaff, AZ 86001
Tel: 928-774-0161
E-mail: danman@danphoto.com
Web Site: www.danphoto.com
Key Personnel
Owner & Photog: Daniel Snyder
Founded: 1988
Commercial people & product photography for advertising & editorial use.
Membership(s): American Society of Media Photographers (ASMP)

Dan Donovan Photography
15005 Valley Ridge Dr, St Louis, MO 63017
Tel: 314-712-0021
E-mail: dan@dandonovan.com
Web Site: www.dandonovan.com
Key Personnel
Owner & Photog: Dan Donovan
Founded: 1989
Photos of people for advertising, corporate, editorial & entertainment assignments. Stock photos of St Louis & fine art prints are also available.
Membership(s): American Society of Media Photographers (ASMP)

Steven Edson Photography
102 Florence Ave, Arlington, MA 02476
Tel: 617-504-4994
E-mail: steve@stevenedson.com
Web Site: stevenedson.com
Key Personnel
Owner & Photog: Steven Edson
Founded: 1988
Commercial & fine art photography. Direct from archives to clients.

Eligh Photographs
Victoria, BC V8R 4B8, Canada
Tel: 250-888-0027
Web Site: www.elighphoto.com; www.facebook.com/pages/category/Photographer/Eligh-Photographs-1550470288586165
Key Personnel
Owner: Gregg Eligh *E-mail:* gregg@elighphoto.com
Founded: 1978
Personality & author photographs for editorial, corporate & publishing.

& SUPPLIERS

Elk Photography
3163 Wisconsin St, Oakland, CA 94602
Tel: 510-531-7469 *Fax:* 510-531-7469
E-mail: cjelk@elkphotography.com
Web Site: www.elkphotography.com
Key Personnel
Owner & Photog: John Elk
Owner & Client Servs: Claude Marie Elk

Ron Elmy Photography
353 Eastern Ave, Suite 104, Toronto, ON M4M 1B7, Canada
Tel: 647-286-7833
E-mail: elmyphotovideo@gmail.com
Web Site: www.ronelmy.com
Founded: 1989
Specialize in jewelry, people, food, corporate, product, events & stock.

Envirovision
733 Cliff Dr, Laguna Beach, CA 92651
Mailing Address: PO Box 4136, Laguna Beach, CA 92652
Tel: 949-689-8794
E-mail: bfactor@beverlyfactor.com
Web Site: www.beverlyfactor.com
Key Personnel
Owner & Photog: Beverly Factor
Founded: 1990
Wildlife photography specializing in underwater stock library of over 10,000 images worldwide. Includes tropical islands & beaches, boating, sailboat racing, sunsets, underwater, wildlife, indigenous people, children, sports, worldwide, Africa to South Pacific & tropical destinations. Available for assignments.
Stock: 10,000 images
Membership(s): American Society of Media Photographers (ASMP)

Sigrid Estrada
902 Broadway, No 1610, New York, NY 10010
Tel: 212-673-4300
E-mail: sigrid@sigridestrada.com
Web Site: www.sigridestrada.com
Photography, portraits of authors & artists. B&W & color stock, also digital photography.
File Begins: 1978
Stock: 2 1/4 format; B&W & color, digital
Membership(s): American Society of Media Photographers (ASMP)

f-stop Fitzgerald Inc
88 James St, Rosendale, NY 12472
E-mail: fstopf@gmail.com
Key Personnel
CEO: Richard Minissali
Author photos, freelance photography, book-packaging, consulting.
Membership(s): American Book Producers Association (ABPA); Professional Photographers of America (PPA)

Lola Troy Fiur
360 E 65 St, Suite 17-A, New York, NY 10065
Tel: 646-247-9044 *Fax:* 212-861-1911
E-mail: ltfoto@yahoo.com
Web Site: www.ltfstudios.com
B&W & color; digital; flowers, scenic landscapes, food, nostalgia, mystery.
Stock: Digital, 35mm; B&W & color
Membership(s): National Association of Photoshop Professionals (NAPP); New York Women in Film & Television (NYWIFT)

Forer Inc
7881 SW 69 Ave, Miami, FL 33143
Tel: 305-495-0838
Web Site: www.forer.com
Key Personnel
Owner & Photog: Dan Forer *E-mail:* dan@forer.com
Founded: 1973
Architectural & interior design photography.
Membership(s): American Institute of Architects (AIA); American Society of Media Photographers (ASMP); International Interior Design Association (ITDA)

Foster Travel Publishing
1623 Martin Luther King Jr Way, Berkeley, CA 94709
Tel: 510-549-2202
Web Site: www.fostertravel.com; stockphotos.fostertravel.com
Key Personnel
Owner & Pres: Lee Foster *E-mail:* lee@fostertravel.com
Founded: 1972
Travel photography (emphasizing 250 worldwide locations, covering attractions, history & nature) especially California, the Western states, then worldwide destinations. Stock or assignment & writing/photography assignments, especially in Western USA (California), Mexico & Europe.
File Begins: 1975
Stock: 250,000 35mm color; 25,000 digital
Membership(s): American Society of Media Photographers (ASMP); Bay Area Independent Publishers Association (BAIPA); Bay Area Travel Writers; Society of American Travel Writers (SATW)

Fotosmith
3539 E 28 St, Tucson, AZ 85713
Tel: 520-882-2033
Web Site: www.jeffsmithusa.com
Key Personnel
Owner & Photog: Jeff Smith *E-mail:* jeffsmithusa@me.com

James Frank Photography Inc
PO Box 3523, Estes Park, CO 80517
Tel: 970-586-3418
E-mail: photos@jamesfrank.com
Web Site: www.jamesfrank.com
Key Personnel
Owner & Photog: James Frank
Founded: 1980
Fine art photography with over 40 years of experience. Specialize in nature & landscape with emphasis on Rocky Mountain National Park & the American West. Thousands of images available for licensing from Colorado & numerous travels.
Agent(s): Alamy; Stock Connection

Fresh Air Photo
152 Sand Valley Ct, Jonesborough, TN 37659
Tel: 423-612-2700
Web Site: www.freshairphoto.com
Key Personnel
Founder & Owner: Tom Raymond *E-mail:* tom@freshairphoto.com
Founded: 1983
All commercial.
File Begins: 2000
Stock: www.cgibackgrounds.com
Agent(s): Bill Messerly
Membership(s): American Society of Media Photographers (ASMP); American Society of Picture Professionals (ASPP)

Robert Fried Photography
610 Eldridge Ct, Novato, CA 94947
Tel: 415-898-6153 *Fax:* 415-897-0353
E-mail: rob@robertfriedphotography.com
Web Site: www.robertfriedphotography.com

PHOTOGRAPHERS

Key Personnel
Owner: Robert Fried
Photographic assignments worldwide for advertising, corporate & editorial clients. Specialize in travel/tourism industry (brochures, catalogs) & editorial markets (magazines, textbooks, religious publishers, calendars); stock photo files include coverage for agriculture, art, cities, ethnic groups, flora & fauna, industry, landmarks, religion, scenics, tourism, underwater.
File Begins: 1983
Stock: 300,000 35mm original color transparencies
Membership(s): American Society of Picture Professionals (ASPP); Society of American Travel Writers (SATW)

Bonnie Geller-Geld
2500 Johnson Ave, Apt 18N, Bronx, NY 10463
Tel: 347-275-4040
E-mail: gellergeldphoto@gmail.com
Web Site: bonniegellergeld.com
Portrait, landscape & documentary photography.
Membership(s): Professional Women Photographers (PWP)

Peter Glass Photography
15 Oakwood St, East Hartford, CT 06108
Tel: 860-528-8559 (off); 860-712-7098 (cell)
E-mail: peter@peterglass.com
Web Site: www.peterglass.com
Commercial photography; specialize in corporate, editorial, public relations & industrial photography.
Stock: 35mm B&W & color, digital

Jeff Gnass Photography™
3042 Nowell Ave, Juneau, AK 99801-1930
Mailing Address: PO Box 35415, Juneau, AK 99803-5415
Tel: 907-789-2002 *Fax:* 206-577-6419
E-mail: office@jeffgnass.com
Web Site: www.jeffgnass.com
Key Personnel
Pres: Jeff Gnass
Founded: 1978
Specialize in digital original & color transparency photography of natural landscapes & natural history for rights-managed commercial, advertising & editorial usage. Available for assignments & documentary projects worldwide. Stock photo library covers many North American places, themes & topics, including arctic, climate-change, clouds, coasts, deserts, environmental impact, flora, forests, geological formations, historic sites, mountains, national parks, Native American ruins, public land use, travel destinations & wilderness areas. Large libraries of Alaska, Hawaii & western US. International coverage of Canada, Patagonia region of Chile & Argentina, Iceland, Czechia, Slovakia, Austria, Australia, Singapore, England & Scotland. Photo coverage emphasizes public lands & travel destinations. Searchable database of stock photo coverage available online.
File Begins: 1976
Stock: 150,000 images, including 80,000 original color transparencies
Agent(s): Geolight™ Stock Images

Beryl Goldberg Photographer
309 W 109 St, Suite 4-F, New York, NY 10025
Tel: 212-222-8215
E-mail: berylgnyc@gmail.com
Web Site: www.berylgoldberg.net
Key Personnel
Owner & Photog: Beryl Goldberg
Assignment & stock photography: Africa, Bangladesh, China, Europe, Israel, Latin America & the US. Health international development families, children.

PHOTOGRAPHERS

File Begins: 1976
Stock: 60,000 35mm B&W & color & digital files

Gomsak Photography
10428 S Hall Dr, Charlotte, NC 28270
Web Site: www.gomsak.com
Key Personnel
Owner & Photog: Brian Gomsak *Tel:* 704-996-3816 (cell) *E-mail:* brian@gomsak.com
Founded: 1996
Membership(s): American Photographic Artists (APA)

Audrey Gottlieb
161 York St, Unit 21, York, ME 03909
Tel: 207-641-7490
E-mail: audreyphoto@gmail.com
Web Site: www.audreygottlieb.com
Founded: 1985
Photography, includes travel & documentary of Greece, Japan, France, UN Operation in Somalia, multicultural America, ethnic festivals, landscapes, citiscapes, seascapes, lighthouses & agricultural fairs in Maine, flowers & gardens, urban street life, New York City landmarks (Queens), etc. Photographer proficient in English, French, Spanish & Greek, accepts travel assignments.
File Begins: 1973
Stock: 1,000,000 35mm B&W & color digital images
Membership(s): American Photography Archives Group (APAG); American Society of Media Photographers (ASMP); American Society of Picture Professionals (ASPP); Professional Women Photographers (PWP); Society for Photographic Education (SPE); United Nations Photographic Society

Tom Graves Photography
400-A Clipper St, San Francisco, CA 94114
Tel: 415-550-7241
E-mail: tom@tomgraves.com
Web Site: www.tomgraves.com; www.twiceheroes.com
Authors' portraits, photo illustration, advertising photography.
File Begins: 1975
Stock: B&W & color
Membership(s): American Photographic Artists (APA); Bay Area Travel Writers; International Association of Business Communicators (IABC); USMC Combat Correspondents Association (USMCCCA)

Greg Johnston Photography
3021 San Jacinto Circle, Sanford, FL 32771
Tel: 305-258-7070
Web Site: www.gregjohnstonphotography.com
Key Personnel
Owner: Greg Johnston *E-mail:* greg@gregjohnston.com
Founded: 1984
Advertising, editorial, stock photography, lifestyle resort, hotel industry.
Agent(s): Danita Delimont; Getty Images; Stock Photography
Membership(s): American Photographic Artists (APA); American Society of Media Photographers (ASMP); Society of American Travel Writers (SATW); Stock Artists Alliance (SAA)

David M Grossman Photography
211 E Seventh St, Brooklyn, NY 11218
Tel: 718-438-5021
E-mail: david@grossmanphotos.com
Web Site: www.davidmgrossmanphotos.com
Key Personnel
Owner: David M Grossman

People photography: depicting the human situation birth through old age, photographic assignments, stock photo library, keyword searchable.
File Begins: 1975
Stock: Digital photography; fully digitized photo library

J S Grove Photography
166 Peace Ave, Tavernier, FL 33070
Tel: 305-393-2817
E-mail: grovejack509@gmail.com
Key Personnel
Photog & Marine Biologist: Jack Stein Grove
Founded: 1990
Membership(s): American Society of Media Photographers (ASMP)

Chris Hamilton Photography
704 Battersea Dr, St Augustine, FL 32095
Tel: 404-355-9411
Web Site: www.hamphoto.com
Key Personnel
Owner: Chris Hamilton *E-mail:* chris@hamphoto.com
Prodr & Rep: Rita Hamilton *E-mail:* rita@hamphoto.com
Founded: 1984
Commercial photography.
Membership(s): American Society of Media Photographers (ASMP)

Milton Heiberg Studios
Subsidiary of Tern Media LLC
1022 Empress Lane, Orlando, FL 32825-8249
Tel: 407-658-4869
E-mail: ternmedia@gmail.com
Web Site: www.miltonheiberg.com
Key Personnel
Owner & Pres: Milton Heiberg
Founded: 1970
Specialize in education, nature, especially birds (natural history), wildlife & environmental photography.
File Begins: 1970
Stock: 95,000 35mm, 4 x 5 & 2 1/4 B&W & color nature & wildlife, over 1,000,000 digital images

Diana Mara Henry
51 Carbonneau Dr, Suite 3, Newport, VT 05855
Tel: 802-334-7054
E-mail: dmh@dianamarahenry.com
Web Site: dianamarahenry.com
Founded: 1967
Traveling exhibits of: The First National Woman's Conference, Houston, 1977, One-room Schools & Schoolteachers of Vermont & New York, Vanishing Jews of Alsace & the Natzweiler-Struthof Concentration Camp, Pompadour-Its French National Stud Farm, People & Celebrities, Harvard College & lifestyles, 1965-1969, NYC-Society & Mores, 1969-1987, Malcolm Forbes balloon meets at the Chateau de Balleroy, Normandy, Carmel, CA, Hawaii, Bali, Kathmandu, Europe & the Caribbean. LIBEL, an exhibit of words & pictures that challenges the acceptance of photographs & captions as truth.
File Begins: 1967
Stock: 100,000 B&W & color

Michal Heron Photography
3806 Easton St, Sarasota, FL 34238
E-mail: michalheronphoto@gmail.com
Web Site: www.michalheron.com
Key Personnel
Owner: Ms Michal Heron
Photojournalism, assignments worldwide. All subjects for general editorial & corporate reportage. Specialize in Native American & Ap-

SERVICES

palachian peoples. Coverage in China, Japan, Mexico, Peru & Spain.
Stock: B&W, color & digital
Membership(s): American Society of Media Photographers (ASMP); American Society of Picture Professionals (ASPP)

Art Holeman Photography
4156 E Cathedral Rock Dr, Phoenix, AZ 85044
Tel: 602-290-7431 (cell)
E-mail: art@artholeman.com; artholeman@cox.net
Web Site: www.artholeman.com; www.fineartholeman.com
Key Personnel
Owner & Photog: Arthur A Holeman
E-mail: art@artholeman.com
Founded: 1986
B&W fine art.
Membership(s): American Society of Media Photographers (ASMP); Through Each Others Eyes (TEOE)

Hollenbeck Productions
13386 FM 2710, Lindale, TX 75771
Tel: 206-444-5314; 206-592-1800
Web Site: www.hollenbeckproductions.com; www.cliffscoolstuff.com
Key Personnel
Founder & Owner: Cliff Hollenbeck
E-mail: pixhot@aol.com; Nancy Hollenbeck
E-mail: cnimages@aol.com
Worldwide photography assignments & creation of image files: advertising, editorial & location, Alaska, Hawaii, Mexico, Far East, Mediterranean, South Pacific & Europe. Specialize in the creation of location, destination & corporation coffee table books. Samples available on request.

Tom Hopkins Studio
2121 Durham Rd, Madison, CT 06443
Tel: 203-350-0530
Web Site: www.tomhopkinsstudio.com
Key Personnel
Owner & Photog: Tom Hopkins
Specialize in fashion, food & travel.

David K Horowitz Studio Inc
920 Chestnut St, No 22, Philadelphia, PA 19107
Studio & location photography: books, catalogs, posters, advertising & architecture.

George H H Huey Photography Inc
382 W Butterfield Rd, Suite 115, Chino Valley, AZ 86323
Tel: 928-308-3460
Web Site: www.georgehhhuey.com
Key Personnel
Owner: George H H Huey *E-mail:* ghhhuey@gmail.com
Assignment & stock photography: landscapes, wildlife, travel, national parks & monuments, historic sites, environmental issues in US & Mexico. Includes Grand Canyon, Arizona, California, Colorado, Texas, New Mexico, Utah, Sonoran desert, Hawaii, Caribbean, all cactus, reptiles, flowers, prehistoric ruins & rock art. People engaged in activities with nature.
Stock: Digital

Richard Hutchings Photography LLC
11 White Well Dr, Rhinebeck, NY 12572
Tel: 914-715-7461
E-mail: richard@hutchingsphotography.com
Web Site: hutchingsphotography.com
Key Personnel
Owner: Richard Hutchings
Contact: Amy Hutchings
E-mail: amyhutchingscastings@gmail.com
Founded: 1969

Photography for the publishing industry, more specifically the educational publishing market. Also write & photograph nonfiction books for early readers. Extensive file of children, teens, families, education, multiethnic, diverse population.
File Begins: 1970
Agent(s): Getty; Photoeditinc.com; Photoresearchers.com

Iverson Science Photos
31 Boss Ave, Portsmouth, NH 03801
Tel: 603-433-8484 *Fax:* 603-433-8484
E-mail: iversonarts@gmail.com
Key Personnel
Owner & Photog: Bruce Iverson
Founded: 1980
Stock & assignment photomicrography, science & medical photographs. Light micrographs, scanning electron micrographs & transmission electron micrographs, in all subjects from anatomy to zoology.
File Begins: 1980
Stock: 10,000, 35mm, 4 x 5 color & B&W & digital

J Brough Schamp Photography
Baltimore, MD 21212
Tel: 443-996-5450 (cell)
Web Site: www.broughschampphotography.com
Key Personnel
Owner & Photog: J Brough Schamp
Founded: 1980
Specialize in architectural, location, environmental portraiture & aerial photography.
Membership(s): American Institute of Architects (AIA); American Society of Media Photographers (ASMP)

Michael Jacobs Photojournalism (MJP)
2105 Vista Oeste NW, Suite 3, No 2057, Albuquerque, NM 87120
Tel: 323-461-0240 *Toll Free Fax:* 866-563-9212
E-mail: michael.mjphoto@gmail.com
Web Site: www.mjphotogallery.com
Key Personnel
Owner: Michael Jacobs
Founded: 1970
Photo assignments accepted worldwide. Editorial, illustrative & general photography for publication. Proficiency in photographing Hollywood/the entertainment industry including production & session work. Public relations, cultural & social events, concerts, international travel (over 70 countries covered), children, annual reports & politics. Album & book covers. Feature films, television & videos.
File Begins: 1970
Stock: Over 2 million multi-format B&W, color & digital; over 1 million 35mm B&W & color

Kerrick James Photography
235 N 22 Place, Unit 560, Mesa, AZ 85213
Mailing Address: PO Box 30639, Mesa, AZ 85275
Tel: 602-276-3111
Web Site: www.kerrickjames.com; www.agpix.com/kerrickjames
Key Personnel
Owner & Photog: Kerrick James
 E-mail: kjames5@cox.net
Photographs from the American West & Pacific Rim for over 25 years as a travel journalist.
Stock: 450,000 digital images
Agent(s): ASAblanca; Getty Images
Membership(s): North American Travel Journalists Association (NATJA); Society of American Travel Writers (SATW); Through Each Others Eyes (TEOE)

John Johnston
1288 Southlyn Dr, Dayton, OH 45409
Tel: 937-681-4309
E-mail: jejphotos@gmail.com
Web Site: www.johnjohnston.co
Founded: 1999
Provide commercial, editorial, corporate, assignment, stock, travel, portrait, event & location photography.
Membership(s): National Press Photographers Association (NPPA)

Johnston Photography, see John Johnston

Lou Jones Studio
44 Breed St, Boston, MA 02128
Tel: 617-561-1194 *Fax:* 617-561-1196
E-mail: fotojones@aol.com
Web Site: www.fotojones.com
Key Personnel
Owner & Photog: Lou Jones
Founded: 1972
Commercial & advertising photography; in studio & on location; fine art; editorial.
File Begins: 1972
Agent(s): Zuma Press
Membership(s): American Society of Media Photographers (ASMP)

Wolfgang Kaehler Photography
723 Third St S, Kirkland, WA 98033
Tel: 425-803-0652
Web Site: www.facebook.com/wolfgang.kaehler
Key Personnel
Owner: Wolfgang Kaehler *E-mail:* wolfgang@phototours.us
Founded: 1977
Available for assignment; photo workshops; worldwide stock photography coverage, wildlife & travel.
File Begins: 1977
Stock: 560,000 digital files

Tom Keck Photos
13393 Landfair Rd, San Diego, CA 92130
Tel: 858-755-2975
E-mail: tomkeckphotos@gmail.com
Web Site: www.tomkeckphotos.com
Key Personnel
Owner & Photog: Tom Keck
Founded: 1963
Photojournalist for 50+ years; sports, surfing, travel, editorial. Includes photo stock of Cuba, Hawaii, Kenya & South Africa. Branch office in Laguna Beach.
Stock: ZUMA Press
Membership(s): American Society of Media Photographers (ASMP); National Press Photographers Association (NPPA); North American Nature Photography Association (NANPA)

Bruce Kluckhohn Photographer
2608 Webster Ave S, Minneapolis, MN 55416-1723
Tel: 612-929-6010
E-mail: bruce@bruceckphoto.com
Web Site: www.bruceckphoto.com
Key Personnel
Photog: Bruce Kluckhohn
Location people photography.

William Koechling Photography
1307 E Harrison Ave, Wheaton, IL 60187
Tel: 630-665-4379
E-mail: koechlingphoto@sbcglobal.net
Web Site: www.facebook.com/koechlingphoto; 500px.com/billkoechling
Key Personnel
Contact: William Koechling
Founded: 1973
Studio & location photography primarily for author/artist portraits; stock photography.

Agent(s): Glasshouse Images
Membership(s): American Society of Media Photographers (ASMP)

Dwight Kuhn
Dexter, ME 04930
E-mail: millacus77@yahoo.com
Web Site: www.kuhnphoto.net
Slides of natural history & biology subjects covering much of the animal & plant kingdom. Macrophotographs & detailed natural history coverage of difficult & small subjects. Biology photos including photomicrographs for textbook & reference uses. Gardening stock also included. Available for assignments.
Stock: 200,000 35mm color & digital images

Mary Langenfeld Photography
3817 Euclid Ave, Madison, WI 53711
Tel: 608-233-9938; 608-334-1375 (cell)
E-mail: madisonfoto@att.net
Web Site: www.langenfeld-photo.com
Founded: 1991
Photojournalist; assignment & stock photography; specialize in education, social issues, sports & agricultural.
File Begins: 1985
Stock: Digital files/B&W negatives
Membership(s): National Press Photographers Association (NPPA)

Jess Lee Photography LLC
13316 Skyview St, Nampa, ID 83686
Tel: 208-521-5170
Web Site: www.jessleephotos.com
Key Personnel
Owner: Jess Lee *E-mail:* jess@jessleephotos.com
Natural history, wildlife, scenics, stock & assignment, western lifestyle.
Stock: 200,000 color slides, digital images

Tom & Pat Leeson
PO Box 2498, Vancouver, WA 98668-2498
Tel: 360-256-0436
E-mail: office@leesonphoto.com
Web Site: www.leesonphoto.com; www.leesonphotoart.com
North American wildlife including eagles, bears, wolves & whales; travel Alaska, Western Canada & Pacific Northwest. African wildlife, elephants, pandas & tigers.
Stock: 14,000 digital images online, backed by over 100,000 transparencies

Steve Leonard Photography
825 W Gunnison St, Chicago, IL 60640-4267
Tel: 312-206-5344
E-mail: steve@steveleonardphoto.com
Web Site: www.steveleonardphoto.com
Founded: 1983
Location photography.
File Begins: 1985
Membership(s): American Society of Media Photographers (ASMP)

LOF Productions
121 Greenwich Rd, Suite 202, Charlotte, NC 28211
Mailing Address: PO Box 11758, Charlotte, NC 28220-1758
Tel: 704-375-8892 *Fax:* 704-375-6316
Web Site: www.lofproductions.com
Key Personnel
Mgr & Photog: John Daughtry
 E-mail: jdaughtry@lofproductions.com
Graphics & Design: Kyle Flory
Founded: 2001
Photography for business to business marketing & communications.

LTF Studios, see Lola Troy Fiur

PHOTOGRAPHERS

MagicLight Productions
4935 McConnell Ave, Suite 1, Marina del Rey, CA 90066
Tel: 310-283-8772 (cell)
Web Site: www.magiclight.com
Key Personnel
CEO & Photog: Robert Reiff *E-mail:* robert@magiclight.com
Founded: 1973
Commercial photography with complete studio. Specialize in food, health & fitness, architecture, fashion, books, travel, cars, women & men.
Membership(s): American Photographic Artists (APA); American Society of Media Photographers (ASMP)

Bruce McMillan
PO Box 85, Shapleigh, ME 04076-0085
Tel: 207-324-9453
E-mail: bruce@brucemcmillan.com
Web Site: www.brucemcmillan.com; theartofbruce.blogspot.com
Photo-illustrated books, book jackets; photo-illustrator/author of more than 45 children's books & 4 adult books; book designer.
Stock: Iceland & Maine, landscapes, scenic & islands

Susan Riva Miller-Alpine Photography
20415 150 Ave SE, Monroe, WA 98272
Tel: 206-679-0475
E-mail: susanrivamiller@hotmail.com
Key Personnel
Owner: Susan Riva Miller
Founded: 1960
Photo assignments & stock photos of aviation, ranching, how-to book illustrations, mountain, aircraft, snow avalanches, aerial photography & snow crystal photography.
File Begins: 1960
Stock: 35mm B&W & color prints, 4 x 5 transparencies, CDs

Clark James Mishler Photography
1815 School St, Calistoga, CA 94515
Tel: 907-351-7863
Web Site: www.mishlerphotos.com
Key Personnel
Owner & Photog: Clark James Mishler *E-mail:* clark@mishlerphotos.com
Founded: 1989
Freelance photographer.
Membership(s): American Society of Media Photographers (ASMP); National Press Photographers Association (NPPA)

Boyd Norton Photography
PO Box 2605, Evergreen, CO 80437-2605
Tel: 303-674-3009 *Fax:* 303-674-3650
Web Site: boydnorton.com; www.facebook.com/boyd.norton; thewildernessphotography.blogspot.com
Key Personnel
Pres: Boyd Norton
Founded: 1968
Stock photo & assignment services. Specialize in travel, adventure, remote areas, wilderness, wildlife, natural history, geography, cultures, cities, environmental & social issues; worldwide coverage. North America: Alaska, Rocky Mountains, Southwest, New England; Asia: Malaysia (Borneo), Indonesia (Bali, Komodo Island, Sumbawa), Siberia; Africa: Democratic Republic of the Congo, Botswana, Kenya, Tanzania, Zaire, Rwanda; South America: Ecuador, Peru, Venezuela & Chile; Antarctica. No research fees.
File Begins: 1966
Stock: 450,000 files
Membership(s): American Society of Media Photographers (ASMP); International League of Conservation Photographers (ILCP); North American Nature Photography Association (NANPA)

Phillip Norton
Subsidiary of County Photographer
4 Chapel St, Picton, ON K0K 2T0, Canada
Tel: 613-827-3214
E-mail: phil@philnorton.com
Web Site: countyphotographer.com; www.countyoutings.com
Founded: 1987
US-Canada issues, Quebec & Ontario Provinces, environment & travel, rural lifestyles. East & West Coast US, Canada, Central Europe & Mexico. Photos accompanied by text (award-winning author). Fluent French & English, web design, teach photojournalism, multimedia, audio & slideshows.
Stock: 100,000 35mm color transparencies & 500,000 digital

Dale O'Dell
1520 Eagle Point Dr, Prescott, AZ 86301
Tel: 928-541-0944
E-mail: dale@cybertrails.com
Web Site: www.dalephoto.com
Stock & assignment photography, digital imaging & author of photography related articles. Stock photography & illustration services specializing in conceptual photography & digital illustration emphasizing story-telling images over simple pictures of things. Stock photographic files also include a wide range of subjects: landscapes, industry, high-tech, medical, computer tech, still life & travel.
Stock: Digital, B&W & color

Arleen Olson Photography
Redway, CA 95560
Tel: 707-923-1974
Web Site: arleenolsonphotography.com
Key Personnel
Photog & Publr: Arleen Olson *E-mail:* aolson@redwoodcoast.net
People, animals, events, landscapes, plants & foreign travel. Stock list available. Photographer & publisher of "Humboldt Wild" photography book.
File Begins: 1970
Stock: Over 20,000 35mm color slides, 35mm & medium format B&W & color prints & digital
Membership(s): National Association of Photoshop Professionals (NAPP); North American Nature Photography Association (NANPA)

Olson Photographic LLC
232 Hunter's Trail, Madison, CT 06443
Tel: 203-245-3752 *Fax:* 203-245-3752
E-mail: info@olsonphotographic.com
Web Site: www.olsonphotographic.com
Key Personnel
Partner: John Olson *E-mail:* john@olsonphotographic.com
Founded: 1999
Photographically capture the essence of interior spaces, exterior structures & designed landscapes. We bring extensive photographic experience & creativity to each assignment. Clients have used our award-winning images to gain industry recognition & build their client bases. In addition to being used in professional portfolios, countless numbers of our images have appeared in major consumer & industrial periodicals, books & in manufacturers' marketing & promotional materials. From secluded country estates to Manhattan townhouses & from high-end automobile dealerships to local bistros, we professionally capture award winning designs with the highest expertise & professional equipment.
File Begins: 2004

SERVICES

Membership(s): American Society of Media Photographers (ASMP); Association of Independent Architectural Photographers (AIAP); IAAP

Danuta Otfinowski
625 "E" St NE, Washington, DC 20002
Tel: 202-546-5646 (studio); 202-744-0333 (cell)
E-mail: danuta@danuta.us
Web Site: www.danuta.us
Founded: 1985
Photo journalist/photographer, events, environmental portraits.

Douglas Peebles Photography
44-527A Kaneohe Bay Dr, Kaneohe, HI 96744
Tel: 808-342-7930
E-mail: douglas@douglaspeebles.com
Web Site: www.douglaspeebles.com
Editorial photography & stock photo file, especially of Hawaii, Mexico, South Pacific & Alaska.

Photographix
1171 Pauline Blvd, Ann Arbor, MI 48103-5319
Tel: 734-476-2068
Key Personnel
Owner: Lance K Burghardt *E-mail:* lkburghardt@comcast.net
Commercial & advertising photography; process or graphic arts photography, copy photography, scientific & technical photography.
Membership(s): American Society of Media Photographers (ASMP)

Photography for Communication & Commerce
3931 S Spruce St, Suite 200, Denver, CO 80237-2152
Tel: 303-829-5678
Web Site: www.howardpaulphotography.com
Key Personnel
Photog: Howard Michael Paul *E-mail:* howard@howardpaulphotography.com
Founded: 1985
Specialize in stock & assignment photography for emergency service & public safety personnel & operations. Specialized stock file of mountain search & rescue operations, fire departments & fire scenes, emergency medical services, Haz-Mat, Chem-Bioterrorism & all areas of rescue operations.
File Begins: 1985
Stock: 16,000 35mm color
Membership(s): American Society of Media Photographers (ASMP)

Geoff Reed Photography
7640 N 22 St, Phoenix, AZ 85020
Tel: 602-432-9065
E-mail: geoff@geoffreedphoto.com
Web Site: www.geoffreedphoto.com
Key Personnel
Owner & Photog: Geoff Reed
Founded: 1989
Business to business corporate location portraiture & travel/outdoor adventure photography.
Membership(s): American Society of Media Photographers (ASMP); Through Each Others Eyes (TEOE)

Sarah Putnam
320 Brookline St, Cambridge, MA 02139
Tel: 617-596-5910
E-mail: sarah@sarahputnam.com
Web Site: www.sarahputnam.com
Editorial & corporate photography, stock, author's portraits, digital & film, multimedia & video.
Stock: B&W & color
Membership(s): National Press Photographers Association (NPPA)

& SUPPLIERS

Laszlo Regos Photography
30601 Woodstream Dr, Farmington Hills, MI 48334
Tel: 248-398-3631
E-mail: laszlo@laszlofoto.com
Web Site: www.laszlofoto.com
Key Personnel
Photog: Laszlo Regos *Tel:* 248-421-1222 (cell)
Founded: 1989
Architectural photographer specializing in retail spaces. Extensive stock library of European cities, Detroit & synagogue architecture.

Carol Robinson Photography
2012 Aldrich Place, Downers Grove, IL 60516
Tel: 630-222-6286
E-mail: goodpix@aol.com
Web Site: carolrobinsonphoto.webs.com; goodpix.zenfolio.com
Founded: 1989
Creative photography with an emphasis on nature & cemeteries.
Stock: Digital
Membership(s): National Association of Photoshop Professionals (NAPP)

Ken Ross Photography
PO Box 4517, Scottsdale, AZ 85261
Tel: 602-319-2974
E-mail: kenrossaz@yahoo.com
Web Site: www.kenrossphotography.com
Key Personnel
Owner & Photog: Ken Ross
Founded: 1985
Commercial/editorial photography, shooting in both Phoenix & Los Angeles. Specialize in travel/location, people & corporate photography.
Membership(s): Through Each Others Eyes (TEOE)

Victoria Roza Research
2454 Adams Ave, San Diego, CA 92116
Tel: 619-295-8082
E-mail: victoriaproza@gmail.com
Photography & photo research.

Sargent Architectural Photography
801 S Olive Ave, Suite 107, West Palm Beach, FL 33401
Tel: 561-881-8887
E-mail: info@sargentphoto.com
Web Site: www.sargentphoto.com
Key Personnel
Owner & Photog: Mr Kim Sargent
Photog: Nick Sargent; Tyler Sargent
Founded: 1987
Commercial photography. Specialize in interiors & architecture.

Carl Schreier
c/o Homestead Publishing & Book Design, Box 193, Moose, WY 83012-0193
Tel: 307-733-6248
Photography & writing assignments for the western states. Specialize in wilderness, travel, nature, national parks, environment & science. Stock photos & historical photographs also available; 80,000 historical Yellowstone & Grand Teton, Glacier National Park B&W photographs. The largest private collection. Search for any period or topic of historical photographs.
Stock: 500,000 35mm, 6 x 7 & 4 x 5, 95% color transparencies & B&W prints, digital, electronic

Cosimo Scianna, Photographer
23407 Milano Ct, Boca Raton, FL 33433
Tel: 917-763-2927
E-mail: cosimoscianna@mac.com
Web Site: www.cosimoscianna.com
Key Personnel
Photog: Cosimo Scianna
Exec Prodr & Contact: Irene Scianna
 E-mail: irenescianna@mac.com
Founded: 1982
Membership(s): American Society of Media Photographers (ASMP); Directors Guild of America (DGA); Society of Illustrators

Seldon Ink Travel Writing & Photography
1513 Riverside Dr, Beaufort, SC 29902
Tel: 910-274-8070
Web Site: www.seldonink.com
Key Personnel
Co-Owner: Cele Seldon *E-mail:* cele@seldonink.com; Lynn Seldon *E-mail:* lynn@seldonink.com
Founded: 1986
Travel writing & photography.
File Begins: 1986
Stock: 200,000
Membership(s): Society of American Travel Writers (SATW)

John Sexton Photography
PO Box 30, Carmel Valley, CA 93924
Tel: 831-659-3130 *Fax:* 831-659-5509
E-mail: info@johnsexton.com
Web Site: www.johnsexton.com
Key Personnel
Owner & Photog: John Sexton
Assoc Dir: Anne Larsen
Founded: 1974
Fine art photography, stock photography.
Membership(s): American Society of Media Photographers (ASMP); North American Nature Photography Association (NANPA)

Ron Sherman Photography
340 Spring Creek Rd, Roswell, GA 30075
Tel: 770-355-8700 (cell)
E-mail: ronsphoto@live.com
Web Site: www.ronsherman.com
Founded: 1971
Location photography, stock photo library & computer imaging. Extensive coverage of Atlanta & Georgia. Archives includes corporate & industrial, college & university, politics, personalities, sports, nature & southeast cities & locations.
File Begins: 1971
Stock: Over 500,000 color & B&W images
Membership(s): American Photographic Artists (APA); American Society of Media Photographers (ASMP)

Frank Siteman Photography
136 Pond St, Winchester, MA 01890
Tel: 781-729-3747
E-mail: frank@franksiteman.com
Web Site: www.franksiteman.com
Advertising & corporate photography; New England scenics & lifestyle.
Stock: 200,000 35mm color transparencies of select stock & digital extensive files
Membership(s): American Society of Media Photographers (ASMP); American Society of Picture Professionals (ASPP); Photographic Resource Center (PRC)

Todd Tarbox
330 Oakhurst Lane, Colorado Springs, CO 80906
Tel: 719-579-9110
E-mail: t_tarbox@msn.com
Key Personnel
Contact: Shirley Tarbox
Founded: 1975
Specialize in people around the world; available for location shooting.

PHOTOGRAPHERS

File Begins: 1965
Stock: B&W & color

Stephen Trimble: Words & Photographs
70 W Apricot Ave, Salt Lake City, UT 84103
Tel: 801-819-2448
E-mail: steve@stephentrimble.net
Web Site: www.stephentrimble.net
Founded: 1970
Editorial photographer & writer with 25 books published. Stock includes Arizona & New Mexico Native people; Pueblo pottery. Wilderness, landscapes, parks, nature, geology: Utah, the Southwest, Rockies, Great Basin, California, Great Plains & Hawaii. Travel, people, architecture: New England, Southeast Asia, Mexico, Ecuador, Galapagos, Guatemala, Cuba, Egypt, France (Provence), Italy (Tuscany) & Spain. Assignments accepted.
Stock: 40,000 35mm & 6 x 7 color transparencies, most scanned, plus many years of digital files

Alvis Upitis Photography
Austin, TX 78701
Tel: 808-937-3173 (cell)
Web Site: www.alvisupitis.com
Image licensing & prints.
Membership(s): American Society of Media Photographers (ASMP)

Visual Pursuit
168 W 86 St, New York, NY 10024
Tel: 212-362-8234
Key Personnel
Owner: Joan Menschenfreund
 E-mail: joanmensch3@aol.com
Founded: 1980
Formerly with *Time Magazine* & *Time For Kids Magazine* staff. Experienced picture editor offers complete visual research & consulting service for all media; Subject specialties: history, current events, art, culture, personalities, travel; wide knowledge of sources; detail & deadline oriented.
Membership(s): American Society of Picture Professionals (ASPP)

Nancy Warner Photographer
Division of Warner-Cotter Co
10 Vinton Ct, San Francisco, CA 94108-2407
Tel: 415-298-0027
Web Site: www.warnerphoto.com
Key Personnel
Owner: Nancy Warner *E-mail:* nancy.warner@gmail.com
Founded: 1980
Portraits - corporate, author or special assignment. Studio or location.

Patrick J Watson
23 Alden Rd, Poughkeepsie, NY 12603
Tel: 845-475-8654
E-mail: info@patrickjwatson.com
Web Site: www.patrickjwatson.com
Founded: 1980
Production, research & management of media for healthcare publishers since 1985.

Jim West Photography
4875 Three Mile Dr, Detroit, MI 48224
E-mail: jim@jimwestphoto.com
Web Site: www.jimwestphoto.com
Key Personnel
Owner & Photog: Jim West
Founded: 1980
Stock & assignment photography, specializing in labor & social issues.
File Begins: 1980
Agent(s): Alamy Images; Science Photo Library; Zuma Press

PHOTOGRAPHERS

Membership(s): American Society of Media Photographers (ASMP); International Labor Communications Association (ILCA); National Press Photographers Association (NPPA)

Chuck Wyrostok
230 Griffith Run Rd, Spencer, WV 25276
Tel: 304-927-2978
E-mail: wyro@appalight.com
Web Site: www.appalight.com
Founded: 1959
Editorial & commercial photography & writing assignments & stock; covering regional, national & international; based near Charleston, WV.
File Begins: 1960
Stock: 22,000 color; 15,000 B&W

Stock Photo Agencies

This section includes agencies whose stock photo files represent the work of many photographers. Individual photographers who maintain and sell their own files of stock and assignment photos are listed in **Photographers**.

Animals Animals/Earth Scenes
17 Railroad Ave, Chatham, NY 12037
Tel: 518-392-5500 *Toll Free Tel:* 800-392-5503
E-mail: info@animalsanimals.com; sales@animalsanimals.com
Web Site: www.animalsanimals.com
Founded: 1976
Comprehensive collection represents entire animal kingdom as well as travel, landscapes & other environmental themes.
File Begins: 1971
Stock: 1 million images
Availability: Web
Membership(s): Digital Media Licensing Association (DMLA)

Anthro-Photo File
133 Washington St, Belmont, MA 02478
Tel: 617-484-6490 *Fax:* 617-484-6490
Web Site: www.anthrophotofile.com
Key Personnel
Image Procurement, Pricing, Billing & Res: Claire DeVore *E-mail:* devoreanthro@gmail.com
Founded: 1970
Specialize in anthropology & behavioral biology.
File Begins: 1934
Stock: 2,018
Availability: Mail & e-mail

AP Images
Division of Associated Press (AP)
200 Liberty St, New York, NY 10281
Toll Free Tel: 844-777-2006
E-mail: info@ap.org
Web Site: newsroom.ap.org/editorial-photos-videos/home
Editorial, sports & entertainment photography, online photo archive, creative stock photos, graphics & interactives.
Stock: 30 million B&W & color
Availability: Online

AppaLight
230 Griffith Run, Spencer, WV 25276
Tel: 304-932-2992
Web Site: www.appalight.com
Key Personnel
Owner & Dir: Chuck Wyrostok *E-mail:* wyro@appalight.com
Founded: 1988
Photo library with emphasis on the people, natural history, culture, commerce, flora, fauna & travel destinations of the Appalachian Mountain region & Eastern Shore of the US.
Number of Photographers Represented: 2
File Begins: 1960
Stock: 40,000 color; 20,000 B&W
Availability: E-mail, walk-in, mail & phone
Restrictions: Holding fees & some research fees may apply

Art Resource Inc
65 Bleeker St, 12th fl, New York, NY 10012
Tel: 212-505-8700 *Toll Free Tel:* 888-505-8666
Fax: 212-505-2053
E-mail: requests@artres.com
Web Site: www.artres.com
Key Personnel
Founder & Pres: Ted Feder
Gen Mgr: Michael Slade *E-mail:* mslade@artres.com
Founded: 1968
Art Resource functions as the official rights & permissions bureau for approximately 200 of the world's major museums & collections including the Metropolitan Museum of Art, Los Angeles County Museum of Art, The National Portrait Gallery, the Smithsonian American Art Museum, the Pierpont Morgan Library, the Jewish Museum of New York, the Newark Museum, the Tate Gallery of London, National Gallery London, Albright-Knox Art Gallery, New York Public Library & Wadsworth Atheneum Art Museum. Also represents a number of major European archives of art & architecture & has a very extensive holdings of works of art from major European museums & world monuments.
Stock: 3 million transparencies & B&W photographs
Availability: Mail, phone, fax & e-mail

Daniel H Bailey - Outdoor/Adventure Photography
3535 E 19 Ave, Anchorage, AK 99508
Tel: 970-484-1632
E-mail: dan@danbaileyphoto.com
Web Site: danbaileyphoto.com
Founded: 1996
Adventure & outdoor photography based in Alaska.
Stock: 20,000
Availability: Order by phone, e-mail or web site

Black Star Publishing Co Inc
333 Mamaroneck Ave, Suite 175, White Plains, NY 10605
Tel: 212-679-3288
Web Site: www.blackstar.com
Founded: 1935
Photojournalism, corporate, editorial & stock photography.
Number of Photographers Represented: 350
Stock: 3 million color transparencies & 1 million B&W prints
Availability: Phone & online

Camerique Inc International
164 Regency Dr, Eagleville, PA 19403
Tel: 610-272-4000 *Fax:* 610-272-4000 (call or e-mail first)
E-mail: info@camerique.com
Web Site: www.camerique.com
Key Personnel
Pres: Christopher C Johnson
Founded: 1972
Photos on all topics except news & personalities. Ask for free picture search.
Number of Photographers Represented: 300
Stock: 600,000 B&W & color
Availability: Mail & phone
Restrictions: As licensed for use

The Canadian Press Images
Division of The Canadian Press/La Presse Canadienne
60 Adelaide St E, Suite 1200, Toronto, ON M5C 3E4, Canada
Tel: 416-507-2198 (photo archives)
Toll Free Tel: 866-599-0599
E-mail: info@cpimages.com
Web Site: www.cpimages.com; www.thecanadianpress.com
Founded: 1917
National news, picture & broadcast wire, photo assignment service & photo archive.
Number of Photographers Represented: 500
File Begins: 1840
Availability: Online

ChinaStock/WorldViews
Division of Dennis Cox LLC
2506 Country Village, Ann Arbor, MI 48103-6500
Tel: 734-680-4660
E-mail: decoxphoto@gmail.com
Web Site: www.denniscox.com
Key Personnel
Pres: Dennis Cox
Founded: 1978
Specialize in stock & historical photos of China by American & Chinese photographers & world travel.
Number of Photographers Represented: 15
Stock: 400,000 color
Availability: Phone & e-mail

ClassicStock.com/Robertstock.com
Division of H Armstrong Roberts Inc
4203 Locust St, Philadelphia, PA 19104
Tel: 215-386-6300 *Toll Free Tel:* 800-786-6300
Toll Free Fax: 800-786-1920
E-mail: sales@classicstock.com; info@classicstock.com; info@robertstock.com
Web Site: www.classicstock.com; www.robertstock.com
Key Personnel
Pres: Bob Roberts
Mgr: Roberta Groves *E-mail:* robertag@classicstock.com
Vintage stock photos for editorial & advertising illustration.
Number of Photographers Represented: 200
File Begins: 1920
Stock: All formats, 2,000,000 B&W & 590,000 color with some earlier illustrations prior to 1920
Availability: Walk-in, mail, phone & web site
Membership(s): Digital Media Licensing Association (DMLA)

CP Images, see The Canadian Press Images

Davis Art Images
Division of Davis Publications Inc
50 Portland St, Worcester, MA 01608
Tel: 508-754-7201 *Toll Free Tel:* 800-533-2847
Fax: 508-753-3834
E-mail: das@davisart.com; contactus@davisart.com
Web Site: www.davisart.com
Key Personnel
Pres: Julian Davis Wade
Curator, Images: Karl Cole *Tel:* 508-754-7201 ext 1745 *E-mail:* kcole@davisart.com
Assoc Curator: Lydia Keene-Kendrick *E-mail:* lkeenekendrick@davisart.com
Founded: 1901
Produce digital images of art & architecture from ancient to contemporary from both old & new worlds, also images on commission from many

STOCK PHOTO AGENCIES

major American museums. Represent 50 museums.
Stock: 20,000 digital images
Availability: Web site

Danita Delimont Stock Photography
4911 Somerset Dr SE, Bellevue, WA 98006
Tel: 425-562-1543
Web Site: www.danitadelimont.com
Key Personnel
CEO: Danita Delimont *E-mail:* danita@danitadelimont.com
CTO: Dave Herbig *E-mail:* dherbig@danitadelimont.com
Founded: 1982
Photo agency. Travel destination specialist, worldwide travel, culture, nature & wildlife. Wall decor specialist.
Number of Photographers Represented: 300
File Begins: 2000
Stock: 1.3 million images
Availability: Online downloads
Membership(s): American Society of Picture Professionals (ASPP); Digital Media Licensing Association (DMLA); North American Nature Photography Association (NANPA)

Diosphere Ltd, see Medical Images

eFootage LLC
530 S Lake Ave, Suite 450, Pasadena, CA 91101
Tel: 626-395-9593
E-mail: info@efootage.com
Web Site: www.efootage.com
Key Personnel
Pres: Paul Lisy
Extensive film & video stockshot library. US/Canada & world stockshot film & video from 1896 to present. 20,000 hours film & video, all formats.
Number of Photographers Represented: 32
File Begins: 1896
Stock: B&W & color, 16mm & 35mm; video, all formats, 22,000 hours
Availability: Mail & phone
Restrictions: Payment

Esto Photographics Inc
36 Waverly Ave, Brooklyn, NY 11205
Tel: 212-505-5454
E-mail: sales@esto.com; assignments@esto.com
Web Site: estostock.com
Key Personnel
Agent: David La Spina *E-mail:* david@esto.com; Alex Nelson *E-mail:* alex@esto.com
Advisor: Erica Stoller *E-mail:* erica@esto.com
Stock photographs of high modern & contemporary architecture & design.
Number of Photographers Represented: 9
Availability: Mail, phone, e-mail & web site

eStock Photo
Long Island City, NY 11101
Tel: 212-689-5580 *Toll Free Tel:* 800-284-3399
E-mail: sales@estockphoto.com; info@estockphoto.com
Web Site: www.estockphoto.com
World travel, lifestyle, nature, landscapes, animals, food & drink.
Number of Photographers Represented: 50
Stock: Over 500,000

FILM Archives Inc
35 W 35 St, Suite 904, New York, NY 10001-2238
Tel: 212-696-2616
E-mail: info@filmarchivesonline.com
Web Site: www.filmarchivesonline.com
Key Personnel
Founding Partner & Pres: Mark Trost

Founded: 1986
Vintage & contemporary stock footage (archival). No photographs.

Foster Travel Publishing
1623 Martin Luther King Jr Way, Berkeley, CA 94709
Tel: 510-549-2202
Web Site: www.fostertravel.com; stockphotos.fostertravel.com
Key Personnel
Owner & Pres: Lee Foster *E-mail:* lee@fostertravel.com
Founded: 1972
Extensive stock photo files of CA & the West, Mexico & 50 other foreign countries. Total of 250 travel destinations worldwide.
Number of Photographers Represented: 1
File Begins: 1975
Stock: 250,000 35mm color. 25,000 stock photos also available online on two web sites
Availability: Walk-in, mail, phone & web site
Membership(s): American Society of Media Photographers (ASMP); Bay Area Independent Publishers Association (BAIPA); Bay Area Travel Writers; Society of American Travel Writers (SATW)

Fundamental Photographs
210 Forsyth St, Suite 2, New York, NY 10002
Tel: 212-473-5770
E-mail: mail@fphoto.com
Web Site: www.fphoto.com
Key Personnel
Partner: Richard Megna; Kip Peticolas
Founded: 1979
Photographic studio with the background & expertise to transform difficult science specs into visually exciting illustrations. Our specialized collection includes science illustration, chemistry principles, physics, optics, magnetism, earth science & stroboscopic images. Offer a specialized stock library of over 40,000 fully-captioned images, with detailed information on our subjects. We can also shoot photos on request.
Number of Photographers Represented: 40
File Begins: 1979
Stock: 40,000 digital files
Availability: Upon request, e-mail, phone & mail. Visit web site to search library
Membership(s): American Society of Picture Professionals (ASPP)

Getty Images Inc
605 Fifth Ave S, Suite 400, Seattle, WA 98104
Tel: 206-925-5000 *Toll Free Tel:* 800-IMAGERY (462-4379); 888-888-5889
Web Site: www.gettyimages.com; www.gettyimages.com/customer-support; engage.gettyimages.com/media-inquiries
Key Personnel
CEO: Craig Peters
CEO, Unsplash: Mikael Cho
CFO: Jennifer Leyden
CTO: Nate Gandert
Chief Mktg & Revenue Offr: Gene Foca
Chief People Offr: Lizanne Vaughan
Chief Prod Offr: Grant Farhall
SVP & Gen Coun: Kjelti Kellough
SVP & Chief of Staff: Michael Teaster
SVP, Content: Ken Mainardis
SVP, Creative Content: Andrew Saunders
SVP, E-Commerce: Daine Weston
SVP, Strategic Devt: Peter Orlowsky
VP, Cust Serv: Matthew J "MJ" Richards
VP, Cust Success: Guy Thorneloe
VP, Sales (Americas): Katie Calhoun
VP, Sales (APAC): Mike Harris
VP, Sales (EMEA): Ken Levernz
VP, Sales Enablement & Opers: Rick Thompson
Founded: 1995

SERVICES

Preeminent global visual content creator & marketplace. Through Getty Images, iStock & Unsplash, we offer a full range of content solutions to meet the needs of any customer, no matter their size, around the globe. Collection of high-quality creative content (imagery & video) for use in advertising, design & editorial. Visual content includes scenes of the US & world, sports, science, technology, business, industry, natural history, human interest, people/lifestyles, animals/wildlife, special effects, etc. B&W includes contemporary images & one of the largest & oldest privately held archives globally dating back to the 1800s. Over 8-10 million news assets added each quarter. Provides a depth, breadth & quality of editorial coverage that is unmatched. From red carpet events to football stadiums to conflict zones & beyond, each year we represent more than 160,000 news, sport & entertainment events around the globe.
Number of Photographers Represented: 115
Stock: 520 million in total assets; over 516,000 contributors
Branch Office(s)
6300 Wilshire Blvd, 16th fl, Los Angeles, CA 90048 *Tel:* 323-202-4200
55 E Monroe St, 17th fl, Chicago, IL 60603 *Tel:* 312-855-0055
195 Broadway, 10th fl, New York, NY 10007 *Tel:* 646-613-4000
Enrique Butty 275 Capital Federal, C1001AFA Buenos Aires, Argentina *Tel:* (011) 59842872
182-186 Blues Point Rd, Level 6, McMahons Point, Sydney, NSW 2060, Australia *Tel:* (02) 9004 2200
LocalMotive Crossing, 1240 20 Ave SE, 3rd fl, Calgary, AB T2G 1M8, Canada *Tel:* 403-265-3062
Unsplash, 5th fl, 400 McGill, Montreal, QC H2Y 2G1, Canada
No 48 Wangjing Xilu, Rm 12A01, Bldg 5, Chaoyang District, Beijing 100102, China *Tel:* (010) 8477 5185
Morning, Bureau 203, 34 rue Laffitte, 75009 Paris, France *Tel:* 01 55 33 66 00
Auenstr 5, 80469 Munich, Germany *Tel:* (089) 20 24 06 0
Off 25, 6/F Luk Kwok Ctr, 72 Gloucester Rd, Wan Chai, Hong Kong *Tel:* 2832 0900
Vaswani Chambers, 2nd fl 264-265, Dr Annie Besant Rd, Worli, Mumbai 400 030, India *Tel:* (022) 40734848
The Herbert Bldg, 1st fl, The Park, Carrickmines, Dublin 18 K8Y4, Ireland *Tel:* (01) 2462700
Via Sant Maria Valle 3, 2012 Milan MI, Italy *Tel:* (02) 36 02 1299
Jingumae Tower Bldg, Level 14, 1-5-8 Jingumae, Shibuya-ku, Tokyo 150-0001, Japan *Tel:* (050) 1790-3930
Varsovia 36, Piso 12 (1202), Colonia Juarez, Delegacion Cuauhtemoc, 06600 Mexico, CDMX, Mexico *Tel:* (0155) 41720159
Generator Level, 10/11 Britomart Place, Auckland CBD, Auckland 1010, New Zealand *Tel:* 0800 462 431
Concept Communications, Oscars Gate 30, 0352 Oslo, Norway *Tel:* 90 87 14 59
120 Robinson Rd, Off S1202, Singapore 068913, Singapore *Tel:* 6410 3300
Lexington, Paseo de la Castellana no 79, Plantas 4, 6, 7 & 8, 28046 Madrid, Spain *Tel:* 91 787 09 00
G Tower, Level 33, 9 Rama Rd, Huaykwang, Bangkok 10310, Thailand *Tel:* (02) 026 0745
Kolektif House, Esentepe Mah Talatpasa Caddesi, Harman Sokak No 5, Levent, Sisli, 34393 Istanbul, Turkey *Tel:* (0850) 441 0939
DSC Tower, Unit 601, Dubai Studio City, Dubai, United Arab Emirates *Tel:* (04) 597-3710
Duo, 6th fl S, 280 Bishopsgate, London EC2M 4AG, United Kingdom

STOCK PHOTO AGENCIES & SUPPLIERS

Glasshouse Images
161 W 15 St, Suite 1-C, New York, NY 10011
Tel: 646-256-1999 (res queries only)
E-mail: agency@glasshouseimages.com
(collection queries only)
Web Site: glasshouseimages.com
Founded: 2002
Dedicated to difference. License images to creatives worldwide. Specialize in model-released RM & RF contemporary & historical/vintage stock images. Accept only the most inspired & inspiring images with a clear commercial spark. We look for classic combination with fresh vision.
Number of Photographers Represented: 100
Membership(s): American Photographic Artists (APA); American Society of Media Photographers (ASMP); American Society of Picture Professionals (ASPP); Digital Media Licensing Association (DMLA); Young Photographers Alliance (YPA)

Globe Entertainment & Media Corp
8500 Beverly Blvd, Suite 683, Los Angeles, CA 90048
Web Site: www.globecorp.co
Key Personnel
CEO: Klaus Moeller
Founded: 1938
Celebrity & historic photography. Custodians of famous archives including the Globe Photo Agency, Movie Star News & the Frank Worth Archive.
Stock: 20 million B&W & color
Availability: Online

Granger - Historical Picture Archive
244 Fifth Ave, Suite 2110, New York, NY 10001
Tel: 212-447-1789 *Fax:* 212-447-1492
E-mail: info@granger.com; research@granger.com
Web Site: www.granger.com
Founded: 1964
Convenient & reliable source for images from prehistoric times through the recent past. Images are available for licensing for professional use. Holdings have grown to encompass millions of engravings, photographs, lithographs & many other forms of illustration. Web site offers instant access to the vast majority of our images, each meticulously keyworded & accurately captioned. In addition to this vast online collection, our archive contains thousands of undigitized images & we represent the collections of a number of institutions & photographers. Any one of our highly-skilled & knowledgeable researchers would be happy to assist you with your search. Granger offers a number of digital services, including custom scans, retouching & custom colorization. For education use, visit GrangerAcademic.com. For personal use, visit GrangerArtonDemand.com.
File Begins: 23,000 BC
Stock: 6,000,000 B&W & 1,000,000 color
Availability: Online
Membership(s): American Society of Picture Professionals (ASPP); Coordination of European Picture Agencies Press Stock Heritage (CEPIC); Digital Media Licensing Association (DMLA)

Grant Heilman Photography Inc
506 W Lincoln Ave, Lititz, PA 17543
Mailing Address: PO Box 317, Lititz, PA 17543
Tel: 717-626-0296 *Toll Free Tel:* 800-622-2046
Fax: 717-626-0971
E-mail: info@heilmanphoto.com
Web Site: www.heilmanphoto.com
Key Personnel
Pres & CEO: Sonia Shaner Wasco *E-mail:* sw@heilmanphoto.com
Founded: 1948
The world's most complete & up-to-date library of American agriculture imagery. Extensive file coverage in natural science, horticulture, wildlife & landscapes. Also featuring the boutique PhotoNetwork collection of travel & lifestyle imagery. Superior quality digital files. A major supplier to the editorial & advertising markets & to textbooks, encyclopedias, magazines, greeting cards & posters. Complete & thorough captions & sales histories; immediate delivery & downloads. Call or e-mail for more information. A fully rights managed image collection with a price for every category.
Number of Photographers Represented: 150
Stock: Over 1,000,000 images with a large historical B&W collection
Availability: Mail, phone, e-mail
Membership(s): American Agricultural Editors' Association (AAEA); American Society of Media Photographers (ASMP); American Society of Picture Professionals (ASPP); Digital Media Licensing Association (DMLA); NAMA; North American Nature Photography Association (NANPA)

Diana Mara Henry
51 Carbonneau Dr, Suite 3, Newport, VT 05855
Tel: 802-334-7054
E-mail: dmh@dianamarahenry.com
Web Site: dianamarahenry.com
Founded: 1967
Traveling exhibits of: The First National Woman's Conference, Houston, 1977, One-room Schools & Schoolteachers of Vermont & New York, Vanishing Jews of Alsace & the Natzweiler-Struthof Concentration Camp, Pompadour-Its French National Stud Farm, People & Celebrities, Harvard College & lifestyles, 1965-1969, NYC-Society & Mores, 1969-1987, Malcolm Forbes Balloon Meets at the Chateau de Balleroy, Normandy, Carmel, CA, Hawaii, Bali, Kathmandu, Europe & the Caribbean. LIBEL, an exhibit of words & pictures that challenges the acceptance of pictures & captions as truth.
Number of Photographers Represented: 1
File Begins: 1967
Stock: 100,000 color slides & B&W prints

Historic Films LLC
211 Third St, Greenport, NY 11944
Tel: 631-477-9700 *Toll Free Tel:* 800-249-1940
Fax: 631-477-9800
E-mail: info@historicfilms.com
Web Site: www.historicfilms.com
Key Personnel
Owner & Pres: Joe Lauro
Res Dir: Kevin Rice *E-mail:* kevin@historicfilms.com
Sales Dir: Mark Heidemann *E-mail:* mark@historicfilms.com
Opers Mgr: Anthea Carr *E-mail:* anthea@historicfilms.com
Founded: 1991
Primarily historical stock footage library covering the years 1895-2010 with over 50,000 hours of logged, copyright cleared footage of all types available for all uses. Modem access to database is available to qualified researchers. Also have over 45,000 individual performances covering all genres of American music form Blues/Jazz to Classical & Rock clips on demand.
Availability: Phone, walk-in, mail & e-mail

Michael Jacobs Photojournalism (MJP)
2105 Vista Oeste NW, Suite 3, No 2057, Albuquerque, NM 87120
Tel: 323-461-0240 *Toll Free Fax:* 866-563-9212
E-mail: michael.mjphoto@gmail.com
Web Site: www.mjphotogallery.com
Key Personnel
Owner: Michael Jacobs
Founded: 1970
Photo assignments accepted worldwide. Editorial, illustrative & general photography for publication. Proficiency in photographing Hollywood/the entertainment industry including production & session work. Public relations, cultural & social events, concerts, international travel (over 70 countries covered), children, annual reports & politics. Album & book covers. Feature films, television & videos.
File Begins: 1970
Stock: Over 2 million multi-format B&W, color & digital; over 1 million 35mm B&W & color
Availability: Mail, phone, fax, e-mail
Restrictions: Research fees apply; model release generally not available

Jeroboam
120 27 St, San Francisco, CA 94110
Tel: 415-637-7840 (cell)
E-mail: jeroboamster@gmail.com
Key Personnel
Owner: Ellen Bunning
Founded: 1972
Stock photographic agency supplying journalistic, documentary & editorial B&W & color transparencies for reproduction; primarily in the educational market. Also available to publishers, art directors, designers & photo researchers.
Number of Photographers Represented: 150
File Begins: 1972
Stock: 200,000 B&W & 200,000 color
Availability: Walk-in, mail, phone & e-mail
Membership(s): American Society of Picture Professionals (ASPP)

Keystone Press Agency Inc
Subsidiary of Zuma Press
408 N El Camino Real, San Clemente, CA 92672
Tel: 949-481-3747 *Fax:* 949-481-3941
E-mail: info@keystonepictures.com
Web Site: www.keystonepictures.com
Key Personnel
Owner: Scott McKiernan *E-mail:* scott@keystonepictures.com
Founded: 1892
News & feature picture service.
Stock: B&W & color
Availability: Mail & phone

Magnum Photos Inc
12 W 23 St, 4th fl, New York, NY 10010
Tel: 212-929-6000
E-mail: photography@magnumphotos.com; contact@magnumphotos.com
Web Site: www.magnumphotos.com; pro.magnumphotos.com
Key Personnel
Sr Licensing Mgr-Edit, Publg, TV & Film (North America): Michael Shulman
Sr Licensing Mgr-Ad & Corp (North America): Diane Raimondo
Founded: 1947
Visual record of the times for editorial, educational or commercial use. B&W & color reportage: nature, science & technology, social & political history, personalities. Selective historical archives.
Number of Photographers Represented: 92
Stock: Over 4 million B&W & color photographs
Availability: Mail & phone, library visit by appt only, images available by digital & analog
Branch Office(s)
68 Rue Leon Frot, Paris 75011, France
Tel: 01 53 42 50 00 *Fax:* 01 53 42 50 01
E-mail: magnum@magnumphotos.fr
63 Gee St, London EC1V 3RS, United Kingdom
Tel: (020) 7490 1771 *Fax:* (020) 7608 0020
E-mail: london@magnumphotos.com

Medical Images
Division of Diomedia Inc USA

1429

STOCK PHOTO AGENCIES

3500 S DuPont Hwy, Suite 300, Dover, DE 19901
Tel: 212-736-2525 *Toll Free Tel:* 800-542-3686
E-mail: sales@medicalimages.com
Web Site: www.medicalimages.com
Key Personnel
CEO: Edwin Redzepagic
Founded: 1982
Medical & health care, biomedical & research, biomedical illustration, science & technology & ideas & effects, clinical & heart science.
Number of Photographers Represented: 450
Stock: 500,000 35mm, 4 x 5 B&W & color, digital image
Availability: Phone, by appt & online

Lawrence Migdale Photography/PIX
23 White Hall Dr, Orinda, CA 94563
Tel: 510-612-2572
E-mail: photopix@migdale.com
Web Site: www.migdale.com
Key Personnel
Owner & Partner: Lawrence Migdale
Founded: 1981
Ethnic families & children in the US. Special emphasis on ethnic holidays & celebrations, the library is geared towards the textbook & children's magazine industries in the US.
File Begins: 1981
Stock: 92,000 color images
Membership(s): American Society of Picture Professionals (ASPP)

Minden Pictures Inc
9565 Soquel Dr, Suite 202, Aptos, CA 95003
Tel: 831-661-5551
E-mail: info@mindenpictures.com
Web Site: www.mindenpictures.com
Key Personnel
Owner: Larry Minden *E-mail:* larry@mindenpictures.com
Gen Mgr: Chris Carey *E-mail:* chris@mindenpictures.com
Founded: 1989
Stock collection includes worldwide wildlife & nature photography.
Number of Photographers Represented: 150
Stock: 600,000 images available for high resolution digital delivery
Restrictions: Rights managed
Membership(s): American Society of Picture Professionals (ASPP); Digital Media Licensing Association (DMLA)

Panoramic Images
4835 Main St, Suite 100, Skokie, IL 60077
Tel: 847-324-7000 *Toll Free Tel:* 800-543-5250
E-mail: info@panoramicimages.com
Web Site: www.panoramicimages.com
Key Personnel
Dir: Doug Segal
Large format & panoramic photo library for graphic design. Professional staff of photo researchers. Ultra Hi res scans from original films, from 100-mb to 2 gig available for immediate download. Specialize in supplying files to custom digital wall covering industry as well as print on demand art & decor print marketplace.
Number of Photographers Represented: 300
Stock: 250,000 color & B&W, 8 x 10, 4 x 10, 6 x 12cm, 6 x 17cm
Availability: Phone, fax & e-mail
Restrictions: Rights managed & royalty free

PhotoEdit Inc
3505 Cadillac Ave, Suite P-101, Costa Mesa, CA 92626
Toll Free Tel: 888-450-0946
Key Personnel
Photo Edit Dir: Tashauna Johnson *Tel:* 714-434-5935 *E-mail:* tashauna.johnson@photoeditinc.com
Founded: 1988
Stock photography agency specializes in children, people & families, especially ethnic & social issues for textbook publishers & magazines; some photographers shoot on spec. Color digital images.
Number of Photographers Represented: 100
Availability: Walk-in, mail, phone, fax & e-mail
Restrictions: Research fees when applicable, permission fees, one-time use
Membership(s): American Society of Picture Professionals (ASPP)

Photofest
East Rutherford, NJ 07073
E-mail: requests@photofestnyc.com
Web Site: www.photofestnyc.com
Key Personnel
Pres: Howard Mandelbaum
Founded: 1981
Photo research; specialize in the performing arts-historic & current.
Stock: 2,000,000 B&W & color
Availability: E-mail

Robertstock.com, see
ClassicStock.com/Robertstock.com

Science Source®
Division of Photo Researchers Inc
307 Fifth Ave, 3rd fl, New York, NY 10016
Tel: 212-758-3420
E-mail: info@sciencesource.com; sales@sciencesource.com; contributor@sciencesource.com
Web Site: www.sciencesource.com
Key Personnel
Pres & Fin Dir: Robert L Zentmaier *Tel:* 212-758-3420 ext 129 *E-mail:* bob@sciencesource.com
VP & Creative Dir: Bug Sutton *Tel:* 212-758-3420 ext 127 *E-mail:* bug@sciencesource.com
Lib Dir: Steve Gerard *E-mail:* steve@sciencesource.com
Rts & Perms: Peter Pagan *E-mail:* peter@sciencesource.com
Founded: 1957
Stocks medical, high technology, electron microscopy, astronomy, chemistry & physics. High resolution scans for reproduction use. Coverage available in all categories, including travel & lifestyle, also the Nature Source collection of wildlife & the Science Source collection of medical, high-tech & scientific photography. Searchable database of over 750,000 images.
Number of Photographers Represented: 700
Availability: Mail, phone, web & digital delivery

Shutterstock Inc
Empire State Bldg, 350 Fifth Ave, 20th fl, New York, NY 10118
E-mail: support@shutterstock.com; press@shutterstock.com
Web Site: www.shutterstock.com
Key Personnel
Founder: Jon Oringer
CEO: Paul Hennessy
CFO: Jarrod Yahes
CIO: Hughes Hervouet
CTO: Sejal Amin
Chief Prod Offr: Meghan Schoen
Gen Coun: John Lapham
Global VP, Shutterstock Edit: Candice Murray
Global Head, Communs: Lori Rodney
Founded: 2003
Premier partner for transformative brands, newsrooms & media companies, empowering the world to create with confidence. Fueled by millions of creators around the world & a fearless approach to product innovation, Shutterstock is the leading global platform for licensing from the most extensive & diverse collection of high quality 3D models, videos, music, photographs, vectors & illustrations. From the world's largest content marketplace, to breaking news & A-list entertainment editorial access, to all-in-one content editing platform & studio production service, all using the latest in innovative technology, Shutterstock offers the most comprehensive selection of resources to bring storytelling to life.

Sovfoto/Eastfoto Inc
263 W 20 St, Suite 3, New York, NY 10011
Tel: 212-727-8170 *Fax:* 212-727-8228
E-mail: info@sovfoto.com; research@sovfoto.com
Web Site: www.sovfoto.com
Founded: 1932
Complete photo coverage of Russia, China, former USSR, Eastern European Republics & former Soviet Republics current & historical. Complete library & current photojournalism from major national news agencies & independent photographers.
Number of Photographers Represented: 30
Stock: B&W & color
Availability: E-mail, mail, fax, phone & by appt
Membership(s): American Society of Picture Professionals (ASPP)

Tom Stack & Associates Inc
7135 N Outrigger Terr, Citrus Springs, FL 34433
Tel: 305-852-5520
E-mail: tomstack@earthlink.net
Web Site: www.tomstackassociates.photoshelter.com
Key Personnel
Pres: Therisa Stack
VP: Tom Stack
High resolution images of all subjects, especially wildlife & marine life. Available for assignments; high resolution downloads available same day.
Number of Photographers Represented: 24
Stock: 200,000 images
Availability: Keyword search & high resolution download from web site

Still Media
PO Box 3362, Santa Barbara, CA 93130
E-mail: info@jeffreyaaronson.com
Web Site: www.stillmedia.com
Licensing & commissioned photography from around the world for editorial & advertising use. Also offers fine art prints by renowned photographers for personal use & corporate clients.
Availability: E-mail & mail

Stock Montage Inc
1817 N Mulligan Ave, Chicago, IL 60639
Key Personnel
Pres: Shirley M Neiman
Dir: Tom Neiman
Stock pictures covering a wide variety of historical people, subjects & events, most prior to 1900.
Stock: Prints & digital image, B&W, color & digital
Availability: E-mail, mail, phone & fax, also see gettyimages.com

Superstock
2401 S Ervay St, Suite 206, Dallas, TX 75215
Tel: 904-565-0066 *Toll Free Tel:* 866-236-0087
E-mail: yourfriends@superstock.com
Web Site: www.superstock.com
General stock picture library; also represents numerous photo stock agencies. Travel, scenic, people, movie personalities, art treasures, religious, Americana, historical, recreation, busi-

ness, domestic & wild animals, European collection, computer & abstract graphics, nostalgia & other miscellaneous stock. Contemporary color photography, vintage, fine art. Royalty free & rights managed images & footage.
Stock: Over 900 million images & footage
Availability: Web site, mail, e-mail & phone
Membership(s): American Society of Picture Professionals (ASPP); Digital Media Licensing Association (DMLA)

University of Southern California - Special Collections, USC Libraries
Doheny Memorial Library, Rm 206, Los Angeles, CA 90089-0189
Tel: 213-740-5900 *Fax:* 213-740-2343
E-mail: specol@usc.edu
Web Site: libraries.usc.edu/locations/special-collections
Maintains a large collection of historical photographs relating to all aspects of life in Southern California, with emphasis on Los Angeles & the surrounding area, between the 1870s & 2000s. The collection includes the work of C C Pierce, a professional photographer in Los Angeles at the turn of the century, George Wharton James, historian & photographer of Southwest Native American groups & the stock photo collection created by the Los Angeles Area Chamber of Commerce in the 1920s, 30s & 40s, to "sell" Los Angeles to potential investors in the area; LA Examiner photograph morgue, Dick Whittington Collection & Wayne Thom Collection.
Number of Photographers Represented: 5
Stock: 3 million B&W & color prints, negatives & duplicates
Availability: Mail & phone
Restrictions: Licensing & reproduction fees for commercial use of photographs

US Naval Institute Photo Archive
291 Wood Rd, Annapolis, MD 21402
Tel: 410-295-1022 *Fax:* 410-295-1049
E-mail: photoservice@usni.org; photoarchive@usni.org; research@usni.org
Web Site: www.usni.org
Key Personnel
Head, Photo Archives: Janis Jorgensen
 E-mail: jjorgensen@usni.org
Digital Archivist: Emily Hegranes
 E-mail: ehegranes@usni.org
Color & B&W photographic collection includes "Our Navy," Miller, James C Fahey, Alfred J Sedivi & Steichen Collections. US & foreign ships & aircraft, weapons, combat scenes & personnel photos. One of the world's largest private collection of over 500,000 US Navy ships & aircraft, of which 15,000 images are available online.
Stock: B&W & color, from 8 x 10 up to 20 x 24, prints
Availability: Online, mail & phone
Restrictions: Reproduction fee to make copies & a usage fee if used for commercial purposes

Viesti Associates Inc
361 S Camino Del Rio, Suite 111, Durango, CO 81303
Tel: 970-403-1000
Key Personnel
CEO: Joseph Viesti
Founded: 1984
International stock photos & assignment photographers available.
Number of Photographers Represented: 110
File Begins: 1973
Stock: 750,000 B&W, color
Availability: Internet, phone & mail
Restrictions: Limited rights to certain photos

WPA Film Library of Stock Footage
16101 S 108 Ave, Orland Park, IL 60467
Tel: 708-460-0555 *Toll Free Tel:* 800-323-0442
E-mail: sales@wpafilmlibrary.com
Web Site: www.wpafilmlibrary.com
Key Personnel
Dir, Sales & Licensing: Diane Paradiso
Founded: 1987

Company Index

Included in this index are the names, addresses, telecommunication numbers and electronic addresses of the organizations included in this volume of *LMP*. Entries also include the page number(s) on which the listings appear.

Sections not represented in this index are **Serials Featuring Books; Radio, TV & Cable Networks; Radio Programs Featuring Books** and **TV Programs Featuring Books.**

A & A, PO Box 16223, Albuquerque, NM 87191-6223 *Tel:* 505-518-3939 *E-mail:* aaartwork@aol.com; aaauthor@aol.com *Web Site:* www.elaineabramson.com, pg 1189, 1411

A B Data Ltd, 600 A B Data Dr, Milwaukee, WI 53217 *Tel:* 414-961-6400 *Toll Free Tel:* 866-217-4470 *Fax:* 414-961-2674 *E-mail:* info@abdata.com; consulting@abdata.com *Web Site:* www.abdata.com, pg 1115

A Good Thing Inc, 333 E 79 St, New York, NY 10075 *Tel:* 212-687-8155 *Web Site:* www.facebook.com/agoodthinginc, pg 1411

A-M Church Supply, 3220 Bay Rd, Suite E, Saginaw, MI 48603 *Tel:* 989-249-9174 *Toll Free Tel:* 800-345-4694 *Web Site:* www.am-church.com, pg 1311

A-R Editions Inc, 1600 Aspen Commons, Suite 100, Middleton, WI 53562 *Tel:* 608-836-9000 *Fax:* 608-831-8200 *E-mail:* info@areditions.com *Web Site:* www.areditions.com, pg 1207, 1221, 1277, 1343, 1411

A to Z Indexing & Bibliographic Services, 20 St James Rd, Shrewsbury, MA 01545 *Tel:* 508-842-5602 *Web Site:* sites.google.com/site/atozindexing, pg 1221

A WordJourney Translation LLC, PO Box 3181, Humble, TX 77347-3181 *Tel:* 281-813-1827 *Fax:* 832-213-2777 *E-mail:* word@wjtranslation.com *Web Site:* www.awordjourneytranslation.com, pg 1399

AAA Fine Translation & Interpretation, 3820 Bowne St, Flushing, NY 11354 *Tel:* 917-582-7456, pg 1399

A&L Express Corp, PO Box 790733, San Antonio, TX 78279-0733 *Tel:* 210-262-6633 *E-mail:* sales@arts-letters.com; support@arts-letters.com *Web Site:* www.arts-letters.com, pg 1363

Aaron Marcus and Associates Inc, 1196 Euclid Ave, Berkeley, CA 94708-1640 *Tel:* 510-599-3195 (cell) *Fax:* 510-527-1994 *Web Site:* www.bamanda.com, pg 1363

Aatrix Software Inc, 2100 Library Circle, Grand Forks, ND 58201 *Tel:* 701-746-6801; 701-746-6814 (Windows); 701-746-6017 (MacIntosh) *Toll Free Tel:* 800-426-0854 (sales) *Fax:* 701-746-4393 *E-mail:* sales@aatrix.com; support@aatrix.com *Web Site:* www.aatrix.com, pg 1363

Abacus Graphics LLC, 15179 Hunger Creek Lane, Bigfork, MT 59911-8313 *Tel:* 406-837-5776 *Web Site:* www.abacusgraphics.com, pg 1411

ABDI Inc, 16 Avenue "A", Leetsdale, PA 15056 *Toll Free Tel:* 800-796-6471 *Fax:* 412-741-4161 *E-mail:* e-fulfillment@abdintl.com *Web Site:* www.abdi-ecommerce10.com/abdintl; www.abdintl.com/abdintl, pg 1117, 1207, 1333

Abraham Associates Inc, 5120-A Cedar Lake Rd, Minneapolis, MN 55416 *Tel:* 952-927-7920 *Toll Free Tel:* 800-701-2489 *Fax:* 952-927-8089 *E-mail:* info@abrahamassociatesinc.com *Web Site:* www.abrahamassociatesinc.com, pg 1285

Russell Abraham Photography, Jack London Sq, 309 Fourth St, Suite 108, Oakland, CA 94607 *Tel:* 510-333-6633 *E-mail:* ra@russellabraham.com *Web Site:* russellabraham.com, pg 1419

Diane Abrams, 71 Faunce St, Providence, RI 02906 *Tel:* 401-274-2149 *Web Site:* www.whitegatefeatures.com, pg 1125

Abridged Readers' Guide to Periodical Literature, 4919 Rte 22, Amenia, NY 12501 *Tel:* 518-789-8700 *Toll Free Tel:* 800-562-2139 *Fax:* 518-789-0556 *E-mail:* books@greyhouse.com *Web Site:* greyhouse.com, pg 1129

Absolut Color, 109 W 27 St, New York, NY 10001 *Tel:* 212-868-0404 *E-mail:* info@absolutcolor.com *Web Site:* www.absolutcolor.com, pg 1247

ACC Distribution Ltd, 6 W 18 St, Suite 4B, New York, NY 10011 *Tel:* 212-645-1111 *Toll Free Tel:* 800-252-5231 *Fax:* 716-242-4911 *E-mail:* ussales@accpublishinggroup.com *Web Site:* www.accpublishinggroup.com/us, pg 1285

Accent Photography Ltd, 1842 31 Ave SW, Calgary, AB T2T 1S7, Canada *Tel:* 403-860-8588 *Toll Free Tel:* 877-470-4120 *Fax:* 403-271-4121 *E-mail:* info@calgaryphotographer.com *Web Site:* www.accentphotography.ca, pg 1419

Access Points Indexing, PO Box 1155, Hood River, OR 97031 *Tel:* 541-806-5436 *Web Site:* www.accesspointsindexing.com, pg 1221

Accredited Language Services (ALS), 15 Maiden Lane, Suite 308, New York, NY 10038 *Toll Free Tel:* 800-322-0284 *E-mail:* interpreting@accreditedlanguage.com; sales@accreditedlanguage.com; translation@accreditedlanguage.com; transcription@accreditedlanguage.com; multimedia@accreditedlanguage.com *Web Site:* www.accreditedlanguage.com, pg 1399

Accurate Writing & More, 16 Barstow Lane, Hadley, MA 01035 *Tel:* 413-586-2388 *Web Site:* www.accuratewriting.com; frugalmarketing.com, pg 1099, 1107, 1343

AccuWeather Inc, 385 Science Park Rd, State College, PA 16803 *Tel:* 814-235-8600; 814-237-0309 *E-mail:* salesmail@accuweather.com; support@accuweather.com *Web Site:* www.accuweather.com; corporate.accuweather.com, pg 1363

ACD Systems International Inc, 129-1335 Bear Mountain Pkwy, Victoria, BC V9B 6T9, Canada *Toll Free Tel:* 800-949-1457 *E-mail:* sales@acdsee.com *Web Site:* www.acdsee.com, pg 1363

Alice B Acheson, PO Box 735, Friday Harbor, WA 98250 *Tel:* 360-378-5850 *Fax:* 360-378-2815 *E-mail:* aliceba7@gmail.com *Web Site:* sites.google.com/view/alice-b-acheson, pg 1107, 1343

AcmeBinding, 8844 Mayfield Rd, Chesterland, OH 44026 *Tel:* 440-729-9411 *Toll Free Tel:* 888-485-5415 *Fax:* 440-729-9415 *Web Site:* www.acmebinding.com, pg 1247

ACT ONE Mailing List Services Inc, 237 Washington St, 2nd fl, Marblehead, MA 01945-3334 *Tel:* 781-639-1919 *Toll Free Tel:* 800-ACT-LIST (228-5478) *Fax:* 781-639-2733 *E-mail:* info@act1lists.com *Web Site:* www.act1lists.com, pg 1119

Actar D, 440 Park Ave S, 17th fl, New York, NY 10016 *Tel:* 212-966-2207 *E-mail:* salesnewyork@actar-d.com *Web Site:* www.actar.com, pg 1285

Action Printing, N6637 Rolling Meadows Dr, Fond du Lac, WI 54937 *Tel:* 920-907-7820 *E-mail:* info@actionprinting.com *Web Site:* www.actionprinting.com, pg 1247

Acxiom, 301 E Dave Ward Dr, Conway, AR 72032 *Toll Free Tel:* 888-322-9466 *Web Site:* www.acxiom.com, pg 1119, 1363

Adair Graphic Communications, 26975 Northline Rd, Taylor, MI 48180 *Tel:* 734-941-6300 *Fax:* 734-942-0920 *E-mail:* adair@printwell.com *Web Site:* www.adairgraphic.com, pg 1207, 1221, 1247, 1277

Adams Book Co Inc, 80 Broad St, 5th fl, New York, NY 10004 *Tel:* 718-875-5464 *Toll Free Tel:* 800-221-0909 *Fax:* 718-852-3212 *Toll Free Fax:* 888-229-2650 *E-mail:* customerservice@adamsbook.com; orders@adamsbook.com; sales@adamsbook.com; returns@adamsbook.com *Web Site:* www.adamsbook.com, pg 1311

Adams Design, 4493 Horseshoe Bend, Murrells Inlet, SC 29576 *Tel:* 843-655-7097 *E-mail:* sa@stephenadamsdesign.com *Web Site:* www.stephenadamsdesign.com, pg 1221

Adams Magnetic Products Co, 888 N Larch Ave, Elmhurst, IL 60126-1133 *Tel:* 630-617-8880 *Toll Free Tel:* 800-747-7543 (sales) *Fax:* 630-617-8881 *Toll Free Fax:* 800-747-1323 *E-mail:* info@adamsmagnetic.com *Web Site:* www.adamsmagnetic.com, pg 1265

Mark A Adams Inc, 425 Riverside Dr, New York, NY 10025 *Tel:* 917-528-3459 *Fax:* 212-864-0416 *E-mail:* mark@markadamsinc.com, pg 1311

Adams Press, 1712 Oakton St, Evanston, IL 60202 *E-mail:* info@adamspress.com, pg 1207, 1221, 1247

J Adel Art & Design, 586 Ramapo Rd, Teaneck, NJ 07666 *Tel:* 201-836-2606 *E-mail:* jadelnj@aol.com, pg 1411

Adler, Corey, Issac, 71 Faunce Dr, Providence, RI 02906 *Tel:* 401-274-2149 *Web Site:* www.whitegatefeatures.com, pg 1125

Jane Adler, 71 Faunce Dr, Providence, RI 02906 *Tel:* 401-274-2149 *Web Site:* www.whitegatefeatures.com, pg 1125

Adobe Systems Inc, 345 Park Ave, San Jose, CA 95110-2704 *Tel:* 408-536-6000 *Fax:* 408-537-6000 *Web Site:* www.adobe.com, pg 1363

Adoption Book Catalog, 131 John Muir Dr, Amherst, NY 14228 *Tel:* 716-639-3900 *Toll Free Tel:* 866-691-3300 *E-mail:* info@tapestrybooks.com *Web Site:* www.tapestrybooks.com, pg 1145

Les Messageries ADP, 2315, rue de la Province, Longueuil, QC J4G 1G4, Canada *Tel:* 450-640-1234 (commercial); 450-640-1237 (sales) *Toll Free Tel:* 800-771-3022 (commercial); 866-874-1237 (sales) *Fax:* 450-640-1251 (commercial); 450-674-6237 (sales) *Toll Free Fax:* 800-603-0433 (commercial); 866-874-6237 (sales) *E-mail:* adpcommandes@messageries-adp.com *Web Site:* www.messageries-adp.com, pg 1285

Advantage Laser Products Inc, 1840 Marietta Blvd NW, Atlanta, GA 30318 *Tel:* 404-351-2700 *Toll Free Tel:* 800-722-2804 (cust serv) *Fax:* 404-351-0911 *Toll Free Fax:* 800-871-3305 *E-mail:* sales@advlaser.com *Web Site:* www.advlaser.com, pg 1363

AdvantageCS, 3850 Ranchero Dr, Ann Arbor, MI 48108 *Tel:* 734-327-3600 *Fax:* 734-327-3620 *E-mail:* sales-na@advantagecs.com *Web Site:* www.advantagecs.com, pg 1363

AEI (Atchity Entertainment International Inc), 400 S Burnside Ave, Suite 11B, Los Angeles, CA 90036 *Tel:* 323-932-1685, pg 1343

Aeon Books, PO Box 396, Accord, NY 12404-0396 *Tel:* 845-658-3068 *E-mail:* aeongroup@msn.com *Web Site:* www.aeongroup.com, pg 1285

Aerial Archives, Lakeport, CA 95453 *Tel:* 415-771-2555 *E-mail:* research@aerialarchives.com *Web Site:* aerialarchives.com, pg 1419

African American Review (AAR), c/o St Louis University, 317 Adorjan Hall, 3800 Lindell Blvd, St Louis, MO 63108 *Tel:* 314-977-3688 *Web Site:* afamreview.org, pg 1129

Agent Research & Evaluation Inc (AR&E), 44 Park Rd, Woodbury, CT 06798 *Tel:* 203-586-1397 *Web Site:* www.agentresearch.org, pg 1343

Agfa Canada Inc, 5975 Falbourne St, Unit 2, Mississauga, ON L5R 3V8, Canada *Tel:* 905-361-6982 *Toll Free Tel:* 800-540-2432 *Fax:* 905-502-9360 *E-mail:* can.customercare@agfa.com (orders) *Web Site:* www.agfa.com/printing/worldwide/north-south-america/canada, pg 1363

Agfa North America, 580 Gotham Pkwy, Carlstadt, NJ 07072 *Tel:* 201-440-2500 *Toll Free Tel:* 888-274-8626 (cust serv) *E-mail:* customercare.us@agfa.com *Web Site:* www.agfa.com/printing/global/usa; www.agfa.com/printing/industrial; www.agfa.com/printing/large-format, pg 1277, 1364

Agincourt Press, 25 Main St, Chatham, NY 12037 *Tel:* 518-392-2898 *E-mail:* aginpress@aol.com, pg 1353

AGS, 4590 Graphics Dr, White Plains, MD 20695 *Tel:* 301-843-1800 *Fax:* 301-843-6339 *E-mail:* info@ags.com *Web Site:* www.ags.com, pg 1207, 1247, 1364

AGS BookWorks, PO Box 460313, San Francisco, CA 94146-0313 *Tel:* 415-285-8799 *Web Site:* www.agsbookworks.com, pg 1353

AIGA, the professional association for design, 228 Park Ave S, Suite 58603, New York, NY 10003 *Tel:* 212-807-1990 *E-mail:* general@aiga.org *Web Site:* www.aiga.org, pg 1139

AIMS International Books Inc, 7709 Hamilton Ave, Cincinnati, OH 45231 *Tel:* 513-521-5590 *Fax:* 513-521-5592 *E-mail:* info@aimsbooks.com *Web Site:* www.aimsbooks.com, pg 1285

Airphoto, 2311 S Prairie Ave, Pueblo, CO 81005 *Tel:* 719-542-5719 *Web Site:* airphotona.com; johnwark.com, pg 1419

AJP Communications Inc, 95 Macdonald Ave, Burnaby, BC V5C 4M4, Canada *Tel:* 604-879-5880 *E-mail:* info@ajpcommunications.com *Web Site:* www.ajpcommunications.com, pg 1221

AK Press, 370 Ryan Ave, Unit 100, Chico, CA 95973 *Tel:* 510-208-1700 *Fax:* 510-208-1701 *E-mail:* info@akpress.org; orders@akpress.org; sales@akpress.org *Web Site:* www.akpress.org, pg 1327

AKJ Education, 4702 Benson Ave, Halethorpe, MD 21227 *Tel:* 410-242-1602 *Toll Free Tel:* 800-922-6066 *Fax:* 410-242-6107 *Toll Free Fax:* 888-770-2338 *E-mail:* info@akjeducation.com *Web Site:* www.akjeducation.com, pg 1286, 1311

Rodelinde Albrecht, 274 Bradley St, Lee, MA 01238 *Tel:* 413-243-4350 *E-mail:* rodelinde@gmail.com, pg 1399

Veronika Albrecht-Rodrigues PhD, PO Box 44, Lovell, ME 04051-0044 *Tel:* 207-925-3117 *E-mail:* vroni@fairpoint.net, pg 1399

ALC Inc, 750 College Rd E, Suite 201, Princeton, NJ 08540 *Tel:* 609-580-2800 *Toll Free Tel:* 800-252-5478 *Fax:* 609-580-2888 *E-mail:* info@alc.com *Web Site:* www.alc.com, pg 1119

alfa CTP Systems Inc, 2503 Spring Ridge Dr, Unit D, Spring Grove, IL 60081 *Tel:* 815-474-7634 *E-mail:* info@alfactp.com *Web Site:* www.alfactp.com, pg 1364

All Craft Digital Inc, 289-C Skidmores Rd, Deer Park, NY 11729 *Tel:* 631-254-8495 *Fax:* 631-254-8496, pg 1221

Allard Inc, 4601 50 St, Suite 204, Lubbock, TX 79414 *Tel:* 214-736-4983 *E-mail:* info@allardinc.com *Web Site:* www.allardinc.com, pg 1221

Allex Indexing, 6039 Sunshine Dr, Ferndale, WA 98248-9234 *Tel:* 360-778-1308 *Web Site:* www.indexpert.com, pg 1221

Alliance Storage Technologies Inc (ASTI), 10045 Federal Dr, Colorado Springs, CO 80908 *Tel:* 719-593-7900 *Toll Free Tel:* 888-567-6332 *Fax:* 719-598-3472 *E-mail:* sales@astiusa.com; info@astiusa.com *Web Site:* www.alliancestoragetechnologies.com, pg 1364

Allied Vaughn, 7600 Parklawn Ave, Suite 300, Minneapolis, MN 55435 *Tel:* 952-832-3100 *Toll Free Tel:* 800-323-0281 *Fax:* 952-832-3203 *Web Site:* www.alliedvaughn.com, pg 1364

Allusion Studios & Pure Wave Audio, 248 W Elm St, Tucson, AZ 85705 *Tel:* 520-622-3895 (Allusion Studios); 520-447-8116 (Pure Wave Audio) *E-mail:* contact@allusionstudios.com *Web Site:* www.allusionstudios.com; www.purewaveaudio.com, pg 1364

AlphaGraphics Inc, 143 Union Blvd, Suite 650, Lakewood, CO 80228 *Toll Free Tel:* 800-955-6246 *Fax:* 801-595-7270 *E-mail:* contactus@alphagraphics.com *Web Site:* www.alphagraphics.com, pg 1364

Marvelia Alpizar, PO Box 4013, Burbank, CA 91503 *Tel:* 213-986-8207 *E-mail:* malpizar@gmail.com, pg 1399

Alps Alpine North America Inc, 3151 Jay St, Suite 101, Santa Clara, CA 95054 *Tel:* 408-361-6400; 408-226-7301 *Fax:* 408-980-9945; 408-226-7301 *E-mail:* alps-pr@jp.alps.com *Web Site:* www.alpsalpine.com/na, pg 1364

Altman Dedicated Direct, 853 Academy St, Rural Hall, NC 27045-9329 *Tel:* 336-969-9538 *Fax:* 336-969-9538 *Web Site:* www.altmandedicateddirect.com, pg 1343

Ambassador Press Inc, 1400 Washington Ave N, Minneapolis, MN 55411 *Tel:* 612-521-0123 *E-mail:* info@ambpress.com *Web Site:* www.ambpress.com, pg 1221, 1247, 1265

Amcorp Ltd, 10 Norden Lane, Huntington Station, NY 11746 *Tel:* 631-271-0548 *Fax:* 631-549-8849 *E-mail:* amcorpltd@aol.com, pg 1327

Amergraph Corp, Rte 15, 520 Lafayette Rd, Sparta, NJ 07871 *Tel:* 973-383-8700 *Fax:* 973-383-9225 *E-mail:* sales@amergraph.com *Web Site:* amergraph.com, pg 1277

American Artist Studio, 1114 W 26 St, Erie, PA 16508-1518 *Tel:* 814-455-4796 *E-mail:* skip@americanartiststudio.com *Web Site:* americanartiststudio.com, pg 1364

American Association for the Advancement of Science (AAAS), 1200 New York Ave NW, Washington, DC 20005 *Tel:* 202-326-6400 *Fax:* 202-371-9526 *Web Site:* www.aaas.org, pg 1145

The American Audio Prose Library Inc, PO Box 842, Columbia, MO 65205 *Tel:* 573-449-7075 *E-mail:* aaplinc@centurytel.net, pg 1364

American Book Publishing Record® Monthly, 4919 Rte 22, Amenia, NY 12501 *Tel:* 518-789-8700 *Toll Free Tel:* 800-562-2139 *Fax:* 518-789-0556 *E-mail:* books@greyhouse.com *Web Site:* greyhouse.com, pg 1129

American Book Review, c/o University of Houston-Victoria College of Liberal Arts & Sciences, 3007 N Ben Wilson St, Victoria, TX 77901 *Tel:* 361-248-8245 *E-mail:* abr@americanbookreview.org; americanbookreview@uhv.org; americanbookreview@gmail.com *Web Site:* americanbookreview.org, pg 1129

American BookWorks Corp, 309 Florida Hill Rd, Ridgefield, CT 06877 *Tel:* 203-431-9620 *Fax:* 203-244-9522 (orders) *E-mail:* info@abwcorporation.com, pg 1353

American Camp Association Inc, 5000 State Rd 67 N, Martinsville, IN 46151-7902 *Tel:* 765-342-8456 *Toll Free Tel:* 800-428-2267 *Fax:* 765-342-2065 *E-mail:* contactus@acacamps.org *Web Site:* www.acacamps.org, pg 1311

The American Collective Stand®, 277 White St, Buchanan, NY 10511 *Tel:* 914-739-7500 *Toll Free Tel:* 800-462-7687 *Fax:* 914-739-7575 *Web Site:* www.americancollectivestand.com, pg 1139

American International Distribution Corp (AIDC), 82 Winter Sport Lane, Williston, VT 05495 *Tel:* 802-862-0095 *Toll Free Tel:* 800-678-2432 *Fax:* 802-864-7749 *Web Site:* www.aidcvt.com, pg 1115, 1117, 1221, 1286, 1311, 1333

American Journal of Philology, 2715 N Charles St, Baltimore, MD 21218-4363 *Tel:* 410-516-6987 (journal orders outside US & CN) *Toll Free Tel:* 800-548-1784 (journal orders) *Fax:* 410-578-2865 (journal orders) *E-mail:* jrnlcirc@jh.edu (journal orders) *Web Site:* www.press.jhu.edu/journals/american-journal-philology, pg 1129

American Language Services Inc (ALSi), 110 Otis St, Cambridge, MA 02141 *E-mail:* info@alsiweb.us *Web Site:* www.americanlanguageservices.us, pg 1399

American Mathematical Society (AMS), 201 Charles St, Providence, RI 02904-2213 *Tel:* 401-455-4000 *Toll Free Tel:* 800-321-4267 *Fax:* 401-331-3842; 401-455-4046 (cust serv) *E-mail:* cust-serv@ams.org; ams@ams.org *Web Site:* www.ams.org, pg 1207, 1221, 1247, 1277

American Quarterly, 2715 N Charles St, Baltimore, MD 21218-4363 *Tel:* 410-516-6987 (journal orders outside US & CN) *Toll Free Tel:* 800-548-1784 (journal orders) *Fax:* 410-578-2865 (journal orders) *E-mail:* jrnlcirc@jh.edu (journal orders) *Web Site:* www.americanquarterly.org; www.press.jhu.edu/journals/american-quarterly, pg 1129

American Translation Partners Inc (ATP), One Trowbridge Rd, Suite 340, Buzzards Bay, MA 02532 *Tel:* 508-823-8892 *Toll Free Tel:* 888-443-2376 (US only) *Fax:* 508-823-8854 *E-mail:* info@atptranslations.com; request@atptranslations.com *Web Site:* atptranslations.com, pg 1399

American Urban Radio Networks (AURN), 938 Penn Ave, Suite 701, Pittsburgh, PA 15222-3811 *Tel:* 412-456-4099 *Fax:* 412-456-4077 *Web Site:* www.aurn.com, pg 1189

Amgraf Inc, 1501 Oak St, Kansas City, MO 64108-1424 *Tel:* 816-474-4797 *Toll Free Tel:* 800-304-4797 (sales & mktg) *Fax:* 816-842-4477 *E-mail:* support@amgraf.com *Web Site:* www.amgraf.com, pg 1364

Ampersand Inc/Professional Publishing Services, 515 Madison St, New Orleans, LA 70116 *Tel:* 312-280-8905 *Fax:* 312-944-1582 *E-mail:* info@ampersandworks.com *Web Site:* www.ampersandworks.com, pg 1343

an ICON Company LLC, 401 Harper Ave SW, Lenoir, NC 28645 *Tel:* 828-758-7260 *Fax:* 828-754-6353 *E-mail:* info@lenoirprinting.com *Web Site:* lenoirprinting.com, pg 1247

Ancient Healing Ways, PO Box 459, Espanola, NM 87532 *Tel:* 505-747-2860 *Toll Free Tel:* 877-753-5351 *Web Site:* www.a-healing.com, pg 1311

Anderberg Innovative Print Solutions, 6999 Oxford St, St Louis Park, MN 55426 *Tel:* 952-848-7300 *Toll Free Tel:* 800-231-9777 *Fax:* 952-920-1103 *E-mail:* sales@anderbergprint.com *Web Site:* www.anderbergprint.com, pg 1247

Anderson & Vreeland Inc, 15348 US Hwy 127 EW, Bryan, OH 43506 *Tel:* 419-636-5002 *Toll Free Tel:* 866-282-7697; 888-832-1600 *Fax:* 419-636-4334 *E-mail:* info@andersonvreeland.com *Web Site:* andersonvreeland.com, pg 1277

Barbara S Anderson, 706 W Davis Ave, Ann Arbor, MI 48103-4855 *Tel:* 734-995-0125; 734-846-3864 *E-mail:* bsa@watercolorbarbara.com, pg 1411

Andrews McMeel Syndication, 1130 Walnut St, Kansas City, MO 64106-2109 *Tel:* 816-581-7300 *Toll Free Tel:* 800-255-6734 *Web Site:* syndication.andrewsmcmeel.com, pg 1189, 1411

Mark Andy Inc, 18081 Chesterfield Airport Rd, Chesterfield, MO 63005 *Tel:* 636-532-4433 *Toll Free Tel:* 800-447-1231 *Toll Free Fax:* 800-447-1231 *Web Site:* www.presstek.com; markandy.com; shop.markandy.com, pg 1364

COMPANY INDEX

Angstrom Graphics Print, 4437 E 49 St, Cleveland, OH 44125 *Tel:* 216-271-5300 *Toll Free Tel:* 800-634-1262 *E-mail:* info@angstromgraphics.com *Web Site:* www.angstromgraphics.com, pg 1247

Animals Animals/Earth Scenes, 17 Railroad Ave, Chatham, NY 12037 *Tel:* 518-392-5500 *Toll Free Tel:* 800-392-5503 *E-mail:* info@animalsanimals.com; sales@animalsanimals.com *Web Site:* www.animalsanimals.com, pg 1427

The ANNALS of The American Academy of Political & Social Science, 2455 Teller Rd, Thousand Oaks, CA 91320 *Toll Free Tel:* 800-818-7243 *Toll Free Fax:* 800-583-2665 *E-mail:* journals@sagepub.com *Web Site:* www.sagepub.com, pg 1129

Anthro-Photo File, 133 Washington St, Belmont, MA 02478 *Tel:* 617-484-6490 *Fax:* 617-484-6490 *Web Site:* www.anthrophotofile.com, pg 1427

Anti-Defamation League, 605 Third Ave, New York, NY 10158-3560 *Tel:* 212-885-7700 *Web Site:* www.adl.org, pg 1145

The Antiquarian Bookstore, 1070 Lafayette Rd, US Rte 1, Portsmouth, NH 03801-5408 *Tel:* 603-436-7250 *Web Site:* www.antiquarianbookstore.com, pg 1311

Antonia Hall Communications, 9663 Santa Monica Blvd, No 1128, Beverly Hills, CA 90210 *Tel:* 707-234-9738 *E-mail:* ahcassociates@gmail.com *Web Site:* www.antoniahallcommunications.com, pg 1107

Any Laminating Service, 13214 Crenshaw Blvd, Gardena, CA 90249 *Tel:* 310-464-8885 *Toll Free Tel:* 800-400-3105 *E-mail:* quoterequest@anylam.com *Web Site:* anylam.com, pg 1247

AP Images, 200 Liberty St, New York, NY 10281 *Toll Free Tel:* 844-777-2006 *E-mail:* info@ap.org *Web Site:* newsroom.ap.org/editorial-photos-videos/home, pg 1103, 1427

Apex CoVantage, 4045 Sheridan Ave, No 266, Miami Beach, FL 33140 *Tel:* 703-709-3000 *Fax:* 703-709-8242 *E-mail:* info@apexcovantage.com *Web Site:* www.apexcovantage.com, pg 1221

Apex Die Corp, 840 Cherry Lane, San Carlos, CA 94070 *Tel:* 650-592-6350 *Fax:* 650-592-5315 *E-mail:* info@apexdie.com *Web Site:* www.apexdie.com, pg 1248

APG Group, 235 Homestead Place, Suite 1A, Park Ridge, NJ 07656 *Tel:* 201-420-8501 *Web Site:* www.apggroupinc.com, pg 1248

APG Sales & Distribution, 1501 County Hospital Rd, Nashville, TN 37218 *Tel:* 615-254-2488 *Toll Free Tel:* 800-327-5113 *Toll Free Fax:* 800-510-3650 *Web Site:* www.apg-sales.com, pg 1286

AppaLight, 230 Griffith Run, Spencer, WV 25276 *Tel:* 304-932-2992 *Web Site:* www.appalight.com, pg 1427

appatura™, A Broadridge Company, 65 Challenger Rd, Suite 400, Ridgefield Park, NJ 07660 *Tel:* 201-508-6000 *Toll Free Tel:* 800-277-2155 *E-mail:* contactus@appatura.com *Web Site:* www.appatura.com, pg 1103, 1115, 1117, 1207, 1221, 1248

Anne Milano Appel, 1364 Virginia St, Alamo, CA 94507 *Tel:* 925-837-5203 *E-mail:* annemilanoappel@gmail.com; amappel@pacbell.net *Web Site:* www.annemilanoappel.com, pg 1400

Apple Inc, One Apple Park Way, Cupertino, CA 95014 *Tel:* 408-996-1010 *Web Site:* www.apple.com, pg 1364

Applied Information Sciences Corp, PO Box 9182, Calabasas, CA 91372-9182 *Tel:* 818-222-0926 *Fax:* 818-222-4329 *E-mail:* sales@aisciences.com *Web Site:* www.aisciences.com; www.searchware.com, pg 1343

Aptara Inc, 2901 Telestar Ct, Suite 522, Falls Church, VA 22042 *Tel:* 703-352-0001 *E-mail:* moreinfo@aptaracorp.com *Web Site:* www.aptaracorp.com, pg 1207, 1222, 1343, 1353, 1364, 1411

Aquent LLC, 101 W Elm St, Suite 300, Conshohocken, PA 19428-2075 *Tel:* 610-828-0900 *Toll Free Fax:* 877-303-5224 *E-mail:* questions@aquent.com *Web Site:* www.aquentstudios.com; aquent.com, pg 1222, 1365, 1381

Arbor Books, 244 Madison Ave, Box 254, New York, NY 10016 *Tel:* 212-956-0950 *Toll Free Tel:* 877-822-2500 *Fax:* 914-401-9385 *E-mail:* info@arborbooks.com; editorial@arborbooks.net *Web Site:* www.arborbooks.com, pg 1207, 1222, 1248, 1265, 1343, 1353

Arbor Books, 244 Madison Ave, Box 254, New York, NY 10016 *Tel:* 212-956-0950 *Toll Free Tel:* 877-822-2500 *Fax:* 914-401-9385 *E-mail:* info@arborbooks.com; editorial@arborbooks.net *Web Site:* www.arborbooks.com; www.arborghostwriters.com; www.arborservices.com, pg 1411

Archetype Inc, 317 N Market St, Lancaster, PA 17603 *Tel:* 717-392-7438 *E-mail:* mail@nmsgbooks.com *Web Site:* nmsgbooks.com, pg 1385

Archetype Press Inc, 11272 N Meadow Sage Dr, Oro Valley, AZ 85737-7250 *Tel:* 302-249-5879 *E-mail:* archepress@aol.com, pg 1353

Ariane Editions Inc, 1504-3460 Blvd St-Elzear W, Laval, QC H7P 0M7, Canada *Tel:* 514-916-8809 *E-mail:* infor@editions-ariane.com *Web Site:* www.editions-ariane.com, pg 1311

Arizona Library Binding Service, 1337 W McKinley, Phoenix, AZ 85007 *Tel:* 602-253-1861 *E-mail:* info@azlbinding.com, pg 1325

Arrow (grades 4-6), 557 Broadway, New York, NY 10012 *Tel:* 212-343-6100; 573-632-1632 (PR, US territories, US military bases) *Toll Free Tel:* 800-541-1097 (US) *Toll Free Fax:* 800-223-4011 *E-mail:* bookclubs@scholastic.com *Web Site:* clubs.scholastic.com, pg 1141

Arrow Graphics Inc, PO Box 380291, Cambridge, MA 02238 *E-mail:* info@arrow1.com *Web Site:* www.arrow1.com, pg 1103, 1208, 1222, 1353, 1365, 1385, 1412

Arrow Publications Inc, 5270 N Park Place NE, Suite 114, Cedar Rapids, IA 52402 *Tel:* 319-395-7833 *Toll Free Tel:* 877-363-6889 *Fax:* 319-395-7353 *Web Site:* www.frangipane.org; www.arrowbookstore.com, pg 1286

Art Consulting Scandinavia: Books on Art & Architecture, 25777 Punto de Vista Dr, Monte Nido, CA 91302-2155 *Tel:* 310-456-8762 *Fax:* 310-456-5714 *E-mail:* info@nordicartbooks.com *Web Site:* nordicartbooks.com, pg 1311

Art Image Publications, PO Box 160, Derby Line, VT 05830 *Toll Free Tel:* 800-361-2598 *Toll Free Fax:* 800-559-2598 *E-mail:* customer.service@artimagepublications; info@artimagepublications.com *Web Site:* www.artimagepublications.com, pg 1311

Art Media Resources Inc, 1965 W Pershing Rd, Chicago, IL 60605 *Tel:* 312-663-5351 *Fax:* 312-663-5177 *E-mail:* paragon@paragonbook.com *Web Site:* www.artmediaresources.com, pg 1286

Art Related Technology Inc, 4 Brattle St, Rm 305, Cambridge, MA 02138 *Tel:* 617-661-1225 *Fax:* 617-491-0618 *E-mail:* artinc@artrelated.com *Web Site:* www.artrelated.com, pg 1222, 1365

Art Resource Inc, 65 Bleeker St, 12th fl, New York, NY 10012 *Tel:* 212-505-8700 *Toll Free Tel:* 888-505-8666 *Fax:* 212-505-2053 *E-mail:* requests@artres.com *Web Site:* www.artres.com, pg 1427

Ascot Media Group Inc, PO Box 2394, Friendswood, TX 77549 *Tel:* 832-334-2733 *Toll Free Tel:* 800-854-1134 *Toll Free Fax:* 800-854-2207 *Web Site:* www.ascotmedia.com, pg 1107

Asia Pacific Offset Inc, 1312 "Q" St NW, Suite B, Washington, DC 20009 *Tel:* 202-462-5436 *Toll Free Tel:* 800-756-4344 *Fax:* 202-986-4030 *Web Site:* www.asiapacificoffset.com, pg 1208, 1222, 1248

Associated Press (AP), 200 Liberty St, New York, NY 10281 *Tel:* 212-621-1500 *E-mail:* info@ap.org *Web Site:* www.ap.org, pg 1189

Association for Childhood Education International, 1875 Connecticut Ave NW, 10th fl, Washington, DC 20009 *Tel:* 202-372-9986 *Toll Free Tel:* 800-423-3563 *E-mail:* headquarters@acei.org *Web Site:* acei.org, pg 1145

Association for Library Service to Children (ALSC), 225 N Michigan Ave, Suite 1300, Chicago, IL 60601 *Tel:* 312-280-2163 *Toll Free Tel:* 800-545-2433 *Fax:* 312-280-5271 *E-mail:* alsc@ala.org *Web Site:* www.ala.org/alsc, pg 1145

Association for PRINT Technologies (APTech), 113 Seaboard Lane, Suite C-250, Franklin, TN 37067 *Tel:* 703-264-7200 *E-mail:* aptech@aptech.org *Web Site:* printtechnologies.org, pg 1277, 1365

The Association of Medical Illustrators (AMI), 201 E Main St, Suite 810, Lexington, KY 40507 *Toll Free Tel:* 866-393-4AMI (393-4264) *E-mail:* hq@ami.org *Web Site:* www.ami.org, pg 1412

Association of Writers & Writing Programs (AWP), 440 Monticello Ave, Suite 1802, PMB 73708, Norfolk, VA 23510-2670 *Tel:* 240-696-7700 *E-mail:* awp@awpwriter.org; press@awpwriter.org *Web Site:* www.awpwriter.org, pg 1381

Athena Productions Inc, 2204 S Ashford Ct, Nashville, TN 37214 *Tel:* 305-807-8607 *E-mail:* atheprod@aol.com, pg 1286

Atlanta Panorama, c/o ALPS Labs, 2579 Lawrenceville Hwy, Suite B, Decatur, GA 30033 *Tel:* 404-872-2577 *Fax:* 404-872-0548 *E-mail:* alps007@mindspring.com *Web Site:* www.alpslabs.com/PANO/index.htm, pg 1419

Audiobook Department, 6429 N Talman Ave, Chicago, IL 60645 *Tel:* 773-312-0554 *Web Site:* www.judithwest.com, pg 1344

Audiobooks.com, an RBmedia company, 935 Sheldon Ct, Burlington, ON L7L 5K6, Canada *E-mail:* customerservice@audiobooks.com *Web Site:* www.audiobooks.com, pg 1141

AudioFile®, 37 Silver St, Portland, ME 04101 *Tel:* 207-774-7563 *Toll Free Tel:* 800-506-1212 *Fax:* 207-775-3744 *E-mail:* info@audiofilemagazine.com *Web Site:* www.audiofilemagazine.com, pg 1129

Auerbach International, Alameda, CA 94501 *Tel:* 415-592-0042 *Fax:* 415-592-0043 *E-mail:* translations@auerbach-intl.com *Web Site:* www.auerbach-intl.com, pg 1400

Augsburg Fortress Publishers, Publishing House of the Evangelical Lutheran Church in America, 510 Marquette Ave S, Minneapolis, MN 55402 *Tel:* 612-330-3300 *Toll Free Tel:* 800-426-0115 (ext 639, subns); 800-328-4648 (orders) *Fax:* 612-330-3455 *Toll Free Fax:* 800-722-7766 (orders) *E-mail:* customercare@augsburgfortress.org; copyright@augsburgfortress.org (reprint permission requests); info@augsburgfortress.org *Web Site:* www.augsburgfortress.org; www.1517.media, pg 1311

Auromere Inc, 2621 W Hwy 12, Lodi, CA 95242 *Toll Free Tel:* 800-735-4691 *E-mail:* contact@auromere.com *Web Site:* www.auromere.com, pg 1286, 1327

AuthorBytes, PO Box 382103, Cambridge, MA 02238-2103 *Tel:* 617-492-0442 *E-mail:* info@authorbytes.com *Web Site:* www.authorbytes.com, pg 1344

Autodesk Inc, 111 McInnis Pkwy, San Rafael, CA 94903 *Tel:* 415-507-5000 *Fax:* 415-507-5100 *Web Site:* www.autodesk.com, pg 1365

AutoGraph International Inc (AGI), 2500 Wilcrest Dr, Suite 324, Houston, TX 77042 *Tel:* 713-954-4848 *E-mail:* sales@myeasycopy.com *Web Site:* myeasycopy.com, pg 1365

Avanti Computer Systems Ltd, 251 Consumers Rd, Suite 600, Toronto, ON M2J 4R3, Canada *Tel:* 416-445-1722 *Toll Free Tel:* 800-482-2908 *Fax:* 416-445-6319 *E-mail:* askavanti@avantisystems.com *Web Site:* www.avantisystems.com, pg 1365

Avanti Enterprises Inc, 18901 Springfield Ave, Flossmoor, IL 60422-1071 *Tel:* 630-850-3245 *Toll Free Tel:* 800-799-6464 *Fax:* 708-799-6474 *Toll Free Fax:* 877-799-6474 *E-mail:* sales@avantiusa.com *Web Site:* www.avantiusa.com, pg 1327

Avery Dennison Corp, 207 N Goode Ave, 6th fl, Glendale, CA 91203-1222 Tel: 626-304-2000 Web Site: www.averydennison.com, pg 1365

AVT Inc, 8601 Dunwoody Place, Bldg 100, Suite 100, Sandy Springs, GA 30350 Tel: 770-541-9780 E-mail: support@avt-inc.com Web Site: www.avt-inc.com, pg 1277

AWT World Trade Inc, 4321 N Knox Ave, Chicago, IL 60641-1906 Tel: 773-777-7100 Fax: 773-777-0909 E-mail: sales@awtworldtrade.com Web Site: www.awt-gpi.com, pg 1277

Azalea Software Inc, PO Box 16660, Seattle, WA 98116-0660 Tel: 206-341-9500; 206-336-9559 (software support); 206-336-9575 (sales & info) Fax: 206-299-5600 E-mail: salesinfo@azaleabarcodes.com Web Site: www.azaleabarcodes.com, pg 1365

AZTEK Inc, 13765-F Alton Pkwy, Irvine, CA 92618 Tel: 949-770-8787 E-mail: mail@aztek.com Web Site: www.aztek.net, pg 1365

AzureGreen, 16 Bell Rd, Middlefield, MA 01243 Tel: 413-623-2155 Fax: 413-623-2156 E-mail: azuregreen@azuregreen.com Web Site: www.azuregreen.net, pg 1286, 1311

B & Z Printing Inc, 1300 E Wakeham Ave, Unit B, Santa Ana, CA 92705 Tel: 714-892-2000 Web Site: www.bandzprinting.com, pg 1208, 1248

Backe Communications, Radnor Corporate Ctr, Bldg 3, Suite 101, 100 Matson Ford Rd, Radnor, PA 19087 Tel: 610-947-6900 Web Site: www.backemarketing.com, pg 1099

Baha'i Distribution Service (BDS), 1233 Central St, Evanston, IL 60201 Tel: 847-853-7899 Toll Free Tel: 800-999-9019 E-mail: bds@usbnc.org Web Site: www.bahaibookstore.com, pg 1286

Daniel H Bailey - Outdoor/Adventure Photography, 3535 E 19 Ave, Anchorage, AK 99508 Tel: 970-484-1632 E-mail: dan@danbaileyphoto.com Web Site: danbaileyphoto.com, pg 1427

Baker & Taylor LLC, 2550 W Tyvola Rd, Suite 300, Charlotte, NC 28217 Tel: 704-998-3100 Toll Free Tel: 800-775-1800 (info servs) Fax: 704-998-3319 Toll Free Fax: 800-775-2600 E-mail: btinfo@baker-taylor.com Web Site: www.baker-taylor.com, pg 1145

Baker & Taylor LLC, 2550 W Tyvola Rd, Suite 300, Charlotte, NC 28217 Tel: 704-998-3100 Toll Free Tel: 800-775-1800 (info servs) Fax: 704-998-3319 E-mail: btinfo@baker-taylor.com Web Site: www.baker-taylor.com, pg 1286, 1312

Baker & Taylor Publisher Services, 30 Amberwood Pkwy, Ashland, OH 44805 Tel: 567-215-0030 Toll Free Tel: 888-814-0208 E-mail: info@btpubservices.com; orders@btpubservices.com Web Site: www.btpubservices.com, pg 1286, 1333, 1400, 1412

Balfour Commercial Printing, 225 E John Carpenter Fwy, Tower 2, Suite 400, Irving, TX 75062 Tel: 214-819-8588 (cust serv) E-mail: printing@balfour.com Web Site: commercial-printing.balfour.com, pg 1208, 1222, 1248, 1265, 1353

Noella Ballenger & Associates, PO Box 457, La Canada, CA 91012 Tel: 818-954-0933 Fax: 818-954-0910 E-mail: noella1b@aol.com Web Site: www.noellaballenger.com, pg 1419

Balogh International Inc, 1911 N Duncan Rd, Champaign, IL 61822 Tel: 217-355-9331 Fax: 217-355-9413 E-mail: balogh@balogh.com Web Site: www.balogh.com, pg 1287

Frank Balthis Photography, PO Box 255, Davenport, CA 95017-0255 Tel: 805-770-3018; 831-426-8205 E-mail: frankbalthisphoto@gmail.com Web Site: frankbalthis.photoshelter.com, pg 1419

Bamboo Ink, 807 Oliver Hill Way, Richmond, VA 23219 Tel: 804-230-4515 E-mail: info@bambooink.com Web Site: www.bambooink.com, pg 1248

Carol Bancroft & Friends, PO Box 2030, Danbury, CT 06813 Tel: 203-730-8270 Fax: 203-730-8275 E-mail: cbfriends@sbcglobal.net Web Site: www.carolbancroft.com, pg 1412

Bang Printing Co Inc, 3323 Oak St, Brainerd, MN 56401 Tel: 218-829-2877 Toll Free Tel: 800-328-0450 Fax: 218-829-7145 E-mail: info@bangprinting.com Web Site: www.bangprinting.com, pg 1208, 1222, 1248, 1265

Bank Street Book Store, 2780 Broadway, New York, NY 10025 Tel: 212-678-1654 Fax: 212-316-7026 E-mail: books@bankstreet.edu Web Site: www.bankstreetbooks.com, pg 1145

Steve Banks Photographer, 14822 Channel Lane, Santa Monica, CA 90402 Tel: 310-998-7062 E-mail: steve@studio6art.com Web Site: www.studio6art.com, pg 1419

Barcode Graphics Inc, 25 Brodie Dr, Unit 5, Richmond Hill, ON L4B 3K7, Canada Tel: 905-770-1154 Toll Free Tel: 800-263-3669 (orders) Fax: 905-787-1575 E-mail: info@barcodegraphics.com Web Site: www.barcodegraphics.com, pg 1222

Stephanie Barko Literary Publicist, Austin, TX 78737 E-mail: stephanie@stephaniebarko.com Web Site: www.stephaniebarko.com; www.diybookplatform.com, pg 1107

Ted Barkus Co Inc, 8017 Anderson St, Philadelphia, PA 19118, pg 1099, 1107

Cynthia Barnhart, 141 E 56 St, New York, NY 10022 Tel: 212-759-8037 E-mail: trans.action@verizon.net, pg 1385

Tim Barnwell Photography, 10 Governors Ct, Asheville, NC 28805 Tel: 828-251-0040 E-mail: barnwellphoto@hotmail.com Web Site: www.barnwellphoto.com, pg 1419

Diana Barth, 535 W 51 St, Suite 3-A, New York, NY 10019 Tel: 212-307-5465 E-mail: diabarth99@gmail.com, pg 1125

Karin Batten, 463 West St, Suite C-617, New York, NY 10014 Tel: 917-405-3595 E-mail: karin.batten@gmail.com Web Site: karinbatten.com, pg 1412

Richard Bauer & Co Inc, 310 Cedar Lane, Teaneck, NJ 07666 Tel: 201-692-1005 Toll Free Tel: 800-995-7881 Fax: 201-692-8626 E-mail: info@richardbauer.com Web Site: www.richardbauer.com, pg 1265

Baumfolder Corp, 1660 Campbell Rd, Sidney, OH 45365 Tel: 937-492-1281 Toll Free Tel: 800-543-6107 Fax: 937-492-7280 E-mail: baumfolder@baumfolder.com Web Site: www.baumfolder.com, pg 1277

BC BookWorld, PO Box 93536, Vancouver, BC V6E 4L7, Canada Tel: 604-736-4011 Fax: 604-736-4011 E-mail: bookworld@telus.net Web Site: www.bcbookworld.com, pg 1130

BCC Software Inc, 75 Josons Dr, Rochester, NY 14623-3494 Toll Free Tel: 800-453-3130; 800-337-0442 (sales) E-mail: marketing@bccsoftware.com Web Site: www.bccsoftware.com, pg 1365

BCH Fulfillment & Distribution, 33 Oakland Ave, Harrison, NY 10528 Tel: 914-835-0015 Toll Free Tel: 800-431-1579 Fax: 914-835-0398 E-mail: bookch@aol.com Web Site: www.bookch.com, pg 1287, 1312

BDT Products Inc, 250 E Rincon St, Suite 101, Corona, CA 92879 Tel: 949-263-6363, pg 1365

Beacon Audiobooks, 132 W 31 St, New York, NY 10001 Toll Free Tel: 800-817-8480 E-mail: info@beaconaudiobooks.com Web Site: www.beaconaudiobooks.com, pg 1287

Tom Bean Photography, PO Box 1567, Flagstaff, AZ 86002-1567 Tel: 928-779-4381 E-mail: tom@tombean.com Web Site: tombean.photoshelter.com, pg 1419

The Bear Wallow Publishing Co, 809 S 12 St, La Grande, OR 97850 Tel: 541-962-7864 Web Site: www.bear-wallow.com, pg 1222, 1277

Bedford Printing Co, 1501 S Blount St, Raleigh, NC 27603 Tel: 919-832-3973 Fax: 919-755-0204 E-mail: info@bedfordprinting.com Web Site: www.bedfordprinting.com, pg 1248

Morton Beebe Photographer/Author, San Francisco, CA 94111 Tel: 415-362-6222; 415-706-0594 (cell) E-mail: morton.beebe@gmail.com Web Site: www.mortonbeebe.com, pg 1419

Beidel Printing House Inc, 225 S Fayette St, Shippensburg, PA 17257 Tel: 717-532-5063 Fax: 717-532-2502 E-mail: customerservice@dreamprint.com Web Site: dreamprint.com, pg 1248, 1344

Beijing Book Co Inc, 701 E Linden Ave, Linden, NJ 07036 Tel: 908-862-0909 Fax: 908-862-4201 E-mail: journals@cnpbbci.com, pg 1312, 1327

Bellevue Literary Review, 149 E 23 St, Suite 1516, New York, NY 10010 Tel: 917-375-5790 E-mail: info@BLReview.org Web Site: www.BLReview.org, pg 1130

Benjamin News Group, 1701 Rankin St, Missoula, MT 59808 Tel: 406-721-7801 Toll Free Tel: 800-823-6397 (MT only); 800-735-8557 (outside MT) E-mail: customerservice@bngmsla.com Web Site: www.bngmsla.com; www.facebook.com/Benjamin-News-Group-168874803126737/, pg 1312

Bentley Publishers, 1734 Massachusetts Ave, Cambridge, MA 02138-1804 Tel: 617-547-4170 E-mail: sales@bentleypubs.com Web Site: www.bentleypublishers.com, pg 1327

Miriam Berkley Photography, 353 W 51 St, Suite 1-A/6, New York, NY 10019-6457 Tel: 212-246-7979 E-mail: miriam.berkley@mac.com; authorpix@aol.com Web Site: www.PublishersMarketplace.com/members/MiriamBerkley; www.miriamberkley.com, pg 1419

David Berman Communications, 340 Selby Ave, Ottawa, ON K2A 3X6, Canada Tel: 613-728-6777 Toll Free Tel: 800-665-1809 E-mail: info@davidberman.com Web Site: www.wcag2.com, pg 1222

Bernan, 4501 Forbes Blvd, Suite 200, Lanham, MD 20706 Tel: 717-794-3800 (cust serv & orders) Toll Free Tel: 800-462-6420 (cust serv & orders) Fax: 717-794-3803 Toll Free Fax: 800-338-4550 E-mail: customercare@rowman.com Web Site: rowman.com/page/bernan, pg 1287, 1312

Berryville Graphics, 25 Jack Enders Blvd, Berryville, VA 22611 Tel: 540-955-2750 Fax: 540-955-2633 E-mail: info@bvgraphics.com Web Site: www.bpg-usa.com, pg 1208, 1222, 1248

Bert Davis Executive Search Inc, 555 Fifth Ave, Suite 302, New York, NY 10017 Tel: 212-838-4000 E-mail: info@bertdavis.com Web Site: www.bertdavis.com, pg 1381

Best Mailing Lists Inc, 7507 E Tanque Verde Rd, Tucson, AZ 85715 Toll Free Tel: 800-692-2378 Fax: 520-885-3100 E-mail: best@bestmailing.com Web Site: www.bestmailing.com, pg 1119

Bethany Press International Inc, 6820 W 115 St, Bloomington, MN 55438 Tel: 952-914-7400 Toll Free Tel: 888-717-7400 Fax: 952-914-7410 E-mail: info@bethanypress.com Web Site: www.bethanypress.com, pg 1248

Biblical Archaeology Society, 4710 41 St NW, Washington, DC 20016-1705 Tel: 202-364-3300 Toll Free Tel: 800-221-4644 Fax: 202-364-2636 E-mail: info@biblicalarchaeology.org Web Site: www.biblicalarchaeology.org, pg 1365

Bien Fait Translations, 104 Seascape, Laguna Niguel, CA 92677 Tel: 781-769-1637 Toll Free Tel: 866-243-6324 Web Site: www.bien-fait.com, pg 1400

Big Vision Art + Design, 251 Hwy 179, Creekside Plaza A1, Sedona, AZ 86336 Tel: 928-202-6320 Web Site: www.bigvisionarts.com, pg 1412

Bilingual Educational Services Inc, 2514 S Grand Ave, Los Angeles, CA 90007 Tel: 213-749-6213 Toll Free Tel: 800-448-6032, pg 1287, 1312

Bindagraphics Inc, 2701 Wilmarco Ave, Baltimore, MD 21223-9922 Tel: 410-362-7200 Toll Free Tel: 800-326-0300 Fax: 410-362-7233 E-mail: info@bindagraphics.com Web Site: www.bindagraphics.com, pg 1222, 1248

Bindery & Distribution Service Inc, 9 Overbrook Rd, South Barrington, IL 60010 Tel: 312-550-7000 Fax: 847-842-8800, pg 1277

COMPANY INDEX

The Bindery Inc, 8201 Brooklyn Blvd, Brooklyn Park, MN 55445 *Tel:* 763-201-2800 *Toll Free Tel:* 800-851-6598 *Fax:* 763-201-2790 *E-mail:* info@thebinderymn.com *Web Site:* www.thebinderymn.com, pg 1249

Birmingham Printing & Publishing Inc, 3101 Sixth Ave S, Birmingham, AL 35233 *Tel:* 205-251-5113 *Toll Free Tel:* 888-276-1192 *Fax:* 205-251-2222 *E-mail:* sales@bhamprinting.com *Web Site:* bhamprinting.com, pg 1249

Jennifer Bishop Photography, 843 W University Pkwy, Baltimore, MD 21210 *Tel:* 410-366-6662 *Web Site:* www.jenniferbishopphotography.com, pg 1419

BJU Press, 1430 Wade Hampton Blvd, Greenville, SC 29609-5046 *Tel:* 864-770-1317; 864-546-4600 *Toll Free Tel:* 800-845-5731 *E-mail:* bjupinfo@bjupress.com *Web Site:* www.bjupress.com, pg 1365

Black Star Publishing Co Inc, 333 Mamaroneck Ave, Suite 175, White Plains, NY 10605 *Tel:* 212-679-3288 *Web Site:* www.blackstar.com, pg 1427

The Blaine Group Inc, 8665 Wilshire Blvd, No 301, Beverly Hills, CA 90211 *Tel:* 310-360-1499 *Fax:* 310-360-1498 *Web Site:* www.blainegroupinc.com, pg 1107

Blanks Printing & Imaging Inc, 2343 N Beckley Ave, Dallas, TX 75208 *Tel:* 214-741-3905 *Toll Free Tel:* 800-325-7651 *E-mail:* sales@blanks.com *Web Site:* www.blanks.com, pg 1222, 1249

Blitzprint Inc, 1235 64 Ave SE, Suite 1, Calgary, AB T2H 2J7, Canada *Toll Free Tel:* 866-479-3248 *Fax:* 403-253-5642 *E-mail:* books@blitzprint.com *Web Site:* www.blitzprint.com, pg 1249

C Blohm & Associates Inc, 5999 Monona Dr, Monona, WI 53716-3531 *Tel:* 608-216-7300 *E-mail:* hello@cblohm.com *Web Site:* www.cblohm.com, pg 1107

The Blue Mouse Studio, 26829 37 St, Gobles, MI 49055 *Tel:* 269-628-5160 *E-mail:* frogville@earthlink.net, pg 1412

Blue Note Publications Inc, 721 North Dr, Suite D, Melbourne, FL 32934 *Tel:* 321-799-2583; 321-622-6289 *Toll Free Tel:* 800-624-0401 (orders) *Fax:* 321-799-1942; 321-622-6830 *E-mail:* bluenotebooks@gmail.com *Web Site:* bluenotepublications.com, pg 1208, 1223, 1249, 1278

Blue Ridge Printing Co, 544 Haywood Rd, Asheville, NC 28806 *Tel:* 828-254-1000 *Toll Free Tel:* 800-633-4298 *Fax:* 828-252-6455 *E-mail:* info@brprinting.com *Web Site:* www.brprinting.com, pg 1249

BMI Educational Services Inc, 26 Haypress Rd, Cranbury, NJ 08512 *Tel:* 732-329-6991 *Toll Free Tel:* 800-222-8100 (orders only) *Fax:* 732-329-6994 *Toll Free Fax:* 800-986-9393 (orders only) *E-mail:* info@bmionline.com *Web Site:* bmionline.com, pg 1312, 1325

Wanda J Boeke, 26 Brown Rd, Corning, NY 14830 *Tel:* 607-207-2786 *E-mail:* wjboeke@gmail.com, pg 1400

Bolger Vision Beyond Print, 3301 Como Ave SE, Minneapolis, MN 55414-2809 *Tel:* 651-645-6311 *Toll Free Tel:* 866-264-3287 *E-mail:* contact@bolgerinc.com *Web Site:* www.bolgerinc.com, pg 1103

Bondarenko Photography, 210 S 41 St, Birmingham, AL 35222 *Tel:* 205-592-8319; 205-243-9910 (cell) *E-mail:* info@bondarenkophoto.com *Web Site:* www.bondarenkophoto.com, pg 1420

Robert Bononno, 109 E Second St, Apt 5, New York, NY 10009 *Tel:* 646-673-6102 *E-mail:* rbononno@twc.com *Web Site:* www.robert-bononno.com, pg 1400

Book Automation Inc, 458 Danbury Rd, Unit B10, New Milford, CT 06776 *Tel:* 860-354-7900 *Toll Free Tel:* 800-429-6305 *E-mail:* info@bookautomation.com *Web Site:* www.bookautomation.com, pg 1278

Book Express, 2440 Viking Way, Richmond, BC V6V 1N2, Canada *Tel:* 604-448-7100 *Toll Free Tel:* 800-663-5714 *Fax:* 604-270-7161 *Toll Free Fax:* 800-565-3770 *E-mail:* info@raincoast.com *Web Site:* raincoast.com, pg 1312

Book Machine Sales Inc, PO Box 297, Hamlin, PA 18427 *Tel:* 570-647-9111 *Web Site:* bookmachinesales.com, pg 1278

Book Publishers Network, 817 238 St SE, Suite G, Bothell, WA 98021 *Tel:* 425-483-3040 *Fax:* 425-483-3098 *Web Site:* www.bookpublishersnetwork.com, pg 1107

Book Sales, 142 W 36 St, 4th fl, New York, NY 10018 *Tel:* 212-779-4971; 212-779-4972 *Fax:* 212-779-6058 *Web Site:* www.quartoknows.com, pg 1312

Book Vine for Children, 3980 Albany St, Suite 7, McHenry, IL 60050-8397 *Tel:* 815-363-8880 *Toll Free Tel:* 800-772-4220 *Fax:* 815-363-8883 *E-mail:* info@bookvine.com *Web Site:* www.bookvine.com, pg 1287

Bookazine Co Inc, 75 Hook Rd, Bayonne, NJ 07002 *Tel:* 201-339-7777 *Toll Free Tel:* 800-221-8112 *Fax:* 201-339-7778 *E-mail:* info@bookazine.com *Web Site:* www.bookazine.com, pg 1312, 1327

BookBaby, 7905 N Crescent Blvd, Pennsauken, NJ 08110 *Tel:* 856-460-8069 *Toll Free Tel:* 877-961-6878 *E-mail:* info@bookbaby.com *Web Site:* www.bookbaby.com/book-printing, pg 1249

BookBaby, 7905 N Crescent Blvd, Pennsauken, NJ 08110 *Toll Free Tel:* 877-961-6878 *E-mail:* info@bookbaby.com *Web Site:* www.bookbaby.com/book-design, pg 1412

BookComp Inc, 6124 Belmont Ave NE, Belmont, MI 49306 *Tel:* 616-774-9700 *E-mail:* production@bookcomp.com *Web Site:* www.bookcomp.com, pg 1223, 1353

Bookcovers.com, c/o Archer Ellison Inc, 7025 CR 46-A, Suite 1071, Lake Mary, FL 32746 *Toll Free Tel:* 800-449-4095 (ext 702) *Toll Free Fax:* 800-366-4086 *E-mail:* info@bookcovers.com *Web Site:* bookcovers.com, pg 1412

theBookDesigners, 454 Las Gallinas Ave, PMB 2015, San Rafael, CA 94903 *Tel:* 415-637-9550 *E-mail:* info@bookdesigners.com *Web Site:* bookdesigners.com, pg 1412

BookFactory, 2302 S Edwin C Moses Blvd, Dayton, OH 45417 *Tel:* 937-226-7100 *Toll Free Tel:* 877-431-2665 *Fax:* 614-388-5635 *E-mail:* sales@bookfactory.com *Web Site:* www.bookfactory.com, pg 1249

Bookforum, 520 Eighth Ave, 21st fl, New York, NY 10018 *E-mail:* editors@bookforum.com; advertising@bookforum.com; circulation@bookforum.com *Web Site:* www.bookforum.com; subscriptions.bookforum.com, pg 1130

Booklist, 225 N Michigan Ave, Suite 1300, Chicago, IL 60601 *Tel:* 312-944-6780 *Toll Free Tel:* 800-545-2433 *Fax:* 312-440-9374 *E-mail:* info@booklistonline.com; ala@ala.org *Web Site:* www.booklistonline.com; www.ala.org, pg 1130

BookLogix, 1264 Old Alpharetta Rd, Alpharetta, GA 30005 *Tel:* 470-239-8547 *E-mail:* info@booklogix.com; publishing@booklogix.com; customerservice@booklogix.com *Web Site:* www.booklogix.com, pg 1208

Bookmasters, 30 Amberwood Pkwy, Ashland, OH 44805 *Tel:* 419-281-5100 *Toll Free Tel:* 800-537-6727 *Fax:* 419-281-0200 *E-mail:* info@btpubservices.com *Web Site:* www.btpubservices.com, pg 1208, 1223, 1249, 1265, 1278

BookMobile, 5120 Cedar Lake Rd, Minneapolis, MN 55416 *Tel:* 763-398-0030 *Toll Free Tel:* 844-488-4477 *Fax:* 763-398-0198 *Web Site:* www.bookmobile.com, pg 1249

BookPage®, 2143 Belcourt Ave, Nashville, TN 37212 *Tel:* 615-292-8926 *Fax:* 615-292-8249 *Web Site:* bookpage.com, pg 1127

Books International Inc, 22883 Quicksilver Dr, Dulles, VA 20166 *Tel:* 703-661-1500 *E-mail:* hdqtrs@booksintl.com *Web Site:* booksintl.presswarehouse.com, pg 1333

Bookshelf Bindery Ltd, 22 Secord Dr, Unit 16, St Catharines, ON L2N 1K8, Canada *Tel:* 905-934-2801 *E-mail:* bookshelfbindery@bellnet.ca, pg 1249

The Booksource Inc, 1230 Macklind Ave, St Louis, MO 63110 *Tel:* 314-647-0600 *Toll Free Tel:* 800-444-0435 *Fax:* 314-647-6850 *Toll Free Fax:* 800-647-1923 *E-mail:* service@booksource.com *Web Site:* www.booksource.com, pg 1312

BookWise Design, 29089 SW Costa Circle W, Wilsonville, OR 97070 *Tel:* 503-542-3551 *Toll Free Tel:* 800-697-9833 *Web Site:* bookwisedesign.com, pg 1223, 1412

Boston Review, PO Box 390568, Cambridge, MA 02139 *Tel:* 617-356-8198 *E-mail:* review@bostonreview.net; customerservice@bostonreview.net *Web Site:* bostonreview.net, pg 1130

David Bouchier, PO Box 763, Stony Brook, NY 11790 *Tel:* 631-751-2660 *E-mail:* davidbouchier5@gmail.com, pg 1125

Bound to Stay Bound Books Inc, 1880 W Morton Rd, Jacksonville, IL 62650 *Tel:* 217-245-5191 *Toll Free Tel:* 800-637-6586 *Fax:* 217-245-0424 *Toll Free Fax:* 800-747-7872 *E-mail:* btsb@btsb.com *Web Site:* www.btsb.com, pg 1312, 1325

Bowen Books LLC, 971 First Ave, New York, NY 10022 *Tel:* 212-421-5797 *E-mail:* bowenbooks@aol.com, pg 1354

BR Printers, 665 Lenfest Rd, San Jose, CA 95133 *Tel:* 408-278-7711 *Fax:* 408-929-8062 *E-mail:* info@brprinters.com *Web Site:* www.brprinters.com, pg 1103, 1249

Brackett Inc, 7115 SE Forbes Ave, Topeka, KS 66619 *Tel:* 785-862-2205 *Toll Free Tel:* 800-255-3506 *Fax:* 785-862-1127 *E-mail:* brackett@brackett-inc.com; sales@brackett-inc.com *Web Site:* brackett-inc.com, pg 1278

Bradford & Bigelow Inc, 3 Perkins Way, Newburyport, MA 01950-4007 *Tel:* 978-904-3100 *E-mail:* sales@bradford-bigelow.com *Web Site:* www.bradford-bigelow.com, pg 1208, 1249

Bradley Ireland Productions, c/o Sea Save Foundation, 20540 Pacific Coast Hwy, Malibu, CA 90265, pg 1420

Brainworks Software, 100 S Main St, Sayville, NY 11782 *Tel:* 631-563-5000 *Toll Free Tel:* 800-755-1111 *Fax:* 631-563-6320 *E-mail:* info@brainworks.com; sales@brainworks.com; support@brainworks.com *Web Site:* www.brainworks.com, pg 1365

Brandtjen & Kluge LLC, 539 Blanding Woods Rd, St Croix Falls, WI 54024 *Tel:* 715-483-3265 *Toll Free Tel:* 800-826-7320 *Fax:* 715-483-1640 *E-mail:* sales@kluge.biz *Web Site:* www.kluge.biz, pg 1278

Art Brewer Photography LLC, 25262 Mainsail Dr, Dana Point, CA 92629 *Tel:* 949-661-8930 *E-mail:* art@artbrewer.com *Web Site:* www.artbrewer.com; www.artbrewergallery.com, pg 1420

Brickman Marketing, 395 Del Monte Ctr, No 250, Monterey, CA 93940 *Tel:* 831-594-1500 *E-mail:* brickman@brickmanmarketing.com *Web Site:* www.brickmanmarketing.com, pg 1107

Bridgeport National Bindery Inc, 662 Silver St, Agawam, MA 01001 *Tel:* 413-789-1981 *Toll Free Tel:* 800-223-5083 *E-mail:* info@bnbindery.com *Web Site:* www.bnbindery.com, pg 1249, 1325

Ashleigh Brilliant Enterprises, 117 W Valerio St, Santa Barbara, CA 93101 *Tel:* 805-682-0531 *Web Site:* www.ashleighbrilliant.com, pg 1189

Broadcast Wire & Audio, c/o The Canadian Press, 36 King St E, Toronto, ON M5C 2L9, Canada *Tel:* 416-507-2126 *Toll Free Tel:* 800-434-7578 (CN only) *Fax:* 416-364-1325 *E-mail:* broadcast@thecanadianpress.com *Web Site:* www.thecanadianpress.com, pg 1189

BroadVision, 460 Seaport Ct, Suite 102, Redwood City, CA 94063 *Tel:* 650-331-1000 *Web Site:* www.broadvision.com, pg 1365

Brodart Books & Library Services, 500 Arch St, Williamsport, PA 17701 *Tel:* 570-326-2461 *Toll Free Tel:* 800-233-8467 *Fax:* 570-651-1639 *Toll Free Fax:* 800-999-6799 *E-mail:* support@brodart.com *Web Site:* www.brodartbooks.com, pg 1313

BRODART BOOKS & LIBRARY SERVICES — COMPANY INDEX

Brodart Books & Library Services, 500 Arch St, Williamsport, PA 17701 *Tel:* 570-326-2461 *Toll Free Tel:* 800-474-9816 *Fax:* 570-651-1639 *Toll Free Fax:* 800-999-6799 *E-mail:* support@brodart.com *Web Site:* www.brodartbooks.com, pg 1325

Brody Public Relations, 145 Kingwood Stockton Rd, Stockton, NJ 08559-1711 *Tel:* 908-295-0600 *Web Site:* www.brodypr.com, pg 1107

Rosalie Brody, 360 E 72 St, New York, NY 10021 *Tel:* 212-988-8951, pg 1108

B Broughton Co Ltd, 322 Consumers Rd, North York, ON M2J 1P8, Canada *Tel:* 416-690-4777 *Toll Free Tel:* 800-268-4449 *Fax:* 416-690-5357 *E-mail:* sales@bbroughton.com *Web Site:* www.bbroughton.com, pg 1287, 1313

Brown Book Co Ltd, 65 Crockford Blvd, Toronto, ON M1R 3B7, Canada *Tel:* 416-504-9696 *Fax:* 416-504-9393 *E-mail:* bbc@brownbook.ca *Web Site:* www.brownbook.ca, pg 1208

Tom Brownold Photography, 801 W Summit Ave, Flagstaff, AZ 86001 *Tel:* 928-779-1583 *E-mail:* tbrownold@tombrownold.com *Web Site:* www.tombrownold.com, pg 1420

Donna Brunet Macro Photography, PO Box 30123, Columbia, MO 65205-3123 *Tel:* 573-999-2178 *Web Site:* www.donnabrunet.com, pg 1420

Brunswick Books, 14 Afton Ave, Toronto, ON M6J 1R7, Canada *Tel:* 416-703-3598 *Fax:* 416-703-6561 *E-mail:* info@brunswickbooks.ca; orders@brunswickbooks.ca *Web Site:* brunswickbooks.ca, pg 1287

JB Bryans Literary, 7 Meetinghouse Ct, Indian Mills, NJ 08088 *Tel:* 609-922-0369 *E-mail:* info@brylit.com *Web Site:* brylit.com, pg 1344

Bulkley Dunton, One Penn Plaza, Suite 2814, 250 W 34 St, New York, NY 10119 *Tel:* 212-863-1800 *Toll Free Tel:* 800-347-9279 *Fax:* 212-863-1872 *Web Site:* www.bulkleydunton.com, pg 1265

Bulletin of the American Schools of Oriental Research (BASOR), James F Strange Ctr, 209 Commerce St, Alexandria, VA 22314 *Tel:* 703-789-9229; 703-789-9230 (pubns) *Fax:* 617-353-6575 *E-mail:* basor@asor.org; info@asor.org; publications@asor.org *Web Site:* www.asor.org, pg 1130

Bulletin of the History of Medicine, 2715 N Charles St, Baltimore, MD 21218-4363 *Tel:* 410-516-6987 (journal orders outside US & CN) *Toll Free Tel:* 800-548-1784 (journal orders) *Fax:* 410-578-2865 (journal orders) *E-mail:* bhm@jhmi.edu; jrnlcirc@jh.edu (journal orders) *Web Site:* www.press.jhu.edu/journals/bulletin-history-medicine, pg 1130

Bunting Magnetics Co, 500 S Spencer Rd, Newton, KS 67114 *Tel:* 316-284-2020 *Toll Free Tel:* 800-835-2526; 877-576-0156 *Fax:* 316-283-4975 *E-mail:* bmc@buntingmagnetics.com *Web Site:* www.buntingmagnetics.com, pg 1278

The Bureau, 2354 English St, Maplewood, MN 55109 *Tel:* 612-788-1000; 612-432-3516 (sales) *Toll Free Tel:* 800-788-9536 *Fax:* 612-788-7792 *E-mail:* sales@thebureau.com *Web Site:* www.thebureau.com, pg 1223, 1249

Burlington News Agency Inc, 382 Hercules Dr, Suite 2, Colchester, VT 05446 *Tel:* 802-655-7000 *Fax:* 802-655-7002 *E-mail:* burlnews@aol.com, pg 1313

Burmar Technical Corp, 106 Ransom Ave, Sea Cliff, NY 11579 *Tel:* 516-484-6000 *Fax:* 516-484-6356 *Web Site:* burmar.net, pg 1223, 1365, 1412

Busch LLC, 516 Viking Dr, Virginia Beach, VA 23452 *Tel:* 757-463-7800 *Toll Free Tel:* 800-USA-PUMP (872-7867) *Fax:* 757-463-7407 *E-mail:* info@buschusa.com; marketing@buschusa.com *Web Site:* www.buschvacuum.com/us, pg 1278

Business Wire, 101 California St, 20th fl, San Francisco, CA 94111 *Tel:* 415-986-4422 *Toll Free Tel:* 800-227-0845 *E-mail:* info@businesswire.com *Web Site:* www.businesswire.com, pg 1189

BW&A Books Inc, 112 W McClanahan St, Oxford, NC 27565 *Tel:* 919-956-9111 *Fax:* 919-956-9112 *E-mail:* bwa@bwabooks.com *Web Site:* www.bwabooks.com, pg 1223

By Design Communications, 144 W 27 St, 3rd fl (rear), New York, NY 10001 *Tel:* 212-366-1740, pg 1412

C & C Offset Printing Co USA Inc, 70 W 36 St, Unit 10C, New York, NY 10018 *Tel:* 212-431-4210 *Toll Free Fax:* 866-540-4134 *Web Site:* www.ccoffset.com, pg 1208, 1223, 1249

C J Traders Inc, 555 Second Ave, Suite C700, Collegeville, PA 19426 *Tel:* 484-902-8057 *Fax:* 484-902-8093 *E-mail:* cjtraders714@gmail.com, pg 1313

Leila Cabib, 8601 Buckhannon Dr, Potomac, MD 20854 *Tel:* 301-299-2659 *E-mail:* leila@leilacabib.com *Web Site:* www.leilacabib.com, pg 1412

Cactus Clyde Productions, PO Box 3624, St Francisville, LA 70775-3624 *Tel:* 225-245-5008 *E-mail:* cactusclyd@aol.com *Web Site:* www.cclockwood.com, pg 1420

Calaf Communications, 10 Warwick Ct, Lawrence, MA 01841 *Tel:* 978-314-3125 *Fax:* 978-686-5960 *Web Site:* www.calafcommunications.com, pg 1400

California Offset Printers Inc, 620 W Elk Ave, Glendale, CA 91204 *Tel:* 818-291-1100 *Toll Free Tel:* 800-280-6446 *Fax:* 818-291-1192 *E-mail:* info@copcomms.com *Web Site:* www.copprints.com, pg 1250

Callaloo, 2715 N Charles St, Baltimore, MD 21218-4363 *Tel:* 410-516-6987 (journal orders outside US & CN) *Toll Free Tel:* 800-548-1784 (journal orders) *Fax:* 410-578-2865 (journal orders) *E-mail:* jrnlcirc@jh.edu (journal orders) *Web Site:* www.press.jhu.edu/journals/callaloo, pg 1130

Calvary Distribution, 3232 W MacArthur Blvd, Santa Ana, CA 92704 *Tel:* 714-545-6548 *Toll Free Tel:* 800-444-7664 *Fax:* 714-641-8201 *E-mail:* info@calvaryd.org *Web Site:* www.calvaryd.org, pg 1287

Camerique Inc International, 164 Regency Dr, Eagleville, PA 19403 *Tel:* 610-272-4000 *Fax:* 610-272-4000 (call or e-mail first) *E-mail:* info@camerique.com *Web Site:* www.camerique.com, pg 1427

The Campbell-Logan Bindery Inc, 7615 Baker St NE, Fridley, MN 55432 *Tel:* 612-332-1313 *Toll Free Tel:* 800-942-6224 *E-mail:* info@campbell-logan.com *Web Site:* www.campbell-logan.com, pg 1325

Canadian Manda Group, 664 Annette St, Toronto, ON M6S 2C8, Canada *Tel:* 416-516-0911 *Fax:* 416-516-0917 *Toll Free Fax:* 888-563-8327 (CN only) *E-mail:* general@mandagroup.com; info@mandagroup.com *Web Site:* www.mandagroup.com, pg 1287

The Canadian Press Images, 60 Adelaide St E, Suite 1200, Toronto, ON M5C 3E4, Canada *Tel:* 416-507-2198 (photo archives) *Toll Free Tel:* 866-599-0599 *E-mail:* info@cpimages.com *Web Site:* www.cpimages.com; www.thecanadianpress.com, pg 1427

The Canadian Press/La Presse Canadienne, 36 King St E, Toronto, ON M5C 2L9, Canada *Tel:* 416-364-0321 *Fax:* 416-364-0207 (newsroom) *E-mail:* sales@thecanadianpress.com *Web Site:* www.thecanadianpress.com, pg 1189

Canon Business Process Services, 261 Madison Ave, 3rd fl, New York, NY 10016 *Tel:* 212-502-2100 *Toll Free Tel:* 888-623-2668 *E-mail:* cbps-info@cbps.canon.com *Web Site:* cbps.canon.com, pg 1333

Canon USA Inc, One Canon Park, Milville, NY 11747 *Tel:* 516-328-5000; 631-330-5000 *Web Site:* www.usa.canon.com, pg 1365

Canterbury Press, 120 Interstate N Pkwy E, Suite 200, Atlanta, GA 30339 *Tel:* 770-952-8309 *Fax:* 770-952-4623 *E-mail:* sales@canterburypress.net *Web Site:* canterburypress.net, pg 1250

Canvys® Visual Technology Solutions, 40W267 Keslinger Rd, LaFox, IL 60147 *Toll Free Tel:* 888-735-7373 *Fax:* 630-208-2350 *Web Site:* www.canvys.com, pg 1365

Cape Cod Compositors Inc, 811 Washington St, Suite 2, Pembroke, MA 02359-2333 *Tel:* 781-826-2100, pg 1223

Capitol News Service, 530 Bercut Dr, Suite E, Sacramento, CA 95811 *Tel:* 916-445-6336 *E-mail:* sacramentobulletin@gmail.com *Web Site:* www.mnc.net/capitol.htm, pg 1189

Cardinal Publishers Group, 2402 N Shadeland Ave, Suite A, Indianapolis, IN 46219 *Tel:* 317-352-8200 *Toll Free Tel:* 800-296-0481 (cust serv) *Fax:* 317-352-8202 *E-mail:* customerservice@cardinalpub.com *Web Site:* cardinalpub.com, pg 1287

Carolina Biological Supply Co, 2700 York Rd, Burlington, NC 27215-3398 *Tel:* 336-586-4399 (intl sales); 336-538-6211 *Toll Free Tel:* 800-334-5551 *Fax:* 336-584-7686 (intl sales) *Toll Free Fax:* 800-222-7112 *E-mail:* quotations@carolina.com; product@carolina.com *Web Site:* www.carolina.com, pg 1313

Michael Carpenter Photography, 7704 Carrleigh Pkwy, Springfield, VA 22152-1304 *Tel:* 703-644-9666 *Web Site:* www.michaelcarpenterphotography.com, pg 1420

R E Carsch, MS-Consultant, 1453 Rhode Island St, San Francisco, CA 94107-3248 *Tel:* 415-533-8356 (cell) *E-mail:* recarsch@mzinfo.com, pg 1344

The Cartoon Bank, A New Yorker Magazine Company, One World Trade Center, 42nd fl, New York, NY 10007 *Tel:* 212-286-2860 *E-mail:* image_licensing@condenast.com; thenewyorkerinfo@condenast.com *Web Site:* www.cartoonbank.com, pg 1413

Casemate | academic, 1950 Lawrence Rd, Havertown, PA 19083 *Tel:* 610-853-9131 *Fax:* 610-853-9146 *E-mail:* info@casemateacademic.com *Web Site:* www.oxbowbooks.com/dbbc, pg 1287

Casemate | IPM, 1950 Lawrence Rd, Havertown, PA 19083 *Tel:* 610-853-9131 *Fax:* 610-853-9146 *E-mail:* casemate@casematepublishers.com *Web Site:* www.casemateipm.com, pg 1108, 1115, 1288, 1344

Wilson Casey, "Trivia" Guinness World Record Holder, 282 Spring Dr, Spartanburg, SC 29302 *Tel:* 864-621-7129 *E-mail:* trivguy@bellsouth.net; wc@triviaguy.com *Web Site:* www.triviaguy.com; www.patreon.com/triviaguy, pg 1125

Elizabeth Castaldini, 927 Winterlochen Dr, Greensboro, NC 27410 *Tel:* 646-247-3190 *E-mail:* eranhec@yahoo.com, pg 1400

Catamount Content LLC, 240 Cummings Rd, Montpelier, VT 05602 *Tel:* 917-512-1962 *E-mail:* info@catamountinternational.com *Web Site:* catamountinternational.com, pg 1288

Cat's Eye Consultancy, 4120 Durham Ct, Eagan, MN 55122 *Tel:* 651-270-3190, pg 1344

Wm Caxton Ltd - Bookseller & Publisher, 12037 Hwy 42, Ellison Bay, WI 54210 *Tel:* 920-854-2955, pg 1313

CCG Marketing Solutions, 14 Henderson Dr, West Caldwell, NJ 07006 *Tel:* 973-808-0009 *E-mail:* info@corpcomm.com *Web Site:* home.corpcomm.com, pg 1115

CC1 Inc, 170 West Rd, Suite 7, Portsmouth, NH 03801 *Tel:* 603-319-2000 *Fax:* 603-319-2200 *E-mail:* customerservice@cc1inc.com *Web Site:* www.cc1inc.com, pg 1278

CD ROM Inc, 3131 E Riverside Dr, Fort Myers, FL 33916 *Tel:* 239-332-2800 *Toll Free Tel:* 866-66-CDROM (662-3766) *E-mail:* info@cdrominc.com *Web Site:* www.cdrominc.com, pg 1366

CD Solutions Inc, 100 W Monument St, Pleasant Hill, OH 45359 *Tel:* 937-676-2376 *Toll Free Tel:* 800-860-2376 *Fax:* 937-676-2478 *E-mail:* contact@cds.com *Web Site:* www.cds.com, pg 1366

CD/Works, 30 Doaks Lane, Marblehead, MA 01945 *Tel:* 978-922-4990 *Toll Free Tel:* 800-CDWORKS (239-6757) *Fax:* 978-922-5110 *Web Site:* www.cdworks.com, pg 1366

COMPANY INDEX

CDS Global, 1901 Bell Ave, Des Moines, IA 50315-1099 *Tel:* 515-247-7500 *Toll Free Tel:* 866-897-7987 *E-mail:* salesinfo@cds-global.com *Web Site:* www.cds-global.com, pg 1117, 1119

CeciBooks Editorial & Publishing Consultation, 7057 26 Ave NW, Seattle, WA 98117 *E-mail:* ceci@cecibooks.com *Web Site:* www.cecibooks.com, pg 1344

Cedar Fort Inc, 2373 W 700 S, Suite 100, Springville, UT 84663 *Tel:* 801-489-4084 *Toll Free Tel:* 800-SKY-BOOK (759-2665) *E-mail:* marketinginfo@cedarfort.com *Web Site:* cedarfort.com, pg 1327

Celtic Castle Photography, 1319 Hardys Creek Rd, Jonesville, VA 24263 *Tel:* 276-346-3625 *E-mail:* celticastlephotography@gmail.com *Web Site:* www.celticastlephotography.com, pg 1420

Dwight Cendrowski Photography LLC, 2870 Easy St, Ann Arbor, MI 48104-6532 *Tel:* 734-330-5230 *Web Site:* www.cendrowski.com, pg 1420

Century Direct Solutions LLC, 15 Enter Lane, Islandia, NY 11749 *Tel:* 212-763-0600 *E-mail:* contact@centurydirect.net *Web Site:* www.centurydirect.net, pg 1103, 1115, 1117, 1278

Cenveo Inc, 200 First Stamford Place, 2nd fl, Stamford, CT 06902 *Tel:* 203-595-3000 *Fax:* 203-595-3070 *E-mail:* info@cenveo.com *Web Site:* www.cenveo.com, pg 1209, 1250, 1265

Cenveo St Louis, 101 Workman Ct, Eureka, MO 63025 *Tel:* 314-966-2000 *Toll Free Tel:* 800-800-8845 *Fax:* 314-966-4725 *Web Site:* www.cenveo.com, pg 1209, 1223, 1250, 1265

CG Book Printers, 1750 Northway Dr, North Mankato, MN 56003 *Tel:* 507-388-3300 *Toll Free Tel:* 800-729-7575 *Fax:* 507-386-6350 *E-mail:* cgbooks@corpgraph.com *Web Site:* www.corpgraph.com, pg 1103, 1115, 1209, 1223, 1250, 1265, 1278, 1354, 1366

Challenge Machinery Co, 6125 Norton Center Dr, Norton Shores, MI 49441 *Tel:* 231-799-8484 *Fax:* 231-798-1275 *E-mail:* info@challengemachinery.com; sales@challengemachinery.com *Web Site:* www.challengemachinery.com, pg 1278

Charlesworth Author Services (USA) Inc, c/o Suite 510 Constitution Place, 325 Chestnut St, Philadelphia, PA 19106 *E-mail:* usa@cwauthors.com *Web Site:* www.cwauthors.com, pg 1366

Alexandra Chciuk-Celt, 392 Maple St, West Hempstead, NY 11552 *Tel:* 516-485-5531 *E-mail:* languagelady@juno.com, pg 1400

Cheneliere Education Inc, 5800, rue St Denis, bureau 900, Montreal, QC H2S 3L5, Canada *Tel:* 514-273-1066 *Toll Free Tel:* 800-565-5531 *Fax:* 514-276-0324 *Toll Free Fax:* 800-814-0324 *E-mail:* info@cheneliere.ca *Web Site:* www.cheneliere.ca, pg 1313

Cheng & Tsui Co Inc, 25 West St, 2nd fl, Boston, MA 02111-1213 *Tel:* 617-988-2400 *Toll Free Tel:* 800-554-1963 *Fax:* 617-426-3669 *E-mail:* service@cheng-tsui.com; orders@cheng-tsui.com; marketing@cheng-tsui.com *Web Site:* www.cheng-tsui.com, pg 1313

Chesapeake & Hudson Inc, 27 Jacks Shop Rd, Rochelle, VA 22738 *Tel:* 301-834-7170 *Toll Free Tel:* 800-231-4469 *E-mail:* office@cheshud.com *Web Site:* www.cheshudinc.com, pg 1288

Chicago Distribution Center (CDC), 11030 S Langley Ave, Chicago, IL 60628 *Tel:* 773-702-7010 *Toll Free Fax:* 800-621-8476 *Web Site:* press.uchicago.edu/cdc, pg 1289

The Children's Book Council (CBC), 54 W 39 St, 14th fl, New York, NY 10018 *E-mail:* cbc.info@cbcbooks.org *Web Site:* www.cbcbooks.org, pg 1145

The Children's Book Store Distribution (CBSD), 23 Griffin St, Waterdown, ON L0R 2H0, Canada *Tel:* 905-690-9397 (ext 237) *Toll Free Tel:* 800-757-8372 (cust serv, CN & US) *Fax:* 905-690-3419 *E-mail:* info@childrensgroup.com; sales@idla.ca *Web Site:* www.childrensgroup.com, pg 1313

The Bulletin of the Center for Children's Books, 2715 N Charles St, Baltimore, MD 21218-4363 *Tel:* 410-516-6900; 410-516-6987 (journal orders outside US & CN); 217-244-0324 (bulletin info) *Toll Free Tel:* 800-548-1784 (journal orders) *Fax:* 410-516-6968; 410-578-2865 (journal orders) *E-mail:* bccb@illinois.edu; jlorder@jhupress.jhu.edu *Web Site:* www.press.jhu.edu/journals/bulletin-center-childrens-books, pg 1130

Children's Books USA Inc, 425 Boardman Ave, Traverse City, MI 49684 *Tel:* 231-933-3699 *E-mail:* info@childrensbooksusa.com *Web Site:* www.childrensbooksusa.com, pg 1139

Children's Bookwatch, 278 Orchard Dr, Oregon, WI 53575-1129 *Tel:* 608-835-7937 *E-mail:* mbr@execpc.com *Web Site:* www.midwestbookreview.com, pg 1131

Children's Braille Book Club, 88 Saint Stephen St, Boston, MA 02115-4312 *Tel:* 617-266-6160 *Toll Free Tel:* 800-548-7323 (cust serv) *Fax:* 617-437-0456 *E-mail:* contact@nbp.org *Web Site:* www.nbp.org, pg 1141

China Books, 360 Swift Ave, Suite 48, South San Francisco, CA 94080 *Fax:* 650-872-7808 *E-mail:* editor.sinomedia@gmail.com, pg 1313, 1327

ChinaStock/WorldViews, 2506 Country Village, Ann Arbor, MI 48103-6500 *Tel:* 734-680-4660 *E-mail:* decoxphoto@gmail.com *Web Site:* www.denniscox.com, pg 1427

Chinese Christian Mission Bookroom, 1269 N McDowell Blvd, Petaluma, CA 94954-1133 *Tel:* 707-762-2688; 707-762-1314 *Fax:* 707-762-1713 *E-mail:* bookroom@ccmusa.org; ccm@ccmusa.org *Web Site:* www.ccmusa.org; www.ccmbookroom.org, pg 1313

Choice, 575 Main St, Suite 300, Middletown, CT 06457 *Tel:* 860-347-6933; 847-504-8803 (subns) *Toll Free Tel:* 844-291-0455 (subns) *Fax:* 860-346-8586 *E-mail:* acrlsubscriptions@omeda.com; support@acrlchoice.freshdesk.com *Web Site:* www.ala.org/acrl-choice; www.choice360.org, pg 1131

Choice Associates, 501 Fifth Ave, Suite 1601, New York, NY 10017 *Tel:* 212-679-2434 *Fax:* 212-213-0984 *E-mail:* info@choicepersonnelinc.com *Web Site:* www.choicepersonnelinc.com, pg 1381

Choice Books, 10100 Piper Lane, Bristow, VA 20136 *Tel:* 703-530-9993 *Fax:* 703-530-9983 *E-mail:* info@choicebooks.com *Web Site:* www.choicebooks.com, pg 1313

Christianbook Inc, 140 Summit St, Peabody, MA 01960-5156 *Tel:* 978-977-5060; 978-977-5000 (intl calls) *Toll Free Tel:* 800-CHRISTIAN (247-4784) *Fax:* 978-977-5010 *E-mail:* customer.service@christianbook.com *Web Site:* www.christianbook.com, pg 1313

Chronicles: A Magazine of American Culture, 8011 34 Ave S, Suite C11, Bloomington, MN 55425 *Web Site:* www.chroniclesmagazine.org, pg 1131

Cimarron Design, 8285 Kincross Dr, Boulder, CO 80301-4228 *Tel:* 303-530-1785 *Web Site:* www.cimarrondesign.com, pg 1223

Circle Graphics Inc, 316 Main St, Suite 1C, Reisters Town, MD 21136 *Tel:* 410-833-2200 *E-mail:* production@circleusa.com *Web Site:* www.circleusa.com, pg 1223

Citation Box & Paper Co, 4700 W Augusta Blvd, Chicago, IL 60651-3397 *Tel:* 773-378-1400 *E-mail:* info@citationbox.com *Web Site:* www.citationbox.com, pg 1337

Citizen Systems America Corp, 363 Van Ness Way, Suite 404, Torrance, CA 90501 *Tel:* 310-781-1460 *Toll Free Tel:* 800-421-6516 *Web Site:* www.citizen-systems.com, pg 1366

City Diecutting Inc, One Cory Rd, Morristown, NJ 07960 *Tel:* 973-270-0370 *Fax:* 973-270-0369 *E-mail:* sales@bookdisplays.com *Web Site:* www.bookdisplays.com, pg 1103, 1344

CJK, 3962 Virginia Ave, Cincinnati, OH 45227 *Tel:* 513-271-6035 *Toll Free Tel:* 800-598-7808 *Fax:* 513-271-6082 *E-mail:* info@cjkusa.com *Web Site:* www.cjkusa.com, pg 1250

Clamco Corp, 775 Berea Industrial Pkwy, Berea, OH 44017 *Tel:* 216-267-1911 *Toll Free Tel:* 800-985-9570 (headquarters) *Fax:* 216-267-8713 *E-mail:* info@clamcopackaging.com *Web Site:* www.pacmachinery.com/clamcopackaging, pg 1278

Clare Printing, 206 S Keystone Ave, Sayre, PA 18840 *Tel:* 570-888-2244 *E-mail:* hr@clareprint.com *Web Site:* www.clareprint.com, pg 1223, 1250, 1278

Claris International Inc, 5201 Patrick Henry Dr, Santa Clara, CA 95054 *Tel:* 408-727-8227 (sales & cust support) *Toll Free Tel:* 800-725-2747 (sales); 800-325-2747 (cust support) *Fax:* 408-987-7447 *E-mail:* claris_sales@claris.com *Web Site:* www.claris.com, pg 1366

Claritas LLC, 8044 Montgomery Rd, Suite 455, Cincinnati, OH 45236 *Toll Free Tel:* 888-981-0040 *E-mail:* findcustomers@claritas.com; marketing@claritas.com *Web Site:* www.claritas.com, pg 1366

Clarity Output Solutions (COS), 860 Honeyspot Rd, Stratford, CT 06615 *Tel:* 203-378-6200 *Toll Free Tel:* 800-414-1624 *E-mail:* info@clarityosl.com *Web Site:* www.clarityosl.com, pg 1115, 1117

ClassicStock.com/Robertstock.com, 4203 Locust St, Philadelphia, PA 19104 *Tel:* 215-386-6300 *Toll Free Tel:* 800-786-6300 *Toll Free Fax:* 800-786-1920 *E-mail:* sales@classicstock.com; info@classicstock.com; info@robertstock.com *Web Site:* www.classicstock.com; www.robertstock.com, pg 1427

CLC Ministries, 701 Pennsylvania Ave, Fort Washington, PA 19034 *Tel:* 215-542-1240 *Toll Free Tel:* 800-659-1240 *Fax:* 215-542-7580 *E-mail:* orders@clcpublications.com *Web Site:* www.clcpublications.com, pg 1313

Clear Concepts, 1329 Federal Ave, Suite 6, Los Angeles, CA 90025 *Tel:* 323-285-0325, pg 1108, 1314, 1344

Clear Print, 9025 Fullbright Ave, Chatsworth, CA 91311 *Tel:* 818-709-1220 *Fax:* 818-709-1320 *E-mail:* info@clearprint.com; sales@clearprint.com *Web Site:* www.clearprint.com, pg 1250

Clerical Plus, 97 Blueberry Lane, Shelton, CT 06484 *Tel:* 203-225-0879 *Fax:* 203-225-0879 *E-mail:* clericalplus@aol.com *Web Site:* www.clericalplus.net, pg 1366

The Cleveland Vibrator Co, 2828 Clinton Ave, Cleveland, OH 44113 *Tel:* 216-241-7157 *Toll Free Tel:* 800-221-3298 *Fax:* 216-241-3480 *E-mail:* sales@clevelandvibrator.com *Web Site:* www.clevelandvibrator.com, pg 1278

Cliff Digital, 14700 S Main St, Gardena, CA 90248 *Tel:* 310-323-5600 *Toll Free Tel:* 866-429-2242 *Fax:* 310-400-3090 *E-mail:* cliff@cliffdigital.com *Web Site:* www.cliffdigital.com, pg 1103

Clotilde's Secretarial & Management Services, PO Box 871926, New Orleans, LA 70187 *Tel:* 504-242-2912; 504-266-9239 (cell) *Fax:* 504-242-2912, pg 1385

Dwight Clough, PO Box 670, Wyocena, WI 53969 *E-mail:* lmp@dwightclough.com *Web Site:* dwightclough.com, pg 1344, 1366

Club Leo (Spanish & bilingual books for all grades), 557 Broadway, New York, NY 10012 *Tel:* 212-343-6100; 573-632-1632 (PR, US territories, US military bases) *Toll Free Tel:* 800-541-1097 (US) *Toll Free Fax:* 800-223-4011 *E-mail:* bookclubs@scholastic.com *Web Site:* clubs.scholastic.com, pg 1141

Coach House Printing, 80 bpNichol Lane, Toronto, ON M5S 3J4, Canada *Tel:* 416-979-2217 *Toll Free Tel:* 800-367-6360 (outside Toronto) *Fax:* 416-977-1158 *E-mail:* mail@chbooks.com *Web Site:* www.chbooks.com, pg 1223, 1250

Codra Enterprises Inc, 17692 Cowan, Suite 200, Irvine, CA 92614 *Tel:* 949-756-8400 *Toll Free Tel:* 888-992-6372 *Fax:* 949-756-8484 *E-mail:* codra@codra.com; sales@codra.com *Web Site:* www.codra.com, pg 1209, 1250

Cohesion®, 511 W Bay St, Suite 480, Tampa, FL 33606 *Tel:* 813-999-3111 *Toll Free Tel:* 866-727-6800 *Web Site:* www.cohesion.com, pg 1344, 1366, 1381

THE COLAD GROUP LLC   COMPANY INDEX

The Colad Group LLC, 693 Seneca St, 5th fl, Buffalo, NY 14210 *Tel:* 716-961-1776 *Toll Free Tel:* 800-950-1755 *Fax:* 716-961-1753 *E-mail:* info@colad.com *Web Site:* www.colad.com, pg 1103

Brandon Cole Marine Photography, 4917 N Boeing Rd, Spokane Valley, WA 99206 *Tel:* 509-535-3489 *E-mail:* brandoncole@msn.com *Web Site:* www.brandoncole.com, pg 1420

Leon Collins, 71 Faunce Dr, Providence, RI 02906 *Tel:* 401-274-2149 *Web Site:* www.whitegatefeatures.com, pg 1125

Color Graphic Press Inc, 42 Main St, Nyack, NY 10960 *Tel:* 845-535-3444 *Fax:* 845-535-3446 *E-mail:* info@cgpny.com *Web Site:* www.cgpny.com, pg 1250

Color House Graphics Inc, 3505 Eastern Ave SE, Grand Rapids, MI 49508 *Toll Free Tel:* 800-454-1916 *Fax:* 616-245-5494 *Web Site:* www.colorhousegraphics.com, pg 1209, 1250, 1344

ColorPage, 81 Ten Broeck Ave, Kingston, NY 12401 *Tel:* 845-331-7581 *Toll Free Tel:* 800-836-7581 *Fax:* 845-331-1571 *E-mail:* sales@colorpageonline.com *Web Site:* www.colorpageonline.com, pg 1209, 1223, 1250, 1265

Colour Technologies, 560 Hensall Circle, Mississauga, ON L5A 1Y1, Canada *Tel:* 416-588-0808 *E-mail:* info@cjgraphics.com *Web Site:* www.cjgraphics.com/services/prepress, pg 1223, 1413

Columbia Finishing Mills Inc, 135 Boundary Rd, Cornwall, ON K6H 5T3, Canada *Tel:* 613-933-1462 *Toll Free Tel:* 800-267-9174 *Fax:* 613-933-7717 *Toll Free Fax:* 800-242-9174 *E-mail:* info@columbiafinishingmills.com *Web Site:* www.columbiafinishingmills.com, pg 1266

Comag Marketing Group LLC (CMG), 155 Village Blvd, Suite 300, Princeton, NJ 08540 *Tel:* 609-524-1800 *Fax:* 609-524-1629 *Web Site:* www.i-cmg.com, pg 1314

The Combined Book Exhibit®, 277 White St, Buchanan, NY 10511 *Tel:* 914-739-7500 *Toll Free Tel:* 800-462-7687 *Fax:* 914-739-7575 *E-mail:* info@combinedbook.com *Web Site:* www.combinedbook.com; www.cbedatabase.com, pg 1139

Communication Abstracts, 10 Estes St, Ipswich, MA 01938 *Tel:* 978-356-6500 *Toll Free Tel:* 800-653-2726 *Fax:* 978-356-6565 *E-mail:* information@ebsco.com *Web Site:* www.ebsco.com, pg 1131

Communication Matters, 48 Aylmer Ave, Ottawa, ON K1S 2X1, Canada *Tel:* 613-233-5423 *Web Site:* www.communicationmatters.ca, pg 1108

Communicorp Inc, 1001 Lockwood Ave, Columbus, GA 31999 *Tel:* 706-324-1182 *E-mail:* mktech@communicorp.com *Web Site:* www.communicorp.com, pg 1224, 1250

Computer Analytics Corp, 999 E Touhy Ave, Suite 130, Des Plaines, IL 60018-2736 *Tel:* 847-297-5290 *Fax:* 847-297-8680 *Web Site:* www.cacorp.com, pg 1366

Concierge Marketing Inc, 4822 S 133 St, Omaha, NE 68137 *Tel:* 402-884-5995 *Web Site:* www.conciergemarketing.com, pg 1345

Concord Editorial & Design LLC, 9450 SW Gemini Dr, Suite 68669, Beaverton, OR 97008 *Tel:* 616-827-7537 *Fax:* 616-825-6048 *E-mail:* info@concordeditorial.com *Web Site:* www.concordeditorial.com, pg 1224, 1354

Conrad Direct Inc, 800 Kinderkamack Rd, Suite 307N, Oradell, NJ 07649 *Tel:* 201-567-3200 *Fax:* 201-567-1530 *E-mail:* listinfo@conraddirect.com *Web Site:* www.conraddirect.com, pg 1115

C Harrison Conroy Co Inc, 501 Penman St, Charlotte, NC 28203 *Tel:* 704-358-0459 *Toll Free Tel:* 800-242-2789 *Fax:* 704-358-0459 *E-mail:* chcphoto@charrisonconroy.com *Web Site:* www.charrisonconroy.com, pg 1209, 1251

Conservation Resources International LLC, 7350 Lockport Place, Suite A, Lorton, VA 22079 *Tel:* 703-321-7730 *Toll Free Tel:* 800-634-6932 *Fax:* 703-321-0629 *E-mail:* sales@conservationresources.com *Web Site:* www.conservationresources.com, pg 1266

Conservative Book Club, 300 New Jersey Ave NW, Suite 500, Washington, DC 20001 *Tel:* 202-216-0601 *Web Site:* www.conservativebookclub.com, pg 1141

Consolidated Printers Inc, 2630 Eighth St, Berkeley, CA 94710 *Tel:* 510-495-3113 (sales); 510-843-8565 (admin) *Web Site:* www.consoprinters.com, pg 1209, 1251

Consortium Book Sales & Distribution, an Ingram brand, The Keg House, Suite 101, 34 13 Ave NE, Minneapolis, MN 55413-1007 *Tel:* 612-746-2600 *Toll Free Tel:* 866-400-5351 (cust serv, Jackson, TN) *E-mail:* cbsdinfo@ingramcontent.com *Web Site:* www.cbsd.com, pg 1289

Conspire Creative, Chicago, IL 60657 *Tel:* 773-562-5499 *Web Site:* www.conspirecreative.com, pg 1345

CONTECH (Converting Technologies), 1756 S 151 St W, Goddard, KS 67052 *Tel:* 316-722-6907 *Fax:* 316-722-2976 *E-mail:* info@contechusa.com *Web Site:* www.contechusa.com, pg 1278

Content Critical Solutions Inc, 10 Fifth St, 2nd fl, Valley Stream, NY 11581 *Tel:* 201-528-2777 *E-mail:* info@contentcritical.com *Web Site:* www.contentcritical.com, pg 1115

Continental Book Co Inc, 7000 Broadway, Suite 102, Denver, CO 80221-2913 *Tel:* 303-289-1761 *Toll Free Fax:* 800-279-1764 *E-mail:* cbc@continentalbook.com *Web Site:* www.continentalbook.com, pg 1289, 1314, 1327

Continental Features/Continental News Service, 501 W Broadway, Plaza A, PMB 265, San Diego, CA 92101 *Tel:* 858-492-8696 *E-mail:* info@continentalnewsservice.com; continentalnewstime@gmail.com *Web Site:* www.continentalnewsservice.com, pg 1189

Continental Sales Inc, 213 W Main St, Barrington, IL 60010 *Tel:* 847-381-6530 *Fax:* 847-382-0385; 847-382-0419 *Web Site:* www.continentalsalesinc.com, pg 1289

Continental Web Press Inc, 1430 Industrial Dr, Itasca, IL 60143-1858 *Tel:* 630-773-1903 *E-mail:* inquiries@continentalweb.com *Web Site:* www.continentalweb.com, pg 1251

Conway Greene Co, 1400 E 30 St, Suite 402, Cleveland, OH 44114 *Tel:* 216-965-3195 *Web Site:* www.conwaygreene.com, pg 1366

Cook Public Relations, 3251 Spear Ave, Arcata, CA 95521 *Tel:* 707-630-3597; 415-302-1752 (cell) *Web Site:* www.cookpr.com, pg 1108

Cookbook Publishers Inc, 11633 W 83 Terr, Lenexa, KS 66285 *Tel:* 913-492-5900 *Toll Free Tel:* 800-227-7282 *Fax:* 913-492-5947 *E-mail:* info@cookbookpublishers.com *Web Site:* www.cookbookpublishers.com, pg 1224, 1251

Robert Cooney Graphic Design, PO Box 362, Half Moon Bay, CA 94019 *Tel:* 650-712-4400, pg 1413

Cooperative Etudiante de Polytechnique, Pavillon Principal Local C-220, 2900 Edouard Mont Petit, Montreal, QC H3T 1J4, Canada *Tel:* 514-340-4851 *Fax:* 514-340-4543 *E-mail:* andre.daneau@polymtl.ca *Web Site:* www.coopoly.ca, pg 1314

Copycats, 216 E 45 St, 10th fl, New York, NY 10017 *Tel:* 212-557-2111 *Toll Free Tel:* 800-404-2679 *Fax:* 212-557-2039 *E-mail:* client@copycats.com *Web Site:* www.copycats.com, pg 1251

Copyright Clearance Center Inc (CCC), 222 Rosewood Dr, Danvers, MA 01923 *Tel:* 978-750-8400 (sales); 978-646-2600 (cust serv) *E-mail:* info@copyright.com *Web Site:* www.copyright.com, pg 1345

Copywriters' Council of America™ (CCA), Linick Bldg, 7 Putter Lane, Middle Island, NY 11953 *Tel:* 631-924-3888; 631-924-8555; 631-604-8599 *E-mail:* linickgroup@gmail.com *Web Site:* www.ccamerica.com, pg 1345

Coral Graphic Services Inc, 840 S Broadway, Hicksville, NY 11801 *Tel:* 516-576-2100 *Fax:* 516-576-2168 *E-mail:* info@coralgraphics.com *Web Site:* www.bpg-usa.com, pg 1224, 1251, 1266

Corder Associates Inc, 2602 W Baseline Rd, Suite 22, Mesa, AZ 85202 *Tel:* 480-752-8533 *Toll Free Tel:* 877-303-7575 *Fax:* 480-752-8534 *E-mail:* info@cordernet.com *Web Site:* cordernet.com, pg 1366

Corel Corporation, 1600 Carling Ave, Ottawa, ON K1Z 8R7, Canada *Toll Free Tel:* 877-582-6735 *Web Site:* www.corel.com, pg 1366

Steve Corey, 71 Faunce Dr, Providence, RI 02906 *Tel:* 401-274-2149 *Web Site:* www.whitegatefeatures.com, pg 1125

Cornell & Company, LLC, 44 Jog Hill Rd, Trumbull, CT 06611 *Tel:* 203-454-4210 *Web Site:* www.cornellandco.com, pg 1413

Coronet Books Inc, 33 Ashley Dr, Schwenksville, PA 19473 *Tel:* 215-925-2762 *Fax:* 215-925-1912 *Web Site:* www.coronetbooks.com, pg 1314

Corporate Disk Co, 4610 Prime Pkwy, McHenry, IL 60050-7005 *Tel:* 815-331-6000 *Toll Free Tel:* 800-634-3475 *Fax:* 815-331-6030 *E-mail:* info@disk.com *Web Site:* www.disk.com, pg 1224, 1251, 1366

Cosmos Communications Inc, 11-05 44 Dr, Long Island City, NY 11101 *Tel:* 718-482-1800 *Toll Free Tel:* 800-223-5751 *Fax:* 718-482-1968 *Web Site:* www.cosmoscommunications.com, pg 1366

The Country Press Inc, One Commercial Dr, Lakeville, MA 02347 *Tel:* 508-947-4485 *Toll Free Tel:* 888-343-2227 *Fax:* 508-947-8989 *E-mail:* info@countrypressinc.com *Web Site:* www.countrypressprinting.com, pg 1209, 1251

Courier Printing, One Courier Place, Smyrna, TN 37167 *Tel:* 615-355-4000 *Toll Free Tel:* 800-467-0444 *Fax:* 615-355-4088 *Web Site:* www.courierprinting.com, pg 1224, 1251

Courier Systems Inc, 180 Pulaski St, Bayonne, NJ 07002 *Tel:* 201-432-0550 *Toll Free Tel:* 800-252-0353 *Fax:* 201-432-9686 *E-mail:* sales@csweb.biz *Web Site:* www.csweb.biz, pg 1333

Coverline Inc, 13 Spruce Pond Rd, Franklin, MA 02038 *Tel:* 508-528-8511 *Fax:* 508-528-6838, pg 1266

Cox-King Multimedia, PO Box 909, Geneva, NY 14456 *Tel:* 315-719-0141 *E-mail:* info@ckmm.com *Web Site:* www.ckmm.com, pg 1413

CQ Roll Call, 1201 Pennsylvania Ave NW, Suite 600, Washington, DC 20004 *Tel:* 202-650-6500; 202-650-6511 (subns); 202-650-6621 (cust serv) *Toll Free Tel:* 800-432-2250; 800-678-8511 (subns) *E-mail:* customerservice@cqrollcall.com *Web Site:* cqrollcall.com; www.rollcall.com, pg 1190

Crafter's Choice®, 34 W 27 St, 10th fl, New York, NY 10001 *Tel:* 716-250-5700 (cust serv) *Toll Free Tel:* 866-250-3166 *E-mail:* customer.service@crafterschoice.com *Web Site:* www.crafterschoice.com, pg 1141

Craftsmen Machinery Co Inc, 1257 Worcester Rd, Unit 167, Framingham, MA 01701 *Tel:* 508-376-2001 *Fax:* 508-376-2603 *E-mail:* sales@craftsmenmachinery.com *Web Site:* www.craftsmenmachinery.com, pg 1278

Crain Communications Inc, 1155 Gratiot Ave, Detroit, MI 48207-2732 *Tel:* 313-446-6000 *Fax:* 313-446-0383 *E-mail:* info@crain.com *Web Site:* crain.com, pg 1190

Crane Duplicating Service Inc, 4915 Rattlesnake Hammock Rd, Suite 207, Naples, FL 34113 *Tel:* 305-280-6742 (help desk) *Fax:* 239-732-8415 *E-mail:* info@craneduplicating.com *Web Site:* www.craneduplicating.com, pg 1209, 1251

Crawshaw Design, 120 Bayview Dr, San Rafael, CA 94901 *Tel:* 415-456-5544 *Fax:* 415-456-4319 *Web Site:* www.crawshawdesign.com, pg 1413

Creative Direct Marketing Group Inc (CDMG), 1313 Fourth Ave N, Nashville, TN 37208 *Tel:* 615-814-6633 *Web Site:* www.cdmginc.com, pg 1345

COMPANY INDEX

The Creative Group®, A Robert Half Company, Oliver Street Tower, 17th fl, 125 High St, Boston, MA 02110 Tel: 617-925-5754 Web Site: www.roberthalf.com/us/en/about/our-company/brands/creative-group, pg 1381, 1413

Creative Trust Inc, 210 Jamestown Park Dr, Suite 200, Brentwood, TN 37027 Tel: 615-297-5010 Fax: 615-297-5020 E-mail: info@creativetrust.com Web Site: creativetrust.com, pg 1345

Creators Syndicate, 737 Third St, Hermosa Beach, CA 90254 Tel: 310-337-7003 E-mail: info@creators.com Web Site: www.creators.com, pg 1190

Crescent Imports, PO Box 721, Union City, CA 94587 Tel: 734-665-3492 Toll Free Tel: 800-521-9744 Fax: 734-677-1717 E-mail: message@crescentimports.com Web Site: crescentimports.com; crescentimports.store, pg 1314

Crescent Imports, PO Box 721, Union City, CA 94587 Tel: 734-665-3492 Toll Free Tel: 800-521-9744 Fax: 734-677-1717 E-mail: message@crescentimports.com Web Site: crescentimports.store; crescentimports.com, pg 1327

The Cricket Letter Inc, PO Box 527, Ardmore, PA 19003-0527 Tel: 610-924-9158 Fax: 610-924-9159 E-mail: crcktinc@aol.com, pg 1190

The Criterion Collection, 215 Park Ave S, 5th fl, New York, NY 10003 Tel: 212-756-8822 E-mail: suggestions@criterion.com Web Site: www.criterion.com, pg 1366

Cromwell Leather, 147 Palmer Ave, Mamaroneck, NY 10543 Tel: 914-381-0100 Fax: 914-381-0046 E-mail: sales@cromwellgroup.com Web Site: www.cromwellgroup.com, pg 1266

Cross Country Computer Corp, 250 Carleton Ave, East Islip, NY 11730-1240 Tel: 631-334-1810 E-mail: inquiry@crosscountrycomputer.com Web Site: www.crosscountrycomputer.com, pg 1119

Cross Cultural Communication Systems Inc, 227 Garfield Ave, Suite B, Woburn, MA 01801 Tel: 781-729-3736 Toll Free Tel: 888-678-CCCS (678-2227 out of state only) Fax: 781-729-1217 Web Site: www.cccsorg.com; www.embracingculture.com, pg 1400

Cross Culture Communications, PO Box 141263, Dallas, TX 75214 Tel: 214-394-3000 E-mail: info@crossculturecommunications.com Web Site: crossculturecommunications.com, pg 1400

The Crowley Co, 5111 Pegasus Ct, Suite M, Frederick, MD 21704 Tel: 240-215-0224 Fax: 240-215-0234 E-mail: webrequest@thecrowleycompany.com Web Site: www.thecrowleycompany.com, pg 1367

Crown Connect, 250 W Rialto Ave, San Bernadino, CA 92408 Tel: 909-888-7531 Fax: 909-889-1639 E-mail: sales@crownconnect.com Web Site: www.crownconnect.com, pg 1209, 1224, 1279

Crown Roll Leaf Inc, 91 Illinois Ave, Paterson, NJ 07503 Tel: 973-742-4000 Toll Free Tel: 800-631-3831 Fax: 973-742-0219 Web Site: www.crownrollleaf.com, pg 1251

CRW Graphics Communications, 9100 Pennsauken Hwy, Pennsauken, NJ 08110 Tel: 856-662-9111 Toll Free Tel: 800-820-3000 Fax: 856-665-1789 E-mail: info@crwgraphics.com Web Site: www.crwgraphics.com, pg 1103, 1367, 1413

Current Biography, 4919 Rte 22, Amenia, NY 12501 Tel: 518-789-8700 Toll Free Tel: 800-562-2139 Fax: 518-789-0556 E-mail: books@greyhouse.com Web Site: greyhouse.com, pg 1131

Cushing-Malloy Inc, 1350 N Main St, Ann Arbor, MI 48104-1045 Tel: 734-663-8554 Fax: 734-663-5731 Web Site: www.cushing-malloy.com; www.c-mbooks.com, pg 1209, 1251

Custom Studios, 77 Main St, Tappan, NY 10983 Tel: 845-365-0414 Toll Free Tel: 800-631-1362 Fax: 845-365-0864 E-mail: customusa@aol.com Web Site: customstudios.com, pg 1224

CyberWolf® Inc, c/o 530-B Harkle Rd, Suite 100, Santa Fe, NM 87505 E-mail: sales@cyberwolf.com Web Site: www.ebookdownloadservice.com, pg 1367

Cypress House, 155 Cypress St, Suite A, Fort Bragg, CA 95437 Tel: 707-964-9520 Toll Free Tel: 800-773-7782 Fax: 707-964-7531 E-mail: office@cypresshouse.com Web Site: www.cypresshouse.com, pg 1104, 1224, 1345, 1413

D C Graphics Inc, 59 Central Ave, Suite 15, Farmingdale, NY 11735 Tel: 631-777-3100 Fax: 631-777-7899 E-mail: prepress@dcgraphicsinc.com Web Site: www.dcgraphicsinc.com, pg 1251

Bob Daemmrich Photography Inc, 1122 Colorado St, Suite 2202, Austin, TX 78701 Tel: 512-469-9700 Web Site: www.bobphoto.com, pg 1420

Dan Daly, 23 Limerock St, Camden, ME 04843-2116 Tel: 207-691-3061 E-mail: dan@dalyart.com Web Site: www.dalyart.com, pg 1413

D&D Sales & Printing, 840 12 St NW, Mason City, IA 50401 Tel: 641-423-9487 Toll Free Tel: 800-325-5308 Fax: 641-423-3068 E-mail: ddsales.service@gmail.com Web Site: www.ddsalesonline.com, pg 1413

D&K Group Inc, 1795 Commerce Dr, Elk Grove Village, IL 60007 Tel: 847-956-0160; 847-956-4757 (tech support) Toll Free Tel: 800-632-2314 Fax: 847-956-8214 E-mail: info@dkgroup.net Web Site: www.dkgroup.com, pg 1251, 1266, 1279

Kent Dannen, 1997 Big Owl Rd, Allenspark, CO 80510 Tel: 303-747-2047 Fax: 303-747-2016 E-mail: kent.dannen@yahoo.com, pg 1420

DANPHOTO, LLC, 408 E Rte 66, Flagstaff, AZ 86001 Tel: 928-774-0161 E-mail: danman@danphoto.com Web Site: www.danphoto.com, pg 1420

Darwill, 11900 W Roosevelt Rd, Hillside, IL 60162 Tel: 708-236-4900 Fax: 708-236-5820 E-mail: info@darwill.com Web Site: www.darwill.com, pg 1224

Data Axle, 13155 Noel Rd, Suite 1750, Dallas, TX 75240 Toll Free Tel: 866-DATAXLE (328-2953) E-mail: sales@data-axle.com; corporate.communications@data-axle.com Web Site: www.data-axle.com, pg 1119

Data Connect/RelComm Inc, 4868 Hwy 4, Suite G, Angels Camp, CA 95222 Tel: 301-924-7400 (ext 17) Fax: 301-924-7403 E-mail: sales@relcomm.com Web Site: www.relcomm.com, pg 1367

Data Conversion Laboratory Inc (DCL), 61-18 190 St, Suite 205, Fresh Meadows, NY 11365 Tel: 718-357-8700 Toll Free Tel: 800-321-2816 (provider problems) E-mail: info@dclab.com Web Site: www.dataconversionlaboratory.com, pg 1224, 1367

Data Index Inc, 13713 NW Indian Springs Dr, Vancouver, WA 98685 Tel: 425-760-9193 Web Site: www.dataindex.com, pg 1224

Data Reproductions Corp, 4545 Glenmeade Lane, Auburn Hills, MI 48326 Tel: 248-371-3700 Toll Free Tel: 800-242-3114 Fax: 248-371-3710 Web Site: datarepro.com, pg 1209, 1251

Datacolor, 5 Princess Rd, Lawrenceville, NJ 08648 Tel: 609-924-2189 Toll Free Tel: 800-982-6496 (support) Fax: 609-895-7414 E-mail: marketing@datacolor.com Web Site: www.datacolor.com, pg 1224

Datalogic USA Inc, 959 Terry St, Eugene, OR 97402-9150 Tel: 541-683-5700 Toll Free Tel: 800-227-2633 Web Site: www.datalogic.com, pg 1279

Datalogics Inc, 101 N Wacker, Suite 1800, Chicago, IL 60606 Tel: 312-853-8200 Fax: 312-853-8282 E-mail: sales@datalogics.com; marketing@datalogics.com Web Site: www.datalogics.com, pg 1367

Jeff Davidson MBA, CMC, Breathing Space Institute, 3202 Ruffin St, Raleigh, NC 27607 Tel: 919-932-1996 E-mail: jeff@breathingspace.com Web Site: www.breathingspace.com, pg 1345

Davis Art Images, 50 Portland St, Worcester, MA 01608 Tel: 508-754-7201 Toll Free Tel: 800-533-2847 Fax: 508-753-3834 E-mail: das@davisart.com; contactus@davisart.com Web Site: www.davisart.com, pg 1427

Jerilyn Glenn Davis, Cathedral Sta, Box 1712, New York, NY 10025 Tel: 212-889-2239 E-mail: jdavisbook@gmail.com, pg 1251

Dayton Daily News, 4805 Meredith Rd, Yellow Springs, OH 45387 Tel: 937-767-1396, pg 1131

DCA Inc, 1515 E Pine St, Cushing, OK 74023 Tel: 918-225-0346 Fax: 918-225-1113 E-mail: sales@dcainc.com Web Site: www.dcainc.com, pg 1367

De Ru's Fine Art, 27762 Antonio Pkwy, No L1103, Ladeira Ranch, CA 92694 Tel: 714-349-8250 E-mail: derusfinearts@yahoo.com Web Site: www.derusfinearts.com, pg 1314

Decker Intellectual Properties Inc, 372 Richmond St W, Toronto, ON M5V 2L7, Canada Tel: 905-522-8526 Toll Free Tel: 855-647-6511 E-mail: customercare@deckermed.com Web Site: www.deckerip.com, pg 1367

Decode, Inc, 1938 11 Ave E, Seattle, WA 98102 Tel: 206-343-9101 E-mail: books@decodebooks.com Web Site: www.decodeinc.com; www.decodebooks.com, pg 1413

Peter L DeGiglio, 6 Overlook Dr, Washingtonville, NY 10992 Tel: 914-850-3803 E-mail: pdegiglio@gmail.com, pg 1345

DeHART's Media Services Inc, 6586 Whitbourne Dr, San Jose, CA 95120 Tel: 408-768-1575 Web Site: www.deharts.com, pg 1251

DeHoff Christian Bookstore, 749 NW Broad St, Murfreesboro, TN 37129 Tel: 615-893-8322 Toll Free Tel: 800-695-5385 Fax: 615-896-7447 E-mail: dehoffbooks@gmail.com Web Site: www.dehoffpublications.com, pg 1314

Dekker Bookbinding Inc, 2941 Clydon Ave SW, Grand Rapids, MI 49519 Tel: 616-538-5160 Toll Free Tel: 800-299-BIND (299-2463) E-mail: hello@dekkerbook.com Web Site: www.dekkerbook.com, pg 1251, 1266

Del Commune Enterprises Inc, 18 Bellport Lane, Bellport, NY 11713 Tel: 212-226-6664 E-mail: mail@dcescouts.com Web Site: www.dcescouts.com, pg 1345

Danita Delimont Stock Photography, 4911 Somerset Dr SE, Bellevue, WA 98006 Tel: 425-562-1543 Web Site: www.danitadelimont.com, pg 1428

Dell EMC, 176 South St, Hopkinton, MA 01748 Tel: 508-435-1000 Toll Free Tel: 866-438-3622 Web Site: www.delltechnologies.com, pg 1367

Dell Magazines, 6 Prowitt St, Norwalk, CT 06855 Tel: 203-866-6688 Toll Free Tel: 800-220-7443 (corp sales) Fax: 203-854-5962 (pubns) E-mail: customerservice@pennypublications.com Web Site: www.pennydellpuzzles.com, pg 1354

Dell Wyse, One Dell Way, Round Rock, TX 78682 Toll Free Tel: 866-438-3622 (sales) Web Site: www.delltechnologies.com, pg 1367

Delmas Typesetting Inc, 461 Hilldale Dr, Ann Arbor, MI 48105 Tel: 734-662-8899 E-mail: delmastype@comcast.net Web Site: www.delmastype.com, pg 1224

Delphax Solutions Inc, 2810 Argentia Rd, Unit 6, Mississauga, ON L5N 8L2, Canada Toll Free Tel: 833-DELPHAX (335-7429) Web Site: www.delphaxsolutions.com, pg 1367

Demand Marketing, 377 Fisher Rd, Suite D, Grosse Pointe, MI 48230 Tel: 313-823-8598 Toll Free Tel: 888-977-2256 E-mail: info@create-demand.com Web Site: www.create-demand.com, pg 1115

Carla Demers, 71 Faunce Dr, Providence, RI 02906 Tel: 401-274-2149 Web Site: www.whitegatefeatures.com, pg 1125

Democrat Printing & Lithographing Co, 6401 Lindsey Rd, Little Rock, AR 72206 Toll Free Tel: 800-622-2216 Fax: 501-907-7953 Web Site: democratprinting.com, pg 1252

Denver Bookbinding Co Inc, 1401 W 47 Ave, Denver, CO 80211 Tel: 303-455-5521 E-mail: dbbc@denverbook.com; info@denverbook.com Web Site: www.denverbook.com, pg 1325

DESIGN PLUS — COMPANY INDEX

Design Plus, 1086 Main Rd, Aquebogue, NY 11931 *Tel:* 631-722-4384 *E-mail:* designplusonline@yahoo.com, pg 1367

Design Science Inc (DSI), 444 W Ocean Blvd, Suite 800, Long Beach, CA 90802 *Tel:* 562-432-2920 *Toll Free Tel:* 800-827-0685 (US sales only) *Fax:* 562-624-2859 *E-mail:* info@wiris.com; sales@wiris.com; support@wiris.com *Web Site:* www.dessci.com, pg 1367

Desktop Miracles Inc, 112 S Main St, Suite 294, Stowe, VT 05672 *Tel:* 802-253-7900 *Toll Free Fax:* 888-293-2676 *E-mail:* info@desktopmiracles.com *Web Site:* www.desktopmiracles.com, pg 1209, 1224, 1266, 1279, 1354, 1413

Devin-Adair Publishers/Seagrace Partners, 525 Flagler Dr, Suite 15A, West Palm Beach, FL 33401 *Tel:* 561-909-7576 *Fax:* 718-359-8568, pg 1314

DeVorss & Co, 1100 Flynn Rd, Unit 104, Camarillo, CA 93012 *Tel:* 805-322-9010 *Toll Free Tel:* 800-843-5743 *Fax:* 805-322-9011 *E-mail:* service@devorss.com *Web Site:* www.devorss.com, pg 1145, 1314

DFI Technologies LLC, 5501 Monte Claire Lane, Loomis, CA 95650 *Tel:* 916-568-1234 *Web Site:* dfitech.com, pg 1367

diacriTech Inc, 4 S Market St, 4th fl, Boston, MA 02109 *Tel:* 617-600-3366 *Fax:* 617-848-2938 *Web Site:* www.diacritech.com, pg 1224, 1354, 1413

Diacritics, 2715 N Charles St, Baltimore, MD 21218-4363 *Tel:* 410-516-6987 (journal orders outside US & CN) *Toll Free Tel:* 800-548-1784 (journal orders) *Fax:* 410-578-2865 (journal orders) *E-mail:* jrnlcirc@jh.edu (journal orders) *Web Site:* www.press.jhu.edu/journals/diacritics, pg 1131

Diamond Book Distributors (DBD), 10150 York Rd, Hunt Valley, MD 21030 *Tel:* 443-318-8001; 443-318-8519 (cust serv) *E-mail:* distribution@diamondbookdistributors.com; dbdreorders@diamondbookdistributors.com (orders); books@diamondbookdistributors.com (cust serv) *Web Site:* diamondbookdistributors.com, pg 1290

Steven Diamond Inc, 104 W 17 St, Suite 3-E, New York, NY 10011 *Tel:* 212-675-0723 *Fax:* 212-675-0762 *E-mail:* steven.diamond@verizon.net, pg 1345

Didona Design, 160 Grandview Rd, Ardmore, PA 19003 *Tel:* 610-649-3110 *E-mail:* didona@didonadesign.com *Web Site:* www.didonadesign.com, pg 1224, 1413

Diecrafters Inc, 1349 S 55 Ct, Cicero, IL 60804-1211 *Tel:* 708-656-3336 *Fax:* 708-656-3386 *E-mail:* info@diecrafters.com *Web Site:* www.diecrafters.com, pg 1252

Diffusion Inter-Livres, 1701 Belleville, Lemoyne, QC J4P 3M2, Canada *Tel:* 450-465-0037 *Toll Free Tel:* 866-465-5579 *E-mail:* interlivres@llbquebec.ca *Web Site:* www.inter-livres.ca, pg 1290

Digimage Arts, 100 S Eighth Ave, Winterset, IA 50273 *Tel:* 515-462-1874 *E-mail:* geninfo@digimagearts.com *Web Site:* www.digimagearts.com, pg 1367

Digital Vista Inc, 24 Amity Place, Massapequa, NY 11758 *Tel:* 516-799-5277 *E-mail:* info@digitalvista.net *Web Site:* www.digitalvista.net, pg 1413

Digital Wisdom Inc, PO Box 11, Tappahannock, VA 22560-0011 *Tel:* 804-443-9000 *Toll Free Tel:* 800-800-8560 *E-mail:* info@digitalwisdom.net *Web Site:* www.digiwis.com; www.mountainhighmaps.com, pg 1367

Dikeman Laminating Corp, 181 Sargeant Ave, Clifton, NJ 07013 *Tel:* 973-473-5696 *Fax:* 973-473-2540 *E-mail:* office@dikemanlaminating.com *Web Site:* www.dikemanlaminating.com, pg 1266

The Dingley Press, 119 Lisbon St, Lisbon, ME 04250 *Tel:* 207-353-4151 *Toll Free Tel:* 800-317-4574 *Fax:* 207-353-9886 *E-mail:* info@dingley.com *Web Site:* www.dingley.com, pg 1252

Direct Link™ Worldwide Inc, 700 Dowd Ave, Elizabeth, NJ 07201 *Tel:* 908-289-0703 *Fax:* 908-289-0705 *E-mail:* infousa@directlink.com *Web Site:* www.directlink.com, pg 1333

Disc Makers, 7905 N Crescent Blvd, Pennsauken, NJ 08110-1402 *Tel:* 856-663-9030 *Toll Free Tel:* 800-468-9353 *Fax:* 856-661-3450 *E-mail:* info@discmakers.com *Web Site:* www.discmakers.com, pg 1367

DisplayMate Technologies Corp, PO Box 550, Amherst, NH 03031 *Tel:* 603-672-8500 *Toll Free Tel:* 800-932-6323 (orders) *E-mail:* info.dm@displaymate.com *Web Site:* www.displaymate.com, pg 1367

Disticor Magazine Distribution Services, 1000 Thornton Rd S, Oshawa, ON L1J 7E2, Canada *Tel:* 905-619-6565 *Web Site:* www.disticor.com; www.magamall.com, pg 1333

Distribooks Inc, 8154 N Ridgeway Ave, Skokie, IL 60076-2911 *Tel:* 847-676-1596 *Toll Free Fax:* 888-266-5713 *E-mail:* info@distribooks.com, pg 1290

Distribooks Inc, 8154 N Ridgeway Ave, Skokie, IL 60076-2911 *Tel:* 847-676-1596 *Toll Free Tel:* 847-676-1195 *Toll Free Fax:* 888-266-5713 *E-mail:* info@distribooks.com; info@schoenhofs.com *Web Site:* www.schoenhofs.com, pg 1314

Distributed Art Publishers Inc, 75 Broad St, Suite 630, New York, NY 10004 *Tel:* 212-627-1999 *Toll Free Tel:* 800-338-2665 (cust serv) *Fax:* 212-627-9484 *E-mail:* orders@dapinc.com *Web Site:* www.artbook.com, pg 1290

Diversified Printing Services Inc, 3425 Cherokee Ave, Columbus, GA 31906 *Tel:* 706-323-2759 *Toll Free Fax:* 888-410-5502 *Web Site:* www.1dps.com, pg 1252

dix! Digital Prepress Inc, 8462 Wayfarer Dr, Cicero, NY 13039 *Tel:* 315-288-5888 *Fax:* 315-288-5898 *E-mail:* info@dixtype.com *Web Site:* www.dixtype.com, pg 1225, 1252

DJD/Golden Advertising, 145 W 28 St, 12th fl, New York, NY 10001 *Tel:* 212-366-5033 *Fax:* 212-243-5044 *E-mail:* call@djdgolden.com *Web Site:* www.djdgolden.com, pg 1099

DNP America LLC, 335 Madison Ave, 3rd fl, New York, NY 10017 *Tel:* 212-503-1060 *E-mail:* gps@dnp-g.com *Web Site:* www.dnpamerica.com, pg 1209, 1225, 1252, 1266

Docunet Corp, 2435 Xenium Lane N, Plymouth, MN 55441 *Tel:* 763-475-9600 *Toll Free Tel:* 800-936-2863 *Fax:* 763-475-1516 *E-mail:* print@docunetworks.com *Web Site:* www.docunetworks.com, pg 1252

DocuWare Corp, 4 Crotty Lane, Suite 200, New Windsor, NY 12553 *Tel:* 845-563-9045 *Toll Free Tel:* 888-565-5907 *Fax:* 845-563-9046 *E-mail:* dwsales@docuware.com; support.americas@docuware.com *Web Site:* www.docuware.com, pg 1367

Domtar Paper Co LLC, 234 Kingsley Park Dr, Fort Mill, SC 29715 *Tel:* 803-802-7500 *Toll Free Tel:* 877-877-4685 *E-mail:* communications@domtar.com; commercialprinting@domtar.com *Web Site:* www.domtar.com, pg 1266

RR Donnelley, 35 W Wacker Dr, Chicago, IL 60601 *Toll Free Tel:* 800-742-4455 *Web Site:* www.rrd.com, pg 1209, 1225, 1252, 1266, 1279

RR Donnelley & Sons Company, 35 W Wacker Dr, Chicago, IL 60601 *Tel:* 312-326-8000 *Toll Free Tel:* 800-742-4455 *Web Site:* www.rrd.com, pg 1333

RR Donnelley Marketing Solutions, 35 W Wacker Dr, Chicago, IL 60601 *Toll Free Tel:* 800-742-4455 *Web Site:* www.rrd.com/services/marketing, pg 1104

Dan Donovan Photography, 15005 Valley Ridge Dr, St Louis, MO 63017 *Tel:* 314-712-0021 *E-mail:* dan@dandonovan.com *Web Site:* www.dandonovan.com, pg 1420

Marcia Nita Doron, 10 Millstone Dr, Concord, NH 03301 *Tel:* 508-735-3454 (cell), pg 1400

Dotronix Technology Inc, 2420 Oakgreen Ave N, West Lakeland, MN 55082 *Tel:* 651-633-1742 *Fax:* 651-633-2152 *E-mail:* sales@dotronix.com *Web Site:* dotronix.com, pg 1368

Double Envelope, 7702 Plantation Rd, Roanoke, VA 24019 *Toll Free Tel:* 800-800-9007 *E-mail:* inquire@double-envelope.com *Web Site:* www.double-envelope.com, pg 1104, 1115

Double Play, 303 Hillcrest Rd, Belton, MO 64012-1852 *Tel:* 816-651-7118, pg 1346

Doubleday Book Club®, 34 W 27 St, 10th fl, New York, NY 10001 *Tel:* 716-250-5700 (cust serv) *E-mail:* customer.service@doubledaybookclub.com; member.services@doubledaybookclub.com *Web Site:* doubledaybookclub.com, pg 1141

Doubleday Large Print Book Club®, 34 W 27 St, 10th fl, New York, NY 10001 *Tel:* 716-250-5700 (cust serv) *E-mail:* customer.service@doubledaylargeprint.com *Web Site:* doubledaylargeprint.com, pg 1141

Dougherty and Associates Public Relations, 1303 Caldwell Mountain Rd, Hot Springs, NC 28743 *Tel:* 828-622-3285 *Fax:* 828-622-3285 *E-mail:* dougherty1515@gmail.com *Web Site:* doughertyandassociatespr.com, pg 1108

Douthitt Corp, 245 Adair St, Detroit, MI 48207-4287 *Tel:* 313-259-1565 *Toll Free Tel:* 800-368-8448 *Fax:* 313-259-6806 *E-mail:* em@douthittcorp.com *Web Site:* www.douthittcorp.com, pg 1279

W R Draper Co, 162 Norfinch Dr, Toronto, ON M3N 1X6, Canada *Tel:* 416-663-6001 *Fax:* 416-663-6043 *E-mail:* info@arthurpress.com *Web Site:* www.arthurpress.com, pg 1210, 1225, 1252, 1267

Spencer Drate, 119 W 80 St, Suite 1-F, New York, NY 10024-7134 *Tel:* 212-799-0535 *E-mail:* spencerdrate@yahoo.com, pg 1413

Drummond, 5664 New Peachtree Rd, Atlanta, GA 30341 *Tel:* 678-597-1050 *Fax:* 678-597-1051 *E-mail:* info@drummond.com *Web Site:* pgc-atl.com, pg 1252

DSM Producers Inc, PO Box 1160, Marco Island, FL 34146-1160 *Tel:* 212-245-0006, pg 1368

D3Logic Inc, 89 Commercial Way, East Providence, RI 02915 *Tel:* 401-435-4300 *Toll Free Tel:* 844-385-5388 *E-mail:* contact@d3-inc.com *Web Site:* www.d3-inc.com, pg 1368

Dual Graphics, 370 Cliffwood Park, Brea, CA 92821 *Tel:* 714-990-3700 *Fax:* 714-990-6818 *Web Site:* www.dualgraphics.com, pg 1225, 1252

Eileen Duhne Public Relations, 203-B Picnic Ave, San Rafael, CA 94901 *Tel:* 415-459-2573 *Fax:* 415-459-2573 *E-mail:* eduhne@comcast.net *Web Site:* eduhne.com, pg 1108

Dukane Corp, Audio Visual Products Division, 2900 Dukane Dr, St Charles, IL 60174 *Tel:* 630-584-2300 *Toll Free Tel:* 888-245-1966; 800-676-2487 (tech support) *Fax:* 630-584-5156 *E-mail:* avsales@dukane.com *Web Site:* dukaneav.com, pg 1368

Dunhill International List Co Inc, 6400 Congress Ave, Suite 1750, Boca Raton, FL 33487-2898 *Tel:* 561-998-7800 *Toll Free Tel:* 800-DUNHILL (386-4455) *Fax:* 561-998-7880 *E-mail:* dunhill@dunhillintl.com *Web Site:* www.dunhills.com, pg 1119

Dunn & Co Inc, 75 Green St, Clinton, MA 01510 *Tel:* 978-368-8505 *Fax:* 978-368-7867 *E-mail:* info@booktrauma.com *Web Site:* www.booktrauma.com, pg 1210, 1252, 1267

Dupli Envelope & Graphics Corp, 6761 Thompson Rd N, Syracuse, NY 13211 *Tel:* 315-472-1316 *Toll Free Tel:* 800-724-2477 *E-mail:* sales@duplionline.com; orders@duplionline.com *Web Site:* www.duplionline.com, pg 1279

Durr MEGTEC LLC, 830 Prosper St, DePere, WI 54115 *Tel:* 920-336-5715 *E-mail:* megtecinquiries@megtec.com *Web Site:* www.durr-megtec.com, pg 1279

Dynabook Americas Inc, 5241 California Ave, Suite 100, Irvine, CA 92617 *Tel:* 949-583-3000 *Web Site:* us.dynabook.com, pg 1368

Dynaric Inc, 5740 Bayside Rd, Virginia Beach, VA 23455 *Tel:* 757-363-5850 *Toll Free Tel:* 800-526-0827 *Fax:* 757-363-8016 *E-mail:* gd@dynaric; order@dynaric.com *Web Site:* www.dynaric.com, pg 1279

COMPANY INDEX

Eaglecrafts Inc, 168 W 12 St, Ogden, UT 84404 *Tel:* 801-393-3991 *Fax:* 801-393-4647 *E-mail:* sales@eaglefeathertrading.com *Web Site:* www.eaglefeathertrading.com, pg 1314

East Mountain Editing Services, PO Box 1895, Tijeras, NM 87059-1895 *Tel:* 505-281-8422 *Web Site:* www.spanishindexing.com, pg 1225

East-West Concepts, PO Box 1435, Kapaa, HI 96746 *Tel:* 808-938-8410 *Fax:* 808-441-8121 *Web Site:* www.eastwestconcepts.com, pg 1400

East-West Health Arts, 45 Academy Circle, Oakland, NJ 07436-0945 *Tel:* 201-337-8787, pg 1314

Eastern Book Co, 7 Lincoln Ave, Scarborough, ME 04074 *Tel:* 207-856-1370 *Toll Free Tel:* 800-937-0331 *Toll Free Fax:* 800-214-3895 *E-mail:* info@ebc.com; sales@ebc.com *Web Site:* www.ebc.com, pg 1314

Eastgate Systems Inc, 134 Main St, Watertown, MA 02472 *Tel:* 617-924-9044 *Toll Free Tel:* 800-562-1638 *E-mail:* info@eastgate.com *Web Site:* www.eastgate.com, pg 1368

Eastman Kodak Co, 343 State St, Rochester, NY 14650 *Tel:* 585-724-4000 *Toll Free Tel:* 866-563-2533 *Web Site:* www.kodak.com, pg 1279

Eastwind Books & Arts Inc, 1435 Stockton St, San Francisco, CA 94133 *Tel:* 415-772-5888 *Fax:* 415-772-5885 *E-mail:* contact@eastwindbooks.com *Web Site:* www.eastwindbooks.com, pg 1314, 1327

Eckhart & Company Inc, 4011 W 54 St, Indianapolis, IN 46254 *Tel:* 317-347-2665 *Toll Free Tel:* 800-443-3791 *Fax:* 317-347-2666 *E-mail:* info@eckhartandco.com *Web Site:* www.eckhartandco.com, pg 1253

Ecological Fibers Inc, 40 Pioneer Dr, Lunenburg, MA 01462 *Tel:* 978-537-0003 *Fax:* 978-537-2238 *E-mail:* info@ecofibers.com *Web Site:* www.ecofibers.com, pg 1210, 1267

ECRM Imaging Systems, 25 Commerce Way, North Andover, MA 01845-1002 *Tel:* 978-851-0207 *Toll Free Tel:* 800-537-ECRM (537-3276) *E-mail:* sales@ecrm.com *Web Site:* www.ecrm.com, pg 1368

Edipresse Inc, 945, ave Beaumont, Montreal, QC H3N 1W3, Canada *Tel:* 514-273-6141 *Toll Free Tel:* 800-361-1043 *Fax:* 514-273-7021 *E-mail:* information@edipresse.ca *Web Site:* www.edipresse.ca, pg 1314

Edison Lithograph & Printing Corp, 3725 Tonnelle Ave, North Bergen, NJ 07047-2421 *Tel:* 201-902-9191 *Fax:* 201-902-0475 *E-mail:* info@edisonlitho.com *Web Site:* www.edisonlitho.com, pg 1225, 1253, 1267

Les Editions Themis, Faculte de droit, Universite de Montreal, CP 6128, Succursale Centreville, Montreal, QC H3C 3J7, Canada *Tel:* 514-343-6627 *Fax:* 514-343-6779 *E-mail:* info@editionsthemis.com *Web Site:* ssl.editionsthemis.com, pg 1315

Steven Edson Photography, 102 Florence Ave, Arlington, MA 02476 *Tel:* 617-504-4994 *E-mail:* steve@stevenedson.com *Web Site:* stevenedson.com, pg 1420

eFootage LLC, 530 S Lake Ave, Suite 450, Pasadena, CA 91101 *Tel:* 626-395-9593 *E-mail:* info@efootage.com *Web Site:* www.efootage.com, pg 1428

eFulfillment Service Inc, 807 Airport Access Rd, Traverse City, MI 49686 *Tel:* 231-276-5057 *Toll Free Tel:* 866-922-6783 *E-mail:* sales@efulfillmentservice.com *Web Site:* www.efulfillmentservice.com, pg 1333

Eizo Inc, 5710 Warland Dr, Cypress, CA 90630 *Tel:* 562-431-5011 *Toll Free Tel:* 800-800-5202 *Fax:* 562-431-4811 *E-mail:* orders@eizo.com *Web Site:* www.eizo.com, pg 1368

Ekus Group LLC, 57 North St, Hatfield, MA 01038 *Tel:* 413-247-9325 *E-mail:* info@ekusgroup.com *Web Site:* ekusgroup.com, pg 1108

Elder's Bookstore, 101 White Bridge Rd, Nashville, TN 37209 *Tel:* 615-352-1562 *E-mail:* info@eldersbookstore.com *Web Site:* eldersbookstore.com, pg 1315

Electronics for Imaging Inc (EFI), 6750 Dumbarton Circle, Fremont, CA 94555 *Tel:* 650-357-3500 *Toll Free Tel:* 800-568-1917; 800-875-7117 (sales) *Fax:* 650-357-3907 *E-mail:* info@efi.com *Web Site:* www.efi.com, pg 1368

1106 Design LLC, 1007 E Orange Dr, Phoenix, AZ 85014 *Tel:* 602-866-3226 *Fax:* 602-866-8166 *E-mail:* md@1106design.com *Web Site:* 1106design.com, pg 1414

Eligh Photographs, Victoria, BC V8R 4B8, Canada *Tel:* 250-888-0027 *Web Site:* www.elighphoto.com; www.facebook.com/pages/category/Photographer/Eligh-Photographs-1550470288586165, pg 1420

Elixir Technologies Corp, 1314 E Ojai Ave, Ojai, CA 93023 *Tel:* 805-641-5900 *Fax:* 805-648-9151 *E-mail:* info_us@elixir.com *Web Site:* www.elixir.com, pg 1368

Elk Photography, 3163 Wisconsin St, Oakland, CA 94602 *Tel:* 510-531-7469 *Fax:* 510-531-7469 *E-mail:* cjelk@elkphotography.com *Web Site:* www.elkphotography.com, pg 1421

Ron Elmy Photography, 353 Eastern Ave, Suite 104, Toronto, ON M4M 1B7, Canada *Tel:* 647-286-7833 *E-mail:* elmyphotovideo@gmail.com *Web Site:* www.ronelmy.com, pg 1421

Ecegul (AJ) Elterman, 18 Sixteenth St, Bayville, NY 11709 *Tel:* 516-661-6525 (cell) *E-mail:* ajelterman@mindspring.com, pg 1401

Embolden Media Group, PO Box 953607, Lake Mary, FL 32795-3607 *E-mail:* info@emboldenmediagroup.com *Web Site:* emboldenmediagroup.com, pg 1346

Emerson, Wajdowicz Studios Inc, 514 W 25 St, New York, NY 10001 *Tel:* 212-807-8144 *E-mail:* info@designews.com *Web Site:* www.designews.com; www.facebook.com/DesignEWS; www.instagram.com/ewsdesign, pg 1414

Emery-Pratt Co, 1966 W M 21, Owosso, MI 48867-1397 *Tel:* 989-723-5291 *Toll Free Tel:* 800-762-5683 (orders); 800-248-3887 (cust serv) *Fax:* 989-723-4677 *Toll Free Fax:* 800-523-6379 (cust serv) *E-mail:* customer.service@emery-pratt.com *Web Site:* www.emery-pratt.com, pg 1315

Emprint®, 5425 Florida Blvd, Baton Rouge, LA 70806 *Tel:* 225-923-2550 *Toll Free Tel:* 800-211-8335 *Web Site:* emprint.com, pg 1210, 1225, 1253

EMT International Inc, 780 Centerline Dr, Hobart, WI 54501 *Tel:* 920-468-5475 *Fax:* 920-468-7991 *E-mail:* info@emtinternational.com *Web Site:* www.emtinternational.com, pg 1279

Encyclopaedia Britannica Inc, 325 N La Salle St, Suite 200, Chicago, IL 60654 *Tel:* 312-347-7000 (all other countries) *Toll Free Tel:* 800-323-1229 (US & CN) *Fax:* 312-294-2104 *E-mail:* contact@eb.com *Web Site:* www.britannica.com, pg 1315

Engineered Software™, PO Box 408, Grafton, MA 01519-0408 *Tel:* 336-299-4843 *E-mail:* info@engsw.com; sales@engsw.com *Web Site:* www.engsw.com, pg 1368

English Literary History (ELH), 2715 N Charles St, Baltimore, MD 21218-4363 *Tel:* 410-516-6987 (journal orders outside US & CN) *Toll Free Tel:* 800-548-1784 (journal orders) *Fax:* 410-578-2865 (journal orders) *E-mail:* jrnlcirc@jh.edu (journal orders) *Web Site:* www.press.jhu.edu/journals/elh, pg 1131

Entro Communications Inc, 33 Harbour Sq, Suite 202, Toronto, ON M5J 2G2, Canada *Tel:* 416-368-6988 *Fax:* 416-368-5616 *E-mail:* toronto@entro.com *Web Site:* www.entro.com, pg 1414

Envirovision, 733 Cliff Dr, Laguna Beach, CA 92651 *Tel:* 949-689-8794 *E-mail:* bfactor@beverlyfactor.com *Web Site:* www.beverlyfactor.com, pg 1421

Envision Peripherals Inc (EPI), 490 N McCarthy Blvd, Suite 120, Milpitas, CA 95035 *Web Site:* us.aoc.com, pg 1368

EP Graphics, 169 S Jefferson St, Berne, IN 46711 *Tel:* 260-589-2145 *Toll Free Tel:* 877-589-2145 *Fax:* 260-589-2810 *Web Site:* www.epgraphics.com, pg 1253

Bob Erdmann, 1116 Oakmont Dr, No 6, Walnut Creek, CA 94595 *Tel:* 925-451-8201 *E-mail:* info@boberdmann.com; columbcomm@gmail.com, pg 1346

Eriako Associates, 1380 Morningside Way, Venice, CA 90291 *Tel:* 310-392-6537 *Fax:* 310-392-6537 *E-mail:* eriakoassociates@gmail.com, pg 1354

Eriksen Translations Inc, 360 Court St, Unit 37, Brooklyn, NY 11231 *Tel:* 718-802-9010 *Fax:* 718-802-0041 *Web Site:* www.eriksen.com, pg 1401

Eska USA BV Inc, 1910 Campostella Rd, Chesapeake, VA 23324 *Tel:* 757-494-7330 *E-mail:* usa@eska.com *Web Site:* www.eska.com, pg 1267

Esko USA, 8535 Gander Creek Dr, Miamisburg, OH 45342 *Tel:* 937-454-1721 *Toll Free Tel:* 800-743-7131 *Fax:* 937-454-1522 *E-mail:* info.usa@esko.com *Web Site:* www.esko.com, pg 1368

Essex Products Group, 30 Industrial Park Rd, Centerbrook, CT 06409-0307 *Tel:* 860-767-7130 *Toll Free Tel:* 800-394-7130 *Fax:* 860-767-9137 *E-mail:* sales@epg-inc.com *Web Site:* www.epg-inc.com, pg 1279

Esto Photographics Inc, 36 Waverly Ave, Brooklyn, NY 11205 *Tel:* 212-505-5454 *E-mail:* sales@esto.com; assignments@esto.com *Web Site:* estostock.com, pg 1428

eStock Photo, Long Island City, NY 11101 *Tel:* 212-689-5580 *Toll Free Tel:* 800-284-3399 *E-mail:* sales@estockphoto.com; info@estockphoto.com *Web Site:* www.estockphoto.com, pg 1428

Sigrid Estrada, 902 Broadway, No 1610, New York, NY 10010 *Tel:* 212-673-4300 *E-mail:* sigrid@sigridestrada.com *Web Site:* www.sigridestrada.com, pg 1421

European Books & Media, 6600 Shattuck Ave, Oakland, CA 94609 *Tel:* 510-922-9157 *E-mail:* info@europeanbook.com *Web Site:* www.europeanbook.com, pg 1315, 1327

Evergreen Engravers, 1819 S Central Ave, Suite 24, Kent, WA 98032 *Tel:* 253-852-6766 *Toll Free Tel:* 800-852-6766 *Fax:* 253-850-3944 *E-mail:* emboss@evergreenengravers.com *Web Site:* www.evergreenengravers.com, pg 1279

Evolution Computing Inc, 4228 E Andrea Dr, Cave Creek, AZ 85331 *Tel:* 602-299-1949 *E-mail:* support@fastcad.com; order_request@fastcad.com *Web Site:* www.fastcad.com, pg 1368

Exhibit Promotions Plus Inc, 11620 Vixens Path, Ellicott City, MD 21042-1539 *Tel:* 410-997-0763 *E-mail:* exhibit@epponline.com *Web Site:* www.epponline.com, pg 1139, 1346

f-stop Fitzgerald Inc, 88 James St, Rosendale, NY 12472 *E-mail:* fstopf@gmail.com, pg 1354, 1421

Taryn Fagerness Agency, 4810 Point Fosdick Dr NW, PMB 34, Gig Harbor, WA 98335 *Tel:* 858-254-7711 *E-mail:* taryn@tarynfagernessagency.com *Web Site:* www.tarynfagernessagency.com, pg 1346

Faherty & Associates Inc, 17548 Redfern Ave, Lake Oswego, OR 97035 *Tel:* 503-639-3113 *Fax:* 503-213-6168 *E-mail:* faherty@fahertybooks.com *Web Site:* www.fahertybooks.com, pg 1290

Linda Fairchild & Company LLC, 101 Lucas Valley Rd, Suite 363, San Rafael, CA 94903 *Tel:* 415-336-6407 *Web Site:* www.lindafairchild.com, pg 1108, 1346, 1354, 1414

Fairfield Marketing Group Inc, 830 Sport Hill Rd, Easton, CT 06112-1241 *E-mail:* info@fairfieldmarketing.com, pg 1104, 1108, 1116, 1117, 1120, 1225, 1253, 1280, 1346, 1368, 1414

Falcon Safety Products Inc, 25 Imclone Dr, Branchburg, NJ 08876 *Tel:* 908-707-4900 *Toll Free Tel:* 800-332-5266 *E-mail:* marketing@falconsafety.com *Web Site:* www.falconsafety.com, pg 1368

Fall River News Co Inc, 144 Robeson St, Fall River, MA 02720 *Tel:* 508-679-5266 *E-mail:* frnewsco@gmail.com, pg 1315

FAR EASTERN BOOKS / COMPANY INDEX

Far Eastern Books, 8889 Yonge St, Richmond Hill, ON L4C 0V3, Canada *Tel:* 905-477-2900 *Toll Free Tel:* 800-291-8886 *E-mail:* books@febonline.com *Web Site:* fareasternbooks.com, pg 1291

Amy E Farrar, 4638 Manchester Rd, Mound, MN 55364 *Tel:* 952-451-5982 *E-mail:* amyfarrar@mchsi.com *Web Site:* www.writeandedit.net, pg 1125

Bryan Farrish Marketing, 1828 Broadway, 2nd fl, Santa Monica, CA 90404 *Tel:* 310-998-8305 *E-mail:* airplay@radio-media.com *Web Site:* www.radio-media.com, pg 1108

FCI Digital, 2032 S Alex Rd, Suite A, West Carrollton, OH 45449 *Tel:* 937-859-9701 *Web Site:* www.fcidigital.com, pg 1225

fd2s, 14205 N Motac Express, Suite 400F, Austin, TX 78728 *Tel:* 512-476-7733 *Web Site:* www.fd2s.com, pg 1414

FedEx Ground, 1000 FedEx Dr, Coraopolis, PA 15108 *Tel:* 412-269-1000 *Toll Free Tel:* 800-762-3725 *Web Site:* www.fedex.com, pg 1333

FedEx Supply Chain, 145 Lt George W Lee Ave, Memphis, TN 38103 *Toll Free Tel:* 800-677-3110 *E-mail:* fsc-leads@fedex.com *Web Site:* www.fedex.com/en-us/logistics/supply-chain.html, pg 1334

Feigenbaum Publishing Consultants Inc, 61 Bounty Lane, Jericho, NY 11753 *Tel:* 516-647-8314 (cell), pg 1346

Feldheim Publishers, 208 Airport Executive Park, Nanuet, NY 10954 *Tel:* 845-356-2282 *Toll Free Tel:* 800-237-7149 (orders) *Fax:* 845-425-1908 *E-mail:* sales@feldheim.com *Web Site:* www.feldheim.com, pg 1315

Alanna Feldman Scouting, 4080 Via Marisol, Apt 135, Los Angeles, CA 90042 *E-mail:* info@afscouting.com *Web Site:* www.afscouting.com, pg 1346

Gayle Feldman, 131 E 74 St, New York, NY 10021 *Tel:* 212-772-8265 *Fax:* 212-517-4020 *E-mail:* feldmangayle@gmail.com *Web Site:* www.gaylefeldman.com; www.thebookseller.com, pg 1125

Fennell Subscription Service Inc, 1002 W Michigan Ave, Jackson, MI 49202 *Tel:* 517-782-3132, pg 1315

Fenway Group, 870 Commonwealth Ave, Boston, MA 02215 *Tel:* 617-226-1900 *Fax:* 617-226-1901 *E-mail:* info@fenwaycommunications.com *Web Site:* www.fenway-group.com, pg 1253

Ferry Associates Inc, 49 Fostertown Rd, Medford, NJ 08055 *Tel:* 609-953-1233 *Toll Free Tel:* 800-257-5258 *Fax:* 609-953-8637 *Web Site:* www.ferryassociates.com, pg 1210, 1225, 1253, 1280

5th Grade Book Club, 557 Broadway, New York, NY 10012 *Tel:* 212-343-6100; 573-632-1632 (PR, US territories, US military bases) *Toll Free Tel:* 800-541-1097 (US) *Toll Free Fax:* 800-223-4011 *E-mail:* bookclubs@scholastic.com *Web Site:* clubs.scholastic.com, pg 1141

Figaro, PO Box 848, Sharon, CT 06069 *Tel:* 860-248-8989; 860-364-0834 *E-mail:* design@figro.com *Web Site:* www.figro.com, pg 1346, 1354, 1368, 1414

FILM Archives Inc, 35 W 35 St, Suite 904, New York, NY 10001-2238 *Tel:* 212-696-2616 *E-mail:* info@filmarchivesonline.com *Web Site:* www.filmarchivesonline.com, pg 1428

Film Quarterly, Journals & Digital Publishing, 155 Grand Ave, Suite 400, Oakland, CA 94612-3758 *E-mail:* info@filmquarterly.org; customerservice@ucpress.edu *Web Site:* www.filmquarterly.org; online.ucpress.edu/fq, pg 1131

FIM, 18 Central Blvd, South Hackensack, NJ 07606 *Tel:* 201-549-1037 *Web Site:* www.fimheadbands.com, pg 1267

Finch Paper LLC, One Glen St, Glens Falls, NY 12801 *Tel:* 518-793-2541 *Toll Free Tel:* 800-833-9983 *Fax:* 518-743-9656 *E-mail:* info@finchpaper.com *Web Site:* www.finchpaper.com, pg 1267

Fine Wordworking, PO Box 3041, Monterey, CA 93942-3041 *Tel:* 831-375-6278 *E-mail:* info@finewordworking.com *Web Site:* marilynch.com, pg 1385

Fire Engineering Books & Videos, Clarion Events LLC, 110 S Hartford, Suite 220, Tulsa, OK 74120 *Tel:* 918-831-9421 *Toll Free Tel:* 800-752-9764 *Fax:* 918-831-9555 *E-mail:* info@fireengineeringbooks.com *Web Site:* fireengineeringbooks.com, pg 1291

Firefly (PreK-K), 557 Broadway, New York, NY 10012 *Tel:* 212-343-6100; 573-632-1632 (PR, US territories, US military bases) *Toll Free Tel:* 800-541-1097 (US) *Toll Free Fax:* 800-223-4011 *E-mail:* bookclubs@scholastic.com *Web Site:* clubs.scholastic.com, pg 1141

Firefly Books Ltd, 50 Staples Ave, Unit 1, Richmond Hill, ON L4B 0A7, Canada *Tel:* 416-499-8412 *Toll Free Tel:* 800-387-6192 (CN); 800-387-5085 (US) *Fax:* 416-499-8313 *Toll Free Fax:* 800-450-0391 (CN); 800-565-6034 (US) *E-mail:* service@fireflybooks.com *Web Site:* www.fireflybooks.com, pg 1291

First Choice Copy, 5208 Grand Ave, Maspeth, NY 11378 *Tel:* 718-381-1480 (ext 200) *Toll Free Tel:* 800-222-COPY (222-2679) *Web Site:* www.firstchoicecopy.com, pg 1117, 1210, 1253, 1368

1st Grade Book Club, 557 Broadway, New York, NY 10012 *Tel:* 212-343-6100; 573-632-1632 (PR, US territories, US military bases) *Toll Free Tel:* 800-541-1097 (US) *Toll Free Fax:* 800-223-4011 *E-mail:* bookclubs@scholastic.com *Web Site:* clubs.scholastic.com, pg 1141

First Things: A Journal of Religion, Culture & Public Life, 9 E 40 St, 10th fl, New York, NY 10016 *Tel:* 212-627-1985 *Fax:* 212-627-2184 *E-mail:* ft@firstthings.com *Web Site:* www.firstthings.com, pg 1131

The Fisher Company, PO Box 89578, Tucson, AZ 85752-9578 *Tel:* 520-547-2460 *Web Site:* www.thefishercompany.com, pg 1346

Lola Troy Fiur, 360 E 65 St, Suite 17-A, New York, NY 10065 *Tel:* 646-247-9044 *Fax:* 212-861-1911 *E-mail:* ltfoto@yahoo.com *Web Site:* www.ltfstudios.com, pg 1421

Flannery Book Service, 20258 Hwy 18, Suite 430-436, Apple Valley, CA 92307 *Toll Free Tel:* 800-456-3400 *Web Site:* fbs-now.com, pg 1346

Flock Tex Inc, 200 Founders Dr, Woonsocket, RI 02895 *Tel:* 401-765-2340 *Toll Free Tel:* 800-556-7286 *Fax:* 401-765-4915 *Web Site:* www.flocktex.com, pg 1267

Flottman Co Inc, 720 Centre View Blvd, Crestview Hills, KY 41017 *Tel:* 859-331-6636 *Fax:* 859-344-7085 *E-mail:* info@flottmanco.com *Web Site:* www.flottmanco.com, pg 1210

Fluke Networks, 6920 Seaway Blvd, Everett, WA 98203 *Tel:* 425-446-5500; 425-446-4519 (sales & support) *Toll Free Tel:* 800-283-5853 *E-mail:* info@flukenetworks.com *Web Site:* www.flukenetworks.com, pg 1369

Flynn Media, 1233 Fitzwater St, Philadelphia, PA 19147 *Tel:* 215-772-3048 *Web Site:* www.flynnmedia.com, pg 1108

Focus Strategic Communications Inc, 15 Hunter Way, Brantford, ON N3T 6S3, Canada *Tel:* 519-756-3265 *E-mail:* info@focussc.com *Web Site:* www.focussc.com, pg 1354

Follett Higher Education Group, 3 Westbrook Corporate Ctr, Suite 200, Westchester, IL 60154 *Tel:* 708-884-0000 *Toll Free Tel:* 800-FOLLETT (365-5388) *Web Site:* www.follett.com/higher-ed, pg 1315

Follett School Solutions Inc, 1340 Ridgeview Dr, McHenry, IL 60050 *Tel:* 815-759-1700 *Toll Free Tel:* 888-511-5114 (cust serv); 877-899-8550 (sales) *Fax:* 815-759-9831 *Toll Free Fax:* 800-852-5458 *E-mail:* info@follettlearning.com; customerservice@follett.com *Web Site:* www.follettlearning.com; www.follett.com/prek12; www.titlewave.com, pg 1291, 1369

The Font Bureau Inc, 151 Beach Rd, Vineyard Haven, MA 02568 *E-mail:* info@fontbureau.com *Web Site:* fontbureau.typenetwork.com, pg 1225

Fontlab Ltd, 403 S Lincoln St, Suite 4-51, Port Angeles, WA 98362 *Tel:* 301-560-3208 *Toll Free Tel:* 866-571-5039 *E-mail:* orders@fontlab.com; contact@fontlab.com *Web Site:* www.fontlab.com, pg 1369

Forecast, 2550 W Tyvola Rd, Suite 300, Charlotte, NC 28217 *Tel:* 704-998-3100 *Toll Free Tel:* 800-775-1800 (info servs); 800-775-1700 (cust serv) *Toll Free Fax:* 866-557-3396 (cust serv) *E-mail:* btinfo@baker-taylor.com *Web Site:* www.baker-taylor.com, pg 1132

Forer Inc, 7881 SW 69 Ave, Miami, FL 33143 *Tel:* 305-495-0838 *Web Site:* www.forer.com, pg 1421

Forest Sales & Distributing Co, 139 Jean Marie St, Reserve, LA 70084 *E-mail:* forestsales@juno.com, pg 1315

Foreword Reviews, 12935 W Bay Shore Rd, Suite 380, Traverse City, MI 49684 *Tel:* 231-933-3699 *Web Site:* www.forewordreviews.com, pg 1132

Forthcoming Books™, 4919 Rte 22, Amenia, NY 12501 *Tel:* 518-789-8700 *Toll Free Tel:* 800-562-2139 *Fax:* 518-789-0556 *E-mail:* books@greyhouse.com *Web Site:* greyhouse.com, pg 1132

Foster Covers, 1401 Wonder Way, Fairfield, IA 52556 *Tel:* 641-919-4367 *E-mail:* info@fostercovers.com *Web Site:* www.fostercovers.com; www.facebook.com/bookcoverdesign, pg 1414

Foster Travel Publishing, 1623 Martin Luther King Jr Way, Berkeley, CA 94709 *Tel:* 510-549-2202 *Web Site:* www.fostertravel.com, pg 1125, 1369

Foster Travel Publishing, 1623 Martin Luther King Jr Way, Berkeley, CA 94709 *Tel:* 510-549-2202 *Web Site:* www.fostertravel.com; stockphotos.fostertravel.com, pg 1421, 1428

Fotofolio, 561 Broadway, New York, NY 10012 *Tel:* 212-226-0923 *Toll Free Tel:* 800-955-FOTO (955-3686) *E-mail:* contact@fotofolio.com *Web Site:* www.fotofolio.com, pg 1291

Fotosmith, 3539 E 28 St, Tucson, AZ 85713 *Tel:* 520-882-2033 *Web Site:* www.jeffsmithusa.com, pg 1421

Four Colour Print Group, 2410 Frankfort Ave, Louisville, KY 40206 *Tel:* 502-896-9644 *Fax:* 502-896-9594 *E-mail:* sales@fourcolour.com *Web Site:* www.fourcolour.com, pg 1210, 1253, 1280

Fournies Associates, 1226 NW 19 Terr, Delray Beach, FL 33445 *Tel:* 561-445-5102, pg 1346

4th Grade Book Club, 557 Broadway, New York, NY 10012 *Tel:* 212-343-6100; 573-632-1632 (PR, US territories, US military bases) *Toll Free Tel:* 800-541-1097 (US) *Toll Free Fax:* 800-223-4011 *E-mail:* bookclubs@scholastic.com *Web Site:* clubs.scholastic.com, pg 1142

James Frank Photography Inc, PO Box 3523, Estes Park, CO 80517 *Tel:* 970-586-3418 *E-mail:* photos@jamesfrank.com *Web Site:* www.jamesfrank.com, pg 1421

Franklin Advertising Associates Inc, 441 Main St, Yarmouth Port, MA 02675 *Tel:* 508-362-7472 *E-mail:* contact@franklinad.com *Web Site:* www.franklinad.com, pg 1099

Franklin & Siegal Associates Inc, 40 Exchange Place, Suite 1703, New York, NY 10005 *Tel:* 212-868-6311 *Web Site:* www.franklinandsiegal.com, pg 1346

Leanne Franson, 4 Poplar Ave, Martensville, SK S0K 2T0, Canada *Tel:* 514-432-4170 *E-mail:* leanne@leannefranson.com *Web Site:* www.leannefranson.com, pg 1225, 1414

Frederic Printing, 14701 E 38 Ave, Aurora, CO 80011-1215 *Tel:* 303-371-7990 *Fax:* 303-371-7959 *Web Site:* www.fredericprinting.com, pg 1225, 1253

Freestyle Software, 9 Campus Dr, Parsippany, NJ 07054 *Toll Free Tel:* 800-474-5760 *Fax:* 973-237-9043 *E-mail:* info@freestylesolutions.com *Web Site:* www.freestylesolutions.com, pg 1369

COMPANY INDEX

French and English Communication Services LLC, 3104 E Camelback Rd, No 124, Phoenix, AZ 85016-4502 *Tel:* 602-870-1000 *E-mail:* RequestFAECS2008@cox.net *Web Site:* www.FrenchAndEnglish.com, pg 1401

French & European Publications Inc, 425 E 58 St, Suite 27-D, New York, NY 10022 *Tel:* 212-581-8810 *Fax:* 212-202-4356 *E-mail:* livresny@gmail.com; frenchbookstore@aol.com *Web Site:* www.frencheuropean.com, pg 1328

French Paper, 100 French St, Niles, MI 49120 *Tel:* 269-683-1100 *Toll Free Tel:* 800-253-5952 *E-mail:* frenchassetorders@frenchpaper.com; frenchpaperco@gmail.com *Web Site:* www.frenchpaper.com, pg 1267

The French Publishers' Agency, PO Box 140, New York, NY 10009 *Tel:* 212-254-4874 *Web Site:* www.frenchrights.com, pg 1346

Fresh Air Photo, 152 Sand Valley Ct, Jonesborough, TN 37659 *Tel:* 423-612-2700 *Web Site:* www.freshairphoto.com, pg 1421

Robert Fried Photography, 610 Eldridge Ct, Novato, CA 94947 *Tel:* 415-898-6153 *Fax:* 415-897-0353 *E-mail:* rob@robertfriedphotography.com *Web Site:* www.robertfriedphotography.com, pg 1421

Friesens Corp, One Printers Way, Altona, MB R0G 0B0, Canada *Tel:* 204-324-6401 *Fax:* 204-324-1333 *E-mail:* book_info@friesens.com *Web Site:* www.friesens.com, pg 1210, 1253

Fry Communications Inc, 800 W Church Rd, Mechanicsburg, PA 17055 *Tel:* 717-766-0211 *Toll Free Tel:* 800-334-1429 *Fax:* 717-691-0341 *E-mail:* info@frycomm.com *Web Site:* www.frycomm.com, pg 1210, 1225, 1253, 1280

Fujifilm North America Corporation, Graphic Systems Division, 850 Central Ave, Hanover Park, IL 60133 *Tel:* 630-259-7200 *Toll Free Tel:* 800-877-0555 *Fax:* 630-259-7078 *Web Site:* www.fujifilmusa.com/products/graphic_arts_printing/index.html; www.fujifilmusa.com, pg 1280

Fujii Associates Inc, 75 Sunny Hill Dr, Troy, MO 63379 *Tel:* 636-528-2546 *Fax:* 636-600-5153 *Web Site:* www.fujiiassociates.com, pg 1291

Fujitsu Computer Products of America Inc, 1250 E Arques Ave, Sunnyvale, CA 94085-4701 *Tel:* 408-746-6000 *Toll Free Tel:* 800-626-4686 *E-mail:* scanner-sales@us.fujitsu.com *Web Site:* www.fujitsu.com/us, pg 1369

Fulfillment by Amazon (FBA), 440 Terry Ave N, Seattle, WA 98109 *Web Site:* services.amazon.com; www.amazon.com/advantage, pg 1291

H B Fuller Co, 1200 Willow Lake Blvd, St Paul, MN 55110-5146 *Tel:* 651-236-5900 *Toll Free Tel:* 888-423-8553 *E-mail:* inquiry@hbfuller.com *Web Site:* www.hbfuller.com, pg 1267, 1280

Fundamental Photographs, 210 Forsyth St, Suite 2, New York, NY 10002 *Tel:* 212-473-5770 *E-mail:* mail@fphoto.com *Web Site:* www.fphoto.com, pg 1428

Fundcraft Publishing, 410 Hwy 72 W, Colliervile, TN 38017 *Tel:* 901-853-7070 *Toll Free Tel:* 800-853-1363 *Fax:* 901-853-6196 *E-mail:* info@fundcraft.com *Web Site:* www.fundcraft.com, pg 1210

Fuse Graphics, 1800 Sandy Plains Pkwy, Suite 124, Marietta, GA 30066 *Tel:* 770-499-7777 *Fax:* 770-499-7778 *E-mail:* info@fusegraphicsatlanta.com *Web Site:* www.fusegraphicsatlanta.com, pg 1253

G & H Soho Inc, 413 Market St, Elmwood Park, NJ 07407 *Tel:* 201-216-9400 *Fax:* 201-216-1778 *E-mail:* print@ghsoho.com *Web Site:* www.ghsoho.com, pg 1210, 1226, 1253, 1267, 1346, 1354, 1414

Gail Leondar Public Relations, 19 Belknap St, Arlington, MA 02474 *Tel:* 781-648-1658 *Web Site:* www.glprbooks.com, pg 1109

Gale Literature: Book Review Index, 27555 Executive Dr, Suite 270, Farmington Hills, MI 48331 *Toll Free Tel:* 800-877-4253 *Toll Free Fax:* 877-363-4253 *E-mail:* gale.customerexperience@cengage.com *Web Site:* www.gale.com/c/literature-book-review-index, pg 1132

Gallus Group, One Ivybrook Blvd, Suite 180, Ivyland, PA 18974 *Tel:* 215-677-9600 *Fax:* 215-677-9700 *E-mail:* info@gallus-group.com *Web Site:* gallus.contento.ch, pg 1280

Gane Brothers & Lane Inc, 1400 Greenleaf Ave, Elk Grove Village, IL 60007 *Tel:* 847-593-3364 *Toll Free Tel:* 800-323-0596 *Toll Free Fax:* 800-784-2464 *E-mail:* sales@ganebrothers.com *Web Site:* www.ganebrothers.com, pg 1267

Gannett News Service, 7950 Jones Branch Dr, McLean, VA 22107-0150 *Tel:* 703-854-6000 *E-mail:* pr@gannett.com *Web Site:* www.gannett.com, pg 1190

Mayra E Garcia, 313 Valley Ct, Sinking Spring, PA 19608 *Tel:* 803-422-5903 *E-mail:* mayra.garcia11@gmail.com, pg 1401

Garcia Publishing Services, 830 Russell Rd, No 8, DeKalb, IL 60115 *Tel:* 815-338-5512 *E-mail:* garpubserv@aol.com, pg 1354

Garlich Printing Co, 525 Rudder Rd, St Louis, MO 63026 *Tel:* 636-349-8000 *Toll Free Tel:* 844-449-4752 *Fax:* 636-349-8080 *E-mail:* customerservice@garlich.com *Web Site:* www.garlich.com, pg 1253

Laurence Gartel, PO Box 4114, Deerfield Beach, FL 33442 *Tel:* 561-302-6774 *E-mail:* gartel@comcast.net *Web Site:* gartelart.com, pg 1414

Garvan Media, Management & Marketing Inc, PO Box 737, Sandpoint, ID 83864 *Tel:* 208-265-1718 *Web Site:* facebook.com/stephen.b.garvan, pg 1347

The Gate Worldwide, 71 Fifth Ave, 8th fl, New York, NY 10003 *Tel:* 212-508-3400 *Fax:* 212-508-3402 (cgi) *E-mail:* contact@thegateworldwide.com *Web Site:* thegateworldwide.com, pg 1099

Liz Gately Book Scouting, 36 W 37 St, Rm 408, New York, NY 10018 *Tel:* 212-244-1441 *E-mail:* liz@lizgately.com *Web Site:* www.lizgately.com, pg 1347

Gaunt Inc, Gaunt Bldg, 3011 Gulf Dr, Holmes Beach, FL 34217 *Tel:* 941-778-5211 *Toll Free Tel:* 800-WGAUNT3 (942-8683) *Fax:* 941-778-5252 *E-mail:* info@gaunt.com *Web Site:* www.gaunt.com, pg 1291

GBS Books, 2321 W Royal Palm Rd, Suite F, Phoenix, AZ 85021 *Tel:* 602-863-6000 *Toll Free Tel:* 800-851-6001 *E-mail:* gbsbooks@gbsbooks.com *Web Site:* www.gbsbooks.com, pg 1315

Gefen Books, c/o Storch, 255 Central Ave, B-206, Lawrence, NY 11559 *Tel:* 516-593-1234 *Fax:* 516-295-2739 *E-mail:* info@gefenpublishing.com *Web Site:* www.gefenpublishing.com, pg 1291, 1328

GEI WideFormat, A Visual Edge Technology Company, 3874 Highland Park NW, North Canton, OH 44720 *Toll Free Tel:* 800-842-8448 (serv); 888-722-6434 (sales) *E-mail:* sales@geiwideformat.com *Web Site:* www.geiwideformat.com; www.visualedgetechnology.com, pg 1369

Bonnie Geller-Geld, 2500 Johnson Ave, Apt 18N, Bronx, NY 10463 *Tel:* 347-275-4040 *E-mail:* gellergeldphoto@gmail.com *Web Site:* bonniegellergeld.com, pg 1421

Gem Guides Book Co, 1155 W Ninth St, Upland, CA 91786 *Tel:* 626-855-1611 *Toll Free Tel:* 800-824-5118 (orders) *Fax:* 626-855-1610 *E-mail:* info@gemguidesbooks.com; sales@gemguidesbooks.com (orders) *Web Site:* www.gemguidesbooks.com, pg 1315

General Cartography Inc, 4 Estate Dr, Boynton Beach, FL 33436 *Tel:* 561-914-6323 *E-mail:* terradata@aol.com *Web Site:* cartographybypaul.com, pg 1414

Genesis Marketing Group Inc, 850 Wade Hampton Blvd, Bldg A, Suite 100, Greenville, SC 29609 *Tel:* 864-233-2651 *Toll Free Tel:* 800-627-2651 *Toll Free Fax:* 800-849-4363 *E-mail:* orders@genesislink.com *Web Site:* www.genesislink.com, pg 1291

German Language Services, 4752 41 Ave SW, Suite B, Seattle, WA 98116 *Tel:* 206-938-3600 *E-mail:* info@germanlanguageservices.com *Web Site:* germanlanguageservices.com, pg 1401

Getty Images Inc, 605 Fifth Ave S, Suite 400, Seattle, WA 98104 *Tel:* 206-925-5000 *Toll Free Tel:* 800-IMAGERY (462-4379); 888-888-5889 *Web Site:* www.gettyimages.com; www.gettyimages.com/customer-support; engage.gettyimages.com/media-inquiries, pg 1369, 1428

GEX Inc, 80 Conley's Grove Rd, Derry, NH 03038 *Tel:* 603-870-9292 *Web Site:* www.gexinc.com, pg 1211, 1226, 1355, 1369, 1414

GGP Publishing Inc, Larchmont, NY 10538 *Tel:* 914-834-8896 *Fax:* 914-834-7566 *Web Site:* www.GGPPublishing.com, pg 1347, 1355, 1401

GHP, 475 Heffernan Dr, West Haven, CT 06516 *Tel:* 203-479-7500 *Fax:* 203-479-7575 *Web Site:* www.ghpmedia.com, pg 1226, 1253

Rosanna M Giammanco Frongia PhD, PO Box 810422, Boca Raton, FL 33481-0422 *Tel:* 718-619-2637 (cell) *E-mail:* giammancorm@gmail.com, pg 1401

Giant Horse Printing Inc, 1336 San Mateo Ave, South San Francisco, CA 94080 *Tel:* 650-875-7137 *Fax:* 650-875-7194 *E-mail:* info@gianthorse.com *Web Site:* www.gianthorse.com, pg 1211

Dot Gibson Publications, PO Box 117, Waycross, GA 31502 *Tel:* 912-285-2848 *Toll Free Tel:* 800-336-8095 (for orders) *Fax:* 912-285-2848 *E-mail:* info@dotgibson.com *Web Site:* www.dotgibson.com, pg 1315

Girol Books Inc, PO Box 5473, LCD Merivale, Ottawa, ON K2C 3M1, Canada *Tel:* 613-233-9044 *E-mail:* info@girol.com *Web Site:* www.girol.com, pg 1291, 1316, 1328

Glasnost Communications, Tallberry Dr, Cincinnati, OH 45230 *Tel:* 513-231-3599 *E-mail:* glasnost@currently.com, pg 1401

Peter Glass Photography, 15 Oakwood St, East Hartford, CT 06108 *Tel:* 860-528-8559 (off); 860-712-7098 (cell) *E-mail:* peter@peterglass.com *Web Site:* www.peterglass.com, pg 1421

Glasshouse Images, 161 W 15 St, Suite 1-C, New York, NY 10011 *Tel:* 646-256-1999 (res queries only) *E-mail:* agency@glasshouseimages.com (collection queries only) *Web Site:* glasshouseimages.com, pg 1429

Glatfelter, Capitol Towers South, 4350 Congress St, Suite 600, Charlotte, NC 28209 *Tel:* 717-850-0170 *Toll Free Tel:* 866-744-7380 *E-mail:* info@glatfelter.com *Web Site:* www.glatfelter.com, pg 1267

Glenbow Museum Shop, 130 Ninth Ave SE, Calgary, AB T2G 0P3, Canada *Tel:* 403-268-4119 *Fax:* 403-262-4045 *E-mail:* shop@glenbow.org *Web Site:* www.glenbow.org, pg 1316

Global Graphics Software Inc, 5996 Clark Center Ave, Sarasota, FL 34238 *Tel:* 941-925-1303 *E-mail:* info@globalgraphics.com; sales@globalgraphics.com *Web Site:* www.globalgraphics.com/globalgraphics-software, pg 1369

Global Interprint Inc, 800 Warrington Rd, Santa Rosa, CA 95403 *Tel:* 707-545-1220 *Fax:* 707-545-1210 *Web Site:* www.globalinterprint.com, pg 1253

Globe Entertainment & Media Corp, 8500 Beverly Blvd, Suite 683, Los Angeles, CA 90048 *Web Site:* www.globecorp.co, pg 1429

GLS Companies, 1280 Energy Park Dr, St Paul, MN 55108-5106 *Tel:* 651-644-3000 *Toll Free Tel:* 800-655-9405 *Web Site:* www.glsmn.com, pg 1226, 1254

The Gluefast Co Inc, 3535 State Rte 66, Bldg No 1, Neptune, NJ 07753 *Tel:* 732-918-4600 *Toll Free Tel:* 800-242-7318 *Fax:* 732-918-4646 *E-mail:* info@gluefast.com *Web Site:* www.gluefast.com, pg 1337

Jeff Gnass Photography™, 3042 Nowell Ave, Juneau, AK 99801-1930 *Tel:* 907-789-2002 *Fax:* 206-577-6419 *E-mail:* office@jeffgnass.com *Web Site:* www.jeffgnass.com, pg 1421

GoalsGuy Learning Systems, 36181 E Lake Rd, Suite 139, Palm Harbor, FL 34685 *Toll Free Tel:* 877-462-5748 *Fax:* 813-435-2022 *Toll Free Fax:* 877-903-2284 *E-mail:* info@goalsguy.com *Web Site:* www.100daychallenge.com, pg 1316

GOBI® Library Solutions from EBSCO, 999 Maple St, Contoocook, NH 03229 *Tel:* 603-746-3102 *Toll Free Tel:* 800-258-3774 (US & CN) *Fax:* 603-746-5628 *E-mail:* information@ebsco.com *Web Site:* gobi.ebsco.com, pg 1316

Celia Godkin, Mod 6, Comp 12, 10 James St, Frankville, ON K0E 1H0, Canada *Tel:* 613-275-7204 *E-mail:* celia@godkin.ca *Web Site:* www.celiagodkin.com, pg 1226

Beryl Goldberg Photographer, 309 W 109 St, Suite 4-F, New York, NY 10025 *Tel:* 212-222-8215 *E-mail:* berylgnyc@gmail.com *Web Site:* www.berylgoldberg.net, pg 1421

Louis Goldberg Library Book Supplier, 45 Belvidere St, Nazareth, PA 18064 *Tel:* 610-759-9458 *E-mail:* orders@goldberg-books.com *Web Site:* www.goldberg-books.com, pg 1316

Gomsak Photography, 10428 S Hall Dr, Charlotte, NC 28270 *Web Site:* www.gomsak.com, pg 1422

The Good Cook®, 34 W 27 St, 10th fl, New York, NY 10001 *Tel:* 716-250-5700 (cust serv) *Toll Free Tel:* 866-250-3166 *E-mail:* customer.service@thegoodcook.com *Web Site:* thegoodcook.com, pg 1142

GoodMinds.com, Six Nations of the Grand River Territory, 188 Mohawk St, Brantford, ON N3S 2X2, Canada *Tel:* 519-753-1185 *Toll Free Tel:* 877-862-8483 (CN & US) *Fax:* 519-751-3136 *E-mail:* helpme@goodminds.com *Web Site:* www.goodminds.com, pg 1292

Goose River Press, 3400 Friendship Rd, Waldoboro, ME 04572-6337 *Tel:* 207-832-6665 *E-mail:* gooseriverpress@gmail.com *Web Site:* gooseriverpress.com, pg 1226, 1254

Andrew S Gordon, PhD, 1230 23 St NW, No 804, Washington, DC 20037 *E-mail:* andgordon@yahoo.com, pg 1401

P M Gordon Associates Inc, 2115 Wallace St, Philadelphia, PA 19130 *Tel:* 215-769-2525 *Web Site:* www.pmgordonassociates.com, pg 1355

Gore Studio Inc, 101 Paxton Ct, Brentwood, TN 37027 *Tel:* 615-519-2262 *E-mail:* gorestudioinc@gmail.com *Web Site:* www.gorestudio.com, pg 1414

Gorham Printing, 3718 Mahoney Dr, Centralia, WA 98531 *Tel:* 360-623-1323 *Toll Free Tel:* 800-837-0970 *E-mail:* info@gorhamprinting.com *Web Site:* www.gorhamprinting.com, pg 1254

Sandra Goroff & Associates, 42 Waterfall Dr, Suite L, Canton, MA 02021 *Tel:* 617-750-0555 *E-mail:* sgma@aol.com *Web Site:* www.sandragoroff.com, pg 1109

Regina Gorzkowska-Rossi, 3349 E Thompson St, Philadelphia, PA 19134 *Tel:* 267-535-1691 *E-mail:* proarterg@yahoo.com, pg 1401

Audrey Gottlieb, 161 York St, Unit 21, York, ME 03909 *Tel:* 207-641-7490 *E-mail:* audreyphoto@gmail.com *Web Site:* www.audreygottlieb.com, pg 1422

Gould Paper Corp, 99 Park Ave, 10th fl, New York, NY 10016 *Tel:* 212-301-0000 *Toll Free Tel:* 800-221-3043 *Fax:* 212-481-0067 *E-mail:* info@gouldpaper.com *Web Site:* www.gouldpaper.com, pg 1267

Stephen Gould Corp, 35 S Jefferson Rd, Whippany, NJ 07981 *Tel:* 973-428-1500; 973-428-1510 *E-mail:* info@stephengould.com *Web Site:* www.stephengould.com, pg 1104, 1337

Gracenote, a Nielsen Company, 2000 Powell St, Suite 1500, Emeryville, CA 94608 *Tel:* 510-428-7200 *Web Site:* www.gracenote.com, pg 1190

Joe & Teresa Graedon, 300 W 57 St, 41st fl, New York, NY 10019 *Toll Free Tel:* 800-708-7311 (FL edit) *Web Site:* www.kingfeatures.com; www.peoplespharmacy.com, pg 1125

Rita Granda, 466 Cambridge St, Peterborough, ON K9H 4T3, Canada *Tel:* 705-748-0943 *E-mail:* rita@ritagranda.com *Web Site:* www.ritagranda.com, pg 1401

Granger - Historical Picture Archive, 244 Fifth Ave, Suite 2110, New York, NY 10001 *Tel:* 212-447-1789 *Fax:* 212-447-1492 *E-mail:* info@granger.com; research@granger.com *Web Site:* www.granger.com, pg 1429

Graphic Composition Inc, N1246 Technical Dr, Greenville, WI 54942 *Tel:* 920-757-6977 *Toll Free Tel:* 800-262-8973 *Fax:* 920-757-9266 *E-mail:* socialmedia@graphiccomp.com *Web Site:* www.graphiccomp.com, pg 1254

Graphic Connections Group LLC, 174 Chesterfield Industrial Blvd, Chesterfield, MO 63005 *Tel:* 636-519-8320 *Toll Free Tel:* 800-378-0378 *Fax:* 636-519-8310 *Web Site:* www.gcfrog.com, pg 1211

GW Illustration & Design, 2290 Ball Dr, St Louis, MO 63146 *Tel:* 314-567-9854 *Web Site:* www.gwinc.com, pg 1414

Graphic Litho, 130 Shepard St, Lawrence, MA 01843 *Tel:* 978-683-2766 *Fax:* 978-681-7588 *E-mail:* sales@graphiclitho.com *Web Site:* www.graphiclitho.com, pg 1104, 1211, 1254

GraphiColor Corp, 3490 N Mill Rd, Vineland, NJ 08360 *Tel:* 856-691-2507 *Toll Free Tel:* 800-552-2507 *Fax:* 856-696-3229 *Web Site:* www.graphicolorcorp.com, pg 1226, 1254

Graphics International, 20475 Bunker Hill Dr, Cleveland, OH 44126 *Tel:* 440-333-9988, pg 1414

Graphics Two, 819 S Main St, Burbank, CA 91506 *Tel:* 818-841-4922, pg 1226, 1280

Tom Graves Photography, 400-A Clipper St, San Francisco, CA 94114 *Tel:* 415-550-7241 *E-mail:* tom@tomgraves.com *Web Site:* www.tomgraves.com; www.twiceheroes.com, pg 1422

Great Lakes Bindery Inc, 3741 Linden Ave SE, Wyoming, MI 49548 *Tel:* 616-245-5264 *Fax:* 616-245-5883 *E-mail:* jeremy@greatlakesbindery.com *Web Site:* www.greatlakesbindery.com, pg 1254

Susannah Greenberg Public Relations, 41 Old Brook Rd, Dix Hills, NY 11746 *Tel:* 646-801-7477 *E-mail:* publicity@bookbuzz.com *Web Site:* bookbuzz.com; linkedin.com/in/susannahgreenberg; www.facebook.com/SusannahGreenbergPublicRelations; x.com/SueGreenbergPR, pg 1109

Greenleaf Book Group LLC, PO Box 91869, Austin, TX 78709 *Tel:* 512-891-6100 *Fax:* 512-891-6150 *E-mail:* contact@greenleafbookgroup.com; orders@greenleafbookgroup.com; foreignrights@greenleafbookgroup.com; media@greenleafbookgroup.com *Web Site:* greenleafbookgroup.com, pg 1292, 1355

Greg Johnston Photography, 3021 San Jacinto Circle, Sanford, FL 32771 *Tel:* 305-258-7070 *Web Site:* www.gregjohnstonphotography.com, pg 1422

David M Grossman Photography, 211 E Seventh St, Brooklyn, NY 11218 *Tel:* 718-438-5021 *E-mail:* david@grossmanphotos.com *Web Site:* www.davidmgrossmanphotos.com, pg 1422

J S Grove Photography, 166 Peace Ave, Tavernier, FL 33070 *Tel:* 305-393-2817 *E-mail:* grovejack509@gmail.com, pg 1422

GSB Digital, 33-01 Hunters Point Ave, Long Island City, NY 11101 *Tel:* 212-684-3600 *Fax:* 212-684-3613 *E-mail:* questions@gsbdigital.com *Web Site:* www.gsbdigital.com, pg 1369

GTCO Calcomp, 14557 N 82 St, Scottsdale, AZ 85260 *Tel:* 480-443-2264 *Toll Free Tel:* 800-220-1137 *Fax:* 480-948-1751 *E-mail:* sales@gtcocalcomp.com *Web Site:* www.gtcocalcomp.com, pg 1369

GTI Graphic Technology Inc, 211 Dupont Ave, Newburgh, NY 12550 *Tel:* 845-562-7066 *Fax:* 845-562-2543 *E-mail:* sales@gtilite.com *Web Site:* www.gtilite.com, pg 1280, 1370

GTxcel Inc, 144 Turnpike Rd, Suite 130, Southborough, MA 01772-2104 *Toll Free Tel:* 800-609-8994 *E-mail:* info@gtxcel.com *Web Site:* www.gtxcel.com, pg 1370

Gulotta Communications Inc, 321 Walnut St, Newton, MA 02460 *Tel:* 617-630-9286 *Fax:* 978-733-6162 *Web Site:* www.booktours.com, pg 1109

Gurarys Israeli Trading Co Inc, 724 Eastern Pkwy, Brooklyn, NY 11213 *Tel:* 718-493-5225 *E-mail:* hebbook@gmail.com, pg 1328

GW Inc, 2290 Ball Dr, St Louis, MO 63146 *Tel:* 314-567-9854 *E-mail:* media@gwinc.com *Web Site:* www.gwinc.com, pg 1226, 1370

Kathryn Hall, Publicist, Los Lunas, NM 87031 *E-mail:* khpbooks@gmail.com *Web Site:* www.kathrynhallpublicist.com; www.linkedin.com/in/kathrynhallpr, pg 1109

Molly Hall, 4338 Mitchell St, Philadelphia, PA 19128 *Tel:* 215-970-1837 *E-mail:* mollyhallindexer@hotmail.com, pg 1226

Chris Hamilton Photography, 704 Battersea Dr, St Augustine, FL 32095 *Tel:* 404-355-9411 *Web Site:* www.hamphoto.com, pg 1422

Hannecke Display Systems Inc, 210 Grove St, Franklin, MA 02038 *Tel:* 774-235-2329 *E-mail:* info@hannecke.com *Web Site:* www.hannecke.com, pg 1104

Hanser Publications LLC, c/o CFAS, 5667 Kyles Lane, Liberty Township, OH 45044 *Toll Free Tel:* 800-950-8977; 888-558-2632 (orders) *E-mail:* publicity@hanserpublications.com *Web Site:* www.hanserpublications.com, pg 1292

Harvard Art Museums, 32 Quincy St, Cambridge, MA 02138 *Tel:* 617-495-9400 *Web Site:* www.harvardartmuseums.org, pg 1316

Harvard Educational Review, 8 Story St, 1st fl, Cambridge, MA 02138 *Tel:* 617-495-3432 *Toll Free Tel:* 888-437-1437 (orders) *Fax:* 617-496-3584 *Web Site:* hepg.org/her-home/home, pg 1132

Hassett Express, 17W775 Butterfield Rd, Suite 109, Oakbrook Terrace, IL 60181 *Tel:* 630-530-6515 *Fax:* 630-530-6538 *Web Site:* www.hassettexpress.com, pg 1334

Haynes North America Inc, 2801 Townsgate Rd, Suite 340, Westlake Village, CA 91361 *Tel:* 805-498-6703 *Toll Free Tel:* 800-4-HAYNES (442-9637) *Fax:* 805-498-2867 *E-mail:* customerservice.haynes@infoprodigital.com *Web Site:* www.haynes.com, pg 1328

HBG Productions/International Publishers Alliance, PO Box 5560, Chico, CA 95927-5560 *Tel:* 530-893-4699 *Web Site:* www.hbgproductions.com, pg 1292

HBP Inc, 952 Frederick St, Hagerstown, MD 21740 *Tel:* 301-733-2000 *Toll Free Tel:* 800-638-3508 *Fax:* 301-733-6586 *E-mail:* contactus@hbp.com *Web Site:* www.hbp.com, pg 1226, 1254, 1280

Hearst Newspapers, 300 W 57 St, New York, NY 10019 *Tel:* 212-649-2000 *Web Site:* www.hearst.com/newspapers, pg 1190

Hedquist Productions Inc, PO Box 1475, Fairfield, IA 52556 *Tel:* 641-472-6708 *Web Site:* www.hedquist.com, pg 1370

Milton Heiberg Studios, 1022 Empress Lane, Orlando, FL 32825-8249 *Tel:* 407-658-4869 *E-mail:* ternmedia@gmail.com *Web Site:* www.miltonheiberg.com, pg 1422

Heidelberg Graphics, 2 Stansbury Ct, Chico, CA 95928 *Tel:* 530-342-6582 *Fax:* 530-342-6582 *E-mail:* heidelberggraphics@gmail.com; service@heidelberggraphics.com *Web Site:* www.heidelberggraphics.com, pg 1226, 1254, 1280, 1347, 1370, 1414

Heidelberg USA Inc, 1000 Gutenberg Dr, Kennesaw, GA 30144 *Tel:* 770-419-6500 *Toll Free Tel:* 800-437-7388 *E-mail:* info@heidelberg.com *Web Site:* www.heidelberg.com/us, pg 1280

COMPANY INDEX

Grant Heilman Photography Inc, 506 W Lincoln Ave, Lititz, PA 17543 Tel: 717-626-0296 Toll Free Tel: 800-622-2046 Fax: 717-626-0971 E-mail: info@heilmanphoto.com Web Site: www.heilmanphoto.com, pg 1429

William S Hein & Co Inc, 2350 N Forest Rd, Suite 10A, Getzville, NY 14068 Tel: 716-882-2600 Toll Free Tel: 800-828-7571 Fax: 716-883-8100 E-mail: mail@wshein.com; marketing@wshein.com; customerservice@wshein.com Web Site: home.heinonline.org, pg 1316

Albert Henderson, 655 West Ave, Milford, CT 06461-3003 Tel: 203-301-0791 E-mail: 70244.1532@compuserve.com, pg 1347

The Hendra Agency Inc, 142 Sterling Place, Brooklyn, NY 11217-3307 Tel: 718-622-3232 Fax: 718-622-3322, pg 1109

Henkel Corp, One Henkel Way, Rocky Hill, CT 06067 Tel: 860-571-5100 Fax: 860-571-5465 E-mail: corp.info@henkel.com Web Site: www.henkel-northamerica.com; www.henkel-adhesives.com, pg 1268

Hennegan Co, 7455 Empire Dr, Florence, KY 41042 Tel: 859-282-3600 Fax: 859-282-3601, pg 1226, 1254

Diana Mara Henry, 51 Carbonneau Dr, Suite 3, Newport, VT 05855 Tel: 802-334-7054 E-mail: dhenry188@gmail.com Web Site: www.natzweiler-struthof.com, pg 1401

Diana Mara Henry, 51 Carbonneau Dr, Suite 3, Newport, VT 05855 Tel: 802-334-7054 E-mail: dmh@dianamarahenry.com Web Site: dianamarahenry.com, pg 1422, 1429

The Henry James Review, 2715 N Charles St, Baltimore, MD 21218-4363 Tel: 410-516-6987 (journal orders outside US & CN) Toll Free Tel: 800-548-1784 (journal orders) Fax: 410-578-2865 (journal orders) E-mail: jrnlcirc@jh.edu (journal orders) Web Site: www.press.jhu.edu/journals/henry-james-review, pg 1132

Heraeus Noblelight America LLC, 910 Clopper Rd, Gaithersburg, MD 20878-1361 Tel: 301-527-2660 Toll Free Tel: 888-276-8600 Fax: 301-527-2661 E-mail: info.hna.uvp@heraeus.com Web Site: www.heraeus-noblelight.com/uvamericas, pg 1280

Mark Herman & Ronnie Apter, Translators, 2222 Westview Dr, Nashville, TN 37212-4123 Tel: 615-942-8462 E-mail: mnh18@columbia.edu, pg 1401

Hermani & Sorrentino Design, 404 Musgrave Rd, Salt Spring Island, BC V8K 1V5, Canada Tel: 250-538-8426 E-mail: hermani2sorrentino@gmail.com Web Site: www.hermanisorrentino.com, pg 1415

Michal Heron Photography, 3806 Easton St, Sarasota, FL 34238 E-mail: michalheronphoto@gmail.com Web Site: www.michalheron.com, pg 1422

Herr's Indexing Service, 76-340 Kealoha St, Kailua Kona, HI 96740-2915 Tel: 808-365-4348 Web Site: www.herrsindexing.com, pg 1226

Hess Print Solutions, 3765 Sunnybrook Rd, Brimfield, OH 44240 Toll Free Tel: 800-678-1222 E-mail: info@hessprintsolutions.com Web Site: www.hessprintsolutions.com, pg 1211, 1254

HF Group LLC, 8844 Mayfield Rd, Chesterland, OH 44026 Tel: 440-729-2445; 440-729-9411 (bindery) E-mail: custservice-oh@hfgroup.com Web Site: www.hfgroup.com, pg 1254, 1268, 1325

HFS, 2715 N Charles St, Baltimore, MD 21218 Tel: 410-516-6965 Toll Free Tel: 800-537-5487 (US & CN) Fax: 410-516-6998 E-mail: hfscustserv@jh.edu Web Site: hfs.jhu.edu; www.hfsbooks.com, pg 1292

The Hibbert Group, 400 Pennington Ave, Trenton, NJ 08650 Tel: 609-394-7500 Toll Free Tel: 888-HIBBERT (442-2378) E-mail: info@hibbertgroup.com Web Site: hibbert.com, pg 1104, 1116, 1117

HID Global, 611 Center Ridge Dr, Austin, TX 78753 Tel: 512-776-9000 Toll Free Tel: 800-872-5359 (cust serv) Fax: 512-776-9930 E-mail: customerservice@hidglobal.com Web Site: www.hidglobal.com, pg 370

HID Ultraviolet LLC, 520 Lafayette Rd, Sparta, NJ 07871 Tel: 973-383-8535 Fax: 973-383-1606 E-mail: sales@hid.com Web Site: www.hid.com, pg 1280

Worth Higgins & Associates Inc, 8770 Park Central Dr, Richmond, VA 23227-1146 Tel: 804-264-2304 Toll Free Tel: 800-883-7768 Fax: 804-264-5733 E-mail: contact@whaprint.com Web Site: www.worthhiggins.com, pg 1226, 1254

Hignell Book Printing Ltd, 488 Burnell St, Winnipeg, MB R3G 2B4, Canada Tel: 204-784-1030 Toll Free Tel: 800-304-5553 Fax: 204-774-4053 E-mail: books@hignell.mb.ca Web Site: www.hignell.mb.ca, pg 1211, 1254

Hill+Knowlton Strategies, 237 Park Ave, 4th fl, New York, NY 10017 Tel: 212-885-0300 Web Site: www.hkstrategies.com, pg 1109

Hilsinger-Mendelson West Inc, 115 N Kings Rd, Los Angeles, CA 90048 Tel: 323-931-5335 (text only) E-mail: hmiwest@aol.com Web Site: www.hilsingermendelson.com, pg 1109

Historic Aviation Books, 640 Taft St NE, Minneapolis, MN 55413-2815 Tel: 612-206-3200 Toll Free Tel: 800-225-5575 Fax: 612-877-3160 E-mail: info@historicaviation.com; customerservice@historicaviation.com Web Site: www.historicaviation.com, pg 1316

Historic Cherry Hill, 523 1/2 S Pearl St, Albany, NY 12202 Tel: 518-434-4791 E-mail: info@historiccherryhill.org Web Site: www.historiccherryhill.org, pg 1316

Historic Films LLC, 211 Third St, Greenport, NY 11944 Tel: 631-477-9700 Toll Free Tel: 800-249-1940 Fax: 631-477-9800 E-mail: info@historicfilms.com Web Site: www.historicfilms.com, pg 1429

The Historical Novels Review, PO Box 1146, Jacksonville, AL 36265 E-mail: reviews@historicalnovelsociety.org; contact@historicalnovelsociety.org Web Site: historicalnovelsociety.org, pg 1132

History Book Club®, 34 W 27 St, 10th fl, New York, NY 10001 Tel: 716-250-5700 (cust serv) E-mail: member.services@historybookclub.com Web Site: www.historybookclub.com, pg 1142

History: Reviews of New Books, 530 Walnut St, Suite 850, Philadelphia, PA 19106 Tel: 215-625-8900 (ext 4) Toll Free Tel: 800-354-1420 Fax: 215-207-0050; 215-207-0046 (cust serv) E-mail: historyreviews@taylorandfrancis.com; support@tandfonline.com Web Site: www.tandfonline.com, pg 1132

HJMT Public Relations Inc, 3280 Sunrise Hwy, Suite 296, Wantagh, NY 11793 Tel: 516-661-2800 E-mail: info@hjmt.com Web Site: www.hjmt.com, pg 1109

Bruce Hoffman, 71 Faunce Dr, Providence, RI 02906 Tel: 401-274-2149 Web Site: www.whitegatefeatures.com, pg 1125

Art Holeman Photography, 4156 E Cathedral Rock Dr, Phoenix, AZ 85044 Tel: 602-290-7431 (cell) E-mail: art@artholeman.com; artholeman@cox.net Web Site: www.artholeman.com; www.fineartholeman.com, pg 1422

Hollenbeck Productions, 13386 FM 2710, Lindale, TX 75771 Tel: 206-444-5314; 206-592-1800 Web Site: www.hollenbeckproductions.com; www.cliffscoolstuff.com, pg 1422

Hollinger Metal Edge Inc, 9401 Northeast Dr, Fredricksburg, VA 22408 Tel: 540-898-7300 Toll Free Tel: 800-634-0491 Fax: 800-947-8814 E-mail: info@hollingermetaledge.com Web Site: www.hollingermetaledge.com, pg 1268

Holliston Holdings LLC, 905 Holliston Mills Rd, Church Hill, TN 37642 Tel: 423-357-6141 Toll Free Tel: 800-251-0451; 800-251-0251 (cust serv) Fax: 423-357-8840 Toll Free Fax: 800-325-0351 (cust serv) E-mail: custserv@holliston.com Web Site: holliston.com, pg 1268

Holmberg Co Inc, 4155 Berkshire Lane N, Minneapolis, MN 55446-3814 Tel: 763-559-4155 Toll Free Tel: 800-328-5101 E-mail: customerservice@holmberg.com Web Site: www.holmberg.com, pg 1254

Holo Image Technology Inc, 101 William Leigh Dr, Tullytown, PA 19007 Tel: 215-946-2190 Fax: 215-946-2129 E-mail: info@holoimagetechnology.com Web Site: www.holoimagetechnology.com, pg 1280

Honeybee (ages 2-4), 557 Broadway, New York, NY 10012 Tel: 212-343-6100; 573-632-1632 (PR, US territories, US military bases) Toll Free Tel: 800-541-1097 (US) Toll Free Fax: 800-223-4011 E-mail: bookclubs@scholastic.com Web Site: clubs.scholastic.com, pg 1142

Tom Hopkins Studio, 2121 Durham Rd, Madison, CT 06443 Tel: 203-350-0530 Web Site: www.tomhopkinsstudio.com, pg 1422

The Horah Group, 351 Manville Rd, Suite 105, Pleasantville, NY 10570 Tel: 914-495-3200 Fax: 914-769-8802 Web Site: www.horah.com, pg 1104

Horizon Paper Co Inc, 1010 Washington Blvd, Stamford, CT 06901 Tel: 203-358-0855 Toll Free Tel: 866-358-0855 E-mail: info@horizonpaper.com Web Site: www.horizonpaper.com, pg 1268

Horn Book Inc, 300 The Fenway, Suite P-311, Palace Road Bldg, Boston, MA 02115 Tel: 617-278-0225 Toll Free Tel: 888-628-0225 Fax: 617-278-6062 E-mail: info@hbook.com Web Site: www.hbook.com, pg 1146

The Horn Book Magazine, 7858 Industrial Pkwy, Plain City, OH 43064 Tel: 614-873-7706 Toll Free Tel: 800-325-9558 E-mail: info@hbook.com Web Site: www.hbook.com, pg 1132

David K Horowitz Studio Inc, 920 Chestnut St, No 22, Philadelphia, PA 19107, pg 1422

Houchen Bindery Ltd, 340 First St, Utica, NE 68456 Tel: 402-534-2261 Toll Free Tel: 800-869-0420 Fax: 402-534-2761 E-mail: email@houchenbindery.com Web Site: www.houchenbindery.com, pg 1325

Joan E Howard, 51 Congress St, Augusta, ME 04330 Tel: 207-622-0580 E-mail: petiteplaisance@acadia.net, pg 1402

HP Inc, 1501 Paige Mill Rd, Palo Alto, CA 94304-1112 Tel: 650-857-1501 Toll Free Tel: 800-282-6672 Web Site: www.hp.com, pg 1370

The Hubbard Co, 612 Clinton St, Defiance, OH 43512 Tel: 419-784-4455 Toll Free Tel: 888-448-2227 Web Site: www.hubbardcompany.com, pg 1316

George H H Huey Photography Inc, 382 W Butterfield Rd, Suite 115, Chino Valley, AZ 86323 Tel: 928-308-3460 Web Site: www.georgehhhuey.com, pg 1422

Cathy Hull, 180 E 79 St, New York, NY 10075 Tel: 212-772-7743 Fax: 212-535-1877 E-mail: cathy@cathyhull.com Web Site: www.cathyhull.com, pg 1415

Human Rights Quarterly, 2715 N Charles St, Baltimore, MD 21218-4363 Tel: 410-516-6987 (journal orders outside US & CN) Toll Free Tel: 800-548-1784 (journal orders) Fax: 410-578-2865 (journal orders) E-mail: jrnlcirc@jh.edu (journal orders) Web Site: www.press.jhu.edu/journals/human-rights-quarterly, pg 1132

HumanEdge, 30 Glenn St, Suite 401, White Plains, NY 10603 Tel: 914-428-2233 Fax: 914-428-5547 E-mail: info@humanedge.com Web Site: www.humanedge.com, pg 1381

HurleyMedia LLC, 1477 Canyon Rd, Santa Fe, NM 87501 Tel: 505-603-6392 Web Site: www.hurleymedia.com, pg 1109, 1347

Richard Hutchings Photography LLC, 11 White Well Dr, Rhinebeck, NY 12572 Tel: 914-715-7461 E-mail: richard@hutchingsphotography.com Web Site: hutchingsphotography.com, pg 1422

The P A Hutchison Co, 400 Penn Ave, Mayfield, PA 18433 Tel: 570-876-4560 Toll Free Tel: 800-USA-PRNT (872-7768) Fax: 570-876-4561 E-mail: sales@pahutch.com Web Site: www.pahutch.com, pg 1211, 1226, 1254, 1268, 1280

1447

I-Web, 175 Bodwell St, Avon, MA 02322 *Tel:* 508-580-5809 *Fax:* 508-580-5632 *E-mail:* info@iwebus.com *Web Site:* iwebus.com, pg 1280

IBM Corp, One New Orchard Rd, Armonk, NY 10504 *Tel:* 914-499-1900 *Toll Free Tel:* 800-426-4968 *E-mail:* askibm@vnet.ibm.com *Web Site:* www.ibm.com, pg 1370

iCAD Inc, 98 Spit Brook Rd, Suite 100, Nashua, NH 03062 *Tel:* 603-882-5200 *Toll Free Tel:* 866-280-2239 *E-mail:* sales@icadmed.com; support@icamed.com *Web Site:* www.icadmed.com, pg 1370

ICSID Review: Foreign Investment Law Journal, 4000 CentreGreen Way, Suite 310, Cary, NC 27513 *Toll Free Tel:* 800-852-7323 (option 1) *E-mail:* jnls.cust.serv@oup.com *Web Site:* academic.oup.com/icsidreview, pg 1133

Idea Architects, 523 Swift St, Santa Cruz, CA 95060 *Tel:* 831-465-9565 *Web Site:* www.ideaarchitects.com, pg 1347

The Idea Logical Co Inc, 300 E 51 St, Apt 17C, New York, NY 10017 *Tel:* 917-680-8598 *E-mail:* info@idealog.com *Web Site:* www.idealog.com, pg 1347

Ideal Foreign Books LLC, 132-10 Hillside Ave, Richmond Hill, NY 11418 *Tel:* 718-297-7477 *Toll Free Tel:* 800-284-2490 *Fax:* 718-297-7645 *E-mail:* idealforeignbooks@att.net, pg 1316

Imago, 110 W 40 St, New York, NY 10018 *Tel:* 212-921-4411 *Fax:* 212-921-8226 *E-mail:* sales@imagousa.com *Web Site:* www.imagousa.com, pg 1211, 1226, 1254, 1268, 1281, 1347, 1370

Impressions Inc, 1050 Westgate Dr, St Paul, MN 55114 *Tel:* 651-646-1050 *Toll Free Tel:* 800-251-4285 *Fax:* 651-646-7228 *E-mail:* info@i-i.com *Web Site:* www.i-i.com, pg 1255

Imprint Group, 2070 Cherry St, Denver, CO 80207 *Toll Free Tel:* 800-738-3961 *Toll Free Fax:* 888-867-3869 *Web Site:* imprintgroupwest.com, pg 1292

IMSI/Design LLC, 384 Bel Marin Keys Blvd, No 150, Novato, CA 94949 *Tel:* 415-483-8000 *Toll Free Tel:* 800-833-8082 (sales) *E-mail:* sales@imsidesign.com; support@imsidesign.com *Web Site:* www.imsidesign.com, pg 1370

Inchworm (ages 3-5), 557 Broadway, New York, NY 10012 *Tel:* 212-343-6100; 573-632-1632 (PR, US territories, US military bases) *Toll Free Tel:* 800-541-1097 (US) *Toll Free Fax:* 800-223-4011 *E-mail:* bookclubs@scholastic.com *Web Site:* clubs.scholastic.com, pg 1142

The Independent Book Publishers Association (IBPA), 1020 Manhattan Beach Blvd, Suite 204, Manhattan Beach, CA 90266 *Tel:* 310-546-1818 *E-mail:* info@ibpa-online.org *Web Site:* www.ibpa-online.org, pg 1116

Independent Publishers Group (IPG), 814 N Franklin St, Chicago, IL 60610 *Tel:* 312-337-0747 *Toll Free Tel:* 800-888-4741 (orders) *Fax:* 312-337-5985 *E-mail:* frontdesk@ipgbook.com; orders@ipgbook.com *Web Site:* www.ipgbook.com, pg 1292, 1328

Indexing by the Book, 5912 E Eastland St, Tucson, AZ 85711-4636 *Tel:* 520-405-8083 *E-mail:* indextran@cox.net *Web Site:* www.indexingbythebook.com, pg 1402

Indexing Research, 620 Park Ave, Suite 183, Rochester, NY 14607 *Tel:* 585-413-1819 *E-mail:* info@indexres.com *Web Site:* www.indexres.com, pg 1370

indiCo, 528 E Lorain St, Oberlin, OH 44074-1298 *Toll Free Tel:* 800-622-7498; 800-321-3883 (orders) *E-mail:* cs@goindico.com; info@goindico.com; orders@goindico.com; service@goindico.com *Web Site:* www.goindico.com, pg 1316

Indigo Books & Music Inc, 468 King St W, Suite 500, Toronto, ON M5V 1L8, Canada *Tel:* 416-364-4499 *E-mail:* cisales@indigo.ca *Web Site:* www.chapters.indigo.ca, pg 1294

InfinitPrint Solutions Inc, 14 N Tenth St, Richmond, IN 47374 *Tel:* 765-962-1507 *Toll Free Tel:* 800-478-4885 *Fax:* 765-962-4997 *E-mail:* info@infinitprint.com *Web Site:* infinitprint.com, pg 1211, 1255

Infinity Graphics, 2277 Science Pkwy, Suite 5, Okemos, MI 48864 *Tel:* 517-349-4635 *Toll Free Tel:* 800-292-2633 *Fax:* 517-349-7608 *E-mail:* barcode@infinitygraphics.com *Web Site:* www.infinitygraphics.com, pg 1227, 1255, 1370

Infocus® Corp, 13190 SW 68 Pkwy, Suite 120, Portland, OR 97223-8368 *Tel:* 503-207-4700 *Toll Free Tel:* 877-388-8360 (cust serv) *E-mail:* salessupport@infocus.com *Web Site:* www.infocus.com, pg 1370

Ingenta, 317 George St, New Brunswick, NJ 08901 *Tel:* 732-563-9292 *Fax:* 732-563-9044 *Web Site:* www.ingenta.com, pg 1370

Ingram Content Group LLC, One Ingram Blvd, La Vergne, TN 37086-1986 *Tel:* 615-793-5000 *Toll Free Tel:* 800-937-8000 (retailers); 800-937-5300 (ext 1, libs) *E-mail:* customerservice@ingramcontent.com *Web Site:* www.ingramcontent.com, pg 1294, 1316

Ingram Micro Inc, 3351 Michelson Dr, Suite 100, Irvin, CA 92612 *Tel:* 714-566-1000 *E-mail:* customerexperience@ingrammicro.com *Web Site:* www.ingrammicro.com, pg 1317

Ingram Publisher Services, an Ingram brand, 14 Ingram Blvd, Mail Stop 631, La Vergne, TN 37086 *Tel:* 615-793-5000 *Toll Free Tel:* 866-400-5351 (cust serv) *E-mail:* ips@ingramcontent.com *Web Site:* www.ingrampublisherservices.com, pg 1294

Inland Press, 2001 W Lafayette Blvd, Detroit, MI 48216 *Tel:* 313-961-6000 *Web Site:* www.inlandpress.com, pg 1104

inlingua Translation Service, 95 Summit Ave, Summit, NJ 07901 *Tel:* 908-522-0622 *E-mail:* summit@inlingua.com *Web Site:* www.inlingua.com, pg 1402

Inman, 1400 Village Square Blvd, Suite 3-80368, Tallahassee, FL 32312 *Tel:* 510-658-9252 *Toll Free Tel:* 800-775-4662 (cust support) *E-mail:* customerservice@inman.com *Web Site:* www.inman.com, pg 1190

Innodata Inc, 55 Challenger Rd, Suite 202, Ridgefield Park, NJ 07660 *Tel:* 201-371-8000 *Toll Free Tel:* 877-454-8400 *E-mail:* info@innodata.com; marketing@innodata.com *Web Site:* innodata.com, pg 1227, 1347, 1370

Innovative Design & Graphics, 1327 Greenleaf St, Evanston, IL 60202 *Tel:* 847-475-7772 *Fax:* 847-475-7784 *E-mail:* info@idgevanston.com *Web Site:* www.idgevanston.com, pg 1227

Institute for the Study of Human Knowledge (ISHK), 1702-L Meridian Ave, No 266, San Jose, CA 95125-5586 *Tel:* 617-497-4124 *Toll Free Tel:* 800-222-4745 (orders) *Fax:* 617-500-0268 *Toll Free Fax:* 800-223-4200 (orders) *E-mail:* ishkadm@aol.com; ishkbooks@aol.com (orders) *Web Site:* www.ishk.com, pg 1295

Institute of Intergovernmental Relations, Queen's University, Robert Sutherland Hall, Rm 301, Kingston, ON K7L 3N6, Canada *Tel:* 613-533-2080 *E-mail:* iigr@queensu.ca *Web Site:* www.queensu.ca/iigr, pg 1317

Integra Software Services Inc, 2021 Midwest Rd, Suite 200, Oak Brook, IL 60523 *Web Site:* www.integranxt.com, pg 1348, 1355

Integrated Distribution Services (IDS), 9431 AllPoints Pkwy, Plainfield, IN 46168 *Toll Free Tel:* 866-232-6533 *E-mail:* cwelch@idsfulfillment.com *Web Site:* www.idsfulfillment.com, pg 1334

Integrated PR Agency (IPR), Penthouse, 9025 Wilshire Blvd, Suite 500, Beverly Hills, CA 90211 *Tel:* 310-858-8230 *Web Site:* www.integrated-pr.com, pg 1109

Intellicor Communications LLC, 330 Eden Rd, Lancaster, PA 17601 *Toll Free Tel:* 800-233-0107 *Web Site:* www.intellicor.com, pg 1104

The Intermarketing Group-Art Licensing Agency, 29 Holt Rd, Amherst, NH 03031 *Tel:* 603-672-0499, pg 1348

International Book Centre Inc, 2391 Auburn Rd, Shelby Township, MI 48317 *Tel:* 586-254-7230 *Fax:* 586-254-7230 *E-mail:* ibc@ibcbooks.com *Web Site:* www.ibcbooks.com, pg 1317

International Book Import Service Inc, 161 Main St, Lynchburg, TN 37352-8300 *Tel:* 931-759-7400 *Toll Free Tel:* 800-277-4247 *Fax:* 931-759-7555 *Toll Free Fax:* 866-277-2722 *E-mail:* ibis@ibiservice.com *Web Site:* www.ibiservice.com, pg 1328

International Institute of Reflexology Inc, PO Box 12642, St Petersburg, FL 33733-2642 *Tel:* 727-343-4811 *E-mail:* info@reflexology-usa.net; orderdept@reflexology-usa.net *Web Site:* reflexology-usa.net, pg 1317, 1328

International Leads (IL), 225 N Michigan Ave, Suite 1300, Chicago, IL 60601 *Tel:* 312-944-6780 *Toll Free Tel:* 800-545-2433 *Fax:* 312-440-9374 *E-mail:* ala.intl.leads@gmail.com; ala@ala.org *Web Site:* www.ala.org/rt/irrt/intlleads/internationalleads; www.ala.org/rt/irrt; www.ala.org, pg 1133

International Literary Properties (ILP), 286 Madison Ave, New York, NY 10017 *Tel:* 646-202-1633 *Fax:* 212-967-0977 *E-mail:* contact@ilpliterary.com *Web Site:* www.internationalliteraryproperties.com, pg 1348

International Mapping Associates, 5300 Dorsey Hall Dr, Suite 201, Ellicott City, MD 21042 *Tel:* 443-367-0050 *E-mail:* frontdesk@internationalmapping.com *Web Site:* internationalmapping.com, pg 1415

International Paper Co, 6400 Poplar Ave, Memphis, TN 38197 *Tel:* 901-419-9000 *Toll Free Tel:* 800-207-4003 *Web Site:* www.internationalpaper.com; facebook.com/internationalpaper; x.com/intlpaperco, pg 1268

International Press Publication Inc, Spadina Rd, Richmond Hill, ON L4B 3C5, Canada *Tel:* 905-883-0343 *E-mail:* sales@ippbooks.com *Web Site:* www.ippbooks.com; www.facebook.com/ippbooks; x.com/ippbooks2, pg 1227, 1281, 1295, 1317

International Service Co, International Service Bldg, 333 Fourth Ave, Indialantic, FL 32903-4295 *Tel:* 321-724-1443 *Fax:* 321-724-1443, pg 1317, 1325, 1328, 1331

International Transactions Inc, 28 Alope Way, Gila, NM 88038 *Tel:* 845-373-9696 *Fax:* 480-393-5162 *E-mail:* info@internationaltransactions.us *Web Site:* www.intltrans.com, pg 1348

Internet Bookwatch, 278 Orchard Dr, Oregon, WI 53575-1129 *Tel:* 608-835-7937 *E-mail:* mbr@execpc.com *Web Site:* www.midwestbookreview.com, pg 1133

Interprint Web Printing, 12350 US 19 N, Clearwater, FL 33764 *Tel:* 727-531-8957 *Toll Free Tel:* 800-749-5152 *Fax:* 727-536-0647 *E-mail:* info@interprintwebprinting.com *Web Site:* www.interprintwebprinting.com, pg 1104

Interstate Books4School, 201 E Badger Rd, Madison, WI 53713 *Tel:* 608-277-2407 *Toll Free Tel:* 800-752-3131 *Fax:* 608-277-2410 *E-mail:* sales@books4school.com *Web Site:* www.books4school.com, pg 1317

Interstate Printing Co, 2002 N 16 St, Omaha, NE 68110 *Tel:* 402-341-8028 *Toll Free Tel:* 800-788-4177 *Web Site:* www.interstateprinting.com, pg 1227, 1255

Intex Solutions Inc, 110 "A" St, Needham, MA 02494 *Tel:* 781-449-6222 *Fax:* 781-444-2318 *E-mail:* sales@intex.com *Web Site:* www.intex.com, pg 1371

Intuit Inc, 2700 Coast Ave, Mountain View, CA 94043 *Tel:* 650-944-6000 *Toll Free Tel:* 800-446-8848 *E-mail:* investor_relations@intuit.com *Web Site:* www.intuit.com, pg 1371

IP Royalty Auditors LLC, 316 Perkins Ave, Oceanside, NY 11572 *Tel:* 516-503-5985 *E-mail:* royalty@aol.com *Web Site:* www.iproyaltyauditors.com, pg 1348

iProbe Multilingual Solutions Inc, 145 W 30 St, 9th fl, New York, NY 10001 *Tel:* 212-489-6035 *Toll Free Tel:* 888-489-6035 *Fax:* 212-202-4790 *E-mail:* info@iprobesolutions.com *Web Site:* iprobesolutions.com, pg 1402

Iranbooks, PO Box 30087, Bethesda, MD 20824 *Tel:* 301-718-8188 *Toll Free Tel:* 888-718-8188 *Fax:* 301-907-8707 *E-mail:* info@iranbooks.com *Web Site:* www.iranbooks.com, pg 1317, 1328

COMPANY INDEX

IRCO-International Language Bank, 10301 NE Glisan St, Portland, OR 97220 Tel: 503-234-0068 (interpretation); 503-505-5186 (translation) Fax: 503-233-4724 E-mail: translation@ircoilb.org; interpretation@ircoilb.org Web Site: www.irco.org/ilb, pg 1402

Ironmark, 9040 Junction Dr, Annapolis Junction, MD 20701 Toll Free Tel: 888-775-3737 E-mail: marketing@ironmarkusa.com Web Site: ironmarkusa.com, pg 1211, 1227, 1255, 1268, 1281

Patti Isaacs Maps, Infographics, Writing, 13720 Paragon Ave N, Stillwater, MN 55082 Tel: 651-430-8127 Web Site: patti-isaacs.com, pg 1415

ISIS Papyrus America, 301 Bank St, South Lake, TX 76092 Tel: 817-416-2345 Fax: 817-416-1223 E-mail: info@isis-papyrus.com Web Site: www.isis-papyrus.com, pg 1371

The Islander Group, 269 Palii St, Mililani, HI 96789 Tel: 808-676-0116 Toll Free Tel: 877-828-4852 Fax: 808-676-5156 E-mail: customerservice@islandergroup.com Web Site: www.islandergroup.com, pg 1317, 1328

ISOMEDIA Inc, 12842 Interurban Ave S, Seattle, WA 98168 Tel: 425-869-5411 Toll Free Tel: 866-838-4389 (sales); 877-638-9277 (support) Fax: 425-869-9437 E-mail: sales@isomedia.com Web Site: www.isomedia.com, pg 1371

Israel's Judaica Center, 441 Clark Ave W, Thornhill, ON L4J 6W7, Canada Tel: 905-881-1010 Toll Free Tel: 877-511-1010 Fax: 905-881-1016 E-mail: contact@israelsjudaica.com; thornhill@israelsjudaica.com (retail store) Web Site: www.israelsjudaica.com, pg 1317

ITW Foils, 5 Malcolm Hoyt Dr, Newburyport, MA 01950 Tel: 978-225-8200 Toll Free Tel: 800-942-9995 Fax: 978-462-0831 E-mail: info@itwsf.com Web Site: www.itwfoils.com, pg 1255, 1415

Itzhack Shelomi Design, 25 Cushman Rd, Scarsdale, NY 10583 Tel: 212-689-7469 E-mail: studio@ishelomi.com; studio@serifes.com Web Site: www.ishelomi.com, pg 1211, 1227, 1371, 1415

Iverson Science Photos, 31 Boss Ave, Portsmouth, NH 03801 Tel: 603-433-8484 Fax: 603-433-8484 E-mail: iversonarts@gmail.com, pg 1423

J Brough Schamp Photography, Baltimore, MD 21212 Tel: 443-996-5450 (cell) Web Site: www.broughschampphotography.com, pg 1423

Michael Jacobs Photojournalism (MJP), 2105 Vista Oeste NW, Suite 3, No 2057, Albuquerque, NM 87120 Tel: 323-461-0240 Toll Free Fax: 866-563-9212 E-mail: michael.mjphoto@gmail.com Web Site: www.mjphotogallery.com, pg 1423, 1429

The James & Law Co, 217 W Main St, Clarksburg, WV 26301 Tel: 304-624-7401 Toll Free Tel: 800-253-5428 Fax: 304-624-9331 E-mail: sales@jamesandlaw.com Web Site: jamesandlaw.com, pg 1317

Kerrick James Photography, 235 N 22 Place, Unit 560, Mesa, AZ 85213 Tel: 602-276-3111 Web Site: www.kerrickjames.com; www.agpix.com/kerrickjames, pg 1423

Jane Wesman Public Relations Inc, 322 Eighth Ave, Suite 1702, New York, NY 10001 Tel: 212-620-4080 Fax: 212-620-0370 Web Site: www.wesmanpr.com, pg 1109

Law Offices of Lloyd J Jassin, The Paramount Bldg, 1501 Broadway, 12th fl, New York, NY 10036 Tel: 212-354-4442 E-mail: jassin@copylaw.com Web Site: www.copylaw.org, pg 1348

Javelin Group, 203 S Union St, Suite 200, Alexandria, VA 22314 Tel: 703-490-8845 E-mail: hello@javelindc.com Web Site: javelindc.com, pg 1348

Jenkins Group Inc, 1129 Woodmere Ave, Suite B, Traverse City, MI 49686 Tel: 231-933-0445; 213-883-5365 E-mail: info@jenkinsgroupinc.com Web Site: www.jenkinsgroupinc.com, pg 1227, 1348, 1355

Jeroboam, 120 27 St, San Francisco, CA 94110 Tel: 415-637-7840 (cell) E-mail: jeroboamster@gmail.com, pg 1429

Jeunesse: Young People, Texts, Cultures, 5201 Dufferin St, Toronto, ON M3H 5T8, Canada Tel: 416-667-7777 (ext 7971) E-mail: journals@utpress.utoronto.ca Web Site: www.utpjournals.press/jeunesse, pg 1133

Jewish Book Council, 520 Eighth Ave, 4th fl, New York, NY 10018 Tel: 212-201-2920 Fax: 212-532-4952 E-mail: info@jewishbooks.org Web Site: www.jewishbookcouncil.org, pg 1146

Jewish Telegraphic Agency, 24 W 30 St, 4th fl, New York, NY 10001 Tel: 646-778-5520 E-mail: info@70facesmedia.org Web Site: www.jta.org; www.70facesmedia.org, pg 1190

JMW Group Inc, 346 Rte 6, No 867, Mahopac, NY 10541 Tel: 914-841-7105 Fax: 914-248-8861 E-mail: jmwgroup@jmwgroup.net Web Site: jmwforlife.com, pg 1348

Bruni Johnson, 457 E Colfax St, Palatine, IL 60074 Tel: 847-359-6839 Fax: 847-359-7075 E-mail: brunijohnson@sbcglobal.net, pg 1402

John Johnston, 1288 Southlyn Dr, Dayton, OH 45409 Tel: 937-681-4309 E-mail: jejphotos@gmail.com Web Site: www.johnjohnston.co, pg 1423

Jonathan David Publishers Inc, 52 Tuscan Way, Suite 202-371, St Augustine, FL 32092 Tel: 718-456-8611 E-mail: customerservice@jdbooks.com Web Site: www.jdbooks.com, pg 1295

Lou Jones Studio, 44 Breed St, Boston, MA 02128 Tel: 617-561-1194 Fax: 617-561-1196 E-mail: fotojones@aol.com Web Site: www.fotojones.com, pg 1423

Journal of Cuneiform Studies (JCS), James F Strange Ctr, 209 Commerce St, Alexandria, VA 22314 Tel: 703-789-9229; 703-789-9230 (pubns) E-mail: info@asor.org; publications@asor.org Web Site: www.asor.org, pg 1133

Journal of Modern Greek Studies, 2715 N Charles St, Baltimore, MD 21218-4363 Tel: 410-516-6987 (journal orders outside US & CN) Toll Free Tel: 800-548-1784 (journal orders) Fax: 410-578-2865 (journal orders) E-mail: jrnlcirc@jh.edu (journal orders) Web Site: www.press.jhu.edu/journal-modern-greek-studies, pg 1133

JP Graphics Inc, 3001 E Venture Dr, Appleton, WI 54911 Tel: 920-733-4483 Fax: 920-733-1700 E-mail: support@jpinc.com Web Site: www.jpinc.com; www.print.jpinc.com, pg 1211, 1227, 1255

JPMC Associates, 7037 Snapdragon Dr, Carlsbad, CA 92011 Tel: 916-203-3693 Fax: 760-931-6878 E-mail: jpmcaso@aol.com, pg 1348

Junior Library Guild, 7858 Industrial Pkwy, Plain City, OH 43064 Tel: 614-733-0312 Toll Free Tel: 800-491-0174 Fax: 614-733-0501 Toll Free Fax: 800-827-3080 E-mail: editorial@juniorlibraryguild.com Web Site: www.juniorlibraryguild.com, pg 1142

K H Marketing Communications, 16205 NE Sixth St, Bellevue, WA 98008 Tel: 425-269-7411 (cell), pg 1110

Kable Product Services Inc, 4275 Thunderbird Lane, Fairfield, OH 45014 Tel: 513-671-2800 E-mail: info@kable.com Web Site: www.kablefulfillment.com, pg 1334

Kachergis Book Design Inc, 575 Stone Wall Rd, Pittsboro, NC 27312 Tel: 919-656-7632 E-mail: goodbooks@kachergisbookdesign.com Web Site: www.kachergisbookdesign.com, pg 1227, 1415

Wolfgang Kaehler Photography, 723 Third St S, Kirkland, WA 98033 Tel: 425-803-0652 Web Site: www.facebook.com/wolfgang.kaehler, pg 1423

Kaplan/DeFiore Rights, 47 E 19 St, 3rd fl, New York, NY 10003 Tel: 212-925-7244 Web Site: kaplanrights.com, pg 1348

Kappa Graphics LLP, 50 Rock St, Hughestown, PA 18640 Tel: 570-655-9681 Toll Free Tel: 800-236-4396 (sales) E-mail: weborders@kappapma.com Web Site: www.kappapma.com/kappagraphics; kappapuzzles.com, pg 1227, 1255

The Karel/Dutton Group, San Francisco, CA 94121 Tel: 415-668-0829 Web Site: kareldutttongroup.com, pg 1295

Dimitri Karetnikov, 221 Ewell Ave, Gettesburg, PA 17325 Tel: 609-468-5627 E-mail: dkare@aol.com, pg 1415

Karen Karibian, 444 Warren St, Apt 1450, Jersey City, NJ 07302 Tel: 914-564-4201 E-mail: karenesque2@aol.com; karenkaribian@gmail.com; karenessence@aol.com Web Site: www.coroflot.com/karenessence/undercurrent-cartoons; www.karenessence.wix.com/undercurrentcartoons.com, pg 1415

Alicja T Kawecki, 4-A Foxwood Dr, Apt D, Morris Plains, NJ 07950 Tel: 973-590-2236 E-mail: atkawecki@optonline.net, pg 1402

Kazi Publications Inc, 3023 W Belmont Ave, Chicago, IL 60618 Tel: 773-267-7001 Fax: 773-267-7002 E-mail: info@kazi.org Web Site: www.kazi.org, pg 1317, 1328

Tom Keck Photos, 13393 Landfair Rd, San Diego, CA 92130 Tel: 858-755-2975 E-mail: tomkeckphotos@gmail.com Web Site: www.tomkeckphotos.com, pg 1423

Keister-Williams Newspaper Services Inc, PO Box 8187, Charlottesville, VA 22906 Tel: 434-293-4709 Toll Free Tel: 800-293-4709 E-mail: kw@kwnews.com Web Site: www.kwnews.com, pg 1190

Kelley & Hall Book Publicity, 5 Briar Lane, Marblehead, MA 01945 Tel: 617-680-1976 Fax: 781-631-5959 Web Site: www.kelleyandhall.com, pg 1110

Kensington Technology Group, 1500 Fashion Island Blvd, Suite 300, San Mateo, CA 94404-1595 Toll Free Tel: 800-535-4242 E-mail: globalmarketing@kensington.com Web Site: www.kensington.com, pg 1371

Ketab Corp, 12701 Van Nuys Blvd, Unit H, Pacoima, CA 91331 Tel: 310-477-7477 Toll Free Tel: 800-FOR-IRAN (367-4726) Fax: 818-908-1457 E-mail: ketab1@ketab.com Web Site: www.ketab.com, pg 1317

Keystone Press Agency Inc, 408 N El Camino Real, San Clemente, CA 92672 Tel: 949-481-3747 Fax: 949-481-3941 E-mail: info@keystonepictures.com Web Site: www.keystonepictures.com, pg 1190, 1429

Kindergarten Book Club, 557 Broadway, New York, NY 10012 Tel: 212-343-6100; 573-632-1632 (PR, US territories, US military bases) Toll Free Tel: 800-541-1097 (US) Toll Free Fax: 800-223-4011 E-mail: bookclubs@scholastic.com Web Site: clubs.scholastic.com, pg 1142

King Features Syndicate, 300 W 57 St, New York, NY 10019-5238 Tel: 212-969-7550 Toll Free Tel: 800-526-5464 Web Site: www.kingfeatures.com, pg 1190

Linda King, 71 Faunce Dr, Providence, RI 02906 Tel: 401-274-2149 Web Site: www.whitegatefeatures.com, pg 1125

King Printing, 181 Industrial Ave E, Lowell, MA 01852-5147 Tel: 978-458-2345 Fax: 978-458-1441 E-mail: inquiries@kingprinting.com Web Site: www.kingprinting.com; www.adibooks.com, pg 1211

Kinokuniya Bookstores of America Co Ltd, 1581 Webster St, San Francisco, CA 94115 Tel: 415-567-6787 Fax: 415-567-4109 E-mail: sales@kinokuniya.com; san_francisco@kinokuniya.com; bookwebusa@kinokuniya.com (cust serv) Web Site: usa.kinokuniya.com, pg 1318, 1328

Kinokuniya Publications Service of New York (KPS-NY), 1073 Avenue of the Americas, New York, NY 10018-3701 Tel: 212-765-1465 Fax: 212-307-5593 E-mail: nyinfo@kinokuniya.com Web Site: www.kinokuniya.co.jp; www.kinokuniya.com, pg 1348

KIPLINGER'S PERSONAL FINANCE

COMPANY INDEX

Kiplinger's Personal Finance/The Kiplinger Washington Editors Inc, 1100 13 St NW, Suite 750, Washington, DC 20005-4364 *Tel:* 202-887-6400 *Toll Free Tel:* 800-544-0155 (cust serv) *E-mail:* feedback@kiplinger.com *Web Site:* www.kiplinger.com, pg 1191

Kirkus, 1140 Broadway, Suite 802, New York, NY 10001 *E-mail:* customercare@kirkus.com *Web Site:* www.kirkusreviews.com, pg 1133

Kitzmiller Sales & Marketing Co, 35 Flint St, Suite 304, Salem, MA 01970-3264 *Tel:* 978-985-1144 (cell) *Fax:* 978-744-0232 *E-mail:* dnd.kitzmiller@gmail.com, pg 1295

Solveig Kjok, 520 Kingsland Ave, Brooklyn, NY 11222 *Web Site:* www.art-texts.plus; www.solkjok.info, pg 1402

Klopotek North America Inc, 19321 US Hwy 19 N, Suite 407, Clearwater, FL 33764 *Tel:* 973-331-1010 *E-mail:* info@klopotek.com *Web Site:* www.klopotek.com, pg 1348

Bruce Kluckhohn Photographer, 2608 Webster Ave S, Minneapolis, MN 55416-1723 *Tel:* 612-929-6010 *E-mail:* bruce@brucekphoto.com *Web Site:* www.brucekphoto.com, pg 1423

Knepper Press Corp, 2251 Sweeney Dr, Clinton, PA 15026 *Tel:* 724-899-4200 *Fax:* 724-899-1331 *Web Site:* www.knepperpress.com, pg 1211, 1227, 1255

knk Software LP, 89 Headquarters Plaza N, No 1478, Morristown, NJ 07960 *Tel:* 908-206-4599 *E-mail:* info@knk.com *Web Site:* www.knkpublishingsoftware.com, pg 1348

Knovel Corp, 230 Park Ave, 8th fl, New York, NY 10169 *Tel:* 212-309-8100 *Web Site:* app.knovel.com/kn, pg 1371

William Koechling Photography, 1307 E Harrison Ave, Wheaton, IL 60187 *Tel:* 630-665-4379 *E-mail:* koechlingphoto@sbcglobal.net *Web Site:* www.facebook.com/koechlingphoto; 500px.com/billkoechling, pg 1423

David W Koehser Attorney at Law, 322 First Ave N, Suite 402, Minneapolis, MN 55401 *Tel:* 612-910-6468 *E-mail:* dk@dklex.com *Web Site:* www.dklex.com, pg 1349

Koenig & Bauer (US) Inc, 2555 Regent Blvd, Dallas, TX 75229 *Tel:* 469-532-8000 *Fax:* 469-532-8190 *Web Site:* us.koenig-bauer.com, pg 1281

Koller Search Partners, 655 Third Ave, 24th fl, New York, NY 10017 *Tel:* 212-661-5250 *E-mail:* ksp@kollersearch.com *Web Site:* www.kollersearch.com, pg 1381

Kontron America Inc, 9477 Waples St, San Diego, CA 92121 *Toll Free Tel:* 888-294-4558 (sales); 800-480-0044 (cust serv, US only) *Fax:* 858-677-0898 *E-mail:* info@kontron.com *Web Site:* www.kontron.com, pg 1371

Jill Kramer - Best of Books, 71 Faunce Dr, Providence, RI 02906 *Tel:* 401-274-2149 *Web Site:* www.whitegatefeatures.com, pg 1126

Kreab, House of Sweden, Suite 504, 2900 "K" St NW, Washington, DC 20007 *Tel:* 202-536-1590 *E-mail:* washingtondc@kreab.com *Web Site:* www.kreab.com/washington-dc, pg 1110

Krishnamurti Publications of America, 1070 McAndrew Rd, Ojai, CA 93023 *Tel:* 805-646-2726 *E-mail:* kfa@kfa.org *Web Site:* www.kfa.org, pg 1329

Kromar Printing Ltd, 725 Portage Ave, Winnipeg, MB R3G 0M8, Canada *Tel:* 204-775-8721 *Fax:* 204-783-8985 *E-mail:* info@kromar.com *Web Site:* www.kromar.com, pg 1212, 1255

Kenneth Kronenberg, 51 Maple Ave, Cambridge, MA 02139 *Tel:* 617-868-8070 *E-mail:* mail@kfkronenberg.com *Web Site:* www.kfkronenberg.com, pg 1402

Kroy LLC, 3830 Kelley Ave, Cleveland, OH 44114 *Tel:* 216-426-5600 *Toll Free Fax:* 800-523-2881 *E-mail:* info@kroy.com; support@kroy.com *Web Site:* www.kroy.com, pg 1371

Dwight Kuhn, Dexter, ME 04930 *E-mail:* millacus77@yahoo.com *Web Site:* www.kuhnphoto.net, pg 1423

Kwikprint Manufacturing Co Inc, 4868 Victor St, Jacksonville, FL 32207 *Tel:* 904-737-3755 *Toll Free Tel:* 800-940-5945 *Fax:* 904-730-0349 *E-mail:* info@kwikprint.net *Web Site:* www.kwik-print.com, pg 1268

KyTek Inc, PO Box 338, Weare, NH 03281 *Tel:* 603-529-2512 *E-mail:* sales@kytek.com *Web Site:* www.kytek.com, pg 1371

La Crosse Graphics Inc, 3025 East Ave S, La Crosse, WI 54601 *Tel:* 608-788-2500 *Toll Free Tel:* 800-832-2503 *Fax:* 608-788-2660 *Web Site:* www.lacrossegraphics.com, pg 1255

Labels Inc, 10 Merrill Industrial Dr, Hampton, NH 03842 *Tel:* 603-929-3088 *Toll Free Tel:* 800-852-2357 *Fax:* 603-929-7305 *E-mail:* sales@labelsinc.com *Web Site:* www.labelsinc.com, pg 1255

Labrecque Creative Sound, 2825 Main St, Becket, MA 01223, pg 1371

Lachina Creative, 3693 Green Rd, Cleveland, OH 44122 *Tel:* 216-292-7959 *E-mail:* info@lachina.com *Web Site:* www.lachina.com, pg 1227, 1355, 1371, 1415

Julie A Laitin Enterprises Inc, 160 West End Ave, Suite 23N, New York, NY 10023 *Tel:* 917-841-8566 *E-mail:* info@julielaitin.com *Web Site:* www.julielaitin.com, pg 1100

Lake Book Manufacturing Inc, 2085 N Cornell Ave, Melrose Park, IL 60160 *Tel:* 708-345-7000 *E-mail:* info@lakebook.com *Web Site:* www.lakebook.com, pg 1212, 1227, 1255, 1268, 1281

Lake Group Media Inc, One Byram Brook Place, Armonk, NY 10504 *Tel:* 914-925-2400 *Fax:* 914-925-2499 *Web Site:* www.lakegroupmedia.com, pg 1120

L+L Printers, 6200 Yarrow Dr, Carlsbad, CA 92011 *Tel:* 760-438-3456; 760-477-0321 *Fax:* 760-929-0853 *E-mail:* info@llprinters.com *Web Site:* www.llprinters.com, pg 1256

The Lane Press Inc, 87 Meadowland Dr, South Burlington, VT 05403 *Tel:* 802-863-5555 *Toll Free Tel:* 877-300-5933 *Fax:* 802-264-1485 *E-mail:* sales@lanepress.com *Web Site:* www.lanepress.com, pg 1227, 1256

Mary Langenfeld Photography, 3817 Euclid Ave, Madison, WI 53711 *Tel:* 608-233-9938; 608-334-1375 (cell) *E-mail:* madisonfoto@att.net *Web Site:* www.langenfeld-photo.com, pg 1423

The Language Center, 62 Brunswick Woods Dr, East Brunswick, NJ 08816 *Tel:* 732-613-4554 *Fax:* 732-238-7659 *Web Site:* www.thelanguagectr.com, pg 1402

LanternMedia, 128 Second Place, Garden Suite, Brooklyn, NY 11231 *Tel:* 212-414-2275 *Web Site:* www.lanternmedia.net, pg 1371

Laplink Software Inc, 600 108 Ave NE, Suite 610, Bellevue, WA 98004 *Tel:* 425-952-6000 *Toll Free Tel:* 800-LAPLINK (527-5465) *E-mail:* info@laplink.com; sales@laplink.com *Web Site:* web.laplink.com, pg 1371

LARB Quarterly Journal, 6671 Sunset Blvd, Suite 1521, Los Angeles, CA 90028 *Tel:* 323-952-3950 *E-mail:* info@lareviewofbooks.org; editorial@lareviewofbooks.org *Web Site:* lareviewofbooks.org, pg 1133

Larson Texts Inc, 1762 Norcross Rd, Erie, PA 16510 *Tel:* 814-824-6365 *Toll Free Tel:* 800-530-2355 *Fax:* 814-824-6377 *Web Site:* www.larsontexts.com, pg 1227, 1269, 1355

Lassco-Wizer Equipment & Supplies, 485 Hague St, Rochester, NY 14606-1296 *Tel:* 585-436-1934 *Toll Free Tel:* 800-854-6595 *Fax:* 585-464-8665 *E-mail:* info@lasscowizer.com; sales@lasscowizer.com *Web Site:* www.lasscowizer.com, pg 1281

The Latin American Book Store Ltd, PO Box 7328, Redlands, CA 92375 *Toll Free Tel:* 800-645-4276 *Fax:* 909-335-9945 *E-mail:* libros@latinamericanbooks.com *Web Site:* www.latinamericanbooks.com, pg 1329

Lawton Connect, 649 Triumph Ct, Orlando, FL 32805 *Tel:* 407-260-0400 *Toll Free Tel:* 877-330-1900 *Fax:* 407-260-1321 *E-mail:* hello@lawtonconnect.com *Web Site:* www.lawtonconnect.com, pg 1256

Lawyers & Judges Publishing Co Inc, 917 N Swan Rd, Suite 300, Tucson, AZ 85711 *Tel:* 520-323-1500 *Fax:* 520-323-0055 *E-mail:* sales@lawyersandjudges.com *Web Site:* www.lawyersandjudges.com, pg 1120

LBS, 1801 Thompson Ave, Des Moines, IA 50316-2751 *Tel:* 515-262-3191 *Toll Free Tel:* 800-247-5323 *Toll Free Fax:* 800-262-4091 *E-mail:* info@lbsbind.com *Web Site:* www.lbsbind.com, pg 1269

LEA Libros de Espana y America, 170-23 83 Ave, Jamaica, NY 11432 *Tel:* 718-291-9891 *Fax:* 718-291-9830 *E-mail:* lea@leabooks.com; orders@leabooks.com *Web Site:* www.leabooks.com, pg 1329

Leading Edge Express, 3651 Robin Lane, Minnetonka, MN 55503 *Tel:* 952-217-4665 *Web Site:* www.leadingedgereview.com, pg 1133

The Learning Source Ltd, 644 Tenth St, Brooklyn, NY 11215 *E-mail:* info@learningsourceltd.com *Web Site:* www.learningsourceltd.com, pg 1355

Learning World Inc, 287 Wycliffe Ave, Vaughan, ON L4L 3N7, Canada, pg 1318

Lectorum Publications Inc, 10 New Maple Ave, Suite 303, Pine Brook, NJ 07058 *Tel:* 201-559-2200 *Toll Free Tel:* 800-345-5946 *E-mail:* lectorum@lectorum.com *Web Site:* www.lectorum.com, pg 1318

Jess Lee Photography LLC, 13316 Skyview St, Nampa, ID 83686 *Tel:* 208-521-5170 *Web Site:* www.jessleephotos.com, pg 1423

Lee Publications, 1100 W Broadway, Louisville, KY 40203 *Tel:* 502-587-6804 *Toll Free Tel:* 800-626-8247 *Fax:* 502-587-6822 *E-mail:* info@leemagicpen.com *Web Site:* www.leemagicpen.com, pg 1256

Tom & Pat Leeson, PO Box 2498, Vancouver, WA 98668-2498 *Tel:* 360-256-0436 *E-mail:* office@leesonphoto.com *Web Site:* www.leesonphoto.com; www.leesonphotoart.com, pg 1423

Leo Paper USA, 1180 NW Maple St, Suite 102, Issaquah, WA 98027 *Tel:* 425-646-8801 *Fax:* 425-646-8805 *E-mail:* info@leousa.com *Web Site:* www.leopaper.com, pg 1212, 1228, 1256

Steve Leonard Photography, 825 W Gunnison St, Chicago, IL 60640-4267 *Tel:* 312-206-5344 *E-mail:* steve@steveleonardphoto.com *Web Site:* www.steveleonardphoto.com, pg 1423

Lerner Publisher Services, 241 First Ave N, Minneapolis, MN 55401 *Tel:* 612-332-3344 *Toll Free Tel:* 800-328-4929 (orders) *Fax:* 612-215-6230 *E-mail:* info@lernerpublisherservices.com; custserve@lernerpublisherservices.com *Web Site:* www.lernerpublisherservices.com, pg 1295

Letterhead Press Inc (LPI), 16800 W Ryerson Rd, New Berlin, WI 53151 *Tel:* 262-787-1717 *Fax:* 262-787-1710; 262-787-7315 (estimating) *E-mail:* contact@letterhead-press.com *Web Site:* www.letterheadpress.com, pg 1256

The Lexington Press Inc, 15 Meriam St, Lexington, MA 02420 *Tel:* 781-862-8900 *Fax:* 781-861-0375 *Web Site:* www.lexingtonpress.com, pg 1228, 1256

LexisNexis®, 9443 Springboro Pike, Dayton, OH 45342 *Toll Free Tel:* 800-227-9597 *E-mail:* information@lexisnexis.com *Web Site:* www.lexisnexis.com, pg 1371

LG Electronics USA, 1000 Sylvan Ave, Englewood Cliffs, NJ 07632 *Tel:* 201-816-2000 *Toll Free Tel:* 800-243-0000 (cust serv) *Web Site:* www.lg.com/us, pg 1371

Maria Liberati, 1250 Bethlehem Pike, Unit 241, Hatfield, PA 19440 *Tel:* 215-436-9524 *E-mail:* maria@marialiberati.com *Web Site:* www.marialiberati.com, pg 1126

COMPANY INDEX

Library Bookwatch, 278 Orchard Dr, Oregon, WI 53575-1129 Tel: 608-835-7937 E-mail: mbr@execpc.com Web Site: www.midwestbookreview.com, pg 1133

Library Bound Inc, 100 Bathurst Dr, Unit 2, Waterloo, ON N2V 1V6, Canada Tel: 519-885-3233 Toll Free Tel: 800-363-4728 Fax: 519-885-2662 Web Site: www.librarybound.com, pg 1318

Library Journal, 123 William St, Suite 802, New York, NY 10038 Tel: 646-380-0700 Toll Free Tel: 800-588-1030 Fax: 646-380-0756 E-mail: ljinfo@mediasourceinc.com Web Site: www.libraryjournal.com, pg 1134

Library of Science® Book Club, 34 W 27 St, 10th fl, New York, NY 10001 Tel: 716-250-5700 (cust serv) E-mail: customer.service@libraryofscience.net Web Site: www.libraryofscience.net, pg 1142

The Library Services Centre, 131 Shoemaker St, Kitchener, ON N2E 3B5, Canada Tel: 519-746-4420 Toll Free Tel: 800-265-3360 (CN only) Fax: 519-746-4425 Web Site: www.lsc.on.ca, pg 1318

Lidec Inc, 800, blvd Industriel, bureau 202, St-Jean-sur-Richlieu, QC J3B 8G4, Canada Tel: 514-843-5991 Toll Free Tel: 800-350-5991 (CN only) Fax: 514-843-5252 E-mail: lidec@lidec.qc.ca Web Site: www.lidec.qc.ca, pg 1212

The Philip Lief Group Inc (PLG), 2976 Pleasant Ridge Rd, Wingdale, NY 12594 Tel: 609-430-1000 Fax: 845-724-7139 E-mail: info@plg.us.com Web Site: plg.us.com, pg 1355

Lightning Source LLC, 1246 Heil Quaker Blvd, La Vergne, TN 37086 Tel: 615-793-5000 (Ingram) Toll Free Tel: 800-378-5508; 800-509-4156 (cust serv) E-mail: lsicustomersupport@ingramcontent.com; contentacquisitioninquiries@ingramcontent.com Web Site: www.ingramcontent.com/publishers/print, pg 1212

Lightning Source LLC, 1246 Heil Quaker Blvd, La Vergne, TN 37086 Tel: 615-793-5000 (Ingram) Toll Free Tel: 800-378-5508; 800-509-4156 (cust serv) E-mail: lsicustomersupport@ingramcontent.com Web Site: www.ingramcontent.com/publishers/print, pg 1256, 1371

Wayne Lim, 2429 Clement St, No 2, San Francisco, CA 94121 Tel: 415-940-3868 E-mail: w_c_lim@yahoo.com, pg 1415

Linda Kittlitz & Associates, 193 Coleridge St, San Francisco, CA 94110-5112 Tel: 415-550-8898 Toll Free Tel: 800-550-8898 Fax: 415-550-7975 Web Site: www.lkandassociates.com, pg 1104

Lindenmeyr Book Publishing Papers, 3 Manhattanville Rd, Purchase, NY 10577 Tel: 914-696-9300 Web Site: www.lindenmeyrbook.com, pg 1269

Linguistic Systems Inc (LSI), 260 Franklin St, Suite 230, Boston, MA 02110 Tel: 617-528-7400 E-mail: clientservice@linguist.com Web Site: www.linguist.com, pg 1228, 1372, 1402, 1415

Linguist's Software, 300 Tineke Way, Travelers Rest, SC 29690-6903 Tel: 425-775-1130 E-mail: sales@linguistsoftware.com Web Site: www.linguistsoftware.com, pg 1372

Link Translations Inc, 60 E 96 St, New York, NY 10128 Toll Free Tel: 866-866-5010 E-mail: info@link-translations.com Web Site: www.link-translations.com, pg 1403

The Lion and the Unicorn, 2715 N Charles St, Baltimore, MD 21218-4363 Tel: 410-516-6987 (journal orders outside US & CN) Toll Free Tel: 800-548-1784 (journal orders) Fax: 410-578-2865 (journal orders) E-mail: jrnlcirc@jh.edu (journal orders) Web Site: www.press.jhu.edu/journals/lion-and-unicorn, pg 1134

Listco Direct Marketing, 1276 46 St, Brooklyn, NY 11219 Tel: 718-871-8400 Fax: 718-871-7692 E-mail: info@listcodirect.com Web Site: www.listcodirect.com, pg 1120

Literary Features Syndicate, 88 Briarcliff Rd, Larchmont, NY 10538 Tel: 914-834-7480, pg 1127

The Literary Guild®, 34 W 27 St, 10th fl, New York, NY 10001 Tel: 716-250-5700 (cust serv) Toll Free Tel: 866-284-3202 E-mail: member.services@literaryguild.com Web Site: literaryguild.com, pg 1142

The Literary Media & Publishing Consultants, 1815 Wynnewood Rd, Philadelphia, PA 19151 Tel: 215-877-2012, pg 1110

Literature & Medicine, 2715 N Charles St, Baltimore, MD 21218-4363 Tel: 410-516-6987 (journal orders outside US & CN) Toll Free Tel: 800-548-1784 (journal orders) Fax: 410-578-2865 (journal orders) E-mail: jrnlcirc@jh.edu (journal orders) Web Site: www.press.jhu.edu/journals/literature-and-medicine, pg 1134

Litzky PR, 33-41 Newark St, 5th fl, Hoboken, NJ 07030 Tel: 201-222-9118 E-mail: inquiries@litzkypr.com Web Site: litzkypr.com, pg 1110

The Live Oak Press LLC, PO Box 60036, Palo Alto, CA 94306-0036 E-mail: info@liveoakpress.com Web Site: www.liveoakpress.com, pg 1349

LK Advertising Agency, Linick Bldg, 7 Putter Lane, Middle Island, NY 11953 Tel: 631-924-3888; 631-924-8555; 631-604-8599 E-mail: topmarketingadvisor@gmail.com; linickgroup@gmail.com, pg 1100

Lo Gatto Bookbinding, 390 Paterson Ave, East Rutherford, NJ 07073 Tel: 201-438-4344 Fax: 201-438-1775 E-mail: bookbindin@aol.com, pg 1212, 1256

LOF Productions, 121 Greenwich Rd, Suite 202, Charlotte, NC 28211 Tel: 704-375-8892 Fax: 704-375-6316 Web Site: www.lofproductions.com, pg 1423

Login Canada, 300 Saulteaux Crescent, Winnipeg, MB R3J 3T2, Canada Tel: 204-837-2987 Toll Free Tel: 800-665-1148 (CN only) Fax: 204-837-3116 Toll Free Fax: 800-665-0103 E-mail: sales@lb.ca Web Site: www.lb.ca, pg 1318

Longleaf Services Inc, 116 S Boundary St, Chapel Hill, NC 27514-3808 Tel: 919-966-7449 Toll Free Tel: 800-848-6224 Fax: 919-962-2704 (24 hours) Toll Free Fax: 800-272-6817 (24 hours) E-mail: customerservice@longleafservices.org; orders@longleafservices.org Web Site: longleafservices.org, pg 1295

Long's Roullet Bookbinders Inc, 2800 Monticello Ave, Norfolk, VA 23504 Tel: 757-623-4244 Fax: 757-627-1404 E-mail: bindlrbi@gmail.com Web Site: longs-roullet.com, pg 1256, 1325

Lorimer Literary Consulting, 1524 SE 46 Ave, Suite A, Portland, OR 97215 Tel: 503-481-5847 E-mail: amnotice@yahoo.com, pg 1349

Love & Logic Institute Inc, 2207 Jackson St, Suite 102, Golden, CO 80401-2300 Tel: 303-278-7552 Toll Free Tel: 800-338-4065 Fax: 303-278-3894 Toll Free Fax: 800-455-7557 E-mail: cservice@loveandlogic.com Web Site: www.loveandlogic.com, pg 1372

Lowe Graphics & Printing, 220 Great Circle Rd, Suite 122, Nashville, TN 37228 Tel: 615-242-6649 Fax: 615-254-8867 Web Site: www.etlowe.com, pg 1228

LSC Global Logistics, 10 New Maple Ave, Suite 304, Pine Brook, NJ 07058 Tel: 973-628-8800 Web Site: www.lsccom.com/clarkgroupinc, pg 1334

Lucky (grades 2-3), 557 Broadway, New York, NY 10012 Tel: 212-343-6100; 573-632-1632 (PR, US territories, US military bases) Toll Free Tel: 800-541-1097 (US) Toll Free Fax: 800-223-4011 E-mail: bookclubs@scholastic.com Web Site: clubs.scholastic.com, pg 1142

Lumina Datamatics Inc, 600 Cordwainer Dr, Unit 103, Norwell, MA 02061 Tel: 508-746-0300 Fax: 508-746-3233 E-mail: marketing@luminad.com Web Site: luminadatamatics.com, pg 1212, 1228, 1349, 1356, 1372, 1415

Lushena Books Inc, 607 Country Club Dr, Unit E, Bensenville, IL 60106 Tel: 630-238-8708 Toll Free Tel: 800-785-1545 Fax: 630-238-8824 E-mail: lushenabks@yahoo.com Web Site: lushenabks.com, pg 1318

MAP RESOURCES

Lynx Media Inc, 13654 Victory Blvd, No 282, Valley Glen, CA 91401 Tel: 818-761-5859 Toll Free Tel: 800-451-5969 Fax: 818-761-7099 E-mail: sales@lynxmedia.com Web Site: www.lynxmedia.com, pg 1372

MacDermid Graphics Solutions LLC, 5210 Phillip Lee Dr, Atlanta, GA 30336 Tel: 404-696-4565 Toll Free Tel: 800-348-7201 E-mail: mpsproductinfo@macdermid.com Web Site: graphics.macdermid.com, pg 1281

Mackin Educational Resources, 3505 County Rd 42 W, Burnsville, MN 55306 Tel: 952-895-9540 Toll Free Tel: 800-245-9540 Fax: 952-894-8806 Toll Free Fax: 800-369-5490 E-mail: mackin@mackin.com Web Site: www.mackin.com, pg 1318

MagicLight Productions, 4935 McConnell Ave, Suite 1, Marina del Rey, CA 90066 Tel: 310-283-8772 (cell) Web Site: www.magiclight.com, pg 1424

Magna Visual Inc, 28271 Cedar Park Blvd, Perrysburg, OH 43551 Tel: 314-843-9000 Toll Free Tel: 800-843-3399 Fax: 314-843-0000 E-mail: magna@magnavisual.com; mvsales@magnavisual.com Web Site: www.magnavisual.com, pg 1281

Magnolia Clipping Service, 298 Commerce Park Dr, Suite A, Ridgeland, MS 39157 Tel: 601-856-0911 Fax: 601-856-3340 E-mail: mail@magnoliaclips.com Web Site: www.magnoliaclips.com, pg 1383

Magnum Book Services LLC, 180 Raritan Center Pkwy, Suite 105, Edison, NJ 08837 Tel: 908-349-2300 E-mail: info@magnumbookservices.com; usoffice@magnumbookservices.com Web Site: www.magnumbookservices.com, pg 1334

Magnum Photos Inc, 12 W 23 St, 4th fl, New York, NY 10010 Tel: 212-929-6000 E-mail: photography@magnumphotos.com; contact@magnumphotos.com Web Site: www.magnumphotos.com; pro.magnumphotos.com, pg 1429

Susan Magrino Agency, 352 Park Ave S, 6th fl, New York, NY 10010 Tel: 212-957-3005 Fax: 212-957-4071 E-mail: info@smapr.com Web Site: www.smapr.com, pg 1110

Maison de l'Education Inc, 10840 Ave Millen, Montreal, QC H0C 0A5, Canada Tel: 514-384-4401 Fax: 514-384-4844 E-mail: librairie@maisondeleducation.com Web Site: maisondeleducation.com, pg 1318

Management Communication Quarterly (MCQ), 2455 Teller Rd, Thousand Oaks, CA 91320 Toll Free Tel: 800-818-7243 Toll Free Fax: 800-583-2665 E-mail: journals@sagepub.com Web Site: www.sagepub.com, pg 1134

Mandel Graphic Solution, 727 W Glendale Ave, Suite 100, Milwaukee, WI 53209 Tel: 414-271-6970 Fax: 414-386-4660 E-mail: info@mandelcompany.com Web Site: www.mandelcompany.com, pg 1228, 1256

Scott Manning & Associates, 2 Horatio St, Suite 16G, New York, NY 10014 Tel: 603-491-0995 Web Site: www.scottmanningpr.com, pg 1110

Manning's Book & Prints, 580-M Crespi Dr, Pacifica, CA 94044 Tel: 415-621-3565 Toll Free Tel: 800-TRY-MAPS (879-6277) Fax: 650-355-1851 E-mail: staff@printsoldandrare.com; manningsbk@aol.com Web Site: www.printsoldandrare.com, pg 1318

manroland Goss web systems Americas LLC, 121 Technology Dr, Durham, NH 03824 Tel: 603-749-6600 Toll Free Tel: 800-323-1200 (parts & serv) Fax: 603-750-6860 E-mail: info@manrolandgoss.com Web Site: www.manrolandgoss.com, pg 1281

Manroland Inc, 800 E Oak Hill Dr, Westmont, IL 60559 Tel: 630-920-2000 E-mail: info.us@manrolandsheetfed.com Web Site: manrolandsheetfed.com, pg 1256, 1281

Map Resources, 151 N Union St, No 4, Lambertville, NJ 08530 Tel: 609-397-1611 Toll Free Tel: 800-334-4291 Fax: 609-751-9378 E-mail: info@mapresources.com; support@mapresources.com Web Site: www.mapresources.com, pg 1372

MAPLE LOGISTICS SOLUTIONS — COMPANY INDEX

Maple Logistics Solutions, 60 Grumbacher Rd, York, PA 17406 *Tel:* 717-764-4596 *E-mail:* info@maplesoln.com *Web Site:* www.maplelogisticssolutions.com, pg 1296, 1334

Maple Press, 480 Willow Springs Lane, York, PA 17406 *Tel:* 717-764-5911 *Toll Free Tel:* 800-999-5911 *Fax:* 717-764-4702 *E-mail:* sales@maplepress.com *Web Site:* www.maplepress.com, pg 1212, 1256, 1281

Mapping Specialists Ltd, 3000 Cahill Main, Suite 220, Fitchburg, WI 53711 *Tel:* 608-274-4004 *Toll Free Tel:* 866-525-2298 *E-mail:* msl@mappingspecialists.com *Web Site:* www.mappingspecialists.com, pg 1416

Maps by Mathison, PO Box 152, Spring Mills, PA 16875 *Tel:* 814-321-7571 *E-mail:* jcmaps6@gmail.com *Web Site:* mapsbymathison.com, pg 1416

Maracle Inc, 1156 King St E, Oshawa, ON L1H 1H8, Canada *Tel:* 905-723-3438 *Toll Free Tel:* 800-558-8604 *Fax:* 905-723-1759 *E-mail:* hello@maracleinc.com *Web Site:* www.maracleinc.com, pg 1212, 1228, 1256

Market Partners International Inc, 232 Madison Ave, Suite 1400, New York, NY 10016 *Tel:* 212-447-0855 *Fax:* 212-447-0785 *E-mail:* info@marketpartnersinternational.com *Web Site:* www.marketpartnersinternational.com, pg 1349

Marketry Inc, 1420 NW Gilman Blvd, No 2558, Issaquah, WA 98027 *Tel:* 425-451-1262 *Toll Free Tel:* 800-346-2013 *Web Site:* www.marketry.com, pg 1120

Markwith Tool Co Inc, 5261 State Rte 49 S, Greenville, OH 45331 *Tel:* 937-548-6808 *Fax:* 937-548-7051 *Web Site:* markwithtool.com, pg 1281

Marquand Books, 3131 Western Ave, Suite 522, Seattle, WA 98121 *Tel:* 206-624-2030 *Web Site:* www.marquandbooks.com, pg 1356

Marquis Book Printing Inc, 350, rue des Entrepreneurs, Montmagny, QC G5V 4T1, Canada *Tel:* 418-246-5666 *Toll Free Tel:* 855-566-1937; 800-246-2468 *E-mail:* marquis@marquisbook.com *Web Site:* www.marquislivre.com; www.marquisbook.com, pg 1256

Marrakech Express Inc, 720 Wesley Ave, No 10, Tarpon Springs, FL 34689 *Tel:* 727-942-2218 *Toll Free Tel:* 800-940-6566 *Fax:* 727-937-4758 *E-mail:* print@marrak.com *Web Site:* www.marrak.com, pg 1212, 1256, 1281

Judith Martin, 1130 Walnut St, Kansas City, MO 64106-2109 *Tel:* 816-581-7300 *Toll Free Tel:* 800-255-6734 *Web Site:* syndication.andrewsmcmeel.com, pg 1126

Martin Printing Co Inc, 1765 Powdersville Rd, Easley, SC 29642 *Toll Free Tel:* 888-985-7330 *Fax:* 864-859-8620 *E-mail:* info@martinprinting.com *Web Site:* www.martinprinting.com, pg 1257

Maryheart Crusaders Inc, 531 W Main St, Meriden, CT 06451-2707 *Tel:* 203-238-9735 *Toll Free Tel:* 800-879-1957 (orders only) *Fax:* 203-235-0059 *E-mail:* maryheart@msn.com *Web Site:* www.maryheartcrusaders.com, pg 1142

Masque Publishing Inc, 8400 Park Meadows Dr, Lonetree, CO 80124 *Tel:* 303-290-9853 *Fax:* 303-290-6303 *E-mail:* support@masque.com *Web Site:* www.masque.com, pg 1372

Master Books®, 3142 Hwy 103 N, Green Forest, AR 72638 *Tel:* 870-438-5288 *Toll Free Tel:* 800-999-3777 *E-mail:* nlp@nlpg.com; sales@masterbooks.com *Web Site:* www.masterbooks.com; www.nlpg.com, pg 1372

Master Flo Technology Inc, 154 Seale Rd, Wentworth, QC J8H 0G9, Canada *Tel:* 450-533-0088 *Fax:* 450-533-4597 *E-mail:* info@mflo.com; sales@mflo.com *Web Site:* www.mflo.com, pg 1281

The Master's Press, 14550 Midway Rd, Dallas, TX 75244 *Tel:* 972-387-0046 *Fax:* 972-404-0317 *Web Site:* www.themasterspress.com, pg 1257

Matrox Graphics Inc, 1055 Saint Regis Blvd, Dorval, QC H9P 2T4, Canada *Tel:* 514-822-6000 *Toll Free Tel:* 800-361-1408 (sales) *Fax:* 514-822-6363 *Web Site:* www.matrox.com/graphics, pg 1372

Matthews Book Co, 11559 Rock Island Ct, Maryland Heights, MO 63043 *Tel:* 314-432-1400 *Toll Free Tel:* 800-633-2665 *Fax:* 314-432-7044 *Toll Free Fax:* 800-421-8816 *E-mail:* orders@mattmccoy.com *Web Site:* www.matthewsbooks.com, pg 1296

Diane Maurer-Hand Marbled Papers, Water St, Spring Mills, PA 16875 *Tel:* 814-308-3685 *E-mail:* dkmaurer1@gmail.com *Web Site:* dianemaurer.com, pg 1416

Maverick Publications LLC, 131 NE Fifth St, Prineville, OR 97754 *Tel:* 541-382-6978 *E-mail:* moreinfo@maverickbooks.com *Web Site:* maverickbooks.com, pg 1212, 1356, 1372

Maxcess International, 222 W Memorial Rd, Oklahoma City, OK 73114 *Tel:* 405-755-1600 *Toll Free Tel:* 800-639-3433 *Fax:* 405-755-8425 *E-mail:* sales@maxcessintl.com *Web Site:* www.maxcessintl.com, pg 1281

The Mazel Co, 31000 Aurora Rd, Solon, OH 44139-2769 *Tel:* 440-248-5200 *Toll Free Tel:* 800-443-4789 *Fax:* 440-349-1931 *Web Site:* www.themazelcompany.com, pg 1318

MBA Computer Service, 1920 Lookout Dr, North Mankato, MN 56003 *Tel:* 507-625-3797, pg 1228

MBR Bookwatch, 278 Orchard Dr, Oregon, WI 53575-1129 *Tel:* 608-835-7937 *E-mail:* mbr@execpc.com *Web Site:* www.midwestbookreview.com, pg 1134

MBS Textbook Exchange Inc, 2711 W Ash, Columbia, MO 65203 *Tel:* 573-445-2243 *Toll Free Tel:* 800-325-0530 (textbook solutions); 800-325-4138 (bookstore systems) *Fax:* 573-446-5256 *E-mail:* cserv@mbsbooks.com *Web Site:* www.mbsbooks.com, pg 1318

McClain Printing Co, 212 Main St, Parsons, WV 26287-1033 *Tel:* 304-478-2881 *Toll Free Tel:* 800-654-7179 *Fax:* 304-478-4658 *E-mail:* mcclain@mcclainprinting.com *Web Site:* www.mcclainprinting.com, pg 1212, 1228, 1257, 1269, 1282

Virginia McCullough, 2527 Telluride Trail, Suite D, Green Bay, WI 54313 *Tel:* 920-662-9633; 920-680-3232 (text) *E-mail:* virginiaauthor47@gmail.com *Web Site:* www.virginiamccullough.com, pg 1349

McGarr & Associates, 5692 Heathwood Ct, Covington, KY 41015 *Tel:* 859-356-9295 *Fax:* 859-356-7804, pg 1296

MCH Strategic Data, 601 E Marshall St, Sweet Springs, MO 65351 *Toll Free Tel:* 800-776-6373 *E-mail:* sales@mchdata.com *Web Site:* www.mchdata.com, pg 1120

McManus & Morgan, 2506 W Seventh St, Los Angeles, CA 90057 *Tel:* 213-387-4433 *Web Site:* www.mcmanusandmorgan.com, pg 1269

Bruce McMillan, PO Box 85, Shapleigh, ME 04076-0085 *Tel:* 207-324-9453 *E-mail:* bruce@brucemcmillan.com *Web Site:* www.brucemcmillan.com; theartofbruce.blogspot.com, pg 1424

MDR, A Dun & Bradstreet Division, 5335 Gate Pkwy, Jacksonville, FL 32256 *Tel:* 973-921-5500 *Toll Free Tel:* 800-333-8802 *E-mail:* mdrinfo@dnb.com *Web Site:* mdreducation.com, pg 1116, 1120

Meadows Design Office, 3800 Yuma St NW, Washington, DC 20016 *Tel:* 202-966-6007 *E-mail:* mdo@mdomedia.com, pg 1212, 1228, 1356, 1416

Meadows Publishing Solutions, 1320 Tower Rd, Schaumburg, IL 60173 *Tel:* 847-882-8202 *Fax:* 847-882-9494 *E-mail:* sales@meadowsps.com *Web Site:* meadowsps.com, pg 1372

Media Connect, 1675 Broadway, New York, NY 10019 *Tel:* 212-715-1600 *Web Site:* www.media-connect.com, pg 1110

Media Cybernetics Inc, 1700 Rockville Pike, Suite 240, Rockville, MD 20852 *Tel:* 301-495-3305 *Toll Free Tel:* 800-263-2088 *E-mail:* support@mediacy.com; marketing@mediacy.com *Web Site:* www.mediacy.com, pg 1372

Media Masters Publicity, 61 Depot St, Tryon, NC 28782 *Tel:* 828-859-9456 *E-mail:* info@mmpublicity.com *Web Site:* www.mmpublicity.com, pg 1110, 1349

Media Relations Agency, 350 W Burnsville Pkwy, Suite 350, Burnsville, MN 55337 *Tel:* 952-697-5220 *Fax:* 952-697-3256 *Web Site:* www.publicity.com, pg 1110

Media Supply Inc, 208 Philips Rd, Exton, PA 19341 *Tel:* 610-884-4400 *Toll Free Tel:* 800-944-4237 *Fax:* 610-884-4500 *E-mail:* info@mediasupply.com *Web Site:* www.mediasupply.com, pg 1372

MediaLocate Inc, 1200 Piedmont Ave, Pacific Grove, CA 93950 *Tel:* 831-655-7500 *E-mail:* info@medialocate.com *Web Site:* www.medialocate.com, pg 1403

Medical Images, 3500 S DuPont Hwy, Suite 300, Dover, DE 19901 *Tel:* 212-736-2525 *Toll Free Tel:* 800-542-3686 *E-mail:* sales@medicalimages.com *Web Site:* www.medicalimages.com, pg 1429

Medievalia et Humanistica: Studies in Medieval & Renaissance Culture, 4501 Forbes Blvd, Suite 200, Lanham, MD 20706 *Tel:* 301-459-3366; 717-794-3800 (cust serv) *Toll Free Tel:* 800-462-6420 (ext 3024, cust serv) *Fax:* 301-429-5748; 717-794-3803 (cust serv) *Toll Free Fax:* 800-338-4550 (cust serv) *E-mail:* customercare@rowman.com *Web Site:* rowman.com, pg 1134

Medina Software Inc, 1441 Oberlin Terr, Suite 1010, Lake Mary, FL 32746 *Tel:* 407-327-4112 *Web Site:* www.medinasoft.com, pg 1372

Megavision Inc, PO Box 60158, Santa Barbara, CA 93160 *Tel:* 805-964-1400 *Toll Free Tel:* 888-324-2580 *E-mail:* info@mega-vision.com *Web Site:* www.mega-vision.com, pg 1372

MEJ Personal Business Services Inc, 245 E 116 St, New York, NY 10029 *Tel:* 212-426-6017 *Toll Free Tel:* 866-557-5336 *Fax:* 646-827-3628 *E-mail:* support@mejpbs.com *Web Site:* www.mejpbs.com, pg 1403

Mekatronics Inc, 85 Channel Dr, Port Washington, NY 11050 *Tel:* 516-883-6805 *Fax:* 516-883-6948 *E-mail:* office@mekatronicsinc.com *Web Site:* mekatronicsinc.com, pg 1269

Donya Melanson Associates, 5 Bisson Lane, Merrimac, MA 01860 *Tel:* 978-346-9240 *Fax:* 978-346-8345 *E-mail:* dmelanson@dmelanson.com *Web Site:* www.dmelanson.com, pg 1100, 1116

Melcher Media Inc, 124 W 13 St, New York, NY 10011 *Tel:* 212-727-2322 *Fax:* 212-627-1973 *E-mail:* info@melcher.com *Web Site:* www.melcher.com, pg 1356

Melissa Data Corp, 22382 Avenida Empresa, Rancho Santa Margarita, CA 92688-2112 *Tel:* 949-858-3000 *Toll Free Tel:* 800-800-6245 *E-mail:* info@melissadata.com *Web Site:* www.melissadata.com, pg 1228

Melissa Turk & the Artist Network, 9 Babbling Brook Lane, Suffern, NY 10901 *Tel:* 845-368-8606 *E-mail:* melissa@melissaturk.com *Web Site:* www.melissaturk.com, pg 1416

Mendon Associates Inc, 44 Glenwood Ave, Suite 210, Toronto, ON M6P 3C6, Canada *Tel:* 416-239-9661 *Toll Free Tel:* 800-361-1325 *E-mail:* info@mendon.com *Web Site:* www.mendon.com, pg 1349

MEP Education, 8154 N Ridgeway Ave, Skokie, IL 60076 *Tel:* 847-676-1596 *Fax:* 847-676-1195 *E-mail:* info@mep-inc.net *Web Site:* www.mepeducation.net, pg 1296

Merrell Enterprises, 3542 E State Rte 73, Waynesville, OH 45068 *Tel:* 202-265-1925 *Fax:* 513-855-4277 *Web Site:* www.merrellenterprises.com, pg 1191

Brian Thomas Merrill, 40 Vandale St, Putnam, CT 06260 *Tel:* 860-315-4638 *E-mail:* zangmerrill@yahoo.com, pg 1416

Le Messager Chretien (The Christian Messenger), 185 Gatineau Ave, Gatineau, QC J8T 4J7, Canada *Tel:* 819-243-8880 *Toll Free Tel:* 800-263-8086 *Fax:* 819-243-1220 *E-mail:* info@messagerchretien.com *Web Site:* www.messagerchretien.com, pg 1319

1452

COMPANY INDEX

MetaComet Systems, 29 College St, South Hadley, MA 01075 *Tel:* 413-536-5989 *Web Site:* www.metacomet.com, pg 1349

Metaphysical Book Club, 18340 Sonoma Hwy, Sonoma, CA 95476 *Tel:* 707-939-9212 *Fax:* 707-938-3515 *E-mail:* warwick@vom.com *Web Site:* www.warwickassociates.com, pg 1142

Metro Editorial Services, 519 Eighth Ave, New York, NY 10018 *Tel:* 212-947-5100 (ext 253, outside US & CN) *Toll Free Tel:* 800-223-1600 *E-mail:* service@metro-email.com *Web Site:* www.mcg.metrocreativeconnection.com, pg 1191

Metro 360, 120 Sinnott Rd, Scarborough, ON M1L 4N1, Canada *Tel:* 416-752-8720 *Toll Free Tel:* 888-260-2208 *Web Site:* www.metro360.ca, pg 1319

Metro Translation Service, 294 De Kalb Ave, Brooklyn, NY 11205 *Tel:* 917-558-0089 (cell) *E-mail:* metrotourservice21@gmail.com *Web Site:* metrotourservice.blogspot.com, pg 1403

Metropolitan Newsclips Service Inc, 1250 Hanley Industrial Ct, St Louis, MO 63144 *Tel:* 314-395-8917 *E-mail:* cheryllm@metronewsclips.com *Web Site:* www.metronewsclips.com, pg 1383

MGP Direct Inc, 17814 Shotley Bridge Place, Olney, MD 20832 *Tel:* 240-755-6976 *Web Site:* www.mgpdirect.com, pg 1349

Miami Wabash Paper LLC, 301 Wedcor Ave, Wabash, IN 46992 *Tel:* 260-563-4181 *Toll Free Tel:* 800-842-9112 *Fax:* 219-563-2724 *E-mail:* miamivalley@mafcote.com *Web Site:* www.mafcote.com, pg 1269

Vick Mickunas, 4805 Meredith Rd, Yellow Springs, OH 45387 *Tel:* 937-767-1396 *E-mail:* vick@vickmickunas.com *Web Site:* www.wyso.org/show/book-nook, pg 1126

Micro Focus, One Irvington Ctr, 700 King Farm Blvd, Suite 125, Rockville, MD 20850-5736 *Tel:* 301-838-5000 *Toll Free Tel:* 877-686-9637 *Web Site:* www.microfocus.com, pg 1372

Microboards Technology Inc, 8150 Mallory Ct, Chanhassen, MN 55317 *Tel:* 952-556-1600; 952-556-1639 (tech support) *Toll Free Tel:* 800-646-8881 *Fax:* 952-556-1620 *E-mail:* sales@microboards.com *Web Site:* www.microboards.com, pg 1372

Microsearch Corp, 101 Western Ave, Gloucester, MA 01930 *Tel:* 781-231-9991 *Toll Free Tel:* 800-895-0212 *E-mail:* info@microsearch.net *Web Site:* www.microsearchcorporation.net, pg 1372

Midland Paper, Packaging & Supplies, 101 E Palatine Rd, Wheeling, IL 60090 *Tel:* 847-777-2700 *Toll Free Tel:* 800-323-8522; 888-564-3526 (cust serv) *Fax:* 847-403-6320 (cust serv) *E-mail:* whl@midlandpaper.com; sales@midlandpaper.com; custservice@midlandpaper.com *Web Site:* www.midlandpaper.com, pg 1269

Midpoint National Inc, 1263 Southwest Blvd, Kansas City, KS 66103 *Tel:* 913-362-7400 *Toll Free Tel:* 800-228-4321 *E-mail:* info@midpt.com *Web Site:* www.midpt.com, pg 1296

Midpoint Trade Books, 814 N Franklin St, Suite 100, Chicago, IL 60610 *Tel:* 312-337-0747 *Fax:* 312-337-5985 *E-mail:* orders@ipgbook.com *Web Site:* www.midpointtrade.com, pg 1297

The Midwest Book Review, 278 Orchard Dr, Oregon, WI 53575-1129 *Tel:* 608-835-7937 *E-mail:* mbr@execpc.com; mwbookrevw@aol.com *Web Site:* www.midwestbookreview.com, pg 1134

Midwest Library Service, 11443 Saint Charles Rock Rd, Bridgeton, MO 63044 *Tel:* 314-739-3100 *Fax:* 314-739-1326 *E-mail:* mail@midwestls.com *Web Site:* www.midwestls.com, pg 1319

Midwest Paper Group, 540 Prospect St, Combined Locks, WI 54113 *Tel:* 920-788-3550 *Toll Free Tel:* 800-828-1987 *Fax:* 920-968-3950 *Web Site:* mwpaper.com, pg 1270

Lawrence Migdale Photography/PIX, 23 White Hall Dr, Orinda, CA 94563 *Tel:* 510-612-2572 *E-mail:* photopix@migdale.com *Web Site:* www.migdale.com, pg 1430

Miles 33 International LLC, 40 Richards Ave, Norwalk, CT 06854 *Tel:* 203-838-2333 *Fax:* 203-838-4473 *E-mail:* info@miles33.com *Web Site:* www.miles33.com, pg 1228, 1282, 1373

Military Book Club®, 34 W 27 St, 10th fl, New York, NY 10001 *Tel:* 716-250-5700 (cust serv) *E-mail:* customer.service@militarybookclub.com *Web Site:* www.militarybookclub.com, pg 1142

Military Update, PO Box 231111, Centreville, VA 20120-1111 *Tel:* 703-830-6863 *E-mail:* milupdate@aol.com *Web Site:* www.militaryupdate.com, pg 1191

Susan Riva Miller-Alpine Photography, 20415 150 Ave SE, Monroe, WA 98272 *Tel:* 206-679-0475 *E-mail:* susanrivamiller@hotmail.com, pg 1424

Miller Trade Book Marketing Inc, 1426 W Carmen Ave, Chicago, IL 60640 *Tel:* 773-307-3446, pg 1298

Minden Pictures Inc, 9565 Soquel Dr, Suite 202, Aptos, CA 95003 *Tel:* 831-661-5551 *E-mail:* info@mindenpictures.com *Web Site:* www.mindenpictures.com, pg 1430

Wendell Minor, 15 Old North Rd, Washington, CT 06793 *Tel:* 860-868-9101 *E-mail:* wendell@minorart.com *Web Site:* www.minorart.com, pg 1416

Clark James Mishler Photography, 1815 School St, Calistoga, CA 94515 *Tel:* 907-351-7863 *Web Site:* www.mishlerphotos.com, pg 1424

Modern Language Notes (MLN), 2715 N Charles St, Baltimore, MD 21218-4363 *Tel:* 410-516-6987 (journal orders outside US & CN) *Toll Free Tel:* 800-548-1784 (journal orders) *Fax:* 410-578-2865 (journal orders) *E-mail:* jrnlcirc@jh.edu (journal orders) *Web Site:* www.press.jhu.edu/journals/mln, pg 1134

Mohawk Fine Papers Inc, 465 Saratoga St, Cohoes, NY 12047 *Tel:* 518-237-1740 *Toll Free Tel:* 800-THE-MILL (843-6455) *Fax:* 518-237-7394 *Web Site:* www.mohawkconnects.com, pg 1270

Monadnock Paper Mills Inc, 117 Antrim Rd, Bennington, NH 03442-4205 *Tel:* 603-588-3311 *Toll Free Tel:* 800-221-2159 (cust serv) *Fax:* 603-588-3158 *E-mail:* info@mpm.com *Web Site:* www.mpm.com, pg 1270

Monotype Imaging Inc, 600 Unicorn Park Dr, Woburn, MA 01801 *Tel:* 781-970-6000 *Web Site:* www.monotype.com, pg 1373

Monteiro & Co Inc, 301 E 57 St, 4th fl, New York, NY 10022 *Tel:* 212-832-8183 *Web Site:* www.monteiroandco.com, pg 1111

Montfort Publications, 26 S Saxon Ave, Bay Shore, NY 11706-8993 *Tel:* 631-665-0726; 631-666-7500 *Fax:* 631-665-0726 *E-mail:* info@montfortpublications.com *Web Site:* www.montfortpublications.com, pg 1319

Morris Press Cookbooks®, 3212 E Hwy 30, Kearney, NE 68847 *Tel:* 308-236-7888; 308-234-1385 *Toll Free Tel:* 800-445-6621 *Fax:* 308-234-3969 *E-mail:* cookbook@morriscookbooks.com *Web Site:* www.morriscookbooks.com, pg 1213

Morris Printing Group Inc, 3212 E Hwy 30, Kearney, NE 68847 *Tel:* 308-236-7888 *Toll Free Tel:* 800-650-7888 *Fax:* 308-237-0263 *Web Site:* www.morrisprintinggroup.com, pg 1257

Morris Publishing®, 3212 E Hwy 30, Kearney, NE 68847 *Tel:* 308-236-7888 *Toll Free Tel:* 800-650-7888 *Fax:* 308-237-0263 *E-mail:* publish@morrispublishing.com *Web Site:* www.morrispublishing.com, pg 1257

Motorbooks, 100 Cummings Ctr, Suite 265D, Beverly, MA 01915 *Tel:* 978-282-9590 *Toll Free Tel:* 800-759-0190 (orders) *Web Site:* www.quartoknows.com/motorbooks, pg 1319, 1329

Mount Ida Press, 111 Washington Ave, Albany, NY 12210-2203 *Tel:* 518-426-5935 *E-mail:* info@mountidapress.com *Web Site:* www.mountidapress.com, pg 1356

MPS North America LLC, 5728 Major Blvd, Suite 528, Orlando, FL 32819 *Tel:* 407-472-1280 *Toll Free Tel:* 866-978-1008 *Fax:* 212-981-2983 *E-mail:* marketing@mpslimited.com *Web Site:* www.mpslimited.com, pg 1228, 1373, 1416

MRC Medical Communications, 12 Lincoln Blvd, Suite 103, Emerson, NJ 07630 *Tel:* 201-986-0247 *E-mail:* info@mrcmedical.net *Web Site:* www.mrcmedical.net, pg 1373

MSC Lists, PO Box 32510, Minneapolis, MN 55432 *Tel:* 763-502-8819, pg 1120

Mary Mueller, 516 Bartram Rd, Moorestown, NJ 08057 *Tel:* 856-778-4769 *E-mail:* mamam49@aol.com, pg 1126

Muller Martini Corp, 456 Wheeler Rd, Hauppauge, NY 11788 *Tel:* 631-582-4343 *Toll Free Tel:* 888-268-5537 *Fax:* 631-348-1961 *E-mail:* info@us.mullermartini.com *Web Site:* www.mullermartiniusa.com, pg 1282

Multi-Reliure, 2112 Ave de la Transmission, Shawinigan, QC G9N 8N8, Canada *Tel:* 819-537-6008 *Toll Free Tel:* 888-735-4873 *Fax:* 819-537-4598 *E-mail:* info@multi-reliure.com; administration@multi-reliure.com *Web Site:* www.multireliure.com, pg 1257

Multi-Tech Systems Inc, 2205 Woodale Dr, Mounds View, MN 55112 *Tel:* 763-785-3500 *Toll Free Tel:* 800-328-9717 *Fax:* 763-785-9874 *E-mail:* info@multitech.com; sales@multitech.com; mtsmktg@multitech.com *Web Site:* www.multitech.com, pg 1373

Multicultural Marketing Resources Inc, 720 Greenwich St, No 7T, New York, NY 10014 *Tel:* 212-242-3351 *Web Site:* www.multicultural.com, pg 1111

Music City Arts Network, PO Box 843, Brentwood, TN 37024 *Toll Free Tel:* 888-80-SHINE (807-4463) *E-mail:* info@musiccityarts.net *Web Site:* www.musiccityartsupdate.com; www.shinetimebooks.com, pg 1111

Myriddian LLC, 8510 Corridor Rd, Suite 100, Savage, MD 20763 *Tel:* 443-285-0271 (cell) *E-mail:* info@myriddian.com *Web Site:* www.myriddian.com, pg 1228, 1373

Mystery Guild®, 34 W 27 St, 10th fl, New York, NY 10001 *Tel:* 716-250-5700 (cust serv) *E-mail:* customer.service@mysteryguild.com *Web Site:* mysteryguild.com, pg 1143

Mystery Readers Journal, 7155 Marlborough Terr, Berkeley, CA 94705 *Tel:* 510-845-3600 *Web Site:* www.mysteryreaders.org, pg 1134

NameBank International, 1001 Cathedral St, Baltimore, MD 21201 *Tel:* 410-864-0854 *Fax:* 410-864-0837 *E-mail:* lists@namebank.com *Web Site:* www.namebank.com, pg 1146

NAPCO Inc, 120 Trojan Ave, Sparta, NC 28675 *Tel:* 336-372-5228 *Toll Free Tel:* 800-854-8621 *Fax:* 336-372-8602 *E-mail:* info@napcousa.com *Web Site:* www.napcousa.com, pg 1257

National Association of Book Entrepreneurs (NABE), PO Box 606, Cottage Grove, OR 97424 *Tel:* 541-942-7455 *Fax:* 541-942-7455 *E-mail:* nabe@bookmarketingprofits.com *Web Site:* www.bookmarketingprofits.com, pg 1139, 1298

National Book Co Inc, Keystone Industrial Park, Dunmore, PA 18512 *Tel:* 570-346-2029 *Toll Free Tel:* 800-233-4830, pg 1319

National Book Network (NBN), 4501 Forbes Blvd, Suite 200, Lanham, MD 20706 *Tel:* 301-459-3366 *Toll Free Tel:* 800-462-6420 (orders only) *Fax:* 301-429-5746 *Toll Free Fax:* 800-338-4550 (orders only) *E-mail:* customercare@nbnbooks.com *Web Site:* nbnbooks.com, pg 1298, 1319

National Council of Teachers of English (NCTE), 340 N Neil St, Suite 104, Champaign, IL 61820 *Tel:* 217-328-3870 *Toll Free Tel:* 877-369-6283 (cust serv) *Fax:* 217-328-9645 *E-mail:* customerservice@ncte.org; permissions@ncte.org *Web Site:* ncte.org, pg 1146

National Learning Corp, 212 Michael Dr, Syosset, NY 11791 *Tel:* 516-921-8888 *Toll Free Tel:* 800-632-8888 *Fax:* 516-921-8743 *E-mail:* info@passbooks.com *Web Site:* www.passbooks.com, pg 1319

NAVIGA

Naviga, 7900 International Dr, Suite 800, Bloomington, MN 55425 Tel: 651-639-0662 E-mail: info@navigaglobal.com Web Site: www.navigaglobal.com, pg 1373

Neenah Inc, 3460 Preston Ridge Rd, Suite 600, Alpharetta, GA 30005 Toll Free Tel: 800-344-5287 E-mail: publishing.team@neenah.com Web Site: www.neenahperformance.com/products/neenah-performance/publishing-products, pg 1270, 1282

Neibauer Press, 20 Industrial Dr, Warminster, PA 18974 Tel: 215-322-6200 Fax: 215-322-2495 E-mail: sales@neibauer.com Web Site: www.neibauer.com, pg 1104, 1116, 1120, 1229, 1257, 1334

Mrs Nelson's Library Services, 1650 W Orange Grove Ave, Pomona, CA 91768 Tel: 909-397-7820 Toll Free Tel: 800-875-9911 Fax: 909-397-7833 E-mail: bookcompany@mrsnelsons.com Web Site: www.mrsnelsons.com, pg 1319

NETS, 2714 Bee Caves Rd, Suite 201, Austin, TX 78746-5682 Web Site: www.netype.com, pg 1229, 1373

Nevada Publications, 4135 Badger Circle, Reno, NV 89519 Tel: 775-747-0800 Web Site: nevadapublicationsonline.com, pg 1282

Iris Nevins Decorative Papers, PO Box 429, Johnsonburg, NJ 07846-0429 Tel: 908-813-8617 E-mail: irisnevins@verizon.net Web Site: www.marblingpaper.com, pg 1270

New Dimensions Radio, 143 Colgan Ave, Suite 1103, Santa Rosa, CA 95404 Tel: 707-468-5215 E-mail: info@newdimensions.org Web Site: www.newdimensions.org, pg 1191

New England Book Service Inc, 7000 Vt Rte 17 W, Addison, VT 05491 Tel: 802-759-3000 Toll Free Tel: 800-356-5772 Fax: 802-759-3220 E-mail: nebs@together.net Web Site: www.nebooks.com, pg 1319

The New England Mobile Book Fair®, 241 Needham St, Newton, MA 02464 Tel: 617-527-5817; 617-964-7440 E-mail: customerservice@nebookfair.com Web Site: nebookfair.com, pg 1319

New Haven Review, 55 Elmwood Rd, New Haven, CT 06515 Tel: 203-494-7018 Web Site: www.newhavenreview.com, pg 1134

New Leaf Distributing Co, 1085 E Lotus Dr, Silver Lake, WI 53170 Tel: 262-889-8501 (ext 162) Toll Free Tel: 800-326-2665 (orders) Fax: 262-889-8598 E-mail: orders@newleafdist.com, pg 1298, 1319

New Literary History, 2715 N Charles St, Baltimore, MD 21218-4363 Tel: 410-516-6987 (journal orders outside US & CN) Toll Free Tel: 800-548-1784 (journal orders) Fax: 410-578-2865 (journal orders) E-mail: jrnlcirc@jh.edu (journal orders) Web Site: www.press.jhu.edu/journals/new-literary-history, pg 1135

New Riders Publishing, 50 California St, 18th fl, San Francisco, CA 94111 Toll Free Tel: 800-428-5331 (cust serv) E-mail: customer-service@informit.com; press@peachpit.com Web Site: www.peachpit.com, pg 1373

New York Legal Publishing Corp, 120 Broadway, Menands, NY 12204 Tel: 518-459-1100 Toll Free Tel: 800-541-2681 Fax: 518-459-9718 E-mail: info@nylp.com Web Site: www.nylp.com, pg 1373

The New York Review of Science Fiction, 206 Valentine St, Yonkers, NY 10704-1814 Tel: 914-965-4861 Web Site: www.nyrsf.com, pg 1135

The New York Times Book Review, 620 Eighth Ave, 5th fl, New York, NY 10018 Tel: 212-556-1234 Toll Free Tel: 800-631-2580 (subns) E-mail: bookreview@nytimes.com; books@nytimes.com Web Site: www.nytimes.com, pg 1135

The New York Times Licensing Group, 620 Eighth Ave, 20th fl, New York, NY 10018 Tel: 212-556-1927 E-mail: nytlg-sales@nytimes.com Web Site: nytlicensing.com, pg 1191

Newborn Enterprises Inc (Altoona News Agency), 808 Green Ave, Altoona, PA 16601 Tel: 814-944-3593, pg 1319

Newgen North America Inc, 2714 Bee Cave Rd, Suite 201, Austin, TX 78746 Tel: 512-478-5341 Fax: 512-476-4756 E-mail: sales@newgen.co Web Site: www.newgen.co, pg 1229

Andrew Newman Design, 9509 W Lilac Rd, Escondido, CA 92026 Tel: 508-221-5101 E-mail: newmandesign@gmail.com Web Site: www.andrewnewmandesign.com, pg 1416

NewTek Inc, 5131 Beckwith Blvd, San Antonio, TX 78249 Tel: 210-370-8000 Toll Free Tel: 800-368-5441 Fax: 210-370-8001 E-mail: sales@newtek.com (cust serv) Web Site: www.newtek.com, pg 1373

Next Chapter Book Club (NCBC), 5909 Cleveland Ave, Columbus, OH 43231 Tel: 614-678-6470 E-mail: 800-674-8390 E-mail: info@nextchapterbookclub.org Web Site: nextchapterbookclub.org, pg 1143

Donald Nicholson-Smith, 50 Plaza St E, Apt 1D, Brooklyn, NY 11238 Tel: 718-636-4732 E-mail: mnr.dns@verizon.net, pg 1403

Nissen Public Relations LLC, 18 Bank St, Suite 101, Summit, NJ 07901 Tel: 908-376-6470 E-mail: info@nissenpr.com Web Site: www.nissenpr.com, pg 1111

Nissha USA Inc, 1051 Perimeter Dr, Suite 600, Schaumburg, IL 60173 Tel: 847-413-2665 Fax: 847-413-4085 Web Site: www.nissha.com, pg 1213, 1229, 1257

Nissho Electronics USA Corp, The Concourse I, 226 Airport Pkwy, Suite 340, San Jose, CA 95110 Tel: 408-969-9700 E-mail: info@nelco.com Web Site: www.nelco.com, pg 1373

Nisus Software Inc, PO Box 1302, Solana Beach, CA 92075-7302 Tel: 858-481-1477 Fax: 858-764-0573 E-mail: info@nisus.com; sales@nisus.com; customerservice@nisus.com Web Site: www.nisus.com, pg 1373

Noble Book Press Corp, 211 Ditmas Ave, Brooklyn, NY 11218 Tel: 718-435-9321 Fax: 718-435-0464, pg 1257

The Nolan/Lehr Group Inc, 214 W 29 St, Suite 1002, New York, NY 10001 Tel: 212-967-8200 E-mail: dblehr@cs.com Web Site: www.nolanlehrgroup.com, pg 1111

North American Color Inc, 5960 S Sprinkle Rd, Portage, MI 49002 Tel: 269-323-0552 Toll Free Tel: 800-537-8296 Fax: 269-323-0190 E-mail: info@nac-mi.com Web Site: www.nac-mi.com, pg 1229

North Atlantic Publishing Systems Inc, 66 Commonwealth Ave, Concord, MA 01742 Tel: 978-371-8989 E-mail: naps@napsys.com Web Site: www.napsys.com, pg 1373

North Carolina Literary Review (NCLR), East Carolina University, English Dept, ECU Mailstop 555 English, Greenville, NC 27858-4353 Tel: 252-328-1537 Fax: 252-328-4889 E-mail: nclrstaff@ecu.edu Web Site: nclr.ecu.edu, pg 1135

North 49 Books, 35 Prince Andrew Place, Toronto, ON M3C 2H2, Canada Tel: 416-449-4000 Toll Free Tel: 800-490-4049 Fax: 416-449-9924 Toll Free Fax: 888-349-2221 E-mail: sales@north49books.com Web Site: www.north49books.com, pg 1320

North Market Street Graphics (NMSG), 317 N Market St, Lancaster, PA 17603 Tel: 717-392-7438 E-mail: mail@nmsgbooks.com Web Site: www.nmsgbooks.com, pg 1229, 1416

Northeast Publishers Reps, Montville Chase, 20 Davenport Rd, Montville, NJ 07045 Tel: 973-299-0085 Fax: 973-263-2363 E-mail: siraksirak@aol.com Web Site: www.nepubreps.com, pg 1298

Boyd Norton Photography, PO Box 2605, Evergreen, CO 80437-2605 Tel: 303-674-3009 Fax: 303-674-3650 Web Site: boydnorton.com; www.facebook.com/boyd.norton; thewildernessphotography.blogspot.com, pg 1424

Phillip Norton, 4 Chapel St, Picton, ON K0K 2T0, Canada Tel: 613-827-3214 E-mail: phil@philnorton.com Web Site: countyphotographer.com; www.countyoutings.com, pg 1424

COMPANY INDEX

Nuance Communications Inc, One Wayside Rd, Burlington, MA 01803 Tel: 781-565-5000 Toll Free Tel: 800-654-1187 (cust serv); 888-372-1908 (orders) Web Site: www.nuance.com, pg 1373

NWinds, One Northgate Sq, Greensburg, PA 15601 Tel: 724-838-8993 Toll Free Fax: 888-315-3711 E-mail: support@nwinds.com Web Site: www.nwinds.com, pg 1374

Caroline O'Connell Communications, 11275 La Maida St, Suite 200, North Hollywood, CA 91601-4514 E-mail: oconnellpr@aol.com Web Site: www.oconnellcommunications.com, pg 1111

OCS America Inc, 195 Anderson Ave, Moonachie, NJ 07074 Tel: 201-460-2888 Toll Free Tel: 800-367-3405 E-mail: info@ocsworld.com Web Site: www.ocsworld.com, pg 1329

Dale O'Dell, 1520 Eagle Point Dr, Prescott, AZ 86301 Tel: 928-541-0944 E-mail: dale@cybertrails.com Web Site: www.dalephoto.com, pg 1424

Odyssey Books, 2421 Redwood Ct, Longmont, CO 80503 Tel: 720-494-1473 Fax: 720-494-1471 E-mail: books@odysseybooks.net, pg 1349

OEC Graphics Inc, 555 W Waukau Ave, Oshkosh, WI 54902 Tel: 920-235-7770 Fax: 920-235-2252 Web Site: www.oecgraphics.com, pg 1229

OGM USA, 4333 46 St, Suite F2, Sunnyside, NY 11104 Tel: 212-964-2430 Web Site: www.ogm.it, pg 1213, 1229, 1257, 1270

The Ohio Blow Pipe Co, 446 E 131 St, Cleveland, OH 44108-1684 Tel: 216-681-7379 Fax: 216-681-7713 E-mail: sales@obpairsystems.com Web Site: www.obpairsystems.com, pg 1282

OKI Data Americas Inc, 8505 Freeport Pkwy, Suite 600, Irving, TX 75063 Tel: 972-815-4800 Toll Free Tel: 800-OKI-DATA (654-3282) E-mail: support@okidata.com Web Site: www.oki.com/us/printing, pg 1374

Oklahoma Press Service Inc, 3601 N Lincoln Blvd, Oklahoma City, OK 73105 Tel: 405-499-0020 Toll Free Tel: 888-815-2672 Web Site: www.okpress.com, pg 1383

Ollis Book Co, 28 E 35 St, Steger, IL 60475 Tel: 708-755-5151 Toll Free Tel: 800-323-0343 (natl) Fax: 708-755-5153, pg 1320

Arleen Olson Photography, Redway, CA 95560 Tel: 707-923-1974 Web Site: arleenolsonphotography.com, pg 1424

Olson Photographic LLC, 232 Hunter's Trail, Madison, CT 06443 Tel: 203-245-3752 Fax: 203-245-3752 E-mail: info@olsonphotographic.com Web Site: www.olsonphotographic.com, pg 1424

Omeda, 4 Overlook Point, Suite A2SE, Lincolnshire, IL 60069 Tel: 847-564-8900 E-mail: getstarted@omeda.com Web Site: www.omeda.com, pg 1334

Omniafiltra LLC, 9567 Main St, Beaver Falls, NY 13305 Tel: 315-346-7300 Web Site: www.omniafiltra.it/inglese/default_en.html, pg 1270

Omnipress, 2600 Anderson St, Madison, WI 53704 Tel: 608-246-2600 Toll Free Tel: 800-828-0305 E-mail: justask@omnipress.com Web Site: www.omnipress.com, pg 1213, 1257

OmniUpdate Inc, 1320 Flynn Rd, Suite 100, Camarillo, CA 93012 Tel: 805-484-9400 Toll Free Tel: 800-362-2605 E-mail: sales@omniupdate.com Web Site: omniupdate.com, pg 1374

OMRON Microscan Systems Inc, 700 SW 39 St, Suite 100, Renton, WA 98057 Tel: 425-226-5700 Toll Free Tel: 800-762-1149 Fax: 425-226-8250 E-mail: info@microscan.com Web Site: www.microscan.com, pg 1374

On Demand Machinery, 150 Broadway, Elizabeth, NJ 07206 Tel: 908-351-6906 Fax: 908-351-7156 E-mail: info@odmachinery.com Web Site: www.odmachinery.com, pg 1282

COMPANY INDEX

One Spirit®, 34 W 27 St, 10th fl, New York, NY 10001 *Tel:* 716-250-5700 (cust serv) *Toll Free Tel:* 866-250-3166 *E-mail:* customer.service@onespirit.com *Web Site:* www.onespirit.com, pg 1143

O'Neil Digital Solutions LLC, 12655 Beatrice St, Los Angeles, CA 90066 *Tel:* 310-448-6400 *E-mail:* sales@oneildata.com *Web Site:* www.oneildata.com, pg 1229, 1257, 1270, 1282

OneTouchPoint, 1225 Walnut Ridge Dr, Hartland, WI 53029 *Tel:* 262-369-6000 *Toll Free Tel:* 800-332-2348 *Fax:* 262-369-5647 *E-mail:* info@1touchpoint.com *Web Site:* www.1touchpoint.com, pg 1105, 1213, 1257, 1374

Open Book Systems Inc®, 21 Broadway, Suite 5, Rockport, MA 01966 *Tel:* 978-546-7346 *E-mail:* info@obs.com *Web Site:* www.obs.com, pg 1350, 1374

Open Horizons Publishing Co, PO Box 271, Dolan Springs, NM 86441 *Tel:* 575-741-1581 *E-mail:* books@bookmarketingbestsellers.com *Web Site:* bookmarketingbestsellers.com, pg 1350

Open Text Corp, 275 Frank Tompa Dr, Waterloo, ON N2L 0A1, Canada *Tel:* 519-888-7111 *Fax:* 519-888-0677 *Web Site:* opentext.com, pg 1374

Oracle America Inc, 500 Oracle Pkwy, Redwood Shores, CA 94065 *Tel:* 650-506-7000 *Toll Free Tel:* 800-392-2999; 800-633-0738 (sales) *Web Site:* www.oracle.com, pg 1374

The Order Fulfillment Group, 7313 Mayflower Park Dr, Zionsville, IN 46077 *Tel:* 317-733-7755 *Web Site:* www.tofg.com, pg 1334

O'Reilly Media Inc, 1005 Gravenstein Hwy N, Sebastopol, CA 95472 *Tel:* 707-827-7019 (cust support); 707-827-7000 *Toll Free Tel:* 800-889-8969; 800-998-9938 *Fax:* 707-829-0104; 707-824-8268 *E-mail:* orders@oreilly.com; support@oreilly.com *Web Site:* www.oreilly.com, pg 1374

Orobora Inc, 644 Greenville Ave, Suite 234, Staunton, VA 24401 *Tel:* 540-324-7023 *E-mail:* info@orobora.com *Web Site:* orobora.com, pg 1350

Osa's Ark Museum Shop, 111 N Lincoln Ave, Chanute, KS 66720 *Tel:* 620-431-2730 *Fax:* 620-431-2730 *E-mail:* osajohns@safarimuseum.com; osasark@yahoo.com *Web Site:* www.safarimuseum.com, pg 1320

Danuta Otfinowski, 625 "E" St NE, Washington, DC 20002 *Tel:* 202-546-5646 (studio); 202-744-0333 (cell) *E-mail:* danuta@danuta.us *Web Site:* www.danuta.us, pg 1424

OTTN Publishing, 16 Risler St, Stockton, NJ 08559 *Tel:* 609-397-4005 *Toll Free Tel:* 866-356-6886 *Fax:* 609-397-4007 *E-mail:* inquiries@ottnpublishing.com; sales@ottnpublishing.com *Web Site:* www.ottnpublishing.com, pg 1356

Outskirts Press Inc, 10940 S Parker Rd, Suite 515, Parker, CO 80134 *Toll Free Tel:* 888-OP-BOOKS (672-6657) *Toll Free Fax:* 888-208-8601 *E-mail:* info@outskirtspress.com *Web Site:* www.outskirtspress.com, pg 1257, 1374

Over the River Public Relations LLC, 116 Gladwin Ave, Leonia, NJ 07605 *Tel:* 201-503-1321 *E-mail:* info@otrpr.com *Web Site:* www.otrpr.com, pg 1111

OverDrive Inc, One OverDrive Way, Cleveland, OH 44125 *Tel:* 216-573-6886 *Fax:* 216-573-6888 *E-mail:* info@overdrive.com *Web Site:* www.overdrive.com, pg 1298

Overseas Printing Corporation, 4040 Civic Center Dr, Suite 200, San Rafael, CA 94903 *Tel:* 415-500-8331 *Fax:* 415-835-9899 *Web Site:* www.overseasprinting.com, pg 1213, 1229, 1257, 1270, 1282

The Ovid Bell Press Inc, 1201 Bluff St, Fulton, MO 65251 *Tel:* 573-642-2256 *Toll Free Tel:* 800-835-8919 *E-mail:* sales@ovidbell.com *Web Site:* ovidbell.com, pg 1229, 1257, 1270, 1282

Pacific Publishing Co Inc, 636 Alaska St S, Seattle, WA 98108 *Tel:* 206-461-1300 *E-mail:* ppcprint@nwlink.com; ppccirc@nwlink.com; ppcbind@nwlink.com *Web Site:* pacificpublishingcompany.com, pg 1258

PadillaCRT, 1101 W River Pkwy, Suite 400, Minneapolis, MN 55415 *Tel:* 612-455-1700 *Fax:* 612-455-1060 *Web Site:* www.padillacrt.com, pg 1111

Page Turner Publicity, 8785 SW 28 St, Miami, FL 33165 *Tel:* 949-254-3214 *E-mail:* pgturnerpub@aol.com *Web Site:* www.pageturnerpublicity.com, pg 1111

Lynne Palmer Executive Recruitment Inc, 295 Madison Ave, Suite 701, New York, NY 10017 *Tel:* 212-883-0203 *Fax:* 212-883-0149 *E-mail:* careers@lpalmer.com *Web Site:* www.lpalmer.com, pg 1381

Panaprint Inc, 7979 NE Industrial Blvd, Macon, GA 31216 *Tel:* 478-788-0676 *Toll Free Tel:* 800-622-0676 *Fax:* 478-788-4276 *Web Site:* www.panaprint.com, pg 1258

Pannonia Bookstore, 300 Sainte Clair Ave W, Suite 103, Toronto, ON M4V 1S4, Canada *Tel:* 416-966-5156 *E-mail:* info@pannonia.ca *Web Site:* www.pannonia.ca, pg 1320, 1329

Panoramic Images, 4835 Main St, Suite 100, Skokie, IL 60077 *Tel:* 847-324-7000 *Toll Free Tel:* 800-543-5250 *E-mail:* info@panoramicimages.com *Web Site:* www.panoramicimages.com, pg 1430

Pantagraph Printing, 217 W Jefferson St, Bloomington, IL 61701 *Tel:* 309-829-1071 *E-mail:* queries1@pantagraphprinting.com *Web Site:* www.pantagraphprinting.com, pg 1229

Pantone Inc, 590 Commerce Blvd, Carlstadt, NJ 07072-3098 *Tel:* 201-935-5500 *Toll Free Tel:* 888-800-9580 *Fax:* 201-896-0242 *E-mail:* pantonesocial@pantone.com *Web Site:* www.pantone.com, pg 1282

Paper Brigade, 520 Eighth Ave, 4th fl, New York, NY 10018 *Tel:* 212-201-2920 *Fax:* 212-532-4952 *E-mail:* info@jewishbooks.org *Web Site:* www.jewishbookcouncil.org, pg 1135

Paperbacks For Educators, 426 W Front St, Washington, MO 63090 *Tel:* 314-960-3015 *E-mail:* paperbacks@usmo.com *Web Site:* www.any-book-in-print.com, pg 1320

Parachute Publishing LLC, PO Box 320249, Fairfield, CT 06825 *Tel:* 203-255-1303, pg 1356

Paraclete Press Inc, 100 Southern Eagle Cartway, Brewster, MA 02631 *Tel:* 508-255-4685 *Toll Free Tel:* 800-451-5006 *E-mail:* customerservice@paracletepress.com *Web Site:* www.paracletepress.com, pg 1213, 1229

Parkhurst Communications Inc, 11 Riverside Dr, Suite 1-TW, New York, NY 10023 *Tel:* 212-362-9722 *Web Site:* www.parkhurstcommunications.com, pg 1111

Parson Weems' Publisher Services LLC, 3811 Canterbury Rd, No 707, Baltimore, MD 21218 *Tel:* 914-948-4259 *Toll Free Tel:* 866-861-0337 *E-mail:* office@parsonweems.com *Web Site:* parsonweems.com, pg 1299

Passwords Communications Inc, 1804 21 St N, Arlington, VA 22209 *Tel:* 703-624-5953 *E-mail:* paellero@aol.com *Web Site:* www.passwords-comm.com, pg 1403

Pathway Book Service, 34 Production Ave, Keene, NH 03431 *Tel:* 603-357-0236 *Toll Free Tel:* 800-345-6665 *Fax:* 603-965-2181 *E-mail:* pbs@pathwaybook.com *Web Site:* www.pathwaybook.com, pg 1320

Patterson Printing Co, 1550 Territorial Rd, Benton Harbor, MI 49022 *Tel:* 269-925-2177 *E-mail:* sales@patterson-printing.com *Web Site:* patterson-printing.com, pg 1213, 1258, 1270, 1282

Paulist Press, 997 Macarthur Blvd, Mahwah, NJ 07430-9990 *Tel:* 201-825-7300 *Toll Free Tel:* 800-218-1903 *Fax:* 201-825-6921 *E-mail:* info@paulistpress.com; publicity@paulistpress.com *Web Site:* www.paulistpress.com, pg 1320, 1374

Paz & Associates: The Bookstore Training & Consulting Group, 1417 Sadler Rd, No 274, Fernandina Beach, FL 32034 *Tel:* 904-277-2664 *Fax:* 904-261-6742 *Web Site:* www.pazbookbiz.com, pg 1350

PBD Worldwide Inc, 1650 Bluegrass Lakes Pkwy, Alpharetta, GA 30004 *Tel:* 470-769-1000 *Toll Free Tel:* 866-998-4PBD (998-4723) *E-mail:* sales.marketing@pbd.com; customerservice@pbd.com *Web Site:* www.pbd.com, pg 1334

PBM Graphics Inc, an RR Donnelley Co, 3700 S Miami Blvd, Durham, NC 27703 *Tel:* 919-544-6222 *Toll Free Tel:* 800-849-8100 *Fax:* 919-544-6695 *E-mail:* info@pbmgraphics.com *Web Site:* pbmgraphics.com, pg 1258

Peace Visions, 18850 Vista del Canon, Suite A, Santa Clarita, CA 91321-4512 *Tel:* 661-251-6669 *Fax:* 661-251-6669, pg 1385

Douglas Peebles Photography, 44-527A Kaneohe Bay Dr, Kaneohe, HI 96744 *Tel:* 808-342-7930 *E-mail:* douglas@douglaspeebles.com *Web Site:* www.douglaspeebles.com, pg 1424

Penfield Books, 215 Brown St, Iowa City, IA 52245 *Tel:* 319-337-9998 *Toll Free Tel:* 800-728-9998 *Fax:* 319-351-6846 *E-mail:* penfield@penfieldbooks.com; orders@penfieldbooks.com *Web Site:* www.penfieldbooks.com, pg 1320

Penguin Random House Canada, a Penguin Random House company, 320 Front St W, Suite 1400, Toronto, ON M5V 3B6, Canada *Tel:* 416-364-4449 *Toll Free Tel:* 888-523-9292 (cust serv) *Fax:* 416-598-7764 *E-mail:* customerservicescanada@penguinrandomhouse.com; publicitycanada@penguinrandomhouse.com; rightscanada@penguinrandomhouse.com *Web Site:* www.penguinrandomhouse.ca, pg 1299

Pennsylvania Literary Journal (PLJ), 1108 W Third St, Quanah, TX 79252 *Tel:* 470-289-6395 *Web Site:* anaphoraliterary.com/journals/plj, pg 1135

The Penworthy Company LLC, 219 N Milwaukee St, 4th fl, Milwaukee, WI 53202 *Tel:* 414-287-4600 *Toll Free Tel:* 800-262-2665 *Fax:* 414-287-4602 *E-mail:* info@penworthy.com *Web Site:* www.penworthy.com, pg 1320, 1325

Peregrine Arts Bindery, 7 Avenida Vista Grande, Suite B-7 119, Santa Fe, NM 87508 *Tel:* 505-466-0490 *Web Site:* www.peregrineartsbindery.etsy.com, pg 1270

Perma-Bound Books, 617 E Vandalia Rd, Jacksonville, IL 62650 *Tel:* 217-243-5451 *Toll Free Tel:* 800-637-6581 *Fax:* 217-243-7505 *Toll Free Fax:* 800-551-1169 *E-mail:* books@perma-bound.com *Web Site:* www.perma-bound.com, pg 1320, 1326

Perma Graphics, 1356 S Jason St, Denver, CO 80223 *Tel:* 303-477-2070 *E-mail:* info@perma-graphics.com *Web Site:* www.perma-graphics.com, pg 1258

Personal TeX Inc, 722 Lombard St, Suite 201, San Francisco, CA 94133 *Tel:* 415-296-7550 *Toll Free Tel:* 800-808-7906 *Fax:* 415-296-7501 *E-mail:* sales@pctex.com *Web Site:* www.pctex.com, pg 1374

Philosophy and Literature, 2715 N Charles St, Baltimore, MD 21218-4363 *Tel:* 410-516-6987 (journal orders outside US & CN) *Toll Free Tel:* 800-548-1784 (journal orders) *Fax:* 410-578-2865 (journal orders) *E-mail:* philandlit@bard.edu; jrnlcirc@jh.edu (journal orders) *Web Site:* www.press.jhu.edu/journals/philosphy-and-literature, pg 1135

Phoenix Media, 29 Miriam Dr, Matawan, NJ 07747 *Tel:* 732-441-1519 *Fax:* 732-566-1913 *Web Site:* www.phoenixmediapr.com, pg 1111

PhotoEdit Inc, 3505 Cadillac Ave, Suite P-101, Costa Mesa, CA 92626 *Toll Free Tel:* 888-450-0946, pg 1430

Photofest, East Rutherford, NJ 07073 *E-mail:* requests@photofestnyc.com *Web Site:* www.photofestnyc.com, pg 1430

Photographix, 1171 Pauline Blvd, Ann Arbor, MI 48103-5319 *Tel:* 734-476-2068, pg 1424

Photography for Communication & Commerce, 3931 S Spruce St, Suite 200, Denver, CO 80237-2152 *Tel:* 303-829-5678 *Web Site:* www.howardpaulphotography.com, pg 1424

Geoff Reed Photography, 7640 N 22 St, Phoenix, AZ 85020 Tel: 602-432-9065 E-mail: geoff@geoffreedphoto.com Web Site: www.geoffreedphoto.com, pg 1424

Emmanuel X Pierreuse, 1830 Avenida del Mundo, Suite 412, Coronado, CA 92118 Tel: 619-435-3931; 619-508-1712 (cell) E-mail: epierreuse@aol.com; franslations@aol.com Web Site: franslations.wixsite.com/website, pg 1403

Law Office of Robert G Pimm Attorney at Law, 2977 Ygnacio Valley Rd, Suite 265, Walnut Creek, CA 94598-3535 Tel: 925-374-1442 Fax: 925-281-2888 Web Site: www.rgpimm.com, pg 1350

Pint Size Productions LLC, 5745 Main St, Amherst, NY 14221 Tel: 716-204-3353 E-mail: sales@pintsizeproductions.com Web Site: www.pintsizeproductions.com, pg 1258

Pivar Computing Services Inc, 1500 Abbott Ct, Buffalo Grove, IL 60089 Tel: 847-478-8000 Toll Free Tel: 800-CONVERT (266-8378) Fax: 847-478-8750 Web Site: www.pivar.com, pg 1374

Robert Pizzo Illustration/Design, 51 Somerset Rd, New Rochelle, NY 10804 Tel: 914-278-9252 E-mail: rp@robertpizzo.com Web Site: www.robertpizzo.com, pg 1416

Planar, 1195 NW Compton Dr, Beaverton, OR 97006-1992 Tel: 503-748-1100 Toll Free Tel: 866-475-2627 E-mail: sales@planar.com Web Site: www.planar.com, pg 1374

PMSI Direct, 242 Old New Brunswick Rd, Suite 350, Piscataway, NJ 08854 Tel: 732-465-1570 Toll Free Tel: 800-238-1316 Web Site: www.pmsidirect.com, pg 1117

POD Print, 2012 E Northern St, Wichita, KS 67216 Tel: 316-522-5599 Toll Free Tel: 800-767-6066 E-mail: info@podprint.com Web Site: www.podprint.com, pg 1213, 1229, 1258

Poetry Flash, 1450 Fourth St, Suite 4, Berkeley, CA 94710 Tel: 510-525-5476 Web Site: www.poetryflash.org, pg 1135

Pointing Robot Studios, 2 Englewood Dr, Suite D3, Harwich, MA 02645 Tel: 774-237-0690 Web Site: nedsonntag.com, pg 1416

Polybook Distributors, 501 Mamaroneck Ave, White Plains, NY 10605 Tel: 914-328-6346, pg 1320

Polyglot Communications Inc, PO Box 1962, Laguna Beach, CA 92652 Tel: 949-497-1544 E-mail: info@polyglot.us.com Web Site: www.polyglot.us.com, pg 1403

Polyglot Translators, PO Box 30087, Bethesda, MD 20824 Fax: 301-907-8707 E-mail: info@polyglottranslators.com Web Site: polyglottranslators.com, pg 1403

Louise B Popkin, 9 Cliff St, Apt 2, Arlington, MA 02476 Tel: 617-281-4649 E-mail: louise@louisebpopkin.com, pg 1403

Porter Novelli, 195 Broadway, 17th fl, New York, NY 10007 Tel: 212-601-8000 Web Site: www.porternovelli.com, pg 1112

Post Bulletin Co LLC, 18 First Ave SE, Rochester, MN 55903 Tel: 507-285-7600 Toll Free Tel: 800-562-1758 E-mail: news@postbulletin.com Web Site: www.postbulletin.com, pg 1191

Power Engineering Books Ltd, 7 Perron St, St Albert, AB T8N 1E3, Canada Tel: 780-458-3155; 780-459-2525 Toll Free Tel: 800-667-3155 Fax: 780-460-2530 E-mail: power@nucleus.com Web Site: www.powerengbooks.com, pg 1299

Powis Parker Inc, 2929 Fifth St, Berkeley, CA 94710 Tel: 510-848-2463 Toll Free Tel: 800-321-BIND (321-2463) Fax: 510-848-2169 E-mail: customerservice@powis.com Web Site: www.powis.com, pg 1374

PR by the Book LLC, PO Box 6226, Round Rock, TX 78683 Tel: 512-501-4399 Fax: 512-501-4399 E-mail: info@prbythebook.com Web Site: www.prbythebook.com, pg 1112

PR Newswire, 350 Hudson St, Suite 300, New York, NY 10014-4504 Toll Free Tel: 888-776-0942; 800-776-8090 Toll Free Fax: 800-793-9313 E-mail: mediainquiries@prnewswire.com Web Site: www.prnewswire.com, pg 1112

PR/PR Public Relations, 2301 Hickory Lane, Orlando, FL 32803 Tel: 407-895-8800 Web Site: www.prpr.net, pg 1112

PrairieView Press, 625 Seventh St, Gretna, MB R0G 0V0, Canada Tel: 204-327-6543 Toll Free Tel: 800-477-7377 Toll Free Fax: 866-480-0253 Web Site: prairieviewpress.com, pg 1229, 1258, 1270, 1282

Pratt Paper Company LLC, 20 Davis Rd, Marblehead, MA 01945 Tel: 781-639-9450 Fax: 781-639-9452, pg 1270

PremierIMS Inc, 11101 Ella Blvd, Houston, TX 77067 Tel: 832-608-6400 Fax: 832-608-6420 E-mail: info@premier-ims.com Web Site: www.premier-ims.com, pg 1117

Press Associates Union News Service, 4000 Cathedral Ave NW, No 535B, Washington, DC 20016 Tel: 312-806-4825 E-mail: paiunionnews@gmail.com, pg 1191

Press Box Publicity, 3920 Duncan Dr, Boca Raton, FL 33434 Tel: 912-658-7860 E-mail: sportspr@smithpublicity.com Web Site: pressboxpublicity-smithpublicity.com, pg 1112

Presskits, PO Box 71, East Walpole, MA 02032 Toll Free Tel: 800-472-3497 E-mail: files@presskits.com; team@presskits.com Web Site: presskits.com, pg 1105

Preston Kelly, 222 First Ave NE, Minneapolis, MN 55413 Tel: 612-843-4000 Fax: 612-843-3900 E-mail: iconicideas@prestonkelly.com Web Site: prestonkelly.com, pg 1100

PrimeArray Systems Inc, 1500 District Ave, Burlington, MA 01803 Tel: 978-455-9488 Toll Free Tel: 800-433-5133 E-mail: info@primearray.com; sales@primearray.com Web Site: www.primearray.com, pg 1375

Print It Plus, 11420 Okeechobee Blvd, Royal Palm Beach, FL 33411 Tel: 561-790-0884 Fax: 561-790-9378 E-mail: info@printitplus.com Web Site: printitplus.com, pg 1258

Printed Matter Inc, 231 11 Ave, Ground fl, New York, NY 10001 Tel: 212-925-0325 Fax: 212-925-0464 E-mail: info@printedmatter.org Web Site: www.printedmatter.org, pg 1299

The Printer, 2810 Cowell Blvd, Davis, CA 95618 Tel: 530-753-2519 Fax: 530-753-2528 E-mail: info@the-printer.net Web Site: the-printer.net, pg 1105, 1258

Printer's Repair Parts, 2706 Edgington St, Franklin Park, IL 60131-3438 Tel: 847-288-9000 Toll Free Tel: 800-444-4338 Fax: 847-288-9010 E-mail: prpsales@printersrepairparts.com Web Site: www.printersrepairparts.com, pg 1282

Printing Corporation of the Americas Inc, 620 SW 12 Ave, Pompano Beach, FL 33069 Tel: 954-781-8100 Toll Free Tel: 866-721-1PCA (721-1722) Web Site: pcaprintingplus.com, pg 1213, 1229, 1258, 1270

Printing Research Inc (PRI), 10760 Shady Trail, Suite 300, Dallas, TX 75220 Tel: 214-353-9000 Toll Free Tel: 800-627-5537 (US only) Fax: 214-357-5847 E-mail: info@superblue.net Web Site: www.printingresearch.com; www.superblue.net, pg 1282

Printronix Inc, 6440 Oak Canyon, Suite 200, Irvine, CA 92618 Tel: 714-368-2300 Toll Free Tel: 800-665-6210 Web Site: www.printronix.com, pg 1375

Printware LLC, 2935 Waters Rd, Suite 160, St Paul, MN 55121-1523 Tel: 651-456-1400 Fax: 651-454-3684 E-mail: sales@printwarellc.com Web Site: www.printwarellc.com, pg 1375

PrintWest, 1111 Eighth Ave, Regina, SK S4R 1C9, Canada Tel: 306-525-2304 Toll Free Tel: 800-236-6438 Fax: 306-757-2439 E-mail: general@printwest.com Web Site: www.printwest.com, pg 1213, 1229, 1270, 1282

Pro-Composition Inc, 2501 Catherine St, Suite 3, York, PA 17408 Tel: 717-965-9872 Web Site: www.pro-composition.com, pg 1229

Pro Laminators, 1511 Avco Blvd, Sellersburg, IN 47172 Tel: 812-246-0900 Toll Free Tel: 800-357-6812 Fax: 812-246-1900 E-mail: customerservice@prolaminators.com Web Site: prolaminators.com, pg 1258

Product Identification & Processing Systems Inc, 10 Midland Ave, Suite M-02, Port Chester, NY 10573-5911 Tel: 212-996-6000 Toll Free Tel: 888-783-7439 Fax: 212-410-7477 Toll Free Fax: 800-241-PIPS (241-7477) E-mail: info@pips.com Web Site: www.pips.com, pg 1230

ProductionPro, 246 Park St, Bensenville, IL 60106 Tel: 847-696-1600 E-mail: sales@productionpro.com; graphics@productionpro.com Web Site: www.productionpro.com, pg 1258, 1375

ProFAX Inc, 20 Max Ave, Hicksville, NY 11801-1419 Toll Free Tel: 877-942-8100 E-mail: sales@profax.com Web Site: www.profax.com, pg 1118

Progress Printing Plus, 2677 Waterlick Rd, Lynchburg, VA 24502 Tel: 434-239-9213 Toll Free Tel: 800-572-7804 Fax: 434-832-7573 E-mail: info@progressprintplus.com Web Site: www.progressprintplus.com, pg 1105, 1213, 1230, 1258

Progressive Publishing Services (PPS), 555 Ryan Run Rd, Suite B, York, PA 17404 Tel: 717-764-5908 Fax: 717-764-5530 E-mail: info@pps-ace.com Web Site: www.pps-ace.com, pg 1230, 1375

Prologue Inc, 3785, Rue La Fayette Ouest, Boisbriand, QC J7H 1N5, Canada Tel: 450-434-0306 Toll Free Tel: 800-363-2864 Toll Free Fax: 800-361-8088 (cust serv) E-mail: prologue@prologue.ca Web Site: www.prologue.ca, pg 1299

Promote A Book Inc, 1753 Rylie Ann Circle, South Jordan, UT 84095 Tel: 512-586-6073 Web Site: promoteabook.com, pg 1350

Promotional Book Co, 12 Cranfield Rd, No 100, Toronto, ON M4B 3G8, Canada Tel: 416-759-2226 Fax: 416-759-2150, pg 1320

Pronk Media Inc, 16 Glen Davis Crescent, Toronto, ON M4E 1X5, Canada Tel: 416-716-9660 (cell) E-mail: info@pronk.com; hello@pronk.com Web Site: www.pronk.com; www.h5engines.com; www.html5alive.com, pg 1230, 1375, 1417

ProQuest LLC, part of Clarivate PLC, 789 E Eisenhower Pkwy, Ann Arbor, MI 48108 Tel: 734-761-4700 Toll Free Tel: 800-521-0600; 877-779-6768 (sales) E-mail: sales@proquest.com Web Site: www.proquest.com, pg 1375

ProtoView, 7515 NE Ambassador Place, Suite A, Portland, OR 97220 Tel: 503-281-9230 E-mail: info@protoview.com Web Site: www.protoview.com, pg 1135, 1146

ps ink LLC, 857 Post Rd, Suite 367, Fairfield, CT 06824 Tel: 203-331-6942 Web Site: www.ps-ink.com, pg 1350

PTC, 121 Seaport Blvd, Boston, MA 02210 Tel: 781-370-5000 Fax: 781-370-6000 Web Site: www.ptc.com, pg 1375

Publication Identification & Processing Systems, 10 Midland Ave, Suite M-02, Port Chester, NY 10573 Tel: 212-996-6000 Toll Free Tel: 888-783-7439 Fax: 212-410-7477 Toll Free Fax: 800-241-7477 E-mail: info@pips.com Web Site: www.pips.com, pg 1230

Publications Professionals LLC, 3603 Chain Bridge Rd, Suite A & B, Fairfax, VA 22030-3244 Tel: 703-934-4499 Fax: 703-591-7289 E-mail: info@pubspros.com Web Site: www.pubspros.com, pg 1381

Publicis North America, 1675 Broadway, New York, NY 10009 Tel: 212-474-5000 Web Site: www.publicisna.com, pg 1112

Publishers Book Bindery (NY), 250 W 16 St, 4th fl, New York, NY 10011 Tel: 917-497-2950, pg 1213, 1258, 1282

COMPANY INDEX

Publishers' Graphics LLC, 131 Fremont St, Chicago, IL 60185 Tel: 630-221-1850 E-mail: contactpg@pubgraphics.com Web Site: pubgraphics.com, pg 1213, 1258, 1282

Publishers Group West (PGW), an Ingram brand, 1700 Fourth St, Berkeley, CA 94710 Tel: 510-809-3700 Toll Free Tel: 866-400-5351 (cust serv) Fax: 510-809-3777 E-mail: info@pgw.com Web Site: www.pgw.com, pg 1300

Publishers Storage & Shipping Corp, 46 Development Rd, Fitchburg, MA 01420 Tel: 978-345-2121 Web Site: www.pssc.com, pg 1334

Publishers Weekly, 49 W 23 St, 9th fl, New York, NY 10010 Tel: 212-377-5500 Fax: 212-377-2733 Web Site: www.publishersweekly.com, pg 1135

Publishing Data Management Inc, 39 Broadway, 28th fl, New York, NY 10006 Tel: 212-673-3210 Fax: 212-673-3390 E-mail: info@pubdata.com Web Site: www.pubdata.com, pg 1230, 1258, 1375

Publishing Management Associates Inc, 129 S Phelps Ave, Suite 312, Rockford, IL 61108 Tel: 815-398-8569 Fax: 815-398-8579 E-mail: pma@pma-inc.net Web Site: www.pma-inc.net, pg 1350

Publishing Trends, 232 Madison Ave, Suite 1400, New York, NY 10016 Tel: 212-447-0855 Fax: 212-447-0785 E-mail: info@publishingtrends.com Web Site: www.marketpartnersinternational.com; www.publishingtrends.com, pg 1136

Puritan Press Inc, 95 Runnells Bridge Rd, Hollis, NH 03049-6565 Tel: 603-889-4500 Toll Free Tel: 800-635-6302 Fax: 603-889-6551 E-mail: print@puritancapital.com Web Site: www.puritanpress.com, pg 1258

Purplegator, 1055 Westlakes Dr, Berwyn, PA 19312 Tel: 610-688-6000 Toll Free Tel: 888-76-GATOR (764-2867) Web Site: www.purplegator.com, pg 1350

The Pushpin Group Inc, 38 W 26 St, New York, NY 10010 Tel: 212-529-7590 Web Site: www.pushpininc.com, pg 1357, 1417

Sarah Putnam, 320 Brookline St, Cambridge, MA 02139 Tel: 617-596-5910 E-mail: sarah@sarahputnam.com Web Site: www.sarahputnam.com, pg 1424

QBR The Black Book Review, 591 Warburton Ave, Unit 170, Hastings-on-Hudson, NY 10706 Tel: 914-231-6778 Web Site: www.qbr.com, pg 1136

QBS Learning, 242 W 30 St, Suite 1100, New York, NY 10001 Tel: 646-668-4645 E-mail: contact@qbslearning.com Web Site: www.qbslearning.com, pg 1357, 1417

Quality Bindery Services Inc, 501 Amherst St, Buffalo, NY 14207 Tel: 716-883-5185 Toll Free Tel: 888-883-1266 Fax: 716-883-1598 E-mail: info@qualitybindery.com Web Site: www.qualitybindery.com, pg 1259

QualityLogic Inc, 9576 W Emerald St, Boise, ID 83704 Tel: 208-424-1905 E-mail: info@qualitylogic.com Web Site: www.qualitylogic.com, pg 1375

Quantum Group, 6511 Oakton St, Morton Grove, IL 60053 Tel: 847-967-3600 Fax: 847-967-3610 E-mail: info@quantumgroup.com Web Site: www.quantumgroup.com, pg 1259

Quark Software Inc, Chrysler Bldg, 405 Lexington Ave, 9th fl, New York, NY 10174 Toll Free Tel: 800-676-4575 Web Site: www.quark.com, pg 1375

Quarto Distribution Services (QDS), 100 Cummings Ctr, Suite 265D, Beverly, MA 01915 Tel: 978-282-9590 E-mail: qds@quarto.com Web Site: www.quartoknows.com/qds, pg 1300

Quiz Features, PO Box 42222, Northwest Sta, Washington, DC 20015-0822 Tel: 202-966-0025 Fax: 202-966-0025, pg 1191

R & R Book Co LLC, 666 Godwin Ave, Suite 120-C, Midland Park, NJ 07432 Tel: 201-337-3400 Web Site: www.rrbookcompany.com, pg 1300

R J Promotions & Advertising, 120 Holton Ave S, Hamilton, ON L8M 2L5, Canada Tel: 905-548-0389 E-mail: rjpromo@cogeco.ca, pg 1350

Rainbo Electronic Reviews, 5405 Cumberland Rd, Minneapolis, MN 55410 Tel: 612-408-4057 Web Site: www.rainboreviews.com, pg 1127

Raincoast Books Distribution Ltd, 2440 Viking Way, Richmond, BC V6V 1N2, Canada Tel: 604-448-7100 Toll Free Tel: 800-663-5714 (CN only) Fax: 604-270-7161 Toll Free Fax: 800-565-3770 E-mail: info@raincoast.com; customerservice@raincoast.com Web Site: www.raincoast.com/distribution, pg 1301

RAM Publications & Distribution Inc, 2525 Michigan Ave, Bldg A2, Santa Monica, CA 90404 Tel: 310-453-0043 Fax: 310-264-4888 E-mail: info@rampub.com; orders@rampub.com Web Site: www.rampub.com, pg 1301

RAmEx Ars Medica Inc, 1714 S Westgate Ave, No 2, Los Angeles, CA 90025-3852 Tel: 310-826-4964 Toll Free Tel: 800-633-9281 Fax: 310-826-9674 E-mail: ars.medica@ramex.com Web Site: www.ramex.com, pg 1301

Rayonier Advanced Materials, 1301 Riverplace Blvd, Suite 2300, Jacksonville, FL 32207 Tel: 904-357-4600 Web Site: rayonieram.com, pg 1270

Readerlink Distribution Services LLC, 1420 Kensington Rd, Suite 300, Oakbrook, IL 60523-2164 Tel: 708-547-4400 Toll Free Tel: 800-549-5389 E-mail: info@readerlink.com; marketingservices@readerlink.com Web Site: www.readerlink.com, pg 1301

Readers' Guide to Periodical Literature, 4919 Rte 22, Amenia, NY 12501 Tel: 518-789-8700 Toll Free Tel: 800-562-2139 Fax: 518-789-0556 E-mail: books@greyhouse.com Web Site: greyhouse.com, pg 1136

Redwing Book Co, 202 Bendix St, Taos, NM 87571 Tel: 575-758-7758 Toll Free Tel: 800-873-3946 (US); 888-873-3947 (CN) Fax: 575-758-7768 E-mail: info@redwingbooks.com; custsrv@redwingbooks.com Web Site: www.redwingbooks.com, pg 1320, 1329

V G Reed & Sons Inc, 1002 S 12 St, Louisville, KY 40210-1302 Toll Free Tel: 800-635-9788 Fax: 502-560-0197 Web Site: www.vgreed.com, pg 1105, 1259

Regal Press, 79 Astor Ave, Norwood, MA 02062 Tel: 781-769-3900 Toll Free Tel: 800-447-3425 Fax: 781-769-7361 E-mail: info@regalpress.com Web Site: www.regalpress.com, pg 1105, 1259

Regent Book Co, PO Box 37, Liberty Corner, NJ 07938 Tel: 973-574-7600 Toll Free Tel: 800-999-9554 Fax: 973-944-5073 Toll Free Fax: 888-597-3661 E-mail: info@regentbook.com Web Site: www.regentbook.com, pg 1320

Regent Press Printers & Publishers, 2747 Regent St, Berkeley, CA 94705 Tel: 510-845-1196 E-mail: regentpress@mindspring.com Web Site: www.regentpress.net, pg 1375

Laszlo Regos Photography, 30601 Woodstream Dr, Farmington Hills, MI 48334 Tel: 248-398-3631 E-mail: laszlo@laszlofoto.com Web Site: www.laszlofoto.com, pg 1425

Reichhold Inc, 1035 Swabia Ct, Durham, NC 27703 Tel: 919-990-7500 Toll Free Tel: 800-448-3482 Fax: 919-990-7749 Web Site: www.reichhold.com, pg 1271

Reindl Bindery Co Inc, W194 N11381 McCormick Dr, Germantown, WI 53022 Tel: 262-293-1444 Toll Free Tel: 800-878-1121 Fax: 262-293-1445 E-mail: info@reindlbindery.com Web Site: www.reindlbindery.com, pg 1259

Ruth & Robert Reld, 71 Faunce Dr, Providence, RI 02906 Tel: 401-274-2149 Web Site: www.whitegatefeatures.com, pg 1126

Religion News Service, c/o University of Missouri's Journalism School, 30 Neff Annex, Columbia, MO 65211 Tel: 573-884-1327 E-mail: info@religionnews.com Web Site: www.religionnews.com, pg 1191

Renaissance Consultations, PO Box 561, Auburn, CA 95604 Tel: 530-362-1339 E-mail: info@marketingandpr.com Web Site: www.MarketingAndPR.com, pg 1112

Renaissance House, 465 Westview Ave, Englewood, NJ 07631 Tel: 201-408-4048 Web Site: www.renaissancehouse.net, pg 1357

Rennert Translation Group, 12 E 41 St, New York, NY 10017 Tel: 212-867-8700 E-mail: translations@rennert.com Web Site: rennerttranslations.com, pg 1404

Reno Typographers, 1020 S Rock Blvd, Suite C, Reno, NV 89502 Tel: 775-852-8800 E-mail: info@renotype.com; work@renotype.com Web Site: www.renotype.com, pg 1230

The Renton Printery Inc, 315 S Third St, Renton, WA 98057-2028 Tel: 425-235-1776 E-mail: info@rentonprintery.com Web Site: www.rentonprintery.com, pg 1230, 1259

Resolute Forest Products, 111 Robert-Bourassa Blvd, Suite 5000, Montreal, QC H3C 2M1, Canada Tel: 514-875-2160 Toll Free Tel: 800-361-2888 E-mail: info@resolutefp.com Web Site: www.resolutefp.com, pg 1271

Retailing Insight Magazine, PO Box 12252, Charlotte, NC 28220 Tel: 704-496-2460 E-mail: circ@retailinginsight.com Web Site: retailinginsight.com, pg 1136

Reviewer Bookwatch, 278 Orchard Dr, Oregon, WI 53575-1129 Tel: 608-835-7937 E-mail: mbr@execpc.com Web Site: www.midwestbookreview.com, pg 1136

Reviews in American History, 2715 N Charles St, Baltimore, MD 21218-4363 Tel: 410-516-6987 (journal orders outside US & CN) Toll Free Tel: 800-548-1784 (journal orders) Fax: 410-578-2865 (journal orders) E-mail: jrnlcirc@jh.edu (journal orders) Web Site: www.press.jhu.edu/journals/reviews-american-history, pg 1136

REX, 13431 SW Scotts Bridge Dr, Tigard, OR 97223-1609 Tel: 503-238-4525 E-mail: info@rexpost.com Web Site: www.rexpost.com, pg 1375

Rex Three Inc, 15431 SW 14 St, Sunrise, FL 33326 Tel: 954-388-8708 Toll Free Tel: 800-782-6509 Fax: 954-452-0569 Web Site: www.rex3.com, pg 1375

Reynolds Design & Management, 52 Piedmont Ave, Waltham, MA 02451-3015 Tel: 781-893-7464 E-mail: rdandm@comcast.net, pg 1417

Nina J Reznick Esq, 28 E Tenth St, New York, NY 10003 Tel: 212-473-6279 E-mail: ninarezesq@icloud.com, pg 1350

Ribolow Associates Inc, 1350 Avenue of the Americas, 2nd fl, New York, NY 10019 Tel: 212-575-2700 Fax: 646-496-9122 E-mail: ribolowstaffingservices@gmail.com Web Site: www.ribolow.com, pg 1382

Ricoh Americas Corp, 300 Eagleview Blvd, Exton, PA 19341 Tel: 610-296-8000 Toll Free Tel: 800-333-2679 (prod support); 800-637-4264 (sales) Web Site: www.ricoh-usa.com, pg 1375

Rights & Distribution Inc, 7519 LaPaz Blvd, Suite C303, Boca Raton, FL 33433 Tel: 954-925-5242 E-mail: rightsinc@aol.com, pg 1301

Rimage Corp, 201 General Mills Blvd, Golden Valley, MN 55427 Tel: 952-944-8144; 952-946-0004 (option 2, tech support) Toll Free Tel: 800-445-8288; 800-553-8312 (option 2, tech support) E-mail: sales@rimage.com Web Site: www.rimage.com, pg 1375

Rising Sun Book Co, 1424 Stony Brook Rd, Stony Brook, NY 11790 Tel: 631-473-7000 Fax: 631-473-7447 Web Site: risingsunbook.com, pg 1320, 1329

RISO Inc, 10 State St, Suite 201, Woburn, MA 01801-2105 Tel: 978-777-7377 Toll Free Tel: 800-942-7476 (cust support) Web Site: us.riso.com, pg 1259, 1376

Judith Riven Literary Agent LLC, 250 W 16 St, Suite 4F, New York, NY 10011, pg 1350

Rivendell Media Inc, 1248 Rte 22 W, Mountainside, NJ 07092 Tel: 908-232-2021 ext 200 Fax: 908-232-0521 E-mail: info@rivendellmedia.com; sales@rivendellmedia.com Web Site: www.rivendellmedia.com, pg 1112

Rizzoli Bookstores, 1133 Broadway, New York, NY 10010 *Tel:* 212-759-2424 *Toll Free Tel:* 800-52-BOOKS (522-6657) *Fax:* 212-826-9754 *Web Site:* rizzolibookstore.com; www.rizzoliusa.com, pg 1320

The John Roberts Company, 9687 East River Rd NW, Minneapolis, MN 55433 *Tel:* 763-755-5500 *Toll Free Tel:* 800-551-1534 *Fax:* 763-755-0394 *E-mail:* success@johnroberts.com *Web Site:* www.johnroberts.com; www.facebook.com/TheJohnRobertsCompany, pg 1105

Richard Owen Roberts, Booksellers & Publishers, 139 N Washington St, Wheaton, IL 60189 *Tel:* 630-752-4122 *E-mail:* sales@rorbooks.com *Web Site:* www.rorbooks.com, pg 1320

Carol Robinson Photography, 2012 Aldrich Place, Downers Grove, IL 60516 *Tel:* 630-222-6286 *E-mail:* goodpix@aol.com *Web Site:* carolrobinsonphoto.webs.com; goodpix.zenfolio.com, pg 1425

Stephanie Rogers & Associates, 8737 Carlitas Joy Ct, Las Vegas, NV 89117 *Tel:* 702-255-9999 *E-mail:* sjrlion@aol.com; write2wow@aol.com *Web Site:* www.write2wow.com, pg 1350

Claudette Roland, Los Angeles, CA 90024 *Tel:* 310-266-6980 *E-mail:* claudette_roland@verizon.net, pg 1404

Roland DGA Corp, 15363 Barranca Pkwy, Irvine, CA 92618-2216 *Tel:* 949-727-2100 *Toll Free Tel:* 800-542-2307 *Fax:* 949-727-2112 *Web Site:* www.rolanddga.com, pg 1376

Rolland Enterprises, 256 JB Rolland W, St-Jerome, QC J7Y 0L6, Canada *Toll Free Tel:* 800-567-9872 (CN); 800-388-0882 (US) *E-mail:* media@rollandinc.com; marketing@rollandinc.com *Web Site:* www.rollandinc.com, pg 1271

Roosevelt Paper Co, One Roosevelt Dr, Mount Laurel, NJ 08054 *Tel:* 856-303-4100 *Toll Free Tel:* 800-523-3470 *Fax:* 856-642-1949 *E-mail:* marketing@rooseveltpaper.com *Web Site:* www.rooseveltpaper.com, pg 1271

Roots & Rhythm Inc, PO Box 837, El Cerrito, CA 94530 *Tel:* 510-965-9503 *Toll Free Tel:* 888-ROOTS-66 (766-8766) *Fax:* 510-526-9001 *E-mail:* roots@toast.net *Web Site:* www.rootsandrhythm.com, pg 1143

Rosemoor House Translations, Rosemoor House, 400 New Bedford Dr, Vallejo, CA 94591 *Tel:* 707-557-8595, pg 1404

Sherri Rosen Publicity Intl NYC, 454 Manhattan Ave, Suite 3-J, New York, NY 10026 *Tel:* 917-699-1284 *E-mail:* sherri@sherrirosen.com *Web Site:* www.sherrirosen.com, pg 1112, 1350

Alex Ross, One World Trade Center, New York, NY 10007 *Tel:* 212-286-2860 *Toll Free Tel:* 800-444-7570 *Web Site:* www.newyorker.com/contributors/alex-ross; www.therestisnoise.com, pg 1126

Ross Gage Inc, 8502 Brookville Rd, Indianapolis, IN 46239 *Tel:* 317-283-2323 *Toll Free Tel:* 800-799-2323 *Fax:* 317-931-2108 *E-mail:* info@rossgage.com *Web Site:* www.rossgage.com, pg 1230, 1259

Ken Ross Photography, PO Box 4517, Scottsdale, AZ 85261 *Tel:* 602-319-2974 *E-mail:* kenrossaz@yahoo.com *Web Site:* www.kenrossphotography.com, pg 1425

Roswell Bookbinding, 2614 N 29 Ave, Phoenix, AZ 85009 *Tel:* 602-272-9338 *Toll Free Tel:* 888-803-8883 *Fax:* 602-272-9786 *Web Site:* www.roswellbookbinding.com, pg 1259, 1326

Roth Advertising Inc, PO Box 96, Sea Cliff, NY 11579 *Tel:* 516-674-8603 *Fax:* 516-368-3885 *Web Site:* www.rothadvertising.com, pg 1100

Round Table Companies, PO Box 1603, Deerfield, IL 60015 *Toll Free Tel:* 833-750-5683 *Web Site:* www.roundtablecompanies.com, pg 1417

Roundtable Press Inc, 20 E Ninth St, New York, NY 10003 *Tel:* 917-597-2183 *Web Site:* www.roundtablepressinc.com, pg 1357

Victoria Roza Research, 2454 Adams Ave, San Diego, CA 92116 *Tel:* 619-295-8082 *E-mail:* victoriaproza@gmail.com, pg 1425

RRD Manchester, 151 Red Stone Rd, Manchester, CT 06042 *Tel:* 860-649-5570 *Fax:* 860-649-7800 *Web Site:* www.rrdonnelley.com/commercial-print/location/rr-donnelley-manchester, pg 1105

Ruder Finn Inc, 425 E 53 St, New York, NY 10022 *Tel:* 212-593-6400 *E-mail:* info@ruderfinn.com *Web Site:* www.ruderfinn.com, pg 1112

Rushmore News Inc, 924 E Saint Andrew, Rapid City, SD 57701 *Tel:* 605-342-2617 *Toll Free Tel:* 800-423-0501, pg 1321

RUSQ: A Journal of Reference and User Experience, 225 N Michigan Ave, Suite 1300, Chicago, IL 60601 *Tel:* 312-280-4395 *Toll Free Tel:* 800-545-2433 *Fax:* 312-280-5273 *E-mail:* rusq@ala.org *Web Site:* www.ala.org/rusa/rusq-journal, pg 1136

S & L Sales Co Inc, 2165 Industrial Blvd, Waycross, GA 31503 *Tel:* 912-283-0210 *Toll Free Tel:* 800-243-3699 *Fax:* 912-283-0261 *Toll Free Fax:* 800-736-7329 *E-mail:* sales@slsales.com *Web Site:* slsales.com, pg 1321

Saferock, 75 Armour Place, Dumont, NJ 07628 *Tel:* 646-535-0110 *E-mail:* info@saferock.com *Web Site:* saferockretail.com, pg 1376

St Armand Paper Mill, 3700 St Patrick, Montreal, QC H4E 1A2, Canada *Tel:* 514-931-8338 *Fax:* 514-931-5953 *Web Site:* www.st-armand.com, pg 1271

St Catharines Museum, 1932 Welland Canals Pkwy, RR 6, St Catharines, ON L2R 7K6, Canada *Tel:* 905-984-8880 *Toll Free Tel:* 800-305-5134 *Fax:* 905-984-6910 *E-mail:* museum@stcatharines.ca *Web Site:* www.stcatharines.ca, pg 1301

St Joseph Communications-Print Group, 50 Macintosh Blvd, Concord, ON L4K 4P3, Canada *Tel:* 905-660-3111 *E-mail:* marketing@stjoseph.com *Web Site:* stjoseph.com, pg 1105, 1259

Sakurai USA Inc, 1700 N Basswood Rd, Schaumburg, IL 60173 *Tel:* 847-490-9400 *Toll Free Tel:* 800-458-4720 *Fax:* 847-490-4200 *E-mail:* inquiry@sakurai.com *Web Site:* www.sakurai.com, pg 1282

Samsung Research America (SRA), 665 Clyde Ave, Mountain View, CA 94043 *Tel:* 650-210-1001 *E-mail:* sra-contact-us@samsung.com *Web Site:* www.sra.samsung.com, pg 1376

Samuel Packaging Systems, 4020 Gault Ave S, Fort Payne, AL 35967 *Tel:* 256-845-1928 *Web Site:* www.samuel.com, pg 1282

San Diego Museum of Art, Balboa Park, 1450 El Prado, San Diego, CA 92112 *Tel:* 619-232-7931 *Web Site:* www.sdmart.org, pg 1321

Sandhill Book Marketing Ltd, Millcreek Industrial Park, Unit 4, 3308 Appaloosa Rd, Kelowna, BC V1V 2W5, Canada *Tel:* 250-491-1446 *Toll Free Tel:* 800-667-3848 (CN only) *Fax:* 250-491-4066 *E-mail:* info@sandhillbooks.com *Web Site:* www.sandhillbooks.com, pg 1321

Santec Corp, 84 Old Gate Lane, Milford, CT 06460 *Tel:* 203-878-1379 *Fax:* 203-876-0949 *E-mail:* info@santeccorp.com *Web Site:* www.santeccorp.com, pg 1282

Sappi Fine Paper North America, 255 State St, Boston, MA 02109 *Tel:* 617-423-7300 *Toll Free Tel:* 800-882-4332 *E-mail:* webqueriesna@sappi.com *Web Site:* www.sappi.com/na, pg 1271

Sargent Architectural Photography, 801 S Olive Ave, Suite 107, West Palm Beach, FL 33401 *Tel:* 561-881-8887 *E-mail:* info@sargentphoto.com *Web Site:* www.sargentphoto.com, pg 1425

Saunders Book Co, PO Box 308, Collingwood, ON L9Y 3Z7, Canada *Tel:* 705-445-4777 *Toll Free Tel:* 800-461-9120 *Fax:* 705-445-9569 *Toll Free Fax:* 800-561-1763 *E-mail:* info@saundersbook.ca *Web Site:* librarybooks.com, pg 1301

Scarf Press, 1385 Baptist Church Rd, Yorktown Heights, NY 10598 *Tel:* 914-245-7811, pg 1357

SCB Distributors, 15608 S New Century Dr, Gardena, CA 90248 *Tel:* 310-532-9400 *Toll Free Tel:* 800-729-6423 *Fax:* 310-532-7001 *E-mail:* scb@scbdistributors.com *Web Site:* www.scbdistributors.com, pg 1302

Sceptre Inc, 16800 Gale Ave, City of Industry, CA 91745 *Tel:* 626-369-3698 *Toll Free Tel:* 800-788-2878 *Fax:* 626-369-3488 *E-mail:* sceptrecs@sceptre.com; scp-marketing@sceptre.com; scp-sales@sceptre.com *Web Site:* www.sceptre.com, pg 1376

Schaefer Machine Co Inc, 200 Commercial Dr, Deep River, CT 06417 *Tel:* 860-526-4000 *Toll Free Tel:* 800-243-5143 *Fax:* 860-526-4654 *E-mail:* schaefer@schaeferco.com *Web Site:* www.schaeferco.com, pg 1283

Schenkman Books Inc, 145 Bethel Mountain Rd, Rochester, VT 05767 *Tel:* 802-767-3104 *E-mail:* schenkmanbooks@gmail.com *Web Site:* www.schenkmanbooks.com, pg 1357

Richard Schneider Language Services (RSLS), 1200 Piedmont Ave, Pacific Grove, CA 93950 *Toll Free Tel:* 800-500-5808 *E-mail:* service@idioms.com *Web Site:* www.idioms.com, pg 1404

Schnoll Media Consulting, 1253 Springfield Ave, PMB 338, New Providence, NJ 07974 *Tel:* 908-522-3190 *Fax:* 908-273-2667 *Web Site:* www.schnollconsult.com, pg 1351

Schoenhof's Foreign Books Inc, 76 A Mount Auburn St, Cambridge, MA 02138 *Tel:* 617-547-8855 *E-mail:* info@schoenhofs.com *Web Site:* www.schoenhofs.com, pg 1321, 1329

Scholarly Book Services Inc, 289 Bridgeland Ave, Unit 105, Toronto, ON M6A 1Z6, Canada *Toll Free Tel:* 800-847-9736 *Toll Free Fax:* 800-220-9895 *E-mail:* customerservice@sbookscan.com *Web Site:* www.sbookscan.com, pg 1302

The Scholar's Choice, 6300 W Port Bay Rd, Suite 101, Wolcott, NY 14590 *Tel:* 315-905-4208 *E-mail:* information@scholarschoice.com *Web Site:* www.scholarschoice.com, pg 1139

Scholar's Choice Ltd, 2323 Trafalgar St, London, ON N5Y 5S7, Canada *Tel:* 519-453-7470 *Toll Free Tel:* 800-265-1095 *Fax:* 519-455-2853 *Toll Free Fax:* 800-363-3398 (CN only) *E-mail:* sales@scholarschoice.ca *Web Site:* www.scholarschoice.ca, pg 1302

Scholastic School Reading Events, 1080 Greenwood Blvd, Lake Mary, FL 32746 *Tel:* 407-829-8000 *Toll Free Tel:* 800-770-4662 *Fax:* 407-829-2600 *E-mail:* custservbf@scholasticbookfairs.com *Web Site:* bookfairs.scholastic.com/content/fairs/home.html, pg 1302, 1321

School Library Journal, 123 William St, Suite 802, New York, NY 10038 *Tel:* 646-380-0752 *Toll Free Tel:* 800-595-1066 *Fax:* 646-380-0756 *E-mail:* slj@mediasourceinc.com; sljsubs@pcspublink.com *Web Site:* www.slj.com; www.facebook.com/schoollibraryjournal; x.com/sljournal, pg 1136

School of World Studies, 312 N Shafer St, Richmond, VA 23284-2021 *Tel:* 804-827-1111 *Web Site:* worldstudies.vcu.edu, pg 1404

Schoolhouse Indexing, 10-B Parade Ground Rd, Etna, NH 03750 *Tel:* 603-359-5826 *Web Site:* schoolhouseindexing.com, pg 1230

Schreiber Translations Inc (STI), 51 Monroe St, Suite 101, Rockville, MD 20850 *Tel:* 301-424-7737 *Toll Free Tel:* 800-822-3213 *Fax:* 301-424-2336 *E-mail:* translation@schreibernet.com *Web Site:* www.schreibernet.com, pg 1404

Carl Schreier, c/o Homestead Publishing & Book Design, Box 193, Moose, WY 83012-0193 *Tel:* 307-733-6248, pg 1425

Bettina Schrewe Literary Scouting, 101 Fifth Ave, Suite 11B, New York, NY 10003 *Tel:* 212-414-2515 *Web Site:* www.bschrewe.com, pg 1351

Schroeder Indexing Services, 23 Camilla Pink Ct, Bluffton, SC 29909 *Tel:* 843-705-9779; 843-415-3900 (cell) *E-mail:* sanindex@schroederindexing.com *Web Site:* www.schroederindexing.com, pg 1230

COMPANY INDEX

Schroeder's Book Haven, 104 Michigan Ave, League City, TX 77573 *Tel:* 281-332-5226 *E-mail:* info@bookhaventexas.com *Web Site:* www.bookhaventexas.com, pg 1321

Lesley M Schuldt, 10153 Bellwether Lane, Lone Tree, CO 80124-5456 *Tel:* 303-619-0310 *E-mail:* stmbt97@aol.com, pg 1404

E C Schultz & Company Inc, 333 Crossen Ave, Elk Grove Village, IL 60007-2001 *Tel:* 847-640-1190 *E-mail:* jobfiles@ecschultz.com *Web Site:* www.ecschultz.com, pg 1283

Marian Schwartz, Austin, TX 78704 *E-mail:* marianschwartz@gmail.com *Web Site:* www.marianschwartz.com, pg 1404

Susan Schwartzman Public Relations, 88 Kings Way, Pawling, NY 12564 *Toll Free Tel:* 877-833-4276 *Toll Free Fax:* 877-833-4276 *E-mail:* susan@susanschwartzmanpublicity.com *Web Site:* www.susanschwartzmanpublicity.com, pg 1113

Cosimo Scianna, Photographer, 23407 Milano Ct, Boca Raton, FL 33433 *Tel:* 917-763-2927 *E-mail:* cosimoscianna@mac.com *Web Site:* www.cosimoscianna.com, pg 1425

Natalia V Sciarini, 219 New England Rd, Guilford, CT 06437 *Tel:* 203-314-7680 *E-mail:* sciarini2009@gmail.com, pg 1404

Science Fiction Book Club®, 34 W 27 St, 10th fl, New York, NY 10001 *Tel:* 716-250-5700 (cust serv) *E-mail:* customer.service@sfbc.com; member.services@sfbc.com *Web Site:* sfbc.com, pg 1143

Science Source®, 307 Fifth Ave, 3rd fl, New York, NY 10016 *Tel:* 212-758-3420 *E-mail:* info@sciencesource.com; sales@sciencesource.com; contributor@sciencesource.com *Web Site:* www.sciencesource.com, pg 1430

Scientific Bindery Inc, 8052 Monticello Ave, Suite 206, Skokie, IL 60076 *Tel:* 847-329-0510 *Fax:* 847-329-0608 *E-mail:* info@scientificbindery.com *Web Site:* www.scientificbindery.com, pg 1259

Scott Publications Inc, 2145 W Sherman Blvd, Norton Shores, MI 49441 *Tel:* 231-755-2200 *Toll Free Tel:* 866-733-9382 *Fax:* 231-755-1003 *E-mail:* contactus@scottpublications.com *Web Site:* scottpublications.com, pg 1105

SCREEN Americas, 5110 Tollview Dr, Rolling Meadows, IL 60008-3715 *Tel:* 847-870-7400 *Toll Free Tel:* 800-372-7737 *E-mail:* info@screenamericas.com *Web Site:* www.screenamericas.com, pg 1283, 1376

Scribe Inc, 765 S Front St, Philadelphia, PA 19147 *Tel:* 215-336-5094; 215-336-5095 *E-mail:* contact@scribenet.com *Web Site:* www.scribenet.com, pg 1230, 1351, 1357, 1376, 1385

SDL, 201 Edgewater Dr, Suite 225, Wakefield, MA 01880 *Tel:* 781-756-4400 *Toll Free Tel:* 800-933-6910 (sales) *Fax:* 781-989-8199 *Web Site:* www.sdl.com, pg 1376

SDP Publishing Solutions LLC, 36 Captain's Way, East Bridgewater, MA 02333 *Tel:* 617-775-0656 *E-mail:* info@sdppublishing.com *Web Site:* sdppublishing.com, pg 1351

2nd Grade Book Club, 557 Broadway, New York, NY 10012 *Tel:* 212-343-6100; 573-632-1632 (PR, US territories, US military bases) *Toll Free Tel:* 800-541-1097 (US) *Toll Free Fax:* 800-223-4011 *E-mail:* bookclubs@scholastic.com *Web Site:* clubs.scholastic.com, pg 1143

SeeSaw (K-1), 557 Broadway, New York, NY 10012 *Tel:* 212-343-6100; 573-632-1632 (PR, US territories, US military bases) *Toll Free Tel:* 800-541-1097 (US) *Toll Free Fax:* 800-223-4011 *E-mail:* bookclubs@scholastic.com *Web Site:* clubs.scholastic.com, pg 1143

Seldon Ink Travel Writing & Photography, 1513 Riverside Dr, Beaufort, SC 29902 *Tel:* 910-274-8070 *Web Site:* www.seldonink.com, pg 1425

SENCOR International, 445 Park Ave, 9th fl, New York, NY 10022 *Tel:* 212-980-6726 *Web Site:* www.sencorinternational.com, pg 1376, 1385

Separa Color, 6951 Oran Circle, Buena Park, CA 90621 *Tel:* 818-988-2882 *Toll Free Tel:* 800-859-0629 *Fax:* 818-988-3882 *E-mail:* sales@separacolor.com *Web Site:* www.separacolor.com; www.simplybrochures.com; www.simplycatalogs.com; www.simplypostcards.com, pg 1105

Sepp Leaf Products Inc, 381 Park Ave S, No 13, New York, NY 10016 *Tel:* 212-683-2840 *Fax:* 212-725-0308 *E-mail:* sales@seppleaf.com *Web Site:* www.seppleaf.com, pg 1271

Christina Sever, PO Box 197, Corvallis, OR 97339 *Tel:* 541-753-3913 *Fax:* 541-757-0640 *E-mail:* csever17@yahoo.com, pg 1404

John Sexton Photography, PO Box 30, Carmel Valley, CA 93924 *Tel:* 831-659-3130 *Fax:* 831-659-5509 *E-mail:* info@johnsexton.com *Web Site:* www.johnsexton.com, pg 1425

SGS International LLC, 626 W Main St, Suite 500, Louisville, KY 40202 *Tel:* 502-637-5443 *E-mail:* info@sgsco.com *Web Site:* www.sgsintl.com, pg 1230

SGW Integrated Marketing Communications Inc, 219 Changebridge Rd, Montville, NJ 07045 *Tel:* 973-299-8000 *E-mail:* info@sgw.com *Web Site:* www.sgw.com, pg 1118

Shaffner's Bindery, 3305 Pattee Canyon Rd, Missoula, MT 59803 *Tel:* 406-251-2699 *E-mail:* shaffnersbindery@centric.net *Web Site:* shaffnersbindery.com, pg 1326

Sharp Electronics Corp, 100 Paragon Dr, Montvale, NJ 07645 *Toll Free Tel:* 800-BE-SHARP (237-4277) *Web Site:* www.sharpusa.com, pg 1376

Shepherd Inc, 2223 Key Way Dr, Suite B, Dubuque, IA 52002 *Tel:* 563-584-0500 *Web Site:* www.shepherd-inc.com, pg 1231, 1259, 1376, 1417

Sheriar Books, 603 Briarwood Dr, Myrtle Beach, SC 29572 *Tel:* 843-272-1339 *Fax:* 843-361-1747 *Web Site:* www.sheriarbooks.org, pg 1321

Sheridan GR, 5100 33 St SE, Grand Rapids, MI 49512 *Tel:* 616-957-5100 *Web Site:* www.sheridan.com, pg 1213, 1259

Sheridan MI, 613 E Industrial Dr, Chelsea, MI 48118 *Tel:* 734-475-9145 *Web Site:* www.sheridan.com, pg 1213, 1259, 1271

Sheridan NH, 69 Lyme Rd, Hanover, NH 03755 *Tel:* 603-643-2220 *Web Site:* www.sheridan.com, pg 1259

Sheridan PA, 450 Fame Ave, Hanover, PA 17331 *Tel:* 717-632-3535 *Toll Free Tel:* 800-352-2210 *Fax:* 717-633-8900 *Web Site:* www.sheridan.com, pg 1259

Sheridan Saline, 960 Woodland Dr, Saline, MI 48176 *Tel:* 734-429-5411 *Web Site:* www.sheridan.com, pg 1214, 1260

Ron Sherman Photography, 340 Spring Creek Rd, Roswell, GA 30075 *Tel:* 770-355-8700 (cell) *E-mail:* ronsphoto@live.com *Web Site:* www.ronsherman.com, pg 1425

Monika Shoffman-Graves, 70 Transylvania Ave, Key Largo, FL 33037 *Tel:* 305-451-1462 *E-mail:* mograv@gmail.com, pg 1404

Shoreline Publishing Group LLC, 125 Santa Rosa Place, Santa Barbara, CA 93109 *Tel:* 805-564-1004 *E-mail:* info@shorelinepublishing.com *Web Site:* shorelinepublishing.com, pg 1357

Shutterstock Inc, Empire State Bldg, 350 Fifth Ave, 20th fl, New York, NY 10118 *E-mail:* support@shutterstock.com; press@shutterstock.com *Web Site:* www.shutterstock.com, pg 1430

Sideshow Media LLC, 315 St Johns Place, 1G, Brooklyn, NY 11238 *Tel:* 917-519-5335 *E-mail:* inquiries@sideshowbooks.com *Web Site:* main.sideshowbooks.com, pg 1357

Signature Book Printing Inc, 8041 Cessna Ave, Gaithersburg, MD 20879 *Tel:* 301-258-8353 *E-mail:* book@sbpbooks.com *Web Site:* sbpbooks.com, pg 1214, 1231, 1260

Signature Print Services, 3565 Sierra Rd, San Jose, CA 95132 *Tel:* 408-213-3393 *Fax:* 408-213-3399 *Web Site:* www.signatureprint.com, pg 1260

Silvermine International Books LLC, 25 Perry Ave, Suite 11, Norwalk, CT 06850 *Tel:* 203-451-2396 *E-mail:* info@jawilsons.com *Web Site:* jawilsons.com/pages/who-we-are, pg 1329

Boris Mark Silversteyn, 700 Cocoanut Ave, Apt 210, Sarasota, FL 34236 *Tel:* 941-552-8310; 941-284-7282 (cell) *E-mail:* bsilversteyn@comcast.net, pg 1404

Simco-Ion, 2257 N Penn Rd, Hatfield, PA 19440 *Tel:* 215-822-6401 *Toll Free Tel:* 800-203-3419 *E-mail:* customerservice@simco-ion.com *Web Site:* www.simco-ion.com, pg 1283

Simon Miller Paper & Packaging, 3409 W Chester Pike, Suite 204, Newton Square, PA 19073 *Tel:* 215-923-3600 *Toll Free Tel:* 800-642-1899 *Fax:* 610-355-9330 *E-mail:* info@simonmiller.com *Web Site:* www.simonmiller.com, pg 1271

Frank Siteman Photography, 136 Pond St, Winchester, MA 01890 *Tel:* 781-729-3747 *E-mail:* frank@franksiteman.com *Web Site:* www.franksiteman.com, pg 1425

SITMA USA Inc, 45 Empire Dr, St Paul, MN 55103-1856 *Tel:* 651-222-2324 *Fax:* 651-222-4652 *E-mail:* sales@sitma.com *Web Site:* www.sitma.it, pg 1283

Six Red Marbles LLC, 101 Station Landing, Medford, MA 02155 *Tel:* 857-588-9000 *E-mail:* info@sixredmarbles.com *Web Site:* www.sixredmarbles.com, pg 1231, 1376

Skylark Co Inc, PO Box 237043, New York, NY 10023-0028 *Tel:* 212-595-0700 *Fax:* 212-595-0700, pg 1329

Small Changes, 1418 NW 53 St, Seattle, WA 98107 *Tel:* 206-382-1980 *Fax:* 206-382-1514 *E-mail:* info@smallchanges.com *Web Site:* www.smallchanges.com, pg 1321

Small Press Bookwatch, 278 Orchard Dr, Oregon, WI 53575-1129 *Tel:* 608-835-7937 *E-mail:* mbr@execpc.com *Web Site:* www.midwestbookreview.com, pg 1136

Smallwood & Stewart Inc, 5 E 20 St, New York, NY 10003 *Tel:* 212-505-3268 *Web Site:* www.smallwoodandstewart.com, pg 1357

Smart Communications Inc, 641 Lexington Ave, 13th fl, New York, NY 10022 *Tel:* 212-486-1894 *E-mail:* info@smartny.com *Web Site:* www.smartny.com, pg 1376

Smith & Sons Printers Inc, 6403 Rutledge Pike, Knoxville, TN 37924 *Tel:* 865-523-1419 *Web Site:* www.ssprintinc.com, pg 1214, 1231, 1260

Smith-Edwards-Dunlap Co, 2867 E Allegheny Ave, Philadelphia, PA 19134 *Tel:* 215-425-8800 *Toll Free Tel:* 800-829-0020 *Fax:* 215-425-9715 *E-mail:* sales@sed.com *Web Site:* www.sed.com, pg 1231, 1260, 1271

Snow Lion Graphics, PO Box 9465, Berkeley, CA 94709-0465 *Tel:* 510-525-1134; 510-816-2840 (cell) *E-mail:* info@slgbooks.com *Web Site:* www.slgbooks.com, pg 1417

Socadis Inc, 420 rue Stinson, Ville St-Laurent, QC H4N 3L7, Canada *Tel:* 514-331-3300 *Toll Free Tel:* 800-361-2847 *Fax:* 514-745-3282; 514-331-8202 (major dist) *Toll Free Fax:* 866-803-5422 *E-mail:* socinfo@socadis.com (cust serv); direction@socadis.com; salesgd@socadis.com (major dist) *Web Site:* www.socadis.com, pg 1302

Social Studies School Service, 10200 Jefferson Blvd, PO Box 802, Culver City, CA 90232 *Tel:* 310-839-2436 *Toll Free Tel:* 800-421-4246 (US & CN) *Fax:* 310-839-2249 *Toll Free Fax:* 800-944-5432 *E-mail:* access@socialstudies.com; customerservice@socialstudies.com *Web Site:* www.socialstudies.com, pg 1302, 1321

Martin Sokolinsky, 60 Pineapple St, Unit 1-F, Brooklyn, NY 11201 *Tel:* 718-643-2747 *E-mail:* cuddys1@verizon.net, pg 1404

Solar-Screen Co Inc, 53-11 105 St, Corona, NY 11368 *Tel:* 718-592-8222 *Toll Free Tel:* 800-347-6527 *Toll Free Fax:* 888-271-0891 *E-mail:* solarscreen@prodigy.net *Web Site:* www.solar-screen.com, pg 1272

SOM Publishing, 163 Moon Valley Rd, Windyville, MO 65783 *Tel:* 417-345-8411 *Fax:* 417-345-6668 *E-mail:* som@som.org; dreams@dreamschool.org *Web Site:* www.som.org; www.dreamschool.org, pg 1321

Sony DADC US Inc, 1800 N Fruitridge Ave, Terre Haute, IN 47804 *Tel:* 818-462-8100 *E-mail:* sales@sonydadc.com *Web Site:* www.sonydadc.com, pg 1376

Sony Electronics Inc, 16535 Via Esprillo, San Diego, CA 92127 *Tel:* 858-942-2400 *E-mail:* selpr@sony.com *Web Site:* www.sony.com/all-electronics, pg 1376

The Sound Lab Inc, 3355 Bee Cave Rd, Bldg 7, Suite 701, Austin, TX 78746 *Tel:* 512-476-2122 *Fax:* 512-476-2127 *E-mail:* info@thesoundlabinc.com *Web Site:* www.thesoundlabinc.com, pg 1376

Southeastern Book Co, 2001 SW 31 Ave, Pembroke Park, FL 33009 *Tel:* 954-985-9400 *Toll Free Tel:* 800-223-3251 *Fax:* 954-987-2200 *E-mail:* staff@sebcobooks.com *Web Site:* www.sebcobooks.com, pg 1321

Southeastern Printing Co, 3601 SE Dixie Hwy, Stuart, FL 34997 *Tel:* 772-287-2141 *Toll Free Tel:* 800-226-8221 *Fax:* 772-288-3988 *E-mail:* sales@seprint.com *Web Site:* www.seprint.com, pg 1231, 1260, 1272, 1283

Southern California Focus, 1720 Oak St, Santa Monica, CA 90405 *Tel:* 310-452-3918 *Web Site:* www.californiafocus.net, pg 1191

Southern Territory Associates, 4508 64 St, Lubbock, TX 79414 *E-mail:* sta77@suddenlink.net *Web Site:* www.southernterritory.com, pg 1302

Southern Tier News Company, Inc, 353 Upper Oakwood Ave, Elmira Heights, NY 14903 *Tel:* 607-734-7108 *Toll Free Tel:* 888-287-4786 *Fax:* 607-734-6825 *Web Site:* www.southerntiernews.com, pg 1321

Southern Wisconsin News Co, 58 Artisan Dr, Edgerton, WI 53534 *Tel:* 608-884-2600 *Fax:* 608-884-2636 *Web Site:* www.southernwisconsinnews.com, pg 1321

Southwest Book Co, 13003 Murphy Rd, Suite H1, Stafford, TX 77477-3934 *Tel:* 281-498-2603 *Fax:* 281-498-7566, pg 1303

Bruce E Southworth Reviews, 1621 Lafond Ave, St Paul, MN 55104-2212 *Tel:* 651-808-1099 *E-mail:* mnbookcritic@yahoo.com, pg 1126

The Souza Agency Inc, PO Box 128, Annapolis, MD 21401-0128 *Tel:* 410-573-1300 *Fax:* 410-573-1305 *E-mail:* info@souza.com *Web Site:* www.souza.com, pg 1100

Sovfoto/Eastfoto Inc, 263 W 20 St, Suite 3, New York, NY 10011 *Tel:* 212-727-8170 *Fax:* 212-727-8228 *E-mail:* info@sovfoto.com; research@sovfoto.com *Web Site:* www.sovfoto.com, pg 1430

Spanish/English Translation & Interpreting Services, 5704 SW 86 Dr, Gainesville, FL 32608-8536 *Tel:* 352-215-7200 *Web Site:* www.afn.org/~vanessa, pg 1404

Special Libraries Association (SLA), 7918 Jones Branch Dr, Suite 300, McLean, VA 22102 *Tel:* 703-647-4900 *Fax:* 703-506-3266 *E-mail:* info@sla.org; sla@sla.org *Web Site:* www.sla.org, pg 1120

Specialist Marketing Services Inc, 777 Terrace Ave, Suite 401, Hasbrouck Heights, NJ 07604 *Tel:* 201-865-5800 *E-mail:* info@sms-inc.com *Web Site:* www.sms-inc.com, pg 1120

Specialty Finishing Group, 1401 Kirk St, Elk Grove Village, IL 60007 *Tel:* 847-290-0110 *Fax:* 847-290-9404 *Web Site:* www.sfgrp.com, pg 1260

Specialty Product Technologies (SPT), 2100 W Broad St, Elizabethtown, NC 28337 *Tel:* 910-862-2511 *Toll Free Tel:* 800-390-6405 *Fax:* 910-879-5486 *Toll Free Fax:* 800-476-5463 *E-mail:* customer.service@sptech.com *Web Site:* www.specialtyproducttechnologies.com, pg 1283

Spectrum PrintGroup Inc, 1535 Farmer's Lane, Suite 254, Santa Rosa, CA 95405 *Tel:* 707-542-6044 *Toll Free Tel:* 888-340-6049 *Fax:* 707-542-6045 *E-mail:* sales@spectrumprintgroup.com *Web Site:* www.spectrumprintgroup.com, pg 1214, 1260, 1272

Spicers Paper, 12310 E Slauson Ave, Santa Fe Springs, CA 90670 *Toll Free Tel:* 800-774-2377 *Fax:* 562-693-8339 *Web Site:* www.spicers.com, pg 1272

Spiral Binding LLC, One Maltese Dr, Totowa, NJ 07511 *Tel:* 973-256-0666 *Toll Free Tel:* 800-631-3572 *Fax:* 973-256-5981 *E-mail:* customerservice@spiralbinding.com; international@spiralbinding.com (outside US) *Web Site:* spiralbinding.com, pg 1260

Spraymation Inc, 4180 NW Tenth Ave, Fort Lauderdale, FL 33309 *Tel:* 954-484-9700 *Toll Free Tel:* 800-327-4985 *Fax:* 954-301-0842 *E-mail:* orders@spraymation.com *Web Site:* www.spraymation.com, pg 1283

Spring Arbor Distributors Inc, One Ingram Blvd, La Vergne, TN 37086-1986 *Toll Free Tel:* 800-395-4340 *Toll Free Fax:* 800-876-0186 *E-mail:* customerservice@ingramcontent.com *Web Site:* www.ingramcontent.com, pg 1283, 1303, 1322

Springdale Bindery LLC, 11411 Landan Lane, Cincinnati, OH 45246 *Tel:* 513-772-8500 *E-mail:* info@springdalebindery.com *Web Site:* www.springdalebindery.com, pg 1260

Barbara Spurll Illustration, 160 Browning Ave, Toronto, ON M4K 1W5, Canada *Tel:* 416-594-6594 *Toll Free Tel:* 800-989-3123 *Web Site:* www.barbaraspurll.com, pg 1231

Square Two Design Inc, 2325 Third St, Suite 305, San Francisco, CA 94107 *Tel:* 415-437-3888 *E-mail:* info@square2.com *Web Site:* www.square2.com, pg 1231, 1376, 1417

SSPR LLC, One Northfield Plaza, Suite 400, Northfield, IL 60093 *Toll Free Tel:* 800-287-2279 *Web Site:* www.sspr.com, pg 1113

Tom Stack & Associates Inc, 7135 N Outrigger Terr, Citrus Springs, FL 34433 *Tel:* 305-852-5520 *E-mail:* tomstack@earthlink.net *Web Site:* www.tomstackassociates.photoshelter.com, pg 1430

Standard Finishing Systems, 10 Connector Rd, Andover, MA 01810 *Tel:* 978-470-1920 *Toll Free Tel:* 877-404-4460 *Fax:* 978-470-0819 *E-mail:* marketing@sdmc.com *Web Site:* www.sdmc.com, pg 1283

Staplex® Electric Stapler Division, 777 Fifth Ave, Brooklyn, NY 11232-1626 *Tel:* 718-768-3333 *Toll Free Tel:* 800-221-0822 *Fax:* 718-965-0750 *E-mail:* info@staplex.com *Web Site:* www.staplex.com, pg 1283

Star Micronics America Inc, 65 Clyde Rd, Suite G, Somerset, NJ 08873-3485 *Tel:* 848-216-3300 (sales) *Toll Free Tel:* 800-782-7636 *Fax:* 848-216-3222 (sales) *E-mail:* sales@starmicronics.com *Web Site:* www.starmicronics.com, pg 1376

StarGroup International Inc, 1194 Old Dixie Hwy, Suite 201, West Palm Beach, FL 33413 *Tel:* 561-547-0667 *E-mail:* info@stargroupinternational.com *Web Site:* stargroupinternational.com, pg 1113

Jane Starr Literary Scouts, 1350 Avenue of the Americas, Suite 1205, New York, NY 10019 *Tel:* 212-421-0777 *E-mail:* jane@janestarr.com, pg 1351

Steeleworks, PO Box 4002, Philadelphia, PA 19118 *Tel:* 215-247-4619 *Web Site:* www.sarasteele.com, pg 1417

Stephenson Printing, 5731 General Washington Dr, Alexandria, VA 22312 *Tel:* 703-642-9000 *Toll Free Tel:* 800-336-4637 *Fax:* 703-354-0384 *Web Site:* www.stephensonprinting.com, pg 1260

Sterling Fulfillment, 100 Quentin Roosevelt Blvd, Suite 205, Garden City, NY 11530 *Tel:* 516-758-2000 *Web Site:* sterlingfulfillment.com, pg 1116

Sterling Pierce Co Inc, 395 Atlantic Ave, East Rockaway, NY 11518 *Tel:* 516-593-1170 *Fax:* 516-593-1401 *Web Site:* www.sterlingpierce.com, pg 1214, 1260

Matt Stewart, 71 Faunce Dr, Providence, RI 02906 *Tel:* 401-274-2149 *Web Site:* www.whitegatefeatures.com, pg 1126

Still Media, PO Box 3362, Santa Barbara, CA 93130 *E-mail:* info@jeffreyaaronson.com *Web Site:* www.stillmedia.com, pg 1430

Stilo Corp, 1900 City Park Dr, Suite 504, Ottawa, ON K1J 1A3, Canada *Tel:* 613-745-4242 *Fax:* 613-745-5560 *E-mail:* contact@stilo.com *Web Site:* www.stilo.com, pg 1377

Stock Montage Inc, 1817 N Mulligan Ave, Chicago, IL 60639, pg 1430

Stoesser Register Systems, 610 Whitetail Blvd, River Falls, WI 54022 *Tel:* 715-425-1900 *Toll Free Tel:* 888-407-4808 *Fax:* 715-425-1901 *E-mail:* info@nela-usa.com *Web Site:* www.nela-usa.com, pg 1283

Stonesong, 270 W 39 St, Suite 201, New York, NY 10018 *Tel:* 212-929-4600 *E-mail:* editors@stonesong.com *Web Site:* www.stonesong.com, pg 1357

StoraEnso North American Sales Inc, Canterbury Green, 201 Broad St, Stamford, CT 06901 *Tel:* 203-541-5100 *Fax:* 203-353-1143 *Web Site:* www.storaenso.com, pg 1272

Story Monsters LLC, 4696 W Tyson St, Chandler, AZ 85226-2903 *Tel:* 480-940-8182 *Fax:* 480-940-8787 *Web Site:* www.StoryMonsters.com; www.StoryMonstersInk.com; www.AuthorBookings.com; www.partnershippublishing.com; www.StoryMonstersBookAwards.com, pg 1113

Story Monsters LLC, 4696 W Tyson St, Chandler, AZ 85226-2903 *Tel:* 480-940-8182 *Fax:* 480-940-8787 *Web Site:* www.StoryMonsters.com; www.StoryMonstersInk.com; www.AuthorBookings.com; www.StoryMonstersBookAwards.com, pg 1351

Story Monsters LLC, 4696 W Tyson St, Chandler, AZ 85226-2903 *Tel:* 480-940-8182 *Fax:* 480-940-8787 *Web Site:* www.StoryMonsters.com, pg 1358

Story Monsters LLC, 4696 W Tyson St, Chandler, AZ 85226-2903 *Tel:* 480-940-8182 *Fax:* 480-940-8787 *Web Site:* www.StoryMonsters.com; www.StoryMonstersInk.com; www.StudioStoryMonster.com, pg 1377

Story Monsters LLC, 4696 W Tyson St, Chandler, AZ 85226-2903 *Tel:* 480-940-8182 *Fax:* 480-940-8787 *Web Site:* www.StoryMonsters.com, pg 1417

Streem Communications LLC, 4949 Harrison Ave, Rockford, IL 61107 *Tel:* 815-282-7695 *Toll Free Tel:* 800-325-7732 *Fax:* 815-639-8931 *Toll Free Fax:* 888-435-2348 *E-mail:* streemsales@cleo.com; sales@cleo.com *Web Site:* www.streem.net, pg 1118

Strictly Spanish Translations LLC, Milford, OH 45150 *E-mail:* info@strictlyspanish.com; quotes@strictlyspanish.com *Web Site:* www.strictlyspanish.com, pg 1404

Hope Strong, 71 Faunce Dr, Providence, RI 02906 *Tel:* 401-274-2149 *Web Site:* www.whitegatefeatures.com, pg 1126

Studio E Book Production, PO Box 20005, Santa Barbara, CA 93120-0005 *Tel:* 805-683-6202 *Fax:* 805-683-6202 *E-mail:* queries@studio-e-books.com *Web Site:* www.studio-e-books.com, pg 1417

The Studley Press Inc, 151 E Housatonic St, Dalton, MA 01226 *Tel:* 413-684-0441 *Toll Free Tel:* 877-684-0441 *Fax:* 413-684-0220 *Web Site:* thestudleypress.com, pg 1260, 1272

Styled Packaging LLC, PO Box 30299, Philadelphia, PA 19103-8299 *Tel:* 610-529-4122 *Fax:* 610-520-9662 *Web Site:* www.taylorbox.com, pg 1260, 1272, 1283, 1335, 1337

COMPANY INDEX

Stylus Publishing LLC, 22883 Quicksilver Dr, Sterling, VA 20166-2019 *Tel:* 703-661-1504 (edit & sales); 703-661-1581 (orders & cust serv); 703-996-1036 *Toll Free Tel:* 800-232-0223 (orders & cust serv) *Fax:* 703-661-1547; 703-661-1501 (orders & cust serv) *E-mail:* stylusinfo@styluspub.com; stylusmail@styluspub.com (orders & cust serv) *Web Site:* styluspub.com, pg 1303

SumTotal Systems LLC, 2850 NW 43 St, Suite 150, Gainesville, FL 32606 *Tel:* 352-264-2800 *Toll Free Tel:* 866-933-1416 *Fax:* 352-374-2257 *E-mail:* customersupport@sumtotalsystems.com *Web Site:* www.sumtotalsystems.com, pg 1377

Sun Chemical Corp, 35 Waterview Blvd, Parsippany, NJ 07054-1285 *Tel:* 973-404-6000 *E-mail:* globalmarketing@sunchemical.com *Web Site:* www.sunchemical.com, pg 1272

Sun Graphics LLC, 1818 Broadway, Parsons, KS 67357 *Toll Free Tel:* 800-835-0588 *Fax:* 620-421-2089 *E-mail:* info@sun-graphics.com *Web Site:* www.sun-graphics.com, pg 1214, 1231, 1260

Sunbelt Publications Inc, 664 Marsat Ct, Suite A, Chula Vista, CA 91911 *Tel:* 619-258-4911 *Toll Free Tel:* 800-626-6579 (cust serv) *Fax:* 619-258-4916 *E-mail:* info@sunbeltpub.com; service@sunbeltpub.com *Web Site:* sunbeltpublications.com, pg 1322

Sunday San Francisco Chronicle Book Review, 901 Mission St, San Francisco, CA 94103 *Tel:* 415-777-1111 *Toll Free Tel:* 866-732-4766 *Web Site:* www.sfgate.com, pg 1137

Superior Printing Ink Co Inc, 100 North St, Teterboro, NJ 07608 *Tel:* 201-478-5600 *Fax:* 201-478-5650 *Web Site:* www.superiorink.com, pg 1272

Superstock, 2401 S Ervay St, Suite 206, Dallas, TX 75215 *Tel:* 904-565-0066 *Toll Free Tel:* 866-236-0087 *E-mail:* yourfriends@superstock.com *Web Site:* www.superstock.com, pg 1430

The Supreme Co, 1909 Lagneaux Rd, Lafayette, LA 70506 *Tel:* 337-453-1028 *Toll Free Tel:* 888-600-4180 *E-mail:* information@supremebooks.com *Web Site:* www.supremebooks.com, pg 1322

Suspension Feeder, 631 E Washington St, St Henry, OH 45883 *Tel:* 419-763-1377 *Toll Free Fax:* 888-210-9654 *Web Site:* www.suspensionfeeder.com, pg 1283

Margaret Swaine, 2 Hawthorn Gardens, Unit 4, Toronto, ON M4W 1P3, Canada *Tel:* 416-961-5328 *E-mail:* m.swaine@rogers.com *Web Site:* www.margaretswaine.com, pg 1126

Swan Packaging Fulfillment Inc, 415 Hamburg Tpke, Wayne, NJ 07470 *Tel:* 973-790-0990 *Fax:* 973-790-0216 *Web Site:* www.swanpackaging.com, pg 1116, 1335, 1337

Swedenborg Foundation, 320 N Church St, West Chester, PA 19380 *Tel:* 610-430-3222 *Toll Free Tel:* 800-355-3222 (cust service) *Fax:* 610-430-7982 *E-mail:* info@swedenborg.com *Web Site:* swedenborg.com, pg 1322

Sweetgrass Books, 2750 Broadway Ave, Helena, MT 59602 *Tel:* 406-422-1255 *Toll Free Tel:* 800-821-3874 *Web Site:* sweetgrassbooks.com, pg 1358

John S Swift Co Inc, 999 Commerce Ct, Buffalo Grove, IL 60089 *Tel:* 847-465-3300 *Fax:* 847-465-3309 *Web Site:* www.johnswiftprint.com, pg 1214, 1231, 1260

Swordsmith Productions, PO Box 242, Pomfret, CT 06258 *Tel:* 860-208-4829 *E-mail:* information@swordsmith.com *Web Site:* www.swordsmith.com, pg 1231

Symbology Inc, 7351 Kirkwood Lane N, Suite 126, Maple Grove, MN 55369 *Tel:* 763-315-8080 *Toll Free Tel:* 800-328-2612 *Fax:* 763-315-8088 *E-mail:* clientservices@symbology.com; sales@symbology.com *Web Site:* www.symbology.com, pg 1232

Symmetry Creative Production, 1300 S Grove Ave, Suite 103, Barrington, IL 60010 *Tel:* 847-382-8750 *E-mail:* information@symmetrycp.com *Web Site:* www.symmetrycp.com, pg 1232

Szablya Consultants Inc, 5300 94 Ave NE, Apt 327, Seattle, WA 98105 *Tel:* 206-465-0482 (cell) *Web Site:* www.helenmszablya.com, pg 1405

T C Public Relations, One N La Salle St, Suite 600, Chicago, IL 60602 *Tel:* 312-422-1333 *Web Site:* www.tcpr.net, pg 1113

TAB (grades 6 & up), 557 Broadway, New York, NY 10012 *Tel:* 212-343-6100; 573-632-1632 (PR, US territories, US military bases) *Toll Free Tel:* 800-541-1097 (US) *Toll Free Fax:* 800-223-4011 *E-mail:* bookclubs@scholastic.com *Web Site:* clubs.scholastic.com, pg 1143

Taconic Wire, 250 Totoket Rd, North Branford, CT 06471 *Tel:* 203-484-2863 *Toll Free Tel:* 800-253-1450 *Fax:* 203-484-2865 *E-mail:* sales@taconicwire.com; taconicwiresales@gmail.com *Web Site:* www.taconicwire.com, pg 1283

Talas, 330 Morgan Ave, Brooklyn, NY 11211 *Tel:* 212-219-0770 *E-mail:* info@talasonline.com; support@talasonline.com *Web Site:* www.talasonline.com, pg 1272, 1322

Tamron USA Inc, 10 Austin Blvd, Commack, NY 11725 *Tel:* 631-858-8400 *Toll Free Tel:* 800-827-8880 *Fax:* 631-543-5666; 631-858-8462 (cust serv) *E-mail:* custserv@tamron.com *Web Site:* www.tamron-usa.com, pg 1377

Johannes Tan, 16682 SW Henderson Ct, Beaverton, OR 97007 *Tel:* 503-642-2586 *Fax:* 503-642-2586 *E-mail:* jt@indotransnet.com *Web Site:* www.indotransnet.com, pg 1405

Tandem Literary, 28 Clinton Rd, Glen Ridge, NJ 07028 *Tel:* 212-629-1990 *Fax:* 212-629-1990 *Web Site:* tandemliterary.com, pg 1113

Tanenbaum International Literary Agency Ltd (TILA), 1035 Fifth Ave, Suite 15D, New York, NY 10028 *Tel:* 212-371-4120 *Fax:* 212-988-0457 *E-mail:* hello@tanenbauminternational.com *Web Site:* tanenbauminternational.com, pg 1351

Todd Tarbox, 330 Oakhurst Lane, Colorado Springs, CO 80906 *Tel:* 719-579-9110 *E-mail:* t_tarbox@msn.com, pg 1425

Tatung Co of America Inc, 2850 El Presidio St, Long Beach, CA 90810 *Tel:* 310-637-2105 *E-mail:* service@tatungusa.com *Web Site:* www.tatungusa.com, pg 1377

Chip Taylor Communications, LLC, 2 East View Dr, Derry, NH 03038 *Tel:* 603-434-9262 *Toll Free Tel:* 800-876-CHIP (876-2447) *Fax:* 603-425-1784 *E-mail:* info@chiptaylor.com *Web Site:* www.chiptaylor.com, pg 1303, 1377

Taylor Communications Inc, 1725 Roe Crest Dr, North Mankato, MN 56003 *Toll Free Tel:* 866-541-0937 *Web Site:* www.taylorcommunications.com, pg 1261, 1377

TEACH Services Inc, 11 Quartermaster Circle, Fort Oglethorpe, GA 30742-3886 *Tel:* 706-504-9192 *Toll Free Tel:* 800-367-1844 (sales) *Toll Free Fax:* 866-757-6023 *E-mail:* sales@teachservices.com; info@teachservices.com *Web Site:* www.teachservices.com, pg 1322, 1377

Teacher's Discovery®, 2741 Paldan Dr, Auburn Hills, MI 48326 *Toll Free Tel:* 800-TEACHER (832-2437) *Toll Free Fax:* 800-287-4509 *E-mail:* help@teachersdiscovery.com; orders@teachersdiscovery.com *Web Site:* www.teachersdiscovery.com, pg 1303, 1322

Tecnau Inc, 4 Suburban Park Dr, Billerica, MA 01821 *Tel:* 978-608-0500 *Fax:* 978-608-0558 *E-mail:* info.us@tecnau.com *Web Site:* www.tecnau.com, pg 1283

TEENS (grades 7 & up), 557 Broadway, New York, NY 10012 *Tel:* 212-343-6100; 573-632-1632 (PR, US territories, US military bases) *Toll Free Tel:* 800-541-1097 (US) *Toll Free Fax:* 800-223-4011 *E-mail:* bookclubs@scholastic.com *Web Site:* clubs.scholastic.com, pg 1143

Teledyne DALSA, 605 McMurray Rd, Waterloo, ON N2V 2E9, Canada *Tel:* 519-886-6000 *Toll Free Tel:* 800-361-4914 *Web Site:* www.teledynedalsa.com, pg 1377

Joan Wagner Teller PhD, Translator, 11625 SE Boise St, Unit 106, Portland, OR 97266-2281 *Tel:* 503-760-1320 *E-mail:* j-teller-11@alumni.uchicago.edu *Web Site:* joantellertranslations.webs.com, pg 1405

Teneo Linguistics Co LLC, 3010 W Parkrow Dr, Pampego, TX 76013 *Tel:* 817-441-9974 *Fax:* 817-953-6424 *E-mail:* info@tlctranslation.com *Web Site:* www.tlctranslation.com, pg 1405

Tennessee Book Co, 1550 Heil Quaker Blvd, La Vergne, TN 37086 *Tel:* 615-793-5040 *Toll Free Tel:* 800-456-0418 *Fax:* 615-213-9545 *Web Site:* www.tennesseebook.com, pg 1322

Terry & Read LLC, 4471 Dean Martin Dr, The Martin 3302, Las Vegas, NV 89103 *Tel:* 510-813-9854 *Toll Free Fax:* 866-214-4762, pg 1303

Texas Art Supply, 2001 Montrose Blvd, Houston, TX 77006 *Tel:* 713-526-5221 *E-mail:* customerservice@texasart.com *Web Site:* www.texasart.com, pg 1322

Texas Book Co, 8501 Technology Circle, Greenville, TX 75402 *Tel:* 903-455-6969 *Toll Free Tel:* 800-527-1016 *E-mail:* customerservice@texasbook.com *Web Site:* www.texasbook.com, pg 1322

Texas Bookman, 2700 Lone Star Dr, Dallas, TX 75212 *Tel:* 214-678-6680 *Toll Free Tel:* 800-566-2665 *Fax:* 214-678-6699 *E-mail:* orders@texasbookman.com *Web Site:* www.texasbookman.com, pg 1322

Texas Graphic Resource Inc, 1234 Round Table Dr, Dallas, TX 75247 *Tel:* 214-630-2800 *Fax:* 214-630-0713 *E-mail:* info@texasgraphics.com *Web Site:* www.texasgraphics.com, pg 1232

TeXnology Inc, 57 Longwood Ave, Brookline, MA 02446 *Tel:* 617-738-8029 *Web Site:* www.texnology.com, pg 1377

Theatre Journal, 2715 N Charles St, Baltimore, MD 21218-4363 *Tel:* 410-516-6987 (journal orders outside US & CN) *Toll Free Tel:* 800-548-1784 (journal orders) *Fax:* 410-578-2865 (journal orders) *E-mail:* tjbooks@athe.org; jrnlcirc@jh.edu (journal orders) *Web Site:* www.press.jhu.edu/journals/theatre-journal, pg 1137

Thinkers' Press Inc, 1524 Le Claire St, Davenport, IA 52803 *Tel:* 563-271-6657 *E-mail:* info@chessbutler.com *Web Site:* www.thinkerspressinc.com, pg 1329

3rd Grade Book Club, 557 Broadway, New York, NY 10012 *Tel:* 212-343-6100; 573-632-1632 (PR, US territories, US military bases) *Toll Free Tel:* 800-541-1097 (US) *Toll Free Fax:* 800-223-4011 *E-mail:* bookclubs@scholastic.com *Web Site:* clubs.scholastic.com, pg 1143

Thistle Printing Ltd, 35 Mobile Dr, Toronto, ON M4A 2P6, Canada *Tel:* 416-288-1288 *Fax:* 416-288-0737 *E-mail:* sales@thistleprinting.com *Web Site:* www.thistleprinting.com, pg 1232, 1261, 1377

The Thomas Tape & Supply Co Inc, 1713 Sheridan Ave, Springfield, OH 45505 *Tel:* 937-325-6414 *Fax:* 937-325-2850 *Web Site:* www.thomastape.com, pg 1272

Thomson Reuters, 3 Times Sq, New York, NY 10036 *Tel:* 646-223-4000; 646-223-6100 (edit); 646-223-6000 (newsroom) *Web Site:* www.thomsonreuters.com, pg 1191

Thomson Reuters, Union Bank Bldg, 50 California St, San Francisco, CA 94111 *Tel:* 424-434-7000 *E-mail:* editorial.booking@tr.com *Web Site:* www.thomsonreuters.com, pg 1377

Three D Graphics Inc, 11340 W Olympic Blvd, Suite 352, Los Angeles, CA 90064 *Tel:* 310-231-3330 *Toll Free Tel:* 800-913-0008 *Fax:* 310-231-3303 *E-mail:* info@threedgraphics.com; orders@threedgraphics.com; sales@threedgraphics.com *Web Site:* www.threedgraphics.com, pg 1377

3M Touch Systems Inc, 501 Griffin Brook Park Dr, Methuen, MA 01844 *Tel:* 978-659-9000 *Web Site:* www.3m.com/3m/en_us/touch-systems-us, pg 1377

Stephen Tiano, 56 Tyler Dr, Riverhead, NY 11901 *Tel:* 631-284-3842; 631-764-2487 (cell) *Fax:* 631-284-3842 *E-mail:* stephen@stephentianobookdesign.com *Web Site:* stephentianobookdesign.com, pg 1417

Times Citizen Communication Inc, 406 Stevens St, Iowa Falls, IA 50126 *Tel:* 641-648-2521 *Toll Free Tel:* 800-798-2691 *Fax:* 641-648-4765 *E-mail:* tcc@iafalls.com *Web Site:* timescitizen.com, pg 1232

Times Printing LLC, 100 Industrial Dr, Random Lake, WI 53075 *Tel:* 920-994-4396 *Toll Free Tel:* 800-236-4396 (sales) *E-mail:* info@kappapma.com *Web Site:* www.kappapma.com, pg 1232, 1261, 1272, 1283

Timsons Inc, 385 Crossen Ave, Elk Grove Village, IL 60007 *Tel:* 847-884-8611 *Fax:* 847-884-8676 *E-mail:* sales@timsonsinc.com *Web Site:* www.timsonsinc.com, pg 1283

TNG, 3320 S Service Rd, Burlington, ON L7N 3M6, Canada *Toll Free Tel:* 800-201-8127 *Toll Free Fax:* 877-664-9732 *E-mail:* cs@tng.com *Web Site:* www.tng.com, pg 1322

To Press & Beyond, 7507 Summersun Dr, Browns Summit, NC 27214 *Tel:* 805-570-8275 *E-mail:* info@topressandbeyond.com *Web Site:* www.topressandbeyond.com, pg 1113, 1351, 1358

Tobias Associates Inc, 50 Industrial Dr, Ivyland, PA 18974 *Tel:* 215-322-1500 *Toll Free Tel:* 800-877-3367 *Fax:* 215-322-1504 *E-mail:* sales@tobiasinc.com *Web Site:* www.densitometer.com, pg 1283

Tompkins Printing Equipment Co, 5050 N Rose St, Schiller Park, IL 60176 *Tel:* 847-671-5050 *Fax:* 847-671-5538 *E-mail:* sales@tompkins.com *Web Site:* www.tompkins.com, pg 1283

Toof American Digital, 4222 Pilot Dr, Memphis, TN 38118 *Tel:* 901-274-3632 *Toll Free Tel:* 800-722-4772 *Web Site:* www.toofamericandigital.com, pg 1214, 1232, 1261, 1272

TOP Engraving, 106 Windsor Way, Berkeley Heights, NJ 07922 *Tel:* 212-239-9170; 201-223-4800, pg 1261

Total Printing Systems, 201 S Gregory Dr, Newton, IL 62448 *Tel:* 618-783-2978 *Toll Free Tel:* 800-465-5200 *Fax:* 618-783-8407 *E-mail:* sales@tps1.com *Web Site:* www.tps1.com, pg 1261

TotalWorks™ Inc, 420 W Huron St, Chicago, IL 60654 *Tel:* 773-489-4313 *E-mail:* production@totalworks.net *Web Site:* www.totalworks.net, pg 1232, 1261

Townsend Communications Inc, 20 E Gregory Blvd, Kansas City, MO 64114 *Tel:* 816-361-0616 *Web Site:* www.townsendcommunications.com; www.townsendprint.com, pg 1232, 1261, 1284

Trade Commission in Miami, Embassy of Spain in the US, 2655 Le Juene Rd, Suite 1114, Miami, FL 33134 *Tel:* 305-446-4387 *Fax:* 305-446-2602 *E-mail:* info@newspanishbooks.com *Web Site:* www.newspanishbooks.us, pg 1146

Transimpex Translators, Interpreters, Editors, Consultants Inc, 2300 Main St, 9th fl, Kansas City, MO 64108 *Tel:* 816-561-3777 *Fax:* 816-561-5515 *E-mail:* translations@transimpex.com *Web Site:* www.transimpex.com, pg 1405

Translations.com, 1250 Broadway, 32nd fl, New York, NY 10001 *Tel:* 212-689-1616 *Fax:* 212-504-8057 *E-mail:* newyork@translations.com; info@translations.com *Web Site:* translations.com, pg 1405

Translingua Associates Inc, 630 Ninth Ave, Suite 708, New York, NY 10036 *Tel:* 212-697-2020 *Fax:* 212-697-2891 *Web Site:* www.translingua.com, pg 1405

Transparent Language Inc, 12 Murphy Dr, Nashua, NH 03062 *Tel:* 603-262-6300 *Toll Free Tel:* 800-567-9619 (cust serv & sales) *E-mail:* info@transparent.com; support@transparent.com (tech support) *Web Site:* www.transparent.com, pg 1377

Treacyfaces Inc, 43 Maltby Ave, West Haven, CT 06516 *Tel:* 203-389-7037 *Web Site:* www.treacyfaces.com, pg 1377

Trend Offset Printing Services, 3791 Catalina St, Los Alamitos, CA 90720 *Tel:* 562-598-2446 *Fax:* 562-493-6840 (sales); 562-430-2373 *E-mail:* salesca@trendoffset.com *Web Site:* www.trendoffset.com, pg 1261

Tri-Fold Books, PO Box 534, King City, ON L7B 1A7, Canada *Tel:* 905-726-0142 *E-mail:* info@trifoldbooks.com *Web Site:* trifoldbooks.com, pg 1303

Tri-Media Integrated Marketing Technologies Inc, 1027 Pelham St, Unit 2, Fonthill, ON L0S 1E0, Canada *E-mail:* think@tri-media.com *Web Site:* tri-media.com, pg 1100

Tribal Print Source, 36146 Pala Temecula Rd, Bldg J, Pala, CA 92059 *Tel:* 760-597-2650 *E-mail:* sales@tribalprintsource.com *Web Site:* www.tribalprintsource.com, pg 1105, 1116, 1261

The Tribune News Service, 160 N Stetson Ave, Chicago, IL 60601 *Tel:* 312-222-4131 *E-mail:* tcanews@trbpub.com *Web Site:* www.mctdirect.com; tribunecontentagency.com/tribune-news-service, pg 1191

Stephen Trimble: Words & Photographs, 70 W Apricot Ave, Salt Lake City, UT 84103 *Tel:* 801-819-2448 *E-mail:* steve@stephentrimble.net *Web Site:* www.stephentrimble.net, pg 1425

Trophy Room Books, PO Box 3041, Agoura, CA 91376 *Tel:* 818-889-2469 *E-mail:* info@trophyroombooks.com *Web Site:* www.trophyroombooks.com, pg 1329

TRUMATCH Inc, PO Box 501, Water Mill, NY 11976-0501 *Tel:* 631-204-9100 *Toll Free Tel:* 800-TRU-9100 (878-9100 US & CN) *E-mail:* info@trumatch.com *Web Site:* www.trumatch.com, pg 1377

TSO General Corp, 79 Emjay Blvd, Brentwood, NY 11717 *Tel:* 631-952-5320 *Fax:* 631-952-5315 *Web Site:* www.tsogeneral.com, pg 1261, 1272

Tukaiz LLC, 2917 N Latoria Lane, Franklin Park, IL 60131 *Tel:* 847-455-1588; 847-288-4968 (sales) *Toll Free Tel:* 800-543-2674 *E-mail:* contacttukaiz@tukaiz.com *Web Site:* www.tukaiz.com, pg 1232, 1261, 1273, 1284

Turtleback Books, 1000 N Second Ave, Logan, IA 51546-0500 *Toll Free Tel:* 800-831-4190 *Toll Free Fax:* 800-543-2745 *E-mail:* turtleback@perfectionlearning.com *Web Site:* turtleback.perfectionlearning.com, pg 1261, 1326

Stan Tusan, 105 Breckinridge Dr, Phoenix, OR 97535 *Tel:* 541-535-6791 *E-mail:* stantoon@charter.net *Web Site:* www.stantoon.com, pg 1417

TWIG One Stop, 10444 White Pinto Ct, Lake Worth, FL 33449 *Tel:* 561-588-0244 *Toll Free Tel:* 855-894-4178 *E-mail:* info@twigonestop.com *Web Site:* www.twigonestop.com, pg 1105

Twin Rivers Paper Co, 82 Bridge Ave, Madawaska, ME 04756 *Tel:* 207-728-3321 *Toll Free Tel:* 800-920-9988 *Fax:* 207-728-8701 *E-mail:* info@twinriverspaper.com *Web Site:* www.twinriverspaper.com, pg 1273

Two Rivers Distribution, an Ingram brand, 1400 Broadway, Suite 520, New York, NY 10018 *Toll Free Tel:* 866-400-5351 *E-mail:* ips@ingramcontent.com (orders, independent bookstores & gift accts) *Web Site:* www.tworiversdistribution.com, pg 1303

Tyler Creative, 1300 S Johnstone Ave, Bartlesville, OK 74003-5624 *Tel:* 918-527-6779 *E-mail:* info@tylercreative.com *Web Site:* tylercreative.com, pg 1417

P Tyrrell Associates, 321 Monica Crescent, Burlington, ON L7N 1Z5, Canada *Tel:* 289-937-6436 *Fax:* 905-639-2640 *E-mail:* pgtyrrell@cogeco.ca, pg 1303

Eric Tyson, 300 W 57 St, 15th fl, New York, NY 10019-5238 *Toll Free Tel:* 800-708-7311 (FL edit) *E-mail:* eric@erictyson.com *Web Site:* www.erictyson.com, pg 1126

Elizabeth Uhlig, 6766 108 St, Suite D-27, Forest Hills, NY 11375 *Tel:* 718-896-4186 *E-mail:* elizabeth.uhlig7@gmail.com *Web Site:* www.marble-house-editions.com, pg 1405

Ulster Linen Co Inc, 383 Moffit Blvd, Islip, NY 11751 *Tel:* 631-859-5244 *Fax:* 631-859-4990 *E-mail:* sales@ulsterlinen.com *Web Site:* www.ulsterlinen.com, pg 1273

Ultimate TechnoGraphics Inc, 480 Blvd St-Laurent, Suite 404, Montreal, QC H2Y 3Y7, Canada *Tel:* 514-938-9050 *E-mail:* customerservice@imposition.com; marketing@imposition.com; sales@imposition.com *Web Site:* www.imposition.com, pg 1378

Ulverscroft Large Print (USA) Inc, 950A Union Rd, Suite 427, West Seneca, NY 14224 *Tel:* 716-674-4270; 905-637-8734 (CN) *Toll Free Tel:* 800-955-9659; 888-860-3365 (CN) *Fax:* 716-674-4195; 905-333-6788 (CN) *E-mail:* sales@ulverscroftusa.com; sales@ulverscroftcanada.com (CN) *Web Site:* www.ulverscroft.com, pg 1303

UniNet Imaging Inc, 3232 W El Segundo Blvd, Hawthorne, CA 90250 *Tel:* 424-675-3300 *Fax:* 424-675-3400 *E-mail:* sales@uninetimaging.com *Web Site:* www.uninetimaging.com, pg 1378

Unisys Corp, 801 Lakeview Dr, Suite 100, Blue Bell, PA 19422 *Tel:* 215-274-2742 *Web Site:* www.unisys.com, pg 1378

UnitechEDI Inc, 220 Winthrop St, Winthrop, MA 02152 *Toll Free Tel:* 800-330-4094 *E-mail:* info@unitechedi.com *Web Site:* www.unitechedi.com, pg 1378

United Library Services Inc, 7140 Fairmount Dr SE, Calgary, AB T2H 0X4, Canada *Tel:* 403-252-4426 *Toll Free Tel:* 888-342-5857 (CN only) *Fax:* 403-258-3426 *Toll Free Fax:* 800-661-2806 (CN only) *E-mail:* info@uls.com *Web Site:* www.uls.com, pg 1323

United Press International (UPI), 1133 19 St NW, Suite 800, Washington, DC 20036 *Tel:* 202-898-8000 *E-mail:* media@upi.com *Web Site:* www.upi.com, pg 1127, 1191

Unitype LLC, 116-A Mockingbird Lane, Lockhart, TX 78644 *Tel:* 512-620-0384 *Toll Free Tel:* 800-697-9186 *E-mail:* info@unitype.com; sales@unitype.com; support@unitype.com *Web Site:* www.unitype.com, pg 1378

Universal Bindery (Sask) Ltd, 516-A Duchess St, Saskatoon, SK S7K 0R1, Canada *Tel:* 306-652-8313 *Toll Free Tel:* 888-JOE-MENU (563-6368) *Fax:* 306-244-2994 *E-mail:* gib@unibindery.com, pg 1105

Universal Bookbindery Inc, 1200 N Colorado, San Antonio, TX 78207 *Tel:* 210-734-9502 *Toll Free Tel:* 800-594-2015 *Fax:* 210-736-0867 *E-mail:* service@universalbookbindery.com *Web Site:* www.universalbookbindery.com, pg 1261

UniversallWilde, 26 Dartmouth St, Westwood, MA 02090 *Tel:* 781-251-2700 *Fax:* 781-251-2613 *Web Site:* www.universalwilde.com, pg 1105, 1116, 1232, 1261

Universe Technical Translation Inc, 9225 Katy Fwy, Suite 400, Houston, TX 77024 *Tel:* 713-827-8800 *Fax:* 713-464-5511 *E-mail:* universe@universe.us *Web Site:* www.universetranslation.com, pg 1405

University Language Services (ULS), 15 Maiden Lane, Suite 308, New York, NY 10038 *Tel:* 212-766-3920 *Toll Free Tel:* 800-419-4601 *E-mail:* clientservices@universitylanguage.com *Web Site:* www.universitylanguage.com, pg 1405

University of Southern California - Special Collections, USC Libraries, Doheny Memorial Library, Rm 206, Los Angeles, CA 90089-0189 *Tel:* 213-740-5900 *Fax:* 213-740-2343 *E-mail:* specol@usc.edu *Web Site:* libraries.usc.edu/locations/special-collections, pg 1431

University of Toronto Press Guidance Centre, 5201 Dufferin St, Toronto, ON M3H 5T8, Canada *Tel:* 416-667-7791 *Toll Free Tel:* 800-565-9523 *Fax:* 416-667-7832 *Toll Free Fax:* 800-221-9985 *E-mail:* utpbooks@utpress.utoronto.ca *Web Site:* www.utpguidancecentre.com, pg 1303

University Products Inc, 517 Main St, Holyoke, MA 01040 *Tel:* 413-532-3372 *Toll Free Tel:* 800-628-1912 (orders) *Fax:* 413-533-4743 *Toll Free Fax:* 800-532-9281 *E-mail:* info@universityproducts.com *Web Site:* www.universityproducts.com, pg 1273

COMPANY INDEX

Alvis Upitis Photography, Austin, TX 78701 *Tel:* 808-937-3173 (cell) *Web Site:* www.alvisupitis.com, pg 1425

UPS Supply Chain Solutions, 12380 Morris Rd, Alpharetta, GA 30005 *Tel:* 913-693-6151 (outside US & CN) *Toll Free Tel:* 800-742-5727 (US & CN) *Web Site:* www.ups.com/us/en/supplychain/Home.page, pg 1335

Upstart Books™, PO Box 7488, Madison, WI 53707 *Tel:* 608-241-1201 *Toll Free Tel:* 800-356-1200 (orders); 800-962-4463 (cust serv) *Toll Free Fax:* 800-245-1329 (orders) *E-mail:* custserv@demco.com; order@demco.com *Web Site:* www.demco.com/upstart, pg 1146, 1323

US Naval Institute Photo Archive, 291 Wood Rd, Annapolis, MD 21402 *Tel:* 410-295-1022 *Fax:* 410-295-1049 *E-mail:* photoservice@usni.org; photoarchive@usni.org; research@usni.org *Web Site:* www.usni.org, pg 1431

US Postal Service International Business Shipping, 475 L'Enfant Plaza SW, Washington, DC 20260 *Web Site:* www.usps.com/business/international-shipping.htm, pg 1335

USCIB International Bookstore, 1212 Avenue of the Americas, 21st fl, New York, NY 10036 *Tel:* 212-703-5066 *Fax:* 212-944-0012 *E-mail:* bookstore@uscib.org *Web Site:* store.internationaltradebooks.org, pg 1304

Liliana Valenzuela, 1103 Maufrais St, Austin, TX 78703 *Tel:* 512-804-8141 *E-mail:* aguafuegolv@gmail.com *Web Site:* www.lilianavalenzuela.com, pg 1405

Valid USA, 1011 Warrenville Rd, Suite 450, Lisle, IL 60532 *Tel:* 630-852-8200 *Toll Free Tel:* 800-773-1588 (cust serv); 855-825-4387 (sales) *Web Site:* www.valid.com, pg 1118

Valley News Co, 1305 Stadium Rd, Mankato, MN 56001 *Tel:* 507-345-4819 *Fax:* 507-345-6793 *Web Site:* www.valleynewscompany.com, pg 1323

Value Added Resources, 7900 Rockville Rd, Indianapolis, IN 46214 *Tel:* 317-899-1000 *E-mail:* info@valueaddedres.com *Web Site:* www.valueaddedres.com, pg 1335

VanDam Inc, The VanDam Bldg, 121 W 27 St, New York, NY 10001 *Tel:* 917-297-5445 *E-mail:* info@vandam.com *Web Site:* www.vandam.com, pg 1358

Vectorworks Inc, 7150 Riverwood Dr, Columbia, MD 21046 *Tel:* 410-290-5114 *Toll Free Tel:* 888-646-4223 (sales) *Fax:* 410-290-7266 *E-mail:* sales@vectorworks.net *Web Site:* www.vectorworks.net, pg 1378

Vedanta Book Center, 14630 S Lemont Rd, Homer Glen, IL 60491 *Tel:* 708-301-9062 *Fax:* 708-301-9063 *E-mail:* info@chicagovedanta.org *Web Site:* www.vedantabooks.com, pg 1323, 1329

Veritiv™ Corporation, 1000 Abernathy Rd, Bldg 400, Suite 1700, Atlanta, GA 30328 *Toll Free Tel:* 844-VERITIV (837-4848); 866-714-8303 (packaging cust serv); 866-714-8306 (print cust serv) *E-mail:* contactus@veritivcorp.com; media@veritivcorp.com *Web Site:* www.veritivcorp.com, pg 1273

VeronaLibri, 124 Willowbrook Ave, Stamford, CT 06902 *Tel:* 203-614-8335 *Web Site:* www.veronalibri.com, pg 1261

Versa Press Inc, 1465 Spring Bay Rd, East Peoria, IL 61611-9788 *Tel:* 309-822-8272 *Toll Free Tel:* 800-447-7829 *Fax:* 309-822-8141 *Web Site:* www.versapress.com, pg 1214, 1232, 1262, 1273

Verso Advertising Inc, 79 Madison Ave, 8th fl, New York, NY 10016 *Tel:* 212-292-2990 *Web Site:* www.versoadvertising.com, pg 1100

ViaTech Publishing Solutions Inc, 11935 N Stemmons Fwy, Dallas, TX 75234 *Tel:* 214-827-8151 *E-mail:* marketing@viatechpub.com *Web Site:* www.viatech.io, pg 1232, 1262

Vicks Lithograph & Printing Corp, 5166 Commercial Dr, Yorkville, NY 13495 *Tel:* 315-736-9344 *E-mail:* info@vicks.biz *Web Site:* www.vicks.biz, pg 1214, 1262

Victory Productions Inc, 55 Linden St, Worcester, MA 01609 *Tel:* 508-755-0051 *E-mail:* victory@victoryprd.com *Web Site:* www.victoryprd.com, pg 1358

Videojet Technologies Inc, 1500 N Mittel Blvd, Wood Dale, IL 60191-1073 *Tel:* 630-860-7300 *Toll Free Tel:* 800-843-3610 *Toll Free Fax:* 800-582-1343 *E-mail:* info@videojet.com *Web Site:* www.videojet.com, pg 1284

Videotex Systems Inc, 10255 Miller Rd, Dallas, TX 75238 *Tel:* 972-231-9200 *Toll Free Tel:* 800-888-4336 *Fax:* 972-231-2420 *E-mail:* info@videotexsystems.com *Web Site:* www.videotexsystems.com, pg 1378

Videx Inc, 1105 NE Circle Blvd, Corvallis, OR 97330 *Tel:* 541-738-5500; 541-738-0521 *Fax:* 541-752-5285 *E-mail:* sales@videx.com; support@videx.com *Web Site:* www.videx.com, pg 1378

Viesti Associates Inc, 361 S Camino Del Rio, Suite 111, Durango, CO 81303 *Tel:* 970-403-1000, pg 1431

VillageSoup®, One Printinghouse Sq, Ellsworth, ME 04605 *Tel:* 207-594-4401 *E-mail:* info@villagesoup.com *Web Site:* www.villagesoup.com; mainestaymedia.com, pg 1351

VIP Digital Print Center, 200 Circle Dr N, Piscataway, NJ 08854 *Tel:* 732-469-5400 *Fax:* 732-469-8414 *E-mail:* info@vipcopycenter.com *Web Site:* www.vipcopycenter.com, pg 1262

Virginia Systems, 5509 W Bay Ct, Midlothian, VA 23112 *Tel:* 804-739-3200 *Fax:* 804-739-8376 *E-mail:* sales@virginiasystems.com *Web Site:* www.virginiasystems.com, pg 1378

Viridiam LLC, 3030 Lowell Dr, Green Bay, WI 54311 *Tel:* 920-465-3030 *Toll Free Tel:* 800-829-6555 *Web Site:* www.viridiam.com, pg 1106, 1232, 1262

VisionWorks, PO Box 92, Greenfield, MA 01302 *Tel:* 413-772-6569 *Toll Free Tel:* 800-933-7326 (orders) *Fax:* 413-772-6559 *E-mail:* dreaming@changingworld.com *Web Site:* www.changingworld.com, pg 1323

VistaBooks LLC, 637 Blue Ridge Rd, Silverthorne, CO 80498-8931 *Tel:* 970-468-7673 *Fax:* 970-468-7673 *E-mail:* email@vistabooks.com *Web Site:* www.vistabooks.com, pg 1323

Visual Pursuit, 168 W 86 St, New York, NY 10024 *Tel:* 212-362-8234, pg 1425

VITEC Multimedia, 931 Benecia Ave, Sunnyvale, CA 94085 *Tel:* 650-230-2400 *Toll Free Tel:* 800-451-5101 *Fax:* 408-739-1706 *E-mail:* sunnyvale@vitec.com *Web Site:* www.vitec.com, pg 1378

VKH Media Resources, 122 S Oneida Ave, Rhinelander, WI 54501 *Tel:* 715-499-6800 (cell) *Web Site:* www.victoriahouston.com, pg 1358

VO2 Mix Audio Post, 116 Spadina Ave, Suite 208, Toronto, ON M5V 2K6, Canada *Tel:* 416-603-3954 *Fax:* 416-603-3957 *E-mail:* info@vo2mix.ca *Web Site:* www.vo2mix.ca, pg 1378

Walker360, 2501 Fifth Ave E, Montgomery, AL 36107 *Tel:* 334-832-4975 *E-mail:* info@walker360.com *Web Site:* walker360.com, pg 1214, 1262

Wallaceburg Bookbinding & Mfg Co Ltd, 95 Arnold St, Wallaceburg, ON N8A 3P3, Canada *Tel:* 519-627-3552 *Toll Free Tel:* 800-214-BIND (214-2463) *Fax:* 519-627-6922 *E-mail:* helpdesk@wbmbindery.com *Web Site:* www.wbmbindery.com, pg 1214, 1232, 1262, 1326

Walsworth, 306 N Kansas Ave, Marceline, MO 64658 *Toll Free Tel:* 800-265-6795 *Web Site:* www.walsworth.com; www.walsworthhistorybooks.com, pg 1214, 1232, 1262

Walter's Publishing, 1750 Northway Dr, North Mankato, MN 56003 *Toll Free Tel:* 800-447-3274 *E-mail:* info@walterspublishing.com *Web Site:* www.walterspublishing.com, pg 1214

Ware-Pak LLC, 2427 Bond St, University Park, IL 60484 *Tel:* 708-534-2600 *E-mail:* sales@ware-pak.com *Web Site:* www.ware-pak.com, pg 1335

Warehouse Books Inc, 1006 Ballantine Blvd, Norfolk, VA 23504 *Tel:* 757-627-4160 *E-mail:* sales@warehousebooksinc.com *Web Site:* www.warehousebooksinc.com, pg 1323

Nancy Warner Photographer, 10 Vinton Ct, San Francisco, CA 94108-2407 *Tel:* 415-298-0027 *Web Site:* www.warnerphoto.com, pg 1425

Warwick Associates, 18340 Sonoma Hwy, Sonoma, CA 95476 *Tel:* 707-939-9212 *Fax:* 707-938-3515 *E-mail:* warwick@vom.com *Web Site:* www.warwickassociates.com, pg 1113, 1351

Wasatch Computer Technology LLC, 333 S 300 E, Salt Lake City, UT 84111 *Tel:* 801-575-8043 *E-mail:* subscription@wasatch.com *Web Site:* www.wasatch.com, pg 1378

Washington Monthly, 1200 18 St NW, Suite 330, Washington, DC 20036 *Tel:* 202-955-9010 *Toll Free Tel:* 855-492-1648 (subns) *Fax:* 202-955-9011 *E-mail:* editors@washingtonmonthly.com *Web Site:* washingtonmonthly.com, pg 1137

Washington Post News Service with Bloomberg News, 1301 "K" St NW, Washington, DC 20071 *Tel:* 202-334-7666 *E-mail:* syndication@washpost.com *Web Site:* www.washingtonpost.com/syndication, pg 1191

Patrick J Watson, 23 Alden Rd, Poughkeepsie, NY 12603 *Tel:* 845-475-8654 *E-mail:* info@patrickjwatson.com *Web Site:* www.patrickjwatson.com, pg 1425

We Need Diverse Books Older (grades 3-6), 557 Broadway, New York, NY 10012 *Tel:* 212-343-6100; 573-632-1632 (PR, US territories, US military bases) *Toll Free Tel:* 800-541-1097 (US) *Toll Free Fax:* 800-223-4011 *E-mail:* bookclubs@scholastic.com *Web Site:* clubs.scholastic.com, pg 1143

We Need Diverse Books Younger (Kindergarten-grade 2), 557 Broadway, New York, NY 10012 *Tel:* 212-343-6100; 573-632-1632 (PR, US territories, US military bases) *Toll Free Tel:* 800-541-1097 (US) *Toll Free Fax:* 800-223-4011 *E-mail:* bookclubs@scholastic.com *Web Site:* clubs.scholastic.com, pg 1143

Webcom Inc, 3480 Pharmacy Ave, Toronto, ON M1W 2S7, Canada *Tel:* 416-496-1000 *Toll Free Tel:* 800-665-9322 *Fax:* 416-496-1537 *E-mail:* webcom@webcomlink.com *Web Site:* www.webcomlink.com, pg 1214, 1262, 1284

Webcrafters Inc, 2211 Fordem Ave, Madison, WI 53704 *Tel:* 608-244-3561 *Toll Free Tel:* 800-356-8200 *Fax:* 608-244-5120 *E-mail:* info@webcrafters-inc.com *Web Site:* www.webcrafters-inc.com, pg 1214, 1262, 1284

Weber Shandwick, 909 Third Ave, New York, NY 10022 *Tel:* 212-445-8000 *Fax:* 212-445-8001 *Web Site:* www.webershandwick.com, pg 1113

Weidner Communications International Inc, 1468 Alton Way, Downingtown, PA 19335 *Tel:* 610-486-6525 *Fax:* 610-486-6527 *Web Site:* www.weidcom.com, pg 1351

Fred Weidner & Daughter Printers, 99 Hudson St, 5th fl, New York, NY 10013 *Tel:* 646-706-5180 *E-mail:* info@fwdprinters.com *Web Site:* www.fwdprinters.com, pg 1232, 1262, 1273, 1284, 1351

Glenn E Weisfeld PhD, 1326 Joliet Place, Detroit, MI 48207 *Tel:* 313-393-2403 *E-mail:* ad4297@wayne.edu *Web Site:* www.clas.wayne.edu, pg 1405

Welcome Enterprises Inc, 50 Plaza St, No 7A, Brooklyn, NY 11238 *Tel:* 212-989-3200 *Web Site:* www.welcomeenterprisesinc.com, pg 1358

WeMakeBooks.ca, 238 Willowdale Ave, North York, ON M2N 4Z5, Canada *Tel:* 416-733-1827 *Fax:* 416-733-7663 *Web Site:* www.wemakebooks.ca, pg 1232

Skye Wentworth Public Relations, 23A Durham Point Rd, Durham, NH 03824 *Tel:* 978-462-4453 *E-mail:* skyewentworth@gmail.com *Web Site:* www.skyewentworth.org/wordpress; www.skyewentworth.org, pg 1113

WERT BOOKBINDING INC

Wert Bookbinding Inc, 9975 Allentown Blvd, Grantville, PA 17028 *Tel:* 717-469-0626 *Toll Free Tel:* 800-344-9378 *Fax:* 717-469-0629 *E-mail:* quotes@wertbookbinding.com *Web Site:* www.wertbookbinding.com, pg 1262

Jim West Photography, 4875 Three Mile Dr, Detroit, MI 48224 *E-mail:* jim@jimwestphoto.com *Web Site:* www.jimwestphoto.com, pg 1425

West Virginia Book Co, 1125 Central Ave, Charleston, WV 25302 *Tel:* 304-342-1848 *Fax:* 304-343-0594 *E-mail:* wvbooks@wvbookco.com *Web Site:* www.wvbookco.com, pg 1304

Westchester Publishing Services, 4 Old Newtown Rd, Danbury, CT 06810 *Tel:* 203-791-0080 *Fax:* 203-791-9286 *E-mail:* info@westchesterpubsvcs.com *Web Site:* www.westchesterpublishingservices.com, pg 1233

Western Printing Machinery Co (WPM), 9228 Ivanhoe St, Schiller Park, IL 60176 *Tel:* 847-678-1740 *Fax:* 847-678-6176 *E-mail:* info@wpm.com *Web Site:* www.wpm.com, pg 1284

Western Telematic Inc (WTI), 5 Sterling, Irvine, CA 92618 *Tel:* 949-586-9950 *Toll Free Tel:* 800-854-7226 *E-mail:* info@wti.com *Web Site:* www.wti.com, pg 1378

Westwind Communications, 1310 Maple St, Plymouth, MI 48170 *Tel:* 734-667-2090 *Web Site:* www.book-marketing-expert.com, pg 1351

WeWrite LLC, 11040 Alba Rd, Ben Lomond, CA 95005 *Tel:* 831-336-3382 *E-mail:* info@wewrite.net *Web Site:* www.wewrite.net, pg 1323, 1378

Wheatmark Inc, 2030 E Speedway Blvd, Suite 106, Tucson, AZ 85719 *Tel:* 520-798-0888 *Toll Free Tel:* 888-934-0888 *Fax:* 520-798-3394 *E-mail:* info@wheatmark.com *Web Site:* www.wheatmark.com, pg 1351

Whitegate Features Syndicate, 71 Faunce Dr, Providence, RI 02906 *Tel:* 401-274-2149 *E-mail:* whitegate.featuressyndicate@gmail.com *Web Site:* www.whitegatefeatures.com, pg 1192

Whitehall Printing Co, 4244 Corporate Sq, Naples, FL 34104 *Tel:* 239-643-6464 *Toll Free Tel:* 800-321-9290 *Fax:* 239-643-6439 *E-mail:* info@whitehallprinting.com *Web Site:* www.whitehallprinting.com, pg 1215, 1233, 1262, 1273

Whitehots Inc, 205 Industrial Pkwy N, Unit 3, Aurora, ON L4G 4C4, Canada *Tel:* 905-727-9188 *Toll Free Tel:* 888-567-9188 *Fax:* 905-727-8756 *Toll Free Fax:* 888-563-0020 *E-mail:* admin@whitehots.com *Web Site:* www.whitehots.com, pg 1323

Whitehurst & Clark Book Fulfillment, 1200 County Rd, Rte 523, Flemington, NJ 08822 *Tel:* 908-782-2323 *Toll Free Tel:* 800-488-8040 *E-mail:* wcbooks@aol.com *Web Site:* www.wcbks.com, pg 1335

Whitman Printing & Creative Services LLC, PO Box 1681, Batavia, NY 14020 *Tel:* 516-294-5350 *Fax:* 516-294-5239 *E-mail:* info@whitmanprinting.com *Web Site:* www.whitmanprinting.com, pg 1106

Widen Enterprises Inc, 6911 Mangrove Lane, Madison, WI 53713 *Tel:* 608-222-1296 *Toll Free Tel:* 800-444-2828 *E-mail:* marketing@widen.com *Web Site:* www.widen.com, pg 1233

Maria Lidia Wilczewski, 228 SW Fernleaf Trail, Port St Lucie, FL 34953 *Tel:* 772-873-9803 *Fax:* 772-873-9803 *E-mail:* lidiaw@bellsouth.net, pg 1406

Wild West Communications Group, PO Box 346, Homewood, CA 96141 *Tel:* 530-412-1096 *Fax:* 530-525-4559 *Web Site:* www.wildwest-tahoe.com, pg 1417

Wiley-Blackwell, 111 River St, Suite 300, Hoboken, NJ 07030-5774 *Tel:* 201-748-6000 *Toll Free Tel:* 800-567-4797 *Fax:* 201-748-6088 *Toll Free Fax:* 800-565-6802 *E-mail:* info@wiley.com *Web Site:* www.wiley.com, pg 1358

Wilshire Book Co, 22647 Ventura Blvd, Suite 314, Woodland Hills, CA 91364 *Tel:* 818-700-1522 *E-mail:* sales@mpowers.com *Web Site:* www.mpowers.com, pg 1323

B W Wilson Paper Co Inc, 2501 Brittons Hill Rd, Richmond, VA 23230 *Tel:* 804-358-6715 *Toll Free Tel:* 800-868-2868 *Fax:* 804-358-4742 *E-mail:* info@bwwilson.com; sales@bwwilson.com *Web Site:* www.bwwilson.com, pg 1273

Windhaven®, 466 Rte 10, Orford, NH 03777 *Tel:* 603-512-9251 (cell) *E-mail:* info@windhavenpress.com *Web Site:* www.windhavenpress.com, pg 1233

Wingo LLC, 12161 Ken Adams Way, Wellington, FL 33414 *Tel:* 561-379-2635 *E-mail:* sat@amerimarketing.com *Web Site:* www.wingopromo.com; www.amerimarketing.com, pg 1192

Krishna Winston, 655 Bow Lane, Middletown, CT 06457 *Tel:* 860-347-0329; 860-918-8713 (cell) *E-mail:* kwinston@wesleyan.edu, pg 1406

Winston Personnel, 122 E 42 St, Suite 320, New York, NY 10168 *Tel:* 212-557-5000 *Web Site:* www.winstonresources.com, pg 1382

Wisconsin Bookwatch, 278 Orchard Dr, Oregon, WI 53575-1129 *Tel:* 608-835-7937 *E-mail:* mbr@execpc.com *Web Site:* www.midwestbookreview.com, pg 1137

Wood & Associates Direct Marketing Services Ltd, 9-1410 Bayly St, Pickering, ON L1W 3R3, Canada *Tel:* 905-831-2511 *E-mail:* clientservices@wood-and-associates.com *Web Site:* www.wood-and-associates.com, pg 1335

Brice Wood, PO Box A, Jerome, AZ 86331 *Tel:* 928-634-3238 *E-mail:* bricewood@yahoo.com *Web Site:* www.bricewood.com, pg 1417

Woodcrafters Lumber Sales Inc, 212 NE Sixth Ave, Portland, OR 97232-2976 *Tel:* 503-231-0226 *Toll Free Tel:* 800-777-3709 *Fax:* 503-232-0511 *Web Site:* www.woodcrafters.us, pg 1323

WordCo Indexing Services Inc, 66 Franklin St, Norwich, CT 06360 *E-mail:* office@wordco.com *Web Site:* www.wordco.com, pg 1233

WordPlayJane, 21 Harrison St, Suite 3, New York, NY 10013 *Tel:* 646-370-9541 (cell), pg 1385

World Literature Today, 630 Parrington Oval, Suite 110, Norman, OK 73019-4033 *Tel:* 405-325-4531 *E-mail:* wlt@ou.edu *Web Site:* www.worldliteraturetoday.org, pg 1137

Worldata, 3000 N Military Trail, Boca Raton, FL 33431-6321 *Tel:* 561-393-8200 *Toll Free Tel:* 800-331-8102 *E-mail:* hello@worldata.com *Web Site:* www.worldata.com, pg 1120

Worldwide Books, 1001 W Seneca St, Ithaca, NY 14850-3342 *Tel:* 607-272-9200 *Toll Free Tel:* 800-473-8146 (US/CN orders only) *Fax:* 607-272-0239 *E-mail:* info@worldwide-artbooks.com *Web Site:* www.worldwide-artbooks.com, pg 1304

Worzalla, 3535 Jefferson St, Stevens Point, WI 54481 *Tel:* 715-344-9608 *Fax:* 715-344-2578 *Web Site:* www.worzalla.com, pg 1215, 1233, 1262

WPA Film Library of Stock Footage, 16101 S 108 Ave, Orland Park, IL 60467 *Tel:* 708-460-0555 *Toll Free Tel:* 800-323-0442 *E-mail:* sales@wpafilmlibrary.com *Web Site:* www.wpafilmlibrary.com, pg 1431

The Writers Lifeline Inc, a Story Merchant company, 400 S Burnside Ave, Suite 11B, Los Angeles, CA 90036 *Tel:* 310-968-1607 *Web Site:* www.thewriterslifeline.com, pg 1352

Writer's Relief, Inc, 18766 John J Williams Hwy, Unit 4, Box 335, Rehoboth Beach, DE 19971 *Toll Free Tel:* 866-405-3003 *Fax:* 201-641-1253 *E-mail:* info@writersrelief.com *Web Site:* www.WritersRelief.com, pg 1233, 1352

Writers' Supercenter, 560 Roland Dr, Norfolk, VA 23509 *Tel:* 757-515-4315 *E-mail:* writerspage@writerspage.com *Web Site:* writersupercenter.com, pg 1378

Wunderman, 3 Columbus Circle, New York, NY 10019 *Tel:* 212-941-3000 *Web Site:* www.wunderman.com, pg 1100

Wybel Marketing Group Inc, 213 W Main St, Barrington, IL 60010 *Tel:* 847-382-0384; 847-382-0382 *Toll Free Tel:* 800-323-5297 *Fax:* 847-382-0385 *Toll Free Fax:* 800-595-5252 *E-mail:* bookreps@wybel.com, pg 1304

Chuck Wyrostok, 230 Griffith Run Rd, Spencer, WV 25276 *Tel:* 304-927-2978 *E-mail:* wyro@appalight.com *Web Site:* www.appalight.com, pg 1426

X-Height Studio, 83 High St, Milford, MA 01757 *Tel:* 508-478-3897 *Toll Free Tel:* 888-474-8973 *E-mail:* info@x-heightstudio.com *Web Site:* www.x-heightstudio.com, pg 1233

X-Rite Inc, 4300 44 St SE, Grand Rapids, MI 49512 *Tel:* 616-803-2100 *Toll Free Tel:* 800-248-9748; 888-800-9580 (sales) *E-mail:* info@xrite.com *Web Site:* www.xrite.com, pg 1284

Xante Corp, 2800 Dauphin St, Suite 100, Mobile, AL 36606 *Tel:* 251-473-6502; 251-473-4920 (tech support) *Fax:* 251-473-6503 *Web Site:* www.xante.com, pg 1378

Xerox Corporation, 201 Merritt 7, Norwalk, CT 06851-1056 *Toll Free Tel:* 800-835-6100 (cust serv) *Web Site:* www.xerox.com, pg 1273

Yeck Brothers Co, 2222 Arbor Blvd, Dayton, OH 45439 *Tel:* 937-294-4000 (ext 207) *Toll Free Tel:* 800-417-2767 *E-mail:* direct@yeck.com *Web Site:* www.yeck.com, pg 1116

Yurchak Printing Inc, 920 Links Ave, Landisville, PA 17538 *Tel:* 717-399-0209 *E-mail:* ypi.info@yurchak.com *Web Site:* www.yurchak.com, pg 1215, 1262, 1284

Z-Axis, 1916 Rte 96, Phelps, NY 14532 *Tel:* 315-548-5000 *Fax:* 315-548-5100 *E-mail:* sales@zaxis.net *Web Site:* www.zaxis.net, pg 1378

Meryl Zegarek Public Relations Inc, 255 W 108 St, Suite 9D1, New York, NY 10025 *Tel:* 917-493-3601 *Web Site:* www.mzpr.com, pg 1113

ZyLAB North America LLC, 7918 Jones Branch Dr, Suite 230, McLean, VA 22102-3366 *Tel:* 703-442-2400 *Toll Free Tel:* 866-995-2262 *Fax:* 703-991-2508 *E-mail:* info@zylab.com *Web Site:* www.zylab.com, pg 1378

Personnel Index

Included in this index are the personnel included in the entries in this volume of *LMP*, along with the page number(s) on which they appear. Not included in this index are those individuals associated with listings in the **Serials Featuring Books; Radio, TV & Cable Networks; Radio Programs Featuring Books** and **TV Programs Featuring Books** sections. Also, personnel associated with secondary addresses within listings (such as branch offices, sales offices, editorial offices, etc.) are not included.

Aaron, Lauren, Bert Davis Executive Search Inc, 555 Fifth Ave, Suite 302, New York, NY 10017 *Tel:* 212-838-4000 *E-mail:* info@bertdavis.com *Web Site:* www.bertdavis.com, pg 1381

Abbate, Salvatore A, Veritiv™ Corporation, 1000 Abernathy Rd, Bldg 400, Suite 1700, Atlanta, GA 30328 *Toll Free Tel:* 844-VERITIV (837-4848); 866-714-8303 (packaging cust serv); 866-714-8306 (print cust serv) *E-mail:* contactus@veritivcorp.com; media@veritivcorp.com *Web Site:* www.veritivcorp.com, pg 1273

Abboud, Dennis, Readerlink Distribution Services LLC, 1420 Kensington Rd, Suite 300, Oakbrook, IL 60523-2164 *Tel:* 708-547-4400 *Toll Free Tel:* 800-549-5389 *E-mail:* info@readerlink.com; marketingservices@readerlink.com *Web Site:* www.readerlink.com, pg 1301

Abdi, Zahra, Penguin Random House Canada, a Penguin Random House company, 320 Front St W, Suite 1400, Toronto, ON M5V 3B6, Canada *Tel:* 416-364-4449 *Toll Free Tel:* 888-523-9292 (cust serv) *Fax:* 416-598-7764 *E-mail:* customerservicescanada@penguinrandomhouse.com; publicitycanada@penguinrandomhouse.com; rightscanada@penguinrandomhouse.com *Web Site:* www.penguinrandomhouse.ca, pg 1299

Abfier, Mel, StarGroup International Inc, 1194 Old Dixie Hwy, Suite 201, West Palm Beach, FL 33413 *Tel:* 561-547-0667 *E-mail:* info@stargroupinternational.com *Web Site:* stargroupinternational.com, pg 1113

Ableman, Brian, The Learning Source Ltd, 644 Tenth St, Brooklyn, NY 11215 *E-mail:* info@learningsourceltd.com *Web Site:* www.learningsourceltd.com, pg 1355

Abraham, Russell, Russell Abraham Photography, Jack London Sq, 309 Fourth St, Suite 108, Oakland, CA 94607 *Tel:* 510-333-6633 *E-mail:* ra@russellabraham.com *Web Site:* russellabraham.com, pg 1419

Abraham, Stu, Abraham Associates Inc, 5120-A Cedar Lake Rd, Minneapolis, MN 55416 *Tel:* 952-927-7920 *Toll Free Tel:* 800-701-2489 *Fax:* 952-927-8089 *E-mail:* info@abrahamassociatesinc.com *Web Site:* www.abrahamassociatesinc.com, pg 1285

Abramek, Brian, Flock Tex Inc, 200 Founders Dr, Woonsocket, RI 02895 *Tel:* 401-765-2340 *Toll Free Tel:* 800-556-7286 *Fax:* 401-765-4915 *Web Site:* www.flocktex.com, pg 1267

Abramek, Edward T Jr, Flock Tex Inc, 200 Founders Dr, Woonsocket, RI 02895 *Tel:* 401-765-2340 *Toll Free Tel:* 800-556-7286 *Fax:* 401-765-4915 *Web Site:* www.flocktex.com, pg 1267

Abramek, Gary, Flock Tex Inc, 200 Founders Dr, Woonsocket, RI 02895 *Tel:* 401-765-2340 *Toll Free Tel:* 800-556-7286 *Fax:* 401-765-4915 *Web Site:* www.flocktex.com, pg 1267

Abrams, Douglas Carlton, Idea Architects, 523 Swift St, Santa Cruz, CA 95060 *Tel:* 831-465-9565 *Web Site:* www.ideaarchitects.com, pg 1347

Abramson, Elaine Sandra, A & A, PO Box 16223, Albuquerque, NM 87191-6223 *Tel:* 505-518-3939 *E-mail:* aaartwork@aol.com; aaauthor@aol.com *Web Site:* www.elaineabramson.com, pg 1189, 1411

Abramson, Martin Stanley, A & A, PO Box 16223, Albuquerque, NM 87191-6223 *Tel:* 505-518-3939 *E-mail:* aaartwork@aol.com; aaauthor@aol.com *Web Site:* www.elaineabramson.com, pg 1189, 1411

Abramson, Steven J, TRUMATCH Inc, PO Box 501, Water Mill, NY 11976-0501 *Tel:* 631-204-9100 *Toll Free Tel:* 800-TRU-9100 (878-9100 US & CN) *E-mail:* info@trumatch.com *Web Site:* www.trumatch.com, pg 1377

Abuhoff, Jack S, Innodata Inc, 55 Challenger Rd, Suite 202, Ridgefield Park, NJ 07660 *Tel:* 201-371-8000 *Toll Free Tel:* 877-454-8400 *E-mail:* info@innodata.com; marketing@innodata.com *Web Site:* innodata.com, pg 1227, 1347, 1371

Acquarola, Amy, Swedenborg Foundation, 320 N Church St, West Chester, PA 19380 *Tel:* 610-430-3222 *Toll Free Tel:* 800-355-3222 (cust serv) *Fax:* 610-430-7982 *E-mail:* info@swedenborg.com *Web Site:* swedenborg.com, pg 1322

Acree, Cat, BookPage®, 2143 Belcourt Ave, Nashville, TN 37212 *Tel:* 615-292-8926 *Fax:* 615-292-8249 *Web Site:* bookpage.com, pg 1127

Adair, Dennis, Adair Graphic Communications, 26975 Northline Rd, Taylor, MI 48180 *Tel:* 734-941-6300 *Fax:* 734-942-0920 *E-mail:* adair@printwell.com *Web Site:* www.adairgraphic.com, pg 1207, 1221, 1247, 1277

Adams, David, Publishers Weekly, 49 W 23 St, 9th fl, New York, NY 10010 *Tel:* 212-377-5500 *Fax:* 212-377-2733 *Web Site:* www.publishersweekly.com, pg 1136

Adams, Joanne, Specialist Marketing Services Inc, 777 Terrace Ave, Suite 401, Hasbrouck Heights, NJ 07604 *Tel:* 201-865-5800 *E-mail:* info@sms-inc.com *Web Site:* www.sms-inc.com, pg 1120

Adams, Katherine, Apple Inc, One Apple Park Way, Cupertino, CA 95014 *Tel:* 408-996-1010 *Web Site:* www.apple.com, pg 1364

Adams, Simon, Gracenote, a Nielsen Company, 2000 Powell St, Suite 1500, Emeryville, CA 94608 *Tel:* 510-428-7200 *Web Site:* www.gracenote.com, pg 1190

Adams, Stephen, Adams Design, 4493 Horseshoe Bend, Murrells Inlet, SC 29576 *Tel:* 843-655-7097 *E-mail:* sa@stephenadamsdesign.com *Web Site:* www.stephenadamsdesign.com, pg 1221

Addison, Tonia, Penguin Random House Canada, a Penguin Random House company, 320 Front St W, Suite 1400, Toronto, ON M5V 3B6, Canada *Tel:* 416-364-4449 *Toll Free Tel:* 888-523-9292 (cust serv) *Fax:* 416-598-7764 *E-mail:* customerservicescanada@penguinrandomhouse.com; publicitycanada@penguinrandomhouse.com; rightscanada@penguinrandomhouse.com *Web Site:* www.penguinrandomhouse.ca, pg 1299

Adel, Judith, J Adel Art & Design, 586 Ramapo Rd, Teaneck, NJ 07666 *Tel:* 201-836-2606 *E-mail:* jadelnj@aol.com, pg 1411

Adelman, Dean A, Veritiv™ Corporation, 1000 Abernathy Rd, Bldg 400, Suite 1700, Atlanta, GA 30328 *Toll Free Tel:* 844-VERITIV (837-4848); 866-714-8303 (packaging cust serv); 866-714-8306 (print cust serv) *E-mail:* contactus@veritivcorp.com; media@veritivcorp.com *Web Site:* www.veritivcorp.com, pg 1273

Adler, Stephen J, Thomson Reuters, 3 Times Sq, New York, NY 10036 *Tel:* 646-223-4000; 646-223-6100 (edit); 646-223-6000 (newsroom) *Web Site:* www.thomsonreuters.com, pg 1191

Adler, Sven, Ricoh Americas Corp, 300 Eagleview Blvd, Exton, PA 19341 *Tel:* 610-296-8000 *Toll Free Tel:* 800-333-2679 (prod support); 800-637-4264 (sales) *Web Site:* www.ricoh-usa.com, pg 1375

Adolphus, Emell, Publishers Weekly, 49 W 23 St, 9th fl, New York, NY 10010 *Tel:* 212-377-5500 *Fax:* 212-377-2733 *Web Site:* www.publishersweekly.com, pg 1136

Agrawal, Indrajeet, QBS Learning, 242 W 30 St, Suite 1100, New York, NY 10001 *Tel:* 646-668-4645 *E-mail:* contact@qbslearning.com *Web Site:* www.qbslearning.com, pg 1357, 1417

Agress, Amy, Innodata Inc, 55 Challenger Rd, Suite 202, Ridgefield Park, NJ 07660 *Tel:* 201-371-8000 *Toll Free Tel:* 877-454-8400 *E-mail:* info@innodata.com; marketing@innodata.com *Web Site:* innodata.com, pg 1227, 1347, 1371

Aguilar, Juan, Penguin Random House Canada, a Penguin Random House company, 320 Front St W, Suite 1400, Toronto, ON M5V 3B6, Canada *Tel:* 416-364-4449 *Toll Free Tel:* 888-523-9292 (cust serv) *Fax:* 416-598-7764 *E-mail:* customerservicescanada@penguinrandomhouse.com; publicitycanada@penguinrandomhouse.com; rightscanada@penguinrandomhouse.com *Web Site:* www.penguinrandomhouse.ca, pg 1299

Ajamian, Vartan, Books International Inc, 22883 Quicksilver Dr, Dulles, VA 20166 *Tel:* 703-661-1500 *E-mail:* hdqtrs@booksintl.com *Web Site:* booksintl.presswarehouse.com, pg 1333

Akins, Jeanna, PBD Worldwide Inc, 1650 Bluegrass Lakes Pkwy, Alpharetta, GA 30004 *Tel:* 470-769-1000 *Toll Free Tel:* 866-998-4PBD (998-4723) *E-mail:* sales.marketing@pbd.com; customerservice@pbd.com *Web Site:* www.pbd.com, pg 1334

Akoury-Ross, Lisa, SDP Publishing Solutions LLC, 36 Captain's Way, East Bridgewater, MA 02333 *Tel:* 617-775-0656 *E-mail:* info@sdppublishing.com *Web Site:* sdppublishing.com, pg 1351

Albanese, Andrew R, Publishers Weekly, 49 W 23 St, 9th fl, New York, NY 10010 *Tel:* 212-377-5500 *Fax:* 212-377-2733 *Web Site:* www.publishersweekly.com, pg 1136

Albert, Kelly, Penguin Random House Canada, a Penguin Random House company, 320 Front St W, Suite 1400, Toronto, ON M5V 3B6, Canada *Tel:* 416-364-4449 *Toll Free Tel:* 888-523-9292 (cust serv) *Fax:* 416-598-7764 *E-mail:* customerservicescanada@penguinrandomhouse.com; publicitycanada@penguinrandomhouse.com; rightscanada@penguinrandomhouse.com *Web Site:* www.penguinrandomhouse.ca, pg 1299

Albright, Nicole, Crown Connect, 250 W Rialto Ave, San Bernadino, CA 92408 *Tel:* 909-888-7531 *Fax:* 909-889-1639 *E-mail:* sales@crownconnect.com *Web Site:* www.crownconnect.com, pg 1209, 1224, 1279

Aldacushion, Richard, Washington Post News Service with Bloomberg News, 1301 "K" St NW, Washington, DC 20071 *Tel:* 202-334-7666 *E-mail:* syndication@washpost.com *Web Site:* www.washingtonpost.com/syndication, pg 1192

Alden, John, Avanti Computer Systems Ltd, 251 Consumers Rd, Suite 600, Toronto, ON M2J 4R3, Canada *Tel:* 416-445-1722 *Toll Free Tel:* 800-482-2908 *Fax:* 416-445-6319 *E-mail:* askavanti@avantisystems.com *Web Site:* www.avantisystems.com, pg 1365

Aldred, Nadene D, Maracle Inc, 1156 King St E, Oshawa, ON L1H 1H8, Canada *Tel:* 905-723-3438 *Toll Free Tel:* 800-558-8604 *Fax:* 905-723-1759 *E-mail:* hello@maracleinc.com *Web Site:* www.maracleinc.com, pg 1212, 1228, 1256

Alexander, Kurt, MediaLocate Inc, 1200 Piedmont Ave, Pacific Grove, CA 93950 *Tel:* 831-655-7500 *E-mail:* info@medialocate.com *Web Site:* www.medialocate.com, pg 1403

Alfano, Carm, TNG, 3320 S Service Rd, Burlington, ON L7N 3M6, Canada *Toll Free Tel:* 800-201-8127 *Toll Free Fax:* 877-664-9732 *E-mail:* cs@tng.com *Web Site:* www.tng.com, pg 1323

Alfaro, Nicole, Penguin Random House Canada, a Penguin Random House company, 320 Front St W, Suite 1400, Toronto, ON M5V 3B6, Canada *Tel:* 416-364-4449 *Toll Free Tel:* 888-523-9292 (cust serv) *Fax:* 416-598-7764 *E-mail:* customerservicescanada@penguinrandomhouse.com; publicitycanada@penguinrandomhouse.com; rightscanada@penguinrandomhouse.com *Web Site:* www.penguinrandomhouse.ca, pg 1299

Ali, Liaquat, Kazi Publications Inc, 3023 W Belmont Ave, Chicago, IL 60618 *Tel:* 773-267-7001 *Fax:* 773-267-7002 *E-mail:* info@kazi.org *Web Site:* www.kazi.org, pg 1317, 1328

Allen, Jennifer, Fujii Associates Inc, 75 Sunny Hill Dr, Troy, MO 63379 *Tel:* 636-528-2546 *Fax:* 636-600-5153 *Web Site:* www.fujiiassociates.com, pg 1291

Allen, Michael, Z-Axis, 1916 Rte 96, Phelps, NY 14532 *Tel:* 315-548-5000 *Fax:* 315-548-5100 *E-mail:* sales@zaxis.net *Web Site:* www.zaxis.net, pg 1378

Allen, Pete, JMW Group Inc, 346 Rte 6, No 867, Mahopac, NY 10541 *Tel:* 914-841-7105 *Fax:* 914-248-8861 *E-mail:* jmwgroup@jmwgroup.net *Web Site:* jmwforlife.com, pg 1348

Allex, Wendy, Allex Indexing, 6039 Sunshine Dr, Ferndale, WA 98248-9234 *Tel:* 360-778-1308 *Web Site:* www.indexpert.com, pg 1221

Allouche, Danny, Avery Dennison Corp, 207 N Goode Ave, 6th fl, Glendale, CA 91203-1222 *Tel:* 626-304-2000 *Web Site:* www.averydennison.com, pg 1365

Allred, Julie, BW&A Books Inc, 112 W McClanahan St, Oxford, NC 27565 *Tel:* 919-956-9111 *Fax:* 919-956-9112 *E-mail:* bwa@bwabooks.com *Web Site:* www.bwabooks.com, pg 1223

Almeida, Alia Maria, Chesapeake & Hudson Inc, 27 Jacks Shop Rd, Rochelle, VA 22738 *Tel:* 301-834-7170 *Toll Free Tel:* 800-231-4469 *E-mail:* office@cheshud.com *Web Site:* www.cheshudinc.com, pg 1289

Almeter, Rebecca L, Whitman Printing & Creative Services LLC, PO Box 1681, Batavia, NY 14020 *Tel:* 516-294-5350 *Fax:* 516-294-5239 *E-mail:* info@whitmanprinting.com *Web Site:* www.whitmanprinting.com, pg 1106

Alperen, Jennifer, The Nolan/Lehr Group Inc, 214 W 29 St, Suite 1002, New York, NY 10001 *Tel:* 212-967-8200 *E-mail:* dblehr@cs.com *Web Site:* www.nolanlehrgroup.com, pg 1111

Altabef, Peter, Unisys Corp, 801 Lakeview Dr, Suite 100, Blue Bell, PA 19422 *Tel:* 215-274-2742 *Web Site:* www.unisys.com, pg 1378

Altman, Amy, The Gluefast Co Inc, 3535 State Rte 66, Bldg No 1, Neptune, NJ 07753 *Tel:* 732-918-4600 *Toll Free Tel:* 800-242-7318 *Fax:* 732-918-4646 *E-mail:* info@gluefast.com *Web Site:* www.gluefast.com, pg 1337

Altman, Shari, Altman Dedicated Direct, 853 Academy St, Rural Hall, NC 27045-9329 *Tel:* 336-969-9538 *Fax:* 336-969-9538 *Web Site:* www.altmandedicateddirect.com, pg 1343

Alvarez, Dr Gloria M, ICSID Review: Foreign Investment Law Journal, 4000 CentreGreen Way, Suite 310, Cary, NC 27513 *Toll Free Tel:* 800-852-7323 (option 1) *E-mail:* jnls.cust.serv@oup.com *Web Site:* academic.oup.com/icsidreview, pg 1133

Ambrose, Albert E Jr, Lowe Graphics & Printing, 220 Great Circle Rd, Suite 122, Nashville, TN 37228 *Tel:* 615-242-6649 *Fax:* 615-254-8867 *Web Site:* www.etlowe.com, pg 1228

Ambrosi, Leigh Ann, Susan Magrino Agency, 352 Park Ave S, 6th fl, New York, NY 10010 *Tel:* 212-957-3005 *Fax:* 212-957-4071 *E-mail:* info@smapr.com *Web Site:* www.smapr.com, pg 1110

Ames, Michael, Puritan Press Inc, 95 Runnells Bridge Rd, Hollis, NH 03049-6565 *Tel:* 603-889-4500 *Toll Free Tel:* 800-635-6302 *Fax:* 603-889-6551 *E-mail:* print@puritancapital.com *Web Site:* www.puritanpress.com, pg 1259

Amick, W Michael Jr, International Paper Co, 6400 Poplar Ave, Memphis, TN 38197 *Tel:* 901-419-9000 *Toll Free Tel:* 800-207-4003 *Web Site:* www.internationalpaper.com; facebook.com/internationalpaper; x.com/intlpaperco, pg 1268

Amin, Sejal, Shutterstock Inc, Empire State Bldg, 350 Fifth Ave, 20th fl, New York, NY 10118 *E-mail:* support@shutterstock.com; press@shutterstock.com *Web Site:* www.shutterstock.com, pg 1430

Ammirata, Mike, Total Printing Systems, 201 S Gregory Dr, Newton, IL 62448 *Tel:* 618-783-2978 *Toll Free Tel:* 800-465-5200 *Fax:* 618-783-8407 *E-mail:* sales@tps1.com *Web Site:* www.tps1.com, pg 1261

Amorese, Cynthia, Julie A Laitin Enterprises Inc, 160 West End Ave, Suite 23N, New York, NY 10023 *Tel:* 917-841-8566 *E-mail:* info@julielaitin.com *Web Site:* www.julielaitin.com, pg 1100

Anagnost, Andrew, Autodesk Inc, 111 McInnis Pkwy, San Rafael, CA 94903 *Tel:* 415-507-5000 *Fax:* 415-507-5100 *Web Site:* www.autodesk.com, pg 1365

Andadari, Chalista, Penguin Random House Canada, a Penguin Random House company, 320 Front St W, Suite 1400, Toronto, ON M5V 3B6, Canada *Tel:* 416-364-4449 *Toll Free Tel:* 888-523-9292 (cust serv) *Fax:* 416-598-7764 *E-mail:* customerservicescanada@penguinrandomhouse.com; publicitycanada@penguinrandomhouse.com; rightscanada@penguinrandomhouse.com *Web Site:* www.penguinrandomhouse.ca, pg 1299

Anderberg, Greg, Anderberg Innovative Print Solutions, 6999 Oxford St, St Louis Park, MN 55426 *Tel:* 952-848-7300 *Toll Free Tel:* 800-231-9777 *Fax:* 952-920-1103 *E-mail:* sales@anderbergprint.com *Web Site:* www.anderbergprint.com, pg 1247

Anderberg, Paul, Anderberg Innovative Print Solutions, 6999 Oxford St, St Louis Park, MN 55426 *Tel:* 952-848-7300 *Toll Free Tel:* 800-231-9777 *Fax:* 952-920-1103 *E-mail:* sales@anderbergprint.com *Web Site:* www.anderbergprint.com, pg 1247

Andersen, Sheila K, Leading Edge Express, 3651 Robin Lane, Minnetonka, MN 55503 *Tel:* 952-217-4665 *Web Site:* www.leadingedgereview.com, pg 1133

Anderson, Bill, L+L Printers, 6200 Yarrow Dr, Carlsbad, CA 92011 *Tel:* 760-438-3456; 760-477-0321 *Fax:* 760-929-0853 *E-mail:* info@llprinters.com *Web Site:* www.llprinters.com, pg 1256

Anderson, Jennifer, Holliston Holdings LLC, 905 Holliston Mills Rd, Church Hill, TN 37642 *Tel:* 423-357-6141 *Toll Free Tel:* 800-251-0451; 800-251-0251 (cust serv) *Fax:* 423-357-8840 *Toll Free Fax:* 800-325-0351 (cust serv) *E-mail:* custserv@holliston.com *Web Site:* holliston.com, pg 1268

Anderson, Joseph, Anderson & Vreeland Inc, 15348 US Hwy 127 EW, Bryan, OH 43506 *Tel:* 419-636-5002 *Toll Free Tel:* 866-282-7697; 888-832-1600 (CN) *Fax:* 419-636-4334 *E-mail:* info@andersonvreeland.com *Web Site:* andersonvreeland.com, pg 1277

Anderson, Rick, Spicers Paper, 12310 E Slauson Ave, Santa Fe Springs, CA 90670 *Toll Free Tel:* 800-774-2377 *Fax:* 562-693-8339 *Web Site:* www.spicers.com, pg 1272

Anderson, Ryan, St Joseph Communications-Print Group, 50 Macintosh Blvd, Concord, ON L4K 4P3, Canada *Tel:* 905-660-3111 *E-mail:* marketing@stjoseph.com *Web Site:* stjoseph.com, pg 1105, 1259

Anderson, Wilda, Modern Language Notes (MLN), 2715 N Charles St, Baltimore, MD 21218-4363 *Tel:* 410-516-6987 (journal orders outside US & CN) *Toll Free Tel:* 800-548-1784 (journal orders) *Fax:* 410-578-2865 (journal orders) *E-mail:* jrnlcirc@jh.edu (journal orders) *Web Site:* www.press.jhu.edu/journals/mln, pg 1134

Andes, Elizabeth, Archetype Inc, 317 N Market St, Lancaster, PA 17603 *Tel:* 717-392-7438 *E-mail:* mail@nmsgbooks.com *Web Site:* nmsgbooks.com, pg 1385

Andes, Elizabeth, North Market Street Graphics (NMSG), 317 N Market St, Lancaster, PA 17603 *Tel:* 717-392-7438 *E-mail:* mail@nmsgbooks.com *Web Site:* www.nmsgbooks.com, pg 1229, 1416

Andonian, Aramais, Arrow Graphics Inc, PO Box 380291, Cambridge, MA 02238 *E-mail:* info@arrow1.com *Web Site:* www.arrow1.com, pg 1103, 1208, 1222, 1353, 1365, 1385, 1412

Andrew, Jan, The Hendra Agency Inc, 142 Sterling Place, Brooklyn, NY 11217-3307 *Tel:* 718-622-3232 *Fax:* 718-622-3322, pg 1109

Andrews, Gaylen, Copywriters' Council of America™ (CCA), Linick Bldg, 7 Putter Lane, Middle Island, NY 11953 *Tel:* 631-924-3888; 631-924-8555; 631-604-8599 *E-mail:* linickgroup@gmail.com, pg 1345

Andujar, Rosa, American Journal of Philology, 2715 N Charles St, Baltimore, MD 21218-4363 *Tel:* 410-516-6987 (journal orders outside US & CN) *Toll Free Tel:* 800-548-1784 (journal orders) *Fax:* 410-578-2865 (journal orders) *E-mail:* jrnlcirc@jh.edu (journal orders) *Web Site:* www.press.jhu.edu/journals/american-journal-philology, pg 1129

Angstrom, Mark, Angstrom Graphics Print, 4437 E 49 St, Cleveland, OH 44125 *Tel:* 216-271-5300 *Toll Free Tel:* 800-634-1262 *E-mail:* info@angstromgraphics.com *Web Site:* www.angstromgraphics.com, pg 1247

Angstrom, Wayne, Angstrom Graphics Print, 4437 E 49 St, Cleveland, OH 44125 *Tel:* 216-271-5300 *Toll Free Tel:* 800-634-1262 *E-mail:* info@angstromgraphics.com *Web Site:* www.angstromgraphics.com, pg 1247

Anson, Matt, Bindagraphics Inc, 2701 Wilmarco Ave, Baltimore, MD 21223-9922 *Tel:* 410-362-7200 *Toll Free Tel:* 800-326-0300 *Fax:* 410-362-7233 *E-mail:* info@bindagraphics.com *Web Site:* www.bindagraphics.com, pg 1222, 1248

Anson, Todd, The Colad Group LLC, 693 Seneca St, 5th fl, Buffalo, NY 14210 *Tel:* 716-961-1776 *Toll Free Tel:* 800-950-1755 *Fax:* 716-961-1753 *E-mail:* info@colad.com *Web Site:* www.colad.com, pg 1103

Ansorge, Jessica, Sheridan MI, 613 E Industrial Dr, Chelsea, MI 48118 *Tel:* 734-475-9145 *Web Site:* www.sheridan.com, pg 1213, 1259, 1271

Antone, Peter, Ingram Publisher Services, an Ingram brand, 14 Ingram Blvd, Mail Stop 631, La Vergne, TN 37086 *Tel:* 615-793-5000 *Toll Free Tel:* 866-400-5351 (cust serv) *E-mail:* ips@ingramcontent.com *Web Site:* www.ingrampublisherservices.com, pg 1294

Aparicio-Ramirez, Rosalind, Bellevue Literary Review, 149 E 23 St, Suite 1516, New York, NY 10010 *Tel:* 917-375-5790 *E-mail:* info@BLReview.org *Web Site:* www.BLReview.org, pg 1130

Apelian, Bill, BJU Press, 1430 Wade Hampton Blvd, Greenville, SC 29609-5046 *Tel:* 864-770-1317; 864-546-4600 *Toll Free Tel:* 800-845-5731 *E-mail:* bjupinfo@bjupress.com *Web Site:* www.bjupress.com, pg 1365

Apter, Ronnie, Mark Herman & Ronnie Apter, Translators, 2222 Westview Dr, Nashville, TN 37212-4123 *Tel:* 615-942-8462 *E-mail:* mnh18@columbia.edu, pg 1401

Aragone, Augusto P, Ingram Micro Inc, 3351 Michelson Dr, Suite 100, Irvin, CA 92612 *Tel:* 714-566-1000 *E-mail:* customerexperience@ingrammicro.com *Web Site:* www.ingrammicro.com, pg 1317

Arambarri, Yolanda, United Library Services Inc, 7140 Fairmount Dr SE, Calgary, AB T2H 0X4, Canada *Tel:* 403-252-4426 *Toll Free Tel:* 888-342-5857 (CN only) *Fax:* 403-258-3426 *Toll Free Fax:* 800-661-2806 (CN only) *E-mail:* info@uls.com *Web Site:* www.uls.com, pg 1323

Araujo-Lane, Zarita, Cross Cultural Communication Systems Inc, 227 Garfield Ave, Suite B, Woburn, MA 01801 *Tel:* 781-729-3736 *Toll Free Tel:* 888-678-CCCS (678-2227 out of state only) *Fax:* 781-729-1217 *Web Site:* www.cccsorg.com; www.embracingculture.com, pg 1400

Arbit, Bruce, A B Data Ltd, 600 A B Data Dr, Milwaukee, WI 53217 *Tel:* 414-961-6400 *Toll Free Tel:* 866-217-4470 *Fax:* 414-961-2674 *E-mail:* info@abdata.com; consulting@abdata.com *Web Site:* www.abdata.com, pg 1115

Arbus, Michelle, Penguin Random House Canada, a Penguin Random House company, 320 Front St W, Suite 1400, Toronto, ON M5V 3B6, Canada *Tel:* 416-364-4449 *Toll Free Tel:* 888-523-9292 (cust serv) *Fax:* 416-598-7764 *E-mail:* customerservicescanada@penguinrandomhouse.com; publicitycanada@penguinrandomhouse.com; rightscanada@penguinrandomhouse.com *Web Site:* www.penguinrandomhouse.ca, pg 1299

Arditte, Edward, AccuWeather Inc, 385 Science Park Rd, State College, PA 16803 *Tel:* 814-235-8600; 814-237-0309 *E-mail:* salesmail@accuweather.com; support@accuweather.com *Web Site:* www.accuweather.com; corporate.accuweather.com, pg 1363

Areglado, R Scott, iCAD Inc, 98 Spit Brook Rd, Suite 100, Nashua, NH 03062 *Tel:* 603-882-5200 *Toll Free Tel:* 866-280-2239 *E-mail:* sales@icadmed.com; support@icamed.com *Web Site:* www.icadmed.com, pg 1370

Armer, Jeremy, Readerlink Distribution Services LLC, 1420 Kensington Rd, Suite 300, Oakbrook, IL 60523-2164 *Tel:* 708-547-4400 *Toll Free Tel:* 800-549-5389 *E-mail:* info@readerlink.com; marketingservices@readerlink.com *Web Site:* www.readerlink.com, pg 1301

Armstrong, Christopher, Universal/Wilde, 26 Dartmouth St, Westwood, MA 02090 *Tel:* 781-251-2700 *Fax:* 781-251-2613 *Web Site:* www.universalwilde.com, pg 1105, 1116, 1232, 1261

Armstrong, Jann, BookWise Design, 29089 SW Costa Circle W, Wilsonville, OR 97070 *Tel:* 503-542-3551 *Toll Free Tel:* 800-697-9833 *Web Site:* bookwisedesign.com, pg 1223, 1412

Armstrong, Kirsten, Penguin Random House Canada, a Penguin Random House company, 320 Front St W, Suite 1400, Toronto, ON M5V 3B6, Canada *Tel:* 416-364-4449 *Toll Free Tel:* 888-523-9292 (cust serv) *Fax:* 416-598-7764 *E-mail:* customerservicescanada@penguinrandomhouse.com; publicitycanada@penguinrandomhouse.com; rightscanada@penguinrandomhouse.com *Web Site:* www.penguinrandomhouse.ca, pg 1299

Armstrong, Sarah, Ingram Publisher Services, an Ingram brand, 14 Ingram Blvd, Mail Stop 631, La Vergne, TN 37086 *Tel:* 615-793-5000 *Toll Free Tel:* 866-400-5351 (cust serv) *E-mail:* ips@ingramcontent.com *Web Site:* www.ingrampublisherservices.com, pg 1294

Armstrong, Tracey L, Copyright Clearance Center Inc (CCC), 222 Rosewood Dr, Danvers, MA 01923 *Tel:* 978-750-8400 (sales); 978-646-2600 (cust serv) *E-mail:* info@copyright.com *Web Site:* www.copyright.com, pg 1345

Armstrong, Walter, Flock Tex Inc, 200 Founders Dr, Woonsocket, RI 02895 *Tel:* 401-765-2340 *Toll Free Tel:* 800-556-7286 *Fax:* 401-765-4915 *Web Site:* www.flocktex.com, pg 1267

Arnold, Kelly, Ingram Content Group LLC, One Ingram Blvd, La Vergne, TN 37086-1986 *Tel:* 615-793-5000 *Toll Free Tel:* 800-937-8000 (retailers); 800-937-5300 (ext 1, libs) *E-mail:* customerservice@ingramcontent.com *Web Site:* www.ingramcontent.com, pg 1294, 1316

Arredondo, Joey, Penguin Random House Canada, a Penguin Random House company, 320 Front St W, Suite 1400, Toronto, ON M5V 3B6, Canada *Tel:* 416-364-4449 *Toll Free Tel:* 888-523-9292 (cust serv) *Fax:* 416-598-7764 *E-mail:* customerservicescanada@penguinrandomhouse.com; publicitycanada@penguinrandomhouse.com; rightscanada@penguinrandomhouse.com *Web Site:* www.penguinrandomhouse.ca, pg 1299

Arrow, Kevin, GW Illustration & Design, 2290 Ball Dr, St Louis, MO 63146 *Tel:* 314-567-9854 *Web Site:* www.gwinc.com, pg 1414

Arrow, Kevin, GW Inc, 2290 Ball Dr, St Louis, MO 63146 *Tel:* 314-567-9854 *E-mail:* media@gwinc.com *Web Site:* www.gwinc.com, pg 1226, 1370

Arsenault, Keith, Chesapeake & Hudson Inc, 27 Jacks Shop Rd, Rochelle, VA 22738 *Tel:* 301-834-7170 *Toll Free Tel:* 800-231-4469 *E-mail:* office@cheshud.com *Web Site:* www.cheshudinc.com, pg 1289

Asen, Matthew, Horizon Paper Co Inc, 1010 Washington Blvd, Stamford, CT 06901 *Tel:* 203-358-0855 *Toll Free Tel:* 866-358-0855 *E-mail:* info@horizonpaper.com *Web Site:* www.horizonpaper.com, pg 1268

Asher, Gary, Maverick Publications LLC, 131 NE Fifth St, Prineville, OR 97754 *Tel:* 541-382-6978 *E-mail:* moreinfo@maverickbooks.com *Web Site:* maverickbooks.com, pg 1212, 1356, 1372

Ashway, Nader, Tri-Media Integrated Marketing Technologies Inc, 1027 Pelham St, Unit 2, Fonthill, ON L0S 1E0, Canada *E-mail:* think@tri-media.com *Web Site:* tri-media.com, pg 1100

Astley, Chris W, Glatfelter, Capitol Towers South, 4350 Congress St, Suite 600, Charlotte, NC 28209 *Tel:* 717-850-0170 *Toll Free Tel:* 866-744-7380 *E-mail:* info@glatfelter.com *Web Site:* www.glatfelter.com, pg 1267

Atchity, Dr Kenneth, AEI (Atchity Entertainment International Inc), 400 S Burnside Ave, Suite 11B, Los Angeles, CA 90036 *Tel:* 323-932-1685, pg 1343

Atchity, Kenneth PhD, The Writers Lifeline Inc, a Story Merchant company, 400 S Burnside Ave, Suite 11B, Los Angeles, CA 90036 *Tel:* 310-968-1607 *Web Site:* www.thewriterslifeline.com, pg 1352

Athey, Jake, Widen Enterprises Inc, 6911 Mangrove Lane, Madison, WI 53713 *Tel:* 608-222-1296 *Toll Free Tel:* 800-444-2828 *E-mail:* marketing@widen.com *Web Site:* www.widen.com, pg 1233

Atkin, Ethan, Catamount Content LLC, 240 Cummings Rd, Montpelier, VT 05602 *Tel:* 917-512-1962 *E-mail:* info@catamountinternational.com *Web Site:* www.catamountinternational.com, pg 1288

Atkin, John, Silvermine International Books LLC, 25 Perry Ave, Suite 11, Norwalk, CT 06850 *Tel:* 203-451-2396 *E-mail:* info@jawilsons.com *Web Site:* jawilsons.com/pages/who-we-are, pg 1329

Atkins, Clay, Progress Printing Plus, 2677 Waterlick Rd, Lynchburg, VA 24502 *Tel:* 434-239-9213 *Toll Free Tel:* 800-572-7804 *Fax:* 434-832-7573 *E-mail:* info@progressprintplus.com *Web Site:* www.progressprintplus.com, pg 1230

Auerbach, Philip B, Auerbach International, Alameda, CA 94501 *Tel:* 415-592-0042 *Fax:* 415-592-0043 *E-mail:* translations@auerbach-intl.com *Web Site:* www.auerbach-intl.com, pg 1400

August, Irene, International Service Co, International Service Bldg, 333 Fourth Ave, Indialantic, FL 32903-4295 *Tel:* 321-724-1443 *Fax:* 321-724-1443, pg 1317, 1325, 1328, 1331

Augustine, Kate, Hill+Knowlton Strategies, 237 Park Ave, 4th fl, New York, NY 10017 *Tel:* 212-885-0300 *Web Site:* www.hkstrategies.com, pg 1109

Aumann, Michael C, Brandtjen & Kluge LLC, 539 Blanding Woods Rd, St Croix Falls, WI 54024 *Tel:* 715-483-3265 *Toll Free Tel:* 800-826-7320 *Fax:* 715-483-1640 *E-mail:* sales@kluge.biz *Web Site:* www.kluge.biz, pg 1278

Ausenda, Marco, Rizzoli Bookstores, 1133 Broadway, New York, NY 10010 *Tel:* 212-759-2424 *Toll Free Tel:* 800-52-BOOKS (522-6657) *Fax:* 212-826-9754 *Web Site:* rizzolibookstore.com; www.rizzoliusa.com, pg 1320

Austin, Kurt, National Council of Teachers of English (NCTE), 340 N Neil St, Suite 104, Champaign, IL 61820 *Tel:* 217-328-3870 *Toll Free Tel:* 877-369-6283 (cust serv) *Fax:* 217-328-9645 *E-mail:* customerservice@ncte.org; permissions@ncte.org *Web Site:* ncte.org, pg 1146

Auth, Mark, The Bureau, 2354 English St, Maplewood, MN 55109 *Tel:* 612-788-1000; 612-432-3516 (sales) *Toll Free Tel:* 800-788-9536 *Fax:* 612-788-7792 *E-mail:* sales@thebureau.com *Web Site:* www.thebureau.com, pg 1223, 1249

Autunnale, Frank, Independent Publishers Group (IPG), 814 N Franklin St, Chicago, IL 60610 *Tel:* 312-337-0747 *Toll Free Tel:* 800-888-4741 (orders) *Fax:* 312-337-5985 *E-mail:* frontdesk@ipgbook.com; orders@ipgbook.com *Web Site:* www.ipgbook.com, pg 1292, 1328

Avery, Cameron, Boston Review, PO Box 390568, Cambridge, MA 02139 *Tel:* 617-356-8198 *E-mail:* review@bostonreview.net; customerservice@bostonreview.net *Web Site:* bostonreview.net, pg 1130

Ay, Evren, Link Translations Inc, 60 E 96 St, New York, NY 10128 *Toll Free Tel:* 866-866-5010 *E-mail:* info@link-translations.com *Web Site:* www.link-translations.com, pg 1403

Ayer, Anne, Sappi Fine Paper North America, 255 State St, Boston, MA 02109 *Tel:* 617-423-7300 *Toll Free Tel:* 800-882-4332 *E-mail:* webqueriesna@sappi.com *Web Site:* www.sappi.com/na, pg 1271

Bacher, Joe, Choice Books, 10100 Piper Lane, Bristow, VA 20136 *Tel:* 703-530-9993 *Fax:* 703-530-9983 *E-mail:* info@choicebooks.com *Web Site:* www.choicebooks.com, pg 1313

Bachner, Andrea, Diacritics, 2715 N Charles St, Baltimore, MD 21218-4363 *Tel:* 410-516-6987 (journal orders outside US & CN) *Toll Free Tel:* 800-548-1784 (journal orders) *Fax:* 410-578-2865 (journal orders) *E-mail:* jrnlcirc@jh.edu (journal orders) *Web Site:* www.press.jhu.edu/journals/diacritics, pg 1131

Backe, John E, Backe Communications, Radnor Corporate Ctr, Bldg 3, Suite 101, 100 Matson Ford Rd, Radnor, PA 19087 *Tel:* 610-947-6900 *Web Site:* www.backemarketing.com, pg 1099

Badalian, Alvart, Arrow Graphics Inc, PO Box 380291, Cambridge, MA 02238 *E-mail:* info@arrow1.com *Web Site:* www.arrow1.com, pg 1103, 1208, 1222, 1353, 1365, 1385, 1412

Bade, Dave, Impressions Inc, 1050 Westgate Dr, St Paul, MN 55114 *Tel:* 651-646-1050 *Toll Free Tel:* 800-251-4285 *Fax:* 651-646-7228 *E-mail:* info@i-i.com *Web Site:* www.i-i.com, pg 1255

Bader, Suzan J, DSM Producers Inc, PO Box 1160, Marco Island, FL 34146-1160 *Tel:* 212-245-0006, pg 1368

Baiamonte, Geno, PremierIMS Inc, 11101 Ella Blvd, Houston, TX 77067 *Tel:* 832-608-6400 *Fax:* 832-608-6420 *E-mail:* info@premier-ims.com *Web Site:* www.premier-ims.com, pg 1118

Baietto, Emma, Independent Publishers Group (IPG), 814 N Franklin St, Chicago, IL 60610 *Tel:* 312-337-0747 *Toll Free Tel:* 800-888-4741 (orders) *Fax:* 312-337-5985 *E-mail:* frontdesk@ipgbook.com; orders@ipgbook.com *Web Site:* www.ipgbook.com, pg 1292, 1328

Bailey, Brenda MLIS, Clotilde's Secretarial & Management Services, PO Box 871926, New Orleans, LA 70187 *Tel:* 504-242-2912; 504-266-9239 (cell) *Fax:* 504-242-2912, pg 1385

Bailey, Jim, Universal/Wilde, 26 Dartmouth St, Westwood, MA 02090 *Tel:* 781-251-2700 *Fax:* 781-251-2613 *Web Site:* www.universalwilde.com, pg 1106, 1116, 1232, 1261

Bailey, Richard, HP Inc, 1501 Paige Mill Rd, Palo Alto, CA 94304-1112 *Tel:* 650-857-1501 *Toll Free Tel:* 800-282-6672 *Web Site:* www.hp.com, pg 1370

Bain, Ralph, Wood & Associates Direct Marketing Services Ltd, 9-1410 Bayly St, Pickering, ON L1W 3R3, Canada *Tel:* 905-831-2511 *E-mail:* clientservices@wood-and-associates.com *Web Site:* www.wood-and-associates.com, pg 1335

Baird, Michele, Six Red Marbles LLC, 101 Station Landing, Medford, MA 02155 *Tel:* 857-588-9000 *E-mail:* info@sixredmarbles.com *Web Site:* www.sixredmarbles.com, pg 1231, 1376

Baker, Eileen, Worldwide Books, 1001 W Seneca St, Ithaca, NY 14850-3342 *Tel:* 607-272-9200 *Toll Free Tel:* 800-473-8146 (US/CN orders only) *Fax:* 607-272-0239 *E-mail:* info@worldwide-artbooks.com *Web Site:* www.worldwide-artbooks.com, pg 1304

Baker, Isabel, Book Vine for Children, 3980 Albany St, Suite 7, McHenry, IL 60050-8397 *Tel:* 815-363-8880 *Toll Free Tel:* 800-772-4220 *Fax:* 815-363-8883 *E-mail:* info@bookvine.com *Web Site:* www.bookvine.com, pg 1287

Baker, Kristine, GOBI® Library Solutions from EBSCO, 999 Maple St, Contoocook, NH 03229 *Tel:* 603-746-3102 *Toll Free Tel:* 800-258-3774 (US & CN) *Fax:* 603-746-5628 *E-mail:* information@ebsco.com *Web Site:* gobi.ebsco.com, pg 1316

Baker, Mike, Midwest Paper Group, 540 Prospect St, Combined Locks, WI 54113 *Tel:* 920-788-3550 *Toll Free Tel:* 800-828-1987 *Fax:* 920-968-3950 *Web Site:* mwpaper.com, pg 1270

Baker, Susan, Westchester Publishing Services, 4 Old Newtown Rd, Danbury, CT 06810 *Tel:* 203-791-0080 *Fax:* 203-791-9286 *E-mail:* info@westchesterpubsvcs.com *Web Site:* www.westchesterpublishingservices.com, pg 1233

Bakhtiar, Mary, Kazi Publications Inc, 3023 W Belmont Ave, Chicago, IL 60618 *Tel:* 773-267-7001 *Fax:* 773-267-7002 *E-mail:* info@kazi.org *Web Site:* www.kazi.org, pg 1317, 1328

Balazs, Lara, Intuit Inc, 2700 Coast Ave, Mountain View, CA 94043 *Tel:* 650-944-6000 *Toll Free Tel:* 800-446-8848 *E-mail:* investor_relations@intuit.com *Web Site:* www.intuit.com, pg 1371

Baldani, Sue, inlingua Translation Service, 95 Summit Ave, Summit, NJ 07901 *Tel:* 908-522-0622 *E-mail:* summit@inlingua.com *Web Site:* www.inlingua.com, pg 1402

Balesh, Chelsea, Independent Publishers Group (IPG), 814 N Franklin St, Chicago, IL 60610 *Tel:* 312-337-0747 *Toll Free Tel:* 800-888-4741 (orders) *Fax:* 312-337-5985 *E-mail:* frontdesk@ipgbook.com; orders@ipgbook.com *Web Site:* www.ipgbook.com, pg 1292

Ballenger, Noella, Noella Ballenger & Associates, PO Box 457, La Canada, CA 91012 *Tel:* 818-954-0933 *Fax:* 818-954-0910 *E-mail:* noella1b@aol.com *Web Site:* www.noellaballenger.com, pg 1419

Ballew, Deanna, Widen Enterprises Inc, 6911 Mangrove Lane, Madison, WI 53713 *Tel:* 608-222-1296 *Toll Free Tel:* 800-444-2828 *E-mail:* marketing@widen.com *Web Site:* www.widen.com, pg 1233

Balogh, Scott Michael, Balogh International Inc, 1911 N Duncan Rd, Champaign, IL 61822 *Tel:* 217-355-9331 *Fax:* 217-355-9413 *E-mail:* balogh@balogh.com *Web Site:* www.balogh.com, pg 1287

Balthis, Frank S, Frank Balthis Photography, PO Box 255, Davenport, CA 95017-0255 *Tel:* 805-770-3018; 831-426-8205 *E-mail:* frankbalthisphoto@gmail.com *Web Site:* frankbalthis.photoshelter.com, pg 1419

Bandrowczak, Steven, Xerox Corporation, 201 Merritt 7, Norwalk, CT 06851-1056 *Toll Free Tel:* 800-835-6100 (cust serv) *Web Site:* www.xerox.com, pg 1273

Banks, Marcus, BCC Software Inc, 75 Josons Dr, Rochester, NY 14623-3494 *Toll Free Tel:* 800-453-3130; 800-337-0442 (sales) *E-mail:* marketing@bccsoftware.com *Web Site:* www.bccsoftware.com, pg 1365

Baranowski, Tony, Times Citizen Communication Inc, 406 Stevens St, Iowa Falls, IA 50126 *Tel:* 641-648-2521 *Toll Free Tel:* 800-798-2691 *Fax:* 641-648-4765 *E-mail:* tcc@iafalls.com *Web Site:* timescitizen.com, pg 1232

Barbetta, Paul, Hearst Newspapers, 300 W 57 St, New York, NY 10019 *Tel:* 212-649-2000 *Web Site:* www.hearst.com/newspapers, pg 1190

Barker, David, Readerlink Distribution Services LLC, 1420 Kensington Rd, Suite 300, Oakbrook, IL 60523-2164 *Tel:* 708-547-4400 *Toll Free Tel:* 800-549-5389 *E-mail:* info@readerlink.com; marketingservices@readerlink.com *Web Site:* www.readerlink.com, pg 1301

Barko, Stephanie, Stephanie Barko Literary Publicist, Austin, TX 78737 *E-mail:* stephanie@stephaniebarko.com *Web Site:* www.stephaniebarko.com; www.diybookplatform.com, pg 1107

Barkus, Allen E, Ted Barkus Co Inc, 8017 Anderson St, Philadelphia, PA 19118, pg 1099, 1107

Barnard, Robert, Ingram Content Group LLC, One Ingram Blvd, La Vergne, TN 37086-1986 *Tel:* 615-793-5000 *Toll Free Tel:* 800-937-8000 (retailers); 800-937-5300 (ext 1, libs) *E-mail:* customerservice@ingramcontent.com *Web Site:* www.ingramcontent.com, pg 1294, 1316

Barnes, Janet, Bentley Publishers, 1734 Massachusetts Ave, Cambridge, MA 02138-1804 *Tel:* 617-547-4170 *E-mail:* sales@bentleypubs.com *Web Site:* www.bentleypublishers.com, pg 1327

Barnes, Jim, Jenkins Group Inc, 1129 Woodmere Ave, Suite B, Traverse City, MI 49686 *Tel:* 231-933-0445; 213-883-5365 *E-mail:* info@jenkinsgroupinc.com *Web Site:* www.jenkinsgroupinc.com, pg 1227, 1355

Barnwell, Tim, Tim Barnwell Photography, 10 Governors Ct, Asheville, NC 28805 *Tel:* 828-251-0040 *E-mail:* barnwellphoto@hotmail.com *Web Site:* www.barnwellphoto.com, pg 1419

Barrenechea, Mark J, Open Text Corp, 275 Frank Tompa Dr, Waterloo, ON N2L 0A1, Canada *Tel:* 519-888-7111 *Fax:* 519-888-0677 *Web Site:* opentext.com, pg 1374

Barresse, Adam, Independent Publishers Group (IPG), 814 N Franklin St, Chicago, IL 60610 *Tel:* 312-337-0747 *Toll Free Tel:* 800-888-4741 (orders) *Fax:* 312-337-5985 *E-mail:* frontdesk@ipgbook.com; orders@ipgbook.com *Web Site:* www.ipgbook.com, pg 1292, 1328

Barrett, Leslie, PR by the Book LLC, PO Box 6226, Round Rock, TX 78683 *Tel:* 512-501-4399 *Fax:* 512-501-4399 *E-mail:* info@prbythebook.com *Web Site:* www.prbythebook.com, pg 1112

Barrett, Liz, National Council of Teachers of English (NCTE), 340 N Neil St, Suite 104, Champaign, IL 61820 *Tel:* 217-328-3870 *Toll Free Tel:* 877-369-6283 (cust serv) *Fax:* 217-328-9645 *E-mail:* customerservice@ncte.org; permissions@ncte.org *Web Site:* ncte.org, pg 1146

Barrett, Robertson, Hearst Newspapers, 300 W 57 St, New York, NY 10019 *Tel:* 212-649-2000 *Web Site:* www.hearst.com/newspapers, pg 1190

Barrett, Trudy, Midwest Library Service, 11443 Saint Charles Rock Rd, Bridgeton, MO 63044 *Tel:* 314-739-3100 *Fax:* 314-739-1326 *E-mail:* mail@midwestls.com *Web Site:* www.midwestls.com, pg 1319

Barrios, James, BR Printers, 665 Lenfest Rd, San Jose, CA 95133 *Tel:* 408-278-7711 *Fax:* 408-929-8062 *E-mail:* info@brprinters.com *Web Site:* www.brprinters.com, pg 1103, 1249

Barry, Jack, The Tribune News Service, 160 N Stetson Ave, Chicago, IL 60601 *Tel:* 312-222-4131 *E-mail:* tcanews@trbpub.com *Web Site:* www.mctdirect.com; tribunecontentagency.com/tribune-news-service, pg 1191

Barry, John, Brainworks Software, 100 S Main St, Sayville, NY 11782 *Tel:* 631-563-5000 *Toll Free Tel:* 800-755-1111 *Fax:* 631-563-6320 *E-mail:* info@brainworks.com; sales@brainworks.com; support@brainworks.com *Web Site:* www.brainworks.com, pg 1365

Bartelme, Kristin, Readerlink Distribution Services LLC, 1420 Kensington Rd, Suite 300, Oakbrook, IL 60523-2164 *Tel:* 708-547-4400 *Toll Free Tel:* 800-549-5389 *E-mail:* info@readerlink.com; marketingservices@readerlink.com *Web Site:* www.readerlink.com, pg 1301

Barvoets, Alex, New York Legal Publishing Corp, 120 Broadway, Menands, NY 12204 *Tel:* 518-459-1100 *Toll Free Tel:* 800-541-2681 *Fax:* 518-459-9718 *E-mail:* info@nylp.com *Web Site:* www.nylp.com, pg 1373

Barvoets, Ernest, New York Legal Publishing Corp, 120 Broadway, Menands, NY 12204 *Tel:* 518-459-1100 *Toll Free Tel:* 800-541-2681 *Fax:* 518-459-9718 *E-mail:* info@nylp.com *Web Site:* www.nylp.com, pg 1373

Basbanes, Nicholas A, Literary Features Syndicate, 88 Briarcliff Rd, Larchmont, NY 10538 *Tel:* 914-834-7480, pg 1127

Basom, Shari, Small Changes, 1418 NW 53 St, Seattle, WA 98107 *Tel:* 206-382-1980 *Fax:* 206-382-1514 *E-mail:* info@smallchanges.com *Web Site:* www.smallchanges.com, pg 1321

Bastion, Cynthia, Chicago Distribution Center (CDC), 11030 S Langley Ave, Chicago, IL 60628 *Tel:* 773-702-7010 *Toll Free Fax:* 800-621-8476 *Web Site:* press.uchicago.edu/cdc, pg 1289

Bates, Dawn, Knepper Press Corp, 2251 Sweeney Dr, Clinton, PA 15026 *Tel:* 724-899-4200 *Fax:* 724-899-1331 *Web Site:* www.knepperpress.com, pg 1211, 1227, 1255

Batra, Vikrant, HP Inc, 1501 Paige Mill Rd, Palo Alto, CA 94304-1112 *Tel:* 650-857-1501 *Toll Free Tel:* 800-282-6672 *Web Site:* www.hp.com, pg 1370

Battersby, Mark E, The Cricket Letter Inc, PO Box 527, Ardmore, PA 19003-0527 *Tel:* 610-924-9158 *Fax:* 610-924-9159 *E-mail:* crcktinc@aol.com, pg 1190

Bauer, Anne Watson, Association for Childhood Education International, 1875 Connecticut Ave NW, 10th fl, Washington, DC 20009 *Tel:* 202-372-9986 *Toll Free Tel:* 800-423-3563 *E-mail:* headquarters@acei.org *Web Site:* acei.org, pg 1145

Bauer, Margaret, North Carolina Literary Review (NCLR), East Carolina University, English Dept, ECU Mailstop 555 English, Greenville, NC 27858-4353 *Tel:* 252-328-1537 *Fax:* 252-328-4889 *E-mail:* nclrstaff@ecu.edu *Web Site:* nclr.ecu.edu, pg 1135

Bauman, Liz, Round Table Companies, PO Box 1603, Deerfield, IL 60015 *Toll Free Tel:* 833-750-5683 *Web Site:* www.roundtablecompanies.com, pg 1417

Baumgartner, Peter, North Atlantic Publishing Systems Inc, 66 Commonwealth Ave, Concord, MA 01742 *Tel:* 978-371-8989 *E-mail:* naps@napsys.com *Web Site:* www.napsys.com, pg 1373

Baumgartner, Rob, Planar, 1195 NW Compton Dr, Beaverton, OR 97006-1992 *Tel:* 503-748-1100 *Toll Free Tel:* 866-475-2627 *E-mail:* sales@planar.com *Web Site:* www.planar.com, pg 1374

Baxter, Nicole, BookMobile, 5120 Cedar Lake Rd, Minneapolis, MN 55416 *Tel:* 763-398-0030 *Toll Free Tel:* 844-488-4477 *Fax:* 763-398-0198 *Web Site:* www.bookmobile.com, pg 1249

Bean, Mike, Allard Inc, 4601 50 St, Suite 204, Lubbock, TX 79414 *Tel:* 214-736-4983 *E-mail:* info@allardinc.com *Web Site:* www.allardinc.com, pg 1221

Bean, Tom, Tom Bean Photography, PO Box 1567, Flagstaff, AZ 86002-1567 *Tel:* 928-779-4381 *E-mail:* tom@tombean.com *Web Site:* tombean.photoshelter.com, pg 1419

Beard, Morgan, Swedenborg Foundation, 320 N Church St, West Chester, PA 19380 *Tel:* 610-430-3222 *Toll Free Tel:* 800-355-3222 (cust serv) *Fax:* 610-430-7982 *E-mail:* info@swedenborg.com *Web Site:* swedenborg.com, pg 1322

Beavers, Nick, Media Cybernetics Inc, 1700 Rockville Pike, Suite 240, Rockville, MD 20852 Tel: 301-495-3305 Toll Free Tel: 800-263-2088 E-mail: support@mediacy.com; marketing@mediacy.com Web Site: www.mediacy.com, pg 1372

Becerra, Nannette, Gem Guides Book Co, 1155 W Ninth St, Upland, CA 91786 Tel: 626-855-1611 Toll Free Tel: 800-824-5118 (orders) Fax: 626-855-1610 E-mail: info@gemguidesbooks.com; sales@gemguidesbooks.com (orders) Web Site: www.gemguidesbooks.com, pg 1315

Beck, Eileen L, Glatfelter, Capitol Towers South, 4350 Congress St, Suite 600, Charlotte, NC 28209 Tel: 717-850-0170 Toll Free Tel: 866-744-7380 E-mail: info@glatfelter.com Web Site: www.glatfelter.com, pg 1267

Becker, Brian, Widen Enterprises Inc, 6911 Mangrove Lane, Madison, WI 53713 Tel: 608-222-1296 Toll Free Tel: 800-444-2828 E-mail: marketing@widen.com Web Site: www.widen.com, pg 1233

Becker, Pamela, Big Vision Art + Design, 251 Hwy 179, Creekside Plaza A1, Sedona, AZ 86336 Tel: 928-202-6320 Web Site: www.bigvisionarts.com, pg 1412

Beebe, Morton, Morton Beebe Photographer/Author, San Francisco, CA 94111 Tel: 415-362-6222; 415-706-0594 (cell) E-mail: morton.beebe@gmail.com Web Site: www.mortonbeebe.com, pg 1419

Beer, Tom, Kirkus, 1140 Broadway, Suite 802, New York, NY 10001 E-mail: customercare@kirkus.com Web Site: www.kirkusreviews.com, pg 1133

Begley, Christine, Dell Magazines, 6 Prowitt St, Norwalk, CT 06855 Tel: 203-866-6688 Toll Free Tel: 800-220-7443 (corp sales) Fax: 203-854-5962 (pubns) E-mail: customerservice@pennypublications.com Web Site: www.pennydellpuzzles.com, pg 1354

Bell, Emma, International Literary Properties (ILP), 286 Madison Ave, New York, NY 10017 Tel: 646-202-1633 Fax: 212-967-0977 E-mail: contact@ilpliterary.com Web Site: www.internationalliteraryproperties.com, pg 1348

Bell, Michael, Ingram Content Group LLC, One Ingram Blvd, La Vergne, TN 37086-1986 Tel: 615-793-5000 Toll Free Tel: 800-937-8000 (retailers); 800-937-5300 (ext 1, libs) E-mail: customerservice@ingramcontent.com Web Site: www.ingramcontent.com, pg 1294, 1316

Bell, Robin, Chesapeake & Hudson Inc, 27 Jacks Shop Rd, Rochelle, VA 22738 Tel: 301-834-7170 Toll Free Tel: 800-231-4469 E-mail: office@cheshud.com Web Site: www.cheshudinc.com, pg 1288

Belsky, Scott, Adobe Systems Inc, 345 Park Ave, San Jose, CA 95110-2704 Tel: 408-536-6000 Fax: 408-537-6000 Web Site: www.adobe.com, pg 1363

Benanzer, Janice, Baumfolder Corp, 1660 Campbell Rd, Sidney, OH 45365 Tel: 937-492-1281 Toll Free Tel: 800-543-6107 Fax: 937-492-7280 E-mail: baumfolder@baumfolder.com Web Site: www.baumfolder.com, pg 1277

Benatar, Raquel, Renaissance House, 465 Westview Ave, Englewood, NJ 07631 Tel: 201-408-4048 Web Site: www.renaissancehouse.net, pg 1357

Bendror, Jack, Mekatronics Inc, 85 Channel Dr, Port Washington, NY 11050 Tel: 516-883-6805 Fax: 516-883-6948 E-mail: office@mekatronicsinc.com Web Site: mekatronicsinc.com, pg 1269

Benedict, Jim, GLS Companies, 1280 Energy Park Dr, St Paul, MN 55108-5106 Tel: 651-644-3000 Toll Free Tel: 800-655-9405 Web Site: www.glsmn.com, pg 1226, 1254

Benenati, Joe, The Gluefast Co Inc, 3535 State Rte 66, Bldg No 1, Neptune, NJ 07753 Tel: 732-918-4600 Toll Free Tel: 800-242-7318 Fax: 732-918-4649 E-mail: info@gluefast.com Web Site: www.gluefast.com, pg 1337

Bengard, Jamie, Dual Graphics, 370 Cliffwood Park, Brea, CA 92821 Tel: 714-990-3700 Fax: 714-990-6818 Web Site: www.dualgraphics.com, pg 1225, 1252

Bengel, Tricia Racke, Ingram Content Group LLC, One Ingram Blvd, La Vergne, TN 37086-1986 Tel: 615-793-5000 Toll Free Tel: 800-937-8000 (retailers); 800-937-5300 (ext 1, libs) E-mail: customerservice@ingramcontent.com Web Site: www.ingramcontent.com, pg 1294, 1317

Benjamin, Mark, Nuance Communications Inc, One Wayside Rd, Burlington, MA 01803 Tel: 781-565-5000 Toll Free Tel: 800-654-1187 (cust serv); 888-372-1908 (orders) Web Site: www.nuance.com, pg 1374

Benner, Deborah J, Goose River Press, 3400 Friendship Rd, Waldoboro, ME 04572-6337 Tel: 207-832-6665 E-mail: gooseriverpress@gmail.com Web Site: gooseriverpress.com, pg 1226, 1254

Benner, Whitney, PR Newswire, 350 Hudson St, Suite 300, New York, NY 10014-4504 Toll Free Tel: 888-776-0942; 800-776-8090 Toll Free Fax: 800-793-9313 E-mail: mediainquiries@prnewswire.com Web Site: www.prnewswire.com, pg 1112

Bennett, Stephen, Esko USA, 8535 Gander Creek Dr, Miamisburg, OH 45342 Tel: 937-454-1721 Toll Free Tel: 800-743-7131 Fax: 937-454-1522 E-mail: info.usa@esko.com Web Site: www.esko.com, pg 1368

Bennett, Steve, AuthorBytes, PO Box 382103, Cambridge, MA 02238-2103 Tel: 617-492-0442 E-mail: info@authorbytes.com Web Site: www.authorbytes.com, pg 1344

Benson, Ken, PrintWest, 1111 Eighth Ave, Regina, SK S4R 1C9, Canada Tel: 306-525-2304 Toll Free Tel: 800-236-6438 Fax: 306-757-2439 E-mail: general@printwest.com Web Site: www.printwest.com, pg 1213, 1229, 1270, 1282

Benson, Scot, MacDermid Graphics Solutions LLC, 5210 Phillip Lee Dr, Atlanta, GA 30336 Tel: 404-696-4565 Toll Free Tel: 800-348-7201 E-mail: mpsproductinfo@macdermid.com Web Site: graphics.macdermid.com, pg 1281

Bentley, Kelvin, Six Red Marbles LLC, 101 Station Landing, Medford, MA 02155 Tel: 857-588-9000 E-mail: info@sixredmarbles.com Web Site: www.sixredmarbles.com, pg 1231, 1376

Bentley, Michael, Bentley Publishers, 1734 Massachusetts Ave, Cambridge, MA 02138-1804 Tel: 617-547-4170 E-mail: sales@bentleypubs.com Web Site: www.bentleypublishers.com, pg 1327

Benton, Bob, International Literary Properties (ILP), 286 Madison Ave, New York, NY 10017 Tel: 646-202-1633 Fax: 212-967-0977 E-mail: contact@ilpliterary.com Web Site: www.internationalliteraryproperties.com, pg 1348

Benton, Polly, International Literary Properties (ILP), 286 Madison Ave, New York, NY 10017 Tel: 646-202-1633 Fax: 212-967-0977 E-mail: contact@ilpliterary.com Web Site: www.internationalliteraryproperties.com, pg 1348

Bentz, Bob, Purplegator, 1055 Westlakes Dr, Berwyn, PA 19312 Tel: 610-688-6000 Toll Free Tel: 888-76-GATOR (764-2867) Web Site: www.purplegator.com, pg 1350

Benyovszky, Chris, Maple Logistics Solutions, 60 Grumbacher Rd, York, PA 17406 Tel: 717-764-4596 E-mail: info@maplesoln.com Web Site: www.maplelogisticssolutions.com, pg 1296, 1334

Benyovszky, Chris, Maple Press, 480 Willow Springs Lane, York, PA 17406 Tel: 717-764-5911 Toll Free Tel: 800-999-5911 Fax: 717-764-4702 E-mail: sales@maplepress.com Web Site: www.maplepress.com, pg 1212, 1256, 1281

Berchenko, Daniel, Publishers Weekly, 49 W 23 St, 9th fl, New York, NY 10010 Tel: 212-377-5500 Fax: 212-377-2733 Web Site: www.publishersweekly.com, pg 1136

Berent, Irwin, Writers' Supercenter, 560 Roland Dr, Norfolk, VA 23509 Tel: 757-515-4315 E-mail: writerspage@writerspage.com Web Site: writersupercenter.com, pg 1378

Bergenholtz, Tom, ViaTech Publishing Solutions Inc, 11935 N Stemmons Fwy, Dallas, TX 75234 Tel: 214-827-8151 E-mail: marketing@viatechpub.com Web Site: www.viatech.io, pg 1232, 1262

Berger, Corey, Readerlink Distribution Services LLC, 1420 Kensington Rd, Suite 300, Oakbrook, IL 60523-2164 Tel: 708-547-4400 Toll Free Tel: 800-549-5389 E-mail: info@readerlink.com; marketingservices@readerlink.com Web Site: www.readerlink.com, pg 1301

Berger, Dick, Cross Country Computer Corp, 250 Carleton Ave, East Islip, NY 11730-1240 Tel: 631-334-1810 E-mail: inquiry@crosscountrycomputer.com Web Site: www.crosscountrycomputer.com, pg 1119

Berger, Elisa PhD, Cross Country Computer Corp, 250 Carleton Ave, East Islip, NY 11730-1240 Tel: 631-334-1810 E-mail: inquiry@crosscountrycomputer.com Web Site: www.crosscountrycomputer.com, pg 1119

Berger, Thomas, Cross Country Computer Corp, 250 Carleton Ave, East Islip, NY 11730-1240 Tel: 631-334-1810 E-mail: inquiry@crosscountrycomputer.com Web Site: www.crosscountrycomputer.com, pg 1119

Berghaum, Lisa, Monadnock Paper Mills Inc, 117 Antrim Rd, Bennington, NH 03442-4205 Tel: 603-588-3311 Toll Free Tel: 800-221-2159 (cust serv) Fax: 603-588-3158 E-mail: info@mpm.com Web Site: www.mpm.com, pg 1270

Berglind, Debra, Book Express, 2440 Viking Way, Richmond, BC V6V 1N2, Canada Tel: 604-448-7100 Toll Free Tel: 800-663-5714 Fax: 604-270-7161 Toll Free Fax: 800-565-3770 E-mail: info@raincoast.com Web Site: www.raincoast.com, pg 1312

Bergstrom, Gerald, Morris Publishing®, 3212 E Hwy 30, Kearney, NE 68847 Tel: 308-236-7888 Toll Free Tel: 800-650-7888 Fax: 308-237-0263 E-mail: publish@morrispublishing.com Web Site: www.morrispublishing.com, pg 1257

Berkowitz, David H, Gould Paper Corp, 99 Park Ave, 10th fl, New York, NY 10016 Tel: 212-301-0000 Toll Free Tel: 800-221-3043 Fax: 212-481-0067 E-mail: info@gouldpaper.com Web Site: www.gouldpaper.com, pg 1267

Berkowitz, Jay, Circle Graphics Inc, 316 Main St, Suite 1C, Reisters Town, MD 21136 Tel: 410-833-2200 E-mail: production@circleusa.com Web Site: www.circleusa.com, pg 1223

Berkowitz, Richard, Circle Graphics Inc, 316 Main St, Suite 1C, Reisters Town, MD 21136 Tel: 410-833-2200 E-mail: production@circleusa.com Web Site: www.circleusa.com, pg 1223

Berlow, David, The Font Bureau Inc, 151 Beach Rd, Vineyard Haven, MA 02568 E-mail: info@fontbureau.com Web Site: fontbureau.typenetwork.com, pg 1225

Berlow, Sam, The Font Bureau Inc, 151 Beach Rd, Vineyard Haven, MA 02568 E-mail: info@fontbureau.com Web Site: fontbureau.typenetwork.com, pg 1225

Berman, David, David Berman Communications, 340 Selby Ave, Ottawa, ON K2A 3X6, Canada Tel: 613-728-6777 Toll Free Tel: 800-665-1809 E-mail: info@davidberman.com Web Site: www.wcag2.com, pg 1222

Bermudes, Peter, Gail Leondar Public Relations, 19 Belknap St, Arlington, MA 02474 Tel: 781-648-1658 Web Site: www.glprbooks.com, pg 1109

Bernard, Peter, Pacific Publishing Co Inc, 636 Alaska St S, Seattle, WA 98108 Tel: 206-461-1300 E-mail: ppcprint@nwlink.com; ppccirc@nwlink.com; ppcbind@nwlink.com Web Site: pacificpublishingcompany.com, pg 1258

Bernhardt, Phil, Scholastic School Reading Events, 1080 Greenwood Blvd, Lake Mary, FL 32746 Tel: 407-829-8000 Toll Free Tel: 800-770-4662 Fax: 407-829-2600 E-mail: custservbf@scholasticbookfairs.com Web Site: bookfairs.scholastic.com/content/fairs/home.html, pg 1302, 1321

Bernstein, David, The Gate Worldwide, 71 Fifth Ave, 8th fl, New York, NY 10003 Tel: 212-508-3400 Fax: 212-508-3402 (cgi) E-mail: contact@thegateworldwide.com Web Site: thegateworldwide.com, pg 1099

Bernstein, Mark, Eastgate Systems Inc, 134 Main St, Watertown, MA 02472 Tel: 617-924-9044 Toll Free Tel: 800-562-1638 E-mail: info@eastgate.com Web Site: www.eastgate.com, pg 1368

Bernstein, Stuart, Liliana Valenzuela, 1103 Maufrais St, Austin, TX 78703 Tel: 512-804-8141 E-mail: aguafuegolv@gmail.com Web Site: www.lilianavalenzuela.com, pg 1405

Berry, Nerry, Bryan Farrish Marketing, 1828 Broadway, 2nd fl, Santa Monica, CA 90404 Tel: 310-998-8305 E-mail: airplay@radio-media.com Web Site: www.radio-media.com, pg 1108

Berry, Savinay, Open Text Corp, 275 Frank Tompa Dr, Waterloo, ON N2L 0A1, Canada Tel: 519-888-7111 Fax: 519-888-0677 Web Site: opentext.com, pg 1374

Berry, Taylor, Penguin Random House Canada, a Penguin Random House company, 320 Front St W, Suite 1400, Toronto, ON M5V 3B6, Canada Tel: 416-364-4449 Toll Free Tel: 888-523-9292 (cust serv) Fax: 416-598-7764 E-mail: customerservicescanada@penguinrandomhouse.com; publicitycanada@penguinrandomhouse.com; rightscanada@penguinrandomhouse.com Web Site: www.penguinrandomhouse.ca, pg 1299

Bertelle, Jeanne, Bert Davis Executive Search Inc, 555 Fifth Ave, Suite 302, New York, NY 10017 Tel: 212-838-4000 E-mail: info@bertdavis.com Web Site: www.bertdavis.com, pg 1381

Bertelli, Eileen, Parson Weems' Publisher Services LLC, 3811 Canterbury Rd, No 707, Baltimore, MD 21218 Tel: 914-948-4259 Toll Free Fax: 866-861-0337 E-mail: office@parsonweems.com Web Site: www.parsonweems.com, pg 1299

Bertuch, Michael, ViaTech Publishing Solutions Inc, 11935 N Stemmons Fwy, Dallas, TX 75234 Tel: 214-827-8151 E-mail: marketing@viatechpub.com Web Site: www.viatech.io, pg 1232, 1262

Berty, Ron, Matrox Graphics Inc, 1055 Saint Regis Blvd, Dorval, QC H9P 2T4, Canada Tel: 514-822-6000 Toll Free Tel: 800-361-1408 (sales) Fax: 514-822-6363 Web Site: www.matrox.com/graphics, pg 1372

Best, Kirby, Penguin Random House Canada, a Penguin Random House company, 320 Front St W, Suite 1400, Toronto, ON M5V 3B6, Canada Tel: 416-364-4449 Toll Free Tel: 888-523-9292 (cust serv) Fax: 416-598-7764 E-mail: customerservicescanada@penguinrandomhouse.com; publicitycanada@penguinrandomhouse.com; rightscanada@penguinrandomhouse.com Web Site: www.penguinrandomhouse.ca, pg 1299

Bethke, Darwin, Action Printing, N6637 Rolling Meadows Dr, Fond du Lac, WI 54937 Tel: 920-907-7820 E-mail: info@actionprinting.com Web Site: www.actionprinting.com, pg 1247

Bethune, Bob, Maple Press, 480 Willow Springs Lane, York, PA 17406 Tel: 717-764-5911 Toll Free Tel: 800-999-5911 Fax: 717-764-4702 E-mail: sales@maplepress.com Web Site: www.maplepress.com, pg 1212, 1256, 1281

Bevington, Stan, Coach House Printing, 80 bpNichol Lane, Toronto, ON M5S 3J4, Canada Tel: 416-979-2217 Toll Free Tel: 800-367-6360 (outside Toronto) Fax: 416-977-1158 E-mail: mail@chbooks.com Web Site: www.chbooks.com, pg 1223, 1250

Beyer, Rodger, Worzalla, 3535 Jefferson St, Stevens Point, WI 54481 Tel: 715-344-9608 Fax: 715-344-2578 Web Site: www.worzalla.com, pg 1215, 1233, 1262

Bible, Maria, Vectorworks Inc, 7150 Riverwood Dr, Columbia, MD 21046 Tel: 410-290-5114 Toll Free Tel: 888-646-4223 (sales) Fax: 410-290-7266 E-mail: sales@vectorworks.net Web Site: www.vectorworks.net, pg 1378

Bicksler, Dennis, North Market Street Graphics (NMSG), 317 N Market St, Lancaster, PA 17603 Tel: 717-392-7438 E-mail: mail@nmsgbooks.com Web Site: www.nmsgbooks.com, pg 1229

Biegel, Brian, D&K Group Inc, 1795 Commerce Dr, Elk Grove Village, IL 60007 Tel: 847-956-0160; 847-956-4757 (tech support) Toll Free Tel: 800-632-2314 Fax: 847-956-8214 E-mail: info@dkgroup.net Web Site: www.dkgroup.com, pg 1251, 1266, 1279

Biesiadecki, Paul J, Mohawk Fine Papers Inc, 465 Saratoga St, Cohoes, NY 12047 Tel: 518-237-1740 Toll Free Tel: 800-THE-MILL (843-6455) Fax: 518-237-7394 Web Site: www.mohawkconnects.com, pg 1270

Bigelow, Topher, Independent Publishers Group (IPG), 814 N Franklin St, Chicago, IL 60610 Tel: 312-337-0747 Toll Free Tel: 800-888-4741 (orders) Fax: 312-337-5985 E-mail: frontdesk@ipgbook.com; orders@ipgbook.com Web Site: www.ipgbook.com, pg 1292, 1328

Biggins, Eric, Sheridan PA, 450 Fame Ave, Hanover, PA 17331 Tel: 717-632-3535 Toll Free Tel: 800-352-2210 Fax: 717-633-8900 Web Site: www.sheridan.com, pg 1260

Bilitzky, Tammy, Data Conversion Laboratory Inc (DCL), 61-18 190 St, Suite 205, Fresh Meadows, NY 11365 Tel: 718-357-8700 Toll Free Tel: 800-321-2816 (provider problems) E-mail: info@dclab.com Web Site: www.dataconversionlaboratory.com, pg 1224, 1367

Bilyard, Celeste, Westchester Publishing Services, 4 Old Newtown Rd, Danbury, CT 06810 Tel: 203-791-0080 Fax: 203-791-9286 E-mail: info@westchesterpubsvcs.com Web Site: www.westchesterpublishingservices.com, pg 1233

Binder, Fred, Smith-Edwards-Dunlap Co, 2867 E Allegheny Ave, Philadelphia, PA 19134 Tel: 215-425-8800 Toll Free Tel: 800-829-0020 Fax: 215-425-9715 E-mail: sales@sed.com Web Site: www.sed.com, pg 1231, 1260, 1272

Bindseil, Heather, Library Bound Inc, 100 Bathurst Dr, Unit 2, Waterloo, ON N2V 1V6, Canada Tel: 519-885-3233 Toll Free Tel: 800-363-4728 Fax: 519-885-2662 Web Site: www.librarybound.com, pg 1318

Bird, Andy, Publicis North America, 1675 Broadway, New York, NY 10009 Tel: 212-474-5000 Web Site: www.publicisna.com, pg 1112

Birdsall, Martin, Purplegator, 1055 Westlakes Dr, Berwyn, PA 19312 Tel: 610-688-6000 Toll Free Tel: 888-76-GATOR (764-2867) Web Site: www.purplegator.com, pg 1350

Birkhead, Shaina, The Children's Book Council (CBC), 54 W 39 St, 14th fl, New York, NY 10018 E-mail: cbc.info@cbcbooks.org Web Site: www.cbcbooks.org, pg 1145

Biscanti, John, Bulkley Dunton, One Penn Plaza, Suite 2814, 250 W 34 St, New York, NY 10119 Tel: 212-863-1800 Toll Free Tel: 800-347-9279 Fax: 212-863-1872 Web Site: www.bulkleydunton.com, pg 1265

Bishop, Jennifer, Jennifer Bishop Photography, 843 W University Pkwy, Baltimore, MD 21210 Tel: 410-366-6662 Web Site: www.jenniferbishopphotography.com, pg 1419

Black, Alison, Ingram Publisher Services, an Ingram brand, 14 Ingram Blvd, Mail Stop 631, La Vergne, TN 37086 Tel: 615-793-5000 Toll Free Tel: 866-400-5351 (cust serv) E-mail: ips@ingramcontent.com Web Site: www.ingrampublisherservices.com, pg 1294

Black, Chris, Rayonier Advanced Materials, 1301 Riverplace Blvd, Suite 2300, Jacksonville, FL 32207 Tel: 904-357-4600 Web Site: rayonieram.com, pg 1270

Black, Roger, The Font Bureau Inc, 151 Beach Rd, Vineyard Haven, MA 02568 E-mail: info@fontbureau.com Web Site: fontbureau.typenetwork.com, pg 1225

Blackie, Michael, Literature & Medicine, 2715 N Charles St, Baltimore, MD 21218-4363 Tel: 410-516-6987 (journal orders outside US & CN) Toll Free Tel: 800-548-1784 (journal orders) Fax: 410-578-2865 (journal orders) E-mail: jrnlcirc@jh.edu (journal orders) Web Site: www.press.jhu.edu/journals/literature-and-medicine, pg 1134

Blackwell, Taylor, Walker360, 2501 Fifth Ave E, Montgomery, AL 36107 Tel: 334-832-4975 E-mail: info@walker360.com Web Site: walker360.com, pg 1214, 1262

Blaine, Devon, The Blaine Group Inc, 8665 Wilshire Blvd, No 301, Beverly Hills, CA 90211 Tel: 310-360-1499 Fax: 310-360-1498 Web Site: www.blainegroupinc.com, pg 1107

Blair, Gary Ryan, GoalsGuy Learning Systems, 36181 E Lake Rd, Suite 139, Palm Harbor, FL 34685 Toll Free Tel: 877-462-5748 Fax: 813-435-2022 Toll Free Fax: 877-903-2284 E-mail: info@goalsguy.com Web Site: www.100daychallenge.com, pg 1316

Blake, Corey Michael, Round Table Companies, PO Box 1603, Deerfield, IL 60015 Toll Free Tel: 833-750-5683 Web Site: www.roundtablecompanies.com, pg 1417

Blanchett, Brian, Canvys® Visual Technology Solutions, 40W267 Keslinger Rd, LaFox, IL 60147 Toll Free Tel: 888-735-7373 Fax: 630-208-2350 Web Site: www.canvys.com, pg 1366

Blanks, Jeff, Blanks Printing & Imaging Inc, 2343 N Beckley Ave, Dallas, TX 75208 Tel: 214-741-3905 Toll Free Tel: 800-325-7651 E-mail: sales@blanks.com Web Site: www.blanks.com, pg 1222, 1249

Blanks, Leron, Blanks Printing & Imaging Inc, 2343 N Beckley Ave, Dallas, TX 75208 Tel: 214-741-3905 Toll Free Tel: 800-325-7651 E-mail: sales@blanks.com Web Site: www.blanks.com, pg 1222, 1249

Blatt, Lou, Open Text Corp, 275 Frank Tompa Dr, Waterloo, ON N2L 0A1, Canada Tel: 519-888-7111 Fax: 519-888-0677 Web Site: opentext.com, pg 1374

Blesch, Susan, North American Color Inc, 5960 S Sprinkle Rd, Portage, MI 49002 Tel: 269-323-0552 Toll Free Tel: 800-537-8296 Fax: 269-323-0190 E-mail: info@nac-mi.com Web Site: www.nac-mi.com, pg 1229

Blevins, Tim, Augsburg Fortress Publishers, Publishing House of the Evangelical Lutheran Church in America, 510 Marquette Ave S, Minneapolis, MN 55402 Tel: 612-330-3300 Toll Free Tel: 800-426-0115 (ext 639, subns); 800-328-4648 (orders) Fax: 612-330-3455 Toll Free Fax: 800-722-7766 (orders) E-mail: customercare@augsburgfortress.org; copyright@augsburgfortress.org (reprint permission requests); info@augsburgfortress.org Web Site: www.augsburgfortress.org; www.1517.media, pg 1311

Blissick, Ed, Sheridan MI, 613 E Industrial Dr, Chelsea, MI 48118 Tel: 734-475-9145 Web Site: www.sheridan.com, pg 1213, 1259, 1271

Blissick, Ed, Sheridan PA, 450 Fame Ave, Hanover, PA 17331 Tel: 717-632-3535 Toll Free Tel: 800-352-2210 Fax: 717-633-8900 Web Site: www.sheridan.com, pg 1260

Blohm, Charlene, C Blohm & Associates Inc, 5999 Monona Dr, Monona, WI 53716-3531 Tel: 608-216-7300 E-mail: hello@cblohm.com Web Site: www.cblohm.com, pg 1107

Blokzyl, Alicia, Clare Printing, 206 S Keystone Ave, Sayre, PA 18840 Tel: 570-888-2244 E-mail: hr@clareprint.com Web Site: www.clareprint.com, pg 1223, 1250, 1278

Bloomgarden, Kathy PhD, Ruder Finn Inc, 425 E 53 St, New York, NY 10022 Tel: 212-593-6400 E-mail: info@ruderfinn.com Web Site: www.ruderfinn.com, pg 1112

Blouin, Ronald, Les Messageries ADP, 2315, rue de la Province, Longueuil, QC J4G 1G4, Canada Tel: 450-640-1234 (commercial); 450-640-1237 (sales) Toll Free Tel: 800-771-3022 (commercial); 866-874-1237 (sales) Fax: 450-640-1251 (commercial); 450-674-6237 (sales) Toll Free Fax: 800-603-0433 (commercial); 866-874-6237 (sales) E-mail: adpcommandes@messageries-adp.com Web Site: www.messageries-adp.com, pg 1285

Blunck, Kay, World Literature Today, 630 Parrington Oval, Suite 110, Norman, OK 73019-4033 Tel: 405-325-4531 E-mail: wlt@ou.edu Web Site: www.worldliteraturetoday.org, pg 1137

Bode, John, Readerlink Distribution Services LLC, 1420 Kensington Rd, Suite 300, Oakbrook, IL 60523-2164 Tel: 708-547-4400 Toll Free Tel: 800-549-5389

E-mail: info@readerlink.com; marketingservices@readerlink.com Web Site: www.readerlink.com, pg 1301

Bodie, Shannon, BookWise Design, 29089 SW Costa Circle W, Wilsonville, OR 97070 Tel: 503-542-3551 Toll Free Tel: 800-697-9833 Web Site: bookwisedesign.com, pg 1223, 1412

Bodziak, Stacy, Bellevue Literary Review, 149 E 23 St, Suite 1516, New York, NY 10010 Tel: 917-375-5790 E-mail: info@BLReview.org Web Site: www.BLReview.org, pg 1130

Boe, Terry, Multi-Tech Systems Inc, 2205 Woodale Dr, Mounds View, MN 55112 Tel: 763-785-3500 Toll Free Tel: 800-328-9717 Fax: 763-785-9874 E-mail: info@multitech.com; sales@multitech.com; mtsmktg@multitech.com Web Site: www.multitech.com, pg 1373

Bogs, Kathy, Fujii Associates Inc, 75 Sunny Hill Dr, Troy, MO 63379 Tel: 636-528-2546 Fax: 636-600-5153 Web Site: www.fujiiassociates.com, pg 1291

Boland, David W III, Fall River News Co Inc, 144 Robeson St, Fall River, MA 02720 Tel: 508-679-5266 E-mail: frnewsco@gmail.com, pg 1315

Bolden, Jevon, Embolden Media Group, PO Box 953607, Lake Mary, FL 32795-3607 E-mail: info@emboldenmediagroup.com Web Site: emboldenmediagroup.com, pg 1346

Bolger, Dik, Bolger Vision Beyond Print, 3301 Como Ave SE, Minneapolis, MN 55414-2809 Tel: 651-645-6311 Toll Free Tel: 866-264-3287 E-mail: contact@bolgerinc.com Web Site: www.bolgerinc.com, pg 1103

Bolin, Mandy, Tennessee Book Co, 1550 Heil Quaker Blvd, La Vergne, TN 37086 Tel: 615-793-5040 Toll Free Tel: 800-456-0418 Fax: 615-213-9545 Web Site: www.tennesseebook.com, pg 1322

Bond, Lynn, Forecast, 2550 W Tyvola Rd, Suite 300, Charlotte, NC 28217 Tel: 704-998-3100 Toll Free Tel: 800-775-1800 (info servs); 800-775-1700 (cust serv) Toll Free Fax: 866-557-3396 (cust serv) E-mail: btinfo@baker-taylor.com Web Site: www.baker-taylor.com, pg 1132

Bondarenko, Marc, Bondarenko Photography, 210 S 41 St, Birmingham, AL 35222 Tel: 205-592-8319; 205-243-9910 (cell) E-mail: info@bondarenkophoto.com Web Site: www.bondarenkophoto.com, pg 1420

Bondell, Martin, Fotofolio, 561 Broadway, New York, NY 10012 Tel: 212-226-0923 Toll Free Tel: 800-955-FOTO (955-3686) E-mail: contact@fotofolio.com Web Site: www.fotofolio.com, pg 1291

Bonner, Erin, Penguin Random House Canada, a Penguin Random House company, 320 Front St W, Suite 1400, Toronto, ON M5V 3B6, Canada Tel: 416-364-4449 Toll Free Tel: 888-523-9292 (cust serv) Fax: 416-598-7764 E-mail: customerservicescanada@penguinrandomhouse.com; publicitycanada@penguinrandomhouse.com; rightscanada@penguinrandomhouse.com Web Site: www.penguinrandomhouse.ca, pg 1299

Boockoff-Bajdek, Michelle, SumTotal Systems LLC, 2850 NW 43 St, Suite 150, Gainesville, FL 32606 Tel: 352-264-2800 Toll Free Tel: 866-933-1416 Fax: 352-374-2257 E-mail: customersupport@sumtotalsystems.com Web Site: www.sumtotalsystems.com, pg 1377

Borden, Garrett, Gorham Printing, 3718 Mahoney Dr, Centralia, WA 98531 Tel: 360-623-1323 Toll Free Tel: 800-837-0970 E-mail: info@gorhamprinting.com Web Site: www.gorhamprinting.com, pg 1254

Borden, Kelly, Love & Logic Institute Inc, 2207 Jackson St, Suite 102, Golden, CO 80401-2300 Tel: 303-278-7552 Toll Free Tel: 800-338-4065 Fax: 303-278-3894 Toll Free Fax: 800-455-7557 E-mail: cservice@loveandlogic.com Web Site: www.loveandlogic.com, pg 1372

Boretz, Adam, Publishers Weekly, 49 W 23 St, 9th fl, New York, NY 10010 Tel: 212-377-5500 Fax: 212-377-2733 Web Site: www.publishersweekly.com, pg 1136

Borg, Paul, Adair Graphic Communications, 26975 Northline Rd, Taylor, MI 48180 Tel: 734-941-6300 Fax: 734-942-0920 E-mail: adair@printwell.com Web Site: www.adairgraphic.com, pg 1207, 1221, 1247, 1277

Borics, David, Quality Bindery Services Inc, 501 Amherst St, Buffalo, NY 14207 Tel: 716-883-5185 Toll Free Tel: 888-883-1266 Fax: 716-883-1598 E-mail: info@qualitybindery.com Web Site: www.qualitybindery.com, pg 1259

Borle, Kim, Power Engineering Books Ltd, 7 Perron St, St Albert, AB T8N 1E3, Canada Tel: 780-458-3155; 780-459-2525 Toll Free Tel: 800-667-3155 Fax: 780-460-2530 E-mail: power@nucleus.com Web Site: www.powerengbooks.com, pg 1299

Boron, Ben, William S Hein & Co Inc, 2350 N Forest Rd, Suite 10A, Getzville, NY 14068 Tel: 716-882-2600 Toll Free Tel: 800-828-7571 Fax: 716-883-8100 E-mail: mail@wshein.com; marketing@wshein.com; customerservice@wshein.com Web Site: home.heinonline.org, pg 1316

Borta, Frank, Hassett Express, 17W775 Butterfield Rd, Suite 109, Oakbrook Terrace, IL 60181 Tel: 630-530-6515 Fax: 630-530-6538 Web Site: www.hassettexpress.com, pg 1334

Borth, DeMar, MBA Computer Service, 1920 Lookout Dr, North Mankato, MN 56003 Tel: 507-625-3797, pg 1228

Bortner, Steve, GHP, 475 Heffernan Dr, West Haven, CT 06516 Tel: 203-479-7500 Fax: 203-479-7575 Web Site: www.ghpmedia.com, pg 1226, 1253

Bossingham, Rob, Omnipress, 2600 Anderson St, Madison, WI 53704 Tel: 608-246-2600 Toll Free Tel: 800-828-0305 E-mail: justask@omnipress.com Web Site: www.omnipress.com, pg 1213, 1257

Bostrom, Annie, Booklist, 225 N Michigan Ave, Suite 1300, Chicago, IL 60601 Tel: 312-944-6780 Toll Free Tel: 800-545-2433 Fax: 312-440-9374 E-mail: info@booklistonline.com; ala@ala.org Web Site: www.booklistonline.com; www.ala.org, pg 1130

Botica, Emily, Diamond Book Distributors (DBD), 10150 York Rd, Hunt Valley, MD 21030 Tel: 443-318-8001; 443-318-8519 (cust serv) E-mail: distribution@diamondbookdistributors.com; dbdreorders@diamondbookdistributors.com (orders); books@diamondbookdistributors.com (cust serv) Web Site: www.diamondbookdistributors.com, pg 1290

Boulerice, Yvan, Art Image Publications, PO Box 160, Derby Line, VT 05830 Toll Free Tel: 800-361-2598 Toll Free Fax: 800-559-2598 E-mail: customer.service@artimagepublications.com; info@artimagepublications.com Web Site: www.artimagepublications.com, pg 1311

Bowen, Barbara, Bowen Books LLC, 971 First Ave, New York, NY 10022 Tel: 212-421-5797 E-mail: bowenbooks@aol.com, pg 1354

Bowen, Lori, Ingram Content Group LLC, One Ingram Blvd, La Vergne, TN 37086-1986 Tel: 615-793-5000 Toll Free Tel: 800-937-8000 (retailers); 800-937-5300 (ext 1, libs) E-mail: customerservice@ingramcontent.com Web Site: www.ingramcontent.com, pg 1317

Bowen, Rickey, WeWrite LLC, 11040 Alba Rd, Ben Lomond, CA 95005 Tel: 831-336-3382 E-mail: info@wewrite.net Web Site: www.wewrite.net, pg 1323, 1378

Bowen, Tom, Fujii Associates Inc, 75 Sunny Hill Dr, Troy, MO 63379 Tel: 636-528-2546 Fax: 636-600-5153 Web Site: www.fujiiassociates.com, pg 1291

Bowles, Gerald, Progress Printing Plus, 2677 Waterlick Rd, Lynchburg, VA 24502 Tel: 434-239-9213 Toll Free Tel: 800-572-7804 Fax: 434-832-7573 E-mail: info@progressprintplus.com Web Site: www.progressprintplus.com, pg 1105, 1213, 1230, 1258

Bowlware, Ben, Maxcess International, 222 W Memorial Rd, Oklahoma City, OK 73114 Tel: 405-755-1600 Toll Free Tel: 800-639-3433 Fax: 405-755-8425 E-mail: sales@maxcessintl.com Web Site: www.maxcessintl.com, pg 1282

Bowman, Benny, Worth Higgins & Associates Inc, 8770 Park Central Dr, Richmond, VA 23227-1146 Tel: 804-264-2304 Toll Free Tel: 800-883-7768 Fax: 804-264-5733 E-mail: contact@whaprint.com Web Site: www.worthhiggins.com, pg 1226, 1254

Boyd, Debby, The John Roberts Company, 9687 East River Rd NW, Minneapolis, MN 55433 Tel: 763-755-5500 Toll Free Tel: 800-551-1534 Fax: 763-755-0394 E-mail: success@johnroberts.com Web Site: www.johnroberts.com; www.facebook.com/TheJohnRobertsCompany, pg 1105

Boydston, Ken, Megavision Inc, PO Box 60158, Santa Barbara, CA 93160 Tel: 805-964-1400 Toll Free Tel: 888-324-2580 E-mail: info@mega-vision.com Web Site: www.mega-vision.com, pg 1372

Boyer, Randy, Yurchak Printing Inc, 920 Links Ave, Landisville, PA 17538 Tel: 717-399-0209 E-mail: ypi.info@yurchak.com Web Site: www.yurchak.com, pg 1215, 1262, 1284

Boyles, Kelly, Copywriters' Council of America™ (CCA), Linick Bldg, 7 Putter Lane, Middle Island, NY 11953 Tel: 631-924-3888; 631-924-8555; 631-604-8599 E-mail: linickgroup@gmail.com, pg 1345

Boyles, Kelly, LK Advertising Agency, Linick Bldg, 7 Putter Lane, Middle Island, NY 11953 Tel: 631-924-3888; 631-924-8555; 631-604-8599 E-mail: topmarketingadvisor@gmail.com; linickgroup@gmail.com, pg 1100

Boynton, Paul G, Rayonier Advanced Materials, 1301 Riverplace Blvd, Suite 2300, Jacksonville, FL 32207 Tel: 904-357-4600 Web Site: rayonieram.com, pg 1270

Bozuwa, Paul, Sheridan MI, 613 E Industrial Dr, Chelsea, MI 48118 Tel: 734-475-9145 Web Site: www.sheridan.com, pg 1213, 1259, 1271

Bozuwa, Paul, Sheridan NH, 69 Lyme Rd, Hanover, NH 03755 Tel: 603-643-2220 Web Site: www.sheridan.com, pg 1259

Bozuwa, Paul, Sheridan PA, 450 Fame Ave, Hanover, PA 17331 Tel: 717-632-3535 Toll Free Tel: 800-352-2210 Fax: 717-633-8900 Web Site: www.sheridan.com, pg 1259

Bozuwa, Paul, Sheridan Saline, 960 Woodland Dr, Saline, MI 48176 Tel: 734-429-5411 Web Site: www.sheridan.com, pg 1214, 1260

Bradley, Bob, Bradford & Bigelow Inc, 3 Perkins Way, Newburyport, MA 01950-4007 Tel: 978-904-3100 E-mail: sales@bradford-bigelow.com Web Site: www.bradford-bigelow.com, pg 1208, 1249

Bradley, Chris, Fundcraft Publishing, 410 Hwy 72 W, Collierville, TN 38017 Tel: 901-853-7070 Toll Free Tel: 800-853-1363 Fax: 901-853-6196 E-mail: info@fundcraft.com Web Site: www.fundcraft.com, pg 1210

Bradley, David, Fundcraft Publishing, 410 Hwy 72 W, Collierville, TN 38017 Tel: 901-853-7070 Toll Free Tel: 800-853-1363 Fax: 901-853-6196 E-mail: info@fundcraft.com Web Site: www.fundcraft.com, pg 1210

Bradley, Georgienne, Bradley Ireland Productions, c/o Sea Save Foundation, 20540 Pacific Coast Hwy, Malibu, CA 90265, pg 1420

Bradley, Lynda, BMI Educational Services Inc, 26 Haypress Rd, Cranbury, NJ 08512 Tel: 732-329-6991 Toll Free Tel: 800-222-8100 (orders only) Fax: 732-329-6994 Toll Free Fax: 800-986-9393 (orders only) E-mail: info@bmionline.com Web Site: bmionline.com, pg 1312, 1325

Brakel-Schutt, Nina, Widen Enterprises Inc, 6911 Mangrove Lane, Madison, WI 53713 Tel: 608-222-1296 Toll Free Tel: 800-444-2828 E-mail: marketing@widen.com Web Site: www.widen.com, pg 1233

Braley, Walt, Independent Publishers Group (IPG), 814 N Franklin St, Chicago, IL 60610 Tel: 312-337-0747 Toll Free Tel: 800-888-4741 (orders) Fax: 312-337-5985 E-mail: frontdesk@ipgbook.com; orders@ipgbook.com Web Site: www.ipgbook.com, pg 1292, 1328

Braman, Carol, Publishers Storage & Shipping Corp, 46 Development Rd, Fitchburg, MA 01420 Tel: 978-345-2121 Web Site: www.pssc.com, pg 1335

Bramson, Scott B, Magnum Book Services LLC, 180 Raritan Center Pkwy, Suite 105, Edison, NJ 08837 *Tel:* 908-349-2300 *E-mail:* info@magnumbookservices.com; usoffice@magnumbookservices.com *Web Site:* www.magnumbookservices.com, pg 1334

Brancati, John, ACC Distribution Ltd, 6 W 18 St, Suite 4B, New York, NY 10011 *Tel:* 212-645-1111 *Toll Free Tel:* 800-252-5231 *Fax:* 716-242-4911 *E-mail:* ussales@accpublishinggroup.com *Web Site:* www.accpublishinggroup.com/us, pg 1285

Branch, Justin, Greenleaf Book Group LLC, PO Box 91869, Austin, TX 78709 *Tel:* 512-891-6100 *Fax:* 512-891-6150 *E-mail:* contact@greenleafbookgroup.com; orders@greenleafbookgroup.com; foreignrights@greenleafbookgroup.com; media@greenleafbookgroup.com *Web Site:* greenleafbookgroup.com, pg 1292, 1355

Brandon, Christine, D C Graphics Inc, 59 Central Ave, Suite 15, Farmingdale, NY 11735 *Tel:* 631-777-3100 *Fax:* 631-777-7899 *E-mail:* prepress@dcgraphicsinc.com *Web Site:* www.dcgraphicsinc.com, pg 1251

Brandt, Suzanne, Feldheim Publishers, 208 Airport Executive Park, Nanuet, NY 10954 *Tel:* 845-356-2282 *Toll Free Tel:* 800-237-7149 (orders) *Fax:* 845-425-1908 *E-mail:* sales@feldheim.com *Web Site:* www.feldheim.com, pg 1315

Branov, Mike, Thistle Printing Ltd, 35 Mobile Dr, Toronto, ON M4A 2P6, Canada *Tel:* 416-288-1288 *Fax:* 416-288-0737 *E-mail:* sales@thistleprinting.com *Web Site:* www.thistleprinting.com, pg 1232, 1261, 1377

Brash, Brian, Actar D, 440 Park Ave S, 17th fl, New York, NY 10016 *Tel:* 212-966-2207 *E-mail:* salesnewyork@actar-d.com *Web Site:* www.actar.com, pg 1285

Brassell, Robert F, Comag Marketing Group LLC (CMG), 155 Village Blvd, Suite 300, Princeton, NJ 08540 *Tel:* 609-524-1800 *Fax:* 609-524-1629 *Web Site:* www.i-cmg.com, pg 1314

Bratton, Jim, AcmeBinding, 8844 Mayfield Rd, Chesterland, OH 44026 *Tel:* 440-729-9411 *Toll Free Tel:* 888-485-5415 *Fax:* 440-729-9415 *Web Site:* www.acmebinding.com, pg 1247

Bratton, Jim, HF Group LLC, 8844 Mayfield Rd, Chesterland, OH 44026 *Tel:* 440-729-2445; 440-729-9411 (bindery) *E-mail:* custservice-oh@hfgroup.com *Web Site:* www.hfgroup.com, pg 1254, 1268, 1325

Brazil, Keith, Translations.com, 1250 Broadway, 32nd fl, New York, NY 10001 *Tel:* 212-689-1616 *Fax:* 212-504-8057 *E-mail:* newyork@translations.com; info@translations.com *Web Site:* translations.com, pg 1405

Breier, Davida, HFS, 2715 N Charles St, Baltimore, MD 21218 *Tel:* 410-516-6965 *Toll Free Tel:* 800-537-5487 (US & CN) *Fax:* 410-516-6998 *E-mail:* hfscustserv@jh.edu *Web Site:* hfs.jhu.edu; www.hfsbooks.com, pg 1292

Breik, Nisreen, Social Studies School Service, 10200 Jefferson Blvd, PO Box 802, Culver City, CA 90232 *Tel:* 310-839-2436 *Toll Free Tel:* 800-421-4246 (US & CN) *Fax:* 310-839-2249 *Toll Free Fax:* 800-944-5432 *E-mail:* access@socialstudies.com; customerservice@socialstudies.com *Web Site:* www.socialstudies.com, pg 1302, 1321

Brenner, Jodi, Pro-Composition Inc, 2501 Catherine St, Suite 3, York, PA 17408 *Tel:* 717-965-9872 *Web Site:* www.pro-composition.com, pg 1230

Brewer, Art, Art Brewer Photography LLC, 25262 Mainsail Dr, Dana Point, CA 92629 *Tel:* 949-661-8930 *E-mail:* art@artbrewer.com *Web Site:* www.artbrewer.com; www.artbrewergallery.com, pg 1420

Brian, Dean, North Market Street Graphics (NMSG), 317 N Market St, Lancaster, PA 17603 *Tel:* 717-392-7438 *E-mail:* mail@nmsgbooks.com *Web Site:* www.nmsgbooks.com, pg 1229

Brickman, Ravelle, Julie A Laitin Enterprises Inc, 160 West End Ave, Suite 23N, New York, NY 10023 *Tel:* 917-841-8566 *E-mail:* info@julielaitin.com *Web Site:* www.julielaitin.com, pg 1100

Brickman, Wendy, Brickman Marketing, 395 Del Monte Ctr, No 250, Monterey, CA 93940 *Tel:* 831-594-1500 *E-mail:* brickman@brickmanmarketing.com *Web Site:* www.brickmanmarketing.com, pg 1107

Briggs, Marian, PadillaCRT, 1101 W River Pkwy, Suite 400, Minneapolis, MN 55415 *Tel:* 612-455-1700 *Fax:* 612-455-1060 *Web Site:* www.padillacrt.com, pg 1111

Brightheart, Harlow, Independent Publishers Group (IPG), 814 N Franklin St, Chicago, IL 60610 *Tel:* 312-337-0747 *Toll Free Tel:* 800-888-4741 (orders) *Fax:* 312-337-5985 *E-mail:* frontdesk@ipgbook.com; orders@ipgbook.com *Web Site:* www.ipgbook.com, pg 1292, 1328

Brilliant, Ashleigh, Ashleigh Brilliant Enterprises, 117 W Valerio St, Santa Barbara, CA 93101 *Tel:* 805-682-0531 *Web Site:* www.ashleighbrilliant.com, pg 1189

Brison, Brandon, Creative Direct Marketing Group Inc (CDMG), 1313 Fourth Ave N, Nashville, TN 37208 *Tel:* 615-814-6633 *Web Site:* www.cdmginc.com, pg 1345

Broad, David M, Digital Wisdom Inc, PO Box 11, Tappahannock, VA 22560-0011 *Tel:* 804-443-9000 *Toll Free Tel:* 800-800-8560 *E-mail:* info@digitalwisdom.net *Web Site:* www.digiwis.com; www.mountainhighmaps.com, pg 1367

Broadhurst, Jamie, Raincoast Books Distribution Ltd, 2440 Viking Way, Richmond, BC V6V 1N2, Canada *Tel:* 604-448-7100 *Toll Free Tel:* 800-663-5714 (CN only) *Fax:* 604-270-7161 *Toll Free Fax:* 800-565-3770 *E-mail:* info@raincoast.com; customerservice@raincoast.com *Web Site:* www.raincoast.com/distribution, pg 1301

Brock, Kara, Independent Publishers Group (IPG), 814 N Franklin St, Chicago, IL 60610 *Tel:* 312-337-0747 *Toll Free Tel:* 800-888-4741 (orders) *Fax:* 312-337-5985 *E-mail:* frontdesk@ipgbook.com; orders@ipgbook.com *Web Site:* www.ipgbook.com, pg 1292

Brockwell, Jason, National Book Network (NBN), 4501 Forbes Blvd, Suite 200, Lanham, MD 20706 *Tel:* 301-459-3366 *Toll Free Tel:* 800-462-6420 (orders only) *Fax:* 301-429-5746 *Toll Free Fax:* 800-338-4550 (orders only) *E-mail:* customercare@nbnbooks.com *Web Site:* www.nbnbooks.com, pg 1298, 1319

Broderick, Tracy, C & C Offset Printing Co USA Inc, 70 W 36 St, Unit 10C, New York, NY 10018 *Tel:* 212-431-4210 *Toll Free Fax:* 866-540-4134 *Web Site:* www.ccoffset.com, pg 1208, 1223, 1249

Brodsky, Steve, Encyclopaedia Britannica Inc, 325 N La Salle St, Suite 200, Chicago, IL 60654 *Tel:* 312-347-7000 (all other countries) *Toll Free Tel:* 800-323-1229 (US & CN) *Fax:* 312-294-2104 *E-mail:* contact@eb.com *Web Site:* www.britannica.com, pg 1315

Brody, Beth, Brody Public Relations, 145 Kingwood Stockton Rd, Stockton, NJ 08559-1711 *Tel:* 908-295-0600 *Web Site:* www.brodypr.com, pg 1108

Brody, Louisa, Ingram Content Group LLC, One Ingram Blvd, La Vergne, TN 37086-1986 *Tel:* 615-793-5000 *Toll Free Tel:* 800-937-8000 (retailers); 800-937-5300 (ext 1, libs) *E-mail:* customerservice@ingramcontent.com *Web Site:* www.ingramcontent.com, pg 1294, 1317

Brody, Louisa, Two Rivers Distribution, an Ingram brand, 1400 Broadway, Suite 520, New York, NY 10018 *Toll Free Tel:* 866-400-5351 *E-mail:* ips@ingramcontent.com (orders, independent bookstores & gift accts) *Web Site:* www.tworiversdistribution.com, pg 1303

Brooks, David, The Country Press Inc, One Commercial Dr, Lakeville, MA 02347 *Tel:* 508-947-4485 *Toll Free Tel:* 888-343-2227 *Fax:* 508-947-8989 *E-mail:* info@countrypressinc.com *Web Site:* www.countrypressprinting.com, pg 1209, 1251

Brooks, Sam, Communication Abstracts, 10 Estes St, Ipswich, MA 01938 *Tel:* 978-356-6500 *Toll Free Tel:* 800-653-2726 *Fax:* 978-356-6565 *E-mail:* information@ebsco.com *Web Site:* www.ebsco.com, pg 1131

Broughton, Brian, B Broughton Co Ltd, 322 Consumers Rd, North York, ON M2J 1P8, Canada *Tel:* 416-690-4777 *Toll Free Tel:* 800-268-4449 *Fax:* 416-690-5357 *E-mail:* sales@bbroughton.com *Web Site:* www.bbroughton.com, pg 1287, 1313

Browdy, Michelle H, IBM Corp, One New Orchard Rd, Armonk, NY 10504 *Tel:* 914-499-1900 *Toll Free Tel:* 800-426-4968 *E-mail:* askibm@vnet.ibm.com *Web Site:* www.ibm.com, pg 1370

Brown, Carol Anne, Tennessee Book Co, 1550 Heil Quaker Blvd, La Vergne, TN 37086 *Tel:* 615-793-5040 *Toll Free Tel:* 800-456-0418 *Fax:* 615-213-9545 *Web Site:* www.tennesseebook.com, pg 1322

Brown, George I, The James & Law Co, 217 W Main St, Clarksburg, WV 26301 *Tel:* 304-624-7401 *Toll Free Tel:* 800-253-5428 *Fax:* 304-624-9331 *E-mail:* sales@jamesandlaw.com *Web Site:* jamesandlaw.com, pg 1317

Brown, Glenn, Gane Brothers & Lane Inc, 1400 Greenleaf Ave, Elk Grove Village, IL 60007 *Tel:* 847-593-3364 *Toll Free Tel:* 800-323-0596 *Toll Free Fax:* 800-784-2464 *E-mail:* sales@ganebrothers.com *Web Site:* www.ganebrothers.com, pg 1267

Brown, Jane, Distributed Art Publishers Inc, 75 Broad St, Suite 630, New York, NY 10004 *Tel:* 212-627-1999 *Toll Free Tel:* 800-338-2665 (cust serv) *Fax:* 212-627-9484 *E-mail:* orders@dapinc.com *Web Site:* www.artbook.com, pg 1290

Brown, Kathy, Sheridan MI, 613 E Industrial Dr, Chelsea, MI 48118 *Tel:* 734-475-9145 *Web Site:* www.sheridan.com, pg 1213, 1259, 1271

Brown, Kortez, Roswell Bookbinding, 2614 N 29 Ave, Phoenix, AZ 85009 *Tel:* 602-272-9338 *Toll Free Tel:* 888-803-8883 *Fax:* 602-272-9786 *Web Site:* www.roswellbookbinding.com, pg 1259, 1326

Brown, Malcolm, Backe Communications, Radnor Corporate Ctr, Bldg 3, Suite 101, 100 Matson Ford Rd, Radnor, PA 19087 *Tel:* 610-947-6900 *Web Site:* www.backemarketing.com, pg 1099

Brown, Melissa, Brown Book Co Ltd, 65 Crockford Blvd, Toronto, ON M1R 3B7, Canada *Tel:* 416-504-9696 *Fax:* 416-504-9393 *E-mail:* bbc@brownbook.ca *Web Site:* www.brownbook.ca, pg 1208

Brown, Robert, Brown Book Co Ltd, 65 Crockford Blvd, Toronto, ON M1R 3B7, Canada *Tel:* 416-504-9696 *Fax:* 416-504-9393 *E-mail:* bbc@brownbook.ca *Web Site:* www.brownbook.ca, pg 1208

Brown, Rose, Clerical Plus, 97 Blueberry Lane, Shelton, CT 06484 *Tel:* 203-225-0879 *Fax:* 203-225-0879 *E-mail:* clericalplus@aol.com *Web Site:* www.clericalplus.net, pg 1366

Brown, Sara, Multi-Tech Systems Inc, 2205 Woodale Dr, Mounds View, MN 55112 *Tel:* 763-785-3500 *Toll Free Tel:* 800-328-9717 *Fax:* 763-785-9874 *E-mail:* info@multitech.com; sales@multitech.com; mtsmktg@multitech.com *Web Site:* www.multitech.com, pg 1373

Browne, Mat, The Bindery Inc, 8201 Brooklyn Blvd, Brooklyn Park, MN 55445 *Tel:* 763-201-2800 *Toll Free Tel:* 800-851-6598 *Fax:* 763-201-2790 *E-mail:* info@thebinderymn.com *Web Site:* www.thebinderymn.com, pg 1249

Browning, Abigail, Dell Magazines, 6 Prowitt St, Norwalk, CT 06855 *Tel:* 203-866-6688 *Toll Free Tel:* 800-220-7443 (corp sales) *Fax:* 203-854-5962 (pubns) *E-mail:* customerservice@pennypublications.com *Web Site:* www.pennydellpuzzles.com, pg 1354

Brownold, Tom, Tom Brownold Photography, 801 W Summit Ave, Flagstaff, AZ 86001 *Tel:* 928-779-1583 *E-mail:* tbrownold@tombrownold.com *Web Site:* www.tombrownold.com, pg 1420

Broze, Gina, Marquand Books, 3131 Western Ave, Suite 522, Seattle, WA 98121 *Tel:* 206-624-2030 *Web Site:* www.marquandbooks.com, pg 1356

Brunet, Donna, Donna Brunet Macro Photography, PO Box 30123, Columbia, MO 65205-3123 *Tel:* 573-999-2178 *Web Site:* www.donnabrunet.com, pg 1420

Bruning, Nat, GOBI® Library Solutions from EBSCO, 999 Maple St, Contoocook, NH 03229 *Tel:* 603-746-3102 *Toll Free Tel:* 800-258-3774 (US & CN) *Fax:* 603-746-5628 *E-mail:* information@ebsco.com *Web Site:* gobi.ebsco.com, pg 1316

Bruns, Amanda, Publishers Weekly, 49 W 23 St, 9th fl, New York, NY 10010 *Tel:* 212-377-5500 *Fax:* 212-377-2733 *Web Site:* www.publishersweekly.com, pg 1136

Bryans, John B, JB Bryans Literary, 7 Meetinghouse Ct, Indian Mills, NJ 08088 *Tel:* 609-922-0369 *E-mail:* info@brylit.com *Web Site:* brylit.com, pg 1344

Bryant, Jonnie, Sheridan Saline, 960 Woodland Dr, Saline, MI 48176 *Tel:* 734-429-5411 *Web Site:* www.sheridan.com, pg 1214, 1260

Bryerman, Cevin, Publishers Weekly, 49 W 23 St, 9th fl, New York, NY 10010 *Tel:* 212-377-5500 *Fax:* 212-377-2733 *Web Site:* www.publishersweekly.com, pg 1135

Buchholz, Miroslawa, The Henry James Review, 2715 N Charles St, Baltimore, MD 21218-4363 *Tel:* 410-516-6987 (journal orders outside US & CN) *Toll Free Tel:* 800-548-1784 (journal orders) *Fax:* 410-578-2865 (journal orders) *E-mail:* jrnlcirc@jh.edu (journal orders) *Web Site:* www.press.jhu.edu/journals/henry-james-review, pg 1132

Buchman, Chris, The Blue Mouse Studio, 26829 37 St, Gobles, MI 49055 *Tel:* 269-628-5160 *E-mail:* frogville@earthlink.net, pg 1412

Buckley, James Jr, Shoreline Publishing Group LLC, 125 Santa Rosa Place, Santa Barbara, CA 93109 *Tel:* 805-564-1004 *E-mail:* info@shorelinepublishing.com *Web Site:* shorelinepublishing.com, pg 1357

Buess, Lani, Bookazine Co Inc, 75 Hook Rd, Bayonne, NJ 07002 *Tel:* 201-339-7777 *Toll Free Tel:* 800-221-8112 *Fax:* 201-339-7778 *E-mail:* info@bookazine.com *Web Site:* www.bookazine.com, pg 1312, 1327

Bulger, Steve, eFulfillment Service Inc, 807 Airport Access Rd, Traverse City, MI 49686 *Tel:* 231-276-5057 *Toll Free Tel:* 866-922-6783 *E-mail:* sales@efulfillmentservice.com *Web Site:* www.efulfillmentservice.com, pg 1333

Bumbaugh, Sue, National Book Network (NBN), 4501 Forbes Blvd, Suite 200, Lanham, MD 20706 *Tel:* 301-459-3366 *Toll Free Tel:* 800-462-6420 (orders only) *Fax:* 301-429-5746 *Toll Free Tel:* 800-338-4550 (orders only) *E-mail:* customercare@nbnbooks.com *Web Site:* www.nbnbooks.com, pg 1298, 1319

Bunning, Ellen, Jeroboam, 120 27 St, San Francisco, CA 94110 *Tel:* 415-637-7840 (cell) *E-mail:* jeroboamster@gmail.com, pg 1429

Bunting, Robert Jr, Bunting Magnetics Co, 500 S Spencer Rd, Newton, KS 67114 *Tel:* 316-284-2020 *Toll Free Tel:* 800-835-2526; 877-576-0156 *Fax:* 316-283-4975 *E-mail:* bmc@buntingmagnetics.com *Web Site:* www.buntingmagnetics.com, pg 1278

Bunting, Robert J Sr, Bunting Magnetics Co, 500 S Spencer Rd, Newton, KS 67114 *Tel:* 316-284-2020 *Toll Free Tel:* 800-835-2526; 877-576-0156 *Fax:* 316-283-4975 *E-mail:* bmc@buntingmagnetics.com *Web Site:* www.buntingmagnetics.com, pg 1278

Buono, Frank, B & Z Printing Inc, 1300 E Wakeham Ave, Unit B, Santa Ana, CA 92705 *Tel:* 714-892-2000 *Web Site:* www.bandzprinting.com, pg 1208, 1248

Burch, Jennifer, ACC Distribution Ltd, 6 W 18 St, Suite 4B, New York, NY 10011 *Tel:* 212-645-1111 *Toll Free Tel:* 800-252-5231 *Fax:* 716-242-4911 *E-mail:* ussales@accpublishinggroup.com *Web Site:* www.accpublishinggroup.com/us, pg 1285

Burden, Matt, eFulfillment Service Inc, 807 Airport Access Rd, Traverse City, MI 49686 *Tel:* 231-276-5057 *Toll Free Tel:* 866-922-6783 *E-mail:* sales@efulfillmentservice.com *Web Site:* www.efulfillmentservice.com, pg 1333

Burghardt, Lance K, Photographix, 1171 Pauline Blvd, Ann Arbor, MI 48103-5319 *Tel:* 734-476-2068, pg 1424

Burgin, Keith, Oklahoma Press Service Inc, 3601 N Lincoln Blvd, Oklahoma City, OK 73105 *Tel:* 405-499-0020 *Toll Free Tel:* 888-815-2672 *Web Site:* www.okpress.com, pg 1383

Burke, Barbara, Jonathan David Publishers Inc, 52 Tuscan Way, Suite 202-371, St Augustine, FL 32092 *Tel:* 718-456-8611 *E-mail:* customerservice@jdbooks.com *Web Site:* www.jdbooks.com, pg 1295

Burke, Suzanne, Augsburg Fortress Publishers, Publishing House of the Evangelical Lutheran Church in America, 510 Marquette Ave S, Minneapolis, MN 55402 *Tel:* 612-330-3300 *Toll Free Tel:* 800-426-0115 (ext 639, subns); 800-328-4648 (orders) *Fax:* 612-330-3455 *Toll Free Tel:* 800-722-7766 (orders) *E-mail:* customercare@augsburgfortress.org; copyright@augsburgfortress.org (reprint permission requests); info@augsburgfortress.org *Web Site:* www.augsburgfortress.org; www.1517.media, pg 1311

Burke, William, Sterling Pierce Co Inc, 395 Atlantic Ave, East Rockaway, NY 11518 *Tel:* 516-593-1170 *Fax:* 516-593-1401 *Web Site:* www.sterlingpierce.com, pg 1214, 1260

Burkhart, Rick, AcmeBinding, 8844 Mayfield Rd, Chesterland, OH 44026 *Tel:* 440-729-9411 *Toll Free Tel:* 888-485-5415 *Fax:* 440-729-9415 *Web Site:* www.acmebinding.com, pg 1247

Burnett, Matia, Publishers Weekly, 49 W 23 St, 9th fl, New York, NY 10010 *Tel:* 212-377-5500 *Fax:* 212-377-2733 *Web Site:* www.publishersweekly.com, pg 1136

Burnett, Sheila, Medievalia et Humanistica: Studies in Medieval & Renaissance Culture, 4501 Forbes Blvd, Suite 200, Lanham, MD 20706 *Tel:* 301-459-3366; 717-794-3800 (cust serv) *Toll Free Tel:* 800-462-6420 (ext 3024, cust serv) *Fax:* 301-429-5748; 717-794-3803 (cust serv) *Toll Free Tel:* 800-338-4550 (cust serv) *E-mail:* customercare@rowman.com *Web Site:* rowman.com, pg 1134

Burnett, Tatrianna, Independent Publishers Group (IPG), 814 N Franklin St, Chicago, IL 60610 *Tel:* 312-337-0747 *Toll Free Tel:* 800-888-4741 (orders) *Fax:* 312-337-5985 *E-mail:* frontdesk@ipgbook.com; orders@ipgbook.com *Web Site:* www.ipgbook.com, pg 1292

Burnham, Jeff, GoodMinds.com, Six Nations of the Grand River Territory, 188 Mohawk St, Brantford, ON N3S 2X2, Canada *Tel:* 519-753-1185 *Toll Free Tel:* 877-862-8483 (CN & US) *Fax:* 519-751-3136 *E-mail:* helpme@goodminds.com *Web Site:* www.goodminds.com, pg 1292

Burnham, Kathy, PadillaCRT, 1101 W River Pkwy, Suite 400, Minneapolis, MN 55415 *Tel:* 612-455-1700 *Fax:* 612-455-1060 *Web Site:* www.padillacrt.com, pg 1111

Burnham, Linda, GoodMinds.com, Six Nations of the Grand River Territory, 188 Mohawk St, Brantford, ON N3S 2X2, Canada *Tel:* 519-753-1185 *Toll Free Tel:* 877-862-8483 (CN & US) *Fax:* 519-751-3136 *E-mail:* helpme@goodminds.com *Web Site:* www.goodminds.com, pg 1292

Burstein, Gerry, G & H Soho Inc, 413 Market St, Elmwood Park, NJ 07407 *Tel:* 201-216-9400 *Fax:* 201-216-1778 *E-mail:* print@ghsoho.com *Web Site:* www.ghsoho.com, pg 1211, 1226, 1253, 1267, 1346, 1354, 1414

Burstein, Jason, G & H Soho Inc, 413 Market St, Elmwood Park, NJ 07407 *Tel:* 201-216-9400 *Fax:* 201-216-1778 *E-mail:* print@ghsoho.com *Web Site:* www.ghsoho.com, pg 1211, 1226, 1253, 1267, 1346, 1354, 1414

Burt, Madelyn, Stonesong, 270 W 39 St, Suite 201, New York, NY 10018 *Tel:* 212-929-4600 *E-mail:* editors@stonesong.com *Web Site:* www.stonesong.com, pg 1357

Burton, Michael, Cenveo Inc, 200 First Stamford Place, 2nd fl, Stamford, CT 06902 *Tel:* 203-595-3000 *Fax:* 203-595-3070 *E-mail:* info@cenveo.com *Web Site:* www.cenveo.com, pg 1209, 1250, 1265

Burton, Robert G Jr, Cenveo Inc, 200 First Stamford Place, 2nd fl, Stamford, CT 06902 *Tel:* 203-595-3000 *Fax:* 203-595-3070 *E-mail:* info@cenveo.com *Web Site:* www.cenveo.com, pg 1209, 1250, 1265

Buser, Jason, All Craft Digital Inc, 289-C Skidmores Rd, Deer Park, NY 11729 *Tel:* 631-254-8495 *Fax:* 631-254-8496, pg 1221

Bush, Nora, Specialist Marketing Services Inc, 777 Terrace Ave, Suite 401, Hasbrouck Heights, NJ 07604 *Tel:* 201-865-5800 *E-mail:* info@sms-inc.com *Web Site:* www.sms-inc.com, pg 1120

Bushell, Ginger, Gracenote, a Nielsen Company, 2000 Powell St, Suite 1500, Emeryville, CA 94608 *Tel:* 510-428-7200 *Web Site:* www.gracenote.com, pg 1190

Buske, Parker, World Literature Today, 630 Parrington Oval, Suite 110, Norman, OK 73019-4033 *Tel:* 405-325-4531 *E-mail:* wlt@ou.edu *Web Site:* www.worldliteraturetoday.org, pg 1137

Butcher, Chantelle, The John Roberts Company, 9687 East River Rd NW, Minneapolis, MN 55433 *Tel:* 763-755-5500 *Toll Free Tel:* 800-551-1534 *Fax:* 763-755-0394 *E-mail:* success@johnroberts.com *Web Site:* www.johnroberts.com; www.facebook.com/TheJohnRobertsCompany, pg 1105

Butier, Mitch, Avery Dennison Corp, 207 N Goode Ave, 6th fl, Glendale, CA 91203-1222 *Tel:* 626-304-2000 *Web Site:* www.averydennison.com, pg 1365

Butler, Butch, StarGroup International Inc, 1194 Old Dixie Hwy, Suite 201, West Palm Beach, FL 33413 *Tel:* 561-547-0667 *E-mail:* info@stargroupinternational.com *Web Site:* stargroupinternational.com, pg 1113

Butler, Doug, Staplex® Electric Stapler Division, 777 Fifth Ave, Brooklyn, NY 11232-1626 *Tel:* 718-768-3333 *Toll Free Tel:* 800-221-0822 *Fax:* 718-965-0750 *E-mail:* info@staplex.com *Web Site:* www.staplex.com, pg 1283

Butler, Rob, Viridiam LLC, 3030 Lowell Dr, Green Bay, WI 54311 *Tel:* 920-465-3030 *Toll Free Tel:* 800-829-6555 *Web Site:* www.viridiam.com, pg 1106, 1232, 1262

Byatt, Lucinda, The Historical Novels Review, PO Box 1146, Jacksonville, AL 36265 *E-mail:* reviews@historicalnovelsociety.org; contact@historicalnovelsociety.org *Web Site:* historicalnovelsociety.org, pg 1132

Byers, Gail, International Institute of Reflexology Inc, PO Box 12642, St Petersburg, FL 33733-2642 *Tel:* 727-343-4811 *E-mail:* info@reflexology-usa.net; orderdept@reflexology-usa.net *Web Site:* reflexology-usa.net, pg 1317, 1328

Byrne, Katie, Nuance Communications Inc, One Wayside Rd, Burlington, MA 01803 *Tel:* 781-565-5000 *Toll Free Tel:* 800-654-1187 (cust serv); 888-372-1908 (orders) *Web Site:* www.nuance.com, pg 1374

Byrne, Simon, Diamond Book Distributors (DBD), 10150 York Rd, Hunt Valley, MD 21030 *Tel:* 443-318-8001; 443-318-8519 (cust serv) *E-mail:* distribution@diamondbookdistributors.com; dbdreorders@diamondbookdistributors.com (orders); books@diamondbookdistributors.com (cust serv) *Web Site:* diamondbookdistributors.com, pg 1290

Cabildo, Suzette, Bookforum, 520 Eighth Ave, 21st fl, New York, NY 10018 *E-mail:* editors@bookforum.com; advertising@bookforum.com; circulation@bookforum.com *Web Site:* www.bookforum.com; subscriptions.bookforum.com, pg 1130

Cafarella, Adair, AzureGreen, 16 Bell Rd, Middlefield, MA 01243 *Tel:* 413-623-2155 *Fax:* 413-623-2156 *E-mail:* azuregreen@azuregreen.com *Web Site:* www.azuregreen.net, pg 1286, 1311

Caglioni, Manrico, Book Automation Inc, 458 Danbury Rd, Unit B10, New Milford, CT 06776 *Tel:* 860-354-7900 *Toll Free Tel:* 800-429-6305 *E-mail:* info@bookautomation.com *Web Site:* www.bookautomation.com, pg 1278

Cai, Liting, Infocus® Corp, 13190 SW 68 Pkwy, Suite 120, Portland, OR 97223-8368 *Tel:* 503-207-4700 *Toll Free Tel:* 877-388-8360 (cust serv) *E-mail:* salessupport@infocus.com *Web Site:* www.infocus.com, pg 1370

Calabra, Christopher, Tukaiz LLC, 2917 N Latoria Lane, Franklin Park, IL 60131 *Tel:* 847-455-1588; 847-288-4968 (sales) *Toll Free Tel:* 800-543-2674 *E-mail:* contacttukaiz@tukaiz.com *Web Site:* www.tukaiz.com, pg 1232, 1261, 1273, 1284

Calaf, Dolores C, Calaf Communications, 10 Warwick Ct, Lawrence, MA 01841 *Tel:* 978-314-3125 *Fax:* 978-686-5960 *Web Site:* www.calafcommunications.com, pg 1400

Calderwood, Daniel B, Veritiv™ Corporation, 1000 Abernathy Rd, Bldg 400, Suite 1700, Atlanta, GA 30328 *Toll Free Tel:* 844-VERITIV (837-4848); 866-714-8303 (packaging cust serv); 866-714-8306 (print cust serv) *E-mail:* contactus@veritivcorp.com; media@veritivcorp.com *Web Site:* www.veritivcorp.com, pg 1273

Caldwell, Tom, Southern Territory Associates, 4508 64 St, Lubbock, TX 79414 *E-mail:* sta77@suddenlink.net *Web Site:* www.southernterritory.com, pg 1302

Calhoun, Katie, Getty Images Inc, 605 Fifth Ave S, Suite 400, Seattle, WA 98104 *Tel:* 206-925-5000 *Toll Free Tel:* 800-IMAGERY (462-4379); 888-888-5889 *Web Site:* www.gettyimages.com; www.gettyimages.com/customer-support; engage.gettyimages.com/media-inquiries, pg 1369, 1428

Calkins, Melanie, Neenah Inc, 3460 Preston Ridge Rd, Suite 600, Alpharetta, GA 30005 *Toll Free Tel:* 800-344-5287 *E-mail:* publishing.team@neenah.com *Web Site:* www.neenahperformance.com/products/neenah-performance/publishing-products, pg 1270, 1282

Callison, Kay, The American Audio Prose Library Inc, PO Box 842, Columbia, MO 65205 *Tel:* 573-449-7075 *E-mail:* aaplinc@centurytel.net, pg 1364

Camacho, Eduarda, PTC, 121 Seaport Blvd, Boston, MA 02210 *Tel:* 781-370-5000 *Fax:* 781-370-6000 *Web Site:* www.ptc.com, pg 1375

Campagna, Frank J II, ColorPage, 81 Ten Broeck Ave, Kingston, NY 12401 *Tel:* 845-331-7581 *Toll Free Tel:* 800-836-7581 *Fax:* 845-331-1571 *E-mail:* sales@colorpageonline.com *Web Site:* www.colorpageonline.com, pg 1209, 1223, 1250, 1266

Campbell, Darby Jo, Progressive Publishing Services (PPS), 555 Ryan Run Rd, Suite B, York, PA 17404 *Tel:* 717-764-5908 *Fax:* 717-764-5530 *E-mail:* info@pps-ace.com *Web Site:* www.pps-ace.com, pg 1230, 1375

Campbell, Duncan, The Campbell-Logan Bindery Inc, 7615 Baker St NE, Fridley, MN 55432 *Tel:* 612-332-1313 *Toll Free Tel:* 800-942-6224 *E-mail:* info@campbell-logan.com *Web Site:* www.campbell-logan.com, pg 1325

Campbell, Greg, The Campbell-Logan Bindery Inc, 7615 Baker St NE, Fridley, MN 55432 *Tel:* 612-332-1313 *Toll Free Tel:* 800-942-6224 *E-mail:* info@campbell-logan.com *Web Site:* www.campbell-logan.com, pg 1325

Campbell, Kathy, Gorham Printing, 3718 Mahoney Dr, Centralia, WA 98531 *Tel:* 360-623-1323 *Toll Free Tel:* 800-837-0970 *E-mail:* info@gorhamprinting.com *Web Site:* www.gorhamprinting.com, pg 1254

Campbell, Mike, PTC, 121 Seaport Blvd, Boston, MA 02210 *Tel:* 781-370-5000 *Fax:* 781-370-6000 *Web Site:* www.ptc.com, pg 1375

Campbell, Sean D, PrimeArray Systems Inc, 1500 District Ave, Burlington, MA 01803 *Tel:* 978-455-9488 *Toll Free Tel:* 800-433-5133 *E-mail:* info@primearray.com; sales@primearray.com *Web Site:* www.primearray.com, pg 1375

Campoli, Leila, Stonesong, 270 W 39 St, Suite 201, New York, NY 10018 *Tel:* 212-929-4600 *E-mail:* editors@stonesong.com *Web Site:* www.stonesong.com, pg 1357

Candelora, Anthony, Taconic Wire, 250 Totoket Rd, North Branford, CT 06471 *Tel:* 203-484-2863 *Toll Free Tel:* 800-253-1450 *Fax:* 203-484-2865 *E-mail:* sales@taconicwire.com; taconicwiresales@gmail.com *Web Site:* www.taconicwire.com, pg 1283

Cann, Jay D Jr, Kwikprint Manufacturing Co Inc, 4868 Victor St, Jacksonville, FL 32207 *Tel:* 904-737-3755 *Toll Free Tel:* 800-940-5945 *Fax:* 904-730-0349 *E-mail:* info@kwikprint.net *Web Site:* www.kwikprint.com, pg 1268

Capellan, Dr Angel, LEA Libros de Espana y America, 170-23 83 Ave, Jamaica, NY 11432 *Tel:* 718-291-9891 *Fax:* 718-291-9830 *E-mail:* lea@leabooks.com; orders@leabooks.com *Web Site:* www.leabooks.com, pg 1329

Capo, James, Omeda, 4 Overlook Point, Suite A2SE, Lincolnshire, IL 60069 *Tel:* 847-564-8900 *E-mail:* getstarted@omeda.com *Web Site:* www.omeda.com, pg 1334

Carbia, Vanessa M, Spanish/English Translation & Interpreting Services, 5704 SW 86 Dr, Gainesville, FL 32608-8536 *Tel:* 352-215-7200 *Web Site:* www.afn.org/~vanessa, pg 1404

Carey, Chris, Minden Pictures Inc, 9565 Soquel Dr, Suite 202, Aptos, CA 95003 *Tel:* 831-661-5551 *E-mail:* info@mindenpictures.com *Web Site:* www.mindenpictures.com, pg 1430

Carey, Tyler M, Westchester Publishing Services, 4 Old Newtown Rd, Danbury, CT 06810 *Tel:* 203-791-0080 *Fax:* 203-791-9286 *E-mail:* info@westchesterpubsvcs.com *Web Site:* www.westchesterpublishingservices.com, pg 1233

Cargill, Robert R, Biblical Archaeology Society, 4710 41 St NW, Washington, DC 20016-1705 *Tel:* 202-364-3300 *Toll Free Tel:* 800-221-4644 *Fax:* 202-364-2636 *E-mail:* info@biblicalarchaeology.org *Web Site:* www.biblicalarchaeology.org, pg 1365

Carlin, James J, Fuse Graphics, 1800 Sandy Plains Pkwy, Suite 124, Marietta, GA 30066 *Tel:* 770-499-7777 *Fax:* 770-499-7778 *E-mail:* info@fusegraphicsatlanta.com *Web Site:* www.fusegraphicsatlanta.com, pg 1253

Carlin, Kelly, Fuse Graphics, 1800 Sandy Plains Pkwy, Suite 124, Marietta, GA 30066 *Tel:* 770-499-7777 *Fax:* 770-499-7778 *E-mail:* info@fusegraphicsatlanta.com *Web Site:* www.fusegraphicsatlanta.com, pg 1253

Carling, Thomas J, Shoreline Publishing Group LLC, 125 Santa Rosa Place, Santa Barbara, CA 93109 *Tel:* 805-564-1004 *E-mail:* info@shorelinepublishing.com *Web Site:* shorelinepublishing.com, pg 1357

Carlini, Matt, Javelin Group, 203 S Union St, Suite 200, Alexandria, VA 22314 *Tel:* 703-490-8845 *E-mail:* hello@javelindc.com *Web Site:* javelindc.com, pg 1348

Carlson, Jennifer, Social Studies School Service, 10200 Jefferson Blvd, PO Box 802, Culver City, CA 90232 *Tel:* 310-839-2436 *Toll Free Tel:* 800-421-4246 (US & CN) *Fax:* 310-839-2249 *Toll Free Fax:* 800-944-5432 *E-mail:* access@socialstudies.com; customerservice@socialstudies.com *Web Site:* www.socialstudies.com, pg 1302, 1321

Carlson, Mark, The John Roberts Company, 9687 East River Rd NW, Minneapolis, MN 55433 *Tel:* 763-755-5500 *Toll Free Tel:* 800-551-1534 *Fax:* 763-755-0394 *E-mail:* success@johnroberts.com *Web Site:* www.johnroberts.com; www.facebook.com/TheJohnRobertsCompany, pg 1105

Carnes, Lance, Personal TeX Inc, 722 Lombard St, Suite 201, San Francisco, CA 94133 *Tel:* 415-296-7550 *Toll Free Tel:* 800-808-7906 *Fax:* 415-296-7501 *E-mail:* sales@pctex.com *Web Site:* www.pctex.com, pg 1374

Carney, Dennis, Roosevelt Paper Co, One Roosevelt Dr, Mount Laurel, NJ 08054 *Tel:* 856-303-4100 *Toll Free Tel:* 800-523-3470 *Fax:* 856-642-1949 *E-mail:* marketing@rooseveltpaper.com *Web Site:* www.rooseveltpaper.com, pg 1271

Carpenter, David, CRW Graphics Communications, 9100 Pennsauken Hwy, Pennsauken, NJ 08110 *Tel:* 856-662-9111 *Toll Free Tel:* 800-820-3000 *Fax:* 856-665-1789 *E-mail:* info@crwgraphics.com *Web Site:* www.crwgraphics.com, pg 1103, 1367, 1413

Carpenter, Michael, Michael Carpenter Photography, 7704 Carrleigh Pkwy, Springfield, VA 22152-1304 *Tel:* 703-644-9666 *Web Site:* www.michaelcarpenterphotography.com, pg 1420

Carr, Anthea, Historic Films LLC, 211 Third St, Greenport, NY 11944 *Tel:* 631-477-9700 *Toll Free Tel:* 800-249-1940 *Fax:* 631-477-9800 *E-mail:* info@historicfilms.com *Web Site:* www.historicfilms.com, pg 1429

Carr, Chris, Alliance Storage Technologies Inc (ASTI), 10045 Federal Dr, Colorado Springs, CO 80908 *Tel:* 719-593-7900 *Toll Free Tel:* 888-567-6332 *Fax:* 719-598-3472 *E-mail:* sales@astiusa.com; info@astiusa.com *Web Site:* www.alliancestoragetechnologies.com, pg 1364

Carreiro, Scotty, Azalea Software Inc, PO Box 16660, Seattle, WA 98116-0660 *Tel:* 206-341-9500; 206-336-9559 (software support); 206-336-9575 (sales & info) *Fax:* 206-299-5600 *E-mail:* salesinfo@azaleabarcodes.com *Web Site:* www.azaleabarcodes.com, pg 1365

Carret Aguero, Catalina, Jane Starr Literary Scouts, 1350 Avenue of the Americas, Suite 1205, New York, NY 10019 *Tel:* 212-421-0777 *E-mail:* jane@janestarr.com, pg 1351

Carrillo, Margarita, Readerlink Distribution Services LLC, 1420 Kensington Rd, Suite 300, Oakbrook, IL 60523-2164 *Tel:* 708-547-4400 *Toll Free Tel:* 800-549-5389 *E-mail:* info@readerlink.com; marketingservices@readerlink.com *Web Site:* www.readerlink.com, pg 1301

Carroll, Scott, NewTek Inc, 5131 Beckwith Blvd, San Antonio, TX 78249 *Tel:* 210-370-8000 *Toll Free Tel:* 800-368-5441 *Fax:* 210-370-8001 *E-mail:* sales@newtek.com (cust serv) *Web Site:* www.newtek.com, pg 1373

Carruthers, David, St Armand Paper Mill, 3700 St Patrick, Montreal, QC H4E 1A2, Canada *Tel:* 514-931-8338 *Fax:* 514-931-5953 *Web Site:* www.st-armand.com, pg 1271

Carson, Doug, DCA Inc, 1515 E Pine St, Cushing, OK 74023 *Tel:* 918-225-0346 *Fax:* 918-225-1113 *E-mail:* sales@dcainc.com *Web Site:* www.dcainc.com, pg 1367

Carter, Barbara, Cardinal Publishers Group, 2402 N Shadeland Ave, Suite A, Indianapolis, IN 46219 *Tel:* 317-352-8200 *Toll Free Tel:* 800-296-0481 (cust serv) *Fax:* 317-352-8202 *E-mail:* customerservice@cardinalpub.com *Web Site:* cardinalpub.com, pg 1287

Carter, Brian, Scholastic School Reading Events, 1080 Greenwood Blvd, Lake Mary, FL 32746 *Tel:* 407-829-8000 *Toll Free Tel:* 800-770-4662 *Fax:* 407-829-2600 *E-mail:* custservbf@scholasticbookfairs.com *Web Site:* bookfairs.scholastic.com/content/fairs/home.html, pg 1302, 1321

Carter, Stuart, Diamond Book Distributors (DBD), 10150 York Rd, Hunt Valley, MD 21030 *Tel:* 443-318-8001; 443-318-8519 (cust serv) *E-mail:* distribution@diamondbookdistributors.com; dbdreorders@diamondbookdistributors.com (orders); books@diamondbookdistributors.com (cust serv) *Web Site:* diamondbookdistributors.com, pg 1290

Cartwright, Dennis, Hassett Express, 17W775 Butterfield Rd, Suite 109, Oakbrook Terrace, IL 60181 *Tel:* 630-530-6515 *Fax:* 630-530-6538 *Web Site:* www.hassettexpress.com, pg 1334

Cary, Britt, Challenge Machinery Co, 6125 Norton Center Dr, Norton Shores, MI 49441 *Tel:* 231-799-8484 *Fax:* 231-798-1275 *E-mail:* info@challengemachinery.com; sales@challengemachinery.com *Web Site:* www.challengemachinery.com, pg 1278

Casey, Lynn, PadillaCRT, 1101 W River Pkwy, Suite 400, Minneapolis, MN 55415 *Tel:* 612-455-1700 *Fax:* 612-455-1060 *Web Site:* www.padillacrt.com, pg 1111

Cassidy, Christi, Publishers Weekly, 49 W 23 St, 9th fl, New York, NY 10010 *Tel:* 212-377-5500 *Fax:* 212-377-2733 *Web Site:* www.publishersweekly.com, pg 1136

Castillanes, John, Penguin Random House Canada, a Penguin Random House company, 320 Front St W, Suite 1400, Toronto, ON M5V 3B6, Canada *Tel:* 416-364-4449 *Toll Free Tel:* 888-523-9292 (cust serv) *Fax:* 416-598-7764 *E-mail:* customerservicescanada@penguinrandomhouse.com; publicitycanada@penguinrandomhouse.com; rightscanada@penguinrandomhouse.com *Web Site:* www.penguinrandomhouse.ca, pg 1299

Castle, Sara, JMW Group Inc, 346 Rte 6, No 867, Mahopac, NY 10541 *Tel:* 914-841-7105 *Fax:* 914-248-8861 *E-mail:* jmwgroup@jmwgroup.net *Web Site:* jmwforlife.com, pg 1348

Castonguay, Genevieve, Socadis Inc, 420 rue Stinson, Ville St-Laurent, QC H4N 3L7, Canada *Tel:* 514-331-3300 *Toll Free Tel:* 800-361-2847 *Fax:* 514-745-3282; 514-331-8202 (major dist) *Toll Free Fax:* 866-803-5422 *E-mail:* socinfo@socadis.com (cust serv); direction@socadis.com; salesgd@socadis.com (major dist) *Web Site:* www.socadis.com, pg 1302

Castro, Luis, Social Studies School Service, 10200 Jefferson Blvd, PO Box 802, Culver City, CA 90232 *Tel:* 310-839-2436 *Toll Free Tel:* 800-421-4246 (US & CN) *Fax:* 310-839-2249 *Toll Free Fax:* 800-944-5432 *E-mail:* access@socialstudies.com; customerservice@socialstudies.com *Web Site:* www.socialstudies.com, pg 1302, 1321

Castro-Klaren, Sara, Modern Language Notes (MLN), 2715 N Charles St, Baltimore, MD 21218-4363 *Tel:* 410-516-6987 (journal orders outside US & CN) *Toll Free Tel:* 800-548-1784 (journal orders) *Fax:* 410-578-2865 (journal orders) *E-mail:* jrnlcirc@jh.edu (journal orders) *Web Site:* www.press.jhu.edu/journals/mln, pg 1134

Catz, Safra A, Oracle America Inc, 500 Oracle Pkwy, Redwood Shores, CA 94065 *Tel:* 650-506-7000 *Toll Free Tel:* 800-392-2999; 800-633-0738 (sales) *Web Site:* www.oracle.com, pg 1374

Cauley, Leslie, Hill+Knowlton Strategies, 237 Park Ave, 4th fl, New York, NY 10017 *Tel:* 212-885-0300 *Web Site:* www.hkstrategies.com, pg 1109

Cauz, Jorge, Encyclopaedia Britannica Inc, 325 N La Salle St, Suite 200, Chicago, IL 60654 *Tel:* 312-347-7000 (all other countries) *Toll Free Tel:* 800-323-1229 (US & CN) *Fax:* 312-294-2104 *E-mail:* contact@eb.com *Web Site:* www.britannica.com, pg 1315

Cee, Nicole, Translingua Associates Inc, 630 Ninth Ave, Suite 708, New York, NY 10036 *Tel:* 212-697-2020 *Fax:* 212-697-2891 *Web Site:* www.translingua.com, pg 1405

Cendrowski, Dwight, Dwight Cendrowski Photography LLC, 2870 Easy St, Ann Arbor, MI 48104-6532 *Tel:* 734-330-5230 *Web Site:* www.cendrowski.com, pg 1420

Cengiz, Mustafa, Link Translations Inc, 60 E 96 St, New York, NY 10128 *Toll Free Tel:* 866-866-5010 *E-mail:* info@link-translations.com *Web Site:* www.link-translations.com, pg 1403

Cerda, Jessy, VanDam Inc, The VanDam Bldg, 121 W 27 St, New York, NY 10001 *Tel:* 917-297-5445 *E-mail:* info@vandam.com *Web Site:* www.vandam.com, pg 1358

Cha, Lee Po, IRCO-International Language Bank, 10301 NE Glisan St, Portland, OR 97220 *Tel:* 503-234-0068 (interpretation); 503-505-5186 (translation) *Fax:* 503-233-4724 *E-mail:* translation@ircoilb.org; interpretation@ircoilb.org *Web Site:* www.irco.org/ilb, pg 1402

Chakravarthy, Anil, Adobe Systems Inc, 345 Park Ave, San Jose, CA 95110-2704 *Tel:* 408-536-6000 *Fax:* 408-537-6000 *Web Site:* www.adobe.com, pg 1363

Chamaillard, Pascal, Edipresse Inc, 945, ave Beaumont, Montreal, QC H3N 1W3, Canada *Tel:* 514-273-6141 *Toll Free Tel:* 800-361-1043 *Fax:* 514-273-7021 *E-mail:* information@edipresse.ca *Web Site:* www.edipresse.ca, pg 1315

Chambers, Joe, Townsend Communications Inc, 20 E Gregory Blvd, Kansas City, MO 64114 *Tel:* 816-361-0616 *Web Site:* www.townsendcommunications.com; www.townsendprint.com, pg 1232, 1261, 1284

Champagne, Mark, Login Canada, 300 Saulteaux Crescent, Winnipeg, MB R3J 3T2, Canada *Tel:* 204-837-2987 *Toll Free Tel:* 800-665-1148 (CN only) *Fax:* 204-837-3116 *Toll Free Fax:* 800-665-0103 *E-mail:* sales@lb.ca *Web Site:* www.lb.ca, pg 1318

Champine, Heather, Media Relations Agency, 350 W Burnsville Pkwy, Suite 350, Burnsville, MN 55337 *Tel:* 952-697-5220 *Fax:* 952-697-3256 *Web Site:* www.publicity.com, pg 1111

Chan, Simon, C & C Offset Printing Co USA Inc, 70 W 36 St, Unit 10C, New York, NY 10018 *Tel:* 212-431-4210 *Toll Free Tel:* 866-540-4134 *Web Site:* www.ccoffset.com, pg 1208, 1223, 1249

Chan, Sylvia, Penguin Random House Canada, a Penguin Random House company, 320 Front St W, Suite 1400, Toronto, ON M5V 3B6, Canada *Tel:* 416-364-4449 *Toll Free Tel:* 888-523-9292 (cust serv) *Fax:* 416-598-7764 *E-mail:* customerservicescanada@penguinrandomhouse.com; publicitycanada@penguinrandomhouse.com; rightscanada@penguinrandomhouse.com *Web Site:* www.penguinrandomhouse.ca, pg 1299

Chan, Terry, O'Neil Digital Solutions LLC, 12655 Beatrice St, Los Angeles, CA 90066 *Tel:* 310-448-6400 *E-mail:* sales@oneildata.com *Web Site:* www.oneildata.com, pg 1229, 1257, 1270, 1282

Chan, Yuk, BroadVision, 460 Seaport Ct, Suite 102, Redwood City, CA 94063 *Tel:* 650-331-1000 *Web Site:* www.broadvision.com, pg 1365

Chaney, Brian, Advantage Laser Products Inc, 1840 Marietta Blvd NW, Atlanta, GA 30318 *Tel:* 404-351-2700 *Toll Free Tel:* 800-722-2804 (cust serv) *Fax:* 404-351-0911 *Toll Free Fax:* 800-871-3305 *E-mail:* sales@advlaser.com *Web Site:* www.advlaser.com, pg 1363

Chang, Beth, Fujii Associates Inc, 75 Sunny Hill Dr, Troy, MO 63379 *Tel:* 636-528-2546 *Fax:* 636-600-5153 *Web Site:* www.fujiiassociates.com, pg 1291

Chang, Richard, Megavision Inc, PO Box 60158, Santa Barbara, CA 93160 *Tel:* 805-964-1400 *Toll Free Tel:* 888-324-2580 *E-mail:* info@mega-vision.com *Web Site:* www.mega-vision.com, pg 1372

Chapman, Amy, AIGA, the professional association for design, 228 Park Ave S, Suite 58603, New York, NY 10003 *Tel:* 212-807-1990 *E-mail:* general@aiga.org *Web Site:* www.aiga.org, pg 1139

Chapman, Kristen, Indigo Books & Music Inc, 468 King St W, Suite 500, Toronto, ON M5V 1L8, Canada *Tel:* 416-364-4499 *E-mail:* cisales@indigo.ca *Web Site:* www.chapters.indigo.ca, pg 1294

Chappo, Louis, GTI Graphic Technology Inc, 211 Dupont Ave, Newburgh, NY 12550 *Tel:* 845-562-7066 *Fax:* 845-562-2543 *E-mail:* sales@gtilite.com *Web Site:* www.gtilite.com, pg 1280, 1370

Charlton, Jeff, Graphic Connections Group LLC, 174 Chesterfield Industrial Blvd, Chesterfield, MO 63005 *Tel:* 636-519-8320 *Toll Free Tel:* 800-378-0378 *Fax:* 636-519-8310 *Web Site:* www.gcfrog.com, pg 1211

Chasman, Deborah, Boston Review, PO Box 390568, Cambridge, MA 02139 *Tel:* 617-356-8198 *E-mail:* review@bostonreview.net; customerservice@bostonreview.net *Web Site:* bostonreview.net, pg 1130

Chaudhari, Piyush, SGS International LLC, 626 W Main St, Suite 500, Louisville, KY 40202 *Tel:* 502-637-5443 *E-mail:* info@sgsco.com *Web Site:* www.sgsintl.com, pg 1230

Chen, Amanda, Bellevue Literary Review, 149 E 23 St, Suite 1516, New York, NY 10010 *Tel:* 917-375-5790 *E-mail:* info@BLReview.org *Web Site:* www.BLReview.org, pg 1130

Chen, Connie, Corel Corporation, 1600 Carling Ave, Ottawa, ON K1Z 8R7, Canada *Toll Free Tel:* 877-582-6735 *Web Site:* www.corel.com, pg 1366

Chen, Gloria, Adobe Systems Inc, 345 Park Ave, San Jose, CA 95110-2704 *Tel:* 408-536-6000 *Fax:* 408-537-6000 *Web Site:* www.adobe.com, pg 1363

Chen, Lucy, Claris International Inc, 5201 Patrick Henry Dr, Santa Clara, CA 95054 *Tel:* 408-727-8227 (sales & cust support) *Toll Free Tel:* 800-725-2747 (sales); 800-325-2747 (cust support) *Fax:* 408-987-7447 *E-mail:* claris_sales@claris.com *Web Site:* www.claris.com, pg 1366

Chen, Dr Pehong, BroadVision, 460 Seaport Ct, Suite 102, Redwood City, CA 94063 *Tel:* 650-331-1000 *Web Site:* www.broadvision.com, pg 1365

Cheng, Doris W, Bellevue Literary Review, 149 E 23 St, Suite 1516, New York, NY 10010 *Tel:* 917-375-5790 *E-mail:* info@BLReview.org *Web Site:* www.BLReview.org, pg 1130

Cheng, Elley, Pantone Inc, 590 Commerce Blvd, Carlstadt, NJ 07072-3098 *Tel:* 201-935-5500 *Toll Free Tel:* 888-800-9580 *Fax:* 201-896-0242 *E-mail:* pantonesocial@pantone.com *Web Site:* www.pantone.com, pg 1282

Cheng, Jill, Cheng & Tsui Co Inc, 25 West St, 2nd fl, Boston, MA 02111-1213 *Tel:* 617-988-2400 *Toll Free Tel:* 800-554-1963 *Fax:* 617-426-3669 *E-mail:* service@cheng-tsui.com; orders@cheng-tsui.com; marketing@cheng-tsui.com *Web Site:* www.cheng-tsui.com, pg 1313

Cheng, Melanie, Penguin Random House Canada, a Penguin Random House company, 320 Front St W, Suite 1400, Toronto, ON M5V 3B6, Canada *Tel:* 416-364-4449 *Toll Free Tel:* 888-523-9292 (cust serv) *Fax:* 416-598-7764 *E-mail:* customerservicescanada@penguinrandomhouse.com; publicitycanada@penguinrandomhouse.com; rightscanada@penguinrandomhouse.com *Web Site:* www.penguinrandomhouse.ca, pg 1299

Cherian, Reney, The Hibbert Group, 400 Pennington Ave, Trenton, NJ 08650 *Tel:* 609-394-7500 *Toll Free Tel:* 888-HIBBERT (442-2378) *E-mail:* info@hibbertgroup.com *Web Site:* hibbert.com, pg 1104, 1116, 1117

Cheteyan, Judy G, ABDI Inc, 16 Avenue "A", Leetsdale, PA 15056 *Toll Free Tel:* 800-796-6471 *Fax:* 412-741-4161 *E-mail:* e-fulfillment@abdintl.com *Web Site:* www.abdi-ecommerce10.com/abdintl; www.abdintl.com/abdintl, pg 1117, 1207, 1333

Cheteyan, Michael D II, ABDI Inc, 16 Avenue "A", Leetsdale, PA 15056 *Toll Free Tel:* 800-796-6471 *Fax:* 412-741-4161 *E-mail:* e-fulfillment@abdintl.com *Web Site:* www.abdi-ecommerce10.com/abdintl; www.abdintl.com/abdintl, pg 1117, 1207, 1333

Chiaia, Nicholas, United Press International (UPI), 1133 19 St NW, Suite 800, Washington, DC 20036 *Tel:* 202-898-8000 *E-mail:* media@upi.com *Web Site:* www.upi.com, pg 1127, 1191

Chiang, Tom, Holo Image Technology Inc, 101 William Leigh Dr, Tullytown, PA 19007 *Tel:* 215-946-2190 *Fax:* 215-946-2129 *E-mail:* info@holoimagetechnology.com *Web Site:* www.holoimagetechnology.com, pg 1280

Chiantera, Michelle, Corel Corporation, 1600 Carling Ave, Ottawa, ON K1Z 8R7, Canada *Toll Free Tel:* 877-582-6735 *Web Site:* www.corel.com, pg 1366

Childress, Penny, BookPage®, 2143 Belcourt Ave, Nashville, TN 37212 *Tel:* 615-292-8926 *Fax:* 615-292-8249 *Web Site:* bookpage.com, pg 1127

Chio, Grace, The Language Center, 62 Brunswick Woods Dr, East Brunswick, NJ 08816 *Tel:* 732-613-4554 *Fax:* 732-238-7659 *Web Site:* www.thelanguagectr.com, pg 1402

Chiu, Clive, Publishers Weekly, 49 W 23 St, 9th fl, New York, NY 10010 *Tel:* 212-377-5500 *Fax:* 212-377-2733 *Web Site:* www.publishersweekly.com, pg 1136

Cho, Alex, HP Inc, 1501 Paige Mill Rd, Palo Alto, CA 94304-1112 *Tel:* 650-857-1501 *Toll Free Tel:* 800-282-6672 *Web Site:* www.hp.com, pg 1370

Cho, Mikael, Getty Images Inc, 605 Fifth Ave S, Suite 400, Seattle, WA 98104 Tel: 206-925-5000 Toll Free Tel: 800-IMAGERY (462-4379); 888-888-5889 Web Site: www.gettyimages.com; www.gettyimages.com/customer-support; engage.gettyimages.com/media-inquiries, pg 1369, 1428

Choudhary, Harsh, appatura™, A Broadridge Company, 65 Challenger Rd, Suite 400, Ridgefield Park, NJ 07660 Tel: 201-508-6000 Toll Free Tel: 800-277-2155 E-mail: contactus@appatura.com Web Site: www.appatura.com, pg 1103, 1115, 1117, 1207, 1221, 1248

Chrisman, Jeffrey R, an ICON Company LLC, 401 Harper Ave SW, Lenoir, NC 28645 Tel: 828-758-7260 Fax: 828-754-6353 E-mail: info@lenoirprinting.com Web Site: lenoirprinting.com, pg 1247

Christiansen, Tapio, Kreab, House of Sweden, Suite 504, 2900 "K" St NW, Washington, DC 20007 Tel: 202-536-1590 E-mail: washingtondc@kreab.com Web Site: www.kreab.com/washington-dc, pg 1110

Christie, Tim, Lindenmeyr Book Publishing Papers, 3 Manhattanville Rd, Purchase, NY 10577 Tel: 914-696-9300 Web Site: www.lindenmeyrbook.com, pg 1269

Chwast, Seymour, The Pushpin Group Inc, 38 W 26 St, New York, NY 10010 Tel: 212-529-7590 Web Site: www.pushpininc.com, pg 1357, 1417

Ciecierski, Andrea, Stylus Publishing LLC, 22883 Quicksilver Dr, Sterling, VA 20166-2019 Tel: 703-661-1504 (edit & sales); 703-661-1581 (orders & cust serv); 703-996-1036 Toll Free Tel: 800-232-0223 (orders & cust serv) Fax: 703-661-1547; 703-661-1501 (orders & cust serv) E-mail: stylusinfo@styluspub.com; stylusmail@styluspub.com (orders & cust serv) Web Site: styluspub.com, pg 1303

Ciesielka, Thomas, T C Public Relations, One N La Salle St, Suite 600, Chicago, IL 60602 Tel: 312-422-1333 Web Site: www.tcpr.net, pg 1113

Cieslicki, Steven, Sterling Pierce Co Inc, 395 Atlantic Ave, East Rockaway, NY 11518 Tel: 516-593-1170 Fax: 516-593-1401 Web Site: www.sterlingpierce.com, pg 1214, 1260

Ciletti, Barbara, Odyssey Books, 2421 Redwood Ct, Longmont, CO 80503 Tel: 720-494-1473 Fax: 720-494-1471 E-mail: books@odysseybooks.net, pg 1349

Cinfio, Janet, Acxiom, 301 E Dave Ward Dr, Conway, AR 72032 Toll Free Tel: 888-322-9466 Web Site: www.acxiom.com, pg 1119

Cipolaro, Robert, Richard Bauer & Co Inc, 310 Cedar Lane, Teaneck, NJ 07666 Tel: 201-692-1005 Toll Free Tel: 800-995-7881 Fax: 201-692-8626 E-mail: info@richardbauer.com Web Site: www.richardbauer.com, pg 1265

Claire, Nicole Basbanes, Literary Features Syndicate, 88 Briarcliff Rd, Larchmont, NY 10538 Tel: 914-834-7480, pg 1127

Clare, Ian, Clare Printing, 206 S Keystone Ave, Sayre, PA 18840 Tel: 570-888-2244 E-mail: hr@clareprint.com Web Site: www.clareprint.com, pg 1223, 1250, 1278

Clark, Jim, Sheridan Saline, 960 Woodland Dr, Saline, MI 48176 Tel: 734-429-5411 Web Site: www.sheridan.com, pg 1214, 1260

Clark, Randy, Laplink Software Inc, 600 108 Ave NE, Suite 610, Bellevue, WA 98004 Tel: 425-952-6000 Toll Free Tel: 800-LAPLINK (527-5465) E-mail: info@laplink.com; sales@laplink.com Web Site: web.laplink.com, pg 1371

Clark, Ted, H B Fuller Co, 1200 Willow Lake Blvd, St Paul, MN 55110-5146 Tel: 651-236-5900 Toll Free Tel: 888-423-8553 E-mail: inquiry@hbfuller.com Web Site: www.hbfuller.com, pg 1267, 1280

Clarke, Andrew, Asia Pacific Offset Inc, 1312 "Q" St NW, Suite B, Washington, DC 20009 Tel: 202-462-5436 Toll Free Tel: 800-756-4344 Fax: 202-986-4030 Web Site: www.asiapacificoffset.com, pg 1208, 1222, 1248

Clarke, Jeff, Dell Wyse, One Dell Way, Round Rock, TX 78682 Toll Free Tel: 866-438-3622 (sales) Web Site: www.delltechnologies.com, pg 1367

Clarke, Jim, GTxcel Inc, 144 Turnpike Rd, Suite 130, Southborough, MA 01772-2104 Toll Free Tel: 800-609-8994 E-mail: info@gtxcel.com Web Site: www.gtxcel.com, pg 1370

Clatterbuck, Michelle, Intuit Inc, 2700 Coast Ave, Mountain View, CA 94043 Tel: 650-944-6000 Toll Free Tel: 800-446-8848 E-mail: investor_relations@intuit.com Web Site: www.intuit.com, pg 1371

Cleland, Robert S, Washington Post News Service with Bloomberg News, 1301 "K" St NW, Washington, DC 20071 Tel: 202-334-7666 E-mail: syndication@washpost.com Web Site: www.washingtonpost.com/syndication, pg 1192

Clements, Bill, West Virginia Book Co, 1125 Central Ave, Charleston, WV 25302 Tel: 304-342-1848 Fax: 304-343-0594 E-mail: wvbooks@wvbookco.com Web Site: www.wvbookco.com, pg 1304

Clements, Dianna, La Crosse Graphics Inc, 3025 East Ave S, La Crosse, WI 54601 Tel: 608-788-2500 Toll Free Tel: 800-832-2503 Fax: 608-788-2660 Web Site: www.lacrossegraphics.com, pg 1255

Clemons, Kim, Cedar Fort Inc, 2373 W 700 S, Suite 100, Springville, UT 84663 Tel: 801-489-4084 Toll Free Tel: 800-SKY-BOOK (759-2665) E-mail: marketinginfo@cedarfort.com Web Site: cedarfort.com, pg 1327

Clifford, Kristin, Media Connect, 1675 Broadway, New York, NY 10019 Tel: 212-715-1600 Web Site: www.media-connect.com, pg 1110

Clifton, Crystal, Progressive Publishing Services (PPS), 555 Ryan Run Rd, Suite B, York, PA 17404 Tel: 717-764-5908 Fax: 717-764-5530 E-mail: info@pps-ace.com Web Site: www.pps-ace.com, pg 1230, 1375

Clos, Laura, Harvard Educational Review, 8 Story St, 1st fl, Cambridge, MA 02138 Tel: 617-495-3432 Toll Free Tel: 888-437-1437 (orders) Fax: 617-496-3584 Web Site: hepg.org/her-home/home, pg 1132

Closson, John, appatura™, A Broadridge Company, 65 Challenger Rd, Suite 400, Ridgefield Park, NJ 07660 Tel: 201-508-6000 Toll Free Tel: 800-277-2155 E-mail: contactus@appatura.com Web Site: www.appatura.com, pg 1103, 1115, 1117, 1207, 1221, 1248

Coan, Cynthia J, Indexing by the Book, 5912 E Eastland St, Tucson, AZ 85711-4636 Tel: 520-405-8083 E-mail: indextran@cox.net Web Site: www.indexingbythebook.com, pg 1402

Cobar, Augusta, Global Interprint Inc, 800 Warrington Rd, Santa Rosa, CA 95403 Tel: 707-545-1220 Fax: 707-545-1210 Web Site: www.globalinterprint.com, pg 1253

Cobb, Michele L, AudioFile®, 37 Silver St, Portland, ME 04101 Tel: 207-774-7563 Toll Free Tel: 800-506-1212 Fax: 207-775-3744 E-mail: info@audiofilemagazine.com Web Site: www.audiofilemagazine.com, pg 1130

Cochrane, Kristin, Penguin Random House Canada, a Penguin Random House company, 320 Front St W, Suite 1400, Toronto, ON M5V 3B6, Canada Tel: 416-364-4449 Toll Free Tel: 888-523-9292 (cust serv) Fax: 416-598-7764 E-mail: customerservicescanada@penguinrandomhouse.com; publicitycanada@penguinrandomhouse.com; rightscanada@penguinrandomhouse.com Web Site: www.penguinrandomhouse.ca, pg 1299

Cockeram, Beth, Penguin Random House Canada, a Penguin Random House company, 320 Front St W, Suite 1400, Toronto, ON M5V 3B6, Canada Tel: 416-364-4449 Toll Free Tel: 888-523-9292 (cust serv) Fax: 416-598-7764 E-mail: customerservicescanada@penguinrandomhouse.com; publicitycanada@penguinrandomhouse.com; rightscanada@penguinrandomhouse.com Web Site: www.penguinrandomhouse.ca, pg 1299

Coe, George, Brodart Books & Library Services, 500 Arch St, Williamsport, PA 17701 Tel: 570-326-2461 Toll Free Tel: 800-233-8467 Fax: 570-651-1639 Toll Free Fax: 800-999-6799 E-mail: support@brodart.com Web Site: www.brodartbooks.com, pg 1313

Coe, George, Brodart Books & Library Services, 500 Arch St, Williamsport, PA 17701 Tel: 570-326-2461 Toll Free Tel: 800-474-9816 Fax: 570-651-1639 Toll Free Fax: 800-999-6799 E-mail: support@brodart.com Web Site: www.brodartbooks.com, pg 1325

Cogan, Jacob Katz, Human Rights Quarterly, 2715 N Charles St, Baltimore, MD 21218-4363 Tel: 410-516-6987 (journal orders outside US & CN) Toll Free Tel: 800-548-1784 (journal orders) Fax: 410-578-2865 (journal orders) E-mail: jrnlcirc@jh.edu (journal orders) Web Site: www.press.jhu.edu/journals/human-rights-quarterly, pg 1133

Cohen, Barbara, International Literary Properties (ILP), 286 Madison Ave, New York, NY 10017 Tel: 646-202-1633 Fax: 212-967-0977 E-mail: contact@ilpliterary.com Web Site: www.internationalliteraryproperties.com, pg 1348

Cohen, Jack, Kromar Printing Ltd, 725 Portage Ave, Winnipeg, MB R3G 0M8, Canada Tel: 204-775-8721 Fax: 204-783-8985 E-mail: info@kromar.com Web Site: www.kromar.com, pg 1212, 1255

Cohen, Joseph, Kromar Printing Ltd, 725 Portage Ave, Winnipeg, MB R3G 0M8, Canada Tel: 204-775-8721 Fax: 204-783-8985 E-mail: info@kromar.com Web Site: www.kromar.com, pg 1212, 1255

Cohen, Joshua, Boston Review, PO Box 390568, Cambridge, MA 02139 Tel: 617-356-8198 E-mail: review@bostonreview.net; customerservice@bostonreview.net Web Site: bostonreview.net, pg 1130

Cohen, Robert, International Service Co, International Service Bldg, 333 Fourth Ave, Indialantic, FL 32903-4295 Tel: 321-724-1443 Fax: 321-724-1443, pg 1317, 1325, 1328, 1331

Cohen, Susan, Bulletin of the American Schools of Oriental Research (BASOR), James F Strange Ctr, 209 Commerce St, Alexandria, VA 22314 Tel: 703-789-9229; 703-789-9230 (pubns) Fax: 617-353-6575 E-mail: basor@asor.org; info@asor.org; publications@asor.org Web Site: www.asor.org, pg 1130

Cole, Karl, Davis Art Images, 50 Portland St, Worcester, MA 01608 Tel: 508-754-7201 Toll Free Tel: 800-533-2847 Fax: 508-753-3834 E-mail: das@davisart.com; contactus@davisart.com Web Site: www.davisart.com, pg 1427

Coles, Sarah, Ruder Finn Inc, 425 E 53 St, New York, NY 10022 Tel: 212-593-6400 E-mail: info@ruderfinn.com Web Site: www.ruderfinn.com, pg 1112

Colin, Graciela Patron, Penguin Random House Canada, a Penguin Random House company, 320 Front St W, Suite 1400, Toronto, ON M5V 3B6, Canada Tel: 416-364-4449 Toll Free Tel: 888-523-9292 (cust serv) Fax: 416-598-7764 E-mail: customerservicescanada@penguinrandomhouse.com; publicitycanada@penguinrandomhouse.com; rightscanada@penguinrandomhouse.com Web Site: www.penguinrandomhouse.ca, pg 1299

Colisto, Nick, Avery Dennison Corp, 207 N Goode Ave, 6th fl, Glendale, CA 91203-1222 Tel: 626-304-2000 Web Site: www.averydennison.com, pg 1365

Collier, Harold, Beidel Printing House Inc, 225 S Fayette St, Shippensburg, PA 17257 Tel: 717-532-5063 Fax: 717-532-2502 E-mail: customerservice@dreamprint.com Web Site: dreamprint.com, pg 1248, 1344

Collinge, Mike, Webcom Inc, 3480 Pharmacy Ave, Toronto, ON M1W 2S7, Canada Tel: 416-496-1000 Toll Free Tel: 800-665-9322 Fax: 416-496-1537 E-mail: webcom@webcomlink.com Web Site: www.webcomlink.com, pg 1214, 1262, 1284

Collings, Andrew, Bookazine Co Inc, 75 Hook Rd, Bayonne, NJ 07002 Tel: 201-339-7777 Toll Free Tel: 800-221-8112 Fax: 201-339-7778 E-mail: info@bookazine.com Web Site: www.bookazine.com, pg 1312, 1327

Collins, Ryan, UniversalWilde, 26 Dartmouth St, Westwood, MA 02090 Tel: 781-251-2700 Fax: 781-251-2613 Web Site: www.universalwilde.com, pg 1106, 1116, 1232, 1261

Collins, Tim, Communication Abstracts, 10 Estes St, Ipswich, MA 01938 *Tel:* 978-356-6500 *Toll Free Tel:* 800-653-2726 *Fax:* 978-356-6565 *E-mail:* information@ebsco.com *Web Site:* www.ebsco.com, pg 1131

Collins, Wanzie, Panaprint Inc, 7979 NE Industrial Blvd, Macon, GA 31216 *Tel:* 478-788-0676 *Toll Free Tel:* 800-622-0676 *Fax:* 478-788-4276 *Web Site:* www.panaprint.com, pg 1258

Colosimo, Terry, Westchester Publishing Services, 4 Old Newtown Rd, Danbury, CT 06810 *Tel:* 203-791-0080 *Fax:* 203-791-9286 *E-mail:* info@westchesterpubsvcs.com *Web Site:* www.westchesterpublishingservices.com, pg 1233

Colwell, Tom, Conrad Direct Inc, 800 Kinderkamack Rd, Suite 307N, Oradell, NJ 07649 *Tel:* 201-567-3200 *Fax:* 201-567-1530 *E-mail:* listinfo@conraddirect.com *Web Site:* www.conraddirect.com, pg 1115

Comer, Dan, Southeastern Book Co, 2001 SW 31 Ave, Pembroke Park, FL 33009 *Tel:* 954-985-9400 *Toll Free Tel:* 800-223-3251 *Fax:* 954-987-2200 *E-mail:* staff@sebcobooks.com *Web Site:* www.sebcobooks.com, pg 1321

Compton, Eric, Scholastic School Reading Events, 1080 Greenwood Blvd, Lake Mary, FL 32746 *Tel:* 407-829-8000 *Toll Free Tel:* 800-770-4662 *Fax:* 407-829-2600 *E-mail:* custservbf@scholasticbookfairs.com *Web Site:* bookfairs.scholastic.com/content/fairs/home.html, pg 1302, 1321

Compton, Laura, Chesapeake & Hudson Inc, 27 Jacks Shop Rd, Rochelle, VA 22738 *Tel:* 301-834-7170 *Toll Free Tel:* 800-231-4469 *E-mail:* office@cheshud.com *Web Site:* www.cheshudinc.com, pg 1288

Conley, James, Bert Davis Executive Search Inc, 555 Fifth Ave, Suite 302, New York, NY 10017 *Tel:* 212-838-4000 *E-mail:* info@bertdavis.com *Web Site:* www.bertdavis.com, pg 1381

Conners, Jim, Encyclopaedia Britannica Inc, 325 N La Salle St, Suite 200, Chicago, IL 60654 *Tel:* 312-347-7000 (all other countries) *Toll Free Tel:* 800-323-1229 (US & CN) *Fax:* 312-294-2104 *E-mail:* contact@eb.com *Web Site:* www.britannica.com, pg 1315

Connor, Mark, Blanks Printing & Imaging Inc, 2343 N Beckley Ave, Dallas, TX 75208 *Tel:* 214-741-3905 *Toll Free Tel:* 800-325-7651 *E-mail:* sales@blanks.com *Web Site:* www.blanks.com, pg 1222, 1249

Conroy, Hal, C Harrison Conroy Co Inc, 501 Penman St, Charlotte, NC 28203 *Tel:* 704-358-0459 *Toll Free Tel:* 800-242-2789 *Fax:* 704-358-0459 *E-mail:* chcphoto@charrisonconroy.com *Web Site:* www.charrisonconroy.com, pg 1209, 1251

Conte, Francesca, Penguin Random House Canada, a Penguin Random House company, 320 Front St W, Suite 1400, Toronto, ON M5V 3B6, Canada *Tel:* 416-364-4449 *Toll Free Tel:* 888-523-9292 (cust serv) *Fax:* 416-598-7764 *E-mail:* customerservicescanada@penguinrandomhouse.com; publicitycanada@penguinrandomhouse.com; rightscanada@penguinrandomhouse.com *Web Site:* www.penguinrandomhouse.ca, pg 1299

Continenza, Jim, Eastman Kodak Co, 343 State St, Rochester, NY 14650 *Tel:* 585-724-4000 *Toll Free Tel:* 866-563-2533 *Web Site:* www.kodak.com, pg 1279

Conway, Barry, Conway Greene Co, 1400 E 30 St, Suite 402, Cleveland, OH 44114 *Tel:* 216-965-3195 *Web Site:* www.conwaygreene.com, pg 1366

Conway, Beth, Nuance Communications Inc, One Wayside Rd, Burlington, MA 01803 *Tel:* 781-565-5000 *Toll Free Tel:* 800-654-1187 (cust serv); 888-372-1908 (orders) *Web Site:* www.nuance.com, pg 1374

Cook, Scott, Intuit Inc, 2700 Coast Ave, Mountain View, CA 94043 *Tel:* 650-944-6000 *Toll Free Tel:* 800-446-8848 *E-mail:* investor_relations@intuit.com *Web Site:* www.intuit.com, pg 1371

Cook, Sharon, Cook Public Relations, 3251 Spear Ave, Arcata, CA 95521 *Tel:* 707-630-3597; 415-302-1752 (cell) *Web Site:* www.cookpr.com, pg 1108

Cook, Tim, Apple Inc, One Apple Park Way, Cupertino, CA 95014 *Tel:* 408-996-1010 *Web Site:* www.apple.com, pg 1364

Cooney, Robert, Robert Cooney Graphic Design, PO Box 362, Half Moon Bay, CA 94019 *Tel:* 650-712-4400, pg 1413

Cooper, Harvey, Cross Country Computer Corp, 250 Carleton Ave, East Islip, NY 11730-1240 *Tel:* 631-334-1810 *E-mail:* inquiry@crosscountrycomputer.com *Web Site:* www.crosscountrycomputer.com, pg 1119

Cooper, Matthew, Washington Monthly, 1200 18 St NW, Suite 330, Washington, DC 20036 *Tel:* 202-955-9010 *Toll Free Tel:* 855-492-1648 (subns) *Fax:* 202-955-9011 *E-mail:* editors@washingtonmonthly.com *Web Site:* washingtonmonthly.com, pg 1137

Copperman, Shirley, Marrakech Express Inc, 720 Wesley Ave, No 10, Tarpon Springs, FL 34689 *Tel:* 727-942-2218 *Toll Free Tel:* 800-940-6566 *Fax:* 727-937-4758 *E-mail:* print@marrak.com *Web Site:* www.marrak.com, pg 1212, 1256, 1281

Coppola, Robert, PR Newswire, 350 Hudson St, Suite 300, New York, NY 10014-4504 *Toll Free Tel:* 888-776-0942; 800-776-8090 *Toll Free Fax:* 800-793-9313 *E-mail:* mediainquiries@prnewswire.com *Web Site:* www.prnewswire.com, pg 1112

Corder, Jennifer D, Corder Associates Inc, 2602 W Baseline Rd, Suite 22, Mesa, AZ 85202 *Tel:* 480-752-8533 *Toll Free Tel:* 877-303-7575 *Fax:* 480-752-8534 *E-mail:* info@cordernet.com *Web Site:* cordernet.com, pg 1366

Corder, Kelly, Corder Associates Inc, 2602 W Baseline Rd, Suite 22, Mesa, AZ 85202 *Tel:* 480-752-8533 *Toll Free Tel:* 877-303-7575 *Fax:* 480-752-8534 *E-mail:* info@cordernet.com *Web Site:* cordernet.com, pg 1366

Corey, Steve, Whitegate Features Syndicate, 71 Faunce Dr, Providence, RI 02906 *Tel:* 401-274-2149 *E-mail:* whitegate.featuressyndicate@gmail.com *Web Site:* www.whitegatefeatures.com, pg 1192

Corkrean, John, H B Fuller Co, 1200 Willow Lake Blvd, St Paul, MN 55110-5146 *Tel:* 651-236-5900 *Toll Free Tel:* 888-423-8553 *E-mail:* inquiry@hbfuller.com *Web Site:* www.hbfuller.com, pg 1267, 1280

Cormier, Beth, Sappi Fine Paper North America, 255 State St, Boston, MA 02109 *Tel:* 617-423-7300 *Toll Free Tel:* 800-882-4332 *E-mail:* webqueriesna@sappi.com *Web Site:* www.sappi.com/na, pg 1271

Cornell, Merial, Cornell & Company, LLC, 44 Jog Hill Rd, Trumbull, CT 06611 *Tel:* 203-454-4210 *Web Site:* www.cornellandco.com, pg 1413

Cornell, Mike, National Book Network (NBN), 4501 Forbes Blvd, Suite 200, Lanham, MD 20706 *Tel:* 301-459-3366 *Toll Free Tel:* 800-462-6420 (orders only) *Fax:* 301-429-5746 *Toll Free Fax:* 800-338-4550 (orders only) *E-mail:* customercare@nbnbooks.com *Web Site:* www.nbnbooks.com, pg 1298, 1319

Correa, Alex, Lectorum Publications Inc, 10 New Maple Ave, Suite 303, Pine Brook, NJ 07058 *Tel:* 201-559-2200 *Toll Free Tel:* 800-345-5946 *E-mail:* lectorum@lectorum.com *Web Site:* www.lectorum.com, pg 1318

Corrette, George, Pathway Book Service, 34 Production Ave, Keene, NH 03431 *Tel:* 603-357-0236 *Toll Free Tel:* 800-345-6665 *Fax:* 603-965-2181 *E-mail:* pbs@pathwaybook.com *Web Site:* www.pathwaybook.com, pg 1320

Corsi, Mark, PMSI Direct, 242 Old New Brunswick Rd, Suite 350, Piscataway, NJ 08854 *Tel:* 732-465-1570 *Toll Free Tel:* 800-238-1316 *Web Site:* www.pmsidirect.com, pg 1117

Cosentino, Jay, Computer Analytics Corp, 999 E Touhy Ave, Suite 130, Des Plaines, IL 60018-2736 *Tel:* 847-297-5290 *Fax:* 847-297-8680 *Web Site:* www.cacorp.com, pg 1366

Costa, Maia, German Language Services, 4752 41 Ave SW, Suite B, Seattle, WA 98116 *Tel:* 206-938-3600 *E-mail:* info@germanlanguageservices.com *Web Site:* germanlanguageservices.com, pg 1401

Costa, Megan, Penguin Random House Canada, a Penguin Random House company, 320 Front St W, Suite 1400, Toronto, ON M5V 3B6, Canada *Tel:* 416-364-4449 *Toll Free Tel:* 888-523-9292 (cust serv) *Fax:* 416-598-7764 *E-mail:* customerservicescanada@penguinrandomhouse.com; publicitycanada@penguinrandomhouse.com; rightscanada@penguinrandomhouse.com *Web Site:* www.penguinrandomhouse.ca, pg 1299

Costache, Irina, Boston Review, PO Box 390568, Cambridge, MA 02139 *Tel:* 617-356-8198 *E-mail:* review@bostonreview.net; customerservice@bostonreview.net *Web Site:* bostonreview.net, pg 1130

Cottle, Aaron, The Master's Press, 14550 Midway Rd, Dallas, TX 75244 *Tel:* 972-387-0046 *Fax:* 972-404-0317 *Web Site:* www.themasterspress.com, pg 1257

Coughlin, Tim, Translations.com, 1250 Broadway, 32nd fl, New York, NY 10001 *Tel:* 212-689-1616 *Fax:* 212-504-8057 *E-mail:* newyork@translations.com; info@translations.com *Web Site:* translations.com, pg 1405

Couret, Nilo, Film Quarterly, Journals & Digital Publishing, 155 Grand Ave, Suite 400, Oakland, CA 94612-3758 *E-mail:* info@filmquarterly.org; customerservice@ucpress.edu *Web Site:* www.filmquarterly.org; online.ucpress.edu/fq, pg 1131

Couturier, Greg, Arizona Library Binding Service, 1337 W McKinley, Phoenix, AZ 85007 *Tel:* 602-253-1861 *E-mail:* info@azlbinding.com, pg 1325

Couturier, Ron, Arizona Library Binding Service, 1337 W McKinley, Phoenix, AZ 85007 *Tel:* 602-253-1861 *E-mail:* info@azlbinding.com, pg 1325

Covas, Laura, Copywriters' Council of America™ (CCA), Linick Bldg, 7 Putter Lane, Middle Island, NY 11953 *Tel:* 631-924-3888; 631-924-8555; 631-604-8599 *E-mail:* linickgroup@gmail.com, pg 1345

Cowles, Gregory, The New York Times Book Review, 620 Eighth Ave, 5th fl, New York, NY 10018 *Tel:* 212-556-1234 *Toll Free Tel:* 800-631-2580 (subns) *E-mail:* bookreview@nytimes.com; books@nytimes.com *Web Site:* www.nytimes.com, pg 1135

Cox, Bryan A, ABDI Inc, 16 Avenue "A", Leetsdale, PA 15056 *Toll Free Tel:* 800-796-6471 *Fax:* 412-741-4161 *E-mail:* e-fulfillment@abdintl.com *Web Site:* www.abdi-ecommerce10.com/abdintl; www.abdintl.com/abdintl, pg 1117, 1207, 1333

Cox, Dennis, ChinaStock/WorldViews, 2506 Country Village, Ann Arbor, MI 48103-6500 *Tel:* 734-680-4660 *E-mail:* decoxphoto@gmail.com *Web Site:* www.denniscox.com, pg 1427

Cox, James A, Children's Bookwatch, 278 Orchard Dr, Oregon, WI 53575-1129 *Tel:* 608-835-7937 *E-mail:* mbr@execpc.com *Web Site:* www.midwestbookreview.com, pg 1131

Cox, James A, Internet Bookwatch, 278 Orchard Dr, Oregon, WI 53575-1129 *Tel:* 608-835-7937 *E-mail:* mbr@execpc.com *Web Site:* www.midwestbookreview.com, pg 1133

Cox, James A, Library Bookwatch, 278 Orchard Dr, Oregon, WI 53575-1129 *Tel:* 608-835-7937 *E-mail:* mbr@execpc.com *Web Site:* www.midwestbookreview.com, pg 1134

Cox, James A, MBR Bookwatch, 278 Orchard Dr, Oregon, WI 53575-1129 *Tel:* 608-835-7937 *E-mail:* mbr@execpc.com *Web Site:* www.midwestbookreview.com, pg 1134

Cox, James A, The Midwest Book Review, 278 Orchard Dr, Oregon, WI 53575-1129 *Tel:* 608-835-7937 *E-mail:* mbr@execpc.com; mwbookrevw@aol.com *Web Site:* www.midwestbookreview.com, pg 1134

Cox, James A, Reviewer Bookwatch, 278 Orchard Dr, Oregon, WI 53575-1129 *Tel:* 608-835-7937 *E-mail:* mbr@execpc.com *Web Site:* www.midwestbookreview.com, pg 1136

Cox, James A, Small Press Bookwatch, 278 Orchard Dr, Oregon, WI 53575-1129 *Tel:* 608-835-7937 *E-mail:* mbr@execpc.com *Web Site:* www.midwestbookreview.com, pg 1137

Cox, James A, Wisconsin Bookwatch, 278 Orchard Dr, Oregon, WI 53575-1129 Tel: 608-835-7937 E-mail: mbr@execpc.com Web Site: www.midwestbookreview.com, pg 1137

Cox, Laura, ProtoView, 7515 NE Ambassador Place, Suite A, Portland, OR 97220 Tel: 503-281-9230 E-mail: info@protoview.com Web Site: www.protoview.com, pg 1146

Coyne, Stephen P, Eastern Book Co, 7 Lincoln Ave, Scarborough, ME 04074 Tel: 207-856-1370 Toll Free Tel: 800-937-0331 Toll Free Fax: 800-214-3895 E-mail: info@ebc.com; sales@ebc.com Web Site: www.ebc.com, pg 1314

Craig, David L, Paperbacks For Educators, 426 W Front St, Washington, MO 63090 Tel: 314-960-3015 E-mail: paperbacks@usmo.com Web Site: www.any-book-in-print.com, pg 1320

Craig, Sean, Maxcess International, 222 W Memorial Rd, Oklahoma City, OK 73114 Tel: 405-755-1600 Toll Free Tel: 800-639-3433 Fax: 405-755-8425 E-mail: sales@maxcessintl.com Web Site: www.maxcessintl.com, pg 1282

Crain, Christopher, Crain Communications Inc, 1155 Gratiot Ave, Detroit, MI 48207-2732 Tel: 313-446-6000 Fax: 313-446-0383 E-mail: info@crain.com Web Site: crain.com, pg 1190

Crain, K C, Crain Communications Inc, 1155 Gratiot Ave, Detroit, MI 48207-2732 Tel: 313-446-6000 Fax: 313-446-0383 E-mail: info@crain.com Web Site: crain.com, pg 1190

Crain, Keith, Crain Communications Inc, 1155 Gratiot Ave, Detroit, MI 48207-2732 Tel: 313-446-6000 Fax: 313-446-0383 E-mail: info@crain.com Web Site: crain.com, pg 1190

Cramer, Phoebe, Publishers Weekly, 49 W 23 St, 9th fl, New York, NY 10010 Tel: 212-377-5500 Fax: 212-377-2733 Web Site: www.publishersweekly.com, pg 1136

Cramp, Beverly, BC BookWorld, PO Box 93536, Vancouver, BC V6E 4L7, Canada Tel: 604-736-4011 Fax: 604-736-4011 E-mail: bookworld@telus.net Web Site: www.bcbookworld.com, pg 1130

Crawford, Sterling, Ingram Content Group LLC, One Ingram Blvd, La Vergne, TN 37086-1986 Tel: 615-793-5000 Toll Free Tel: 800-937-8000 (retailers); 800-937-5300 (ext 1, libs) E-mail: customerservice@ingramcontent.com Web Site: www.ingramcontent.com, pg 1294, 1317

Crawshaw, Todd, Crawshaw Design, 120 Bayview Dr, San Rafael, CA 94901 Tel: 415-456-5544 Fax: 415-456-4319 Web Site: www.crawshawdesign.com, pg 1413

Crecca, Paul J, Westchester Publishing Services, 4 Old Newtown Rd, Danbury, CT 06810 Tel: 203-791-0080 Fax: 203-791-9286 E-mail: info@westchesterpubsvcs.com Web Site: www.westchesterpublishingservices.com, pg 1233

Cripps, Paul, Electronics for Imaging Inc (EFI), 6750 Dumbarton Circle, Fremont, CA 94555 Tel: 650-357-3500 Toll Free Tel: 800-568-1917; 800-875-7117 (sales) Fax: 650-357-3907 E-mail: info@efi.com Web Site: www.efi.com, pg 1368

Crochetiere, Chris, BW&A Books Inc, 112 W McClanahan St, Oxford, NC 27565 Tel: 919-956-9111 Fax: 919-956-9112 E-mail: bwa@bwabooks.com Web Site: www.bwabooks.com, pg 1223

Crockett, Chris, VillageSoup®, One Printinghouse Sq, Ellsworth, ME 04605 Tel: 207-594-4401 E-mail: info@villagesoup.com Web Site: www.villagesoup.com; mainestaymedia.com, pg 1351

Crockett, Samuel, Worzalla, 3535 Jefferson St, Stevens Point, WI 54481 Tel: 715-344-9608 Fax: 715-344-2578 Web Site: www.worzalla.com, pg 1215, 1233, 1262

Cronshaw, Francine, East Mountain Editing Services, PO Box 1895, Tijeras, NM 87059-1895 Tel: 505-281-8422 Web Site: www.spanishindexing.com, pg 1225

Croom, Darren, Texas Book Co, 8501 Technology Circle, Greenville, TX 75402 Tel: 903-455-6969 Toll Free Tel: 800-527-1016 E-mail: customerservice@texasbook.com Web Site: www.texasbook.com, pg 1322

Cross, Tim, Westchester Publishing Services, 4 Old Newtown Rd, Danbury, CT 06810 Tel: 203-791-0080 Fax: 203-791-9286 E-mail: info@westchesterpubsvcs.com Web Site: www.westchesterpublishingservices.com, pg 1233

Crowell, David, AIMS International Books Inc, 7709 Hamilton Ave, Cincinnati, OH 45231 Tel: 513-521-5590 Fax: 513-521-5592 E-mail: info@aimsbooks.com Web Site: www.aimsbooks.com, pg 1286

Crowell, Georgia W, AIMS International Books Inc, 7709 Hamilton Ave, Cincinnati, OH 45231 Tel: 513-521-5590 Fax: 513-521-5592 E-mail: info@aimsbooks.com Web Site: www.aimsbooks.com, pg 1286

Crowley, Kevin, The Crowley Co, 5111 Pegasus Ct, Suite M, Frederick, MD 21704 Tel: 240-215-0224 Fax: 240-215-0234 E-mail: webrequest@thecrowleycompany.com Web Site: www.thecrowleycompany.com, pg 1367

Crowley, Pat, The Crowley Co, 5111 Pegasus Ct, Suite M, Frederick, MD 21704 Tel: 240-215-0224 Fax: 240-215-0234 E-mail: webrequest@thecrowleycompany.com Web Site: www.thecrowleycompany.com, pg 1367

Croy, Michael, Consortium Book Sales & Distribution, an Ingram brand, The Keg House, Suite 101, 34 13 Ave NE, Minneapolis, MN 55413-1007 Tel: 612-746-2600 Toll Free Tel: 866-400-5351 (cust serv, Jackson, TN) E-mail: cbsdinfo@ingramcontent.com Web Site: www.cbsd.com, pg 1289

Cruz, Gilbert, The New York Times Book Review, 620 Eighth Ave, 5th fl, New York, NY 10018 Tel: 212-556-1234 Toll Free Tel: 800-631-2580 (subns) E-mail: bookreview@nytimes.com; books@nytimes.com Web Site: www.nytimes.com, pg 1135

Crystal, Scott M, American Translation Partners Inc (ATP), One Trowbridge Rd, Suite 340, Buzzards Bay, MA 02532 Tel: 508-823-8892 Toll Free Tel: 888-443-2376 (US only) Fax: 508-823-8854 E-mail: info@atptranslations.com; request@atptranslations.com Web Site: atptranslations.com, pg 1399

Cue, Eddy, Apple Inc, One Apple Park Way, Cupertino, CA 95014 Tel: 408-996-1010 Web Site: www.apple.com, pg 1364

Cullen, Teddee, Apex Die Corp, 840 Cherry Lane, San Carlos, CA 94070 Tel: 650-592-6350 Fax: 650-592-5315 E-mail: info@apexdie.com Web Site: www.apexdie.com, pg 1248

Culver, Russ, Whitehots Inc, 205 Industrial Pkwy N, Unit 3, Aurora, ON L4G 4C4, Canada Tel: 905-727-9188 Toll Free Tel: 888-567-9188 Fax: 905-727-8756 Toll Free Fax: 888-563-0020 E-mail: admin@whitehots.com Web Site: www.whitehots.com, pg 1323

Culver, Sharon, Whitehots Inc, 205 Industrial Pkwy N, Unit 3, Aurora, ON L4G 4C4, Canada Tel: 905-727-9188 Toll Free Tel: 888-567-9188 Fax: 905-727-8756 Toll Free Fax: 888-563-0020 E-mail: admin@whitehots.com Web Site: www.whitehots.com, pg 1323

Cummings, Eva, Apex Die Corp, 840 Cherry Lane, San Carlos, CA 94070 Tel: 650-592-6350 Fax: 650-592-5315 E-mail: info@apexdie.com Web Site: www.apexdie.com, pg 1248

Curley, Sandra, The Supreme Co, 1909 Lagneaux Rd, Lafayette, LA 70506 Tel: 337-453-1028 Toll Free Fax: 888-600-4180 E-mail: information@supremebooks.com Web Site: www.supremebooks.com, pg 1322

Curran, Kevin, SITMA USA Inc, 45 Empire Dr, St Paul, MN 55103-1856 Tel: 651-222-2324 Fax: 651-222-4652 E-mail: sales@sitma.com Web Site: www.sitma.it, pg 1283

Curry, Clare, Distributed Art Publishers Inc, 75 Broad St, Suite 630, New York, NY 10004 Tel: 212-627-1999 Toll Free Tel: 800-338-2665 (cust serv) Fax: 212-627-9484 E-mail: orders@dapinc.com Web Site: www.artbook.com, pg 1290

Curtin, Rose, Reviews in American History, 2715 N Charles St, Baltimore, MD 21218-4363 Tel: 410-516-6987 (journal orders outside US & CN) Toll Free Tel: 800-548-1784 (journal orders) Fax: 410-578-2865 (journal orders) E-mail: jrnlcirc@jh.edu (journal orders) Web Site: www.press.jhu.edu/journals/reviews-american-history, pg 1136

Cushing, Connie M, Cushing-Malloy Inc, 1350 N Main St, Ann Arbor, MI 48104-1045 Tel: 734-663-8554 Fax: 734-663-5731 Web Site: www.cushing-malloy.com; www.c-mbooks.com, pg 1209, 1251

Cushinsky, Steven M, ACT ONE Mailing List Services Inc, 237 Washington St, 2nd fl, Marblehead, MA 01945-3334 Tel: 781-639-1919 Toll Free Tel: 800-ACT-LIST (228-5478) Fax: 781-639-2733 E-mail: info@act1lists.com Web Site: www.act1lists.com, pg 1119

Cushman, Tori, Ingram Content Group LLC, One Ingram Blvd, La Vergne, TN 37086-1986 Tel: 615-793-5000 Toll Free Tel: 800-937-8000 (retailers); 800-937-5300 (ext 1, libs) E-mail: customerservice@ingramcontent.com Web Site: www.ingramcontent.com, pg 1294, 1317

Cusick, Kate, Porter Novelli, 195 Broadway, 17th fl, New York, NY 10007 Tel: 212-601-8000 Web Site: www.porternovelli.com, pg 1112

Cusick, Molly, International Literary Properties (ILP), 286 Madison Ave, New York, NY 10017 Tel: 646-202-1633 Fax: 212-967-0977 E-mail: contact@ilpliterary.com Web Site: www.internationalliteraryproperties.com, pg 1348

Cusson, Charles, Les Messageries ADP, 2315, rue de la Province, Longueuil, QC J4G 1G4, Canada Tel: 450-640-1234 (commercial); 450-640-1237 (sales) Toll Free Tel: 800-771-3022 (commercial); 866-874-1237 (sales) Fax: 450-640-1251 (commercial); 450-674-6237 (sales) Toll Free Fax: 800-603-0433 (commercial); 866-874-6237 (sales) E-mail: adpcommandes@messageries-adp.com Web Site: www.messageries-adp.com, pg 1285

Custard, Jill, The Ovid Bell Press Inc, 1201 Bluff St, Fulton, MO 65251 Tel: 573-642-2256 Toll Free Tel: 800-835-8919 E-mail: sales@ovidbell.com Web Site: ovidbell.com, pg 1229, 1258, 1270, 1282

Czerwinski, Diane, Scientific Bindery Inc, 8052 Monticello Ave, Suite 206, Skokie, IL 60076 Tel: 847-329-0510 Fax: 847-329-0608 E-mail: info@scientificbindery.com Web Site: www.scientificbindery.com, pg 1259

D'Angelo, Allen, Bookcovers.com, c/o Archer Ellison Inc, 7025 CR 46-A, Suite 1071, Lake Mary, FL 32746 Toll Free Tel: 800-449-4095 (ext 702) Toll Free Fax: 800-366-4086 E-mail: info@bookcovers.com Web Site: bookcovers.com, pg 1412

D'Angelo, Louise, Maryheart Crusaders Inc, 531 W Main St, Meriden, CT 06451-2707 Tel: 203-238-9735 Toll Free Tel: 800-879-1957 (orders only) Fax: 203-235-0059 E-mail: maryheart@msn.com Web Site: www.maryheartcrusaders.com, pg 1142

D'Angelo, Michael, Maryheart Crusaders Inc, 531 W Main St, Meriden, CT 06451-2707 Tel: 203-238-9735 Toll Free Tel: 800-879-1957 (orders only) Fax: 203-235-0059 E-mail: maryheart@msn.com Web Site: www.maryheartcrusaders.com, pg 1142

D'Antonio, Ray, St Joseph Communications-Print Group, 50 Macintosh Blvd, Concord, ON L4K 4P3, Canada Tel: 905-660-3111 E-mail: marketing@stjoseph.com Web Site: stjoseph.com, pg 1105, 1259

D'Aquila, Greg, Dunhill International List Co Inc, 6400 Congress Ave, Suite 1750, Boca Raton, FL 33487-2898 Tel: 561-998-7800 Toll Free Tel: 800-DUNHILL (386-4455) Fax: 561-998-7880 E-mail: dunhill@dunhillintl.com Web Site: www.dunhills.com, pg 1120

D'Onofrio, Joseph, Chicago Distribution Center (CDC), 11030 S Langley Ave, Chicago, IL 60628 Tel: 773-702-7010 Toll Free Fax: 800-621-8476 Web Site: press.uchicago.edu/cdc, pg 1289

PERSONNEL INDEX

Daemmrich, Bob, Bob Daemmrich Photography Inc, 1122 Colorado St, Suite 2202, Austin, TX 78701 *Tel:* 512-469-9700 *Web Site:* www.bobphoto.com, pg 1420

Daemmrich, Janis, Bob Daemmrich Photography Inc, 1122 Colorado St, Suite 2202, Austin, TX 78701 *Tel:* 512-469-9700 *Web Site:* www.bobphoto.com, pg 1420

Daigneault, Yves, Cooperative Etudiante de Polytechnique, Pavillon Principal Local C-220, 2900 Edouard Mont Petit, Montreal, QC H3T 1J4, Canada *Tel:* 514-340-4851 *Fax:* 514-340-4543 *E-mail:* andre.daneau@polymtl.ca *Web Site:* www.coopoly.ca, pg 1314

Daniel, Kaan, Link Translations Inc, 60 E 96 St, New York, NY 10128 *Toll Free Tel:* 866-866-5010 *E-mail:* info@link-translations.com *Web Site:* www.link-translations.com, pg 1403

Daniel, William, Ingram Content Group LLC, One Ingram Blvd, La Vergne, TN 37086-1986 *Tel:* 615-793-5000 *Toll Free Tel:* 800-937-8000 (retailers); 800-937-5300 (ext 1, libs) *E-mail:* customerservice@ingramcontent.com *Web Site:* www.ingramcontent.com, pg 1294, 1316

Daniels, Tracey, Media Masters Publicity, 61 Depot St, Tryon, NC 28782 *Tel:* 828-859-9456 *E-mail:* info@mmpublicity.com *Web Site:* www.mmpublicity.com, pg 1110, 1349

Danz, Emma, Franklin & Siegal Associates Inc, 40 Exchange Place, Suite 1703, New York, NY 10005 *Tel:* 212-868-6311 *Web Site:* www.franklinandsiegal.com, pg 1346

Danziger, Karen, Koller Search Partners, 655 Third Ave, 24th fl, New York, NY 10017 *Tel:* 212-661-5250 *E-mail:* ksp@kollersearch.com *Web Site:* www.kollersearch.com, pg 1381

Dar, Mahnaz, Kirkus, 1140 Broadway, Suite 802, New York, NY 10001 *E-mail:* customercare@kirkus.com *Web Site:* www.kirkusreviews.com, pg 1133

Dart, Jeremiah, Creative Direct Marketing Group Inc (CDMG), 1313 Fourth Ave N, Nashville, TN 37208 *Tel:* 615-814-6633 *Web Site:* www.cdmginc.com, pg 1345

Dauber, Miri Pomerantz, Jewish Book Council, 520 Eighth Ave, 4th fl, New York, NY 10018 *Tel:* 212-201-2920 *Fax:* 212-532-4952 *E-mail:* info@jewishbooks.org *Web Site:* www.jewishbookcouncil.org, pg 1146

Dauber, Miri Pomerantz, Paper Brigade, 520 Eighth Ave, 4th fl, New York, NY 10018 *Tel:* 212-201-2920 *Fax:* 212-532-4952 *E-mail:* info@jewishbooks.org *Web Site:* www.jewishbookcouncil.org, pg 1135

Daubert, Fred, Universal Bookbindery Inc, 1200 N Colorado, San Antonio, TX 78207 *Tel:* 210-734-9502 *Toll Free Tel:* 800-594-2015 *Fax:* 210-736-0867 *E-mail:* service@universalbookbindery.com *Web Site:* www.universalbookbindery.com, pg 1261

Daughtry, John, LOF Productions, 121 Greenwich Rd, Suite 202, Charlotte, NC 28211 *Tel:* 704-375-8892 *Fax:* 704-375-6316 *Web Site:* www.lofproductions.com, pg 1423

Dauphin, Brian, Ingram Content Group LLC, One Ingram Blvd, La Vergne, TN 37086-1986 *Tel:* 615-793-5000 *Toll Free Tel:* 800-937-8000 (retailers); 800-937-5300 (ext 1, libs) *E-mail:* customerservice@ingramcontent.com *Web Site:* www.ingramcontent.com, pg 1294, 1316

Dauphin, Brian, Lightning Source LLC, 1246 Heil Quaker Blvd, La Vergne, TN 37086 *Tel:* 615-793-5000 (Ingram) *Toll Free Tel:* 800-378-5508; 800-509-4156 (cust serv) *E-mail:* lsicustomersupport@ingramcontent.com; contentacquisitioninquiries@ingramcontent.com *Web Site:* www.ingramcontent.com/publishers/print, pg 1212

Dauphin, Brian, Lightning Source LLC, 1246 Heil Quaker Blvd, La Vergne, TN 37086 *Tel:* 615-793-5000 (Ingram) *Toll Free Tel:* 800-378-5508; 800-509-4156 (cust serv) *E-mail:* lsicustomersupport@ingramcontent.com *Web Site:* www.ingramcontent.com/publishers/print, pg 1256, 1371

Davenport, Angela, eFulfillment Service Inc, 807 Airport Access Rd, Traverse City, MI 49686 *Tel:* 231-276-5057 *Toll Free Tel:* 866-922-6783 *E-mail:* sales@efulfillmentservice.com *Web Site:* www.efulfillmentservice.com, pg 1333

Davey, Kate, Chicago Distribution Center (CDC), 11030 S Langley Ave, Chicago, IL 60628 *Tel:* 773-702-7010 *Toll Free Fax:* 800-621-8476 *Web Site:* press.uchicago.edu/cdc, pg 1289

Davidson, Jeff, Jeff Davidson MBA, CMC, Breathing Space Institute, 3202 Ruffin St, Raleigh, NC 27607 *Tel:* 919-932-1996 *Web Site:* www.breathingspace.com, pg 1345

Davies, Gordon A, Open Text Corp, 275 Frank Tompa Dr, Waterloo, ON N2L 0A1, Canada *Tel:* 519-888-7111 *Fax:* 519-888-0677 *Web Site:* opentext.com, pg 1374

Daving, Kyle, William S Hein & Co Inc, 2350 N Forest Rd, Suite 10A, Getzville, NY 14068 *Tel:* 716-882-2600 *Toll Free Tel:* 800-828-7571 *Fax:* 716-883-8100 *E-mail:* mail@wshein.com; marketing@wshein.com; customerservice@wshein.com *Web Site:* home.heinonline.org, pg 1316

Davis, Allan, Bookazine Co Inc, 75 Hook Rd, Bayonne, NJ 07002 *Tel:* 201-339-7777 *Toll Free Tel:* 800-221-8112 *Fax:* 201-339-7778 *E-mail:* info@bookazine.com *Web Site:* www.bookazine.com, pg 1312, 1327

Davis, Bailey, Lightning Source LLC, 1246 Heil Quaker Blvd, La Vergne, TN 37086 *Tel:* 615-793-5000 (Ingram) *Toll Free Tel:* 800-378-5508; 800-509-4156 (cust serv) *E-mail:* lsicustomersupport@ingramcontent.com; contentacquisitioninquiries@ingramcontent.com *Web Site:* www.ingramcontent.com/publishers/print, pg 1212

Davis, Bailey, Lightning Source LLC, 1246 Heil Quaker Blvd, La Vergne, TN 37086 *Tel:* 615-793-5000 (Ingram) *Toll Free Tel:* 800-378-5508; 800-509-4156 (cust serv) *E-mail:* lsicustomersupport@ingramcontent.com *Web Site:* www.ingramcontent.com/publishers/print, pg 1256, 1371

Davis, Bert, Bert Davis Executive Search Inc, 555 Fifth Ave, Suite 302, New York, NY 10017 *Tel:* 212-838-4000 *E-mail:* info@bertdavis.com *Web Site:* www.bertdavis.com, pg 1381

Davis, Gary, The Learning Source Ltd, 644 Tenth St, Brooklyn, NY 11215 *E-mail:* info@learningsourceltd.com *Web Site:* www.learningsourceltd.com, pg 1355

Davis, Gilbert, Universal Bindery (Sask) Ltd, 516-A Duchess St, Saskatoon, SK S7K 0R1, Canada *Tel:* 306-652-8313 *Toll Free Tel:* 888-JOE-MENU (563-6368) *Fax:* 306-244-2994 *E-mail:* gib@unibindery.com, pg 1105

Davis, Ken, Christianbook Inc, 140 Summit St, Peabody, MA 01960-5156 *Tel:* 978-977-5060; 978-977-5000 (intl calls) *Toll Free Tel:* 800-CHRISTIAN (247-4784) *Fax:* 978-977-5010 *E-mail:* customer.service@christianbook.com *Web Site:* www.christianbook.com, pg 1313

Davis, Larry, Ironmark, 9040 Junction Dr, Annapolis Junction, MD 20701 *Toll Free Tel:* 888-775-3737 *E-mail:* marketing@ironmarkusa.com *Web Site:* ironmarkusa.com, pg 1211, 1227, 1255, 1268, 1281

Davis, Sandy, The Philip Lief Group Inc (PLG), 2976 Pleasant Ridge Rd, Wingdale, NY 12594 *Tel:* 609-430-1000 *Fax:* 845-724-7139 *E-mail:* info@plg.us.com *Web Site:* plg.us.com, pg 1355

Davis, Shelly, LBS, 1801 Thompson Ave, Des Moines, IA 50316-2751 *Tel:* 515-262-3191 *Toll Free Tel:* 800-247-5323 *Toll Free Fax:* 800-262-4091 *E-mail:* info@lbsbind.com *Web Site:* www.lbsbind.com, pg 1269

Davis, Tammy, Videx Inc, 1105 NE Circle Blvd, Corvallis, OR 97330 *Tel:* 541-738-5500; 541-738-0521 *Fax:* 541-752-5285 *E-mail:* sales@videx.com; support@videx.com *Web Site:* www.videx.com, pg 1378

Davis, Tieshena, The Independent Book Publishers Association (IBPA), 1020 Manhattan Beach Blvd, Suite 204, Manhattan Beach, CA 90266 *Tel:* 310-546-1818 *E-mail:* info@ibpa-online.org *Web Site:* www.ibpa-online.org, pg 1116

Davis, Wayne, Digimage Arts, 100 S Eighth Ave, Winterset, IA 50273 *Tel:* 515-462-1874 *E-mail:* geninfo@digimagearts.com *Web Site:* www.digimagearts.com, pg 1367

Davis, Wendy, The Learning Source Ltd, 644 Tenth St, Brooklyn, NY 11215 *E-mail:* info@learningsourceltd.com *Web Site:* www.learningsourceltd.com, pg 1355

Davis-Undiano, Robert Con, World Literature Today, 630 Parrington Oval, Suite 110, Norman, OK 73019-4033 *Tel:* 405-325-4531 *E-mail:* wlt@ou.edu *Web Site:* www.worldliteraturetoday.org, pg 1137

Davison, Nicole, Vectorworks Inc, 7150 Riverwood Dr, Columbia, MD 21046 *Tel:* 410-290-5114 *Toll Free Tel:* 888-646-4223 (sales) *Fax:* 410-290-7266 *E-mail:* sales@vectorworks.net *Web Site:* www.vectorworks.net, pg 1378

Dawson, Effie, Washington Post News Service with Bloomberg News, 1301 "K" St NW, Washington, DC 20071 *Tel:* 202-334-7666 *E-mail:* syndication@washpost.com *Web Site:* www.washingtonpost.com/syndication, pg 1192

Dayton, Gary, Baker & Taylor LLC, 2550 W Tyvola Rd, Suite 300, Charlotte, NC 28217 *Tel:* 704-998-3100 *Toll Free Tel:* 800-775-1800 (info servs) *Fax:* 704-998-3319 *Toll Free Fax:* 800-775-2600 *E-mail:* btinfo@baker-taylor.com *Web Site:* www.baker-taylor.com, pg 1145

Dayton, Gary, Baker & Taylor LLC, 2550 W Tyvola Rd, Suite 300, Charlotte, NC 28217 *Tel:* 704-998-3100 *Toll Free Tel:* 800-775-1800 (info servs) *Fax:* 704-998-3319 *E-mail:* btinfo@baker-taylor.com *Web Site:* www.baker-taylor.com, pg 1286, 1312

De Anda, Julie, Eizo Inc, 5710 Warland Dr, Cypress, CA 90630 *Tel:* 562-431-5011 *Toll Free Tel:* 800-800-5202 *Fax:* 562-431-4811 *E-mail:* orders@eizo.com *Web Site:* www.eizo.com, pg 1368

De Filippo, Michele, 1106 Design LLC, 1007 E Orange Dr, Phoenix, AZ 85014 *Tel:* 602-866-3226 *Fax:* 602-866-8166 *E-mail:* md@1106design.com *Web Site:* 1106design.com, pg 1414

De Jesus, John, Coach House Printing, 80 bpNichol Lane, Toronto, ON M5S 3J4, Canada *Tel:* 416-979-2217 *Toll Free Tel:* 800-367-6360 (outside Toronto) *Fax:* 416-977-1158 *E-mail:* mail@chbooks.com *Web Site:* www.chbooks.com, pg 1223, 1250

de los Reyes, Monica, The Horn Book Magazine, 7858 Industrial Pkwy, Plain City, OH 43064 *Toll Free Tel:* 800-325-9558 *E-mail:* info@hbook.com *Web Site:* www.hbook.com, pg 1132

de Mendonca, A Jorge, Mendon Associates Inc, 44 Glenwood Ave, Suite 210, Toronto, ON M6P 3C6, Canada *Tel:* 416-239-9661 *Toll Free Tel:* 800-361-1325 *E-mail:* info@mendon.com *Web Site:* www.mendon.com, pg 1349

De Pape, Lawrence, Accent Photography Ltd, 1842 31 Ave SW, Calgary, AB T2T 1S7, Canada *Tel:* 403-860-8588 *Toll Free Tel:* 877-470-4120 *Fax:* 403-271-4121 *E-mail:* info@calgaryphotographer.com *Web Site:* www.accentphotography.ca, pg 1419

De Spirito, Sal, Encyclopaedia Britannica Inc, 325 N La Salle St, Suite 200, Chicago, IL 60654 *Tel:* 312-347-7000 (all other countries) *Toll Free Tel:* 800-323-1229 (US & CN) *Fax:* 312-294-2104 *E-mail:* contact@eb.com *Web Site:* www.britannica.com, pg 1315

De Vos, Eric, City Diecutting Inc, One Cory Rd, Morristown, NJ 07960 *Tel:* 973-270-0370 *Fax:* 973-270-0369 *E-mail:* sales@bookdisplays.com *Web Site:* www.bookdisplays.com, pg 1103, 1344

Deacon, Cherry, Glenbow Museum Shop, 130 Ninth Ave SE, Calgary, AB T2G 0P3, Canada *Tel:* 403-268-4119 *Fax:* 403-262-4045 *E-mail:* shop@glenbow.org *Web Site:* www.glenbow.org, pg 1316

Deady, John F, Symmetry Creative Production, 1300 S Grove Ave, Suite 103, Barrington, IL 60010 Tel: 847-382-8750 E-mail: information@symmetrycp.com Web Site: www.symmetrycp.com, pg 1232

Deahl, Rachel, Publishers Weekly, 49 W 23 St, 9th fl, New York, NY 10010 Tel: 212-377-5500 Fax: 212-377-2733 Web Site: www.publishersweekly.com, pg 1136

Deal, Barbara, Copywriters' Council of America™ (CCA), Linick Bldg, 7 Putter Lane, Middle Island, NY 11953 Tel: 631-924-3888; 631-924-8555; 631-604-8599 E-mail: linickgroup@gmail.com, pg 1345

Deal, Barbara, LK Advertising Agency, Linick Bldg, 7 Putter Lane, Middle Island, NY 11953 Tel: 631-924-3888; 631-924-8555; 631-604-8599 E-mail: topmarketingadvisor@gmail.com; linickgroup@gmail.com, pg 1100

Deaton, Steve, LBS, 1801 Thompson Ave, Des Moines, IA 50316-2751 Tel: 515-262-3191 Toll Free Tel: 800-247-5323 Toll Free Fax: 800-262-4091 E-mail: info@lbsbind.com Web Site: www.lbsbind.com, pg 1269

DeCaires, Angela, BookLogix, 1264 Old Alpharetta Rd, Alpharetta, GA 30005 Tel: 470-239-8547 E-mail: info@booklogix.com; publishing@booklogix.com; customerservice@booklogix.com Web Site: www.booklogix.com, pg 1208

DeChantal, Rick, The Tribune News Service, 160 N Stetson Ave, Chicago, IL 60601 Tel: 312-222-4131 E-mail: tcanews@trbpub.com Web Site: www.mctdirect.com; tribunecontentagency.com/tribune-news-service, pg 1191

Dechow, Chloe, C Blohm & Associates Inc, 5999 Monona Dr, Monona, WI 53716-3531 Tel: 608-216-7300 E-mail: hello@cblohm.com Web Site: www.cblohm.com, pg 1107

Decker, Jeffrey B, Decker Intellectual Properties Inc, 372 Richmond St W, Toronto, ON M5V 2L7, Canada Tel: 905-522-8526 Toll Free Tel: 855-647-6511 E-mail: customercare@deckermed.com Web Site: www.deckerip.com, pg 1367

Decker, Ryan T, Decker Intellectual Properties Inc, 372 Richmond St W, Toronto, ON M5V 2L7, Canada Tel: 905-522-8526 Toll Free Tel: 855-647-6511 E-mail: customercare@deckermed.com Web Site: www.deckerip.com, pg 1367

DeFabis, Mark, Integrated Distribution Services (IDS), 9431 AllPoints Pkwy, Plainfield, IN 46168 Toll Free Tel: 866-232-6533 E-mail: cwelch@idsfulfillment.com Web Site: www.idsfulfillment.com, pg 1334

DeFabis, Mike, Integrated Distribution Services (IDS), 9431 AllPoints Pkwy, Plainfield, IN 46168 Toll Free Tel: 866-232-6533 E-mail: cwelch@idsfulfillment.com Web Site: www.idsfulfillment.com, pg 1334

Defino, Daniel, Tukaiz LLC, 2917 N Latoria Lane, Franklin Park, IL 60131 Tel: 847-455-1588; 847-288-4968 (sales) Toll Free Tel: 800-543-2674 E-mail: contacttukaiz@tukaiz.com Web Site: www.tukaiz.com, pg 1232, 1261, 1273, 1284

Defino, Frank Jr, Tukaiz LLC, 2917 N Latoria Lane, Franklin Park, IL 60131 Tel: 847-455-1588; 847-288-4968 (sales) Toll Free Tel: 800-543-2674 E-mail: contacttukaiz@tukaiz.com Web Site: www.tukaiz.com, pg 1232

Defino, Frank Sr, Tukaiz LLC, 2917 N Latoria Lane, Franklin Park, IL 60131 Tel: 847-455-1588; 847-288-4968 (sales) Toll Free Tel: 800-543-2674 E-mail: contacttukaiz@tukaiz.com Web Site: www.tukaiz.com, pg 1232

Defino, Frank Jr, Tukaiz LLC, 2917 N Latoria Lane, Franklin Park, IL 60131 Tel: 847-455-1588; 847-288-4968 (sales) Toll Free Tel: 800-543-2674 E-mail: contacttukaiz@tukaiz.com Web Site: www.tukaiz.com, pg 1261

Defino, Frank Sr, Tukaiz LLC, 2917 N Latoria Lane, Franklin Park, IL 60131 Tel: 847-455-1588; 847-288-4968 (sales) Toll Free Tel: 800-543-2674 E-mail: contacttukaiz@tukaiz.com Web Site: www.tukaiz.com, pg 1261

Defino, Frank Jr, Tukaiz LLC, 2917 N Latoria Lane, Franklin Park, IL 60131 Tel: 847-455-1588; 847-288-4968 (sales) Toll Free Tel: 800-543-2674 E-mail: contacttukaiz@tukaiz.com Web Site: www.tukaiz.com, pg 1273

Defino, Frank Sr, Tukaiz LLC, 2917 N Latoria Lane, Franklin Park, IL 60131 Tel: 847-455-1588; 847-288-4968 (sales) Toll Free Tel: 800-543-2674 E-mail: contacttukaiz@tukaiz.com Web Site: www.tukaiz.com, pg 1273

Defino, Frank Jr, Tukaiz LLC, 2917 N Latoria Lane, Franklin Park, IL 60131 Tel: 847-455-1588; 847-288-4968 (sales) Toll Free Tel: 800-543-2674 E-mail: contacttukaiz@tukaiz.com Web Site: www.tukaiz.com, pg 1284

Defino, Frank Sr, Tukaiz LLC, 2917 N Latoria Lane, Franklin Park, IL 60131 Tel: 847-455-1588; 847-288-4968 (sales) Toll Free Tel: 800-543-2674 E-mail: contacttukaiz@tukaiz.com Web Site: www.tukaiz.com, pg 1284

Deger, Dave, Twin Rivers Paper Co, 82 Bridge Ave, Madawaska, ME 04756 Tel: 207-728-3321 Toll Free Tel: 800-920-9988 Fax: 207-728-8701 E-mail: info@twinriverspaper.com Web Site: www.twinriverspaper.com, pg 1273

DeHamer, Steve, Springdale Bindery LLC, 11411 Landan Lane, Cincinnati, OH 45246 Tel: 513-772-8500 E-mail: info@springdalebindery.com Web Site: www.springdalebindery.com, pg 1260

DeHart, Don, DeHART's Media Services Inc, 6586 Whitbourne Dr, San Jose, CA 95120 Tel: 408-768-1575 Web Site: www.deharts.com, pg 1251

Dehmler, Mari Lynch, Fine Wordworking, PO Box 3041, Monterey, CA 93942-3041 Tel: 831-375-6278 E-mail: info@finewordworking.com Web Site: marilynch.com, pg 1385

Dekker, Chris, Dekker Bookbinding Inc, 2941 Clydon Ave SW, Grand Rapids, MI 49519 Tel: 616-538-5160 Toll Free Tel: 800-299-BIND (299-2463) E-mail: hello@dekkerbook.com Web Site: www.dekkerbook.com, pg 1251, 1266

Dekker, Corbin, Dekker Bookbinding Inc, 2941 Clydon Ave SW, Grand Rapids, MI 49519 Tel: 616-538-5160 Toll Free Tel: 800-299-BIND (299-2463) E-mail: hello@dekkerbook.com Web Site: www.dekkerbook.com, pg 1251, 1266

del Commune, Lauri, Del Commune Enterprises Inc, 18 Bellport Lane, Bellport, NY 11713 Tel: 212-226-6664 E-mail: mail@dcescouts.com Web Site: www.dcescouts.com, pg 1345

Delanoy, Randy, ColorPage, 81 Ten Broeck Ave, Kingston, NY 12401 Tel: 845-331-7581 Toll Free Tel: 800-836-7581 Fax: 845-331-1571 E-mail: sales@colorpageonline.com Web Site: www.colorpageonline.com, pg 1209, 1223, 1250, 1266

DeLetto, Ralph, Midland Paper, Packaging & Supplies, 101 E Palatine Rd, Wheeling, IL 60090 Tel: 847-777-2700 Toll Free Tel: 800-323-8522; 888-564-3526 (cust serv) Fax: 847-403-6320 (cust serv) E-mail: whl@midlandpaper.com; sales@midlandpaper.com; custservice@midlandpaper.com Web Site: www.midlandpaper.com, pg 1269

Delimont, Danita, Danita Delimont Stock Photography, 4911 Somerset Dr SE, Bellevue, WA 98006 Tel: 425-562-1543 Web Site: www.danitadelimont.com, pg 1428

Dell, Michael S, Dell Wyse, One Dell Way, Round Rock, TX 78682 Toll Free Tel: 866-438-3622 (sales) Web Site: www.delltechnologies.com, pg 1367

Delmonico, Ralph R Jr, D3Logic Inc, 89 Commercial Way, East Providence, RI 02915 Tel: 401-435-4300 Toll Free Tel: 844-385-5388 E-mail: contact@d3-inc.com Web Site: www.d3-inc.com, pg 1252

Delnero, Paul, Journal of Cuneiform Studies (JCS), James F Strange Ctr, 209 Commerce St, Alexandria, VA 22314 Tel: 703-789-9229; 703-789-9230 (pubns) E-mail: info@asor.org; publications@asor.org Web Site: www.asor.org, pg 1133

DeLuca, Mike, Hearst Newspapers, 300 W 57 St, New York, NY 10019 Tel: 212-649-2000 Web Site: www.hearst.com/newspapers, pg 1190

DeLuca, Salvatore, Specialty Product Technologies (SPT), 2100 W Broad St, Elizabethtown, NC 28337 Tel: 910-862-2511 Toll Free Tel: 800-390-6405 Fax: 910-879-5486 Toll Free Fax: 800-476-5463 E-mail: customer.service@sptech.com Web Site: www.specialtyproducttechnologies.com, pg 1283

DeMaestri, Adam, BR Printers, 665 Lenfest Rd, San Jose, CA 95133 Tel: 408-278-7711 Fax: 408-929-8062 E-mail: info@brprinters.com Web Site: www.brprinters.com, pg 1103, 1249

DeMatteo, Patti, JMW Group Inc, 346 Rte 6, No 867, Mahopac, NY 10541 Tel: 914-841-7105 Fax: 914-248-8861 E-mail: jmwgroup@jmwgroup.net Web Site: jmwforlife.com, pg 1348

DeMusis, Anthony III, Boston Review, PO Box 390568, Cambridge, MA 02139 Tel: 617-356-8198 E-mail: review@bostonreview.net; customerservice@bostonreview.net Web Site: bostonreview.net, pg 1130

Deng, Cat, Eastwind Books & Arts Inc, 1435 Stockton St, San Francisco, CA 94133 Tel: 415-772-5888 Fax: 415-772-5885 E-mail: contact@eastwindbooks.com Web Site: www.eastwindbooks.com, pg 1314, 1327

Dennewitz-Hobson, Denise, GEI WideFormat, A Visual Edge Technology Company, 3874 Highland Park NW, North Canton, OH 44720 Toll Free Tel: 800-842-8448 (serv); 888-722-6434 (sales) E-mail: sales@geiwideformat.com Web Site: www.geiwideformat.com; www.visualedgetechnology.com, pg 1369

Denney, Rob, Readerlink Distribution Services LLC, 1420 Kensington Rd, Suite 300, Oakbrook, IL 60523-2164 Tel: 708-547-4400 Toll Free Tel: 800-549-5389 E-mail: info@readerlink.com; marketingservices@readerlink.com Web Site: www.readerlink.com, pg 1301

Dennis, Gil, Indigo Books & Music Inc, 468 King St W, Suite 500, Toronto, ON M5V 1L8, Canada Tel: 416-364-4499 E-mail: cisales@indigo.ca Web Site: www.chapters.indigo.ca, pg 1294

Deos, Tim, Copywriters' Council of America™ (CCA), Linick Bldg, 7 Putter Lane, Middle Island, NY 11953 Tel: 631-924-3888; 631-924-8555; 631-604-8599 E-mail: linickgroup@gmail.com, pg 1345

Derie, Kate, Mystery Readers Journal, 7155 Marlborough Terr, Berkeley, CA 94705 Tel: 510-845-3600 Web Site: www.mysteryreaders.org, pg 1134

Derosa, Peter, ALC Inc, 750 College Rd E, Suite 201, Princeton, NJ 08540 Tel: 609-580-2800 Toll Free Tel: 800-252-5478 Fax: 609-580-2888 E-mail: info@alc.com Web Site: www.alc.com, pg 1119

Dertien, Jon F, BookComp Inc, 6124 Belmont Ave NE, Belmont, MI 49306 Tel: 616-774-9700 E-mail: production@bookcomp.com Web Site: www.bookcomp.com, pg 1223, 1353

DeSalvo, Domenica, The Karel/Dutton Group, San Francisco, CA 94121 Tel: 415-668-0829 Web Site: karelduttongroup.com, pg 1295

Deschenes, Luc, Le Messager Chretien (The Christian Messenger), 185 Gatineau Ave, Gatineau, QC J8T 4J7, Canada Tel: 819-243-8880 Toll Free Tel: 800-263-8086 Fax: 819-243-1220 E-mail: info@messagerchretien.com Web Site: www.messagerchretien.com, pg 1319

Desharnais, Jacques, Cooperative Etudiante de Polytechnique, Pavillon Principal Local C-220, 2900 Edouard Mont Petit, Montreal, QC H3T 1J4, Canada Tel: 514-340-4851 Fax: 514-340-4543 E-mail: andre.daneau@polymtl.ca Web Site: www.coopoly.ca, pg 1314

Desjardins, Francoise, Art Image Publications, PO Box 160, Derby Line, VT 05830 Toll Free Tel: 800-361-2598 Toll Free Fax: 800-559-2598 E-mail: customer.service@artimagepublications.com; info@artimagepublications.com Web Site: www.artimagepublications.com, pg 1311

Desormeaux, Daniel, Modern Language Notes (MLN), 2715 N Charles St, Baltimore, MD 21218-4363 *Tel:* 410-516-6987 (journal orders outside US & CN) *Toll Free Tel:* 800-548-1784 (journal orders) *Fax:* 410-578-2865 (journal orders) *E-mail:* jrnlcirc@jh.edu (journal orders) *Web Site:* www.press.jhu.edu/journals/mln, pg 1134

Deuel, Kim, Worzalla, 3535 Jefferson St, Stevens Point, WI 54481 *Tel:* 715-344-9608 *Fax:* 715-344-2578 *Web Site:* www.worzalla.com, pg 1215, 1233, 1262

DeVore, Claire, Anthro-Photo File, 133 Washington St, Belmont, MA 02478 *Tel:* 617-484-6490 *Fax:* 617-484-6490 *Web Site:* www.anthrophotofile.com, pg 1427

DeVries, Peter, OmniUpdate Inc, 1320 Flynn Rd, Suite 100, Camarillo, CA 93012 *Tel:* 805-484-9400 *Toll Free Tel:* 800-362-2605 *E-mail:* sales@omniupdate.com *Web Site:* omniupdate.com, pg 1374

Dew, Allison, Dell Wyse, One Dell Way, Round Rock, TX 78682 *Toll Free Tel:* 866-438-3622 (sales) *Web Site:* www.delltechnologies.com, pg 1367

DeWeerd, Steve, Sheridan GR, 5100 33 St SE, Grand Rapids, MI 49512 *Tel:* 616-957-5100 *Web Site:* www.sheridan.com, pg 1213, 1259

DeWester, Nanette, Parkhurst Communications Inc, 11 Riverside Dr, Suite 1-TW, New York, NY 10023 *Tel:* 212-362-9722 *Web Site:* www.parkhurstcommunications.com, pg 1111

Dextor, Roger, Copywriters' Council of America™ (CCA), Linick Bldg, 7 Putter Lane, Middle Island, NY 11953 *Tel:* 631-924-3888; 631-924-8555; 631-604-8599 *E-mail:* linickgroup@gmail.com, pg 1345

Dextor, Roger, LK Advertising Agency, Linick Bldg, 7 Putter Lane, Middle Island, NY 11953 *Tel:* 631-924-3888; 631-924-8555; 631-604-8599 *E-mail:* topmarketingadvisor@gmail.com; linickgroup@gmail.com, pg 1100

Dhamee, Saleem, Chicago Distribution Center (CDC), 11030 S Langley Ave, Chicago, IL 60628 *Tel:* 773-702-7010 *Toll Free Fax:* 800-621-8476 *Web Site:* press.uchicago.edu/cdc, pg 1289

Dhawan, Sandeep, Lumina Datamatics Inc, 600 Cordwainer Dr, Unit 103, Norwell, MA 02061 *Tel:* 508-746-0300 *Fax:* 508-746-3233 *E-mail:* marketing@luminad.com *Web Site:* luminadatamatics.com, pg 1212, 1228, 1349, 1356, 1372, 1415

Di Bianco, Laura, Modern Language Notes (MLN), 2715 N Charles St, Baltimore, MD 21218-4363 *Tel:* 410-516-6987 (journal orders outside US & CN) *Toll Free Tel:* 800-548-1784 (journal orders) *Fax:* 410-578-2865 (journal orders) *E-mail:* jrnlcirc@jh.edu (journal orders) *Web Site:* www.press.jhu.edu/journals/mln, pg 1134

Di Leo, Dr Jeffrey R, American Book Review, c/o University of Houston-Victoria College of Liberal Arts & Sciences, 3007 N Ben Wilson St, Victoria, TX 77901 *Tel:* 361-248-8245 *E-mail:* abr@americanbookreview.org; americanbookreview@uhv.org; americanbookreview@gmail.com *Web Site:* americanbookreview.org, pg 1129

Di Leo, Orlando, American Book Review, c/o University of Houston-Victoria College of Liberal Arts & Sciences, 3007 N Ben Wilson St, Victoria, TX 77901 *Tel:* 361-248-8245 *E-mail:* abr@americanbookreview.org; americanbookreview@uhv.org; americanbookreview@gmail.com *Web Site:* americanbookreview.org, pg 1129

Di Silvio, Rich, Digital Vista Inc, 24 Amity Place, Massapequa, NY 11758 *Tel:* 516-799-5277 *E-mail:* info@digitalvista.net *Web Site:* www.digitalvista.net, pg 1413

Diamond, Steven, Steven Diamond Inc, 104 W 17 St, Suite 3-E, New York, NY 10011 *Tel:* 212-675-0723 *Fax:* 212-675-0762 *E-mail:* steven.diamond@verizon.net, pg 1345

Diarra, Alpha, appatura™, A Broadridge Company, 65 Challenger Rd, Suite 400, Ridgefield Park, NJ 07660 *Tel:* 201-508-6000 *Toll Free Tel:* 800-277-2155 *E-mail:* contactus@appatura.com *Web Site:* www.appatura.com, pg 1103, 1115, 1117, 1207, 1221, 1248

DiCanio, Theresa, Videojet Technologies Inc, 1500 N Mittel Blvd, Wood Dale, IL 60191-1073 *Tel:* 630-860-7300 *Toll Free Tel:* 800-843-3610 *Toll Free Fax:* 800-582-1343 *E-mail:* info@videojet.com *Web Site:* www.videojet.com, pg 1284

Dick, George C, Four Colour Print Group, 2410 Frankfort Ave, Louisville, KY 40206 *Tel:* 502-896-9644 *Fax:* 502-896-9594 *E-mail:* sales@fourcolour.com *Web Site:* www.fourcolour.com, pg 1210, 1253, 1280

Dick, Jason, CQ Roll Call, 1201 Pennsylvania Ave NW, Suite 600, Washington, DC 20004 *Tel:* 202-650-6500; 202-650-6511 (subns); 202-650-6621 (cust serv) *Toll Free Tel:* 800-432-2250; 800-678-8511 (subns) *E-mail:* customerservice@cqrollcall.com *Web Site:* cqrollcall.com; www.rollcall.com, pg 1190

Dickey, Bob, Gannett News Service, 7950 Jones Branch Dr, McLean, VA 22107-0150 *Tel:* 703-854-6000 *E-mail:* pr@gannett.com *Web Site:* www.gannett.com, pg 1190

Dickie, Matthew, Ingram Publisher Services, an Ingram brand, 14 Ingram Blvd, Mail Stop 631, La Vergne, TN 37086 *Tel:* 615-793-5000 *Toll Free Tel:* 866-400-5351 (cust serv) *E-mail:* ips@ingramcontent.com *Web Site:* www.ingrampublisherservices.com, pg 1294

Didona, Cathy, Didona Design, 160 Grandview Rd, Ardmore, PA 19003 *Tel:* 610-649-3110 *E-mail:* didona@didonadesign.com *Web Site:* www.didonadesign.com, pg 1224, 1413

Didona, Lawrence R, Didona Design, 160 Grandview Rd, Ardmore, PA 19003 *Tel:* 610-649-3110 *E-mail:* didona@didonadesign.com *Web Site:* www.didonadesign.com, pg 1224, 1413

Dieckman, Tom, Finch Paper LLC, One Glen St, Glens Falls, NY 12801 *Tel:* 518-793-2541 *Toll Free Tel:* 800-833-9983 *Fax:* 518-743-9656 *E-mail:* info@finchpaper.com *Web Site:* www.finchpaper.com, pg 1267

Dietz, Jeff, Koenig & Bauer (US) Inc, 2555 Regent Blvd, Dallas, TX 75229 *Tel:* 469-532-8000 *Fax:* 469-532-8190 *Web Site:* us.koenig-bauer.com, pg 1281

Dill, Richard, Brodart Books & Library Services, 500 Arch St, Williamsport, PA 17701 *Tel:* 570-326-2461 *Toll Free Tel:* 800-233-8467 *Fax:* 570-651-1639 *Toll Free Fax:* 800-999-6799 *E-mail:* support@brodart.com *Web Site:* www.brodartbooks.com, pg 1313

Dill, Richard, Brodart Books & Library Services, 500 Arch St, Williamsport, PA 17701 *Tel:* 570-326-2461 *Toll Free Tel:* 800-474-9816 *Fax:* 570-651-1639 *Toll Free Fax:* 800-999-6799 *E-mail:* support@brodart.com *Web Site:* www.brodartbooks.com, pg 1325

Dillon, Cecile, The Library Services Centre, 131 Shoemaker St, Kitchener, ON N2E 3B5, Canada *Tel:* 519-746-4420 *Toll Free Tel:* 800-265-3360 (CN only) *Fax:* 519-746-4425 *Web Site:* www.lsc.on.ca, pg 1318

DiMartino, Sunny, Round Table Companies, PO Box 1603, Deerfield, IL 60015 *Toll Free Tel:* 833-750-5683 *Web Site:* www.roundtablecompanies.com, pg 1417

Dion, Danielle, Maison de l'Education Inc, 10840 Ave Millen, Montreal, QC H2C 0A5, Canada *Tel:* 514-384-4401 *Fax:* 514-384-4844 *E-mail:* librairie@maisondeleducation.com *Web Site:* maisondeleducation.com, pg 1318

Diponio, Anthony, Crain Communications Inc, 1155 Gratiot Ave, Detroit, MI 48207-2732 *Tel:* 313-446-6000 *Fax:* 313-446-0383 *E-mail:* info@crain.com *Web Site:* crain.com, pg 1190

Dirks, Paul, Valley News Co, 1305 Stadium Rd, Mankato, MN 56001 *Tel:* 507-345-4819 *Fax:* 507-345-6793 *Web Site:* www.valleynewscompany.com, pg 1323

Dispenziere, Dennis, Ricoh Americas Corp, 300 Eagleview Blvd, Exton, PA 19341 *Tel:* 610-296-8000 *Toll Free Tel:* 800-333-2679 (prod support); 800-637-4264 (sales) *Web Site:* www.ricoh-usa.com, pg 1375

Ditty, Dean, Microboards Technology Inc, 8150 Mallory Ct, Chanhassen, MN 55317 *Tel:* 952-556-1600; 952-556-1639 (tech support) *Toll Free Tel:* 800-646-8881 *Fax:* 952-556-1620 *E-mail:* sales@microboards.com *Web Site:* www.microboards.com, pg 1372

Ditullio, Michael, PTC, 121 Seaport Blvd, Boston, MA 02210 *Tel:* 781-370-5000 *Fax:* 781-370-6000 *Web Site:* www.ptc.com, pg 1375

Dobiel, Maryrita, Historic Cherry Hill, 523 1/2 S Pearl St, Albany, NY 12202 *Tel:* 518-434-4791 *E-mail:* info@historiccherryhill.org *Web Site:* www.historiccherryhill.org, pg 1316

Dobratz, Tim, The Bureau, 2354 English St, Maplewood, MN 55109 *Tel:* 612-788-1000; 612-432-3516 (sales) *Toll Free Tel:* 800-788-9536 *Fax:* 612-788-7792 *E-mail:* sales@thebureau.com *Web Site:* www.thebureau.com, pg 1223, 1249

Dockter, Gregory R, PBD Worldwide Inc, 1650 Bluegrass Lakes Pkwy, Alpharetta, GA 30004 *Tel:* 470-769-1000 *Toll Free Tel:* 866-998-4PBD (998-4723) *E-mail:* sales.marketing@pbd.com; customerservice@pbd.com *Web Site:* www.pbd.com, pg 1334

Dockter, Scott A, PBD Worldwide Inc, 1650 Bluegrass Lakes Pkwy, Alpharetta, GA 30004 *Tel:* 470-769-1000 *Toll Free Tel:* 866-998-4PBD (998-4723) *E-mail:* sales.marketing@pbd.com; customerservice@pbd.com *Web Site:* www.pbd.com, pg 1334

Dodge, Elizabeth K, AudioFile®, 37 Silver St, Portland, ME 04101 *Tel:* 207-774-7563 *Toll Free Tel:* 800-506-1212 *Fax:* 207-775-3744 *E-mail:* info@audiofilemagazine.com *Web Site:* www.audiofilemagazine.com, pg 1130

Doherty, Adriane, Cardinal Publishers Group, 2402 N Shadeland Ave, Suite A, Indianapolis, IN 46219 *Tel:* 317-352-8200 *Toll Free Tel:* 800-296-0481 (cust serv) *Fax:* 317-352-8202 *E-mail:* customerservice@cardinalpub.com *Web Site:* cardinalpub.com, pg 1287

Doherty, Thomas, Cardinal Publishers Group, 2402 N Shadeland Ave, Suite A, Indianapolis, IN 46219 *Tel:* 317-352-8200 *Toll Free Tel:* 800-296-0481 (cust serv) *Fax:* 317-352-8202 *E-mail:* customerservice@cardinalpub.com *Web Site:* cardinalpub.com, pg 1287

Dolan, Linda Harris, Bellevue Literary Review, 149 E 23 St, Suite 1516, New York, NY 10010 *Tel:* 917-375-5790 *E-mail:* info@BLReview.org *Web Site:* www.BLReview.org, pg 1130

Dolan, Mike, Pantagraph Printing, 217 W Jefferson St, Bloomington, IL 61701 *Tel:* 309-829-1071 *E-mail:* queries1@pantagraphprinting.com *Web Site:* www.pantagraphprinting.com, pg 1229

Donnelly, Karena, Communication Abstracts, 10 Estes St, Ipswich, MA 01938 *Tel:* 978-356-6500 *Toll Free Tel:* 800-653-2726 *Fax:* 978-356-6565 *E-mail:* information@ebsco.com *Web Site:* www.ebsco.com, pg 1131

Donohue, Mike, AGS, 4590 Graphics Dr, White Plains, MD 20695 *Tel:* 301-843-1800 *Fax:* 301-843-6339 *E-mail:* info@ags.com *Web Site:* www.ags.com, pg 1207, 1247, 1364

Donohue, Prentiss, Open Text Corp, 275 Frank Tompa Dr, Waterloo, ON N2L 0A1, Canada *Tel:* 519-888-7111 *Fax:* 519-888-0677 *Web Site:* opentext.com, pg 1374

Donovan, Dan, Dan Donovan Photography, 15005 Valley Ridge Dr, St Louis, MO 63017 *Tel:* 314-712-0021 *E-mail:* dan@dandonovan.com *Web Site:* www.dandonovan.com, pg 1420

Doolin, Desi, Next Chapter Book Club (NCBC), 5909 Cleveland Ave, Columbus, OH 43231 *Toll Free Tel:* 800-674-8390 *E-mail:* info@nextchapterbookclub.org *Web Site:* nextchapterbookclub.org, pg 1143

Doornbos, Scott, Dukane Corp, Audio Visual Products Division, 2900 Dukane Dr, St Charles, IL 60174 *Tel:* 630-584-2300 *Toll Free Tel:* 888-245-1966; 800-676-2487 (tech support) *Fax:* 630-584-5156 *E-mail:* avsales@dukane.com *Web Site:* dukaneav.com, pg 1368

Dorsch, Jeff, eFulfillment Service Inc, 807 Airport Access Rd, Traverse City, MI 49686 *Tel:* 231-276-5057 *Toll Free Tel:* 866-922-6783 *E-mail:* sales@efulfillmentservice.com *Web Site:* www.efulfillmentservice.com, pg 1333

Dotson, David, ALC Inc, 750 College Rd E, Suite 201, Princeton, NJ 08540 *Tel:* 609-580-2800 *Toll Free Tel:* 800-252-5478 *Fax:* 609-580-2888 *E-mail:* info@alc.com *Web Site:* www.alc.com, pg 1119

Doucet, Marc, Webcom Inc, 3480 Pharmacy Ave, Toronto, ON M1W 2S7, Canada *Tel:* 416-496-1000 *Toll Free Tel:* 800-665-9322 *Fax:* 416-496-1537 *E-mail:* webcom@webcomlink.com *Web Site:* www.webcomlink.com, pg 1214, 1262, 1284

Dougherty, Michael J, Dougherty and Associates Public Relations, 1303 Caldwell Mountain Rd, Hot Springs, NC 28743 *Tel:* 828-622-3285 *Fax:* 828-622-3285 *E-mail:* dougherty1515@gmail.com *Web Site:* doughertyandassociatespr.com, pg 1108

Douglass, Roy, Electronics for Imaging Inc (EFI), 6750 Dumbarton Circle, Fremont, CA 94555 *Tel:* 650-357-3500 *Toll Free Tel:* 800-568-1917; 800-875-7117 (sales) *Fax:* 650-357-3907 *E-mail:* info@efi.com *Web Site:* www.efi.com, pg 1368

Dove, Veronica M, Bernan, 4501 Forbes Blvd, Suite 200, Lanham, MD 20706 *Tel:* 717-794-3800 (cust serv & orders) *Toll Free Tel:* 800-462-6420 (cust serv & orders) *Fax:* 717-794-3803 *Toll Free Tel:* 800-338-4550 *E-mail:* customercare@rowman.com *Web Site:* rowman.com/page/bernan, pg 1287, 1312

Dowbnia, George, The Hibbert Group, 400 Pennington Ave, Trenton, NJ 08650 *Tel:* 609-394-7500 *Toll Free Tel:* 888-HIBBERT (442-2378) *E-mail:* info@hibbertgroup.com *Web Site:* hibbert.com, pg 1104, 1116, 1117

Dowd, Katie, Sunday San Francisco Chronicle Book Review, 901 Mission St, San Francisco, CA 94103 *Tel:* 415-777-1111 *Toll Free Tel:* 866-732-4766 *Web Site:* www.sfgate.com, pg 1137

Dowdell, Chris, Devin-Adair Publishers/Seagrace Partners, 525 Flagler Dr, Suite 15A, West Palm Beach, FL 33401 *Tel:* 561-909-7576 *Fax:* 718-359-8568, pg 1314

Dowell, Jennifer M, AudioFile®, 37 Silver St, Portland, ME 04101 *Tel:* 207-774-7563 *Toll Free Tel:* 800-506-1212 *Fax:* 207-775-3744 *E-mail:* info@audiofilemagazine.com *Web Site:* www.audiofilemagazine.com, pg 1130

Downes, Debbie, ColorPage, 81 Ten Broeck Ave, Kingston, NY 12401 *Tel:* 845-331-7581 *Toll Free Tel:* 800-836-7581 *Fax:* 845-331-1571 *E-mail:* sales@colorpageonline.com *Web Site:* www.colorpageonline.com, pg 1209, 1223, 1250, 1266

Drake, Cary, Six Red Marbles LLC, 101 Station Landing, Medford, MA 02155 *Tel:* 857-588-9000 *E-mail:* info@sixredmarbles.com *Web Site:* www.sixredmarbles.com, pg 1231, 1376

Dralyuk, Boris, LARB Quarterly Journal, 6671 Sunset Blvd, Suite 1521, Los Angeles, CA 90028 *Tel:* 323-952-3950 *E-mail:* info@lareviewofbooks.org; editorial@lareviewofbooks.org *Web Site:* lareviewofbooks.org, pg 1133

Draper, John, Double Envelope, 7702 Plantation Rd, Roanoke, VA 24019 *Toll Free Tel:* 800-800-9007 *E-mail:* inquire@double-envelope.com *Web Site:* www.double-envelope.com, pg 1104, 1116

Drate, Spencer, Spencer Drate, 119 W 80 St, Suite 1-F, New York, NY 10024-7134 *Tel:* 212-799-0535 *E-mail:* spencerdrate@yahoo.com, pg 1413

Dreshfield, Richard, Koenig & Bauer (US) Inc, 2555 Regent Blvd, Dallas, TX 75229 *Tel:* 469-532-8000 *Fax:* 469-532-8190 *Web Site:* us.koenig-bauer.com, pg 1281

Drew, Michael R, Promote A Book Inc, 1753 Rylie Ann Circle, South Jordan, UT 84095 *Tel:* 512-586-6073 *Web Site:* promoteabook.com, pg 1350

Drinkwater, Simone, Casemate | academic, 1950 Lawrence Rd, Havertown, PA 19083 *Tel:* 610-853-9131 *Fax:* 610-853-9146 *E-mail:* info@casemateacademic.com *Web Site:* www.oxbowbooks.com/dbbc, pg 1287

Driscoll, Jim, EMT International Inc, 780 Centerline Dr, Hobart, WI 54155 *Tel:* 920-468-5475 *Fax:* 920-468-7991 *E-mail:* info@emtinternational.com *Web Site:* www.emtinternational.com, pg 1279

Droll, Francesca, Abacus Graphics LLC, 15179 Hunger Creek Lane, Bigfork, MT 59911-8313 *Tel:* 406-837-5776 *Web Site:* www.abacusgraphics.com, pg 1411

Dryl, Mariel, Northeast Publishers Reps, Montville Chase, 20 Davenport Rd, Montville, NJ 07045 *Tel:* 973-299-0085 *Fax:* 973-263-2363 *E-mail:* siraksirak@aol.com *Web Site:* www.nepubreps.com, pg 1298

Dubin, Jordan, Association for Library Service to Children (ALSC), 225 N Michigan Ave, Suite 1300, Chicago, IL 60601 *Tel:* 312-280-2163 *Toll Free Tel:* 800-545-2433 *Fax:* 312-280-5271 *E-mail:* alsc@ala.org *Web Site:* www.ala.org/alsc, pg 1145

Dubuque, Don, Standard Finishing Systems, 10 Connector Rd, Andover, MA 01810 *Tel:* 978-470-1920 *Toll Free Tel:* 877-404-4460 *Fax:* 978-470-0819 *E-mail:* marketing@sdmc.com *Web Site:* www.sdmc.com, pg 1283

Duckworth, Jennifer, The Association of Medical Illustrators (AMI), 201 E Main St, Suite 810, Lexington, KY 40507 *Toll Free Tel:* 866-393-4AMI (393-4264) *E-mail:* hq@ami.org *Web Site:* www.ami.org, pg 1412

Duffes, Melissa, Marquand Books, 3131 Western Ave, Suite 522, Seattle, WA 98121 *Tel:* 206-624-2030 *Web Site:* www.marquandbooks.com, pg 1356

Duffy, Tim, Master Flo Technology Inc, 154 Seale Rd, Wentworth, QC J8H 0G9, Canada *Tel:* 450-533-0088 *Fax:* 450-533-4597 *E-mail:* info@mflo.com; sales@mflo.com *Web Site:* www.mflo.com, pg 1281

Dufour, Michelle, Data Index Inc, 13713 NW Indian Springs Dr, Vancouver, WA 98685 *Tel:* 425-760-9193 *Web Site:* www.dataindex.com, pg 1224

Dugan, Andrew, Alanna Feldman Scouting, 4080 Via Marisol, Apt 135, Los Angeles, CA 90042 *E-mail:* info@afscouting.com *Web Site:* www.afscouting.com, pg 1346

Duggan, Paul, Open Text Corp, 275 Frank Tompa Dr, Waterloo, ON N2L 0A1, Canada *Tel:* 519-888-7111 *Fax:* 519-888-0677 *Web Site:* opentext.com, pg 1374

Duignam, Dianne, Louis Goldberg Library Book Supplier, 45 Belvidere St, Nazareth, PA 18064 *Tel:* 610-759-9458 *E-mail:* orders@goldberg-books.com *Web Site:* www.goldberg-books.com, pg 1316

Dumas, Kellie, Tennessee Book Co, 1550 Heil Quaker Blvd, La Vergne, TN 37086 *Tel:* 615-793-5040 *Toll Free Tel:* 800-456-0418 *Fax:* 615-213-9545 *Web Site:* www.tennesseebook.com, pg 1322

Duncan, Kenneth, Independent Publishers Group (IPG), 814 N Franklin St, Chicago, IL 60610 *Tel:* 312-337-0747 *Toll Free Tel:* 800-888-4741 (orders) *Fax:* 312-337-5985 *E-mail:* frontdesk@ipgbook.com; orders@ipgbook.com *Web Site:* www.ipgbook.com, pg 1292, 1328

Dunham, Joe, LBS, 1801 Thompson Ave, Des Moines, IA 50316-2751 *Tel:* 515-262-3191 *Toll Free Tel:* 800-247-5323 *Fax:* 800-262-4091 *E-mail:* info@lbsbind.com *Web Site:* www.lbsbind.com, pg 1269

Dunhill, Candy, Dunhill International List Co Inc, 6400 Congress Ave, Suite 1750, Boca Raton, FL 33487-2898 *Tel:* 561-998-7800 *Toll Free Tel:* 800-DUNHILL (386-4455) *Fax:* 561-998-7880 *E-mail:* dunhill@dunhillintl.com *Web Site:* www.dunhills.com, pg 1120

Dunhill, Cindy, Dunhill International List Co Inc, 6400 Congress Ave, Suite 1750, Boca Raton, FL 33487-2898 *Tel:* 561-998-7800 *Toll Free Tel:* 800-DUNHILL (386-4455) *Fax:* 561-998-7880 *E-mail:* dunhill@dunhillintl.com *Web Site:* www.dunhills.com, pg 1120

Dunhill, Robert, Dunhill International List Co Inc, 6400 Congress Ave, Suite 1750, Boca Raton, FL 33487-2898 *Tel:* 561-998-7800 *Toll Free Tel:* 800-DUNHILL (386-4455) *Fax:* 561-998-7880 *E-mail:* dunhill@dunhillintl.com *Web Site:* www.dunhills.com, pg 1119

Dunn, David M, Dunn & Co Inc, 75 Green St, Clinton, MA 01510 *Tel:* 978-368-8505 *Fax:* 978-368-7867 *E-mail:* info@booktrauma.com *Web Site:* www.booktrauma.com, pg 1210, 1252, 1267

Dunn, Frank, Circle Graphics Inc, 316 Main St, Suite 1C, Reisters Town, MD 21136 *Tel:* 410-833-2200 *E-mail:* production@circleusa.com *Web Site:* www.circleusa.com, pg 1223

Dunphy, John A, University Products Inc, 517 Main St, Holyoke, MA 01040 *Tel:* 413-532-3372 *Toll Free Tel:* 800-628-1912 (orders) *Fax:* 413-533-4743 *Toll Free Tel:* 800-532-9281 *E-mail:* info@universityproducts.com *Web Site:* www.universityproducts.com, pg 1273

Dupuis, Tom, Dual Graphics, 370 Cliffwood Park, Brea, CA 92821 *Tel:* 714-990-3700 *Fax:* 714-990-6818 *Web Site:* www.dualgraphics.com, pg 1225, 1252

Dupuis-Jones, Trish, Falcon Safety Products Inc, 25 Imclone Dr, Branchburg, NJ 08876 *Tel:* 908-707-4900 *Toll Free Tel:* 800-332-5266 *E-mail:* marketing@falconsafety.com *Web Site:* www.falconsafety.com, pg 1368

Duran, Victor, SCB Distributors, 15608 S New Century Dr, Gardena, CA 90248 *Tel:* 310-532-9400 *Toll Free Tel:* 800-729-6423 *Fax:* 310-532-7001 *E-mail:* scb@scbdistributors.com *Web Site:* www.scbdistributors.com, pg 1302

Durham, Rusty, StarGroup International Inc, 1194 Old Dixie Hwy, Suite 201, West Palm Beach, FL 33413 *Tel:* 561-547-0667 *E-mail:* info@stargroupinternational.com *Web Site:* stargroupinternational.com, pg 1113

Durkee, Jim, Tri-Media Integrated Marketing Technologies Inc, 1027 Pelham St, Unit 2, Fonthill, ON L0S 1E0, Canada *E-mail:* think@tri-media.com *Web Site:* tri-media.com, pg 1100

Dutton, Dory, The Karel/Dutton Group, San Francisco, CA 94121 *Tel:* 415-668-0829 *Web Site:* kareldutongroup.com, pg 1295

Duvieusart, Guillaume, Diffusion Inter-Livres, 1701 Belleville, Lemoyne, QC J4P 3M2, Canada *Tel:* 450-465-0037 *Toll Free Tel:* 866-465-5579 *E-mail:* interlivres@llbquebec.ca *Web Site:* www.inter-livres.ca, pg 1290

Dyer, C Brent, Texas Book Co, 8501 Technology Circle, Greenville, TX 75402 *Tel:* 903-455-6969 *Toll Free Tel:* 800-527-1016 *E-mail:* customerservice@texasbook.com *Web Site:* www.texasbook.com, pg 1322

Dyer, Gordon, OmniUpdate Inc, 1320 Flynn Rd, Suite 100, Camarillo, CA 93012 *Tel:* 805-484-9400 *Toll Free Tel:* 800-362-2605 *E-mail:* sales@omniupdate.com *Web Site:* omniupdate.com, pg 1374

Dyer, Stacy, Texas Book Co, 8501 Technology Circle, Greenville, TX 75402 *Tel:* 903-455-6969 *Toll Free Tel:* 800-527-1016 *E-mail:* customerservice@texasbook.com *Web Site:* www.texasbook.com, pg 1322

Dykhouse, Clarence, Wallaceburg Bookbinding & Mfg Co Ltd, 95 Arnold St, Wallaceburg, ON N8A 3P3, Canada *Tel:* 519-627-3552 *Toll Free Tel:* 800-214-BIND (214-2463) *Fax:* 519-627-6922 *E-mail:* helpdesk@wbmbindery.com *Web Site:* www.wbmbindery.com, pg 1262, 1326

Dykhouse, Gerrit, Wallaceburg Bookbinding & Mfg Co Ltd, 95 Arnold St, Wallaceburg, ON N8A 3P3, Canada *Tel:* 519-627-3552 *Toll Free Tel:* 800-214-BIND (214-2463) *Fax:* 519-627-6922 *E-mail:* helpdesk@wbmbindery.com *Web Site:* www.wbmbindery.com, pg 1262, 1326

Dziesietnik, Ghilad, Electronics for Imaging Inc (EFI), 6750 Dumbarton Circle, Fremont, CA 94555 *Tel:* 650-357-3500 *Toll Free Tel:* 800-568-1917; 800-875-7117 (sales) *Fax:* 650-357-3907 *E-mail:* info@efi.com *Web Site:* www.efi.com, pg 1368

PERSONNEL INDEX

Eads, Carol, Ross Gage Inc, 8502 Brookville Rd, Indianapolis, IN 46239 *Tel:* 317-283-2323 *Toll Free Tel:* 800-799-2323 *Fax:* 317-931-2108 *E-mail:* info@rossgage.com *Web Site:* www.rossgage.com, pg 1230, 1259

Eakin, Emily, The New York Times Book Review, 620 Eighth Ave, 5th fl, New York, NY 10018 *Tel:* 212-556-1234 *Toll Free Tel:* 800-631-2580 (subns) *E-mail:* bookreview@nytimes.com; books@nytimes.com *Web Site:* www.nytimes.com, pg 1135

Ealy, C Cato, International Paper Co, 6400 Poplar Ave, Memphis, TN 38197 *Tel:* 901-419-9000 *Toll Free Tel:* 800-207-4003 *Web Site:* www.internationalpaper.com; facebook.com/internationalpaper; x.com/intlpaperco, pg 1268

Earls, G Scott, Simon Miller Paper & Packaging, 3409 W Chester Pike, Suite 204, Newton Square, PA 19073 *Tel:* 215-923-3600 *Toll Free Tel:* 800-642-1899 *Fax:* 610-355-9330 *E-mail:* info@simonmiller.com *Web Site:* www.simonmiller.com, pg 1271

Eastman, Daniel, Distribooks Inc, 8154 N Ridgeway Ave, Skokie, IL 60076-2911 *Tel:* 847-676-1596 *Toll Free Fax:* 888-266-5713 *E-mail:* info@distribooks.com, pg 1290

Eastman, Daniel, Distribooks Inc, 8154 N Ridgeway Ave, Skokie, IL 60076-2911 *Tel:* 847-676-1596 *Fax:* 847-676-1195 *Toll Free Fax:* 888-266-5713 *E-mail:* info@distribooks.com; info@schoenhofs.com *Web Site:* www.schoenhofs.com, pg 1314

Eastman, Daniel, Schoenhof's Foreign Books Inc, 76 A Mount Auburn St, Cambridge, MA 02138 *Tel:* 617-547-8855 *E-mail:* info@schoenhofs.com *Web Site:* www.schoenhofs.com, pg 1321, 1329

Easton, Elmer, Three D Graphics Inc, 11340 W Olympic Blvd, Suite 352, Los Angeles, CA 90064 *Tel:* 310-231-3330 *Toll Free Tel:* 800-913-0008 *Fax:* 310-231-3303 *E-mail:* info@threedgraphics.com; orders@threedgraphics.com; sales@threedgraphics.com *Web Site:* www.threedgraphics.com, pg 1377

Easton, Kaylie, Litzky PR, 33-41 Newark St, 5th fl, Hoboken, NJ 07030 *Tel:* 201-222-9118 *E-mail:* inquiries@litzkypr.com *Web Site:* litzkypr.com, pg 1110

Eastwood, Mike, Thomson Reuters, 3 Times Sq, New York, NY 10036 *Tel:* 646-223-4000; 646-223-6100 (edit); 646-223-6000 (newsroom) *Web Site:* www.thomsonreuters.com, pg 1191

Ebrahimi, Katie, Unisys Corp, 801 Lakeview Dr, Suite 100, Blue Bell, PA 19422 *Tel:* 215-274-2742 *Web Site:* www.unisys.com, pg 1378

Echter, Tammy, GBS Books, 2321 W Royal Palm Rd, Suite F, Phoenix, AZ 85021 *Tel:* 602-863-6000 *Toll Free Tel:* 800-851-6001 *E-mail:* gbsbooks@gbsbooks.com *Web Site:* www.gbsbooks.com, pg 1315

Eckhart, Chris, Eckhart & Company Inc, 4011 W 54 St, Indianapolis, IN 46254 *Tel:* 317-347-2665 *Toll Free Tel:* 800-443-3791 *Fax:* 317-347-2666 *E-mail:* info@eckhartandco.com *Web Site:* www.eckhartandco.com, pg 1253

Eckstein, Meyer, Listco Direct Marketing, 1276 46 St, Brooklyn, NY 11219 *Tel:* 718-871-8400 *Fax:* 718-871-7692 *E-mail:* info@listcodirect.com *Web Site:* www.listcodirect.com, pg 1120

Eckstein, Shlomo, Listco Direct Marketing, 1276 46 St, Brooklyn, NY 11219 *Tel:* 718-871-8400 *Fax:* 718-871-7692 *E-mail:* info@listcodirect.com *Web Site:* www.listcodirect.com, pg 1120

Edelboim, Jason, PR Newswire, 350 Hudson St, Suite 300, New York, NY 10014-4504 *Toll Free Tel:* 888-776-0942; 800-776-8090 *Toll Free Fax:* 800-793-9313 *E-mail:* mediainquiries@prnewswire.com *Web Site:* www.prnewswire.com, pg 1112

Edelstein, Gabriele Freydank, Tri-Fold Books, PO Box 534, King City, ON L7B 1A7, Canada *Tel:* 905-726-0142 *E-mail:* info@trifoldbooks.com *Web Site:* trifoldbooks.com, pg 1303

Edmonds, Scott, International Mapping Associates, 5300 Dorsey Hall Dr, Suite 201, Ellicott City, MD 21042 *Tel:* 443-367-0050 *E-mail:* frontdesk@internationalmapping.com *Web Site:* internationalmapping.com, pg 1415

Edmondson, Laura, Theatre Journal, 2715 N Charles St, Baltimore, MD 21218-4363 *Tel:* 410-516-6987 (journal orders outside US & CN) *Toll Free Tel:* 800-548-1784 (journal orders) *Fax:* 410-578-2865 (journal orders) *E-mail:* tjbooks@athe.org; jrnlcirc@jh.edu (journal orders) *Web Site:* www.press.jhu.edu/journals/theatre-journal, pg 1137

Edson, Durga, Amcorp Ltd, 10 Norden Lane, Huntington Station, NY 11746 *Tel:* 631-271-0548 *Fax:* 631-549-8849 *E-mail:* amcorpltd@aol.com, pg 1327

Edson, Steven, Steven Edson Photography, 102 Florence Ave, Arlington, MA 02476 *Tel:* 617-504-4994 *E-mail:* steve@stevenedson.com *Web Site:* stevenedson.com, pg 1420

Edwards, Adrianna, Focus Strategic Communications Inc, 15 Hunter Way, Brantford, ON N3T 6S3, Canada *Tel:* 519-756-3265 *E-mail:* info@focussc.com *Web Site:* www.focussc.com, pg 1354

Edwards, Alicia, Penguin Random House Canada, a Penguin Random House company, 320 Front St W, Suite 1400, Toronto, ON M5V 3B6, Canada *Tel:* 416-364-4449 *Toll Free Tel:* 888-523-9292 (cust serv) *Fax:* 416-598-7764 *E-mail:* customerservicescanada@penguinrandomhouse.com; publicitycanada@penguinrandomhouse.com; rightscanada@penguinrandomhouse.com *Web Site:* www.penguinrandomhouse.ca, pg 1299

Edwards, Melissa, Stonesong, 270 W 39 St, Suite 201, New York, NY 10018 *Tel:* 212-929-4600 *E-mail:* editors@stonesong.com *Web Site:* www.stonesong.com, pg 1357

Edwards, Ron, Focus Strategic Communications Inc, 15 Hunter Way, Brantford, ON N3T 6S3, Canada *Tel:* 519-756-3265 *E-mail:* info@focussc.com *Web Site:* www.focussc.com, pg 1354

Egan, Dean T, Roosevelt Paper Co, One Roosevelt Dr, Mount Laurel, NJ 08054 *Tel:* 856-303-4100 *Toll Free Tel:* 800-523-3470 *Fax:* 856-642-1949 *E-mail:* marketing@rooseveltpaper.com *Web Site:* www.rooseveltpaper.com, pg 1271

Egan, Elisabeth, The New York Times Book Review, 620 Eighth Ave, 5th fl, New York, NY 10018 *Tel:* 212-556-1234 *Toll Free Tel:* 800-631-2580 (subns) *E-mail:* bookreview@nytimes.com; books@nytimes.com *Web Site:* www.nytimes.com, pg 1135

Egginton, William, Modern Language Notes (MLN), 2715 N Charles St, Baltimore, MD 21218-4363 *Tel:* 410-516-6987 (journal orders outside US & CN) *Toll Free Tel:* 800-548-1784 (journal orders) *Fax:* 410-578-2865 (journal orders) *E-mail:* jrnlcirc@jh.edu (journal orders) *Web Site:* www.press.jhu.edu/journals/mln, pg 1134

Ehmann, Stephanie, Penguin Random House Canada, a Penguin Random House company, 320 Front St W, Suite 1400, Toronto, ON M5V 3B6, Canada *Tel:* 416-364-4449 *Toll Free Tel:* 888-523-9292 (cust serv) *Fax:* 416-598-7764 *E-mail:* customerservicescanada@penguinrandomhouse.com; publicitycanada@penguinrandomhouse.com; rightscanada@penguinrandomhouse.com *Web Site:* www.penguinrandomhouse.ca, pg 1299

Ehrlich, Serena, Business Wire, 101 California St, 20th fl, San Francisco, CA 94111 *Tel:* 415-986-4422 *Toll Free Tel:* 800-227-0845 *E-mail:* info@businesswire.com *Web Site:* www.businesswire.com, pg 1189

Eidel, Lindsay, Consortium Book Sales & Distribution, an Ingram brand, The Keg House, Suite 101, 34 13 Ave NE, Minneapolis, MN 55413-1007 *Tel:* 612-746-2600 *Toll Free Tel:* 866-400-5351 (cust serv, Jackson, TN) *E-mail:* cbsdinfo@ingramcontent.com *Web Site:* www.cbsd.com, pg 1289

Ekren, Hannah, Alanna Feldman Scouting, 4080 Via Marisol, Apt 135, Los Angeles, CA 90042 *E-mail:* info@afscouting.com *Web Site:* www.afscouting.com, pg 1346

Ekus, Sally, Ekus Group LLC, 57 North St, Hatfield, MA 01038 *Tel:* 413-247-9325 *E-mail:* info@ekusgroup.com *Web Site:* ekusgroup.com, pg 1108

Elancheran, Maran, Newgen North America Inc, 2714 Bee Cave Rd, Suite 201, Austin, TX 78746 *Tel:* 512-478-5341 *Fax:* 512-476-4756 *E-mail:* sales@newgen.co *Web Site:* www.newgen.co, pg 1229

Elder, David C, Glatfelter, Capitol Towers South, 4350 Congress St, Suite 600, Charlotte, NC 28209 *Tel:* 717-850-0170 *Toll Free Tel:* 866-744-7380 *E-mail:* info@glatfelter.com *Web Site:* www.glatfelter.com, pg 1267

Elder, Randy, Elder's Bookstore, 101 White Bridge Rd, Nashville, TN 37209 *Tel:* 615-352-1562 *E-mail:* info@eldersbookstore.com *Web Site:* eldersbookstore.com, pg 1315

Eldon, Bonnie, Melcher Media Inc, 124 W 13 St, New York, NY 10011 *Tel:* 212-727-2322 *Fax:* 212-627-1973 *E-mail:* info@melcher.com *Web Site:* www.melcher.com, pg 1356

Eldred, Tanya, Sheridan GR, 5100 33 St SE, Grand Rapids, MI 49512 *Tel:* 616-957-5100 *Web Site:* www.sheridan.com, pg 1213, 1259

Elias, Thomas D, Southern California Focus, 1720 Oak St, Santa Monica, CA 90405 *Tel:* 310-452-3918 *Web Site:* www.californiafocus.net, pg 1191

Eligh, Gregg, Eligh Photographs, Victoria, BC V8R 4B8, Canada *Tel:* 250-888-0027 *Web Site:* www.elighphoto.com; www.facebook.com/pages/category/Photographer/Eligh-Photographs-1550470288586165, pg 1420

Elk, Claude Marie, Elk Photography, 3163 Wisconsin St, Oakland, CA 94602 *Tel:* 510-531-7469 *Fax:* 510-531-7469 *E-mail:* cjelk@elkphotography.com *Web Site:* www.elkphotography.com, pg 1421

Elk, John, Elk Photography, 3163 Wisconsin St, Oakland, CA 94602 *Tel:* 510-531-7469 *Fax:* 510-531-7469 *E-mail:* cjelk@elkphotography.com *Web Site:* www.elkphotography.com, pg 1421

Elkalai, Khalid, MetaComet Systems, 29 College St, South Hadley, MA 01075 *Tel:* 413-536-5989 *Web Site:* www.metacomet.com, pg 1349

Ellis, Duncan, Avanti Computer Systems Ltd, 251 Consumers Rd, Suite 600, Toronto, ON M2J 4R3, Canada *Tel:* 416-445-1722 *Toll Free Tel:* 800-482-2908 *Fax:* 416-445-6319 *E-mail:* askavanti@avantisystems.com *Web Site:* www.avantisystems.com, pg 1365

Ellison, Larry, Oracle America Inc, 500 Oracle Pkwy, Redwood Shores, CA 94065 *Tel:* 650-506-7000 *Toll Free Tel:* 800-392-2999; 800-633-0738 (sales) *Web Site:* www.oracle.com, pg 1374

Ellsworth, Kate, Tanenbaum International Literary Agency Ltd (TILA), 1035 Fifth Ave, Suite 15D, New York, NY 10028 *Tel:* 212-371-4120 *Fax:* 212-988-0457 *E-mail:* hello@tanenbauminternational.com *Web Site:* tanenbauminternational.com, pg 1351

Elmore, Tina, Ingram Content Group LLC, One Ingram Blvd, La Vergne, TN 37086-1986 *Tel:* 615-793-5000 *Toll Free Tel:* 800-937-8000 (retailers); 800-937-5300 (ext 1, libs) *E-mail:* customerservice@ingramcontent.com *Web Site:* www.ingramcontent.com, pg 1294, 1316

Elsayed, Danya, Penguin Random House Canada, a Penguin Random House company, 320 Front St W, Suite 1400, Toronto, ON M5V 3B6, Canada *Tel:* 416-364-4449 *Toll Free Tel:* 888-523-9292 (cust serv) *Fax:* 416-598-7764 *E-mail:* customerservicescanada@penguinrandomhouse.com; publicitycanada@penguinrandomhouse.com; rightscanada@penguinrandomhouse.com *Web Site:* www.penguinrandomhouse.ca, pg 1299

Embury, Emily, C Blohm & Associates Inc, 5999 Monona Dr, Monona, WI 53716-3531 *Tel:* 608-216-7300 *E-mail:* hello@cblohm.com *Web Site:* www.cblohm.com, pg 1107

Emmons-Andarawis, Deborah, Historic Cherry Hill, 523 1/2 S Pearl St, Albany, NY 12202 *Tel:* 518-434-4791 *E-mail:* info@historiccherryhill.org *Web Site:* www.historiccherryhill.org, pg 1316

Endugesick, Sharon, Brown Book Co Ltd, 65 Crockford Blvd, Toronto, ON M1R 3B7, Canada *Tel:* 416-504-9696 *Fax:* 416-504-9393 *E-mail:* bbc@brownbook.ca *Web Site:* www.brownbook.ca, pg 1208

Engelgau, Chad, Acxiom, 301 E Dave Ward Dr, Conway, AR 72032 *Toll Free Tel:* 888-322-9466 *Web Site:* www.acxiom.com, pg 1363

Engle, Harold, Ambassador Press Inc, 1400 Washington Ave N, Minneapolis, MN 55411 *Tel:* 612-521-0123 *E-mail:* info@ambpress.com *Web Site:* www.ambpress.com, pg 1221, 1247, 1265

Engle-Fieldman, Candice, Ambassador Press Inc, 1400 Washington Ave N, Minneapolis, MN 55411 *Tel:* 612-521-0123 *E-mail:* info@ambpress.com *Web Site:* www.ambpress.com, pg 1221, 1247, 1265

Enomoto, Mizuki, Nissho Electronics USA Corp, The Concourse I, 226 Airport Pkwy, Suite 340, San Jose, CA 95110 *Tel:* 408-969-9700 *E-mail:* info@nelco.com *Web Site:* www.nelco.com, pg 1373

Epping, Robert, GTxcel Inc, 144 Turnpike Rd, Suite 130, Southborough, MA 01772-2104 *Toll Free Tel:* 800-609-8994 *E-mail:* info@gtxcel.com *Web Site:* www.gtxcel.com, pg 1370

Erf, Keith, KyTek Inc, PO Box 338, Weare, NH 03281 *Tel:* 603-529-2512 *E-mail:* sales@kytek.com *Web Site:* www.kytek.com, pg 1371

Eriksen, Vigdis, Eriksen Translations Inc, 360 Court St, Unit 37, Brooklyn, NY 11231 *Tel:* 718-802-9010 *Fax:* 718-802-0041 *Web Site:* www.eriksen.com, pg 1401

Ermelino, Louisa, Publishers Weekly, 49 W 23 St, 9th fl, New York, NY 10010 *Tel:* 212-377-5500 *Fax:* 212-377-2733 *Web Site:* www.publishersweekly.com, pg 1136

Errera, Stacie, Tamron USA Inc, 10 Austin Blvd, Commack, NY 11725 *Tel:* 631-858-8400 *Toll Free Tel:* 800-827-8880 *Fax:* 631-543-5666; 631-858-8462 (cust serv) *E-mail:* custserv@tamron.com *Web Site:* www.tamron-usa.com, pg 1377

Errico, Joe, VIP Digital Print Center, 200 Circle Dr N, Piscataway, NJ 08854 *Tel:* 732-469-5400 *Fax:* 732-469-8414 *E-mail:* info@vipcopycenter.com *Web Site:* www.vipcopycenter.com, pg 1262

Erwin, Rick, ALC Inc, 750 College Rd E, Suite 201, Princeton, NJ 08540 *Tel:* 609-580-2800 *Toll Free Tel:* 800-252-5478 *Fax:* 609-580-2888 *E-mail:* info@alc.com *Web Site:* www.alc.com, pg 1119

Esguerra, Dennis, OmniUpdate Inc, 1320 Flynn Rd, Suite 100, Camarillo, CA 93012 *Tel:* 805-484-9400 *Toll Free Tel:* 800-362-2605 *E-mail:* sales@omniupdate.com *Web Site:* omniupdate.com, pg 1374

Eskenazi, Brian, Skylark Co Inc, PO Box 237043, New York, NY 10023-0028 *Tel:* 212-595-0700 *Fax:* 212-595-0700, pg 1329

Ethier, Melanie, Multi-Reliure, 2112 Ave de la Transmission, Shawinigan, QC G9N 8N8, Canada *Tel:* 819-537-6008 *Toll Free Tel:* 888-735-4873 *Fax:* 819-537-4598 *E-mail:* info@multi-reliure.com; administration@multi-reliure.com *Web Site:* www.multireliure.com, pg 1257

Etlin, Alexander (Sasha), Glasnost Communications, Tallberry Dr, Cincinnati, OH 45230 *Tel:* 513-231-3599 *E-mail:* glasnost@currently.com, pg 1401

Evans, Craig, Dual Graphics, 370 Cliffwood Park, Brea, CA 92821 *Tel:* 714-990-3700 *Fax:* 714-990-6818 *Web Site:* www.dualgraphics.com, pg 1225, 1252

Evans, Daryl, Miami Wabash Paper LLC, 301 Wedcor Ave, Wabash, IN 46992 *Tel:* 260-563-4181 *Toll Free Tel:* 800-842-9112 *Fax:* 219-563-2724 *E-mail:* miamivalley@mafcote.com *Web Site:* www.mafcote.com, pg 1269

Evans, Todd, Rivendell Media Inc, 1248 Rte 22 W, Mountainside, NJ 07092 *Tel:* 908-232-2021 ext 200 *Fax:* 908-232-0521 *E-mail:* info@rivendellmedia.com; sales@rivendellmedia.com *Web Site:* www.rivendellmedia.com, pg 1112

Evans-Lombe, Monica, Special Libraries Association (SLA), 7918 Jones Branch Dr, Suite 300, McLean, VA 22102 *Tel:* 703-647-4900 *Fax:* 703-506-3266 *E-mail:* info@sla.org; sla@sla.org *Web Site:* www.sla.org, pg 1120

Eveleigh, Douglas, Encyclopaedia Britannica Inc, 325 N La Salle St, Suite 200, Chicago, IL 60654 *Tel:* 312-347-7000 (all other countries) *Toll Free Tel:* 800-323-1229 (US & CN) *Fax:* 312-294-2104 *E-mail:* contact@eb.com *Web Site:* www.britannica.com, pg 1315

Everett, Amy, Independent Publishers Group (IPG), 814 N Franklin St, Chicago, IL 60610 *Tel:* 312-337-0747 *Toll Free Tel:* 800-888-4741 (orders) *Fax:* 312-337-5985 *E-mail:* frontdesk@ipgbook.com; orders@ipgbook.com *Web Site:* www.ipgbook.com, pg 1292

Everson, Shawn, Ingram Content Group LLC, One Ingram Blvd, La Vergne, TN 37086-1986 *Tel:* 615-793-5000 *Toll Free Tel:* 800-937-8000 (retailers); 800-937-5300 (ext 1, libs) *E-mail:* customerservice@ingramcontent.com *Web Site:* www.ingramcontent.com, pg 1294, 1316

Eykemans, Tom, Marquand Books, 3131 Western Ave, Suite 522, Seattle, WA 98121 *Tel:* 206-624-2030 *Web Site:* www.marquandbooks.com, pg 1356

Fabian, Erika, Eriako Associates, 1380 Morningside Way, Venice, CA 90291 *Tel:* 310-392-6537 *Fax:* 310-392-6537 *E-mail:* eriakoassociates@gmail.com, pg 1354

Factor, Beverly, Envirovision, 733 Cliff Dr, Laguna Beach, CA 92651 *Tel:* 949-689-8794 *E-mail:* bfactor@beverlyfactor.com *Web Site:* www.beverlyfactor.com, pg 1421

Faherty, Kevin L, Lorimer Literary Consulting, 1524 SE 46 Ave, Suite A, Portland, OR 97215 *Tel:* 503-481-5847 *E-mail:* amnotice@yahoo.com, pg 1349

Fahr, Jean, Crane Duplicating Service Inc, 4915 Rattlesnake Hammock Rd, Suite 207, Naples, FL 34113 *Tel:* 305-280-6742 (help desk) *Fax:* 239-732-8415 *E-mail:* info@craneduplicating.com *Web Site:* www.craneduplicating.com, pg 1209, 1251

Fairchild, Linda, Linda Fairchild & Company LLC, 101 Lucas Valley Rd, Suite 363, San Rafael, CA 94903 *Tel:* 415-336-6407 *Web Site:* www.lindafairchild.com, pg 1108, 1346, 1354, 1414

Fairfield, Jay, HF Group LLC, 8844 Mayfield Rd, Chesterland, OH 44026 *Tel:* 440-729-2445; 440-729-9411 (bindery) *E-mail:* custservice-oh@hfgroup.com *Web Site:* www.hfgroup.com, pg 1254, 1268, 1325

Fakeris, Edward G, The Ohio Blow Pipe Co, 446 E 131 St, Cleveland, OH 44108-1684 *Tel:* 216-681-7379 *Fax:* 216-681-7713 *E-mail:* sales@obpairsystems.com *Web Site:* www.obpairsystems.com, pg 1282

Fakes, Bonnie, DeHoff Christian Bookstore, 749 NW Broad St, Murfreesboro, TN 37129 *Tel:* 615-893-8322 *Toll Free Tel:* 800-695-5385 *Fax:* 615-896-7447 *E-mail:* dehoffbooks@gmail.com *Web Site:* www.dehoffpublications.com, pg 1314

Faktorovich, Anna PhD, Pennsylvania Literary Journal (PLJ), 1108 W Third St, Quanah, TX 79252 *Tel:* 470-289-6395 *Web Site:* anaphoraliterary.com/journals/plj, pg 1135

Falvey, Kate, Bellevue Literary Review, 149 E 23 St, Suite 1516, New York, NY 10010 *Tel:* 917-375-5790 *E-mail:* info@BLReview.org *Web Site:* www.BLReview.org, pg 1130

Fancher, Chris, Adoption Book Catalog, 131 John Muir Dr, Amherst, NY 14228 *Tel:* 716-639-3900 *Toll Free Tel:* 866-691-3300 *E-mail:* info@tapestrybooks.com *Web Site:* www.tapestrybooks.com, pg 1145

Fareed, Faisal, appatura™, A Broadridge Company, 65 Challenger Rd, Suite 400, Ridgefield Park, NJ 07660 *Tel:* 201-508-6000 *Toll Free Tel:* 800-277-2155 *E-mail:* contactus@appatura.com *Web Site:* www.appatura.com, pg 1103, 1115, 1117, 1207, 1221, 1248

Fargis, Alison, Stonesong, 270 W 39 St, Suite 201, New York, NY 10018 *Tel:* 212-929-4600 *E-mail:* editors@stonesong.com *Web Site:* www.stonesong.com, pg 1357

Fargnoli, Jayne M, Harvard Educational Review, 8 Story St, 1st fl, Cambridge, MA 02138 *Tel:* 617-495-3432 *Toll Free Tel:* 888-437-1437 (orders) *Fax:* 617-496-3584 *Web Site:* hepg.org/her-home/home, pg 1132

Farhall, Grant, Getty Images Inc, 605 Fifth Ave S, Suite 400, Seattle, WA 98104 *Tel:* 206-925-5000 *Toll Free Tel:* 800-IMAGERY (462-4379); 888-888-5889 *Web Site:* www.gettyimages.com; www.gettyimages.com/customer-support; engage.gettyimages.com/media-inquiries, pg 1369, 1428

Farley, Kelly, dix! Digital Prepress Inc, 8462 Wayfarer Dr, Cicero, IN 13039 *Tel:* 315-288-5888 *Fax:* 315-288-5898 *E-mail:* info@dixtype.com *Web Site:* www.dixtype.com, pg 1225, 1252

Farmer, Greg, OverDrive Inc, One OverDrive Way, Cleveland, OH 44125 *Tel:* 216-573-6886 *Fax:* 216-573-6888 *E-mail:* info@overdrive.com *Web Site:* www.overdrive.com, pg 1298

Farmer, Tessin, BookFactory, 2302 S Edwin C Moses Blvd, Dayton, OH 45417 *Tel:* 937-226-7100 *Toll Free Tel:* 877-431-2665 *Fax:* 614-388-5635 *E-mail:* sales@bookfactory.com *Web Site:* www.bookfactory.com, pg 1249

Farnell, Sharon, Media Connect, 1675 Broadway, New York, NY 10019 *Tel:* 212-715-1600 *Web Site:* www.media-connect.com, pg 1110

Farnham, Kyle, Porter Novelli, 195 Broadway, 17th fl, New York, NY 10007 *Tel:* 212-601-8000 *Web Site:* www.porternovelli.com, pg 1112

Farr, Clay, Longleaf Services Inc, 116 S Boundary St, Chapel Hill, NC 27514-3808 *Tel:* 919-966-7449 *Toll Free Tel:* 800-848-6224 *Fax:* 919-962-2704 (24 hours) *Toll Free Fax:* 800-272-6817 (24 hours) *E-mail:* customerservice@longleafservices.org; orders@longleafservices.org *Web Site:* longleafservices.org, pg 1295

Farris, Ryan, AlphaGraphics Inc, 143 Union Blvd, Suite 650, Lakewood, CO 80228 *Toll Free Tel:* 800-955-6246 *Fax:* 801-595-7270 *E-mail:* contactus@alphagraphics.com *Web Site:* www.alphagraphics.com, pg 1364

Farrish, Bryan, Bryan Farrish Marketing, 1828 Broadway, 2nd fl, Santa Monica, CA 90404 *Tel:* 310-998-8305 *E-mail:* airplay@radio-media.com *Web Site:* www.radio-media.com, pg 1108

Fattman, Kelly, Harvard Educational Review, 8 Story St, 1st fl, Cambridge, MA 02138 *Tel:* 617-495-3432 *Toll Free Tel:* 888-437-1437 (orders) *Fax:* 617-496-3584 *Web Site:* hepg.org/her-home/home, pg 1132

Faulkner, Cassandra, Cat's Eye Consultancy, 4120 Durham Ct, Eagan, MN 55122 *Tel:* 651-270-3190, pg 1344

Fautsch, Carolina, English Literary History (ELH), 2715 N Charles St, Baltimore, MD 21218-4363 *Tel:* 410-516-6987 (journal orders outside US & CN) *Toll Free Tel:* 800-548-1784 (journal orders) *Fax:* 410-578-2865 (journal orders) *E-mail:* jrnlcirc@jh.edu (journal orders) *Web Site:* www.press.jhu.edu/journals/elh, pg 1131

Fazakerley, Richard, Pacific Publishing Co Inc, 636 Alaska St S, Seattle, WA 98108 *Tel:* 206-461-1300 *E-mail:* ppcprint@nwlink.com; ppccirc@nwlink.com; ppcbind@nwlink.com *Web Site:* pacificpublishingcompany.com, pg 1258

Fazekas, Zsolt Bede, Pannonia Bookstore, 300 Sainte Clair Ave W, Suite 103, Toronto, ON M4V 1S4, Canada *Tel:* 416-966-5156 *E-mail:* info@pannonia.ca *Web Site:* www.pannonia.ca, pg 1320, 1329

Febus, Fernando, Lectorum Publications Inc, 10 New Maple Ave, Suite 303, Pine Brook, NJ 07058 *Tel:* 201-559-2200 *Toll Free Tel:* 800-345-5946 *E-mail:* lectorum@lectorum.com *Web Site:* www.lectorum.com, pg 1318

Feder, Rosalie Brody, Rosalie Brody, 360 E 72 St, New York, NY 10021 *Tel:* 212-988-8951, pg 1108

Feder, Ted, Art Resource Inc, 65 Bleeker St, 12th fl, New York, NY 10012 Tel: 212-505-8700 Toll Free Tel: 888-505-8666 Fax: 212-505-2053 E-mail: requests@artres.com Web Site: www.artres.com, pg 1427

Federighi, Craig, Apple Inc, One Apple Park Way, Cupertino, CA 95014 Tel: 408-996-1010 Web Site: www.apple.com, pg 1364

Fegan, Trudy, Penguin Random House Canada, a Penguin Random House company, 320 Front St W, Suite 1400, Toronto, ON M5V 3B6, Canada Tel: 416-364-4449 Toll Free Tel: 888-523-9292 (cust serv) Fax: 416-598-7764 E-mail: customerservicescanada@penguinrandomhouse.com; publicitycanada@penguinrandomhouse.com; rightscanada@penguinrandomhouse.com Web Site: www.penguinrandomhouse.ca, pg 1299

Feigenbaum, Laurie, Feigenbaum Publishing Consultants Inc, 61 Bounty Lane, Jericho, NY 11753 Tel: 516-647-8314 (cell), pg 1346

Feldheim, Yitzchak, Feldheim Publishers, 208 Airport Executive Park, Nanuet, NY 10954 Tel: 845-356-2282 Toll Free Tel: 800-237-7149 (orders) Fax: 845-425-1908 E-mail: sales@feldheim.com Web Site: www.feldheim.com, pg 1315

Feldman, Alanna, Alanna Feldman Scouting, 4080 Via Marisol, Apt 135, Los Angeles, CA 90042 E-mail: info@afscouting.com Web Site: www.afscouting.com, pg 1346

Felt, Robert, Redwing Book Co, 202 Bendix St, Taos, NM 87571 Tel: 575-758-7758 Toll Free Tel: 800-873-3946 (US); 888-873-3947 (CN) Fax: 575-758-7768 E-mail: info@redwingbooks.com; custsrv@redwingbooks.com Web Site: www.redwingbooks.com, pg 1320, 1329

Felts, James W, Comag Marketing Group LLC (CMG), 155 Village Blvd, Suite 300, Princeton, NJ 08540 Tel: 609-524-1800 Fax: 609-524-1629 Web Site: www.i-cmg.com, pg 1314

Feng, Kelly, China Books, 360 Swift Ave, Suite 48, South San Francisco, CA 94080 Fax: 650-872-7808 E-mail: editor.sinomedia@gmail.com, pg 1313, 1327

Fenkel, William R, Styled Packaging LLC, PO Box 30299, Philadelphia, PA 19103-8299 Tel: 610-529-4122 Fax: 610-520-9662 Web Site: www.taylorbox.com, pg 1260, 1272, 1283, 1335, 1337

Fennell, Laura, Intuit Inc, 2700 Coast Ave, Mountain View, CA 94043 Tel: 650-944-6000 Toll Free Tel: 800-446-8848 E-mail: investor_relations@intuit.com Web Site: www.intuit.com, pg 1371

Fennell, Reginald F, Fennell Subscription Service Inc, 1002 W Michigan Ave, Jackson, MI 49202 Tel: 517-782-3132, pg 1315

Fenton-Hathaway, Anna, Literature & Medicine, 2715 N Charles St, Baltimore, MD 21218-4363 Tel: 410-516-6987 (journal orders outside US & CN) Toll Free Tel: 800-548-1784 (journal orders) Fax: 410-578-2865 (journal orders) E-mail: jrnlcirc@jh.edu (journal orders) Web Site: www.press.jhu.edu/journals/literature-and-medicine, pg 1134

Ferguson, David S, PBD Worldwide Inc, 1650 Bluegrass Lakes Pkwy, Alpharetta, GA 30004 Tel: 470-769-1000 Toll Free Tel: 866-998-4PBD (998-4723) E-mail: sales.marketing@pbd.com; customerservice@pbd.com Web Site: www.pbd.com, pg 1334

Ferreyra, Gonzalo, Ingram Publisher Services, an Ingram brand, 14 Ingram Blvd, Mail Stop 631, La Vergne, TN 37086 Tel: 615-793-5000 Toll Free Tel: 866-400-5351 (cust serv) E-mail: ips@ingramcontent.com Web Site: www.ingrampublisherservices.com, pg 1294

Ferry, Kevin, Ferry Associates Inc, 49 Fostertown Rd, Medford, NJ 08055 Tel: 609-953-1233 Toll Free Tel: 800-257-5258 Fax: 609-953-8637 Web Site: www.ferryassociates.com, pg 1210, 1225, 1253, 1280

Fetaya, Alain, Ideal Foreign Books LLC, 132-10 Hillside Ave, Richmond Hill, NY 11418 Tel: 718-297-7477 Toll Free Tel: 800-284-2490 Fax: 718-297-7645 E-mail: idealforeignbooks@att.net, pg 1316

Fetherston, James, Worzalla, 3535 Jefferson St, Stevens Point, WI 54481 Tel: 715-344-9608 Fax: 715-344-2578 Web Site: www.worzalla.com, pg 1215, 1233, 1262

Fideler, David PhD, Concord Editorial & Design LLC, 9450 SW Gemini Dr, Suite 68669, Beaverton, OR 97008 Tel: 616-827-7537 Fax: 616-825-6048 E-mail: info@concordeditorial.com Web Site: www.concordeditorial.com, pg 1224, 1354

Field, David C, Separa Color, 6951 Oran Circle, Buena Park, CA 90621 Tel: 818-988-2882 Toll Free Tel: 800-859-0629 Fax: 818-988-3882 E-mail: sales@separacolor.com Web Site: www.separacolor.com; www.simplybrochures.com; www.simplycatalogs.com; www.simplypostcards.com, pg 1105

Field, Diane, Continental Web Press Inc, 1430 Industrial Dr, Itasca, IL 60143-1858 Tel: 630-773-1903 E-mail: inquiries@continentalweb.com Web Site: www.continentalweb.com, pg 1251

Field, Ken Jr, Continental Web Press Inc, 1430 Industrial Dr, Itasca, IL 60143-1858 Tel: 630-773-1903 E-mail: inquiries@continentalweb.com Web Site: www.continentalweb.com, pg 1251

Field, Ken Sr, Continental Web Press Inc, 1430 Industrial Dr, Itasca, IL 60143-1858 Tel: 630-773-1903 E-mail: inquiries@continentalweb.com Web Site: www.continentalweb.com, pg 1251

Fields, Marty, Interstate Books4School, 201 E Badger Rd, Madison, WI 53713 Tel: 608-277-2407 Toll Free Tel: 800-752-3131 Fax: 608-277-2410 E-mail: sales@books4school.com Web Site: www.books4school.com, pg 1317

Fieler, Steve, HP Inc, 1501 Paige Mill Rd, Palo Alto, CA 94304-1112 Tel: 650-857-1501 Toll Free Tel: 800-282-6672 Web Site: www.hp.com, pg 1370

Fillmore, Laura, Open Book Systems Inc®, 21 Broadway, Suite 5, Rockport, MA 01966 Tel: 978-546-7346 E-mail: info@obs.com Web Site: www.obs.com, pg 1350, 1374

Finger, Lea, Marquand Books, 3131 Western Ave, Suite 522, Seattle, WA 98121 Tel: 206-624-2030 Web Site: www.marquandbooks.com, pg 1356

Finken, Zach, The Tribune News Service, 160 N Stetson Ave, Chicago, IL 60601 Tel: 312-222-4131 E-mail: tcanews@trbpub.com Web Site: www.mctdirect.com; tribunecontentagency.com/tribune-news-service, pg 1191

Fiore, Carol A, ISIS Papyrus America, 301 Bank St, South Lake, TX 76092 Tel: 817-416-2345 Fax: 817-416-1223 E-mail: info@isis-papyrus.com Web Site: www.isis-papyrus.com, pg 1371

Fiorelli, Paolo, AlphaGraphics Inc, 143 Union Blvd, Suite 650, Lakewood, CO 80228 Toll Free Tel: 800-955-6246 Fax: 801-595-7270 E-mail: contactus@alphagraphics.com Web Site: www.alphagraphics.com, pg 1364

Fish, Thomas PhD, Next Chapter Book Club (NCBC), 5909 Cleveland Ave, Columbus, OH 43231 Toll Free Tel: 800-674-8390 E-mail: info@nextchapterbookclub.org Web Site: nextchapterbookclub.org, pg 1143

Fisher, Cory, Krishnamurti Publications of America, 1070 McAndrew Rd, Ojai, CA 93023 Tel: 805-646-2726 E-mail: kfa@kfa.org Web Site: www.kfa.org, pg 1329

Fisher, Howard W, The Fisher Company, PO Box 89578, Tucson, AZ 85752-9578 Tel: 520-547-2460 Web Site: www.thefishercompany.com, pg 1346

Fisher, Lilly, American Quarterly, 2715 N Charles St, Baltimore, MD 21218-4363 Tel: 410-516-6987 (journal orders outside US & CN) Toll Free Tel: 800-548-1784 (journal orders) Fax: 410-578-2865 (journal orders) E-mail: jrnlcirc@jh.edu (journal orders) Web Site: www.americanquarterly.org; www.press.jhu.edu/journals/american-quarterly, pg 1129

Fiske, Mr Kelly M, Worldwide Books, 1001 W Seneca St, Ithaca, NY 14850-3342 Tel: 607-272-9200 Toll Free Tel: 800-473-8146 (US/CN orders only) Fax: 607-272-0239 E-mail: info@worldwide-artbooks.com Web Site: www.worldwide-artbooks.com, pg 1304

Fitzwilliam, Grant, Spraymation Inc, 4180 NW Tenth Ave, Fort Lauderdale, FL 33309 Tel: 954-484-9700 Toll Free Tel: 800-327-4985 Fax: 954-301-0842 E-mail: orders@spraymation.com Web Site: www.spraymation.com, pg 1283

Flaherty, Jack, Clarity Output Solutions (COS), 860 Honeyspot Rd, Stratford, CT 06615 Tel: 203-378-6200 Toll Free Tel: 800-414-1624 E-mail: info@clarityosl.com Web Site: www.clarityosl.com, pg 1115, 1117

Flatow, Bob, Lake Book Manufacturing Inc, 2085 N Cornell Ave, Melrose Park, IL 60160 Tel: 708-345-7000 E-mail: info@lakebook.com Web Site: www.lakebook.com, pg 1212, 1227, 1255, 1268, 1281

Flatt, Doug, PR by the Book LLC, PO Box 6226, Round Rock, TX 78683 Tel: 512-501-4399 Fax: 512-501-4399 E-mail: info@prbythebook.com Web Site: www.prbythebook.com, pg 1112

Flatt, Marika, PR by the Book LLC, PO Box 6226, Round Rock, TX 78683 Tel: 512-501-4399 Fax: 512-501-4399 E-mail: info@prbythebook.com Web Site: www.prbythebook.com, pg 1112

Flavin, Bill, Lake Book Manufacturing Inc, 2085 N Cornell Ave, Melrose Park, IL 60160 Tel: 708-345-7000 E-mail: info@lakebook.com Web Site: www.lakebook.com, pg 1212, 1227, 1256, 1269, 1281

Fleck-Nisbet, Andrea, The Independent Book Publishers Association (IBPA), 1020 Manhattan Beach Blvd, Suite 204, Manhattan Beach, CA 90266 Tel: 310-546-1818 E-mail: info@ibpa-online.org Web Site: www.ibpa-online.org, pg 1116

Fleeman, Mark, Fujii Associates Inc, 75 Sunny Hill Dr, Troy, MO 63379 Tel: 636-528-2546 Fax: 636-600-5153 Web Site: www.fujiiassociates.com, pg 1291

Fleisch, Thomas, Cromwell Leather, 147 Palmer Ave, Mamaroneck, NY 10543 Tel: 914-381-0100 Fax: 914-381-0046 E-mail: sales@cromwellgroup.com Web Site: www.cromwellgroup.com, pg 1266

Fleming, Tom, ALC Inc, 750 College Rd E, Suite 201, Princeton, NJ 08540 Tel: 609-580-2800 Toll Free Tel: 800-252-5478 Fax: 609-580-2888 E-mail: info@alc.com Web Site: www.alc.com, pg 1119

Flint, Alan, AGS, 4590 Graphics Dr, White Plains, MD 20695 Tel: 301-843-1800 Fax: 301-843-6339 E-mail: info@ags.com Web Site: www.ags.com, pg 1207, 1247, 1364

Flood, Stephen, Universal|Wilde, 26 Dartmouth St, Westwood, MA 02090 Tel: 781-251-2700 Fax: 781-251-2613 Web Site: www.universalwilde.com, pg 1105, 1116, 1232, 1261

Flory, Kyle, LOF Productions, 121 Greenwich Rd, Suite 202, Charlotte, NC 28211 Tel: 704-375-8892 Fax: 704-375-6316 Web Site: www.lofproductions.com, pg 1423

Flottman, Peter, Flottman Co Inc, 720 Centre View Blvd, Crestview Hills, KY 41017 Tel: 859-331-6636 Fax: 859-344-7085 E-mail: info@flottmanco.com Web Site: www.flottmanco.com, pg 1210

Flynn, Kathleen, Indigo Books & Music Inc, 468 King St W, Suite 500, Toronto, ON M5V 1L8, Canada Tel: 416-364-4499 E-mail: cisales@indigo.ca Web Site: www.chapters.indigo.ca, pg 1294

Flynn, Kitty, The Horn Book Magazine, 7858 Industrial Pkwy, Plain City, OH 43064 Toll Free Tel: 800-325-9558 E-mail: info@hbook.com Web Site: www.hbook.com, pg 1132

Flynn, Rosemary, Sony Electronics Inc, 16535 Via Esprillo, San Diego, CA 92127 Tel: 858-942-2400 E-mail: selpr@sony.com Web Site: www.sony.com/all-electronics, pg 1376

Flynn, Tanya, Cedar Fort Inc, 2373 W 700 S, Suite 100, Springville, UT 84663 Tel: 801-489-4084 Toll Free Tel: 800-SKY-BOOK (759-2665) E-mail: marketinginfo@cedarfort.com Web Site: cedarfort.com, pg 1327

Foca, Gene, Getty Images Inc, 605 Fifth Ave S, Suite 400, Seattle, WA 98104 *Tel:* 206-925-5000 *Toll Free Tel:* 800-IMAGERY (462-4379); 888-888-5889 *Web Site:* www.gettyimages.com; www.gettyimages.com/customer-support; engage.gettyimages.com/media-inquiries, pg 1369, 1428

Fogel, David, Worldwide Books, 1001 W Seneca St, Ithaca, NY 14850-3342 *Tel:* 607-272-9200 *Toll Free Tel:* 800-473-8146 (US/CN orders only) *Fax:* 607-272-0239 *E-mail:* info@worldwide-artbooks.com *Web Site:* www.worldwide-artbooks.com, pg 1304

Foley, Joe D, Corporate Disk Co, 4610 Prime Pkwy, McHenry, IL 60050-7005 *Tel:* 815-331-6000 *Toll Free Tel:* 800-634-3475 *Fax:* 815-331-6030 *E-mail:* info@disk.com *Web Site:* www.disk.com, pg 1224, 1251, 1366

Foley, William, Westchester Publishing Services, 4 Old Newtown Rd, Danbury, CT 06810 *Tel:* 203-791-0080 *Fax:* 203-791-9286 *E-mail:* info@westchesterpubsvcs.com *Web Site:* www.westchesterpublishingservices.com, pg 1233

Follante, Carina, BR Printers, 665 Lenfest Rd, San Jose, CA 95133 *Tel:* 408-278-7711 *Fax:* 408-929-8062 *E-mail:* info@brprinters.com *Web Site:* www.brprinters.com, pg 1103, 1249

Follett, Britten, Follett School Solutions Inc, 1340 Ridgeview Dr, McHenry, IL 60050 *Tel:* 815-759-1700 *Toll Free Tel:* 888-511-5114 (cust serv); 877-899-8550 (sales) *Fax:* 815-759-9831 *Toll Free Fax:* 800-852-5458 *E-mail:* info@follettlearning.com; customerservice@follett.com *Web Site:* www.follettlearning.com; www.follett.com/prek12; www.titlewave.com, pg 1291, 1369

Fontaine, Adrienne, Media Connect, 1675 Broadway, New York, NY 10019 *Tel:* 212-715-1600 *Web Site:* www.media-connect.com, pg 1110

Ford, Ted, Knepper Press Corp, 2251 Sweeney Dr, Clinton, PA 15026 *Tel:* 724-899-4200 *Fax:* 724-899-1331 *Web Site:* www.knepperpress.com, pg 1211, 1227, 1255

Ford, Tony, alfa CTP Systems Inc, 2503 Spring Ridge Dr, Unit D, Spring Grove, IL 60081 *Tel:* 815-474-7634 *E-mail:* info@alfactp.com *Web Site:* www.alfactp.com, pg 1364

Fordyce, Barbara, Map Resources, 151 N Union St, No 4, Lambertville, NJ 08530 *Tel:* 609-397-1611 *Toll Free Tel:* 800-334-4291 *Fax:* 609-751-9378 *E-mail:* info@mapresources.com; support@mapresources.com *Web Site:* www.mapresources.com, pg 1372

Forer, Dan, Forer Inc, 7881 SW 69 Ave, Miami, FL 33143 *Tel:* 305-495-0838 *Web Site:* www.forer.com, pg 1421

Forgey, Mike, Unitype LLC, 116-A Mockingbird Lane, Lockhart, TX 78644 *Tel:* 512-620-0384 *Toll Free Tel:* 800-697-9186 *E-mail:* info@unitype.com; sales@unitype.com; support@unitype.com *Web Site:* www.unitype.com, pg 1378

Formby, Scott, Indigo Books & Music Inc, 468 King St W, Suite 500, Toronto, ON M5V 1L8, Canada *Tel:* 416-364-4499 *E-mail:* cisales@indigo.ca *Web Site:* www.chapters.indigo.ca, pg 1294

Forrest, Julie, Penguin Random House Canada, a Penguin Random House company, 320 Front St W, Suite 1400, Toronto, ON M5V 3B6, Canada *Tel:* 416-364-4449 *Toll Free Tel:* 888-523-9292 (cust serv) *Fax:* 416-598-7764 *E-mail:* customerservicescanada@penguinrandomhouse.com; publicitycanada@penguinrandomhouse.com; rightscanada@penguinrandomhouse.com *Web Site:* www.penguinrandomhouse.ca, pg 1299

Fortuna, Nadia, United Library Services Inc, 7140 Fairmount Dr SE, Calgary, AB T2H 0X4, Canada *Tel:* 403-252-4426 *Toll Free Tel:* 888-342-5857 (CN only) *Fax:* 403-258-3426 *Toll Free Fax:* 800-661-2806 (CN only) *E-mail:* info@uls.com *Web Site:* www.uls.com, pg 1323

Foster, George, Foster Covers, 1401 Wonder Way, Fairfield, IA 52556 *Tel:* 641-919-4367 *E-mail:* info@fostercovers.com *Web Site:* www.fostercovers.com; www.facebook.com/bookcoverdesign, pg 1414

Foster, John W, The Antiquarian Bookstore, 1070 Lafayette Rd, US Rte 1, Portsmouth, NH 03801-5408 *Tel:* 603-436-7250 *Web Site:* www.antiquarianbookstore.com, pg 1311

Foster, Lee, Foster Travel Publishing, 1623 Martin Luther King Jr Way, Berkeley, CA 94709 *Tel:* 510-549-2202 *Web Site:* www.fostertravel.com, pg 1125, 1369

Foster, Lee, Foster Travel Publishing, 1623 Martin Luther King Jr Way, Berkeley, CA 94709 *Tel:* 510-549-2202 *Web Site:* www.fostertravel.com; stockphotos.fostertravel.com, pg 1421, 1428

Fournies, Sandra, Fournies Associates, 1226 NW 19 Terr, Delray Beach, FL 33445 *Tel:* 561-445-5102, pg 1346

Fowler, Allen, Blue Ridge Printing Co, 544 Haywood Rd, Asheville, NC 28806 *Tel:* 828-254-1000 *Toll Free Tel:* 800-633-4298 *Fax:* 828-252-6455 *E-mail:* info@brprinting.com *Web Site:* www.brprinting.com, pg 1249

Fowler, Bruce, Blue Ridge Printing Co, 544 Haywood Rd, Asheville, NC 28806 *Tel:* 828-254-1000 *Toll Free Tel:* 800-633-4298 *Fax:* 828-252-6455 *E-mail:* info@brprinting.com *Web Site:* www.brprinting.com, pg 1249

Fowler, Steve, Inland Press, 2001 W Lafayette Blvd, Detroit, MI 48216 *Tel:* 313-961-6000 *Web Site:* www.inlandpress.com, pg 1104

Fox, Bette-Lee, Library Journal, 123 William St, Suite 802, New York, NY 10038 *Tel:* 646-380-0700 *Toll Free Tel:* 800-588-1030 *Fax:* 646-380-0756 *E-mail:* ljinfo@mediasourceinc.com *Web Site:* www.libraryjournal.com, pg 1134

Fox, Michael, knk Software LP, 89 Headquarters Plaza N, No 1478, Morristown, NJ 07960 *Tel:* 908-206-4599 *E-mail:* info@knk.com *Web Site:* www.knkpublishingsoftware.com, pg 1348

Fox, Nancy, Gem Guides Book Co, 1155 W Ninth St, Upland, CA 91786 *Tel:* 626-855-1611 *Toll Free Tel:* 800-824-5118 (orders) *Fax:* 626-855-1610 *E-mail:* info@gemguidesbooks.com; sales@gemguidesbooks.com (orders) *Web Site:* www.gemguidesbooks.com, pg 1315

Franceschi, Adrienne, Fujii Associates Inc, 75 Sunny Hill Dr, Troy, MO 63379 *Tel:* 636-528-2546 *Fax:* 636-600-5153 *Web Site:* www.fujiiassociates.com, pg 1291

Franco, Vivian, Ascot Media Group Inc, PO Box 2394, Friendswood, TX 77549 *Tel:* 832-334-2733 *Toll Free Tel:* 800-854-1134 *Toll Free Fax:* 800-854-2207 *Web Site:* www.ascotmedia.com, pg 1107

Frank, Cynthia, Cypress House, 155 Cypress St, Suite A, Fort Bragg, CA 95437 *Tel:* 707-964-9520 *Toll Free Tel:* 800-773-7782 *Fax:* 707-964-7531 *E-mail:* office@cypresshouse.com *Web Site:* www.cypresshouse.com, pg 1104, 1224, 1345, 1413

Frank, Eric, Koenig & Bauer (US) Inc, 2555 Regent Blvd, Dallas, TX 75229 *Tel:* 469-532-8000 *Fax:* 469-532-8190 *Web Site:* us.koenig-bauer.com, pg 1281

Frank, James, James Frank Photography Inc, PO Box 3523, Estes Park, CO 80517 *Tel:* 970-586-3418 *E-mail:* photos@jamesfrank.com *Web Site:* www.jamesfrank.com, pg 1421

Franklin, Lori, OverDrive Inc, One OverDrive Way, Cleveland, OH 44125 *Tel:* 216-573-6886 *Fax:* 216-573-6888 *E-mail:* info@overdrive.com *Web Site:* www.overdrive.com, pg 1298

Franklin, MJ, The New York Times Book Review, 620 Eighth Ave, 5th fl, New York, NY 10018 *Tel:* 212-556-1234 *Toll Free Tel:* 800-631-2580 (subns) *E-mail:* bookreview@nytimes.com; books@nytimes.com *Web Site:* www.nytimes.com, pg 1135

Fraser, Beau, The Gate Worldwide, 71 Fifth Ave, 8th fl, New York, NY 10003 *Tel:* 212-508-3400 *Fax:* 212-508-3402 (cgi) *E-mail:* contact@thegateworldwide.com *Web Site:* thegateworldwide.com, pg 1099

Frechette, Pierre, Marquis Book Printing Inc, 350, rue des Entrepreneurs, Montmagny, QC G5V 4T1, Canada *Tel:* 418-246-5666 *Toll Free Tel:* 855-566-1937; 800-246-2468 *E-mail:* marquis@marquisbook.com *Web Site:* www.marquislivre.com; www.marquisbook.com, pg 1256

Frederick, Bill, Printware LLC, 2935 Waters Rd, Suite 160, St Paul, MN 55121-1523 *Tel:* 651-456-1400 *Fax:* 651-454-3684 *E-mail:* sales@printwarellc.com *Web Site:* www.printwarellc.com, pg 1375

Frederick, John, SumTotal Systems LLC, 2850 NW 43 St, Suite 150, Gainesville, FL 32606 *Tel:* 352-264-2800 *Toll Free Tel:* 866-933-1416 *Fax:* 352-374-2257 *E-mail:* customersupport@sumtotalsystems.com *Web Site:* www.sumtotalsystems.com, pg 1377

Frederico, Carmen, Bradford & Bigelow Inc, 3 Perkins Way, Newburyport, MA 01950-4007 *Tel:* 978-904-3100 *E-mail:* sales@bradford-bigelow.com *Web Site:* www.bradford-bigelow.com, pg 1208, 1249

Freeman, Jane, WordPlayJane, 21 Harrison St, Suite 3, New York, NY 10013 *Tel:* 646-370-9541 (cell), pg 1385

Freeman, Kent, Ingram Content Group LLC, One Ingram Blvd, La Vergne, TN 37086-1986 *Tel:* 615-793-5000 *Toll Free Tel:* 800-937-8000 (retailers); 800-937-5300 (ext 1, libs) *E-mail:* customerservice@ingramcontent.com *Web Site:* www.ingramcontent.com, pg 1294, 1316

Freeman, Nancy, VeronaLibri, 124 Willowbrook Ave, Stamford, CT 06902 *Tel:* 203-614-8335 *Web Site:* www.veronalibri.com, pg 1261

Freese, Michael, Rushmore News Inc, 924 E Saint Andrew, Rapid City, SD 57701 *Tel:* 605-342-2617 *Toll Free Tel:* 800-423-0501, pg 1321

Freet, Veronica, eFulfillment Service Inc, 807 Airport Access Rd, Traverse City, MI 49686 *Tel:* 231-276-5057 *Toll Free Tel:* 866-922-6783 *E-mail:* sales@efulfillmentservice.com *Web Site:* www.efulfillmentservice.com, pg 1333

Freitag, Brad, Claris International Inc, 5201 Patrick Henry Dr, Santa Clara, CA 95054 *Tel:* 408-727-8227 (sales & cust support) *Toll Free Tel:* 800-725-2747 (sales); 800-325-2747 (cust support) *Fax:* 408-987-7447 *E-mail:* claris_sales@claris.com *Web Site:* www.claris.com, pg 1366

Freund, Ron, Midpoint National Inc, 1263 Southwest Blvd, Kansas City, KS 66103 *Tel:* 913-362-7400 *Toll Free Tel:* 800-228-4321 *E-mail:* info@midpt.com *Web Site:* www.midpt.com, pg 1296

Frew, Lena, C & C Offset Printing Co USA Inc, 70 W 36 St, Unit 10C, New York, NY 10018 *Tel:* 212-431-4210 *Toll Free Fax:* 866-540-4134 *Web Site:* www.ccoffset.com, pg 1208, 1223, 1249

Frey, Christiane, Modern Language Notes (MLN), 2715 N Charles St, Baltimore, MD 21218-4363 *Tel:* 410-516-6987 (journal orders outside US & CN) *Toll Free Tel:* 800-548-1784 (journal orders) *Fax:* 410-578-2865 (journal orders) *E-mail:* jrnlcirc@jh.edu (journal orders) *Web Site:* www.press.jhu.edu/journals/mln, pg 1134

Fried, Robert, Robert Fried Photography, 610 Eldridge Ct, Novato, CA 94947 *Tel:* 415-898-6153 *Fax:* 415-897-0353 *E-mail:* rob@robertfriedphotography.com *Web Site:* www.robertfriedphotography.com, pg 1421

Friedenberg, Michael, Thomson Reuters, 3 Times Sq, New York, NY 10036 *Tel:* 646-223-4000; 646-223-6100 (edit); 646-223-6000 (newsroom) *Web Site:* www.thomsonreuters.com, pg 1191

Friedman, Dina, Accurate Writing & More, 16 Barstow Lane, Hadley, MA 01035 *Tel:* 413-586-2388 *Web Site:* www.accuratewriting.com; frugalmarketing.com, pg 1099, 1107, 1343

Friesen, Chad, Friesens Corp, One Printers Way, Altona, MB R0G 0B0, Canada *Tel:* 204-324-6401 *Fax:* 204-324-1333 *E-mail:* book_info@friesens.com *Web Site:* www.friesens.com, pg 1210, 1253

Friesen, Russell, Login Canada, 300 Saulteaux Crescent, Winnipeg, MB R3J 3T2, Canada *Tel:* 204-837-2987 *Toll Free Tel:* 800-665-1148 (CN only) *Fax:* 204-837-3116 *Toll Free Fax:* 800-665-0103 *E-mail:* sales@lb.ca *Web Site:* www.lb.ca, pg 1318

Fritsch, Janet, The American Collective Stand®, 277 White St, Buchanan, NY 10511 *Tel:* 914-739-7500 *Toll Free Tel:* 800-462-7687 *Fax:* 914-739-7575 *Web Site:* www.americancollectivestand.com, pg 1139

Fritz, Thomas M, Beidel Printing House Inc, 225 S Fayette St, Shippensburg, PA 17257 *Tel:* 717-532-5063 *Fax:* 717-532-2502 *E-mail:* customerservice@dreamprint.com *Web Site:* dreamprint.com, pg 1248, 1344

Froehlich, Conrad G, Osa's Ark Museum Shop, 111 N Lincoln Ave, Chanute, KS 66720 *Tel:* 620-431-2730 *Fax:* 620-431-2730 *E-mail:* osajohns@safarimuseum.com; osasark@yahoo.com *Web Site:* www.safarimuseum.com, pg 1320

Frogh, Thomas, International Mapping Associates, 5300 Dorsey Hall Dr, Suite 201, Ellicott City, MD 21042 *Tel:* 443-367-0050 *E-mail:* frontdesk@internationalmapping.com *Web Site:* internationalmapping.com, pg 1415

Froman, Craig, Master Books®, 3142 Hwy 103 N, Green Forest, AR 72638 *Tel:* 870-438-5288 *Toll Free Tel:* 800-999-3777 *E-mail:* nlp@nlpg.com; sales@masterbooks.com *Web Site:* www.masterbooks.com; www.nlpg.com, pg 1372

Fry, David S, Fry Communications Inc, 800 W Church Rd, Mechanicsburg, PA 17055 *Tel:* 717-766-0211 *Toll Free Tel:* 800-334-1429 *Fax:* 717-691-0341 *E-mail:* info@frycomm.com *Web Site:* www.frycomm.com, pg 1210, 1226, 1253, 1280

Fry, Henry, Fry Communications Inc, 800 W Church Rd, Mechanicsburg, PA 17055 *Tel:* 717-766-0211 *Toll Free Tel:* 800-334-1429 *Fax:* 717-691-0341 *E-mail:* info@frycomm.com *Web Site:* www.frycomm.com, pg 1210, 1225, 1253, 1280

Fujiwara, Sho, RISO Inc, 10 State St, Suite 201, Woburn, MA 01801-2105 *Tel:* 978-777-7377 *Toll Free Tel:* 800-942-7476 (cust support) *Web Site:* us.riso.com, pg 1259, 1376

Funches, Devin, Diamond Book Distributors (DBD), 10150 York Rd, Hunt Valley, MD 21030 *Tel:* 443-318-8001; 443-318-8519 (cust serv) *E-mail:* distribution@diamondbookdistributors.com; dbdreorders@diamondbookdistributors.com (orders); books@diamondbookdistributors.com (cust serv) *Web Site:* diamondbookdistributors.com, pg 1290

Gaafar, Sean, Rimage Corp, 201 General Mills Blvd, Golden Valley, MN 55427 *Tel:* 952-944-8144; 952-946-0004 (option 2, tech support) *Toll Free Tel:* 800-445-8288; 800-553-8312 (option 2, tech support) *E-mail:* sales@rimage.com *Web Site:* www.rimage.com, pg 1376

Gaerlan, Diane, Omeda, 4 Overlook Point, Suite A2SE, Lincolnshire, IL 60069 *Tel:* 847-564-8900 *E-mail:* getstarted@omeda.com *Web Site:* www.omeda.com, pg 1334

Gaffin, Elizabeth, Distributed Art Publishers Inc, 75 Broad St, Suite 630, New York, NY 10004 *Tel:* 212-627-1999 *Toll Free Tel:* 800-338-2665 (cust serv) *Fax:* 212-627-9484 *E-mail:* orders@dapinc.com *Web Site:* www.artbook.com, pg 1290

Gagliano, John, St Joseph Communications-Print Group, 50 Macintosh Blvd, Concord, ON L4K 4P3, Canada *Tel:* 905-660-3111 *E-mail:* marketing@stjoseph.com *Web Site:* stjoseph.com, pg 1105, 1259

Gainous, Doug, Omeda, 4 Overlook Point, Suite A2SE, Lincolnshire, IL 60069 *Tel:* 847-564-8900 *E-mail:* getstarted@omeda.com *Web Site:* www.omeda.com, pg 1334

Gaither, John, Reichhold Inc, 1035 Swabia Ct, Durham, NC 27703 *Tel:* 919-990-7500 *Toll Free Tel:* 800-448-3482 *Fax:* 919-990-7749 *Web Site:* www.reichhold.com, pg 1271

Galasso, Al, National Association of Book Entrepreneurs (NABE), PO Box 606, Cottage Grove, OR 97424 *Tel:* 541-942-7455 *Fax:* 541-942-7455 *E-mail:* nabe@bookmarketingprofits.com *Web Site:* www.bookmarketingprofits.com, pg 1139, 1298

Galbraith, Ali, Lightning Source LLC, 1246 Heil Quaker Blvd, La Vergne, TN 37086 *Tel:* 615-793-5000 (Ingram) *Toll Free Tel:* 800-378-5508; 800-509-4156 (cust serv) *E-mail:* lsicustomersupport@ingramcontent.com; contentacquisitioninquiries@ingramcontent.com *Web Site:* www.ingramcontent.com/publishers/print, pg 1212

Galbraith, Ali, Lightning Source LLC, 1246 Heil Quaker Blvd, La Vergne, TN 37086 *Tel:* 615-793-5000 (Ingram) *Toll Free Tel:* 800-378-5508; 800-509-4156 (cust serv) *E-mail:* lsicustomersupport@ingramcontent.com *Web Site:* www.ingramcontent.com/publishers/print, pg 1256, 1371

Galbreath, Howard, The Printer, 2810 Cowell Blvd, Davis, CA 95618 *Tel:* 530-753-2519 *Fax:* 530-753-2528 *E-mail:* info@the-printer.net *Web Site:* the-printer.net, pg 1105, 1258

Gall, David, BR Printers, 665 Lenfest Rd, San Jose, CA 95133 *Tel:* 408-278-7711 *Fax:* 408-929-8062 *E-mail:* info@brprinters.com *Web Site:* www.brprinters.com, pg 1103, 1249

Gallagher, Bill, Alliance Storage Technologies Inc (ASTI), 10045 Federal Dr, Colorado Springs, CO 80908 *Tel:* 719-593-7900 *Toll Free Tel:* 888-567-6332 *Fax:* 719-598-3472 *E-mail:* sales@astiusa.com; info@astiusa.com *Web Site:* www.alliancestoragetechnologies.com, pg 1364

Gallagher, Jim, OTTN Publishing, 16 Risler St, Stockton, NJ 08559 *Tel:* 609-397-4005 *Toll Free Tel:* 866-356-6886 *Fax:* 609-397-4007 *E-mail:* inquiries@ottnpublishing.com; sales@ottnpublishing.com *Web Site:* www.ottnpublishing.com, pg 1356

Gallagher, Kelly, Ingram Content Group LLC, One Ingram Blvd, La Vergne, TN 37086-1986 *Tel:* 615-793-5000 *Toll Free Tel:* 800-937-8000 (retailers); 800-937-5300 (ext 1, libs) *E-mail:* customerservice@ingramcontent.com *Web Site:* www.ingramcontent.com, pg 1294, 1316

Gallagher, Sharon Helgason, Distributed Art Publishers Inc, 75 Broad St, Suite 630, New York, NY 10004 *Tel:* 212-627-1999 *Toll Free Tel:* 800-338-2665 (cust serv) *Fax:* 212-627-9484 *E-mail:* orders@dapinc.com *Web Site:* www.artbook.com, pg 1290

Gallagher, Thomas L, Religion News Service, c/o University of Missouri's Journalism School, 30 Neff Annex, Columbia, MO 65211 *Tel:* 573-884-1327 *E-mail:* info@religionnews.com *Web Site:* www.religionnews.com, pg 1191

Gallant, Barry, Penguin Random House Canada, a Penguin Random House company, 320 Front St W, Suite 1400, Toronto, ON M5V 3B6, Canada *Tel:* 416-364-4449 *Toll Free Tel:* 888-523-9292 (cust serv) *Fax:* 416-598-7764 *E-mail:* customerservicescanada@penguinrandomhouse.com; publicitycanada@penguinrandomhouse.com; rightscanada@penguinrandomhouse.com *Web Site:* www.penguinrandomhouse.ca, pg 1299

Galletta, Gregg, ALC Inc, 750 College Rd E, Suite 201, Princeton, NJ 08540 *Tel:* 609-580-2800 *Toll Free Tel:* 800-252-5478 *Fax:* 609-580-2888 *E-mail:* info@alc.com *Web Site:* www.alc.com, pg 1119

Galligan, John, Bradford & Bigelow Inc, 3 Perkins Way, Newburyport, MA 01950-4007 *Tel:* 978-904-3100 *E-mail:* sales@bradford-bigelow.com *Web Site:* www.bradford-bigelow.com, pg 1208, 1249

Gallin-Dwyer, Alice J, Washington Monthly, 1200 18 St NW, Suite 330, Washington, DC 20036 *Tel:* 202-955-9010 *Toll Free Tel:* 855-492-1648 (subns) *Fax:* 202-955-9011 *E-mail:* editors@washingtonmonthly.com *Web Site:* washingtonmonthly.com, pg 1137

Gallo, Jamie, Wunderman, 3 Columbus Circle, New York, NY 10019 *Tel:* 212-941-3000 *Web Site:* www.wunderman.com, pg 1100

Gallo, Jim, Specialty Finishing Group, 1401 Kirk St, Elk Grove Village, IL 60007 *Tel:* 847-290-0110 *Fax:* 847-290-9404 *Web Site:* www.sfgrp.com, pg 1260

Gallup, Stuart, Mark Andy Inc, 18081 Chesterfield Airport Rd, Chesterfield, MO 63005 *Tel:* 636-532-4433 *Toll Free Tel:* 800-447-1231 *Toll Free Fax:* 800-447-1231 *Web Site:* www.presstek.com; markandy.com; shop.markandy.com, pg 1364

Gammons, Robert, Schaefer Machine Co Inc, 200 Commercial Dr, Deep River, CT 06417 *Tel:* 860-526-4000 *Toll Free Tel:* 800-243-5143 *Fax:* 860-526-4654 *E-mail:* schaefer@schaeferco.com *Web Site:* www.schaeferco.com, pg 1283

Gandert, Nate, Getty Images Inc, 605 Fifth Ave S, Suite 400, Seattle, WA 98104 *Tel:* 206-925-5000 *Toll Free Tel:* 800-IMAGERY (462-4379); 888-888-5889 *Web Site:* www.gettyimages.com/customer-support; engage.gettyimages.com/media-inquiries, pg 1369, 1428

Ganser, Doris, Transimpex Translators, Interpreters, Editors, Consultants Inc, 2300 Main St, 9th fl, Kansas City, MO 64108 *Tel:* 816-561-5515 *Fax:* 816-561-5515 *E-mail:* translations@transimpex.com *Web Site:* www.transimpex.com, pg 1405

Garcia, Michael, Domtar Paper Co LLC, 234 Kingsley Park Dr, Fort Mill, SC 29715 *Tel:* 803-802-7500 *Toll Free Tel:* 877-877-4685 *E-mail:* communications@domtar.com; commercialprinting@domtar.com *Web Site:* www.domtar.com, pg 1266

Garcia, Nancy, Garcia Publishing Services, 830 Russell Rd, No 8, DeKalb, IL 60115 *Tel:* 815-338-5512 *E-mail:* garpubserv@aol.com, pg 1354

Garcia, Robert T, Garcia Publishing Services, 830 Russell Rd, No 8, DeKalb, IL 60115 *Tel:* 815-338-5512 *E-mail:* garpubserv@aol.com, pg 1354

Garda, Donna, Sterling Fulfillment, 100 Quentin Roosevelt Blvd, Suite 205, Garden City, NY 11530 *Tel:* 516-758-2000 *Web Site:* sterlingfulfillment.com, pg 1116

Garfinkel, David, Nuance Communications Inc, One Wayside Rd, Burlington, MA 01803 *Tel:* 781-565-5000 *Toll Free Tel:* 800-654-1187 (orders); 888-372-1908 (orders) *Web Site:* www.nuance.com, pg 1374

Gargioli, Stefano, BroadVision, 460 Seaport Ct, Suite 102, Redwood City, CA 94063 *Tel:* 650-331-1000 *Web Site:* www.broadvision.com, pg 1365

Garlich, Brad, Garlich Printing Co, 525 Rudder Rd, St Louis, MO 63026 *Tel:* 636-349-8000 *Toll Free Tel:* 844-449-4752 *Fax:* 636-349-8080 *E-mail:* customerservice@garlich.com *Web Site:* www.garlich.com, pg 1253

Garlich, Greg, Garlich Printing Co, 525 Rudder Rd, St Louis, MO 63026 *Tel:* 636-349-8000 *Toll Free Tel:* 844-449-4752 *Fax:* 636-349-8080 *E-mail:* customerservice@garlich.com *Web Site:* www.garlich.com, pg 1253

Garner, Frank III, Amgraf Inc, 1501 Oak St, Kansas City, MO 64108-1424 *Tel:* 816-474-4797 *Toll Free Tel:* 800-304-4797 (sales & mktg) *Fax:* 816-842-4477 *E-mail:* support@amgraf.com *Web Site:* www.amgraf.com, pg 1364

Garner, Gary, GLS Companies, 1280 Energy Park Dr, St Paul, MN 55108-5106 *Tel:* 651-644-3000 *Toll Free Tel:* 800-655-9405 *Web Site:* www.glsmn.com, pg 1226, 1254

Garner, Jonathan, Amgraf Inc, 1501 Oak St, Kansas City, MO 64108-1424 *Tel:* 816-474-4797 *Toll Free Tel:* 800-304-4797 (sales & mktg) *Fax:* 816-842-4477 *E-mail:* support@amgraf.com *Web Site:* www.amgraf.com, pg 1364

Garner, Raymond L, Amgraf Inc, 1501 Oak St, Kansas City, MO 64108-1424 *Tel:* 816-474-4797 *Toll Free Tel:* 800-304-4797 (sales & mktg) *Fax:* 816-842-4477 *E-mail:* support@amgraf.com *Web Site:* www.amgraf.com, pg 1364

Garnett, Missy, Cape Cod Compositors Inc, 811 Washington St, Suite 2, Pembroke, MA 02359-2333 *Tel:* 781-826-2100, pg 1223

Garrett, Shaun, Overseas Printing Corporation, 4040 Civic Center Dr, Suite 200, San Rafael, CA 94903 *Tel:* 415-500-8331 *Fax:* 415-835-9899 *Web Site:* www.overseasprinting.com, pg 1213, 1229, 1257, 1270, 1282

Garvan, Stephen Bond, Garvan Media, Management & Marketing Inc, PO Box 737, Sandpoint, ID 83864 *Tel:* 208-265-1718 *Web Site:* facebook.com/stephen.b.garvan, pg 1347

Gasanz, Marcela, UniNet Imaging Inc, 3232 W El Segundo Blvd, Hawthorne, CA 90250 *Tel:* 424-675-3300 *Fax:* 424-675-3400 *E-mail:* sales@uninetimaging.com *Web Site:* www.uninetimaging.com, pg 1378

Gasiorowski, Mary Beth, Symmetry Creative Production, 1300 S Grove Ave, Suite 103, Barrington, IL 60010 *Tel:* 847-382-8750 *E-mail:* information@symmetrycp.com *Web Site:* www.symmetrycp.com, pg 1232

Gasser-Ellis, Gretchen L, Copyright Clearance Center Inc (CCC), 222 Rosewood Dr, Danvers, MA 01923 *Tel:* 978-750-8400 (sales); 978-646-2600 (cust serv) *E-mail:* info@copyright.com *Web Site:* www.copyright.com, pg 1345

Gately, Liz, Liz Gately Book Scouting, 36 W 37 St, Rm 408, New York, NY 10018 *Tel:* 212-244-1441 *E-mail:* liz@lizgately.com *Web Site:* www.lizgately.com, pg 1347

Gazzarolle, Roberta, Retailing Insight Magazine, PO Box 12252, Charlotte, NC 28220 *E-mail:* circ@retailinginsight.com *Web Site:* retailinginsight.com, pg 1136

Gebhart, David, Independent Publishers Group (IPG), 814 N Franklin St, Chicago, IL 60610 *Tel:* 312-337-0747 *Toll Free Tel:* 800-888-4741 (orders) *Fax:* 312-337-5985 *E-mail:* frontdesk@ipgbook.com; orders@ipgbook.com *Web Site:* www.ipgbook.com, pg 1292

Gecht, Guy, Electronics for Imaging Inc (EFI), 6750 Dumbarton Circle, Fremont, CA 94555 *Tel:* 650-357-3500 *Toll Free Tel:* 800-568-1917; 800-875-7117 (sales) *Fax:* 650-357-3907 *E-mail:* info@efi.com *Web Site:* www.efi.com, pg 1368

Gedman, Kent, Midpoint National Inc, 1263 Southwest Blvd, Kansas City, KS 66103 *Tel:* 913-362-7400 *Toll Free Tel:* 800-228-4321 *E-mail:* info@midpt.com *Web Site:* www.midpt.com, pg 1296

Gelfand, Dr Sergei, American Mathematical Society (AMS), 201 Charles St, Providence, RI 02904-2213 *Tel:* 401-455-4000 *Toll Free Tel:* 800-321-4267 *Fax:* 401-331-3842; 401-455-4046 (cust serv) *E-mail:* cust-serv@ams.org; ams@ams.org *Web Site:* www.ams.org, pg 1207, 1221, 1247, 1277

Geller, Martha Ferro, Translations.com, 1250 Broadway, 32nd fl, New York, NY 10001 *Tel:* 212-689-1616 *Fax:* 212-504-8057 *E-mail:* newyork@translations.com; info@translations.com *Web Site:* translations.com, pg 1405

Gendler, Joel, Victory Productions Inc, 55 Linden St, Worcester, MA 01609 *Tel:* 508-755-0051 *E-mail:* victory@victoryprd.com *Web Site:* www.victoryprd.com, pg 1358

Gendreau, Peter, Omniafiltra LLC, 9567 Main St, Beaver Falls, NY 13305 *Tel:* 315-346-7300 *Web Site:* www.omniafiltra.it/inglese/default_en.html, pg 1270

Genovese, Dan, Lake Book Manufacturing Inc, 2085 N Cornell Ave, Melrose Park, IL 60160 *Tel:* 708-345-7000 *E-mail:* info@lakebook.com *Web Site:* www.lakebook.com, pg 1212, 1227, 1255, 1268, 1281

Genovese, Paul, Lake Book Manufacturing Inc, 2085 N Cornell Ave, Melrose Park, IL 60160 *Tel:* 708-345-7000 *E-mail:* info@lakebook.com *Web Site:* www.lakebook.com, pg 1212, 1227, 1256, 1269, 1281

George, David, Aptara Inc, 2901 Telestar Ct, Suite 522, Falls Church, VA 22042 *Tel:* 703-352-0001 *E-mail:* moreinfo@aptaracorp.com *Web Site:* www.aptaracorp.com, pg 1365

George, David, Genesis Marketing Group Inc, 850 Wade Hampton Blvd, Bldg A, Suite 100, Greenville, SC 29609 *Tel:* 864-233-2651 *Toll Free Tel:* 800-627-2651 *Toll Free Fax:* 800-849-4363 *E-mail:* orders@genesislink.com *Web Site:* www.genesislink.com, pg 1291

Georges, Patrick, Penguin Random House Canada, a Penguin Random House company, 320 Front St W, Suite 1400, Toronto, ON M5V 3B6, Canada *Tel:* 416-364-4449 *Toll Free Tel:* 888-523-9292 (cust serv) *Fax:* 416-598-7764 *E-mail:* customerservicescanada@penguinrandomhouse.com; publicitycanada@penguinrandomhouse.com; rightscanada@penguinrandomhouse.com *Web Site:* www.penguinrandomhouse.ca, pg 1299

Gerard, Steve, Science Source®, 307 Fifth Ave, 3rd fl, New York, NY 10016 *Tel:* 212-758-3420 *E-mail:* info@sciencesource.com; sales@sciencesource.com; contributor@sciencesource.com *Web Site:* www.sciencesource.com, pg 1430

Gerardi, Mark, Horizon Paper Co Inc, 1010 Washington Blvd, Stamford, CT 06901 *Tel:* 203-358-0855 *Toll Free Tel:* 866-358-0855 *E-mail:* info@horizonpaper.com *Web Site:* www.horizonpaper.com, pg 1268

Gerhold, Chris, BR Printers, 665 Lenfest Rd, San Jose, CA 95133 *Tel:* 408-278-7711 *Fax:* 408-929-8062 *E-mail:* info@brprinters.com *Web Site:* www.brprinters.com, pg 1103, 1249

Gershowitz, Elissa, The Horn Book Magazine, 7858 Industrial Pkwy, Plain City, OH 43064 *Toll Free Tel:* 800-325-9558 *E-mail:* info@hbook.com *Web Site:* www.hbook.com, pg 1132

Gerson, Johnathan, Copywriters' Council of America™ (CCA), Linick Bldg, 7 Putter Lane, Middle Island, NY 11953 *Tel:* 631-924-3888; 631-924-8555; 631-604-8599 *E-mail:* linickgroup@gmail.com, pg 1345

Gerson, Linda, The Intermarketing Group-Art Licensing Agency, 29 Holt Rd, Amherst, NH 03031 *Tel:* 603-672-0499, pg 1348

Gessmann, Nancy, CDS Global, 1901 Bell Ave, Des Moines, IA 50315-1099 *Tel:* 515-247-7500 *Toll Free Tel:* 866-897-7987 *E-mail:* salesinfo@cds-global.com *Web Site:* www.cds-global.com, pg 1117, 1119

Gherson, Diane, IBM Corp, One New Orchard Rd, Armonk, NY 10504 *Tel:* 914-499-1900 *Toll Free Tel:* 800-426-4968 *E-mail:* askibm@vnet.ibm.com *Web Site:* www.ibm.com, pg 1370

Giampietro, Susan, Specialist Marketing Services Inc, 777 Terrace Ave, Suite 401, Hasbrouck Heights, NJ 07604 *Tel:* 201-865-5800 *E-mail:* info@sms-inc.com *Web Site:* www.sms-inc.com, pg 1120

Giannandrea, John, Apple Inc, One Apple Park Way, Cupertino, CA 95014 *Tel:* 408-996-1010 *Web Site:* www.apple.com, pg 1364

Giarratano, Frank, SGW Integrated Marketing Communications Inc, 219 Changebridge Rd, Montville, NJ 07045 *Tel:* 973-299-8000 *E-mail:* info@sgw.com *Web Site:* www.sgw.com, pg 1118

Gibbs, Jim, The Dingley Press, 119 Lisbon St, Lisbon, ME 04250 *Tel:* 207-353-4151 *Toll Free Tel:* 800-317-4574 *Fax:* 207-353-9886 *E-mail:* info@dingley.com *Web Site:* www.dingley.com, pg 1252

Gibbs, Michael D, InfinitPrint Solutions Inc, 14 N Tenth St, Richmond, IN 47374 *Tel:* 765-962-1507 *Toll Free Tel:* 800-478-4885 *Fax:* 765-962-4997 *E-mail:* info@infinitprint.com *Web Site:* infinitprint.com, pg 1211, 1255

Gibson, Dot, Dot Gibson Publications, PO Box 117, Waycross, GA 31502 *Tel:* 912-285-2848 *Toll Free Tel:* 800-336-8095 (for orders) *Fax:* 912-285-2848 *E-mail:* info@dotgibson.com *Web Site:* www.dotgibson.com, pg 1315

Gibson, N Gilbert Jr, Dot Gibson Publications, PO Box 117, Waycross, GA 31502 *Tel:* 912-285-2848 *Toll Free Tel:* 800-336-8095 (for orders) *Fax:* 912-285-2848 *E-mail:* info@dotgibson.com *Web Site:* www.dotgibson.com, pg 1315

Gibson, Phil, Diamond Book Distributors (DBD), 10150 York Rd, Hunt Valley, MD 21030 *Tel:* 443-318-8001; 443-318-8519 (cust serv) *E-mail:* distribution@diamondbookdistributors.com; dbdreorders@diamondbookdistributors.com (orders); books@diamondbookdistributors.com (cust serv) *Web Site:* diamondbookdistributors.com, pg 1290

Gicewicz, Jonathan, HJMT Public Relations Inc, 3280 Sunrise Hwy, Suite 296, Wantagh, NY 11793 *Tel:* 516-661-2800 *E-mail:* info@hjmt.com *Web Site:* www.hjmt.com, pg 1109

Giella, Miguel Angel, Girol Books Inc, PO Box 5473, LCD Merivale, Ottawa, ON K2C 3M1, Canada *Tel:* 613-233-9044 *E-mail:* info@girol.com *Web Site:* www.girol.com, pg 1292, 1316, 1328

Gildemeister, Cathy, The Bear Wallow Publishing Co, 809 S 12 St, La Grande, OR 97850 *Tel:* 541-962-7864 *Web Site:* www.bear-wallow.com, pg 1222, 1277

Gildemeister, Jerry, The Bear Wallow Publishing Co, 809 S 12 St, La Grande, OR 97850 *Tel:* 541-962-7864 *Web Site:* www.bear-wallow.com, pg 1222, 1277

Giles, Ericka D, ABDI Inc, 16 Avenue "A", Leetsdale, PA 15056 *Toll Free Tel:* 800-796-6471 *Fax:* 412-741-4161 *E-mail:* e-fulfillment@abdintl.com *Web Site:* www.abdi-ecommerce10.com/abdintl; www.abdintl.com/abdintl, pg 1117, 1207, 1333

Gill, Stacey, Publishers Weekly, 49 W 23 St, 9th fl, New York, NY 10010 *Tel:* 212-377-5500 *Fax:* 212-377-2733 *Web Site:* www.publishersweekly.com, pg 1136

Gillen, Michael, Comag Marketing Group LLC (CMG), 155 Village Blvd, Suite 300, Princeton, NJ 08540 *Tel:* 609-524-1800 *Fax:* 609-524-1629 *Web Site:* www.i-cmg.com, pg 1314

Gillies, Ron, Printronix Inc, 6440 Oak Canyon, Suite 200, Irvine, CA 92618 *Tel:* 714-368-2300 *Toll Free Tel:* 800-665-6210 *Web Site:* www.printronix.com, pg 1375

Gillman, Bob, Videotex Systems Inc, 10255 Miller Rd, Dallas, TX 75238 *Tel:* 972-231-9200 *Toll Free Tel:* 800-888-4336 *Fax:* 972-231-2420 *E-mail:* info@videotexsystems.com *Web Site:* www.videotexsystems.com, pg 1378

Giovannelli, Rosemary, Hassett Express, 17W775 Butterfield Rd, Suite 109, Oakbrook Terrace, IL 60181 *Tel:* 630-530-6515 *Fax:* 630-530-6538 *Web Site:* www.hassettexpress.com, pg 1334

Giroux, Steve, Teacher's Discovery®, 2741 Paldan Dr, Auburn Hills, MI 48326 *Toll Free Tel:* 800-TEACHER (832-2437) *Toll Free Fax:* 800-287-4509 *E-mail:* help@teachersdiscovery.com; orders@teachersdiscovery.com *Web Site:* www.teachersdiscovery.com, pg 1303, 1322

Giulianelli, Derek, BR Printers, 665 Lenfest Rd, San Jose, CA 95133 *Tel:* 408-278-7711 *Fax:* 408-929-8062 *E-mail:* info@brprinters.com *Web Site:* www.brprinters.com, pg 1103, 1249

Glassman, Will, CRW Graphics Communications, 9100 Pennsauken Hwy, Pennsauken, NJ 08110 *Tel:* 856-662-9111 *Toll Free Tel:* 800-820-3000 *Fax:* 856-665-1789 *E-mail:* info@crwgraphics.com *Web Site:* www.crwgraphics.com, pg 1103, 1367, 1413

Glastris, Paul, Washington Monthly, 1200 18 St NW, Suite 330, Washington, DC 20036 *Tel:* 202-955-9010 *Toll Free Tel:* 855-492-1648 (subns) *Fax:* 202-955-9011 *E-mail:* editors@washingtonmonthly.com *Web Site:* washingtonmonthly.com, pg 1137

Gleichman, Eve, Liz Gately Book Scouting, 36 W 37 St, Rm 408, New York, NY 10018 *Tel:* 212-244-1441 *E-mail:* liz@lizgately.com *Web Site:* www.lizgately.com, pg 1347

Gleisner, Nichole, New Haven Review, 55 Elmwood Rd, New Haven, CT 06515 *Tel:* 203-494-7018 *Web Site:* www.newhavenreview.com, pg 1134

Glenn, Thomas R, A B Data Ltd, 600 A B Data Dr, Milwaukee, WI 53217 *Tel:* 414-961-6400 *Toll Free Tel:* 866-217-4470 *Fax:* 414-961-2674 *E-mail:* info@abdata.com; consulting@abdata.com *Web Site:* www.abdata.com, pg 1115

Glover, Kelly, Penguin Random House Canada, a Penguin Random House company, 320 Front St W, Suite 1400, Toronto, ON M5V 3B6, Canada *Tel:* 416-

364-4449 *Toll Free Tel:* 888-523-9292 (cust serv) *Fax:* 416-598-7764 *E-mail:* customerservicescanada@penguinrandomhouse.com; publicitycanada@penguinrandomhouse.com; rightscanada@penguinrandomhouse.com *Web Site:* www.penguinrandomhouse.ca, pg 1299

Glynn, Jen, Greenleaf Book Group LLC, PO Box 91869, Austin, TX 78709 *Tel:* 512-891-6100 *Fax:* 512-891-6150 *E-mail:* contact@greenleafbookgroup.com; orders@greenleafbookgroup.com; foreignrights@greenleafbookgroup.com; media@greenleafbookgroup.com *Web Site:* greenleafbookgroup.com, pg 1355

Gnass, Jeff, Jeff Gnass Photography™, 3042 Nowell Ave, Juneau, AK 99801-1930 *Tel:* 907-789-2002 *Fax:* 206-577-6419 *E-mail:* office@jeffgnass.com *Web Site:* www.jeffgnass.com, pg 1421

Go, Jonathan, iCAD Inc, 98 Spit Brook Rd, Suite 100, Nashua, NH 03062 *Tel:* 603-882-5200 *Toll Free Tel:* 866-280-2239 *E-mail:* sales@icadmed.com; support@icamed.com *Web Site:* www.icadmed.com, pg 1370

Gochberg, Elise, Spectrum PrintGroup Inc, 1535 Farmer's Lane, Suite 254, Santa Rosa, CA 95405 *Tel:* 707-542-6044 *Toll Free Tel:* 888-340-6049 *Fax:* 707-542-6045 *E-mail:* sales@spectrumprintgroup.com *Web Site:* www.spectrumprintgroup.com, pg 1214, 1260, 1272

Godfrey, Alice, The James & Law Co, 217 W Main St, Clarksburg, WV 26301 *Tel:* 304-624-7401 *Toll Free Tel:* 800-253-5428 *Fax:* 304-624-9331 *E-mail:* sales@jamesandlaw.com *Web Site:* jamesandlaw.com, pg 1317

Goedegebuure, Petra M, Journal of Cuneiform Studies (JCS), James F Strange Ctr, 209 Commerce St, Alexandria, VA 22314 *Tel:* 703-789-9229; 703-789-9230 (pubns) *E-mail:* info@asor.org; publications@asor.org *Web Site:* www.asor.org, pg 1133

Goelman, Ron, Promotional Book Co, 12 Cranfield Rd, No 100, Toronto, ON M4B 3G8, Canada *Tel:* 416-759-2226 *Fax:* 416-759-2150, pg 1320

Goff, Michaela, Casemate | academic, 1950 Lawrence Rd, Havertown, PA 19083 *Tel:* 610-853-9131 *Fax:* 610-853-9146 *E-mail:* info@casemateacademic.com *Web Site:* www.oxbowbooks.com/dbbc, pg 1287

Goff, Michaela, Casemate | IPM, 1950 Lawrence Rd, Havertown, PA 19083 *Tel:* 610-853-9131 *Fax:* 610-853-9146 *E-mail:* casemate@casematepublishers.com *Web Site:* www.casemateipm.com, pg 1288

Goldberg, Beryl, Beryl Goldberg Photographer, 309 W 109 St, Suite 4-F, New York, NY 10025 *Tel:* 212-222-8215 *E-mail:* berylgnyc@gmail.com *Web Site:* berylgoldberg.net, pg 1421

Goldberg, Steven, Bookazine Co Inc, 75 Hook Rd, Bayonne, NJ 07002 *Tel:* 201-339-7777 *Toll Free Tel:* 800-221-8112 *Fax:* 201-339-7778 *E-mail:* info@bookazine.com *Web Site:* www.bookazine.com, pg 1312, 1327

Golden, John, Stephen Gould Corp, 35 S Jefferson Rd, Whippany, NJ 07981 *Tel:* 973-428-1500; 973-428-1510 *E-mail:* info@stephengould.com *Web Site:* www.stephengould.com, pg 1104, 1337

Golden, Justin, Stephen Gould Corp, 35 S Jefferson Rd, Whippany, NJ 07981 *Tel:* 973-428-1500; 973-428-1510 *E-mail:* info@stephengould.com *Web Site:* www.stephengould.com, pg 1104, 1337

Golden, Marcia, DJD/Golden Advertising, 145 W 28 St, 12th fl, New York, NY 10001 *Tel:* 212-366-5033 *Fax:* 212-243-5044 *E-mail:* call@djdgolden.com *Web Site:* www.djdgolden.com, pg 1099

Golden, Michael, Stephen Gould Corp, 35 S Jefferson Rd, Whippany, NJ 07981 *Tel:* 973-428-1500; 973-428-1510 *E-mail:* info@stephengould.com *Web Site:* www.stephengould.com, pg 1104, 1337

Golden, Patrick, Multi-Tech Systems Inc, 2205 Woodale Dr, Mounds View, MN 55112 *Tel:* 763-785-3500 *Toll Free Tel:* 800-328-9717 *Fax:* 763-785-9874 *E-mail:* info@multitech.com; sales@multitech.com; mtsmktg@multitech.com *Web Site:* www.multitech.com, pg 1373

Goldman, Ed, Publishers Book Bindery (NY), 250 W 16 St, 4th fl, New York, NY 10011 *Tel:* 917-497-2950, pg 1213, 1258, 1282

Goldsmith, Richard, The Horah Group, 351 Manville Rd, Suite 105, Pleasantville, NY 10570 *Tel:* 914-495-3200 *Fax:* 914-769-8802 *Web Site:* www.horah.com, pg 1104

Goldstein, Alyosha, American Quarterly, 2715 N Charles St, Baltimore, MD 21218-4363 *Tel:* 410-516-6987 (journal orders outside US & CN) *Toll Free Tel:* 800-548-1784 (journal orders) *Fax:* 410-578-2865 (journal orders) *E-mail:* jrnlcirc@jh.edu (journal orders) *Web Site:* www.americanquarterly.org; www.press.jhu.edu/journals/american-quarterly, pg 1129

Goldstein, Jeff, Coronet Books Inc, 33 Ashley Dr, Schwenksville, PA 19473 *Tel:* 215-925-2762 *Fax:* 215-925-1912 *Web Site:* www.coronetbooks.com, pg 1314

Gomsak, Brian, Gomsak Photography, 10428 S Hall Dr, Charlotte, NC 28270 *Web Site:* www.gomsak.com, pg 1422

Gonnering, Matthew, Widen Enterprises Inc, 6911 Mangrove Lane, Madison, WI 53713 *Tel:* 608-222-1296 *Toll Free Tel:* 800-444-2828 *E-mail:* marketing@widen.com *Web Site:* www.widen.com, pg 1233

Gonzalez, Eduardo, Modern Language Notes (MLN), 2715 N Charles St, Baltimore, MD 21218-4363 *Tel:* 410-516-6987 (journal orders outside US & CN) *Toll Free Tel:* 800-548-1784 (journal orders) *Fax:* 410-578-2865 (journal orders) *E-mail:* jrnlcirc@jh.edu (journal orders) *Web Site:* www.press.jhu.edu/journals/mln, pg 1134

Gonzalez, Gina, Heraeus Noblelight America LLC, 910 Clopper Rd, Gaithersburg, MD 20878-1361 *Tel:* 301-527-2660 *Toll Free Tel:* 888-276-8600 *Fax:* 301-527-2661 *E-mail:* info.hna.uvp@heraeus.com *Web Site:* www.heraeus-noblelight.com/uvamericas, pg 1280

Gonzalez, Marta, The Library Services Centre, 131 Shoemaker St, Kitchener, ON N2E 3B5, Canada *Tel:* 519-746-4420 *Toll Free Tel:* 800-265-3360 (CN only) *Fax:* 519-746-4425 *Web Site:* www.lsc.on.ca, pg 1318

Gonzalez, Neil, Greenleaf Book Group LLC, PO Box 91869, Austin, TX 78709 *Tel:* 512-891-6100 *Fax:* 512-891-6150 *E-mail:* contact@greenleafbookgroup.com; orders@greenleafbookgroup.com; foreignrights@greenleafbookgroup.com; media@greenleafbookgroup.com *Web Site:* greenleafbookgroup.com, pg 1355

Gonzalez, Paola, Penguin Random House Canada, a Penguin Random House company, 320 Front St W, Suite 1400, Toronto, ON M5V 3B6, Canada *Tel:* 416-364-4449 *Toll Free Tel:* 888-523-9292 (cust serv) *Fax:* 416-598-7764 *E-mail:* customerservicescanada@penguinrandomhouse.com; publicitycanada@penguinrandomhouse.com; rightscanada@penguinrandomhouse.com *Web Site:* www.penguinrandomhouse.ca, pg 1299

Goodarzi, Sasan, Intuit Inc, 2700 Coast Ave, Mountain View, CA 94043 *Tel:* 650-944-6000 *Toll Free Tel:* 800-446-8848 *E-mail:* investor_relations@intuit.com *Web Site:* www.intuit.com, pg 1371

Goodman, David, Six Red Marbles LLC, 101 Station Landing, Medford, MA 02155 *Tel:* 857-588-9000 *E-mail:* info@sixredmarbles.com *Web Site:* www.sixredmarbles.com, pg 1231, 1376

Goodman, Noah, International Literary Properties (ILP), 286 Madison Ave, New York, NY 10017 *Tel:* 646-202-1633 *Fax:* 212-967-0977 *E-mail:* contact@ilpliterary.com *Web Site:* www.internationalliteraryproperties.com, pg 1348

Goossen, Chester, PrairieView Press, 625 Seventh St, Gretna, MB R0G 0V0, Canada *Tel:* 204-327-6543 *Toll Free Tel:* 800-477-7377 *Toll Free Fax:* 866-480-0253 *Web Site:* prairieviewpress.com, pg 1229, 1258, 1270, 1282

Gordon, Amy, Bettina Schrewe Literary Scouting, 101 Fifth Ave, Suite 11B, New York, NY 10003 *Tel:* 212-414-2515 *Web Site:* www.bschrewe.com, pg 1351

Gordon, Douglas C, P M Gordon Associates Inc, 2115 Wallace St, Philadelphia, PA 19130 *Tel:* 215-769-2525 *Web Site:* www.pmgordonassociates.com, pg 1355

Gordon, John Jr, Roosevelt Paper Co, One Roosevelt Dr, Mount Laurel, NJ 08054 *Tel:* 856-303-4100 *Toll Free Tel:* 800-523-3470 *Fax:* 856-642-1949 *E-mail:* marketing@rooseveltpaper.com *Web Site:* www.rooseveltpaper.com, pg 1271

Gordon, Lisa, HJMT Public Relations Inc, 3280 Sunrise Hwy, Suite 296, Wantagh, NY 11793 *Tel:* 516-661-2800 *E-mail:* info@hjmt.com *Web Site:* www.hjmt.com, pg 1109

Gordon, Peggy M, P M Gordon Associates Inc, 2115 Wallace St, Philadelphia, PA 19130 *Tel:* 215-769-2525 *Web Site:* www.pmgordonassociates.com, pg 1355

Gordon, Peter, Absolut Color, 109 W 27 St, New York, NY 10001 *Tel:* 212-868-0404 *E-mail:* info@absolutcolor.com *Web Site:* www.absolutcolor.com, pg 1247

Gordon, Susan, Lynne Palmer Executive Recruitment Inc, 295 Madison Ave, Suite 701, New York, NY 10017 *Tel:* 212-883-0203 *Fax:* 212-883-0149 *E-mail:* careers@lpalmer.com *Web Site:* www.lpalmer.com, pg 1381

Gore, Bruce, Gore Studio Inc, 101 Paxton Ct, Brentwood, TN 37027 *Tel:* 615-519-2262 *E-mail:* gorestudioinc@gmail.com *Web Site:* www.gorestudio.com, pg 1414

Gore, Kiran, ICSID Review: Foreign Investment Law Journal, 4000 CentreGreen Way, Suite 310, Cary, NC 27513 *Toll Free Tel:* 800-852-7323 (option 1) *E-mail:* jnls.cust.serv@oup.com *Web Site:* academic.oup.com/icsidreview, pg 1133

Gorham, Kurt, Gorham Printing, 3718 Mahoney Dr, Centralia, WA 98531 *Tel:* 360-623-1323 *Toll Free Tel:* 800-837-0970 *E-mail:* info@gorhamprinting.com *Web Site:* www.gorhamprinting.com, pg 1254

Gorham, Norma, Gorham Printing, 3718 Mahoney Dr, Centralia, WA 98531 *Tel:* 360-623-1323 *Toll Free Tel:* 800-837-0970 *E-mail:* info@gorhamprinting.com *Web Site:* www.gorhamprinting.com, pg 1254

Goroff, Sandra, Sandra Goroff & Associates, 42 Waterfall Dr, Suite L, Canton, MA 02021 *Tel:* 617-750-0555 *E-mail:* sgma@aol.com *Web Site:* www.sandragoroff.com, pg 1109

Gorowsky, John, Symbology Inc, 7351 Kirkwood Lane N, Suite 126, Maple Grove, MN 55369 *Tel:* 763-315-8080 *Toll Free Tel:* 800-328-2612 *Fax:* 763-315-8088 *E-mail:* clientservices@symbology.com; sales@symbology.com *Web Site:* www.symbology.com, pg 1232

Gorsline, Russell, REX, 13431 SW Scotts Bridge Dr, Tigard, OR 97223-1609 *Tel:* 503-238-4525 *E-mail:* info@rexpost.com *Web Site:* www.rexpost.com, pg 1375

Gospodarek, Bob, Baker & Taylor Publisher Services, 30 Amberwood Pkwy, Ashland, OH 44805 *Tel:* 567-215-0030 *Toll Free Tel:* 888-814-0208 *E-mail:* info@btpubservices.com; orders@btpubservices.com *Web Site:* www.btpubservices.com, pg 1286, 1333, 1400, 1412

Gossen, Jeff, Symbology Inc, 7351 Kirkwood Lane N, Suite 126, Maple Grove, MN 55369 *Tel:* 763-315-8080 *Toll Free Tel:* 800-328-2612 *Fax:* 763-315-8088 *E-mail:* clientservices@symbology.com; sales@symbology.com *Web Site:* www.symbology.com, pg 1232

Gottesman, Jan, Spicers Paper, 12310 E Slauson Ave, Santa Fe Springs, CA 90670 *Toll Free Tel:* 800-774-2377 *Fax:* 562-693-8339 *Web Site:* www.spicers.com, pg 1272

Gougherty, Dan, Capitol News Service, 530 Bercut Dr, Suite E, Sacramento, CA 95811 *Tel:* 916-445-6336 *E-mail:* sacramentobulletin@gmail.com *Web Site:* www.mnc.net/capitol.htm, pg 1189

Gould, Donna, Phoenix Media, 29 Miriam Dr, Matawan, NJ 07747 Tel: 732-441-1519 Fax: 732-566-1913 Web Site: www.phoenixmediapr.com, pg 1111

Goullard, Diane, French and English Communication Services LLC, 3104 E Camelback Rd, No 124, Phoenix, AZ 85016-4502 Tel: 602-870-1000 E-mail: RequestFAECS2008@cox.net Web Site: www.FrenchAndEnglish.com, pg 1401

Gow, Val, Penguin Random House Canada, a Penguin Random House company, 320 Front St W, Suite 1400, Toronto, ON M5V 3B6, Canada Tel: 416-364-4449 Toll Free Tel: 888-523-9292 (cust serv) Fax: 416-598-7764 E-mail: customerservicescanada@penguinrandomhouse.com; publicitycanada@penguinrandomhouse.com; rightscanada@penguinrandomhouse.com Web Site: www.penguinrandomhouse.ca, pg 1299

Gowen, George, Ricoh Americas Corp, 300 Eagleview Blvd, Exton, PA 19341 Tel: 610-296-8000 Toll Free Tel: 800-333-2679 (prod support); 800-637-4264 (sales) Web Site: www.ricoh-usa.com, pg 1375

Grab, Alex K, Electronics for Imaging Inc (EFI), 6750 Dumbarton Circle, Fremont, CA 94555 Tel: 650-357-3500 Toll Free Tel: 800-568-1917; 800-875-7117 (sales) Fax: 650-357-3907 E-mail: info@efi.com Web Site: www.efi.com, pg 1368

Graf, Michael, Letterhead Press Inc (LPI), 16800 W Ryerson Rd, New Berlin, WI 53151 Tel: 262-787-1717 Fax: 262-787-1710; 262-787-7315 (estimating) E-mail: contact@letterhead-press.com Web Site: www.letterheadpress.com, pg 1256

Grant, Kyrell, Penguin Random House Canada, a Penguin Random House company, 320 Front St W, Suite 1400, Toronto, ON M5V 3B6, Canada Tel: 416-364-4449 Toll Free Tel: 888-523-9292 (cust serv) Fax: 416-598-7764 E-mail: customerservicescanada@penguinrandomhouse.com; publicitycanada@penguinrandomhouse.com; rightscanada@penguinrandomhouse.com Web Site: www.penguinrandomhouse.ca, pg 1299

Grant, Nathan L, African American Review (AAR), c/o St Louis University, 317 Adorjan Hall, 3800 Lindell Blvd, St Louis, MO 63108 Tel: 314-977-3688 Web Site: afamreview.org, pg 1129

Grant, Patricia, VanDam Inc, The VanDam Bldg, 121 W 27 St, New York, NY 10001 Tel: 917-297-5445 E-mail: info@vandam.com Web Site: www.vandam.com, pg 1358

Grantz, Peter, Crain Communications Inc, 1155 Gratiot Ave, Detroit, MI 48207-2732 Tel: 313-446-6000 Fax: 313-446-0383 E-mail: info@crain.com Web Site: crain.com, pg 1190

Granville, Chris, Longleaf Services Inc, 116 S Boundary St, Chapel Hill, NC 27514-3808 Tel: 919-966-7449 Toll Free Tel: 800-848-6224 Fax: 919-962-2704 (24 hours) Toll Free Fax: 800-272-6817 (24 hours) E-mail: customerservice@longleafservices.org; orders@longleafservices.org Web Site: longleafservices.org, pg 1295

Graves, Mike, Midland Paper, Packaging & Supplies, 101 E Palatine Rd, Wheeling, IL 60090 Tel: 847-777-2700 Toll Free Tel: 800-323-8522; 888-564-3526 (cust serv) Fax: 847-403-6320 (cust serv) E-mail: whl@midlandpaper.com; sales@midlandpaper.com; custservice@midlandpaper.com Web Site: www.midlandpaper.com, pg 1269

Grayson, Fred N, American BookWorks Corp, 309 Florida Hill Rd, Ridgefield, CT 06877 Tel: 203-431-9620 Fax: 203-244-9522 (orders) E-mail: info@abwcorporation.com, pg 1353

Green, Brandy, Electronics for Imaging Inc (EFI), 6750 Dumbarton Circle, Fremont, CA 94555 Tel: 650-357-3500 Toll Free Tel: 800-568-1917; 800-875-7117 (sales) Fax: 650-357-3907 E-mail: info@efi.com Web Site: www.efi.com, pg 1368

Green, Eve, Whitegate Features Syndicate, 71 Faunce Dr, Providence, RI 02906 Tel: 401-274-2149 E-mail: whitegate.featuressyndicate@gmail.com Web Site: www.whitegatefeatures.com, pg 1192

Green, Fran, ALC Inc, 750 College Rd E, Suite 201, Princeton, NJ 08540 Tel: 609-580-2800 Toll Free Tel: 800-252-5478 Fax: 609-580-2888 E-mail: info@alc.com Web Site: www.alc.com, pg 1119

Green, Heidi, Upstart Books™, PO Box 7488, Madison, WI 53707 Tel: 608-241-1201 Toll Free Tel: 800-356-1200 (orders); 800-962-4463 (cust serv) Toll Free Fax: 800-245-1329 (orders) E-mail: custserv@demco.com; order@demco.com Web Site: www.demco.com/upstart, pg 1146, 1323

Green, Joel, L+L Printers, 6200 Yarrow Dr, Carlsbad, CA 92011 Tel: 760-438-3456; 760-477-0321 Fax: 760-929-0853 E-mail: info@llprinters.com Web Site: www.llprinters.com, pg 1256

Green, Michael, AWT World Trade Inc, 4321 N Knox Ave, Chicago, IL 60641-1906 Tel: 773-777-7100 Fax: 773-777-0909 E-mail: sales@awtworldtrade.com Web Site: www.awt-gpi.com, pg 1277

Green, Ted, International Literary Properties (ILP), 286 Madison Ave, New York, NY 10017 Tel: 646-202-1633 Fax: 212-967-0977 E-mail: contact@ilpliterary.com Web Site: www.internationalliteraryproperties.com, pg 1348

Greenawalt, Marc, Publishers Weekly, 49 W 23 St, 9th fl, New York, NY 10010 Tel: 212-377-5500 Fax: 212-377-2733 Web Site: www.publishersweekly.com, pg 1136

Greenberg, Susannah, Susannah Greenberg Public Relations, 41 Old Brook Rd, Dix Hills, NY 11746 Tel: 646-801-7477 E-mail: publicity@bookbuzz.com Web Site: bookbuzz.com; linkedin.com/in/susannahgreenberg; www.facebook.com/SusannahGreenbergPublicRelations; x.com/SueGreenbergPR, pg 1109

Greenblatt, Jonathan, Anti-Defamation League, 605 Third Ave, New York, NY 10158-3560 Tel: 212-885-7700 Web Site: www.adl.org, pg 1145

Greene, Jeremey A, Bulletin of the History of Medicine, 2715 N Charles St, Baltimore, MD 21218-4363 Tel: 410-516-6987 (journal orders outside US & CN) Toll Free Tel: 800-548-1784 (journal orders) Fax: 410-578-2865 (journal orders) E-mail: bhm@jhmi.edu; jrnlcirc@jh.edu (journal orders) Web Site: www.press.jhu.edu/journals/bulletin-history-medicine, pg 1130

Greenhouse, Meredith, Ingram Publisher Services, an Ingram brand, 14 Ingram Blvd, Mail Stop 631, La Vergne, TN 37086 Tel: 615-793-5000 Toll Free Tel: 866-400-5351 (cust serv) E-mail: ips@ingramcontent.com Web Site: www.ingrampublisherservices.com, pg 1294

Greenleaf, Clint, Greenleaf Book Group LLC, PO Box 91869, Austin, TX 78709 Tel: 512-891-6100 Fax: 512-891-6150 E-mail: contact@greenleafbookgroup.com; orders@greenleafbookgroup.com; foreignrights@greenleafbookgroup.com; media@greenleafbookgroup.com Web Site: greenleafbookgroup.com, pg 1292, 1355

Greer, Derrick, Tennessee Book Co, 1550 Heil Quaker Blvd, La Vergne, TN 37086 Tel: 615-793-5040 Toll Free Tel: 800-456-0418 Fax: 615-213-9545 Web Site: www.tennesseebook.com, pg 1322

Gregory, Cam, Bookshelf Bindery Ltd, 22 Secord Dr, Unit 16, St Catharines, ON L2N 1K8, Canada Tel: 905-934-2801 E-mail: bookshelfbindery@bellnet.ca, pg 1249

Griffin, Andrew, Metro Editorial Services, 519 Eighth Ave, New York, NY 10018 Tel: 212-947-5100 (ext 253, outside US & CN) Toll Free Tel: 800-223-1600 E-mail: service@metro-email.com Web Site: www.mcg.metrocreativeconnection.com, pg 1191

Griffin, Kelly, Aquent LLC, 101 W Elm St, Suite 300, Conshohocken, PA 19428-2075 Tel: 610-828-0900 Toll Free Fax: 877-303-5224 E-mail: questions@aquent.com Web Site: aquentstudios.com; aquent.com, pg 1222, 1365, 1381

Griffin, Peter, Essex Products Group, 30 Industrial Park Rd, Centerbrook, CT 06409-0307 Tel: 860-767-7130 Toll Free Tel: 800-394-7130 Fax: 860-767-9137 E-mail: sales@epg-inc.com Web Site: www.epg-inc.com, pg 1279

Griffith, Mike, DCA Inc, 1515 E Pine St, Cushing, OK 74023 Tel: 918-225-0346 Fax: 918-225-1113 E-mail: sales@dcainc.com Web Site: www.dcainc.com, pg 1367

Grima, Tony, Children's Braille Book Club, 88 Saint Stephen St, Boston, MA 02115-4312 Tel: 617-266-6160 Toll Free Tel: 800-548-7323 (cust serv) Fax: 617-437-0456 E-mail: contact@nbp.org Web Site: www.nbp.org, pg 1141

Groschup-Black, Maria, Sunbelt Publications Inc, 664 Marsat Ct, Suite A, Chula Vista, CA 91911 Tel: 619-258-4911 Toll Free Tel: 800-626-6579 (cust serv) Fax: 619-258-4916 E-mail: info@sunbeltpub.com; service@sunbeltpub.com Web Site: sunbeltpublications.com, pg 1322

Groschup-Black, Nichole, Sunbelt Publications Inc, 664 Marsat Ct, Suite A, Chula Vista, CA 91911 Tel: 619-258-4911 Toll Free Tel: 800-626-6579 (cust serv) Fax: 619-258-4916 E-mail: info@sunbeltpub.com; service@sunbeltpub.com Web Site: sunbeltpublications.com, pg 1322

Gross, Gail R, IP Royalty Auditors LLC, 316 Perkins Ave, Oceanside, NY 11572 Tel: 516-503-5985 E-mail: royalty@aol.com Web Site: www.iproyaltyauditors.com, pg 1348

Gross, Judy, Data Conversion Laboratory Inc (DCL), 61-18 190 St, Suite 205, Fresh Meadows, NY 11365 Tel: 718-357-8700 Toll Free Tel: 800-321-2816 (provider problems) E-mail: info@dclab.com Web Site: www.dataconversionlaboratory.com, pg 1224, 1367

Gross, Lisa M, Choice, 575 Main St, Suite 300, Middletown, CT 06457 Tel: 860-347-6933; 847-504-8803 (subns) Toll Free Tel: 844-291-0455 (subns) Fax: 860-346-8586 E-mail: acrlsubscriptions@omeda.com; support@acrlchoice.freshdesk.com Web Site: www.ala.org/acrl-choice; www.choice360.org, pg 1131

Gross, Mark, Data Conversion Laboratory Inc (DCL), 61-18 190 St, Suite 205, Fresh Meadows, NY 11365 Tel: 718-357-8700 Toll Free Tel: 800-321-2816 (provider problems) E-mail: info@dclab.com Web Site: www.dataconversionlaboratory.com, pg 1224, 1367

Gross, Mike, Data Conversion Laboratory Inc (DCL), 61-18 190 St, Suite 205, Fresh Meadows, NY 11365 Tel: 718-357-8700 Toll Free Tel: 800-321-2816 (provider problems) E-mail: info@dclab.com Web Site: www.dataconversionlaboratory.com, pg 1224, 1367

Grossman, David M, David M Grossman Photography, 211 E Seventh St, Brooklyn, NY 11218 Tel: 718-438-5021 E-mail: david@grossmanphotos.com Web Site: www.davidmgrossmanphotos.com, pg 1422

Grossman, Leigh, Swordsmith Productions, PO Box 242, Pomfret, CT 06258 Tel: 860-208-4829 E-mail: information@swordsmith.com Web Site: www.swordsmith.com, pg 1232

Grote, Traci, POD Print, 2012 E Northern St, Wichita, KS 67216 Tel: 316-522-5599 Toll Free Tel: 800-767-6066 E-mail: info@podprint.com Web Site: www.podprint.com, pg 1213, 1229, 1258

Groton, John, Quarto Distribution Services (QDS), 100 Cummings Ctr, Suite 265D, Beverly, MA 01915 Tel: 978-282-9590 E-mail: qds@quarto.com Web Site: www.quartoknows.com/qds, pg 1300

Grove, Jack Stein, J S Grove Photography, 166 Peace Ave, Tavernier, FL 33070 Tel: 305-393-2817 E-mail: grovejack509@gmail.com, pg 1422

Groves, Roberta, ClassicStock.com/Robertstock.com, 4203 Locust St, Philadelphia, PA 19104 Tel: 215-386-6300 Toll Free Tel: 800-786-6300 Toll Free Fax: 800-786-1920 E-mail: sales@classicstock.com; info@classicstock.com; info@robertstock.com Web Site: www.classicstock.com; www.robertstock.com, pg 1427

Gruenberg, Mark, Press Associates Union News Service, 4000 Cathedral Ave NW, No 535B, Washington, DC 20016 Tel: 312-806-4825 E-mail: paiunionnews@gmail.com, pg 1191

Grzybowski, Tracy, Omnipress, 2600 Anderson St, Madison, WI 53704 Tel: 608-246-2600 Toll Free Tel: 800-828-0305 E-mail: justask@omnipress.com Web Site: www.omnipress.com, pg 1213, 1257

Guerin, Eric J, Veritiv™ Corporation, 1000 Abernathy Rd, Bldg 400, Suite 1700, Atlanta, GA 30328 Toll Free Tel: 844-VERITIV (837-4848); 866-714-8303 (packaging cust serv) E-mail: contactus@veritivcorp.com; media@veritivcorp.com Web Site: www.veritivcorp.com, pg 1273

Guerins, Ken, Faherty & Associates Inc, 17548 Redfern Ave, Lake Oswego, OR 97035 Tel: 503-639-3113 Fax: 503-213-6168 E-mail: faherty@fahertybooks.com Web Site: www.fahertybooks.com, pg 1290

Guglielmelli, Rachel, Penguin Random House Canada, a Penguin Random House company, 320 Front St W, Suite 1400, Toronto, ON M5V 3B6, Canada Tel: 416-364-4449 Toll Free Tel: 888-523-9292 (cust serv) Fax: 416-598-7764 E-mail: customerservicescanada@penguinrandomhouse.com; publicitycanada@penguinrandomhouse.com; rightscanada@penguinrandomhouse.com Web Site: www.penguinrandomhouse.ca, pg 1299

Guillespie, Hugh, Montfort Publications, 26 S Saxon Ave, Bay Shore, NY 11706-8993 Tel: 631-665-0726; 631-666-7500 Fax: 631-665-0726 E-mail: info@montfortpublications.com Web Site: www.montfortpublications.com, pg 1319

Gul, Rachel Tarlow, Over the River Public Relations LLC, 116 Gladwin Ave, Leonia, NJ 07605 Tel: 201-503-1321 E-mail: info@otrpr.com Web Site: www.otrpr.com, pg 1111

Gulick, Lisa, Sunbelt Publications Inc, 664 Marsat Ct, Suite A, Chula Vista, CA 91911 Tel: 619-258-4911 Toll Free Tel: 800-626-6579 (cust serv) Fax: 619-258-4916 E-mail: info@sunbeltpub.com; service@sunbeltpub.com Web Site: sunbeltpublications.com, pg 1322

Gullette, Nancy, Creative Direct Marketing Group Inc (CDMG), 1313 Fourth Ave N, Nashville, TN 37208 Tel: 615-814-6633 Web Site: www.cdmginc.com, pg 1345

Gulotta, Renee, Hilsinger-Mendelson West Inc, 115 N Kings Rd, Los Angeles, CA 90048 Tel: 323-931-5335 (text only) E-mail: hmiwest@aol.com Web Site: www.hilsingermendelson.com, pg 1109

Gulotta, Victor, Gulotta Communications Inc, 321 Walnut St, Newton, MA 02460 Tel: 617-630-9286 Fax: 978-733-6162 Web Site: www.booktours.com, pg 1109

Gupta, Margaret, Apex CoVantage, 4045 Sheridan Ave, No 266, Miami Beach, FL 33140 Tel: 703-709-3000 Fax: 703-709-8242 E-mail: info@apexcovantage.com Web Site: www.apexcovantage.com, pg 1221

Gupta, Shalabh, Unisys Corp, 801 Lakeview Dr, Suite 100, Blue Bell, PA 19422 Tel: 215-274-2742 Web Site: www.unisys.com, pg 1378

Gupta, Dr Shashikant, Apex CoVantage, 4045 Sheridan Ave, No 266, Miami Beach, FL 33140 Tel: 703-709-3000 Fax: 703-709-8242 E-mail: info@apexcovantage.com Web Site: www.apexcovantage.com, pg 1221

Gupta, Vishal, Unisys Corp, 801 Lakeview Dr, Suite 100, Blue Bell, PA 19422 Tel: 215-274-2742 Web Site: www.unisys.com, pg 1378

Gurrapu, Srini, Claris International Inc, 5201 Patrick Henry Dr, Santa Clara, CA 95054 Tel: 408-727-8227 (sales & cust support) Toll Free Tel: 800-725-2747 (sales); 800-325-2747 (cust support) Fax: 408-987-7447 E-mail: claris_sales@claris.com Web Site: www.claris.com, pg 1366

Gutierrez, Mark, Social Studies School Service, 10200 Jefferson Blvd, PO Box 802, Culver City, CA 90232 Tel: 310-839-2436 Toll Free Tel: 800-421-4246 (US & CN) Fax: 310-839-2249 Toll Free Fax: 800-944-5432 E-mail: access@socialstudies.com; customerservice@socialstudies.com Web Site: www.socialstudies.com, pg 1302, 1321

Gutmann, Kate, UPS Supply Chain Solutions, 12380 Morris Rd, Alpharetta, GA 30005 Tel: 913-693-6151 (outside US & CN) Toll Free Tel: 800-742-5727 (US & CN) Web Site: www.ups.com/us/en/supplychain/Home.page, pg 1335

Haase, Carlos, Catamount Content LLC, 240 Cummings Rd, Montpelier, VT 05602 Tel: 917-512-1962 E-mail: info@catamountinternational.com Web Site: catamountinternational.com, pg 1288

Hafenbredl, Saul, C Blohm & Associates Inc, 5999 Monona Dr, Monona, WI 53716-3531 Tel: 608-216-7300 E-mail: hello@cblohm.com Web Site: www.cblohm.com, pg 1107

Hagberg, Garry L, Philosophy and Literature, 2715 N Charles St, Baltimore, MD 21218-4363 Tel: 410-516-6987 (journal orders outside US & CN) Toll Free Tel: 800-548-1784 (journal orders) Fax: 410-578-2865 (journal orders) E-mail: philandlit@bard.edu; jrnlcirc@jh.edu (journal orders) Web Site: www.press.jhu.edu/journals/philosophy-and-literature, pg 1135

Hagerty, Mark, Translations.com, 1250 Broadway, 32nd fl, New York, NY 10001 Tel: 212-689-1616 Fax: 212-504-8057 E-mail: newyork@translations.com; info@translations.com Web Site: translations.com, pg 1405

Hahn, David, Media Connect, 1675 Broadway, New York, NY 10019 Tel: 212-715-1600 Web Site: www.media-connect.com, pg 1110

Hale, Chris, CQ Roll Call, 1201 Pennsylvania Ave NW, Suite 600, Washington, DC 20004 Tel: 202-650-6500; 202-650-6511 (subns); 202-650-6621 (cust serv) Toll Free Tel: 800-432-2250; 800-678-8511 (subns) E-mail: customerservice@cqrollcall.com Web Site: cqrollcall.com; www.rollcall.com, pg 1190

Hale, Travis, Independent Publishers Group (IPG), 814 N Franklin St, Chicago, IL 60610 Tel: 312-337-0747 Toll Free Tel: 800-888-4741 (orders) Fax: 312-337-5985 E-mail: frontdesk@ipgbook.com; orders@ipgbook.com Web Site: www.ipgbook.com, pg 1292, 1328

Halkerston, Michelle, Hassett Express, 17W775 Butterfield Rd, Suite 109, Oakbrook Terrace, IL 60181 Tel: 630-530-6515 Fax: 630-530-6538 Web Site: www.hassettexpress.com, pg 1334

Hall, Antonia, Antonia Hall Communications, 9663 Santa Monica Blvd, No 1128, Beverly Hills, CA 90210 Tel: 707-234-9738 E-mail: ahcassociates@gmail.com Web Site: www.antoniahallcommunications.com, pg 1107

Hall, Carson, Distributed Art Publishers Inc, 75 Broad St, Suite 630, New York, NY 10004 Tel: 212-627-1999 Toll Free Tel: 800-338-2665 (cust serv) Fax: 212-627-9484 E-mail: orders@dapinc.com Web Site: www.artbook.com, pg 1290

Hall, Cindy, University of Toronto Press Guidance Centre, 5201 Dufferin St, Toronto, ON M3H 5T8, Canada Tel: 416-667-7791 Toll Free Tel: 800-565-9523 Fax: 416-667-7832 Toll Free Fax: 800-221-9985 E-mail: utpbooks@utpress.utoronto.ca Web Site: www.utpguidancecentre.com, pg 1304

Hall, Martha, Julie A Laitin Enterprises Inc, 160 West End Ave, Suite 23N, New York, NY 10023 Tel: 917-841-8566 E-mail: info@julielaitin.com Web Site: www.julielaitin.com, pg 1100

Hall, Megan Kelley, Kelley & Hall Book Publicity, 5 Briar Lane, Marblehead, MA 01945 Tel: 617-680-1976 Fax: 781-631-5959 Web Site: www.kelleyandhall.com, pg 1110

Hall, Tanya, Greenleaf Book Group LLC, PO Box 91869, Austin, TX 78709 Tel: 512-891-6100 Fax: 512-891-6150 E-mail: contact@greenleafbookgroup.com; orders@greenleafbookgroup.com; foreignrights@greenleafbookgroup.com; media@greenleafbookgroup.com Web Site: greenleafbookgroup.com, pg 1292, 1355

Hallinger, Linda Herr, Herr's Indexing Service, 76-340 Kealoha St, Kailua Kona, HI 96740-2915 Tel: 808-365-4348 Web Site: www.herrsindexing.com, pg 1226

Hamilton, Chris, Chris Hamilton Photography, 704 Battersea Dr, St Augustine, FL 32095 Tel: 404-355-9411 Web Site: www.hamphoto.com, pg 1422

Hamilton, David M, The Live Oak Press LLC, PO Box 60036, Palo Alto, CA 94306-0036 E-mail: info@liveoakpress.com Web Site: www.liveoakpress.com, pg 1349

Hamilton, Doug, Pro Laminators, 1511 Avco Blvd, Sellersburg, IN 47172 Tel: 812-246-0900 Toll Free Tel: 800-357-6812 Fax: 812-246-1900 E-mail: customerservice@prolaminators.com Web Site: prolaminators.com, pg 1258

Hamilton, Duncan, Library Bound Inc, 100 Bathurst Dr, Unit 2, Waterloo, ON N2V 1V6, Canada Tel: 519-885-3233 Toll Free Tel: 800-363-4728 Fax: 519-885-2662 Web Site: www.librarybound.com, pg 1318

Hamilton, Rita, Chris Hamilton Photography, 704 Battersea Dr, St Augustine, FL 32095 Tel: 404-355-9411 Web Site: www.hamphoto.com, pg 1422

Hamilton, Roland, Eric Tyson, 300 W 57 St, 15th fl, New York, NY 10019-5238 Toll Free Tel: 800-708-7311 (FL edit) E-mail: eric@erictyson.com Web Site: www.erictyson.com, pg 1126

Hamlin, Kurt, Frederic Printing, 14701 E 38 Ave, Aurora, CO 80011-1215 Tel: 303-371-7990 Fax: 303-371-7959 Web Site: www.fredericprinting.com, pg 1225, 1253

Hammett, John, Sun Graphics LLC, 1818 Broadway, Parsons, KS 67357 Toll Free Tel: 800-835-0588 Fax: 620-421-2089 E-mail: info@sun-graphics.com Web Site: www.sun-graphics.com, pg 1214, 1231, 1260

Hanebrink, Anton, Intuit Inc, 2700 Coast Ave, Mountain View, CA 94043 Tel: 650-944-6000 Toll Free Tel: 800-446-8848 E-mail: investor_relations@intuit.com Web Site: www.intuit.com, pg 1371

Haney, Mike, Allied Vaughn, 7600 Parklawn Ave, Suite 300, Minneapolis, MN 55435 Tel: 952-832-3100 Toll Free Tel: 800-323-0281 Fax: 952-832-3203 Web Site: www.alliedvaughn.com, pg 1364

Hang, Sherry, Yeck Brothers Co, 2222 Arbor Blvd, Dayton, OH 45439 Tel: 937-294-4000 (ext 207) Toll Free Tel: 800-417-2767 E-mail: direct@yeck.com Web Site: www.yeck.com, pg 1116

Hanger, Nancy C, Windhaven®, 466 Rte 10, Orford, NH 03777 Tel: 603-512-9251 (cell) E-mail: info@windhavenpress.com Web Site: www.windhavenpress.com, pg 1233

Hannigan, Deece, Sappi Fine Paper North America, 255 State St, Boston, MA 02109 Tel: 617-423-7300 Toll Free Tel: 800-882-4332 E-mail: webqueriesna@sappi.com Web Site: www.sappi.com/na, pg 1271

Hansen, Jan, WeWrite LLC, 11040 Alba Rd, Ben Lomond, CA 95005 Tel: 831-336-3382 E-mail: info@wewrite.net Web Site: www.wewrite.net, pg 1323, 1378

Hansen, Jeffrey, Horizon Paper Co Inc, 1010 Washington Blvd, Stamford, CT 06901 Tel: 203-358-0855 Toll Free Tel: 866-358-0855 E-mail: info@horizonpaper.com Web Site: www.horizonpaper.com, pg 1268

Hansen, Lena Torslow, Art Consulting Scandinavia: Books on Art & Architecture, 25777 Punto de Vista Dr, Monte Nido, CA 91302-2155 Tel: 310-456-8762 Fax: 310-456-5714 E-mail: info@nordicartbooks.com Web Site: www.nordicartbooks.com, pg 1311

Hansinger, Mark, OKI Data Americas Inc, 8505 Freeport Pkwy, Suite 600, Irving, TX 75063 Tel: 972-815-4800 Toll Free Tel: 800-OKI-DATA (654-3282) E-mail: support@okidata.com Web Site: www.oki.com/us/printing, pg 1374

Hara, Sheryn, Book Publishers Network, 817 238 St SE, Suite G, Bothell, WA 98021 Tel: 425-483-3040 Fax: 425-483-3098 Web Site: www.bookpublishersnetwork.com, pg 1107

1491

Hardell, Joyce, Ecological Fibers Inc, 40 Pioneer Dr, Lunenburg, MA 01462 Tel: 978-537-0003 Fax: 978-537-2238 E-mail: info@ecofibers.com Web Site: www.ecofibers.com, pg 1210, 1267

Harding, Peter, Lindenmeyr Book Publishing Papers, 3 Manhattanville Rd, Purchase, NY 10577 Tel: 914-696-9300 Web Site: www.lindenmeyrbook.com, pg 1269

Hargest, Scott, Ironmark, 9040 Junction Dr, Annapolis Junction, MD 20701 Toll Free Tel: 888-775-3737 E-mail: marketing@ironmarkusa.com Web Site: ironmarkusa.com, pg 1211, 1227, 1255, 1268, 1281

Harkness, Frances, C & C Offset Printing Co USA Inc, 70 W 36 St, Unit 10C, New York, NY 10018 Tel: 212-431-4210 Toll Free Fax: 866-540-4134 Web Site: www.ccoffset.com, pg 1208, 1223, 1249

Harlan, Jennifer, The New York Times Book Review, 620 Eighth Ave, 5th fl, New York, NY 10018 Tel: 212-556-1234 Toll Free Tel: 800-631-2580 (subns) E-mail: bookreview@nytimes.com; books@nytimes.com Web Site: www.nytimes.com, pg 1135

Harper, Mary, Access Points Indexing, PO Box 1155, Hood River, OR 97031 Tel: 541-806-5436 Web Site: www.accesspointsindexing.com, pg 1221

Harrington, Dr Robert M, American Mathematical Society (AMS), 201 Charles St, Providence, RI 02904-2213 Tel: 401-455-4000 Toll Free Tel: 800-321-4267 Fax: 401-331-3842; 401-455-4046 (cust serv) E-mail: cust-serv@ams.org; ams@ams.org Web Site: www.ams.org, pg 1207, 1221, 1247, 1277

Harris, Debbie, The Crowley Co, 5111 Pegasus Ct, Suite M, Frederick, MD 21704 Tel: 240-215-0224 Fax: 240-215-0234 E-mail: webrequest@thecrowleycompany.com Web Site: www.thecrowleycompany.com, pg 1367

Harris, Mary Ann, Xante Corp, 2800 Dauphin St, Suite 100, Mobile, AL 36606 Tel: 251-473-6502; 251-473-4920 (tech support) Fax: 251-473-6503 Web Site: www.xante.com, pg 1378

Harris, Mike, Getty Images Inc, 605 Fifth Ave S, Suite 400, Seattle, WA 98104 Tel: 206-925-5000 Toll Free Tel: 800-IMAGERY (462-4379); 888-888-5889 Web Site: www.gettyimages.com; www.gettyimages.com/customer-support; engage.gettyimages.com/media-inquiries, pg 1369, 1428

Harrison, Margaret, Ingram Content Group LLC, One Ingram Blvd, La Vergne, TN 37086-1986 Tel: 615-793-5000 Toll Free Tel: 800-937-8000 (retailers); 800-937-5300 (ext 1, libs) E-mail: customerservice@ingramcontent.com Web Site: www.ingramcontent.com, pg 1294, 1316

Harrison, Simon "Ted", Open Text Corp, 275 Frank Tompa Dr, Waterloo, ON N2L 0A1, Canada Tel: 519-888-7111 Fax: 519-888-0677 Web Site: opentext.com, pg 1374

Harrison, Ted, Fontlab Ltd, 403 S Lincoln St, Suite 4-51, Port Angeles, WA 98362 Tel: 301-560-3208 Toll Free Tel: 866-571-5039 E-mail: orders@fontlab.com; contact@fontlab.com Web Site: www.fontlab.com, pg 1369

Harry, Tarek, Elixir Technologies Corp, 1314 E Ojai Ave, Ojai, CA 93023 Tel: 805-641-5900 Fax: 805-648-9151 E-mail: info_us@elixir.com Web Site: www.elixir.com, pg 1368

Hart, Barbara B, Publications Professionals LLC, 3603 Chain Bridge Rd, Suite A & B, Fairfax, VA 22030-3244 Tel: 703-934-4499 Fax: 703-591-7389 E-mail: info@pubspros.com Web Site: www.pubspros.com, pg 1381

Hartford, Charles, Victory Productions Inc, 55 Linden St, Worcester, MA 01609 Tel: 508-755-0051 E-mail: victory@victoryprd.com Web Site: www.victoryprd.com, pg 1358

Hartland, Julia, Penguin Random House Canada, a Penguin Random House company, 320 Front St W, Suite 1400, Toronto, ON M5V 3B6, Canada Tel: 416-364-4449 Toll Free Tel: 888-523-9292 (cust serv) Fax: 416-598-7764 E-mail: customerservicescanada@penguinrandomhouse.com; publicitycanada@penguinrandomhouse.com; rightscanada@penguinrandomhouse.com Web Site: www.penguinrandomhouse.ca, pg 1299

Hartmans, Kathleen, Quality Bindery Services Inc, 501 Amherst St, Buffalo, NY 14207 Tel: 716-883-5185 Toll Free Tel: 888-883-1266 Fax: 716-883-1598 E-mail: info@qualitybindery.com Web Site: www.qualitybindery.com, pg 1259

Hartnett, Kate, GOBI® Library Solutions from EBSCO, 999 Maple St, Contoocook, NH 03229 Tel: 603-746-3102 Toll Free Tel: 800-258-3774 (US & CN) Fax: 603-746-5628 E-mail: information@ebsco.com Web Site: gobi.ebsco.com, pg 1316

Harwood, Josh, Bookazine Co Inc, 75 Hook Rd, Bayonne, NJ 07002 Tel: 201-339-7777 Toll Free Tel: 800-221-8112 Fax: 201-339-7778 E-mail: info@bookazine.com Web Site: www.bookazine.com, pg 1312, 1327

Hasker, Steve, Thomson Reuters, 3 Times Sq, New York, NY 10036 Tel: 646-223-4000; 646-223-6100 (edit); 646-223-6000 (newsroom) Web Site: www.thomsonreuters.com, pg 1191

Hauser, Matt, Translations.com, 1250 Broadway, 32nd fl, New York, NY 10001 Tel: 212-689-1616 Fax: 212-504-8057 E-mail: newyork@translations.com; info@translations.com Web Site: translations.com, pg 1405

Hawkinberry, Jennifer, Chesapeake & Hudson Inc, 27 Jacks Shop Rd, Rochelle, VA 22738 Tel: 301-834-7170 Toll Free Tel: 800-231-4469 E-mail: office@cheshud.com Web Site: www.cheshudinc.com, pg 1289

Hawkins, Lawrence A, Consolidated Printers Inc, 2630 Eighth St, Berkeley, CA 94710 Tel: 510-495-3113 (sales); 510-843-8565 (admin) Web Site: www.consoprinters.com, pg 1209, 1251

Hawkins, Tom, American Journal of Philology, 2715 N Charles St, Baltimore, MD 21218-4363 Tel: 410-516-6987 (journal orders outside US & CN) Toll Free Tel: 800-548-1784 (journal orders) Fax: 410-578-2865 (journal orders) E-mail: jrnlcirc@jh.edu (journal orders) Web Site: www.press.jhu.edu/journals/american-journal-philology, pg 1129

Hawkinson, Lynnette, Holmberg Co Inc, 4155 Berkshire Lane N, Minneapolis, MN 55446-3814 Tel: 763-559-4155 Toll Free Tel: 800-328-5101 E-mail: customerservice@holmberg.com Web Site: www.holmberg.com, pg 1254

Hawley, Merry, eFulfillment Service Inc, 807 Airport Access Rd, Traverse City, MI 49686 Tel: 231-276-5057 Toll Free Tel: 866-922-6783 E-mail: sales@efulfillmentservice.com Web Site: www.efulfillmentservice.com, pg 1333

Haws, Mike, Sappi Fine Paper North America, 255 State St, Boston, MA 02109 Tel: 617-423-7300 Toll Free Tel: 800-882-4332 E-mail: webqueriesna@sappi.com Web Site: www.sappi.com/na, pg 1271

Hayat, Linette, Continental Book Co Inc, 7000 Broadway, Suite 102, Denver, CO 80221-2913 Tel: 303-289-1761 Toll Free Fax: 800-279-1764 E-mail: cbc@continentalbook.com Web Site: www.continentalbook.com, pg 1289, 1314, 1327

Hayes, Trish, The Library Services Centre, 131 Shoemaker St, Kitchener, ON N2E 3B5, Canada Tel: 519-746-4420 Toll Free Tel: 800-265-3360 (CN only) Fax: 519-746-4425 Web Site: www.lsc.on.ca, pg 1318

Haywood, Jack, Pro Laminators, 1511 Avco Blvd, Sellersburg, IN 47172 Tel: 812-246-0900 Toll Free Tel: 800-357-6812 Fax: 812-246-1900 E-mail: customerservice@prolaminators.com Web Site: prolaminators.com, pg 1258

Haywood, Karen, Pro Laminators, 1511 Avco Blvd, Sellersburg, IN 47172 Tel: 812-246-0900 Toll Free Tel: 800-357-6812 Fax: 812-246-1900 E-mail: customerservice@prolaminators.com Web Site: prolaminators.com, pg 1258

Hazaert, Jenna, Impressions Inc, 1050 Westgate Dr, St Paul, MN 55114 Tel: 651-646-1050 Toll Free Tel: 800-251-4285 Fax: 651-646-7228 E-mail: info@i-i.com Web Site: www.i-i.com, pg 1255

Headley, Jennifer, BJU Press, 1430 Wade Hampton Blvd, Greenville, SC 29609-5046 Tel: 864-770-1317; 864-546-4600 Toll Free Tel: 800-845-5731 E-mail: bjupinfo@bjupress.com Web Site: www.bjupress.com, pg 1365

Healy, Michael, Copyright Clearance Center Inc (CCC), 222 Rosewood Dr, Danvers, MA 01923 Tel: 978-750-8400 (sales); 978-646-2600 (cust serv) E-mail: info@copyright.com Web Site: www.copyright.com, pg 1345

Hearley, Randy, JP Graphics Inc, 3001 E Venture Dr, Appleton, WI 54911 Tel: 920-733-4483 Fax: 920-733-1700 E-mail: support@jpinc.com Web Site: www.jpinc.com; www.print.jpinc.com, pg 1211, 1227, 1255

Hebel, Alan Dino, theBookDesigners, 454 Las Gallinas Ave, PMB 2015, San Rafael, CA 94903 Tel: 415-637-9550 E-mail: info@bookdesigners.com Web Site: bookdesigners.com, pg 1412

Hecht, Michael, Graphic Connections Group LLC, 174 Chesterfield Industrial Blvd, Chesterfield, MO 63005 Tel: 636-519-8320 Toll Free Tel: 800-378-0378 Fax: 636-519-8310 Web Site: www.gcfrog.com, pg 1211

Hedquist, Jeffrey P, Hedquist Productions Inc, PO Box 1475, Fairfield, IA 52556 Tel: 641-472-6708 Web Site: www.hedquist.com, pg 1370

Heelan, Peter R, Dunn & Co Inc, 75 Green St, Clinton, MA 01510 Tel: 978-368-8505 Fax: 978-368-7867 E-mail: info@booktrauma.com Web Site: www.booktrauma.com, pg 1210, 1252, 1267

Heffernan, Daniel D, AdvantageCS, 3850 Ranchero Dr, Ann Arbor, MI 48108 Tel: 734-327-3600 Fax: 734-327-3620 E-mail: sales-na@advantagecs.com Web Site: www.advantagecs.com, pg 1363

Heffner, Donna, Forecast, 2550 W Tyvola Rd, Suite 300, Charlotte, NC 28217 Tel: 704-998-3100 Toll Free Tel: 800-775-1800 (info servs); 800-775-1700 (cust serv) Toll Free Fax: 866-557-3396 (cust serv) E-mail: btinfo@baker-taylor.com Web Site: www.baker-taylor.com, pg 1132

Hegranes, Emily, US Naval Institute Photo Archive, 291 Wood Rd, Annapolis, MD 21402 Tel: 410-295-1022 Fax: 410-295-1049 E-mail: photoservice@usni.org; photoarchive@usni.org; research@usni.org Web Site: www.usni.org, pg 1431

Heiberg, Milton, Milton Heiberg Studios, 1022 Empress Lane, Orlando, FL 32825-8249 Tel: 407-658-4869 E-mail: ternmedia@gmail.com Web Site: www.miltonheiberg.com, pg 1422

Heid, Werner, Printronix Inc, 6440 Oak Canyon, Suite 200, Irvine, CA 92618 Tel: 714-368-2300 Toll Free Tel: 800-665-6210 Web Site: www.printronix.com, pg 1375

Heidemann, Eric, Fujii Associates Inc, 75 Sunny Hill Dr, Troy, MO 63379 Tel: 636-528-2546 Fax: 636-600-5153 Web Site: www.fujiiassociates.com, pg 1291

Heidemann, Mark, Historic Films LLC, 211 Third St, Greenport, NY 11944 Tel: 631-477-9700 Toll Free Tel: 800-249-1940 Fax: 631-477-9800 E-mail: info@historicfilms.com Web Site: www.historicfilms.com, pg 1429

Heidt, Eleanor, Whitehots Inc, 205 Industrial Pkwy N, Unit 3, Aurora, ON L4G 4C4, Canada Tel: 905-727-9188 Toll Free Tel: 888-567-9188 Fax: 905-727-8756 Toll Free Fax: 888-563-0020 E-mail: admin@whitehots.com Web Site: www.whitehots.com, pg 1323

Heimann, Alexandra, Bettina Schrewe Literary Scouting, 101 Fifth Ave, Suite 11B, New York, NY 10003 Tel: 212-414-2515 Web Site: www.bschrewe.com, pg 1351

Heimann, Gail, Weber Shandwick, 909 Third Ave, New York, NY 10022 Tel: 212-445-8000 Fax: 212-445-8001 Web Site: www.webershandwick.com, pg 1113

Hein, William S Jr, William S Hein & Co Inc, 2350 N Forest Rd, Suite 10A, Getzville, NY 14068 Tel: 716-882-2600 Toll Free Tel: 800-828-7571 Fax: 716-883-8100 E-mail: mail@wshein.com; marketing@wshein.com; customerservice@wshein.com Web Site: home.heinonline.org, pg 1316

Heiss, Xavier, Xerox Corporation, 201 Merritt 7, Norwalk, CT 06851-1056 *Toll Free Tel:* 800-835-6100 (cust serv) *Web Site:* www.xerox.com, pg 1273

Helgeland, Dale, D&D Sales & Printing, 840 12 St NW, Mason City, IA 50401 *Tel:* 641-423-9487 *Toll Free Tel:* 800-325-5308 *Fax:* 641-423-3068 *E-mail:* ddsales. service@gmail.com *Web Site:* www.ddsalesonline.com, pg 1413

Helgeland, Sue, D&D Sales & Printing, 840 12 St NW, Mason City, IA 50401 *Tel:* 641-423-9487 *Toll Free Tel:* 800-325-5308 *Fax:* 641-423-3068 *E-mail:* ddsales. service@gmail.com *Web Site:* www.ddsalesonline.com, pg 1413

Helman, Terry, Diamond Book Distributors (DBD), 10150 York Rd, Hunt Valley, MD 21030 *Tel:* 443-318-8001; 443-318-8519 (cust serv) *E-mail:* distribution@diamondbookdistributors.com; dbdreorders@diamondbookdistributors.com (orders); books@diamondbookdistributors.com (cust serv) *Web Site:* diamondbookdistributors.com, pg 1290

Helmers, Kathryn A, Creative Trust Inc, 210 Jamestown Park Dr, Suite 200, Brentwood, TN 37027 *Tel:* 615-297-5010 *Fax:* 615-297-5020 *E-mail:* info@creativetrust.com *Web Site:* creativetrust.com, pg 1345

Helton, John, CQ Roll Call, 1201 Pennsylvania Ave NW, Suite 600, Washington, DC 20004 *Tel:* 202-650-6500; 202-650-6511 (subns); 202-650-6621 (cust serv) *Toll Free Tel:* 800-432-2250; 800-678-8511 (subns) *E-mail:* customerservice@cqrollcall.com *Web Site:* cqrollcall.com; www.rollcall.com, pg 1190

Henderson, Bob, Hollinger Metal Edge Inc, 9401 Northeast Dr, Fredricksburg, VA 22408 *Tel:* 540-898-7300 *Toll Free Tel:* 800-634-0491 *Toll Free Fax:* 800-947-8814 *E-mail:* info@hollingermetaledge.com *Web Site:* www.hollingermetaledge.com, pg 1268

Henderson, John, The Bureau, 2354 English St, Maplewood, MN 55109 *Tel:* 612-788-1000; 612-432-3516 (sales) *Toll Free Tel:* 800-788-9536 *Fax:* 612-788-7792 *E-mail:* sales@thebureau.com *Web Site:* www.thebureau.com, pg 1223, 1249

Henderson, Mark, MBS Textbook Exchange Inc, 2711 W Ash, Columbia, MO 65203 *Tel:* 573-445-2243 *Toll Free Tel:* 800-325-0530 (textbook solutions); 800-325-4138 (bookstore systems) *Fax:* 573-446-5256 *E-mail:* cserv@mbsbooks.com *Web Site:* www.mbsbooks.com, pg 1319

Hendra, Barbara J, The Hendra Agency Inc, 142 Sterling Place, Brooklyn, NY 11217-3307 *Tel:* 718-622-3232 *Fax:* 718-622-3322, pg 1109

Hendrick, Rachel, Choice, 575 Main St, Suite 300, Middletown, CT 06457 *Tel:* 860-347-6933; 847-504-8803 (subns) *Toll Free Tel:* 844-291-0455 (subns) *Fax:* 860-346-8586 *E-mail:* acrlsubscriptions@omeda.com; support@acrlchoice.freshdesk.com *Web Site:* www.ala.org/acrl-choice; www.choice360. org, pg 1131

Hendrickson, Amy, TeXnology Inc, 57 Longwood Ave, Brookline, MA 02446 *Tel:* 617-738-8029 *Web Site:* www.texnology.com, pg 1377

Hendrickson, Kevin, Christianbook Inc, 140 Summit St, Peabody, MA 01960-5156 *Tel:* 978-977-5060; 978-977-5000 (intl calls) *Toll Free Tel:* 800-CHRISTIAN (247-4784) *Fax:* 978-977-5010 *E-mail:* customer.service@christianbook.com *Web Site:* www.christianbook.com, pg 1313

Hendrickson, Ray, Christianbook Inc, 140 Summit St, Peabody, MA 01960-5156 *Tel:* 978-977-5060; 978-977-5000 (intl calls) *Toll Free Tel:* 800-CHRISTIAN (247-4784) *Fax:* 978-977-5010 *E-mail:* customer.service@christianbook.com *Web Site:* www.christianbook.com, pg 1313

Henley, Jeffrey O, Oracle America Inc, 500 Oracle Pkwy, Redwood Shores, CA 94065 *Tel:* 650-506-7000 *Toll Free Tel:* 800-392-2999; 800-633-0738 (sales) *Web Site:* www.oracle.com, pg 1374

Hennessy, Paul, Shutterstock Inc, Empire State Bldg, 350 Fifth Ave, 20th fl, New York, NY 10118 *E-mail:* support@shutterstock.com; press@shutterstock.com *Web Site:* www.shutterstock.com, pg 1430

Henning, Robert D, FedEx Ground, 1000 FedEx Dr, Coraopolis, PA 15108 *Tel:* 412-269-1000 *Toll Free Tel:* 800-762-3725 *Web Site:* www.fedex.com, pg 1333

Henrie, Sam, Wheatmark Inc, 2030 E Speedway Blvd, Suite 106, Tucson, AZ 85719 *Tel:* 520-798-0888 *Toll Free Tel:* 888-934-0888 *Fax:* 520-798-3394 *E-mail:* info@wheatmark.com *Web Site:* www.wheatmark.com, pg 1351

Henry, Georgia, Penguin Random House Canada, a Penguin Random House company, 320 Front St W, Suite 1400, Toronto, ON M5V 3B6, Canada *Tel:* 416-364-4449 *Toll Free Tel:* 888-523-9292 (cust serv) *Fax:* 416-598-7764 *E-mail:* customerservicescanada@penguinrandomhouse.com; publicitycanada@penguinrandomhouse.com; rightscanada@penguinrandomhouse.com *Web Site:* www.penguinrandomhouse.ca, pg 1299

Henry, Jay, ProtoView, 7515 NE Ambassador Place, Suite A, Portland, OR 97220 *Tel:* 503-281-9230 *E-mail:* info@protoview.com *Web Site:* www.protoview.com, pg 1146

Henry, Kirti, Penguin Random House Canada, a Penguin Random House company, 320 Front St W, Suite 1400, Toronto, ON M5V 3B6, Canada *Tel:* 416-364-4449 *Toll Free Tel:* 888-523-9292 (cust serv) *Fax:* 416-598-7764 *E-mail:* customerservicescanada@penguinrandomhouse.com; publicitycanada@penguinrandomhouse.com; rightscanada@penguinrandomhouse.com *Web Site:* www.penguinrandomhouse.ca, pg 1299

Henzell, Peter, Marrakech Express Inc, 720 Wesley Ave, No 10, Tarpon Springs, FL 34689 *Tel:* 727-942-2218 *Toll Free Tel:* 800-940-6566 *Fax:* 727-937-4758 *E-mail:* print@marrak.com *Web Site:* www.marrak.com, pg 1212, 1256, 1281

Heppelman, James, PTC, 121 Seaport Blvd, Boston, MA 02210 *Tel:* 781-370-5000 *Fax:* 781-370-6000 *Web Site:* www.ptc.com, pg 1375

Herbig, Dave, Danita Delimont Stock Photography, 4911 Somerset Dr SE, Bellevue, WA 98006 *Tel:* 425-562-1543 *Web Site:* www.danitadelimont.com, pg 1428

Herman, Chacho, San Diego Museum of Art, Balboa Park, 1450 El Prado, San Diego, CA 92112 *Tel:* 619-232-7931 *Web Site:* www.sdmart.org, pg 1321

Herman, Gretchen, Brodart Books & Library Services, 500 Arch St, Williamsport, PA 17701 *Tel:* 570-326-2461 *Toll Free Tel:* 800-233-8467 *Fax:* 570-651-1639 *Toll Free Fax:* 800-999-6799 *E-mail:* support@brodart.com *Web Site:* www.brodartbooks.com, pg 1313

Herman, Gretchen, Brodart Books & Library Services, 500 Arch St, Williamsport, PA 17701 *Tel:* 570-326-2461 *Toll Free Tel:* 800-474-9816 *Fax:* 570-651-1639 *Toll Free Fax:* 800-999-6799 *E-mail:* support@brodart.com *Web Site:* www.brodartbooks.com, pg 1325

Herman, Mark, Mark Herman & Ronnie Apter, Translators, 2222 Westview Dr, Nashville, TN 37212-4123 *Tel:* 615-942-8462 *E-mail:* mnh18@columbia.edu, pg 1401

Hermann, Kathy, Specialist Marketing Services Inc, 777 Terrace Ave, Suite 401, Hasbrouck Heights, NJ 07604 *Tel:* 201-865-5800 *E-mail:* info@sms-inc.com *Web Site:* www.sms-inc.com, pg 1120

Hernandez, Adrianna, Greenleaf Book Group LLC, PO Box 91869, Austin, TX 78709 *Tel:* 512-891-6100 *Fax:* 512-891-6150 *E-mail:* contact@greenleafbookgroup.com; orders@greenleafbookgroup.com; foreignrights@greenleafbookgroup.com; media@greenleafbookgroup.com *Web Site:* greenleafbookgroup.com, pg 1355

Herndon, Rick, Lee Publications, 1100 W Broadway, Louisville, KY 40203 *Tel:* 502-587-6804 *Toll Free Tel:* 800-626-8247 *Fax:* 502-587-6822 *E-mail:* info@leemagicpen.com *Web Site:* www.leemagicpen.com, pg 1256

Heron, Ms Michal, Michal Heron Photography, 3806 Easton St, Sarasota, FL 34238 *E-mail:* michalheronphoto@gmail.com *Web Site:* www.michalheron.com, pg 1422

Herrick, Greg E, Historic Aviation Books, 640 Taft St NE, Minneapolis, MN 55413-2815 *Tel:* 612-206-3200 *Toll Free Tel:* 800-225-5575 *Fax:* 612-877-3160 *E-mail:* info@historicaviation.com; customerservice@historicaviation.com *Web Site:* www.historicaviation.com, pg 1316

Herrin, Ann, MSC Lists, PO Box 32510, Minneapolis, MN 55432 *Tel:* 763-502-8819, pg 1120

Herring, Ellen, Trophy Room Books, PO Box 3041, Agoura, CA 91376 *Tel:* 818-889-2469 *E-mail:* info@trophyroombooks.com *Web Site:* www.trophyroombooks.com, pg 1329

Herring, Jim, Trophy Room Books, PO Box 3041, Agoura, CA 91376 *Tel:* 818-889-2469 *E-mail:* info@trophyroombooks.com *Web Site:* www.trophyroombooks.com, pg 1329

Herrington, Michael P, Comag Marketing Group LLC (CMG), 155 Village Blvd, Suite 300, Princeton, NJ 08540 *Tel:* 609-524-1800 *Fax:* 609-524-1629 *Web Site:* www.i-cmg.com, pg 1314

Herrold, Kelly, Scott Publications Inc, 2145 W Sherman Blvd, Norton Shores, MI 49441 *Tel:* 231-755-2200 *Toll Free Tel:* 866-733-9382 *Fax:* 231-755-1003 *E-mail:* contactus@scottpublications.com *Web Site:* scottpublications.com, pg 1105

Hershberg, Neil, Business Wire, 101 California St, 20th fl, San Francisco, CA 94111 *Tel:* 415-986-4422 *Toll Free Tel:* 800-227-0845 *E-mail:* info@businesswire.com *Web Site:* www.businesswire.com, pg 1189

Hervouet, Hughes, Shutterstock Inc, Empire State Bldg, 350 Fifth Ave, 20th fl, New York, NY 10118 *E-mail:* support@shutterstock.com; press@shutterstock.com *Web Site:* www.shutterstock.com, pg 1430

Herzig, John, Barcode Graphics Inc, 25 Brodie Dr, Unit 5, Richmond Hill, ON L4B 3K7, Canada *Tel:* 905-770-1154 *Toll Free Tel:* 800-263-3669 (orders) *Fax:* 905-787-1575 *E-mail:* info@barcodegraphics.com *Web Site:* www.barcodegraphics.com, pg 1222

Hess, Frank L, Journal of Modern Greek Studies, 2715 N Charles St, Baltimore, MD 21218-4363 *Tel:* 410-516-6987 (journal orders outside US & CN) *Toll Free Tel:* 800-548-1784 (journal orders) *Fax:* 410-578-2865 (journal orders) *E-mail:* jrnlcirc@jh.edu (journal orders) *Web Site:* www.press.jhu.edu/journal-modern-greek-studies, pg 1133

Hettler, Kurt, Ingram Content Group LLC, One Ingram Blvd, La Vergne, TN 37086-1986 *Tel:* 615-793-5000 *Toll Free Tel:* 800-937-8000 (retailers); 800-937-5300 (ext 1, libs) *E-mail:* customerservice@ingramcontent.com *Web Site:* www.ingramcontent.com, pg 1294, 1316

Heyerdahl, Doug, Blanks Printing & Imaging Inc, 2343 N Beckley Ave, Dallas, TX 75208 *Tel:* 214-741-3905 *Toll Free Tel:* 800-325-7651 *E-mail:* sales@blanks.com *Web Site:* www.blanks.com, pg 1222, 1249

Hieber, Adam, Cushing-Malloy Inc, 1350 N Main St, Ann Arbor, MI 48104-1045 *Tel:* 734-663-8554 *Fax:* 734-663-5731 *Web Site:* www.cushing-malloy.com; www.c-mbooks.com, pg 1209, 1251

Hilberer, David, Sheridan Saline, 960 Woodland Dr, Saline, MI 48176 *Tel:* 734-429-5411 *Web Site:* www.sheridan.com, pg 1214, 1260

Hill, Anne, Avery Dennison Corp, 207 N Goode Ave, 6th fl, Glendale, CA 91203-1222 *Tel:* 626-304-2000 *Web Site:* www.averydennison.com, pg 1365

Hill, Jeffrey A, Horizon Paper Co Inc, 1010 Washington Blvd, Stamford, CT 06901 *Tel:* 203-358-0855 *Toll Free Tel:* 866-358-0855 *E-mail:* info@horizonpaper.com *Web Site:* www.horizonpaper.com, pg 1268

Hillard, Samuel L, Glatfelter, Capitol Towers South, 4350 Congress St, Suite 600, Charlotte, NC 28209 *Tel:* 717-850-0170 *Toll Free Tel:* 866-744-7380 *E-mail:* info@glatfelter.com *Web Site:* www.glatfelter.com, pg 1267

Hilsinger, Judy, Hilsinger-Mendelson West Inc, 115 N Kings Rd, Los Angeles, CA 90048 *Tel:* 323-931-5335 (text only) *E-mail:* hmiwest@aol.com *Web Site:* www.hilsingermendelson.com, pg 1109

Hilton, Jeff, Evergreen Engravers, 1819 S Central Ave, Suite 24, Kent, WA 98032 *Tel:* 253-852-6766 *Toll Free Tel:* 800-852-6766 *Fax:* 253-850-3944 *E-mail:* emboss@evergreenengravers.com *Web Site:* www.evergreenengravers.com, pg 1280

Hiltwein, Mark, Cenveo Inc, 200 First Stamford Place, 2nd fl, Stamford, CT 06902 *Tel:* 203-595-3000 *Fax:* 203-595-3070 *E-mail:* info@cenveo.com *Web Site:* www.cenveo.com, pg 1209, 1250, 1265

Hinchcliffe, Max, International Literary Properties (ILP), 286 Madison Ave, New York, NY 10017 *Tel:* 646-202-1633 *Fax:* 212-967-0977 *E-mail:* contact@ilpliterary.com *Web Site:* www.internationalliteraryproperties.com, pg 1348

Hindman, Gene, Drummond, 5664 New Peachtree Rd, Atlanta, GA 30341 *Tel:* 678-597-1050 *Fax:* 678-597-1051 *E-mail:* info@drummond.com *Web Site:* pgc-atl.com, pg 1252

Hirsch, Alan, knk Software LP, 89 Headquarters Plaza N, No 1478, Morristown, NJ 07960 *Tel:* 908-206-4599 *E-mail:* info@knk.com *Web Site:* www.knkpublishingsoftware.com, pg 1348

Hirsch, Emil G, Whitehall Printing Co, 4244 Corporate Sq, Naples, FL 34104 *Tel:* 239-643-6464 *Toll Free Tel:* 800-321-9290 *Fax:* 239-643-6439 *E-mail:* info@whitehallprinting.com *Web Site:* www.whitehallprinting.com, pg 1215, 1233, 1262, 1273

Hirsch, Jeff, Whitehall Printing Co, 4244 Corporate Sq, Naples, FL 34104 *Tel:* 239-643-6464 *Toll Free Tel:* 800-321-9290 *Fax:* 239-643-6439 *E-mail:* info@whitehallprinting.com *Web Site:* www.whitehallprinting.com, pg 1215, 1233, 1262, 1273

Hirsch, Mike, Whitehall Printing Co, 4244 Corporate Sq, Naples, FL 34104 *Tel:* 239-643-6464 *Toll Free Tel:* 800-321-9290 *Fax:* 239-643-6439 *E-mail:* info@whitehallprinting.com *Web Site:* www.whitehallprinting.com, pg 1215, 1233, 1262, 1273

Hirschtick, Jon, PTC, 121 Seaport Blvd, Boston, MA 02210 *Tel:* 781-370-5000 *Fax:* 781-370-6000 *Web Site:* www.ptc.com, pg 1375

Hischar, Mark, Koenig & Bauer (US) Inc, 2555 Regent Blvd, Dallas, TX 75229 *Tel:* 469-532-8000 *Fax:* 469-532-8190 *Web Site:* us.koenig-bauer.com, pg 1281

Hite, Daniel, Arrow Publications Inc, 5270 N Park Place NE, Suite 114, Cedar Rapids, IA 52402 *Tel:* 319-395-7833 *Toll Free Tel:* 877-363-6889 *Fax:* 319-395-7353 *Web Site:* www.frangipane.org; www.arrowbookstore.com, pg 1286

Ho, Edward, OCS America Inc, 195 Anderson Ave, Moonachie, NJ 07074 *Tel:* 201-460-2888 *Toll Free Tel:* 800-367-3405 *E-mail:* info@ocsworld.com *Web Site:* www.ocsworld.com, pg 1329

Ho, Francis, C & C Offset Printing Co USA Inc, 70 W 36 St, Unit 10C, New York, NY 10018 *Tel:* 212-431-4210 *Toll Free Fax:* 866-540-4134 *Web Site:* www.ccoffset.com, pg 1208, 1223, 1249

Hoadley, Katherine, Louis Goldberg Library Book Supplier, 45 Belvidere St, Nazareth, PA 18064 *Tel:* 610-759-9458 *E-mail:* orders@goldberg-books.com *Web Site:* www.goldberg-books.com, pg 1316

Hochman, Joel, Arbor Books, 244 Madison Ave, Box 254, New York, NY 10016 *Tel:* 212-956-0950 *Toll Free Tel:* 877-822-2500 *Fax:* 914-401-9385 *E-mail:* info@arborbooks.com; editorial@arborbooks.net *Web Site:* www.arborbooks.com, pg 1207, 1222, 1248, 1265, 1344, 1353

Hochman, Joel, Arbor Books, 244 Madison Ave, Box 254, New York, NY 10016 *Tel:* 212-956-0950 *Toll Free Tel:* 877-822-2500 *Fax:* 914-401-9385 *E-mail:* info@arborbooks.com; editorial@arborbooks.net *Web Site:* www.arborbooks.com; www.arborghostwriters.com; www.arborservices.com, pg 1411

Hockenbury, Don, Garlich Printing Co, 525 Rudder Rd, St Louis, MO 63026 *Tel:* 636-349-8000 *Toll Free Tel:* 844-449-4752 *Fax:* 636-349-8080 *E-mail:* customerservice@garlich.com *Web Site:* www.garlich.com, pg 1253

Hodge, Barbara, Foreword Reviews, 12935 W Bay Shore Rd, Suite 380, Traverse City, MI 49684 *Tel:* 231-933-3699 *Web Site:* www.forewordreviews.com, pg 1132

Hodge, Camden, AlphaGraphics Inc, 143 Union Blvd, Suite 650, Lakewood, CO 80228 *Toll Free Tel:* 800-955-6246 *Fax:* 801-595-7270 *E-mail:* contactus@alphagraphics.com *Web Site:* www.alphagraphics.com, pg 1364

Hoffman, Scott, International Literary Properties (ILP), 286 Madison Ave, New York, NY 10017 *Tel:* 646-202-1633 *Fax:* 212-967-0977 *E-mail:* contact@ilpliterary.com *Web Site:* www.internationalliteraryproperties.com, pg 1348

Hogan, Bruce M, Mohawk Fine Papers Inc, 465 Saratoga St, Cohoes, NY 12047 *Tel:* 518-237-1740 *Toll Free Tel:* 800-THE-MILL (843-6455) *Fax:* 518-237-7394 *Web Site:* www.mohawkconnects.com, pg 1270

Hogan, Lauren, Franklin & Siegal Associates Inc, 40 Exchange Place, Suite 1703, New York, NY 10005 *Tel:* 212-868-6311 *Web Site:* www.franklinandsiegal.com, pg 1346

Hoge, Kurt, Reno Typographers, 1020 S Rock Blvd, Suite C, Reno, NV 89502 *Tel:* 775-852-8800 *E-mail:* info@renotype.com; work@renotype.com *Web Site:* www.renotype.com, pg 1230

Hoggan, Kathy D, K H Marketing Communications, 16205 NE Sixth St, Bellevue, WA 98008 *Tel:* 425-269-7411 (cell), pg 1110

Hohenshell, John, Sun Graphics LLC, 1818 Broadway, Parsons, KS 67357 *Toll Free Tel:* 800-835-0588 *Fax:* 620-421-2089 *E-mail:* info@sun-graphics.com *Web Site:* www.sun-graphics.com, pg 1214, 1231, 1260

Holcomb, Andy, Fujii Associates Inc, 75 Sunny Hill Dr, Troy, MO 63379 *Tel:* 636-528-2546 *Fax:* 636-600-5153 *Web Site:* www.fujiiassociates.com, pg 1291

Holden, Oliver, knk Software LP, 89 Headquarters Plaza N, No 1478, Morristown, NJ 07960 *Tel:* 908-206-4599 *E-mail:* info@knk.com *Web Site:* www.knkpublishingsoftware.com, pg 1349

Holder, Kelly, MCH Strategic Data, 601 E Marshall St, Sweet Springs, MO 65351 *Toll Free Tel:* 800-776-6373 *E-mail:* sales@mchdata.com *Web Site:* www.mchdata.com, pg 1120

Holeman, Arthur A, Art Holeman Photography, 4156 E Cathedral Rock Dr, Phoenix, AZ 85044 *Tel:* 602-290-7431 (cell) *E-mail:* art@artholeman.com; artholeman@cox.net *Web Site:* www.artholeman.com; www.fineartholeman.com, pg 1422

Holland, Dave, OneTouchPoint, 1225 Walnut Ridge Dr, Hartland, WI 53029 *Tel:* 262-369-6000 *Toll Free Tel:* 800-332-2348 *Fax:* 262-369-5647 *E-mail:* info@1touchpoint.com *Web Site:* www.1touchpoint.com, pg 1105, 1213, 1257, 1374

Hollander, Eli M, Feldheim Publishers, 208 Airport Executive Park, Nanuet, NY 10954 *Tel:* 845-356-2282 *Toll Free Tel:* 800-237-7149 (orders) *Fax:* 845-425-1908 *E-mail:* sales@feldheim.com *Web Site:* www.feldheim.com, pg 1315

Hollenbeck, Cliff, Hollenbeck Productions, 13386 FM 2710, Lindale, TX 75771 *Tel:* 206-444-5314; 206-592-1800 *Web Site:* www.hollenbeckproductions.com; www.cliffscoolstuff.com, pg 1422

Hollenbeck, Nancy, Hollenbeck Productions, 13386 FM 2710, Lindale, TX 75771 *Tel:* 206-444-5314; 206-592-1800 *Web Site:* www.hollenbeckproductions.com; www.cliffscoolstuff.com, pg 1422

Hollinger, Catherine, Conservation Resources International LLC, 7350 Lockport Place, Suite A, Lorton, VA 22079 *Tel:* 703-321-7730 *Toll Free Tel:* 800-634-6932 *Fax:* 703-321-0629 *E-mail:* sales@conservationresources.com *Web Site:* www.conservationresources.com, pg 1266

Hollinger, Lavonia, Conservation Resources International LLC, 7350 Lockport Place, Suite A, Lorton, VA 22079 *Tel:* 703-321-7730 *Toll Free Tel:* 800-634-6932 *Fax:* 703-321-0629 *E-mail:* sales@conservationresources.com *Web Site:* www.conservationresources.com, pg 1266

Hollinger, William K Jr, Conservation Resources International LLC, 7350 Lockport Place, Suite A, Lorton, VA 22079 *Tel:* 703-321-7730 *Toll Free Tel:* 800-634-6932 *Fax:* 703-321-0629 *E-mail:* sales@conservationresources.com *Web Site:* www.conservationresources.com, pg 1266

Holmberg, Steve, The Islander Group, 269 Palii St, Mililani, HI 96789 *Tel:* 808-676-0116 *Toll Free Tel:* 877-828-4852 *Fax:* 808-676-5156 *E-mail:* customerservice@islandergroup.com *Web Site:* www.islandergroup.com, pg 1317, 1328

Holmes, James, ProQuest LLC, part of Clarivate PLC, 789 E Eisenhower Pkwy, Ann Arbor, MI 48108 *Tel:* 734-761-4700 *Toll Free Tel:* 800-521-0600; 877-779-6768 (sales) *E-mail:* sales@proquest.com *Web Site:* www.proquest.com, pg 1375

Holsinger, Bruce, New Literary History, 2715 N Charles St, Baltimore, MD 21218-4363 *Tel:* 410-516-6987 (journal orders outside US & CN) *Toll Free Tel:* 800-548-1784 (journal orders) *Fax:* 410-578-2865 (journal orders) *E-mail:* jrnlcirc@jh.edu (journal orders) *Web Site:* www.press.jhu.edu/journals/new-literary-history, pg 1135

Holzschuh, Douglas, Hess Print Solutions, 3765 Sunnybrook Rd, Brimfield, OH 44240 *Toll Free Tel:* 800-678-1222 *E-mail:* info@hessprintsolutions.com *Web Site:* www.hessprintsolutions.com, pg 1211, 1254

Hooge, Tim, William S Hein & Co Inc, 2350 N Forest Rd, Suite 10A, Getzville, NY 14068 *Tel:* 716-882-2600 *Toll Free Tel:* 800-828-7571 *Fax:* 716-883-8100 *E-mail:* mail@wshein.com; marketing@wshein.com; customerservice@wshein.com *Web Site:* home.heinonline.org, pg 1316

Hoogwerf, Robin, United Library Services Inc, 7140 Fairmount Dr SE, Calgary, AB T2H 0X4, Canada *Tel:* 403-252-4426 *Toll Free Tel:* 888-342-5857 (CN only) *Fax:* 403-258-3426 *Toll Free Fax:* 800-661-2806 (CN only) *E-mail:* info@uls.com *Web Site:* www.uls.com, pg 1323

Hook, Ruth Alden, R & R Book Co LLC, 666 Godwin Ave, Suite 120-C, Midland Park, NJ 07432 *Tel:* 201-337-3400 *Web Site:* www.rrbookcompany.com, pg 1300

Hopkins, Michelle, PTC, 121 Seaport Blvd, Boston, MA 02210 *Tel:* 781-370-5000 *Fax:* 781-370-6000 *Web Site:* www.ptc.com, pg 1375

Hopkins, Tom, Tom Hopkins Studio, 2121 Durham Rd, Madison, CT 06443 *Tel:* 203-350-0530 *Web Site:* www.tomhopkinsstudio.com, pg 1422

Horikawa, Sergio, OKI Data Americas Inc, 8505 Freeport Pkwy, Suite 600, Irving, TX 75063 *Tel:* 972-815-4800 *Toll Free Tel:* 800-OKI-DATA (654-3282) *E-mail:* support@okidata.com *Web Site:* www.oki.com/us/printing, pg 1374

Horowitz, Devoiry, Listco Direct Marketing, 1276 46 St, Brooklyn, NY 11219 *Tel:* 718-871-8400 *Fax:* 718-871-7692 *E-mail:* info@listcodirect.com *Web Site:* www.listcodirect.com, pg 1120

Horowitz, Eileen S, Exhibit Promotions Plus Inc, 11620 Vixens Path, Ellicott City, MD 21042-1539 *Tel:* 410-997-0763 *E-mail:* exhibit@epponline.com *Web Site:* www.epponline.com, pg 1139, 1346

Horowitz, Harve C Esq, Exhibit Promotions Plus Inc, 11620 Vixens Path, Ellicott City, MD 21042-1539 *Tel:* 410-997-0763 *E-mail:* exhibit@epponline.com *Web Site:* www.epponline.com, pg 1139, 1346

Horowitz, Shel, Accurate Writing & More, 16 Barstow Lane, Hadley, MA 01035 *Tel:* 413-586-2388 *Web Site:* www.accuratewriting.com; frugalmarketing.com, pg 1099, 1107, 1343

PERSONNEL INDEX

Hoskin, Christine, Schoolhouse Indexing, 10-B Parade Ground Rd, Etna, NH 03750 *Tel:* 603-359-5826 *Web Site:* schoolhouseindexing.com, pg 1230

Hough, Suzi, Imprint Group, 2070 Cherry St, Denver, CO 80207 *Toll Free Tel:* 800-738-3961 *Toll Free Fax:* 888-867-3869 *Web Site:* imprintgroupwest.com, pg 1292

Houston, Victoria, VKH Media Resources, 122 S Oneida Ave, Rhinelander, WI 54501 *Tel:* 715-499-6800 (cell) *Web Site:* www.victoriahouston.com, pg 1358

Hovsepian, Ronald, SumTotal Systems LLC, 2850 NW 43 St, Suite 150, Gainesville, FL 32606 *Tel:* 352-264-2800 *Toll Free Tel:* 866-933-1416 *Fax:* 352-374-2257 *E-mail:* customersupport@sumtotalsystems.com *Web Site:* www.sumtotalsystems.com, pg 1377

Howard, Carey, OneTouchPoint, 1225 Walnut Ridge Dr, Hartland, WI 53029 *Tel:* 262-369-6000 *Toll Free Tel:* 800-332-2348 *Fax:* 262-369-5647 *E-mail:* info@1touchpoint.com *Web Site:* www.1touchpoint.com, pg 1105, 1213, 1257, 1374

Howard, Mari, Diane Abrams, 71 Faunce Dr, Providence, RI 02906 *Tel:* 401-274-2149 *Web Site:* www.whitegatefeatures.com, pg 1125

Howard, Mari, Adler, Corey, Issac, 71 Faunce Dr, Providence, RI 02906 *Tel:* 401-274-2149 *Web Site:* www.whitegatefeatures.com, pg 1125

Howard, Mari, Jane Adler, 71 Faunce Dr, Providence, RI 02906 *Tel:* 401-274-2149 *Web Site:* www.whitegatefeatures.com, pg 1125

Howard, Mari, Leon Collins, 71 Faunce Dr, Providence, RI 02906 *Tel:* 401-274-2149 *Web Site:* www.whitegatefeatures.com, pg 1125

Howard, Mari, Steve Corey, 71 Faunce Dr, Providence, RI 02906 *Tel:* 401-274-2149 *Web Site:* www.whitegatefeatures.com, pg 1125

Howard, Mari, Carla Demers, 71 Faunce Dr, Providence, RI 02906 *Tel:* 401-274-2149 *Web Site:* www.whitegatefeatures.com, pg 1125

Howard, Mari, Bruce Hoffman, 71 Faunce Dr, Providence, RI 02906 *Tel:* 401-274-2149 *Web Site:* www.whitegatefeatures.com, pg 1125

Howard, Mari, Linda King, 71 Faunce Dr, Providence, RI 02906 *Tel:* 401-274-2149 *Web Site:* www.whitegatefeatures.com, pg 1125

Howard, Mari, Jill Kramer - Best of Books, 71 Faunce Dr, Providence, RI 02906 *Tel:* 401-274-2149 *Web Site:* www.whitegatefeatures.com, pg 1126

Howard, Mari, Ruth & Robert Reld, 71 Faunce Dr, Providence, RI 02906 *Tel:* 401-274-2149 *Web Site:* www.whitegatefeatures.com, pg 1126

Howard, Mari, Matt Stewart, 71 Faunce Dr, Providence, RI 02906 *Tel:* 401-274-2149 *Web Site:* www.whitegatefeatures.com, pg 1126

Howard, Mari, Hope Strong, 71 Faunce Dr, Providence, RI 02906 *Tel:* 401-274-2149 *Web Site:* www.whitegatefeatures.com, pg 1126

Howard, Mari, Whitegate Features Syndicate, 71 Faunce Dr, Providence, RI 02906 *Tel:* 401-274-2149 *E-mail:* whitegate.featuressyndicate@gmail.com *Web Site:* www.whitegatefeatures.com, pg 1192

Howell, Bill, Double Envelope, 7702 Plantation Rd, Roanoke, VA 24019 *Toll Free Tel:* 800-800-9007 *E-mail:* inquire@double-envelope.com *Web Site:* www.double-envelope.com, pg 1104, 1116

Hoxsie, Fred, GHP, 475 Heffernan Dr, West Haven, CT 06516 *Tel:* 203-479-7500 *Fax:* 203-479-7575 *Web Site:* www.ghpmedia.com, pg 1226, 1253

Hreha, Bob, Knepper Press Corp, 2251 Sweeney Dr, Clinton, PA 15026 *Tel:* 724-899-4200 *Fax:* 724-899-1331 *Web Site:* www.knepperpress.com, pg 1212, 1227, 1255

Hsieh, Ryk, Publishers Weekly, 49 W 23 St, 9th fl, New York, NY 10010 *Tel:* 212-377-5500 *Fax:* 212-377-2733 *Web Site:* www.publishersweekly.com, pg 1136

Hu, Huver, Amgraf Inc, 1501 Oak St, Kansas City, MO 64108-1424 *Tel:* 816-474-4797 *Toll Free Tel:* 800-304-4797 (sales & mktg) *Fax:* 816-842-4477 *E-mail:* support@amgraf.com *Web Site:* www.amgraf.com, pg 1364

Hubbard, Greg, Omnipress, 2600 Anderson St, Madison, WI 53704 *Tel:* 608-246-2600 *Toll Free Tel:* 800-828-0305 *E-mail:* justask@omnipress.com *Web Site:* www.omnipress.com, pg 1213, 1257

Hubbard, Thomas K, The Hubbard Co, 612 Clinton St, Defiance, OH 43512 *Tel:* 419-784-4455 *Toll Free Tel:* 888-448-2227 *Web Site:* www.hubbardcompany.com, pg 1316

Hudson, Scott, Worth Higgins & Associates Inc, 8770 Park Central Dr, Richmond, VA 23227-1146 *Tel:* 804-264-2304 *Toll Free Tel:* 800-883-7768 *Fax:* 804-264-5733 *E-mail:* contact@whaprint.com *Web Site:* www.worthhiggins.com, pg 1226, 1254

Huey, Caleb, Creative Direct Marketing Group Inc (CDMG), 1313 Fourth Ave N, Nashville, TN 37208 *Tel:* 615-814-6633 *Web Site:* www.cdmginc.com, pg 1345

Huey, Craig, Creative Direct Marketing Group Inc (CDMG), 1313 Fourth Ave N, Nashville, TN 37208 *Tel:* 615-814-6633 *Web Site:* www.cdmginc.com, pg 1345

Huey, George H H, George H H Huey Photography Inc, 382 W Butterfield Rd, Suite 115, Chino Valley, AZ 86323 *Tel:* 928-308-3460 *Web Site:* www.georgehhhuey.com, pg 1422

Huffaker, Dru, Cedar Fort Inc, 2373 W 700 S, Suite 100, Springville, UT 84663 *Tel:* 801-489-4084 *Toll Free Tel:* 800-SKY-BOOK (759-2665) *E-mail:* marketinginfo@cedarfort.com *Web Site:* cedarfort.com, pg 1327

Hughes, Annette, Midpoint Trade Books, 814 N Franklin St, Suite 100, Chicago, IL 60610 *Tel:* 312-337-0747 *Fax:* 312-337-5985 *E-mail:* orders@ipgbook.com *Web Site:* www.midpointtrade.com, pg 1297

Hughes, Karen, UniNet Imaging Inc, 3232 W El Segundo Blvd, Hawthorne, CA 90250 *Tel:* 424-675-3300 *Fax:* 424-675-3400 *E-mail:* sales@uninetimaging.com *Web Site:* www.uninetimaging.com, pg 1378

Hughes, Tony, The Order Fulfillment Group, 7313 Mayflower Park Dr, Zionsville, IN 46077 *Tel:* 317-733-7755 *Web Site:* www.tofg.com, pg 1334

Huhn, William, Midpoint Trade Books, 814 N Franklin St, Suite 100, Chicago, IL 60610 *Tel:* 312-337-0747 *Fax:* 312-337-5985 *E-mail:* orders@ipgbook.com *Web Site:* www.midpointtrade.com, pg 1297

Hullquist, Timothy, TEACH Services Inc, 11 Quartermaster Circle, Fort Oglethorpe, GA 30742-3886 *Tel:* 706-504-9192 *Toll Free Tel:* 800-367-1844 (sales) *Toll Free Fax:* 866-757-6023 *E-mail:* sales@teachservices.com; info@teachservices.com *Web Site:* www.teachservices.com, pg 1322, 1377

Humrich, Rebecca, Sheridan MI, 613 E Industrial Dr, Chelsea, MI 48118 *Tel:* 734-475-9145 *Web Site:* www.sheridan.com, pg 1213, 1259, 1271

Hunter, Clint, Cedar Fort Inc, 2373 W 700 S, Suite 100, Springville, UT 84663 *Tel:* 801-489-4084 *Toll Free Tel:* 800-SKY-BOOK (759-2665) *E-mail:* marketinginfo@cedarfort.com *Web Site:* cedarfort.com, pg 1327

Hunter, Liz, Lightning Source LLC, 1246 Heil Quaker Blvd, La Vergne, TN 37086 *Tel:* 615-793-5000 (Ingram) *Toll Free Tel:* 800-378-5508; 800-509-4156 (cust serv) *E-mail:* lsicustomersupport@ingramcontent.com; contentacquisitioninquiries@ingramcontent.com *Web Site:* www.ingramcontent.com/publishers/print, pg 1212

Hunter, Liz, Lightning Source LLC, 1246 Heil Quaker Blvd, La Vergne, TN 37086 *Tel:* 615-793-5000 (Ingram) *Toll Free Tel:* 800-378-5508; 800-509-4156 (cust serv) *E-mail:* lsicustomersupport@ingramcontent.com *Web Site:* www.ingramcontent.com/publishers/print, pg 1256, 1371

Hunter, Sarah, Booklist, 225 N Michigan Ave, Suite 1300, Chicago, IL 60601 *Tel:* 312-944-6780 *Toll Free Tel:* 800-545-2433 *Fax:* 312-440-9374 *E-mail:* info@booklistonline.com; ala@ala.org *Web Site:* www.booklistonline.com; www.ala.org, pg 1130

Hurd, Charlie, CLC Ministries, 701 Pennsylvania Ave, Fort Washington, PA 19034 *Tel:* 215-542-1240 *Toll Free Tel:* 800-659-1240 *Fax:* 215-542-7580 *E-mail:* orders@clcpublications.com *Web Site:* www.clcpublications.com, pg 1314

Hurley, Joanna Thorne, HurleyMedia LLC, 1477 Canyon Rd, Santa Fe, NM 87501 *Tel:* 505-603-6392 *Web Site:* www.hurleymedia.com, pg 1109, 1347

Hurley, Michael P, Horizon Paper Co Inc, 1010 Washington Blvd, Stamford, CT 06901 *Tel:* 203-358-0855 *Toll Free Tel:* 866-358-0855 *E-mail:* info@horizonpaper.com *Web Site:* www.horizonpaper.com, pg 1268

Hussey, John, Ingram Content Group LLC, One Ingram Blvd, La Vergne, TN 37086-1986 *Tel:* 615-793-5000 *Toll Free Tel:* 800-937-8000 (retailers); 800-937-5300 (ext 1, libs) *E-mail:* customerservice@ingramcontent.com *Web Site:* www.ingramcontent.com, pg 1294, 1316

Hutcheson, Deborah, Agfa North America, 580 Gotham Pkwy, Carlstadt, NJ 07072 *Tel:* 201-440-2500 *Toll Free Tel:* 888-274-8626 (cust serv) *E-mail:* customercare.us@agfa.com *Web Site:* www.agfa.com/printing/global/usa; www.agfa.com/printing/industrial; www.agfa.com/printing/large-format, pg 1277, 1364

Hutchings, Amy, Richard Hutchings Photography LLC, 11 White Well Dr, Rhinebeck, NY 12572 *Tel:* 914-715-7461 *E-mail:* richard@hutchingsphotography.com *Web Site:* hutchingsphotography.com, pg 1422

Hutchings, Richard, Richard Hutchings Photography LLC, 11 White Well Dr, Rhinebeck, NY 12572 *Tel:* 914-715-7461 *E-mail:* richard@hutchingsphotography.com *Web Site:* hutchingsphotography.com, pg 1422

Hutchison, Chris, The P A Hutchison Co, 400 Penn Ave, Mayfield, PA 18433 *Tel:* 570-876-4560 *Toll Free Tel:* 800-USA-PRNT (872-7768) *Fax:* 570-876-4561 *E-mail:* sales@pahutch.com *Web Site:* www.pahutch.com, pg 1211, 1226, 1254, 1268, 1280

Hutchison, Roger, CD ROM Inc, 3131 E Riverside Dr, Fort Myers, FL 33916 *Tel:* 239-332-2800 *Toll Free Tel:* 866-66-CDROM (662-3766) *E-mail:* info@cdrominc.com *Web Site:* www.cdrominc.com, pg 1366

Hutto, Eric, Unisys Corp, 801 Lakeview Dr, Suite 100, Blue Bell, PA 19422 *Tel:* 215-274-2742 *Web Site:* www.unisys.com, pg 1378

Hynes, Johanna, Ingram Publisher Services, an Ingram brand, 14 Ingram Blvd, Mail Stop 631, La Vergne, TN 37086 *Tel:* 615-793-5000 *Toll Free Tel:* 866-400-5351 (cust serv) *E-mail:* ips@ingramcontent.com *Web Site:* www.ingrampublisherservices.com, pg 1294

Hyzy, Karen, Chicago Distribution Center (CDC), 11030 S Langley Ave, Chicago, IL 60628 *Tel:* 773-702-7010 *Toll Free Fax:* 800-621-8476 *Web Site:* press.uchicago.edu/cdc, pg 1289

Iannantuono, Albert, Tri-Media Integrated Marketing Technologies Inc, 1027 Pelham St, Unit 2, Fonthill, ON L0S 1E0, Canada *E-mail:* think@tri-media.com *Web Site:* tri-media.com, pg 1100

Iarrera, Linda, Penguin Random House Canada, a Penguin Random House company, 320 Front St W, Suite 1400, Toronto, ON M5V 3B6, Canada *Tel:* 416-364-4449 *Toll Free Tel:* 888-523-9292 (cust serv) *Fax:* 416-598-7764 *E-mail:* customerservicescanada@penguinrandomhouse.com; publicitycanada@penguinrandomhouse.com; rightscanada@penguinrandomhouse.com *Web Site:* www.penguinrandomhouse.ca, pg 1299

Ibrahim, Gulshan, Crescent Imports, PO Box 721, Union City, CA 94587 *Tel:* 734-665-3492 *Toll Free Tel:* 800-521-9744 *Fax:* 734-677-1717 *E-mail:* message@crescentimports.com *Web Site:* crescentimports.com; crescentimports.store, pg 1314

Ibrahim, Gulshan, Crescent Imports, PO Box 721, Union City, CA 94587 *Tel:* 734-665-3492 *Toll Free Tel:* 800-521-9744 *Fax:* 734-677-1717 *E-mail:* message@crescentimports.com *Web Site:* crescentimports.store; crescentimports.com, pg 1327

Ibrahim, Sabir, Crescent Imports, PO Box 721, Union City, CA 94587 *Tel:* 734-665-3492 *Toll Free Tel:* 800-521-9744 *Fax:* 734-677-1717 *E-mail:* message@crescentimports.com *Web Site:* crescentimports.com; crescentimports.store, pg 1314

Ibrahim, Sabir, Crescent Imports, PO Box 721, Union City, CA 94587 *Tel:* 734-665-3492 *Toll Free Tel:* 800-521-9744 *Fax:* 734-677-1717 *E-mail:* message@crescentimports.com *Web Site:* crescentimports.store; crescentimports.com, pg 1327

Ilse, Paul, Follett School Solutions Inc, 1340 Ridgeview Dr, McHenry, IL 60050 *Tel:* 815-759-1700 *Toll Free Tel:* 888-511-5114 (cust serv); 877-899-8550 (sales) *Fax:* 815-759-9831 *Toll Free Fax:* 800-852-5458 *E-mail:* info@follettlearning.com; customerservice@follett.com *Web Site:* www.follettlearning.com; www.follett.com/prek12; www.titlewave.com, pg 1291, 1369

Ingle, Stephen, WordCo Indexing Services Inc, 66 Franklin St, Norwich, CT 06360 *E-mail:* office@wordco.com *Web Site:* www.wordco.com, pg 1233

Ingram, John, Ingram Content Group LLC, One Ingram Blvd, La Vergne, TN 37086-1986 *Tel:* 615-793-5000 *Toll Free Tel:* 800-937-8000 (retailers); 800-937-5300 (ext 1, libs) *E-mail:* customerservice@ingramcontent.com *Web Site:* www.ingramcontent.com, pg 1294, 1316

Ingram, Ken, SCREEN Americas, 5110 Tollview Dr, Rolling Meadows, IL 60008-3715 *Tel:* 847-870-7400 *Toll Free Tel:* 800-372-7737 *E-mail:* info@screenamericas.com *Web Site:* www.screenamericas.com, pg 1283, 1376

Ings, Kim, Stephen Gould Corp, 35 S Jefferson Rd, Whippany, NJ 07981 *Tel:* 973-428-1500; 973-428-1510 *E-mail:* info@stephengould.com *Web Site:* www.stephengould.com, pg 1104, 1337

Inkles, Anita, Cross Country Computer Corp, 250 Carleton Ave, East Islip, NY 11730-1240 *Tel:* 631-334-1810 *E-mail:* inquiry@crosscountrycomputer.com *Web Site:* www.crosscountrycomputer.com, pg 1119

Inman, Brad, Inman, 1400 Village Square Blvd, Suite 3-80368, Tallahassee, FL 32312 *Tel:* 510-658-9252 *Toll Free Tel:* 800-775-4662 (cust support) *E-mail:* customerservice@inman.com *Web Site:* www.inman.com, pg 1190

Inwood, Qassye "Q", Independent Publishers Group (IPG), 814 N Franklin St, Chicago, IL 60610 *Tel:* 312-337-0747 *Toll Free Tel:* 800-888-4741 (orders) *Fax:* 312-337-5985 *E-mail:* frontdesk@ipgbook.com; orders@ipgbook.com *Web Site:* www.ipgbook.com, pg 1292, 1328

Ireland, Jay, Bradley Ireland Productions, c/o Sea Save Foundation, 20540 Pacific Coast Hwy, Malibu, CA 90265, pg 1420

Isaac, Ed, Diane Abrams, 71 Faunce Dr, Providence, RI 02906 *Tel:* 401-274-2149 *Web Site:* www.whitegatefeatures.com, pg 1125

Isaac, Ed, Adler, Corey, Issac, 71 Faunce Dr, Providence, RI 02906 *Tel:* 401-274-2149 *Web Site:* www.whitegatefeatures.com, pg 1125

Isaac, Ed, Jane Adler, 71 Faunce Dr, Providence, RI 02906 *Tel:* 401-274-2149 *Web Site:* www.whitegatefeatures.com, pg 1125

Isaac, Ed, Leon Collins, 71 Faunce Dr, Providence, RI 02906 *Tel:* 401-274-2149 *Web Site:* www.whitegatefeatures.com, pg 1125

Isaac, Ed, Steve Corey, 71 Faunce Dr, Providence, RI 02906 *Tel:* 401-274-2149 *Web Site:* www.whitegatefeatures.com, pg 1125

Isaac, Ed, Carla Demers, 71 Faunce Dr, Providence, RI 02906 *Tel:* 401-274-2149 *Web Site:* www.whitegatefeatures.com, pg 1125

Isaac, Ed, Bruce Hoffman, 71 Faunce Dr, Providence, RI 02906 *Tel:* 401-274-2149 *Web Site:* www.whitegatefeatures.com, pg 1125

Isaac, Ed, Linda King, 71 Faunce Dr, Providence, RI 02906 *Tel:* 401-274-2149 *Web Site:* www.whitegatefeatures.com, pg 1125

Isaac, Ed, Jill Kramer - Best of Books, 71 Faunce Dr, Providence, RI 02906 *Tel:* 401-274-2149 *Web Site:* www.whitegatefeatures.com, pg 1126

Isaac, Ed, Ruth & Robert Reld, 71 Faunce Dr, Providence, RI 02906 *Tel:* 401-274-2149 *Web Site:* www.whitegatefeatures.com, pg 1126

Isaac, Ed, Matt Stewart, 71 Faunce Dr, Providence, RI 02906 *Tel:* 401-274-2149 *Web Site:* www.whitegatefeatures.com, pg 1126

Isaac, Ed, Hope Strong, 71 Faunce Dr, Providence, RI 02906 *Tel:* 401-274-2149 *Web Site:* www.whitegatefeatures.com, pg 1126

Isaac, Ed, Whitegate Features Syndicate, 71 Faunce Dr, Providence, RI 02906 *Tel:* 401-274-2149 *E-mail:* whitegate.featuressyndicate@gmail.com *Web Site:* www.whitegatefeatures.com, pg 1192

Isaacs, Patricia, Patti Isaacs Maps, Infographics, Writing, 13720 Paragon Ave N, Stillwater, MN 55082 *Tel:* 651-430-8127 *Web Site:* patti-isaacs.com, pg 1415

Isaacs, Suzanne T, Ampersand Inc/Professional Publishing Services, 515 Madison St, New Orleans, LA 70116 *Tel:* 312-280-8905 *Fax:* 312-944-1582 *E-mail:* info@ampersandworks.com *Web Site:* www.ampersandworks.com, pg 1343

Ishatmananda, Swami, Vedanta Book Center, 14630 S Lemont Rd, Homer Glen, IL 60491 *Tel:* 708-301-9062 *Fax:* 708-301-9063 *E-mail:* info@chicagovedanta.org *Web Site:* www.vedantabooks.com, pg 1323, 1329

Ishiwata, Shuichi, Citizen Systems America Corp, 363 Van Ness Way, Suite 404, Torrance, CA 90501 *Tel:* 310-781-1460 *Toll Free Tel:* 800-421-6516 *Web Site:* www.citizen-systems.com, pg 1366

Ishizuka, Kathy, School Library Journal, 123 William St, Suite 802, New York, NY 10038 *Tel:* 646-380-0752 *Toll Free Tel:* 800-595-1066 *Fax:* 646-380-0756 *E-mail:* sljsubs@mediasourceinc.com; sljsubs@pcspublink.com *Web Site:* www.slj.com; www.facebook.com/schoollibraryjournal; x.com/sljournal, pg 1136

Iverson, Bruce, Iverson Science Photos, 31 Boss Ave, Portsmouth, NH 03801 *Tel:* 603-433-8484 *Fax:* 603-433-8484 *E-mail:* iversonarts@gmail.com, pg 1423

Iwanicki, Jennifer, PadillaCRT, 1101 W River Pkwy, Suite 400, Minneapolis, MN 55415 *Tel:* 612-455-1700 *Fax:* 612-455-1060 *Web Site:* www.padillacrt.com, pg 1111

Iwasutiak, Adria, Penguin Random House Canada, a Penguin Random House company, 320 Front St W, Suite 1400, Toronto, ON M5V 3B6, Canada *Tel:* 416-364-4449 *Toll Free Tel:* 888-523-9292 (cust serv) *Fax:* 416-598-7764 *E-mail:* customerservicescanada@penguinrandomhouse.com; publicitycanada@penguinrandomhouse.com; rightscanada@penguinrandomhouse.com *Web Site:* www.penguinrandomhouse.ca, pg 1299

Iyer, Karthik, Claritas LLC, 8044 Montgomery Rd, Suite 455, Cincinnati, OH 45236 *Toll Free Tel:* 888-981-0040 *E-mail:* findcustomers@claritas.com; marketing@claritas.com *Web Site:* www.claritas.com, pg 1366

Izold, Don, Graphics International, 20475 Bunker Hill Dr, Cleveland, OH 44126 *Tel:* 440-333-9988, pg 1414

Jacik, Donna, Beijing Book Co Inc, 701 E Linden Ave, Linden, NJ 07036 *Tel:* 908-862-0909 *Fax:* 908-862-4201 *E-mail:* journals@cnpbbci.com, pg 1312, 1327

Jackel, Michael, Brunswick Books, 14 Afton Ave, Toronto, ON M6J 1R7, Canada *Tel:* 416-703-3598 *Fax:* 416-703-6561 *E-mail:* info@brunswickbooks.ca; orders@brunswickbooks.ca *Web Site:* brunswickbooks.ca, pg 1287

Jackson, Jeanne-Marie, English Literary History (ELH), 2715 N Charles St, Baltimore, MD 21218-4363 *Tel:* 410-516-6987 (journal orders outside US & CN) *Toll Free Tel:* 800-548-1784 (journal orders) *Fax:* 410-578-2865 (journal orders) *E-mail:* jrnlcirc@jh.edu (journal orders) *Web Site:* www.press.jhu.edu/journals/elh, pg 1131

Jackson, Larry S, Heidelberg Graphics, 2 Stansbury Ct, Chico, CA 95928 *Tel:* 530-342-6582 *Fax:* 530-342-6582 *E-mail:* heidelberggraphics@gmail.com; service@heidelberggraphics.com *Web Site:* www.heidelberggraphics.com, pg 1226, 1254, 1280, 1347, 1370, 1414

Jackson, Lisa, Apple Inc, One Apple Park Way, Cupertino, CA 95014 *Tel:* 408-996-1010 *Web Site:* www.apple.com, pg 1364

Jacobs, John, C J Traders Inc, 555 Second Ave, Suite C700, Collegeville, PA 19426 *Tel:* 484-902-8057 *Fax:* 484-902-8093 *E-mail:* cjtraders714@gmail.com, pg 1313

Jacobs, Michael, Michael Jacobs Photojournalism (MJP), 2105 Vista Oeste NW, Suite 3, No 2057, Albuquerque, NM 87120 *Tel:* 323-461-0240 *Toll Free Fax:* 866-563-9212 *E-mail:* michael.mjphoto@gmail.com *Web Site:* www.mjphotogallery.com, pg 1423, 1429

Jacobsen, Bruce F, Bridgeport National Bindery Inc, 662 Silver St, Agawam, MA 01001 *Tel:* 413-789-1981 *Toll Free Tel:* 800-223-5083 *E-mail:* info@bnbindery.com *Web Site:* www.bnbindery.com, pg 1249, 1325

Jacobson, Kyle, Monotype Imaging Inc, 600 Unicorn Park Dr, Woburn, MA 01801 *Tel:* 781-970-6000 *Web Site:* www.monotype.com, pg 1373

Jaffe, Gary, The Booksource Inc, 1230 Macklind Ave, St Louis, MO 63110 *Tel:* 314-647-0600 *Toll Free Tel:* 800-444-0435 *Fax:* 314-647-6850 *Toll Free Fax:* 800-647-1923 *E-mail:* service@booksource.com *Web Site:* www.booksource.com, pg 1312

Jaffe, Neil, The Booksource Inc, 1230 Macklind Ave, St Louis, MO 63110 *Tel:* 314-647-0600 *Toll Free Tel:* 800-444-0435 *Fax:* 314-647-6850 *Toll Free Fax:* 800-647-1923 *E-mail:* service@booksource.com *Web Site:* www.booksource.com, pg 1312

Jahromi, Neima, The New York Times Book Review, 620 Eighth Ave, 5th fl, New York, NY 10018 *Tel:* 212-556-1234 *Toll Free Tel:* 800-631-2580 (subns) *E-mail:* bookreview@nytimes.com; books@nytimes.com *Web Site:* www.nytimes.com, pg 1135

James, Gary, QualityLogic Inc, 9576 W Emerald St, Boise, ID 83704 *Tel:* 208-424-1905 *E-mail:* info@qualitylogic.com *Web Site:* www.qualitylogic.com, pg 1375

James, Kerrick, Kerrick James Photography, 235 N 22 Place, Unit 560, Mesa, AZ 85213 *Tel:* 602-276-3111 *Web Site:* www.kerrickjames.com; www.agpix.com/kerrickjames, pg 1423

Jamieson, David, Open Text Corp, 275 Frank Tompa Dr, Waterloo, ON N2L 0A1, Canada *Tel:* 519-888-7111 *Fax:* 519-888-0677 *Web Site:* opentext.com, pg 1374

Janezich, Marnie, The John Roberts Company, 9687 East River Rd NW, Minneapolis, MN 55433 *Tel:* 763-755-5500 *Toll Free Tel:* 800-551-1534 *Fax:* 763-755-0394 *E-mail:* success@johnroberts.com *Web Site:* www.johnroberts.com; www.facebook.com/TheJohnRobertsCompany, pg 1105

Janosi, Nick, Data Reproductions Corp, 4545 Glenmeade Lane, Auburn Hills, MI 48326 *Tel:* 248-371-3700 *Toll Free Tel:* 800-242-3114 *Fax:* 248-371-3710 *Web Site:* datarepro.com, pg 1209, 1251

Janulewicz, Tony, Roosevelt Paper Co, One Roosevelt Dr, Mount Laurel, NJ 08054 *Tel:* 856-303-4100 *Toll Free Tel:* 800-523-3470 *Fax:* 856-642-1949 *E-mail:* marketing@rooseveltpaper.com *Web Site:* www.rooseveltpaper.com, pg 1271

Janus, Rev Mark-David PhD, Paulist Press, 997 Macarthur Blvd, Mahwah, NJ 07430-9990 *Tel:* 201-825-7300 *Toll Free Tel:* 800-218-1903 *Fax:* 201-825-6921 *E-mail:* info@paulistpress.com; publicity@paulistpress.com *Web Site:* www.paulistpress.com, pg 1320, 1374

PERSONNEL INDEX

Jay, Erin Flynn, Flynn Media, 1233 Fitzwater St, Philadelphia, PA 19147 *Tel:* 215-772-3048 *Web Site:* www.flynnmedia.com, pg 1109

Jenkins, A Diehl, Pratt Paper Company LLC, 20 Davis Rd, Marblehead, MA 01945 *Tel:* 781-639-9450 *Fax:* 781-639-9452, pg 1270

Jenkins, Bobby, SumTotal Systems LLC, 2850 NW 43 St, Suite 150, Gainesville, FL 32606 *Tel:* 352-264-2800 *Toll Free Tel:* 866-933-1416 *Fax:* 352-374-2257 *E-mail:* customersupport@sumtotalsystems.com *Web Site:* www.sumtotalsystems.com, pg 1377

Jenkins, Jerrold R, Jenkins Group Inc, 1129 Woodmere Ave, Suite B, Traverse City, MI 49686 *Tel:* 231-933-0445; 213-883-5365 *E-mail:* info@jenkinsgroupinc.com *Web Site:* www.jenkinsgroupinc.com, pg 1227, 1348, 1355

Jenkins, John III, Decode, Inc, 1938 11 Ave E, Seattle, WA 98102 *Tel:* 206-343-9101 *E-mail:* books@decodebooks.com *Web Site:* www.decodeinc.com; www.decodebooks.com, pg 1413

Jenkins, Joyce, Poetry Flash, 1450 Fourth St, Suite 4, Berkeley, CA 94710 *Tel:* 510-525-5476 *Web Site:* www.poetryflash.org, pg 1135

Jenkins, Ralph, Mark Andy Inc, 18081 Chesterfield Airport Rd, Chesterfield, MO 63005 *Tel:* 636-532-4433 *Toll Free Tel:* 800-447-1231 *Toll Free Fax:* 800-447-1231 *Web Site:* www.presstek.com; markandy.com; shop.markandy.com, pg 1364

Jennette, Alyssa, Stonesong, 270 W 39 St, Suite 201, New York, NY 10018 *Tel:* 212-929-4600 *E-mail:* editors@stonesong.com *Web Site:* www.stonesong.com, pg 1357

Jensen, Bruce, TotalWorks™ Inc, 420 W Huron St, Chicago, IL 60654 *Tel:* 773-489-4313 *E-mail:* production@totalworks.net *Web Site:* www.totalworks.net, pg 1232, 1261

Jensen, Christine, Burmar Technical Corp, 106 Ransom Ave, Sea Cliff, NY 11579 *Tel:* 516-484-6000 *Fax:* 516-484-6356 *Web Site:* burmar.net, pg 1223, 1365, 1412

Jensen, Janine, Chesapeake & Hudson Inc, 27 Jacks Shop Rd, Rochelle, VA 22738 *Tel:* 301-834-7170 *Toll Free Tel:* 800-231-4469 *E-mail:* office@cheshud.com *Web Site:* www.cheshudinc.com, pg 1288

Jensen, Michael Jon, Westchester Publishing Services, 4 Old Newtown Rd, Danbury, CT 06810 *Tel:* 203-791-0080 *Fax:* 203-791-9286 *E-mail:* info@westchesterpubsvcs.com *Web Site:* www.westchesterpublishingservices.com, pg 1233

Jernigan, Ms S A "Sam", Renaissance Consultations, PO Box 561, Auburn, CA 95604 *Tel:* 530-362-1339 *E-mail:* info@marketingandpr.com *Web Site:* www.MarketingAndPR.com, pg 1112

Jesse, Joanne, Cape Cod Compositors Inc, 811 Washington St, Suite 2, Pembroke, MA 02359-2333 *Tel:* 781-826-2100, pg 1223

Jessen, Dale C, Computer Analytics Corp, 999 E Touhy Ave, Suite 130, Des Plaines, IL 60018-2736 *Tel:* 847-297-5290 *Fax:* 847-297-8680 *Web Site:* www.cacorp.com, pg 1366

Jewett, Brad, Corel Corporation, 1600 Carling Ave, Ottawa, ON K1Z 8R7, Canada *Toll Free Tel:* 877-582-6735 *Web Site:* www.corel.com, pg 1366

Jobson, Leslie, Ingram Publisher Services, an Ingram brand, One Ingram Blvd, Mail Stop 631, La Vergne, TN 37086 *Tel:* 615-793-5000 *Toll Free Tel:* 866-400-5351 (cust serv) *E-mail:* ips@ingramcontent.com *Web Site:* www.ingrampublisherservices.com, pg 1295

Joesel, Kevin, Heraeus Noblelight America LLC, 910 Clopper Rd, Gaithersburg, MD 20878-1361 *Tel:* 301-527-2660 *Toll Free Tel:* 888-276-8600 *Fax:* 301-527-2661 *E-mail:* info.hna.uvp@heraeus.com *Web Site:* www.heraeus-noblelight.com/uvamericas, pg 1280

Johansson, Kay, Gracenote, a Nielsen Company, 2000 Powell St, Suite 1500, Emeryville, CA 94608 *Tel:* 510-428-7200 *Web Site:* www.gracenote.com, pg 1190

Johnson, Bennie F, AIGA, the professional association for design, 228 Park Ave S, Suite 58603, New York, NY 10003 *Tel:* 212-807-1990 *E-mail:* general@aiga.org *Web Site:* www.aiga.org, pg 1139

Johnson, Bert, Graphics Two, 819 S Main St, Burbank, CA 91506 *Tel:* 818-841-4922, pg 1226, 1280

Johnson, Christopher C, Camerique Inc International, 164 Regency Dr, Eagleville, PA 19403 *Tel:* 610-272-4000 *Fax:* 610-272-4000 (call or e-mail first) *E-mail:* info@camerique.com *Web Site:* www.camerique.com, pg 1427

Johnson, Connie, Double Play, 303 Hillcrest Rd, Belton, MO 64012-1852 *Tel:* 816-651-7118, pg 1346

Johnson, Elizabeth, MEJ Personal Business Services Inc, 245 E 116 St, New York, NY 10029 *Tel:* 212-426-6017 *Toll Free Tel:* 866-557-5336 *Fax:* 646-827-3628 *E-mail:* support@mejpbs.com *Web Site:* www.mejpbs.com, pg 1403

Johnson, Emily, Abraham Associates Inc, 5120-A Cedar Lake Rd, Minneapolis, MN 55416 *Tel:* 952-927-7920 *Toll Free Tel:* 800-701-2489 *Fax:* 952-927-8089 *E-mail:* info@abrahamassociatesinc.com *Web Site:* www.abrahamassociatesinc.com, pg 1285

Johnson, Greg, Intuit Inc, 2700 Coast Ave, Mountain View, CA 94043 *Tel:* 650-944-6000 *Toll Free Tel:* 800-446-8848 *E-mail:* investor_relations@intuit.com *Web Site:* www.intuit.com, pg 1371

Johnson, Jeffrey M, Hearst Newspapers, 300 W 57 St, New York, NY 10019 *Tel:* 212-649-2000 *Web Site:* www.hearst.com/newspapers, pg 1190

Johnson, Lloyd, Double Play, 303 Hillcrest Rd, Belton, MO 64012-1852 *Tel:* 816-651-7118, pg 1346

Johnson, Melvin, MEJ Personal Business Services Inc, 245 E 116 St, New York, NY 10029 *Tel:* 212-426-6017 *Toll Free Tel:* 866-557-5336 *Fax:* 646-827-3628 *E-mail:* support@mejpbs.com *Web Site:* www.mejpbs.com, pg 1403

Johnson, Michelle, World Literature Today, 630 Parrington Oval, Suite 110, Norman, OK 73019-4033 *Tel:* 405-325-4531 *E-mail:* wlt@ou.edu *Web Site:* www.worldliteraturetoday.org, pg 1137

Johnson, Paolo, Cliff Digital, 14700 S Main St, Gardena, CA 90248 *Tel:* 310-323-5600 *Toll Free Tel:* 866-429-2242 *Fax:* 310-400-3090 *E-mail:* cliff@cliffdigital.com *Web Site:* www.cliffdigital.com, pg 1103

Johnson, Peter H, Book Machine Sales Inc, PO Box 297, Hamlin, PA 18427 *Tel:* 570-647-9111 *Web Site:* www.bookmachinesales.com, pg 1278

Johnson, Rich, Diamond Book Distributors (DBD), 10150 York Rd, Hunt Valley, MD 21030 *Tel:* 443-318-8001; 443-318-8519 (cust serv) *E-mail:* distribution@diamondbookdistributors.com; dbdreorders@diamondbookdistributors.com (orders); books@diamondbookdistributors.com (cust serv) *Web Site:* diamondbookdistributors.com, pg 1290

Johnson, Sarah, The Historical Novels Review, PO Box 1146, Jacksonville, AL 36265 *E-mail:* reviews@historicalnovelsociety.org; contact@historicalnovelsociety.org *Web Site:* historicalnovelsociety.org, pg 1132

Johnson, Scott, Pivar Computing Services Inc, 1500 Abbott Ct, Buffalo Grove, IL 60089 *Tel:* 847-478-8000 *Toll Free Tel:* 800-CONVERT (266-8378) *Fax:* 847-478-8750 *Web Site:* www.pivar.com, pg 1374

Johnson, Stephanie, AlphaGraphics Inc, 143 Union Blvd, Suite 650, Lakewood, CO 80228 *Toll Free Tel:* 800-955-6246 *Fax:* 801-595-7270 *E-mail:* contactus@alphagraphics.com *Web Site:* www.alphagraphics.com, pg 1364

Johnson, Steve, Vectorworks Inc, 7150 Riverwood Dr, Columbia, MD 21046 *Tel:* 410-290-5114 *Toll Free Tel:* 888-646-4223 (sales) *Fax:* 410-290-7266 *E-mail:* sales@vectorworks.net *Web Site:* www.vectorworks.net, pg 1378

Johnson, Tashauna, PhotoEdit Inc, 3505 Cadillac Ave, Suite P-101, Costa Mesa, CA 92626 *Toll Free Tel:* 888-450-0946, pg 1430

Johnston, Andrea, Corel Corporation, 1600 Carling Ave, Ottawa, ON K1Z 8R7, Canada *Toll Free Tel:* 877-582-6735 *Web Site:* www.corel.com, pg 1366

Johnston, Charidy, Penguin Random House Canada, a Penguin Random House company, 320 Front St W, Suite 1400, Toronto, ON M5V 3B6, Canada *Tel:* 416-364-4449 *Toll Free Tel:* 888-523-9292 (cust serv) *Fax:* 416-598-7764 *E-mail:* customerservicescanada@penguinrandomhouse.com; publicitycanada@penguinrandomhouse.com; rightscanada@penguinrandomhouse.com *Web Site:* www.penguinrandomhouse.ca, pg 1299

Johnston, Greg, Greg Johnston Photography, 3021 San Jacinto Circle, Sanford, FL 32771 *Tel:* 305-258-7070 *Web Site:* www.gregjohnstonphotography.com, pg 1422

Johnston, Jamie, Distributed Art Publishers Inc, 75 Broad St, Suite 630, New York, NY 10004 *Tel:* 212-627-1999 *Toll Free Tel:* 800-338-2665 (cust serv) *Fax:* 212-627-9484 *E-mail:* orders@dapinc.com *Web Site:* www.artbook.com, pg 1290

Johnston, Kristi, Bert Davis Executive Search Inc, 555 Fifth Ave, Suite 302, New York, NY 10017 *Tel:* 212-838-4000 *E-mail:* info@bertdavis.com *Web Site:* www.bertdavis.com, pg 1381

Jones, Carla, Thomson Reuters, 3 Times Sq, New York, NY 10036 *Tel:* 646-223-4000; 646-223-6100 (edit); 646-223-6000 (newsroom) *Web Site:* www.thomsonreuters.com, pg 1191

Jones, Carrie, Greenleaf Book Group LLC, PO Box 91869, Austin, TX 78709 *Tel:* 512-891-6100 *Fax:* 512-891-6150 *E-mail:* contact@greenleafbookgroup.com; orders@greenleafbookgroup.com; foreignrights@greenleafbookgroup.com; media@greenleafbookgroup.com *Web Site:* greenleafbookgroup.com, pg 1292, 1355

Jones, Christopher, Chicago Distribution Center (CDC), 11030 S Langley Ave, Chicago, IL 60628 *Tel:* 773-702-7010 *Toll Free Fax:* 800-621-8476 *Web Site:* press.uchicago.edu/cdc, pg 1289

Jones, Cindy, Four Colour Print Group, 2410 Frankfort Ave, Louisville, KY 40206 *Tel:* 502-896-9644 *Fax:* 502-896-9594 *E-mail:* sales@fourcolour.com *Web Site:* www.fourcolour.com, pg 1210, 1253, 1280

Jones, Erin, The P A Hutchison Co, 400 Penn Ave, Mayfield, PA 18433 *Tel:* 570-876-4560 *Toll Free Tel:* 800-USA-PRNT (872-7768) *Fax:* 570-876-4561 *E-mail:* sales@pahutch.com *Web Site:* www.pahutch.com, pg 1211, 1226, 1254, 1268, 1280

Jones, Jan, PBD Worldwide Inc, 1650 Bluegrass Lakes Pkwy, Alpharetta, GA 30004 *Tel:* 470-769-1000 *Toll Free Tel:* 866-998-4PBD (998-4723) *E-mail:* sales.marketing@pbd.com; customerservice@pbd.com *Web Site:* www.pbd.com, pg 1334

Jones, Lou, Lou Jones Studio, 44 Breed St, Boston, MA 02128 *Tel:* 617-561-1194 *Fax:* 617-561-1196 *E-mail:* fotojones@aol.com *Web Site:* www.fotojones.com, pg 1423

Jones, Mike, Integrated Distribution Services (IDS), 9431 AllPoints Pkwy, Plainfield, IN 46168 *Toll Free Tel:* 866-232-6533 *E-mail:* cwelch@idsfulfillment.com *Web Site:* www.idsfulfillment.com, pg 1334

Jones, Phillip, Printing Research Inc (PRI), 10760 Shady Trail, Suite 300, Dallas, TX 75220 *Tel:* 214-353-9000 *Toll Free Tel:* 800-627-5537 (US only) *Fax:* 214-357-5847 *E-mail:* info@superblue.net *Web Site:* www.printingresearch.com; www.superblue.net, pg 1282

Jones, Roger L, Bedford Printing Co, 1501 S Blount St, Raleigh, NC 27603 *Tel:* 919-832-3973 *Fax:* 919-755-0204 *Web Site:* www.bedfordprinting.com, pg 1248

Jones, Stephanie, Cookbook Publishers Inc, 11633 W 83 Terr, Lenexa, KS 66285 *Tel:* 913-492-5900 *Toll Free Tel:* 800-227-7282 *Fax:* 913-492-5947 *E-mail:* info@cookbookpublishers.com *Web Site:* www.cookbookpublishers.com, pg 1224, 1251

Jones, Steve, Roswell Bookbinding, 2614 N 29 Ave, Phoenix, AZ 85009 *Tel:* 602-272-9338 *Toll Free Tel:* 888-803-8883 *Fax:* 602-272-9786 *Web Site:* www.roswellbookbinding.com, pg 1259, 1326

Jones, Suzanne, International Service Co, International Service Bldg, 333 Fourth Ave, Indialantic, FL 32903-4295 *Tel:* 321-724-1443 *Fax:* 321-724-1443, pg 1317, 1325, 1328, 1331

Jones, William R, VistaBooks LLC, 637 Blue Ridge Rd, Silverthorne, CO 80498-8931 *Tel:* 970-468-7673 *Fax:* 970-468-7673 *E-mail:* email@vistabooks.com *Web Site:* www.vistabooks.com, pg 1323

Jordan, Tina, The New York Times Book Review, 620 Eighth Ave, 5th fl, New York, NY 10018 *Tel:* 212-556-1234 *Toll Free Tel:* 800-631-2580 (subns) *E-mail:* bookreview@nytimes.com; books@nytimes.com *Web Site:* www.nytimes.com, pg 1135

Jordan-Smith, Gavin, Ricoh Americas Corp, 300 Eagleview Blvd, Exton, PA 19341 *Tel:* 610-296-8000 *Toll Free Tel:* 800-333-2679 (prod support); 800-637-4264 (sales) *Web Site:* www.ricoh-usa.com, pg 1375

Jorgensen, Janis, US Naval Institute Photo Archive, 291 Wood Rd, Annapolis, MD 21402 *Tel:* 410-295-1022 *Fax:* 410-295-1049 *E-mail:* photoservice@usni.org; photoarchive@usni.org; research@usni.org *Web Site:* www.usni.org, pg 1431

Jorgensen, Mike, Impressions Inc, 1050 Westgate Dr, St Paul, MN 55114 *Tel:* 651-646-1050 *Toll Free Tel:* 800-251-4285 *Fax:* 651-646-7228 *E-mail:* info@i-i.com *Web Site:* www.i-i.com, pg 1255

Joseph, Miles, Solar-Screen Co Inc, 53-11 105 St, Corona, NY 11368 *Tel:* 718-592-8222 *Toll Free Tel:* 800-347-6527 *Toll Free Fax:* 888-271-0891 *E-mail:* solarscreen@prodigy.net *Web Site:* www.solar-screen.com, pg 1272

Joseph, Tommy S, International Paper Co, 6400 Poplar Ave, Memphis, TN 38197 *Tel:* 901-419-9000 *Toll Free Tel:* 800-207-4003 *Web Site:* www.internationalpaper.com; facebook.com/internationalpaper; x.com/intlpaperco, pg 1268

Joyce, Jim, Dual Graphics, 370 Cliffwood Park, Brea, CA 92821 *Tel:* 714-990-3700 *Fax:* 714-990-6818 *Web Site:* www.dualgraphics.com, pg 1225, 1252

Judge, Amrit, Hilsinger-Mendelson West Inc, 115 N Kings Rd, Los Angeles, CA 90048 *Tel:* 323-931-5335 (text only) *E-mail:* hmiwest@aol.com *Web Site:* www.hilsingermendelson.com, pg 1109

Jungen, Mark, Graphic Composition Inc, N1246 Technical Dr, Greenville, WI 54942 *Tel:* 920-757-6977 *Toll Free Tel:* 800-262-8973 *Fax:* 920-757-9266 *E-mail:* socialmedia@graphiccomp.com *Web Site:* www.graphiccomp.com, pg 1254

Juris, Carolyn, Publishers Weekly, 49 W 23 St, 9th fl, New York, NY 10010 *Tel:* 212-377-5500 *Fax:* 212-377-2733 *Web Site:* www.publishersweekly.com, pg 1136

Jutkowitz, Alexander, Hill+Knowlton Strategies, 237 Park Ave, 4th fl, New York, NY 10017 *Tel:* 212-885-0300 *Web Site:* www.hkstrategies.com, pg 1109

Kacala, Julie, Balfour Commercial Printing, 225 E John Carpenter Fwy, Tower 2, Suite 400, Irving, TX 75062 *Tel:* 214-819-8588 (cust serv) *E-mail:* printing@balfour.com *Web Site:* commercial-printing.balfour.com, pg 1208, 1222, 1248, 1265, 1353

Kachergis, Anne, Kachergis Book Design Inc, 575 Stone Wall Rd, Pittsboro, NC 27312 *Tel:* 919-656-7632 *E-mail:* goodbooks@kachergisbookdesign.com *Web Site:* www.kachergisbookdesign.com, pg 1227, 1415

Kaefer, Chris, Six Red Marbles LLC, 101 Station Landing, Medford, MA 02155 *Tel:* 857-588-9000 *E-mail:* info@sixredmarbles.com *Web Site:* www.sixredmarbles.com, pg 1231, 1376

Kaehler, Wolfgang, Wolfgang Kaehler Photography, 723 Third St S, Kirkland, WA 98033 *Tel:* 425-803-0652 *Web Site:* www.facebook.com/wolfgang.kaehler, pg 1423

Kahanec, Cheryl, Quantum Group, 6511 Oakton St, Morton Grove, IL 60053 *Tel:* 847-967-3600 *Fax:* 847-967-3610 *E-mail:* info@quantumgroup.com *Web Site:* www.quantumgroup.com, pg 1259

Kahn, Karen, HP Inc, 1501 Paige Mill Rd, Palo Alto, CA 94304-1112 *Tel:* 650-857-1501 *Toll Free Tel:* 800-282-6672 *Web Site:* www.hp.com, pg 1370

Kaiman, Athena Millas, Athena Productions Inc, 2204 S Ashford Ct, Nashville, TN 37214 *Tel:* 305-807-8607 *E-mail:* atheprod@aol.com, pg 1286

Kaiman, Ken, Athena Productions Inc, 2204 S Ashford Ct, Nashville, TN 37214 *Tel:* 305-807-8607 *E-mail:* atheprod@aol.com, pg 1286

Kakar, Samir, Aptara Inc, 2901 Telestar Ct, Suite 522, Falls Church, VA 22042 *Tel:* 703-352-0001 *E-mail:* moreinfo@aptaracorp.com *Web Site:* www.aptaracorp.com, pg 1207, 1222, 1343, 1353, 1364, 1411

Kalajian, James, Jenkins Group Inc, 1129 Woodmere Ave, Suite B, Traverse City, MI 49686 *Tel:* 231-933-0445; 213-883-5365 *E-mail:* info@jenkinsgroupinc.com *Web Site:* www.jenkinsgroupinc.com, pg 1227, 1348, 1355

Kalina, Sarah, Kirkus, 1140 Broadway, Suite 802, New York, NY 10001 *E-mail:* customercare@kirkus.com *Web Site:* www.kirkusreviews.com, pg 1133

Kallek, Nikki, Crain Communications Inc, 1155 Gratiot Ave, Detroit, MI 48207-2732 *Tel:* 313-446-6000 *Fax:* 313-446-0383 *E-mail:* info@crain.com *Web Site:* crain.com, pg 1190

Kallman, Richard, Bookazine Co Inc, 75 Hook Rd, Bayonne, NJ 07002 *Tel:* 201-339-7777 *Toll Free Tel:* 800-221-8112 *Fax:* 201-339-7778 *E-mail:* info@bookazine.com *Web Site:* www.bookazine.com, pg 1312, 1327

Kallman, Robert, Bookazine Co Inc, 75 Hook Rd, Bayonne, NJ 07002 *Tel:* 201-339-7777 *Toll Free Tel:* 800-221-8112 *Fax:* 201-339-7778 *E-mail:* info@bookazine.com *Web Site:* www.bookazine.com, pg 1312, 1327

Kalvin, William, Delmas Typesetting Inc, 461 Hilldale Dr, Ann Arbor, MI 48105 *Tel:* 734-662-8899 *E-mail:* delmastype@comcast.net *Web Site:* www.delmastype.com, pg 1224

Kamaliddin, Hala, Penguin Random House Canada, a Penguin Random House company, 320 Front St W, Suite 1400, Toronto, ON M5V 3B6, Canada *Tel:* 416-364-4449 *Toll Free Tel:* 888-523-9292 (cust serv) *Fax:* 416-598-7764 *E-mail:* customerservicescanada@penguinrandomhouse.com; publicitycanada@penguinrandomhouse.com; rightscanada@penguinrandomhouse.com *Web Site:* www.penguinrandomhouse.ca, pg 1299

Kampmann, Alex, Independent Publishers Group (IPG), 814 N Franklin St, Chicago, IL 60610 *Tel:* 312-337-0747 *Toll Free Tel:* 800-888-4741 (orders) *Fax:* 312-337-5985 *E-mail:* frontdesk@ipgbook.com; orders@ipgbook.com *Web Site:* www.ipgbook.com, pg 1292, 1328

Kampmann, Alex, Midpoint Trade Books, 814 N Franklin St, Suite 100, Chicago, IL 60610 *Tel:* 312-337-0747 *Fax:* 312-337-5985 *E-mail:* orders@ipgbook.com *Web Site:* www.midpointtrade.com, pg 1297

Kampmann, Alison, Midpoint Trade Books, 814 N Franklin St, Suite 100, Chicago, IL 60610 *Tel:* 312-337-0747 *Fax:* 312-337-5985 *E-mail:* orders@ipgbook.com *Web Site:* www.midpointtrade.com, pg 1297

Kampmann, Eric, Midpoint Trade Books, 814 N Franklin St, Suite 100, Chicago, IL 60610 *Tel:* 312-337-0747 *Fax:* 312-337-5985 *E-mail:* orders@ipgbook.com *Web Site:* www.midpointtrade.com, pg 1297

Kang, Steve, QualityLogic Inc, 9576 W Emerald St, Boise, ID 83704 *Tel:* 208-424-1905 *E-mail:* info@qualitylogic.com *Web Site:* www.qualitylogic.com, pg 1375

Kanter, Peter, Dell Magazines, 6 Prowitt St, Norwalk, CT 06855 *Tel:* 203-866-6688 *Toll Free Tel:* 800-220-7443 (corp sales) *Fax:* 203-854-5962 (pubns) *E-mail:* customerservice@pennypublications.com *Web Site:* www.pennydellpuzzles.com, pg 1354

Kantor, Becca, Paper Brigade, 520 Eighth Ave, 4th fl, New York, NY 10018 *Tel:* 212-201-2920 *Fax:* 212-532-4952 *E-mail:* info@jewishbooks.org *Web Site:* www.jewishbookcouncil.org, pg 1135

Kantor, Emma, Publishers Weekly, 49 W 23 St, 9th fl, New York, NY 10010 *Tel:* 212-377-5500 *Fax:* 212-377-2733 *Web Site:* www.publishersweekly.com, pg 1136

Kantor, Russell, Social Studies School Service, 10200 Jefferson Blvd, PO Box 802, Culver City, CA 90232 *Tel:* 310-839-2436 *Toll Free Tel:* 800-421-4246 (US & CN) *Fax:* 310-839-2249 *Toll Free Fax:* 800-944-5432 *E-mail:* access@socialstudies.com; customerservice@socialstudies.com *Web Site:* www.socialstudies.com, pg 1302, 1321

Kaplan, Dan, Booklist, 225 N Michigan Ave, Suite 1300, Chicago, IL 60601 *Tel:* 312-944-6780 *Toll Free Tel:* 800-545-2433 *Fax:* 312-440-9374 *E-mail:* info@booklistonline.com; ala@ala.org *Web Site:* www.booklistonline.com; www.ala.org, pg 1130

Kaplan, Linda, Kaplan/DeFiore Rights, 47 E 19 St, 3rd fl, New York, NY 10003 *Tel:* 212-925-7244 *Web Site:* kaplanrights.com, pg 1348

Kapolnek, Paul, Western Printing Machinery Co (WPM), 9228 Ivanhoe St, Schiller Park, IL 60176 *Tel:* 847-678-1740 *Fax:* 847-678-6176 *E-mail:* info@wpm.com *Web Site:* www.wpm.com, pg 1284

Kapoor, Prashant, Aptara Inc, 2901 Telestar Ct, Suite 522, Falls Church, VA 22042 *Tel:* 703-352-0001 *E-mail:* moreinfo@aptaracorp.com *Web Site:* www.aptaracorp.com, pg 1207, 1222, 1343, 1353, 1364, 1411

Karabots, Nick, Kappa Graphics LLP, 50 Rock St, Hughestown, PA 18640 *Tel:* 570-655-9681 *Toll Free Tel:* 800-236-4396 (sales) *E-mail:* weborders@kappapma.com *Web Site:* www.kappapma.com/kappagraphics; kappapuzzles.com, pg 1227, 1255

Karabulut, Asli Merve, Link Translations Inc, 60 E 96 St, New York, NY 10128 *Toll Free Tel:* 866-866-5010 *E-mail:* info@link-translations.com *Web Site:* www.link-translations.com, pg 1403

Karamsetty, Pardha, Apex CoVantage, 4045 Sheridan Ave, No 266, Miami Beach, FL 33140 *Tel:* 703-709-3000 *Fax:* 703-709-8242 *E-mail:* info@apexcovantage.com *Web Site:* www.apexcovantage.com, pg 1221

Karancak, Ilge, MediaLocate Inc, 1200 Piedmont Ave, Pacific Grove, CA 93950 *Tel:* 831-655-7500 *E-mail:* info@medialocate.com *Web Site:* www.medialocate.com, pg 1403

Karancak-Splane, Ilge, Richard Schneider Language Services (RSLS), 1200 Piedmont Ave, Pacific Grove, CA 93950 *Toll Free Tel:* 800-500-5808 *E-mail:* service@idioms.com *Web Site:* www.idioms.com, pg 1404

Karel, Howard, The Karel/Dutton Group, San Francisco, CA 94121 *Tel:* 415-668-0829 *Web Site:* kareldultongroup.com, pg 1295

Karim, Shah, Saferock, 75 Armour Place, Dumont, NJ 07628 *Tel:* 646-535-0110 *E-mail:* info@saferock.com *Web Site:* saferockretail.com, pg 1376

Karmelich, Robert, Design Science Inc (DSI), 444 W Ocean Blvd, Suite 800, Long Beach, CA 90802 *Tel:* 562-432-2920 *Toll Free Tel:* 800-827-0685 (US sales only) *Fax:* 562-624-2859 *E-mail:* info@wiris.com; sales@wiris.com; support@wiris.com *Web Site:* www.dessci.com, pg 1367

Kastner, Suzanne, GW Illustration & Design, 2290 Ball Dr, St Louis, MO 63146 *Tel:* 314-567-9854 *Web Site:* www.gwinc.com, pg 1414

Kastner, Suzanne, GW Inc, 2290 Ball Dr, St Louis, MO 63146 *Tel:* 314-567-9854 *E-mail:* media@gwinc.com *Web Site:* www.gwinc.com, pg 1226, 1370

Katagiri, Takehito, OKI Data Americas Inc, 8505 Freeport Pkwy, Suite 600, Irving, TX 75063 *Tel:* 972-815-4800 *Toll Free Tel:* 800-OKI-DATA (654-3282) *E-mail:* support@okidata.com *Web Site:* www.oki.com/us/printing, pg 1374

Katano, Hiroaki, Tamron USA Inc, 10 Austin Blvd, Commack, NY 11725 *Tel:* 631-858-8400 *Toll Free Tel:* 800-827-8880 *Fax:* 631-543-5666; 631-858-8462 (cust serv) *E-mail:* custserv@tamron.com *Web Site:* www.tamron-usa.com, pg 1377

Katzenberger, Amy, American Camp Association Inc, 5000 State Rd 67 N, Martinsville, IN 46151-7902 *Tel:* 765-342-8456 *Toll Free Tel:* 800-428-2267 *Fax:* 765-342-2065 *E-mail:* contactus@acacamps.org *Web Site:* www.acacamps.org, pg 1311

Kaufman, Carol, Jewish Book Council, 520 Eighth Ave, 4th fl, New York, NY 10018 *Tel:* 212-201-2920 *Fax:* 212-532-4952 *E-mail:* info@jewishbooks.org *Web Site:* www.jewishbookcouncil.org, pg 1146

Kaufman, Carol, Paper Brigade, 520 Eighth Ave, 4th fl, New York, NY 10018 *Tel:* 212-201-2920 *Fax:* 212-532-4952 *E-mail:* info@jewishbooks.org *Web Site:* www.jewishbookcouncil.org, pg 1135

Kaufman, Carol E, Paper Brigade, 520 Eighth Ave, 4th fl, New York, NY 10018 *Tel:* 212-201-2920 *Fax:* 212-532-4952 *E-mail:* info@jewishbooks.org *Web Site:* www.jewishbookcouncil.org, pg 1135

Kaufman, Cecile, X-Height Studio, 83 High St, Milford, MA 01757 *Tel:* 508-478-3897 *Toll Free Tel:* 888-474-8973 *E-mail:* info@x-heightstudio.com *Web Site:* www.x-heightstudio.com, pg 1233

Kaufman, Donna Paz, Paz & Associates: The Bookstore Training & Consulting Group, 1417 Sadler Rd, No 274, Fernandina Beach, FL 32034 *Tel:* 904-277-2664 *Fax:* 904-261-6742 *Web Site:* www.pazbookbiz.com, pg 1350

Kaufman, Doris, DSM Producers Inc, PO Box 1160, Marco Island, FL 34146-1160 *Tel:* 212-245-0006, pg 1368

Kaufman, Mark, Paz & Associates: The Bookstore Training & Consulting Group, 1417 Sadler Rd, No 274, Fernandina Beach, FL 32034 *Tel:* 904-277-2664 *Fax:* 904-261-6742 *Web Site:* www.pazbookbiz.com, pg 1350

Kaufman, Roy S, Copyright Clearance Center Inc (CCC), 222 Rosewood Dr, Danvers, MA 01923 *Tel:* 978-750-8400 (sales); 978-646-2600 (cust serv) *E-mail:* info@copyright.com *Web Site:* www.copyright.com, pg 1345

Kaufman, Susie V, Peace Visions, 18850 Vista del Canon, Suite A, Santa Clarita, CA 91321-4512 *Tel:* 661-251-6669 *Fax:* 661-251-6669, pg 1385

Kavanagh, Dennis, Data Reproductions Corp, 4545 Glenmeade Lane, Auburn Hills, MI 48326 *Tel:* 248-371-3700 *Toll Free Tel:* 800-242-3114 *Fax:* 248-371-3710 *Web Site:* datarepro.com, pg 1209, 1251

Kavanagh, Kimberly, Data Reproductions Corp, 4545 Glenmeade Lane, Auburn Hills, MI 48326 *Tel:* 248-371-3700 *Toll Free Tel:* 800-242-3114 *Fax:* 248-371-3710 *Web Site:* datarepro.com, pg 1209, 1251

Kavanaugh, James J, IBM Corp, One New Orchard Rd, Armonk, NY 10504 *Tel:* 914-499-1900 *Toll Free Tel:* 800-426-4968 *E-mail:* askibm@vnet.ibm.com *Web Site:* www.ibm.com, pg 1370

Kaye, Gregg, Winston Personnel, 122 E 42 St, Suite 320, New York, NY 10168 *Tel:* 212-557-5000 *Web Site:* www.winstonresources.com, pg 1382

Kaye, Sy, Winston Personnel, 122 E 42 St, Suite 320, New York, NY 10168 *Tel:* 212-557-5000 *Web Site:* www.winstonresources.com, pg 1382

Kaye, Todd, Winston Personnel, 122 E 42 St, Suite 320, New York, NY 10168 *Tel:* 212-557-5000 *Web Site:* www.winstonresources.com, pg 1382

Kean, Carla, Penguin Random House Canada, a Penguin Random House company, 320 Front St W, Suite 1400, Toronto, ON M5V 3B6, Canada *Tel:* 416-364-4449 *Toll Free Tel:* 888-523-9292 (cust serv) *Fax:* 416-598-7764 *E-mail:* customerservicescanada@penguinrandomhouse.com; publicitycanada@penguinrandomhouse.com; rightscanada@penguinrandomhouse.com *Web Site:* www.penguinrandomhouse.ca, pg 1299

Kearns, Gail M, To Press & Beyond, 7507 Summersun Dr, Browns Summit, NC 27214 *Tel:* 805-570-8275 *E-mail:* info@topressandbeyond.com *Web Site:* www.topressandbeyond.com, pg 1113, 1351, 1358

Keck, Tom, Tom Keck Photos, 13393 Landfair Rd, San Diego, CA 92130 *Tel:* 858-755-2975 *E-mail:* tomkeckphotos@gmail.com *Web Site:* www.tomkeckphotos.com, pg 1423

Kecskemethy, Thomas A, The ANNALS of The American Academy of Political & Social Science, 2455 Teller Rd, Thousand Oaks, CA 91320 *Toll Free Tel:* 800-818-7243 *Toll Free Fax:* 800-583-2665 *E-mail:* journals@sagepub.com *Web Site:* www.sagepub.com, pg 1129

Keegan, Wayne, Ingram Content Group LLC, One Ingram Blvd, La Vergne, TN 37086-1986 *Tel:* 615-793-5000 *Toll Free Tel:* 800-937-8000 (retailers); 800-937-5300 (ext 1, libs) *E-mail:* customerservice@ingramcontent.com *Web Site:* www.ingramcontent.com, pg 1294, 1316

Keenan, Aileen, Theatre Journal, 2715 N Charles St, Baltimore, MD 21218-4363 *Tel:* 410-516-6987 (journal orders outside US & CN) *Toll Free Tel:* 800-548-1784 (journal orders) *Fax:* 410-578-2865 (journal orders) *E-mail:* tjbooks@athe.org; jrnlcirc@jh.edu (journal orders) *Web Site:* www.press.jhu.edu/journals/theatre-journal, pg 1137

Keenan, Aileen M, African American Review (AAR), c/o St Louis University, 317 Adorjan Hall, 3800 Lindell Blvd, St Louis, MO 63108 *Tel:* 314-977-3688 *Web Site:* afamreview.org, pg 1129

Keenan, Timothy, H B Fuller Co, 1200 Willow Lake Blvd, St Paul, MN 55110-5146 *Tel:* 651-236-5900 *Toll Free Tel:* 888-423-8553 *E-mail:* inquiry@hbfuller.com *Web Site:* www.hbfuller.com, pg 1267, 1280

Keene, Michael, The John Roberts Company, 9687 East River Rd NW, Minneapolis, MN 55433 *Tel:* 763-755-5500 *Toll Free Tel:* 800-551-1534 *Fax:* 763-755-0394 *E-mail:* success@johnroberts.com *Web Site:* www.johnroberts.com; www.facebook.com/TheJohnRobertsCompany, pg 1105

Keene-Kendrick, Lydia, Davis Art Images, 50 Portland St, Worcester, MA 01608 *Tel:* 508-754-7201 *Toll Free Tel:* 800-533-2847 *Fax:* 508-753-3834 *E-mail:* das@davisart.com; contactus@davisart.com *Web Site:* www.davisart.com, pg 1427

Keessen, Robert H, Scott Publications Inc, 2145 W Sherman Blvd, Norton Shores, MI 49441 *Tel:* 231-755-2200 *Toll Free Tel:* 866-733-9382 *Fax:* 231-755-1003 *E-mail:* contactus@scottpublications.com *Web Site:* scottpublications.com, pg 1105

Keessen, Ruth M, Scott Publications Inc, 2145 W Sherman Blvd, Norton Shores, MI 49441 *Tel:* 231-755-2200 *Toll Free Tel:* 866-733-9382 *Fax:* 231-755-1003 *E-mail:* contactus@scottpublications.com *Web Site:* scottpublications.com, pg 1105

Keller, Kim, GTxcel Inc, 144 Turnpike Rd, Suite 130, Southborough, MA 01772-2104 *Toll Free Tel:* 800-609-8994 *E-mail:* info@gtxcel.com *Web Site:* www.gtxcel.com, pg 1370

Kelley, Gloria, Kelley & Hall Book Publicity, 5 Briar Lane, Marblehead, MA 01945 *Tel:* 617-680-1976 *Fax:* 781-631-5959 *Web Site:* www.kelleyandhall.com, pg 1110

Kelley, Jocelyn, Kelley & Hall Book Publicity, 5 Briar Lane, Marblehead, MA 01945 *Tel:* 617-680-1976 *Fax:* 781-631-5959 *Web Site:* www.kelleyandhall.com, pg 1110

Kelley, Sarah, Jane Wesman Public Relations Inc, 322 Eighth Ave, Suite 1702, New York, NY 10001 *Tel:* 212-620-4080 *Fax:* 212-620-0370 *Web Site:* www.wesmanpr.com, pg 1110

Kellough, Kjelti, Getty Images Inc, 605 Fifth Ave S, Suite 400, Seattle, WA 98104 *Tel:* 206-925-5000 *Toll Free Tel:* 800-IMAGERY (462-4379); 888-888-5889 *Web Site:* www.gettyimages.com; www.gettyimages.com/customer-support; engage.gettyimages.com/media-inquiries, pg 1369, 1428

Kelly, Charles J, Microsearch Corp, 101 Western Ave, Gloucester, MA 01930 *Tel:* 781-231-9991 *Toll Free Tel:* 800-895-0212 *E-mail:* info@microsearch.net *Web Site:* www.microsearchcorporation.net, pg 1372

Kelly, Chuck, Preston Kelly, 222 First Ave NE, Minneapolis, MN 55413 *Tel:* 612-843-4000 *Fax:* 612-843-3900 *E-mail:* iconicideas@prestonkelly.com *Web Site:* prestonkelly.com, pg 1100

Kelly, David, The New York Times Book Review, 620 Eighth Ave, 5th fl, New York, NY 10018 *Tel:* 212-556-1234 *Toll Free Tel:* 800-631-2580 (subns) *E-mail:* bookreview@nytimes.com; books@nytimes.com *Web Site:* www.nytimes.com, pg 1135

Kelly, Erin, Penguin Random House Canada, a Penguin Random House company, 320 Front St W, Suite 1400, Toronto, ON M5V 3B6, Canada *Tel:* 416-364-4449 *Toll Free Tel:* 888-523-9292 (cust serv) *Fax:* 416-598-7764 *E-mail:* customerservicescanada@penguinrandomhouse.com; publicitycanada@penguinrandomhouse.com; rightscanada@penguinrandomhouse.com *Web Site:* www.penguinrandomhouse.ca, pg 1299

Kelly, Heather, SSPR LLC, One Northfield Plaza, Suite 400, Northfield, IL 60093 *Toll Free Tel:* 800-287-2279 *Web Site:* www.sspr.com, pg 1113

Kelly, Henry Boon, DCA Inc, 1515 E Pine St, Cushing, OK 74023 *Tel:* 918-225-0346 *Fax:* 918-225-1113 *E-mail:* sales@dcainc.com *Web Site:* www.dcainc.com, pg 1367

Kelly, Susan, Microsearch Corp, 101 Western Ave, Gloucester, MA 01930 *Tel:* 781-231-9991 *Toll Free Tel:* 800-895-0212 *E-mail:* info@microsearch.net *Web Site:* www.microsearchcorporation.net, pg 1372

Kelman, Ari, Reviews in American History, 2715 N Charles St, Baltimore, MD 21218-4363 *Tel:* 410-516-6987 (journal orders outside US & CN) *Toll Free Tel:* 800-548-1784 (journal orders) *Fax:* 410-578-2865 (journal orders) *E-mail:* jrnlcirc@jh.edu (journal orders) *Web Site:* www.press.jhu.edu/journals/reviews-american-history, pg 1136

Kemp, R Douglas, Innodata Inc, 55 Challenger Rd, Suite 202, Ridgefield Park, NJ 07660 *Tel:* 201-371-8000 *Toll Free Tel:* 877-454-8400 *E-mail:* info@innodata.com; marketing@innodata.com *Web Site:* innodata.com, pg 1227, 1347, 1371

Kempf, Adam, Action Printing, N6637 Rolling Meadows Dr, Fond du Lac, WI 54937 *Tel:* 920-907-7820 *E-mail:* info@actionprinting.com *Web Site:* www.actionprinting.com, pg 1247

Kendall, George, Booklist, 225 N Michigan Ave, Suite 1300, Chicago, IL 60601 *Tel:* 312-944-6780 *Toll Free Tel:* 800-545-2433 *Fax:* 312-440-9374 *E-mail:* info@booklistonline.com; ala@ala.org *Web Site:* www.booklistonline.com; www.ala.org, pg 1130

Kendziora, Laurie, Wybel Marketing Group Inc, 213 W Main St, Barrington, IL 60010 *Tel:* 847-382-0384; 847-382-0382 *Toll Free Tel:* 800-323-5297 *Fax:* 847-382-0385 *Toll Free Fax:* 800-595-5252 *E-mail:* bookreps@wybel.com, pg 1304

Kennedy, Kyle, The John Roberts Company, 9687 East River Rd NW, Minneapolis, MN 55433 *Tel:* 763-755-5500 *Toll Free Tel:* 800-551-1534 *Fax:* 763-755-0394 *E-mail:* success@johnroberts.com *Web Site:* www.johnroberts.com; www.facebook.com/TheJohnRobertsCompany, pg 1105

Kennedy, Mary, Institute of Intergovernmental Relations, Queen's University, Robert Sutherland Hall, Rm 301, Kingston, ON K7L 3N6, Canada *Tel:* 613-533-2080 *E-mail:* iigr@queensu.ca *Web Site:* www.queensu.ca/iigr, pg 1317

Kennedy, Tom, AlphaGraphics Inc, 143 Union Blvd, Suite 650, Lakewood, CO 80228 *Toll Free Tel:* 800-955-6246 *Fax:* 801-595-7270 *E-mail:* contactus@alphagraphics.com *Web Site:* www.alphagraphics.com, pg 1364

Kennell, Joseph F, Versa Press Inc, 1465 Spring Bay Rd, East Peoria, IL 61611-9788 *Tel:* 309-822-8272 *Toll Free Tel:* 800-447-7829 *Fax:* 309-822-8141 *Web Site:* www.versapress.com, pg 1214, 1232, 1261, 1273

Kennell, Matthew, Versa Press Inc, 1465 Spring Bay Rd, East Peoria, IL 61611-9788 *Tel:* 309-822-8272 *Toll Free Tel:* 800-447-7829 *Fax:* 309-822-8141 *Web Site:* www.versapress.com, pg 1214, 1232, 1261, 1273

Kennell, Steven J, Versa Press Inc, 1465 Spring Bay Rd, East Peoria, IL 61611-9788 *Tel:* 309-822-8272 *Toll Free Tel:* 800-447-7829 *Fax:* 309-822-8141 *Web Site:* www.versapress.com, pg 1214, 1232, 1261, 1273

Kenney, Elaine, Communication Matters, 48 Aylmer Ave, Ottawa, ON K1S 2X1, Canada *Tel:* 613-233-5423 *Web Site:* www.communicationmatters.ca, pg 1108

Kenney, Gerald P, Unisys Corp, 801 Lakeview Dr, Suite 100, Blue Bell, PA 19422 *Tel:* 215-274-2742 *Web Site:* www.unisys.com, pg 1378

Kenney, John, Six Red Marbles LLC, 101 Station Landing, Medford, MA 02155 *Tel:* 857-588-9000 *E-mail:* info@sixredmarbles.com *Web Site:* www.sixredmarbles.com, pg 1231, 1376

Keogh, Tracy, HP Inc, 1501 Paige Mill Rd, Palo Alto, CA 94304-1112 *Tel:* 650-857-1501 *Toll Free Tel:* 800-282-6672 *Web Site:* www.hp.com, pg 1370

Kepler, James A, Adams Press, 1712 Oakton St, Evanston, IL 60202 *E-mail:* info@adamspress.com, pg 1207, 1221, 1247

Kerr, Chris, Parson Weems' Publisher Services LLC, 3811 Canterbury Rd, No 707, Baltimore, MD 21218 *Tel:* 914-948-4259 *Toll Free Fax:* 866-861-0337 *E-mail:* office@parsonweems.com *Web Site:* www.parsonweems.com, pg 1299

Kerr, Fran, The Hibbert Group, 400 Pennington Ave, Trenton, NJ 08650 *Tel:* 609-394-7500 *Toll Free Tel:* 888-HIBBERT (442-2378) *E-mail:* info@hibbertgroup.com *Web Site:* hibbert.com, pg 1104, 1116, 1117

Kerrigan, Barry T, Desktop Miracles Inc, 112 S Main St, Suite 294, Stowe, VT 05672 *Tel:* 802-253-7900 *Toll Free Fax:* 888-293-2676 *E-mail:* info@desktopmiracles.com *Web Site:* www.desktopmiracles.com, pg 1209, 1224, 1266, 1279, 1354, 1413

Kerrigan, Virginia, Desktop Miracles Inc, 112 S Main St, Suite 294, Stowe, VT 05672 *Tel:* 802-253-7900 *Toll Free Fax:* 888-293-2676 *E-mail:* info@desktopmiracles.com *Web Site:* www.desktopmiracles.com, pg 1209, 1224, 1266, 1279, 1354, 1413

Kessel, Charlene, Ulverscroft Large Print (USA) Inc, 950A Union Rd, Suite 427, West Seneca, NY 14224 *Tel:* 716-674-4710; 905-637-8734 (CN) *Toll Free Tel:* 800-955-9659; 888-860-3365 (CN) *Fax:* 716-674-4195; 905-333-6788 (CN) *E-mail:* sales@ulverscroftusa.com; sales@ulverscroftcanada.com (CN) *Web Site:* www.ulverscroft.com, pg 1303

Ketcham, Jenelle, NameBank International, 1001 Cathedral St, Baltimore, MD 21201 *Tel:* 410-864-0854 *Fax:* 410-864-0837 *E-mail:* lists@namebank.com *Web Site:* www.namebank.com, pg 1146

Ketkar, Prashant, Corel Corporation, 1600 Carling Ave, Ottawa, ON K1Z 8R7, Canada *Toll Free Tel:* 877-582-6735 *Web Site:* www.corel.com, pg 1366

Kettler, C J, King Features Syndicate, 300 W 57 St, New York, NY 10019-5238 *Tel:* 212-969-7550 *Toll Free Tel:* 800-526-5464 *Web Site:* www.kingfeatures.com, pg 1190

Kettler, CJ, Eric Tyson, 300 W 57 St, 15th fl, New York, NY 10019-5238 *Toll Free Tel:* 800-708-7311 (FL edit) *E-mail:* eric@erictyson.com *Web Site:* www.erictyson.com, pg 1126

Key, Curtis, Casemate | academic, 1950 Lawrence Rd, Havertown, PA 19083 *Tel:* 610-853-9131 *Fax:* 610-853-9146 *E-mail:* info@casemateacademic.com *Web Site:* www.oxbowbooks.com/dbbc, pg 1287

Khalili, Bijan, Ketab Corp, 12701 Van Nuys Blvd, Unit H, Pacoima, CA 91331 *Tel:* 310-477-7477 *Toll Free Tel:* 800-FOR-IRAN (367-4726) *Fax:* 818-908-1457 *E-mail:* ketab1@ketab.com *Web Site:* www.ketab.com, pg 1318

Khan, Sabih, Apple Inc, One Apple Park Way, Cupertino, CA 95014 *Tel:* 408-996-1010 *Web Site:* www.apple.com, pg 1364

Khuri, Ronny, Booklist, 225 N Michigan Ave, Suite 1300, Chicago, IL 60601 *Tel:* 312-944-6780 *Toll Free Tel:* 800-545-2433 *Fax:* 312-440-9374 *E-mail:* info@booklistonline.com; ala@ala.org *Web Site:* www.booklistonline.com; www.ala.org, pg 1130

Kiesler, Michael, Widen Enterprises Inc, 6911 Mangrove Lane, Madison, WI 53713 *Tel:* 608-222-1296 *Toll Free Tel:* 800-444-2828 *E-mail:* marketing@widen.com *Web Site:* www.widen.com, pg 1233

Kilani, Marwan, Bulletin of the American Schools of Oriental Research (BASOR), James F Strange Ctr, 209 Commerce St, Alexandria, VA 22314 *Tel:* 703-789-9229; 703-789-9230 (pubns) *Fax:* 617-353-6575 *E-mail:* basor@asor.org; info@asor.org; publications@asor.org *Web Site:* www.asor.org, pg 1130

Kim, Dave, The New York Times Book Review, 620 Eighth Ave, 5th fl, New York, NY 10018 *Tel:* 212-556-1234 *Toll Free Tel:* 800-631-2580 (subns) *E-mail:* bookreview@nytimes.com; books@nytimes.com *Web Site:* www.nytimes.com, pg 1135

Kim, Gary, Codra Enterprises Inc, 17692 Cowan, Suite 200, Irvine, CA 92614 *Tel:* 949-756-8400 *Toll Free Tel:* 888-992-6372 *Fax:* 949-756-8484 *E-mail:* codra@codra.com; sales@codra.com *Web Site:* www.codra.com, pg 1209, 1250

Kincade, Jason, Parson Weems' Publisher Services LLC, 3811 Canterbury Rd, No 707, Baltimore, MD 21218 *Tel:* 914-948-4259 *Toll Free Fax:* 866-861-0337 *E-mail:* office@parsonweems.com *Web Site:* www.parsonweems.com, pg 1299

Kincaid, Paul, Freestyle Software, 9 Campus Dr, Parsippany, NJ 07054 *Toll Free Tel:* 800-474-5760 *Fax:* 973-237-9043 *E-mail:* info@freestylesolutions.com *Web Site:* www.freestylesolutions.com, pg 1369

King, Charles, Cox-King Multimedia, PO Box 909, Geneva, NY 14456 *Tel:* 315-719-0141 *E-mail:* info@ckmm.com *Web Site:* www.ckmm.com, pg 1413

Kingdon, Rose, Broadcast Wire & Audio, c/o The Canadian Press, 36 King St E, Toronto, ON M5C 2L9, Canada *Tel:* 416-507-2126 *Toll Free Tel:* 800-434-7578 (CN only) *Fax:* 416-364-1325 *E-mail:* broadcast@thecanadianpress.com *Web Site:* www.thecanadianpress.com, pg 1189

Kirk, Malcolm, The Canadian Press/La Presse Canadienne, 36 King St E, Toronto, ON M5C 2L9, Canada *Tel:* 416-364-0321 *Fax:* 416-364-0207 (newsroom) *E-mail:* sales@thecanadianpress.com *Web Site:* www.thecanadianpress.com, pg 1189

Kirk, Steve, GLS Companies, 1280 Energy Park Dr, St Paul, MN 55108-5106 *Tel:* 651-644-3000 *Toll Free Tel:* 800-655-9405 *Web Site:* www.glsmn.com, pg 1226, 1254

Kirkpatrick, Emily, National Council of Teachers of English (NCTE), 340 N Neil St, Suite 104, Champaign, IL 61820 *Tel:* 217-328-3870 *Toll Free Tel:* 877-369-6283 (cust serv) *Fax:* 217-328-9645 *E-mail:* customerservice@ncte.org; permissions@ncte.org *Web Site:* ncte.org, pg 1146

Kirsch, Herbert, Best Mailing Lists Inc, 7507 E Tanque Verde Rd, Tucson, AZ 85715 *Toll Free Tel:* 800-692-2378 *Fax:* 520-885-3100 *E-mail:* best@bestmailing.com *Web Site:* www.bestmailing.com, pg 1119

Kirsch, Karen J, Best Mailing Lists Inc, 7507 E Tanque Verde Rd, Tucson, AZ 85715 *Toll Free Tel:* 800-692-2378 *Fax:* 520-885-3100 *E-mail:* best@bestmailing.com *Web Site:* www.bestmailing.com, pg 1119

Kisel, Robert, Amgraf Inc, 1501 Oak St, Kansas City, MO 64108-1424 *Tel:* 816-474-4797 *Toll Free Tel:* 800-304-4797 (sales & mktg) *Fax:* 816-842-4477 *E-mail:* support@amgraf.com *Web Site:* www.amgraf.com, pg 1364

Kitt, Tyler, EP Graphics, 169 S Jefferson St, Berne, IN 46711 *Tel:* 260-589-2145 *Toll Free Tel:* 877-589-2145 *Fax:* 260-589-2810 *Web Site:* www.epgraphics.com, pg 1253

Kittlitz, Linda G, Linda Kittlitz & Associates, 193 Coleridge St, San Francisco, CA 94110-5112 *Tel:* 415-550-8898 *Toll Free Tel:* 800-550-8898 *Fax:* 415-550-7975 *Web Site:* www.lkandassociates.com, pg 1104

Kitzmiller, David E, Kitzmiller Sales & Marketing Co, 35 Flint St, Suite 304, Salem, MA 01970-3264 *Tel:* 978-985-1144 (cell) *Fax:* 978-744-0232 *E-mail:* dnd.kitzmiller@gmail.com, pg 1295

Klauer, Michael, Sheridan PA, 450 Fame Ave, Hanover, PA 17331 *Tel:* 717-632-3535 *Toll Free Tel:* 800-352-2210 *Fax:* 717-633-8900 *Web Site:* www.sheridan.com, pg 1260

Klauer, Mike, Sheridan NH, 69 Lyme Rd, Hanover, NH 03755 *Tel:* 603-643-2220 *Web Site:* www.sheridan.com, pg 1259

Klein, Michael, iCAD Inc, 98 Spit Brook Rd, Suite 100, Nashua, NH 03062 *Tel:* 603-882-5200 *Toll Free Tel:* 866-280-2239 *E-mail:* sales@icadmed.com; support@icamed.com *Web Site:* www.icadmed.com, pg 1370

Klein, Steve, Choice Associates, 501 Fifth Ave, Suite 1601, New York, NY 10017 *Tel:* 212-679-2434 *Fax:* 212-213-0984 *E-mail:* info@choicepersonnelinc.com *Web Site:* www.choicepersonnelinc.com, pg 1381

Kleiner, Karen, Clear Concepts, 1329 Federal Ave, Suite 6, Los Angeles, CA 90025 *Tel:* 323-285-0325, pg 1108, 1314, 1344

Kleinschmidt, Caitlin, Lightning Source LLC, 1246 Heil Quaker Blvd, La Vergne, TN 37086 *Tel:* 615-793-5000 (Ingram) *Toll Free Tel:* 800-378-5508; 800-509-4156 (cust serv) *E-mail:* lsicustomersupport@ingramcontent.com; contentacquisitioninquiries@ingramcontent.com *Web Site:* www.ingramcontent.com/publishers/print, pg 1212

Kleinschmidt, Caitlin, Lightning Source LLC, 1246 Heil Quaker Blvd, La Vergne, TN 37086 *Tel:* 615-793-5000 (Ingram) *Toll Free Tel:* 800-378-5508; 800-509-4156 (cust serv) *E-mail:* lsicustomersupport@ingramcontent.com *Web Site:* www.ingramcontent.com/publishers/print, pg 1256, 1371

Klouda, Lauren, Independent Publishers Group (IPG), 814 N Franklin St, Chicago, IL 60610 *Tel:* 312-337-0747 *Toll Free Tel:* 800-888-4741 (orders) *Fax:* 312-337-5985 *E-mail:* frontdesk@ipgbook.com; orders@ipgbook.com *Web Site:* www.ipgbook.com, pg 1292

Kluckhohn, Bruce, Bruce Kluckhohn Photographer, 2608 Webster Ave S, Minneapolis, MN 55416-1723 *Tel:* 612-929-6010 *E-mail:* bruce@brucekphoto.com *Web Site:* www.brucekphoto.com, pg 1423

Knab, Phil L, B W Wilson Paper Co Inc, 2501 Brittons Hill Rd, Richmond, VA 23230 *Tel:* 804-358-6715 *Toll Free Tel:* 800-868-2868 *Fax:* 804-358-4742 *E-mail:* info@bwwilson.com; sales@bwwilson.com *Web Site:* www.bwwilson.com, pg 1273

Knaggs, Tammy, Pacific Publishing Co Inc, 636 Alaska St S, Seattle, WA 98108 *Tel:* 206-461-1300 *E-mail:* ppcprint@nwlink.com; ppccirc@nwlink.com; ppcbind@nwlink.com *Web Site:* pacificpublishingcompany.com, pg 1258

Knight, Phil, Color House Graphics Inc, 3505 Eastern Ave SE, Grand Rapids, MI 49508 *Toll Free Tel:* 800-454-1916 *Fax:* 616-245-5494 *Web Site:* www.colorhousegraphics.com, pg 1209, 1250, 1345

Knipfer, David R, Mapping Specialists Ltd, 3000 Cahill Main, Suite 220, Fitchburg, WI 53711 *Tel:* 608-274-4004 *Toll Free Tel:* 866-525-2298 *E-mail:* msl@mappingspecialists.com *Web Site:* www.mappingspecialists.com, pg 1416

Knotts, Daniel L, RR Donnelley, 35 W Wacker Dr, Chicago, IL 60601 *Toll Free Tel:* 800-742-4455 *Web Site:* www.rrd.com, pg 1210, 1225, 1252, 1266, 1279

Knotts, Daniel L, RR Donnelley & Sons Company, 35 W Wacker Dr, Chicago, IL 60601 *Tel:* 312-326-8000 *Toll Free Tel:* 800-742-4455 *Web Site:* www.rrd.com, pg 1333

Knudson, Serena, Independent Publishers Group (IPG), 814 N Franklin St, Chicago, IL 60610 *Tel:* 312-337-0747 *Toll Free Tel:* 800-888-4741 (orders) *Fax:* 312-337-5985 *E-mail:* frontdesk@ipgbook.com; orders@ipgbook.com *Web Site:* www.ipgbook.com, pg 1292, 1328

Kobberger, Brian, QBS Learning, 242 W 30 St, Suite 1100, New York, NY 10001 *Tel:* 646-668-4645 *E-mail:* contact@qbslearning.com *Web Site:* www.qbslearning.com, pg 1357, 1417

Koch, Brad, Webcrafters Inc, 2211 Fordem Ave, Madison, WI 53704 *Tel:* 608-244-3561 *Toll Free Tel:* 800-356-8200 *Fax:* 608-244-5120 *E-mail:* info@webcrafters-inc.com *Web Site:* www.webcrafters-inc.com, pg 1215, 1262, 1284

Kochar, Amandeep, Baker & Taylor LLC, 2550 W Tyvola Rd, Suite 300, Charlotte, NC 28217 *Tel:* 704-998-3100 *Toll Free Tel:* 800-775-1800 (info servs) *Fax:* 704-998-3319 *Toll Free Fax:* 800-775-2600 *E-mail:* btinfo@baker-taylor.com *Web Site:* www.baker-taylor.com, pg 1145

Kochar, Amandeep, Baker & Taylor LLC, 2550 W Tyvola Rd, Suite 300, Charlotte, NC 28217 *Tel:* 704-998-3100 *Toll Free Tel:* 800-775-1800 (info servs) *Fax:* 704-998-3319 *E-mail:* btinfo@baker-taylor.com *Web Site:* www.baker-taylor.com, pg 1286, 1312

Kocina, Lonny, Media Relations Agency, 350 W Burnsville Pkwy, Suite 350, Burnsville, MN 55337 *Tel:* 952-697-5220 *Fax:* 952-697-3256 *Web Site:* www.publicity.com, pg 1111

Koecher, Molly, Longleaf Services Inc, 116 S Boundary St, Chapel Hill, NC 27514-3808 *Tel:* 919-966-7449 *Toll Free Tel:* 800-848-6224 *Fax:* 919-962-2704 (24 hours) *Toll Free Fax:* 800-272-6817 (24 hours) *E-mail:* customerservice@longleafservices.org; orders@longleafservices.org *Web Site:* longleafservices.org, pg 1295

Koechling, William, William Koechling Photography, 1307 E Harrison Ave, Wheaton, IL 60187 *Tel:* 630-665-4379 *E-mail:* koechlingphoto@sbcglobal.net *Web Site:* www.facebook.com/koechlingphoto; 500px.com/billkoechling, pg 1423

Koenigsknecht, Michelle, AIGA, the professional association for design, 228 Park Ave S, Suite 5803, New York, NY 10003 *Tel:* 212-807-1990 *E-mail:* general@aiga.org *Web Site:* www.aiga.org, pg 1139

Koffler, Lionel, Firefly Books Ltd, 50 Staples Ave, Unit 1, Richmond Hill, ON L4B 0A7, Canada *Tel:* 416-499-8412 *Toll Free Tel:* 800-387-6192 (CN); 800-387-5085 (US) *Fax:* 416-499-8313 *Toll Free Fax:* 800-450-0391 (CN); 800-565-6034 (US) *E-mail:* service@fireflybooks.com *Web Site:* www.fireflybooks.com, pg 1291

Kohan, Deborah, Media Connect, 1675 Broadway, New York, NY 10019 *Tel:* 212-715-1600 *Web Site:* www.media-connect.com, pg 1110

Kolady, Emmanuel, Follett Higher Education Group, 3 Westbrook Corporate Ctr, Suite 200, Westchester, IL 60154 *Tel:* 708-884-0000 *Toll Free Tel:* 800-FOLLETT (365-5388) *Web Site:* www.follett.com/higher-ed, pg 1315

Kolatch, David, Jonathan David Publishers Inc, 52 Tuscan Way, Suite 202-371, St Augustine, FL 32092 *Tel:* 718-456-8611 *E-mail:* customerservice@jdbooks.com *Web Site:* www.jdbooks.com, pg 1295

Koll, Thomas, Laplink Software Inc, 600 108 Ave NE, Suite 610, Bellevue, WA 98004 *Tel:* 425-952-6000 *Toll Free Tel:* 800-LAPLINK (527-5465) *E-mail:* info@laplink.com; sales@laplink.com *Web Site:* web.laplink.com, pg 1371

Koller, Edward III, Koller Search Partners, 655 Third Ave, 24th fl, New York, NY 10017 *Tel:* 212-661-5250 *E-mail:* ksp@kollersearch.com *Web Site:* www.kollersearch.com, pg 1381

Koller, Edward R Jr, Koller Search Partners, 655 Third Ave, 24th fl, New York, NY 10017 *Tel:* 212-661-5250 *E-mail:* ksp@kollersearch.com *Web Site:* www.kollersearch.com, pg 1381

Konecky, Steven, Printing Corporation of the Americas Inc, 620 SW 12 Ave, Pompano Beach, FL 33069 *Tel:* 954-781-8100 *Toll Free Tel:* 866-721-1PCA (721-1722) *Web Site:* pcaprintingplus.com, pg 1213, 1229, 1258, 1270

Konzelman, Megan, Penguin Random House Canada, a Penguin Random House company, 320 Front St W, Suite 1400, Toronto, ON M5V 3B6, Canada *Tel:* 416-364-4449 *Toll Free Tel:* 888-523-9292 (cust serv) *Fax:* 416-598-7764 *E-mail:* customerservicescanada@penguinrandomhouse.com; publicitycanada@penguinrandomhouse.com; rightscanada@penguinrandomhouse.com *Web Site:* www.penguinrandomhouse.ca, pg 1299

Koon, Tyler, Lawton Connect, 649 Triumph Ct, Orlando, FL 32805 *Tel:* 407-260-0400 *Toll Free Tel:* 877-330-1900 *Fax:* 407-260-1321 *E-mail:* hello@lawtonconnect.com *Web Site:* www.lawtonconnect.com, pg 1256

Koonse, Emma, Publishers Weekly, 49 W 23 St, 9th fl, New York, NY 10010 *Tel:* 212-377-5500 *Fax:* 212-377-2733 *Web Site:* www.publishersweekly.com, pg 1136

Kopp, Darby, GOBI® Library Solutions from EBSCO, 999 Maple St, Contoocook, NH 03229 *Tel:* 603-746-3102 *Toll Free Tel:* 800-258-3774 (US & CN) *Fax:* 603-746-5628 *E-mail:* information@ebsco.com *Web Site:* gobi.ebsco.com, pg 1316

Koschmann, Matthew, Management Communication Quarterly (MCQ), 2455 Teller Rd, Thousand Oaks, CA 91320 *Toll Free Tel:* 800-818-7243 *Toll Free Fax:* 800-583-2665 *E-mail:* journals@sagepub.com *Web Site:* www.sagepub.com, pg 1134

Kosloff, David, Roosevelt Paper Co, One Roosevelt Dr, Mount Laurel, NJ 08054 *Tel:* 856-303-4100 *Toll Free Tel:* 800-523-3470 *Fax:* 856-642-1949 *E-mail:* marketing@rooseveltpaper.com *Web Site:* www.rooseveltpaper.com, pg 1271

Kosloff, Ted, Roosevelt Paper Co, One Roosevelt Dr, Mount Laurel, NJ 08054 *Tel:* 856-303-4100 *Toll Free Tel:* 800-523-3470 *Fax:* 856-642-1949 *E-mail:* marketing@rooseveltpaper.com *Web Site:* www.rooseveltpaper.com, pg 1271

Kosnik, Kenneth R, Computer Analytics Corp, 999 E Touhy Ave, Suite 130, Des Plaines, IL 60018-2736 *Tel:* 847-297-5290 *Fax:* 847-297-8680 *Web Site:* www.cacorp.com, pg 1366

Koss, Gretchen, Tandem Literary, 28 Clinton Rd, Glen Ridge, NJ 07028 *Tel:* 212-629-1990 *Fax:* 212-629-1990 *Web Site:* tandemliterary.com, pg 1113

Kostiuk, Tony, Citation Box & Paper Co, 4700 W Augusta Blvd, Chicago, IL 60651-3397 *Tel:* 773-378-1400 *E-mail:* info@citationbox.com *Web Site:* www.citationbox.com, pg 1337

Kotze, Alaine, Omeda, 4 Overlook Point, Suite A2SE, Lincolnshire, IL 60069 *Tel:* 847-564-8900 *E-mail:* getstarted@omeda.com *Web Site:* www.omeda.com, pg 1334

Koviak, Ian, theBookDesigners, 454 Las Gallinas Ave, PMB 2015, San Rafael, CA 94903 *Tel:* 415-637-9550 *E-mail:* info@bookdesigners.com *Web Site:* bookdesigners.com, pg 1412

Kraus, Dennis, Chicago Distribution Center (CDC), 11030 S Langley Ave, Chicago, IL 60628 *Tel:* 773-702-7010 *Toll Free Fax:* 800-621-8476 *Web Site:* press.uchicago.edu/cdc, pg 1289

Krause, Rayner, Southern Territory Associates, 4508 64 St, Lubbock, TX 79414 *E-mail:* sta77@suddenlink.net *Web Site:* www.southernterritory.com, pg 1302

Kravitz, Scott, Ironmark, 9040 Junction Dr, Annapolis Junction, MD 20701 *Toll Free Tel:* 888-775-3737 *E-mail:* marketing@ironmarkusa.com *Web Site:* ironmarkusa.com, pg 1211, 1227, 1255, 1268, 1281

Kravtin, Teresa Rolfe, Southern Territory Associates, 4508 64 St, Lubbock, TX 79414 *E-mail:* sta77@suddenlink.net *Web Site:* www.southernterritory.com, pg 1302

Kremer, John, Open Horizons Publishing Co, PO Box 271, Dolan Springs, NM 86441 *Tel:* 575-741-1581 *E-mail:* books@bookmarketingbestsellers.com *Web Site:* bookmarketingbestsellers.com, pg 1350

Krickett, J D, The Cricket Letter Inc, PO Box 527, Ardmore, PA 19003-0527 *Tel:* 610-924-9158 *Fax:* 610-924-9159 *E-mail:* crcktinc@aol.com, pg 1190

Kriho, John, Meadows Publishing Solutions, 1320 Tower Rd, Schaumburg, IL 60173 *Tel:* 847-882-8202 *Fax:* 847-882-9494 *E-mail:* sales@meadowsps.com *Web Site:* meadowsps.com, pg 1372

Krinsky, Santosh, New Leaf Distributing Co, 1085 E Lotus Dr, Silver Lake, WI 53170 *Tel:* 262-889-8501 (ext 162) *Toll Free Tel:* 800-326-2665 (orders) *Fax:* 262-889-8598 *E-mail:* orders@newleafdist.com, pg 1298, 1319

Krishna, Arvind, IBM Corp, One New Orchard Rd, Armonk, NY 10504 *Tel:* 914-499-1900 *Toll Free Tel:* 800-426-4968 *E-mail:* askibm@vnet.ibm.com *Web Site:* www.ibm.com, pg 1370

Krofick, Randolph S PhD, NWinds, One Northgate Sq, Greensburg, PA 15601 *Tel:* 724-838-8993 *Toll Free Fax:* 888-315-3711 *E-mail:* support@nwinds.com *Web Site:* www.nwinds.com, pg 1374

Kronsberg, Ashley, Diamond Book Distributors (DBD), 10150 York Rd, Hunt Valley, MD 21030 *Tel:* 443-318-8001; 443-318-8519 (cust serv) *E-mail:* distribution@diamondbookdistributors.com; dbdreorders@diamondbookdistributors.com (orders); books@diamondbookdistributors.com (cust serv) *Web Site:* diamondbookdistributors.com, pg 1290

Krueger, Ray, The New York Times Licensing Group, 620 Eighth Ave, 20th fl, New York, NY 10018 *Tel:* 212-556-1927 *E-mail:* nytlg-sales@nytimes.com *Web Site:* nytlicensing.com, pg 1191

Kruk, Ondrej, X-Rite Inc, 4300 44 St SE, Grand Rapids, MI 49512 *Tel:* 616-803-2100 *Toll Free Tel:* 800-248-9748; 888-800-9580 (sales) *E-mail:* info@xrite.com *Web Site:* www.xrite.com, pg 1284

Kubinec, Jessica, LARB Quarterly Journal, 6671 Sunset Blvd, Suite 1521, Los Angeles, CA 90028 *Tel:* 323-952-3950 *E-mail:* info@lareviewofbooks.org; editorial@lareviewofbooks.org *Web Site:* lareviewofbooks.org, pg 1133

Kucharski, Matt, PadillaCRT, 1101 W River Pkwy, Suite 400, Minneapolis, MN 55415 *Tel:* 612-455-1700 *Fax:* 612-455-1060 *Web Site:* www.padillacrt.com, pg 1111

Kuehn, Meg LaBorde, Kirkus, 1140 Broadway, Suite 802, New York, NY 10001 *E-mail:* customercare@kirkus.com *Web Site:* www.kirkusreviews.com, pg 1133

Kui, Barnabas, Hearst Newspapers, 300 W 57 St, New York, NY 10019 *Tel:* 212-649-2000 *Web Site:* www.hearst.com/newspapers, pg 1190

Kumar, Nilima, Avanti Enterprises Inc, 18901 Springfield Ave, Flossmoor, IL 60422-1071 *Tel:* 630-850-3245 *Toll Free Tel:* 800-799-6464 *Fax:* 708-799-6474 *Toll Free Fax:* 877-799-6474 *E-mail:* sales@avantiusa.com *Web Site:* www.avantiusa.com, pg 1327

Kupec, Lolly, Wild West Communications Group, PO Box 346, Homewood, CA 96141 *Tel:* 530-412-1096 *Fax:* 530-525-4559 *Web Site:* www.wildwest-tahoe.com, pg 1417

Kuriyqua, Toshihiro, Alps Alpine North America Inc, 3151 Jay St, Suite 101, Santa Clara, CA 95054 *Tel:* 408-361-6400; 408-226-7301 *Fax:* 408-980-9945; 408-226-7301 *E-mail:* alps-pr@jp.alps.com *Web Site:* www.alpsalpine.com/na, pg 1329

Kurtaran, Dilara, Penguin Random House Canada, a Penguin Random House company, 320 Front St W, Suite 1400, Toronto, ON M5V 3B6, Canada *Tel:* 416-364-4449 *Toll Free Tel:* 888-523-9292 (cust serv)

Fax: 416-598-7764 E-mail: customerservicescanada@penguinrandomhouse.com; publicitycanada@penguinrandomhouse.com; rightscanada@penguinrandomhouse.com Web Site: www.penguinrandomhouse.ca, pg 1299

Kurtis, Matthew, Ware-Pak LLC, 2427 Bond St, University Park, IL 60484 Tel: 708-534-2600 E-mail: sales@ware-pak.com Web Site: www.ware-pak.com, pg 1335

Kurtzman, Chris, Webcrafters Inc, 2211 Fordem Ave, Madison, WI 53704 Tel: 608-244-3561 Toll Free Tel: 800-356-8200 Fax: 608-244-5120 E-mail: info@webcrafters-inc.com Web Site: www.webcrafters-inc.com, pg 1215, 1262, 1284

Kurz, Dave, Stoesser Register Systems, 610 Whitetail Blvd, River Falls, WI 54022 Tel: 715-425-1900 Toll Free Tel: 888-407-4808 Fax: 715-425-1901 E-mail: info@nela-usa.com Web Site: www.nela-usa.com, pg 1283

Kuzyk, Andrew, Entro Communications Inc, 33 Harbour Sq, Suite 202, Toronto, ON M5J 2G2, Canada Tel: 416-368-6988 Fax: 416-368-5616 E-mail: toronto@entro.com Web Site: www.entro.com, pg 1414

Kvasnicka, Dan, CG Book Printers, 1750 Northway Dr, North Mankato, MN 56003 Tel: 507-388-3300 Toll Free Tel: 800-729-7575 Fax: 507-386-6350 E-mail: cgbooks@corpgraph.com Web Site: www.corpgraph.com, pg 1103, 1115, 1209, 1223, 1250, 1265, 1278, 1354, 1366

Kyberd, Tony, Freestyle Software, 9 Campus Dr, Parsippany, NJ 07054 Toll Free Tel: 800-474-5760 Fax: 973-237-9043 E-mail: info@freestylesolutions.com Web Site: www.freestylesolutions.com, pg 1369

Kyle, Shane, Scholastic School Reading Events, 1080 Greenwood Blvd, Lake Mary, FL 32746 Tel: 407-829-8000 Toll Free Tel: 800-770-4662 Fax: 407-829-2600 E-mail: custservbf@scholasticbookfairs.com Web Site: bookfairs.scholastic.com/content/fairs/home.html, pg 1302, 1321

La Reau, Rick, Worth Higgins & Associates Inc, 8770 Park Central Dr, Richmond, VA 23227-1146 Tel: 804-264-2304 Toll Free Tel: 800-883-7768 Fax: 804-264-5733 E-mail: contact@whaprint.com Web Site: www.worthhiggins.com, pg 1226

La Spina, David, Esto Photographics Inc, 36 Waverly Ave, Brooklyn, NY 11205 Tel: 212-505-5454 E-mail: sales@esto.com; assignments@esto.com Web Site: estostock.com, pg 1428

Labrecque, David, Labrecque Creative Sound, 2825 Main St, Becket, MA 01223, pg 1371

Lach, Will, Eriksen Translations Inc, 360 Court St, Unit 37, Brooklyn, NY 11231 Tel: 718-802-9010 Fax: 718-802-0041 Web Site: www.eriksen.com, pg 1401

Lachina, Jeff, Lachina Creative, 3693 Green Rd, Cleveland, OH 44122 Tel: 216-292-7959 E-mail: info@lachina.com Web Site: www.lachina.com, pg 1227, 1355, 1371, 1415

Laden, Susan, Biblical Archaeology Society, 4710 41 St NW, Washington, DC 20016-1705 Tel: 202-364-3300 Toll Free Tel: 800-221-4644 Fax: 202-364-2636 E-mail: info@biblicalarchaeology.org Web Site: www.biblicalarchaeology.org, pg 1365

Ladewski, Bill, RUSQ: A Journal of Reference and User Experience, 225 N Michigan Ave, Suite 1300, Chicago, IL 60601 Tel: 312-280-4395 Toll Free Tel: 800-545-2433 Fax: 312-280-5273 E-mail: rusq@ala.org Web Site: www.ala.org/rusa/rusq-journal, pg 1136

Lafave, John, Resolute Forest Products, 111 Robert-Bourassa Blvd, Suite 5000, Montreal, QC H3C 2M1, Canada Tel: 514-875-2160 Toll Free Tel: 800-361-2888 E-mail: info@resolutefp.com Web Site: www.resolutefp.com, pg 1271

Laflamme, Yves, Resolute Forest Products, 111 Robert-Bourassa Blvd, Suite 5000, Montreal, QC H3C 2M1, Canada Tel: 514-875-2160 Toll Free Tel: 800-361-2888 E-mail: info@resolutefp.com Web Site: www.resolutefp.com, pg 1271

Lafranier, John, Disticor Magazine Distribution Services, 1000 Thornton Rd S, Oshawa, ON L1J 7E2, Canada Tel: 905-619-6565 Web Site: www.disticor.com; www.magamall.com, pg 1333

Lagunarajan, Ankanee, Penguin Random House Canada, a Penguin Random House company, 320 Front St W, Suite 1400, Toronto, ON M5V 3B6, Canada Tel: 416-364-4449 Toll Free Tel: 888-523-9292 (cust serv) Fax: 416-598-7764 E-mail: customerservicescanada@penguinrandomhouse.com; publicitycanada@penguinrandomhouse.com; rightscanada@penguinrandomhouse.com Web Site: www.penguinrandomhouse.ca, pg 1299

Laib, James, Allied Vaughn, 7600 Parklawn Ave, Suite 300, Minneapolis, MN 55435 Tel: 952-832-3100 Toll Free Tel: 800-323-0281 Fax: 952-832-3203 Web Site: www.alliedvaughn.com, pg 1364

Lair, Dave, AcmeBinding, 8844 Mayfield Rd, Chesterland, OH 44026 Tel: 440-729-9411 Toll Free Tel: 888-485-5415 Fax: 440-729-9415 Web Site: www.acmebinding.com, pg 1247

Laitin, Julie A, Julie A Laitin Enterprises Inc, 160 West End Ave, Suite 23N, New York, NY 10023 Tel: 917-841-8566 E-mail: info@julielaitin.com Web Site: www.julielaitin.com, pg 1100

Lake, Karen, Lake Group Media Inc, One Byram Brook Place, Armonk, NY 10504 Tel: 914-925-2400 Fax: 914-925-2499 Web Site: www.lakegroupmedia.com, pg 1120

Lake, Ryan, Lake Group Media Inc, One Byram Brook Place, Armonk, NY 10504 Tel: 914-925-2400 Fax: 914-925-2499 Web Site: www.lakegroupmedia.com, pg 1120

Lamkin, Bryan, Adobe Systems Inc, 345 Park Ave, San Jose, CA 95110-2704 Tel: 408-536-6000 Fax: 408-537-6000 Web Site: www.adobe.com, pg 1363

Lamy, Dr Francis, X-Rite Inc, 4300 44 St SE, Grand Rapids, MI 49512 Tel: 616-803-2100 Toll Free Tel: 800-248-9748; 888-800-9580 (sales) E-mail: info@xrite.com Web Site: www.xrite.com, pg 1284

Lance, Jim, MSC Lists, PO Box 32510, Minneapolis, MN 55432 Tel: 763-502-8819, pg 1120

Landers, Scott, Monotype Imaging Inc, 600 Unicorn Park Dr, Woburn, MA 01801 Tel: 781-970-6000 Web Site: www.monotype.com, pg 1373

Landheer, Matt, Great Lakes Bindery Inc, 3741 Linden Ave SE, Wyoming, MI 49548 Tel: 616-245-5264 Fax: 616-245-5883 E-mail: jeremy@greatlakesbindery.com Web Site: www.greatlakesbindery.com, pg 1254

Landheer, Steve, Color House Graphics Inc, 3505 Eastern Ave SE, Grand Rapids, MI 49508 Toll Free Tel: 800-454-1916 Fax: 616-245-5494 Web Site: www.colorhousegraphics.com, pg 1209, 1250

Landheer, Steve, Great Lakes Bindery Inc, 3741 Linden Ave SE, Wyoming, MI 49548 Tel: 616-245-5264 Fax: 616-245-5883 E-mail: jeremy@greatlakesbindery.com Web Site: www.greatlakesbindery.com, pg 1254

Lane, Dave, D&D Sales & Printing, 840 12 St NW, Mason City, IA 50401 Tel: 641-423-9487 Toll Free Tel: 800-325-5308 Fax: 641-423-3068 E-mail: ddsales.service@gmail.com Web Site: www.ddsalesonline.com, pg 1413

Lane, Eric, The Dingley Press, 119 Lisbon St, Lisbon, ME 04250 Tel: 207-353-4151 Toll Free Tel: 800-317-4574 Fax: 207-353-9886 E-mail: info@dingley.com Web Site: www.dingley.com, pg 1252

Lane, Lisa, D&D Sales & Printing, 840 12 St NW, Mason City, IA 50401 Tel: 641-423-9487 Toll Free Tel: 800-325-5308 Fax: 641-423-3068 E-mail: ddsales.service@gmail.com Web Site: www.ddsalesonline.com, pg 1413

Langerman, Alisha, AudioFile®, 37 Silver St, Portland, ME 04101 Tel: 207-774-7563 Toll Free Tel: 800-506-1212 Fax: 207-775-3744 E-mail: info@audiofilemagazine.com Web Site: www.audiofilemagazine.com, pg 1130

Langley, Paul, Coverline Inc, 13 Spruce Pond Rd, Franklin, MA 02038 Tel: 508-528-8511 Fax: 508-528-6838, pg 1266

Langston, Keitha, United Library Services Inc, 7140 Fairmount Dr SE, Calgary, AB T2H 0X4, Canada Tel: 403-252-4426 Toll Free Tel: 888-342-5857 (CN only) Fax: 403-258-3426 Toll Free Fax: 800-661-2806 (CN only) E-mail: info@uls.com Web Site: www.uls.com, pg 1323

Lansdon, Jason, Communicorp Inc, 1001 Lockwood Ave, Columbus, GA 31999 Tel: 706-324-1182 E-mail: mktech@communicorp.com Web Site: www.communicorp.com, pg 1224, 1250

Lantz, Heather, Ingenta, 317 George St, New Brunswick, NJ 08901 Tel: 732-563-9292 Fax: 732-563-9044 Web Site: www.ingenta.com, pg 1370

Lanuke, Kevin, Blitzprint Inc, 1235 64 Ave SE, Suite 1, Calgary, AB T2H 2J7, Canada Toll Free Tel: 866-479-3248 Fax: 403-253-5642 E-mail: books@blitzprint.com Web Site: www.blitzprint.com, pg 1249

Lapham, John, Shutterstock Inc, Empire State Bldg, 350 Fifth Ave, 20th fl, New York, NY 10118 E-mail: support@shutterstock.com; press@shutterstock.com Web Site: www.shutterstock.com, pg 1430

LaPierre, Jim, GEX Inc, 80 Conley's Grove Rd, Derry, NH 03038 Tel: 603-870-9292 Web Site: www.gexinc.com, pg 1211, 1226, 1355, 1369, 1414

Lapointe, Denise, St Armand Paper Mill, 3700 St Patrick, Montreal, QC H4E 1A2, Canada Tel: 514-931-8338 Fax: 514-931-5953 Web Site: www.st-armand.com, pg 1271

Laredo, Sam, Renaissance House, 465 Westview Ave, Englewood, NJ 07631 Tel: 201-408-4048 Web Site: www.renaissancehouse.net, pg 1357

Larmor, Joseph H, Ulster Linen Co Inc, 383 Moffit Blvd, Islip, NY 11751 Tel: 631-859-5244 Fax: 631-859-4990 E-mail: sales@ulsterlinen.com Web Site: www.ulsterlinen.com, pg 1273

LaRoche, JP, eFulfillment Service Inc, 807 Airport Access Rd, Traverse City, MI 49686 Tel: 231-276-5057 Toll Free Tel: 866-922-6783 E-mail: sales@efulfillmentservice.com Web Site: www.efulfillmentservice.com, pg 1333

LaRochelle, Lisa, Emerson, Wajdowicz Studios Inc, 514 W 25 St, New York, NY 10001 Tel: 212-807-8144 E-mail: info@designews.com Web Site: www.designews.com; www.facebook.com/DesignEWS; www.instagram.com/ewsdesign, pg 1414

Larsen, Anne, John Sexton Photography, PO Box 30, Carmel Valley, CA 93924 Tel: 831-659-3130 Fax: 831-659-5509 E-mail: info@johnsexton.com Web Site: www.johnsexton.com, pg 1425

Larsen, James M, Bridgeport National Bindery Inc, 662 Silver St, Agawam, MA 01001 Tel: 413-789-1981 Toll Free Tel: 800-223-5083 E-mail: info@bnbindery.com Web Site: www.bnbindery.com, pg 1249, 1325

Larsen, Jill, PTC, 121 Seaport Blvd, Boston, MA 02210 Tel: 781-370-5000 Fax: 781-370-6000 Web Site: www.ptc.com, pg 1375

Larson, Dave, Nisus Software Inc, PO Box 1302, Solana Beach, CA 92075-7302 Tel: 858-481-1477 Fax: 858-764-0573 E-mail: info@nisus.com; sales@nisus.com; customerservice@nisus.com Web Site: www.nisus.com, pg 1373

Larson, Eric C, Studio E Book Production, PO Box 20005, Santa Barbara, CA 93120-0005 Tel: 805-683-6202 Fax: 805-683-6202 E-mail: queries@studio-e-books.com Web Site: www.studio-e-books.com, pg 1417

Larson, John, Cohesion®, 511 W Bay St, Suite 480, Tampa, FL 33606 Tel: 813-999-3111 Toll Free Tel: 866-727-6800 Web Site: www.cohesion.com, pg 1344, 1366, 1381

Larson, Kent, Bridgeport National Bindery Inc, 662 Silver St, Agawam, MA 01001 *Tel:* 413-789-1981 *Toll Free Tel:* 800-223-5083 *E-mail:* info@bnbindery.com *Web Site:* www.bnbindery.com, pg 1249, 1325

Larson, Pete, Bethany Press International Inc, 6820 W 115 St, Bloomington, MN 55438 *Tel:* 952-914-7400 *Toll Free Tel:* 888-717-7400 *Fax:* 952-914-7410 *E-mail:* info@bethanypress.com *Web Site:* www.bethanypress.com, pg 1248

Larson, Tim, Larson Texts Inc, 1762 Norcross Rd, Erie, PA 16510 *Tel:* 814-824-6365 *Toll Free Tel:* 800-530-2355 *Fax:* 814-824-6377 *Web Site:* www.larsontexts.com, pg 1228, 1269, 1355

Lashkari, Shahab, OmniUpdate Inc, 1320 Flynn Rd, Suite 100, Camarillo, CA 93012 *Tel:* 805-484-9400 *Toll Free Tel:* 800-362-2605 *E-mail:* sales@omniupdate.com *Web Site:* omniupdate.com, pg 1374

Latham, Bethany, The Historical Novels Review, PO Box 1146, Jacksonville, AL 36265 *E-mail:* reviews@historicalnovelsociety.org; contact@historicalnovelsociety.org *Web Site:* historicalnovelsociety.org, pg 1132

Latimer, Len, Lynx Media Inc, 13654 Victory Blvd, No 282, Valley Glen, CA 91401 *Tel:* 818-761-5859 *Toll Free Tel:* 800-451-5969 *Fax:* 818-761-7099 *E-mail:* sales@lynxmedia.com *Web Site:* www.lynxmedia.com, pg 1372

Latimer, Matt, Javelin Group, 203 S Union St, Suite 200, Alexandria, VA 22314 *Tel:* 703-490-8845 *E-mail:* hello@javelindc.com *Web Site:* javelindc.com, pg 1348

Lau, Travis Chi Wing, Literature & Medicine, 2715 N Charles St, Baltimore, MD 21218-4363 *Tel:* 410-516-6987 (journal orders outside US & CN) *Toll Free Tel:* 800-548-1784 (journal orders) *Fax:* 410-578-2865 (journal orders) *E-mail:* jrnlcirc@jh.edu (journal orders) *Web Site:* www.press.jhu.edu/journals/literature-and-medicine, pg 1134

Lau, Victoria, Jane Wesman Public Relations Inc, 322 Eighth Ave, Suite 1702, New York, NY 10001 *Tel:* 212-620-4080 *Fax:* 212-620-0370 *Web Site:* www.wesmanpr.com, pg 1110

Laurenzo, Hana, Teneo Linguistics Co LLC, 3010 W Parkrow Dr, Pampego, TX 76013 *Tel:* 817-441-9974 *Fax:* 817-953-6424 *E-mail:* info@tlctranslation.com *Web Site:* www.tlctranslation.com, pg 1405

Laures, Wolfgang, Glatfelter, Capitol Towers South, 4350 Congress St, Suite 600, Charlotte, NC 28209 *Tel:* 717-850-0170 *Toll Free Tel:* 866-744-7380 *E-mail:* info@glatfelter.com *Web Site:* www.glatfelter.com, pg 1267

Lauro, Joe, Historic Films LLC, 211 Third St, Greenport, NY 11944 *Tel:* 631-477-9700 *Toll Free Tel:* 800-249-1940 *Fax:* 631-477-9800 *E-mail:* info@historicfilms.com *Web Site:* www.historicfilms.com, pg 1429

Lauzon, Rachelle, eFulfillment Service Inc, 807 Airport Access Rd, Traverse City, MI 49686 *Tel:* 231-276-5057 *Toll Free Tel:* 866-922-6783 *E-mail:* sales@efulfillmentservice.com *Web Site:* www.efulfillmentservice.com, pg 1333

Law, Sandra, Abraham Associates Inc, 5120-A Cedar Lake Rd, Minneapolis, MN 55416 *Tel:* 952-927-7920 *Toll Free Tel:* 800-701-2489 *Fax:* 952-927-8089 *E-mail:* info@abrahamassociatesinc.com *Web Site:* www.abrahamassociatesinc.com, pg 1285

Lawlor, Owen, Victory Productions Inc, 55 Linden St, Worcester, MA 01609 *Tel:* 508-755-0051 *E-mail:* victory@victoryprd.com *Web Site:* www.victoryprd.com, pg 1358

Lawrance, Heidy, WeMakeBooks.ca, 238 Willowdale Ave, North York, ON M2N 4Z5, Canada *Tel:* 416-733-1827 *Fax:* 416-733-7663 *Web Site:* www.wemakebooks.ca, pg 1233

Lawrence, Bill, Powis Parker Inc, 2929 Fifth St, Berkeley, CA 94710 *Tel:* 510-848-2463 *Toll Free Tel:* 800-321-BIND (321-2463) *Fax:* 510-848-2169 *E-mail:* customerservice@powis.com *Web Site:* www.powis.com, pg 1375

Lawrence, Derek, Imprint Group, 2070 Cherry St, Denver, CO 80207 *Toll Free Tel:* 800-738-3961 *Toll Free Fax:* 888-867-3869 *Web Site:* imprintgroupwest.com, pg 1292

Lawton-Koon, Kimberly, Lawton Connect, 649 Triumph Ct, Orlando, FL 32805 *Tel:* 407-260-0400 *Toll Free Tel:* 877-330-1900 *Fax:* 407-260-1321 *E-mail:* hello@lawtonconnect.com *Web Site:* www.lawtonconnect.com, pg 1256

Lazzaro, Erica, OverDrive Inc, One OverDrive Way, Cleveland, OH 44125 *Tel:* 216-573-6886 *Fax:* 216-573-6888 *E-mail:* info@overdrive.com *Web Site:* www.overdrive.com, pg 1298

Leah, Deanna, HBG Productions/International Publishers Alliance, PO Box 5560, Chico, CA 95927-5560 *Tel:* 530-893-4699 *Web Site:* www.hbgproductions.com, pg 1292

Leathem, Jane, Stylus Publishing LLC, 22883 Quicksilver Dr, Sterling, VA 20166-2019 *Tel:* 703-661-1504 (edit & sales); 703-661-1581 (orders & cust serv); 703-996-1036 *Toll Free Tel:* 800-232-0223 (orders & cust serv) *Fax:* 703-661-1547; 703-661-1501 (orders & cust serv) *E-mail:* stylusinfo@styluspub.com; stylusmail@styluspub.com (orders & cust serv) *Web Site:* styluspub.com, pg 1303

LeBlanc, Hailey, Penguin Random House Canada, a Penguin Random House company, 320 Front St W, Suite 1400, Toronto, ON M5V 3B6, Canada *Tel:* 416-364-4449 *Toll Free Tel:* 888-523-9292 (cust serv) *Fax:* 416-598-7764 *E-mail:* customerservicescanada@penguinrandomhouse.com; publicitycanada@penguinrandomhouse.com; rightscanada@penguinrandomhouse.com *Web Site:* www.penguinrandomhouse.ca, pg 1299

Lebrun, Denise, Design Plus, 1086 Main Rd, Aquebogue, NY 11931 *Tel:* 631-722-4384 *E-mail:* designplusonline@yahoo.com, pg 1367

Lee, Amy, Art Media Resources Inc, 1965 W Pershing Rd, Chicago, IL 60605 *Tel:* 312-663-5351 *Fax:* 312-663-5177 *E-mail:* paragon@paragonbook.com *Web Site:* www.artmediaresources.com, pg 1286

Lee, Eddie, Square Two Design Inc, 2325 Third St, Suite 305, San Francisco, CA 94107 *Tel:* 415-437-3888 *E-mail:* info@square2.com *Web Site:* www.square2.com, pg 1231, 1376, 1417

Lee, Jess, Jess Lee Photography LLC, 13316 Skyview St, Nampa, ID 83686 *Tel:* 208-521-5170 *Web Site:* www.jessleephotos.com, pg 1423

Lee, Joon, Samsung Research America (SRA), 665 Clyde Ave, Mountain View, CA 94043 *Tel:* 650-210-1001 *E-mail:* sra-contact-us@samsung.com *Web Site:* www.sra.samsung.com, pg 1376

Lee, Richard, Delphax Solutions Inc, 2810 Argentia Rd, Unit 6, Mississauga, ON L5N 8L2, Canada *Toll Free Tel:* 833-DELPHAX (335-7429) *Web Site:* www.delphaxsolutions.com, pg 1367

Lee, Richard, The Historical Novels Review, PO Box 1146, Jacksonville, AL 36265 *E-mail:* reviews@historicalnovelsociety.org; contact@historicalnovelsociety.org *Web Site:* historicalnovelsociety.org, pg 1132

Lee, Roger, Ingram Content Group LLC, One Ingram Blvd, La Vergne, TN 37086-1986 *Tel:* 615-793-5000 *Toll Free Tel:* 800-937-8000 (retailers); 800-937-5300 (ext 1, libs) *E-mail:* customerservice@ingramcontent.com *Web Site:* www.ingramcontent.com, pg 1294, 1316

Leeper, Don, BookMobile, 5120 Cedar Lake Rd, Minneapolis, MN 55416 *Tel:* 763-398-0030 *Toll Free Tel:* 844-488-4477 *Fax:* 763-398-0198 *Web Site:* www.bookmobile.com, pg 1249

Lehr, Donald B, The Nolan/Lehr Group Inc, 214 W 29 St, Suite 1002, New York, NY 10001 *Tel:* 212-967-8200 *Fax:* 212-967-4602 *E-mail:* dblehr@cs.com *Web Site:* www.nolanlehrgroup.com, pg 1111

Leibfried, Deb, Shepherd Inc, 2223 Key Way Dr, Suite B, Dubuque, IA 52002 *Tel:* 563-584-0500 *Web Site:* www.shepherd-inc.com, pg 1231, 1259, 1376, 1417

Leichman, Larry, Arbor Books, 244 Madison Ave, Box 254, New York, NY 10016 *Tel:* 212-956-0950 *Toll Free Tel:* 877-822-2500 *Fax:* 914-401-9385 *E-mail:* info@arborbooks.com; editorial@arborbooks.net *Web Site:* www.arborbooks.com, pg 1207, 1222, 1248, 1265, 1344, 1353

Leichman, Larry, Arbor Books, 244 Madison Ave, Box 254, New York, NY 10016 *Tel:* 212-956-0950 *Toll Free Tel:* 877-822-2500 *Fax:* 914-401-9385 *E-mail:* info@arborbooks.com; editorial@arborbooks.net *Web Site:* www.arborbooks.com; www.arborghostwriters.com; www.arborservices.com, pg 1411

Leiferman, Troy, Valley News Co, 1305 Stadium Rd, Mankato, MN 56001 *Tel:* 507-345-4819 *Fax:* 507-345-6793 *Web Site:* www.valleynewscompany.com, pg 1323

Leisner, Debby, Widen Enterprises Inc, 6911 Mangrove Lane, Madison, WI 53713 *Tel:* 608-222-1296 *Toll Free Tel:* 800-444-2828 *E-mail:* marketing@widen.com *Web Site:* www.widen.com, pg 1233

Leite, Denis, Berryville Graphics, 25 Jack Enders Blvd, Berryville, VA 22611 *Tel:* 540-955-2750 *Fax:* 540-955-2633 *E-mail:* info@bvgraphics.com *Web Site:* www.bpg-usa.com, pg 1208, 1222, 1248

Leite, Denis, Coral Graphic Services Inc, 840 S Broadway, Hicksville, NY 11801 *Tel:* 516-576-2100 *Fax:* 516-576-2168 *E-mail:* info@coralgraphics.com *Web Site:* www.bpg-usa.com, pg 1224, 1251, 1266

Leitman, Jennifer, OverDrive Inc, One OverDrive Way, Cleveland, OH 44125 *Tel:* 216-573-6886 *Fax:* 216-573-6888 *E-mail:* info@overdrive.com *Web Site:* www.overdrive.com, pg 1298

Leland, David, Print It Plus, 11420 Okeechobee Blvd, Royal Palm Beach, FL 33411 *Tel:* 561-790-0884 *Fax:* 561-790-9378 *E-mail:* info@printitplus.com *Web Site:* printitplus.com, pg 1258

Leland, Kimberly, Print It Plus, 11420 Okeechobee Blvd, Royal Palm Beach, FL 33411 *Tel:* 561-790-0884 *Fax:* 561-790-9378 *E-mail:* info@printitplus.com *Web Site:* printitplus.com, pg 1258

Lemieux, Drew J, Pratt Paper Company LLC, 20 Davis Rd, Marblehead, MA 01945 *Tel:* 781-639-9450 *Fax:* 781-639-9452, pg 1270

Lemke, Meg, Publishers Weekly, 49 W 23 St, 9th fl, New York, NY 10010 *Tel:* 212-377-5500 *Fax:* 212-377-2733 *Web Site:* www.publishersweekly.com, pg 1136

Lempereur, Yves, OmniUpdate Inc, 1320 Flynn Rd, Suite 100, Camarillo, CA 93012 *Tel:* 805-484-9400 *Toll Free Tel:* 800-362-2605 *E-mail:* sales@omniupdate.com *Web Site:* omniupdate.com, pg 1374

Lennertz, Carl, The Children's Book Council (CBC), 54 W 39 St, 14th fl, New York, NY 10018 *E-mail:* cbc.info@cbcbooks.org *Web Site:* www.cbcbooks.org, pg 1145

Lennie, Frances S, Indexing Research, 620 Park Ave, Suite 183, Rochester, NY 14607 *Tel:* 585-413-1819 *E-mail:* info@indexres.com *Web Site:* www.indexres.com, pg 1370

Leonhartsberger, Laura, Strictly Spanish Translations LLC, Milford, OH 45150 *E-mail:* info@strictlyspanish.com; quotes@strictlyspanish.com *Web Site:* www.strictlyspanish.com, pg 1404

Leontis, Artemis, Journal of Modern Greek Studies, 2715 N Charles St, Baltimore, MD 21218-4363 *Tel:* 410-516-6987 (journal orders outside US & CN) *Toll Free Tel:* 800-548-1784 (journal orders) *Fax:* 410-578-2865 (journal orders) *E-mail:* jrnlcirc@jh.edu (journal orders) *Web Site:* www.press.jhu.edu/journal-modern-greek-studies, pg 1133

Lepore, Bernie, Electronics for Imaging Inc (EFI), 6750 Dumbarton Circle, Fremont, CA 94555 *Tel:* 650-357-3500 *Toll Free Tel:* 800-568-1917; 800-875-7117 (sales) *Fax:* 650-357-3907 *E-mail:* info@efi.com *Web Site:* www.efi.com, pg 1368

Lerner, Ilene, HBP Inc, 952 Frederick St, Hagerstown, MD 21740 *Tel:* 301-733-2000 *Toll Free Tel:* 800-638-3508 *Fax:* 301-733-6586 *E-mail:* contactus@hbp.com *Web Site:* www.hbp.com, pg 1226, 1254, 1280

LeSage, Danielle, Penguin Random House Canada, a Penguin Random House company, 320 Front St W, Suite 1400, Toronto, ON M5V 3B6, Canada *Tel:* 416-364-4449 *Toll Free Tel:* 888-523-9292 (cust serv) *Fax:* 416-598-7764 *E-mail:* customerservicescanada@penguinrandomhouse.com; publicitycanada@penguinrandomhouse.com; rightscanada@penguinrandomhouse.com *Web Site:* www.penguinrandomhouse.ca, pg 1299

Leslie, Jack, Weber Shandwick, 909 Third Ave, New York, NY 10022 *Tel:* 212-445-8000 *Fax:* 212-445-8001 *Web Site:* www.webershandwick.com, pg 1113

Lesser, Herbert M, Midwest Library Service, 11443 Saint Charles Rock Rd, Bridgeton, MO 63044 *Tel:* 314-739-3100 *Fax:* 314-739-1326 *E-mail:* mail@midwestls.com *Web Site:* www.midwestls.com, pg 1319

Lesser, Howard N, Midwest Library Service, 11443 Saint Charles Rock Rd, Bridgeton, MO 63044 *Tel:* 314-739-3100 *Fax:* 314-739-1326 *E-mail:* mail@midwestls.com *Web Site:* www.midwestls.com, pg 1319

Lessne, Donald L, Rights & Distribution Inc, 7519 LaPaz Blvd, Suite C303, Boca Raton, FL 33433 *Tel:* 954-925-5242 *E-mail:* rightsinc@aol.com, pg 1301

Letchinger, Richard, Worzalla, 3535 Jefferson St, Stevens Point, WI 54481 *Tel:* 715-344-9608 *Fax:* 715-344-2578 *Web Site:* www.worzalla.com, pg 1215, 1233, 1262

Leto, Tim, North American Color Inc, 5960 S Sprinkle Rd, Portage, MI 49002 *Tel:* 269-323-0552 *Toll Free Tel:* 800-537-8296 *Fax:* 269-323-0190 *E-mail:* info@nac-mi.com *Web Site:* www.nac-mi.com, pg 1229

Letson, Jacqueline, Ingram Content Group LLC, One Ingram Blvd, La Vergne, TN 37086-1986 *Tel:* 615-793-5000 *Toll Free Tel:* 800-937-8000 (retailers); 800-937-5300 (ext 1, libs) *E-mail:* customerservice@ingramcontent.com *Web Site:* www.ingramcontent.com, pg 1294, 1316

Leung, Jackson, C & C Offset Printing Co USA Inc, 70 W 36 St, Unit 10C, New York, NY 10018 *Tel:* 212-431-4210 *Toll Free Fax:* 866-540-4134 *Web Site:* www.ccoffset.com, pg 1208, 1223, 1249

Leurpecht, Dr Christian, Institute of Intergovernmental Relations, Queen's University, Robert Sutherland Hall, Rm 301, Kingston, ON K7L 3N6, Canada *Tel:* 613-533-2080 *E-mail:* iigr@queensu.ca *Web Site:* www.queensu.ca/iigr, pg 1317

Levernz, Ken, Getty Images Inc, 605 Fifth Ave S, Suite 400, Seattle, WA 98104 *Tel:* 206-925-5000 *Toll Free Tel:* 800-IMAGERY (462-4379); 888-888-5889 *Web Site:* www.gettyimages.com; www.gettyimages.com/customer-support; engage.gettyimages.com/media-inquiries, pg 1369, 1428

Levin, Shane, TOP Engraving, 106 Windsor Way, Berkeley Heights, NJ 07922 *Tel:* 212-239-9170; 201-223-4800, pg 1261

Levine, Mark L, Scarf Press, 1385 Baptist Church Rd, Yorktown Heights, NY 10598 *Tel:* 914-245-7811, pg 1357

LeVines, George, CQ Roll Call, 1201 Pennsylvania Ave NW, Suite 600, Washington, DC 20004 *Tel:* 202-650-6500; 202-650-6511 (subns); 202-650-6621 (cust serv) *Toll Free Tel:* 800-432-2250; 800-678-8511 (subns) *E-mail:* customerservice@cqrollcall.com *Web Site:* cqrollcall.com; www.rollcall.com, pg 1190

Levit, Henri C, Simon Miller Paper & Packaging, 3409 W Chester Pike, Suite 204, Newton Square, PA 19073 *Tel:* 215-923-3600 *Toll Free Tel:* 800-642-1899 *Fax:* 610-355-9330 *E-mail:* sales@simonmiller.com *Web Site:* www.simonmiller.com, pg 1271

Levit, Jeffrey, Simon Miller Paper & Packaging, 3409 W Chester Pike, Suite 204, Newton Square, PA 19073 *Tel:* 215-923-3600 *Toll Free Tel:* 800-642-1899 *Fax:* 610-355-9330 *E-mail:* sales@simonmiller.com *Web Site:* www.simonmiller.com, pg 1271

Levy-Grayson, Valerie, American BookWorks Corp, 309 Florida Hill Rd, Ridgefield, CT 06877 *Tel:* 203-431-9620 *Fax:* 203-244-9522 (orders) *E-mail:* info@abwcorporation.com, pg 1353

Lewak, Jerzy PhD, Nisus Software Inc, PO Box 1302, Solana Beach, CA 92075-7302 *Tel:* 858-481-1477 *Fax:* 858-764-0573 *E-mail:* info@nisus.com; sales@nisus.com; customerservice@nisus.com *Web Site:* www.nisus.com, pg 1373

Lewis, Kathleen, Publishers' Graphics LLC, 131 Fremont St, Chicago, IL 60185 *Tel:* 630-221-1850 *E-mail:* contactpg@pubgraphics.com *Web Site:* pubgraphics.com, pg 1213, 1258, 1282

Lewis, Nick A, Publishers' Graphics LLC, 131 Fremont St, Chicago, IL 60185 *Tel:* 630-221-1850 *E-mail:* contactpg@pubgraphics.com *Web Site:* pubgraphics.com, pg 1213, 1258, 1282

Lewis, Scott, Adams Magnetic Products Co, 888 N Larch Ave, Elmhurst, IL 60126-1133 *Tel:* 630-617-8880 *Toll Free Tel:* 800-747-7543 (sales) *Fax:* 630-617-8881 *Toll Free Fax:* 800-747-1323 *E-mail:* info@adamsmagnetic.com *Web Site:* www.adamsmagnetic.com, pg 1265

Lewis, Tanisha, American Association for the Advancement of Science (AAAS), 1200 New York Ave NW, Washington, DC 20005 *Tel:* 202-326-6400 *Fax:* 202-371-9526 *Web Site:* www.aaas.org, pg 1145

Lewnes, Ann, Adobe Systems Inc, 345 Park Ave, San Jose, CA 95110-2704 *Tel:* 408-536-6000 *Fax:* 408-537-6000 *Web Site:* www.adobe.com, pg 1363

Leyden, Jennifer, Getty Images Inc, 605 Fifth Ave S, Suite 400, Seattle, WA 98104 *Tel:* 206-925-5000 *Toll Free Tel:* 800-IMAGERY (462-4379); 888-888-5889 *Web Site:* www.gettyimages.com; www.gettyimages.com/customer-support; engage.gettyimages.com/media-inquiries, pg 1369, 1428

Liebenau, Jim, Business Wire, 101 California St, 20th fl, San Francisco, CA 94111 *Tel:* 415-986-4422 *Toll Free Tel:* 800-227-0845 *E-mail:* info@businesswire.com *Web Site:* www.businesswire.com, pg 1189

Lieberman, Hyam, Gurarys Israeli Trading Co Inc, 724 Eastern Pkwy, Brooklyn, NY 11213 *Tel:* 718-493-5225 *E-mail:* hebbook@gmail.com, pg 1328

Lief, Philip, The Philip Lief Group Inc (PLG), 2976 Pleasant Ridge Rd, Wingdale, NY 12594 *Tel:* 609-430-1000 *Fax:* 845-724-7139 *E-mail:* info@plg.us.com *Web Site:* plg.us.com, pg 1355

Lien, Chris, BCC Software Inc, 75 Josons Dr, Rochester, NY 14623-3494 *Toll Free Tel:* 800-453-3130; 800-337-0442 (sales) *E-mail:* marketing@bccsoftware.com *Web Site:* www.bccsoftware.com, pg 1365

Lienau, Anthony, Trend Offset Printing Services, 3791 Catalina St, Los Alamitos, CA 90720 *Tel:* 562-598-2446 *Fax:* 562-493-6840 (sales); 562-430-2373 *E-mail:* salesca@trendoffset.com *Web Site:* www.trendoffset.com, pg 1261

Lienau, Robert Jr, Trend Offset Printing Services, 3791 Catalina St, Los Alamitos, CA 90720 *Tel:* 562-598-2446 *Fax:* 562-493-6840 (sales); 562-430-2373 *E-mail:* salesca@trendoffset.com *Web Site:* www.trendoffset.com, pg 1261

Lilian, Farnaz, Penguin Random House Canada, a Penguin Random House company, 320 Front St W, Suite 1400, Toronto, ON M5V 3B6, Canada *Tel:* 416-364-4449 *Toll Free Tel:* 888-523-9292 (cust serv) *Fax:* 416-598-7764 *E-mail:* customerservicescanada@penguinrandomhouse.com; publicitycanada@penguinrandomhouse.com; rightscanada@penguinrandomhouse.com *Web Site:* www.penguinrandomhouse.ca, pg 1299

Lindberg, Jason, eFulfillment Service Inc, 807 Airport Access Rd, Traverse City, MI 49686 *Tel:* 231-276-5057 *Toll Free Tel:* 866-922-6783 *E-mail:* sales@efulfillmentservice.com *Web Site:* www.efulfillmentservice.com, pg 1333

Lindemann, Rick, Total Printing Systems, 201 S Gregory Dr, Newton, IL 62448 *Tel:* 618-783-2978 *Toll Free Tel:* 800-465-5200 *Fax:* 618-783-8407 *E-mail:* sales@tps1.com *Web Site:* www.tps1.com, pg 1261

Lindemann, RJ, Total Printing Systems, 201 S Gregory Dr, Newton, IL 62448 *Tel:* 618-783-2978 *Toll Free Tel:* 800-465-5200 *Fax:* 618-783-8407 *E-mail:* sales@tps1.com *Web Site:* www.tps1.com, pg 1261

Linden, Jeremy, Marquand Books, 3131 Western Ave, Suite 522, Seattle, WA 98121 *Tel:* 206-624-2030 *Web Site:* www.marquandbooks.com, pg 1356

Linden, Judy, Stonesong, 270 W 39 St, Suite 201, New York, NY 10018 *Tel:* 212-929-4600 *E-mail:* editors@stonesong.com *Web Site:* www.stonesong.com, pg 1357

Lindley, Gail, Denver Bookbinding Co Inc, 1401 W 47 Ave, Denver, CO 80211 *Tel:* 303-455-5521 *E-mail:* dbbc@denverbook.com; info@denverbook.com *Web Site:* www.denverbook.com, pg 1325

Lindman, Kim, Stonesong, 270 W 39 St, Suite 201, New York, NY 10018 *Tel:* 212-929-4600 *E-mail:* editors@stonesong.com *Web Site:* www.stonesong.com, pg 1357

Lindsay, Carol, Keister-Williams Newspaper Services Inc, PO Box 8187, Charlottesville, VA 22906 *Tel:* 434-293-4709 *Toll Free Tel:* 800-293-4709 *E-mail:* kw@kwnews.com *Web Site:* www.kwnews.com, pg 1190

Lindsay, Ky, Keister-Williams Newspaper Services Inc, PO Box 8187, Charlottesville, VA 22906 *Tel:* 434-293-4709 *Toll Free Tel:* 800-293-4709 *E-mail:* kw@kwnews.com *Web Site:* www.kwnews.com, pg 1190

Lindvall, Stefan, Multi-Tech Systems Inc, 2205 Woodale Dr, Mounds View, MN 55112 *Tel:* 763-785-3500 *Toll Free Tel:* 800-328-9717 *Fax:* 763-785-9874 *E-mail:* info@multitech.com; sales@multitech.com; mtsmktg@multitech.com *Web Site:* www.multitech.com, pg 1373

Lingl, Herb, Aerial Archives, Lakeport, CA 95453 *Tel:* 415-771-2555 *E-mail:* research@aerialarchives.com *Web Site:* aerialarchives.com, pg 1419

Linick, Andrew S PhD, Copywriters' Council of America™ (CCA), Linick Bldg, 7 Putter Lane, Middle Island, NY 11953 *Tel:* 631-924-3888; 631-924-8555; 631-604-8599 *E-mail:* linickgroup@gmail.com, pg 1345

Linick, Andrew S PhD, LK Advertising Agency, Linick Bldg, 7 Putter Lane, Middle Island, NY 11953 *Tel:* 631-924-3888; 631-924-8555; 631-604-8599 *E-mail:* topmarketingadvisor@gmail.com; linickgroup@gmail.com, pg 1100

Lins, Stephan, MediaLocate Inc, 1200 Piedmont Ave, Pacific Grove, CA 93950 *Tel:* 831-655-7500 *E-mail:* info@medialocate.com *Web Site:* www.medialocate.com, pg 1403

Lins, Stephan, Richard Schneider Language Services (RSLS), 1200 Piedmont Ave, Pacific Grove, CA 93950 *Toll Free Tel:* 800-500-5808 *E-mail:* service@idioms.com *Web Site:* www.idioms.com, pg 1404

Lippenholz, Michael, National Book Network (NBN), 4501 Forbes Blvd, Suite 200, Lanham, MD 20706 *Tel:* 301-459-3366 *Toll Free Tel:* 800-462-6420 (orders only) *Fax:* 301-429-5746 *Toll Free Fax:* 800-338-4550 (orders only) *E-mail:* customercare@nbnbooks.com *Web Site:* www.nbnbooks.com, pg 1298, 1319

Lippisch, Bettina, Omeda, 4 Overlook Point, Suite A2SE, Lincolnshire, IL 60069 *Tel:* 847-564-8900 *E-mail:* getstarted@omeda.com *Web Site:* www.omeda.com, pg 1334

Lisy, Paul, eFootage LLC, 530 S Lake Ave, Suite 450, Pasadena, CA 91101 *Tel:* 626-395-9593 *E-mail:* info@efootage.com *Web Site:* www.efootage.com, pg 1428

Litty, Tedd, Cushing-Malloy Inc, 1350 N Main St, Ann Arbor, MI 48104-1045 *Tel:* 734-663-8554 *Fax:* 734-663-5731 *Web Site:* www.cushing-malloy.com; www.c-mbooks.com, pg 1209, 1251

PERSONNEL INDEX

Lizza, Fred, Freestyle Software, 9 Campus Dr, Parsippany, NJ 07054 *Toll Free Tel:* 800-474-5760 *Fax:* 973-237-9043 *E-mail:* info@freestylesolutions.com *Web Site:* www.freestylesolutions.com, pg 1369

Lloyd-Sgambati, Vanesse, The Literary Media & Publishing Consultants, 1815 Wynnewood Rd, Philadelphia, PA 19151 *Tel:* 215-877-2012, pg 1110

Lo Gatto, Michael, Lo Gatto Bookbinding, 390 Paterson Ave, East Rutherford, NJ 07073 *Tel:* 201-438-4344 *Fax:* 201-438-1775 *E-mail:* bookbindin@aol.com, pg 1212, 1256

Locascio, James, Dukane Corp, Audio Visual Products Division, 2900 Dukane Dr, St Charles, IL 60174 *Tel:* 630-584-2300 *Toll Free Tel:* 888-245-1966; 800-676-2487 (tech support) *Fax:* 630-584-5156 *E-mail:* avsales@dukane.com *Web Site:* dukaneav.com, pg 1368

Lockley, Beth, Penguin Random House Canada, a Penguin Random House company, 320 Front St W, Suite 1400, Toronto, ON M5V 3B6, Canada *Tel:* 416-364-4449 *Toll Free Tel:* 888-523-9292 (cust serv) *Fax:* 416-598-7764 *E-mail:* customerservicescanada@penguinrandomhouse.com; publicitycanada@penguinrandomhouse.com; rightscanada@penguinrandomhouse.com *Web Site:* www.penguinrandomhouse.ca, pg 1299

Lockwood, Bert, Human Rights Quarterly, 2715 N Charles St, Baltimore, MD 21218-4363 *Tel:* 410-516-6987 (journal orders outside US & CN) *Toll Free Tel:* 800-548-1784 (journal orders) *Fax:* 410-578-2865 (journal orders) *E-mail:* jrnlcirc@jh.edu (journal orders) *Web Site:* www.press.jhu.edu/journals/human-rights-quarterly, pg 1133

Lockwood, C C, Cactus Clyde Productions, PO Box 3624, St Francisville, LA 70775-3624 *Tel:* 225-245-5008 *E-mail:* cactusclyd@aol.com *Web Site:* www.cclockwood.com, pg 1420

Loeffler, Katherine, Peregrine Arts Bindery, 7 Avenida Vista Grande, Suite B-7 119, Santa Fe, NM 87508 *Tel:* 505-466-0490 *Web Site:* www.peregrineartsbindery.etsy.com, pg 1270

Loerke, Ellen, Books International Inc, 22883 Quicksilver Dr, Dulles, VA 20166 *Tel:* 703-661-1500 *E-mail:* hdqtrs@booksintl.com *Web Site:* booksintl.presswarehouse.com, pg 1333

Loewen-Young, Anais, Penguin Random House Canada, a Penguin Random House company, 320 Front St W, Suite 1400, Toronto, ON M5V 3B6, Canada *Tel:* 416-364-4449 *Toll Free Tel:* 888-523-9292 (cust serv) *Fax:* 416-598-7764 *E-mail:* customerservicescanada@penguinrandomhouse.com; publicitycanada@penguinrandomhouse.com; rightscanada@penguinrandomhouse.com *Web Site:* www.penguinrandomhouse.ca, pg 1299

Lombardo, Laura M, Santec Corp, 84 Old Gate Lane, Milford, CT 06460 *Tel:* 203-878-1379 *Fax:* 203-876-0949 *E-mail:* info@santeccorp.com *Web Site:* www.santeccorp.com, pg 1283

Lombardo, Vito, Santec Corp. 84 Old Gate Lane, Milford, CT 06460 *Tel:* 203-878-1379 *Fax:* 203-876-0949 *E-mail:* info@santeccorp.com *Web Site:* www.santeccorp.com, pg 1283

Long, Bob, Thinkers' Press Inc, 1524 Le Claire St, Davenport, IA 52803 *Tel:* 563-271-6657 *E-mail:* info@chessbutler.com *Web Site:* www.thinkerspressinc.com, pg 1329

Long, Peter, MCH Strategic Data, 601 E Marshall St, Sweet Springs, MO 65351 *Toll Free Tel:* 800-776-6373 *E-mail:* sales@mchdata.com *Web Site:* mchdata.com, pg 1120

Long, Thayer, Association for PRINT Technologies (APTech), 113 Seaboard Lane, Suite C-250, Franklin, TN 37067 *Tel:* 703-264-7200 *E-mail:* aptech@aptech.org *Web Site:* printtechnologies.org, pg 1277, 1365

Long, William S, Maple Logistics Solutions, 60 Grumbacher Rd, York, PA 17406 *Tel:* 717-764-4596 *E-mail:* info@maplesoln.com *Web Site:* www.maplelogisticssolutions.com, pg 1296

Longman, Phillip, Washington Monthly, 1200 18 St NW, Suite 330, Washington, DC 20036 *Tel:* 202-955-9010 *Toll Free Tel:* 855-492-1648 (subns) *Fax:* 202-955-9011 *E-mail:* editors@washingtonmonthly.com *Web Site:* washingtonmonthly.com, pg 1137

Longworth, Jo-Ann, Resolute Forest Products, 111 Robert-Bourassa Blvd, Suite 5000, Montreal, QC H3C 2M1, Canada *Tel:* 514-875-2160 *Toll Free Tel:* 800-361-2888 *E-mail:* info@resolutefp.com *Web Site:* www.resolutefp.com, pg 1271

Loomis, Dan, Omnipress, 2600 Anderson St, Madison, WI 53704 *Tel:* 608-246-2600 *Toll Free Tel:* 800-828-0305 *E-mail:* justask@omnipress.com *Web Site:* www.omnipress.com, pg 1213, 1257

Loomis, Mike, GW Illustration & Design, 2290 Ball Dr, St Louis, MO 63146 *Tel:* 314-567-9854 *Web Site:* www.gwinc.com, pg 1414

Lord, Matt, Boston Review, PO Box 390568, Cambridge, MA 02139 *Tel:* 617-356-8198 *E-mail:* review@bostonreview.net; customerservice@bostonreview.net *Web Site:* bostonreview.net, pg 1130

Lorence, Mauricio, Metro Translation Service, 294 De Kalb Ave, Brooklyn, NY 11205 *Tel:* 917-558-0089 (cell) *E-mail:* metrotourservice21@gmail.com *Web Site:* metrotourservice.blogspot.com, pg 1403

Lorenz, Scott, Westwind Communications, 1310 Maple St, Plymouth, MI 48170 *Tel:* 734-667-2090 *Web Site:* www.book-marketing-expert.com, pg 1351

Lores, Enrique, HP Inc, 1501 Paige Mill Rd, Palo Alto, CA 94304-1112 *Tel:* 650-857-1501 *Toll Free Tel:* 800-282-6672 *Web Site:* www.hp.com, pg 1370

Lory, Irene, Cross Country Computer Corp, 250 Carleton Ave, East Islip, NY 11730-1240 *Tel:* 631-334-1810 *E-mail:* inquiry@crosscountrycomputer.com *Web Site:* www.crosscountrycomputer.com, pg 1119

Losch, Brian, Worth Higgins & Associates Inc, 8770 Park Central Dr, Richmond, VA 23227-1146 *Tel:* 804-264-2304 *Toll Free Tel:* 800-883-7768 *Fax:* 804-264-5733 *E-mail:* contact@whaprint.com *Web Site:* www.worthhiggins.com, pg 1226, 1254

Loubier, Serge, Marquis Book Printing Inc, 350, rue des Entrepreneurs, Montmagny, QC G5V 4T1, Canada *Tel:* 418-246-5666 *Toll Free Tel:* 855-566-1937; 800-246-2468 *E-mail:* marquis@marquisbook.com *Web Site:* www.marquislivre.com; www.marquisbook.com, pg 1256

Louie, Jon, Haynes North America Inc, 2801 Townsgate Rd, Suite 340, Westlake Village, CA 91361 *Tel:* 805-498-6703 *Toll Free Tel:* 800-4-HAYNES (442-9637) *Fax:* 805-498-2867 *E-mail:* customerservice.haynes@infopro-digital.com *Web Site:* www.haynes.com, pg 1328

Lourie, Roger H, Devin-Adair Publishers/Seagrace Partners, 525 Flagler Dr, Suite 15A, West Palm Beach, FL 33401 *Tel:* 561-909-7576 *Fax:* 718-359-8568, pg 1314

Love, Brian, DocuWare Corp, 4 Crotty Lane, Suite 200, New Windsor, NY 12553 *Tel:* 845-563-9045 *Toll Free Tel:* 888-565-5907 *Fax:* 845-563-9046 *E-mail:* dwsales@docuware.com; support.americas@docuware.com *Web Site:* www.docuware.com, pg 1367

Love, Cody, Idea Architects, 523 Swift St, Santa Cruz, CA 95060 *Tel:* 831-465-9565 *Web Site:* www.ideaarchitects.com, pg 1347

Love, Dave, Cross Country Computer Corp, 250 Carleton Ave, East Islip, NY 11730-1240 *Tel:* 631-334-1810 *E-mail:* inquiry@crosscountrycomputer.com *Web Site:* www.crosscountrycomputer.com, pg 1119

Love, Ty Gideon, Idea Architects, 523 Swift St, Santa Cruz, CA 95060 *Tel:* 831-465-9565 *Web Site:* www.ideaarchitects.com, pg 1347

Lovins, Greg, Avery Dennison Corp, 207 N Goode Ave, 6th fl, Glendale, CA 91203-1222 *Tel:* 626-304-2000 *Web Site:* www.averydennison.com, pg 1365

Low, Carey, Canadian Manda Group, 664 Annette St, Toronto, ON M6S 2C8, Canada *Tel:* 416-516-0911 *Fax:* 416-516-0917 *Toll Free Fax:* 888-563-8327 (CN only) *E-mail:* general@mandagroup.com; info@mandagroup.com *Web Site:* www.mandagroup.com, pg 1287

Lowe, Kurtis, Imprint Group, 2070 Cherry St, Denver, CO 80207 *Toll Free Tel:* 800-738-3961 *Toll Free Fax:* 888-867-3869 *Web Site:* imprintgroupwest.com, pg 1292

Loy, Paul, Sheridan MI, 613 E Industrial Dr, Chelsea, MI 48118 *Tel:* 734-475-9145 *Web Site:* www.sheridan.com, pg 1213, 1259, 1271

Loy, Paul, Sheridan NH, 69 Lyme Rd, Hanover, NH 03755 *Tel:* 603-643-2220 *Web Site:* www.sheridan.com, pg 1259

Loy, Paul, Sheridan PA, 450 Fame Ave, Hanover, PA 17331 *Tel:* 717-632-3535 *Toll Free Tel:* 800-352-2210 *Fax:* 717-633-8900 *Web Site:* www.sheridan.com, pg 1260

Loy, Paul, Sheridan Saline, 960 Woodland Dr, Saline, MI 48176 *Tel:* 734-429-5411 *Web Site:* www.sheridan.com, pg 1214, 1260

Lozada, Avery, Distributed Art Publishers Inc, 75 Broad St, Suite 630, New York, NY 10004 *Tel:* 212-627-1999 *Toll Free Tel:* 800-338-2665 (cust serv) *Fax:* 212-627-9484 *E-mail:* orders@dapinc.com *Web Site:* www.artbook.com, pg 1290

Lu, David, DFI Technologies LLC, 5501 Monte Claire Lane, Loomis, CA 95650 *Tel:* 916-568-1234 *Web Site:* dfitech.com, pg 1367

Luchene, Annette, Sappi Fine Paper North America, 255 State St, Boston, MA 02109 *Tel:* 617-423-7300 *Toll Free Tel:* 800-882-4332 *E-mail:* webqueriesna@sappi.com *Web Site:* www.sappi.com/na, pg 1271

Luchterhand, Kubet, Wm Caxton Ltd - Bookseller & Publisher, 12037 Hwy 42, Ellison Bay, WI 54210 *Tel:* 920-854-2955, pg 1313

Ludewig, Gail, TotalWorks™ Inc, 420 W Huron St, Chicago, IL 60654 *Tel:* 773-489-4313 *E-mail:* production@totalworks.net *Web Site:* www.totalworks.net, pg 1232, 1261

Ludwig, Christof, Berryville Graphics, 25 Jack Enders Blvd, Berryville, VA 22611 *Tel:* 540-955-2750 *Fax:* 540-955-2633 *E-mail:* info@bvgraphics.com *Web Site:* www.bpg-usa.com, pg 1208, 1222, 1248

Ludwig, Christof, Coral Graphic Services Inc, 840 S Broadway, Hicksville, NY 11801 *Tel:* 516-576-2100 *Fax:* 516-576-2168 *E-mail:* info@coralgraphics.com *Web Site:* www.bpg-usa.com, pg 1224, 1251, 1266

Lui, Adeline, The Independent Book Publishers Association (IBPA), 1020 Manhattan Beach Blvd, Suite 204, Manhattan Beach, CA 90266 *Tel:* 310-546-1818 *E-mail:* info@ibpa-online.org *Web Site:* www.ibpa-online.org, pg 1116

Luisotti, Theresa, RAM Publications & Distribution Inc, 2525 Michigan Ave, Bldg A2, Santa Monica, CA 90404 *Tel:* 310-453-0043 *Fax:* 310-264-4888 *E-mail:* info@rampub.com; orders@rampub.com *Web Site:* www.rampub.com, pg 1301

Lukas, Mike, Fry Communications Inc, 800 W Church Rd, Mechanicsburg, PA 17055 *Tel:* 717-766-0211 *Toll Free Tel:* 800-334-1429 *Fax:* 717-691-0341 *E-mail:* info@frycomm.com *Web Site:* www.frycomm.com, pg 1210, 1225, 1253, 1280

Lundgren, Laura, Scholastic School Reading Events, 1080 Greenwood Blvd, Lake Mary, FL 32746 *Tel:* 407-829-8000 *Toll Free Tel:* 800-770-4662 *Fax:* 407-829-2600 *E-mail:* custservbf@scholasticbookfairs.com *Web Site:* bookfairs.scholastic.com/content/fairs/home.html, pg 1302, 1321

Lunseth, Steve, Aatrix Software Inc, 2100 Library Circle, Grand Forks, ND 58201 *Tel:* 701-746-6801; 701-746-6814 (Windows); 701-746-6017 (MacIntosh) *Toll Free Tel:* 800-426-0854 (sales) *Fax:* 701-746-4393 *E-mail:* sales@aatrix.com; support@aatrix.com *Web Site:* www.aatrix.com, pg 1363

Lupo, Anthony, Stephen Gould Corp, 35 S Jefferson Rd, Whippany, NJ 07981 *Tel:* 973-428-1500; 973-428-1510 *E-mail:* info@stephengould.com *Web Site:* www.stephengould.com, pg 1104, 1337

Lussier, Gary, Christianbook Inc, 140 Summit St, Peabody, MA 01960-5156 Tel: 978-977-5060; 978-977-5000 (intl calls) Toll Free Tel: 800-CHRISTIAN (247-4784) Fax: 978-977-5010 E-mail: customer.service@christianbook.com Web Site: www.christianbook.com, pg 1313

Lutkus, Tony, Diamond Book Distributors (DBD), 10150 York Rd, Hunt Valley, MD 21030 Tel: 443-318-8001; 443-318-8519 (cust serv) E-mail: distribution@diamondbookdistributors.com; dbdreorders@diamondbookdistributors.com (orders); books@diamondbookdistributors.com (cust serv) Web Site: diamondbookdistributors.com, pg 1290

Lutz, Tom, LARB Quarterly Journal, 6671 Sunset Blvd, Suite 1521, Los Angeles, CA 90028 Tel: 323-952-3950 E-mail: info@lareviewofbooks.org; editorial@lareviewofbooks.org Web Site: lareviewofbooks.org, pg 1133

Lutzy, Patrick, Cheneliere Education Inc, 5800, rue St Denis, bureau 900, Montreal, QC H2S 3L5, Canada Tel: 514-273-1066 Toll Free Tel: 800-565-5531 Fax: 514-276-0324 Toll Free Fax: 800-814-0324 E-mail: info@cheneliere.ca Web Site: www.cheneliere.ca, pg 1313

Lynch, Brian, Columbia Finishing Mills Inc, 135 Boundary Rd, Cornwall, ON K6H 5T3, Canada Tel: 613-933-1462 Toll Free Tel: 800-267-9174 Fax: 613-933-7717 Toll Free Fax: 800-242-9174 E-mail: info@columbiafinishingmills.com Web Site: www.columbiafinishingmills.com, pg 1266

Lynch, Susan, Melcher Media Inc, 124 W 13 St, New York, NY 10011 Tel: 212-727-2322 Fax: 212-627-1973 E-mail: info@melcher.com Web Site: www.melcher.com, pg 1356

Lyon, Darin, Anderson & Vreeland Inc, 15348 US Hwy 127 EW, Bryan, OH 43506 Tel: 419-636-5002 Toll Free Tel: 866-282-7697; 888-832-1600 (CN) Fax: 419-636-4334 E-mail: info@andersonvreeland.com Web Site: andersonvreeland.com, pg 1277

Lyons, Jed, National Book Network (NBN), 4501 Forbes Blvd, Suite 200, Lanham, MD 20706 Tel: 301-459-3366 Toll Free Tel: 800-462-6420 (orders only) Fax: 301-429-5746 Toll Free Fax: 800-338-4550 (orders only) E-mail: customercare@nbnbooks.com Web Site: www.nbnbooks.com, pg 1298, 1319

Lyons, Stephen, Decode, Inc, 1938 11 Ave E, Seattle, WA 98102 Tel: 206-343-9101 E-mail: books@decodebooks.com Web Site: www.decodeinc.com; www.decodebooks.com, pg 1413

Lyons, Tom, The New England Mobile Book Fair®, 241 Needham St, Newton, MA 02464 Tel: 617-527-5817; 617-964-7440 E-mail: customerservice@nebookfair.com Web Site: nebookfair.com, pg 1319

Ma, Chiu Bing, Giant Horse Printing Inc, 1336 San Mateo Ave, South San Francisco, CA 94080 Tel: 650-875-7137 Fax: 650-875-7194 E-mail: info@gianthorse.com Web Site: www.gianthorse.com, pg 1211

Ma, Karen, Penguin Random House Canada, a Penguin Random House company, 320 Front St W, Suite 1400, Toronto, ON M5V 3B6, Canada Tel: 416-364-4449 Toll Free Tel: 888-523-9292 (cust serv) Fax: 416-598-7764 E-mail: customerservicescanada@penguinrandomhouse.com; publicitycanada@penguinrandomhouse.com; rightscanada@penguinrandomhouse.com Web Site: www.penguinrandomhouse.ca, pg 1299

MacAskill, Jennifer, Universal|Wilde, 26 Dartmouth St, Westwood, MA 02090 Tel: 781-251-2700 Fax: 781-251-2613 Web Site: www.universalwilde.com, pg 1105, 1116, 1232, 1261

MacDonald, Brian A, Children's Braille Book Club, 88 Saint Stephen St, Boston, MA 02115-4312 Tel: 617-266-6160 Toll Free Tel: 800-548-7323 (cust serv) Fax: 617-437-0456 E-mail: contact@nbp.org Web Site: www.nbp.org, pg 1141

MacDonald, Bryan, ALC Inc, 750 College Rd E, Suite 201, Princeton, NJ 08540 Tel: 609-580-2800 Toll Free Tel: 800-252-5478 Fax: 609-580-2888 E-mail: info@alc.com Web Site: www.alc.com, pg 1119

MacDougall, Peter, Raincoast Books Distribution Ltd, 2440 Viking Way, Richmond, BC V6V 1N2, Canada Tel: 604-448-7100 Toll Free Tel: 800-663-5714 (CN only) Fax: 604-270-7161 Toll Free Fax: 800-565-3770 E-mail: info@raincoast.com; customerservice@raincoast.com Web Site: www.raincoast.com/distribution, pg 1301

MacKenzie, Julia, American Association for the Advancement of Science (AAAS), 1200 New York Ave NW, Washington, DC 20005 Tel: 202-326-6400 Fax: 202-371-9526 Web Site: www.aaas.org, pg 1145

Macy, John P, Mohawk Fine Papers Inc, 465 Saratoga St, Cohoes, NY 12047 Tel: 518-237-1740 Toll Free Tel: 800-THE-MILL (843-6455) Fax: 518-237-7394 Web Site: www.mohawkconnects.com, pg 1270

Madan, Ashish, Aptara Inc, 2901 Telestar Ct, Suite 522, Falls Church, VA 22042 Tel: 703-352-0001 E-mail: moreinfo@aptaracorp.com Web Site: www.aptaracorp.com, pg 1207, 1222, 1343, 1353, 1365, 1411

Maddex, Diane, Archetype Press Inc, 11272 N Meadow Sage Dr, Oro Valley, AZ 85737-7250 Tel: 302-249-5879 E-mail: archepress@aol.com, pg 1353

Mader, Don, Southeastern Printing Co, 3601 SE Dixie Hwy, Stuart, FL 34997 Tel: 772-287-2141 Toll Free Tel: 800-226-8221 Fax: 772-288-3988 E-mail: sales@seprint.com Web Site: www.seprint.com, pg 1231, 1260, 1272, 1283

Madera-Zapf, Zobeida, The Hibbert Group, 400 Pennington Ave, Trenton, NJ 08650 Tel: 609-394-7500 Toll Free Tel: 888-HIBBERT (442-2378) E-mail: info@hibbertgroup.com Web Site: hibbert.com, pg 1104, 1116, 1117

Maestri, Luca, Apple Inc, One Apple Park Way, Cupertino, CA 95014 Tel: 408-996-1010 Web Site: www.apple.com, pg 1364

Magrino, Ms Allyn, Susan Magrino Agency, 352 Park Ave S, 6th fl, New York, NY 10010 Tel: 212-957-3005 Fax: 212-957-4071 E-mail: info@smapr.com Web Site: www.smapr.com, pg 1110

Maguire, Susan, Booklist, 225 N Michigan Ave, Suite 1300, Chicago, IL 60601 Tel: 312-944-6780 Toll Free Tel: 800-545-2433 Fax: 312-440-9374 E-mail: info@booklistonline.com; ala@ala.org Web Site: www.booklistonline.com; www.ala.org, pg 1130

Maher, John, Publishers Weekly, 49 W 23 St, 9th fl, New York, NY 10010 Tel: 212-377-5500 Fax: 212-377-2733 Web Site: www.publishersweekly.com, pg 1136

Mahtani, Chandru, Amcorp Ltd, 10 Norden Lane, Huntington Station, NY 11746 Tel: 631-271-0548 Fax: 631-549-8849 E-mail: amcorpltd@aol.com, pg 1327

Maier, Henry J, FedEx Ground, 1000 FedEx Dr, Coraopolis, PA 15108 Tel: 412-269-1000 Toll Free Tel: 800-762-3725 Web Site: www.fedex.com, pg 1333

Maier, Steve, Conrad Direct Inc, 800 Kinderkamack Rd, Suite 307N, Oradell, NJ 07649 Tel: 201-567-3200 Fax: 201-567-1530 E-mail: listinfo@conraddirect.com Web Site: www.conraddirect.com, pg 1115

Main, Bill, Ross Gage Inc, 8502 Brookville Rd, Indianapolis, IN 46239 Tel: 317-283-2323 Toll Free Tel: 800-799-2323 Fax: 317-931-2108 E-mail: info@rossgage.com Web Site: www.rossgage.com, pg 1230, 1259

Mainardis, Ken, Getty Images Inc, 605 Fifth Ave S, Suite 400, Seattle, WA 98104 Tel: 206-925-5000 Toll Free Tel: 800-IMAGERY (462-4379); 888-888-5889 Web Site: www.gettyimages.com; www.gettyimages.com/customer-support; engage.gettyimages.com/media-inquiries, pg 1369, 1428

Majkowski, Mary, The Language Center, 62 Brunswick Woods Dr, East Brunswick, NJ 08816 Tel: 732-613-4554 Fax: 732-238-7659 Web Site: www.thelanguagectr.com, pg 1402

Majzoub, Muhi, Open Text Corp, 275 Frank Tompa Dr, Waterloo, ON N2L 0A1, Canada Tel: 519-888-7111 Fax: 519-888-0677 Web Site: opentext.com, pg 1374

Makanoff, Daniel, PolyBook Distributors, 501 Mamaroneck Ave, White Plains, NY 10605 Tel: 914-328-6346, pg 1320

Makuch, Jay, Whitehurst & Clark Book Fulfillment, 1200 County Rd, Rte 523, Flemington, NJ 08822 Tel: 908-782-2323 Toll Free Tel: 800-488-8040 E-mail: wcbooks@aol.com Web Site: www.wcbks.com, pg 1335

Malandrakis, Kirk, TSO General Corp, 79 Emjay Blvd, Brentwood, NY 11717 Tel: 631-952-5320 Fax: 631-952-5315 Web Site: www.tsogeneral.com, pg 1261, 1273

Malen, Ms Michal Hoschander, Paper Brigade, 520 Eighth Ave, 4th fl, New York, NY 10018 Tel: 212-201-2920 Fax: 212-532-4952 E-mail: info@jewishbooks.org Web Site: www.jewishbookcouncil.org, pg 1135

Malhotra, Aakanksha, Penguin Random House Canada, a Penguin Random House company, 320 Front St W, Suite 1400, Toronto, ON M5V 3B6, Canada Tel: 416-364-4449 Toll Free Tel: 888-523-9292 (cust serv) Fax: 416-598-7764 E-mail: customerservicescanada@penguinrandomhouse.com; publicitycanada@penguinrandomhouse.com; rightscanada@penguinrandomhouse.com Web Site: www.penguinrandomhouse.ca, pg 1299

Malik, Jeff, Miles 33 International LLC, 40 Richards Ave, Norwalk, CT 06854 Tel: 203-838-2333 Fax: 203-838-4473 E-mail: info@miles33.com Web Site: www.miles33.com, pg 1228, 1282, 1373

Malik, Virender, Far Eastern Books, 8889 Yonge St, Richmond Hill, ON L4C 0V3, Canada Tel: 905-477-2900 Toll Free Tel: 800-291-8886 E-mail: books@febonline.com Web Site: fareasternbooks.com, pg 1291

Malinowski, Chris, The Combined Book Exhibit®, 277 White St, Buchanan, NY 10511 Tel: 914-739-7500 Toll Free Tel: 800-462-7687 Fax: 914-739-7575 E-mail: info@combinedbook.com Web Site: www.combinedbook.com; www.cbedatabase.com, pg 1139

Malinowski, Jon, The American Collective Stand®, 277 White St, Buchanan, NY 10511 Tel: 914-739-7500 Toll Free Tel: 800-462-7687 Fax: 914-739-7575 Web Site: www.americancollectivestand.com, pg 1139

Malinowski, Jon, The Combined Book Exhibit®, 277 White St, Buchanan, NY 10511 Tel: 914-739-7500 Toll Free Tel: 800-462-7687 Fax: 914-739-7575 E-mail: info@combinedbook.com Web Site: www.combinedbook.com; www.cbedatabase.com, pg 1139

Mallet, Lester, The Gluefast Co Inc, 3535 State Rte 66, Bldg No 1, Neptune, NJ 07753 Tel: 732-918-4600 Toll Free Tel: 800-242-7318 Fax: 732-918-4646 E-mail: info@gluefast.com Web Site: www.gluefast.com, pg 1337

Mallozzi, Frank, Electronics for Imaging Inc (EFI), 6750 Dumbarton Circle, Fremont, CA 94555 Tel: 650-357-3500 Toll Free Tel: 800-568-1917; 800-875-7117 (sales) Fax: 650-357-3907 E-mail: info@efi.com Web Site: www.efi.com, pg 1368

Maluccio, Paul, Blue Note Publications Inc, 721 North Dr, Suite D, Melbourne, FL 32934 Tel: 321-799-2583; 321-622-6289 Toll Free Tel: 800-624-0401 (orders) Fax: 321-799-1942; 321-622-6830 E-mail: bluenotebooks@gmail.com Web Site: bluenotepublications.com, pg 1208, 1223, 1249, 1278

Manchester, Sarah, Sappi Fine Paper North America, 255 State St, Boston, MA 02109 Tel: 617-423-7300 Toll Free Tel: 800-882-4332 E-mail: webqueriesna@sappi.com Web Site: www.sappi.com/na, pg 1271

Mandarino, Jay, Colour Technologies, 560 Hensall Circle, Mississauga, ON L5A 1Y1, Canada Tel: 416-588-0808 E-mail: info@cjgraphics.com Web Site: www.cjgraphics.com/services/prepress, pg 1224, 1413

Mandel, Rick, Mandel Graphic Solution, 727 W Glendale Ave, Suite 100, Milwaukee, WI 53209 Tel: 414-271-6970 Fax: 414-386-4660 E-mail: info@mandelcompany.com Web Site: www.mandelcompany.com, pg 1228, 1256

PERSONNEL INDEX

Mandelbaum, Howard, Photofest, East Rutherford, NJ 07073 E-mail: requests@photofestnyc.com Web Site: www.photofestnyc.com, pg 1430

Mandell, Lon, Specialist Marketing Services Inc, 777 Terrace Ave, Suite 401, Hasbrouck Heights, NJ 07604 Tel: 201-865-5800 E-mail: info@sms-inc.com Web Site: www.sms-inc.com, pg 1120

Maniaci, Greg, Tamron USA Inc, 10 Austin Blvd, Commack, NY 11725 Tel: 631-858-8400 Toll Free Tel: 800-827-8880 Fax: 631-543-5666; 631-858-8462 (cust serv) E-mail: custserv@tamron.com Web Site: www.tamron-usa.com, pg 1377

Mann, Jim, BCC Software Inc, 75 Josons Dr, Rochester, NY 14623-3494 Toll Free Tel: 800-453-3130; 800-337-0442 (sales) E-mail: marketing@bccsoftware.com Web Site: www.bccsoftware.com, pg 1365

Manning, Kathleen, Manning's Book & Prints, 580-M Crespi Dr, Pacifica, CA 94044 Tel: 415-621-3565 Toll Free Tel: 800-TRY-MAPS (879-6277) Fax: 650-355-1851 E-mail: staff@printsoldandrare.com; manningsbk@aol.com Web Site: www.printsoldandrare.com, pg 1318

Manning, Scott, Scott Manning & Associates, 2 Horatio St, Suite 16G, New York, NY 10014 Tel: 603-491-0995 Web Site: www.scottmanningpr.com, pg 1110

Mannix, Erin, Unisys Corp, 801 Lakeview Dr, Suite 100, Blue Bell, PA 19422 Tel: 215-274-2742 Web Site: www.unisys.com, pg 1378

Manoliu, Connie, Walker360, 2501 Fifth Ave E, Montgomery, AL 36107 Tel: 334-832-4975 E-mail: info@walker360.com Web Site: walker360.com, pg 1214, 1262

Mansoor, Leah, Encyclopaedia Britannica Inc, 325 N La Salle St, Suite 200, Chicago, IL 60654 Tel: 312-347-7000 (all other countries) Toll Free Tel: 800-323-1229 (US & CN) Fax: 312-294-2104 E-mail: contact@eb.com Web Site: www.britannica.com, pg 1315

Mantilla, Antonio, Busch LLC, 516 Viking Dr, Virginia Beach, VA 23452 Tel: 757-463-7800 Toll Free Tel: 800-USA-PUMP (872-7867) Fax: 757-463-7407 E-mail: info@buschusa.com; marketing@buschusa.com Web Site: www.buschvacuum.com/us, pg 1278

Manwiller, Jeffrey, The Crowley Co, 5111 Pegasus Ct, Suite M, Frederick, MD 21704 Tel: 240-215-0224 Fax: 240-215-0234 E-mail: webrequest@thecrowleycompany.com Web Site: www.thecrowleycompany.com, pg 1367

Manzer, William R, Rayonier Advanced Materials, 1301 Riverplace Blvd, Suite 2300, Jacksonville, FL 32207 Tel: 904-357-4600 Web Site: rayonieram.com, pg 1270

Marciano, Joseph R, Canon Business Process Services, 261 Madison Ave, 3rd fl, New York, NY 10016 Tel: 212-502-2100 Toll Free Tel: 888-623-2668 E-mail: cbps-info@cbps.canon.com Web Site: cbps.canon.com, pg 1333

Marcus, Aaron, Aaron Marcus and Associates Inc, 1196 Euclid Ave, Berkeley, CA 94708-1640 Tel: 510-599-3195 (cell) Fax: 510-527-1994 Web Site: www.bamanda.com, pg 1363

Marek, Grant, Sunday San Francisco Chronicle Book Review, 901 Mission St, San Francisco, CA 94103 Tel: 415-777-1111 Toll Free Tel: 866-732-4766 Web Site: www.sfgate.com, pg 1137

Marino, Pamela, Choice, 575 Main St, Suite 300, Middletown, CT 06457 Tel: 860-347-6933; 847-504-8803 (subns) Toll Free Tel: 844-291-0455 (subns) Fax: 860-346-8586 E-mail: acrlsubscriptions@omeda.com; support@acrlchoice.freshdesk.com Web Site: www.ala.org/acrl/acrl-choice; www.choice360.org, pg 1131

Markley, Chris, Tecnau Inc, 4 Suburban Park Dr, Billerica, MA 01821 Tel: 978-608-0500 Fax: 978-608-0558 E-mail: info.us@tecnau.com Web Site: www.tecnau.com, pg 1283

Marks, Meredith, Hill+Knowlton Strategies, 237 Park Ave, 4th fl, New York, NY 10017 Tel: 212-885-0300 Web Site: www.hkstrategies.com, pg 1109

Marks, Sherwin, Craftsmen Machinery Co Inc, 1257 Worcester Rd, Unit 167, Framingham, MA 01701 Tel: 508-376-2001 Fax: 508-376-2003 E-mail: sales@craftsmenmachinery.com Web Site: www.craftsmenmachinery.com, pg 1279

Marlin, David, MetaComet Systems, 29 College St, South Hadley, MA 01075 Tel: 413-536-5989 Web Site: www.metacomet.com, pg 1349

Marmanis, Haralambos "Babis", Copyright Clearance Center Inc (CCC), 222 Rosewood Dr, Danvers, MA 01923 Tel: 978-750-8400 (sales); 978-646-2600 (cust serv) E-mail: info@copyright.com Web Site: www.copyright.com, pg 1345

Marmion, Shane, William S Hein & Co Inc, 2350 N Forest Rd, Suite 10A, Getzville, NY 14068 Tel: 716-882-2600 Toll Free Tel: 800-828-7571 Fax: 716-883-8100 E-mail: mail@wshein.com; marketing@wshein.com; customerservice@wshein.com Web Site: home.heinonline.org, pg 1316

Marocchino, Kathryn D, Rosemoor House Translations, Rosemoor House, 400 New Bedford Dr, Vallejo, CA 94591 Tel: 707-557-8595, pg 1404

Maroney, Kevin, The New York Review of Science Fiction, 206 Valentine St, Yonkers, NY 10704-1814 Tel: 914-965-4861 Web Site: www.nyrsf.com, pg 1135

Marsh, Robert S, National Book Network (NBN), 4501 Forbes Blvd, Suite 200, Lanham, MD 20706 Tel: 301-459-3366 Toll Free Tel: 800-462-6420 (orders only) Fax: 301-429-5746 Toll Free Fax: 800-338-4550 (orders only) E-mail: customercare@nbnbooks.com Web Site: www.nbnbooks.com, pg 1298, 1319

Marshall, Kelly K, Exhibit Promotions Plus Inc, 11620 Vixens Path, Ellicott City, MD 21042-1539 Tel: 410-997-0763 E-mail: exhibit@epponline.com Web Site: www.epponline.com, pg 1109, 1346

Marshall, Steve, Ingram Content Group LLC, One Ingram Blvd, La Vergne, TN 37086-1986 Tel: 615-793-5000 Toll Free Tel: 800-937-8000 (retailers); 800-937-5300 (ext 1, libs) E-mail: customerservice@ingramcontent.com Web Site: www.ingramcontent.com, pg 1294, 1316

Marston, Susan, Junior Library Guild, 7858 Industrial Pkwy, Plain City, OH 43064 Tel: 614-733-0312 Toll Free Tel: 800-491-0174 Fax: 614-733-0501 Toll Free Fax: 800-827-3080 E-mail: editorial@juniorlibraryguild.com Web Site: www.juniorlibraryguild.com, pg 1142

Martel, George, SENCOR International, 445 Park Ave, 9th fl, New York, NY 10022 Tel: 212-980-6726 Web Site: www.sencorinternational.com, pg 1376, 1385

Martin, Alice, Adams Magnetic Products Co, 888 N Larch Ave, Elmhurst, IL 60126-1133 Tel: 630-617-8880 Toll Free Tel: 800-747-7543 (sales) Fax: 630-617-8881 Toll Free Fax: 800-747-1323 E-mail: info@adamsmagnetic.com Web Site: www.adamsmagnetic.com, pg 1265

Martin, Amy, Four Colour Print Group, 2410 Frankfort Ave, Louisville, KY 40206 Tel: 502-896-9644 Fax: 502-896-9594 E-mail: sales@fourcolour.com Web Site: www.fourcolour.com, pg 1210, 1253, 1280

Martin, Beth, Northeast Publishers Reps, Montville Chase, 20 Davenport Rd, Montville, NJ 07045 Tel: 973-299-0085 Fax: 973-263-2363 E-mail: siraksirak@aol.com Web Site: www.nepubreps.com, pg 1298

Martin, Beverly Swerling, Agent Research & Evaluation Inc (AR&E), 44 Park Rd, Woodbury, CT 06798 Tel: 203-586-1397 Web Site: www.agentresearch.org, pg 1343

Martin, Jack, Hill+Knowlton Strategies, 237 Park Ave, 4th fl, New York, NY 10017 Tel: 212-885-0300 Web Site: www.hkstrategies.com, pg 1109

Martin, Jan, Domtar Paper Co LLC, 234 Kingsley Park Dr, Fort Mill, SC 29715 Tel: 803-802-7500 Toll Free Tel: 877-877-4685 E-mail: communications@domtar.com; commercialprinting@domtar.com Web Site: www.domtar.com, pg 1266

Martin, Ken, Crown Connect, 250 W Rialto Ave, San Bernadino, CA 92408 Tel: 909-888-7531 Fax: 909-889-1639 E-mail: sales@crownconnect.com Web Site: www.crownconnect.com, pg 1209, 1224, 1279

Martin, Lesley A, Printed Matter Inc, 231 11 Ave, Ground fl, New York, NY 10001 Tel: 212-925-0325 Fax: 212-925-0464 E-mail: info@printedmatter.org Web Site: www.printedmatter.org, pg 1299

Martin, Peter B, Signature Print Services, 3565 Sierra Rd, San Jose, CA 95132 Tel: 408-213-3393 Fax: 408-213-3399 Web Site: www.signatureprint.com, pg 1260

Martinelli, Rob, Tri-Media Integrated Marketing Technologies Inc, 1027 Pelham St, Unit 2, Fonthill, ON L0S 1E0, Canada E-mail: think@tri-media.com Web Site: tri-media.com, pg 1100

Martinez, Amanda, The Crowley Co, 5111 Pegasus Ct, Suite M, Frederick, MD 21704 Tel: 240-215-0224 Fax: 240-215-0234 E-mail: webrequest@thecrowleycompany.com Web Site: www.thecrowleycompany.com, pg 1367

Martinez, Joseph, Dynaric Inc, 5740 Bayside Rd, Virginia Beach, VA 23455 Tel: 757-363-5850 Toll Free Tel: 800-526-0827 Fax: 757-363-8016 E-mail: gd@dynaric.com; order@dynaric.com Web Site: www.dynaric.com, pg 1279

Martino, Lisa, Dunhill International List Co Inc, 6400 Congress Ave, Suite 1750, Boca Raton, FL 33487-2898 Tel: 561-998-7800 Toll Free Tel: 800-DUNHILL (386-4455) Fax: 561-998-7880 E-mail: dunhill@dunhillintl.com Web Site: www.dunhills.com, pg 1120

Martsching, Robert, H B Fuller Co, 1200 Willow Lake Blvd, St Paul, MN 55110-5146 Tel: 651-236-5900 Toll Free Tel: 888-423-8553 E-mail: inquiry@hbfuller.com Web Site: www.hbfuller.com, pg 1267, 1280

Marty, Jeff, Scholastic School Reading Events, 1080 Greenwood Blvd, Lake Mary, FL 32746 Tel: 407-829-8000 Toll Free Tel: 800-770-4662 Fax: 407-829-2600 E-mail: custservbf@scholasticbookfairs.com Web Site: bookfairs.scholastic.com/content/fairs/home.html, pg 1302, 1321

Marusic, Mike, Sharp Electronics Corp, 100 Paragon Dr, Montvale, NJ 07645 Toll Free Tel: 800-BE-SHARP (237-4277) Web Site: www.sharpusa.com, pg 1376

Marx, Kyle, Readerlink Distribution Services LLC, 1420 Kensington Rd, Suite 300, Oakbrook, IL 60523-2164 Tel: 708-547-4400 Toll Free Tel: 800-549-5389 E-mail: info@readerlink.com; marketingservices@readerlink.com Web Site: www.readerlink.com, pg 1301

Marzullo, Chris, Ironmark, 9040 Junction Dr, Annapolis Junction, MD 20701 Toll Free Tel: 888-775-3737 E-mail: marketing@ironmarkusa.com Web Site: ironmarkusa.com, pg 1211, 1227, 1255, 1268, 1281

Marzullo, Matt, Ironmark, 9040 Junction Dr, Annapolis Junction, MD 20701 Toll Free Tel: 888-775-3737 E-mail: marketing@ironmarkusa.com Web Site: ironmarkusa.com, pg 1211, 1227, 1255, 1268, 1281

Masaaki, Yamamoto, C & C Offset Printing Co USA Inc, 70 W 36 St, Unit 10C, New York, NY 10018 Tel: 212-431-4210 Toll Free Fax: 866-540-4134 Web Site: www.ccoffset.com, pg 1208, 1223, 1249

Mashumba, Kwangu, Penguin Random House Canada, a Penguin Random House company, 320 Front St W, Suite 1400, Toronto, ON M5V 3B6, Canada Tel: 416-364-4449 Toll Free Tel: 888-523-9292 (cust serv) Fax: 416-598-7764 E-mail: customerservicescanada@penguinrandomhouse.com; publicitycanada@penguinrandomhouse.com; rightscanada@penguinrandomhouse.com Web Site: www.penguinrandomhouse.ca, pg 1299

Mast, E Dale, Choice Books, 10100 Piper Lane, Bristow, VA 20136 Tel: 703-530-9993 Fax: 703-530-9983 E-mail: info@choicebooks.com Web Site: www.choicebooks.com, pg 1313

Mastantuono, Gina, Ingram Micro Inc, 3351 Michelson Dr, Suite 100, Irvin, CA 92612 *Tel:* 714-566-1000 *E-mail:* customerexperience@ingrammicro.com *Web Site:* www.ingrammicro.com, pg 1317

Masterson, Neil, Thomson Reuters, 3 Times Sq, New York, NY 10036 *Tel:* 646-223-4000; 646-223-6100 (edit); 646-223-6000 (newsroom) *Web Site:* www.thomsonreuters.com, pg 1191

Mater, James, QualityLogic Inc, 9576 W Emerald St, Boise, ID 83704 *Tel:* 208-424-1905 *E-mail:* info@qualitylogic.com *Web Site:* www.qualitylogic.com, pg 1375

Mateski, Kristin, Walsworth, 306 N Kansas Ave, Marceline, MO 64658 *Toll Free Tel:* 800-265-6795 *Web Site:* www.walsworth.com; www.walsworthhistorybooks.com, pg 1214, 1232, 1262

Mathews, Kaitlyn, The Association of Medical Illustrators (AMI), 201 E Main St, Suite 810, Lexington, KY 40507 *Toll Free Tel:* 866-393-4AMI (393-4264) *E-mail:* hq@ami.org *Web Site:* www.ami.org, pg 1412

Mathis, Craig, Printed Matter Inc, 231 11 Ave, Ground fl, New York, NY 10001 *Tel:* 212-925-0325 *Fax:* 212-925-0464 *E-mail:* info@printedmatter.org *Web Site:* www.printedmatter.org, pg 1299

Mathison, Jeff, Maps by Mathison, PO Box 152, Spring Mills, PA 16875 *Tel:* 814-321-7571 *E-mail:* jcmaps6@gmail.com *Web Site:* mapsbymathison.com, pg 1416

Matlock, Trevin, Faherty & Associates Inc, 17548 Redfern Ave, Lake Oswego, OR 97035 *Tel:* 503-639-3113 *Fax:* 503-213-6168 *E-mail:* faherty@fahertybooks.com *Web Site:* www.fahertybooks.com, pg 1290

Matonti, Frank, City Diecutting Inc, One Cory Rd, Morristown, NJ 07960 *Tel:* 973-270-0370 *Fax:* 973-270-0369 *E-mail:* sales@bookdisplays.com *Web Site:* www.bookdisplays.com, pg 1103, 1344

Matsliach, Gaby, Electronics for Imaging Inc (EFI), 6750 Dumbarton Circle, Fremont, CA 94555 *Tel:* 650-357-3500 *Toll Free Tel:* 800-568-1917; 800-875-7117 (sales) *Fax:* 650-357-3907 *E-mail:* info@efi.com *Web Site:* www.efi.com, pg 1368

Matsuoka, Eigi, Kinokuniya Publications Service of New York (KPS-NY), 1073 Avenue of the Americas, New York, NY 10018-3701 *Tel:* 212-765-1465 *Fax:* 212-307-5593 *E-mail:* nyinfo@kinokuniya.com *Web Site:* www.kinokuniya.co.jp; www.kinokuniya.com, pg 1348

Matt, J Kemper Jr, Dupli Envelope & Graphics Corp, 6761 Thompson Rd N, Syracuse, NY 13211 *Tel:* 315-472-1316 *Toll Free Tel:* 800-724-2477 *E-mail:* sales@duplionline.com; orders@duplionline.com *Web Site:* www.duplionline.com, pg 1252

Matthews, Joe, Independent Publishers Group (IPG), 814 N Franklin St, Chicago, IL 60610 *Tel:* 312-337-0747 *Toll Free Tel:* 800-888-4741 (orders) *Fax:* 312-337-5985 *E-mail:* frontdesk@ipgbook.com; orders@ipgbook.com *Web Site:* www.ipgbook.com, pg 1292, 1328

Mattina, Nick, Cross Country Computer Corp, 250 Carleton Ave, East Islip, NY 11730-1240 *Tel:* 631-334-1810 *E-mail:* inquiry@crosscountrycomputer.com *Web Site:* www.crosscountrycomputer.com, pg 1119

Mattscheck, Karen, National Book Network (NBN), 4501 Forbes Blvd, Suite 200, Lanham, MD 20706 *Tel:* 301-459-3366 *Toll Free Tel:* 800-462-6420 (orders only) *Fax:* 301-429-5746 *Toll Free Fax:* 800-338-4550 (orders only) *E-mail:* customercare@nbnbooks.com *Web Site:* www.nbnbooks.com, pg 1298, 1319

Matuska, Todd, GLS Companies, 1280 Energy Park Dr, St Paul, MN 55108-5106 *Tel:* 651-644-3000 *Toll Free Tel:* 800-655-9405 *Web Site:* www.glsmn.com, pg 1226, 1254

Mauritz, Rob, LBS, 1801 Thompson Ave, Des Moines, IA 50316-2751 *Tel:* 515-262-3191 *Toll Free Tel:* 800-247-5323 *Toll Free Fax:* 800-262-4091 *E-mail:* lbsbind.com *Web Site:* www.lbsbind.com, pg 1269

Mayer, Robert, IMSI/Design LLC, 384 Bel Marin Keys Blvd, No 150, Novato, CA 94949 *Tel:* 415-483-8000 *Toll Free Tel:* 800-833-8082 (sales) *E-mail:* sales@imsidesign.com; support@imsidesign.com *Web Site:* www.imsidesign.com, pg 1370

Mayerle, Stephanie E, Veritiv™ Corporation, 1000 Abernathy Rd, Bldg 400, Suite 1700, Atlanta, GA 30328 *Toll Free Tel:* 844-VERITIV (837-4848); 866-714-8303 (packaging cust serv); 866-714-8306 (print cust serv) *E-mail:* contactus@veritivcorp.com; media@veritivcorp.com *Web Site:* www.veritivcorp.com, pg 1273

Mayers, Glen, Kiplinger's Personal Finance/The Kiplinger Washington Editors Inc, 1100 13 St NW, Suite 750, Washington, DC 20005-4364 *Tel:* 202-887-6400 *Toll Free Tel:* 800-544-0155 (cust serv) *E-mail:* feedback@kiplinger.com *Web Site:* www.kiplinger.com, pg 1191

Mayland, Chris, Encyclopaedia Britannica Inc, 325 N La Salle St, Suite 200, Chicago, IL 60654 *Tel:* 312-347-7000 (all other countries) *Toll Free Tel:* 800-323-1229 (US & CN) *Fax:* 312-294-2104 *E-mail:* contact@eb.com *Web Site:* www.britannica.com, pg 1315

Maylander, Heather, Lake Group Media Inc, One Byram Brook Place, Armonk, NY 10504 *Tel:* 914-925-2400 *Fax:* 914-925-2499 *Web Site:* www.lakegroupmedia.com, pg 1120

Mazer, Norm, Applied Information Sciences Corp, PO Box 9182, Calabasas, CA 91372-9182 *Tel:* 818-222-0926 *Fax:* 818-222-4329 *E-mail:* sales@aisciences.com *Web Site:* www.aisciences.com; www.searchware.com, pg 1343

McAndrew, Karen, alfa CTP Systems Inc, 2503 Spring Ridge Dr, Unit D, Spring Grove, IL 60081 *Tel:* 815-474-7634 *E-mail:* info@alfactp.com *Web Site:* www.alfactp.com, pg 1364

McAvoy, Jack, PTC, 121 Seaport Blvd, Boston, MA 02210 *Tel:* 781-370-5000 *Fax:* 781-370-6000 *Web Site:* www.ptc.com, pg 1375

McCabe, Matthew, The Crowley Co, 5111 Pegasus Ct, Suite M, Frederick, MD 21704 *Tel:* 240-215-0224 *Fax:* 240-215-0234 *E-mail:* webrequest@thecrowleycompany.com *Web Site:* www.thecrowleycompany.com, pg 1367

McCafferty, Jim, Ecological Fibers Inc, 40 Pioneer Dr, Lunenburg, MA 01462 *Tel:* 978-537-0003 *Fax:* 978-537-2238 *E-mail:* info@ecofibers.com *Web Site:* www.ecofibers.com, pg 1210, 1267

McCaffrey, Kalah, Franklin & Siegal Associates Inc, 40 Exchange Place, Suite 1703, New York, NY 10005 *Tel:* 212-868-6311 *Web Site:* www.franklinandsiegal.com, pg 1346

McCall, Clint, De Ru's Fine Art, 27762 Antonio Pkwy, No L1103, Ladeira Ranch, CA 92694 *Tel:* 714-349-8250 *E-mail:* derusfinearts@yahoo.com *Web Site:* www.derusfinearts.com, pg 1314

McCall, Kim, Ascot Media Group Inc, PO Box 2394, Friendswood, TX 77549 *Tel:* 832-334-2733 *Toll Free Tel:* 800-854-1134 *Toll Free Fax:* 800-854-2207 *Web Site:* www.ascotmedia.com, pg 1107

McCall, Tim, Independent Publishers Group (IPG), 814 N Franklin St, Chicago, IL 60610 *Tel:* 312-337-0747 *Toll Free Tel:* 800-888-4741 (orders) *Fax:* 312-337-5985 *E-mail:* frontdesk@ipgbook.com; orders@ipgbook.com *Web Site:* www.ipgbook.com, pg 1292, 1328

McCallum, Duncan, Spectrum PrintGroup Inc, 1535 Farmer's Lane, Suite 254, Santa Rosa, CA 95405 *Tel:* 707-542-6044 *Toll Free Tel:* 888-340-6049 *Fax:* 707-542-6045 *E-mail:* sales@spectrumprintgroup.com *Web Site:* www.spectrumprintgroup.com, pg 1214, 1260, 1272

McCann, Ryan, Claris International Inc, 5201 Patrick Henry Dr, Santa Clara, CA 95054 *Tel:* 408-727-8227 (sales & cust support) *Toll Free Tel:* 800-725-2747 (sales); 800-325-2747 (cust support) *Fax:* 408-987-7447 *E-mail:* claris_sales@claris.com *Web Site:* www.claris.com, pg 1366

McCarthy, Pete, Ingram Content Group LLC, One Ingram Blvd, La Vergne, TN 37086-1986 *Tel:* 615-793-5000 *Toll Free Tel:* 800-937-8000 (retailers); 800-937-5300 (ext 1, libs) *E-mail:* customerservice@ingramcontent.com *Web Site:* www.ingramcontent.com, pg 1294, 1316

McCarthy, Rob, SGS International LLC, 626 W Main St, Suite 500, Louisville, KY 40202 *Tel:* 502-637-5443 *E-mail:* info@sgsco.com *Web Site:* www.sgsintl.com, pg 1230

McCloat, Keith, King Features Syndicate, 300 W 57 St, New York, NY 10019-5238 *Tel:* 212-969-7550 *Toll Free Tel:* 800-526-5464 *Web Site:* www.kingfeatures.com, pg 1190

McConnell, Marilyn, American International Distribution Corp (AIDC), 82 Winter Sport Lane, Williston, VT 05495 *Tel:* 802-862-0095 *Toll Free Tel:* 800-678-2432 *Fax:* 802-864-7749 *Web Site:* www.aidcvt.com, pg 1115, 1117, 1221, 1286, 1311, 1333

McConnell, Suzanne, Bellevue Literary Review, 149 E 23 St, Suite 1516, New York, NY 10010 *Tel:* 917-375-5790 *E-mail:* info@BLReview.org *Web Site:* www.BLReview.org, pg 1130

McCourtney, Carolynn, Walter's Publishing, 1750 Northway Dr, North Mankato, MN 56003 *Toll Free Tel:* 800-447-3274 *E-mail:* info@walterspublishing.com *Web Site:* www.walterspublishing.com, pg 1214

McCracken, Leah Rex, Ingram Publisher Services, an Ingram brand, 14 Ingram Blvd, Mail Stop 631, La Vergne, TN 37086 *Tel:* 615-793-5000 *Toll Free Tel:* 866-400-5351 (cust serv) *E-mail:* ips@ingramcontent.com *Web Site:* www.ingrampublisherservices.com, pg 1294

McCray, Alicia, Independent Publishers Group (IPG), 814 N Franklin St, Chicago, IL 60610 *Tel:* 312-337-0747 *Toll Free Tel:* 800-888-4741 (orders) *Fax:* 312-337-5985 *E-mail:* frontdesk@ipgbook.com; orders@ipgbook.com *Web Site:* www.ipgbook.com, pg 1292, 1328

McCurdy, Robert, GTI Graphic Technology Inc, 211 Dupont Ave, Newburgh, NY 12550 *Tel:* 845-562-7066 *Fax:* 845-562-2543 *E-mail:* sales@gtilite.com *Web Site:* www.gtilite.com, pg 1280, 1370

McCutcheon, Wayne, Entro Communications Inc, 33 Harbour Sq, Suite 202, Toronto, ON M5J 2G2, Canada *Tel:* 416-368-6988 *Fax:* 416-368-5616 *E-mail:* toronto@entro.com *Web Site:* www.entro.com, pg 1414

McDonough, Judy, PR by the Book LLC, PO Box 6226, Round Rock, TX 78683 *Tel:* 512-501-4399 *Fax:* 512-501-4399 *E-mail:* info@prbythebook.com *Web Site:* www.prbythebook.com, pg 1112

McFadden, Stillman, Toof American Digital, 4222 Pilot Dr, Memphis, TN 38118 *Tel:* 901-274-3632 *Toll Free Tel:* 800-722-4772 *Web Site:* www.toofamericandigital.com, pg 1214, 1232, 1261, 1272

McGarr, Bill, Wybel Marketing Group Inc, 213 W Main St, Barrington, IL 60010 *Tel:* 847-382-0384; 847-382-0382 *Toll Free Tel:* 800-323-5297 *Fax:* 847-382-0385 *Toll Free Fax:* 800-595-5252 *E-mail:* bookreps@wybel.com, pg 1304

McGarr, William D, McGarr & Associates, 5692 Heathwood Ct, Covington, KY 41015 *Tel:* 859-356-9295 *Fax:* 859-356-7804, pg 1296

McGarrity, Andrew, Tennessee Book Co, 1550 Heil Quaker Blvd, La Vergne, TN 37086 *Tel:* 615-793-5040 *Toll Free Tel:* 800-456-0418 *Fax:* 615-213-9545 *Web Site:* www.tennesseebook.com, pg 1322

McGee, Thomas, Horizon Paper Co Inc, 1010 Washington Blvd, Stamford, CT 06901 *Tel:* 203-358-0855 *Toll Free Tel:* 866-358-0855 *E-mail:* info@horizonpaper.com *Web Site:* www.horizonpaper.com, pg 1268

McGonagle, Chuck, Transparent Language Inc, 12 Murphy Dr, Nashua, NH 03062 *Tel:* 603-262-6300 *Toll Free Tel:* 800-567-9619 (cust serv & sales) *E-mail:* info@transparent.com; support@transparent.com (tech support) *Web Site:* www.transparent.com, pg 1377

McGough, Jim, JPMC Associates, 7037 Snapdragon Dr, Carlsbad, CA 92011 *Tel:* 916-203-3693 *Fax:* 760-931-6878 *E-mail:* jpmcaso@aol.com, pg 1348

McGourlay, James, Open Text Corp, 275 Frank Tompa Dr, Waterloo, ON N2L 0A1, Canada *Tel:* 519-888-7111 *Fax:* 519-888-0677 *Web Site:* opentext.com, pg 1374

McInerney, Linda, University Products Inc, 517 Main St, Holyoke, MA 01040 *Tel:* 413-532-3372 *Toll Free Tel:* 800-628-1912 (orders) *Fax:* 413-533-4743 *Toll Free Fax:* 800-532-9281 *E-mail:* info@universityproducts.com *Web Site:* www.universityproducts.com, pg 1273

McKee, Jeff, X-Rite Inc, 4300 44 St SE, Grand Rapids, MI 49512 *Tel:* 616-803-2100 *Toll Free Tel:* 800-248-9748; 888-800-9580 (sales) *E-mail:* info@xrite.com *Web Site:* www.xrite.com, pg 1284

McKenna, Graham, Gracenote, a Nielsen Company, 2000 Powell St, Suite 1500, Emeryville, CA 94608 *Tel:* 510-428-7200 *Web Site:* www.gracenote.com, pg 1190

McKeon, John C, Hearst Newspapers, 300 W 57 St, New York, NY 10019 *Tel:* 212-649-2000 *Web Site:* www.hearst.com/newspapers, pg 1190

McKiernan, Scott, Keystone Press Agency Inc, 408 N El Camino Real, San Clemente, CA 92672 *Tel:* 949-481-3747 *Fax:* 949-481-3941 *E-mail:* info@keystonepictures.com *Web Site:* www.keystonepictures.com, pg 1190, 1429

McKinley, Brian, Ingram Content Group LLC, One Ingram Blvd, La Vergne, TN 37086-1986 *Tel:* 615-793-5000 *Toll Free Tel:* 800-937-8000 (retailers); 800-937-5300 (ext 1, libs) *E-mail:* customerservice@ingramcontent.com *Web Site:* www.ingramcontent.com, pg 1294, 1316

McKinnie, Michelle, McClain Printing Co, 212 Main St, Parsons, WV 26287-1033 *Tel:* 304-478-2881 *Toll Free Tel:* 800-654-7179 *Fax:* 304-478-4658 *E-mail:* mcclain@mcclainprinting.com *Web Site:* www.mcclainprinting.com, pg 1212, 1228, 1257, 1269, 1282

McKown-Finken, Amber, Independent Publishers Group (IPG), 814 N Franklin St, Chicago, IL 60610 *Tel:* 312-337-0747 *Toll Free Tel:* 800-888-4741 (orders) *Fax:* 312-337-5985 *E-mail:* frontdesk@ipgbook.com; orders@ipgbook.com *Web Site:* www.ipgbook.com, pg 1292

McLachlan, Prof Campbell, ICSID Review: Foreign Investment Law Journal, 4000 CentreGreen Way, Suite 310, Cary, NC 27513 *Toll Free Tel:* 800-852-7323 (option 1) *E-mail:* jnls.cust.serv@oup.com *Web Site:* academic.oup.com/icsidreview, pg 1133

McLaughlin, Carolyn, Bulletin of the History of Medicine, 2715 N Charles St, Baltimore, MD 21218-4363 *Tel:* 410-516-6987 (journal orders outside US & CN) *Toll Free Tel:* 800-548-1784 (journal orders) *Fax:* 410-578-2865 (journal orders) *E-mail:* bhm@jhmi.edu; jrnlcirc@jh.edu (journal orders) *Web Site:* www.press.jhu.edu/journals/bulletin-history-medicine, pg 1130

McLean, Kerry, Intuit Inc, 2700 Coast Ave, Mountain View, CA 94043 *Tel:* 650-944-6000 *Toll Free Tel:* 800-446-8848 *E-mail:* investor_relations@intuit.com *Web Site:* www.intuit.com, pg 1371

McLeester, Dick, VisionWorks, PO Box 92, Greenfield, MA 01302 *Tel:* 413-772-6569 *Toll Free Tel:* 800-933-7326 (orders) *Fax:* 413-772-6559 *E-mail:* dreaming@changingworld.com *Web Site:* www.changingworld.com, pg 1323

McLoraine, Jack, Gane Brothers & Lane Inc, 1400 Greenleaf Ave, Elk Grove Village, IL 60007 *Tel:* 847-593-3364 *Toll Free Tel:* 800-323-0596 *Toll Free Fax:* 800-784-2464 *E-mail:* sales@ganebrothers.com *Web Site:* www.ganebrothers.com, pg 1267

McManus, Brian, Worzalla, 3535 Jefferson St, Stevens Point, WI 54481 *Tel:* 715-344-9608 *Fax:* 715-344-2578 *Web Site:* www.worzalla.com, pg 1215, 1233, 1262

McMillen, Jim, Spraymation Inc, 4180 NW Tenth Ave, Fort Lauderdale, FL 33309 *Tel:* 954-484-9700 *Toll Free Tel:* 800-327-4985 *Fax:* 954-301-0842 *E-mail:* orders@spraymation.com *Web Site:* www.spraymation.com, pg 1283

McMurtrie, John, Kirkus, 1140 Broadway, Suite 802, New York, NY 10001 *Fax:* customercare@kirkus.com *Web Site:* www.kirkusreviews.com, pg 1133

McNeace, Richard, Faherty & Associates Inc, 17548 Redfern Ave, Lake Oswego, OR 97035 *Tel:* 503-639-3113 *Fax:* 503-213-6168 *E-mail:* faherty@fahertybooks.com *Web Site:* www.fahertybooks.com, pg 1290

McNeill, Kevin, Datalogics Inc, 101 N Wacker, Suite 1800, Chicago, IL 60606 *Tel:* 312-853-8200 *Fax:* 312-853-8282 *E-mail:* sales@datalogics.com; marketing@datalogics.com *Web Site:* www.datalogics.com, pg 1367

McNulty, Timothy, C & C Offset Printing Co USA Inc, 70 W 36 St, Unit 10C, New York, NY 10018 *Tel:* 212-431-4210 *Toll Free Fax:* 866-540-4134 *Web Site:* www.ccoffset.com, pg 1208, 1223, 1249

McNutty, Aidan, The New York Times Licensing Group, 620 Eighth Ave, 20th fl, New York, NY 10018 *Tel:* 212-556-1927 *E-mail:* nytlg-sales@nytimes.com *Web Site:* nytlicensing.com, pg 1191

McPhate, Chris, Crown Connect, 250 W Rialto Ave, San Bernadino, CA 92408 *Tel:* 909-888-7531 *Fax:* 909-889-1639 *E-mail:* sales@crownconnect.com *Web Site:* www.crownconnect.com, pg 1209, 1224, 1279

McPherson, Bill, AlphaGraphics Inc, 143 Union Blvd, Suite 650, Lakewood, CO 80228 *Toll Free Tel:* 800-955-6246 *Fax:* 801-595-7270 *E-mail:* contactus@alphagraphics.com *Web Site:* www.alphagraphics.com, pg 1364

McWilliams, Scott, Independent Publishers Group (IPG), 814 N Franklin St, Chicago, IL 60610 *Tel:* 312-337-0747 *Toll Free Tel:* 800-888-4741 (orders) *Fax:* 312-337-5985 *E-mail:* frontdesk@ipgbook.com; orders@ipgbook.com *Web Site:* www.ipgbook.com, pg 1292

McWilliams, Skip, Teacher's Discovery®, 2741 Paldan Dr, Auburn Hills, MI 48326 *Toll Free Tel:* 800-TEACHER (832-2437) *Toll Free Fax:* 800-287-4509 *E-mail:* help@teachersdiscovery.com; orders@teachersdiscovery.com *Web Site:* www.teachersdiscovery.com, pg 1303, 1322

Mead, Jim, Walsworth, 306 N Kansas Ave, Marceline, MO 64658 *Toll Free Tel:* 800-265-6795 *Web Site:* www.walsworth.com; www.walsworthhistorybooks.com, pg 1214, 1232, 1262

Meadows, Amy, Meadows Design Office, 3800 Yuma St NW, Washington, DC 20016 *Tel:* 202-966-6007 *E-mail:* mdo@mdomedia.com, pg 1212, 1228, 1356, 1416

Meadows, Marc, Meadows Design Office, 3800 Yuma St NW, Washington, DC 20016 *Tel:* 202-966-6007 *E-mail:* mdo@mdomedia.com, pg 1212, 1228, 1356, 1416

Medeiros, George, The Country Press Inc, One Commercial Dr, Lakeville, MA 02347 *Tel:* 508-947-4485 *Toll Free Tel:* 888-343-2227 *Fax:* 508-947-8989 *E-mail:* info@countrypressinc.com *Web Site:* www.countrypressprinting.com, pg 1209, 1251

Medina, Carmen, Medina Software Inc, 1441 Oberlin Terr, Suite 1010, Lake Mary, FL 32746 *Tel:* 407-227-4112 *Web Site:* www.medinasoft.com, pg 1372

Medina, Jorge, Medina Software Inc, 1441 Oberlin Terr, Suite 1010, Lake Mary, FL 32746 *Tel:* 407-227-4112 *Web Site:* www.medinasoft.com, pg 1372

Megna, Richard, Fundamental Photographs, 210 Forsyth St, Suite 2, New York, NY 10002 *Tel:* 212-473-5770 *E-mail:* mail@fphoto.com *Web Site:* www.fphoto.com, pg 1428

Meisner, Joe, First Choice Copy, 5208 Grand Ave, Maspeth, NY 11378 *Tel:* 718-381-1480 (ext 200) *Toll Free Tel:* 800-222-COPY (222-2679) *Web Site:* www.firstchoice-copy.com, pg 1117, 1210, 1253, 1368

Melanson, Donya, Donya Melanson Associates, 5 Bisson Lane, Merrimac, MA 01860 *Tel:* 978-346-9240 *Fax:* 978-346-8345 *E-mail:* dmelanson@dmelanson.com *Web Site:* www.dmelanson.com, pg 1100, 1116

Melcher, Charles, Melcher Media Inc, 124 W 13 St, New York, NY 10011 *Tel:* 212-727-2322 *Fax:* 212-627-1973 *E-mail:* info@melcher.com *Web Site:* www.melcher.com, pg 1356

Melendez, John, RAM Publications & Distribution Inc, 2525 Michigan Ave, Bldg A2, Santa Monica, CA 90404 *Tel:* 310-453-0043 *Fax:* 310-264-4888 *E-mail:* info@rampub.com; orders@rampub.com *Web Site:* www.rampub.com, pg 1301

Melissa, Raymond F, Melissa Data Corp, 22382 Avenida Empresa, Rancho Santa Margarita, CA 92688-2112 *Tel:* 949-858-3000 *Toll Free Tel:* 800-800-6245 *E-mail:* info@melissadata.com *Web Site:* www.melissadata.com, pg 1228

Melnick, Marsha, Roundtable Press Inc, 20 E Ninth St, New York, NY 10003 *Tel:* 917-597-2183 *Web Site:* www.roundtablepressinc.com, pg 1357

Melville, Kirsty, Andrews McMeel Syndication, 1130 Walnut St, Kansas City, MO 64106-2109 *Tel:* 816-581-7300 *Toll Free Tel:* 800-255-6734 *Web Site:* syndication.andrewsmcmeel.com, pg 1189, 1411

Melvin, Terrence, HFS, 2715 N Charles St, Baltimore, MD 21218 *Tel:* 410-516-6965 *Toll Free Tel:* 800-537-5487 (US & CN) *Fax:* 410-516-6998 *E-mail:* hfscustserv@jh.edu *Web Site:* hfs.jhu.edu; www.hfsbooks.com, pg 1292

Mendelson, Sandi, Hilsinger-Mendelson West Inc, 115 N Kings Rd, Los Angeles, CA 90048 *Tel:* 323-931-5335 (text only) *E-mail:* hmiwest@aol.com *Web Site:* www.hilsingermendelson.com, pg 1109

Mendez, Manny, Emerson, Wajdowicz Studios Inc, 514 W 25 St, New York, NY 10001 *Tel:* 212-807-8144 *E-mail:* info@designews.com *Web Site:* www.designews.com; www.facebook.com/DesignEWS; www.instagram.com/ewsdesign, pg 1414

Menezes, Andrew, CQ Roll Call, 1201 Pennsylvania Ave NW, Suite 600, Washington, DC 20004 *Tel:* 202-650-6500; 202-650-6511 (subns); 202-650-6621 (cust serv) *Toll Free Tel:* 800-432-2250; 800-678-8511 (subns) *E-mail:* customerservice@cqrollcall.com *Web Site:* cqrollcall.com; www.rollcall.com, pg 1190

Mengin, Nicolas, Distribooks Inc, 8154 N Ridgeway Ave, Skokie, IL 60076-2911 *Tel:* 847-676-1596 *Toll Free Fax:* 888-266-5713 *E-mail:* info@distribooks.com, pg 1290

Mengin, Nicolas, Distribooks Inc, 8154 N Ridgeway Ave, Skokie, IL 60076-2911 *Tel:* 847-676-1596 *Fax:* 847-676-1195 *Toll Free Fax:* 888-266-5713 *E-mail:* info@distribooks.com; info@schoenhofs.com *Web Site:* www.schoenhofs.com, pg 1314

Mengin, Nicolas, Schoenhof's Foreign Books Inc, 76 A Mount Auburn St, Cambridge, MA 02138 *Tel:* 617-547-8855 *E-mail:* info@schoenhofs.com *Web Site:* www.schoenhofs.com, pg 1321, 1329

Menke, Jim, Roswell Bookbinding, 2614 N 29 Ave, Phoenix, AZ 85009 *Tel:* 602-272-9338 *Toll Free Tel:* 888-803-8883 *Fax:* 602-272-9786 *Web Site:* www.roswellbookbinding.com, pg 1259, 1326

Menschenfreund, Joan, Visual Pursuit, 168 W 86 St, New York, NY 10024 *Tel:* 212-362-8234, pg 1425

Mercer, Rachel, ALC Inc, 750 College Rd E, Suite 201, Princeton, NJ 08540 *Tel:* 609-580-2800 *Toll Free Tel:* 800-252-5478 *Fax:* 609-580-2888 *E-mail:* info@alc.com *Web Site:* www.alc.com, pg 1119

Merker, Lance, OmniUpdate Inc, 1320 Flynn Rd, Suite 100, Camarillo, CA 93012 *Tel:* 805-484-9400 *Toll Free Tel:* 800-362-2605 *E-mail:* sales@omniupdate.com *Web Site:* omniupdate.com, pg 1374

Merrell, Jesse H, Merrell Enterprises, 3542 E State Rte 73, Waynesville, OH 45068 *Tel:* 202-265-1925 *Fax:* 513-855-4277 *Web Site:* www.merrellenterprises.com, pg 1191

Mersmann, Peter, StoraEnso North American Sales Inc, Canterbury Green, 201 Broad St, Stamford, CT 06901 Tel: 203-541-5100 Fax: 203-353-1143 Web Site: www.storaenso.com, pg 1272

Mesjak, Alice, Abraham Associates Inc, 5120-A Cedar Lake Rd, Minneapolis, MN 55416 Tel: 952-927-7920 Toll Free Tel: 800-701-2489 Fax: 952-927-8089 E-mail: info@abrahamassociatesinc.com Web Site: www.abrahamassociatesinc.com, pg 1285

Mesjak, John, Abraham Associates Inc, 5120-A Cedar Lake Rd, Minneapolis, MN 55416 Tel: 952-927-7920 Toll Free Tel: 800-701-2489 Fax: 952-927-8089 E-mail: info@abrahamassociatesinc.com Web Site: www.abrahamassociatesinc.com, pg 1285

Messenger, Jeff, EMT International Inc, 780 Centerline Dr, Hobart, WI 54155 Tel: 920-468-5475 Fax: 920-468-7991 E-mail: info@emtinternational.com Web Site: www.emtinternational.com, pg 1279

Metz, Steve, The Sound Lab Inc, 3355 Bee Cave Rd, Bldg 7, Suite 701, Austin, TX 78746 Tel: 512-476-2122 Fax: 512-476-2127 E-mail: info@thesoundlabinc.com Web Site: www.thesoundlabinc.com, pg 1376

Metzger, Heather, Biblical Archaeology Society, 4710 41 St NW, Washington, DC 20016-1705 Tel: 202-364-3300 Toll Free Tel: 800-221-4644 Fax: 202-364-2636 E-mail: info@biblicalarchaeology.org Web Site: www.biblicalarchaeology.org, pg 1365

Meurice, Stephen, The Canadian Press/La Presse Canadienne, 36 King St E, Toronto, ON M5C 2L9, Canada Tel: 416-364-0321 Fax: 416-364-0207 (newsroom) E-mail: sales@thecanadianpress.com Web Site: www.thecanadianpress.com, pg 1189

Meyer, Cheryll A, Metropolitan Newsclips Service Inc, 1250 Hanley Industrial Ct, St Louis, MO 63144 Tel: 314-395-8917 E-mail: cheryllm@metronewsclips.com Web Site: www.metronewsclips.com, pg 1383

Meyerhoff, Deanna, Baker & Taylor Publisher Services, 30 Amberwood Pkwy, Ashland, OH 44805 Tel: 567-215-0030 Toll Free Tel: 888-814-0208 E-mail: info@btpubservices.com; orders@btpubservices.com Web Site: www.btpubservices.com, pg 1286, 1333, 1400, 1412

Mezzetti, Phil, The Sound Lab Inc, 3355 Bee Cave Rd, Bldg 7, Suite 701, Austin, TX 78746 Tel: 512-476-2122 Fax: 512-476-2127 E-mail: info@thesoundlabinc.com Web Site: www.thesoundlabinc.com, pg 1376

Micaelian, Fadi, BroadVision, 460 Seaport Ct, Suite 102, Redwood City, CA 94063 Tel: 650-331-1000 Web Site: www.broadvision.com, pg 1365

Michailidis, Parisa, Firefly Books Ltd, 50 Staples Ave, Unit 1, Richmond Hill, ON L4B 0A7, Canada Tel: 416-499-8412 Toll Free Tel: 800-387-6192 (CN); 800-387-5085 (US) Fax: 416-499-8313 Toll Free Fax: 800-450-0391 (CN); 800-565-6034 (US) E-mail: service@fireflybooks.com Web Site: www.fireflybooks.com, pg 1291

Michaud, Ann, Association for Library Service to Children (ALSC), 225 N Michigan Ave, Suite 1300, Chicago, IL 60601 Tel: 312-280-2163 Toll Free Tel: 800-545-2433 Fax: 312-280-5271 E-mail: alsc@ala.org Web Site: www.ala.org/alsc, pg 1145

Mickey, Bill, Choice, 575 Main St, Suite 300, Middletown, CT 06457 Tel: 860-347-6933; 847-504-8803 (subns) Toll Free Tel: 844-291-0455 (subns) Fax: 860-346-8586 E-mail: acrlsubscriptions@omeda.com; support@acrlchoice.freshdesk.com Web Site: www.ala.org/acrl-choice; www.choice360.org, pg 1131

Mickunas, Vick, Dayton Daily News, 4805 Meredith Rd, Yellow Springs, OH 45387 Tel: 937-767-1396, pg 1131

Migdale, Lawrence, Lawrence Migdale Photography/PIX, 23 White Hall Dr, Orinda, CA 94563 Tel: 510-612-2572 E-mail: photopix@migdale.com Web Site: www.migdale.com, pg 1430

Mihaley, Jackie, Ulster Linen Co Inc, 383 Moffit Blvd, Islip, NY 11751 Tel: 631-859-5244 Fax: 631-859-4990 E-mail: sales@ulsterlinen.com Web Site: www.ulsterlinen.com, pg 1273

Mikell, Troy, Mackin Educational Resources, 3505 County Rd 42 W, Burnsville, MN 55306 Tel: 952-895-9540 Toll Free Tel: 800-245-9540 Fax: 952-894-8806 Toll Free Fax: 800-369-5490 E-mail: mackin@mackin.com Web Site: www.mackin.com, pg 1318

Mikos, Peter, North 49 Books, 35 Prince Andrew Place, Toronto, ON M3C 2H2, Canada Tel: 416-449-4000 Toll Free Tel: 800-490-4049 Fax: 416-449-9924 Toll Free Fax: 888-349-2221 E-mail: sales@north49books.com Web Site: www.north49books.com, pg 1320

Milano, Chrissi, Dunhill International List Co Inc, 6400 Congress Ave, Suite 1750, Boca Raton, FL 33487-2898 Tel: 561-998-7800 Toll Free Tel: 800-DUNHILL (386-4455) Fax: 561-998-7880 E-mail: dunhill@dunhillintl.com Web Site: www.dunhills.com, pg 1120

Milano, Denise, New Leaf Distributing Co, 1085 E Lotus Dr, Silver Lake, WI 53170 Tel: 262-889-8501 (ext 162) Toll Free Tel: 800-326-2665 (orders) Fax: 262-889-8598 E-mail: orders@newleafdist.com, pg 1298, 1319

Miles, Terry, Longleaf Services Inc, 116 S Boundary St, Chapel Hill, NC 27514-3808 Tel: 919-966-7449 Toll Free Tel: 800-848-6224 Fax: 919-962-2704 (24 hours) Toll Free Fax: 800-272-6817 (24 hours) E-mail: customerservice@longleafservices.org; orders@longleafservices.org Web Site: longleafservices.org, pg 1295

Miller, Bruce, Miller Trade Book Marketing Inc, 1426 W Carmen Ave, Chicago, IL 60640 Tel: 773-307-3446, pg 1298

Miller, Candysse, Independent Publishers Group (IPG), 814 N Franklin St, Chicago, IL 60610 Tel: 312-337-0747 Toll Free Tel: 800-888-4741 (orders) Fax: 312-337-5985 E-mail: frontdesk@ipgbook.com; orders@ipgbook.com Web Site: www.ipgbook.com, pg 1292, 1328

Miller, Ceci, CeciBooks Editorial & Publishing Consultation, 7057 26 Ave NW, Seattle, WA 98117 E-mail: ceci@cecibooks.com Web Site: www.cecibooks.com, pg 1344

Miller, Edward, Wild West Communications Group, PO Box 346, Homewood, CA 96141 Tel: 530-412-1096 Fax: 530-525-4559 Web Site: www.wildwest-tahoe.com, pg 1417

Miller, Hannah, Diacritics, 2715 N Charles St, Baltimore, MD 21218-4363 Tel: 410-516-6987 (journal orders outside US & CN) Toll Free Tel: 800-548-1784 (journal orders) Fax: 410-578-2865 (journal orders) E-mail: jrnlcirc@jh.edu (journal orders) Web Site: www.press.jhu.edu/journals/diacritics, pg 1131

Miller, Jeff, MBS Textbook Exchange Inc, 2711 W Ash, Columbia, MO 65203 Tel: 573-445-2243 Toll Free Tel: 800-325-0530 (textbook solutions); 800-325-4138 (bookstore systems) Fax: 573-446-5256 E-mail: cserv@mbsbooks.com Web Site: www.mbsbooks.com, pg 1319

Miller, Joelle Silverman, By Design Communications, 144 W 27 St, 3rd fl (rear), New York, NY 10001 Tel: 212-366-1740, pg 1412

Miller, John, Advantage Laser Products Inc, 1840 Marietta Blvd NW, Atlanta, GA 30318 Tel: 404-351-2700 Toll Free Tel: 800-722-2804 (cust serv) Fax: 404-351-0911 Toll Free Fax: 800-871-3305 E-mail: sales@advlaser.com Web Site: www.advlaser.com, pg 1363

Miller, Merlin, Markwith Tool Co Inc, 5261 State Rte 49 S, Greenville, OH 45331 Tel: 937-548-6808 Fax: 937-548-7051 Web Site: markwithtool.com, pg 1281

Miller, Michael, Bookforum, 520 Eighth Ave, 21st fl, New York, NY 10018 E-mail: editors@bookforum.com; advertising@bookforum.com; circulation@bookforum.com Web Site: www.bookforum.com; subscriptions.bookforum.com, pg 1130

Miller, Rebecca, International Leads (IL), 225 N Michigan Ave, Suite 1300, Chicago, IL 60601 Tel: 312-944-6780 Toll Free Tel: 800-545-2433 Fax: 312-440-9374 E-mail: ala.intl.leads@gmail.com; ala@ala.org Web Site: www.ala.org/rt/irrt/intlleads/internationalleads; www.ala.org/rt/irrt; www.ala.org, pg 1133

Miller, Rebecca T, Horn Book Inc, 300 The Fenway, Suite P-311, Palace Road Bldg, Boston, MA 02115 Tel: 617-278-0225 Toll Free Tel: 888-628-0225 Fax: 617-278-6062 E-mail: info@hbook.com Web Site: www.hbook.com, pg 1146

Miller, Rebecca T, The Horn Book Magazine, 7858 Industrial Pkwy, Plain City, OH 43064 Toll Free Tel: 800-325-9558 E-mail: info@hbook.com Web Site: www.hbook.com, pg 1132

Miller, Rebecca T, Library Journal, 123 William St, Suite 802, New York, NY 10038 Tel: 646-380-0700 Toll Free Tel: 800-588-1030 Fax: 646-380-0756 E-mail: ljinfo@mediasourceinc.com Web Site: www.libraryjournal.com, pg 1134

Miller, Rebecca T, School Library Journal, 123 William St, Suite 802, New York, NY 10038 Tel: 646-380-0752 Toll Free Tel: 800-595-1066 Fax: 646-380-0756 E-mail: slj@mediasourceinc.com; sljsubs@pcspublink.com Web Site: www.slj.com; www.facebook.com/schoollibraryjournal; x.com/sljournal, pg 1136

Miller, Sue, Avery Dennison Corp, 207 N Goode Ave, 6th fl, Glendale, CA 91203-1222 Tel: 626-304-2000 Web Site: www.averydennison.com, pg 1365

Miller, Susan Riva, Susan Riva Miller-Alpine Photography, 20415 150 Ave SE, Monroe, WA 98272 Tel: 206-679-0475 E-mail: susanrivamiller@hotmail.com, pg 1424

Miller, Zack, Motorbooks, 100 Cummings Ctr, Suite 265D, Beverly, MA 01915 Tel: 978-282-9590 Toll Free Tel: 800-759-0190 (orders) Web Site: www.quartoknows.com/motorbooks, pg 1319, 1329

Milliot, Jim, Publishers Weekly, 49 W 23 St, 9th fl, New York, NY 10010 Tel: 212-377-5500 Fax: 212-377-2733 Web Site: www.publishersweekly.com, pg 1136

Milne, Lindsey, Del Commune Enterprises Inc, 18 Bellport Lane, Bellport, NY 11713 Tel: 212-226-6664 E-mail: mail@dcescouts.com Web Site: www.dcescouts.com, pg 1345

Milton, Steve, ISOMEDIA Inc, 12842 Interurban Ave S, Seattle, WA 98168 Tel: 425-869-5411 Toll Free Tel: 866-838-4389 (sales); 877-638-9277 (support) Fax: 425-869-9437 E-mail: sales@isomedia.com Web Site: www.isomedia.com, pg 1371

Minden, Larry, Minden Pictures Inc, 9565 Soquel Dr, Suite 202, Aptos, CA 95003 Tel: 831-661-5551 E-mail: info@mindenpictures.com Web Site: www.mindenpictures.com, pg 1430

Minguez, Patrice, Resolute Forest Products, 111 Robert-Bourassa Blvd, Suite 5000, Montreal, QC H3C 2M1, Canada Tel: 514-875-2160 Toll Free Tel: 800-361-2888 E-mail: info@resolutefp.com Web Site: www.resolutefp.com, pg 1271

Minissali, Richard, f-stop Fitzgerald Inc, 88 James St, Rosendale, NY 12472 E-mail: fstopf@gmail.com, pg 1354, 1421

Minkow, Andrew, International Literary Properties (ILP), 286 Madison Ave, New York, NY 10017 Tel: 646-202-1633 Fax: 212-967-0977 E-mail: contact@ilpliterary.com Web Site: www.internationalliteraryproperties.com, pg 1348

Minor, Florence, Wendell Minor, 15 Old North Rd, Washington, CT 06793 Tel: 860-868-9101 E-mail: wendell@minorart.com Web Site: www.minorart.com, pg 1416

Mishler, Clark James, Clark James Mishler Photography, 1815 School St, Calistoga, CA 94515 Tel: 907-351-7863 Web Site: www.mishlerphotos.com, pg 1424

Mishra, Ashok Kumar, Innodata Inc, 55 Challenger Rd, Suite 202, Ridgefield Park, NJ 07660 Tel: 201-371-8000 Toll Free Tel: 877-454-8400 E-mail: info@innodata.com; marketing@innodata.com Web Site: innodata.com, pg 1227, 1347, 1371

Misiewicz, Megan, The Philip Lief Group Inc (PLG), 2976 Pleasant Ridge Rd, Wingdale, NY 12594 Tel: 609-430-1000 Fax: 845-724-7139 E-mail: info@plg.us.com Web Site: plg.us.com, pg 1355

Mitchell, Jack, Lumina Datamatics Inc, 600 Cordwainer Dr, Unit 103, Norwell, MA 02061 Tel: 508-746-0300 Fax: 508-746-3233 E-mail: marketing@luminad.com Web Site: luminadatamatics.com, pg 1212, 1228, 1349, 1356, 1372, 1415

Mitford, Kathleen, PTC, 121 Seaport Blvd, Boston, MA 02210 Tel: 781-370-5000 Fax: 781-370-6000 Web Site: www.ptc.com, pg 1375

Mittelsdorf, Carol, Fred Weidner & Daughter Printers, 99 Hudson St, 5th fl, New York, NY 10013 Tel: 646-706-5180 E-mail: info@fwdprinters.com Web Site: www.fwdprinters.com, pg 1232, 1262, 1273, 1284, 1351

Mo, David, Envision Peripherals Inc (EPI), 490 N McCarthy Blvd, Suite 120, Milpitas, CA 95035 Web Site: us.aoc.com, pg 1368

Moeller, Klaus, Globe Entertainment & Media Corp, 8500 Beverly Blvd, Suite 683, Los Angeles, CA 90048 Web Site: www.globecorp.co, pg 1429

Molho, Emanuel, French & European Publications Inc, 425 E 58 St, Suite 27-D, New York, NY 10022 Tel: 212-581-8810 Fax: 212-202-4356 E-mail: livresny@gmail.com, frenchbookstore@aol.com Web Site: www.frencheuropean.com, pg 1328

Monahan, Michael, The Library Services Centre, 131 Shoemaker St, Kitchener, ON N2E 3B5, Canada Tel: 519-746-4420 Toll Free Tel: 800-265-3360 (CN only) Fax: 519-746-4425 Web Site: www.lsc.on.ca, pg 1318

Monie, Alain, Ingram Micro Inc, 3351 Michelson Dr, Suite 100, Irvin, CA 92612 Tel: 714-566-1000 E-mail: customerexperience@ingrammicro.com Web Site: www.ingrammicro.com, pg 1317

Monteiro, Barbara, Monteiro & Co Inc, 301 E 57 St, 4th fl, New York, NY 10022 Tel: 212-832-8183 Web Site: www.monteiroandco.com, pg 1111

Moochalla, Hussain, The Hibbert Group, 400 Pennington Ave, Trenton, NJ 08650 Tel: 609-394-7500 Toll Free Tel: 888-HIBBERT (442-2378) E-mail: info@hibbertgroup.com Web Site: hibbert.com, pg 1104, 1116, 1117

Moonan, Thomas J, The Hibbert Group, 400 Pennington Ave, Trenton, NJ 08650 Tel: 609-394-7500 Toll Free Tel: 888-HIBBERT (442-2378) E-mail: info@hibbertgroup.com Web Site: hibbert.com, pg 1104, 1116, 1117

Moonan, Timothy J, The Hibbert Group, 400 Pennington Ave, Trenton, NJ 08650 Tel: 609-394-7500 Toll Free Tel: 888-HIBBERT (442-2378) E-mail: info@hibbertgroup.com Web Site: hibbert.com, pg 1104, 1116, 1117

Moore, Erica, Follett School Solutions Inc, 1340 Ridgeview Dr, McHenry, IL 60050 Tel: 815-759-1700 Toll Free Tel: 888-511-5114 (cust serv); 877-899-8550 (sales) Tel: 815-759-9831 Toll Free Fax: 800-852-5458 E-mail: info@follettlearning.com; customerservice@follett.com Web Site: www.follettlearning.com; www.follett.com/prek12; www.titlewave.com, pg 1291, 1369

Moore, Marc, Sheridan Saline, 960 Woodland Dr, Saline, MI 48176 Tel: 734-429-5411 Web Site: www.sheridan.com, pg 1214, 1260

Moore, Michael, Augsburg Fortress Publishers, Publishing House of the Evangelical Lutheran Church in America, 510 Marquette Ave S, Minneapolis, MN 55402 Tel: 612-330-3300 Toll Free Tel: 800-426-0115 (ext 639, subns); 800-328-4648 (orders) Fax: 612-330-3455 Toll Free Fax: 800-722-7766 (orders) E-mail: customercare@augsburgfortress.org; copyright@augsburgfortress.org (reprint permission requests); info@augsburgfortress.org Web Site: www.augsburgfortress.org; www.1517.media, pg 1311

Morales, Jessica, Two Rivers Distribution, an Ingram brand, 1400 Broadway, Suite 520, New York, NY 10018 Toll Free Tel: 866-400-5351 E-mail: ips@ingramcontent.com (orders, independent bookstores & gift accts) Web Site: www.tworiversdistribution.com, pg 1303

Moran, Kevin, Parson Weems' Publisher Services LLC, 3811 Canterbury Rd, No 707, Baltimore, MD 21218 Tel: 914-948-4259 Toll Free Fax: 866-861-0337 E-mail: office@parsonweems.com Web Site: www.parsonweems.com, pg 1299

Moran, Michael, Gem Guides Book Co, 1155 W Ninth St, Upland, CA 91786 Tel: 626-855-1611 Toll Free Tel: 800-824-5118 (orders) Fax: 626-855-1610 E-mail: info@gemguidesbooks.com; sales@gemguidesbooks.com (orders) Web Site: www.gemguidesbooks.com, pg 1315

Moran, Michael, Spraymation Inc, 4180 NW Tenth Ave, Fort Lauderdale, FL 33309 Tel: 954-484-9700 Toll Free Tel: 800-327-4985 Fax: 954-301-0842 E-mail: orders@spraymation.com Web Site: www.spraymation.com, pg 1283

Morcom, David, Hignell Book Printing Ltd, 488 Burnell St, Winnipeg, MB R3G 2B4, Canada Tel: 204-784-1030 Toll Free Tel: 800-304-5553 Fax: 204-774-4053 E-mail: books@hignell.mb.ca Web Site: www.hignell.mb.ca, pg 1211, 1254

Morehead, Tod, Indigo Books & Music Inc, 468 King St W, Suite 500, Toronto, ON M5V 1L8, Canada Tel: 416-364-4499 E-mail: cisales@indigo.ca Web Site: www.chapters.indigo.ca, pg 1294

Morgan, Emmanuelle, Stonesong, 270 W 39 St, Suite 201, New York, NY 10018 Tel: 212-929-4600 E-mail: editors@stonesong.com Web Site: www.stonesong.com, pg 1357

Morgan, Tim, Genesis Marketing Group Inc, 850 Wade Hampton Blvd, Bldg A, Suite 100, Greenville, SC 29609 Tel: 864-233-2651 Toll Free Tel: 800-627-2651 Toll Free Fax: 800-849-4363 E-mail: orders@genesislink.com Web Site: www.genesislink.com, pg 1291

Morgan, Tim, La Crosse Graphics Inc, 3025 East Ave S, La Crosse, WI 54601 Tel: 608-788-2500 Toll Free Tel: 800-832-2503 Fax: 608-788-2660 Web Site: www.lacrossegraphics.com, pg 1255

Moriarty, Amy, WordCo Indexing Services Inc, 66 Franklin St, Norwich, CT 06360 E-mail: office@wordco.com Web Site: www.wordco.com, pg 1233

Morical, Wendy, Docunet Corp, 2435 Xenium Lane N, Plymouth, MN 55441 Tel: 763-475-9600 Toll Free Tel: 800-936-2863 Fax: 763-475-1516 E-mail: print@docunetworks.com Web Site: www.docunetworks.com, pg 1252

Morin, Michel, Les Editions Themis, Faculte de droit, Universite de Montreal, CP 6128, Succursale Centreville, Montreal, QC H3C 3J7, Canada Tel: 514-343-6627 Fax: 514-343-6779 E-mail: info@editionsthemis.com Web Site: ssl.editionsthemis.com, pg 1315

Morin, Shawn, Ingram Content Group LLC, One Ingram Blvd, La Vergne, TN 37086-1986 Tel: 615-793-5000 Toll Free Tel: 800-937-8000 (retailers); 800-937-5300 (ext 1, libs) E-mail: customerservice@ingramcontent.com Web Site: www.ingramcontent.com, pg 1294, 1316

Morris, Jamie, Specialty Finishing Group, 1401 Kirk St, Elk Grove Village, IL 60007 Tel: 847-290-0110 Fax: 847-290-9404 Web Site: www.sfgrp.com, pg 1260

Morris, Melody, Sun Graphics LLC, 1818 Broadway, Parsons, KS 67357 Toll Free Tel: 800-835-0588 Fax: 620-421-2089 E-mail: info@sun-graphics.com Web Site: www.sun-graphics.com, pg 1214, 1231, 1260

Morris, Michael, Publishers Weekly, 49 W 23 St, 9th fl, New York, NY 10010 Tel: 212-377-5500 Fax: 212-377-2733 Web Site: www.publishersweekly.com, pg 1136

Morris, Ryan, Morris Printing Group Inc, 3212 E Hwy 30, Kearney, NE 68847 Tel: 308-236-7888 Toll Free Tel: 800-650-7888 Fax: 308-237-0263 Web Site: www.morrisprintinggroup.com, pg 1257

Morris, Scott, Morris Printing Group Inc, 3212 E Hwy 30, Kearney, NE 68847 Tel: 308-236-7888 Toll Free Tel: 800-650-7888 Fax: 308-237-0263 Web Site: www.morrisprintinggroup.com, pg 1257

Morrison, Beth, Symmetry Creative Production, 1300 S Grove Ave, Suite 103, Barrington, IL 60010 Tel: 847-382-8750 E-mail: information@symmetrycp.com Web Site: www.symmetrycp.com, pg 1232

Morrison, Dan, Western Telematic Inc (WTI), 5 Sterling, Irvine, CA 92618 Tel: 949-586-9950 Toll Free Tel: 800-854-7226 E-mail: info@wti.com Web Site: www.wti.com, pg 1378

Morrissey, Caitlyn, Bank Street Book Store, 2780 Broadway, New York, NY 10025 Tel: 212-678-1654 Fax: 212-316-7026 E-mail: books@bankstreet.edu Web Site: www.bankstreetbooks.com, pg 1145

Morrissey, Patrick, Electronics for Imaging Inc (EFI), 6750 Dumbarton Circle, Fremont, CA 94555 Tel: 650-357-3500 Toll Free Tel: 800-568-1917; 800-875-7117 (sales) Fax: 650-357-3907 E-mail: info@efi.com Web Site: www.efi.com, pg 1368

Morrow, Dee, New England Book Service Inc, 7000 Vt Rte 17 W, Addison, VT 05491 Tel: 802-759-3000 Toll Free Tel: 800-356-5772 Fax: 802-759-3220 E-mail: nebs@together.net Web Site: www.nebooks.com, pg 1319

Morrow, Fred, New England Book Service Inc, 7000 Vt Rte 17 W, Addison, VT 05491 Tel: 802-759-3000 Toll Free Tel: 800-356-5772 Fax: 802-759-3220 E-mail: nebs@together.net Web Site: www.nebooks.com, pg 1319

Mortee, Marvin, Art Related Technology Inc, 4 Brattle St, Rm 305, Cambridge, MA 02138 Tel: 617-661-1225 Fax: 617-491-0618 E-mail: artinc@artrelated.com Web Site: www.artrelated.com, pg 1222, 1365

Morten, Scott J, Interprint Web Printing, 12350 US 19 N, Clearwater, FL 33764 Tel: 727-531-8957 Toll Free Tel: 800-749-5152 Fax: 727-536-0647 E-mail: info@interprintwebprinting.com Web Site: www.interprintwebprinting.com, pg 1104

Mortimer, Bryce, Cedar Fort Inc, 2373 W 700 S, Suite 100, Springville, UT 84663 Tel: 801-489-4084 Toll Free Tel: 800-SKY-BOOK (759-2665) E-mail: marketinginfo@cedarfort.com Web Site: cedarfort.com, pg 1327

Moser, Paul, Direct Link™ Worldwide Inc, 700 Dowd Ave, Elizabeth, NJ 07201 Tel: 908-289-0703 Fax: 908-289-0705 E-mail: infousa@directlink.com Web Site: www.directlink.com, pg 1333

Moss, Anne Eakin, Modern Language Notes (MLN), 2715 N Charles St, Baltimore, MD 21218-4363 Tel: 410-516-6987 (journal orders outside US & CN) Toll Free Tel: 800-548-1784 (journal orders) Fax: 410-578-2865 (journal orders) E-mail: jrnlcirc@jh.edu (journal orders) Web Site: www.press.jhu.edu/journals/mln, pg 1134

Moss, Monique, Integrated PR Agency (IPR), Penthouse, 9025 Wilshire Blvd, Suite 500, Beverly Hills, CA 90211 Tel: 310-858-8230 Web Site: www.integrated-pr.com, pg 1109

Moster, Meg, Chesapeake & Hudson Inc, 27 Jacks Shop Rd, Rochelle, VA 22738 Tel: 301-834-7170 Toll Free Tel: 800-231-4469 E-mail: office@cheshud.com Web Site: www.cheshudinc.com, pg 1289

Moyer, Josh, Purplegator, 1055 Westlakes Dr, Berwyn, PA 19312 Tel: 610-688-6000 Toll Free Tel: 888-76-GATOR (764-2867) Web Site: www.purplegator.com, pg 1350

Muchnick, Laurie, Kirkus, 1140 Broadway, Suite 802, New York, NY 10001 E-mail: customercare@kirkus.com Web Site: www.kirkusreviews.com, pg 1133

Mueller, Felix, Heidelberg USA Inc, 1000 Gutenberg Dr, Kennesaw, GA 30144 Tel: 770-419-6500 Toll Free Tel: 800-437-7388 E-mail: info@heidelberg.com Web Site: www.heidelberg.com/us, pg 1280

Muertens, Gunther, Agfa North America, 580 Gotham Pkwy, Carlstadt, NJ 07072 Tel: 201-440-2500 Toll Free Tel: 888-274-8626 (cust serv)

E-mail: customercare.us@agfa.com Web Site: www.agfa.com/printing/global/usa; www.agfa.com/printing/industrial; www.agfa.com/printing/large-format, pg 1277, 1364

Mugambi, Florence, International Leads (IL), 225 N Michigan Ave, Suite 1300, Chicago, IL 60601 Tel: 312-944-6780 Toll Free Tel: 800-545-2433 Fax: 312-440-9374 E-mail: ala.intl.leads@gmail.com; ala@ala.org Web Site: www.ala.org/rt/irrt/intlleads/internationalleads; www.ala.org/rt/irrt; www.ala.org, pg 1133

Mukalla, Doris, International Book Centre Inc, 2391 Auburn Rd, Shelby Township, MI 48317 Tel: 586-254-7230 Fax: 586-254-7230 E-mail: ibc@ibcbooks.com Web Site: www.ibcbooks.com, pg 1317

Mukherjee, Debabrata, Finch Paper LLC, One Glen St, Glens Falls, NY 12801 Tel: 518-793-2541 Toll Free Tel: 800-833-9983 Fax: 518-743-9656 E-mail: info@finchpaper.com Web Site: www.finchpaper.com, pg 1267

Mulvaney, Jon, The Criterion Collection, 215 Park Ave S, 5th fl, New York, NY 10003 Tel: 212-756-8822 E-mail: suggestions@criterion.com Web Site: www.criterion.com, pg 1367

Mummert, Nicole, Sheridan MI, 613 E Industrial Dr, Chelsea, MI 48118 Tel: 734-475-9145 Web Site: www.sheridan.com, pg 1213, 1259, 1271

Mummert, Nicole, Sheridan NH, 69 Lyme Rd, Hanover, NH 03755 Tel: 603-643-2220 Web Site: www.sheridan.com, pg 1259

Mummert, Nicole, Sheridan PA, 450 Fame Ave, Hanover, PA 17331 Tel: 717-632-3535 Toll Free Tel: 800-352-2210 Fax: 717-633-8900 Web Site: www.sheridan.com, pg 1259

Munday, Evan, Penguin Random House Canada, a Penguin Random House company, 320 Front St W, Suite 1400, Toronto, ON M5V 3B6, Canada Tel: 416-364-4449 Toll Free Tel: 888-523-9292 (cust serv) Fax: 416-598-7764 E-mail: customerservicescanada@penguinrandomhouse.com; publicitycanada@penguinrandomhouse.com; rightscanada@penguinrandomhouse.com Web Site: www.penguinrandomhouse.ca, pg 1299

Munford, Robert, Pacific Publishing Co Inc, 636 Alaska St S, Seattle, WA 98108 Tel: 206-461-1300 E-mail: ppcprint@nwlink.com; ppccirc@nwlink.com; ppcbind@nwlink.com Web Site: pacificpublishingcompany.com, pg 1258

Murad, Richard, Courier Systems Inc, 180 Pulaski St, Bayonne, NJ 07002 Tel: 201-432-0550 Toll Free Tel: 800-252-0353 Fax: 201-432-9686 E-mail: sales@csweb.biz Web Site: www.csweb.biz, pg 1333

Murphy, Brian T, Burlington News Agency Inc, 382 Hercules Dr, Suite 2, Colchester, VT 05446 Tel: 802-655-7000 Fax: 802-655-7002 E-mail: burlnews@aol.com, pg 1313

Murphy, Cynthia, Independent Publishers Group (IPG), 814 N Franklin St, Chicago, IL 60610 Tel: 312-337-0747 Toll Free Tel: 800-888-4741 (orders) Fax: 312-337-5985 E-mail: frontdesk@ipgbook.com; orders@ipgbook.com Web Site: www.ipgbook.com, pg 1292, 1328

Murphy, Glenn E, Burlington News Agency Inc, 382 Hercules Dr, Suite 2, Colchester, VT 05446 Tel: 802-655-7000 Fax: 802-655-7002 E-mail: burlnews@aol.com, pg 1313

Murphy, John, Adobe Systems Inc, 345 Park Ave, San Jose, CA 95110-2704 Tel: 408-536-6000 Fax: 408-537-6000 Web Site: www.adobe.com, pg 1363

Murphy, Paul, Independent Publishers Group (IPG), 814 N Franklin St, Chicago, IL 60610 Tel: 312-337-0747 Toll Free Tel: 800-888-4741 (orders) Fax: 312-337-5985 E-mail: frontdesk@ipgbook.com; orders@ipgbook.com Web Site: www.ipgbook.com, pg 1292, 1328

Murphy, Tim, Printware LLC, 2935 Waters Rd, Suite 160, St Paul, MN 55121-1523 Tel: 651-456-1400 Fax: 651-454-3684 E-mail: sales@printwarellc.com Web Site: www.printwarellc.com, pg 1375

Murray, Candice, Shutterstock Inc, Empire State Bldg, 350 Fifth Ave, 20th fl, New York, NY 10118 E-mail: support@shutterstock.com; press@shutterstock.com Web Site: www.shutterstock.com, pg 1430

Murray, J M "Mike", Brackett Inc, 7115 SE Forbes Ave, Topeka, KS 66619 Tel: 785-862-2205 Toll Free Tel: 800-255-3506 Fax: 785-862-1127 E-mail: brackett@brackett-inc.com; sales@brackett-inc.com Web Site: brackett-inc.com, pg 1278

Murray, Joe, Publishers Weekly, 49 W 23 St, 9th fl, New York, NY 10010 Tel: 212-377-5500 Fax: 212-377-2733 Web Site: www.publishersweekly.com, pg 1136

Murray, Sharon, Login Canada, 300 Saulteaux Crescent, Winnipeg, MB R3J 3T2, Canada Tel: 204-837-2987 Toll Free Tel: 800-665-1148 (CN only) Fax: 204-837-3116 Toll Free Fax: 800-665-0103 E-mail: sales@lb.ca Web Site: www.lb.ca, pg 1318

Musanti, Joe, UniversallWilde, 26 Dartmouth St, Westwood, MA 02090 Tel: 781-251-2700 Fax: 781-251-2613 Web Site: www.universalwilde.com, pg 1105, 1116, 1232, 1261

Musk, Howard, Imago, 110 W 40 St, New York, NY 10018 Tel: 212-921-4411 Fax: 212-921-8226 E-mail: sales@imagousa.com Web Site: www.imagousa.com, pg 1211, 1226, 1255, 1268, 1281, 1347, 1370

Musto, Diane, BCH Fulfillment & Distribution, 33 Oakland Ave, Harrison, NY 10528 Tel: 914-835-0015 Toll Free Tel: 800-431-1579 Fax: 914-835-0398 E-mail: bookch@aol.com Web Site: www.bookch.com, pg 1287, 1312

Myers, Evan, AccuWeather Inc, 385 Science Park Rd, State College, PA 16803 Tel: 814-235-8600; 814-237-0309 E-mail: salesmail@accuweather.com; support@accuweather.com Web Site: www.accuweather.com; corporate.accuweather.com, pg 1363

Myers, Jason, Myriddian LLC, 8510 Corridor Rd, Suite 100, Savage, MD 20763 Tel: 443-285-0271 (cell) E-mail: info@myriddian.com Web Site: www.myriddian.com, pg 1228, 1373

Myers, Dr Joel N, AccuWeather Inc, 385 Science Park Rd, State College, PA 16803 Tel: 814-235-8600; 814-237-0309 E-mail: salesmail@accuweather.com; support@accuweather.com Web Site: www.accuweather.com; corporate.accuweather.com, pg 1363

Myhren, Tor, Apple Inc, One Apple Park Way, Cupertino, CA 95014 Tel: 408-996-1010 Web Site: www.apple.com, pg 1364

Mynarova, Jana, Bulletin of the American Schools of Oriental Research (BASOR), James F Strange Ctr, 209 Commerce St, Alexandria, VA 22314 Tel: 703-789-9229; 703-789-9230 (pubns) Fax: 617-353-6575 E-mail: basor@asor.org; www@asor.org; publications@asor.org Web Site: www.asor.org, pg 1130

Myrden, Andrew, Penguin Random House Canada, a Penguin Random House company, 320 Front St W, Suite 1400, Toronto, ON M5V 3B6, Canada Tel: 416-364-4449 Toll Free Tel: 888-523-9292 (cust serv) Fax: 416-598-7764 E-mail: customerservicescanada@penguinrandomhouse.com; publicitycanada@penguinrandomhouse.com; rightscanada@penguinrandomhouse.com Web Site: www.penguinrandomhouse.ca, pg 1299

Naasz, Christophe, Star Micronics America Inc, 65 Clyde Rd, Suite G, Somerset, NJ 08873-3485 Tel: 848-216-3300 (sales) Toll Free Tel: 800-782-7636 Fax: 848-216-3222 (sales) E-mail: sales@starmicronics.com Web Site: www.starmicronics.com, pg 1377

Naegeli, Werner, Muller Martini Corp, 456 Wheeler Rd, Hauppauge, NY 11788 Tel: 631-582-4343 Toll Free Tel: 888-268-5537 Fax: 631-348-1961 E-mail: info@us.mullermartini.com Web Site: www.mullermartiniusa.com, pg 1282

Nagaoka, Yasuhiko, Fujitsu Computer Products of America Inc, 1250 E Arques Ave, Sunnyvale, CA 94085-4701 Tel: 408-746-6000 Toll Free Tel: 800-626-4686 E-mail: scanner-sales@us.fujitsu.com Web Site: www.fujitsu.com/us, pg 1369

Nakamura, Norikatsu, DNP America LLC, 335 Madison Ave, 3rd fl, New York, NY 10017 Tel: 212-503-1060 E-mail: gps@dnp-g.com Web Site: www.dnpamerica.com, pg 1209, 1225, 1252, 1266

Nanzetta, Phil, Signature Book Printing Inc, 8041 Cessna Ave, Gaithersburg, MD 20879 Tel: 301-258-8353 E-mail: book@sbpbooks.com Web Site: sbpbooks.com, pg 1214, 1231, 1260

Napoleone, Tony, Omeda, 4 Overlook Point, Suite A2SE, Lincolnshire, IL 60069 Tel: 847-564-8900 E-mail: getstarted@omeda.com Web Site: www.omeda.com, pg 1334

Narasimhan, Lavanya, Penguin Random House Canada, a Penguin Random House company, 320 Front St W, Suite 1400, Toronto, ON M5V 3B6, Canada Tel: 416-364-4449 Toll Free Tel: 888-523-9292 (cust serv) Fax: 416-598-7764 E-mail: customerservicescanada@penguinrandomhouse.com; publicitycanada@penguinrandomhouse.com; rightscanada@penguinrandomhouse.com Web Site: www.penguinrandomhouse.ca, pg 1299

Narayen, Shantanu, Adobe Systems Inc, 345 Park Ave, San Jose, CA 95110-2704 Tel: 408-536-6000 Fax: 408-537-6000 Web Site: www.adobe.com, pg 1363

Narowski, Eric, BCC Software Inc, 75 Josons Dr, Rochester, NY 14623-3494 Toll Free Tel: 800-453-3130; 800-337-0442 (sales) E-mail: marketing@bccsoftware.com Web Site: www.bccsoftware.com, pg 1365

Nash, Douglas, Spiral Binding LLC, One Maltese Dr, Totowa, NJ 07511 Tel: 973-256-0666 Toll Free Tel: 800-631-3572 Fax: 973-256-5981 E-mail: customerservice@spiralbinding.com; international@spiralbinding.com (outside US) Web Site: spiralbinding.com, pg 1260

Nash, Linda, Matthews Book Co, 11559 Rock Island Ct, Maryland Heights, MO 63043 Tel: 314-432-1400 Toll Free Tel: 800-633-2665 Fax: 314-432-7044 Toll Free Fax: 800-421-8816 E-mail: orders@mattmccoy.com Web Site: www.matthewsbooks.com, pg 1296

Nason, Charles, Worzalla, 3535 Jefferson St, Stevens Point, WI 54481 Tel: 715-344-9608 Fax: 715-344-2578 Web Site: www.worzalla.com, pg 1215, 1233, 1262

Nathan, Lauren, Melcher Media Inc, 124 W 13 St, New York, NY 10011 Tel: 212-727-2322 Fax: 212-627-1973 E-mail: info@melcher.com Web Site: www.melcher.com, pg 1356

Nathan, Terry, The Independent Book Publishers Association (IBPA), 1020 Manhattan Beach Blvd, Suite 204, Manhattan Beach, CA 90266 Tel: 310-546-1818 E-mail: info@ibpa-online.org Web Site: www.ibpa-online.org, pg 1116

Naughton, Kevin, Cookbook Publishers Inc, 11633 W 83 Terr, Lenexa, KS 66285 Tel: 913-492-5900 Toll Free Tel: 800-227-7282 Fax: 913-492-5947 E-mail: info@cookbookpublishers.com Web Site: www.cookbookpublishers.com, pg 1224, 1251

Navin, Jennifer, OEC Graphics Inc, 555 W Waukau Ave, Oshkosh, WI 54902 Tel: 920-235-7770 Fax: 920-235-2252 Web Site: www.oecgraphics.com, pg 1229

Nawotka, Ed, Publishers Weekly, 49 W 23 St, 9th fl, New York, NY 10010 Tel: 212-377-5500 Fax: 212-377-2733 Web Site: www.publishersweekly.com, pg 1136

Nay, Meta L, Keister-Williams Newspaper Services Inc, PO Box 8187, Charlottesville, VA 22906 Tel: 434-293-4709 Toll Free Tel: 800-293-4709 E-mail: kw@kwnews.com Web Site: www.kwnews.com, pg 1190

Nazzaro, Mike, Claritas LLC, 8044 Montgomery Rd, Suite 455, Cincinnati, OH 45236 Toll Free Tel: 888-981-0040 E-mail: findcustomers@claritas.com; marketing@claritas.com Web Site: www.claritas.com, pg 1366

Neibauer-Baker, Ruth, Neibauer Press, 20 Industrial Dr, Warminster, PA 18974 *Tel:* 215-322-6200 *Fax:* 215-322-2495 *E-mail:* sales@neibauer.com *Web Site:* www.neibauer.com, pg 1105, 1116, 1120, 1229, 1257, 1334

Neidlinger, Gary, Eckhart & Company Inc, 4011 W 54 St, Indianapolis, IN 46254 *Tel:* 317-347-2665 *Toll Free Tel:* 800-443-3791 *Fax:* 317-347-2666 *E-mail:* info@eckhartandco.com *Web Site:* www.eckhartandco.com, pg 1253

Neiman, Shirley M, Stock Montage Inc, 1817 N Mulligan Ave, Chicago, IL 60639, pg 1430

Neiman, Tom, Stock Montage Inc, 1817 N Mulligan Ave, Chicago, IL 60639, pg 1430

Nelson, Alex, Esto Photographics Inc, 36 Waverly Ave, Brooklyn, NY 11205 *Tel:* 212-505-5454 *E-mail:* sales@esto.com; assignments@esto.com *Web Site:* estostock.com, pg 1428

Nelson, Brant, Docunet Corp, 2435 Xenium Lane N, Plymouth, MN 55441 *Tel:* 763-475-9600 *Toll Free Tel:* 800-936-2863 *Fax:* 763-475-1516 *E-mail:* print@docunetworks.com *Web Site:* www.docunetworks.com, pg 1252

Nelson, Jason, Sheridan GR, 5100 33 St SE, Grand Rapids, MI 49512 *Tel:* 616-957-5100 *Web Site:* www.sheridan.com, pg 1213, 1259

Nelson, Judy, Mrs Nelson's Library Services, 1650 W Orange Grove Ave, Pomona, CA 91768 *Tel:* 909-397-7820 *Toll Free Tel:* 800-875-9911 *Fax:* 909-397-7833 *E-mail:* bookcompany@mrsnelsons.com *Web Site:* www.mrsnelsons.com, pg 1319

Nelson, Patrick, Mrs Nelson's Library Services, 1650 W Orange Grove Ave, Pomona, CA 91768 *Tel:* 909-397-7820 *Toll Free Tel:* 800-875-9911 *Fax:* 909-397-7833 *E-mail:* bookcompany@mrsnelsons.com *Web Site:* www.mrsnelsons.com, pg 1319

Nelson, Peter, Claris International Inc, 5201 Patrick Henry Dr, Santa Clara, CA 95054 *Tel:* 408-727-8227 (sales & cust support) *Toll Free Tel:* 800-725-2747 (sales); 800-325-2747 (cust support) *Fax:* 408-987-7447 *E-mail:* claris_sales@claris.com *Web Site:* www.claris.com, pg 1366

Nelson, Todd, Trend Offset Printing Services, 3791 Catalina St, Los Alamitos, CA 90720 *Tel:* 562-598-2446 *Fax:* 562-493-6840 (sales); 562-430-2373 *E-mail:* salesca@trendoffset.com *Web Site:* www.trendoffset.com, pg 1261

Nelson, Tony, LBS, 1801 Thompson Ave, Des Moines, IA 50316-2751 *Tel:* 515-262-3191 *Toll Free Tel:* 800-247-5323 *Toll Free Fax:* 800-262-4091 *E-mail:* info@lbsbind.com *Web Site:* www.lbsbind.com, pg 1269

Nereson, Ariel, Theatre Journal, 2715 N Charles St, Baltimore, MD 21218-4363 *Tel:* 410-516-6987 (journal orders outside US & CN) *Toll Free Tel:* 800-548-1784 (journal orders) *Fax:* 410-578-2865 (journal orders) *E-mail:* tjbooks@athe.org; jrnlcirc@jh.edu (journal orders) *Web Site:* www.press.jhu.edu/journals/theatre-journal, pg 1137

Netburn, Malcolm, CDS Global, 1901 Bell Ave, Des Moines, IA 50315-1099 *Tel:* 515-247-7500 *Toll Free Tel:* 866-897-7987 *E-mail:* salesinfo@cds-global.com *Web Site:* www.cds-global.com, pg 1117, 1119

Nevins, Iris, Iris Nevins Decorative Papers, PO Box 429, Johnsonburg, NJ 07846-0429 *Tel:* 908-813-8617 *E-mail:* irisnevins@verizon.net *Web Site:* www.marblingpaper.com, pg 1270

Newborn, Barry, Newborn Enterprises Inc (Altoona News Agency), 808 Green Ave, Altoona, PA 16601 *Tel:* 814-944-3593, pg 1319

Newcombe, Jack, Creators Syndicate, 737 Third St, Hermosa Beach, CA 90254 *Tel:* 310-337-7003 *E-mail:* info@creators.com *Web Site:* www.creators.com, pg 1190

Newcombe, Rick, Creators Syndicate, 737 Third St, Hermosa Beach, CA 90254 *Tel:* 310-337-7003 *E-mail:* info@creators.com *Web Site:* www.creators.com, pg 1190

Newman, Andrew, Andrew Newman Design, 9509 W Lilac Rd, Escondido, CA 92026 *Tel:* 508-221-5101 *E-mail:* newmandesign@gmail.com *Web Site:* www.andrewnewmandesign.com, pg 1416

Newman, Bill, TEACH Services Inc, 11 Quartermaster Circle, Fort Oglethorpe, GA 30742-3886 *Tel:* 706-504-9192 *Toll Free Tel:* 800-367-1844 (sales) *Toll Free Fax:* 866-757-6023 *E-mail:* sales@teachservices.com; info@teachservices.com *Web Site:* www.teachservices.com, pg 1322, 1377

Newman, Helen, Custom Studios, 77 Main St, Tappan, NY 10983 *Tel:* 845-365-0414 *Toll Free Tel:* 800-631-1362 *Fax:* 845-365-0864 *E-mail:* customusa@aol.com *Web Site:* customstudios.com, pg 1224

Ng, Yu-Kai, Translations.com, 1250 Broadway, 32nd fl, New York, NY 10001 *Tel:* 212-689-1616 *Fax:* 212-504-8057 *E-mail:* newyork@translations.com; info@translations.com *Web Site:* translations.com, pg 1405

Nicewarner, Angie, Chesapeake & Hudson Inc, 27 Jacks Shop Rd, Rochelle, VA 22738 *Tel:* 301-834-7170 *Toll Free Tel:* 800-231-1469 *E-mail:* office@cheshud.com *Web Site:* www.cheshudinc.com, pg 1288

Nicholls, Tim S, International Paper Co, 6400 Poplar Ave, Memphis, TN 38197 *Tel:* 901-419-9000 *Toll Free Tel:* 800-207-4003 *Web Site:* www.internationalpaper.com; facebook.com/internationalpaper; x.com/intlpaperco, pg 1268

Nichols, Jane E, TRUMATCH Inc, PO Box 501, Water Mill, NY 11976-0501 *Tel:* 631-204-9100 *Toll Free Tel:* 800-TRU-9100 (878-9100 US & CN) *E-mail:* info@trumatch.com *Web Site:* www.trumatch.com, pg 1378

Nichols, Jim, Consortium Book Sales & Distribution, an Ingram brand, The Keg House, Suite 101, 34 13 Ave NE, Minneapolis, MN 55413-1007 *Tel:* 612-746-2600 *Toll Free Tel:* 866-400-5351 (cust serv, Jackson, TN) *E-mail:* cbsdinfo@ingramcontent.com *Web Site:* www.cbsd.com, pg 1289

Nichols, Stephen G, Modern Language Notes (MLN), 2715 N Charles St, Baltimore, MD 21218-4363 *Tel:* 410-516-6987 (journal orders outside US & CN) *Toll Free Tel:* 800-548-1784 (journal orders) *Fax:* 410-578-2865 (journal orders) *E-mail:* jrnlcirc@jh.edu (journal orders) *Web Site:* www.press.jhu.edu/journals/mln, pg 1134

Nicholson, Leah, Jenkins Group Inc, 1129 Woodmere Ave, Suite B, Traverse City, MI 49686 *Tel:* 231-933-0445; 213-883-5365 *E-mail:* info@jenkinsgroupinc.com *Web Site:* www.jenkinsgroupinc.com, pg 1227, 1348, 1355

Nickels, Nancy, Valley News Co, 1305 Stadium Rd, Mankato, MN 56001 *Tel:* 507-345-4819 *Fax:* 507-345-6793 *Web Site:* www.valleynewscompany.com, pg 1323

Niebauer, Skip, American Artist Studio, 1114 W 26 St, Erie, PA 16508-1518 *Tel:* 814-455-4796 *E-mail:* skip@americanartiststudio.com *Web Site:* americanartiststudio.com, pg 1364

Niel, Michele Olson, C & C Offset Printing Co USA Inc, 70 W 36 St, Unit 10C, New York, NY 10018 *Tel:* 212-431-4210 *Toll Free Fax:* 866-540-4134 *Web Site:* www.ccoffset.com, pg 1208, 1223, 1249

Nielsen, Markie, GTCO Calcomp, 14557 N 82 St, Scottsdale, AZ 85260 *Tel:* 480-443-2264 *Toll Free Tel:* 800-220-1137 *Fax:* 480-948-1751 *E-mail:* sales@gtcocalcomp.com *Web Site:* www.gtcocalcomp.com, pg 1369

Nip, Charlotte, Penguin Random House Canada, a Penguin Random House company, 320 Front St W, Suite 1400, Toronto, ON M5V 3B6, Canada *Tel:* 416-364-4449 *Toll Free Tel:* 888-523-9292 (cust serv) *Fax:* 416-598-7764 *E-mail:* customerservicescanada@penguinrandomhouse.com; publicitycanada@penguinrandomhouse.com; rightscanada@penguinrandomhouse.com *Web Site:* www.penguinrandomhouse.ca, pg 1299

Nissen, Rob, Nissen Public Relations LLC, 18 Bank St, Suite 101, Summit, NJ 07901 *Tel:* 908-376-6470 *E-mail:* info@nissenpr.com *Web Site:* www.nissenpr.com, pg 1111

Nivens, Michele R, Copyright Clearance Center Inc (CCC), 222 Rosewood Dr, Danvers, MA 01923 *Tel:* 978-750-8400 (sales); 978-646-2600 (cust serv) *E-mail:* info@copyright.com *Web Site:* www.copyright.com, pg 1345

Noble, Mark, Independent Publishers Group (IPG), 814 N Franklin St, Chicago, IL 60610 *Tel:* 312-337-0747 *Toll Free Tel:* 800-888-4741 (orders) *Fax:* 312-337-5985 *E-mail:* frontdesk@ipgbook.com; orders@ipgbook.com *Web Site:* www.ipgbook.com, pg 1292, 1328

Noble, Max, PremierIMS Inc, 11101 Ella Blvd, Houston, TX 77067 *Tel:* 832-608-6400 *Fax:* 832-608-6420 *E-mail:* info@premier-ims.com *Web Site:* www.premier-ims.com, pg 1118

Nock, Beth, King Features Syndicate, 300 W 57 St, New York, NY 10019-5238 *Tel:* 212-969-7550 *Toll Free Tel:* 800-526-5464 *Web Site:* www.kingfeatures.com, pg 1190

Nolan, Karen, Intuit Inc, 2700 Coast Ave, Mountain View, CA 94043 *Tel:* 650-944-6000 *Toll Free Tel:* 800-446-8848 *E-mail:* investor_relations@intuit.com *Web Site:* www.intuit.com, pg 1371

Nole, Diana, Nuance Communications Inc, One Wayside Rd, Burlington, MA 01803 *Tel:* 781-565-5000 *Toll Free Tel:* 800-654-1187 (cust serv); 888-372-1908 (orders) *Web Site:* www.nuance.com, pg 1374

Noon, Kristen, Independent Publishers Group (IPG), 814 N Franklin St, Chicago, IL 60610 *Tel:* 312-337-0747 *Toll Free Tel:* 800-888-4741 (orders) *Fax:* 312-337-5985 *E-mail:* frontdesk@ipgbook.com; orders@ipgbook.com *Web Site:* www.ipgbook.com, pg 1292, 1328

Noorlander, Mary, Tanenbaum International Literary Agency Ltd (TILA), 1035 Fifth Ave, Suite 15D, New York, NY 10028 *Tel:* 212-371-4120 *Fax:* 212-988-0457 *E-mail:* hello@tanenbauminternational.com *Web Site:* tanenbauminternational.com, pg 1351

Norman, Chanelle, Franklin & Siegal Associates Inc, 40 Exchange Place, Suite 1703, New York, NY 10005 *Tel:* 212-868-6311 *Web Site:* www.franklinandsiegal.com, pg 1346

Norris, Jill, Electronics for Imaging Inc (EFI), 6750 Dumbarton Circle, Fremont, CA 94555 *Tel:* 650-357-3500 *Toll Free Tel:* 800-568-1917; 800-875-7117 (sales) *Fax:* 650-357-3907 *E-mail:* info@efi.com *Web Site:* www.efi.com, pg 1368

Norris, John, Readerlink Distribution Services LLC, 1420 Kensington Rd, Suite 300, Oakbrook, IL 60523-2164 *Tel:* 708-547-4400 *Toll Free Tel:* 800-549-5389 *E-mail:* info@readerlink.com; marketingservices@readerlink.com *Web Site:* www.readerlink.com, pg 1301

Norton, Boyd, Boyd Norton Photography, PO Box 2605, Evergreen, CO 80437-2605 *Tel:* 303-674-3009 *Fax:* 303-674-3650 *Web Site:* boydnorton.com; www.facebook.com/boyd.norton; thewildernessphotography.blogspot.com, pg 1424

Norton, Grael, Wheatmark Inc, 2030 E Speedway Blvd, Suite 106, Tucson, AZ 85719 *Tel:* 520-798-0888 *Toll Free Tel:* 888-934-0888 *Fax:* 520-798-3394 *E-mail:* info@wheatmark.com *Web Site:* www.wheatmark.com, pg 1352

Notarainni, Mark, Intuit Inc, 2700 Coast Ave, Mountain View, CA 94043 *Tel:* 650-944-6000 *Toll Free Tel:* 800-446-8848 *E-mail:* investor_relations@intuit.com *Web Site:* www.intuit.com, pg 1371

Nuffer, Pam, Publishers Storage & Shipping Corp, 46 Development Rd, Fitchburg, MA 01420 *Tel:* 978-345-2121 *Web Site:* www.pssc.com, pg 1335

Nugeren, Nils, ZyLAB North America LLC, 7918 Jones Branch Dr, Suite 230, McLean, VA 22102-3366 *Tel:* 703-442-2400 *Toll Free Tel:* 866-995-2262 *Fax:* 703-991-2508 *E-mail:* info@zylab.com *Web Site:* www.zylab.com, pg 1378

Nunez, Peter, Superior Printing Ink Co Inc, 100 North St, Teterboro, NJ 07608 *Tel:* 201-478-5600 *Fax:* 201-478-5650 *Web Site:* www.superiorink.com, pg 1272

Nurse, Cheryl, Penguin Random House Canada, a Penguin Random House company, 320 Front St W, Suite 1400, Toronto, ON M5V 3B6, Canada Tel: 416-364-4449 Toll Free Tel: 888-523-9292 (cust serv) Fax: 416-598-7764 E-mail: customerservicescanada@penguinrandomhouse.com; publicitycanada@penguinrandomhouse.com; rightscanada@penguinrandomhouse.com Web Site: www.penguinrandomhouse.ca, pg 1299

O'Brien, Deidre, Apple Inc, One Apple Park Way, Cupertino, CA 95014 Tel: 408-996-1010 Web Site: www.apple.com, pg 1364

O'Brien, Ken, RR Donnelley, 35 W Wacker Dr, Chicago, IL 60601 Toll Free Tel: 800-742-4455 Web Site: www.rrd.com, pg 1210, 1225, 1252, 1266, 1279

O'Brien, Ken, RR Donnelley & Sons Company, 35 W Wacker Dr, Chicago, IL 60601 Tel: 312-326-8000 Toll Free Tel: 800-742-4455 Web Site: www.rrd.com, pg 1333

O'Bries, Elizabeth, Consortium Book Sales & Distribution, an Ingram brand, The Keg House, Suite 101, 34 13 Ave NE, Minneapolis, MN 55413-1007 Tel: 612-746-2600 Toll Free Tel: 866-400-5351 (cust serv, Jackson, TN) E-mail: cbsdinfo@ingramcontent.com Web Site: www.cbsd.com, pg 1289

O'Connell, Caroline, Caroline O'Connell Communications, 11275 La Maida St, Suite 200, North Hollywood, CA 91601-4514 E-mail: oconnellpr@aol.com Web Site: www.oconnellcommunications.com, pg 1111

O'Connell, Daniel, Content Critical Solutions Inc, 10 Fifth St, 2nd fl, Valley Stream, NY 11581 Tel: 201-528-2777 E-mail: info@contentcritical.com Web Site: www.contentcritical.com, pg 1115

O'Connor, Kirsten, Celtic Castle Photography, 1319 Hardys Creek Rd, Jonesville, VA 24263 Tel: 276-346-3625 E-mail: celticastlephotography@gmail.com Web Site: www.celticastlephotography.com, pg 1420

O'Connor, Ryan, Parson Weems' Publisher Services LLC, 3811 Canterbury Rd, No 707, Baltimore, MD 21218 Tel: 914-948-4259 Toll Free Fax: 866-861-0337 E-mail: office@parsonweems.com Web Site: www.parsonweems.com, pg 1299

O'Connor Sr, Dr John William PhD, Celtic Castle Photography, 1319 Hardys Creek Rd, Jonesville, VA 24263 Tel: 276-346-3625 E-mail: celticastlephotography@gmail.com Web Site: www.celticastlephotography.com, pg 1420

O'Connor, Thomas D Jr, Mohawk Fine Papers Inc, 465 Saratoga St, Cohoes, NY 12047 Tel: 518-237-1740 Toll Free Tel: 800-THE-MILL (843-6455) Fax: 518-237-7394 Web Site: www.mohawkconnects.com, pg 1270

O'Donley, David, The Ovid Bell Press Inc, 1201 Bluff St, Fulton, MO 65251 Tel: 573-642-2256 Toll Free Tel: 800-835-8919 E-mail: sales@ovidbell.com Web Site: ovidbell.com, pg 1229, 1258, 1270, 1282

O'Donnell, Brooke, Independent Publishers Group (IPG), 814 N Franklin St, Chicago, IL 60610 Tel: 312-337-0747 Toll Free Tel: 800-888-4741 (orders) Fax: 312-337-5985 E-mail: frontdesk@ipgbook.com; orders@ipgbook.com Web Site: www.ipgbook.com, pg 1292, 1328

O'Donnell, Paul, Religion News Service, c/o University of Missouri's Journalism School, 30 Neff Annex, Columbia, MO 65211 Tel: 573-884-1327 E-mail: info@religionnews.com Web Site: www.religionnews.com, pg 1191

O'Grady, John, Eastman Kodak Co, 343 State St, Rochester, NY 14650 Tel: 585-724-4000 Toll Free Tel: 866-563-2533 Web Site: www.kodak.com, pg 1279

O'Keefe, Steve, Orobora Inc, 644 Greenville Ave, Suite 234, Staunton, VA 24401 Tel: 540-324-7023 E-mail: info@orobora.com Web Site: orobora.com, pg 1350

O'Leyne, Eithne, ProtoView, 7515 NE Ambassador Place, Suite A, Portland, OR 97220 Tel: 503-281-9230 E-mail: info@protoview.com Web Site: www.protoview.com, pg 1135, 1146

O'Meara, Kelvin, Western Printing Machinery Co (WPM), 9228 Ivanhoe St, Schiller Park, IL 60176 Tel: 847-678-1740 Fax: 847-678-6176 E-mail: info@wpm.com Web Site: www.wpm.com, pg 1284

O'Neal, Mark, The Karel/Dutton Group, San Francisco, CA 94121 Tel: 415-668-0829 Web Site: kareldutongroup.com, pg 1295

O'Reilly, Tim, O'Reilly Media Inc, 1005 Gravenstein Hwy N, Sebastopol, CA 95472 Tel: 707-827-7019 (cust support); 707-827-7000 Toll Free Tel: 800-889-8969; 800-998-9938 Fax: 707-829-0104; 707-824-8268 E-mail: orders@oreilly.com; support@oreilly.com Web Site: www.oreilly.com, pg 1374

O'Sullivan, Dan, Translations.com, 1250 Broadway, 32nd fl, New York, NY 10001 Tel: 212-689-1616 Fax: 212-504-8057 E-mail: newyork@translations.com; info@translations.com Web Site: translations.com, pg 1405

O'Toole, Jim, Midland Paper, Packaging & Supplies, 101 E Palatine Rd, Wheeling, IL 60090 Tel: 847-777-2700 Toll Free Tel: 800-323-8522; 888-564-3526 (cust serv) Fax: 847-403-6320 (cust serv) E-mail: whl@midlandpaper.com; sales@midlandpaper.com; custservice@midlandpaper.com Web Site: www.midlandpaper.com, pg 1269

Obarski, Kevin, Translations.com, 1250 Broadway, 32nd fl, New York, NY 10001 Tel: 212-689-1616 Fax: 212-504-8057 E-mail: newyork@translations.com; info@translations.com Web Site: translations.com, pg 1405

Oberdorf, Anya, Penguin Random House Canada, a Penguin Random House company, 320 Front St W, Suite 1400, Toronto, ON M5V 3B6, Canada Tel: 416-364-4449 Toll Free Tel: 888-523-9292 (cust serv) Fax: 416-598-7764 E-mail: customerservicescanada@penguinrandomhouse.com; publicitycanada@penguinrandomhouse.com; rightscanada@penguinrandomhouse.com Web Site: www.penguinrandomhouse.ca, pg 1299

Oberman, Aaron, Omeda, 4 Overlook Point, Suite A2SE, Lincolnshire, IL 60069 Tel: 847-564-8900 E-mail: getstarted@omeda.com Web Site: www.omeda.com, pg 1334

Obernier, Robert B, Horizon Paper Co Inc, 1010 Washington Blvd, Stamford, CT 06901 Tel: 203-358-0855 Toll Free Tel: 866-358-0855 E-mail: info@horizonpaper.com Web Site: www.horizonpaper.com, pg 1268

Ocher, Medaya, LARB Quarterly Journal, 6671 Sunset Blvd, Suite 1521, Los Angeles, CA 90028 Tel: 323-952-3950 E-mail: info@lareviewofbooks.org; editorial@lareviewofbooks.org Web Site: lareviewofbooks.org, pg 1133

Ochoa, Gladys, Lectorum Publications Inc, 10 New Maple Ave, Suite 303, Pine Brook, NJ 07058 Tel: 201-559-2200 Toll Free Tel: 800-345-5946 E-mail: lectorum@lectorum.com Web Site: www.lectorum.com, pg 1318

Ofri, Dr Danielle, Bellevue Literary Review, 149 E 23 St, Suite 1516, New York, NY 10010 Tel: 917-375-5790 E-mail: info@BLReview.org Web Site: www.BLReview.org, pg 1130

Ogawa, Kazuto, Canon USA Inc, One Canon Park, Milville, NY 11747 Tel: 516-328-5000; 631-330-5000 Web Site: www.usa.canon.com, pg 1365

Ogden, Max, CONTECH (Converting Technologies), 1756 S 151 St W, Goddard, KS 67052 Tel: 316-722-6907 Fax: 316-722-2976 E-mail: info@contechusa.com Web Site: www.contechusa.com, pg 1278

Oglesby, John, Data Index Inc, 13713 NW Indian Springs Dr, Vancouver, WA 98685 Tel: 425-760-9193 Web Site: www.dataindex.com, pg 1224

Oglesby, Scott, Bellevue Literary Review, 149 E 23 St, Suite 1516, New York, NY 10010 Tel: 917-375-5790 E-mail: info@BLReview.org Web Site: www.BLReview.org, pg 1130

Ogushwitz, Mary Blanton, Susan Magrino Agency, 352 Park Ave S, 6th fl, New York, NY 10010 Tel: 212-957-3005 Fax: 212-957-4071 E-mail: info@smapr.com Web Site: www.smapr.com, pg 1110

Okhai, Adam, Learning World Inc, 287 Wycliffe Ave, Vaughan, ON L4L 3N7, Canada, pg 1318

Olin, Marc, Electronics for Imaging Inc (EFI), 6750 Dumbarton Circle, Fremont, CA 94555 Tel: 650-357-3500 Toll Free Tel: 800-568-1917; 800-875-7117 (sales) Fax: 650-357-3907 E-mail: info@efi.com Web Site: www.efi.com, pg 1368

Olinsky, David, Disc Makers, 7905 N Crescent Blvd, Pennsauken, NJ 08110-1402 Tel: 856-663-9030 Toll Free Tel: 800-468-9353 Fax: 856-661-3450 E-mail: info@discmakers.com Web Site: www.discmakers.com, pg 1367

Olive, Sarah, Jeunesse: Young People, Texts, Cultures, 5201 Dufferin St, Toronto, ON M3H 5T8, Canada Tel: 416-667-7777 (ext 7971) E-mail: journals@utpress.utoronto.ca Web Site: www.utpjournals.press/jeunesse, pg 1133

Oliver, Kirk, The Library Services Centre, 131 Shoemaker St, Kitchener, ON N2E 3B5, Canada Tel: 519-746-4420 Toll Free Tel: 800-265-3360 (CN only) Fax: 519-746-4425 Web Site: www.lsc.on.ca, pg 1318

Oliver, Matthew J, Dupli Envelope & Graphics Corp, 6761 Thompson Rd N, Syracuse, NY 13211 Tel: 315-472-1316 Toll Free Tel: 800-724-2477 E-mail: sales@duplionline.com; orders@duplionline.com Web Site: www.duplionline.com, pg 1252

Olko, Steve, Data Reproductions Corp, 4545 Glenmeade Lane, Auburn Hills, MI 48326 Tel: 248-371-3700 Toll Free Tel: 800-242-3114 Fax: 248-371-3710 Web Site: datarepro.com, pg 1209, 1251

Ollila, Phil, Ingram Content Group LLC, One Ingram Blvd, La Vergne, TN 37086-1986 Tel: 615-793-5000 Toll Free Tel: 800-937-8000 (retailers); 800-937-5300 (ext 1, libs) E-mail: customerservice@ingramcontent.com Web Site: www.ingramcontent.com, pg 1294, 1316

Ollila, Phil, Lightning Source LLC, 1246 Heil Quaker Blvd, La Vergne, TN 37086 Tel: 615-793-5000 (Ingram) Toll Free Tel: 800-378-5508; 800-509-4156 (cust serv) E-mail: lsicustomersupport@ingramcontent.com; contentacquisitioninquiries@ingramcontent.com Web Site: www.ingramcontent.com/publishers/print, pg 1212

Ollila, Phil, Lightning Source LLC, 1246 Heil Quaker Blvd, La Vergne, TN 37086 Tel: 615-793-5000 (Ingram) Toll Free Tel: 800-378-5508; 800-509-4156 (cust serv) E-mail: lsicustomersupport@ingramcontent.com Web Site: www.ingramcontent.com/publishers/print, pg 1256, 1371

Ollis, Kenneth R, Ollis Book Co, 28 E 35 St, Steger, IL 60475 Tel: 708-755-5151 Toll Free Tel: 800-323-0343 (natl) Fax: 708-755-5153, pg 1320

Olmsted, Christina, eFulfillment Service Inc, 807 Airport Access Rd, Traverse City, MI 49686 Tel: 231-276-5057 Toll Free Tel: 866-922-6783 E-mail: sales@efulfillmentservice.com Web Site: www.efulfillmentservice.com, pg 1333

Olsen, Bevan, Cedar Fort Inc, 2373 W 700 S, Suite 100, Springville, UT 84663 Tel: 801-489-4084 Toll Free Tel: 800-SKY-BOOK (759-2665) E-mail: marketinginfo@cedarfort.com Web Site: cedarfort.com, pg 1327

Olsen, Teresa, Emerson, Wajdowicz Studios Inc, 514 W 25 St, New York, NY 10001 Tel: 212-807-8144 E-mail: info@designews.com Web Site: www.designews.com; www.facebook.com/DesignEWS; www.instagram.com/ewsdesign, pg 1414

Olshan, Alex, RISO Inc, 10 State St, Suite 201, Woburn, MA 01801-2105 Tel: 978-777-7377 Toll Free Tel: 800-942-7476 (cust support) Web Site: us.riso.com, pg 1259, 1376

Olson, Arleen, Arleen Olson Photography, Redway, CA 95560 Tel: 707-923-1974 Web Site: arleenolsonphotography.com, pg 1424

Olson, John, Olson Photographic LLC, 232 Hunter's Trail, Madison, CT 06443 *Tel:* 203-245-3752 *Fax:* 203-245-3752 *E-mail:* info@olsonphotographic.com *Web Site:* www.olsonphotographic.com, pg 1424

Olson, Peter, TNG, 3320 S Service Rd, Burlington, ON L7N 3M6, Canada *Toll Free Tel:* 800-201-8127 *Toll Free Fax:* 877-664-9732 *E-mail:* cs@tng.com *Web Site:* www.tng.com, pg 1323

Olzenak, Doug, Allied Vaughn, 7600 Parklawn Ave, Suite 300, Minneapolis, MN 55435 *Tel:* 952-832-3100 *Toll Free Tel:* 800-323-0281 *Fax:* 952-832-3203 *Web Site:* www.alliedvaughn.com, pg 1364

Ong, Yi-Ping, Modern Language Notes (MLN), 2715 N Charles St, Baltimore, MD 21218-4363 *Tel:* 410-516-6987 (journal orders outside US & CN) *Toll Free Tel:* 800-548-1784 (journal orders) *Fax:* 410-578-2865 (journal orders) *E-mail:* jrnlcirc@jh.edu (journal orders) *Web Site:* www.press.jhu.edu/journals/mln, pg 1134

Onisk, Mark, SumTotal Systems LLC, 2850 NW 43 St, Suite 150, Gainesville, FL 32606 *Tel:* 352-264-2800 *Toll Free Tel:* 866-933-1416 *Fax:* 352-374-2257 *E-mail:* customersupport@sumtotalsystems.com *Web Site:* www.sumtotalsystems.com, pg 1377

Oppenheimer, Michael, Creative Direct Marketing Group Inc (CDMG), 1313 Fourth Ave N, Nashville, TN 37208 *Tel:* 615-814-6633 *Web Site:* www.cdmginc.com, pg 1345

Oransky, Andrew, Roland DGA Corp, 15363 Barranca Pkwy, Irvine, CA 92618-2216 *Tel:* 949-727-2100 *Toll Free Tel:* 800-542-2307 *Fax:* 949-727-2112 *Web Site:* www.rolanddga.com, pg 1376

Orellana, Carlos, Booklist, 225 N Michigan Ave, Suite 1300, Chicago, IL 60601 *Tel:* 312-944-6780 *Toll Free Tel:* 800-545-2433 *Fax:* 312-440-9374 *E-mail:* info@booklistonline.com; ala@ala.org *Web Site:* www.booklistonline.com; www.ala.org, pg 1130

Orf, Steve, FCI Digital, 2032 S Alex Rd, Suite A, West Carrollton, OH 45449 *Tel:* 937-859-9701 *Web Site:* www.fcidigital.com, pg 1225

Oringer, Jon, Shutterstock Inc, Empire State Bldg, 350 Fifth Ave, 20th fl, New York, NY 10118 *E-mail:* support@shutterstock.com; press@shutterstock.com *Web Site:* www.shutterstock.com, pg 1430

Orlowsky, Peter, Getty Images Inc, 605 Fifth Ave S, Suite 400, Seattle, WA 98104 *Tel:* 206-925-5000 *Toll Free Tel:* 800-IMAGERY (462-4379); 888-888-5889 *Web Site:* www.gettyimages.com; www.gettyimages.com/customer-support; engage.gettyimages.com/media-inquiries, pg 1369, 1428

Ornstein, Robert PhD, Institute for the Study of Human Knowledge (ISHK), 1702-L Meridian Ave, No 266, San Jose, CA 95125-5586 *Tel:* 617-497-4124 *Toll Free Tel:* 800-222-4745 (orders) *Fax:* 617-500-0268 *Toll Free Fax:* 800-223-4200 (orders) *E-mail:* ishkadm@aol.com; ishkbooks@aol.com (orders) *Web Site:* www.ishk.com, pg 1295

Orr, James, Perma-Bound Books, 617 E Vandalia Rd, Jacksonville, IL 62650 *Tel:* 217-243-5451 *Toll Free Tel:* 800-637-6581 *Fax:* 217-243-7505 *Toll Free Fax:* 800-551-1169 *E-mail:* books@perma-bound.com *Web Site:* www.perma-bound.com, pg 1320, 1326

Ortega, Claribel, The Combined Book Exhibit®, 277 White St, Buchanan, NY 10511 *Tel:* 914-739-7500 *Toll Free Tel:* 800-462-7687 *Fax:* 914-739-7575 *E-mail:* info@combinedbook.com *Web Site:* www.combinedbook.com; www.cbedatabase.com, pg 1139

Ortolani, Terry, Pint Size Productions LLC, 5745 Main St, Amherst, NY 14221 *Tel:* 716-204-3353 *E-mail:* sales@pintsizeproductions.com *Web Site:* www.pintsizeproductions.com, pg 1258

Osborne, H Damon, Houchen Bindery Ltd, 340 First St, Utica, NE 68456 *Tel:* 402-534-2261 *Toll Free Tel:* 800-869-0420 *Fax:* 402-534-2761 *E-mail:* email@houchenbindery.com *Web Site:* www.houchenbindery.com, pg 1325

Osman, Dr A, Learning World Inc, 287 Wycliffe Ave, Vaughan, ON L4L 3N7, Canada, pg 1318

Ostenso, Jeff, Ironmark, 9040 Junction Dr, Annapolis Junction, MD 20701 *Toll Free Tel:* 888-775-3737 *E-mail:* marketing@ironmarkusa.com *Web Site:* ironmarkusa.com, pg 1211, 1227, 1255, 1268, 1281

Ostrander, Brian, Maracle Inc, 1156 King St E, Oshawa, ON L1H 1H8, Canada *Tel:* 905-723-3438 *Toll Free Tel:* 800-558-8604 *Fax:* 905-723-1759 *E-mail:* hello@maracleinc.com *Web Site:* www.maracleinc.com, pg 1212, 1228, 1256

Ostreicher, Joseph, Edison Lithograph & Printing Corp, 3725 Tonnelle Ave, North Bergen, NJ 07047-2421 *Tel:* 201-902-9191 *Fax:* 201-902-0475 *E-mail:* info@edisonlitho.com *Web Site:* www.edisonlitho.com, pg 1225, 1253, 1267

Otis, Martha Stillman, Verso Advertising Inc, 79 Madison Ave, 8th fl, New York, NY 10016 *Tel:* 212-292-2990 *Web Site:* www.versoadvertising.com, pg 1100

Ottman, Lance, A-R Editions Inc, 1600 Aspen Commons, Suite 100, Middleton, WI 53562 *Tel:* 608-836-9000 *Fax:* 608-831-8200 *E-mail:* info@areditions.com *Web Site:* www.areditions.com, pg 1221

Ouellet, Daniel, Resolute Forest Products, 111 Robert-Bourassa Blvd, Suite 5000, Montreal, QC H3C 2M1, Canada *Tel:* 514-875-2160 *Toll Free Tel:* 800-361-2888 *E-mail:* info@resolutefp.com *Web Site:* www.resolutefp.com, pg 1271

Owens, Jim, H B Fuller Co, 1200 Willow Lake Blvd, St Paul, MN 55110-5146 *Tel:* 651-236-5900 *Toll Free Tel:* 888-423-8553 *E-mail:* inquiry@hbfuller.com *Web Site:* www.hbfuller.com, pg 1267, 1280

Owens, John, Cohesion®, 511 W Bay St, Suite 480, Tampa, FL 33606 *Tel:* 813-999-3111 *Toll Free Tel:* 866-727-6800 *Web Site:* www.cohesion.com, pg 1344, 1366, 1381

Ownby, Stephen, Smith & Sons Printers Inc, 6403 Rutledge Pike, Knoxville, TN 37924 *Tel:* 865-523-1419 *Web Site:* www.ssprintinc.com, pg 1214, 1231, 1260

Paasche, Carl, Woodcrafters Lumber Sales Inc, 212 NE Sixth Ave, Portland, OR 97232-2976 *Tel:* 503-231-0226 *Toll Free Tel:* 800-777-3709 *Fax:* 503-232-0511 *Web Site:* www.woodcrafters.us, pg 1323

Packles, Arlene, APG Group, 235 Homestead Place, Suite 1A, Park Ridge, NJ 07656 *Tel:* 201-420-8501 *Web Site:* www.apggroupinc.com, pg 1248

Pagan, Peter, Science Source®, 307 Fifth Ave, 3rd fl, New York, NY 10016 *Tel:* 212-758-3420 *E-mail:* info@sciencesource.com; sales@sciencesource.com; contributor@sciencesource.com *Web Site:* www.sciencesource.com, pg 1430

Paglia, Storm, Conservative Book Club, 300 New Jersey Ave NW, Suite 500, Washington, DC 20001 *Tel:* 202-216-0601 *Web Site:* www.conservativebookclub.com, pg 1141

Paher, Stanley W, Nevada Publications, 4135 Badger Circle, Reno, NV 89519 *Tel:* 775-747-0800 *Web Site:* nevadapublicationsonline.com, pg 1282

Paine, Penelope C, To Press & Beyond, 7507 Summersun Dr, Browns Summit, NC 27214 *Tel:* 805-570-8275 *E-mail:* info@topressandbeyond.com *Web Site:* www.topressandbeyond.com, pg 1113, 1351, 1358

Pak, Hoyoung, SGS International LLC, 626 W Main St, Suite 500, Louisville, KY 40202 *Tel:* 502-637-5443 *E-mail:* info@sgsco.com *Web Site:* www.sgsintl.com, pg 1230

Pakzad, Behzad, Leo Paper USA, 1180 NW Maple St, Suite 102, Issaquah, WA 98027 *Tel:* 425-646-8801 *Fax:* 425-646-8805 *E-mail:* info@leousa.com *Web Site:* www.leopaper.com, pg 1212, 1228, 1256

Palacheck, Del, Multi-Tech Systems Inc, 2205 Woodale Dr, Mounds View, MN 55112 *Tel:* 763-785-3500 *Toll Free Tel:* 800-328-9717 *Fax:* 763-785-9874 *E-mail:* info@multitech.com; sales@multitech.com; mtsmktg@multitech.com *Web Site:* www.multitech.com, pg 1373

Palicki, Jeff, Independent Publishers Group (IPG), 814 N Franklin St, Chicago, IL 60610 *Tel:* 312-337-0747 *Toll Free Tel:* 800-888-4741 (orders) *Fax:* 312-337-5985 *E-mail:* frontdesk@ipgbook.com; orders@ipgbook.com *Web Site:* www.ipgbook.com, pg 1292, 1328

Palizzolo, Bill, Northeast Publishers Reps, Montville Chase, 20 Davenport Rd, Montville, NJ 07045 *Tel:* 973-299-0085 *Fax:* 973-263-2363 *E-mail:* siraksirak@aol.com *Web Site:* www.nepubreps.com, pg 1298

Palmer, Delores L, WeWrite LLC, 11040 Alba Rd, Ben Lomond, CA 95005 *Tel:* 831-336-3382 *E-mail:* info@wewrite.net *Web Site:* www.wewrite.net, pg 1323, 1378

Palmer, Ian, Copyright Clearance Center Inc (CCC), 222 Rosewood Dr, Danvers, MA 01923 *Tel:* 978-750-8400 (sales); 978-646-2600 (cust serv) *E-mail:* info@copyright.com *Web Site:* www.copyright.com, pg 1345

Palmer, Terry, Library Bound Inc, 100 Bathurst Dr, Unit 2, Waterloo, ON N2V 1V6, Canada *Tel:* 519-885-3233 *Toll Free Tel:* 800-363-4728 *Fax:* 519-885-2662 *Web Site:* www.librarybound.com, pg 1318

Panek, Kathleen, AlphaGraphics Inc, 143 Union Blvd, Suite 650, Lakewood, CO 80228 *Toll Free Tel:* 800-955-6246 *Fax:* 801-595-7270 *E-mail:* contactus@alphagraphics.com *Web Site:* www.alphagraphics.com, pg 1364

Panzarella, Nancy, Timsons Inc, 385 Crossen Ave, Elk Grove Village, IL 60007 *Tel:* 847-884-8611 *Fax:* 847-884-8676 *E-mail:* sales@timsonsinc.com *Web Site:* www.timsonsinc.com, pg 1283

Papamichael, Haris, Victory Productions Inc, 55 Linden St, Worcester, MA 01609 *Tel:* 508-755-0051 *E-mail:* victory@victoryprd.com *Web Site:* www.victoryprd.com, pg 1358

Papas, Sabrina, Penguin Random House Canada, a Penguin Random House company, 320 Front St W, Suite 1400, Toronto, ON M5V 3B6, Canada *Tel:* 416-364-4449 *Toll Free Tel:* 888-523-9292 (cust serv) *Fax:* 416-598-7764 *E-mail:* customerservicescanada@penguinrandomhouse.com; publicitycanada@penguinrandomhouse.com; rightscanada@penguinrandomhouse.com *Web Site:* www.penguinrandomhouse.ca, pg 1299

Papp, Hortenzia, Pannonia Bookstore, 300 Sainte Clair Ave W, Suite 103, Toronto, ON M4V 1S4, Canada *Tel:* 416-966-5156 *E-mail:* info@pannonia.ca *Web Site:* www.pannonia.ca, pg 1320, 1329

Paquet, Patrick, Multi-Reliure, 2112 Ave de la Transmission, Shawinigan, QC G9N 8N8, Canada *Tel:* 819-537-6008 *Toll Free Tel:* 888-735-4873 *Fax:* 819-537-4598 *E-mail:* info@multi-reliure.com; administration@multi-reliure.com *Web Site:* www.multireliure.com, pg 1257

Paquet, Sonia, Multi-Reliure, 2112 Ave de la Transmission, Shawinigan, QC G9N 8N8, Canada *Tel:* 819-537-6008 *Toll Free Tel:* 888-735-4873 *Fax:* 819-537-4598 *E-mail:* info@multi-reliure.com; administration@multi-reliure.com *Web Site:* www.multireliure.com, pg 1257

Paquette, Emily, Inman, 1400 Village Square Blvd, Suite 3-80368, Tallahassee, FL 32312 *Tel:* 510-658-9252 *Toll Free Tel:* 800-775-4662 (cust support) *E-mail:* customerservice@inman.com *Web Site:* www.inman.com, pg 1190

Paradiso, Diane, WPA Film Library of Stock Footage, 16101 S 108 Ave, Orland Park, IL 60467 *Tel:* 708-460-0555 *Toll Free Tel:* 800-323-0442 *E-mail:* sales@wpafilmlibrary.com *Web Site:* www.wpafilmlibrary.com, pg 1431

Parasnis, Abhay, Adobe Systems Inc, 345 Park Ave, San Jose, CA 95110-2704 *Tel:* 408-536-6000 *Fax:* 408-537-6000 *Web Site:* www.adobe.com, pg 1363

Parikh, Sudip, American Association for the Advancement of Science (AAAS), 1200 New York Ave NW, Washington, DC 20005 *Tel:* 202-326-6400 *Fax:* 202-371-9526 *Web Site:* www.aaas.org, pg 1145

Parizadeh, Bo, Indigo Books & Music Inc, 468 King St W, Suite 500, Toronto, ON M5V 1L8, Canada *Tel:* 416-364-4499 *E-mail:* cisales@indigo.ca *Web Site:* www.chapters.indigo.ca, pg 1294

Park, Casey, Independent Publishers Group (IPG), 814 N Franklin St, Chicago, IL 60610 *Tel:* 312-337-0747 *Toll Free Tel:* 800-888-4741 (orders) *Fax:* 312-337-5985 *E-mail:* frontdesk@ipgbook.com; orders@ipgbook.com *Web Site:* www.ipgbook.com, pg 1292, 1328

Park, Casey, Midpoint Trade Books, 814 N Franklin St, Suite 100, Chicago, IL 60610 *Tel:* 312-337-0747 *Fax:* 312-337-5985 *E-mail:* orders@ipgbook.com *Web Site:* www.midpointtrade.com, pg 1297

Parke, Frank III, Democrat Printing & Lithographing Co, 6401 Lindsey Rd, Little Rock, AR 72206 *Toll Free Tel:* 800-622-2216 *Fax:* 501-907-7953 *Web Site:* democratprinting.com, pg 1252

Parker, Douglas "Doug" M, Open Text Corp, 275 Frank Tompa Dr, Waterloo, ON N2L 0A1, Canada *Tel:* 519-888-7111 *Fax:* 519-888-0677 *Web Site:* opentext.com, pg 1374

Parker, Kevin Powis, Powis Parker Inc, 2929 Fifth St, Berkeley, CA 94710 *Tel:* 510-848-2463 *Toll Free Tel:* 800-321-BIND (321-2463) *Fax:* 510-848-2169 *E-mail:* customerservice@powis.com *Web Site:* www.powis.com, pg 1375

Parker, Nick, Ingram Publisher Services, an Ingram brand, 14 Ingram Blvd, Mail Stop 631, La Vergne, TN 37086 *Tel:* 615-793-5000 *Toll Free Tel:* 866-400-5351 (cust serv) *E-mail:* ips@ingramcontent.com *Web Site:* www.ingrampublisherservices.com, pg 1294

Parker, Troy Scott, Cimarron Design, 8285 Kincross Dr, Boulder, CO 80301-4228 *Tel:* 303-530-1785 *Web Site:* www.cimarrondesign.com, pg 1223

Parkhurst, William, Parkhurst Communications Inc, 11 Riverside Dr, Suite 1-TW, New York, NY 10023 *Tel:* 212-362-9722 *Web Site:* www.parkhurstcommunications.com, pg 1111

Parmet, David, HJMT Public Relations Inc, 3280 Sunrise Hwy, Suite 296, Wantagh, NY 11793 *Tel:* 516-661-2800 *E-mail:* info@hjmt.com *Web Site:* www.hjmt.com, pg 1109

Parmley, Jasmine, Boston Review, PO Box 390568, Cambridge, MA 02139 *Tel:* 617-356-8198 *E-mail:* review@bostonreview.net; customerservice@bostonreview.net *Web Site:* bostonreview.net, pg 1130

Parrini, Dante C, Glatfelter, Capitol Towers South, 4350 Congress St, Suite 600, Charlotte, NC 28209 *Tel:* 717-850-0170 *Toll Free Tel:* 866-744-7380 *E-mail:* info@glatfelter.com *Web Site:* www.glatfelter.com, pg 1267

Parrish, Jim, Carolina Biological Supply Co, 2700 York Rd, Burlington, NC 27215-3398 *Tel:* 336-586-4399 (intl sales); 336-538-6211 *Toll Free Tel:* 800-334-5551 *Fax:* 336-584-7686 (intl sales) *Toll Free Fax:* 800-222-7112 *E-mail:* quotations@carolina.com; product@carolina.com *Web Site:* www.carolina.com, pg 1313

Parrott, Kiera, School Library Journal, 123 William St, Suite 802, New York, NY 10038 *Tel:* 646-380-0752 *Toll Free Tel:* 800-595-1066 *Fax:* 646-380-0756 *E-mail:* slj@mediasourceinc.com; sljsubs@pcspublink.com *Web Site:* www.slj.com; www.facebook.com/schoollibraryjournal; x.com/sljournal, pg 1136

Pasanen, Jennifer, Verso Advertising Inc, 79 Madison Ave, 8th fl, New York, NY 10016 *Tel:* 212-292-2990 *Web Site:* www.versoadvertising.com, pg 1100

Pasqua, Dominique, DJD/Golden Advertising, 145 W 28 St, 12th fl, New York, NY 10001 *Tel:* 212-366-5033 *Fax:* 212-243-5044 *E-mail:* call@djdgolden.com *Web Site:* www.djdgolden.com, pg 1099

Patil, Galina, Business Wire, 101 California St, 20th fl, San Francisco, CA 94111 *Tel:* 415-986-4422 *Toll Free Tel:* 800-227-0845 *E-mail:* info@businesswire.com *Web Site:* www.businesswire.com, pg 1189

Patten, Barbara L, International Book Import Service Inc, 161 Main St, Lynchburg, TN 37352-8300 *Tel:* 931-759-7400 *Toll Free Tel:* 800-277-4247 *Fax:* 931-759-7555 *Toll Free Fax:* 866-277-2722 *E-mail:* ibis@ibiservice.com *Web Site:* www.ibiservice.com, pg 1328

Patterson, William, Demand Marketing, 377 Fisher Rd, Suite D, Grosse Pointe, MI 48230 *Tel:* 313-823-8598 *Toll Free Tel:* 888-977-2256 *E-mail:* info@create-demand.com *Web Site:* www.create-demand.com, pg 1115

Patti, Chris, AccuWeather Inc, 385 Science Park Rd, State College, PA 16803 *Tel:* 814-235-8600; 814-237-0309 *E-mail:* salesmail@accuweather.com; support@accuweather.com *Web Site:* www.accuweather.com; corporate.accuweather.com, pg 1363

Patton, Rob, Clamco Corp, 775 Berea Industrial Pkwy, Berea, OH 44017 *Tel:* 216-267-1911 *Toll Free Tel:* 800-985-9570 (headquarters) *Fax:* 216-267-8713 *E-mail:* info@clamcopackaging.com *Web Site:* www.pacmachinery.com/clamcopackaging, pg 1278

Paul, Howard Michael, Photography for Communication & Commerce, 3931 S Spruce St, Suite 200, Denver, CO 80237-2152 *Tel:* 303-829-5678 *Web Site:* www.howardpaulphotography.com, pg 1424

Paul, Tammy, Chicago Distribution Center (CDC), 11030 S Langley Ave, Chicago, IL 60628 *Tel:* 773-702-7010 *Toll Free Fax:* 800-621-8476 *Web Site:* press.uchicago.edu/cdc, pg 1289

Paulsen, Eric, Dynabook Americas Inc, 5241 California Ave, Suite 100, Irvine, CA 92617 *Tel:* 949-583-3000 *Web Site:* us.dynabook.com, pg 1368

Paulson, Tim, Augsburg Fortress Publishers, Publishing House of the Evangelical Lutheran Church in America, 510 Marquette Ave S, Minneapolis, MN 55402 *Tel:* 612-330-3300 *Toll Free Tel:* 800-426-0115 (ext 639, subns); 800-328-4648 (orders) *Fax:* 612-330-3455 *Toll Free Fax:* 800-722-7766 (orders) *E-mail:* customercare@augsburgfortress.org; copyright@augsburgfortress.org (reprint permission requests); info@augsburgfortress.org *Web Site:* www.augsburgfortress.org; www.1517.media, pg 1311

Pauly, Louise, TotalWorks™ Inc, 420 W Huron St, Chicago, IL 60654 *Tel:* 773-489-4313 *E-mail:* production@totalworks.net *Web Site:* www.totalworks.net, pg 1232, 1261

Pautz, Michael, E C Schultz & Company Inc, 333 Crossen Ave, Elk Grove Village, IL 60007-2001 *Tel:* 847-640-1190 *E-mail:* jobfiles@ecschultz.com *Web Site:* www.ecschultz.com, pg 1283

Pavett, Jim, Allusion Studios & Pure Wave Audio, 248 W Elm St, Tucson, AZ 85705 *Tel:* 520-622-3895 (Allusion Studios); 520-447-8116 (Pure Wave Audio) *E-mail:* contact@allusionstudios.com *Web Site:* www.allusionstudios.com; www.purewaveaudio.com, pg 1364

Pavlin, Maryanne, Datalogics Inc, 101 N Wacker, Suite 1800, Chicago, IL 60606 *Tel:* 312-853-8200 *Fax:* 312-853-8282 *E-mail:* sales@datalogics.com; marketing@datalogics.com *Web Site:* www.datalogics.com, pg 1367

Pavri, Farishteh, Penguin Random House Canada, a Penguin Random House company, 320 Front St W, Suite 1400, Toronto, ON M5V 3B6, Canada *Tel:* 416-364-4449 *Toll Free Tel:* 888-523-9292 (cust serv) *Fax:* 416-598-7764 *E-mail:* customerservicescanada@penguinrandomhouse.com; publicitycanada@penguinrandomhouse.com; rightscanada@penguinrandomhouse.com *Web Site:* www.penguinrandomhouse.ca, pg 1299

Paxson, Chris, LBS, 1801 Thompson Ave, Des Moines, IA 50316-2751 *Tel:* 515-262-3191 *Toll Free Tel:* 800-247-5323 *Toll Free Fax:* 800-262-4091 *E-mail:* info@lbsbind.com *Web Site:* www.lbsbind.com, pg 1269

Payne, Philip B, Linguist's Software, 300 Tineke Way, Travelers Rest, SC 29690-6903 *Tel:* 425-775-1130 *E-mail:* sales@linguistsoftware.com *Web Site:* www.linguistsoftware.com, pg 1372

Pearce, Jerry, NAPCO Inc, 120 Trojan Ave, Sparta, NC 28675 *Tel:* 336-372-5228 *Toll Free Tel:* 800-854-8621 *Fax:* 336-372-8602 *E-mail:* info@napcousa.com *Web Site:* www.napcousa.com, pg 1257

Pearl, George S, Atlanta Panorama, c/o ALPS Labs, 2579 Lawrenceville Hwy, Suite B, Decatur, GA 30033 *Tel:* 404-872-2577 *Fax:* 404-872-0548 *E-mail:* alps007@mindspring.com *Web Site:* www.alpslabs.com/PANO/index.htm, pg 1419

Peattie, Gary R, DeVorss & Co, 1100 Flynn Rd, Unit 104, Camarillo, CA 93012 *Tel:* 805-322-9010 *Toll Free Tel:* 800-843-5743 *Fax:* 805-322-9011 *E-mail:* service@devorss.com *Web Site:* www.devorss.com, pg 1145, 1314

Pecaric, John, RR Donnelley, 35 W Wacker Dr, Chicago, IL 60601 *Toll Free Tel:* 800-742-4455 *Web Site:* www.rrd.com, pg 1210, 1225, 1252, 1266, 1279

Pecaric, John, RR Donnelley & Sons Company, 35 W Wacker Dr, Chicago, IL 60601 *Tel:* 312-326-8000 *Toll Free Tel:* 800-742-4455 *Web Site:* www.rrd.com, pg 1333

Peccarelli, Brian, Thomson Reuters, 3 Times Sq, New York, NY 10036 *Tel:* 646-223-4000; 646-223-6100 (edit); 646-223-6000 (newsroom) *Web Site:* www.thomsonreuters.com, pg 1191

Peccatori, Stefano, Rizzoli Bookstores, 1133 Broadway, New York, NY 10010 *Tel:* 212-759-2424 *Toll Free Tel:* 800-52-BOOKS (522-6657) *Fax:* 212-826-9754 *Web Site:* rizzolibookstore.com; www.rizzoliusa.com, pg 1320

Peck, Tom, Ingram Micro Inc, 3351 Michelson Dr, Suite 100, Irvin, CA 92612 *Tel:* 714-566-1000 *E-mail:* customerexperience@ingrammicro.com *Web Site:* www.ingrammicro.com, pg 1317

Peel, Alan, L+L Printers, 6200 Yarrow Dr, Carlsbad, CA 92011 *Tel:* 760-438-3456; 760-477-0321 *Fax:* 760-929-0853 *E-mail:* info@llprinters.com *Web Site:* www.llprinters.com, pg 1256

Pegram, Norm, PremierIMS Inc, 11101 Ella Blvd, Houston, TX 77067 *Tel:* 832-608-6400 *Fax:* 832-608-6420 *E-mail:* info@premier-ims.com *Web Site:* www.premier-ims.com, pg 1118

Pelczar, Anne H, Conservative Book Club, 300 New Jersey Ave NW, Suite 500, Washington, DC 20001 *Tel:* 202-216-0601 *Web Site:* www.conservativebookclub.com, pg 1141

Pelikan, Karl, Horizon Paper Co Inc, 1010 Washington Blvd, Stamford, CT 06901 *Tel:* 203-358-0855 *Toll Free Tel:* 866-358-0855 *E-mail:* info@horizonpaper.com *Web Site:* www.horizonpaper.com, pg 1268

Pelland, Michael, American International Distribution Corp (AIDC), 82 Winter Sport Lane, Williston, VT 05495 *Tel:* 802-862-0095 *Toll Free Tel:* 800-678-2432 *Fax:* 802-864-7749 *Web Site:* www.aidcvt.com, pg 1115, 1117, 1221, 1286, 1311, 1333

Pellegrino, Mike, SumTotal Systems LLC, 2850 NW 43 St, Suite 150, Gainesville, FL 32606 *Tel:* 352-264-2800 *Toll Free Tel:* 866-933-1416 *Fax:* 352-374-2257 *E-mail:* customersupport@sumtotalsystems.com *Web Site:* www.sumtotalsystems.com, pg 1377

Pellerin, Nicolas, European Books & Media, 6600 Shattuck Ave, Oakland, CA 94609 *Tel:* 510-922-9157 *E-mail:* info@europeanbook.com *Web Site:* www.europeanbook.com, pg 1315, 1327

Pelto, Lisa K, Concierge Marketing Inc, 4822 S 133 St, Omaha, NE 68137 *Tel:* 402-884-5995 *Web Site:* www.conciergemarketing.com, pg 1345

Peluso, Michelle, IBM Corp, One New Orchard Rd, Armonk, NY 10504 *Tel:* 914-499-1900 *Toll Free Tel:* 800-426-4968 *E-mail:* askibm@vnet.ibm.com *Web Site:* www.ibm.com, pg 1370

Penberthy, Stephen, Woodcrafters Lumber Sales Inc, 212 NE Sixth Ave, Portland, OR 97232-2976 *Tel:* 503-231-0226 *Toll Free Tel:* 800-777-3709 *Fax:* 503-232-0511 *Web Site:* www.woodcrafters.us, pg 1323

Penichet, Jeff, Bilingual Educational Services Inc, 2514 S Grand Ave, Los Angeles, CA 90007 *Tel:* 213-749-6213 *Toll Free Tel:* 800-448-6032, pg 1287, 1312

Penny, Saleem Hue, Bellevue Literary Review, 149 E 23 St, Suite 1516, New York, NY 10010 *Tel:* 917-375-5790 *E-mail:* info@BLReview.org *Web Site:* www.BLReview.org, pg 1130

Perez, Amilcar, Gracenote, a Nielsen Company, 2000 Powell St, Suite 1500, Emeryville, CA 94608 *Tel:* 510-428-7200 *Web Site:* www.gracenote.com, pg 1190

Perez, Javier, Page Turner Publicity, 8785 SW 28 St, Miami, FL 33165 *Tel:* 949-254-3214 *E-mail:* pgturnerpub@aol.com *Web Site:* www.pageturnerpublicity.com, pg 1111

Perez, McKenzie, AlphaGraphics Inc, 143 Union Blvd, Suite 650, Lakewood, CO 80228 *Toll Free Tel:* 800-955-6246 *Fax:* 801-595-7270 *E-mail:* contactus@alphagraphics.com *Web Site:* www.alphagraphics.com, pg 1364

Perica, Adrian, Apple Inc, One Apple Park Way, Cupertino, CA 95014 *Tel:* 408-996-1010 *Web Site:* www.apple.com, pg 1364

Perkins, Lori, Total Printing Systems, 201 S Gregory Dr, Newton, IL 62448 *Tel:* 618-783-2978 *Toll Free Tel:* 800-465-5200 *Fax:* 618-783-8407 *E-mail:* sales@tps1.com *Web Site:* www.tps1.com, pg 1261

Pernu, Dennis, Motorbooks, 100 Cummings Ctr, Suite 265D, Beverly, MA 01915 *Tel:* 978-282-9590 *Toll Free Tel:* 800-759-0190 (orders) *Web Site:* www.quartoknows.com/motorbooks, pg 1319, 1329

Perritt, Rickey L, S & L Sales Co Inc, 2165 Industrial Blvd, Waycross, GA 31503 *Tel:* 912-283-0210 *Toll Free Tel:* 800-243-3699 *Fax:* 912-283-0261 *Toll Free Fax:* 800-736-7329 *E-mail:* sales@slsales.com *Web Site:* slsales.com, pg 1321

Perron, Michel Carl, Cheneliere Education Inc, 5800, rue St Denis, bureau 900, Montreal, QC H2S 3L5, Canada *Tel:* 514-273-1066 *Toll Free Tel:* 800-565-5531 *Fax:* 514-276-0324 *Toll Free Fax:* 800-814-0324 *E-mail:* info@cheneliere.ca *Web Site:* www.cheneliere.ca, pg 1313

Perrotti, Theresa, Maryheart Crusaders Inc, 531 W Main St, Meriden, CT 06451-2707 *Tel:* 203-238-9735 *Toll Free Tel:* 800-879-1957 (orders only) *Fax:* 203-235-0059 *E-mail:* maryheart@msn.com *Web Site:* www.maryheartcrusaders.com, pg 1142

Perry, Brian, Infinity Graphics, 2277 Science Pkwy, Suite 5, Okemos, MI 48864 *Tel:* 517-349-4635 *Toll Free Tel:* 800-292-2633 *Fax:* 517-349-7608 *E-mail:* barcode@infinitygraphics.com *Web Site:* www.infinitygraphics.com, pg 1227, 1255, 1370

Perry, Connie, Monteiro & Co Inc, 301 E 57 St, 4th fl, New York, NY 10022 *Tel:* 212-832-8183 *Web Site:* www.monteiroandco.com, pg 1111

Perry, Glynn, RR Donnelley, 35 W Wacker Dr, Chicago, IL 60601 *Toll Free Tel:* 800-742-4455 *Web Site:* www.rrd.com, pg 1210, 1225, 1252, 1266, 1279

Perry, Glynn, RR Donnelley & Sons Company, 35 W Wacker Dr, Chicago, IL 60601 *Tel:* 312-326-8000 *Toll Free Tel:* 800-742-4455 *Web Site:* www.rrd.com, pg 1333

Perry, Suzette, Infinity Graphics, 2277 Science Pkwy, Suite 5, Okemos, MI 48864 *Tel:* 517-349-4635 *Toll Free Tel:* 800-292-2633 *Fax:* 517-349-7608 *E-mail:* barcode@infinitygraphics.com *Web Site:* www.infinitygraphics.com, pg 1227, 1255, 1370

Peters, Craig, Getty Images Inc, 605 Fifth Ave S, Suite 400, Seattle, WA 98104 *Tel:* 206-925-5000 *Toll Free Tel:* 800-IMAGERY (462-4379); 888-888-5889 *Web Site:* www.gettyimages.com; www.gettyimages.com/customer-support; engage.gettyimages.com/media-inquiries, pg 1369, 1428

Peters, Kevin, Imprint Group, 2070 Cherry St, Denver, CO 80207 *Toll Free Tel:* 800-738-3961 *Toll Free Fax:* 888-867-3869 *Web Site:* imprintgroupwest.com, pg 1292

Petersen, Ryan, Follett Higher Education Group, 3 Westbrook Corporate Ctr, Suite 200, Westchester, IL 60154 *Tel:* 708-884-0000 *Toll Free Tel:* 800-FOLLETT (365-5388) *Web Site:* www.follett.com/higher-ed, pg 1315

Peterson, Kurt A, Puritan Press Inc, 95 Runnells Bridge Rd, Hollis, NH 03049-6565 *Tel:* 603-889-4500 *Toll Free Tel:* 800-635-6302 *Fax:* 603-889-6551 *E-mail:* print@puritancapital.com *Web Site:* www.puritanpress.com, pg 1259

Peterson, Terry D, RR Donnelley, 35 W Wacker Dr, Chicago, IL 60601 *Toll Free Tel:* 800-742-4455 *Web Site:* www.rrd.com, pg 1210, 1225, 1252, 1266, 1279

Peterson, Terry D, RR Donnelley & Sons Company, 35 W Wacker Dr, Chicago, IL 60601 *Tel:* 312-326-8000 *Toll Free Tel:* 800-742-4455 *Web Site:* www.rrd.com, pg 1333

Peticolas, Kip, Fundamental Photographs, 210 Forsyth St, Suite 2, New York, NY 10002 *Tel:* 212-473-5770 *E-mail:* mail@fphoto.com *Web Site:* www.fphoto.com, pg 1428

Petric-Black, Alexis, OverDrive Inc, One OverDrive Way, Cleveland, OH 44125 *Tel:* 216-573-6886 *Fax:* 216-573-6888 *E-mail:* info@overdrive.com *Web Site:* www.overdrive.com, pg 1298

Petriw, Les, National Book Network (NBN), 4501 Forbes Blvd, Suite 200, Lanham, MD 20706 *Tel:* 301-459-3366 *Toll Free Tel:* 800-462-6420 (orders only) *Fax:* 301-429-5746 *Toll Free Fax:* 800-338-4550 (orders only) *E-mail:* customercare@nbnbooks.com *Web Site:* www.nbnbooks.com, pg 1298, 1319

Petro, Joe, Nuance Communications Inc, One Wayside Rd, Burlington, MA 01803 *Tel:* 781-565-5000 *Toll Free Tel:* 800-654-1187 (cust serv); 888-372-1908 (orders) *Web Site:* www.nuance.com, pg 1374

Petrook, Malcolm, DJD/Golden Advertising, 145 W 28 St, 12th fl, New York, NY 10001 *Tel:* 212-366-5033 *Fax:* 212-243-5044 *E-mail:* call@djdgolden.com *Web Site:* www.djdgolden.com

Petrucci, Anthony, HID Global, 611 Center Ridge Dr, Austin, TX 78753 *Tel:* 512-776-9000 *Toll Free Tel:* 800-872-5359 (cust serv) *Fax:* 512-776-9930 *E-mail:* customerservice@hidglobal.com *Web Site:* www.hidglobal.com, pg 1370

Petruch, Myron, Sun Chemical Corp, 35 Waterview Blvd, Parsippany, NJ 07054-1285 *Tel:* 973-404-6000 *E-mail:* globalmarketing@sunchemical.com *Web Site:* www.sunchemical.com, pg 1272

Petty, Shea, Faherty & Associates Inc, 17548 Redfern Ave, Lake Oswego, OR 97035 *Tel:* 503-639-3113 *Fax:* 503-213-6168 *E-mail:* faherty@fahertybooks.com *Web Site:* www.fahertybooks.com, pg 1290

Peyton, Jonathan M, Double Envelope, 7702 Plantation Rd, Roanoke, VA 24019 *Toll Free Tel:* 800-800-9007 *E-mail:* inquire@double-envelope.com *Web Site:* www.double-envelope.com, pg 1104, 1116

Pfeil, Suzanne, Creative Direct Marketing Group Inc (CDMG), 1313 Fourth Ave N, Nashville, TN 37208 *Tel:* 615-814-6633 *Web Site:* www.cdmginc.com, pg 1345

Pfister, Erin, Perma Graphics, 1356 S Jason St, Denver, CO 80223 *Tel:* 303-477-2070 *E-mail:* info@perma-graphics.com *Web Site:* www.perma-graphics.com, pg 1258

Phadnis, Atul, Gracenote, a Nielsen Company, 2000 Powell St, Suite 1500, Emeryville, CA 94608 *Tel:* 510-428-7200 *Web Site:* www.gracenote.com, pg 1190

Pharr, Paul, Vectorworks Inc, 7150 Riverwood Dr, Columbia, MD 21046 *Tel:* 410-290-5114 *Toll Free Tel:* 888-646-4223 (sales) *Fax:* 410-290-7266 *E-mail:* sales@vectorworks.net *Web Site:* www.vectorworks.net, pg 1274

Philipp, Whitney, Lachina Creative, 3693 Green Rd, Cleveland, OH 44122 *Tel:* 216-292-7959 *E-mail:* info@lachina.com *Web Site:* www.lachina.com, pg 1227, 1355, 1371, 1415

Phillips, Andrew V, Windhaven®, 466 Rte 10, Orford, NH 03777 *Tel:* 603-512-9251 (cell) *E-mail:* info@windhavenpress.com *Web Site:* www.windhavenpress.com, pg 1233

Phillips, Burt, Hess Print Solutions, 3765 Sunnybrook Rd, Brimfield, OH 44240 *Toll Free Tel:* 800-678-1222 *E-mail:* info@hessprintsolutions.com *Web Site:* www.hessprintsolutions.com, pg 1211, 1254

Philpott, Tom, Military Update, PO Box 231111, Centreville, VA 20120-1111 *Tel:* 703-830-6863 *E-mail:* milupdate@aol.com *Web Site:* www.militaryupdate.com, pg 1191

Pick, Geoffrey, Clear Print, 9025 Fullbright Ave, Chatsworth, CA 91311 *Tel:* 818-709-1220 *Fax:* 818-709-1320 *E-mail:* info@clearprint.com; sales@clearprint.com *Web Site:* www.clearprint.com, pg 1250

Pickert, Jeffrey, GOBI® Library Solutions from EBSCO, 999 Maple St, Contoocook, NH 03229 *Tel:* 603-746-3102 *Toll Free Tel:* 800-258-3774 (US & CN) *Fax:* 603-746-5628 *E-mail:* information@ebsco.com *Web Site:* gobi.ebsco.com, pg 1316

Pidgeon, Tom, D&K Group Inc, 1795 Commerce Dr, Elk Grove Village, IL 60007 *Tel:* 847-956-0160; 847-956-4757 (tech support) *Toll Free Tel:* 800-632-2314 *Fax:* 847-956-8214 *E-mail:* info@dkgroup.net *Web Site:* www.dkgroup.com, pg 1251, 1266, 1279

Pierre, Leah, Greenleaf Book Group LLC, PO Box 91869, Austin, TX 78709 *Tel:* 512-891-6100 *Fax:* 512-891-6150 *E-mail:* contact@greenleafbookgroup.com; editorial@greenleafbookgroup.com; foreignrights@greenleafbookgroup.com; media@greenleafbookgroup.com *Web Site:* greenleafbookgroup.com, pg 1355

Piestrzynska, Isabella, To Press & Beyond, 7507 Summersun Dr, Browns Summit, NC 27214 *Tel:* 805-570-8275 *E-mail:* info@topressandbeyond.com *Web Site:* www.topressandbeyond.com, pg 1113, 1351, 1358

Pieters, Jeff, Post Bulletin Co LLC, 18 First Ave SE, Rochester, MN 55903 *Tel:* 507-285-7600 *Toll Free Tel:* 800-562-1758 *E-mail:* news@postbulletin.com *Web Site:* www.postbulletin.com, pg 1191

Pimm, Robert G, Law Office of Robert G Pimm Attorney at Law, 2977 Ygnacio Valley Rd, Suite 265, Walnut Creek, CA 94598-3535 *Tel:* 925-374-1442 *Fax:* 925-281-2888 *Web Site:* www.rgpimm.com, pg 1350

Pinero, Miranda, Azalea Software Inc, PO Box 16660, Seattle, WA 98116-0660 *Tel:* 206-341-9500; 206-336-9559 (software support); 206-336-9575 (sales & info) *Fax:* 206-299-5600 *E-mail:* salesinfo@azaleabarcodes.com *Web Site:* www.azaleabarcodes.com, pg 1365

Ping, Trisha, BookPage®, 2143 Belcourt Ave, Nashville, TN 37212 *Tel:* 615-292-8926 *Fax:* 615-292-8249 *Web Site:* bookpage.com, pg 1127

Pinn, Naomi, Penguin Random House Canada, a Penguin Random House company, 320 Front St W, Suite 1400, Toronto, ON M5V 3B6, Canada *Tel:* 416-364-4449 *Toll Free Tel:* 888-523-9292 (cust serv) *Fax:* 416-598-7764 *E-mail:* customerservicescanada@penguinrandomhouse.com; publicitycanada@penguinrandomhouse.com; rightscanada@penguinrandomhouse.com *Web Site:* www.penguinrandomhouse.ca, pg 1299

Pinto, Mike, The Country Press Inc, One Commercial Dr, Lakeville, MA 02347 *Tel:* 508-947-4485 *Toll Free Tel:* 888-343-2227 *Fax:* 508-947-8989 *E-mail:* info@countrypressinc.com *Web Site:* www.countrypressprinting.com, pg 1209, 1251

Piquion, Deena LaMarque, Xerox Corporation, 201 Merritt 7, Norwalk, CT 06851-1056 *Toll Free Tel:* 800-835-6100 (cust serv) *Web Site:* www.xerox.com, pg 1273

Pisanie, Taylor, Bettina Schrewe Literary Scouting, 101 Fifth Ave, Suite 11B, New York, NY 10003 *Tel:* 212-414-2515 *Web Site:* www.bschrewe.com, pg 1351

Pistone, Dennis, Westchester Publishing Services, 4 Old Newtown Rd, Danbury, CT 06810 *Tel:* 203-791-0080 *Fax:* 203-791-9286 *E-mail:* info@westchesterpubsvcs.com *Web Site:* www.westchesterpublishingservices.com, pg 1233

Pitman, Jim, CLC Ministries, 701 Pennsylvania Ave, Fort Washington, PA 19034 *Tel:* 215-542-1240 *Toll Free Tel:* 800-659-1240 *Fax:* 215-542-7580 *E-mail:* orders@clcpublications.com *Web Site:* www.clcpublications.com, pg 1314

Pizar, Charles, Forecast, 2550 W Tyvola Rd, Suite 300, Charlotte, NC 28217 Tel: 704-998-3100 Toll Free Tel: 800-775-1800 (info servs); 800-775-1700 (cust serv) Toll Free Fax: 866-557-3396 (cust serv) E-mail: btinfo@baker-taylor.com Web Site: www.baker-taylor.com, pg 1132

Plantz, Julie, The Penworthy Company LLC, 219 N Milwaukee St, 4th fl, Milwaukee, WI 53202 Tel: 414-287-4600 Toll Free Tel: 800-262-2665 Fax: 414-287-4602 E-mail: info@penworthy.com Web Site: www.penworthy.com, pg 1320, 1325

Plath, Thomas J, International Paper Co, 6400 Poplar Ave, Memphis, TN 38197 Tel: 901-419-9000 Toll Free Tel: 800-207-4003 Web Site: www.internationalpaper.com; facebook.com/internationalpaper; x.com/intlpaperco, pg 1268

Plechaty, Corby, Ware-Pak LLC, 2427 Bond St, University Park, IL 60484 Tel: 708-534-2600 E-mail: sales@ware-pak.com Web Site: www.ware-pak.com, pg 1335

Plotka, Richard, appatura™, A Broadridge Company, 65 Challenger Rd, Suite 400, Ridgefield Park, NJ 07660 Tel: 201-508-6000 Toll Free Tel: 800-277-2155 E-mail: contactus@appatura.com Web Site: www.appatura.com, pg 1103, 1115, 1117, 1207, 1221, 1248

Plourde, Dan, Columbia Finishing Mills Inc, 135 Boundary Rd, Cornwall, ON K6H 5T3, Canada Tel: 613-933-1462 Toll Free Tel: 800-267-9174 Fax: 613-933-7717 Toll Free Fax: 800-242-9174 E-mail: info@columbiafinishingmills.com Web Site: www.columbiafinishingmills.com, pg 1266

Polansky, Andy, Weber Shandwick, 909 Third Ave, New York, NY 10022 Tel: 212-445-8000 Fax: 212-445-8001 Web Site: www.webershandwick.com, pg 1113

Polasek, Martina, ICSID Review: Foreign Investment Law Journal, 4000 CentreGreen Way, Suite 310, Cary, NC 27513 Toll Free Tel: 800-852-7323 (option 1) E-mail: jnls.cust.serv@oup.com Web Site: academic.oup.com/icsidreview, pg 1133

Polich, Ryan, Marquand Books, 3131 Western Ave, Suite 522, Seattle, WA 98121 Tel: 206-624-2030 Web Site: www.marquandbooks.com, pg 1356

Poll, Debra, Amgraf Inc, 1501 Oak St, Kansas City, MO 64108-1424 Tel: 816-474-4797 Toll Free Tel: 800-304-4797 (sales & mktg) Fax: 816-842-4477 E-mail: support@amgraf.com Web Site: www.amgraf.com, pg 1364

Pollard, Scott, Hill+Knowlton Strategies, 237 Park Ave, 4th fl, New York, NY 10017 Tel: 212-885-0300 Web Site: www.hkstrategies.com, pg 1109

Polley, Kevin, Hignell Book Printing Ltd, 488 Burnell St, Winnipeg, MB R3G 2B4, Canada Tel: 204-784-1030 Toll Free Tel: 800-304-5553 Fax: 204-774-4053 E-mail: books@hignell.mb.ca Web Site: www.hignell.mb.ca, pg 1211, 1254

Pollock, Ian, Mark Andy Inc, 18081 Chesterfield Airport Rd, Chesterfield, MO 63005 Tel: 636-532-4433 Toll Free Tel: 800-447-1231 Toll Free Fax: 800-447-1231 Web Site: www.presstek.com; markandy.com; shop.markandy.com, pg 1364

Pollock, Michele, Taconic Wire, 250 Totoket Rd, North Branford, CT 06471 Tel: 203-484-2863 Toll Free Tel: 800-253-1450 Fax: 203-484-2865 E-mail: sales@taconicwire.com; taconicwiresales@gmail.com Web Site: www.taconicwire.com, pg 1283

Polus, Paul, CDS Global, 1901 Bell Ave, Des Moines, IA 50315-1099 Tel: 515-247-7500 Toll Free Tel: 866-897-7987 E-mail: salesinfo@cds-global.com Web Site: www.cds-global.com, pg 1117, 1119

Pon, Amy, AJP Communications Inc, 95 Macdonald Ave, Burnaby, BC V5C 4M4, Canada Tel: 604-879-5880 E-mail: info@ajpcommunications.com Web Site: www.ajpcommunications.com, pg 1221

Poole, M Kenzie, Human Rights Quarterly, 2715 N Charles St, Baltimore, MD 21218-4363 Tel: 410-516-6987 (journal orders outside US & CN) Toll Free Tel: 800-548-1784 (journal orders) Fax: 410-578-2865 (journal orders) E-mail: jnlcirc@jh.edu (journal orders) Web Site: www.press.jhu.edu/journals/human-rights-quarterly, pg 1133

Popa, Maya C, Publishers Weekly, 49 W 23 St, 9th fl, New York, NY 10010 Tel: 212-377-5500 Fax: 212-377-2733 Web Site: www.publishersweekly.com, pg 1136

Popp, Bruce D PhD, Bien Fait Translations, 104 Seascape, Laguna Niguel, CA 92677 Tel: 781-769-1637 Toll Free Tel: 866-243-6324 Web Site: www.bien-fait.com, pg 1400

Popp, Jonny, Omnipress, 2600 Anderson St, Madison, WI 53704 Tel: 608-246-2600 Toll Free Tel: 800-828-0305 E-mail: justask@omnipress.com Web Site: www.omnipress.com, pg 1213, 1257

Porras, Raul, Victory Productions Inc, 55 Linden St, Worcester, MA 01609 Tel: 508-755-0051 E-mail: victory@victoryprd.com Web Site: www.victoryprd.com, pg 1358

Porras, Victoria, Victory Productions Inc, 55 Linden St, Worcester, MA 01609 Tel: 508-755-0051 E-mail: victory@victoryprd.com Web Site: www.victoryprd.com, pg 1358

Porter, Dred Jr, Magnolia Clipping Service, 298 Commerce Park Dr, Suite A, Ridgeland, MS 39157 Tel: 601-856-0911 Fax: 601-856-3340 E-mail: mail@magnoliaclips.com Web Site: magnoliaclips.com, pg 1383

Porter, Dred Sr, Magnolia Clipping Service, 298 Commerce Park Dr, Suite A, Ridgeland, MS 39157 Tel: 601-856-0911 Fax: 601-856-3340 E-mail: mail@magnoliaclips.com Web Site: magnoliaclips.com, pg 1383

Porter, Joe, Magnolia Clipping Service, 298 Commerce Park Dr, Suite A, Ridgeland, MS 39157 Tel: 601-856-0911 Fax: 601-856-3340 E-mail: mail@magnoliaclips.com Web Site: magnoliaclips.com, pg 1383

Porter, Jonathan, AccuWeather Inc, 385 Science Park Rd, State College, PA 16803 Tel: 814-235-8600; 814-237-0309 E-mail: salesmail@accuweather.com; support@accuweather.com Web Site: www.accuweather.com; corporate.accuweather.com, pg 1363

Porter, Michael, QBS Learning, 242 W 30 St, Suite 1100, New York, NY 10001 Tel: 646-668-4645 E-mail: contact@qbslearning.com Web Site: www.qbslearning.com, pg 1357, 1417

Poston, Neal, The Dingley Press, 119 Lisbon St, Lisbon, ME 04250 Tel: 207-353-4151 Toll Free Tel: 800-317-4574 Fax: 207-353-9886 E-mail: info@dingley.com Web Site: www.dingley.com, pg 1252

Potash, Steve, OverDrive Inc, One OverDrive Way, Cleveland, OH 44125 Tel: 216-573-6886 Fax: 216-573-6888 E-mail: info@overdrive.com Web Site: www.overdrive.com, pg 1298

Potcoava, Virginia, A WordJourney Translation LLC, PO Box 3181, Humble, TX 77347-3181 Tel: 281-813-1827 Fax: 832-213-2777 E-mail: word@wjtranslation.com Web Site: www.awordjourneytranslation.com, pg 1399

Potente, Ralph, ProFAX Inc, 20 Max Ave, Hicksville, NY 11801-1419 Toll Free Tel: 877-942-8100 E-mail: sales@profax.com Web Site: www.profax.com, pg 1118

Poticny, Carol, Steven Diamond Inc, 104 W 17 St, Suite 3-E, New York, NY 10011 Tel: 212-675-0723 Fax: 212-675-0762 E-mail: steven.diamond@verizon.net, pg 1345

Pouliot, Donna, Copyright Clearance Center Inc (CCC), 222 Rosewood Dr, Danvers, MA 01923 Tel: 978-750-8400 (sales); 978-646-2600 (cust serv) E-mail: info@copyright.com Web Site: www.copyright.com, pg 1345

Powell, Frank, GLS Companies, 1280 Energy Park Dr, St Paul, MN 55108-5106 Tel: 651-644-3000 Toll Free Tel: 800-655-9405 Web Site: www.glsmn.com, pg 1226, 1254

Powell, Jeremy, Vectorworks Inc, 7150 Riverwood Dr, Columbia, MD 21046 Tel: 410-290-5114 Toll Free Tel: 888-646-4223 (sales) Fax: 410-290-7266 E-mail: sales@vectorworks.net Web Site: www.vectorworks.net, pg 1378

Powell, Kathleen, St Catharines Museum, 1932 Welland Canals Pkwy, RR 6, St Catharines, ON L2R 7K6, Canada Tel: 905-984-8880 Toll Free Tel: 800-305-5134 Fax: 905-984-6910 E-mail: museum@stcatharines.ca Web Site: www.stcatharines.ca, pg 1301

Powers, Marcia, Wilshire Book Co, 22647 Ventura Blvd, Suite 314, Woodland Hills, CA 91364 Tel: 818-700-1522 E-mail: sales@mpowers.com Web Site: www.mpowers.com, pg 1323

Pratt, Jane, Association for PRINT Technologies (APTech), 113 Seaboard Lane, Suite C-250, Franklin, TN 37067 Tel: 703-264-7200 E-mail: aptech@aptech.org Web Site: printtechnologies.org, pg 1277, 1365

Pratt, Randy, Master Books®, 3142 Hwy 103 N, Green Forest, AR 72638 Tel: 870-438-5288 Toll Free Tel: 800-999-3777 E-mail: nlp@nlpg.com; sales@masterbooks.com Web Site: www.masterbooks.com; www.nlpg.com, pg 1372

Prazuch, Ron, Continental Sales Inc, 213 W Main St, Barrington, IL 60010 Tel: 847-381-6530 Fax: 847-382-0385; 847-382-0419 Web Site: www.continentalsalesinc.com, pg 1289

Prazuch, Ronald J, Wybel Marketing Group Inc, 213 W Main St, Barrington, IL 60010 Tel: 847-382-0384; 847-382-0382 Toll Free Tel: 800-323-5297 Fax: 847-382-0385 Toll Free Fax: 800-595-5252 E-mail: bookreps@wybel.com, pg 1304

Prentice, Don, Hassett Express, 17W775 Butterfield Rd, Suite 109, Oakbrook Terrace, IL 60181 Tel: 630-530-6515 Fax: 630-530-6538 Web Site: www.hassettexpress.com, pg 1334

Prentiss, Winnie, Motorbooks, 100 Cummings Ctr, Suite 265D, Beverly, MA 01915 Tel: 978-282-9590 Toll Free Tel: 800-759-0190 (orders) Web Site: www.quartoknows.com/motorbooks, pg 1319, 1329

Preston, Chris, Preston Kelly, 222 First Ave NE, Minneapolis, MN 55413 Tel: 612-843-4000 Fax: 612-843-3900 E-mail: iconicideas@prestonkelly.com Web Site: prestonkelly.com, pg 1100

Previn, Fletcher, IBM Corp, One New Orchard Rd, Armonk, NY 10504 Tel: 914-499-1900 Toll Free Tel: 800-426-4968 E-mail: askibm@vnet.ibm.com Web Site: www.ibm.com, pg 1370

Price, Richard W, Crane Duplicating Service Inc, 4915 Rattlesnake Hammock Rd, Suite 207, Naples, FL 34113 Tel: 305-280-6742 (help desk) Fax: 239-732-8415 E-mail: info@craneduplicating.com Web Site: www.craneduplicating.com, pg 1209, 1251

Prickett, Byron, Panaprint Inc, 7979 NE Industrial Blvd, Macon, GA 31216 Tel: 478-788-0676 Toll Free Tel: 800-622-0676 Fax: 478-788-4276 Web Site: www.panaprint.com, pg 1258

Priede, Mark, Xante Corp, 2800 Dauphin St, Suite 100, Mobile, AL 36606 Tel: 251-473-6502; 251-473-4920 (tech support) Fax: 251-473-6503 Web Site: www.xante.com, pg 1378

Prieto, Kimberly, OmniUpdate Inc, 1320 Flynn Rd, Suite 100, Camarillo, CA 93012 Tel: 805-484-9400 Toll Free Tel: 800-362-2605 E-mail: sales@omniupdate.com Web Site: omniupdate.com, pg 1374

Primo, Jim, Douthitt Corp, 245 Adair St, Detroit, MI 48207-4287 Tel: 313-259-1565 Toll Free Tel: 800-368-8448 Fax: 313-259-6806 E-mail: em@douthittcorp.com Web Site: www.douthittcorp.com, pg 1279

Prince, Boo, Idea Architects, 523 Swift St, Santa Cruz, CA 95060 Tel: 831-465-9565 Web Site: www.ideaarchitects.com, pg 1347

Prins, Thomas, The Scholar's Choice, 6300 W Port Bay Rd, Suite 101, Wolcott, NY 14590 Tel: 315-905-4208 E-mail: information@scholarschoice.com Web Site: www.scholarschoice.com, pg 1139

Pritzkat, Carl, Publishers Weekly, 49 W 23 St, 9th fl, New York, NY 10010 Tel: 212-377-5500 Fax: 212-377-2733 Web Site: www.publishersweekly.com, pg 1135

Proffit, James R, NAPCO Inc, 120 Trojan Ave, Sparta, NC 28675 Tel: 336-372-5228 Toll Free Tel: 800-854-8621 Fax: 336-372-8602 E-mail: info@napcousa.com Web Site: www.napcousa.com, pg 1257

Prohaske, Eugene, D C Graphics Inc, 59 Central Ave, Suite 15, Farmingdale, NY 11735 Tel: 631-777-3100 Fax: 631-777-7899 E-mail: prepress@dcgraphicsinc.com Web Site: www.dcgraphicsinc.com, pg 1251

Pronk, Gord, Pronk Media Inc, 16 Glen Davis Crescent, Toronto, ON M4E 1X5, Canada Tel: 416-716-9660 (cell) E-mail: info@pronk.com; hello@pronk.com Web Site: www.pronk.com; www.h5engines.com; www.html5alive.com, pg 1230, 1375, 1417

Protano, Generosa Gina, GGP Publishing Inc, Larchmont, NY 10538 Tel: 914-834-8896 Fax: 914-834-7566 Web Site: www.GGPPublishing.com, pg 1347, 1355, 1401

Pruitt, Charles, A B Data Ltd, 600 A B Data Dr, Milwaukee, WI 53217 Tel: 414-961-6400 Toll Free Tel: 866-217-4470 Fax: 414-961-2674 E-mail: info@abdata.com; consulting@abdata.com Web Site: www.abdata.com, pg 1115

Pruitt, Gary, Associated Press (AP), 200 Liberty St, New York, NY 10281 Tel: 212-621-1500 E-mail: info@ap.org Web Site: www.ap.org, pg 1189

Pruzsinszky, Regine, Bulletin of the American Schools of Oriental Research (BASOR), James F Strange Ctr, 209 Commerce St, Alexandria, VA 22314 Tel: 703-789-9229; 703-789-9230 (pubns) Fax: 617-353-6575 E-mail: basor@asor.org; info@asor.org; publications@asor.org Web Site: www.asor.org, pg 1130

Pucher, Annmarie, ISIS Papyrus America, 301 Bank St, South Lake, TX 76092 Tel: 817-416-2345 Fax: 817-416-1223 E-mail: info@isis-papyrus.com Web Site: www.isis-papyrus.com, pg 1371

Pugliese, Paul, General Cartography Inc, 4 Estate Dr, Boynton Beach, FL 33436 Tel: 561-914-6323 E-mail: terradata@aol.com Web Site: cartographybypaul.com, pg 1414

Purakayastha, Apratim, SumTotal Systems LLC, 2850 NW 43 St, Suite 150, Gainesville, FL 32606 Tel: 352-264-2800 Toll Free Tel: 866-933-1416 Fax: 352-374-2257 E-mail: customersupport@sumtotalsystems.com Web Site: www.sumtotalsystems.com, pg 1377

Purdy, Judy, Saunders Book Co, PO Box 308, Collingwood, ON L9Y 3Z7, Canada Tel: 705-445-4777 Toll Free Tel: 800-461-9120 Fax: 705-445-9569 Toll Free Fax: 800-561-1763 E-mail: info@saundersbook.ca Web Site: librarybooks.com, pg 1301

Purnell, Thomas, Southern Wisconsin News Co, 58 Artisan Dr, Edgerton, WI 53534 Tel: 608-884-2600 Fax: 608-884-2636 Web Site: www.southernwisconsinnews.com, pg 1322

Quagliato, Steve, Lake Book Manufacturing Inc, 2085 N Cornell Ave, Melrose Park, IL 60160 Tel: 708-345-7000 E-mail: info@lakebook.com Web Site: www.lakebook.com, pg 1212, 1227, 1255, 1269, 1281

Quant, Daniel, Multi-Tech Systems Inc, 2205 Woodale Dr, Mounds View, MN 55112 Tel: 763-785-3500 Toll Free Tel: 800-328-9717 Fax: 763-785-9874 E-mail: info@multitech.com; sales@multitech.com; mtsmktg@multitech.com Web Site: www.multitech.com, pg 1373

Quarles, Christa, Corel Corporation, 1600 Carling Ave, Ottawa, ON K1Z 8R7, Canada Toll Free Tel: 877-582-6735 Web Site: www.corel.com, pg 1366

Quental, Carla, National Book Network (NBN), 4501 Forbes Blvd, Suite 200, Lanham, MD 20706 Tel: 301-459-3366 Toll Free Tel: 800-462-6420 (orders only) Fax: 301-429-5746 Toll Free Fax: 800-338-4550 (orders only) E-mail: customercare@nbnbooks.com Web Site: www.nbnbooks.com, pg 1298, 1319

Quigley, Rich, CRW Graphics Communications, 9100 Pennsauken Hwy, Pennsauken, NJ 08110 Tel: 856-662-9111 Toll Free Tel: 800-820-3000 Fax: 856-665-1789 E-mail: info@crwgraphics.com Web Site: www.crwgraphics.com, pg 1103, 1367, 1413

Quill, John A, Ecological Fibers Inc, 40 Pioneer Dr, Lunenburg, MA 01462 Tel: 978-537-0003 Fax: 978-537-2238 E-mail: info@ecofibers.com Web Site: www.ecofibers.com, pg 1210, 1267

Quinlan, Michael, Transparent Language Inc, 12 Murphy Dr, Nashua, NH 03062 Tel: 603-262-6300 Toll Free Tel: 800-567-9619 (cust serv & sales) E-mail: info@transparent.com; support@transparent.com (tech support) Web Site: www.transparent.com, pg 1377

Quinlisk, Frank, Media Supply Inc, 208 Philips Rd, Exton, PA 19341 Tel: 610-884-4400 Toll Free Tel: 800-944-4237 Fax: 610-884-4500 E-mail: info@mediasupply.com Web Site: www.mediasupply.com, pg 1372

Quinn, Kevin, Fry Communications Inc, 800 W Church Rd, Mechanicsburg, PA 17055 Tel: 717-766-0211 Toll Free Tel: 800-334-1429 Fax: 717-691-0341 E-mail: info@frycomm.com Web Site: www.frycomm.com, pg 1210, 1226, 1253, 1280

Quinn, Tony, Fire Engineering Books & Videos, Clarion Events LLC, 110 S Hartford, Suite 220, Tulsa, OK 74120 Tel: 918-831-9421 Toll Free Tel: 800-752-9764 Fax: 918-831-9555 E-mail: info@fireengineeringbooks.com Web Site: fireengineeringbooks.com, pg 1291

Quinton, Sasha, Arrow (grades 4-6), 557 Broadway, New York, NY 10012 Tel: 212-343-6100; 573-632-1632 (PR, US territories, US military bases) Toll Free Tel: 800-541-1097 (US) Toll Free Fax: 800-223-4011 E-mail: bookclubs@scholastic.com Web Site: clubs.scholastic.com, pg 1141

Quinton, Sasha, Club Leo (Spanish & bilingual books for all grades), 557 Broadway, New York, NY 10012 Tel: 212-343-6100; 573-632-1632 (PR, US territories, US military bases) Toll Free Tel: 800-541-1097 (US) Toll Free Fax: 800-223-4011 E-mail: bookclubs@scholastic.com Web Site: clubs.scholastic.com, pg 1141

Quinton, Sasha, 5th Grade Book Club, 557 Broadway, New York, NY 10012 Tel: 212-343-6100; 573-632-1632 (PR, US territories, US military bases) Toll Free Tel: 800-541-1097 (US) Toll Free Fax: 800-223-4011 E-mail: bookclubs@scholastic.com Web Site: clubs.scholastic.com, pg 1141

Quinton, Sasha, Firefly (PreK-K), 557 Broadway, New York, NY 10012 Tel: 212-343-6100; 573-632-1632 (PR, US territories, US military bases) Toll Free Tel: 800-541-1097 (US) Toll Free Fax: 800-223-4011 E-mail: bookclubs@scholastic.com Web Site: clubs.scholastic.com, pg 1141

Quinton, Sasha, 1st Grade Book Club, 557 Broadway, New York, NY 10012 Tel: 212-343-6100; 573-632-1632 (PR, US territories, US military bases) Toll Free Tel: 800-541-1097 (US) Toll Free Fax: 800-223-4011 E-mail: bookclubs@scholastic.com Web Site: clubs.scholastic.com, pg 1141

Quinton, Sasha, 4th Grade Book Club, 557 Broadway, New York, NY 10012 Tel: 212-343-6100; 573-632-1632 (PR, US territories, US military bases) Toll Free Tel: 800-541-1097 (US) Toll Free Fax: 800-223-4011 E-mail: bookclubs@scholastic.com Web Site: clubs.scholastic.com, pg 1141

Quinton, Sasha, Honeybee (ages 2-4), 557 Broadway, New York, NY 10012 Tel: 212-343-6100; 573-632-1632 (PR, US territories, US military bases) Toll Free Tel: 800-541-1097 (US) Toll Free Fax: 800-223-4011 E-mail: bookclubs@scholastic.com Web Site: clubs.scholastic.com, pg 1142

Quinton, Sasha, Inchworm (ages 3-5), 557 Broadway, New York, NY 10012 Tel: 212-343-6100; 573-632-1632 (PR, US territories, US military bases) Toll Free Tel: 800-541-1097 (US) Toll Free Fax: 800-223-4011 E-mail: bookclubs@scholastic.com Web Site: clubs.scholastic.com, pg 1142

Quinton, Sasha, Kindergarten Book Club, 557 Broadway, New York, NY 10012 Tel: 212-343-6100; 573-632-1632 (PR, US territories, US military bases) Toll Free Tel: 800-541-1097 (US) Toll Free Fax: 800-223-4011 E-mail: bookclubs@scholastic.com Web Site: clubs.scholastic.com, pg 1142

Quinton, Sasha, Lucky (grades 2-3), 557 Broadway, New York, NY 10012 Tel: 212-343-6100; 573-632-1632 (PR, US territories, US military bases) Toll Free Tel: 800-541-1097 (US) Toll Free Fax: 800-223-4011 E-mail: bookclubs@scholastic.com Web Site: clubs.scholastic.com, pg 1142

Quinton, Sasha, Scholastic School Reading Events, 1080 Greenwood Blvd, Lake Mary, FL 32746 Tel: 407-829-8000 Toll Free Tel: 800-770-4662 Fax: 407-829-2600 E-mail: custservbf@scholasticbookfairs.com Web Site: bookfairs.scholastic.com/content/fairs/home.html, pg 1302, 1321

Quinton, Sasha, 2nd Grade Book Club, 557 Broadway, New York, NY 10012 Tel: 212-343-6100; 573-632-1632 (PR, US territories, US military bases) Toll Free Tel: 800-541-1097 (US) Toll Free Fax: 800-223-4011 E-mail: bookclubs@scholastic.com Web Site: clubs.scholastic.com, pg 1143

Quinton, Sasha, SeeSaw (K-1), 557 Broadway, New York, NY 10012 Tel: 212-343-6100; 573-632-1632 (PR, US territories, US military bases) Toll Free Tel: 800-541-1097 (US) Toll Free Fax: 800-223-4011 E-mail: bookclubs@scholastic.com Web Site: clubs.scholastic.com, pg 1143

Quinton, Sasha, TAB (grades 6 & up), 557 Broadway, New York, NY 10012 Tel: 212-343-6100; 573-632-1632 (PR, US territories, US military bases) Toll Free Tel: 800-541-1097 (US) Toll Free Fax: 800-223-4011 E-mail: bookclubs@scholastic.com Web Site: clubs.scholastic.com, pg 1143

Quinton, Sasha, TEENS (grades 7 & up), 557 Broadway, New York, NY 10012 Tel: 212-343-6100; 573-632-1632 (PR, US territories, US military bases) Toll Free Tel: 800-541-1097 (US) Toll Free Fax: 800-223-4011 E-mail: bookclubs@scholastic.com Web Site: clubs.scholastic.com, pg 1143

Quinton, Sasha, 3rd Grade Book Club, 557 Broadway, New York, NY 10012 Tel: 212-343-6100; 573-632-1632 (PR, US territories, US military bases) Toll Free Tel: 800-541-1097 (US) Toll Free Fax: 800-223-4011 E-mail: bookclubs@scholastic.com Web Site: clubs.scholastic.com, pg 1143

Quinton, Sasha, We Need Diverse Books Older (grades 3-6), 557 Broadway, New York, NY 10012 Tel: 212-343-6100; 573-632-1632 (PR, US territories, US military bases) Toll Free Tel: 800-541-1097 (US) Toll Free Fax: 800-223-4011 E-mail: bookclubs@scholastic.com Web Site: clubs.scholastic.com, pg 1143

Quinton, Sasha, We Need Diverse Books Younger (Kindergarten-grade 2), 557 Broadway, New York, NY 10012 Tel: 212-343-6100; 573-632-1632 (PR, US territories, US military bases) Toll Free Tel: 800-541-1097 (US) Toll Free Fax: 800-223-4011 E-mail: bookclubs@scholastic.com Web Site: clubs.scholastic.com, pg 1143

Radke, Linda F, Story Monsters LLC, 4696 W Tyson St, Chandler, AZ 85226-2903 Tel: 480-940-8182 Fax: 480-940-8787 Web Site: www.StoryMonsters.com; www.StoryMonstersInk.com; www.AuthorBookings.com; www.partnershippublishing.com; www.StoryMonstersBookAwards.com, pg 1113

Radke, Linda F, Story Monsters LLC, 4696 W Tyson St, Chandler, AZ 85226-2903 Tel: 480-940-8182 Fax: 480-940-8787 Web Site: www.StoryMonsters.com; www.StoryMonstersInk.com; www.AuthorBookings.com; www.StoryMonstersBookAwards.com, pg 1351

Radke, Linda F, Story Monsters LLC, 4696 W Tyson St, Chandler, AZ 85226-2903 Tel: 480-940-8182 Fax: 480-940-8787 Web Site: www.StoryMonsters.com, pg 1358

Radke, Linda F, Story Monsters LLC, 4696 W Tyson St, Chandler, AZ 85226-2903 Tel: 480-940-8182 Fax: 480-940-8787 Web Site: www.StoryMonsters.com; www.StoryMonstersInk.com; www.StudioStoryMonster.com, pg 1377

Radke, Linda F, Story Monsters LLC, 4696 W Tyson St, Chandler, AZ 85226-2903 Tel: 480-940-8182 Fax: 480-940-8787 Web Site: www.StoryMonsters.com, pg 1417

Rafanello, Krista, Publishers Weekly, 49 W 23 St, 9th fl, New York, NY 10010 Tel: 212-377-5500 Fax: 212-377-2733 Web Site: www.publishersweekly.com, pg 1136

Ragsdale, Craig, Martin Printing Co Inc, 1765 Powdersville Rd, Easley, SC 29642 Toll Free Tel: 888-985-7330 Fax: 864-859-8620 E-mail: info@martinprinting.com Web Site: www.martinprinting.com, pg 1257

Ragsdale, William, Martin Printing Co Inc, 1765 Powdersville Rd, Easley, SC 29642 Toll Free Tel: 888-985-7330 Fax: 864-859-8620 E-mail: info@martinprinting.com Web Site: www.martinprinting.com, pg 1257

Ragusa, Mario, Content Critical Solutions Inc, 10 Fifth St, 2nd fl, Valley Stream, NY 11581 Tel: 201-528-2777 E-mail: info@contentcritical.com Web Site: www.contentcritical.com, pg 1115

Raimondo, Diane, Magnum Photos Inc, 12 W 23 St, 4th fl, New York, NY 10010 Tel: 212-929-6000 E-mail: photography@magnumphotos.com; contact@magnumphotos.com Web Site: www.magnumphotos.com, pro.magnumphotos.com, pg 1429

Raines, Daniel, Creative Trust Inc, 210 Jamestown Park Dr, Suite 200, Brentwood, TN 37027 Tel: 615-297-5010 Fax: 615-297-5020 E-mail: info@creativetrust.com Web Site: creativetrust.com, pg 1345

Rainone, Sarah, Idea Architects, 523 Swift St, Santa Cruz, CA 95060 Tel: 831-465-9565 Web Site: www.ideaarchitects.com, pg 1347

Raiton, Cindy, Bookazine Co Inc, 75 Hook Rd, Bayonne, NJ 07002 Tel: 201-339-7777 Toll Free Tel: 800-221-8112 Fax: 201-339-7778 E-mail: info@bookazine.com Web Site: www.bookazine.com, pg 1312, 1327

Raja, Gautham, Penguin Random House Canada, a Penguin Random House company, 320 Front St W, Suite 1400, Toronto, ON M5V 3B6, Canada Tel: 416-364-4449 Toll Free Tel: 888-523-9292 (cust serv) Fax: 416-598-7764 E-mail: customerservicescanada@penguinrandomhouse.com; publicitycanada@penguinrandomhouse.com; rightscanada@penguinrandomhouse.com Web Site: www.penguinrandomhouse.ca, pg 1299

Rajamani, Madhu, diacriTech Inc, 4 S Market St, 4th fl, Boston, MA 02109 Tel: 617-600-3366 Fax: 617-848-2938 Web Site: www.diacritech.com, pg 1224, 1354, 1413

Rajasekharan, Mahesh PhD, Streem Communications LLC, 4949 Harrison Ave, Rockford, IL 61107 Tel: 815-282-7695 Toll Free Tel: 800-325-7732 Fax: 815-639-8931 Toll Free Fax: 888-435-2348 E-mail: streemsales@cleo.com; sales@cleo.com Web Site: www.streem.net, pg 1118

Rambo, Amy, MCH Strategic Data, 601 E Marshall St, Sweet Springs, MO 65351 Toll Free Tel: 800-776-6373 E-mail: sales@mchdata.com Web Site: www.mchdata.com, pg 1120

Rameau, Ms Leone Giannone, Edipresse Inc, 945, ave Beaumont, Montreal, QC H3N 1W3, Canada Tel: 514-273-6141 Toll Free Tel: 800-361-1043 Fax: 514-273-7021 E-mail: information@edipresse.ca Web Site: www.edipresse.ca, pg 1315

Ramirez, Amanda, Publishers Weekly, 49 W 23 St, 9th fl, New York, NY 10010 Tel: 212-377-5500 Fax: 212-377-2733 Web Site: www.publishersweekly.com, pg 1136

Rampertab, Ramesh, RAmEx Ars Medica Inc, 1714 S Westgate Ave, No 2, Los Angeles, CA 90025-3852 Tel: 310-826-4964 Toll Free Tel: 800-633-9281 Fax: 310-826-9674 E-mail: ars.medica@ramex.com Web Site: www.ramex.com, pg 1301

Ramsahai, Sharon, Penguin Random House Canada, a Penguin Random House company, 320 Front St W, Suite 1400, Toronto, ON M5V 3B6, Canada Tel: 416-364-4449 Toll Free Tel: 888-523-9292 (cust serv) Fax: 416-598-7764 E-mail: customerservicescanada@penguinrandomhouse.com; publicitycanada@penguinrandomhouse.com; rightscanada@penguinrandomhouse.com Web Site: www.penguinrandomhouse.ca, pg 1299

Randall, Dorian, Franklin & Siegal Associates Inc, 40 Exchange Place, Suite 1703, New York, NY 10005 Tel: 212-868-6311 Web Site: www.franklinandsiegal.com, pg 1346

Ranganathan, Madhu, Open Text Corp, 275 Frank Tompa Dr, Waterloo, ON N2L 0A1, Canada Tel: 519-888-7111 Fax: 519-888-0677 Web Site: opentext.com, pg 1374

Rangel, Nicholas, Eastman Kodak Co, 343 State St, Rochester, NY 14650 Tel: 585-724-4000 Toll Free Tel: 866-563-2533 Web Site: www.kodak.com, pg 1279

Rankin, Alisha, Bulletin of the History of Medicine, 2715 N Charles St, Baltimore, MD 21218-4363 Tel: 410-516-6987 (journal orders outside US & CN) Toll Free Tel: 800-548-1784 (journal orders) Fax: 410-578-2865 (journal orders) E-mail: bhm@jhmi.edu; jrnlcirc@jh.edu (journal orders) Web Site: www.press.jhu.edu/journals/bulletin-history-medicine, pg 1130

Rankin, Kelly, Penguin Random House Canada, a Penguin Random House company, 320 Front St W, Suite 1400, Toronto, ON M5V 3B6, Canada Tel: 416-364-4449 Toll Free Tel: 888-523-9292 (cust serv) Fax: 416-598-7764 E-mail: customerservicescanada@penguinrandomhouse.com; publicitycanada@penguinrandomhouse.com; rightscanada@penguinrandomhouse.com Web Site: www.penguinrandomhouse.ca, pg 1299

Rao, Dana, Adobe Systems Inc, 345 Park Ave, San Jose, CA 95110-2704 Tel: 408-536-6000 Fax: 408-537-6000 Web Site: www.adobe.com, pg 1363

Rao, Karthik, Gracenote, a Nielsen Company, 2000 Powell St, Suite 1500, Emeryville, CA 94608 Tel: 510-428-7200 Web Site: www.gracenote.com, pg 1190

Rapin-Klopp, Karrie, A-M Church Supply, 3220 Bay Rd, Suite E, Saginaw, MI 48603 Tel: 989-249-9174 Toll Free Tel: 800-345-4694 Web Site: www.am-church.com, pg 1311

Rapp, Ken, Sheridan MI, 613 E Industrial Dr, Chelsea, MI 48118 Tel: 734-475-9145 Web Site: www.sheridan.com, pg 1213, 1259, 1271

Rapp, Ken, Sheridan NH, 69 Lyme Rd, Hanover, NH 03755 Tel: 603-643-2220 Web Site: www.sheridan.com, pg 1259

Rappaport, Jennifer, Falcon Safety Products Inc, 25 Imclone Dr, Branchburg, NJ 08876 Tel: 908-707-4900 Toll Free Tel: 800-332-5266 E-mail: marketing@falconsafety.com Web Site: www.falconsafety.com, pg 1368

Rappaport, Susan Rice, ALC Inc, 750 College Rd E, Suite 201, Princeton, NJ 08540 Tel: 609-580-2800 Toll Free Tel: 800-252-5478 Fax: 609-580-2888 E-mail: info@alc.com Web Site: www.alc.com, pg 1119

Rascher, Linda, Bert Davis Executive Search Inc, 555 Fifth Ave, Suite 302, New York, NY 10017 Tel: 212-838-4000 E-mail: info@bertdavis.com Web Site: www.bertdavis.com, pg 1381

Rauppius, Lawrence H Jr, B W Wilson Paper Co Inc, 2501 Brittons Hill Rd, Richmond, VA 23230 Tel: 804-358-6715 Toll Free Tel: 800-868-2868 Fax: 804-358-4742 E-mail: info@bwwilson.com; sales@bwwilson.com Web Site: www.bwwilson.com, pg 1273

Rayas, Betsy, Independent Publishers Group (IPG), 814 N Franklin St, Chicago, IL 60610 Tel: 312-337-0747 Toll Free Tel: 800-888-4741 (orders) Fax: 312-337-5985 E-mail: frontdesk@ipgbook.com; orders@ipgbook.com Web Site: www.ipgbook.com, pg 1292, 1328

Raymond, Tom, Fresh Air Photo, 152 Sand Valley Ct, Jonesborough, TN 37659 Tel: 423-612-2700 Web Site: www.freshairphoto.com, pg 1421

Read, Alan, Terry & Read LLC, 4471 Dean Martin Dr, The Martin 3302, Las Vegas, NV 89103 Tel: 510-813-9854 Toll Free Fax: 866-214-4762, pg 1303

Reagan, Maggie, Booklist, 225 N Michigan Ave, Suite 1300, Chicago, IL 60601 Tel: 312-944-6780 Toll Free Tel: 800-545-2433 Fax: 312-440-9374 E-mail: info@booklistonline.com; ala@ala.org Web Site: www.booklistonline.com; www.ala.org, pg 1130

Reasoner, Jason, Independent Publishers Group (IPG), 814 N Franklin St, Chicago, IL 60610 Tel: 312-337-0747 Toll Free Tel: 800-888-4741 (orders) Fax: 312-337-5985 E-mail: frontdesk@ipgbook.com; orders@ipgbook.com Web Site: www.ipgbook.com, pg 1292

Recchia, Bob, Crain Communications Inc, 1155 Gratiot Ave, Detroit, MI 48207-2732 Tel: 313-446-6000 Fax: 313-446-0383 E-mail: info@crain.com Web Site: crain.com, pg 1190

Rech, David Alan, Scribe Inc, 765 S Front St, Philadelphia, PA 19147 Tel: 215-336-5094; 215-336-5095 E-mail: contact@scribenet.com Web Site: www.scribenet.com, pg 1230, 1351, 1357, 1376, 1385

Reckamp, Renee, Western Printing Machinery Co (WPM), 9228 Ivanhoe St, Schiller Park, IL 60176 Tel: 847-678-1740 Fax: 847-678-6176 E-mail: info@wpm.com Web Site: www.wpm.com, pg 1284

Reckinger, Michael, ALC Inc, 750 College Rd E, Suite 201, Princeton, NJ 08540 Tel: 609-580-2800 Toll Free Tel: 800-252-5478 Fax: 609-580-2888 E-mail: info@alc.com Web Site: www.alc.com, pg 1119

Rector, Amy PhD, School of World Studies, 312 N Shafer St, Richmond, VA 23284-2021 Tel: 804-827-1111 Web Site: worldstudies.vcu.edu, pg 1404

Rector, David J, MRC Medical Communications, 12 Lincoln Blvd, Suite 103, Emerson, NJ 07630 Tel: 201-986-0247 E-mail: info@mrcmedical.net Web Site: www.mrcmedical.net, pg 1373

Rector, Susan, MRC Medical Communications, 12 Lincoln Blvd, Suite 103, Emerson, NJ 07630 Tel: 201-986-0247 E-mail: info@mrcmedical.net Web Site: www.mrcmedical.net, pg 1373

Redwood, Joan, Cross Country Computer Corp, 250 Carleton Ave, East Islip, NY 11730-1240 Tel: 631-334-1810 E-mail: inquiry@crosscountrycomputer.com Web Site: www.crosscountrycomputer.com, pg 1119

Redzepagic, Edwin, Medical Images, 3500 S DuPont Hwy, Suite 300, Dover, DE 19901 Tel: 212-736-2525 Toll Free Tel: 800-542-3686 E-mail: sales@medicalimages.com Web Site: www.medicalimages.com, pg 1430

Reed, Bobby Sr, V G Reed & Sons Inc, 1002 S 12 St, Louisville, KY 40210-1302 Toll Free Tel: 800-635-9788 Fax: 502-560-0197 Web Site: www.vgreed.com, pg 1105, 1259

Reed, Geoff, Geoff Reed Photography, 7640 N 22 St, Phoenix, AZ 85020 Tel: 602-432-9065 E-mail: geoff@geoffreedphoto.com Web Site: www.geoffreedphoto.com, pg 1424

Reed, Mary, Dunhill International List Co Inc, 6400 Congress Ave, Suite 1750, Boca Raton, FL 33487-2898 Tel: 561-998-7800 Toll Free Tel: 800-DUNHILL (386-4455) Fax: 561-998-7880 E-mail: dunhill@dunhillintl.com Web Site: www.dunhills.com, pg 1120

Reed, Scott W, V G Reed & Sons Inc, 1002 S 12 St, Louisville, KY 40210-1302 Toll Free Tel: 800-635-9788 Fax: 502-560-0197 Web Site: www.vgreed.com, pg 1105, 1259

Rego, Martin A, Century Direct Solutions LLC, 15 Enter Lane, Islandia, NY 11749 Tel: 212-763-0600 E-mail: contact@centurydirect.net Web Site: www.centurydirect.net, pg 1103, 1115, 1117, 1278

Regos, Laszlo, Laszlo Regos Photography, 30601 Woodstream Dr, Farmington Hills, MI 48334 Tel: 248-398-3631 E-mail: laszlo@laszlofoto.com Web Site: www.laszlofoto.com, pg 1425

Reid, Tracy, Library Bound Inc, 100 Bathurst Dr, Unit 2, Waterloo, ON N2V 1V6, Canada Tel: 519-885-3233 Toll Free Tel: 800-363-4728 Fax: 519-885-2662 Web Site: www.librarybound.com, pg 1318

Reiff, Robert, MagicLight Productions, 4935 McConnell Ave, Suite 1, Marina del Rey, CA 90066 Tel: 310-283-8772 (cell) Web Site: www.magiclight.com, pg 1424

Reindl, David C, Reindl Bindery Co Inc, W194 N11381 McCormick Dr, Germantown, WI 53022 Tel: 262-293-1444 Toll Free Tel: 800-878-1121 Fax: 262-293-1445 E-mail: info@reindlbindery.com Web Site: www.reindlbindery.com, pg 1259

Reindl, Dick, Letterhead Press Inc (LPI), 16800 W Ryerson Rd, New Berlin, WI 53151 Tel: 262-787-1717 Fax: 262-787-1710; 262-787-7315 (estimating) E-mail: contact@letterhead-press.com Web Site: www.letterheadpress.com, pg 1256

Reinhard, Cordell, Universal Bookbindery Inc, 1200 N Colorado, San Antonio, TX 78207 Tel: 210-734-9502 Toll Free Tel: 800-594-2015 Fax: 210-736-0867 E-mail: service@universalbookbindery.com Web Site: www.universalbookbindery.com, pg 1261

Reisman, Heather, Indigo Books & Music Inc, 468 King St W, Suite 500, Toronto, ON M5V 1L8, Canada Tel: 416-364-4499 E-mail: cisales@indigo.ca Web Site: www.chapters.indigo.ca, pg 1294

Remington, Paul, DocuWare Corp, 4 Crotty Lane, Suite 200, New Windsor, NY 12553 Tel: 845-563-9045 Toll Free Tel: 888-565-5907 Fax: 845-563-9046 E-mail: dwsales@docuware.com; support.americas@docuware.com Web Site: www.docuware.com, pg 1367

Renaud, Beth, The Lane Press Inc, 87 Meadowland Dr, South Burlington, VT 05403 Tel: 802-863-5555 Toll Free Tel: 877-300-5933 Fax: 802-264-1485 E-mail: sales@lanepress.com Web Site: www.lanepress.com, pg 1227, 1256

Renner, Karen K, Veritiv™ Corporation, 1000 Abernathy Rd, Bldg 400, Suite 1700, Atlanta, GA 30328 Toll Free Tel: 844-VERITIV (837-4848); 866-714-8303 (packaging cust serv); 866-714-8306 (print cust serv) E-mail: contactus@veritivcorp.com; media@veritivcorp.com Web Site: www.veritivcorp.com, pg 1273

Rennert, Cesar, Rennert Translation Group, 12 E 41 St, New York, NY 10017 Tel: 212-867-8700 E-mail: translations@rennert.com Web Site: rennerttranslations.com, pg 1404

Rennie, Kathryn, Penguin Random House Canada, a Penguin Random House company, 320 Front St W, Suite 1400, Toronto, ON M5V 3B6, Canada Tel: 416-364-4449 Toll Free Tel: 888-523-9292 (cust serv) Fax: 416-598-7764 E-mail: customerservicescanada@penguinrandomhouse.com; publicitycanada@penguinrandomhouse.com; rightscanada@penguinrandomhouse.com Web Site: www.penguinrandomhouse.ca, pg 1299

Reno, R R, First Things: A Journal of Religion, Culture & Public Life, 9 E 40 St, 10th fl, New York, NY 10016 Tel: 212-627-1985 Fax: 212-627-2184 E-mail: ft@firstthings.com Web Site: www.firstthings.com, pg 1131

Renzi, Jeff, Unisys Corp, 801 Lakeview Dr, Suite 100, Blue Bell, PA 19422 Tel: 215-274-2742 Web Site: www.unisys.com, pg 1378

Resk, Patrick, Porter Novelli, 195 Broadway, 17th fl, New York, NY 10007 Tel: 212-601-8000 Web Site: www.porternovelli.com, pg 1112

Resnik, Josh, CQ Roll Call, 1201 Pennsylvania Ave NW, Suite 600, Washington, DC 20004 Tel: 202-650-6500; 202-650-6511 (subns); 202-650-6621 (cust serv) Toll Free Tel: 800-432-2250; 800-678-8511 (subns) E-mail: customerservice@cqrollcall.com Web Site: cqrollcall.com; www.rollcall.com, pg 1190

Retta, Edward, Cross Culture Communications, PO Box 141263, Dallas, TX 75214 Tel: 214-394-3000 E-mail: info@crossculturecommunications.com Web Site: crossculturecommunications.com, pg 1400

Retta, Marilyn, Cross Culture Communications, PO Box 141263, Dallas, TX 75214 Tel: 214-394-3000 E-mail: info@crossculturecommunications.com Web Site: crossculturecommunications.com, pg 1400

Reyes, Crystal, Texas Bookman, 2700 Lone Star Dr, Dallas, TX 75212 Tel: 214-678-6680 Toll Free Tel: 800-566-2665 Fax: 214-678-6699 E-mail: orders@texasbookman.com Web Site: www.texasbookman.com, pg 1322

Reynolds, Christine, Reynolds Design & Management, 52 Piedmont Ave, Waltham, MA 02451-3015 Tel: 781-893-7464 E-mail: rdandm@comcast.net, pg 1417

Rhodes, Amy, Market Partners International Inc, 232 Madison Ave, Suite 1400, New York, NY 10016 Tel: 212-447-0855 Fax: 212-447-0785 E-mail: info@marketpartnersinternational.com Web Site: www.marketpartnersinternational.com, pg 1349

Rhodes, Amy, Publishing Trends, 232 Madison Ave, Suite 1400, New York, NY 10016 Tel: 212-447-0855 Fax: 212-447-0785 E-mail: info@publishingtrends.com Web Site: www.marketpartnersinternational.com; www.publishingtrends.com, pg 1136

Rhodes, Brooke, Bamboo Ink, 807 Oliver Hill Way, Richmond, VA 23219 Tel: 804-230-4515 E-mail: info@bambooink.com Web Site: www.bambooink.com, pg 1248

Rhodes, Robert, Bamboo Ink, 807 Oliver Hill Way, Richmond, VA 23219 Tel: 804-230-4515 E-mail: info@bambooink.com Web Site: www.bambooink.com, pg 1248

Ribas, Maria, Stonesong, 270 W 39 St, Suite 201, New York, NY 10018 Tel: 212-929-4600 E-mail: editors@stonesong.com Web Site: www.stonesong.com, pg 1357

Ribolow, Adele, Ribolow Associates Inc, 1350 Avenue of the Americas, 2nd fl, New York, NY 10019 Tel: 212-575-2700 Fax: 646-496-9122 E-mail: ribolowstaffingservices@gmail.com Web Site: www.ribolow.com, pg 1382

Riccio, Dan, Apple Inc, One Apple Park Way, Cupertino, CA 95014 Tel: 408-996-1010 Web Site: www.apple.com, pg 1364

Rice, Kevin, Historic Films LLC, 211 Third St, Greenport, NY 11944 Tel: 631-477-9700 Toll Free Tel: 800-249-1940 Fax: 631-477-9800 E-mail: info@historicfilms.com Web Site: www.historicfilms.com, pg 1429

Rice, Taylor, Penguin Random House Canada, a Penguin Random House company, 320 Front St W, Suite 1400, Toronto, ON M5V 3B6, Canada Tel: 416-364-4449 Toll Free Tel: 888-523-9292 (cust serv) Fax: 416-598-7764 E-mail: customerservicescanada@penguinrandomhouse.com; publicitycanada@penguinrandomhouse.com; rightscanada@penguinrandomhouse.com Web Site: www.penguinrandomhouse.ca, pg 1299

Rich, B Ruby, Film Quarterly, Journals & Digital Publishing, 155 Grand Ave, Suite 400, Oakland, CA 94612-3758 E-mail: info@filmquarterly.org; customerservice@ucpress.edu Web Site: www.filmquarterly.org; online.ucpress.edu/fq, pg 1131

Rich, Hallie, Library Journal, 123 William St, Suite 802, New York, NY 10038 Tel: 646-380-0700 Toll Free Tel: 800-588-1030 Fax: 646-380-0756 E-mail: ljinfo@mediasourceinc.com Web Site: www.libraryjournal.com, pg 1134

Richard, Brent, Penguin Random House Canada, a Penguin Random House company, 320 Front St W, Suite 1400, Toronto, ON M5V 3B6, Canada Tel: 416-364-4449 Toll Free Tel: 888-523-9292 (cust serv) Fax: 416-598-7764 E-mail: customerservicescanada@penguinrandomhouse.com; publicitycanada@penguinrandomhouse.com; rightscanada@penguinrandomhouse.com Web Site: www.penguinrandomhouse.ca, pg 1299

Richard, Traci, Hassett Express, 17W775 Butterfield Rd, Suite 109, Oakbrook Terrace, IL 60181 Tel: 630-530-6515 Fax: 630-530-6538 Web Site: www.hassettexpress.com, pg 1334

Richards, Bill, Lake Book Manufacturing Inc, 2085 N Cornell Ave, Melrose Park, IL 60160 Tel: 708-345-7000 E-mail: info@lakebook.com Web Site: www.lakebook.com, pg 1212, 1227, 1255, 1268, 1281

Richards, Jennifer, Over the River Public Relations LLC, 116 Gladwin Ave, Leonia, NJ 07605 Tel: 201-503-1321 E-mail: info@otrpr.com Web Site: www.otrpr.com, pg 1111

Richards, Matthew J "MJ", Getty Images Inc, 605 Fifth Ave S, Suite 400, Seattle, WA 98104 Tel: 206-925-5000 Toll Free Tel: 800-IMAGERY (462-4379); 888-888-5889 Web Site: www.gettyimages.com; www.gettyimages.com/customer-support; engage.gettyimages.com/media-inquiries, pg 1369, 1428

Richardson, Scott, GLS Companies, 1280 Energy Park Dr, St Paul, MN 55108-5106 Tel: 651-644-3000 Toll Free Tel: 800-655-9405 Web Site: www.glsmn.com, pg 1226, 1254

Richardson, Seth, Journal of Cuneiform Studies (JCS), James F Strange Ctr, 209 Commerce St, Alexandria, VA 22314 Tel: 703-789-9229; 703-789-9230 (pubns) E-mail: info@asor.org; publications@asor.org Web Site: www.asor.org, pg 1133

Richardson, Tashina, Independent Publishers Group (IPG), 814 N Franklin St, Chicago, IL 60610 Tel: 312-337-0747 Toll Free Tel: 800-888-4741 (orders) Fax: 312-337-5985 E-mail: frontdesk@ipgbook.com; orders@ipgbook.com Web Site: www.ipgbook.com, pg 1292, 1328

Richman, Aaron J, A Good Thing Inc, 333 E 79 St, New York, NY 10075 Tel: 212-687-8155 Web Site: www.facebook.com/agoodthinginc, pg 1411

Richter, Barbara Basbanes, Literary Features Syndicate, 88 Briarcliff Rd, Larchmont, NY 10538 Tel: 914-834-7480, pg 1127

Rickerby, Joan, Promotional Book Co, 12 Cranfield Rd, No 100, Toronto, ON M4B 3G8, Canada Tel: 416-759-2226 Fax: 416-759-2150, pg 1320

Riddle, Michael, Evolution Computing Inc, 4228 E Andrea Dr, Cave Creek, AZ 85331 Tel: 602-299-1949 E-mail: support@fastcad.com; order_request@fastcad.com Web Site: www.fastcad.com, pg 1368

Ridpath, Angela, MCH Strategic Data, 601 E Marshall St, Sweet Springs, MO 65351 Toll Free Tel: 800-776-6373 E-mail: sales@mchdata.com Web Site: www.mchdata.com, pg 1120

Riemenschneider, Jennifer, Sheridan MI, 613 E Industrial Dr, Chelsea, MI 48118 Tel: 734-475-9145 Web Site: www.sheridan.com, pg 1214, 1259, 1271

Riez, Krisztina, Penguin Random House Canada, a Penguin Random House company, 320 Front St W, Suite 1400, Toronto, ON M5V 3B6, Canada Tel: 416-364-4449 Toll Free Tel: 888-523-9292 (cust serv) Fax: 416-598-7764 E-mail: customerservicescanada@penguinrandomhouse.com; publicitycanada@penguinrandomhouse.com; rightscanada@penguinrandomhouse.com Web Site: www.penguinrandomhouse.ca, pg 1299

Rifenberick, Adam, Press Box Publicity, 3920 Duncan Dr, Boca Raton, FL 33434 Tel: 912-658-7860 E-mail: sportspr@smithpublicity.com Web Site: pressboxpublicity-smithpublicity.com, pg 1112

Rifkind, Marion, Universe Technical Translation Inc, 9225 Katy Fwy, Suite 400, Houston, TX 77024 Tel: 713-827-8800 Fax: 713-464-5511 E-mail: universe@universe.us Web Site: www.universetranslation.com, pg 1405

Rigelman, Tony, Twin Rivers Paper Co, 82 Bridge Ave, Madawaska, ME 04756 Tel: 207-728-3321 Toll Free Tel: 800-920-9988 Fax: 207-728-8701 E-mail: info@twinriverspaper.com Web Site: www.twinriverspaper.com, pg 1273

Riggins, Kathy, ColorPage, 81 Ten Broeck Ave, Kingston, NY 12401 Tel: 845-331-7581 Toll Free Tel: 800-836-7581 Fax: 845-331-1571 E-mail: sales@colorpageonline.com Web Site: www.colorpageonline.com, pg 1209, 1223, 1250, 1266

Riley, Estella, Walker360, 2501 Fifth Ave E, Montgomery, AL 36107 Tel: 334-832-4975 E-mail: info@walker360.com Web Site: walker360.com, pg 1214, 1262

Rishel, Grace, POD Print, 2012 E Northern St, Wichita, KS 67216 *Tel:* 316-522-5599 *Toll Free Tel:* 800-767-6066 *E-mail:* info@podprint.com *Web Site:* www.podprint.com, pg 1213, 1229, 1258

Rishel, Jim, POD Print, 2012 E Northern St, Wichita, KS 67216 *Tel:* 316-522-5599 *Toll Free Tel:* 800-767-6066 *E-mail:* info@podprint.com *Web Site:* www.podprint.com, pg 1213, 1229, 1258

Ritacco, Robby, Publishers Weekly, 49 W 23 St, 9th fl, New York, NY 10010 *Tel:* 212-377-5500 *Fax:* 212-377-2733 *Web Site:* www.publishersweekly.com, pg 1136

Ritchie, Ken, Finch Paper LLC, One Glen St, Glens Falls, NY 12801 *Tel:* 518-793-2541 *Toll Free Tel:* 800-833-9983 *Fax:* 518-743-9656 *E-mail:* info@finchpaper.com *Web Site:* www.finchpaper.com, pg 1267

Rithcreek, Chris, King Features Syndicate, 300 W 57 St, New York, NY 10019-5238 *Tel:* 212-969-7550 *Toll Free Tel:* 800-526-5464 *Web Site:* www.kingfeatures.com, pg 1190

Rittman, Carliann, Publishers Weekly, 49 W 23 St, 9th fl, New York, NY 10010 *Tel:* 212-377-5500 *Fax:* 212-377-2733 *Web Site:* www.publishersweekly.com, pg 1136

Rittwage, William, California Offset Printers Inc, 620 W Elk Ave, Glendale, CA 91204 *Tel:* 818-291-1100 *Toll Free Tel:* 800-280-6446 *Fax:* 818-291-1192 *E-mail:* info@copcomms.com *Web Site:* www.copprints.com, pg 1250

Ritz, Holly, The Penworthy Company LLC, 219 N Milwaukee St, 4th fl, Milwaukee, WI 53202 *Tel:* 414-287-4600 *Toll Free Tel:* 800-262-2665 *Fax:* 414-287-4602 *E-mail:* info@penworthy.com *Web Site:* www.penworthy.com, pg 1320, 1325

Riva, Peter, International Transactions Inc, 28 Alope Way, Gila, NM 88038 *Tel:* 845-373-9696 *Fax:* 480-393-5162 *E-mail:* info@internationaltransactions.us *Web Site:* www.intltrans.com, pg 1348

Rivas, Tracy, Omeda, 4 Overlook Point, Suite A2SE, Lincolnshire, IL 60069 *Tel:* 847-564-8900 *E-mail:* getstarted@omeda.com *Web Site:* www.omeda.com, pg 1334

Riven, Judith, Judith Riven Literary Agent LLC, 250 W 16 St, Suite 4F, New York, NY 10011, pg 1350

Rivera, Kim M, HP Inc, 1501 Paige Mill Rd, Palo Alto, CA 94304-1112 *Tel:* 650-857-1501 *Toll Free Tel:* 800-282-6672 *Web Site:* www.hp.com, pg 1370

Rivers, Alena, Association for Library Service to Children (ALSC), 225 N Michigan Ave, Suite 1300, Chicago, IL 60601 *Tel:* 312-280-2163 *Toll Free Tel:* 800-545-2433 *Fax:* 312-280-5271 *E-mail:* alsc@ala.org *Web Site:* www.ala.org/alsc, pg 1145

Rizzo, Geoff, Southern Territory Associates, 4508 64 St, Lubbock, TX 79414 *E-mail:* sta77@suddenlink.net *Web Site:* www.southernterritory.com, pg 1302

Roark, Micah, OmniUpdate Inc, 1320 Flynn Rd, Suite 100, Camarillo, CA 93012 *Tel:* 805-484-9400 *Toll Free Tel:* 800-362-2605 *E-mail:* sales@omniupdate.com *Web Site:* omniupdate.com, pg 1374

Roback, Diane, Publishers Weekly, 49 W 23 St, 9th fl, New York, NY 10010 *Tel:* 212-377-5500 *Fax:* 212-377-2733 *Web Site:* www.publishersweekly.com, pg 1136

Robbins, Dave, Ecological Fibers Inc, 40 Pioneer Dr, Lunenburg, MA 01462 *Tel:* 978-537-0003 *Fax:* 978-537-2238 *E-mail:* info@ecofibers.com *Web Site:* www.ecofibers.com, pg 1210, 1297

Robbins, Harold, Choice Associates, 501 Fifth Ave, Suite 1601, New York, NY 10017 *Tel:* 212-679-2434 *Fax:* 212-213-0984 *E-mail:* info@choicepersonnelinc.com *Web Site:* www.choicepersonnelinc.com, pg 1381

Robbins, Kelley A, Callaloo, 2715 N Charles St, Baltimore, MD 21218-4363 *Tel:* 410-516-6987 (journal orders outside US & CN) *Toll Free Tel:* 800-548-1784 (journal orders) *Fax:* 410-578-2865 (journal orders) *E-mail:* jrnlcirc@jh.edu (journal orders) *Web Site:* www.press.jhu.edu/journals/callaloo, pg 1130

Roberts, Bill, The Ohio Blow Pipe Co, 446 E 131 St, Cleveland, OH 44108-1684 *Tel:* 216-681-7379 *Fax:* 216-681-7713 *E-mail:* sales@obpairsystems.com *Web Site:* www.obpairsystems.com, pg 1282

Roberts, Bob, ClassicStock.com/Robertstock.com, 4203 Locust St, Philadelphia, PA 19104 *Tel:* 215-386-6300 *Toll Free Tel:* 800-786-6300 *Toll Free Fax:* 800-786-1920 *E-mail:* sales@classicstock.com; info@classicstock.com; info@robertstock.com *Web Site:* www.classicstock.com; www.robertstock.com, pg 1427

Roberts, Dr Catherine A, American Mathematical Society (AMS), 201 Charles St, Providence, RI 02904-2213 *Tel:* 401-455-4000 *Toll Free Tel:* 800-321-4267 *Fax:* 401-331-3842; 401-455-4046 (cust serv) *E-mail:* cust-serv@ams.org; ams@ams.org *Web Site:* www.ams.org, pg 1207, 1221, 1247, 1277

Roberts, Curtis, fd2s, 14205 N Motac Express, Suite 400F, Austin, TX 78728 *Tel:* 512-476-7733 *Web Site:* www.fd2s.com, pg 1414

Roberts, Gillian, CQ Roll Call, 1201 Pennsylvania Ave NW, Suite 600, Washington, DC 20004 *Tel:* 202-650-6500; 202-650-6511 (subns); 202-650-6621 (cust serv) *Toll Free Tel:* 800-432-2250; 800-678-8511 (subns) *E-mail:* customerservice@cqrollcall.com *Web Site:* cqrollcall.com; www.rollcall.com, pg 1190

Roberts, Margaret J, Richard Owen Roberts, Booksellers & Publishers, 139 N Washington St, Wheaton, IL 60189 *Tel:* 630-752-4122 *E-mail:* sales@rorbooks.com *Web Site:* www.rorbooks.com, pg 1321

Roberts, Martin, Linguistic Systems Inc (LSI), 260 Franklin St, Suite 230, Boston, MA 02110 *Tel:* 617-528-7400 *E-mail:* clientservice@linguist.com *Web Site:* www.linguist.com, pg 1228, 1372, 1402, 1415

Roberts, Richard Owen, Richard Owen Roberts, Booksellers & Publishers, 139 N Washington St, Wheaton, IL 60189 *Tel:* 630-752-4122 *E-mail:* sales@rorbooks.com *Web Site:* www.rorbooks.com, pg 1321

Robertson, Brett, Management Communication Quarterly (MCQ), 2455 Teller Rd, Thousand Oaks, CA 91320 *Toll Free Tel:* 800-818-7243 *Toll Free Fax:* 800-583-2665 *E-mail:* journals@sagepub.com *Web Site:* www.sagepub.com, pg 1134

Robertson, Nicholle, BookComp Inc, 6124 Belmont Ave NE, Belmont, MI 49306 *Tel:* 616-774-9700 *E-mail:* production@bookcomp.com *Web Site:* www.bookcomp.com, pg 1223

Robinson, Catherine, Ingram Content Group LLC, One Ingram Blvd, La Vergne, TN 37086-1986 *Tel:* 615-793-5000 *Toll Free Tel:* 800-937-8000 (retailers); 800-937-5300 (ext 1, libs) *E-mail:* customerservice@ingramcontent.com *Web Site:* www.ingramcontent.com, pg 1294, 1307

Robinson, Jennifer, eFulfillment Service Inc, 807 Airport Access Rd, Traverse City, MI 49686 *Tel:* 231-276-5057 *Toll Free Tel:* 866-922-6783 *E-mail:* sales@efulfillmentservice.com *Web Site:* www.efulfillmentservice.com, pg 1333

Robinson, Joe, Lake Group Media Inc, One Byram Brook Place, Armonk, NY 10504 *Tel:* 914-925-2400 *Fax:* 914-925-2499 *Web Site:* www.lakegroupmedia.com, pg 1120

Robinson, John, GHP, 475 Heffernan Dr, West Haven, CT 06516 *Tel:* 203-479-7500 *Fax:* 203-479-7575 *Web Site:* www.ghpmedia.com, pg 1226, 1253

Robitaille, Lyne, Les Messageries ADP, 2315, rue de la Province, Longueuil, QC J4G 1G4, Canada *Tel:* 450-640-1234 (commercial); 450-640-1237 (sales) *Toll Free Tel:* 800-771-3022 (commercial); 866-874-1237 (sales); 450-640-1251 (commercial); 450-674-6237 (sales) *Toll Free Fax:* 800-603-0433 (commercial); 866-874-6237 (sales) *E-mail:* adpcommandes@messageries-adp.com *Web Site:* www.messageries-adp.com, pg 1285

Robyn, Chris, China Books, 360 Swift Ave, Suite 48, South San Francisco, CA 94080 *Fax:* 650-872-7808 *E-mail:* editor.sinomedia@gmail.com, pg 1313, 1327

Roche, Bonnie, Crain Communications Inc, 1155 Gratiot Ave, Detroit, MI 48207-2732 *Tel:* 313-446-6000 *Fax:* 313-446-0383 *E-mail:* info@crain.com *Web Site:* crain.com, pg 1190

Rocheleau, Kathleen, A to Z Indexing & Bibliographical Services, 20 St James Rd, Shrewsbury, MA 01545 *Tel:* 508-842-5602 *Web Site:* sites.google.com/site/atozindexing, pg 1221

Rochman, Paul, Color Graphic Press Inc, 42 Main St, Nyack, NY 10960 *Tel:* 845-535-3444 *Fax:* 845-535-3446 *E-mail:* info@cgpny.com *Web Site:* www.cgpny.com, pg 1250

Rock, Britta Meyer, Claris International Inc, 5201 Patrick Henry Dr, Santa Clara, CA 95054 *Tel:* 408-727-8227 (sales & cust support) *Toll Free Tel:* 800-725-2747 (sales); 800-325-2747 (cust support) *Fax:* 408-987-7447 *E-mail:* claris_sales@claris.com *Web Site:* www.claris.com, pg 1366

Rodney, Lori, Shutterstock Inc, Empire State Bldg, 350 Fifth Ave, 20th fl, New York, NY 10118 *E-mail:* support@shutterstock.com; press@shutterstock.com *Web Site:* www.shutterstock.com, pg 1430

Rodriguez, Bianca, Independent Publishers Group (IPG), 814 N Franklin St, Chicago, IL 60610 *Tel:* 312-337-0747 *Toll Free Tel:* 800-888-4741 (orders) *Fax:* 312-337-5985 *E-mail:* frontdesk@ipgbook.com; orders@ipgbook.com *Web Site:* www.ipgbook.com, pg 1292, 1328

Rodriguez, Diego, Intuit Inc, 2700 Coast Ave, Mountain View, CA 94043 *Tel:* 650-944-6000 *Toll Free Tel:* 800-446-8848 *E-mail:* investor_relations@intuit.com *Web Site:* www.intuit.com, pg 1371

Rodriguez, Max, QBR The Black Book Review, 591 Warburton Ave, Unit 170, Hastings-on-Hudson, NY 10706 *Tel:* 914-231-6778 *Web Site:* www.qbr.com, pg 1136

Roeske, Keith, alfa CTP Systems Inc, 2503 Spring Ridge Dr, Unit D, Spring Grove, IL 60081 *Tel:* 815-474-7634 *E-mail:* info@alfactp.com *Web Site:* www.alfactp.com, pg 1364

Roessner, Jeff, Suspension Feeder, 631 E Washington St, St Henry, OH 45883 *Tel:* 419-763-1377 *Toll Free Fax:* 888-210-9654 *Web Site:* www.suspensionfeeder.com, pg 1283

Rogalski, Margaret, Hilsinger-Mendelson West Inc, 115 N Kings Rd, Los Angeles, CA 90048 *Tel:* 323-931-5335 (text only) *E-mail:* hmiwest@aol.com *Web Site:* www.hilsingermendelson.com, pg 1109

Rogers, Fran, Alliance Storage Technologies Inc (ASTI), 10045 Federal Dr, Colorado Springs, CO 80908 *Tel:* 719-593-7900 *Toll Free Tel:* 888-567-6332 *Fax:* 719-598-3472 *E-mail:* sales@astiusa.com; info@astiusa.com *Web Site:* www.alliancestoragetechnologies.com, pg 1364

Rogers, Dr Montra L, Social Studies School Service, 10200 Jefferson Blvd, PO Box 802, Culver City, CA 90232 *Tel:* 310-839-2436 *Toll Free Tel:* 800-421-4246 (US & CN) *Fax:* 310-839-2249 *Toll Free Fax:* 800-944-5432 *E-mail:* access@socialstudies.com; customerservice@socialstudies.com *Web Site:* www.socialstudies.com, pg 1302, 1321

Rogers, Stephanie, Stephanie Rogers & Associates, 8737 Carlitas Joy Ct, Las Vegas, NV 89117 *Tel:* 702-255-9999 *E-mail:* sjrlion@aol.com; write2wow@aol.com *Web Site:* www.write2wow.com, pg 1350

Rogers, Sydney, Idea Architects, 523 Swift St, Santa Cruz, CA 95060 *Tel:* 831-465-9565 *Web Site:* www.ideaarchitects.com, pg 1347

Rogers-Naff, Shirley, Osa's Ark Museum Shop, 111 N Lincoln Ave, Chanute, KS 66720 *Tel:* 620-431-2730 *Fax:* 620-431-2730 *E-mail:* osajohns@safarimuseum.com; osasark@yahoo.com *Web Site:* www.safarimuseum.com, pg 1320

Roks, Edwin, Teledyne DALSA, 605 McMurray Rd, Waterloo, ON N2V 2E9, Canada *Tel:* 519-886-6000 *Toll Free Tel:* 800-361-4914 *Web Site:* www.teledynedalsa.com, pg 1377

Roland, David, Ingram Content Group LLC, One Ingram Blvd, La Vergne, TN 37086-1986 *Tel:* 615-793-5000 *Toll Free Tel:* 800-937-8000 (retailers); 800-937-5300 (ext 1, libs) *E-mail:* customerservice@ingramcontent.com *Web Site:* www.ingramcontent.com, pg 1294, 1316

Romano, Jen, Casemate | academic, 1950 Lawrence Rd, Havertown, PA 19083 *Tel:* 610-853-9131 *Fax:* 610-853-9146 *E-mail:* info@casemateacademic.com *Web Site:* www.oxbowbooks.com/dbbc, pg 1287

Rosado, Adrienne, Stonesong, 270 W 39 St, Suite 201, New York, NY 10018 *Tel:* 212-929-4600 *E-mail:* editors@stonesong.com *Web Site:* www.stonesong.com, pg 1357

Rosales, Dulce, Penguin Random House Canada, a Penguin Random House company, 320 Front St W, Suite 1400, Toronto, ON M5V 3B6, Canada *Tel:* 416-364-4449 *Toll Free Tel:* 888-523-9292 (cust serv) *Fax:* 416-598-7764 *E-mail:* customerservicescanada@penguinrandomhouse.com; publicitycanada@penguinrandomhouse.com; rightscanada@penguinrandomhouse.com *Web Site:* www.penguinrandomhouse.ca, pg 1299

Rosario, Jason, Stephen Gould Corp, 35 S Jefferson Rd, Whippany, NJ 07981 *Tel:* 973-428-1500; 973-428-1510 *E-mail:* info@stephengould.com *Web Site:* www.stephengould.com, pg 1104, 1337

Rosato, Steve, OverDrive Inc, One OverDrive Way, Cleveland, OH 44125 *Tel:* 216-573-6886 *Fax:* 216-573-6888 *E-mail:* info@overdrive.com *Web Site:* www.overdrive.com, pg 1298

Rose, David, Sakurai USA Inc, 1700 N Basswood Rd, Schaumburg, IL 60173 *Tel:* 847-490-9400 *Toll Free Tel:* 800-458-4720 *Fax:* 847-490-4200 *E-mail:* inquiry@sakurai.com *Web Site:* www.sakurai.com, pg 1282

Rosean, Grace, Booklist, 225 N Michigan Ave, Suite 1300, Chicago, IL 60601 *Tel:* 312-944-6780 *Toll Free Tel:* 800-545-2433 *Fax:* 312-440-9374 *E-mail:* info@booklistonline.com; ala@ala.org *Web Site:* www.booklistonline.com; www.ala.org, pg 1130

Roseberry, Dawn, Chesapeake & Hudson Inc, 27 Jacks Shop Rd, Rochelle, VA 22738 *Tel:* 301-834-7170 *Toll Free Tel:* 800-231-4469 *E-mail:* office@cheshud.com *Web Site:* www.cheshudinc.com, pg 1289

Roseman, Donald, Ingram Content Group LLC, One Ingram Blvd, La Vergne, TN 37086-1986 *Tel:* 615-793-5000 *Toll Free Tel:* 800-937-8000 (retailers); 800-937-5300 (ext 1, libs) *E-mail:* customerservice@ingramcontent.com *Web Site:* www.ingramcontent.com, pg 1294, 1316

Rosen, Jamie, Publicis North America, 1675 Broadway, New York, NY 10009 *Tel:* 212-474-5000 *Web Site:* www.publicisna.com, pg 1112

Rosen, Sherri, Sherri Rosen Publicity Intl NYC, 454 Manhattan Ave, Suite 3-J, New York, NY 10026 *Tel:* 917-699-1284 *E-mail:* sherri@sherrirosen.com *Web Site:* www.sherrirosen.com, pg 1112, 1350

Rosenbaum, Emily, The Tribune News Service, 160 N Stetson Ave, Chicago, IL 60601 *Tel:* 312-222-4131 *E-mail:* tcanews@trbpub.com *Web Site:* www.mctdirect.com; tribunecontentagency.com/tribune-news-service, pg 1191

Rosenbaum, Nanette, Stephen Gould Corp, 35 S Jefferson Rd, Whippany, NJ 07981 *Tel:* 973-428-1500; 973-428-1510 *E-mail:* info@stephengould.com *Web Site:* www.stephengould.com, pg 1104, 1337

Rosenberg, Roberta, MGP Direct Inc, 17814 Shotley Bridge Place, Olney, MD 20832 *Tel:* 240-755-6976 *Web Site:* www.mgpdirect.com, pg 1349

Rosenberger, Jim, Any Laminating Service, 13214 Crenshaw Blvd, Gardena, CA 90249 *Tel:* 310-464-8885 *Toll Free Tel:* 800-400-3105 *E-mail:* quoterequest@anylam.com *Web Site:* anylam.com, pg 1247

Ross, Ken, Ken Ross Photography, PO Box 4517, Scottsdale, AZ 85261 *Tel:* 602-319-2974 *E-mail:* kenrossaz@yahoo.com *Web Site:* www.kenrossphotography.com, pg 1425

Ross, Maureen, diacriTech Inc, 4 S Market St, 4th fl, Boston, MA 02109 *Tel:* 617-600-3366 *Fax:* 617-848-2938 *Web Site:* www.diacritech.com, pg 1224, 1354, 1413

Ross, Robert C Jr, Xante Corp, 2800 Dauphin St, Suite 100, Mobile, AL 36606 *Tel:* 251-473-6502; 251-473-4920 (tech support) *Fax:* 251-473-6503 *Web Site:* www.xante.com, pg 1378

Ross, Thomas W, Ross Gage Inc, 8502 Brookville Rd, Indianapolis, IN 46239 *Tel:* 317-283-2323 *Toll Free Tel:* 800-799-2323 *Fax:* 317-931-2108 *E-mail:* info@rossgage.com *Web Site:* www.rossgage.com, pg 1230, 1259

Rosson, Mark, O'Neil Digital Solutions LLC, 12655 Beatrice St, Los Angeles, CA 90066 *Tel:* 310-448-6400 *E-mail:* sales@oneildata.com *Web Site:* www.oneildata.com, pg 1229, 1257, 1270, 1282

Roster, Leslie, Girol Books Inc, PO Box 5473, LCD Merivale, Ottawa, ON K2C 3M1, Canada *Tel:* 613-233-9044 *E-mail:* info@girol.com *Web Site:* www.girol.com, pg 1292, 1316, 1328

Roster, Peter, Girol Books Inc, PO Box 5473, LCD Merivale, Ottawa, ON K2C 3M1, Canada *Tel:* 613-233-9044 *E-mail:* info@girol.com *Web Site:* www.girol.com, pg 1292, 1316, 1328

Roswell, Michael, Roswell Bookbinding, 2614 N 29 Ave, Phoenix, AZ 85009 *Tel:* 602-272-9338 *Toll Free Tel:* 888-803-8883 *Fax:* 602-272-9786 *Web Site:* www.roswellbookbinding.com, pg 1259, 1326

Roth, Charles A, Roth Advertising Inc, PO Box 96, Sea Cliff, NY 11579 *Tel:* 516-674-8603 *Fax:* 516-368-3885 *Web Site:* www.rothadvertising.com, pg 1100

Roth, Daniel J, Roth Advertising Inc, PO Box 96, Sea Cliff, NY 11579 *Tel:* 516-674-8603 *Fax:* 516-368-3885 *Web Site:* www.rothadvertising.com, pg 1100

Roth, Robert, Spiral Binding LLC, One Maltese Dr, Totowa, NJ 07511 *Tel:* 973-256-0666 *Toll Free Tel:* 800-631-3572 *Fax:* 973-256-5981 *E-mail:* customerservice@spiralbinding.com; international@spiralbinding.com (outside US) *Web Site:* spiralbinding.com, pg 1260

Roth, Steve, Motorbooks, 100 Cummings Ctr, Suite 265D, Beverly, MA 01915 *Tel:* 978-282-9590 *Toll Free Tel:* 800-759-0190 (orders) *Web Site:* www.quartoknows.com/motorbooks, pg 1319, 1329

Roth, Tom, Fluke Networks, 6920 Seaway Blvd, Everett, WA 98203 *Tel:* 425-446-5500; 425-446-4519 (sales & support) *Toll Free Tel:* 800-283-5853 *E-mail:* info@flukenetworks.com *Web Site:* www.flukenetworks.com, pg 1369

Rotterman, Jacqueline, R J Promotions & Advertising, 120 Holton Ave S, Hamilton, ON L8M 2L5, Canada *Tel:* 905-548-0389 *E-mail:* rjpromo@cogeco.ca, pg 1350

Roukas, Marie, Warehouse Books Inc, 1006 Ballantine Blvd, Norfolk, VA 23504 *Tel:* 757-627-4160 *E-mail:* sales@warehousebooksinc.com *Web Site:* www.warehousebooksinc.com, pg 1323

Roullet, Alain, Long's Roullet Bookbinders Inc, 2800 Monticello Ave, Norfolk, VA 23504 *Tel:* 757-623-4244 *Fax:* 757-627-1404 *E-mail:* bindlrbi@gmail.com *Web Site:* longs-roullet.com, pg 1256, 1325

Roullet, Eileen, Long's Roullet Bookbinders Inc, 2800 Monticello Ave, Norfolk, VA 23504 *Tel:* 757-623-4244 *Fax:* 757-627-1404 *E-mail:* bindlrbi@gmail.com *Web Site:* longs-roullet.com, pg 1256, 1325

Roush, Sue, Andrews McMeel Syndication, 1130 Walnut St, Kansas City, MO 64106-2109 *Tel:* 816-581-7300 *Toll Free Tel:* 800-255-6734 *Web Site:* syndication.andrewsmcmeel.com, pg 1189, 1411

Rousseau, Stephane, Les Editions Themis, Faculte de droit, Universite de Montreal, CP 6128, Succursale Centreville, Montreal, QC H3C 3J7, Canada *Tel:* 514-343-6627 *Fax:* 514-343-6779 *E-mail:* info@editionsthemis.com *Web Site:* ssl.editionsthemis.com, pg 1315

Roverano, Addison, Publishing Data Management Inc, 39 Broadway, 28th fl, New York, NY 10006 *Tel:* 212-673-3210 *Fax:* 212-673-3390 *E-mail:* info@pubdata.com *Web Site:* www.pubdata.com, pg 1230, 1258, 1375

Rowe, Martin, LanternMedia, 128 Second Place, Garden Suite, Brooklyn, NY 11231 *Tel:* 212-414-2275 *Web Site:* www.lanternmedia.net, pg 1371

Rowe-Richardson, Joshleigh, Independent Publishers Group (IPG), 814 N Franklin St, Chicago, IL 60610 *Tel:* 312-337-0747 *Toll Free Tel:* 800-888-4741 (orders) *Fax:* 312-337-5985 *E-mail:* frontdesk@ipgbook.com; orders@ipgbook.com *Web Site:* www.ipgbook.com, pg 1292, 1328

Rowell, Charles Henry, Callaloo, 2715 N Charles St, Baltimore, MD 21218-4363 *Tel:* 410-516-6987 (journal orders outside US & CN) *Toll Free Tel:* 800-548-1784 (journal orders) *Fax:* 410-578-2865 (journal orders) *E-mail:* jrnlcirc@jh.edu (journal orders) *Web Site:* www.press.jhu.edu/journals/callaloo, pg 1130

Rowland, Catherine Zaller, Copyright Clearance Center Inc (CCC), 222 Rosewood Dr, Danvers, MA 01923 *Tel:* 978-750-8400 *Fax:* 978-646-2600 (cust serv) *E-mail:* info@copyright.com *Web Site:* www.copyright.com, pg 1345

Royal, Kathy, NAPCO Inc, 120 Trojan Ave, Sparta, NC 28675 *Tel:* 336-372-5228 *Toll Free Tel:* 800-854-8621 *Fax:* 336-372-8602 *E-mail:* info@napcousa.com *Web Site:* www.napcousa.com, pg 1257

Ruback, Martin S, East-West Health Arts, 45 Academy Circle, Oakland, NJ 07436-0945 *Tel:* 201-337-8787, pg 1314

Rubel, David, Agincourt Press, 25 Main St, Chatham, NY 12037 *Tel:* 518-392-2898 *E-mail:* aginpress@aol.com, pg 1353

Rubin, Jeff, Southern Tier News Company, Inc, 353 Upper Oakwood Ave, Elmira Heights, NY 14903 *Tel:* 607-734-7108 *Toll Free Tel:* 888-287-4786 *Fax:* 607-734-6825 *Web Site:* www.southerntiernews.com, pg 1230

Ruckstuhl, Ann Sung, Unisys Corp, 801 Lakeview Dr, Suite 100, Blue Bell, PA 19422 *Tel:* 215-274-2742 *Web Site:* www.unisys.com, pg 1378

Ruda, Layne, Independent Publishers Group (IPG), 814 N Franklin St, Chicago, IL 60610 *Tel:* 312-337-0747 *Toll Free Tel:* 800-888-4741 (orders) *Fax:* 312-337-5985 *E-mail:* frontdesk@ipgbook.com; orders@ipgbook.com *Web Site:* www.ipgbook.com, pg 1292

Rudat, Petra, Transimpex Translators, Interpreters, Editors, Consultants Inc, 2300 Main St, 9th fl, Kansas City, MO 64108 *Tel:* 816-561-3777 *Fax:* 816-561-5515 *E-mail:* translations@transimpex.com *Web Site:* www.transimpex.com, pg 1405

Ruddick, Heath, PadillaCRT, 1101 W River Pkwy, Suite 400, Minneapolis, MN 55415 *Tel:* 612-455-1700 *Fax:* 612-455-1060 *Web Site:* www.padillacrt.com, pg 1111

Rudman, Michael P, National Learning Corp, 212 Michael Dr, Syosset, NY 11791 *Tel:* 516-921-8888 *Toll Free Tel:* 800-632-8888 *Fax:* 516-921-8743 *E-mail:* info@passbooks.com *Web Site:* www.passbooks.com, pg 1319

Rudolph, Janet A, Mystery Readers Journal, 7155 Marlborough Terr, Berkeley, CA 94705 *Tel:* 510-845-3600 *Web Site:* www.mysteryreaders.org, pg 1134

Ruf, Richard A, Copyright Clearance Center Inc (CCC), 222 Rosewood Dr, Danvers, MA 01923 *Tel:* 978-750-8400 (sales); 978-646-2600 (cust serv) *E-mail:* info@copyright.com *Web Site:* www.copyright.com, pg 1345

Ruppert, Jens, Canvys® Visual Technology Solutions, 40W267 Keslinger Rd, LaFox, IL 60147 *Toll Free Tel:* 888-735-7373 *Fax:* 630-208-2350 *Web Site:* www.canvys.com, pg 1366

Ruppert, Tim, CJK, 3962 Virginia Ave, Cincinnati, OH 45227 *Tel:* 513-271-6035 *Toll Free Tel:* 800-598-7808 *Fax:* 513-271-6082 *E-mail:* info@cjkusa.com *Web Site:* www.cjkusa.com, pg 1250

Rusert, Britt, American Quarterly, 2715 N Charles St, Baltimore, MD 21218-4363 *Tel:* 410-516-6987 (journal orders outside US & CN) *Toll Free Tel:* 800-548-1784 (journal orders) *Fax:* 410-578-2865 (journal orders) *E-mail:* jrnlcirc@jh.edu (journal orders) *Web Site:* www.americanquarterly.org; www.press.jhu.edu/journals/american-quarterly, pg 1129

Russell, David L, The Lion and the Unicorn, 2715 N Charles St, Baltimore, MD 21218-4363 *Tel:* 410-516-6987 (journal orders outside US & CN) *Toll Free Tel:* 800-548-1784 (journal orders) *Fax:* 410-578-2865 (journal orders) *E-mail:* jrnlcirc@jh.edu (journal orders) *Web Site:* www.press.jhu.edu/journals/lion-and-unicorn, pg 1134

Russell, Gary, GEX Inc, 80 Conley's Grove Rd, Derry, NH 03038 *Tel:* 603-870-9292 *Web Site:* www.gexinc.com, pg 1211, 1226, 1355, 1369, 1414

Russo, Elena, Modern Language Notes (MLN), 2715 N Charles St, Baltimore, MD 21218-4363 *Tel:* 410-516-6987 (journal orders outside US & CN) *Toll Free Tel:* 800-548-1784 (journal orders) *Fax:* 410-578-2865 (journal orders) *E-mail:* jrnlcirc@jh.edu (journal orders) *Web Site:* www.press.jhu.edu/journals/mln, pg 1134

Rust, Laura, Scholarly Book Services Inc, 289 Bridgeland Ave, Unit 105, Toronto, ON M6A 1Z6, Canada *Toll Free Tel:* 800-847-9736 *Toll Free Fax:* 800-220-9895 *E-mail:* customerservice@sbookscan.com *Web Site:* www.sbookscan.com, pg 1302

Rutberg, Steve, knk Software LP, 89 Headquarters Plaza N, No 1478, Morristown, NJ 07960 *Tel:* 908-206-4599 *E-mail:* info@knk.com *Web Site:* www.knkpublishingsoftware.com, pg 1348

Rutt, Sheila, RR Donnelley, 35 W Wacker Dr, Chicago, IL 60601 *Toll Free Tel:* 800-742-4455 *Web Site:* www.rrd.com, pg 1210, 1225, 1252, 1266, 1279

Rutt, Sheila, RR Donnelley & Sons Company, 35 W Wacker Dr, Chicago, IL 60601 *Tel:* 312-326-8000 *Toll Free Tel:* 800-742-4455 *Web Site:* www.rrd.com, pg 1333

Ryan, Doug, RR Donnelley, 35 W Wacker Dr, Chicago, IL 60601 *Toll Free Tel:* 800-742-4455 *Web Site:* www.rrd.com, pg 1210, 1225, 1252, 1266, 1279

Ryan, Doug, RR Donnelley & Sons Company, 35 W Wacker Dr, Chicago, IL 60601 *Tel:* 312-326-8000 *Toll Free Tel:* 800-742-4455 *Web Site:* www.rrd.com, pg 1333

Ryan, Doug, RR Donnelley Marketing Solutions, 35 W Wacker Dr, Chicago, IL 60601 *Toll Free Tel:* 800-742-4455 *Web Site:* www.rrd.com/services/marketing, pg 1104

Ryan, Sharon R, International Paper Co, 6400 Poplar Ave, Memphis, TN 38197 *Tel:* 901-419-9000 *Toll Free Tel:* 800-207-4003 *Web Site:* www.internationalpaper.com; facebook.com/internationalpaper; x.com/intlpaperco, pg 1268

Ryan, Shawn, BCC Software Inc, 75 Josons Dr, Rochester, NY 14623-3494 *Toll Free Tel:* 800-453-3130; 800-337-0442 (sales) *E-mail:* marketing@bccsoftware.com *Web Site:* www.bccsoftware.com, pg 1365

Ryoo, Catherine, Penguin Random House Canada, a Penguin Random House company, 320 Front St W, Suite 1400, Toronto, ON M5V 3B6, Canada *Tel:* 416-364-4449 *Toll Free Tel:* 888-523-9292 (cust serv) *Fax:* 416-598-7764 *E-mail:* customerservicescanada@penguinrandomhouse.com; publicitycanada@penguinrandomhouse.com; rightscanada@penguinrandomhouse.com *Web Site:* www.penguinrandomhouse.ca, pg 1299

Sacco, Josephine, Microsearch Corp, 101 Western Ave, Gloucester, MA 01930 *Tel:* 781-231-9991 *Toll Free Tel:* 800-895-0212 *E-mail:* info@microsearch.net *Web Site:* www.microsearchcorporation.net, pg 1373

Sacco, Robert F, The Lexington Press Inc, 15 Meriam St, Lexington, MA 02420 *Tel:* 781-862-8900 *Fax:* 781-861-0375 *Web Site:* www.lexingtonpress.com, pg 1228, 1256

Sadler, Kurt, Dotronix Technology Inc, 2420 Oakgreen Ave N, West Lakeland, MN 55082 *Tel:* 651-633-1742 *Fax:* 651-633-2152 *E-mail:* sales@dotronix.com *Web Site:* dotronix.com, pg 1368

Sagsen-Ercel, Elif, RR Donnelley, 35 W Wacker Dr, Chicago, IL 60601 *Toll Free Tel:* 800-742-4455 *Web Site:* www.rrd.com, pg 1210, 1225, 1252, 1266, 1279

Sagsen-Ercel, Elif, RR Donnelley & Sons Company, 35 W Wacker Dr, Chicago, IL 60601 *Tel:* 312-326-8000 *Toll Free Tel:* 800-742-4455 *Web Site:* www.rrd.com, pg 1333

Saiber, Arielle, Modern Language Notes (MLN), 2715 N Charles St, Baltimore, MD 21218-4363 *Tel:* 410-516-6987 (journal orders outside US & CN) *Toll Free Tel:* 800-548-1784 (journal orders) *Fax:* 410-578-2865 (journal orders) *E-mail:* jrnlcirc@jh.edu (journal orders) *Web Site:* www.press.jhu.edu/journals/mln, pg 1134

Saiko, Joe, Bang Printing Co Inc, 3323 Oak St, Brainerd, MN 56401 *Tel:* 218-829-2877 *Toll Free Tel:* 800-328-0450 *Fax:* 218-829-7145 *E-mail:* info@bangprinting.com *Web Site:* www.bangprinting.com, pg 1208, 1222, 1248, 1265

Sakurai, Ryuta, Sakurai USA Inc, 1700 N Basswood Rd, Schaumburg, IL 60173 *Tel:* 847-490-9400 *Toll Free Tel:* 800-458-4720 *Fax:* 847-490-4200 *E-mail:* inquiry@sakurai.com *Web Site:* www.sakurai.com, pg 1282

Salamone, Gary P, Continental Features/Continental News Service, 501 W Broadway, Plaza A, PMB 265, San Diego, CA 92101 *Tel:* 858-492-8696 *E-mail:* info@continentalnewsservice.com; continentalnewstime@gmail.com *Web Site:* www.continentalnewsservice.com, pg 1189

Salavetz, Judith, Spencer Drate, 119 W 80 St, Suite 1-F, New York, NY 10024-7134 *Tel:* 212-799-0535 *E-mail:* spencerdrate@yahoo.com, pg 1413

Salazar, Benito, Greenleaf Book Group LLC, PO Box 91869, Austin, TX 78709 *Tel:* 512-891-6100 *Fax:* 512-891-6150 *E-mail:* contact@greenleafbookgroup.com; orders@greenleafbookgroup.com; foreignrights@greenleafbookgroup.com; media@greenleafbookgroup.com *Web Site:* greenleafbookgroup.com, pg 1355

Salczer, Blima, Listco Direct Marketing, 1276 46 St, Brooklyn, NY 11219 *Tel:* 718-871-8400 *Fax:* 718-871-7692 *E-mail:* info@listcodirect.com *Web Site:* www.listcodirect.com, pg 1120

Sales, Jerry, Knepper Press Corp, 2251 Sweeney Dr, Clinton, PA 15026 *Tel:* 724-899-4200 *Fax:* 724-899-1331 *Web Site:* www.knepperpress.com, pg 1211, 1227, 1255

Salih, Mohammad, GTxcel Inc, 144 Turnpike Rd, Suite 130, Southborough, MA 01772-2104 *Toll Free Tel:* 800-609-8994 *E-mail:* info@gtxcel.com *Web Site:* www.gtxcel.com, pg 1370

Salik, Aarol, Talas, 330 Morgan Ave, Brooklyn, NY 11211 *Tel:* 212-219-0770 *E-mail:* info@talasonline.com; support@talasonline.com *Web Site:* www.talasonline.com, pg 1272, 1322

Salik, Jillian, Talas, 330 Morgan Ave, Brooklyn, NY 11211 *Tel:* 212-219-0770 *E-mail:* info@talasonline.com; support@talasonline.com *Web Site:* www.talasonline.com, pg 1272, 1322

Salinetti, Suzanne K, The Studley Press Inc, 151 E Housatonic St, Dalton, MA 01226 *Tel:* 413-684-0441 *Toll Free Tel:* 877-684-0441 *Fax:* 413-684-0220 *Web Site:* thestudleypress.com, pg 1260, 1272

Salistean, John C, Houchen Bindery Ltd, 340 First St, Utica, NE 68456 *Tel:* 402-534-2261 *Toll Free Tel:* 800-869-0420 *Fax:* 402-534-2761 *E-mail:* email@houchenbindery.com *Web Site:* www.houchenbindery.com, pg 1325

Salow, Betty, Sheridan Saline, 960 Woodland Dr, Saline, MI 48176 *Tel:* 734-429-5411 *Web Site:* www.sheridan.com, pg 1214, 1260

Salt, Edmund, Whitehots Inc, 205 Industrial Pkwy N, Unit 3, Aurora, ON L4G 4C4, Canada *Tel:* 905-727-9188 *Toll Free Tel:* 888-567-9188 *Fax:* 905-727-8756 *Toll Free Fax:* 888-563-0020 *E-mail:* admin@whitehots.com *Web Site:* www.whitehots.com, pg 1323

Saltz, Donald, Quiz Features, PO Box 42222, Northwest Sta, Washington, DC 20015-0822 *Tel:* 202-966-0025 *Fax:* 202-966-0025, pg 1191

Salyer, Susan B, Veritiv™ Corporation, 1000 Abernathy Rd, Bldg 400, Suite 1700, Atlanta, GA 30328 *Toll Free Tel:* 844-VERITIV (837-4848); 866-714-8303 (packaging cust serv); 866-714-8306 (print cust serv) *E-mail:* contactus@veritivcorp.com; media@veritivcorp.com *Web Site:* www.veritivcorp.com, pg 1273

Sam, Vicki, Electronics for Imaging Inc (EFI), 6750 Dumbarton Circle, Fremont, CA 94555 *Tel:* 650-357-3500 *Toll Free Tel:* 800-568-1917; 800-875-7117 (sales) *Fax:* 650-357-3907 *E-mail:* info@efi.com *Web Site:* www.efi.com, pg 1368

Samejima, Shark, Ricoh Americas Corp, 300 Eagleview Blvd, Exton, PA 19341 *Tel:* 610-296-8000 *Toll Free Tel:* 800-333-2679 (prod support); 800-637-4264 (sales) *Web Site:* www.ricoh-usa.com, pg 1375

Samper, Marjorie, Lectorum Publications Inc, 10 New Maple Ave, Suite 303, Pine Brook, NJ 07058 *Tel:* 201-559-2200 *Toll Free Tel:* 800-345-5946 *E-mail:* lectorum@lectorum.com *Web Site:* www.lectorum.com, pg 1318

Sampson, Brent, Outskirts Press Inc, 10940 S Parker Rd, Suite 515, Parker, CO 80134 *Toll Free Tel:* 888-OP-BOOKS (672-6657) *Toll Free Fax:* 888-208-8601 *E-mail:* info@outskirtspress.com *Web Site:* www.outskirtspress.com, pg 1257, 1374

Sampson, Jeanine, Outskirts Press Inc, 10940 S Parker Rd, Suite 515, Parker, CO 80134 *Toll Free Tel:* 888-OP-BOOKS (672-6657) *Toll Free Fax:* 888-208-8601 *E-mail:* info@outskirtspress.com *Web Site:* www.outskirtspress.com, pg 1257, 1374

Sampson, Lynn, Outskirts Press Inc, 10940 S Parker Rd, Suite 515, Parker, CO 80134 *Toll Free Tel:* 888-OP-BOOKS (672-6657) *Toll Free Fax:* 888-208-8601 *E-mail:* info@outskirtspress.com *Web Site:* www.outskirtspress.com, pg 1257, 1374

Samu, Krisztina, East-West Concepts, PO Box 1435, Kapaa, HI 96746 *Tel:* 808-938-8410 *Fax:* 808-441-8121 *Web Site:* www.eastwestconcepts.com, pg 1400

Samuel, Alicia, Lightning Source LLC, 1246 Heil Quaker Blvd, La Vergne, TN 37086 *Tel:* 615-793-5000 (Ingram) *Toll Free Tel:* 800-378-5508; 800-509-4156 (cust serv) *E-mail:* lsicustomersupport@ingramcontent.com; contentacquisitioninquiries@ingramcontent.com *Web Site:* www.ingramcontent.com/publishers/print, pg 1212

Samuel, Alicia, Lightning Source LLC, 1246 Heil Quaker Blvd, La Vergne, TN 37086 *Tel:* 615-793-5000 (Ingram) *Toll Free Tel:* 800-378-5508; 800-509-4156 (cust serv) *E-mail:* lsicustomersupport@ingramcontent.com *Web Site:* www.ingramcontent.com/publishers/print, pg 1256, 1371

Samuels, Ann C, International Service Co, International Service Bldg, 333 Fourth Ave, Indialantic, FL 32903-4295 *Tel:* 321-724-1443 *Fax:* 321-724-1443, pg 1317, 1325, 1328, 1331

Samuels, Dennis, International Service Co, International Service Bldg, 333 Fourth Ave, Indialantic, FL 32903-4295 *Tel:* 321-724-1443 *Fax:* 321-724-1443, pg 1317, 1325, 1328, 1331

Sander, Brian, Post Bulletin Co LLC, 18 First Ave SE, Rochester, MN 55903 *Tel:* 507-285-7600 *Toll Free Tel:* 800-562-1758 *E-mail:* news@postbulletin.com *Web Site:* www.postbulletin.com, pg 1191

Sandoval, Jorge, Creative Direct Marketing Group Inc (CDMG), 1313 Fourth Ave N, Nashville, TN 37208 *Tel:* 615-814-6633 *Web Site:* www.cdmginc.com, pg 1345

Sands, Rick, Fenway Group, 870 Commonwealth Ave, Boston, MA 02215 *Tel:* 617-226-1900 *Fax:* 617-226-1901 *E-mail:* info@fenwaycommunications.com *Web Site:* www.fenway-group.com, pg 1253

Sank, Michael, Translations.com, 1250 Broadway, 32nd fl, New York, NY 10001 *Tel:* 212-689-1616 *Fax:* 212-504-8057 *E-mail:* newyork@translations.com; info@translations.com *Web Site:* translations.com, pg 1405

Saphire-Bernstein, Evie, Jewish Book Council, 520 Eighth Ave, 4th fl, New York, NY 10018 *Tel:* 212-201-2920 *Fax:* 212-532-4952 *E-mail:* info@jewishbookcouncil.org *Web Site:* www.jewishbookcouncil.org, pg 1146

Saporiti, Nestor, UniNet Imaging Inc, 3232 W El Segundo Blvd, Hawthorne, CA 90250 *Tel:* 424-675-3300 *Fax:* 424-675-3400 *E-mail:* sales@uninetimaging.com *Web Site:* www.uninetimaging.com, pg 1378

Sappenfield, Darrin, Total Printing Systems, 201 S Gregory Dr, Newton, IL 62448 *Tel:* 618-783-2978 *Toll Free Tel:* 800-465-5200 *Fax:* 618-783-8407 *E-mail:* sales@tps1.com *Web Site:* www.tps1.com, pg 1261

Sargent, Mr Kim, Sargent Architectural Photography, 801 S Olive Ave, Suite 107, West Palm Beach, FL 33401 *Tel:* 561-881-8887 *E-mail:* info@sargentphoto.com *Web Site:* www.sargentphoto.com, pg 1425

Sargent, Nick, Sargent Architectural Photography, 801 S Olive Ave, Suite 107, West Palm Beach, FL 33401 *Tel:* 561-881-8887 *E-mail:* info@sargentphoto.com *Web Site:* www.sargentphoto.com, pg 1425

Sargent, Tyler, Sargent Architectural Photography, 801 S Olive Ave, Suite 107, West Palm Beach, FL 33401 *Tel:* 561-881-8887 *E-mail:* info@sargentphoto.com *Web Site:* www.sargentphoto.com, pg 1425

Sarkar, Dr Biplab, Vectorworks Inc, 7150 Riverwood Dr, Columbia, MD 21046 *Tel:* 410-290-5114 *Toll Free Tel:* 888-646-4223 (sales) *Fax:* 410-290-7266 *E-mail:* sales@vectorworks.net *Web Site:* www.vectorworks.net, pg 1378

Sartain, Jeffrey A, American Book Review, c/o University of Houston-Victoria College of Liberal Arts & Sciences, 3007 N Ben Wilson St, Victoria, TX 77901 *Tel:* 361-248-8245 *E-mail:* abr@americanbookreview.org; americanbookreview@uhv.org; americanbookreview@gmail.com *Web Site:* americanbookreview.org, pg 1129

Sass, Brian, Double Envelope, 7702 Plantation Rd, Roanoke, VA 24019 *Toll Free Tel:* 800-800-9007 *E-mail:* inquire@double-envelope.com *Web Site:* www.double-envelope.com, pg 1104, 1116

Sauer, Scott, Omniafiltra LLC, 9567 Main St, Beaver Falls, NY 13305 *Tel:* 315-346-7300 *Web Site:* www.omniafiltra.it/inglese/default_en.html, pg 1270

Saunders, Andrew, Getty Images Inc, 605 Fifth Ave S, Suite 400, Seattle, WA 98104 *Tel:* 206-925-5000 *Toll Free Tel:* 800-IMAGERY (462-4379); 888-888-5889 *Web Site:* www.gettyimages.com; www.gettyimages.com/customer-support; engage.gettyimages.com/media-inquiries, pg 1369, 1428

Saunders, Carol, Saunders Book Co, PO Box 308, Collingwood, ON L9Y 3Z7, Canada *Tel:* 705-445-4777 *Toll Free Tel:* 800-461-9120 *Fax:* 705-445-9569 *Toll Free Fax:* 800-561-1763 *E-mail:* info@saundersbook.ca *Web Site:* librarybooks.com, pg 1301

Saunders, James, Saunders Book Co, PO Box 308, Collingwood, ON L9Y 3Z7, Canada *Tel:* 705-445-4777 *Toll Free Tel:* 800-461-9120 *Fax:* 705-445-9569 *Toll Free Fax:* 800-561-1763 *E-mail:* info@saundersbook.ca *Web Site:* librarybooks.com, pg 1301

Saunders, John, Saunders Book Co, PO Box 308, Collingwood, ON L9Y 3Z7, Canada *Tel:* 705-445-4777 *Toll Free Tel:* 800-461-9120 *Fax:* 705-445-9569 *Toll Free Fax:* 800-561-1763 *E-mail:* info@saundersbook.ca *Web Site:* librarybooks.com, pg 1301

Saunders, Neil, Victory Productions Inc, 55 Linden St, Worcester, MA 01609 *Tel:* 508-755-0051 *E-mail:* victory@victoryprd.com *Web Site:* www.victoryprd.com, pg 1358

Sauter, Megan, Biblical Archaeology Society, 4710 41 St NW, Washington, DC 20016-1705 *Tel:* 202-364-3300 *Toll Free Tel:* 800-221-4644 *Fax:* 202-364-2636 *E-mail:* info@biblicalarchaeology.org *Web Site:* www.biblicalarchaeology.org, pg 1365

Sauvageau, Yvon, Multi-Reliure, 2112 Ave de la Transmission, Shawinigan, QC G9N 8N8, Canada *Tel:* 819-537-6008 *Toll Free Tel:* 888-735-4873 *Fax:* 819-537-4598 *E-mail:* info@multi-reliure.com; administration@multi-reliure.com *Web Site:* www.multireliure.com, pg 1257

Savage, Owen, OmniUpdate Inc, 1320 Flynn Rd, Suite 100, Camarillo, CA 93012 *Tel:* 805-484-9400 *Toll Free Tel:* 800-362-2605 *E-mail:* sales@omniupdate.com *Web Site:* omniupdate.com, pg 1374

Sawatzki, Cory, AlphaGraphics Inc, 143 Union Blvd, Suite 650, Lakewood, CO 80228 *Toll Free Tel:* 800-955-6246 *Fax:* 801-595-7270 *E-mail:* contactus@alphagraphics.com *Web Site:* www.alphagraphics.com, pg 1364

Sawyer, John, Book Express, 2440 Viking Way, Richmond, BC V6V 1N2, Canada *Tel:* 604-448-7100 *Toll Free Tel:* 800-663-5714 *Fax:* 604-270-7161 *Toll Free Fax:* 800-565-3770 *E-mail:* info@raincoast.com *Web Site:* www.raincoast.com, pg 1312

Sawyer, John, Raincoast Books Distribution Ltd, 2440 Viking Way, Richmond, BC V6V 1N2, Canada *Tel:* 604-448-7100 *Toll Free Tel:* 800-663-5714 (CN only) *Fax:* 604-270-7161 *Toll Free Fax:* 800-565-3770 *E-mail:* info@raincoast.com; customerservice@raincoast.com *Web Site:* www.raincoast.com/distribution, pg 1301

Saxe, Dr Karen, American Mathematical Society (AMS), 201 Charles St, Providence, RI 02904-2213 *Tel:* 401-455-4000 *Toll Free Tel:* 800-321-4267 *Fax:* 401-331-3842; 401-455-4046 (cust serv) *E-mail:* cust-serv@ams.org; ams@ams.org *Web Site:* www.ams.org, pg 1207, 1221, 1247, 1277

Scelba, Dave, SGW Integrated Marketing Communications Inc, 219 Changebridge Rd, Montville, NJ 07045 *Tel:* 973-299-8000 *E-mail:* info@sgw.com *Web Site:* www.sgw.com, pg 1118

Schaff, Gema M, American Language Services Inc (ALSi), 110 Otis St, Cambridge, MA 02141 *E-mail:* info@alsiweb.us *Web Site:* www.americanlanguageservices.us, pg 1399

Schamp, J Brough, J Brough Schamp Photography, Baltimore, MD 21212 *Tel:* 443-996-5450 (cell) *Web Site:* www.broughschampphotography.com, pg 1423

Schaper, Julie, Consortium Book Sales & Distribution, an Ingram brand, The Keg House, Suite 101, 34 13 Ave NE, Minneapolis, MN 55413-1007 *Tel:* 612-746-2600 *Toll Free Tel:* 866-400-5351 (cust serv, Jackson, TN) *E-mail:* cbsdinfo@ingramcontent.com *Web Site:* www.cbsd.com, pg 1289

Schattner, Glen, Adams Book Co Inc, 80 Broad St, 5th fl, New York, NY 10004 *Tel:* 718-875-5464 *Toll Free Tel:* 800-221-0909 *Fax:* 718-852-3212 *Toll Free Fax:* 888-229-2650 *E-mail:* customerservice@adamsbook.com; orders@adamsbook.com; sales@adamsbook.com; returns@adamsbook.com *Web Site:* www.adamsbook.com, pg 1311

Schauer, Justin, SGS International LLC, 626 W Main St, Suite 500, Louisville, KY 40202 *Tel:* 502-637-5443 *E-mail:* info@sgsco.com *Web Site:* www.sgsintl.com, pg 1230

Schauffler, Rob, Forest Sales & Distributing Co, 139 Jean Marie St, Reserve, LA 70084 *E-mail:* forestsales@juno.com, pg 1315

Schechner, Chaya, Kirkus, 1140 Broadway, Suite 802, New York, NY 10001 *E-mail:* customercare@kirkus.com *Web Site:* www.kirkusreviews.com, pg 1133

Schelberger, Ken, Printer's Repair Parts, 2706 Edgington St, Franklin Park, IL 60131-3438 *Tel:* 847-288-9000 *Toll Free Tel:* 800-444-4338 *Fax:* 847-288-9010 *E-mail:* prpsales@printersrepairparts.com *Web Site:* www.printersrepairparts.com, pg 1282

Schell, Christopher, HP Inc, 1501 Paige Mill Rd, Palo Alto, CA 94304-1112 *Tel:* 650-857-1501 *Toll Free Tel:* 800-282-6672 *Web Site:* www.hp.com, pg 1370

Schenkman, Joe, Schenkman Books Inc, 145 Bethel Mountain Rd, Rochester, VT 05767 *Tel:* 802-767-3104 *E-mail:* schenkmanbooks@gmail.com *Web Site:* www.schenkmanbooks.com, pg 1357

Schenkman, Kathryn, Schenkman Books Inc, 145 Bethel Mountain Rd, Rochester, VT 05767 *Tel:* 802-767-3104 *E-mail:* schenkmanbooks@gmail.com *Web Site:* www.schenkmanbooks.com, pg 1357

Scherba, Nancy, Roswell Bookbinding, 2614 N 29 Ave, Phoenix, AZ 85009 *Tel:* 602-272-9338 *Toll Free Tel:* 888-803-8883 *Fax:* 602-272-9786 *Web Site:* www.roswellbookbinding.com, pg 1259, 1326

Scherstuhl, Alan, Publishers Weekly, 49 W 23 St, 9th fl, New York, NY 10010 *Tel:* 212-377-5500 *Fax:* 212-377-2733 *Web Site:* www.publishersweekly.com, pg 1136

Schiele, Nichole, Motorbooks, 100 Cummings Ctr, Suite 265D, Beverly, MA 01915 *Tel:* 978-282-9590 *Toll Free Tel:* 800-759-0190 (orders) *Web Site:* www.quartoknows.com/motorbooks, pg 1319, 1329

Schiller, Philip W, Apple Inc, One Apple Park Way, Cupertino, CA 95014 *Tel:* 408-996-1010 *Web Site:* www.apple.com, pg 1364

Schilling, Derek, Modern Language Notes (MLN), 2715 N Charles St, Baltimore, MD 21218-4363 *Tel:* 410-516-6987 (journal orders outside US & CN) *Toll Free Tel:* 800-548-1784 (journal orders); 410-578-2865 (journal orders) *E-mail:* jrnlcirc@jh.edu (journal orders) *Web Site:* www.press.jhu.edu/journals/mln, pg 1134

Schingler, Michelle Anne, Foreword Reviews, 12935 W Bay Shore Rd, Suite 380, Traverse City, MI 49684 *Tel:* 231-933-3699 *Web Site:* www.forewordreviews.com, pg 1132

Schloesser, Jack, OEC Graphics Inc, 555 W Waukau Ave, Oshkosh, WI 54902 *Tel:* 920-235-7770 *Fax:* 920-235-2252 *Web Site:* www.oecgraphics.com, pg 1229

Schloesser, Jeff, OEC Graphics Inc, 555 W Waukau Ave, Oshkosh, WI 54902 *Tel:* 920-235-7770 *Fax:* 920-235-2252 *Web Site:* www.oecgraphics.com, pg 1229

Schmalzbach, Jonathan, QBS Learning, 242 W 30 St, Suite 1100, New York, NY 10001 *Tel:* 646-668-4645 *E-mail:* contact@qbslearning.com *Web Site:* www.qbslearning.com, pg 1357, 1417

Schmidt, Adam, Planar, 1195 NW Compton Dr, Beaverton, OR 97006-1992 *Tel:* 503-748-1100 *Toll Free Tel:* 866-475-2627 *E-mail:* sales@planar.com *Web Site:* www.planar.com, pg 1374

Schmidt, Ysobel, Ware-Pak LLC, 2427 Bond St, University Park, IL 60484 *Tel:* 708-534-2600 *E-mail:* sales@ware-pak.com *Web Site:* www.ware-pak.com, pg 1335

Schmitt, Mike, CG Book Printers, 1750 Northway Dr, North Mankato, MN 56003 *Tel:* 507-388-3300 *Toll Free Tel:* 800-729-7575 *Fax:* 507-386-6350 *E-mail:* cgbooks@corpgraph.com *Web Site:* www.corpgraph.com, pg 1103, 1115, 1209, 1223, 1250, 1265, 1278, 1354, 1366

Schneider, F, International Service Co, International Service Bldg, 333 Fourth Ave, Indialantic, FL 32903-4295 *Tel:* 321-724-1443 *Fax:* 321-724-1443, pg 1317, 1325, 1328, 1331

Schneider, Rex, The Blue Mouse Studio, 26829 37 St, Gobles, MI 49055 *Tel:* 269-628-5160 *E-mail:* frogville@earthlink.net, pg 1412

Schnoll, Steven, Schnoll Media Consulting, 1253 Springfield Ave, PMB 338, New Providence, NJ 07974 *Tel:* 908-522-3190 *Fax:* 908-273-2667 *Web Site:* www.schnollconsult.com, pg 1351

Schoen, Meghan, Shutterstock Inc, Empire State Bldg, 350 Fifth Ave, 20th fl, New York, NY 10118 *E-mail:* support@shutterstock.com; press@shutterstock.com *Web Site:* www.shutterstock.com, pg 1430

Schonwald, Barbara, Conrad Direct Inc, 800 Kinderkamack Rd, Suite 307N, Oradell, NJ 07649 Tel: 201-567-3200 Fax: 201-567-1530 E-mail: listinfo@conraddirect.com Web Site: www.conraddirect.com, pg 1115

Schreider, Ilene, Independent Publishers Group (IPG), 814 N Franklin St, Chicago, IL 60610 Tel: 312-337-0747 Toll Free Tel: 800-888-4741 (orders) Fax: 312-337-5985 E-mail: frontdesk@ipgbook.com; orders@ipgbook.com Web Site: www.ipgbook.com, pg 1292, 1328

Schreiner, Mike, The Bureau, 2354 English St, Maplewood, MN 55109 Tel: 612-788-1000; 612-432-3516 (sales) Toll Free Tel: 800-788-9536 Fax: 612-788-7792 E-mail: sales@thebureau.com Web Site: www.thebureau.com, pg 1223, 1249

Schrewe, Bettina, Bettina Schrewe Literary Scouting, 101 Fifth Ave, Suite 11B, New York, NY 10003 Tel: 212-414-2515 Web Site: www.bschrewe.com, pg 1351

Schriver, Amy, Sheridan PA, 450 Fame Ave, Hanover, PA 17331 Tel: 717-632-3535 Toll Free Tel: 800-352-2210 Fax: 717-633-8900 Web Site: www.sheridan.com, pg 1260

Schroeder, Bert, Schroeder's Book Haven, 104 Michigan Ave, League City, TX 77573 Tel: 281-332-5226 E-mail: info@bookhaventexas.com Web Site: www.bookhaventexas.com, pg 1321

Schroeder, Sandi, Schroeder Indexing Services, 23 Camilla Pink Ct, Bluffton, SC 29909 Tel: 843-705-9779; 843-415-3900 (cell) E-mail: sanindex@schroederindexing.com Web Site: www.schroederindexing.com, pg 1230

Schroeder, Yannic, Berryville Graphics, 25 Jack Enders Blvd, Berryville, VA 22611 Tel: 540-955-2750 Fax: 540-955-2633 E-mail: info@bvgraphics.com Web Site: www.bpg-usa.com, pg 1208, 1222, 1248

Schroeder, Yannic, Coral Graphic Services Inc, 840 S Broadway, Hicksville, NY 11801 Tel: 516-576-2100 Fax: 516-576-2168 E-mail: info@coralgraphics.com Web Site: www.bpg-usa.com, pg 1224, 1251, 1266

Schubert, Michael, Ruder Finn Inc, 425 E 53 St, New York, NY 10022 Tel: 212-593-6400 E-mail: info@ruderfinn.com Web Site: www.ruderfinn.com, pg 1112

Schuler, Angie, Midwest Library Service, 11443 Saint Charles Rock Rd, Bridgeton, MO 63044 Tel: 314-739-3100 Fax: 314-739-1326 E-mail: mail@midwestls.com Web Site: www.midwestls.com, pg 1319

Schulman, Marla, Schreiber Translations Inc (STI), 51 Monroe St, Suite 101, Rockville, MD 20850 Tel: 301-424-7737 Toll Free Tel: 800-822-3213 Fax: 301-424-2336 E-mail: translation@schreibernet.com Web Site: www.schreibernet.com, pg 1404

Schulman, Steven A, Miami Wabash Paper LLC, 301 Wedcor Ave, Wabash, IN 46992 Tel: 260-563-4181 Toll Free Tel: 800-842-9112 Fax: 219-563-2724 E-mail: miamivalley@mafcote.com Web Site: www.mafcote.com, pg 1269

Schultz, Prof David, AAA Fine Translation & Interpretation, 3820 Bowne St, Flushing, NY 11354 Tel: 917-582-7456, pg 1399

Schultz, Emily, The John Roberts Company, 9687 East River Rd NW, Minneapolis, MN 55433 Tel: 763-755-5500 Toll Free Tel: 800-551-1534 Fax: 763-755-0394 E-mail: success@johnroberts.com Web Site: www.johnroberts.com; www.facebook.com/TheJohnRobertsCompany, pg 1105

Schultz, Mike, Sappi Fine Paper North America, 255 State St, Boston, MA 02109 Tel: 617-423-7300 Toll Free Tel: 800-882-4332 E-mail: webqueriesna@sappi.com Web Site: www.sappi.com/na, pg 1271

Schumacher, Paul, RAM Publications & Distribution Inc, 2525 Michigan Ave, Bldg A2, Santa Monica, CA 90404 Tel: 310-453-0043 Fax: 310-264-4888 E-mail: info@rampub.com; orders@rampub.com Web Site: www.rampub.com, pg 1301

Schurer, Kelsey, Round Table Companies, PO Box 1603, Deerfield, IL 60015 Toll Free Tel: 833-750-5683 Web Site: www.roundtablecompanies.com, pg 1417

Schurig, Tiia, AIGA, the professional association for design, 228 Park Ave S, Suite 58603, New York, NY 10003 Tel: 212-807-1990 E-mail: general@aiga.org Web Site: www.aiga.org, pg 1139

Schutte, Kim, Ingram Content Group LLC, One Ingram Blvd, La Vergne, TN 37086-1986 Tel: 615-793-5000 Toll Free Tel: 800-937-8000 (retailers); 800-937-5300 (ext 1, libs) E-mail: customerservice@ingramcontent.com Web Site: www.ingramcontent.com, pg 1294, 1316

Schwabe, Paul, HumanEdge, 30 Glenn St, Suite 401, White Plains, NY 10603 Tel: 914-428-2233 Fax: 914-428-5547 E-mail: info@humanedge.com Web Site: www.humanedge.com, pg 1381

Schwartz, Jerry, Associated Press (AP), 200 Liberty St, New York, NY 10281 Tel: 212-621-1500 E-mail: info@ap.org Web Site: www.ap.org, pg 1189

Schwartz, Rodney, Durr MEGTEC LLC, 830 Prosper St, DePere, WI 54115 Tel: 920-336-5715 E-mail: megtecinquiries@megtec.com Web Site: www.durr-megtec.com, pg 1279

Schwarz, Walter, Figaro, PO Box 848, Sharon, CT 06069 Tel: 860-248-8989; 860-364-0834 E-mail: design@figro.com Web Site: www.figro.com, pg 1346, 1354, 1368, 1414

Schwedelson, Jay, Worldata, 3000 N Military Trail, Boca Raton, FL 33431-6321 Tel: 561-393-8200 Toll Free Tel: 800-331-8102 E-mail: hello@worldata.com Web Site: www.worldata.com, pg 1120

Scianna, Cosimo, Cosimo Scianna, Photographer, 23407 Milano Ct, Boca Raton, FL 33433 Tel: 917-763-2927 E-mail: cosimoscianna@mac.com Web Site: www.cosimoscianna.com, pg 1425

Scianna, Irene, Cosimo Scianna, Photographer, 23407 Milano Ct, Boca Raton, FL 33433 Tel: 917-763-2927 E-mail: cosimoscianna@mac.com Web Site: www.cosimoscianna.com, pg 1425

Scordato, Ellen, Stonesong, 270 W 39 St, Suite 201, New York, NY 10018 Tel: 212-929-4600 E-mail: editors@stonesong.com Web Site: www.stonesong.com, pg 1357

Scorzelli, Frank, L+L Printers, 6200 Yarrow Dr, Carlsbad, CA 92011 Tel: 760-438-3456; 760-477-0321 Fax: 760-929-0853 E-mail: info@llprinters.com Web Site: www.llprinters.com, pg 1256

Scott, AO, The New York Times Book Review, 620 Eighth Ave, 5th fl, New York, NY 10018 Tel: 212-556-1234 Toll Free Tel: 800-631-2580 (subns) E-mail: bookreview@nytimes.com; books@nytimes.com Web Site: www.nytimes.com, pg 1135

Scott, Beverly, Masque Publishing Inc, 8400 Park Meadows Dr, Lonetree, CO 80124 Tel: 303-290-9853 Fax: 303-290-6303 E-mail: support@masque.com Web Site: www.masque.com, pg 1372

Scott, Frank, Roots & Rhythm Inc, PO Box 837, El Cerrito, CA 94530 Tel: 510-965-9503 Toll Free Tel: 888-ROOTS-66 (766-8766) Fax: 510-526-9001 E-mail: roots@toast.net Web Site: www.rootsandrhythm.com, pg 1143

Scott, Michael, Aptara Inc, 2901 Telestar Ct, Suite 522, Falls Church, VA 22042 Tel: 703-352-0001 E-mail: moreinfo@aptaracorp.com Web Site: www.aptaracorp.com, pg 1207, 1222, 1343, 1353, 1365, 1411

Scott-Noennig, Nancy, Roots & Rhythm Inc, PO Box 837, El Cerrito, CA 94530 Tel: 510-965-9503 Toll Free Tel: 888-ROOTS-66 (766-8766) Fax: 510-526-9001 E-mail: roots@toast.net Web Site: www.rootsandrhythm.com, pg 1143

Scotti, Chris, Codra Enterprises Inc, 17692 Cowan, Suite 200, Irvine, CA 92614 Tel: 949-756-8400 Toll Free Tel: 888-992-6372 Fax: 949-756-8484 E-mail: codra@codra.com; sales@codra.com Web Site: www.codra.com, pg 1209, 1250

Scroggie, Bill, Six Red Marbles LLC, 101 Station Landing, Medford, MA 02155 Tel: 857-588-9000 E-mail: info@sixredmarbles.com Web Site: www.sixredmarbles.com, pg 1231, 1376

Scruggs, Jim, Carolina Biological Supply Co, 2700 York Rd, Burlington, NC 27215-3398 Tel: 336-586-4399 (intl sales); 336-538-6211 Toll Free Tel: 800-334-5551 Fax: 336-584-7686 (intl sales) Toll Free Fax: 800-222-7112 E-mail: quotations@carolina.com; product@carolina.com Web Site: www.carolina.com, pg 1313

Seagram, Mike, Publishers Storage & Shipping Corp, 46 Development Rd, Fitchburg, MA 01420 Tel: 978-345-2121 Web Site: www.pssc.com, pg 1334

Seaman, Donna, Booklist, 225 N Michigan Ave, Suite 1300, Chicago, IL 60601 Tel: 312-944-6780 Toll Free Tel: 800-545-2433 Fax: 312-440-9374 E-mail: info@booklistonline.com; ala@ala.org Web Site: www.booklistonline.com; www.ala.org, pg 1130

Searles, Bradley J, Whitehurst & Clark Book Fulfillment, 1200 County Rd, Rte 523, Flemington, NJ 08822 Tel: 908-782-2323 Toll Free Tel: 800-488-8040 E-mail: wcbooks@aol.com Web Site: www.wcbks.com, pg 1335

Secrest, John F, Lightning Source LLC, 1246 Heil Quaker Blvd, La Vergne, TN 37086 Tel: 615-793-5000 (Ingram) Toll Free Tel: 800-378-5508; 800-509-4156 (cust serv) E-mail: lsicustomersupport@ingramcontent.com; contentacquisitioninquiries@ingramcontent.com Web Site: www.ingramcontent.com/publishers/print, pg 1212

Secrest, John F, Lightning Source LLC, 1246 Heil Quaker Blvd, La Vergne, TN 37086 Tel: 615-793-5000 (Ingram) Toll Free Tel: 800-378-5508; 800-509-4156 (cust serv) E-mail: lsicustomersupport@ingramcontent.com Web Site: www.ingramcontent.com/publishers/print, pg 1256, 1371

Segal, Doug, Panoramic Images, 4835 Main St, Suite 100, Skokie, IL 60077 Tel: 847-324-7000 Toll Free Tel: 800-543-5250 E-mail: info@panoramicimages.com Web Site: www.panoramicimages.com, pg 1430

Segal, Joseph, Israel's Judaica Center, 441 Clark Ave W, Thornhill, ON L4J 6W7, Canada Tel: 905-881-1010 Toll Free Tel: 877-511-1010 Fax: 905-881-1016 E-mail: contact@israelsjudaica.com; thornhill@israelsjudaica.com (retail store) Web Site: www.israelsjudaica.com, pg 1317

Segedin, Ben, Booklist, 225 N Michigan Ave, Suite 1300, Chicago, IL 60601 Tel: 312-944-6780 Toll Free Tel: 800-545-2433 Fax: 312-440-9374 E-mail: info@booklistonline.com; ala@ala.org Web Site: www.booklistonline.com; www.ala.org, pg 1130

Seguin, Becquer, Modern Language Notes (MLN), 2715 N Charles St, Baltimore, MD 21218-4363 Tel: 410-516-6987 (journal orders outside US & CN) Toll Free Tel: 800-548-1784 (journal orders) Fax: 410-578-2865 (journal orders) E-mail: jrnlcirc@jh.edu (journal orders) Web Site: www.press.jhu.edu/journals/mln, pg 1134

Segura, Jonathan, Publishers Weekly, 49 W 23 St, 9th fl, New York, NY 10010 Tel: 212-377-5500 Fax: 212-377-2733 Web Site: www.publishersweekly.com, pg 1135

Sekler, Marvin, Jonathan David Publishers Inc, 52 Tuscan Way, Suite 202-371, St Augustine, FL 32092 Tel: 718-456-8611 E-mail: customerservice@jdbooks.com Web Site: www.jdbooks.com, pg 1295

Seldon, Cele, Seldon Ink Travel Writing & Photography, 1513 Riverside Dr, Beaufort, SC 29902 Tel: 910-274-8070 Web Site: www.seldonink.com, pg 1425

Seldon, Eric, Communicorp Inc, 1001 Lockwood Ave, Columbus, GA 31999 Tel: 706-324-1182 E-mail: mktech@communicorp.com Web Site: www.communicorp.com, pg 1224, 1250

Seldon, Lynn, Seldon Ink Travel Writing & Photography, 1513 Riverside Dr, Beaufort, SC 29902 Tel: 910-274-8070 Web Site: www.seldonink.com, pg 1425

Self, Dennis, Acxiom, 301 E Dave Ward Dr, Conway, AR 72032 Toll Free Tel: 888-322-9466 Web Site: www.acxiom.com, pg 1119

Sepp, Peter, Sepp Leaf Products Inc, 381 Park Ave S, No 13, New York, NY 10016 Tel: 212-683-2840 Fax: 212-725-0308 E-mail: sales@seppleaf.com Web Site: www.seppleaf.com, pg 1271

Serrano, Carla, Publicis North America, 1675 Broadway, New York, NY 10009 Tel: 212-474-5000 Web Site: www.publicisna.com, pg 1112

Serrano, Elizabeth, Association for Library Service to Children (ALSC), 225 N Michigan Ave, Suite 1300, Chicago, IL 60601 Tel: 312-280-2163 Toll Free Tel: 800-545-2433 Fax: 312-280-5271 E-mail: alsc@ala.org Web Site: www.ala.org/alsc, pg 1145

Seshadri, Jana, United Library Services Inc, 7140 Fairmount Dr SE, Calgary, AB T2H 0X4, Canada Tel: 403-252-4426 Toll Free Tel: 888-342-5857 (CN only) Fax: 403-258-3426 Toll Free Fax: 800-661-2806 (CN only) E-mail: info@uls.com Web Site: www.uls.com, pg 1323

Setbon, Julie H, iProbe Multilingual Solutions Inc, 145 W 30 St, 9th fl, New York, NY 10001 Tel: 212-489-6035 Toll Free Tel: 888-489-6035 Fax: 212-202-4790 E-mail: info@iprobesolutions.com Web Site: iprobesolutions.com, pg 1402

Sethi, Bali, International Press Publication Inc, Spadina Rd, Richmond Hill, ON L4B 3C5, Canada Tel: 905-883-0343 E-mail: sales@ippbooks.com Web Site: www.ippbooks.com; www.facebook.com/ippbooks; x.com/ippbooks2, pg 1227, 1281, 1295, 1317

Seto, Sarah, Penguin Random House Canada, a Penguin Random House company, 320 Front St W, Suite 1400, Toronto, ON M5V 3B6, Canada Tel: 416-364-4449 Toll Free Tel: 888-523-9292 (cust serv) Fax: 416-598-7764 E-mail: customerservicescanada@penguinrandomhouse.com; publicitycanada@penguinrandomhouse.com; rightscanada@penguinrandomhouse.com Web Site: www.penguinrandomhouse.ca, pg 1299

Sevoz, Philippe, Glatfelter, Capitol Towers South, 4350 Congress St, Suite 600, Charlotte, NC 28209 Tel: 717-850-0170 Toll Free Tel: 866-744-7380 E-mail: info@glatfelter.com Web Site: www.glatfelter.com, pg 1267

Sexton, John, John Sexton Photography, PO Box 30, Carmel Valley, CA 93924 Tel: 831-659-3130 Fax: 831-659-5509 E-mail: info@johnsexton.com Web Site: www.johnsexton.com, pg 1425

Sexton, Paul, Electronics for Imaging Inc (EFI), 6750 Dumbarton Circle, Fremont, CA 94555 Tel: 650-357-3500 Toll Free Tel: 800-568-1917; 800-875-7117 (sales) Fax: 650-357-3907 E-mail: info@efi.com Web Site: www.efi.com, pg 1368

Seykora, Ted, Abraham Associates Inc, 5120-A Cedar Lake Rd, Minneapolis, MN 55416 Tel: 952-927-7920 Toll Free Tel: 800-701-2489 Fax: 952-927-8089 E-mail: info@abrahamassociatesinc.com Web Site: abrahamassociatesinc.com, pg 1285

Shaffer, Julie, Association for PRINT Technologies (APTech), 113 Seaboard Lane, Suite C-250, Franklin, TN 37067 Tel: 703-264-7200 E-mail: aptech@aptech.org Web Site: printtechnologies.org, pg 1277, 1365

Shaffner, Carol, Shaffner's Bindery, 3305 Pattee Canyon Rd, Missoula, MT 59803 Tel: 406-251-2699 E-mail: shaffnersbindery@centric.net Web Site: shaffnersbindery.com, pg 1326

Shaffner, Jeff, Shaffner's Bindery, 3305 Pattee Canyon Rd, Missoula, MT 59803 Tel: 406-251-2699 E-mail: shaffnersbindery@centric.net Web Site: shaffnersbindery.com, pg 1326

Shaifer, Norman, Custom Studios, 77 Main St, Tappan, NY 10983 Tel: 845-365-0414 Toll Free Tel: 800-631-1362 Fax: 845-365-0864 E-mail: customusa@aol.com Web Site: customstudios.com, pg 1224

Shanbhag, Arun, Rising Sun Book Co, 1424 Stony Brook Rd, Stony Brook, NY 11790 Tel: 631-473-7000 Fax: 631-473-7447 Web Site: risingsunbook.com, pg 1320, 1329

Shanks, Gwyneth, Theatre Journal, 2715 N Charles St, Baltimore, MD 21218-4363 Tel: 410-516-6987 (journal orders outside US & CN) Toll Free Tel: 800-548-1784 (journal orders) Fax: 410-578-2865 (journal orders) E-mail: tjbooks@athe.org; jrnlcirc@jh.edu (journal orders) Web Site: www.press.jhu.edu/journals/theatre-journal, pg 1137

Shanley, Lorraine W, Market Partners International Inc, 232 Madison Ave, Suite 1400, New York, NY 10016 Tel: 212-447-0855 Fax: 212-447-0785 E-mail: info@marketpartnersinternational.com Web Site: www.marketpartnersinternational.com, pg 1349

Shanley, Lorraine W, Publishing Trends, 232 Madison Ave, Suite 1400, New York, NY 10016 Tel: 212-447-0855 Fax: 212-447-0785 E-mail: info@publishingtrends.com Web Site: www.marketpartnersinternational.com; www.publishingtrends.com, pg 1136

Shapiro, Daniel, Metro 360, 120 Sinnott Rd, Scarborough, ON M1L 4N1, Canada Tel: 416-752-8720 Toll Free Tel: 888-260-2208 Web Site: www.metro360.ca, pg 1319

Shapiro, Ira, AlphaGraphics Inc, 143 Union Blvd, Suite 650, Lakewood, CO 80228 Toll Free Tel: 800-955-6246 Fax: 801-595-7270 E-mail: contactus@alphagraphics.com Web Site: www.alphagraphics.com, pg 1364

Shapiro, Jonathan, Smith-Edwards-Dunlap Co, 2867 E Allegheny Ave, Philadelphia, PA 19134 Tel: 215-425-8800 Toll Free Tel: 800-829-0020 Fax: 215-425-9715 E-mail: sales@sed.com Web Site: www.sed.com, pg 1231, 1260, 1271

Sharma, Patricia, Multi-Tech Systems Inc, 2205 Woodale Dr, Mounds View, MN 55112 Tel: 763-785-3500 Toll Free Tel: 800-328-9717 Fax: 763-785-9874 E-mail: info@multitech.com; sales@multitech.com; mtsmktg@multitech.com Web Site: www.multitech.com, pg 1373

Sharp, Brad, Bookmasters, 30 Amberwood Pkwy, Ashland, OH 44805 Tel: 419-281-5100 Toll Free Tel: 800-537-6727 Fax: 419-281-0200 E-mail: info@btpubservices.com Web Site: www.btpubservices.com, pg 1208, 1223, 1249, 1265, 1278

Sharp, Michael J, RR Donnelley, 35 W Wacker Dr, Chicago, IL 60601 Toll Free Tel: 800-742-4455 Web Site: www.rrd.com, pg 1210, 1225, 1252, 1266, 1279

Sharp, Michael J, RR Donnelley & Sons Company, 35 W Wacker Dr, Chicago, IL 60601 Tel: 312-326-8000 Toll Free Tel: 800-742-4455 Web Site: www.rrd.com, pg 1333

Sharpe, Lindsay, Brunswick Books, 14 Afton Ave, Toronto, ON M6J 1R7, Canada Tel: 416-703-3598 Fax: 416-703-6561 E-mail: info@brunswickbooks.ca; orders@brunswickbooks.ca Web Site: brunswickbooks.ca, pg 1224

Shattuck, Byron, Emery-Pratt Co, 1966 W M 21, Owosso, MI 48867-1397 Tel: 989-723-5291 Toll Free Tel: 800-762-5683 (orders); 800-248-3887 (cust serv) Fax: 989-723-4677 Toll Free Fax: 800-523-6379 (cust serv) E-mail: customer.service@emery-pratt.com Web Site: www.emery-pratt.com, pg 1315

Shattuck, Maurie, Emery-Pratt Co, 1966 W M 21, Owosso, MI 48867-1397 Tel: 989-723-5291 Toll Free Tel: 800-762-5683 (orders); 800-248-3887 (cust serv) Fax: 989-723-4677 Toll Free Fax: 800-523-6379 (cust serv) E-mail: customer.service@emery-pratt.com Web Site: www.emery-pratt.com, pg 1315

Shattuck, Mo, Emery-Pratt Co, 1966 W M 21, Owosso, MI 48867-1397 Tel: 989-723-5291 Toll Free Tel: 800-762-5683 (orders); 800-248-3887 (cust serv) Fax: 989-723-4677 Toll Free Fax: 800-523-6379 (cust serv) E-mail: customer.service@emery-pratt.com Web Site: www.emery-pratt.com, pg 1315

Shatzkin, Mike, The Idea Logical Co Inc, 300 E 51 St, Apt 17C, New York, NY 10017 Tel: 917-680-8598 E-mail: info@idealog.com Web Site: www.idealog.com, pg 1347

Shaw, Joe, Cypress House, 155 Cypress St, Suite A, Fort Bragg, CA 95437 Tel: 707-964-9520 Toll Free Tel: 800-773-7782 Fax: 707-964-7531 E-mail: office@cypresshouse.com Web Site: www.cypresshouse.com, pg 1104, 1224, 1345, 1413

Shawe, Phil, Translations.com, 1250 Broadway, 32nd fl, New York, NY 10001 Tel: 212-689-1616 Fax: 212-504-8057 E-mail: newyork@translations.com; info@translations.com Web Site: translations.com, pg 1405

Sheahan, Emily, Copyright Clearance Center Inc (CCC), 222 Rosewood Dr, Danvers, MA 01923 Tel: 978-750-8400 (sales); 978-646-2600 (cust serv) E-mail: info@copyright.com Web Site: www.copyright.com, pg 1345

Sheehy, Terence, Bulkley Dunton, One Penn Plaza, Suite 2814, 250 W 34 St, New York, NY 10119 Tel: 212-863-1800 Toll Free Tel: 800-347-9279 Fax: 212-863-1872 Web Site: www.bulkleydunton.com, pg 1265

Sheere, Dara, Penguin Random House Canada, a Penguin Random House company, 320 Front St W, Suite 1400, Toronto, ON M5V 3B6, Canada Tel: 416-364-4449 Toll Free Tel: 888-523-9292 (cust serv) Fax: 416-598-7764 E-mail: customerservicescanada@penguinrandomhouse.com; publicitycanada@penguinrandomhouse.com; rightscanada@penguinrandomhouse.com Web Site: www.penguinrandomhouse.ca, pg 1299

Sheffield, Jon, Ingenta, 317 George St, New Brunswick, NJ 08901 Tel: 732-563-9292 Fax: 732-563-9044 Web Site: www.ingenta.com, pg 1370

Shell, Sharon, Independent Publishers Group (IPG), 814 N Franklin St, Chicago, IL 60610 Tel: 312-337-0747 Toll Free Tel: 800-888-4741 (orders) Fax: 312-337-5985 E-mail: frontdesk@ipgbook.com; orders@ipgbook.com Web Site: www.ipgbook.com, pg 1292, 1328

Shelomi, Itzhack, Itzhack Shelomi Design, 25 Cushman Rd, Scarsdale, NY 10583 Tel: 212-689-7469 E-mail: studio@ishelomi.com; studio@serifes.com Web Site: www.ishelomi.com, pg 1211, 1227, 1371, 1415

Shelton, David, Progress Printing Plus, 2677 Waterlick Rd, Lynchburg, VA 24502 Tel: 434-239-9213 Toll Free Tel: 800-572-7804 Fax: 434-832-7573 E-mail: info@progressprintplus.com Web Site: www.progressprintplus.com, pg 1230

Shenk, Patricia, Datacolor, 5 Princess Rd, Lawrenceville, NJ 08648 Tel: 609-924-2189 Toll Free Tel: 800-982-6496 (support) Fax: 609-895-7414 E-mail: marketing@datacolor.com Web Site: www.datacolor.com, pg 1224

Shepherd, Scott, TNG, 3320 S Service Rd, Burlington, ON L7N 3M6, Canada Toll Free Tel: 800-201-8127 Toll Free Fax: 877-664-9732 E-mail: cs@tng.com Web Site: www.tng.com, pg 1323

Sheppard, Emily, Penguin Random House Canada, a Penguin Random House company, 320 Front St W, Suite 1400, Toronto, ON M5V 3B6, Canada Tel: 416-364-4449 Toll Free Tel: 888-523-9292 (cust serv) Fax: 416-598-7764 E-mail: customerservicescanada@penguinrandomhouse.com; publicitycanada@penguinrandomhouse.com; rightscanada@penguinrandomhouse.com Web Site: www.penguinrandomhouse.ca, pg 1299

Sheppard, Scott, Creative Direct Marketing Group Inc (CDMG), 1313 Fourth Ave N, Nashville, TN 37208 Tel: 615-814-6633 Web Site: www.cdmginc.com, pg 1345

Sherbow, Bruce W, Dell Magazines, 6 Prowitt St, Norwalk, CT 06855 Tel: 203-866-6688 Toll Free Tel: 800-220-7443 (corp sales) Fax: 203-854-5962 (pubns) E-mail: customerservice@pennypublications.com Web Site: www.pennydellpuzzles.com, pg 1354

Sherman, Bruce, Specialist Marketing Services Inc, 777 Terrace Ave, Suite 401, Hasbrouck Heights, NJ 07604 Tel: 201-865-5800 E-mail: info@sms-inc.com Web Site: www.sms-inc.com, pg 1120

Sherman, Matt, Hassett Express, 17W775 Butterfield Rd, Suite 109, Oakbrook Terrace, IL 60181 Tel: 630-530-6515 Fax: 630-530-6538 Web Site: www.hassettexpress.com, pg 1334

Sherman, Scott D, Ingram Micro Inc, 3351 Michelson Dr, Suite 100, Irvin, CA 92612 Tel: 714-566-1000 E-mail: customerexperience@ingrammicro.com Web Site: www.ingrammicro.com, pg 1317

Sherwood, Mark, Nuance Communications Inc, One Wayside Rd, Burlington, MA 01803 Tel: 781-565-5000 Toll Free Tel: 800-654-1187 (cust serv); 888-372-1908 (orders) Web Site: www.nuance.com, pg 1374

Shibata, Tsukasa, OCS America Inc, 195 Anderson Ave, Moonachie, NJ 07074 Tel: 201-460-2888 Toll Free Tel: 800-367-3405 E-mail: info@ocsworld.com Web Site: www.ocsworld.com, pg 1329

Shibusawa, Masanori, Fujitsu Computer Products of America Inc, 1250 E Arques Ave, Sunnyvale, CA 94085-4701 Tel: 408-746-6000 Toll Free Tel: 800-626-4686 E-mail: scanner-sales@us.fujitsu.com Web Site: www.fujitsu.com/us, pg 1369

Shill, Dan, Absolut Color, 109 W 27 St, New York, NY 10001 Tel: 212-868-0404 E-mail: info@absolutcolor.com Web Site: www.absolutcolor.com, pg 1247

Shimizu, Yasunari, Fujitsu Computer Products of America Inc, 1250 E Arques Ave, Sunnyvale, CA 94085-4701 Tel: 408-746-6000 Toll Free Tel: 800-626-4686 E-mail: scanner-sales@us.fujitsu.com Web Site: www.fujitsu.com/us, pg 1369

Shine, Jeffrey, Naviga, 7900 International Dr, Suite 800, Bloomington, MN 55425 Tel: 651-639-0662 E-mail: info@navigaglobal.com Web Site: www.navigaglobal.com, pg 1373

Shirzad, Farhad, Iranbooks, PO Box 30087, Bethesda, MD 20824 Tel: 301-718-8188 Toll Free Tel: 888-718-8188 Fax: 301-907-8707 E-mail: info@iranbooks.com Web Site: www.iranbooks.com, pg 1317, 1328

Shorett, Denny, Crown Connect, 250 W Rialto Ave, San Bernadino, CA 92408 Tel: 909-888-7531 Fax: 909-889-1639 E-mail: sales@crownconnect.com Web Site: www.crownconnect.com, pg 1209, 1224, 1279

Shulman, Michael, Magnum Photos Inc, 12 W 23 St, 4th fl, New York, NY 10010 Tel: 212-929-6000 E-mail: photography@magnumphotos.com; contact@magnumphotos.com Web Site: www.magnumphotos.com; pro.magnumphotos.com, pg 1429

Shutter, John, Communicorp Inc, 1001 Lockwood Ave, Columbus, GA 31999 Tel: 706-324-1182 E-mail: mktech@communicorp.com Web Site: www.communicorp.com, pg 1224, 1251

Sibert, Robert L, Bound to Stay Bound Books Inc, 1880 W Morton Rd, Jacksonville, IL 62650 Tel: 217-245-5191 Toll Free Tel: 800-637-6586 Fax: 217-245-0424 Toll Free Fax: 800-747-7872 E-mail: btsb@btsb.com Web Site: www.btsb.com, pg 1313, 1325

Siefker, Kayla, Gale Literature: Book Review Index, 27555 Executive Dr, Suite 270, Farmington Hills, MI 48331 Toll Free Tel: 800-877-4253 Toll Free Fax: 877-363-4253 E-mail: gale.customerexperience@cengage.com Web Site: www.gale.com/c/literature-book-review-index, pg 1132

Siegal, Todd R, Franklin & Siegal Associates Inc, 40 Exchange Place, Suite 1703, New York, NY 10005 Tel: 212-868-6311 Web Site: www.franklinandsiegal.com, pg 1346

Sifton, Sam, The New York Times Book Review, 620 Eighth Ave, 5th fl, New York, NY 10018 Tel: 212-556-1234 Toll Free Tel: 800-631-2580 (subns) E-mail: bookreview@nytimes.com; books@nytimes.com Web Site: www.nytimes.com, pg 1135

Sigmund, Steen, Marrakech Express Inc, 720 Wesley Ave, No 10, Tarpon Springs, FL 34689 Tel: 727-942-2218 Toll Free Tel: 800-940-6566 Fax: 727-937-4758 E-mail: print@marrak.com Web Site: www.marrak.com, pg 1212, 1256, 1281

Sikkes, JoAnn, BookComp Inc, 6124 Belmont Ave NE, Belmont, MI 49306 Tel: 616-774-9700 E-mail: production@bookcomp.com Web Site: www.bookcomp.com, pg 1223, 1353

Silberg, Richard, Poetry Flash, 1450 Fourth St, Suite 4, Berkeley, CA 94710 Tel: 510-525-5476 Web Site: www.poetryflash.org, pg 1135

Silcott, Aleyois, Transimpex Translators, Interpreters, Editors, Consultants Inc, 2300 Main St, 9th fl, Kansas City, MO 64108 Tel: 816-561-3777 Fax: 816-561-5515 E-mail: translations@transimpex.com Web Site: www.transimpex.com, pg 1405

Silow-Carroll, Andy, Jewish Telegraphic Agency, 24 W 30 St, 4th fl, New York, NY 10001 Tel: 646-778-5520 E-mail: info@70facesmedia.org Web Site: www.jta.org; www.70facesmedia.org, pg 1190

Silva, Carla, King Features Syndicate, 300 W 57 St, New York, NY 10019-5238 Tel: 212-969-7550 Toll Free Tel: 800-526-5464 Web Site: www.kingfeatures.com, pg 1190

Silva, Carla, Eric Tyson, 300 W 57 St, 15th fl, New York, NY 10019-5238 Toll Free Tel: 800-708-7311 (FL edit) E-mail: eric@erictyson.com Web Site: www.erictyson.com, pg 1126

Silverman, Aaron, SCB Distributors, 15608 S New Century Dr, Gardena, CA 90248 Tel: 310-532-9400 Toll Free Tel: 800-729-6423 Fax: 310-532-7001 E-mail: scb@scbdistributors.com Web Site: www.scbdistributors.com, pg 1302

Silverstein, Lee, Jewish Telegraphic Agency, 24 W 30 St, 4th fl, New York, NY 10001 Tel: 646-778-5520 E-mail: info@70facesmedia.org Web Site: www.jta.org; www.70facesmedia.org, pg 1190

Simard, Hugues, Indigo Books & Music Inc, 468 King St W, Suite 500, Toronto, ON M5V 1L8, Canada Tel: 416-364-4499 E-mail: cisales@indigo.ca Web Site: www.chapters.indigo.ca, pg 1294

Simeon, Laura, Kirkus, 1140 Broadway, Suite 802, New York, NY 10001 E-mail: customercare@kirkus.com Web Site: www.kirkusreviews.com, pg 1133

Simon, Daniel, World Literature Today, 630 Parrington Oval, Suite 110, Norman, OK 73019-4033 Tel: 405-325-4531 E-mail: wlt@ou.edu Web Site: www.worldliteraturetoday.org, pg 1137

Simone, Mike, Regal Press, 79 Astor Ave, Norwood, MA 02062 Tel: 781-769-3900 Toll Free Tel: 800-447-3425 Fax: 781-769-7361 E-mail: info@regalpress.com Web Site: www.regalpress.com, pg 1105, 1259

Simonean, Joanne, AudioFile®, 37 Silver St, Portland, ME 04101 Tel: 207-774-7563 Toll Free Tel: 800-506-1212 Fax: 207-775-3744 E-mail: info@audiofilemagazine.com Web Site: www.audiofilemagazine.com, pg 1130

Simonetti, Pat, Tamron USA Inc, 10 Austin Blvd, Commack, NY 11725 Tel: 631-858-8400 Toll Free Tel: 800-827-8880 Fax: 631-543-5666; 631-858-8462 (cust serv) E-mail: custserv@tamron.com Web Site: www.tamron-usa.com, pg 1377

Simonnet, Antoine, HP Inc, 1501 Paige Mill Rd, Palo Alto, CA 94304-1112 Tel: 650-857-1501 Toll Free Tel: 800-282-6672 Web Site: www.hp.com, pg 1370

Simons, Jeffrey I, Superior Printing Ink Co Inc, 100 North St, Teterboro, NJ 07608 Tel: 201-478-5600 Fax: 201-478-5650 Web Site: www.superiorink.com, pg 1272

Simonton, David, The Thomas Tape & Supply Co Inc, 1713 Sheridan Ave, Springfield, OH 45505 Tel: 937-325-6414 Fax: 937-325-2850 Web Site: www.thomastape.com, pg 1272

Simpson, Hunter, Liz Gately Book Scouting, 36 W 37 St, Rm 408, New York, NY 10018 Tel: 212-244-1441 E-mail: liz@lizgately.com Web Site: www.lizgately.com, pg 1347

Sims, Charlene, The Master's Press, 14550 Midway Rd, Dallas, TX 75244 Tel: 972-387-0046 Fax: 972-404-0317 Web Site: www.themasterspress.com, pg 1257

Simunek, Thomas, Kappa Graphics LLP, 50 Rock St, Hughestown, PA 18640 Tel: 570-655-9681 Toll Free Tel: 800-236-4396 (sales) E-mail: weborders@kappapma.com Web Site: www.kappapma.com/kappagraphics; kappapuzzles.com, pg 1227, 1255

Singer, Karl, D&K Group Inc, 1795 Commerce Dr, Elk Grove Village, IL 60007 Tel: 847-956-0160; 847-956-4757 (tech support) Toll Free Tel: 800-632-2314 Fax: 847-956-8214 E-mail: info@dkgroup.net Web Site: www.dkgroup.com, pg 1251, 1266, 1279

Singh, Hanut, QBS Learning, 242 W 30 St, Suite 1100, New York, NY 10001 Tel: 646-668-4645 E-mail: contact@qbslearning.com Web Site: www.qbslearning.com, pg 1357, 1417

Singh, Reggie Chua, QBS Learning, 242 W 30 St, Suite 1100, New York, NY 10001 Tel: 646-668-4645 E-mail: contact@qbslearning.com Web Site: www.qbslearning.com, pg 1357, 1417

Singh, Siri Ram, Ancient Healing Ways, PO Box 459, Espanola, NM 87532 Tel: 505-747-2860 Toll Free Tel: 877-753-5351 Web Site: www.a-healing.com, pg 1311

Sirak, James F, Northeast Publishers Reps, Montville Chase, 20 Davenport Rd, Montville, NJ 07045 Tel: 973-299-0085 Fax: 973-263-2363 E-mail: siraksirak@aol.com Web Site: www.nepubreps.com, pg 1298

Sirak, Lisa, Northeast Publishers Reps, Montville Chase, 20 Davenport Rd, Montville, NJ 07045 Tel: 973-299-0085 Fax: 973-263-2363 E-mail: siraksirak@aol.com Web Site: www.nepubreps.com, pg 1298

Sit, Jenny, Chinese Christian Mission Bookroom, 1269 N McDowell Blvd, Petaluma, CA 94954-1133 Tel: 707-762-2688; 707-762-1314 Fax: 707-762-1713 E-mail: bookroom@ccmusa.org; ccm@ccmusa.org Web Site: www.ccmusa.org; www.ccmbookroom.org, pg 1313

Sittlinger, George, Maracle Inc, 1156 King St E, Oshawa, ON L1H 1H8, Canada Tel: 905-723-3438 Toll Free Tel: 800-558-8604 Fax: 905-723-1759 E-mail: hello@maracleinc.com Web Site: www.maracleinc.com, pg 1212, 1228, 1256

Sivils, Dan, ISOMEDIA Inc, 12842 Interurban Ave S, Seattle, WA 98168 Tel: 425-869-5411 Toll Free Tel: 866-838-4389 (sales); 877-638-9277 (support) Fax: 425-869-9437 E-mail: sales@isomedia.com Web Site: www.isomedia.com, pg 1371

Skelton, Samantha, The Writers Lifeline Inc, a Story Merchant company, 400 S Burnside Ave, Suite 11B, Los Angeles, CA 90036 Tel: 310-968-1607 Web Site: www.thewriterslifeline.com, pg 1352

Skillman, Richard, Allied Vaughn, 7600 Parklawn Ave, Suite 300, Minneapolis, MN 55435 Tel: 952-832-3100 Toll Free Tel: 800-323-0281 Fax: 952-832-3203 Web Site: www.alliedvaughn.com, pg 1364

Skriloff, Lisa, Multicultural Marketing Resources Inc, 720 Greenwich St, No 7T, New York, NY 10014 Tel: 212-242-3351 Web Site: www.multicultural.com, pg 1111

Slade, Michael, Art Resource Inc, 65 Bleeker St, 12th fl, New York, NY 10012 Tel: 212-505-8700 Toll Free Tel: 888-505-8666 Fax: 212-505-2053 E-mail: requests@artres.com Web Site: www.artres.com, pg 1427

Slaney, John, Content Critical Solutions Inc, 10 Fifth St, 2nd fl, Valley Stream, NY 11581 Tel: 201-528-2777 E-mail: info@contentcritical.com Web Site: www.contentcritical.com, pg 1115

Slater, George, CRW Graphics Communications, 9100 Pennsauken Hwy, Pennsauken, NJ 08110 Tel: 856-662-9111 Toll Free Tel: 800-820-3000 Fax: 856-665-1789 E-mail: info@crwgraphics.com Web Site: www.crwgraphics.com, pg 1103, 1367, 1413

Slater, Jacob, Independent Publishers Group (IPG), 814 N Franklin St, Chicago, IL 60610 Tel: 312-337-0747 Toll Free Tel: 800-888-4741 (orders) Fax: 312-337-5985 E-mail: frontdesk@ipgbook.com; orders@ipgbook.com Web Site: www.ipgbook.com, pg 1292, 1328

Sleder, Steve, eFulfillment Service Inc, 807 Airport Access Rd, Traverse City, MI 49686 Tel: 231-276-5057 Toll Free Tel: 866-922-6783 E-mail: sales@efulfillmentservice.com Web Site: www.efulfillmentservice.com, pg 1333

PERSONNEL INDEX

Slowik, George Jr, Publishers Weekly, 49 W 23 St, 9th fl, New York, NY 10010 *Tel:* 212-377-5500 *Fax:* 212-377-2733 *Web Site:* www.publishersweekly.com, pg 1136

Sluijter, Jaap, Krishnamurti Publications of America, 1070 McAndrew Rd, Ojai, CA 93023 *Tel:* 805-646-2726 *E-mail:* kfa@kfa.org *Web Site:* www.kfa.org, pg 1329

Small, Ian, Audiobooks.com, an RBmedia company, 935 Sheldon Ct, Burlington, ON L7L 5K6, Canada *E-mail:* customerservice@audiobooks.com *Web Site:* www.audiobooks.com, pg 1141

Smart, John M, Smart Communications Inc, 641 Lexington Ave, 13th fl, New York, NY 10022 *Tel:* 212-486-1894 *E-mail:* info@smartny.com *Web Site:* www.smartny.com, pg 1376

Smee, Joanne Collins, Xerox Corporation, 201 Merritt 7, Norwalk, CT 06851-1056 *Toll Free Tel:* 800-835-6100 (cust serv) *Web Site:* www.xerox.com, pg 1273

Smeltz, Emilie, Purplegator, 1055 Westlakes Dr, Berwyn, PA 19312 *Tel:* 610-688-6000 *Toll Free Tel:* 888-76-GATOR (764-2867) *Web Site:* www.purplegator.com, pg 1350

Smietana, Bob, Religion News Service, c/o University of Missouri's Journalism School, 30 Neff Annex, Columbia, MO 65211 *Tel:* 573-884-1327 *E-mail:* info@religionnews.com *Web Site:* www.religionnews.com, pg 1191

Smith, Adam, Yeck Brothers Co, 2222 Arbor Blvd, Dayton, OH 45439 *Tel:* 937-294-4000 (ext 207) *Toll Free Tel:* 800-417-2767 *E-mail:* direct@yeck.com *Web Site:* www.yeck.com, pg 1116

Smith, Bowen, Kable Product Services Inc, 4275 Thunderbird Lane, Fairfield, OH 45014 *Tel:* 513-671-2800 *E-mail:* info@kable.com *Web Site:* www.kablefulfillment.com, pg 1334

Smith, Brad, Intuit Inc, 2700 Coast Ave, Mountain View, CA 94043 *Tel:* 650-944-6000 *Toll Free Tel:* 800-446-8848 *E-mail:* investor_relations@intuit.com *Web Site:* www.intuit.com, pg 1371

Smith, Jeff, Fotosmith, 3539 E 28 St, Tucson, AZ 85713 *Tel:* 520-882-2033 *Web Site:* www.jeffsmithusa.com, pg 1421

Smith, Jeff, Kensington Technology Group, 1500 Fashion Island Blvd, Suite 300, San Mateo, CA 94404-1595 *Toll Free Tel:* 800-535-4242 *E-mail:* globalmarketing@kensington.com *Web Site:* www.kensington.com, pg 1371

Smith, Jill, Penguin Random House Canada, a Penguin Random House company, 320 Front St W, Suite 1400, Toronto, ON M5V 3B6, Canada *Tel:* 416-364-4449 *Toll Free Tel:* 888-523-9292 (cust serv) *Fax:* 416-598-7764 *E-mail:* customerservicescanada@penguinrandomhouse.com; publicitycanada@penguinrandomhouse.com; rightscanada@penguinrandomhouse.com *Web Site:* www.penguinrandomhouse.ca, pg 1299

Smith, Julia, Booklist, 225 N Michigan Ave, Suite 1300, Chicago, IL 60601 *Tel:* 312-944-6780 *Toll Free Tel:* 800-545-2433 *Fax:* 312-440-9374 *E-mail:* info@booklistonline.com; ala@ala.org *Web Site:* www.booklistonline.com; www.ala.org, pg 1130

Smith, Kenneth E, McClain Printing Co, 212 Main St, Parsons, WV 26287-1033 *Tel:* 304-478-2881 *Toll Free Tel:* 800-654-7179 *Fax:* 304-478-4658 *E-mail:* mcclain@mcclainprinting.com *Web Site:* www.mcclainprinting.com, pg 1212, 1228, 1257, 1269, 1282

Smith, Kristal, Ingram Publisher Services, an Ingram brand, 14 Ingram Blvd, Mail Stop 631, La Vergne, TN 37086 *Tel:* 615-793-5000 *Toll Free Tel:* 866-400-5351 (cust serv) *E-mail:* ips@ingramcontent.com *Web Site:* www.ingrampublisherservices.com, pg 1294

Smith, Laura, Sheriar Books, 603 Briarwood Dr, Myrtle Beach, SC 29572 *Tel:* 843-272-1339 *Fax:* 843-361-1747 *Web Site:* www.sheriarbooks.org, pg 1321

Smith, Megan, Ingram Content Group LLC, One Ingram Blvd, La Vergne, TN 37086-1986 *Tel:* 615-793-5000 *Toll Free Tel:* 800-937-8000 (retailers); 800-937-5300 (ext 1, libs) *E-mail:* customerservice@ingramcontent.com *Web Site:* www.ingramcontent.com, pg 1294, 1317

Smith, Monte, Eaglecrafts Inc, 168 W 12 St, Ogden, UT 84404 *Tel:* 801-393-3991 *Fax:* 801-393-4647 *E-mail:* sales@eaglefeathertrading.com *Web Site:* www.eaglefeathertrading.com, pg 1314

Smith, Nick, Canadian Manda Group, 664 Annette St, Toronto, ON M6S 2C8, Canada *Tel:* 416-516-0911 *Fax:* 416-516-0917 *Toll Free Fax:* 888-563-8327 (CN only) *E-mail:* general@mandagroup.com; info@mandagroup.com *Web Site:* www.mandagroup.com, pg 1287

Smith, Rob, TNG, 3320 S Service Rd, Burlington, ON L7N 3M6, Canada *Toll Free Tel:* 800-201-8127 *Toll Free Fax:* 877-664-9732 *E-mail:* cs@tng.com *Web Site:* www.tng.com, pg 1323

Smith, Ronnie L, Writer's Relief, Inc, 18766 John J Williams Hwy, Unit 4, Box 335, Rehoboth Beach, DE 19971 *Toll Free Tel:* 866-405-3003 *Fax:* 201-641-1253 *E-mail:* info@writersrelief.com *Web Site:* www.WritersRelief.com, pg 1233, 1352

Smith, Steven, AccuWeather Inc, 385 Science Park Rd, State College, PA 16803 *Tel:* 814-235-8600; 814-237-0309 *E-mail:* salesmail@accuweather.com; support@accuweather.com *Web Site:* www.accuweather.com; corporate.accuweather.com, pg 1363

Smith, Sue, Eaglecrafts Inc, 168 W 12 St, Ogden, UT 84404 *Tel:* 801-393-3991 *Fax:* 801-393-4647 *E-mail:* sales@eaglefeathertrading.com *Web Site:* www.eaglefeathertrading.com, pg 1314

Smith, Victoria, The Lion and the Unicorn, 2715 N Charles St, Baltimore, MD 21218-4363 *Tel:* 410-516-6987 (journal orders outside US & CN) *Toll Free Tel:* 800-548-1784 (journal orders) *Fax:* 410-578-2865 (journal orders) *E-mail:* jrnlcirc@jh.edu (journal orders) *Web Site:* www.press.jhu.edu/journals/lion-and-unicorn, pg 1134

Smits, Angie, Southern Territory Associates, 4508 64 St, Lubbock, TX 79414 *E-mail:* sta77@suddenlink.net *Web Site:* www.southernterritory.com, pg 1302

Smolin, Ronald P, Coronet Books Inc, 33 Ashley Dr, Schwenksville, PA 19473 *Tel:* 215-925-2762 *Fax:* 215-925-1912 *Web Site:* www.coronetbooks.com, pg 1314

Smyth, Judy, The Children's Book Store Distribution (CBSD), 23 Griffin St, Waterdown, ON L0R 2H0, Canada *Tel:* 905-690-9397 (ext 237) *Toll Free Tel:* 800-757-8372 (cust serv, CN & US) *Fax:* 905-690-3419 *E-mail:* info@childrensgroup.com; sales@idla.ca *Web Site:* www.childrensgroup.com, pg 1313

Smyth, Sam, StarGroup International Inc, 1194 Old Dixie Hwy, Suite 201, West Palm Beach, FL 33413 *Tel:* 561-547-0667 *E-mail:* info@stargroupinternational.com *Web Site:* stargroupinternational.com, pg 1113

Snow, Chris, Labels Inc, 10 Merrill Industrial Dr, Hampton, NH 03842 *Tel:* 603-929-3088 *Toll Free Tel:* 800-852-2357 *Fax:* 603-929-7305 *E-mail:* sales@labelsinc.com *Web Site:* www.labelsinc.com, pg 1255

Snyder, Daniel, DANPHOTO, LLC, 408 E Rte 66, Flagstaff, AZ 86001 *Tel:* 928-774-0161 *E-mail:* danman@danphoto.com *Web Site:* www.danphoto.com, pg 1420

Snyder, Jake, American Book Review, c/o University of Houston-Victoria College of Liberal Arts & Sciences, 3007 N Ben Wilson St, Victoria, TX 77901 *Tel:* 361-248-8245 *E-mail:* abr@americanbookreview.org; americanbookreview@uhv.org; americanbookreview@gmail.com *Web Site:* americanbookreview.org, pg 1129

Snyder, Jeffrey W, Dikeman Laminating Corp, 181 Sargeant Ave, Clifton, NJ 07013 *Tel:* 973-473-5696 *Fax:* 973-473-2540 *E-mail:* office@dikemanlaminating.com *Web Site:* dikemanlaminating.com, pg 1266

Snyder, John, HBP Inc, 952 Frederick St, Hagerstown, MD 21740 *Tel:* 301-733-2000 *Toll Free Tel:* 800-638-3508 *Fax:* 301-733-6586 *E-mail:* contactus@hbp.com *Web Site:* www.hbp.com, pg 1226, 1254, 1280

Soden, Dave, manroland Goss web systems Americas LLC, 121 Technology Dr, Durham, NH 03824 *Tel:* 603-749-6600 *Toll Free Tel:* 800-323-1200 (parts & serv) *Fax:* 603-750-6860 *E-mail:* info@manrolandgoss.com *Web Site:* www.manrolandgoss.com, pg 1281

Solherm, Mark, Kiplinger's Personal Finance/The Kiplinger Washington Editors Inc, 1100 13 St NW, Suite 750, Washington, DC 20005-4364 *Tel:* 202-887-6400 *Toll Free Tel:* 800-544-0155 (cust serv) *E-mail:* feedback@kiplinger.com *Web Site:* www.kiplinger.com, pg 1191

Solmson, Jim, Canterbury Press, 120 Interstate N Pkwy E, Suite 200, Atlanta, GA 30339 *Tel:* 770-952-8309 *Fax:* 770-952-4623 *E-mail:* sales@canterburypress.net *Web Site:* canterburypress.net, pg 1250

Solomon, Lisa, The Karel/Dutton Group, San Francisco, CA 94121 *Tel:* 415-668-0829 *Web Site:* kareldruttongroup.com, pg 1295

Solyom, Lori, T C Public Relations, One N La Salle St, Suite 600, Chicago, IL 60602 *Tel:* 312-422-1333 *Web Site:* www.tcpr.net, pg 1113

Sonder, Tim, Innovative Design & Graphics, 1327 Greenleaf St, Evanston, IL 60202 *Tel:* 847-475-7772 *Fax:* 847-475-7784 *E-mail:* info@idgevanston.com *Web Site:* www.idgevanston.com, pg 1227

Soneira, Dr Raymond, DisplayMate Technologies Corp, PO Box 550, Amherst, NH 03031 *Tel:* 603-672-8500 *Toll Free Tel:* 800-932-6323 (orders) *E-mail:* info.dm@displaymate.com *Web Site:* www.displaymate.com, pg 1367

Sonntag, Ned, Pointing Robot Studios, 2 Englewood Dr, Suite D3, Harwich, MA 02645 *Tel:* 774-237-0690 *Web Site:* nedsonntag.com, pg 1416

Sonobe, Koji, RISO Inc, 10 State St, Suite 201, Woburn, MA 01801-2105 *Tel:* 978-777-7377 *Toll Free Tel:* 800-942-7476 (cust support) *Web Site:* us.riso.com, pg 1259, 1376

Sood, Tej PS, Newgen North America Inc, 2714 Bee Cave Rd, Suite 201, Austin, TX 78746 *Tel:* 512-478-5341 *Fax:* 512-476-4756 *E-mail:* sales@newgen.co *Web Site:* www.newgen.co, pg 1229

Sorna, Linda, eFulfillment Service Inc, 807 Airport Access Rd, Traverse City, MI 49686 *Tel:* 231-276-5057 *Toll Free Tel:* 866-922-6783 *E-mail:* sales@efulfillmentservice.com *Web Site:* www.efulfillmentservice.com, pg 1333

Sorrentino, Michela, Hermani & Sorrentino Design, 404 Musgrave Rd, Salt Spring Island, BC V8K 1V5, Canada *Tel:* 250-538-8426 *E-mail:* hermani2sorrentino@gmail.com *Web Site:* www.hermanisorrentino.com, pg 1415

Sosinsky, Milt, Copywriters' Council of America™ (CCA), Linick Bldg, 7 Putter Lane, Middle Island, NY 11953 *Tel:* 631-924-3888; 631-924-8555; 631-604-8599 *E-mail:* linickgroup@gmail.com, pg 1345

Soto Laveaga, Gabriela, Bulletin of the History of Medicine, 2715 N Charles St, Baltimore, MD 21218-4363 *Tel:* 410-516-6987 (journal orders outside US & CN) *Toll Free Tel:* 800-548-1784 (journal orders) *Fax:* 410-578-2865 (journal orders) *E-mail:* bhm@jhmi.edu; jrnlcirc@jh.edu (journal orders) *Web Site:* www.press.jhu.edu/journals/bulletin-history-medicine, pg 1130

Souers, Dan, Victory Productions Inc, 55 Linden St, Worcester, MA 01609 *Tel:* 508-755-0051 *E-mail:* victory@victoryprd.com *Web Site:* www.victoryprd.com, pg 1358

Southworth, Bruce E, Bruce E Southworth Reviews, 1621 Lafond Ave, St Paul, MN 55104-2212 *Tel:* 651-808-1099 *E-mail:* mnbookcritic@yahoo.com, pg 1126

Souza, Anthony, The Souza Agency Inc, PO Box 128, Annapolis, MD 21401-0128 *Tel:* 410-573-1300 *Fax:* 410-573-1305 *E-mail:* info@souza.com *Web Site:* www.souza.com, pg 1100

Souza, Meg, Total Printing Systems, 201 S Gregory Dr, Newton, IL 62448 *Tel:* 618-783-2978 *Toll Free Tel:* 800-465-5200 *Fax:* 618-783-8407 *E-mail:* sales@tps1.com *Web Site:* www.tps1.com, pg 1261

Souza, Roseanne, The Souza Agency Inc, PO Box 128, Annapolis, MD 21401-0128 *Tel:* 410-573-1300 *Fax:* 410-573-1305 *E-mail:* info@souza.com *Web Site:* www.souza.com, pg 1100

Spangler, Joyce, Six Red Marbles LLC, 101 Station Landing, Medford, MA 02155 *Tel:* 857-588-9000 *E-mail:* info@sixredmarbles.com *Web Site:* www.sixredmarbles.com, pg 1231, 1376

Spanos, Jason, knk Software LP, 89 Headquarters Plaza N, No 1478, Morristown, NJ 07960 *Tel:* 908-206-4599 *E-mail:* info@knk.com *Web Site:* www.knkpublishingsoftware.com, pg 1349

Spedding, Michelle, The Hibbert Group, 400 Pennington Ave, Trenton, NJ 08650 *Tel:* 609-394-7500 *Toll Free Tel:* 888-HIBBERT (442-2378) *E-mail:* info@hibbertgroup.com *Web Site:* hibbert.com, pg 1104, 1116, 1117

Speer, Ren, United Library Services Inc, 7140 Fairmount Dr SE, Calgary, AB T2H 0X4, Canada *Tel:* 403-252-4426 *Toll Free Tel:* 888-342-5857 (CN only) *Fax:* 403-258-3426 *Toll Free Fax:* 800-661-2806 (CN only) *E-mail:* info@uls.com *Web Site:* www.uls.com, pg 1323

Spiegel, Tom, Presskits, PO Box 71, East Walpole, MA 02032 *Toll Free Tel:* 800-472-3497 *E-mail:* files@presskits.com; team@presskits.com *Web Site:* presskits.com, pg 1105

Spielman, Rachel, Ruder Finn Inc, 425 E 53 St, New York, NY 10022 *Tel:* 212-593-6400 *E-mail:* info@ruderfinn.com *Web Site:* www.ruderfinn.com, pg 1112

Spretnjak, Dr Christine, SOM Publishing, 163 Moon Valley Rd, Windyville, MO 65783 *Tel:* 417-345-8411 *Fax:* 417-345-6668 *E-mail:* som@som.org; dreams@dreamschool.org *Web Site:* www.som.org; www.dreamschool.org, pg 1321

Springett, Sean, Manroland Inc, 800 E Oak Hill Dr, Westmont, IL 60559 *Tel:* 630-920-2000 *E-mail:* info.us@manrolandsheetfed.com *Web Site:* manrolandsheetfed.com, pg 1256, 1281

Springmeyer, Kathy, Sweetgrass Books, 2750 Broadway Ave, Helena, MT 59602 *Tel:* 406-422-1255 *Toll Free Tel:* 800-821-3874 *Web Site:* sweetgrassbooks.com, pg 1358

Spurgeon, Heath W, Flannery Book Service, 20258 Hwy 18, Suite 430-436, Apple Valley, CA 92307 *Toll Free Tel:* 800-456-3400 *Web Site:* fbs-now.com, pg 1346

Spurll, Barbara, Barbara Spurll Illustration, 160 Browning Ave, Toronto, ON M4K 1W5, Canada *Tel:* 416-594-6594 *Toll Free Tel:* 800-989-3123 *Web Site:* www.barbaraspurll.com, pg 1231

Spurlock, Tammy, Ingram Content Group LLC, One Ingram Blvd, La Vergne, TN 37086-1986 *Tel:* 615-793-5000 *Toll Free Tel:* 800-937-8000 (retailers); 800-937-5300 (ext 1, libs) *E-mail:* customerservice@ingramcontent.com *Web Site:* www.ingramcontent.com, pg 1294, 1316

Srouji, Johnny, Apple Inc, One Apple Park Way, Cupertino, CA 95014 *Tel:* 408-996-1010 *Web Site:* www.apple.com, pg 1364

St Clair, David, BDT Products Inc, 250 E Rincon St, Suite 101, Corona, CA 92879 *Tel:* 949-263-6363, pg 1365

St Clement, Courtney, DJD/Golden Advertising, 145 W 28 St, 12th fl, New York, NY 10001 *Tel:* 212-366-5033 *Fax:* 212-243-5044 *E-mail:* call@djdgolden.com *Web Site:* www.djdgolden.com, pg 1099

Stachowiak, Charles Jr, Quality Bindery Services Inc, 501 Amherst St, Buffalo, NY 14207 *Tel:* 716-883-5185 *Toll Free Tel:* 888-883-1266 *Fax:* 716-883-1598 *E-mail:* info@qualitybindery.com *Web Site:* www.qualitybindery.com, pg 1259

Stack, Therisa, Tom Stack & Associates Inc, 7135 N Outrigger Terr, Citrus Springs, FL 34433 *Tel:* 305-852-5520 *E-mail:* tomstack@earthlink.net *Web Site:* www.tomstackassociates.photoshelter.com, pg 1430

Stack, Tom, Tom Stack & Associates Inc, 7135 N Outrigger Terr, Citrus Springs, FL 34433 *Tel:* 305-852-5520 *E-mail:* tomstack@earthlink.net *Web Site:* www.tomstackassociates.photoshelter.com, pg 1430

Stackhouse, Amy M, Washington Monthly, 1200 18 St NW, Suite 330, Washington, DC 20036 *Tel:* 202-955-9010 *Toll Free Tel:* 855-492-1648 (subns) *Fax:* 202-955-9011 *E-mail:* editors@washingtonmonthly.com *Web Site:* washingtonmonthly.com, pg 1137

Stadnik, Ron, Library Bound Inc, 100 Bathurst Dr, Unit 2, Waterloo, ON N2V 1V6, Canada *Tel:* 519-885-3233 *Toll Free Tel:* 800-363-4728 *Fax:* 519-885-2662 *Web Site:* www.librarybound.com, pg 1318

Stallings, Lisa, Longleaf Services Inc, 116 S Boundary St, Chapel Hill, NC 27514-3808 *Tel:* 919-966-7449 *Toll Free Tel:* 800-848-6224 *Fax:* 919-962-2704 (24 hours) *Toll Free Fax:* 800-272-6817 (24 hours) *E-mail:* customerservice@longleafservices.org; orders@longleafservices.org *Web Site:* longleafservices.org, pg 1295

Stamper, Steven L, fd2s, 14205 N Motac Express, Suite 400F, Austin, TX 78728 *Tel:* 512-476-7733 *Web Site:* www.fd2s.com, pg 1414

Stanley, Deirdre, Thomson Reuters, 3 Times Sq, New York, NY 10036 *Tel:* 646-223-4000; 646-223-6100 (edit); 646-223-6000 (newsroom) *Web Site:* www.thomsonreuters.com, pg 1191

Stanley, Todd, Engineered Software™, PO Box 408, Grafton, MA 01519-0408 *Tel:* 336-299-4843 *E-mail:* info@engsw.com; sales@engsw.com *Web Site:* www.engsw.com, pg 1368

Star, Brenda, StarGroup International Inc, 1194 Old Dixie Hwy, Suite 201, West Palm Beach, FL 33413 *Tel:* 561-547-0667 *E-mail:* info@stargroupinternational.com *Web Site:* stargroupinternational.com, pg 1113

Starfield, Jeffrey, CD/Works, 30 Doaks Lane, Marblehead, MA 01945 *Tel:* 978-922-4990 *Toll Free Tel:* 800-CDWORKS (239-6757) *Fax:* 978-922-5110 *Web Site:* www.cdworks.com, pg 1366

Starling, Jaime, Consortium Book Sales & Distribution, an Ingram brand, The Keg House, Suite 101, 34 13 Ave NE, Minneapolis, MN 55413-1007 *Tel:* 612-746-2600 *Toll Free Tel:* 866-400-5351 (cust serv, Jackson, TN) *E-mail:* cbsdinfo@ingramcontent.com *Web Site:* www.cbsd.com, pg 1289

Starr, Jane, Jane Starr Literary Scouts, 1350 Avenue of the Americas, Suite 1205, New York, NY 10019 *Tel:* 212-421-0777 *E-mail:* jane@janestarr.com, pg 1351

Stecher, Patricia, ALC Inc, 750 College Rd E, Suite 201, Princeton, NJ 08540 *Tel:* 609-580-2800 *Toll Free Tel:* 800-252-5478 *Fax:* 609-580-2888 *E-mail:* info@alc.com *Web Site:* www.alc.com, pg 1119

Steele, Jennifer, AudioFile®, 37 Silver St, Portland, ME 04101 *Tel:* 207-774-7563 *Toll Free Tel:* 800-506-1212 *Fax:* 207-775-3744 *E-mail:* info@audiofilemagazine.com *Web Site:* www.audiofilemagazine.com, pg 1130

Steele, Julia, BookPage®, 2143 Belcourt Ave, Nashville, TN 37212 *Tel:* 615-292-8926 *Fax:* 615-292-8249 *Web Site:* bookpage.com, pg 1127

Steele, Sara, Steeleworks, PO Box 4002, Philadelphia, PA 19118 *Tel:* 215-247-4619 *Web Site:* www.sarasteele.com, pg 1417

Steen, John, Evolution Computing Inc, 4228 E Andrea Dr, Cave Creek, AZ 85331 *Tel:* 602-299-1949 *E-mail:* support@fastcad.com; order_request@fastcad.com *Web Site:* www.fastcad.com, pg 1368

Steep, Jamie, Penguin Random House Canada, a Penguin Random House company, 320 Front St W, Suite 1400, Toronto, ON M5V 3B6, Canada *Tel:* 416-364-4449 *Toll Free Tel:* 888-523-9292 (cust serv) *Fax:* 416-598-7764 *E-mail:* customerservicescanada@penguinrandomhouse.com; publicitycanada@penguinrandomhouse.com; rightscanada@penguinrandomhouse.com *Web Site:* www.penguinrandomhouse.ca, pg 1299

Stehle, Causten, Parson Weems' Publisher Services LLC, 3811 Canterbury Rd, No 707, Baltimore, MD 21218 *Tel:* 914-948-4259 *Toll Free Fax:* 866-861-0337 *E-mail:* office@parsonweems.com *Web Site:* www.parsonweems.com, pg 1299

Stein, Andrea J, Jane Wesman Public Relations Inc, 322 Eighth Ave, Suite 1702, New York, NY 10001 *Tel:* 212-620-4080 *Fax:* 212-620-0370 *Web Site:* www.wesmanpr.com, pg 1110

Stein, Jennifer, Walter's Publishing, 1750 Northway Dr, North Mankato, MN 56003 *Toll Free Tel:* 800-447-3274 *E-mail:* info@walterspublishing.com *Web Site:* www.walterspublishing.com, pg 1214

Stein, Sadie, The New York Times Book Review, 620 Eighth Ave, 5th fl, New York, NY 10018 *Tel:* 212-556-1234 *Toll Free Tel:* 800-631-2580 (subns) *E-mail:* bookreview@nytimes.com; books@nytimes.com *Web Site:* www.nytimes.com, pg 1135

Steinbuch, Jack, The Cleveland Vibrator Co, 2828 Clinton Ave, Cleveland, OH 44113 *Tel:* 216-241-7157 *Toll Free Tel:* 800-221-3298 *Fax:* 216-241-3480 *E-mail:* sales@clevelandvibrator.com *Web Site:* www.clevelandvibrator.com, pg 1278

Steiner, Deborah, RR Donnelley, 35 W Wacker Dr, Chicago, IL 60601 *Toll Free Tel:* 800-742-4455 *Web Site:* www.rrd.com, pg 1210, 1225, 1252, 1266, 1279

Steiner, Deborah, RR Donnelley & Sons Company, 35 W Wacker Dr, Chicago, IL 60601 *Tel:* 312-326-8000 *Toll Free Tel:* 800-742-4455 *Web Site:* www.rrd.com, pg 1333

Steiner, Stephan S, GSB Digital, 33-01 Hunters Point Ave, Long Island City, NY 11101 *Tel:* 212-684-3600 *Fax:* 212-684-3613 *E-mail:* questions@gsbdigital.com *Web Site:* www.gsbdigital.com, pg 1369

Steller, Sue F, Flottman Co Inc, 720 Centre View Blvd, Crestview Hills, KY 41017 *Tel:* 859-331-6636 *Fax:* 859-344-7085 *E-mail:* info@flottmanco.com *Web Site:* www.flottmanco.com, pg 1210

Stenger, Robert W Jr, GraphiColor Corp, 3490 N Mill Rd, Vineland, NJ 08360 *Tel:* 856-691-2507 *Toll Free Tel:* 800-552-2507 *Fax:* 856-696-3229 *Web Site:* www.graphicolorcorp.com, pg 1226, 1254

Stephenson, George W, Stephenson Printing, 5731 General Washington Dr, Alexandria, VA 22312 *Tel:* 703-642-9000 *Toll Free Tel:* 800-336-4637 *Fax:* 703-354-0384 *Web Site:* www.stephensonprinting.com, pg 1260

Stephenson, Sandy, Stephenson Printing, 5731 General Washington Dr, Alexandria, VA 22312 *Tel:* 703-642-9000 *Toll Free Tel:* 800-336-4637 *Fax:* 703-354-0384 *Web Site:* www.stephensonprinting.com, pg 1260

Steuben, Alex, Rex Three Inc, 15431 SW 14 St, Sunrise, FL 33326 *Tel:* 954-388-8708 *Toll Free Tel:* 800-782-6509 *Fax:* 954-452-0569 *Web Site:* www.rex3.com, pg 1375

Stevens, Melissa, Mohawk Fine Papers Inc, 465 Saratoga St, Cohoes, NY 12047 *Tel:* 518-237-1740 *Toll Free Tel:* 800-THE-MILL (843-6455) *Fax:* 518-237-7394 *Web Site:* www.mohawkconnects.com, pg 1270

Stevens, Stacey, iCAD Inc, 98 Spit Brook Rd, Suite 100, Nashua, NH 03062 *Tel:* 603-882-5200 *Toll Free Tel:* 866-280-2239 *E-mail:* sales@icadmed.com; support@icadmed.com *Web Site:* www.icadmed.com, pg 1370

Stevens, Trish, Ascot Media Group Inc, PO Box 2394, Friendswood, TX 77549 *Tel:* 832-334-2733 *Toll Free Tel:* 800-854-1134 *Toll Free Fax:* 800-854-2207 *Web Site:* www.ascotmedia.com, pg 1107

Stevenson, Deborah, The Bulletin of the Center for Children's Books, 2715 N Charles St, Baltimore, MD 21218-4363 *Tel:* 410-516-6900; 410-516-6987 (journal orders outside US & CN); 217-244-0324 (bulletin info) *Toll Free Tel:* 800-548-1784 (journal orders) *Fax:* 410-516-6968; 410-578-2865 (journal orders)

E-mail: bccb@illinois.edu; jlorder@jhupress.jhu.edu Web Site: www.press.jhu.edu/journals/bulletin-center-childrens-books, pg 1131

Stevenson, Judy, Southern Territory Associates, 4508 64 St, Lubbock, TX 79414 E-mail: sta77@suddenlink.net Web Site: www.southernterritory.com, pg 1302

Stewart, Jay, Puritan Press Inc, 95 Runnells Bridge Rd, Hollis, NH 03049-6565 Tel: 603-889-4500 Toll Free Tel: 800-635-6302 Fax: 603-889-6551 E-mail: print@puritancapital.com Web Site: www.puritanpress.com, pg 1259

Stewart, Mark, Chicago Distribution Center (CDC), 11030 S Langley Ave, Chicago, IL 60628 Tel: 773-702-7010 Toll Free Fax: 800-621-8476 Web Site: press.uchicago.edu/cdc, pg 1289

Stilson, Peter, GTxcel Inc, 144 Turnpike Rd, Suite 130, Southborough, MA 01772-2104 Toll Free Tel: 800-609-8994 E-mail: info@gtxcel.com Web Site: www.gtxcel.com, pg 1370

Stilwell, Craig, Open Text Corp, 275 Frank Tompa Dr, Waterloo, ON N2L 0A1, Canada Tel: 519-888-7111 Fax: 519-888-0677 Web Site: opentext.com, pg 1374

Stinson, Sherry L, Tyler Creative, 1300 S Johnstone Ave, Bartlesville, OK 74003-5624 Tel: 918-527-6779 E-mail: info@tylercreative.com Web Site: tylercreative.com, pg 1417

Stipe, LeRoy R Jr, Archetype Inc, 317 N Market St, Lancaster, PA 17603 Tel: 717-392-7438 E-mail: mail@nmsgbooks.com Web Site: nmsgbooks.com, pg 1385

Stipe, LeRoy R Jr, North Market Street Graphics (NMSG), 317 N Market St, Lancaster, PA 17603 Tel: 717-392-7438 E-mail: mail@nmsgbooks.com Web Site: www.nmsgbooks.com, pg 1229, 1416

Stire, Rob, The Bindery Inc, 8201 Brooklyn Blvd, Brooklyn Park, MN 55445 Tel: 763-201-2800 Toll Free Tel: 800-851-6598 Fax: 763-201-2790 E-mail: info@thebinderymn.com Web Site: www.thebinderymn.com, pg 1249

Stocking, Derek, LBS, 1801 Thompson Ave, Des Moines, IA 50316-2751 Tel: 515-262-3191 Toll Free Tel: 800-247-5323 Toll Free Fax: 800-262-4091 E-mail: info@lbsbind.com Web Site: www.lbsbind.com, pg 1269

Stoffel, Rod, JP Graphics Inc, 3001 E Venture Dr, Appleton, WI 54911 Tel: 920-733-4483 Fax: 920-733-1700 E-mail: support@jpinc.com Web Site: www.jpinc.com; www.print.jpinc.com, pg 1211, 1227, 1255

Stoller, Erica, Esto Photographics Inc, 36 Waverly Ave, Brooklyn, NY 11205 Tel: 212-505-5454 E-mail: sales@esto.com; assignments@esto.com Web Site: estostock.com, pg 1428

Stone, Ben, Scholastic School Reading Events, 1080 Greenwood Blvd, Lake Mary, FL 32746 Tel: 407-829-8000 Toll Free Tel: 800-770-4662 Fax: 407-829-2600 E-mail: custservbf@scholasticbookfairs.com Web Site: bookfairs.scholastic.com/content/fairs/home.html, pg 1302, 1321

Stone, Jenn, Chicago Distribution Center (CDC), 11030 S Langley Ave, Chicago, IL 60628 Tel: 773-702-7010 Toll Free Fax: 800-621-8476 Web Site: press.uchicago.edu/cdc, pg 1289

Stor, Robert, Copycats, 216 E 45 St, 10th fl, New York, NY 10017 Tel: 212-557-2111 Toll Free Tel: 800-404-2679 Fax: 212-557-2039 E-mail: client@copycats.com Web Site: www.copycats.com, pg 1251

Stradinger, Kristen, Bolger Vision Beyond Print, 3301 Como Ave SE, Minneapolis, MN 55414-2809 Tel: 651-645-6311 Toll Free Tel: 866-264-3287 E-mail: contact@bolgerinc.com Web Site: www.bolgerinc.com, pg 1103

Strang, Ward B, FedEx Ground, 1000 FedEx Dr, Coraopolis, PA 15108 Tel: 412-269-1000 Toll Free Tel: 800-762-3725 Web Site: www.fedex.com, pg 1333

Straughan, Bruce, ISOMEDIA Inc, 12842 Interurban Ave S, Seattle, WA 98168 Tel: 425-869-5411 Toll Free Tel: 866-838-4389 (sales); 877-638-9277 (support) Fax: 425-869-9437 E-mail: sales@isomedia.com Web Site: www.isomedia.com, pg 1371

Straw, Steve, Chesapeake & Hudson Inc, 27 Jacks Shop Rd, Rochelle, VA 22738 Tel: 301-834-7170 Toll Free Tel: 800-231-4469 E-mail: office@cheshud.com Web Site: www.cheshudinc.com, pg 1288

Stringer, Linda L, Publications Professionals LLC, 3603 Chain Bridge Rd, Suite A & B, Fairfax, VA 22030-3244 Tel: 703-934-4499 Fax: 703-591-7389 E-mail: info@pubspros.com Web Site: www.pubspros.com, pg 1381

Strong, Kathi, Emery-Pratt Co, 1966 W M 21, Owosso, MI 48867-1397 Tel: 989-723-5291 Toll Free Tel: 800-762-5683 (orders); 800-248-3887 (cust serv) Fax: 989-723-4677 Toll Free Fax: 800-523-6379 (cust serv) E-mail: customer.service@emery-pratt.com Web Site: www.emery-pratt.com, pg 1315

Stubblefield, Terri D, World Literature Today, 630 Parrington Oval, Suite 110, Norman, OK 73019-4033 Tel: 405-325-4531 E-mail: wlt@ou.edu Web Site: www.worldliteraturetoday.org, pg 1137

Sturtz, Don, Fujii Associates Inc, 75 Sunny Hill Dr, Troy, MO 63379 Tel: 636-528-2546 Fax: 636-600-5153 Web Site: www.fujiiassociates.com, pg 1291

Subel, Janine, Bert Davis Executive Search Inc, 555 Fifth Ave, Suite 302, New York, NY 10017 Tel: 212-838-4000 E-mail: info@bertdavis.com Web Site: www.bertdavis.com, pg 1381

Suchomel, Mark, Baker & Taylor Publisher Services, 30 Amberwood Pkwy, Ashland, OH 44805 Tel: 567-215-0030 Toll Free Tel: 888-814-0208 E-mail: info@btpubservices.com; orders@btpubservices.com Web Site: www.btpubservices.com, pg 1286, 1333, 1400, 1412

Suckno, Elayne, Whitehurst & Clark Book Fulfillment, 1200 County Rd, Rte 523, Flemington, NJ 08822 Tel: 908-782-2323 Toll Free Tel: 800-488-8040 E-mail: wcbooks@aol.com Web Site: www.wcbks.com, pg 1335

Sullivan, Patty, ps ink LLC, 857 Post Rd, Suite 367, Fairfield, CT 06824 Tel: 203-331-6942 Web Site: www.ps-ink.com, pg 1350

Summerfield, Martin A, Franklin Advertising Associates Inc, 441 Main St, Yarmouth Port, MA 02675 Tel: 508-362-7472 E-mail: contact@franklinad.com Web Site: www.franklinad.com, pg 1099

Summers, Tim, Alliance Storage Technologies Inc (ASTI), 10045 Federal Dr, Colorado Springs, CO 80908 Tel: 719-593-7900 Toll Free Tel: 888-567-6332 Fax: 719-598-3472 E-mail: sales@astiusa.com; info@astiusa.com Web Site: www.alliancestoragetechnologies.com, pg 1364

Sun, Christina, Tatung Co of America Inc, 2850 El Presidio St, Long Beach, CA 90810 Tel: 310-637-2105 E-mail: service@tatungusa.com Web Site: www.tatungusa.com, pg 1377

Sutherland, Charles, Lowe Graphics & Printing, 220 Great Circle Rd, Suite 122, Nashville, TN 37228 Tel: 615-242-6649 Fax: 615-254-8867 Web Site: www.etlowe.com, pg 1228

Sutherland, Linda, GTI Graphic Technology Inc, 211 Dupont Ave, Newburgh, NY 12550 Tel: 845-562-7066 Fax: 845-562-2543 E-mail: sales@gtilite.com Web Site: www.gtilite.com, pg 1280, 1370

Sutherland, Matt, Children's Books USA Inc, 425 Boardman Ave, Traverse City, MI 49684 Tel: 231-933-3699 E-mail: info@childrensbooksusa.com Web Site: www.childrensbooksusa.com, pg 1139

Sutherland, Matt, Foreword Reviews, 12935 W Bay Shore Rd, Suite 380, Traverse City, MI 49684 Tel: 231-933-3699 Web Site: www.forewordreviews.com, pg 1132

Sutherland, Victoria, Children's Books USA Inc, 425 Boardman Ave, Traverse City, MI 49684 Tel: 231-933-3699 E-mail: info@childrensbooksusa.com Web Site: www.childrensbooksusa.com, pg 1139

Sutherland, Victoria, Foreword Reviews, 12935 W Bay Shore Rd, Suite 380, Traverse City, MI 49684 Tel: 231-933-3699 Web Site: www.forewordreviews.com, pg 1132

Sutton, Bug, Science Source®, 307 Fifth Ave, 3rd fl, New York, NY 10016 Tel: 212-758-3420 E-mail: info@sciencesource.com; sales@sciencesource.com; contributor@sciencesource.com Web Site: www.sciencesource.com, pg 1430

Sutton, Mark S, International Paper Co, 6400 Poplar Ave, Memphis, TN 38197 Tel: 901-419-9000 Toll Free Tel: 800-207-4003 Web Site: www.internationalpaper.com; facebook.com/internationalpaper; x.com/intlpaperco, pg 1268

Suurd, Rhonda, Webcom Inc, 3480 Pharmacy Ave, Toronto, ON M1W 2S7, Canada Tel: 416-496-1000 Toll Free Tel: 800-665-9322 Fax: 416-496-1537 E-mail: webcom@webcomlink.com Web Site: www.webcomlink.com, pg 1214, 1262, 1284

Suzuki, Hidekazu, Tamron USA Inc, 10 Austin Blvd, Commack, NY 11725 Tel: 631-858-8400 Toll Free Tel: 800-827-8880 Fax: 631-543-5666; 631-858-8462 (cust serv) E-mail: custserv@tamron.com Web Site: www.tamron-usa.com, pg 1377

Suzuki, Junya, Nissha USA Inc, 1051 Perimeter Dr, Suite 600, Schaumburg, IL 60173 Tel: 847-413-2665 Fax: 847-413-4085 Web Site: www.nissha.com, pg 1213, 1229, 1257

Svec, Todd, Tennessee Book Co, 1550 Heil Quaker Blvd, La Vergne, TN 37086 Tel: 615-793-5040 Toll Free Tel: 800-456-0418 Fax: 615-213-9545 Web Site: www.tennesseebook.com, pg 1322

Swados, Sharon, Ingram Content Group LLC, One Ingram Blvd, La Vergne, TN 37086-1986 Tel: 615-793-5000 Toll Free Tel: 800-937-8000 (retailers); 800-937-5300 (ext 1, libs) E-mail: customerservice@ingramcontent.com Web Site: www.ingramcontent.com, pg 1294, 1316

Swain, P K, Heraeus Noblelight America LLC, 910 Clopper Rd, Gaithersburg, MD 20878-1361 Tel: 301-527-2660 Toll Free Tel: 888-276-8600 Fax: 301-527-2661 E-mail: info.hna.uvp@heraeus.com Web Site: www.heraeus-noblelight.com/uvamericas, pg 1280

Swan, Amy, Washington Monthly, 1200 18 St NW, Suite 330, Washington, DC 20036 Tel: 202-955-9010 Toll Free Tel: 855-492-1648 (subns) Fax: 202-955-9011 E-mail: editors@washingtonmonthly.com Web Site: washingtonmonthly.com, pg 1137

Swanberg, Katherine, International Service Co, International Service Bldg, 333 Fourth Ave, Indialantic, FL 32903-4295 Tel: 321-724-1443 Fax: 321-724-1443, pg 1317, 1325, 1328, 1331

Swanzy, Mark, Xante Corp, 2800 Dauphin St, Suite 100, Mobile, AL 36606 Tel: 251-473-6502; 251-473-4920 (tech support) Fax: 251-473-6503 Web Site: www.xante.com, pg 1378

Swartz, Bryan, Omeda, 4 Overlook Point, Suite A2SE, Lincolnshire, IL 60069 Tel: 847-564-8900 E-mail: getstarted@omeda.com Web Site: www.omeda.com, pg 1334

Swartz, Jeff, The Islander Group, 269 Palii St, Mililani, HI 96789 Tel: 808-676-0116 Toll Free Tel: 877-828-4852 Fax: 808-676-5156 E-mail: customerservice@islandergroup.com Web Site: www.islandergroup.com, pg 1317, 1328

Sweeney, Brian, Open Text Corp, 275 Frank Tompa Dr, Waterloo, ON N2L 0A1, Canada Tel: 519-888-7111 Fax: 519-888-0677 Web Site: opentext.com, pg 1374

Sweeney, Richard, The Renton Printery Inc, 315 S Third St, Renton, WA 98057-2028 Tel: 425-235-1776 E-mail: info@rentonprintery.com Web Site: www.rentonprintery.com, pg 1230, 1259

Swenson, Linda, Figaro, PO Box 848, Sharon, CT 06069 Tel: 860-248-8989; 860-364-0834 E-mail: design@figro.com Web Site: www.figro.com, pg 1346, 1354, 1368, 1414

Swent, Greg, Marketry Inc, 1420 NW Gilman Blvd, No 2558, Issaquah, WA 98027 *Tel:* 425-451-1262 *Toll Free Tel:* 800-346-2013 *Web Site:* www.marketry.com, pg 1120

Swiatkowski, Kenneth J, The Hibbert Group, 400 Pennington Ave, Trenton, NJ 08650 *Tel:* 609-394-7500 *Toll Free Tel:* 888-HIBBERT (442-2378) *E-mail:* info@hibbertgroup.com *Web Site:* hibbert.com, pg 1104, 1116, 1117

Swift, John S, John S Swift Co Inc, 999 Commerce Ct, Buffalo Grove, IL 60089 *Tel:* 847-465-3300 *Fax:* 847-465-3309 *Web Site:* www.johnswiftprint.com, pg 1214, 1231, 1261

Swingle, Bob, BookWise Design, 29089 SW Costa Circle W, Wilsonville, OR 97070 *Tel:* 503-542-3551 *Toll Free Tel:* 800-697-9833 *Web Site:* bookwisedesign.com, pg 1223, 1412

Sylve, Elvira C, Clotilde's Secretarial & Management Services, PO Box 871926, New Orleans, LA 70187 *Tel:* 504-242-2912; 504-266-9239 (cell) *Fax:* 504-242-2912, pg 1385

Sylve, Kelly M, Clotilde's Secretarial & Management Services, PO Box 871926, New Orleans, LA 70187 *Tel:* 504-242-2912; 504-266-9239 (cell) *Fax:* 504-242-2912, pg 1385

Symington, Doug, Friesens Corp, One Printers Way, Altona, MB R0G 0B0, Canada *Tel:* 204-324-6401 *Fax:* 204-324-1333 *E-mail:* book_info@friesens.com *Web Site:* www.friesens.com, pg 1210, 1253

Szablya, Helen M, Szablya Consultants Inc, 5300 94 Ave NE, Apt 327, Seattle, WA 98105 *Tel:* 206-465-0482 (cell) *Web Site:* www.helenmszablya.com, pg 1405

Szenda, Stefani, Independent Publishers Group (IPG), 814 N Franklin St, Chicago, IL 60610 *Tel:* 312-337-0747 *Toll Free Tel:* 800-888-4741 (orders) *Fax:* 312-337-5985 *E-mail:* frontdesk@ipgbook.com; orders@ipgbook.com *Web Site:* www.ipgbook.com, pg 1292

Szwet, Gail, Chicago Distribution Center (CDC), 11030 S Langley Ave, Chicago, IL 60628 *Tel:* 773-702-7010 *Toll Free Fax:* 800-621-8476 *Web Site:* press.uchicago.edu/cdc, pg 1289

Tabori, Lena, Welcome Enterprises Inc, 50 Plaza St, No 7A, Brooklyn, NY 11238 *Tel:* 212-989-3200 *Web Site:* www.welcomeenterprisesinc.com, pg 1358

Tacit, Melody, Penguin Random House Canada, a Penguin Random House company, 320 Front St W, Suite 1400, Toronto, ON M5V 3B6, Canada *Tel:* 416-364-4449 *Toll Free Tel:* 888-523-9292 (cust serv) *Fax:* 416-598-7764 *E-mail:* customerservicescanada@penguinrandomhouse.com; publicitycanada@penguinrandomhouse.com; rightscanada@penguinrandomhouse.com *Web Site:* www.penguinrandomhouse.ca, pg 1299

Tadokoro, Shigeaki, OKI Data Americas Inc, 8505 Freeport Pkwy, Suite 600, Irving, TX 75063 *Tel:* 972-815-4800 *Toll Free Tel:* 800-OKI-DATA (654-3282) *E-mail:* support@okidata.com *Web Site:* www.oki.com/us/printing, pg 1374

Tagler, John, Bert Davis Executive Search Inc, 555 Fifth Ave, Suite 302, New York, NY 10017 *Tel:* 212-838-4000 *E-mail:* info@bertdavis.com *Web Site:* www.bertdavis.com, pg 1381

Taiwo, Ayomikun, Penguin Random House Canada, a Penguin Random House company, 320 Front St W, Suite 1400, Toronto, ON M5V 3B6, Canada *Tel:* 416-364-4449 *Toll Free Tel:* 888-523-9292 (cust serv) *Fax:* 416-598-7764 *E-mail:* customerservicescanada@penguinrandomhouse.com; publicitycanada@penguinrandomhouse.com; rightscanada@penguinrandomhouse.com *Web Site:* www.penguinrandomhouse.ca, pg 1299

Talvitie, Kristian, PTC, 121 Seaport Blvd, Boston, MA 02210 *Tel:* 781-370-5000 *Fax:* 781-370-6000 *Web Site:* www.ptc.com, pg 1375

Tambellini, Mike, Symmetry Creative Production, 1300 S Grove Ave, Suite 103, Barrington, IL 60010 *Tel:* 847-382-8750 *E-mail:* information@symmetrycp.com *Web Site:* www.symmetrycp.com, pg 1232

Tanenbaum, Ann, Tanenbaum International Literary Agency Ltd (TILA), 1035 Fifth Ave, Suite 15D, New York, NY 10028 *Tel:* 212-371-4120 *Fax:* 212-988-0457 *E-mail:* hello@tanenbauminternational.com *Web Site:* tanenbauminternational.com, pg 1351

Tang, Adrienne, Penguin Random House Canada, a Penguin Random House company, 320 Front St W, Suite 1400, Toronto, ON M5V 3B6, Canada *Tel:* 416-364-4449 *Toll Free Tel:* 888-523-9292 (cust serv) *Fax:* 416-598-7764 *E-mail:* customerservicescanada@penguinrandomhouse.com; publicitycanada@penguinrandomhouse.com; rightscanada@penguinrandomhouse.com *Web Site:* www.penguinrandomhouse.ca, pg 1299

Tarbox, Shirley, Todd Tarbox, 330 Oakhurst Lane, Colorado Springs, CO 80906 *Tel:* 719-579-9110 *E-mail:* t_tarbox@msn.com, pg 1425

Tassel, Alice, The French Publishers' Agency, PO Box 140, New York, NY 10009 *Tel:* 212-254-4874 *Web Site:* www.frenchrights.com, pg 1346

Taylor, Chip, Chip Taylor Communications, LLC, 2 East View Dr, Derry, NH 03038 *Tel:* 603-434-9262 *Toll Free Tel:* 800-876-CHIP (876-2447) *Fax:* 603-425-1784 *E-mail:* info@chiptaylor.com *Web Site:* www.chiptaylor.com, pg 1303, 1377

Taylor, Glen, Taylor Communications Inc, 1725 Roe Crest Dr, North Mankato, MN 56003 *Toll Free Tel:* 866-541-0937 *Web Site:* www.taylorcommunications.com, pg 1261, 1377

Teaster, Michael, Getty Images Inc, 605 Fifth Ave S, Suite 400, Seattle, WA 98104 *Tel:* 206-925-5000 *Toll Free Tel:* 800-IMAGERY (462-4379); 888-888-5889 *Web Site:* www.gettyimages.com; www.gettyimages.com/customer-support; engage.gettyimages.com/media-inquiries, pg 1369, 1428

Tello, Douglas, ProductionPro, 246 Park St, Bensenville, IL 60106 *Tel:* 847-696-1600 *E-mail:* sales@productionpro.com; graphics@productionpro.com *Web Site:* www.productionpro.com, pg 1258, 1375

Tempesta, Dan, Nuance Communications Inc, One Wayside Rd, Burlington, MA 01803 *Tel:* 781-565-5000 *Toll Free Tel:* 800-654-1187 (cust serv); 888-372-1908 (orders) *Web Site:* www.nuance.com, pg 1374

Temple, Scott, FedEx Supply Chain, 145 Lt George W Lee Ave, Memphis, TN 38103 *Toll Free Tel:* 800-677-3110 *E-mail:* fsc-leads@fedex.com *Web Site:* www.fedex.com/en-us/logistics/supply-chain.html, pg 1334

Terry, David M, Terry & Read LLC, 4471 Dean Martin Dr, The Martin 3302, Las Vegas, NV 89103 *Tel:* 510-813-9854 *Toll Free Fax:* 866-214-4762, pg 1303

Tessel, Marianna, Intuit Inc, 2700 Coast Ave, Mountain View, CA 94043 *Tel:* 650-944-6000 *Toll Free Tel:* 800-446-8848 *E-mail:* investor_relations@intuit.com *Web Site:* www.intuit.com, pg 1371

Tessier, Julien, SGS International LLC, 626 W Main St, Suite 500, Louisville, KY 40202 *Tel:* 502-637-5443 *E-mail:* info@sgsco.com *Web Site:* www.sgsintl.com, pg 1230

Tez, Oytun, Link Translations Inc, 60 E 96 St, New York, NY 10128 *Toll Free Tel:* 866-866-5010 *E-mail:* info@link-translations.com *Web Site:* www.link-translations.com, pg 1403

Thacker, Ben, Kensington Technology Group, 1500 Fashion Island Blvd, Suite 300, San Mateo, CA 94404-1595 *Toll Free Tel:* 800-535-4242 *E-mail:* globalmarketing@kensington.com *Web Site:* www.kensington.com, pg 1371

Thaler, Ike, TWIG One Stop, 10444 White Pinto Ct, Lake Worth, FL 33449 *Tel:* 561-588-0244 *Toll Free Tel:* 855-894-4178 *E-mail:* info@twigonestop.com *Web Site:* www.twigonestop.com, pg 1105

Thessman, Sami, Wunderman, 3 Columbus Circle, New York, NY 10019 *Tel:* 212-941-3000 *Web Site:* www.wunderman.com, pg 1100

Thews, Mike, The John Roberts Company, 9687 East River Rd NW, Minneapolis, MN 55433 *Tel:* 763-755-5500 *Toll Free Tel:* 800-551-1534 *Fax:* 763-755-0394 *E-mail:* success@johnroberts.com *Web Site:* www.johnroberts.com; www.facebook.com/TheJohnRobertsCompany, pg 1105

Thiede, Brian, Action Printing, N6637 Rolling Meadows Dr, Fond du Lac, WI 54937 *Tel:* 920-907-7820 *E-mail:* info@actionprinting.com *Web Site:* www.actionprinting.com, pg 1247

Thomas, Dave, Cliff Digital, 14700 S Main St, Gardena, CA 90248 *Tel:* 310-323-5600 *Toll Free Tel:* 866-429-2242 *Fax:* 310-400-3090 *E-mail:* cliff@cliffdigital.com *Web Site:* www.cliffdigital.com, pg 1103

Thomas, Jared, Omeda, 4 Overlook Point, Suite A2SE, Lincolnshire, IL 60069 *Tel:* 847-564-8900 *E-mail:* getstarted@omeda.com *Web Site:* www.omeda.com, pg 1334

Thomas, Lyra, North Carolina Literary Review (NCLR), East Carolina University, English Dept, ECU Mailstop 555 English, Greenville, NC 27858-4353 *Tel:* 252-328-1537 *Fax:* 252-328-4889 *E-mail:* nclrstaff@ecu.edu *Web Site:* nclr.ecu.edu, pg 1135

Thomas, Mike, Communicorp Inc, 1001 Lockwood Ave, Columbus, GA 31999 *Tel:* 706-324-1182 *E-mail:* mktech@communicorp.com *Web Site:* www.communicorp.com, pg 1224, 1250

Thomason, Ted, Naviga, 7900 International Dr, Suite 800, Bloomington, MN 55425 *Tel:* 651-639-0662 *E-mail:* info@navigaglobal.com *Web Site:* www.navigaglobal.com, pg 1373

Thompson, Anne, MediaLocate Inc, 1200 Piedmont Ave, Pacific Grove, CA 93950 *Tel:* 831-655-7500 *E-mail:* info@medialocate.com *Web Site:* www.medialocate.com, pg 1403

Thompson, Bradley L II, Inland Press, 2001 W Lafayette Blvd, Detroit, MI 48216 *Tel:* 313-961-6000 *Web Site:* www.inlandpress.com, pg 1104

Thompson, Daryl, Wingo LLC, 12161 Ken Adams Way, Wellington, FL 33414 *Tel:* 561-379-2635 *E-mail:* sat@amerimarketing.com *Web Site:* www.wingopromo.com; www.amerimarketing.com, pg 1192

Thompson, Matt, Adobe Systems Inc, 345 Park Ave, San Jose, CA 95110-2704 *Tel:* 408-536-6000 *Fax:* 408-537-6000 *Web Site:* www.adobe.com, pg 1363

Thompson, Rick, Getty Images Inc, 605 Fifth Ave S, Suite 400, Seattle, WA 98104 *Tel:* 206-925-5000 *Toll Free Tel:* 800-IMAGERY (462-4379); 888-888-5889 *Web Site:* www.gettyimages.com; www.gettyimages.com/customer-support; engage.gettyimages.com/media-inquiries, pg 1369, 1428

Thompson, Scott, Wingo LLC, 12161 Ken Adams Way, Wellington, FL 33414 *Tel:* 561-379-2635 *E-mail:* sat@amerimarketing.com *Web Site:* www.wingopromo.com; www.amerimarketing.com, pg 1192

Thompson, Sidney, Independent Publishers Group (IPG), 814 N Franklin St, Chicago, IL 60610 *Tel:* 312-337-0747 *Toll Free Tel:* 800-888-4741 (orders) *Fax:* 312-337-5985 *E-mail:* frontdesk@ipgbook.com; orders@ipgbook.com *Web Site:* www.ipgbook.com, pg 1292, 1328

Thompson, Tim, AKJ Education, 4702 Benson Ave, Halethorpe, MD 21227 *Tel:* 410-242-1602 *Toll Free Tel:* 800-922-6066 *Fax:* 410-242-6107 *Toll Free Fax:* 888-770-2338 *E-mail:* info@akjeducation.com *Web Site:* www.akjeducation.com, pg 1286, 1311

Thomson, Joe, Sheridan GR, 5100 33 St SE, Grand Rapids, MI 49512 *Tel:* 616-957-5100 *Web Site:* www.sheridan.com, pg 1213, 1259

Thomson, Joe, Sheridan MI, 613 E Industrial Dr, Chelsea, MI 48118 *Tel:* 734-475-9145 *Web Site:* www.sheridan.com, pg 1213, 1259, 1271

Thomson, Joe, Sheridan Saline, 960 Woodland Dr, Saline, MI 48176 *Tel:* 734-429-5411 *Web Site:* www.sheridan.com, pg 1214, 1260

Thomson, Mike, Unisys Corp, 801 Lakeview Dr, Suite 100, Blue Bell, PA 19422 *Tel:* 215-274-2742 *Web Site:* www.unisys.com, pg 1378

Thorn, Jeremy, W R Draper Co, 162 Norfinch Dr, Toronto, ON M3N 1X6, Canada *Tel:* 416-663-6001 *Fax:* 416-663-6043 *E-mail:* info@arthurpress.com *Web Site:* www.arthurpress.com, pg 1210, 1225, 1252, 1267

Thorne, Mark, Hill+Knowlton Strategies, 237 Park Ave, 4th fl, New York, NY 10017 *Tel:* 212-885-0300 *Web Site:* www.hkstrategies.com, pg 1109

Thorneloe, Guy, Getty Images Inc, 605 Fifth Ave S, Suite 400, Seattle, WA 98104 *Tel:* 206-925-5000 *Toll Free Tel:* 800-IMAGERY (462-4379); 888-888-5889 *Web Site:* www.gettyimages.com; www.gettyimages.com/customer-support; engage.gettyimages.com/media-inquiries, pg 1369, 1428

Thornton, Jan, Blanks Printing & Imaging Inc, 2343 N Beckley Ave, Dallas, TX 75208 *Tel:* 214-741-3905 *Toll Free Tel:* 800-325-7651 *E-mail:* sales@blanks.com *Web Site:* www.blanks.com, pg 1222, 1249

Thornton, Michael, Progress Printing Plus, 2677 Waterlick Rd, Lynchburg, VA 24502 *Tel:* 434-239-9213 *Toll Free Tel:* 800-572-7804 *Fax:* 434-832-7573 *E-mail:* info@progressprintplus.com *Web Site:* www.progressprintplus.com, pg 1105, 1213, 1230, 1258

Tiburcio, Chastery, Lectorum Publications Inc, 10 New Maple Ave, Suite 303, Pine Brook, NJ 07058 *Tel:* 201-559-2200 *Toll Free Tel:* 800-345-5946 *E-mail:* lectorum@lectorum.com *Web Site:* www.lectorum.com, pg 1318

Tidwell, Andrew, SGS International LLC, 626 W Main St, Suite 500, Louisville, KY 40202 *Tel:* 502-637-5443 *E-mail:* info@sgsco.com *Web Site:* www.sgsintl.com, pg 1230

Tillander, Roger, Symmetry Creative Production, 1300 S Grove Ave, Suite 103, Barrington, IL 60010 *Tel:* 847-382-8750 *E-mail:* information@symmetrycp.com *Web Site:* www.symmetrycp.com, pg 1232

Tillman, Lillian Gail, Clotilde's Secretarial & Management Services, PO Box 871926, New Orleans, LA 70187 *Tel:* 504-242-2912; 504-266-9239 (cell) *Fax:* 504-242-2912, pg 1385

Timms, Ed, CQ Roll Call, 1201 Pennsylvania Ave NW, Suite 600, Washington, DC 20004 *Tel:* 202-650-6500; 202-650-6511 (subns); 202-650-6621 (cust serv) *Toll Free Tel:* 800-432-2250; 800-678-8511 (subns) *E-mail:* customerservice@cqrollcall.com *Web Site:* cqrollcall.com; www.rollcall.com, pg 1190

Ting, Alice, The New York Times Licensing Group, 620 Eighth Ave, 20th fl, New York, NY 10018 *Tel:* 212-556-1927 *E-mail:* nytlg-sales@nytimes.com *Web Site:* nytlicensing.com, pg 1191

Tingley, Paul, Paraclete Press Inc, 100 Southern Eagle Cartway, Brewster, MA 02631 *Tel:* 508-255-4685 *Toll Free Tel:* 800-451-5006 *E-mail:* customerservice@paracletepress.com *Web Site:* www.paracletepress.com, pg 1213, 1229

Tipper, Bryan, Stilo Corp, 1900 City Park Dr, Suite 504, Ottawa, ON K1J 1A3, Canada *Tel:* 613-745-4242 *Fax:* 613-745-5560 *E-mail:* contact@stilo.com *Web Site:* www.stilo.com, pg 1377

Title, Harry, Custom Studios, 77 Main St, Tappan, NY 10983 *Tel:* 845-365-0414 *Toll Free Tel:* 800-631-1362 *Fax:* 845-365-0864 *E-mail:* custumusa@aol.com *Web Site:* customstudios.com, pg 1224

Tobias, Eric, Tobias Associates Inc, 50 Industrial Dr, Ivyland, PA 18974 *Tel:* 215-322-1500 *Toll Free Tel:* 800-877-3367 *Fax:* 215-322-1504 *E-mail:* sales@tobiasinc.com *Web Site:* www.densitometer.com, pg 1283

Tobias, Rochelle, Modern Language Notes (MLN), 2715 N Charles St, Baltimore, MD 21218-4363 *Tel:* 410-516-6987 (journal orders outside US & CN) *Toll Free Tel:* 800-548-1784 (journal orders) *Fax:* 410-578-2865 (journal orders) *E-mail:* jrnlcirc@jh.edu (journal orders) *Web Site:* www.press.jhu.edu/journals/mln, pg 1134

Tobin, Mark, Printronix Inc, 6440 Oak Canyon, Suite 200, Irvine, CA 92618 *Tel:* 714-368-2300 *Toll Free Tel:* 800-665-6210 *Web Site:* www.printronix.com, pg 1375

Tokunaga, Joji, Ricoh Americas Corp, 300 Eagleview Blvd, Exton, PA 19341 *Tel:* 610-296-8000 *Toll Free Tel:* 800-333-2679 (prod support); 800-637-4264 (sales) *Web Site:* www.ricoh-usa.com, pg 1375

Toles, Eve Flannery, Flannery Book Service, 20258 Hwy 18, Suite 430-436, Apple Valley, CA 92307 *Toll Free Tel:* 800-456-3400 *Web Site:* fbs-now.com, pg 1346

Tomasello, Lisa, Ingram Content Group LLC, One Ingram Blvd, La Vergne, TN 37086-1986 *Tel:* 615-793-5000 *Toll Free Tel:* 800-937-8000 (retailers); 800-937-5300 (ext 1, libs) *E-mail:* customerservice@ingramcontent.com *Web Site:* www.ingramcontent.com, pg 1294, 1316

Tompkins, Bill, Tompkins Printing Equipment Co, 5050 N Rose St, Schiller Park, IL 60176 *Tel:* 847-671-5050 *Fax:* 847-671-5538 *E-mail:* sales@tompkins.com *Web Site:* www.tompkins.com, pg 1284

Tompkins, Steve, Tompkins Printing Equipment Co, 5050 N Rose St, Schiller Park, IL 60176 *Tel:* 847-671-5050 *Fax:* 847-671-5538 *E-mail:* sales@tompkins.com *Web Site:* www.tompkins.com, pg 1284

Toms, Justine, New Dimensions Radio, 143 Colgan Ave, Suite 1103, Santa Rosa, CA 95404 *Tel:* 707-468-5215 *E-mail:* info@newdimensions.org *Web Site:* www.newdimensions.org, pg 1191

Tondera, Steve, Translations.com, 1250 Broadway, 32nd fl, New York, NY 10001 *Tel:* 212-689-1616 *Fax:* 212-504-8057 *E-mail:* newyork@translations.com; info@translations.com *Web Site:* translations.com, pg 1405

Toner, Michael, Business Wire, 101 California St, 20th fl, San Francisco, CA 94111 *Tel:* 415-986-4422 *Toll Free Tel:* 800-227-0845 *E-mail:* info@businesswire.com *Web Site:* www.businesswire.com, pg 1189

Tophoff, Vincent, Eska USA BV Inc, 1910 Campostella Rd, Chesapeake, VA 23324 *Tel:* 757-494-7330 *E-mail:* usa@eska.com *Web Site:* www.eska.com, pg 1267

Topper, Hilary, HJMT Public Relations Inc, 3280 Sunrise Hwy, Suite 296, Wantagh, NY 11793 *Tel:* 516-661-2800 *E-mail:* info@hjmt.com *Web Site:* www.hjmt.com, pg 1109

Torre, Kathryn, BR Printers, 665 Lenfest Rd, San Jose, CA 95133 *Tel:* 408-278-7711 *Fax:* 408-929-8062 *E-mail:* info@brprinters.com *Web Site:* www.brprinters.com, pg 1103, 1249

Torres, Angel, Superior Printing Ink Co Inc, 100 North St, Teterboro, NJ 07608 *Tel:* 201-478-5600 *Fax:* 201-478-5650 *Web Site:* www.superiorink.com, pg 1272

Torres, Anna, Independent Publishers Group (IPG), 814 N Franklin St, Chicago, IL 60610 *Tel:* 312-337-0747 *Toll Free Tel:* 800-888-4741 (orders) *Fax:* 312-337-5985 *E-mail:* frontdesk@ipgbook.com; orders@ipgbook.com *Web Site:* www.ipgbook.com, pg 1292, 1328

Torres, Louis Force, The Independent Book Publishers Association (IBPA), 1020 Manhattan Beach Blvd, Suite 204, Manhattan Beach, CA 90266 *Tel:* 310-546-1818 *E-mail:* info@ibpa-online.org *Web Site:* www.ibpa-online.org, pg 1116

Toth, Christian, Verso Advertising Inc, 79 Madison Ave, 8th fl, New York, NY 10016 *Tel:* 212-292-2990 *Web Site:* www.versoadvertising.com, pg 1100

Toth, Luann, School Library Journal, 123 William St, Suite 802, New York, NY 10038 *Tel:* 646-380-0752 *Toll Free Tel:* 800-595-1066 *Fax:* 646-380-0756 *E-mail:* slj@mediasourceinc.com; sljsubs@pcspublink.com *Web Site:* www.slj.com; www.facebook.com/schoollibraryjournal; x.com/sljournal, pg 1136

Totske, Matt, Larson Texts Inc, 1762 Norcross Rd, Erie, PA 16510 *Tel:* 814-824-6365 *Toll Free Tel:* 800-530-2355 *Fax:* 814-824-6377 *Web Site:* www.larsontexts.com, pg 1227, 1269, 1355

Towell, Ellen, The Karel/Dutton Group, San Francisco, CA 94121 *Tel:* 415-668-0829 *Web Site:* kareldutongroup.com, pg 1295

Towey, Brian, Microboards Technology Inc, 8150 Mallory Ct, Chanhassen, MN 55317 *Tel:* 952-556-1600; 952-556-1639 (tech support) *Toll Free Tel:* 800-646-8881 *Fax:* 952-556-1620 *E-mail:* sales@microboards.com *Web Site:* www.microboards.com, pg 1372

Townsend, Guy III, Townsend Communications Inc, 20 E Gregory Blvd, Kansas City, MO 64114 *Tel:* 816-361-0616 *Web Site:* www.townsendcommunications.com; www.townsendprint.com, pg 1232, 1261, 1284

Trahan, Russell, PR/PR Public Relations, 2301 Hickory Lane, Orlando, FL 32803 *Tel:* 407-895-8800 *Web Site:* www.prpr.net, pg 1112

Traina, Sharon, Conrad Direct Inc, 800 Kinderkamack Rd, Suite 307N, Oradell, NJ 07649 *Tel:* 201-567-3200 *Fax:* 201-567-1530 *E-mail:* listinfo@conraddirect.com *Web Site:* www.conraddirect.com, pg 1115

Tran, Tuan, HP Inc, 1501 Paige Mill Rd, Palo Alto, CA 94304-1112 *Tel:* 650-857-1501 *Toll Free Tel:* 800-282-6672 *Web Site:* www.hp.com, pg 1370

Trank, Megan, Independent Publishers Group (IPG), 814 N Franklin St, Chicago, IL 60610 *Tel:* 312-337-0747 *Toll Free Tel:* 800-888-4741 (orders) *Fax:* 312-337-5985 *E-mail:* frontdesk@ipgbook.com; orders@ipgbook.com *Web Site:* www.ipgbook.com, pg 1292, 1328

Trant, Meg, Six Red Marbles LLC, 101 Station Landing, Medford, MA 02155 *Tel:* 857-588-9000 *E-mail:* info@sixredmarbles.com *Web Site:* www.sixredmarbles.com, pg 1231, 1376

Trask, Tami, Cape Cod Compositors Inc, 811 Washington St, Suite 2, Pembroke, MA 02359-2333 *Tel:* 781-826-2100, pg 1223

Travettoo, David, Readerlink Distribution Services LLC, 1420 Kensington Rd, Suite 300, Oakbrook, IL 60523-2164 *Tel:* 708-547-4400 *Toll Free Tel:* 800-549-5389 *E-mail:* info@readerlink.com; marketingservices@readerlink.com *Web Site:* www.readerlink.com, pg 1301

Treacy, Joseph, Treacyfaces Inc, 43 Maltby Ave, West Haven, CT 06516 *Tel:* 203-389-7037 *Web Site:* www.treacyfaces.com, pg 1377

Tremblay, Joseph, Faherty & Associates Inc, 17548 Redfern Ave, Lake Oswego, OR 97035 *Tel:* 503-639-3113 *Fax:* 503-213-6168 *E-mail:* faherty@fahertybooks.com *Web Site:* www.fahertybooks.com, pg 1290

Tremblay, Marc, Fluke Networks, 6920 Seaway Blvd, Everett, WA 98203 *Tel:* 425-446-5500; 425-446-4519 (sales & support) *Toll Free Tel:* 800-283-5853 *E-mail:* info@flukenetworks.com *Web Site:* www.flukenetworks.com, pg 1369

Tremblay, Richard, Resolute Forest Products, 111 Robert-Bourassa Blvd, Suite 5000, Montreal, QC H3C 2M1, Canada *Tel:* 514-875-2160 *Toll Free Tel:* 800-361-2888 *E-mail:* info@resolutefp.com *Web Site:* www.resolutefp.com, pg 1271

Trethewey, Richard, Rainbo Electronic Reviews, 5405 Cumberland Rd, Minneapolis, MN 55410 *Tel:* 612-408-4057 *Web Site:* www.rainboreviews.com, pg 1127

Tricarico, Joy Elton, Carol Bancroft & Friends, PO Box 2030, Danbury, CT 06813 *Tel:* 203-730-8270 *Fax:* 203-730-8275 *E-mail:* cbfriends@sbcglobal.net *Web Site:* www.carolbancroft.com, pg 1412

Triest, Mark, OmniUpdate Inc, 1320 Flynn Rd, Suite 100, Camarillo, CA 93012 *Tel:* 805-484-9400 *Toll Free Tel:* 800-362-2605 *E-mail:* sales@omniupdate.com *Web Site:* omniupdate.com, pg 1374

Triffo, Corie, PrintWest, 1111 Eighth Ave, Regina, SK S4R 1C9, Canada *Tel:* 306-525-2304 *Toll Free Tel:* 800-236-6438 *Fax:* 306-757-2439 *E-mail:* general@printwest.com *Web Site:* www.printwest.com, pg 1213, 1229, 1270, 1282

Trombley, Brian, Data Conversion Laboratory Inc (DCL), 61-18 190 St, Suite 205, Fresh Meadows, NY 11365 *Tel:* 718-357-8700 *Toll Free Tel:* 800-321-2816 (provider problems) *E-mail:* info@dclab.com *Web Site:* www.dataconversionlaboratory.com, pg 1224, 1367

Trost, Mark, FILM Archives Inc, 35 W 35 St, Suite 904, New York, NY 10001-2238 Tel: 212-696-2616 E-mail: info@filmarchivesonline.com Web Site: www.filmarchivesonline.com, pg 1428

Troup, Peter C, Veritiv™ Corporation, 1000 Abernathy Rd, Bldg 400, Suite 1700, Atlanta, GA 30328 Toll Free Tel: 844-VERITIV (837-4848); 866-714-8303 (packaging cust serv); 866-714-8306 (print cust serv) E-mail: contactus@veritivcorp.com; media@veritivcorp.com Web Site: www.veritivcorp.com, pg 1273

Trujillo, Roy B, Translations.com, 1250 Broadway, 32nd fl, New York, NY 10001 Tel: 212-689-1616 Fax: 212-504-8057 E-mail: newyork@translations.com; info@translations.com Web Site: translations.com, pg 1405

Tsakiris, Natasha, Penguin Random House Canada, a Penguin Random House company, 320 Front St W, Suite 1400, Toronto, ON M5V 3B6, Canada Tel: 416-364-4449 Toll Free Tel: 888-523-9292 (cust serv) Fax: 416-598-7764 E-mail: customerservicescanada@penguinrandomhouse.com; publicitycanada@penguinrandomhouse.com; rightscanada@penguinrandomhouse.com Web Site: www.penguinrandomhouse.ca, pg 1299

Tschumper, Heath, La Crosse Graphics Inc, 3025 East Ave S, La Crosse, WI 54601 Tel: 608-788-2500 Toll Free Tel: 800-832-2503 Fax: 608-788-2660 Web Site: www.lacrossegraphics.com, pg 1255

Tuchman, Buddy, Printing Corporation of the Americas Inc, 620 SW 12 Ave, Pompano Beach, FL 33069 Tel: 954-781-8100 Toll Free Tel: 866-721-1PCA (721-1722) Web Site: pcaprintingplus.com, pg 1213, 1229, 1258, 1270

Tucker, Daniel, Sideshow Media LLC, 315 St Johns Place, 1G, Brooklyn, NY 11238 Tel: 917-519-5335 E-mail: inquiries@sideshowbooks.com Web Site: main.sideshowbooks.com, pg 1357

Tulloch, Lauren, Copyright Clearance Center Inc (CCC), 222 Rosewood Dr, Danvers, MA 01923 Tel: 978-750-8400 (sales); 978-646-2600 (cust serv) E-mail: info@copyright.com Web Site: www.copyright.com, pg 1345

Turk, Melissa, Melissa Turk & the Artist Network, 9 Babbling Brook Lane, Suffern, NY 10901 Tel: 845-368-8606 E-mail: melissa@melissaturk.com Web Site: www.melissaturk.com, pg 1416

Twardoch, Adam, Fontlab Ltd, 403 S Lincoln St, Suite 4-51, Port Angeles, WA 98362 Tel: 301-560-3208 Toll Free Tel: 866-571-5039 E-mail: orders@fontlab.com; contact@fontlab.com Web Site: www.fontlab.com, pg 1369

Twiss, Cynthia M, AdvantageCS, 3850 Ranchero Dr, Ann Arbor, MI 48108 Tel: 734-327-3600 Fax: 734-327-3620 E-mail: sales-na@advantagecs.com Web Site: www.advantagecs.com, pg 1363

Tyillian, Jon, VanDam Inc, The VanDam Bldg, 121 W 27 St, New York, NY 10001 Tel: 917-297-5445 E-mail: info@vandam.com Web Site: www.vandam.com, pg 1358

Tyree, J M, Film Quarterly, Journals & Digital Publishing, 155 Grand Ave, Suite 400, Oakland, CA 94612-3758 E-mail: info@filmquarterly.org; customerservice@ucpress.edu Web Site: www.filmquarterly.org; online.ucpress.edu/fq, pg 1131

Tyrrell, Jason, OverDrive Inc, One OverDrive Way, Cleveland, OH 44125 Tel: 216-573-6886 Fax: 216-573-6888 E-mail: info@overdrive.com Web Site: www.overdrive.com, pg 1298

Tyrrell, Paul, P Tyrrell Associates, 321 Monica Crescent, Burlington, ON L7N 1Z5, Canada Tel: 289-937-6436 Fax: 905-639-2640 E-mail: pgtyrrell@cogeco.ca, pg 1303

Uchimoto, Dennis, Bindery & Distribution Service Inc, 9 Overbrook Rd, South Barrington, IL 60010 Tel: 312-550-7000 Fax: 847-842-8800, pg 1278

Uenishi, Hiroyuki, Nissha USA Inc, 1051 Perimeter Dr, Suite 600, Schaumburg, IL 60173 Tel: 847-413-2665 Fax: 847-413-4085 Web Site: www.nissha.com, pg 1213, 1229, 1257

Ulanowicz, Anastasia, The Lion and the Unicorn, 2715 N Charles St, Baltimore, MD 21218-4363 Tel: 410-516-6987 (journal orders outside US & CN) Toll Free Tel: 800-548-1784 (journal orders) Fax: 410-578-2865 (journal orders) E-mail: jrnlcirc@jh.edu (journal orders) Web Site: www.press.jhu.edu/journals/lion-and-unicorn, pg 1134

Urbahn, Keith, Javelin Group, 203 S Union St, Suite 200, Alexandria, VA 22314 Tel: 703-490-8845 E-mail: hello@javelindc.com Web Site: javelindc.com, pg 1348

Urey, Jill L, Glatfelter, Capitol Towers South, 4350 Congress St, Suite 600, Charlotte, NC 28209 Tel: 717-850-0170 Toll Free Tel: 866-744-7380 E-mail: info@glatfelter.com Web Site: www.glatfelter.com, pg 1267

Utomo, Ricky, Penguin Random House Canada, a Penguin Random House company, 320 Front St W, Suite 1400, Toronto, ON M5V 3B6, Canada Tel: 416-364-4449 Toll Free Tel: 888-523-9292 (cust serv) Fax: 416-598-7764 E-mail: customerservicescanada@penguinrandomhouse.com; publicitycanada@penguinrandomhouse.com; rightscanada@penguinrandomhouse.com Web Site: www.penguinrandomhouse.ca, pg 1299

Uttam, Lal, Amcorp Ltd, 10 Norden Lane, Huntington Station, NY 11746 Tel: 631-271-0548 Fax: 631-549-8849 E-mail: amcorpltd@aol.com, pg 1327

Vachon, Jacques, Resolute Forest Products, 111 Robert-Bourassa Blvd, Suite 5000, Montreal, QC H3C 2M1, Canada Tel: 514-875-2160 Toll Free Tel: 800-361-2888 E-mail: info@resolutefp.com Web Site: www.resolutefp.com, pg 1271

Valdivia, Arturo, Polyglot Communications Inc, PO Box 1962, Laguna Beach, CA 92652 Tel: 949-497-1544 E-mail: info@polyglot.us.com Web Site: www.polyglot.us.com, pg 1403

Vallee, Marc, Ariane Editions Inc, 1504-3460 Blvd St-Elzear W, Laval, QC H7P 0M7, Canada Tel: 514-916-8809 E-mail: info@editions-ariane.com Web Site: www.editions-ariane.com, pg 1311

Vallette, Alexandre, Six Red Marbles LLC, 101 Station Landing, Medford, MA 02155 Tel: 857-588-9000 E-mail: info@sixredmarbles.com Web Site: www.sixredmarbles.com, pg 1231, 1376

Van Alstyne, Frederick, Content Critical Solutions Inc, 10 Fifth St, 2nd fl, Valley Stream, NY 11581 Tel: 201-528-2777 E-mail: info@contentcritical.com Web Site: www.contentcritical.com, pg 1115

Van Cleave, Margaret, Virginia Systems, 5509 W Bay Ct, Midlothian, VA 23112 Tel: 804-739-3200 Fax: 804-739-8376 E-mail: sales@virginiasystems.com Web Site: www.virginiasystems.com, pg 1378

Van Cleave, Philip, Virginia Systems, 5509 W Bay Ct, Midlothian, VA 23112 Tel: 804-739-3200 Fax: 804-739-8376 E-mail: sales@virginiasystems.com Web Site: www.virginiasystems.com, pg 1378

Van Dam, Stephan, VanDam Inc, The VanDam Bldg, 121 W 27 St, New York, NY 10001 Tel: 917-297-5445 E-mail: info@vandam.com Web Site: www.vandam.com, pg 1358

Van Dyke, Brandon, Darwill, 11900 W Roosevelt Rd, Hillside, IL 60162 Tel: 708-236-4900 Fax: 708-236-5820 E-mail: info@darwill.com Web Site: www.darwill.com, pg 1224

Van Dyke, Troy, Darwill, 11900 W Roosevelt Rd, Hillside, IL 60162 Tel: 708-236-4900 Fax: 708-236-5820 E-mail: info@darwill.com Web Site: www.darwill.com, pg 1224

Van Horn, James R, Sun Chemical Corp, 35 Waterview Blvd, Parsippany, NJ 07054-1285 Tel: 973-404-6000 E-mail: globalmarketing@sunchemical.com Web Site: www.sunchemical.com, pg 1272

van Kralingen, Bridget, IBM Corp, One New Orchard Rd, Armonk, NY 10504 Tel: 914-499-1900 Toll Free Tel: 800-426-4968 E-mail: askibm@vnet.ibm.com Web Site: www.ibm.com, pg 1370

Van Leeuwen, Mitzi, Reichhold Inc, 1035 Swabia Ct, Durham, NC 27703 Tel: 919-990-7500 Toll Free Tel: 800-448-3482 Fax: 919-990-7749 Web Site: www.reichhold.com, pg 1271

Van Sprang, Andrew J, Maple Logistics Solutions, 60 Grumbacher Rd, York, PA 17406 Tel: 717-764-4596 E-mail: info@maplesoln.com Web Site: www.maplelogisticssolutions.com, pg 1296, 1334

Van Sprang, Andrew J, Maple Press, 480 Willow Springs Lane, York, PA 17406 Tel: 717-764-5911 Toll Free Tel: 800-999-5911 Fax: 717-764-4702 E-mail: sales@maplepress.com Web Site: www.maplepress.com, pg 1212, 1256, 1281

Vance, Becky, Emprint®, 5425 Florida Blvd, Baton Rouge, LA 70806 Tel: 225-923-2550 Toll Free Tel: 800-211-8335 Web Site: emprint.com, pg 1210, 1225, 1253

Vanek, Todd, Bang Printing Co Inc, 3323 Oak St, Brainerd, MN 56401 Tel: 218-829-2877 Toll Free Tel: 800-328-0450 Fax: 218-829-7145 E-mail: info@bangprinting.com Web Site: www.bangprinting.com, pg 1208, 1222, 1248, 1265

Vanek, Todd, Sheridan Saline, 960 Woodland Dr, Saline, MI 48176 Tel: 734-429-5411 Web Site: www.sheridan.com, pg 1214, 1260

Varno, David, Publishers Weekly, 49 W 23 St, 9th fl, New York, NY 10010 Tel: 212-377-5500 Fax: 212-377-2733 Web Site: www.publishersweekly.com, pg 1136

Varrasso, Rino, OGM USA, 4333 46 St, Suite F2, Sunnyside, NY 11104 Tel: 212-964-2430 Web Site: www.ogm.it, pg 1213, 1229, 1257, 1270

Vatne, Britt, ALC Inc, 750 College Rd E, Suite 201, Princeton, NJ 08540 Tel: 609-580-2800 Toll Free Tel: 800-252-5478 Fax: 609-580-2888 E-mail: info@alc.com Web Site: www.alc.com, pg 1119

Vaughan, Lizanne, Getty Images Inc, 605 Fifth Ave S, Suite 400, Seattle, WA 98104 Tel: 206-925-5000 Toll Free Tel: 800-IMAGERY (462-4379); 888-888-5889 Web Site: www.gettyimages.com; www.gettyimages.com/customer-support; engage.gettyimages.com/media-inquiries, pg 1369, 1428

Vaughan, Richard A, Publishing Management Associates Inc, 129 S Phelps Ave, Suite 312, Rockford, IL 61108 Tel: 815-398-8569 Fax: 815-398-8579 E-mail: pma@pma-inc.net Web Site: www.pma-inc.net, pg 1350

Vazinski, Shawn, Lachina Creative, 3693 Green Rd, Cleveland, OH 44122 Tel: 216-292-7959 E-mail: info@lachina.com Web Site: www.lachina.com, pg 1227, 1355, 1371, 1415

Vekony, Atilla, Wheatmark Inc, 2030 E Speedway Blvd, Suite 106, Tucson, AZ 85719 Tel: 520-798-0888 Toll Free Tel: 888-934-0888 Fax: 520-798-3394 E-mail: info@wheatmark.com Web Site: www.wheatmark.com, pg 1351

Venable, Donna, Ricoh Americas Corp, 300 Eagleview Blvd, Exton, PA 19341 Tel: 610-296-8000 Toll Free Tel: 800-333-2679 (prod support); 800-637-4264 (sales) Web Site: www.ricoh-usa.com, pg 1375

Verant, Cindy, Allied Vaughn, 7600 Parklawn Ave, Suite 300, Minneapolis, MN 55435 Tel: 952-832-3100 Toll Free Tel: 800-323-0281 Fax: 952-832-3203 Web Site: www.alliedvaughn.com, pg 1364

Vergoth, Nick, Lake Book Manufacturing Inc, 2085 N Cornell Ave, Melrose Park, IL 60160 Tel: 708-345-7000 E-mail: info@lakebook.com Web Site: www.lakebook.com, pg 1212, 1227, 1256, 1269, 1281

Verma, Pallavi, QBS Learning, 242 W 30 St, Suite 1100, New York, NY 10001 Tel: 646-668-4645 E-mail: contact@qbslearning.com Web Site: www.qbslearning.com, pg 1357, 1417

Vettel, Rich, UnitechEDI Inc, 220 Winthrop St, Winthrop, MA 02152 Toll Free Tel: 800-330-4094 E-mail: info@unitechedi.com Web Site: www.unitechedi.com, pg 1378

Vicks, Dwight E III, Vicks Lithograph & Printing Corp, 5166 Commercial Dr, Yorkville, NY 13495 Tel: 315-736-9344 E-mail: info@vicks.biz Web Site: www.vicks.biz, pg 1214, 1262

Viesti, Joseph, Viesti Associates Inc, 361 S Camino Del Rio, Suite 111, Durango, CO 81303 *Tel:* 970-403-1000, pg 1431

Vijil, Alfonso, The Latin American Book Store Ltd, PO Box 7328, Redlands, CA 92375 *Toll Free Tel:* 800-645-4276 *Fax:* 909-335-9945 *E-mail:* libros@latinamericanbooks.com *Web Site:* www.latinamericanbooks.com, pg 1329

Viktorin, Brian, Greenleaf Book Group LLC, PO Box 91869, Austin, TX 78709 *Tel:* 512-891-6100 *Fax:* 512-891-6150 *E-mail:* contact@greenleafbookgroup.com; orders@greenleafbookgroup.com; foreignrights@greenleafbookgroup.com; media@greenleafbookgroup.com *Web Site:* greenleafbookgroup.com, pg 1292, 1355

Villavicencio-Eschinger, Deb, Choice, 575 Main St, Suite 300, Middletown, CT 06457 *Tel:* 860-347-6933; 847-504-8803 (subns) *Toll Free Tel:* 844-291-0455 (subns) *Fax:* 860-346-8586 *E-mail:* acrlsubscriptions@omeda.com; support@acrlchoice.freshdesk.com *Web Site:* www.ala.org/acrl-choice; www.choice360.org, pg 1131

Viskovic, Hilda, Lectorum Publications Inc, 10 New Maple Ave, Suite 303, Pine Brook, NJ 07058 *Tel:* 201-559-2200 *Toll Free Tel:* 800-345-5946 *E-mail:* lectorum@lectorum.com *Web Site:* www.lectorum.com, pg 1318

Vivona, John, Andrews McMeel Syndication, 1130 Walnut St, Kansas City, MO 64106-2109 *Tel:* 816-581-7300 *Toll Free Tel:* 800-255-6734 *Web Site:* syndication.andrewsmcmeel.com, pg 1189, 1411

Vladi, Olga, Arbor Books, 244 Madison Ave, Box 254, New York, NY 10016 *Tel:* 212-956-0950 *Toll Free Tel:* 877-822-2500 *Fax:* 914-401-9385 *E-mail:* info@arborbooks.com; editorial@arborbooks.net *Web Site:* www.arborbooks.com, pg 1208, 1222, 1248, 1265, 1344, 1353

Vladi, Olga, Arbor Books, 244 Madison Ave, Box 254, New York, NY 10016 *Tel:* 212-956-0950 *Toll Free Tel:* 877-822-2500 *Fax:* 914-401-9385 *E-mail:* info@arborbooks.com; editorial@arborbooks.net *Web Site:* www.arborbooks.com; www.arborghostwriters.com; www.arborservices.com, pg 1411

Vlazny, Jeanne, Graphics Two, 819 S Main St, Burbank, CA 91506 *Tel:* 818-841-4922, pg 1226, 1280

Vogel, Brian, The Language Center, 62 Brunswick Woods Dr, East Brunswick, NJ 08816 *Tel:* 732-613-4554 *Fax:* 732-238-7659 *Web Site:* www.thelanguagectr.com, pg 1402

Vollink, Ron, Sheridan Saline, 960 Woodland Dr, Saline, MI 48176 *Tel:* 734-429-5411 *Web Site:* www.sheridan.com, pg 1214, 1260

Vollmar, Robert, World Literature Today, 630 Parrington Oval, Suite 110, Norman, OK 73019-4033 *Tel:* 405-325-4531 *E-mail:* wlt@ou.edu *Web Site:* www.worldliteraturetoday.org, pg 1137

von Knorring, John, Stylus Publishing LLC, 22883 Quicksilver Dr, Sterling, VA 20166-2019 *Tel:* 703-661-1504 (edit & sales); 703-661-1581 (orders & cust serv); 703-996-1036 *Toll Free Tel:* 800-232-0223 (orders & cust serv) *Fax:* 703-661-1547; 703-661-1501 (orders & cust serv) *E-mail:* stylusinfo@styluspub.com; stylusmail@styluspub.com (orders & cust serv) *Web Site:* styluspub.com, pg 1303

Von Olenhusen, Cuno, Hannecke Display Systems Inc, 210 Grove St, Franklin, MA 02038 *Tel:* 774-235-2329 *E-mail:* info@hannecke.com *Web Site:* www.hannecke.com, pg 1104

Von Staats, Aaron, PTC, 121 Seaport Blvd, Boston, MA 02210 *Tel:* 781-370-5000 *Fax:* 781-370-6000 *Web Site:* www.ptc.com, pg 1375

Voorhees, Barry, Bunting Magnetics Co, 500 S Spencer Rd, Newton, KS 67114 *Tel:* 316-284-2020 *Toll Free Tel:* 800-835-2526; 877-576-0156 *Fax:* 316-283-4975 *E-mail:* bmc@buntingmagnetics.com *Web Site:* www.buntingmagnetics.com, pg 1278

Vosburgh, Andy, GW Inc, 2290 Ball Dr, St Louis, MO 63146 *Tel:* 314-567-9854 *E-mail:* media@gwinc.com *Web Site:* www.gwinc.com, pg 1226, 1370

Votaw, John, Imprint Group, 2070 Cherry St, Denver, CO 80207 *Toll Free Tel:* 800-738-3961 *Toll Free Fax:* 888-867-3869 *Web Site:* imprintgroupwest.com, pg 1292

Votel, Kevin, Publishers Group West (PGW), an Ingram brand, 1700 Fourth St, Berkeley, CA 94710 *Tel:* 510-809-3700 *Toll Free Tel:* 866-400-5351 (cust serv) *Fax:* 510-809-3777 *E-mail:* info@pgw.com *Web Site:* www.pgw.com, pg 1300

Vreeland, Howard Jr, Anderson & Vreeland Inc, 15348 US Hwy 127 EW, Bryan, OH 43506 *Tel:* 419-636-5002 *Toll Free Tel:* 866-282-7697; 888-832-1600 (CN) *Fax:* 419-636-4334 *E-mail:* info@andersonvreeland.com *Web Site:* andersonvreeland.com, pg 1277

Vuicic, Mary Alice, Thomson Reuters, 3 Times Sq, New York, NY 10036 *Tel:* 646-223-4000; 646-223-6100 (edit); 646-223-6000 (newsroom) *Web Site:* www.thomsonreuters.com, pg 1191

Vuolo, Tim, Scholastic School Reading Events, 1080 Greenwood Blvd, Lake Mary, FL 32746 *Tel:* 407-829-8000 *Toll Free Tel:* 800-770-4662 *Fax:* 407-829-2600 *E-mail:* custservbf@scholasticbookfairs.com *Web Site:* bookfairs.scholastic.com/content/fairs/home.html, pg 1302, 1321

Wade, Julian Davis, Davis Art Images, 50 Portland St, Worcester, MA 01608 *Tel:* 508-754-7201 *Toll Free Tel:* 800-533-2847 *Fax:* 508-753-3834 *E-mail:* das@davisart.com; contactus@davisart.com *Web Site:* www.davisart.com, pg 1427

Wagner, Jerry, BMI Educational Services Inc, 26 Haypress Rd, Cranbury, NJ 08512 *Tel:* 732-329-6991 *Toll Free Tel:* 800-222-8100 (orders only) *Fax:* 732-329-6994 *Toll Free Fax:* 800-986-9393 (orders only) *E-mail:* info@bmionline.com *Web Site:* bmionline.com, pg 1312, 1325

Waite, Diana S, Mount Ida Press, 111 Washington Ave, Albany, NY 12210-2203 *Tel:* 518-426-5935 *E-mail:* info@mountidapress.com *Web Site:* www.mountidapress.com, pg 1356

Waitts, George, Crown Roll Leaf Inc, 91 Illinois Ave, Paterson, NJ 07503 *Tel:* 973-742-4000 *Toll Free Tel:* 800-631-3831 *Fax:* 973-742-0219 *Web Site:* www.crownrollleaf.com, pg 1251

Wajdowicz, Jurek, Emerson, Wajdowicz Studios Inc, 514 W 25 St, New York, NY 10001 *Tel:* 212-807-8144 *E-mail:* info@designews.com *Web Site:* www.designews.com; www.facebook.com/DesignEWS; www.instagram.com/ewsdesign, pg 1414

Wakabayashi, H Clark, Welcome Enterprises Inc, 50 Plaza St, No 7A, Brooklyn, NY 11238 *Tel:* 212-989-3200 *Web Site:* www.welcomeenterprisesinc.com, pg 1358

Waletzki, Dave, Eizo Inc, 5710 Warland Dr, Cypress, CA 90630 *Tel:* 562-431-5011 *Toll Free Tel:* 800-800-5202 *Fax:* 562-431-4811 *E-mail:* orders@eizo.com *Web Site:* www.eizo.com, pg 1368

Walkenhorst, Michael D, Veritiv™ Corporation, 1000 Abernathy Rd, Bldg 400, Suite 1700, Atlanta, GA 30328 *Toll Free Tel:* 844-VERITIV (837-4848); 866-714-8303 (packaging cust serv); 866-714-8306 (print cust serv) *E-mail:* contactus@veritivcorp.com; media@veritivcorp.com *Web Site:* www.veritivcorp.com, pg 1273

Walker, Meg, Tandem Literary, 28 Clinton Rd, Glen Ridge, NJ 07028 *Tel:* 212-629-1990 *Fax:* 212-629-1990 *Web Site:* tandemliterary.com, pg 1113

Walker, Ruth, Datalogics Inc, 101 N Wacker, Suite 1800, Chicago, IL 60606 *Tel:* 312-853-8200 *Fax:* 312-853-8282 *E-mail:* sales@datalogics.com; marketing@datalogics.com *Web Site:* www.datalogics.com, pg 1367

Wall, Patrick, A-R Editions Inc, 1600 Aspen Commons, Suite 100, Middleton, WI 53562 *Tel:* 608-836-9000 *Fax:* 608-831-8200 *E-mail:* info@areditions.com *Web Site:* www.areditions.com, pg 1207, 1221, 1277, 1343, 1411

Wallace, Terri, Washington Monthly, 1200 18 St NW, Suite 330, Washington, DC 20036 *Tel:* 202-955-9010 *Toll Free Tel:* 855-492-1648 (subns) *Fax:* 202-955-9011 *E-mail:* editors@washingtonmonthly.com *Web Site:* washingtonmonthly.com, pg 1137

Waller, Cameron, Penguin Random House Canada, a Penguin Random House company, 320 Front St W, Suite 1400, Toronto, ON M5V 3B6, Canada *Tel:* 416-364-4449 *Toll Free Tel:* 888-523-9292 (cust serv) *Fax:* 416-598-7764 *E-mail:* customerservicescanada@penguinrandomhouse.com; publicitycanada@penguinrandomhouse.com; rightscanada@penguinrandomhouse.com *Web Site:* www.penguinrandomhouse.ca, pg 1299

Walsworth, Don Jr, Walsworth, 306 N Kansas Ave, Marceline, MO 64658 *Toll Free Tel:* 800-265-6795 *Web Site:* www.walsworth.com; www.walsworthhistorybooks.com, pg 1214, 1232, 1262

Walsworth, Don O, Walsworth, 306 N Kansas Ave, Marceline, MO 64658 *Toll Free Tel:* 800-265-6795 *Web Site:* www.walsworth.com; www.walsworthhistorybooks.com, pg 1214, 1232, 1262

Walter, Bill, Social Studies School Service, 10200 Jefferson Blvd, PO Box 802, Culver City, CA 90232 *Tel:* 310-839-2436 *Toll Free Tel:* 800-421-4246 (US & CN) *Toll Free Fax:* 800-944-5432 *E-mail:* access@socialstudies.com; customerservice@socialstudies.com *Web Site:* www.socialstudies.com, pg 1302, 1321

Walters, Doug, Bang Printing Co Inc, 3323 Oak St, Brainerd, MN 56401 *Tel:* 218-829-2877 *Toll Free Tel:* 800-328-0450 *Fax:* 218-829-7145 *E-mail:* info@bangprinting.com *Web Site:* www.bangprinting.com, pg 1208, 1222, 1248, 1265

Walters, Eric, Crain Communications Inc, 1155 Gratiot Ave, Detroit, MI 48207-2732 *Tel:* 313-446-6000 *Fax:* 313-446-0383 *E-mail:* info@crain.com *Web Site:* crain.com, pg 1190

Waricha, Joan, Parachute Publishing LLC, PO Box 320249, Fairfield, CT 06825 *Tel:* 203-255-1303, pg 1357

Wark, John, Airphoto, 2311 S Prairie Ave, Pueblo, CO 81005 *Tel:* 719-542-5719 *Web Site:* airphotona; johnwark.com, pg 1419

Warner, Jerry, CD Solutions Inc, 100 W Monument St, Pleasant Hill, OH 45359 *Tel:* 937-676-2376 *Toll Free Tel:* 800-860-2376 *Fax:* 937-676-2478 *E-mail:* contact@cds.com *Web Site:* www.cds.com, pg 1366

Warner, Luther A, Lushena Books Inc, 607 Country Club Dr, Unit E, Bensenville, IL 60106 *Tel:* 630-238-8708 *Toll Free Tel:* 800-785-1545 *Fax:* 630-238-8824 *E-mail:* lushenabks@yahoo.com *Web Site:* lushenabks.com, pg 1318

Warner, Matt, Gem Guides Book Co, 1155 W Ninth St, Upland, CA 91786 *Tel:* 626-855-1611 *Toll Free Tel:* 800-824-5118 (orders) *Fax:* 626-855-1610 *E-mail:* info@gemguidesbooks.com; sales@gemguidesbooks.com (orders) *Web Site:* www.gemguidesbooks.com, pg 1315

Warner, Nancy, Nancy Warner Photographer, 10 Vinton Ct, San Francisco, CA 94108-2407 *Tel:* 415-298-0027 *Web Site:* www.warnerphoto.com, pg 1425

Warren, Erin, Crown Connect, 250 W Rialto Ave, San Bernadino, CA 92408 *Tel:* 909-888-7531 *Fax:* 909-889-1639 *E-mail:* sales@crownconnect.com *Web Site:* www.crownconnect.com, pg 1209, 1224, 1279

Warrick, Mike, Specialty Product Technologies (SPT), 2100 W Broad St, Elizabethtown, NC 28381 *Tel:* 910-862-2511 *Toll Free Tel:* 800-390-6405 *Fax:* 910-879-5486 *Toll Free Fax:* 800-476-5463 *E-mail:* customer.service@sptech.com *Web Site:* www.specialtyproducttechnologies.com, pg 1283

Warwick-Smith, Simon, Metaphysical Book Club, 18340 Sonoma Hwy, Sonoma, CA 95476 *Tel:* 707-939-9212 *Fax:* 707-938-3515 *E-mail:* warwick@vom.com *Web Site:* www.warwickassociates.com, pg 1142

Warwick-Smith, Simon, Warwick Associates, 18340 Sonoma Hwy, Sonoma, CA 95476 Tel: 707-939-9212 Fax: 707-938-3515 E-mail: warwick@vom.com Web Site: www.warwickassociates.com, pg 1113, 1351

Wasco, Sonia Shaner, Grant Heilman Photography Inc, 506 W Lincoln Ave, Lititz, PA 17543 Tel: 717-626-0296 Toll Free Tel: 800-622-2046 Fax: 717-626-0971 E-mail: info@heilmanphoto.com Web Site: www.heilmanphoto.com, pg 1429

Washburne, Mollie H, New Literary History, 2715 N Charles St, Baltimore, MD 21218-4363 Tel: 410-516-6987 (journal orders outside US & CN) Toll Free Tel: 800-548-1784 (journal orders) Fax: 410-578-2865 (journal orders) E-mail: jrnlcirc@jh.edu (journal orders) Web Site: www.press.jhu.edu/journals/new-literary-history, pg 1135

Washchilla, Edward P Jr, Fairfield Marketing Group Inc, 830 Sport Hill Rd, Easton, CT 06112-1241 E-mail: info@fairfieldmarketing.com, pg 1104, 1108, 1116, 1117, 1120, 1225, 1253, 1280, 1346, 1368, 1414

Washington, Kaylynn, Essex Products Group, 30 Industrial Park Rd, Centerbrook, CT 06409-0307 Tel: 860-767-7130 Toll Free Tel: 800-394-7130 Fax: 860-767-9137 E-mail: sales@epg-inc.com Web Site: www.epg-inc.com, pg 1279

Watrous, Angela, Taconic Wire, 250 Totoket Rd, North Branford, CT 06471 Tel: 203-484-2863 Toll Free Tel: 800-253-1450 Fax: 203-484-2865 E-mail: sales@taconicwire.com; taconicwiresales@gmail.com Web Site: www.taconicwire.com, pg 1283

Watson, Amber, Data Conversion Laboratory Inc (DCL), 61-18 190 St, Suite 205, Fresh Meadows, NY 11365 Tel: 718-357-8700 Toll Free Tel: 800-321-2816 (provider problems) E-mail: info@dclab.com Web Site: www.dataconversionlaboratory.com, pg 1224, 1367

Watson, Julie, Ultimate TechnoGraphics Inc, 480 Blvd St-Laurent, Suite 404, Montreal, QC H2Y 3Y7, Canada Tel: 514-938-9050 E-mail: customerservice@imposition.com; marketing@imposition.com; sales@imposition.com Web Site: www.imposition.com, pg 1378

Wawrzyniak, Chris, Fry Communications Inc, 800 W Church Rd, Mechanicsburg, PA 17055 Tel: 717-766-0211 Toll Free Tel: 800-334-1429 Fax: 717-691-0341 E-mail: info@frycomm.com Web Site: www.frycomm.com, pg 1210, 1225, 1253, 1280

Way, Bryan, Roswell Bookbinding, 2614 N 29 Ave, Phoenix, AZ 85009 Tel: 602-272-9338 Toll Free Tel: 888-803-8883 Fax: 602-272-9786 Web Site: www.roswellbookbinding.com, pg 1259, 1326

Webb, B Joanne, The Henry James Review, 2715 N Charles St, Baltimore, MD 21218-4363 Tel: 410-516-6987 (journal orders outside US & CN) Toll Free Tel: 800-548-1784 (journal orders) Fax: 410-578-2865 (journal orders) E-mail: jrnlcirc@jh.edu (journal orders) Web Site: www.press.jhu.edu/journals/henry-james-review, pg 1132

Webb, Patricia, Stylus Publishing LLC, 22883 Quicksilver Dr, Sterling, VA 20166-2019 Tel: 703-661-1504 (edit & sales); 703-661-1581 (orders & cust serv); 703-996-1036 Toll Free Tel: 800-232-0223 (orders & cust serv) Fax: 703-661-1547; 703-661-1501 (orders & cust serv) E-mail: stylusinfo@styluspub.com; stylusmail@styluspub.com (orders & cust serv) Web Site: styluspub.com, pg 1303

Webster, John R, Abacus Graphics LLC, 15179 Hunger Creek Lane, Bigfork, MT 59911-8313 Tel: 406-837-5776 Web Site: www.abacusgraphics.com, pg 1411

Webster, Scott, Scholar's Choice Ltd, 2323 Trafalgar St, London, ON N5Y 5S7, Canada Tel: 519-453-7470 Toll Free Tel: 800-265-1095 Fax: 519-455-2853 Toll Free Tel: 800-363-3398 (CN only) E-mail: sales@BLReview.org Web Site: www.scholarschoice.ca, pg 1302

Wedel, Terry, VO2 Mix Audio Post, 116 Spadina Ave, Suite 208, Toronto, ON M5V 2K6, Canada Tel: 416-603-3954 Fax: 416-603-3957 E-mail: info@vo2mix.ca Web Site: www.vo2mix.ca, pg 1378

Weerasooriya, Supipi, Penguin Random House Canada, a Penguin Random House company, 320 Front St W, Suite 1400, Toronto, ON M5V 3B6, Canada Tel: 416-364-4449 Toll Free Tel: 888-523-9292 (cust serv) Fax: 416-598-7764 E-mail: customerservicescanada@penguinrandomhouse.com; publicitycanada@penguinrandomhouse.com; rightscanada@penguinrandomhouse.com Web Site: www.penguinrandomhouse.ca, pg 1299

Wegenstein, Bernadette, Modern Language Notes (MLN), 2715 N Charles St, Baltimore, MD 21218-4363 Tel: 410-516-6987 (journal orders outside US & CN) Toll Free Tel: 800-548-1784 (journal orders) Fax: 410-578-2865 (journal orders) E-mail: jrnlcirc@jh.edu (journal orders) Web Site: www.press.jhu.edu/journals/mln, pg 1134

Weidner, Cynthia, Fred Weidner & Daughter Printers, 99 Hudson St, 5th fl, New York, NY 10013 Tel: 646-706-5180 E-mail: info@fwdprinters.com Web Site: www.fwdprinters.com, pg 1232, 1262, 1273, 1284, 1351

Weidner, Matthew T, Weidner Communications International Inc, 1468 Alton Way, Downingtown, PA 19335 Tel: 610-486-6525 Fax: 610-486-6527 Web Site: www.weidcom.com, pg 1351

Weiler, Heidi, H B Fuller Co, 1200 Willow Lake Blvd, St Paul, MN 55110-5146 Tel: 651-236-5900 Toll Free Tel: 888-423-8553 E-mail: inquiry@hbfuller.com Web Site: www.hbfuller.com, pg 1267, 1280

Weiman, Mark, Regent Press Printers & Publishers, 2747 Regent St, Berkeley, CA 94705 Tel: 510-845-1196 E-mail: regentpress@mindspring.com Web Site: www.regentpress.net, pg 1375

Weiner, David, Social Studies School Service, 10200 Jefferson Blvd, PO Box 802, Culver City, CA 90232 Tel: 310-839-2436 Toll Free Tel: 800-421-4246 (US & CN) Fax: 310-839-2249 Toll Free Tel: 800-944-5432 E-mail: access@socialstudies.com; customerservice@socialstudies.com Web Site: www.socialstudies.com, pg 1302, 1321

Weingarten, Jon, FIM, 18 Central Blvd, South Hackensack, NJ 07606 Tel: 201-549-1037 Web Site: www.fimheadbands.com, pg 1267

Weinreich, Philip B, Noble Book Press Corp, 211 Ditmas Ave, Brooklyn, NY 11218 Tel: 718-435-9321 Fax: 718-435-0464, pg 1257

Weinschreider, Jennifer, Lassco-Wizer Equipment & Supplies, 485 Hague St, Rochester, NY 14606-1296 Tel: 585-436-1934 Toll Free Tel: 800-854-6595 Fax: 585-464-8665 E-mail: info@lasscowizer.com; sales@lasscowizer.com Web Site: www.lasscowizer.com, pg 1281

Weintraub, Steve, Lawyers & Judges Publishing Co Inc, 917 N Swan Rd, Suite 300, Tucson, AZ 85711 Tel: 520-323-1500 Fax: 520-323-0055 E-mail: sales@lawyersandjudges.com Web Site: www.lawyersandjudges.com, pg 1120

Weiss, Emily, Ingram Content Group LLC, One Ingram Blvd, La Vergne, TN 37086-1986 Tel: 615-793-5000 Toll Free Tel: 800-937-8000 (retailers); 800-937-5300 (ext 1, libs) E-mail: customerservice@ingramcontent.com Web Site: www.ingramcontent.com, pg 1294, 1316

Weiss, Jack, Cosmos Communications Inc, 11-05 44 Dr, Long Island City, NY 11101 Tel: 718-482-1800 Toll Free Tel: 800-223-5751 Fax: 718-482-1968 Web Site: www.cosmoscommunications.com, pg 1366

Weiss, Toby, Electronics for Imaging Inc (EFI), 6750 Dumbarton Circle, Fremont, CA 94555 Tel: 650-357-3500 Toll Free Tel: 800-568-1917; 800-875-7117 (sales) Fax: 650-357-3907 E-mail: info@efi.com Web Site: www.efi.com, pg 1368

Weissman, Alanna, Bellevue Literary Review, 149 E 23 St, Suite 1516, New York, NY 10010 Tel: 917-375-5790 E-mail: info@BLReview.org Web Site: www.BLReview.org, pg 1130

Welch, Brian, Greenleaf Book Group LLC, PO Box 91869, Austin, TX 78709 Tel: 512-891-6100 Fax: 512-891-6150 E-mail: contact@greenleafbookgroup.com; orders@greenleafbookgroup.com; foreignrights@greenleafbookgroup.com; media@greenleafbookgroup.com Web Site: greenleafbookgroup.com, pg 1355

Welch, Josslynne, Litzky PR, 33-41 Newark St, 5th fl, Hoboken, NJ 07030 Tel: 201-222-9118 E-mail: inquiries@litzkypr.com Web Site: litzkypr.com, pg 1110

Welch, Laura, Master Books®, 3142 Hwy 103 N, Green Forest, AR 72638 Tel: 870-438-5288 Toll Free Tel: 800-999-3777 E-mail: nlp@nlpg.com; sales@masterbooks.com Web Site: www.masterbooks.com; www.nlpg.com, pg 1372

Welhouse, Abigail, Scott Manning & Associates, 2 Horatio St, Suite 16G, New York, NY 10014 Tel: 603-491-0995 Web Site: www.scottmanningpr.com, pg 1110

Wells, Huey, Independent Publishers Group (IPG), 814 N Franklin St, Chicago, IL 60610 Tel: 312-337-0747 Toll Free Tel: 800-888-4741 (orders) Fax: 312-337-5985 E-mail: frontdesk@ipgbook.com; orders@ipgbook.com Web Site: www.ipgbook.com, pg 1292, 1328

Wells, Jeff, PBD Worldwide Inc, 1650 Bluegrass Lakes Pkwy, Alpharetta, GA 30004 Tel: 470-769-1000 Toll Free Tel: 866-998-4PBD (998-4723) E-mail: sales.marketing@pbd.com; customerservice@pbd.com Web Site: www.pbd.com, pg 1334

Welsch, Edward, Chronicles: A Magazine of American Culture, 8011 34 Ave S, Suite C11, Bloomington, MN 55425 Web Site: www.chroniclesmagazine.org, pg 1131

Wemyss, Courtney, StoraEnso North American Sales Inc, Canterbury Green, 201 Broad St, Stamford, CT 06901 Tel: 203-541-5100 Fax: 203-353-1143 Web Site: www.storaenso.com, pg 1272

Wenger, Scott, dix! Digital Prepress Inc, 8462 Wayfarer Dr, Cicero, NY 13039 Tel: 315-288-5888 Fax: 315-288-5898 E-mail: info@dixtype.com Web Site: www.dixtype.com, pg 1225, 1252

Wentworth, Skye, Skye Wentworth Public Relations, 23A Durham Point Rd, Durham, NH 03824 Tel: 978-462-4453 E-mail: skyewentworth@gmail.com Web Site: www.skyewentworth.org/wordpress; www.skyewentworth.org, pg 1113

Werdehausen, Kevin, The Ovid Bell Press Inc, 1201 Bluff St, Fulton, MO 65251 Tel: 573-642-2256 Toll Free Tel: 800-835-8919 E-mail: sales@ovidbell.com Web Site: ovidbell.com, pg 1229, 1258, 1270, 1282

Werkley, Timothy S, Swan Packaging Fulfillment Inc, 415 Hamburg Tpke, Wayne, NJ 07470 Tel: 973-790-0990 Fax: 973-790-0216 Web Site: www.swanpackaging.com, pg 1116, 1335, 1337

Wert, Gary L, Wert Bookbinding Inc, 9975 Allentown Blvd, Grantville, PA 17028 Tel: 717-469-0626 Toll Free Tel: 800-344-9378 Fax: 717-469-0629 E-mail: quotes@wertbookbinding.com Web Site: www.wertbookbinding.com, pg 1262

Wert, Kathryn E, Wert Bookbinding Inc, 9975 Allentown Blvd, Grantville, PA 17028 Tel: 717-469-0626 Toll Free Tel: 800-344-9378 Fax: 717-469-0629 E-mail: quotes@wertbookbinding.com Web Site: www.wertbookbinding.com, pg 1262

Wert, Rodney D, Wert Bookbinding Inc, 9975 Allentown Blvd, Grantville, PA 17028 Tel: 717-469-0626 Toll Free Tel: 800-344-9378 Fax: 717-469-0629 E-mail: quotes@wertbookbinding.com Web Site: www.wertbookbinding.com, pg 1262

Wert, Scott A, Wert Bookbinding Inc, 9975 Allentown Blvd, Grantville, PA 17028 Tel: 717-469-0626 Toll Free Tel: 800-344-9378 Fax: 717-469-0629 E-mail: quotes@wertbookbinding.com Web Site: www.wertbookbinding.com, pg 1262

Werthamer, Cynthia, Philosophy and Literature, 2715 N Charles St, Baltimore, MD 21218-4363 Tel: 410-516-6987 (journal orders outside US & CN) Toll Free Tel: 800-548-1784 (journal orders) Fax: 410-578-2865 (journal orders) E-mail: philandlit@bard.edu; jrnlcirc@jh.edu (journal orders) Web Site: www.press.jhu.edu/journals/philosophy-and-literature, pg 1135

PERSONNEL INDEX

Wesman, Jane, Jane Wesman Public Relations Inc, 322 Eighth Ave, Suite 1702, New York, NY 10001 *Tel:* 212-620-4080 *Fax:* 212-620-0370 *Web Site:* www.wesmanpr.com, pg 1110

West, Jim, Jim West Photography, 4875 Three Mile Dr, Detroit, MI 48224 *E-mail:* jim@jimwestphoto.com *Web Site:* www.jimwestphoto.com, pg 1425

West, Judith, Audiobook Department, 6429 N Talman Ave, Chicago, IL 60645 *Tel:* 773-312-0554 *Web Site:* www.judithwest.com, pg 1344

Westbrook, Mr Courtney, Emprint®, 5425 Florida Blvd, Baton Rouge, LA 70806 *Tel:* 225-923-2550 *Toll Free Tel:* 800-211-8335 *Web Site:* emprint.com, pg 1210, 1225, 1253

Westman, Karin E, The Lion and the Unicorn, 2715 N Charles St, Baltimore, MD 21218-4363 *Tel:* 410-516-6987 (journal orders outside US & CN) *Toll Free Tel:* 800-548-1784 (journal orders) *Fax:* 410-578-2865 (journal orders) *E-mail:* jrnlcirc@jh.edu (journal orders) *Web Site:* www.press.jhu.edu/journals/lion-and-unicorn, pg 1134

Weston, Daine, Getty Images Inc, 605 Fifth Ave S, Suite 400, Seattle, WA 98104 *Tel:* 206-925-5000 *Toll Free Tel:* 800-IMAGERY (462-4379); 888-888-5889 *Web Site:* www.gettyimages.com; www.gettyimages.com/customer-support; engage.gettyimages.com/media-inquiries, pg 1369, 1428

Wexler, David, Lerner Publisher Services, 241 First Ave N, Minneapolis, MN 55401 *Tel:* 612-332-3344 *Toll Free Tel:* 800-328-4929 (orders) *Fax:* 612-215-6230 *E-mail:* info@lernerpublisherservices.com; custserve@lernerpublisherservices.com *Web Site:* www.lernerpublisherservices.com, pg 1295

Wheaton, Robert, Penguin Random House Canada, a Penguin Random House company, 320 Front St W, Suite 1400, Toronto, ON M5V 3B6, Canada *Tel:* 416-364-4449 *Toll Free Tel:* 888-523-9292 (cust serv) *Fax:* 416-598-7764 *E-mail:* customerservicescanada@penguinrandomhouse.com; publicitycanada@penguinrandomhouse.com; rightscanada@penguinrandomhouse.com *Web Site:* www.penguinrandomhouse.ca, pg 1299

Wheeler, Brad, Diversified Printing Services Inc, 3425 Cherokee Ave, Columbus, GA 31906 *Tel:* 706-323-2759 *Toll Free Fax:* 888-410-5502 *Web Site:* www.1dps.com, pg 1252

Whitcomb, Pamela, A-R Editions Inc, 1600 Aspen Commons, Suite 100, Middleton, WI 53562 *Tel:* 608-836-9000 *Fax:* 608-831-8200 *E-mail:* info@areditions.com *Web Site:* www.areditions.com, pg 1411

White, Brian, Transimpex Translators, Interpreters, Editors, Consultants Inc, 2300 Main St, 9th fl, Kansas City, MO 64108 *Tel:* 816-561-3777 *Fax:* 816-561-5515 *E-mail:* translations@transimpex.com *Web Site:* www.transimpex.com, pg 1405

White, Terry, eFulfillment Service Inc, 807 Airport Access Rd, Traverse City, MI 49686 *Tel:* 231-276-5057 *Toll Free Tel:* 866-922-6783 *E-mail:* sales@efulfillmentservice.com *Web Site:* www.efulfillmentservice.com, pg 1333

Whitehead, Diane, Association for Childhood Education International, 1875 Connecticut Ave NW, 10th fl, Washington, DC 20009 *Tel:* 202-372-9986 *Toll Free Tel:* 800-423-3563 *E-mail:* headquarters@acei.org *Web Site:* acei.org, pg 1145

Whitehurst, Jim, IBM Corp, One New Orchard Rd, Armonk, NY 10504 *Tel:* 914-499-1900 *Toll Free Tel:* 800-426-4968 *E-mail:* askibm@vnet.ibm.com *Web Site:* www.ibm.com, pg 1370

Whiting, Chuck, Music City Arts Network, PO Box 843, Brentwood, TN 37024 *Toll Free Tel:* 888-80-SHINE (807-4463) *E-mail:* info@musiccityarts.net *Web Site:* www.musiccityartsupdate.com; www.shinetimebooks.com, pg 1111

Whiting, Jerry, Azalea Software Inc, PO Box 16660, Seattle, WA 98116-0660 *Tel:* 206-341-9500; 206-336-9559 (software support); 206-336-9575 (sales & info) *Fax:* 206-299-5600 *E-mail:* salesinfo@azaleabarcodes.com *Web Site:* www.azaleabarcodes.com, pg 1365

Whitney, Haynes, Democrat Printing & Lithographing Co, 6401 Lindsey Rd, Little Rock, AR 72206 *Toll Free Tel:* 800-622-2216 *Fax:* 501-907-7953 *Web Site:* democratprinting.com, pg 1252

Whitney, Thomas, Democrat Printing & Lithographing Co, 6401 Lindsey Rd, Little Rock, AR 72206 *Toll Free Tel:* 800-622-2216 *Fax:* 501-907-7953 *Web Site:* democratprinting.com, pg 1252

Whitten, Robin F, AudioFile®, 37 Silver St, Portland, ME 04101 *Tel:* 207-774-7563 *Toll Free Tel:* 800-506-1212 *Fax:* 207-775-3744 *E-mail:* info@audiofilemagazine.com *Web Site:* www.audiofilemagazine.com, pg 1129

Whobrey, Larry A, International Service Co, International Service Bldg, 333 Fourth Ave, Indialantic, FL 32903-4295 *Tel:* 321-724-1443 *Fax:* 321-724-1443, pg 1317, 1325, 1328, 1331

Wiese, Kris, Ingram Content Group LLC, One Ingram Blvd, La Vergne, TN 37086-1986 *Tel:* 615-793-5000 *Toll Free Tel:* 800-937-8000 (retailers); 800-937-5300 (ext 1, libs) *E-mail:* customerservice@ingramcontent.com *Web Site:* www.ingramcontent.com, pg 1294, 1317

Wilbur, Ralph E, Graphic Litho, 130 Shepard St, Lawrence, MA 01843 *Tel:* 978-683-2766 *Fax:* 978-681-7588 *E-mail:* sales@graphiclitho.com *Web Site:* www.graphiclitho.com, pg 1104, 1211, 1254

Wilcox, Alana, Coach House Printing, 80 bpNichol Lane, Toronto, ON M5S 3J4, Canada *Tel:* 416-979-2217 *Toll Free Tel:* 800-367-6360 (outside Toronto) *Fax:* 416-977-1158 *E-mail:* mail@chbooks.com *Web Site:* www.chbooks.com, pg 1223, 1250

Wilcox, Bruce, Carolina Biological Supply Co, 2700 York Rd, Burlington, NC 27215-3398 *Tel:* 336-586-4399 (intl sales); 336-538-6211 *Toll Free Tel:* 800-334-5551 *Fax:* 336-584-7686 (intl sales) *Toll Free Fax:* 800-222-7112 *E-mail:* quotations@carolina.com; product@carolina.com *Web Site:* www.carolina.com, pg 1313

Willemstyn, Brian, Great Lakes Bindery Inc, 3741 Linden Ave SE, Wyoming, MI 49548 *Tel:* 616-245-5264 *Fax:* 616-245-5883 *E-mail:* jeremy@greatlakesbindery.com *Web Site:* www.greatlakesbindery.com, pg 1254

Willette, E David, Allied Vaughn, 7600 Parklawn Ave, Suite 300, Minneapolis, MN 55435 *Tel:* 952-832-3100 *Toll Free Tel:* 800-323-0281 *Fax:* 952-832-3203 *Web Site:* www.alliedvaughn.com, pg 1364

Willette, Emily, Hilsinger-Mendelson West Inc, 115 N Kings Rd, Los Angeles, CA 90048 *Tel:* 323-931-5335 (text only) *E-mail:* hmiwest@aol.com *Web Site:* www.hilsingermendelson.com, pg 1109

Williams, Abigail, GBS Books, 2321 W Royal Palm Rd, Suite F, Phoenix, AZ 85021 *Tel:* 602-863-6000 *Toll Free Tel:* 800-851-6001 *E-mail:* gbsbooks@gbsbooks.com *Web Site:* www.gbsbooks.com, pg 1315

Williams, Amy, Data Conversion Laboratory Inc (DCL), 61-18 190 St, Suite 205, Fresh Meadows, NY 11365 *Tel:* 718-357-8700 *Toll Free Tel:* 800-321-2816 (provider problems) *E-mail:* info@dclab.com *Web Site:* www.dataconversionlaboratory.com, pg 1224, 1367

Williams, Amy Cox, Ingram Content Group LLC, One Ingram Blvd, La Vergne, TN 37086-1986 *Tel:* 615-793-5000 *Toll Free Tel:* 800-937-8000 (retailers); 800-937-5300 (ext 1, libs) *E-mail:* customerservice@ingramcontent.com *Web Site:* www.ingramcontent.com, pg 1294, 1316

Williams, Dirk, L+L Printers, 6200 Yarrow Dr, Carlsbad, CA 92011 *Tel:* 760-438-3456; 760-477-0321 *Fax:* 760-929-0853 *E-mail:* info@llprinters.com *Web Site:* www.llprinters.com, pg 1256

Williams, Frances, Snow Lion Graphics, PO Box 9465, Berkeley, CA 94709-0465 *Tel:* 510-525-1134; 510-816-2840 (cell) *E-mail:* info@slgbooks.com *Web Site:* www.slgbooks.com, pg 1417

Williams, Jeff, Apple Inc, One Apple Park Way, Cupertino, CA 95014 *Tel:* 408-996-1010 *Web Site:* www.apple.com, pg 1364

Williams, Kathleen, Larson Texts Inc, 1762 Norcross Rd, Erie, PA 16510 *Tel:* 814-824-6365 *Toll Free Tel:* 800-530-2355 *Fax:* 814-824-6377 *Web Site:* www.larsontexts.com, pg 1227, 1269, 1355

Williams, Lenore, American Urban Radio Networks (AURN), 938 Penn Ave, Suite 701, Pittsburgh, PA 15222-3811 *Tel:* 412-456-4099 *Fax:* 412-456-4077 *Web Site:* www.aurn.com, pg 1189

Williams, Lisa, PBD Worldwide Inc, 1650 Bluegrass Lakes Pkwy, Alpharetta, GA 30004 *Tel:* 470-769-1000 *Toll Free Tel:* 866-998-4PBD (998-4723) *E-mail:* sales.marketing@pbd.com; customerservice@pbd.com *Web Site:* www.pbd.com, pg 1334

Williams, Mary K, DocuWare Corp, 4 Crotty Lane, Suite 200, New Windsor, NY 12553 *Tel:* 845-563-9045 *Toll Free Tel:* 888-565-5907 *Fax:* 845-563-9046 *E-mail:* dwsales@docuware.com; support.americas@docuware.com *Web Site:* www.docuware.com, pg 1367

Williams, Matt, Ingenta, 317 George St, New Brunswick, NJ 08901 *Tel:* 732-563-9292 *Fax:* 732-563-9044 *Web Site:* www.ingenta.com, pg 1370

Williams, Richard T, Independent Publishers Group (IPG), 814 N Franklin St, Chicago, IL 60610 *Tel:* 312-337-0747 *Toll Free Tel:* 800-888-4741 (orders) *Fax:* 312-337-5985 *E-mail:* frontdesk@ipgbook.com; orders@ipgbook.com *Web Site:* www.ipgbook.com, pg 1292, 1328

Williams, Robert, I-Web, 175 Bodwell St, Avon, MA 02322 *Tel:* 508-580-5809 *Fax:* 508-580-5632 *E-mail:* info@iwebus.com *Web Site:* iwebus.com, pg 1281

Williams, Roger Dale, Snow Lion Graphics, PO Box 9465, Berkeley, CA 94709-0465 *Tel:* 510-525-1134; 510-816-2840 (cell) *E-mail:* info@slgbooks.com *Web Site:* www.slgbooks.com, pg 1417

Williams, Sylvia, National Book Network (NBN), 4501 Forbes Blvd, Suite 200, Lanham, MD 20706 *Tel:* 301-459-3366 *Toll Free Tel:* 800-462-6420 (orders only) *Fax:* 301-429-5746 *Toll Free Fax:* 800-338-4550 (orders only) *E-mail:* customercare@nbnbooks.com *Web Site:* www.nbnbooks.com, pg 1298, 1319

Williams, Troy, GBS Books, 2321 W Royal Palm Rd, Suite F, Phoenix, AZ 85021 *Tel:* 602-863-6000 *Toll Free Tel:* 800-851-6001 *E-mail:* gbsbooks@gbsbooks.com *Web Site:* www.gbsbooks.com, pg 1315

Williams, Troy, The Ovid Bell Press Inc, 1201 Bluff St, Fulton, MO 65251 *Tel:* 573-642-2256 *Toll Free Tel:* 800-835-8919 *E-mail:* sales@ovidbell.com *Web Site:* ovidbell.com, pg 1229, 1258, 1270, 1282

Willis, Dr Aaron, Social Studies School Service, 10200 Jefferson Blvd, PO Box 802, Culver City, CA 90232 *Tel:* 310-839-2436 *Toll Free Tel:* 800-421-4246 (US & CN) *Fax:* 310-839-2249 *Toll Free Fax:* 800-944-5432 *E-mail:* access@socialstudies.com; customerservice@socialstudies.com *Web Site:* www.socialstudies.com, pg 1302, 1321

Willis, Chris, Ingram Content Group LLC, One Ingram Blvd, La Vergne, TN 37086-1986 *Tel:* 615-793-5000 *Toll Free Tel:* 800-937-8000 (retailers); 800-937-5300 (ext 1, libs) *E-mail:* customerservice@ingramcontent.com *Web Site:* www.ingramcontent.com, pg 1294, 1316

Willoughby, Vanessa, Publishers Weekly, 49 W 23 St, 9th fl, New York, NY 10010 *Tel:* 212-377-5500 *Fax:* 212-377-2733 *Web Site:* www.publishersweekly.com, pg 1136

Wilmoth, Gabriel, SCB Distributors, 15608 S New Century Dr, Gardena, CA 90248 *Tel:* 310-532-9400 *Toll Free Tel:* 800-729-6423 *Fax:* 310-532-7001 *E-mail:* scb@scbdistributors.com *Web Site:* www.scbdistributors.com, pg 1302

Wilner, Jim, Intex Solutions Inc, 110 "A" St, Needham, MA 02494 *Tel:* 781-449-6222 *Fax:* 781-444-2318 *E-mail:* sales@intex.com *Web Site:* www.intex.com, pg 1371

Wilson, Dan, Roland DGA Corp, 15363 Barranca Pkwy, Irvine, CA 92618-2216 *Tel:* 949-727-2100 *Toll Free Tel:* 800-542-2307 *Fax:* 949-727-2112 *Web Site:* www.rolanddga.com, pg 1376

Wilson, Jack, Laplink Software Inc, 600 108 Ave NE, Suite 610, Bellevue, WA 98004 *Tel:* 425-952-6000 *Toll Free Tel:* 800-LAPLINK (527-5465) *E-mail:* info@laplink.com; sales@laplink.com *Web Site:* web.laplink.com, pg 1371

Wilson, Jennifer, The New York Times Book Review, 620 Eighth Ave, 5th fl, New York, NY 10018 *Tel:* 212-556-1234 *Toll Free Tel:* 800-631-2580 (subns) *E-mail:* bookreview@nytimes.com; books@nytimes.com *Web Site:* www.nytimes.com, pg 1135

Wilson, Scott, Value Added Resources, 7900 Rockville Rd, Indianapolis, IN 46214 *Tel:* 317-899-1000 *E-mail:* info@valueaddedres.com *Web Site:* www.valueaddedres.com, pg 1335

Wilson, Stacy, Progress Printing Plus, 2677 Waterlick Rd, Lynchburg, VA 24502 *Tel:* 434-239-9213 *Toll Free Tel:* 800-572-7804 *Fax:* 434-832-7573 *E-mail:* info@progressprintplus.com *Web Site:* www.progressprintplus.com, pg 1230

Wilson, Steven, Book Sales, 142 W 36 St, 4th fl, New York, NY 10018 *Tel:* 212-779-4971; 212-779-4972 *Fax:* 212-779-6058 *Web Site:* www.quartoknows.com, pg 1312

Winchester, Dawn, Publicis North America, 1675 Broadway, New York, NY 10009 *Tel:* 212-474-5000 *Web Site:* www.publicisna.com, pg 1112

Wind, Lee, The Independent Book Publishers Association (IBPA), 1020 Manhattan Beach Blvd, Suite 204, Manhattan Beach, CA 90266 *Tel:* 310-546-1818 *E-mail:* info@ibpa-online.org *Web Site:* www.ibpa-online.org, pg 1116

Windler, Robert, Diecrafters Inc, 1349 S 55 Ct, Cicero, IL 60804-1211 *Tel:* 708-656-3336 *Fax:* 708-656-3386 *E-mail:* info@diecrafters.com *Web Site:* www.diecrafters.com, pg 1252

Windover, Rocco, Dunn & Co Inc, 75 Green St, Clinton, MA 01510 *Tel:* 978-368-8505 *Fax:* 978-368-7867 *E-mail:* info@booktrauma.com *Web Site:* www.booktrauma.com, pg 1210, 1252, 1267

Wine, Lauren, GTxcel Inc, 144 Turnpike Rd, Suite 130, Southborough, MA 01772-2104 *Toll Free Tel:* 800-609-8994 *E-mail:* info@gtxcel.com *Web Site:* www.gtxcel.com, pg 1370

Winkler, Simon, Listco Direct Marketing, 1276 46 St, Brooklyn, NY 11219 *Tel:* 718-871-8400 *Fax:* 718-871-7692 *E-mail:* info@listcodirect.com *Web Site:* www.listcodirect.com, pg 1120

Winner, Scott, Ingenta, 317 George St, New Brunswick, NJ 08901 *Tel:* 732-563-9292 *Fax:* 732-563-9044 *Web Site:* www.ingenta.com, pg 1370

Winslow, Ted, SumTotal Systems LLC, 2850 NW 43 St, Suite 150, Gainesville, FL 32606 *Tel:* 352-264-2800 *Toll Free Tel:* 866-933-1416 *Fax:* 352-374-2257 *E-mail:* customersupport@sumtotalsystems.com *Web Site:* www.sumtotalsystems.com, pg 1377

Winterhalter, Ken, Twin Rivers Paper Co, 82 Bridge Ave, Madawaska, ME 04756 *Tel:* 207-728-3321 *Toll Free Tel:* 800-920-9988 *Fax:* 207-728-8701 *E-mail:* info@twinriverspaper.com *Web Site:* www.twinriverspaper.com, pg 1273

Wirtz, Cathrin, Liz Gately Book Scouting, 36 W 37 St, Rm 408, New York, NY 10018 *Tel:* 212-244-1441 *E-mail:* liz@lizgately.com *Web Site:* www.lizgately.com, pg 1347

Wise, LaDonna, O'Neil Digital Solutions LLC, 12655 Beatrice St, Los Angeles, CA 90066 *Tel:* 310-448-6400 *E-mail:* sales@oneildata.com *Web Site:* www.oneildata.com, pg 1229, 1257, 1270, 1282

Wise, Nancy, Sandhill Book Marketing Ltd, Millcreek Industrial Park, Unit 4, 3308 Appaloosa Rd, Kelowna, BC V1V 2W5, Canada *Tel:* 250-491-1446 *Toll Free Tel:* 800-667-3848 (CN only) *Fax:* 250-491-4066 *E-mail:* info@sandhillbooks.com *Web Site:* www.sandhillbooks.com, pg 1321

Wisniewski, Cassie, Chicago Distribution Center (CDC), 11030 S Langley Ave, Chicago, IL 60628 *Tel:* 773-702-7010 *Toll Free Tel:* 800-621-8476 *Web Site:* press.uchicago.edu/cdc, pg 1289

Wisotzkey, James S, Maple Logistics Solutions, 60 Grumbacher Rd, York, PA 17406 *Tel:* 717-764-4596 *E-mail:* info@maplesoln.com *Web Site:* www.maplelogisticssolutions.com, pg 1296, 1334

Wisotzkey, James S, Maple Press, 480 Willow Springs Lane, York, PA 17406 *Tel:* 717-764-5911 *Toll Free Tel:* 800-999-5911 *Fax:* 717-764-4702 *E-mail:* sales@maplepress.com *Web Site:* www.maplepress.com, pg 1212, 1256, 1281

Wolf, Lawrence, CyberWolf® Inc, c/o 530-B Harkle Rd, Suite 100, Santa Fe, NM 87505 *E-mail:* sales@cyberwolf.com *Web Site:* www.ebookdownloadservice.com, pg 1367

Wolf, Linda Masco, CyberWolf® Inc, c/o 530-B Harkle Rd, Suite 100, Santa Fe, NM 87505 *E-mail:* sales@cyberwolf.com *Web Site:* www.ebookdownloadservice.com, pg 1367

Wolfe, Lainey, North Market Street Graphics (NMSG), 317 N Market St, Lancaster, PA 17603 *Tel:* 717-392-7438 *E-mail:* mail@nmsgbooks.com *Web Site:* www.nmsgbooks.com, pg 1229, 1416

Wolff, Harvey, Haynes North America Inc, 2801 Townsgate Rd, Suite 340, Westlake Village, CA 91361 *Tel:* 805-498-6703 *Toll Free Tel:* 800-4-HAYNES (442-9637) *Fax:* 805-498-2867 *E-mail:* customerservice.haynes@infopro-digital.com *Web Site:* www.haynes.com, pg 1328

Wolff, Richard J, Kreab, House of Sweden, Suite 504, 2900 "K" St NW, Washington, DC 20007 *Tel:* 202-536-1590 *E-mail:* washingtondc@kreab.com *Web Site:* www.kreab.com/washington-dc, pg 1110

Wolfson, Milt, FIM, 18 Central Blvd, South Hackensack, NJ 07606 *Tel:* 201-549-1037 *Web Site:* www.fimheadbands.com, pg 1267

Wolin, Gary, McManus & Morgan, 2506 W Seventh St, Los Angeles, CA 90057 *Tel:* 213-387-4433 *Web Site:* www.mcmanusandmorgan.com, pg 1269

Woliner, Tal, American Association for the Advancement of Science (AAAS), 1200 New York Ave NW, Washington, DC 20005 *Tel:* 202-326-6400 *Fax:* 202-371-9526 *Web Site:* www.aaas.org, pg 1145

Wong, Ms Chi-Li, AEI (Atchity Entertainment International Inc), 400 S Burnside Ave, Suite 11B, Los Angeles, CA 90036 *Tel:* 323-932-1685, pg 1343

Wong, Kit, C & C Offset Printing Co USA Inc, 70 W 36 St, Unit 10C, New York, NY 10018 *Tel:* 212-431-4210 *Toll Free Tel:* 866-540-4134 *Web Site:* www.ccoffset.com, pg 1208, 1223, 1249

Wong, Lan, International Literary Properties (ILP), 286 Madison Ave, New York, NY 10017 *Tel:* 646-202-1633 *Fax:* 212-967-0977 *E-mail:* contact@ilpliterary.com *Web Site:* www.internationalliteraryproperties.com, pg 1348

Wood, Glenn, Fujitsu Computer Products of America Inc, 1250 E Arques Ave, Sunnyvale, CA 94085-4701 *Tel:* 408-746-6000 *Toll Free Tel:* 800-626-4686 *E-mail:* scanner-sales@us.fujitsu.com *Web Site:* www.fujitsu.com/us, pg 1369

Wood, Jeff, Data Conversion Laboratory Inc (DCL), 61-18 190 St, Suite 205, Fresh Meadows, NY 11365 *Tel:* 718-357-8700 *Toll Free Tel:* 800-321-2816 (provider problems) *E-mail:* info@dclab.com *Web Site:* www.dataconversionlaboratory.com, pg 1224, 1367

Wood, Linda, Signature Book Printing Inc, 8041 Cessna Ave, Gaithersburg, MD 20879 *Tel:* 301-258-8353 *E-mail:* book@sbpbooks.com *Web Site:* sbpbooks.com, pg 1214, 1231, 1260

Wood, Naomi J, The Lion and the Unicorn, 2715 N Charles St, Baltimore, MD 21218-4363 *Tel:* 410-516-6987 (journal orders outside US & CN) *Toll Free Tel:* 800-548-1784 (journal orders) *Fax:* 410-578-2865 (journal orders) *E-mail:* jrnlcirc@jh.edu (journal orders) *Web Site:* www.press.jhu.edu/journals/lion-and-unicorn, pg 1134

Wood, Tara, Litzky PR, 33-41 Newark St, 5th fl, Hoboken, NJ 07030 *Tel:* 201-222-9118 *E-mail:* inquiries@litzkypr.com *Web Site:* litzkypr.com, pg 1110

Woodhouse, Sharon, Conspire Creative, Chicago, IL 60657 *Tel:* 773-562-5499 *Web Site:* www.conspirecreative.com, pg 1345

Woolforde, Marlon, Printronix Inc, 6440 Oak Canyon, Suite 200, Irvine, CA 92618 *Tel:* 714-368-2300 *Toll Free Tel:* 800-665-6210 *Web Site:* www.printronix.com, pg 1375

Worden, Trip, Universal Bookbindery Inc, 1200 N Colorado, San Antonio, TX 78207 *Tel:* 210-734-9502 *Toll Free Tel:* 800-594-2015 *Fax:* 210-736-0867 *E-mail:* service@universalbookbindery.com *Web Site:* www.universalbookbindery.com, pg 1261

Worman, Megan, Melcher Media Inc, 124 W 13 St, New York, NY 10011 *Tel:* 212-727-2322 *Fax:* 212-627-1973 *E-mail:* info@melcher.com *Web Site:* www.melcher.com, pg 1356

Wortman, Shawn, La Crosse Graphics Inc, 3025 East Ave S, La Crosse, WI 54601 *Tel:* 608-788-2500 *Toll Free Tel:* 800-832-2503 *Fax:* 608-788-2660 *Web Site:* www.lacrossegraphics.com, pg 1255

Wren, Mark, Texas Bookman, 2700 Lone Star Dr, Dallas, TX 75212 *Tel:* 214-678-6680 *Toll Free Tel:* 800-566-2665 *Fax:* 214-678-6699 *E-mail:* orders@texasbookman.com *Web Site:* www.texasbookman.com, pg 1322

Wrenn, Kevin, PTC, 121 Seaport Blvd, Boston, MA 02210 *Tel:* 781-370-5000 *Fax:* 781-370-6000 *Web Site:* www.ptc.com, pg 1375

Wright, George IV, Publication Identification & Processing Systems, 10 Midland Ave, Suite M-02, Port Chester, NY 10573 *Tel:* 212-996-6000 *Toll Free Tel:* 888-783-7439 *Fax:* 212-410-7477 *Toll Free Fax:* 800-241-7477 *E-mail:* info@pips.com *Web Site:* www.pips.com, pg 1230

Wright, Randy, Product Identification & Processing Systems Inc, 10 Midland Ave, Suite M-02, Port Chester, NY 10573-5911 *Tel:* 212-996-6000 *Toll Free Tel:* 888-783-7439 *Fax:* 212-410-7477 *Toll Free Fax:* 800-241-PIPS (241-7477) *E-mail:* info@pips.com *Web Site:* www.pips.com, pg 1230

Wyatt, Neal, Library Journal, 123 William St, Suite 802, New York, NY 10038 *Tel:* 646-380-0700 *Toll Free Tel:* 800-588-1030 *Fax:* 646-380-0756 *E-mail:* ljinfo@mediasourceinc.com *Web Site:* www.libraryjournal.com, pg 1134

Wybel, Sheryl L, Wybel Marketing Group Inc, 213 W Main St, Barrington, IL 60010 *Tel:* 847-382-0384; 847-382-0382 *Toll Free Tel:* 800-323-5297 *Fax:* 847-382-0385 *Toll Free Fax:* 800-595-5252 *E-mail:* bookreps@wybel.com, pg 1304

Wyrostok, Chuck, AppaLight, 230 Griffith Run, Spencer, WV 25276 *Tel:* 304-932-2992 *Web Site:* www.appalight.com, pg 1427

Xu, Meifang, Signature Print Services, 3565 Sierra Rd, San Jose, CA 95132 *Tel:* 408-213-3393 *Fax:* 408-213-3399 *Web Site:* www.signatureprint.com, pg 1260

Yahes, Jarrod, Shutterstock Inc, Empire State Bldg, 350 Fifth Ave, 20th fl, New York, NY 10118 *E-mail:* support@shutterstock.com; press@shutterstock.com *Web Site:* www.shutterstock.com, pg 1430

Yahr, Andrea, Round Table Companies, PO Box 1603, Deerfield, IL 60015 *Toll Free Tel:* 833-750-5683 *Web Site:* www.roundtablecompanies.com, pg 1417

Yake, Sarah, International Literary Properties (ILP), 286 Madison Ave, New York, NY 10017 *Tel:* 646-202-1633 *Fax:* 212-967-0977 *E-mail:* contact@ilpliterary.com *Web Site:* www.internationalliteraryproperties.com, pg 1348

Yambao, Mariluz, FIM, 18 Central Blvd, South Hackensack, NJ 07606 Tel: 201-549-1037 Web Site: www.fimheadbands.com, pg 1267

Yanez, Danny, Franklin & Siegal Associates Inc, 40 Exchange Place, Suite 1703, New York, NY 10005 Tel: 212-868-6311 Web Site: www.franklinandsiegal.com, pg 1346

Yang, Cecilia, Penguin Random House Canada, a Penguin Random House company, 320 Front St W, Suite 1400, Toronto, ON M5V 3B6, Canada Tel: 416-364-4449 Toll Free Tel: 888-523-9292 (cust serv) Fax: 416-598-7764 E-mail: customerservicescanada@penguinrandomhouse.com; publicitycanada@penguinrandomhouse.com; rightscanada@penguinrandomhouse.com Web Site: www.penguinrandomhouse.ca, pg 1299

Yang, Mai, Independent Publishers Group (IPG), 814 N Franklin St, Chicago, IL 60610 Tel: 312-337-0747 Toll Free Tel: 800-888-4741 (orders) Fax: 312-337-5985 E-mail: frontdesk@ipgbook.com; orders@ipgbook.com Web Site: www.ipgbook.com, pg 1292, 1328

Yarmola, Yuri, Fontlab Ltd, 403 S Lincoln St, Suite 4-51, Port Angeles, WA 98362 Tel: 301-560-3208 Toll Free Tel: 866-571-5039 E-mail: orders@fontlab.com; contact@fontlab.com Web Site: www.fontlab.com, pg 1369

Yates, Keith, Copywriters' Council of America™ (CCA), Linick Bldg, 7 Putter Lane, Middle Island, NY 11953 Tel: 631-924-3888; 631-924-8555; 631-604-8599 E-mail: linickgroup@gmail.com, pg 1345

Yeager, Michael A, Lindenmeyr Book Publishing Papers, 3 Manhattanville Rd, Purchase, NY 10577 Tel: 914-696-9300 Web Site: www.lindenmeyrbook.com, pg 1269

Yeager, Riff, PadillaCRT, 1101 W River Pkwy, Suite 400, Minneapolis, MN 55415 Tel: 612-455-1700 Fax: 612-455-1060 Web Site: www.padillacrt.com, pg 1111

Yenne, Bill, AGS BookWorks, PO Box 460313, San Francisco, CA 94146-0313 Tel: 415-285-8799 Web Site: www.agsbookworks.com, pg 1353

Yip, Steve, Pacific Publishing Co Inc, 636 Alaska St S, Seattle, WA 98108 Tel: 206-461-1300 E-mail: ppcprint@nwlink.com; ppccirc@nwlink.com; ppcbind@nwlink.com Web Site: pacificpublishingcompany.com, pg 1258

Yoder, Madison, Human Rights Quarterly, 2715 N Charles St, Baltimore, MD 21218-4363 Tel: 410-516-6987 (journal orders outside US & CN) Toll Free Tel: 800-548-1784 (journal orders) Fax: 410-578-2865 (journal orders) E-mail: jrnlcirc@jh.edu (journal orders) Web Site: www.press.jhu.edu/journals/human-rights-quarterly, pg 1133

Yogachandra, Nat, Baha'i Distribution Service (BDS), 1233 Central St, Evanston, IL 60201 Tel: 847-853-7899 Toll Free Tel: 800-999-9019 E-mail: bds@usbnc.org Web Site: www.bahaibookstore.com, pg 1286

Yoon, Thomas, LG Electronics USA, 1000 Sylvan Ave, Englewood Cliffs, NJ 07632 Tel: 201-816-2000 Toll Free Tel: 800-243-0000 (cust serv) Web Site: www.lg.com/us, pg 1371

Yorimitsu, Megan, Calvary Distribution, 3232 W MacArthur Blvd, Santa Ana, CA 92704 Tel: 714-545-6548 Toll Free Tel: 800-444-7664 Fax: 714-641-8201 E-mail: info@calvaryd.org Web Site: www.calvaryd.org, pg 1287

Yoshida-Carrera, Yoko, Emerson, Wajdowicz Studios Inc, 514 W 25 St, New York, NY 10001 Tel: 212-807-8144 E-mail: info@designews.com Web Site: www.designews.com; www.facebook.com/DesignEWS; www.instagram.com/ewsdesign, pg 1414

Yoshihara, Mari, American Quarterly, 2715 N Charles St, Baltimore, MD 21218-4363 Tel: 410-516-6987 (journal orders outside US & CN) Toll Free Tel: 800-548-1784 (journal orders) Fax: 410-578-2865 (journal orders) E-mail: jrnlcirc@jh.edu (journal orders) Web Site: www.americanquarterly.org; www.press.jhu.edu/journals/american-quarterly, pg 1129

Young, Debi, Sunbelt Publications Inc, 664 Marsat Ct, Suite A, Chula Vista, CA 91911 Tel: 619-258-4911 Toll Free Tel: 800-626-6579 (cust serv) Fax: 619-258-4916 E-mail: info@sunbeltpub.com; service@sunbeltpub.com Web Site: sunbeltpublications.com, pg 1322

Young, Joseph L, Magna Visual Inc, 28271 Cedar Park Blvd, Perrysburg, OH 43551 Tel: 314-843-9000 Toll Free Tel: 800-843-3399 Fax: 314-843-0000 E-mail: magna@magnavisual.com; mvsales@magnavisual.com Web Site: www.magnavisual.com, pg 1281

Yun, Michelle, Courier Printing, One Courier Place, Smyrna, TN 37167 Tel: 615-355-4000 Toll Free Tel: 800-467-0444 Fax: 615-355-4088 Web Site: www.courierprinting.com, pg 1224, 1251

Yungen, Sophia, Claris International Inc, 5201 Patrick Henry Dr, Santa Clara, CA 95054 Tel: 408-727-8227 (sales & cust support) Toll Free Tel: 800-325-2747 (sales); 800-325-2747 (cust support) Fax: 408-987-7447 E-mail: claris_sales@claris.com Web Site: www.claris.com, pg 1366

Yurchak, Jason, Yurchak Printing Inc, 920 Links Ave, Landisville, PA 17538 Tel: 717-399-0209 E-mail: ypi.info@yurchak.com Web Site: www.yurchak.com, pg 1215, 1262, 1284

Yurchak, John Jr, Yurchak Printing Inc, 920 Links Ave, Landisville, PA 17538 Tel: 717-399-0209 E-mail: ypi.info@yurchak.com Web Site: www.yurchak.com, pg 1215, 1262, 1284

Yurchak, John W, Yurchak Printing Inc, 920 Links Ave, Landisville, PA 17538 Tel: 717-399-0209 E-mail: ypi.info@yurchak.com Web Site: www.yurchak.com, pg 1215, 1262, 1284

Zaccardo, Robin, Six Red Marbles LLC, 101 Station Landing, Medford, MA 02155 Tel: 857-588-9000 E-mail: info@sixredmarbles.com Web Site: www.sixredmarbles.com, pg 1231, 1376

Zacharias, Greg, The Henry James Review, 2715 N Charles St, Baltimore, MD 21218-4363 Tel: 410-516-6987 (journal orders outside US & CN) Toll Free Tel: 800-548-1784 (journal orders) Fax: 410-578-2865 (journal orders) E-mail: jrnlcirc@jh.edu (journal orders) Web Site: www.press.jhu.edu/journals/henry-james-review, pg 1132

Zaeh, Brion, PBD Worldwide Inc, 1650 Bluegrass Lakes Pkwy, Alpharetta, GA 30004 Tel: 470-769-1000 Toll Free Tel: 866-998-4PBD (998-4723) E-mail: sales.marketing@pbd.com; customerservice@pbd.com Web Site: www.pbd.com, pg 1334

Zak, Ken, Durr MEGTEC LLC, 830 Prosper St, DePere, WI 54115 Tel: 920-336-5715 E-mail: megtecinquiries@megtec.com Web Site: www.durr-megtec.com, pg 1279

Zales, Steve, Library Journal, 123 William St, Suite 802, New York, NY 10038 Tel: 646-380-0700 Toll Free Tel: 800-588-1030 Fax: 646-380-0756 E-mail: ljinfo@mediasourceinc.com Web Site: www.libraryjournal.com, pg 1214

Zamiska, Gene, Electronics for Imaging Inc (EFI), 6750 Dumbarton Circle, Fremont, CA 94555 Tel: 650-357-3500 Toll Free Tel: 800-568-1917; 800-875-7117 (sales) Fax: 650-357-3907 E-mail: info@efi.com Web Site: www.efi.com, pg 1368

Zangri, Ann, Ingram Content Group LLC, One Ingram Blvd, La Vergne, TN 37086-1986 Tel: 615-793-5000 Toll Free Tel: 800-937-8000 (retailers); 800-937-5300 (ext 1, libs) E-mail: customerservice@ingramcontent.com Web Site: www.ingramcontent.com, pg 1294, 1316

Zanou, Konstantina, Journal of Modern Greek Studies, 2715 N Charles St, Baltimore, MD 21218-4363 Tel: 410-516-6987 (journal orders outside US & CN) Toll Free Tel: 800-548-1784 (journal orders) Fax: 410-578-2865 (journal orders) E-mail: jrnlcirc@jh.edu (journal orders) Web Site: www.press.jhu.edu/journal-modern-greek-studies, pg 1133

Zant, Tom, Challenge Machinery Co, 6125 Norton Center Dr, Norton Shores, MI 49441 Tel: 231-799-8484 Fax: 231-798-1275 E-mail: info@challengemachinery.com; sales@challengemachinery.com Web Site: www.challengemachinery.com, pg 1278

Zegarek, Meryl, Meryl Zegarek Public Relations Inc, 255 W 108 St, Suite 9D1, New York, NY 10025 Tel: 917-493-3601 Web Site: www.mzpr.com, pg 1113

Zelezny, Carol A, Jonathan David Publishers Inc, 52 Tuscan Way, Suite 202-371, St Augustine, FL 32092 Tel: 718-456-8611 E-mail: customerservice@jdbooks.com Web Site: www.jdbooks.com, pg 1295

Zentmaier, Robert L, Science Source®, 307 Fifth Ave, 3rd fl, New York, NY 10016 Tel: 212-758-3420 E-mail: info@sciencesource.com; sales@sciencesource.com; contributor@sciencesource.com Web Site: www.sciencesource.com, pg 1430

Zhang, Ellen, Penguin Random House Canada, a Penguin Random House company, 320 Front St W, Suite 1400, Toronto, ON M5V 3B6, Canada Tel: 416-364-4449 Toll Free Tel: 888-523-9292 (cust serv) Fax: 416-598-7764 E-mail: customerservicescanada@penguinrandomhouse.com; publicitycanada@penguinrandomhouse.com; rightscanada@penguinrandomhouse.com Web Site: www.penguinrandomhouse.ca, pg 1299

Zibart, Mary Claire, BookPage®, 2143 Belcourt Ave, Nashville, TN 37212 Tel: 615-292-8926 Fax: 615-292-8249 Web Site: bookpage.com, pg 1127

Zibart, Michael A, BookPage®, 2143 Belcourt Ave, Nashville, TN 37212 Tel: 615-292-8926 Fax: 615-292-8249 Web Site: bookpage.com, pg 1127

Ziff, Dorothy, Melissa Turk & the Artist Network, 9 Babbling Brook Lane, Suffern, NY 10901 Tel: 845-368-8606 E-mail: melissa@melissaturk.com Web Site: www.melissaturk.com, pg 1416

Zimmerling, Beth, Litzky PR, 33-41 Newark St, 5th fl, Hoboken, NJ 07030 Tel: 201-222-9118 E-mail: inquiries@litzkypr.com Web Site: litzkypr.com, pg 1110

Zimmerman, Brianna, Franklin & Siegal Associates Inc, 40 Exchange Place, Suite 1703, New York, NY 10005 Tel: 212-868-6311 Web Site: www.franklinandsiegal.com, pg 1346

Zipoli, Robert, Pathway Book Service, 34 Production Ave, Keene, NH 03431 Tel: 603-357-0236 Toll Free Tel: 800-345-6665 Fax: 603-965-2181 E-mail: pbs@pathwaybook.com Web Site: www.pathwaybook.com, pg 1320

Ziv, Christie, Litzky PR, 33-41 Newark St, 5th fl, Hoboken, NJ 07030 Tel: 201-222-9118 E-mail: inquiries@litzkypr.com Web Site: litzkypr.com, pg 1110

Zorn, Scott, The John Roberts Company, 9687 East River Rd NW, Minneapolis, MN 55433 Tel: 763-755-5500 Toll Free Tel: 800-551-1534 Fax: 763-755-0394 E-mail: success@johnroberts.com Web Site: www.johnroberts.com; www.facebook.com/TheJohnRobertsCompany, pg 1105

Zosel, Andy, OMRON Microscan Systems Inc, 700 SW 39 St, Suite 100, Renton, WA 98057 Tel: 425-226-5700 Toll Free Tel: 800-762-1149 Fax: 425-226-8250 E-mail: info@microscan.com Web Site: www.microscan.com, pg 1374

Zucker, Janice, Regent Book Co, PO Box 37, Liberty Corner, NJ 07938 Tel: 973-574-7600 Toll Free Tel: 800-999-9554 Fax: 973-944-5073 Toll Free Fax: 888-597-3661 E-mail: info@regentbook.com Web Site: www.regentbook.com, pg 1320

Zucker, Josh, Regent Book Co, PO Box 37, Liberty Corner, NJ 07938 Tel: 973-574-7600 Toll Free Tel: 800-999-9554 Fax: 973-944-5073 Toll Free Fax: 888-597-3661 E-mail: info@regentbook.com Web Site: www.regentbook.com, pg 1320

Zulkowsky, Margaret, Cromwell Leather, 147 Palmer Ave, Mamaroneck, NY 10543 Tel: 914-381-0100 Fax: 914-381-0046 E-mail: sales@cromwellgroup.com Web Site: www.cromwellgroup.com, pg 1266

Zuznicki, Matt, Datalogics Inc, 101 N Wacker, Suite 1800, Chicago, IL 60606 *Tel:* 312-853-8200 *Fax:* 312-853-8282 *E-mail:* sales@datalogics.com; marketing@datalogics.com *Web Site:* www.datalogics.com, pg 1367

Zwergel, Gerrit, Koenig & Bauer (US) Inc, 2555 Regent Blvd, Dallas, TX 75229 *Tel:* 469-532-8000 *Fax:* 469-532-8190 *Web Site:* us.koenig-bauer.com, pg 1281

Zwollo, Kim, Copyright Clearance Center Inc (CCC), 222 Rosewood Dr, Danvers, MA 01923 *Tel:* 978-750-8400 (sales); 978-646-2600 (cust serv) *E-mail:* info@copyright.com *Web Site:* www.copyright.com, pg 1345

Zychowicz, James, A-R Editions Inc, 1600 Aspen Commons, Suite 100, Middleton, WI 53562 *Tel:* 608-836-9000 *Fax:* 608-831-8200 *E-mail:* info@areditions.com *Web Site:* www.areditions.com, pg 1207, 1221, 1277, 1343, 1411

Index to Sections

A

Abstracting 429
Accounts - Bookstores—Wholesalers 1305
Accounts - Libraries—Wholesalers 1305
Accounts - Schools—Wholesalers 1305
Ad Placement – Software 1359
Adaptations, Novelizations 429
Adhesive Binding - Hard 1235
Adhesive Binding - Soft 1235
Advertising & Promotion Copywriting 429
Advertising - Promotional Associations 489
Advertising Agencies 1099
Advertising, Promotion Consultants 1339
App Development – Software 1359
Approval Plans—Wholesalers 1306
Art & Design 1217
Art Editing 1407
Artists & Art Services 1411
    Artists & Art Services — Activity Index 1407
        Art Editing 1407
        Book Design 1407
        Calligraphy 1407
        Cartoons 1407
        Cover Design 1407
        Electronic Layout 1407
        Film Animation 1407
        Icon Design 1407
        Illustration 1408
        Jacket Design 1408
        Layout 1408
        Letterheads 1408
        Lettering 1408
        Logos & Corporate Identity 1409
        Map Design 1409
        Paste-up 1409
        Pictorial Statistics 1409
        Poster Design 1409
        Prototyping 1409
        Retouching 1409
        Silk Screen 1409
        Spot Drawings 1409
        Technical Illustration 1409
        Templating 1409
        Trademarks 1410
        Typesetting 1410
Audiobook Production – Services 1361
AV Materials—Wholesalers 1306
Awards, Prize Contests, Fellowships & Grants 569

B

Bibliographies 429
Binders 1101
Binding Supplies 1263
Binding 1101
Book Clubs 1141
Book Clubs Consultants 1339
Book Covers 1263
Book Design 1407
Book Distributors & Sales Representatives 1285
Book Exhibits 1139
Book Exporters & Importers 1327
Book Jackets 1263
Book Lists & Catalogs 1145
Book Manufacturing Associations 489
Book Manufacturing Equipment 1275
Book Printing - Hardbound 1235
Book Printing - Mass Market 1236
Book Printing - Professional 1236
Book Printing - Softbound 1236
Book Producers 1353
Book Review & Index Journals & Services 1129
Book Review Syndicates 1127
Book Trade & Allied Associations 493
    Book Trade & Allied Associations — Index 489
        Advertising - Promotional 489
        Book Manufacturing 489
        Book Trade Suppliers 489
        Bookselling 489
        Editorial 489
        Library 489
        Literacy 490
        Literary 490
        Magazine & Press 490
        Media - Communications 490
        Publishing 490
        Publishing Services 491
        Writers 491
Book Trade Suppliers Associations 489
Booklets 1101
Bookselling Associations 489
Bound Galleys 1236
Brochures, Pamphlets 1101
Broker for Manufacturing 429
Burst Binding 1237
Business, Finance Consultants 1339

C

Calendar of Book Trade & Promotional Events 535
    Alphabetical Index of Events 531
    Alphabetical Index of Sponsors 527
Calendar Printing 1237
Calligraphy 1407
Canadian Publishers 395
Cartoons 1407
Casebinding 1237
Catalog Cards & Kits—Wholesalers 1306
Catalog Printing 1237
Cataloging & Processing—Wholesalers 1306
CD-ROM – Services 1362
CD-ROM Authoring – Software 1359

INDEX TO SECTIONS

CD-ROM Mastering – Hardware 1359
Chart & Graph – Software 1360
Clip Art – Software 1360
Clipping Bureaus 1383
Color Separation – Software 1360
Color Separations 1217
Columnists & Commentators 1125
   Columnists & Commentators — Subject Index 1123
      Animals, Pets 1123
      Art, Antiques 1123
      Automotive 1123
      Books 1123
      Business, Finance 1123
      Consumer Education 1123
      Fashion 1123
      Film, Radio, TV, Video 1123
      Food, Wine 1123
      Gardening, Plants 1123
      General Commentary 1123
      Health, Nutrition 1123
      House & Home 1123
      Humor 1123
      Inspirational 1123
      Music, Dance, Theater 1123
      National & World Affairs 1123
      Personal Advice, Counseling 1123
      Personalities 1123
      Photography 1123
      Politics 1123
      Science, Technology 1123
      Sports, Recreation 1123
      Travel, Resorts 1123
Comic Book Printing 1238
Company Index 709, 1433
Complete Book Manufacturing 1207
Composition – Systems 1361
Computer Software—Wholesalers 1306
Computer Technology Consultants 1339
Computerized Typesetting 1217
Condensations 429
Consultants 1343
   Consultants — Activity Index 1339
      Advertising, Promotion 1339
      Book Clubs 1339
      Business, Finance 1339
      Computer Technology 1339
      Electronic Publishing 1339
      Legal Services 1339
      Libraries 1339
      Literary Scout 1339
      Management 1340
      Manufacturing, Production 1340
      Marketing 1340
      Mergers, Acquisitions 1340
      Paper, Paper Products 1340
      Printing 1340
      Publishing 1340
      Recruiter 1341
      Rights, Permissions 1341
Conversion – Systems 1361
Copy-Editing 429

Courses for the Book Trade 561
Cover Design 1407

D

Data Processing Services 1218
Desktop Publishing – Services 1362
Desktop Publishing – Systems 1361
Dictionaries & Reference Books—Wholesalers 1306
Die-Cutting 1101, 1238
Digital Printing 1238
Direct Mail Specialists 1115
Display Devices – Hardware 1359
Displays 1101
Distribution & Mailing 1275
Draw & Paint – Software 1360
Drop Shipping—Wholesalers 1306

E

Ebook Conversion – Services 1362
Editing – Systems 1361
Edition (Hardcover) Binding 1238
Editorial Associations 489
Editorial Services 435
   Editorial Services — Activity Index 429
      Abstracting 429
      Adaptations, Novelizations 429
      Advertising & Promotion Copywriting 429
      Bibliographies 429
      Broker for Manufacturing 429
      Condensations 429
      Copy-Editing 429
      Fact Checking 430
      Ghostwriting 430
      Indexing 430
      Interviewing 430
      Line Editing 431
      Manuscript Analysis 431
      Permissions 431
      Photo Research 431
      Proofreading 432
      Research 432
      Rewriting 432
      Special Assignment Writing 433
      Statistics 433
      Technical Writing 433
      Transcription Editing 433
      Typemarking 433
Educational Kits 1101
Electronic Layout 1407
Electronic Publishing Consultants 1339
Embossing 1238
Employment Agencies 1381
Engraving 1101, 1239
EP Utility – Software 1360
Export Representatives 1331

F

Fact Checking 430
File Conversion – Software 1360
Film Animation 1407
Film Laminating 1239

1542

INDEX TO SECTIONS

Foiling 1239
Folders 1101
Font Editors – Software 1360
Font Editors – Systems 1361
Fonts & Faces – Software 1360
Foreign Language & Bilingual Materials—
   Wholesalers 1306
Foreign Language Composition 1218
Foundations 525
Front End Systems – Systems 1361

G

General Trade Books - Hardcover—Wholesalers 1307
Ghostwriting 430
Gilding 1239
Glue or Paste Binding 1239
Government Publications—Wholesalers 1307
Graphic Systems – Systems 1361
Gravure 1240

H

Hand Bookbinding 1240
Hardware 1359
Holograms 1240

I

Icon Design 1407
Illustration Agents 485
Illustration 1408
Imports—Wholesalers 1307
Imprinting 1101
Imprints, Subsidiaries & Distributors 333
Index to Sections 1089, 1541
Indexing 430, 1218
Input Devices – Hardware 1359
Interfaces – Hardware 1359
Interviewing 430

J

Jacket Design 1408
Journal Printing 1240
Juvenile & Young Adult Books—Wholesalers ... 1307

L

Large Print & Braille Materials—Wholesalers 1307
Layout 1408
Lecture Agents 487
Legal Services Consultants 1339
Letterheads 1408
Lettering 1408
Letterpress 1240
Libraries Consultants 1339
Library Associations 489
Line Editing 431
Literacy Associations 490
Literary Agents 447
Literary Associations 490
Literary Scout Consultants 1339
Litho Printing 1240

Logos & Corporate Identity 1409
Looseleaf Binding 1240

M

Magazine & Press Associations 490
Magazines for the Trade 699
Mailing List Brokers & Services 1119
Mailing, Duplicating & Fax Services 1117
Management Consultants 1340
Manual Printing 1240
Manufacturing Brokers or Brokering 1275
Manufacturing Materials 1265
   Manufacturing Materials Index 1263
      Binding Supplies 1263
      Book Covers 1263
      Book Jackets 1263
      Paper Merchants 1263
      Paper Mills 1263
      Printing Ink 1263
Manufacturing Services & Equipment 1277
   Manufacturing Services & Equipment Index 1275
      Book Manufacturing Equipment 1275
      Distribution & Mailing 1275
      Manufacturing Brokers or Brokering ... 1275
Manufacturing, Production Consultants 1340
Manuscript Analysis 431
Map Design 1409
Map Printing 1241
Maps & Atlases—Wholesalers 1308
Marketing Consultants 1340
Mathematics & Chemistry Composition 1218
McCain Sewn Binding 1241
Media - Communications Associations 490
Mergers, Acquisitions Consultants 1340
Metal Composition 1241
Microforms—Wholesalers 1308
Modems – Hardware 1359
Mounting & Finishing 1101
Music Composition 1218

N

News Services & Feature Syndicates 1189
Non-Roman Alphabets 1218
Notch Binding 1241

O

OCR – Hardware 1359
Offset Printing - Sheetfed 1241
Offset Printing - Web 1242
On Demand Printing 1242
Online Ordering—Wholesalers 1308
OP Search—Wholesalers 1308
Other – Hardware 1359
Other – Services 1362
Other – Software 1361
Other – Systems 1361

P

Page Composition – Software 1360
Paper Merchants 1263
Paper Mills 1263

1543

INDEX TO SECTIONS

Paper, Paper Products Consultants	1340
Paperback Books - Mass Market—Wholesalers	1308
Paperback Books - Trade—Wholesalers	1308
Paste-up	1409
Perfect (Adhesive) Binding	1242
Periodicals—Wholesalers	1309
Permissions	431
Personnel Index	785, 1465
Photo Research	431
Photocomposition	1243
Photographers	1419
Photography	1101
Phototypesetters – Hardware	1359
Pictorial Statistics	1409
Plastic Comb Binding	1243
Platforms – Hardware	1359
Poster Design	1409
Posters	1101
Prebinders to Schools & Libraries	1325
Prebinding—Wholesalers	1309
Prepress Services	1221
Prepress Services Index	1217
Art & Design	1217
Color Separations	1217
Computerized Typesetting	1217
Data Processing Services	1218
Foreign Language Composition	1218
Indexing	1218
Mathematics & Chemistry Composition	1218
Music Composition	1218
Non-Roman Alphabets	1218
Production Services	1218
Proofing	1219
Scientific Composition	1219
UPC & Bar Code Services	1219
Word Processing Interface	1219
Printers (Laser & Non-Impact) – Hardware	1359
Printing Consultants	1340
Printing Ink	1263
Printing, Binding & Book Finishing	1247
Printing, Binding & Book Finishing Index	1235
Adhesive Binding - Hard	1235
Adhesive Binding - Soft	1235
Book Printing - Hardbound	1235
Book Printing - Mass Market	1236
Book Printing - Professional	1236
Book Printing - Softbound	1236
Bound Galleys	1236
Burst Binding	1237
Calendar Printing	1237
Casebinding	1237
Catalog Printing	1237
Comic Book Printing	1238
Die-Cutting	1238
Digital Printing	1238
Edition (Hardcover) Binding	1238
Embossing	1238
Engraving	1239
Film Laminating	1239
Foiling	1239
Gilding	1239
Glue or Paste Binding	1239
Gravure	1240
Hand Bookbinding	1240
Holograms	1240
Journal Printing	1240
Letterpress	1240
Litho Printing	1240
Looseleaf Binding	1240
Manual Printing	1240
Map Printing	1241
McCain Sewn Binding	1241
Metal Composition	1241
Notch Binding	1241
Offset Printing - Sheetfed	1241
Offset Printing - Web	1242
On Demand Printing	1242
Perfect (Adhesive) Binding	1242
Photocomposition	1243
Plastic Comb Binding	1243
Saddle Stitch Binding	1243
Short Run Printing	1244
Side Stitch Binding	1244
Smyth-type Sewn Binding	1245
Specialty Binding	1245
Spiral Binding	1245
Struck-Image Composition	1245
Textbook Printing - College	1245
Textbook Printing - El-Hi	1245
Wire-O Binding	1246
Workbook Printing	1246
Printing	1101
Production Services	1218
Promotional Boxes	1101
Promotional Printing & Allied Services	1103
Promotional Printing & Allied Services — Activity Index	1101
Binders	1101
Binding	1101
Booklets	1101
Brochures, Pamphlets	1101
Die-Cutting	1101
Displays	1101
Educational Kits	1101
Engraving	1101
Folders	1101
Imprinting	1101
Mounting & Finishing	1101
Photography	1101
Posters	1101
Printing	1101
Promotional Boxes	1101
Silk Screen	1101
Slip Cases	1102
Typography	1102
Varnishing	1102
Proofing	1219
Proofreading	432
Prototyping	1409
Public Relations Services	1107
Publishing Associations	490
Publishing Consultants	1340

INDEX TO SECTIONS

Publishing Services Associations 491
Publishing Systems, Services & Technology 1363
    Publishing Systems, Services & Technology Index 1359
        Hardware 1359
            CD-ROM Mastering 1359
            Display Devices 1359
            Input Devices 1359
            Interfaces 1359
            Modems 1359
            OCR 1359
            Other 1359
            Phototypesetters 1359
            Platforms 1359
            Printers (Laser & Non-Impact) 1359
            Scanners & Digitizers 1359
        Services 1361
            Audiobook Production 1361
            CD-ROM 1362
            Desktop Publishing 1362
            Ebook Conversion 1362
            Other 1362
            SGML 1362
            Web Development 1362
        Software 1359
            Ad Placement 1359
            App Development 1359
            CD-ROM Authoring 1359
            Chart & Graph 1360
            Clip Art 1360
            Color Separation 1360
            Draw & Paint 1360
            EP Utility 1360
            File Conversion 1360
            Font Editors 1360
            Fonts & Faces 1360
            Other 1361
            Page Composition 1360
            SGML Programs 1360
            Text Formatters 1360
            Tracking 1360
            Word Processing & Text Editing 1360
        Systems 1361
            Composition 1361
            Conversion 1361
            Desktop Publishing 1361
            Editing 1361
            Font Editors 1361
            Front End Systems 1361
            Graphic Systems 1361
            Other 1361

R

Radio Programs Featuring Books 1197
Radio, TV & Cable Networks 1193
Recruiter Consultants 1341
Reference Books for the Trade 681
Remainders & Overstock—Wholesalers 1309
Research 432
Retouching 1409
Rewriting 432
Rights, Permissions Consultants 1341

S

Saddle Stitch Binding 1243
Scanners & Digitizers – Hardware 1359
Scholarly Books—Wholesalers 1309
Sci-Tech & Medicine—Wholesalers 1309
Scientific Composition 1219
Serials Featuring Books 1147
Services 1361
SGML – Services 1362
SGML Programs – Software 1360
Shipping Services 1333
Shipping Suppliers 1337
Short Run Printing 1244
Side Stitch Binding 1244
Silk Screen 1101, 1409
Slip Cases 1102
Smyth-type Sewn Binding 1245
Software 1359
Special Assignment Writing 433
Specialty Binding 1245
Spiral Binding 1245
Spot Drawings 1409
Standing Orders & Continuations—Wholesalers 1309
Statistics 433
Stock Photo Agencies 1427
Struck-Image Composition 1245
Systems 1361

T

Technical Illustration 1409
Technical Writing 433
Templating 1409
Text Formatters – Software 1360
Textbook Printing - College 1245
Textbook Printing - El-Hi 1245
Textbooks - College—Wholesalers 1310
Textbooks - Elementary—Wholesalers 1309
Textbooks - Secondary—Wholesalers 1309
Toll Free Directory, Publishers 1079
Tracking – Software 1360
Trademarks 1410
Transcription Editing 433
Translators & Interpreters 1399
    Translators & Interpreters — Source Language
        Index 1387
        Afrikaans 1387
        Albanian 1387
        Arabic 1387
        Armenian 1387
        Belarussian 1387
        Bengali 1387
        Bulgarian 1387
        Burmese 1387
        Catalan 1387
        Chinese 1387
        Czech 1387
        Danish 1387
        Dutch 1387
        English 1387

INDEX TO SECTIONS

Esperanto	1388
Estonian	1388
Finnish	1388
Flemish	1388
French	1388
Gaelic	1388
Georgian	1388
German	1388
Greek	1388
Hebrew	1389
Hindi	1389
Hungarian	1389
Icelandic	1389
Indonesian	1389
Italian	1389
Japanese	1389
Javanese	1389
Khmer	1389
Korean	1389
Kurdish	1389
Latin	1389
Latvian	1389
Lithuanian	1389
Macedonian	1390
Malagasy	1390
Malayalam	1390
Malaysian	1390
Nepali	1390
Norwegian	1390
Persian	1390
Polish	1390
Portuguese	1390
Provencal	1390
Punjabi	1390
Romanian	1390
Russian	1390
Serbo-Croatian	1390
Sinhalese	1390
Slovak	1390
Slovene	1391
Spanish	1391
Swahili	1391
Swedish	1391
Tagalog	1391
Tamil	1391
Telugu	1391
Thai	1391
Turkish	1391
Ukrainian	1391
Urdu	1391
Vietnamese	1391
Welsh	1391
Yiddish	1391

Translators & Interpreters — Target Language

Index	1393
Afrikaans	1393
Albanian	1393
Arabic	1393
Armenian	1393
Belarussian	1393
Bengali	1393
Bulgarian	1393
Burmese	1393
Catalan	1393
Chinese	1393
Czech	1393
Danish	1393
Dutch	1393
English	1393
Esperanto	1394
Estonian	1394
Finnish	1394
Flemish	1394
French	1394
Gaelic	1394
Georgian	1394
German	1394
Greek	1394
Hebrew	1394
Hindi	1395
Hungarian	1395
Icelandic	1395
Indonesian	1395
Italian	1395
Japanese	1395
Javanese	1395
Khmer	1395
Korean	1395
Kurdish	1395
Latin	1395
Latvian	1395
Lithuanian	1395
Macedonian	1395
Malagasy	1395
Malayalam	1396
Malaysian	1396
Nepali	1396
Norwegian	1396
Persian	1396
Polish	1396
Portuguese	1396
Provencal	1396
Punjabi	1396
Romanian	1396
Russian	1396
Serbo-Croatian	1396
Sinhalese	1396
Slovak	1396
Slovene	1396
Spanish	1396
Swahili	1397
Swedish	1397
Tagalog	1397
Tamil	1397
Telugu	1397
Thai	1397
Turkish	1397
Ukrainian	1397
Urdu	1397
Vietnamese	1397
Welsh	1397
Yiddish	1397

INDEX TO SECTIONS

TV Programs Featuring Books 1201
Typemarking 433
Typesetting 1410
Typing & Word Processing Services 1385
Typography 1102

U

U.S. Publishers 1
   U.S. Publishers — Geographic Index 239
   U.S. Publishers — Subject Index 277
      Accounting 277
      Advertising 277
      Aeronautics, Aviation 277
      African American Studies 277
      Agriculture 278
      Alternative 278
      Americana, Regional 278
      Animals, Pets 279
      Anthropology 279
      Antiques 280
      Archaeology 280
      Architecture & Interior Design 280
      Art 281
      Asian Studies 282
      Astrology, Occult 282
      Astronomy 282
      Automotive 282
      Behavioral Sciences 283
      Biblical Studies 283
      Biography, Memoirs 284
      Biological Sciences 285
      Business 285
      Career Development 287
      Chemistry, Chemical Engineering 287
      Child Care & Development 287
      Civil Engineering 288
      Communications 288
      Computer Science 288
      Computers 288
      Cookery 289
      Crafts, Games, Hobbies 289
      Criminology 290
      Developing Countries 290
      Disability, Special Needs 290
      Drama, Theater 291
      Earth Sciences 291
      Economics 291
      Education 292
      Electronics, Electrical Engineering 293
      Energy 294
      Engineering (General) 294
      English as a Second Language 294
      Environmental Studies 294
      Erotica 295
      Ethnicity 295
      Fashion 296
      Fiction 296
      Film, Video 298
      Finance 298
      Foreign Countries 299
      Gardening, Plants 299
      Genealogy 299
      Geography, Geology 299
      Government, Political Science 300
      Health, Nutrition 301
      History 302
      House & Home 304
      How-to 304
      Human Relations 305
      Humor 305
      Inspirational, Spirituality 306
      Journalism 306
      Labor, Industrial Relations 306
      Language Arts, Linguistics 307
      Law 307
      LGBTQ+ 308
      Library & Information Sciences 308
      Literature, Literary Criticism, Essays 308
      Management 310
      Maritime 310
      Marketing 310
      Mathematics 311
      Mechanical Engineering 311
      Medicine, Nursing, Dentistry 311
      Military Science 312
      Music, Dance 312
      Mysteries, Suspense 313
      Native American Studies 313
      Natural History 314
      Nonfiction (General) 314
      Outdoor Recreation 316
      Parapsychology 316
      Philosophy 317
      Photography 317
      Physical Sciences 318
      Physics 318
      Poetry 318
      Pop Culture 319
      Psychology, Psychiatry 320
      Public Administration 320
      Publishing & Book Trade Reference 320
      Radio, TV 321
      Real Estate 321
      Regional Interests 321
      Religion - Buddhist 321
      Religion - Catholic 322
      Religion - Hindu 322
      Religion - Islamic 322
      Religion - Jewish 322
      Religion - Other 323
      Religion - Protestant 323
      Romance 324
      Science (General) 324
      Science Fiction, Fantasy 325
      Securities 326
      Self-Help 326
      Social Sciences, Sociology 327
      Sports, Athletics 328
      Technology 328
      Theology 329
      Transportation 329
      Travel & Tourism 330

INDEX TO SECTIONS

Veterinary Science 330
Western Fiction 330
Wine & Spirits 331
Women's Studies 331
U.S. Publishers — Type of Publication Index 247
    Association Presses 247
    Audiobooks 247
    AV Materials 248
    Belles Lettres 248
    Bibles 248
    Bibliographies 248
    Braille Books 249
    Children's Books 249
    Computer Software 250
    Databases 250
    Dictionaries, Encyclopedias 251
    Directories, Reference Books 251
    Ebooks or CD-ROMs 252
    Fine Editions, Illustrated Books 255
    Foreign Language & Bilingual Books 255
    General Trade Books - Hardcover 256
    Juvenile & Young Adult Books 258
    Large Print Books 260
    Maps, Atlases 260
    Paperback Books - Mass Market 260
    Paperback Books - Trade 261
    Periodicals, Journals 264
    Professional Books 266
    Reprints 268
    Scholarly Books 269
    Sidelines 271
    Subscription & Mail Order Books 271
    Textbooks - College 272
    Textbooks - Elementary 271
    Textbooks - Secondary 272
    Translations 273
    University Presses 274
    Videos, DVDs 275
University Press Books—Wholesalers 1310
UPC & Bar Code Services 1219

V

Varnishing 1102

W

Web Development – Services 1362
Wholesalers 1311
    Wholesalers — Activity Index 1305
    Accounts - Bookstores 1305
    Accounts - Libraries 1305
    Accounts - Schools 1305
    Approval Plans 1306
    AV Materials 1306
    Catalog Cards & Kits 1306
    Cataloging & Processing 1306
    Computer Software 1306
    Dictionaries & Reference Books 1306
    Drop Shipping 1306
    Foreign Language & Bilingual Materials 1306
    General Trade Books - Hardcover 1307
    Government Publications 1307
    Imports 1307
    Juvenile & Young Adult Books 1307
    Large Print & Braille Materials 1307
    Maps & Atlases 1308
    Microforms 1308
    Online Ordering 1308
    OP Search 1308
    Paperback Books - Mass Market 1308
    Paperback Books - Trade 1308
    Periodicals 1309
    Prebinding 1309
    Remainders & Overstock 1309
    Scholarly Books 1309
    Sci-Tech & Medicine 1309
    Standing Orders & Continuations 1309
    Textbooks - College 1310
    Textbooks - Elementary 1309
    Textbooks - Secondary 1309
    University Press Books 1310
Wire-O Binding 1246
Word Processing & Text Editing – Software 1360
Word Processing Interface 1219
Workbook Printing 1246
Writers Associations 491
Writers' Conferences & Workshops 553